TEACHER'S EDITION

GRADE TEN

PEARSON

Upper Saddle River, New Jersey
Boston, Massachusetts
Chandler, Arizona
Glenview, Illinois
Shoreview, Minnesota

13-digit ISBN 978-0-13-366643-4
10-digit ISBN 0-13-366643-3
1 2 3 4 5 6 7 8 9 10   12 11 10 09 08

Remember when you first started teaching? You imagined students pouring into class eager to talk about your favorite stories. The reality is a little different—students' packed schedules, their growing pains, pressures at home, and the buzzing digital world make those great discussions a huge challenge. Yet every now and then you experience those break-through moments. You remember why you love teaching. Let *Prentice Hall Literature* rekindle your love of teaching. Live your dream.

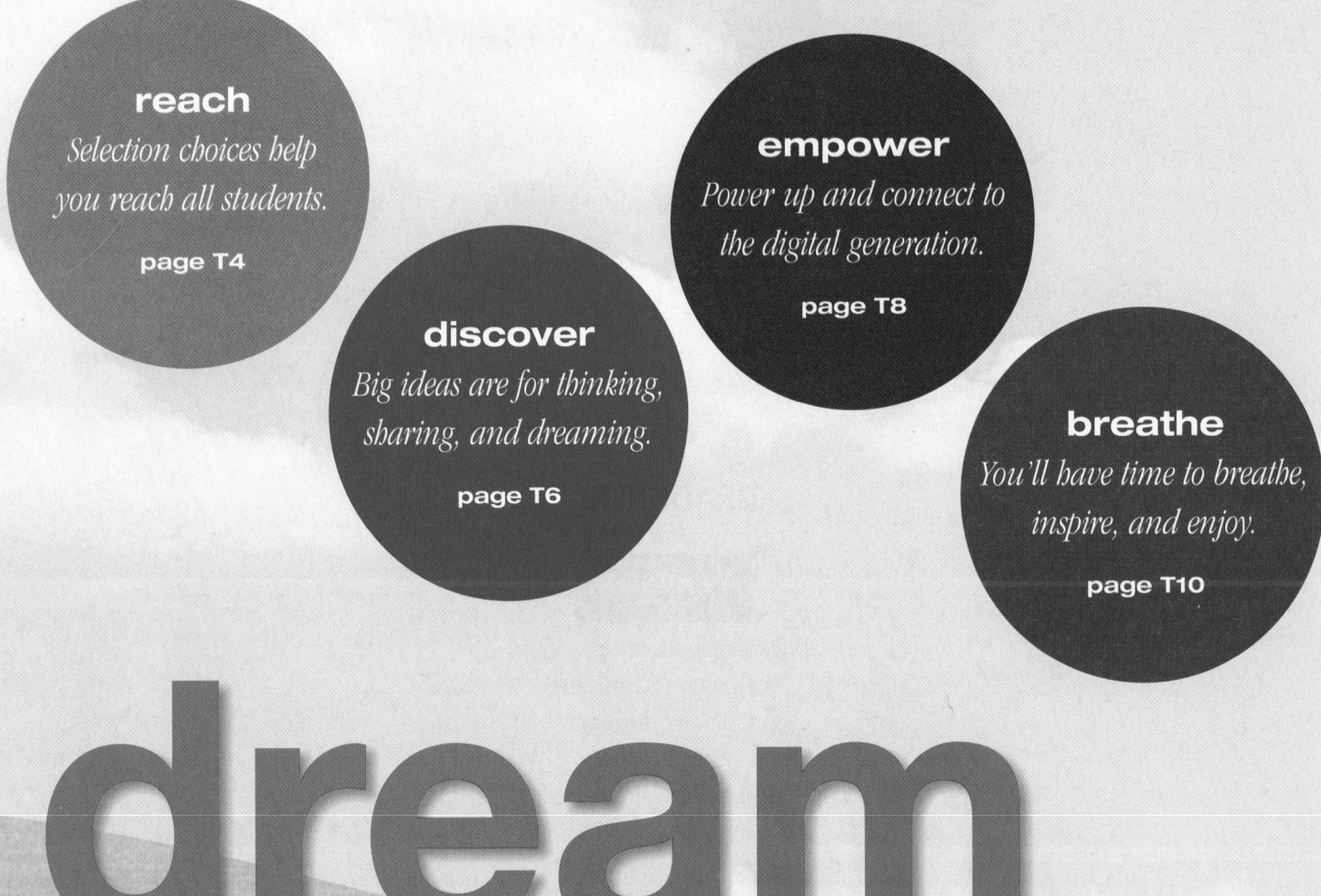

reach
Selection choices help you reach all students.
page T4

discover
Big ideas are for thinking, sharing, and dreaming.
page T6

empower
Power up and connect to the digital generation.
page T8

breathe
You'll have time to breathe, inspire, and enjoy.
page T10

dream

Dreaming is where all good things begin.

PEARSON

Hello, Literature Teachers

Pearson is a company devoted to teachers, to learners, to all those with a dream. We share your determination, your belief, to change the world through education. From Kindergarten through Grade 12, Pearson aligns instruction, assessment, and digital media, because the learning that takes place in the elementary years leads to success in high school. Is there such a thing as a dream partner? Let us show you.

Pearson Literacy Programs

Kindergarten–Grade 5

Scott Foresman Reading Street

Grades K–5

Comprehensive reading/language arts program

Grades 6–12

Prentice Hall Literature

Grades 6–12

Comprehensive literature/language arts program

Partnership for 21st Century Skills

Pearson and companies such as Apple, Microsoft, Dell, and AT&T are members of the leading advocacy organization infusing 21st century skills into education.

reach

Leveled selections let you respond to students' needs and interests.

Choose a Leveled Selection

More Accessible | **More Challenging**

Student Edition, Grade 7

Selection Choices

Only *Prentice Hall Literature* lets you choose the literature you teach based on students' backgrounds, needs, and interests. Use the accessibility chart to guide your selection.

Differentiated Instruction for Universal Access

Accessibility at a Glance: Selection Choices

	The Cask of Amontillado	Sonata for Harp and Bicycle
Context	Setting: gothic; set in eighteenth-century Europe	Setting: haunted office building in London
Language/ Vocabulary	• Numerous long sentences with embedded clauses • Difficult diction	• Accessible vocabulary • Conversational dialogue
Concept Level	Challenging (ghastly quest for revenge)	Accessible (determination to solve a mystery and to win another's love)
Literary Merit	Classic	Contemporary
Lexile/Length	Lexile: 800L Word Count: 1,976	Lexile: 960L Word Count: 3,141
Overall Rating	**More challenging**	**More accessible**

Because a number of factors determine the relative accessibility of paired selections, in some cases the Lexile rating of the more challenging selection will be lower than that of the more accessible selection.

Focus on the Standards

Leveled Support

A full complement of leveled support is provided for each selection to help you attend to varied learning needs.

- Leveled Reading Warm-Ups
- Leveled Vocabulary Warm-Ups
- Leveled Graphic Organizers
- Leveled Assessment
- Leveled Trade Books
- Leveled Online Practice
- Leveled Reader's Notebook

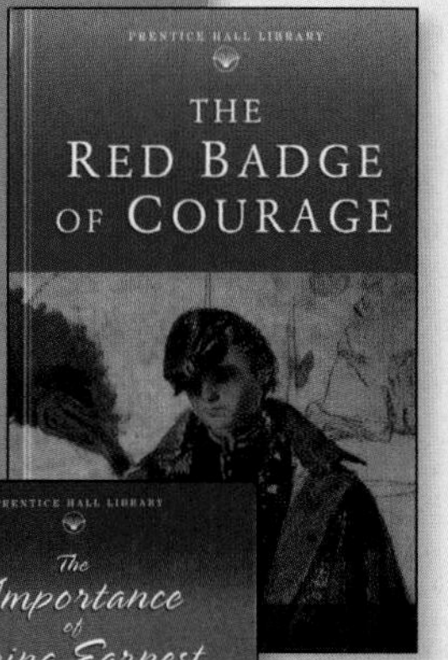

Over 300 titles with a range of readabilities!

More Reach

Get Real Appeal
Reality Central is provocative, edgy, and (dare we say) cool. The high-interest, real-world readings are written at a slightly lower readability level and are organized around the same big questions as *Prentice Hall Literature.*

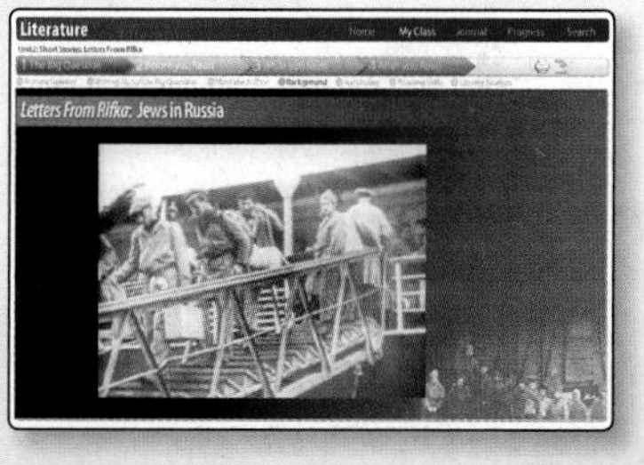

Personalized Learning
PHLit Online assesses, diagnoses, and auto-assigns reading materials and practice at each student's level.

"The big-idea questions signal that education is not just about learning 'the answer' but about learning how to learn."

Grant Wiggins
Contributing Author

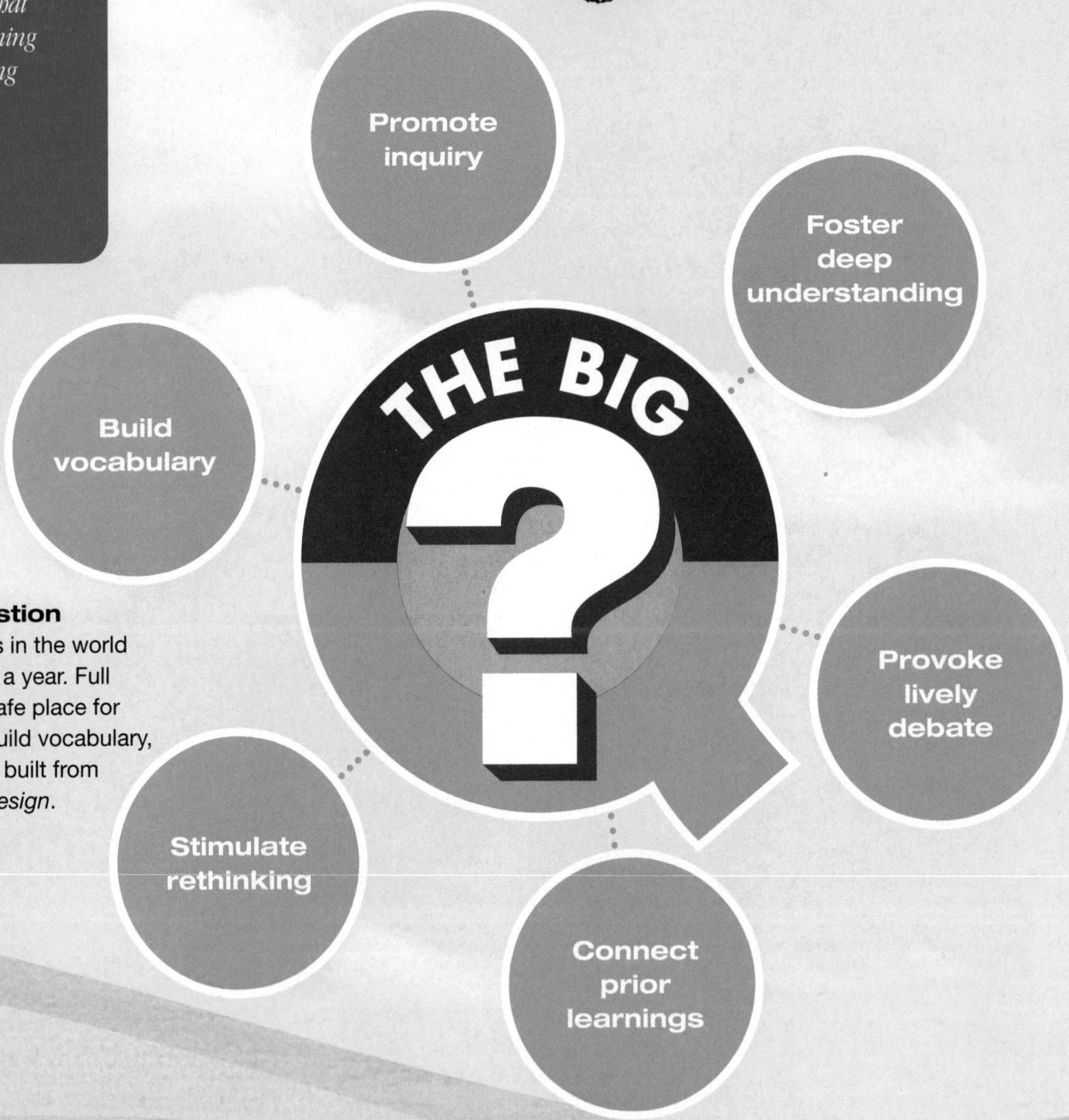

Go Deep with One Big Question

Prentice Hall Literature puts students in the world of a concept for six weeks, six times a year. Full immersion in a concept provides a safe place for all learners to connect knowledge, build vocabulary, and learn how to learn. Instruction is built from Grant Wiggins's *Understanding by Design*.

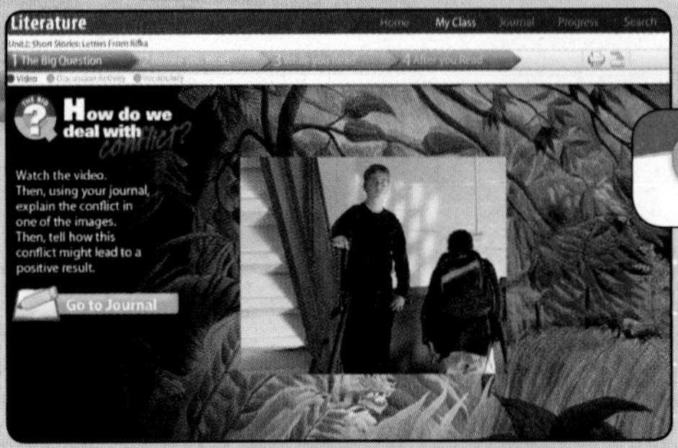

PHLit Online!

Turn an ordinary lesson into a cinema-quality experience! Big Question Videos give students motivation to discover and learn.

Students explore big ideas and deepen understanding.

discover

Diagnose Readiness

This is the springboard for responsive instruction. Brief assessments help you diagnose student readiness and implement personalized instruction.

Monitor Progress

Progress monitoring occurs with every selection, so you stay in touch with students' needs and can make adjustments on the fly.

Benchmark Mastery

Only *Prentice Hall Literature* provides benchmark tests every three weeks to help you catch small learning problems before they become big ones.

"The Internet is this generation's defining technology for literacy and learning."

Donald Leu
Contributing Author

Welcome to the digital world!

Tech-savvy students live in a world teeming with iPods, blogs, and Facebook. *Prentice Hall Literature* lets students seamlessly integrate with their digital world. The Student Edition is online with exciting ways to access content, video, and audio. An online teacher center helps you work smarter every day.

Student Edition, Grade 9

Digital media ingeniously connects students to their world.

empower

Organization 24/7
Introducing your new best friend! PHLit Online helps you prepare lessons, monitor progress, manage reports, and personalize your teaching.

Hear It!

Hip-hop, folk, and alternative music featuring Big Question vocabulary

See It!

Archival footage

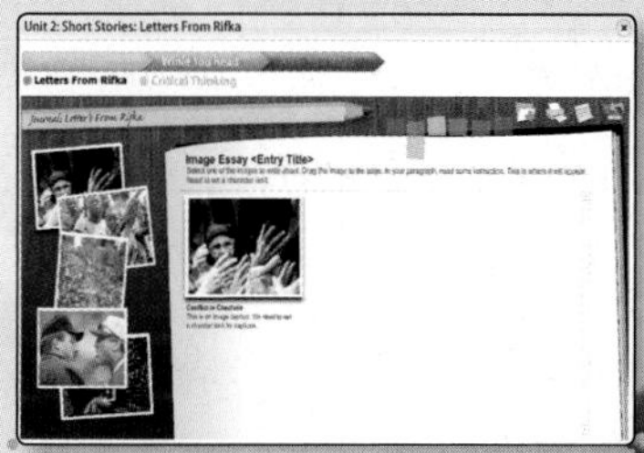

Interactive journal

Do It!

From the Author's Desk Videos

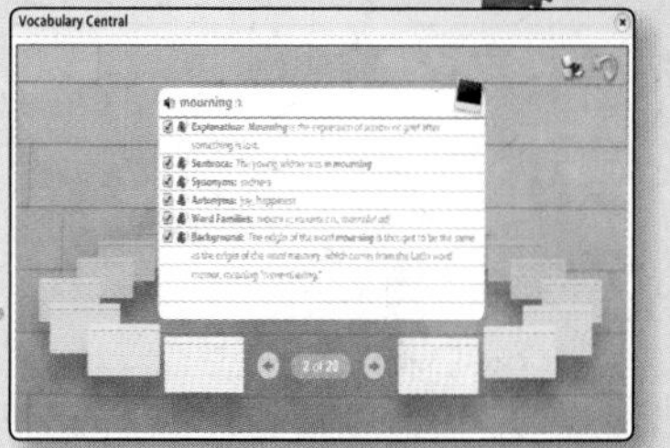

Vocabulary builders

Complete audiobook in English

Have a wonderful journey!

Teaching isn't easy. It's sacrifice and hard work. It's standing alone in front of the classroom every day. It's all you do after the last bell has rung. We want to say "thank you." (And thank you again!) You are America's true hero. All of us at Pearson stand behind you. We want to take some of your worry away and lighten the load. Breathe. Enjoy every minute, because you put so much of yourself into each day. *For the love of teaching.*

breathe

Don't believe anyone who says teaching is easy.

Components

Core Program

Student Edition

Teacher's Edition

All-in-One Workbook

- Writing support for every selection
- Standards review worksheets
- Grammar workshops
- Vocabulary builders
- Support for each selection
- Development worksheets

Differentiated Instruction

Reader's Notebook

Reader's Notebook, Adapted Version

Reader's Notebook, English Learner's Version

Reader's Notebook Teaching Guide

Reading Kit: Reading and Literacy

Independent Reading

Literature Library Novels

Prentice Hall Discoveries Readers

Readings in the Real World

Reality Central Student Anthology

Reality Central Writing Journal

Reality Central Teacher's Manual

Technology

PHLit Online

- Online Student Edition
- Online Teacher's Edition
- Online Success Tracker

Hear It!

- Selection summary audio
- Complete selection audio in English
- BQ Tunes

See It!

- Penguin author videos
- Big Question videos
- Get Connected videos
- Background videos
- More about the authors
- Illustrated vocabulary words
- Vocabulary flashcards

Do It!

- Interactive journal
- Interactive graphic organizers
- Grammar tutorials
- Interactive vocabulary games
- Test practice

Exam*View*® Assessment Suite CD-ROM

Hear It! Prentice Hall Audio Program CD

See It! Prentice Hall Video Program CD

Virtual Art Museum CD-ROM

Professional Development

Professional Development Guidebook

Classroom Strategies and Teaching Routines

Classroom Management

Unit Resources

Daily Bellringer Activities

Graphic Organizer Transparencies

WordWALL Vocabulary Builder

Professional Development Handbook

National Teacher Board Members

Heather Barnes
Language Arts Instructor
Central Crossing High School
Grove City, Ohio

Lee Bromberger
English Department Chairperson
Mukwonago High School
Mukwonago, Wisconsin

Cathy Cassy
Communication Arts Curriculum Supervisor 6-12
St. Louis Public Schools
St. Louis, Missouri

Judy Castrogiavanni
English Teacher
Abington Heights School
Clarks Summit, Pennsylvania

Ann Catrillo
Sr. English & AP Teacher; Department Chairperson
East Stroudsburg High School South
East Stroudsburg, Pennsylvania

Susan Cisna
Instructor Middle School Education
Eastern Illinois University
Charleston, Illinois

Linda Fund
Reading Specialist
Ezra L. Nolan Middle School #40
Jersey City, New Jersey

Gail Hacker
Adjunct Professor
Springfield College School of Human Services
North Charleston, South Carolina

Patricia Matysik
English Department Chairperson
Belleville West Middle School
Belleville, Illinois

Gail Phelps
Literacy Intervention Coach
Oak Grove High School
Little Rock, Arkansas

Julie Rucker
Literacy Coach/English Teacher
Tift County High School
Tifton, Georgia

Kathy Ryan
Curriculum Coordinator
Rockwood Schools
St. Louis, Missouri

Matthew Scanlon
Vice Principal
Kinnelon High School
Kinnelon, New Jersey

Renee Trotier
Freshman Principal
Lafayette High School
Wildwood, Missouri

Carolyn Waters
Language Arts Supervisor
Cobb County Schools
Marietta, Georgia

Martha Wildman
Social Studies Teacher
Las Cruces Public Schools
Las Cruces, New Mexico

Melissa Williams
District Supervisor
Delsea Regional Schools
Franklinville, New Jersey

Charles Youngs
English Language Arts Facilitator
Bethel Park High School
Bethel Park, Pennsylvania

Contributing Authors

The contributing authors guided the direction and philosophy of Prentice Hall Literature. *Working with the development team, they helped to build the pedagogical integrity of the program and to ensure its relevance for today's teachers and students.*

Grant Wiggins, Ed.D, is the President of Authentic Education in Hopewell, New Jersey. He earned his Ed.D. from Harvard University and his B. A. from St. John's College in Annapolis. Grant consults with schools, districts and state education departments on a variety of reform matters; organizes conferences and workshops; and develops print materials and Web resources on curricular change. He is the co-author, with Jay McTighe, of *Understanding By Design* and *The Understanding By Design Handbook*, the award-winning and highly successful materials on curriculum published by ASCD. His work has been supported by the Pew Charitable Trusts, the Geraldine R. Dodge Foundation, and the National Science Foundation.

Jeff Anderson has worked with struggling writers and readers for almost 20 years. Anderson's specialty is the integration of grammar and editing instruction into the processes of reading and writing. He has published two books, *Mechanically Inclined: Building Grammar, Usage, and Style into Writer's Workshop* and *Everyday Editing: Inviting Students to Develop Skill and Craft in Writer's Workshop* as well as a DVD, *The Craft of Grammar.* Anderson's work has appeared in *The English Journal.* Anderson won the NCTE Paul and Kate Farmer Award for his *English Journal* article on teaching grammar in context.

Maria V. Balderrama, Ph.D, is a Professor at California State University, San Bernardino's College of Education. She is a bilingual, multicultural educator and researcher with more than 25 years in public education. Professor Balderrama's experiences include work with diverse youth, their families, teachers and school administrators. Her recent book *Teacher Performance Expectations for Educating English Learners* (with L.T. Díaz-Rico). Her work is frequently widely recognized for its contributions to the field.

Arnetha F. Ball, Ph.D, is a Professor at Stanford University. Her areas of expertise include language and literacy studies of diverse student populations, research on writing instruction, and the teacher preparation to work with diverse populations. She is the author of *African American Literacies Unleashed* with Dr. Ted Lardner, and *Multicultural Strategies for Education and Social Change.*

Sheridan Blau is Professor of Education and English at the University of California, Santa Barbara, where he directs the South Coast Writing Project and the Literature Institute for Teachers. He has served in senior advisory roles for such groups as the National Board for Professional Teaching Standards, the College Board, and the American Board for Teacher Education. Blau served for twenty years on the National Writing Project Advisory Board and Task Force, and is a former President of NCTE. Blau is the author of *The Literature Workshop: Teaching Texts and Their Readers,* which was named by the Conference on English Education as the 2004 Richard Meade Award for outstanding research in English education.

Doug Buehl is a teacher, author, and national literacy consultant. He taught in the Madison Metropolitan School District, Madison, WI, for 33 years. Buehl is the author of *Classroom Strategies for Interactive Learning,* and co-author of *Reading and the High School Student: Strategies to Enhance Literacy; and Strategies to Enhance Literacy and Learning in Middle School Content Area Classrooms.* He was a member of the IRA Commission on Adolescent Literacy, and served on the task force that drafted the National Standards for Middle and High School Literacy Coaches.

Harvey Daniels, Ph.D, has been a classroom teacher, writing project director, author, and university professor. "Smokey," serves as an international consultant to schools, districts, and educational agencies. He is known for his work on student-led book clubs, as recounted in *Literature Circles: Voice and Choice in Book Clubs & Reading Groups* and *Mini Lessons for Literature Circles.* Recent works include *Subjects Matter: Every Teacher's Guide to Content-Area Reading* and *Content Area Writing: Every Teacher's Guide.*

Tradition and innovation in research-based, classroom tested strategies from the best minds in the field

Jane Feber is the author of *Creative Book Reports* and *Active Word Play.* A classroom teacher for 35 years, Feber currently teaches language arts at Mandarin Middle School in Jacksonville, Florida, where she serves as department chair. Feber plays an active role in the Florida Council of Teachers of English. She was the 2006 recipient of NCTE's Edwin A. Hoey Award and received the Gladys Prior Award for Teaching Excellence. In 2003, she was the Florida Council of Teachers of English Teacher of the Year.

Danling Fu, Ph.D, is Professor of Language and Culture, in the College of Education in the University of Florida. She researches and provides inservice to public schools nationally, focusing on literacy instruction for new immigrant students. Fu's books include *My Trouble is My English* and *An Island of English* addressing English language learners in the secondary schools. She has authored chapters in the *Handbook of Adolescent Literacy Research* and in *Adolescent Literacy: Turning Promise to Practice.*

Kelly Gallagher is a full-time English teacher at Magnolia High School in Anaheim, California. He is the former co-director of the South Basin Writing Project at California State University, Long Beach. Gallagher wrote *Reading Reasons: Motivational Mini-Lessons for the Middle and High School; Deeper Reading: Comprehending Challenging Texts 4-12;* and *Teaching Adolescent Writers.* Gallagher won the Secondary Award of Classroom Excellence from the California Association of Teachers of English—the state's top English teacher honor.

Sharroky Hollie, Ph.D, is an assistant professor at California State University, Dominguez Hills, and an urban literacy visiting professor at Webster University, St. Louis. Hollie's work focuses on professional development, African American education, and second language methodology. He is a contributing author in two texts on culturally and linguistically responsive teaching. He is the Executive Director of the Center for Culturally Responsive Teaching and Learning and the co-founding director of the Culture and Language Academy of Success, an independent charter school in Los Angeles.

Dr. Donald J. Leu, Ph.D, teaches at University of Connecticut and holds a joint appointment in Curriculum and Instruction and Educational Psychology. He directs the New Literacies Research Lab and is a member of the Board of Directors of the International Reading Association. Leu studies the skills required to read, write, and learn with Internet technologies. His research has been funded by groups including the U.S. Department of Education, the National Science Foundation, and the Bill & Melinda Gates Foundation.

Julie Maravilla is an elementary school principal for the Los Angeles Unified School District. As an expert in English Language Development, she served as a member of the Curriculum Development. Maravilla was chair of the Reading Language Arts/ English Language Development Subject Matter Committee that developed criteria for instructional materials for the 2008 Language Arts adoption. She has served as a literacy coach and professional development provider for California teachers and administrators.

Jon Scieszka founded GUYS READ, a nonprofit literacy initiative for boys to call attention to the problem of getting boys connected with reading. In 2008, he was named the first U.S. National Ambassador for Young People's Literature by the Library of Congress. Scieszka taught from first grade to eighth grade for ten years in New York City, drawing inspiration from his students to write *The True Story of the 3 Little Pigs!, The Stinky Cheese Man,* the *Time Warp Trio* series of chapter books, and the *Trucktown* series of books for beginning readers.

Sharon Vaughn, Ph.D, Sharon Vaughn teaches at the University of Texas at Austin. She is the previous Editor-in-Chief of the *Journal of Learning Disabilities* and the Co-Editor of *Learning Disabilities Research and Practice.* She is the recipient of the American Education Research Association SIG Award for Outstanding Researcher. Vaughn's work focuses on effective practices for enhancing reading outcomes for students with reading difficulties. She is the author of more than 100 articles, and numerous books designed to improve research-based practices in the classroom.

Unit Authors

An award-winning contemporary author hosts each unit in each level of Prentice Hall Literature. *Serving as guides for your students, these authors introduce literary concepts, answer questions about their work, and discuss their own writing processes, using their works as models. Following are the featured unit authors for Grade 10.*

Susan Vreeland (b. 1946)

Unit 1: Fiction and Nonfiction Susan Vreeland has extensive experience in writing both fiction and nonfiction. Her book *Girl in Hyacinth Blue*, which describes the successive owners of an imaginary painting by Vermeer, received the San Diego Book Awards' Best Novel of the Year prize. Other novels include *The Forest Lover* and *The Passion of Artemisia*. Ms. Vreeland has also written about 250 nonfiction articles on a variety of subjects.

C. J. Cherryh (b. 1942)

Unit 2: Short Stories C. J. Cherryh is the ideal guide for the short-story unit. A popular and critically acclaimed fantasy and science-fiction writer, she has won numerous prizes for her short stories and for her more than forty novels. For example, she received the coveted Hugo Award for both her short story "Cassandra" and her novels *Downbelow Station* and *Cyteen*. Her hobbies include traveling, weaving, and ice skating, in addition to studying marine life, dinosaurs, and art.

Erik Weihenmayer (b. 1968)

Unit 3: Types of Nonfiction: Essays and Speeches As an athlete and motivational speaker, Erik Weihenmayer has experience in writing various types of nonfiction, including informal essays and an autobiography. On May 25, 2001, he became the first blind climber in history to reach the summit of Mt. Everest. He wrote about his life and the experience of climbing Everest in *Touch the Top of the World*, a best-seller that *Publishers Weekly* called "moving and adventure packed."

Cornelius Eady (b. 1954)

Unit 4: Poetry Cornelius Eady is a well-known poet and teacher of poetry, making him an ideal guide for this unit. His books includes *Victims of the Latest Dance Craze*, which was named a Lamont Poetry Selection by the Academy of American Poets, and *The Gathering of My Name*, which was nominated for a Pulitzer Prize. A music-theater piece he collaborated on was a finalist for a Pulitzer Prize in Drama. In addition, his work frequently draws inspiration from African American musical traditions.

David Henry Hwang (b. 1957)

Unit 5: Drama As a dramatist, David Henry Hwang achieved early success in the theater with his first play, *FOB (Fresh Off the Boat)*. It won the 1981 Obie Award as the best new off-Broadway play of the season. He established himself as a major talent with *M. Butterfly*, which won a Tony Award for best play on Broadway. His recent work includes *Tibet Through the Red Box*, a play that appeals to both young people and adults.

John Phillip Santos (b. 1957)

Unit 6: Themes in Literature: Heroes and Dreamers John Phillip Santos is well suited to serve as a guide for this unit by virtue of his memoir, *Places Left Unfinished at the Time of Creation*, a National Book Award Finalist. This lyrical book weaves together family history, literary references, and reflections to explore a variety of themes. Mr. Santos, the first Mexican American to win a Rhodes scholarship, has also written documentary films.

Contents in Brief

THE BIG ?

Each Unit addresses a BIG Question to enrich exploration of literary concepts and reading strategies.

UNIT 1

Fiction and Nonfiction

Six units per grade explore specific genres while focusing on a Big Question.

Is there a difference between *reality* and truth?

Each unit develops reading and literary skills, teaching them to mastery.

Selection Choices

Leveled selection pairs let you choose text that is appropriate for your students' abilities without skipping essential skills.

Selection Choices

Grammar, Writing, and Activities link to selection content.

Frequent progress monitoring catches small learning problems before they become big ones.

PHLit Online!
www.PHLitOnline.com

Interactive resources provide personalized instruction and activities online.

UNIT 1

Fiction and Nonfiction

Test Practice allows you to confirm skill mastery twice per unit

THE BIG ?

Program pacing allows for 3, 6, or 9-week intervals.

Skills at a Glance

This page provides a quick look at the skills you will learn and practice in Unit 1.

Reading Skills

Make Predictions
- Use Your Prior Knowledge
- Ask Questions

Cause and Effect
- Reflect on Key Details
- Reread

Informational Reading
- Analyze Structure and Format
- Evaluate Sources

Literary Analysis

Plot and Foreshadowing
Author's Perspective
Comparing Style
Conflict and Resolution
Author's Purpose
Comparing Irony and Paradox

Vocabulary

Big Question Vocabulary
Prefixes: *pro-*, *super-*, *inter-*, *ab-*
Roots: *-cred-*, *-strict-*, *-ver-*, *-ven-*
Using a Dictionary and Thesaurus
Independent Reading

Grammar

Common and Proper Nouns
Abstract and Concrete Nouns
Using Possessive Nouns Correctly
Personal Pronouns
Relative Pronouns
Revising Pronoun-Antecedent Agreement

Writing

Writing About the Big Question
Sequel
Description
Anecdote
Proposal
Timed Writing
Writing Workshop: Autobiographical Narrative
Writing Workshop: Exposition: Cause-and-Effect Essay

Listening and Speaking

Interview
Problem-Solving Group
Analyzing Media Presentations

Research and Technology

Daily Observation Journal
Spreadsheet

UNIT 2

Short Stories

A Big Question drives instruction, shaping the unit around a critical issue.

Award-winning authors introduce genres and guide students through key literary and writing concepts.

Can progress be made without conflict?

Grant Wiggins, author of *Understanding By Design*, worked with the Pearson development team to identify the Big Questions that drive the instruction in this program.

Leveled selections let you teach skills with either text.

Informational Texts appears twice per unit.

PHLit Online! www.PHLitOnline.com

Interactive resources provide personalized instruction and activities online.

UNIT 2

Short Stories

Skills at a Glance

This page provides a quick look at the skills you will learn and practice in Unit 2.

Reading Skills

Make Inferences

- Use Your Own Prior Knowledge and Experience
- Read On

Draw Conclusions

- Recognize Key Details
- Identify Patterns

Informational Reading

- Analyze Texts to Extend Ideas
- Paraphrase

Literary Analysis

- Character and Characterization
- Setting
- Comparing Points of View
- Theme
- Symbolism and Allegory
- Comparing Tone
- Independent Reading

Vocabulary

- Big Question Vocabulary
- Prefixes: *dis-*, *com-*
- Suffixes: *-ence*, *-able*, *-ity*, *-ic*, *-tion*, *-id*
- Word Origins

Grammar

- The Principal Parts of Regular Verbs
- Irregular Verbs
- Revising to Apply Consistent Verb Tense
- Action and Linking Verbs
- Active and Passive Voice
- Subject-Verb Agreement

Writing

- Writing About the Big Question
- Retelling
- Letter / Book Review
- Character Analysis
- Narrative
- Timed Writing
- Writing Workshop: Narration: Short Story
- Writing Workshop: Exposition: Problem-and-Solution Essay

Listening and Speaking

- Oral Reading
- Group Discussion
- Viewing and Evaluating a Speech

Research and Technology

- Report on Sources
- Research Summary

UNIT 3

Types of Nonfiction

Introducing the Big Question features academic vocabulary that is reinforced throughout the unit.

What kind of *knowledge* changes our lives?

Selection Choices

Selection Choices

Assessment practice includes writing on demand.

Informational Texts: Real-Life Reading

Informational Texts present nonfiction with warranties, contracts, editorials, Web sites, and other real-life readings.

Writer's Toolbox focuses on the Six Traits of writing.

Literature in Context notes provide point-of-use cross curricular nonfiction links to literature.

All program resources are available online for classroom presentation or individual study.

PHLit Online! www.PHLitOnline.com

Interactive resources provide personalized instruction and activities online.

UNIT 3 Types of Nonfiction

Informational texts include test practice.

Skills at a Glance

This page provides a quick look at the skills you will learn and practice in Unit 3.

Reading Skills

Main Idea
- Summarize
- Ask Questions

Evaluate Persuasion
- Persuasive Techniques
- Distinguish Between Fact and Opinion

Informational Reading
- Follow and Critique Technical Directions
- Analyze Text Structures

Literary Analysis

Expository Essay
Reflective Essay
Comparing Humorous Writing
Persuasive Writing and Rhetorical Devices
Analytic and Interpretive Essays
Comparing Authors' Purposes
Independent Reading

Vocabulary

Big Question Vocabulary
Prefixes: *suc-, para-, em-, im-*
Roots: *-tact-, -tang-, -fig-, -scend-, -jur-*
Words With Multiple Meanings

Grammar

Direct and Indirect Objects
Subject Complements
Revising to Combine Short Sentences
Degrees of Adverbs
Degrees of Adjectives
Revising to Create Parallelism

Writing

Writing About the Big Question
Business Letter
Memoir
Letter
Critique
Timed Writing
Writing Workshop: Persuasion: Letter to the Editor
Writing Workshop: Persuasion: Persuasive Essay

Listening and Speaking

Humorous Persuasive Speech
Oral Recollection
Debate
Delivering a Persuasive Speech

Research and Technology

Cover Letter and Résumé

UNIT 4

Poetry

Does all *communication* serve a positive purpose?

Selection Choices

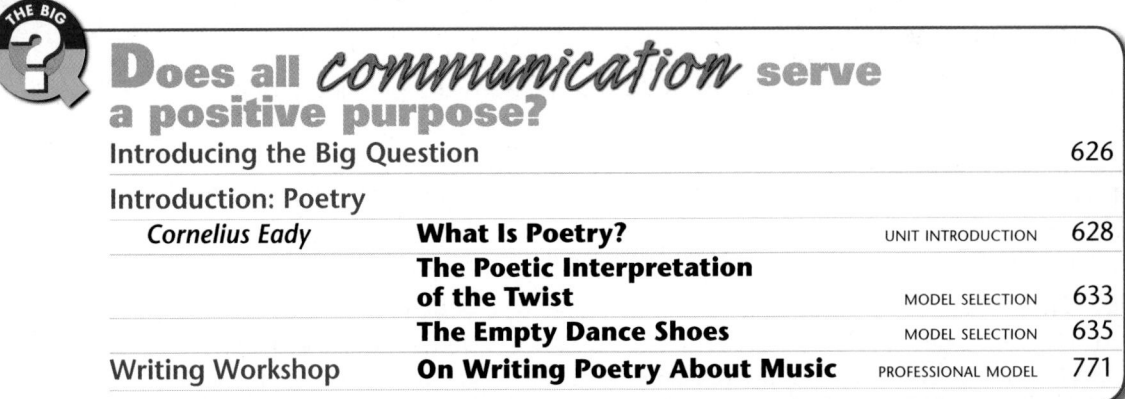

Poetry is organized in collections to allow students to practice skills with either group.

Selection Choices

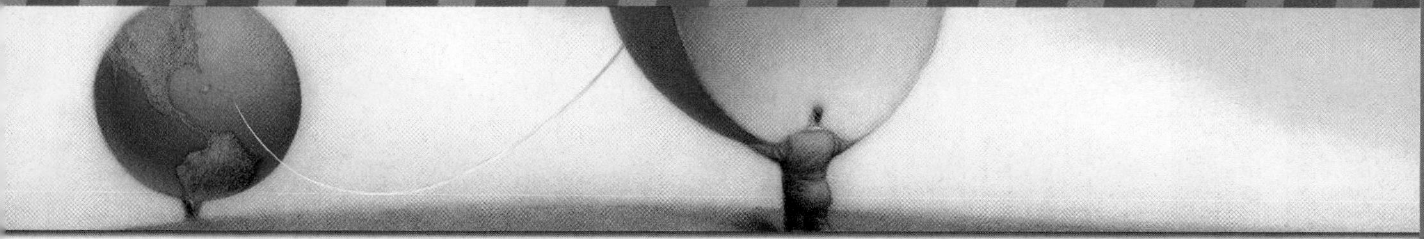

A perfect mix of classic and contemporary selections provide a rich variety of choices.

PHLit Online! www.PHLitOnline.com

Interactive resources provide personalized instruction and activities online.

UNIT 4

Poetry

Selection Choices

Informational Texts provide support for prompt-based writing, including a planning guide for students.

THE BIG ?

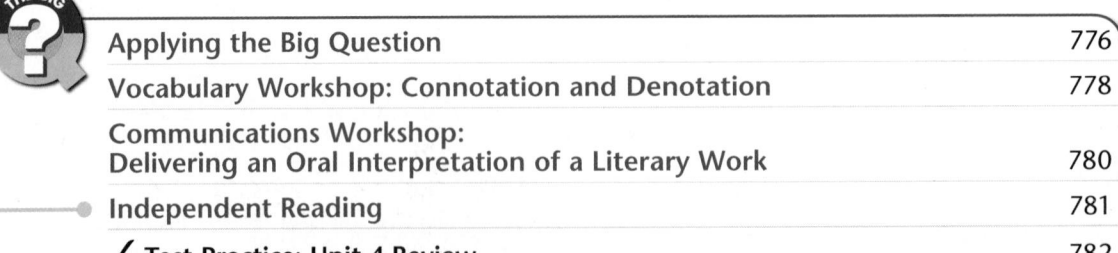

Each unit includes leveled titles for independent reading or literature circles.

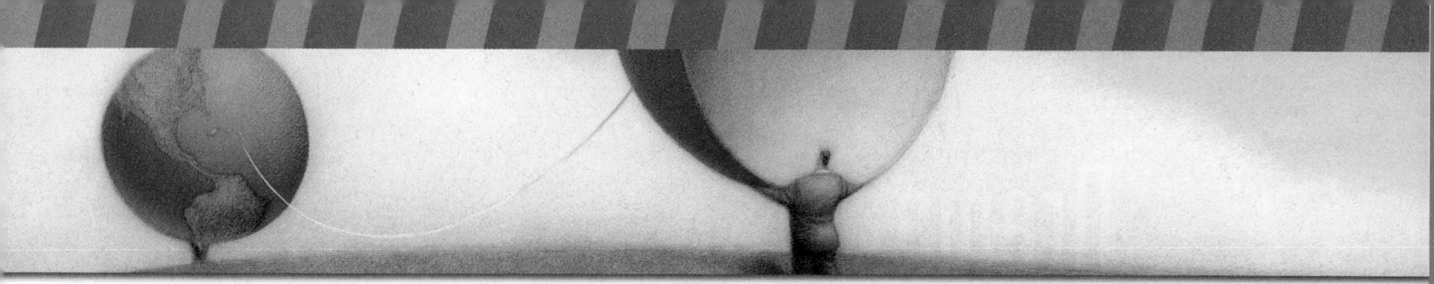

Skills at a Glance

This page provides a quick look at the skills you will learn and practice in Unit 4. The abbreviations listed after each skill refer to your state's corresponding language arts standards. You will find a more detailed description of your language arts standards throughout this book.

Reading Skills

Read Fluently
- Adjust Your Reading Rate
- Preview

Paraphrase
- Picture the Imagery
- Break Down Long Sentences

Informational Reading
- Make Predictions: Purpose
- Synthesize: Make Generalizations

Literary Analysis

- The Speaker in Poetry
- Poetic Forms
- Comparing Tone and Mood
- Figurative Language
- Sound Devices
- Comparing Theme
- Independent Reading

Vocabulary

- Big Question Vocabulary
- Prefixes: *fore-*, *re-*
- Suffixes: *-ary*, *-ous*, *-or*, *-ial*
- Roots: *-lun-*, *-temp-*
- Connotation and Denotation

Grammar

- Prepositions and Prepositional Phrases
- Direct Objects
- Revising to Vary Sentence Patterns
- Prepositional Phrases
- Infinitives
- Revising Common Usage Problems

Writing

- Writing About the Big Question
- Lyric Poem
- Tanka
- Critical Essay
- Poems
- Timed Writing
- Writing Workshop: Description: Descriptive Essay
- Writing Workshop: Analytic Response to Literature

Listening and Speaking

- Oral Interpretation
- Poetry Reading Discussion
- Delivering an Oral Interpretation of a Literary Work

Research and Technology

- Literary History Report
- Visual Arts Presentation

UNIT 5

Drama

THE BIG ?

To what extent does *experience* determine what we perceive?

Featured unit author presents writing strategies.

UNIT 5

Drama

Writing Workshop supports writing process instructions.

Skills Workshops provide practice with key language arts standards.

Skills at a Glance

This page provides a quick look at the skills you will learn and practice in Unit 5.

Reading Skills

Summarize
- Retell
- Take Notes

Reading Shakespearean Drama
- Use Text Aids
- Paraphrase
- Analyze Imagery
- Read Between the Lines
- Compare and Contrast Characters

Informational Reading
- Synthesize: Connect Ideas
- Analyze Workplace Documents

Literary Analysis

- Protagonist and Antagonist
- Greek Tragedies
- Comparing Universal and Culturally Specific Themes
- Shakespeare's Tragedies
- Blank Verse
- Dramatic Speeches
- External and Internal Conflict
- Tragic Heroes
- Comparing Character Motivation

Vocabulary

- Big Question Vocabulary
- Prefixes: *en-*
- Suffixes: *-ile*
- Roots: *-dict-*, *-fer-*, *-spect-*, *-sum-*, *-stru-*
- Borrowed and Foreign Words

Grammar

- Participles and Gerunds
- Independent and Subordinate Clauses
- Revising to Combine Sentences With Verbal Phrases
- Absolutes and Absolute Phrases
- Revising to Combine Sentences Using Adverb Clauses

Writing

- Writing About the Big Question
- Essay
- Reflective Essay
- Editorial
- Obituary
- Timed Writing
- Writing Workshop: Narration: Reflective Essay
- Writing Workshop: Research Writing: Research Report

Listening and Speaking

- Oral Report
- Mock Trial
- Dramatic Reading
- Group Screening

Research and Technology

- Women's History Report
- Advertising Poster
- Multimedia Presentation
- Delivering a Multimedia Presentation of a Research Report

UNIT 6

Themes in Literature: Heroes and Dreamers

THE BIG ? Can anyone be a *hero?*

Selection Choices

Selection Choices

Informational Texts: Real-Life Reading

PHLit Online!
www.PHLitOnline.com

Interactive resources provide personalized instruction and activities online.

UNIT 6

Themes in Literature: Heroes and Dreamers

Comparing Literary Works features support genre and style study.

THE BIG ?

Skills at a Glance

This page provides a quick look at the skills you will learn and practice in Unit 6.

Reading Skills

Analyze Cultural Context

Generate Questions

Acquire Background Knowledge

Compare Worldviews

Identify Details and Draw a Conclusion

Compare Worldview: Compare and Contrast

Informational Reading

Generate Questions

Critique Generalizations and Evidence

Literary Analysis

Myths

Epic and Epic Hero

Comparing Archetypal Narrative Patterns

Legends and Legendary Heroes

Parody

Comparing Themes and Worldviews

Independent Reading

Vocabulary

Big Question Vocabulary

Prefixes: *multi-*, *ex-*

Suffixes: *-ive*, *-tude*, *-ate*, *-ment*

Roots: *-dur-*, *-fus-*

Idioms, Jargon, and Technical Terms

Grammar

Simple and Compound Sentences

Complex and Compound-Complex Sentences

Revising to Correct Fragments and Run-on Sentences

Commas and Dashes

Semicolons, Colons, and Ellipsis Points

Revising to Vary Sentence Structure and Length

Writing

Writing About the Big Question

Myth

Newspaper Report

Script

Parody

Timed Writing

Writing Workshop: Technical Document

Writing Workshop: Comparison-and-Contrast Essay

Listening and Speaking

Retelling

Improvised Dialogue

Comparing Media Coverage

Research and Technology

Influences Chart

Biographical Brochure

Selections by Reading Skill

▶ Unit 1

▶ Unit 2

Unit 3

Main Idea

Summarize

Main Idea

Ask Questions

Evaluate Persuasion

Persuasive Techniques

Evaluate Persuasion

Distinguish Between Fact and Opinion

Unit 4

Read Fluently

Adjust Your Reading Rate

Read Fluently

Preview

(Continued on the next page)

Selections by Reading Skill

▶ Unit 4

▶ Unit 5

(Continued on the next page)

▶ Unit 5

▶ Unit 6

Nonfiction and Informational Texts

Reading Informational Materials

Additional Nonfiction

Literature in Context—Reading in the Content Areas

Comparing Literary Works

Comparing Style

Comparing Irony and Paradox

Comparing Points of View

Comparing Tone

Comparing Humorous Writing

Comparing Authors' Purposes

Comparing Tone and Mood

Comparing Theme

Comparing Universal and Culturally Specific Themes

Comparing Character Motivation

Comparing Archetypal Narrative Patterns

Comparing Themes and Worldviews

Skills Workshops

Writing Workshops

Vocabulary Workshops

Communications Workshops

Skills Navigator Overview

Unit	Featured Unit Author	Assessment	Informational Texts
1. Fiction and Nonfiction	**Susan Vreeland,** pp. 4–27, 203	**Test Practice: Unit Review,** pp. 214–219	**Feature Article/Newsletter:** Analyze Structure and Format, p. 90 **Web Site/Primary Source:** Evaluate Sources, p. 182
2. Short Stories	**C.J. Cherryh,** pp. 224–337, 423	**Test Practice: Unit Review,** pp. 434–439	**Technical Article/News Release:** Analyze Texts to Extend Ideas, p. 298 **Newspaper Editorial/Primary Source:** Paraphrase to Conect Ideas, p. 402
3. Essays	**Eric Weihenmayer,** pp. 444–459, 607	**Test Practice: Unit Review,** pp. 618–623	**Technical Directions/User's Guide:** Follow and Critique Technical Directions, p. 512 **Research Source/Course Catalog:** Analyze Text Structure, p. 578
4. Poetry	**Cornelius Eady,** pp. 628–637, 771	**Test Practice: Unit Review,** pp. 782–787	**Signs/Web Site:** Make Predictions, p. 694 **Atlas Entry/Magazine Article:** Make Generalizations, p. 752
5. Drama	**David Henry Hwang,** pp. 792–807, 1024	**Test Practice: Unit Review,** pp. 1038–1043	**Drama Reviews:** Synthesize: Connect Ideas, p. 864 **Job Application/Public Document:** Analyze Workplace Documents, p. 1008
6. Themes in Literature	**John Phillip Santos,** pp. 1048–1061, 1245	**Test Practice: Unit Review,** pp. 1256–1261	**Interview/Public Document:** Generate Questions, p. 1122 **Book Review/Movie Review:** Critique Generalizations and Evidence, p. 1222

PHLit Online!
www.PHLitOnline.com

• Big Question Video • Vocabulary Central • BQ Tunes	**PHLitOnline** **From the Author's Desk Video** Bring real writers into your classroom	**PHLitOnline** Interactive Online Test Practice	

Writing Workshop	Vocabulary Workshop	Communications Workshop
Autobiographical Narrative, pp. 57, 87, 108 **Work in Progress:** pp. 57, 87, 108–113 **Cause-and-Effect Essay,** pp. 151, 179, 200–207 **Work in Progress:** pp. 151, 179	**Using a Dictionary and Thesaurus,** pp. 210–211	**Analyzing Media Presentations,** p. 212
Short Story, pp. 267, 328–333 **Work in Progress:** pp. 267, 295, 328 **Problem-and-Solution Essay,** pp. 367, 399, 420–427 **Work in Progress:** pp. 367, 399, 420	**Word Origins,** pp. 430–431	**Viewing and Evaluating a Speech,** p. 432
Letter to the Editor, pp. 532–537 **Work in Progress:** pp. 532–537 **Persuasive Essay,** pp. 605–611 **Work in Progress:** p. 604	**Words with Multiple Meanings,** pp. 614–615	**Delivering a Persuasive Speech,** p. 616
Descriptive Essay, pp. 708–713 **Work in Progress:** pp. 669, 691 **Analytic Response to Literature,** pp. 768–775 **Work in Progress:** pp. 731, 749	**Connotation and Denotation,** pp. 778–779	**Delivering an Oral Interpretation of a Literary Work,** p. 780
Reflective Essay, p. 810 **Work in Progress:** pp. 741, 793, 810 **Research Report,** p. 942 **Work in Progress:** p. 942	**Borrowed and Foreign Words,** pp. 1034–1035	**Delivering a Multimedia Presentation,** p. 1036
Technical Document, pp. 1146–1151 **Work in Progress:** pp. 1089, 1119 **Comparison-and-Contrast Essay,** pp. 1242–1249 **Work in Progress:** pp. 1187, 1219	**Idioms, Jargon, and Technical Terms,** pp. 1252–1253	**Comparing Media Coverage,** p. 1254

PHLitOnline **Essay Scorer:** score essays in seconds	**PHLitOnline** Vocabulary Central: • Games • Audio • Flash cards • Images	

Unit 1: Fiction and Nonfiction

		Selection	Page	Reading Skill	Literary Analysis	Word Study
UNIT INTRO		**Magdalena Looking from *Girl in Hyacinth Blue*** Susan Vreeland	9		**Fiction and Nonfiction,** pp. 4–8, 20, 27	
		Artful Research Susan Vreeland	21			
READING FOCUS **PREDICTION**	MA	**The Monkey's Paw** W.W. Jacobs	32	**Using Prior Knowledge to Make Predictions,** pp. 29, 36, 39, 43, 48, 51, 52, 55 **UR** pp. 36, 54	**Plot,** pp. 29, 33, 35, 37, 38, 40, 42, 43, 49, 54, 55 **UR** pp. 35, 53	**Latin root *-cred-*,** pp. 30, 43 **Latin root *-strict-*,** pp. 44, 55 **UR** pp. 37, 55
	MC	**The Leap** Louise Erdrich	46			
	MA	**from *Swimming to Antarctica*** Lynne Cox	62	**Using Prior Knowledge to Make Predictions,** pp. 59, 63, 65, 68, 72, 75, 82, 85 **UR** pp. 75, 93	**Author's Perspective,** pp. 59, 63, 64, 65, 67, 69, 71, 72, 74, 75, 80, 85 **UR** pp. 74, 92	**Latin prefix *pro-*,** pp. 60, 75 **Latin prefix *super-*,** pp. 76, 85 **UR** pp. 76, 94
	MC	**Occupation: Conductorette** Maya Angelou	79			
		Informational Texts Feature Article/Newsletter	90	**Analyze Structure and Format,** p. 90		
		Comparing Literary Works **Marian Anderson, Famous Concert Singer** Langston Hughes	96		**Comparing Literary Works: Comparing Style,** pp. 96, 107 **UR** p. 113	
		Tepeyac Sandra Cisneros	104			
READING FOCUS **CAUSE AND EFFECT**	MA	**Contents of the Dead Man's Pocket** Jack Finney	118	**Reflecting on Key Details to Analyze Cause and Effect,** pp. 115, 120, 122, 125, 126, 128, 131, 132, 134, 135, 141, 147, 149 **UR** pp. 140, 158	**Conflict and Resolution,** pp. 115, 119, 121, 125, 127, 130, 133, 134, 135, 140, 144, 146, 149 **UR** pp. 139, 157	**Latin root *-ver-*,** pp. 116, 135 **Latin root *-ven-*,** pp. 136, 149 **UR** pp. 141, 159
	MC	**Games at Twilight** Anita Desai	139			
	MA	**The Marginal World** Rachel Carson	156	**Reflecting on Key Details to Analyze Cause and Effect,** pp. 153, 159, 162, 165, 168, 173, 175, 176, 177 **UR** pp. 179, 197	**Author's Purpose,** pp. 153, 158, 160, 164, 165, 168, 171, 176, 177 **UR** pp. 178, 196	**Latin prefix *inter-*,** pp. 154, 165 **Latin prefix *ob-*,** pp. 166, 177 **UR** pp. 180, 198
	MC	**Making History with Vitamin C** Penny LeCouteur and Jay Burreson	168			
		Informational Texts Web Site/Primary Source	182	**Evaluate Credibility of Sources,** p. 182		
		Comparing Literary Works **Like the Sun** R.K. Narayan	190		**Comparing Literary Works: Irony and Paradox,** pp. 188, 192, 194, 197, 199	
		The Open Window Saki	195			

Key: UR: *Unit Resources* **MA:** More Accessible **MC:** More Challenging
See Accessibility at a Glance chart on Time and Resource Manager

Writing	Grammar	Extension Activity	Assessment
Writing Workshop: Narration: Autobiographical Narrative, pp. 57, 87, 108–113 **Writing Workshop:** Cause-and-Effect Essay, pp. 151, 179, 200–207		• **Research the Author: Bulletin Board Display,** p. 27	**Selection Tests, UR** pp. 24–29
Sequel, p. 57 **UR** p. 58 **Writing Workshop:** Work in Progress: Prewriting for Autobiographical Narrative, p. 57	**Common Nouns and Proper Nouns,** p. 56 **UR** p. 57	• **Listening and Speaking: Interview,** p. 57 **UR** p. 59	**Selection Tests, UR** pp. 42–47, 63–68
Description, p. 87 **UR** p. 97 **Writing Workshop:** Work in Progress: Prewriting for Autobiographical Narrative, p. 87	**Abstract and Concrete Nouns,** p. 86 **UR** p. 96	• **Research and Technology: Daily Observation Journal,** p. 87 **UR** p. 98	**Test Practice: Reading,** pp. 88–89 **Selection Tests, UR** pp. 81–86, 102–107
			Test Practice: Informational Texts, p. 95
Writing to Compare Styles, p. 107			**Selection Tests, UR** pp. 119–124
Anecdote, p. 151 **UR** p. 162 **Writing Workshop:** Work in Progress: Prewriting for Cause-and-Effect Essay, p. 151	**Personal Pronouns,** p. 150; **UR** p. 161	• **Listening and Speaking:** Problem-Solving Group, p. 151; **UR** p. 163	**Selection Tests, UR** pp. 167–172
Documentary Proposal, p. 179 **UR** p. 201 **Writing Workshop:** Work in Progress: Prewriting for Cause and Effect, p. 179	**Relative Pronouns,** p. 178 **UR** p. 200	• **Research and Technology:** Spreadsheets, p. 179 **UR** p. 202	**Test Practice: Reading,** pp. 180–181 **Selection Tests, UR** pp. 206–211
			Test Practice: Informational Texts, p. 187
Writing to Compare Literary Works, p. 199			**Selection Tests, UR** pp. 223–228

All selections are supported in the *Reader's Notebooks.*

Unit 2: Short Stories

		Selection	Page	Reading Skill	Literary Analysis	Word Study
UNIT INTRO		**The Threads of Time** C. J. Cherryh	229		**Short Stories,** pp. 224–228, 237	
READING FOCUS **INFERENCES**	MA	**A Visit to Grandmother** William Melvin Kelley	243	**Relate to Your Experiences to Make Inferences,** pp. 239, 244, 250, 253, 259, 262, 265 **UR** pp. 29, 47	**Character and Characterization,** pp. 239, 244, 245, 248, 251, 253, 258, 260, 262, 264, 265 **UR** pp. 28, 46	**Latin suffix *-ence*,** pp. 240, 253 **Latin suffix *-able*,** pp. 254, 265 **UR** pp. 30, 48
	MC	**A Problem** Anton Chekhov	256			
	MA	**The Street of the Cañon** Josephina Niggli	272	**Reading Ahead to Confirm Inferences,** pp. 269, 273, 277, 280, 281, 286, 291, 293 **UR** pp. 68, 86	**Setting,** pp. 269, 273, 278, 281, 286, 288, 293 **UR** pp. 67, 85	**Latin suffix *-ity*,** pp. 270, 281 **Greek suffix *-ic*,** pp. 282, 293 **UR** pp. 69, 87
	MC	**There Will Come Soft Rains** Ray Bradbury	284			
		Informational Texts Technical Article/News Release	298	**Analyze Texts to Extend Ideas,** p. 298		
		Comparing Literary Works **One Thousand Dollars** O. Henry **By the Waters of Babylon** Stephen Vincent Benét	308 314		**Comparing Literary Works: Point of View,** pp. 306, 309, 310, 312, 313, 315, 316, 317, 318,	
READING FOCUS **DRAWING CONCLUSIONS**	MA	**How Much Land Does a Man Need?** Leo Tolstoy	338	**Drawing Conclusions,** pp. 335, 341, 342, 343, 347, 348, 351, 352, 355, 361, 365 **UR** pp. 133, 151	**Theme and Universal,** pp. 335, 339, 344, 353, 355, 359, 365 **UR** pp. 132, 150	**Latin prefix *dis-*,** pp. 336, 356 **Latin prefix *com-*,** p. 365 **UR** pp. 134, 152
	MC	**Civil Peace** Chinua Achebe	358			
	MA	**The Masque of the Red Death** Edgar Allan Poe	372	**Drawing Conclusions and Identifying Patterns,** pp. 369, 373, 374, 377, 380, 381, 386, 390, 394, 397 **UR** pp. 172, 190	**Symbolism and Allegory,** pp. 369, 380, 381, 385, 389, 392, 397 **UR** pp. 171, 189	**Latin suffix *-tion*** pp. 370, 381 **Latin suffix *-id*,** pp. 382, 397 **UR** pp. 173, 191
	MC	**The Garden of Stubborn Cats** Italo Calvino	384			
		Informational Texts Newspaper Editorial/ Primary Source	403	**Paraphrase to Connect Ideas,** p. 402		
		Comparing Literary Works **The Censors** Luisa Valenzuela **The Leader in the MIrror** Pat Mora	410 414		**Comparing Literary Works: Tone in Fiction and Nonfiction,** pp. 408, 411, 412, 413, 415, 417, 419	

Key: UR: *Unit Resources* **MA:** More Accessible **MC:** More Challenging
See Accessibility at a Glance chart on Time and Resource Manager

Writing	Grammar	Extension Activity	Assessment
Writing Workshop: Short Story, pp. 267, 295, 328–333 **Writing Workshop:** Problem-and-Solution Essay, pp. 367, 399, 420–427		• **Research the Author: Report,** p. 237	**Selection Tests, UR** pp. 18–22
Retellings, p. 267 **UR** p. 51 **Writing Workshop:** Work in Progress: Prewriting for a Short Story, p. 267	**Regular Verbs,** p. 266 **UR** p. 50	• **Research and Technology: Report of Sources,** p. 267 **UR** p. 52	**Selection Tests, UR** pp. 56–61
Letter to a Friend, p. 295 **UR** p. 90 **Writing Workshop:** Work in Progress: Prewriting for Narration, p. 295	**Irregular Verbs,** p. 294 **UR** p. 89	• **Listening and Speaking: Oral Reading,** p. 295 **UR** p. 91	**Test Practice: Reading,** pp. 296–297 **Selection Tests, UR** pp. 95–100
			Test Practice: Informational Texts, p. 305
Writing to Compare Points of View, p. 327			**Selection Tests, UR** pp. 112–117
Character Analysis, p. 367 **UR** p. 155 **Writing Workshop:** Work in Progress: Prewriting for Problem-and-Solution Essay, p. 367	**Action and Linking Verbs,** p. 366 **UR** p. 154	• **Listening and Speaking: Group Discussion,** p. 367 **UR** p. 156	**Selection Tests, UR** pp. 160–165
Narrative, p. 399 **UR** p. 194 **Writing Workshop:** Work in Progress: Prewriting for Problem-and-Solution Essay, p. 399	**Active and Passive Voice,** p. 398 **UR** p. 193	• **Research and Technology: Research Summary,** p. 399 **UR** p. 195	**Test Practice: Reading,** pp. 400–401 **Selection Tests, UR** pp. 199–204
			Test Practice: Informational Texts, p. 407
Writing to Compare Tone, p. 419			**Selection Tests, UR** pp. 216–221

All selections are supported in the *Reader's Notebooks.*

Unit 3: Essays

		Selection	Page	Reading Skill	Literary Analysis	Word Study
UNIT INTRO		from Everest from *Touch the Top of the World* Eric Weihenmayer	449		**Nonfiction,** pp. 444–448, 459	
READING FOCUS MAIN IDEA	MA	**The Spider and the Wasp** Alexander Petrunkevitch	464	**Main Idea,** pp. 461, 466, 470, 471, 477, 479, 483 **UR** pp. 29, 47	**Expository Essay,** pp. 461, 465, 469, 471, 480, 483 **UR** pp. 28, 46	**Latin roots *-tact-* and *-tang-*,** pp. 462, 471 **Latin root *-fig-*,** pp. 472, 483 **UR** pp. 30, 48
	MC	**from *Longitude*** Dava Sobel	474			
	MA	**The Sun Parlor** Dorothy West	490	**Analyze Main Ideas and Supporting Details,** pp. 487, 492, 494, 497, 502, 504, 507 **UR** pp. 68, 86	**Reflective Essay,** pp. 487, 492, 494, 496, 497, 502, 503, 505, 507 **UR** pp. 67, 85	**Latin prefix *suc-*,** pp. 488, 497 **Greek prefix *para-*,** p. 498 **UR** pp. 69, 87
	MC	**from In Commemoration: *One Million Volumes*** Rudolfo Anaya	500			
		Informational Texts Technical Directions/ User's Guide	512	**Follow and Critique Technical Directions,** p. 512		
		Comparing Literary Works **The Weather of New England** Mark Twain **The Dog That Bit People** James Thurber	520 525		**Comparing Literary Works: Humorous Writing,** pp. 518, 521, 523, 524, 526, 529, 530, 531	
READING FOCUS PREDICTION	MA	**Keep Memory Alive** Elie Wiesel	542	**Evaluate Persuasion,** pp. 539, 545, 552, 553 **UR** pp. 133, 151	**Persuasive Writing,** pp. 539, 543, 545, 549, 553 **UR** pp. 132, 150	**Latin root *-scend-*,** pp. 540, 545 **Latin root *-jur-*,** p. 546 **UR** pp. 134, 152
	MC	**from Nobel Lecture** Alexander Solzhenitsyn	548			
	MA	**The American Idea** Theodore H. White	560	**Evaluate Persuasion,** pp. 557, 562, 565, 573 **UR** pp. 172, 190	**Analytic and Interpretive Essays,** pp. 557, 561, 565, 569, 573 **UR** pp. 171, 189	**Greek prefix *em-*,** pp. 558, 565 **Latin prefix *im-*,** pp. 566, 573 **UR** pp. 173, 191
	MC	**What Makes a Degas a Degas?** Richard Mühlberger	568			
		Informational Texts Research Source/Course Catalog	578	**Analyzing Text Structures,** p. 578		
		Comparing Literary Works **from *Desert Exile: The Uprooting of a Japanese-American Family*** Yoshiko Uchida **from *The Way to Rainy Mountain*** N. Scott Momaday	586 595		**Comparing Literary Works: Author's Purpose,** pp. 584, 587, 588, 589, 590, 593, 594, 597, 598, 600, 601, 602,	

Key: UR: *Unit Resources* **MA:** More Accessible **MC:** More Challenging
See Accessibility at a Glance chart on Time and Resource Manager

Writing	Grammar	Extension Activity	Assessment
Writing Workshop: Persuasion: Letter to the Editor, pp. 532–537		• **Research the Author: Write a Report,** p. 459	**Selection Tests, UR** pp. 18–22
Business Letter, p. 485 **UR** p. 51 **Writing Workshop:** Work in Progress: Prewriting for a Letter to the Editor, p. 485	**Direct and Indirect Objects,** p. 484 **UR** p. 50	• **Listening and Speaking: Humorous Persuasive Speech,** pp. 435, 445 **UR** p. 52	**Selection Tests, UR** pp. 56–61
Brief Memoir, p. 509 **UR** p. 90 **Writing Workshop:** Work in Progress: Prewriting for a Letter to the Editor, p. 509	**Predicate Nominatives and Predicate Adjectives,** p. 508 **UR** p. 89	• **Listening and Speaking: Oral Recollection,** p. 509 **UR** p. 91	**Test Practice: Reading,** pp. 510–511 **Selection Tests, UR** pp. 95–100
			Test Practice: Informational Texts, pp. 517–518
Writing to Compare Humorous Writing, p. 531			**Selection Tests, UR** pp. 112–117
Letter, p. 555 **UR** p. 155 **Writing Workshop:** Work in Progress: Prewriting for Persuasive Essay, p. 555	**Degrees of Adverbs,** p. 554 **UR** p. 154	• **Listening and Speaking: Debate,** p. 555 **UR** p. 156	**Selection Tests, UR** pp. 160–165
Critique p. 575 **UR** p. 194 **Writing Workshop:** Work in Progress: Prewriting for Persuasive Essay, p. 575	**Degrees of Adjectives,** p. 574 **UR** p. 193	• **Research and Technology: Cover Letter and Résumé,** p. 575 **UR** p. 195	**Test Practice: Reading,** pp. 576–577 **Selection Tests, UR** pp. 200–204
			Test Practice: Informational Texts, p. 583
Writing to Compare Author's Purpose, p. 603; **Standards refs**			**Selection Tests, UR** pp. 216–221

All selections are supported in the *Reader's Notebooks.*

Unit 4: Poetry

	Selection	Page	Reading Skill	Literary Analysis	Word Study
UNIT INTRO	**The Poetic Interpretation of the Twist** Cornelius Eady	633		**Exploring Poetry,** pp. 628–632	
	The Empty Dance Shoes Cornelius Eady	635			
READING FOCUS **READING FLUENCY** — MA	**Poetry Collection 1**	642, 649, 650, 652	**Read Fluently,** pp. 639, 644, 650, 653, 655, 665, 667 **UR** pp. 29, 47	**The Speaker in Poetry,** pp. 639, 643, 657, 649, 651, 655, 659, 660, 662, 663, 664, 665, 667 **UR** pp. 28, 46	**Old English prefix *fore-*,** pp. 640, 655 **Latin prefix *re-*,** pp. 656, 667 **UR** pp. 30, 48
MC	**Poetry Collection 2**	658, 659, 664, 665			
MA	**Poetry Collection 1**	677, 679, 680	**Read Fluently,** pp. 673, 679, 681, 688, 689 **UR** pp. 68, 86	**Poetic Forms,** pp. 671, 677, 679, 681, 685, 687, 689; **UR** pp. 67, 85	**Latin root *-lun-*,** pp. 674, 681 **Latin root *-temp-*,** pp. 682, 689 **UR** pp. 69, 87
MC	**Poetry Collection 2**	685, 687, 688			
	Informational Texts Signs/Web Site	694	**Make Predictions: Purpose,** p. 694		
	Comparing Literary Works **Fear** Gabriela Mistral; **The Bean Eaters** Gwendolyn Brooks; **How to React to Familiar Faces** Umberto Eco	702, 703, 704		**Comparing Literary Works: Tone and Mood,** pp. 700, 702, 703, 705, 706, 707; **UR** p. 106	**UR** p. 107
READING FOCUS **PARAPHRASING** — MA	**Poetry Collection 1**	718, 720, 722	**Paraphrase,** pp. 715, 718, 723, 728, 729 **UR** pp. 133, 151	**Figurative Language,** pp. 715, 722, 723, 726, 729 **UR** pp. 132, 150	**Latin suffix *-ous*,** pp. 716, 723 **Latin suffix *-ary*,** pp. 724, 729 **UR** pp. 134, 152
MC	**Poetry Collection 2**	726, 727, 728			
MA	**Poetry Collection 1**	736, 738, 739	**Paraphrase,** pp. 733, 739, 741, 745, 747 **UR** pp. 172, 190	**Sound Devices,** pp. 733, 737, 741, 744, 747 **UR** pp. 171, 189	**Latin suffix *-or*,** pp. 734, 741 **Latin suffix *-ial*,** pp. 742, 747 **UR** pp. 173, 191
MC	**Poetry Collection 2**	744, 745, 746			
	Informational Texts Atlas/Magazine Article	752	**Make Generalizations,** p. 752		
	Comparing Literary Works **Hold Fast Your Dreams** Billy Joel; **All** Bei Dao; **Also All** Shu Ting	760, 764, 765		**Comparing Literary Works: Theme,** pp. 758, 762, 763, 764, 767 **UR** p. 211	

Key: UR: *Unit Resources* **MA:** More Accessible **MC:** More Challenging
See Accessibility at a Glance chart on Time and Resource Manager

Writing	Grammar	Extension Activity	Assessment
Writing Workshop: Description: Descriptive Essay, pp. 708–713 **Writing Workshop:** Analytic Response to Literature, pp. 768–775		• **Research the Author: Annotated Poster,** p. 637	**Selection Tests, UR** pp. 18–22
Lyric Poem, p. 669 **UR** p. 51 **Writing Workshop:** Work in Progress: Prewriting for Descriptive Essay, p. 669	**Prepositions and Prepositional Phrases,** p. 668 **UR** p. 50	• **Listening and Speaking: Oral Interpretation,** p. 669 **UR** p. 52	**Selection Tests, UR** pp. 57–61
Tanka, p. 691 **UR** p. 90 **Writing Workshop:** Work in Progress: Prewriting for Descriptive Essay, p. 691	**Direct Objects,** p. 690 **UR** p. 89	• **Listening and Speaking: Poetry Reading Discussion,** p. 691 **UR** p. 91	**Test Practice: Reading,** pp. 692–693 **Selection Tests, UR** pp. 95–100
Writing to Compare Tone and Mood, p. 707 **UR** p. 108			**Test Practice: Informational Text,** p. 699 **Selection Tests, UR** pp. 112–117
Critical Essay, p. 731; **UR** p. 155 **Writing Workshop:** Work in Progress: Prewriting for an Analytical Response, p. 731	**Prepositional Phrases,** p. 730 **UR** p. 154	• **Research and Technology: Literary History Report,** p. 731 **UR** p. 156	**Selection Tests, UR** pp. 161–165
Poem, p. 749 **UR** p. 194 **Writing Workshop:** Work in Progress: Prewriting for Analytical Response, p. 749	**Infinitives,** p. 748 **UR** p. 193	• **Research and Technology: Visual Arts Presentation,** p. 749 **UR** p. 195	**Test Practice: Reading,** pp. 750–751 **Selection Tests, UR** pp. 199–204
Writing to Compare Theme, p. 767 **UR** p. 212			**Test Practice: Informational Text,** p. 757 **Selection Tests, UR** pp. 216–221

All selections are supported in the *Reader's Notebooks.*

Unit 5: Drama

Focus	Level	Selection	Page	Reading Skill	Literary Analysis	Word Study
UNIT INTRO		*from* **Tibet Through the Red Box** David Henry Hwang	**797**		**Drama,** pp. 792–796	
READING FOCUS **SUMMARY**	MA	**Antigone** Part 1 Sophocles	**814**	**Retelling to Summarize,** pp. 811, 816, 818, 820, 822, 825, 829, 832, 833; **UR** p. 29	**Protagonist and Antagonist,** pp. 811, 815, 816, 820, 822, 826, 827, 830, 833; **UR** p. 28	**Latin root** ***-dict-*,** pp. 812, 833; **UR** p. 30
	MA	**Antigone** Part 2 Sophocles	**839**	**Taking Notes to Summarize,** pp. 837, 840, 845, 855, 859; **UR** p. 50	**Greek Tragedies,** pp. 837, 840, 841, 843, 846, 851, 856, 859; **UR** p. 49	**Latin root** ***-fer-*,** pp. 838, 859 **UR** p. 51
		Informational Texts Drama Reviews	**864**	**Synthesize by Connecting Ideas,** p. 864		
		Comparing Literary Works ***scene from*** **An Enemy of the People** Henrik Ibsen	**870**		**Comparing Literary Works: Comparing Universal and Culturally Specific Themes,** pp. 868, 871, 872, 873, 875, 876, 877	
READING FOCUS **COMPARE AND CONTRAST**	MC	**Julius Caesar** Act I William Shakespeare	**886**	**Using Text Aids,** pp. 887, 894, 897, 902, 904, 907, 910, 913; **UR** p. 97	**Shakespeare's Tragedies,** pp. 887, 897, 900, 902, 909, 913 **UR** p. 96	**Latin suffix** ***-ile*,** pp. 888, 913; **UR** p. 98
	MC	**Julius Caesar** Act II William Shakespeare	**917**	**Paraphrasing when Reading Shakespearean Drama,** pp. 915, 920, 924, 928, 929, 932, 937; **UR** p. 115	**Blank Verse,** pp. 915, 917, 919, 924, 927, 935, 937; **UR** p. 114	**Latin prefix** ***-en*,** pp. 914, 937; **UR** p. 11
	MC	**Julius Caesar** Act III William Shakespeare	**941**	**Analyzing the Imagery,** pp. 939, 945, 946, 948, 950, 956, 957, 959, 960, 961, 962, 963; **UR** p. 133	**Dramatic Speeches,** pp. 939, 941, 947, 948, 949, 950, 952, 953, 955, 963; **UR** p. 132	**Latin root** ***-spect-*,** pp. 938, 963; **UR** p. 134
	MC	**Julius Caesar** Act IV William Shakespeare	**967**	**Reading Between the Lines,** pp. 965, 970, 971, 975, 978, 979, 981 **UR** p. 151	**External and Internal Conflict,** pp. 965, 976, 977, 981, 983; **UR** p. 150	**Latin root** ***-sum-*,** pp. 964, 983; **UR** p. 152
	MC	**Julius Caesar** Act V William Shakespeare	**987**	**Comparing and Contrasting Characters,** pp. 985, 987, 990, 998, 1001; **UR** p. 169	**Tragic Heroes,** pp. 985, 988, 990, 992, 994, 997, 1001 **UR** p. 168	**Latin root** ***-stru-*,** pp. 984, 1001; **UR** p. 170
		Informational Texts Job Application/ Public Document	**1008**	**Analyzing Workplace Documents,** p. 1008		
		Comparing Literary Works ***scene from*** **A Raisin in the Sun** Lorraine Hansberry	**1016**	**Comparing Literary Works: Character Motive,** pp. 1014, 1017, 1019		

Key: UR: *Unit Resources* **MA:** More Accessible **MC:** More Challenging
See Accessibility at a Glance chart on Time and Resource Manager

Writing	Grammar	Extension Activity	Assessment
Writing Workshop: Essay: Reflective Essay, pp. 835, 878–883 **Writing Workshop:** Research Report, pp. 1020–1031		• **Research the Author: Poster,** p. 807	**Selection Tests, UR** pp. 17–22
Reflective Essay p. 835 **UR** p. 33 **Writing Workshop:** Work in Progress: Prewriting for a Reflective Essay, p. 835	**Participles and Participle Phrasing,** p. 834 **UR** p. 32	• **Listening and Speaking: Oral Report,** p. 835; **UR** p. 34	**Selection Tests, UR** p. 38–43
Description, p. 861; **UR** p. 54 **Writing Workshop:** Work in Progress: Prewriting for a Reflective Essay, p. 861	**Independent and Subordinate Clauses,** p. 860 **UR** p. 53	• **Listening and Speaking: Mock Trial,** p. 861 **UR** p. 55	**Test Practice: Reading,** pp. 862–863 **Selection Tests** **UR** pp. 59–64
			Test Practice: Informational Texts, p. 864
Writing to Compare Themes, p. 877			**Selection Tests, UR** pp. 76–81
		• **Listening and Speaking: Dramatic Reading,** p. 1004 **UR** pp. 174–175	**Selection Tests, UR** pp. 103–108
		• **Research and Technology: Women's History Report,** p. 1004; **UR** pp. 174–175	**Selection Tests, UR** pp. 121–126
		• **Research and Technology: Advertising Poster,** p. 1004 **UR** pp. 174–175	**Selection Tests, UR** pp. 139–144
		• **Research and Technology: Multimedia Presentation,** p. 1004; **UR** pp. 174–175	**Selection Tests, UR** pp. 157–162
Editorial, p. 1003; **UR** p. 173 **Obituary,** p. 1003; **UR** p. 173 **Writing Workshop:** Work in Progress: Prewriting for a Research Report, p. 1003	**Absolutes and Absolute Phrases,** p. 1002; **UR** p. 172		**Test Practice: Reading,** pp. 1006–1007 **Selection Tests, UR** pp. 179–184
			Test Practice: Informational Text, p. 1013
Writing to Compare Characters' Motivations, p.1019			**Selection Tests** **UR** pp. 196–201

All selections are supported in the *Reader's Notebooks.*

Unit 6: Themes in Literature

		Selection	Page	Reading Skill	Literary Analysis	Word Study
UNIT INTRO		from ***Places Left Unfinished at the Time of Creation*** John Phillip Santos	**1053**		**Themes in Literature,** pp. 1048–1052, 1061	
READING FOCUS **CULTURAL CONTEXT**	MA	**Prometheus and the First People** Greek Myth retold by Olivia E. Coolidge	**1066**	**Analyze Cultural Context,** pp. 1063, 1067, 1073, 1077, 1082, 1085, 1087 **UR** pp. 29, 47	**Myths,** pp. 1063, 1067, 1072, 1073, 1079, 1080, 1086, 1087 **UR** pp. 28, 46	**Latin root *-dur-*,** pp. 1064, 1073 **Latin root *-fus-*,** pp. 1074, 1087 **UR** pp. 30, 48
	MC	**The Orphan Boy and the Elk Dog** Native American Myth from the Blackfeet Tribe	**1076**			
	MA	**Sundiata, An Epic of Old Mali** D. T. Niane	**1094**	**Analyze Cultural Context,** pp. 1091, 1096, 1097, 1099, 1102, 1104, 1105, 1110, 1113, 1116, 1117 **UR** pp. 68, 86	**Epic and Epic Heroes,** pp. 1091, 1096, 1100, 1103, 1105, 1110, 1111, 1115, 1117 **UR** pp. 67, 85	**Latin suffix *-ive*,** pp. 1092, 1105 **Latin suffix *-tude*,** pp. 1106, 1117 UR pp. 69, 87
	MC	**from the *Ramayana*** R. K. Narayan	**1108**			
		Informational Texts Interview/Public Document	**1122**	**Generate Questions,** p. 1122		
		Comparing Literary Works **Cupid and Psyche** retold by Sally Benson **Ashputtle** Jakob and Wilhelm Grimm	**1130** **1138**		**Comparing Literary Works: Archetypal Narrative Patterns,** pp. 1128, 1131, 1132, 1134, 1136, 1139, 1140, 1143, 1144, 1145 **UR** p. 106	**UR** p. 107
READING FOCUS **WORLD VIEWS**	MC	**Arthur Becomes King of Britain from *The Once and Future King*** T. H. White	**1156**	**Compare Worldviews,** pp. 1153, 1157, 1160, 1163, 1166, 1168, 1169, 1171, 1175, 1177, 1178, 1182, 1185 **UR** pp. 133, 151	**Legends and Legendary Heroes,** pp. 1153, 1158, 1160, 1165, 1167, 1168, 1170, 1171, 1181, 1182, 1184, 1185 **UR** pp. 132, 150	**Latin suffix *-ate*,** pp. 1154, 1171 **Latin suffix *-ment*,** pp. 1172, 1185 **UR** pp. 134, 152
	MA	**Morte d'Arthur** Alfred, Lord Tennyson	**1174**			
	MC	**from *A Connecticut Yankee in King Arthur's Court*** Mark Twain	**1192**	**Compare Worldviews,** pp. 1189, 1193, 1196, 1198, 1203, 1205, 1210, 1212, 1214, 1216, 1217 **UR** pp. 172, 190	**Parody,** pp. 1189, 1194, 1196, 1197, 1200, 1203, 1205, 1209, 1212, 1215, 1217 **UR** pp. 171, 189	**Latin prefix *multi-*,** pp. 1190, 1205 **Latin prefix *ex-*,** pp. 1206, 1217 **UR** pp. 173, 191
	MA	**from *Don Quixote*** Miguel de Cervantes	**1208**			
		Informational Texts Book Review/Movie Review	**1222**	**Critique Generalizations and Evidence,** p. 1222		
		Comparing Literary Works **Damon and Pythias** retold by William F. Russell **Two Friends** Guy de Maupassant	**1230** **1233**		**Comparing Literary Works: Comparing Themes and Worldviews,** pp. 1228, 1230, 1232, 1234, 1236, 1237, 1239, 1240, 1241 **UR** p. 210	**UR** p. 211

Key: UR: *Unit Resources* **MA:** More Accessible **MC:** More Challenging
See Accessibility at a Glance chart on Time and Resource Manager

Writing	Grammar	Extension Activity	Assessment
Writing Workshop: Technical Document, pp. 1146–1151 **Writing Workshop:** Comparison-and-Contrast Essay, pp. 1242–1249		• **Research the Author: Annotated Map,** p. 1061	**Selection Tests, UR** pp. 18–22
Myth, p. 1089 **UR** p. 51 **Writing Workshop:** Work in Progress: Prewriting for a Technical Document, p. 1089	**Simple and Compound Sentences,** p. 1088 **UR** p. 50	• **Listening and Speaking: Retell,** p. 1089 **UR** p. 52	**Selection Tests, UR** pp. 35–40
Newspaper Report, p. 1119 **UR** p. 90 **Writing Workshop:** Work in Progress: Prewriting for a Technical Document, p. 1119	**Complex and Compound-Complex Sentences,** p. 1118 **UR** p. 89	• **Listening and Speaking: Improvised Dialogue,** p. 1119 **UR** p. 91	**Test Practice: Reading,** pp. 1120–1121 **Selection Tests, UR** pp. 95–100
			Test Practice: Informational Text, p. 1127
Writing to Compare Archetypal Narrative Patterns, p. 1145 **UR** p. 108			**Selection Tests, UR** pp. 112–117
Script, p. 1187 **UR** p. 155 **Writing Workshop:** Work in Progress: Prewriting for a Comparison-and-Contrast Essay, p. 1187	**Commas and Dashes,** p. 1186 **UR** p. 154	• **Research and Technology: "Influences" Chart,** p. 1187 **UR** p. 156	**Selection Tests, UR** pp. 160–165
Parody, p. 1219 **UR** p. 194 **Writing Workshop:** Work in Progress: Prewriting for a Comparison-and-Contrast Essay, p. 1219	**Semicolons, Colons, and Ellipsis Points,** p. 1218 **UR** p. 193	• **Research and Technology: Biographical Brochure,** p. 1219 **UR** p. 195	**Test Practice: Reading,** pp. 1220–1221 **Selection Tests, UR** pp. 199–204
			Test Practice: Informational Text, p. 1227
Writing to Compare Theme and Worldview, p. 1241 **UR** p. 212			**Selection Tests, UR** pp. 216–221

All selections are supported in the *Reader's Notebooks.*

Research Bibliography

Reading and Concept Driven Instruction

Alexander, Patricia A., and Tamara Jetton. "Learning from Text: A Multidimensional and Developmental Perspective." *Handbook of Reading Research,* vol. 3, eds. M. L. Kamil, P. B. Mosenthal, P. D. Pearson, and R. Barr, 285–310. Mahwah, NJ: Lawrence Erlbaum Associates, 2000.

Blau, Sheridan. *The Literature Workshop: Teaching Texts and Their Readers.* Portsmouth, ME: Heinemann Press, 2003.

Buehl, Doug, Judith L. Irvin, and Ronald M. Klemp. *Reading and the High School Student: Strategies to Enhance Literacy.* Boston, MA: Allyn and Bacon, 2007.

Buehl, Doug, Judith L. Irvin, and Barbara J. Radcliffe. *Strategies to Enhance Literacy and Learning in Middle School Content Area Classrooms.* Boston, MA: Allyn and Bacon, 2007.

Daniels, Harvey. *Literature Circles: Voice and Choice in Book Clubs and Reading Groups.* Portland, ME: Stenhouse Publishers, 2002.

———*Mini-Lessons for Literature Circles.* Portsmouth, ME: Heinemann Press, 2005.

Gallagher, Kelly. *Reading Reasons: Motivational Mini-Lessons for the Middle and High School.* Portland, ME: Stenhouse Publishers, 2003.

Guthrie, John T. and Allan Wigfield. "Engagement and Motivation in Reading." *Handbook of Reading Research,* vol. 3, eds. M. L. Kamil, P. B. Mosenthal, P. D. Pearson, and R. Barr, 403–422. Mahwah, NJ: Lawrence Erlbaum Associates, 2000.

Harvey, Stephanie, and Anne Goudvis. "Determining Importance in Text: The Nonfiction Connection." *Strategies That Work: Teaching Comprehension to Enhance Understanding.* Portland, ME: Stenhouse Publishers, 2000.

Langer, Judith. "Beating the Odds: Teaching Middle and High School Students to Read and Write Well," 1999. Center on English Learning and Achievement. May 2003. http://cela.albany.edu/eie2/main.html>

National Reading Panel. *Teaching Children to Read: An Evidence-Based Assessment of the Scientific Research on Reading and Its Implications for Reading Instruction.* NIH Publication 00–4769. Bethesda, MD: U.S. Department of Health and Human Services, 2000.

Pressley, Michael. "What Should Comprehension Instruction Be the Instruction Of?" *Handbook of Reading Research,* vol. 3, eds. M. L. Kamil, P. B. Mosenthal, P. D. Pearson, and R. Barr, 545–562. Mahwah, NJ: Lawrence Erlbaum Associates, 2000.

Scieszka, Jon. *Guys Write for Guys Read.* New York: Penguin Group, 2005.

Wiggins, Grant P. and Jay McTighe. *Understanding By Design.* Alexandria, VA: Association for Supervision and Curriculum Development, 2006.

Vocabulary, Writing, and Grammar

Anderson, Jeff. *Mechanically Inclined: Building Grammar, Usage, and Style into Writer's Workshop.* Portland, ME: Stenhouse Publishers, 2005.

Baumann, J. F. and E. J. Kame' enui. *Vocabulary Instruction: From Research to Practice.* New York: Guilford Press, 2004.

Blachowicz, Camille, and Peter Fisher. *Teaching Vocabulary in All Classrooms,* Second Edition. Upper Saddle River, NJ: Merrill, 2002.

Feber, Jane. *Creative Book Reports: Fun Projects With Rubrics for Fiction and Nonfiction.* Gainesville, FL: Maupin House Publishing, Inc., 2004.

———*Active Word Play.* Gainesville, FL: Maupin House Publishing, Inc., 2008.

Kinsella, Kate. "Strategies to Teach Academic Vocabulary." *Strategies to Promote Academic Literacy for Second Language Learners Within the English Language Arts Classroom.* 2005.

Kinsella, Kate and Kevin Feldman. *Narrowing the Language Gap: The Case for Explicit Vocabulary Instruction.* New York: Scholastic, Inc., 2005.

Marzano, Robert J. "The Developing Vision of Vocabulary Instruction." *Vocabulary Instruction: From Research to Practice.* New York: Guilford Press, 2004.

Differentiated Instruction for Universal Access

Allington, Richard L. *What Really Matters for Struggling Readers: Designing Research Based Programs.* New York: Longman, 2001.

Armbruster, Bonnie, and Thomas H. Anderson. "On Selecting 'Considerate' Content Area Textbooks." *Remedial and Special Education*, vol. 9 (1): 47–52.

Balderrama, María V. and Lynne T. Díaz-Rico. *Teacher Performance Expectations for Educating English Learners*. Boston, MA: Allyn and Bacon, 2006.

Ball, Arnetha F. and Ted Lardner. *African American Literacies Unleashed: Vernacular English and the Composition Classroom*. Carbondale, IL: Southern Illinois University Press, 2005.

Carnie, Douglas, Jerry Silbert, and Edward J. Kame' enui. *Direct Instruction Reading*. 3rd ed. Upper Saddle River, NJ: Prentice Hall, 1997.

Deshler, Donald D., Keith B. Lenz, and Brenda R. Kissam. *Teaching Content to All: Evidence-Based Inclusive Practices in Middle and Secondary Schools*. Boston: Allyn and Bacon, 2004.

Francis, David, Mabel Rivera, Nonie Lesuax, Michael Kieffer, and Hector Rivera. *Practical Guidelines for the Education of English Language Learners*, RMC Research Corporation, Center on Instruction, 2006.

Vaughn, Sharon, Candace S. Bos, and Jeanne Shay Schumm. *Teaching Exceptional, Diverse, and At-Risk Students in the General Education Classroom*. Boston: Allyn and Bacon, 2002.

Pearson Prentice Hall Literature: A Rich Tradition of Learning Success

The Research Process

Since 1988, *Pearson Prentice Hall Literature* has been at the forefront of language arts instruction, providing teachers and their students with quality instruction and assessment tools to ensure success. Each successive edition builds on the strong heritage of the program. Our research comprised these three design stages:

1. EXPLORATORY NEEDS ASSESSMENT

In conjunction with Pearson Prentice Hall authors, we conducted research proven to explore educational reading methodologies. This research was incorporated into our instructional strategy and pedagogy to create a more effective literature program. This stage included:

- reading research
- review of state standards
- teacher interviews

2. FORMATIVE RESEARCH, DEVELOPMENT, AND FIELD-TESTING

During this phase of the research, we developed and field-tested prototype material with students and teachers. Results informed revisions to the final design and pedagogy. Formative research included:

- field testing of prototypes in classroom pilots
- classroom observations
- teacher reviews
- supervisor reviews
- educator advisory panels

3. SUMMATIVE RESEARCH AND VALIDATION RESEARCH

Finally, we have conducted and will continue to conduct longer-term research under actual classroom conditions. Research at this phase includes:

- pilot-testing
- prepublication learner verification research
- postpublication validation studies, including validation of test questions
- evaluation of results on standardized tests

Pearson Prentice Hall Literature: Proven to Get Results

Claremont University Randomized Control Trial

The need to determine whether educational curricula and products are effective at improving student achievement has grown throughout the past decade. To measure the extent to which *Pearson Prentice Hall Literature* curriculum impacted student learning in grades 7 and 9 in English Languages Arts, Pearson Education hired researchers from Claremont Graduate University to conduct a research study that meets the highest standard of "what works" in Language Arts curriculum by implementing a Randomized Controlled Trial (RCT) to test the efficacy of the program. A total of seven schools across three states (California, Colorado, Illinois), with diverse populations and ability levels participated in the RCT study. The study was conducted incorporating 1,722 students in schools from different locations and with differnent ethnic compositions, economic backgrounds, school sizes, and performances. The results show gains in achievement in language, reading, and writing.

All students were tested at the start of the study with a nationally-normed standardized test, the ITBS (middle grades) or ITED (high school).

English Language Arts Achievement Pre-test and Post-test Scores (Grade 7)

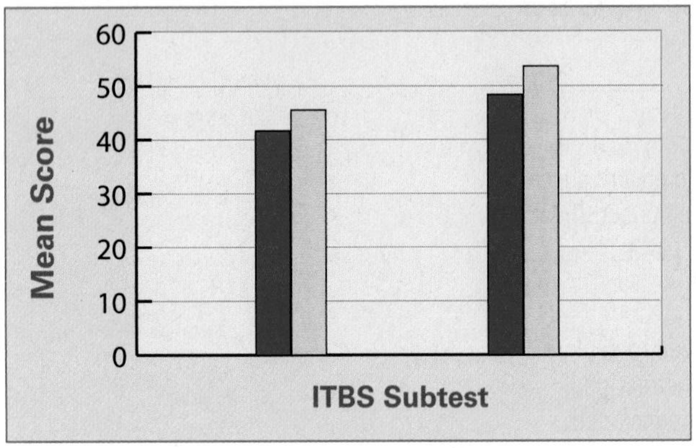

English Language Arts Achievement Pre-test and Post-test Scores (Grade 9)

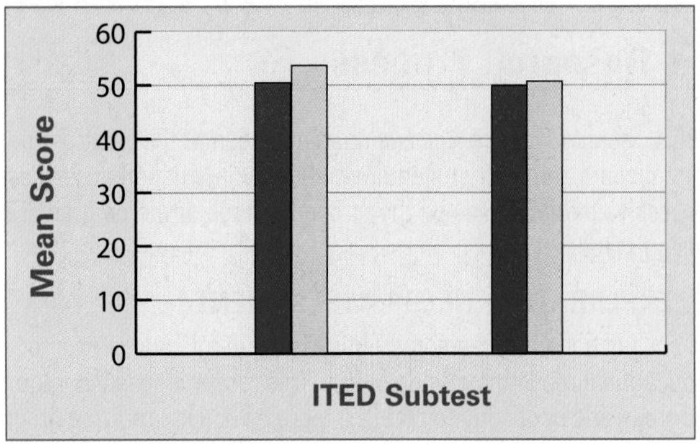

In addition, participating students completed persuasive essays at both the pre-test and post-test. To achieve sufficient reliability, two raters coded each essay on four dimensions: content, organization, voice, and convention. Analysis of writing scores requires that inter-rater reliability is achieved as measured by Cohen's kappa (Stemler, 2004). Calculation of Cohen's kappa indicates a high level of inter-rater reliability as most rater pairs were in agreement above 90.

Writing Assessment Pre-test and Post-test Scores (Grade 7)

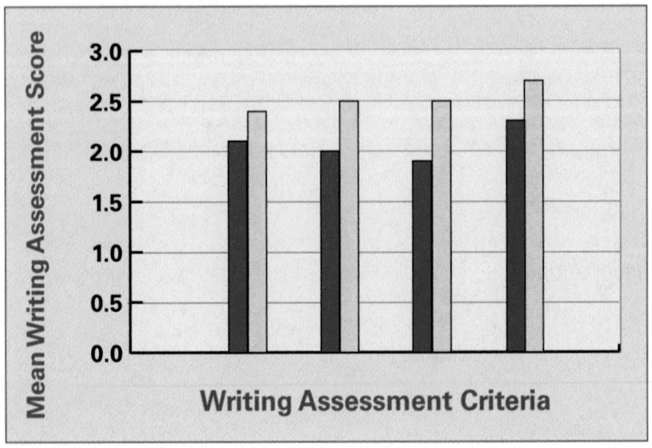

Writing Assessment Pre-test and Post-test Scores (Grade 9)

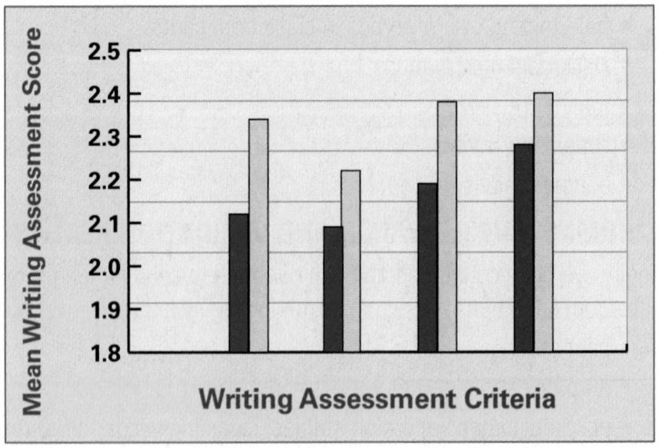

KEY: Pre-test Scores | Post-test Scores

National Effect-Size Study: Student Performance of *Pearson Prentice Hall Literature*, Users vs. Non-Users

This quasi-experimental study examined longitudinal test results of 976 closely matched user and non-user districts as a point of comparison across the same time periods and achievement tests.

Pearson Prentice Hall Literature users performed as well or better than their counterparts, achieving approximately a 56 percent gain in the percentage of students meeting or exceeding state reading/ELA standards and a 62 percent gain in national percentile ranking after one or more years of program implementation. A sustained gain was noted in districts that have implemented the program for two or more years.

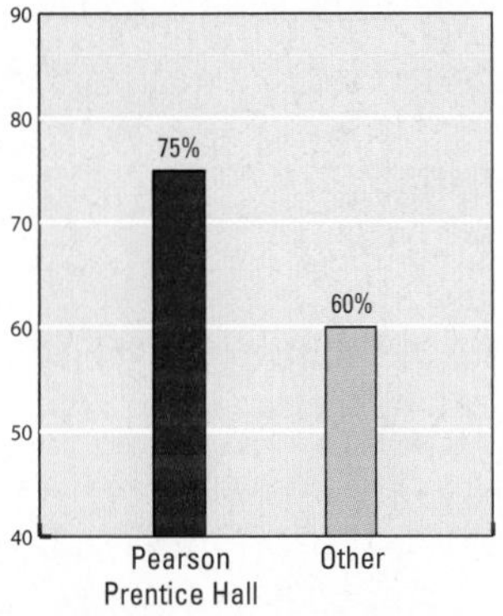

State: Colorado
Number of Districts: 10
Assessment: CSAP

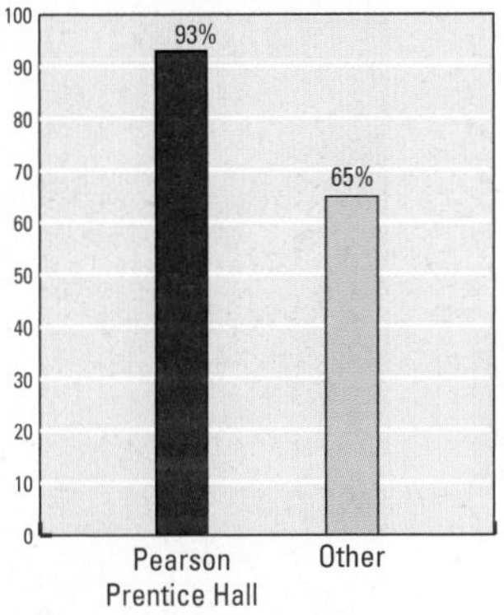

State: Arizona
Number of Districts: 34
Assessment: Stanford

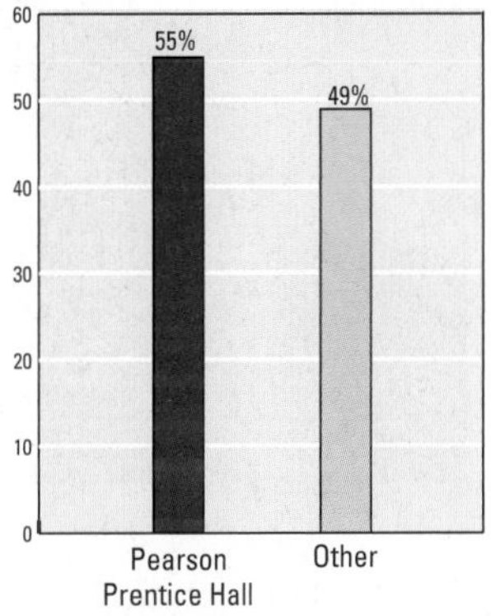

State: Tennessee
Number of Districts: 117
Assessment: Terra Nova

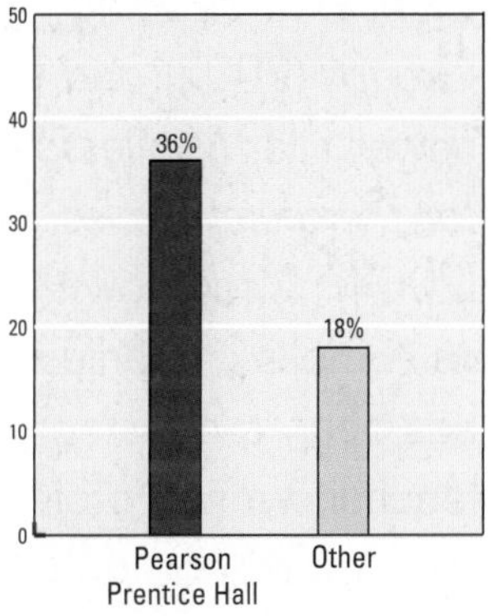

State: Ohio
Number of Districts: 43
Assessment: OPT

Learner Verification Research

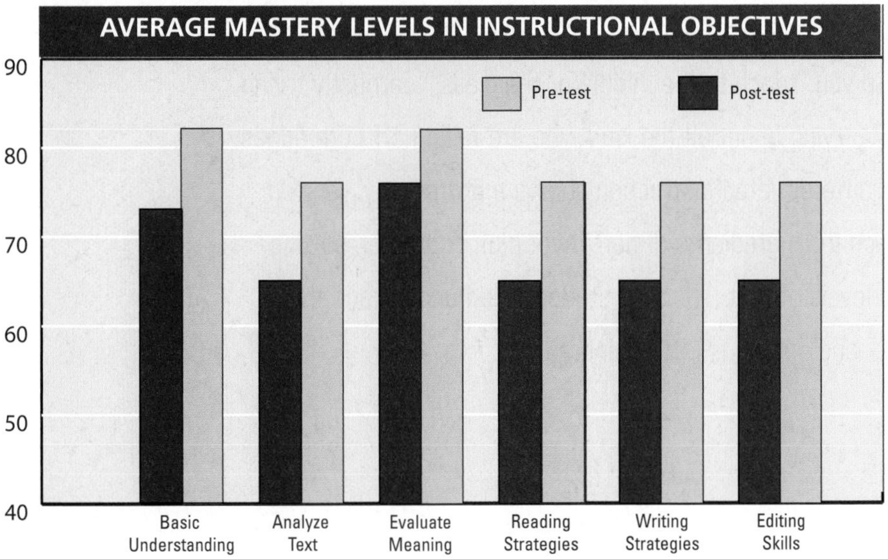

In a yearlong learner verification study, students using *Pearson Prentice Hall Literature* increased their mastery levels in several diagnostic skill areas for reading/language arts.

All students were tested at the start of the year with a nationally-normed standardized test, the TerraNova Complete Battery Plus exam. At the end of the study period, students were retested with the same standardized test. Only students who completed both the pre-tests and post-tests were included in this analysis. All tests were scored by CTB/McGraw Hill, publisher of the TerraNova.

LEVELED READING SELECTIONS

A Key to Differentiation

Harvey Daniels

An advocate for literature and reading, Harvey Daniels is known for his passionate work on literacy and student-led book clubs, as recounted in *Literature Circles: Voice and Choice in Book Clubs and Reading Groups* (2002) and his newer title, *Minilessons for Literature Circles* (2004). Also known as "Smokey," Daniels has been a classroom teacher, writing project director, author, and university professor.

"Decades of research warn us that students grow fastest when they study text that's precisely leveled to provide challenge without frustration. That's why *Pearson Prentice Hall Literature* offers two leveled-selections for almost every lesson—one more accessible and one more challenging."

We have all watched it unfold. You select a wonderful book or article for your class to read. You hand it out to the students and what happens? The text is way too hard for some kids, and far too easy for others. So you "teach to the middle of the class," earnestly trying to keep everyone on board, but always worrying about all the kids who are falling off both edges. Not a good feeling. Happily, research on differentiated instruction shows a better way: *leveled selections.* Let's say that we want to teach the ingredients of narrative: plot, character, setting, and theme. To do this, we can offer two levels of text. Then, all students can understand their selection and learn the necessary skills—and no one is left behind.

Why Leveled Readings Are So Important

The whole-class study of "common texts" is a staple of language arts teaching, for some good reasons. But decades of research warn us that students grow fastest when they study text that's precisely leveled to provide challenge without frustration. That's why *Pearson Prentice Hall Literature* offers two leveled selections for almost every lesson—one more accessible and one more challenging. With these choices, you can teach the same literary skills (and meet all the relevant standards) using either reading selection, or both. Every student learns the same skills, but each works in a text that's accessible. Following are research findings that support this approach:

- If we expect kids to try hard at literacy, they must spend at least part of each school day with *text they can read.* Kids cannot learn, retain, and apply skills if they cannot understand the print in front of them. (Allington, 2001)
- A prime determinant of comprehension is prior knowledge. The more a reader knows about the setting, topic, focus, or theme, the better his or her comprehension will be. Having a choice of texts means more kids will have the needed background. (Keene and Zimmerman, 2007).
- Student interests can weigh more in determining text difficulty than a Lexile score. Even kids who flounder with academic selections often read quite challenging text outside of school. (Smith and Wilhelm, 2002)
- Offering leveled selections helps us to meet the needs of students with reading difficulties or disabilities, as well as our non-readers and won't-readers. Giving a choice, even the modest one of deciding between two alternatives, can create a sense of ownership and control for kids who feel powerless, overwhelmed, or bored. For advanced learners, consistently having a more challenging selection to study provides an advantage as well. Here's the best part: when we make accommodations like leveled selections, we often find that such accommodations make learning work better for *everyone.* (Schwarz, 2005)

Strategies for Using Leveled Texts in the Classroom

Pick One Selection for the Whole Class. If you are committed to a common text, you can decide which of the two offered selections matches the general reading level of your class. If you have a group filled with below grade-level readers, you may wish to use the more accessible selection for everyone. Similarly, if you have an honors or mostly above grade-level group, the more challenging selection may be just the ticket. The Teacher's Edition provides all the support you need to introduce, teach, and assess either choice.

Match Selections to Individual Students. With your knowledge of your kids as readers, along with the help the program provides (see the Accessibility at a Glance Charts in the TE), assign the best selection for each student. Even better, let students make their own choices, thus bringing topic interest and prior knowledge into play. Though most of the leveled selections share a common genre, many differ greatly in their content. Letting kids choose can double your chances that students will be engaged in the selection they are reading.

Once Students Have Chosen or Been Assigned a Text, How Do You Teach Two Different Selections at Once?

Approach One: Splitting the Class

Before Reading: Because the skills taught with either selection are the same, you can introduce the target skills (making predictions, paraphrasing, analyzing plot) as shown in the TE. Encourage students to use their text-reading strategies in the margins, both to record personal responses and to address the provided prompts about literary analysis, reading skills, factual recall, critical viewing of visual elements, and vocabulary building.

During Reading: As students read and study the text, make quiet check-in visits with individuals, pulling a chair up close and asking questions about the text so far, discussing marginal notes, and answering questions. Aim for one-to two-minute conferences, so that with a typical lesson, you'll be able to meet with five or more students during the reading time. Keep quick notes of your conferences, both as raw material for assessment and also to help you remember ideas to share or students to call upon later.

After Reading: Place students in pairs who have read the same selection. Suggest two steps of discussion: first, students should share personal responses to the selection; next, they should review the selection in light of the focus skills of the lesson. They can use their own text markings to develop a list or chart of key passages where key elements appear. Finally, re-gather the whole class to elicit examples from both texts as a way of summarizing the lesson focus.

Approach 2: Setting Up Heterogeneous Group Workshops

Mini-lesson: Begin with a short mini-lesson that can apply to both selections. Whatever topic your mini-lesson addresses, it will involve your modeling, explaining, or thinking aloud for students. You might focus on key elements of the genre being studied (rhythm in poetry, text structures in nonfiction). You might teach about a particular strategy that smart readers use (visualizing, inferring). Or you could show specific literary devices that are common to both pieces (character development, figurative language). There are plenty of such suggestions in the Before You Read page for each selection.

Guided and Collaborative Practice: Now have kids read their chosen text, applying the concepts from the mini-lesson and jotting down their thinking as they read. After reading, form heterogeneous groups of four, with kids who have read different selections. Tell groups to have a two-step discussion: first, they should offer a quick summary of their piece. Then, members should take turns pointing out examples of where their selection manifests the target skill or literary element. During these meetings, move around the room listening in on a few groups, coaching, assessing and redirecting where necessary (you may want to jot down some notes as you go). Invite students with interesting work to share with the whole group later.

Debriefing and Wrap-up: Finally, pull students back together for a whole class meeting. Reiterate the day's target structure or skill, and then ask students who have read both texts to offer examples and share their thinking. Reinforce the mini-lesson focus.

Have All Students Read Both Selections. There are several reasons why you might have everyone read both pieces:

To deepen understanding. If you want to teach the genre under study more thoroughly, then reading both selections can help kids dig deeper, even in a heterogeneous class. Start with the more accessible piece to establish a core understanding, using the ample apparatus provided in the TE. Then move on to the more challenging text. Read aloud key passages to the whole class to enhance access for all, and use brief paired "turn and talk" activities along the way to help students think out loud as you read. Next, invite students to search back through both texts to locate common, genre-specific elements as well as note any structural, content, or value differences between the two readings.

To prepare students for standardized tests, college and work. In some areas of the country, high-stakes state exams feature pairs or even "triplets" of related pieces which kids must first read, and then seek connections, draw inferences, and make comparisons across texts. This kind of reading is both challenging and true to real-life tasks. Coordinating our thinking among multiple texts is one skill that proficient readers rely upon every day, in school, at work, and as citizens.

For enrichment or independent reading. Let kids read the other text for pleasure and to build their background knowledge for future reading. Make any accountability measures gentle—perhaps just a quick conference, so students can really read "just for fun."

Supporting Research

Allington, Richard. 2001. *What Really Matters for Struggling Readers: Designing Research Based Programs.* Boston, MA: Allyn and Bacon.

Beers, Kylene. 2005. *When Kids Can't Read, What Teachers Can Do.* Portsmouth, NH: Heinemann.

Keene, Ellin and Susan Zimmerman. 2007. *The Mosaic Of Thought.* Portsmouth, NH: Heinemann.

Schwarz, Patrick. 2006. *From Disability To Possibility: The Power of Inclusive Classrooms.* Portsmouth, NH: Heinemann.

Smith, Michael and Jeffrey Wilhelm. 2002. *Reading Don't Fix No Chevies: Literacy In the Lives Of Young Men.* Portsmouth, NH: Heinemann.

Zemelman, Steven, Harvey Daniels, and Arthur Hyde. 2005. Best Practice: *Today's Standards For Teaching and Learning In America's Schools (Third Edition).* Portsmouth, NH: Heinemann.

BIG QUESTIONS

Teaching Literature by Design: Introducing the Big Questions

Grant Wiggins, Ed. D.

As the co-author of *Understanding By Design,* Grant Wiggins advocates the use of Big Questions to ensure learning. During the development of *Pearson Prentice Hall Literature,* Wiggins advised the product team in the creation of the big questions and pedagogy that supports them.

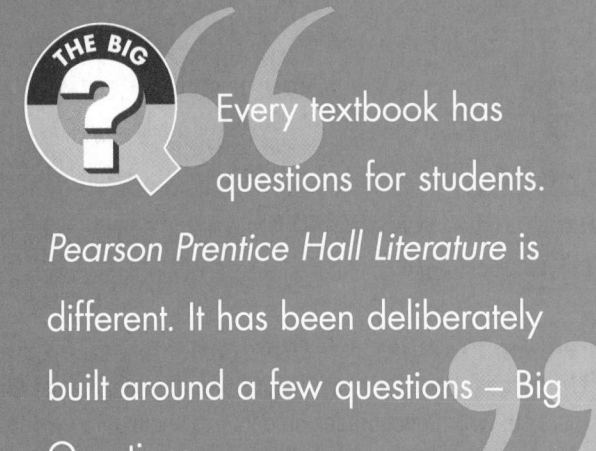

> Every textbook has questions for students. *Pearson Prentice Hall Literature* is different. It has been deliberately built around a few questions – Big Questions.

What *is* a "Big Question"? A Big Question is important, vital, at the heart of the matter. Whether in our teaching or our personal lives, when we wonder, for example: "Which relationships matter most?" "How do we decide what is true?" "Who shall we become?" "Who shall we trust?" "Do we see people for who they really are?" "Do we know who we are and how we seem to others?" "What is perception and what is reality?" "Can our doubts be avoided or conflicts resolved?"—then, we are pondering Big Questions. Such questions form the basis of this textbook.

A Big Question is different from many of the questions teachers typically ask students in class. The most commonly asked questions in school are what may be called academic questions—questions that seek or underscore a correct answer. There are definitive responses to academic questions, and they can typically be found in the textbook. For example, in leading a discussion on a short story, teachers are constantly asking questions to elicit recall of prior learning or to call attention to some part of the current story: "So, when did the character's motive change?" "Who was lurking in the shadows, and why?" "Why would the author use language like this?" There is nothing wrong with this type of question, of course. It just doesn't fit what we mean when we say: Let's consider the Big Questions.

What makes a question "big"? "Big" connotes "substantial"—occupying a considerable amount of space and time. A question is "big" or "weighty" if it has significant depth and breadth —occupying a good deal of our psychic "space," such as our thoughts and feelings. Another aspect of "bigness" is the time it consumes. Vital issues and inquiries remain alive over days, months, and years, unlike simple or superficial queries. Important questions recur over and through time, as we rethink and reflect on our present and past experiences.

Defining and Developing Big Questions. In my writing over the years with Jay McTighe, we have described Big Questions as "essential" and defined them as follows:

To what extent is the question meant to—

- cause genuine and relevant inquiry into the big ideas and core content?
- provoke deep thought, lively discussion, sustained inquiry, and new understanding as well as more questions?
- require students to consider alternatives, weigh evidence, support their ideas, and justify their answers?
- stimulate vital, on-going rethinking of big ideas, assumptions, and prior lessons?
- spark meaningful connections with prior learning and personal experiences?
- naturally recur, creating opportunities for transfer to other situations and subjects?

Understanding by Design, 2nd edition (ASCD: 2006), p. 110

GRADE 10

Unit 1: Is there a difference between reality and truth?

Unit 2: Can progress be made without conflict?

Unit 3: What kind of knowledge changes our lives?

Unit 4: Does all communication serve a positive purpose?

Unit 5: To what extent does experience determine what we perceive?

Unit 6: Can anyone be a hero?

***Pearson Prentice Hall Literature*—Based on such Big Questions** Each unit begins with Introducing the Big Question, which encourages students to begin a serious consideration of the topic before they even approach the literature. Here, questions and activities help students measure what they already know and decide what they may already think. In each unit, literature selections illuminate and take us deeper into these inquiries. For each reading selection there is a Writing About the Big Question pre-reading prompt, which presents students with a unique angle on the question. After reading the selection, students consider a question designed to focus their thinking and expand their understanding of the issue. Most importantly, at the end of each unit, Applying the Big Question requires students to relate the Big Question to other subjects and to revisit their first thoughts about it, explaining how their thoughts may have changed after completing the Unit. A **Challenge** question encourages students to continue their exploration by identifying the issues that spark their interest and that require further thought, discovery, and reflection.

The aim of working with Big Questions The teacher has a different intent when asking a "big" as opposed to an "academic" question. A Big Question is more of a "why?" or "so what?" question, rather than a "what?" or "where?" question. We are not looking for an answer, really; we are inviting inquiry and reflection. The teacher needs to clearly signal learners that we are not really trying to find "the answer" to a Big Question once and for all. Although we might sometimes wish for an easy answer, the task is to keep wondering and to continue asking the question. In a way, a typical academic question isn't really a question at all. It can usefully be thought of as a prompt, or as a cue for remembering something. "So, what does the main character do when he finds out the news?" is really just a recall question, a technique used to highlight something deemed important to remember.

A Big Question is different; and this difference sometimes confuses students who are so used to academic questions. The Big Question is asked seriously! We are opening the subject up. The Big Question is supposed to slow students down, make them stop and think! It invites more questions. This goal is made most clear when a teacher continues asking the same question across the discussion and across various texts, as this book was designed to help you do. The more we re-ask the Big Question and encourage students to do so also, the more it demonstrates that we actually learn from reconsidering the same important question as we read, discuss, experience, and reflect further. That's what keeps Big Questions alive.

A key long-term purpose of the Big Question is to make the question the student's own. As teachers, we ask Big Questions repeatedly and build activities and assessments around them to cause transfer. We succeed in the long term, only if and when the Big Questions are persistently and confidently asked and pursued by students own their own, without our prompts. Isn't that really what we mean by talking about the goal of critical thinking? A thoughtful person keeps sifting the evidence, attending to other points of view, arguments and assumptions, pondering "what if . . .?"—in other words, keeps asking questions. Thoughtful people keep the Big Questions alive in the face of the constant temptation to settle for the first plausible answer. Only by learning the discipline of questioning, is the bad habit of intellectual laziness undercut.

The Big Question as a focus of lesson and unit design: Understanding by Design This approach to organizing instruction around a question is a centerpiece of a more general and comprehensive approach to planning entitled Understanding by Design (UbD). As the title suggests, the two big ideas in UbD are: aim for understanding, not "coverage"; and aim at understanding by design—in other words, by deliberately crafting assessments and activities "backward" from the goal of understanding, not content recall, to make understanding more likely. In short, content mastery is the means, not the long-term goal of education. The point of education is to learn to use content wisely (transfer) and to be able to make sense of new tasks, situations, and texts on one's own. So, we must design backward from such transfer and sense-making, or it will only happen "by good fortune," not "by design."

It's really about common sense, then. If we want students to end up asking the Big Questions on their own, then our courses have to be designed "backward" from that goal, using this text as a resource. Along the way in *Pearson Prentice Hall Literature*, teachers are expected to help students become more proficient and discerning readers, using various skills and strategies. But those are the short-term goals. *The point of literacy is not to learn to read, but to read to learn.* That shift depends upon becoming a better questioner. So, we have to plan to meet this more challenging, long-term goal from the start. If we want students to learn from their reading, our methods have to foster that questioning and meaning-making. If we aim to have students ponder the Big Questions and transfer their prior thinking to new texts and discussions, then the course has to be planned to make that happen. Alas, too many teachers expect thoughtful reading and good student questioning to happen by osmosis; it doesn't work that way. So, in UbD, there is a deliberate process for achieving long-term understanding goals.

A key to "backward" design from understanding: Make sure your assessments reflect the long-term goal of understanding. Backward design, in UbD, means at its essence—honor your goals by embodying them in your assessments. So, design your assessments before designing your lessons. This is easily done: Make the Big Questions central to the assessments. "Is it going to be on the test?" This classic question signals, in no uncertain terms, that we had best practice what we preach, or the Big Questions will be lost. Yes, it is more challenging to assess progress when asking and pursuing good questions. But it must be done. The mantra in UbD is: More practically, the kinds of essays, oral presentations, and seminars implied in such a call for higher-order assessment based on Big Questions is what occurs in every good college in America.

In other words, the Big Questions can be said to be the actual content of a model literature course. A teacher challenge is to make this fact clear to students—that a major goal of reading is to pursue important questions via text—so that the questions are as much the course as the readings. If the readings are organized around the questions, if the questions can and do recur, and if assessment requires the student to respond to them often and to improve in their response over time, then that understanding about the purpose of class occurs. *Pearson Prentice Hall Literature* has been designed to help teachers make this aim and framework more transparent.

A postscript: "Why read?" A Big Question for you and your students Reading is difficult. "Why read?" "Why make the effort?" For all but a few learners— and thus for every teacher—this is always a Big Question! What your course should do is help students find an answer. You cannot merely tell them, they must experience it "by design."

There is a practical reason, then, for organizing courses in literature around Big Questions. The pursuit of vital questions, via stimulating literature (and discussion and writing), is often the key to reluctant readers becoming more interested in reading. Why? Because the Big Questions awaken curiosity and thus provide a purpose for reading that is often missing in typical classes. If students start to see that key questions are going to be taken seriously, and that reading shows some promise of helping each one to pursue them, then students are more likely to make the effort to become better readers. More importantly, if the class makes clear that questions matter more than quick answers, each student will feel there is room for him or her as an unsure reader.

Thus, while many of our students may not be confident of their technical abilities as readers, each one can ask good questions. The more confident students become in pursuing questions—seeing that questions, not glib answers, are valued—the more willing they will be to risk the effort of reading and share their about what the text means.

The challenge and the opportunity The teacher of literature, therefore, has a great challenge and an exciting opportunity. The challenge is twofold: overcoming the student view that a teacher or textbook question requires a "correct" answer, and making students overcome their reluctance to question for fear of looking ignorant. A primary goal in a literature class focused on Big Questions is to overcome this natural reticence. Our task as teachers of inquiry is to help students see the irony that is as old as Socrates—the more you realize you do not understand and admit it, the more you ask, and the more you find.

The opportunity is exciting because teachers of literature have endless chances to have lively, thoughtful, and life-changing discussions. We read literature together and discuss its possible meaning to provide students with a safe and enjoyable place to ponder vital questions about life, death, self, and relationships. Adolescents are natural philosophers, with a desire to consider the issues. Language Arts classes provide one of the few places in the curriculum where such inquiry is central, not tangential, to the "content" to be learned. What an advantage we teachers of literature have!

We have done our work well when students, on their own, see the value of reading in order to pursue the most vital questions. We ultimately don't read because we have to. We read because we feel the urge to—when Big Questions have truly become our own, and literature holds out the promise of opening up new worlds for exploring them.

Supporting Research

Adler, M. (1984). *The Paideia Program: An Educational Syllabus.* New York: Macmillan.

Adler, M. and C. Van Doren,. (1940). *How to Read a Book.* New York: Simon and Schuster.

Bransford, J., A. Brown, and R. Cocking, (eds.). (2001). *How People Learn: Brain, Mind, Experience, and School.* Washington, D.C.: National Research Council.

Bruner, J. (1960). *The Process of Education.* Cambridge, MA: Harvard University Press.

Chapman, A. (ed.). (1993). *Making Sense: Teaching Critical Reading Across the Curriculum.* New York: The College Entrance Examination Board.

Dewey, J. (1933). *How We Think: A Restatement of the Relation of Reflective Thinking to the Educative Process.* Boston, MA: Henry Holt.

Erickson, L. (1998). *Concept-Based Curriculum and Instruction: Teaching Beyond the Facts.* Thousand Oaks, CA: Corwin Press.

Gardner, H. (1991). *The Unschooled Mind: How Children Think and How Schools Should Teach.* New York: Basic Books.

Goodlad, J. (1984). *A Place Called School.* New York: McGraw-Hill.

Kasulis, T. (1986). *"Questioning."* M. M. Gilette (ed.). *The Art and Craft of Teaching.* Cambridge, MA: Harvard University Press.

Light, R. J. (2001). *Making the Most of College: Students Speak Their Minds.* Cambridge, MA and London: Harvard University Press.

Mansilla, V. B., and H.Gardner. (1997). *"Of Kinds of Disciplines and Kinds of Understanding."* Phi Delta Kappa, 78,5: 381–386.

Newmann, F. N., and Associates. (1997). *Authentic Achievement: Restructuring Schools For Intellectual Quality.* San Francisco, CA: Jossey-Bass Publishers.

Perkins, D. (1992). *Smart Schools: From Training Memories to Educating Minds.* New York: Free Press.

Sizer, T. (1984). *Horace's Compromise: The Dilemma of the American High School.* Boston, MA: Houghton-Mifflin.

Tyler, Ralph W. (1949) *Basic Principles of Curriculum and Instruction.* Chicago, IL: University of Chicago Press.

White, Richard and Gunstone, Richard (1992) *Probing Understanding.* London: The Falmer Press.

Wiggins, Grant. (1987). "Creating A Thought-Provoking Curriculum", *American Educator.* 11,4: 10–17. (Winter)

——(1989). "The Futility of Teaching Everything of Importance", *Educational Leadership.* 47,3: 44–59. (November)

——(1998). *Educative Assessment: Designing Assessments to Inform and Improve Performance.* San Francisco, CA: Jossey-Bass Publishers

Wiggins, Grant and Jay McTighe. (2006). *Understanding by Design, 2nd edition* revised. Alexandria, VA: ASCD.

Wiske, Martha Stone. (1997). *Teaching For Understanding: Linking Research With Practice.* San Francisco, CA: Jossey-Bass Publishers.

Wolf, D. (1987). "The Art of Questioning." *Academic Connections.* (Winter) The College Board.

Introduction to Linguistics: Transference

Pronunciation

All languages build on the same fundamentals. All languages contrast voiced and voiceless sound, and have stops and fricatives. Many languages use the same places of articulation for consonants as well. The majority of sounds will easily transfer from another language to English.

However, there will always be some sounds that are not found in a person's native language that can pose a challenge to the English language learner. English has a few relatively rare sounds, such as the interdental sounds spelled with *th*, /θ/ and /ð/. The /r/ sound in English is also a very rare type of sound. Most other languages use a tap or trill articulation for an /r/ sound.

In some languages, the /l/ and /r/ sounds belong to one psychological category. This means that they count as the same sound in that language. In this case, it is not the articulation that is difficult, but the perception of the difference and consistent use of one versus the other in any word context. This type of psychological category is called a *phoneme*, and multiple speech sounds all can be categorized as the same phoneme in that language.

Grammar

Pronouncing English is not the only stumbling block for English learners. The grammar and usage, or syntax, of English may present distinctions that are unique to the language. For example, English syntax requires adjectives to precede the nouns they modify, as in *the tall girl*. In other languages, such as Spanish, Hmong, and Vietnamese, adjectives follow nouns, as in *la chica alta* (literally *the girl tall* in Spanish). This may cause word-order problems, particularly for less advanced English learners.

Other syntactic differences are less obvious and may cause problems even for advanced learners. For example, many East Asian languages (such as Mandarin, Cantonese, and Korean) do not mark agreement between subject and verb. Speakers of these languages may therefore leave out agreement markers such as the -s in *The girl like cats.*

The use of articles varies across languages. For instance, Spanish uses the definite article more often than English, while Mandarin and Cantonese do not have articles. A Spanish-speaking English learner might say *The girl likes the cats* instead of *The girl likes cats*, and a Mandarin or Cantonese speaker might say *Girl like cat.*

Plural marking is another potential trouble spot: Vietnamese, Filipino, Cantonese, and Mandarin do not add plural markers to nouns. Learners speaking these languages may have difficulty with English plurals, saying *cat* instead of *cats.*

Common First Languages

In the Common First Languages section, you will find details of some common non-English languages spoken in the United States. They are Spanish, Vietnamese, Cantonese, Hmong, Filipino, Korean, and Mandarin.

You can use the fundamentals of speech articulation already covered to help you understand where the languages differ from English. Differences in the spoken language and in the writing systems are explored as well. These sections pinpoint common trouble spots specific to learners of English.

African American Vernacular English

While not a non-English language, African American Vernacular English (AAVE) is spoken commonly in many student populations and can present barriers to success in reading and writing similar to those facing English language learners. This section provides details on this unique English dialect and suggestions for addressing potential learning problems you may encounter with speakers of AAVE.

Linguistic Contrastive Analysis

The Linguistic Contrastive Analysis Charts provide a quick reference for comparing English sounds with those of other languages. The charts allow you to check at a glance which sounds have equivalents in other languages. For those sounds that don't have equivalents, you can find the closest sound used as a substitute and suggestions for helping someone gain a native English articulation.

In these charts, the sounds are notated using the International Phonetic Alphabet (IPA). This is the most widely recognized and used standard for representing speech sounds in any language. A guiding principle of the IPA across all languages is that each sound is uniquely represented by one symbol, and each symbol represents only one sound.

The chart has columns for each native language with rows corresponding to each English phoneme. Each cell in the chart gives an example word using that sound in the native language, a definition in parenthesis, and transference tips below. If there is no sound equivalent to English, a common substitution used by speakers of that language may be provided.

English Sounds

These charts give the International Phonetic Alphabet (IPA) symbol for each English consonant and vowels.

Consonants of English		
IPA	**Articulation**	
p	voiceless bilabial stop	**p**it
b	voiced bilabial stop	**b**it
m	voiced bilabial nasal stop	**m**an
w	voiced labio-velar approximant	**w**in
f	voiceless labio-dental fricative	**f**un
v	voiced labio-dental fricative	**v**ery
θ	voiceless interdental fricative	**th**ing
ð	voiced interdental fricative	**th**ere
t	voiceless alveolar stop	**t**ime
d	voiced alveolar stop	**d**ime
n	voiced alveolar nasal stop	**n**ame
s	voiceless alveolar fricative	**s**oy
z	voiced alveolar fricative	**z**eal
ɾ	voiced alveolar tap	bu**tt**er
l	voiced alveolar lateral approximant	**l**oop
ɹ	voiced alveolar central approximant	**r**ed
ʃ	voiceless palato-alveolar fricative	
ʒ	voiced palato-alveolar fricative	vi**s**ion
ʧ	voiceless palato-alveolar affricate	**ch**irp
ʤ	voiced palato-alveolar affricate	**j**oy
j	voiced palatal approximant	**y**ou
k	voiceless velar stop	**k**ite
g	voiced velar stop	**g**oat
ŋ	voiced velar nasal stop	ki**ng**
h	voiceless glottal fricative	**h**ope

Vowels of English		
IPA	**Sound**	**Example**
i	ē	b**ea**t
ɪ	ĭ	b**i**t
e	ā	b**ai**t
ɛ	ĕ	b**e**t
æ	ă	b**a**t
u	o͞o	b**oo**t
ʊ	o͝o	c**ou**ld
o	ō	b**oa**t
ɔ	aw	l**aw**
ɑ	ŏ	h**o**t
ə	ə	**a**bout
ʌ	ŭ	c**u**t
ɝ	er	b**ir**d
ɑ ʊ	ow	h**ou**se
ɔ ɪ	oy	b**oy**
ɑ ɪ	ī	b**i**te

Spanish

BACKGROUND Spanish is the second most widely spoken language in the world. There are more than 400 million native Spanish speakers in 20-plus countries on three continents. Spanish vocabulary and pronunciation differ from country to country. While most dialect differences in English are in vowel sounds, Spanish dialects differ in their consonants.

SPOKEN Spanish sounds are similar to those found in English, so there is a strong foundation for the native Spanish speaker learning English. However, there are three key differences between English and Spanish consonants:

Culture Clues

The Spanish language covers many countries, dialects, and cultures. Always encourage students to share special things about their culture, such as foods, festivals, or social customs.

1. Most of the alveolar sounds in English, such as /t/, /d/, and /n/ are produced farther forward in the mouth in Spanish. Instead of the tongue touching the alveolar ridge as in English, in Spanish it touches the back of the teeth.
2. Another difference is that the /r/ sound in English is not found in Spanish. There are two /r/ sounds in Spanish. One is the tap /ɾ/, which occurs in English as the quick sound in the middle of the name *Betty*. Psychologically, this tap sound is a kind of /t/ or /d/ sound in English, while in Spanish it is perceived as an /r/. The other /r/ sound in Spanish is a trill, or series of tongue taps on the alveolar ridge. This does not occur in English.
3. The third key difference between English and Spanish can be found in the English production of the voiceless stops /p/, /t/, and /k/. In English these sounds are aspirated, with an extra puff of air at the end, when the sound occurs at the beginning of a word or stressed syllable. So, /p/ is aspirated in *pit*. Learners can add a puff of air to such sounds to sound more like native English speakers.

There are five vowels in Spanish, which are a subset of the English vowels. Spanish vowels include tense vowel sounds /a/ /e/ /i/ /o/ /u/. Lax vowel sounds in English are the problematic ones for native Spanish speakers.

WRITTEN Like English, written Spanish uses the Roman alphabet, so both writing systems are similar. There are a few orthographic differences to note, however:

- The letter *h* in Spanish is silent, but the sound /h/ is written as *j* or *g*.
- A single letter *r* in Spanish represents a tap, while the double *rr* represents a trill.
- Accents are used to show the stress on a syllable when the stress is different from the usual rules. In some cases, words change meaning according to the accents. For example, *el* means *the* while *él* means *he*.

Written Spanish vowels are pronounced like the symbols in the IPA. So, the Spanish "i" is pronounced with the long **e** as in the word *beat*. The IPA and Spanish symbol for this letter is the same: /i/.

Grammar Hot Spots

- Double negatives are part of standard grammar in Spanish. Stress the single negative construction in English.
- English prepositions are a common stumbling block for Spanish speakers.

Vietnamese

BACKGROUND Approximately eighty million people in Vietnam speak Vietnamese. The northern dialect is the standard, though central and southern dialects also exist. Most Vietnamese speakers in the United States are from southern Vietnam and speak the southern dialect.

SPOKEN Vietnamese is a tonal language, so each syllable is pronounced with a distinctive tone that affects meaning. Vietnamese has a complex vowel system of 12 vowels and 26 diphthongs. Its consonants are simpler, but Vietnamese syllable structure allows few possibilities for final consonants.

> **Culture Clues**
>
> In traditional Vietnamese education, there is a strict division between the roles of student and teacher. Students may be confused if asked to direct a part of their own study, so encourage group work.

Students may need help noticing and learning to reproduce final consonant sounds in English words and syllables. Vietnamese syllable structure allows for limited combinations of initial consonants. Students also may need help with the more complex initial consonant clusters of English words and syllables.

WRITTEN Since the 1600s, Vietnamese has used a Romanized alphabet. Many characters written in Vietnamese have different sounds than their English counterparts, such as *d, x, ch, nh, kh, g, tr, r, and e.*

> **Grammar Hot Spots**
>
> - Like English, Vietnamese uses Subject-Verb-Object (SVO) syntax, or word order.
> - Vietnamese does not use affixes; instead, syntax expresses number, case, and tense.

Cantonese

BACKGROUND Cantonese is one of the seven major Chinese languages, not all of which are mutually intelligible. Cantonese is mostly spoken in China's southern provinces, Hong Kong, and Macau by about 66 million people. It is a tonal language, and the same sequence of letters can have different meanings depending on their pitch.

SPOKEN Cantonese has six stops, aspirated and non-aspirated /p/, /t/, /k/; three fricatives /f/, /s/, /h/, and two affricates /ts/, /ts^h/. Some sounds which do not exist in Cantonese can be difficult for the English language learner. The /v/ often gets pronounced as /f/ or /w/; the /z/ is often said as /s/, the sounds spelled with th are often said as /t/, /d/, or /f/. Cantonese speakers have difficulty distinguishing between /l/ and /r/, since /r/ is not present in their language. They tend to produce an /l/-like sound for both English sounds in words such as *ride* and *lied.*

Cantonese has 11 vowels and 10 diphthongs. One of the major problems for Cantonese speakers is distinguishing between English tense and lax vowels, because the distribution of Cantonese short and long vowels is determined by the sound context.

Syllables in Cantonese don't have consonant clusters. English consonant clusters are often deleted or broken up by vowel insertion (e.g., *list* becomes *lis*). This may be especially problematic when producing English past tense (e.g. *baked*).

WRITTEN Cantonese is written with standard Chinese characters known as *Hànzi* where each character represents a syllable and has a meaning. Additional Cantonese-specific characters were also added. Cantonese speakers may have difficulty with sound-letter correspondences in English.

> **Grammar Hot Spots**
>
> - English articles and prepositions are difficult for Cantonese speakers. *In, on,* and *at,* for instance, can be translated as the same pronoun in Cantonese.
> - Plurals, tenses, and gerund endings are difficult for Cantonese speakers to transfer to English.

Hmong

BACKGROUND Hmong is a group of approximately 18 languages within the Hmong-Mien family. There are roughly four million speakers of Hmong, including 200,000 in the United States. They are mainly from two groups with mutually intelligible dialects—Hmong Daw and Mong Leng.

SPOKEN Hmong vowels are few and simple, but its consonants are complex and differ from those of English. Notable features of Hmong phonology absent from English include consonantal pre-nasalization (the /m/n/ŋ/ sound before a consonant), and the contrast between nasalized and non-nasalized vowels. Hmong is tonal. Each syllable is pronounced with a distinctive pitch.

WRITTEN The Romanized Popular Alphabet (RPA), developed in the 1950s, is the usual way of transcribing Hmong. Syllable-final consonants are absent in pronunciation, but are used to represent orthographically the tonal value of a given syllable. Students may need particular help in identifying and learning to reproduce the final consonant sounds of English words and syllables.

Culture Clues

In traditional Hmong culture, learning takes place through hands-on experience. Students may find it difficult to adjust to the use of graphics or print media. Competition, personal achievement, and self-directed instruction may be unfamiliar concepts, so students may prefer group work.

Grammar Hot Spots

- Like English, Hmong is an SVO language. Personal pronouns are marked for number, including inflection for singular, dual, and plural, though they are not marked for case.
- Because Hmong and English prepositions often have different semantic qualities, students may need help mastering uses of English prepositions. For example, it is correct to say "think about [something]" rather than "think on [something]."

Filipino

BACKGROUND Filipino and English are the official languages of the Philippines, where 175 languages are spoken. There are about 24 million native speakers of Filipino, and more than 50 million people speak Filipino as a second language. You may hear the terms Filipino and Tagalog being used interchangeably.

SPOKEN Filipino has many similar speech sounds to English. The notable exceptions are the lack of the consonant sounds /f/, /v/, and those spelled with th. Of these, the English /f/ and /v/ cause the most difficulty for learners. The distinction between long *e* (as in *beat*) and short i (as in *bit*) is also a trouble spot. Filipino does not allow consonant clusters at the end of syllables, so *detect* may be simplified to just one consonant (*detec*).

Culture Clues

Most people from the Philippines can speak Filipino, but for many it is not their first language. Ask Filipino students about other languages they speak. Because English is used alongside Filipino as the language of instruction in the Philippines, most Filipinos are familiar with English.

WRITTEN The Filipino alphabet has 28 letters and is based on the Spanish alphabet, so the English writing system poses little problem.

Grammar Hot Spots

- Filipino word order is Verb-Subject-Object (VSO), which does not transfer well to English.
- Inflectional verb endings, such as *-s, -en, -ed,* and *-ing* do not exist in Filipino, so it is common to leave out the third person singular verb marker ("He *walk,*" not "He *walks*").

Korean

BACKGROUND Korean is spoken by 71 million people in North and South Korea. Standard Korean is based on the speech in and around Seoul.

SPOKEN Korean does not have corresponding sounds for English /f/, /v/, /ɵ/, /ð/, and /ʤ/. In word-initial position, all Korean stops are voiceless. Voiced stops /b/, /d/, and /g/ are only produced between two vowels. Korean speakers may have difficulty producing /s/, /ʃ/, and /z/ in some contexts, in addition to English /r/ and /l/ sounds (e.g., *rock* and *lock*). They may have problems in producing English consonant clusters (e.g., *str-*, *sk-*). These problems can often be eliminated by vowel insertion or consonant deletion. In addition, the distinction between English tense and lax vowels (e.g. /i/ as in *beat* vs. /ɪ/ as in *bit*) may be problematic for Korean speakers.

Culture Clues

Korean uses a complex system of honorifics, so it is unusual for Korean students to use the pronoun *you* or call their teachers by their first name.

WRITTEN Modern Korean uses the Korean alphabet (*Hangul*) or a mixed script of *Hangul* and Chinese. *Hangul* is an alphabetic script organized into syllabic blocks.

Grammar Hot Spots

- In contrast to English, Korean word order is Subject-Object-Verb (SOV). The verb always comes at the end of a sentence.
- Korean syllable stress is different, so learners may have difficulties with the rhythm of English.

Mandarin

BACKGROUND Chinese encompasses a wide range of dialects and is the native language of two-thirds of China. There are approximately 870 million Mandarin speakers worldwide. North Mandarin, as found in Beijing, is the basis of the modern standard language.

SPOKEN Mandarin Chinese and English differ substantially in their sound structure. Mandarin lacks voiced obstruent consonants (/b/, /d/, /g/, /ʤ/), causing difficulty for speakers in perceiving and producing English voiced consonants (e.g., *buy* may be pronounced and perceived as *pie*). The sounds spelled with *th* are not present in Mandarin, so they are often substituted with /s/ or /t/ causing, for example, *fourth* to be pronounced as *fours*. Mandarin Chinese has five vowels. Due to the relatively small vowel inventory and contextual effects on vowels in Mandarin, many English vowels and tense/lax distinctions present problems for speakers of Mandarin Chinese. Mandarin allows only a very simple syllable structure, causing problems in producing consonant clusters in English. Speakers may drop consonants or insert vowels between them (e.g., film may become /filəm/. The use of tones in Mandarin may result in the rising and falling of pitch when speaking English.

WRITTEN Chinese is written with characters known as Hànzi. Each character represents a syllable and also has a meaning. A Romanized alphabet called Pinyin marks pronunciation of characters. Chinese speakers may have problems mastering letter-sound correspondences in written English, especially for sounds that are not present in Mandarin.

Grammar Hot Spots

- The non-inflected nature of Chinese causes Mandarin speakers to have problems with plurals, past tense markers, and gerund forms (*-s, -ed, -ing*).
- Mastering English tenses and passive is difficult. Students should be familiarized with correct lexical and syntactic features as well as appropriate situations for the use of various tenses and passives.

Linguistic Contrastive Analysis Chart

The Consonants of English

IPA	ENGLISH	SPANISH	VIETNAMESE	CANTONESE
p	*pit* Aspirated at the start of a word or stressed syllable	*pato* (duck) Never aspirated	*pin* (battery)	*p^ha* (to lie prone) Always aspirated
b	*bit*	*barco* (boat) Substitute voiced bilabial fricative/ β/ in between vowels	*ba* (three) Implosive (air moves into the mouth during articulation)	NO EQUIVALENT Substitute word-initial/ p/
m	*man*	*mundo* (world)	*mot* (one)	*ma* (mother)
w	*win*	*agua* (water)	NO EQUIVALENT Substitute word-initial/ u/	*wa* (frog)
f	*fun*	*flor* (flower)	*phu o ng (phoenix)* Substitute sound made with both lips, rather than with the upper lip and the teeth like English /f/	*fa* (flower) Only occurs at the beginning of syllables
v	*very*	NO EQUIVALENT Learners can use correct sound	*Vie t* Nam (Vietnam)	NO EQUIVALENT Substitute /f/
ɵ	*thing* Rare in other languages. When done correctly, the tongue will stick out between the teeth.	NO EQUIVALENT Learners can use correct sound	NO EQUIVALENT Substitute /t^h/ or /f/	NO EQUIVALENT Substitute /t^h/ or /f/
о	*there* Rare in other languages. When done correctly, the tongue will stick out between the teeth.	*cada* (every) Sound exists in Spanish only between vowels; sometimes substitute voiceless /ɵ/.	NO EQUIVALENT Substitute /d/	NO EQUIVALENT Substitute /t/ or /f/
t	*time* Aspirated at the start of a word or stressed syllable English tongue-touch. Is a little farther back in the mouth than the other languages.	*tocar* (touch) Never aspirated	*tám* (eight) Distinguishes aspirated and non-aspirated	*t^ha* (he/she) Distinguishes aspirated and non-aspirated
d	*dime* English tongue-touch is a little farther back in the mouth than the other languages.	*dos* (two)	Dō *ng* (Dong = unit of currency) Vietnamese /d/ is implosive (air moves into the mouth during articulation)	NO EQUIVALENT Substitute /t/
n	*name* English tongue-touch is a little farther back in the mouth than the other languages.	*nube* (cloud)	*nam* (south)	*na* (take)
s	*soy*	*seco* (dry)	*xem* (to see)	*sa* (sand) Substitute *sh*- sound before /u/ Difficult at ends of syllables and words

IPA	HMONG	FILIPINO	KOREAN	MANDARIN
p	*p*eb (we/us/our) Distinguishes aspirated and non-aspirated	*p*aalam (goodbye) Never aspirated	*pal* (sucking)	p^hei (cape) Always aspirated
b	NO EQUIVALENT Substitute /p/	*b*aka (beef)	NO EQUIVALENT /b/ said between vowels Substitute /p/ elsewhere	NO EQUIVALENT
m	*m*us (to go)	*m*abuti (good)	*m*al (horse)	*m*ei (rose)
w	NO EQUIVALENT Substitute word-initial /*u*/	*w*alo (eight)	g*we* (box)	*w*en (mosquito)
f	*f*aib (to divide)	NO EQUIVALENT Substitute /p/	NO EQUIVALENT Substitute /p/	*f*a (issue)
v	*V*aj ('Vang' clan name)	NO EQUIVALENT Substitute /b/	NO EQUIVALENT Substitute /b/	NO EQUIVALENT Substitute /w/ or /f/
θ	NO EQUIVALENT Substitute /t^h/ or /f/	NO EQUIVALENT Learners can use correct sound, but sometimes mispronounce voiced /ð/.	NO EQUIVALENT Substitute /t/	NO EQUIVALENT Substitute /t/ or /s/
ð	NO EQUIVALENT Substitute /d/	NO EQUIVALENT Learners can use correct sound	NO EQUIVALENT Substitute /d/	NO EQUIVALENT Substitute /t/ or /s/
t	*th*em (to pay) Distinguishes aspirated and non-aspirated	*t*akbo (run) Never aspirated	*t*al (daughter)	*t*a (wet) Distinguishes aspirated and non-aspirated
d	*d*ev (dog)	*d*eretso (straight)	NO EQUIVALENT Substitute /d/ when said between vowels and /t/ elsewhere.	NO EQUIVALENT Substitute /t/
n	*n*oj (to eat)	*n*aman (too)	*n*al (day)	*n*i (you) May be confused with /l/
s	*x*a (to send)	*s*ila (they)	*s*al (rice) Substitute ***shi***- sound before /i/ and /z/ after a nasal consonant	*s*an (three)

The Consonants of English (continued)

IPA	ENGLISH	SPANISH	VIETNAMESE	CANTONESE
z	*zeal*	NO EQUIVALENT Learners can use correct sound	*rồi* (already) In northern dialect only Southern dialect, substitute /y/	NO EQUIVALENT Substitute /s/
ɾ	*butter* Written 't' and 'd' are pronounced with a quick tongue-tip tap.	*rana* (toad) Written as single *r* and thought of as an /r/ sound.	NO EQUIVALENT Substitute /t/	NO EQUIVALENT Substitute /t/
l	*loop* English tongue-touch is a little farther back in the mouth than the other languages. At the ends of syllables, the /l/ bunches up the back of the tongue, becoming velarized / / or dark-l as in the word *ball*.	*libro* (book)	cú *l*ao (island) /l/ does not occur at the ends of syllables	*lau* (angry) /l/ does not occur at the ends of syllables
ɹ	*red* Rare sound in the world Includes lip-rounding	NO EQUIVALENT Substitute /ɾ/ sound such as the tap /ɾ/ or the trilled /r/	NO EQUIVALENT Substitute /l/	NO EQUIVALENT Substitute /l/
ʃ	*shallow* Often said with lip-rounding	NO EQUIVALENT Substitute /s/ or /ʧ/	*sieu* thi (supermarket) southern dialect only	NO EQUIVALENT Substitute /s/
ʒ	*vision* rare sound in English	NO EQUIVALENT Substitute /z/ or /ʤ/	NO EQUIVALENT Substitute /s/	NO EQUIVALENT Substitute /s/
ʧ	*chirp*	*chico* (boy)	*chính* ph u (government) Pronounced harder than English *ch*	NO EQUIVALENT Substitute /ts/
ʤ	*joy*	NO EQUIVALENT Sometimes substituted with /ʃ/ sound Some dialects have this sound for the *ll* spelling as in llamar	NO EQUIVALENT Substitute /c/, the equivalent sound, but voiceless	NO EQUIVALENT Substitute /ts/ Only occurs at beginnings of syllables
j	*you*	*cielo* (sky) Often substitute /ʤ/	*yeu* (to love)	*jau* (worry)
k	*kite* Aspirated at the start of a word or stressed syllable	*casa* (house) Never aspirated	*com* (rice) Never aspirated	*kʰa* (family) Distinguishes aspirated and non-aspirated
g	*goat*	*gato* (cat)	NO EQUIVALENT Substitute /k/	NO EQUIVALENT Substitute /k/
ŋ	*king*	*man*go (mango)	*Ng*u yen (proper last name)	phaŋ (to cook)
h	*hope*	*g*ente (people) Sometimes substitute sound with friction higher in the vocal tract as velar /x/ or uvular /χ/	*hoa* (flower)	*ha* (shrimp)

IPA	HMONG	FILIPINO	KOREAN	MANDARIN
z	NO EQUIVALENT Learners can use correct sound	NO EQUIVALENT Learners can use correct sound	NO EQUIVALENT Learners can use correct sound	NO EQUIVALENT Substitute /ts/ or /tsh/
ɾ	NO EQUIVALENT Substitute /t/	*r*in/din (too) Variant of the /d/ sound	Only occurs only between two vowels Considered an /l/ sound	NO EQUIVALENT
l	*l*os (to come) /l/ does not occur at the ends of syllables	sa*l*amat (thank you)	ba*l*am (wind)	*l*an (blue) Can be confused and substituted with /r/
ɹ	NO EQUIVALENT Substitute /l/	NO EQUIVALENT Substitute the tap /ɾ/	NO EQUIVALENT Substitute the tap or /l/ confused with /l/	*r*an (caterpillar) Tongue tip curled further backward than for English /r/
ʃ	*s*au (to write)	*s*iya (s/he)	Only occurs before /i/; Considered an /s/ sound	*sh*i (wet)
ʒ	*z*os (village)	NO EQUIVALENT Learners can use correct sound	NO EQUIVALENT	NO EQUIVALENT Substitute palatal affricate /tþ/
ʧ	*ch*eb (to sweep)	*ts*a (tea)	*c*ʰal (kicking)	*ch*eng (red)
ʤ	NO EQUIVALENT Substitute *ch* sound	*D*ios (God)	NO EQUIVALENT Substitute ***ch*** sound	NO EQUIVALENT Substitute /ts/
j	*Y*aj (Yang, clan name)	ta*y*o (we)	je:zan (budget)	*y*an (eye)
k	*K*oo (Kong, clan name) Distinguishes aspirated and non-aspirated	*k*alian (when) Never aspirated	*k*al (spreading)	*k*e (nest) Distinguishes aspirated and non-aspirated
g	NO EQUIVALENT Substitute /k/	*g*ulay (vegetable)	NO EQUIVALENT Substitute /k/ Learners use correct sound between two vowels	NO EQUIVALENT Substitute /k/
ŋ	*g*us (goose)	a*ng*aw (one million)	ba*ŋ* (room)	tan*g* (gong) Sometimes add /k/ sound to the end
h	*h*ais (to speak)	*h*indi (no)	*h*al (doing)	NO EQUIVALENT Substitute velar fricative /x/

Linguistic Contrastive Analysis Chart

The Vowels of English

IPA	ENGLISH	SPANISH	VIETNAMESE	CANTONESE
i	***beat***	***hijo*** (son)	***di*** (to go)	***si*** (silk)
ɪ	*bit;* Rare in other languages Usually confused with /i/ (*meat* vs. *mit*)	NO EQUIVALENT Substitute /i/	NO EQUIVALENT Substitute /i/	***sik*** (color); Only occurs before velars Substitute /i/
e	*bait;* End of vowel diphthongized —tongue moves up to /i/ or /ɪ/ position	***eco*** (echo)	***kê*** (millet)	***se*** (to lend)
ɛ	*bet;* Rare in other languages Learners may have difficulty distinguishing /e/ and /ɛ/: pain vs. pen	NO EQUIVALENT Substitute /e/	NO EQUIVALENT Substitute /e/	***seŋ*** (sound); Only occurs before velars; difficult to distinguish from /e/ in all positions
æ	*bat;* Rare in other languages Learners may have trouble getting the tongue farther forward in the mouth	NO EQUIVALENT Substitute mid central /ʌ/ or low front tense /a/	***ghe*** (boat)	NO EQUIVALENT Hard to distinguish between /æ/ and /e/
u	***boot***	***uva*** (grape)	***mua*** (to buy)	***fu*** (husband)
ʊ	*could;* Rare in other languages Learners may have difficulty distinguishing /u/ and /ʊ/; wooed vs. wood	NO EQUIVALENT Substitute /ù/	NO EQUIVALENT Substitute ư (high back unrounded)	***suk*** (uncle); Only occurs before velars Difficult to distinguish from /u/ in all positions
o	*boat;* End of vowel diphthongized – tongue moves up to /u/ or / / position	***ojo*** (eye)	***cô*** (aunt)	***so*** (comb)
ɔ	***law***	NO EQUIVALENT Substitute /o/ or /ɑ/ Substituting /o/ will cause confusion (low vs. law); substituting /ɑ/ will not	***cá*** (fish)	***hok*** (shell); Only occurs before velars Difficult to distinguish from /o/ in all positions
ɑ	***hot***	***mal*** (bad)	***con*** (child)	***sa*** (sand)
ɑ ʊ	*house;* Diphthong starts /ɑ/ and moves to /ʊ/	***pauta***	***dao*** (knife)	***sau*** (basket)
ɔ ɪ	*boy;* Diphthong starts at /ɔ/ and moves to / /	***hoy*** (today)	***rồi*** (already)	***soi*** (grill)
ɑ ɪ	*bite;* Diphthong starts at /ɑ/ and moves to /ɪ/	***baile*** (dance)	***hai*** (two)	***sai*** (to waste)
ə	*about;* Most common vowel in English; only in unstressed syllables Learners may have difficulty keeping it very short	NO EQUIVALENT Substitute /ʌ/ or the full vowel from the word's spelling	***mua*** (to buy)	NO EQUIVALENT
ʌ	*cut;* very similar to schwa /ə/	NO EQUIVALENT Substitute /a/	*gio* (time)	***san*** (new)
ɝ	*bird;* Difficult articulation, unusual in the world but common in American English Learners must bunch the tongue and constrict the throat	NO EQUIVALENT Substitute /ʌ/ or /er/ with trill	NO EQUIVALENT Substitute /ɨ/	***hæ*** (boot)

IPA	HMONG	FILIPINO	KOREAN	MANDARIN
i	***ib*** (one)	*ikaw* (you); This vowel is interchangeable with /ɪ/; hard for speakers to distinguish these	z-ɩ:ʄaŋ (market)	***ti*** (ladder); Sometimes English /i/ can be produced shorter
ɪ	NO EQUIVALENT Substitute /i/	*limampu* (fifty); This vowel is interchangeable with /i/; hard for speakers to distinguish these	NO EQUIVALENT Substitute /i/	NO EQUIVALENT
e	***tes*** (hand)	***sero*** (zero)	***be:****da* (to cut)	***te*** (nervous); Sometimes substitute English schwa /ə/
ɛ	NO EQUIVALENT Substitute /e/	***sero*** (zero); This vowel interchanges with /e/ like *bait*; not difficult for speakers to learn	*th :do* (attitude)	NO EQUIVALENT
æ	NO EQUIVALENT Substitute /ɛ/	NO EQUIVALENT Substitute /ɑ/ as in hot	NO EQUIVALENT	NO EQUIVALENT Substitute /ə/ or /ʌ/
u	***kub*** (hot or gold)	***tu****nay* (actual); This vowel interchanges with /ʊ/ like *could;* not difficult for speakers to learn	***zu:****bag* (watermelon)	***lu*** (hut); Sometimes English /u/ can be produced shorter
ʊ	NO EQUIVALENT Substitute /ɨ/ (mid central with lips slightly rounded)	***gu****mawa* (act); This vowel interchanges with /u/ like *boot;* not difficult for speakers to learn	NO EQUIVALENT	NO EQUIVALENT
o	NO EQUIVALENT	***ubo*** (cough)	***bo:****zu* (salary)	***mo*** (sword); This vowel is a little lower than English vowel
ɔ	***Yaj*** (Yang clan name)	NO EQUIVALENT Spoken as /ɑ/ as in *hot*	NO EQUIVALENT	NO EQUIVALENT Substitute /o/
ɑ	***mov*** (cooked rice)	*t****a****lim* (blade)	***ma:****l* (speech)	***ta*** (he/she); Sometimes substitute back /o/ or /u/
ɑ ʊ	*pl****au****b* (four)	*ik****aw*** (you)	NO EQUIVALENT	NO EQUIVALENT
ɔ ɪ	NO EQUIVALENT	*ap****oy*** (fire)	NO EQUIVALENT	NO EQUIVALENT
ɑ ɪ	*q****ai****b* (chicken)	himatay (faint)	NO EQUIVALENT	NO EQUIVALENT
ə	NO EQUIVALENT	NO EQUIVALENT Spoken as /ɑ/ as in hot	NO EQUIVALENT Difficult sound for learners	NO EQUIVALENT
ʌ	NO EQUIVALENT	NO EQUIVALENT Spoken as /ɑ/ as in *hot*	NO EQUIVALENT	NO EQUIVALENT
ɝ	NO EQUIVALENT Substitute diphthong /əɨ/	NO EQUIVALENT Spoken as many different vowels (depending on English spelling) plus tongue tap /ɾ/	NO EQUIVALENT	NO EQUIVALENT

Culturally Responsive Instruction

What is Culturally Responsive Instruction?

Students entering the classroom bring with them a variety of experiences, traditions, interpretive frameworks, and learning styles. Culturally responsive instruction begins when a teacher acknowledges this variety as a positive resource for education—not as the static interrupting a mainstream message, but as a prospectively rich harmony of voices; not as the rough edges hiding a jewel's luster, but as a treasure in its own right. By capitalizing on the student's own resources, a teacher ensures success.

Build From Strength A key premise for culturally responsive pedagogy is that education proceeds from students' strengths, not students' weaknesses. To make academic progress, a student must build one success on to another. In defining culturally responsive teaching, Geneva Gay calls for an educational paradigm "that teaches *to and through* [students'] personal and cultural strengths, their intellectual capabilities, and their prior accomplishments" (Gay, 2000, p. 24).

- At a minimum, culturally responsive instruction transpires whenever a teacher builds a bridge from what students already know or have experienced to new knowledge or skills.
- At a maximum, the culturally responsive classroom is a cooperative learning environment rich in affirmations of students' heritages—a classroom that builds, not just on students' individual strengths, but on the new strength that emerges when individuals join together in a community that respects their diversity.

Provide Bridges to Mastery Aristotle confidently claims in his *Metaphysics*, "All men desire by nature to know." While the instinct for knowledge may be universal, learning is also culturally inflected. The authorities a learner acknowledges, the teaching styles the learner responds to, the kinds of learning the learner recognizes as a good—all are to some degree shaped by community and culture. Learners in an urban environment may pride themselves on different types of knowledge than learners in the suburbs. Some learners comes from a family that places a premium on cultural literacy, others do not. Learners from a tradition that privileges associative, interactive conversational styles may not respond as readily to traditional classroom interactions as others do.

To address the cultural component of learning, culturally responsive instruction builds bridges between students' background knowledge and discourse styles to academic content and discourse. Providing background knowledge the student may require to understand a selection is a step to understanding; relating this background knowledge to the student's own world and experiences builds a bridge. Giving students instruction and practice in linear, critical thinking is a step to mastery; providing scaffolding and visual correlates to reasoning, such as graphic organizers, builds a bridge.

Culturally Responsive Instruction in *Prentice Hall Literature*

Pearson Prentice Hall consistently supports culturally responsive instruction with each selection in the anthology. (S. Hollie. professional consultations, November 2007 to Feburary 2008). Opportunities for culturally responsive instruction are called out with this icon CRI in the Lesson Pacing Guide preceding each leveled selection pair.

Lesson Pacing Guide

DAY 1 Preteach

- Administer the Reading and Vocabulary Warm-ups (*Unit 1 Resources*, pp. 30–33 or 48–51) as necessary.
- Introduce the Reading Skill: Context Clues. FT
- Introduce the Literary Analysis concept: Narrative Text. FT
- Distribute copies of the appropriate graphic organizer for the Reading Skill (*Graphic Organizer Transparencies*, pp. 6–8). CRI
- Distribute copies of the appropriate graphic organizer for Literary Analysis (*Graphic Organizer Transparencies*, pp. 3–5). CRI
- Teach the selection vocabulary. FT CRI
- Introduce the Word Study skill.

Some lesson features, such as the graphic organizers, are in their nature culturally responsive: They provide bridges from students' own background and learning styles to academic mastery. Other lesson features may be easily transposed into culturally responsive instruction once the teacher brings students' background into play.

In the Student Edition, culturally responsive instruction is supported by

- **Background notes** By building background before reading, and by relating this background to a student's own world, the teacher builds a bridge between what students already know and what they will encounter in a selection.

> BACKGROUND FOR THE STORY
>
> **Amateur Boxing**
>
> In "Amigo Brothers," two teenage boys want to compete in the annual Golden Gloves tournament. This competition is probably the most famous amateur boxing event in the United States. Each year, local and regional elimination bouts lead to final championship matches.

- **Graphic organizers** Students' repertoire of communicative competencies may privilege nonlinear, "participatory–interactive," or "topic-chaining" discursive styles—communication as performance in a group, as collective storytelling, or as conversation that circles from topic to topic (Gay, 2000, pp. 77–110). By providing a visual component for tracking and reasoning skills, the skill-specific graphic organizers with every selection form a natural bridge between nonlinear thinking and conversational styles and academic critical thinking skills.
- **Reading Skill and Literary Analysis Instruction** The Reading Skill instruction presented with each selection helps develop critical thinking skills and thus serves as a bridge between students' own discursive styles and academic mastery. In addition, the Reading and Literary Analysis prompts can be rendered culturally responsive by 1) addressing language issues in students' responses while affirming the validity of their ideas and 2) using them as opportunities to build bridges from the selection to students' own experiences.
- **Vocabulary Instruction** By using activities such as the Personal Thesaurus in the *Reader's Notebook* series, the teacher aids the student in "owning" words by helping students connect new words to words they already know.
- **Extension Activities** Listening and Speaking, and Research and Technology activities address a variety of cultural styles, including discourse-as-performance and collaborative and cooperative learning.

In the Teacher's Edition, culturally responsive instruction is supported by

- **Culturally Responsive Instruction Notes** Notes focusing on language, culture, and background-building provide concrete strategies for addressing the needs of students of diverse backgrounds.

> **Differentiated Instruction** for Universal Access
>
> **Culturally Responsive Instruction:**
>
> **Culture Focus** Storytellers are important in cultures around the world, including the African culture from which this story comes. Ask students: Who are the storytellers in your family or community?
>
> Invite students to relate family stories that they can recall. Discuss as a class how students' stories are similar to and different from "Why
>
> Monkeys Live in Trees."
> what role humor plays
> mals appear in student
> how their behavior co
> Lester's story. Finally, h
> ways in which stories
> ber their history and h
> close to each other.

- **English Learners Notes** Notes providing support for English learners help teachers help students to gain entry to the text.
- **Think Aloud Notes** By modeling the application of skills, teachers provide a bridge to mastery via imitation.
- **Activating Prior Knowledge Notes** By engaging students' own experiences, knowledge, and values, teachers prepare them for understanding and lead them deeper into a selection.

References

Culturally responsive teaching: Theory, research, and practice. New York: Teachers College Press.

How To Use This Program

1 Where Do I Start?

Right here! These pages will guide you through the program's unique organization and describe the many resources that will enrich your teaching.

2 How Do I Teach the Unit?

Begin each unit with **Introducing the Big Question** to present an overarching big idea that will guide students' reading. Have students use the academic vocabulary to think, talk, and write about this question throughout the unit.

At the end of the unit, use **Applying the Big Question** to help students explore how their ideas about the Big Question have deepened or changed as a result of their reading.

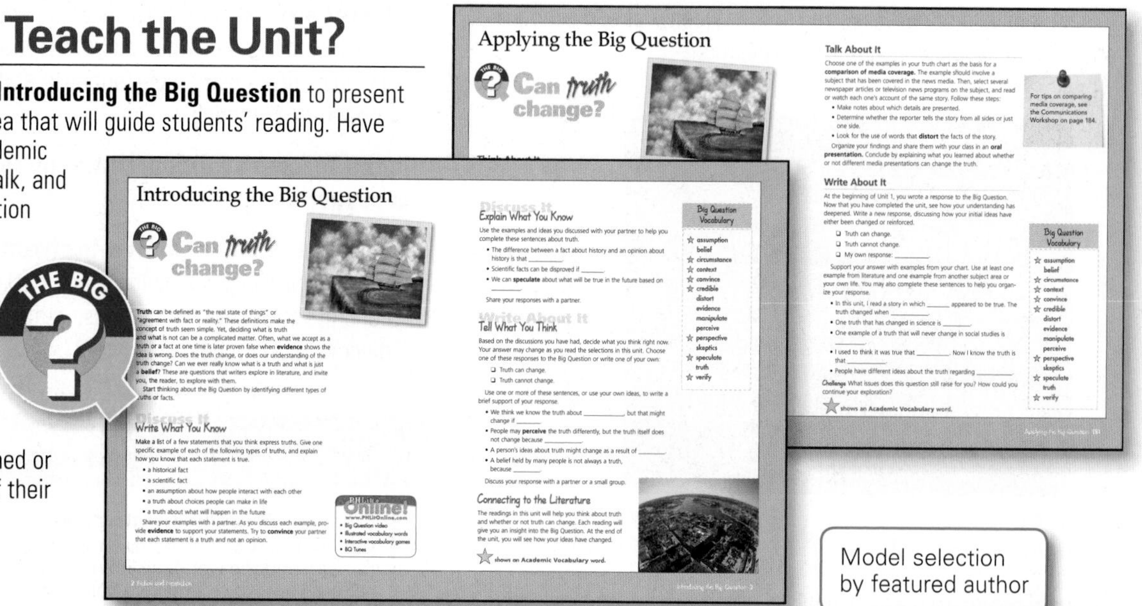

Each of the six units focuses on a different genre and is hosted by a featured contemporary author. Use the **Introduction** to teach your students about each genre by introducing important characteristics, key concepts, and literary terms.

Then, read the unit author's **Model Selection** to help students apply their understanding of the literary forms and concepts. Use the **Author's Insight** notes that accompany the selection to enhance students' understanding of the literary concepts taught in the unit.

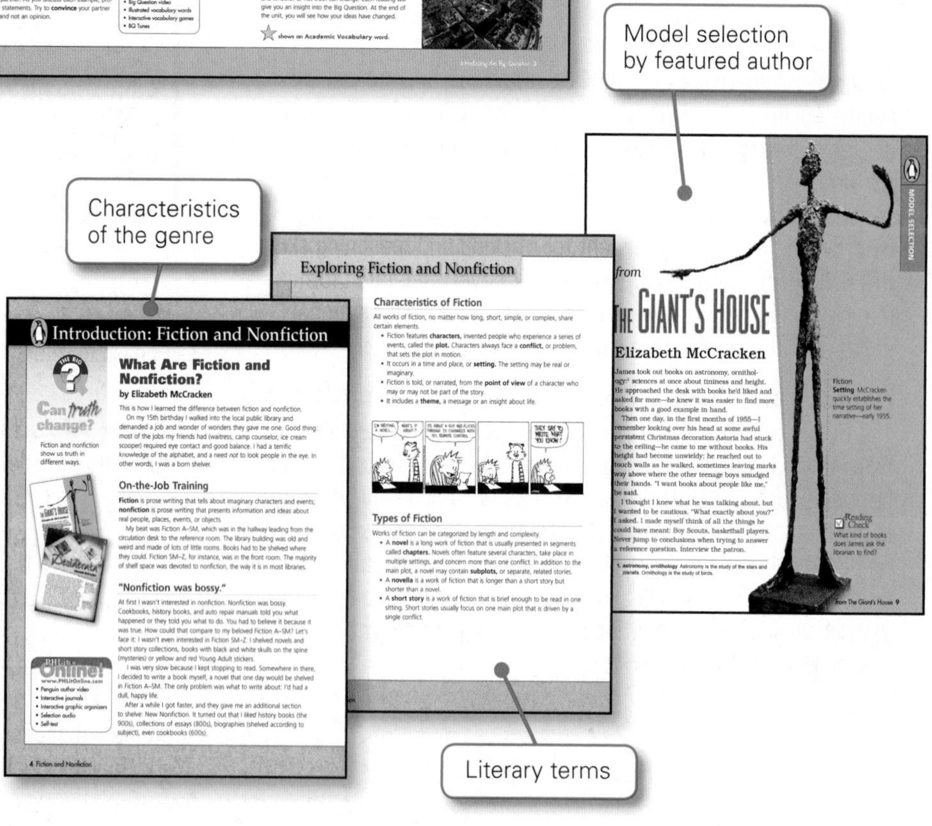

Technology

PHLit Online!

See It! Pearson Prentice Hall Literature Video Program

Stimulate student interest with this engaging DVD featuring in-depth interviews with the unit authors.

3 What Should I Use to Plan and Prepare?

Start your planning with the **Pacing Plan** at the beginning of each unit and the **Time and Resource Manager** before every leveled selection pair.

The Time and Resource Manager provides

- a detailed lesson plan.
- a list of the standards covered in the lesson.
- suggestions for incorporating program resources into your instruction.

Resources
Suggested resources for differentiated instruction

Lesson Pacing Guide
Suggested pacing information

Meeting Your Standards
Standard coverage information

TIME AND RESOURCE MANAGER

The Washwoman • New Directions

Lesson Pacing Guide

DAY 1 Preteach

- Administer the Reading and Vocabulary Warm-ups (*Unit 9 Resources*, pp. 30–33 or 48–51) as necessary.
- Introduce the Reading Skill: Make Predictions. FT
- Introduce the Literary Analysis concept: Narrative Essay. FT
- Distribute copies of the graphic organizer for the Reading Skill (*Graphic Organizer Transparencies*, pp. 3–5). CRI
- Distribute copies of the graphic organizer for Literary Analysis (*Graphic Organizer Transparencies*, pp. 6–8). CRI
- Teach the selection vocabulary. FT CRI
- Introduce the Word Study skill.

DAYS 2–3 Preteach/Teach

- Build Background with the Background feature. CRI
- Develop thematic vocabulary and thematic thinking with Writing About the Big Question.
- Prepare students to read with the Activating Prior Knowledge activities (TE). CRI
- Informally monitor comprehension while students read. FT
- Use the Reading Check questions to confirm comprehension.
- Develop students' ability to make predictions, using the Reading Skills questions.
- Develop students' understanding ofnarrative essays, using the Literary Analysis questions. CRI
- Reinforce vocabulary with the Vocabulary notes. CRI

DAY 4 Assess

- Assess students' comprehension and mastery of the skills by having them answer the Thinking About the Selection, Reading Skill, and Literary Analysis questions. FT
- Have students complete the Vocabulary Practice activities. FT
- Have students complete the Word Study activities.

DAY 5 Extend/Assess

- Have students complete the Grammar lesson. CRI
- Have students complete the Writing activity and write an an anecdote. (You may assign as homework.) FT
- Extend learning by having students complete the Listening and Speaking activity, an interview. As an alternateive assign them "As Long As They Can Play" or "Riding the Wave" in *Reality Central*. CRI
- Administer Selection Test A or B (Unit 9 Resources, pp. 42–47 or 63–68). FT

Meeting Your Standards

Reading Process LA.910.1.7.1 Use to make and confirm complex predictions of content of a reading selection. *(Reading Skill: Make Predictions)*

Literary Analysis LA.910.2.1.1 Analyze and compare historically and culturally significant works of literature, identifying the relationships among the major genres and the literary devices unique to each, and analyze how they support and enhance the theme and main ideas of the text. *(Literary Analysis: Narrative Essay)*

Writing Process LA.910.3.3.3 Create precision and interest by elaborating ideas through supporting details. *(Writing: Anecdote)*

Communication LA.910.5.2.1 Select and use appropriate listening strategies according to the intended purposes. *(Listening and Speaking: Interview)*

Additional standards addressed:

Reading Process LA.910.1.7.8 *(Reading Skill: Make Predictions)*

Literary Analysis LA.910.2.2.2 *(Literary Analysis: Narrative Essay)*

Writing Applications

LA.910.4.1.1 *(Writing: Anecdote)*

CRI For a full explanation of Culturally Responsive Instruction opportunities in this lesson, see p. FL 106.

FT For an accelerated lesson, use the Fast Track strategies and activities.

Managing Differentiated Instruction
This leveled selection pairing groups a more accessible with a more challenging selection. Choose either one to teach the lesson skills. For classroom management suggestions for using the pairing in a mixed-ability class, see pp. FL 100–FL 102.

Daily Block Scheduling
Each day in this Lesson Pacing Guide represents a 40–50 minute period. Teachers using block scheduling may combine days to revise pacing. In addition, teachers may differentiate and support core instruction by integrating components for extended and intensive support as students require. See the Guide to Selected Leveled Resources (facing page).

22a

Guide to Selected Leveled Resources

EL English Learners			The Washwoman	New Direction
CORE COURSE	*Unit 1 Resources*	Selection Test A	pp. 42–44	pp. 63–65
	Graphic Organizer Transparencies	Reading Skill Graphic Organizer A	p. 3	p. 4
		Literary Analysis Graphic Organizer A	p. 6	p.7
EXTENDED SUPPORT (Level 2)	*Unit 1 Resources*	Reading and Vocabulary Warm-ups A or B	pp. 30–33	pp. 48-51
	Reader's Notebook: English Learner's Version		adapted instruction and selection	adapted instruction and summary
	Hear It! Audio CD		selection and summaries	selection and summaries
	Hear It! Audio CD (adapted text)		adapted selection and summaries	—
INTENSIVE SUPPORT (Level 1)	*Reality Central*		"As Long As They Can Play"	"Riding the Wave
	Real-World Writing Journal		Lesson 1, pp. 2–5	Lesson 2, pp. 6–9

Below-Level Students			The Washwoman	New Direction
CORE COURSE	*Unit 1 Resources*	Selection Test A	pp. 42–44	pp. 63–65
	Graphic Organizer Transparencies	Reading Skill Graphic Organizer A	p. 3	p. 4
		Literary Analysis Graphic Organizer A	p. 6	p.7
EXTENDED SUPPORT (Level 2)	*Unit 1 Resources*	Reading and Vocabulary Warm-ups A or B	pp. 30–33	pp. 48-51
	Reader's Notebook		adapted instruction and selection	adapted instruction and summary
	Listening to Literature Audio CD		selection and summaries	selection and summaries
INTENSIVE SUPPORT (Level 1)	*Reality Central*		"As Long As They Can Play"	"Riding the Wave"
	Real-World Writing Journal		Lesson 1, pp. 2–5	Lesson 2, pp. 6–9
	Reading Kit		Reteaching worksheets	Reteaching worksheets

Special Needs Students			The Washwoman	New Direction
CORE COURSE	*Unit 2 Resources*	Selection Test A	pp. 42–44	pp. 63–65
	Graphic Organizer Transparencies	Reading Skill Graphic Organizer A	p. 3	p. 4
		Literary Analysis Graphic Organizer A	p. 6	p.7
EXTENDED SUPPORT (Level 2)	*Unit 2 Resources*	Reading and Vocabulary Warm-ups A or B	pp. 30–33	pp. 48-51
	Reader's Notebook: Adapted Version		adapted instruction and selection	adapted instruction and summary
	Adapted Reader's Notebook Online Audio		adapted selection and summaries	—
INTENSIVE SUPPORT (Level 1)	*Real-Life Readings*		"As Long As They Can Play"	"Riding the Wave"
	My Real-Life Reading Journal		Lesson 1, pp. 2–5	Lesson 2, pp. 6–9
	Reading Kit		Reteaching worksheets	Reteaching worksheets

The program also includes resources for these students: L1 L2 L3 On-Level L4 Advanced All All
For a complete guide to program resources for selection pairings, see 118–120.

NOTE: All print materials are also available online at *www.PHLitOnline.com*.

22b

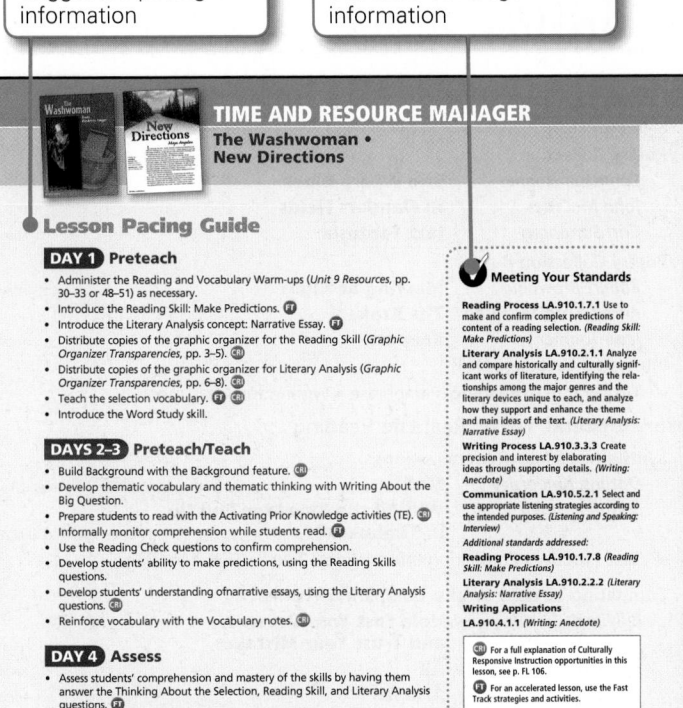

For an at-a-glance look at selection resources, see the **Visual Guide to Featured Selection Resources** that precedes each leveled selection pair.

4 How Does the Program Help Me With Pacing?

The program is organized into three-week instructional blocks, with each block focusing on core skills and standards. This consistent organization ensures thorough skills coverage presented in manageable chunks. A benchmark test is provided at the middle and end of each unit, allowing you to administer assessment at 3-, 6-, or 9-week intervals. This systematic, logical organization with built-in progress monitoring allows you to make sound instructional choices for your class without skipping or missing any skills or standards.

5 How Do I Use Each Feature in a Unit?

A Choose a selection from the **leveled selection pair** to teach and practice core skills and strategies. See p. T 91 for how to choose the most appropriate selection for your class.

B Use **Test Practice** to assess students' grasp of the reading skill.

C Show your students how to apply informational reading skills to real-life reading situations with the **Informational Texts** feature.

D Use **Test Practice** to assess students' grasp of the informational reading skill and to give them practice with timed writing.

E Deepen students' understanding of the genre with the **Comparing Literary Works** feature, which provides an opportunity for students to analyze a specific literary element at work in two or more selections.

F Use the **Workshops** to provide opportunities for skills practice. See p. T 92 for more details about the Writing Workshop.

G Develop students' ability to read independently and make their own reading choices with the **Independent Reading feature.**

H Use the **Test Practice: Unit Review** to check students' competency with the core skills before administering a benchmark.

UNIT 4

Poetry

xxii Contents

6 How Do I Use the Leveled Selection Pairs?

Pearson Prentice Hall Literature addresses the challenges of today's mixed ability classrooms through its unique combination of differentiated instruction, online activities, and skills support. When planning lessons for a diverse group of students, look for the **Accessibility-at-a-Glance** grid on the Before You Read pages. Take advantage of the following useful features:

The chart provides a **Lexile** score. Lexile uses factors such as sentence length and vocabulary difficulty to determine a score that can help you predict student comprehension.

This grid also provides a variety of qualitative measures to help you match your students to the literature that is most appropriate for them.

Differentiated Instruction for Universal Access

Accessibility at a Glance: Selection Choices

	The Real Story of a Cowboy's Life		Rattlesnake Hunt		
Context	Historical: Late 1800s		Florida Everglades		Because a number of factors determine the relative accessibility of leveled selections, in some cases the Lexile rating of the more challenging selection will be lower than that of the more accessible selection.
Language/ Vocabulary	• Both formal and informal (colloquial) diction • Grade-level vocabulary		• Both formal and conversational diction • Above-level vocabulary is footnoted		
Concept Level	Accessible (the truth about cowboys' lives)		Accessible (overcoming a fear)		
Literary Merit	Factual account		Personal experience		
Lexile/Length	Lexile: 1160L	Word Count: 1,208	Lexile: 1030L	Word Count: 1,981	
Overall Rating	**More accessible**		**More challenging**		

Use the **Overall Rating** as the final tool for deciding which selection is appropriate for your students.

7 How Do I Differentiate Instruction?

Pearson Prentice Hall Literature provides unprecedented opportunities for differentiated instruction:

- **Teacher's Edition:** Use the strategies and techniques geared toward different reading levels and learning styles.
- **Reader's Notebooks:** Customize instruction for every selection with reading support for struggling readers and English learners.
- **Leveled Vocabulary and Reading Warm-ups:** For each selection, build background, fluency, and vocabulary.
- **Leveled Selection Tests:** Choose from two tests for each selection, according to your students' ability levels.
- **Graphic Organizers:** Give struggling readers additional support with completed versions of all organizers in the Student Edition.

Differentiated Instruction for Universal Access

Background for Special Needs Students
Point out that author Amy Tan uses nonstandard English for the mother's dialogue. Explain that this type of "broken" English is not intended to be derogatory; it represents the communication of a person whose first language is not English and who has not had much instruction in English. The author uses nonstandard English to make the character seem real to readers. Help students identify the nonstandard elements in the mother's speech, adding missing words to complete the thoughts in standard English.

EL Strategy for English Learners
Students may have difficulty understanding the descriptions in the story because of the use of unfamiliar phrases. Help students by using gestures and body language to communicate the meaning of descriptive phrases such as "pursing her lips" (p. 261) and "performed listlessly" (p. 263). Tell students to record these phrases as they read further and to take time to reread and visualize them or act them out.

8 When Do I Teach Writing?

This program incorporates opportunities in every unit for both process writing and writing for assessment.

Writing Process: To help students prepare for every **Writing Workshop,** *Work in Progress* features appear with each leveled selection pair. These focused prewriting activities encourage students to practice prewriting strategies such as these:

- choosing and narrowing a topic
- gathering details
- preparing a thesis statement

Twice per unit, a **Writing Workshop** with step-by-step instruction guides students to develop their ideas into full-length compositions, addressing these key stages in the writing process:

- Prewriting
- Drafting
- Revising
- Editing and Proofreading
- Publishing and Presenting

Writing Workshop

Exposition: Cause-and-Effect Essay

Defining the Form Whether the subject is human nature, historical trends, or weather patterns, cause-and-effect reasoning explains why things happen. A **cause-and-effect essay** examines the relationship between or among two or more events, explaining how one causes another. You may use elements of this type of writing in science reports, history papers, and health articles, for example.

Assignment Write a cause-and-effect essay to explain an event or a condition in a subject area that interests you, such as business, the arts, technology, history, sports, or music. Include these elements:

- ✔ a clear *identification of a cause-and-effect relationship*
- ✔ an *analysis of specific aspects of the cause* or causes that produce the effects
- ✔ *facts, details, examples, and reasons that support your assertions and anticipate readers' questions*
- ✔ a *logical organization* clarified by smooth transitions
- ✔ error-free grammar, including correct *subject-verb agreement*

To preview the criteria on which your cause-and-effect essay may be judged, see the rubric on page 409.

Writing Workshop: *Work in Progress*

If you have completed the Work-in-Progress assignments on pages 345 and 373, you already have many ideas to use in your cause-and-effect essay. Work with these ideas, or explore a new one as you complete the Writing Workshop.

Reading Writing Connection
To get a feel for cause-and-effect essays, read the excerpt from *Silent Spring* by Rachel Carson on page 167.

FCAT Reading Performance Tasks: To help students prepare for short-response and extended-response performance tasks on the FCAT Reading, many **Informational Texts** features conclude with an annotated FCAT Reading performance task that includes a step-by-step planner to help students complete the assignment.

Test Practice: Informational Texts

Comparing Informational Texts

(a) Paraphrase the first paragraphs of both the newspaper editorial and the primary source. **(b)** State the **main idea** of each paraphrase. **(c)** In what ways does the main idea in the editorial paraphrase **connect** with the main idea of the primary source paraphrase? Explain your answer.

Timed Writing

Write a Response to Literature

Format
The prompt directs you to write a response to literature. Therefore, you must discuss your thoughts about a text you have read.

Each of these texts presents a different perspective on the same historical event, the fall of the Berlin Wall in 1989. Choose one of the texts and write a response to literature in which you describe what you found compelling about the text. Explain what effect the author's writing had on you, citing and paraphrasing sections of text to support your response. (40 minutes)

Academic Vocabulary
When you *cite* a section or passage from a text, you quote it as support for the argument or ideas you are presenting.

5-Minute Planner

Complete these steps before you begin to write:

1. Read the prompt carefully and completely. Look for key words that will help you understand the assignment.
2. Review the editorial and primary source. Think about the authors' perspectives and opinions. Consider your response to the texts when you first read them. Decide which article is more compelling. **TIP** Paraphrase any sections of text that are unclear to gain a better understanding of the information and locate main ideas.
3. Skim the text you have chosen and take notes about details and information you will include as support in your response.
4. Use your notes to draft an outline. Then use your outline and notes to draft your response.

Test Practice: Informational Text 407

Technology

PH Online Essay Scorer

Score student essays in seconds.

Finally, to facilitate your teaching of writing, the **Pearson Prentice Hall Online Essay Scorer** provides instant scoring and feedback, plus tips for revision. You save time, and your students become better writers!

9 How Do I Monitor Student Progress?

Pearson Prentice Hall makes progress monitoring easy with frequent opportunities to evaluate student progress and to reteach material.

- Use the **Diagnostic Tests** at the beginning of the school year to determine entry-level reading skills. You will find frequent **reading checks** and suggestions in the Teacher's Edition for monitoring student progress during reading.
- After reading selections, use the **Open Book Tests** and leveled **Selection Tests** to assess comprehension and mastery of the literary, reading, and vocabulary skills.
- As you teach the unit, use the **Test Practice** pages in standardized-test format to give students practice in applying core unit skills and in writing for assessment under test-taking conditions.
- Use the **Benchmark Tests** to monitor progress at regular, frequent intervals. For your convenience, both mid-unit and end-of-unit tests are provided.

ExamView test generator

Use the electronic test generator to customize assessment.

10 How Does the Program Help Me Develop as a Teacher?

The Teacher's Edition provides these built-in professional development features:

- **Step-by-Step Teaching:** Margin notes provide strategies, tips, and examples for teaching skills.
- **Differentiated Instruction:** Notes provide support, strategies, and enrichment for learners of varied abilities.
- **Vocabulary Development:** A variety of strategies helps you expand students' vocabulary.
- **Professional Development:** The **Professional Development Guidebook** and Professional Development essays and notes in the Teacher's Edition provide pedagogical explanations of specific techniques that will enhance your effectiveness as a teacher.

11 How Can I Use Technology In My Classroom?

PHLit Online!

PHLitOnline allows you to teach the entire program without using the print products. It contains all of the components of the program in one central location: all of the print and activity-based materials PLUS integrated videos, animations, interactive practice activities, songs, and audio. You will navigate through the program by the Table of Contents, exactly as you would in the textbook.

In addition to serving as a stand-alone, the digital product can also support a print-based approach, providing material for classroom presentations, assessment, lesson planning, and reporting.

Differentiated Instruction for Universal Access

Background for Special Needs Students
Point out that author Amy Tan uses nonstandard English for the mother's dialogue. Explain that this type of "broken" English is not intended to be derogatory; it represents the communication of a person whose first language is not English and who has not had much instruction in English. The author uses nonstandard English to make the character seem real to readers. Help students identify the nonstandard elements in the mother's speech, adding missing words to complete the thoughts in standard English.

EL Strategy for English Learners
Students may have difficulty understanding the descriptions in the story because of the use of unfamiliar phrases. Help students by using gestures and body language to communicate the meaning of descriptive phrases such as "pursing her lips" (p. 261) and "performed listlessly" (p. 263). Tell students to record these phrases as they read further and to take time to reread and visualize them or act them out.

Using *Pearson Prentice Hall Literature* for Test Preparation

National and state assessments typically present a variety of multiple-choice and written response questions that address literary concepts, reading comprehension, writing, language conventions, and vocabulary. *Pearson Prentice Hall Literature* provides assessment practice for each of these domains throughout the student editions.

1

Reinforce the strategies students will use to tackle multiple-choice questions each and every day.

TIP 1

Encourage students to read the passage carefully and refer to it if the question requires them to do so.

TIP 2

Look for key words or facts before looking for the correct answer. For example, a question may ask students to define a word as it is used in a passage or to provide a synonym or antonym for the word.

TIP 3

Remind students that words receiving special type treatment in a test question indicate that the word is important in determining the correct answer.

TIP 4

Always remind students to be sure that the question number on the answer sheet is the same as the question they are answering. One way to reinforce this skill is to provide bubble-sheets for daily assessments.

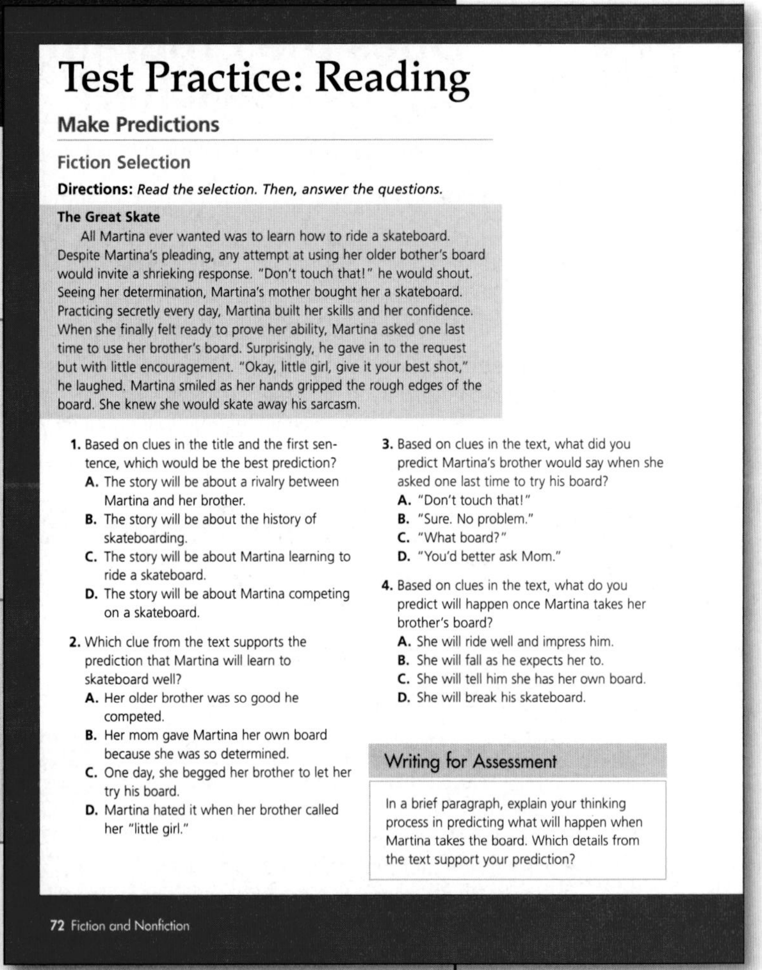

Test Practice: Reading

Make Predictions

Fiction Selection

Directions: *Read the selection. Then, answer the questions.*

The Great Skate

All Martina ever wanted was to learn how to ride a skateboard. Despite Martina's pleading, any attempt at using her older bother's board would invite a shrieking response. "Don't touch that!" he would shout. Seeing her determination, Martina's mother bought her a skateboard. Practicing secretly every day, Martina built her skills and her confidence. When she finally felt ready to prove her ability, Martina asked one last time to use her brother's board. Surprisingly, he gave in to the request but with little encouragement. "Okay, little girl, give it your best shot," he laughed. Martina smiled as her hands gripped the rough edges of the board. She knew she would skate away his sarcasm.

1. Based on clues in the title and the first sentence, which would be the best prediction?
   A. The story will be about a rivalry between Martina and her brother.
   B. The story will be about the history of skateboarding.
   C. The story will be about Martina learning to ride a skateboard.
   D. The story will be about Martina competing on a skateboard.
2. Which clue from the text supports the prediction that Martina will learn to skateboard well?
   A. Her older brother was so good he competed.
   B. Her mom gave Martina her own board because she was so determined.
   C. One day, she begged her brother to let her try his board.
   D. Martina hated it when her brother called her "little girl."
3. Based on clues in the text, what did you predict Martina's brother would say when she asked one last time to try his board?
   A. "Don't touch that!"
   B. "Sure. No problem."
   C. "What board?"
   D. "You'd better ask Mom."
4. Based on clues in the text, what do you predict will happen once Martina takes her brother's board?
   A. She will ride well and impress him.
   B. She will fall as he expects her to.
   C. She will tell him she has her own board.
   D. She will break his skateboard.

Writing for Assessment

In a brief paragraph, explain your thinking process in predicting what will happen when Martina takes the board. Which details from the text support your prediction?

72 Fiction and Nonfiction

2

Use **After You Read** questions to provide writing experiences on a daily basis.

Most national and state assessments include writing prompts in addition to multiple-choice questions. The ability to explain an answer in writing will help students clarify their thinking about a selection.

Daily writing practice is key to developing students' communication and writing skills. Hold students accountable for clearly expressing their understanding in each response. *Pearson Prentice Hall Literature* features the following **After You Read** exercises four times per unit. Use them to provide the writing practice students need:

- Literary Analysis Questions
- Reading Skill Questions
- Vocabulary Questions

After You Read | Sonata for Harp and Bicycle

Literary Analysis: Plot

1. Using a chart like this one, identify two key events in the **rising action,** one that marks the **climax,** and one in the **falling action.** Trade charts with a partner and discuss why you chose the events that you did.
2. **(a)** Identify a statement or event that **foreshadows** Jason's decision to enter the Grimes Buildings after closing hours. **(b)** Explain how the use of foreshadowing increases the story's **suspense.**

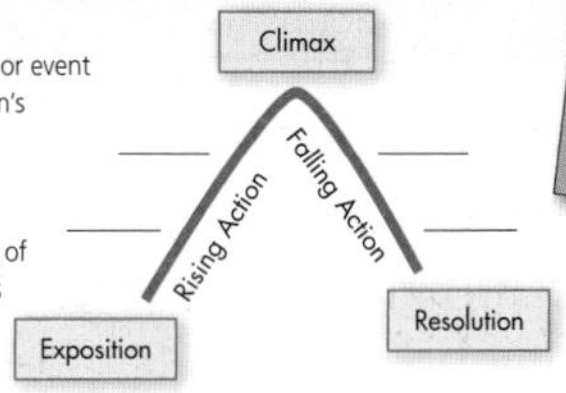

Reading Skill: Make Predictions

3. What **prediction** did you make when Jason entered the Grimes Buildings after closing and heard a bicycle bell? **(b)** What details helped you make your prediction?
4. Was your prediction **verified** by later story events? Explain.

Vocabulary

Practice An **analogy** shows the relationship between pairs of words. Use a word from the vocabulary list on page 44 to complete each analogy. For each case, your choice should create a word pair that matches the relationship between the first two words.

1. angry : shout :: _____ : whisper
2. steal : take :: _____ : give
3. hopelessly : far :: _____ : near
4. ending : concluding :: _____ : infringing
5. criticizing : praising :: _____ : comforting
6. funny : serious :: _____ : reasonable

Word Study Use the context of the sentences and what you know about the **suffix *-ate*** to explain your answer to each question.

1. What does someone do if they *participate* in an activity?
2. If a question is *complicated,* is it easy?

Word Study

The **suffix *-ate*** means "to become or form."

Challenge Explain how the suffix *-ate* contributes to the meaning of these words. Use a dictionary if necessary.

depreciate
captivate
duplicate

Sonata for Harp and Bicycle **57**

3

Provide ongoing practice with prompts similar to those students will encounter on state and national assessments.

To de-mystify tests and alleviate anxiety related to testing situations, provide frequent practice opportunities for writing.

Use the exercises in the twelve **Writing Workshops** and well as the **Work-in-Progress** features leading up to each workshop to help students hone their writing skills.

Writing Workshop

Narration: Autobiographical Narrative

Defining the Form An **autobiographical narrative** describes real events in the writer's life and shares the lessons or wisdom the writer gained from the experiences. You might use elements of autobiographical narration in letters, journals, reflective essays, or persuasive essays.

Assignment Write an autobiographical narrative about an event that taught you a valuable lesson. Include the following elements:

- ✔ a *sequence of events* involving you, the writer
- ✔ a *problem, or conflict,* and a lesson you learned from it
- ✔ details that locate scenes and incidents in specific places
- ✔ your thoughts, feelings, or views about the significance of events
- ✔ error-free grammar, including *correct use of possessive nouns*

To preview the criteria on which your autobiographical narrative may be judged, see the rubric on page 99.

Writing Workshop: *Work-in-Progress*

Review the work you did on pages 41 and 71.

PREPARING FOR STANDARDIZED TESTS

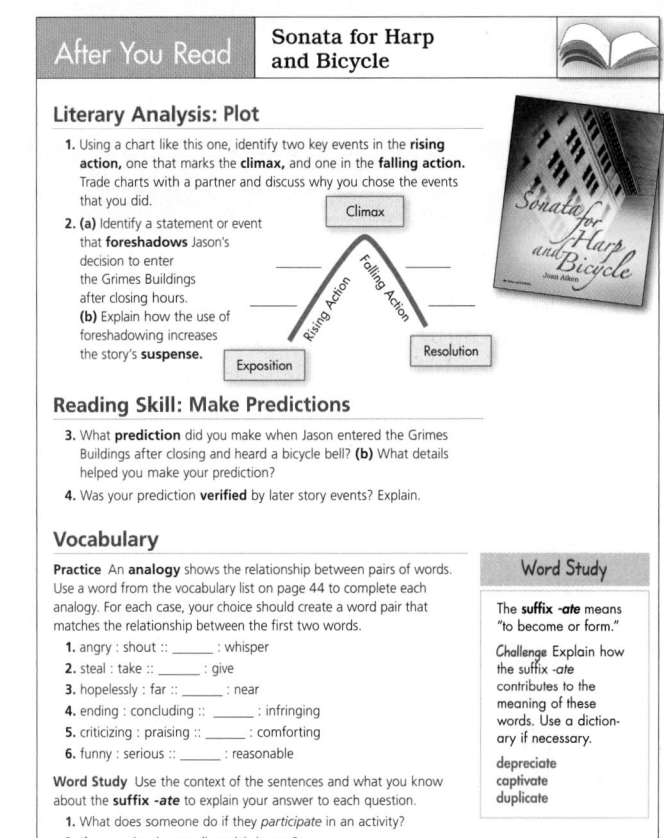

4

Familiarize students with the rubric scoring system.

In addition to familiarizing students with the types of prompts to which they will be required to respond, it is also important that students be exposed to the criteria against which their written responses will be assessed.

Each rubric is aligned to an individual writing assessment.

Once students are familiar with these criteria, you should also offer models of what constitutes the various points on the rubric scale. You may also ask students to use the rubrics to assess their peers' writing.

Criteria	Rating Scale (not very – very)				
Focus: How central are you to the action of the story?	1	2	3	4	5
Organization: How clearly organized is the sequence of events?	1	2	3	4	5
Support/Elaboration: How powerfully are sensory details used to locate scenes in specific places?	1	2	3	4	5
Style: How clearly do you convey your insights, thoughts, and feelings?	1	2	3	4	5
Conventions: How correct is your grammar, especially your use of possessive nouns?	1	2	3	4	5
Word Choice: How precise is the language used to describe the people, places, and events in your narrative?	1	2	3	4	5

5

Provide practice writing timed responses.

Alleviate the stress often associated with taking timed writing tests by providing ongoing practice. *Pearson Prentice Hall Literature* provides twelve timed-writing exercises per grade level.

Each timed-writing activity includes a prompt, annotations, and tips to help students budget time for their prewriting and writing activities.

Timed Writing

Write an Essay

Format
The prompt directs you to write an essay. Therefore, you should write an expository composition that has an introduction, body, and conclusion.

Many stories contain factual information to establish the setting or support the plot. Review the information given in the recipe and the how-to article. Write an essay of a few short paragraphs in which you explain how using this information might make a fiction piece more believable or realistic. (15 minutes)

Academic Vocabulary
When you *explain* something, you make it clear using examples, descriptions, details, and facts.

5-Minute Planner

Complete these steps before you begin to write:

1. Read the prompt carefully and completely to make sure you understand the assignment and the format to use for your writing.

6

Monitor your students' skills on an ongoing basis.

Multiple opportunities to monitor progress can be found in each unit.

- Use the **Before You Read** section at the beginning of every selection pairing to familiarize students with the literary analysis, comprehenson, and vocabulary skills that they will be using in conjunction with a particular selection.

Literary Analysis: Plot

Plot is the sequence of events in a narrative. It is structured around a **conflict,** or problem, and it can be divided into the following parts:

- **Exposition:** characters and setting are introduced
- **Rising Action:** central conflict begins
- **Climax:** high point of intensity in the conflict is reached
- **Falling Action:** conflict's intensity lessens
- **Resolution:** conflict concludes and loose ends are tied up

Writers use a variety of techniques, or *stylistic devices,* to keep readers interested in the plot. One of these devices, **foreshadowing,** is the use of clues to hint at events that will happen later in a story. Authors use this technique to create **suspense,** a feeling of tension that keeps readers wondering what will happen next.

Reading Skill: Make Predictions

A **prediction** is an idea you develop about what will happen later in a narrative. It is based on details in the text combined with your own experience. As you read, notice details that may foreshadow future events. Next, make predictions based on those details, and then **read ahead to verify your predictions.** If a prediction turns out to be wrong, evaluate your reasoning by asking questions like these:

- Did you misread details?
- Did the author purposely create false expectations in order to surprise you later in the story?

Revise, or change, your prediction based on your evaluation.

Using the Strategy: Predictions Map

Use a chart like the one shown to record and evaluate your predictions. Analyze any inaccurate predictions to determine why they were incorrect.

Prediction	Outcome	Analysis of Prediction
The butler will be exposed as the criminal.	The gardener is exposed as the criminal.	The author created a surprise ending by misleading readers.

PHLit Online!
www.PHLitOnline.com

Hear It!
- Selection summary audio
- Selection audio

See It!
- Get Connected video
- Background video
- More about the author
- Vocabulary flashcards

Do It!
- Interactive journals
- Interactive graphic organizers
- Self-test
- Internet activity
- Grammar tutorial
- Interactive vocabulary games

Before You Read: Sonata for Harp and Bicycle • The Cask of Amontillado 43

Vocabulary
furtive (fur' tiv) *adj.* sneaky; hidden

Literary Analysis
Plot
How do Jason's actions increase the suspense of the narrative?

▼ Critical Viewing
What advantages would patrolling corridors on a bicycle offer as opposed to patrolling on foot? **[Evaluate]**

snowy chrysanthemums, and up Glass Street. A tiny furtive wedge of darkness beckoned him, a snicket, a hacket, an alley carved into the thickness of the building. It was so narrow that at any moment, it seemed, the overtopping walls would come together and squeeze it out of existence.

Walking as softly as an Indian, Jason passed through it, slid by a file of dustbins,[5] and found the foot of the fire escape. Iron treads rose into the mist, like an illustration to a Gothic[6] fairy tale.

He began to climb.

When he had mounted to the ninth story he paused for breath. It was a lonely place. The lighting consisted of a dim bulb at the foot of every flight. A well of gloom sank beneath him. The cold fingers of the wind nagged and fluttered at the tails of his jacket, and he pulled the string of the fire door and edged inside.

Grimes Buildings were triangular, with the street forming the base of the triangle, and the fire escape the point. Jason could see two long passages coming toward him, meeting at an acute angle where he stood. He started down the left-hand one, tiptoeing in the cavelike silence. Nowhere was there any sound, except for the faraway drip of a tap. No night watchman would stay in the building; none was needed. Burglars gave the place a wide berth.

Jason opened a door at random; then another. Offices lay everywhere about him, empty and forbidding. Some held lipstick-stained tissues, spilled powder, and orange peels; others were still foggy with cigarette smoke. Here was a Director's suite of rooms—a desk like half an acre of frozen lake, inch-thick carpet, roses, and the smell of cigars. Here was a conference room with scattered squares of doodled blotting paper. All equally empty.

He was not sure when he first began to notice the bell. Telephone, he thought at first, and then he remembered that all the outside lines were disconnected at five. And

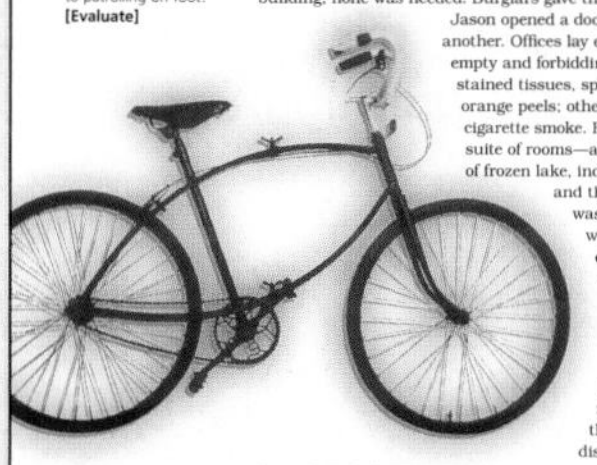

5. **dustbins** *n.* British term for garbage cans.
6. **Gothic** *adj.* mysterious.

50 Fiction and Nonfiction

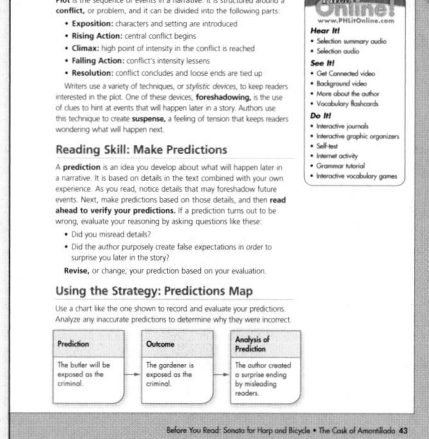

- Use side-column notes with a selection and the **After You Read** questions to informally monitor student understanding.

- Use the **Test Practice: Reading** sections and **Unit Reviews** to assess students' mastery of key skills and concepts.

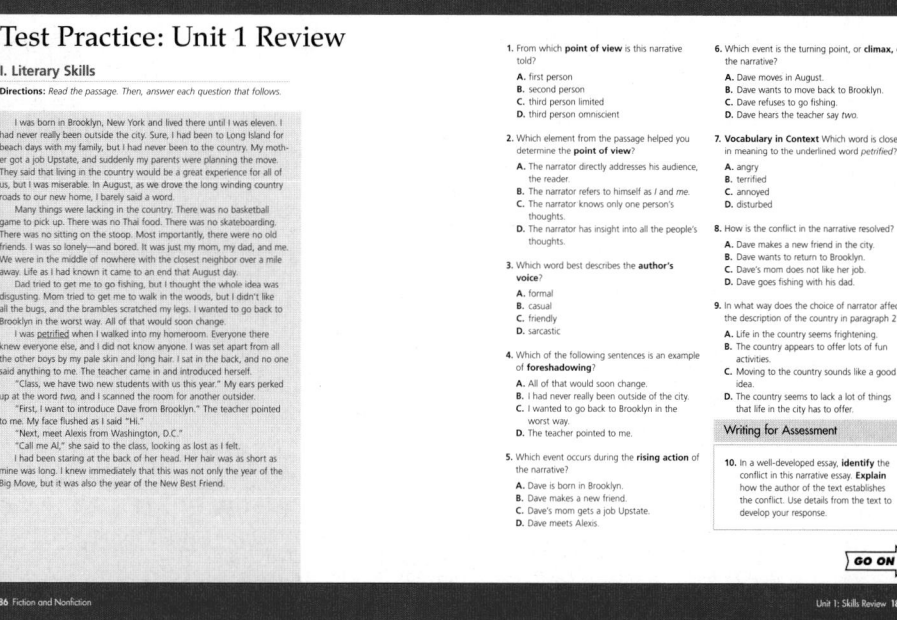

Test Practice: Unit 1 Review

I. Literary Skills

Directions: *Read the passage. Then, answer each question that follows.*

I was born in Brooklyn, New York and lived there until I was eleven. I had never really been outside the city. Sure, I had been to Long Island for beach days with my family, but I had never been to the country. My mother got a job Upstate, and suddenly my parents were planning the move. They said that living in the country would be a great experience for all of us, but I was miserable. In August, as we drove the long winding country roads to our new home, I barely said a word.

Many things were lacking in the country. There was no basketball game to pick up. There was no Thai food. There was no skateboarding. There was no sitting on the stoop. Most importantly, there were no old friends. I was so lonely—and bored. It was just my mom, my dad, and me. We were in the middle of nowhere with the closest neighbor over a mile away. Life as I had known it came to an end that August day.

Dad tried to get me to go fishing, but I thought the whole idea was disgusting. Mom tried to get me to walk in the woods, but I didn't like all the bugs, and the brambles scratched my legs. I wanted to go back to Brooklyn in the worst way. All of that would soon change.

I was petrified when I walked into my homeroom. Everyone there knew everyone else, and I did not know anyone. I was set apart from all the other boys by my pale skin and long hair. I sat in the back, and no one said anything to me. The teacher came in and introduced herself.

"Class, we have two new students with us this year." My ears perked up at the word *two,* and I scanned the room for another outsider.

"First, I want to introduce Dave from Brooklyn." The teacher pointed to me. My face flushed as I said "Hi."

"Next, meet Alexis from Washington, D.C."

"Call me Al," she said to the class, looking as lost as I felt.

I had been staring at the back of her head. Her hair was as short as mine was long. I knew immediately that this was not only the year of the Big Move, but it was also the year of the New Best Friend.

186 Fiction and Nonfiction

1. From which **point of view** is this narrative told?
   A. first person
   B. second person
   C. third person limited
   D. third person omniscient

2. Which element from the passage helped you determine the **point of view**?
   A. The narrator directly addresses his audience, the reader.
   B. The narrator refers to himself as *I* and *me.*
   C. The narrator knows only one person's thoughts.
   D. The narrator has insight into all the people's thoughts.

3. Which word best describes the **author's voice**?
   A. formal
   B. casual
   C. friendly
   D. sarcastic

4. Which of the following sentences is an example of **foreshadowing**?
   A. All of that would soon change.
   B. I had never really been outside of the city.
   C. I wanted to go back to Brooklyn in the worst way.
   D. The teacher pointed to me.

5. Which event occurs during the **rising action** of the narrative?
   A. Dave is born in Brooklyn.
   B. Dave makes a new friend.
   C. Dave's mom gets a job Upstate.
   D. Dave meets Alexis.

6. Which event is the turning point, or **climax,** of the narrative?
   A. Dave moves in August.
   B. Dave wants to move back to Brooklyn.
   C. Dave refuses to go fishing.
   D. Dave hears the teacher say *two.*

7. **Vocabulary in Context** Which word is closest in meaning to the underlined word *petrified*?
   A. angry
   B. terrified
   C. annoyed
   D. disturbed

8. How is the conflict in the narrative resolved?
   A. Dave makes a new friend in the city.
   B. Dave wants to return to Brooklyn.
   C. Dave's mom does not like her job.
   D. Dave goes fishing with his dad.

9. In what way does the choice of narrator affect the description of the country in paragraph 2?
   A. Life in the country seems frightening.
   B. The country appears to offer lots of fun activities.
   C. Moving to the country sounds like a good idea.
   D. The country seems to lack a lot of things that life in the city has to offer.

Writing for Assessment

10. In a well-developed essay, **identify** the conflict in this narrative essay. **Explain** how the author of the text establishes the conflict. Use details from the text to develop your response.

GO ON

Unit 1: Skills Review 187

How to Use This Book

How is this book organized?

- **There are six units, each focusing on a specific genre.**
- **Each unit has a Big Question to get you thinking about important ideas and to guide your reading.**

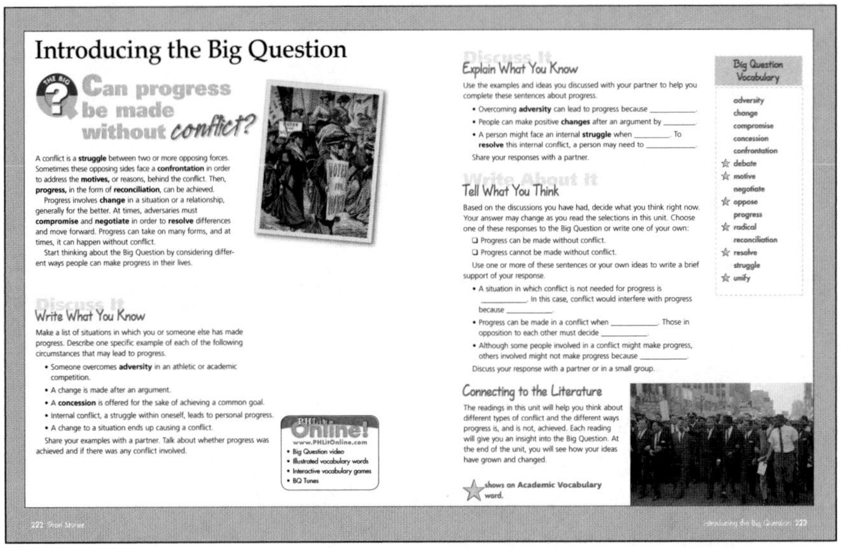

Introducing the Big Question

THE BIG ? Can progress be made without conflict?

A conflict is a **struggle** between two or more opposing forces. Sometimes these opposing sides face a **confrontation** in order to address the **motives,** or reasons, behind the conflict. Then, **progress,** in the form of **reconciliation**, can be achieved.

Progress involves **change** in a situation or a relationship, generally for the better. At times, adversaries must **compromise** and **negotiate** in order to **resolve** differences and move forward. Progress can take on many forms, and at times, it can happen without conflict.

Start thinking about the Big Question by considering different ways people can make progress in their lives.

Discuss It

Write What You Know

Make a list of situations in which you or someone else has made progress. Describe one specific example of each of the following circumstances that may lead to progress.

- Someone overcomes **adversity** in an athletic or academic competition.
- A change is made after an argument.
- A **concession** is offered for the sake of achieving a common goal.
- Internal conflict, a struggle within oneself, leads to personal progress.
- A change to a situation ends up causing a conflict.

Share your examples with a partner. Talk about whether progress was achieved and if there was any conflict involved.

PHLit Online! www.PHLitOnline.com
- Big Question video
- Illustrated vocabulary words
- Interactive vocabulary games
- BQ Tunes

Discuss It

Explain What You Know

Use the examples and ideas you discussed with your partner to help you complete these sentences about progress.

- Overcoming **adversity** can lead to progress because ________.
- People can make positive **changes** after an argument by ________.
- A person might face an internal **struggle** when ________. To **resolve** this internal conflict, a person may need to ________.

Share your responses with a partner.

Write About It

Tell What You Think

Based on the discussions you have had, decide what you think right now. Your answer may change as you read the selections in this unit. Choose one of these responses to the Big Question or write one of your own:

❑ Progress can be made without conflict.
❑ Progress cannot be made without conflict.

Use one or more of these sentences or your own ideas to write a brief support of your response.

- A situation in which conflict is not needed for progress is ________. In this case, conflict would interfere with progress because ________.
- Progress can be made in a conflict when ________. Those in opposition to each other must decide ________.
- Although some people involved in a conflict might make progress, others involved might not make progress because ________.

Discuss your response with a partner or in a small group.

Connecting to the Literature

The readings in this unit will help you think about different types of conflict and the different ways progress is, and is not, achieved. Each reading will give you an insight into the Big Question. At the end of the unit, you will see how your ideas have grown and changed.

☆ shows an **Academic Vocabulary** word.

Big Question Vocabulary

adversity
change
compromise
concession
confrontation
☆ debate
☆ motive
negotiate
☆ oppose
progress
☆ radical
reconciliation
☆ resolve
struggle
☆ unify

◀ At the beginning of the unit—**Introducing the Big Question** provides a reading focus for the entire unit. Use **academic vocabulary** to think, talk, and write about this question.

At the end of the unit—**Applying the Big Question** gives you an opportunity to reflect on what you have read and learned. See how your ideas about the Big Question have deepened or changed as a result of your work throughout the unit. ▶

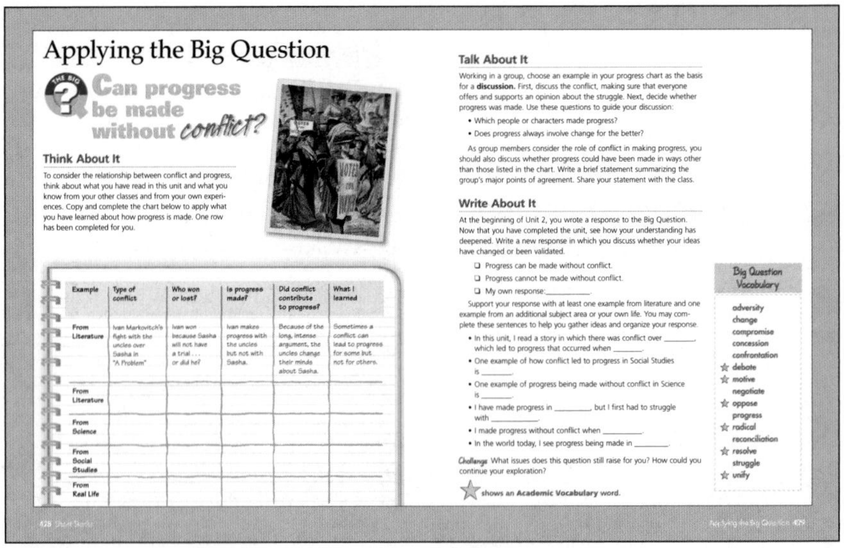

Applying the Big Question

THE BIG ? Can progress be made without conflict?

Think About It

To consider the relationship between conflict and progress, think about what you have read in this unit and what you know from your other classes and from your own experiences. Copy and complete the chart below to apply what you have learned about how progress is made. One row has been completed for you.

Example	Type of conflict	Who won or lost?	Is progress made?	Did conflict contribute to progress?	What I learned
From Literature	Ivan Markovitch's fight with the uncles over Sasha in "A Problem"	Ivan won because Sasha will not have a trial . . . or did he?	Ivan makes progress with the uncles but not with Sasha.	Because of the long, intense argument, the uncles change their minds about Sasha.	Sometimes a conflict can lead to progress for some but not for others.
From Literature					
From Science					
From Social Studies					
From Real Life					

Talk About It

Working in a group, choose an example in your progress chart as the basis for a **discussion.** First, discuss the conflict, making sure that everyone offers and supports an opinion about the struggle. Next, decide whether progress was made. Use these questions to guide your discussion:

- Which people or characters made progress?
- Does progress always involve change for the better?

As group members consider the role of conflict in making progress, you should also discuss whether progress could have been made in ways other than those listed in the chart. Write a brief statement summarizing the group's major points of agreement. Share your statement with the class.

Write About It

At the beginning of Unit 2, you wrote a response to the Big Question. Now that you have completed the unit, see how your understanding has deepened. Write a new response in which you discuss whether your ideas have changed or been validated.

❑ Progress can be made without conflict.
❑ Progress cannot be made without conflict.
❑ My own response: ________.

Support your response with at least one example from literature and one example from an additional subject area or your own life. You may complete these sentences to help you gather ideas and organize your response.

- In this unit, I read a story in which there was conflict over ________, which led to progress that occurred when ________.
- One example of how conflict led to progress in Social Studies is ________.
- One example of progress being made without conflict in Science is ________.
- I have made progress in ________, but I first had to struggle with ________.
- I made progress without conflict when ________.
- In the world today, I see progress being made in ________.

Challenge What issues does this question still raise for you? How could you continue your exploration?

☆ shows an **Academic Vocabulary** word.

Big Question Vocabulary

adversity
change
compromise
concession
confrontation
☆ debate
☆ motive
negotiate
☆ oppose
progress
☆ radical
reconciliation
☆ resolve
struggle
☆ unify

How are the literary selections organized?

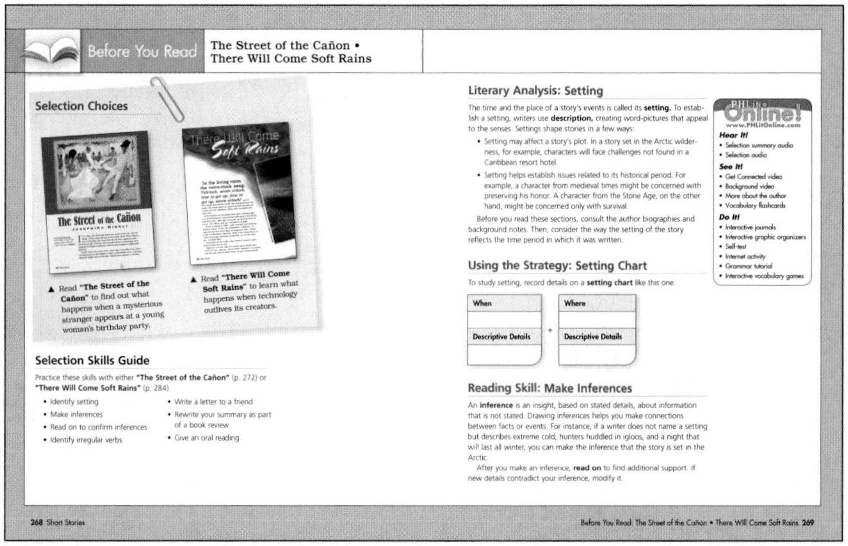

◀ **Before You Read** introduces two selection choices that both teach the same skills. Your teacher will help you choose the selection that is right for you.

Writing About the Big Question is a quick-writing activity that helps you connect the Big Question to the selection you are about to read.

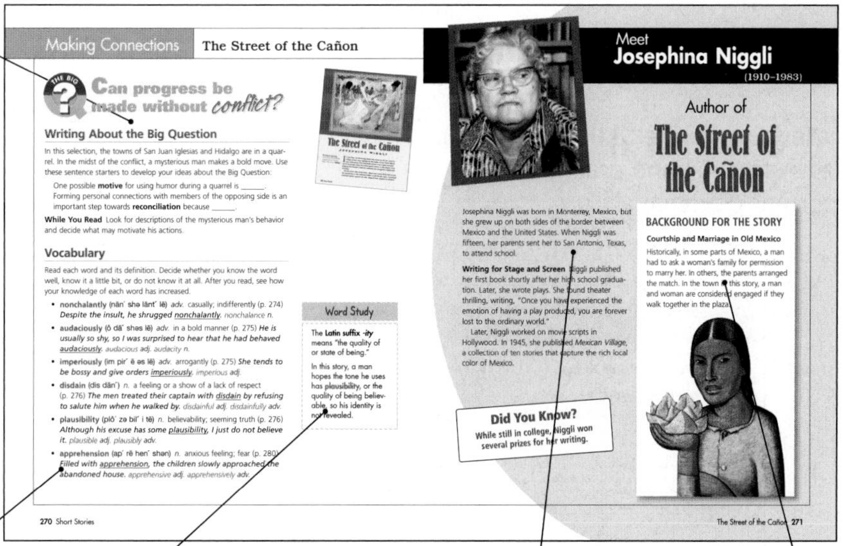

Vocabulary and Word Study introduce important selection vocabulary words and teach you about prefixes, suffixes, and roots.

Meet the Author and Background teach you about the author's life, and provide information that will help you understand the selection.

How are the literary selections organized? *(continued)*

After You Read helps you practice the skills you have learned. ▼

Critical Thinking questions help you reflect on what you have read, and apply the Big Question to the selection.

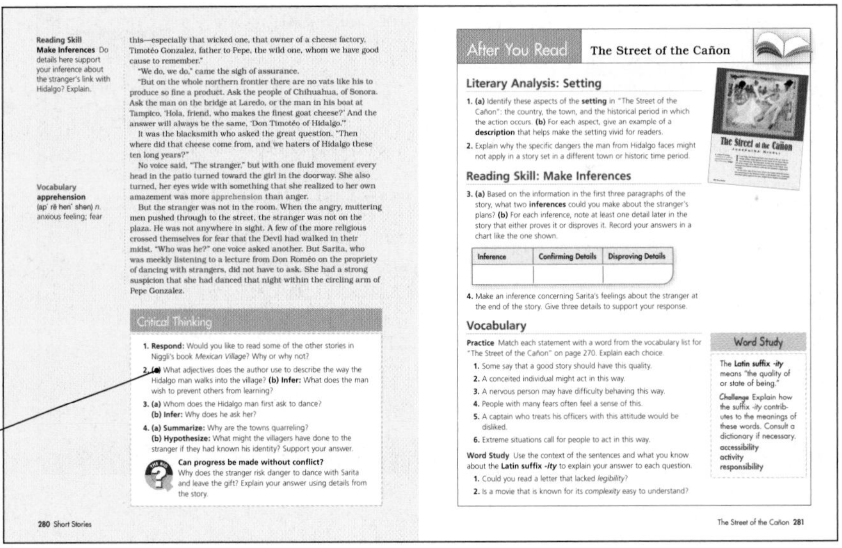

Reading Skill
Make Inferences Do details here support your inference about the stranger's link with Hidalgo? Explain.

Vocabulary
apprehension (ap' rē hen' shən) *n.* anxious feeling; fear

this—especially that wicked one, that owner of a cheese factory, Timotéo Gonzalez, father to Pepe, the wild one, whom we have good cause to remember."

"We do, we do," came the sigh of assurance.

"But on the whole northern frontier there are no vats like his to produce so fine a product. Ask the people of Chihuahua, of Sonora. Ask the man on the bridge at Laredo, or the man in his boat at Tampico, 'Hola, friend, who makes the finest goat cheese?' And the answer will always be the same, 'Don Timotéo of Hidalgo.'"

It was the blacksmith who asked the great question. "Then where did that cheese come from, and we haters of Hidalgo these ten long years?"

No voice said, "The stranger," but with one fluid movement every head in the patio turned toward the girl in the doorway. She also turned, her eyes wide with something that she realized to her own amazement was more apprehension than anger.

But the stranger was not in the room. When the angry, muttering men pushed through to the street, the stranger was not on the plaza. He was not anywhere in sight. A few of the more religious crossed themselves for fear that the Devil had walked in their midst. "Who was he?" one voice asked another. But Sarita, who was meekly listening to a lecture from Don Roméo on the propriety of dancing with strangers, did not have to ask. She had a strong suspicion that she had danced that night within the circling arm of Pepe Gonzalez.

Critical Thinking

1. **Respond:** Would you like to read some of the other stories in Niggli's book *Mexican Village*? Why or why not?
2. **(a)** What adjectives does the author use to describe the way the Hidalgo man walks into the village? **(b) Infer:** What does the man wish to prevent others from learning?
3. **(a)** Whom does the Hidalgo man first ask to dance? **(b) Infer:** Why does he ask her?
4. **(a) Summarize:** Why are the towns quarreling? **(b) Hypothesize:** What might the villagers have done to the stranger if they had known his identity? Support your answer.

Can progress be made without conflict? Why does the stranger risk danger to dance with Sarita and leave the gift? Explain your answer using details from the story.

280 Short Stories

After You Read **The Street of the Cañon**

Literary Analysis: Setting

1. **(a)** Identify these aspects of the **setting** in "The Street of the Cañon": the country, the town, and the historical period in which the action occurs. **(b)** For each aspect, give an example of a **description** that helps make the setting vivid for readers.
2. Explain why the specific dangers the man from Hidalgo faces might not apply in a story set in a different town or historic time period.

Reading Skill: Make Inferences

3. **(a)** Based on the information in the first three paragraphs of the story, what two **inferences** could you make about the stranger's plans? **(b)** For each inference, note at least one detail later in the story that either proves it or disproves it. Record your answers in a chart like the one shown.

Inference	Confirming Details	Disproving Details

4. Make an inference concerning Sarita's feelings about the stranger at the end of the story. Give three details to support your response.

Vocabulary

Practice Match each statement with a word from the vocabulary list for "The Street of the Cañon" on page 270. Explain each choice.

1. Some say that a good story should have this quality.
2. A conceited individual might act in this way.
3. A nervous person may have difficulty behaving this way.
4. People with many fears often feel a sense of this.
5. A captain who treats his officers with this attitude would be disliked.
6. Extreme situations call for people to act in this way.

Word Study Use the context of the sentences and what you know about the **Latin suffix -*ity*** to explain your answer to each question.

1. Could you read a letter that lacked *legibility*?
2. Is a movie that is known for its *complexity* easy to understand?

Word Study

The **Latin suffix -*ity*** means "the quality of or state of being."

Challenge Explain how the suffix -*ity* contributes to the meanings of these words. Consult a dictionary if necessary.
accessibility
activity
responsibility

The Street of the Cañon 281

Integrated Language Skills provides instruction and practice for important grammar skills.

Projects and activities help you deepen your understanding of the selection while strengthening your **writing, listening, speaking, and research skills.**

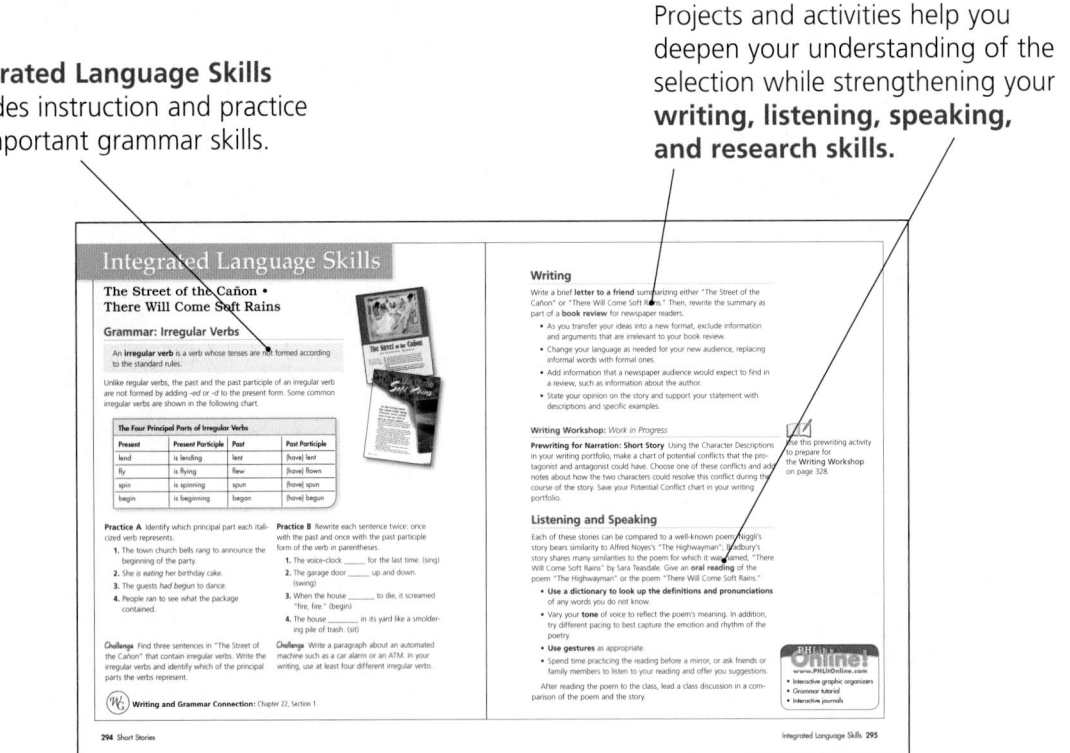

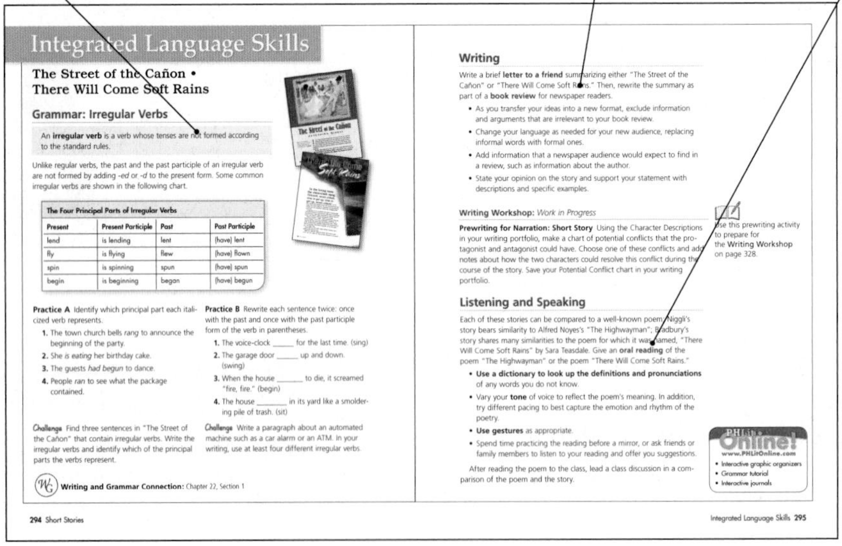

Integrated Language Skills

The Street of the Cañon • There Will Come Soft Rains

Grammar: Irregular Verbs

An **irregular verb** is a verb whose tenses are not formed according to the standard rules.

Unlike regular verbs, the past and the past participle of an irregular verb are not formed by adding *-ed* or *-d* to the present form. Some common irregular verbs are shown in the following chart.

The Four Principal Parts of Irregular Verbs

Present	Present Participle	Past	Past Participle
lend	is lending	lent	(have) lent
fly	is flying	flew	(have) flown
spin	is spinning	spun	(have) spun
begin	is beginning	began	(have) begun

Practice A Identify which principal part each italicized verb represents.

1. The town church bells *rang* to announce the beginning of the party.
2. She *is eating* her birthday cake.
3. The guests *had begun* to dance.
4. People *ran* to see what the package contained.

Challenge Find three sentences in "The Street of the Cañon" that contain irregular verbs. Write the irregular verbs and identify which of the principal parts the verbs represent.

Practice B Rewrite each sentence twice: once with the past and once with the past participle form of the verb in parentheses.

1. The voice-clock ______ for the last time. (sing)
2. The garage door ______ up and down. (swing)
3. When the house ______ to die, it screamed "fire, fire." (begin)
4. The house ______ in its yard like a smoldering pile of trash. (sit)

Challenge Write a paragraph about an automated machine such as a car alarm or an ATM. In your writing, use at least four different irregular verbs.

Writing and Grammar Connection: Chapter 22, Section 1

294 Short Stories

Writing

Write a brief **letter to a friend** summarizing either "The Street of the Cañon" or "There Will Come Soft Rains." Then, rewrite the summary as part of a **book review** for newspaper readers.

- As you transfer your ideas into a new format, exclude information and arguments that are irrelevant to your book review.
- Change your language as needed for your new audience, replacing informal words with formal ones.
- Add information that a newspaper audience would expect to find in a review, such as information about the author.
- State your opinion on the story and support your statement with descriptions and specific examples.

Writing Workshop: *Work in Progress*

Prewriting for Narration: Short Story Using the Character Descriptions in your writing portfolio, make a chart of potential conflicts that the protagonist and antagonist could have. Choose one of these conflicts and add notes about how the two characters could resolve this conflict during the course of the story. Save your Potential Conflict chart in your writing portfolio.

Use this prewriting activity to prepare for the **Writing Workshop** on page 328.

Listening and Speaking

Each of these stories can be compared to a well-known poem. Niggli's story bears similarity to Alfred Noyes's "The Highwayman"; Bradbury's story shares many similarities to the poem for which it was named, "There Will Come Soft Rains" by Sara Teasdale. Give an **oral reading** of the poem "The Highwayman" or the poem "There Will Come Soft Rains."

- **Use a dictionary to look up the definitions and pronunciations** of any words you do not know.
- Vary your **tone** of voice to reflect the poem's meaning. In addition, try different pacing to best capture the emotion and rhythm of the poetry.
- **Use gestures** as appropriate.
- Spend time practicing the reading before a mirror, or ask friends or family members to listen to your reading and offer you suggestions.

After reading the poem to the class, lead a class discussion in a comparison of the poem and the story.

PHLit Online! www.PHLitOnline.com
- Interactive graphic organizers
- Grammar tutorial
- Interactive journals

Integrated Language Skills 295

What special features will I find in this book?

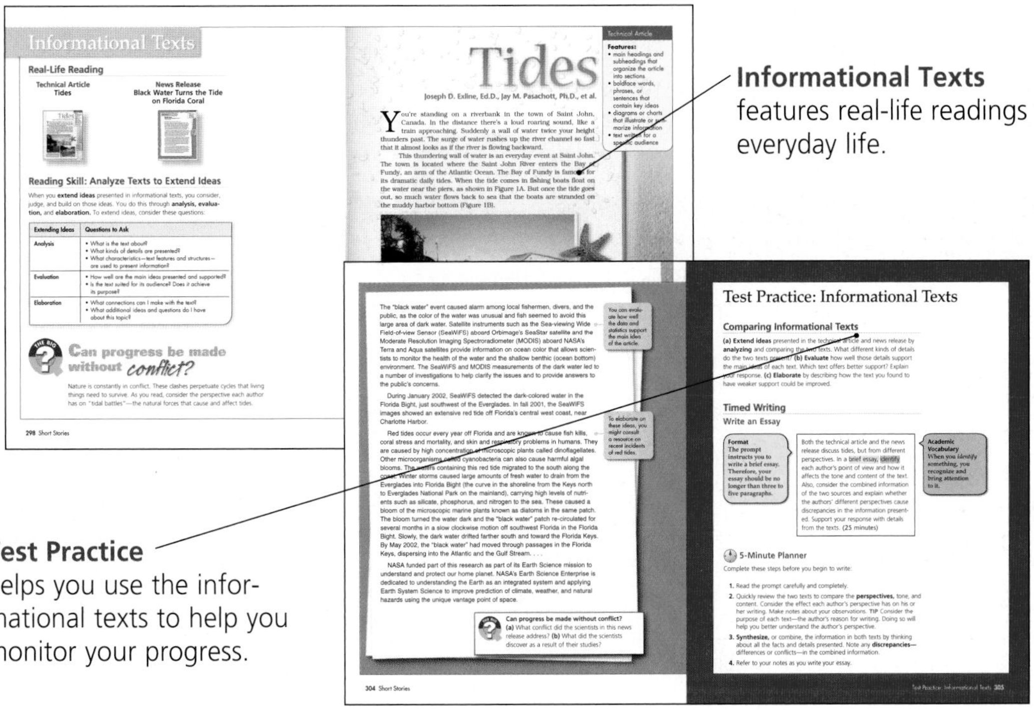

Informational Texts features real-life readings from everyday life.

Test Practice helps you use the informational texts to help you monitor your progress.

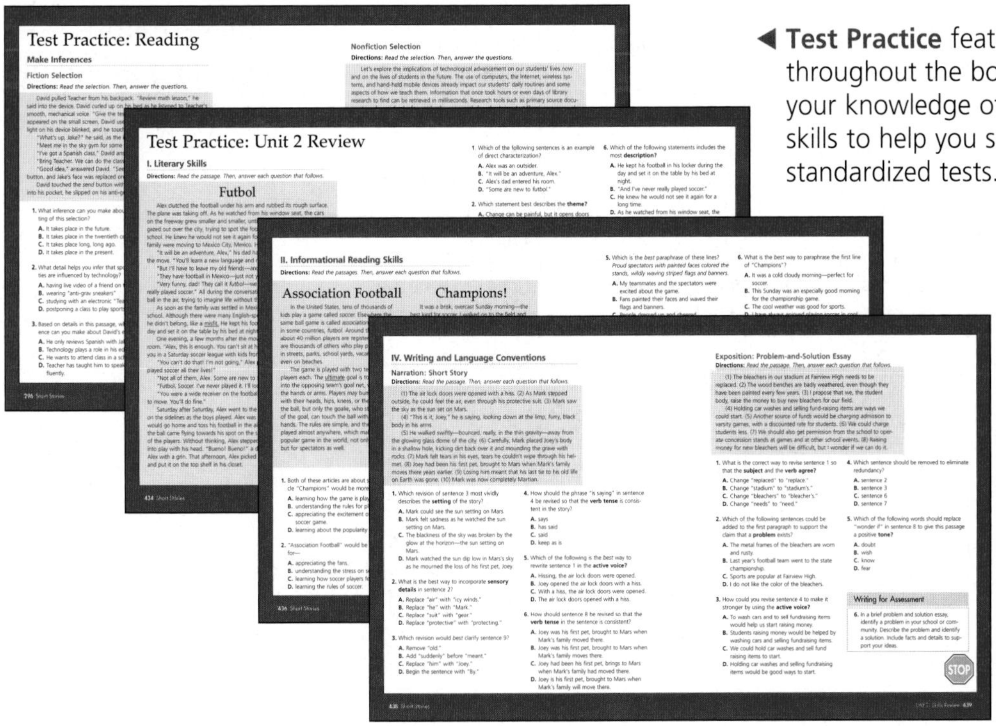

◀ **Test Practice** features throughout the book test your knowledge of all major skills to help you succeed on standardized tests.

Building Your Vocabulary

Academic Vocabulary

Academic vocabulary is the language you encounter in textbooks and on standardized tests. Understanding these words and using them in your classroom discussions and writing will help you communicate your ideas clearly and effectively. The words listed in this chart appear throughout your literature book.

Word	Definition	Related Words	Word in Context
adapt (uh DAPT) v.	change or adjust	adaptable adaptation	Remember to adapt your reading rate to the text.
anticipate (an TIHS uh payt) v.	look forward to	anticipation anticipatory	Look for clues that anticipate future events.
awareness (uh WAIR nuhs) n.	having knowledge	aware	The author has a great awareness of his readers' interests.
background (BAK grownd) n.	conditions that surround or come before something		An author's background shapes his or her writing.
bias (BY uhs) n.	point of view one has before the facts are known	biased	The speaker tried not to allow his bias against fast food to show.
character (KAR ihk tuhr) n.	moral strength; self-discipline	characteristic characteristically	The hero in the myth shows her character through dialogue.
comprehend (kom prih HEHND) v.	grasp mentally; understand	comprehension	The side notes will help you comprehend new vocabulary.
conduct (KON duhkt) n.	the way a person acts; behavior		A speaker's conduct affects how the audience views the speech.
confirm (kuhn FURM) v.	establish the truth or correctness of something	confirmation confirmatory	Confirm whether the predictions are accurate.
context (KON tehkst) n.	circumstances that form the setting of an event	contextual	The context of a story may be historical.
convey (kuhn VAY) v.	communicate or make known		The poet uses imagery to convey feelings.
debate (dih BAYT) v.	argue or discuss	debatable debater	In a debate, always support your arguments.
differentiate (dihf uh REHN shee ayt) v.	distinguish between	differ different	When reading an essay, differentiate between fact and opinion.

Ordinary Language:
I will **fix** my thesis before handing the paper in.

Academic Language:
I will **revise** my thesis before handing the paper in.

Word	Definition	Related Words	Word in Context
discern (duh ZURN) v.	tell the difference between two or more things; perceive	discernable discerning	Until I reached the end of the story, I couldn't discern the character's motives.
discourse (DIHS kawrs) n.	ongoing communication of ideas and information	discourser	Discourse in a group is an important way to hear different opinions.
distortion (dihs TAWR shuhn) n.	anything that shows something in an untrue way	distort	Avoid using unreliable sources that exhibit a distortion of facts.
evaluate (ih VAL yoo ayt) v.	determine the worth of something	evaluation	Rubrics help students evaluate their essays.
evolve (ih VOLV) v.	develop through gradual changes	evolution	Dealing with conflict allows Sam to evolve and grow.
explanation (ehks pluh NAY shuhn) n.	clarifying statement	explain explanatory	A technical document provides an explanation.
individual (ihn duh VIHJ oo uhl) adj.	relating to a single person or thing	individualism individuality	Work on an individual response, and then discuss the question.
inherent (ihn HIHR uhnt) adj.	existing naturally in something	inherence inherently	Revising is an inherent part of the writing process.
insight (ihn syt) n.	clear idea of the nature of things	insightful	A preface provides insight into an author's purpose.
integrity (ihn TEHG ruh tee) n.	willingness to stand by moral principles		Heroes typically display great integrity.
interact (ihn tuhr AKT) v.	relate to one another; affect another	interaction interactive	The characters interact with one another in the play.
interpretation (ihn tur pruh TAY shuhn) n.	explanation of the meaning of something	interpret interpretive	Sonnets may have more than one interpretation.
isolation (y suh LAY shuhn) n.	being alone or set apart	isolate isolated	Poems address complex feelings such as isolation.
manipulate (muh NIHP yuh layt) v.	control by use of influence, often in an unfair way	manipulation manipulative	Some speakers use bias to manipulate their audiences.
meaning (MEE nihng) n.	significance of something	meaningful	Break down long sentences to help determine their meaning.
misinterpret (mihs ihn TUR priht) v.	not understand correctly	interpret misinterpretation	If you misinterpret the instructions, you will build it wrong.

BUILDING YOUR VOCABULARY

Ordinary Language:
After reading further, I **changed** my original prediction.

Academic Language:
After reading further, I **modified** my original prediction.

Building Your Vocabulary

Word	Definition	Related Words	Word in Context
modified (MOD uh fyd) v.	changed; altered slightly	modification modifier	The cross-outs revealed that he had modified his essay.
motive (MOH tihv) n.	something that causes a person to act in a certain way	motivate motivation	The character's motive was revealed in the conclusion.
objective (uhb JEHK tihv) adj.	not dependent on another's point of view	objectively	Critics should take an objective and unbiased stance.
oppose (uh POHZ) v.	to set against; disagree with	opposing opposition	If you oppose another student's opinion, reply respectfully.
perspective (puhr SPEHK tihv) n.	the way one sees things; viewpoint		I enjoy an essay more if I understand the author's perspective.
principles (PRIHN suh puhlz) n.	rules for right conduct; basics	principled	The principles of spelling are simple.
radical (RAD uh kuhl) adj.	extreme change	radicalism radically	Beat poetry was a radical departure from classic poetry.
resolute (REHZ uh loot) adj.	showing a fixed purpose	resolutely	He is resolute about being honest in his article.
resolve (rih ZOLV) v.	reach a conclusion or decision	resolution resolved	How do the enemies resolve their conflict?
respond (rih SPOND) v.	answer	respondent response	How do you respond to the suspense?
responsibility (rih spon suh BIHL uh tee) n.	having to answer to someone; being accountable for success or failure	responsible	It is your responsibility to cite your sources when writing a research report.
revise (rih VYZ) v.	reconsider; modify	revision	Revise your paper by fixing any errors.
subjective (suhb JEHK tihv) adj.	based on or influenced by a person's feelings or point of view	subjectively subjectivity	It is difficult not to be subjective when debating.
unify (YOO nuh fy) v.	combine into one	unification	To unify the ideas, we should add transitions.

Ordinary Language: The author presents a unique **view** on the subject.

Academic Language: The author presents a unique **perspective** on the subject.

Increasing Your Word Knowledge

Increase your word knowledge and chances of success by taking an active role in developing your vocabulary. Here are some tips for you.

To own a word, follow these steps:

Steps to Follow	Model
1. Learn to identify the word and its basic meaning.	The word *examine* means "to look at closely."
2. Take note of the word's spelling.	*Examine* begins and ends with an *e*.
3. Practice pronouncing the word so that you can use it in conversation.	The *e* on the end of the word is silent. Its second syllable gets the most stress.
4. Visualize the word and illustrate its key meaning.	When I think of the word *examine*, I visualize a doctor checking a patient's health.
5. Learn the various forms of the word and its related words.	*Examination* and *exam* are forms of the word *examine*.
6. Compare the word with similar words.	*Examine*, *peruse*, and *study* are synonyms.
7. Contrast the word with similar words.	When you peruse materials, you do a more casual kind of examination. *Study* is often used to describe preparing for a test.
8. Use the word in various contexts.	"I'd like to *examine* the footprints more closely." "I will *examine* the use of imagery in this poem."

BUILDING YOUR VOCABULARY

Building Your Speaking Vocabulary

Language gives us the ability to express ourselves. The more words you know, the better able you will be to get your points across. There are two main aspects of language: reading and speaking. Using the steps above will help you to acquire a rich vocabulary. Follow these steps to help you learn to use this rich vocabulary in discussions, speeches, and conversations.

Steps	Tip
1. Practice pronouncing the word.	Become familiar with pronunciation guides to allow you to sound out unfamilar words. Listening to audio books as you read the text will help you learn prounciations of words.
2. Learn word forms.	Dictionaries often list forms of words following the main word entry. Practice saying word families aloud: "generate," "generated," "generation," "regenerate," "generator."
3. Translate your thoughts.	Restate your own thoughts and ideas in a variety of way, to inject formality or to change your tone, for example.
4. Hold discussions.	With a classmate, practice using academic vocabulary words in discussions about the text. Choose one term to practice at a time, and see how many statements you can create using that term.
5. Tape-record yourself.	Analyze your word choices by listening to yourself objectively. Note places your word choice could be strengthened or changed.

Overview of Resources

Selection and Skills Support

Every selection is fully supported with worksheets in *Unit Resources*, differentiated for various groups of learners. The Visual Guide to Selected Resources preceding each leveled selection pair gives a sample of the worksheets available. The full complement is presented on these pages.

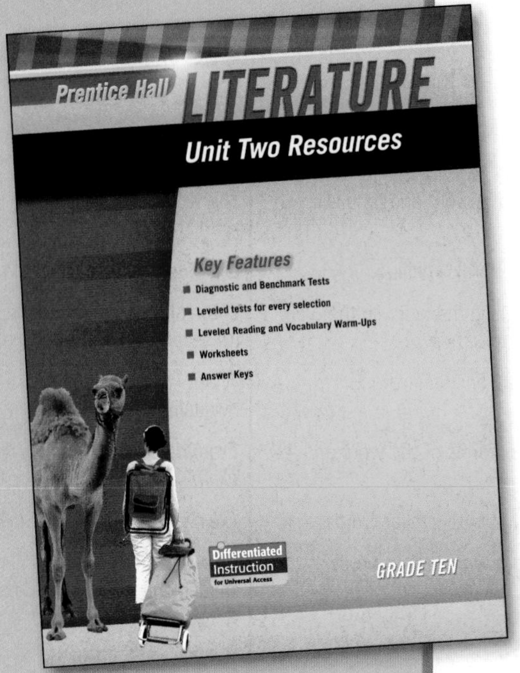

RESOURCES FOR:

- **L1** Special Needs Students
- **L2** Below-Level Students
- **EL** English Learners
- **L3** On-Level
- **L4** Advanced Students
- **All** All Students

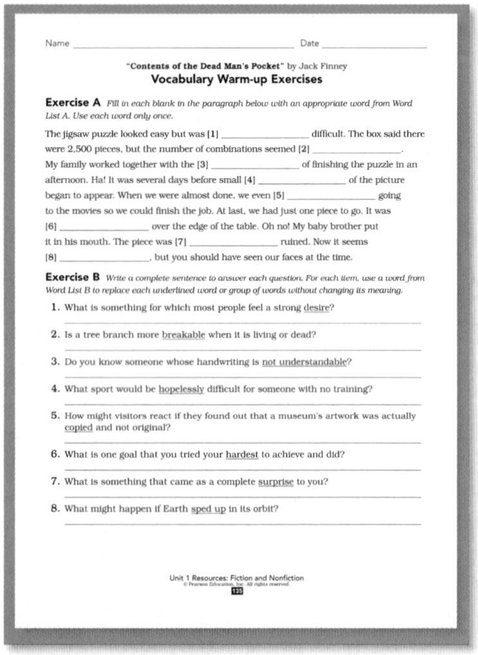

Name ______________________ Date __________

"Contents of the Dead Man's Pocket" by Jack Finney

Vocabulary Warm-up Exercises

Exercise A *Fill in each blank in the paragraph below with an appropriate word from Word List A. Use each word only once.*

The jigsaw puzzle looked easy but was [1] ____________ difficult. The box said there were 2,500 pieces, but the number of combinations seemed [2] ____________. My family worked together with the [3] ____________ of finishing the puzzle in an afternoon. Ha! It was several days before small [4] ____________ of the picture began to appear. When we were almost done, we even [5] ____________ going to the movies so we could finish the job. At last, we had just one piece to go. It was [6] ____________ over the edge of the table. Oh no! My baby brother put it in his mouth. The piece was [7] ____________ ruined. Now it seems [8] ____________, but you should have seen our faces at the time.

Exercise B *Write a complete sentence to answer each question. For each item, use a word from Word List B to replace each underlined word or group of words without changing its meaning.*

1. What is something for which most people feel a strong desire?
2. Is a tree branch more breakable when it is living or dead?
3. Do you know someone whose handwriting is not understandable?
4. What sport would be hopelessly difficult for someone with no training?
5. How might visitors react if they found out that a museum's artwork was actually copied and not original?
6. What is one goal that you tried your hardest to achieve and did?
7. What is something that came as a complete surprise to you?
8. What might happen if Earth sped up in its orbit?

Unit 1 Resources: Fiction and Nonfiction
© Pearson Education, Inc. All rights reserved.
135

EL L1 L2 Vocabulary Warm-ups A and B

vocabulary and reading practice for lower-level students and English learners

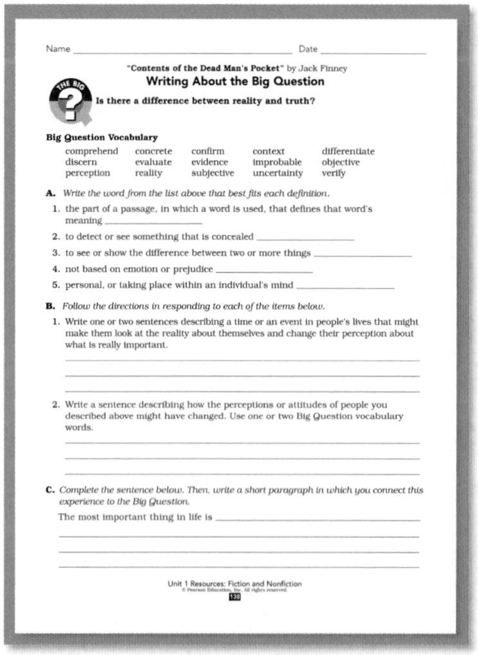

Name ______________________ Date __________

"Contents of the Dead Man's Pocket" by Jack Finney

Writing About the Big Question

THE BIG ? **Is there a difference between reality and truth?**

Big Question Vocabulary

comprehend	concrete	confirm	context	differentiate
discern	evaluate	evidence	improbable	objective
perception	reality	subjective	uncertainty	verify

A. *Write the word from the list above that best fits each definition.*

1. the part of a passage, in which a word is used, that defines that word's meaning ____________
2. to detect or see something that is concealed ____________
3. to see or show the difference between two or more things ____________
4. not based on emotion or prejudice ____________
5. personal, or taking place within an individual's mind ____________

B. *Follow the directions in responding to each of the items below.*

1. Write one or two sentences describing a time or an event in people's lives that might make them look at the reality about themselves and change their perception about what is really important.
2. Write a sentence describing how the perceptions or attitudes of people you described above might have changed. Use one or two Big Question vocabulary words.

C. *Complete the sentence below. Then, write a short paragraph in which you connect this experience to the Big Question.*

The most important thing in life is ____________

Unit 1 Resources: Fiction and Nonfiction
© Pearson Education, Inc. All rights reserved.
138

All Writing About the Big Question

thematic vocabulary and thought-provoking activities centered around the unit Big Question

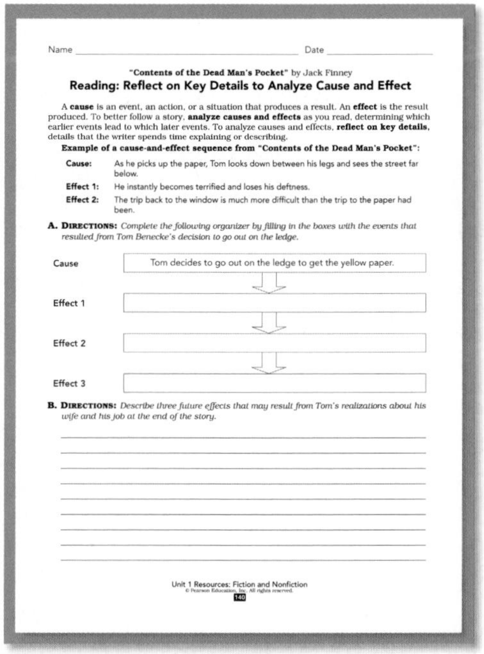

Name ______________________ Date __________

"Contents of the Dead Man's Pocket" by Jack Finney

Reading: Reflect on Key Details to Analyze Cause and Effect

A **cause** is an event, an action, or a situation that produces a result. An **effect** is the result produced. To better follow a story, **analyze causes and effects** as you read, determining which earlier events lead to which later events. To analyze causes and effects, **reflect on key details**, details that the writer spends time explaining or describing.

Example of a cause-and-effect sequence from "Contents of the Dead Man's Pocket":

Cause: As he picks up the paper, Tom looks down between his legs and sees the street far below.

Effect 1: He instantly becomes terrified and loses his deftness.

Effect 2: The trip back to the window is much more difficult than the trip to the paper had been.

A. Directions: *Complete the following organizer by filling in the boxes with the events that resulted from Tom Benecke's decision to go out on the ledge.*

Cause	Tom decides to go out on the ledge to get the yellow paper.
Effect 1	
Effect 2	
Effect 3	

B. Directions: *Describe three future effects that may result from Tom's realizations about his wife and his job at the end of the story.*

Unit 1 Resources: Fiction and Nonfiction
© Pearson Education, Inc. All rights reserved.
140

All Reading

a full page of support for the Reading Skill taught with the selection

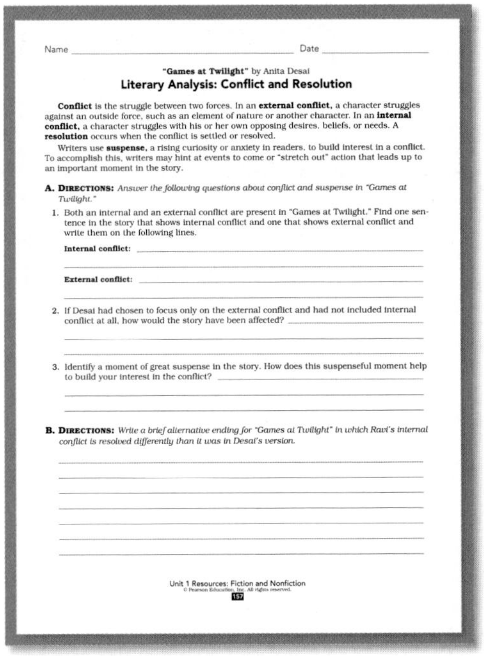

Name ______ Date ______

"Games at Twilight" by Anita Desai

Literary Analysis: Conflict and Resolution

Conflict is the struggle between two forces. In an **external conflict,** a character struggles against an outside force, such as an element of nature or another character. In an **internal conflict,** a character struggles with his or her own opposing desires, beliefs, or needs. A **resolution** occurs when the conflict is settled or resolved.

Writers use **suspense,** a rising curiosity or anxiety in readers, to build interest in a conflict. To accomplish this, writers may hint at events to come or "stretch out" action that leads up to an important moment in the story.

A. Directions: *Answer the following questions about conflict and suspense in "Games at Twilight."*

1. Both an internal and an external conflict are present in "Games at Twilight." Find one sentence in the story that shows internal conflict and one that shows external conflict and write them on the following lines.

   Internal conflict: ______

   External conflict: ______

2. If Desai had chosen to focus only on the external conflict and had not included internal conflict at all, how would the story have been affected? ______

3. Identify a moment of great suspense in the story. How does this suspenseful moment help to build your interest in the conflict? ______

B. Directions: *Write a brief alternative ending for "Games at Twilight" in which Ravi's internal conflict is resolved differently than it was in Desai's version.*

Unit 1 Resources: Fiction and Nonfiction

© Pearson Education, Inc. All rights reserved.

157

All Literary Analysis

a full page of support for the Literary Analysis concept taught with the selection

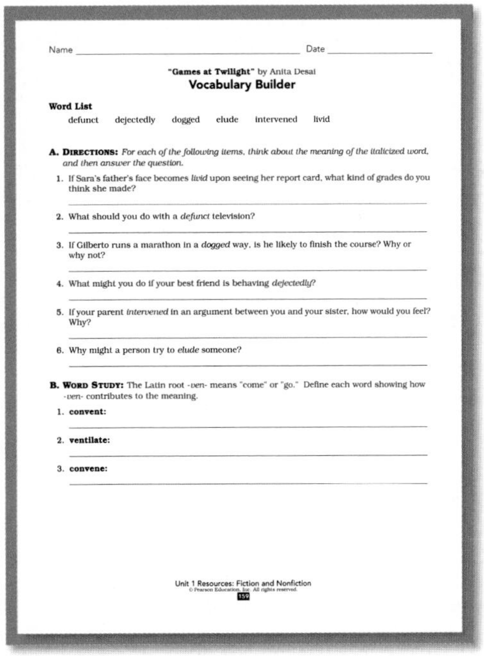

Name ______ Date ______

"Games at Twilight" by Anita Desai

Vocabulary Builder

Word List

defunct dejectedly dogged elude intervened livid

A. Directions: *For each of the following items, think about the meaning of the italicized word, and then answer the question.*

1. If Sara's father's face becomes *livid* upon seeing her report card, what kind of grades do you think she made?
2. What should you do with a *defunct* television?
3. If Gilberto runs a marathon in a *dogged* way, is he likely to finish the course? Why or why not?
4. What might you do if your best friend is behaving *dejectedly*?
5. If your parent *intervened* in an argument between you and your sister, how would you feel? Why?
6. Why might a person try to *elude* someone?

B. Word Study: The Latin root *-ven-* means "come" or "go." Define each word showing how *-ven-* contributes to the meaning.

1. **convent:**
2. **ventilate:**
3. **convene:**

Unit 1 Resources: Fiction and Nonfiction

© Pearson Education, Inc. All rights reserved.

159

All Vocabulary Builder

selection vocabulary and Word Study skill practice

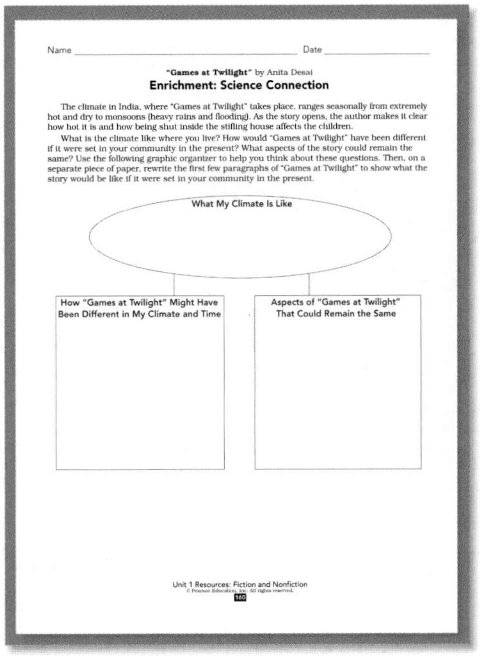

Name ______ Date ______

"Games at Twilight" by Anita Desai

Enrichment: Science Connection

The climate in India, where "Games at Twilight" takes place, ranges seasonally from extremely hot and dry to monsoons (heavy rains and flooding). As the story opens, the author makes it clear how hot it is and how being shut inside the stifling house affects the children.

What is the climate like where you live? How would "Games at Twilight" have been different if it were set in your community in the present? What aspects of the story could remain the same? Use the following graphic organizer to help you think about these questions. Then, on a separate piece of paper, rewrite the first few paragraphs of "Games at Twilight" to show what the story would be like if it were set in your community in the present.

Unit 1 Resources: Fiction and Nonfiction

© Pearson Education, Inc. All rights reserved.

160

L4 Enrichment

a selection-related challenge for advanced learners

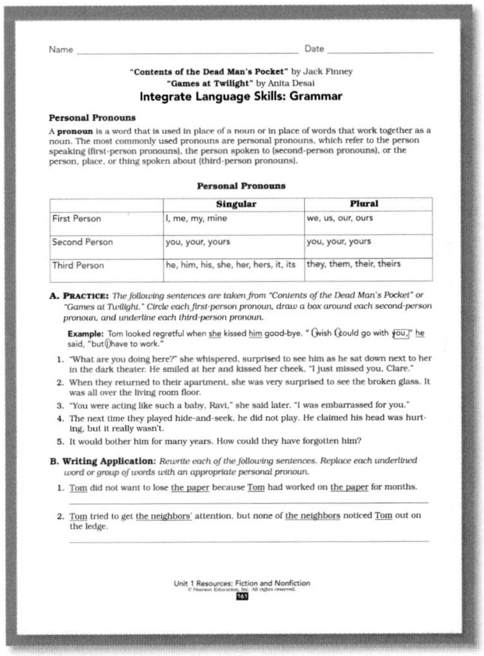

Name ______ Date ______

"Contents of the Dead Man's Pocket" by Jack Finney

"Games at Twilight" by Anita Desai

Integrate Language Skills: Grammar

Personal Pronouns

A **pronoun** is a word that is used in place of a noun or in place of words that work together as a noun. The most commonly used pronouns are personal pronouns, which refer to the person speaking (first-person pronouns), the person spoken to (second-person pronouns), or the person, place, or thing spoken about (third-person pronouns).

Personal Pronouns

	Singular	Plural
First Person	I, me, my, mine	we, us, our, ours
Second Person	you, your, yours	you, your, yours
Third Person	he, him, his, she, her, hers, it, its	they, them, their, theirs

A. Practice: *The following sentences are taken from "Contents of the Dead Man's Pocket" or "Games at Twilight." Circle each first-person pronoun, draw a box around each second-person pronoun, and underline each third-person pronoun.*

Example: Tom looked regretful when she kissed him good-bye. "I wish I could go with you," he said, "but I have to work."

1. "What are you doing here?" she whispered, surprised to see him as he sat down next to her in the dark theater. He smiled at her and kissed her cheek. "I just missed you, Clare."
2. When they returned to their apartment, she was very surprised to see the broken glass. It was all over the living room floor.
3. "You were acting like such a baby, Ravi," she said later. "I was embarrassed for you."
4. The next time they played hide-and-seek, he did not play. He claimed his head was hurting, but it really wasn't.
5. It would bother him for many years. How could they have forgotten him?

B. Writing Application: *Rewrite each of the following sentences. Replace each underlined word or group of words with an appropriate personal pronoun.*

1. Tom did not want to lose the paper because Tom had worked on the paper for months.
2. Tom tried to get the neighbors' attention, but none of the neighbors noticed Tom out on the ledge.

Unit 1 Resources: Fiction and Nonfiction

© Pearson Education, Inc. All rights reserved.

161

L3 L4 Grammar

more practice with the grammar skill taught with the selection

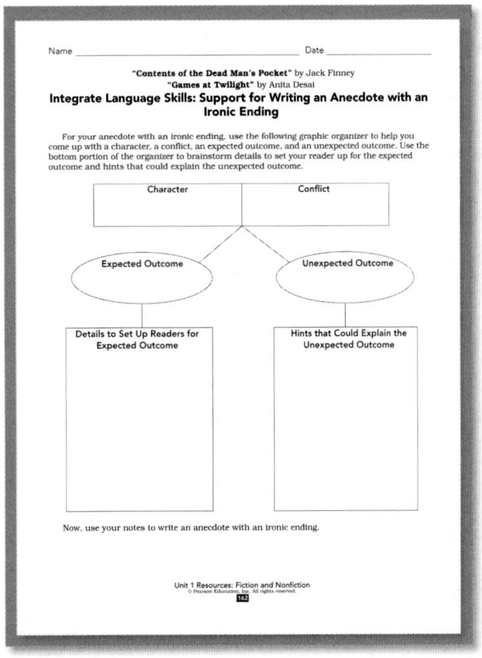

Name ______ Date ______

"Contents of the Dead Man's Pocket" by Jack Finney

"Games at Twilight" by Anita Desai

Integrate Language Skills: Support for Writing an Anecdote with an Ironic Ending

For your anecdote with an ironic ending, use the following graphic organizer to help you come up with a character, a conflict, an expected outcome, and an unexpected outcome. Use the bottom portion of the organizer to brainstorm details to set your reader up for the expected outcome and hints that could explain the unexpected outcome.

Now, use your notes to write an anecdote with an ironic ending.

Unit 1 Resources: Fiction and Nonfiction

© Pearson Education, Inc. All rights reserved.

162

L3 L4 Writing

support for the Writing activity accompanying the selection

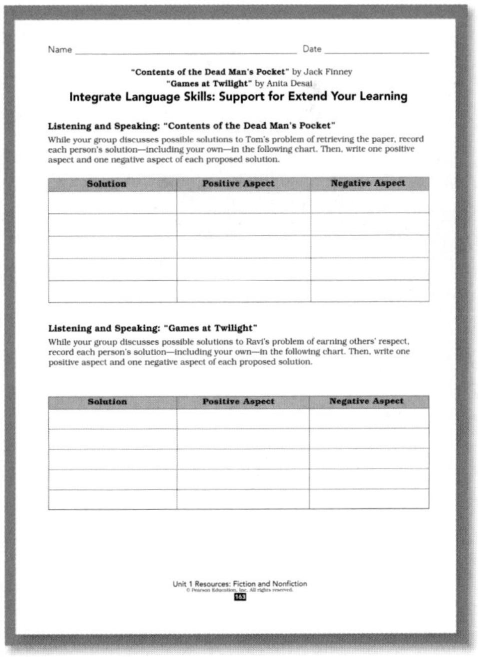

Name ______ Date ______

"Contents of the Dead Man's Pocket" by Jack Finney

"Games at Twilight" by Anita Desai

Integrate Language Skills: Support for Extend Your Learning

Listening and Speaking: "Contents of the Dead Man's Pocket"

While your group discusses possible solutions to Tom's problem of retrieving the paper, record each person's solution—including your own—in the following chart. Then, write one positive aspect and one negative aspect of each proposed solution.

Solution	Positive Aspect	Negative Aspect

Listening and Speaking: "Games at Twilight"

While your group discusses possible solutions to Ravi's problem of earning others' respect, record each person's solution—including your own—in the following chart. Then, write one positive aspect and one negative aspect of each proposed solution.

Solution	Positive Aspect	Negative Aspect

Unit 1 Resources: Fiction and Nonfiction

© Pearson Education, Inc. All rights reserved.

163

L3 L4 Extend Your Learning

customized support for the Listening and Speaking or Research and Technology activity related to the selection

Overview of Resources

Selection Support

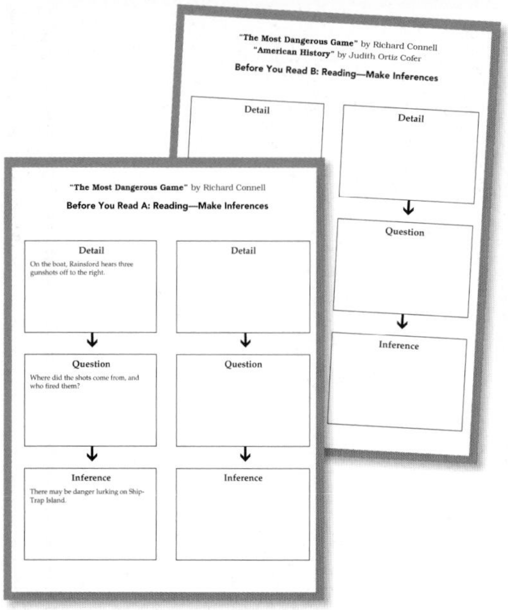

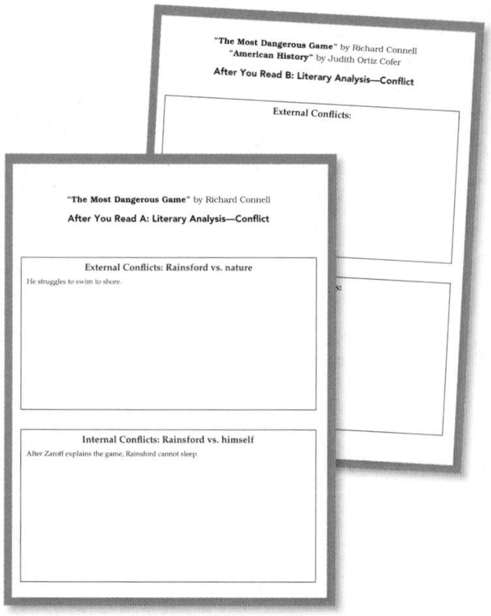

EL L1 L2 Reading Graphic Organizer A

a partially filled-in graphic organizer to model or scaffold the use of the organizer

L3 Reading Graphic Organizer B

the blank version of the organizer

EL L1 L2 Literary Analysis Graphic Organizer A

a partially filled-in graphic organizer to model or scaffold the use of the organizer

L3 Literary Analysis Organizer B

the blank version of the organizer

Assessment

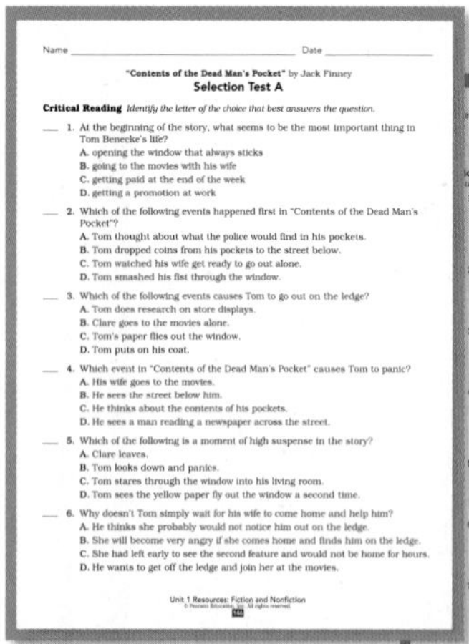

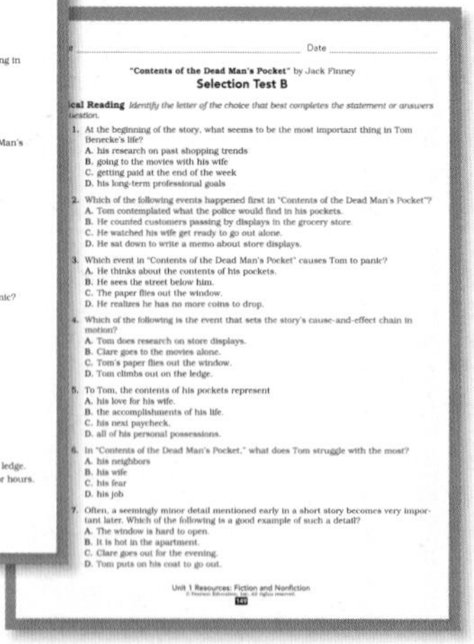

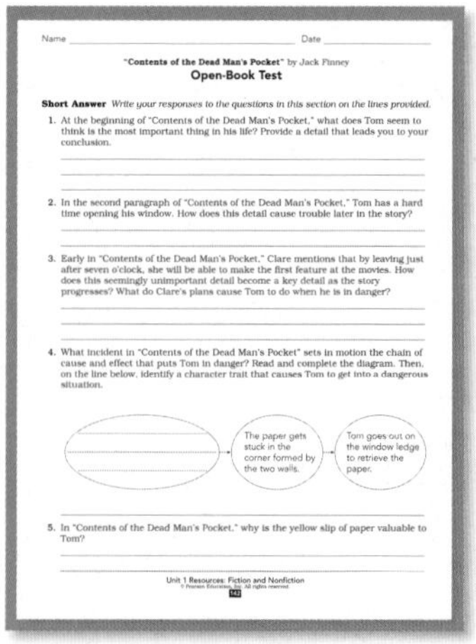

EL L1 L2 Selection Test A

selection test with complete skills coverage, adapted for lower-level students and English learners

L3 L4 Selection Test B

selection test with complete skills coverage, including multiple choice and essay items

L3 L4 Open-Book Test

an alternative assessment format for on-level and advanced students

Prentice Hall

LITERATURE

Language and Literacy

PEARSON

Upper Saddle River, New Jersey
Boston, Massachusetts
Chandler, Arizona
Glenview, Illinois
Shoreview, Minnesota

Acknowledgments appear on p. R75, which constitutes an extension of this copyright page.

PEARSON

13-digit ISBN 978-0-13-366648-9
10-digit ISBN 0-13-366648-4
1 2 3 4 5 6 7 8 9 10 12 11 10 09 08

Prentice Hall

LITERATURE

Language and Literacy

Grade Ten

Unit 1 Overview

Unit Genre and Unit Big Question

Explain to students that throughout this unit, they will read and analyze fiction and nonfiction. As they read, they will think about and discuss answers to the Unit Big Question: Is there a difference between reality and truth?

Students will learn more about the Big Question on pp. 2–3. Then, on pp. 4-27, Susan Vreeland introduces the unit literary form, fiction and nonfiction, and presents a model short story of her own.

Using the Unit Selections

Teach Skills Instructional selections are presented in leveled pairs. To teach the skills and meet the objectives, you need to complete only one selection in each pairing.

Differentiate and Reinforce Choose the selection in a pair that is best suited for your students. The selections are listed by accessibility in the Differentiated Instruction box on the next page. You may use the other selection in the pairing to reinforce comprehension and skills or to provide enrichment.

Integrate Skills Each selection pair presents students with a reading strategy, a literary analysis concept, and a vocabulary skill, as well as vocabulary development opportunities and grammar instruction. In addition, students have opportunities to extend learning in the Writing and extension (Research and Technology or Listening and Speaking) activities.

Unit Features

Informational Texts Students learn to use and evaluate various types of informational texts.

Comparing Literary Works Students compare the use of a literary element in two or more works.

To help you plan your use of the unit, see the Unit Overview and Pacing Plan on pp. 2a–2b and the Time and Resource Manager preceding each selection pairing

Fiction and Nonfiction

THE BIG ?

Is there a difference between *reality* and *truth?*

PHLit Online!

www.PHLitOnline.com

Teaching from Technology

Enriched Online Student Edition
- full narration of selections
- interactive graphic organizers
- linked Get Connected! and Background videos
- all worksheets and other student resources

Professional Development
- the *Professional Development Guidebook* online
- additional professional development articles by program authors

Planning, Assigning, and Monitoring
- software for online assignment of work to students, individually or to the whole class
- a system for tracking and grading students' work

UNIT 1

PHLit Online!
www.PHLitOnline.com

Hear It!
- Selection summary audio
- Selection audio
- BQ Tunes

See It!
- Penguin author video
- Big Question video
- Get Connected videos
- Background videos
- More about the authors
- Illustrated vocabulary words
- Vocabulary flashcards

Do It!
- Interactive journals
- Interactive graphic organizers
- Grammar tutorials
- Interactive vocabulary games
- Test practice

1

Instructional Resources

Unit 1 Resources supports unit skills with pages of the following types:

- **Benchmark Tests** assess and monitor students' progress at mid-unit and at unit's end.
- **Vocabulary and Reading Warm-ups** provide additional vocabulary support, based on Lexile rankings of words, for each selection. "A" **Warm-ups** are for students reading two grades below level. "B" **Warm-ups** are for students reading one grade below level.
- **Selection Support** These practice pages are available for each selection:
  - **Reading Skill**
  - **Literary Analysis**
  - **Writing About the Big Question**
  - **Vocabulary**
  - **Support for Writing**
  - **Support for Extend Your Learning**
  - **Enrichment**

PHLit Online!
All worksheets and other student resources are also available at **www.PHLitOnline.com**.

Differentiated Instruction for Universal Access

Accessibility for Various Ability Levels
This chart gives a general accessibility rating to help you decide which selection in each leveled pair is more appropriate for your students. **Choose one selection in each pair or choose to teach both.** You will meet the objectives for the pair when you teach either of the two selections. For additional guidance on factors that affect the accessibility of each selection, see the Selection Choices page for each selection set.

Accessibility for English Learners
EL This icon indicates support for English learners at point of use in this Teacher's Edition.

	More Accessible	More Challenging
Pair 1	The Monkey's Paw	The Leap
Pair 2	*from* Swimming to Antarctica	Occupation: Conductorette
Pair 3	Contents of the Dead Man's Pocket	Games at Twilight
Pair 4	The Marginal World	Making History With Vitamin C

UNIT OVERVIEW AND PACING PLAN

Meeting Your Standards

Students will

1. recognize and appreciate fiction and nonfiction as literary forms.
2. read and analyze a variety of fiction and nonfiction.
3. apply reading skills.
   - Use prior knowledge to make predictions
   - Revise and verify predictions
   - Analyze cause and effect
   - Use a sequence of events chart to analyze cause and effect
4. analyze literary elements.
   - Plot and foreshadowing
   - Author's perspective
   - Conflict and resolution
   - Author's purpose
5. build vocabulary and vocabulary concepts.
   - Roots
   - Prefixes
   - Use a dictionary and a thesaurus
6. learn elements of grammar, mechanics, and usage.
   - Common and proper nouns
   - Abstract and concrete nouns
   - Possessive nouns
   - Personal pronouns
   - Relative pronouns
   - Pronoun-antecedent agreement
7. use a recursive writing process to write in a variety of forms.
   - Autobiographical narrative
   - Cause-and-effect essay
8. read informational materials.
   - Analyze structure and format of an article and a newsletter
   - Analyze the credibility of a Web site and a primary source
9. compare literary works.
   - Compare style
   - Compare irony and paradox
10. develop research and technology skills.
    - Create a spreadsheet
11. develop listening and speaking skills.
    - Interview
    - Daily observation journal
    - Problem-solving group
    - Analyze media presentations

	Week 1					Week 2					Week 3				
	1	2	3	4	5	1	2	3	4	5	1	2	3	4	5
Administer the Diagnostic Test, ***Unit 1 Resources***, (pp. 5–10).	●														
Introduce the Unit Big Question (pp. 2–3).	●														
Introduce the Unit author and the Unit forms, fiction and nonfiction (pp 4–7).		●													
Teach the Model selections (pp. 8–7).		●	●												
Teach one selection from Pairing 1 (pp. 28–57).			●	●	●	●	●								
Teach one selection from Pairing 2 (pp. 58–87).							●	●	●	●					
Complete the Test Practice: Reading (pp. 88–89).										●					
Teach Informational Texts (pp. 90–95).											●				
Teach Comparing Literary Works (pp. 96–107).												●	●		
Have students complete the Writing Workshop (pp. 108–113).											●	●	●	●	●
Administer **Benchmark Test 1** (***Unit 1 Resources,*** pp. 127–132).														●	
Reteach skills, judging which skills to reteach by evaluating students' performance on **Benchmark Test 1**.															●

	Week 4					Week 5					Week 6				
	1	2	3	4	5	1	2	3	4	5	1	2	3	4	5
Teach one selection from Pairing 3 (pp. 114–151).	●	●	●	●											
Teach one selection from Pairing 4 (pp. 152–179).					●	●	●	●							
Complete the Test-Practice: Reading (pp. 180–181).								●							
Teach Informational Texts (pp. 182–187).									●						
Teach Comparing Literary Works (pp. 188–199).										●	●				
Have students complete the Writing Workshop (pp. 200–207).									●	●	●	●	●		
Have students complete Applying the Big Question (pp. 208–209).												●			
Have students complete the Vocabulary Workshop (pp. 210–211).												●			
Have students complete the Communications Workshop (p. 212).													●		
Complete the Test Practice: Unit 1 Review (pp. 214–219).													●		
Administer **Benchmark Test 2** (*Unit 1 Resources*, pp. 234–243).														●	
Reteach skills, judging which skills to reteach by evaluating students' performance on **Benchmark Test 2.**															●

Block and Daily Scheduling

The assignments and activities in this Unit planner are organized by week. You may adjust them to your daily or block schedule. The Time and Resource Manager for each selection set gives specific pacing suggestions, or you may use the comprehensive lesson planning support online at **www.PHLitOnline.com.**

Monitoring Progress

Diagnose Each main selection pairing in the Unit contains a more accessible and a more challenging selection. To determine which selection to assign to students, administer the **Diagnostic Test, *Unit 1 Resources,*** pp. 5–10. Use the **Interpretation Guide** to interpret the results of the diagnostic portion of the test.

Preteach and Prepare As indicated by the diagnostic, prepare students for reading by assigning the **Vocabulary Practice** and **Reading Warm-ups** for the selections you assign.

Teach Follow this Pacing Plan and use the resources to teach the skills and selections. For specific pacing suggestions and a list of resources, see the Time and Resource Manager and the Visual Guide to Featured Selection Resources preceding each selection pairing.

Assess After students have completed the first half of the Unit, administer **Benchmark Test 1**. Administer **Benchmark Test 2** at the end of the Unit. **Note:** For the most accurate diagnosis of students who score in the middle range of the diagnostic portion of the test, administer the additional diagnostic questions online at **www.PHLitOnline.com.**

Intervention and Reteach After administering each test, use the **Interpretation Guide** for the tests to determine which reteaching pages, if any, you should assign from the ***Reading Kit.*** The appropriate pages are also available through the online Progress Monitoring software.

Independent Reading

To differentiate, reinforce, and extend your instruction, have students choose a full-length work from the Independent Reading page, page 213, and read it while working on this Unit. Consult the Sensitivity Issues notes for the page to guide students' choices.

Teaching Vocabulary **Sharon Vaughn**

"Genuine and lasting word knowledge is not a result of asking students to look up words in the dictionary."

"How can I expect my students to understand the themes in a text and provide interpretations when they don't know the meaning of the words?" A critical connection to understanding is having a deep and facile understanding of the important words in the text. What meaningful ways can teachers promote word meaning so that students are adept users of the word in their oral and written language? We know that genuine and lasting word knowledge is not a result of asking students to look up words in the dictionary, nor mentioning words and their meanings briefly during class. We know that when teachers use extensive and research-proven practices to facilitate vocabulary development, students learn more words.

Improving Vocabulary Learning

Deciding Words to Teach Deciding which vocabulary words to teach is no easy decision. There are so many words to choose from, it is useful to have the most important words selected for us. Fortunately, the critical vocabulary words you need to teach in depth are highlighted and usually defined for you in the Teacher's Edition.

In their book, *Bringing Words to Life*, the authors (Beck, McKeown, & Kucan, 2002) indicate that vocabulary words students need to learn can be categorized based on their impact on their learning, how frequently they are likely to encounter them, and the extent to which they are related to our understanding. They identify three tiers of words.

- **Tier 1** are **common words** that can be readily learned by listening and talking to others. These words typically do not require instruction by the teacher. These include such words as painting, ribbon, excitement, and wish.
- **Tier 3** vocabulary words are ones that are not readily recognized words and also do not typically need to be taught at this grade level. Tier 3 words are more **content-specific words** that are highly specialized and relate to the discipline students are studying – for example, narrative, literary analysis, context clues, morphology and linguistics.
- The most important words to teach are **Tier 2 words, academic words**. These are more complex words that occur in academic listening or reading. For example words like: enlighten, speculate, infirm, tenuous, oratory, and poignant.

Teaching Academic Vocabulary

Teaching students to use and understand the Tier 2 words and to expand their independent word learning requires implementing all of the following instructional practices (Denton, Bryan, Wexler, Reed, & Vaughn, 2007; Graves, 2006):

1. Modeling and supporting using words that are as descriptive and accurate as possible. For example, instead of stating that a child deliberately did not follow directions the teacher can use the word "defiant".
2. Promoting word learning by "looking" for new, unusual, unknown, or interesting words. For example, praise students when they bring in new words like "parchment", "apparel", and "smug". Talk about words that mean the same thing or something very different.
3. Developing a verbal learning environment that focuses on improving word and world knowledge. Use every opportunity to teach more about words and how they relate to the world. For example, "import" and "export" are excellent ways to talk about new words related to commerce.
4. Promoting meta-linguistic awareness. Teach students how to use affixes such as prefixes and suffixes to further understand word use and meaning.
5. Making connections among words. Link new words to words previously known, similar words, and words that are the opposite.

Other Ways to Promote Word Learning

- Teaching several new words each day.
- Reviewing previously learned words regularly.
- Teaching students to use context clues by reading the sentence before the unknown word and after the unknown word (as well as the sentence the unknown word is in) to figure out its meaning.
- Providing vocabulary word walls where key words are listed.
- Asking students to maintain vocabulary journals.

Modeled Strategy

See pp. 103 and 171 for point-of-use notes modeling these strategies.

Teacher Resources

- ***Professional Development Guidebook***
- ***Classroom Strategies and Teaching Routines* cards**

PHLit Online!

Log on as a teacher at **www.PHLitOnline.com** to access a library of all Professional Development articles by the Contributing Authors of Pearson Prentice Hall *Literature*.

Sharon Vaughn, Ph.D.

Sharon Vaughn is the H.E. Hartfelder/Southland Corporation Regents Chair of Human Development and Professor, University of Texas at Austin. She is the author of numerous books and articles on effective practices for enhancing reading outcomes for students with reading difficulties. She is currently the P.I. or Co-P.I. on numerous Institute for Education Sciences and National Institute of Child Health and Human Development research grants.

Supporting Research

Beck, I.L., & McKeown, M.G. (2002). *Bringing words to life: Robust vocabulary instruction.* New York: Guilford.

Denton, C., Bryan, D., Wexler, J., Reed, D., & Vaughn, S. (2007). *Effective instruction for middle school students with reading difficulties: The reading teacher's sourcebook.* University of Texas System/Texas Education Agency.

Graves, M.F. (2006). The Vocabulary Book: Learning and Instruction. Teachers College, Columbia University. New York, NY.

Introducing the Big Question

1. To help students differentiate between *truth* and *reality,* give the following example: People once believed that the Sun revolves around the Earth. They based this truth on their observations of reality—natural phenomena, such as the Sun's movement across the Earth's sky. Explain to students that other people challenged this truth using astronomy and mathematical calculations—observations of reality—to prove that Earth revolves around the Sun. Though the reality remained the same (natural phenomena), people's perceptions of it changed.
2. Discuss with students other examples in which truths changed due to advances in science or technology.
3. **Ask** the Big Question, "Is there a difference between reality and truth?" **Possible responses:** Yes. Reality is the same whether or not we perceive it correctly. Truth varies.
4. Explain that the stories in this unit present ideas about truth and reality. Students should think about these concepts as they read.

Introducing the Big Question Vocabulary

1. Point out the Big Question Vocabulary on the facing page. Explain that these words are useful in discussing the Big Question.
2. Review the meaning of each word. (Definitions appear on the teacher edition on p. 3.)
3. Have students complete the **Big Question Vocabulary** worksheets, *Unit 1 Resources,* pp. 7–9.

Write What You Know

1. Review the assignment with students, using the instruction on the student page.
2. Urge students to think of examples from their own lives, and have them discuss the examples with their partners.

Introducing the Big Question

THE BIG ?

Is there a difference between *reality* and *truth?*

Reality and truth may seem like abstract ideas, but your expectations and everyday experiences can influence the way you see the world.

The truth is something that has been proven or that we believe is so. However, what is true to one person might not be true to another. The truth can be **subjective,** or influenced by each person's **perceptions** or life experiences. In contrast, reality refers to all the things that exist in the world. Our senses, such as sight and touch, help us **discern** what is real. However, things that are not **concrete** and observable can still exist.

Two people might watch the same event, for example, but observe different things. What is true about the event to one person is not true to the other. A video or photograph might more **objectively** reveal the reality of the situation.

Start thinking about the Big Question by discussing the way one person's truth may be different from another's.

Discuss It

Write What You Know

Make a list of things that are true for some but may differ from reality or from other people's perception of the truth. Describe one specific example of each of the following. Add more examples if you like.

- Something that is easy for you and difficult for a friend
- Something that you and your parents see differently
- The solution to a political issue
- The importance of the outcome of a game
- A scientific theory that has some **uncertainty**

Share your examples with a partner. **Evaluate** and discuss whether or not truth differs from reality in each case.

PHLit Online!
www.PHLitOnline.com

- Big Question video
- Illustrated vocabulary words
- Interactive vocabulary games
- BQ Tunes

Understanding by Design

The Big Question

Explain to students that they will continue to consider the Big Question as they work through the unit.

- At the beginning of each selection, they will write a response to a Writing About the Big Question sentence frame.
- As they read the selection, they will look for details related to the Big Question.
- At the end of the selection, they will answer a Critical Thinking question that is related to the Big Question.
- At the end of Unit 1, they will complete an Applying the Big Question workshop (pp. 208–209). In the workshop, they will review literature in the unit and think about real-world examples that shed light on the Big Question. They will also have a chance to reflect on their first answers, thinking about how their ideas have changed.
- Tell students that their goal will be to gain a deeper understanding of literature and a more sophisticated way of discussing the Big Question.

Explain What You Know

Use the examples and ideas you discussed with your partner to help you complete these sentences about truth and reality.

- People's life experiences influence their perceptions of reality and truth by _________.
- An individual may see something differently than a family member because _________.
- A person may learn something new about him- or herself when _________. When this happens, he or she may feel ____________.

Share your responses with a partner.

Tell What You Think

Based on the discussions you have had, decide what you think right now. Your answer may change as you read the selections in this unit. Choose one of these responses to the Big Question or write one of your own:

- ❑ Truth and reality are the same.
- ❑ Truth and reality are different.

Use one or more of these sentences or your own ideas to write a paragraph that supports your response.

- Reality and truth are the same when ____________.
- Reality and truth can be different when ____________.
- People may disagree about what they believe is true because ____________.

Discuss your response with a partner or a small group.

Connecting to the Literature

The readings in this unit will help you think about reality and truth and whether or not these two concepts differ. Each reading will give you an insight into the Big Question. At the end of the unit, you will have a chance to revisit this concept to see how your ideas have changed.

☆ shows an **Academic Vocabulary** word.

Big Question Vocabulary

- ☆ comprehend
- concrete
- ☆ confirm
- ☆ context
- ☆ differentiate
- ☆ discern
- ☆ evaluate
- evidence
- improbable
- ☆ objective
- perception
- reality
- ☆ subjective
- uncertainty
- verify

Explain What You Know

1. Introduce the assignment, using the instruction on the student page.
2. Have students review their lists to find examples of different perceptions of reality and truth. As needed, use the definitions from the Big Question Vocabulary box below to clarify meaning.
3. Guide students to complete the sentence frames and share their responses with partners.

Tell What You Think

1. Introduce the assignment. Guide students to review the examples of reality and truth on their lists. Then, have them decide whether they think reality and truth are the same or different. Have students mark their answers on their student pages.
2. Explain to students that they will now write a paragraph to support their decision. Have students complete the sentence frames, basing their responses on their previous work. Encourage students to use the sentence frames to help them write their responses.
3. As they write their paragraphs, have students give examples from previous activities to support their decisions.
4. Have volunteers discuss their completed responses within small groups.

Connecting to the Literature

Explain the structure of the Big Question strand in the unit, referring to the Understanding by Design box on the previous page.

Big Question Vocabulary

comprehend* (käm′prē hend′) *v.* to grasp mentally; understand
concrete (kän′krēt′, kän krēt′) *adj.* something specific or tangible
confirm* (kən furm′) *v.* to establish the truth or correctness of something
context* (kän′tekst′) *n.* the circumstances that form the setting of an event
differentiate* (dif′ər en shē āt′) *v.* to distinguish between
discern* (di surn′, di zurn′) *v.* to separate one thing from another
evaluate* (ē val′ yo͞o āt′) *v.* to determine the worth of something
evidence (ev′ə dəns) *n.* information that indicates whether something is true or valid
improbable (im präb′ə bəl) *adj.* not likely to happen or be true
objective* (əb jek′tiv) *adj.* not dependent on a person's point of view
perception (pər sep′shən) *n.* the way one understands the world through the senses
reality (rē al′ə tē) *n.* the quality of being true to life
subjective* (səb jek′tiv) adj. based on or influenced by a person's feelings or point of view
uncertainty (un surt′'n tē) *n.* inability to be sure
verify (ver′ə fī′) *v.* to prove that something is true

Meeting Your Standards

Students will

1. understand the characteristics, types, and purposes of fiction and nonfiction.
2. analyze foreshadowing
3. compare a writer's critical statements with the writer's own works

❶ Is there a difference between reality and truth?

Remind students that they will think more about the Unit Big Question as they read and discuss the fiction and nonfiction selections in this unit.

❷ What Are Fiction and Nonfiction?

Introduce Susan Vreeland

1. Inform students that Vreeland has written acclaimed novels, such as *Girl in Hyacinth Blue.*
2. Show Segment 1 of ***See It!* DVD** to provide insight into ways that Vreeland prepares to write historical fiction. **Ask:** How does Vreeland prepare to write a historical fiction book? **Answer:** She begins by becoming interested in a certain person or time in history. Then she chooses a focus, tracks down information, and invents parts when necessary.
3. Interested students might enjoy *The Forest Lover* by Vreeland; this novel is based on Canadian painter Emily Carr's life. (We recommend that you preview the book before recommending it to students.)

Introduce Fiction and Nonfiction

1. Create a two-column chart headed *Fiction* and *Nonfiction.* Brainstorm media types that fit into each category. Record their ideas. **Possible responses:** *Fiction*—TV sitcom, novel; *Nonfiction*—newspaper, math textbook.
2. Have students discuss purposes for creating each type.

Introduction: Fiction and Nonfiction

THE BIG ?

Is there a difference between *reality* and *truth?*

Fiction and nonfiction let readers question whether reality and truth are always the same. ❶

PHLit Online!
www.PHLitOnline.com

- Penguin author video
- Interactive journals
- Interactive graphic organizers
- Selection audio
- Self-test

❷ What Are Fiction and Nonfiction?

by Susan Vreeland

You've probably heard that nonfiction is true and fiction is not true. More precisely, **nonfiction** reports on real people, events, and ideas, while **fiction** narrates an imagined story. Nonfiction aims to inform, while fiction aims to generate feeling. You read fiction to inhabit the world of another person; that is, to live the fictive dream and feel the emotions of the characters. Along the way, you might discover some truth about people or life.

Characters to Care About

What I look for in fiction is a character whom I care about, one who grows as a result of the conflicts and experiences narrated. I like to contemplate how I would have felt or acted in a similar situation. As a young reader, I came to love the characters in Harper Lee's novel *To Kill a Mockingbird.* Because of them, I began to think about issues of conscience and racial prejudice. It's important, then, to choose your reading wisely so its effect will be a deepening of your heart.

❸ Connecting Fiction and Nonfiction

I love **historical novels**—fictional stories with real historical settings—because they allow me to imagine what it was like to live in a culturally different time, or in a foreign setting. They give me a better understanding of the present by showing the stages society has gone through. Authors of historical fiction do research in nonfiction sources, so that characters play out their personal stories against an accurate picture of the time.

Such novels are not **biographies,** narratives of a person's life that include everything from birth to death, revealing these facts in an outsider's objective tone. Instead, a historical novel develops selected themes with invented scenes and dialogue delivered in what sounds like the subject's own voice.

The passage here is from a biography of the seventeenth-century Dutch painter Johannes Vermeer, a character in my story "Magdalena Looking." The biography reports a fact that I expanded into the plot of

Teaching Resources

The following resources can be used to enrich, extend, or differentiate the instruction.

- All *Unit 1 Resources,* pp. 13–29
- All *Professional Development Guidebook,* p. 33
- All *See It!* DVD **Susan Vreeland,** Segments 1 and 2
- All *Graphic Organizer Transparencies,* pp. 1, 2, 235
- All **Enriched Online Student Edition**
- L2 L3 *Reader's Notebook*
- L1 *Hear It!* **Audio CD** (adapted text)
- EL *Reader's Notebook: English Learner's Version*
- L2 EL *Hear It!* **Audio CD**
- L1 EL *Hear It!* **Audio CD** (adapted text)

PHLit Online! All resources, including print and video, are available at **www.PHLitOnline.com.**

my story. When the historical record doesn't reveal an element I need, such as someone with whom my historic person can interact, I have to invent it. In this case, I chose one of Vermeer's daughters, named her Magdalena, and gave her characteristics that would develop my theme.

> *Catharina and Vermeer did well in that eleven of their fifteen children lived, and had to be cared for, fed, clothed, and schooled. . . . [H]ow Vermeer dealt with these interruptions we can only guess. His paintings reflect a turning-away from the messiness of life to a perfected state where there is no discordant clatter, crying or shouting. . . .*
>
> **from *Vermeer, A View of Delft***
> —Anthony Bailey

Meet **Susan Vreeland** (b. 1946)

Author of "Magdalena Looking" and "Artful Research"

Susan Vreeland was a high school English teacher in California for thirty years. She got her start as a writer by publishing articles in magazines and newspapers. Then, she won acclaim for her novel *Girl in Hyacinth Blue.* This award-winning book was made into the Hallmark Hall of Fame movie *Brush with Fate,* starring Glenn Close.

Did You Know?

To research one of her travel articles, Vreeland trekked in the Himalayas, near Mt. Everest.

❸ Connecting Fiction and Nonfiction (pp. 4–5)

1. Make sure that students understand Vreeland's process of using historical nonfiction as a way of inspiring her to write fiction. Discuss with students what writers and readers can glean from historical fiction.
2. Direct students' attention to the paragraph from *A View of Delft* by Anthony Bailey. **Ask** students to identify the biographical information about Vermeer included in this paragraph.
   Answer: Vermeer was a painter with fifteen children, eleven of whom survived to adulthood. Vermeer was married to a woman named Catharina.
3. **Ask** students to speculate about which fact in the paragraph caught Vreeland's attention and inspired her to write a work of historical fiction.
   Possible responses: Students may cite the loss of four children or the fact that Vermeer was able to paint while raising a large family.

PHLit Online!

Show or assign the Penguin author video segments for these pages, available at **www.PHLitOnline.com.**

❹ Elements of Fiction

1. Remind students that the term *narrative* applies to both fiction and nonfiction. Humans have long used the idea of narratives (stories) to pass on information about traditions and historical events.
2. Remind students that *setting* refers to the time and place of the action.
3. Introduce the Plot Diagram, p. 235 in the ***Graphic Organizer Transparencies.*** Have students complete the diagram as they read the selection.
4. Explain that an author can define a character by using the character's words, thoughts, feelings, actions, and interactions with others. As they read, have students pay attention to the main character's traits. Prompt them to identify ways in which the author conveys the characters' traits.
5. Discuss with students the advantages and limitations of each *point of view.* For example, first-person narrators can relay only their own thoughts and experiences. Ask students which point of view would be most effective in an epic story with multiple characters.
   Answer: The most effective point of view would be third person.
6. Remind students that a *theme* is more than a single idea such as *freedom* or *peace.* A theme is a message that conveys the central insight of a story and is supported by details from the work.

❺ Types of Fiction

Help students understand that length is one of the primary differences among different types of fiction. **Ask** students to cite other differences.

Possible response: Novels may include subplots and many characters, while novellas and short stories are likely to focus on primary plots and fewer characters.

Exploring Fiction and Nonfiction

❹ Elements of Fiction

Fiction is narrative prose about characters and events from the author's imagination. All works of fiction share the following basic elements:

Setting is the time and place in which a story takes place.

Plot is the progression of events in a work of fiction. Plot originates in a **conflict,** or problem, that sets off a sequence of actions, rises to a **climax,** or point of greatest intensity, and ends with a **resolution,** or conclusion.

Characters are the individuals who take part in the action.

Dialogue is conversation between or among characters. In some literary works, characters speak in a **dialect,** a way of speaking particular to a group or region. Characters may also use **idiomatic expressions,** phrases that mean something different from their individual words and help a writer to show a character's personality. For example, "raining cats and dogs" is an idiomatic expression used to describe a heavy rain.

Point of view is the perspective from which a story is told. The voice and persona of the narrator can affect the tone and plot of a text.

- **First-person point of view:** The story is told by a narrator who participates in the action of the story.
- **Third-person point of view:** The story is told by a narrator outside the story.

Theme is the underlying meaning or insight that an author conveys in a story. A **universal theme** is one that applies to all people in all cultures.

❺ Types of Fiction

Novels are extended works of fiction that are usually organized into segments called chapters. Novels may include *subplots* in addition to the main story line and may explore a number of characters in depth.

Novellas are intermediate works of fiction that are longer than short stories but are more concise and focused than novels.

Short Stories are brief narratives, with carefully limited action that allows the writer to focus on one main plot complication.

Speed Bump

Understanding by Design

Clarifying Expected Outcomes

Explain to students that pages 6–7 set out their goals in this unit. By the end of the unit, they will understand the elements of fiction (including setting, plot, characters, dialogue, point of view, and theme) and the elements of nonfiction (including tone and perspective). They will be able to identify and discuss these elements in specific fiction and nonfiction selections. They will also be able to use some of these elements in writing their own pieces in the Writing Workshop on pp. 200–207.

Remind students that in addition, they will explore different ways of defining *reality* and *truth* as they work toward an answer to the Unit Big Question, "Is there a difference between reality and truth?" They will also add words to their vocabulary that will help them when discussing reality and truth. (See Introducing the Big Question, pp. 2–3.)

❻ Elements of Nonfiction

In addition to conveying information, a nonfiction writer may offer a particular view of his or her subject, using elements such as the following:

Tone expresses an author's attitude toward the subject and the readers. It is conveyed through choice of words and details.

Perspective is the author's point of view on the subject, including the opinions that the author expresses and the source of the author's information—whether general research, for example, or personal experience.

❼ Purposes of Nonfiction

Nonfiction is written for a variety of purposes, including those listed here:

- **To persuade:** Editorials, speeches, and reviews are often written to influence the opinions or actions of an audience.
- **To inform:** Articles, news reports, and instructions present facts to increase the knowledge and understanding of an audience.
- **To entertain:** Humor columns and many biographies and autobiographies are written for the enjoyment of an audience.
- **To describe:** Some essays or articles are written to help a reader understand the look, feel, or experience of a person, place, or event.

Put Yourself in the Picture

Use these sentence starters to help you describe how this picture could relate to pieces of fiction and nonfiction.

- A nonfiction piece based on this picture might try to **persuade** someone to ____________________.
- If the scene were the **setting** of a novel, I would expect __________.
- **Dialogue** between two people in this picture might reveal that one person is wondering ____________________.

Challenge Imagine you are one of the figures in this picture. Use as many details as possible to describe what is happening as you or people around you participate in these virtual reality games.

Differentiated Instruction for Universal Access

Support for Special Needs Students
Have students read the **Exploring Fiction and Nonfiction** page in the ***Reader's Notebook: Adapted Version***. This version provides a basic-level introduction to fiction and nonfiction.

Support for Less Proficient Readers
Have students read the **Exploring Fiction and Nonfiction** page in the ***Reader's Notebook***. This version provides a basic-level introduction to fiction and nonfiction.

EL Support for English Learners
Have students read the **Exploring Fiction and Nonfiction** page in the ***Reader's Notebook: English Learner's Version***. This version provides a basic-level introduction to fiction and nonfiction.

❻ Elements of Nonfiction

1. In discussing tone, explain that subtle changes in words and details can affect the way a reader perceives a subject. Write the following sentences on the board: *The weather was warm. The brilliant sunshine lured me from my desk. The annoying sunshine provoked a headache.* Discuss how the tone changes in each sentence.
2. Tell students that the author's vantage point, or perspective, makes a crucial difference in the way he or she writes a piece of nonfiction.
3. Provide the following tips for reading nonfiction: (a) figure out whether the information is organized in order of importance, chronological order, or spatial order; (b) identify the author's purpose; (c) distinguish between facts and opinions; (d) evaluate whether the author adequately supports his or her argument.

❼ Purposes of Nonfiction

Provide students with samples of nonfiction works that illustrate each purpose. Then, ask student groups to write examples of statements meant to persuade, to inform, and to entertain. Invite groups to share their statements with the class. Have them identify the purpose for each.

ASSESS

Answers

Put Yourself in the Picture

Possible response: A nonfiction piece based on this picture might try to **persuade** someone to play virtual reality games. If the scene were the **setting** of a novel, I would expect it to be a work of science fiction. **Dialogue** between two people in this picture might reveal that one person is wondering whether the virtual reality game might turn out to be real.

Challenge

Possible response: The landscape on the virtual screen passes by as I pedal and guide my bicycle around a sharp turn in the road. Friends are yelling off to the side and lights are shining on the screen, but all I can see is the hill ahead.

PRETEACH

❶ Introducing the Selection

1. Have students read Susan Vreeland's introduction to "Magdalena Looking."
2. **Ask** students to predict an event in the story based on Vreeland's introduction.
   Possible response: A daughter of Vermeer's will dream of becoming an artist, too, but she will have to do housework instead.
3. Call students' attention to terms used to discuss fiction: *setting, conflict,* and *theme*. Have students identify these elements in "Magdalena Looking" as they read.

❷ Background

Johannes Vermeer The seventeenth century is often referred to as the Golden Age of Dutch art. A group of painters, now called the Dutch Masters, dominated the artistic scene. Johannes (also known as Jan) Vermeer was one of these painters. Although he was successful during his lifetime, the latter part of his life was marred by financial difficulty.

❸ Connecting to the Big Question

1. Prepare students to apply the Big Question, "Is there a difference between reality and truth?" to the Model Selection.
2. Explain to students that in "Magdalena Looking," Vermeer paints a portrait of his daughter.
3. Have students complete this sentence starter, featuring thematic vocabulary from pp. 2–3:
   Portrait painters are somewhat subjective, because to be completely objective they would . . .
   Possible response: have to ignore feelings they have about their subjects.
4. Discuss responses as a class. Then have students look for examples of subjectivity as they read the selection.

Concept Connector

After reading, students will discuss differences between Magdalena's view of herself and her father's view of her.

Model Selection: Fiction

Susan Vreeland

Introduces "Magdalena Looking" ❶ ❷ ❸

When I was nine, my great-grandfather, a painter, guided my hand holding a watercolor brush until a lily appeared on the paper before me. How many girls throughout history would have longed to be taught that, but had to do washing and mending instead?

Paintings Inspire Stories

Now, whenever I look at paintings of people, stories rise in my imagination. I wonder, What was the relationship between artist and model? Was the artist sick with dread over how he would feed his family? What did his children want from him the day he painted that? These questions, and my desire to explore my heritage, prompted me to create Magdalena, the fictional daughter of the seventeenth-century Dutch painter Johannes Vermeer.

Settings and Conflicts from Paintings

While looking through a book of his paintings, wondering who owned them and feeling moved by their survival through time, I felt I was seeing **settings** for stories. He had repeated items in several paintings—a wall map, a woman's blue silk jacket, a Turkish rug, a luminous window of pale yellow glass—that told me he had a reverence for beautiful things, as I do. The expressions on some of the faces suggested yearnings and inner **conflicts** that I could use for characters like Magdalena.

Inventing a Painting, Discovering a Theme

I felt compelled to invent a painting made by Vermeer, using elements from his real paintings, and to add objects from my own imagination—a glass of milk, a sewing basket, Magdalena's shoes with square gold buckles. I imagined tracing this painting through centuries, and having the characters who encountered it live their most important moments under its influence, ending with the day it was painted, in a story called "Magdalena Looking." The title of my novel would be the name of the painting, *Girl in Hyacinth Blue,* and the power of great art to offer a moving experience would be my **theme.**

Vocabulary Development

Vocabulary Knowledge Rating

Create a **Vocabulary Knowledge Rating Chart (*Professional Development Guidebook,* p. 33),** with these words from the selection:

defiance *parchment*

Give students a copy of the chart. Read the words aloud and have students mark their rating in the Before Reading column. Urge them to be aware of these words as they read and discuss "Magdalena Looking," because they will rate their knowledge of the words again after they finish.

Ask how many students think they know a word so you can gauge how much instruction to provide. As students read, point out the words in their context.

PHLit Online! **Vocabulary Central,** featuring student tools for recording and studying vocabulary, is available at **www.PHLitOnline.com.**

4 # Magdalena
5 # Looking

6

Susan Vreeland

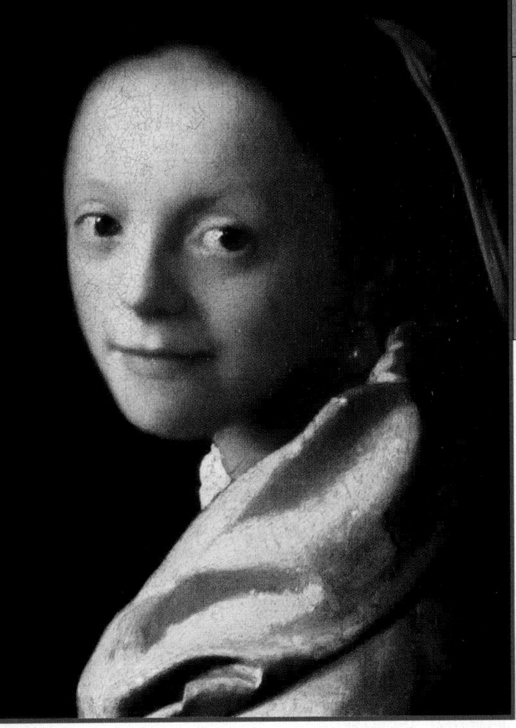

MODEL SELECTION

8 Late one afternoon when Magdalena finished the clothes washing and her mother let her go out, she ran from their house by the Nieuwe Kerk across the market square, past van Buyten's bakery, over two cobbled bridges across the canals, past the blacksmith's all the way to Kethelstraat and the town wall where she climbed up and up the ochre stone steps, each one as high as her knee, to her favorite spot in all of Delft,[1] the round sentry post. From that great height, oh, what she could see. If only she could paint it. In one direction Schiedam Gate and beyond it the twin towers of Rotterdam Gate, and ships with odd-shaped sails the color of brown eggshells coming up the great Schie River from the sea, and in another direction strips of potato fields with wooden plows casting shadows over the soil like long fingers, and orchards, rows of rounded green as ordered as Mother wished their eleven young lives to be, and the smoke of the potteries and brickeries, and beyond that, she didn't know. She didn't know.

1. **Nieuwe Kerk** (nü´ e kärk) . . . **van Buyten's** (fän bī´ tens) . . . **Kethelstraat** (kä´ tel strät) . . . **Delft** . . . *Nieuwe Kirk* means "New Church"; Kethelstraat is a street in the city; Delft is a manufacturing city on the Schie River in the Netherlands.

▲ Critical Viewing 7
This Vermeer portrait inspired the character of Magdalena. What impression of the character does it convey? **[Interpret]**

Fiction
Character and Setting
In her opening paragraph, Vreeland quickly establishes the setting of the story and gives the reader a strong first impression of the main character.

TEACH

4 Activating Prior Knowledge

Tell students they will use textbooks, library books, or Internet images to show examples of paintings that feature people. Then, have students make up fictional answers to the following question: What is the relationship between the artist and model(s)?

Concept Connector →

Students will follow up on this activity after completing the story.

5 About the Selection

Magdalena, a young girl living in Delft, wishes to see the world beyond the town wall and to be free of her chores. Her most fervent wish, however, is to paint like her father.

6 Humanities

Detail of *Study of a Young Woman* by Jan Vermeer

One of the most distinctive features of Vermeer's portrait *Study of a Young Woman* is the pearl earring in the young girl's left ear. **Ask:** What does the pearl suggest about the girl who is wearing it?

Possible answer: The pearl suggests that the girl is from a family of wealth and status.

7 Critical Viewing

Possible response: Magdalena's large eyes suggest her gift for seeing.

8 Fiction

Character and Setting

Ask students to describe their first impressions of Magdalena.

Possible response: Magdalena seems to be a restless girl with boundless energy and curiosity.

Differentiated Instruction for Universal Access

Strategy for Special Needs Students
Have students read the adapted version of "Magdalena Looking" in the ***Reader's Notebook: Adapted Version.*** They may also listen to the adapted version on the ***Hear It!* Audio CD** (adapted text).

Strategy for Less Proficient Readers
Have students read "Magdalena Looking" in the ***Reader's Notebook.*** After students finish the selection in the ***Reader's Notebook,*** have them complete the questions and activities in the student edition.

EL Strategy for English Learners
Have students read "Magdalena Looking" in the ***Reader's Notebook: English Learner's Version.*** English learners may also read the selection as they listen to the recorded version on the ***Hear It!* Audio CD.**

PHLit Online!

Enriched Online Student Edition To have students read the selection in interactive format, with narration and point-of-use interactive graphic organizers, go online at **www.PHLitOnline.com.**

9 Humanities

The Lacemaker by Jan Vermeer

Lace making is the creation of ornamental openwork fabric by looping and interlacing thread. It requires good eyesight, close concentration, and a sense of pattern. The birthplace of this art form is generally believed to be Flanders or Italy. Lace making was one of the best-known ways for a respectable young woman to make a living in times when their options for paid employment were few. Use these questions for discussion:

Ask: Does the painting suggest that Vermeer respected lace making as a form of art or is he depicting a woman going about her everyday household chores, one of them being lace making?
Possible response: At the least, Vermeer seems to respect the amount of attention required by lace making.

Ask: How might Vermeer have reacted if he had recognized Magdalena's artistic ability?
Possible response: Vermeer probably would have ignored her talent because it was not socially acceptable to groom a woman to become an artist.

10 Critical Viewing

Possible response: Students may identify shades of gold, yellow, brown, red, blue, and gray in the painting.

11 Point of View

1. Tell students that a character's thoughts often reveal important details about him or her.
2. **Ask** students which point of view Vreeland uses and to explain how they know.
   Possible response: Magdalena does not speak in the first person; however, the reader is made aware of her inner thoughts and wishes. Any narrative on the thoughts of other characters is based on Magdalena's knowledge. This presentation illustrates the third-person point of view.

10 ▼ **Critical Viewing** Magdalena is very aware of color. What do you think is the dominant color in this painting by her father, Johannes Vermeer? What colors complement it? **[Analyze]**

She stood there looking, looking, and behind her she heard the creak and thrum of the south windmill turning like her heart in the sea wind, and she breathed the brine[2] that had washed here from other shores. Below her the Schie lay like a pale yellow ribbon along the town wall. The longer she looked, the more it seemed to borrow its color from the sky. In the wind, the boats along the Schie docks with their fasteners clanking and their hollow bellies nudging one another made a kind of low rattling music she loved. It wasn't just today. She loved the sentry post in every kind of weather. To see rain pocking the gray sea and shimmering the stone bridge, to feel its cold strings of water on her face and hands, filled her to bursting.

9

She moved to a notch in the wall and just then a gust of wind lifted her skirts. The men on the bridge waiting with their bundles to go to sea shouted something in words she did not understand. She'd never tell Mother. Mother did not want her going there. The sentry post was full of guards smoking tobacco, Mother had said. There was some dark thing in her voice, as though she thought Magdalena should be afraid, but Magdalena did not know how to feel that then, or there. 11

Up there, high up above the town, she had longings no one in the family knew. No one would ever know them, she thought, unless perhaps a soul would read her face or she herself would have soul enough to speak

2. **brine** (brīn) saltwater.

Vocabulary Development

Thematic Vocabulary: The Big Question

As students are discussing "Magdalena Looking," encourage them to use the thematic vocabulary presented in Introducing the Big Question, pp. 2–30. You might encourage them with sentence starters like these:

1. One person's *perception* of the color ultramarine might be . . .
2. Sometimes it's hard to *differentiate* between shades of one color . . .
3. There may be *uncertainty* about the way two people will describe a certain color because . . .

of them. Wishes had the power to knock the breath out of her. Some were large and throbbing and persistent, some mere pinpricks of golden light, short-lived as fireflies but keenly felt. She wished for her chores to be done so she'd have time to race to the town wall every day before supper, or to the Oude Kerk[3] to lift the fallen leaves from her brother's grave. She wished her baby sisters wouldn't cry so, and the boys wouldn't quarrel and wrestle underfoot or run shouting through the house. Father wished that too, she knew. She wished there were not so many bowls to wash, thirteen each meal. She wished her hair shone flaxen in the sunlight of the market square like little Geertruida's.[4] She wished she could travel in a carriage across borders to all the lands drawn on her father's map.

12

She wished the grocer wouldn't treat her so gruffly when he saw her hand open out to offer four guilders,[5] all that her mother gave her to pay the grocery bill that was mounting into the hundreds, as far as she could tell. She wished he wouldn't shout; it sent his garlic breath straight into her nostrils. The baker, Hendrick van Buyten, was kinder. Two times so far he let Father pay with a painting so they could start over. Sometimes he gave her a still-warm bun to eat while walking home. And sometimes he put a curl of honey on it. She wished the grocer was like him.

She wished Father would take the iceboat to the Schie more often. He'd bought a fine one with a tall ivory sail. "Eighty guilders," Mother grumbled. "Better a winter's worth of bread and meat." On winter Sundays if the weather was clear, and if he was between paintings, it whisked them skimming across the white glass of the canal. She'd never known such speed. The sharp cold air blew life and hope and excitement into her ears and open mouth.

13

She remembered wishing, one particular morning when Father mixed lead white with the smallest dot of lead-tin yellow[6] for the goose quill in a painting of Mother writing a letter, that she might someday have someone to write to, that she could write at the end of a letter full of love and news, "As ever, your loving Magdalena Elisabeth."

He painted Mother often, and Maria he painted once, draped her head in a golden mantle and her shoulders in a white satin shawl. She was older, fifteen, though only by eleven months. It might be fun to dress up like Maria did, and wear pearl earrings and have

3. **Oude Kerk** (ou´ de kärk)
4. **Geertruida's** (kher trī´ das)
5. **guilders** (gil´ dərz) The guilder is the basic unit of Dutch currency.
6. **lead white . . . lead-tin yellow** references to pigments made from lead and tin and mixed with oil to produce paints of various colors.

Susan Vreeland
Author's Insight
With the list of Magdalena's wishes, I reveal her character, as well as give a great deal of background needed to understand the story.

Susan Vreeland
Author's Insight
Important to my story is the fact that in the seventeenth century and earlier, it was extremely unlikely that a young woman would be trained as an artist.

14 Reading Check
How do you know that Magdalena's family does not have a lot of money?

MODEL SELECTION

12 Author's Insight
Susan Vreeland

1. Remind students that they can learn about characters based on their actions.
2. **Ask** students to make lists of each wish that Magdalena makes, noting what they learn about her character and the story background from each wish.
   Possible responses: Magdalena's wishes include the following: she wishes her baby sister would not cry; she wishes she could travel; she wishes that the grocer would not treat her badly. Possible conclusions to be drawn from these wishes include the following: Magdalena comes from a poor family that is deeply in debt; she is a free spirit who enjoys adventure; and she longs for love.

13 Author's Insight

1. A young woman's inability to become a painter is just one of the historical facts Vreeland used to create this story.
2. **Ask** students to identify other historical facts that Vreeland used to create this story.
   Possible answer: Painters in the seventeenth century used pigments made from lead and tin, and they wrote with goose quill pens.

14 Reading Check

Answer: Magdalena's mother gave her only four guilders to pay their mounting grocery bill.

Differentiated Instruction for Universal Access

Strategy for Less Proficient Readers

Remind students that in the seventeenth century, people sometimes had difficulty paying for items. Magdalena's family is suffering from debt like so many other families of the time. Reread the first paragraph on this page. Point out that the reactions of the grocer and the baker contribute to their characterizations.

Ask: How do the grocer and the baker differ in their treatment of Magdalena?

Answer: The grocer treats Magdalena poorly because her family owes him money; however, the baker, who is in the same situation, is able to show kindness.

Ask: Do you think Magdalena is more like the grocer or the baker? Why?

Possible response: Magdalena resembles the baker because she is sensitive and thoughtful.

⓯ Humanities

The Allegory of Painting
by Jan Vermeer

The Allegory of Painting is one of Vermeer's best-known works. The young girl in the painting is dressed as Clio, the muse of history, and the map, chandelier, tapestry, and artist at his easel are as much the focus of the work as the girl is. The title reveals that to Vermeer, this was not just another of his many indoor scenes of people and objects but a comment on what art is and ought to be.

Despite the family's financial difficulties, Vermeer never sold this painting, and his wife took steps to ensure that it remained in the family after his death. Use this question for discussion:

Ask: If Magdalena had been the girl in the painting, how do you think she would have felt when she realized that she was not the central focus of the painting?
Possible response: Magdalena might have felt mad or sad that her father didn't see her for what she was but just as another element in one of his paintings.

⓰ Critical Viewing

Possible response: In the story, Magdalena poses for her father in the act of sewing her brother's shirt; a tapestry, a sewing basket, and a glass of milk are on the table.

⓰

▼ Critical Viewing
How is the scene in this painting different from Magdalena's description of the time her father paints? **[Contrast]**

Father position her just so, but the only part she really wished for was that he would look and look and pay attention.

More than all those wishes, she had one pulsing wish that outshone all the others. She wished to paint. Yes, me, she thought, leaning out over the stone wall. I want to paint. This and everything. The world from that vantage point stretched so grandly. Up there, beauty was more than color and shapes, but openness, light, the air itself, and because of that, it seemed untouchable. If only the act of wishing would make her able. Father only

⓯

Think Aloud

Vocabulary: Using Context
Direct students' attention to the word *apothecary* on page 13. Use the following "think aloud" to model how to use context to infer the meaning of an unknown word. Say to students:

I can figure out the meaning of the word *apothecary* by using context clues.

In the sentence, the author says Vermeer sent Magdalena to the apothecary to pick up bricks of lead-tin yellow and linseed oil. I know that Magdalena went to a person or place that could provide her with these items. In the seventeenth century, pharmacists carried medicine, chemicals, and oils. From this fact, I can assume that an apothecary is a pharmacist.

smiled queerly when she told him she wanted to paint, just as if she'd said she wanted to sail the seas, which, of course, she also wished, in order to paint what she would see. When she said so, that she wished to paint, Mother thrust into her hands the basket of mending to do.

Often from the edge of the room, she'd watch him work. Because he was always asking for quiet, with the little ones running through the room laughing or shouting, she didn't ask him many questions. He rarely answered anyway. Still, she studied how much linseed oil he used to thin the ultramarine,[7] and watched him apply it over a glassy layer of reddish brown. By magic, it made the dress he painted warmer than the blue on the palette. He would not let her go with him to the attic where he ground lead-tin yellow to powder, but he did send her to the apothecary[8] for the small bricks of it, and for linseed oil. Always there was money for that, but she didn't know what to answer when the apothecary demanded the guilders for her brother's potions still owed after he died.

17 If only she could have colors of her own, and brushes. She wouldn't just paint pictures of women inside cramped little rooms. She'd paint them out in marketplaces, bending in the potato fields, talking in doorways in the sunlight, in boats on the Schie, or praying in the Oude Kerk. Or she'd paint people skating, fathers teaching their children on the frozen Schie.

Fathers teaching their children. The thought stopped her.

18 Looking from the sentry tower at a cloud darkening the river, she knew, just as she knew she'd always have washing and mending to do, that it would not be so. She'd worn herself out with wishing, and turned to go. She had to be home to help with supper.

On a spring day that began in no special way, except that she had climbed the town wall the afternoon before, and all over Delft lime trees lining the canals had burst into chartreuse[9] leaves, and light shone through them and made them yellower except where one leaf crossed over another and so was darker—on that spring-certain day, out of some unknown, unborn place came that scream. "I hate to mend," she shouted to the walls, to Mother, to anyone. "It's not making anything."

Father stepped into the room, looked at Mother and then scowled at Magdalena. It had been her job to keep her little brothers quiet for him, or shoo them out of doors, and here she was,

7. **linseed oil . . . ultramarine** Linseed oil, made from the seed of the flax plant, can be used as the base for oil paint. Ultramarine is a rich blue.

8. **apothecary** (ə päth′ ə ker′ ē) historical term for a pharmacist; a dealer in medicines and various other preparations and chemicals.

9. **chartreuse** (shär trōōz′) pale, yellowish green.

Fiction

Plot Here, Vreeland raises the tension in Magdalena's conflict with her own role in life. This conflict will move the plot, or sequence of events, along.

19 **Reading Check**

What is Magdalena's greatest wish?

17 Fiction

Setting

1. Point out to students that, although Magdalena desperately wants to learn to paint, she wants to paint subjects that are very different from those her father paints.
2. Have students read the bracketed text. **Ask:** What do the comparisons between Magdalena's wishes and her father's work suggest about the role of women during this time period?
   Possible response: Vermeer's works mirror the limited, restricted lives of women during the time period. Magdalena desires to show women who are free and active, even if she still sees them in the traditional settings of the marketplace and the garden. Vermeer paints the world as it is; Magdalena wishes to paint the world as she would like it to be—a world in which she would be allowed to paint.

18 Fiction

Plot

1. Tell students that characters can experience both internal and external conflict. External conflicts occur when a character struggles against another character, nature, or fate. An internal conflict occurs when a character struggles within himself or herself.
2. **Ask:** What are the external and internal conflicts that Magdalena faces in the story?
   Possible response: Magdalena wishes to be a painter and see the world; however, external obstacles such as her father and her social circumstances stand in her way. Internally, she struggles with her need to be herself and her fears of being trapped in an unhappy life.

19 Reading Check

Answer: Magdalena's greatest wish is to have colors and brushes of her own so she could paint people doing things outdoors, not "women inside cramped little rooms."

Differentiated Instruction for Universal Access

EL Background for English Learners

Explain to English learners that during the 1600s, when Vermeer was painting, artists did not go to the store to buy tubes of paint made at a factory as painters do today. These artists mixed their paint colors by hand. They experimented with oils, berries, and powders to create shades of red, blue, and other colors.

Strategy for Advanced Readers

To further explore how point of view affects what readers know, have students rewrite a portion of the story from Vermeer's point of view. Remind students that they can use the first-person point of view or the third-person point of view. These versions may give students insight into Vermeer's character and even shift their sympathy toward a father who seems distant and indifferent in the original telling.

20 Fiction

Character and Point of View

1. Explain to students there are several types of third-person point of view. This story is told from third-person limited—the narrator reveals the thoughts of one character using the pronoun *he* or *she*.
2. Discuss with students why the author chooses to use a third-person limited narrator in "Magdalena Looking" rather than an omniscient narrator, which reveals the thoughts of all the characters in the story.
3. **Ask:** How would the story change if it were written from an omniscient point of view? **Possible response:** Although the characters in Magdalena's life might become more apparent to the reader through an omniscient narrator, the reader's almost personal relationship with Magdalena would fade.

Vocabulary
defiance (dē fi′ əns) *n.* the act of defying; open resistance to authority

the noisy one. No one moved. Even the boys were still. At first she looked only at Father's hand smeared with ultramarine powder, not in his eyes, too surprised by the echo of her voice to fling out any additional **defiance.** She loved him, loved what he did with that hand, and even, she suspected, loved what he loved, though they had not spoken of it. When that thought lifted her face to his, she saw his cheeks grow softer, as if he noticed her in his house for the first time. He drew her over to the table by the window, brought the sewing basket, placed on her lap her brother's shirt that needed buttons, adjusted the chair, opened the window, a little more, then less, and discovered that at a certain angle, it reflected her face. "If you sit here mending, I will paint you, Magdalena. But only if you stop that shouting." He positioned her shoulders, and his hands resting a moment were warm through the muslin[10] of her smock and seemed to settle her.

20

Mother rushed over to take away Geertruida's glass of milk.

"No, leave it, Catharina. Right there in the light."

For days she sat there, still as she could for Father, and yet sewing a few stitches every so often to satisfy Mother. In that mood of stillness, all the things within her line of vision touched her deeply. The tapestry laid across the table, the sewing basket, the same glass repoured each day to the same level, the amber-toned map of the world on the wall—it plucked a lute string in her heart that these things she'd touched, grown as familiar to her as her own skin, would be looked at, marveled at, maybe even loved by viewers of his painting.

Vocabulary
parchment (parch′ mənt) *adj.* creamy or yellowish color of the paper used for special documents, letters, or artwork

On sunny days the panes of window glass glistened before her. Like jewels melted into flat squares, she thought. Each one was slightly different in its pale transparent color—ivory, **parchment,** the lightest of wines and the palest of tulips. She wondered how glass was made, but she didn't ask. It would disturb him.

Fiction
Character and Point of View
Although Vreeland tells the story in the third person, the narrator sees deep into Magdalena and helps the reader understand her.

Outside the window the market chattered with the selling of apples and lard and brooms and wooden buckets. She liked the cheese porters in their flat-brimmed red hats and stark white clothes. Their curved yellow carrying platforms stacked neatly with cheese rounds were suspended on ropes between pairs of them, casting brown shadows on the paving stones. Two platforms diagonally placed in the midground between their carriers would make a nice composition with the repeated shapes of those bulging cheese rounds. She'd put a delivery boy wheeling his cart of silver cod in the background against the guild hall, and maybe in the foreground a couple of lavender gray pigeons pecking crumbs.

10. muslin (muz′ lin) strong, plain cotton cloth.

Vocabulary Development

Adjectives

Ask students to reread the last paragraph on this page. The author uses many adjectives to describe the scene outside the window. Have students make a list of the adjectives used in this paragraph. Have students look out the windows in their classroom or another room in the school. Ask them to use the adjectives on their list and other adjectives to write paragraphs describing the scene they see outside the window. Compare and contrast students' descriptions to that created by Vreeland.

The carillon[11] from Nieuwe Kerk ringing out the hour sounded something profound in her chest. All of it is ordinary to everyone but me, she thought.

All that month she did not speak, the occasion too momentous to dislodge it with words. He said he'd paint her as long as she didn't shout, and so she did not speak a word. Her chest ached like a dull wound when she realized that her silence did not cause him a moment's reflection or curiosity. When she looked out the corner of her eye at him, she could not tell what she meant to him. Slowly, she came to understand that he looked at her with the same interest he gave to the glass of milk.

Maybe it was because she wasn't pretty like Maria. She knew her jaws protruded and her watery, pale eyes were too widely set. She had a mole on her forehead that she always tried to hide by tugging at her cap. What if no one would want the painting? What then? It might be her fault, because she wasn't pretty. She wished he'd say something about her, but all he said, not to her directly, more to himself, was how the sunlight whitened her cap at the forehead, how the shadow at the nape of her neck reflected blue from her collar, or how the sienna of her skirt deepened to Venetian red[12] in the folds. It was never her, she cried to herself, only something surrounding her that she did not make or even contribute to knowingly. Another wish that never would come true, she saw then, even if she lived forever, was that he, that someone, would look at her not as an artistic study, but

22

▼ Critical Viewing
In this painting by Vermeer, which details suggest the same care in arranging a scene that the character of Vermeer shows in the story? Explain. **[Connect]**

21

11. **carillon** (kar′ ə län′) a set of tuned church bells.
12. **sienna** (sē en′ ə) . . . **Venetian** (və nē′ shən) **red** colors; sienna is a reddish or yellowish brown, and Venetian red is a brownish red.

MODEL SELECTION

21 Humanities

Young Woman With a Water Jug
by Jan Vermeer

During the sixteenth century, art played an important role in European society. Highly trained male painters, printmakers, and sculptors had as their patrons the political, religious, scientific, and intellectual leaders of the day. Women, however, were largely barred from the art world; they were homemakers whose responsibilities were everyday household chores. This portrait depicts a woman performing one of those chores. **Ask:** If this portrait were of Magdalena, what might she be thinking about as she pours water from the jug?

Possible response: Magdalena might be thinking about the artist she wishes to become. She might be thinking about the colors and shapes around her.

22 Critical Viewing

Possible response: The young woman is posed beside a carefully angled window; ordinary household objects are on the table.

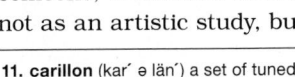

Differentiated Instruction for Universal Access

Strategy for Special Needs Students

When Vermeer dies, Magdalena spends time washing and preparing his body for burial. During this time, the narrator reveals Magdalena's desire to paint the picture of her father in his death. Discuss with students why Magdalena would want to do this. Talk about how pictures preserve the memories of the past. Ask students whether they have any pictures that are special to them. Talk about why they keep these pictures and what they think about when they look at them. Discuss how they would feel if these pictures did not exist or if they were to lose them. On the day before this discussion, you may want to suggest that students bring important pictures to class to share.

23 Humanities

Franz Hanfstaengl Muchery by Jan Vermeer

Of the paintings attributed to Vermeer, most portray figures in interiors and all are admired for the use of light and color. It is possible that Leonaert Bramer, a Dutch artist who was a witness at Vermeer's wedding, may have tutored him in painting. Vermeer, his wife, and eleven children lived in debt during the artist's final years. Use this question for discussion:

1. What is noteworthy about Vermeer's use of color and light? **Possible response:** Vermeer's use of color and light is so natural and vibrant that it creates a vivid sense of reality within his paintings.

24 Critical Viewing

Possible response: Students may agree that the painting shows a love of color and light, particularly in the sun-lit brilliant colors of the window, the woman's dress, the tablecloth, and the sky-blue drapery in the left corner.

with love. If two people love the same thing, she reasoned, then they must love each other, at least a little, even if they never say it. Nevertheless, because he painted with such studied concentration, and because she held him in awe, she practiced looking calm for him as she looked out the window, but when she saw the canvas, what she intended as calm looked more like wistfulness.[13]

The painting was not bought by the brewer, Pieter Claesz van Ruijven,[14] who bought most of her father's work. He saw it, but passed over it for another. Disgrace seared her so that she could not speak that night. The painting hung without a frame in the outer kitchen where the younger children slept. Eventually the

24 ▼ **Critical Viewing** What details in this painting by Vermeer confirm the descriptions in the story of his love of color and light? Explain. **[Connect]**

13. **wistfulness** a mood of wishfulness or vague longing.
14. **Pieter Claesz van Ruijven** (pē ter kläs fän rī fen)

23

Vocabulary Development

Currency Terminology

This story takes place in a small town in Holland. As a result, the author uses Dutch currency when discussing the exchange of money; for example, on page 17, when Magdalena offers the paintings in exchange for paying off a debt of more than six hundred guilders. A *guilder* is the basic unit of Dutch currency. A *stuiver* is a fraction of a guilder, roughly a dime. Lead students in a discussion regarding how these references to Dutch money contribute to the setting of the story.

family had to give up their lodgings at Mechelen on the square, and take smaller rooms with Grandmother Maria on the Oude Langendijck.[15] Her father stopped taking the iceboat out to the Schie, sold it, in fact. He rarely painted, the rooms were so cramped and dark, the younger children boisterous, and a few years later, he died.

When she washed him in his bed that last time, his fingers already cold, she had a thought, the shame of which prevented her from uttering: It would make a fine painting, a memorial, the daughter with towel and blue-figured washing bowl at bedside, her hand covering his, the wife exhausted on the Spanish chair clutching a crucifix, the father-husband, eyes glazed, looking to another landscape. While he painted everyone else, no one was there to paint him, to make him remembered. She yearned to do it, but the task was too fearsome. She lacked the skill, and the one to teach her had never offered.

Even though she asked for them, Mother sold his paints and brushes to the Guild of St. Luke. It helped to pay a debt. When Mother became sick with worry, Magdalena had the idea to take the painting to Hendrick van Buyten, the baker, because she knew he liked her. And he accepted it, along with one of a lady playing a guitar, for the debt of six hundred seventeen guilders, six stuivers,[16] more than two years' worth of bread. He smiled at her and gave her a bun.

25 Within a year, she married a saddlemaker named Nicolaes, the first man to notice her, a hard worker whose pores smelled of leather and grease, who taught her a pleasure not of the eyes, but, she soon realized, a man utterly without imagination. They moved to Amsterdam and she didn't see the painting again for twenty years.

In 1696, just after their only living child, Magritte, damp with fever, stopped breathing in her arms, Magdalena read in the *Amsterdamsche Courant* of a public auction of one hundred thirty-four paintings by various artists. "Several outstandingly artful paintings," the notice said, "including twenty-one works most powerfully and splendidly painted by the late J. Vermeer of Delft, will be auctioned May 16, 1:00, at the Oude Heeren Logement."[17] Only a week away. She thought of Hendrick. Of course he couldn't be expected to keep those paintings forever. Hers might be there. The possibility kept her awake nights.

15. **Mechelen** (me´ khe len) . . . **Oude Langendijck** (ou´ de läŋ en dīk) The Mechelen was an inn owned by the Vermeer family. The Oude Langendijck is a canal in Delft.
16. **stuivers** (stī´ fers) coins worth a fraction of a guilder; roughly, a dime.
17. **Oude Heeren Logement** (ou´ de her´ en lōzh mōn)

Fiction

Character By filling in the sad events that occur between the death of Magdalena's father and the auction, Vreeland inspires compassion for the main character.

26 **Reading Check**

What event does Magdalena attend?

MODEL SELECTION

25 Fiction

Character

1. Have students briefly review the wishes that Magdalena had expressed as a young girl.
2. Then have students read the bracketed text, two sentences that sum up Magdalena's adult life.
3. **Ask** students: What feelings are created by the harsh contrast between Magdalena's youthful wishes and the reality of her adult life?
   Possible response: Students may note that the contrast evokes feelings of pity and regret for the colorless life Magdalena has had to live.

26 Reading Check

Answer: Magdalena attends an art auction.

Differentiated Instruction for Universal Access

Strategy for Special Needs Students

To monitor comprehension, have students pause at points in the story to make predictions about what will happen. For instance, have students predict what is going to happen when the bidding starts on Magdalena's portrait. Have students record their predictions on sheets of paper. Read the auction scene with the students. Have students review their predictions for accuracy. If students were not correct in their predictions, instruct them to write about what really happened at the auction.

Enrichment for Gifted/Talented Students

Students may enjoy bringing Vreeland's words to life by creating a visual image from her explicit descriptions. Have students use Vreeland's description of Delft to create a visual image of the town. Students could draw, paint, build a collage, or use other mediums to create their image. You may want to create an art gallery in the classroom to display students' work.

㉗ Author's Insight

1. Vreeland says that she consciously keeps the reader guessing about whether or not Magdalena has talent to make her life seem less painful.
2. **Ask** students to list the sorrows of Magdalena's life.
   Possible responses: The sorrows in Magdalena's life include suffering her father's indifference, marrying a man with no imagination, leading a life she does not want, and mourning the death of her only living child.
3. Discuss Vreeland's insight as to why she portrays Magdalena in this way. **Ask:** Do you agree or disagree with Vreeland's idea that not knowing whether she is talented makes the sorrows in Magdalena's life easier to bear? Explain why.
   Possible response: Students may disagree, because doubt and unfulfilled dreams can lead to disenchantment with one's life just as easily as unfulfilled potential.

Concept Connector

Connecting to the Big Question

Have students discuss the differences they see in Magdalena's view of herself and her father's view of her. Did their views change when their relationship was that of model and artist? You might have students complete statements such as this one:

Before reading this story, I thought Magdalena saw herself as . . . Now I see that . . .

Have volunteers share their work.

Susan Vreeland
Author's Insight
Here's what I wanted to convey about Magdalena: If it had been evident that she had talent, her limited life might have been more painful to her because she'd be conscious of unfulfilled possibility. Not knowing if she had talent made her life of sorrows more bearable.

Entering the auction gallery, she was struck again by that keenest of childhood wishes—to make a record not only of what she saw, but how. The distance she'd come from that, and not even a child to show for it! She shocked herself by asking, involuntarily, what had been the point of having lived? Wishing had not been enough. Was it a mistake that she didn't beg him to teach her? Maybe not. If she'd seen that eventually, with help, she could paint, it might have made the years of birthing and dying harder. But then the birthing and dying would have been painted and the pain given. It would have served a purpose. Would that have been enough—to tell a truth in art? ㉗

She didn't know.

To see again so many of Father's paintings was like walking down an avenue of her childhood. The honey-colored window, the Spanish chair, the map she'd stared at, dreaming, hanging on the wall, Grandmother Maria's golden water pitcher, Mother's pearls and yellow satin jacket—they commanded such a reverence for her now that she felt they all had souls.

And suddenly there she was on canvas, framed. Her knees went weak.

Hendrick hadn't kept it. Even though he liked her, he hadn't kept it.

Almost a child she was, it seemed to her, gazing out the window instead of doing her mending, as if by the mere act of looking she could send her spirit out into the world. And those shoes! She had forgotten. How she loved the buckles, and thought they made her such a lady. Eventually she'd worn the soles right through, but now, brand-new, the buckles glinted on the canvas, each with a point of golden light. A bubble of joy surged upward right through her.

"Would that have been enough—to tell a truth in art?"

No, she wasn't beautiful, she owned, but there was a simplicity in her young face that she knew the years had eroded, a stilled longing in the forward lean of her body, a wishing in the intensity of her eyes. The painting showed she did not yet know that lives end abruptly, that much of living is repetition and separation, that buttons forever need resewing no matter how ferociously one works the thread, that nice things almost happen. Still a woman overcome with wishes, she wished Nicolaes would have come with her to see her in the days of her sentry post wonder when life and hope were new and full of possibility, but he had seen no reason to close up the shop on such a whim.

She stood on tiptoe and didn't breathe when her painting was announced. Her hand in her pocket closed tight around the twenty-four guilders, some of it borrowed from two neighbor

Vocabulary Development

Vocabulary Knowledge Rating

When students have completed reading and discussing "Magdalena Looking," have them take out their **Vocabulary Knowledge Rating Chart** for this selection. Read the words aloud once more, and have students rate their knowledge of the words again in the After Reading column. Clarify any words that are still problematic. Have students write their own definitions and example sentence in the appropriate column. Encourage students to use the words in further discussion and written work about this selection. Remind them that they will be accountable for these words on the **Selection Test, *Unit 1 Resources*,** pp. 24–26 or 27–29.

women, some of it taken secretly from the box where Nicolaes kept money for leather supplies. It was all she could find, and she didn't dare ask for more. He would have thought it foolish.

"Twenty," said a man in front of her.

"Twenty-two," said another.

"Twenty-four," she said so loud and fast the auctioneer was startled. Did he see something similar in her face? He didn't call for another bid. The painting was hers!

"Twenty-five."

Her heart cracked.

The rest was a blur of sound. It finally went to a man who kept conferring with his wife, which she took as a good sign that it was going to a nice family. Forty-seven guilders. Most of the paintings sold for much more, but forty-seven was fine, she thought. In fact, it filled her momentarily with what she'd been taught was the sin of pride. Then she thought of Hendrick and a pain lashed through her. Forty-seven guilders minus the auctioneer's fee didn't come close to what her family had owed him.

She followed the couple out into the drizzle of Herengracht,[18] wanting to make herself known to them, just to have a few words, but then dropped back. She had such bad teeth now, and they were people of means. The woman wore stockings. What would she say to them? She didn't want them to think she wanted anything.

28 She walked away slowly along a wet stone wall that shone iridescent, and the wetness of the street reflected back the blue of her best dress. Water spots appeared fast, turning the cerulean[19] to deep ultramarine, Father's favorite blue. Light rain pricked the charcoal green canal water into delicate, dark lace, and she wondered if it had ever been painted just that way, or if the life of something as inconsequential as a water drop could be arrested and given to the world in a painting, or if the world would care.

She thought of all the people in all the paintings she had seen that day, not just Father's, in all the paintings of the world, in fact. Their eyes, the particular turn of a head, their loneliness or suffering or grief was borrowed by an artist to be seen by other people throughout the years who would never see them face to face. People who would be that close to her, she thought, a matter of a few arms' lengths, looking, looking, and they would never know her.

18. Herengracht (her´ en khräkht) the "Gentleman's Canal;" one of the three main canals in the center of the city of Amsterdam.

19. cerulean (sə ro͞o´ lē ən) sky-blue.

Susan Vreeland
Author's Insight
Magdalena has changed from a girl with many wishes to a woman who didn't want the buyers "to think she wanted anything." Despite this fading of desire, she can still take quiet, private joy in the look of things.

Fiction
Plot In many stories, the resolution is a clear win or certain loss. Magdalena's concluding thoughts represent a little of both.

MODEL SELECTION

28 Author's Insight

1. Lead students in a discussion regarding whether the new owners of Magdalena's portrait would have wanted Magdalena to introduce herself to them. Why or why not?
2. **Ask:** How do you know that Magdalena still takes private joy in the look of things?
   Possible response: As she walks along, she notices the street has reflected back the blue of her dress; water spots on her cerulean blue dress have turned to ultramarine, her father's favorite color; and light rain falling on the dark-green canal is making lacy shapes.

29 Fiction

Plot

1. Explain to students that the resolution in a story is not always clear. Generally, readers like a satisfactory ending; however, greater depth and complexity can come from more subtle conclusions.
2. Discuss with students the conflict and resolution in this story. **Ask** students whether the conflict is resolved in a positive or negative way.
   Possible response: The tragic resolution of this story is that no one really knows Magdalena, not the people who view her portrait and not the real people in her life.

30 Fiction

Theme

1. Remind students that the theme is a complete statement that conveys the insight a story offers about people or life.
2. Vreeland states on p. 8 that "the power of great art to offer a moving experience would be my theme." **Ask** students to think of other themes conveyed in "Magdalena Looking."
   Possible response: Unfulfilled dreams can lead to a life of unhappiness.

Fluency

Pair more fluent readers with less fluent readers. Distribute copies of page 19. Have partners take turns reading paragraphs aloud. While one student reads, the other should mark words that are difficult for his or her partner to read. Circulate to monitor the fluency of students' reading. Collect students' marked-up copies of the page, and review difficult words with the class. These spots may pose problems:

- If students have difficulty with the word *momentarily*, point out that the word features the common base word *moment*. Have students define the word *moment* (a very brief period of time). Then have them read the sentence again, and ask if the word makes sense in the context of the sentence.
- If students have difficulty with the word *inconsequential*, practice oral cloze with the sentence. First, read the sentence, replacing the word *inconsequential* with a synonym such as *unimportant*. Then read the sentence omitting the word *inconsequential*: ". . . or if the life of something as *blank* as a water drop . . . ." Finally, reread the sentence, asking student to "fill in the blank" with the word from the story.

PRETEACH

❸❶ Introducing the Selection

1. Have students read Susan Vreeland's introduction to this nonfiction article.
2. **Ask** students to explain whether the introduction increases their interest in reading the selection and, if so, why.
3. Call students' attention to the terms used in discussing nonfiction: *expository, audience, thesis, purpose,* and *hook*. **Prompt** students to identify these terms in "Artful Research" as they read.

❸❷ Background

James Joyce Joyce was one of the most important and influential fiction writers of the twentieth century. Joyce's depictions of Dublin streets and landmarks in *Ulysses* are so vivid and accurate that fans of his writings can visit the tavern that the main character, Leopold Bloom, patronizes in the Siren scene.

❸❸ Connecting to the Big Question

1. Prepare students to apply the Big Question, "Is there a difference between reality and truth?" to the Model Selection.
2. Explain to students that in "Artful Research," Vreeland uses many different resources in her research before writing.
3. Have students complete this sentence frame, featuring thematic vocabulary from pp. 2–3:
   Nonfiction writers have to be able to clearly comprehend what they read as they research so they can differentiate between . . .
   Possible response: what information is factual and what information is not.
4. Discuss responses as a class. Then have students list resources they would use to differentiate between factual and nonfactual information.

Concept Connector →

After reading, students will discuss Vreeland's resource list on p. 25 and choose two resources from the list they think would have been most helpful to her when writing "Magdalena Looking."

Model Selection: Nonfiction

Susan Vreeland

Introduces "Artful Research" ❸❶ ❸❷ ❸❸

I suppose I'll always be a teacher in one way or another. Even while writing, I'm teaching, whether I'm writing fiction which teaches about life, or nonfiction, which teaches by explaining something. In both cases, my "class" is invisible, so I have to fire up their curiosity and make the writing clear without me being there.

Expository Nonfiction: "An Invisible Class"

In my **expository article,** "Artful Research," I'm teaching an invisible class of fiction writers, my **audience.** I want them to learn how they can make their own stories better by doing specific research.

Article Versus Essay

An **article** differs from an **essay** in that its main intent is to provide useful information, while the main intent of an essay is to put forth an argument on an issue. There is some overlap, however. Both can use a **thesis** and examples. Among other **purposes,** an article can present the necessity or advantages of a certain course of action and can then provide methods to carry out that action.

Techniques of Nonfiction: The "Hook"

That's what "Artful Research" does. Because I'm not in the room with them, my audience might at any moment turn the page and ignore me. As a **hook** to catch their attention, I begin with a curious example of a writer needing to know something that might seem odd. Then, I tell them what I want them to remember: my *thesis,* followed by examples from the writing of *Girl in Hyacinth Blue,* the novel that includes "Magdalena Looking." Because the novel spans 350 years, I needed to do a lot of research, so it's a good example.

After I get readers to agree to the necessity and benefits of research, particularly for a historical novel but not exclusively, I offer them some research methods that I've discovered, including possible sources for information.

Vocabulary Development

Vocabulary Knowledge Rating

Create a **Vocabulary Knowledge Rating Chart** ***(Professional Development Guidebook, p. 33),*** with these words from the selection:

revealing *crucial* *interesting* *direction*

Give students a copy of the chart. Read the words aloud, and have students mark their rating in the Before Reading column. Urge them to be aware of these words as they read and discuss "Artful Research," because they will rate their knowledge of the words again after they finish.

Ask how many students think they know a word so you can gauge how much instruction to provide. As students read, point out the words in their context.

PHLit Online! **Vocabulary Central,** featuring student tools for recording and studying vocabulary, is available at **www.PHLitOnline.com.**

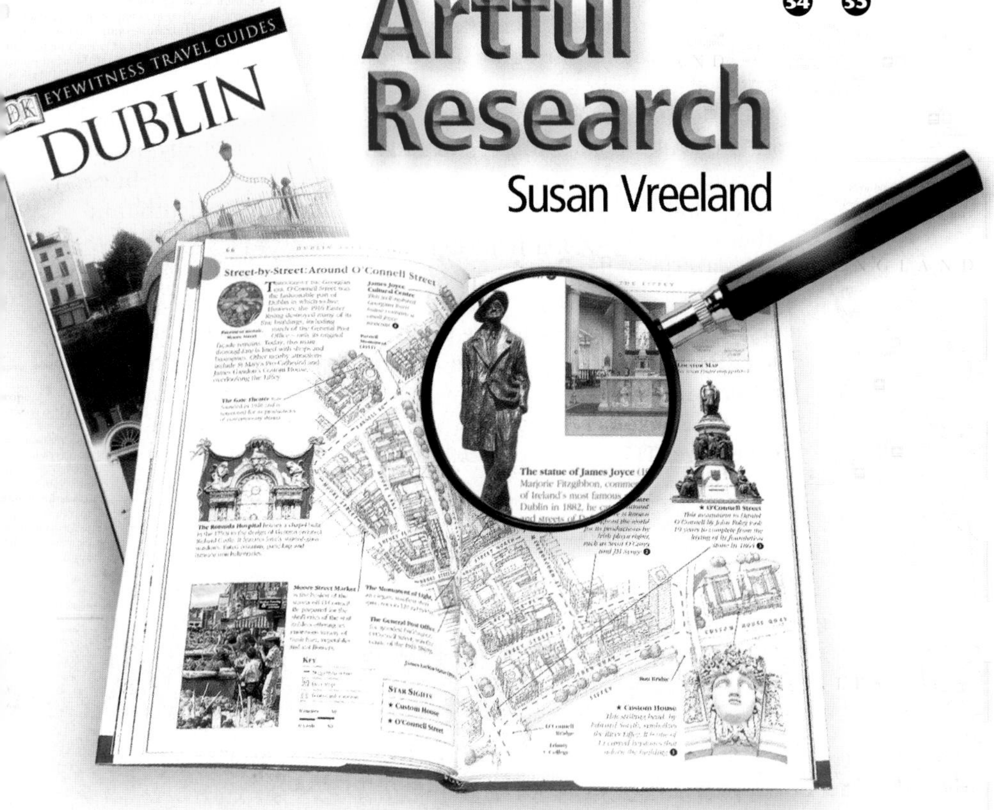

Artful Research (34) (35)

Susan Vreeland

MODEL SELECTION

Is it possible for an ordinary person to climb over the area railings of #7 Eccles Street, either from the path or the steps, lower himself down from the lowest part of the railings till his feet are within two feet or three of the ground and drop unhurt? I saw it done myself but by a man of rather athletic build. I require this information in detail in order to determine the wording of a paragraph.

(36) James Joyce[1] wrote this to his aunt once when he was out of Dublin. Can't you just imagine her muttering, "That boy! What will he think of next?" as she looks for her umbrella to go out in the rain and take the trolley to Eccles Street?

Excessive? Unnecessary? Stalling from the act of writing? Joyce's letter is instructive and revealing.

Susan Vreeland
Author's Insight
I use this type of question, called a rhetorical question, to direct readers' thinking toward an answer I want them to have.

1. **James Joyce** (1882–1941) famed Irish writer noted for *Dubliners* (1914), a collection of short stories, and *Ulysses* (1922), a novel, among other works.

TEACH

(34) Focusing Reading

1. Tell students that Susan Vreeland credits viewing images from a Vermeer Exhibition as the inspiration for her novel *Girl in Hyacinth Blue*. Emphasize how her appreciation of and research into art are the basis of much of the detail in "Magdalena Looking."
2. Inform students that Vreeland explains how she transforms research into fiction by stating that artists "are not gods, they must be humanized by this writing." **Ask** students to recall examples of this humanizing process in "Magdalena Looking."
   Possible response: Although his talent as a painter is awe-inspiring, Johannes Vermeer is portrayed as a real person with ordinary problems such as debt and noisy children

(35) About the Selection

In the expository piece "Artful Research," Susan Vreeland defends her philosophy on research. She provides information as to why research was so important in the development of her novel *Girl in Hyacinth Blue*. She also provides a list of her favorite reference materials.

(36) Author's Insight

1. Tell students that a rhetorical question is a question to which no answer is expected.
2. Have students read the rhetorical questions in the bracketed text. **Ask** students how the effect would have been different if the rhetorical questions had been deleted.
   Possible response: Vreeland uses the questions as vertical steps to heighten the impact of her point. Without the questions, the statement regarding Joyce's letter falls flat.

Differentiated Instruction for Universal Access

Strategy for Special Needs Students
Have students read the adapted version of "Artful Research" in the ***Reader's Notebook: Adapted Version.*** They may also listen to the adapted version on the ***Hear It!* Audio CD** (adapted text).

Strategy for Less Proficient Readers
Have students read "Artful Research" in the ***Reader's Notebook.*** After students finish the selection in the ***Reader's Notebook,*** have them complete the questions and activities in the student edition.

EL Strategy for English Learners
Have students read "Artful Research" in the ***Reader's Notebook: English Learner's Version.*** English learners may also read the selection as they listen to the recorded version on the ***Hear It!* Audio CD.**

PHLit Online!

Enriched Online Student Edition To have students read the selection in interactive format, with narration and point-of-use interactive graphic organizers, go online at **www.PHLitOnline.com.**

37 **Nonfiction**

Perspective

1. Remind students that perspective is the author's point of view on a subject.
2. Perspective is based on personal experience or general research. **Ask** students from which perspective Vreeland writes in "Artful Research."
   Possible response: Although the article is about research, it is based on Vreeland's personal experience.

Similarly, I must admit that I sent my French translator on a mission to find out whether the carvings of heads on the façade of the Ministère de la Défense[2] on Boulevard Saint-Germain in Paris are repeats of the same face or different faces. Among other things, she told me I had the wrong street!

While some writers may be more cavalier, claiming that it's fiction, after all, I hold with the meticulous Joyce, not wholly out of allegiance to a recognized master, but for the sake of the richness of story that results. For me, research gives direction, depth, and authority to the writing; it doesn't just decorate a preconceived story with timely trivia.

37 Early research tends to be scattered, while one searches for the story, but later, usually during or after a first draft when one discovers in the work some needed information, it becomes pinpoint precise. At either time, an array of interesting material, some of it crucial, some merely useable, will emerge—and sometimes leap off the page. The results can be exciting. A single unexpected line

2. **Ministère de la Défense** (mēn i stār′ də lȧ dā fäns′) the Ministry of Defense building in Paris, France.

Susan Vreeland's Historical Fiction

These are the type of books I hunt down in used bookstores:

- history of art by time period and country
- history of music
- history of costume
- history of transportation, manufacture, household devices
- books of names of things, including tools and architecture
- atlases with street maps of cities
- foreign-language dictionaries
- time-sequence histories
- field guides to birds, flowers, and trees

These are the reference books on my shelves that I turn to often:

- *The Oxford English Dictionary.* Crowning every historical fiction writer's wish list is the mother of all dictionaries, *The Oxford English Dictionary,* which indicates when individual words came in to use and how and when their meanings changed. There are three versions that won't break the bank: The Shorter OED, two volumes; The Compact OED, small print with magnifying glass; and The OED on CD-ROM.
- *Timetables of History: A Horizontal Linkage of People and Events,* by Bernard Grun (Touchstone Press). The entire book is an indexed grid, with years beginning at 5000 B.C. down the left column and categories across the top: History and Politics; Literature and Theater; Religion and Philosophy; Visual Arts; Music; Science and Technology; Daily Life. If I'm looking for whether I

can prompt a whole story. For example, the line in Jacob Presser's grim history, *Ashes in the Wind: The Destruction of Dutch Jewry*, 37 indicating that in 1941, Jews were not allowed to keep pigeons, provided the genesis of my story "A Night Different from All Other Nights."

That story is one of eight linked narratives comprising my composite novel, *Girl in Hyacinth Blue*, which traces an alleged Vermeer[3] painting in reverse chronology through the centuries, showing how defining moments in people's lives are lived under its influence. Besides the present, six time periods and numerous 38 locales in the Netherlands are evoked: 1942 in Amsterdam; 1896 in Vreeland (yes, a real village located between Amsterdam and Utrecht); 1798 in The Hague during French rule: 1717 in Oling, Delfzijl, Westerbork, and Groningen (which I learned had been a university town since 1614, prompting my focal character to be a student); 1665 in Delft; and 1685 in Amsterdam. Naive in understanding what such a project entailed, I found that by the end, I had consulted seventy-six books.

3. **Vermeer** (vər mir′) Jan (yän) Vermeer (1632–1675), renowned Dutch painter.

39 **Reading Check**

What is Susan Vreeland's attitude about research?

MODEL SELECTION

Writer's Research Wish List

can have a character turn on a water faucet in a Paris flat in 1883 (indexed under Plumbing), this is the first book I turn to.

- *Timelines: Day by Day and Trend by Trend from the Dawn of the Atomic Age to the Close of the Cold War,* by Paul Dickson (Addison Wesley). Besides news items by date, this book gives fads, innovations, hot topics, additions to the national lexicon, and phrases typical of the time.
- *The Writer's Digest Books Reference Series,* which includes
  - *Everyday Life in the 1800s,* Marc McCutcheon
  - *The Writer's Guide to Everyday Life in Renaissance England,* Kathy Lynn Emerson
  - *The Writer's Guide to Everyday Life in the Middle Ages,* Sherrilyn Kenyon
- *English Through the Ages,* by William Brohaugh, gives approximate dates of the first recorded use of words, by category.
- *Roget's International Thesaurus,* edited by Barbara Ann Kipfer (HarperCollins). The index lists items of apparel, fabrics, furniture, hairstyles, tools and machinery, vehicles, vessels, musical instruments, animals, plants, stones, minerals, woods, colors, types of glass, manners of cooking, foods—all of which can be checked against historical references.

38 Critical Thinking

Analyze

1. Have students read the bracketed passage. **Ask** a volunteer to define the word *naive*.
   Answer: The word *naive* means "lacking critical insight or ability."
2. Point out the time periods and locations in which the novel takes place. To help students grasp the concept of the varied differences in locations, list six areas of your state that have obvious differences. For example, you could list these: factories, farmlands, tall buildings, or coastline.
3. **Ask** students to explain why Vreeland said she was naive in understanding what such a project entailed when she began research for her novel.
   Possible response: Vreeland might have begun her research thinking that the different locales in her novel were in the Netherlands, so details would be the same throughout. While researching, she found this was not true and that each location had its own individuality.

39 Reading Check

Possible response: Vreeland believes that research is a vital part of writing successful historical fiction.

Differentiated Instruction for Universal Access

EL Strategy for English Learners

Explain to students that pronouns have three cases, or forms, which are dependent on the pronoun's function in a sentence. Tell students that possessive pronouns function to show ownership. Introduce the following list:

possessive pronouns: *my, mine, your, yours, his, her, hers, its, our, ours, their, theirs*

Have students identify several sentences in the article that use possessive pronouns.

Strategy for Less Proficient Readers

Students may have difficulty identifying critical details in the selection that will help them comprehend what they are reading. Preteach the following vocabulary: *chronology, defining, present,* and *time periods*. Then make a timeline with students to show how Vreeland's one novel covers different places and times. You might want to use a map to follow the route the novel takes. This will help students comprehend the extent of Vreeland's research on many different time periods and places.

40 Nonfiction

Purposes of Nonfiction

1. Remind students that the purpose of nonfiction is to persuade, to inform, to describe or to entertain. Discuss with students how successful Vreeland is in fulfilling each purpose with this article.
Possible response: Vreeland is probably more successful at informing readers about the variety of resources available to researchers than she is at persuading or entertaining them.
2. Have students read the first paragraph on this page. **Ask:** Why would Vreeland read so many different types of books on the Netherlands?
Possible answer: By reading different types of books, Vreeland gains a depth of knowledge not possible from a single book. Such a depth of knowledge gives her own writing more credibility. Also, she exposes herself to a variety of perspectives and tones on the topics.

41 Critical Viewing

Possible response: The books and the telescope enrich the figure's journey, allowing him to appreciate more deeply the colorful world around him. In the same way, background knowledge serves to enrich the reading experience.

41 ▲ **Critical Viewing**
In what way does this illustration represent Vreeland's claim that research enriches fiction? **[Connect]**

I'd been to the Netherlands only once, twenty-five years ago for three days, and I had never seen a Vermeer painting face to face. Blithely, I went ahead. I read books on Vermeer, Dutch art and social and cultural history, the Holocaust[4] as experienced in the Netherlands, the changing geography of the Netherlands as more land was reclaimed from the sea,[5] Erasmus' adages,[6] the history of costume, Passover and the practice of Jewish customs, Amsterdam's diamond trade, Dutch superstitions and treatment of witches, the French occupation, and the engineering of windmills and dikes.

Twenty printout pages from the Internet on the engineering of windmills (they vary regionally), on gears, wallowers, Archimedean screws, and drive shafts yielded one paragraph establishing the authority of my character the windmill engineer. More importantly, the research also suggested a metaphor appropriate for him:

> *I had fancied love a casual adjunct and not the central turning shaft making all parts move. I had not stood astonished at the power of its turning.*

I would not have arrived at his critical self-assessment and the epiphany of the story without meandering through gears and drive shafts.

Here are ten research sources and approaches, beginning with the most obvious and ending with the ultimate—travel—that I used for either *Girl in Hyacinth Blue* or my subsequent novel,

4. **the Holocaust**(häl´ ə kôst´) the persecution, imprisonment, and mass murder of Jews by Nazi Germany before and during the Second World War (1939–1945).
5. **reclaimed from the sea** Significant portions of the Netherlands were originally covered by water. To drain water from this land, the Dutch built a system of dikes (dams) and canals.
6. **Erasmus' adages** (i raz´ məs əz a´ di jəz) the sayings or brief observations of Desiderius (des´ ə dir´ ē əs) Erasmus (1469–1536), an influential Dutch scholar.

Think Aloud

Vocabulary: Using Context

Model the use of context clues for students. Direct students' attention to the word *adjunct* in the italicized passage on this page. Say to students:

> I am going to think aloud to show you how I can use context to discover the meaning of an unfamiliar word.
>
> The word *adjunct* appears in the sentence "I had fancied love a casual adjunct and not the central turning shaft making all the parts move." In the preceding text, Vreeland says that this sentence is a metaphor, a comparison of two things. Here, love is being compared to the machinery of a windmill. She says what love is: "a casual adjunct;" then, she follows by saying what it is not: "the central turning shaft." I can picture love as a minor gear in the machinery, part of the process of turning but not essential to making all the parts move like the turning shaft would. So, in this sentence, *adjunct* must mean "something additional rather than an essential part."

The Passion of Artemisia, which takes place in seventeenth-century Italy.

1. **Works on history, politics, and social conditions** A couple of titles might serve to show how I approached possible narratives from different angles: on the one hand, *Daily Life in Rembrandt's Holland;* on the other, *The Embarrassment of Riches: An Interpretation of Dutch Culture in the Golden Age.* Some I used as browser books; others, for specific information. Their bibliographies proved to be good sources for characters' names.
2. **Biography, autobiography, personal narrative, and oral history** The mere memory of *Anne Frank's Diary of a Young Girl* suggested that I create a young character the antithesis of Anne in terms of self-expression, yet suffering similar revelations.
3. **Geography books** These can give information about weather, topography, crops, industry, indigenous plants, birds, and other animals.
4. **Maps** Besides those available in travel bookstores, universities often have historical map collections. This was essential for *Girl* because I had to know if certain villages and canals existed at the time of each of the stories.
5. **Travel books** Those of the descriptive sort, the older the better, provide visual and cultural detail.
6. **Novels** Novels written at the time, written about the time, or set in the same place can be helpful in revealing attitudes, concerns, expressions, syntax, and diction.
7. **Paintings** Paintings done in the same time and place as one's fiction are excellent sources of information about costume, hairstyles, jewelry, household furnishings, landscape, available foods, flowers typical of the region, even the quality of light in a region, Vermeer's "trademark."
8. **Children's and juvenile fiction and nonfiction** Works for younger readers are sufficient in some cases and have the advantages of providing evocative illustrations and simplifying complicated political histories.
9. **Interviews and phone calls** Don't neglect the importance of interviews and phone calls. People are intrigued by novelists and are usually delighted to be consulted. For *Girl in Hyacinth Blue,* I consulted a pigeon breeder to learn why the owning of pigeons was prohibited to Jews under the German occupation and how homing pigeons "worked."
10. **Going there!** While travel is not always practical (I wrote *Girl in Hyacinth Blue* entirely while undergoing cancer treatment and could not travel), it will yield unexpected insights.

MODEL SELECTION

Susan Vreeland
Author's Insight
While writing *Girl in Hyacinth Blue,* I had a serious illness. Unable to leave the house, I couldn't do necessary research on windmill engineering. A concerned former student, who knew that writing was the key to my survival, did the research for me without my asking. The love metaphor, which I quote on page 24, was the result.

43
Reading Check
Why does Vreeland think novels are useful for research?

42 Author's Insight

1. Have students read the bracketed passage on p. 24.
2. Point out that attention to detail is clearly evident in Vreeland's writing and her research. **Ask** students which elements of fiction would be most affected if Vreeland were not so meticulous in her research and why.
   Possible response: Setting and character, which rely on detail and description, would be significantly changed.

43 Reading Check

Answer: Vreeland believes that novels are useful for research because they reveal attitudes, concerns, expressions, syntax, and diction of a particular time period.

Differentiated Instruction for Universal Access

Strategy for Gifted/Talented Students
Students may enjoy reversing the process of using art to inspire fiction. Have students think about favorite works of fiction. Ask students to use these works to inspire their own works of art. Emphasize that students may use a variety of mediums to create paintings, sketches, sculptures, collages, videos, or musical compositions.

Enrichment for Advanced Readers
To further explore the role of research in writing fiction, have students read Vreeland's lists on pp. 22–23 and p. 25. Take the students to the library to find their own reference books. These books may or may not be recommended by Vreeland. Have students browse through the books to find a word, idea, or fact that they will use as a prompt to write stories of their own. Encourage students to share their stories as well as the process they go through to move from research to fiction.

44 Literature in Context

History Connection *L'Encyclopédie* was the consummate work of a group of French thinkers called *philosophes*, but the information contained in it was extremely practical rather than purely philosophical. Modern scholars, recognizing the continuing importance of this historic work, have translated the text into English and made it available through a portal on the World Wide Web.

Connect to the Literature
Students may be surprised to learn that reference books such as encyclopedias and dictionaries have not always existed and only recently reached their modern forms. The concept may be more understandable if you discuss with students the ongoing evolution in reference sources that has occurred with the increased availability of computer technology. For example, online or CD-ROM dictionaries now often include audio clips of pronunciation, and electronic encyclopedias now offer instant links to other articles within the encyclopedia. Then direct students' attention to the Connect to the Literature question: What resources might have been available to writers before encyclopedias?
Possible response: Before encyclopedias, writers could have used novels, diaries, letters, biographies, and public records to conduct research.

Concept Connector

Now that students have read "Artful Research," have them write down the two resources from Vreeland's list that they think were most helpful to her research. Ask them to explain whether their choices changed as they read the selection and why they think these are the two most helpful resources for doing the type of research Vreeland did for her historical novel.

Connecting to the Big Question
Ask: How does factual information included as details in fiction help to make fiction seem more truthful?
Possible response: Even though fiction comes from the writer's imagination, there might be parts of the story, such as a real place, that are based on reality. These details help to make the story seem more convincing and authentic.

So when does one stop researching and start writing? You write when the story comes to life, when it assumes some structure, when you can't help but start, not when you know everything you'll need to know. That's impossible to anticipate before you get into the heart of the writing. You might need to push yourself away from the safer act of research and leap into a first draft.

Don't get bogged down with fears of historical inaccuracy when writing a first draft. In one of the flood stories in *Girl in Hyacinth Blue*, the student needs to write a note. He's in a rowboat. He can't dip a pen in an inkwell. Did they have pencils in 1717? Look it up later. Keep writing. Keep the momentum going. If you don't know what they ate, leave it blank and get down the more important elements of the scene.

One caveat: Even if you put into your manuscript some fact delectable to you, recalling your delight in discovering it, if the story does not justify it, take it out. Type it up. Pin it on your wall. Use it elsewhere. But don't include it! The book is about characters, not about research.

44

LITERATURE IN CONTEXT

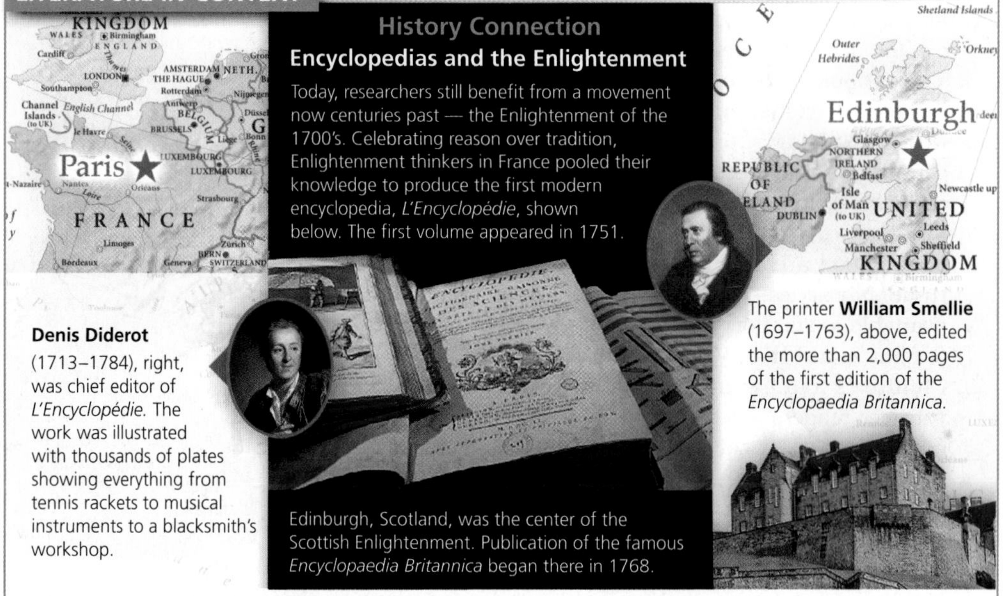

History Connection
Encyclopedias and the Enlightenment
Today, researchers still benefit from a movement now centuries past — the Enlightenment of the 1700's. Celebrating reason over tradition, Enlightenment thinkers in France pooled their knowledge to produce the first modern encyclopedia, *L'Encyclopédie*, shown below. The first volume appeared in 1751.

Denis Diderot (1713–1784), right, was chief editor of *L'Encyclopédie*. The work was illustrated with thousands of plates showing everything from tennis rackets to musical instruments to a blacksmith's workshop.

The printer **William Smellie** (1697–1763), above, edited the more than 2,000 pages of the first edition of the *Encyclopaedia Britannica*.

Edinburgh, Scotland, was the center of the Scottish Enlightenment. Publication of the famous *Encyclopaedia Britannica* began there in 1768.

Connect to the Literature What resources might have been available to writers before encyclopedias?

Vocabulary Development

Vocabulary Knowledge Rating
When students have completed reading and discussing "Artful Research," have them take out their **Vocabulary Knowledge Rating Chart** for this selection. Read the words aloud once more, and have students rate their knowledge of the words again in the After Reading column. Clarify any words that are still problematic. Have students write their own definition and example sentence in the appropriate column. Encourage students to use the words in discussion and written work about his selection. Remind them that they will be accountable for these words on the **Selection Test, *Unit 1 Resources*,** pp. 24–26 or 27–29.

After You Read

Magdalena Looking • Artful Research

Critical Thinking

1. **Respond:** Do you sympathize with Magdalena? Why or why not?
2. **(a)** What is Magdalena's "one pulsing wish"? **(b) Interpret:** What obstacles prevent Magdalena from fulfilling her wish?
   (c) Evaluate: Are Magdalena's disappointments due more to her own behavior or to circumstances beyond her control? Explain.
3. **(a) Draw Conclusions:** Did Magdalena demonstrate artistic talent? Explain. **(b) Support:** Identify the characteristics that show Magdalena's artistic ability. Then, identify any opposing evidence that suggests that she does not have talent.
4. In "Artful Research," Vreeland writes, "For me, research gives direction, depth, and authority to the writing. . . ." Complete a chart like the one shown by noting three passages from "Magdalena Looking" that show what Vreeland means and explaining your choices.

How Research Helps in Fiction

"Magdalena Looking" Passage	Why You Chose It

Is there a difference between reality and truth?
(a) How does the reality of a time and place change for Vreeland when she researches? **(b)** How is Magdalena's understanding of the painting different from the perception of the people who see it at the auction?

Fiction and Nonfiction Review

1. **(a)** How does the time and cultural **setting** of "Magdalena Looking" influence the **conflict** that she experiences? **(b)** Do you think she would experience similar conflicts if she lived today? Explain.
2. Which aspect of **nonfiction** is more developed in "Artful Research," exploration of ideas or sharing information? Support your answer.

Research the Author

Use the Internet and library resources to find other Vreeland works, both fiction and nonfiction, that focus on art. Present your findings as a **bulletin board display.**

- Provide summaries of Vreeland's works that relate to art and artists.
- Add quotations from Vreeland's interviews and writing.
- If possible, add images of paintings, artists, and Vreeland herself.

ASSESS/EXTEND

Answers

Critical Thinking

1. Students may not sympathize with Magdalena because she should have created her destiny.
2. (a) To paint. (b) In Holland's society at this time, women are not allowed to become painters.
   (c) **Possible response:** Both. She could not control the values of the society, but she could have asked her father to teach her to paint.
3. (a) **Possible response:** Magdalena displays an artistic eye for colors. (b) Descriptions of her father's painting. She does not try painting, so this could illustrate a lack of talent.
4. **Possible response:** "Father mixed lead white with the smallest dot of lead-tin yellow for the goose quill." Research on artist's paints in the seventeenth century would have allowed Vreeland the knowledge to truthfully describe how artists mixed their own colors.

Is there a difference between reality and truth?
(a) It changes over the years. Research tells of physical changes in geography or cultural details.
(b) Magdalena sees the painting as a record of her childhood; whereas, the other people simply see it as another "artful painting."

Fiction and Nonfiction Review

1. (a) In Holland during the seventeenth century, it was unacceptable for Magdalena to become a painter. (b) No, because society is more accepting of women's changing roles.
2. Exploring ideas, because Vreeland discusses the importance of allowing research to lead the process of writing fiction.

Research the Author

Students may complete this research assignment for homework. Tell them that they can find information about Vreeland in the library or online.

Assessment Resources

The following resources can be used to assess students' knowledge and skills.

Unit 1 Resources

L1 L2 EL **Selection Test A,** pp. 24–26
L3 L4 **Selection Test B,** pp. 27–29
L3 L4 **Open-Book Test,** pp. 21–23

PHLit Online! Students may use the **Self-test,** online at **www.PHLitOnline.com,** to prepare for Selection Test A or Selection Test B.

PHLit Online! Students can find more about the author at **www.PHLitOnline.com.**

TIME AND RESOURCE MANAGER

The Monkey's Paw • The Leap

Lesson Pacing Guide

DAY 1 Preteach

- Administer the Reading and Vocabulary Warm-ups (*Unit 1 Resources*, pp. 30–33 or 48–51) as necessary.
- Introduce the Reading Skill: Make Predictions FT
- Introduce the Literary Analysis concept: Plot and Foreshadowing FT
- Distribute copies of the appropriate graphic organizer for the Reading Skill (*Graphic Organizer Transparencies*, pp. 6–8). CRI
- Distribute copies of the appropriate graphic organizer for Literary Analysis (*Graphic Organizer Transparencies*, pp. 3–5). CRI
- Teach the selection vocabulary. FT CRI
- Introduce the Word Study skill.

DAYS 2–3 Preteach/Teach

- Build background with the Background feature. CRI
- Develop thematic vocabulary and thematic thinking with Writing About the Big Question.
- Prepare students to read with the Activating Prior Knowledge activities (TE). CRI
- Informally monitor comprehension while students read. FT
- Use the Reading Check questions to confirm comprehension.
- Develop students' ability to predict a logical idea about what will happen using the Reading Skill questions. CRI
- Develop students' understanding of plot and foreshadowing using the Literary Analysis questions. CRI
- Reinforce vocabulary with the Vocabulary notes. CRI

DAY 4 Assess

- Assess students' comprehension and mastery of the skills by having them answer the Critical Thinking, Reading Skill, and Literary Analysis questions. FT
- Have students complete the Vocabulary Practice activities. FT
- Have students complete the Word Study activities.

DAY 5 Extend/Assess

- Have students complete the Grammar lesson. CRI
- Have students complete the Writing activity and write a sequel. (You may assign as homework.) FT
- Extend learning by having students complete the Listening and Speaking activity, an interview. As an alternative, assign them "Unlucky Winners" or "High Flyers" in *Reality Central*. CRI
- Administer Selection Test A or B (*Unit 1 Resources*, pp. 42–47 or 63–68). FT

"The Monkey's Paw" is a short story presented unedited and in its entirety.
"The Leap" is a short story presented unedited and in its entirety.

Meeting Your Standards

Students will

1. analyze and respond to literary elements.
   - Literary Analysis: Character and Characterization
2. read, comprehend, and analyze short stories.
   - Reading Skill: Make Inferences
   - Reading Check questions
   - Apply the Skills questions
   - Assessment Practice
3. develop vocabulary.
   - Vocabulary
   - Word Study
4. apply grammar skills.
   - Principal Parts of Regular Verbs
   - Author's perspective
   - Conflict and resolution
   - Author's purpose
5. Develop writing proficiency.
   - Work in Progress: Short Story
   - retellings
6. strengthen research and technology skills.
   - report on sources

CRI For a full explanation of Culturally Responsive Instruction opportunities in this lesson, see p. T86–T87.

FT For an accelerated lesson, use the Fast Track strategies and activities.

Managing Differentiated Instruction
This leveled selection pairing groups a more accessible with a more challenging selection. Choose either one to teach the lesson skills. For classroom management suggestions for using the pairing in a mixed-ability class, see pp. T68–T69.

Daily Block Scheduling
Each day in this Lesson Pacing Guide represents a 40–50 minute period. Teachers using block scheduling may combine days to revise pacing. In addition, teachers may differentiate and support core instruction by integrating components for extended and intensive support as students require. See the Guide to Selected Leveled Resources (facing page).

Guide to Selected Leveled Resources

EL English Learners

			The Monkey's Paw	The Leap
CORE COURSE	*Unit 1 Resources*	Selection Test A	pp. 42–44	pp. 63–65
	Graphic Organizer Transparencies	Reading Skill Graphic Organizer A	p. 6	p. 7
		Literary Analysis Graphic Organizer A	p. 3	p. 4
EXTENDED SUPPORT (Level 2)	*Unit 1 Resources*	Reading and Vocabulary Warm-ups A or B	pp. 30–33	pp. 48–51
	Reader's Notebook: English Learner's Version		adapted instruction and adapted selection	adapted instruction and summary
	Hear It! Audio CD		selection and summaries	selection and summaries
	Hear It! Audio CD (adapted text)		adapted selection and summaries	—
INTENSIVE SUPPORT (Level 1)	*Reality Central*		"Unlucky Winners"	"High Flyers"
	Real-World Writing Journal		Lesson 1, pp. 2–5	Lesson 2, pp. 6–9

L2 Below-Level Students

			The Monkey's Paw	The Leap
CORE COURSE	*Unit 1 Resources*	Selection Test A	pp. 42–44	pp. 63–65
	Graphic Organizer Transparencies	Reading Skill Graphic Organizer A	p. 6	p. 7
		Literary Analysis Graphic Organizer A	p. 3	p. 4
EXTENDED SUPPORT (Level 2)	*Unit 1 Resources*	Reading and Vocabulary Warm-ups A or B	pp. 30–33	pp. 48–51
	Reader's Notebook		adapted instruction and full selection	adapted instruction and summary
	Hear It! Audio CD		selection and summaries	selection and summaries
INTENSIVE SUPPORT (Level 1)	*Reality Central*		"Unlucky Winners"	"High Flyers"
	Real-World Writing Journal		Lesson 1, pp. 2–5	Lesson 2, pp. 6–9
	Reading Kit		Reteaching worksheets	Reteaching worksheets

L1 Special Needs Students

			The Monkey's Paw	The Leap
CORE COURSE	*Unit 1 Resources*	Selection Test A	pp. 42–44	pp. 63–65
	Graphic Organizer Transparencies	Reading Skill Graphic Organizer A	p. 6	p. 7
		Literary Analysis Graphic Organizer A	p. 3	p. 4
EXTENDED SUPPORT (Level 2)	*Unit 1 Resources*	Reading and Vocabulary Warm-ups A or B	pp. 30–33	pp. 48–51
	Reader's Notebook: Adapted Version		adapted instruction and adapted selection	adapted instruction and summary
	Hear It! Audio CD (adapted text)		selection and summaries	selection and summaries
INTENSIVE SUPPORT (Level 1)	*Reality Central*		"Unlucky Winners"	"High Flyers"
	Real-World Writing Journal		Lesson 1, pp. 2–5	Lesson 2, pp. 6–9
	Reading Kit		Reteaching worksheets	Reteaching worksheets

The program includes resources for these students: L3 On-Level L4 Advanced All All
For a complete guide to selection support, see pp. T106–T108.

NOTE: All print materials are also available online at *www.PHLitOnline.com.*

VISUAL GUIDE to Featured Selection Resources

- **The Monkey's Paw**
- **The Leap**

RESOURCES FOR:

- EL English Learners
- L1 Special Needs Students
- L2 Below-Level Students
- L3 On-Level Students
- L4 Advanced Students
- All All Students

Vocabulary/Fluency/Prior Knowledge

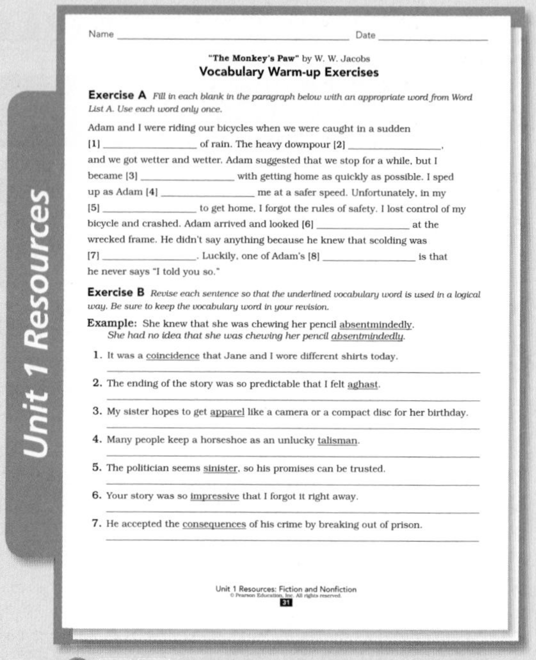

Name ______________ Date ______________

"The Monkey's Paw" by W. W. Jacobs

Vocabulary Warm-up Exercises

Exercise A *Fill in each blank in the paragraph below with an appropriate word from Word List A. Use each word only once.*

Adam and I were riding our bicycles when we were caught in a sudden [1] ______________ of rain. The heavy downpour [2] ______________, and we got wetter and wetter. Adam suggested that we stop for a while, but I became [3] ______________ with getting home as quickly as possible. I sped up as Adam [4] ______________ me at a safer speed. Unfortunately, in my [5] ______________ to get home, I forgot the rules of safety. I lost control of my bicycle and crashed. Adam arrived and looked [6] ______________ at the wrecked frame. He didn't say anything because he knew that scolding was [7] ______________. Luckily, one of Adam's [8] ______________ is that he never says "I told you so."

Exercise B *Revise each sentence so that the underlined vocabulary word is used in a logical way. Be sure to keep the vocabulary word in your revision.*

Example: She knew that she was chewing her pencil absentmindedly.
She had no idea that she was chewing her pencil absentmindedly.

1. It was a coincidence that Jane and I wore different shirts today.
2. The ending of the story was so predictable that I felt aghast.
3. My sister hopes to get apparel like a camera or a compact disc for her birthday.
4. Many people keep a horseshoe as an unlucky talisman.
5. The politician seems sinister, so his promises can be trusted.
6. Your story was so impressive that I forgot it right away.
7. He accepted the consequences of his crime by breaking out of prison.

Unit 1 Resources: Fiction and Nonfiction
© Pearson Education, Inc. All rights reserved.
31

EL L1 L2 **Vocabulary Warm-ups A and B, pp. 30–31, 48–49**

Also available for these selections:

- EL L1 L2 **Reading Warm-ups A and B, pp. 32–33, 50–51**
- All **Vocabulary Builder, pp. 37, 55**
- All **Writing About the Big Question, pp. 34, 52**

Reader's Notebooks

Pre- and postreading pages for both selections, as well as "The Monkey's Paw," appear in an interactive format in the *Reader's Notebooks*. Each *Notebook* is differentiated for a different group of learners. The selections in the Adapted and English Learner's versions are abridged.

L2 L3 ***Reader's Notebook***

L1 ***Reader's Notebook: Adapted Version***

EL ***Reader's Notebook: English Learner's Version***

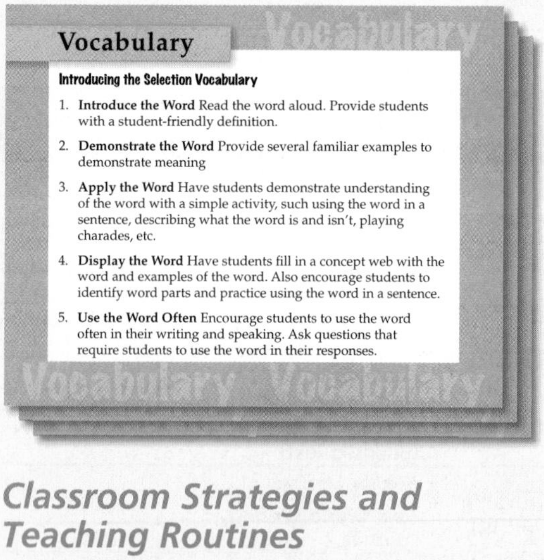

Introducing the Selection Vocabulary

1. **Introduce the Word** Read the word aloud. Provide students with a student-friendly definition.
2. **Demonstrate the Word** Provide several familiar examples to demonstrate meaning
3. **Apply the Word** Have students demonstrate understanding of the word with a simple activity, such using the word in a sentence, describing what the word is and isn't, playing charades, etc.
4. **Display the Word** Have students fill in a concept web with the word and examples of the word. Also encourage students to identify word parts and practice using the word in a sentence.
5. **Use the Word Often** Encourage students to use the word often in their writing and speaking. Ask questions that require students to use the word in their responses.

Classroom Strategies and Teaching Routines

- core classroom routines outlined step-by-step
- convenient format for easy reference while teaching

Graphic Organizer Transparencies

Selection Support

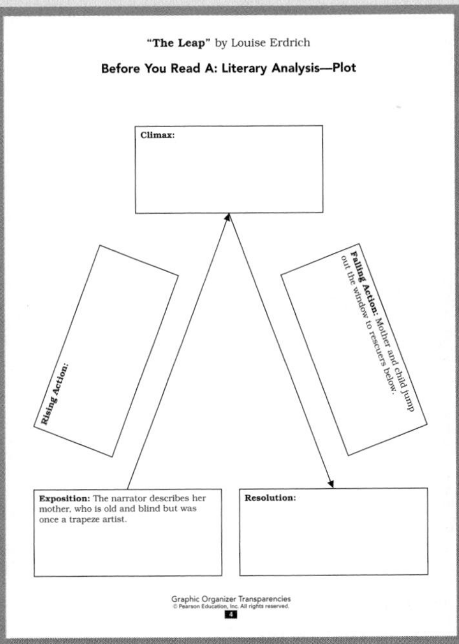
"The Leap" by Louise Erdrich

Before You Read A: Literary Analysis—Plot

Climax:

Rising Action:

Falling Action: Mother and child jump out the window to rescuers below.

Exposition: The narrator describes her mother, who is old and blind but was once a trapeze artist.

Resolution:

Graphic Organizer Transparencies
© Pearson Education, Inc. All rights reserved.
4

EL L1 L2 **Literary Analysis: Graphic Organizer A,** pp. 3, 4 (partially filled in)

Also available for these selections:

EL L1 L2 Reading: Graphic Organizer A, pp. 6, 7 (partially filled in)

L3 Reading: Graphic Organizer B, p. 8

L3 Literary Analysis: Graphic Organizer B, p. 5

Skills Development/Extension

Unit 1 Resources

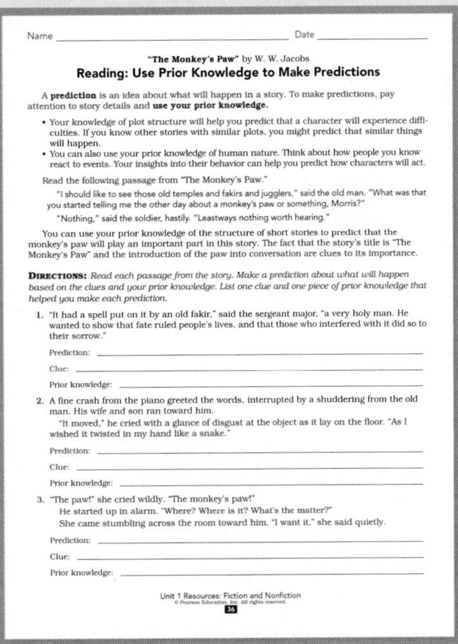
Name ______________ Date ______________

"**The Monkey's Paw**" by W. W. Jacobs

Reading: Use Prior Knowledge to Make Predictions

A **prediction** is an idea about what will happen in a story. To make predictions, pay attention to story details and **use your prior knowledge.**

- Your knowledge of plot structure will help you predict that a character will experience difficulties. If you know other stories with similar plots, you might predict that similar things will happen.
- You can also use your prior knowledge of human nature. Think about how people you know react to events. Your insights into their behavior can help you predict how characters will act.

Read the following passage from "The Monkey's Paw."

"I should like to see those old temples and fakirs and jugglers," said the old man. "What was that you started telling me the other day about a monkey's paw or something, Morris?"

"Nothing," said the soldier, hastily. "Leastways nothing worth hearing."

You can use your prior knowledge of the structure of short stories to predict that the monkey's paw will play an important part in this story. The fact that the story's title is "The Monkey's Paw" and the introduction of the paw into conversation are clues to its importance.

Directions: *Read each passage from the story. Make a prediction about what will happen based on the clues and your prior knowledge. List one clue and one piece of prior knowledge that helped you make each prediction.*

1. "It had a spell put on it by an old fakir," said the sergeant major, "a very holy man. He wanted to show that fate ruled people's lives, and that those who interfered with it did so to their sorrow."

   Prediction: ______________

   Clue: ______________

   Prior knowledge: ______________

2. A fine crash from the piano greeted the words, interrupted by a shuddering from the old man. His wife and son ran toward him.

   "It moved," he cried with a glance of disgust at the object as it lay on the floor. "As I wished it twisted in my hand like a snake."

   Prediction: ______________

   Clue: ______________

   Prior knowledge: ______________

3. "The paw!" she cried wildly. "The monkey's paw!"

   He started up in alarm. "Where? Where is it? What's the matter?"

   She came stumbling across the room toward him. "I want it," she said quietly.

   Prediction: ______________

   Clue: ______________

   Prior knowledge: ______________

Unit 1 Resources: Fiction and Nonfiction
© Pearson Education, Inc. All rights reserved.
36

All **Reading: Make Predictions,** pp. 36, 54

Also available for these selections:

All Literary Analysis: Plot and Foreshadowing, pp. 35, 53

L4 Enrichment, pp. 38, 56

L3 L4 Grammar, p. 57

L3 L4 Support for Writing, p. 58

L3 L4 Support for Extend Your Learning, p. 59

Assessment

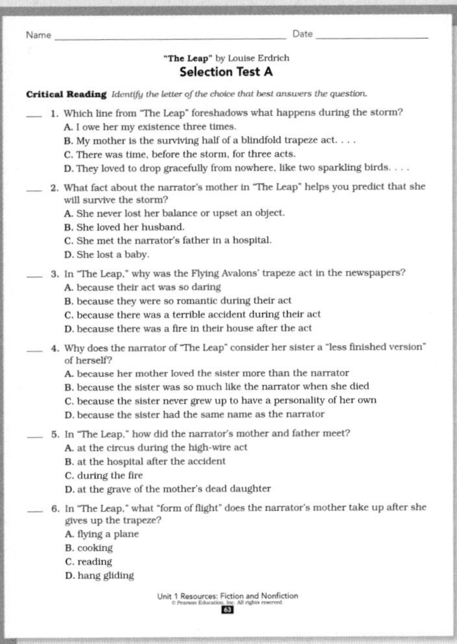
Name ______________ Date ______________

"**The Leap**" by Louise Erdrich

Selection Test A

Critical Reading *Identify the letter of the choice that best answers the question.*

___ 1. Which line from "The Leap" foreshadows what happens during the storm?
A. I owe her my existence three times.
B. My mother is the surviving half of a blindfold trapeze act. . . .
C. There was time, before the storm, for three acts.
D. They loved to drop gracefully from nowhere, like two sparkling birds. . . .

___ 2. What fact about the narrator's mother in "The Leap" helps you predict that she will survive the storm?
A. She never lost her balance or upset an object.
B. She loved her husband.
C. She met the narrator's father in a hospital.
D. She lost a baby.

___ 3. In "The Leap," why was the Flying Avalons' trapeze act in the newspapers?
A. because their act was so daring
B. because they were so romantic during their act
C. because there was a terrible accident during their act
D. because there was a fire in their house after the act

___ 4. Why does the narrator of "The Leap" consider her sister a "less finished version" of herself?
A. because her mother loved the sister more than the narrator
B. because the sister was so much like the narrator when she died
C. because the sister never grew up to have a personality of her own
D. because the sister had the same name as the narrator

___ 5. In "The Leap," how did the narrator's mother and father meet?
A. at the circus during the high-wire act
B. at the hospital after the accident
C. during the fire
D. at the grave of the mother's dead daughter

___ 6. In "The Leap," what "form of flight" does the narrator's mother take up after she gives up the trapeze?
A. flying a plane
B. cooking
C. reading
D. hang gliding

Unit 1 Resources: Fiction and Nonfiction
© Pearson Education, Inc. All rights reserved.
63

EL L1 L2 **Selection Test A,** pp. 42–44, 63–65

Also available for these selections:

L3 L4 Selection Test B, pp. 45–47, 66–68

L3 L4 Open-Book Test, pp. 39–41, 60–62

PHLit Online!

www.PHLitOnline.com

- complete narrated selection text
- a thematically related video with writing prompt
- an interactive graphic organizer
- highlighting feature
- access to all student print resources, adapted to individual student needs
- Spanish and English summaries

Background video

Also available:

Get Connected! (thematic video with writing prompt)

Vocabulary Central (tools, activities, and songs for studying vocabulary)

Also available:

Writer's Journal (with graphics feature)

DIFFERENTIATE/PRETEACH

❶ Selection Choices

You may use either "The Monkey's Paw" or "The Leap" to meet the lesson standards. Skills instruction for both selections appears on p. 29. Choose one selection to teach (or choose to teach both). The Accessibility at a Glance chart at the bottom of this page will help you determine which of the two selections is more appropriate for your students.

❷ Selection Skills

1. With the class, preview the selection skills. (The lesson meets the lesson objectives given on p. 28a.)
2. Explain that students will learn to use the skill of making predictions to better understand and enjoy the selection. By examining plot and foreshadowing as they read, they will gain deeper insight into the selection.
3. To introduce the Writing and Listening and Speaking activities (p. 57), tell students that when they have finished reading the selection, they will write a sequel and conduct an interview related to the selection.
4. Tell students that they will also study a grammar concept: common and proper nouns. By mastering this concept, they will improve their reading fluency and the quality of their own writing.

Before You Read

The Monkey's Paw • The Leap

❶ Selection Choices

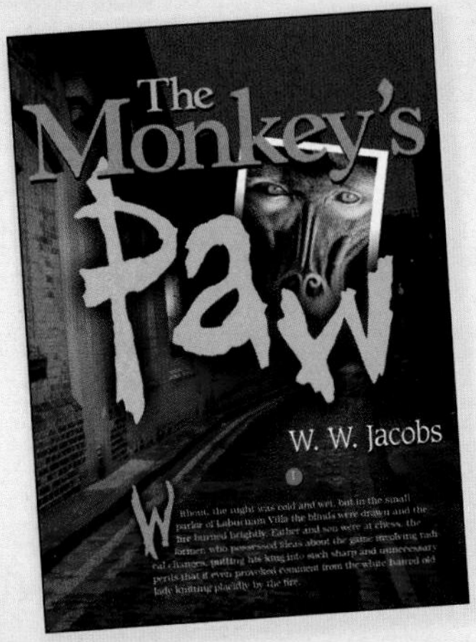

▲ Read **"The Monkey's Paw"** to see how a mysterious object changes the lives of those who possess it.

▲ Read **"The Leap"** to find out how a mother draws on her past as a circus performer to help her daughter.

❷ Selection Skills Guide

Practice these skills with either **"The Monkey's Paw"** (p. 32) or **"The Leap"** (p. 46).

- Understand plot
- Recognize foreshadowing and flashback
- Make predictions
- Use your prior knowledge
- Identify common nouns and proper nouns
- Write a sequel
- Conduct an interview

Differentiated Instruction for Universal Access

Accessibility at a Glance: Selection Choices

	The Monkey's Paw	The Leap
Context	Historical: Britain at turn of twentieth century	Contemporary: family history
Language/ Vocabulary	• Dialogue heavy • Language from the period is footnoted • Grade-level vocabulary	• Accessible vocabulary • No dialogue • Some challenging vocabulary
Concept Level	Accessible (desire for fortune through wishes)	Challenging (responsibility to family)
Literary Merit	Classic	Noted contemporary author
Lexile/Length	Lexile: 980L Word Count: 3,928	Lexile: 1260L Word Count: 2,878
Other	Suspenseful	
Overall Rating	**More accessible**	**More challenging**

Because a number of factors determine the relative accessibility of paired selections, in some cases the Lexile rating of the more challenging selection will be lower than that of the more accessible selection.

❸ Literary Analysis: Plot and Foreshadowing

A **plot** is the sequence of related events in a story. A typical plot revolves around a **conflict**—a struggle between opposing forces—and follows a pattern like the one shown in the diagram below. Elements of plot include the following:

- **Exposition:** background on the characters and situation
- **Rising action:** events that intensify the conflict
- **Climax:** highest point of story tension at which outcome of conflict is revealed
- **Falling action:** events following climax
- **Resolution:** remaining issues resolved; conclusions or insights revealed by narrator

Writers use various techniques to add tension to a story. One technique is **foreshadowing**—giving details that hint at upcoming events.

To provide background on characters and their experiences, some authors use **flashback,** an interruption in the plot to describe an action of the past. After the flashback, the story returns to the present time of the action.

PHLit Online!
www.PHLitOnline.com

Hear It!
- Selection summary audio
- Selection audio

See It!
- Get Connected video
- Background video
- More about the author
- Vocabulary flashcards

Do It!
- Interactive journals
- Interactive graphic organizers
- Self-test
- Internet activity
- Grammar tutorial
- Interactive vocabulary games

❹ Using the Strategy: Plot Diagram

Use a diagram like the one here to help you track the plot of the story.

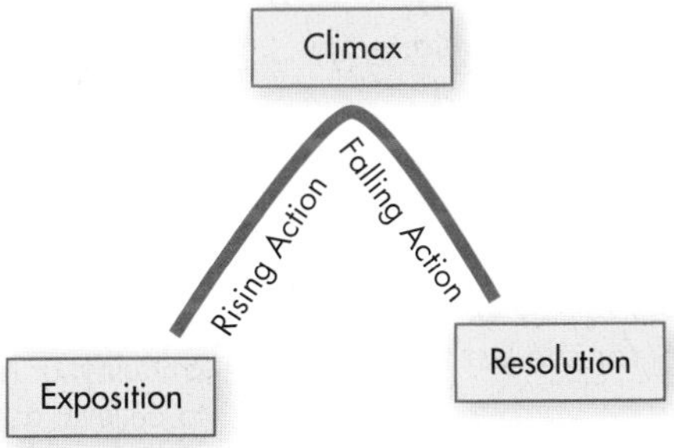

❺ Reading Skill: Make Predictions

A **prediction** is a logical idea about what will happen. To make predictions, pay attention to story details and **use your prior knowledge.**

- Use knowledge of stories with similar plots to help you predict events.
- Use knowledge of human nature to help you predict how characters will act.

Differentiated Instruction for Universal Access

Preparing Students for the More Challenging Selection

If you wish to prepare lower-level readers to read "The Leap," the more challenging selection, follow these steps:

- Review strategies for reading long sentences. Suggest that when students encounter a long sentence, they first identify the main action, and then break the rest of the sentence down into smaller parts for interpretation. Point out the sentence on the first page of the selection that begins, "I would, in fact . . ." Write the sentence on the board, and work with students to break it into multiple simpler sentences.
- Read several sentences that contain difficult diction. You might choose the sentence on page 48 that begins, "When extremes of temperature collide . . ." Review difficult vocabulary with students. Then, call on volunteers to restate the sentences in their own words.
- Discuss with students how a single event or decision can alter the course of a person's life.

PRETEACH

❸ Literary Analysis

Plot and Foreshadowing

1. Introduce the skill, using the instruction on the student page.
2. Tell students that they will identify plot and foreshadowing as they read.

Think Aloud: Model the Skill

Model the skill of analyzing plot and foreshadowing. Say to students:

> Suppose I am writing about a man who slays a dragon. I follow a specific plot pattern. The man's background is given in the *exposition.* In the *rising action,* the man looks for the dragon. In the *climax,* he slays it. In the *falling action,* he takes it's tail. In the *resolution,* he returns home a hero.

❹ Using the Strategy

Give students a copy of either **Literary Analysis Graphic Organizer A** or **B** ***(Graphic Organizer Transparencies***, pp. 3–5) to record their ideas about plot and foreshadowing as they read. Use the examples in **Literary Analysis Graphic Organizer A**, which is partially filled in, to model the process of completing the organizer.

❺ Reading Skill

1. Introduce the skill, using the instruction on the student page.
2. Tell students that they will make predictions as they read.

Think Aloud: Model the Skill

Model the skill of making predictions. Say to students:

> Suppose I am reading about a poor man who is offered a wish. He wishes to be rich. I can make predictions about what will happen to him based on what I know: when people are offered an attractive opportunity, many seize it without considering the consequences. I predict that he will regret his wish.

❶ Writing About the Big Question

1. Review the assignment with the class.
2. Ask students to think of times they have disagreed with a friend about something they believed to be true. Discuss with students the methods for verifying who is right.
3. Have students complete the sentence starter. Review responses as a class. (**Possible response:** People may try to verify the truth by looking it up in a book.)
4. Remind students that their answers will help them think about the Big Question, "Is there a difference between reality and truth?"

While You Read

Tell students that as they read, they should look for ways the characters explain the truth behind the events in the story.

❷ Vocabulary

1. Have students preview the selection vocabulary.
2. For each word, have students say the word aloud.
3. Then, use the word in a sentence that defines the word.
4. Finally, repeat your definitional sentence or a similar sentence with the word missing and have the class "fill in the blank" chorally. Here are some examples:

   Something done furtively is done in secret. The girl looked at the boy she secretly liked [students say "furtively"].

   Apathy is an I-don't-care attitude. The girl who did not care about the weather noticed the rain with [students say "apathy"].

❸ Word Study

1. Introduce the skill, using the instruction in the box.
2. Using their knowledge of the root *-cred-*, ask students to describe someone who is "credible." (**Possible response:** Someone who is credible can be believed or trusted.)

Making Connections | The Monkey's Paw

Is there a difference between *reality* and *truth?*

❶ Writing About the Big Question

In "The Monkey's Paw," a family learns the truth behind a mysterious monkey's paw. Use this sentence starter to help you develop your ideas about the Big Question:

People may try to **verify** the truth by ____________________.

While You Read Look for explanations the characters offer to explain the truth behind the events in "The Monkey's Paw."

❷ Vocabulary

Read each word and its definition. Decide whether you know the word well, know it a little bit, or do not know it at all. After you read, see how your knowledge of each word has increased.

- **grave** (grāv) *adj.* very serious and worrying (p. 35) ***The doctor had a grave expression on her face when she gave John's family the bad news.*** *gravely adv. gravity n.*
- **maligned** (mə līnd′) *adj.* spoken ill of (p. 36) ***The CD, maligned by critics, was still a tremendous hit.*** *malign v. malignant adj.*
- **credulity** (krə do͞o′ lə tē) *n.* tendency to believe too readily (p. 36) ***Due to his credulity, Tim was unaware that the news report was fake.*** *credulous adj. incredulous adj.*
- **furtively** (fur′ tiv lē) *adv.* secretively; sneakily; stealthily (p. 38) ***When no one was looking, she reached furtively for the last slice of pie.*** *furtive adj.*
- **apathy** (ap′ ə thē) *n.* lack of interest or emotion (p. 39) ***The bored audience looked at the speaker with apathy.*** *apathetic adj. apathetically adv.*
- **oppressive** (ə pres′ iv) *adj.* causing great discomfort; distressing (p. 41) ***The heat was so oppressive that they finally opened a window.*** *oppress v. oppression n.*

❸ Word Study

The **Latin root *-cred-*** means "believe."

In this story, a character must monitor his **credulity,** or readiness to believe, as he hears a wild story about a supernatural object.

30 Fiction and Nonfiction

Vocabulary Development

Vocabulary Knowledge Rating

Create a **Vocabulary Knowledge Rating Chart** (***Professional Development Guidebook***, p. 33) for this selection. Include the selection vocabulary and the Big Question word that appears in the Writing About the Big Question sentence starter on this page. (The Big Question vocabulary is introduced on pp. 2–3.)

Give students a copy of the chart. Read the words aloud, and have students mark their rating in the Before Reading column. Urge them to be alert to these words as they read and discuss the selection.

Tally how many students think they know a word to gauge how much instruction to provide. As students read and discuss the selection, point out the words and their context.

PHLit Online! **Vocabulary Central,** featuring tools, activities, and songs for studying vocabulary, is available at **www.PHLitOnline.com.**

Meet
W. W. Jacobs
(1863–1943)

Author of
The Monkey's Paw

As a boy, William Wymark Jacobs traveled far and wide in his imagination. He lived in London, England, in a house near the docks, and he listened eagerly to the tales of adventure told by sailors whom he met there. These tales shaped the stories he wrote as an adult—stories in which everyday life is disrupted by strange and fantastic events. "The Monkey's Paw" is his most famous tale of the supernatural.

More Than Horror Although today W. W. Jacobs is best known for this tale of suspense, in his own lifetime he was famous as a humorist. In fact, he wrote works of various kinds, and he wrote them in quantity. When a collection of his works was published in 1931, it contained seventeen books!

BACKGROUND FOR THE STORY

The British View of India

4 "The Monkey's Paw" tells of an eerie object that arrives in England from India. From the late 1700s until 1947, India was a British colony. In letters and visits back home, British soldiers passed on information and misinformation about India's culture. Before long, India came to represent the mysterious and supernatural, as this story shows.

DID YOU KNOW?

Moviemakers have told the strange tale of "The Monkey's Paw" eight times! The first film version of the story was made in 1915. More recent remakes came out in 1996 and 2003.

Daily Bellringer

For each class during which you will teach this selection, have students complete one of the five Quick Write activities for Week 1 in the ***Daily Bellringer Activities*** booklet.

4 Background
The British View of India

The English East India Company settled in India by 1611 and exported tea and textiles to England. The English quickly became fascinated with Indian culture. Elephants, tigers, and monkeys were great novelties. Rajahs had outrageous wealth and many wives, fakirs did astonishing feats such as lying on beds of nails, and many people wore exotic clothing and jewelry. There were ornate temples and artwork, new foods, and unfamiliar beliefs, along with dreadful diseases, poisonous snakes, and mysterious cults.

Multidraft Reading

This icon ● marks natural pauses in the selection. To assist struggling readers and to deepen reading for all, assign the text in "chunks," having students read from one icon to the next, and apply multidraft reading protocols. For each reading, have students set the purpose indicated:

- **First reading**—literal comprehension: answering the Reading Check questions.
- **Second reading**—application of skills: answering the Make Predictions and Plot and Foreshadowing prompts.
- **Third reading**—interpretation: answering the end-of-selection questions.

For more guidance, refer to the ***Classroom Strategies and Teaching Routines*** card on multidraft reading.

Differentiated Instruction — Additional Instruction

EL Extended Support—English Learners
Have students complete the **Reading and Vocabulary Warm-ups, *Unit 1 Resources*,** pp. 30–33, before they read. Assign the prereading pages and the adapted selection in the ***Reader's Notebook: English Learner's Version.*** Then, have students listen to portions of the selection on the ***Hear It!*** **Audio CD.**

L1 L2 Extended Support—Struggling Readers
Have students complete the **Reading and Vocabulary Warm-ups, *Unit 1 Resources*,** pp. 19–22, before they read. Assign the prereading pages and adapted selection in the ***Reader's Notebook: Adapted Version.*** Then, have students listen to portions of the selection on the ***Hear It!*** **Audio CD** (adapted text).

Extended Support—Reluctant Readers
To build motivation and engagement before assigning the selection, have students read "Unlucky Winners," a thematically related selection in ***Reality Central.*** Then, use the questions at the conclusion of the related selection to guide discussion.

PHLit Online!
For more about the author, practice with the selection vocabulary, and more background, go online at **www.PHLitOnline.com.**

❶ Activating Prior Knowledge

1. Prepare an **Anticipation Guide** (see ***Professional Development Guidebook***, pp. 36–38) with the following statements:
   - One should be content with his or her life as it is.
   - People should not play games with fate.
   - You should never be afraid to be the master of your own destiny.
   - There is no such thing as a free lunch.
2. Give students copies of the prepared **Anticipation Guide.** Have students mark their responses in the Me column. Then, have students discuss the statements in pairs or groups and mark the Guides again, this time in the Group column.
3. For further guidance, use the ***Classroom Strategies and Teaching Routines*** card: **Using an Anticipation Guide.**

Concept Connector →

Students will return to the **Anticipation Guide** after completing "The Monkey's Paw."

Individual Activity

Numerous sounds and noises echo through "The Monkey's Paw," from the wind at the beginning of the story to Mrs. White's "long loud wail of disappointment" at the end. Ask students to list these sounds as they read and to identify how they help to create the story's mood.

❷ About the Selection

"The Monkey's Paw" is a chilling version of the "three wishes" tale told the world over. Like many renditions of the tale, it offers lessons in morality, but it distinguishes itself from other such tales through its aura of terror and suspense. Students will be taken on an emotional roller-coaster ride as the Whites are pushed to the brink of desperation, trying to reverse their wish and bring their son back from the dead.

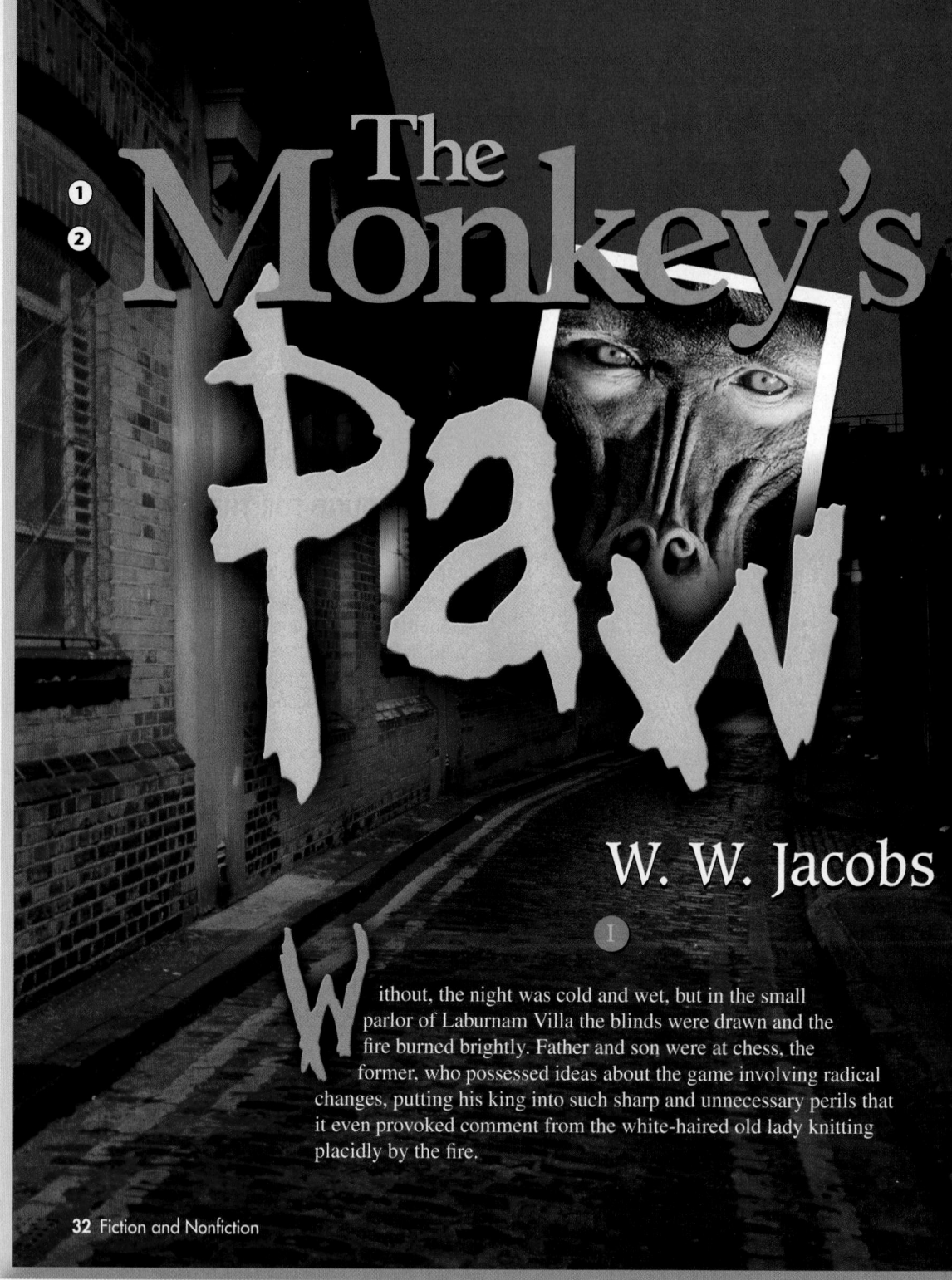

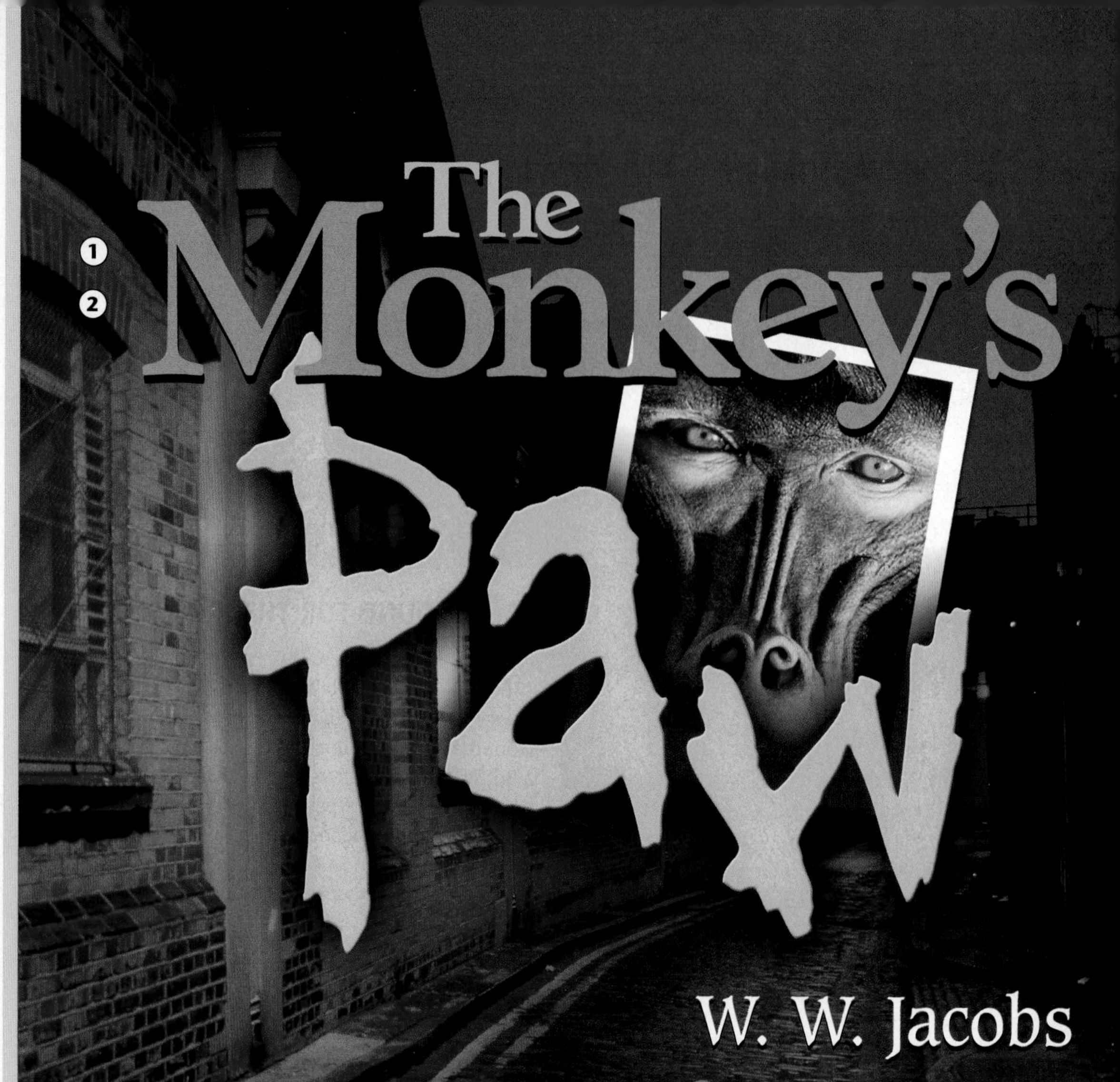

① ②

The Monkey's Paw

W. W. Jacobs

I

Without, the night was cold and wet, but in the small parlor of Laburnam Villa the blinds were drawn and the fire burned brightly. Father and son were at chess, the former, who possessed ideas about the game involving radical changes, putting his king into such sharp and unnecessary perils that it even provoked comment from the white-haired old lady knitting placidly by the fire.

32 Fiction and Nonfiction

Vocabulary Development

Former* and *Latter

Point out the terms *former* and *latter* in the first few paragraphs of this story. Tell students that these words, used together, are a common way to refer to or to contrast the first and last named of two people or things. *Former* refers to the first of two things mentioned. *Latter* refers to the second. They are often used with *the*, the nouns to which they refer being understood.

In this story, W. W. Jacobs is writing about the father and the son: "Father and son were at chess . . ." When he later refers to the two, he says "the former" to refer to the father and "the latter" to refer to the son.

Ask students to use *former* and *latter* in the following sentences:

1. Maria and Shawna are both interested in athletics; the _____ is a basketball player, and the _____ likes tennis.
2. Chess and checkers are played on the same board, but the _____ is more challenging than the _____.

"Hark at the wind," said Mr. White, who, having seen a fatal mistake after it was too late, was amiably desirous of preventing his son from seeing it.

"I'm listening," said the latter, grimly surveying the board as he stretched out his hand. "Check."

"I should hardly think that he'd come tonight," said his father,
3 with his hand poised over the board.

"Mate,"[1] replied the son.

"That's the worst of living so far out," bawled Mr. White, with sudden and unlooked-for violence; "of all the beastly, slushy, out-of-the-way places to live in, this is the worst. Pathway's a bog, and the road's a torrent. I don't know what people are thinking about. I suppose because only two houses on the road are let, they think it doesn't matter."

"Never mind, dear," said his wife, soothingly; "perhaps you'll win the next one."

Mr. White looked up sharply, just in time to intercept a knowing glance between mother and son. The words died away on his lips, and he hid a guilty grin in his thin gray beard.

"There he is," said Herbert White, as the gate banged to loudly and heavy footsteps came toward the door.

The old man rose with hospitable haste, and opening the door, was heard condoling with the new arrival. The new arrival also condoled with himself, so that Mrs. White said, "Tut, tut!" and coughed gently as her husband entered the room, followed by a tall, burly man, beady of eye and rubicund of visage.[2]

"Sergeant Major Morris," he said, introducing him.

4 The sergeant major shook hands, and taking the proffered seat by the fire, watched contentedly while his host got out tumblers and stood a small copper kettle on the fire.

At the third glass his eyes got brighter, and he began to talk, the little family circle regarding with eager interest this visitor from distant parts, as he squared his broad shoulders in the chair and spoke of wild scenes and doughty[3] deeds; of wars and plagues and strange peoples.

"Twenty-one years of it," said Mr. White, nodding at his wife and son. "When he went away he was a slip of a youth in the warehouse. Now look at him."

"He don't look to have taken much harm," said Mrs. White, politely.

1. **mate** *n.* checkmate, a chess move that prevents the opponent's king from escaping capture and so ends the game.
2. **rubicund** (ro͞o′ bə kund′) **of visage** (viz′ ij) having a red face.
3. **doughty** (dout′ ē) *adj.* brave.

Literary Analysis
Plot What important background information about the characters and their home is given in the exposition of this story?

5 **Reading Check**
Who has arrived at the White's house?

3 Literary Analysis
Plot
1. Have students read the bracketed passage. Point out that this stage of the plot is called the *exposition*. **Ask** students what role the exposition plays in the plot.
   Answer: In the exposition, the writer gives background information about the setting, characters, and situation.
2. **Ask** students the Literary Analysis question: What important background information about the characters and their home is given in the exposition of this story?
   Possible response: The White family lives in a remote villa. The wife teases her husband as he loses a chess game with the son.
3. Remind students that in a short story, every detail in the exposition plays a key role in the plot. Encourage them to keep these details in mind as they read on.

4 Critical Thinking
Analyze
1. Have students read the bracketed passage.
2. **Ask** students what the description reveals about Morris.
   Possible response: Morris appears to be a serious man who has had some extraordinary experiences.
3. Encourage students to keep their impressions of Morris in mind as they continue to read. Students should consider how Morris might change the atmosphere of the Whites' home.

5 Reading Check
Answer: The visitor is Sergeant Major Morris, a friend of Mr. White's who has been serving abroad in the military—possibly in India.

Differentiated Instruction for Universal Access

Strategy for Special Needs Students
Students may have difficulty understanding the role exposition plays in plot. To model plot structure, show them **Literary Analysis Graphic Organizer A** (*Graphic Organizer Transparencies,* p. 3). Use the completed Plot Diagram to explain to students how the information given in the beginning of the story establishes the background for the plot.

Enrichment for Gifted/Talented Students
As these students approach the Literary Analysis exercise, point out that there is a contrast between the tone created by the story's exposition and the mood suggested by the image on the previous page. Encourage students to create an illustration for the opening scene of "The Monkey's Paw." Instruct them to represent all of the information they find in the exposition, taking into the account the foreshadowing provided by the opening image.

PHLit Online!
This selection is available in interactive format in the **Enriched Online Student Edition**, which includes a thematically related video with writing prompt and an interactive graphic organizer.

❻ Critical Thinking

Analyze

1. Have students read the bracketed passage, looking for details that describe Sergeant Major Morris's body language and gestures.
2. **Ask** students what these details reveal about Morris.
   Possible response: Morris's sighs and gestures with his glass reveal that he is deeply uncomfortable talking about some of his experiences.
3. Encourage students to think about the impact Morris's contrasting tone has on the story.

❼ Critical Viewing

Possible response: He has a traditional marking on his head and wears beads that may have religious uses.

❽ Reading Skill

Make Predictions

1. Remind students that they can make predictions based on details in the story and their prior knowledge of plot structure and human nature.
2. Have students read the bracketed passage. Make sure they understand that *fate* is the power that determines the outcome of events before they occur. Explain that one's fate is similar to one's destiny.
3. Suggest to students that Sergeant Major Morris's use of the word *fate* is a detail that could be the basis for a prediction. Have students think about who might be hurt by the paw and how.
4. Beginning with this passage, encourage students to create Prediction Charts. You may use **Reading Skill Graphic Organizer B** (*Graphic Organizer Transparencies*, p. 6) to model the chart for students.
5. As they continue reading, students will gather information to validate or invalidate the predictions in their charts.

"I'd like to go to India myself," said the old man, "just to look round a bit, you know."

"Better where you are," said the sergeant major, shaking his head. He put down the empty glass, and sighing softly, shook it again.

"I should like to see those old temples and fakirs and jugglers," said the old man. "What was that you started telling me the other day about a monkey's paw or something, Morris?"

"Nothing," said the soldier, hastily. "Leastways nothing worth

❻ hearing."

"Monkey's paw?" said Mrs. White, curiously.

"Well, it's just a bit of what you might call magic, perhaps," said the sergeant major, offhandedly.

His three listeners leaned forward eagerly. The visitor absent-mindedly put his empty glass to his lips and then set it down again. His host filled it for him.

"To look at," said the sergeant major, fumbling in his pocket, "it's just an ordinary little paw, dried to a mummy."

He took something out of his pocket and proffered it. Mrs. White drew back with a grimace, but her son, taking it, examined it curiously.

"And what is there special about it?" inquired Mr. White as he took it from his son, and having examined it, placed it upon the table.

"It had a spell put on it by an old fakir," said the sergeant major, "a very holy man. He wanted to show that fate ruled ❽ people's lives, and that those who interfered with it did so to their sorrow. He put a spell on it so that three separate men could each have three wishes from it."

His manner was so impressive that his hearers were conscious that their light laughter jarred somewhat.

"Well, why don't you have three, sir?" said Herbert White, cleverly.

The soldier regarded him in the way that middle age is wont to regard presumptuous youth. "I have," he said, quietly, and his blotchy face whitened.

"And did you really have the three wishes granted?" asked Mrs. White.

"I did," said the sergeant major, and his glass tapped against his strong teeth.

"And has anybody else wished?" persisted the old lady.

"The first man had his three wishes, yes," was the reply; "I don't know what the first

❼

▼ **Critical Viewing**
What details of this man's appearance might make you think that he is "a very holy man"? **[Support]**

Think Aloud

Vocabulary: Using Context

Direct students' attention to Sergeant Major Morris's use of the word *fakir* on this page. Using the following "think aloud," model how to use context to infer the meaning of an unknown word.

Sergeant Major Morris says that a *fakir* put a spell on the monkey's paw. Also, I know that Morris has been in India for the past twenty-one years. So I can assume that a *fakir* is a person in India with supernatural powers. Are there any more context clues? There is one at the end of the sentence. Morris describes the *fakir* as "a very holy man." This tells me that the *fakir* is a religious figure. I think that a *fakir* is an Indian high priest who is believed to have the ability to cast spells and work wonders.

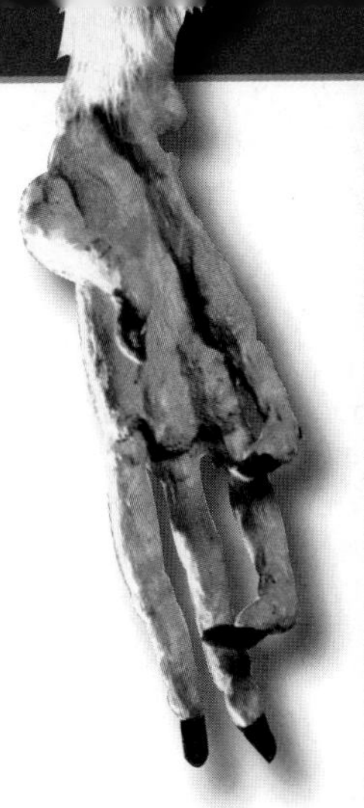

two were, but the third was for death. That's how I got the paw."

His tones were so **grave** that a hush fell upon the group.

"If you've had your three wishes, it's no good to you now, then, Morris," said the old man at last. "What do you keep it for?"

The soldier shook his head. "Fancy, I suppose," he said, slowly. "I did have some idea of selling it, but I don't think I will. It has caused enough mischief already. Besides, people won't buy. They think it's a fairy tale, some of them, and those who do think anything of it want to try it first and pay me afterward."

"If you could have another three wishes," said the old man, eyeing him keenly, "would you have them?"

"I don't know," said the other. "I don't know."

He took the paw, and dangling it between his forefinger and thumb, suddenly threw it upon the fire. White, with a slight cry, stooped down and snatched it off.

"Better let it burn," said the soldier, solemnly.

9 "If you don't want it, Morris," said the other, "give it to me."

"I won't," said his friend doggedly. "I threw it on the fire. If you keep it, don't blame me for what happens. Pitch it on the fire again, like a sensible man."

The other shook his head and examined his new possession closely. "How do you do it?" he inquired.

"Hold it up in your right hand and wish aloud," said the sergeant major, "but I warn you of the consequences."

"Sounds like the *Arabian Nights*,"[4] said Mrs. White, as she rose and began to set the supper. "Don't you think you might wish for four pairs of hands for me?"

Her husband drew the talisman from his pocket, and then all three burst into laughter as the sergeant major, with a look of alarm on his face, caught him by the arm. "If you must wish," he said, gruffly, "wish for something sensible."

Mr. White dropped it back in his pocket, and placing chairs, motioned his friend to the table. In the business of supper the talisman was partly forgotten, and afterward the three sat listening in an enthralled fashion to a second installment of the soldier's adventures in India.

"If the tale about the monkey's paw is not more truthful than those he has been telling us," said Herbert, as the door closed behind their guest, just in time for him to catch the last train, "we shan't make much out of it."

"Did you give him anything for it, Father?" inquired Mrs. White,

4. ***Arabian Nights*** collection of stories from the ancient Near East telling of fantastical adventures and supernatural beings.

Vocabulary
grave (grāv) *adj.* very serious and worrying

Literary Analysis
Plot How does the information about the previous wishers foreshadow danger for the Whites?

10 **Reading Check**
According to the sergeant major, what is special about the monkey's paw?

9 Literary Analysis
Plot

1. **Ask** students what they have learned already about the previous wisher.
   Answer: The first man had three wishes, and his third was for death, which was granted.
2. Have students read the bracketed passage. Then, **ask** the Literary Analysis question: How does the information about the previous wishers foreshadow danger for the Whites?
   Possible response: The story of the man who wishes for his own death, as well as Sergeant Major Morris's somber tone, hints that nothing good can come from this paw. The Whites' interest suggests that they will ignore these signs and make wishes of their own.

10 Reading Check

Answer: A fakir has put a spell on the monkey's paw, giving it the power to grant three wishes to three different people.

Differentiated Instruction for Universal Access

Strategy for Less Proficient Readers
Students may have trouble identifying foreshadowing in this section of the story. Tell students that Sergeant Major Morris gives readers many hints that the paw will cause danger. They should recognize that Morris's dialogue suggests the paw possesses terrible powers. Then, have them reread the scene, paying special attention to the descriptions of Morris's appearance, body language, and mood. Help them to understand that Morris is hesitant to talk about the monkey's paw, suggesting that he is afraid of it.

EL Strategy for English Learners
Students may find the foreshadowing in this scene especially challenging. The description of Sergeant Major Morris is important because his appearance, body language, and mood reveal his feelings about the monkey's paw. Have students list words used to describe his actions, such as "hastily," "offhandedly," and "absent-mindedly." Give students time to find the meaning of each word before asking them to explain how these details foreshadow events to come.

⓫ Reading Skill

Make Predictions

1. Remind students that when they make predictions about what will happen in a story, they should draw upon their prior knowledge of the plot structure and of human nature.
2. Have students reread the bracketed passage. Have students **interpret** Herbert's emotions in his quip about the wish.
   Possible response: He is afraid of the paw and the wishes it might grant. His cynicism is a way to dispel that fear.
3. **Ask** students the Reading Skill question: What do characters in stories about wishes usually learn? Predict the results of Mr. White's wish.
   Possible response: They learn that human attempts to alter fate usually have dangerous and unpredictable consequences. His wish will bring misfortune.

⓬ THE BIG ? Connecting to the Big Question

1. Explain that myths are one example of people's struggle to deal with questions about *reality* and *truth*. Discuss the following:
   - Myths are retold by many people within a culture. The details may differ, but the main point remains the same.
   - Myths include supernatural events or ideas. Some people believe them; others do not.
   - There are often local stories. Individuals tell about experiences that "prove" the myth's validity.
2. Have students read the bracketed passage. **Ask:** Are the Whites acting as if they believe this myth is true? Explain.
   Possible response: Mr. and Mrs. White grow quiet. They may be worried about what will happen if the myth is true. Herbert speaks as if he thinks the myth is not true.
3. **Ask:** How do the characters demonstrate the human longing to know the truth?
   Possible response: They wish they could be sure that the myth is either true or false. They are worried because they do not know what will happen.

regarding her husband closely.

"A trifle," said he, coloring slightly. "He didn't want it, but I made him take it. And he pressed me again to throw it away."

"Likely," said Herbert, with pretended horror. "Why, we're going to be rich, and famous and happy. Wish to be an emperor, Father, to begin with; then you can't be bossed around."

He darted round the table, pursued by the **maligned** Mrs. White armed with an antimacassar.[5]

Mr. White took the paw from his pocket and eyed it dubiously. "I don't know what to wish for, and that's a fact," he said, slowly. "It seems to me I've got all I want."

"If you only cleared the house, you'd be quite happy, wouldn't you?" said Herbert, with his hand on his shoulder. "Well, wish for two hundred pounds,[6] then; that'll just do it."

His father, smiling shamefacedly at his own **credulity**, held up the talisman, as his son, with a solemn face somewhat marred by a wink at his mother, sat down at the piano and struck a few impressive chords.

"I wish for two hundred pounds," said the old man distinctly.

A fine crash from the piano greeted the words, interrupted by a shuddering cry from the old man. His wife and son ran toward him.

"It moved," he cried, with a glance of disgust at the object as it lay on the floor. "As I wished it twisted in my hand like a snake."

"Well, I don't see the money," said his son as he picked it up and placed it on the table, "and I bet I never shall."

"It must have been your fancy, Father," said his wife, regarding him anxiously.

He shook his head. "Never mind, though; there's no harm done, but it gave me a shock all the same."

They sat down by the fire again while the two men finished their pipes. Outside, the wind was higher than ever, and the old man started nervously at the sound of a door banging upstairs. A silence unusual and depressing settled upon all three, which lasted until the old couple rose to retire for the night.

⓫ "I expect you'll find the cash tied up in a big bag in the middle of your bed," said Herbert, as he bade them good night, "and something horrible squatting up on top of the wardrobe watching you as you pocket your ill-gotten gains."

⓬ Herbert sat alone in the darkness, gazing at the dying fire, and seeing faces in it. The last face was so horrible and so simian[7] that he gazed at it in amazement. It got so vivid that, with a little uneasy

Vocabulary
maligned (mə līnd′) *adj.* spoken ill of
credulity (krə do͞o′ lə tē) *n.* tendency to believe too readily

Reading Skill
Make Predictions
What do characters in stories about wishes usually learn? Predict the results of Mr. White's wish.

5. **antimacassar** (an′ ti mə kas′ ər) *n.* small cover for the arms or back of a chair or sofa.
6. **pounds** *n.* units of English currency, roughly comparable to dollars.
7. **simian** (sim′ ē ən) *adj.* monkeylike.

Vocabulary Development

THE BIG ? Thematic Vocabulary: The Big Question

As students are discussing "The Monkey's Paw," have them use the thematic vocabulary presented in Introducing the Big Question, pp. 2–3. You might encourage them with sentence starters like these:

1. Mr. White's initial *perception* of the sergeant major is . . .
2. Mr. White began to *comprehend* the effect of his first wish when . . .
3. The *evidence* Mr. and Mrs. White receive that the paw's powers are real comes when . . .
4. The most *improbable* event from the story occurs when . . .

12 laugh, he felt on the table for a glass containing a little water to throw over it. His hand grasped the monkey's paw, and with a little shiver he wiped his hand on his coat and went up to bed.

II

In the brightness of the wintry sun next morning as it streamed over the breakfast table Herbert laughed at his fears. There was an air of prosaic wholesomeness about the room which it had lacked on the previous night, and the dirty, shriveled little paw was pitched on the sideboard with a carelessness which betokened no great belief in its virtues.

"I suppose all old soldiers are the same," said Mrs. White. "The idea of our listening to such nonsense! How could wishes be granted in these days? And if they could, how could two hundred pounds hurt you, Father?"

"Might drop on his head from the sky," said the frivolous Herbert.

"Morris said the things happened so naturally," said his father, "that you might if you so wished attribute it to coincidence."

"Well, don't break into the money before I come back," said Herbert, as he rose from the table. "I'm afraid it'll turn you into a mean, avaricious[8] man, and we shall have to disown you."

13 His mother laughed, and following him to the door, watched him down the road, and, returning to the breakfast table, was very happy at the expense of her husband's credulity. All of which did not prevent her from scurrying to the door at the postman's knock, nor prevent her from referring somewhat shortly to retired sergeant majors of bibulous habits when she found that the post brought a tailor's bill.

"Herbert will have some more of his funny remarks, I expect, when he comes home," she said, as they sat at dinner.

"I dare say," said Mr. White, "but for all that, the thing moved in my hand; that I'll swear to."

"You thought it did," said the old lady soothingly.

"I say it did," replied the other. "There was no thought about it; I had just—What's the matter?"

His wife made no reply. She was watching the mysterious movements of a man outside, who, peering in an undecided fashion at the house, appeared to be trying to make up his mind to enter. In mental connection with the two hundred pounds, she noticed that the stranger was well dressed, and wore a silk hat of glossy newness. Three times he paused at the gate, and then walked on

8. **avaricious** (av´ ə rish´ əs) *adj.* greedy for wealth.

Literary Analysis
Plot How does the conversation about the money foreshadow a problem?

14 **Reading Check**

For what does Mr. White wish?

13 Literary Analysis

Plot

1. Instruct students to pause before they begin reading Part II. Have students **summarize** what has happened in the story so far.
 Possible response: Sergeant Major Morris, who carries a monkey's paw, visits the Whites. Morris claims the paw has the power to grant three wishes but that the wishes have consequences. Reluctantly, Morris gives the paw to Mr. White, who gives him a small "trifle" in return. Encouraged by his son, Mr. White wishes for 200 pounds.
2. Have students read the bracketed passage. Then, **ask** them the Literary Analysis question: How does the conversation about the money foreshadow a problem?
 Possible response: During the discussion about the wish for 200 pounds, Mrs. White questions how the money could hurt her husband, and Herbert "frivolously" says that the money might drop on his father's head from the sky; these comments foreshadow harm to Mr. White as a result of the wish.

▶ **Monitor Progress:** Lead students in a discussion regarding how the writer's use of foreshadowing builds tension and helps the plot's action rise. **Ask** them to describe examples of foreshadowing that have already taken place in the story; have students use these examples to predict upcoming events.
Possible responses: Examples of foreshadowing include the warnings that Sergeant Major Morris gives to the Whites, including the description of the man who wishes for death. Possible future events include the arrival of the 200 pounds and subsequent grave consequences.

▶ **Reteach** Remind students that in most plots, tension builds as the action rises toward a climax. Use **Literary Analysis Graphic Organizer A** to model plot structure for students who are having difficulty understanding the elements of plot.

14 Reading Check

Answer: Mr. White wishes for 200 pounds, a considerable sum of money.

PROFESSIONAL DEVELOPMENT

APPLY THE STRATEGY

Before reading the story, direct students to the paragraphs that have highlighted Tier 2 vocabulary words. For this story, the highlighted vocabulary words are *maligned, furtively* and *apathy.* Start with the paragraph that contains word *maligned.* Ask students to read the paragraph and try to figure out what *maligned* means from its context. Give students an opportunity to define the word. Then, clarify, by providing them with a clear definition and example. For example, say to students, "Maligned means spoken ill of. I was maligned when . . ." Ask students for additional examples.

Follow this procedure with the other words. Also, give examples of what the word does not mean. For *maligned,* you could say, "I was not maligned when my grandmother told my mother what a good dinner I cooked."

For more of Sharon Vaughn's strategies, see the Professional Development essay, pp. 2c–2d.

15 Critical Thinking

Infer

1. Have students read the bracketed passage. Encourage them to pay close attention to the detailed description of the stranger's appearance and bearing.
2. **Ask** students what they can infer, or guess, about the stranger based on these details.
   Possible response: The stranger is bearing bad news, which makes him feel awkward and uncomfortable in the Whites' home.

16 Literary Analysis

Plot

1. Remind students that writers can use dialogue to move the plot along and create the rising action. Have students read the bracketed passage, specifically noting the dialogue. **Ask:** How do the mother's words show her feelings?
   Possible response: She immediately asks if something is wrong. Then, she jumps to the conclusion that everything is okay. She is nervous and worried about her son, but does not want to think the worst.
2. **Ask** students the Literary Analysis question: In what way does the stranger's answer increase the tension of the rising action?
   Possible response: The stranger's answer shows readers that Mr. White's wish has come true and that Herbert's death is the consequence. This event builds tension because there are still two wishes left.

---

again. The fourth time he stood with his hand upon it, and then with sudden resolution flung it open and walked up the path. Mrs. White at the same moment placed her hands behind her, and hurriedly unfastening the strings of her apron, put that useful article of apparel beneath the cushion of her chair.

Vocabulary
furtively (fur´ tiv lē) *adv.* secretively; sneakily; stealthily

15 She brought the stranger, who seemed ill at ease, into the room. He gazed at her **furtively,** and listened in a preoccupied fashion as the old lady apologized for the appearance of the room, and her husband's coat, a garment which he usually reserved for the garden. She then waited patiently for him to broach his business, but he was at first strangely silent.

"I—was asked to call," he said at last, and stooped and picked a piece of cotton from his trousers. "I come from 'Maw and Meggins.'"

16 The old lady started. "Is anything the matter?" she asked, breathlessly. "Has anything happened to Herbert? What is it? What is it?"

Her husband interposed. "There, there, mother," he said, hastily. "Sit down, and don't jump to conclusions. You've not brought bad news, I'm sure, sir," and he eyed the other wistfully.

"I'm sorry—" began the visitor.

"Is he hurt?" demanded the mother, wildly.

The visitor bowed in assent. "Badly hurt," he said quietly, "but he is not in any pain."

Literary Analysis
Plot In what way does the stranger's answer increase the tension of the rising action?

"Oh, thank God!" said the old woman, clasping her hands. "Thank God for that! Thank—"

She broke off suddenly as the sinister meaning of the assurance dawned upon her and she saw the awful confirmation of her fears in the other's averted face. She caught her breath, and turning to her husband, laid her trembling old hand upon his. There was a long silence.

"He was caught in the machinery," said the visitor at length, in a low voice.

"Caught in the machinery," repeated Mr. White, in a dazed fashion, "yes."

He sat staring blankly out at the window, and taking his wife's hand between his own, pressed it as he had been wont to do in their old courting days nearly forty years before.

"He was the only one left to us," he said, turning gently to the visitor. "It is hard."

The other coughed, and, rising, walked slowly to the window. "The firm wished me to convey their sincere sympathy with you in your great loss," he said, without looking round. "I beg that you will understand I am only their servant and merely obeying orders."

Vocabulary Development

Word Forms

Expand students' vocabulary by helping them learn related forms of the vocabulary words.

Give students a blank **Word Form Chart** (***Professional Development Guidebook***, pp. 41–42) with *furtively, oppressive,* and *apathy* listed in the correct columns. Instruct students to complete the charts. Work with the class, or have students work in pairs, to determine all of the related forms. The final chart should look like the one shown.

Noun	Verb	Adjective	Adverb
furtiveness		furtive	**furtively**
oppressiveness	oppress	**oppressive**	oppressively
apathy		apathetic	apathetically

There was no reply; the old woman's face was white, her eyes staring, and her breath inaudible; on the husband's face was a look such as his friend the sergeant might have carried into his first action.

17 "I was to say that Maw and Meggins disclaim all responsibility," continued the other. "They admit no liability at all, but in consideration of your son's services they wish to present you with a certain sum as compensation."

Mr. White dropped his wife's hand, and rising to his feet, gazed with a look of horror at his visitor. His dry lips shaped the words, "How much?"

"Two hundred pounds," was the answer.

Unconscious of his wife's shriek, the old man smiled faintly, put out his hands like a sightless man, and dropped, a senseless heap, to the floor.

III

18 In the huge new cemetery, some two miles distant, the old people buried their dead, and came back to a house steeped in shadow and silence. It was all over so quickly that at first they could hardly realize it, and remained in a state of expectation as though of something else to happen—something else which was to lighten this load, too heavy for old hearts to bear.

But the days passed, and expectation gave place to resignation—the hopeless resignation of the old, sometimes miscalled apathy. Sometimes they hardly exchanged a word, for now they had nothing to talk about, and their days were long to weariness.

It was about a week after that the old man, waking suddenly in the night, stretched out his hand and found himself alone. The room was in darkness, and the sound of subdued weeping came from the window. He raised himself in bed and listened.

"Come back," he said, tenderly. "You will be cold."

"It is colder for my son," said the old woman, and wept afresh.

The sound of her sobs died away on his ears. The bed was warm, and his eyes heavy with sleep. He dozed fitfully, and then slept until a sudden wild cry from his wife awoke him with a start.

"*The paw!*" she cried wildly. "The monkey's paw!"

He started up in alarm. "Where? Where is it? What's the matter?"

She came stumbling across the room toward him. "I want it," she said quietly. "You've not destroyed it?"

"It's in the parlor, on the bracket," he replied, marveling. "Why?"

She cried and laughed together, and bending over, kissed his cheek.

Reading Skill
Make Predictions
Do you think the Whites will make another wish? Why or why not?

Vocabulary
apathy (ap′ə thē) *n.* lack of interest or emotion

19 Reading Check
How do the Whites get their money?

17 Literary Analysis

Plot

1. Before students read the bracketed passage, make sure they understand that Herbert White has been killed in an accident at work.
2. Now, have students read the bracketed passage. Discuss why Mrs. White shrieks when they hear the sum of money that they will receive as a result of their son's death.

18 Reading Skill

Make Predictions

1. Have students review their earlier predictions about the outcome of Mr. White's first wish. Encourage discussion of whether or not these predictions are accurate. Guide students to recognize the role of their prior knowledge in the accuracy of their predictions.
2. Have students read the bracketed passage. **Ask** them to describe the states of mind of both Mr. White and Mrs. White.
Possible response: The Whites are devastated by the death of their son, so much so that they can barely speak to each other. They do not blame themselves or the paw for his death, but they seem to be afraid to speak about the paw and its power.
3. **Ask** students the Reading Skill question: Do you think the Whites will make another wish? Why or why not?
Possible response: Despite Mr. White's reservations, students may predict that the Whites' desire to see their son will convince them to make another wish.

19 Reading Check

Answer: The White's son is killed in an accident, and they receive 200 pounds as compensation.

Differentiated Instruction for Universal Access

Enrichment for Advanced Readers

At this point in the story, the consequences of wishing, of which Sergeant Major Morris warns, have become terribly apparent. To enrich the story, explain to these students that the theme of wishing reappears again and again in the folklore of various cultures.

One common variation features characters who have three wishes granted and who use them so foolishly that in the end, their lives do not change for the better. For example, in a Jewish folk tale from Eastern Europe, a man is helped by a magical wishing ring, but he nearly dies when he reveals its existence to others.

Many cultures also have proverbs about wishing. The Chinese, for example, warn, "Be careful what you wish for; you might get it." Have students write short essays explaining the universal appeal of this plot structure. Why aren't the stories about getting wishes *without* consequences?

20 Critical Thinking

Infer

1. Have students read the bracketed passage. Then, **ask** them why Mr. White is afraid of his wife. **Possible response:** Mr. White fears Mrs. White's unnatural obsession with using the monkey's paw to bring their son back. He is afraid of further consequences.
2. Point out that the monkey's paw causes another problem for Mr. and Mrs. White: It creates distance between them.

21 Literary Analysis

Plot

1. Point out that Mr. White and Mrs. White's feelings about the monkey's paw have begun to change. As students read the dialogue at the beginning of this page, encourage them to pay special attention to each character's attitude toward the paw.
2. **Ask** students to analyze Mr. White's attitudes and Mrs. White's attitudes toward the paw. **Possible response:** Mrs. White, in her desperation, believes in the power of the paw but disregards the consequences of using it. Mr. White, on the other hand, no longer wants anything to do with the paw.
3. Point out that at this point in the plot, the conflict has deepened to the point where the Whites are struggling with each other, as well as against the power of the paw. Help students recognize that the tension in the house is building to an almost unbearable level.
4. **Ask** students the Literary Analysis question: In what way does this new wish increase the tension at the end of the story? **Possible response:** The likelihood that the wish will come true but will have a terrible consequence, as Mr. White fears, builds the tension. The struggle of Mr. and Mrs. White over the wish also adds to the tension.
5. Make sure students understand that they have nearly reached the climax—the point at which the tension reaches its highest point. After the climax, the outcome of the conflict will be revealed.

"The other two wishes," she replied rapidly. "We've only had one."

"I only just thought of it," she said hysterically. "Why didn't I think of it before? Why didn't *you* think of it?"

"Think of what?" he questioned.

"The other two wishes," she replied rapidly. "We've only had one."

"Was not that enough?" he demanded, fiercely.

"No," she cried triumphantly; "we'll have one more. Go down and get it quickly, and wish our boy alive again."

The man sat up in bed and flung the bedclothes from his quaking limbs. "You are mad!" he cried, aghast.

"Get it," she panted; "get it quickly, and wish—Oh, my boy, my boy!"

Her husband struck a match and lit the candle. "Get back to bed," he said unsteadily. "You don't know what you are saying."

"We had the first wish granted," said the old woman feverishly; "why not the second?"

"A coincidence," stammered the old man.

"Go and get it and wish," cried his wife, quivering with excitement.

The old man turned and regarded her, and his voice shook. "He has been dead ten days, and besides he—I would not tell you else, but—I could only recognize him by his clothing. If he was too terrible for you to see then, how now?" 20

"Bring him back," cried the old woman, and dragged him toward the door. "Do you think I fear the child I have nursed?"

He went down in the darkness, and felt his way to the parlor, and then to the mantelpiece. The talisman was in its place, and a horrible fear that the unspoken wish might bring his mutilated son before him ere he could escape from the room seized upon him, and he caught his breath as he found that he had lost the direction of the door. His brow cold with sweat, he felt his way round the table, and groped along the wall until he found himself in the small passage with the unwholesome thing in his hand.

Even his wife's face seemed changed as he entered the room. It was white and expectant, and to his fears seemed to have an unnatural look upon it. He was afraid of her.

"*Wish!*" she cried, in a strong voice.

"It is foolish and wicked," he faltered.

"*Wish!*" repeated his wife.

He raised his hand. "I wish my son alive again."

The talisman fell to the floor, and he regarded it fearfully. Then he sank trembling into a chair as the old woman, with burning eyes, walked to the window and raised the blind.

Literary Analysis
Plot In what way does this new wish increase the tension of the story?

21 He sat until he was chilled with the cold, glancing occasionally

Vocabulary Development

Vocabulary Knowledge Rating

When students have completed reading and discussing "The Monkey's Paw," have them take out their **Vocabulary Knowledge Rating Chart** for this selection. Read the words aloud once more, and have students rate their knowledge of the words again in the After Reading column. Clarify any words that are still problematic. Have students write their own definition and example or sentence in the appropriate column. Then have students complete the Vocabulary Practice activities on page 43. Encourage students to use the words in further discussion and written work about this selection. Remind them that they will be accountable for these words on the **Selection Test, *Unit 1 Resources,*** pp. 42–44 or 45–47.

21 at the figure of the old woman peering through the window. The candle-end, which had burned below the rim of the china candlestick, was throwing pulsating shadows on the ceiling and walls, until, with a flicker larger than the rest, it expired. The old man, with an unspeakable sense of relief at the failure of the talisman, crept back to his bed, and a minute or two afterward the old woman came silently and apathetically beside him.

Neither spoke, but lay silently listening to the ticking of the clock. A stair creaked, and a squeaky mouse scurried noisily through the wall. The darkness was **oppressive**, and after lying for some time screwing up his courage, he took the box of matches, and striking one, went downstairs for a candle.

At the foot of the stairs the match went out, and he paused to strike another; and at the same moment a knock, so quiet and stealthy as to be scarcely audible, sounded on the front door.

The matches fell from his hand and spilled in the passage. He stood motionless, his breath suspended until the knock was repeated. Then he turned and fled swiftly back to his room, and closed the door behind him. A third knock sounded through the house.

"*What's that?*" cried the old woman, starting up.

"A rat," said the old man in shaking tones—"a rat. It passed me on the stairs."

His wife sat up in bed listening. A loud knock resounded through the house.

22 "It's Herbert!" she screamed. "It's Herbert!"

She ran to the door, but her husband was before her, and catching her by the arm, held her tightly.

"What are you going to do?" he whispered hoarsely.

"It's my boy; it's Herbert!" she cried, struggling mechanically. "I forgot it was two miles away. What are you holding me for? Let go. I must open the door."

"Don't let it in," cried the old man, trembling.

"You're afraid of your own son," she cried, struggling. "Let me go. I'm coming, Herbert, I'm coming."

24 There was another knock, and another. The old woman with a sudden wrench broke free and ran from the room. Her husband followed to the landing, and called after her appealingly as she hurried downstairs. He heard the chain rattle back and the bottom bolt drawn slowly and stiffly from the socket. Then the old woman's voice, strained and panting.

"The bolt," she cried, loudly. "Come down. I can't reach it."

But her husband was on his hands and knees groping wildly on

Vocabulary
oppressive (ə pres′ iv) *adj.* causing great discomfort; distressing

23 **Reading Check**
Why is Mr. White afraid?

22 Critical Thinking

Infer

1. Have students read the bracketed passage. **Ask:** What can you infer about Herbert's location from Mrs. White's statement, "I forgot it was two miles away"?
   Possible response: Mrs. White reasons that Herbert did not arrive at the house immediately after the wish was made because he had to travel from the cemetery where he was buried, which is two miles away from the house.
2. Discuss with students the state in which Herbert will be if the Whites see him. Have them explain what clues allow them to make this inference.
   Possible response: Herbert will arrive as a mangled corpse, the state in which he died. Mrs. White realizes he has not come immediately because he has had to walk two miles from the cemetery. If he is coming from the cemetery, he must be in the same state as he was when he died. Mr. White realizes this horrible truth—that the thing is not his son but a risen corpse—for he says, "Don't let it in."

23 Reading Check

Possible response: Mr. White is afraid that his son will be some type of monster or zombie.

Concept Connector

Anticipation Guide

Have students return to their **Anticipation Guides** and respond to the statements again, this time in the After Reading column. They may do this individually, or you may wish to have them work in their original pairs or groups. Guide students to recognize how their responses have changed—or remained the same—after reading "The Monkey's Paw." Encourage students to cite specific details or evidence from the text to support their new responses to the statements.

Writing About the Big Question

Have students compare the sentence starter they completed before reading the story with the ideas raised by the story. Ask them to explain how they might finish the sentence differently now.

Reading Skill Graphic Organizer

Ask students to review the graphic organizers they completed to follow the plot while reading. You may want to use the partially completed **Literary Analysis Graphic Organizer A** (p. 6 in ***Graphic Organizer Transparencies***) as an example. Then, have students share their graphic organizers.

24 Literary Analysis
Plot

1. Remind students that the plot reaches its climax when the tension is at its highest point.
2. **Ask** students the Literary Analysis question: How does the difference between what Mr. and Mrs. White are trying to do bring events to a climax?
   Possible response: Mrs. White hopes to find her son on the other side of the door. Mr. White, who wants to prevent further tragedy, is forced into a climactic confrontation over the paw.
3. Have students read the final paragraph. Then, lead them in discussing how the conflict is resolved at the end of the story.

ASSESS
Answers

Critical Thinking

1. **Possible response:** Students may respond that the most frightening moment is when there is a knock at the door in the middle of the night. It might be the mutilated Herbert.
2. (a) At first, Mr. White believes in the paw, Mrs. White is dubious, and Herbert is cynical and amused. (b) Mr. White comes to fear the paw; Mrs. White hopes it will restore her son.
3. (a) "I wish for two hundred pounds." (b) Mr. White fails to include a qualifier in his wish to prevent tragic consequences.
   (c) Students are not likely to think that any wording is foolproof.

Is there a difference between reality and truth?

(a) Yes, they think the legend is true. (b) Mrs. White shows this when she excitedly demands that they make a second wish to save their son.

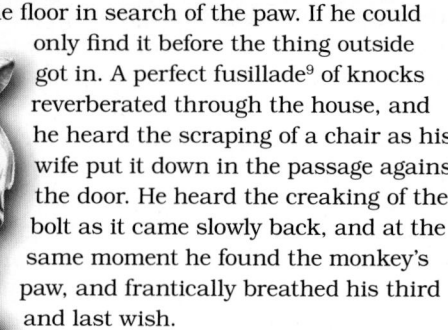

Literary Analysis
Plot How does the difference between what Mr. and Mrs. White are trying to do bring events to a climax?

the floor in search of the paw. If he could only find it before the thing outside got in. A perfect fusillade[9] of knocks reverberated through the house, and he heard the scraping of a chair as his wife put it down in the passage against the door. He heard the creaking of the bolt as it came slowly back, and at the same moment he found the monkey's paw, and frantically breathed his third and last wish. 24

The knocking ceased suddenly, although the echoes of it were still in the house. He heard the chair drawn back and the door opened. A cold wind rushed up the staircase, and a long loud wail of disappointment and misery from his wife gave him courage to run down to her side, and then to the gate beyond. The street lamp flickering opposite shone on a quiet and deserted road.

9. **fusillade** (fyo͞o′ sə lād′) *n.* rapid firing, as of gunshots.

Critical Thinking

1. **Respond:** What is the most frightening moment in the story for you? Why?
2. **(a)** How does each of the Whites react when first hearing the legend of the monkey's paw? **(b) Contrast:** How do the reactions of the mother and the father change?
3. **(a)** How does Mr. White word his first wish? **(b) Infer:** What painful outcome seems to follow from his wording?
   (c) Discuss: In a group, discuss the strengths and weaknesses of other ways the wish could have been worded. Decide whether any version is foolproof. Share your decision with the class.

THE BIG ?
Is there a difference between reality and truth?
(a) Do the Whites begin to think that the legend of the monkey's paw is true? **(b)** Which of their actions support your answer?

Assessment Resources

Unit 1 Resources

L1 L2 EL **Selection Test A,** pp. 42–44. Administer Text A to less advanced readers and English learners.

L3 L4 **Selection Test B,** pp. 45–47. Administer Text B to on-level and more advanced students.

L3 L4 **Open-Book Test,** pp. 60–62. As an alternative, give the Open-Book Test.

All **Customizable Test Bank**

All **Self-tests**
Students may prepare for the **Selection Test** by taking the **Self-test** online.

PHLit Online! All assessment resources are available at **www.PHLitOnline.com**.

After You Read | The Monkey's Paw

Literary Analysis: Plot and Foreshadowing

1. What information about the paw is given in the **exposition?**
2. **(a)** Describe three events in the **rising action** that increase the tension in the **plot. (b)** Where does the story reach its **climax?**
3. Identify two details that **foreshadow** the tragic outcome of the first wish.

Reading Skill: Make Predictions

4. **(a)** Using a chart like the one shown, indicate how you used your prior knowledge to **make a prediction** about one of the wishes.

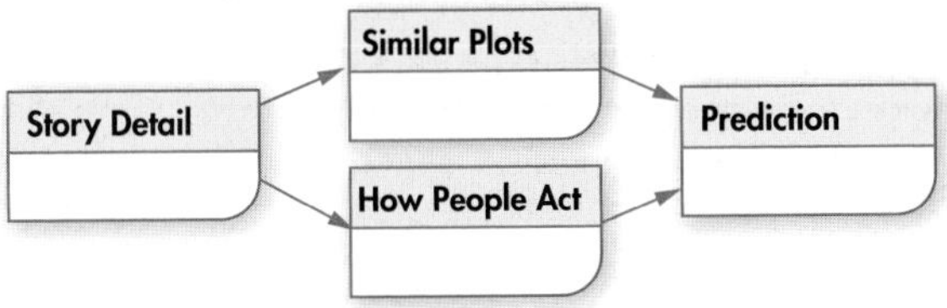

(b) How close was your prediction to the actual outcome? Explain your answer.

Vocabulary

Practice An **analogy** shows the relationship between pairs of words. Use a word from the vocabulary list for "The Monkey's Paw" on page 30 to complete each analogy. Your choice should create a word pair that matches the relationship between the first two words given. Explain the relationship in each analogy.

1. ran : rapidly :: crept : ____________
2. kindness : cruelty :: passion : ____________
3. nourished : starved :: praised : ____________
4. lighthearted : cheerful :: serious : ____________
5. happiness : sadness :: doubt : ____________
6. cautious : reckless :: unburdened : ____________

Word Study Use the context of the sentences and what you know about the **Latin root *-cred-*** to explain your answer to each question.

1. Would you believe an *incredible* rumor?
2. Does someone who tells lies have *credibility?*

Word Study

The **Latin root *-cred-*** means "believe."

Challenge Explain how the root *-cred-* contributes to the meanings of these words. Consult a dictionary if necessary.

credence
credo
discredit

Literary Analysis

1. Readers are told that the monkey's paw has been enchanted by a fakir and that it has the power to grant three wishes to each of three people.
2. (a) **Possible response:** Rising action includes Mr. White's first wish, Mr. White's realization that his son's death is the consequence of his wish, and Mrs. White's insistence that Mr. White wish for Herbert's return. (b) The story reaches its climax when Mr. White makes the last wish and Mrs. White struggles to open the door.
3. **Possible response:** Morris's grim words and manner, Mr. White dropping the paw with a "shuddering cry," and the faces Herbert sees in the fire foreshadow the tragic outcome of the wish.

Reading Skill

4. (a) **Possible response:** Story Detail: Mr. White wishes for two hundred pounds. Similar Plots: When characters are warned there will be consequences, it foreshadows a tragic outcome. How People Act: People as cynical as Herbert are often taken by surprise. Prediction: The wish will be granted, but something bad will happen to Herbert.
(b) Students' predictions are likely to be fairly accurate.
For other sample answers, see ***Graphic Organizer Transparencies,* Reading Skill Graphic Organizer A**, p. 3, and the **Additional Answers** section.

Vocabulary

Practice

Sample answers:

1. furtively; adverb to describe the action
2. apathy; antonym
3. maligned; antonym
4. grave; synonym
5. credulity; antonym
6. oppressive; antonym

Word Study

Sample answers:

1. No, the root *-cred-* means "believe," so *incredible* means "unbelievable." An incredible rumor would be too wild to believe.
2. No, the root *-cred-* means "believe," so *credibility* means "believability." If someone is known to tell lies, people will stop believing him or her.

Word Study: Challenge

Sample answers: *Credence* is a belief in something. A *credo* is a statement of what you believe. To *discredit* is to show why something cannot be believed.

PRETEACH

*Skills instruction for the **Reading Skill** and the **Literary Analysis** concept for this selection appear on p. 29.*

❶ Writing About the Big Question

1. Review the assignment with the class.
2. Discuss important decisions that students have made. What effects did the decision have on their life? What would their life be like if they had chosen differently?
3. Have students complete the sentence starters. Review responses as a class. (**Possible response:** Decisions that people make can affect the reality of their lives by changing what will happen to them in the future. The choices people make can have concrete effects on their level of happiness and success.)
4. Remind students that their answers will help them think about the Big Question.

While You Read

Tell students that as they read, they should consider the impact of the characters' choices on their lives.

❷ Vocabulary

1. Have students preview the selection vocabulary.
2. For each word, have students say the word aloud.
3. Then, use the word in a sentence that defines the word.
4. Repeat your definitional sentence or a similar sentence with the word missing, and have the class "fill in the blank" chorally. For example:

   A tentative action is an uncertain or experimental one. The timid student was unsure of the correct answer, so her response was [students say "tentative"].

❸ Word Study

1. Introduce the skill, using the instruction in the box.
2. Ask students to think of and define a word that includes the root *-strict-*. (**Possible response:** *Boa constrictor:* The root *-strict-* means "squeeze," so a *boa constrictor* is "a large snake that squeezes its prey.")

Making Connections | The Leap

❶ **Is there a difference between *reality* and *truth*?**

Writing About the Big Question

In "The Leap," a daughter thinks about the truth of her life by contemplating how much she owes her mother. Use these sentence starters to develop your ideas about the Big Question.

Decisions that people make can affect the **reality** of their lives by ____.
The choices people make can have **concrete** effects on ______.

While You Read Think about the choices that the characters make and how their choices affect their own lives and the lives of others.

❷ Vocabulary

Read each word and its definition. Decide whether you know the word well, know it a little bit, or do not know it at all. After you read, see how your knowledge of each word has increased.

- **encroaching** (en krōch′ iŋ) *adj.* intruding on, especially in a gradual way (p. 47) *Toward afternoon, the encroaching clouds dimmed the sun.* *encroach v. encroachment n.*
- **commemorates** (kə mem′ ə rāts′) *v.* honors a memory (p. 47) *The memorial commemorates the soldiers who died defending their country.* *commemoration n. memorial n. memory n.*
- **extricating** (eks′ tri kāt′ iŋ) *n.* setting free; removing from a difficult situation (p. 50) *Extricating the kite from the tree proved to be very difficult.* *extricate v. extrication n.*
- **constricting** (kən strikt′ iŋ) *adj.* preventing freedom of movement; limiting (p. 51) *He found the sweater to be too constricting, so he bought a larger size.* *constrict v. constriction n.*
- **perpetually** (pər pech′ o͞o əl lē) *adv.* continuing forever; constantly (p. 52) *He was fired for being perpetually late to work.* *perpetual adj. perpetuate v.*
- **tentative** (ten′ tə tiv) *adj.* hesitant; not confident (p. 53) *I took a tentative bite of the odd dessert.* *tentatively adv.*

❸ **Word Study**

The **Latin root *-strict-*** means "confine" or "squeeze."

In this story, a character thinks living in a small town can be **constricting,** because his experiences are confined within the boundaries of this small area.

Vocabulary Development

Vocabulary Knowledge Rating

Create a **Vocabulary Knowledge Rating Chart** (***Professional Development Guidebook,*** p. 33) for this selection. Include the selection vocabulary and the Big Question words that appear in the Writing About the Big Question sentence starters on this page. (The Big Question vocabulary is introduced on pp. 2–3.)

Give students a copy of the chart. Read the words aloud, and have students mark their rating in the Before Reading column. Urge them to be alert to these words as they read and discuss the selection.

Tally how many students think they know a word to gauge how much instruction to provide. As students read and discuss the selection, point out the words and their context.

PHLit Online! **Vocabulary Central,** featuring tools, activities, and songs for studying vocabulary, is available at **www.PHLitOnline.com.**

Meet Louise Erdrich (b. 1954)

Author of The Leap

Louise Erdrich's fiction and poetry celebrate life's richness. Born to a German American father and a French-Native American mother, Erdrich writes from the complex perspective of two distinct cultures.

A Family Tradition Erdrich grew up in North Dakota, where she often visited with her relatives in the Turtle Mountain Band of Chippewa, a Native American people. With little exposure to television or movies, Erdrich became fascinated by the storytelling tradition that surrounded her. "The people in our families made everything into a story," she explains. Her first published book, *Love Medicine*, a group of interrelated stories, brought Erdrich national acclaim.

DID YOU KNOW?

***Love Medicine* was rejected by the first twenty-eight publishers to whom Erdrich sent it. When finally published, the book won rave reviews and the National Book Critics Circle Award.**

4

BACKGROUND FOR THE STORY

Circus Families

Circus families often develop their own acts. They pass the specific skills involved, such as acrobatics or juggling, from one generation to the next. Many young circus performers, like the mother in "The Leap," bypass traditional schooling to develop the remarkable physical talents that they display to amazed audiences.

Differentiated Instruction — Additional Instruction

EL Extended Support—English Learners
Have students complete the **Reading and Vocabulary Warm-ups, *Unit 1 Resources,*** pp. 48–51, before they read. Assign the prereading pages for the selection in the ***Reader's Notebook: English Learner's Version.*** Then, have students listen to portions of the selection on the ***Hear It!* Audio CD**.

L1 L2 Extended Support—Struggling Readers
Have students complete the **Reading and Vocabulary Warm-ups, *Unit 1 Resources,*** pp. 48–51, before they read. Assign the prereading pages in the ***Reader's Notebook: Adapted Version.*** Then, have students listen to portions of the selection on the ***Hear It!* Audio CD** (adapted text).

Extended Support—Reluctant Readers
To build motivation and engagement before assigning the selection, have students read "High Flyers," a thematically related selection in ***Reality Central.*** Then, use the questions at the conclusion of the related selection to guide discussion.

Daily Bellringer

For each class during which you will teach this selection, have students complete one of the five Quick Write activities for Week 1 in the ***Daily Bellringer Activities*** booklet.

4 Background

Circus Families

The American circus world in which the mother in "The Leap" once lived is almost as old as the nation itself. The Ricketts circus, America's first, was initially staged in 1792. George Washington is believed to have sold the Ricketts circus a horse. American circuses grew in size and popularity through the nineteenth century. Circus tents, like the one commemorated in the narrator's hometown in "The Leap," date back to the 1820s. The trapeze that was the mother's specialty was invented in 1859 and became a key circus act. Circuses—and the families that performed in them—continued to travel and perform in tents well into the twentieth century.

Multidraft Reading

This icon ● marks natural pauses in the selection. To assist struggling readers and to deepen reading for all, assign the text in "chunks," following the icons, and apply multidraft reading protocols. For each reading, have students set the purpose indicated:

- **First reading**—literal comprehension: answering the Reading Check questions.
- **Second reading**—application of skills: answering the Make Predictions and Plot and Foreshadowing prompts.
- **Third reading**—interpretation: answering the end-of-selection questions.

For more guidance, refer to the ***Classroom Strategies and Teaching Routines*** card on multidraft reading.

PHLit Online!
For more about the author, practice with the selection vocabulary, and more background, go online at **www.PHLitOnline.com**.

TEACH

❶ Activating Prior Knowledge

1. Prepare an **Anticipation Guide** (see ***Professional Development Guidebook***, pp. 36–38) with the following statements:
   - Family is the most important thing in life.
   - People's secrets are their own.
   - Destiny brings people together.
   - Saving yourself instead of a family member in a deadly situation is selfish.
2. Give students copies of the prepared **Anticipation Guide.** Have students mark their responses in the Me column. Then, have students discuss the statements in pairs or groups and mark the Guides again, this time in the Group column.
3. For further guidance, use the *Classroom Strategies and Teaching Routines* card: **Using an Anticipation Guide.**

Concept Connector →

Students will return to the **Anticipation Guide** after completing "The Leap."

Whole-Class Activity

While it would be dangerous for students to attempt the feats of the mother in "The Leap," they can approximate the sensation of leaping and falling by practicing high and long jumps. Discuss with the class the appeal of flying through the air.

❷ About the Selection

"The Leap" paints an emotionally rich portrait of the bond between mother and daughter. The narrator recounts her now blind mother's past as a trapeze artist, focusing on the accident that took her first husband's life. The daughter then turns to the fire that almost took her own young life and the daring leap her mother made to save her.

46 Fiction and Nonfiction

Vocabulary Development

Thematic Vocabulary: The Big Question

As students are discussing "The Leap," have them use the thematic vocabulary presented in Introducing the Big Question, pp. 2–3. You might encourage them with sentence starters like these:

1. The narrator's opinions of her mother are *subjective* because . . .
2. There is *uncertainty* over whether the narrator would have been born if . . .
3. As the narrator's mother was flying through the air, she was able to *comprehend* that . . .
4. The narrator's *perception* of her mother is probably affected by the fact that . . .

1

2

The Leap

Louise Erdrich

My mother is the surviving half of a blindfold trapeze act, not a fact I think about much even now that she is sightless, the result of encroaching and stubborn cataracts.

3 She walks slowly through her house here in New Hampshire, lightly touching her way along walls and running her hands over knickknacks, books, the drift of a grown child's belongings and castoffs. She has never upset an object or as much as brushed a magazine onto the floor. She has never lost her balance or bumped into a closet door left carelessly open.

It has occurred to me that the catlike precision of her movements in old age might be the result of her early training, but she shows so little of the drama or flair one might expect from a performer that I tend to forget the Flying Avalons. She has kept no sequined costume, no photographs, no fliers or posters from that part of her youth. I would, in fact, tend to think that all memory of double somersaults and heart-stopping catches had left her arms and legs were it not for the fact that sometimes, as I sit sewing in the room of the rebuilt house in which I slept as a child, I hear the crackle, catch a whiff of smoke from the stove downstairs, and suddenly the room goes dark, the stitches burn beneath my fingers, and I am sewing with a needle of hot silver, a thread of fire.

5 I owe her my existence three times. The first was when she saved herself. In the town square a replica tent pole, cracked and splintered, now stands cast in concrete. It commemorates the disaster that put our town smack on the front page of the Boston and New York tabloids. It is from those old newspapers, now

Vocabulary

encroaching (en krōch′ iŋ) *adj.* intruding on, especially in a gradual way

commemorates (kə mem′ ə rāts′) *v.* honors a memory

4 **Reading Check**

What was the narrator's mother's profession?

3 Critical Thinking

Infer

1. Tell students to read the bracketed passage, paying attention to the description of the mother.
2. **Ask** students what these details reveal about the mother. **Possible response:** She has had wide-ranging experiences and yet is very comfortable in the familiar space of her home.

4 Reading Check

Answer: The mother was a trapeze artist.

Differentiated Instruction for Universal Access

Strategy for Less Proficient Readers

Point out to students that one key to the structure of this story is the narrator's statement on this page: "I owe her my existence three times." Have students create a three-column chart. As they read, ask them to identify each episode in which the mother's actions contributed to her daughter's life. In the first column, for example, they should describe the circus accident and tell how the narrator owes her life to her mother's decision in that event.

Enrichment for Gifted/Talented Students

Students begin to get an indication of what the narrator's mother did for a living before the narrator was born. To better understand an act such as the Flying Avalons, have students do some research on circuses and trapeze artists of the time. Why do they think that circuses were so popular then? Were trapeze acts more or less safe at that time than they are now? They can illustrate what they learn by making posters or flyers, such as those mentioned by the narrator.

PHLit Online!

This selection is available in interactive format in the **Enriched Online Student Edition, www.PHLitOnline.com,** which includes a thematically related video with writing prompt and an interactive graphic organizer.

❺ Literary Analysis

Plot

1. Remind students that foreshadowing is often an important part of plot. In foreshadowing, details hint at coming events. Point out that writers use this technique to build tension as the action of the plot rises.
2. Have students read the bracketed passage. Then, **ask** them to explain what the narrator is describing.
   Answer: The narrator is describing how she learned of an event in the past, before she was born, when her mother saved her own life.
3. Point out that the passage leaves out a great deal of information about what happened. For example, it mentions the mother and her first husband's particular act, but it does not describe the act. Encourage students to consider what else the narrator leaves unstated and why.
4. Tell students that details in this passage foreshadow events the narrator has not yet described. Call their attention to the quotation from a news account that ends the passage.
5. **Ask:** How does the statement from the news account foreshadow a tragic event?
   Answer: By letting readers know that a "deadly gale" struck by surprise on the day in question, the statement hints that the weather will create a crisis that will threaten the mother's life.

❻ Reading Skill

Make Predictions

1. Have students read the bracketed passage. Instruct them to pay close attention to threatening details.
2. Then, **ask** the Reading Skill question: What details help you predict that something will go wrong?
   Possible response: The news quotation about lips that were "never again to meet" and the description of rising wind and rumbling thunder create a sense of growing danger.

---

❺ historical records, that I get my information. Not from my mother, Anna of the Flying Avalons, nor from any of her in-laws, nor certainly from the other half of her particular act, Harold Avalon, her first husband. In one news account it says, "The day was mildly overcast, but nothing in the air or temperature gave any hint of the sudden force with which the deadly gale would strike."

I have lived in the West, where you can see the weather coming for miles, and it is true that out here we are at something of a disadvantage. When extremes of temperature collide, a hot and cold front, winds generate instantaneously behind a hill and crash upon you without warning. That, I think, was the likely situation on that day in June. People probably commented on the pleasant air, grateful that no hot sun beat upon the striped tent that stretched over the entire center green. They bought their tickets and surrendered them in anticipation. They sat. They ate caramelized popcorn and roasted peanuts. There was time, before the storm, for three acts. The White Arabians[1] of Ali-Khazar rose on their hind legs and waltzed. The Mysterious Bernie folded himself into a painted cracker tin, and the Lady of the Mists made herself appear and disappear in surprising places. As the clouds gathered outside, unnoticed, the ringmaster cracked his whip, shouted his introduction, and pointed to the ceiling of the tent, where the Flying Avalons were perched.

They loved to drop gracefully from nowhere, like two sparkling birds, and blow kisses as they threw off their plumed helmets and high-collared capes. They laughed and flirted openly as they beat their way up again on the trapeze bars. In the final vignette of their act, they actually would kiss in midair, pausing, almost hovering as they swooped past one another. On the ground, between bows, Harry Avalon would skip quickly to the front rows and point out the smear of my mother's lipstick, just off the edge of his mouth. They made a romantic pair all right, especially in the blindfold sequence.

❼ That afternoon, as the anticipation increased, as Mr. and Mrs. Avalon tied sparkling strips of cloth onto each other's face and as they puckered their lips in mock kisses, lips destined "never again to meet," as one long breathless article put it, the wind rose, miles off, wrapped itself into a cone, and howled. There came a rumble of electrical energy, drowned out by the sudden roll of drums.

❻ Reading Skill
Make Predictions What details help you predict that something will go wrong?

1. **Arabians** horses of the Arabian breed.

Vocabulary Development

Circus Terminology

The narrator describes her mother's last performance in the circus. You may wish to clarify with students the terms related to the circus that are used in this section of "The Leap."

ringmaster: person in charge of the performances in the circus; a master of ceremonies

trapeze: a bar hung between two parallel ropes, used for acrobatic stunts and performances

vignette: a short scene; in this context, an individual trick or stunt in an acrobatic routine

main pole: the primary support holding up the tent under which the circus performs

guy wires: a cable of braided metal used to steady equipment inside the circus tent

7 One detail not mentioned by the press, perhaps unknown—Anna was pregnant at the time, seven months and hardly showing, her stomach muscles were that strong. It seems incredible that she would work high above the ground when any fall could be so dangerous, but the explanation—I know from watching her go blind—is that my mother lives comfortably in extreme elements. She is one with the constant dark now, just as the air was her home, familiar to her, safe, before the storm that afternoon.

From opposite ends of the tent they waved, blind and smiling, to the crowd below. The ringmaster removed his hat and called for silence, so that the two above could concentrate. They rubbed their hands in chalky powder, then Harry launched himself and swung, once, twice, in huge calibrated beats across space. He hung from his knees and on the third swing stretched wide his arms, held his hands out to receive his pregnant wife as she dove from her shining bar.

It was while the two were in midair, their hands about to meet, that lightning struck the main pole and sizzled down the guy wires, filling the air with a blue radiance that Harry Avalon must certainly have seen through the cloth of his blindfold as the tent buckled and the edifice[2] toppled him forward, the swing continuing and not returning in its sweep, and Harry going down, down into the crowd with his last thought, perhaps, just a prickle of surprise at his empty hands.

10 My mother once said that I'd be amazed at how many things a person can do within the act of falling. Perhaps, at the time, she

2. **edifice** (ed´ i fis) *n.* large structure or building.

8 ▲ **Critical Viewing**
What feelings might a scene like this inspire in an onlooker? **[Infer]**

Literary Analysis
Plot In what way do these descriptions of events increase the tension in the rising action?

9 **Reading Check**
What happens to Harry on the day of the gale?

7 Literary Analysis

Plot

1. Remind students that the main purpose of the *rising action* section of a story's plot is to build tension and increase the conflict. Use **Literary Analysis Graphic Organizer A** (*Graphic Organizer Transparencies*, p. 4) to demonstrate the role rising action plays in plot development. Encourage students to complete Plot Diagrams of their own as they read.
2. **Ask** students to identify ways a writer can build tension in this part of a plot.
   Possible response: To build tension, writers can hint at things to come. For instance, the narrator of "The Leap" describes the Avalons getting ready to perform, mentions the weather's drastic change, and then jumps to the present. This leaves readers wondering just what happened to the Avalons.
3. Have students read the bracketed passage. Instruct them to pay special attention to the detailed descriptions of each event.
4. **Ask** students the Literary Analysis question: In what way do these descriptions of events increase the tension in the rising action?
   Possible response: The detailed descriptions emphasize just how dangerous the Flying Avalons' act is to perform. They also give readers a sense of foreboding.

8 Critical Viewing

Possible response: The scene would probably make an onlooker feel frightened and horrified.

9 Reading Check

Answer: Harry falls to his death when lightning strikes the main tent pole during the trapeze act.

Differentiated Instruction for Universal Access

Strategy for Special Needs Students
Students may need help remembering the elements of plot structure. To review, use **Literary Analysis Graphic Organizer B** (*Graphic Organizer Transparencies,* p. 5) to review plot structure. Have students use copies of the blank Plot Diagram to record instances of foreshadowing and rising action in "The Leap."

Strategy for Less Proficient Readers
Students may have difficulty understanding how elements such as foreshadowing and rising action fit into the plot of "The Leap." For support, show them **Literary Analysis Graphic Organizer A** (*Graphic Organizer Transparencies,* p. 4). Use the completed Plot Diagram to demonstrate how the bracketed passages fit into the story's plot.

⑩ Critical Thinking

Interpret

1. Have students read the bracketed passage.
2. **Ask** students what life-altering decision Anna makes while falling.
   Answer: Anna's daughter believes that her mother decides to save herself—and her unborn child—instead of dying with her husband. Anna does not give her daughter any information about the accident. The narrator draws her own conclusions based on newspaper articles and her personal experience.

⑪ Connecting to the Big Question

1. Remind students that people have different ways of viewing the world and the events that go on around them. In this way, *reality* can be personal. On the one hand, there are the facts. On the other hand, people interpret the facts differently.
2. Have students think about the plot of the story to this point.
   Ask: How does the narrator interpret these events from her mother's life?
   Possible response: She looks at these events as reasons for her own existence. She takes her mother's story and makes it into her own story.
3. Have students read the bracketed passage. **Ask:** What does the narrator mean when she says that her "vision [is] shifting"?
   Possible response: She sees things differently from the way she saw them before. She now sees the past as more important than the present or the future.

⑩ was teaching me to dive off a board at the town pool, for I associate the idea with midair somersaults. But I also think she meant that even in that awful doomed second one could think, for she certainly did. When her hands did not meet her husband's, my mother tore her blindfold away. As he swept past her on the wrong side, she could have grasped his ankle, the toe-end of his tights, and gone down clutching him. Instead, she changed direction. Her body twisted toward a heavy wire and she managed to hang on to the braided metal, still hot from the lightning strike. Her palms were burned so terribly that once healed they bore no lines, only the blank scar tissue of a quieter future. She was lowered, gently, to the sawdust ring just underneath the dome of the canvas roof, which did not entirely settle but was held up on one end and jabbed through, torn, and still on fire in places from the giant spark, though rain and men's jackets soon put that out.

Three people died, but except for her hands my mother was not seriously harmed until an overeager rescuer broke her arm in extricating her and also, in the process, collapsed a portion of the tent bearing a huge buckle that knocked her unconscious. She was taken to the town hospital, and there she must have hemorrhaged,[3] for they kept her, confined to her bed, a month and a half before her baby was born without life.

Vocabulary
extricating (eks´ tri kāt´ iŋ) *n.* setting free; removing from a difficult situation

Harry Avalon had wanted to be buried in the circus cemetery next to the original Avalon, his uncle, so she sent him back with his brothers. The child, however, is buried around the corner, beyond this house and just down the highway. Sometimes I used to walk there just to sit. She was a girl, but I rarely thought of her as a sister or even as a separate person really. I suppose you could call it the egocentrism[4] of a child, of all young children, but I considered her a less finished version of myself.

⑪ When the snow falls, throwing shadows among the stones, I can easily pick hers out from the road, for it is bigger than the others and in the shape of a lamb at rest, its legs curled beneath. The carved lamb looms larger as the years pass, though it is probably only my eyes, the vision shifting, as what is close to me blurs and distances sharpen. In odd moments, I think it is the edge drawing near, the edge of everything, the unseen horizon we do not really speak of in the eastern woods. And it also seems to me, although this is probably an idle fantasy, that the statue is growing more sharply etched, as if, instead of weathering itself into a porous mass, it is hardening on the hillside with each snowfall, perfecting itself. ●

3. **hemorrhaged** (hem´ ər ij'd´) *v.* bled heavily.
4. **egocentrism** (ē´ gō sen´ triz əm) *n.* self-centeredness; inability to distinguish one's own needs and interests from those of others.

Vocabulary Development

Expressive Vocabulary

To help students broaden their expressive vocabulary, encourage them to use the following words as they discuss the selection: *demonstrates, devote, enrich, enlighten.* Have them complete these sentence starters:

1. The narrator's father *demonstrates* his love by . . .
2. To *devote* the time and attention it takes to teach someone to read . . .
3. Books *enrich* Anna's life so much that . . .
4. An emotional gift can *enlighten* someone by . . .

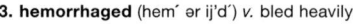

It was during her confinement in the hospital that my mother met my father. He was called in to look at the set of her arm, which was complicated. He stayed, sitting at her bedside, for he was something of an armchair traveler and had spent his war quietly, at an air force training grounds, where he became a specialist in
12 arms and legs broken during parachute training exercises. Anna Avalon had been to many of the places he longed to visit—Venice, Rome, Mexico, all through France and Spain. She had no family of her own and was taken in by the Avalons, trained to perform from a very young age. They toured Europe before the war, then based themselves in New York. She was illiterate.

It was in the hospital that she finally learned to read and write, as a way of overcoming the boredom and depression of those weeks, and it was my father who insisted on teaching her. In return for stories of her adventures, he graded her first exercises. He bought her her first book, and over her bold letters, which the pale guides of the penmanship pads could not contain, they fell in love.

I wonder if my father calculated the exchange he offered: one form of flight for another. For after that, and for as long as I can remember, my mother has never been without a book. Until now, that is, and it remains the greatest difficulty of her blindness. Since my father's recent death, there is no one to read to her, which is why I returned, in fact, from my failed life where the land is flat. I came home to read to my mother, to read out loud, to read long into the dark if I must, to read all night.

Once my father and mother married, they moved onto the old farm he had inherited but didn't care much for. Though he'd been thinking of moving to a larger city, he settled down and broadened his practice in this valley. It still seems odd to me, when they could
13 have gone anywhere else, that they chose to stay in the town where the disaster had occurred, and which my father in the first place had found so **constricting**. It was my mother who insisted upon it, after her child did not survive. And then, too, she loved the sagging

Literary Analysis
Plot Which details in this paragraph provide additional exposition?

Vocabulary
constricting (kən strikt′ iŋ) *adj.* preventing freedom of movement; limiting

14 **Reading Check**
How do the narrator's mother and father first meet?

12 Literary Analysis
Plot

1. Have students read the bracketed passage. Then, **ask** students the Literary Analysis question: Which details in this paragraph provide additional exposition?
Answer: The paragraph introduces the narrator's father as an Air Force doctor who specializes in treating fractures and who longs to travel.

13 Literary Analysis
Plot

1. Have students read the bracketed passage. **Ask** them to explain what this passage describes.
Answer: It describes the narrator's parents' decision to live in her father's hometown, moving—at Anna's insistence—onto a farm he has inherited.
2. Instruct students to reread the passage, looking closely for foreshadowing. **Ask** students to identify details that hint at events to come.
Possible response: The description of the peaceful farm and "sagging farmhouse" suggest that something will happen involving the property. Also, the fact that moving there is Anna's idea hints that something will threaten the narrator.

▶ **Monitor Progress:** Have students make foreshadowing charts by drawing lines down the center of sheets of paper. On the left, have them write details from the bracketed passage. On the right, have them write the events these details foreshadow. Students should explain the connections between the details and the events.

▶ **Reteach:** If students are having difficulty understanding foreshadowing, present sample details, such as: *A character says she hopes it will not rain on her picnic, or a character says "The only thing that could go wrong is . . ."*

14 Reading Check

Answer: Her father is a doctor who treats her mother's arm in the hospital where she recovers from the accident.

Differentiated Instruction for Universal Access

EL Strategy for English Learners
Students may need help reading, understanding, and interpreting the bracketed passages. Before addressing the Reading Skill and Literary Analysis exercises, preview this part of "The Leap" with ***Hear It!* Audio CD**. Have students read along as they listen. They may need particular help with metaphoric expressions. For example, explain that "one form of flight for another" refers to Anna giving up her trapeze performance while learning to read and love books. For some people, reading is the flight of the imagination.

Enrichment for Advanced Readers
To enrich students' knowledge of the historical context, call students' attention to the narrator's brief description of her parents' experiences surrounding the war. The war is probably World War II, given the description of her father's time in the war at an Air Force training ground, setting the broken bones of parachutists, and the fact that the circus traveled through Europe before the war. Encourage students to research the historical context for Anna and her second husband's experiences.

⓯ Critical Thinking

Analyze/Interpret

1. Have students read the bracketed passage. **Ask** them to explain the significance of the paragraph.
   Possible response: The narrator may want to believe that her mother makes the choice to "save her" on this second occasion. However, the opening sentence suggests that the controlling force in Anna's life is fate rather than her own decisions.
2. **Ask** students what this statement reveals about the narrator.
   Possible response: The narrator is experiencing an inner conflict over whether life is controlled by fate or free will. She wants to believe that people control their own destinies, but the events of her life may suggest otherwise.

⓰ Reading Skill

Make Predictions

1. Instruct students to read the bracketed passage. **Ask** them to describe the situation the narrator's mother faces.
   Answer: The mother's house is on fire, and her daughter is trapped in an upstairs bedroom. There is no way for the firefighters to rescue the girl. A tree near the daughter's window catches her eye.
2. Have students use their knowledge about plots, Anna, and how people act in emergencies to make predictions about what will happen in the story. Invite students to discuss their ideas or write them in their Prediction Charts.
3. **Ask** students the Reading Skill question: Based on facts in the story about Anna's past, what do you predict she will do next?
   Possible response: Anna is a trained trapeze performer and has a fierce, protective love for her daughter. She will climb the tree and try to leap from it into the narrator's window.

⓭ farmhouse with its scrap of what was left of a vast acreage of woods and hidden hay fields that stretched to the game park.

⓯ I owe my existence, the second time then, to the two of them and the hospital that brought them together. That is the debt we take for granted since none of us asks for life. It is only once we have it that we hang on so dearly. ●

I was seven the year the house caught fire, probably from standing ash. It can rekindle, and my father, forgetful around the house and perpetually exhausted from night hours on call, often emptied what he thought were ashes from cold stoves into wooden or cardboard containers. The fire could have started from a flaming box, or perhaps a buildup of creosote inside the chimney was the culprit. It started right around the stove, and the heart of the house was gutted. The baby-sitter, fallen asleep in my father's den on the first floor, woke to find the stairway to my upstairs room cut off by flames. She used the phone, then ran outside to stand beneath my window.

Vocabulary
perpetually (pər pech′ o͞o əl lē) *adv.* continuing forever; constantly

When my parents arrived, the town volunteers had drawn water from the fire pond and were spraying the outside of the house, preparing to go inside after me, not knowing at the time that there was only one staircase and that it was lost. On the other side of the house, the superannuated[5] extension ladder broke in half. Perhaps the clatter of it falling against the walls woke me, for I'd been asleep up to that point.

As soon as I awakened, in the small room that I now use for sewing, I smelled the smoke. I followed things by the letter then, was good at memorizing instructions, and so I did exactly what was taught in the second-grade home fire drill. I got up, I touched the back of my door before opening it. Finding it hot, I left it closed and stuffed my rolled-up rug beneath the crack. I did not hide under my bed or crawl into my closet. I put on my flannel robe, and then I sat down to wait.

⓰ Outside, my mother stood below my dark window and saw clearly that there was no rescue. Flames had pierced one side wall, and the glare of the fire lighted the massive limbs and trunk of the vigorous old elm that had probably been planted the year the house was built, a hundred years ago at least. No leaf touched the wall, and just one thin branch scraped the roof. From below, it looked as though even a squirrel would have had trouble jumping from the tree onto the house, for the breadth of that small branch was no bigger than my mother's wrist.

Reading Skill
Make Preditions Based on facts in the story about Anna's past, what do you predict she will do next?

Standing there, beside Father, who was preparing to rush back around to the front of the house, my mother asked him to unzip her dress. When he wouldn't be bothered, she made him understand.

5. **superannuated** (so͞o′ pər an′ yo͞o āt′ əd) *adj.* too old to be usable.

52 Fiction and Nonfiction

Vocabulary Development

Vocabulary Knowledge Rating

When students have completed reading and discussing "The Leap," have them take out their **Vocabulary Knowledge Rating Chart** for this selection. Read the words aloud once more, and have students rate their knowledge of the words again in the After Reading column. Clarify any words that are still problematic. Have students write their own definition and example or sentence in the appropriate column. Then, have students complete the Vocabulary Practice at the end of the selection. Encourage students to use the words in further discussion and written work about this selection. Remind them that they will be accountable for these words on the **Selection Test, *Unit 1 Resources,*** pp. 63–65 or 66–68.

He couldn't make his hands work, so she finally tore it off and stood there in her pearls and stockings. She directed one of the men to lean the broken half of the extension ladder up against the trunk of the tree. In surprise, he complied. She ascended. She vanished. Then she could be seen among the leafless branches of late November as she made her way up and, along her stomach, inched the length of a bough that curved above the branch that brushed the roof.

17 Once there, swaying, she stood and balanced. There were plenty of people in the crowd and many who still remember, or think they do, my mother's leap through the ice-dark air toward that thinnest extension, and how she broke the branch falling so that it cracked in her hands, cracked louder than the flames as she vaulted with it toward the edge of the roof, and how it hurtled down end over end without her, and their eyes went up, again, to see where she had flown.

I didn't see her leap through air, only heard the sudden thump and looked out my window. She was hanging by the backs of her heels from the new gutter we had put in that year, and she was smiling. I was not surprised to see her, she was so matter-of-fact. She tapped on the window. I remember how she did it, too. It was the friendliest tap, a bit tentative, as if she was afraid she had arrived too early at a friend's house. Then she gestured at the latch, and when I opened the window she told me to

Vocabulary
tentative (ten´ tə tiv) *adj.* hesitant; not confident

18 **Reading Check**

What steps does the narrator take when she realizes that there is a fire?

17 Critical Thinking

Support

1. Have students read the bracketed passage. **Ask** them to explain why this paragraph contains the *climax*, the point at which the conflict reaches its highest point.
Possible response: Anna's daughter is trapped in the burning house and will surely die if someone does not save her. Anna plans to save her daughter by climbing a nearby tree and leaping to her daughter's window. This paragraph describes, with much suspense, Anna's balancing act on the bough and the start of her leap, causing the branch to break. The climax is reached when it is uncertain that Anna will reach the house. If Anna does not make it, she and her daughter will probably perish.

18 Reading Check

Answer: The narrator follows the directions she learned in grade school. She checks to see if the door is hot before opening it. When she finds the door is hot, she does not open it. Instead, she rolls a rug and stuffs it under the door. Then, she sits on her bed and waits.

Concept Connector

Anticipation Guide

Have students return to their **Anticipation Guides** and respond to the statements again, this time in the After Reading column. They may do this individually, or you may wish to have them work in their original pairs or groups. Then, lead a class discussion. Start by putting responses from the Me and Group columns on the board. Guide students to recognize how their responses have changed—or remained the same—after reading "The Leap." Encourage students to cite specific details or evidence from the text to support their new responses to the statements.

Writing About the Big Question

Have students compare their responses to the sentence starters they completed before reading the story with their ideas afterward. Ask them to explain whether their thoughts have changed.

Literary Analysis Graphic Organizer

Ask students to review the graphic organizers they completed to follow the plot while reading. You may want to use the **Literary Analysis Graphic Organizer A** (p. 4 in *Graphic Organizer Transparencies*) as an example. Then, have students share their graphic organizers and the plot developments they found in the selection.

19 Literary Analysis

Plot

1. Have students read the bracketed passage.
2. **Ask** students the Literary Analysis question: How is the conflict resolved?
   Answer: The narrator's mother, clad in her underwear, calmly faces great danger by leaping to her daughter's window and rescuing her from the burning house.

ASSESS

Answers

Critical Thinking

1. **Possible response:** Anna's leap to save her daughter's life may be the most surprising because her trapeze days are far behind her.
2. (a) Anna changes direction and grabs onto a wire. (b) If Anna had not acted in this way, she would have died.
3. (a) The narrator owes her birth to her mother and is later saved from a burning house by her.
   (b) **Possible response:** Only one of the three events actually involves the narrator; the first two help make her birth possible. One similarity is that all three represent choices her mother makes.
4. (a) The family's house is on fire. The narrator is trapped inside.
   (b) She realizes no one else can save her daughter. (c) **Possible response:** Qualities and ideas may include courage, strength, skill, and maternal love.

Is there a difference between reality and truth?

Possible response: The choices the narrator's mother has made lead the narrator to believe that a single decision can change the course of a person's life.

raise it wider and prop it up with the stick so it wouldn't crush her fingers. She swung down, caught the ledge, and crawled through the opening. Once she was in my room, I realized she had on only underclothing, a bra of the heavy stitched cotton women used to wear and step-in, lace-trimmed drawers. I remember feeling light-headed, of course, terribly relieved, and then embarrassed for her to be seen by the crowd undressed.

I was still embarrassed as we flew out the window, toward earth, me in her lap, her toes pointed as we skimmed toward the painted target of the fire fighter's net.

Literary Analysis
Plot How is the conflict resolved?

19 I know that she's right. I knew it even then. As you fall there is time to think. Curled as I was, against her stomach, I was not startled by the cries of the crowd or the looming faces. The wind roared and beat its hot breath at our back, the flames whistled. I slowly wondered what would happen if we missed the circle or bounced out of it. Then I wrapped my hands around my mother's hands. I felt the brush of her lips and heard the beat of her heart in my ears, loud as thunder, long as the roll of drums.

Critical Thinking

1. **Respond:** Which of the events in Anna's life surprised you the most? Why?
2. **(a)** What does Anna decide to do when the circus tent pole is struck by lightning? **(b) Interpret:** In what sense does the narrator owe her life to her mother's decision?
3. **(a)** Using details from the story, identify the two other ways in which the narrator owes her life to her mother.
   (b) Compare and Contrast: Compare the three ways in which the narrator owes her life to her mother. Identify at least one difference and one similarity among them.
4. **(a) Summarize:** Describe the scene at the end in which the mother leaps. **(b) Infer:** Why does the mother make the leap?
   (c) Discuss: In a group, discuss the qualities or ideas that the leap might represent. Choose one idea to share with the class.

Is there a difference between reality and truth?
In what ways is the narrator's view of reality shaped by the choices her mother has made?

Assessment Resources

Unit 1 Resources

L1 L2 EL **Selection Test A,** pp. 63–65. Administer Test A to less advanced readers and English learners.

L3 L4 **Selection Test B,** pp. 66–68. Administer Test B to on-level and more advanced students.

L3 L4 **Open-Book Test,** pp. 60–62. As an alternative, give the Open-Book test.

All **Customizable Test Bank**

All **Self-tests**
Students may prepare for the **Selection Test** by taking the **Self-test** online.

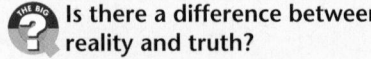

PHLit Online! All assessment resources are available at **www.PHLitOnline.com.**

After You Read — The Leap

Literary Analysis: Plot and Foreshadowing

1. What information about the mother is given in the **exposition?**
2. **(a)** Describe three events in the **rising action** that increase the tension in the **plot. (b)** Where does the story reach its **climax?** Explain.
3. What insight about the relationship between mother and daughter is presented in the **resolution** of the story?
4. Give two examples of **foreshadowing** in the story. Give one example of a **flashback.**

Reading Skill: Make Predictions

5. **(a)** Using a chart like the one shown, indicate how you used prior knowledge to **make a prediction** about the outcome of the story.

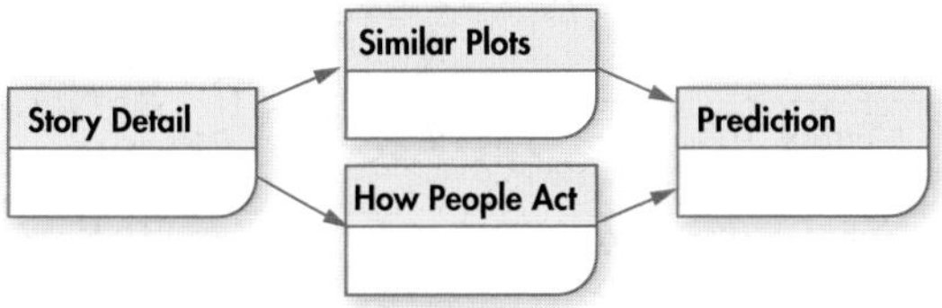

   (b) How close was your prediction to the actual outcome of the story? Explain your answer.

Vocabulary

Practice An **analogy** shows the relationship between pairs of words. Use a word from the vocabulary list for "The Leap," on page 44, to complete each analogy. Your choice should create a word pair that matches the relationship between the first two words given. Explain the relationship in each analogy.

1. happiness : cheerful :: insecurity : ___________
2. knowledge : teaching :: freedom : ___________
3. receiving : giving :: retreating : ___________
4. helps : aids :: honors : ___________
5. towering : small :: expansive : ___________
6. quickly : rapidly :: constantly : ___________

Word Study Use the context of the sentences and what you know about the **Latin root *-strict-*** to explain your answer to each question.

1. Would a *strict* parent have many or few rules?
2. How would a *constrictor* snake kill its prey?

Word Study

The **Latin root *-strict-*** means "confine" or "squeeze."

Challenge Explain how the root *-strict-* contributes to the meanings of these words. Consult a dictionary if necessary.

district
restrict
stricture

ASSESS/EXTEND

Answers

Literary Analysis

1. The mother is old and blind but still moves with "catlike precision."
2. (a) Rising action includes the deadly lightning strike, Anna falling in love with and marrying the narrator's father, and the fire. (b) The story's climax occurs when Anna leaps to save her daughter. This is the moment Anna's struggle to save her daughter reaches its peak.
3. **Possible response:** Students may say that the narrator's life is bound to her mother's.
4. Foreshadowing includes the mention of the "rebuilt" house in New Hampshire and the narrator's collection of a newspaper account of a circus tragedy. The story of the mother's leap on the trapeze is an example of a flashback.

Reading Skill

5. **Possible response:** (a) Story Detail: The Avalons are about to perform their blindfolded leap. Similar Plots: Details such as the reference to a storm and the narrator's claim that her mother saved her life foreshadow a disaster. How People Act: People who do dangerous things sometimes have accidents. Prediction: The storm will cause the stunt to go awry.
   (b) Students' predictions are likely to be fairly accurate because the major events in the plot are heavily foreshadowed.

   For other sample answers, see ***Graphic Organizer Transparencies*, Reading Skill Graphic Organizer A**, p. 7, and the **Additional Answers** section.

Vocabulary

Practice

1. tentative; adjective to describe the noun
2. extricating; verb to describe the action associated with the noun
3. encroaching; antonym
4. commemorates; synonym
5. constricting; antonym
6. perpetually; synonym

Word Study

1. The root *-strict-* means "confine," and *strict* means "exacting or confining in enforcing rules." A strict parent would have many rules that would be constantly enforced.
2. The root *-strict-* means "squeeze," and *constrictor* means "a snake with the ability to squeeze and suffocate its prey." It would kill its prey by wrapping its body tightly around its victim.

Word Study: Challenge

A *district* is a <u>confined</u> area. A *stricture* <u>confines</u> a person to certain behaviors. When you *restrict* something, you are holding it back or <u>confining</u> it.

Answers

Grammar

1. Introduce the skill, using the instruction on the student page.
2. Discuss the definitions and the chart.

Think Aloud: Model the Skill

Model the skill of using common and proper nouns correctly. Say to students:

> I find it easy to recognize proper nouns, because they are always capitalized. The capital letter signals that the noun refers to a specific person, place, or thing rather than any person, place, or thing of that kind. For example, *Cleveland* is the name of a particular place, but *city* is a general name for all such places.

WG Writing and Grammar, Grade 10

Students will find further instruction on and practice with common and proper nouns in Chapter 16, Section 1.

Practice A

1. Morris—proper; paw, monkey, pocket—common
2. Mr. White—proper; legend, money—common
3. Herbert—proper; job, parents, money, employers—common
4. Mrs. White, Herbert—proper; life, magic—common

Challenge

Sample answer: common nouns: supper, friend, door; proper nouns: India, Herbert, Morris

Practice B

Sample answer:

1. The narrator's mother was part of the trapeze act. Anna was part of the Flying Avalons.
2. The mother had traveled to many countries. Anna had traveled to Italy, Mexico, France, and Spain.
3. The storm that caused the circus tent to collapse occurred in the summer.
4. The narrator moved back to her hometown.

Challenge

Sample answer: My brother Danny plays baseball in Central Park.

Integrated Language Skills

The Monkey's Paw • The Leap

Grammar: Common Nouns and Proper Nouns

A **noun** is a word that names a person, a place, or a thing. A **common noun** refers to any one of a certain kind of person, place, or thing. A **proper noun** names a specific person, place, or thing. Proper nouns always begin with capital letters. Look at these examples:

Common Nouns	Proper Nouns
writer	Louise Erdrich, W. W. Jacobs
city	St. Louis, Nairobi
athlete	Derek Jeter, Venus Williams

Practice A Identify the nouns in each sentence, and indicate whether they are common nouns or proper nouns.

1. Morris kept the withered paw of a monkey in his pocket.
2. Mr. White believes the legend and wishes for money.
3. When Herbert is killed at his job, his parents receive money from his employers.
4. Mrs. White tries to bring Herbert back to life using magic.

Challenge In "The Monkey's Paw," find three common nouns and three proper nouns.

Practice B Underline the common nouns in the following sentences. Then, substitute a proper noun, if possible, to make the sentence more precise.

1. The narrator's mother was part of the trapeze act.
2. The mother had traveled to many countries.
3. The storm that caused the circus tent to collapse occurred in the summer.
4. The narrator moved back to her hometown.

Challenge Use this sentence as a model to write two sentences that include both common and proper nouns: *Anna's home in New Hampshire contains few mementos of her life in the circus.*

WG **Writing and Grammar Connection:** Chapter 16, Section 1

56 Fiction and Nonfiction

Extend the Lesson

Sentence Modeling

Choose the sentence given from the selection students have read:

> "Sounds like the *Arabian Nights*," said Mrs. White, as she rose and began to set the supper. ("The Monkey's Paw")
>
> The Mysterious Bernie folded himself into a painted cracker tin, and the Lady of the Mists made herself appear and disappear in surprising places. ("The Leap")

Ask students what they notice about the sentence. Elicit from them that at least one noun is a proper noun. Then, ask what else they notice. ("The Monkey's Paw": the italicized proper noun is also the title of a collection of stories. "The Leap": proper nouns add detail to the circus acts, making the setting seem more real.)

Have students imitate the sentence in a sentence on a topic of their own choosing, matching each grammatical and stylistic feature discussed. Collect the sentences, and share them with the class.

Writing

Write a brief **sequel** to the story you read. For example, if you read "The Monkey's Paw," write about what might happen if someone else finds the paw. If you read "The Leap," develop a description of the mother's next daring rescue.

- Use a plot outline or map to plan the details for your story.
- As you draft and revise, work to capture the author's writing style. Use descriptive details to create an appropriate tone for the story.
- Use foreshadowing to build suspense.
- Add information in a flashback to help explain the characters' present actions.

Writing Workshop: *Work in Progress*

Prewriting for Autobiographical Narrative To prepare for a narrative you may write later, develop a list of places that you have visited. Next to each item, list three words or names you associate with the place. Keep this Place List in your writing portfolio for later development.

Use this prewriting activity to prepare for the Writing Workshop on page 108.

Listening and Speaking

In a small group, conduct an **interview** between a journalist and some of the characters in the story you read.

- If you read "The Monkey's Paw," prepare an interview between a journalist and the Whites after the tragedy. Plan questions that will focus the Whites' retelling of the story.
- If you read "The Leap," prepare an interview between a journalist who is writing about circus families and the narrator. Plan questions that help the narrator retell the main events of the story.

Follow these steps while role-playing the interview:

- **Make notes of responses** to specific interview questions.
- **Respond appropriately to questions.**
- **Demonstrate a knowledge of the subject or organization** through the questions asked and the responses given.

After the interview, prepare an evaluation of the presentation. Discuss which questions and responses were most effective, using **language that conveys maturity and respect. Compile and report your responses.** Then, have each team member offer one suggestion for improving the interview.

PHLit Online!
www.PHLitOnline.com
- Interactive graphic organizers
- Grammar tutorial
- Interactive journals

EXTEND/ASSESS

Answers

Writing

1. Review the assignment, using the instruction on the student page.
2. To give students guidance for writing a sequel, give them the **Support for Writing**, p. 58 in ***Unit 1 Resources.***
3. To evaluate students' sequels, use the Short Story rubrics, pp. 226–227 in ***Professional Development Guidebook.***

Six Traits Focus

✔	Ideas	✔	Word Choice
✔	Organization		Sentence Fluency
✔	Voice		Conventions

Writing and Grammar, Grade 10

Students will find additional instruction on short-story writing in Chapter 5.

Writing Workshop
Work in Progress

Have students save their completed Place Lists in their portfolios. They will use them later as they continue this Work-in-Progress assignment (see p. 101). The assignment prepares them to complete the Writing Workshop (see pp. 108–113).

Listening and Speaking

1. Review the assignment, using the instruction on the student page.
2. Have students complete the **Support for Extend Your Learning** page (***Unit 1 Resources,*** p. 59).

Teaching Resources

Unit 1 Resources

L3 L4 **Integrated Language Skills: Grammar,** p. 57

L3 L4 **Support for Writing,** p. 58

L3 L4 **Support for Extend Your Learning,** p. 59

L4 **Enrichment,** pp. 38, 56

Enriched Online Student Edition

Available under After You Read for this selection:

All **Interactive Grammar Tutorial**

L3 L4 **Internet Research Activity**

Professional Development Guidebook

Rubrics for Short Story, pp. 226–227.

PHLit Online! All print and digital resources are available online at **www.PHLitOnline.com.** Online resources accessible to students are noted on the student page.

TIME AND RESOURCE MANAGER

from *Swimming to Antarctica* • Occupation: Conductorette

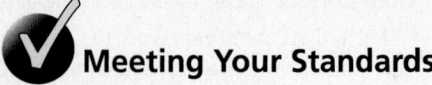

Lesson Pacing Guide

DAY 1 Preteach

- Administer the Reading and Vocabulary Warm-ups (*Unit 1 Resources*, pp. 69–72 or 87–90) as necessary.
- Introduce the Reading Skill: Make Predictions FT
- Introduce the Literary Analysis concept: Author's Perspective FT
- Distribute copies of the appropriate graphic organizer for the Reading Skill (*Graphic Organizer Transparencies*, pp. 9–11). CRI
- Distribute copies of the appropriate graphic organizer for Literary Analysis (*Graphic Organizer Transparencies*, pp. 12–14). CRI
- Teach the selection vocabulary. FT CRI
- Introduce the Word Study skill.

DAYS 2–3 Preteach/Teach

- Build background with the Background feature. CRI
- Develop thematic vocabulary and thematic thinking with Writing About the Big Question.
- Prepare students to read with the Activating Prior Knowledge activities (TE). CRI
- Informally monitor comprehension while students read. FT
- Use the Reading Check questions to confirm comprehension.
- Develop students' ability to predict what will happen next using the Reading Skill questions. CRI
- Develop students' understanding of author's perspective using the Literary Analysis questions. CRI
- Reinforce vocabulary with the Vocabulary notes. CRI

DAY 4 Assess

- Assess students' comprehension and mastery of the skills by having them answer the Critical Thinking, Reading Skill, and Literary Analysis questions. FT
- Have students complete the Vocabulary Practice activities. FT
- Have students complete the Word Study activities.

DAY 5 Extend/Assess

- Have students complete the Grammar lesson. CRI
- Have students complete the Writing activity and write a description. (You may assign as homework.) FT
- Extend learning by having students complete the Research and Technology activity *A Daily Observation Journal*. (You may assign as homework.) As an alternative, assign them "Going to Extremes" or "Women's Wage Gap" in *Reality Central*. CRI
- Administer Selection Test A or B (*Unit 1 Resources*, pp. 81–86 or 102–107). FT

The selection from Swimming to Antarctica is an unedited excerpt from a book-length memoir. "Occupation: Conductorette" is an excerpt from a memoir, edited for sensitivity issues.

Meeting Your Standards

Students will

1. **analyze and respond to literary elements.**
   - **Literary Analysis: Author's Perspective**
2. **read, comprehend, and analyze autobiographies.**
   - **Reading Skill: Make Predictions**
   - **Reading Check questions**
   - **Apply the Skills questions**
   - **Assessment Practice**
3. **develop vocabulary.**
   - **Vocabulary**
   - **Word Study**
4. **apply grammar skills.**
   - **Abstract and Concrete Nouns**
5. **Develop writing proficiency.**
   - **Work in Progress: Autobiographical Narrative**
   - **description**
6. **strengthen research and technology skills.**
   - **daily observation journal**

CRI For a full explanation of Culturally Responsive Instruction opportunities in this lesson, see p. T86–T87.

FT For an accelerated lesson, use the Fast Track strategies and activities.

Managing Differentiated Instruction

This leveled selection pairing groups a more accessible with a more challenging selection. Choose either one to teach the lesson skills. For classroom management suggestions for using the pairing in a mixed-ability class, see pp. T68–T69.

Daily Block Scheduling

Each day in this Lesson Pacing Guide represents a 40–50 minute period. Teachers using block scheduling may combine days to revise pacing. In addition, teachers may differentiate and support core instruction by integrating components for extended and intensive support as students require. See the Guide to Selected Leveled Resources (facing page).

Guide to Selected Leveled Resources

EL English Learners

			from *Swimming to Antarctica*	Occupation: Conductorette
CORE COURSE	*Unit 1 Resources*	Selection Test A	pp. 81–83	pp. 102–104
	Graphic Organizer Transparencies	Reading Skill Graphic Organizer A	p. 9	p. 10
		Literary Analysis Graphic Organizer A	p. 12	p. 13
EXTENDED SUPPORT (Level 2)	*Unit 1 Resources*	Reading and Vocabulary Warm-ups A or B	pp. 69–72	pp. 87–90
	Reader's Notebook: English Learner's Version		adapted instruction and adapted selection	adapted instruction and summary
	Hear It! Audio CD		selection and summaries	selection and summaries
	Hear It! Audio CD (adapted text)		adapted selection and summaries	—
INTENSIVE SUPPORT (Level 1)	*Reality Central*		"Going to Extremes"	"Women's Wage Gap"
	Real-World Writing Journal		Lesson 3, pp. 10–13	Lesson 4, pp. 14–17

L2 Below-Level Students

			from *Swimming to Antarctica*	Occupation: Conductorette
CORE COURSE	*Unit 1 Resources*	Selection Test A	pp. 81–83	pp. 102–104
	Graphic Organizer Transparencies	Reading Skill Graphic Organizer A	p. 9	p. 10
		Literary Analysis Graphic Organizer A	p. 12	p. 13
EXTENDED SUPPORT (Level 2)	*Unit 1 Resources*	Reading and Vocabulary Warm-ups A or B	pp. 69–72	pp. 87–90
	Reader's Notebook		adapted instruction and full selection	adapted instruction and summary
	Hear It! Audio CD		selection and summaries	selection and summaries
INTENSIVE SUPPORT (Level 1)	*Reality Central*		"Going to Extremes"	"Women's Wage Gap"
	Real-World Writing Journal		Lesson 3, pp. 10–13	Lesson 4, pp. 14–17
	Reading Kit		Reteaching worksheets	Reteaching worksheets

L1 Special Needs Students

			from *Swimming to Antarctica*	Occupation: Conductorette
CORE COURSE	*Unit 1 Resources*	Selection Test A	pp. 81–83	pp. 102–104
	Graphic Organizer Transparencies	Reading Skill Graphic Organizer A	p. 9	p. 10
		Literary Analysis Graphic Organizer A	p. 12	p. 13
EXTENDED SUPPORT (Level 2)	*Unit 1 Resources*	Reading and Vocabulary Warm-ups A or B	pp. 69–72	pp. 87–90
	Reader's Notebook: Adapted Version		adapted instruction and adapted selection	adapted instruction and summary
	Hear It! Audio CD (adapted text)		adapted selection and summaries	—
INTENSIVE SUPPORT (Level 1)	*Reality Central*		"Going to Extremes"	"Women's Wage Gap"
	Real-World Writing Journal		Lesson 3, pp. 10–13	Lesson 4, pp. 14–17
	Reading Kit		Reteaching worksheets	Reteaching worksheets

The program includes resources for these students: L3 On-Level L4 Advanced All All
For a complete guide to selection support, see pp. T106–T108.

NOTE: All print materials are also available online at *www.PHLitOnline.com.*

VISUAL GUIDE to Featured Selection Resources

• from *Swimming to Antarctica*
• Occupation: Conductorette

RESOURCES FOR:

- EL English Learners
- L1 Special Needs Students
- L2 Below-Level Students
- L3 On-Level Students
- L4 Advanced Students
- All All Students

Vocabulary/Fluency/Prior Knowledge

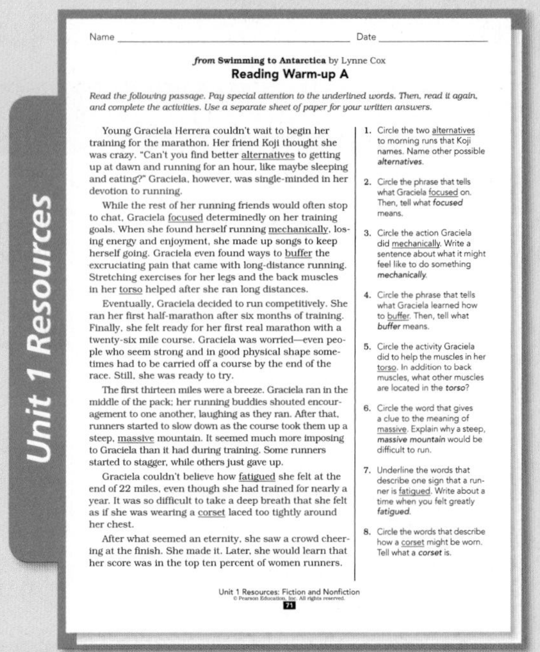

Unit 1 Resources

Name ______________________ Date ______________

***from* Swimming to Antarctica** by Lynne Cox
Reading Warm-up A

Read the following passage. Pay special attention to the underlined words. Then, read it again, and complete the activities. Use a separate sheet of paper for your written answers.

Young Graciela Herrera couldn't wait to begin her training for the marathon. Her friend Koji thought she was crazy. "Can't you find better alternatives to getting up at dawn and running for an hour, like maybe sleeping and eating?" Graciela, however, was single-minded in her devotion to running.

While the rest of her running friends would often stop to chat, Graciela focused determinedly on her training goals. When she found herself running mechanically, losing energy and enjoyment, she made up songs to keep herself going. Graciela even found ways to buffer the excruciating pain that came with long-distance running. Stretching exercises for her legs and the back muscles in her torso helped after she ran long distances.

Eventually, Graciela decided to run competitively. She ran her first half-marathon after six months of training. Finally, she felt ready for her first real marathon with a twenty-six mile course. Graciela was worried—even people who seem strong and in good physical shape sometimes had to be carried off a course by the end of the race. Still, she was ready to try.

The first thirteen miles were a breeze. Graciela ran in the middle of the pack; her running buddies shouted encouragement to one another, laughing as they ran. After that, runners started to slow down as the course took them up a steep, massive mountain. It seemed much more imposing to Graciela than it had during training. Some runners started to stagger, while others just gave up.

Graciela couldn't believe how fatigued she felt at the end of 22 miles, even though she had trained for nearly a year. It was so difficult to take a deep breath that she felt as if she was wearing a corset laced too tightly around her chest.

After what seemed an eternity, she saw a crowd cheering at the finish. She made it. Later, she would learn that her score was in the top ten percent of women runners.

1. Circle the two alternatives to morning runs that Koji names. Name other possible *alternatives*.
2. Circle the phrase that tells what Graciela focused on. Then, tell what *focused* means.
3. Circle the action Graciela did mechanically. Write a sentence about what it might feel like to do something *mechanically*.
4. Circle the phrase that tells what Graciela learned how to buffer. Then, tell what *buffer* means.
5. Circle the activity Graciela did to help the muscles in her torso. In addition to back muscles, what other muscles are located in the *torso*?
6. Circle the word that gives a clue to the meaning of massive. Explain why a steep, *massive mountain* would be difficult to run.
7. Underline the words that describe one sign that a runner is fatigued. Write about a time when you felt greatly *fatigued*.
8. Circle the words that describe how a corset might be worn. Tell what a *corset* is.

Unit 1 Resources: Fiction and Nonfiction
© Pearson Education, Inc. All rights reserved.
71

L2 **Reading Warm-ups A and B, pp. 71–72, 89–90**

Also available for these selections:

- EL L1 L2 **Vocabulary Warm-ups A and B, pp. 69–70, 87–88**
- All **Vocabulary Builder, pp. 76, 94**
- All **Writing About the Big Question, pp. 73, 91**

Reader's Notebooks

Pre- and postreading pages for both selections, as well as the selection from *Swimming to Antarctica*, appear in an interactive format in the *Reader's Notebooks*. Each *Notebook* is differentiated for a different group of learners. The selections in the Adapted and English Learner's versions are abridged.

L2 L3 ***Reader's Notebook***

L1 ***Reader's Notebook: Adapted Version***

EL ***Reader's Notebook: English Learner's Version***

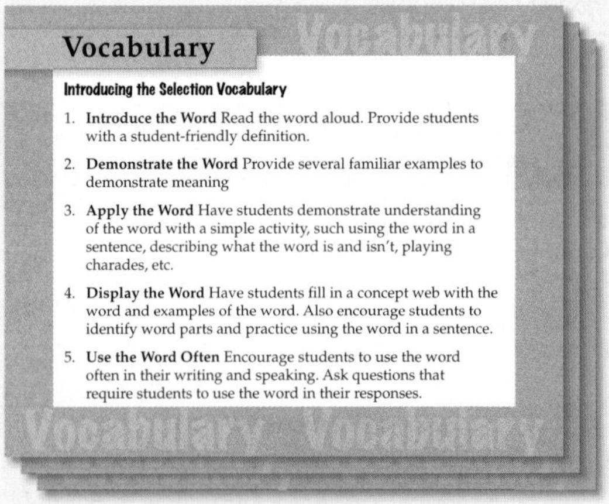

Vocabulary

Introducing the Selection Vocabulary

1. **Introduce the Word** Read the word aloud. Provide students with a student-friendly definition.
2. **Demonstrate the Word** Provide several familiar examples to demonstrate meaning
3. **Apply the Word** Have students demonstrate understanding of the word with a simple activity, such using the word in a sentence, describing what the word is and isn't, playing charades, etc.
4. **Display the Word** Have students fill in a concept web with the word and examples of the word. Also encourage students to identify word parts and practice using the word in a sentence.
5. **Use the Word Often** Encourage students to use the word often in their writing and speaking. Ask questions that require students to use the word in their responses.

Classroom Strategies and Teaching Routines

- core classroom routines outlined step-by-step
- convenient format for easy reference while teaching

Selection Support

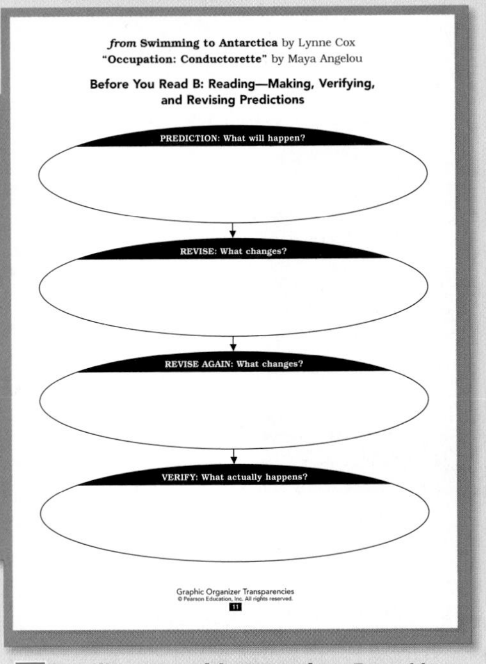

from **Swimming to Antarctica** by Lynne Cox
"Occupation: Conductorette" by Maya Angelou

Before You Read B: Reading—Making, Verifying, and Revising Predictions

PREDICTION: What will happen?

REVISE: What changes?

REVISE AGAIN: What changes?

VERIFY: What actually happens?

Graphic Organizer Transparencies

11

Graphic Organizer Transparencies

L3 Reading: Graphic Organizer B, p. 11

Also available for these selections:

EL L1 L2 Reading: Graphic Organizer A, pp. 9, 10 (partially filled in)

EL L1 L2 Literary Analysis: Graphic Organizer A pp. 12, 13 (partially filled in)

L3 Literary Analysis: Graphic Organizer B p. 14

Skills Development/Extension

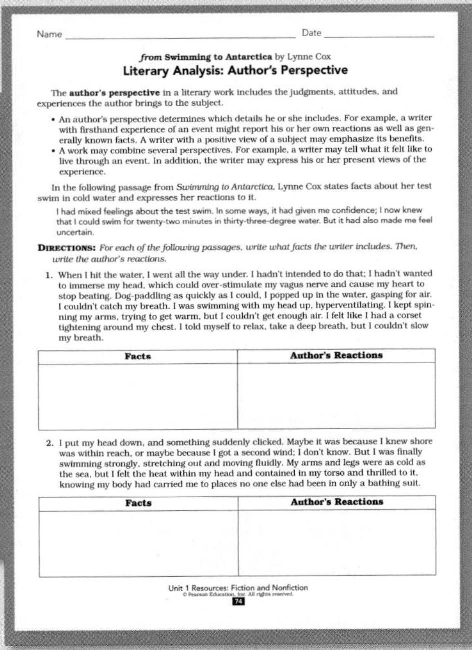

Name ______________________ Date ____________

from **Swimming to Antarctica** by Lynne Cox
Literary Analysis: Author's Perspective

The **author's perspective** in a literary work includes the judgments, attitudes, and experiences the author brings to the subject.

- An author's perspective determines which details he or she includes. For example, a writer with firsthand experience of an event might report his or her own reactions as well as generally known facts. A writer with a positive view of a subject may emphasize its benefits.
- A work may combine several perspectives. For example, a writer may tell what it felt like to live through an event. In addition, the writer may express his or her present views of the experience.

In the following passage from *Swimming to Antarctica*, Lynne Cox states facts about her test swim in cold water and expresses her reactions to it.

I had mixed feelings about the test swim. In some ways, it had given me confidence; I now knew that I could swim for twenty-two minutes in thirty-three-degree water. But it had also made me feel uncertain.

Directions: *For each of the following passages, write what facts the writer includes. Then, write the author's reactions.*

1. When I hit the water, I went all the way under. I hadn't intended to do that; I hadn't wanted to immerse my head, which could over-stimulate my vagus nerve and cause my heart to stop beating. Dog-paddling as quickly as I could, I popped up in the water, gasping for air. I couldn't catch my breath. I was swimming with my head up, hyperventilating. I kept spinning my arms, trying to get warm, but I couldn't get enough air. I felt like I had a corset tightening around my chest. I told myself to relax, take a deep breath, but I couldn't slow my breath.

Facts	Author's Reactions

2. I put my head down, and something suddenly clicked. Maybe it was because I knew shore was within reach, or maybe because I got a second wind; I don't know. But I was finally swimming strongly, stretching out and moving fluidly. My arms and legs were as cold as the sea, but I felt the heat within my head and contained in my torso and thrilled to it, knowing my body had carried me to places no one else had been in only a bathing suit.

Facts	Author's Reactions

Unit 1 Resources: Fiction and Nonfiction

74

Unit 1 Resources

All Literary Analysis: Author's Perspective, pp. 74, 92

Also available for these selections:

All Reading: Make Predictions, pp. 75, 93

L4 Enrichment, pp. 77, 95

L3 L4 Grammar, p. 96

L3 L4 Support for Writing, p. 97

L3 L4 Support for Extend Your Learning, p. 98

Assessment

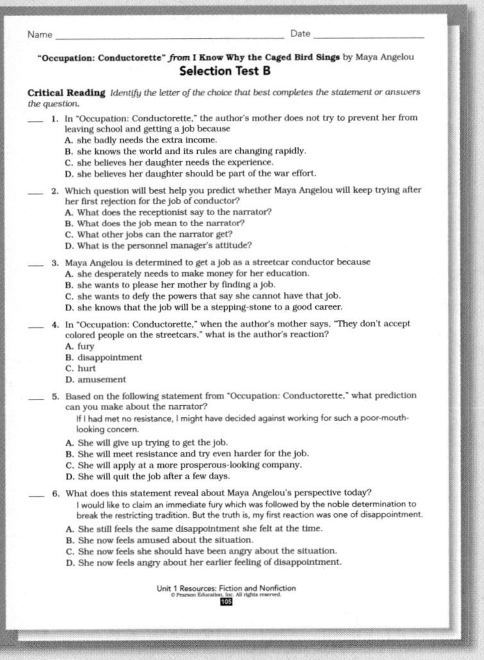

Name ______________________ Date ____________

"Occupation: Conductorette" *from* **I Know Why the Caged Bird Sings** by Maya Angelou
Selection Test B

Critical Reading *Identify the letter of the choice that best completes the statement or answers the question.*

___ 1. In "Occupation: Conductorette," the author's mother does not try to prevent her from leaving school and getting a job because
A. she badly needs the extra income.
B. she knows the world and its rules are changing rapidly.
C. she believes her daughter needs the experience.
D. she believes her daughter should be part of the war effort.

___ 2. Which question will best help you predict whether Maya Angelou will keep trying after her first rejection for the job of conductor?
A. What does the receptionist say to the narrator?
B. What does the job mean to the narrator?
C. What other jobs can the narrator get?
D. What is the personnel manager's attitude?

___ 3. Maya Angelou is determined to get a job as a streetcar conductor because
A. she desperately needs to make money for her education.
B. she wants to please her mother by finding a job.
C. she wants to defy the powers that say she cannot have that job.
D. she knows that the job will be a stepping-stone to a good career.

___ 4. In "Occupation: Conductorette," when the author's mother says, "They don't accept colored people on the streetcars," what is the author's reaction?
A. fury
B. disappointment
C. hurt
D. amusement

___ 5. Based on the following statement from "Occupation: Conductorette," what prediction can you make about the narrator?
If I had met no resistance, I might have decided against working for such a poor-mouth-looking concern.
A. She will give up trying to get the job.
B. She will meet resistance and try even harder for the job.
C. She will apply at a more prosperous-looking company.
D. She will quit the job after a few days.

___ 6. What does this statement reveal about Maya Angelou's perspective today?
I would like to claim an immediate fury which was followed by the noble determination to break the restricting tradition. But the truth is, my first reaction was one of disappointment.
A. She still feels the same disappointment she felt at the time.
B. She now feels amused about the situation.
C. She now feels she should have been angry about the situation.
D. She now feels angry about her earlier feeling of disappointment.

Unit 1 Resources: Fiction and Nonfiction

105

L3 L4 Selection Test B, pp. 84–86, 105–107

Also available for these selections:

EL L1 L2 Selection Test A, pp. 81–83, 102–104

L3 L4 Open-Book Test, pp. 78–80, 99–101

PHLit Online!
www.PHLitOnline.com

- complete narrated selection text
- a thematically related video with writing prompt
- an interactive graphic organizer
- highlighting feature
- access to all student print resources, adapted to individual student needs
- Spanish and English summaries

Get Connected Video
Instructions
Watch the video. Then, use your journal to respond to the prompt at the end of the clip.

Get Connected! (thematic video with writing prompt)

Also available:

Background video

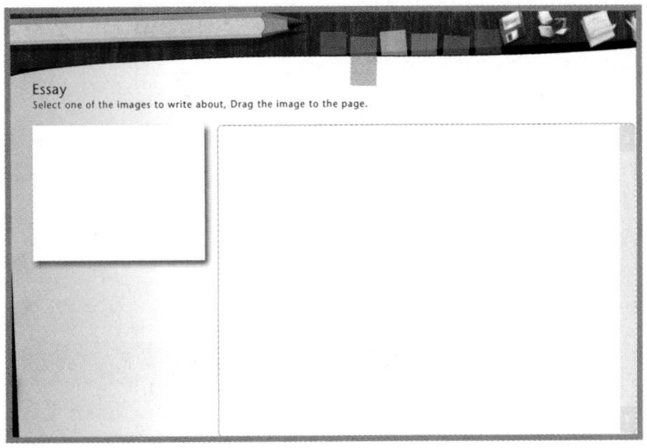
Essay
Select one of the images to write about. Drag the image to the page.

Writer's Journal (with graphics feature)

Also available:

Vocabulary Central (tools, activities, and songs for studying vocabulary)

❶ Selection Choices

You may use either the selection *Swimming to Antarctica* or "Occupation: Conductorette" to meet the lesson standards. Skills instruction for both selections appears on p. 59. Choose one selection to teach (or choose to teach both). The Accessibility at a Glance chart at the bottom of this page will help you determine which of the two selections is more appropriate for your students.

❷ Selection Skills

1. With the class, preview the selection skills. (The lesson meets the lesson objectives given on p. 58a.)
2. Explain that students will develop the skill of making predictions (introduced on p. 29) as they read to better understand and enjoy the selection you choose. By examining the author's perspective as they read, they will gain deeper insight into the selection.
3. To introduce the Writing and Research and Technology activities (p. 87), tell students that when they have finished reading the selection, they will write a brief description of a scene and keep a daily observation journal related to the selection.
3. Tell students that they will also study a grammar concept: abstract and concrete nouns. By mastering this concept, they will improve their reading fluency and the quality of their own writing.

Before You Read

from Swimming to Antarctica • Occupation: Conductorette

❶ Selection Choices

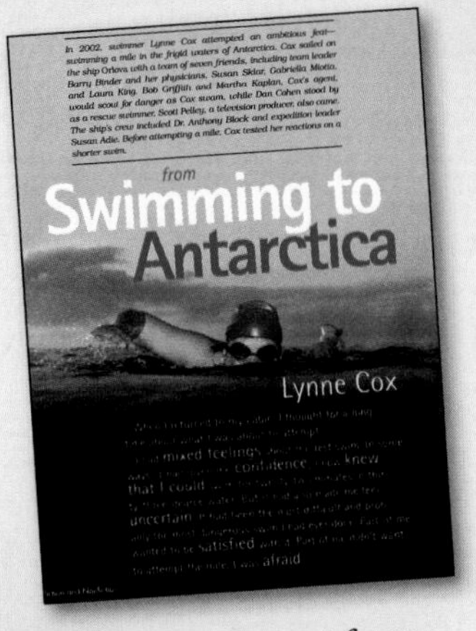

▲ Read the excerpt from ***Swimming to Antarctica*** to find out how one woman's fierce determination helps her complete a dangerous swim.

▲ Read **"Occupation: Conductorette"** to see how a young girl's persistence helps her when she is faced with discrimination.

❷ Selection Skills Guide

Practice these skills with either the excerpt from ***Swimming to Antarctica*** (p. 62) or **"Occupation: Conductorette"** (p. 78).

- Identify the author's perspective
- Make predictions
- Ask questions to revise and verify predictions
- Identify abstract and concrete nouns
- Write a brief description
- Keep a daily observation journal

Differentiated Instruction for Universal Access

Accessibility at a Glance: Selection Choices

	from Swimming to Antarctica	Occupation: Conductorette	
Context	Record-breaking swim	Fight against prejudice	Because a number of factors determine the relative accessibility of paired selections, in some cases the Lexile rating of the more challenging selection will be lower than that of the more accessible selection.
Language/ Vocabulary	• Conversational • Scientific terms defined • Below-level vocabulary	• Some complicated syntax • Grade-appropriate vocabulary	
Concept Level	Accessible (pushing oneself in a sport)	Challenging (understanding segregation)	
Literary Merit	Fast-paced, factual account	Prize-winning author	
Lexile/Length	Lexile: 850L Word Count: 4,483	Lexile: 1050L Word Count: 1,946	
Overall Rating	**More accessible**	**More challenging**	

❸ Literary Analysis: Author's Perspective

The **author's perspective** in a literary work includes the judgments, attitudes, and experiences the author brings to the subject. An author's perspective determines which details he or she includes, as in these examples:

- A writer with firsthand experience of an event might report his or her own reactions as well as generally known facts.
- A writer with a positive view of a subject may emphasize its benefits.

A work may combine several perspectives. For example, a writer may tell what it felt like to live through an event. In addition, the writer may express his or her present views of the experience. As you read, look for details that suggest the author's perspective.

PHLit Online!
www.PHLitOnline.com

Hear It!
- Selection summary audio
- Selection audio

See It!
- Get Connected video
- Background video
- More about the author
- Vocabulary flashcards

Do It!
- Interactive journals
- Interactive graphic organizers
- Self-test
- Internet activity
- Grammar tutorial
- Interactive vocabulary games

❹ Reading Skill: Make Predictions

As you read, **make predictions,** or develop ideas, about what will happen next. These predictions can be based on details in the text combined with your own background and experiences. You can check your predictions as you read.

- **Revise,** or adjust, your predictions as you gather more information.
- **Verify,** or confirm, predictions by comparing the outcome you predicted to the actual outcome.

To help you make, verify, and revise predictions, **ask questions** such as "Why did that happen?" and "What will be the result?"

❺ Using the Strategy: Prediction Chart

Record your questions on a **prediction chart** like this one.

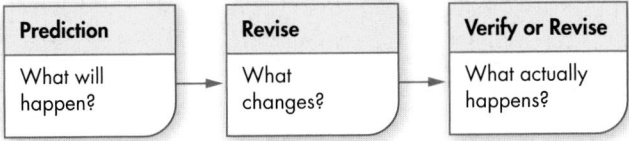

Prediction
What will happen?
→
Revise
What changes?
→
Verify or Revise
What actually happens?

PRETEACH

❸ Literary Analysis

1. Introduce the skill, using the instruction on the student page.
2. Tell students that they will examine the author's perspective as they read.

Think Aloud: Model the Skill

Model the skill of determining the author's perspective, using the following "think aloud":

I know that the details an author includes in a work reflect his or her personal beliefs, judgments, and attitudes. If a writer lists all of the things she hated during her first year at college, I know that she is giving her perspective from that time: She didn't like school. If she then tells me how valuable the experience turned out to be, I realize that she is sharing her present perspective.

❹ Reading Skill

1. Introduce the skill, using the instruction on the student page.
2. Tell students that they will practice making predictions as they read.

Think Aloud: Model the Skill

Model the skill of making predictions, using the following "think aloud":

Suppose a snowstorm is approaching. I can ask myself: *What will happen if I drive home during the snowstorm?* I predict that it will take me longer than usual to get home. When I arrive home and check the time, I verify whether or not my prediction matches the actual outcome.

I can follow these steps as I read. First, I make a prediction about what will happen by asking myself questions; then, I revise my prediction as I have more information; finally, I confirm my prediction by comparing it to the actual outcome.

❺ Using the Strategy

Give students a copy of either **Reading Skill Graphic Organizer A** or **B** (*Graphic Organizer Transparencies,* pp. 9–11) to record predictions as they read. Use the examples in **Graphic Organizer A,** which is partially filled in, to model the process of completing the organizer.

Differentiated Instruction for Universal Access

Preparing Students for the More Challenging Selection

If you wish to prepare lower level readers to read "Occupation: Conductorette," the more challenging selection, follow these steps:

- Review strategies for reading sentences with complicated syntax. When students have difficulty understanding a sentence, guide them to identify the subject and predicate of the sentence first. Reading the sentence aloud can also help them recognize a sentence's meaning more clearly.
- Point out that the story is told from the first-person point of view, interspersing the narrator's thoughts as an adult with her thoughts as a teenager. Direct students to page 80, and have them read the paragraphs describing the narrator's reaction to her mother's news that African Americans were not permitted to work as conductorettes. Guide them in distinguishing the adult Angelou's perspective from that of her teenage self.

PRETEACH

❶ Writing About the Big Question

1. Review the assignment with the class.
2. Point out that truth and reality might vary depending on a person's perspective and background.
3. Have students compete the sentence starter. Review responses as a class.
(**Possible response:** Facing <u>uncertainty</u> about your ability to accomplish a difficult task is an opportunity to prove yourself and overcome adversity.)
4. Remind students that their answers will help them think about the Big Question, "Is there a difference between reality and truth?"

While You Read

Tell students that as they read, they should look for details that show the realities Cox faces while she swims.

❷ Vocabulary

1. Have students preview the selection vocabulary.
2. For each word, have students say the word aloud.
3. Then, use the word in a sentence that defines the word.
4. Finally, repeat your definitional sentence or a similar sentence with the word missing and have the class "fill in the blank" chorally. Here are some examples:

Something <u>prolonged</u> is stretched out or extended. When our cat returned after six weeks, we wondered about its [students say "prolonged"] *absence.*

<u>Equilibrium</u> is the same as balance. Tightrope walkers need to maintain their [students say "equilibrium"].

❸ Word Study

1. Introduce the skill, using the instruction in the box.
2. Ask students to think of other words that contain the Latin prefix *pro-*. (**Sample answers:** *protect, propose, prologue*) Define them together as a class.

Making Connections | *from* Swimming to Antarctica

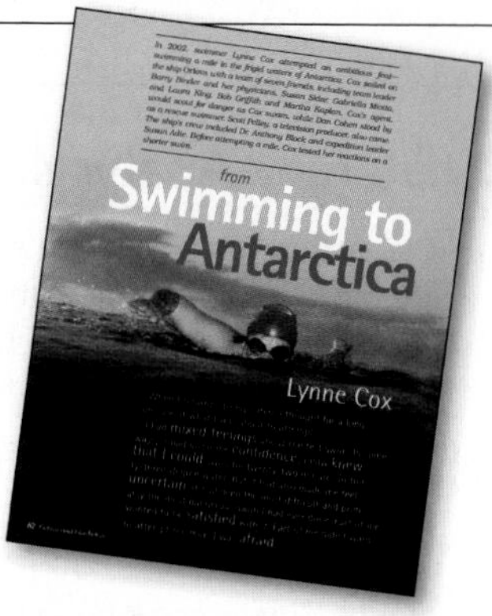

Is there a difference between *reality* and *truth?*

❶ Writing About the Big Question

In the excerpt from *Swimming to Antarctica,* a swimmer discovers how hard she can push her body to achieve a remarkable goal. Use this sentence starter to develop your ideas abut the Big Question.

Facing **uncertainty** about your ability to accomplish a difficult task is an opportunity to ________________________.

While You Read Look for details that reveal the realities Cox faces during her swim.

❷ Vocabulary

Read each word and its definition. Decide whether you know the word well, know it a little bit, or do not know it at all. After you read, see how your knowledge of each word has increased.

- **venturing** (ven′ chər iŋ) *v.* attempting to do something that involves taking risks (p. 63) ***The astronauts will be <u>venturing</u> into space next Tuesday.*** *adventure n. venture n. venturesome adj.*
- **prolonged** (prō lôŋd′) *adj.* extended; lengthy (p. 65) ***His <u>prolonged</u> absence is due to serious illness.*** *prolong v.*
- **equilibrium** (ē′ kwi lib′ rē əm) *n.* a state of balance (p. 68) ***See how well she keeps her <u>equilibrium</u> while walking on the balance beam!*** *equilibrate v.*
- **abruptly** (ə brupt′ lē) *adv. happening suddenly; unexpectedly (p. 68)* ***The diner <u>abruptly</u> stood up and ran from the restaurant.*** *abrupt adj. abruptness n.*
- **gauge** (gāj) *v.* measure something's size, amount, extent or capacity (p. 70) ***Use the map to <u>gauge</u> the distance between the two museums.*** *gauge n.*
- **buffer** (buf′ ər) *v.* lessen a shock; cushion (p. 73) ***A helmet helps <u>buffer</u> the impact of a fall.*** *buffer n.*

❸ Word Study

The **Latin prefix *pro-*** means "forth" or "forward."

In this story, the narrator endures **prolonged** exposure, or an extended amount of time, to water that is freezing.

Vocabulary Development

Vocabulary Knowledge Rating

Create a **Vocabulary Knowledge Rating Chart** (***Professional Development Guidebook,*** p. 33) for this selection. Include the selection vocabulary from this page and the Big Question words that appear in the Writing About the Big Question sentence frame on this page. (The Big Question vocabulary is introduced on pp. 2–3.)

Give students a copy of the chart. Read the words aloud, and have students mark their rating in the Before Reading column. Urge them to be alert to these words as they read and discuss the selection.

Tally how many students think they know a word to gauge how much instruction to provide. As students read and discuss the selection, point out the words and their context.

PHLit Online! **Vocabulary Central**, featuring tools, activities, and songs for studying vocabulary, is available at **www.PHLitOnline.com.**

Meet Lynne Cox

(b. 1957)

Raised in California, Lynne Cox got started breaking records when she was young. At age fourteen, she swam twenty-six miles from Catalina Island to the California coast. The next year, she broke the men's and the women's records swimming the English Channel.

Made to Swim Cox has a high percentage of body fat, evenly distributed around her body. This fat helps her float and provides insulation. Her unique body has allowed her to swim in waters ranging from the Bering Strait to Antarctica. Today, Lynne Cox stands as the most successful cold-water long-distance swimmer ever.

DID YOU KNOW?

During her swim around the Cape of Good Hope, Cox was chased by a shark.

Author of

Swimming to Antarctica

❹ **BACKGROUND FOR THE AUTOBIOGRAPHY**

Cold-Water Swimming

Swimming in frigid water, as Lynne Cox does, puts great stress on the body. The body's core—the heart, lungs, and brain—must stay warm or normal muscle and brain function will be impaired, a condition called *hypothermia.* Water temperatures as "warm" as forty-four degrees Fahrenheit would kill most swimmers.

Daily Bellringer

For each class during which you will teach this selection, have students complete one of the five Sentence Modeling activities for Week 2 in the ***Daily Bellringer Activities*** booklet.

❹ Background

Cold-Water Swimming

Hypothermia is a dangerous reaction of the body to exposure to cold. In this condition, blood stops flowing to the body's surface. As a result, body temperature drops dramatically. This is a dangerous condition, and, as Lynne Cox explains, it can cause permanent damage even in the young and fit. The treatment for hypothermia is to slowly raise the body's temperature again, allowing normal blood flow to resume.

Interestingly, hypothermia does have medical uses. The shutting off of blood flow can reduce bleeding. Doctors may induce hypothermia as an aid for some types of surgery.

Multidraft Reading

This icon ● marks natural pauses in the selection. To assist struggling readers and to deepen reading for all, assign the text in "chunks," following the icons, and apply multidraft reading protocols. For each reading, have students set the purpose indicated:

- **First reading**—literal comprehension: answering the Reading Check questions.
- **Second reading**—application of skills: answering the Make Predictions and Author's Perspective prompts.
- **Third reading**—interpretation: answering the end-of-selection questions.

For more guidance, refer to the ***Classroom Strategies and Teaching Routines*** card on multidraft reading.

Differentiated Instruction — Additional Instruction

EL Extended Support—English Learners

Have students complete the **Reading and Vocabulary Warm-Ups, *Unit 1 Resources,*** pp. 69–72, before they read. Assign the prereading pages and the adapted selection in the ***Reader's Notebook: English Learner's Version.*** Then, have students listen to portions of the selection on the ***Hear It!* Audio CD.**

L1 L2 Extended Support—Struggling Readers

Have students complete the **Reading and Vocabulary Warm-ups, *Unit 1 Resources,*** pp. 69–72, before they read. Assign the prereading pages and the adapted selection in the ***Reader's Notebook: Adapted Version.*** Then, have students listen to portions of the selection on the ***Hear It!* Audio CD** (adapted text).

Extended Support—Reluctant Readers

To build motivation and engagement before assigning the selection, have students read "Going to Extremes," a thematically related selection in ***Reality Central.*** Then, use the questions at the conclusion of the related selection to guide discussion.

PHLit Online!

For more about the author, practice with the selection vocabulary, and more background, go to **www.PHLitOnline.com.**

TEACH

❶ Activating Prior Knowledge

Explain to students that *Swimming to Antarctica* is about the challenge Lynne Cox faces to swim a mile in the Antarctic Ocean. Emphasize that even though Cox has a support crew, including a doctor, she is in the water alone. Ask students to describe a physical or intellectual challenge they have faced alone. Then, **ask** students whether they had a team of supporters to encourage and assist in this challenge. Did students depend on family members for support and assistance? Was the support from a coach? Does a challenge faced alone hold more importance than one faced as part of a team?

Concept Connector →

Students will follow up on this activity after completing the story.

Individual Activity

If students swim, ask them to write down details about the physical sensations they experience while swimming. If they do not swim, have them write down details about another form of physical exertion in cold temperatures, such as doing outside chores, running, or playing team sports. Tell students to compare the details they listed to those described by Cox in the excerpt from *Swimming to Antarctica.*

❷ About the Selection

In *Swimming to Antarctica,* champion swimmer Lynne Cox recounts her record-setting one-mile swim off the shores of Antarctica. Cox describes the steps she took to prepare herself, physically and psychologically, for the challenge. She also gives a riveting, detailed description of the experience itself. What does water that is 32 degrees do to a swimmer's body and mind? What drives a champion to face such an ordeal? All these questions, and more, are answered in *Swimming to Antarctica.*

In 2002, swimmer Lynne Cox attempted an ambitious feat—swimming a mile in the frigid waters of Antarctica. Cox sailed on the ship Orlova *with a team of seven friends, including team leader Barry Binder and her physicians, Susan Sklar, Gabriella Miotta, and Laura King. Bob Griffith and Martha Kaplan, Cox's agent, would scout for danger as Cox swam, while Dan Cohen stood by as a rescue swimmer. Scott Pelley, a television producer, also came. The ship's crew included Dr. Anthony Block and expedition leader Susan Adie. Before attempting a mile, Cox tested her reactions on a shorter swim.*

❶ ❷

from Swimming to Antarctica

Lynne Cox

When I returned to my cabin, I thought for a long time about what I was about to attempt.

❸ I had mixed feelings about the test swim. In some ways, it had given me confidence; I now knew that I could swim for twenty-two minutes in thirty-three-degree water. But it had also made me feel uncertain. It had been the most difficult and probably the most dangerous swim I had ever done. Part of me wanted to be satisfied with it. Part of me didn't want to attempt the mile. I was afraid.

Vocabulary Development

Thematic Vocabulary: The Big Question

As students are discussing the excerpt from *Swimming to Antarctica*, encourage them to use the thematic vocabulary presented in Introducing the Big Question, pp. 2–3. You might encourage them with sentence starters like these:

1. Cox sees glaciers ahead of her but cannot *comprehend* . . .
2. The crew has a different *perception* of . . .
3. Cox experiences *uncertainty* about . . .

3 The water temperature on the big swim would be a degree colder. Thirty-two degrees. That was a magic number, the temperature at which freshwater froze. I wondered if in thirty-two-degree water the water in my cells would freeze, if my body's tissues would become permanently damaged. I wondered if my mind would function better this time, if I would be able to be more aware of what was happening, or if it would be further dulled by the cold. Would my core temperature drop faster, more quickly than I could recognize? Would I be able to tell if I needed to get out? Did I really want to risk my life for this? Or did I want to risk failure?

The other part of me wanted to try, wanted to do what I had trained for, wanted to explore and reach beyond what I had done. That part of me was excited about **venturing** into the unknown. That part of me knew I would have felt a tremendous letdown if I didn't get a chance to try. I wanted to do it now.

The next morning, on December 15, 2002, Susan called me up to the bridge. She pointed out Water Boat Point. The tiny gray beach between steep glaciers was completely blocked by icebergs and brash ice.[1] There was no place to land.

We continued sailing south through the Gerlache Strait, past mountain-high glaciers and by ship-sized icebergs ranging in shades of blue from juniper berry to robin's-egg to light powder blue. In the protection of the Antarctic Peninsula, the wind dropped off and the sea grew calmer. When we reached Neko Harbor, about an hour later, Susan called me up to the bridge. She was excited. The beach was free of icebergs and brash ice. A landing was possible.

Now I would have a chance to swim the first Antarctic mile. I was thrilled and scared, but I tried to remain calm; I knew that the weather could suddenly change and the swim would be off. I met with Barry Binder, who said, "I'll get the crew into the Zodiacs[2] and come and get you when everything's set."

4 I walked to the ship's library, drank four eight-ounce cups of hot water, and ate two small croissants for breakfast—they were high in fat and carbohydrates, two sources of energy I would need for the swim. Then I started through the hallway to my cabin, where many of the *Orlova's* passengers were waiting, eager to find out if I was going to swim. They wished me luck and said they would wait for me at the finish. I stopped by Dan's cabin to ask him if he would jump into the water with me at the end of the swim. He was already in his dry suit, prepared to go. Everyone was doing what we had practiced. All I could do was to go back to my room and wait. Gabriella came in to take a core temperature; it was up to 100.4 degrees. Knowing I was venturing into unknown waters, I must have psyched myself

1. **brash ice** *n.* floating fragments of ice.
2. **Zodiacs** *n.* speedboats.

Literary Analysis
Author's Perspective
What do the opening sentences indicate about the author's attitude toward her swim?

Vocabulary
venturing (ven´ chər iŋ) *v.* attempting to do something that involves taking risks

Reading Skill
Make Predictions
Use details from the narrative to predict whether Cox will succeed or fail.

5 **Reading Check**
What will Cox attempt to do?

3 Literary Analysis
Author's Perspective

1. Remind students that the author's perspective includes the author's judgments and attitudes as well as her experiences.
2. Call students' attention to the background note on the previous page. **Ask** students what they learn about Lynne Cox.
   Possible response: Cox is a very experienced swimmer who comes to the Antarctic well prepared and with a full support team. She enjoys challenging herself mentally and physically.
3. Have students read the bracketed passage. **Ask** the Literary Analysis question: What do the opening sentences indicate about the author's attitude toward her swim?
   Possible response: Cox is nervous about what could happen to her body, but despite all that she is confident in herself.
4. Make sure students understand that Cox's feelings about the swim are a part of the author's perspective.

4 Reading Skill
Make Predictions

1. Remind students that they can use details to make predictions about the selection.
2. **Ask** students to respond to the Reading Skill prompt: Use details from the narrative to predict whether Cox will succeed or fail.
   Possible response: The details suggest that the swim will be difficult, but Cox is so well prepared that she will probably succeed.
3. Encourage students to record their predictions so they can verify and revise them as necessary.

5 Reading Check

Answer: Cox will attempt to be the first person to swim one mile off the coast of Antarctica.

Differentiated Instruction for Universal Access

Enrichment for Advanced Readers

Students may find it rewarding to base their predictions about the outcome of Lynne Cox's adventure on research. After they read the bracketed passage for the Reading Skill exercise on this page, encourage students to do further research on the risks of swimming in the Antarctic waters. Suggest such topics as the geography of the Antarctic coast, the marine life of Antarctica, and the effect on the human body of exposure to extremely cold water.

Motivate students by asking questions such as these: *At what temperature does sea water freeze? Are there animals in the waters off the Antarctic shore that could threaten a swimmer? How do animals survive swimming in these waters when humans often do not?* Have students present their research to the class as part of the Reading Skill exercise.

PHLit Online!

This selection is available in interactive format in the **Enriched Online Student Edition,** which includes a thematically related video with writing prompt and an interactive graphic organizer.

❻ Literary Analysis

Author's Perspective

1. Explain to students that an author's perspective determines which details he or she includes. These details reveal the author's perspective to the reader.
2. Before students read the bracketed passage, **ask** them to describe Cox's perspective based on what they have read so far.
   Possible response: Cox's perspective is that of a highly trained and experienced swimmer who knows what she is doing.
3. Have students read the bracketed passage. Instruct them to pay special attention to any details that might give them insight into Cox's perspective on the swim.
4. **Ask** students the Literary Analysis question: What details indicate that the writer feels fear and doubt before the swim?
   Possible response: The following details suggest that Cox is afraid and doubtful of her swim: her attention to the glaciers' placement so that she can keep on course and the fact that the doctor traces her veins in magic marker, giving her "the creeps."

❼ Critical Thinking

Speculate

1. **Ask** students how Cox feels at this point about the swim.
   Possible response: Cox says that she is nervous, but she feels excitement building up within her.
2. Have students think about individuals who have reached an advanced level of dedication to a particular goal. Have students listen to a volunteer read the bracketed passage. Instruct them to pay close attention to details that may affect Cox's chances for success. Then, **ask** students to discuss whether or not Cox's fears might overpower her motivation to succeed.
   Possible response: Although Cox is nervous before the swim, she is determined to be the first person to swim an Antarctic mile. Her will to succeed, coupled with knowing that she will be disappointed with herself if she does not, will subdue her feelings of fear.

---

4 up so much that I increased my body temperature. Gabriella left me alone while I put on my swimsuit and sweats. I rubbed sunscreen on my face, but not on my arms or legs; it could make my skin slippery, and if my crew needed me to get out of the water quickly, that would create a problem. The night before, three of the crew had spotted a pod of eight killer whales swimming into the Gerlache Strait. They hadn't been moving fast. I hoped they were still north of us.

I stared out the window at the brown crescent-shaped beach. There were snow-covered hills directly above the beach, and massive glaciers on either side. I picked out landmarks, places I could aim for, so I'd know if I was on or off course.

Literary Analysis
Author's Perspective
What details indicate that the writer feels fear and doubt before the swim?

6 Dr. Block caught me at the top of the stairs, just before we stepped out the door and onto the ramp, and asked if I would sit down on a step so he could trace two veins on my hands with a blue Magic Marker. It was just a precaution, he said, in case I needed emergency assistance; this way he would easily be able to find a vein to start an IV. I gave him my right hand and watched him draw the blue lines for the television camera. It gave me the creeps. Why did he have to do this now, right before I swam? Didn't he realize this kind of stuff psychs people out? *I know the swim is dangerous, but he could have done this hours ago, not just before I swam. Get over it,* I told myself. *Shake it off. Take a deep breath. Refocus. Take another breath. Good. Now think about the swim.* I smiled. *I'm so ready for this.*

Why did he have to do this now, right before I swam?

7 Walking to the door, I peeked out and felt a blast of icy wind hit my face from the northwest. It was blowing in off the glaciers in gusts to twenty-five knots,[3] and the air temperature was thirty-two degrees. I felt the hair rising on my arms and my jaw tighten to suppress a shiver. I was much more nervous than I had been during my first swim. I had greater expectations of myself now. I wanted to swim the first Antarctic mile, and I knew I would be very disappointed if I didn't succeed.

8 I stared across the icy water at Neko Harbor's beach and felt excitement building within me. Quickly, before I could lose my chance, I pulled off my sweat suit and shoes and stuck them in a corner of the ship, climbed down the gangway, sat on the platform,

3. **knots** (näts) *n.* a rate of speed. One knot equals one nautical mile (6,076.12 feet) per hour.

Think Aloud

Vocabulary: Using Context

Direct students' attention to Cox's use of the word *tourniquet* in the last paragraph on p. 65. Using a think-aloud process, model how to use context to infer the meaning of an unknown word.

In this sentence, Cox uses the word *tourniquet* to describe what the ice-cold water feels like on her body. I know that the cold does not feel good, so a *tourniquet* does not provide a pleasant sensation. Cox says that her body feels tight and pressurized by the cold. This suggests that a *tourniquet* is something that applies pressure. Cox also says the cold water is squeezing her blood deep into her core. Based on this sentence, I think a *tourniquet* is something that squeezes blood.

Students may wish to look up the definition of *tourniquet* in a dictionary.

and dangled my feet in the water. Surprisingly, it didn't feel any colder than it had two days before. I didn't realize then that the nerves on my skin's surface had been damaged from the first swim. I didn't know that the nerves that signaled danger weren't firing. I wasn't aware that my first line of defense was gone. I had no idea that prolonged exposure in thirty-two-degree water could cause
8 permanent nerve and muscle damage. And I didn't know then that when an untrained person is immersed in water colder than forty degrees, their nerves are cooled down so they can't fire at the neuromuscular level. After only seven or eight minutes the person's body seizes up and [he or she] can't move. It was a good thing I didn't know any of this. All I knew was that I was ready. I took a deep breath, leaned back, and threw myself forward into the thirty-two-degree water.

When I hit the water, I went all the way under. I hadn't intended to do that; I hadn't wanted to immerse my head, which could over-stimulate my vagus nerve[4] and cause my heart to stop beating. Dog-paddling as quickly as I could, I popped up in the water, gasping for air. I couldn't catch my breath. I was swimming with my head up, hyperventilating.[5] I kept spinning my arms, trying to get warm, but I couldn't get enough air. I felt like I had a corset tightening around my chest. I told myself to relax, take a deep breath, but I couldn't
9 slow my breath. And I couldn't get enough air in. I tried again. My body wanted air, and it wanted it now. I had to override that reaction of hyperventilating. I had to concentrate on my breath, to press my chest out against the cold water and draw the icy air into my lungs.

My body resisted it. The air was too cold. My body didn't want to draw the cold air deep into my lungs and cool myself from the inside. It wanted to take short breaths so the cold air would be warmed in my mouth before it reached my lungs. I was fighting against myself.

I noticed my arms. They were bright red, and I felt like I was swimming through slush. My arms were thirty-two degrees, as cold as the sea. They were going numb, and so were my legs. I pulled my hands right under my chest so that I was swimming on the upper inches of the sea, trying to minimize my contact with the water. I was swimming fast and it was hard to get enough air. I began to notice that the cold was pressurizing my body like a giant tourniquet. It was squeezing the blood from the exterior part of my body and pushing it into the core. Everything felt tight. *Focus on your breath,* I told myself. *Slow it down. Let it fill your lungs. You're*

4. **vagus** (vāg´ əs) **nerve** *n.* either of a pair of nerves running from the brain to the heart that regulate the heartbeat.
5. **hyperventilating** *v.* breathing so rapidly or deeply as to cause dizziness or fainting.

Vocabulary
prolonged (prō lôŋd´)
adj. extended; lengthy

Literary Analysis
Author's Perspective
How does this passage reflect both how it felt to live through the event and how it feels to look back on it?

Reading Skill
Make Predictions
Do these details verify your original prediction or lead you to revise it?

10 **Reading Check**
List two dangers Cox faces on her swim.

Differentiated Instruction for Universal Access

Strategy for Special Needs Students
Tell students that an author's perspective is how the author "sees" or understands his or her subject. Use **Literary Analysis Graphic Organizer B** (*Graphic Organizer Transparencies,* p. 14) and help students complete an Author's Perspective chart using details on these pages. A partially completed chart can be found in *Graphic Organizer Transparencies*, **Literary Analysis Graphic Organizer A**, p. 12.

Strategy for Less Proficient Readers
Students may need assistance understanding the elements that make up an author's perspective. Use **Literary Analysis Graphic Organizer A** to demonstrate that perspective includes knowledge gained from research and personal experiences. Using details from these pages, help students complete an Author's Perspective chart.

8 Literary Analysis
Author's Perspective

1. Remind students that author Lynne Cox actually lived through everything she describes in *Swimming to Antarctica*. These experiences shape her perspective as an author.
2. Point out to students that Cox's perspective is also shaped by information she did not have at the time of her swim.
3. Encourage students to share a time when they faced a challenge and then found out more about the situation after it was over. **Ask** how their perspectives changed after they learned more. **Possible response:** Knowing more about the situation made me question the confidence I had at the time of the challenge.
4. Have students read the bracketed passage. Then, **ask** them the Literary Analysis question: How does this passage reflect both how it felt to live through the event and how it feels to look back on it? **Possible response:** As she lives through the experience, Cox stays focused on the swim and does not think about the details she later describes. Looking back, she recognizes how dangerous the swim was and how lucky she is to have come through it unharmed.

9 Reading Skill
Make Predictions

1. Have students read the bracketed passage. **Ask** students the Reading Skill question: Do these details verify your original prediction or lead you to revise it? **Possible response:** The details make it seem less likely that Cox will succeed, because she is having trouble breathing.
2. Have students enter these details in **Reading Skill Graphic Organizer B** (*Graphic Organizer Transparencies*, p. 11).

10 Reading Check

Possible response: Cox faces the danger of doing permanent damage to her muscles and nerves. She also risks being attacked by killer whales.

11 Connecting to the Big Question

1. Point out that a writer can contrast one character's experience or perception with the view of other characters. Doing so can help readers see the different views people can have of reality.
2. Have students read the bracketed text. **Ask:** What is actually happening to Cox at this point? How does she feel?
   Possible response: She is having trouble breathing because the water is so cold. She is almost panicking.
3. **Ask:** What do people around Cox seem to think about what is happening?
   Possible response: They do not know that there is a problem. They see Cox swimming and think everything is all right.
4. **Ask:** What does this suggest about people's perception of reality?
   Possible response: It suggests that people do not always "see" the same reality. In this case, the reality is that Cox is struggling. What people see, or believe is true, is that she is doing all right.

12 Critical Viewing

Answer: The picture does not show the dangers, such as how cold the water was or how difficult it was for Cox to breathe.

not going to be able to make it if you keep going at this rate.

It wasn't working. I was laboring for breath harder than on the test swim. I was in oxygen debt,[6] panting, gasping. My breath was inefficient, and the oxygen debt was compounding. In an attempt to create heat, I was spinning my arms wildly, faster than I'd ever turned them over before. Laura later told me that I was swimming at a rate of ninety strokes per minute, thirty strokes per minute quicker than my normal rate. My body was demanding more oxygen, but I couldn't slow down. Not for a nanosecond. Or I would freeze up and the swim would be over.

11 An icy wave slapped my face: I choked and felt a wave of panic rise within me. My throat tightened. I tried to clear my throat and breathe. My breath didn't come out. I couldn't get enough air in to clear my throat. I glanced at the crew. They couldn't tell I was in trouble. If I stopped, Dan would jump in and pull me out. I still couldn't get a good breath. I thought of rolling on my back to give myself time to breathe, but I couldn't. It was too cold. I closed my mouth, overrode everything my body was telling me to do, held my breath, and gasped, coughed, cleared my windpipe, and relaxed just a little, just enough to let my guard down and catch another wave in the face. I choked again. I put my face down into the water, hoping this time I could slow my heart rate down. I held my face in the water for two strokes and told myself, *Relax, just turn your head and breathe.*

12 ▼ Critical Viewing Explain whether or not any of the dangers faced by Cox are represented in this photograph. **[Connect]**

6. **oxygen debt** *n.* an increased need for oxygen in the body brought on by intensive activity.

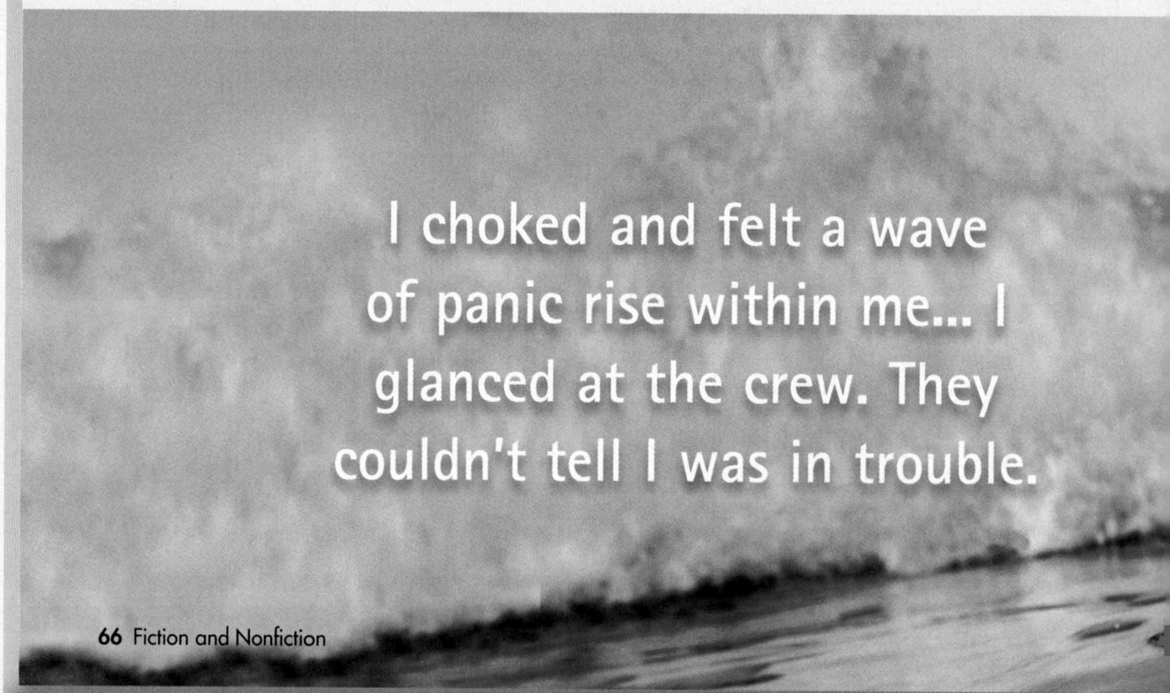
I choked and felt a wave of panic rise within me... I glanced at the crew. They couldn't tell I was in trouble.

Vocabulary Development

Vocabulary Reinforcement

To reinforce students' comprehension of the selection vocabulary words as they read "Swimming to Antarctica," give them "show-you-know" sentences. The first part of each sentence uses the vocabulary word in an appropriate context.

1. His instructions were needlessly *prolonged*; ____________.
   Sample response: we already knew all of the background information.
2. It took me a while to regain my *equilibrium*; ____________.
   Sample response: the bad news really threw me off balance.
3. I looked for something to *buffer* the force of the blast; ____________.
   Sample response: an old mattress was all I could find.

13 It was easier to breathe in a more horizontal position. I thought it might be helping. I drew in a deep breath and put my face down again. I knew I couldn't do this for long. I was losing too much heat through my face. The intensity of the cold was as sharp as broken glass. I'd thought that swimming across the Bering Strait[7] in thirty-eight-degree water had been tough, but there was a world of difference between thirty-eight degrees and thirty-two. In a few seconds, the cold pierced my skin and penetrated into my muscles. It felt like freezer burn, like touching wet fingers to frozen metal.

Finally I was able to gain control of my breath. I was inhaling and exhaling so deeply I could hear the breath moving in and out of my mouth even though I was wearing earplugs. I kept thinking about breathing, working on keeping it deep and even; that way I didn't have time to think about the cold.

My brain wasn't working as it normally did. It wasn't flowing freely from one idea to another—it was moving mechanically, as if my awareness came from somewhere deep inside my brain. Maybe it was because my body was being assaulted with so many sensations, too different and too complex to recognize. Or maybe it was because my blood and oxygen were going out to the working muscles. I didn't know.

For the next five or six minutes, I continued swimming, telling myself that I was doing well, telling myself that this was what I

7. **Bering Strait** (ber′ iŋ strāt) *n.* the body of water between Russia and Alaska, joining the Pacific and Arctic oceans.

Literary Analysis
Author's Perspective
Name one way in which the details in this paragraph might be different if presented by a crew member on the boat.

14 **Reading Check**
List two effects of the cold water on Cox's mind and body.

13 Literary Analysis

Author's Perspective

1. Remind students that an author who experienced an event will write about it from a different perspective from one written by an author who did not experience the event.
2. Explain to students that after doing proper research, any author can write what exposure to cold water does to the human body. Because she swam in the Antarctic, however, Lynne Cox can describe what that exposure actually feels like.
3. Have students read the bracketed passage. Instruct them to pay close attention to the details that reveal the author's perspective.
4. **Ask** students to respond to the Literary Analysis prompt: Name one way in which the details in this paragraph might be different if presented by a crew member on the boat.
   Possible response: While Cox gives a detailed description of her troubled breathing, a crew member might say only that she seemed to be having a little trouble getting into the rhythm of the swim.
5. **Ask** students what Cox's perspective adds to this account of her Antarctic swim.
   Possible response: The details Cox is able to draw from her experience make the account much more suspenseful and vivid, which is important because very few readers will ever experience a long swim in 32 degree waters.

14 Reading Check

Possible response: The cold water makes it very difficult for Cox to breathe and seems to induce a state of panic against which she must fight.

Fluency

Distribute copies of pages 66 and 67 and put students into small groups. Place one or two fluent readers in each group. Have students take turns reading paragraphs aloud. While one student is reading, have another student mark words with which the one reading has difficulty. Circulate to monitor the fluency of students' reading. Collect students' marked up copies, and then write the difficult words and passages on the board. Review these with the class. Look for these problem spots:

- If students have difficulty with the word *inefficient* (p. 66), point out that the word features a common prefix, *in-*. Have students cover up parts of the word with their thumb to sound out each syllable in turn. Then explain that *inefficient* means "not producing the desired effect with minimum energy."
- If students have difficulty with the word *earplugs* (p. 67), point out that the word is a compound word. Have students cover up one of the two words, *ear* or *plug*. Ask a student to define the word. Repeat with the second word. Then, have a student combine the words and tell the meaning of the word *earplug*.

15 Critical Thinking

Interpret

1. Have students read the bracketed passage. Point out that few people would understand their body the way Lynne Cox does.
2. **Ask** students what this passage reveals about Cox.
   Possible responses: Cox understands her body can work like a tool that can help her achieve her goals.

16 Reading Skill

Make Predictions

1. Have students pause before reading the bracketed passage. **Ask** them to summarize what has happened so far in Cox's account.
   Answer: As she prepares for the swim, Cox is excited as well as nervous and frightened. In the water, she finds that the cold affects her more strongly than she expected. She has trouble breathing, thinking, and moving. Finally, she regains control of her breath and begins to swim fairly steadily.
2. Tell students to return to their predictions about Cox's success or failure in their Prediction Charts.
3. Instruct students to read the bracketed passage. Have them look for information that either supports their predictions or leads them to think about revising them.
4. **Ask** students the Reading Skill question: Do the details in this paragraph verify or lead you to revise your predictions about whether Cox will succeed?
   Possible response: These details make it seem that Cox will not succeed. She seems confused. She is swimming toward glaciers, which does not seem right. She is also having trouble swimming and cannot get a good pace or rhythm.
5. Have students write details, revisions, and verifications on their Prediction Charts at any point in the text, not only in response to Reading Skill questions.

Vocabulary
equilibrium (ē´ kwi lib´ rē əm) *n.* a state of balance

had trained for. Then something clicked, as if my body had gained **equilibrium**. It had fully closed down the blood flow in my skin and fingers and toes. My arms and legs were as cold as the water, but I could feel the heat radiating deep within my torso and head, and this gave me confidence. I knew that my body was protecting my brain and vital organs. Staring through the clear, silver-blue water, I examined my fingers; they were red and swollen. They were different than when I'd been swimming in the Bering Strait, when they'd looked like the fingers of a dead person. They looked healthy, and I thought their swollenness would give me more surface area, more to pull with. **15**

I smiled and looked up at the crew, who were in the Zodiacs on either side of me. Each of them was leaning forward, willing me ahead. Their faces were filled with tension. Gabriella, Barry, Dan, and Scott were leaning so far over the Zodiac's pontoon I felt as if they were swimming right beside me. I was sprinting faster than I ever had before, moving faster than the Zodiac, and I was getting fatigued quickly. The water was thicker than on the test swim, and it took more force to pull through on each stroke. My arms ached. I didn't feel right; I couldn't seem to get into any kind of a rhythm. Then I sensed that something was wrong.

We were heading to the left, toward some glaciers. This didn't make sense; we couldn't land there. It was too dangerous. The glaciers could calve[8] and kill us.

"Barry, where are we going?" I shouted, using air I needed for breathing.

Reading Skill
Make Predictions
Do the details in this paragraph verify or lead you to revise your prediction about whether Cox will succeed?

He pointed out our direction—right toward the glaciers. I didn't understand. I didn't want to go that way. I wanted to aim for the beach. I was confused. I was moving my arms as fast as they would go, and it was taking all I had. From each moment to the next, I had to tell myself to keep going. The water felt so much colder than on the test swim. It had already worked its way deep into my muscles. My arms and legs were stiff. My strokes were short and choppy. But I kept going, telling myself to trust the crew and focus on the glaciers to watch the outcropping of rocks that was growing larger. I couldn't get into any kind of pace. **16**

Vocabulary
abruptly (ə brupt´ lē) *adv.* happening suddenly; unexpectedly

Abruptly the Zodiacs zagged to the right. I looked up and thought, *Wow, okay; we're heading for the beach now.* For a moment, I started to feel better. I was able to extend my reach farther, and I

8. **calve** (käv) *v.* to give birth to young; used here to refer to the "birth" of a new ice mass when a piece of a glacier splits off.

Vocabulary Development

Word Analysis: *equilibrium*

Have students further examine the parts of the selection vocabulary word *equilibrium* at the top of this page. Point out the familiar word part *-equi-*, which students will recognize in words like *equilateral* ("having all sides equal") and *equate* ("assert that one thing is equal to or the same as another"). You might also teach these words:

- *equinox*: when day and night are of equal length in all parts of the Earth
- *equitable*: fair; just
- *equality*: the condition of being equal
- *equivalent*: equal in quantity, value, and so on

The other part of *equilibrium* comes from the root word *libra*, which means "scale" or "balance." The word *deliberate* is also formed from this word. *Deliberate* means "to consider carefully" or "to weigh thoroughly." Students might recognize the scales as the symbol of the constellation Libra.

17 **LITERATURE IN CONTEXT**

Geography Connection

Antarctica: The Coldest Place On Earth

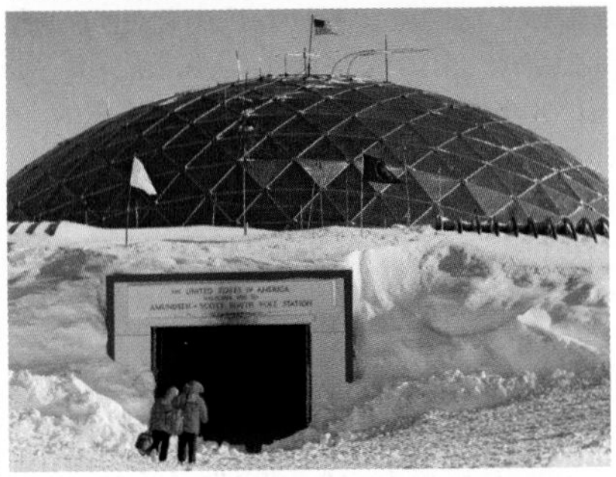

▲ The Amundsen-Scott South Pole Station was established by the United States in 1956.

- Antarctica is an ice-covered continent that covers the South Pole.
- Antarctica is the coldest place on Earth. Temperatures have reached a record 120° F below zero in the winter.
- Antarctica has no native population.
- The Antarctic icecap is the largest reserve of freshwater or snow in the world.

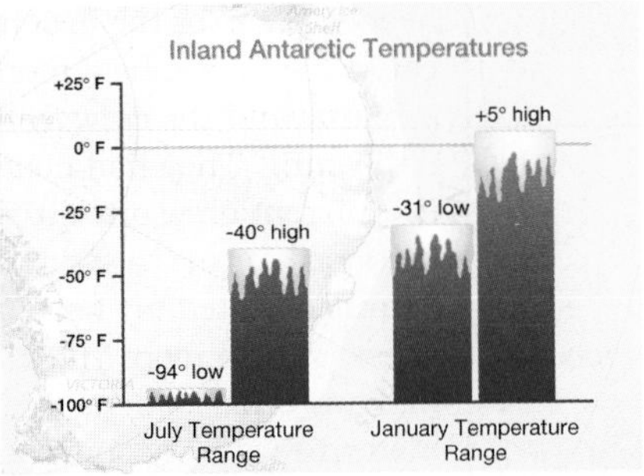

Connect to the Literature

What does this information suggest about the significance of Cox's endeavor?

could see passengers from the *Orlova* walking along the snowbanks. In the distance, their clothes lost their color and they looked black, like giant penguins. I saw smaller black figures, too—real penguins nesting near the edge of the shore. For a few moments, I felt like I was going to be okay, like I was going to make it in to shore, but then the Zodiacs abruptly turned farther to the right, and we were headed past the beach for another range of glaciers.

18 Finally, it occurred to me that the *Orlova* had anchored too close to shore for me to swim a mile, so Barry was adding distance by altering the course. And the ship's captain was on the bridge monitoring our course on his GPS[9] and radioing our Zodiacs, updating them on the distance we had traveled. One of the passengers, Mrs. Stokie, who was on the bridge with him, told me later, "The captain was watching you and he was shaking his head. He was an older man, and he had experienced everything. And now he was seeing something new. It was good for him. Still, I think he couldn't believe it."

We continued on right past the beach, toward more glaciers.

"How long have I been swimming?" I asked.

"Fifteen minutes," Barry said.

9. **GPS** "Global Positioning System," referring here to a portable device that provides information about the bearer's location and speed.

Literary Analysis
Author's Perspective
Identify one detail in this paragraph that shows Cox's past perspective and one that comes from her present perspective.

19 **Reading Check**
What new obstacle does Cox face on her swim?

17 Literature in Context

Geography Connection Antarctica was the last continent discovered. Explorers reached the continent at the beginning of the nineteenth century. By the century's end, only parts of its shoreline had been explored. An expedition reached the South Pole in 1911, but permanent stations for scientific research were not established until the 1940s. Although people have explored Antarctica's surface and made claims on its territory, for most of us it remains a mysterious, uninhabited frontier.

Connect to the Literature Remind students that Cox's goal is to be the first to swim one mile in the Antarctic Ocean. Then, **ask** the Connect to the Literature question: What does this information suggest about the significance of Lynne Cox's endeavor?
Possible response: By swimming to Antarctica, Cox is acting as an explorer, stretching human frontiers.

18 Literary Analysis

Author's Perspective

1. Remind students that in the excerpt from *Swimming to Antarctica*, Cox describes the swim as she experienced it. She also includes information she learned after the experience ended.
2. Have students read the bracketed passage. Then, **ask** them to respond to the Literary Analysis prompt: Identify one detail in this paragraph that shows Cox's past perspective and one that comes from her present perspective.
Possible response: Cox's realization that the Zodiacs change course comes from the past. The captain's surprised reaction to the swim, which a passenger tells her later, comes from the present.
3. Explain that Cox's inclusion of both details from the swim itself and details she learned later is part of her perspective. Her perspective shifted between the day of the swim and the time she wrote this text.

19 Reading Check

Answer: A new obstacle for Cox is the glaciers.

Differentiated Instruction for Universal Access

Enrichment for Advanced Readers
As students read the Literature in Context feature on this page, use the additional background information to call their attention to the limited human presence in Antarctica. Encourage students to research the history of Antarctic exploration and settlement. Have students work in groups to assemble reports on one or more aspects of this subject. Possible report topics include the first expedition to the South Pole, types of scientific work conducted in Antarctica, and strategies for human survival in Antarctica.

Enrichment for Gifted and Talented Students
The Literature in Context feature on this page focuses on the uniqueness of Antarctica and of Lynne Cox's endeavor. Ask these students to create artwork representing this unique, dangerous, otherworldly place. Students should draw on the details described in the Literature in Context feature, as well as details from Cox's descriptions. Encourage them to use media suited to capturing the extremities of the Antarctic environment. Have students present their work to the class.

⓴ Reading Skill

Make Predictions

1. Before students begin reading the bracketed passage, **ask** them to evaluate how well Cox is doing at this point.
   Answer: Cox is just past the halfway point, but she is not doing well. She is experiencing a problem she cannot seem to identify.
2. Have students read the bracketed passage. Encourage them to think carefully about the new information Cox reveals at this point and to consider how it might affect their predictions.
3. **Ask** students whether the new information in this passage verifies their predictions about the outcome of Cox's swim or whether it leads them to revise their predictions.
   Possible response: The new information reveals that the swim is in serious jeopardy. While Cox is still likely to complete the swim, it will be even more difficult than students may have predicted.
4. Have students record any changes they have made to their predictions based on the new information.

➤**Monitor Progress:** Point out to students that Cox is about to swim across a narrow channel where she may encounter a dangerous current. Instruct students to predict what will happen using their Prediction Charts. Have them read the next three paragraphs and **ask** them to explain whether their predictions are accurate.
Possible response: I predicted Cox would be hampered by the current but would be able to save herself, which proved to be true.

➤**Reteach:** If students have difficulty making predictions for this section, have them reread the bracketed section. **Ask** students to record any descriptions on which they can base predictions. Then have them read the next three paragraphs again while they record details that verify their predictions or lead them to revise their charts. Then, break the class into small groups to review the charts.

I had swum a little more than half a mile. I looked up at the shore. If I turned left, I could make it in. I could reach the shore. This struggle could be over. But I wouldn't complete the mile. I had swum farther two days before. But I was tired now, and this was so much harder. I just didn't feel right. I couldn't figure out what the problem was. I kept talking to myself, coaching myself to keep going. Then I felt it; it was the water pressure, and it was increasing on my back. It meant there was a strong current behind me. I looked at the glaciers onshore, using the fixed points to gauge how fast the current was flowing. It was flowing at over a knot. I wondered if I would have enough strength to fight it when we turned around and headed back for the beach. It would cut my speed by half and could cause me to lose heat more rapidly.

Vocabulary
gauge (gāj) *v.* measure something's size, amount, extent or capacity

⓴ Barry and the crew in the Zodiacs couldn't feel what was happening. They had no idea we were moving into a risky area. If the current grew any stronger, it could cost us the swim. Barry motioned for me to swim past a peninsula and across a narrow channel. I lifted my head and pulled my hands directly under my chest, to gain more lift, so I could look across the bay and see if we had any other options for landing. There were no alternatives. This made me very uncomfortable. Chances were good that there would be a strong current flowing into or out of the narrow bay. And if we got caught in that current, all would be lost. ●

We started across the inlet, and within a moment I could feel that second current, slamming into our right side at two knots, pushing us into the inlet. Without any explanation, I spun around, put my head down, dug my arms into the water, and crabbed[10] into the current. I focused on repositioning myself so I

And if we got caught in that current, all would be lost.

Vocabulary Development

Marine Terminology

On pages 70–71, Lynne Cox is nearing the end of her Antarctic swim. As she gets closer to shore, she describes a number of features and phenomena of the coastal waters that begin to affect her progress. Clarify with students the marine terms that are used in this section of *Swimming to Antarctica.*

- *current:* part of a body of water that flows in one direction
- *peninsula:* a projection of land into a body of water
- *channel:* a deep part of a harbor
- *bay:* a body of water that is partially enclosed by land but has a wide opening onto the sea
- *inlet:* a stream or bay leading inland from the ocean
- *harbor:* a sheltered area in a body of water that is deep enough for ships to anchor
- *pontoon:* a floating base for a bridge or boat

could parallel shore again and head toward Neko Harbor. Barry knew I knew what I was doing. But the abrupt course change caught the Zodiac drivers by surprise. They scattered in different directions, trying to avoid ramming into each other and trying to catch up with me. The motor on the lead Zodiac on my left sputtered and stopped. The second Zodiac immediately pulled up beside me. I sprinted against the current.

"How long have I been swimming?"

"Twenty-one minutes," Barry said. He and all the crew were watching me intently, their faces filled with tension and concern.

21 I put my head down, and something suddenly clicked. Maybe it was because I knew shore was within reach, or maybe because I got a second wind; I don't know. But I was finally swimming strongly, stretching out and moving fluidly. My arms and legs were as cold as the sea, but I felt the heat within my head and contained in my torso and I thrilled to it, knowing my body had carried me to places no one else had been in only a bathing suit. I looked down into the water; it was a bright blue-gray and so clear that it appeared as if I were swimming through air. The viscosity of the water was different, too; it was thicker than any I had ever swum in. It felt like I was swimming through gelato. And I got more push out of each arm stroke than I ever had before. I looked at the crew. They were leaning so far over the pontoons, as if they were right there with me. I needed to let them know I was okay.

I lifted my head, took a big breath, and shouted, "Barry, I'm swimming to Antarctica!"

I saw the smiles, heard the cheers and laughs, and I felt their energy lift me. They were as thrilled as I was. I swam faster, extending my arms, pulling more strongly, reaching for the shores of Antarctica. Now I knew we were almost there.

The crew was shouting warnings about ice. I swerved around two icebergs. Some chunks looked sharp, but I was too tired to care. I swam into whatever was in my path. It hurt, but all I wanted now was to finish.

As we neared shore, I lifted my head and saw the other passengers from the *Orlova*, in their bright red and yellow hats and parkas, tromping down the snowbanks, spreading their feet and arms wide for balance, racing to the water's edge to meet us. I lifted my foot and waved and saw my crew break into bigger smiles.

23 *I'm almost done,* I thought. *I feel okay. I feel strong. I feel warm inside. My arms and legs are thirty-two degrees. But I feel good. I can stretch out my strokes and put my face in the water. Maybe I can go a little farther. Maybe I can see what more I can do. Maybe I can swim five or ten more minutes. Or maybe I should be happy with what I've*

10. crabbed *v.* moved sideways or diagonally.

Literary Analysis
Author's Perspective
What information here reveals the writer's swimming expertise?

22 **Reading Check**
What changes for Cox after she shifts her course?

21 Literary Analysis

Author's Perspective

1. Remind students that Lynne Cox has approached her subject from more than one perspective.
2. **Ask** students to identify the perspectives from which Cox has written up to this point.
   Possible response: Cox describes the swim itself from the perspective of living through the event. She also has the perspective of a writer looking back at past events.
3. Have students read the bracketed passage. Instruct them to pay close attention to Cox's perspective.
4. **Ask** students to respond to the Literary Analysis question: What information here reveals the writer's swimming expertise?
   Answer: She describes the different moves, such as putting her head down, stretching out, and moving fluidly. She also thinks about each stroke.
5. Make sure students understand that the change in Cox's attitude about the swim is a change in perspective.

Monitor Progress: Have students write short paragraphs describing how Cox's perspective has evolved throughout the selection. Evaluate the paragraphs based on how clearly students recognize that Cox draws on her anxieties before the swim and her fears up until the final stretch to heighten the drama and suspense of her account.

Reteach: If students do not understand the shifts in Cox's perspective, have them chart the major turning points she describes. Then have them identify how her attitude shifts at each point.

22 Reading Check

Answer: After changing course, Cox finds her swimming rhythm and regains confidence.

Differentiated Instruction for Universal Access

EL Pronunciation for English Learners

Some students might have difficulty pronouncing words with the soft "th" sound, as in *with*, *thrilled*, and *breath*, replacing it with the "z" sound. The following strategy can help students to pronounce the soft "th" sound:
Pair English learners with fluent speakers. Have partners take turns reading the paragraphs on p. 71. When English learners have difficulty with a word, have fluent speakers carefully pronounce the word, guiding English learners to the correct sound.

23 Literary Analysis

Author's Perspective

1. Point out that the author wrote this piece long after her swim. She writes in the present tense to show how she felt at each moment along the way. Have students read the bracketed text, specifically looking for any change in the writer's perspective.
2. **Ask** students the Literary Analysis prompt: Explain in what way the author's perspective on her swim changes as she nears the shore.
   Answer: She no longer doubts whether she will accomplish her goal. Instead, she wonders if she should swim even farther. Then, she reviews the dangers of prolonged exposure and decides that she should remain satisfied with what she has already accomplished.

24 Reading Skill

Make Predictions

1. Instruct students to pause before reading the bracketed passage. Ask them to summarize Cox's account of her Antarctic swim up to this point.
   Answer: Cox has difficulty breathing and moving at first. Her crew shifts her course, which adds to her confusion. Currents make her swim more difficult as well. When she changes course on her own, she finally hits her stride and can soon see the shore.
2. Tell students to return to their Prediction Charts. Lead students in discussing any revisions they made as they read.
3. Have students read the bracketed passage. Then **ask** them the Reading Skill question: How does this outcome match up with your predictions?
   Possible response: Cox's success will probably match the initial predictions of students. However, they may not have imagined that the swim would be so difficult. Students should have revised and fine-tuned their predictions as they read.
4. For additional sample answers, use **Reading Skill Graphic Organizer A** (***Graphic Organizer Transparencies,*** p. 12).

done. My skin is so cold I can't feel it, and when I stop swimming, I don't know how far my temperature's going to drop. I looked at my watch. Twenty-three minutes. I'd been in a minute longer than two days before. *How much difference would a minute make? I asked myself. How much difference is there between thirty-two-degree and thirty-three-degree water? Remember what Dr. Keatinge*[11] *said: once your temperature starts to drop, it will drop very fast. If you continue swimming, you're going to cool down even more. Remember how hard you shivered last time? Remember how much work it was? Remember how uncomfortable you were? This is the place where people make mistakes, when they're tired and cold and they push too far into the unknown.*

You could really hurt yourself. Finish now. You've done a good job. Be satisfied with what you've done. Go celebrate with your friends.

Literary Analysis
Author's Perspective
Explain in what way the author's perspective on her swim changes as she nears the shore.

23

My skin is so cold I can't feel it.

Turning in toward shore, I again lifted my foot and waved it, and my friends waved back and cheered. One hundred yards from shore, I saw chinstrap penguins sliding headfirst, like tiny black toboggans, down a steep snowbank. When they reached the base of the hill, they used their bristly tails like brakes, sticking them into the snow to stop their momentum. They waddled across the beach at full tilt, holding their wings out at their sides for balance. Reaching the water, they dove in headfirst, then porpoised across it, clearing it by one or two feet with each surface dive. They tucked their wings back by their sides so they would be more aerodynamic. When they neared the Zodiacs, they dove and flapped their wings under the water as if they were flying through air. It was amazing to think this was the only place they would fly. They zoomed under me in bursts of speed, and their bubbles exploded like white fireworks. More penguins joined in. One cannonballed off a ledge, another slipped on some ice and belly flopped, and three penguins swam within inches of my hands. I reached out to touch one, but he swerved and flapped his wings, so he moved just beyond my fingertips. I had no idea why they were swimming with me, but I knew it was a good sign; it meant there were no killer whales or leopard seals in the area.

24

Reading Skill
Make Predictions
How does this outcome match up with your predictions?

11. **Dr. Keatinge** Cox's doctor on her swim across the Bering Strait.

Vocabulary Development

Vocabulary Knowledge Rating

When students have completed reading and discussing the excerpt from *Swimming to Antarctica*, have them take out their **Vocabulary Knowledge Rating Chart** for this selection. Read the words aloud once more, and have students rate their knowledge of the words again in the After Reading column. Clarify any words that are still problematic. Have students write their own definition and example or sentence in the appropriate column. Then have students complete the Vocabulary Practice at the end of the selection. Encourage students to use the words in further discussion and written work about this selection. Remind them that they will be accountable for these words on the **Selection Test**, ***Unit 1 Resources***, pp. 81–83 or 84–86.

25 Critical Viewing

Possible response: My image of the chinstrap penguins matches closely to what Cox describes. They are balancing themselves with their wings spread out at their sides, and one is diving in headfirst, just as she described, although I did not imagine they traveled that in such a large group!

26 Reading Check

Sample answer: Cox swims a little farther than a mile. She has succeeded.

24 When I reached knee-deep water, Dan jumped in, ran through the water, looped his arm through mine, and helped me stand. "Are you okay?" he asked.

"Yes. We made it!" I said.

Everyone around me was crying. Susan Adie helped Dan pull me up the incline. Martha wrapped a towel around my shoulders. Barry hugged me tightly. Laura and Susan began drying me off. I was so cold I was already starting to shiver hard. My legs were stiffer than after the other swim. The crew helped me into the Zodiac and I flopped onto the floor. Laura and Susan piled on top of me to protect me from the wind, and we pounded across the water, my head slamming into the Zodiac's floor. I managed to lift my head so that someone could place a hand under it to **buffer** the impact. I was so cold and stiff and shaking harder than before.

When we reached the Orlova, it took me a minute to stand, to gain my balance, and as I climbed the ramp's steps I clung to the railing and pulled myself up, shaking hard. By the time I reached the top of the ramp, my teeth were chattering and I was breathing harder and faster than when I had been swimming. I didn't like being so cold. I didn't like my body having to work so hard. My temperature had dropped to 95.5 degrees, and I couldn't control my shaking. I just let go, and my body bounced up and down with shakes and shivers.

Quickly Martha and Dan and the three doctors huddled around me like emperor penguins, and their combined comfort and body heat began to warm me. It seemed as if I would never stop shaking,

25 ▲ **Critical Viewing**
Does this image of chinstrap penguins match what you imagined based on Cox's descriptions? Explain. **[Connect]**

Vocabulary
buffer (buf´ ər) *v.* lessen a shock; cushion

26 **Reading Check**
What is the outcome of Cox's attempt to swim a mile?

Concept Connector

Activating Prior Knowledge

Ask students to recall their responses to the question: Does a challenge faced alone hold more importance than one faced as part of a team? Have the students' responses changed after reading the selection? Invite students to cite examples from the story to support their responses.

Writing About the Big Question

Have students compare their responses to the sentence starter they completed before reading with their ideas afterward. Have them explain whether their thoughts have changed.

Reading Skill Graphic Organizer

Have students review their Prediction charts. Ask how many students were able to verify their predictions and how many revised their predictions. Show students **Reading Skill Graphic Organizer A**, (*Graphic Organizer Transparencies*, p. 12) as an example of a partially filled-in chart. You may want to have students work in pairs to compare their predictions, verifications, and revisions.

27 Literary Analysis

Author's Perspective

Have students read the bracketed passage. **Ask** students the Literary Analysis question: Which details show the difference between Cox's perspective before and after her swim?

Possible response: During the swim, she focused on the challenge of the moment and on her own ability to succeed. After the swim, she looks back and focuses on how other people helped her.

ASSESS

Answers

Critical Thinking

1. Students may cite the moment Cox changes course on her own as the most exciting because it is a dramatic turning point.
2. (a) Preparations include taking a test swim, eating croissants, and finding landmarks. (b) The test swim is intended to give a sense of the water's impact. The croissants give her energy. The landmarks are meant to keep her on course.
3. (a) She cannot control her breathing. (b) She forces her breathing to slow, showing her willpower.
4. (a) She talks after her session with the doctor and as she nears the end of her swim. (b) First talk: Focus on the swim. Second talk: Finish now; be satisfied. (c) Both talks enable Cox to concentrate and succeed.
5. (a) Cox desires to be first, and she wants to test human limits. (b) Cox faces the dangers of death from hypothermia, permanent injury, attack by sea animals, and drowning. (c) Students are likely to think the swim was worth the effort.

Is there a difference between reality and truth?

(a) Cox is determined, and her training makes it possible to push herself. She does not want to give up without achieving the goal. (b) She now looks back and sees that people need the help of others when they set out to achieve great things.

and I was completely exhausted. Within half an hour my shivering had subsided to small body shudders. Once I was able to stand and maintain my balance, the doctors helped me pull on a special top and pants that had been designed by a friend. She had sewn pockets under the arms, in the groin area, and into a scarf and had placed chemical packs that emitted heat inside the pockets. Their placement in the clothing warmed the major blood-flow areas of my body so that I was heated from the inside out. It was effective, and within an hour my temperature was back to normal.

That night we celebrated with everyone aboard the Orlova. I had swum the first Antarctic mile—a distance of 1.06 miles, in fact—in thirty-two-degree water in twenty-five minutes. I had been able to do what had seemed impossible because I'd had a crew who believed in me and in what we as human beings were capable of. It was a great dream, swimming to Antarctica.

Literary Analysis 27
Author's Perspective
Which details show the difference between Cox's perspective before and after her swim?

Critical Thinking

1. **Respond:** Which part of Cox's story did you find the most exciting? Why?
2. **(a)** Using details from the selection, list three ways in which Cox prepares for her swim. **(b) Analyze Causes and Effects:** For each method of preparation, explain the effect it has or is intended to have.
3. **(a)** What physical challenge causes Cox to struggle at the start of her swim? **(b) Analyze:** What does Cox's ability to overcome this challenge reveal about her?
4. **(a)** Identify two instances in which Cox gives herself a pep talk. **(b) Summarize:** What is the main point Cox makes in each pep talk? **(c) Analyze:** Is each pep talk effective? Why?
5. **(a) Speculate:** Identify two reasons Cox may have had for making the swim. **(b) Summarize:** List the dangers that Cox faces. **(c) Evaluate:** Explain whether the swim was worth the effort.

Is there a difference between reality and truth?
(a) What makes Cox able to push herself harder than she thought she could? **(b)** How does the reality of Cox's Antarctic swim differ from what she predicted it would be like?

Assessment Resources

Unit 1 Resources

L1 L2 EL **Selection Test A,** pp. 81–83. Administer Test A to less advanced readers and English learners.

L3 L4 **Selection Test B,** pp. 84–86. Administer Test B to on-level and more advanced students.

L3 L4 **Open-Book Test,** pp. 78–80. As an alternative, give the Open-Book Test.

All **Customizable Test Bank**

All **Self-tests**
Students may prepare for the **Selection Test** by taking the **Self-test** online.

PHLit Online! All assessment resources are available at **www.PHLitOnline.com.**

After You Read | *from* Swimming to Antarctica

Literary Analysis: Author's Perspective

1. **(a)** Using a chart like the one shown, analyze the **author's perspective** in the selection.

Author's Perspective	
Types of Details Included	**Examples of Each**
❑ researched facts	
❑ personal experiences	
❑ opinions	
❑ attitudes	

   (b) Referring to your chart, briefly describe Cox's perspective.

2. **(a)** List two ways in which Cox's story would be different if told by a news reporter. **(b)** Do you think Cox's firsthand perspective adds to the story's drama? Explain.

Reading Skill: Make Predictions

3. Identify details in the selection that you used to **verify a prediction.**
4. **(a)** Identify one prediction you **revised** as you read. **(b)** In a small group, discuss your predictions and explain why you revised them.

Vocabulary

Practice Explain whether each sentence makes sense given the meaning of the underlined word. If a sentence does not make sense, revise it using the word correctly.

1. After <u>prolonged</u> workouts at the gym, he is finally back in shape.
2. The best tightrope walkers have no sense of <u>equilibrium</u>.
3. Open the windows; I need to <u>buffer</u> myself from the outside noise.
4. <u>Venturing</u> into the forest without a map is not a good idea.
5. After it is defrosted, <u>abruptly</u> cook the turkey for three hours.
6. An odometer helps you <u>gauge</u> how many miles you drive.

Word Study Use the context of the sentences and what you know about the **Latin prefix *pro-*** to explain your answer to each question.

1. If a runner *proceeds* to the finish line, has she finished the race?
2. Would a *progressive* idea look toward the future or the past?

Word Study

The **Latin prefix *pro-*** means "forth" or "forward."

Challenge Explain how the prefix *pro-* contributes to the meanings of these words. Consult a dictionary if necessary.

projectile
propeller
proficient

ASSESS/EXTEND

Answers

Literary Analysis

1. (a) **Possible response: researched facts:** Prolonged exposure . . . could cause permanent . . . damage; **personal experiences:** [Watching Dr. Block draw my veins] gave me the creeps; **opinions:** It was a great dream, swimming to Antarctica. **attitudes:** That part of me was excited about venturing into the unknown.

   For other sample answers, see ***Graphic Organizer Transparencies,* Literary Analysis Graphic Organizer A**, p. 12, and the **Additional Answers** section.

   (b) Students may note that Cox writes about the Antarctic as she experienced it and as she reflects upon the experience.

2. (a) A reporter's story would lack Cox's emotions and thoughts as well as her physical sensations. (b) **Possible response:** Knowing Cox's thoughts and feelings adds to the story's drama because she realizes the potential danger she is in which adds suspense.

Reading Skill

3. **Possible response:** At 21 minutes, something "clicks" for Cox; she begins swimming more strongly. Prediction: Cox will make it to the beach.
4. (a) Students may have revised predictions that Cox would fail. (b) Have students share their reasons for revising predictions.

Vocabulary

Practice

Sample answers:

1. This sentence does make sense because lengthy workouts would help someone get in shape.
2. This sentence does not make sense because tightrope walkers have a good sense of balance. "I need <u>equilibrium</u> to balance on such a small rope without falling."
3. This sentence does not make sense because the closed windows would be a buffer. "My headphones <u>buffer</u> me from the noise."

Answers continued

4. This sentence makes sense because risking a walk into a forest is even more of a risk without a map.
5. This sentence does not make sense because the turkey would take a long time to cook. "After fifteen minutes of steady walking, Marcia <u>abruptly</u> stopped."
6. This sentence makes sense because an odometer measures the number of miles you drive.

Word Study

Sample answers:

1. No; if she *proceeds*, she has not yet reached the end, she is going forward to it.
2. A *progressive* idea would look <u>forward</u> to the future.

Word Study: Challenge

Sample answers: A *projectile* is something that is shot <u>forward</u>. A *propeller* moves an airplane <u>forward</u>. If you are *proficient* at something, you are able to move <u>forward</u> through it easily.

PRETEACH

*Skills instruction for the **Reading Skill** and the **Literary Analysis** concept for this selection appears on p. 59.*

❶ Writing About the Big Question

1. Review the assignment with the class.
2. Discuss with students cases in which social realities, such as unfairness or prejudice, can conflict with truths, such as justice and decency.
3. Have students complete the sentence starter. Revise responses as a class. (**Possible response:** People who are able to <u>comprehend</u> the truth behind problems in society must decide whether to fight hard for change or allow the problems to remain.)
4. Remind students that their answers will help them think about the Big Question, "Is there a difference between reality and truth?"

While You Read

Tell students that as they read, they should look for ways the author challenges reality to reach her goal.

❷ Vocabulary

1. Have students preview the selection vocabulary.
2. For each word, have students say the word aloud.
3. Then, use the word in a sentence that defines the word.
4. Repeat your definitional sentence or a similar sentence with the word missing, and have the class "fill in the blank" chorally. Here is an example:

   You might show <u>indignation</u> when you react with anger to an injustice. When she cut in front of me in line, I could barely hide my [students say "indignation"].

❸ Word Study

1. Introduce the skill, using the instruction in the box.
2. Ask students to restate the definition of *supercilious*, using the word "above." (**Sample answer:** "behaving as though one feels above others in status").

Making Connections

Occupation: Conductorette

THE BIG ? Is there a difference between reality and truth?

❶ Writing About the Big Question

In "Occupation: Conductorette," a young girl experiences the harsh reality of prejudice. Use this sentence starter to develop your ideas about the Big Question.

People who are able to **comprehend** the truth behind problems in society must decide whether to ________________________ or ________________________.

While You Read Look for the ways the author challenges reality to fight for the job of streetcar conductor.

❷ Vocabulary

Read each word and its definition. Decide whether you know the word well, know it a little bit, or do not know it at all. After you read, see how your knowledge of each word has increased.

- **self-sufficiency** (self′ sə fish′ ən sē) *n.* independence (p. 79) ***His <u>self-sufficiency</u> helped him survive in the woods.*** *sufficient adj.*
- **indignation** (in′ dig nā′ shən) *n.* anger that is a reaction to injustice or meanness (p. 80) ***The <u>indignation</u> she felt towards the thief who stole her wallet was hard to put into words.*** *indignant adj.*
- **dingy** (din′ jē) *adj.* dirty-looking; shabby (p. 81) ***The dark walls made the room look <u>dingy</u>.*** *dingily adv. dinginess n.*
- **supercilious** (so͞o′pər sil′ ē əs) *adj.* expressing an attitude of superiority; contemptuous (p. 81) ***The queen gave the peasant a <u>supercilious</u> smile.*** *superciliously adv. superciliousness n.*
- **hypocrisy** (hi päk′ rə sē) *n.* the act of saying one thing but doing another (p. 81) ***The environmentalist's hypocrisy was revealed when he littered.*** *hypocrite n. hypocritical adj.*
- **dexterous** (deks′ tər əs) *adj.* having or showing mental skill (p. 83) ***She showed how <u>dexterous</u> she was by quickly answering all the questions with ease.*** *dexterity n.*

❸ Word Study

The **Latin prefix *super-*** means "above."

In this excerpt, a young Maya Angelou tries to project confidence and show that she is above others by speaking in a **supercilious** manner, but she is really quite nervous.

Vocabulary Development

Vocabulary Knowledge Rating

Create a **Vocabulary Knowledge Rating Chart** (***Professional Development Guidebook***, p. 33) for this selection. Include the selection vocabulary and the Big Question words that appear in the Writing About the Big Question sentence starter on this page. (The Big Question vocabulary is introduced on pp. 2–3.)

Give students a copy of the chart. Read the words aloud, and have students mark their rating in the Before Reading column. Urge them to be alert to these words as they read and discuss the selection.

Tally how many students think they know a word to gauge how much instruction to provide. As students read and discuss the selection, point out the words and their context.

PHLit Online! **Vocabulary Central**, featuring tools, activities, and songs for studying vocabulary, is available at **www.PHLitOnline.com**.

Meet
Maya Angelou
(b. 1928)

Author of
Occupation: Conductorette

Maya Angelou was born Marguerite Johnson in St. Louis, Missouri. *I Know Why the Caged Bird Sings,* the work from which this selection comes, is the first part of her autobiography.

Up From Hard Times Some of the communities in which Angelou grew up were segregated—African Americans were excluded from facilities, including schools, used by whites. Yet, Angelou rejects bitterness, saying, "The honorary duty of a human being is to love."

Angelou has had diverse experiences in life. She worked with Dr. Martin Luther King, Jr., in the civil rights movement. Afterward, she moved to Africa, where she lived from 1961 to 1966. Her literary success came in the 1970s.

DID YOU KNOW?
Angelou read one of her poems at President William Jefferson Clinton's inauguration in 1993.

❹ BACKGROUND FOR THE AUTOBIOGRAPHY

Jobs and World War II

During the 1940s, the time Maya Angelou recalls, millions of American men went overseas to fight World War II. Their absence created new opportunities at home. Six million women went to work in industry to aid the war effort, taking jobs newly open to them. Although African Americans still faced prejudice, some found—or made—new opportunities for themselves.

Daily Bellringer

For each class during which you will teach this selection, have students complete one of the five Sentence Modeling activities for Week 2 in the ***Daily Bellringer Activities*** booklet.

❹ Background

Jobs and World War II

At the start of World War II, the American economy still suffered the lingering effects of the Great Depression. That began to change even before the United States entered the war. American industry turned toward military needs, such as manufacturing airplanes, tanks, and weapons, plus such goods as synthetic rubber. Suddenly, labor, not jobs, was in short supply. The Great Depression was over.

The wartime economy produced major social change, particularly for African Americans. Many thousands moved from the rural, agricultural South to northern cities. There, African Americans found work in war industries. Along with increased economic opportunity, they found a new access to civil rights that white Americans took for granted.

Multidraft Reading

This icon ● marks natural pauses in the selection. To assist struggling readers and to deepen reading for all, assign the text in "chunks," following the icons, and apply multidraft reading protocols. For each reading, have students set the purpose indicated:

- **First reading**—literal comprehension: answering the Reading Check questions.
- **Second reading**—application of skills: answering the Make Predictions and Author's Perspective prompts.
- **Third reading**—interpretation: answering the end-of-selection questions.

For more guidance, refer to the **Classroom Strategies and Teaching Routines** on multidraft reading.

Differentiated Instruction — Additional Instruction

EL Extended Support—English Learners
Have students complete the **Reading and Vocabulary Warm-ups, *Unit 1 Resources,*** pp. 87–90, before they read. Assign the prereading pages in the ***Reader's Notebook: English Learner's Version.*** Then, have students listen to portions of the selection on the ***Hear It!*** **Audio CD.**

L1 L2 Extended Support—Struggling Readers
Have students complete the **Reading and Vocabulary Warm-ups, *Unit 1 Resources,*** pp. 87–90, before they read. Assign the prereading pages in the ***Reader's Notebook: Adapted Version.*** Then, have students listen to portions of the selection on the ***Hear It!*** **Audio CD** (adapted text).

Extended Support—Reluctant Readers
To build motivation and engagement before assigning the selection, have students read "Women's Wage Gap," a thematically related selection in ***Reality Central.*** Then, use the questions at the conclusion of the related selection to guide discussion.

PHLit Online!
For more about the author, practice with the selection vocabulary, and more background, go to at **www.PHLitOnline.com.**

TEACH

❶ Activating Prior Knowledge

1. Ask students what they know about the civil rights movement. Explain that this story takes place during World War II and that the civil rights movement did not take place until after the war. Point out that segregation—laws prohibiting African Americans and whites from using many of the same public facilities—was still in place at the time the story takes place.
2. Explain that this story is about the author as a young black girl and her personal struggle against social injustices. Ask students to consider these questions as they read:
   - What does the historical context reveal about the character in the story?
   - Would the story be less powerful if it did not take place in this context?
3. Guide students to keep in mind that this is Angelou's personal story. She learns about herself within the context of her world.

Concept Connector ⟶

Students will follow up on this activity after completing the story.

Whole-Class Activity

A key scene in "Occupation: Conductorette" focuses on a formal, almost ritualized, interaction between Angelou and a receptionist. Ask students to consider the unstated rules that govern interactions between people, especially in the workplace. If students have jobs or have applied for them, have them describe an encounter in which awkwardness and emotional response were hidden behind formalities.

❷ About the Selection

In "Occupation: Conductorette," fifteen-year-old Maya Angelou decides she wants to be a streetcar conductorette in World War II-era San Francisco. The fact that the streetcar company does not employ African Americans only increases her determination. In her battle against segregation and complacency, Angelou learns about her mother, herself, and the society in which she lives.

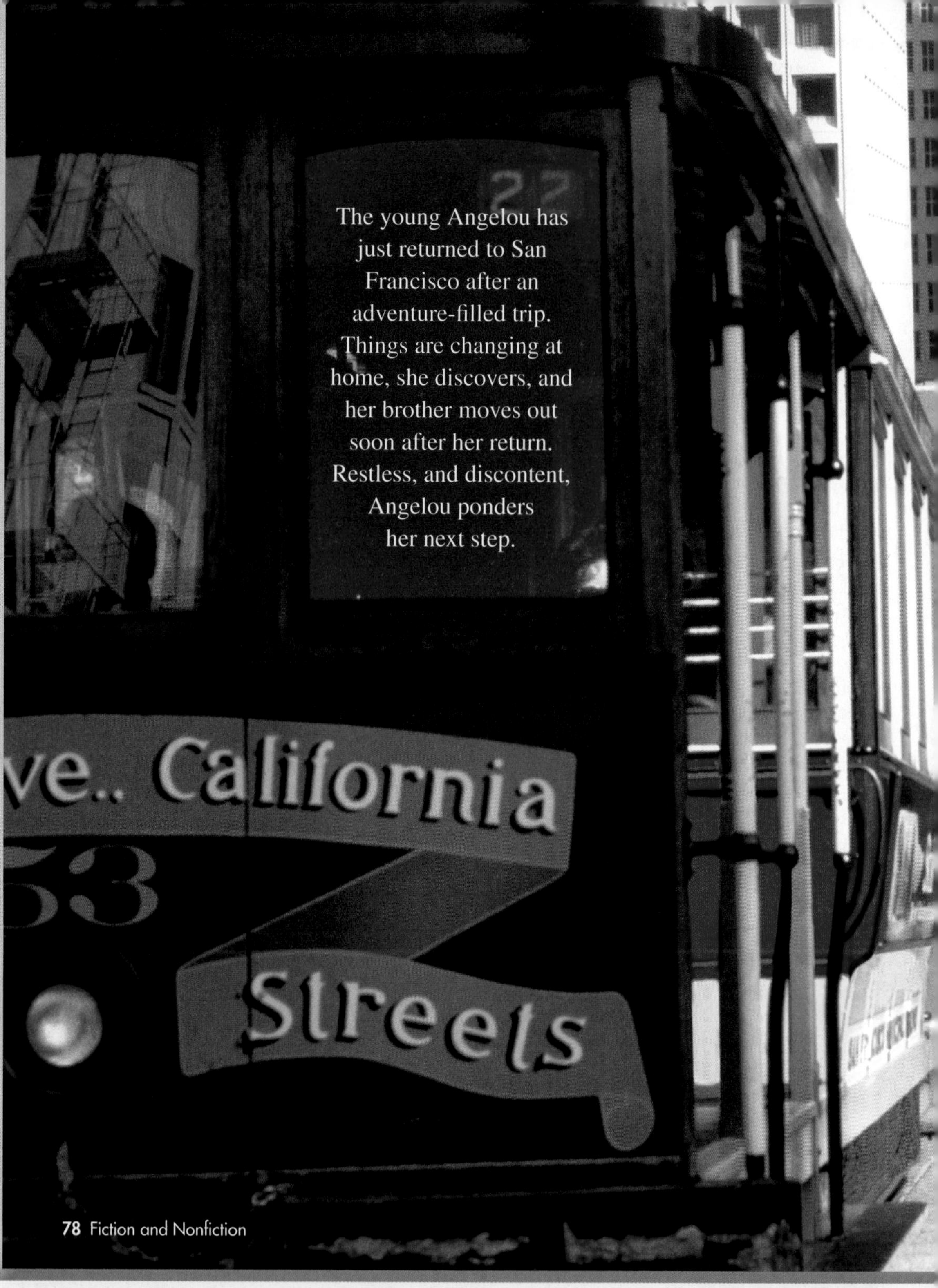

The young Angelou has just returned to San Francisco after an adventure-filled trip. Things are changing at home, she discovers, and her brother moves out soon after her return. Restless, and discontent, Angelou ponders her next step.

78 Fiction and Nonfiction

Vocabulary Development

Thematic Vocabulary: The Big Question

As students are discussing "Occupation: Conductorette," have them use the thematic vocabulary presented in Introducing the Big Question, pp. 2–3. You might encourage them with sentence starters like these:

1. At first, Angelou does not *comprehend* how difficult . . .
2. Angelou's *objective* is to . . .
3. Many people thought it was *improbable* that Angelou . . .
4. Angelou's mother's actions are *evidence* that she . . .

1 2

Occupation: Conductorette

from

I Know Why the Caged Bird Sings

Maya Angelou

3 **I had it.** The answer came to me with the suddenness of a collision. I would go to work. Mother wouldn't be difficult to convince; after all, in school I was a year ahead of my grade and Mother was a firm believer in self-sufficiency. In fact, she'd be pleased to think that I had that much gumption, that much of her in my character. (She liked to speak of herself as the original "do-it-yourself girl.")

Vocabulary
self-sufficiency
(self´ sə fish´ ən sē)
n. independence

3 Critical Thinking

Speculate

1. Reminds students that as they read, they should develop ideas about what will occur in the story based on details that they encounter in a text.
2. Have students read the bracketed text of the story. **Ask:** Based on the first paragraph, what do you think the story will be about? **Possible response:** This story will be about Angelou's struggle to find a job.
3. **Ask:** What do you think will be the outcome of the story? **Possible response:** Some students may say that Angelou will succeed in finding employment because she is motivated and intelligent. Other students may say that Angelou will not get a job because, although she has decided to find a job, she appears to be making an impulsive decision.

Differentiated Instruction for Universal Access

Culturally Responsive Instruction

Culture Connection Point out to students that, even when she was only fifteen years old, Maya Angelou sought to overcome the prevalent racial prejudice against African Americans. Since then, Maya Angelou has been a strong proponent of equal rights for African Americans, spreading her messages through her award-winning books, poetry, speeches, essays, and plays.

Explain to students that it is often passionate, strong people like Maya Angelou who help to bring about necessary social, cultural, and economic change. Ask students to identify prominent figures from their own cultures who have accomplished or are working to create positive change for their people. Then, have students discuss how society has benefited from these individuals' dedicated work.

PHLit Online!

This selection is available in interactive format in the **Enriched Online Student Edition**, **www.PHLitOnline.com**, which includes a thematically related video with writing prompt and an interactive graphic organizer.

❹ Critical Viewing

Answer: The picture of the ticket suggests that the conductorette marks the ticket to show what station a person got on and at what time.

❺ Literary Analysis

Author's Perspective

1. Remind students that an author who has experienced an event can write from the perspective of the event as it is happening and from the perspective of looking back in time at the event.
2. **Ask** students to describe the perspective Maya Angelou chose to use to tell of the events she describes in "Occupation: Conductorette."
   Possible response: Angelou is an adult reflecting on the experience of her teenage years.
3. Have students read the bracketed passage. **Ask:** Which details show Angelou's teenage personality? Which show her attitude as an adult?
   Possible response: Angelou's impulsive decision to leave school at fifteen and her attraction to the job of streetcar conductor based on her liking of the uniform are examples of her teenage personality. Angelou's comment on her youthful failure to become instantly angry at racial discrimination represents an adult perspective.

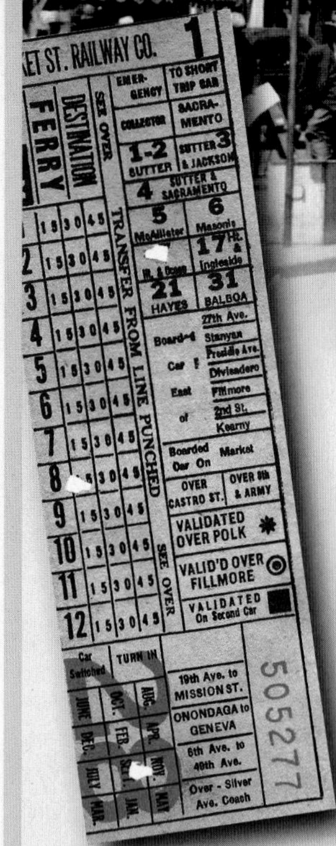

❹ ▲ **Critical Viewing**
Based on this ticket, what do you think might be one of the tasks of a conductorette? Explain. **[Infer]**

Vocabulary
indignation (in′ dig nā′ shən) *n.* anger that is a reaction to injustice or meanness

Literary Analysis
Author's Perspective
Which details show Angelou's teenage personality? Which show her attitude as an adult?

Once I had settled on getting a job, all that remained was to decide which kind of job I was most fitted for. My intellectual pride had kept me from selecting typing, shorthand or filing as subjects in school, so office work was ruled out. War plants and shipyards demanded birth certificates, and mine would reveal me to be fifteen, and ineligible for work. So the well-paying defense jobs were also out. Women had replaced men on the streetcars as conductors and motormen, and the thought of sailing up and down the hills of San Francisco in a dark-blue uniform, with a money changer at my belt, caught my fancy.

❺ Mother was as easy as I had anticipated. The world was moving so fast, so much money was being made, so many people were dying in Guam, and Germany,[1] that hordes of strangers became good friends overnight. Life was cheap and death entirely free. How could she have the time to think about my academic career?

To her question of what I planned to do, I replied that I would get a job on the streetcars. She rejected the proposal with: "They don't accept colored people on the streetcars."

I would like to claim an immediate fury which was followed by the noble determination to break the restricting tradition. But the truth is, my first reaction was one of disappointment. I'd pictured myself, dressed in a neat blue serge suit, my money changer swinging jauntily at my waist, and a cheery smile for the passengers which would make their own work day brighter.

From disappointment, I gradually ascended the emotional ladder to haughty **indignation,** and finally to that state of stubbornness where the mind is locked like the jaws of an enraged bulldog.

I would go to work on the streetcars and wear a blue serge suit. Mother gave me her support with one of her usual terse asides, "That's what you want to do? Then nothing beats a trial but a failure. Give it everything you've got. I've told you many times, 'Can't do is like Don't Care.' Neither of them have a home."

Translated, that meant there was nothing a person can't do, and there should be nothing a human being didn't care about. It was the most positive encouragement I could have hoped for.

1. **Guam** (gwäm), and Germany places where World War II (1939–1945) was fought. Guam is an island in the Pacific Ocean.

Vocabulary Development

Vocabulary Reinforcement

Reinforce students' comprehension of the vocabulary word using "show-you-know" sentences in which the first part of the sentence uses the vocabulary word in an appropriate context. The second part of the sentence clarifies the first. Model the strategy using the word *indignation.*

The woman's letter expressed her *indignation;* she explained that she wanted a full refund and she would not be coming back to the store any time soon.

Then give students these sentence prompts, and coach them to complete the sentences.

1. My eyes glanced around the *dingy* room; _____.
   Sample answer: even in the poor lighting, I could see that the paint was peeling.
2. I saw the *supercilious* expression on the man's face; ______.
   Sample answer: he clearly did not have a high opinion of me.

In the offices of the Market Street Railway Company, the receptionist seemed as surprised to see me there as I was surprised to find the interior **dingy** and the décor drab. Somehow I had expected waxed surfaces and carpeted floors. If I had met no resistance, I might have decided against working for such a poor-mouth-looking concern. As it was, I explained that I had come to see about a job. She asked, was I sent by an agency, and when I replied that I was not, she told me they were only accepting applicants from agencies.

The classified pages of the morning papers had listed
6 advertisements for motorettes and conductorettes and I reminded her of that. She gave me a face full of astonishment that my suspicious nature would not accept.

"I am applying for the job listed in this morning's *Chronicle* and I'd like to be presented to your personnel manager." While I spoke in **supercilious** accents, and looked at the room as if I had an oil well in my own backyard, my armpits were being pricked by millions of hot pointed needles. She saw her escape and dived into it.

"He's out. He's out for the day. You might call tomorrow and if he's in, I'm sure you can see him." Then she swiveled her chair around on its rusty screws and with that I was supposed to be dismissed.

"May I ask his name?"

She half turned, acting surprised to find me still there.

"His name? Whose name?"

"Your personnel manager."

We were firmly joined in the **hypocrisy** to play out the scene.

"The personnel manager? Oh, he's Mr. Cooper, but I'm not sure you'll find him here tomorrow. He's . . . Oh, but you can try."

"Thank you."

"You're welcome."

And I was out of the musty room and into the even mustier lobby. In the street I saw the receptionist and myself going faithfully through paces that were stale with familiarity, although I had never encountered that kind of situation before and, probably, neither had 7 she. We were like actors who, knowing the play by heart, were still able to cry afresh over the old tragedies and laugh spontaneously at the comic situations.

8 ↓ The miserable little encounter had nothing to do with me, the me

Vocabulary

dingy (din′ jē) *adj.* dirty-looking; shabby

supercilious (so͞o′ pər sil′ ē əs) *adj.* expressing an attitude of superiority; contemptuous

hypocrisy (hi päk′ rə sē) *n.* the act of saying one thing but doing another

Reading Check

What major obstacle does Angelou face in her job quest?

6 Connecting to the Big Question

1. Explain that coming-of-age stories tell about real challenges and experiences that can transform a young person into an adult. One common theme in coming-of-age stories is the reality that the character ends up looking at himself or herself very differently.
2. Have students read the bracketed passage. **Ask** students how Angelou balances youthful and adult perspectives in describing this incident.
   Possible response: Angelou's expectation of "waxed surfaces and carpeted floors," her suspicion of the receptionist, and her own supercilious manner show her teenage personality. Her recognition that she would have walked away from fighting for the job if she had not met resistance and the "hot pointed needles" she felt in her armpits show her adult attitude.
3. Discuss with students how the dual perspective affects the text. Suggest that Angelou is able to capture both the serious reality of the challenge she faced and her naivete as a teenager.
4. As they continue reading, direct students to pay close attention to clues about how Angelou's challenge helps change her into an adult.

7 Reading Check

Answer: The major obstacle she faces is the Market Street Railway Company's policy against hiring African Americans.

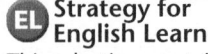

Differentiated Instruction for Universal Access

EL Strategy for English Learners

This selection contains several idioms that may prove difficult for English learners. Explain to students that an idiom is an expression that means something more or different from the meaning of the words that make it up. For example, the idiom "reach for the stars" does not literally mean to stretch one's arm toward the sky, but to have ambitious goals. Direct students' attention to the following idioms in the selection:

- On p. 80, Angelou says that she "settled on" getting a job. Explain to students that this idiom does not refer to moving to a place or to sitting down, as the word *settled* might suggest. Instead, it means to choose one of a number of alternatives.
- When Angelou says on p. 81 that she and the receptionist were "going faithfully through paces," she does not mean they were walking. *Going through paces*, like *going through the motions*, refers to a pattern of activity that is routine, formalized, or automatic but that is not sincerely meant. A related expression, *putting someone through his or her paces*, means to require someone to demonstrate what they know or can do as a test or challenge.

8 Reading Skill

Make Predictions

Remind students of the historical context of the memoir. Have students read the bracketed text. **Ask** the Reading Skill prompt: Explain whether the details in this paragraph verify or lead you to revise your prediction about whether Angelou will get the job.

Possible response: Angelou describes a continuous struggle between two forces that inevitably ends with one side standing victorious. She is aware that the peculiar interaction with the secretary has nothing to do with either of them; it is a product of decisions made in the past. This makes me think that she will not get the job.

Reading Skill
Make Predictions
Explain whether the details in this paragraph verify or lead you to revise your prediction about whether Angelou will get the job. 8

of me, any more than it had to do with that silly clerk. The incident was a recurring dream, concocted years before by stupid whites and it eternally came back to haunt us all. The secretary and I were like Hamlet and Laertes[2] in the final scene, where, because of harm done by one ancestor to another, we were bound to duel to the death. Also because the play must end somewhere.

I went further than forgiving the clerk, I accepted her as a fellow victim of the same puppeteer.

On the streetcar, I put my fare into the box and the conductorette looked at me with the usual hard eyes of white contempt. "Move into the car, please move on in the car." She patted her money changer.

Her Southern nasal accent sliced my meditation and I looked deep into my thoughts. All lies, all comfortable lies. The receptionist was not innocent and neither was I. The whole charade we had played out in that crummy waiting room had directly to do with me, Black, and her, white.

I wouldn't move into the streetcar but stood on the ledge over the conductor, glaring. My mind shouted so energetically that the announcement made my veins stand out, and my mouth tighten into a prune.

I WOULD HAVE THE JOB. I WOULD BE A CONDUCTORETTE AND SLING A FULL MONEY CHANGER FROM MY BELT. I WOULD.

The next three weeks were a honeycomb[3] of determination with apertures for the days to go in and out. The Negro organizations to whom I appealed for support bounced me back and forth like a shuttlecock on a badminton court. Why did I insist on that particular job? Openings were going begging that paid nearly twice the money. The minor officials with whom I was able to win an audience thought me mad. Possibly I was.

Downtown San Francisco became alien and cold, and the streets I had loved in a personal familiarity were unknown lanes that twisted with malicious intent. Old buildings, whose gray rococo façades[4] housed my memories of the Forty-Niners, and Diamond Lil, Robert Service, Sutter and Jack London, were then imposing structures viciously joined to keep me out. My trips to the streetcar office were of the frequency of a person on salary. The struggle expanded. I was no longer in conflict only with the Market Street Railway

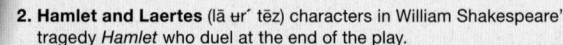

2. **Hamlet and Laertes** (lā ʉr´ tēz) characters in William Shakespeare's tragedy *Hamlet* who duel at the end of the play.
3. **honeycomb** (hun´ ē kōm´) *n.* wax structure, filled with holes, that bees build to store honey.
4. **rococo façades** (rə kō´ kō fə sädz´) elaborately designed building fonts.

Vocabulary Development

Vocabulary Knowledge Rating

When students have completed reading and discussing "Occupation: Conductorette," have them take out their **Vocabulary Knowledge Rating Chart** for this selection. Read the words aloud once more, and have students rate their knowledge of the words again in the After Reading column. Clarify any words that are still problematic. Have students write their own definition and example or sentence in the appropriate column. Then, have students complete the Vocabulary Practice at the end of the selection. Encourage students to use the words in further discussion and written work about this selection. Remind them that they will be accountable for these words on the **Selection Test, *Unit 1 Resources*,** pp. 102–104 or pp. 105–107.

but with the marble lobby of the building which housed its offices, and elevators and their operators.

During this period of strain Mother and I began our first steps on the long path toward mutual adult admiration. She never asked for reports and I didn't offer any details. But every morning she made breakfast, gave me carfare and lunch money, as if I were going to work. She comprehended the perversity of life, that in the struggle lies the joy. That I was no glory seeker was obvious to her, and that I had to exhaust every possibility before giving in was also clear.

On my way out of the house one morning she said, "Life is going to give you just what you put in it. Put your whole heart in everything you do, and pray, then you can wait." Another time she reminded me that "God helps those who help themselves." She had a store of aphorisms which she dished out as the occasion demanded. Strangely, as bored as I was with clichés, her inflection gave them something new, and set me thinking for a little while at least. Later when asked how I got my job, I was never able to say exactly. I only knew that
10 one day, which was tiresomely like all the others before it, I sat in the Railway office, ostensibly waiting to be interviewed. The receptionist called me to her desk and shuffled a bundle of papers to me. They were job application forms. She said they had to be filled in triplicate. I had little time to wonder if I had won or not, for the standard questions reminded me of the necessity for **dexterous** lying. How old was I? List my previous jobs, starting from the last held and go backward to the first. How much money did I earn, and why did I leave the position? Give two references (not relatives).

Sitting at a side table my mind and I wove a cat's ladder of near truths and total lies. I kept my face blank (an old art) and wrote quickly the fable of Marguerite Johnson, aged nineteen, former companion and driver for Mrs. Annie Henderson (a White Lady) in Stamps, Arkansas.

I was given blood tests, aptitude tests, physical coordination tests, and Rorschachs,[5] then on a blissful day I was hired as the first Negro on the San Francisco streetcars.

Mother gave me the money to have my blue serge suit tailored, and I learned to fill out work cards, operate the money changer and punch transfers. The time crowded together and at an End of Days I was swinging on the back of the rackety trolley, smiling sweetly and persuading my charges to "step forward in the car, please."

5. **Rorschachs** (rôr′ shäks′) The Rorschach test is a method of analyzing an individual's personality using abstract images.

9 LITERATURE IN CONTEXT

History Connection

San Francisco and the Gold Rushes When she looks at the buildings of San Francisco, Angelou thinks of names associated with the gold rushes of the 1800s:

- **Forty-Niners** were the prospectors who poured into the San Francisco area in the California Gold Rush of 1849. They transformed San Francisco from a small town of 800 to a rough-and-tumble city of 25,000.
- **Diamond Lil** was a flashy entertainer.
- **Robert Service** was a Canadian poet who portrayed the miners of the Yukon Gold Rush of the 1890s.
- **Robert Sutter** was the owner of the land where gold was first discovered in California.
- **Jack London** was a writer who re-created his experiences in the Yukon Gold Rush in stories and the novel *Call of the Wild* (1903).

Connect to the Literature

How does Angelou feel about the buildings she associates with these historical figures?

Vocabulary
dexterous (deks′ tər əs) *adj.* having or showing mental skill

9 Literature in Context

History Connection The great Gold Rush of 1849 started with the discovery of gold on John Sutter's land in 1848. Hundreds of thousands of people traveled to California in hopes of finding sudden riches. Most of the prospectors, known as Forty-Niners, were individuals searching for gold on their own. By the early 1850s, however, industrial mining corporations had taken over. The wild days were over. Despite its short span, the Gold Rush transformed California and the entire United States. Trails were blazed, and new roads were built. Industry gained a stronger foothold in the nation.

Connect to the Literature After students discuss the historical associations of San Francisco, **ask** the Connect to the Literature question: How does Angelou feel about the buildings she associates with these historical figures?
Possible response: Angelou regards these historic buildings as "imposing structures viciously joined" to exclude her.

10 Reading Skill

Make Predictions

Before students read the bracketed passage, have them **summarize** what happens to Angelou as she seeks to become a conductorette.
Answer: Angelou tries to apply at the Market Street Railway Company and is put off by the receptionist, increasing her determination. Seeking an interview, she returns daily. Meanwhile, she and her mother gain new respect for each other.

▶ **Monitor Progress:** Have students use their Prediction Charts to predict what the final outcome of Angelou's battle will be. Then, after students complete the selection, **ask** them if the final paragraphs verified their predictions or led them to revise.
Possible response: Angelou got the job, which may verify the predictions of many students. However, she quits after a few months, which may lead students to revise.

▶ **Reteach:** If students have difficulty using new information to revise their predictions, model revising a prediction using **Reading Skill Graphic Organizer A** in *Graphic Organizer Transparencies*, p. 13.

Concept Connector

Activating Prior Knowledge
Ask students to recall their responses to these questions: What does the historical context reveal about the character in the story? Would the story be less powerful if it did not take place in this context? Invite students to cite examples from the story to support their responses.

Writing About the Big Question
Have students compare their responses to the sentence starter they completed before reading "Occupation: Conductorette" with their ideas afterward. Ask them to explain whether their thoughts have changed.

Reading Skill Graphic Organizer
Have students review their Prediction charts. Ask how many students were able to verify their predictions and how many revised their predictions based on information they learned after making them. Show students **Reading Skill Graphic Organizer A** (*Graphic Organizer Transparencies*, p. 13) as an example. You may want to have students work in pairs to compare their predictions, verifications, and revisions.

ASSESS

Answers

Critical Thinking

1. Most students will say they hoped Angelou would get the job because it would be a victory over racism.
2. (a) Angelou compares the encounter to the final duel between Hamlet and Laertes. (b) The conductorette's contempt brings home the personal reality racism has for Angelou, and she no longer views the earlier encounter to be ritualized and impersonal.
3. She insists on becoming a conductorette because of the stubborn, dishonest resistance she encounters at the streetcar company. She also likes the uniform.
4. (a) The mother says, "Can't do is like Don't Care," and she tells Angelou to "Put your whole heart in everything you do, and pray, then you can wait." Both show she understands life to be a struggle one must undertake with perseverance. (b) She never stops supporting Angelou's determination to succeed.

Is there a difference between reality and truth?

The accepted reality in San Francisco was that African Americans were not, and were not allowed to be, streetcar conductors. Angelou challenged this reality by becoming a conductor.

For one whole semester the street cars and I shimmied up and scooted down the sheer hills of San Francisco. I lost some of my need for the Black ghetto's shielding-sponge quality, as I clanged and cleared my way down Market Street, with its honky-tonk homes for homeless sailors, past the quiet retreat of Golden Gate Park and along closed undwelled-in-looking dwellings of the Sunset District.

My work shifts were split so haphazardly that it was easy to believe that my superiors had chosen them maliciously. Upon mentioning my suspicions to Mother, she said, "Don't worry about it. You ask for what you want, and you pay for what you get. And I'm going to show you that it ain't no trouble when you pack double."

You ask for what you want, and you pay for what you get.

She stayed awake to drive me out to the car barn at four thirty in the mornings, or to pick me up when I was relieved just before dawn. Her awareness of life's perils convinced her that while I would be safe on the public conveyances, she "wasn't about to trust a taxi driver with her baby."

When the spring classes began, I resumed my commitment with formal education. I was so much wiser and older, so much more independent, with a bank account and clothes that I had bought for myself, that I was sure that I had learned and earned the magic formula which would make me a part of the gay life my contemporaries led.

Critical Thinking

1. **Respond:** Did you hope Angelou would get the conductorette job? Explain.
2. **(a)** To what does Angelou compare her first encounter with the secretary at the railway company? **(b) Analyze Cause and Effect:** Explain how the greeting of the streetcar conductorette changes Angelou's view of the meeting.
3. **Interpret:** Explain why Angelou insists on becoming a conductorette. List details from the selection to support your answer.
4. **(a) Interpret:** Find two passages in which Angelou's mother reacts to her quest, and explain what each shows about her mother's view of life. **(b) Draw Conclusions:** In what ways does her mother contribute to Angelou's success?

Is there a difference between reality and truth? In what ways does Angelou's attempt to become a streetcar conductor challenge the accepted reality for African Americans in San Francisco?

Assessment Resources

Unit 1 Resources

L1 L2 EL **Selection Test A,** pp. 102–104. Administer Test A to less advanced readers and English learners.

L3 L4 **Selection Test B,** pp. 105–107. Administer Test B to on-level and more advanced students.

L3 L4 **Open-Book Test,** pp. 78–80. As an alternative, give the Open-Book Test.

All **Customizable Test Bank**

All **Self-tests**

Students may prepare for the **Selection Test** by taking the **Self-test** online.

PHLit Online! All assessment resources are available at **www.PHLitOnline.com.**

After You Read | Occupation: Conductorette

Literary Analysis: Author's Perspective

1. **(a)** Using a chart like the one shown, analyze the **author's perspective** in the selection.

Author's Perspective	
Types of Details Included	**Examples of Each**
❑ researched facts ❑ personal experiences ❑ opinions ❑ attitudes	

   (b) Referring to your chart, briefly describe Angelou's perspective.
2. What is Angelou's present attitude toward her younger self? In your answer, consider her use of phrases such as "haughty indignation" to describe her reactions at the time.

Reading Skill: Make Predictions

3. Identify details in the selection that you used to **verify a prediction.**
4. **(a)** Identify one prediction you **revised** as you read. **(b)** In a small group, discuss your predictions and explain why you revised them.

Vocabulary

Practice Explain whether each sentence makes sense given the meaning of the underlined word. If a sentence does not make sense, revise it using the word correctly.

1. She whines until her little brother makes her lunch for her—a clear sign of her self-sufficiency.
2. I painted the room a bright white to add to its dingy feeling.
3. When you ask him for help, give him a supercilious look.
4. Reading the thank you letter gave him a great sense of indignation.
5. Known for his hypocrisy, he always said exactly what he felt.
6. Pat is such a dexterous thinker that she is never at a loss for words.

Word Study Use the context of the sentences and what you know about the **Latin prefix *super-*** to explain your answer to each question.

1. If a pet requires *supervision,* should it be left alone?
2. Does a *supervisor* generally give or receive orders?

Word Study

The **Latin prefix *super-*** means "above."

Challenge Explain how the prefix *super-* contributes to the meanings of these words. Consult a dictionary if necessary.

superimpose
superintendent
supersonic

EXTEND/ASSESS

Answers

Literary Analysis

1. (a) **Possible response: researched facts:** war plants and shipyards demanded birth certificates; **personal experiences**: She told me they were only accepting applications from agencies. **opinions:** The receptionist seemed . . . surprised to see me there. **attitudes:** A face full of astonishment that my suspicious nature would not accept.

   For other sample answers, see *Graphic Organizer Transparencies,* **Literary Analysis Graphic Organizer A**, p. 13, and the **Additional Answers** section.

   (b) Angelou's perspective combines the determined, if naive, idealism she has as a teenager with the amusement and the pride of an adult looking back at her struggle.
2. Angelou is aware of the limits of her youthful idealism. She is also very proud of her determination.

Reading Skill

3. **Possible response:** Students who predicted that she would have difficulty with the job may note that details describing Angelou's struggles verified their predictions.
4. (a) Students may say they revised their predictions when they noted details about Angelou's determination. (b) Students should describe specific reasons for revising their predictions.

Vocabulary

Practice

Sample answers:

1. The sentence does not make sense because the actions show dependence. "Her *self-sufficiency* keeps her from feeling lonely and bored."
2. The sentence does not make sense because bright white is not dingy. "The room, once clean, was now terribly *dingy.*"
3. The sentence does not make sense because contempt will not encourage anyone. "His *supercilious* manner showed his dislike of most people."

Answers continued

4. The sentence does not make sense because a thank you letter would make someone pleased, not angry. "Reading the angry letter gave him a great sense of *indignation.*"
5. The sentence does not make sense because *hypocrisy* means "saying one thing and doing something else." "Known for his hypocrisy, he always said one thing and did something else."
6. This sentence does make sense because someone who is *dexterous* can do things easily. "Pat is such a dexterous thinker that she is never at a loss for words."

Word Study

Sample answers:

1. No, it should be watched over.
2. A supervisor gives orders because he or she is in charge of watching over someone.

Word Study: Challenge

Sample answers: When you *superimpose* something, you put it above or on top of something else. A *superintendent* is in a position above others. *Supersonic* is above the speed of sound.

EXTEND/ASSESS

Answers

Grammar

1. Introduce the skill, using the instruction on the student page.
2. Discuss the definitions and the examples in the chart.

Think Aloud: Model the Skill

Say to students:

I can make my writing more interesting by using abstract and concrete nouns. I might write *Justice belongs to all humanity*, using two abstract nouns. My sentence is more interesting, though, if I include concrete nouns: *Justice belongs to the window washer as well as to the president.* The concrete nouns *window washer* and *president* add vividness to my sentence.

WG Writing and Grammar, Grade 10

Students will find further instruction and practice in abstract and concrete nouns in Chapter 16, Section 1.

Practice A

1. water: concrete; endurance: abstract
2. Lynne Cox, team: concrete; goal: abstract
3. swimmer, wet suit, dry suit: concrete
4. Cox: concrete; faith, determination: abstract

Challenge

Sample answer: Concrete: hands, glacier, Antarctica; abstract: expectations, excitement, panic

Practice B

Sample answers:

1. abstract; He had the gumption to walk right up to me!
2. concrete; I arrived just as the streetcar was pulling away.
3. abstract; Tom made a commitment to help his brother.
4. concrete; The tall building loomed over the street.
5. abstract; The woman's determination impressed her employers.

Challenge

Sample answer: Maria fell into her chair in exhaustion.

Integrated Language Skills

from Swimming to Antarctica • Occupation: Conductorette

Grammar: Abstract and Concrete Nouns

A **noun** is a word that names a person, a place, or a thing.

Concrete nouns name specific things that can be directly experienced or perceived by the senses. The word *airplane* is a concrete noun because it names something you can see, feel, and hear.

Abstract nouns name ideas or concepts that cannot be seen, heard, felt, tasted, smelled, or directly experienced. *Justice* is an abstract noun because it is a concept that cannot be directly perceived by the senses.

Concrete Nouns	Abstract Nouns
The *pancakes* are still hot.	*Honesty* is an important trait for everyone.
My sister wanted a small *dog* with soft, fluffy fur and a wet nose.	Her greatest wish was for *peace* around the world.
The *car* was so loud I could not hear what my mother was saying.	*Democracy* is an important tradition in the United States.

Practice A Identify the noun or nouns in each sentence, and indicate whether they are concrete or abstract nouns. There are eleven in all.

1. To swim in cold water takes much endurance.
2. Lynne Cox needed a team to help her reach her goal.
3. A cold-water swimmer usually wears a wetsuit or a drysuit.
4. Cox relied on faith and determination.

Challenge Find three concrete nouns and three abstract nouns in *Swimming to Antarctica.*

Practice B Label each noun as concrete or abstract. Then, use each word in a sentence.

1. gumption
2. streetcar
3. commitment
4. building
5. determination

Challenge Using this sentence as a model, write two more sentences that feature both concrete and abstract nouns: *Today is a basket of joy.*

WG Writing and Grammar Connection: Chapter 16, Section 1

Extend the Lesson

Sentence Modeling

Choose the sentence given from the selection students have read:

- I began to notice that the cold was pressurizing my body like a giant tourniquet. (from *Swimming to Antarctica*)
- From disappointment, I gradually climbed the emotional ladder to haughty indignation, and finally to the state of stubbornness where the mind is locked like the jaws of an enraged bulldog. ("Occupation: Conductorette")

Ask students what they notice about the sentence. Elicit that it contains abstract and concrete nouns. (*Swimming to Antarctica:* concrete noun *tourniquet* helps to describe *cold.* "Occupation: Conductorette": concrete noun *ladder* helps to describe *disappointment*, *indignation*, and *stubbornness.*)

Have students imitate each grammatical and stylistic feature discussed in a sentence on a topic of their choosing. Have them share with the class.

Writing

Each selection provides information to help readers imagine an important scene. Write a brief **description** of either a scene in Antarctica or a 1940s streetcar ride.

- Use your prior knowledge and the information you learned from reading Cox's or Angelou's work to help you write your description.
- Identify the mood, or atmosphere, you want to create. For example, consider whether you want to convey danger, beauty, or frustration.
- Use precise words and sensory details to capture the scene and to create your chosen mood.

Writing Workshop: *Work in Progress*

Prewriting for Autobiographical Narrative Review the Place List in your writing portfolio. Use your notes to write three to four lines about each item. Choose the one that is most meaningful to you and write a few sentences telling why. Save this Place Description in your writing portfolio for later development.

Use this prewriting activity to prepare for the **Writing Workshop** on page 108.

Research and Technology

Keep a **daily observation journal** and use it to chart one of the following situations, depending on the story you read.

- If you read *Swimming to Antarctica*, keep a daily observation journal charting your speed or accomplishments in some activity, such as the number of miles you run in a day or the number of words you can type in a minute.
- If you read "Occupation: Conductorette," observe someone who has a job you might be interested in some day. Keep a journal to chart the person's work, recording the important tasks of the day and the time each task takes.

Follow these steps to complete the assignment:

- Using computer software, create a **graph** or **chart** that maps the information you discover.
- At the end of the observation, write a paragraph based on your journal that **summarizes** your findings.
- Share your summary with a classmate.

PHLit Online!
www.PHLitOnline.com
- Interactive graphic organizers
- Grammar tutorial
- Interactive journals

EXTEND/ASSESS

Writing

1. Review the assignment, using the instruction on the student page.
2. To guide students in writing a description of a scene, give them **Support for Writing**, p. 97 in *Unit 1 Resources.*
3. To evaluate students' descriptions, use the Descriptive Essay rubrics, pp. 220–221 in ***Professional Development Guidebook***. In addition, you might evaluate descriptions on how effectively the details create and sustain a mood. Encourage students to use sensory language and detail.

Six Traits Focus

✔	Ideas	✔	Word Choice
	Organization		Sentence Fluency
✔	Voice		Conventions

Writing and Grammar, Grade 10

Students will additional instruction on descriptive writing in Chapter 6.

Writing Workshop
Work in Progress

Have students save their completed scene descriptions in their portfolios. They will use the descriptions later as they complete the Writing Workshop assignment (see pp. 108–113).

Research and Technology

1. Review the assignment, using the instruction on the student page.
2. Have students complete the **Support for Extend Your Learning** page (*Unit 1 Resources*, p. 98)

Teaching Resources

Unit 1 Resources
L3 L4 **Integrated Language Skills: Grammar,** p. 96
L3 L4 **Support for Writing,** p. 97
L3 L4 **Support for Extend Your Learning,** p. 98
L4 **Enrichment,** pp. 77, 95

Enriched Online Student Edition
Available under After You Read for this selection:
All **Interactive Grammar Tutorial**
L3 L4 **Internet Research Activity**

Professional Development Guidebook
Rubrics for Descriptive Essay, pp. 220–221

PHLit Online! All print and digital resources are available at **www.PHLitOnline.com.** Online resources accessible by students are noted on the student page.

MONITORING PROGRESS

Using the Test Practice

In this two-page Test Practice, students apply the reading skill for the first half of Unit 1 to a passage of fiction and a passage of nonfiction.

Review this skill, making predictions, and then administer the test. For more guidance, consult the ***Classroom Strategies and Teaching Routines*** card on administering timed tests.

ASSESS

Answers

Answers With Explanations

1. A—The sunny sky darkened rapidly, and then Jack's father told him a tornado was coming. *Incorrect answers:* B—A sighting does not suggest whether the tornado formed quickly or slowly. C—Swirling debris only suggests fast movement. D—A quickly passing roar only suggests fast movement.
2. B—Jack and his father hid in a cellar; knowing that it was a safe place would lead you predict their escape from harm. *Incorrect answers:* A—A tornado's speed is evidence of danger, not safety. C—The way tornadoes form is not related to safety or harm. D—Damage from tornadoes is evidence of danger, not safety.
3. A—Tracking tornadoes can help people to take quick action and thus avoid harm. *Incorrect answers:* B—This statement is untrue; tornadoes do cause damage, as the story's last paragraph describes. C— This statement is untrue; tornadoes do damage houses, as the story's last paragraph describes. D—This statement is untrue; Jack and his father might have been hurt, if they hadn't taken precautions.
4. B—Jack's last statement shows that he has learned from experience; he would likely stay inside if he saw a tornado. *Incorrect answers:* A—Jack's experience will likely give him a healthy fear of tornadoes. C— Jack may or may not help his neighbors; there is no evidence for this prediction. D— Jack may or may not study tornadoes; there is no evidence for this prediction.

Test Practice: Reading

Make Predictions

Fiction Selection

Directions: *Read the selection. Then, answer the questions*

The day had been sunny, but as Jack was leaving his house, he noticed the sky was rapidly darkening. He heard his father calling.

"What's up, Dad?"

"Hurry," his father said. "To the cellar. A tornado is headed this way."

"Cool!" Jack responded.

"Not cool, Jack." Jack's father glanced outside. "Look—you can see it now!" Jack followed his father's gaze. A funnel-shaped cloud was swirling along the ground, twisting and pushing forward, absorbing debris as it moved. Jack and his father bolted to the cellar and huddled in a storage room. The wind howled overhead. When the roaring passed, Jack and his father peeked outside.

They were shocked to see that the house next door was missing its roof. Cars lay upside down in the street. When Jack and his father inspected their home, the only damage was a broken window. Jack looked at his father. "We're very lucky, aren't we?"

1. What information leads you to predict that a storm is coming?

A. The sky was rapidly darkening.
B. Jack heard his father calling.
C. Debris was swirling in the funnel cloud.
D. The roar of the tornado passed quickly.

2. What prior knowledge do you need to have to predict that Jack and his father will escape harm from the tornado?

A. knowing how fast tornadoes can move
B. knowing that the cellar is the safest place to be during a tornado
C. knowing how tornadoes are formed
D. knowing the damage tornadoes can cause

3. Which infomation does *not* help you predict that the tornado will cause damage?

A. prior knowledge about tornadoes
B. the description of the funnel cloud
C. the description of the wind howling
D. Jack's comment about being lucky.

4. Based on the passage, you can predict that Jack—

A. will never fear tornadoes.
B. will not go outside if he sees a tornado.
C. will rebuild his neighbor's roof.
D. will study tornadoes to learn more.

Writing for Assessment

What do you predict Jack and his father will do immediately after the tornado? Write a short paragraph explaining your prediction.

Writing for Assessment

In their responses, students should use evidence from the story to support their prediction. They should keep in mind what they know about the two characters and consider the condition of the neighborhood after the tornado.

Strategies for Test Taking

Remind students to first eliminate answer choices which they know are incorrect. Then they should think carefully about each of the remaining choices, keeping in mind that predictions draw on details presented in the selection as well as prior knowledge.

ASSESS

Nonfiction Selection

Directions: *Read the selection. Then, answer the questions.*

A tornado, or twister, is a very violent type of storm. When it touches down on the ground, it can cause terrible devastation. A tornado's rotational, or twisting, speed is usually estimated at about 300 miles per hour but can reach nearly 500 miles per hour. A tornado can be recognized by its funnel cloud, which dips downward from the clouds of a strong thunderstorm. The funnel becomes darker as it touches the earth because of the debris it has sucked up.

A tornado moves forward at about 30 to 40 miles per hour, but can travel as fast as 70 miles per hour. Most tornadoes are only about 300 yards wide; however, one of the most destructive tornadoes ever to strike the United States was about one mile wide. Even though a tornado passes quickly, it can cause extreme destruction. The wind is so strong that blades of straw have been embedded in fence posts by tornadoes. In one case, a school with eighty-five students was destroyed and the students were carried about 450 feet by the twister. Surprisingly, not one of the students was injured.

1. Which of the following can you predict would suffer the most destruction from a tornado?

A. a concrete apartment building
B. an underground shelter
C. an outdoor carnival
D. a school's basement

2. If you knew exactly where a tornado was first sighted, which of the following details could help you predict how quickly to take cover?

A. Tornadoes are usually about 300 yards wide.
B. Winds can reach 300 miles per hour.
C. Tornadoes can move at 30 miles per hour.
D. Tornadoes cause terrible destruction.

3. Based on the passage, you can reasonably predict that—

A. small items such as pencils or pens can become deadly in a tornado.
B. most tornadoes will pass by without doing harm.
C. tornadoes do not usually injure people.
D. faster tornadoes pick up more debris.

4. What information is most helpful for predicting how much damage a tornado will cause?

A. the amount of debris that it picks up
B. the tornado's rotational speed
C. the shape of the funnel cloud
D. which storm generated the tornado

Writing for Assessment

Connecting Across Texts
What dangers might Jack have faced if he had not taken safety precautions? In a paragraph, use details from the two passages to support your answer.

PHLit Online!
www.PHLitOnline.com
- Online practice
- Instant feedback

Differentiated Instruction for Universal Access

Strategy for Special Needs Students
The nonfiction selection contains difficult vocabulary related to the destructive power of tornadoes. These words are crucial to understanding the text and answering the questions that follow. Create a word web with the word *damage* in a middle circle. Invite students to find words form the story with the same or similar meaning (devastation, destructive, destruction, destroyed). Add these words to the web with other synonymous words, such as *injury, harm, hurt, ruin*. Review other difficult vocabulary from the nonfiction selection such as *rotational, debris*, and *embedded*. Encourage students to practice using the reviewed vocabulary by including some of the words in their Writing for Assessment paragraphs.

Answers

Answers With Explanations

1. C—A carnival is vulnerable, being aboveground with structures that may be flimsy. *Incorrect answers:* A—Concrete is sturdy and often holds up under stress. C—An underground shelter is not exposed. D— A basement is not exposed and wouldn't be as vulnerable.
2. C—Knowing its speed, you could figure out the time it would take to travel a given distance. *Incorrect answers:* A—Knowing its width does not give insight into how fast it would travel to you. B—Wind speed does not help with predicting time or distance. D—This detail would not help in predicting a tornado's movement.
3. A—The fact that tornadoes can embed straw in a fence suggests that they could turn pencils or pens into dangerous missiles. *Incorrect answers:* B—The passage says that tornadoes touching down may cause damage. C—The passage does not support this prediction. D—The passage does not say whether speed affects the amount of debris sucked up.
4. B—Greater speed will cause more damage; therefore, rotational speed is predictive. *Incorrect answers:* A—The time amount of debris may show the power of a tornado but it is not the clearest predictor. C—A funnel cloud is always indicative of a tornado. D—How it is formed is not as helpful in predicting damage as speed or width.

Writing for Assessment

Students should use details from both passages, drawing on the information presented in the nonfiction selection to make predictions about the fiction selection. Remind students keep in mind the description of tornadoes and causes of damage presented in the nonfiction selection.

PHLit Online!
Students may take the test in interactive format with instant feedback online at **www.PHLitOnline.com**.

PRE1TEACH

Meeting Your Standards

Students will

1. analyze the structure and format in a text.
2. read a feature article and a newsletter.

Log on as a teacher at ***www.PHLitOnline.com*** for a detailed lesson plan for Informational Texts.

Reading Skill

1. Introduce the skill, using the instruction on the student page.
2. Review the chart.
3. Tell students that they will analyze structure and format as they read.

Think Aloud: Model the Skill

Model the skill of analyzing structure and format, using the following "think aloud." Say to students:

To better understand an article, I look at the text features before I read. For example, when I see the title on page 91, "Feel the City's Pulse?", I know the article will be about be-bop music in the city.

As I read, I note other text features, such as subheads and boldfaced text, which help me locate and analyze the information provided.

Is there a difference between reality and truth?

Have students consider ways features such as maps, photographs, and illustration represent truth or reality in a way that the text cannot.

Multidraft Reading

Have students follow a multidraft reading protocol after they read.

- **First reading:** Have students read for general understanding.
- **Second reading:** Have students explain how structure and format help them understand an article.
- **Third reading:** Have students look for ways in which text features help them determine truth or reality

Informational Texts

Real-Life Reading

Feature Article
Feel the City's Pulse? It's Be-bop, Man!

Newsletter
The Healdsburg Jazz Festival

Reading Skill: Analyze Structure and Format

When you **analyze structure** and **format** in a text, you examine how the information is organized and presented. Authors make decisions about how words appear on a page in order to achieve specific **purposes.** Understanding how authors use structural features, or text features, can help you locate and analyze the information provided.

This chart shows some common structural features and their purposes.

Structural Feature	Purpose
Main heading	• provides an overview of content
Subheading	• introduces a specific topic within the main topic • helps readers to quickly locate information
Bold or italic text	• separates text on a page, making it easier to read • calls attention to certain information
Illustration or other graphic	• conveys visual information • adds visual interest to a page

THE BIG ?

Is there a difference between *reality* and *truth?*

The feature article uses a map with annotations and the newsletter uses photographs and illustrations to support the information in the text. As you read, think about how these text features represent truth or reality.

Differentiated Instruction for Universal Access

Reading Support

Give students reading support with the appropriate version of the ***Reader's Notebooks:***

L2 L3 ***Reader's Notebook***

L1 ***Reader's Notebook: Adapted Version***

EL ***Reader's Notebook: English Learner's Version***

PHLit Online! All student resources are available online at **www.PHLitOnline.com.**

Feel the City's Pulse? It's Be-bop man!

By Ann Douglass

Feature Article

Features:

- a focused topic
- quotations from experts, participants, or observers
- photos, maps, or other informative graphics

The main heading tells you that the article will be about be-bop music in the city.

In 1964, Thelonious Monk, one of the pioneers of be-bop and perhaps jazz's greatest composer, was asked by an interviewer to define jazz. Though Monk disliked questions and usually ignored them, this time he didn't miss a beat: "New York, man. You can feel it. It's around in the air. . . ."

Be-Bop (bop for short) was sometimes labeled "New York Jazz," and it is, in fact, the only major school of jazz to which the city can lay proprietary claim. Jazz of the 20's, dominated by Louis Armstrong, originated in New Orleans, migrating to New York only after a formative detour in Chicago. Armstrong inspired 30's swing, the music of the big bands led by Benny Goodman, Artie Shaw, Glenn Miller, Count Basie and Duke Ellington, the "mother bands," as Gillespie called them, whose music the be-boppers both emulated and revolutionized.

. . . Bop's wide-ranging allusiveness, its quicksilver expressivity, angular dissonance and shockingly extended palette of pitches and rhythms echoed the international mix, the fluidity and speed of New York life.

Jamming After Hours

The subheading breaks up the text for easier reading and explains what material will follow.

Bop began at roughly the same time as World War II, in 1940 when Monk, then 23, was hired to play with Kenny (Klook) Clarke, the man who transformed jazz drumming, at Minton's Playhouse in Harlem. Gillespie jammed with them after his regular engagement, and Parker joined them a year later. When Minton's closed for the night, they adjourned to Clark Monroe's Uptown House, an after-hours club where an extraordinary teen-age drummer named Max Roach played in the band.

The nation's entrance into the war in late 1941 imposed gas rationing, entertainment taxes and curfews, sharply restricting travel. The swing bands were touring bands, and some of them continued to tour, but now everyone was looking for a long-term base in a big city, easily accessible by public transit. What hurt swing helped be-bop. The expense and risks of touring (especially down South) had been far greater for black musicians than for white.

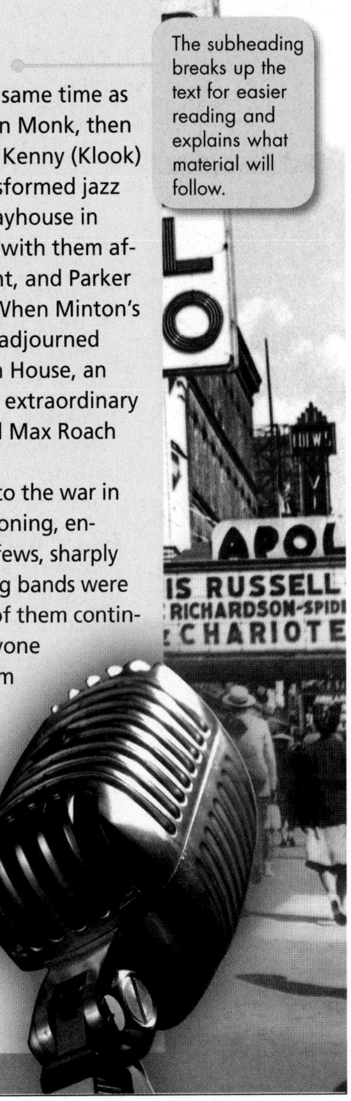

TEACH

About Feature Articles

1. Review the information in the Feature Article box on this page.
2. Explain that feature articles typically provide a great deal of information about a topic. The information is usually from a particular point of view and provides a new look at the topic.
3. Point out that the feature articles are often found in newspapers, magazines, and newsletters. **Ask** students to tell about feature articles they have read. Have them describe how the article provided information that was different from other sources on the topic.
   Possible response: I read an article on the winner of the Tour de France. It had information on the race, but it also gave a lot of information on the rider's personal training habits.
4. Remind students that it is important to consider the sources of information used in an article.

Analyze Structure and Format

1. Have students read "Feel the City's Pulse? It's Be-bop, man!" **Ask** students to identify text features in the feature article.
   Sample answer: Heading, subheading, photographs, map, and annotations.
2. **Ask** students to think about how these features help them understand the article.
   Possible response: The heading tells what the article will be about. The photographs give the reader clues that the music is both instrumental and vocal.
3. Direct students' attention to the subheading "Jamming After Hours." Then, **ask** them what they think the text under the subheading will be about.
   Possible response: The text will be about the musicians playing be-bop because *jamming* means "informally playing with other musicians." *After hours* means "late into the night after places have closed," so it will also be about where the musicians played once the clubs were closed.

Differentiated Instruction for Universal Access

Support for Special Needs Students

Not all students have an understanding of the terms *jazz* and *be-bop*. Without this understanding, this feature article is not very meaningful. Try to find an example of each type of music and play it for the students.

Enrichment for Advanced Readers

Instruct students to research one of the artists or subgenres of the jazz scene mentioned in the feature article. Have them include the information on the history of the time and the struggles many artists encountered while trying to create their music. Tell students that they will prepare a final report to present to the class orally. Encourage students to use video, collage, or music in their presentation.

Analyze Structure and Format

1. Remind students that feature articles often include graphic elements that support the information in the article.
2. Review with students that along with New York, Douglas mentions New Orleans and Chicago as cities that were important to the evolution of jazz. Explain that jazz does not necessarily define Chicago as much as it does New Orleans, where the music is a major component of entertainment and a tourist attraction. **Ask:** Why is there only a map of New York in this article?
   Possible response: Douglas chose to focus on the New York jazz scene and, in particular, bebop music, which began in New York City.
3. **Ask** students why they think Douglas chose a map rather than a picture of Monk and some of his jazz peers.
   Possible response: Douglas wanted to clarify not only that be-bop began in New York City, but also that its foundation was within a very small area of the city. Also, the map shows that Monk and other jazz musicians lived, worked, and died in this area.
4. **Ask** students to discuss the importance of the annotations that accompany the map.
   Possible response: They provide specific details that support the article's description of the New York be-bop scene.

The cramped quarters of many city clubs suited the young bop musicians, eager to work with the small ensembles that maximized opportunities for experimentation. . . .

The word "be-bop," which both Monk and Gillespie claimed to have coined, described the music's unconventional stop-and-start form, especially Gillespie and Parker's witty eighth-note pair conclusions. The purpose of bop's irregular phrasings, side-sliding harmonies and whirlwind pace, was, in Kenny Clarke's words, to "raise the standards of musicianship," to tell people, "Whatever you go into, go into it intelligently." The be-boppers were the real New York intellectuals, the hippest, smartest men in town.

The map shows the locations of sites mentioned in the text.

SITES OF BOP'S TRIUMPHS AND TRAGEDIES

1. **Savoy Ballroom**, Lenox Avenue and 140th Street, Harlem. Charlie Parker played in this legendary jazz and dance hall with the Jay McShann Orchestra in his early days in New York.
2. **Minton's Playhouse**, 210 West 118th Street, Morningside Heights. Charlie Christian, Kenny Clarke, Thelonious Monk, Parker and Gillespie made musical history here in the early 1940s.
3. **St. Peter's Church**, 54th Street and Lexington Avenue, Manhattan (also its current site). Monk's funeral took place here on Feb. 22, 1982, with musicians playing for three hours.
4. **52nd Street**, between Fifth and Sixth Avenues, known as "The Street." A magical block of jazz clubs . . . including the Onyx, Spotlite, Three Deuces and Kelly's Stable.
5. **Birdland**, 1678 Broadway, at 53rd Street, Manhattan. It opened on Dec. 15, 1949, with dozens of (caged) birds on view and Charlie (Bird) Parker presiding.
6. **216 West 19th Street**
   Eager to become "a New York musician," Gillespie lived here with his brother, . . . when he first came to town from Philadelphia in 1937, eating for 25 cents a day.

Bold text helps to separate this list into clear sections.

THE BIG ? **Is there a difference between reality and truth?** Does the final sentence of the main text express reality or the author's feelings? Explain.

ASSESS/EXTEND

Answers

THE BIG ? **Is there a difference between reality and truth?**

Possible response: The final sentence reflects the author's opinion. It displays her personal belief that the be-boppers were the hippest and most intelligent people in New York.

Vocabulary Development

Vocabulary from Feature Articles

Point out that feature articles often use vocabulary that is specific to one particular topic; in this case, be-bop history. Guide students to understand the meaning of the following words that are used in "Feel the City's Pulse?":

pioneer: a person or group that originates a new line of thought or a new method
emulated: imitated; strived to equal
dissonance: clashing of unresolved musical intervals or chords
allusiveness: characterized by indirect references
palette: range, quality, or use of available elements

PHLit Online! **Vocabulary Central**, featuring tools, activities, and songs for studying vocabulary, is available at **www.PHLitOnline.com.**

THE Grapevine Rag

THE NEWSLETTER OF THE

HEALDSBURG JAZZ FESTIVAL

WINTER 2007
VOLUME 7
ISSUE 1

Newsletter

Features:

- regular publication intervals
- information about upcoming activities and events
- text written for a specific audience

Dig Deeper into Jazz

The title indicates a specific area of interest—learning more about jazz.

JAZZ APPRECIATION COURSE STARTS IN HEALDSBURG

What is this "jazz" thing all about, anyway? Though we all know what we like—and we like jazz!—most of us don't know as much about it as we wish. Whether you're a novice or a fan, if you dig jazz, this is your chance to dig it deeper. Three fun, informative, and inexpensive mid-week Jazz Appreciation classes will begin February 28 at the Raven Film Center. The classes will mix live and recorded music with the expertise of the guest instructor to bring jazz history alive.

"Adult education has always been a missing component in the Healdsburg Jazz Festival," said artistic director Jessica Felix as she announced a new grant from the Healdsburg Area Affiliate of the Community Foundation, Sonoma County. The grant makes it possible to offer this three-part series on the history of jazz for area adults, extending the reach of the Festival's Jazz Education Program out of the schools and into the community at large."

"The goal of this series is to bring us all closer to understanding the depth and history of an art form that has grown out of the American experience," Jessica Felix explained.

Take three giant steps toward jazz enjoyment with our first-ever Jazz Appreciation Series, starting the last day of February. To learn more, see page 2 of this newsletter.

About Newsletters

1. Review the features listed in the Newsletter box on page 93. **Ask** students how a newsletter serves the interests of a specific audience. **Answer:** A newsletter provides comprehensive and detailed information on a specific area of interest. It is published at regular intervals, so the audience is kept current on upcoming events and activities.
2. Explain to students that many clubs and organizations have newsletters. **Ask** students if they are involved in a club or organization that publishes a newsletter. If so, **ask** whether they find these newsletters helpful or informative.
3. Remind students that they will not find all newsletters interesting or relevant to their lives because they are created for audiences with specific interests.

Analyze Structure and Format

1. Have students read "Dig Deeper into Jazz." **Ask** students which features first caught their attention.
   Possible response: Students may say that they noticed the title first, because it stands out on the page.
2. **Ask** students if the title helped them gain a better understanding of the newsletter's content.
   Possible response: Students may say that the title helped them understand which topic the newsletter would cover because it states the focus of the newsletter's first page.
3. Point out other text features that students might have overlooked. Remind them that images are included to help visualize the main idea of the text as well as add interest to the page. Explain that the piano is an important instrument in jazz music.

Differentiated Instruction for Universal Access

Culturally Responsive Instruction: Culture Connection

Explain to students that jazz began hundreds of years ago and has garnered a loyal following throughout the years. The origins of jazz date back to the eighteenth century, when African American slaves would sing together while working the plantation fields. They would improvise tunes and lyrics. This improvisation became a signature quality to the music of jazz. Encourage students to think of people in their own community's who have contributed to an aspect of American culture, such as music, art, or literature. Have students work in groups to research their culture's contribution. Have them present and compare their findings with other groups.

Analyze Structure and Format

1. **Ask** students to point out text features that make this page easy to understand.
   Answer: Text features include a heading, a subhead, and boldfaced dates introducing each event.
2. **Ask** students how the boldfaced dates are helpful to understanding the newsletter's purpose and content.
   Possible response: Students may say that since a newsletter's purpose is to provide information about events for a specific audience, boldfacing dates compartmentalizes each event chronologically, allowing readers to easily find and categorize the different events.

Reflecting on the Reading Skill

After students have finished reading both selections, discuss with them the various text features that can help them understand the informational text. **Ask** if they found some text features better suited to aiding comprehension than others.
Possible response: Students may say that boldfaced text helped them to locate information quickly.

ASSESS/EXTEND

Answers

Is there a difference between reality and truth?

Possible response: The headings and subheadings clearly state what information will be covered in the news release.

THE Grapevine Rag

THE NEWSLETTER OF THE

HEALDSBURG JAZZ FESTIVAL

LEARN MORE ABOUT *Jazz Music With The*

HEALDSBURG JAZZ FESTIVAL'S JAZZ APPRECIATION COURSE

A subheading introduces the topic covered in the second section of the newsletter.

THREE-PART SERIES AT THE RAVEN FILM CENTER, THEATER 2, 415 CENTER STREET

February 28th, March 28th, and May 9th. 6:30 to 9:30 pm

Open to all Ages, $10 per class, 3 for $25, half price for Senior Citizens (65 and over) and Students. Financial assistance available.

This class is made possible in part by a generous grant from the Healdsburg Area Affiliate of the Community Foundation, Sonoma County.

Class 1, February 28: Jazz History and Jazz Styles
Jazz educator, Ali Jackson explores the origins of jazz music with his celebrated *What is Jazz?*, a class, designed to make "America's Classical Music" accessible to a wide audience. What is jazz? Where did jazz come from? Who are the true pioneers and innovators of jazz? If you or a friend have asked these questions, *What is Jazz?* will provide the answers.
Class will use audio (CDs) and visual materials (DVDs).

Boldface dates are followed by details for each event in the schedule.

Class 2, March 28: The Music Making Process
Dr. James Newton, internationally acclaimed musician, composer, educator and jazz historian, will introduce the class to the essential concepts of interaction within a jazz ensemble. The class will also demonstrate how a jazz combo approaches the interpretation of a composition, and Newton will be joined by a rhythm section to illustrate these concepts.
CDs, DVDs, and live music will be used as part of this class.

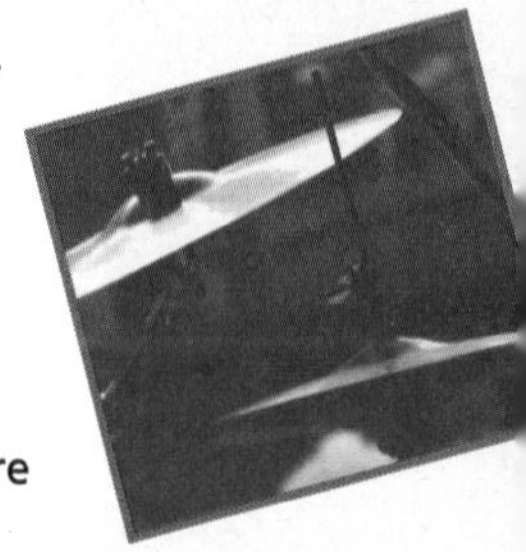

Class 3, May 9: Artists and Music of the Healdsburg Jazz Festival
Also taught by Dr. James Newton, this class will give participants a more informed perspective on the bands appearing at the 2007 Healdsburg Jazz Festival. The class will cover the stylistic practices of the artists and highlights of their careers, and explore the use of different size ensembles particularly as they relate to the jazz repertoire.
CDs and DVDs will be used as part of this class.

Is there a difference between reality and truth?
Do the headings and subheadings in this newsletter point out truth or reality?

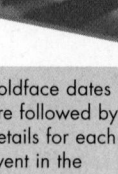

Test Practice: Informational Texts

Comparing Informational Texts

(a) What is the author's **purpose** in each of the two documents? **(b)** How do the **structure and format** of each document support that purpose? **(c)** Which document do you think uses structural features more effectively to achieve the author's purpose? Explain your response.

Timed Writing

Write a Persuasive Essay

Format
The prompt directs you to write a persuasive essay. Therefore, you should express an opinion and convince readers to agree with you.

Write a persuasive essay in which you take a position on the following quotation: "Music reflects culture. It is a central means by which a group asserts its relationship to past generations, distinguishes insiders from outsiders, and addresses the future." Support your response with details from the two texts. (25 minutes)

Academic Vocabulary
When you *take a position,* you state your opinion on an issue. You *support* your position by defending it with evidence and examples.

5-Minute Planner

Complete these steps before you begin to write:

1. Read the prompt carefully to make sure you understand the assignment. Pay special attention to highlighted key words and phrases.
2. Review the article and newsletter, keeping in mind the quotation in the assignment. **TIP** Use structural features to help you navigate the content of the documents.
3. Decide what position you will take on the quotation.
4. Note details from the two texts that you can use to support your position.
5. Prepare a quick outline for your essay. Then, refer to your notes and outline as you write.

Extend the Lesson

Connecting to the Students' World

To give students more practice with newsletters, and to help them apply the lesson to their own world, divide students into small groups. Have each group decide upon a particular area of interest. Divide these tasks among the members in each group: writing articles; creating a title, headings, and subheadings appropriate to the topic; developing graphics to go along with the articles.

Have students work together to compile research about the chosen topic. Emphasize that students work together to help make the newsletter focused and targeted toward their intended audience. Prompt students to make copies of their finished newsletters, and distribute them to their target audience. Invite groups to critique one another's newsletter.

ASSESS/EXTEND

Answers

Comparing Informational Texts

(a) **Possible response:** The first document aims to educate readers about the history of jazz music and be-bop in New York City. The second document aims to inform readers about jazz appreciation classes being offered during the Healdsburg Jazz Festival.

(b) **Possible response:** The headings and subheadings allow for a quick understanding of the information in each selection. The boldfaced subheadings clarify the content that will follow, making it easy to determine whether the selection is something you want to read or skip over. The photographs and graphics help to support the points that are made in both texts.

(c) **Possible response:** The second document uses text features more effectively. The author utilizes features to highlight essential information for the reader, making the document easier to navigate and understand.

Timed Writing

1. Before students complete the activity, guide them in identifying and analyzing key words and phrases in the prompt, highlighted on the student page.
2. Work with students to draw up guidelines for their essays based on the key words in the prompt:
   - **Focus** The essay should clearly take a position on the quotation provided.
   - **Organization** The essay should present a position and support it with details from the two texts.
   - **Elaboration** The essay should provide specific details and examples from the two texts.
   - **Style** The audience is not specified, so a formal style is appropriate.
3. Have students use the 5-Minute Planner to structure their time.
4. Allow students 25 minutes to complete the assignment. Evaluate their work using the guidelines they have developed.

PRETEACH

Meeting Your Standards

Students will

1. analyze and respond to the author's writing style.
2. compare the writing style of two authors.
3. write a comparison of styles.

Log on as a teacher at ***www.PHLitOnline.com*** *for a detailed lesson plan for Comparing Literary Works.*

❶ Comparing Style

1. Introduce the skill to students, using the instruction on the student page.
2. Discuss the chart.
3. Give students a copy of **Comparing Style Graphic Organizer B** (***Graphic Organizer Transparencies,*** p. 16). Tell them they will fill it in to compare style as they read.

Think Aloud: Model the Skill

Model a way to identify a writer's style. Say to students:

I look at a writer's words and sentence structure to identify his or her style. The sentences "He darted across the busy intersection" and "Before you could bat an eyelash, he was across," mean the same thing, but are written in different styles. The first is direct while the second uses indirect, poetic language.

❷ Vocabulary

1. Have students say each word aloud.
2. Then, use the word in a sentence that defines the word. Repeat the sentence, now with the word missing, and have the class "fill in the blank"chorally.

For more guidance, see the ***Classroom Strategies and Teaching Routines*** card, **Introducing Selection Vocabulary.**

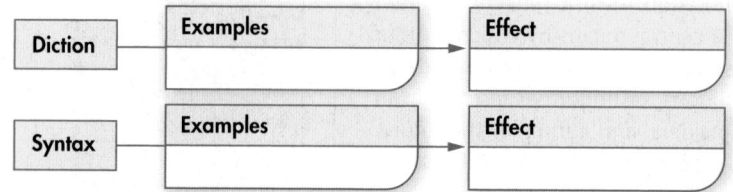

Comparing Literary Works

Marian Anderson, Famous Concert Singer • Tepeyac

❶ Comparing Style

A writer's **style** is made up of the features that make his or her expression of ideas distinctive. Writers may use various styles, depending on their **purpose,** or reason for writing. Here are two important elements of style:

- **Diction,** or word choice, involves the type of words the writer uses. Writers can choose to use words that are difficult or simple, abstract or concrete, old-fashioned or modern.
- **Syntax,** or sentence structure, is related to the way words are organized to express ideas. One writer may write a series of short, punchy sentences, driving home each new idea. Another may play with readers, putting a key idea at the end of a long, twisty sentence.

Use a chart like the one shown to compare the writers' styles and purposes in "Marian Anderson, Famous Concert Singer" and "Tepeyac."

	Examples	Effect
Diction		
Syntax		

❷ Vocabulary

- **staunch** (stônch) *adj.* steadfast; loyal (p. 99) *James is a staunch supporter of his sister.*
- **lucrative** (lo͞o´ krə tiv) *adj.* producing wealth; profitable (p. 100) *He closed the business when it was no longer lucrative.*
- **debut** (dā byo͞o´) *n.* first public appearance (p. 100) *The ballerina was nervous before her debut.* debuted *v.* debuting *v.*
- **repertoire** (rep´ ər twär´) *n.* a stock of works, such as songs, that a performer is prepared to present (p. 103) *The singer's repertoire was limited to show tunes.* repertory *n.*
- **canopied** (kan´ ə pēd) *adj.* covered by a cloth suspended from poles or a framework (p. 104) *If it rains, stay in the canopied area.* canopy *n.* canopying *v.*
- **dimpled** (dim´ pəld) *adj.* marked with small hollows or indentations (p. 105) *The baby's dimpled cheeks invited nonstop pinching.* dimple *n.* dimpling *v.*
- **irretrievable** (ir´ i trēv´ ə bəl) *adj.* impossible to regain or recover (p. 106) *After the computer crashed, the files were irretrievable.* retrieve *v.* irretrievability *n.* irretrievably *adv.*

PHLit Online! www.PHLitOnline.com
- Vocabulary flashcards
- Interactive journals
- More about the authors
- Selection audio
- Interactive graphic organizers

Vocabulary Development

Vocabulary Knowledge Rating

Create a **Vocabulary Knowledge Rating Chart** (***Professional Development Guidebook,*** p. 33) for this selection. Include the selection vocabulary and the Big Question word that appears in the Writing About the Big Question sentence starter on the next page. (The Big Question vocabulary is introduced on pp. 2–3.)

Give students a copy of the chart. Read the words aloud, and have students mark their rating in the Before Reading column. Urge them to be alert to these words as they read and discuss the selections.

Tally how many students think they know a word to gauge how much instruction to provide. As students read and discuss the selections, point out the words and their context.

PHLit Online! **Vocabulary Central,** featuring tools, activities, and songs for studying vocabulary, is available at **www.PHLitOnline.com.**

Is there a difference between *reality* and *truth?*

❸ Writing About the Big Question

These selections show characters who grow as a result of the reality around them. Use this sentence starter to develop your ideas.

One person's idea of **truth** can be challenged when ________.

Meet the Authors

Langston Hughes (1902–1967)

Author of "Marian Anderson, Famous Concert Singer"

In the 1920s and 1930s, African American writers, artists, and musicians based in Harlem, a neighborhood in New York City, gave vivid, intense expression to the African American experience. The period is known as the Harlem Renaissance, and Langston Hughes is acknowledged as one of its dominant forces.

Jazz Rhythms on the Page Harlem Renaissance artists dedicated themselves to finding authentically African American styles. Hughes crafted a style, especially in his poetry, that reflected the rhythms and moods of jazz and blues music. (You can read one of Hughes's poems on page 736.)

Sandra Cisneros (b. 1954)

Author of "Tepeyac"

Born to a Mexican father and a Mexican American mother, Sandra Cisneros spent her childhood shuttling between Chicago and Mexico City. The only girl among seven children, Cisneros felt as if she had "seven fathers." Struggling to find her identity, she took refuge in reading and writing.

Winning Honors Although her family was not well-off, Cisneros managed to attend the prestigious Writers' Workshop at the University of Iowa. Her first novel, the autobiographical *The House on Mango Street* (1984), was a commercial and critical success, earning her the American Book Award from the Before Columbus Foundation in 1985.

Teaching Resources

The following resources can be used to enrich, extend, or differentiate the instruction.

- All *Unit 1 Resources,* pp. 108–124
- All *Graphic Organizer Transparencies,* pp. 15–16
- All Enriched Online Student Edition

PHLit Online! All resources, including print and audio, are available at **www.PHLitOnline.com.**

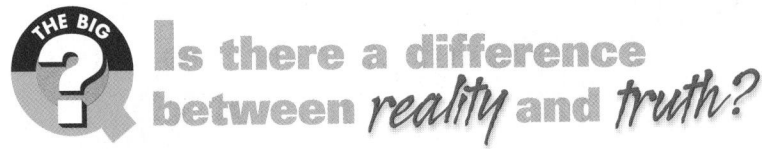

Daily Bellringer

For each class during which you will teach this selection, have students complete one of the five vocabulary activities for Week 3 in the ***Daily Bellringer Activities*** booklet.

❸ Writing About the Big Question

1. Review the assignment with the class.
2. Ask students to consider what it might be like to meet a kindergarten friend after many years apart. Would they expect their ideas of this friend to still hold true?
3. Have students complete the sentence starter. Review responses as a class. (**Possible response:** One person's idea of truth can be challenged when he sees evidence to the contrary.)
4. Remind students that their answers will help them think about the Big Question, "Is there a difference between reality and truth?"

Concept Connector →

Students will return to their responses to the sentence starter after they have finished reading the selections.

Multidraft Reading

To assist struggling readers and to deepen reading for all, apply multidraft reading protocols. For each reading, have students set the purpose indicated:

- **First reading**—literal comprehension: answering the Reading Check questions
- **Second reading**—application of skills: answering the Comparing Style prompts
- **Third reading**—interpretation: answering the end-of-selection questions

For more guidance, refer to the ***Classroom Strategies and Teaching Routines*** card on multidraft reading.

PHLit Online!

For more about the authors, practice with the selection vocabulary, and more background, go online at **www.PHLitOnline.com.**

TEACH

❶ Background
Marian Anderson

In this selection, author Langston Hughes chronicles the life of singer Marian Anderson (1897–1993), who became one of the first African American singers to gain widespread recognition as a performer of classical music, including opera. Hughes's account ends in 1943, but Anderson accomplished much after that time. She broke many barriers early in her career, and later, in 1955, she became the first African American to sing on stage at the Metropolitan Opera. She received many awards in her lifetime, including the Presidential Medal of Freedom in 1963.

❷ Activating Prior Knowledge

In this selection, students will learn more about Marian Anderson's struggle and how she handled herself in the face of obstacles such as racial prejudice and segregation. **Ask** students: What traits do you admire in others? Do you think that these traits are inborn or are they developed? Have students explain their answers.

Concept Connector →

Students will return to their responses once they have read the selection.

❸ About the Selection

Langston Hughes, an African American best known for his poetry, admired Marian Anderson and wrote this short biography as a tribute to her. In a straightforward, journalistic style, he begins with her birth and describes the major milestones of her life in chronological order, pausing occasionally to clarify and amplify with anecdotes. He consolidates Anderson's struggles against racial prejudice in one section near the end of the selection, and then uses her open-air performance in Washington, D.C., in front of a huge audience as proof of her success and broad appeal.

❹ Critical Viewing

Possible response: Students may predict that they will learn about a performer completely devoted to and passionate about her music.

❶ ❷ ❸ Marian Anderson
Famous Concert Singer

Langston Hughes

❹ ▲ **Critical Viewing** Judging from this photograph, what do you predict you will learn about Marian Anderson's personality? **[Predict]**

Background Marian Anderson (1897?–1993) was one of the first African American singers to gain widespread recognition as a performer of classical music, including opera.

When Marian Anderson was born in a little red brick house in Philadelphia, a famous group of Negro singers, the Fisk Jubilee Singers, had already carried the spirituals all over Europe. And a colored woman billed as "Black Patti" had become famous on variety programs as a singer of both folk songs and the classics. Both

Vocabulary Development

Thematic Vocabulary: The Big Question

As students are discussing "Marian Anderson, Famous Concert Singer," ask them to use the thematic vocabulary presented in Introducing the Big Question, pp. 2–3. You might encourage them with sentence starters like these:

1. In 1939, Marian Anderson was faced with the *reality* of racial prejudice when . . .
2. The historical *context* of Anderson's Washington, D.C. performance was . . .
3. The *objective* of Anderson's congregation was to . . .
4. Anderson's success as a performer of classical music changed people's *perception* of . . .

Negro and white minstrels had popularized American songs. The all-Negro musical comedies of Bert Williams and George Walker had been successful on Broadway. But no well-trained colored singers performing the great songs of Schubert, Handel, and the other masters, or the arias from famous operas, had become successful on the concert stage. And most people thought of Negro vocalists only in connection with spirituals. Roland Hayes[1] and Marian Anderson were the first to become famous enough to break this stereotype.

Marian Anderson's mother was a **staunch** church worker who loved to croon the hymns of her faith about the house, as did the aunt who came to live with them when Marian's father died. Both parents were from Virginia. Marian's mother had been a schoolteacher there, and her father a farm boy. Shortly after they moved to Philadelphia where three daughters were born, the father died, and the mother went to work at Wanamaker's department store. But she saw to it that her children attended school and church regularly. The father had been an usher in the Union Baptist Church, so the congregation took an interest in his three little girls. Marian was the oldest and, before she was eight, singing in the Sunday school choir, she had already learned a great many hymns and spirituals by heart.

5 One day Marian saw an old violin in a pawnshop window marked $3.45. She set her mind on that violin, and began to save the nickels and dimes neighbors would give her for scrubbing their white front steps—the kind of stone steps so characteristic of Philadelphia and Baltimore houses—until she had $3.00. The pawnshop man let her take the violin at a reduced price. Marian never became very good on the violin. A few years later her mother bought a piano, so the child forgot all about it in favor of their newer instrument. By that time, too, her unusual singing voice had attracted the attention of her choir master, and at the age of fourteen she was promoted to a place in the main church choir. There she learned all four parts of all the hymns and anthems and could easily fill in anywhere from bass to soprano.

Sensing that she had exceptional musical talent, some of the church members began to raise money so that she might have singing lessons. But her first teacher, a colored woman, refused to accept any pay for instructing so talented a child. So the church folks put their money into a trust fund called "Marian Anderson's Future," banking it until the time came for her to have advanced training. Meanwhile, Marian attended South Philadelphia High School for Girls and took part in various group concerts, usually doing the solo parts. When she was fifteen she sang a group of

1. **Roland Hayes** (1887–1977) famous African American tenor.

Vocabulary
staunch (stônch) *adj.* steadfast; loyal

Literary Analysis
Style Identify an example of a direct, down-to-earth word or phrase in this passage.

6 **Reading Check**
What organization supported the development of Anderson's talent?

5 Literary Analysis

Style

1. Have students read the bracketed passage, paying attention to diction. **Ask** students to respond to the Literary Analysis prompt: Identify an example of a direct, down-to-earth word or phrase in this passage.
   Possible response: The word *folks* is an informal, familiar way of saying *people.*
2. For reinforcement, **ask** students to identify other synonyms for *people* and to discuss their connotations.
   Possible responses: Synonyms for *people* include *human beings, persons, neighbors,* and *community. Human beings,* for instance, would give the passage a very clinical or scientific style.

6 Reading Check

Answer: Anderson's church group supported her by raising money for singing lessons.

Differentiated Instruction for Universal Access

Accessibility at a Glance
Use this information to guide your teaching of "Marian Anderson, Famous Concert Singer."

Context	Biography of African American opera singer
Language/Vocabulary	• Conversational • Grade-appropriate vocabulary
Concept Level	Accessible
Literary Merit	Noted author
Lexile/Length	Lexile: 1230L Word Count: 1,825

PHLit Online!
This selection is available in interactive format in the **Enriched Online Student Edition**, online at **www.PHLitOnline.com**, which includes an interactive graphic organizer.

❼ Literary Analysis

Style

1. Remind students that syntax is the structure of a sentence and that an author will use long, short, simple, or complex sentences depending on the purpose of a piece of writing. However, explain that length does not necessarily mean complexity. To illustrate this concept, have students read the bracketed passage. Then, **ask** them to count the words in each of the three sentences.
   Answer: The first sentence has 18 words; the second has 15; and the third has 32.
2. Next, **ask** students whether the length of these sentences is directly related to the difficulty of comprehension and to explain their responses.
   Possible response: While these sentences are long, they are not hard to understand. Hughes writes with a conversational quality, and the vocabulary is simple.

❽ Literary Analysis

Style

1. Remind students that diction is an author's choice of words that contributes to the style of any piece of writing. To reinforce this concept, **ask** students whether the words *sure enough* in the bracketed passage are essential to the meaning of the sentence.
   Answer: No; these words are expressive and not necessary to the sentence's meaning.
2. **Ask** students the Literary Analysis question: How do the words *sure enough* contribute to the informal, conversational diction?
   Answer: Because *sure enough* is unnecessary to the meaning of the sentence, one would expect to hear the phrase in conversation but would expect it to have been deleted from formal writing.

songs alone at a Sunday School Convention in Harrisburg and word of her talent began to spread about the state. When she was graduated from high school, the Philadelphia Choral Society, a Negro group, sponsored her further study and secured for her one of the best local teachers. Then in 1925 she journeyed to New York to take part, with three hundred other young singers, in the New York Philharmonic Competitions, where she won first place, and appeared with the orchestra at Lewisohn Stadium.

Vocabulary
lucrative (lo͞o´ krə tiv) *adj.* producing wealth; profitable
debut (dā byo͞o´) *n.* first public appearance

❼ This appearance was given wide publicity, but very few **lucrative** engagements came in, so Marian continued to study. A Town Hall concert was arranged for her in New York, but it was unsuccessful. Meanwhile, she kept on singing with various choral groups, and herself gave concerts in churches and at some of the Negro colleges until, in 1930, a Rosenwald Fellowship made European study possible. During her first year abroad she made her **debut** in Berlin. A prominent Scandinavian concert manager read of this concert, but was attracted more by the name, *Anderson*, than by what the critics said about her voice. "Ah," he said, "a Negro singer with a Swedish name! She is bound to be a success in Scandinavia." He sent two of his friends to Germany to hear her, one of them being Kosti Vehanen who shortly became her accompanist and remained with her for many years.

Literary Analysis
Style How do the words *sure enough* contribute to the informal, conversational diction?

❽ Sure enough, Marian Anderson did become a great success in the Scandinavian countries, where she learned to sing in both Finnish and Swedish, and her first concert tour of Europe became a critical triumph. When she came back home to America, she gave several programs and appeared as soloist with the famous Hall Johnson Choir, but without financial success. However, the Scandinavian people, who had fallen in love with her, kept asking her to come back there. So, in 1933, she went again to Europe for 142 concerts in Norway, Sweden, Denmark, and Finland. She was decorated by the King of Denmark and the King of Sweden. Sibelius[2] dedicated a song to her. And the following spring she made her debut in Paris where she was so well received that she had to give three concerts that season at the Salle Gaveau.[3] Great successes followed in all the European capitals. In 1935 the famous conductor, Arturo Toscanini, listened to her sing at Salzburg.[4] He said, "What I heard today one is privileged to hear only once in a hundred years." It was in Europe that Marian Anderson began to be acclaimed by critics as "the greatest singer in the world."

When Marian Anderson again returned to America, she was a seasoned artist. News of her tremendous European successes

2. **Sibelius** (si bä´ lē o͞os) Jean Sibelius (1865–1957), a Finnish composer.
3. **Salle Gaveau** (sål ga vō´) concert hall in Paris, France.
4. **Salzburg** city in Austria noted for its music festivals.

Think Aloud

Making Inferences

Use the last paragraph on page 100 as a model to show students how to make inferences. Say to students:

> Reading the paragraph that begins "When Marian Anderson again" tells me a lot about Anderson's character. I learn that although she has a broken ankle she is determined to perform in New York. I also read that she decides to hide her injury from her audience by wearing a long dress and propping herself against the piano.
>
> By combining the information I read with what I already know, I can make an inference. I know that it can take great courage to do something difficult while injured. I also know that hiding an injury can be a sign of pride. I can thus infer that Anderson is a courageous and proud woman.

had preceded her, so a big New York concert was planned. But a few days before she arrived at New York, in a storm on the liner crossing the Atlantic, Marian fell and broke her ankle. She refused to allow this to interfere with her concert, however, nor did she even want people to know about it. She wore a very long evening gown that night so that no one could see the plaster cast on her leg. She propped herself in a curve of the piano before the curtains parted, and gave her New York concert standing on one foot! The next day Howard Taubman wrote enthusiastically in *The New York Times*:

> Marian Anderson has returned to her native land one of the great singers of our time. . . . There is no doubt of it, she was mistress of all she surveyed. . . . It was music making that probed too deep for words.

A coast-to-coast American tour followed. And, from that season on, Marian Anderson has been one of our country's favorite singers, rated, according to *Variety*,[5] among the top ten of the concert stage who earn over $100,000 a year. Miss Anderson has sung with the great symphony orchestras, and appeared on all the major radio and television networks many times, being a particular favorite with the millions of listeners to the Ford Hour. During the years she has returned often to Europe for concerts, and

9 ▲ **Critical Viewing**
Does this photograph of Anderson's concert in Washington, D.C., support Hughes's description of her success? Explain.
[Support]

10 ☑ **Reading Check**
In which region of the world did Anderson first find success?

5. ***Variety*** a show-business newspaper.

9 Critical Viewing

Possible response: Yes; the audience spreads as far as the photographer's lens can capture. Many people are standing. Camera operators on the middle right record the performance, and loud speakers at the upper left amplify her voice so that it can be heard from a distance. Additionally, many of the people in the audience are Caucasian, supporting Hughes' claim that Anderson is famous in communities other than her own.

10 Reading Check

Answer: Anderson first achieved success in Scandinavia.

Differentiated Instruction for Universal Access

EL Background for English Learners

Explain to English Learners that America experienced widespread prejudice and racial segregation during the first half of the 20th century. Define segregation, and explain that segregation took place in public schools as well as restaurants, hotels, and even buses. It will aid students' understanding to view photographs from this time period in American history.

Enrichment for Advanced Readers

Suggest that students read additional works by Langston Hughes. Best known today as a poet (see p. 736), Hughes wrote prolifically in many genres, including fiction and drama. Challenge students to read poetry collections by Hughes in order to select one or two poems that touch on the same themes as his biography of Marian Anderson and could serve as companion pieces to this tribute.

11 Humanities

Incident in Contemporary American Life by Mitchell Jamieson (1917–1965)

Mitchell Jamieson was a combat artist for the Navy during World War II and was present at the D-Day Invasion, which he represented in his paintings. This mural of tempera on canvas hangs at the entrance to the cafeteria of the Department of the Interior in Washington, D.C. Painted in 1942, the mural is focused on a group of concertgoers near the back of the crowd at Marian Anderson's famous 1939 concert at the Lincoln Memorial.

1. **Ask** students why they think that Jamieson focused on the crowd instead of painting Anderson on stage.
   Possible response: Students may say that by showing the crowd, Jamieson shows the mix of people who came to the concert. Although everyone is there to hear Anderson, the fact that 75,000 people attended is more important in this mural than the singer herself.
2. Have students focus on the woman sitting on the chair holding the child. **Ask** them how her sitting might be significant, considering that most everyone else is standing.
   Possible response: Students may point out that Anderson's singing was amplified on speakers, which meant that she could be heard from very far back in the crowd. This could symbolize that Anderson did not need to be seen to have influence. Students may also point out that Anderson was a pathbreaker and that the child may symbolize the future to which she contributed.

12 Critical Viewing

Possible response: The presence of African Americans, families, and attendees of all ages at Anderson's concert creates feelings of respect and admiration that many people had for her. The painting shows people listening intently and quietly. Their focus on the performance illustrates how moved they are by Anderson's performance.

11

12 ▲ **Critical Viewing** What mood does this painting of Anderson's famous Washington, D.C., concert capture? **[Interpret]**

among the numerous honors accorded her abroad was a request for a command performance before the King and Queen of England, and a decoration from the government of Finland. Her concerts in South America and Asia have been as successful as those elsewhere. Since 1935 she has averaged over one hundred programs a year in cities as far apart as Vienna, Buenos Aires, Moscow, and Tokyo. Her recordings have sold millions of copies around the world. She has been invited more than once to sing at the White House. She has appeared in concert at the Paris Opera and at the Metropolitan Opera House in New York. Several colleges have granted her honorary degrees, and in 1944 Smith College made her a Doctor of Music.

In spite of all this, as a Negro, Marian Anderson has not been immune from those aspects of racial segregation which affect most traveling artists of color in the United States. In his book, *Marian Anderson*, her longtime accompanist, Vehanen, tells of hotel accommodations being denied her, and service in dining rooms often refused. Once after a concert in a Southern city, Vehanen writes that some white friends drove Marian to the railroad station and took her into the main waiting room. But a policeman ran them out, since Negroes were not allowed in that part of the station. Then they went into the smaller waiting room marked, COLORED. But again they were ejected, because white people were not permitted in the cubby hole allotted to Negroes. So they all had to stand on the platform until the train arrived.

The most dramatic incident of prejudice in all Marian Anderson's career occurred in 1939 when the Daughters of the American Revolution, who own Constitution Hall in Washington, refused to allow her to sing there. The newspapers headlined this and many Americans were outraged. In protest a committee of prominent people, including a number of great artists and distinguished figures in the government, was formed. Through the efforts of this committee, Marian Anderson sang in Washington, anyway—before the statue of Abraham Lincoln—to one of the largest crowds ever to hear a singer at one time in the history of the world. Seventy-five thousand people stood in the open air on a cold clear Easter Sunday afternoon to hear her. And millions more listened to Marian Anderson that day over the radio or heard her in the newsreels that

Vocabulary Development

Vocabulary Selection Reinforcement

Students will benefit from additional examples and practice with the selection vocabulary. Reinforce their comprehension with "show-you-know" sentences. The first part of the sentence uses the vocabulary word in an appropriate context. The second part of the sentence—the "show-you-know" part—clarifies the first:

> The comedian gave his *debut* stand-up act in front of a sold-out crowd; he would always remember the first time he heard laughter from so many people.

Then, give students these sentence prompts, and coach them to complete the sentences:

1. Capt. Rodriguez knew he could trust Private Saunders' *staunch* nature; _______________.
   Possible response: the private displayed loyalty and strength to his commanding officer.
2. Before investing in a company, be sure that it is *lucrative;* _______________.
   Possible response: you will only make money if the company is profitable.

recorded the event. Harold Ickes, then Secretary of the Interior, presented Miss Anderson to that enormous audience standing in the plaza to pay honor, as he said, not only to a great singer, but to the basic ideals of democracy and equality.

In 1943 Marian Anderson married Orpheus H. Fisher, an architect, and settled down—between tours—in a beautiful country house in Connecticut where she rehearses new songs to add to her already vast repertoire. Sometimes her neighbors across the fields can hear the rich warm voice that covers three octaves singing in English, French, Finnish, or German. And sometimes they hear in the New England air that old Negro spiritual, "Honor, honor unto the dying Lamb. . . ."

Friends say that Marian Anderson has invested her money in real estate and in government bonds. Certainly, throughout her career, she has lived very simply, traveled without a maid or secretary, and carried her own sewing machine along by train,
13 ship, or plane to mend her gowns. When in 1941 in Philadelphia she was awarded the coveted Bok Award for outstanding public service, the $10,000 that came with the medallion she used to establish a trust fund for "talented American artists without regard to race or creed." Now, each year from this fund promising young musicians receive scholarships.

Vocabulary
repertoire (rep´ ər twär´) *n.* a stock of works, such as songs, that a performer is prepared to present

Literary Analysis
Style Which words and phrases here give a direct illustration of Anderson's lifestyle?

Critical Thinking

1. **Respond:** What most impressed you about Anderson's life? Explain.
2. **(a)** According to Hughes, in what area had African American singers not received recognition before Anderson?
   (b) Infer: How can you explain this lack of recognition?
3. **(a)** Identify one action Anderson's congregation took to help her career. **(b) Infer:** What does their decision to help suggest about Anderson's talent as a young girl? Explain.
4. **(a) Summarize:** What type of difficulties did Anderson face when traveling in the United States? **(b) Infer:** What attitude led to these difficulties? **(c) Analyze:** In what sense was Anderson's outdoor concert in Washington, D.C., a response to this attitude?

Is there a difference between reality and truth?
In this biography, the narrator describes the reality of racial segregation practices during the 1930s and 1940s. How did Marian Anderson's career help expose the truth about racism during this time? Using details from the text, explain your answer.

13 Literary Analysis

Style

1. Remind students that a writer's diction reflects the purpose and subject of the selection.
2. **Ask** the Literary Analysis question.
   Answer: The phrases *lived very simply, traveled without a maid or secretary,* and *carried her own sewing machine* describe the simplicity of her life in direct terms.

Concept Connector

Have students compare their Writing About the Big Question and Activating Prior Knowledge responses with their ideas after reading the selection.

ASSESS

Answers

1. **Possible response:** Students may be impressed with Anderson's dedication to her music and her humble approach to success.
2. (a) African American singers had not gained recognition for performing classical music. (b) African Americans had not had formal training before Anderson.
3. (a) The congregation raised money to pay for her training.
   (b) The extent of her talent was so obvious at a very early age that members of the church were committed to helping her succeed.
4. (a) She was denied accommodations in hotels, service in dining rooms, and the right to perform in certain performance halls.
   (b) Prejudice against African Americans was responsible.
   (c) **Possible response:** The concert was performed at the Lincoln Memorial, itself a symbol of the fight against racial prejudice; additionally, the crowd included African Americans, who might not have been allowed into certain concert halls.

Is there a difference between reality and truth?

Possible response: Her career showed that people could exist together, regardless of color. Students may point out that following the 1939 Constitution Hall incident, many prominent Americans protested the Hall's decision.

⓮ Background

Tepeyac

As a child, author Sandra Cisneros (1954–), a first-generation American, lived in Chicago but regularly visited her paternal grandmother in Mexico City, Mexico. This selection is set around 1960 in Tepeyac, on a hill outside of Mexico City.

⓯ Activating Prior Knowledge

Have students think of a place they visited as a child. Do they remember many details? Are some things clearer than others? Are there people that they remember more clearly than others? How do they think these memories will change over time?

Concept Connector →

Students will return to their responses once they have read the selection.

⓰ About the Selection

"Tepeyac" focuses on a young girl's relationship with her grandfather, beginning on a single evening in her youth but moving ahead to a time when she returns to Tepeyac as a woman after her grandfather's death. In the end, Cisneros abruptly punctuates her flowing style of writing with a short sentence emphasizing that the narrator realizes that no one remembers her childhood as she does—she is now the one responsible for that vanished world.

⓱ Literary Analysis

Style

1. To introduce students to Cisneros's style of writing, **ask** students to define *syntax*.
   Answer: Syntax is sentence structure.
2. Now, **ask** the Literary Analysis question: How many sentences are included in this first paragraph?
   Answer: The first paragraph is a single, lengthy sentence.
3. For reinforcement, discuss the author's purpose for this syntax.
   Possible response: The paragraph cites a collection of childhood memories. Often, one memory triggers another and so on, without regard for the conventions of grammar. This syntax mimics the movement of the narrator's mind as these memories come flooding back to her.

⓮ ⓯ ⓰

TEPEYAC

Sandra Cisneros

Vocabulary
canopied (kan´ ə pēd) *adj.* covered by a cloth suspended from poles or a framework

Literary Analysis
Style How many sentences are included in this first paragraph?

When the sky of Tepeyac[1] opens its first thin stars and the dark comes down in an ink of Japanese blue above the bell towers of La Basílica de Nuestra Señora,[2] above the plaza photographers and their souvenir backdrops of La Virgen de Guadalupe, above the balloon vendors and their balloons wearing paper hats, above the red-**canopied** thrones of the shoeshine stands, above the wooden booths of the women frying lunch in vats of oil, above the *tlapalería*[3] on the corner of Misterios and Cinco de Mayo, when the photographers have toted up their tripods ⓱ and big box cameras, have rolled away the wooden ponies I don't know where, when the balloon men have sold all but the ugliest balloons and herded these last few home, when the shoeshine men have grown tired of squatting on their little wooden boxes, and the women frying lunch have finished packing dishes, tablecloth, pots, in the big straw basket in which they came, then Abuelito[4] tells the boy with dusty hair, *Arturo, we are closed,* and in crooked shoes and purple elbows Arturo pulls down with a pole the corrugated metal curtains—first the one on Misterios, then the other on Cinco de Mayo—like an eyelid over each door, before Abuelito tells him he can go.

This is when I arrive, one shoe and then the next, over the sagging door stone, worn smooth in the middle from the huaraches of those who have come for tins of glue and to have their scissors sharpened, who have asked for candles and cans of boot polish,

1. **Tepeyac** (tep ā yäk´) Tepeyac Hill lies in the northern part of Mexico City.
2. **La Basílica de Nuestra Señora** (lä bä sil´ ē kä dā nwās´ trä sen yō´ rä) the Basilica [Church] of Our Lady, lying at the foot of Tepeyac Hill on the site where, according to legend, Juan Diego had a vision in 1531.
3. **tlapalería** (tlä pä lā rē´ ä) *n.* the Mexican equivalent of a hardware store.
4. **Abuelito** (ä bwā lē´ tō) *n.* affectionate Spanish term for "grandfather."

Think Aloud

Vocabulary: Using Context

Direct students' attention to the word *huaraches* on this page. Explain to students that it is sometimes possible to use context clues to figure out how to translate foreign words. Model how to use context to infer the meaning of an unknown word, using the following "think aloud." Say to students:

> In this sentence, the narrator describes herself as walking into the store, "one shoe and then the next." She then goes on to describe how the door stone is worn smooth because of the many people who have come to buy things such as nails and string. I know that the door stone is the part of the floor underneath the door and the place where many people take their first steps when entering a room. Using these clues and the knowledge that the author is probably describing Mexico, I can ascertain that *huaraches* is a Spanish word for a type of shoe.

a half-kilo sack of nails, turpentine, blue-specked spoons, paintbrushes, photographic paper, a spool of picture wire, lamp oil, and string.

Abuelito under a bald light bulb, under a ceiling dusty with flies, puffs his cigar and counts money soft and wrinkled as old Kleenex, money earned by the plaza women serving lunch on flat tin plates, by the souvenir photographers and their canvas Recuerdo[5] de Tepeyac backdrops, by the shoeshine men sheltered beneath their fringed and canopied kingdoms, by the blessed vendors of the holy cards, rosaries, scapulars, little plastic altars, by the good sisters who live in the convent across the street, counts and recounts in a whisper and puts the money in a paper sack we carry home.

I take Abuelito's hand, fat and **dimpled** in the center like a valentine, and we walk past the basilica, where each Sunday the Abuela[6] lights the candles for the soul of Abuelito. Past the very same spot where long ago Juan Diego brought down from the *cerro*[7] the miracle that has drawn everyone, except my Abuelito, on their knees, down the avenue one block past the bright lights of
18 the *sastrería*[8] of Señor Guzmán who is still at work at his sewing machine, past the candy store where I buy my milk-and-raisin gelatins, past La Providencia *tortillería* where every afternoon Luz María and I are sent for the basket of lunchtime tortillas, past the house of the widow Márquez whose husband died last winter of a tumor the size of her little white fist, past La Muñeca's mother watering her famous dahlias with a pink rubber hose and a skinny string of water, to the house on La Fortuna, number 12, that has always been our house. Green iron gates that arabesque[9] and scroll like the initials of my name, familiar whine and clang, familiar lacework of ivy growing over and between except for one small clean square for the hand of the postman whose face I have never seen, up the twenty-two steps we count out loud together—*uno, dos, tres*—to the supper of *sopa de fideo* and *carne guisada*—*cuatro, cinco, seis*—the glass of *café con leche*—*siete, ocho, nueve*—shut the door against the mad parrot voice of the Abuela—*diez, once, doce*—fall asleep as we always do, with the television mumbling—*trece, catorce, quince*—the Abuelito snoring—*dieciséis, diecisiete, dieciocho*—the grandchild, the one who will leave soon for that borrowed country—

5. **Recuerdo** (rā kwer′ tho) Spanish for "souvenir."
6. **Abuela** (ä bwā′ lä) *n.* Spanish for "grandmother."
7. **cerro** (se′ rō) *n.* Spanish for "hill."
8. **sastrería** (säs tre rē′ ä) *n.* tailor's shop.
9. **arabesque** (ar′ ə besk′) *v.* branch out in complex, intertwining lines (usually a noun referring to such lines).

Vocabulary
dimpled (dim′ pəld) *adj.* marked with small hollows or indentations

19 **Reading Check**

With whom does the narrator live in Tepeyac?

18 Literary Analysis

Style

1. To further familiarize students with Cisneros's style of writing, **ask** students to define diction.
   Answer: Diction is the words an author chooses to use.
2. Now, have students read the bracketed passage. **Ask** students how Cisneros helps readers follow this very long sentence.
   Answer: She uses the words *past* and *down* to lead readers from one idea to the next.
3. To help students further analyze Cisneros's word choices, **ask** them how the word *past* can function on two levels in this passage.
   Answer: *Past* can be used as a directional indicator, explaining where the narrator is going; it can also be an indicator of time when it highlights something that happened previously to the people that the narrator is describing.

19 Reading Check

Answer: The narrator lives with her Abuelito, her grandfather.

Differentiated Instruction for Universal Access

Accessibility at a Glance

Context	Memories of the writer's ancestral country
Language/Vocabulary	• Very long sentences • Foreign words • Above-level vocabulary
Concept Level	Challenging
Literary Merit	Prize-winning author
Lexile/Length	Lexile: 2690L Word Count: 876

PHLit Online!

This selection is available in interactive format in the **Enriched Online Student Edition,** online at **www.PHLitOnline.com,** which includes an interactive graphic organizer.

20 Literary Analysis

Style

1. Help students recognize the shift in time that occurs at the end of the selection.
2. **Ask** the Literary Analysis question: What contrast does Cisneros create by ending the story with a shorter sentence?
   Answer: This form of syntax stops the flow of memory, creating an abrupt ending that suggests another shift in the story and in the narrator's feelings.

Concept Connector

Have students recall the Activating Prior Knowledge exercise. Discuss with students how the memories they recalled compare with those recalled by the narrator in "Tepeyac." Then, have them connect their Writing About the Big Question responses to the story.

ASSESS

Answers

1. **Possible response:** Yes; her attention to detail would help me know the place.
2. (a) **Possible response:** She remembers balloons wearing paper hats; the red-canopied thrones of the shoeshine stands; and women frying lunch. (b) The details give the impression of a busy, crowded marketplace.
3. She is referring to her own journey to the United States.
4. (a) **Possible responses:** Her grandfather's shop has become a pharmacy and the basilica is closed. (b) The narrator discovers that she shares her grandfather's ability to savor the beauty and liveliness of the marketplace. The narrator finally understands the irretrievable loss of her grandfather's power in her life and is left feeling empty.

Is there a difference between reality and truth?

Possible response: She conveys that the reality of the past is held only in memory and that the "adult world" a child knows growing up survives only in the child when he or she becomes an adult.

---

diecinueve, veinte, veintiuno—the one he will not remember, the one he is least familiar with—*veintidós, veintitrés, veinticuatro*—years later when the house on La Fortuna, number 12, is sold, when the *tlapalería*, corner of Misterios and Cinco de Mayo, changes owners, when the courtyard gate of arabesques and scrolls is taken off its hinges and replaced with a corrugated sheet metal door instead, when the widow Márquez and La Muñeca's mother move away, when Abuelito falls asleep one last time—*veinticinco, veintiséis, veintisiete*—years afterward when I return to the shop on the corner of Misterios and Cinco de Mayo, repainted and redone as a pharmacy, to the basilica that is crumbling and closed, to the plaza photographers, the balloon vendors and shoeshine thrones, the women whose faces I do not recognize serving lunch in the wooden booths, to the house on La Fortuna, number 12, smaller and darker than when we lived there, with the rooms boarded shut and rented to strangers, the street suddenly dizzy with automobiles and diesel fumes, the house fronts scuffed and the gardens frayed, the children who played kickball all grown and moved away.

Vocabulary
irretrievable
(ir′ i trēv′ ə bəl) *adj.* impossible to regain or recover

Who would've guessed, after all this time, it is me who will remember when everything else is forgotten, you who took with you to your stone bed something irretrievable without a name.

Literary Analysis 20
Style What contrast does Cisneros create by ending the story with a shorter sentence?

Critical Thinking

1. **Respond:** Would you have liked visiting Tepeyac with the narrator? Why or why not?
2. **(a)** List three details the narrator remembers about the market at Tepeyac. **(b) Synthesize:** What overall impression about the market do these details create? Explain your answer.
3. **Interpret:** To what event is the narrator referring when she says, "the grandchild, the one who will leave soon for that borrowed country"?
4. **(a) Analyze:** List two things that have changed in Tepeyac when the narrator returns. **(b) Draw a Conclusion:** Why is the narrator surprised to discover at the end that "it is me who will remember"?

Is there a difference between reality and truth? In this selection, the narrator describes Tepeyac very realistically. What overall truth is she trying to convey with her detailed description? Explain.

Vocabulary Development

Vocabulary Knowledge Rating

When students have completed reading and discussing "Marian Anderson, Famous Concert Singer" and "Tepeyac," have them take out their **Vocabulary Knowledge Rating Chart.** Read the words aloud once more and have students rate their knowledge of the words again in the After Reading column. Clarify any words that are still problematic. Have students write their own definition and example or sentence in the appropriate column. Then, have students complete the Vocabulary Practice activities at the end of the selection. Encourage students to use the words in further discussion and written work about these selections. Remind them that they will be accountable for these words in the **Selection Test** (*Unit 1 Resources,* pp. 119–121 or 122–124).

After You Read | Marian Anderson, Famous Concert Singer • Tepeyac

Comparing Styles

1. **(a)** Explain how Hughes's **style** helps make Anderson seem accessible or sympathetic to readers, despite her fame. **(b)** Explain how Cisneros's style helps re-create the rushing flow of memories.
2. **(a)** Using a chart like the one shown, compare each writer's style at the dramatic moment indicated.

	Hughes	Cisneros
Moment	**Washington, D.C., Concert**	**Concluding Realization**
type of words		
type of sentences		
similar to/different from rest of work?		

(b) Based on your chart, explain the way in which each writer's style—or a shift in the writer's style—adds dramatic effect.

Writing to Compare Styles

An author's style is often related to his or her **purpose,** or reason for writing. Evaluate each selection to decide which style is more effective in meeting the author's purpose. In an essay, support your view with examples and quotations from the selections. Consider these questions:

- What is the writer trying to accomplish in each selection?
- How does the writer's style help achieve this purpose?
- Are there places in which the style gets in the way of the purpose?

Vocabulary

Practice In each set of words, identify the word that does not belong. Explain how the meaning of the italicized word helped determine your answer.

1. *staunch* / courage / stain
2. *lucrative* / music / notes
3. *debut* / retirement / argument
4. *repertoire* / journal / book
5. *canopied* / dessert / cloth
6. *dimpled* / indented / dry
7. *irretrievable* / lost / unusual

ASSESS

Answers

Comparing Styles

1. (a) Hughes's direct style and simple syntax reflect Anderson's character and makes her story accessible. (b) Cisneros's long, flowing sentences and repetitive phrases give the reader the sense of remembering.
2. (a) **Sample answer:** Hughes: Matter-of-fact words; Cicernos: Descriptive, colorful words
   (b) A conversational style makes Anderson's extraordinary life accessible to the reader. Spanish words reinforce the Mexican setting.

   For other sample answers, see ***Graphic Organizer Transparencies,*** **Reading Skill Graphic Organizer A**, p. 17, and the **Additional Answers** section.

Writing to Compare Style

Review the assignment criteria. Have students note examples from the selections in which the diction and syntax support the purpose. Then, discuss the ways in which students may choose to organize their essays.

Six Traits Focus

✔	Ideas		Word Choice
✔	Organization		Sentence Fluency
	Voice		Conventions

Vocabulary

1. Stain. The word *staunch* means strong or loyal, and the word *courage* relates to this quality.
2. Lucrative. The word *lucrative* does not have a direct relationship with *music,* or musical *notes.*
3. Argument. The word *debut* relates to a time in life, as does the word *retirement.*
4. Repertoire. A *repertoire* of songs has nothing to do with a *journal* or a *book.*
5. Dessert. When something is *canopied,* it is covered by *cloth.*
6. Dry. *Dimpled* and *indented* are synonyms.
7. Unusual. When something is *irretrievable,* it is forever *lost.*

Assessment Resources

Unit 1 Resources

L1 L2 EL **Selection Test A,** pp. 119–121. Administer **Selection Test A** to less advanced students and English Learners.

L3 L4 **Selection Test B,** pp. 122–124. Administer **Selection Test B** to on-level and more advanced students.

L3 L4 **Open-Book Test,** pp. 116–118. As an alternative, give the **Open-Book Test.**

All **Customizable Test Bank**

All **Self-tests**
Students may prepare for the **Selection Test** by taking the **Self-test** online.

PHLit Online! All assessment resources are available at **www.PHLitOnline.com.**

PRETEACH

Meeting Your Standards

Students will

1. write an autobiographical narrative.
2. use writing strategies to generate ideas and to plan, organize, evaluate, and revise an autobiographical narrative.
3. organize the order of ideas, events, and actions in your narrative.
4. apply grammar skills.

Introducing the Writing Assignment

Review the assignment and the criteria, using the instruction on the student page.

Connecting to Real-Life Writing

Point out to students that autobiographical narration is often incorporated into other types of writing. For example, college applications often require students to explain significant events from their lives.

Writing Workshop *Work in Progress*

If students have done the Work-in-Progress assignments on pp. 57 and 87, suggest that they examine their recorded ideas as they begin prewriting. They may wish to develop these ideas in an autobiographical narrative.

Writing Workshop

Narration: Autobiographical Narrative

Defining the Form **Autobiographical narratives** tell a story from the writer's own life. They can be as simple as a remembrance of a weekend vacation or as complex as the entire story of the writer's life. You might use elements of autobiographical narratives in journals, eyewitness accounts, and persuasive essays.

Assignment Write an autobiographical narrative about an event in your life that changed you or helped you grow. Include these elements:

- ✔ a *clear sequence of events* involving you, the writer
- ✔ a *problem or conflict*
- ✔ *effective descriptions* of people, places, and events
- ✔ use of *dialogue* to show character
- ✔ an insight you gained as a result of this experience
- ✔ error-free grammar, including *correct use of possessive nouns*

To preview the criteria on which your autobiographical narrative may be judged, see the rubric on page 113.

Writing Workshop: *Work in Progress*

Review the work you did on pages 57 and 87.

Prewriting Strategy

Create character and setting cards. To select a story from your life, consider events that were funny, exciting, unusual, or puzzling. Choose one and prepare to focus your narrative by identifying the main conflict or insight you want to explain. Write an index card for each important character or setting.

- For characters, include facts like name, age, and appearance. Also note personality, habits, and the person's role in your story.
- For settings, jot down physical details to use in your descriptions.

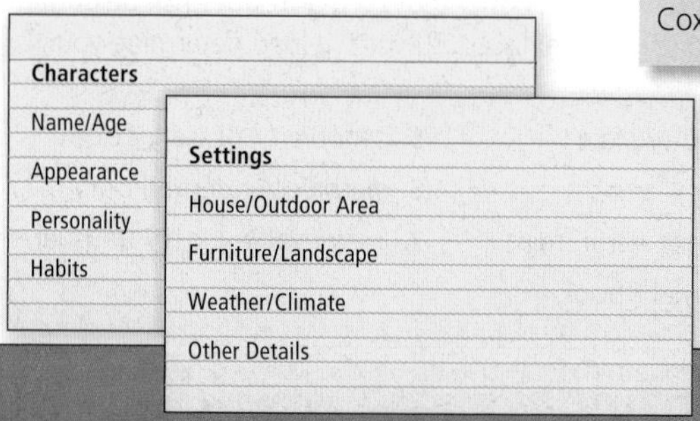

Characters
Name/Age
Appearance
Personality
Habits
Settings
House/Outdoor Area
Furniture/Landscape
Weather/Climate
Other Details

Reading Writing Connection
To get a feel for narrative nonfiction, read the excerpt from *Swimming to Antarctica* by Lynne Cox on page 62.

TEACH

Prewriting Strategies

1. Introduce the Prewriting Strategies, using the instruction on the student page.
2. Have students apply the strategies to choose a topic.

Six Traits Focus

✔	Ideas	Word Choice
✔	Organization	Sentence Fluency
	Voice	Conventions

Teaching Resources

The following resources can be used to enrich or extend the instruction.

- All *Unit 1 Resources* **Writing Workshop,** pp. 125–126
- All *Professional Development Guidebook,* **Rubric for Self-Assessment: Autobiographical Narrative,** pp. 222–223
- All *Graphic Organizer Transparencies* **Rubric for Self-Assessment: Autobiographical Narrative,** p. 19

PHLit Online! All resources are available at **www.PHLitOnline.com.**

WRITER'S TOOLBOX

SIX TRAITS

Organization | Word Choice | Ideas | Conventions | Sentence Fluency | Voice

Telling the Story

Organization is the order in which you present your ideas or the events and actions in your narrative. The most common form of organization for narratives is *chronological.* Writers begin by setting the scene and introducing the characters. Then, they describe the action or event that occurs first in time and continue presenting the details of the narrative in the order that they took place.

Writers of narratives do not simply list details of the action in sequence. Occasionally, writers will use *flashbacks,* or go back in time to describe an event that has an impact on their narrative. Writers also pace the presentation of the actions to show the changes in time and in the mood of the characters. For example, the first part of a narrative contains the rising action, or the actions and events that lead to the *climax*—the point of highest interest. After reaching the climax, writers reduce the suspense of their narrative until they reach a resolution, or tie up the loose ends.

Prentice Hall Writing and Grammar Connection: Chapter 4

Decide the point you want to make. Before you begin, decide what impression you want to make on your readers. You may want to show how another person influenced your life. You might want to describe a suspenseful and frightening incident in which you narrowly escaped from injury. Perhaps you want to show how you reached an important decision in your life.

Choose your details. Remember that telling every single detail of an event usually bores the reader. Choose only those details that help readers understand the point you are making.

Pace the action. Be sure to identify the climax before you begin writing. Then, pace the presentation of the events or actions to create tension or suspense as you build to the key moment of the climax.

Devise a plan for telling your story. As you write your narrative, tell only the important events in a logical order. Use this plot diagram to help structure your narrative.

Apply It!

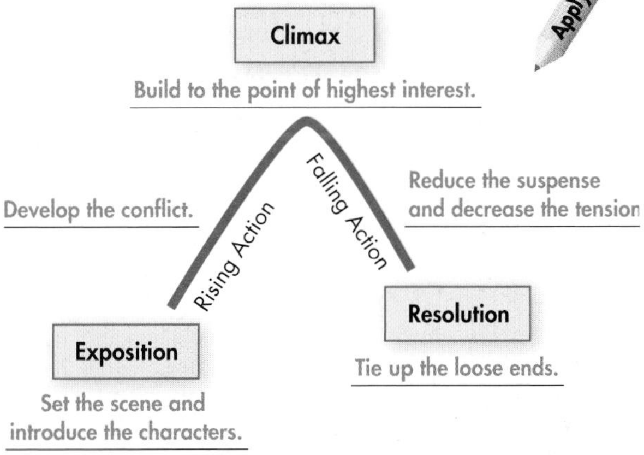

Climax
Build to the point of highest interest.
Develop the conflict.
Rising Action
Falling Action
Reduce the suspense and decrease the tension
Exposition
Set the scene and introduce the characters.
Resolution
Tie up the loose ends.

Telling the Story

1. Introduce the writing skill, using the instruction on the student page.
2. Discuss the tips and strategies for planning, organizing, and pacing an autobiographical narrative.

Teaching the Writing Skill

1. Remind students that an autobiographical narrative is a story from the writer's life. It can span a time as long as years or as short as a day. Have students determine the time frame of their stories by asking themselves these questions: *When did the series of events begin? How long did they last?* Then, have each student sketch a rough timeline to show the chronology of events.
2. Explain to students that the literary technique of flashback is useful to a writer in several ways: It provides background information on an event or a character, it can develop a character, and it can create suspense. Emphasize that when a writer does use a flashback, he or she inserts it seamlessly into the plot, introducing it with a sentence like this one: "The game began just as it had two years ago, when . . ." Encourage students to experiment with flashbacks, but emphasize that they should use flashbacks only when the story would benefit from them.

OES Online Essay Scorer

A writing prompt for this mode of writing can be found on the *PH Essay Scorer* at www.PHLitOnline.com.

Writing and Grammar Interactive Textbook Online

Students can use the following tools as they complete their autobiographical narratives:

- Self-interview
- Exploding the moment (Chapter 4, Section 3)
- Color-coding to achieve sentence variety (Chapter 4, Section 3)

Differentiated Instruction for Universal Access

Strategy for Special Needs Students

Review with students the structure of the plot diagram on p. 109. Work with students to create plot diagrams for their autobiographical narratives.

On a separate sheet of paper, have students list the important events in their narratives. Point out that the climax is the turning point of the story. Have students choose their climaxes and circle them. Then have them circle and label events that relate to the exposition and resolution.

On another sheet of paper, have each student draw a blank plot diagram. Students should then write the climax at the top and events related to the exposition and resolution at the beginning and end. Have student finish by filling in events related to the rising and falling action. Once students start drafting their narratives, they can use their diagrams as a guide.

Drafting Strategy

1. Introduce the Drafting Strategy, using the instruction on the student page.
2. Have students apply the strategy as they draft.

Teaching the Strategy

1. Remind students that once they choose a specific point of view, they must use it consistently throughout their narratives.
2. Using the examples of narration and dialogue, call students' attention to the difference between *telling* and *showing* writing. Ask students to identify places in their narratives that would benefit from dialogue.

Think Aloud: Model Dialogue

Model the strategy, using the following "think aloud":

> Suppose I want to show that my character Delia is surprised. I wrote, "Delia gasped and asked if the car really was for her." This sentence *describes* what Delia says. If I use dialogue instead of narration, I can make this portrayal much stronger and more effective: "Delia gasped, 'Is the car really for me?'"
>
> I can also show Delia's thoughts and feelings in an interior *monologue*. I could write, "*I'll never take the bus again,* Delia thought." This shows her feelings clearly without explaining them.

Six Traits Focus

✔	Ideas	✔	Word Choice
✔	Organization		Sentence Fluency
✔	Voice		Conventions

Revising Strategies

1. Introduce the Revising Strategies, using the instruction on the student page.
2. Have students apply the strategies as they review their drafts.

Six Traits Focus

✔	Ideas	✔	Word Choice
✔	Organization	✔	Sentence Fluency
✔	Voice	✔	Conventions

WG Writing and Grammar, Grade 10

Students will find additional instruction on drafting and revising an autobiographical narrative in Chapter 4, Sections 3 and 4.

Drafting Strategy

Apply It!

Use dialogue. *Dialogue*—the conversations among people in a narrative—can add interest to your writing. Use dialogue to advance the plot and show what characters are like. You might also create *interior monologues*: statements that reveal your exact thoughts at the time.

Narration	Dialogue
She told me not to go into the cave without a flashlight.	"Don't go into that cave without a flashlight," she warned me.

Dialogue also reflects the *point of view*, or perspective from which the narrative is told. In a *third-person* point of view, a voice outside the story relates the narrative. In a *first-person* point of view, the narrator or speaker is a character in the narrative. With a first-person point of view, the readers learn only what this character sees or hears.

Revising Strategies

Revise to clarify insight. Review your draft to make sure that you have clearly communicated the importance of the event you narrate. Underline sentences that show your reader what you learned. If necessary, add more of these sentences to explain your insight.

Vary sentence length. Add interest by including both long and short sentences in your narrative. If you find a series of short, choppy sentences, combine some of them. Adding a short, energetic sentence to a passage of longer sentences can emphasize an exciting moment.

Varying Sentence Length	
I was lying in the hammock in the front yard. I was nearly asleep. The wind rustled in the trees. Cicadas were buzzing.	I was lying in the hammock in the front yard, nearly asleep. Wind rustled in the trees, and cicadas were buzzing.

Combining short sentences into single longer ones adds interest. Keeping a short sentence adds emphasis to the moment.

Understanding by Design

Clarifying Expected Outcomes: Using Rubrics

- Before students begin working on this assignment, have them preview the Rubric for Self-Assessment (p. 113) to learn what qualities their autobiographical narrative must have. A copy of this rubric appears in ***Graphic Organizer Transparencies,*** p. 19.
- Review the criteria in the rubric with the class. Before students use the rubric to assess their writing, work with them to rate the Student Model (p. 112) using the rubric.
- If you wish to assess students' autobiographical narrative with either a 4-point or a 6-point scoring rubric, see ***Professional Development Guidebook,*** pp. 222–223.

SIX TRAITS WRITER'S TOOLBOX SIX TRAITS

Conventions | Sentence Fluency | Voice | Organization | Word Choice | Ideas

Using Possessive Nouns Correctly

A **possessive noun** indicates possession or ownership. An apostrophe must be used to form a possessive noun.

Identifying Incorrect Possessive Nouns You might find these three kinds of mistakes involving possessive nouns:

- nouns that are possessive but do not have an apostrophe
- possessive nouns that have an apostrophe in the wrong place
- nouns that are not possessive but include an apostrophe

Clarifying Your Meaning Thinking about what you mean will help you choose the correct possessive noun.

The student's essays were due on Friday. *(one student, many essays)*

The students' essays were due on Friday. *(more than one student)*

In the following example, the plural noun is not possessive. It should not have an apostrophe.

Wrong: The student's laughed.

Right: The students laughed.

Fixing Incorrect Possessive Nouns To fix the possessive nouns in your writing, look for any nouns that show ownership.

1. **Ask yourself whether the noun is singular or plural.**
2. **Follow these rules to place the apostrophe correctly:**

Apply It!

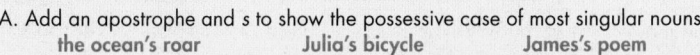

A. Add an apostrophe and *s* to show the possessive case of most singular nouns.
the ocean's roar   Julia's bicycle   James's poem

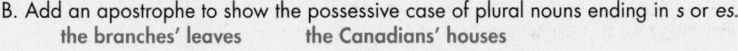

B. Add an apostrophe to show the possessive case of plural nouns ending in *s* or *es*.
the branches' leaves   the Canadians' houses

C. Add an apostrophe and *s* to show the possessive case of plural nouns that do not end in *s* or *es*.
the people's stories   the children's department

WG *Prentice Hall Writing and Grammar Connection: Chapter 28, Section 6*

Grammar in Your Writing

Scan your writing for apostrophes. You might find some in abbreviations, but others will be used in possessive nouns. Check that each possessive noun is punctuated correctly. Then, review your writing for possessives that are missing their apostrophes.

Using Possessive Nouns Correctly

1. Introduce the grammar skill, using the instruction on the student page.
2. Discuss the examples and the strategies for fixing incorrect usage of possessive nouns.
3. Have students follow the instruction under Grammar in Your Writing to correct errors in their drafts.

Teaching the Grammar Skill

1. Review how to form regular singular and plural possessive nouns. Provide students with examples such as these:
   Singular: *It was the **teacher's** decision.*
   Plural: *It was the **teachers'** decision.*
2. Write the following on the board. Have students identify any errors in the underlined possessive nouns. Have them provide the correctly formed possessive noun.

   Everything in the room was <u>Roberts</u>, even the dust bunnies.
   Answer: Robert's

   The <u>Jone's</u> yard sale was a great success.
   Answer: Jones's

   The <u>womens'</u> room was locked.
   Answer: women's
3. Point out to students that possessive pronouns such as *his, hers,* and *its* do not have apostrophes. Also point out that apostrophes can be used to form contractions, such as *don't, shouldn't,* and *you'll.*

WG **Writing and Grammar, Grade 10**

Students will find additional instruction on using possessive nouns in Chapter 28, Section 6.

Strategies for Using Technology in Writing

If students are using word processors to draft and revise their autobiographical narratives, explain to them that spell-check programs will not recognize the most common types of possessive noun errors. If the apostrophe in a singular possessive noun is placed after the *-s*, it appears to be a correctly spelled plural possessive. Likewise, if the apostrophe in a plural possessive is placed *before* the *-s*, it appears singular. The absence of the apostrophe forms a correctly spelled plural noun.

Instruct students using word processors to check their autobiographical narratives carefully for possessive noun errors. Some errors may be spotted by grammar-check software, but this is not a foolproof strategy. Requiring students to manually check their use of possessive nouns will also encourage more careful proofreading in general. Make sure students understand that the technology of word processing does have its limitations.

Student Model

Review the Student Model with the class, using the annotations to analyze the writer's use of the elements of an autobiographical narrative.

Teaching From the Student Model

1. Explain to students that the Student Model is a sample and that their autobiographical narratives may be longer.
2. Tell students that there are three ways to begin a narrative: action, dialogue, or reaction.
   Ask which type of introduction this writer uses and how effective it is.
   Possible response: The writer uses a reaction lead. The lead is effective because the reader wonders why the writer has lost consciousness.
3. Point out instances in the narrative where the writer uses humor.
   Ask what comedic techniques the writer employs in her narrative.
   Answer: The writer uses exaggeration and sarcasm.
4. Point out references to the introduction in the conclusion.
   Ask why it is an effective technique to echo portions of the introduction in the conclusion.
   Possible response: Referencing the beginning of the story in the conclusion calls attention to the structure of the story, reminding readers of the story's beginning and preparing them for the end.

Connecting to Real-Life Writing

Explain that students may be asked to tell about significant events in their lives when filling out college or job applications. Point out that a problem or change that a student has faced is often an excellent focus for such an essay. Discuss why a school or company might ask a potential student or employee to write about an important event in his or her life. Then, have students imagine that they are applying for admission to college or for a job. What event would they choose to write about and why? Invite students to share their ideas.

Student Model: Alexandria Symonds, Royersford, PA

The Collision, or Hardly Extreme

Some people are simply not meant for extreme athletics, I thought to myself as I slowly regained consciousness. I am one of those people. I will never compete in the X Games; I should just stick to my orderly world where "sports" include Scrabble. I would have continued in this thought pattern, but a feeling like someone stabbing me in the eye with a dozen dull forks grabbed my attention instead.

> Alexandria's thoughts provide an intriguing beginning for the narrative.

I was bored that Saturday afternoon in May of 1998–so bored, in fact, that it seemed like a bright and creative idea to see if my old girly purple bike could be used for off-roading. The "off-road" in question was to be our front and back yards (the latter of which happened, incidentally, to back up to the North Carolina woods). I planned a fairly straightforward circuit around the house, complicated only slightly by the fact that our house sat on a hill.

> Specific details about Alexandria's state of mind and her bicycle add color and interest to the tale.

It is prophesied that if the earth ever loses its gravitational pull, the moon will abandon its orbit and spin, instead, in a straight line into infinity. Something similar happened to me after a couple of laps around the house. I had reached a speed so high that I concentrated solely on pedaling to maintain it—forgetting, as it were, to turn at a pivotal point in the round. The difference, however, between the moon and me is that while the moon could spin into infinity unobstructed, there was a forest in my way.

> Alexandria's sense of humor gives a spark to the narrative.

I realized a split second too late that I hadn't made the turn and knew there was no use trying to do it now. In retrospect, I could have jumped off the bike, but logical thoughts rarely occur when one is hurtling toward a giant oak tree at 25 miles per hour. Instead, I stopped pedaling, closed my eyes, and braced myself for the impact.

I never actually felt it. When I opened my eyes, I was crumpled on the grass in a position I'm sure humans were never intended to take. My bike was tangled in my limbs, and a searing pain in my left eye was the only thing I could feel. After a bit of reflection about my "extreme" lack of foresight, I decided the best response was to scream as loudly as I could.

> Key details create a vivid picture and also keep the story moving.

The events immediately following my ill-fated rendezvous with the tree are a blur; but I know that somehow I made it to the hospital, where I endured what seemed like endless tests and injections. I would be okay, but my recovery was a painful process. While the rest of me suffered only surface cuts and deep bruises, my left eye was swollen shut for a week. It was distended for months afterwards, and I still have some puffy scar tissue that causes my left eye to close more than the right when I smile.

Still, every time I get photos developed and notice this phenomenon, it serves as a reminder that I was simply not meant for any kind of physical activity more "extreme" than skipping.

> Details here echo the beginning of the narrative and bring the story full circle.

Differentiated Instruction for Universal Access

Strategy for Special Needs Students

Before students read the Student Model, provide a quick tour of the model's features. Call students' attention to the title. Next, have students place blank self-sticking notes next to each paragraph of the model.

Read the first paragraph aloud. Then, encourage students to reread the paragraph aloud. Explain that this paragraph serves to introduce the topic of the narrative. Have students label their first self-sticking note *Introduction*. Provide a one-sentence summary that states the main idea of the first paragraph.

Read the following four paragraphs. Emphasize that these paragraphs include the most detail because they serve to support the main idea in the introduction. Have students label their self-sticking notes *Body* for body paragraphs. For each paragraph, provide a one-sentence summary of its content.

Read the final paragraph, the narrative's conclusion. Instruct students to write *Conclusion* on their notes. Provide a one-sentence summary of its content. Encourage students to use this narrative's structure as a model for their own work.

Editing and Proofreading

Check your draft for errors in spelling, grammar, and punctuation.

Focus on Punctuating Dialogue: Check that you have punctuated dialogue correctly. Quotation marks should surround a character's exact words or thoughts. As you edit, make sure that there is a closing quotation mark for every opening quotation mark. (For more on punctuating dialogue, see Quotation Marks on page XX.)

Publishing and Presenting

Consider one of the following ways to share your writing:

Illustrate your narrative. Use photographs or drawings to illustrate people, places, or events in your narrative. Assemble a clean copy of your narrative, choosing an appropriate title and cover.

Deliver a narrative presentation. Rehearse reading your narrative aloud. Using a copy as a reading script, underline words that you will emphasize. Note places where you will vary your reading rate.

Reflecting on Your Writing

Jot down your answer to this question.

How did writing about the work help you to understand it?

Rubric for Self-Assessment

Find evidence in your writing to address each category. Then, use the rating scale to grade your work.

Criteria	Rating Scale (*not very* — *very*)
Focus: How clearly do you explain the insight gained from this experience?	1 2 3 4 5
Organization: How clear and effectively paced is the sequence of events?	1 2 3 4 5
Support/Elaboration: How effective are your descriptions of people, places, and events?	1 2 3 4 5
Style: How effective is your use of dialogue?	1 2 3 4 5
Conventions: How correct is your grammar, especially your use of possessive nouns?	1 2 3 4 5

Differentiated Instruction for Universal Access

EL Strategy for English Learners

Although giving a dramatic reading may be challenging for students, it provides them with an opportunity to practice reading and speaking English. Work on fluency with individual students. Read each sentence of the student's narrative aloud. Tell the student to echo the sentence, adopting your speed, intonation, and pronunciation.

Strategy for Gifted/Talented Students

Encourage students to create and present illustrations for their autobiographical narratives. Students may wish to explore a range of mediums for their illustrations, including pen and ink, paint, photography, and collage. If students wish to work with sculpture, have them photograph their work and include the photographs with their narratives.

Editing and Proofreading

1. Introduce the Editing and Proofreading focus, using the instruction on the student page.
2. Have students edit and proofread their autobiographical narratives, correcting grammar, spelling, punctuation, and word choice. Make sure they check for errors of the type noted on the student page.

Teaching the Editing Focus

1. Remind students that editing is not the same as revising. In the revising stage, writers change their work's content. In the editing stage, they correct errors in usage, grammar, and spelling.
2. Review punctuation conventions for dialogue. Spoken words are enclosed in quotation marks. End punctuation of dialogue goes inside the closing quotation marks.

Six Traits Focus

	Ideas		Word Choice
	Organization		Sentence Fluency
	Voice	✔	Conventions

ASSESS

Publishing and Presenting

1. Explain that carefully chosen visual images can help readers connect with the characters, settings, and events in a narrative.
2. Students giving dramatic readings can find guidance in the **Communications Workshop, p. 212.**

Reflecting on Your Writing

Encourage students to reflect on how the stages of the writing process—especially revising—affected their perspectives on the real-life events in their narratives.

WG Writing and Grammar, Grade 10

Students will find additional guidance for editing and proofreading and publishing and presenting in Chapter 4, Sections 5 and 6.

TIME AND RESOURCE MANAGER

Contents of the Dead Man's Pocket • Games at Twilight

Lesson Pacing Guide

DAY 1 Preteach

- Administer the Reading and Vocabulary Warm-ups (*Unit 1 Resources*, pp. 134–137 or 152–155) as necessary.
- Introduce the Reading Skill: Cause and Effect FT
- Introduce the Literary Analysis concept: Conflict and Resolution FT
- Distribute copies of the appropriate graphic organizer for the Reading Skill (*Graphic Organizer Transparencies*, pp. 23–25). CRI
- Distribute copies of the appropriate graphic organizer for Literary Analysis (*Graphic Organizer Transparencies*, pp. 20–22). CRI
- Teach the selection vocabulary. FT CRI
- Introduce the Word Study skill.

DAYS 2–3 Preteach/Teach

- Build background with the Background feature. CRI
- Develop thematic vocabulary and thematic thinking with Writing About the Big Question.
- Prepare students to read with the Activating Prior Knowledge activities (TE). CRI
- Informally monitor comprehension while students read. FT
- Use the Reading Check questions to confirm comprehension.
- Develop students' ability to analyze cause and effect as well as reflect on key details using the Reading Skills questions. CRI
- Develop students' understanding of conflict and resolution using the Literary Analysis questions. CRI
- Reinforce vocabulary with the Vocabulary notes. CRI

DAY 4 Assess

- Assess students' comprehension and mastery of the skills by having them answer the Critical Thinking, Reading Skill, and Literary Analysis questions. FT
- Have students complete the Vocabulary Practice activities. FT
- Have students complete the Word Study activities.

DAY 5 Extend/Assess

- Have students complete the Grammar lesson. CRI
- Have students complete the Writing activity and write an anecdote. (You may assign as homework.) FT
- Extend learning by having students complete the Listening and Speaking activity, a problem-solving group. As an alternative, assign them "Happy Together" or "Winners and Losers" in *Reality Central*. CRI
- Administer Selection Test A or B (*Unit 1 Resources*, pp. 146–151 or 167–172). FT

"Contents of the Dead Man's Pocket" is a short story edited for sensitivity issues. "Games at Twilight" is a short story, presented unedited and in its entirety.

Meeting Your Standards

Students will

1. **analyze and respond to literary elements.**
   - **Literary Analysis: Conflict and Resolution**
2. **read, comprehend, and analyze short stories.**
   - **Reading Skill: Cause and Effect**
   - **Reading Check questions**
   - **Apply the Skills questions**
   - **Assessment Practice**
3. **develop vocabulary.**
   - **Vocabulary**
   - **Word Study**
4. **apply grammar skills.**
   - **Personal Pronouns**
5. **Develop writing proficiency.**
   - **Work in Progress: Cause-and-Effect Essay**
   - **anecdote**
6. **strengthen research and technology skills.**
   - **problem-solving group**

CRI For a full explanation of Culturally Responsive Instruction opportunities in this lesson, see p. T86–T87.

FT For an accelerated lesson, use the Fast Track strategies and activities.

Managing Differentiated Instruction

This leveled selection pairing groups a more accessible with a more challenging selection. Choose either one to teach the lesson skills. For classroom management suggestions for using the pairing in a mixed-ability class, see pp. T68–T69.

Daily Block Scheduling

Each day in this Lesson Pacing Guide represents a 40–50 minute period. Teachers using block scheduling may combine days to revise pacing. In addition, teachers may differentiate and support core instruction by integrating components for extended and intensive support as students require. See the Guide to Selected Leveled Resources (facing page).

Guide to Selected Leveled Resources

EL English Learners

			Contents of the Dead Man's Pocket	Games at Twilight
CORE COURSE	*Unit 1 Resources*	Selection Test A	pp. 146–148	pp. 167–169
	Graphic Organizer Transparencies	Reading Skill Graphic Organizer A	p. 23	p. 24
		Literary Analysis Graphic Organizer A	p. 20	p. 21
EXTENDED SUPPORT (Level 2)	*Unit 1 Resources*	Reading and Vocabulary Warm-ups A or B	pp. 134–137	pp. 152–155
	Reader's Notebook: English Learner's Version		adapted instruction and adapted selection	adapted instruction and summary
	Hear It! Audio CD		selection and summaries	selection and summaries
	Hear It! Audio CD (adapted text)		adapted selection and summaries	—
INTENSIVE SUPPORT (Level 1)	*Reality Central*		"Happy Together"	"Winners and Losers"
	Real-World Writing Journal		Lesson 5, pp. 18–21	Lesson 6, pp. 22–25

L2 Below-Level Students

			Contents of the Dead Man's Pocket	Games at Twilight
CORE COURSE	*Unit 1 Resources*	Selection Test A	pp. 146–148	pp. 167–169
	Graphic Organizer Transparencies	Reading Skill Graphic Organizer A	p. 23	p. 24
		Literary Analysis Graphic Organizer A	p. 20	p. 21
EXTENDED SUPPORT (Level 2)	*Unit 1 Resources*	Reading and Vocabulary Warm-ups A or B	pp. 134–137	pp. 152–155
	Reader's Notebook		adapted instruction and full selection	adapted instruction and summary
	Hear It! Audio CD		selection and summaries	selection and summaries
INTENSIVE SUPPORT (Level 1)	*Reality Central*		"Happy Together"	"Winners and Losers"
	Real-World Writing Journal		Lesson 5, pp. 18–21	Lesson 6, pp. 22–25
	Reading Kit		Reteaching worksheets	Reteaching worksheets

L1 Special Needs Students

			Contents of the Dead Man's Pocket	Games at Twilight
CORE COURSE	*Unit 1 Resources*	Selection Test A	pp. 146–148	pp. 167–169
	Graphic Organizer Transparencies	Reading Skill Graphic Organizer A	p. 23	p. 24
		Literary Analysis Graphic Organizer A	p. 20	p. 21
EXTENDED SUPPORT (Level 2)	*Unit 1 Resources*	Reading and Vocabulary Warm-ups A or B	pp. 134–137	pp. 152–155
	Reader's Notebook: Adapted Version		adapted instruction and adapted selection	adapted instruction and summary
	Hear It! Audio CD (adapted text)		adapted selection and summaries	—
INTENSIVE SUPPORT (Level 1)	*Reality Central*		"Happy Together"	"Winners and Losers"
	Real-World Writing Journal		Lesson 5, pp. 18–21	Lesson 6, pp. 22–25
	Reading Kit		Reteaching worksheets	Reteaching worksheets

The program includes resources for these students: L3 On-Level L4 Advanced All All
For a complete guide to selection support, see pp. T106–T108.

NOTE: All print materials are also available online at *www.PHLitOnline.com.*

VISUAL GUIDE to Featured Selection Resources

• Contents of the Dead Man's Pocket
• Games at Twilight

RESOURCES FOR:

- EL English Learners
- L1 Special Needs Students
- L2 Below-Level Students
- L3 On-Level Students
- L4 Advanced Students
- All All Students

Vocabulary/Fluency/Prior Knowledge

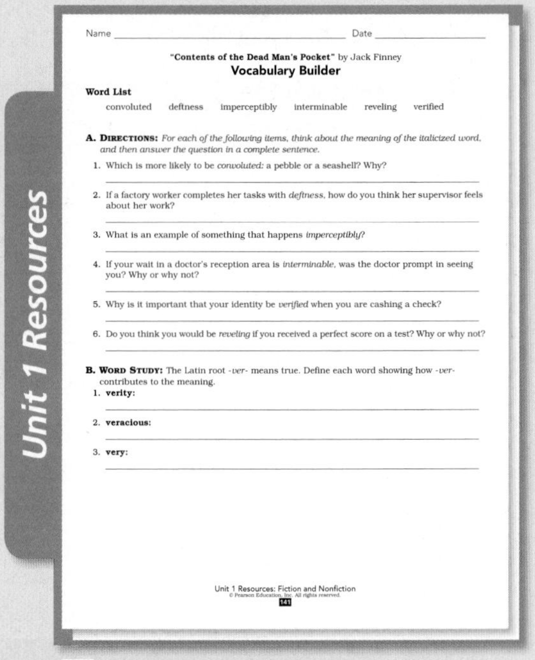

Unit 1 Resources

Name ______________________ Date ____________

"Contents of the Dead Man's Pocket" by Jack Finney

Vocabulary Builder

Word List

convoluted deftness imperceptibly interminable reveling verified

A. Directions: *For each of the following items, think about the meaning of the italicized word, and then answer the question in a complete sentence.*

1. Which is more likely to be *convoluted:* a pebble or a seashell? Why?
2. If a factory worker completes her tasks with *deftness*, how do you think her supervisor feels about her work?
3. What is an example of something that happens *imperceptibly?*
4. If your wait in a doctor's reception area is *interminable*, was the doctor prompt in seeing you? Why or why not?
5. Why is it important that your identity be *verified* when you are cashing a check?
6. Do you think you would be *reveling* if you received a perfect score on a test? Why or why not?

B. Word Study: The Latin root *-ver-* means true. Define each word showing how *-ver-* contributes to the meaning.

1. **verity:**
2. **veracious:**
3. **very:**

Unit 1 Resources: Fiction and Nonfiction
© Pearson Education, Inc. All rights reserved.
141

All **Vocabulary Builder,** pp. 141, 159

Also available for these selections:

EL L1 L2 Reading Warm-ups A and B, pp. 136–137, 154–155

EL L1 L2 Vocabulary Warm-ups A and B, pp. 134–135, 152–153

All Writing About the Big Question, pp. 138, 156

L2 L3 ***Reader's Notebook***

L1 ***Reader's Notebook: Adapted Version***

EL ***Reader's Notebook: English Learner's Version***

Reader's Notebooks

Pre- and postreading pages for both selections, as well as "Contents of the Dead Man's Pocket," appear in an interactive format in the *Reader's Notebooks*. Each *Notebook* is differentiated for a different group of learners.

The selections in the Adapted and English Learner's versions are abridged.

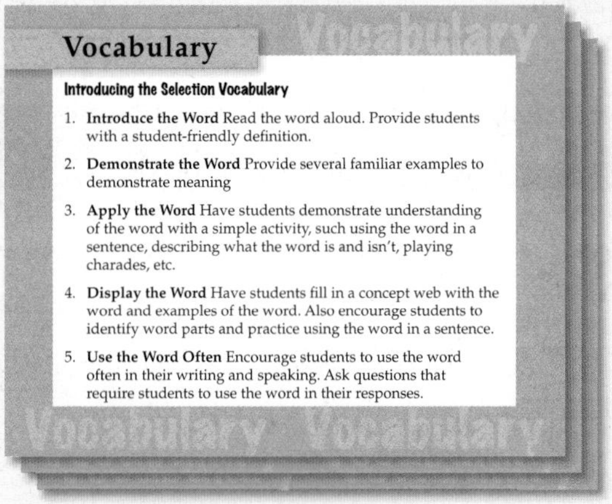

Vocabulary

Introducing the Selection Vocabulary

1. **Introduce the Word** Read the word aloud. Provide students with a student-friendly definition.
2. **Demonstrate the Word** Provide several familiar examples to demonstrate meaning
3. **Apply the Word** Have students demonstrate understanding of the word with a simple activity, such using the word in a sentence, describing what the word is and isn't, playing charades, etc.
4. **Display the Word** Have students fill in a concept web with the word and examples of the word. Also encourage students to identify word parts and practice using the word in a sentence.
5. **Use the Word Often** Encourage students to use the word often in their writing and speaking. Ask questions that require students to use the word in their responses.

Classroom Strategies and Teaching Routines

- core classroom routines outlined step-by-step
- convenient format for easy reference while teaching

Graphic Organizer Transparencies

Selection Support

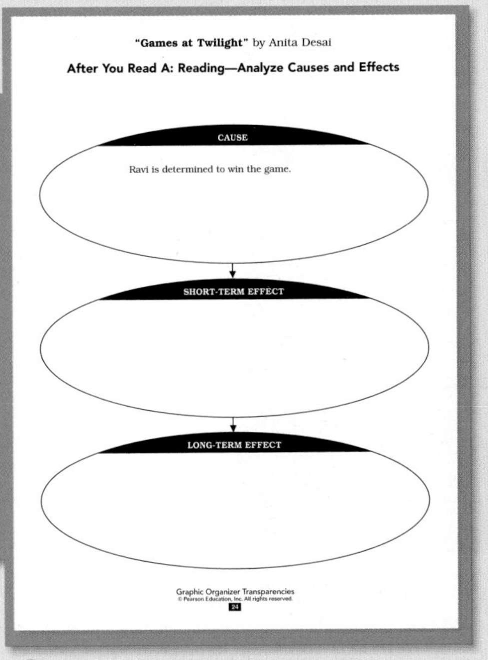
"Games at Twilight" by Anita Desai

After You Read A: Reading—Analyze Causes and Effects

Graphic Organizer Transparencies
© Pearson Education, Inc. All rights reserved.
24

EL L1 L2 **Reading: Graphic Organizer A, pp. 23, 24 (partially filled in)**

Also available for these selections:

L3 Reading: Graphic Organizer B, p. 25

EL L1 L2 Literary Analysis: Graphic Organizer A, pp. 20, 21 (partially filled in)

L3 Literary Analysis: Graphic Organizer B, p. 22

Skills Development/Extension

Unit 1 Resources

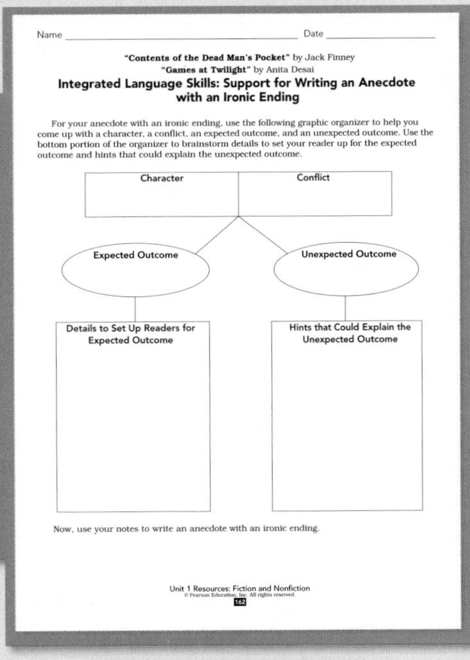
Name ______ Date ______

"Contents of the Dead Man's Pocket" by Jack Finney
"Games at Twilight" by Anita Desai

Integrated Language Skills: Support for Writing an Anecdote with an Ironic Ending

For your anecdote with an ironic ending, use the following graphic organizer to help you come up with a character, a conflict, an expected outcome, and an unexpected outcome. Use the bottom portion of the organizer to brainstorm details to set your reader up for the expected outcome and hints that could explain the unexpected outcome.

Now, use your notes to write an anecdote with an ironic ending.

Unit 1 Resources: Fiction and Nonfiction
© Pearson Education, Inc. All rights reserved.
162

L3 L4 **Support for Writing,** p. 162

Also available for these selections:

All Literary Analysis: Conflict and Resolution, pp. 139, 157

All Reading: Cause and Effect, pp. 140, 158

L4 Enrichment, pp. 142, 160

L3 L4 Grammar, p. 161

L3 L4 Support for Extend Your Learning, p. 163

Assessment

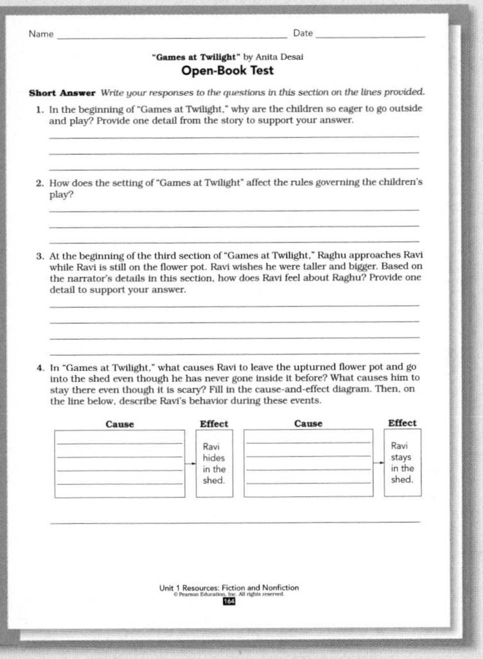
Name ______ Date ______

"Games at Twilight" by Anita Desai

Open-Book Test

Short Answer *Write your responses to the questions in this section on the lines provided.*

1. In the beginning of "Games at Twilight," why are the children so eager to go outside and play? Provide one detail from the story to support your answer.

2. How does the setting of "Games at Twilight" affect the rules governing the children's play?

3. At the beginning of the third section of "Games at Twilight," Raghu approaches Ravi while Ravi is still on the flower pot. Ravi wishes he were taller and bigger. Based on the narrator's details in this section, how does Ravi feel about Raghu? Provide one detail to support your answer.

4. In "Games at Twilight," what causes Ravi to leave the upturned flower pot and go into the shed even though he has never gone inside it before? What causes him to stay there even though it is scary? Fill in the cause-and-effect diagram. Then, on the line below, describe Ravi's behavior during these events.

Unit 1 Resources: Fiction and Nonfiction
© Pearson Education, Inc. All rights reserved.
164

L3 L4 **Open-Book Test,** pp. 143–145, 164–166

Also available for these selections:

EL L1 L2 Selection Test A, pp. 146–148, 167–169

L3 L4 Selection Test B, pp. 149–151, 170–172

PHLit Online!

www.PHLitOnline.com

- complete narrated selection text
- a thematically related video with writing prompt
- an interactive graphic organizer
- highlighting feature
- access to all student print resources, adapted to individual student needs
- Spanish and English summaries

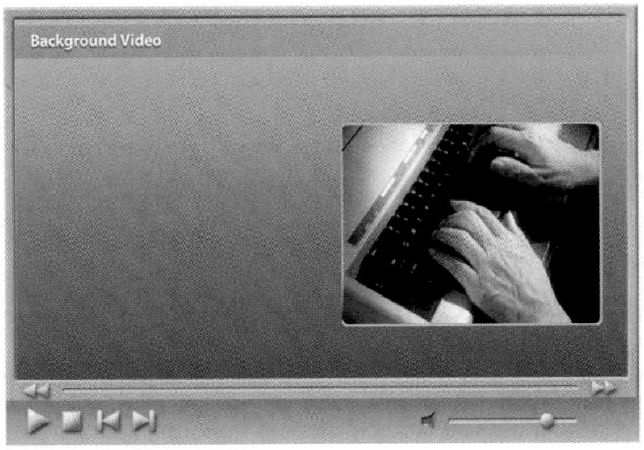

Background video

Also available:

Get Connected! (thematic video with writing prompt)

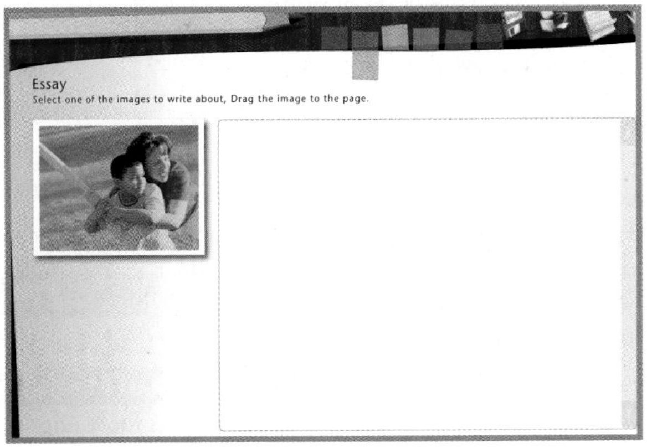

Writer's Journal (with graphics feature)

Also available:

Vocabulary Central (tools, activities, and songs for studying vocabulary)

DIFFERENTIATE/PRETEACH

❶ Selection Choices

You may use either "Contents of the Dead Man's Pocket" or "Games at Twilight" to meet the lesson standards. Skills instruction for both selections appears on p. 115. Choose one selection to teach (or choose to teach both). The Accessibility at a Glance chart at the bottom of this page will help you determine which selection is more appropriate for your students.

❷ Selection Skills

1. With the class, preview the selection skills. (The lesson meets the lesson objectives given on p. 114a.)
2. Explain that students will learn to use the skill analyzing cause and effect as they read to better understand and enjoy the selection you choose. By examining conflict and resolution as they read, they will gain deeper insight into the selection.
3. To introduce the Writing and Listening and Speaking activities (p. 151), tell students that when they have finished reading the selection, they will write an anecdote and form a problem-solving group. In these activities, they will explore ideas, people, or situations that they encountered in the selection.
4. Tell students that they will also study a grammar concept: personal pronouns. By mastering this concept, they will improve their reading fluency and the quality of their own writing.

Before You Read

Contents of the Dead Man's Pocket • Games at Twilight

❶ Selection Choices

▲ Read **"Contents of the Dead Man's Pocket"** to find out why a man risks his life on the ledge of a tall building.

▲ Read **"Games at Twilight"** to experience the drama of a game of hide-and-seek from the point of view of a child.

❷ Selection Skills Guide

Practice these skills with either **Contents of the Dead Man's Pocket** (p. 118) or **Games at Twilight** (p. 139).

- Identify conflict and resolution
- Understand external conflict and internal conflict
- Analyze causes and effects
- Reflect on key details
- Identify personal pronouns
- Write an anecdote using irony
- Form a problem-solving group

Differentiated Instruction for Universal Access

Accessibility at a Glance: Selection Choices

	Contents of the Dead Man's Pocket	Games at Twilight
Context	Man realizes that life is more important than work	Young boy tries to earn respect through hide-and seek game
Language/ Vocabulary	• Some long, complex descriptions • Some imaginary sequences • On-level vocabulary	• Many simple sentences • Difficult vocabulary defined • Below-level vocabulary
Concept Level	Accessible (man faces death in struggle to retrieve lost paper)	Challenging (recognizing how one is viewed by others)
Literary Merit	Suspenseful	Cross-generational
Lexile/Length	Lexile: 1180L Word Count: 6,667	Lexile: 1200L Word Count: 2,995
Overall Rating	**More accessible**	**More challenging**

Because a number of factors determine the relative accessibility of paired selections, in some cases the Lexile rating of the more challenging selection will be lower than that of the more accessible selection.

❸ Literary Analysis: Conflict and Resolution

The **conflict** in a short story is a struggle between two forces. Conflict usually drives the plot of a story.

- In an **external conflict,** a character struggles against an outside force, such as an element of nature or another character.
- In an **internal conflict,** a character struggles with his or her own opposing desires, beliefs, or needs.

In many stories, the conflict intensifies until one force wins and a **resolution** of the conflict occurs. To build interest in a story's conflict, writers may hint at events to come or "stretch out" episodes that lead up to a crucial moment. In these ways, they create **suspense,** a rising curiosity or anxiety in readers.

❹ Using the Strategy: Conflict Chart

As you read, use a chart like this one to record conflicts.

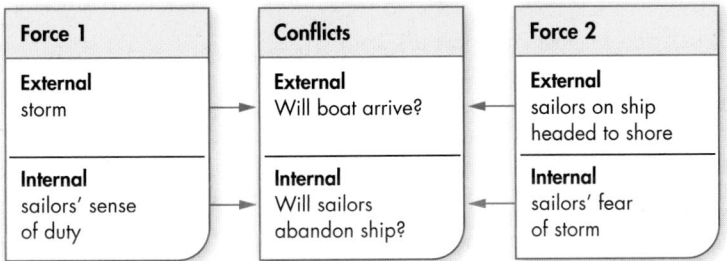

Force 1	→	Conflicts	←	Force 2
External storm	→	**External** Will boat arrive?	←	**External** sailors on ship headed to shore
Internal sailors' sense of duty	→	**Internal** Will sailors abandon ship?	←	**Internal** sailors' fear of storm

❺ Reading Skill: Cause and Effect

A **cause** is an event, an action, or a situation that produces a result. An **effect** is the result produced. To better follow a story, **analyze causes and effects** as you read, determining which earlier events lead to which later events. Many stories are chains of cause and effect, in which one event leads to the next.

To analyze causes and effects, **reflect on key details** that the writer spends time explaining or describing. For example, a writer's description of a dangerous coastline prepares you to understand the cause-and-effect relationships leading to the sinking of a ship.

PHLit Online!
www.PHLitOnline.com

Hear It!
- Selection summary audio
- Selection audio

See It!
- Get Connected video
- Background video
- More about the author
- Vocabulary flashcards

Do It!
- Interactive journals
- Interactive graphic organizers
- Self-test
- Internet activity
- Grammar tutorial
- Interactive vocabulary games

PRETEACH

❸ Literary Analysis

Conflict

1. Introduce the skill, using the instruction on the student page.
2. Tell students that they will identify different types of conflict as they read.

Think Aloud: Model the Skill

Model the skill of identifying conflict and resolution. Say to students:

> Before we can resolve any conflict, we need to understand exactly what that conflict is. I know that conflict is a struggle between two forces.
>
> Suppose that I am driving, and my car gets a flat tire. The conflict is that I can't drive the car with a flat tire. The opposing forces are me and the flat tire. I can't drive unless I resolve the conflict. The resolution is to fix the flat tire.

❹ Using the Strategy

Give students a copy of either **Literary Analysis Graphic Organizer A or B** (*Graphic Organizer Transparencies,* pp. 20–21) to record their ideas about conflict and resolution as they read. Use the examples in **Literary Analysis Graphic Organizer A,** which is partially filled in, to model the process of completing the organizer.

❺ Reading Skill

1. Introduce the skill, using the instruction on the student page.
2. Tell students that they will analyze cause and effect as they read.

Think Aloud: Model the Skill

Model the skill of relating cause and effect. Say to students:

> Almost everything in real life can be described through cause and effect. For example, let's say I install solar panels on my house. The panels generate enough energy to power my appliances. As a result, I use less electricity all year round. Installing the solar panels is the cause, and using less electricity is the effect.

Differentiated Instruction for Universal Access

Preparing Students for the More Challenging Selection

If you wish to prepare lower-level readers to read "Games at Twilight," the more challenging selection, follow these steps:

- Review strategies for unlocking word meanings. Although the most difficult vocabulary words in the selection are defined, students may not understand a word's meaning as it relates to the text. Encourage students to put the definition in their own words. Then, have students read the text in which the word appears, substituting the word with their own definition.
- Discuss the main concept of the selection. Prompt students to think of a time when they were aware of how others viewed them. Encourage students to determine how important their views of themselves are compared to how others see them.
- Practice strategies for reading long sentences. Select several sentences to use as examples. Have students identify the main action(s), and then break down the smaller parts for interpretation.

PRETEACH

❶ Writing About the Big Question

1. Review the assignment with the class.
2. Remind students that a person's idea of truth and reality can alter when they have new experiences. Invite students to think of a situation that could cause them to re-evaluate their goals and ideas.
3. Have students complete the sentence starter. Review responses as a class. **Possible response:** Life-threatening situations may cause people to evaluate whether they are happy with their lives because they realize how short life is.
4. Remind students that their answers will help them think about the Big Question, "Is there a difference between reality and truth?"

While You Read

Tell students that as they read, they should look for moments in which Tom experiences changes in his perception of reality or truth.

❷ Vocabulary

1. Have students preview the selection vocabulary.
2. For each word, have students say the word aloud.
3. Then, use the word in a sentence that defines the word.
4. Finally, repeat your definitional sentence or a similar sentence with the word missing and have the class "fill in the blank" chorally. Here are some examples:

Something convoluted is knotty, complex, and intricate. Why is this story, with multiple narrators and changing perspective, so [students say "convoluted"]?

Deftness is skillfulness. The master woodworker was so familiar with his tools that he carved into wood the most complex details with what seemed a natural [students say "deftness"].

❸ Word Study

1. Introduce the skill, using the instruction in the box.
2. Ask students to think of other words containing the Latin root *-ver-*. (**Sample answers:** *very, verily, aver*)

Making Connections

Contents of the Dead Man's Pocket

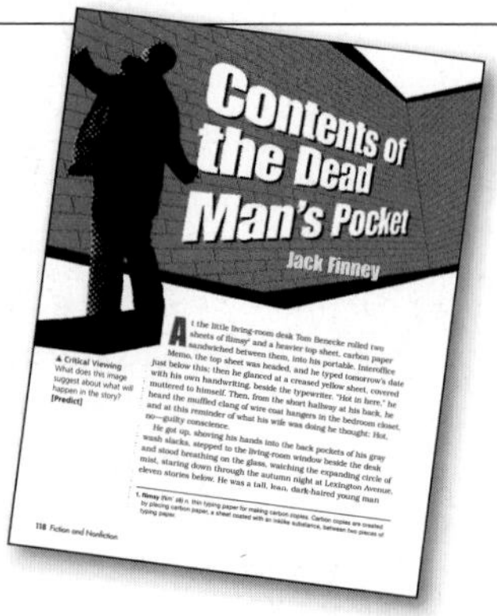

Is there a difference between *reality* and *truth?*

❶ Writing About the Big Question

In "Contents of the Dead Man's Pocket," a man's perception of reality shifts because of a terrifying experience. He discovers the truth about his life and his priorities. Use this sentence starter to develop your ideas about the Big Question.

Life-threatening situations may cause people to **evaluate** ___________ because ___________.

While You Read Look for moments when the main character experiences changes in his understanding of reality or truth.

❷ Vocabulary

Read each word and its definition. Decide whether you know the word well, know it a little bit, or do not know it at all. After you read, see how your knowledge of each word has increased.

- **convoluted** (kän′ və lo͞ot′ əd) *adj.* twisted in a complicated way (p. 121) ***The convoluted maze confused us.*** convolution *n.*
- **verified** (ver′ ə fīd) *v.* proved to be true (p. 122) ***He verified the results of the test by double-checking the scores.*** verification *n.* verifiable *adj.*
- **deftness** (deft′ nis) *n.* skillfulness (p. 126) ***She climbed with the deftness of a mountain goat.*** deftly *adv.* deft *adj.*
- **imperceptibly** (im′ pər sep′ tə blē) *adv.* so slowly or slightly as to be barely noticeable (p. 127) ***I did not notice when the fish nibbled imperceptibly at my bait.*** imperceptible *adj.* perception *n.*
- **reveling** (rev′ əl iŋ) *v.* taking great pleasure or delight (p. 127) ***When she got her first job, she could not stop reveling in her newfound independence.*** revel *v.* reveler *n.* revelry *v.*
- **interminable** (in tʉr′ mi nə bəl) *adj.* endless or seeming endless (p. 130) ***The wait seemed interminable to the impatient shopper.*** interminably *adv.* terminate *v.*

❸ Word Study

The **Latin root *-ver-*** means "true."

In this story, Tom **verified** a situation when he made sure that it was true.

Vocabulary Development

Vocabulary Knowledge Rating

Create a **Vocabulary Knowledge Rating Chart** (***Professional Development Guidebook***, p. 33) for this selection. Include the selection vocabulary and the Big Question words that appear in the Writing About the Big Question sentence starters on this page. (The Big Question vocabulary is introduced on pp. 2–3.)

Give students a copy of the chart. Read the words aloud, and have students mark their rating in the Before Reading column. Urge them to be alert to these words as they read and discuss the selection.

Tally how many students think they know a word to gauge how much instruction to provide. As students read and discuss the selection, point out the words and their context.

PHLit Online! **Vocabulary Central**, featuring tools, activities, and songs for studying vocabulary, is available at **www.PHLitOnline.com**.

Meet Jack Finney (1911–1995)

Author of

Contents of the Dead Man's Pocket

While working at an advertising agency, Jack Finney dreamed of becoming a writer. He realized his dream when he entered his first short story in a contest sponsored by a magazine—and won!

Tales of Time Finney became especially well known for blending realistic and imaginary details into tales of time travel. In his popular works, the hero often escapes from the present into a simpler and calmer time in the past. However, Finney was happy to live in the present. "There's no past time I'd like to stay in," he said. "I want to stay here permanently."

DID YOU KNOW?

Finney's novel *Invasion of the Body Snatchers* has been made into a movie three times.

4 BACKGROUND FOR THE STORY

Before Computers

In the 1950s, when this story takes place, there were no computers or photocopiers. To make copies, people used carbon paper—black-coated sheets that transferred written or typed marks onto blank paper below. Without a carbon copy, a lost document might be gone forever—a possibility the main character in this story dreads.

Daily Bellringer

For each class during which you will teach this selection, have students complete one of the five Revision activities for Week 4 in the ***Daily Bellringer Activities*** booklet.

4 Background

Before Computers

Today's offices have laser printers, faxes, and high-tech hard drives that store information electronically for instant retrieval. Whereas in the 1950s a single document was often unique, multiple copies of a document can be made in seconds today. Our fast-paced information-based society is a contrast to the 1950s in the story.

Multidraft Reading

This icon ● marks natural pauses in the selection. To assist struggling readers and to deepen reading for all, assign the text in "chunks," following the icons, and apply multidraft reading protocols. For each reading, have students set the purpose indicated:

- **First reading**—literal comprehension: answering the Reading Check questions.
- **Second reading**—application of skills: answering the Cause-and-Effect prompt and the Conflict prompt.
- **Third reading**—interpretation: answering the end-of-selection questions.

For more guidance, refer to the ***Classroom Strategies and Teaching Routines*** card on multidraft reading.

Differentiated Instruction — Additional Instruction

EL Extended Support—English Learners

Have students complete the **Reading and Vocabulary Warm-ups, *Unit 1 Resources,*** pp. 134–137, before they read. Assign the prereading pages and the adapted selection in the ***Reader's Notebook: English Learner's Version.*** Then, have students listen to portions of the selection on the ***Hear It!* Audio CD** (adapted text).

L1 L2 Extended Support—Struggling Readers

Have students complete the **Reading and Vocabulary Warm-ups, *Unit 1 Resources,*** pp. 134–137, before they read. Assign the prereading pages and the adapted selection in the ***Reader's Notebook: Adapted Version.*** Then, have students listen to portions of the selection on the ***Hear It!* Audio CD** (adapted text).

Extended Support—Reluctant Readers

To build motivation and engagement before assigning the selection, have students read "Happy Together," a thematically related selection in ***Reality Central.*** Then, use the questions at the conclusion of the related selection to guide discussion.

PHLit Online!

For more about the author, practice with the selection vocabulary, and more background, go online at **www.PHLitOnline.com**.

TEACH

❶ Activating Prior Knowledge

1. Prepare an **Anticipation Guide** (see ***Professional Development Guidebook,*** pp. 36–38) with the following statements:
   - What people do for work is the most important part of their lives.
   - We all struggle when making decisions.
   - An action we take today will not have much of an effect on our lives in the future.
   - People should take risks in their lives.
   - Competition helps people perform their best.
2. Give students a copy of the prepared **Anticipation Guide,** and have them mark their responses in the Me column. Have students discuss the statements in pairs or groups, and mark the Guide again in the Group Column.
3. For further guidance, use the ***Classroom Strategies and Teaching Routines*** card: **Using an Anticipation Guide.**

Concept Connector ➔

Students will return to the **Anticipation Guide** after completing the story.

Small-Group Activity

Have students work in groups to write screenplays based on one scene from Finney's story. Encourage them to study how Finney's verbal and visual effects should be essential aspects of a screenplay.

❷ About the Selection

In "Contents of the Dead Man's Pocket," Tom Benecke stays home to work on a business proposal while his wife goes to the movies alone. When Tom has a harrowing experience on the ledge of his apartment building, he is forced to reexamine his life and reshape his outlook.

❸ Critical Viewing

Answer: The image suggests that a man will be outside a building on a ledge.

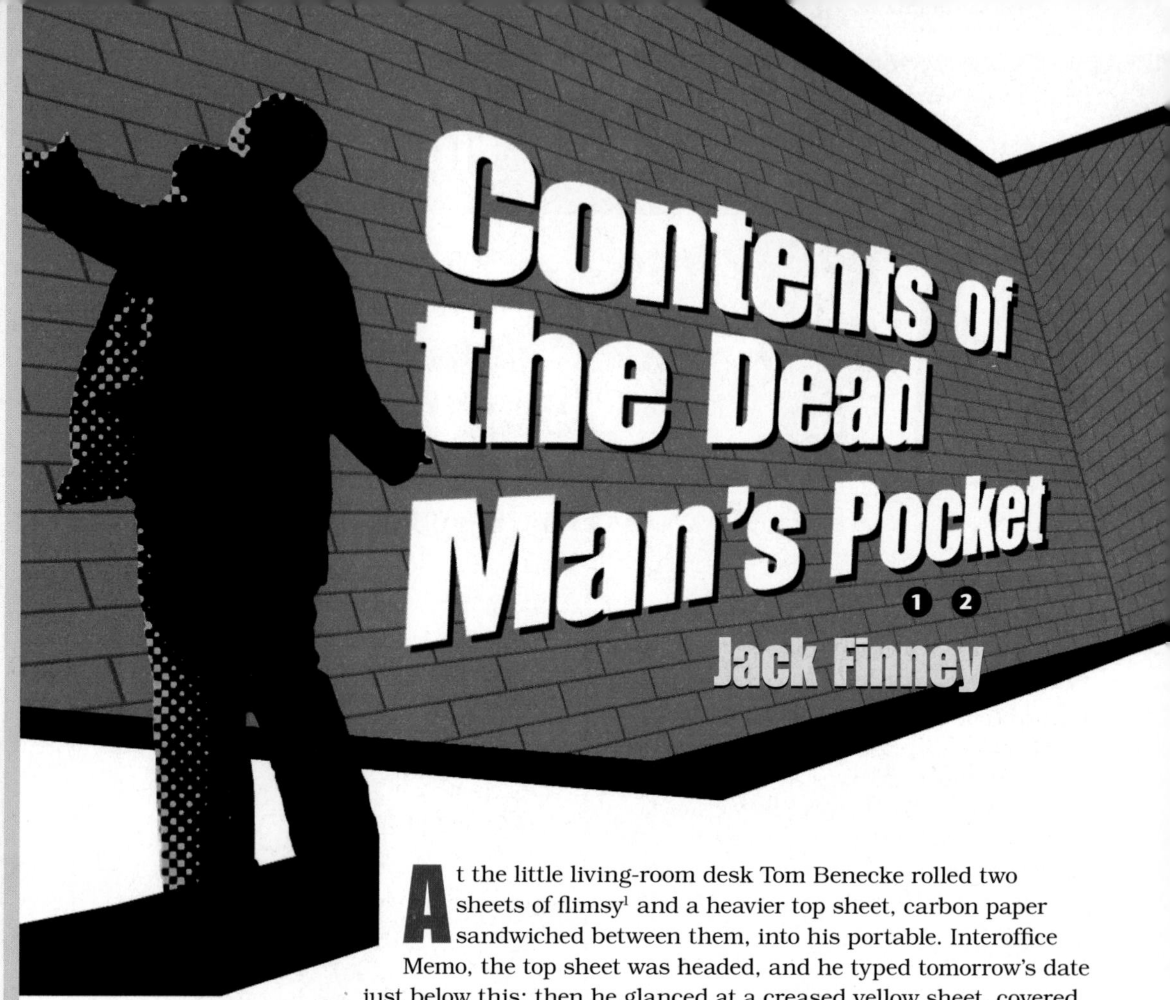

Contents of the Dead Man's Pocket ❶ ❷

Jack Finney

❸ ▲ **Critical Viewing** What does this image suggest about what will happen in the story? **[Predict]**

At the little living-room desk Tom Benecke rolled two sheets of flimsy[1] and a heavier top sheet, carbon paper sandwiched between them, into his portable. Interoffice Memo, the top sheet was headed, and he typed tomorrow's date just below this; then he glanced at a creased yellow sheet, covered with his own handwriting, beside the typewriter. "Hot in here," he muttered to himself. Then, from the short hallway at his back, he heard the muffled clang of wire coat hangers in the bedroom closet, and at this reminder of what his wife was doing he thought: Hot, no—guilty conscience.

He got up, shoving his hands into the back pockets of his gray wash slacks, stepped to the living-room window beside the desk and stood breathing on the glass, watching the expanding circle of mist, staring down through the autumn night at Lexington Avenue, eleven stories below. He was a tall, lean, dark-haired young man

1. **flimsy** (flim′ zē) *n.* thin typing paper for making carbon copies. Carbon copies are created by placing carbon paper, a sheet coated with an inklike substance, between two pieces of typing paper.

Vocabulary Development

Thematic Vocabulary

As students are discussing "Contents of the Dead Man's Pocket," encourage them to use the thematic vocabulary presented in Introducing the Big Question, pp. 2–3. You might encourage them with sentence starters like these:

1. When the paper first flies out the window, Tom cannot *comprehend* that . . .
2. Tom decides to go out on the ledge, but he does not *discern* . . .
3. Tom wants the paper because the information on it can *verify* . . .
4. Based on his *perception* of his job, Tom feels he must . . .

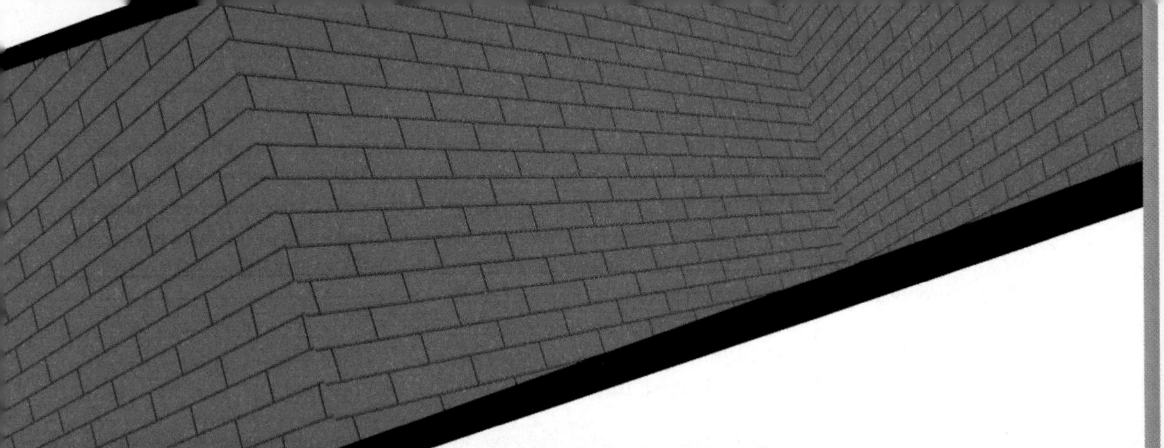

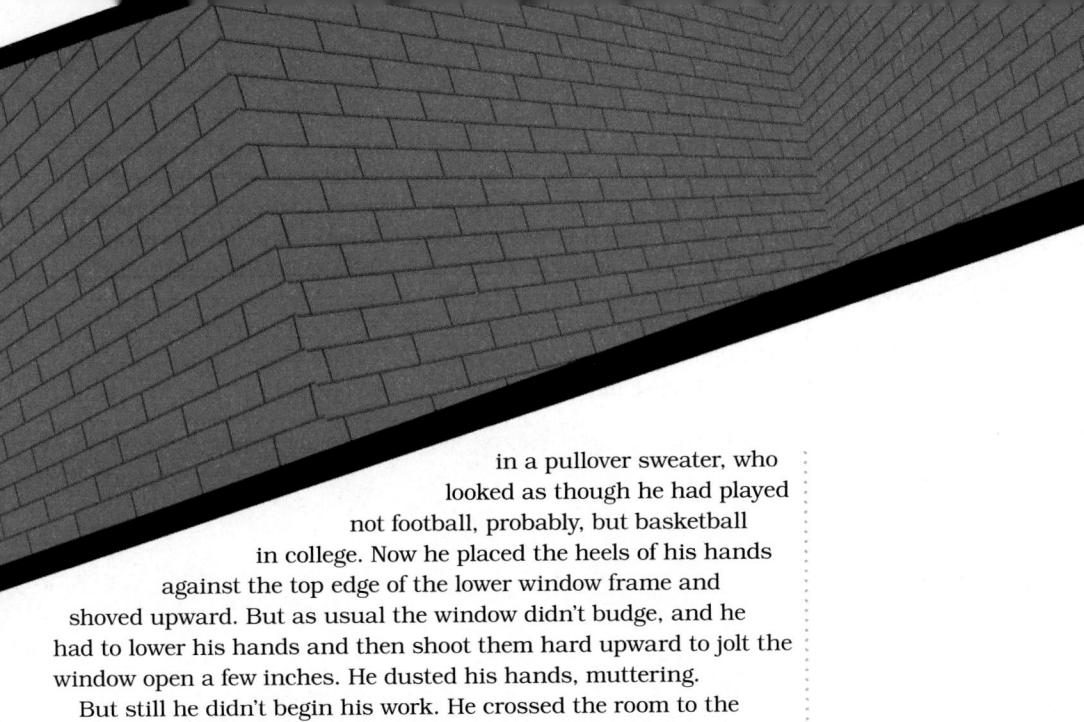

in a pullover sweater, who looked as though he had played not football, probably, but basketball in college. Now he placed the heels of his hands against the top edge of the lower window frame and shoved upward. But as usual the window didn't budge, and he had to lower his hands and then shoot them hard upward to jolt the window open a few inches. He dusted his hands, muttering.

But still he didn't begin his work. He crossed the room to the hallway entrance and, leaning against the doorjamb, hands shoved into his back pockets again, he called, "Clare?" When his wife answered, he said, "Sure you don't mind going alone?"

"No." Her voice was muffled, and he knew her head and shoulders were in the bedroom closet. Then the tap of her high heels sounded on the wood floor and she appeared at the end of the little hallway, wearing a slip, both hands raised to one ear, clipping on an earring. She smiled at him—a slender, very pretty girl with light brown, almost blonde, hair—her prettiness emphasized by the pleasant nature that showed in her face. "It's just that I hate you to miss this movie; you wanted to see it too."

❹ "Yeah, I know." He ran his fingers through his hair. "Got to get this done though."

She nodded, accepting this. Then, glancing at the desk across the living room, she said, "You work too much, though, Tom—and too hard."

He smiled. "You won't mind though, will you, when the money comes rolling in and I'm known as the Boy Wizard of Wholesale Groceries?"

"I guess not." She smiled and turned back toward the bedroom. ❺

At his desk again, Tom lighted a cigarette, then a few moments later as Clare appeared, dressed and ready to leave, he set it on the

Literary Analysis
Conflict What internal conflict of Tom's does this paragraph show?

Reading Check
Why has Tom decided to stay home?

❹ Literary Analysis
Conflict

1. Tell students that stories revolve around conflicts that a character must face. Explain that sometimes a conflict is settled quickly, but, more often, the conflict does not get resolved until the end of the story, creating suspense.
2. Have students read the bracketed passage, and then **ask** the Literary Analysis question: What internal conflict of Tom's does this paragraph show?
   Answer: Tom runs his hands through his hair, which shows stress or distraction, and his words show that he is torn between going to the movies and doing work.

❺ Reading Check

Answer: Tom decides not to go to the movies because he wants to write an interoffice memo that will bolster his reputation at work.

Differentiated Instruction for Universal Access

Strategy for Less Proficient Students
Students might have difficulty understanding which causes lead to which effects. Ask students to reread the beginning of the story, making a list of details that may play an important role in the plot. Make sure they include the jammed window and the fact that Tom will be spending the evening alone. As they read ahead, encourage students to track how these details develop. To further assist their comprehension of cause and effect, you may want to show students the **Reading Skill Graphic Organizer A** (*Graphic Organizer Transparencies,* p. 23).

EL Strategy for English Learners
Before they read ahead, make sure students have a thorough understanding of the introduction. Ask them to reread this page, making a list of unfamiliar words. Help them obtain the definitions by rereading, reading ahead, or consulting dictionaries. Encourage students to keep lists of new words in their notebooks.

PHLit Online!
This selection is available in interactive format in the **Enriched Online Student Edition, www.PHLitOnline.com**, which includes a thematically related video and writing prompt and an interactive graphic organizer.

❻ Critical Viewing

Answer: The image captures the danger of falling from a narrow ledge to the busy city street below.

❼ Connecting to the Big Question

1. Explain that a character's view of the world is revealed through his or her words, thoughts, and actions.
2. Have students read the bracketed text. **Ask:** What does Tom think will happen if he stays home to finish his work instead of going to the movies with his wife? **Answer:** Tom's boss will be able to read his ideas over the weekend rather than on Monday.
3. **Ask:** Why is it important to know that Tom does not "have to work tonight"? **Possible response:**
4. Work is very important to Tom. Remind students to keep this explanation in mind as they continue to read.

❽ Reading Skill
Cause and Effect

1. Have students fill out their **Reading Skill Graphic Organizer B** (*Graphic Organizer Transparencies,* p. 22) with details from the bracketed passage, including the open window and Clare's leaving to go to the movies.
2. Then **ask** the Reading Skill question: Which key details explain why the paper drops out of the window?
   Possible response: The door does not close right away. An air current suddenly rushes into the room, creating a force that lifts papers off Tom's desk. The yellow paper makes its way to the window ledge before the current dies, and then the paper disappears outside.

rim of the ash tray. "Just after seven," she said. "I can make the beginning of the first feature."

❼ He walked to the front-door closet to help her on with her coat. He kissed her then and, for an instant, holding her close, smelling the perfume she had used, he was tempted to go with her; it was not actually true that he had to work tonight, though he very much wanted to. This was his own project, unannounced as yet in his office, and it could be postponed. But then they won't see it till Monday, he thought once again, and if I give it to the boss tomorrow he might read it over the weekend . . . "Have a good time," he said aloud. He gave his wife a little swat and opened the door for her,

❻ ▼ **Critical Viewing**
How does this image suggest suspense and danger? **[Interpret]**

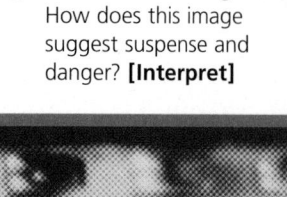

feeling the air from the building hallway, smelling faintly of floor wax, stream gently past his face.

He watched her walk down the hall, flicked a hand in response as she waved, and then he started to close the door, but it resisted for a moment. As the door opening narrowed, the current of warm air from the hallway, channeled through this smaller opening now, suddenly rushed past him with accelerated force. Behind him he heard the slap of the window curtains against the wall and the sound of paper fluttering from his desk, and he had to push to close the door.

Turning, he saw a sheet of white paper drifting to the floor in a series of arcs, and another sheet, yellow, moving toward the window, caught in the dying current flowing through the narrow

Reading Skill
Cause and Effect ❽
Which key details explain why the paper floats off the desk?

Vocabulary Development

Vocabulary Reinforcement

Students will benefit from additional examples and practice with the selection vocabulary words. Reinforce their comprehension with "show-you-know" sentences. The first part of the sentence uses the vocabulary word in an appropriate context. The second part of the sentence—the "show-you-know" part—clarifies the first:

> Finding the way through the *convoluted* maze challenged the participants; they made many wrong turns and ran into several dead ends before reaching the end.

1. Maria's *convoluted* directions to her house were hard to follow; ____________.
   Sample answer: they required several turns without signs, one U-turn, and finding a driveway hidden by two large trees.
2. The snail crawled *imperceptibly* across the road; ____________.
   Sample answer: two hours later, it seemed to be in the same place.

8 opening. As he watched, the paper struck the bottom edge of the window and hung there for an instant, plastered against the glass and wood. Then as the moving air stilled completely, the curtains swinging back from the wall to hang free again, he saw the yellow sheet drop to the window ledge and slide over out of sight.

He ran across the room, grasped the bottom edge of the window and tugged, staring through the glass. He saw the yellow sheet, dimly now in the darkness outside, lying on the ornamental ledge a yard below the window. Even as he watched, it was moving, scraping slowly along the ledge, pushed by the breeze that pressed steadily against the building wall. He heaved on the window with all his strength and it shot open with a bang, the window weight rattling in the casing. But the paper was past his reach and, leaning out into the night, he watched it scud steadily along the ledge to the south, half plastered against the building wall. Above the muffled sound of the street traffic far below, he could hear the dry scrape of its movement, like a leaf on the pavement.

9 The living room of the next apartment to the south projected a yard or more farther out toward the street than this one; because of this the Beneckes paid seven and a half dollars less rent than their neighbors. And now the yellow sheet, sliding along the stone ledge, nearly invisible in the night, was stopped by the projecting blank wall of the next apartment. It lay motionless, then, in the corner formed by the two walls—a good five yards away, pressed firmly against the ornate corner ornament of the ledge, by the breeze that moved past Tom Benecke's face.

He knelt at the window and stared at the yellow paper for a full minute or more, waiting for it to move, to slide off the ledge and fall, hoping he could follow its course to the street, and then hurry down in the elevator and retrieve it. But it didn't move, and then he saw that the paper was caught firmly between a projection of the convoluted corner ornament and the ledge. He thought about the poker from the fireplace, then the broom, then the mop—discarding each thought as it occurred to him. There was nothing in the apartment long enough to reach that paper.

11 It was hard for him to understand that he actually had to abandon it—it was ridiculous—and he began to curse. Of all the papers on his desk, why did it have to be this one in particular! On four long Saturday afternoons he had stood in supermarkets counting the people who passed certain displays, and the results were scribbled on that yellow sheet. From stacks of trade publications, gone over page by page in snatched half hours at work and during evenings at home, he had copied facts, quotations, and figures onto that sheet. And he had carried it with him to the Public

Literary Analysis
Conflict Explain how an external conflict here helps create suspense.

Vocabulary
convoluted (kän′ və lo͞ot′ id) *adj.* twisted in a complicated way

10 **Reading Check**
What problem does Tom face?

9 Literary Analysis
Conflict

1. Explain to students that prolonging a situation, rather than immediately telling the reader what will happen next, is one way that authors create suspense.
2. Have two students alternately read aloud the sentences in the bracketed passage. Then **ask** the Literary Analysis prompt: Explain how an external conflict here helps create suspense.
   Possible response: Tom's problem is that he cannot reach the paper, which is on a ledge several stories above a city street. This conflict of a character versus the environment creates suspense when Tom begins to panic and mentally inventory things in his house, such as a broom handle, that he can use to reach the paper. However, the only way it seems that Tom can get the paper back is to go after it, but he could fall and die.

10 Reading Check

Answer: The information Tom needs to finish a project and gain notice at work is out of reach on a ledge 15 feet away.

Differentiated Instruction for Universal Access

Strategy for Special Needs Students
Students may have difficulty picturing where the paper has landed. Have students reread the paragraph that begins, "He knelt at the window . . ." on page 121. As a class, make of sketch of the ledge, showing the location of Tom's window, the corner, and other details. Then, make sure students understand exactly where the paper has landed by having them mark each of the paper's movements.

Enrichment for Gifted/Talented Students
Students may be interested in the science behind how the paper "flies" out the window. After students reread the paragraph that begins, "He watched her walk . . ." on page 120, have them explain exactly how the force of the warm and cold air currents could draw the paper outside the room. Students may wish to use diagrams, charts, or other graphic organizers to demonstrate this effect.

⓫ Reading Skill
Cause and Effect

1. Have students reread the paragraph that begins with "It was hard for him . . ." **Ask:** What does this paragraph say about Tom's attitude toward his project? Explain.
   Possible response: Tom is very dedicated to his project because he has spent his spare time on it.
2. Now remind students that an author puts in particular details in order to stress the causes for certain effects. **Ask** students to identify the details that show Tom's dedication to his project by listing the specific words or phrases used in the paragraph.
   Possible responses: Details such as spending *four long* Saturday afternoons counting customers; reading *stacks* of trade publications; *snatched* half hours; copied *facts, quotations, and figures*; spent a *dozen* lunch hours; and *countless hours of work* all describe Tom's dedication to his work.
3. After students read the bracketed passage, **ask** the Reading Skill question: What might cause Tom to go after the paper?
   Possible response: Without the information on the paper and the proposal it supports, Tom believes that he will not get a chance to rise to the top of his company because it will take too long to duplicate his work.

⓬ Reading Skill
Cause and Effect

1. Remind students that an event, an action, or a situation is a cause that creates an effect.
2. Direct students to read the bracketed passage silently. Then ask students whether they have ever recounted a scary or an exciting or even a funny story to their friends. Have volunteers describe their reasons for telling the story.
3. **Ask** the Reading Skill question: What effect does Tom hope the story of his adventure will have on listeners?
   Possible response: Tom hopes the story will make people at the office notice him and, at the same time, add importance to his grocery store display proposal.

Library on Fifth Avenue, where he'd spent a dozen lunch hours and early evenings adding more. All were needed to support and lend authority to his idea for a new grocery-store display method; without them his idea was a mere opinion. And there they all lay, in his own improvised shorthand—countless hours of work—out there on the ledge. ⓫

For many seconds he believed he was going to abandon the yellow sheet, that there was nothing else to do. The work could be duplicated. But it would take two months, and the time to present this idea . . . was *now*, for use in the spring displays. He struck his fist on the window ledge. Then he shrugged. Even if his plan were adopted, he told himself, it wouldn't bring him a raise in pay—not immediately, anyway, or as a direct result. It won't bring me a promotion either, he argued—not of itself.

Reading Skill
Cause and Effect What might cause Tom to go after the paper?

But just the same, and he couldn't escape the thought, this and other independent projects, some already done and others planned for the future, would gradually mark him out from the score of other young men in his company. They were the way to change from a name on the payroll to a name in the minds of the company officials. They were the beginning of the long, long climb to where he was determined to be, at the very top. And he knew he was going out there in the darkness, after the yellow sheet fifteen feet beyond his reach.

By a kind of instinct, he instantly began making his intention acceptable to himself by laughing at it. The mental picture of himself sidling along the ledge outside was absurd—it was actually comical—and he smiled. He imagined himself describing it; it would make a good story at the office and, it occurred to him, would add a special interest and importance to his memorandum, which would do it no harm at all. ⓬

Reading Skill
Cause and Effect What effect does Tom hope the story of his adventure will have on listeners?

To simply go out and get his paper was an easy task—he could be back here with it in less than two minutes—and he knew he wasn't deceiving himself. The ledge, he saw, measuring it with his eye, was about as wide as the length of his shoe, and perfectly flat. And every fifth row of brick in the face of the building, he remembered—leaning out, he verified this—was indented half an inch, enough for the tips of his fingers, enough to maintain balance easily. It occurred to him that if this ledge and wall were only a yard aboveground—as he knelt at the window staring out, this thought was the final confirmation of his intention—he could move along the ledge indefinitely.

Vocabulary
verified (ver′ ə fīd) *v.* proved to be true

⓭ On a sudden impulse, he got to his feet, walked to the front closet and took out an old tweed jacket; it would be cold outside. He put

Vocabulary Development

Word Forms
Some of the selection vocabulary words for "Contents of the Dead Man's Pocket" have related forms. Give students a blank **Word Form Chart** (***Professional Development Guidebook***, p. 42), with *convoluted*, *imperceptibly*, and *deftness* in the correct columns. Work with the class, or have students work with a partner, to determine the related forms. The final chart should look like the one shown.

Noun	Verb	Adjective	Adverb
convolution		**convoluted**	convolutedly
deftness		deft	deftly
imperceptibleness		imperceptible	**imperceptibly**

13 it on and buttoned it as he crossed the room rapidly toward the open window. In the back of his mind he knew he'd better hurry and get this over with before he thought too much, and at the window he didn't allow himself to hesitate.

He swung a leg over the sill, then felt for and found the ledge a yard below the window with his foot. Gripping the bottom of the window frame very tightly and carefully, he slowly ducked his head under it, feeling on his face the sudden change from the warm air of the room to the chill outside. With infinite care he brought out his other leg, his mind concentrating on what he was doing. Then he slowly stood erect. Most of the putty, dried out and brittle, had dropped off the bottom edging of the window frame, he found, and the flat wooden edging provided a good gripping surface, a half inch or more deep, for the tips of his fingers.

Now, balanced easily and firmly, he stood on the ledge outside in the slight, chill breeze, eleven stories above the street, staring into his own lighted apartment, odd and different-seeming now.

14 First his right hand, then his left, he carefully shifted his fingertip grip from the puttyless window edging to an indented row of bricks directly to his right. It was hard to take the first shuffling sideways step then—to make himself move—and the fear stirred in his stomach, but he did it, again by not allowing himself time to think. And now—with his chest, stomach, and the left side of his face pressed against the rough cold brick—his lighted apartment was suddenly gone, and it was much darker out here than he had thought.

17 Without pause he continued—right foot, left foot, right foot, left—his shoe soles shuffling and scraping along the rough stone, never lifting from it, fingers sliding along the exposed edging of brick. He moved on the balls of his feet, heels lifted slightly; the ledge was not quite as wide as he'd expected. But leaning slightly inward toward the face of the building and pressed against it, he could feel his balance firm and secure, and moving along the ledge was quite as easy as he had thought it would be. He could hear the buttons of his jacket scraping steadily along the rough bricks and feel them

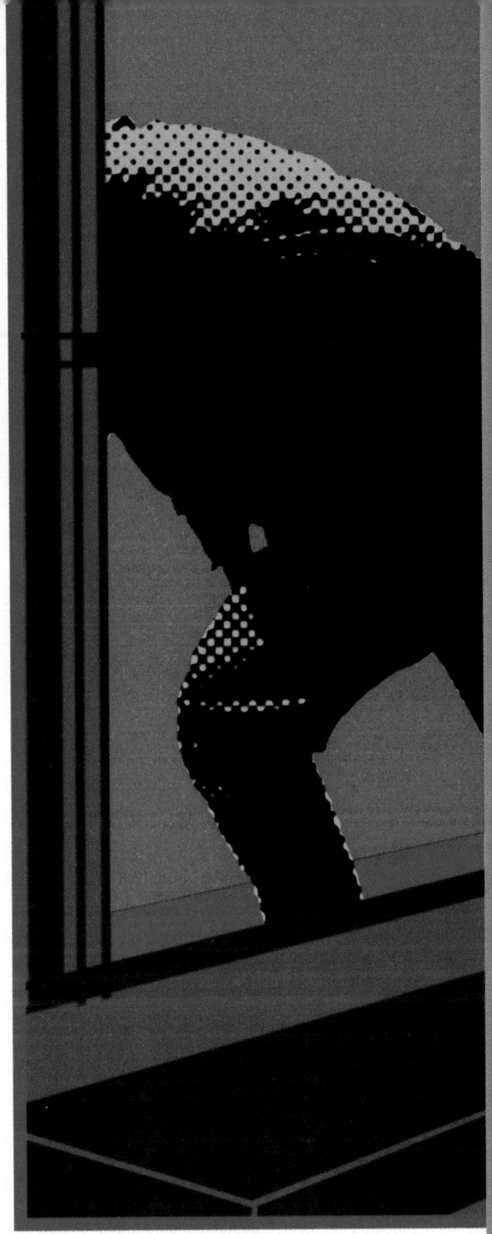

15 **Reading Check**

Describe Tom's progress on the first part of his journey.

13 Critical Thinking
Draw Conclusions

1. Have students reread the bracketed passage. **Ask** for a volunteer to define the word *impulse*.
   Answer: An *impulse* is a sudden or spontaneous action.
2. Next, point out that when Tom decides to go after the paper, Finney writes that "he knew he'd better hurry and get this over with before he thought too much."
3. Based on these details, **ask** students how Tom feels about going out on the ledge.
   Possible response: Though he seems to understand that it will be risky and dangerous, Tom seems to want to go about it quickly so that he cannot talk himself out of it.

14 Literary Analysis
Conflict

Monitor Progress: To determine whether or not students understand the types of conflicts, **ask**, What are the two kinds of conflict a character can face?
Answer: Characters can face external and internal conflicts.

Ask students to define these types of conflicts.
Answer: An external conflict is a struggle between the character and an outside force. An internal conflict is a struggle between the character and his or her opposing desires, beliefs, or needs.

Have a student read the bracketed passage aloud. Discuss the external and internal conflicts Tom faces.

Reteach: If students have difficulty understanding the internal conflict, direct them to the line that begins the passage, "It was hard to take the first shuffling step. . . ." After reading the sentence, point out that getting out on the ledge has created a feeling in Tom. Help students identify that the feeling is fear, and that it creates a conflict about whether to continue or go back. As a visual aid, show students the completed **Literary Analysis Graphic Organizer A** (*Graphic Organizer Transparencies*, p. 20).

15 Reading Check

Answer: Tom moves slowly and carefully as he shuffles along the ledge with his body pressed against the building, but he makes progress.

Differentiated Instruction for Universal Access

EL Strategy for English Learners

Students can benefit from Finney's descriptions of the senses involved in Tom's walk along the ledge. Have students make a list of words that describe what Tom feels, hears, and sees. To help students better follow Tom's adventure, play this portion of Finney's story on the ***Hear It!* Audio CD** as students read along in their books. Ask students to pay attention to descriptions that convey the senses.

Enrichment for Advanced Readers

First-person point of view allows readers to experience directly the world through a character's actions and feelings. Ask students to write paragraphs from Tom's point of view about his feelings as he walks along the ledge. Challenge them to include details that appeal to all five senses: touch, taste, smell, sight, and sound.

⑯ Critical Viewing

Possible response: The picture helps the reader understand Tom's fear because it shows how narrow the ledge is and how far down the street is below.

⑰ Critical Thinking

Speculate

1. Have a student read aloud the bracketed section, beginning on p. 123, while the class reads along.
2. **Ask** students if they have ever found themselves in a situation where they have been afraid of heights. Allow students to compare their reactions to these situations.
3. **Ask** students to speculate on what might happen if Tom permits himself to look down while he is on the ledge.
   Possible response: If Tom looks down and sees how high above the ground he actually is, then he might freeze and not be able to continue. Also, he might be so afraid that he will make a mistake and fall off the ledge.

⑯ ▲ **Critical Viewing** Explain how this picture helps you understand Tom's feelings in the story. **[Relate]**

⑰

catch momentarily, tugging a little, at each mortared crack. He simply did not permit himself to look down, though the compulsion to do so never left him; nor did he allow himself actually to think. Mechanically—right foot, left foot, over and again—he shuffled along crabwise, watching the projecting wall ahead loom steadily closer . . .

Then he reached it, and, at the corner—he'd decided how he was going to pick up the paper—he lifted his right foot and placed it carefully on the ledge that ran along the projecting wall at a right angle to the ledge on which his other foot rested. And now, facing the building, he stood in the corner formed by the two walls, one foot on the ledging of each, a hand on the shoulder-high indentation of each wall. His forehead was pressed directly into the corner against the cold bricks, and now he carefully lowered first one hand, then the other, perhaps a foot farther down, to the next indentation in the rows of bricks.

Very slowly, sliding his forehead down the trough of the brick corner and bending his knees, he lowered his body toward the paper lying between his outstretched feet. Again he lowered his fingerholds another foot and bent his knees still more, thigh muscles taut, his forehead sliding and bumping down the

Think Aloud

Vocabulary: Using Context

Using a think-aloud process, model how to use context to infer the meaning of *spasmodic*, located in the middle of p. 125.

In this sentence, *spasmodic* is used to describe the way Tom's body moves after he glimpses the street far below him. At the beginning of the sentence, I find a clue: "In the fractional moment before horror paralyzed him." Because it is the moment before he is paralyzed by horror, I understand that he is still able to move. Another clue is the noun that *spasmodic* modifies, the word *jerk*. A jerking motion is sudden, almost unconscious. Also, the description of what happens to Tom after this movement imply actions he has no control over and would not normally do. So, in its context, I think that *spasmodic* refers to the sudden, uncontrollable, irregular movement of Tom's body.

brick V. Half squatting now, he dropped his left hand to the next indentation and then slowly reached with his right hand toward the paper between his feet.

He couldn't quite touch it, and his knees now were pressed against the wall; he could bend them no farther. But by ducking his head another inch lower, the top of his head now pressed against the bricks, he lowered his right shoulder and his fingers had the paper by a corner, pulling it loose. At the same instant he saw, between his legs and far below, Lexington Avenue stretched out for miles ahead.

He saw, in that instant, the Loew's theater sign, blocks ahead past Fiftieth Street; the miles of traffic signals, all green now; the lights of cars and street lamps; countless neon signs; and the moving black dots of people. And a violent instantaneous explosion of absolute terror roared through him. For a motionless instant he saw himself externally—bent practically double, balanced on this narrow ledge, nearly half his body projecting out above the street far below—and he began to tremble violently, panic flaring through his mind and muscles, and he felt the blood rush from the surface of his skin.

18 In the fractional moment before horror paralyzed him, as he stared between his legs at that terrible length of street far beneath him, a fragment of his mind raised his body in a spasmodic jerk to an upright position again, but so violently that his head scraped hard against the wall, bouncing off it, and his body swayed outward to the knife edge of balance, and he very nearly plunged backward and fell. Then he was leaning far into the corner again, squeezing and pushing into it, not only his face but his chest and stomach, his back arching; and his fingertips clung with all the pressure of his pulling arms to the shoulder-high half-inch indentation in the bricks.

He was more than trembling now; his whole body was racked with a violent shuddering beyond control, his eyes squeezed so tightly shut it was painful, though he was past awareness of that. His teeth were exposed in a frozen grimace, the strength draining like water from his knees and calves. 19 It was extremely likely, he knew, that he would faint, to slump down along the wall, his face scraping, and then drop backward, a limp weight, out into nothing. And to save his life he concentrated on holding onto consciousness, drawing deliberate deep breaths of cold air into his lungs, fighting to keep his senses aware.

Then he knew that he would not faint, but he could neither stop shaking nor open his eyes. He stood where he was, breathing deeply, trying to hold back the terror of the glimpse he had had of

Reading Skill
Cause and Effect What is the effect of Tom's glimpse of the avenue below?

Literary Analysis
Conflict What internal conflict does Tom's external conflict cause?

20 **Reading Check**
What event introduces a new obstacle in Tom's journey?

18 Reading Skill
Cause and Effect

1. Read the bracketed passage aloud. **Ask:** What has Tom done that he has not done before?
   Answer: Tom sees the street below.
2. Now **ask** the Reading Skill question: What is the effect of Tom's glimpse of the avenue below?
   Answer: He begins to tremble, and he feels blood rush from his skin. He jerks upright. His head scrapes against the wall and bounces off it, and he almost falls off the ledge. Then he clings more strongly to the indentations in the wall.

19 Literary Analysis
Conflict

1. Remind students that an external conflict is a struggle between a character and an outside force.
2. Remind students that an internal conflict is a struggle that a character has with his or her desires, beliefs, or needs.
   Ask: What does Tom want?
   Answer: He wants to retrieve the yellow piece of paper.
3. Have students read the bracketed passage silently. Then **ask** the Literary Analysis question: What internal conflict does Tom's external conflict cause?
   Answer: Tom's external conflict of trying to hold on to the ledge and then nearly falling causes him to almost pass out with fear. He then fights an internal conflict when he tries to hold on to consciousness.

20 Reading Check

Answer: Tom glances down, and the sight paralyzes him with panic; he is unable to move.

Differentiated Instruction for Universal Access

Strategy for Less Proficient Readers
In order to create suspense, Finney includes numerous details of both the actual scene and the scene in Tom's imagination. Students may have a difficult time separating real events from those imagined in "Contents of the Dead Man's Pocket." Help students separate the real events from those occurring in Tom's mind. In their notebooks, have them label one column on a sheet of paper "Reality" and the other "Tom's Mind." Then, as they read, help them list each image in the proper column.

Enrichment for Advanced Readers
Finney's story is an excellent example of suspenseful writing. Help students appreciate his craft by asking them to list words and images that create the tense, white-knuckled atmosphere. Have students keep this list in their notebooks for future reference in their own writing.

㉑ Reading Skill
Cause and Effect

1. Explain to students that, sometimes, it is an event or a situation beyond the character's control that creates an effect on that character. Brainstorm for a few of those types of situations.
   Possible responses: Weather, actions of others, physical obstacles, or deadlines might create effects that are not within a character's control.
2. Then, explain that a character can, with his or her decisions, thoughts, or actions, create an effect. Have students refer to **Literary Analysis Graphic Organizer A** or **B** (*Graphic Organizer Transparencies*, pp. 20–22) and identify which forces they have listed that are beyond Tom's control and which he may be able to control.
3. Then refer back to the story and **ask:** What thoughts does Tom just have on the previous page that cause him to stop moving?
   Answer: Tom imagines falling off the ledge.
4. Have students read the bracketed passage. Then **ask** the Reading Skill question: What causes Tom to begin moving?
   Answer: Tom is afraid that the things he imagines will happen if he does not move, so he forces himself not to think about anything but moving along the ledge.

---

what lay below him; and he knew he had made a mistake in not making himself stare down at the street, getting used to it and accepting it, when he had first stepped out onto the ledge.

It was impossible to walk back. He simply could not do it. He couldn't bring himself to make the slightest movement. The strength was gone from his legs; his shivering hands—numb, cold and desperately rigid—had lost all **deftness**; his easy ability to move and balance was gone. Within a step or two, if he tried to move, he knew that he would stumble clumsily and fall.

Vocabulary
deftness (deft′ nis) *n.* skillfulness

Seconds passed, with the chill faint wind pressing the side of his face, and he could hear the toned-down volume of the street traffic far beneath him. Again and again it slowed and then stopped, almost to silence; then presently, even this high, he would hear the click of the traffic signals and the subdued roar of the cars starting up again. During a lull in the street sounds, he called out. Then he was shouting "*Help!*" so loudly it rasped his throat. But he felt the steady pressure of the wind, moving between his face and the blank wall, snatch up his cries as he uttered them, and he knew they must sound directionless and distant. And he remembered how habitually, here in New York, he himself heard and ignored shouts in the night. If anyone heard him, there was no sign of it, and presently Tom Benecke knew he had to try moving; there was nothing else he could do.

Eyes squeezed shut, he watched scenes in his mind like scraps of motion-picture film—he could not stop them. He saw himself stumbling suddenly sideways as he crept along the ledge and saw his upper body arc outward, arms flailing. He saw a dangling shoestring caught between the ledge and the sole of his other shoe, saw a foot start to move, to be stopped with a jerk, and felt his balance leaving him. He saw himself falling with a terrible speed as his body revolved in the air, knees clutched tight to his chest, eyes squeezed shut, moaning softly.

Reading Skill
Cause and Effect ㉑
What causes Tom to begin moving?

Out of utter necessity, knowing that any of these thoughts might be reality in the very next seconds, he was slowly able to shut his mind against every thought but what he now began to do. With fear-soaked slowness, he slid his left foot an inch or two toward his own impossibly distant window. Then he slid the fingers of his shivering left hand a corresponding distance. For a moment he could not bring himself to lift his right foot from one ledge to the other; then he did it, and became aware of the harsh exhalation of air from his throat and realized that he was panting. As his right hand, then, began to slide along the brick edging, he was astonished to feel the yellow paper pressed to the bricks underneath his stiff fingers, and he uttered a terrible, abrupt bark

---

Vocabulary Development

Vocabulary Reinforcement

To reinforce and assess students' comprehension of the selection vocabulary words, give them sentences using the words in which the word may or may not be used correctly. Students must tell whether the use is correct and explain their answers.

1. The snake was coiled quietly in the grass, with only its eyes moving back and forth *imperceptibly*.
   Answer: Yes, *imperceptibly* is used correctly because it means barely moving, and only the snake's eyes are moving.
2. Toby quickly ran straight from one end of the *convoluted* hall to the other.
   Answer: No, *convoluted* is not used correctly because the hall is straight, and *convoluted* means "twisted."

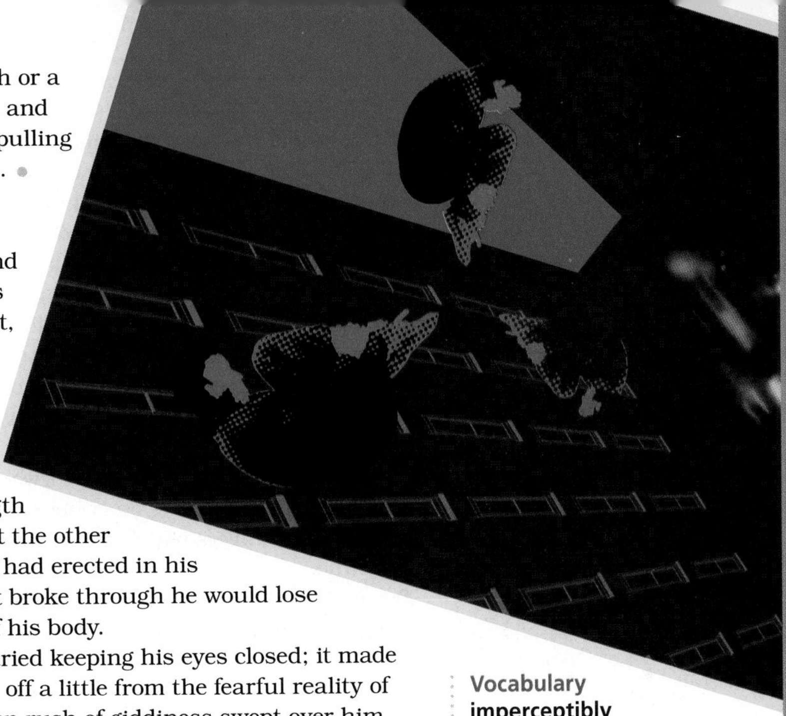

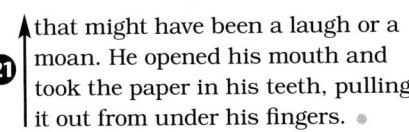

21 that might have been a laugh or a moan. He opened his mouth and took the paper in his teeth, pulling it out from under his fingers.

22 By a kind of trick—by concentrating his entire mind on first his left foot, then his left hand, then the other foot, then the other hand—he was able to move, almost imperceptibly, trembling steadily, very nearly without thought. But he could feel the terrible strength of the pent-up horror on just the other side of the flimsy barrier he had erected in his mind; and he knew that if it broke through he would lose this thin artificial control of his body.

During one slow step he tried keeping his eyes closed; it made him feel safer, shutting him off a little from the fearful reality of where he was. Then a sudden rush of giddiness swept over him and he had to open his eyes wide, staring sideways at the cold rough brick and angled lines of mortar, his cheek tight against the building. He kept his eyes open then, knowing that if he once let them flick outward, to stare for an instant at the lighted windows across the street, he would be past help.

He didn't know how many dozens of tiny sidling steps he had taken, his chest, belly, and face pressed to the wall; but he knew the slender hold he was keeping on his mind and body was going to break. He had a sudden mental picture of his apartment on just the other side of this wall—warm, cheerful, incredibly spacious. And he saw himself striding through it, lying down on the floor on his back, arms spread wide, reveling in its unbelievable security. The impossible remoteness of this utter safety, the contrast between it and where he now stood, was more than he could bear. And the barrier broke then, and the fear of the awful height he stood on coursed through his nerves and muscles.

A fraction of his mind knew he was going to fall, and he began taking rapid blind steps with no feeling of what he was doing, sidling with a clumsy desperate swiftness, fingers scrabbling along the brick, almost hopelessly resigned to the sudden backward pull and swift motion outward and down. Then his moving left hand slid

Vocabulary

imperceptibly (im´ pər sep´ tə blē) *adv.* so slowly or slightly as to be barely noticeable

reveling (rev´ əl iŋ) *v.* taking great pleasure or delight

23 **Reading Check**

Why does Tom stop calling for help?

22 Critical Thinking

Analyze

1. Have students analyze Tom's character in terms of his response to the pressure he feels.
   Possible response: Some students may realize that the pressure Tom is under causes him to feel paralyzed; they may take his loss of control as a normal response to a dangerous situation. Other students may think that a stronger character would be able to master his body's response to terror.
2. **Ask** students why Finney spends so much time describing Tom's thoughts and feelings, rather than focusing entirely on the action.
   Possible response: The events in Tom's mind become as threatening as his actual movements. This intensifies the suspense for the reader.

23 Reading Check

Answer: Tom stops calling for help because he realizes that, ordinarily, he ignores any shouts he hears in the night. He thinks other New Yorkers will do the same.

Differentiated Instruction for Universal Access

Strategy for Special Needs Students

Students may have difficulty understanding the difference between internal and external conflict in this section of the story. Have students draw two columns on sheets of paper, one labeled "Internal" and the other "External." Then, have them reread this page and the previous page, making note of every time Tom is described as thinking something; tell students that the word *mind* is a good indication of this. Difficulties Tom faces as he moves along the ledge happen outside of his mind, so those details are external.

Enrichment for Gifted/Talented Students

Ask students to consider whether this story could occur in a modern-day setting. Point out that modern digital devices make it unlikely that anyone would keep vital data on only one sheet of paper; cellphones make it unlikely that a person could be completely out of touch with help. Most modern, air-conditioned buildings do not have ledges or windows that open. Have students work in groups to propose changes in the story that would make Tom's predicament plausible in the present day.

㉔ Literary Analysis
Conflict

1. Have students read the bracketed passage. Next, **ask** students to list details in the passage that convey action.
   Possible response: Descriptions such as *smashed, began falling, dropped shudderingly*, and *body swaying* are some examples of details that convey action in this passage.
2. **Ask:** How long does the action in the bracketed passage last?
   Possible response: The action probably happens in only a few seconds.
3. Next **ask** the Literary Analysis question: Why does this lengthy description at a moment of excitement add to the suspense?
   Possible response: The description stretches the episode and increases the reader's curiosity and anxiety about what will happen.

㉕ Reading Skill
Cause and Effect

1. Explain to students that some situations described at one point in a story can have an effect on a character later in the story. Suggest that Tom's ambition to get ahead at work is just one situation that continues to have an effect on Tom's actions later in the story.
2. Have students read the bracketed passage silently. Then **ask** the Reading Skill question: What key detail from the beginning of the story helps you understand the cause of Tom's situation?
   Answer: The sticky window from the beginning of the story is now stuck and will not open without great effort.

onto not brick but sheer emptiness, an impossible gap in the face of the wall, and he stumbled.

His right foot smashed into his left anklebone; he staggered sideways, began falling, and the claw of his hand cracked against glass and wood, slid down it, and his fingertips were pressed hard on the puttyless edging of his window. His right hand smacked gropingly beside it as he fell to his knees; and, under the full weight and direct downward pull of his sagging body, the open window dropped shudderingly in its frame till it closed and his wrists struck the sill and were jarred off.

Literary Analysis ㉔
Conflict Why does this lengthy description at a moment of excitement add to the suspense?

For a single moment he knelt, knee bones against stone on the very edge of the ledge, body swaying and touching nowhere else, fighting for balance. Then he lost it, his shoulders plunging backward, and he flung his arms forward, his hands smashing against the window casing on either side; and—his body moving backward—his fingers clutched the narrow wood stripping of the upper pane.

For an instant he hung suspended between balance and falling, his fingertips pressed onto the quarter-inch wood strips. Then, with utmost delicacy, with a focused concentration of all his senses, he increased even further the strain on his fingertips hooked to these slim edgings of wood. Elbows slowly bending, he began to draw the full weight of his upper body forward, knowing that the instant his fingers slipped off these quarter-inch strips he'd plunge backward and be falling. Elbows imperceptibly bending, body shaking with the strain, the sweat starting from his forehead in great sudden drops, he pulled, his entire being and thought concentrated in his fingertips. Then suddenly, the strain slackened and ended, his chest touching the window sill, and he was kneeling on the ledge, his forehead pressed to the glass of the closed window.

Reading Skill ㉕
Cause and Effect
What key detail from the beginning of the story helps you understand the cause of Tom's situation?

Dropping his palms to the sill, he stared into his living room—at the red-brown davenport[2] across the room, and a magazine he had left there; at the pictures on the walls and the gray rug; the entrance to the hallway; and at his papers, typewriter and desk, not two feet from his nose. A movement from his desk caught his eye and he saw that it was a thin curl of blue smoke; his cigarette, the ash long, was still burning in the ash tray where he'd left it—this was past all belief—only a few minutes before.

His head moved, and in faint reflection from the glass before him he saw the yellow paper clenched in his front teeth. Lifting a hand from the sill he took it from his mouth; the moistened corner parted from the paper, and he spat it out.

2. **davenport** (dav´ ən pôrt´) *n.* large couch.

Vocabulary Development

Expressive Vocabulary
To help students broaden their expressive vocabulary, encourage them to use the following words as they discuss the selection: *consequences, maximize, compromise*, and *experimentally*. Have them complete these sentence starters:

1. A person must deal with the *consequences* when . . .
2. You can *maximize* your chances of success by . . .
3. Sometimes it is smart to *compromise* because . . .
4. When you act *experimentally*, you . . .

For a moment, in the light from the living room, he stared wonderingly at the yellow sheet in his hand and then crushed it into the side pocket of his jacket.

He couldn't open the window. It had been pulled not completely closed, but its lower edge was below the level of the outside sill; there was no room to get his fingers underneath it. Between the upper sash and the lower was a gap not wide enough—reaching up, he tried—to get his fingers into; he couldn't push it open. The upper window panel, he knew from long experience, was impossible to move, frozen tight with dried paint.

Very carefully observing his balance, the fingertips of his left hand again hooked to the narrow stripping of the window casing, he drew back his right hand, palm facing the glass, and then struck the glass with the heel of his hand.

His arm rebounded from the pane, his body tottering, and he knew he didn't dare strike a harder blow.

27 But in the security and relief of his new position, he simply smiled; with only a sheet of glass between him and the room just before him, it was not possible that there wasn't a way past it. Eyes narrowing, he thought for a few moments about what to do. Then his eyes widened, for nothing occurred to him. But still he felt calm: the trembling, he realized, had stopped. At the back of his mind there still lay the thought that once he was again in his home, he could give release to his feelings. He actually would lie on the floor, rolling, clenching tufts of the rug in his hands. He would literally run across the room, free to move as he liked, jumping on the floor, testing and reveling in its absolute security, letting the relief flood through him, draining the fear from his mind and body. His yearning for this was astonishingly intense, and somehow he understood that he had better keep this feeling at bay.

He took a half dollar from his pocket and struck it against the pane, but without any hope that the glass would break and with very little disappointment when it did not. After a few moments of thought he drew his leg up onto the ledge and picked loose the knot of his shoelace. He slipped off the shoe and, holding it across the instep, drew back his arm as far as he dared and struck the leather heel against the glass. The pane rattled, but he knew he'd been a long way from breaking it. His foot was cold and he slipped the shoe back on. He shouted again experimentally, and then once more, but there was no answer.

26 LITERATURE IN CONTEXT

Science Connection

Physics

Tom is on the ledge with only a pane of glass between him and safety. Yet he is reluctant to hit the window to break the glass—with good reason. Tom understands Newton's third law of motion: for every action, there is an equal and opposite reaction. For example, the *action* of throwing a ball against a wall has the opposite *reaction* of the ball bouncing away from the wall.

Connect to the Literature

What opposite reaction does Tom fear will result if he hits the glass hard but does not break it?

28 **Reading Check**

In what way has Tom's situation improved? In what way does it remain the same?

26 Literature in Context

Science Connection In his calculations, Tom uses the science of physics, which concerns itself with the fundamental elements of the universe, the forces they exert on each other, and the results produced by these forces.

The Greek mathematician Archimedes designed devices to deal with force and motion, such as the lever. It was not until 1687, however, that the English mathematician Sir Isaac Newton stated the principles of mechanics. The subsequent development of physics owes much to Newton's laws of motion.

Connect to the Literature After students discuss the Science Connection, **ask** the Connect to the Literature question: What opposite reaction does Tom fear will result if he hits the glass hard but does not break it?

Answer: If Tom hits the glass without enough force to break it, the opposite reaction of his hand bouncing off the glass will have enough force to throw him backward off the ledge.

27 Literary Analysis

Conflict

1. Read aloud the bracketed passage. **Ask:** What new internal conflict does Tom experience?
   Answer: Although Tom seems to have calmed his fears, he is now overcome with imagining how excited he will be when he gets into his apartment. He is afraid that this feeling might cause him to relax too much and that he will not be able to get inside.
2. Make note of Tom's change in attitude toward his situation. Alert students to look for other moments in the story when Tom's feelings about his situation shift and how that shift affects Tom.

28 Reading Check

Answer: Tom has retrieved the paper and has made his way back to the window, but he is still out on the ledge with the window stuck closed.

Differentiated Instruction for Universal Access

Enrichment for Gifted/Talented Students

Students may be interested in exploring in detail how the principles of physics affect Tom's attempts to break the window with the half dollar and the shoe on the previous page. Have them research how Sir Isaac Newton's laws of motion, notably the second and third, affect Tom's chances of success. Have them write their findings and make recommendations to Tom about the safest and most effective way to break the window.

Enrichment for Advanced Readers

After students review all of Tom's ideas and efforts to save himself, ask students to consider other options that Tom might have tried. Would it have been feasible for Tom to go along the ledge to a neighboring apartment window? Could he have climbed or descended to another floor? Could he have used the contents of his pockets in other ways to attract attention? Remind students that their alternatives must be compatible with the physical details given in the story. Encourage them to share their solutions to Tom's dilemma with classmates.

29 Literary Analysis
Conflict

1. Explain to students that in trying to resolve one conflict, another conflict might arise. Before a resolution can be made, then, all consequences must be considered.
2. Have students read the bracketed passage silently. **Ask** the Literary Analysis question: What new internal conflict does Tom experience?
   Possible response: Tom struggles over whether to wait for Clare (whose reaction might embarrass him) to come home and help him, or to find another way in.

30 Critical Thinking
Infer

1. Explain to students that clues or details in this passage can allow them to make educated guesses, or inferences, about the actions or reactions of Tom and other people.
2. Have students read the bracketed passage. **Ask:** What details in the first paragraph describe what people are doing in the apartments across the street?
   Answer: A man is reading the newspaper, someone is watching television, and another person is walking from one room to the next.
3. **Ask:** Why is it not surprising that these people do not notice Tom on the ledge?
   Possible response: They are going about their normal routines, which do not include checking for people on the ledge, and people in a city tend to mind their own business.
4. Have students reread the final paragraph on this page. **Ask:** Why does Tom think he sees a man look toward him?
   Answer: Tom is so desperate to catch someone's attention that he probably sees something that has not happened.

Literary Analysis
Conflict What new internal conflict does Tom experience?

29 The realization suddenly struck him that he might have to wait here till Clare came home, and for a moment the thought was funny. He could see Clare opening the front door, withdrawing her key from the lock, closing the door behind her, and then glancing up to see him crouched on the other side of the window. He could see her rush across the room, face astounded and frightened, and hear himself shouting instructions: "Never mind how I got here! Just open the wind—" She couldn't open it, he remembered, she'd never been able to; she'd always had to call him. She'd have to get the building superintendent or a neighbor, and he pictured himself smiling and answering their questions as he climbed in. "I just wanted to get a breath of fresh air, so—"

He couldn't possibly wait here till Clare came home. It was the second feature she'd wanted to see, and she'd left in time to see the first. She'd be another three hours or—He glanced at his watch; Clare had been gone eight minutes. It wasn't possible, but only eight minutes ago he had kissed his wife goodbye. She wasn't even at the theater yet!

It would be four hours before she could possibly be home, and he tried to picture himself kneeling out here, fingertips hooked to these narrow strippings, while first one movie, preceded by a slow listing of credits, began, developed, reached its climax and then finally ended. There'd be a newsreel next, maybe, and then an animated cartoon, and then **interminable** scenes from coming pictures. And then, once more, the beginning of a full-length picture—while all the time he hung out here in the night.

Vocabulary
interminable (in tʉr′ mi nə bəl) *adj.* endless or seemingly endless

He might possibly get to his feet, but he was afraid to try. Already his legs were cramped, his thigh muscles tired; his knees hurt, his feet felt numb and his hands were stiff. He couldn't possibly stay out here for four hours, or anywhere near it. Long before that his legs and arms would give out; he would be forced to try changing his position often—stiffly, clumsily, his coordination and strength gone—and he would fall. Quite realistically, he knew that he would fall; no one could stay out here on this ledge for four hours.

30 A dozen windows in the apartment building across the street were lighted. Looking over his shoulder, he could see the top of a man's head behind the newspaper he was reading; in another window he saw the blue-gray flicker of a television screen. No more than twenty-odd yards from his back were scores of people, and if just one of them would walk idly to his window and glance out. . . . For some moments he stared over his shoulder at the lighted rectangles, waiting. But no one appeared. The man reading

Think Aloud

Vocabulary: Using Context
Direct students' attention to the word *interminable* on page 130. Using a think-aloud process, model how to use context to infer the meaning of an unknown word. Say to students:

I'm going to think aloud to show you how to figure out the meaning of *interminable* from its context.

In this sentence, *interminable* is being used to describe scenes of coming attractions Tom's wife would be viewing at the theater. I already know that Tom is desperately anxious for his wife to return; he knows that 4 long hours must pass before she does. Tom is thinking through, in tedious detail, what will occur in the theater, including a "slow listing of credits" and another "full-length picture." Given this emphasis, I think *interminable* might refer to Tom's feeling that the scenes would be dragged out, long, or endless.

30 his paper turned a page and then continued his reading. A figure passed another of the windows and was immediately gone.

In the inside pocket of his jacket he found a little sheaf of papers, and he pulled one out and looked at it in the light from the living room. It was an old letter, an advertisement of some sort; his name and address, in purple ink, were on a label pasted to the envelope. Gripping one end of the envelope in his teeth, he twisted it into a tight curl. From his shirt pocket he brought out a book of matches. He didn't dare let go the casing with both hands, but, with the twist of paper in his teeth, he opened the matchbook with his free hand; then he bent one of the matches in two without tearing it from the folder, its red-tipped end now touching the striking surface. With his thumb, he rubbed the red tip across the striking area.

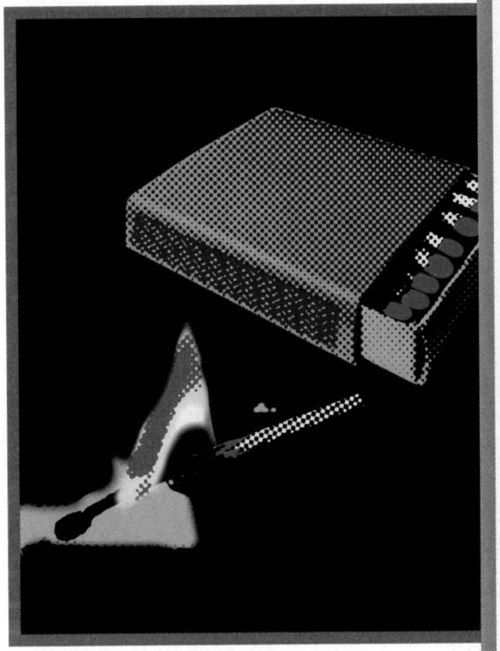

He did it again, then again, and still again, pressing harder each time, and the match suddenly flared, burning his thumb. But he kept it alight, cupping the matchbook in his hand and shielding it with his body. He held the flame to the paper in his mouth till it caught. Then he snuffed out the match flame with his thumb and forefinger, careless of the burn, and replaced the book in his pocket. Taking the paper twist in his hand, he held it flame down, watching the flame crawl up the paper, till it flared bright. Then he held it behind him over the street, moving it from side to side, watching it over his shoulder, the flame flickering and guttering in the wind.

31 There were three letters in his pocket and he lighted each of them, holding each till the flame touched his hand and then dropping it to the street below. At one point, watching over his shoulder while the last of the letters burned, he saw the man across the street put down his paper and stand—even seeming, to Tom, to glance toward his window. But when he moved, it was only to walk across the room and disappear from sight.

Reading Skill
Cause and Effect
What effect does Tom hope the burning papers and the falling coins will have?

There were a dozen coins in Tom Benecke's pocket and he dropped them, three or four at a time. But if they struck anyone, or if anyone noticed their falling, no one connected them with their source, and no one glanced upward.

His arms had begun to tremble from the steady strain of clinging to this narrow perch, and he did not know what to do now and was terribly frightened. Clinging to the window stripping with one hand, he again searched his pockets. But now—he had left his wallet

32 **Reading Check**
Why can't Tom wait for Clare to come home?

31 Reading Skill
Cause and Effect

1. Explain to students that sometimes people take actions that they hope will have certain effects.
2. Have students read the bracketed passage. Now **ask** the Reading Skill question: What effect does Tom hope the burning papers and the falling coins will have?
Answer: He hopes someone will see the burning papers or someone will be hit by a coin, look up from the street, and see him.

32 Reading Check

Possible response: Tom has been outside for only 8 minutes. Clare won't be back for another 4 hours. Tom thinks it's almost physically impossible to stay outside on the ledge, kneeling and cramped, for that long.

Differentiated Instruction for Universal Access

Strategy for Less Proficient Readers

Students may not understand exactly what chain of causes and effects Tom hopes for when he drops the coins and burning paper to the street. Discuss with students what will happen to a coin when dropped from a height to a sidewalk. Next, discuss with students what will happen when someone is hit by a falling coin. When students answer "the person will look up," repeat the chain of cause and effect to students so that they understand how one effect can become a cause for another effect.

EL Strategy for English Learners

In the scene in which Tom drops the burning letters to the street, Finney uses a variety of verbs relating to the fires, such as *flare, snuff,* and *flicker*. Explain how each one describes the action of the flame at different moments and in different conditions. Then, have students use dictionaries or thesauruses to add at least two related verbs to the list. Examples include *blaze, ignite,* and *kindle*.

㉝ Reading Skill

Cause and Effect

1. Point out the phrase, "Contents of the dead man's pockets." **Ask** what effect the phrase has on Tom now.
   Possible responses: He realizes that if he does die, his life will have been wasted because no one will know who he really is or what his plans for the future are.
2. Explain that an author purposely includes particular details in a story to support a character's state of mind.
3. Have students read the bracketed passage silently. Now **ask** the Reading Skill question: What key details explain why Tom grows angry?
   Answer: The facts that his wife has gone out alone, he spends time away from his wife during evenings working, and all the hours he spends on the yellow sheet that may be the cause of his death make Tom angry with himself.

Reading Skill
Cause and Effect
What key details explain why Tom grows angry?

on his dresser when he'd changed clothes—there was nothing left but the yellow sheet. It occurred to him irrelevantly that his death on the sidewalk below would be an eternal mystery; the window closed—why, how, and from where could he have fallen? No one would be able to identify his body for a time, either—the thought was somehow unbearable and increased his fear. All they'd find in his pockets would be the yellow sheet. *Contents of the dead man's pockets,* he thought, *one sheet of paper bearing penciled notations—incomprehensible.*

He understood fully that he might actually be going to die; his arms, maintaining his balance on the ledge, were trembling steadily now. And it occurred to him then with all the force of a revelation that, if he fell, all he was ever going to have out of life he would then, abruptly, have had. Nothing, then, could ever be changed; and nothing more—no least experience or pleasure—could ever be added to his life. ㉝ He wished, then, that he had not allowed his wife to go off by herself tonight—and on similar nights. He thought of all the evenings he had spent away from her, working; and he regretted them. He thought wonderingly of his fierce ambition and of the direction his life had taken; he thought of the hours he'd spent by himself, filling the yellow sheet that had brought him out here. *Contents of the dead man's pockets,* he thought with sudden fierce anger, *a wasted life.*

He was simply not going to cling here till he slipped and fell; he told himself that now. There was one last thing he could try; he had been aware of it for some moments, refusing to think about it, but now he faced it. Kneeling here on the ledge, the fingertips of one hand pressed to the narrow strip of wood, he could, he knew, draw his other hand back a yard perhaps, fist clenched tight, doing it very slowly till he sensed the outer limit of balance, then, as hard as he was able from the distance, he could drive his fist forward against the glass. If it broke, his fist smashing through, he was safe; he might cut himself badly, and probably would, but with his arm inside the room, he would be secure. But if the glass did not break, the rebound, flinging his arm back, would topple him off the ledge. He was certain of that.

He tested his plan. The fingers of his left hand clawlike on the little stripping, he drew back his other fist until his body began teetering backward. But he had no leverage now—he could feel that there would be no force to his swing—and he moved his fist slowly forward till he rocked forward on his knees again and could sense that his swing would carry its greatest force. Glancing down, however, measuring the distance from his fist to the glass, he saw that it was less than two feet.

Vocabulary Development

Vocabulary Knowledge Rating

When students have completed reading and discussing "Contents of the Dead Man's Pocket," have them take out their **Vocabulary Knowledge Rating Chart** for this selection. Read the words aloud once more and have students rate their knowledge of the words again in the After Reading column. Clarify any words that are still problematic. Have students write their own definition and example or sentence in the appropriate column. Then have students complete the Vocabulary Practice at the end of the selection. Encourage students to use the words in further discussion and written work about this selection. Remind them that they will be accountable for these words on the **Selection Test,** ***Unit 1 Resources,*** pp. 122–124 or 125–127.

It occurred to him that he could raise his arm over his head, to bring it down against the glass. But, experimenting in slow motion, he knew it would be an awkward . . . blow without the force of a driving punch, and not nearly enough to break the glass.

Literary Analysis
Conflict
How do Tom's imaginings of what might happen build suspense?

Facing the window, he had to drive a blow from the shoulder, he knew now, at a distance of less than two feet; and he did not know whether it would break through the heavy glass. It might; he could picture it happening, he could feel it in the nerves of his arm. And it might not; he could feel that too—feel his fist striking this glass
34 and being instantaneously flung back by the unbreaking pane, feel the fingers of his other hand breaking loose, nails scraping along the casing as he fell.

He waited, arm drawn back, fist balled, but in no hurry to strike; this pause, he knew, might be an extension of his life. And to live even a few seconds longer, he felt, even out here on this ledge in the night, was infinitely better than to die a moment earlier than he had to. His arm grew tired, and he brought it down and rested it.

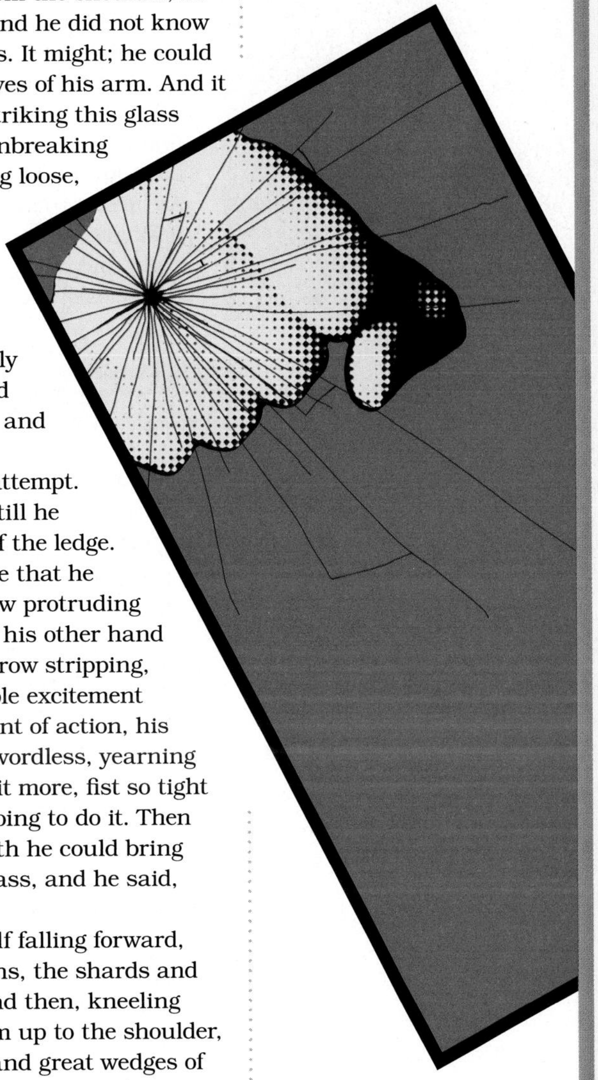

Then he knew that it was time to make the attempt. He could not kneel here hesitating indefinitely till he lost all courage to act, waiting till he slipped off the ledge. Again he drew back his arm, knowing this time that he would not bring it down till he struck. His elbow protruding over Lexington Avenue far below, the fingers of his other hand pressed down bloodlessly tight against the narrow stripping,
35 he waited, feeling the sick tenseness and terrible excitement building. It grew and swelled toward the moment of action, his nerves tautening. He thought of Clare—just a wordless, yearning thought—and then drew his arm back just a bit more, fist so tight his fingers pained him, and knowing he was going to do it. Then with full power, with every last scrap of strength he could bring to bear, he shot his arm forward toward the glass, and he said, "*Clare!*"

He heard the sound, felt the blow, felt himself falling forward, and his hand closed on the living-room curtains, the shards and fragments of glass showering onto the floor. And then, kneeling there on the ledge, an arm thrust into the room up to the shoulder, he began picking away the protruding slivers and great wedges of glass from the window frame, tossing them in onto the rug. And, as he grasped the edges of the empty window frame and climbed into his home, he was grinning in triumph.

34 Literary Analysis
Conflict

1. Have students read the bracketed passage. **Ask:** Why is this a crucial moment in the story?
   Answer: Tom will either break the window and enter his home or his fist will bounce off the window and he will fall.
2. **Ask** the Literary Analysis question: Why do Tom's imaginings of what might happen build suspense?
   Possible response: Tom's imaginings prolong the episode and suggest both good and bad possibilities, making the reader curious to find out what will happen.

35 Reading Skill
Cause and Effect

1. Have students read the bracketed passage. **Ask:** What is so important about this moment in the story?
   Answer: If Tom fails to break the window, he will most likely fall off the ledge.
2. Have students identify whom Tom is thinking about as he draws his arm back to hit the window pane.
   Answer: He is thinking about his wife, Clare.
3. **Ask** students to define the verb *to yearn*.
   Answer: *To yearn* means to "long for persistently," or to "feel tenderness or compassion for."
4. Now, **ask**: What effect does Tom hope for by calling out his wife's name while striking the window?
   Possible response: He hopes his desire to see her again will give him greater strength and allow him to break the glass.

Concept Connector

Anticipation Guide
Have students return to their **Anticipation Guides** and respond to the statement again in the After Reading column. They may do this individually or in their original pairs or groups. Then, lead a class discussion, probing for what students have learned that confirms or invalidates each statement. Encourage students to cite specific details, quotations, or other evidence from the text to support their responses to each statement.

Writing About the Big Question
Have students compare their responses to the sentence starter they completed before reading the story with their ideas afterward. Ask them to explain whether their thoughts have changed.

Literary Analysis Graphic Organizer
Ask students to review the graphic organizers they completed to define the forces of conflicts while reading. Show them the partially completed **Literary Analysis Graphic Organizer A** as an example. Then have students share the graphic organizers they did and the conflicts they described.

ASSESS

Answers

Critical Thinking

1. Students may approve of Tom's choice to break through the window. Students may criticize his choice to go out the window in the first place.
2. (a) Tom is working on a proposal for a new grocery-store display method. (b) He hopes it will advance his career. (c) **Possible response:** Tom is ambitious and cares deeply about his work.
3. (a) Tom goes out on the ledge to retrieve a sheet of statistics. (b) **Possible response:** No, Tom seems to be completely consumed with ambition.
4. (a) At the beginning, Tom is interested only in his work; at the end, he realizes that his relationship with his wife is more important. (b) His close encounter with death makes him realize what is important to him. (c) **Possible response:** He will probably spend more time enjoying life with his wife.
5. (a) Students may say a movie version would be difficult because so much "action" takes place in Tom's mind. (b) In discussion, students might note that there is only one main character and little dialogue.

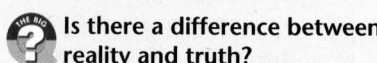

Is there a difference between reality and truth?

(a) **Possible response:** At first, Tom feels safe and secure in his environment and place in life. Then, when he is out on the ledge, he realizes how dangerous reality can be and how insignificant and small he is in the world.

(b) **Possible response:** Tom discovers that work, making money, and getting recognition are all superficial priorities. He realizes that his own life and, more important, sharing his life with his wife, are his real priorities.

He did not lie down on the floor or run through the apartment, as he had promised himself; even in the first few moments it seemed to him natural and normal that he should be where he was. He simply turned to his desk, pulled the crumpled yellow sheet from his pocket and laid it down where it had been, smoothing it out; then he absently laid a pencil across it to weight it down. He shook his head wonderingly, and turned to walk toward the closet.

There he got out his topcoat and hat and, without waiting to put them on, opened the front door and stepped out, to go find his wife. He turned to pull the door closed and the warm air from the hall rushed through the narrow opening again. As he saw the yellow paper, the pencil flying, scooped off the desk and, unimpeded by the glassless window, sail out into the night and out of his life, Tom Benecke burst into laughter and then closed the door behind him.

Critical Thinking

1. **Respond:** Which of Tom's choices did you think were good? Which did you think were foolish? Explain.
2. **(a)** What document is Tom working on at the start of the story? **(b) Analyze Cause and Effect:** What long-term goals does he hope to achieve by this work? **(c) Draw Conclusions:** What does his plan tell you about his character?
3. **(a)** Why does Tom go out on the ledge? **(b) Connect:** Is his decision surprising? Explain using details from the story.
4. **(a) Compare and Contrast:** Contrast Tom's attitude toward life at the beginning of the story with his attitude at the end. **(b) Infer:** What causes his attitude to change? **(c) Speculate:** What changes, if any, will Tom make as a result of this experience?
5. **(a) Evaluate:** Do you think that a movie based on Finney's story would be as effective as the story itself? Why or why not? **(b) Discuss:** Share and discuss responses with a partner. Then, discuss whether your partner's response has changed or expanded your own thinking.

Is there a difference between reality and truth? **(a)** How do Tom's perceptions of reality change during the course of the story? **(b)** What truth about priorities in life does he discover through his experience?

Assessment Resources

Unit 1 Resources

L1 L2 EL **Selection Test A,** pp. 146–148. Administer Test A to less advanced students and English learners.

L3 L4 **Selection Test B,** pp. 149–151. Administer Test B to on-level and more advanced students.

L3 L4 **Open-Book Test,** pp. 143–145. As an alternative, give the Open-Book Test.

All **Customizable Test Bank**

All **Self-tests**

Students may prepare for the **Selection Test** by taking the **Self-test** online.

PHLit Online! All assessment resources are available at **www.PHLitOnline.com.**

After You Read — Contents of the Dead Man's Pocket

Literary Analysis: Conflict

1. **(a)** What is the main **external conflict** in this story? Explain. **(b)** What is the main **internal conflict** in the story? Explain.
2. **(a)** Identify a moment in the story that has great **suspense.** **(b)** Which conflict helps to create this suspense? Explain.
3. **(a)** How are Tom's conflicts resolved? **(b)** Describe an alternative **resolution** the story might have had.

Reading Skill: Cause and Effect

4. **(a)** In your opinion, which single **cause** sets the story's cause-and-effect chain in motion? **(b)** Identify two **effects**—one short-term and one long-term—of this event. Use a diagram like this one to record your answer.

Cause	→	Cause/Effect	→	Effect

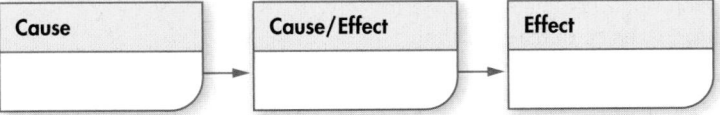

5. **(a)** Identify a key detail early in the story that becomes important later on. **(b)** Analyze the causes and effects linked to this detail.

Vocabulary

Practice Answer each question. Explain your responses.

1. Should directions for dealing with an emergency be <u>convoluted</u>?
2. Can you trust information that has been <u>verified</u>?
3. Would you want a surgeon to display <u>deftness</u>?
4. If the temperature fell <u>imperceptibly</u>, would most people notice?
5. Is someone who is <u>reveling</u> expressing joy?
6. Would you be happy if your school day was <u>interminable</u>?

Word Study Use the context of the sentences and what you know about the **Latin root *-ver-*** to explain your answer to each question.

1. Does a judge expect *veracity* from those testifying in court?
2. Would you feel proud if your personal narrative was a *veritable* masterpiece?

Word Study

The **Latin root *-ver-*** means "true."

Challenge Explain how the root *-ver-* contributes to the meanings of these words. Consult a dictionary if necessary.

verification
aver
verdict

ASSESS/EXTEND

Answers

Literary Analysis

1. (a) The main external conflict is Tom's struggle to get back into his apartment. (b) The main internal conflict is between Tom's ambition and his love for his wife.
2. (a) **Possible response:** A moment of great suspense is when Tom strikes the window with his fist. (b) The conflict is literally a matter of life (breaking the glass) and death (bouncing off the ledge).
3. (a) Tom's external conflict is resolved when he breaks the window. His internal conflict is resolved when he lets the yellow sheet float back out the window. (b) **Possible response:** The yellow sheet stays in the room, Tom gets a promotion, but his wife gets tired of being alone and leaves him.

Reading Skill

4. **Possible response:** (a) Students may say that Tom's decision to stay home and work sets the chain in motion. (b) Short-term: The paper flies out the window as he shuts the door behind his wife. Long-term: Tom realizes that his life is more important than his work.

   For other sample answers, see ***Graphic Organizer Transparencies,* Reading Skill Graphic Organizer** A, p. 23, and the **Additional Answers** section.
5. (a) Key detail: Clare goes to the movies. (b) Effect: She will not return in time to help Tom.

Vocabulary

Practice

Sample answers:

1. No, emergency directions should be clear and direct.
2. Yes, <u>verified</u> information has been checked for accuracy and correctness, so it is true.
3. Yes, a surgeon should display skillfulness.
4. No, most people would not notice such a small drop in temperature.
5. Yes, someone who is filled with delight and happiness would also be feeling joy.
6. No, if my school day were <u>interminable</u>, it would never end.

Word Study

Sample answers:

1. Yes, the root *-ver-* means "true," so *veracity* means "truth." It is a law for people who testify in court to tell the truth, so a judge would expect <u>veracity</u>.
2. Yes, the root *-ver-* means "true," so *veritable* means "being truly." I would be proud if my personal narrative were truly a masterpiece.

Word Study: Challenge

Sample answers: *Verification* is the act of checking whether something is <u>true</u> or not. *Aver* is to state firmly as the <u>truth</u>. A *verdict* is a lawful decision based on <u>truths</u> known.

PRETEACH

Teaching notes introducing the ***Reading Skill*** *and the* ***Literary Analysis*** *concept for this selection appear on p. 115.*

❶ Writing About the Big Question

1. Review the assignment with the class.
2. Remind students that every situation or experience can change the way we perceive our reality and the truths about ourselves.
3. Have students complete the sentence starter. Revise answers as a class. (**Possible response:** Playing a game can change a person's perception of his or her abilities because he or she might not do as well as previously thought.)
4. Remind students that their answers will help them think about the Big Question, "Is there a difference between reality and truth?"

While You Read

Tell students that as they read, they should look for moments in which Ravi experiences changes in his perception of reality or truth.

❷ Vocabulary

1. Have students preview the selection vocabulary.
2. For each word, have students say the word aloud.
3. Then, use the word in a sentence that defines the word.
4. Finally, repeat your definitional sentence or a similar sentence with the word missing, and have the class "fill in the blank" chorally. Here is an example:

   Something livid is discolored, usually a combination of blue, red, and purple. As the athlete's broken ankle swelled, the bruised skin around it turning sickeningly [students say "livid"].

❸ Word Study

1. Introduce the skill, using the instruction in the box.
2. Ask students to give the meaning of *convene* in this sentence: *Once all members of the court have* convened, *the case will be presented.* (**Answer:** *Convene* means "to come together.")

Making Connections | Games at Twilight

Is there a difference between *reality* and *truth?*

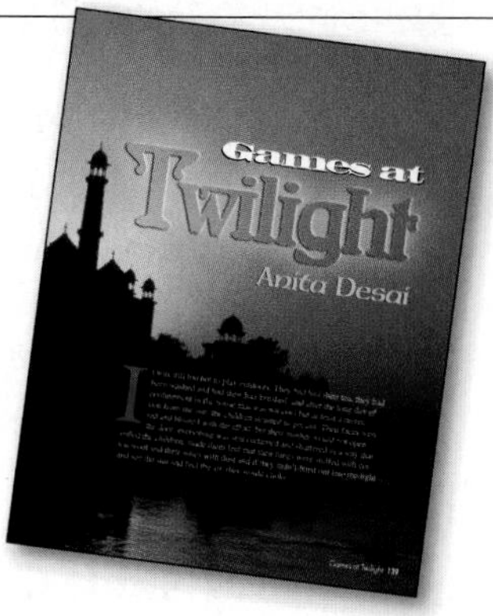

❶ Writing About the Big Question

In "Games at Twilight," a boy tries to gain the respect of the older children by winning a game of hide-and-seek. Though it is just a game, it gives him a glimpse of a harsh reality. Use this sentence starter to develop your ideas about the Big Question.

Playing a game can change a person's **perception** of **reality** because _______________.

While You Read Look for moments when the main character experiences changes in his understanding of reality or truth.

❷ Vocabulary

Read each word and its definition. Decide whether you know the word well, know it a little bit, or do not know it at all. After you read, see how your knowledge of each word has increased.

- **livid** (liv´ id) *adj.* discolored, as by a bruise; red with anger (p. 140) ***She became livid when she saw the bully bothering the first grade students.*** *lividly adv. lividness n.*
- **intervened** (in´ tər vēnd´) *v.* came between (p. 140) ***The moderator intervened because the two lawyers could not come to an agreement.*** *intervention n. interval n.*
- **dejectedly** (dē jek´ tid lē) *adv.* in a depressed way (p. 142) ***After losing the game, the players walked away dejectedly.*** *dejection n. dejected adj.*
- **defunct** (dē fuŋkt´) *adj.* no longer in use or existence (p. 142) ***The defunct computer now gathers cobwebs.*** *function v.*
- **dogged** (dôg´ id) *adj.* stubborn (p. 146) ***It took a day of dogged efforts to solve the puzzle.*** *doggedness n. doggedly adv.*
- **elude** (ē lo͞od´) *v.* escape or avoid (p. 146) ***The toddler tried to elude us by hiding under a blanket.*** *elusion n. elusive adj.*

❸ Word Study

The **Latin root *-ven-*** means "come" or "go."

In this story, an adult **intervened**, or came between, arguing children.

Vocabulary Development

Vocabulary Knowledge Rating

Create a **Vocabulary Knowledge Rating Chart** (***Professional Development Guidebook***, p. 33) for this selection. Include the selection vocabulary and the Big Question words that appear in the Writing About the Big Question sentence starter on this page. (The Big Question vocabulary is introduced on pp. 2–3.)

Give students a copy of the chart. Read the words aloud, and have students mark their rating in the Before Reading column. Urge them to be alert to these words as they read and discuss the selection.

Tally how many students think they know a word to gauge how much instruction to provide. As students read and discuss the selection, point out the words and their context.

PHLit Online! **Vocabulary Central,** featuring student tools, activities, and songs for studying vocabulary, is available at **www.PHLitOnline.com.**

Meet
Anita Desai
(b. 1937)

Anita Desai was born in India to a German mother and an Indian father. As a child, she learned German, Hindi, and English. Today, Desai writes in English and is widely regarded as one of India's foremost novelists.

Family and Familiarity Desai's stories are often about the relationships among family members—in the words of one critic, "the tug and pull of Indian family life." Desai has been praised for her ability to create vivid portraits of her characters and for her powerful images.

DID YOU KNOW?
Anita Desai published her first story at the age of nine.

Author of *Games at Twilight*

❹ BACKGROUND FOR THE STORY

India's Hot Season

"Games at Twilight" is set in India during the 1940s—a time and a place in which air conditioning is unknown. From the story's first sentence, you can almost feel the heat of India's hot season rising off the page. The hot season is one of three main south Asian seasons. Falling between the wet season and the cool season, the hot season lasts from early March to mid-June.

Daily Bellringer
For each class during which you will teach this selection, have students complete one of the five Revision activities for Week 4 in the ***Daily Bellringer Activities*** booklet.

❹ Background
India's Hot Season

In Calcutta, the largest city in India, the hot season begins in April when the mean temperature is 86 degrees F and the humidity averages 70 percent. The mean temperature rises to 88 degrees F in May and stays in the 80s until November. Humidity averages around 80 percent through September.

Multidraft Reading
This icon ● marks natural pauses in the selection. To assist struggling readers and to deepen reading for all, assign the text in "chunks," following the icons, and apply multidraft reading protocols. For each reading, have students set the purpose indicated:

- **First reading**—literal comprehension: answering the Reading Check questions.
- **Second reading**—application of skills: answering the Cause-and-Effect prompt and the Conflict prompt.
- **Third reading**—interpretation: answering the end-of-selection questions.

For further guidance, use the ***Classroom Strategies and Teaching Routines*** card on multidraft reading.

Differentiated Instruction
Additional Instruction

EL Extended Support—English Learners
Have students complete the **Reading and Vocabulary Warm-ups, *Unit 1 Resources*,** pp. 152–155 before they read. Assign the prereading pages for the selection in the ***Reader's Notebook: English Learner's Version***. Then, have students listen to portions of the selection on the ***Hear It!* Audio CD.**

L1 L2 Extended Support—Struggling Readers
Have students complete the **Reading and Vocabulary Warm-ups, *Unit 1 Resources*,** pp. 152–155, before they read. Assign the prereading pages for the selection in the ***Reader's Notebook: Adapted Version***. Then, have students listen to portions of the selection on the ***Hear It!* Audio CD** (adapted text).

Extended Support for—Reluctant Readers
To build motivation and engagement before assigning the selection, have students read "Winners and Losers," a thematically related selection in ***Reality Central***. Then, use the questions at the conclusion of the related selection to guide discussion.

PHLit Online!
For more about the author, practice with the selection vocabulary, and more background, go online at **www.PHLitOnline.com**.

TEACH

❶ Activating Prior Knowledge

1. Prepare an **Anticipation Guide** (see ***Professional Development Guidebook,*** pp. 36–38) with the following statements:
   - We should always play games to win.
   - How other people think about us is important in how we feel about ourselves.
   - People should respect their elders.
   - At some point, you have to let go of some of your dreams.
2. Give students a copy of the prepared **Anticipation Guide** and have students mark their responses in the Me column. Have students discuss the statements in pairs or groups and mark the guides again in the Group column.
3. For further guidance, use the ***Classroom Strategies and Teaching Routines*** card: **Using an Anticipation Guides.**

Concept Connector →

Students will return to the **Anticipation Guide** after completing the story.

Individual Activity

Have students notice the vivid imagery in the story's exposition. Ask them to create visual representations, such as drawings or paintings, of the way the children feel on this intensely hot afternoon. Their representations should include details from the text.

❷ About the Selection

In "Games at Twilight," Ravi plays a game of hide-and-seek with his siblings and cousins. To prove that he can win, Ravi decides to hide in a dark and forbidding shed. He stays there all afternoon. Finally, when it starts to get dark, Ravi emerges from the shed to claim his victory, only to find that the game had ended long ago and no one noticed his absence.

Vocabulary Development

Thematic Vocabulary: The Big Question

As students are discussing "Games at Twilight," encourage them to use the thematic vocabulary presented in Introducing the Big Question, pp. 2–3. You might encourage them with sentence starters like these:

1. "Games at Twilight" shows the *uncertainty* that younger children feel when . . .
2. Ravi thinks it is *improbable* that he will . . .
3. Ravi does not achieve his *objective* because . . .
4. The other children do not *comprehend* that Ravi . . .

1
2

Games at Twilight

Anita Desai

3 It was still too hot to play outdoors. They had had their tea, they had been washed and had their hair brushed, and after the long day of confinement in the house that was not cool but at least a protection from the sun, the children strained to get out. Their faces were red and bloated with the effort, but their mother would not open the door, everything was still curtained and shuttered in a way that stifled the children, made them feel that their lungs were stuffed with cotton wool and their noses with dust and if they didn't burst out into the light and see the sun and feel the air, they would choke.

3 Critical Thinking

Connect

1. Have students read the bracketed passage. Emphasize the sensory details Desai uses to describe the heat of the day.
2. **Ask:** Based on the clues given in this paragraph, at what time of day does the story begin?
Possible response: The story starts later on in the day, because the children have already completed their mundane activities, such as bathing and brushing their hair. Also, Desai characterizes the children's mood as frenzied with impatience ". . . after the long day of confinement in the house. . . ."
3. Direct student's attention to the title of the story. **Ask:** How can you connect the title's significance to the information provided in the first paragraph?
Possible response: Since it is too hot for the children to play outside during the day, the children will be able to play during twilight, when the scorching day cools into a chilly night.

Differentiated Instruction for Universal Access

Strategy for Special Needs Students

Students may benefit from a quick "selection tour" before reading. Focus students' attention on the title first, and discuss the time of day it describes. Next, have students look through the selection at the pictures. To prompt discussion, **ask** students what they can guess about the story from the pictures. **Possible response:** Students may say that it looks like children are playing and that maybe there is an old building where they are playing.

EL Strategy for English Learners

Students may have difficulty understanding idioms and figurative language. Explain figurative expressions such as "the children strained to get out," and "bloated with the effort." Then, have the students rewrite them in their own words. Encourage them to identify and define figurative expressions as they continue to read.

PHLit Online!

This selection is available in interactive format in the **Enriched Online Student Edition**, **www.PHLitOnline.com**, which includes a thematically related video and writing prompt and an interactive graphic organizer.

❹ Literary Analysis
Conflict

1. Remind students that conflict in a story is a struggle between characters and one or more forces. Those forces can be external, such as nature or another character, or internal, such as contradictory beliefs or needs.
2. **Ask** the Literary Analysis question: What two external forces do the children struggle against? **Answer:** The children struggle against the stifling heat inside the house and the mother who will not let them go outside to play.

❺ Reading Skill
Cause and Effect

1. Have students reread the first paragraph in the story. Emphasize the fact that the mother decides it is too hot to play outside.
2. Now have students read the bracketed passage. Have a student look up the word *horrendously* in a dictionary and share the meaning with the class. **Answer:** It means "dreadfully" or "horridly."
3. **Ask** what effect the children's wailing has on the mother. **Answer:** She lets them out of the house and then she cools off with a bath.
4. Reinforce the concept of cause and effect by pointing out that the children's complaints, the tight quarters of the house, and the heat are all reasons why the mother decides to let them play outside.

Literary Analysis ❹
Conflict What two external forces create conflict for the children?

"Please, Ma, please," they begged. "We'll play in the veranda and porch—we won't go a step out of the porch."

"You will, I know you will, and then—"

"No—we won't, we won't," they wailed so horrendously that she actually let down the bolt of the front door so that they burst out like seeds from a crackling, over-ripe pod into the veranda, with such wild, maniacal yells that she retreated to her bath and the shower of talcum powder and the fresh sari[1] that were to help her face the summer evening. ❺

Vocabulary
livid (liv′ id) *adj.* discolored, as by a bruise; red with anger

They faced the afternoon. It was too hot. Too bright. The white walls of the veranda glared stridently in the sun. The bougainvillea hung about it, purple and magenta, in livid balloons. The garden outside was like a tray made of beaten brass, flattened out on the red gravel and the stony soil in all shades of metal—aluminum, tin, copper and brass. No life stirred at this arid time of day—the birds still drooped, like dead fruit, in the papery tents of the trees; some squirrels lay limp on the wet earth under the garden tap. The outdoor dog lay stretched as if dead on the veranda mat, his paws and ears and tail all reaching out like dying travelers in search of water. He rolled his eyes at the children—two white marbles rolling in the purple sockets, begging for sympathy—and attempted to lift his tail in a wag but could not. It only twitched and lay still.

Then, perhaps roused by the shrieks of the children, a band of parrots suddenly fell out of the eucalyptus tree, tumbled frantically in the still, sizzling air, then sorted themselves out into battle formation and streaked away across the white sky.

The children, too, felt released. They too began tumbling, shoving, pushing against each other, frantic to start. Start what? Start their business. The business of the children's day which is—play.

"Let's play hide-and-seek."

"Who'll be It?"

"You be It."

"Why should I? You be—"

"You're the eldest—"

"That doesn't mean—"

Vocabulary
intervened (in′ tər vēnd′) *v.* came between

The shoves became harder. Some kicked out. The motherly Mira intervened. She pulled the boys roughly apart. There was a tearing sound of cloth but it was lost in the heavy panting and angry grumbling and no one paid attention to the small sleeve hanging loosely off a shoulder.

❻ "Make a circle, make a circle!" she shouted, firmly pulling and pushing till a kind of vague circle was formed. "Now clap!" she

1. **sari** (sä′ rē) *n.* a long piece of cloth wrapped around the body, forming a skirt and draped over one shoulder; the main garment of Indian women.

Vocabulary Development

Word Forms

Expand students' vocabulary by helping them learn related forms of selection vocabulary words. Give students a blank **Word Form Chart** (***Professional Development Guidebook,*** p. 42) with *livid* and *dogged* in their appropriate columns. Work with the class, or have students work with partners, to determine the related forms. The final chart should look like the one shown.

Noun	Verb	Adjective	Adverb
doggedness		**dogged**	doggedly
lividity or lividness		**livid**	lividly

6 roared and, clapping, they all chanted in melancholy unison: "Dip, dip, dip—my blue ship—" and every now and then one or the other saw he was safe by the way his hands fell at the crucial moment—palm on palm, or back of hand on palm—and dropped out of the circle with a yell and a jump of relief and jubilation.

Raghu was It. He started to protest, to cry "You cheated—Mira cheated—Anu cheated—" but it was too late, the others had all already streaked away. There was no one to hear when he called out, "Only in the veranda—the porch—Ma said—Ma said to stay in the porch!" No one had stopped to listen, all he saw were their brown legs flashing through the dusty shrubs, scrambling up brick walls, leaping over compost heaps and hedges, and then the porch stood empty in the purple shade of the bougainvillea and the garden was as empty as before; even the limp squirrels had whisked away, leaving everything gleaming, brassy and bare.

Only small Manu suddenly reappeared, as if he had dropped out of an invisible cloud or from a bird's claws, and stood for a moment in the center of the yellow lawn, chewing his finger and near to tears as he heard Raghu shouting, with his head pressed against the veranda wall, "Eighty-three, eighty-five, eighty-nine, ninety . . ." and then made off in a panic, half of him wanting to fly north, the other half counseling south. Raghu turned just in time to see the flash of his white shorts and the uncertain skittering of his red sandals, and charged after him with such a bloodcurdling yell that Manu

Reading Skill
Cause and Effect What key details suggest that the children use this rhyming game to choose who will be "it"?

7 **Reading Check**
What game do the children decide to play?

6 Reading Skill
Cause and Effect

1. Remind students that actions taken at one point in a story can create an effect, or result, later in the story. **Ask:** What do the children want to do at the beginning of the story? How do they get what they want?
   Answer: They want to get out of the house, so they complain and beg.
2. Note that the author uses details, in the form of direct quotations from several of the children, to illustrate the children's complaining and begging.
3. After students read the bracketed passage, **ask** the Reading Skill question: What key details suggest that the children use this rhyming game to choose who will be "it"?
   Answer: At certain moments when a child's hands fall the right way, that child drops out of the circle and is very happy, indicating that he or she does not want to be "it."

7 Reading Check

Answer: The children decide to play hide-and-seek.

Differentiated Instruction for Universal Access

EL Pronunciation for English Learners

Some students might have difficulty pronouncing words with the initial untrilled English "r," as in *Raghu*, *red*, and *rubber*, replacing it with a uvular "hr" sound. The following strategies can help students to pronounce the "r" sound.

- Write the words *Raghu*, *red*, and *rubber* on the board. Pronounce each word in turn, having students repeat each. Then, call out the words at random, having student volunteers circle the called word on the board. Discuss the results with the class.
- Pair English learners with fluent speakers. Have partners take turns reading from the last paragraph on p. 141, containing the words *Raghu*, *red*, and *rubber*. Ask fluent speakers to assist English learners by pronouncing carefully each problem word, guiding the English learners to the correct sound.

8 Literary Analysis
Conflict

Have students read the bracketed passage silently. Then remind them that some conflicts exist between the needs or desires within a single character, such as Ravi. Then have them recall the definition of *suspense*: a rising curiosity or anxiety in readers.

9 Literary Analysis
Conflict

1. Remind students that characters can face both internal and external conflicts during the course of a story. Emphasize that both types of conflict can be difficult to resolve for a character.
2. Have students read the bracketed passage. Then **ask:** What characteristic prevents Ravi from entering the garage? What type of conflict is this?
   Answer: Ravi is too short to reach the key. This conflict is an external conflict between Ravi's lack of height and the height of the key.
3. Turn students' attention to the shed. **Ask:** What internal conflict does Ravi experience in relation to the shed?
   Answer: The shed is dark and scary, and Ravi fights his fear.
4. Emphasize to students that sometimes internal and external conflicts act in opposition to one another. Occasionally, a character's desire for something is so strong that one conflict is ignored for the time being.
5. **Ask:** How do Ravi's external and internal conflicts compete here? Make a prediction about which conflict will win.
   Possible response: Ravi's external conflicts are not having a hiding place and not being able to get into the locked garage because he is too short to reach the key. The internal conflict of being afraid of the dark shed competes with his external conflicts because he needs somewhere to hide as soon as possible. Students may say that they think that his desire to find a hiding place is much stronger than his internal conflict relating to his fear of the dark shed.

stumbled over the hosepipe, fell into its rubber coils and lay there weeping, "I won't be It—you have to find them all—all—All!"

"I know I have to, idiot," Raghu said, superciliously[2] kicking him with his toe. "You're dead," he said with satisfaction, licking the beads of perspiration off his upper lip, and then stalked off in search of worthier prey, whistling spiritedly so that the hiders should hear and tremble. •

Ravi heard the whistling and picked his nose in a panic, trying to find comfort by burrowing the finger deep—deep into that soft tunnel. He felt himself too exposed, sitting on an upturned flower pot behind the garage. Where could he burrow? He could run around the garage if he heard Raghu come—around and around and around—but he hadn't much faith in his short legs when 8 matched against Raghu's long, hefty, hairy footballer legs. Ravi had a frightening glimpse of them as Raghu combed the hedge of crotons and hibiscus, trampling delicate ferns underfoot as he did so. Ravi looked about him desperately, swallowing a small ball of snot in his fear.

The garage was locked with a great heavy lock to which the driver had the key in his room, hanging from a nail on the wall under his work-shirt. Ravi had peeped in and seen him still sprawling on his string-cot in his vest and striped underpants, the hair on his chest and the hair in his nose shaking with the vibrations of his phlegm-obstructed snores. Ravi had wished he were tall enough, big enough to reach the key on the nail, but it was impossible, beyond his reach for years to come. He had sidled away and sat **dejectedly** on the flower pot. That at least was cut to his own size.

But next to the garage was another shed with a big green door. 9 Also locked. No one even knew who had the key to the lock. That shed wasn't opened more than once a year when Ma turned out all the old broken bits of furniture and rolls of matting and leaking buckets, and the white ant hills were broken and swept away and Flit sprayed into the spider webs and rat holes so that the whole operation was like the looting of a poor, ruined and conquered city. The green leaves of the door sagged. They were nearly off their rusty hinges. The hinges were large and made a small gap between the door and the walls—only just large enough for rats, dogs, and, possibly, Ravi to slip through.

Ravi had never cared to enter such a dark and depressing mortuary of **defunct** household goods seething with such

Vocabulary
dejectedly (dē jek′ tid lē) *adv.* in a depressed way

defunct (dē fuŋkt′) *adj.* no longer in use or existence

2. **superciliously** (sōō′ pər sil′ ē əs lē) *adv.* haughtily; in a manner expressing pride in oneself and scorn for the other person.

Vocabulary Development

Word Analysis

Draw students' attention to the word *superciliously* at the top of this page and its definition, "acting as though one is above, or better than, others." Explain that the Latin prefix *super-* means "above" or "extra." Have students name and define other words that contain this root, such as *superhuman*, "having powers above those of humans"; *superfluous*, "above what is necessary;" *superstar*, "a performer above all others"; or *supersonic*, "faster than the speed of sound."

Provide students with the following tips for determining the meaning of an unfamiliar word:

- Substitute the meaning of the prefix for the prefix itself.
- Then think of possible definitions for the entire word. Make sure the definition makes sense in the context.
- Check the definition in a dictionary.

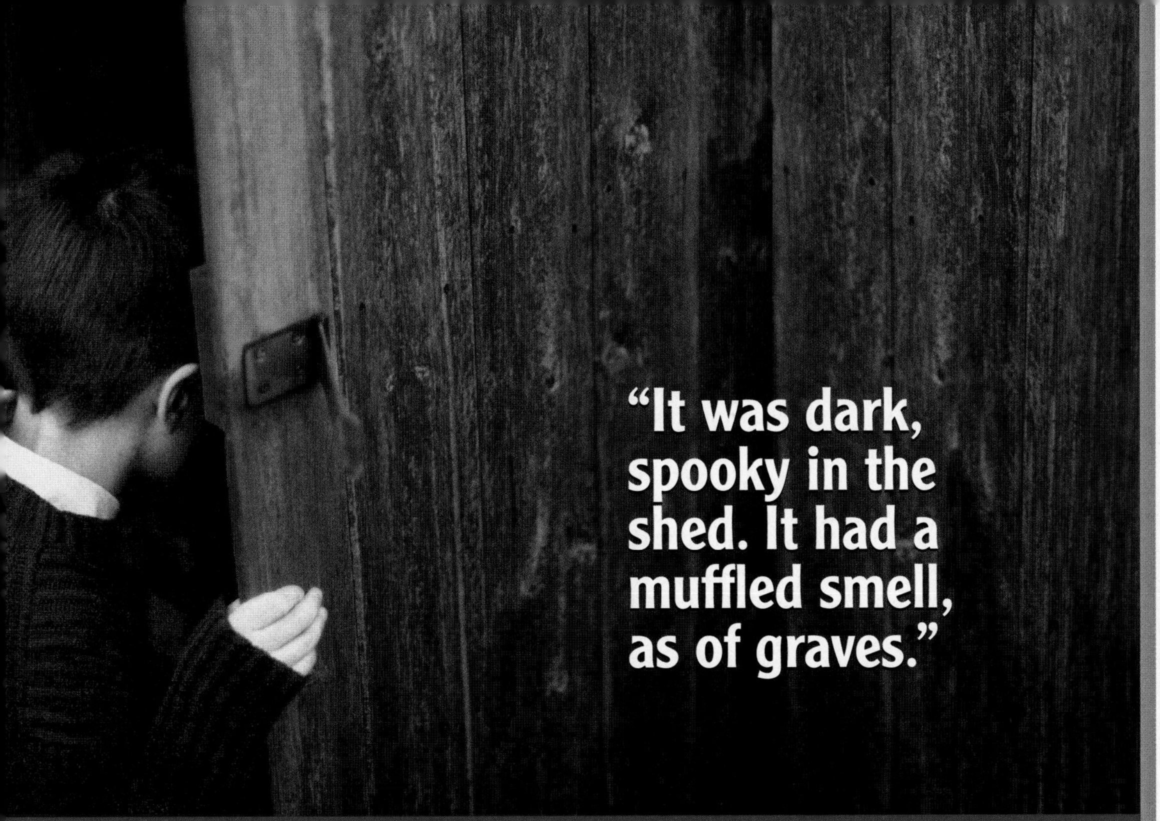

"It was dark, spooky in the shed. It had a muffled smell, as of graves."

unspeakable and alarming animal life but, as Raghu's whistling grew angrier and sharper and his crashing and storming in the hedge wilder, Ravi suddenly slipped off the flower pot and through the crack and was gone. He chuckled aloud with astonishment at his own temerity[3] so that Raghu came out of the hedge, stood silent with his hands on his hips, listening, and finally shouted "I heard you! I'm coming! Got you—" and came charging round the garage only to find the upturned flower pot, the yellow dust, the crawling of white ants in a mud-hill against the closed shed door—nothing. Snarling, he bent to pick up a stick and went off, whacking it against the garage and shed walls as if to beat out his prey.

12 Ravi shook, then shivered with delight, with self-congratulation. Also with fear. It was dark, spooky in the shed. It had a muffled smell, as of graves. Ravi had once got locked into the linen cupboard and sat there weeping for half an hour before he was rescued. But at least that had been a familiar place, and even

3. **temerity** (tə mer´ ə tē) *n.* recklessness; foolish boldness.

10 ▲ **Critical Viewing**
What might Ravi find in a shed like the one shown in the photograph? **[Speculate]**

11 **Reading Check**
Where does Ravi decide to hide?

10 Critical Viewing

Possible response: Ravi may find old, unused tools in the shed, or the shed may be empty because it is old and deteriorated. Wildlife and insects may inhabit the shed.

11 Reading Check

Answer: He decides to hide in an old shed next to the garage.

Differentiated Instruction for Universal Access

Strategy for Less Proficient Readers

Have students make a chart with one column labeled "Now" and another labeled "Past." Then, have them reread the bracketed passage for the Literary Analysis question on p. 142, looking for time clues, such as *wasn't opened more than once a year when*, to understand that Ma having the shed cleaned is Past. Emphasize to students to remember that Ravi is in the yard, looking for somewhere to hide. This belongs in the "Now" column. Students can use this chart as they continue to read to keep track of shifts in time in the selection.

Enrichment for Advanced Readers

Desai's story is filled with rich sensory details that make the setting and the action more vivid. Ask students to identify the sensory details in the story, explain to which sense each detail appeals, and describe how these details contribute to the story. They might make sensory details charts that have columns for sight, sound, smell, touch, and taste.

⓬ Reading Skill
Cause and Effect

After reading aloud the bracketed passage, have students make lists of the details in the passage that suggest that Ravi should not stay in the old shed.

Possible responses: The shed is dark, and Ravi is afraid of the dark. The shed smells of rats and insects. Ravi imagines that snakes live in the shed.

▶**Monitor Progress:** To assess whether students understand cause-and-effect relationships, have them fill out **Reading Skill Graphic Organizer B** (*Graphic Organizer Transparencies,* p. 25). Have students fill out the chart with causes and effects found in the bracketed passage.

▶**Reteach:** For those students who have difficulty identifying cause and effect, direct them to the completed **Reading Skill Graphic Organizer A** (*Graphic Organizer Transparencies,* p. 24). Explain to students that a character's actions often result in another action of some sort, and that these actions and reactions relate to causes and effects. Have them reread the bracketed passage, paying close attention to how Ravi acts in the shed. Make sure that students understand that Ravi's behavior is an effect and that the cause is his own imagination telling him that there are bugs and snakes in the shed.

⓭ Literary Analysis
Conflict

1. Have students read the passage silently. Then **ask** students how Ravi's state of mind is changing as the game progresses.
   Possible responses: Ravi is beginning to feel uncomfortable. He is starting to imagine life outside the shed, and he is getting lonely.
2. Then **ask** the Literary Analysis question: What internal conflict does Ravi now experience?
   Answer: Ravi struggles with his desire to stay in the shed and win the game and his need to return to the outdoors, his family, and his friends.

smelled pleasantly of starch, laundry and, reassuringly, of his mother. But the shed smelled of rats, ant hills, dust and spider webs. Also of less definable, less recognizable horrors. And it was dark. Except for the white-hot cracks along the door, there was no light. The roof was very low. Although Ravi was small, he felt as if he could reach up and touch it with his finger tips. But he ⓬ didn't stretch. He hunched himself into a ball so as not to bump into anything, touch or feel anything. What might there not be to touch him and feel him as he stood there, trying to see in the dark? Something cold, or slimy—like a snake. Snakes! He leapt up as Raghu whacked the wall with his stick—then quickly realizing what it was, felt almost relieved to hear Raghu, hear his stick. It made him feel protected.

But Raghu soon moved away. There wasn't a sound once his footsteps had gone around the garage and disappeared. Ravi stood frozen inside the shed. Then he shivered all over. Something had tickled the back of his neck. It took him a while to pick up the courage to lift his hand and explore. It was an insect—perhaps a spider—exploring him. He squashed it and wondered how many more creatures were watching him, waiting to reach out and touch him, the stranger.

There was nothing now. After standing in that position—his hand still on his neck, feeling the wet splodge of the squashed spider gradually dry—for minutes, hours, his legs began to tremble with the effort, the inaction. By now he could see enough in the dark to make out the large solid shapes of old wardrobes, broken buckets and bedsteads piled on top of each other around him. He recognized an old bathtub—patches of enamel glimmered at him and at last he lowered himself onto its edge.

Literary Analysis
Conflict What internal conflict does Ravi now experience?

He contemplated slipping out of the shed and into the fray. He wondered if it would not be better to be captured by Raghu and be returned to the milling crowd as long as he could be in the sun, the light, the free spaces of the garden and the familiarity of his brothers, sisters and cousins. It would be evening soon. Their games would become legitimate. The parents would sit out on the lawn on cane basket chairs and watch them as they tore around ⓭ the garden or gathered in knots to share a loot of mulberries or black, teeth-splitting jamun from the garden trees. The gardener would fix the hosepipe to the water tap and water would fall lavishly through the air to the ground, soaking the dry yellow grass and the red gravel and arousing the sweet, the intoxicating scent of water on dry earth—that loveliest scent in the world. Ravi sniffed for a whiff of it. He half-rose from the bathtub, then heard the despairing scream of one of the girls as Raghu bore down upon her. There

Think Aloud

Cause and Effect

Draw students' attention to this sentence on page 145: "Ravi sat back on the harsh edge of the tub, deciding to hold out a bit longer." Use the following "think aloud" to model analyzing cause and effect:

> I realize this sentence describes an action—Ravi sits back down—but more specifically, it describes an effect: Because of some cause, Ravi decides to stay in the shed longer. I know that when people make decisions, they make them based on information they already have. Some cause, then, made Ravi decide to stay in the shed.
>
> If I look back in the text, I know that Ravi wishes to be outside, enjoying the sun and air. Ravi wants to enjoy the evening as the other children are, so he rises, ready to leave, but then he hears Raghu capture one of the girls. Upon hearing Raghu, the cause, Ravi does not want to be caught anytime soon, like the girl was, so he sits back down and decides to wait.

13 was the sound of a crash, and of rolling about in the bushes, the shrubs, then screams and accusing sobs of, "I touched the den—" "You did not—" "I did—" "You liar, you did not" and then a fading away and silence again.

Ravi sat back on the harsh edge of the tub, deciding to hold out a bit longer. What fun if they were all found and caught—he alone left unconquered! He had never known that sensation. Nothing more wonderful had ever happened to him than being taken out by an uncle and bought a whole slab of chocolate all to himself, or being flung into the soda-man's pony cart and driven up to the gate by the friendly driver with the red beard and pointed ears. To defeat Raghu—that hirsute,[4] hoarse-voiced football champion—and to be the winner in a circle of older, bigger, luckier children—that would be thrilling beyond imagination. He hugged his knees together and smiled to himself almost shyly at the thought of so much victory, such laurels.[5]

14 ▲ **Critical Viewing**
Contrast the time of day in this image with the time of day at the beginning of the story. **[Contrast]**

15 **Reading Check**
What does Ravi hope happens?

4. **hirsute** (hʉr´ so͞ot´) *adj.* hairy.
5. **laurels** (lôr´ əlz) *n.* leaves of the laurel tree; worn in a crown as an ancient symbol of victory in a contest.

14 Critical Viewing

Answer: The image shows dusk or sunset. The story begins in the late afternoon, when the sun is still high in the sky and it is very hot.

15 Reading Check

Answer: Ravi looks forward to defeating the bigger, older Raghu and receiving the congratulations of his family and friends.

Differentiated Instruction for Universal Access

Strategy for Special Needs Students

Students may have difficulty visualizing Ravi's surroundings. Help students visualize the shed in which Ravi hides by first having them go back and look at any pictures of a shed in the selection. Next, have students draw a picture of the inside of the shed where Ravi is hiding. To make sure that students include details from the text, have them label their drawings with items, such as the bathtub and the insect on Ravi's back. Point out to students that other senses, such as smell, are also used to describe the shed.

Enrichment for Gifted/Talented Students

Reading about Ravi's internal and external conflicts may remind some students of similar situations they faced during their own childhoods. Have students write journal entries about challenging childhood experiences. Have them answer the following questions: What was the challenge? Did you meet it successfully and why? What did you learn from it? Ask for volunteers to share journal entries with the class.

⓰ Literary Analysis
Conflict

1. Help students recall that Ravi must engage in conflicts that are the result of external forces, such as the hot weather or Raghu as "it" in the game, and internal forces, such as his desire to impress the older children and his fears inside the shed.
2. After students read the bracketed passage, **ask** the Literary Analysis question: What new internal conflict does Ravi face?
Answer: Ravi realizes that his desire to find the best hiding place causes him to forget to run to the goal and win the game.

⓱ Connecting to the Big Question

1. Remind students that, like us, a character can perceive the world in a unique way, and the perceptions of people and characters can change.
2. Have students think about how Ravi feels about himself when he hides in the shed. **Ask:** How does Ravi feel when he enters the shed? **Answer:** Ravi feels confident and smug that he has escaped Raghu.
3. Have students read the bracketed passage. **Ask:** How does Ravi feel when he reaches the Den? Why?
Possible response: Ravi feels ashamed and angry that he waited so long to leave the shed. He realizes that, because he waited so long, his victory is not as impressive or even important anymore.

⓲ Critical Viewing

Possible response: The children in this image look happy and friendly. They are dancing and holding hands. In contrast, Ravi is alone and is upset.

Vocabulary
dogged (dôg′ id) *adj.* stubborn

elude (ē lo͞od′) *v.* escape or avoid

There he sat smiling, knocking his heels against the bathtub, now and then getting up and going to the door to put his ear to the broad crack and listening for sounds of the game, the pursuer and the pursued, and then returning to his seat with the dogged determination of the true winner, a breaker of records, a champion.

It grew darker in the shed as the light at the door grew softer, fuzzier, turned to a kind of crumbling yellow pollen that turned to yellow fur, blue fur, gray fur. Evening. Twilight. The sound of water gushing, falling. The scent of earth receiving water, slaking its thirst in great gulps and releasing that green scent of freshness, coolness. Through the crack Ravi saw the long purple shadows of the shed and the garage lying still across the yard. Beyond that, the white walls of the house. The bougainvillea had lost its lividity, hung in dark bundles that quaked and twittered and seethed with masses of homing sparrows. The lawn was shut off from his view. Could he hear the children's voices? It seemed to him that he could. It seemed to him that he could hear them chanting, singing, laughing. But what about the game? What had happened? Could it be over? How could it when he was still not found?

Literary Analysis
Conflict What new internal conflict does Ravi face? ⓰

It then occurred to him that he could have slipped out long ago, dashed across the yard to the veranda and touched the "den." It was necessary to do that to win. He had forgotten. He had only remembered the part of hiding and trying to elude the seeker. He had done that so successfully, his success had occupied him so wholly that he had quite forgotten that success had to be clinched by that final dash to victory and the ringing cry of "Den!"

⓲ ▼ **Critical Viewing** Contrast the feelings the children express in this image with Ravi's feelings. **[Contrast]**

⓱ With a whimper he burst through the crack, fell on his knees, got up and stumbled on stiff, benumbed legs across the shadowy yard, crying heartily by the time he reached the veranda so that when he flung himself at the white pillar and bawled, "Den! Den! Den!" his voice broke with rage and pity at the disgrace of it all and he felt himself flooded with tears and misery.

Vocabulary Development

Vocabulary Knowledge Rating

When student have completed reading and discussing "Games at Twilight," have them take out their **Vocabulary Knowledge Rating Chart** for this selection. Read the words aloud once more, and have students rate their knowledge of the words again in the After Reading column. Clarify any words that are still problematic. Have students write their own definition and example or sentence in the appropriate column. Then have students complete the Vocabulary Practice at the end of the selection. Encourage students to use the words in further discussion and written work about this selection. Remind them that they will be accountable for these words on the **Selection Test**, ***Unit 1 Resources***, pp. 167–169 or 170–172.

19 Out on the lawn, the children stopped chanting. They all turned to stare at him in amazement. Their faces were pale and triangular in the dusk. The trees and bushes around them stood inky and sepulchral,[6] spilling long shadows across them. They stared, wondering at his reappearance, his passion, his wild animal howling. Their mother rose from her basket chair and came toward him, worried, annoyed, saying, "Stop it, stop it, Ravi. Don't be a baby. Have you hurt yourself?" Seeing him attended to, the children went back to clasping their hands and chanting "The grass is green, the rose is red. . . . "

But Ravi would not let them. He tore himself out of his mother's grasp and pounded across the lawn into their midst, charging at them with his head lowered so that they scattered in surprise. "I won, I won, I won," he bawled, shaking his head so that the big tears flew. "Raghu didn't find me. I won, I won—"

20 It took them a minute to grasp what he was saying, even who he was. They had quite forgotten him. Raghu had found all the others long ago. There had been a fight about who was to be It next. It had been so fierce that their mother had emerged from her bath and made them change to another game. Then they had played another and another. Broken mulberries from the tree and eaten them. Helped the driver wash the car when their father returned from work. Helped the gardener water the beds till he roared at them and swore he would complain to their parents. The parents had come out, taken up their positions on the cane chairs. They had begun to play again, sing and chant. All this time no one had remembered Ravi. Having disappeared from the scene, he had disappeared from their minds. Clean. 21

"Don't be a fool," Raghu said roughly, pushing him aside, and even Mira said, "Stop howling, Ravi. If you want to play, you can

6. **sepulchral** (sə pul′ krəl) *adj.* of the tomb; gloomy.

Reading Skill
Cause and Effect
What effect had Ravi hoped for in hiding so well? What effect has it actually caused?

21 **Reading Check**
What rule of the game does Ravi forget?

19 Critical Thinking
Infer

1. Have students read the bracketed passage and describe what the other children do first when Ravi appears.
   Answer: They stop their game to stare at him.
2. Then **ask**: What is the mother's first response to Ravi's sudden appearance?
   Answer: She tells him to be quiet.
3. Using these responses as support, **ask** students to describe the opinion that the other children and the mother have of Ravi.
   Possible response: Students may say that because the other children are surprised to see Ravi but quickly turn back to their game, they have a low opinion of him. Because the mother first scolds Ravi for making so much noise, she thinks Ravi's efforts to win the game are worthless.

20 Reading Skill
Cause and Effect

1. Remind students that actions, situations, or events that occur near the beginning of a story often create effects later on in the story. Have them recall how anxious Ravi is at the start of the hide-and-seek game.
2. After students read the bracketed passage, **ask** the Reading Skill question: What effect had Ravi hoped for in hiding so well? What effect has it actually caused?
   Possible response: Ravi hoped he would win the game by finding the best hiding place. In reality, when Raghu does not find Ravi, Raghu and the other children forget about him. In the end, not being found results in Ravi's feeling insignificant.

21 Reading Check

Answer: Ravi forgets that he cannot win unless he touches the veranda and yells "Den" before he gets caught.

Concept Connector

Anticipation Guide
Have students return to their **Anticipation Guides** and respond to the statement again in the After Reading column. They may do this individually or in their original pairs or groups. Then, lead a class discussion, probing for what students have learned that confirms or invalidates each statement. Encourage students to cite specific details, quotations, or other evidence from the text to support their responses to each statement.

Writing About the Big Question
Have students compare their responses to the sentence starters they completed before reading the story with their ideas afterward. Ask them to explain whether their thoughts have changed.

Literary Analysis Graphic Organizer
Ask students to review the graphic organizers they completed to define the forces of conflicts while reading. Show them the partially completed **Literary Analysis Graphic Organizer A** as an example. Then have students share the graphic organizers they did and the conflicts they described.

ASSESS

Answers

Critical Thinking

1. Some students will say that they would have stayed in the shed; others would have left the shed immediately.
2. (a) Ravi thinks it will be thrilling. (b) **Possible response:** Ravi's feelings show that he thinks the other children are superior to him in many ways.
3. (a) The other children are too busy enjoying themselves at other games to be concerned with Ravi. (b) They think Ravi is foolish and immature. Raghu and Mira scold him for causing a scene.
4. (a) Ravi learns that he can easily be forgotten. (b) **Possible response:** Ravi might continue to feel insignificant if the older children continue to treat him that way.

Is there a difference between reality and truth?

(a) **Possible response:** Ravi discovers his ideas about reality are not true when he bursts in upon the children playing, yelling "I won, I won," only to find that the children all but ignore him. Raghu and Mira further trivialize Ravi's claims of winning by pushing him aside and making him stand at the end of the line of the game they are now playing. This discovery crushes Ravi. (b) **Possible response:** Ravi discovers that among this group of children, his presence or participation is not valued.

stand at the end of the line," and she put him there very firmly.

The game proceeded. Two pairs of arms reached up and met in an arc. The children trooped under it again and again in a lugubrious[7] circle, ducking their heads and intoning

"The grass is green,
The rose is red;
Remember me
When I am dead, dead, dead, dead . . ."

And the arc of thin arms trembled in the twilight, and the heads were bowed so sadly, and their feet tramped to that melancholy refrain so mournfully, so helplessly, that Ravi could not bear it. He would not follow them, he would not be included in this funereal game. He had wanted victory and triumph—not a funeral. But he had been forgotten, left out and he would not join them now. The ignominy[8] of being forgotten—how could he face it? He felt his heart go heavy and ache inside him unbearably. He lay down full length on the damp grass, crushing his face into it, no longer crying, silenced by a terrible sense of his insignificance.

He would not follow them, he would not be included in this funereal game.

7. **lugubrious** (lə gōō′ brē əs) *adj.* very sad, especially in an exaggerated or ridiculous way.
8. **ignominy** (ig′ nə min′ ē) *n.* shame and dishonor.

Critical Thinking

1. **Respond:** Put yourself in Ravi's place. What would you have done after Raghu left the shed area? Explain your answer.
2. **(a)** What does Ravi think it would feel like to be "the winner in a circle of older, bigger, luckier children"?
   (b) Draw Conclusions: What do his feelings show about his view of the other children?
3. **(a) Infer:** Why do the other children stop searching for Ravi?
   (b) Draw Conclusions: What do the other children think of Ravi? Give details from the story to support your answer.
4. **(a) Interpret:** What bitter lesson does Ravi learn at the end of the story? **(b) Apply:** Do you think that Ravi's sense of his "insignificance" will remain strong? Explain.

Is there a difference between reality and truth?
(a) When does Ravi discover that his ideas about reality are not true? How does this discovery affect him?
(b) What truth about life does Ravi discover?

Assessment Resources

Unit 1 Resources

L1 L2 EL **Selection Test A,** pp. 167–169. Administer Test A to less advanced readers and English learners.

L3 L4 **Selection Test B,** pp. 170–172. Administer Test B to on-level and more advanced students.

L3 L4 **Open-Book Test,** pp. 164–166. As an alternative, give the Open-Book Test.

All **Customizable Test Bank**

All **Self-tests**
Students may prepare for the **Selection Test** by taking the **Self-test** online.

PHLit Online! All assessment resources are available at **www.PHLitOnline.com.**

After You Read — Games at Twilight

Literary Analysis: Conflict and Resolution

1. **(a)** What is the main **external conflict** in this story? Explain. **(b)** What is the main **internal conflict** in the story? Explain.
2. **(a)** Identify a moment in the story that has great **suspense. (b)** Which conflict helps to create this suspense? Why?
3. **(a)** Are Ravi's conflicts settled by the end of the story? Explain. **(b)** Describe an alternative **resolution** the story might have.

Reading Skill: Cause and Effect

4. **(a)** In your opinion, which **cause** sets the story's cause-and-effect chain in motion? **(b)** Identify two **effects** that depend on this event. Use a diagram like this one to record your answer.

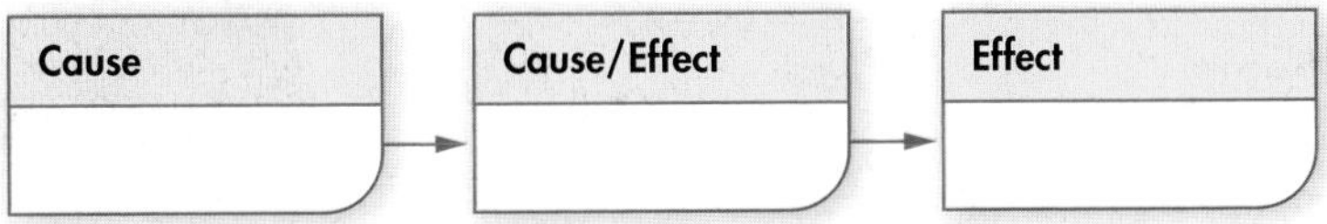

5. **(a)** Identify a key detail about the shed that is linked to later events. **(b)** Explain the causes and effects to which this detail is linked.

Vocabulary

Practice Answer each question. Explain your responses.

1. To inspire calm, would you paint a room in <u>livid</u> colors?
2. If a neutral person <u>intervened</u> in an argument, could it help the two sides resolve their differences?
3. Would an athlete sigh <u>dejectedly</u> after a game if she had won?
4. How many calls can you make on a <u>defunct</u> cell phone?
5. Is a lazy person likely to make a <u>dogged</u> effort?
6. Would you want to <u>elude</u> someone who has a gift for you?

Word Study Follow the directions for using a word that has the **Latin root *-ven-*.**

1. Use the verb *venture* to tell about a person who takes a risk.
2. Use the verb *convene* to tell about a group coming together.

Word Study

The **Latin root *-ven-*** means "come" or "go."

Challenge Explain how the root *-ven-* contributes to the meaning of these words. Consult a dictionary if necessary.

event
adventure
avenue

ASSESS/EXTEND

Answers

Literary Analysis

1. (a) The main external conflict in the story is Ravi's trying not to be found by Raghu. (b) The main internal conflict is between Ravi's desire to win the game and his fears and discomfort in the shed.
2. (a) **Possible response:** A moment of suspense occurs when Ravi is trying to decide whether to run or hide in the shed.
   (b) **Possible response:** The conflict of Ravi's desire to win the game and his fears make this moment particularly suspenseful.
3. (a) No, Ravi does not win the game, does not rejoin the children in their games, and does not get respect from the other children.
   (b) **Possible response:** Ravi finally leaves the shed, touches the goal, and is hailed as the winner.

Reading Skill

4. **Possible responses:** (a) When Ravi decides to go into the shed, the story's cause-and-effect chain is set in motion. (b) No one finds him. The other children forget about him.

   For other sample answers, see ***Graphic Organizer Transparencies*, Reading Skill Graphic Organizer A**, p. 25, and the **Additional Answers** section.
5. (a) The shed has a lock on it.
   (b) Because it is locked, Raghu decides that no one is inside and goes away. After Raghu leaves the shed, he catches the other children and forgets about Ravi. Because he is forgotten, Ravi ends up feeling "insignificant."

Vocabulary

Practice

1. No, <u>livid</u> colors make one feel angry or excited.
2. Yes, a neutral person coming between two opposing people might help them to resolve their conflict.
3. No, an athlete would not be depressed if she had won a game.
4. None, when something is <u>defunct</u>, it no longer functions.
5. No, a lazy person gives up easily, and a <u>dogged</u> person would keep trying.
6. No, I would not want to avoid a person who has a gift for me.

Word Study

Sample answers:

1. She <u>ventured</u> into the new business, hoping that it would succeed.
2. The board members <u>convened</u> at the regularly scheduled time to discuss next month's events.

Word Study: Challenge

Sample answers: An *event* is something to which people <u>come</u> in order to experience it. An *adventure* is something, often dangerous or risky, on which people <u>go</u> to experience new things. An *avenue* is a route by which people <u>come</u> and <u>go</u>.

EXTEND/ASSESS

Answers

Grammar

1. Introduce the skill, using the instruction on the student page.
2. Discuss the items in the chart.

Think Aloud: Model the Skill

Model the skill of determining when to use personal pronouns. Say to students:

> I use personal pronouns in my speech and in my writing to avoid unnecessary repetition. Consider this sentence: "Tim was worried, because Tim needed Tim's bike." The name Tim is used over and over again. You can use personal pronouns instead. Consider this new sentence: "Tim was worried, because he needed his bike." This sentence sounds better because it isn't repetitive.

WG Writing and Grammar, Grade 10

Students will find further instruction and practice on personal pronouns in Chapter 16, Section 2.

Practice A

1. his (third person); it (third person)
2. He (third person); it (third person)
3. You (second person); he (third person); himself (third person)
4. him (third person)

Challenge

Sample answer:

"But he still didn't begin his work." third-person pronouns

"'Sure you don't mind going alone?'" second-person pronoun

"'Yeah, I know.'" first-person pronoun."

Practice B

Sample answers:

1. They hoped to elude him. It is not clear who is avoiding whom.
2. He has never won it before. It is not clear who has never won what.
3. Though Ravi is frightened in the shed, he hides in it for a long time. The meaning of the sentence does not change.
4. "Victory will be his," thought Ravi. It is not clear whose victory it will be.

Challenge

Students should observe that inserting pronouns might make the sentences vague or difficult to understand.

Integrated Language Skills

Contents of the Dead Man's Pocket • Games at Twilight

Grammar: Personal Pronouns

Pronouns are words that are used in place of nouns or of words that work together as a noun.

The most common pronouns are **personal pronouns.** First-person pronouns refer to the person speaking. Second-person pronouns refer to the person being spoken to. Third-person pronouns refer to the person, place, or thing being spoken about. Look at the chart below to see first-, second-, and third-person pronouns in both singular and plural forms.

Personal Pronouns	Singular	Plural
First Person	I, me, my, mine	we, us, our, ours
Second Person	you, your, yours	you, your, yours
Third Person	he, him, his, she, her, hers, it, its	they, them, their, theirs

Practice A Identify the personal pronoun or pronouns in each sentence. Then, indicate whether they are first-, second-, or third-person pronouns.

1. Tom loses his paper when the wind blows it out the window.
2. He goes out on the ledge to retrieve it.
3. "You will not die today," he tells himself.
4. Tom wishes Clare was there to save him.

Challenge In "Contents of the Dead Man's Pocket," find one example of each type of personal pronoun. Write the sentences in which they appear, circling and labeling the pronouns.

Practice B Rewrite each sentence, using a pronoun for each underlined word or words. Then, explain how the effect of the sentence changes.

1. The children hope to elude Raghu.
2. Ravi has never won the game before.
3. Though Ravi is frightened in the shed, Ravi hides in the shed for a long time.
4. "Victory will be Ravi's," thought Ravi.

Challenge Find three sentences in "Games at Twilight" in which you could replace a noun or nouns with a personal pronoun. Rewrite these sentences with the substituting pronoun. What effect do these changes have?.

WG **Writing and Grammar Connection:** Chapter 16, Section 2

Extend the Lesson

Sentence Modeling

Choose the sentence given from the selection students have read:

His teeth were exposed in a frozen grimace, the strength draining like water from his knees and calves. ("Contents of the Dead Man's Pocket")

It was an insect—perhaps a spider—exploring him. ("Games at Twilight")

Ask students what they notice about the sentence. Elicit from them the personal pronouns used. Then, ask what else they notice. ("Contents of the Dead Man's Pocket": vivid details, like "frozen grimace," and the simile, "strength draining like water," make Tom's fear easy to picture; "Games at Twilight": the pronouns begin and end the sentence, emphasizing the details in the middle: "insect" and "spider." The dash adds information, presented as a speculation, that interrupts Ravi's flow of thought.)

Have students imitate the sentence in a sentence on a topic of their own choosing, matching each grammatical and stylistic feature discussed. Collect the sentences, and share them with the class.

Writing

Both "Contents of the Dead Man's Pocket" and "Games at Twilight" end with **irony**—a strong contrast between a characters efforts and expectations and what actually happens. Write an **anecdote,** or brief story, that has an ironic ending.

- Pick a character, a conflict, an expected end, and a twist.
- As you draft, include details to set up the expected outcome, but include hints that could explain an unexpected one.
- Be sure to pace the presentation of actions to accommodate time or mood changes.
- Finally, resolve the conflict with your ironic ending. Ask a classmate to read a draft and tell you how effective your ending is. Consider revising based on your reader's feedback.

Writing Workshop: *Work in Progress*

Prewriting for Cause-and-Effect Essay For an essay you may write, jot down three *why* questions on topics that interest you. Note one or two sources you think might have information on each topic. Keep this Why List in your writing portfolio.

Use this prewriting activity to prepare for the **Writing Workshop** on page 200.

Listening and Speaking

With other students in your class, form a **problem-solving group** to explore and find solutions to either Tom's or Ravi's problem.

- Identify the problem the character faces.
- **Generate questions** about the problem to determine an appropriate approach.
- Discuss strategies, **supporting your ideas** with reasons and examples.
- **Summarize and evaluate** comments as the discussion unfolds. Respond to one another respectfully and ask for clarification of any points you do not understand.
- At the end of the discussion, **formulate one or two possible conclusions.**
- **Produce concise notes** summarizing the main points of your discussion to aid you as you explain the potential solutions to your classmates.

Share your ideas with the rest of the class.

PHLit Online!
www.PHLitOnline.com
- Interactive graphic organizers
- Grammar tutorial
- Interactive journals

EXTEND/ASSESS

Writing

1. Review the assignment, using the instruction on the student page.
2. To guide students in writing an anecdote, give them **Support for Writing**, p. 162 in ***Unit 1 Resources***. In addition, encourage students to pace their narratives to accommodate changes in time or mood.
3. To evaluate students' anecdotes, use the Short Story rubric, pp. 226–227 in ***Professional Development Guidebook***. In addition, you might also evaluate the anecdote for an ironic ending.

Six Traits Focus

✓	Ideas		Word Choice
	Organization		Sentence Fluency
✓	Voice	✓	Conventions

Writing and Grammar, Grade 10

Students will find guidance on narrative writing in Chapter 5.

Writing Workshop
Work in Progress

Have students save their completed cause-and-effect essay notes in their portfolios. They will use them later as they continue this Work-in-Progress assignment (see pp. 178–179). These assignments prepare them to complete the Writing Workshop (see pp. 200–207).

Listening and Speaking

1. Review the assignment, using the instruction on the student page.
2. Have students complete the **Support for Extend Your Learning** page (*Unit 1 Resources*, p. 163).

Teaching Resources

Unit 1 Resources
- L3 L4 **Integrated Language Skills: Grammar,** p. 161
- L3 L4 **Support for Writing,** p. 162
- L3 L4 **Support for Extend Your Learning,** p. 163
- L4 **Enrichment,** pp. 121, 137

Enriched Online Student Edition
Available under After You Read for this selection:
- All **Interactive Grammar Tutorial**
- L3 L4 **Internet Research Activity**

Professional Development Guidebook
Rubrics for Short Story, pp. 226–227

PHLit Online! All print and digital resources are available at **www.PHLitOnline.com.** Online resources accessible by students are noted on the student page.

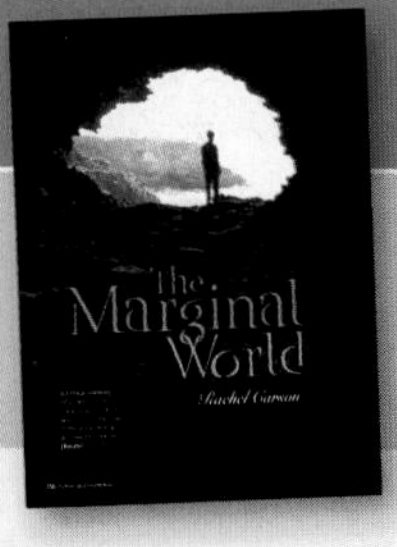

TIME AND RESOURCE MANAGER

The Marginal World • Making History With Vitamin C

Lesson Pacing Guide

DAY 1 Preteach

- Administer the Reading and Vocabulary Warm-ups (*Unit 1 Resources*, pp. 173–176 or 191–194) as necessary.
- Introduce the Reading Skill: Cause and Effect FT
- Introduce the Literary Analysis concept: Author's Purpose FT
- Distribute copies of the appropriate graphic organizer for the Reading Skill (*Graphic Organizer Transparencies*, pp. 26–28). CRI
- Distribute copies of the appropriate graphic organizer for Literary Analysis (*Graphic Organizer Transparencies*, pp. 29–31). CRI
- Teach the selection vocabulary. FT CRI
- Introduce the Word Study skill.

DAYS 2–3 Preteach/Teach

- Build background with the Background feature. CRI
- Develop thematic vocabulary and thematic thinking with Writing About the Big Question.
- Prepare students to read with the Activating Prior Knowledge activities (TE). CRI
- Informally monitor comprehension while students read. FT
- Use the Reading Check questions to confirm comprehension.
- Develop students' ability to analyze cause and effect using the Reading Skill questions. CRI
- Develop students' understanding of the author's purpose using the Literary Analysis questions. CRI
- Reinforce vocabulary with the Vocabulary notes. CRI

DAY 4 Assess

- Assess students' comprehension and mastery of the skills by having them answer the Critical Thinking, Reading Skill, and Literary Analysis questions. FT
- Have students complete the Vocabulary Practice activities. FT
- Have students complete the Word Study activities.

DAY 5 Extend/Assess

- Have students complete the Grammar lesson. CRI
- Have students complete the Writing activity and write a proposal for a documentary. (You may assign as homework.) FT
- Extend learning by having students complete the Research and Technology activity, a spreadsheet. (You may assign as homework.) As an alternative, assign them "Shark Story" or "The ABCs of Antioxidants" in *Reality Central*. CRI
- Administer Selection Test A or B (*Unit 1 Resources*, pp. 185–190 or 206–211). FT

"The Marginal World" is an unedited excerpt from a nonfiction book. "Making History With Vitamin C" is an excerpt from a book on history and science, edited for length.

Meeting Your Standards

Students will

1. **analyze and respond to literary elements.**
   - **Literary Analysis: Author's Purpose**
2. **read, comprehend, and analyze nonfiction.**
   - **Reading Skill: Cause and Effect**
   - **Reading Check questions**
   - **Apply the Skills questions**
   - **Assessment Practice**
3. **develop vocabulary.**
   - **Vocabulary**
   - **Word Study**
4. **apply grammar skills.**
   - **Relative Pronouns**
5. **Develop writing proficiency.**
   - **Work in Progress: Cause-and-Effect Essay**
   - **proposal for a documentary**
6. **strengthen research and technology skills.**
   - **spreadsheet**

CRI For a full explanation of Culturally Responsive Instruction opportunities in this lesson, see p. T86–T87.

FT For an accelerated lesson, use the Fast Track strategies and activities.

Managing Differentiated Instruction

This leveled selection pairing groups a more accessible with a more challenging selection. Choose either one to teach the lesson skills. For classroom management suggestions for using the pairing in a mixed-ability class, see pp. T68–T69.

Daily Block Scheduling

Each day in this Lesson Pacing Guide represents a 40–50 minute period. Teachers using block scheduling may combine days to revise pacing. In addition, teachers may differentiate and support core instruction by integrating components for extended and intensive support as students require. See the Guide to Selected Leveled Resources (facing page).

Guide to Selected Leveled Resources

EL English Learners

			The Marginal World	Making History With Vitamin C
CORE COURSE	*Unit 1 Resources*	Selection Test A	pp. 185–187	pp. 206–211
	Graphic Organizer Transparencies	Reading Skill Graphic Organizer A	p. 27	p. 26
		Literary Analysis Graphic Organizer A	p. 30	p. 29
EXTENDED SUPPORT (Level 2)	*Unit 1 Resources*	Reading and Vocabulary Warm-ups A or B	pp. 173–176	pp. 191–194
	Reader's Notebook: English Learner's Version		adapted instruction and adapted selection	adapted instruction and summary
	Hear It! Audio CD		selection and summaries	selection and summaries
	Hear It! Audio CD (adapted text)		adapted selection and summaries	—
INTENSIVE SUPPORT (Level 1)	*Reality Central*		"Shark Story"	"The ABCs of Antioxidants"
	Real-World Writing Journal		Lesson 7, pp. 26–29	Lesson 8, pp. 30–33

Below-Level Students

			The Marginal World	Making History With Vitamin C
CORE COURSE	*Unit 1 Resources*	Selection Test A	pp. 185–187	pp. 206–211
	Graphic Organizer Transparencies	Reading Skill Graphic Organizer A	p. 27	p. 26
		Literary Analysis Graphic Organizer A	p. 30	p. 29
EXTENDED SUPPORT (Level 2)	*Unit 1 Resources*	Reading and Vocabulary Warm-ups A or B	pp. 173–176	pp. 191–194
	Reader's Notebook		adapted instruction and full selection	adapted instruction and summary
	Hear It! Audio CD		selection and summaries	selection and summaries
INTENSIVE SUPPORT (Level 1)	*Reality Central*		"Shark Story"	"The ABCs of Antioxidants"
	Real-World Writing Journal		Lesson 7, pp. 26–29	Lesson 8, pp. 30–33
	Reading Kit		Reteaching worksheets	Reteaching worksheets

Special Needs Students

			The Marginal World	Making History With Vitamin C
CORE COURSE	*Unit 1 Resources*	Selection Test A	pp. 185–187	pp. 206–211
	Graphic Organizer Transparencies	Reading Skill Graphic Organizer A	p. 27	p. 26
		Literary Analysis Graphic Organizer A	p. 30	p. 29
EXTENDED SUPPORT (Level 2)	*Unit 1 Resources*	Reading and Vocabulary Warm-ups A or B	pp. 173–176	pp. 191–194
	Reader's Notebook: Adapted Version		adapted instruction and adapted selection	adapted instruction and summary
	Hear It! Audio CD (adapted text)		adapted selection and summaries	—
INTENSIVE SUPPORT (Level 1)	*Reality Central*		"Shark Story"	"The ABCs of Antioxidants"
	Real-World Writing Journal		Lesson 7, pp. 26–29	Lesson 8, pp. 30–33
	Reading Kit		Reteaching worksheets	Reteaching worksheets

The program includes resources for these students: L3 On-Level L4 Advanced All All
For a complete guide to selection support, see pp. T106–T108.

NOTE: All print materials are also available online at *www.PHLitOnline.com.*

VISUAL GUIDE to Featured Selection Resources

• The Marginal World
• Making History With Vitamin C

RESOURCES FOR:

- **EL** English Learners
- **L1** Special Needs Students
- **L2** Below-Level Students
- **L3** On-Level Students
- **L4** Advanced Students
- **All** All Students

Vocabulary/Fluency/Prior Knowledge

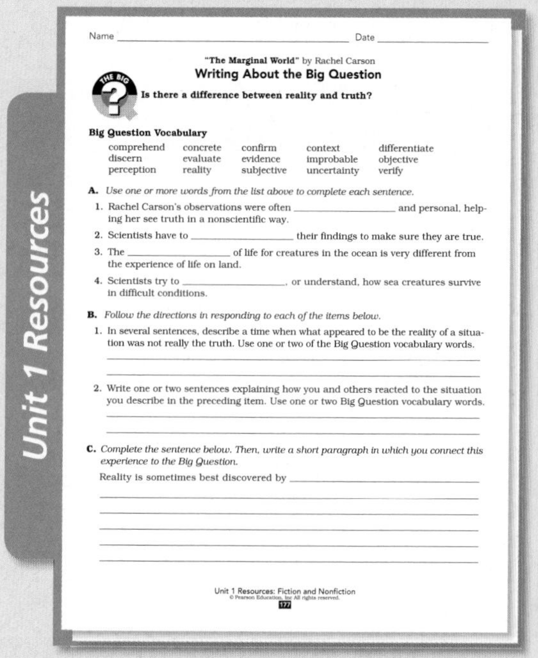

Name ______ Date ______

"The Marginal World" by Rachel Carson
Writing About the Big Question

Is there a difference between reality and truth?

Big Question Vocabulary

comprehend	concrete	confirm	context	differentiate
discern	evaluate	evidence	improbable	objective
perception	reality	subjective	uncertainty	verify

A. *Use one or more words from the list above to complete each sentence.*

1. Rachel Carson's observations were often ______ and personal, helping her see truth in a nonscientific way.
2. Scientists have to ______ their findings to make sure they are true.
3. The ______ of life for creatures in the ocean is very different from the experience of life on land.
4. Scientists try to ______, or understand, how sea creatures survive in difficult conditions.

B. *Follow the directions in responding to each of the items below.*

1. In several sentences, describe a time when what appeared to be the reality of a situation was not really the truth. Use one or two of the Big Question vocabulary words.
2. Write one or two sentences explaining how you and others reacted to the situation you describe in the preceding item. Use one or two Big Question vocabulary words.

C. *Complete the sentence below. Then, write a short paragraph in which you connect this experience to the Big Question.*

Reality is sometimes best discovered by ______

Unit 1 Resources: Fiction and Nonfiction
© Pearson Education, Inc. All rights reserved.
177

All **Writing About the Big Question, pp. 177, 195**

Also available for these selections:

- **EL** **L1** **L2** Vocabulary Warm-ups A and B, pp. 173–174, 191–192
- **EL** **L1** **L2** Reading Warm-ups A and B, pp. 175–176, 193–194
- **All** Vocabulary Builder, pp. 180, 198

Reader's Notebooks

Pre- and postreading pages for both selections, as well as "The Marginal World," appear in an interactive format in the *Reader's Notebooks*. Each *Notebook* is differentiated for a different group of learners. The selections in the Adapted and English Learner's versions are abridged.

L2 **L3** ***Reader's Notebook***

L1 ***Reader's Notebook: Adapted Version***

EL ***Reader's Notebook: English Learner's Version***

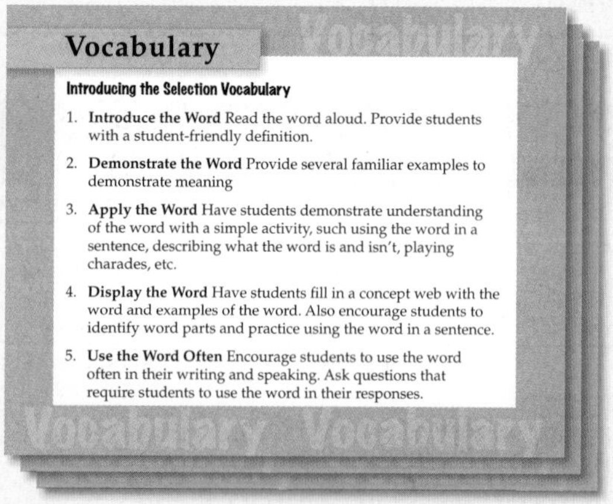

Vocabulary

Introducing the Selection Vocabulary

1. **Introduce the Word** Read the word aloud. Provide students with a student-friendly definition.
2. **Demonstrate the Word** Provide several familiar examples to demonstrate meaning
3. **Apply the Word** Have students demonstrate understanding of the word with a simple activity, such using the word in a sentence, describing what the word is and isn't, playing charades, etc.
4. **Display the Word** Have students fill in a concept web with the word and examples of the word. Also encourage students to identify word parts and practice using the word in a sentence.
5. **Use the Word Often** Encourage students to use the word often in their writing and speaking. Ask questions that require students to use the word in their responses.

Classroom Strategies and Teaching Routines

- core classroom routines outlined step-by-step
- convenient format for easy reference while teaching

Selection Support

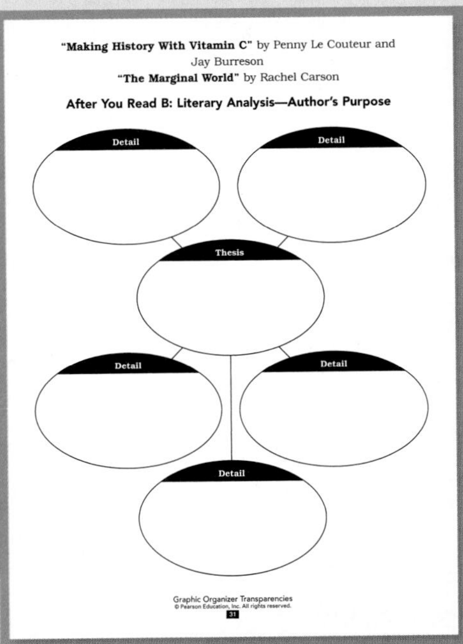

L3 Literary Analysis: Graphic Organizer B, p. 31

Also available for these selections:

EL L1 L2 Reading: Graphic Organizer A, pp. 26, 27 (partially filled in)

L3 Reading: Graphic Organizer B p. 28

EL L1 L2 Literary Analysis: Graphic Organizer A, pp. 29, 30 (partially filled in)

Skills Development/Extension

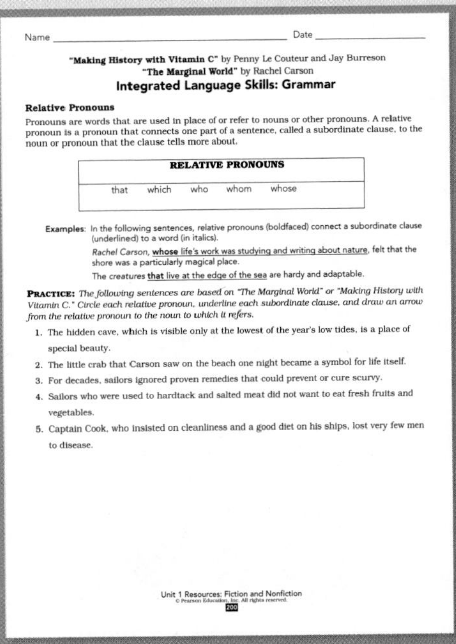

Name ______________________ Date ____________

"Making History with Vitamin C" by Penny Le Couteur and Jay Burreson
"The Marginal World" by Rachel Carson

Integrated Language Skills: Grammar

Relative Pronouns

Pronouns are words that are used in place of or refer to nouns or other pronouns. A relative pronoun is a pronoun that connects one part of a sentence, called a subordinate clause, to the noun or pronoun that the clause tells more about.

RELATIVE PRONOUNS
that which who whom whose

Examples: In the following sentences, relative pronouns (boldfaced) connect a subordinate clause (underlined) to a word (in italics).

Rachel Carson, **whose** life's work was studying and writing about nature, felt that the shore was a particularly magical place.

The *creatures* **that** live at the edge of the sea are hardy and adaptable.

PRACTICE: *The following sentences are based on "The Marginal World" or "Making History with Vitamin C." Circle each relative pronoun, underline each subordinate clause, and draw an arrow from the relative pronoun to the noun to which it refers.*

1. The hidden cave, which is visible only at the lowest of the year's low tides, is a place of special beauty.
2. The little crab that Carson saw on the beach one night became a symbol for life itself.
3. For decades, sailors ignored proven remedies that could prevent or cure scurvy.
4. Sailors who were used to hardtack and salted meat did not want to eat fresh fruits and vegetables.
5. Captain Cook, who insisted on cleanliness and a good diet on his ships, lost very few men to disease.

Unit 1 Resources: Fiction and Nonfiction
© Pearson Education, Inc. All rights reserved.
200

L3 L4 Grammar, p. 200

Also available for these selections:

All Literary Analysis: Author's Purpose, pp. 178, 196

All Reading: Cause and Effect, pp. 179, 197

L4 Enrichment, pp. 181, 199

L3 L4 Support for Writing, p. 201

L3 L4 Support for Extend Your Learning, p. 202

Assessment

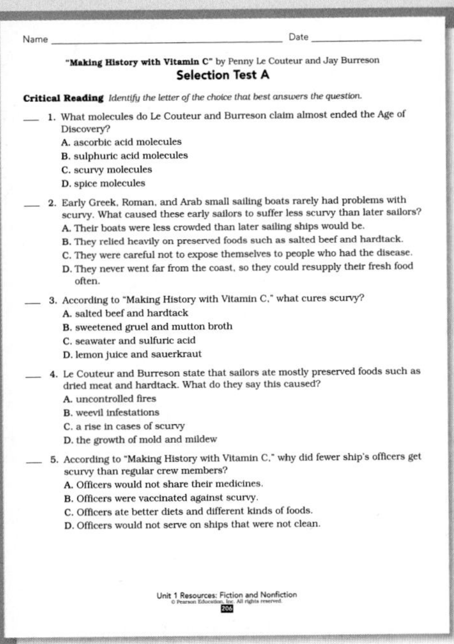

Name ______________________ Date ____________

"Making History with Vitamin C" by Penny Le Couteur and Jay Burreson

Selection Test A

Critical Reading *Identify the letter of the choice that best answers the question.*

___ 1. What molecules do Le Couteur and Burreson claim almost ended the Age of Discovery?
A. ascorbic acid molecules
B. sulphuric acid molecules
C. scurvy molecules
D. spice molecules

___ 2. Early Greek, Roman, and Arab small sailing boats rarely had problems with scurvy. What caused these early sailors to suffer less scurvy than later sailors?
A. Their boats were less crowded than later sailing ships would be.
B. They relied heavily on preserved foods such as salted beef and hardtack.
C. They were careful not to expose themselves to people who had the disease.
D. They never went far from the coast, so they could resupply their fresh food often.

___ 3. According to "Making History with Vitamin C," what cures scurvy?
A. salted beef and hardtack
B. sweetened gruel and mutton broth
C. seawater and sulfuric acid
D. lemon juice and sauerkraut

___ 4. Le Couteur and Burreson state that sailors ate mostly preserved foods such as dried meat and hardtack. What do they say this caused?
A. uncontrolled fires
B. weevil infestations
C. a rise in cases of scurvy
D. the growth of mold and mildew

___ 5. According to "Making History with Vitamin C," why did fewer ship's officers get scurvy than regular crew members?
A. Officers would not share their medicines.
B. Officers were vaccinated against scurvy.
C. Officers ate better diets and different kinds of foods.
D. Officers would not serve on ships that were not clean.

Unit 1 Resources: Fiction and Nonfiction
© Pearson Education, Inc. All rights reserved.
206

EL L1 L2 Selection Test A, pp. 185–187, 206–208

Also available for these selections:

L3 L4 Open-Book Test, pp. 182–184, 203–205

L3 L4 Selection Test B, pp. 188–190, 209–211

PHLit Online!

www.PHLitOnline.com

- complete narrated selection text
- a thematically related video with writing prompt
- an interactive graphic organizer
- highlighting feature
- access to all student print resources, adapted to individual student needs
- Spanish and English summaries

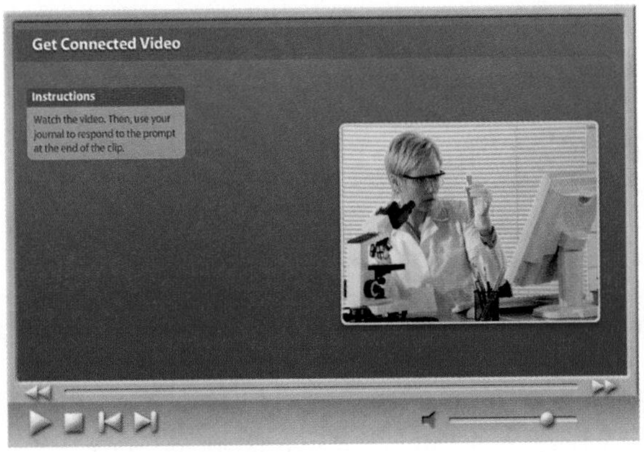

Get Connected! (thematic video with writing prompt)

Also available:

Background video

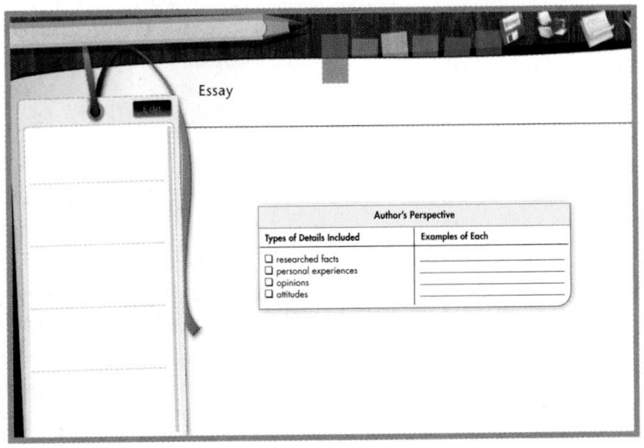

Writer's Journal (with graphics feature)

Also available:

Vocabulary Central (tools, activities, and songs for studying vocabulary)

DIFFERENTIATE/PRETEACH

❶ Selection Choices

You may use either "The Marginal World" or "Making History With Vitamin C" to meet the lesson standards. Skills instruction for both selections appears on p. 153. Choose one selection to teach (or choose to teach both). The Accessibility at a Glance chart at the bottom of this page will help you determine which of the two selections is more appropriate for your students.

❷ Selection Skills

1. With the class, preview the selection skills. (The lesson meets the lesson objectives given on p. 152a.)
2. Explain that students will develop the skill of analyzing cause and effect (introduced on p. 115) as they read to better understand and enjoy the selection you choose. By examining the author's purpose as they read, they will gain deeper insight into nonfiction.
3. To introduce the Writing and Research and Technology activities (p. 179), tell students that when they have finished reading the selection, they will write a proposal for a documentary and compile a spreadsheet related to the selection.
4. Tell students that they will also study a grammar concept: relative pronouns. By mastering this concept, they will improve their reading fluency and the quality of their own writing.

Before You Read

The Marginal World • Making History With Vitamin C

❶ Selection Choices

▲ Read **"The Marginal World"** to learn about the enormous vitality of life at the edge of the sea.

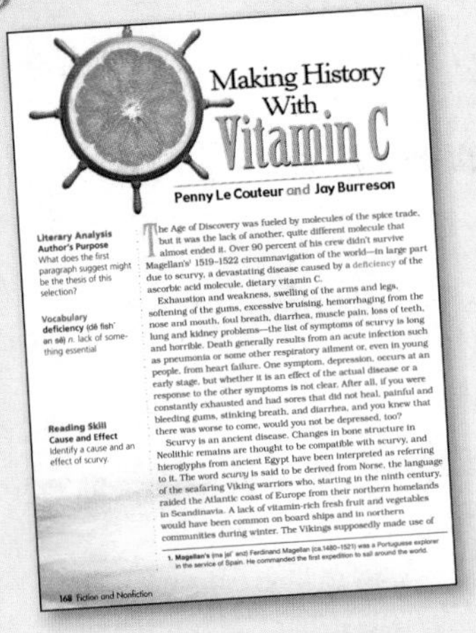

▲ Read **"Making History With Vitamin C"** to learn about the role vitamin C played in sea travel.

❷ Selection Skills Guide

Practice these skills with either **"The Marginal World"** (p. 156) or **"Making History With Vitamin C"** (p. 168).

- Understand the author's purpose
- Identify the author's style
- Analyze cause and effect
- Reread to analyze causes and effects
- Identify relative pronouns
- Write a proposal for a documentary
- Create a spreadsheet

Differentiated Instruction for Universal Access

Accessibility at a Glance: Selection Choices

	The Marginal World	Making History With Vitamin C	
Context	Exploring the environment of the seashore	Finding the reason and a treatment for scurvy	Because a number of factors determine the relative accessibility of paired selections, in some cases the Lexile rating of the more challenging selection will be lower than that of the more accessible selection.
Language/ Vocabulary	• Some scientific terms • Above-level vocabulary	• Some scientific terms • Subject-specific vocabulary	
Concept Level	Challenging (the seashore is full of wonder)	Accessible (events from historic sea voyages lead to support of thesis)	
Literary Merit	Noted author	Historical; scientific	
Lexile/Length	Lexile: 1220L Word Count: 2,517	Lexile: 1380L Word Count: 3,099	
Overall Rating	**More challenging**	**More accessible**	

Nonfiction Selection

Directions: *Read the selection. Then, answer the questions.*

3 Recycling saves on the amount of garbage we make and helps us keep our planet healthy. Even if you recycle just a small amount of material, you can have a positive impact on the environment. Some materials can be reused in their present state, such as using a tire for a flower planter. Other materials can be recycled into new products. Plastic, for example, is processed and reused to create new plastic items. Whatever way you choose to recycle, you do the earth a favor. Recycling helps lower greenhouse gases and decreases the space we need for landfills. Overall, recycling is a friend to the environment. You can make a difference. Why not recycle something today?

1. What is the general purpose of this article?
A. to entertain
B. to reflect
C. to describe
D. to persuade

4 **2.** Why do you think the author ends the article with a question?
A. to call the audience to action
B. to make the audience look for an answer
C. to teach the audience about landfills
D. to eliminate the need for questioning the author

3. For what purpose does the author give examples of how materials can be recycled?
A. to provide ideas for recycling plastic
B. to explain how recycling works
C. to convince the reader to do Earth a favor
D. to show the advantages of reusing products

4. Which sentence *best* reveals the author's purpose in this selection?
A. Some materials can be reused in their present state, such as using a tire for a flower planter.
B. Other materials can be recycled into new products.
C. Whatever way you choose to recycle, you do the earth a favor.
D. Recycling is expensive and unnecessary.

5. What would be the *best* title for this article?
A. The Environment
B. Recycling Saves Lives
C. How I Started Recycling
D. Why Everyone Should Recycle

5

Writing for Assessment

Connecting Across Texts
In what ways would this article be helpful to Juan as he completes his science fair project? Write a paragraph in which you use specific details from both passages to explain why Juan should read this article as he prepares his presentation on recycling.

PHLit Online!
www.PHLitOnline.com
- Online practice
- Instant feedback

Differentiated Instruction for Universal Access

Preparing Students for the More Challenging Selection
If you wish to prepare lower-level readers to read "The Marginal World," the more challenging selection, follow these steps:

- Carson describes the shore as "belonging now to the land, now to the sea." To help students understand this idea, work with them to imagine these two worlds, each bounded by the shoreline. On a large sheet of paper, draw the world of the sand, dune, grasses, and marsh; draw the shoreline as the boundary; for the world of the sea, elicit from students examples of sea life. Explain to students that as the tide goes in and out, it exposes parts of each world in turn.
- Remind students that they can use context to find the meaning of difficult words. Invite students to read the third paragraph on p. 158, using context to suggest definitions for *vitality* and *niche*.
- Elicit from students their own experiences at the shore. Discuss the plant life and animal life they observed, as well as the sounds, smells, and textures they experienced.

3 Literary Analysis

Author's Purpose

1. Introduce the skill, using the instruction on the student page.
2. Tell students that they will examine the author's purpose as they read.

Think Aloud: Model the Skill

Model the skill of identifying the author's purpose. Say to students:

> Suppose I am reading an essay in which the author describes an ocean ecosystem. The essay contains examples, facts, and details, so I know the author's purpose is to inform the reader of sea life.
>
> The author, though, does not explain every detail known about sea life, because there is too much to include. Instead, the author has refined the topic by organizing information around a thesis, the main point about a subject.

4 Reading Skill

1. Introduce the skill, using the instruction on the student page.
2. Tell students that they will practice recording causes and effects as they read.

Think Aloud: Model the Skill

Model the skill of rereading to analyze cause and effect. Say to students:

> Suppose I read an article about cars run by hydrogen fuel cells. I know the basic idea: hydrogen pumped into the fuel cell causes a reaction. The article describes the effects, some of which become causes. I can reread the passage, underlining the causes once, and then underlining the effects twice, to help me see the relationship among the ideas.

5 Using the Strategy

Give students a copy of either **Reading Skill Graphic Organizer A** or **B** (*Graphic Organizer Transparencies*, pp. 27–28) to record their ideas about cause and effect as they read. Use the examples in **Reading Skill Graphic Organizer A**, which is partially filled in, to model the process of completing the organizer.

❶ Writing About the Big Question

1. Review the assignment with the class.
2. Discuss with students why *reality* and *truth* might be important terms for a scientist. Elicit that *evidence* is information that a scientist needs to collect in order to prove his or her work.
3. Have students complete the sentence starters. Review responses as a class. (**Possible response:** Reality is sometimes best discovered by thinking about things from someone else's point of view. Scientists can find evidence of the wonders that exist in nature by making careful observations.)
4. Remind students that their answers will help them think about the Big Question, "Is there a difference between reality and truth?"

While You Read

Tell students that as they read, they should consider the truth in the way the author describes the tidal pool.

❷ Vocabulary

1. Have students preview the selection vocabulary.
2. For each word, have students say the word aloud.
3. Then, use the word in a sentence that defines the word.
4. Finally, repeat your definitional sentence or a similar sentence with the word missing and have the class "fill in the blank" chorally. Here are some examples:

   Something mutable is changeable over time. The smoothing of rocks by stream water shows that even stone is [students say "mutable"].

   Manifestations are outward indications or proofs. Symptoms of illness, such as rashes, are a disease's [students say "manifestations"].

❸ Word Study

1. Introduce the skill, using the instruction in the box.
2. Have students define the word *intermediate* using "between" or "among." (**Answer:** between two things)

Making Connections | **The Marginal World**

Is there a difference between *reality* and *truth?*

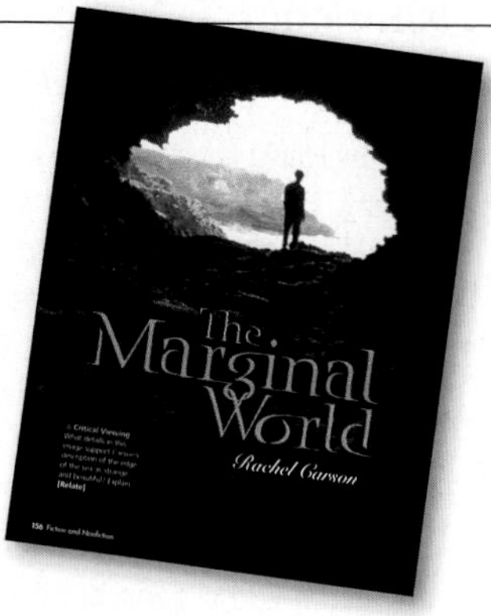

❶ Writing About the Big Question

Successful scientists, such as Rachel Carson, seek to discover truths through scientific inquiry. Use these sentence starters to develop your ideas about the Big Question.

Reality is sometimes best discovered by ____________________.

Scientists can find **evidence** of the wonders that exist in nature by ____________________.

While You Read Decide what "truth" the author is expressing by describing real things in the tidal pool in an imaginative way.

❷ Vocabulary

Read each word and its definition. Decide whether you know the word well, know it a little bit, or do not know it at all. After you read, see how your knowledge of each word has increased.

- **elusive** (ē lo͞o′ siv) *adj.* hard to grasp mentally (p. 158) *The twisted plot made the movie too elusive for many viewers.* elude *v.*
- **mutable** (myo͞ot′ ə bəl) *adj.* changeable (p. 158) *His personality is mutable, and I never know how he will react.* mutability *n.* mutation *n.*
- **intertidal** (in′ tər tīd′'l) *adj.* pertaining to a shore zone bounded by the levels of low and high tide (p. 158) *When the tide is high, the intertidal zone is covered with water.* tide *n.* tidal *adj.*
- **ephemeral** (e fem′ ər əl) *adj.* short-lived (p. 160) *The fog was ephemeral; it lifted just after sunrise.*
- **marginal** (mär′ jə nəl) *adj.* at, on, or near the edge (p. 163) *The teacher wrote a few marginal comments on my final draft.* margin *n.* marginally *adv.*
- **manifestations** (man′ ə fes tā′ shənz) *n.* appearances; forms (p. 164) *Steam and ice are different manifestations of water.* manifest *v.*

❸ Word Study

The **Latin prefix *inter-*** means "between" or "among."

In this selection, the author focuses on the part of the sea that is between the high tide and the low tide mark. Many plants and animals live in this **intertidal** zone.

Vocabulary Development

Vocabulary Knowledge Rating

Create a **Vocabulary Knowledge Rating Chart** (***Professional Development Guidebook***, p. 33) for this selection. Include the selection vocabulary and the Big Question words that appear in the Writing About the Big Question sentence starters on this page. (The Big Question vocabulary is introduced on pp. 2–3.)

Give students a copy of the chart. Read the words aloud, and have students mark their rating in the Before Reading column. Urge them to be alert to these words as they read and discuss the selection.

Tally how many students think they know a word to gauge how much instruction to provide. As students read and discuss the selection, point out the words and their context.

PHLit Online! **Vocabulary Central**, featuring tools, activities, and songs for studying vocabulary, is available at **www.PHLitOnline.com**.

Meet
Rachel Carson
(1907–1964)

Author of
The Marginal World

A lifelong lover of nature, Rachel Carson trained as a marine biologist at a time when few women pursued the study of the sea. She worked for the United States Fish and Wildlife Service and wrote poetically about nature in books like *The Sea Around Us,* which won the National Book Award.

A Crusade One day a friend wrote to complain that many birds had died on her property after it was sprayed for insects. Carson decided she had to show the world that people were damaging the environment with insecticides. In 1962, she published *Silent Spring,* a pioneering environmental work.

DID YOU KNOW?
As a result of Carson's book *Silent Spring,* the insecticide DDT was eventually banned.

4 BACKGROUND FOR THE ESSAY
Tides

The pull of the moon's gravity is strongest on the part of Earth that is closest to the moon. As the Earth rotates, the area that is closest to the moon changes. The result is tides, the daily changes in the water level at the ocean shore. Each day, the edge of the shore is flooded and then exposed by the tides. Rachel Carson explores the creatures that live in this special zone.

Daily Bellringer
For each class during which you will teach this selection, have students complete one of the five Revision activities for Week 5 in the ***Daily Bellringer Activities*** booklet.

4 Background
Tides

Knowing when the tide will come in, how high it will be, and how far it will reach along a shoreline has many practical applications. Ship captains, who must navigate into harbors or along waterways such as river estuaries, choose their routes and schedules according to the depth of tidal waters. A falling tide gives construction crews building structures on the water access to certain areas of their projects. Also, water-sports enthusiasts, such as boaters and surfers, rely on tidal charts.

Multidraft Reading
This icon ● marks natural pauses in the selection. To assist struggling readers and to deepen reading for all, assign the text in "chunks," following the icons, and apply multidraft reading protocols. For each reading, have students set the purpose indicated:

- **First reading**—literal comprehension: answering the Reading Check questions.
- **Second reading**—application of skills: answering the Cause-and-Effect and Author's Purpose prompts.
- **Third reading**—interpretation: answering the end-of-selection questions.

For more guidance, refer to the ***Classroom Strategies and Teaching Routines*** card on multidraft reading.

Differentiated Instruction — Additional Instruction

EL Extended Support—English Learners
Have students complete the **Reading and Vocabulary Warm-ups, *Unit 1 Resources,*** pp. 173–176, before they read. Assign the prereading pages and the adapted selection in the ***Reader's Notebook: English Learner's Version.*** Then, have students listen to portions of the selection on the ***Hear It!*** **Audio CD.**

L1 L2 Extended Support—Struggling Readers
Have students complete the **Reading and Vocabulary Warm-ups, *Unit 1 Resources,*** pp. 173–176, before they read. Assign the prereading pages and the adapted selection in the ***Reader's Notebook: Adapted Version.*** Then, have students listen to portions of the selection on the ***Hear It!*** **Audio CD** (adapted text).

Extended Support—Reluctant Readers
To build motivation and engagement before assigning the selection, have students read "Shark Story," a thematically related selection in ***Reality Central.*** Then, use the questions at the conclusion of the related selection to guide discussion.

PHLit Online!
For more about the author, practice with the selection vocabulary, and more background, go online at **www.PHLitOnline.com.**

❶ Activating Prior Knowledge

1. Prepare an **Anticipation Guide** (see ***Professional Development Guidebook***, pp. 36–38) with the following statements:
   - The diversity of life forms is what makes nature so appealing.
   - We can identify and define the boundaries among different environments.
   - As human beings, we influence conditions in the natural world.
   - No two creatures in nature look or act the same.
2. Give students a copy of the prepared **Anticipation Guide,** and have students mark their responses in the Me column. Have students discuss the statements in pairs or groups and mark the Guides again in the Group column.
3. For further guidance, use the ***Classroom Strategies and Teaching Routines*** card: **Using an Anticipation Guide.**

Concept Connector →

Students will return to the **Anticipation Guide** after completing the story.

Small-Group Activity

Carson's descriptions of the sea can call to mind aspects of music: "rush of water," "surge of surf," "pressure of incoming tides." Suggest that students find descriptions in the selection that remind them of music. In small groups, have students create their own musical descriptions of the sea.

❷ About the Selection

Although Carson imparts a great deal of scientific knowledge about tidal zones in "The Marginal World," the main focus is philosophical. In language that is more often poetic than scientific, Carson describes the sights, sounds, and feelings that contribute to her appreciation of this delicate and changeable region.

❸ Critical Viewing

Possible response: The perspective of the photo—taken from within the dark cave and allowing in only the blinding light from outside—creates a stark contrast, both strange and beautiful, between the worlds of land and sea.

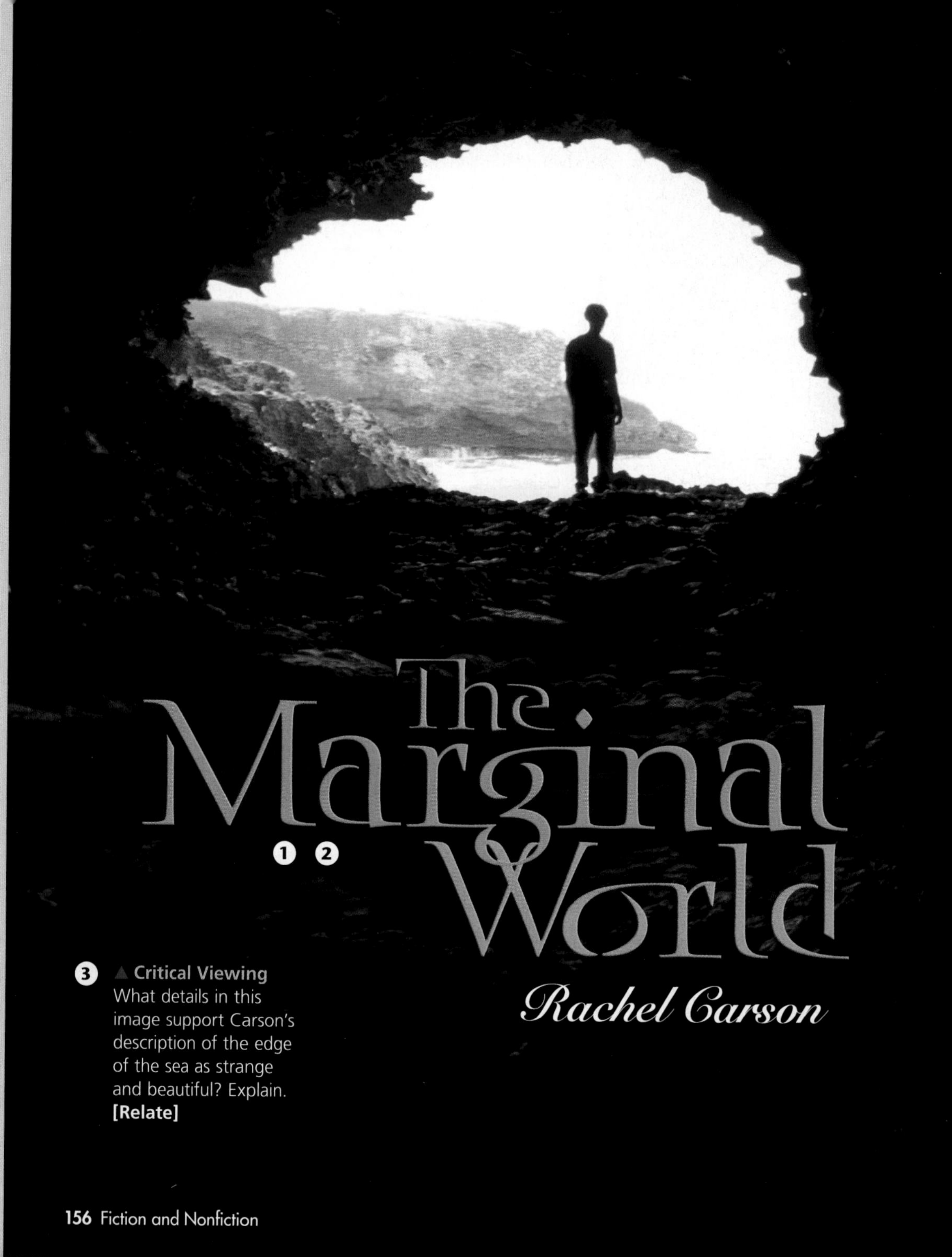

The Marginal World

❶ ❷

Rachel Carson

❸ ▲ **Critical Viewing**
What details in this image support Carson's description of the edge of the sea as strange and beautiful? Explain. **[Relate]**

Vocabulary Development

Thematic Vocabulary: The Big Question

As students are discussing "The Marginal World," encourage them to use the thematic vocabulary presented in Introducing the Big Question, pp. 2–3. You might encourage them with sentence starters like these:

1. Carson *differentiates* the dual nature of the shore by describing it as . . .
2. Along the shore, one can easily *discern* life . . .
3. Carson's *perception* of the enchanted world of the shore is different from . . .
4. The shore at night contains no *evidence* of life except for . . .

4 The edge of the sea is a strange and beautiful place. All through the long history of Earth it has been an area of unrest where waves have broken heav-

5 ily against the land, where the tides have pressed forward over the continents, receded, and then returned. For no two successive days is the shoreline precisely the same.

❹ Critical Thinking

Infer

1. Explain to students that details in this paragraph suggest that the rhythms of life about which the author writes apply to more than just the tides. Point out to them that the word "unrest" in the first paragraph suggests a state of constant movement.
2. Have students read the bracketed passage. **Ask:** What does the "unrest" of the tides suggest about the challenges of living at the edge of the sea?
   Possible response: The tides' continual movement suggests that any organisms, plant life, or animals that live at the edge of the sea must be well suited to survive in this ever-changing environment.

Differentiated Instruction for Universal Access

Strategy for Less Proficient Readers

Students may not have much experience with the sea and may have difficulty understanding what Carson is describing. Point out the phrases in the first paragraph that describe motion: "area of unrest"; "waves have broken heavily"; "pressed forward." Explain that the essay will describe the actions in the region where the ocean meets the land. Suggest that students look for words and phrases in the essay that describe movement. They can use these descriptions in tandem with the photographs shown to visualize how the ocean moves.

Enrichment for Advanced Readers

Invite students to work together to create a classification chart of the animal and plant life cited in "The Marginal World." For example, the phylum *Mollusca* includes the species lobster and ghost crab. Have students describe the plants and animals and list where each is found. Have students find pictures of the creatures and plants that they can use to illustrate their chart. Invite students to display their chart, which can be used as a visual learning tool for classmates.

PHLit Online!

This selection is available in interactive format in the **Enriched Online Student Edition**, **www.PHLitOnline.com**, which includes a thematically related video and writing prompt and an interactive graphic organizer.

❺ Literary Analysis
Author's Purpose

1. Remind students that an essay can have one or more purposes, such as to inform and to persuade. Have them fill in **Literary Analysis Graphic Organizer B** (***Graphic Organizer Transparencies***, p. 31) as they read the selection.
2. Have students read the bracketed text. Then, **ask:** From this passage, which type of essay do you think Carson is writing?
Possible response: Some students may say the essay describes, while others may say it informs or explains.
3. Then, **ask** the Literary Analysis question: Which sentence in the opening paragraph states the author's thesis?
Answer: The author states her thesis in the sentence "Always the edge of the sea remains an elusive and indefinable boundary."

❻ Reading Skill
Cause and Effect

1. Remind students that cause-and-effect relationships link events, actions, or situations to the consequences they produce.
2. Ask students to reread the bracketed text, focusing on the changes described by the author. **Ask:** What causes the "dual nature" of the shore?
Answer: The rise and fall of the tides cause the dual nature of the shore.

❼ Critical Viewing

Possible response: Students may say that Carson says creatures must be hardy and adaptable to survive in a mutable environment. The starfish uses tiny suction cups to hold onto the clam's shell against the motion of the sea. The clam's hard shell protects its organs from outside pressures.

Literary Analysis
Author's Purpose
Which sentence in the opening paragraph states the author's thesis? ❺

Vocabulary
elusive (ē lo͞o′ siv) *adj.* hard to grasp mentally ❻
mutable (myo͞ot′ ə bəl) *adj.* changeable
intertidal (in tər tīd′ ′l) *adj.* pertaining to a shore zone bounded by the levels of low and high tide

Not only do the tides advance and retreat in their eternal rhythms, but the level of the sea itself is never at rest. It rises or falls as the glaciers melt or grow, as the floor of the deep ocean basins shifts under its increasing load of sediments, or as the earth's crust along the continental margins warps up or down in adjustment to strain and tension. Today a little more land may belong to the sea, tomorrow a little less. Always the edge of the sea remains an **elusive** and indefinable boundary.

The shore has a dual nature, changing with the swing of the tides, belonging now to the land, now to the sea. On the ebb tide it knows the harsh extremes of the land world, being exposed to heat and cold, to wind, to rain and drying sun. On the flood tide it is a water world, returning briefly to the relative stability of the open sea.

❽ Only the most hardy and adaptable can survive in a region so **mutable**, yet the area between the tide lines is crowded with plants and animals. In this difficult world of the shore, life displays its enormous toughness and vitality by occupying almost every conceivable niche. Visibly, it carpets the **intertidal** rocks; or half hidden, it descends into fissures and crevices, or hides under boulders, or lurks in the wet gloom of sea caves. Invisibly, where the casual observer would say there is no life, it lies deep in the sand, in burrows and tubes and passageways. It tunnels into solid rock and bores into peat and clay. It encrusts weeds or drifting spars[1] or the hard, chitinous[2] shell of a lobster. It exists minutely, as the film of bacteria that spreads over a rock surface or a wharf piling; as spheres of protozoa, small as pinpricks, sparkling at the surface of the sea; and as Lilliputian[3] beings swimming through dark pools that lie between the grains of sand.

❼ ▼ **Critical Viewing**
In what way are these creatures prepared for the life along the shore Carson describes? **[Draw Conclusions]**

1. **spars** (spärz) *n.* pieces of wood or metal, such as masts or booms, for supporting sails on a ship.
2. **chitinous** (kī′ tin əs) *adj.* of the material that forms the tough outer covering of insects, crustaceans, and so on.
3. **Lilliputian** (lil′ ə pyo͞o′ shən) *adj.* tiny (from the name of the tiny people who inhabit Lilliput in *Gulliver's Travels* by Jonathan Swift).

Think Aloud

Author's Purpose
Draw students' attention to the sentence on page 159: "In my thoughts of the shore, one place stands apart for its revelation of exquisite beauty." Use the following "think aloud" to model identifying the author's purpose:

I know that every author writes for a reason, and that every sentence and every word serve the author's purpose.

I know this sentence is important for two reasons. It is the first sentence of the paragraph about the hidden pool, so it must be a main idea. I know from reading some of the selection that the author is describing the world of the shore. This sentence and the rest of the paragraph provide more details about a unique part of the shore.

Also, this sentence reveals the author's personal thoughts about a special place along the shore. The author says that this place "stands apart" for its "exquisite beauty." Clearly, this place has special meaning for the author, which she wants to share with her readers.

8 The shore is an ancient world, for as long as there has been an earth and sea there has been this place of the meeting of land and water. Yet it is a world that keeps alive the sense of continuing creation and of the relentless drive of life. Each time that I enter it, I gain some new awareness of its beauty and its deeper meanings, sensing that intricate fabric of life by which one creature is linked with another, and each with its surroundings.

9 In my thoughts of the shore, one place stands apart for its revelation of exquisite beauty. It is a pool hidden within a cave that one can visit only rarely and briefly when the lowest of the year's low tides fall below it, and perhaps from that very fact it acquires some of its special beauty. Choosing such a tide, I hoped for a glimpse of the pool. The ebb was to fall early in the morning. I knew that if the wind held from the northwest and no interfering swell ran in from a distant storm the level of the sea should drop below the entrance to the pool. There had been sudden ominous showers in the night, with rain like handfuls of gravel flung on the roof. When I looked out into the early morning the sky was full of a gray dawn light but the sun had not yet risen. Water and air were pallid. Across the bay the moon was a luminous disc in the western sky, suspended above the dim line of distant shore—the full August moon, drawing the tide to the low, low levels of the threshold of the alien sea world. As I watched, a gull flew by, above the spruces. Its breast was rosy with the light of the unrisen sun. The day was, after all, to be fair.

Later, as I stood above the tide near the entrance to the pool, the promise of that rosy light was sustained. From the base of the steep wall of rock on which I stood, a moss-covered ledge jutted seaward

Reading Skill
Cause and Effect What effect does the changing region have on the creatures that live there?

The shore is an ancient world, for as long as there has been an earth and sea there has been this place of the meeting of land and water.

10 **Reading Check**
Name three places creatures may live along the shore.

Differentiated Instruction for Universal Access

EL Pronunciation for English Learners

Some students might have difficulty pronouncing words with the short "u" sound, as in *sudden*, *gull*, *such*, and *sun*, replacing it with the short "o" sound (as in *cop*) or the broad "o" (as in *caught*). The following strategies can help students to pronounce the short "u" sound.

- Call out the words *sudden*, *gull*, *such*, and *sun*, pronouncing each carefully. Then, have students repeat each word. Have student volunteers come to the board and write them as you say each word again. Discuss any errors made.
- Write *sudden*, *gull*, *such*, and *sun* on the board. Then, play a game of "telephone" with the class, passing (saying) each word first to an English-fluent student, who then pronounces it to another student, until every student has said the word.

8 Reading Skill
Cause and Effect

1. Explain to students that although Carson's essay is informative, she writes in a creative way, so her ideas are more abstract. As a result, identifying causes and effects might be challenging.
2. Have students reread the bracketed text. Then, **ask:** What has allowed so much life to settle in this changing region? **Answer:** Because there is a diverse landscape of rock, plant, sand, and water, there is plenty of room for life to thrive.
3. Then, **ask** the Reading Skill question: What effect does the changing region have on the creatures that live there?
   Possible response: Creatures have had to be hardy and adaptable in order to survive in a mutable environment.

9 The Big Question: Connecting to the Big Question

1. Explain that our perception influences how we understand reality and truth.
2. Have students read the bracketed text. **Ask:** What "truth" is Carson imaginatively expressing by describing life along the tidal line?
   Possible response: Even in the harshest, most inhospitable environments, life can thrive.
3. **Ask:** Through her description, what is Carson implying about the reality of the shore? Is this reality different from the truth she expresses in the passage?
   Possible response: Carson implies that the shore is teeming with life, although one might not see all of it. This reality matches the truth that in any harsh environment, life can survive.

10 Reading Check

Possible response: Students may say that creatures may cling to plants, rocks, or other animals. They may hide in small crevices, under rocks, or in underground tunnels. They may live in pools left behind by the receding tide.

⑪ Literary Analysis
Author's Purpose

1. Recall that the opening paragraph stated a thesis for the essay about the beauty and mystery of the marginal world, where land meets sea. Remind students that each paragraph of an essay has a purpose that supports the larger purpose of the essay.
2. Have students read the bracketed text.
3. Now, **ask** the Literary Analysis question: Which details indicate that the author's purpose here is to show the beauty of sea life?
   Answer: Carson shows the beauty of sea life with the following details: the water is as clear as glass; the colonies of coral are a pale apricot color; a starfish hangs by the merest thread, projecting a perfect reflection; sea creatures are as colorful and delicate as flowers.
4. For students who need help with this concept, show the completed **Literary Analysis Graphic Organizer A** (***Graphic Organizer Transparencies***, p. 30). Have them fill out their own charts as they read the selection.

into deep water. In the surge at the rim of the ledge the dark fronds of oarweeds swayed, smooth and gleaming as leather. The projecting ledge was the path to the small hidden cave and its pool. Occasionally a swell, stronger than the rest, rolled smoothly over the rim and broke in foam against the cliff. But the intervals between such swells were long enough to admit me to the ledge and long enough for a glimpse of that fairy pool, so seldom and so briefly exposed.

And so I knelt on the wet carpet of sea moss and looked back into the dark cavern that held the pool in a shallow basin. The floor of the cave was only a few inches below the roof, and a mirror had been created in which all that grew on the ceiling was reflected in the still water below.

Literary Analysis
Author's Purpose
Which details indicate that the author's purpose here is to show the beauty of sea life?

Under water that was clear as glass the pool was carpeted with green sponge. Gray patches of sea squirts glistened on the ceiling and colonies of soft coral were a pale apricot color. In the moment when I looked into the cave a little elfin starfish hung down, suspended by the merest thread, perhaps by only a single tube foot. It reached down to touch its own reflection, so perfectly delineated that there might have been, not one starfish, but two. The beauty of the reflected images and of the limpid pool itself was the poignant beauty of things that are ephemeral, existing only until the sea should return to fill the little cave.

Vocabulary
ephemeral
(e fem´ ər əl) *adj.*
short-lived

Whenever I go down into this magical zone of the low water of the spring tides, I look for the most delicately beautiful of all the shore's inhabitants—flowers that are not plant but animal, blooming on the threshold of the deeper sea. In that fairy cave I was not disappointed. Hanging from its roof were the pendent[4] flowers of the hydroid Tubularia, pale pink, fringed and delicate as the wind flower. Here were creatures so exquisitely fashioned that they seemed unreal, their beauty too fragile to exist in a world of crushing force. Yet every detail was functionally useful, every stalk and hydranth[5] and petallike tentacle fashioned for dealing with the realities of existence. I knew that they were merely waiting, in that moment of the tide's ebbing, for the return of the sea. Then in the rush of water, in the surge of surf and the pressure of the incoming tide, the delicate flower heads would stir with life. They would sway on their slender stalks, and their long tentacles would sweep the returning water, finding in it all that they needed for life. ⑪

And so in that enchanted place on the threshold

4. **pendent** (pen´ dənt) *adj.* dangling; hanging like a pendant on a necklace or charm.
5. **hydranth** (hī´ dranth´) *n.* one of the feeding individuals in a hydroid colony; the individuals are all attached at the base to a common tube.

Vocabulary Development

Expressive Vocabulary

To help students broaden their expressive vocabulary, encourage them to use the following words as they discuss the selection: *boundary, appreciate, contrast, interdependence,* and *observant.* Have them complete these sentence starters:

1. The *boundary* between sea and land . . .
2. Rachel Carson's description helps readers better *appreciate* . . .
3. The environment of the seashore is in stark *contrast* to . . .
4. The *interdependence* of life in the tidal zone . . .
5. Because she is so *observant,* Rachel Carson . . .

Challenge students to use these words as you continue to discuss the essay.

of the sea the realities that possessed my mind were far from those of the land world I had left an hour before. In a different way the same sense of remoteness and of a world apart came to me in a twilight hour on a great beach on the coast of Georgia. I had come down after sunset and walked far out over sands that lay wet and gleaming, to the very edge of the retreating sea. Looking back across that immense flat, crossed by winding, waterfilled gullies and here and there holding shallow pools left by the tide, I was filled with awareness that this intertidal area, although abandoned briefly and rhythmically by the sea, is always reclaimed by the rising tide. There at the edge of low water the beach with its reminders of the land seemed far away. The only sounds were those of the wind and the sea and the birds. There was one sound of wind moving over water, and another of water sliding over the sand and tumbling down the faces of its own wave forms. The flats were astir with birds, and the voice of the willet[6] rang insistently. One of them stood at the edge of the water and gave its loud, urgent cry; an answer came from far up the beach and the two birds flew to join each other.

The flats took on a mysterious quality as dusk approached and the last evening light was reflected from the scattered pools and creeks. Then birds became only dark shadows, with no color discernible. Sanderlings[7] scurried across the beach like little ghosts, and here and there the darker forms
12 of the willets stood out. Often I could come very close to them before they would start up in alarm—the sanderlings running, the willets flying up, crying. Black skimmers[8] flew along the ocean's edge silhouetted against the dull, metallic gleam, or they went flitting above the sand like large, dimly seen moths. Sometimes they "skimmed" the winding creeks of tidal water, where little spreading surface ripples marked the presence of small fish.

The shore at night is a different world, in which the very darkness that hides the distractions of daylight brings into sharper focus the elemental realities. Once, exploring the night beach, I surprised a small ghost crab in the searching beam of my torch. He was lying in a pit he had dug just above the surf, as though watching the sea and waiting. The blackness of the night possessed water, air, and beach. It was the darkness of an older world, before

13 ▲ **Critical Viewing** What features might make the skimmer particularly adept at catching fish? **[Interpret]**

14 **Reading Check** What main qualities does Carson associate with life along the seashore?

6. **willet** (wil′ it) *n.* shorebird, about 16 inches long, with a long bill, found by shallow shores and other waters of North and South America.
7. **sanderlings** (san′ dər liŋz) *n.* small, gray-and-white shorebirds.
8. **skimmers** (skim′ ərz) *n.* shorebirds with bladelike bills, which they use to skim the surface of the water for small fish and crustaceans.

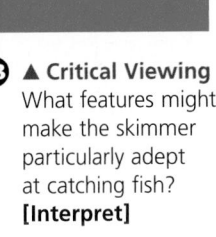

12 Reading Skill
Cause and Effect

1. Have students brainstorm for effects that are caused by sunrise. **Possible response:** People wake up. Birds eat. Nocturnal animals find places to sleep. The temperature usually warms.
2. Have students read the bracketed passage.
3. **Ask:** What effect does the coming of dusk have on the flats? **Answer:** The coming of dusk makes birds in the air and on the shore look like shadows.

13 Critical Viewing

Possible response: The skimmer has a long, thick beak that might allow it to skim the surface of the water for fish.

14 Reading Check

Possible response: Carson describes life along the shore as diverse, beautiful, and always changing.

Differentiated Instruction for Universal Access

Strategy for Special Needs Students

Students may have difficulty following the descriptions in this essay because Carson moves from place to place. Students may find it helpful to identify the author's pattern of organization. Have students create three-column charts with headings that indicate the three places she describes: the pool in the cave, the Georgia beach, and the Florida island described on the following page. Have students list descriptive details under each heading as they read, including animal and plant life, colors, the time of day that is described, and even what Carson does at each place. Encourage students to use this same strategy when reading other essays or stories that take place in a new environment to better help them understand the author's organizational pattern.

Reading Skill
Cause and Effect

1. **Ask:** How is a cause-and-effect relationship similar to cause-and-effect reasoning?
   Answer: A cause-and-effect relationship names the cause and effect, while cause-and-effect reasoning describes how the cause produces the effect.
2. Have a student read the bracketed text aloud. Then, **ask** students to respond to the Reading Skill question: Which details in this passage indicate cause-and-effect relationships?
   Possible response: Students may cite the growth of mangrove roots, which hold the mud, causing islands to form. The retreating tide exposes shellfish, causing birds and animals to come to the shore to feed.

Monitor Progress: To determine whether or not students understand cause-and-effect reasoning, **ask:** What is the relationship between a cause and an effect? **Answer:** A cause is an event, an action, or a situation that produces a result, called the effect.

Reteach: If students have difficulty understanding cause-and-effect reasoning, direct them to the line that begins the passage, "The sense of creation comes with memories of a southern coast. . . . " After reading the sentence, point out several key words that indicate a cause-and-effect relationship between the mangroves and the islands: "sea and the mangroves," "building," and "thousands of small islands." Then, emphasize the mangroves' branches, "grasping and holding the mud, building the land out a little more. . . . " For additional guidance, show students the partially completed **Reading Skill Graphic Organizer A** (*Graphic Organizer Transparencies*, p. 30.

Man. There was no sound but the all-enveloping, primeval sounds of wind blowing over water and sand, and of waves crashing on the beach. There was no other visible life—just one small crab near the sea. I have seen hundreds of ghost crabs in other settings, but suddenly I was filled with the odd sensation that for the first time I knew the creature in its own world—that I understood, as never before, the essence of its being. In that moment time was suspended; the world to which I belonged did not exist and I might have been an onlooker from outer space. The little crab alone with the sea became a symbol that stood for life itself—for the delicate, destructible, yet incredibly vital force that somehow holds its place amid the harsh realities of the inorganic world.

Reading Skill
Cause and Effect
Which details in this passage indicate cause-and-effect relationships?

15 The sense of creation comes with memories of a southern coast, where the sea and the mangroves,[9] working together, are building a wilderness of thousands of small islands off the southwestern coast of Florida, separated from each other by a tortuous[10] pattern of bays, lagoons, and narrow waterways. I remember a winter day when the sky was blue and drenched with sunlight; though there was no wind one was conscious of flowing air like cold clear crystal. I had landed on the surf-washed tip of one of those islands, and then worked my way around to the sheltered bay side. There I found the tide far out, exposing the broad mud flat of a cove bordered by the mangroves with their twisted branches, their glossy leaves, and their long prop roots reaching down, grasping and holding the mud, building the land out a little more, then again a little more.

The mud flats were strewn with the shells of that small, exquisitely colored mollusk,[11] the rose tellin, looking like scattered

9. **mangroves** (maŋ´ grōvz) *n.* tropical trees that grow in swampy ground with spreading branches. The branches send down additional roots, forming a cluster of trunks for each tree.
10. **tortuous** (tôr´ cho͞o əs) *adj.* full of twists and turns.
11. **mollusk** (mäl´ əsk) *n.* one of a large group of soft-bodied animals with shells, including clams and snails.

Vocabulary Development

Vocabulary Knowledge Rating

When students have completed reading and discussing "The Marginal World," have them take out their **Vocabulary Knowledge Rating Chart** for this selection. Read the words aloud once more, and have students rate their knowledge of the words again in the After Reading column. Clarify any words that are still problematic. Have students write their own definition and example or sentence in the appropriate column. Then, have students complete the Vocabulary Practice at the end of the selection. Encourage students to use the words in further discussion and written work about this selection. Remind them that they will be accountable for these words on the **Selection Test**, ***Unit 1 Resources***, pp. 185–187 or 188–190.

petals of pink roses. There must have been a colony nearby, living buried just under the surface of the mud. At first the only creature visible was a small heron in gray and rusty plumage—a reddish egret that waded across the flat with the stealthy, hesitant movements of its kind. But other land creatures had been there, for a line of fresh tracks wound in and out among the mangrove roots, marking the path of a raccoon feeding on the oysters that gripped the supporting roots with projections from their shells. Soon I found the tracks of a shore bird, probably a sanderling, and followed them a little; then they turned toward the water and were lost, for the tide had erased them and made them as though they had never been. 15

Looking out over the cove I felt a strong sense of the interchangeability of land and sea in this **marginal** world of the shore, and of the links between the life of the two. There was also an awareness of the past and of the continuing flow of time, obliterating much that had gone before, as the sea had that morning washed away the tracks of the bird.

The sequence and meaning of the drift of time were quietly summarized in the existence of hundreds of small snails—the mangrove periwinkles—browsing on the branches and roots of the trees. Once their ancestors had been sea dwellers, bound to the salt waters by every tie of their life processes. Little by little over the thousands and millions of years the ties had been broken, the snails had adjusted themselves to life out of water, and now today they were living many feet above the tide to which they only occasionally returned. And perhaps, who could say how many ages hence, there would be in their descendants not even this gesture of remembrance for the sea. 17

The spiral shells of other snails—these quite minute—left
16 winding tracks on the mud as they moved about in search of food. They were horn shells, and when I saw them I had a nostalgic

Vocabulary
marginal (mär′ jə nəl) *adj.* at, on, or near the edge

17 Reading Check
What realization does Carson come to during her encounter with the crab?

16 Critical Thinking
Speculate

1. Have a student read aloud the bracketed text while the other students read along. **Ask:** What prompts Carson to imagine flocks of flamingos?
   Answer: She is thinking about how the snails on the beach had once lived in the sea.
2. **Ask:** Why would she relate these two creatures?
   Possible response: They both lived in the same environment, the flamingos feeding on the snails.
3. Have students speculate as to why the flamingos apparently no longer live in this location.
   Possible responses: Students may say that the flamingos are no longer abundant in this place because their sources of food and shelter have shifted; predators have appeared; or outside forces, such as a changing climate or pollution, have endangered their survival.

17 Reading Check
Answer: Carson realizes that even in the ever-changing and difficult world of the shore, the relationship between life and environment is an intimate one in which both life and environment are perfectly suited to each other.

Concept Connector
Anticipation Guide
Have students return to their **Anticipation Guides** and respond to the statements again in the After Reading column. They may do this individually or in their original groups. Then, lead a class discussion, probing for what students have learned that confirms or invalidates each statement. Encourage students to cite specific details, quotations, or other evidence from the text to support their responses to each statement.

Writing About the Big Question
Have students compare their responses to the sentence starters they completed before reading "The Marginal World" with their ideas afterwards. Ask them to explain whether their thoughts have changed.

Reading Skill Graphic Organizer
Ask students to review the graphic organizers they completed to recognize causes and effects while reading. Show them the partially completed **Reading Skill Graphic Organizer A** (***Graphic Organizer Transparencies***, page 27) as an example. Then, have students share the graphic organizers they did and the inferences they made about other creatures and places.

18 Literary Analysis
Author's Purpose

Ask the Literary Analysis question: In what way does this final paragraph relate to the thesis identified in the first paragraph?

Possible response: In the first paragraph, Carson indicates that the essay will be about the beauty and mystery of tidal zones. In the last paragraph, she echoes this language as she describes the "beauty of the spectacle" and the "elusiveness of that meaning," or mystery, that keeps people returning to the natural world again and again.

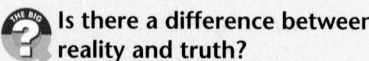

ASSESS
Answers

Critical Thinking

1. **Possible responses:** Students may name any aspect of nature: underwater life, stars and planets, woodland life.
2. (a) Carson first visits a pool hidden in a cave in the early morning.
   (b) Access to the cave is rare and difficult; it contains beautiful, tiny creatures.
3. (a) Carson describes the starfish in the cave pool, the hanging flowers in the cave pool, and the sanderling shorebirds.
   (b) **Possible response:** These seemingly delicate creatures survive in darkness, on land, and in water.
4. **Possible response:** Carson communicates a lesson that all nature is related—to each other and to past and future things. She describes how mudflats created by the ebb and flow of the tides become home to shellfish, which are food for shorebirds.

Is there a difference between reality and truth?

Possible response: The realities that Carson wrote about have not changed, because the beauty, diversity, and mystery of nature are still a part of us.

---

16 moment when I wished I might see what Audubon[12] saw, a century and more ago. For such little horn shells were the food of the flamingo, once so numerous on this coast, and when I half closed my eyes I could almost imagine a flock of these magnificent flame birds feeding in that cove, filling it with their color. It was a mere yesterday in the life of the earth that they were there; in nature, time and space are relative matters, perhaps most truly perceived subjectively in occasional flashes of insight, sparked by such a magical hour and place.

Vocabulary
manifestations (man′ ə fes tā′ shənz) *n.* appearances; forms

Literary Analysis
Author's Purpose
In what way does this final paragraph relate to the thesis identified in the first paragraph?

18 There is a common thread that links these scenes and memories—the spectacle of life in all its varied **manifestations** as it has appeared, evolved, and sometimes died out. Underlying the beauty of the spectacle there is meaning and significance. It is the elusiveness of that meaning that haunts us, that sends us again and again into the natural world where the key to the riddle is hidden. It sends us back to the edge of the sea, where the drama of life played its first scene on earth and perhaps even its prelude; where the forces of evolution are at work today, as they have been since the appearance of what we know as life; and where the spectacle of living creatures faced by the cosmic realities of their world is crystal clear.

12. **Audubon** (ôd′ ə bän′) John James Audubon (1785–1851), an ornithologist, a naturalist, and a painter famous for his paintings of North American birds.

Critical Thinking

1. **Respond:** Which aspects of nature that Carson describes do you find the most intriguing? Why?
2. **(a)** Which place does Carson first visit? **(b) Infer:** Which details make the place special to her?
3. **(a)** Name three creatures that Carson describes at length.
   (b) Compare and Contrast: For each, explain how it demonstrates or symbolizes the power of life to endure in a harsh world.
4. **Interpret:** What lesson about life does Carson draw from her observation of the "marginal world"? Support your answer with details from the work.

Is there a difference between reality and truth?
Carson wrote this essay about fifty years ago. Do you think she expresses a truth that is valid today? Explain your answer.

Assessment Resources

Unit 1 Resources

L1 L2 EL **Selection Test A,** pp. 185–187. Administer Test A to less advanced readers and English learners.

L3 L4 **Selection Test B,** pp. 188–190. Administer Test B to on-level and more advanced students.

L3 L4 **Open-Book Test,** pp. 182–184. As an alternative, give the Open-Book Test.

All **Customizable Test Bank**

All **Self-tests**
Students may prepare for the **Selection Test** by taking the **Self-test** online.

PHLit Online! All assessment resources are available at **www.PHLitOnline.com.**

After You Read | The Marginal World

Literary Analysis: Author's Purpose

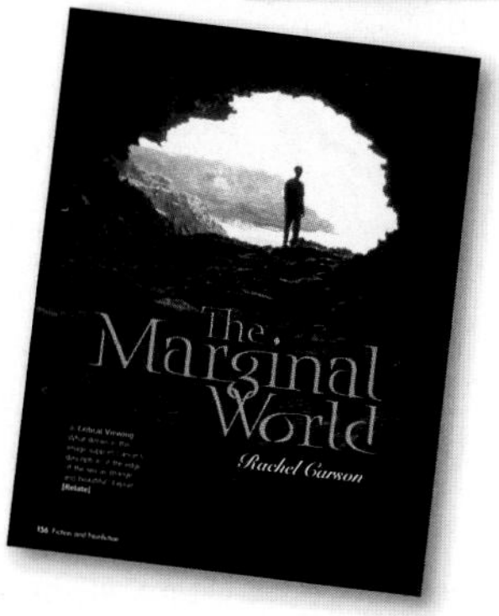

1. **(a)** Explain Carson's main **purpose.** **(b)** Write one sentence describing the author's subject and her **thesis,** or main point.
2. **(a)** Use a diagram like the one shown to record details that **support** the author's thesis. Include at least five details. **(b)** Explain how each detail supports the thesis.

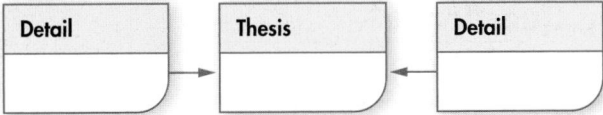

Detail	→ Thesis ←	Detail

3. Identify two examples to show how Carson's descriptions of creatures or places help make her thesis about the "spectacle of life" more convincing to readers. Explain your choices.

Reading Skill: Cause and Effect

4. Identify the **cause** of water level changes in the "marginal world."
5. **(a)** Name two **effects** on creatures in the tidal zone caused by the changing water level. **(b)** For each effect, explain how the changing water level brings it about.

Vocabulary

Practice In vocabulary study, **antonyms** are words with opposite meanings, such as *day* and *night.* For each numbered word, choose the best antonym. Then, use each pair of antonyms in a sentence.

1. elusive: (a) unreal, (b) indefinable, (c) understandable
2. marginal: (a) buttery, (b) outside, (c) central
3. ephemeral: (a) enduring, (b) weak, (c) healthy
4. manifestations: (a) upheavals, (b) absences, (c) questions
5. mutable: (a) worried, (b) noisy, (c) permanent
6. intertidal: (a) watery, (b) deep-sea, (c) moving

Word Study Use the context of the sentences and what you know about the **Latin prefix *inter-*** to explain your answer to each question.

1. Would an *intermediate* course be very easy?
2. Does an *interstate* truck stay within the state?

Word Study

The **Latin prefix *inter-*** means "between" or "among."

Challenge Explain how the prefix *inter-* contributes to the meanings of these words. Consult a dictionary if necessary.

interfere
international
intermission

Word Study
Sample answers:

1. No, it would be neither very easy nor very difficult, but in between.
2. No, it goes between states.

Word Study: Challenge
Sample answers:

When you *interfere* with something, you come between it and its goal. Something that is *international* exists among different nations.
An *intermission* comes between acts.

ASSESS/EXTEND
Answers

Literary Analysis

1. (a) Carson's main purpose for writing this essay is to describe the life in tidal zones. (b) Where land and sea meet creates a complex zone of animal and plant life that symbolizes the power, diversity, and adaptability of nature.
2. **Possible response: Detail:** the mudflats are created by the ebb and flow of the tides. This detail shows the power of the tides.

   For other sample answers, see ***Graphic Organizer Transparencies,*** **Literary Analysis Graphic Organizer A,** p. 30, and the **Additional Answers** section.
3. **Possible response:** Carson gives examples of current and extinct species of the sea, including periwinkle snails that moved from sea to land.

Reading Skill

4. The tides cause the water level to change in the "marginal world."
5. (a) The creatures can roam the mudflats, beaches, and exposed rocks for food. Creatures thrive in tidal pools. (b) The ebb tide exposes land that is submerged during the high tide. The receding tide leaves behind water that is captured in low points.

Vocabulary
Practice

1. *(c) understandable.* When the word's meaning proved elusive, a dictionary made it more *understandable.*
2. *(c) central. Central* to life in the tidal zones on the marginal areas of the shore is the continuing ebb and flow of the tides.
3. *(a) enduring.* Shooting stars, so ephemeral in the night sky, are an *enduring* symbol of good luck.
4. *(b) absences.* The witness's *absences* from court resulted in the manifestation of a police escort at her door.
5. *(c) permanent.* Though we may wish for spring to be *permanent,* the seasons are mutable, and summer inevitably comes.
6. *(b) deep-sea.* A *deep-sea* fish could never survive in an intertidal area.

PRETEACH

*Teaching notes introducing the **Reading Skill** and the **Literary Analysis** concept for this selection appear on p. 153.*

❶ Writing About the Big Question

1. Review the assignment with the class.
2. Ask students to come up with ways in which the truth can be discovered.
3. Have students complete the sentence starter. Review responses as a class. (**Possible response:** Even in the face of evidence, some people refuse to face the truth because they want to believe something else.)
4. Remind students that their answers will help them think about the Big Question, "Is there a difference between reality and truth?"

While You Read

Tell students that as they read, they should look for reasons why sailors ignored the scurvy problem.

❷ Vocabulary

1. Have students preview the selection vocabulary.
2. For each word, have students say the word aloud.
3. Then, use the word in a sentence that defines the word.
4. Finally, repeat your definitional sentence or a similar sentence with the word missing, and have the class "fill in the blank" chorally. For example:

   Incessant means "not ending." *We were bothered by Rex's* [students say "incessant"] *barking.*

❸ Word Study

1. Introduce the skill, using the instruction in the box.
2. Say the word *obstruct,* and provide its definition. Have students use the word to create a sentence. (**Sample answer:** I hope the tall person sitting in front of me at the theater does not obstruct my view of the screen.)

Making Connections — Making History With Vitamin C

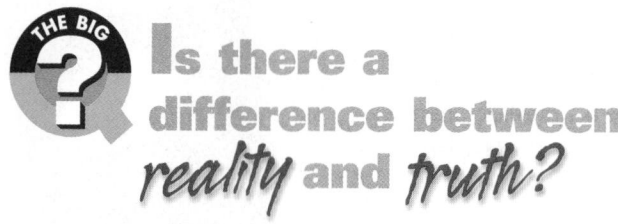

Making History With Vitamin C
Penny Le Couteur and Jay Burreson

Is there a difference between *reality* and *truth?*

❶ Writing About the Big Question

In "Making History With Vitamin C," you will learn that although there was proof that vitamin C prevented a terrible disease called scurvy, many people did not use this knowledge! Use this sentence starter to develop your ideas about the Big Question.

Even in the face of **evidence,** some people refuse to face the truth because ________________________.

While You Read Look for reasons that explain why many sailors ignored advice on avoiding scurvy.

❷ Vocabulary

Read each word and its definition. Decide whether you know the word well, know it a little bit, or do not know it at all. After you read, see how your knowledge of each word has increased.

- **deficiency** (dē fish′ ən sē) *n.* lack of something essential (p. 168) ***A calcium deficiency can cause weak bones.*** *deficient adj.*
- **replenished** (ri plen′ isht) *v.* made complete or full again (p. 169) ***She replenished the bowl with pretzels before it was empty.*** *replenishment n. replenish v.*
- **incessant** (in ses′ ənt) *adj.* not stopping; constant (p. 169) ***His incessant chatter gave me a headache.*** *incessantly adv. cease v.*
- **alleviate** (ə lē′ vē āt′) *v.* lighten or relieve (p. 170) ***The medicine should alleviate your headache and you will feel better.*** *alleviation n.*
- **obscured** (əb skyoord′) *v.* made dark; blocked from view; hid (p. 171) ***The tall person sitting in front of me obscured my view of the screen.*** *obscurely adv. obscurity n. obscure v., adj.*
- **compulsory** (kəm pul′ sə rē) *adj.* required, mandatory (p. 172) ***It is compulsory that the hikers stay on the safe trail, or they must leave the park.*** *compulsion n. compulsive adj. compel v.*

❸ Word Study

The **Latin prefix *ob-*** means "against," "over," or "in front of."

In this selection, the authors explain that the use of ineffective remedies for scurvy may have **obscured,** or covered over, our understanding of the power of vitamin C.

Vocabulary Development

Vocabulary Knowledge Rating

Create a **Vocabulary Knowledge Rating Chart** (***Professional Development Guidebook***, p. 33) for this selection. Include the selection vocabulary and the Big Question words that appear in the Writing About the Big Question sentence starter on this page. (The Big Question vocabulary is introduced on pp. 2–3.)

Give students a copy of the chart. Read the words aloud, and have students mark their rating in the Before Reading column. Urge them to be alert to these words as they read and discuss the selection.

Tally how many students think they know a word to gauge how much instruction to provide. As students read and discuss the selection, point out the words and their context.

PHLit Online! **Vocabulary Central**, featuring tools, activities, and songs for studying vocabulary, is available at **www.PHLitOnline.com.**

Making History With Vitamin C

Penny Le Couteur (b. 1943)
Jay Burreson (b. 1942)

Authors of "Making History With Vitamin C"

Born in New Zealand, Penny Le Couteur (lə ko͞o´ tər) has taught chemistry for more than thirty years. Jay Burreson is also a chemist and runs a high-tech company. The two met in graduate school and have remained friends ever since.

Teaming Up The two friends decided to work together on a book "to tell the stories of the fascinating connections between chemical structures and historical episodes." Each chapter in this book, *Napoleon's Buttons*, examines a different molecule and its role in history.

Napoleon's Buttons takes its title from the chapter on tin. In extreme cold, tin will crumble. When the French leader Napoleon invaded Russia in 1812, his soldiers' tin buttons disintegrated in the freezing air. Many perished of cold in this defeat—some, perhaps, because of their tin buttons.

DID YOU KNOW?

These two chemists propose that molecules helped shape history. For example, they claim that the pursuit of sugar led to the slave trade and the Industrial Revolution.

❹ BACKGROUND FOR THE ESSAY

The Age of Discovery

In the 1300s, Europeans began sailing the known world in search of spices and other goods to trade. As navigation improved, they traveled farther. These adventurers risked shipwreck and losing their way. They also risked scurvy, the illness resulting from a lack of vitamin C, as "Making History With Vitamin C" explains.

Daily Bellringer

For each class during which you will teach this selection, have students complete one of the five Research activities for Week 5 in the ***Daily Bellringer Activities*** booklet.

❹ Background

The Age of Discovery From the beginning of the history of ocean exploration, navigators struggled to ascertain how far they had sailed. To determine their position from one point to the next, they needed a way of relating to a fixed point in the sky while measuring their time of travel. For centuries, navigators relied upon crude instruments for positioning themselves relative to the North Star and the sun.

Finally, in the eighteenth century, a better way of calculating longitude was invented. An English mathematician and an American inventor developed a sextant for celestial sighting. Then, an English watchmaker produced the first chronometer, a portable, accurate timepiece.

Multidraft Reading

This icon ● marks natural pauses in the selection. To assist struggling readers and to deepen reading for all, assign the text in "chunks," following the icons, and apply multidraft reading protocols. For each reading, have students set the purpose indicated:

- **First reading**—literal comprehension: answering the Reading Check questions.
- **Second reading**—application of skills: answering the Cause-and-Effect and the Author's Purpose prompts.
- **Third reading**—interpretation: answering the end-of-selection questions.

For more guidance, refer to the ***Classroom Strategies and Teaching Routines*** card on multidraft reading.

Differentiated Instruction — Additional Instruction

EL Extended Support—English Learners
Have students complete the **Reading and Vocabulary Warm-ups, *Unit 1 Resources*,** pp. 191–194, before they read. Assign the prereading pages for the selection in the ***Reader's Notebook: English Learner's Version***. Then, have students listen to portions of the selection on the ***Hear It!* Audio CD.**

L1 L2 Extended Support—Struggling Readers
Have students complete the **Reading and Vocabulary Warm-ups, *Unit 1 Resources*,** pp. 191–194, before they read. Assign the prereading pages for the selection in the ***Reader's Notebook: Adapted Version***. Then, have students listen to portions of the selection on the ***Hear It!* Audio CD** (adapted text).

Extended Support—Reluctant Readers
To build motivation and engagement before assigning the selection, have students read "The ABCs of Antioxidants," a thematically related selection in ***Reality Central***. Then, use the questions at the conclusion of the related selection to guide discussion.

PHLit Online!

For more about the author, practice with the selection vocabulary, and more background, go online at **www.PHLitOnline.com**.

TEACH

❶ Activating Prior Knowledge

1. Prepare an **Anticipation Guide** (see ***Professional Development Guidebook,*** pp. 36–38) with the following statements:
   - Human lives should be sacrificed in the name of great discoveries.
   - Major scientific discoveries rarely affect the daily lives of people.
2. Give students a copy of the prepared **Anticipation Guide,** and have them mark their responses in the Me column. Have students discuss the statements in pairs or groups and mark the Guides again in the Group column.
3. For further guidance, use the **Classroom Strategies and Teaching Routines card: Using an Anticipation Guide.**

Concept Connector →

Students will return to the **Anticipation Guide** after completing the story.

Individual Activity

Have students with scientific and mathematical interests create timelines of the discoveries described.

❷ About the Selection

Two chemists examine how scurvy dictated the success or failure of early oceanic explorations.

❸ Literary Analysis
Author's Purpose

1. Tell students that the selection's purpose is to inform readers about scurvy.
2. **Ask** the Literary Analysis question.
   Answer: The lack of vitamin C in sailors' diets affected early explorations of the world.

❹ Reading Skill
Analyzing Cause and Effect

1. Remind students that past actions or situations almost always have future effects.
2. **Ask** the Reading Skill question.
   Possible response: A lack of vitamin C is a cause and depression is an effect.

❶ ❷

Making History With Vitamin C

Penny Le Couteur and Jay Burreson

Literary Analysis
Author's Purpose ❸
What does the first paragraph suggest might be the thesis of this selection?

Vocabulary
deficiency (dē fish′ ən sē) *n.* lack of something essential

❹

Reading Skill
Cause and Effect
Identify a cause and an effect of scurvy.

The Age of Discovery was fueled by molecules of the spice trade, but it was the lack of another, quite different molecule that almost ended it. Over 90 percent of his crew didn't survive Magellan's[1] 1519–1522 circumnavigation of the world—in large part due to scurvy, a devastating disease caused by a **deficiency** of the ascorbic acid molecule, dietary vitamin C.

Exhaustion and weakness, swelling of the arms and legs, softening of the gums, excessive bruising, hemorrhaging from the nose and mouth, foul breath, diarrhea, muscle pain, loss of teeth, lung and kidney problems—the list of symptoms of scurvy is long and horrible. Death generally results from an acute infection such as pneumonia or some other respiratory ailment or, even in young people, from heart failure. One symptom, depression, occurs at an early stage, but whether it is an effect of the actual disease or a response to the other symptoms is not clear. After all, if you were constantly exhausted and had sores that did not heal, painful and bleeding gums, stinking breath, and diarrhea, and you knew that there was worse to come, would you not be depressed, too?

Scurvy is an ancient disease. Changes in bone structure in Neolithic remains are thought to be compatible with scurvy, and hieroglyphs from ancient Egypt have been interpreted as referring to it. The word *scurvy* is said to be derived from Norse, the language of the seafaring Viking warriors who, starting in the ninth century, raided the Atlantic coast of Europe from their northern homelands in Scandinavia. A lack of vitamin-rich fresh fruit and vegetables would have been common on board ships and in northern communities during winter. The Vikings supposedly made use of

1. **Magellan's** (mə jel′ ənz) Ferdinand Magellan (ca.1480–1521) was a Portuguese explorer in the service of Spain. He commanded the first expedition to sail around the world.

Vocabulary Development

Thematic Vocabulary: The Big Question

As students are discussing "Making History With Vitamin C," encourage them to use the thematic vocabulary presented in Introducing the Big Question, pp. 2–3. You might encourage them with sentence starters like these:

1. One piece of *evidence* that indicates someone might have scurvy is . . .
2. Before scientific studies *confirmed* scurvy's cure, other peoples, for example, the Chinese . . .
3. Cook *comprehended* the negative effects of scurvy on his crew, so he . . .
4. Being onboard a ship for months was a harsh *reality,* because the crew often experienced . . .

scurvy grass, a form of Arctic cress, on their way to America via Greenland. The first real descriptions of what was probably scurvy date from the Crusades in the thirteenth century.

Scurvy at Sea

In the fourteenth and fifteenth centuries, as longer voyages were made possible by the development of more efficient sets of sails and fully rigged ships, scurvy became commonplace at sea. Oar-propelled galleys, such as those used by the Greeks and Romans, and the small sailing boats of Arab traders had stayed fairly close to the coast. These vessels were not seaworthy enough to withstand
5 the rough waters and huge swells of the open ocean. Consequently, they would seldom venture far from the coast, and supplies could be replenished every few days or weeks. Access to fresh food on a regular basis meant that scurvy was seldom a major problem. But in the fifteenth century, long ocean voyages in large sailing ships heralded not only the Age of Discovery but also reliance on preserved food.

Bigger ships had to carry cargo and arms, a larger crew to handle the more complicated rigging and sails, and food and water for months at sea. An increase in the number of decks and men and the amount of supplies inevitably translated into cramped sleeping and living conditions for the crew, poor ventilation, and a subsequent increase in infectious diseases and respiratory conditions. Consumption (tuberculosis) and the "bloody flux" (a pernicious form of diarrhea) were common as, no doubt, were body and head lice, scabies, and other contagious skin conditions.

The standard sailor's food did nothing to improve his health. Two major factors dictated the seafaring diet. Firstly, aboard wooden ships it was extremely difficult to keep anything, including food, dry and mold free. Water was absorbed through wooden hulls, as the only water-proofing material available was pitch, a dark-colored, sticky resin obtained as a by-product of charcoal manufacture, applied to the outside of the hull. The inside of the hull, particularly where ventilation was poor, would have been extremely humid. Many accounts of sailing journeys describe incessant dampness, as mold and mildew grew on clothing, on leather boots and belts, on bedding, and on books. The standard sailor's fare was salted beef or pork and ship's biscuits known as hardtack, a mixture of flour and water without salt that was baked rock hard and used as a substitute for bread. Hardtack had the desirable characteristic of being relatively immune to mildew. It was baked to such a degree of hardness that it remained edible for

Vocabulary
replenished (ri plen′ isht) *v.* made complete or full again

incessant (in ses′ ənt) *adj.* not stopping; constant

6 **Reading Check**
What problems did the lack of vitamin C in sailors' diets cause?

5 Reading Skill
Cause and Effect

1. Have students read the bracketed text silently. Then, **ask:** Why did the oar-propelled ships and small sailing boats stay close to land?
   Answer: These vessels could not handle the rough seas and swells of the open ocean.
2. **Ask** students: What effect did the use of oar-propelled ships and small sailing boats have on food supplies for sailors in the past?
   Answer: By having to stay close to the land, sailors were able to replenish their fresh food supplies regularly.
3. Have students suggest other effects that this situation may have caused.
   Possible response: Sailors could sleep on land, overcome seasickness, or maintain contact with the people living on the land.

6 Reading Check
Answer: The lack of vitamin C brought on scurvy, which caused many physical symptoms, depression, and usually death by infection or heart failure.

Differentiated Instruction for Universal Access

Strategy for Less Proficient Readers
Students may have difficulty understanding the authors' purpose in an essay. Ask students to reread this page, making lists of details that the authors have included. Explain that these details early in the essay will probably play an important role in the authors' purpose. Make sure students note that ships were bigger, crews were larger, and more food and water had to be on board for months at sea. As students read ahead, encourage them to track how these details contribute to future effects.

EL Support for English Learners
"Making History With Vitamin C" contains some unfamiliar vocabulary, including seafaring and medical terms. Students will benefit from following along in their text as they listen to the recording of the selection on the ***Hear It!* Audio CD**. Pause the recording as necessary to clarify particular words and phrases.

PHLit Online!
This selection is available in interactive format in the **Enriched Online Student Edition**, **www.PHLitOnline.com**, which includes a thematically related video and writing prompt and an interactive graphic organizer.

7 Connecting to the Big Question

1. Explain that even when certain truths are known or widely accepted, some people still choose to deny them.
2. Have students read the bracketed text. Ask volunteers to describe the information available about the dangers of scurvy and the ways of preventing it.
3. **Ask:** If these measures had been taken, what do you think the impact would have been on a country's ability to operate its ships? Explain.
   Possible response: A country would have been able to operate more ships because there would have been more people willing to sail on voyages.
4. Invite students to discuss why people might have resorted to violent measures such as press-gangs rather than paying attention to the realities of scurvy prevention.

Vocabulary
alleviate (ə lē′ vē āt′)
v. to lighten or relieve

decades, but it was extremely difficult to bite into, especially for those whose gums were inflamed by the onset of scurvy. Typically, ship's biscuits were weevil-infested, a circumstance that was actually welcomed by sailors as the weevil holes increased porosity and made the biscuits easier to break and chew.

The second factor governing diet on wooden ships was the fear of fire. Wooden construction and liberal use of highly combustible pitch meant that constant diligence was necessary to prevent fire at sea. For this reason the only fire permitted on board was in the galley and then only in relatively calm weather. At the first sign of foul weather, galley fires would be extinguished until the storm was over. Cooking was often not possible for days at a time. Salted meat could not be simmered in water for the hours necessary to reduce its saltiness; nor could ship's biscuits be made at least somewhat palatable by dunking them in hot stew or broth.

At the outset of a voyage provisions would be taken on board: butter, cheese, vinegar, bread, dried peas, beer, and rum. The butter was soon rancid, the bread moldy, the dried peas weevil infested, the cheeses hard, and the beer sour. None of these items provided vitamin C, so signs of scurvy were often evident after as little as six weeks out of port. Was it any wonder that the navies of European countries had to resort to the press-gang[2] as a means of manning their ships?

Scurvy's toll on the lives and health of sailors is recorded in the logs of early voyages. By the time the Portuguese explorer Vasco da Gama sailed around the southern tip of Africa in 1497, one hundred of his 160-member crew had died from scurvy. Reports exist of the discovery of ships adrift at sea with entire crews dead from 7
the disease. It is estimated that for centuries scurvy was responsible for more death at sea than all other causes; more than the combined total of naval battles, piracy, shipwrecks, and other illnesses.

Astonishingly, preventives and remedies for scurvy during these years were known—but largely ignored. As early as the fifth century, the Chinese were growing fresh ginger in pots on board their ships. The idea that fresh fruit and vegetables could alleviate symptoms of scurvy was, no doubt, available to other countries in Southeast Asia in contact with Chinese trading vessels. It would have been passed on to the Dutch

2. **press-gang** men who round up other men to force them into naval or military service.

Vocabulary Development

Expressive Vocabulary

To help students broaden their expressive vocabulary, encourage them to use the following words as they discuss the selection: *unknowingly*, *relied*, *dependent*, and *revolutionize*. Have them complete these sentence starters:

1. Shipowners *unknowingly* sacrificed . . .
2. To sail for distances, sea captains *relied* on . . .
3. European navies became *dependent* upon press-gangs to man their ships because . . .
4. An onboard cure for scurvy would *revolutionize* . . .

Challenge students to use these words as you continue to discuss the essay.

and been reported by them to other Europeans as, by 1601, the first fleet of the English East India Company is known to have collected oranges and lemons at Madagascar[3] on their way to the East. This small squadron of four ships was under the command of Captain James Lancaster, who carried bottled lemon juice with him on his flagship, the *Dragon*. Anyone who showed signs of scurvy was dosed with three teaspoons of lemon juice every morning.
8 On arrival at the Cape of Good Hope, none of the men on board the *Dragon* was suffering from scurvy, but the toll on the other three ships was significant. Despite Lancaster's instructions and example, nearly a quarter of the total crew of this expedition died from scurvy—and not one of these deaths was on his flagship.

Some sixty-five years earlier the crew members on French explorer Jacques Cartier's second expedition to Newfoundland and Quebec were badly affected by a severe outbreak of scurvy, resulting in many deaths. An infusion of needles of the spruce tree, a remedy suggested by the local Indians, was tried with seemingly miraculous results. Almost overnight the symptoms were said to lessen and the disease rapidly disappeared. In 1593 Sir Richard Hawkins, an admiral of the British navy, claimed that within his own experience at least ten thousand men had died at sea from scurvy, but that lemon juice would have been an immediately effective cure.

There were even published accounts of successful treatments of scurvy. In 1617, John Woodall's *The Surgeon's Mate* described lemon juice as being prescribed for both cure and prevention. Eighty years later Dr. William Cockburn's *Sea Diseases, or the Treatise of their Nature, Cause and Cure* recommended fresh fruits and vegetables. Other suggestions such as vinegar, salt water, cinnamon, and whey were quite useless and may have **obscured** the correct action.

It was not until the middle of the following century that the effectiveness of citrus juice was proven in the first controlled clinical studies of scurvy. Although the numbers involved were very small, the conclusion was obvious. In 1747, James Lind, a Scottish naval surgeon at sea in the *Salisbury*, chose twelve of the crew suffering from scurvy for his experiment. He selected men whose symptoms seemed as similar as possible. He had them all eat the same diet: not the standard salted meat and hardtack, which these patients would have found very difficult to chew, but sweetened gruel, mutton broth, boiled biscuits, barley, sago, rice, raisins, currants, and wine. Lind added various supplements to this

3. **Madagascar** (mad´ ə gas´ kər) an island in the Indian Ocean off the southeast coast of Africa.

Literary Analysis
Author's Purpose Which details in this paragraph support the idea that vitamin C is important?

Vocabulary
obscured (əb skyo͞ord´) *v.* made dark; blocked from view; hid

9 **Reading Check**
What factors limited sailors' diets on board a ship?

8 Literary Analysis
Author's Purpose

Have students recall the thesis of the essay.
Answer: Vitamin C, or the lack of it, had an effect on early explorations of the world.

Monitor Progress: Remind students that the authors are concerned not only with describing the effect of scurvy on sailors, but also how it was treated and cured. Point out to students that lemon juice has vitamin C. Then, **ask** the Literary Analysis question: Which details in this paragraph support the idea that vitamin C is important?
Answer: The importance of vitamin C is demonstrated by the fact that sailors who took lemon juice, which is high in vitamin C, survived, while those who did not, died.

Reteach: If students have difficulty identifying the details that support the thesis statement, have them reread the bracketed text. Help them to see that there are several facts, or details, in the passage. Have students write down the details, and then have them chart whether each detail informs the reader, whether it also persuades the reader, and whether or not the detail supports the thesis. To help students better understand this concept, show them the completed **Literary Analysis Graphic Organizer A** (*Graphic Organizer Transparencies*, p. 29).

9 Reading Check

Answer: Spoilage, distance between supply points, and limited onboard storage space were all factors that limited sailors' diets.

PROFESSIONAL DEVELOPMENT
APPLY THE STRATEGY

Before reading "Making History with Vitamin C", write the Tier 2 vocabulary words *deficiency, replenished, incessant, obscured* on the board. Read the words aloud to the students. Then ask students to read the words as you point to them. Have students look for these words in the text and ask them to interpret the meaning of the words from their context. Then, in their vocabulary journal, have students write down the word and their interpretation of its meaning.

After reading, ask students to explain what they think each word means. Provide feedback, assuring that students are correct.

Ask students to listen for words that mean the same thing as *deficiency, replenished, incessant*, and *obscured* as they hear people talk at home or on television. Ask them to keep a list of these words.

For more of Sharon Vaughn's strategies, see the Professional Development essay, pp. 2c–2d.

⑩ Literary Analysis
Author's Purpose

1. Remind students that sometimes an author's purpose is not revealed right at the beginning of a piece of writing.
2. Read aloud the bracketed text. Then, **ask**: What words suggest that the authors' purpose here is to comment on events, not just to give information?
Answer: The words "why wasn't it acted upon," "sadly," and "though proven" indicate that the authors are commenting on the situation of scurvy treatments being ignored.

carbohydrate-based regime. Two of the sailors each received a quart of cider daily. Two others were dosed with vinegar, and another unfortunate pair received diluted elixir of vitriol (or sulfuric acid). Two more were required to drink half a pint of seawater daily, and another two were fed a concoction of nutmeg, garlic, mustard seed, gum myrrh, cream of tartar, and barley water. The lucky remaining pair was issued daily two oranges and one lemon each.

The results were sudden and visible and what we would expect with today's knowledge. Within six days the men who received the citrus fruit were fit for duty. Hopefully, the other ten sailors were then taken off their seawater, nutmeg, or sulfuric acid regimes and also supplied with lemons and oranges. Lind's results were published in *A Treatise of Scurvy*, but it was another forty years before the British navy began the **compulsory** issue of lemon juice.

Vocabulary
compulsory (kəm pul′ sə rē) *adj.* required, mandatory

⑩ If an effective treatment for scurvy was known, why wasn't it acted upon and used routinely? Sadly, the remedy for scurvy, though proven, seems to have not been recognized or believed. A widely held theory blamed scurvy on a diet of either too much salted meat or not enough fresh meat rather than a lack of fresh fruit and vegetables. Also, there was a logistical problem: it was difficult to keep fresh citrus fruit or juice for weeks at a time. Attempts were made to concentrate and preserve lemon juice, but such procedures were time consuming, costly, and perhaps not very effective, as we now know that vitamin C is easily destroyed by heat and light and that long-term storage reduces the amount in fruits and vegetables.

Because of expense and inconvenience, naval officers, physicians, the British admiralty, and shipowners could see no way of growing sufficient greens or citrus fruit on heavily manned vessels. Precious cargo space would have to be used for this purpose. Fresh or preserved citrus fruit was expensive, especially if it was to be allocated daily as a preventive measure. Economy and the profit margin ruled—although, in hindsight, it does seem that this was a false economy. Ships had to be manned above capacity to allow for a 30, 40 or even 50 percent death rate from scurvy. Even without a high death rate, the effectiveness of a crew suffering from scurvy would have been remarkably low. And then there was the humane factor—rarely considered during these centuries.

Think Aloud

Vocabulary: Using Context
Direct students' attention to the word *intransigence* at the beginning of the first paragraph on p. 173. Use the following "think aloud" to model how to use context to infer the meaning of an unknown word:

In this sentence, the word *intransigence* is used to describe something about an average crew. The phrases "They were used to eating" and "although they complained" indicate something about the crew's eating habits that was not helpful in curbing the spread of scurvy. Further into the paragraph, I see that the crews "would not have been interested" in fresh vegetables, and they "wanted meat and more meat." From previous information in the essay, I know that meat is not a source of vitamin C, and vitamin C stops the spread of scurvy.

So I think the word *intransigence* means "a stubbornness or unwillingness" by the crew to change their diet.

Another element was the intransigence of the average crew. They were used to eating the standard ship's fare, and although they complained about the monotonous diet of salt meat and ship's biscuit when they were at sea, what they wanted in port was lots of fresh meat, fresh bread, cheese, butter, and good beer. Even if fresh fruit and vegetables were available, the majority of the crew would not have been interested in a quick stir-fry of tender crunchy greens. They wanted meat and more meat—boiled, stewed, or roasted. ⓫ The officers, who generally came from a higher social class, where a wider and more varied diet was common, would have found eating fruit and vegetables in port to be normal and probably highly acceptable. It would not have been unusual for them to be interested in trying exotic new foodstuffs to be found in the locales where they made landfall. Tamarinds, limes, and other fruits high in vitamin C would have been used in the local cuisine that they, unlike the crew, might try. Scurvy was thus usually less of a problem among a ship's officers.

Reading Skill
Cause and Effect
In your own words, explain why the crew's food preferences were a cause of scurvy.

> If an effective treatment for scurvy was known, why wasn't it acted upon and used routinely?

Cook: Hundreds—Scurvy: Nil

James Cook of the British Royal Navy was the first ship's captain to ensure that his crews remained scurvy free. Cook is sometimes associated with the discovery of antiscorbutics, as scurvy-curing foods are called, but his true achievement lay in the fact that he insisted on maintaining high levels of diet and hygiene aboard all his vessels. The result of his meticulous standards was an extraordinarily good level of health and a low mortality rate among his crew. Cook entered the navy at the relatively late age of twenty-seven, but his previous nine years of experience sailing as a merchant seaman mate in the North Sea and the Baltic, his intelligence, and his innate seamanship combined to ensure his rapid promotion within the naval ranks. His first experience with scurvy came aboard the *Pembroke*, in 1758, on his initial voyage across the Atlantic Ocean to Canada to challenge the French hold on the St. Lawrence River. Cook was alarmed by the devastation this common affliction caused and appalled that the deaths of so many crew, the dangerous reduction of working efficiency, and even actual loss of ships were generally accepted as inevitable.

His experience exploring and mapping around Nova Scotia, the Gulf of St. Lawrence, and Newfoundland and his accurate observations of the eclipse of the sun greatly impressed the Royal Society, a body founded in 1645 with the aim of "improving natural knowledge." He was granted command of the ship *Endeavour* and instructed to explore and chart the southern oceans, to investigate

⓬ **Reading Check**
What was James Cook's contribution to maintaining sailors' health?

⓫ Reading Skill
Cause and Effect

1. Remind students that an effect can result due to a combination of many actions or behaviors. Note that the lack of sources of vitamin C on ships was the result of many factors.
2. Read aloud the bracketed text. Then, **ask** the Reading Skill question: In your own words, explain why the crew's food preferences were a cause of scurvy.
Possible response: Sailors were used to a meat and biscuit diet. When they had the chance to eat fresh food, they preferred fresh meat, bread, cheese, butter, and beer, all foods that do not contain sufficient amounts of vitamin C.

⓬ Reading Check

Answer: He insisted upon high levels of diet and hygiene aboard his vessels.

Fluency

Distribute copies of p. 173, and pair students. Have partners take turns reading paragraphs aloud. While one partner reads, the other should mark any words with which the one reading has difficulty. Circulate to monitor the fluency of students' reading. Collect students' marked-up copies of the story, and review difficult words and passages with the class. The word *meticulous* might be challenging for some students:

If students have difficulty pronouncing the word *meticulous*, show them how to cover up parts of the word with their thumb. Then, show students how to pronounce each part, moving their thumb along the word to the right as they do. Finally, have them read the word again, this time blending the parts together.

⓭ Humanities

James Cook (1728–1779)
by Nathaniel Dance

Nathaniel Dance (1735–1811) was born in London. He began as a portrait painter, based in Rome, but he wanted to paint historical enactments. During most of his career, he combined the two by painting portraits of famous people, including the Duke of York, King George III, and Queen Charlotte.

Use these questions for discussion:

- Because Dance painted portraits of historical figures, what details in this portrait of Cook hint at the time period in which it was painted?
  Possible response: Cook's wig and the style of his formal military wear give hints as to when the painting might have been created.
- What does the painting suggest about Dance's impression of Cook?
  Possible response: Dance likely had a good impression of Cook because he creates a handsome image of an explorer who has a ruddy complexion from sun and sea.

⓮ Critical Viewing

Answer: Yes; in the portrait, Cook appears to be clean and healthy, and he has a look of firm but gentle authority on his face.

new plants and animals, and to make astronomical observations of the transit of planets across the sun.

Less known but nonetheless compelling reasons for this voyage and for Cook's subsequent later voyages were political. Taking possession in the name of Britain of already discovered lands; claiming of new lands still to be discovered, including Terra Australis Incognita, the great southern continent; and the hopes of finding a Northwest Passage were all on the minds of the admiralty. That Cook was able to complete so many of these objectives depended to a large degree on ascorbic acid.

⓭

Consider the scenario on June 10, 1770, when the *Endeavour* ran aground on coral of the Great Barrier Reef just south of present-day Cooktown, in northern Queensland, Australia. It was a near catastrophe. The ship had struck at high water; a resulting hole in the hull necessitated drastic measures. In order to lighten the ship, the entire crew heaved overboard everything that could be spared. For twenty-three hours straight they manned the pumps as seawater leaked inexorably into the hold, hauling desperately on cables and anchor in an attempt to plug the hole by fothering, a temporary method of mending a hole by drawing a heavy sail under the hull. Incredible effort, superb seamanship, and good fortune prevailed. The ship eventually slid off the reef and was beached for repairs. It had been a very close call—one that an exhausted, scurvy-inflicted crew could not have summoned the energy to answer.

⓮ ▲ **Critical Viewing**
Do the actions of James Cook described in the essay seem to fit with his personality as suggested by this painting? Explain. **[Connect]**

⓯ A healthy, well-functioning crew was essential for Cook to accomplish what he did on his voyages. This fact was recognized by the Royal Society when it awarded him its highest honor, the Copley gold medal, not for his navigational feats but for his demonstration that scurvy was not an inevitable companion on long ocean voyages. Cook's methods were simple. He insisted on maintaining cleanliness throughout the ship, especially in the tight confines of the seamen's quarters. All hands were required to wash their clothes regularly, to air and dry their bedding when the weather permitted, to fumigate between decks, and in general to live up to the meaning of the term *shipshape*. When it was not possible to obtain the fresh fruit and vegetables he thought necessary for a balanced diet, he required that his men eat the sauerkraut he had included in the ship's provisions. Cook touched land at every

Vocabulary Development

Vocabulary Knowledge Rating
When students have completed reading and discussing "Making History With Vitamin C," have them take out their **Vocabulary Knowledge Rating Chart** for this essay. Read the words aloud once more, and have students rate their knowledge of the words again in the After Reading column. Clarify any words that are still problematic. Have students write their own definition and example or sentence in the appropriate column. Then, have students complete the Vocabulary Practice activities at the end of the selection. Encourage students to use the words in further discussion and written work about this essay. Remind them that they will be accountable for these words on the **Selection Test**, ***Unit 1 Resources***, pp. 206–208 or 209–211.

possible opportunity to replenish stores and gather local grasses (celery grass, scurvy grass) or plants from which he brewed teas.

This diet was not at all popular with the crew, accustomed as they were to the standard seamen's fare and reluctant to try anything new. But Cook was adamant. He and his officers also adhered to this diet, and it was by his example, authority, and
15 determination that his regimen was followed. There is no record that Cook had anyone flogged for refusing to eat sauerkraut or celery grass, but the crew knew the captain would not hesitate to prescribe the lash for opposing his rules. Cook also made use of a more subtle approach. He records that a "Sour Kroutt" prepared from local plants was initially made available only to the officers; within a week the lower ranks were clamoring for their share.

Success no doubt helped convince Cook's crew that their captain's strange obsession with what they ate was worthwhile. Cook never lost a single man to scurvy. On his first voyage of
17 almost three years, one-third of his crew died after contracting malaria or dysentery in Batavia (now Jakarta) in the Dutch East Indies (now Indonesia). On his second voyage from 1772 to 1775,
16

Reading Skill
Cause and Effect
What factors caused Cook to be successful in the Navy?

LITERATURE IN CONTEXT

History Connection

The Voyages of Captain James Cook (1728–1779)

First Voyage to the Pacific, 1768–1771: As first lieutenant of the ship *Endeavor,* Cook sails around the world from east to west; in New Zealand, he surveys the coast and proves it is not part of a vast southern continent.

Second Voyage to the Pacific, 1772–1775: As commander of the ship *Resolution,* he becomes the first navigator to cross the Antarctic Circle; he also charts Easter Island.

Third Voyage to the Pacific, 1776–1780: As commander of the *Resolution,* he explores Hawaii, which he names the Sandwich Islands.

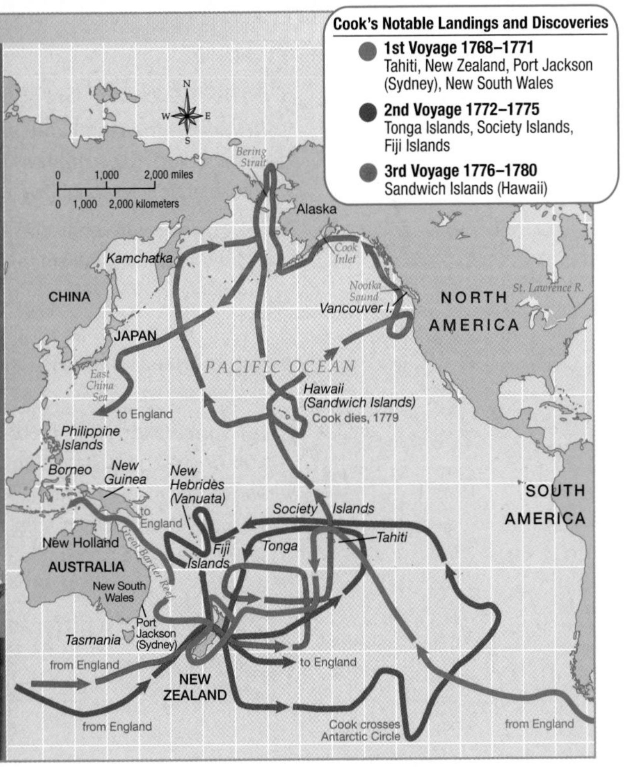

Connect to the Literature What important point in the essay does the length of Cook's voyages, shown on the map, support?

15 Reading Skill
Cause and Effect

1. Have students read the bracketed text, paying close attention to the number of details the authors include about James Cook.
2. Then, **ask** the Reading Skill question: What factors caused Cook to be successful in the Navy?
Possible response: Students may cite Cook's intelligence and seamanship and the fact that he maintained high standards of diet and hygiene on his ships.

16 Literature in Context

History Connection Students may notice a discrepancy in the dates in the Literature in Context feature. Captain James Cook's life ended in 1779, but his third voyage to the Pacific lasted until 1780. Cook's participation in this long voyage ended when he died in Hawaii as a result of a scuffle over a stolen boat. Cook's crew continued the voyage, stopping in China before continuing on to England.

Connect to Literature After students have reviewed Cook's voyages, **ask** the Connect to the Literature question: What important point in the essay does the length of Cook's voyages, shown on the map, support?

Possible response: The authors argue that scurvy was a cause of the widespread illness and death of sailors, resulting in ships being shorthanded, and shorthanded ships could not sail far. Cook, however, insisted on certain measures to prevent and treat scurvy; therefore, he was able to undertake long voyages to far-off lands, as shown on the map.

Concept Connector

Anticipation Guide

Have students return to their **Anticipation Guides** and respond to the statements again in the After Reading column. They may do this individually or in their original groups. Then, lead a class discussion, probing for what students have learned that confirms or invalidates each statement. Encourage students to cite specific details, quotations, or other evidence from the text to support their responses to each statement.

Writing About the Big Question

Have students compare their responses to the sentence starter they completed before reading "Making History With Vitamin C" with their ideas afterwards. Ask them to explain whether their thoughts have changed.

Reading Skill Graphic Organizer

Ask students to review the graphic organizers they completed to recognize causes and effects while reading. Show them the partially completed **Reading Skill Graphic Organizer A** (*Graphic Organizer Transparencies*, p. 26) as an example. Then, have students share the graphic organizers they completed.

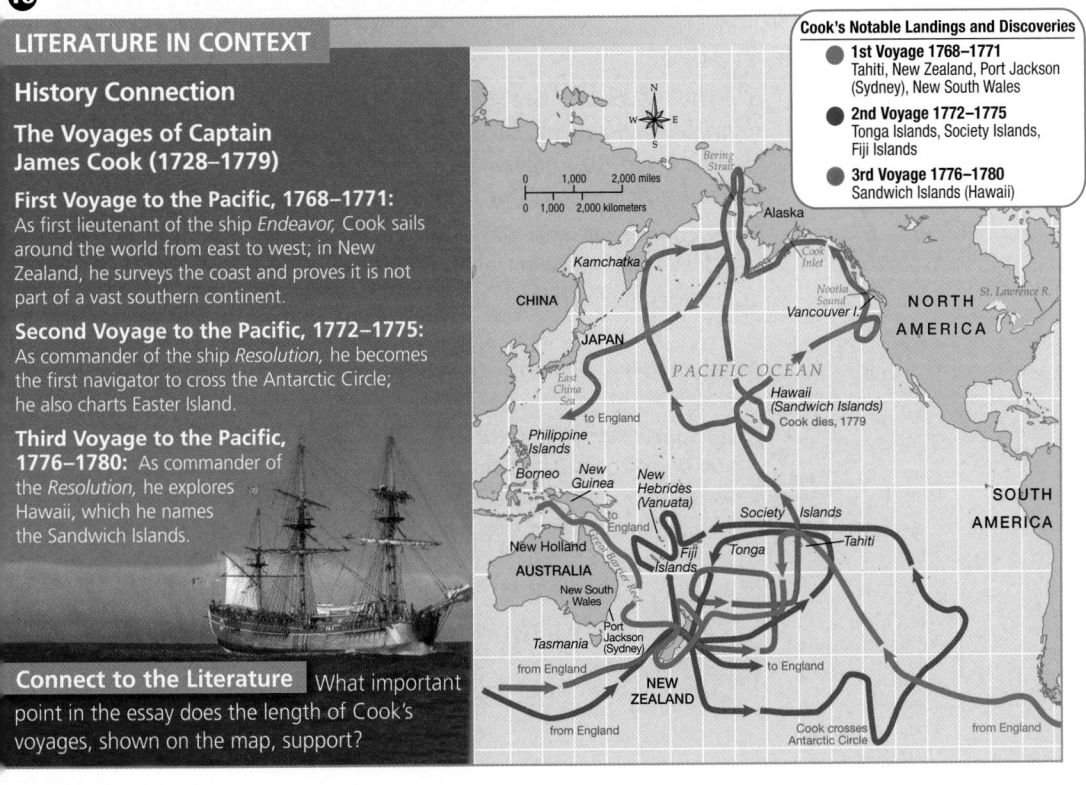

⑰ Literary Analysis
Author's Purpose

1. Have students read the bracketed text.
2. **Ask** the Literary Analysis question: What details about Captain Cook support the authors' thesis about the importance of vitamin C for the Age of Discovery?
   Possible response: Because Cook found ways to curb scurvy by keeping sources of vitamin C on his ships, he and his crews made many of the major explorations during the Age of Discovery.

ASSESS
Answers

Critical Thinking

1. **Possible response:** The most surprising fact was how quickly scurvy disappeared once vitamin C was introduced to sailors' diets.
2. (a) The standard sailor's diet included salted meat and hardtack. (b) The diet lacked vitamin C, which protected against scurvy.
3. (a) Shipowners wanted to load as much cargo as they could onto ships, so they avoided efforts to supply fresh fruit and vegetables. (b) **Possible response:** Often people have a stronger desire to make money than to save individual lives.
4. Captain Cook insisted on regular hygiene and good diets for his sailors, which reduced the spread of disease, including scurvy.
5. **Possible response:** (a) and (b) Refrigeration, freeze-drying, and air-tight containers would have helped preserve healthful foods.

Is there a difference between reality and truth?

Possible response: Sailors preferred meat and other foods lacking in vitamin C. Captains failed to see the truth about vitamin C's effectiveness because they had few opportunities to bring food with vitamin C on their long voyages.

Literary Analysis
Author's Purpose What details about Captain Cook support the authors' thesis about the importance of vitamin C for the Age of Discovery?

he lost one member of his crew to illness—but not to scurvy. Yet on that trip the crew of his companion vessel was badly affected by the problem. The commander, Tobias Furneaux, was severely reprimanded and instructed yet again by Cook on the need for preparation and administration of antiscorbutics. Thanks to vitamin C, the ascorbic acid molecule, Cook was able to compile an impressive list of accomplishments: the discovery of the Hawaiian Islands and the Great Barrier Reef, the first circumnavigation of New Zealand, the first charting of the coast of the Pacific Northwest, and first crossing of the Antarctic Circle. ⑰

Critical Thinking

1. **Respond:** Which fact in this essay most surprised you? Why?
2. **(a)** Before the eighteenth century, what was included in a typical sailor's diet? **(b) Analyze Cause and Effect:** Using details from the selection, explain why this diet led to widespread illness.
3. **(a) Connect:** In what way did shipowners' concern about saving money add to the problem of scurvy? **(b) Interpret:** What does the delay in preventing and treating scurvy reveal about human nature?
4. **Summarize:** What was Captain James Cook's contribution to eliminating scurvy?
5. **(a) Speculate:** What modern inventions related to food preparation or storage do you think would have been most helpful to navigators in the Age of Discovery? Why? **(b) Discuss:** Share your ideas with classmates in a group. Discuss the inventions, and select the three you think are most important. Present them to the class, explaining why the group chose them.

THE BIG ? **Is there a difference between reality and truth?** What are some reasons sailors and ships' captains failed to see the truth about the effectiveness of vitamin C?

Assessment Resources

Unit 1 Resources

L1 L2 EL **Selection Test A**, pp. 185–187. Administer Test A to less advanced readers and English learners.

L3 L4 **Selection Test B**, pp. 188–190. Administer Test B to on-level and more advanced students.

L3 L4 **Open-Book Test**, pp. 182–184. As an alternative, give the Open-Book Test.

All **Customizable Test Bank**

All **Self-tests**
Students may prepare for the **Selection Test** by taking the **Self-test** online.

PHLit Online! All assessment resources are available at **www.PHLitOnline.com.**

After You Read | Making History With Vitamin C

Literary Analysis: Author's Purpose

1. **(a)** What is the authors' main **purpose** for writing? Explain.
   (b) Write one sentence describing the authors' subject and their **thesis,** or main point.
2. **(a)** Use a diagram like the one shown to record details that **support** the authors' thesis. Include at least five details.
   (b) Explain how each detail supports the thesis.

3. Identify two examples that show how the writers' choice of words helps them accomplish their purpose.

Reading Skill: Cause and Effect

4. Why was scurvy was such a problem during the Age of Discovery? Name two **causes** from the text.
5. Explain the **effect** Captain Cook's shipboard dietary policies had on his voyages in the 1770s.

Vocabulary

Practice Words that have opposite meanings, such as *day* and *night* are called **antonyms.** For each numbered word here, choose the best antonym. Then, use each pair of antonyms in a sentence.

1. deficiency: (a) shortage, (b) obstacle, (c) surplus
2. replenished: (a) emptied, (b) forgave, (c) allowed
3. incessant: (a) failing, (b) brief, (c) filthy
4. alleviate: (a) oppose, (b) destroy, (c) increase
5. obscured: (a) revealed, (b) darkened, (c) pierced
6. compulsory: (a) necessary, (b) optional, (c) thoughtless

Word Study Use the context of the sentences and what you know about the **Latin prefix *ob-*** to explain your answer to each question.

1. Would a person who is *obstinate* be easily persuaded?
2. Would a lawyer *object* to a ruling in his favor?

Word Study

The **Latin prefix *ob-*** means "against," "over," or "in front of."

Challenge Explain how the prefix *ob-* contributes to the meanings of these words. Consult a dictionary if necessary.

obliterate
obstruction
obstacle

Answers

Literary Analysis

1. (a) The authors wanted to show how the level of vitamin C in the diet of early seafaring explorers affected the extent of exploration. (b) The lack of dietary vitamin C had important effects on exploration during the Age of Discovery.
2. **Possible response:** (a) **Detail:** Magellan lost 90 percent of his crew to scurvy. (b) This demonstrates the effects of scurvy on long voyages.

   For other sample answers, see ***Graphic Organizer Transparencies,*** **Literary Analysis Graphic Organizer A**, p. 29, and the **Additional Answers** section.
3. **Possible response:** In the first paragraph, the authors use the word *devastating* to emphasize the severity of scurvy. In addition, the authors use the word *astonishingly* to show that the primary concern of European shipowners was trade, not saving lives.

Reading Skill

4. The lack of knowledge about the cause of scurvy and long periods of time at sea were causes of scurvy's spread during the Age of Discovery.
5. Cook insisted on a high-quality diet on his ships, which kept his crew healthy and able to perform its tasks.

Vocabulary

Practice

1. (c) *surplus.* The ships left port with a *surplus* of salted meat, but by the time they reached America, the storage areas showed a deficiency of supplies.
2. (a) *emptied.* After a day of hard work, the grain silo that had been *emptied* by the end of winter was again replenished.
3. (b) *brief.* The neighbor's incessant hammering ended for a *brief* time late last night.
4. (c) *increase.* When the pain of my headache *increased,* I took medicine to alleviate the symptoms.
5. (a) *revealed.* When she took off the blindfold that obscured her

Answers continued

vision, a surprise birthday party was *revealed.*

6. (b) *optional.* I will not take the class if it is *optional,* but I will have no choice if it is compulsory.

Word Study

Sample answers:

1. No, the prefix *ob-* means "against," and *obstinate* means "stubborn or against yielding to persuasion." An obstinate person would be too stubborn to yield.
2. No, the prefix *ob-* means "against," and *object* means "to be against or oppose." A lawyer would gladly accept a ruling in his favor.

Word Study: Challenge

Sample answers:

When you *obliterate* something, you knock it over and destroy it. Standing in front of something is a form of *obstruction.* An *obstacle* is something that stands in front of something to block a path.

EXTEND/ASSESS

Answers

Grammar

1. Introduce the skill, using the instruction on the student page.
2. Discuss the definitions and the examples in the chart.

Think Aloud: Model the Skill

Model the skill of identifying relative pronouns, using the following "think aloud." Say to students:

> I use a shortcut to remember what the relative pronouns are. I call it *TW4*. It stands for *that* (the *T*) and *which, who, whom,* and *whose* (the 4 *W* words). When I write, TW4 reminds me to insert the proper pronouns:
>
> My dad, *who* is a writer, knows lots of words.
>
> The show, *which* lasted an hour, was interesting.

Think of TW4 as you complete the exercises.

WG Writing and Grammar, Grade 10

Students will find further instruction and practice with relative pronouns in Chapter 16, Section 2.

Practice A

1. circle *that*; underline *life* and *exists at the shore's edge*
2. circle *whose*; underline *starfish* and *reflection appears in the water*
3. circle *which*; underline *crab* and *was scurrying near the water*
4. circle *whose*; underline *Creatures* and *ancestors inhabited the sea for millions of years*

Challenge

Sample answers: under water that was clear as glass; the realities that possessed my mind

Practice B

Sample answers:

1. that helps us stay healthy
2. who did not eat well
3. who suffered greatly
4. whose crew ate better than most

Challenge

Sample answers: My breakfast, which I eat every morning, includes cereal. My Dad, who takes us to school, makes sure we have our lunch.

Integrated Language Skills

The Marginal World • Making History With Vitamin C

Grammar: Relative Pronouns

A **relative pronoun** is a pronoun that begins a subordinate clause. The relative pronoun relates the information in the clause to a noun or pronoun in the sentence.

Relative Pronouns

that	which	who	whom	whose
This is the shell ***that*** my brother gave me.	Cook insisted his crew drink lemon juice, ***which*** saved many lives.	Carson is the author ***who*** ignited environmental awareness in the public.	Cook was the captain with ***whom*** men preferred to serve.	Captains ***whose*** crews suffered from scurvy could have saved their men with lemon juice.

Practice A Copy the sentences. Circle the relative pronoun. Underline the noun and the clause that are connected by this relative pronoun.

1. Low tides expose the myriad of life that exists at the shore's edge.
2. A delicate starfish, whose reflection appears in the water, clings to the roof of the cave.
3. The little crab, which was scurrying near the water, was the only visible sign of life.
4. Creatures whose ancestors inhabited the sea for millions of years still exist in tidal waters.

Challenge In "The Marginal World," find two sentences that contain a relative pronoun. Write the relative pronouns and the nouns to which the relative pronouns relate.

Practice B Complete the following sentences using a relative pronoun and a clause that relates to the noun.

1. Vitamin C is an important nutrient ___________.
2. Early sailors, ___________, often died from scurvy.
3. Victims of scurvy, ___________, could have been saved by drinking lemon juice.
4. Captain Cook was a man ___________.

Challenge Using this sentence as a model, write two more sentences that contain relative pronouns and a clause. *Eating oranges, which contain a lot of vitamin C, prevents scurvy.*

WG Writing and Grammar Connection: Chapter 16, Section 2

Extend the Lesson

Sentence Modeling

I have seen hundreds of ghost crabs . . . but suddenly, I was filled with the odd sensation that for the first time I knew the creature in its own world—that I understood . . . ("The Marginal World")

The word *scurvy* is said to be derived from Norse, the language of the seafaring Viking warriors who, starting in the nineteenth century, raided . . . ("Making History With Vitamin C")

Ask students what they notice about the sentence. Elicit from them that the sentence has relative pronouns. Then, ask what else they notice. ("The Marginal World": The repeated pronoun *that* sets up a parallel structure and adds drama to the final clause. "Making History With Vitamin C": The pronoun *who* acts as a marker that readers will recall after the pause introduced by the phrase *starting in the ninth century*.)

Have students imitate the sentence in a sentence on a topic of their own choosing, matching each grammatical and stylistic feature discussed. Collect the sentences and share them with the class.

Writing

Both of these essays are on topics that could be presented well in a film version. Write a **proposal for a documentary** on life at the edge of the sea or on Cook's efforts to prevent scurvy. First, reread the essay you chose for ideas. Then, write your own essay describing the documentary you propose to create. Include these elements:

- the main impression you want to convery
- details about objects to be filmed and the places to be filmed
- summaries of the actions
- topics for comment by the narrator and actors
- quotations to use from the essay

Writing Workshop: *Work in Progress*

Prewriting for Cause and Effect Look at the Why List in your writing portfolio and identify a question to research. While researching, note the progression of causes and effects that produced the final result. Keep these Cause-Effect Notes in your writing portfolio.

Use this prewriting activity to prepare for the **Writing Workshop** on page 200.

Research and Technology

Using computer software, create a **spreadsheet** based on one of the selections you read.

- If you read "The Marginal World," create a **wildlife spreadsheet** to record information about living things you observe in your area. Include dates, times, and your observations. At the end of a week, record a conclusion about your environment, and compare your conclusion to Carson's.
- If you read "Making History With Vitamin C," create a personal **diet spreadsheet** by keeping track of what you eat for one week. Record the foods you eat at each meal. Review your log and compare your diet to that of typical sailors in Cook's day.

Use these suggestions when working on the assignment.

- Be sure to record as many details as possible for each observation. For example, if you are creating a wildlife spreadsheet, make sure to include detailed descriptions of all the plants, animals, and insects you observe. If you are creating a diet spreadsheet, record the ingredients of packaged foods.
- Review all your data carefully and check to be sure that your conclusions follow logically from the data you have recorded.

PHLit Online!
www.PHLitOnline.com
- Interactive graphic organizers
- Grammar tutorial
- Interactive journals

EXTEND/ASSESS

Writing

1. Review the assignment, using the instruction on the student page.
2. To guide students in writing a documentary proposal, give them the **Support for Writing**, p. 201 in *Unit 1 Resources.*
3. To evaluate students' proposals, use the Persuasive Essay rubrics, pp. 230–231 in *Professional Development Guidebook*. In addition, you might also evaluate the proposal for professional tone.

Six Traits Focus

✔	Ideas	✔	Word Choice
✔	Organization		Sentence Fluency
	Voice		Conventions

Writing and Grammar, Grade 10

Students will find additional instruction on persuasive writing in Chapter 7.

Writing Workshop
Work in Progress

Have students save their completed Cause-Effect Notes in their portfolios. They will use them later as they complete the Writing Workshop assignment (see pp. 200–207).

Research and Technology

1. Review the assignment, using the instruction on the student page.
2. Have students complete the **Support for Extend Your Learning** page (*Unit 1 Resources*, p. 202).

Teaching Resources

Unit 1 Resources
- L3 L4 **Integrated Language Skills: Grammar,** p. 200
- L3 L4 **Support for Writing,** p. 201
- L3 L4 **Support for Extend Your Learning,** p. 202
- L4 **Enrichment,** pp. 181 and 199

Enriched Online Student Edition
Available under After You Read for this selection:
- All **Interactive Grammar Tutorial**
- L3 L4 **Internet Research Activity**

Professional Development Guidebook
Rubrics for Persuasive Essay, pp. 230–231

PHLit Online! All print and digital resources are available at **www.PHLitOnline.com.** Online resources accessible by students are noted on the student page.

MONITORING PROGRESS

Using the Test Practice

In this two-page Test Practice, students apply the reading skill for the first half of Unit 1 to a passage of fiction and a passage of nonfiction.

Review this skill, recognizing cause and effect, and then administer the test. For more guidance, consult the ***Classroom Strategies and Teaching Routines*** card on administering timed tests.

ASSESS

Answers

Answers With Explanations

1. B—Lisa catches George's cold, which leads to her missing the exam. *Incorrect answers:* A—Lisa never studied with Keisha because of her cold. C—Lisa missed the exam, one effect of her cold. D—Missing school was the effect of Lisa's cold; not its cause.
2. A—Lisa's nervousness may have made her more susceptible to catching a cold. *Incorrect answers:* B—Lisa woke up with a cold after a night's rest. C—George's cold is the direct cause of Lisa's cold, not indirect. D—A sore throat is a symptom, not a cause of a cold.
3. A—Lisa's cold is the effect of George's cold; it is also the cause of her missing school and an exam. *Incorrect answers:* B—George's cold is the cause of Lisa's cold; it is the effect of an earlier event not told in the story. C— Having to make up the exam is only an effect of Lisa's cold; not a cause of anything. D—Keisha staying in bed is an effect of catching a cold; not a cause of anything.
4. C—Both Keisha and Lisa stay home from school because of the cold. *Incorrect answers:* A—A sick brother, George, is the cause of both colds; not an effect. B— The story doesn't mention a trip to the doctor. D— The story doesn't say how the girls do on the test.

Test Practice: Reading

Cause and Effect

Fiction Selection

Directions: *Read the selection. Then, answer the questions.*

"Ah-choo!" Lisa heard her brother George sneezing. He had been ill for two days, and Lisa could feel her throat getting itchy. "I knew I'd catch his cold," Lisa told her friend Keisha. "If he has a virus, I get it." Still, Lisa knew she could not miss school. "I need to review for the geometry exam tomorrow," she told her mother. "Keisha and I are studying after class."

"Okay, but be home early. If you don't get more rest, you will catch George's cold," her mother replied.

The next morning Lisa woke up with a throbbing headache. Her throat ached and she began sneezing and coughing.

"It looks like you're staying home today," her mother said. "You'll just have to miss the exam and make it up later."

That evening, Lisa phoned Keisha. "How was the exam?" asked Lisa.

"I didn't go to school," Keisha replied, wheezing. "I have a cold, too."

"Great!" said Lisa. "We'll both spend the weekend in bed and then have to make up the exam on Monday. And all because of George!"

1. Which event occurs first?

A. Lisa studies with Keisha for the exam.
B. George has a cold.
C. Lisa has a geometry exam.
D. Lisa misses school.

2. What does Lisa suspect is causing her itchy throat?

A. anxiety about her geometry exam
B. lack of rest.
C. an oncoming cold
D. a sore throat

3. Which event is both a cause and an effect?

A. Lisa catches a cold.
B. George has a cold.
C. Lisa makes up a math exam.
D. Keisha spends the weekend in bed.

4. Which effect of the cold do both Lisa and Keisha experience?

A. a sick brother
B. a trip to the doctor
C. a day home from school
D. a failed geometry exam

Writing for Assessment

In a paragraph, describe the chain of events that occurs in this passage. What additional effects might George's cold have on his school, community, or family?

Writing for Assessment

Students should connect George's cold to Lisa and Keisha getting sick, staying home, and missing an exam. They should recognize the potential risk of transmitting the cold to family, school members, and others in the community, as well as other related effects such as the parents needing to miss work to take care of their sick children.

Strategies for Test Taking

Remind students to use their time wisely. They should not spend too much time on one item. If they are not sure of an answer, they can eliminate one or more wrong choices and choose the best answer. Or, they can skip a question and go back if they have time.

Nonfiction Selection

Directions: *Read the selection. Then, answer the questions.*

Most people occasionally suffer from the common cold. Although a cold is rarely serious, it can be uncomfortable and downright annoying. The first signs of a cold are a runny nose and sneezing, which are often followed by coughing, headache, fatigue, sore throat, and sometimes chills. Usually, no fever is involved.

Colds are caused by viruses. As many as 200 different viruses can cause colds. Colds are passed from one person to another. In fact, people can be carriers of cold viruses without having cold symptoms themselves. It takes only a short time to catch a cold from another person—as little as one to four days. Many colds are contracted in the fall, and cold epidemics can continue throughout the winter months. Scientists believe most colds occur during the cooler months because people spend more time indoors and have closer contact with people carrying cold viruses. No medicine is available that can cure the cold. Cold medicines simply help relieve cold symptoms. The most common treatment is resting and drinking fluids.

1. Which of the following is the direct cause of a cold?

A. contact with a sick person
B. staying indoors
C. a virus
D. cold weather

2. Which of the following is an effect of a cold?

A. a high fever
B. being confined to bed
C. headache and tiredness
D. drinking more fluids

3. According to the selection, which of the following causes people to catch colds?

A. change of seasons
B. contact with someone carrying the cold virus
C. being outside in cold weather
D. sneezing and coughing

4. Which of the following helps cure a cold?

A. getting plenty of rest
B. taking cold medicine
C. staying indoors
D. none of the above

Writing for Assessment

Connecting Across Texts
Lisa gets angry with her brother when she misses a geometry exam. In a paragraph, explain whether she is right to feel this way. Use details from each passage to support your response.

PHLit Online!
www.PHLitOnline.com
- Online practice
- Instant feedback

Differentiated Instruction for Universal Access

EL Strategy for English Learners

Explain difficult vocabulary and terms to ensure that students understand each question. Tell them that the word *initial* (item 1, page 180) means "original" or "first"; the story has several causes but the item asks about the first cause. Also clarify the difference between "indirect" causes and "direct" cause. Tell students that a direct cause leads immediately to an effect without anything in-between, while an indirect cause leads to an effect that is not immediate.

Strategy for Less Proficient Readers

Students may have difficulty with the Writing for Assessment assignment provided on page 181. Remind them that in order to successfully compare the two selections they must have a full understanding of what each selection is about and how they relate to one another. Suggest that students reread the fiction selection to draw parallels and form an opinion as to whether or not Lisa has the right to be angry with her brother.

ASSESS

Answers

Answers With Explanations

1. C—A virus is the direct cause, as stated in paragraph 2, sentence 1. *Incorrect answers:* A—Contact with a sick person indirectly leads to contact with the virus. C—Being indoors with a sick person indirectly leads to contact with the virus. D— Cold weather indirectly leads to more contact with people who have a virus.
2. C—According to the third sentence, these are signs, or effects, of a cold. *Incorrect answers:* A—According to the last sentence in paragraph 1, a fever is not typically an effect. B—Staying in bed is a helpful treatment, not an effect. D—Drinking fluids is a helpful treatment, not an effect.
3. B—Paragraph 2, sentence 3 states that colds are passed from other people. *Incorrect answers:* A—Contact with a cold virus causes colds; not change of seasons. C— Contact with people carrying cold virus is more common in cold weather, not the cold weather itself. D—Sneezing and coughing are symptoms, not causes, of colds.
4. D—There is no cure, only treatments, as the last three sentences show. *Incorrect answers:* A—The last sentence states that resting is a treatment, not a cure. B—Paragraph 2, sentence 7 states that medicines do not cure colds. C— Staying indoors is a possible treatment, not a cure.

Writing for Assessment

In their responses, students should reflect an understanding that cold viruses are passed from person to person and take only a short time to spread. If George treated his cold responsibly, he was not at fault. If he did not treat his cold responsibly, then he put Lisa at a greater risk which would give her the right to be angry.

PHLit Online!
Students may take the test in interactive format with instant feedback online at **www.PHLitOnline.com.**

Informational Texts

Meeting Your Standards

Students will

1. evaluate sources.
2. read and understand a Web site and a primary source.

Log on at *www.PHLitOnline.com* as a teacher for a lesson plan for Informational Texts.

Reading Skill

1. Introduce the skill, using the instruction on the student page.
2. Tell students that they will be learning how to evaluate sources as they read.

Think Aloud: Model the Skill

Model evaluating sources, using the following "think aloud." Say:

Suppose I am researching artificial sweeteners and I find a Web site claiming that they are a healthy alternative to sugar. Before I trust the information, I will examine the source. If it is a ".com" site that sells sweeteners, I will suspect that it is biased. If it is a ".org" site that researches nutrition, I will be more confident that the sources is reliable.

Is there a difference between reality and truth?

Have students look for details that describe life in ancient Egypt.

Multidraft Reading

Have students follow a multidraft reading protocol after they preview:

- **First reading:** Have students read for general understanding.
- **Second reading:** Have students evaluate the credibility of sources as they read.
- **Third reading:** Have students look for ways in which the author's perception of the truth may differ from their own.

Real-Life Reading

Web Site **Egyptology Resources**	Primary Source **Interactive Dig**

Reading Skill: Evaluate Sources

When researching a topic, remember that not all the material you find will be completely accurate. Before you use material from a Web site or a primary source, **analyze the credibility** of the source. Do this by evaluating the text's validity and reliability. Use the following checklist to help draw your conclusions.

Checklist for Evaluating Credibility of Sources

- ❑ Consider the author or sponsor. Might the source be biased?
- ❑ Check the information against another reliable source.
- ❑ Check the date of the document or the "last updated" field on the Web page.
- ❑ For Web sites, check the ending of the URL.
  - Educational and governmental (".edu" and ".gov")—generally reliable
  - Nonprofit (".org")—may be unbiased, or they may present only a specific point of view
  - Businesses and individuals (".com")—information of varying quality

THE BIG ?

Is there a difference between *reality* and *truth?*

The Web site and the primary source both give information about ancient Egypt. As you read, think about whether it is possible to get a completely accurate representation of what life in ancient Egypt was like.

Differentiated Instruction for Universal Access

Reading Support

Give students reading support with the appropriate version of the ***Reader's Notebooks:***

L2 L3 *Reader's Notebook*

L1 *Reader's Notebook: Adapted Version*

EL *Reader's Notebook: English Learner's Version*

PHLit Online! All student resources are available online at **www.PHLitOnline.com.**

The URL, or address, of the Web site, appears in the browser here. Check the ending of the URL to evaluate the site's credibility.

Web Site

Features:

- home page with links to other pages
- informative text for research or leisure reading
- photos or other images
- audio or video content may be included

EGYPTOLOGY RESOURCES

Popular local items

News & Gossip

Announcements

Bulletin Board

E-mail Addresses

Tomb of Sennefen

Beinlich Wordlist

Wilbour Library Acquisitions

Online Publications

Commercial Items

Server statistics

The first Egyptology site on the web

This page is set up with the kind assistance of the Newton Institute in the University of Cambridge to provide a World Wide Web resource for Egyptological information. The pages are not a publication of the Newton Institute, and all matters concerning them (e.g., comments, criticisms, and suggestions for items to include) should be sent to Nigel Strudwick.

Click here for guidelines on the format of material.

Click here for site history.

Main pages

Essential Resources

Institutions

Museums

Digs

Publishers, Booksellers

Journals, Magazines

Organizations, Societies

Interesting Egypt Pages

Personal Egypt Pages

Other Resources of Interest

Information on the individual who maintains this Web site is available by clicking his name. This information will help you evaluate the credibility of the site.

Differentiated Instruction for Universal Access

Strategy for Less Proficient Readers

Tell students that Web sites are often "busy," crammed with images and information that often make it hard to find the facts needed. Tell students to follow this general plan each time they open a Web site that is new to them:

1. Look at the URL address to make sure you are where you mean to be.
2. Read the different menu buttons. Look for these buttons on the top or at the sides.
3. Look for hot links, words (printed in color) or graphics that link to other information. (Don't click on them, just look at the options for now.)
4. Scroll to the bottom of the page to view everything significant.
5. Decide whether you want to look around only on the current page or which, if any, links or menu buttons you want to check out.
6. After you have found the information for which you are looking, close the Web site.

TEACH

About Web Sites

1. Review the features listed in the Web Site box with the class. **Ask** students to define the terms *Web site* and *URL*. **Possible response:** A Web site is a location connected to the Internet where pages are maintained, and a URL is the address, or location of, a file on the Web.
2. Tell students they will probably use Web sites as sources of information for school projects, so evaluating the sites' credibility will be important. **Ask** students which Web sites they enjoy. Encourage them to share the types of sites they enjoy, such as news, sports, and reference sites.
3. Talk to students about how to use a Web site. Suggest that for casual viewing, students may want to skim the information. In contrast, when doing research, they will need to read more carefully.

Evaluate Sources

1. Have students read "Egyptology Resources." **Ask** how they would evaluate the credibility of the source. Remind students to use the checklist on page 182. **Possible response:** Nigel Strudwick is the source of the information. He is affiliated with the University of Cambridge. The university would probably not lend its name to someone who is not reputable, so he is probably a reliable source.
2. **Ask** students whether they would check Nigel's details or just accept them as fact. **Possible response:** I would check his facts since he is an individual.
3. Direct students' attention to the links listed under the heading "Main pages." **Ask** students to identify a link that is likely to be reliable and one that is less likely to be reliable. Have them explain their choices. **Possible response:** The "Essential Resources" link is probably more reliable than the "Personal Egypt Pages." This seems like a personal site, whereas "Essential Resources" might be used regularly by people doing research.

Evaluate Sources

1. Remind students that this page is a link from the main "Egyptology Resources" page.
2. **Ask** students which sites would be most difficult for the typical American student to use.
   Possible response: Typical American students would probably find it difficult to get information from the Musées royaux, Museo Egizio, and Agyyptishes Museum Web sites because these are likely to be foreign language sites.
3. **Ask** students to infer how credible the museums' sites might be.
   Possible response: The museum sites probably contain credible information.
4. Point out to students that if the information they want is not on the Museums page, the link at the bottom will take them back to the main Egyptology Resources page.
5. **Ask** students if they know what the ABZU indexes are. If no one knows, have someone look it up on the Internet.
   Answer: The ABZU indexes is an Internet guide to resources for the study of the ancient Near East.

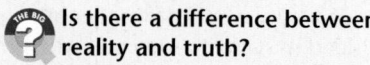

ASSESS/EXTEND

Answers

Is there a difference between reality and truth?

(a) **Possible response:** The university links should provide accurate and reliable information, as they are organizations dedicated to education. Additionally, the Egyptian links should provide the viewer with a truthful "insider's" perspective.

(b) **Possible response:** Some of the art museums may be more focused on art appreciation rather than providing factual information about life in ancient Egypt.

Egyptology Resources--resources for Ancient Egypt

Google

MUSEUMS ONLINE WITH EGYPTIAN COLLECTIONS

Many museums, of course, have WWW pages now. I have tried to select some of those which have more specific information on their Egyptian Collections, but I do also include the general Web presences of major museums with relevant material. Some of these links often go directly to the Egypt pages and bypass the home page. A more general set of links will be found in the ABZU indexes.

Each of these links brings users to the Web site of a museum that has Egyptian artifacts in its collection. Evaluate the credibility of any site you visit.

Egypt

- The Egyptian Museum, Cairo
- The Coptic Museum, Cairo

North America

- Museum of Fine Arts, Boston
- Metropolitan Museum, New York
- Michael C. Carlos Museum, Emory University, Atlanta
- Brooklyn Museum
- Oriental Institute, University of Chicago

Europe

- The British Museum, London COMPASS Project
- The Louvre, Paris
- Musées royaux d'art et d'art historie, Brussels
- Museo Egizio, Torino
- Agyptisches Museum und Papyrussammlung Berlin-Charlottenburg
- Allard Pierson Museum
- Carsten Niebuhr Institute, University of Copenhagen, Papyrus Collection

Back to Egyptology Resources home page

Is there a difference between reality and truth?

(a) Which links on this Web site would help you find the truth about ancient Egypt? **(b)** Which sites might be less reliable? Explain your responses.

Vocabulary Development

Vocabulary from Web Sites

Point out that Web sites often use vocabulary that is specific to one particular setting, in this case Egyptology. Guide students to understand the meaning of the following words that are used in "Egyptology Resources":

Egyptology: The study of Egyptian antiquities
acquisitions: something gained or brought into possession
presence: the condition of being at hand or existing.
relevant: being significant to
artifacts: something created by humans, usually for a practical purpose, that is of archaeological or historical significance

PHLit Online! **Vocabulary Development**, featuring tools, activities, and songs for studying vocabulary, is available at **www.PHLitOnline.com.**

Interactive Dig

Primary Source

Features:

- informative text used for reference or research
- first-person perspective
- accounts of events given by an active participant or an eyewitness

Narmer's Temple: Week 1

by Renée Friedman

After a hiatus of 13 years, we've returned to the Predynastic Temple at Hierakonpolis. Dating to around 3500 B.C., it is Egypt's oldest. Excavations here in 1985, 1986–1987, and 1989 had revealed about half of a large (presumably) oval courtyard walled by a wooden fence, onto which fronted a main shrine with a façade composed of four large wooden pillars—now marked by four enormous postholes.

Our first order of business was to remove the sand that had accumulated over the millennia over the unexcavated portion of the courtyard floor in order to determine the full architectural layout of the vast complex. Of special interest was the area between the entrance to the compound and the entrance to the main shrine, as this might be where important things happened. With over 80cm of sand and debris covering this possible processional corridor, it is no wonder that the area was not cleared earlier. The volume of debris meant a lot of work, but it also, we hope, meant that the temple deposits below had a good chance of being undisturbed.

We got to work immediately. With Ramadan coming up, it was a race against time. We excavate with local workmen, who have worked with us for over 30 years. They come from the nearby village and ride their donkeys to work each day, since we can provide miles of free parking. Michael Hoffman, who directed the excavations, began training the villagers in 1969 and working for the expedition has become a family tradition. Now we are working with the sons and grandsons of the original crew, who have worked their way up from basket boy to valued excavator. They are not only skilled, but also interested and proud of their own local heritage. Trained to note the slightest change in the soil, they can point out areas of compaction, or texture differences, disturbance, etc. In a sandy site, where excavation balks are hard to maintain, and a prehistoric site, where detailed observation is critical, they make our work possible.

The dig is described from a first-person perspective, which suggests the information is reliable.

About Primary Sources

1. Review Primary Sources with students. Explain that a primary source is an account of an experience written by a person who took part in or was present during an event.
2. **Ask** students when they might use primary sources. **Possible response:** Students may use primary sources when researching a topic or writing a report. Then, **ask** them to explain why a primary source would be the best source to use. **Possible response:** The information provided in the source is specific to their topic and most likely factual and reliable.
3. **Ask:** What is the most important characteristic of a primary source? **Answer:** The person writing the account has to be an eyewitness to the event. In some cases, such as a recording, it must be an authentic and unaltered record.

Evaluate Sources

1. Have students read "Interactive Dig." **Ask** students what details in the story can help them confirm that the account is a primary source. **Sample answer:** Dates and photographs can help prove the reliability of the source. Also, references to the other people who were present at the event can confirm an eyewitness account.
2. **Ask:** How does the vivid description of the activity in "Interactive Dig" indicate that it is a primary source? **Possible response:** The description is told in the first person and includes many details, so it is likely that the author participated in the activity.
3. **Ask** students if a primary source has to be written in the first person in order to be authentic. **Possible responses:** Many primary sources are written in the third person; not all primary sources are written, such as photographs or recordings taken at an event.

Differentiated Instruction for Universal Access

Enrichment for Gifted/Talented Students

Tell students that they will make a primary source account of an event or a special occasion in their own life. Point out that primary sources can be written, visual, or auditory. Suggest that students use photos, recordings, images, diary entries, letters, or anything that will show evidence of their eyewitness account. Students may want to include interviews or create drawings to go along with their account. Instruct students to be prepared to verify the credibility of their facts and details. Allow students to present their accounts in front of the class.

Evaluate Sources

1. **Ask:** What graphic elements do you see in the article, "Interactive Dig?" **Sample answer:** Pictures of objects, photos of the crew working, a journal account of "Week 1."
2. Next, have students think about the importance of these elements in a primary source. **Ask:** How do the elements help verify that this is a primary source? **Possible response:** The elements give evidence that the people the author describes were present at the events covered in the article.
3. **Ask** students to think about ways in which the primary source differs from the Web site. **Possible response:** The Web site offers a variety of research options. In contrast, the primary source offers a focused examination of an isolated experience.

Reflecting on the Reading Skill

Discuss with students the methods of evaluating sources. **Ask** if they found it easier to judge the credibility of a Web site or a primary source. Have them explain why.

Possible response: Students might say that they found is easier to judge the credibility of the Web site because it is affiliated with the University of Cambridge. Others may say they found the primary source to be more credible because it chronicles a firsthand account of the dig.

ASSESS/EXTEND

Answers

Is there a difference between reality and truth?

Possible response: The discoveries provide insight into the daily life and activities of ancient Egyptians. The author mentions popular everyday objects—stone vessels, potsherds, and lithics—and tells readers about a common tool they used: a crescent-shaped flint.

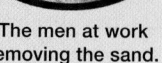

Interactive Dig

Our workers are very good-natured. During the first week, the plan was to remove as much of the windblown sand and mixed debris as possible. This made for somewhat boring work as once we reached a level that looked good, I made them stop, and move over to the next square (we dig in 10×10m squares divided into 5×5m subunits) and begin again, saving the detailed work, brush work, sieving, and other less arduous tasks for the fasting days of Ramadan.

In the first six digging days, working from six in the morning until noon, we managed to clear seven 5×5m squares of about 50cm of sand to layers that look promising. The sand over the courtyard floor, however, was not entirely devoid of interesting things. We found a number of fragments of once beautifully polished stone vessels made of exotic stones imported from the Red Sea hills—diorite, basalt, alabaster, marble. We also recovered a crescent drill of flint used in the manufacture of these stone vessels. It probably originated from the workshops that surround the temple complex. Microdrills for boring out beads, and fragments of carefully knapped bifacial knives also turned up. The fine micro-retouch on the edge of what may have been a lance is amazing.

These objects, however, are no longer in their original place because of fertilizer digging. In the early part of the last century and before, farmers mined the rich soil of archaeological deposits as fertilizer for their fields, which is called *sebakh* in Arabic. The decayed organic debris of ancient sites provided a supply of nitrogen, necessary for the crops and before chemical fertilizer was easily available, mining the ancient levels was the only alternative. As a result, the low desert at Hierakonpolis looks like the valleys of the moon, with sand-filled pits surrounded by mountains of discarded predynastic artifacts that were of no interest to the farmers, who only wanted the midden in which they were found. Piles of potsherds, animal bone, grinding stones, lithics, and assorted other wonderful things cover the site—over two square miles. It was years before I ever looked up while walking to work here—the wealth of goodies on the ground was riveting and after a good rain (like the one we had on our very first day this season!) or a major sand storm, new wonders can always be found.

The author demonstrates reliability by describing in detail how objects were found.

The photo and caption indicate that the author was present for the work being described.

The men at work removing the sand.

Is there a difference between reality and truth?
How do the discoveries described in this article help you understand the realities of life in ancient Egypt?

Vocabulary Development

Vocabulary from Earth Science

Students may benefit from identifying words in the selection that relate to the topic of Earth Science. Have students work in pairs to create a list of words that are unfamiliar to them. Then have them use a dictionary to define the words.

Possible words students might be unfamiliar with are: *soil, compaction, midden, diorite, basalt,* and *fertilizer.*

Test Practice: Informational Texts

Comparing Informational Texts

(a) Compare and contrast the possible disadvantages of using Web sites and primary sources for research. **(b)** Under what circumstances would you use either of these two sources?

Timed Writing

Write an Expository Essay

Format
The prompt calls for a brief essay. Therefore, you will need to present and support your ideas in three to five paragraphs.

Write a brief essay in which you evaluate the credibility of the Web site and the primary source document as sources of information on ancient Egypt. Note the features or techniques that make each source seem credible, as well as improvements that would make each source seem more credible. (20 minutes)

Academic Vocabulary
When you *evaluate* the credibility of a source, you analyze and make judgments about the source's quality and reliability.

5-Minute Planner

Complete these steps before you begin to write:

1. Read the prompt carefully. Notice the essay should **evaluate the sources,** not the content of the Web site and article.
2. Review the Web site and primary source document. Make notes about clues to each author's credibility and the features and techniques that make each source seem more cedible. **TIP** Credibility of primary sources written in the first person often depends upon the author's purpose in writing or biases the author may have.
3. Decide what elements of these two sources might be improved or what could be added to the sources that would improve their credibility. Note your observations and refer to your notes as you draft your essay.

ASSESS/EXTEND

Answers

Comparing Informational Texts

(a) **Possible responses:** Some Web sites might not be credible because they can be created and published by anyone. The disadvantages of using a primary source in research is that it might not include an outsider's unbiased perspective.
(b) **Possible response:** Web sites can be used as a quick and convenient way to locate many sources on a single topic. Primary source material can be used to get a focused eyewitness view when researching a particular historical topic.

Timed Writing

1. Before students complete the activity, guide them in identifying and analyzing key words and phrases in the prompt, highlighted on the student page.
2. Work with students to draw up guidelines for their essay based on the following key words:
   - **Focus** The essay should clearly evaluate the credibility of the Web site and the primary source.
   - **Organization** The essay should explain ways each source is credible and then provide suggestions on how to improve the credibility of each.
   - **Elaboration** The essay should cite details and features from each text that establish credibility and offer suggestions for improving credibility.
   - **Style** The audience is not specified, so a formal style is appropriate.
3. Have students use the 5-Minute Planner to structure their time.
4. Allow students 10 minutes to complete the assignment. Evaluate their work using the guidelines they have developed.

Extend the Lesson

Connecting to the Students' World

To give students more practice with Web sites and maps and to help them apply the lesson to their own world, divide students into small groups. Have each group select a local area or site to research. Have members of the group find articles about the area, maps of the area, and Web links related to the area. Students can look for information from the Internet, their Town Hall, local visitors' bureau, or their school office.

First, have students create a map of their area. Then, have members work together to create a Web site home page (or a representation of a Web site home page) about the area. Emphasize to students that their Web page should include graphic aids for navigation. For example, a search feature on the Web site and a legend on the map would be helpful to archaeologists who investigate the area in the future. Invite students to browse one another's home pages.

PRETEACH

Meeting Your Standards

Students will

1. analyze and respond to irony and paradox.
2. compare the effect of irony and paradox in fiction.
3. write a comparison of the authors' use of irony and paradox.

Log on as a teacher at ***www.PHLitOnline.com*** *for a detailed lesson plan for Comparing Literary Works.*

❶ Comparing Irony and Paradox

1. Introduce the skill, using the instruction on the student page.
2. Discuss the bulleted items.
3. Give students a copy of **Comparing Irony and Paradox Graphic Organizer B, *Graphic Organizer Transparencies*, p. 33.** Tell them they will fill it in with examples as they read.

Think Aloud: Model the Skill

Model a way of understanding irony and paradox. Say to the students:

Situational irony is when I search everywhere for my glasses—while I'm wearing them! Verbal irony is when I say "Thanks" for something being snatched out of my hand. Dramatic irony is when a cartoon character strikes a match to see why a room smells like gas. Boom! A paradox is when my friend tells me he's lying—is that a truth or a lie?

❷ Vocabulary

1. Have students say each word aloud.
2. Then, use the word in a sentence that defines the word. Repeat the sentence, now with the word missing, and have the class "fill in the blank" chorally.

For more guidance, see the ***Classroom Strategies and Teaching Routines*** card on introducing vocabulary.

Comparing Literary Works

Like the Sun • The Open Window

❶ Comparing Irony and Paradox

Irony is the effect created when a writer contrasts expectations and reality.

- In **situational irony,** an event directly contradicts strong expectations.
- **Verbal irony** when a character states the opposite of what is meant.
- In **dramatic irony,** the reader knows something a character does not.

In addition to irony, writers may use **paradox**—an expression of two contradictory ideas that reveals a truth. For example, the following paradox shows the harm of not telling a painful truth: "It is cruel to be kind."

In "Like the Sun" and "The Open Window," the writers use irony and paradox to explore contradictory ideas of honesty and deceit. Note examples of irony and paradox in the stories using a diagram like the one shown.

Like the Sun

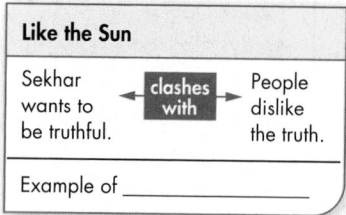

Sekhar wants to be truthful. ← **clashes with** → People dislike the truth.

Example of ______________

The Open Window

Mr. Nuttel needs calm. ← **clashes with** → Vera enjoys scaring him.

Example of ______________

❷ Vocabulary

- **tempering** (tem′ pər iŋ) *n.* changing to make more suitable, usually by mixing with something (p. 191) *Even when I am angry, I try tempering my remarks with politeness.* temper *v.* temperature *n.* temperance *n.*
- **ingratiating** (in grā′ shē āt′ iŋ) *adj.* acting in a way intended to win someone's favor (p. 192) *Her ingratiating ways charmed us.* grateful *adj.* gratitude *n.* ingratiated *v.*
- **scrutinized** (skro͞ot′ 'n īzd) *v.* examined carefully (p. 194) *I scrutinized my face, looking for wrinkles.* scrutiny *n.* inscrutable *adj.*
- **endeavored** (en dev′ ərd) *v.* tried to achieve a set goal (p. 195) *Though shy, he endeavored to make new friends.* endeavors *n.*
- **falteringly** (fôl′ tər iŋ lē) *adv.* spoken hesitatingly or with a wavering voice (p. 196) *Marisol's voice becomes falteringly soft if she is nervous.* falter *v.* unfaltering *adj.*
- **delusion** (di lo͞o′ zhən) *n.* an erroneous belief that is held despite evidence to the contrary (p. 197) *Jackson optimistically clung to the delusion that nothing could ever go wrong for him.* delusional *adj.* delude *v.*

PHLit Online! www.PHLitOnline.com

- Vocabulary flashcards
- Interactive journals
- More about the authors
- Selection audio
- Interactive graphic organizers

Vocabulary Development

Vocabulary Knowledge Rating

Create a **Vocabulary Knowledge Rating Chart** (***Professional Development Guidebook***, p. 33) for this selection. Include the selection vocabulary and the Big Question words that appear in the Writing About the Big Question sentence starters on the next page. (The Big Question vocabulary is introduced on pp. 2–3.)

Give students a copy of the chart. Read the words aloud, and have students mark their rating in the Before Reading column. Urge them to be alert to these words as they read and discuss the selection.

Tally how many students think they know a word to gauge how much instruction to provide. As students read and discuss the selections, point out the words and their context.

PHLit Online! **Vocabulary Central**, featuring tools, activities, and songs for studying vocabulary, is available online at **www.PHLitOnline.com.**

Is there a difference between *reality* and *truth?*

Writing About the Big Question

In these stories, characters plan reasonable goals, but the outcomes are far from what they expect. Think about a time when things did not turn out as you had planned. Use these sentence starters to develop your ideas.

My **perception** of the situation was that ________________.

In **reality,** though, ________________.

Meet the Authors

R. K. Narayan (1906–2001)

Author of "Like the Sun"

R. K. Narayan spun his tales from the stuff of real life. His hometown of Mysore in southern India probably served as the basis for Malgudi, the setting for much of his fiction. Like the main character in "Like the Sun," Narayan's father was a schoolteacher, and Narayan studied music, a key element of the story, as a youth.

Crossing Languages A native Tamil speaker, Narayan wrote his novels and stories in English, a second language to many Indians. In addition to fiction, he wrote a memoir, *My Days,* and a noted English translation of the ancient Indian epic the *Mahabharata.*

Saki (1870–1916)

Author of "The Open Window"

Saki is the pen name of Hector Hugh Munro. Born to British parents in Burma (now Myanmar), Saki lived in England for most of his life. He began his career writing political satires for newspapers and later turned to fiction.

Humor and Wit Today, Saki is best known for his witty, sometimes cruel short stories, many of which feature humorous surprise endings. Many readers consider "The Open Window" to be one of the best examples of Saki's style.

Teaching Resources

The following resources can be used to enrich, extend, or differentiate the instruction.

All *Unit 1 Resources,* pp. 212–228

All *Graphic Organizer Transparencies,* pp. 33, 34

All **Enriched Online Student Edition**

PHLit Online! All resources, including print and audio, are available at **www.PHLitOnline.com.**

Daily Bellringer

For each class during which you will teach this selection, have students complete one of the five Sentence Combining activities for Week 6 in the *Daily Bellringer Activities* booklet.

Writing About the Big Question

1. Review the assignment with the class.
2. Ask students for examples of times when their plans failed.
3. Have students complete the sentence starters. Review responses as a class. (**Possible responses:** My perception of the situation was that I would not enjoy my summer away from home. In reality, though, I had a great time and made a lot of friends.)
4. Remind students that their answers will help them think about the Big Question, "Is there a difference between reality and truth?"

Concept Connector

Students will return to their responses to the sentence starters they completed before reading.

Multidraft Reading

To assist struggling readers and to deepen reading for all, apply multidraft reading protocols. For each reading, have students set the purpose intended:

- **First reading**—literal comprehension: answering the Reading Check questions
- **Second reading**—application of skills: responding to the side-column notes
- **Third reading**—interpretation: answering the end-of-selection questions

For more guidance, refer to the *Classroom Strategies and Teaching Routines* card on multidraft reading.

PHLit Online!

For more about the authors, practice with the selection vocabulary, and more background, go online at **www.PHLitOnline.com.**

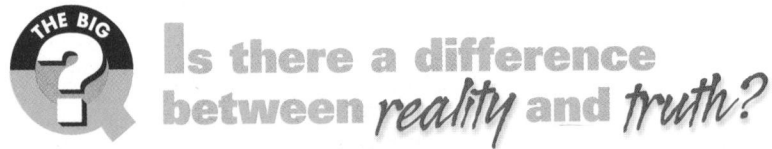

❶ Background

Indian Music Southern Indian music features such instruments as the violin, the double-headed drum known as *mridangam,* and the *ghatam*, a clay pot that the player may sometimes toss into the air. These instruments produce the *raga*, a rhythm or series of sounds. (The Hindu/Urdu word *rag* comes from the Sanskrit word *raga*, which means "color" or "passions." *Rag* may be thought of as an acoustic method of coloring the mind of listeners with an emotion.) Some ragas are believed to have magical or curative powers, and are traditionally played at specific hours or during specific seasons; it is believed that departing from this timetable would be harmful to both the performer and the audience.

❷ Activating Prior Knowledge

On the board, write the word *truth*. **Ask** students what they consider truth to be. Then, lead the class in a discussion of whether it is possible or desirable to tell the truth at all times. Then, read aloud the first paragraph of "Like the Sun." Tell students that this story will allow them to watch the adventures of a man who decides to do just that.

Concept Connector →

Students will return to the above discussion once they have read the selection.

❸ About the Selection

When Sekhar decides to tell the whole truth for one day in "Like the Sun," he hurts his wife's feelings, alienates a colleague, and insults the headmaster at his school. Through the experiences of the main character, Narayan explores whether it is possible or wise to tell the unvarnished truth at all times.

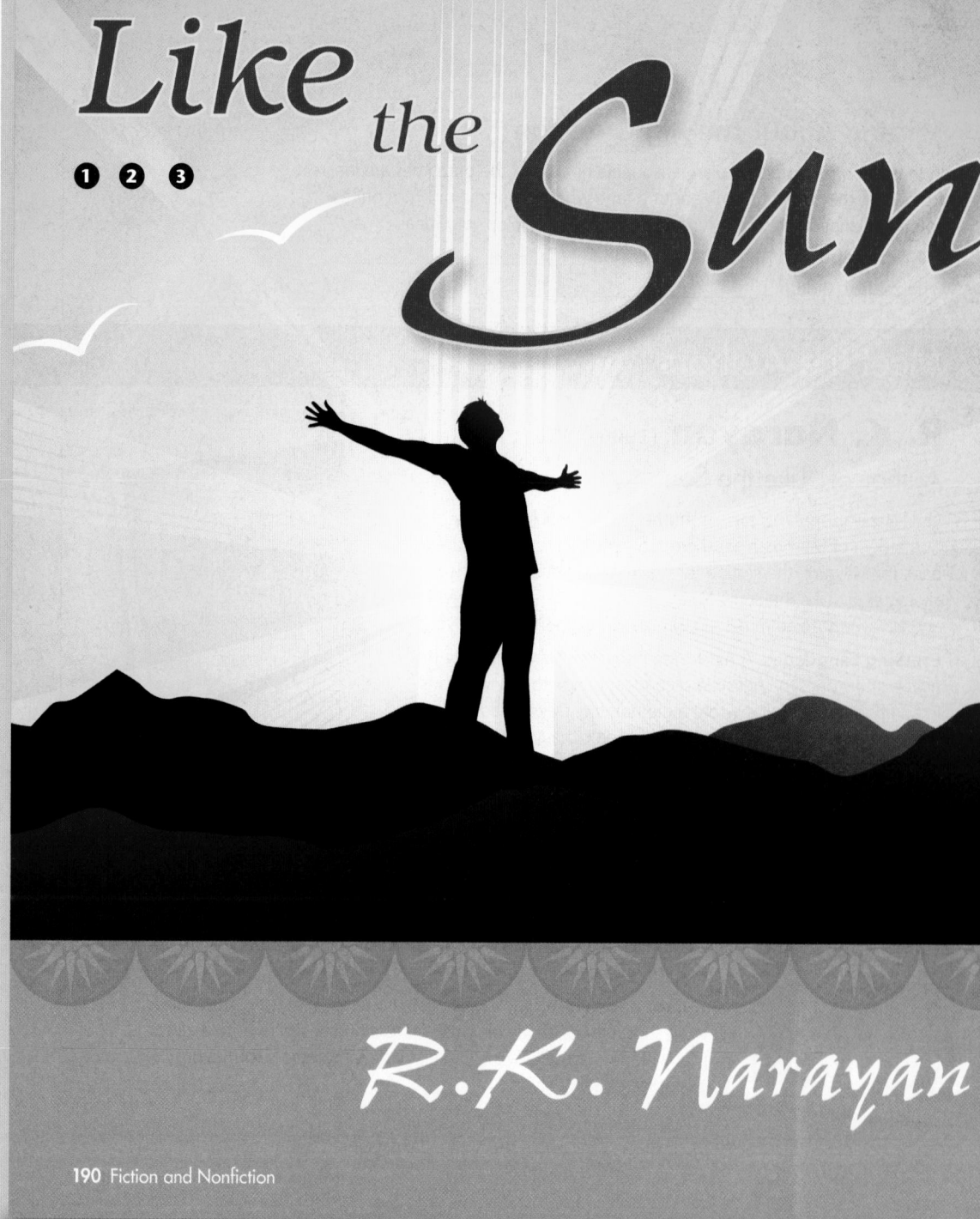

Like the Sun

❶ ❷ ❸

R.K. Narayan

Think Aloud

Comparing Irony and Paradox

Model the skill of comparing irony and paradox, using the following "think aloud." Say to students:

> We are faced with irony and paradox in our everyday lives. Suppose I am on my way to purchase a new tire for my car and I get a flat tire. That would be an example of irony. Now, suppose that I am interviewing for my first job and I'm told that I don't have enough experience for the position. But without the position, I cannot gain the experience. I am describing a paradoxical situation.

Truth, Sekhar reflected, is like the sun. I suppose no human being can ever look it straight in the face without blinking or being dazed. He realized that, morning till night, the essence of human relationships consisted in tempering truth so that it might not shock. This day he set apart as a unique day—at least one day in the year we must give and take absolute Truth whatever may happen. Otherwise life is not worth living. The day ahead seemed to him full of possibilities. He told no one
4 of his experiment. It was a quiet resolve, a secret pact between him and eternity.

The very first test came while his wife served him his morning meal. He showed hesitation over a tidbit, which she had thought was her culinary masterpiece. She asked, "Why, isn't it good?" At other times he would have said, considering her feelings in the matter, "I feel full up, that's all." But today he said, "It isn't good. I'm unable to swallow it." He saw her wince and said to himself, Can't be helped. Truth is like the sun.

Vocabulary
tempering (tem´ pər iŋ)
n. changing to make more suitable, usually by mixing with something

4 Connecting to the Big Question

1. Discuss with students situations in which speaking the truth is less than desirable.
2. Have students read the bracketed text. **Ask:** What "truth" is Narayan trying to convey by presenting Sekhar's perception of honesty?
   Possible response: Life, however challenging, is best lived when a person is honest.
3. **Ask:** Through the interaction that Sekhar has with his wife, what reality is Narayan conveying about telling the "absolute truth"?
   Possible response: The truth can be a difficult thing for people to hear.

Differentiated Instruction for Universal Access

Accessibility at a Glance

Use this information to guide your teaching of "Like the Sun."

Context	Experiment with human behavior
Language/Vocabulary	• Accessible vocabulary • Some complicated sentences • Grade-appropriate vocabulary
Concept Level	Accessible (the impact of telling the truth on others)
Literary Merit	Cross-cultural experience
Lexile/Length	Lexile: 670L Word Count: 1,257

PHLit Online!

This selection is available in interactive format in the **Enriched Online Student Edition**, online at **www.PHLitOnline.com**, which includes an interactive graphic organizer.

❺ Literary Analysis
Irony and Paradox

1. Explain that irony occurs when we expect one thing to happen and then are surprised that it does not occur.
2. **Ask** students the Literary Analysis question: Why is it ironic that this is the day the headmaster will ask for Sekhar's opinion about his musical abilities?
   Possible response: Sekhar never expected that his resolve to tell the truth would collide with the headmaster's musical aspirations.

He always struck me as a mean and selfish brute.

His next trial was in the common room when one of his colleagues came up and said, "Did you hear of the death of so-and-so? Don't you think it a pity?" "No," Sekhar answered. "He was such a fine man—" the other began. But Sekhar cut him short with: "Far from it. He always struck me as a mean and selfish brute."

During the last period when he was teaching geography for Third Form A,[1] Sekhar received a note from the headmaster: "Please see me before you go home." Sekhar said to himself: It must be about these horrible test papers. A hundred papers in the boys' scrawls; he had shirked this work for weeks, feeling all the time as if a sword were hanging over his head. The bell rang, and the boys burst out of the class.

Sekhar paused for a moment outside the headmaster's room to button up his coat; that was another subject the headmaster always sermonized about.

He stepped in with a very polite "Good evening, sir."

The headmaster looked up at him in a very friendly manner and asked, "Are you free this evening?"

Sekhar replied, "Just some outing which I have promised the children at home."

"Well, you can take them out another day. Come home with me now."

"Oh . . . yes, sir, certainly. . ." And then he added timidly, "anything special, sir?"

"Yes," replied the headmaster, smiling to himself. . . ."You didn't know my weakness for music?"

"Oh, yes, sir. . ."

"I've been learning and practicing secretly, and now I want you to hear me this evening. I've engaged a drummer and a violinist to accompany me—this is the first time I'm doing it full-dress, and I want your opinion. I know it will be valuable." ❺

Sekhar's taste in music was well known. He was one of the most dreaded music critics in the town. But he never anticipated his musical inclinations would lead him to this trial. . . . "Rather a surprise for you, isn't it?" asked the headmaster. "I've spent a fortune on it behind closed doors. . . ."

They started for the headmaster's house.

"God hasn't given me a child, but at least let him not deny me the consolation of music," the headmaster said, pathetically, as they walked. He incessantly chattered about music: how he began one day out of sheer boredom; how his teacher at first laughed at him and then gave him hope; how his ambition in life was to forget himself in music.

At home the headmaster proved very **ingratiating**. He sat Sekhar on a red silk carpet, set before him several dishes of delicacies, and

Literary Analysis
Irony and Paradox
Why is it ironic that this is the day the headmaster will ask for Sekhar's opinion about his musical abilities?

Vocabulary
ingratiating (in grā′ shē āt′ iŋ) *adj.* acting in a way intended to win someone's favor

1. **Third Form A** in British-style schools, an advanced class roughly equivalent to eighth grade in the United States school system.

Vocabulary Development

Thematic Vocabulary: The Big Question

As students are discussing "Like the Sun," ask them to use the thematic vocabulary presented in Introducing the Big Question, pp. 2–3. You might encourage them with sentence starters like these:

1. If Sekhar had *evaluated* his wife's reaction to his telling the truth, he might have . . .
2. A conscientious teacher would be able to *differentiate* . . .
3. In *reality*, Sekhar's truth test . . .
4. Sekhar would be able to *verify* that . . .

fussed over him as if he were a son-in-law of the house. He even said, "Well, you must listen with a free mind. Don't worry about these test papers." He added half humorously, "I will give you a week's time."

"Make it ten days, sir," Sekhar pleaded.

"All right, granted," the headmaster said generously. Sekhar felt really relieved now—he would attack them at the rate of ten a day and get rid of the nuisance.

The headmaster lighted incense sticks. "Just to create the right atmosphere," he explained. A drummer and a violinist, already seated on a Rangoon mat, were waiting for him. The headmaster sat down between them like a professional at a concert, cleared his throat and began an alapana[2], and paused to ask, "Isn't it good Kalyani[3]?" Sekhar pretended not to have heard the question. The headmaster went on to sing a full song composed by Thyagaraja[4] and followed it with two more. All the time the headmaster was singing, Sekhar went on commenting within himself, He croaks like a dozen frogs. He is bellowing like a buffalo. Now he sounds like loose window shutters in a storm.

The incense sticks burnt low. Sekhar's head throbbed with the medley of sounds that had assailed his eardrums for a couple of hours now. He felt half stupefied. The headmaster had gone nearly hoarse, when he paused to ask, "Shall I go on?" Sekhar replied, "Please don't, sir; I think this will do. . . ." The headmaster looked stunned. His face was beaded with perspiration. Sekhar felt the greatest pity for him. But he felt he could not help it. No judge delivering a sentence felt more pained and helpless. Sekhar noticed that the headmaster's wife peeped in from the kitchen, with eager curiosity. The drummer and the violinist put away their burdens with an air of relief. The headmaster removed his spectacles, mopped his brow, and asked, "Now, come out with your opinion."

"Can't I give it tomorrow, sir?" Sekhar asked tentatively.

"No. I want it immediately—your frank opinion. Was it good?"

"No, sir. . . ." Sekhar replied.

"Oh! . . . Is there any use continuing my lessons?"

"Absolutely none, sir. . . ." Sekhar said with his voice trembling. He felt very unhappy that he could not speak more soothingly. Truth, he reflected, required as much strength to give as to receive. All the way home he felt worried. He felt that his official life was not going to be smooth sailing hereafter. There were questions of increment and

2. **alapana** (äl ä′ pä nä) in classical Indian music, an improvisational exploration of a melody, without a defined beat, and intended to showcase the talent of a singer.
3. **Kalyani** (käl yä′ nē) traditional Indian folk songs.
4. **Thyagaraja** (tē ä′ gä rä′ jä) (1767–1847) revered composer of Indian devotional songs.

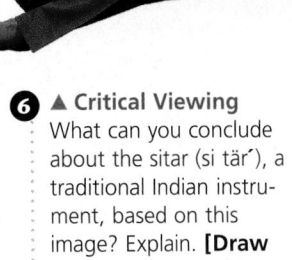

6 ▲ Critical Viewing
What can you conclude about the sitar (si tär′), a traditional Indian instrument, based on this image? Explain. **[Draw Conclusions]**

7 Reading Check
What does the headmaster request that Sekhar do that evening?

6 Critical Viewing

Possible response: The sitar is a stringed instrument with a long neck—similar to a guitar. A person plays it while seated. It is played by plucking the strings. Men play the sitar. (Students may know that women do, too.) Sitar music could be soothing. Also, it could be enjoyable to play—the musician looks happy.

7 Reading Check

Answer: The headmaster asks Sekhar to give an opinion of the headmaster's musical ability.

Differentiated Instruction for Universal Access

Strategy for Special Needs Students

Draw a cause-and-effect chain on the board to help students evaluate the events of the story. For the title of the chart write, "Sekhar insults the headmaster." Have volunteers make suggestions about the causes of the event. Then, ask volunteers to explain the effects of the insult. Have students work in small groups to record their ideas on their own cause-and-effect charts. Ask a volunteer to summarize the chart. Display the charts together in the class.

Enrichment for Advanced Readers

Challenge students to find information about traditional Indian music. They might visit the local library or search the Internet for information from credible Web sites. Students might find it useful to research the variety of instruments used in Indian music, famous Indian artists, including vocalists and musicians, or the progression of musical style throughout the years. When they have concluded their research, have students give a brief presentation about their findings.

8 Literary Analysis
Irony and Paradox

Ask students the Literary Analysis question: How does Sekhar's experience contradict the idea that "honesty is the best policy"?
Answer: Sekhar's actions have hurt and angered his wife, upset a colleague, made Sekhar uncomfortable, and ended the headmaster's musical ambitions.

Concept Connector

Have students compare their Writing About the Big Question and Activating Prior Knowledge responses with their ideas after reading the selection.

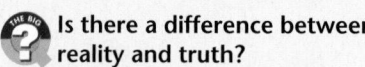

ASSESS
Answers

1. Students will probably reply that they do feel sorry for the headmaster. The headmaster says that, "God hasn't given me a child, but at least let him not deny me the consolation of music." He is now denied that, too.
2. (a) Sekhar plans to tell the absolute truth for one day.
(b) Sekhar realizes that it is difficult for people to hear the absolute truth.
3. (a) Yes, but perhaps not in the way that Sekhar had anticipated.
(b) The headmaster appreciates no longer wasting his money on music lessons. Sekhar won't have to eat the food or listen to the music from his headmaster. Sekhar will grade the tests and they will no longer be weighing on his conscience.
4. **Possible response:** The headmaster is angry with Sekhar. I can tell because he changes his mind about the length of time Sekhar has to grade the papers.

Is there a difference between reality and truth?
(a) **Possible response:** People tend to prefer tempered truth. Both Sekhar's wife and the headmaster react negatively to Sekhar's truthful responses. (b) **Possible response:** No. Often, truth can be more hurtful to a person than being told a lie.

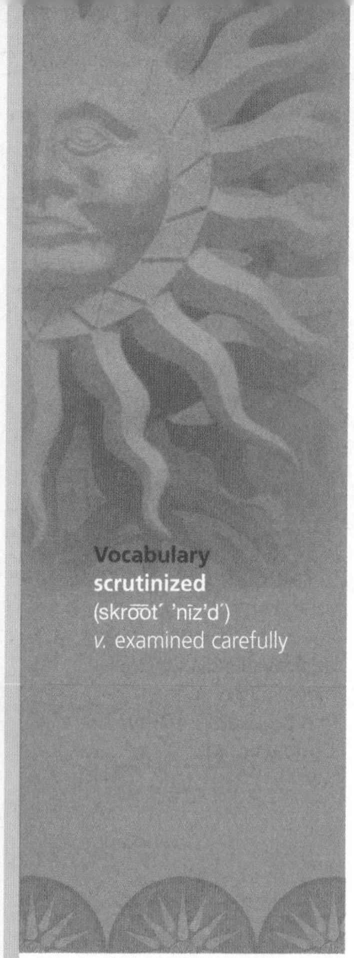

confirmation[5] and so on, all depending upon the headmaster's goodwill. All kinds of worries seemed to be in store for him. . . . Did not Harishchandra[6] lose his throne, wife, child, because he would speak nothing less than the absolute Truth whatever happened?

At home his wife served him with a sullen face. He knew she was still angry with him for his remark of the morning. Two casualties for today, Sekhar said to himself. If I practice it for a week, I don't think I shall have a single friend left.

He received a call from the headmaster in his classroom next day. He went up apprehensively.

"Your suggestion was useful. I have paid off the music master. No one would tell me the truth about my music all these days. Why such antics at my age! Thank you. By the way, what about those test papers?" 8

"You gave me ten days, sir, for correcting them."

"Oh, I've reconsidered it. I must positively have them here tomorrow. . . ." A hundred papers in a day! That meant all night's sitting up! "Give me a couple of days, sir. . . ."

"No. I must have them tomorrow morning. And remember, every paper must be thoroughly **scrutinized**."

"Yes, sir," Sekhar said, feeling that sitting up all night with a hundred test papers was a small price to pay for the luxury of practicing Truth.

Vocabulary
scrutinized (skrōōt´ 'nīz'd´) *v.* examined carefully

Literary Analysis
Irony and Paradox
How does Sekhar's experience contradict the idea that "honesty is the best policy"?

5. **increment and confirmation** salary increase and job security.
6. **Harischchandra** (he rish chen´ dra) legendary Hindu king who was subject of many Indian stories. His name has come to symbolize truth and integrity.

Critical Thinking

1. **Respond:** Did you sympathize with the headmaster after reading Sekhar's critique? Explain.
2. **(a)** What experiment does Sekhar plan at the beginning of the story? **(b) Connect:** What conflict does this create for him?
3. **(a) Draw Conclusions:** Are there any benefits to Sekhar's truth telling? **(b) Support:** Cite story details and logical reasons to support your conclusion.
4. **Infer:** Is the headmaster pleased or angry that Sekhar has told him the truth about his music? Explain your conclusions.

Is there a difference between reality and truth?
(a) Based on the results of Sekhar's experiment, do people prefer to hear reality through absolute truths, or do they prefer tempered truth? Explain your answer using details from the story. **(b)** Would you be willing to conduct Sekhar's truth experiment? Why or why not?

THE OPEN WINDOW

❾ ❿ ⓫

Saki (H.H. Munro)

"My aunt will be down presently, Mr. Nuttel," said a very self-possessed young lady of fifteen; "in the meantime you must try and put up with me."

Framton Nuttel endeavored to say the correct something that should duly flatter the niece of the moment without unduly discounting the aunt that was to come. Privately he doubted more than ever whether these formal visits on a succession of total strangers would do much towards helping the nerve cure which he was supposed to be undergoing.

"I know how it will be," his sister had said when he was preparing to migrate to this rural retreat; "you will bury yourself down there and not speak to a living soul, and your nerves will be worse than ever from moping. I shall just give you letters of introduction[1] to all the people I know there. Some of them, as far as I can remember, were quite nice."

Vocabulary
endeavored (en dev′ ərd) *v.* tried to achieve a set goal

1. **letters of introduction** letters introducing two strangers, written by someone who knows them both. The person to whom such a letter is written is obliged to provide hospitality to the person carrying the letter.

❾ Background

Victorian-Edwardian Period

The Victorian-Edwardian period was an era in the United Kingdom known for its prestige and elegant fashion. Society was segregated based on economic standing. The aristocracy was the highest, most prominent class, followed by the bourgeoisie, the working class, and the poor. Such apparent financial distinctions led classes to look poorly upon those below them. Victorian-Edwardian society was very polite, but it could conceal tensions and cruelty that might not have been apparent to the casual observer. On the whole, it was a private, exclusive society that greeted newcomers with hatred and disdain.

❿ Activating Prior Knowledge

Write the words *deception* and *honesty* on the board. **Ask** students how they would define the words based on their life experiences. Then, have students think about times they have made up stories. Discuss their reasons for doing so and how it affected someone's perception.

Concept Connector →

Students will follow up on this activity after completing the story.

⓫ About the Selection

In "The Open Window," a young girl tests her power to change the look of things by telling tales. When Mr. Nuttel arrives at the home of Mrs. Sappleton he first encounters Vera, the niece of the woman that he is intending to meet. Quickly, he is drawn into a tale of unsolved disappearances and terror by the cruel story that Vera recounts.

Differentiated Instruction for Universal Access

Accessibility at a Glance

Use this information to guide your teaching of "The Open Window."

Context	Historical: nineteenth-century Britain
Language/Vocabulary	• Some complicated sentences • Grade-appropriate vocabulary
Concept Level	Accessible
Literary Merit	Noted author
Lexile/Length	Lexile: 1030L — Word Count: 1,202

PHLit Online!

This selection is available in interactive format in the **Enriched Online Student Edition**, online at **www.PHLitOnline.com**, which includes an interactive graphic organizer.

12 Connecting to the Big Question

1. Explain that sometimes reality can appear to be different for different people, depending on the way they see the world.
2. Have students read the bracketed text. **Ask:** How does the niece's story of the tragedy affect the way Framton perceives the reality of the home?
   Possible response: The home suddenly appears to be a sad place where something terrible has happened.
3. **Ask:** What is one way a person or an author can affect the way we perceive reality?
   Possible response: A person can change our views by providing new information about a given situation.
4. Encourage students to consider how the perceived reality of the story changes as the author provides new information.

Framton wondered whether Mrs. Sappleton, the lady to whom he was presenting one of the letters of introduction, came into the nice division.

"Do you know many of the people round here?" asked the niece, when she judged that they had had sufficient silent communion.

"Hardly a soul," said Framton. "My sister was staying here, at the rectory, you know, some four years ago, and she gave me letters of introduction to some of the people here."

He made the last statement in a tone of distinct regret.

"Then you know practically nothing about my aunt?" pursued the self-possessed young lady.

12 "Only her name and address," admitted the caller. He was wondering whether Mrs. Sappleton was in the married or widowed state. An undefinable something about the room seemed to suggest masculine habitation.

"Her great tragedy happened just three years ago," said the child; "that would be since your sister's time."

"Her tragedy?" asked Framton; somehow in this restful country spot tragedies seemed out of place.

"You may wonder why we keep that window wide open on an October afternoon," said the niece, indicating a large French window that opened on to a lawn.

"It is quite warm for the time of the year," said Framton; "but has that window got anything to do with the tragedy?"

"Out through that window, three years ago to a day, her husband and her two young brothers went off for their day's shooting. They never came back. In crossing the moor to their favorite snipe-shooting ground[2] they were all three engulfed in a treacherous piece of bog.[3] It had been that dreadful wet summer, you know, and places that were safe in other years gave way suddenly without warning. Their bodies were never recovered. That was the dreadful part of it." Here the child's voice lost its self-possessed note and became **falteringly** human. "Poor aunt always thinks that they will come back some day,

Vocabulary
falteringly (fôl′ tər iŋ lē) adv. spoken hesitatingly or with a wavering voice

2. **snipe-shooting ground** area for hunting snipe—wading birds that live chiefly in marshy places and have long, flexible bills.
3. **bog** small swamp; wet, spongy ground.

they and the little brown spaniel that was lost with them, and walk in at that window just as they used to do. That is why the window is kept open every evening till it is quite dusk. Poor dear aunt, she has often told me how they went out, her husband with his white waterproof coat over his arm, and Ronnie, her youngest brother, singing, 'Bertie, why do you bound?' as he always did to tease her, because she said it got on her nerves. Do you know, sometimes on still, quiet evenings like this, I almost get a creepy feeling that they will walk in through that window—"

She broke off with a little shudder. It was a relief to Framton when the aunt bustled into the room with a whirl of apologies for being late in making her appearance.

"I hope Vera has been amusing you?" she said.

"She has been very interesting," said Framton.

"I hope you don't mind the open window," said Mrs. Sappleton briskly; "my husband and brothers will be home directly from shooting, and they always come in this way. They've been out for snipe in the marshes today, so they'll make a fine mess over my poor carpets. So like you menfolk, isn't it?"

13 She rattled on cheerfully about the shooting and the scarcity of birds, and the prospects for duck in the winter. To Framton, it was all purely horrible. He made a desperate but only partially successful effort to turn the talk on to a less ghastly topic; he was conscious that his hostess was giving him only a fragment of her attention, and her eyes were constantly straying past him to the open window and the lawn beyond. It was certainly an unfortunate coincidence that he should have paid his visit on this tragic anniversary.

"The doctors agree in ordering me complete rest, an absence of mental excitement, and avoidance of anything in the nature of violent physical exercise," announced Framton, who labored under the tolerably widespread **delusion** that total strangers and chance acquaintances are hungry for the least detail of one's ailments and infirmities, their cause and cure. "On the matter of diet they are not so much in agreement," he continued.

"No?" said Mrs. Sappleton, in a voice which only replaced a yawn at the last moment. Then she suddenly brightened into alert attention—but not to what Framton was saying.

"Here they are at last!" she cried. "Just in time for tea, and don't they look as if they were muddy up to the eyes!"

Framton shivered slightly and turned towards the niece with a look intended to convey sympathetic comprehension. The child was staring out through the open window with dazed horror in her eyes. In a chill shock of nameless fear Framton swung round in his seat and looked in the same direction.

Literary Analysis
Irony and Paradox
What kind of irony is involved when Mrs. Sappleton does not know about the tall tale Vera told Mr. Nuttel?

Vocabulary
delusion (di lo͞o′ zhan) *n.* an erroneous belief that is held despite evidence to the contrary

14 **Reading Check**
What does Vera say is her aunt's great tragedy?

13 Literary Analysis
Irony and Paradox

1. To help students identify types of irony, remind them that there are various forms of irony.
2. Have a volunteer read the bracketed passage aloud. **Ask:** What do you know that one of the characters in the passage does not know?
   Answer: Mrs. Sappleton is unaware of the story that Vera has told Mr. Nuttel.
3. **Ask** students the Literary Analysis question: What kind of irony is involved when Mrs. Sappleton does not know about the tall tale Vera told Mr. Nuttel?
   Answer: dramatic irony

14 Reading Check

Answer: Vera tells Mr. Nuttel that her aunt's great tragedy is the disappearance of her husband and two brothers.

Differentiated Instruction for Universal Access

Strategy for Less Proficient Readers
Remind students that to analyze the effect of culture on characters and their actions, they must identify the culture within which the characters live. Guide students to consider aspects of the cultures within this story such as time period, country, position in life, and ages of the characters. Make sure they identify the timing of the story to be around the late 1800s, the country to be England, the position in life to be wealthy and comfortable for the Sappletons and uncertain for Nuttel, and the ages of the characters to range from teenage to midlife.

Once they have a picture of the culture in mind, tell them that they can consider what different characters will find to be normal versus shocking. Explain that they can then use these opinions to decide which behaviors are culturally acceptable. Lead them through discussing cultural aspects of actions such as the niece's fabrications, letters of introduction, snipe shooting, crossing the moor, running late to greet a guest, visiting rural homes on foot, and running out of a house without saying farewells.

Concept Connector

Have students recall the Activating Prior Knowledge exercise and compare their responses before reading. Then, have them connect their Writing About the Big Question responses to the story.

ASSESS

Answers

1. **Answer:** The hunters are actually returning from a day of snipe hunting. Mr. Nuttel is shocked because Vera told him that the hunters were dead.
2. (a) Mr Nuttel is undergoing a cure for frayed nerves. (b) It is crucial because, ironically, he is subjected to the very thing he is trying to recover from.
3. (a) **Possible response:** Vera enjoys being mean-spirited. (b) No (c) **Possible response:** By saying, "in the meantime you must try and put up with me," Vera is implying that she has a tendency to misbehave.
4. **Possible response:** Both Mr. Nuttel and Vera follow the same social conventions. They are extremely polite. Mr. Nuttel is innocent and trusting while Vera is vindictive.

Is there a difference between reality and truth?

(a) **Possible response:** Vera incorporates the open window, the hunting trip, and the white raincoat into her factitious tale knowing the impact that each will have upon the hunters' return. (b) Mr. Nuttel believes that the missing hunters have returned when in actuality they were never missing.

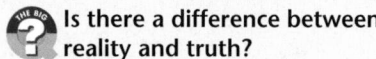

In the deepening twilight three figures were walking across the lawn towards the window...

In the deepening twilight three figures were walking across the lawn towards the window; they all carried guns under their arms, and one of them was additionally burdened with a white coat hung over his shoulders. A tired brown spaniel kept close at their heels. Noiselessly they neared the house, and then a hoarse young voice chanted out of the dusk: "I said, Bertie, why do you bound?"

Framton grabbed wildly at his stick and hat; the hall door, the gravel drive, and the front gate were dimly noted stages in his headlong retreat. A cyclist coming along the road had to run into the hedge to avoid imminent collision.

"Here we are, my dear," said the bearer of the white mackintosh,[4] coming in through the window; "fairly muddy, but most of it's dry. Who was that who bolted out as we came up?"

"A most extraordinary man, a Mr. Nuttel," said Mrs. Sappleton; "could only talk about his illnesses, and dashed off without a word of goodbye or apology when you arrived. One would think he had seen a ghost."

"I expect it was the spaniel," said the niece calmly; "he told me he had a horror of dogs. He was once hunted into a cemetery somewhere on the banks of the Ganges[5] by a pack of pariah dogs, and had to spend the night in a newly dug grave with the creatures snarling and grinning and foaming just above him. Enough to make anyone lose their nerve."

4. **mackintosh** (mak´ in täsh´) *n.* waterproof raincoat.
5. **Ganges** (gan´ jēz) river in northern India and Bangladesh.

Critical Thinking

1. **Respond:** When Mrs. Sappleton announces that she sees the hunters returning, what do you think is actually happening? Explain.
2. **(a)** Why is Mr. Nuttel visiting the country? **(b) Interpret**: Why is this detail critical to the story?
3. **(a) Speculate:** Why does Vera tell Mr. Nuttel the story about the hunters' deaths? **(b) Connect:** Is it unusual for her to tell such stories? **(c) Support:** How do you know?
4. **Compare and Contrast:** How are Mr. Nuttel and Vera similar and different? Use details from the story to support your answer.

Is there a difference between reality and truth? **(a)** How does Vera use aspects of reality to shape her story? **(b)** How is Mr. Nuttel's perception of the situation at the end of the story different from reality?

Vocabulary Development

Vocabulary Knowledge Rating

When students have completed reading "Like the Sun" and "The Open Window," have them take out their **Vocabulary Knowledge Rating Chart**. Read the words aloud once more and have students rate their knowledge of the words again in the After Reading column. Clarify any words that are still problematic. Have students write their own definition and example or sentence in the appropriate column. Then, have students complete the Vocabulary Practice activities on the next page. Encourage students to use the words in further discussion and written work about the selection. Remind them that they will be accountable for these words in the **Selection Test** (*Unit 1 Resources*, pp. 223–225 or 226–228).

After You Read | Like the Sun • The Open Window

Comparing Irony and Paradox

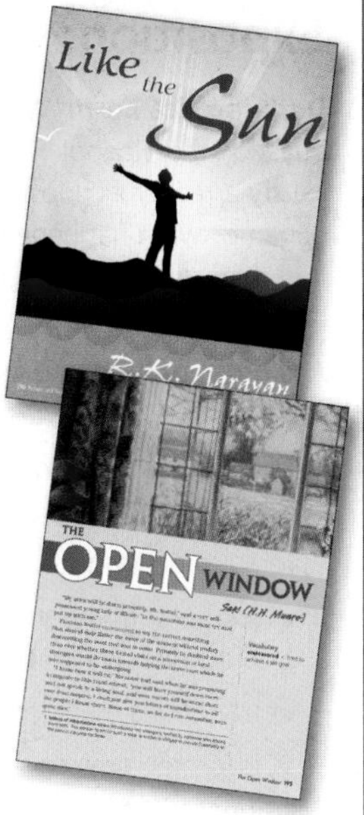

1. **(a)** Analyze one example of **irony** in "Like the Sun" and one in "The Open Window." In your analysis, identify and explain the elements in the examples that contrast with one another. **(b)** Did you identify situational, verbal, or dramatic irony? Explain.
2. Explain in what ways each story explores the **paradox** stated:
   (a) "Like the Sun": Telling the truth is a virtue that leads to punishment.
   (b) "The Open Window": The cure for Mr. Nuttel's illness makes him worse.
3. Compare the effect of irony and paradox in the two stories. Consider whether these devices simply add humor or whether they emphasize the impossible dilemmas facing a character. Complete a diagram like this one to show how irony and paradox affect each story.

Like the Sun	The Open Window
Effect of Irony and Paradox:	Effect of Irony and Paradox:

Writing to Compare Irony and Paradox

Both Narayan and Saki use irony or paradox to explore ideas of truth, deception, and honesty. In an essay, compare and contrast the concepts of honesty and deception in the stories. Support your answer with details from the stories. Use these suggestions to get started:

- Identify a few examples of irony or paradox in each story.
- Decide what message each writer is trying to convey about truth, deception, and honesty.
- Explain how using irony and paradox helps each writer convey an idea.

Vocabulary

Practice For each item, write a sentence in which you use both words correctly.

1. tempering; response
2. delusion; perfection
3. scrutinized; report
4. ingratiating; interview
5. endeavored; sincerity
6. falteringly; nervous

Assessment Resources

Unit 1 Resources

L1 L2 EL **Selection Test A,** pp. 223–225. Administer Test A to less advanced students and English learners.

L3 L4 **Selection Test B,** pp. 226–228. Administer Test B to on-level and more advanced students.

L3 L4 **Open-Book Test,** pp. 220–222. As an alternative, give the Open-Book Test.

All **Customizable Test Bank**

All **Self-tests**

Students may prepare for the **Selection Test** by taking the **Self-test** online.

PHLit Online! All assessment resources are available at **www.PHLitOnline.com**.

ASSESS

Answers

Comparing Irony and Paradox

1. (a) **Possible response:** Students' responses should choose one example of irony and explain the reversal. (b) **Possible response:** The reversals are examples of situational irony.
   Other sample answers appear in ***Graphic Organizer Transparencies,*** **Comparing Irony and Paradox Graphic Organizer A (After You Read),** p. 34, and the **Additional Answers** section.
2. (a) Pursuing absolute virtue can lead to inflexibility and unkindness. (b) Searching for answers might not have the intended result.
3. "Like the Sun" effect: Dilemmas are emphasized to show how good intentions can result in bad ends; "The Open Window" effect: They add humor by surprising the reader.

Writing to Compare Irony and Paradox

1. Review the assignment criteria with students.
2. Students could organize their essays by comparing and contrasting the concept of deception and honesty in each story or by analyzing first one story and then the other.

Six Traits Focus

✔	Ideas		Word Choice
✔	Organization		Sentence Fluency
	Voice		Conventions

Vocabulary

1. She avoided hurting his feelings by tempering her response.
2. Her delusions kept her from achieving the perfection she hoped to attain.
3. Although highly scrutinized, the report revealed numerous flaws in the administration's plans.
4. He spoke in such an ingratiating manner that he was asked to return for a second interview.
5. She showed sincerity as she endeavored to mend their friendship.
6. We were nervous as we watched him walk falteringly across the tightrope.

PREACH

Meeting Your Standards

Students will

1. write a cause-and-effect essay.
2. use writing strategies to generate ideas and to plan, organize, evaluate, and revise a cause-and-effect essay.
3. apply grammar skills.

Introducing the Writing Assignment

Review the assignment and the criteria, using the instruction on the student page.

Connecting to Real-Life Writing

Point out that analysis of cause-and-effect relationships is often used in other types of writing. For example: A chemistry lab report might describe the effects of combining specific chemicals.

Susan Vreeland on Cause-and-Effect Essays

Show students Segment 3 on Susan Vreeland on *See It!* DVD or from this page in the **Enriched Online Student Edition,** at **www.PHLitOnline.com.** Discuss the use of sensory language to elaborate on details.

Writing Workshop
Work in Progress

If students have done the Work-in-Progress assignments on pp. 151 and 179, suggest that they examine their recorded ideas as they begin prewriting. They may wish to develop these ideas in a cause-and-effect essay.

OES Online Essay Scorer

A writing prompt for this mode of writing can be found on the *PH Online Essay Scorer* at **www.PHLitOnline.com.**

Writing Workshop

Exposition: Cause-and-Effect Essay

Defining the Form Whenever something unusual happens, the first question most people ask is, "Why?" A **cause-and-effect essay** can satisfy a reader's curiosity. It might explain why a weird new fashion fad began or what happened as a result of a groundbreaking court decision. You might use elements of this form in news articles, process explanations, and reflective essays.

Assignment Write an essay in which you explain a cause-and-effect relationship. Include these elements:

- ✔ a clearly stated *thesis* that identifies the cause-and-effect relationships to be explored
- ✔ an effective and *logical method of organization*
- ✔ *supporting evidence* and examples that suit your audience and purpose
- ✔ *transitions* that smoothly and clearly connect your ideas
- ✔ error-free grammar, including *correct use of pronouns*

To preview the criteria on which your cause-and-effect essay may be judged, see the rubric on page 207.

Writing Workshop: *Work in Progress*

If you have completed the Work-in-Progress assignments on pages 151 and 179, you already have many ideas you can use in your cause-and-effect essay. Work with these ideas, or explore a new idea as you complete the Writing Workshop.

Reading Writing Connection
To get a feel for cause-and-effect essays, read "Making History With Vitamin C" by Penny Le Couteur and Jay Burreson on page 168.

Teaching Resources

The following resources can be used to enrich or extend the instruction.

- All *Unit 1 Resources* **Writing Workshop,** pp. 193–194
- All *Professional Development Guidebook,* **Rubric for Self-Assessment: Cause-and-Effect Essay,** pp. 238–239
- All *Graphic Organizer Transparencies* **Rubric for Self-Assessment: Cause-and-Effect Essay,** p. 36
- All *See It!* **DVD**
  Susan Vreeland, Segments 3 and 4

PHLit Online! All resources, including print and video, are available at **www.PHLitOnline.com.**

Prewriting Strategies

Make a list. With a partner, brainstorm for a list of scientific phenomena, historic events, or popular trends that you find interesting, important, or even confusing. Look over your list to choose a topic you would like to explore in an essay.

Scan a newspaper or magazine. Review print or online articles, looking for ideas that make you ask, "Why?" Keep notes of possible topics and then focus on the subjects that make you most curious. Review your notes and choose a topic to address.

Narrow your topic. Once you have a topic, make sure that you will be able to discuss it fully in your essay. If your topic is too broad, you may need to focus it. For example, you might not be able to answer "Why did the Great Depression happen?" in a short essay. Instead, your essay could focus on why the stock market crashed in October of 1929.

Make a cause-and-effect chart. Organizing your ideas and details in a cause-and-effect chart can help you form a clear picture of the relationship you will discuss. One chart shown here presents three possible causes of one effect. The other chart classifies the possible effects of one cause.

PHLit Online!
www.PHLitOnline.com
- Author video: Writing Process
- Author video: Rewards of Writing

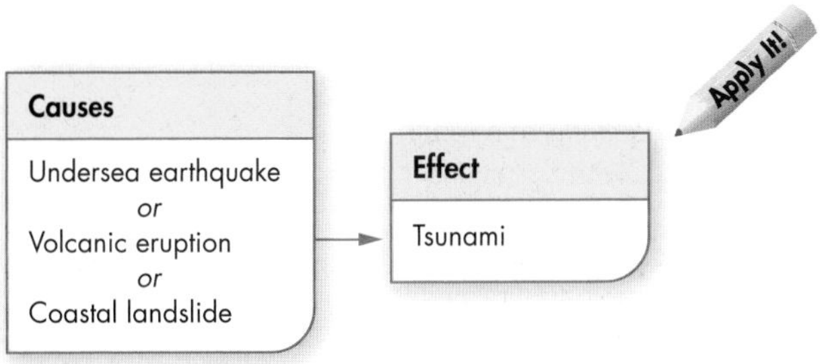

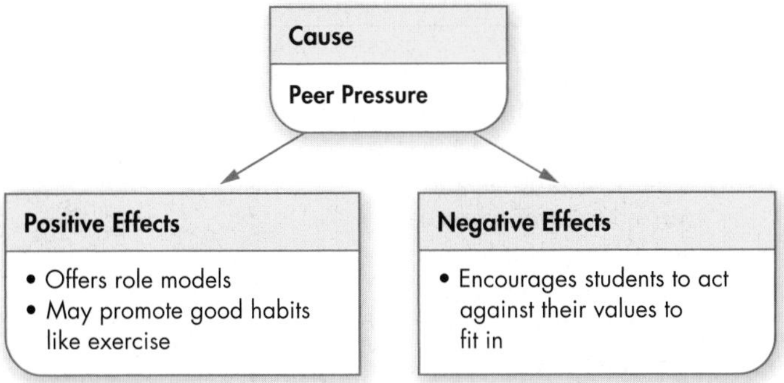

Understanding by Design

Clarifying Expected Outcomes: Using Rubrics

- Before students begin work on this assignment, have them preview the Rubric for Self-Assessment on p. 207 to learn what qualities their cause-and-effect essay must have. A copy of this rubric appears in ***Graphic Organizer Transparencies,*** p. 36.
- Review the criteria in the rubric with the class. Before students use the rubric to assess their own writing, work with them to rate the Student Model (p. 206) using the rubric.
- If you wish to assess students' cause-and-effect essays with a 4-point or a 6-point scoring rubric, see ***Professional Development Guidebook,*** pp. 238–239.

TEACH

Prewriting Strategies

1. Introduce the Prewriting Strategies, using the instruction on the student page.
2. Have students apply the strategies to choose a topic.

Teaching the Strategies

1. Bring newspapers and magazines to class for students to use in choosing a topic.
2. Ask students to consider the scale of their topics. Subtopics they suggest may help to **narrow their topics.**

Think Aloud: Model Making a Cause-and-Effect Chart

Model the strategy, using the following "think aloud":

> If there are many causes and effects, they can be difficult to organize in an essay. To help me I can use a cause-and-effect chart.
>
> Let's say my topic is how an oil spill damages the ocean environment. I'll start with the cause, "oil spill." One possible effect is "ruined shellfish bed." I enter it in my chart under the heading "Effect" and connect it to its cause with an arrow. That effect is the cause of another effect: "fewer shellfish for fishermen to harvest." I enter this effect in my chart and connect it with an arrow to its cause. I can continue in this manner, stating other effects. Then, I review my chart and change the head "Effect" to "Effect/Cause" wherever an effect of one event causes another.

Six Traits Focus

✔	Ideas		Word Choice
✔	Organization		Sentence Fluency
	Voice		Conventions

WG Writing and Grammar, Grade 10

Students will find additional instruction on prewriting for a cause-and-effect essay in Chapter 10, Section 2.

Writing and Grammar Interactive Textbook Online

Students can use the following tools at **www.pearsonsuccessnet.com** as they complete their essay:

- Make a List (Chapter 10, Section 2)
- Use the SEE Technique for Elaboration (Chapter 10, Section 3)

Drafting Strategies

1. Introduce the Drafting Strategies, using the instruction on the student page.
2. Have students apply the strategies as they draft.

Teaching the Strategies

1. Before they begin drafting, have students review the cause-and-effect charts they created. Tell students to highlight the most important causes and effects on their charts. Encourage them to identify one element, either cause or effect, to focus on in their introductions.
2. Tell students that in choosing organizational structures for their essays, they should consider the structure that is the easiest to explain to readers.
3. Explain that transitions are especially important in cause-and-effect essays. Write some of the given transitional words and phrases on the board. Ask volunteers to write sentences using these examples.

Think Aloud: Model Choosing a Logical Organization

Model choosing a logical organization, using the following "think aloud"

Suppose I'm writing an essay about the events that granted women the right to vote. I know that this event is the effect of multiple causes; for example, the movement to free the slaves in the nineteenth century inspired many to think about human rights. At the same time, educational opportunities for women were increasing. The main point will be to show how the movement began and then grew, so it makes sense to give a sequence of events. I decide to use chronological organization.

Six Traits Focus

✔	Ideas	✔	Word Choice
✔	Organization		Sentence Fluency
✔	Voice		Conventions

WG Writing and Grammar, Grade 10

Students will find additional instruction on drafting a cause-and-effect article in Chapter 10, Section 3.

Drafting Strategies

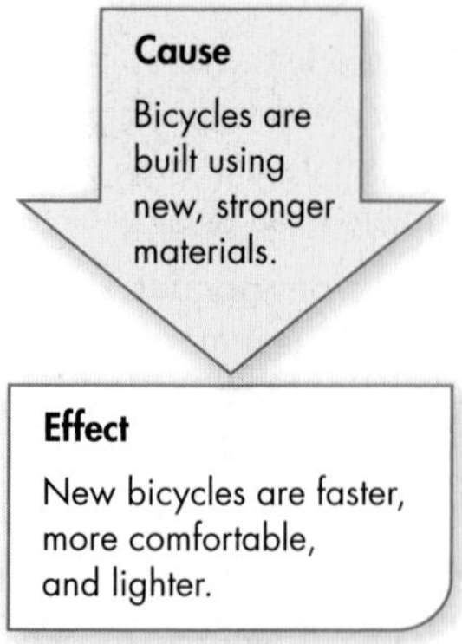

Cause
Bicycles are built using new, stronger materials.
Effect
New bicycles are faster, more comfortable, and lighter.

Clarify your analysis. Even if you are describing a complicated chain of effects, you will need a clear and direct introduction. Prepare a simplified cause-and-effect chart like the one shown here to organize your prewriting ideas. The chart can show you which ideas are essential to your topic and which are less critical.

Choose a logical organization. The structure you choose for your essay depends on the information you have.

- **Chronological order** makes sense for many cause-and-effect essays. You can start with the cause and then continue by describing its effects, or you could start with the effect and then work through its causes one at a time.
- If you are describing multiple causes, consider using an **order of importance organization.** You might begin with your most important cause or save the most important cause for last.

When developing your organization, make sure your essay includes introductory, body, and concluding paragraphs.

Consider your audience. Think about how much your audience of readers already knows about your topic. Be sure to provide full explanations for any unfamiliar words or events.

Use clear transitions. Many words and phrases will help you introduce causes and effects. For example, use *therefore, consequently, as a result,* or *for that reason* to introduce effects. Refer to causes with transitions such as *because, since, as,* or *for the reason that.*

As you write, also look for phrases that help you connect, contrast, and compare ideas. You might use *not only . . . but also* to join two related ideas. Other transitions, such as *however* and *on the other hand,* can introduce contrasting ideas.

Using Transitions

The buffalo nearly became extinct in the nineteenth century. George Grinnell worked to save the animal and protect it for future generations. Today several herds are thriving in the wild.	*Because* the buffalo nearly became extinct in the nineteenth century, George Grinnell worked to save the animal and protect it for future generations. *As a result,* several herds are thriving in the wild today.

Strategies for Using the Graphic Organizer

A cause-and-effect chart can be a very useful tool for students drafting cause-and-effect articles. To ensure that students understand how to use this tool, model using the Cause-and-Effect Flowchart in **Graphic Organizer Transparencies**, p. 230. Point out that the model summarizes multiple effects (bicycles are faster, more comfortable, and lighter) in clear terms. The writer might begin the essay by illustrating the drawbacks of earlier bicycles and going on to explain how these drawbacks caused the development of new materials.

Using the model, instruct students to create cause-and-effect charts of their own. Students may enjoy working on their charts together in peer review groups. After the charts are completed, have students begin drafting.

Susan Vreeland

On Showing Causes and Effects

My story "Crayon, 1955" is drawn from a time in my childhood when my great-grandfather, an artist, came to our house to die. What occurred there in that intense time was magical: He introduced me to his world of art. The experience narrated here was the cause of my lifelong interest in art, and resulted, ultimately, in writing *Girl in Hyacinth Blue.*

"Re-visioning . . . is a coaxing process."
—Susan Vreeland

Professional Model:
from "Crayon, 1955"

"Jenny," he said the next day. His voice scraped [like a Popsicle stick across the sidewalk]. "Let me teach you to paint."

I wasn't sure I wanted him to. The room smelled bad, but not just because of his . . . paints. Once Mom said Gramp's blood ran with turpentine, which I thought was what made his skin waxy and yellow.

Practicing a secret style of shallow breathing, I sat on the edge of the bed and he held my hand inside his [spidery one] while I held the long brush. He squeezed so tightly, directing where my hand should go, that his long yellow nails jabbed into my palm. I curled up my toes and kept quiet. [Like a miracle,] in front of me appeared an unrolled white flower with an orange finger inside. "There's nothing so cheerful as a calla lily," he said as we worked. "They grow tall and graceful just like you, and one day, they open themselves to the world."

In my revision, I inserted images that a young girl might think — the simile of a Popsicle stick, and the visual adjective "spidery."

To convey sharply the resulting change in Jenny, in my revision I added, "like a miracle," an exaggerated simile revealing her astonishment.

In fiction, cause and effect are subtle, sometimes only a suggestion. Jenny's negative reactions to her grandfather change when the painting resulting from his teaching pleases her.

Susan Vreeland on Showing Causes and Effects

Review the passage on the student page with the class, using Susan Vreeland's comments to illuminate the process of writing a cause-and-effect essay.

Teaching From the Professional Model

1. Show students Segment 3 on Susan Vreeland on ***See It!* DVD** or from this page in the **Enriched Online Student Edition.** Discuss Vreeland's use of figurative language to provide specific details to support her main points.
2. Read the quotation by Susan Vreeland aloud to students.
   Ask: Why does she use the word *re-visioning instead of revision?*
   Possible response: The word *re-visioning* suggests an active and ongoing process.
   Ask: What does she mean when she calls re-visioning "a coaxing process"?
   Possible response: The word *coaxing* suggests that Vreeland is in a partnership with her writing. For example, she creates the character of the girl and then must coax from the character the images and associations that she makes about her grandfather.
3. **Ask:** How are cause-and-effect relationships important in fiction?
   Possible response: Cause-and-effect relationships are important to characterization in fiction. These relationships help to illustrate why characters act as they do and how and why characters change.

Strategies for Adding Details

Although Susan Vreeland's story is fiction, she uses details to clearly depict the connections between the causes and effects in her story. Like Vreeland, students can benefit from adding details to their own essays. Have students reread their drafts, adding descriptive details to help sharpen their presentation of causes and effects. For example, the addition of adjectives such as *powerful* and *overwhelming* to an essay on the effects of a tsunami can help make clear to readers the magnitude of the forces at work.

Have students exchange essays with partners. Partners should read each other's essays, underlining the details that describe causes and effects and suggesting where details could be added.

PHLit Online!
Show or assign the video online at **www.PHLITOnline.com**

Revising Strategies

1. Introduce the Revising Strategies, using the instruction on the student page.
2. Have students apply the strategies as they revise.

Teaching the Strategies

1. Write this short paragraph on the board: *Health insurance costs too much for too little coverage. My aunt once had surgery on her knee. The government needs to take steps to provide everyone with comprehensive coverage at a minimum cost. There are many countries, such as Canada, whose health-care systems might serve as a model for a new health-care system.*
2. Ask a volunteer to circle the topic sentence. In a different color, ask another volunteer to circle supportive details. **Ask:** Can the uncircled details be revised to support the topic sentence, or should they be eliminated from the paragraph?
   Possible response: The detail, "My aunt once had surgery on her knee" can be revised to support the topic sentence if the writer can add the appropriate information. If the aunt paid a high heath insurance premium and then found that her surgery was still not fully covered, then her case can be used as evidence in support of the topic sentence. If not, the detail is irrelevant and should be cut.

Six Traits Focus

✔	Ideas	✔	Word Choice
✔	Organization		Sentence Fluency
✔	Voice		Conventions

WG Writing and Grammar, Grade 10

Students will find additional instruction on revising a cause-and-effect essay in Chapter 10, Section 4.

Revising Strategies

Look for careless repetition. Effective use of repetition helps to emphasize key ideas and create a memorable impact. Sloppy repetition, however, weakens your writing. Look for words that appear too often or too close together. Use a thesaurus to find words with related meanings or use a pronoun to replace a noun that appears over and over again.

Too Much Repetition: Bees *buzz* as a result of beating their wings *rapidly.* When an intruder approaches, bees beat their wings even more *rapidly.* As a result, *the bees' buzzing rapidly* grows louder.

More Effective: Bees *buzz* as a result of beating their wings *rapidly.* When an intruder approaches, bees beat their wings *faster* and their *buzzing* grows louder.

Color-code to identify related details. Each paragraph in your essay should have a strong, single focus. First, circle the topic sentence of each paragraph. If you cannot find a topic sentence, consider adding one. Then, underline the details that support the topic of the paragraph.

Peer Review

After identifying topic sentences and supporting details, take a close look at the sentences that are neither circled nor underlined. With a partner, discuss whether you should rewrite or delete these sentences. You might also consider moving those sentences to another paragraph where they would support the topic more effectively. After revising, explain your decisions to your partner.

Model: Revising to Strengthen Focus

Ice storms caused devastation throughout the Northeast. Power lines were downed by the heavy coating of ice, causing widespread electric outages. ~~People became bored without access to television.~~ Roads coated with ice became impassable.

The writer deleted a sentence that offered useful information but did not relate to the topic of the paragraph.

Strategies for Test Taking

On most writing-assessment tests, students are instructed to work through the major steps of the writing process: prewriting, drafting, and revising. Some tests provide time and space for complete first and final drafts; others do not.

Remind students that no matter how much time and space they have, paragraph focus is very important. If students are making revisions directly on the draft they will turn in, they might mark topic sentences with a small dot instead of circling them.

On writing tests, students should try to be conscious of words they are likely to overuse, especially key terms in a cause-and-effect relationship. If they are making changes directly on the draft they will turn in, carefully crossing out some uses of these words and replacing them with synonyms or pronouns is an appropriate approach.

WRITER'S TOOLBOX

Word Choice | Ideas | Conventions | Sentence Fluency | Voice | Organization

Revising Pronoun-Antecedent Agreement

Antecedents are the nouns for which pronouns stand. A pronoun must agree with its antecedent in number, person, and gender.

Identifying Incorrect Pronoun-Antecedent Agreement In your writing, check each pronoun to make sure it agrees with its antecedent. Ask three things about the antecedent:

- *Number:* Is it singular or plural?
- *Person:* Is it first person (the one speaking), second person (the one being spoken to), or third person (the one spoken about)?
- *Gender:* Is it masculine, feminine, or neuter?

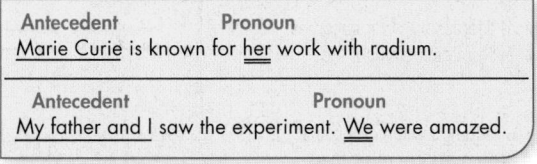

Antecedent — Pronoun
Marie Curie is known for her work with radium.

Antecedent — Pronoun
My father and I saw the experiment. We were amazed.

Apply It!

Prentice Hall Writing and Grammar Connection: Chapter 24, Section 2

Special Problems with Agreement Use a plural personal pronoun with two or more antecedents joined by *and.*

Lewis and Clark described the expedition in their journal.

Use a singular personal pronoun with two or more antecedents joined by *or* or *nor.*

Neither Lewis nor Clark regretted his journey.

Fixing Agreement Errors To fix a pronoun and antecedent that do not agree, choose the pronoun that has the correct number, person, and gender.

1. **Describe the number, person, and gender of the antecedent.**
2. **Choose a pronoun with the same number, person, and gender.** Be sure you use the right pronoun case: nominative, objective, or possessive.

Grammar in Your Writing

Circle the pronouns in two paragraphs of your draft. Draw an arrow to the antecedent for each pronoun. Evaluate whether or not the pronoun and antecedent agree. Replace any incorrect pronouns.

Revising Pronoun-Antecedent Agreement

1. Introduce the grammar skill, using the instruction on the student page.
2. Discuss the rules, the examples in the box, and the strategies for fixing agreement errors.
3. Have students follow the instruction under Grammar in Your Writing to correct errors in their drafts.

Teaching the Grammar Skill

1. Demonstrate asking the questions under Identifying Incorrect Pronoun-Antecedent Agreement by applying them to the sentences in the chart.
2. Have students fix incorrect pronoun-antecedent agreement in the following sentences.

   Bettie went home early to get started on our homework.
   Answer: her homework

   Neither she nor her mom could spare an hour for their chores.
   Answer: her chores

   Tom and Bettie are close friends. We often do homework together.
   Answer: They
3. As students begin to apply the skill, you may ask volunteers to copy and correct sentences from their essays on the board.

Writing and Grammar, Grade 10

Students will find additional instruction on pronoun-antecedent agreement in Chapter 24, Section 2.

Strategies for Test Taking

On writing tests, students will need to avoid pronoun-antecedent errors and correct them when they occur. With slight modification, the Grammar in Your Writing strategy may be useful in a test-taking situation. Students should practice identifying antecedents with their fingers.

On reading tests, students may encounter multiple-choice questions that require them to identify and correct errors in pronoun-antecedent agreement. On such questions, students will also have to distinguish pronoun-antecedent agreement errors from other errors of grammar, usage, and spelling. Have students practice with this example:

Roberta raced home to walk they're dog.

A. walked their dog
B. walk there dog
C. walk her dog
D. The sentence is correct.

The correct answer is **C.**

Student Model

Review the Student Model with the class, using the annotations to analyze the writer's use of the elements of a cause-and-effect essay.

Teaching From the Student Model

1. Explain to students that the Student Model is a sample, and that their own cause-and-effect essays may be longer.
2. Tell students that in addition to helping the writer organize information, subheads are also useful for readers. **Ask:** How might readers benefit from subheads?
   Answer: Subheads are useful to readers in the following ways: (1) they help readers understand the writer's organizational pattern, which facilitates comprehension; (2) they help readers locate specific information within an essay.
3. **Ask** students why the writer breaks the information about the effects of hurricanes into two sections.
   Answer: By categorizing the types of damage that may be caused by a hurricane, the writer helps the reader understand and remember the information in the essay.
4. **Ask** students why writers should include specific details to support broader claims.
   Answer: Specific details strengthen a writer's argument.

Connecting to Real-Life Writing

Explain to students that a newspaper editorial might focus in large part on a cause-and-effect relationship. Point out that many editorials deal with social, political, or community problems that are in need of solutions. Often, editorials will explain the factors that caused a problem and the effect of the problem on the community. The writer may go on to suggest a solution to the problem and to describe the potential effects of the proposed solution. Ask students to consider issues in their school or community that might be addressed in an editorial using a cause-and-effect text structure.

Student Model: Andrew Vanover
Raleigh, NC

Hurricane: Causes and Effects

Everyone dreads the hurricane season. When that time of year comes around, we all lock down and get ready for the harsh winds and power outages. The 2004 season started out with a bang. Large parts of the coast were torn apart as storms rolled in, one after another.

Causes of Hurricanes

Hurricanes form when weather patterns of different temperatures run into each other and start spinning. When a cold front out in the ocean, moving in one direction, comes in contact with a warm front moving in the opposite direction, winds start. These winds start moving in circular motions. As they spin, they pick up speed. These large areas of fast-moving winds generate tornadoes that pull water up into the storm. Hurricanes have high winds with tornadoes, and carry large amounts of water.

When it starts, the storm is classified as a tropical depression. As it becomes stronger, it is called a tropical storm. If the wind speeds get high enough, the tropical storm is categorized as a hurricane.

Effects of Hurricanes: Damage to Property

When the storm hits land, it dumps all its water, and that is when it becomes the most destructive. Some of the water soaks into the ground, but often there is more water than the land can absorb. As a result, the water quickly runs off to lower areas. These run-offs are called flash floods. Flash floods can wash away land and possessions or destroy them by filling them with water. At the same time, hurricane winds can blow over trees and power lines. With the power out, repairs are hard to make quickly. This means power can be out for a week or longer. Hurricanes also bring lightning, which can cause fires in trees or houses.

Effects of Hurricanes: Damage to Business

During the late summer and fall of 2004, the state of Florida was hit by four major hurricanes: Charley, Frances, Ivan, and Jeanne. Each hurricane caused so much damage that it could not be repaired before the next storm hit. The damage was so bad that President Bush asked Congress for 7.1 billion dollars for repairs in Florida. Many people had to board up stores and wait in line for electric generators. In addition, relief workers were sent down to Florida to help deliver meals, water, and ice.

These storms not only caused trouble for the insurance companies, but also affected the citrus and tourism industries. The citrus growers in Florida lost about half of their grapefruit crop during Hurricane Frances. Tourism was also hurt because people do not want to travel into a disaster zone.

Conclusion

The hurricane season of 2004 was more intense than previous years. This is said to be from warm temperatures in the Atlantic Ocean and a decrease in wind shear. We hope that in the future we will better be able to predict and prepare for these hurricanes.

Andrew uses subheads to clearly organize the information. This paragraph explains what causes hurricanes.

Andrew breaks his discussion of the effects of hurricanes into two sections.

In addition, Andrew uses a specific detail to support his broader claims.

Strategies for Using Technology in Writing

Make any available technology accessible to students for their presentations. If computer projectors are available, encourage students to create illustrations, charts and graphs, and even text to display. Students can also generate their presentations at home and bring disks to class. If computer projectors are not available, students can use blank transparencies and markers to create graphics for the overhead projector. Students may also enjoy using slide projectors.

Editing and Proofreading

Review your draft to correct errors in grammar, spelling, and punctuation.

Focus on Usage Errors: Check your writing for commonly confused words. Remember that *then* refers to time and *than* is used for comparisons. Use *since* to refer to a previous time, not to mean "because." If you are unsure about a word, consult a dictionary or usage guide.

Publishing and Presenting

Consider one of the following ways to share your writing:

Give a class presentation. Use your essay as the basis of a presentation. Use photographs, charts, maps, or diagrams to make the cause-and-effect relationships clear. Practice combining visuals with your writing, deciding when you will show each visual as you share the ideas from your essay.

Use e-mail. Share your writing electronically. Type the essay using word-processing software. Attach the file to an e-mail to a friend or relative. Save printouts of the essay and any responses in your writing portfolio.

Reflecting on Your Writing

Writer's Journal Jot down your answers to this question:
How did writing about the work help you to understand it?

Rubric for Self-Assessment

Find evidence in your writing to address each category. Then, use the rating scale to grade your work.

Criteria	Rating Scale				
	not very				*very*
Focus: How clearly do you identify the cause-and-effect relationship you explore?	1	2	3	4	5
Organization: How effectively do you organize your information?	1	2	3	4	5
Support/Elaboration: How strong are the details and examples you use as support?	1	2	3	4	5
Style: How effectively do you use transitions to connect your ideas?	1	2	3	4	5
Conventions: How correct is your grammar, especially your use of pronouns?	1	2	3	4	5

Differentiated Instruction for Universal Access

Support for Special Needs Students
It is important for students to recognize how different parts of the Student Model essay convey aspects of the cause-and-effect relationship. Make copies of the Student Model, cutting the side notes away from the model and into separate notes. Ask pairs of students to place the side notes next to the appropriate text. Ask volunteers to share where they placed each note and why.

Enrichment for Advanced Readers
Have students analyze the strengths and weaknesses of the Student Model. Encourage them to use self-sticking notes to mark places where the cause-and-effect relationship could be explained more clearly or more information could be included. Then, have students suggest better ways of explaining the relationship.

Editing and Proofreading

1. Introduce the Editing and Proofreading focus, using the instruction on the student page.
2. Have students edit and proofread their cause-and-effect essays, correcting grammar, spelling, punctuation, and word choice. Make sure they check for errors of the type noted on the student page.

Teaching the Editing Focus

Note common usage problems, such as confusing *affect* ("to influence") with *effect* ("result"), using the reason *because* for the reason *that,* and using *different than* for *different from.*

Six Traits Focus

	Ideas		Word Choice
	Organization		Sentence Fluency
	Voice	✓	Conventions

ASSESS

Publishing and Presenting

1. Point out that audiences outside the class may be interested in the topics of students' cause-and-effect essays.
2. Encourage students to construct presentations that would appeal to broader audiences.
3. If students choose to e-mail their essays to members of this larger audience, encourage them to send their essays to people with a range of different perspectives on their topics.

Reflecting on Your Writing

1. Suggest to students that working through the writing process may have changed their perspectives on their topics.
2. Before they begin writing in their journals, encourage students to discuss how their ideas have changed and evolved.

WG Writing and Grammar, Grade 10

Students will find additional guidance for editing and proofreading, publishing and presenting, and reflecting on cause-and-effect essays in Chapter 10, Sections 5 and 6.

MONITORING PROGRESS

Think About It

1. Remind students that the Unit Big Question is "Is there a difference between reality and truth?"
2. Direct students' attention to the selections they have read in Unit 1. Point out that the selections help answer the Big Question. **Ask** students for examples in the selections that show the difference between reality and truth.
   Possible response: In "Swimming to Antarctica," Cox feels that, due to the shock of the frigid water on her body, her progress is slow. However, the crew, who watch her from the boat, believe she is swimming well and is all right.
3. Explain to students that the Big Question applies in areas other than literature. For example, students may learn in social studies that people are required to tell the truth in court. **Ask** students how the truth that someone tells might be different from reality.
   Possible response: The person might say what he or she believes to be true but may not be aware of other realities of a situation.
4. Review the headings on the chart. Emphasize that distinguishing between reality and truth can be very important when coming to a conclusion about a situation.
5. Have students copy over and complete the chart on the student page. If they have difficulty finding examples from science, suggest the following starting points:
   - What are some different truths and realities about global warming?
   - What studies in space exploration have caused debate about what is truth and what is reality?
6. Have students discuss their answers in small groups and then present their examples to the class.

Applying the Big Question

Is there a difference between reality and truth?

Think About It

Think about what you have read in this unit and what you know about the differences between reality and truth from your other classes and your own experiences. Copy and complete the chart below to apply what you have learned about differences between reality and truth. One row has been completed for you.

Example	Reality	Truth	Difference Between Truth and Reality	What I learned
From Literature	The game of hide-and-seek in "Games at Twilight" is just a game and does not really matter.	Winning the game carries a deep life lesson for Ravi about how insignificant he really is.	In reality the game is just a game; but the truth to Ravi is that the game is proof of his place in the world.	A person's perception of reality is often subjective.
From Literature				
From Science				
From Social Studies				
From Real Life				

Teaching Resources

Unit 1 Resources

All *Applying the Big Question*, p. 11

PHLit Online! All print resources are also avaliable online at www.PHLitOnline.com.

Talk About It

Choose one of the examples in your chart as the basis for a **group discussion.** On note cards, write details about the example you chose. Include specific facts and details that support the ideas of reality and truth as they pertain to your example. Be prepared to explain how these two concepts are similar or different in the topic you chose. Then, take turns with a small group of classmates discussing each member's example. Invite group members to challenge your interpretation or contribute their own ideas about the relationship between reality and truth.

For tips on identifying verbal and nonverbal clues conveyed by a speaker, see the Communications Workshop on page 212.

Write About It

At the beginning of Unit 1, you wrote a response to the Big Question. Now that you have completed the unit, see how your understanding has deepened or changed. Write a new response, discussing how your initial ideas have been either changed or reinforced.

- ❑ Truth and reality are the same.
- ❑ Truth and reality are different.
- ❑ My own reponse:____________.

Support your answer with two or more of the ideas in your chart—one from literature, and one from another subject area or from your own life. You may also complete these sentences to help you organize your response.

- In this unit, I read a selection that included a difference between reality and a character's perception of truth. The character believed __________ , but the reality was _________ .
- One example of a similarity between reality and truth in Science is __________ because ____________.
- An example in which people have very different perceptions of the truth about a current political issue is ___________. The facts behind the issue are ____________. I believe the truth of the issue is _______.
- An example of a situation in which a friend and I see different truths based on the same reality, is ______________. When this happens, it creates a problem because ______________, but we can overcome our differences by __________.

Challenge What issues does this question still raise for you? How could you continue your exploration?

Big Question Vocabulary

- ☆ comprehend
- concrete
- ☆ confirm
- ☆ context
- ☆ differentiate
- ☆ discern
- ☆ evaluate
- evidence
- improbable
- ☆ objective
- perception
- reality
- ☆ subjective
- uncertainty
- verify

☆ **shows an Academic Vocabulary word.**

Strategies for Listening and Speaking

Remind students to follow these rules for partaking in a group discussion.

- Do not interrupt while someone is speaking. Instead, wait until he or she is finished.
- Offer criticism, but do it in a helpful, constructive way.
- Build on others' contributions whenever possible.

MONITORING PROGRESS

Talk About It

1. Have students complete the assignment, following the instruction on the student page.
2. Have students review their notecards before discussing them in small groups.

Write About It

1. Introduce the assignment, using the instruction on the student page.
2. Review the thematic vocabulary with the class (see pp. 2–3).

Teaching Prewriting

1. Point out that students may have read a selection in Unit 1 that shifted their viewpoints on the Big Question.
2. Encourage students to reflect on their new ideas about reality and truth and explain how these ideas have changed or been reinforced.
3. Have students complete the sentence starters on the student page. Guide them to compare their responses from Introducing the Big Question on pp. 2–3 with their new ideas.

Teaching Drafting

1. Review the elements of an essay: it focuses on a single topic and contains an introduction, a body, and a conclusion.
2. Have each student begin to draft by writing a thesis statement using a new or reinforced idea. Advise students to support their theses with a variety of details and examples.

Teaching Revising/Editing

1. Have students revise their essays. Encourage them to check for organization and logical decisive word choice.
2. Have students work with partners for peer review. Encourage partners to point to areas that are especially well done, as well as areas that could use improvement.

Guiding Student Publishing

Students might share their essays by submitting them to the school newspaper.

EXTEND/ASSESS

Answers

Meeting Your Standards

Students will

1. use a dictionary and a thesaurus as resources.
2. understand word origins and derivations.

Using a Dictionary and Thesaurus

1. Introduce the skill, using the instruction on the student page.
2. Review the definitions and examples.

Think Aloud: Model the Skill

Model the use of a dictionary. Say to students:

When I come across a word I don't recognize or a word I want to know more about, I can look it up in a dictionary.

Suppose I want to know more about the word *mollify*. First, I locate the word in a dictionary. The boldfaced word is followed by its pronunciation and then by the different verb forms it takes: *mollified, mollifying,* and *mollifies.* The word has more than one definition, but, in general, it means "to calm" or "to soften." When I check the word's etymology, I see how the word's definitions connect to its origin. *Mollify* comes from the Late Latin *mollificare* and *mollis,* which mean "soft." Finally, the entry provides the different parts of speech of the word: *mollifiable* (adj.), *mollification* (noun), *mollifier* (noun), and *mollifyingly* (adverb).

Practice A

Sample answers:

1. displeasure; discontent
2. calmness; forbearance
3. address; speak
4. endlessly; recurrently
5. recall; recollect
6. mischief; prank

Vocabulary Workshop

Using a Dictionary and Thesaurus

A **dictionary** is an alphabetical listing of words. It gives definitions, parts of speech, etymologies, and more. Notice the information given in this dictionary entry.

Dictionary

Part of speech — Etymology — Definition

narrate (nar′āt; na āt′, nə-) ***vt., vi.*** **-rat′ed, -rat′ing** [< L *narratus*, pp. of *narrare*, to tell, akin to *gnarus*, acquainted with < IE **gnoro-* < base **gen-*, to KNOW] **1.** to tell (a story) in writing or speech **2.** to give an account of (happenings, etc.)

In addition to information about the work, a dictionary includes a guide to pronunciation. Most dictionaries provide a key to the symbols at the bottom of the page or in the front of the dictionary.

There are many kinds of dictionaries. One to know about is the *Oxford English Dictionary,* or OED. It tracks the usage of most English words over the past thousand years. The latest edition is available online and in a twenty-volume set. It is a very useful tool if you are studying the etymology, or origin, of a word in English.

A **thesaurus** is a reference book that lists synonyms, or words with similar meanings. You can use a thesaurus to increase your vocabulary or to find alternative words to express your meaning. Here's an example of a thesaurus entry:

Thesaurus

entertainer ***n.*** **1.** entertainer, performer, artist, dancer, hoofer **2.** actor, actress, player, thespian, mime, villain, character ***v.*** entertain, act, perform, dramatize, dance, play

Both dictionaries and thesauruses are available in print, in computer programs, and on the Internet.

Practice A Look up each word in a thesaurus. For each, write two words that have almost the same meaning.

1. disapproval
2. patience
3. talk
4. repeatedly
5. remember
6. joke

Teaching Resources

Unit 1 Resources

All *Using a Dictionary and Thesaurus* pp. 229–230

PHLit Online! **Vocabulary Central,** featuring definitions, audio pronunciations, Word Families, and activities, is available at **www.PHLitOnline.com.**

Practice B Use a dictionary to answer questions 1–7 and a thesaurus to respond to questions 8 and 9.

1. Some words have more than one dictionary definition. **(a)** What is the definition of *idle* in this sentence? Eliot sat *idle* all afternoon. **(b)** What is another definition for this word?
2. **(a)** What is the adverb form of the word *sleepy*? **(b)** How would you use it in a sentence?
3. What is the meaning of the word *cuff* when used as a verb?
4. If the situation is *fraught* with danger, is it safe? Explain.
5. Which dictionary definition is correct for *sorry* as it is used in this sentence? In Aunt Sarah's opinion, I was one *sorry* entertainer.
6. Is it possible use the word *revise* as a noun? Explain.
7. How many definitions does your dictionary give for the word *frost*?
8. Find three synonyms for *deadly.*
9. Rewrite this sentence twice using synonyms for *genuine*. The painting turned out to be a *genuine* Van Gogh.

PHLit Online!
www.PHLitOnline.com

- Illustrated vocabulary words
- Interactive vocabulary games
- Vocabulary flashcards

Activity Create a note card like the one shown for each of these words.

allay unkempt linear quandary naive

Word:

Definition:

Pronunciation:

Sentence:

Read your sentences aloud. Then, in a group, trade cards and read each other's sentences. Check one another's pronunciations and usage. Refer to a dictionary if you disagree on the pronunciation or word meaning.

Challenge

Look up the following words in a dictionary or reliable online source. Find the earliest usage of each word and its definition. Then, locate a more modern definition of each word. Talk with a group about how the meaning of each word has changed over the years. Is the original meaning still used?

flaunt
cab
fragile
vandal

Differentiated Instruction for Universal Access

Special Needs Students
Have students work in small groups. Give each group a word to look up in the dictionary. Once students have located the word, have students copy the entry on a large piece of paper. Have students use self-sticking notes to identify the word's pronunciation, definition(s), and parts of speech. Have groups present their words, including pronunciations and definitions.

Gifted/Talented Students
Have students work in pairs. Provide each pair with a word that they can use to create their own dictionary entry. Encourage students to use music or art to illustrate the meaning of their word. Make sure students include the word, pronunciation, definition(s), and parts of speech in their creative presentation of the word.

EXTEND/ASSESS

Answers

Practice B
Sample answers:

1. (a) In this sentence, idle means "doing nothing." (b) Another definition is "having no basis or reason."
2. (a) sleepily (b) After a long yawn, Miranda sleepily took out a bowl, some cereal and milk, and ate breakfast.
3. When cuff is used as a verb, its meaning is "to put handcuffs on."
4. To be *fraught* with something means "to be full of that thing," so a situation fraught with danger would be dangerous.
5. In this sentence, sorry means "poor" or "pitiful."
6. No, revise is the verb form; *revision* is the noun form.
7. 15
8. dangerous; harmful; fatal
9. The painting turned out to be an *authentic* Van Gogh. The painting turned out to be a *real* Van Gogh.

Activity

To prepare students for the Activity, give each student a dictionary and five notecards. Then, guide students in using a dictionary to identify the pronunciation, which generally follows the word and precedes the part of speech. Encourage students to use the pronunciation guide in the dictionary to determine the meanings of symbols.

Challenge

Divide the class into groups, and ensure that each group has access to a dictionary. The following are some similarities and differences your students may note.

flaunt: The meaning has changed little.

cab: While the origin is from *cabriolet*, *cab* today refers to a similar vehicle that transports people.

fragile: The meaning is the same: "easily broken."

vandal: The name comes from a Germanic tribe that ransacked Rome. Today's definition, "any person that destroys or spoils public or private property," is similar.

Meeting Your Standards

Students will

1. analyze the content of media presentations by identifying and analyzing evidence.
2. evaluate the delivery of media presentations.

Introducing Analyzing Media Presentations

Introduce the assignment and the strategies, using the instruction on the student page.

Evaluate the Content

1. Explain that evidence is the information used to support a claim. Ask students to imagine that a newspaper journalist uses an interview and public records as evidence to support a claim. **Ask** students to identify the evidence. **Answer:** The interview would appear in the form of quotations, and the public records would provide facts or statistics.
2. Explain that it is particularly important to identify whether the presentation is biased or impartial. One way to identify bias is to ask why the person or organization is making the presentation.
3. Explain that statements that are not true and damage someone's reputation are legally considered either slander (if spoken) or libel (if written).

Evaluate the Presentation

1. Tell students that charged language and stereotypes are signals that a presentation is biased.
2. **Ask** students to identify the cultural assumption in a television commercial for a luxury car. **Possible response:** The cultural assumption may be that cars are status symbols rather than mere modes of transportation.

Assess the Activity

To evaluate students' delivery, use the Listening: Evaluating a Media Presentation rubric, p. 268 in the *Professional Development Guidebook.*

Communications Workshop

Analyzing Media Presentations

Some television, radio, and Internet sources are truthful, thorough, and objective. Others offer information that is inaccurate, incomplete, or reported in a biased way. To evaluate media, stay alert and analyze claims critically. Use the following strategies.

Evaluate Content

To evaluate the information, listen or read for facts, statistics, quotations, and other evidence. If no support is provided, decide whether you have any reason to accept the claims in the presentation.

Consider relevance. A fact or image may be attention-grabbing, but if it has nothing to do with the main idea, it is not evidence.

Consider bias. People quoted in media may present biased, or distorted, evidence. Consider the reasons a source might have to favor one version of events over another.

Consider inconsistencies or ambiguities. Ask yourself whether the claims made are contradictory or vague. Consider whether any viewpoints have been left out.

Look out for illegal statements. There are laws to protect people from libel, false written statements, and slander, false spoken statements.

Evaluate the Presentation

Once you know a presentation's content, notice how the information is delivered. Some media techniques sway viewers or misrepresent ideas.

Be alert to charged or manipulative language. Listen for words and phrases that are meant to manipulate or affect your emotions.

Be aware of stereotypes. Watch for stereotypes, or oversimplified ideas about a group of people. Many stereotypes are negative images based on race, gender, age, or role.

Avoid cultural assumptions. Media presentations can reflect basic assumptions about what is important or good. Think about whether you agree with such value judgments.

Activity: Analyze a Newscast or Advertisement

Analyze a television newscast or advertisement using the Feedback Form as a guide. Share your conclusions in a class discussion.

Rating System

Poor				Excellent
1	2	3	4	5

Purpose
What is the main purpose? ______

Use of Facts
___ Relevant Support
___ Reliable Support
___ Complete Support

Options
___ Reasonableness
___ Breadth

Presentation
___ Speaker's Clarity
___ Graphics
___ Speaker's Tone
___ Music
Does the presentation include charged language? ______
Does it include charged images? ______
Does it present stereotypes? ______

Conclusions
Was the presentation objective? ______
Was it reliable? ______

Independent Reading

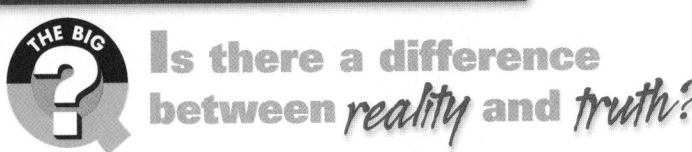

Is there a difference between *reality* and *truth?*

The Fall of the House of Usher and Other Tales
Edgar Allan Poe
Signet, 1960

Edgar Allan Poe's nightmarish visions lead readers to the darkest places in the human heart. From a family confronting an ancient curse to a murderer losing his grasp on sanity, characters in Poe's stories may leave you wondering what is real and what is not.

Girl in Hyacinth Blue
Susan Vreeland
MacMurray & Beck, 2000

When a mysterious painting surfaces after being hidden for years, secrets begin to unravel. As the work passes from owner to owner, it illuminates the changing realities that it has witnessed during its journey through people's lives.

Illustrated Dictionary of Mythology: Heroes, Heroines, Gods, and Goddesses From Around the World
Philip Wilkinson
DK Publishing, 1998

Do you believe that fire started when it was stolen from the gods? Does a good harvest depend on special ceremonies? Are the moon and the sun a sister and brother who fled the earth in shame? In this illustrated reference book of myths and fables from around the world, you can immerse yourself in times when the realities of science and nature were explained differently from the way they are today.

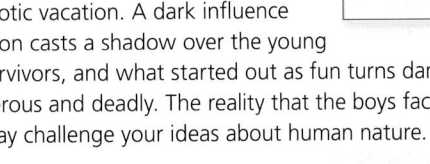

Lord of the Flies
William Golding
Berkley Publishing Group, 1954

When a plane crash leaves a group of boys stranded without adults on a deserted island, life feels like an exotic vacation. A dark influence soon casts a shadow over the young survivors, and what started out as fun turns dangerous and deadly. The reality that the boys face may challenge your ideas about human nature.

Animal Farm
George Orwell
Signet Classic, 1996

With idealism and stirring slogans, mistreated animals take over a farm and try to create a paradise of progress, justice, and equality. As the story progresses however, the reality of the situation points to far different truths.

41 Stories
O. Henry
Signet, 1984

This collection of O. Henry's finest stories whisks readers from a bustling city to a seedy saloon to a prison shoe shop. Wherever the talented O. Henry takes you, you will find yourself discovering that reality and truth may not always be as they appear. Lose yourself in this collection and you may find something you did not expect.

Consult your teacher before choosing one of these books.

Planning Students' Further Reading

Have students choose a book for independent reading from those listed. Before recommending a work to students, preview it, taking into account the values of your community as well as the maturity of your students. The following notes offer some guidance. Because a variety of factors play a role in determining the accessibility of a work, a book with a higher readability rating may be deemed more accessible than a book with a lower rating.

L4 ***The Fall of the House of Usher*** These tales contain violence, murder, insanity, and other irrational behavior, as well as incidental mentions of drinking and drugs. Ethnic or racial groups are sometimes portrayed in prejudiced or highly inaccurate ways.
Level suitable for high school students

L3 ***Girl in Hyacinth Blue*** The Nazi brutality in the first two stories may upset some readers. In some of the other stories, married people are unfaithful to each other. A woman bears twins and kills one of them.
Lexile: 950L

L2 ***The Illustrated Dictionary of Mythology: Heroes, Heroines, Gods, and Goddesses from Around the World*** Some students may be disturbed by creation myths that differ from their own beliefs, the idea of spirits, multiple gods and goddesses, and pictures of classic statues.
Level suitable for high school students

L2 ***Lord of the Flies*** Sensitive issues include the violence that occurs and the sexual imagery that is used when the pig is slaughtered.
Lexile: 770

L3 ***Animal Farm*** Some students may be troubled by the corruption and immorality among figures of authority, the scenes of the animal's executions, description of Frederick's cruelty to his animals, the Battle of the Windmill and Boxer being sent to the knackers.
Level suitable for high school students

L3 ***41 Stories*** Students may react to comments about ethnic or racial groups that reflect the culture in which O. Henry lived.
Level suitable for high school students

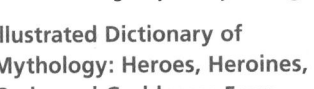

Connecting to the Big Question

Have students form literature circles in which to discuss the books they read independently. See *Professional Development Guidebook*, pp. 47–49, for guidance in running literature circles.

Suggest that students discuss these questions:

- What is the reality, or the facts, that you found in this work?
- What do the main characters believe is the truth?
- Is there a difference between the reality you found and the main character's definition of the truth? Explain.

Challenge

The following titles for advanced readers are available in the Penguin Literature Library.

***Don Quixote* by Miguel de Cervantes** Sensitive issues include ethnic labels and sexual promiscuity. Lower-class woman are treated very poorly.

***Their Eyes Were Watching God* by Zora Neale Hurston** The novel includes language and attitudes toward African Americans that are considered offensive today, extramarital sex, and disobedience to authority figures

MONITORING PROGRESS

Using the Unit Review

In this Test Practice workshop (pp. 214–219), students apply the skills in Unit 1. The practice is divided into four sections.

1. Before assigning each section, review the relevant Unit skills with students.
2. Set a time limit for the multiple choice items in each section, allowing a little over one minute per question. Allow ten to fifteen minutes for any Writing for Assessment questions.
3. Administer each section. Have students write the starting time at the top of their papers. When half the time for the multiple choice items has run out, ask students to write the time next to an answer on which they are working. Have them do the same when time is three quarters through and again when time is up. Have them note the start and end times for any Writing for Assessment questions as well.
4. Review with students the pacing reflected in their notes.

Reteaching Skills

1. For each practice, use the Reteach chart on the same page as the answers to determine which skills require reteaching, based on which items students answered incorrectly.
2. Reteach these skills prior to assigning the **Benchmark Test** for the second half of Unit 1 (***Unit 1 Resources***, pp. 233–239).

Test Practice: Unit 1 Review

I. Literary Skills

Directions: *Read the passage. Then, answer each question that follows.*

The Mummy's Curse

Death Shall Come on Swift Wings to Him Who Disturbs the Peace of the King.

These words, supposedly inscribed on the tomb of Egyptian King Tutankhamen, did not deter the intrepid English archaeologist, Howard Carter. After years of searching, in 1922 Carter located King Tut's tomb. Archaeologists had long known that pharaohs were mummified at death and buried with riches to accompany them to the afterworld. To protect them from grave robbers, tombs were sealed with stone blocks or contained false passages. In some cases, the tombs were guarded by a curse.

After visiting England, Carter brought a canary back to Egypt. When Carter returned to his house after locating the tomb, his servant met him holding the dead bird. The servant claimed the bird had been killed by a cobra, a symbol of ancient Egyptian royalty, because Carter had violated the tomb. Carter ignored the warning. Upon the arrival in Egypt of his wealthy backer, Lord Carnarvon, Carter prepared to open the tomb.

Lord Carnarvon watched as Carter drilled a hole in the tomb door. Carter leaned through the hole, a candle in his hand.

"Can you see anything?" asked Lord Carnarvon.

"Yes, wonderful things," answered Carter.

The tomb contained a treasure trove, including a stone sarcophagus in which rested three gold coffins, nested inside each other. The innermost coffin held the mummy of King Tut. Everyone was excited about the find, and no one considered the curse. According to rumor, Carter had found a tablet inscribed with the curse, but hid it from his superstitious workers.

Shortly after the tomb was opened, the curse struck. Lord Carnarvon died from an infected bug bite. When King Tut's mummy was unwrapped, it had a wound in the same position as Lord Carnarvon's bug bite.

Within ten years, eleven people related to the discovery of King Tut's tomb had died of unnatural causes. Newspapers sensationalized the "mummy's curse," and claimed there were as many as twenty-one victims of the curse. Was this the hype of a sensationalist press, or did the curse exist?

Later investigation showed that of twenty-two people present when the tomb was opened, only six had died by 1934. Carter himself lived to the age of sixty-six, dying of natural causes.

Strategies for Test Taking

Remind students to focus on the key words in the question, such as those in the practice test that are highlighted in boldface. In question 1, for instance, they are to find the detail that appears first. Locating each detail in the story should guide them to the answer. Similarly, in question 2, they must focus on an event that foreshadows another event. Explain that answer options that cite incidents that do not reflect on later incidents can be eliminated.

1. Which event in the selection occurs first?

A. The canary dies.
B. King Tut's tomb is discovered.
C. Lord Carnarvon dies.
D. King Tut's mummy is unwrapped.

2. Which event is an example of **foreshadowing?**

A. the death of Lord Carnarvon
B. the arrival of Lord Carnarvon in Egypt
C. the discovery of King Tut's tomb
D. the death of the canary

3. Which of the following represents an **internal conflict** of a character?

A. The servant fears the Mummy's curse.
B. Carter dismisses the superstition.
C. Lord Carnarvon pays for Carter's work.
D. The reporters tell stories about the "curse."

4. **Vocabulary in Context** Which word is closest in meaning to the underlined word *deter*?

A. encourage
B. destroy
C. stop
D. include

5. Which of the following best states the **author's purpose?**

A. to persuade readers that the "mummy's curse" may have been exaggerated
B. to persuade readers to study archaeology
C. to entertain readers with a comic tale
D. to inform readers about King Tut

6. Which of the following best describes the **author's perspective?**

A. The author believes in the "mummy's curse."
B. The author supports archaeological studies.
C. The author views the story objectively.
D. The author wants tombs to be undisturbed.

7. Which of the following is an example of **irony?**

A. Carter eventually locates King Tut's tomb after years of searching.
B. Lord Carnarvon attends the tomb's opening.
C. The canary dies when the tomb is found.
D. The mummy has a wound in the same location as Lord Carnarvon's bug bite.

8. Which of these sentences *best* increases the tension in the selection?

A. Carter leaned through the hole, a candle in his hand.
B. After years of searching, in 1922 Carter located King Tut's tomb.
C. On one of his trips to England, Carter had brought a yellow canary back to Egypt.
D. Carter himself lived to the age of sixty-six, dying of natural causes.

9. Which element of a short story is *not* represented in this selection?

A. character
B. dialogue
C. suspense
D. exposition

Writing for Assessment

10. In a paragraph, **explain** how the syntax and diction in the opening quotation reinforces the mysteriousness of the curse as described in the passage. **Support** your answer with details from the passage.

GO ON

Answers

Answers With Explanations

1. B—This event is in paragraph 1. *Incorrect answers:* A—This event is in paragraph 2. C—This event is in paragraph 7. D—same explanation as for C.
2. D—The bird's death foreshadows others. *Incorrect answers:* A—Carnarvon's is the chief death foreshadowed by the bird's. B—This event does not hint at later events. C—same explanation as for B.
3. B—Carter's personal beliefs cause him to dismiss the curse. *Incorrect answers:* A—The servant is fearful of an external, the curse. C—This fact does not represent conflict. D—same explanation as for C.
4. C—The warnings did not "stop" Carter from continuing. *Incorrect answers:* A—To *deter* is to get someone to stop, not to "encourage" them. B—Deterring stops an action; it does not "destroy" the actor. D—*Deterring* does not include someone in a group.
5. A—The ending makes clear that the author does not believe in the curse. *Incorrect answers:* B—This purpose would have been better served with an account of Carter's satisfaction with his work. C—The story is not meant to be funny. D—The author dwells on the excavation of the tomb, not Tut's life.
6. C—The author weighs evidence for and against the curse. *Incorrect answers:* A—The ending shows this is not the case. B—That may be true, but is not the point of the passage. D—The author does not condemn Carter for his excavation.
7. D—The similar locations would surprise the skeptical reader. *Incorrect answers:* A—Archaeology often requires years of searching. B—Carnarvon would have interest in seeing the results. C—That something will happen to the bird is suggested by its being mentioned in the first place.
8. A—The reader wonders if something will happen to Carter as he looks in. *Incorrect answers:* B—This statement does not build tension. C—same explanation as for B. D—This statement defuses tension.

Answers continued

9. C—There is question as to whether the "curse" will strike Carter and others, but it does not build suspense as a story would. *Incorrect answers:* A—Carter and Lord Carnarvon are characters. B—There is dialogue. D—Description of background offers exposition.

Writing for Assessment

Students might suggest that the foreboding language used in the quotation, such as *Death* and *Swift*, contribute to the mystery over whether the deaths of the team members that discovered Tut's tomb were in fact part of the curse or just coincidence.

Reteach

Question	Instructional Pages to Reteach
1	29
2	29
3	115
4	153
5	59
6	188
7	29
8	6
9	96

ASSESS

Answers

Answers With Explanations

1. **D**—This subhead indicates that the text below describes the ghost crab's physical features. *Incorrect answers:* A—The title is too general to be useful for this specific purpose. B—*Habitat* refers to where the ghost crab lives, not its physical features. C—The bulleted list contains interesting facts, but mostly address behavior.
2. **C**—Since the ghost crab's habitat is a beach, the photograph would be most helpful in this section. *Incorrect answers:* A—This feature does not address the ghost crab's environment. B—same explanation as for A. D—same explanation as for A.
3. **D**—Text details make clear that ghost crabs eat both animals and plants. *Incorrect answers:* A—This would not explain the text that follows regarding its diet. B—An animal that only eats animals is a *carnivore.* C—The term *omnivore* is applied to many different animals.
4. **C**—A detailed discussion of the ghost crab's behavior would be a useful addition. *Incorrect answers:* A—This heading simply refers to one feature of the ghost crab's appearance. B—This heading refers to information that does not apply to current ghost crabs. D—This heading refers to a broader category and would not be an appropriate subheading.
5. **C**—The publisher of the article could give clues to the reliability of the source. *Incorrect answers:* A—The author's name would not be sufficient to reveal credibility, though his or her credentials would. B—This additional information does not reflect on the article's credibility. D—same explanation as for B.
6. **A**—This encyclopedia has a reputation for accuracy. *Incorrect answers:* B—An activist is likely to have solid information about ghost crabs, but that might be colored by political views. C—Such a Web site is not necessarily deeply researched. D—same explanation as for C.

II. Informational Reading Skills

Directions: *Read the passage. Then, answer each question that follows.*

The Ghost Crab

Have you ever taken an evening stroll on the beach and seen a small ghostly figure scurry across the sand and suddenly disappear? This was most probably a ghost crab, or *Ocypode quadrata,* also known as a sand crab. The name *ghost crab* comes from the creature's ability to blend in with the sand and to suddenly appear out of and disappear into the sand.

Habitat

Ghost crabs live on the sandy beaches along the eastern coastline of North America and South America. They live in burrows that can be as deep as three feet. Older crabs live farther from the water than younger crabs:

Appearance

Their body shell, or carapace, is usually square and can be up to two inches wide. They are gray or yellow-white on their top surface, but their underside is white. Ghost crabs have white or lavender pincers, are uneven in size, and have hairy legs. Their eyes, which sit atop long stalks, sense changes in light.

Diet

Ghost crabs are omnivorous. They will eat clams, insects, other crabs, and vegetation, as well as plant and animal detritus that washes up on the shore. They feed at night and burrow into the sand during daylight hours.

The following list shows some interesting facts about ghost crabs.

- At night, they face the moon when it is full.
- They can run up to ten miles per hour.
- At night, they wash water over their gills for oxygen.
- Their "periscope" eyes can see 360°.

1. If you wanted to draw a ghost crab, which feature in the text would help you locate the most useful information?

A. the title
B. the subhead *Habitat*
C. the bulleted list
D. the subhead *Appearance*

2. Where in the article would a photograph of a beach be most useful?

A. the bulleted list
B. the subhead *Diet*
C. the subhead *Habitat*
D. the subhead *Appearance*

Reteach

Question	Instructional Pages to Reteach
1	90
2	90
4	90
5	182
6	182

3. **Vocabulary in Context** The underlined word *omnivorous* best describes which animal?

A. a burrowing animal
B. an animal that eats other animals
C. a type of crab
D. an animal that eats both plants and animals

4. Which of the following additional subheads might logically fit under the main heading?

A. *Carapace*
B. *Prehistoric Fossilized Ghost Crabs*
C. *Behavior*
D. *Ocean Creatures*

5. To verify the credibility of this source, which is the most useful question to ask?

A. What is the name of the author?
B. Where can most crabs be found?
C. Where was this article published?
D. Where can other articles on crabs be found?

6. Which of the following sources on ghost crabs would be most credible?

A. an article in the *Encyclopedia Britannica*
B. a speech by an activist for ghost crab rights
C. an entry found at *www.funnyanimals.com*
D. a web site entitled *Fun on the Beach*

III. Vocabulary

Directions: *Read each question. Then, choose the best answer.*

1. Which sentence uses the word *concrete* correctly?

A. The concrete defense argued well.
B. The concrete discussion solved the dispute.
C. Jackie refused to concrete to the rules.
D. The court had concrete evidence against Jan.

2. The word *improbable* most nearly means—

A. inadequate
B. unlikely
C. insufficient
D. unjust

3. Which sentence uses the word *confirm* correctly?

A. I could confirm that the answer was right.
B. Andre felt he should confirm to his peers.
C. Lisa wanted to confirm her computer.
D. The computer confirmed to my expectations.

4. Which pair of words are **antonyms?**

A. perception, view
B. reality, fantasy
C. uncertainty, confusion
D. comprehend, understand

5. Which pair of words are **synonyms?**

A. discern, neglect
B. differentiate, distinguish
C. context, belief
D. evaluate, reject

6. Which sentence uses an **antonym** of *subjective?*

A. The reviewer gave his personal judgment.
B. Bill has an introverted personality.
C. The solution must be objective and fair.
D. The bill for the party was substantial.

7. Which sentence uses the word *verify* correctly?

A. The reporter needed to verify the details.
B. The verify of the evidence convicted her.
C. Your verify shows you are an honest person.
D. When you verify your cousin, be patient.

8. The word *evaluate* most nearly means—

A. confuse
B. overlook
C. neglect
D. judge

GO ON

ASSESS

Answers

1. D—Evidence that is *concrete* is solid and convincing. *Incorrect answers:* A—A defense might be "tightly constructed," but not *concrete.* B—A discussion might include "concrete details," but that would not make it a *concrete discussion.* C—A verb is needed here, not an adjective.
2. B—Something *improbable* most likely will not take place. *Incorrect answers:* A—*Inadequate* and *insufficient* are synonyms, but do not means the same as *improbable.* C—same explanation as for A. D—*Unjust* means "unfair," not "unlikely. "
3. A—*Confirm* means "to verify the accuracy" of something. *Incorrect answers:* B—Andre might "confirm a statement," but he cannot simply *confirm.* C—The computer itself cannot be confirmed, though an operation it did could be. D—It is the performance of the computer that may or may not meet expectations, not the machine itself.
4. B—*Reality* refers to the actual world, *fantasy* to the imaginary. *Incorrect answers:* A—Both *perception* and *view* refer to how a person sees things. C—*Uncertainty* and *confusion* are synonyms for something lacking definition. D—*Comprehend* and *understand* are synonyms for grasping something.
5. B—Both words refer to the ability to see differences. *Incorrect answers:* A—*Discern* means "to see underlying meaning or significance"; *neglect* means "to leave alone." C—A *context* is the environment of something; a *belief* is something thought to be true. D—To *evaluate* is "to analyze critically"; to *reject* is "to turn down."
6. C—*Objective,* meaning "in reference to external criteria," is the opposite of *subjective,* or "personal and idiosyncratic." *Incorrect answers:* A—*Personal* is close in meaning to *subjective.* B—No word in the sentence has any relation to *subjective.* D—same explanation as for B.

Answers continued

7. A—A reporter tries to confirm, or *verify,* facts before publishing them. *Incorrect answers:* B—The noun *verification* is needed here. C—A noun is required here. D—Someone might need patience if he or she *judged* a cousin's actions or words in a negative way, but *verify* is not appropriate here.
8. D—Someone *evaluating* an actor's performance judges it. *Incorrect answers:* A—An evaluation aims at clarifying, not creating confusion. B—Someone evaluating a situation is not ignoring it. C—same explanation as for B.

Reteach

Question	Instructional Pages to Reteach
1	2–3
2	2–3
3	2–3
4	2–3
5	2–3
6	2–3
7	2–3
8	2–3

ASSESS

Answers

Answers With Explanations

1. C—The story focuses on the narrator's surprise at seeing the bear. *Incorrect answers:* A—The narrator expresses no such fear. B—The narrator enjoys this camping trip with his father. D—The narrator does not express major concern for Charlie.
2. C—This revision, using irony and playing along with the job, effectively reveals the narrator's attitude. *Incorrect answers:* A—This version suggests irony, but is more heavy-handed than carefree. B—This version suggests the narrator was really concerned there might be bears. D—This version is not as light-hearted; a speaker saying this would be more annoyed than amused.
3. A—The replacement would appeal to the sense of smell ("fragrant"), sight ("green"), and touch ("pines"). *Incorrect answers:* B—This change would be less clear and no more vivid than the original. C—This change would simply be wordy. D—This change would simply add words.
4. B—It would be helpful to the reader to identify Charlie as the dog in this sentence. *Incorrect answers:* A—The dog's name is not Joe. C—It was the dog, not the narrator's father, who followed. D—*Trail* is not a proper noun, and not a suitable replacement for anything in the sentence.
5. C—This replacement would be much more succinct than the original. *Incorrect answers:* A—The narrator might have felt exhilaration, but *joy* is not suitable. B—The narrator was certainly not bored, but rather excited. D—The narrator was not melancholy, but excited.
6. D—The dog belonged to only one family, so the singular possessive shown in the original is the correct form. *Incorrect answers:* A—The plural *families* is incorrect, and this version has no apostrophe indicating possession. B—The plural *familys* is doubly incorrect: the plural is wrong, and it is spelled incorrectly as well. C— The plural *families* is incorrect.

IV. Writing and Language Conventions

Narration: Autobiographical Narrative

Directions: *Read the passage. Then, answer each question that follows.*

(1) My dad and I had looked forward to our camping trip in the mountains for weeks. (2) Charlie, the family's black Labrador pup, was going along. (3) It was our first visit to the mountains.

(4) Our campsite was thickly lined with trees. (5) I inhaled the fresh mountain air, and grabbing my fishing tackle, I strolled down the path to the lake with my dog. (6) The dog ran after me, ready for fun.

(7) "Watch out for bears, Joe," Dad called.

(8) "Okay!" I said, laughing. (9) As I rounded a bend, though, right in front of me was a small black bear ambling along the path. (10) Charlie's fur bristled. (11) The bear stopped cold, staring at me. (12) I froze, holding my breath until the bear finally turned and hurried off down the path.

(13) I've been camping a lot since then, but I'll never forget the dramatic events of that first trip.

1. Which of the following revisions to sentence 10 enhances the story's **conflict** and increases suspense?

A. Charlie's black fur bristled.
B. Charlie's fur bristled, his senses on full predator alert.
C. Charlie stopped and his fur bristled.
D. Charlie, his fur bristling, stopped suddenly.

2. How would you revise the **dialogue** in sentence 8 to better convey Joe's carefree attitude?

A. "Yeah, sure!" I said, laughing.
B. "Do you really think so?" I asked.
C. "Thanks for the reminder!" I said.
D. "Stop fooling around!" I cried.

3. What is the *best* way to add **sensory description** to sentence 4?

A. Replace "trees" with "fragrant green pines."
B. Replace "lined" with "wooded."
C. Replace "campsite" with "camping area."
D. Replace "Our campsite" with "Our chosen campsite."

4. Which **proper noun** should replace the **common noun** in sentence 6 for clarity?

A. Joe
B. Charlie
C. Dad
D. trail

5. Which **abstract noun** should be substituted for the phrase "the lively feelings and dramatic events" in sentence 13 in order to use precise language?

A. joy
B. boredom
C. excitement
D. melancholy

6. What is the correct way to write the **possessive noun** in sentence 2?

A. the families black Labrador pup
B. the familys' black Labrador pup
C. the families' black Labradoor pup
D. Leave as is.

Reteach

Question	Instructional Pages to Reteach
1	115
2	110
3	87
4	56
5	86
6	111

Exposition: Cause and Effect Essay

Directions: *Read the passage. Then, answer each question that follows.*

(1) Coral reefs are built by tiny sea-anemone polyps that secrete hard, limestone skeletons. (2) Algae live on the polyps of coral reefs and feed the polyps by changing sunlight and carbon dioxide into sugar. (3) In turn, the polyps secrete waste products that feed the algae. (4) These reefs are fragile. (5) They are home to about 25 percent of all marine species.

(6) Today, 15 percent of the world's reefs have been damaged by the warming climate. (7) Warmer waters stifle the algae. (8) As algae stop using carbon dioxide, polyps stop secreting skeletons, and they "bleach," turning a ghostly white. (9) The coral reefs die, and marine life goes away. (10) The warming climate has dramatic effects upon marine life.

1. Which of the following reflects the **sequence of events** causing the destruction of coral reefs?

A. sea water warms • algae stop growing • marine life becomes scarcer
B. coral reefs die • algae die • reefs are fragile
C. algae absorb sunlight • marine life goes away • polyps secrete skeletons
D. coral reefs die • algae die • waters warm

2. Which revision of sentence 2 has a **personal pronoun** that correctly refers to its **antecedent?**

A. Algae live on them and feed them.
B. Algae live on the polyps of coral reefs and feed them by changing sunlight and carbon dioxide into sugar.
C. Algae live on the them and feed them by changing them into sugar.
D. Algae live on them and feed the polyps by changing sunlight and carbon dioxide.

3. Which revision would *best* improve the flow of the passage?

A. Delete sentence 3.
B. Move sentence 5 before sentence 4.
C. Break sentence 2 into two shorter sentences.
D. Combine sentences 4 and 5.

4. Of the choices below, all of which include **relative pronouns,** which revision best elaborates on the ideas in sentence 7?

A. Warmer waters which stifle the algae.
B. Warmer waters whose stifling of the algae is directly caused by warming climate.
C. Warming climate causes warmer waters, which stifle the algae.
D. Waters whom are warm stifle the algae.

5. Which **transition** would be the *best* addition to sentence 10?

A. today
B. these reefs
C. as coral reefs die
D. thus

Writing for Assessment

6. Write an **autobiographical essay** that relates a series of **causes and effects.** Use **descriptive details** and **dialogue** to make the events come to life for readers.

STOP

ASSESS

Answers

Answers With Explanations

1. **A**—The warming sea water harms algae, and their death harms the reefs, which makes marine life leave. *Incorrect answers:* B—Algae die first, and the fragility of reefs is an underlying condition. C—Items 1 and 3 are parts of a healthy reef system; item 2 is not. D—This sequence is in reverse order.
2. **B**—The polyps the algae live on are the "them" that the algae feed. *Incorrect answers:* A—The antecedents are not clear. C—The antecedents are not clear, and the sentence as a whole is incorrect. D—Placing the pronoun before the antecedent is unclear.
3. **B**—This change would effectively place the statement of the reef's fragility before the last paragraph, about how they are being damaged. *Incorrect answers:* A—The sentence is necessary to the cause-and-effect chain. C—The sentence is fine as is. D—This could be effective, but option B is better.
4. **C**—This version has a clear sequence of events and correctly uses and punctuates *which.* *Incorrect answers:* A—This version is a sentence fragment. B—This version is wordy and awkward. D—This version incorrectly uses *whom.*
5. **D**—The addition would so how the preceding material applies to the last sentence. *Incorrect answers:* A—*Today* would not reveal the logic of the concluding statement. B—This is not a transitional statement. C—same explanation as for B.

Writing for Assessment

Students' essays should be lively and describe chains of events that they have personally experienced. Essays should be organized as a series of causes and effects, utilize descriptive details, and include dialogue as a way of recounting the stories. Students might write about funny trips or experiences or focus on more serious times in their lives. They should allot time to make revisions to their essays.

Reteach

Question	Instructional Pages to Reteach
1	201
2	205
3	202
4	178
5	202

Benchmark

Reteach skills as indicated by students' performance, following the Reteach charts on pp. 215–219 administer the end-of-unit **Benchmark Test** (***Unit 1 Resources***, pp. 233–239). Follow the **Interpretation Guide** for the test (***Unit 1 Resources***, pp. 243–248) to assign reteaching pages as necessary in the ***Reading Kit***. Use **Success Tracker** online to automatically assign these pages.

PHLit Online!

The **Benchmark Tests** and **Success Tracker** are available online at **www.PHLitOnline.com.**

Unit 2 Overview

Unit Genre and Unit Big Question

Explain to students that throughout this unit, they will read and analyze short stories. As they read, they will think about and discuss answers to the Unit Big Question: Can progress be made without conflict?

Students will learn more about the Big Question on pp. 222–223. Then, on pp. 224–237, C.J. Cherryh introduces the unit literary genre, the short story, and presents a model short story of her own.

Using the Unit Selections

Teach Skills Instructional selections are presented in leveled pairs. To teach the skills and meet the objectives, you need to complete only one selection in each pairing.

Differentiate and Reinforce Choose the selection in a pairing that is best suited for your students. The selections are listed by accessibility in the Differentiated Instruction box on the next page. You may use the other selection in the pairing to reinforce comprehension and skills or to provide enrichment.

Integrate Skills Each selection pairing presents students with a reading strategy, a literary analysis concept, and a vocabulary skill, as well as vocabulary development opportunities and grammar instruction. In addition, students have opportunities to extend learning in the Writing and extension (Research and Technology or Listening and Speaking) activities.

Unit Features

Informational Texts Students learn to use and evaluate various types of informational texts.

Comparing Literary Works Students compare the use of a literary element in two or more works.

To help you plan your use of the unit, see the Unit Overview and Pacing Plan on pp. 222a–222b and the Time and Resource Manager preceding each selection pairing.

Short Stories
THE BIG ?
Can progress be made without conflict?
220 Short Stories

PHLit Online!
www.PHLitOnline.com

Teaching From Technology

Enriched Online Student Edition
- full narration of selections
- interactive graphic organizers
- linked Get Connected! and Background videos
- all worksheets and other student resources

Professional Development
- the *Professional Development Guidebook* online
- additional professional development articles by program authors

Planning, Assigning, and Monitoring
- software for online assignment of work to students, individually or to the whole class
- a system for tracking and grading students' work

UNIT 2

PHLit Online!
www.PHLitOnline.com

Hear It!
- Selection summary audio
- Selection audio
- BQ Tunes

See It!
- Penguin author video
- Big Question video
- Get Connected videos
- Background videos
- More about the authors
- Illustrated vocabulary words
- Vocabulary flashcards

Do It!
- Interactive journals
- Interactive graphic organizers
- Grammar tutorials
- Interactive vocabulary games
- Test practice

221

Instructional Resources

Unit 2 Resources supports unit skills with pages of the following types:

- **Benchmark Tests** assess and monitor students' progress at mid-unit and at unit's end.
- **Vocabulary and Reading Warm-ups** provide additional vocabulary support, based on Lexile rankings of words, for each selection. "A" **Warm-ups** are for students reading two grades below level. "B" **Warm-ups** are for students reading one grade below level.
- **Selection Support** These practice pages are available for each selection:
  - **Reading Skill**
  - **Literary Analysis**
  - **Writing About the Big Question**
  - **Vocabulary**
  - **Support for Writing**
  - **Support for Extend Your Learning**
  - **Enrichment**

PHLit Online!
All worksheets and other student resources are also available at www.PHLitOnline.com.

Differentiated Instruction for Universal Access

Accessibility for Various Ability Levels
This chart gives a general accessibility rating to help you decide which selection in each leveled pair is more appropriate for your students. **Choose one selection in each pair or choose to teach both.** You will meet the objectives for the pair when you teach either of the two selections. For additional guidance on factors that affect the accessibility of each selection, see the Selection Choices page for each selection set.

Accessibility for English Learners
EL This icon indicates support for English learners at point of use in this Teacher's Edition.

	More Accessible	More Challenging
Pair 1	A Visit to Grandmother	A Problem
Pair 2	The Street of the Cañon	There Will Come Soft Rains
Pair 3	How Much Land Does a Man Need?	Civil Peace
Pair 4	The Masque of the Red Death	The Garden of Stubborn Cats

UNIT OVERVIEW AND PACING PLAN

Meeting Your Standards

Students will
1. recognize and appreciate the short story as a literary genre.
2. read and analyze a variety of short stories.
3. apply reading skills.
   - Relate characters and events to prior experience to make predictions
   - Read ahead to support inferences
   - Recognize key details to draw conclusions
   - Identify patterns to draw conclusions
4. analyze literary elements.
   - Character and characterization
   - Setting
   - Theme
   - Symbolism and allegory
5. build vocabulary and vocabulary concepts.
   - Suffixes
   - Prefixes
   - Word origins
6. learn elements of grammar, mechanics, and usage.
   - Principal parts of regular verbs
   - Irregular verbs
   - Consistent verb tense
   - Action and linking verbs
   - Active and passive voice
   - Subject-verb agreement
7. use a recursive writing process to write in a variety of forms.
   - Short story
   - Problem-and-solution essay
8. read informational materials.
   - Analyze texts to extend ideas in a technical article and a news release
   - Paraphrase to connect ideas in an editorial and a primary source
9. compare literary works.
   - Compare point of view
   - Compare tone
10. develop research and technology skills.
    - Report on sources
    - Research summary
11. develop listening and speaking skills.
    - Oral reading
    - Group discussion
    - View and evaluate a speech

	Week 1					Week 2					Week 3				
	1	2	3	4	5	1	2	3	4	5	1	2	3	4	5
Introduce the Unit Big Question (pp. 222–223).	●														
Introduce the Unit author and the Unit forms, fiction and nonfiction (pp 224–227).	●														
Teach the Model selections (pp. 228–237).	●	●													
Teach one selection from Pairing 1 (pp. 238–267).		●	●	●	●	●									
Teach one selection from Pairing 2 (pp. 268–295).						●	●	●	●						
Complete the Test Practice: Reading (pp. 296–297).									●						
Teach Informational Texts (pp. 298–305).										●					
Teach Comparing Literary Works (pp. 306–327).											●	●			
Have students complete the Writing Workshop (pp. 328–333).										●	●	●	●	●	
Administer **Benchmark Test 3** (*Unit 2 Resources,* pp. 120–125).														●	
Reteach skills, judging which skills to reteach by evaluating students' performance on **Benchmark Test 3**.															●

	Week 4					Week 5					Week 6				
	1	2	3	4	5	1	2	3	4	5	1	2	3	4	5
Teach one selection from Pairing 3 (pp. 334–367).	●	●	●	●											
Teach one selection from Pairing 4 (pp. 368–399).					●	●	●	●							
Complete the Test-Practice: Reading (pp. 400–401).								●							
Teach Informational Texts (pp. 402–407).									●						
Teach Comparing Literary Works (pp. 408-419).										●	●				
Have students complete the Writing Workshop (pp. 420–427).									●	●	●	●	●		
Have students complete Applying the Big Question (pp. 428–429).												●			
Have students complete the Vocabulary and Communications Workshops (pp. 430–431, 432).													●		
Complete the Test Practice: Unit 2 Review (pp. 434–439).													●		
Administer **Benchmark Test 4** (***Unit 2 Resources***, pp. 227–235).														●	
Reteach skills, judging which skills to reteach by evaluating students' performance on **Benchmark Test 4**.															●

Block and Daily Scheduling

The assignments and activities in this Unit planner are organized by week. You may adjust them to your daily or block schedule. The Time and Resource Manager for each selection set gives specific pacing suggestions, or you may use the comprehensive lesson planning support online at **www.PHLitOnline.com.**

Monitoring Progress

Diagnose Each main selection pairing in the Unit contains a more accessible and a more challenging selection. To determine which selection in each pairing to assign, refer to students' results on **Benchmark Test 2, *Unit 1 Resources,*** pp. 234–243 (administered at the end of the previous Unit). Use the **Interpretation Guide** to interpret the results of the diagnostic portion of the test. **Note:** For the most accurate diagnosis of students who score in the middle range, administer the additional diagnostic questions online at **www.PHLitOnline.com.**

Preteach and Prepare As indicated by the diagnostic, prepare students for reading by assigning the **Vocabulary** and **Reading Warm-ups** for the selections you assign.

Teach Follow this Pacing Plan and use the resources to teach the skills and selections. For specific pacing suggestions and a list of resources, see the Time and Resource Manager and the Visual Guide to Featured Selection Resources preceding each selection pairing.

Assess After students have completed the first half of the Unit, administer **Benchmark Test 3**. Administer **Benchmark Test 4** at the end of the Unit.

Intervention and Reteach After administering each test, use the **Interpretation Guide** for the tests to determine which reteaching pages, if any, you should assign from the ***Reading Kit.*** The appropriate pages are also available through the online Progress Monitoring software.

Independent Reading

To differentiate, reinforce, and extend your instruction, have students choose a full-length work from the Independent Reading page, page 433, and read it while working on this Unit. Consult the Sensitivity Issues notes for the page to guide students' choices.

CLASSROOM STRATEGIES

Engaging Students in the Study of Literary Elements **Jane Feber**

> As text becomes more difficult in high school, students must be provided with engaging activities that help them access and analyze the text.

The stakes are high in secondary school. Graduation is the light at the end of the tunnel. In order to enter the work force, students must be able to apply the skills they learn in school. As teachers, we must engage students through the use of purposeful talk, movement, and autonomy. These are indicators of best practices that lessen lecturing and allow for a richer array of activities (Zemelman, Daniel, and Hyde, 1998). What better way to engage students at the application level then through activities where they are actively engaged?

Fostering Engagement

As text becomes more difficult in high school, students must be provided with engaging activities that help them access and analyze the text. Keeping students engaged helps them focus on the content of what they are reading. One of my most successful, and popular, activities is a mini-book which my students use as a learning log.

Creating a Mini-Book

How to Make a Mini-Book

1. Provide each student with one sheet of 12″ × 18″ construction paper.
2. Holding the construction paper with the 18″ side at the top, fold the paper in half from left to right.
3. Make a second fold from top to bottom.
4. Make a third fold from left to right.
5. Open up the paper. There should be eight equal segments.
6. Fold the paper in half again from the 12″ side to the other 12″ side. They then make a cut on the center crease starting from the fold to the center of the sheet. They cut only to the center of the paper.
7. Open up the paper again, and fold it from the 18″ top side to the bottom The cut they made should now be on the top fold.
8. Hold the paper with one hand on each end of the paper and push inward. The central segments with the cut top will flare out on each side and then come together to make four equal segments.

The Mini-Book as a Learning Log

Have students organize the mini-book based on the skills you want to teach. For example, I use the mini-book to teach literary elements, character analysis, reader response and vocabulary.

Literacy Elements Mini-Book To focus on literary elements, instruct students to write the title and author on the front cover and then label and organize the pages as follows:

- **Pages 1–2:** Characters Pages
  Take notes describing the characters:
  - What they look like
  - How they behave
  - What others think of them
- **Pages 3–4:** Plot Summary
  List details as the plot develops
- **Pages 5–6:** Conflicts/Resolutions
  Note the conflicts as they occur, and their resolutions as the conflicts are solved
- **Page 7:** Setting
  Describe where the story takes place

Students can illustrate the front cover to reflect the theme of the story. Students make extensive use of the notes in their mini-book during literature discussions.

A Diary Tell the students that they will be keeping a diary written from the perspective of a character in the selection. They will write this diary from the first person point of view. I usually chunk the reading and tell the students that their first diary entry should reflect the events from so many pages or paragraphs of the selection. The following entries will be for other specified chunks of text. I provide the students with a bookmark telling them which chunks of text will be read for each diary entry. Upon completion of the selection, students can use the diary entries to describe how the character changed during the course of the story.

A Reaction Journal In some selections, the characters undergo emotional turmoil. When reading these selections, students need to digest what is happening and talk about how they feel. I call this mini-book a reaction journal. This reaction journal tells how the reader feels about what is taking place to the characters in the story. Students' reactions can be based on assigned "chunks" of text.

Vocabulary Mini-Book As students read a selection, they often come across words they are unfamiliar with. For the vocabulary mini-book, students write these unfamiliar words and the sentences in which they occur. They then write what they think the word means using context clues from the surrounding text. They will write these clues that assist them in determining the words' meanings. They will then write what they think the word means. During reading, I often walk around the classroom checking the students' vocabulary books to see if they need assistance deciphering vocabulary in order to comprehend the text. Upon completion of the selection, students can place their words on the class' word wall.

Engaging students as they read a selection allows them to take ownership of the text. Loose notebook paper is often found on the floor of my classroom, but I rarely find students' mini-books. It's easy to slap some words on a sheet of paper; it's a little more work for them to recreate their mini-books. Students take pride in what they create.

Modeled Strategy

See pp. 277 and 339 for point-of-use notes modeling these strategies.

Teacher Resources

- ***Professional Development Guidebook***
- ***Classroom Strategies and Teaching Routines*** **cards**

PHLit Online!

Log on as a teacher at **www.PHLitOnline.com** to access a library of all Professional Development articles by the Contributing Authors of Pearson Prentice Hall *Literature.*

Jane Feber

Jane Feber has taught language arts for 35 years in Jacksonville, FL. She is a National Board Certified Teacher and was the 2006 NCTE Edwin A. Hoey Award winner.

Supporting Research

Feber, Jane. (2004). Creative Book Reports: Fun Projects with Rubrics for Fiction and Nonfiction. Florida: Maupin House.

Zemelman, S., Daniels, H., Hyde, A. (1998). *Best practice: New standards for teaching and learning in America's schools.* Portsmouth, NH: Heinemann.

INTRODUCE

Introducing the Big Question

1. Give the following example of progress resulting from compromise: Two friends want to use the same idea for a science competition. They discuss other topics until they think of an idea that one friend likes better.
2. **Ask:** How did the confrontation in this example bring about progress? **Possible response:** It helped one friend think of a new idea so they could move forward.
3. **Ask** students the Big Question, "Can progress be made without conflict?" **Possible response:** Yes, a group might be in agreement from the start, allowing them to move forward.
4. Tell students that the stories in this unit involve conflicts people faced in order to make progress. As they read, have students reconsider their answers to the Big Question.

Introducing the Big Question Vocabulary

1. Point out the Big Question Vocabulary on the facing page. Explain that these words are useful in discussing the Big Question.
2. Review the meaning of each word. (Definitions appear in the teacher edition on p. 223.)
3. Have students complete the **Big Question Vocabulary** worksheets, ***Unit 2 Resources***, pp. 1–3.

Write What You Know

1. Review the assignment, using the instruction on the page.
2. Have students work with partners to complete their lists. Encourage them to use examples of conflicts that brought about progress in their own lives.

PHLit Online!

Show the Big Question video, online at **www.PHLitOnline.com.**

Introducing the Big Question

THE BIG ? Can progress be made without *conflict?*

A conflict is a **struggle** between two or more opposing forces. Sometimes these opposing sides face a **confrontation** in order to address the **motives,** or reasons, behind the conflict. Then, **progress,** in the form of **reconciliation**, can be achieved.

Progress involves **change** in a situation or a relationship, generally for the better. At times, adversaries must **compromise** and **negotiate** in order to **resolve** differences and move forward. Progress can take on many forms, and at times, it can happen without conflict.

Start thinking about the Big Question by considering different ways people can make progress in their lives.

Write What You Know

Make a list of situations in which you or someone else has made progress. Describe one specific example of each of the following circumstances that may lead to progress.

- Someone overcomes **adversity** in an athletic or academic competition.
- A change is made after an argument.
- A **concession** is offered for the sake of achieving a common goal.
- Internal conflict, a struggle within oneself, leads to personal progress.
- A change to a situation ends up causing a conflict.

Share your examples with a partner. Talk about whether progress was achieved and if there was any conflict involved.

PHLit Online!
www.PHLitOnline.com
- Big Question video
- Illustrated vocabulary words
- Interactive vocabulary games
- BQ Tunes

Understanding by Design

The Big Question

Explain to students that they will continue to consider the Big Question as they work through the Unit.

- At the beginning of each selection, they will write a response to a Writing About the Big Question sentence starter.
- As they read the selection, they will look for details related to the Big Question.
- At the end of the selection, they will answer a Critical Thinking question that is related to the Big Question.
- At the end of Unit 2, they will complete an Applying the Big Question workshop (pp. 428–429). In the workshop, they will review literature in the Unit and think about real-world examples that shed light on the Big Question. They will also have a chance to reflect on their first answers, thinking about how their ideas have changed.

Tell students that their goal will be to gain a deeper understanding of literature and a more sophisticated way of discussing the Big Question.

Discuss It
Explain What You Know

Use the examples and ideas you discussed with your partner to help you complete these sentences about progress.

- Overcoming **adversity** can lead to progress because ___________.
- People can make positive **changes** after an argument by ________.
- A person might face an internal **struggle** when ________. To **resolve** this internal conflict, a person may need to ___________.

Share your responses with a partner.

Write About It
Tell What You Think

Based on the discussions you have had, decide what you think right now. Your answer may change as you read the selections in this unit. Choose one of these responses to the Big Question or write one of your own:

- ❑ Progress can be made without conflict.
- ❑ Progress cannot be made without conflict.

Use one or more of these sentences or your own ideas to write a brief support of your response.

- A situation in which conflict is not needed for progress is ___________. In this case, conflict would interfere with progress because ___________.
- Progress can be made in a conflict when ___________. Those in opposition to each other must decide ___________.
- Although some people involved in a conflict might make progress, others involved might not make progress because ___________.

Discuss your response with a partner or in a small group.

Big Question Vocabulary

adversity
change
compromise
concession
confrontation
☆ debate
☆ motive
negotiate
☆ oppose
progress
☆ radical
reconciliation
☆ resolve
struggle
☆ unify

Connecting to the Literature

The readings in this unit will help you think about different types of conflict and the different ways progress is, and is not, achieved. Each reading will give you an insight into the Big Question. At the end of the unit, you will see how your ideas have grown and changed.

☆ shows an **Academic Vocabulary** word.

Explain What You Know

1. Introduce the assignment, using the instruction on the student page.
2. Have students work with partner, using their lists to find motives that prompted people to seek change or progress. Give definitions to the Big Question Vocabulary words as needed. (See definitions below in the Big Question Vocabulary box.)
3. Guide students to complete the sentence starters and share their responses with partners.

Tell What You Think

1. Introduce the assignment. Ask students to review the examples of progress from their lists. Have them decide whether or not progress can be made without conflict. Instruct students to mark their pages.
2. Have students write brief paragraphs supporting their decisions. First, guide them to complete the sentence starters and encourage them to base their responses on their previous work. Then, remind students to use the sentence starters while writing their responses.
3. As they write, have students support their decisions with examples from previous activities.
4. Instruct students to discuss their writing in small groups.

Connecting to the Literature

Explain the structure of the Big Question strand in the Unit, referring to the Understanding by Design box on the previous page.

Big Question Vocabulary

adversity (ad vur′sə tē) *n.* a state of difficulty or misfortune
change (chānj) *v.* to become different or transform
compromise (käm′prə mīz′) *n.* an agreement in which both sides give something up
concession (kən sesh′ən) *n.* an act of granting
confrontation (kän′frən tā′shən) *n.* the clashing of forces or ideas
debate (dē bāt′) *v.* to argue or discuss
motive (mōt′iv) *n.* something that causes a person to act in a certain way
negotiate (ni gō′shē āt′) *v.* to bargain with the hope of reaching an agreement
oppose (ə pōz′) *v.* to set against
progress (präg′res) *n.* moving forward to a better state
radical (rad′i kəl) *adj.* tending to make extreme changes in existing views, conditions, or institutions
reconciliation (rek′ən sil′ē ā′shən) *n.* restoring friendship and harmony
resolve (ri zälv′′, -zôlv) *v.* to reach a conclusion or decision
struggle (strug′əl) *v.* to face difficulty
unify (yo͞o′nə fī′) *v.* to combine into one

PREACH

Meeting Your Standards

Students will

1. understand the characteristics of short stories, such as setting, character, them, plot, and conflict.
2. learn about author C. J. Cherryh
3. read and analyze an example of a science fiction.
4. relate visuals to characteristics of short stories.

❶ Can progress be made without conflict?

Remind students that they will think more about the Unit Big Question as they read and discuss the short stories in this unit.

❷ What Is a Short Story?

Introduce C. J. Cherryh

1. C. J. Cherryh knew she wanted to be a writer when she began writing at the age of ten . Today, she is a popular writer of science fiction and fantasy who has won numerous awards for her short stories and novels.
2. Use the *See It! DVD* to introduce the author and the genre. Show Segment 2 to provide insight into Cherryh's attitude toward writing science-fiction short stories. **Ask:** Why does C. J. Cherryh believe that a short story is a good vehicle for expressing science-fiction plots? **Answer:** Cherryh believes that short stories are a good way to express science-fiction plots because they add mystery with their brevity, focus on important details, and use concise language.
3. Interested students might enjoy this work by C. J. Cherryh: *Downbelow Station*, a novel about interstellar conflict

Introduce Short Stories

1. Explore students' prior knowledge of short stories: if students view their lives today as novels, the short stories are the many encounters they have during the day with people, places, and events.
2. Have students read C. J. Cherryh's discussion on short stories.

Introduction: Short Stories

THE BIG ?

Can progress be made without *conflict?*

❶ Conflicts often drive the plots of short stories.

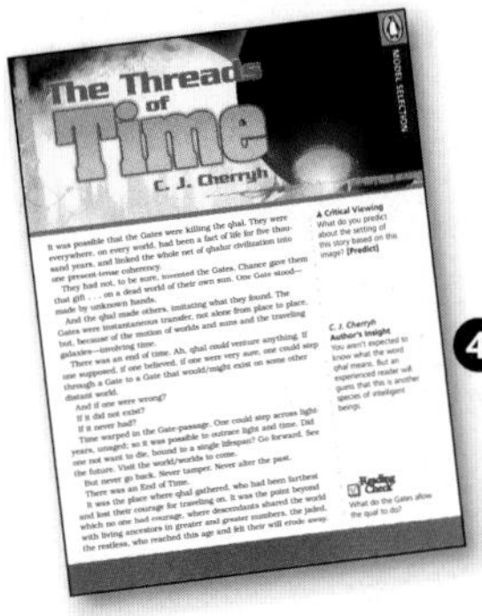

❷ What Is a Short Story?

by C. J. Cherryh

The **short story** isn't my native medium. I'm a novelist. Novels use very different rules than the short story: novels, unlike stories, have elaborately developed **characters** and an involved **plot** that produces change in the central characters.

❸ "Compression of Time and Place"

I wanted to try the short story, and knew it was different, but I hadn't been able to produce a good short story idea until I heard Mr. Harlan Ellison, an excellent writer, speak on the basic characteristics of the short story, namely compression of time and place.

Ideally, in Mr. Ellison's words, a short story arranges matters so that the **conflict** comes to a head in one single encounter between individuals who don't know they know as much as they do—and their whole world shakes in that encounter. So a short story, unlike a novel, doesn't have deeply complex characters, doesn't have a complicated **plot,** and doesn't use many **settings.**

❹ "Follow No Rule Off a Cliff"

Now my own proverb is this: follow no rule off a cliff . . . meaning, don't carry any rule to the point of absurdity. So you will see that, in my story "The Threads of Time," while I have an encounter which creates a shock in two lives, the matter of time is somewhat wider in scope. I took Mr. Ellison's definition for a good guide and applied it at need.

I write **science fiction**, meaning fiction in which science is important. What is science? Knowledge. And what is fiction? Fiction is what-if, in modern Brooklyn or in 1800s' London.

Dare we what-if about something as certain as science? Yes—precisely because science should never be too sure of itself, as the quotation shown on the next page indicates.

PHLit Online!
www.PHLitOnline.com

- Penguin author video
- Interactive journals
- Interactive graphic organizers
- Selection audio
- Self-test

Teaching Resources

- **All** *Unit 2 Resources,* pp. 1–13
- **All** *Professional Development Guidebook,* pp. 33, 42
- **All** *See It!* DVD
  C. J. **Cherryh,** Segments 1 and 2
- **All** *Graphic Organizer Transparencies,* pp. 37–38
- **All** Enriched Online Student Edition
- **L2 L3** *Reader's Notebook*
- **L1** *Hear It!* Audio CD (adapted text)
- **EL** *Reader's Notebook: English Learner's Version*
- **L2 EL** *Hear It!* Audio CD
- **L1 EL** *Hear It!* Audio CD

PHLit Online! All resources, including print and video, are available online at **www.PHLitOnline.com.**

4 What-if is how science makes progress. What-if breaks us out of the stale daily rut and makes us look at the world in a different way, and scientists read science fiction because it makes them follow trails their knowledge doesn't encourage them to use.

So science fiction is a literature of questions and what-ifs, but it's not a new literature. The first hunters sitting around the fire, telling the first tall tales and what-ifs in the world—that began what we now call science fiction.

It is less than five hundred years since an entire half of the world was discovered. . . . The sciences of chemistry and physics go back scarcely one century. The science of aviation goes back forty years. The science of atomics is being born.

And yet we think we know a lot.

—from "Mimic," by Donald A. Wollheim

Meet C. J. Cherryh (b. 1942)

Author of "The Threads of Time"

C. J. Cherryh is known for her space opera series—books filled with romantic adventure, vivid details of alien cultures, and interstellar conflict.

She enjoys excitement in her real life on Earth as well. Her adventures include outrunning a dog pack in Thebes, Greece, and falling down a chute in a cave on Crete. Referring to her home in the Pacific Northwest, she says, "I choose to live downwind of five active volcanoes."

Did You Know?

Cherryh took up figure skating when she was 61 and won a silver medal in a competition six months later.

3 Compression of Time and Place (p. 224)

Review the meaning of the word *compression* with students. **Ask:** Why did the author use the word *compression* in describing the writing of a short story?

Possible response: In writing a short story, the author has to compress the element of a story by using fewer words and less space than that of a novel. A short story is a brief work that is meant to be read over a short period of time.

4 Follow No Rule Off a Cliff (pp. 224–225)

1. Cherryh states that the definition of science fiction is "what-if knowledge." **Ask** students to discuss what she means by this definition.
   Possible response: Science-fiction stories question what people think they know.
2. Direct students' attention to the quotation from "Mimic" by Donald A. Wollheim. **Ask** students to identify the irony of this quotation.
   Possible response: In this quotation, Wollheim points out that people think they have a great deal of knowledge, although scientific discovery is only a recent development in modern civilization. In fact, it is probable that people know very little. People may know a great deal about the past, but the future is uncertain. So much about the world has changed in such a short time that, as stated by Cherryh, science should not be too sure of itself.

PHLit Online!

Show or assign the Penguin author video segments for these pages online at **www.PHLitOnline.com.**

❺ Elements of Short Stories

1. Show students the Plot Diagram in *Graphic Organizer Transparencies,* pp. 37–38, to illustrate elements of plot. Prompt students to think of their favorite books, movies, or plays. For each example, talk through the plot and discuss the climax and resolution.
2. Review the different types of external conflict: character vs. character; character vs. environment or nature; character vs. supernatural forces or fate. **Ask** students to brainstorm for examples of each type of external conflict.
   Possible responses: ***Character vs. character:*** a story about two boxers in a match; ***Character vs. environment or nature:*** an account of someone who is stranded on an island or lost in a forest; ***Character vs. supernatural forces or fate:*** a character struggles against an alien or a ghost.
3. Tell students that an internal conflict exists only when a character struggles within his or her own mind regarding a desire or a moral choice of some kind. Emphasize that it is not an internal struggle when a character wonders whether to eat a salad or a sandwich for lunch.
4. Have students read the definition of an *epiphany* and volunteer examples of times in their lives when they may have experienced epiphanies.
5. Have students recall the settings in a familiar story, such as *The Wizard of Oz.* **Ask:** How do the settings add to the plot and theme of the story?
   Possible response: There are two primary settings in *The Wizard of Oz:* Kansas and Oz. Kansas serves to illustrate Dorothy's familiar and mundane life. Oz serves to illustrate the magical and the supernatural, a place where anything can happen. The two settings help to further the theme of the story when Dorothy encounters elements of her familiar life in Kansas within the magical context of Oz.

Exploring Short Stories

❺ Elements of Short Stories

A **short story** is a brief work of fiction intended to be read in one sitting. Due to the brevity of a short story, writers usually limit the number of characters, the range of settings, and the scope of the action.

"I thought it had a pretty good story and interesting characters, but I really didn't like the font."

Following are some of the key elements of a short story:

Plot A story's **plot** is the sequence of events that make up the action. As a story's plot moves forward, events unfold, develop to a climax (or high point), and are resolved, or sorted out, during the **resolution.**

Conflict Most plots center around a **conflict,** a problem or struggle. There are two main types of conflict in literature.

- An **external conflict** is a struggle between two characters, between an individual and a group, or between a character and a force, such as nature or fate.
- An **internal conflict** is a struggle within the mind of one character.

In traditional stories, the conflict ends at the resolution. However, in modern stories, characters may experience an **epiphany,** or sudden insight, that changes their feelings about the conflict without necessarily resolving it.

Setting The **setting** of a story is the time and place of the action. Setting provides a context or backdrop for the action. It can also add complications to the plot or contribute to the mood of the short story.

- The setting can be past, present, or future, and it can also include a specific year, season, or time of day.
- The setting can include the social, economic, or cultural circumstances that affect the characters and their specific geographic location.

Understanding by Design

Clarifying Expected Outcomes

Explain to students that pages 226–227 set out their goals in this Unit. By the end of the Unit, they will understand the elements of the short story (including setting, plot, characters, dialogue, point of view, and theme). They will be able to identify and discuss these elements in specific short stories. They will also be able to use some of these elements in writing their own pieces in the Writing Workshop on pp. 420–427.

Remind students that in addition, they will explore ways in which progress is made with or without *conflict* as they work toward an answer to the Unit Big Question, "Can progress be made without conflict?" They will also add words to their vocabulary that will help them when discussing progress/conflict. (See Introducing the Big Question, pp. 222–223.)

Character The **characters** in a story are the individuals who participate in the action. Types of characters include the **protagonist** and **antagonist**—the main character and his or her adversary. The **hero,** a character who exhibits positive traits, is often the protagonist.

Characterization is the writer's process of revealing a character's traits to the reader. Writers reveal characters both directly and indirectly.

- **Direct:** Writers make direct statements about a character's personality, appearance, habits, goals, values, or beliefs.
- **Indirect:** Writers can report a character's words, thoughts, actions, and interactions with other characters without commenting on them.

The process of showing how a character changes or of revealing different sides of a character's personality is called **character development.**

Theme The **theme** of a story is its central message or insight. A theme is not a summary of "what happens" in a story. Instead, it is a generalization about what the events mean. Themes may be stated or implied.

- A **stated theme** is expressed directly by the author.
- An **implied theme** is suggested indirectly through the experiences of the characters or through the events and the setting of the work.

Put Yourself in the Picture

Use these sentence starters to imagine a short story based on this photograph.

- **Characters** in a story based on this picture might be motivated by ________________.
- In the **plot** of a short story based on this picture, this moment could be followed by _______________.
- The **setting** of this story might include _______________________.

Challenge Imagine that you are a participant in this event. Decide what might have occurred before the moment in this picture. In a short paragraph, relate a sequence of events that could have led up to this photograph. In your writing, reveal more about the people pictured by using examples of **direct** and **indirect characterization.**

Differentiated Instruction for Universal Access

Support for Special Needs Students
Have students read the **Build Skills** page for "The Threads of Time" in the ***Reader's Notebook: Adapted Version.*** This version provides a basic-level introduction to fiction and nonfiction.

Support for Less Proficient Readers
Have students read the **Build Skills** page for "The Threads of Time" in the ***Reader's Notebook.*** This version provides a basic-level introduction to fiction and nonfiction.

EL Support for English Learners
Have students read the **Build Skills** page for "The Threads of Time" in the ***Reader's Notebook: English Learner's Version.*** This version provides a basic-level introduction to fiction and nonfiction.

5 Elements of Short Stories (cont.)

6. Discuss how authors reveal their characters to the reader through direct and indirect characterization. **Ask** students to consider the reasons that authors may use each kind of characterization.
   Possible response: Direct characterization means greater clarity for the reader; however, the author loses the element of reader discovery. Indirect characterization may make a story more interesting, but the writer gives up some control and risks reader misunderstanding.
7. Discuss stated and implied theme with students. **Ask:** Why would an author choose to use an implied theme instead of a stated theme?
   Possible response: An implied theme is used to create a complex statement about life or existence. A stated theme is more limited in its ability to inspire readers.

ASSESS

Answers

Put Yourself in the Picture

Possible response: Characters in a story based on this picture might be motivated by their worry about being separated from their friends and sent to a new school. In the **plot** of a short story based on this picture, this moment in the photo could have been followed by an administrator trying to convince the students to return to the school. The setting of this story might include a meeting between school officials, parents, and a company that wants to buy the old school.

Challenge

Possible response: The students reacted against the idea of losing their school by planning a walkout. After learning about the prospect of losing the school, the students decided to voice their opinion. Kate, the instigator, was angry at not being included in any of the talks about their school. She aggressively sought to convince the other students to fight to save their school. The students eagerly joined in the walkout.

PRETEACH

❶ Introducing the Selection

1. Invite students to read C. J. Cherryh's introduction to "The Threads of Time."
2. Call students' attention to the terms used in discussing the short story: *setting, character, antagonist, hero,* and *science fiction*. Have students identify these elements in "The Threads of Time" as they read.
3. **Ask** students to explain whether the section "Combining What's Real and What-If" increases their interest in reading the selection.
   Possible response: No, it makes me think the plot will be confusing.

❷ Background

Time Travel When Einstein published his Theory of Relativity in 1920, the idea of traveling through time became a mathematical possibility. Time travel has since become a staple of science-fiction literature.

❸ Connecting to the Big Question

1. Prepare students to apply the Big Question, "Can progress be made without conflict?" to the Model Selection.
2. Explain to students that in "The Threads of Time," Harrh is struggling between his roles: a time-mender who enforces the laws of time travel and a family man.
3. Have students complete this sentence starter, featuring thematic vocabulary from pp. 222–223:
   When faced with a conflict, the motive a person has for doing something is often ______.
   Possible response: the desire to reach a resolution.
4. Discuss students' responses. Then, have students look for examples of conflicts as they read the story.

Concept Connector →

Students will discuss the conflicts in the story when they have concluded reading.

Model Selection: Short Story

❶ C. J. Cherryh
❷ Introduces "The Threads of Time"

❸ This little story is a good example of why one should never throw creative work away. In the year this was written, I was using a typewriter, which produces paper, and because it was on paper, I filed it. When you use a computer, it's natural simply to highlight and delete something that doesn't fit where it is—or to delete the outtake files when you finish a project.

An Introductory Scene Becomes a Short Story

"The Threads of Time" was the introductory scene for my first published novel, back in 1975. It's set in a very futuristic world, and while one of the characters does appear in the novel that follows, the **setting** of the novel itself is a feudal age. So my editor, Don Wollheim, said the introduction had to go.

I cut it, he published the book—*Gate of Ivrel*—and the little snippet I'd clipped off lay in a manila folder for nearly ten years until someone needed a short-short for a convention program book. I polished the snippet into what you see before you. It's interesting to note that the **central character** in this story became the **antagonist,** not the **hero,** in the novel that followed.

Combining What's Real and What-if

"The Threads of Time" is a time-travel story. It is **science fiction.** But you don't have to believe time travel exists. In fact, to be a good science fiction reader, you need two things: first, a "sense of wonder," which means being able to look at the real world and say, "But—what if . . .?" And second, you need to engage in "willing suspension of disbelief" as you read. This means you know what part of the story is real, and what part is what-if. Then, you enter into the what-if for the duration of the tale, with your imagination given free rein.

Once you let yourself imagine time travel, for instance, you can think of all the strange effects that might follow. It's so human to wish to relive yesterday, or to leap ahead to a longed-for event. Science fiction allows you to fulfill that wish.

Vocabulary Development

Vocabulary Knowledge Rating

Create a **Vocabulary Knowledge Rating Chart** (*Professional Development Guidebook*, p. 33) with these words from the selection:

somber *mementoes* *confounded*

Give students a copy. Introduce the words by reading them aloud and having students mark their rating in the Before Reading column. Urge them to be alert to these words as they read and discuss the selection, because they will rate their knowledge of the words again after they finish.

If you wish, you may tally how many students know (or think they know) a word to gauge how much instruction you need to provide. As students read, point out the words and their context.

PHLit Online! **Vocabulary Central**, featuring student tools for recording and studying vocabulary, is available online at **www.PHLitOnline.com**.

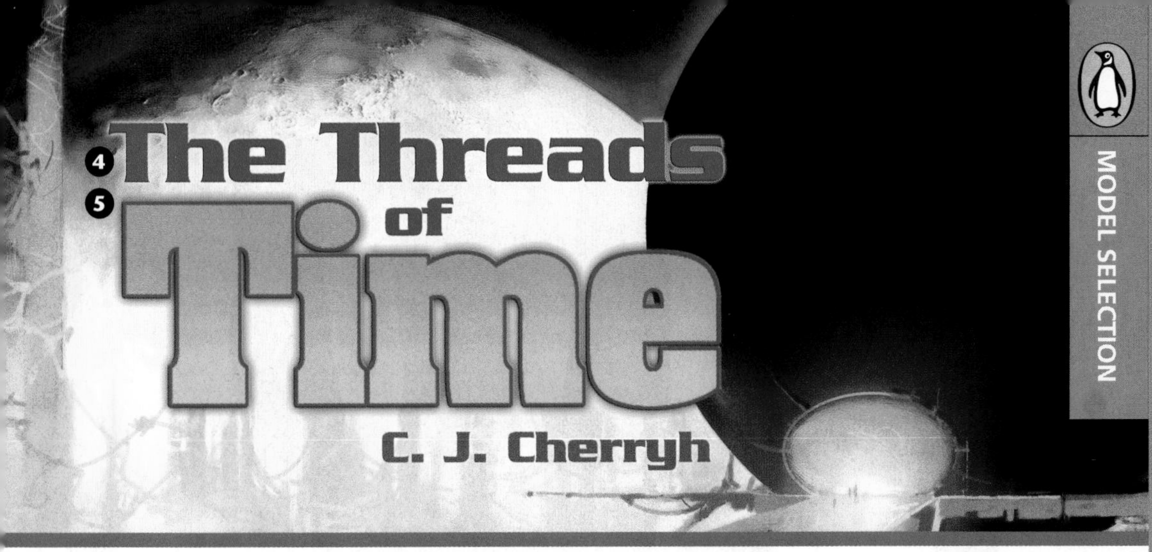

4 5 The Threads of Time

C. J. Cherryh

MODEL SELECTION

It was possible that the Gates were killing the qhal. They were everywhere, on every world, had been a fact of life for five thousand years, and linked the whole net of qhalur civilization into one present-tense coherency.

They had not, to be sure, invented the Gates. Chance gave them that gift . . . on a dead world of their own sun. One Gate stood—made by unknown hands.

And the qhal made others, imitating what they found. The Gates were instantaneous transfer, not alone from place to place, but, because of the motion of worlds and suns and the traveling galaxies—involving time.

There was an end of time. Ah, qhal *could* venture anything. If one supposed, if one believed, if one were very *sure*, one could step through a Gate to a Gate that would/might exist on some other distant world.

And if one were wrong?

If it did not exist?

If it never had?

Time warped in the Gate-passage. One could step across light-years, unaged; so it was possible to outrace light and time. Did one not want to die, bound to a single lifespan? Go forward. See the future. Visit the world/worlds to come.

But never go back. Never tamper. Never alter the past.

There was an End of Time.

It was the place where qhal gathered, who had been farthest and lost their courage for traveling on. It was the point beyond which no one had courage, where descendants shared the world with living ancestors in greater and greater numbers, the jaded, the restless, who reached this age and felt their will erode away.

6 ▲ **Critical Viewing**
What do you predict about the setting of this story based on this image? **[Predict]**

C. J. Cherryh
Author's Insight
You aren't expected to know what the word *qhal* means. But an experienced reader will guess that this is another species of intelligent beings.

7 **Reading Check**
What do the Gates allow the qhal to do?

TEACH

4 Activating Prior Knowledge

Based on what students know about different historical periods and their predictions about the future, have them discuss whether they would travel to the past or to the future if they were given the opportunity and to explain why.

Concept Connector →
Students will return to this discussion point when they have completed reading "The Threads of Time."

5 About the Selection

"The Threads of Time" explores the idea of time travel. For over 5,000 years, Gates have linked qhalur civilization into one present-tense coherency. Agent Harrh, a time-mender, is one of the few responsible for policing the laws that bind the Gates. Although he is acutely aware of the dangers of time-mending, he does not escape the vast complexities of time.

6 Critical Viewing

Possible Response: Students may predict the story will have a futuristic setting, possibly one of going to an unknown place.

7 Reading Check

Possible Response: The Gates allow the qhal to transfer instantaneously through time.

Differentiated Instruction for Universal Access

Strategy for Special Needs Students
Have students read the adapted version of "The Threads of Time" in the ***Reader's Notebook: Adapted Version.*** They may also listen to the adapted version on the ***Hear It!* Audio CD** (adapted text).

Support for Less Proficient Readers
Have students read "The Threads of Time" in the ***Reader's Notebook.*** After students finish the selection in the ***Reader's Notebook,*** have them complete the questions and activities in the student edition.

EL Support for English Learners
Have students read "The Threads of Time" in the ***Reader's Notebook: English Learner's Version.*** English learners may also read the selection as they listen to the recorded version on the ***Hear It!* Audio CD.**

PHLit Online!
Enriched Online Student Edition
To have students read the selection in interactive format, with narration and point-of-use interactive graphic organizers, go online at **www.PHLitOnline.com**

❽ Visual Connections

Whole-Class/Individual Activity

1. **Ask** students to describe the mood of the artwork—what feelings does it inspire?
   Possible responses: It is eerie; it is funny.
2. Then, **ask** students to explain which details in the painting contribute to this mood.
   Possible responses: The appearance of an eye surrounded by gears in the middle of a palm is unexpected and grotesque. The textures and details in the hand suggest exposed nerves and blood vessels. The faded clock face in the background seems to represent the impersonal force of time.
3. Guide students to appreciate the contrast between the flesh-and-blood hand and the mechanical gears and clock face. Discuss what this contrast suggests about the nature of time.
4. Have students to write a brief reflective paragraph on the theme of time, based on their discussion of the painting.

❽

Vocabulary Development

Thematic Vocabulary

As students are discussing "The Threads of Time," encourage them to use the thematic vocabulary presented in Introducing the Big Question, pp. 222–223. You might encourage them with sentence starters like these:

1. Harrh had to deal with his internal *struggle* of . . .
2. Harrh was uneasy about the *reconciliation* between himself and Alhir because . . .
3. The *debate* between Alhir and Harrh took place because . . .
4. Harrh was forced to *resolve* his belief that he was immortal because . . .

It was the place where hope ended. Oh, a few went farther, and the age saw them—no more. They were gone. They did not return.

They went beyond, whispered those who had lost their courage. They went out a Gate and found nothing there.

They died.

Or was it death—to travel without end? And what was death? And was the universe finite at all?

Some went, and vanished, and the age knew nothing more of them.

Those who were left were in agony—of desire to go; of fear to go farther.

Of changes.

This age—did change. It rippled with possibilities. Memories deceived. One remembered, or remembered that one had remembered, and the fact grew strange and dim, contradicting what obviously *was*. People remembered things that never had been true.

And one must never go back to see. Backtiming—had direst possibilities. It made paradox.

But some tried, seeking a time as close to their original exit point as possible. Some came too close, and involved themselves in time-loops, a particularly distressing kind of accident and unfortunate equally for those involved as bystanders.

Among qhal, between the finding of the first Gate and the End of Time, a new kind of specialist evolved: time-menders, who in most extreme cases of disturbance policed the Gates and carefully researched afflicted areas. They alone were licensed to violate the back-time barrier, passing back and forth under strict non-involvement regulations, exchanging intelligence only with each other, to minutely adjust reality.

Evolved.

Agents recruited other agents at need—but at whose instance? There might be some who knew. It might have come from the far end of time—in that last (or was it last?) age beyond which nothing seemed certain, when the years since the First Gate were more than five thousand, and the Now in which all Gates existed was—very distant. Or it might have come from those who had found the Gate, overseeing their invention. Someone knew, somewhen, somewhere along the course of the stars toward the end of time.

But no one said.

10 It was hazardous business, this time-mending, in all senses. Precisely *what* was done was something virtually unknowable after it was done, for alterations in the past produced (one believed) changes in future reality. Whole time-fields, whose events

9 ◄ **Critical Viewing** Which details in this illustration suggest the life the qhal lead? **[Connect]**

Short Story
Conflict The information here reveals one of the story's conflicts—the hazards of time travel.

11 **Reading Check**

What special job do time-menders do?

MODEL SELECTION

9 Critical Viewing

Possible response: As shown through the clock, the life of the qhal is dominated by the efforts to control time, and the hand and the eye show the conflict of the qhal's decision to go forward in time or to live in a single lifespan.

10 Short Story

Conflict

1. Remind students that there may be more than one conflict in a short story.
2. **Ask** students to describe the conflict presented in the bracketed passage.
   Possible response: The narrator describes an external conflict between the beings and the force of time. It is impossible to know that time has been altered, and the alterations of time change history.

11 Reading Check

Answer: Time-menders police the Gates by passing back and forth through time, exchanging intelligence only with each other to minutely adjust reality.

Differentiated Instruction for Universal Access

EL Strategy for English Learners

Use simpler language to help explain the concept of time travel. Define the words *finite* (having limits or boundaries), *contradicting* (asserting the opposite of a statement), and *alterations* (the process of being altered). Read the sentences where each word appears. Then, have students replace each word with a more familiar word or phrase to show their understanding of the author's word choice.

Strategy for Less Proficient Readers

To make sense of this science-fiction world, suggest that students create timelines. Tell students to place three Gates on their timelines: one each in the past, the present, and the future. In each Gate, tell students to record appropriate details from the story. For example, students may record the creation of the Gates in the past, a man having breakfast in a house on a hill in the present, and the destruction caused by time stretched thin in possibilities in the future.

12 Author's Insight

C. J. Cherryh

1. Read the following line aloud to students: "alterations in the past produced (one believed) changes in future reality." **Ask** students to think of situations where seemingly small mistakes change the course of events.
   Possible response: Forgetting to set an alarm, misplacing a set of keys, or missing a bus are everyday situations that trigger alterations in daily life.
2. Discuss the little girl's possible relationship with the man on the hill. Focusing first on the stranger, suggest that students create sequence-of-events charts that demonstrate causality among the items and people on the list.
3. Lead students in a discussion about how "a thread of causality strings" together events in their own lives.

13 Short Story

Character

1. The main character is introduced late in this story. **Ask** students to think about why Cherryh might have chosen to delay the reader's introduction to Harrh.
   Possible response: This late introduction makes Harrh seem unimportant, an afterthought. This first impression proves to be prophetic.
2. **Ask:** What does Cherryh reveal about Agent Harrh's character?
   Possible response: Harrh is a time-mender who loves his wife and family and is desperate to live in his own present of 1003.

C. J. Cherryh
Author's Insight A thread of causality strings these events together. The little girl might have been the man on the hill's great-grandmother. A chain of events led her to become what she was. Small events could lead us in many possible directions, but the single path we do take defines the future.

10 could be wiped and redone, with effects which widened the farther down the timeline they proceeded. Detection of time-tampering was almost impossible.

A stranger wanted something to eat, a long time ago. He shot himself his dinner.

A small creature was not where it had been, when it had been.

A predator missed a meal and took another . . . likewise small.

A child lost a pet.

12 *And found another.*

And a friend she would not have had. She was happier for it.

She met many people she had never/would never meet.

A man in a different age had breakfast in a house on a hill.

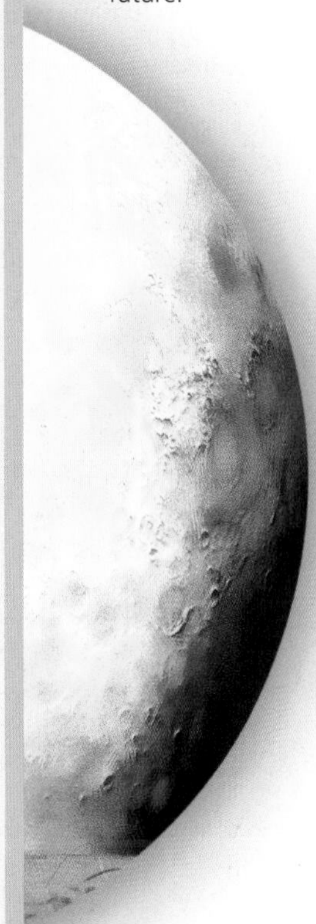

Short Story
Character The details here develop the character of Agent Harrh.

Agent Harrh had acquired a sense about disruptions, a kind of extrasensory queasiness about a just-completed timewarp. He was not alone in this. But the time-menders (Harrh knew three others of his own age) never reported such experiences outside their own special group. Such reports would have been meaningless to his own time, involving a past which (as a result of the warp) was neither real nor valid nor perceptible to those in Time Present. Some time-menders would reach the verge of insanity because of this. This was future fact. Harrh knew this.

He had been there.

13 And he refused to go again to Now, that Now to which time had advanced since the discovery of the Gate—let alone to the End of Time, which was the farthest that anyone imagined. He was one of a few, a very few, licensed to do so, but he refused.

He lived scattered lives in ages to come, and remembered the future with increasing melancholy.

He had visited the End of Time, and left it in the most profound despair. He had seen what was there, and when he had contemplated going beyond, that most natural step out the Gate which stood and beckoned—

He fled. He had never run from anything but that. It remained, a recollection of shame at his fear.

A sense of a limit which he had never had before.

Think Aloud

Vocabulary: Using Context

Use a think-aloud process to model for students how to find the meaning of *somber* using the context of a sentence. Read the following sentence from p. 233.

He caught her hand on the crystal table, held slender fingers, not speaking his thoughts, which were far too somber *for the morning.*

I can use the context of this sentence to figure out the meaning of *somber.* The narrator says that Harrh's thoughts are far too *somber* to share with his beloved wife over breakfast. If Harrh is having happy thoughts, he would probably want to share his thoughts with his wife. Harrh is probably having unhappy thoughts because he does not want to spoil the scene or his wife's mood over breakfast. Given the context of the sentence, I think that *somber* means unhappy.

And this in itself was terrible, to a man who had thought time infinite and himself immortal.

In his own present of 1003 since the First Gate, Harrh had breakfast, a quiet meal. The children were off to the beach. His wife shared tea with him and thought it would be a fine morning.

"Yes," he said. "Shall we take the boat out? We can fish a little, take the sun."

"Marvelous," she said. Her gray eyes shone. He loved her—for herself, for her patience. He caught her hand on the crystal table, held slender fingers, not speaking his thoughts, which were far too somber for the morning.

They spent their mornings and their days together. He came back to her, time after shifting time. He might be gone a month; and home a week; and gone two months next time. He never dared cut it too close. They lost a great deal of each other's lives, and so much—so much he could not share with her. "The island," he said. "Mhreihrrinn, I'd like to see it again."

"I'll pack," she said.

And went away.

He came back to her never aged; and she bore their two sons; and reared them; and managed the accounts: and explained his absences to relatives and the world. *He travels*, she would say, with that right amount of secrecy that protected secrets.

14 And even to her he could never confide what he knew.

"I trust you," she would say—knowing what he was, but never what he did.

He let her go. She went off to the hall and out the door— He imagined happy faces, holiday, the boys making haste to run the boat out and put on the bright colored sail. She would keep them busy carrying this and that, fetching food and clothes—things happened in shortest order when Mhreihrrinn set her hand to them. He wanted that, wanted the familiar, the orderly, the homely. He was, if he let his mind dwell on things—afraid. He had the notion never to leave again.

He had been to the Now most recently—5045, and his flesh crawled at the memory. There was recklessness there. There was disquiet. The Now had traveled two decades and more since he had first begun, and he felt it more and more. The whole decade of the 5040's had a queasiness about it, ripples of instability as if the whole fabric of the Now were shifting like a kaleidoscope.

And it headed for the End of Time. It had become more and more like that age, confirming it by its very collapse.

People had illusions in the Now. They perceived what had not been true.

Vocabulary
somber (säm′ bər)
adj. dark and gloomy

15 **Reading Check**
From what challenge did Agent Harrh flee?

MODEL SELECTION

14 Short Story
Conflict

1. Remind students that most plots center around a conflict and that characters can experience internal and external conflict. Emphasize that an internal conflict is a struggle within the mind of one character and an external conflict is a struggle against another character, nature, or fate.
2. **Ask:** What internal and external conflicts does Harrh face in "The Threads of Time"?
Possible response: Harrh struggles internally when he thinks about having to make a decision to stay in the present with his family or to do his job as time-mender. Externally, Harrh struggles with the state of the Now—the disquiet and instability he has seen of the time period.

15 Reading Check

Answer: Agent Harrh refuses to go beyond the End of Time.

Fluency

Distribute copies of page 233. Read the page aloud as students follow along. Divide the class into small groups of fluent and less fluent readers. Have students take turns reading paragraphs. Have other students circle words with which the reader has difficulty. Collect the marked-up copies. Review difficult words with the class. Look for these problem spots:

- If students have difficulty with the word *infinite,* point out the common prefix *in-*. Then explain that *in-* means "not" and *finite* means "having limits or boundaries." **Ask** what the word *infinite* means. **Sample answer:** "something that doesn't have limits." Discuss what the author means when she says Harrh thought time was *finite*. Repeat the same exercise with the word *immortal.*
- If students have difficulty with the word *kaleidoscope,* remind them to use context clues. Point out that if they read the whole sentence, the words *ripples, instability,* and *shifting* can help them determine the meaning of the word.

16 Critical Viewing

Possible response: The artwork gives the feeling of getting smaller and smaller while at the same time becoming translucent and almost air-like. This might be what it feels like to get drawn away, or disappear, from the present time.

17 Short Story

Conflict

1. Discuss the conflict between Harrh and the time-menders.
2. **Ask:** Why does Harrh refuse to travel to the Now?
   Possible response: He has seen too much and seems afraid to face the dreadful consequences of time-mending.

16 ▶ **Critical Viewing**
What does this artwork suggest about how it might feel to travel through time? **[Infer]**

And yet it *was* when he came home.

It had grown to be so—while he was gone.

A university stood in Morurir, which he did not remember.

A hedge of trees grew where a building had been in Morurir.

A man was in the Council who had died.

17 He would not go back to Now. He had resolved that this morning.

He had children, begotten before his first time-traveling. He had so very much to keep him—this place, this home, this stability—He was very well to do. He had invested well—his own small tampering. He had no lack, no need. He was mad to go on and on. He was done.

But a light distracted him, an opal shimmering beyond his breakfast nook, arrival in that receptor which his fine home afforded, linked to the master gate at Pyvrrhn.

A young man materialized there, opal and light and then solidity, a distraught young man.

"Harrh," the youth said, disregarding the decencies of meeting, and strode forward unasked. "Harrh, is everything all right here?"

Harrh arose from the crystal table even before the shimmer died, beset by that old queasiness of things out of joint. This was Alhir from 390 Since the Gate, an experienced man in the force: he had used a Master Key to come here—had such access, being what he was.

"Alhir," Harrh said, perplexed. "What's wrong?"

"You don't know." Alhir came as far as the door.

18 "A cup of tea?" Harrh said. Alhir had been here before. They were friends. There were oases along the course of suns, friendly years, places where houses served as rest-stops. In this too Mhreihrrinn was patient. "I've got to tell you— No, don't tell me. I don't want to know. I'm through. I've made up my mind. You can carry that where you're going. —But if you want the breakfast—"

"There's been an accident."

"I don't want to hear."

"He got past us."

"I don't want to know." He walked over to the cupboard, took another cup. "Mhreihrrinn's with the boys down at the beach. You just caught us." He set the cup down and poured the tea, where Mhreihrrinn had sat. "Won't you? You're always welcome here. Mhreihrrinn has no idea what you are. My young friend, she calls you. She doesn't know. Or she suspects. She'd never say.—Sit *down*."

Short Story
Conflict In this paragraph, the author provides more detail about the conflict between Harrh and the time-menders.

C. J. Cherryh
Author's Insight
When Harrh hears this, he is afraid. Why? Look back at the line "a university stood in Morurir" at the top of this page.

Vocabulary Development

Word Forms

Expand students' vocabulary by helping them learn related forms of the selection words called out on teacher's page 228. Two of these words have related forms. Give students a blank **Word Form Chart** (***Professional Development Guidebook***, p. 42) with *somber* and *confounded* in the correct columns. Work with the class, or have students work with a partner, to determine the related forms. The final chart should look like the one shown.

Hold students accountable for integrating the related forms of the words into their speaking and writing.

Noun	Verb	Adjective	Adverb
somberness		**somber**	somberly
confoundedness	confound	confounded	

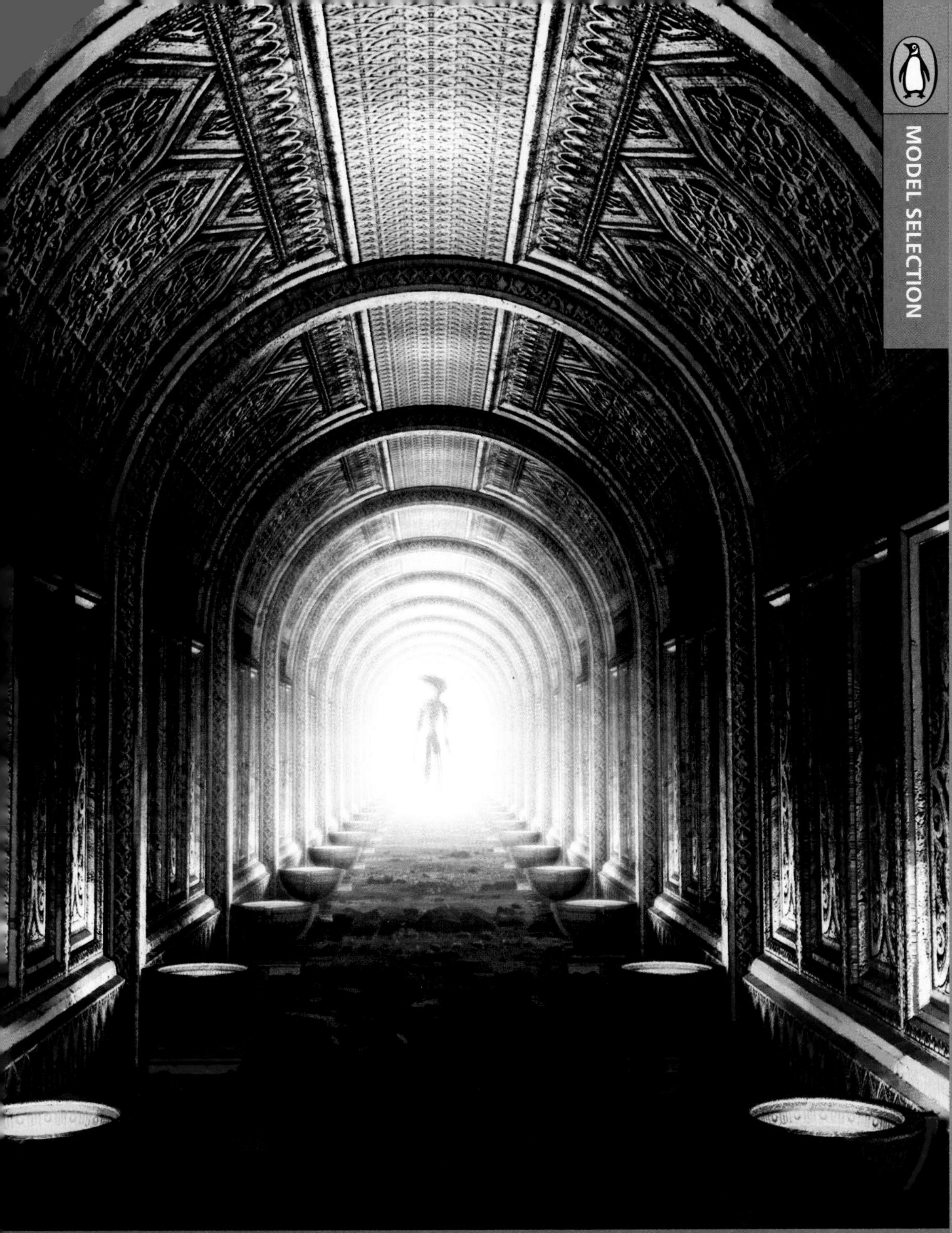

MODEL SELECTION

⓲ Author's Insight

C. J. Cherryh

1. Read the passage on page 234 aloud to students.
2. **Ask:** What is Harrh afraid of when he realizes that there are things in the present he doesn't remember and then he hears there has been an accident? **Possible response:** Harrh is afraid that life in the Now is affecting what happened in the past. He wants to hold on to the life that he loves surrounded by his wife and children. He is afraid that the Now is going to take that life away from him.

Differentiated Instruction for Universal Access

Strategy for Advanced Readers
Time travel is a common element in science-fiction stories and films. Have students review and compare the time-travel plots with which they are familiar. What makes time travel possible—machines, gateways, or other devices? Is time travel viewed as beneficial or harmful? What "rules" or "laws" are connected with time travel? Once students have made some generalizations about time-travel literature, have them discuss the ways in which "The Threads of Time" is similar to or different from other time-travel plots.

Strategy for Gifted/Talented Students
Cherryh created the qhal and their imaginary civilization for "The Threads of Time." Students may enjoy creating their own fictional civilizations. Ask students to brainstorm for the characteristics of their new worlds and the inhabitants. Then have students create artistic representations of their ideas. These representations may take the form of stories, poems, paintings, models, or songs. Invite students to share their work.

19 Author's Insight

C. J. Cherryh

Discuss how the progress of time slips slowly away from Harrh's grasp. **Ask:** Why do you think Cherryh chooses to take the memories away from Harrh in this order?
Possible answer: Cherryh chooses to take away Harrh's memories in order from the most important to the least important. In the end, like all other time-menders, he is left with nothing but the will to live.

Concept Connector

Have students return to their remarks about time travel. Ask students if their ideas have changed after reading the story. Invite students to share their altered views with the class.

Connecting to the Big Question

Ask students to identify the conflicts Harrh faces throughout the story. (**Answer:** internal conflict between staying in the present and continuing to time travel; external conflict between himself and Alhir) Then, have them compare their completed sentence starters with their thoughts after reading the story.

Vocabulary
mementoes (mə men′ tōz) *n.* souvenirs; objects that serve as reminders

Alhir had strayed aside, where a display case sat along the wall, a lighted case of mementoes of treasures, of crystal. "Harrh, there was a potsherd here."

"No," Harrh said, less and less comfortable. "Just the glasses. I'm quite sure."

"Harrh, it was very old."

"No," he said. "—I promised Mhreihrrinn and the boys—I mean it. I'm through. I don't want to know."

"It came from Silen. From the digs at the First Gate, Harrh. It was a very valuable piece. You valued it very highly.—You don't remember."

"No," Harrh said, feeling fear thick about him, like a change in atmosphere. "I don't know of such a piece. I never had such a thing. Check your memory, Alhir."

"It was from the ruins by the *First Gate*, don't you understand?"

And then Alhir did not exist.

Harrh blinked, remembered pouring a cup of tea. But he was sitting in the chair, his breakfast before him.

He poured the tea and drank.

He was sitting on rock, amid the grasses blowing gently in the wind, on a clifftop by the sea.

He was standing there. "Mhreihrrinn," he said, in the first chill touch of fear.

C. J. Cherryh
Author's Insight
After Harrh's initial fear, something has changed. What follows is all his perception, as the orderly progress of time rips loose around him. 19

But that memory faded. He had never had a wife, nor children. He forgot the house as well.

Trees grew and faded.

Rocks moved at random.

The time-menders were in most instances the only ones who survived even a little while.

Wrenched loose from time and with lives rooted in many parts of it, they felt it first and lived it longest, and not a few were trapped in backtime and did not die, but survived the horror of it and begot children who further confounded the time-line.

Vocabulary
confounded (kən foun′ did) *v.* confused; bewildered

Time, stretched thin in possibilities, adjusted itself.

He was Harrh.

But he was many possibilities and many names.

In time none of them mattered.

He was many names; he lived. He had many bodies; and the souls stained his own.

In the end he remembered nothing at all, except the drive to live.

And the dreams.

And none of the dreams were true.

Vocabulary Development

Vocabulary Knowledge Rating

When students have completed reading and discussing "The Threads of Time," have them take out their **Vocabulary Knowledge Rating Chart** for this selection. Read the words aloud once more and have students rate their knowledge of the words again in the After Reading column. Clarify any words that are still problematic. Have students write their own definitions or examples in the appropriate column. Encourage students to use the words in further discussion and written work about this selection. Remind them that they will be accountable for these words on the **Selection Test, *Unit 2 Resources,*** pp. 17–19 or 20–22.

After You Read | The Threads of Time

Critical Thinking

1. **Respond:** If you could travel in time, what or whom would you want to see? Why?
2. **(a)** How did the qhal acquire the ability to travel in time? **(b) Infer:** In what ways does this circumstance suggest that the qhal may not have fully understood the consequences of time travel?
3. **(a)** In his present of 1003, what changes does Harrh notice? **(b) Draw Conclusions:** Why are these changes significant?
4. **(a) Speculate:** What is the "accident" that Alhir reports to Harrh? **(b) Analyze Cause and Effect:** How does this accident affect Harrh?
5. **(a) Define:** Use a chart like the one shown to analyze key terms from the story. **(b) Discuss:** In a group, share and discuss your definitions. Then, revise your work based on the discussion.

Term	What It Means	Why It Is Important
the qual		
Gate		
time-mender		
the Now		
End of Time		

Can progress be made without conflict?
(a) How do the gates cause conflict for Harrh? **(b)** In what ways did the gates change Harrh's society? **(c)** Did the gates lead to progress in the story? Explain.

Short Story Review

1. Which aspect of the story—**plot, setting,** or **character**—does the author emphasize? Support your answer with details.
2. A common **theme** of science fiction is the warning against a misuse of technology. What warning or warnings do you find in this story?

Research the Author

Using the Internet and library sources, write a **report** about one of the several science-fiction worlds that C. J. Cherryh has created. Follow these steps:

- Identify the specific novels in one series.
- Describe the universe and the lives of the beings who populate it.
- Present your findings to the class.

ASSESS/EXTEND

Answers

Critical Thinking

1. Students may want to go back in time to change something or go to the future to discover something.
2. (a) Upon finding the First Gate, the qhal created others by imitating what they had found. (b) The qhal were unaware of the consequences of time travel as they built multiple Gates.
3. (a) Harrh notices that a university stands in a place he doesn't remember, a hedge of trees grew where a building had been, and a man in the Council is someone who had already died.
   (b) **Possible response:** These changes inform the characters that changes in the past affect the present and future.
4. (a) **Possible response:** The "accident" may be that a time-mender has gone back in time and destroyed the First Gate.
   (b) Without the existence of the First Gate, Harrh's life and his civilization would never have existed.
5. (a) **Possible response: Term:** the qhal; **What It Means:** beings who discover the Gates; **Why It Is Important:** They are the people whom the story is about.
   (b) Allow students time to discuss the terms.

Can progress be made without conflict?

(a) The Gates are the cause of the struggle Harrh has between staying in the present and returning to time travel. (b) **Possible response:** The Gates allowed people to see the future and the past so they could never live each day in the present. (c) **Possible response:** The Gates led to progress in time travel, but the progress gained seemed to be coming undone after the "accident."

Short Story Review

1. The author emphasizes the setting in her descriptions of the qhal civilization, the history of the Gates, and the references to time periods.
2. The warning is about the dangers of tampering with time while not considering the consequences.

Research the Author

Students may complete this research assignment for homework. Tell them they can find information about Cherryh's works in a library or online. They can find more about the author at **www.PHLitOnline.com.**

Assessment Resources

The following resources can be used to assess students' knowledge and skills.

Unit 2 Resources

L1 L2 EL **Selection Test A**, pp. 17–19
L3 L4 **Selection Test B**, pp. 20–22
L3 L4 **Open-Book Test**, pp. 14–16

PHLit Online! Students may use the **Self-test**, online at **www.PhLitOnline.com**, to prepare for **Selection Test A** or **Selection Test B.**

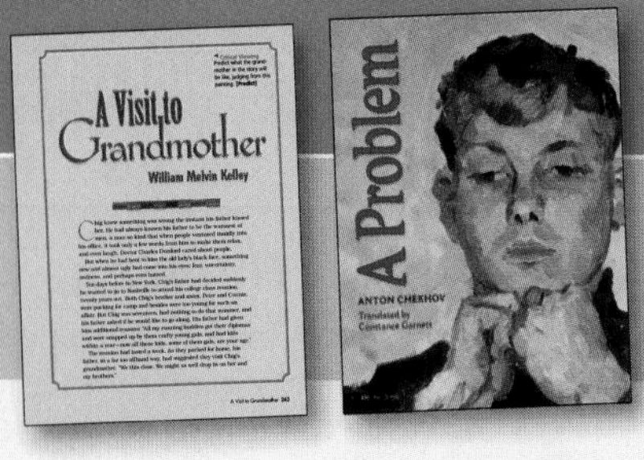

TIME AND RESOURCE MANAGER

A Visit to Grandmother • A Problem

Lesson Pacing Guide

DAY 1 Preteach

- Administer the Reading and Vocabulary Warm-ups (*Unit 2 Resources*, pp. 23–26 or 41–44) as necessary.
- Introduce the Reading Skill: Make Inferences FT
- Introduce the Literary Analysis concept: Character and Characterization FT
- Distribute copies of the appropriate graphic organizer for the Reading Skill (*Graphic Organizer Transparencies*, pp. 39–41). CRI
- Distribute copies of the appropriate graphic organizer for Literary Analysis (*Graphic Organizer Transparencies*, pp. 42–44). CRI
- Teach the selection vocabulary. FT CRI
- Introduce the Word Study skill.

DAYS 2–3 Preteach/Teach

- Build background with the Background feature. CRI
- Develop thematic vocabulary and thematic thinking with Writing About the Big Question.
- Prepare students to read with the Activating Prior Knowledge activities (TE). CRI
- Informally monitor comprehension while students read. FT
- Use the Reading Check questions to confirm comprehension.
- Develop students' ability to infer using the Reading Skill questions. CRI
- Develop students' understanding of character and characterization using the Literary Analysis questions. CRI
- Reinforce vocabulary with the Vocabulary notes. CRI

DAY 4 Assess

- Assess students' comprehension and mastery of the skills by having them answer the Critical Thinking, Reading Skill, and Literary Analysis questions. FT
- Have students complete the Vocabulary Practice activities. FT
- Have students complete the Word Study activities.

DAY 5 Extend/Assess

- Have students complete the Grammar lesson. CRI
- Have students complete the Writing activity and write retellings. (You may assign as homework.) FT
- Extend learning by having students complete the Research and Technology activity, a report on sources. (You may assign as homework.) As an alternative, assign them "Sibling Strife" or "Holding Parents Responsible" in *Reality Central*. CRI
- Administer Selection Test A or B (*Unit 2 Resources*, pp. 35–40 or 56–61). FT

"A Visit to Grandmother" is a short story edited for sensitivity issues.
"A Problem" is an adapted short story presented in its entirety.

Meeting Your Standards

Students will

1. **analyze and respond to literary elements.**
   - **Literary Analysis: Character and Characterization**
2. **read, comprehend, and analyze short stories.**
   - **Reading Skill: Make Inferences**
   - **Reading Check questions**
   - **Apply the Skills questions**
   - **Assessment Practice**
3. **develop vocabulary.**
   - **Vocabulary**
   - **Word Study**
4. **apply grammar skills.**
   - **Principal Parts of Regular Verbs**
   - **Author's perspective**
   - **Conflict and resolution**
   - **Author's purpose**
5. **Develop writing proficiency.**
   - **Work in Progress: Short Story**
   - **retellings**
6. **strengthen research and technology skills.**
   - **report on sources**

CRI For a full explanation of Culturally Responsive Instruction opportunities in this lesson, see p. T86–T87.

FT For an accelerated lesson, use the Fast Track strategies and activities.

Managing Differentiated Instruction

This leveled selection pairing groups a more accessible with a more challenging selection. Choose either one to teach the lesson skills. For classroom management suggestions for using the pairing in a mixed-ability class, see pp. T68–T69.

Daily Block Scheduling

Each day in this Lesson Pacing Guide represents a 40–50 minute period. Teachers using block scheduling may combine days to revise pacing. In addition, teachers may differentiate and support core instruction by integrating components for extended and intensive support as students require. See the Guide to Selected Leveled Resources (facing page).

Guide to Selected Leveled Resources

EL English Learners

			A Visit to Grandmother	A Problem
CORE COURSE	*Unit 2 Resources*	Selection Test A	pp. 35–37	pp. 56–58
	Graphic Organizer Transparencies	Reading Skill Graphic Organizer A	p. 39	p. 40
		Literary Analysis Graphic Organizer A	p. 42	p. 43
EXTENDED SUPPORT (Level 2)	*Unit 2 Resources*	Reading and Vocabulary Warm-ups A or B	pp. 23–26	pp. 56–61
	Reader's Notebook: English Learner's Version		adapted instruction and adapted selection	adapted instruction and summary
	Hear It! Audio CD		selection and summaries	selection and summaries
	Hear It! Audio CD (adapted text)		adapted selection and summaries	—
INTENSIVE SUPPORT (Level 1)	*Reality Central*		"Sibling Strife"	"Holding Parents Responsible"
	Real-World Writing Journal		Lesson 1, pp. 36–39	Lesson 2, pp. 40–43

L2 Below-Level Students

			A Visit to Grandmother	A Problem
CORE COURSE	*Unit 2 Resources*	Selection Test A	pp. 35–37	pp. 56–58
	Graphic Organizer Transparencies	Reading Skill Graphic Organizer A	p. 39	p. 40
		Literary Analysis Graphic Organizer A	p. 42	p. 43
EXTENDED SUPPORT (Level 2)	*Unit 2 Resources*	Reading and Vocabulary Warm-ups A or B	pp. 23–26	pp. 56–61
	Reader's Notebook		adapted instruction and full selection	adapted instruction and summary
	Hear It! Audio CD		selection and summaries	selection and summaries
INTENSIVE SUPPORT (Level 1)	*Reality Central*		"Sibling Strife"	"Holding Parents Responsible"
	Real-World Writing Journal		Lesson 1, pp. 36–39	Lesson 2, pp. 40–43
	Reading Kit		Reteaching worksheets	Reteaching worksheets

L1 Special Needs Students

			A Visit to Grandmother	A Problem
CORE COURSE	*Unit 2 Resources*	Selection Test A	pp. 35–37	pp. 56–58
	Graphic Organizer Transparencies	Reading Skill Graphic Organizer A	p. 39	p. 40
		Literary Analysis Graphic Organizer A	p. 42	p. 43
EXTENDED SUPPORT (Level 2)	*Unit 2 Resources*	Reading and Vocabulary Warm-ups A or B	pp. 23–26	pp. 56–61
	Reader's Notebook: Adapted Version		adapted instruction and adapted selection	adapted instruction and summary
	Hear It! Audio CD (adapted text)		adapted selection and summaries	—
INTENSIVE SUPPORT (Level 1)	*Reality Central*		"Sibling Strife"	"Holding Parents Responsible"
	Real-World Writing Journal		Lesson 1, pp. 36–39	Lesson 2, pp. 40–43
	Reading Kit		Reteaching worksheets	Reteaching worksheets

The program includes resources for these students: L3 On-Level L4 Advanced All All
For a complete guide to selection support, see pp. T106–T108.

NOTE: All print materials are also available online at *www.PHLitOnline.com*.

• A Visit to Grandmother
• A Problem

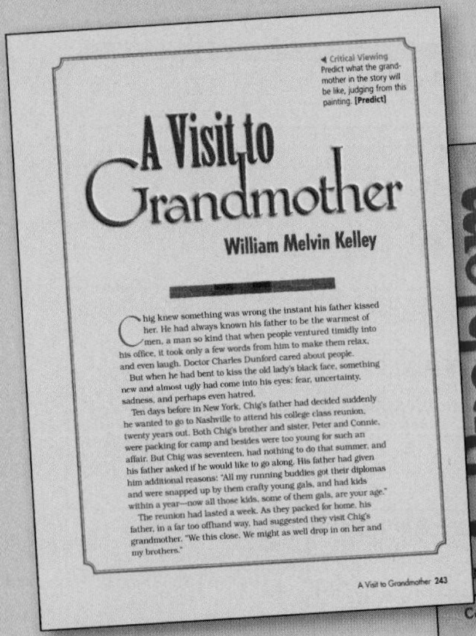

◀ Critical Viewing Predict what the grandmother in the story will be like, judging from this painting. **[Predict]**

A Visit to Grandmother

William Melvin Kelley

Chig knew something was wrong the instant his father kissed her. He had always known his father to be the warmest of men, a man so kind that when people ventured timidly into his office, it took only a few words from him to make them relax, and even laugh. Doctor Charles Dunford cared about people.

But when he had bent to kiss the old lady's black face, something new and almost ugly had come into his eyes: fear, uncertainty, sadness, and perhaps even hatred.

Ten days before in New York, Chig's father had decided suddenly he wanted to go to Nashville to attend his college class reunion, twenty years out. Both Chig's brother and sister, Peter and Connie, were packing for camp and besides were too young for such an affair. But Chig was seventeen, had nothing to do that summer, and his father asked if he would like to go along. His father had given him additional reasons: "All my running buddies got their diplomas and were snapped up by them crafty young gals, and had kids within a year—now all those kids, some of them gals, are your age."

The reunion had lasted a week. As they packed for home, his father, in a far too offhand way, had suggested they visit Chig's grandmother. "We this close. We might as well drop in on her and my brothers."

A Visit to Grandmother 243

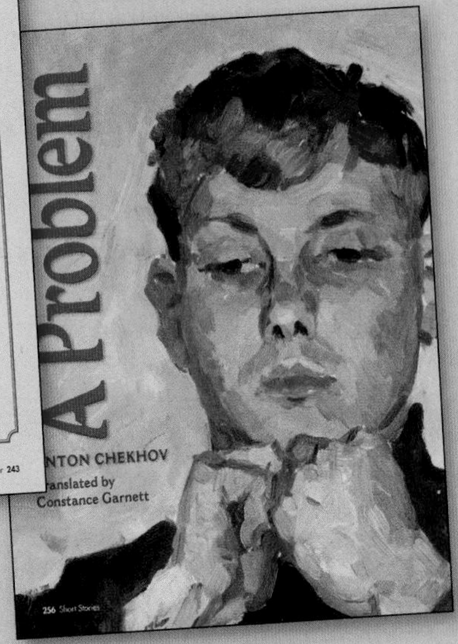

A Problem

NTON CHEKHOV

ranslated by Constance Garnett

256 Short Stories

RESOURCES FOR:

- EL English Learners
- L1 Special Needs Students
- L2 Below-Level Students
- L3 On-Level Students
- L4 Advanced Students
- All All Students

Vocabulary/Fluency/Prior Knowledge

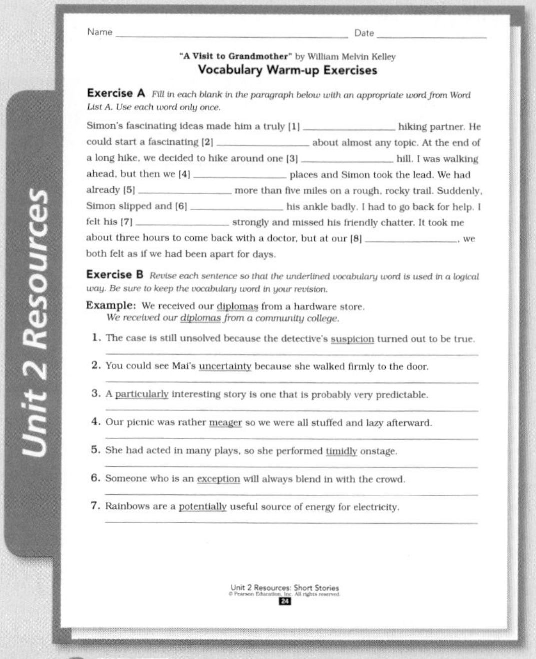

Unit 2 Resources

Name ______________________ Date ______________

"**A Visit to Grandmother**" by William Melvin Kelley

Vocabulary Warm-up Exercises

Exercise A *Fill in each blank in the paragraph below with an appropriate word from Word List A. Use each word only once.*

Simon's fascinating ideas made him a truly [1] ____________ hiking partner. He could start a fascinating [2] ____________ about almost any topic. At the end of a long hike, we decided to hike around one [3] ____________ hill. I was walking ahead, but then we [4] ____________ places and Simon took the lead. We had already [5] ____________ more than five miles on a rough, rocky trail. Suddenly, Simon slipped and [6] ____________ his ankle badly. I had to go back for help. I felt his [7] ____________ strongly and missed his friendly chatter. It took me about three hours to come back with a doctor, but at our [8] ____________, we both felt as if we had been apart for days.

Exercise B *Revise each sentence so that the underlined vocabulary word is used in a logical way. Be sure to keep the vocabulary word in your revision.*

Example: We received our diplomas from a hardware store.
We received our diplomas from a community college.

1. The case is still unsolved because the detective's suspicion turned out to be true.
2. You could see Mai's uncertainty because she walked firmly to the door.
3. A particularly interesting story is one that is probably very predictable.
4. Our picnic was rather meager so we were all stuffed and lazy afterward.
5. She had acted in many plays, so she performed timidly onstage.
6. Someone who is an exception will always blend in with the crowd.
7. Rainbows are a potentially useful source of energy for electricity.

Unit 2 Resources: Short Stories

24

EL L1 L2 **Vocabulary Warm-ups A and B, pp. 23–24, 41–42**

Also available for these selections:

EL L1 L2 **Reading Warm-ups A and B, pp. 25–26, 43–44**

All **Vocabulary Builder, pp. 30, 48**

All **Writing About the Big Question, pp. 27, 45**

Reader's Notebooks

Pre- and postreading pages for both selections, as well as "A Visit to Grandmother," appear in an interactive format in the *Reader's Notebooks*. Each *Notebook* is differentiated for a different group of learners.

The selections in the Adapted and English Learner's versions are abridged.

L2 L3 ***Reader's Notebook***

L1 ***Reader's Notebook: Adapted Version***

EL ***Reader's Notebook: English Learner's Version***

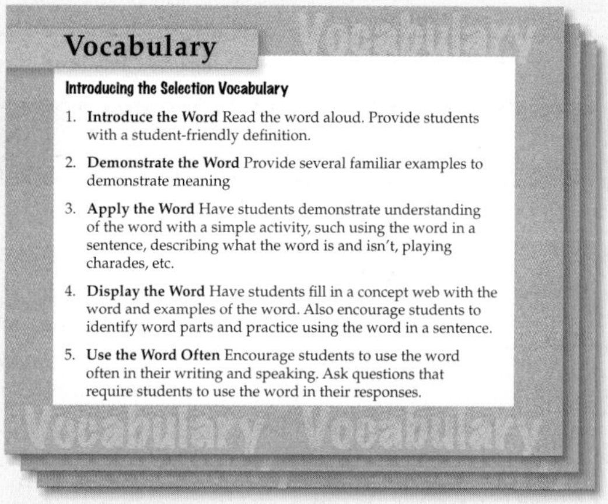

Vocabulary

Introducing the Selection Vocabulary

1. **Introduce the Word** Read the word aloud. Provide students with a student-friendly definition.
2. **Demonstrate the Word** Provide several familiar examples to demonstrate meaning
3. **Apply the Word** Have students demonstrate understanding of the word with a simple activity, such using the word in a sentence, describing what the word is and isn't, playing charades, etc.
4. **Display the Word** Have students fill in a concept web with the word and examples of the word. Also encourage students to identify word parts and practice using the word in a sentence.
5. **Use the Word Often** Encourage students to use the word often in their writing and speaking. Ask questions that require students to use the word in their responses.

Vocabulary Vocabulary

Classroom Strategies and Teaching Routines

- core classroom routines outlined step-by-step
- convenient format for easy reference while teaching

Selection Support

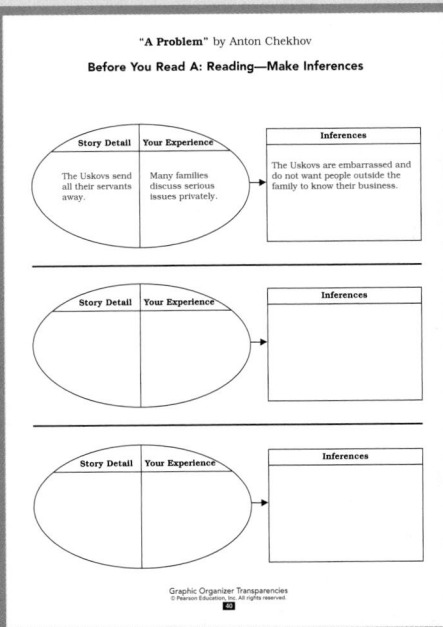

Graphic Organizer Transparencies

"**A Problem**" by Anton Chekhov

Before You Read A: Reading—Make Inferences

Story Detail	Your Experience	Inferences
The Uskovs send all their servants away.	Many families discuss serious issues privately.	The Uskovs are embarrassed and do not want people outside the family to know their business.

Story Detail	Your Experience	Inferences

Story Detail	Your Experience	Inferences

Graphic Organizer Transparencies

40

EL L1 L2 Reading: Graphic Organizer A, pp. 39, 40 (partially filled in)

Also available for these selections:

- **L3 Reading: Graphic Organizer B, p. 41**
- **EL L1 L2 Literary Analysis: Graphic Organizer A, pp. 42, 43 (partially filled in)**
- **L3 Literary Analysis: Graphic Organizer B, p. 44**

Skills Development/Extension

Unit 2 Resources

Name ______________________ Date ____________

"**A Visit to Grandmother**" by William Melvin Kelley

Enrichment: Connecting to the Performing Arts Through Storytelling

Storytelling is the art of sharing an experience with an audience. As with any other art form, it requires special tools and the skills to use these tools effectively. The storyteller's tools are language and his or her own voice and body. Whether they are performing on stage or sharing an experience at a family party, great storytellers are able to use words, voice, and body language to create vivid pictures in the minds of their listeners.

A. Directions: *Answer the following questions.*

1. What specific elements do you think are important in the art of storytelling?
2. What story does Chig's grandmother share in "A Visit to Grandmother"? How do people react to her story?
3. What elements of effective storytelling can be found in Chig's grandmother's tale? What specific details does she use to make the story visual for her audience? At what moments in the story is her own, unique perspective most noticeable?

B. *Practice your skills as a storyteller. First, take a few moments to think about an experience you would like to share with your classmates. Your story can be humorous, frightening, sad, or exciting. Then, practice telling your story. You may practice with a partner if you wish so that you can give each other suggestions and feedback. Use specific, interesting details to make the story come alive for your audience. Practice changing the level of loudness and softness in your voice at appropriate moments. Then, decide where to use movement and hand gestures to emphasize parts of your story. When everyone has finished rehearsing, gather in a circle with your classmates and share your stories. After each story is told, discuss which elements of good storytelling were used by the performer.*

Unit 2 Resources: Short Stories

31

L4 Enrichment, pp. 31, 49

Also available for these selections:

- **All Literary Analysis: Character and Characterization, pp. 28, 46**
- **All Reading: Make Inferences, pp. 29, 47**
- **L3 L4 Grammar, p. 50**
- **L3 L4 Support for Writing, p. 51**
- **L3 L4 Support for Extend Your Learning, p. 52**

Assessment

Name ______________________ Date ____________

"**A Problem**" by Anton Chekhov

Selection Test B

Critical Reading *Identify the letter of the choice that best completes the statement or answers the question.*

___ 1. At the beginning of "A Problem," the Uskov family is very careful to keep the servants from finding out the family secret. Which of the following would best help you understand why this is important to the Uskovs?
A. thinking about a time when you had a particularly fun day with your friends
B. thinking about how things have changed between the time the story was written and now
C. thinking about how the servants must feel about being sent away
D. thinking about a situation that your family prefers to keep to itself and not share with others

___ 2. Which of the following is NOT a reason that Sasha cashed a false promissory note in "A Problem"?
A. His friends were getting tired of him sponging off them.
B. He wanted money to spend while partying with his friends.
C. He wanted to pay his friends back for their generosity and kindness.
D. His friends cashed false notes regularly, so he believed it was normal and acceptable.

___ 3. What does Sasha's uncle mean when he says that it would be "civic cowardice" to help Sasha?
A. that Sasha is a coward
B. that the family should not hide behind Sasha's problems
C. that civic duty is more important than family honor
D. that by protecting Sasha from punishment they would be breaking the law

___ 4. What does the Colonel argue the uncles should do about Sasha in "A Problem"?
A. pay the debt to save the family's honor and keep the story out of the papers
B. not pay the debt because he believes Sasha will do the same thing again
C. make him work off the debt by becoming a servant in the family's household
D. send him to military school to learn some discipline

___ 5. While listening to his uncles' discussion, Sasha feels indifferent about his fate. How does the author reveal this aspect of Sasha's character?
A. through his actions
B. through his dialogue
C. through his appearance
D. through his thoughts

___ 6. While he is sitting by the door listening to his uncles argue, Sasha experiences several negative emotions. Which of the following would most help you understand his reactions?
A. thinking about how many people are in debt in the United States today
B. thinking about a time you overheard strangers arguing in a public place
C. thinking about how the uncles must feel as they discuss their nephew's fate
D. thinking about a time you got in trouble and had to wait for your punishment

Unit 2 Resources: Short Stories

59

L3 L4 Selection Test B, pp. 38–40, 59–61

Also available for these selections:

- **EL L1 L2 Selection Test A, pp. 35–37, 56–58**
- **L3 L4 Open-Book Test, pp. 32–34, 53–55**

PHLit Online!
www.PHLitOnline.com

- complete narrated selection text
- a thematically related video with writing prompt
- an interactive graphic organizer
- highlighting feature
- access to all student print resources, adapted to individual student needs
- Spanish and English summaries

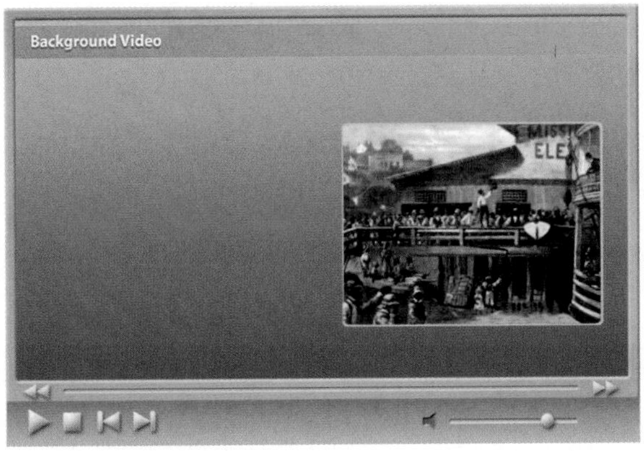

Background video

Also available:

Get Connected! (thematic video with writing prompt)

Vocabulary Central (tools, activities, and songs for studying vocabulary)

Also available:

Writer's Journal (with graphics feature)

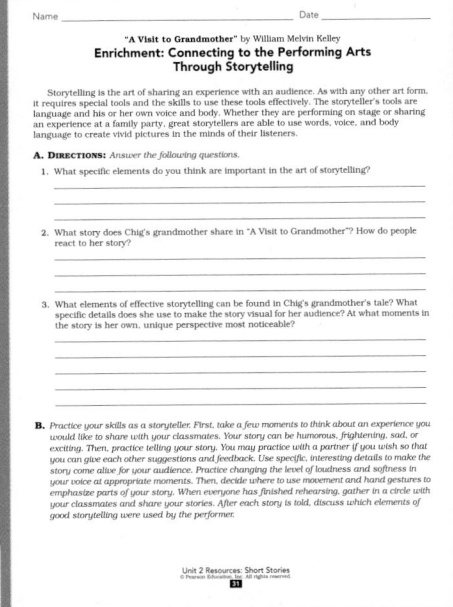

DIFFERENTIATE/PRETEACH

❶ Selection Choices

You may use either "A Visit to Grandmother" or "A Problem" to meet the lesson standards. Skills instruction for both selections appears on p. 239. Choose one selection to teach (or choose to teach both). The Accessibility at a Glance chart at the bottom of this page will help you determine which of the two selections is more appropriate for your students.

❷ Selection Skills

1. With the class, preview the selection skills. (The lesson meets the lesson objectives given on p. 238a.)
2. Explain that students will learn to use the skill of making inferences as they read to better understand and enjoy the selection you choose. By examining character and characterization as they read, they will gain a deeper insight into the selection.
3. To introduce the Writing and Research and Technology activities (p. 267), tell students that when they have finished reading the selection, they will write a retelling and a report related to the selection.
4. Tell students that they will also study a grammar concept: principal parts of regular verbs. By mastering this concept, they will improve their reading fluency and the quality of their own writing.

Before You Read

A Visit to Grandmother • A Problem

❶ Selection Choices

▲ Read **"A Visit to Grandmother"** to see what happens when a son confronts his mother about his childhood.

▲ Read **"A Problem"** to see how a group of uncles debate the fate of their irresponsible nephew.

❷ Selection Skills Guide

Practice these skills with either **"A Visit to Grandmother"** (p. 242) or **"A Problem"** (p. 256).

- Identify characters and character development
- Distinguish between direct and indirect characterization
- Make inferences
- Relate characters and events to your own experience
- Identify principal parts of regular verbs
- Write retellings of a story
- Write a report on sources

Differentiated Instruction for Universal Access

Accessibility at a Glance: Selection Choices

	A Visit to Grandmother	A Problem	
Context	Historical: The Great Migration, 1917–1930	Historical: Russia	Because a number of factors determine the relative accessibility of paired selections, in some cases the Lexile rating of the more challenging selection will be lower than that of the more accessible selection.
Language/ Vocabulary	• Accessible vocabulary and sentence structure • Southern dialect • Regionalisms	• Numerous long and complex sentences • Challenging vocabulary; historical and foreign terms footnoted • Above-level vocabulary	
Concept Level	Accessible (family relationships)	• Challenging (family honor and relationships; keeping up appearances; failure to accept responsibility for actions)	
Literary Merit	Regional; character-driven story	Noted author; universal theme	
Lexile/Length	Lexile: 700L Word Count: 3,263	Lexile: 800 Word Count: 2,639	
Overall Rating	**More accessible**	**More challenging**	

❸ Literary Analysis: Character and Characterization

Story **characters** are the people, animals, or even objects who perform the actions and experience the events of a narrative. Writers use two main types of **characterization** to bring characters to life:

- **Direct characterization:** The writer tells readers exactly what a character is like. For example, "Hugo is generous to a fault."
- **Indirect characterization:** The writer reveals a character's traits through **dialogue** (the character's words), the character's actions and thoughts, and the effect the character has on others.

To better understand characters and gain insight into the message of a story, take note of the **character development**—changes the character undergoes or new aspects of the character the writer reveals.

❹ Reading Skill: Make Inferences

An **inference** is a logical assumption based on details in a story. Making inferences helps you more fully understand story characters and why they act as they do. To make inferences about a character, **relate characters and events to your own experience,** and make assumptions based on that information.

For example, if a story character mumbles and avoids eye contact, you may think of people that you know who act this way and infer that the character is shy.

❺ Using the Strategy: Inference Chart

Use an **inference chart** like this one to help you relate your reading to your experiences.

Story Detail		Your Experience		Inference
The new captain's palms are sweating as she addresses the crew.	+	New camp counselors are nervous about whether campers will obey them.	→	The new captain is unsure of herself.

PHLit Online!
www.PHLitOnline.com

Hear It!
- Selection summary audio
- Selection audio

See It!
- Get Connected video
- Background video
- More about the author
- Vocabulary flashcards

Do It!
- Interactive journals
- Interactive graphic organizers
- Self-test
- Internet activity
- Grammar tutorial
- Interactive vocabulary games

PRETEACH

❸ Literary Analysis

1. Introduce the skill, using the instruction on the student page.
2. Tell students that they will analyze character as they read.

Think Aloud: Model the Skill

Model direct and indirect characterization using the following "think aloud." Say to students:

Suppose I am writing about a character named Bob. I want to reveal a character trait: his cautious behavior. I can do this through direct characterization by stating his traits: "Bob always thought deeply before acting." Also, I can use indirect characterization, showing his personality through his thoughts and actions: "Peter didn't rush forward. He remained in his seat, considering his options."

❹ Reading Skill

1. Introduce the skill, using the instruction on the student page.
2. Tell students that they will make inferences as they read.

Think Aloud: Model the Skill

Model the skill of making inferences, using the following "think aloud." Say to students:

To fully understand a piece of writing, I have to read between the lines, or make inferences.

Let's say I'm reading a story about a man awaiting a phone call. The man is holding his cellphone and pacing across his office. I know that when people pace, they are usually nervous about something. Because the man is holding his phone, I can infer that he is nervous about the phone call. Whenever I read, I connect clues like these to make inferences, using my own prior knowledge.

❺ Using the Strategy

Give students a copy of **Reading Skill Graphic Organizer A** or **B** (***Graphic Organizer Transparencies,*** pp. 39–40) to record their inferences as they read. Use the examples in **Reading Skill Graphic Organizer A** (partially filled in) to model the process of completing the organizer.

Differentiated Instruction for Universal Access

Preparing Students for the More Challenging Selection

If you wish to prepare lower-level readers to read "A Problem," the more challenging selection, follow these steps:

- Students might have difficulty comprehending why the Uskov family name is at stake. Discuss with students the significance of the family name in aristocratic society. Explain that a family's prominence in society and influence on cultural, economic, and government affairs depended on several factors, including the family's ancestry, its wealth, and the respectable behavior of its members.
- Review the Background note on p. 255. Make sure students understand the concept of forging an IOU and of selling it to a third party.
- Discuss with students what they believe makes one a criminal. Ask students to consider whether certain behaviors or actions define a criminal or whether a person's attitude counts. Lead them in discussing cases of people who do not believe they are criminals, despite their crimes, because "everyone's doing it" or because they think it doesn't harm anyone.

PRETEACH

❶ Writing About the Big Question

1. Review the assignment with the class.
2. Lead students in discussing cases in which open conflict can bring people to "have it out," or express their true feelings.
3. Have students complete the sentence starters. Review responses as a class. (**Possible response:** When people experience a misunderstanding, a confrontation may be helpful because it will allow people to communicate their and feelings. Following a conflict, relationships might change because a problem might have been resolved.)
4. Remind students that their answers will help them think about the Big Question, "Can progress be made without conflict?"

While You Read

Tell students to note, as they read, details that reveal a growing confrontation.

❷ Vocabulary

1. Have students preview the selection vocabulary.
2. For each word, have students say the word aloud.
3. Then, use the word in a sentence that defines the word.
4. Finally, repeat your definitional sentence or a similar sentence with the word missing and have the class "fill in the blank" chorally. Here is an example:

   To be meager is to be of poor quality or a small amount. Customers looking for a bountiful assortment of cakes will be disappointed if the selection is [students say "meager"].

❸ Word Study

1. Introduce the skill, using the instruction in the box.
2. Ask students how the meaning of *-ence* contributes to the meaning of *magnificence*. (**Answer:** *Magnificence* means "the state of being magnificent.")

Can progress be made without conflict?

A Visit to Grandmother
William Melvin Kelley

❶ Writing About the Big Question

In "A Visit to Grandmother," a man must decide if he can believe his mother's version of a longstanding family conflict. Use these sentence starters to develop your ideas about the Big Question:

When people experience a misunderstanding, a **confrontation** may be helpful because ________________.

Following a conflict, relationships might **change** because ____________ ____________.

While You Read Look for details that build up to a confrontation and decide whether progress can be made.

❷ Vocabulary

Read each word and its definition. Decide whether you know the word well, know it a little bit, or do not know it at all. After you read, see how your knowledge of each word has increased.

- **indulgence** (in dul′ jəns) *n.* leniency; readiness to tolerate or forgive bad behavior (p. 244) ***If you show the child too much indulgence, you may spoil her.*** *indulge v. indulgent adj.*
- **grimacing** (grim′ is iŋ) *v.* making a twisted face showing disgust or pain (p. 244) ***She is grimacing because she has a splinter in her toe.*** *grimace n.*
- **meager** (mē′ gər) *adj.* of poor quality or small amount (p. 250) ***Due to poor rainfall, there was only a meager crop.*** *meagerly adv. meagerness n.*
- **trace** (trās) *n.* tiny amount; hint (p. 250) ***There was not even a trace of cake left.***
- **fraud** (frôd) *n.* deceit; trickery (p. 251) ***There are strict penalties for insurance fraud.*** *fraudulent adj. fraudulently adv.*
- **engaging** (en gāj′ iŋ) *adj.* attractive; pleasant (p. 252) ***The doctor's engaging personality puts his patients at ease.*** *engage v. engagingly adv. engagement n.*

❸ Word Study

The **Latin suffix *-ence*** means "quality of" or "state of."

In this story, a mother treats one of her sons with **indulgence,** or the state of yielding to his wishes, by not punishing him for improper behavior.

Vocabulary Development

Vocabulary Knowledge Rating

Create a **Vocabulary Knowledge Rating Chart** (***Professional Development Guidebook***, p. 33) for this selection. Include the selection vocabulary and the Big Question words that appear in the Writing About the Big Question sentence starters on this page. (The Big Question vocabulary is introduced on pp. 222–223.)

Give students a copy of the chart. Read the words aloud, and have students mark their rating in the Before Reading column. Urge them to be alert to these words as they read and discuss the selection.

Tally how many students think they know a word to gauge how much instruction to provide. As students read and discuss the selection, point out the words and their context.

PHLit Online! **Vocabulary Central,** featuring tools, activities, and songs for studying vocabulary, is available at **www.PHLitOnline.com**

Meet William Melvin Kelley (b. 1937)

Author of

A Visit to Grandmother

William Melvin Kelley is a man of questions. He says, "I am not a sociologist or a politician or a spokesman. Such people try to give answers. A writer, I think, should ask questions."

Kelley's questions often explore the problems of belonging to a group. His first novel, *A Different Drummer,* reflects his belief in individualism.

A Community Artist At the same time, Kelley's work shows a strong connection to community. He belongs to the Black Arts Movement, the generation of writers, artists, dancers, and musicians that emerged in the 1960s and 1970s. Like others in the movement, he often addresses the moral, cultural, and political questions African Americans face.

4 BACKGROUND FOR THE STORY

Dialect

Dialect is the variety of a language spoken in a region or community. Some characters in "A Visit to Grandmother" speak in a southern dialect. In this dialect, *I reckon* means "I believe." *Fixin' to* replaces "about to."

DID YOU KNOW?

Introducing his class on writing fiction, Kelley notes that "Art may come from the heart, but craft comes from the brain."

Daily Bellringer

For each class during which you will teach this selection, have students complete one of the five Quick Write activities for Week 7 in the ***Daily Bellringer Activities*** booklet.

4 Background

The Great Migration

As a mass movement, the Great Migration had several "push" and "pull" factors. Poverty, racism, and violence pushed African Americans out of the South. Better jobs in factories and the chance for more freedom and better education pulled African Americans to Chicago, Detroit, New York, and other northern cities. Northern factory owners sent agents to recruit African American workers, and railroad companies needing workers paid African Americans' fares north.

African American writers responded to the Great Migration with novels and short stories about urban life and freedom. Ralph Ellison's *Invisible Man,* James Baldwin's *Go Tell It on the Mountain,* and Gloria Naylor's *The Women of Brewster Place* are migration narratives.

Multidraft Reading

This icon ● marks natural pauses in the selection. To assist struggling readers and to deepen reading for all, assign the text in "chunks," following the icons, and apply multidraft reading protocols. For each reading, have students set the purpose indicated:

- **First reading**—literal comprehension: answer the Reading Check questions.
- **Second reading**—application of skills: answering the Make Inferences and the Character and Characterization prompts.
- **Third reading**—interpretation: answering the end-of-selection questions.

For more guidance, refer to the ***Classroom Strategies and Teaching Routines*** card on multidraft reading.

Differentiated Instruction — Additional Instruction

EL Extended Support—English Learners
Have students complete the **Reading and Vocabulary Warm-ups,** ***Unit 2 Resources,*** pp. 23–26, before they read. Assign the prereading pages and the adapted selection in the ***Reader's Notebook: English Learner's Version.*** Then, have students listen to portions of the selection on the ***Hear It!*** **Audio CD.**

L1 L2 Extended Support—Struggling Readers
Have students complete the **Reading and Vocabulary Warm-ups,** ***Unit 2 Resources,*** pp. 23–26, before they read. Assign the prereading pages and the adapted selection in the ***Reader's Notebook: Adapted Version.*** Then, have students listen to portions of the selection on the ***Hear It!*** **Audio CD** (adapted text).

Extended Support—Reluctant Readers
To build motivation and engagement before assigning the selection, have students read "Sibling Strife," a thematically related selection in ***Reality Central.*** Then, use the questions at the conclusion of the related selection to guide discussion.

PHLit Online!
For more about the author, practice with the selection vocabulary, or more background, go online at **www.PHLitOnline.com**

TEACH

❶ Activating Prior Knowledge

1. Prepare an **Anticipation Guide** (see ***Professional Development Guidebook,*** pp. 36–38) with the following statements:
   - Parents love all their children equally.
   - Sibling rivalry is a natural accompaniment to having brothers and sisters.
   - Every family has a black sheep, or a member who brings disgrace.
   - It's never too late to make amends or right a wrong.
2. Give students a copy of the prepared **Anticipation Guide** and have them respond in the Me column. Have them discuss the statements in groups and mark the Guide again in the Group column.
3. For further guidance, use the ***Classroom Strategies and Teaching Routines*** card: **Using an Anticipation Guide.**

Concept Connector →

Students will return to the **Anticipation Guide** after completing the story.

Individual Activity

Have students preview the illustrations on pages 242, 245, and 246 on their own. Have them list expectations these pictures create about the characters and their ways of life.

❷ About the Selection

"A Visit to Grandmother" shows how old grievances and tensions within a family can persist through the years, affecting even the most capable and accomplished people.

Vocabulary Development

Latin Word Origins

- Call students' attention to the word *ventured* in line 3 of the story. Model the use of context clues to determine the meaning of the word: "to proceed despite possible danger or risk." Then tell them that the word comes from the Latin word *aventura*, meaning "a happening."
- Invite students to brainstorm for a list of English words that derive from the Latin word *aventura,* such as *adventure, misadventure, venturesome,* and *venturous.* Have students discuss what the words have in common and make educated guesses about each word's meaning. Finally, have them check the dictionary definition for each word.

3 ◀ Critical Viewing
Predict what the grandmother in the story will be like, judging from this painting. **[Predict]**

1 2 A Visit to Grandmother

William Melvin Kelley

4 Chig knew something was wrong the instant his father kissed her. He had always known his father to be the warmest of men, a man so kind that when people ventured timidly into his office, it took only a few words from him to make them relax, and even laugh. Doctor Charles Dunford cared about people.

But when he had bent to kiss the old lady's black face, something new and almost ugly had come into his eyes: fear, uncertainty, sadness, and perhaps even hatred.

Ten days before in New York, Chig's father had decided suddenly he wanted to go to Nashville to attend his college class reunion, twenty years out. Both Chig's brother and sister, Peter and Connie, were packing for camp and besides were too young for such an affair. But Chig was seventeen, had nothing to do that summer, and his father asked if he would like to go along. His father had given him additional reasons: "All my running buddies got their diplomas and were snapped up by them crafty young gals, and had kids within a year—now all those kids, some of them gals, are your age."

The reunion had lasted a week. As they packed for home, his father, in a far too offhand way, had suggested they visit Chig's grandmother. "We this close. We might as well drop in on her and my brothers."

3 Critical Viewing

Possible response: The grandmother will be patient, gentle, and wise.

4 Connecting to the Big Question

1. Explain that the way people resolve their conflicts with another often determines the success or failure of their relationship.
2. Have students read the bracketed text. **Ask:** How does Chig's father reveal that he is uneasy around his mother?
   Answer: Chig describes his father as being the "warmest of men," but when his father kisses Chig's grandmother, Chig notices a combination of fear, uncertainty, sadness, and hatred present in his father's eyes.
3. **Ask:** What can you infer about Chig's father's uneasiness?
   Possible response: Chig's father's uneasiness indicates that something about his mother is bothering him, so there may be a conflict between them. The resolution, however, might not benefit the relationship; if it does not, then progress has not been made.
4. Then, **ask:** How might his feeling result in progress in his relationship with his mother?
   Possible response: If Chig's father explains what is bothering him, it may lead to a discussion that resolves the conflict.

Differentiated Instruction for Universal Access

Support for Special Needs Students

Students may have a difficult time with the southern dialect in "A Visit to Grandmother." Have them read the story in the **Adapted Reader's Notebook** to get a basic understanding of the plot. Then, have students listen to the recording of the selection on the ***Hear It!* Audio CD** (adapted text) as they follow along in the text.

EL Strategy for English Learners

"A Visit to Grandmother" contains challenging vocabulary and dialect that may be unfamiliar to some students. Students will benefit from following along in their text as they listen to the recording of the selection on the ***Hear It!* Audio CD**. Pause the recording as necessary to clarify particular words and phrases.

PHLit Online!

This selection is available in interactive format in the **Enriched Online Student Edition,** online at **www.PHLitOnline.com,** which includes a thematically related video and writing prompt and an interactive graphic organizer.

❺ Literary Analysis

Character and Characterization

1. Have a volunteer read aloud the bracketed text.
2. Review with students the definition of direct characterization and remind them that it involves telling rather than showing.
3. Then **ask** students the Literary Analysis question: What do you learn about GL through direct characterization?
   Answer: GL is funny, impractical, immoral, and untrustworthy.
4. **Ask** students what Dr. Dunford's attitude toward GL shows about their relationship.
   Answer: Dr. Dunford must care for GL since GL is the only member of the family he talks about. However, Dr. Dunford seems to feel superior to his brother, not expecting much from him.

❻ Reading Skill

Make Inferences

1. Remind students that their inferences need to derive from the clues in the text as well as their prior knowledge.
2. Have students use their **Reading Skill Graphic Organizer B** (*Graphic Organizer Transparencies*, p. 41) with details from this scene showing his mother's reaction to his visit.
3. Then, **ask** students the Reading Skill question: What feelings does the grandmother have upon seeing her son? Which details support your inference?
   Possible response: She is surprised, thrilled, and overwhelmed. At first, when she is trying to figure out who is there, she eliminates Charles because she never hears from him. Then, when she realizes it is really him, she cries and hugs him. She does not seem to want to let go.

Literary Analysis
Character and Characterization What do you learn about GL through direct characterization? ❺

Vocabulary
indulgence (in dul′ jəns) *n.* leniency; readiness to tolerate or forgive bad behavior

So, instead of going north, they had gone farther south, had just entered her house. And Chig had a suspicion now that the reunion had been only an excuse to drive south, that his father had been heading to this house all the time.

His father had never talked much about his family, with the exception of his brother, GL, who seemed part con man, part practical joker and part Don Juan;[1] he had spoken of GL with the kind of **indulgence** he would have shown a cute, but ill-behaved and potentially dangerous, five-year-old.

Chig's father had left home when he was fifteen. When asked why, he would answer: "I wanted to go to school. They didn't have a Negro high school at home, so I went up to Knoxville and lived with a cousin and went to school."

They had been met at the door by Aunt Rose, GL's wife, and ushered into the living room. The old lady had looked up from her seat by the window. Aunt Rose stood between the visitors.

The old lady eyed his father. "Rose, who that? Rose?" She squinted. She looked like a doll, made of black straw, the wrinkles in her face running in one direction like the head of a broom. Her hair was white and coarse and grew out straight from her head. Her eyes were brown—the whites, too, seemed light brown—and were hidden behind thick glasses, which remained somehow on a tiny nose. "That Hiram?" That was another of his father's brothers. "No, it ain't Hiram; too big for Hiram." She turned then to Chig. "Now that man, he look like Eleanor, Charles's wife, but Charles wouldn't never send my grandson to see me. I never even hear from Charles." She stopped again.

Reading Skill ❻
Make Inferences What feelings does the grandmother have upon seeing her son? Which details support your inference?

"It Charles, Mama. That who it is." Aunt Rose, between them, led them closer. "It Charles come all the way from New York to see you, and brung little Charles with him."

The old lady stared up at them. "Charles? Rose, that really Charles?" She turned away, and reached for a handkerchief in the pocket of her clean, ironed, flowered housecoat, and wiped her eyes. "God have mercy, Charles." She spread her arms up to him, and he bent down and kissed her cheek. That was when Chig saw his face, **grimacing**. She hugged him; Chig watched the muscles in her arms as they tightened around his father's neck. She half rose out of her chair. "How are you, son?"

Vocabulary
grimacing (grim′ is iŋ) *v.* making a twisted face showing disgust or pain

Chig could not hear his father's answer.

She let him go, and fell back into her chair, grabbing the arms. Her hands were as dark as the wood, and seemed to become part of it. "Now, who that standing there? Who that man?"

---

1. **Don Juan** (dän′ wän′) a legendary nobleman, idle and immoral, who fascinates women.

Vocabulary Development

Thematic Vocabulary: The Big Question

As students are discussing "A Visit to Grandmother," encourage them to use the thematic vocabulary presented in Introducing the Big Question, pp. 222–223. You might encourage them with sentence starters like these:

1. GL *negotiates* with the man who has the horses and soon realizes that the man . . .
2. Chig's father's *motive* for bringing up differences in the way his mother treated him and GL is . . .
3. Once Chig's father demands the truth of his mother, we see him *struggle* to . . .
4. The *confrontation* between Chig's father and Chig's grandmother seems unsuccessful because . . .

"That's one of your grandsons, Mama." His father's voice cracked. "Charles Dunford, junior. You saw him once, when he was a baby, in Chicago. He's grown now."

"I can see that, boy!" She looked at Chig squarely. "Come here, son, and kiss me once." He did. "What they call you? Charles too?"

"No, ma'am, they call me Chig."

She smiled. She had all her teeth, but they were too perfect to be her own. "That's good. Can't have two boys answering to Charles in the same house. Won't nobody at all come. So you that little boy. You don't remember me, do you. I used to take you to church in Chicago, and you'd get up and hop in time to the music. You studying to be a preacher?"

"No, ma'am. I don't think so. I might be a lawyer."

"You'll be an honest one, won't you?"

"I'll try."

"Trying ain't enough! You be honest, you hear? Promise me. You be honest like your daddy."

"All right. I promise."

"Good. Rose, where's GL at? Where's that thief? He gone again?"

"I don't know, Mama." Aunt Rose looked embarrassed. "He say he was going by the store. He'll be back."

"Well, then where's Hiram? You call up those boys, and get them over here—now! You got enough to eat? Let me go see." She started to get up. Chig reached out his hand. She shook him off. "What they tell you about me, Chig? They tell you I'm all laid up? Don't believe it. They don't know nothing about old ladies. When I want help, I'll let you know. Only time I'll need help getting anywheres is when I dies and they lift me into the ground."

She was standing now, her back and shoulders straight. She came only to Chig's chest. She squinted up at him. "You eat much? Your daddy ate like two men."

"Yes, ma'am."

"That's good. That means you ain't nervous. Your mama, she ain't nervous. I remember that. In Chicago,

8

Literary Analysis
Character and Characterization
Name one trait of the grandmother that is suggested in the dialogue.

9 **Reading Check**
How does the grandmother react to the surprise visit?

7 Literary Analysis

Character and Characterization

1. Have two volunteers read the bracketed text as Chig and his grandmother might have held the conversation.
2. Point out to students that one way authors develop characters is to show them in action. What characters say as well as how they say it conveys a great deal about their personalities.
3. **Ask** students the Literary Analysis question: Name one trait of the grandmother that is suggested through dialogue.
   Possible responses: She is practical, nostalgic, curious, caring, and somewhat authoritative. Students should indicate the line or lines of dialogue from which they draw their inferences and explain how their own experiences support their inferences.

8 Humanities

Detail from *Young Man in Blue Suit* by Alice Kent Stoddard (1885–1976)

Born in Watertown, Connecticut, Alice Kent Stoddard painted landscapes and seascapes as well as portraits. She studied at the Pennsylvania Academy of Fine Arts with the American realist painters Thomas Eakins, Thomas Anshutz, and William Merritt Chase and later at the Philadelphia School of Design for Women. In Philadelphia, she captured famous faces of federal and Supreme Court Justices. During World War I, Stoddard served with the French YMCA, painting battlefield scenes. Use this question for discussion:

What conclusions can you draw about the man in the portrait?
Possible response: The young man is well dressed, as if he might be a professional. He looks slightly tired with half-shuttered eyes and his head propped up on his hand, but he is intent on watching or listening to something as he sits forward in his chair.

9 Reading Check

Answer: The grandmother is thrilled with the surprise visit. She obviously loves to have her family around her.

Differentiated Instruction for Universal Access

EL Pronunciation for English Learners

Some students might have difficulty pronouncing words with the initial "th" sound, as in *that* and *they,* replacing it with the "b" or "f" sounds. The following strategies can help students to pronounce the "th" sound.

- Write the words *that/bat, they/bay,* and *that/fat* on the board. Pronounce each word pair in turn, having students repeat each. Then, call out the words at random, having student volunteers circle the called word on the board. Discuss the results with the class, noting what might have led to incorrect choices.
- Pronounce the word pairs again with students. Then, call out a word and have students write out the word. Have students compare and discuss results, noting what might have led to any discrepancies in their spellings.

⑩ Humanities

Haystack by Thomas Hart Benton

Thomas Hart Benton (1889–1975) was a leader of the American artistic movement, Regionalism, which rejected modernism and focused its attention on portraying the everyday life of the American people. Benton's most well-known paintings depict scenes of rural life and focus on laboring figures. His work is characterized by vivid colors, cartoon-like figures, and undulating forms.

Use the following questions for discussion:

Why do you think Benton made a haystack the focus of his painting? What do you notice about the people working near the haystack?
Possible response: Benton chose to focus on the haystack as a symbol of rural life. The painting accentuates the labor, not the people themselves. In fact, we cannot see the people's faces and thus cannot identify or personalize them.

Think Aloud

Vocabulary: Using Context
Direct students' attention to the word *footloose* on p. 247. Using the following "think aloud," model how to use context to infer the meaning of an unknown word. Say to students:

> I'm going to think aloud to show you how I would figure out the meaning of *footloose* from its context.
>
> In this sentence, *footloose* is used to describe how Uncle GL used to be. We know from the rest of the sentence that he is getting older. This indicates that being *footloose* might have something to do with being young. We also know from the previous sentence that Uncle GL tends to disappear and do whatever he wants to do, such as go to Chicago and see a boxing match. These descriptions of Uncle GL make me think that *footloose* means "free" or "not tied down."

she'd sit down by a window all afternoon and never say nothing, just knit." She smiled. "Let me see what we got to eat."

"I'll do that, Mama." Aunt Rose spoke softly. "You haven't seen Charles in a long time. You sit and talk."

The old lady squinted at her. "You can do the cooking if you promise it ain't because you think I can't."

Aunt Rose chuckled. "I know you can do it, Mama."

"All right. I'll just sit and talk a spell." She sat again and arranged her skirt around her short legs.

Chig did most of the talking, told all about himself before she asked. His father spoke only when he was spoken to, and then, only one word at a time, as if by coming back home, he had become a small boy again, sitting in the parlor while his mother spoke with her guests.

When Uncle Hiram and Mae, his wife, came they sat down to eat. Chig did not have to ask about Uncle GL's absence; Aunt Rose volunteered an explanation: "Can't never tell where the man is at. One Thursday morning he left here and next thing we knew, he was calling from Chicago, saying he went up to see Joe Louis[2] fight. He'll be here though; he ain't as young and footloose as he used to be." Chig's father had mentioned driving down that GL was about five years older than he was, nearly fifty.

Uncle Hiram was somewhat smaller than Chig's father; his short-cropped kinky hair was half gray, half black. One spot, just off his forehead, was totally white. Later, Chig found out it had been that way since he was twenty. Mae (Chig could not bring himself to call her Aunt) was a good deal younger than Hiram, pretty enough so that Chig would have looked at her twice on the street. She was a honey-colored woman, with long eyelashes. She was wearing a white sheath.

12 At dinner, Chig and his father sat on one side, opposite Uncle Hiram and Mae; his grandmother and Aunt Rose sat at the ends. The food was good; there was a lot and Chig ate a lot. All through the meal, they talked about the family as it had been thirty years before, and particularly about the young GL. Mae and Chig asked questions; the old lady answered; Aunt Rose directed the discussion, steering the old lady onto the best stories; Chig's father laughed from time to time; Uncle Hiram ate.

"Why don't you tell them about the horse, Mama?" Aunt Rose, over Chig's weak protest, was spooning mashed potatoes onto his plate. "There now, Chig."

2. **Joe Louis** (1914–1981) U.S. boxer and the world heavyweight champion from 1937 to 1949.

11 ◀ Critical Viewing
What does this image suggest about the life the grandmother and her family lead?
[Connect]

13 Reading Check
How does Chig's father act during their visit?

11 Critical Viewing

Possible response: The painting suggests that life was hard and filled with work for the grandmother and the rest of the family who remained in the South.

12 Reading Skill

Make Inferences

1. Remind students that making inferences means putting together clues in order to make educated guesses.
2. Direct students to read the bracketed text silently. Then, **ask** them to make inferences about which member of the family is least involved in the dinner table conversation. Have them support their inferences with specific details from the passage.
   Answer: Uncle Hiram is the least involved because he simply eats. Mae and Chig ask questions, the grandmother answers the questions, Aunt Rose steers the grandmother to the best stories, and even Chig's father laughs occasionally.

13 Reading Check

Answer: Chig's father does not speak much during dinner, but he laughs from time to time.

Fluency

Students might have difficulty reading the paragraph beginning with "Uncle Hiram was somewhat smaller . . ." because it contains several compound adjectives and words with which students may not be familiar. To model fluent reading, read the passage to students with expression as students track, or follow along by pointing at each word in the text as you read. Then, have students read the passage back to you. Look for this problem spot:

Students may stumble with the phrase *short-cropped kinky hair.* Point out that *short-cropped* is a compound adjective that describes Uncle Hiram's hair. Remind students that this adjective, as well as *honey-colored,* helps the reader to visualize what the characters look like. Encourage students to sound out the phrases, repeating them until they can read the paragraph smoothly.

⑭ Literary Analysis

Character and Characterization

1. Have students silently review the text, this time looking for details of indirect characterization.
2. Then, **ask** students the Literary Analysis question: How does the writer use indirect characterization to reveal GL's character? **Answer:** Through the grandmother's story about the chair and the horse, the author indirectly characterizes GL. GL is a liar and a swindler, ready to manipulate any situation in which he feels he can take advantage of someone else.

▶ **Monitor Progress Ask** students why this passage is an example of indirect characterization. **Answer:** The story reveals GL's character through the grandmother's words and perceptions, not through the author's direct statements.

▶ **Reteach** If students have difficulty explaining why the passage is an instance of indirect characterization, review with them the differences between the methods: In direct characterization, the author tells what the characters are like. In indirect characterization, the author shows personality through thoughts, actions, words, and feelings, as well as through other characters' comments.

"I'm trying to think." The old lady was holding her fork halfway to her mouth, looking at them over her glasses. "Oh, you talking about that crazy horse GL brung home that time."

"That's right, Mama." Aunt Rose nodded and slid another slice of white meat on Chig's plate.

Mae started to giggle. "Oh, I've heard this. This is funny, Chig."

Literary Analysis Character and Characterization How does the writer use indirect characterization to reveal GL's character?

The old lady put down her fork and began: Well, GL went out of the house one day with an old, no-good chair I wanted him to take over to the church for a bazaar, and he met up with this man who'd just brung in some horses from out West. Now, I reckon you can expect one swindler[3] to be in every town, but you don't rightly think there'll be two, and God forbid they should ever meet—but they did, GL and his chair, this man and his horses. Well, I wished I'd-a been there; there must-a been some mighty high-powered talking going on. ⑭ That man with his horses, he told GL them horses was half-Arab, half-Indian, and GL told that man the chair was an antique he'd stole from some rich white folks. So they swapped. Well, I was a-looking out the window and seen GL dragging this animal to the house. It looked pretty gentle and its eyes was most closed and its feet was shuffling.

"GL, where'd you get that thing?" I says.

"I swapped him for that old chair, Mama," he says. "And made myself a bargain. This is even better than Papa's horse."

Well, I'm a-looking at this horse and noticing how he be looking more and more wide awake every minute, sort of warming up like a teakettle until, I swears to you, that horse is blowing steam out its nose.

"Come on, Mama," GL says, "come on and I'll take you for a ride." Now George, my husband, God rest his tired soul, he'd brung home this white folks' buggy which had a busted wheel and fixed it and was to take it back that day and GL says: "Come on, Mama, we'll use this fine buggy and take us a ride."

"GL," I says, "no, we ain't. Them white folks'll burn us alive if we use their buggy. You just take that horse right on back." You see, I was sure that boy'd come by that animal ungainly.

"Mama, I can't take him back," GL says.

"Why not?" I says.

"Because I don't rightly know where that man is at," GL says.

"Oh," I says. "Well, then I reckon we stuck with it." And I turned around to go back into the house because it was getting late, near dinner time, and I was cooking for ten.

"Mama," GL says to my back. "Mama, ain't you coming for a ride with me?"

3. **swindler** (swind´ lər) *n.* a cheater; a person who takes the money or property of others using deception.

Vocabulary Development

Word Form Chart

Expand students' vocabulary by helping them learn related forms of the selection vocabulary. Give students a blank **Word Form Chart** (***Professional Development Guidebook,*** pp. 41–42), with *indulgence, trace,* and *grimacing* in their appropriate columns. Work with the class, or have students work with a partner, to determine the related forms. The final chart should look like the one shown.

Noun	Verb	Adjective	Adverb
indulgence	indulge	indulgent	indulgently
trace	traced		
grimace	**grimacing**		grimacingly

15 LITERATURE IN CONTEXT

History Connection

The Great Migration

When Chig's father was a young man, he left the South and moved to a northern city. In the early twentieth century, many Aftican Americans made similiar decisions in a trend than historians call the Great Migration.

- In 1910, 89 percent of all African Americans lived in the South. The majority were sharecroppers or tenant farmers–they did not own the land they farmed.
- Between 1917 and 1930, almost 2 million African Americans moved from rural areas of the South to northern cities.
- By 1930, the percentage of African Americans living in the South had fallen to 80 percent.

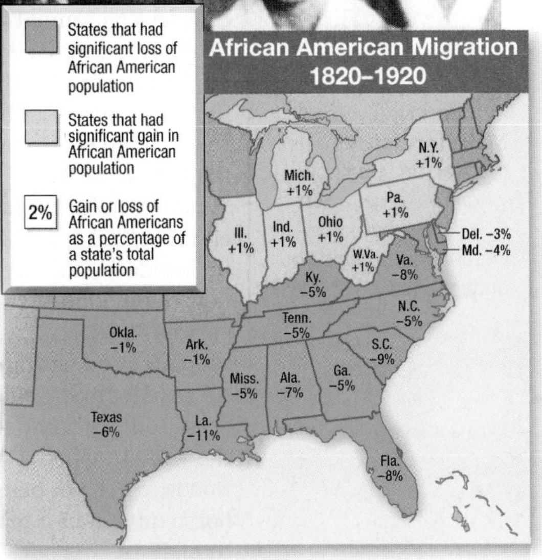

Connect to the Literature Find evidence in the story that Charles's life in the North has made him different from family members who stayed in the South.

"Go on, boy. You ain't getting me inside kicking range of that animal." I was eying that beast and it was boiling hotter all the time. I reckon maybe that man had drugged it. "That horse is wild, GL," I says.

"No, he ain't. He ain't. That man say he is buggy and saddle broke[4] and as sweet as the inside of a apple."

My oldest girl, Essie, had-a come out on the porch and she says: "Go on, Mama. I'll cook. You ain't been out the house in weeks."

"Sure, come on, Mama," GL says. "There ain't nothing to be fidgety about. This horse is gentle as a rose petal." And just then that animal snorts so hard it sets up a little dust storm around its feet.

"Yes, Mama," Essie says, "you can see he gentle." Well, I looked at Essie and then at that horse because I didn't think we could be

16 **Reading Check**
What is the subject of the grandmother's story?

4. **buggy and saddle broke** trained to carry a mounted rider or to pull a carriage.

15 Literature in Context

History Connection Though the Great Migration is often viewed as a phenomenon of the early twentieth century, African Americans continued to move north well into the 1970s. The migration waned during the Depression years and accelerated during World War II, due to the great demand for workers in the war industries.

Connect to the Literature Direct students to review the story to collect details about how life in the South differed from life in the North. Then **ask** students to respond to the Connect to Literature prompt: Find evidence in the story that Charles's life in the North has made him different from the family members who stayed in the South.
Answer: Charles Dunford has had advantages that his family in the South has lacked: He has been more or less independent since he was fifteen when he left home to go to school; he has had a college education; he has become a professional; and he has made enough money to send his children to camp and to take time off for a week-long reunion. The family that remains in the South has had none of these advantages—everyone, except perhaps GL, works hard and has little leisure time. Also, the family in the South has remained connected to one another, while Charles and his family have become outsiders.

16 Reading Check

Answer: The subject of the story is the way GL and a man swindle each other by exchanging a worthless chair for a worthless horse.

Differentiated Instruction for Universal Acces

Culturally Responsive Instruction

Culture Connection Some students may have personal experience with the effects of a geographical relocation—moving from one country to another, from one region to another, or from one city to another. Using Charles Dunford's experience as a starting point, discuss the motives people have in making a major relocation. What benefits do people seek? What risks do they take? What changes do they experience? Encourage students to draw from their own experiences as well as Dunford's as they respond.

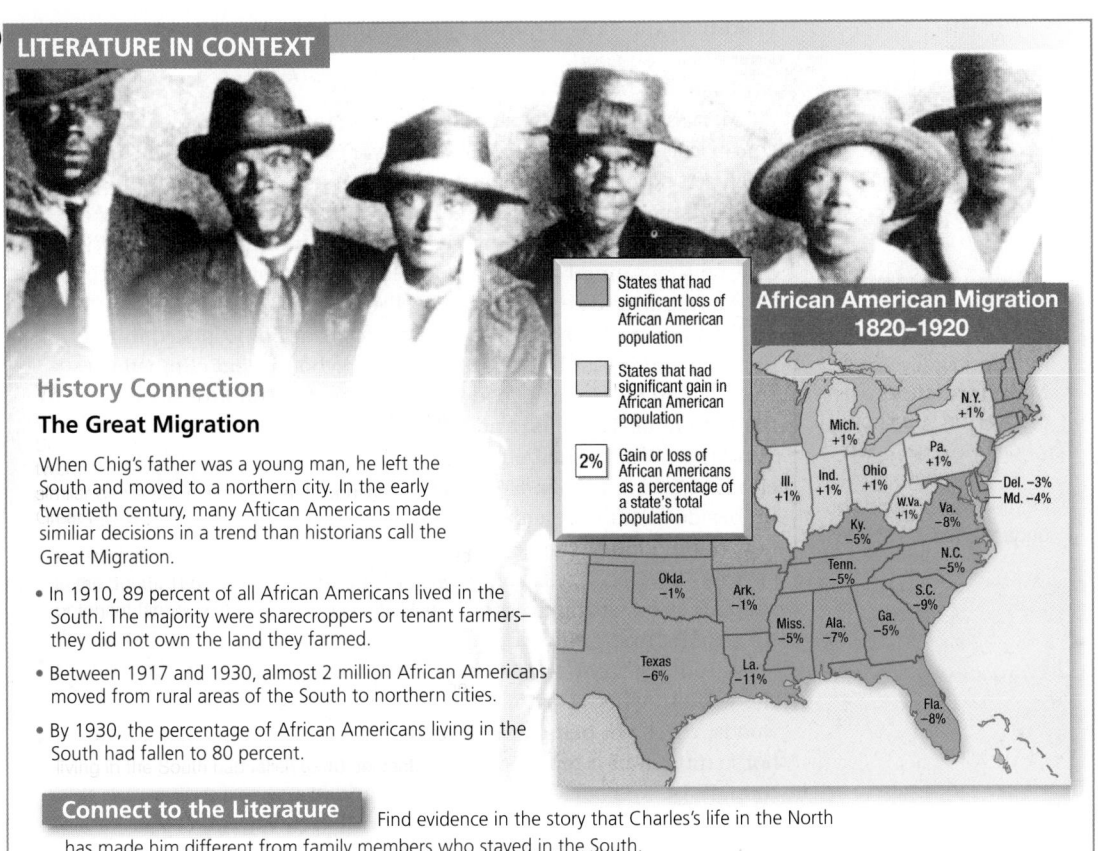

17 Reading Skill

Make Inferences

1. Remind students that prior knowledge refers to what they already know or have already experienced before reading. By connecting the experiences in their own lives with what they read, students can make inferences and predictions, both of which broaden their understanding of what they read.
2. Then, **ask** students the Reading Skill question: Think of a person you know who likes to get attention. How does knowing this person help you understand GL's actions?
   Possible response: I know a boy who is always playing tricks on other students. One day, another student played a trick on the boy. Although everyone found the trick funny and thought that the boy got what he deserved, he would never acknowledge that he had been duped. GL also values his skills as a conman. He never entertains the thought that anyone might con him. This sense of superiority keeps GL from recognizing the truth about the horse.

looking at the same animal. I should-a figured how Essie's eyes ain't never been so good.

"Come on, Mama," GL says.

"All right," I says. So I stood on the porch and watched GL hitching that horse up to the white folks' buggy. For a while there, the animal was pretty quiet, pawing a little, but not much. And I was feeling a little better about riding with GL behind that crazy-looking horse. I could see how GL was happy I was going with him. He was scurrying around that animal buckling buckles and strapping straps, all the time smiling, and that made me feel good.

Reading Skill
Make Inferences Think of a person you know who likes to get attention. How does knowing this person help you understand GL's actions? 17

Then he was finished, and I must say, that horse looked mighty fine hitched to that buggy and I knew anybody what climbed up there would look pretty good too. GL came around and stood at the bottom of the steps, and took off his hat and bowed and said: "Madam," and reached out his hand to me and I was feeling real elegant like a fine lady. He helped me up to the seat and then got up beside me and we moved out down our alley. And I remember how colored folks come out on their porches and shook their heads, saying: "Lord now, will you look at Eva Dunford, the fine lady! Don't she look good sitting up there!" And I pretended not to hear and sat up straight and proud.

We rode on through the center of town, up Market Street, and all the way out where Hiram is living now, which in them days was all woods, there not being even a farm in sight and that's when that horse must-a first realized he weren't at all broke or tame or maybe thought he was back out West again, and started to gallop.

Vocabulary
meager (mē´ gər) *adj.* of poor quality or small amount

trace (trās) *n.* tiny amount; hint

"GL," I says, "now you ain't joking with your mama, is you? Because if you is, I'll strap you purple if I live through this."

Well, GL was pulling on the reins with all his meager strength, and yelling, "Whoa, you. Say now, whoa!" He turned to me just long enough to say, "I ain't fooling with you, Mama. Honest!"

I reckon that animal weren't too satisfied with the road, because it made a sharp right turn just then, down into a gulley and struck out across a hilly meadow. "Mama," GL yells. "Mama, do something!"

I didn't know what to do, but I figured I had to do something so I stood up, hopped down onto the horse's back and pulled it to a stop. Don't ask me how I did that; I reckon it was that I was a mother and my baby asked me to do something, is all.

"Well, we walked that animal all the way home; sometimes I had to club it over the nose with my fist to make it come, but we made it, GL and me. You remember how tired we was, Charles?"

"I wasn't here at the time." Chig turned to his father and found his face completely blank, without even a trace of a smile or a laugh.

Vocabulary Development

Vocabulary Knowledge Rating

When students have completed reading and discussing "A Visit to Grandmother," have them take out their **Vocabulary Knowledge Rating Chart** for this selection. Read the words aloud once more and have students rate their knowledge of the words again in the After Reading column. Clarify any words that are still problematic. Have students write their own definition and example or sentence in the appropriate column. Then have students complete the Vocabulary Practice at the end of the selection. Encourage students to use the words in further discussion and written work about this selection. Remind them that they will be accountable for these words on the **Selection Test, *Unit 2 Resources,*** pp. 35–37 or 38–40.

"Well, of course you was, son. That happened in . . . in . . . it was a hot summer that year and—"

"I left here in June of that year. You wrote me about it."

The old lady stared past Chig at him. They all turned to him; Uncle Hiram looked up from his plate.

"Then you don't remember how we all laughed?"

"No, I don't, Mama. And I probably wouldn't have laughed. I don't think it was funny." They were staring into each other's eyes.

"Why not, Charles?"

"Because in the first place, the horse was gained by fraud. And in the second place, both of you might have been seriously injured or even killed." He broke off their stare and spoke to himself more than to any of them: "And if I'd done it, you would've beaten me good for it."

"Pardon?" The old lady had not heard him; only Chig had heard.

Chig's father sat up straight as if preparing to debate. "I said that if I had done it, if I had done just exactly what GL did, you would have beaten me good for it, Mama." He was looking at her again.

"Why you say that, son?" She was leaning toward him.

"Don't you know? Tell the truth. It can't hurt me now." His voice cracked, but only once. "If GL and I did something wrong, you'd beat me first and then be too tired to beat him. At dinner, he'd always get seconds and I wouldn't. You'd do things with him, like ride in that buggy, but if I wanted you to do something with me, you were always too busy." He paused and considered whether to say what he finally did say: "I cried when I left here. Nobody loved me, Mama. I cried all the way up to Knoxville. That was the last time I ever cried in my life."

"Oh, Charles." She started to get up, to come around the table to him.

He stopped her. "It's too late."

"But you don't understand."

"What don't I understand? I understood then; I understand now."

Tears now traveled down the lines in her face, but when she spoke, her voice was clear. "I thought you knew. I had ten children. I had to give all of them what they needed most." She nodded. "I paid more mind to GL. I had to. GL could-a ended up swinging if I hadn't.

18 But you was smarter. You was more growed up than GL when you was five and he was ten, and I tried to show you that by letting you do what you wanted to do."

"That's not true, Mama. You know it. GL was light-skinned and had good hair and looked almost white and you loved him for that." 19

"Charles, no. No, son. I didn't love any one of you more than any other."

"That can't be true." His father was standing now, his fists

Vocabulary
fraud (frôd) *n.* deceit; trickery

Literary Analysis
Character and Characterization
What new information helps to develop Charles's character?

Reading Check
What happens when GL takes his mother for a buggy ride?

18 Literary Analysis

Character and Characterization

1. Ask a volunteer to read the passage aloud. Direct the class to consider, as they listen, what Charles and his mother are thinking and feeling during the exchange. Briefly discuss with students what these thoughts and feelings might be.
   Possible responses: Charles's mother may be thinking that she tried her best for her son and believed that she was giving him what she thought he most needed—the freedom to do what he wanted. Honesty is very important to her, and she is devastated that Charles does not believe her. Charles thinks his mother has shown favoritism to his older brother because GL looks whiter than he (Charles) does. He has been hurt for so long that he can barely believe the truth and accept his own responsibility for the estrangement from his family.
2. Then, **ask** students the Literary Analysis question: What new information helps to develop Charles's character?
   Answer: By the end of the story, Charles is not the strong and uncaring figure he has appeared to be. In spite of how he might have seemed mature to his mother at age five, he was only a sad little boy who did not believe that he was loved. He asks for the truth, but he does not want to believe it. If his mother really loves him, then he has wasted thirty years being angry. When he says that his mother is thirty years too late, he is rejecting her response and choosing to hold on to his anger.

19 Reading Check

Answer: At first, the horse is calm, as if it has been drugged to sedate its wild nature. Then, it becomes livelier and begins to gallop, taking GL and his mother off the road and into the meadow.

Concept Connector

Anticipation Guide

Have students return to their **Anticipation Guides** and respond to the statements again in the After Reading column. They may do this individually or in their original groups. Then, lead a class discussion, probing for what students have learned that confirms or invalidates each statement. Encourage students to cite specific details, quotations, or other evidence from the text to support their responses to each statement.

Writing About the Big Question

Have students compare their responses to the sentence starters they completed before reading the essay with their ideas afterwards. Ask them to explain whether their thoughts have changed.

Reading Skill Graphic Organizer

Ask students to review the graphic organizers they completed to make inferences about characters while reading. Show them the partially completed **Reading Skill Graphic Organizer A** (*Graphic Organizer Transparencies,* p. 39) as an example. Then have students share the graphic organizers they did.

ASSESS

Answers

Critical Thinking

1. Some students may sympathize with the grandmother because she is such a likable character.
2. (a) He says he left home because there was no high school for African Americans. (b) **Possible response:** He may have been unhappy at home. The jealousy he feels for GL, which he reveals at the end, supports this explanation.
3. (a) Charles becomes angry. (b) The grandmother thinks the story is funny. She recalls the event as an adventure, while Charles condemns GL's behavior as irresponsible. (c) Charles is jealous that his mother remembers the incident fondly and that she has overlooked the dangerous aspects of it. His reaction is caused by his frustration and sadness over feeling unloved.
4. Some students may say that Charles and his mother will reconcile their differences now that Charles's feelings are in the open. Others may feel that it is too late.
5. (a) Mama tried to give her children what she thought they needed most. (b) Some students may say that Mama's intentions were good, but she needed to communicate better with her sons.

Can progress be made without conflict?

Possible response: No, Chig's father has not made any progress in repairing his relationship with his family. When Chig's father asserts that his mother treated GL and him differently, his mother denies any favoritism. Chig's father feels so strongly about this supposed favoritism that he has convinced himself of its truth; therefore, anything his mother says he does not accept. Their relationship, as it is at the end of the story, is still strained.

clenched tight. "Admit it, Mama . . . please!" Chig looked at him, shocked; the man was actually crying.

"It may not-a been right what I done, but I ain't no liar." Chig knew she did not really understand what had happened, what he wanted of her. "I'm not lying to you, Charles."

18

Chig's father had gone pale. He spoke very softly. "You're about thirty years too late, Mama." He bolted from the table. Silverware and dishes rang and jumped. Chig heard him hurrying up to their room.

They sat in silence for a while and then heard a key in the front door. A man with a new, lacquered[5] straw hat came in. He was wearing brown and white two-tone shoes with very pointed toes and a white summer suit. "Say now! Man! I heard my brother was in town. Where he at? Where that rascal?"

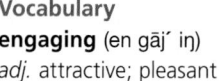

Vocabulary
engaging (en gāj´ iŋ) *adj.* attractive; pleasant

He stood in the doorway, smiling broadly, an **engaging**, open, friendly smile, the innocent smile of a five-year-old.

5. **lacquered** (lak´ ərd) *adj.* coated with a hardened protective layer of resinous material, which gives a shine.

Critical Thinking

1. **Respond:** With which character in the story do you sympathize most strongly? Share your responses in a small group. Record members' thoughts about each character. Then, review the notes and explain how others' responses affected your viewpoint.
2. **(a)** What reason does Charles give for leaving home when he was fifteen? **(b) Hypothesize:** What other reasons might he have had? Support your answer with story details.
3. **(a)** How does Charles react to Mama's story about GL and the horse? **(b) Compare and Contrast:** In what way does his reaction contrast with the way Mama feels about the story? **(c) Connect:** Explain why the story has this effect on Charles.
4. **Speculate:** What might Charles's relationship with his mother be like in the future? Explain.
5. **(a) Summarize:** Describe Mama's approach to raising her children. **(b) Evaluate:** Is her approach sound? Explain.

Can progress be made without conflict?
By finally confronting his mother about his feelings, has Chig's father made progress in repairing his relationship with his family? Explain.

Assessment Resources

Unit 2 Resources

L1 L2 EL **Selection Test A,** pp. 35–37. Administer Test A to less advanced students and English Learners.

L3 L4 **Selection Test B,** pp. 38–40. Administer Test B to on-level and more advanced students.

L3 L4 **Open-Book Test,** pp. 32–34. As an alternative, give the Open-Book Test.

All **Customizable Test Bank**

All **Self-tests**
Students may prepare for the **Selection Test** by taking the **Self-test** online.

PHLit Online! All assessment resources are available at **www.PHLitOnline.com**

After You Read | A Visit to Grandmother

Literary Analysis: Character and Characterization

A Visit to Grandmother
William Melvin Kelley

1. Compare and contrast the **characters** of Charles and GL. Use details from the story to support your answer.
2. Identify three examples of **indirect characterization** used to portray Charles. Use a chart like the one shown.

What He Says	What He Does	What Others Say About Him

3. **(a)** What does Charles say is his reason for visiting Mama? **(b)** In what way is his character **developed** at the end?
4. **(a)** Give two examples of **dialogue** from Mama and two from Charles. **(b)** What do your examples show about how they differ?

Reading Skill: Make Inferences

5. **Make an inference** about Charles's feelings toward GL. On which story details is your inference based?
6. Make an inference about Chig's feelings toward his family. Support your inference with story details and your own experiences.

Vocabulary

Practice Answer each question, and explain how the meaning of the underlined vocabulary word influences your answer.

1. Would unlimited playtime be an <u>indulgence</u> for a child?
2. On what occasions might you see someone <u>grimacing</u>?
3. If there is a <u>trace</u> of mud on the rug, is a big cleanup necessary?
4. Would a child with a <u>meager</u> allowance have a large savings?
5. Would a bank allow a man known as a <u>fraud</u> to open an account?
6. Why would a politician want to have an <u>engaging</u> personality?

Word Study Use the context of the sentences and what you know about the **Latin suffix *-ence*** to explain your answer to each question.

1. Would a person's *negligence* help or hurt others?
2. Would you trust someone who demonstrates *competence*?

Word Study

The **Latin suffix *-ence*** means "quality of" or "state of."

Challenge Explain how the suffix *-ence* contributes to the meanings of these words. Consult a dictionary if necessary.

fraudulence
dependence
diligence

ASSESS/EXTEND

Answers

Literary Analysis

1. **Possible response:** Charles is a doctor and a kind-hearted man. GL is immature and unreliable, as shown in his last-minute trip to Chicago and the story of the swindle he uses to obtain a horse.
2. **Possible response:**
   What He Says: "I cried when I left here. Nobody loved me, Mama."
   What He Does: Charles grimaces when he kisses his mother's cheek.
   What Others Say About Him: His mother says, "You was more growed up than GL when you was five and he was ten. . . ."

   For other sample answers, see ***Graphic Organizer Transparencies,*** **Literary Analysis Graphic Organizer A**, p. 42, and the **Additional Answers** section.
3. (a) Charles says he and Chig might as well make the visit since they are close by. (b) **Possible response:** When Charles confronts his mother, the reader has the chance to understand the reasons for his anger and resentment.
4. (a) and (b) Students should cite examples of Mama's dialogue that reflect her dialect, good humor, and spirit. They should contrast her lively speech with Charles's choppier, less revealing dialogue, which shows him to hold his feelings inside and conceal them from others. Mama's dialogue, by contrast, shows her to be open and straightforward.

Reading Skill

5. **Possible response:** Charles is jealous of the attention GL gets from Mama. Mama treated both boys differently, leading Charles to think GL was the favorite. Supporting details include his anger over the story of the horse and his accusation that his mother loved GL more.
6. Students may infer that Chig respects his father because he is well behaved, but that he is capable of independent observation: He suspects his father's true motive for the trip.

Vocabulary

Practice

Sample answers:

1. Yes, unlimited playtime would spoil a child.
2. I might see someone <u>grimacing</u>, or wincing in pain, when he or she is injured.
3. No, because a <u>trace</u> is only a small amount.
4. No, a child with a <u>meager</u> allowance would not have much money.
5. No, a <u>fraud</u> would be a dishonest man.
6. A politician would want to have an <u>engaging</u>, or amiable, personality to woo the voters.

Word Study

Sample answers:

1. A person who has <u>the quality of</u> neglectfulness and does not think of the welfare of others hurts them.
2. Yes, I would trust a person who has <u>the quality of</u> being competent, or is experienced and skillful.

Word Study: Challenge

Sample answers:

Fraudulence means "<u>the state of</u> being deceitful."
Dependence means "<u>the state of</u> relying on others."
Diligence means "<u>the quality of</u> working hard."

PRETEACH

Skills instruction for the ***Reading Skill*** *and* ***Literary Analysis*** *concept appears on p. 239.*

❶ Writing About the Big Question

1. Review the assignment with the class.
2. Lead students in discussing why people may have difficulty changing old bad habits. Then, help them brainstorm for ways others can help. Have them identify any suggestions that involve conflict.
3. Have students complete the sentence starter. Review responses as a class. (**Possible response:** In order to help a loved one make an important change in his or life, one should offer support and understanding.)
4. Remind students that their answers will help them think about the Big Question, "Can progress be made without conflict?"

While You Read

Tell students to look for clues as they read that show that Ivan's efforts to help Sasha are successful.

❷ Vocabulary

1. Have students preview the selection vocabulary.
2. For each word, have students say the word aloud.
3. Then, use the word in a sentence that defines the word.
4. Finally, repeat your definitional sentence or a similar sentence with the word missing, and have the class "fill in the blank" chorally. Here are some examples:

   Something edifying instructs in a moral or intellectual way. A book that teaches you how to be a good person is meant to be [students say "edifying"].

❸ Word Study

1. Introduce the skill, using the instruction in the box.
2. Instruct students to explain what *arguable* means, given the meaning of the suffix. (**Answer:** worthy of being argued, as a point that can be supported or debated)

Making Connections — A Problem

Can progress be made without *conflict?*

❶ Writing About the Big Question

In "A Problem," an uncle argues with other family members to give his wayward nephew a second chance. Use this sentence starter to develop your ideas about the Big Question.

In order to help a loved one make an important **change** in his or her life, one should ______________________.

While You Read Look for clues that suggest Ivan Markovitch is successful in his efforts to help his nephew.

❷ Vocabulary

Read each word and its definition. Decide whether you know the word well, know it a little bit, or do not know it at all. After you read, see how your knowledge of each word has increased.

- **pretense** (prē tens′) *n.* a pretending; a false show of something (p. 257) ***She maintained a pretense of being friendly, but was really quite mean.*** *pretend v. pretentious adj.*
- **candid** (kan′ did) *adj.* honest; direct (p. 257) ***Stop telling tales, and give me a candid answer.*** *candidly adv. candor n.*
- **lofty** (lôf′ tē) *adj.* elevated in character; noble (p. 258) ***The dignitary's lofty ideals, such as equality and peace, are admirable.*** *loftily adv. loftiness n. aloft adj.*
- **detestable** (dē tes′ tə bəl) *adj.* deserving hate or scorn; offensive (p. 259) ***The factory's thick, foul-smelling smoke was detestable to her.*** *detest v. detestation n.*
- **subdued** (səb do͞od′) *adj.* quiet; lacking energy (p. 262) ***The boy was subdued after he was scolded.*** *subdue v.*
- **edifying** (ed′ i fī′ iŋ) *adj.* instructive in such a way as to improve morally or intellectually (p. 263) ***The counselor's advice was generally quite helpful and edifying.*** *edify v. edification n.*

❸ Word Study

The **Latin suffix *-able*** means "worthy of; capable of being."

In this story, a character thinks his uncles are **detestable,** or worthy of being disliked, because they will not give in to his wishes.

Vocabulary Development

Vocabulary Knowledge Rating

Create a **Vocabulary Knowledge Rating Chart** (***Professional Development Guidebook,*** p. 33) for this selection. Include the selection vocabulary and the Big Question words that appear in the Writing About the Big Question sentence starter on this page. (The Big Question vocabulary is introduced on pp. 222–223.)

Give students a copy of the chart. Read the words aloud, and have students mark their rating in the Before Reading column. Urge them to be alert to these words as they read and discuss the selection.

Tally how many students think they know a word to gauge how much instruction to provide. As students read and discuss the selection, point out the words and their context.

PHLit Online! **Vocabulary Central,** featuring tools, activities, and songs for studying vocabulary, is available at **www.PHLitOnline.com**

Meet
Anton Chekhov
(1860–1904)

Author of
A Problem

Anton Chekhov grew up in the small coastal town of Taganrog in southern Russia. When the family moved to Moscow, he helped support them by writing comic sketches and light short stories. Although he attended medical school and became a doctor, Chekhov devoted himself to writing short stories and dramas.

A Diagnosis Chekhov said that "a writer is not a confectioner, a cosmetic dealer, or an entertainer. He is a man who has signed a contract with his conscience and his sense of duty." Some of Chekhov's works offer a diagnosis of nineteenth-century Russian society, showing how it trapped individuals into hopeless, unproductive lives. Other works humorously reveal universal human weaknesses. Today, he is regarded as one of the greatest modern writers and one of the most important dramatists of all time.

❹ BACKGROUND FOR THE STORY

Money Lending

An IOU, or promissory note, is a promise to pay money or goods. In Russia at the time of this story, a person could "discount" an IOU, selling it to a moneylender for less than full value. Later, the person could "redeem" the note, buying it back by a certain date. In this story, a character commits a crime by forging an IOU and selling it to a moneylender.

DID YOU KNOW?

Chekhov's study of prisoner's lives, *The Island of Sakhalin,* helped reform the Russian prison system.

PRETEACH

Daily Bellringer

For each class during which you will teach this selection, have students complete one of the five Quick Write activities for Week 7 in the ***Daily Bellringer Activities*** booklet.

❹ Background
Money Lending

Debt figured prominently in Chekhov's life, so it is not surprising that the subject appears in his stories. In 1875, his father's business failed, and the threat of imprisonment loomed. The family lost their home to a wealthy local man who posed as a friend. Chekhov started writing not to express ideas but to support his family. He continued, throughout his career, to pay the debts of his older brothers.

Multidraft Reading

This icon ● marks natural pauses in the selection. To assist struggling readers and to deepen reading for all, assign the text in "chunks," following the icons, and apply multidraft reading protocols. For each reading, have students set the purpose indicated:

- **First reading**—literal comprehension: answering the Reading Check questions.
- **Second reading**—application of skills: answering the Make Inferences and Character and Characterization prompts.
- **Third reading**—interpretation: answering the end-of-selection questions.

For more guidance, refer to the ***Classroom Strategies and Teaching Routines*** card on multidraft reading.

Differentiated Instruction   Additional Instruction

EL Extended Support— English Learners
Have students complete the **Reading and Vocabulary Warm-ups, *Unit 2 Resources,*** pp. 41–44, before they read. Assign the prereading pages for the selection in the ***Reader's Notebook: English Learner's Version.*** Then, have students listen to portions of the selection on the ***Hear It!* Audio CD.**

L1 L2 Extended Support— Struggling Readers
Have students complete the **Reading and Vocabulary Warm-ups, *Unit 2 Resources,*** pp. 41–44, before they read. Assign the prereading pages for the selection in the ***Reader's Notebook: Adapted Version.*** Then, have students listen to portions of the selection on the ***Hear It!* Audio CD** (adapted text).

Extended Support— Reluctant Readers
To build motivation and engagement before assigning the selection, have students read "Holding Parents Responsible," a thematically related selection in ***Reality Central.*** Then, use the questions at the conclusion of the related selection to guide discussion.

PHLit Online!
For more about the author, practice with the selection vocabulary, or more background, go online at **www.PHLitOnline.com**

❶ Activating Prior Knowledge

1. Prepare an **Anticipation Guide** (see ***Professional Development Guidebook***, pp. 36–37) with the following statements:
   - It is the responsibility of adults to take care of young people.
   - One should not have to bear responsibility for all one's actions.
   - All actions have consequences.
   - "Spare the rod, spoil the child."
2. Give students a copy of the prepared **Anticipation Guide** and have them respond in the Me column. Have them discuss the statements in groups and mark the Guide again in the Group column.
3. For further guidance, use the ***Classroom Strategies and Teaching Routines*** card: **Using an Anticipation Guide.**

Concept Connector →

Students will return to the **Anticipation Guide** after completing the story.

Individual Activity

Ask students to review the second paragraph of the story on the next page. They should note that this is one compound-complex sentence—it contains dependent clauses within the structure of a compound sentence. Have students analyze the sentence and produce another that has the same structure.

❷ About the Selection

In "A Problem," three uncles grapple with the question of what to do about their errant nephew, Sasha. Instead of welcoming their leniency as an opportunity to mend his ways, Sasha seizes it as an opportunity to continue his irresponsible habits, with just one difference—he gains self-knowledge. He now sees how he can manipulate his relatives and avoid facing the consequences he deserves. The story raises important questions about forgiveness and responsibility.

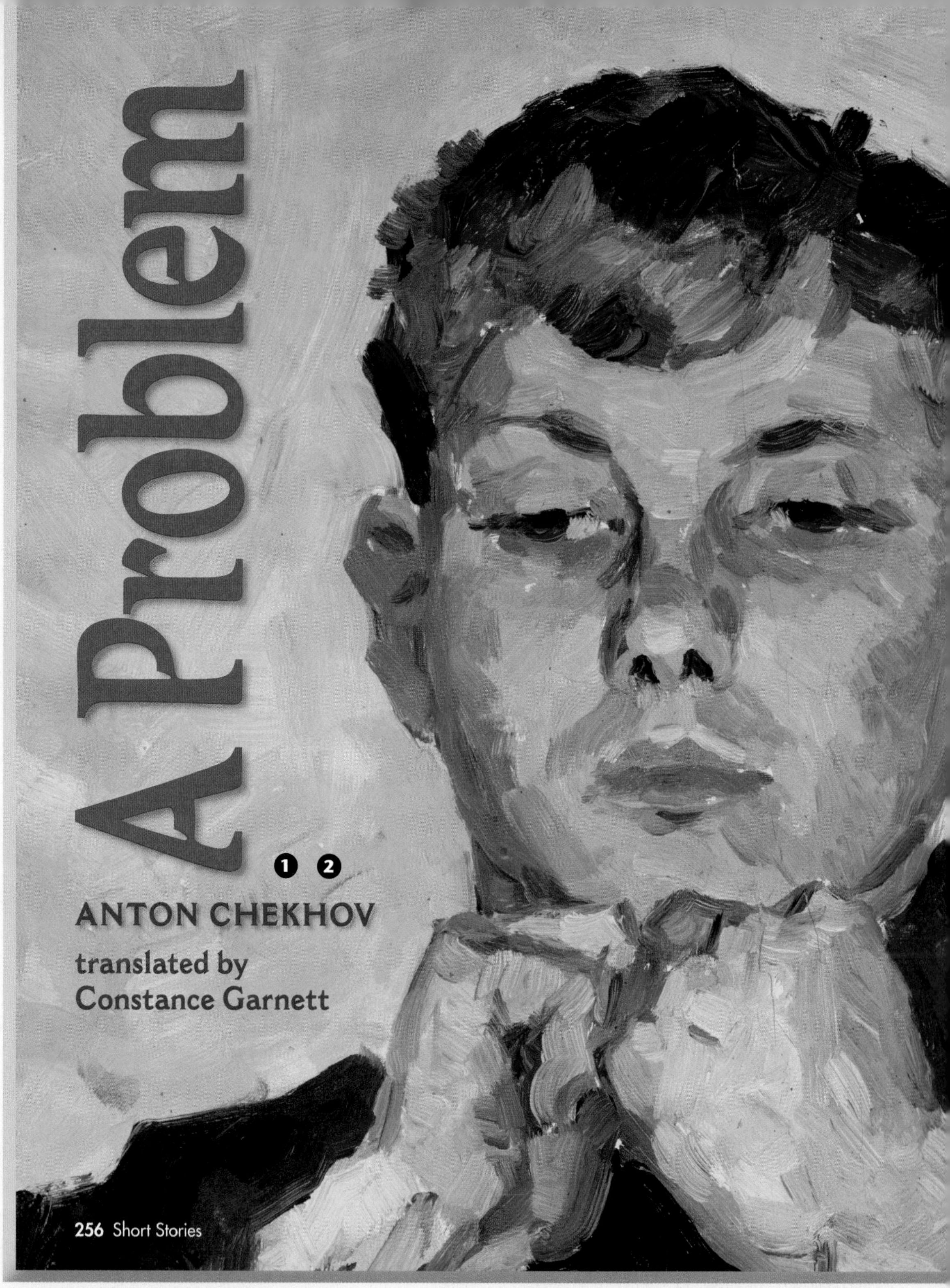

A Problem ❶ ❷

ANTON CHEKHOV

translated by Constance Garnett

Vocabulary Development

Thematic Vocabulary: The Big Question

As students are discussing "A Problem," encourage them to use the thematic vocabulary presented in Introducing the Big Question, pp. 222–223. You might encourage them with sentence starters like these:

1. The *adversity* Sasha has already experienced in his young life has . . .
2. In the family council, Ivan Markovitch and the Uskov uncles *debate* . . .
3. Sasha's *motive* for forging the IOU is . . .
4. The *compromise* Ivan Markovitch reaches with the Uskov uncles is . . .

The strictest measures were taken that the Uskovs' family secret might not leak out and become generally known. Half of the servants were sent off to the theater or the circus; the other half were sitting in the kitchen and not allowed to leave it. Orders were given that no one was to be admitted. The wife of the Colonel, her sister, and the governess, though they had been initiated into the secret, kept up a pretense of knowing nothing; they sat in the dining room and did not show themselves in the drawing room or the hall.

4 Sasha Uskov, the young man of twenty-five who was the cause of all the commotion, had arrived some time before, and by the advice of kind-hearted Ivan Markovitch, his uncle, who was taking his part, he sat meekly in the hall by the door leading to the study, and prepared himself to make an open, candid explanation.

The other side of the door, in the study, a family council was being held. The subject under discussion was an exceedingly disagreeable and delicate one. Sasha Uskov had cashed at one of the banks a false promissory note,[1] and it had become due for payment three days before, and now his two paternal uncles and Ivan Markovitch, the brother of his dead mother, were deciding the question whether they should pay the money and save the family honor, or wash their hands of it and leave the case to go to trial.

To outsiders who have no personal interest in the matter such questions seem simple; for those who are so unfortunate as to have to decide them in earnest they are extremely difficult. The uncles had been talking for a long time, but the problem seemed no nearer decision.

"My friends!" said the uncle who was a colonel, and there was a note of exhaustion and bitterness in his voice. "Who says that family honor is a mere convention? I don't say that at all. I am only warning you against a false view; I am pointing out the possibility of an unpardonable mistake. How can you fail to see it? I am not speaking Chinese; I am speaking Russian!"

6 "My dear fellow, we do understand," Ivan Markovitch protested mildly.

"How can you understand if you say that I don't believe in family honor? I repeat once more; fa-mil-y ho-nor false-ly un-der-stood is a prejudice! Falsely understood! That's what I say: whatever may be the motives for screening a scoundrel, whoever he may be, and helping him to escape punishment, it is contrary to law and unworthy of a gentleman. It's not saving the family honor; it's civic cowardice! Take the army, for instance. . . . The honor of the army is more precious to us than any other honor, yet we don't screen

1. **promissory note** written promise to pay a specified sum on demand; an IOU.

3 ◀ **Critical Viewing**
Based on this painting, what do you expect the mood of the story will be? **[Predict]**

Vocabulary
pretense (prē tens´) *n.* a pretending; a false show of something

candid (kan´ did) *adj.* honest; direct

5 **Reading Check**
Why is Sasha in trouble?

3 Critical Viewing

Possible response: The painting shows a smug-looking and pensive young man. Based on the painting, I expect the mood of the story to be serious.

4 Reading Skill
Make Inferences

1. Draw students' attention to the description of Sasha sitting meekly in the hall. **Ask** students to define the word *meekly*.
   Answer: The word *meekly* means "submissively."
2. Then, **ask** students what they can infer about Sasha based on his behavior at this point in the story.
   Possible response: Sasha appears to be obedient because he fulfills his uncle's request. He also seems sorry about his wrongdoings because he sits meekly and prepares to speak honestly about his actions.
3. As they continue to read, have students to determine whether their first impression of Sasha is accurate.

5 Reading Check

Answer: Sasha borrowed money on false pretenses. He could not redeem the promissory note when it came due because he did not have the money.

Differentiated Instruction for Universal Access

Strategy for Less Proficient Readers
This story contains long and complex sentences that may pose difficulty for students. Using examples from the story, model how to break such sentences into smaller parts. Remind students to use punctuation marks, as well as signal words such as *if, that,* and *so,* as clues to the logic of the sentence.

Enrichment for Advanced Readers
As students read the works of well-known and respected authors, encourage them to expand their own vocabulary by appreciating the author's choice of words and phrases. Have students make a list of interesting language in "A Problem," such as *purely anatomical peculiarities, dissipated,* and *paltry,* and analyze how the language affects the story's tone.

PHLit Online!
This selection is available in interactive format in the **Enriched Online Student Edition, www.PHLitOnline.com,** which includes a thematically related video with writing prompt and an interactive graphic organizer.

❻ Literary Analysis
Characters and Characterization

1. Have students read the bracketed text on pages 257 and 258, paying close attention to the differing views of the Colonel and Ivan Markovitch.
2. Invite volunteers to summarize the position of each man.
Answer: The Colonel does not believe in covering up another person's wrongdoing. Regardless of the circumstances, he thinks it is wrong. Ivan Markovitch, on the other hand, says that everyone makes mistakes and that Sasha has already been punished by his own conscience and by having to wait for the uncles' decision.
3. Then, **ask** students the Literary Analysis question: Contrast the Colonel's position with Ivan Markovitch's. What does this contrast indirectly reveal about the two?
Possible response: The Colonel is a stickler for detail and discipline. Regardless of family honor or any other mitigating circumstances, he believes it is their civic duty to punish a wrongdoing. Ivan Markovitch, however, is a soft-hearted man, willing to forgive and forget. He is compassionate and optimistic, believing in the inherent goodness of people.

Literary Analysis
Character and Characterization
Contrast the Colonel's position with Ivan Markovitch's. What does this contrast indirectly reveal about the two?

Vocabulary
lofty (lôf′ tē) *adj.* elevated in character; noble

our guilty members, but condemn them. And does the honor of the army suffer in consequence? Quite the opposite!"

The other paternal uncle, an official in the Treasury, a taciturn, dull-witted, and rheumatic man, sat silent, or spoke only of the fact that the Uskovs' name would get into the newspapers if the case went for trial. His opinion was that the case ought to be hushed up from the first and not become public property; but, apart from publicity in the newspapers, he advanced no other argument in support of this opinion.

The maternal uncle, kind-hearted Ivan Markovitch, spoke smoothly, softly, and with a tremor in his voice. He began with saying that youth has its rights and its peculiar temptations. Which of us has not been young, and who has not been led astray? 6
To say nothing of ordinary mortals, even great men have not escaped errors and mistakes in their youth. Take, for instance, the biography of great writers. Did not every one of them gamble, drink, and draw down upon himself the anger of right-thinking people in his young days? If Sasha's error bordered upon crime, they must remember that Sasha had received practically no education; he had been expelled from the high school in the fifth class; he had lost his parents in early childhood, and so had been left at the tenderest age without guidance and good, benevolent influences. He was nervous, excitable, had no firm ground under his feet, and, above all, he had been unlucky. Even if he were guilty, anyway he deserved indulgence[2] and the sympathy of all compassionate souls. He ought, of course, to be punished, but he was punished as it was by his conscience and the agonies he was enduring now while awaiting the sentence of his relations. The comparison with the army made by the Colonel was delightful, and did credit to his lofty intelligence; his appeal to their feeling of public duty spoke for the chivalry of his soul, but they must not forget that in each individual the citizen is closely linked with the Christian. . . .

"Shall we be false to civic duty," Ivan Markovitch exclaimed passionately, "if instead of punishing an erring boy we hold out to him a helping hand?"

Ivan Markovitch talked further of family honor. He had not the honor to belong to the Uskov family himself, but he knew their distinguished family went back to the thirteenth century; he did

2. **indulgence** (in dul′ jəns) *n.* forgiveness; tolerance.

Vocabulary Development

Word Analysis

Point out to students that knowing the prefix *in-* and its variants *il-, im-,* and *ir-* can help them determine the meanings of unfamiliar words. Although the prefix *in-* may mean "in" in some circumstances (*internal, invert*), it generally means "not." Have students pick out words on page 259 that include the prefix (*immoral, insufferably, inextricably, indifferent*) and use their knowledge of the prefix to determine the meaning of each word.

Provide students with the following tips:
- Substitute the meaning of the prefix for the prefix itself.
- Then think of possible definitions for the entire word. Make sure the definition makes sense in the context because *in-* can also mean "in."
- Check your definition in the dictionary.

not forget for a minute, either, that his precious, beloved sister had been the wife of one of the representatives of that name. In short, the family was dear to him for many reasons, and he refused to admit the idea that, for the sake of a paltry fifteen hundred rubles,[3] a blot should be cast on the escutcheon[4] that was beyond all price. If all the motives he had brought forward were not sufficiently convincing, he, Ivan Markovitch, in conclusion, begged his listeners to ask themselves what was meant by crime? Crime is an immoral act founded upon ill-will. But is the will of man free? Philosophy has not yet given a positive answer to that question. Different views were held by the learned. The latest school of Lombroso,[5] for instance, denies the freedom of the will, and considers every crime as the product of the purely anatomical peculiarities of the individual.

"Ivan Markovitch," said the Colonel, in a voice of entreaty, "we are talking seriously about an important matter, and you bring in Lombroso, you clever fellow. Think a little, what are you saying all this for? Can you imagine that all your thunderings and rhetoric will furnish an answer to the question?"

Sasha Uskov sat at the door and listened. He felt neither terror, shame, nor depression, but only weariness and inward emptiness. It seemed to him that it made absolutely no difference to him whether they forgave him or not; he had come here to hear his sentence and to explain himself simply because kind-hearted Ivan Markovitch had begged him to do so. He was not afraid of the future. It made no difference to him where he was: here in the hall, in prison, or in Siberia.

"If Siberia, then let it be Siberia, damn it all!"

He was sick of life and found it insufferably hard. He was inextricably involved in debt; he had not a farthing[6] in his pocket; his family had become **detestable** to him; he would have to part from his friends and his women sooner or later, as they had begun to be too contemptuous of his sponging on them. The future looked black.

Sasha was indifferent, and was only disturbed by one circumstance; the other side of the door they were calling him a scoundrel and a criminal. Every minute he was on the point of jumping up, bursting into the study and shouting in answer to the detestable metallic voice of the Colonel:

"You are lying!"

---

3. **rubles** (ro͞o´ belz) *n.* A ruble is the basic unit of Russian currency.
4. **escutcheon** (e skuch´ ən) *n.* shield displaying a family's coat of arms, symbol of its nobility.
5. **Lombroso** Cesare Lombroso (1835–1909), an Italian criminologist who believed that criminals were of a distinct human type and were led to crime by hereditary, inborn characteristics.
6. **farthing** (fär´ thiŋ) *n.* coin of little value.

Reading Skill
Make Inferences Based on Sasha's thoughts, what can you infer about how mature he is?

Vocabulary
detestable (dē tes´ tə bəl) *adj.* deserving hate or scorn; offensive

8 **Reading Check**
What is one reason Ivan Markovitch wants to help Sasha?

7 Reading Skill
Make Inferences

1. Remind students that inferences are based on details in their reading as well as on their own experiences.
2. Read the bracketed text aloud to students, urging them to listen for the ways in which Sasha justifies his actions.
3. Then, **ask** students the Reading Skill question: Based on Sasha's thoughts, what can you infer about how mature he is?
   Possible response: Sasha is not mature. He does not understand the difference between being in debt and acting illegally to get out of debt. Rather than taking responsibility, he pouts and pities himself.

8 Reading Check

Answer: Sasha lost his parents when he was young and has had a hard life. Ivan Markovitch, Sasha's maternal uncle, thinks Sasha could use some compassion and support from a caring family member.

Differentiated Instruction for Universal Access

Strategy for Special Needs Students
To help students keep track of the different views of the three uncles, work with students to create a two-column chart, with columns headed **Key Issue** and **Solution.** For each uncle, list his main concern and his proposed solution. For the Colonel, the key issue is honor; Sasha must be punished. For the Treasury official, the key issue is family reputation; the scandal must be hidden. For Ivan Markovitch, Sasha has made a youthful mistake; Sasha should be helped instead of punished. Ask students with which viewpoint they agree.

Strategy for Advanced Readers
After reading the passage reflecting the three uncles' views about the problem, ask students to analyze each man's motives. Why might the Colonel be so concerned about honor? Why might the Treasury official be so concerned about secrecy? Why might Ivan Markovitch be so compassionate? After discussing their motives, ask students to identify which uncle they think will prevail in the debate over Sasha's fate.

❾ Critical Viewing

Possible response: Students may say the painting is similar to the way they picture the Uskov's home. The painting shows an opulent and lushly decorated hallway and room. Also, the furnishings, such as the candelabra and ornate furniture, match those used around the time the story was written.

❿ Literary Analysis

Character and Characterization

1. Ask students to describe Sasha's attitude toward his misdeed at this point.
   Answer: Sasha feels neither ashamed nor guilty about cashing the false promissory note.
2. Then, **ask** students the Literary Analysis question: How do Sasha's thoughts about himself compare to what you have learned about his character?
   Possible response: Sasha's thoughts complement his actions and what others say about him. He makes excuses for himself and feels no responsibility for what he does. He claims to have had no intention of causing anyone damage or loss; his only motive is to get money by whatever means he can. He sees himself as innocent and put upon; the reader sees him as self-pitying, self-deceived, and immature.

❾ ▶ **Critical Thinking** How is the painting similar to or different from how you pictured the Uskov's home? **[Compare and Contrast]**

❼

❿ **Literary Analysis Character and Characterization** How do Sasha's thoughts about himself compare to what you have learned about his character?

"Criminal" is a dreadful word—that is what murderers, thieves, robbers are; in fact, wicked and morally hopeless people. And Sasha was very far from being all that. . . . It was true he owed a great deal and did not pay his debts. But debt is not a crime, and it is unusual for a man not to be in debt. The Colonel and Ivan Markovitch were both in debt. . . .

"What have I done wrong besides?" Sasha wondered.

He had discounted a forged note. But all the young men he knew did the same. Handrikov and Von Burst always forged IOU's from their parents or friends when their allowances were not paid at the regular time, and then when they got their money from home they redeemed them before they became due. Sasha had done the same, but had not redeemed the IOU because he had not got the money which Handrikov had promised to lend him. He was not to blame; it was the fault of circumstances. It was true that the use of another person's signature was considered reprehensible; but, still, it was not a crime but a generally accepted dodge, an ugly formality which injured no one and was quite harmless, for in forging the Colonel's signature Sasha had had no intention of causing anybody damage or loss.

"No, it doesn't mean that I am a criminal . . ." thought Sasha. "And it's not in my character to bring myself to commit a crime. I am soft, emotional. . . . When I have the money I help the poor. . . ."

Sasha was musing after this fashion while they went on talking the other side of the door.

"But, my friends, this is endless," the Colonel declared, getting excited. "Suppose we were to forgive him and pay the money. You know he would not give up leading a dissipated life, squandering money, making debts, going to our tailors and ordering suits in our names! Can you guarantee that this will be his last prank? As far as I am concerned, I have no faith whatever in his reforming!"

The official of the Treasury muttered something in reply; after him Ivan Markovitch began talking blandly and suavely again. The Colonel moved his chair impatiently and drowned the other's words with his detestable metallic voice. At last the door opened and Ivan Markovitch came out of the study; there were patches of red on his cleanshaven face.

"Come along," he said, taking Sasha by the hand. "Come and speak frankly from your heart. Without pride, my dear boy, humbly and from your heart."

Sasha went into the study. The official of the Treasury was sitting down; the Colonel was standing before the table with one hand in his pocket and one knee on a chair. It was smoky and stifling in the study. Sasha did not look at the official or the Colonel; he felt

Vocabulary Development

Word Forms

Expand students' vocabulary by helping them learn related forms of the selection vocabulary. Two of the selection vocabulary words for "A Problem" have related forms. Give students a blank **Word Form Chart** (*Professional Development Guidebook,* p. 42), with *lofty* and *candid* in the adjective column. Work with the class, or have students work with a partner, to determine the related forms. The final chart should look like the one shown.

Noun	Verb	Adjective	Adverb
candor		**candid**	candidly
loftiness		**lofty**	loftily

11

A Problem 261

11 Humanities

Candelabra by William Ireland

A graduate of the Glasgow School of Art, William Ireland is a contemporary painter best known for his representations of tranquil interiors. His works demonstrate a distinctive use of color and are noted for their warmth and exuberance. Currently he resides in Scotland.

Use the following questions for discussion:

What room in the story could the painting represent?
Possible response: The painting could represent the study.

Do you think representation in the painting is accurate? Explain.
Possible response: No, it is not an accurate representation. The painting seems welcoming and full of warmth, while the study in the story seems unwelcoming and stifling.

Differentiated Instruction for Universal Access

EL Support for English Learners

Make sure students understand that a promissory note is an IOU (I Owe You), or a promise to pay an amount of money. In the story, Sasha forges his uncle's signature and cashes the note at a bank. If he cannot pay back the money he has received, he will be charged with a crime.

Enrichment for Gifted/Talented Students

Have students do research about the practice of sending criminals to Siberia. Give them questions like these to guide their research: What types of crimes were punished by sending criminals to the region? What did they do while they were there? What were conditions like in Siberia?

⓬ Literary Analysis
Character and Characterization

1. Have students read the bracketed text to themselves.
2. Then, **ask** the Literary Analysis question: How does the writer reveal without directly stating it that Sasha is not sorry?
   Possible response: Sasha's only reaction to his aunt's tears and the upset voices he hears from behind the door is to shrug his shoulders. He is surprised that his relatives are so upset over a matter he sees as insignificant.

⓭ Reading Skill
Make Inferences

1. **Ask** students to speculate about the argument that convinces the uncles to pay Sasha's debt.
   Answer: Sasha's dead mother will not have peace beyond her grave unless they help her son.
2. Then, **ask** students to respond to the Reading Skill prompt: Based on Ivan's response and your knowledge of families, make an inference about the uncles' feelings for Sasha's mother.
   Possible responses: They care deeply about her, or perhaps they are exhausted and looking for a reason to rescue their nephew. Perhaps they feel that things with Sasha would have been different if she had not died.

▶ **Monitor Progress Ask** students to list the details from the story that lead them to make their inferences.
Possible response: The Uskov uncles change their minds only when Ivan Markovitch begins sobbing over his sister. Sasha was very young when he lost both of his parents. His mother was probably young, too, so her brothers-in-law feel her loss quite strongly.

▶ **Reteach** If students have difficulty recalling supporting details, have them return to the text on this page and on page 258. Direct their attention to the third and fourth paragraphs on the page. Help them to pick out the details to be used in making inferences.

suddenly ashamed and uncomfortable. He looked uneasily at Ivan Markovitch and muttered:

"I'll pay it . . . I'll give it back. . . ."

"What did you expect when you discounted the IOU?" he heard a metallic voice.

"I . . . Handrikov promised to lend me the money before now."

Sasha could say no more. He went out of the study and sat down again on the chair near the door. He would have been glad to go away altogether at once, but he was choking with hatred and he awfully wanted to remain, to tear the Colonel to pieces, to say something rude to him. He sat trying to think of something violent and effective to say to his hated uncle, and at that moment a woman's figure, shrouded in the twilight, appeared at the drawing room door. It was the Colonel's wife. She beckoned Sasha to her, and, wringing her hands, said, weeping:

"*Alexandre*, I know you don't like me, but . . . listen to me; listen, I beg you. . . . But, my dear, how can this have happened? Why, it's awful, awful! For goodness' sake, beg them, defend yourself, entreat them."

Literary Analysis
Character and Characterization How does the writer reveal without directly stating it that Sasha is not sorry? ⓬

Sasha looked at her quivering shoulders, at the big tears that were rolling down her cheeks, heard behind his back the hollow, nervous voices of worried and exhausted people, and shrugged his shoulders. He had not in the least expected that his aristocratic relations would raise such a tempest over a paltry fifteen hundred rubles! He could not understand her tears nor the quiver of their voices.

An hour later he heard that the Colonel was getting the best of it; the uncles were finally inclining to let the case go for trial.

"The matter's settled," said the Colonel, sighing. "Enough."

After this decision all the uncles, even the emphatic Colonel, became noticeably depressed. A silence followed.

Vocabulary
subdued (səb do͞od′) *adj.* quiet; lacking energy

"Merciful Heavens!" sighed Ivan Markovitch. "My poor sister!"

And he began saying in a **subdued** voice that most likely his sister, Sasha's mother, was present unseen in the study at that moment. He felt in his soul how the unhappy, saintly woman was weeping, grieving, and begging for her boy. For the sake of her peace beyond the grave, they ought to spare Sasha.

⓭ **Reading Skill**
Make Inferences Based on Ivan's response and your knowledge of families, make an inference about the uncles' feelings for Sasha's mother.

The sound of a muffled sob was heard. Ivan Markovitch was weeping and muttering something which it was impossible to catch through the door. The Colonel got up and paced from corner to corner. The long conversation began over again.

But then the clock in the drawing room struck two. The family council was over. To avoid seeing the person who had moved him to

Vocabulary Development

Vocabulary Knowledge Rating

When students have completed reading and discussing "A Problem," have them take out their **Vocabulary Knowledge Rating Chart** for this selection. Read the words aloud once more and have students rate their knowledge of the words again in the After Reading column. Clarify any words that are still problematic. Have students write their own definition and example or sentence in the appropriate column. Then have students complete the Vocabulary Practice at the end of the selection.

Encourage students to use the words in further discussion and written work about this selection. Remind them that they will be accountable for these words on the **Selection Test,** ***Unit 2 Resources,*** pp. 56–58 or 59–61.

such wrath, the Colonel went from the study, not into the hall, but into the vestibule. . . . Ivan Markovitch came out into the hall. . . . He was agitated and rubbing his hands joyfully. His tear-stained eyes looked good-humored and his mouth was twisted into a smile.

"Capital," he said to Sasha. "Thank God! You can go home, my dear, and sleep tranquilly. We have decided to pay the sum, but on condition that you repent and come with me tomorrow into the country and set to work."

A minute later Ivan Markovitch and Sasha in their greatcoats and caps were going down the stairs. The uncle was muttering something edifying. Sasha did not listen, but felt as though some uneasy weight were gradually slipping off his shoulders. They had forgiven him; he was free! A gust of joy sprang up within him and sent a sweet chill to his heart. He longed to breathe, to move swiftly, to live! Glancing at the street lamps and the black sky, he remembered that Von Burst was celebrating his name day[7] that evening at the "Bear," and again a rush of joy flooded his soul. . . .

"I am going!" he decided.

But then he remembered he had not a farthing, that the companions he was going to would despise him at once for his empty pockets. He must get hold of some money, come what may!

"Uncle, lend me a hundred rubles," he said to Ivan Markovitch.

His uncle, surprised, looked into his face and backed against a lamppost.

"Give it to me," said Sasha, shifting impatiently from one foot to the other and beginning to pant. "Uncle, I entreat you, give me a hundred rubles."

7. **name day** feast day of the saint after whom a person is named.

Vocabulary
edifying (ed′ i fī′ iŋ) *adj.* instructive in such a way as to improve morally or intellectually

They had forgiven him; he was free! A gust of joy sprang up within him and sent a sweet chill to his heart. He longed to breathe, to move swiftly, to live!

15 **Reading Check**
What decision do the uncles come to regarding Sasha?

14 Connecting to the Big Question

1. Explain to students that a conflict's resolution can be considered successful if the desired outcome is met.
2. **Ask:** What is the conflict and what is Ivan Markovitch's desired outcome?
   Answer: Sasha cashed a false promissory note, which, if made public, might tarnish the family name. Ivan Markovitch hopes to convince the uncles to give Sasha a second chance. He also hopes Sasha will learn from his mistake.
3. Have students read the bracketed text. **Ask:** What clues from Ivan Markovitch's behavior and dialogue suggest that he is successful in helping his nephew?
   Possible response: When Ivan Markovitch exits the study, he rubs his hands "joyfully," his eyes are "good-humored," and he is smiling. These clues suggest that he is happy about something; because he just came from the meeting, he must have managed to persuade the others to help Sasha. Then, Ivan Markovitch explicitly states that the family has decided to pay the sum.
4. **Ask:** What clues from Sasha's thoughts suggest that Ivan Markovitch is successful in helping him?
   Possible response: Sasha feels a burden lift off him. The realization that the family had forgiven him brings a wave of joy through him. Sasha feels free and alive again.
5. **Ask:** students: Based on these clues, was progress made through conflict? Explain.
   Possible response: Yes, because Ivan Markovitch has succeeded in convincing the family to give the boy a second chance. This decision implies that the family, which had not thought well of Sasha's behavior before, feels compassion for his unfortunate situation. Ivan Markovitch, then, has managed to better the relations among family members.

15 Reading Check

Answer: They decide to pay his debt provided that he admits his wrongdoing and works on Ivan Markovitch's estate.

Concept Connector

Anticipation Guide

Have students return to their **Anticipation Guides** and respond to the statements again in the After Reading column. They may do this individually or in their original groups. Then, lead a class discussion, probing for what students have learned that confirms or invalidates each statement. Encourage students to cite specific details, quotations, or other evidence from the text to support their responses to each statement.

Writing About the Big Question

Have students compare their responses to the sentence starter they completed before reading the essay with their ideas afterwards. Ask them to explain whether their thoughts have changed.

Reading Skill Graphic Organizer

Ask students to review the graphic organizers they completed to make inferences about characters while reading. Show them the partially completed **Reading Skill Graphic Organizer A** (*Graphic Organizer Transparencies*, p. 40) as an example. Then have students share the graphic organizers they did.

16 Literary Analysis
Character and Characterization

Ask students the Literary Analysis question: In what way does Sasha's character develop at the end of the story?

Possible response: Although Sasha ultimately realizes that he is a criminal, the realization does not change his behavior. He seems reconciled to being wicked.

ASSESS
Answers

Critical Thinking
1. Students may say that they sympathize with Ivan Markovitch because his trust and kindness are betrayed by his nephew. After discussion, they should explain whether their views changed.
2. (a) Sasha is in trouble because he has cashed a false promissory note. (b) Ivan Markovitch is the only one who is sympathetic. The other two uncles, the Colonel and the official in the Treasury, are not.
3. Ivan reminds the Colonel that his dead sister would be terribly upset if she knew how they were treating her son.
4. (a) Students may say that Ivan is enabling Sasha to continue his irresponsible ways. (b) Most students will say that Ivan should have refused the request.
5. (a) Most students will consider writing a false promissory note a crime. (b) Encourage students to think carefully about the effect of their actions.

Can progress be made without conflict?

Possible response: (a) Yes, Ivan Markovitch made progress with the other uncles. The uncles wanted a heavier punishment for Sasha, but Ivan convinced the uncles to show mercy.

(b) Sasha did not learn his lesson. As soon as he learns of his lighter punishment, he thinks immediately of money, realizes he is still in debt, and demands money from Ivan Markovitch. His conflict with his uncles has not led him to progress.

His face worked; he trembled, and seemed on the point of attacking his uncle. . . .

"Won't you?" he kept asking, seeing that his uncle was still amazed and did not understand. "Listen. If you don't, I'll give myself up tomorrow! I won't let you pay the IOU! I'll present another false note tomorrow!"

Petrified, muttering something incoherent in his horror, Ivan Markovitch took a hundred-ruble note out of his pocketbook and gave it to Sasha. The young man took it and walked rapidly away from him. . . .

Literary Analysis Character and Characterization In what way does Sasha's character develop at the end of the story? 16

Taking a sledge, Sasha grew calmer, and felt a rush of joy within him again. The "rights of youth" of which kind-hearted Ivan Markovitch had spoken at the family council woke up and asserted themselves. Sasha pictured the drinking party before him, and, among the bottles, the women, and his friends, the thought flashed through his mind:

"Now I see that I am a criminal; yes, I am a criminal."

Critical Thinking
1. **Respond:** With which character in the story do you sympathize most strongly? Share your responses in a small group. Record members' thoughts about each character. Then, review the notes and explain how others' responses affected your viewpoint.
2. **(a)** Why is Sasha in trouble? **(b) Compare and Contrast:** Use details from the story to compare the position each uncle takes toward Sasha's problem.
3. **Infer:** How does Ivan Markovitch change the Colonel's mind?
4. **(a) Evaluate:** Does Ivan Markovitch's attitude help or harm Sasha? Explain. **(b) Take a Position:** What should he have done when Sasha asked him for money after the family meeting?
5. **(a) Evaluate:** Do you think what Sasha did should be punished as a crime? Why or why not? **(b) Relate:** What would you have done if you were one of Sasha's uncles? Explain.

Can progress be made without conflict?
(a) Did Ivan Markovitch make progress with the other uncles in his fight for Sasha? Explain. **(b)** Explain why you think Sasha did or did not learn his lesson after being given a second chance.

Assessment Resources
Unit 2 Resources

- L1 L2 EL **Selection Test A,** pp. 56–58. Administer Test A to less advanced readers and English Learners.
- L3 L4 **Selection Test B,** pp. 59–61. Administer Test B to on-level and more advanced students.
- L3 L4 **Open-Book Test,** pp. 53–55. As an alternative, give the Open-Book Test.

All **Customizable Test Bank**

All **Self-tests**
Students may prepare for the **Selection Test** by taking the **Self-test** online.

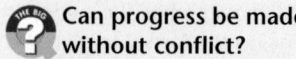

PHLit Online! All assessment resources are available at **www.PHLitOnline.com**

After You Read | A Problem

Literary Analysis: Character and Characterization

1. Compare and contrast the **characters** of Ivan Markovitch and the Colonel. Use details from the story to support your answer.
2. Identify three examples of **indirect characterization** used to portray Sasha. Use a chart like the one shown.

What He Says	What He Does	What Others Say About Him

3. **(a)** What is Sasha's reason for cashing a false note? **(b)** Explain how his character is **developed** by the end of the story.
4. **(a)** Give two examples of **dialogue** from Sasha and two from Ivan. **(b)** What do your examples reveal about their differences?

Reading Skill: Make Inferences

5. **Make an inference** about how Sasha feels having been caught doing wrong. On which story details is your inference based?
6. Make an inference about Ivan's feelings at the end of the story. Support your inference with story details and your own experience.

Vocabulary

Practice Answer each question, and explain how the meaning of the underlined word influences your answer.

1. Why might you expect a candid answer from a good friend?
2. When might it be a good idea to keep your conversation subdued?
3. Is someone who displays a pretense of wealth actually rich?
4. What lofty goals might an aspiring actor have?
5. Would you want to spend a lot of time with a detestable person?
6. When might a child expect an edifying speech from an adult?

Word Study Use the context of the sentences and what you know about the **Latin suffix *-able*** to explain your answer to each question.

1. If you have a *curable* disease, will you feel better soon?
2. When an athlete makes a *remarkable* play, do spectators cheer?

Word Study

The **Latin suffix *-able*** means "worthy of; capable of being."

Challenge Explain how the suffix *-able* contributes to the meanings of these words. Consult a dictionary if necessary.

admirable
calculable
negotiable

ASSESS/EXTEND

Answers

Literary Analysis

1. Ivan Markovitch is compassionate, shown in his efforts to defend Sasha. The Colonel is a disciplinarian, shown in his desire to see the boy punished.
2. **Possible response: What He Says:** Sasha shows himself to be self-pitying, as when he thinks " '. . . it's not in my character to bring myself to commit a crime. I am soft, emotional. . . .' " **What He Does:** Sasha's request at the end of the story shows that he is still lost in his life of immediate gratification. **What Others Say About Him:** Ivan Markovitch's descriptions show that Sasha has lacked guidance.

   For other sample answers, see ***Graphic Organizer Transparencies,* Literary Analysis Graphic Organizer A**, p. 43, and the **Additional Answers** section.
3. (a) Sasha cashes the note because he is in debt. (b) **Possible response:** When told that his uncles will forgive him, Sasha asks Ivan Markovitch for a loan. He still sees life as a series of parties funded by other people. However, his final thought, " 'Now I see that I am a criminal . . . ,' " indicates that he now accepts his own immorality.
4. (a) *Sasha:* " 'Give it to me. . . . Uncle, I entreat you, give me a hundred roubles.' " " 'Listen, if you don't, I'll give myself up tomorrow!' " *Ivan Markovitch:* " 'Merciful Heavens! My poor sister!' " " 'Thank God, my dear, you can go home, and sleep tranquilly.' " (b) Sasha thinks only of himself; Ivan Markovitch sympathizes with others.

Vocabulary

Practice

1. A friend would be candid, or honest, with me because she is concerned with my welfare.
2. It might be a good idea to keep a conversation subdued in a quiet place like a library.
3. Someone who displays a pretense, or fakes being wealthy, is not rich.
4. A lofty goal an aspiring actor might have is to win an Oscar.
5. I would not want to spend time with a detestable, or offensive, person.
6. A child might expect an edifying speech, after he or she has misbehaved.

Word Study

1. If I have a disease that can be cured, I will probably feel better soon.
2. Spectators cheer because the athlete's play is worthy of remark or praise.

Word Study: Challenge

To be *admirable* is to be "capable of being admired." To be *calculable* means "to be capable of being calculated." To be *negotiable* means "to be capable of being negotiated."

Reading Skill

5. **Possible response:** Sasha feels some shame and spends much time denying to himself that he is a criminal. He is not ashamed by his action itself, shown in his failure to acknowledge wrongdoing.
6. **Possible response:** Ivan is shocked by Sasha's request. He stands "Petrified, muttering something incoherent in his horror. . . ."

Answers

Grammar

1. Introduce the skill, using the instruction on the student page.
2. Discuss the examples in the chart.

Think Aloud: Model the Skill

Model the skill of forming principal parts of verbs, using the following "think aloud":

> To form the principal parts of regular verbs, I use the following rules: The present form of a verb is the same as the verb itself, so the present form of the verb *cook* is *cook.* To form the present participle of cook I add *-ing* to the end of the verb—*cooking.* To form both the past and the past participle I add *-ed* to the end of the verb—*cooked.*

Writing and Grammar, Grade 10

Students will find further instruction and practice on regular verbs in Chapter 22, Section 1.

Practice A

1. has traveled; past participle
2. tells; present
3. are passing; present participle
4. confronted; past

Challenge

Sample answer: The reunion had lasted a week (past p); The old lady eyed his father (past); "How are you, son?" (present); "I'm trying to think." (present p)

Practice B

Sample answers:

1. present participle; Sasha waited for his uncles to finish their discussion.
2. present; "I have always borrowed money," Sasha explained.
3. past; Sasha is jumping into a sledge and driving off.
4. past participle; Ivan Markovitch pleaded Sasha's case to the uncles.

Challenge

Answer: Sasha prepares a candid explanation; Sasha is preparing a candid explanation; Sasha has prepared a candid explanation.

Integrated Language Skills

A Visit to Grandmother • A Problem

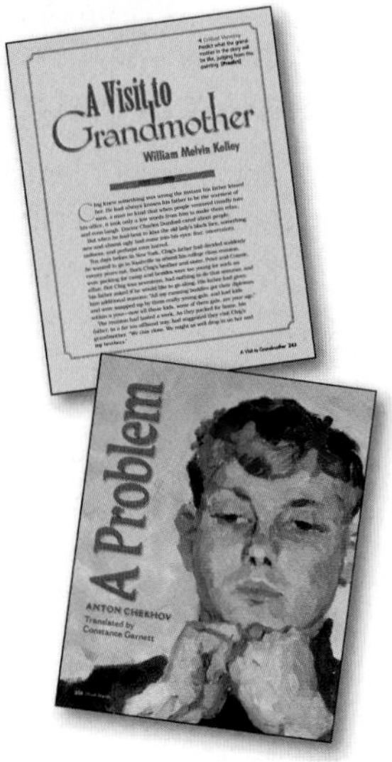

Grammar: Principal Parts of Regular Verbs

A **verb** is a word that expresses existence, action, or occurrence in a sentence. A verb has four **principal parts:** the present, the present participle, the past, and the past participle.

Most of the verbs in the English language form the present participle by adding *-ing* to the present. The past and the past participle of most verbs add *-ed* or *-d* to the present.

The Four Principal Parts of Verbs

Present	Present Participle	Past	Past Participle
talk	(is) talking	talked	(have) talked
type	(is) typing	typed	(have) typed

Practice A Identify the verb in each sentence, and indicate whether it is the present, present participle, past, or past participle.

1. Chig has traveled with his father to the South.
2. Chig's grandmother tells stories about the past.
3. The aunts are passing the food to Chig.
4. Chig's father confronted his mother about his childhood.

Challenge In "A Visit to Grandmother," find one example of each principal verb part.

Practice B Identify the principal part of the italicized verb in each sentence. Then, rewrite each sentence using a different principal part.

1. Sasha *is waiting* for his uncles to finish their discussion.
2. "I always *borrow* money," Sasha explained.
3. Sasha *jumped* into a sledge and drove off.
4. Ivan Markovitch *has pleaded* Sasha's case to the uncles.

Challenge Rewrite this model sentence three times using the other principal parts of the verb: *Sasha prepared a candid explanation.*

Writing and Grammar Connection: Chapter 22, Section 1

Extend the Lesson

Sentence Modeling

Choose the sentences given from the selection students have read:

"Why don't you tell them about the horse, Mama?" Aunt Rose, over Chig's weak protest, was spooning mashed potatoes onto his plate. ("A Visit to Grandmother")

"Uncle, lend me a hundred rubles," he said to Ivan Markovitch. His uncle, surprised, looked into his face and backed against the lamppost. ("A Problem")

Ask students what they notice about the sentence. Elicit from them that the dialogue is in the form of a command, with the verb in the present tense. Then, ask what else they notice. ("A Visit to Grandmother": Aunt Rose uses a negative phrase to gently command Mama to tell the story; the next sentence describes Aunt Rose's current action. "A Problem": dialogue is short and to the point and uses direct address. The next sentence gives his uncle's reaction.)

Have students imitate the sentences in sentences on a topic of their own choosing, matching each feature discussed.

Writing

Each of these two selections describes a family conflict. Write two brief **retellings** of the events that took place in the selection you read. For "A Visit to Grandmother," retell the story first as Mama would tell it and then retell the story from GL's viewpoint. For "A Problem," retell the story from the perspective of one of the uncles and then from Sasha's perspective.

- Use a story map or plot diagram to list the main events.
- Identify details that will show the difference between the characters' perspectives.
- Use the first-person pronoun *I* to write from the character's point of view.
- When you have completed a first draft, evaluate the draft for appropriate point of view.

Writing Workshop: *Work in Progress*

Prewriting for a Short Story Select a character trait that would be suitable for a protagonist in a short story. Then, choose a trait for an antagonist. Provide brief descriptions of these two characters based on these traits. Save your Character Descriptions in your writing portfolio.

Use this prewriting activity to prepare for the **Writing Workshop** on page 328.

Research and Technology

Write a **report on sources** for a research project about either the Great Migration from the rural South to northern cities or social status in Russia during the nineteenth century.

Follow these steps to complete the assignment:

- Find three to four sources of varied types, including books, online material, CD-ROM references, or audiovisual materials.
- **Evaluate the accuracy and reliability** of each source. Consider the date of the source, the author's credentials, and whether the details are verified or contradicted by other sources.
- **Identify and evaluate each source's text features,** such as the table of contents, glossary, index, charts, and graphs.
- **Identify complexities and discrepancies** in the information found in each source.
- As you review the material, jot down the thoughts, opinions, and questions that occur to you.
- In your report, explain the value of each resource you found. Describe the type of research you would conduct using these materials.

PHLit Online!
www.PHLitOnline.com
- Interactive graphic organizers
- Grammar tutorial
- Interactive journals

EXTEND/ASSESS

Answers

Writing

1. Review the assignment, using the instruction on the student page.
2. To guide students in writing their retellings of the story, give them **Support for Writing**, p. 51 in ***Unit 2 Resources.***
3. To evaluate students' retellings, use the **Narration: Short Story** rubrics on pp. 226–227 in ***Professional Development Guidebook.*** In addition, evaluate how well students use point of view to show different interpretations of story events.

Six Traits Focus

✓	Ideas	✓	Word Choice
	Organization		Sentence Fluency
✓	Voice		Conventions

Writing and Grammar, Grade 10

Students will find guidance on narrative writing in Chapter 5.

Writing Workshop
Work in Progress

Have students save their completed Character Descriptions in their portfolios. They will use the Character Descriptions later as they continue this Work-in-Progress assignment (see p. 295). These assignments prepare them to complete the Writing Workshop assignment (see pp. 328–333).

Research and Technology

1. Review the assignment, using the instruction on the student page.
2. Have students complete the **Support for Extend Your Learning** page (***Unit 2 Resources,*** p. 52).

Teaching Resources

All *Unit 2 Resources*

L3 L4 **Integrated Language Skills: Grammar,** p. 50

L3 L4 **Support for Writing,** p. 51

L3 L4 **Support for Extend Your Learning,** p. 52

L4 **Enrichment,** pp. 31, 49

All **Enriched Online Student Edition**
Available under After You Read for this selection:

All **Interactive Grammar Tutorial**

L3 L4 **Internet Research Activity**

Professional Development Guidebook
Rubrics for Narration: Short Story, pp. 226–227

PHLit Online! All print and digital resources are available at **www.PHLitOnline.com.** Online resources accessible by students are noted on the student page.

TIME AND RESOURCE MANAGER

The Street of the Cañon • There Will Come Soft Rains

Lesson Pacing Guide

DAY 1 Preteach

- Administer the Reading and Vocabulary Warm-ups (*Unit 2 Resources*, pp. 62–65 or 80–83) as necessary.
- Introduce the Reading Skill: Make Inferences FT
- Introduce the Literary Analysis concept: Setting FT
- Distribute copies of the appropriate graphic organizer for the Reading Skill (*Graphic Organizer Transparencies*, pp. 48–50). CRI
- Distribute copies of the appropriate graphic organizer for Literary Analysis (*Graphic Organizer Transparencies*, pp. 45–47). CRI
- Teach the selection vocabulary. FT CRI
- Introduce the Word Study skill.

DAYS 2–3 Preteach/Teach

- Build background with the Background feature. CRI
- Develop thematic vocabulary and thematic thinking with Writing About the Big Question.
- Prepare students to read with the Activating Prior Knowledge activities (TE). CRI
- Informally monitor comprehension while students read. FT
- Use the Reading Check questions to confirm comprehension.
- Develop students' ability to infer using the Reading Skill questions. CRI
- Develop students' understanding of setting using the Literary Analysis questions. CRI
- Reinforce vocabulary with the Vocabulary notes. CRI

DAY 4 Assess

- Assess students' comprehension and mastery of the skills by having them answer the Critical Thinking, Reading Skill, and Literary Analysis questions. FT
- Have students complete the Vocabulary Practice activities. FT
- Have students complete the Word Study activities.

DAY 5 Extend/Assess

- Have students complete the Grammar lesson. CRI
- Have students complete the Writing activity and write a letter to a friend. (You may assign as homework.) FT
- Extend learning by having students complete the Listening and Speaking activity, an oral reading. As an alternative, assign them "Identity Theft" or "Tracking Teen Drivers" in *Reality Central*. CRI
- Administer Selection Test A or B (*Unit 2 Resources*, pp. 74–79 or 95–100). FT

"The Street of the Cañon" is a short story presented unedited and in its entirety. "There Will Come Soft Rains" is a short story presented unedited and in its entirety.

Meeting Your Standards

Students will

1. **analyze and respond to literary elements.**
   - **Literary Analysis: Setting**
2. **read, comprehend, and analyze short stories.**
   - **Reading Skill: Make Inferences**
   - **Reading Check questions**
   - **Apply the Skills questions**
   - **Assessment Practice**
3. **develop vocabulary.**
   - **Vocabulary**
   - **Word Study**
4. **apply grammar skills.**
   - **Irregular Verbs**
5. **Develop writing proficiency.**
   - **Work in Progress: Short Story**
   - **letter to a friend**
   - **book review**
6. **strengthen listening and speaking skills.**
   - **oral reading**

CRI For a full explanation of Culturally Responsive Instruction opportunities in this lesson, see p. T86–T87.

FT For an accelerated lesson, use the Fast Track strategies and activities.

Managing Differentiated Instruction

This leveled selection pairing groups a more accessible with a more challenging selection. Choose either one to teach the lesson skills. For classroom management suggestions for using the pairing in a mixed-ability class, see pp. T68–T69.

Daily Block Scheduling

Each day in this Lesson Pacing Guide represents a 40–50 minute period. Teachers using block scheduling may combine days to revise pacing. In addition, teachers may differentiate and support core instruction by integrating components for extended and intensive support as students require. See the Guide to Selected Leveled Resources (facing page).

Guide to Selected Leveled Resources

EL English Learners

			The Street of the Cañon	There Will Come Soft Rains
CORE COURSE	*Unit 2 Resources*	Selection Test A	pp. 74–76	pp. 95–97
	Graphic Organizer Transparencies	Reading Skill Graphic Organizer A	p. 48	p. 49
		Literary Analysis Graphic Organizer A	p. 45	p. 46
EXTENDED SUPPORT (Level 2)	*Unit 2 Resources*	Reading and Vocabulary Warm-ups A or B	pp. 62–65	pp. 80–83
	Reader's Notebook: English Learner's Version		adapted instruction and adapted selection	adapted instruction and summary
	***Hear It!* Audio CD**		selection and summaries	selection and summaries
	***Hear It!* Audio CD (adapted text)**		adapted selection and summaries	—
INTENSIVE SUPPORT (Level 1)	*Reality Central*		"Identity Theft"	"Tracking Teen Drivers"
	Real-World Writing Journal		Lesson 3, pp. 44–47	Lesson 4, pp. 48–51

L2 Below-Level Students

			The Street of the Cañon	There Will Come Soft Rains
CORE COURSE	*Unit 2 Resources*	Selection Test A	pp. 74–76	pp. 95–97
	Graphic Organizer Transparencies	Reading Skill Graphic Organizer A	p. 48	p. 49
		Literary Analysis Graphic Organizer A	p. 45	p. 46
EXTENDED SUPPORT (Level 2)	*Unit 2 Resources*	Reading and Vocabulary Warm-ups A or B	pp. 62–65	pp. 80–83
	Reader's Notebook		adapted instruction and full selection	adapted instruction and summary
	***Hear It!* Audio CD**		selection and summaries	selection and summaries
INTENSIVE SUPPORT (Level 1)	*Reality Central*		"Identity Theft"	"Tracking Teen Drivers"
	Real-World Writing Journal		Lesson 3, pp. 44–47	Lesson 4, pp. 48–51
	Reading Kit		Reteaching worksheets	Reteaching worksheets

L1 Special Needs Students

			The Street of the Cañon	There Will Come Soft Rains
CORE COURSE	*Unit 2 Resources*	Selection Test A	pp. 74–76	pp. 95–97
	Graphic Organizer Transparencies	Reading Skill Graphic Organizer A	p. 48	p. 49
		Literary Analysis Graphic Organizer A	p. 45	p. 46
EXTENDED SUPPORT (Level 2)	*Unit 2 Resources*	Reading and Vocabulary Warm-ups A or B	pp. 62–65	pp. 80–83
	Reader's Notebook: Adapted Version		adapted instruction and adapted selection	adapted instruction and summary
	***Hear It!* Audio CD (adapted text)**		adapted selection and summaries	—
INTENSIVE SUPPORT (Level 1)	*Reality Central*		"Identity Theft"	"Tracking Teen Drivers"
	Real-World Writing Journal		Lesson 3, pp. 44–47	Lesson 4, pp. 48–51
	Reading Kit		Reteaching worksheets	Reteaching worksheets

The program includes resources for these students: L3 On-Level L4 Advanced All All
For a complete guide to selection support, see pp. T106–T108.

NOTE: All print materials are also available online at *www.PHLitOnline.com.*

VISUAL GUIDE to Featured Selection Resources

• The Street of the Cañon
• There Will Come Soft Rains

RESOURCES FOR:

- EL English Learners
- L1 Special Needs Students
- L2 Below-Level Students
- L3 On-Level Students
- L4 Advanced Students
- All All Students

Vocabulary/Fluency/Prior Knowledge

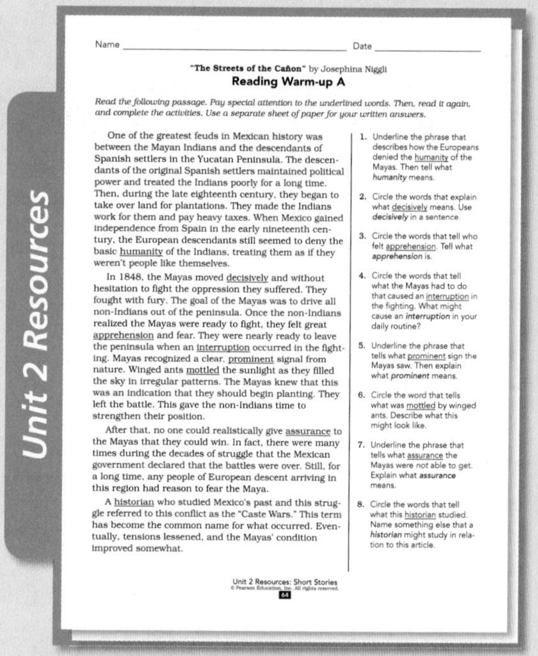

Unit 2 Resources

Name ______________________ Date ____________

"The Streets of the Cañon" by Josephina Niggli

Reading Warm-up A

Read the following passage. Pay special attention to the underlined words. Then, read it again, and complete the activities. Use a separate sheet of paper for your written answers.

One of the greatest feuds in Mexican history was between the Mayan Indians and the descendants of Spanish settlers in the Yucatan Peninsula. The descendants of the original Spanish settlers maintained political power and treated the Indians poorly for a long time. Then, during the late eighteenth century, they began to take over land for plantations. They made the Indians work for them and pay heavy taxes. When Mexico gained independence from Spain in the early nineteenth century, the European descendants still seemed to deny the basic humanity of the Indians, treating them as if they weren't people like themselves.

In 1848, the Mayas moved decisively and without hesitation to fight the oppression they suffered. They fought with fury. The goal of the Mayas was to drive all non-Indians out of the peninsula. Once the non-Indians realized the Mayas were ready to fight, they felt great apprehension and fear. They were nearly ready to leave the peninsula when an interruption occurred in the fighting. Mayas recognized a clear, prominent signal from nature. Winged ants mottled the sunlight as they filled the sky in irregular patterns. The Mayas knew that this was an indication that they should begin planting. They left the battle. This gave the non-Indians time to strengthen their position.

After that, no one could realistically give assurance to the Mayas that they could win. In fact, there were many times during the decades of struggle that the Mexican government declared that the battles were over. Still, for a long time, any people of European descent arriving in this region had reason to fear the Maya.

A historian who studied Mexico's past and this struggle referred to this conflict as the "Caste Wars." This term has become the common name for what occurred. Eventually, tensions lessened, and the Mayas' condition improved somewhat.

1. Underline the phrase that describes how the Europeans denied the humanity of the Mayas. Then tell what *humanity* means.
2. Circle the words that explain what decisively means. Use *decisively* in a sentence.
3. Circle the words that tell who felt apprehension. Tell what *apprehension* is.
4. Circle the words that tell what the Mayas had to do that caused an interruption in the fighting. What might cause an *interruption* in your daily routine?
5. Underline the phrase that tells what prominent sign the Mayas saw. Then explain what *prominent* means.
6. Circle the word that tells what was mottled by winged ants. Describe what this might look like.
7. Underline the phrase that tells what assurance the Mayas were not able to get. Explain what *assurance* means.
8. Circle the words that tell what this historian studied. Name something else that a *historian* might study in relation to this article.

Unit 2 Resources: Short Stories
© Pearson Education, Inc. All rights reserved.
64

EL L1 L2 **Reading Warm-ups A and B, pp. 64–65, 82–83**

Also available for these selections:

- EL L1 L2 **Vocabulary Warm-ups A and B, pp. 62–63, 80–81**
- All **Vocabulary Builder, pp. 69, 87**
- All **Writing About the Big Question, pp. 66, 84**

Reader's Notebooks

Pre- and postreading pages for both selections, as well as "The Street of the Cañon," appear in an interactive format in the *Reader's Notebooks*. Each *Notebook* is differentiated for a different group of learners.
The selections in the Adapted and English Learner's versions are abridged.

L2 L3 ***Reader's Notebook***

L1 ***Reader's Notebook: Adapted Version***

EL ***Reader's Notebook: English Learner's Version***

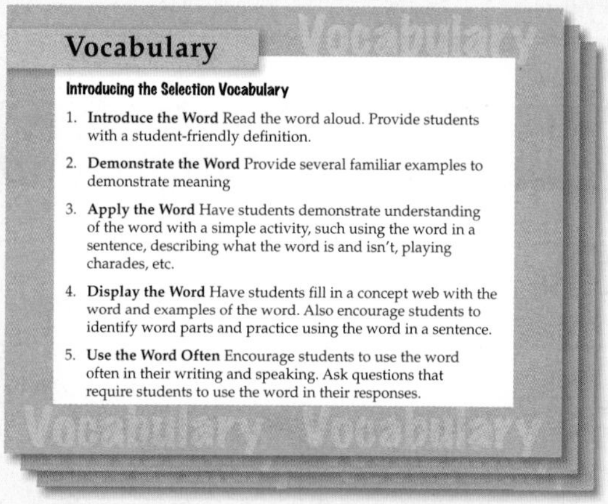

Vocabulary

Introducing the Selection Vocabulary

1. **Introduce the Word** Read the word aloud. Provide students with a student-friendly definition.
2. **Demonstrate the Word** Provide several familiar examples to demonstrate meaning
3. **Apply the Word** Have students demonstrate understanding of the word with a simple activity, such using the word in a sentence, describing what the word is and isn't, playing charades, etc.
4. **Display the Word** Have students fill in a concept web with the word and examples of the word. Also encourage students to identify word parts and practice using the word in a sentence.
5. **Use the Word Often** Encourage students to use the word often in their writing and speaking. Ask questions that require students to use the word in their responses.

Classroom Strategies and Teaching Routines

- core classroom routines outlined step-by-step
- convenient format for easy reference while teaching

Selection Support

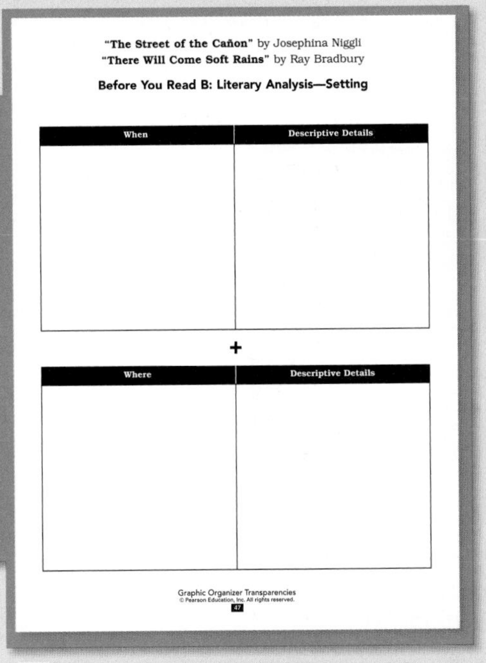

"The Street of the Cañon" by Josephina Niggli
"There Will Come Soft Rains" by Ray Bradbury

Before You Read B: Literary Analysis—Setting

When	Descriptive Details

+

Where	Descriptive Details

Graphic Organizer Transparencies
© Pearson Education, Inc. All rights reserved.
47

L3 Literary Analysis: Graphic Organizer B, p. 47

Also available for these selections:

EL L1 L2 Literary Analysis: Graphic Organizer A, pp. 45, 46 (partially filled in)

EL L1 L2 Reading: Graphic Organizer A, pp. 48, 49 (partially filled in)

L3 Reading: Graphic Organizer B, p. 50

Skills Development/Extension

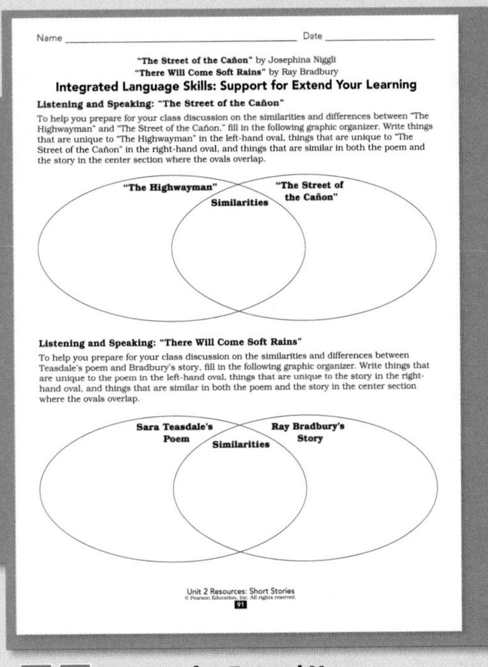

Name ______________________ Date ______________

"The Street of the Cañon" by Josephina Niggli
"There Will Come Soft Rains" by Ray Bradbury

Integrated Language Skills: Support for Extend Your Learning

Listening and Speaking: "The Street of the Cañon"

To help you prepare for your class discussion on the similarities and differences between "The Highwayman" and "The Street of the Cañon," fill in the following graphic organizer. Write things that are unique to "The Highwayman" in the left-hand oval, things that are unique to "The Street of the Cañon" in the right-hand oval, and things that are similar in both the poem and the story in the center section where the ovals overlap.

Listening and Speaking: "There Will Come Soft Rains"

To help you prepare for your class discussion on the similarities and differences between Teasdale's poem and Bradbury's story, fill in the following graphic organizer. Write things that are unique to the poem in the left-hand oval, things that are unique to the story in the right-hand oval, and things that are similar in both the poem and the story in the center section where the ovals overlap.

Unit 2 Resources: Short Stories
© Pearson Education, Inc. All rights reserved.
91

L3 L4 Support for Extend Your Learning, p. 91

Also available for these selections:

All Literary Analysis: Setting, pp. 67, 85

All Reading: Make Inferences, pp. 68, 86

L4 Enrichment, pp. 70, 88

L3 L4 Grammar, p. 89

L3 L4 Support for Writing, p. 90

Assessment

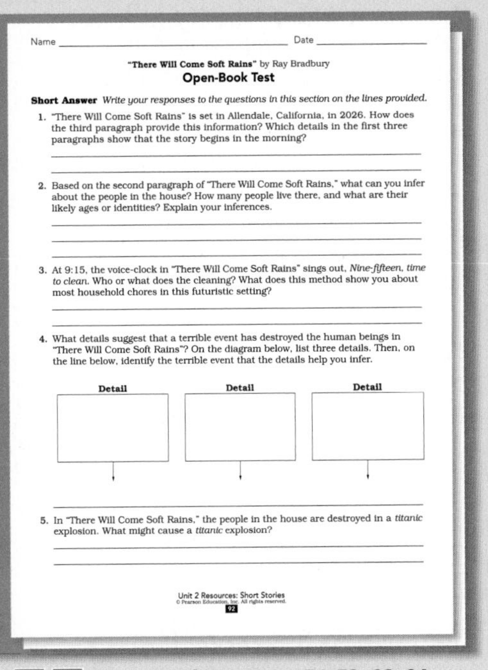

Name ______________________ Date ______________

"There Will Come Soft Rains" by Ray Bradbury

Open-Book Test

Short Answer *Write your responses to the questions in this section on the lines provided.*

1. "There Will Come Soft Rains" is set in Allendale, California, in 2026. How does the third paragraph provide this information? Which details in the first three paragraphs show that the story begins in the morning?
2. Based on the second paragraph of "There Will Come Soft Rains," what can you infer about the people in the house? How many people live there, and what are their likely ages or identities? Explain your inferences.
3. At 9:15, the voice-clock in "There Will Come Soft Rains" sings out, *Nine-fifteen, time to clean.* Who or what does the cleaning? What does this method show you about most household chores in this futuristic setting?
4. What details suggest that a terrible event has destroyed the human beings in "There Will Come Soft Rains"? On the diagram below, list three details. Then, on the line below, identify the terrible event that the details help you infer.

5. In "There Will Come Soft Rains," the people in the house are destroyed in a *titanic* explosion. What might cause a *titanic* explosion?

Unit 2 Resources: Short Stories
© Pearson Education, Inc. All rights reserved.
92

L3 L4 Open-Book Test, pp. 71–73, 92–94

Also available for these selections:

EL L1 L2 Selection Test A, pp. 74–76, 95–97

L3 L4 Selection Test B, pp. 77–79, 98–100

PHLit Online!
www.PHLitOnline.com

- complete narrated selection text
- a thematically related video with writing prompt
- an interactive graphic organizer
- highlighting feature
- access to all student print resources, adapted to individual student needs
- Spanish and English summaries

Get Connected! (thematic video with writing prompt)

Also available:

Background video

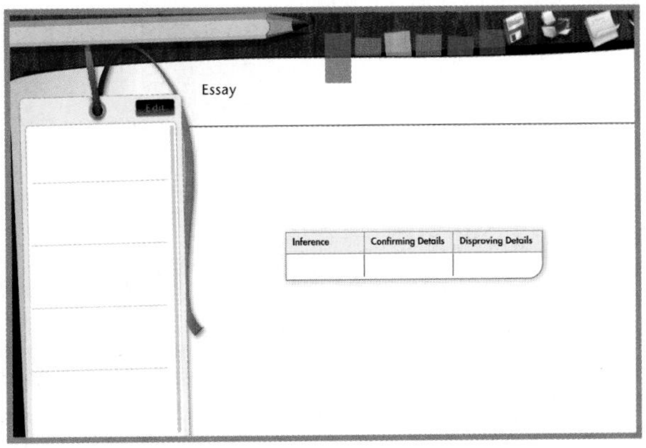

Writer's Journal (with graphics feature)

Also available:

Vocabulary Central (tools, activities, and songs for studying vocabulary)

❶ Selection Choices

You may use either "The Street of the Cañon" or "There Will Come Soft Rains" to meet the lesson standards. Skills instruction for both selections appears on p. 269. Choose one selection to teach (or choose to teach both). The Accessibility at a Glance chart at the bottom of this page will help you determine which of the two selections is more appropriate for your students.

❷ Selection Skills

1. With the class, preview the selection skills. (The lesson meets the lesson objectives given on p. 268a.)
2. Explain that students will develop the skill of making inferences (introduced on p. 239) as they read to better understand and enjoy the selection. By examining the setting of the story, they will gain deeper insight into short stories.
3. To introduce the Writing and Listening and Speaking activities (p. 295), tell students that when they have finished reading the selection, they will write a letter to a friend, a book review, and give an oral reading related to the selection.
4. Tell students that they will also study a grammar concept: irregular verbs. By mastering this concept, they will improve their reading fluency and the quality of their own writing.

Before You Read

The Street of the Cañon • There Will Come Soft Rains

❶ Selection Choices

▲ Read **"The Street of the Cañon"** to find out what happens when a mysterious stranger appears at a young woman's birthday party.

▲ Read **"There Will Come Soft Rains"** to learn what happens when technology outlives its creators.

❷ Selection Skills Guide

Practice these skills with either **"The Street of the Cañon"** (p. 272) or **"There Will Come Soft Rains"** (p. 284).

- Identify setting
- Make inferences
- Read on to confirm inferences
- Identify irregular verbs
- Write a letter to a friend
- Rewrite your summary as part of a book review
- Give an oral reading

268 Short Stories

Differentiated Instruction for Universal Access

Accessibility at a Glance: Selection Choices

	The Street of the Cañon	There Will Come Soft Rains
Context	Historical: early Mexico	Future: aftermath of an atomic bomb
Language/ Vocabulary	• Accessible vocabulary and sentence structure • Spanish words taught in feature • Below-level vocabulary	• Accessible vocabulary and sentence structure • Below-level vocabulary
Concept Level	Accessible (uninvited mystery man; town rivalry; male/female relationships)	Challenging (depicts a world in which humans have been destroyed; people vs. technology)
Literary Merit	Multicultural; local customs and traditions	Irony; science fiction encompassing moral and philosophical issues
Lexile/Length	Lexile: 770L Word Count: 2,884	Lexile: 800L Word Count: 2,074
Overall Rating	**More accessible**	**More challenging**

Because a number of factors determine the relative accessibility of paired selections, in some cases the Lexile rating of the more challenging selection will be lower than that of the more accessible selection.

❸ Literary Analysis: Setting

The time and the place of a story's events is called its **setting.** To establish a setting, writers use **description,** creating word-pictures that appeal to the senses. Settings shape stories in a few ways:

- Setting may affect a story's plot. In a story set in the Arctic wilderness, for example, characters will face challenges not found in a Caribbean resort hotel.
- Setting helps establish issues related to its historical period. For example, a character from medieval times might be concerned with preserving his honor. A character from the Stone Age, on the other hand, might be concerned only with survival.

Before you read these sections, consult the author biographies and background notes. Then, consider the way the setting of the story reflects the time period in which it was written.

❹ Using the Strategy: Setting Chart

To study setting, record details on a **setting chart** like this one.

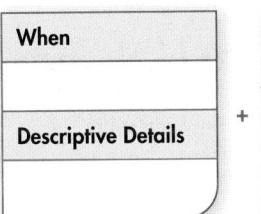

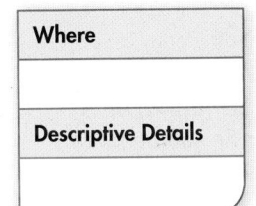

When
Descriptive Details

+

Where
Descriptive Details

❺ Reading Skill: Make Inferences

An **inference** is an insight, based on stated details, about information that is not stated. Drawing inferences helps you make connections between facts or events. For instance, if a writer does not name a setting but describes extreme cold, hunters huddled in igloos, and a night that will last all winter, you can make the inference that the story is set in the Arctic.

After you make an inference, **read on** to find additional support. If new details contradict your inference, modify it.

PHLit Online!
www.PHLitOnline.com

Hear It!
- Selection summary audio
- Selection audio

See It!
- Get Connected video
- Background video
- More about the author
- Vocabulary flashcards

Do It!
- Interactive journals
- Interactive graphic organizers
- Self-test
- Internet activity
- Grammar tutorial
- Interactive vocabulary games

Differentiated Instruction for Universal Access

If you wish to prepare lower-level readers to read "There Will Come Soft Rains," the more challenging selection, follow these steps:

- Help students grasp the central idea of the story by having them list items in their lives that are "automatic," "user friendly," or "interactive." Explain that the house in the story is fully automated. Ask students to list features they would expect such a house to have.
- Build background before students read, using the Background note on p. 283. Explore with students the possible consequences of a nuclear war. Have students list movies or books they may know describing life after a nuclear war. Then, explain that this story imagines such a future—while sending a message about technology in our lives.

PRETEACH

❸ Literary Analysis

Setting

1. Introduce the skill, using the instruction on the student page.
2. Tell students that they will identify the setting as they read.

Think Aloud: Model the Skill

Model the skill of identifying the setting, using the following "think aloud." Say to students:

> When reading a story, I want to know the setting, which is where and when the story takes place. Description can help me imagine what the setting is like.
>
> Consider this description: "A black cloud of starlings wavered like a mirage in the moist, warm summer sky." This statement appeals to the senses of sight and touch, making the setting vivid and easy to picture. Every setting, whether it is a farm or a big city, shapes the problems that characters face. As I read, I note ways setting influences events.

❹ Using the Strategy

Give students a copy of either **Literary Analysis Graphic Organizer** A or B (*Graphic Organizer Transparencies,* pp. 46–47) to record details of the setting as they read. Use the examples in **Literary Analysis Graphic Organizer A,** which is partially filled in, to model the process of completing the organizer.

❺ Reading Skill

1. Introduce the skill, using the instruction on the student page.
2. Tell students that they will make inferences as they read.

Think Aloud: Model the Skill

Model the skill of making inferences, using the following "think aloud." Say to students:

> Often, when I read, I must use details to infer the setting of a story.
>
> Suppose the author gives details about thick vegetation, exotic birds, and sweltering heat. I can infer from this information that the setting is a tropical place, such as a rain forest or jungle.

❶ Writing About the Big Question

1. Review the assignment with the class.
2. Have students list ways of resolving a quarrel or of defusing a tense situation, such as an argument between friends at a party.
3. Have students complete the sentence starters. Review responses as a class. (**Possible response:** One possible <u>motive</u> for using humor during a quarrel is to ease the tension created by the people quarreling. Forming personal connections with members of the opposing side is an important step toward <u>reconciliation</u> because people who are emotionally close are more likely to compromise.
4. Remind students that their answers will help them think about the Big Question, "Can progress be made without conflict?"

While You Read

Tell students that as they read, they should look for descriptions of the stranger's behavior.

❷ Vocabulary

1. Have students preview the selection vocabulary.
2. For each word, have students say the word aloud.
3. Then, use the word in a sentence that defines the word.
4. Finally, repeat your definitional sentence or a similar sentence with the word missing and have the class "fill in the blank" chorally. Here are some examples:

   To do something <u>nonchalantly</u> is to do it casually or indifferently. Even though he was very nervous, he tried to hide it by acting [students say "nonchalantly"].

   To act <u>audaciously</u> is to act in a bold manner. If a dog openly tries to snatch scraps from the dinner table, it is behaving [students say "audaciously"].

❸ Word Study

1. Introduce the skill, using the instruction in the box.
2. Ask students to think of an *-ity* word that means "lawful power." (**Answer:** authority)

Can progress be made without *conflict?*

❶ Writing About the Big Question

In this selection, the towns of San Juan Iglesias and Hidalgo are in a quarrel. In the midst of the conflict, a mysterious man makes a bold move. Use these sentence starters to develop your ideas about the Big Question:

One possible **motive** for using humor during a quarrel is ______.
Forming personal connections with members of the opposing side is an important step towards **reconciliation** because ______.

While You Read Look for descriptions of the mysterious man's behavior and decide what may motivate his actions.

❷ Vocabulary

Read each word and its definition. Decide whether you know the word well, know it a little bit, or do not know it at all. After you read, see how your knowledge of each word has increased.

- **nonchalantly** (nän′ shə länt′ lē) *adv.* casually; indifferently (p. 274) ***Despite the insult, he shrugged <u>nonchalantly</u>.*** *nonchalance n.*
- **audaciously** (ô dā′ shəs lē) *adv.* in a bold manner (p. 275) ***He is usually so shy, so I was surprised to hear that he had behaved <u>audaciously</u>.*** *audacious adj. audacity n.*
- **imperiously** (im pir′ ē əs lē) *adv.* arrogantly (p. 275) ***She tends to be bossy and give orders <u>imperiously</u>.*** *imperious adj.*
- **disdain** (dis dān′) *n.* a feeling or a show of a lack of respect (p. 276) ***The men treated their captain with <u>disdain</u> by refusing to salute him when he walked by.*** *disdainful adj. disdainfully adv.*
- **plausibility** (plô′ zə bil′ i tē) *n.* believability; seeming truth (p. 276) ***Although his excuse has some <u>plausibility</u>, I just do not believe it.*** *plausible adj. plausibly adv.*
- **apprehension** (ap′ rē hen′ shən) *n.* anxious feeling; fear (p. 280) ***Filled with <u>apprehension</u>, the children slowly approached the abandoned house.*** *apprehensive adj. apprehensively adv.*

❸ Word Study

The **Latin suffix *-ity*** means "the quality of or state of being."

In this story, a man hopes the tone he uses has **plausibility**, or the quality of being believable, so his identity is not revealed.

Vocabulary Development

Vocabulary Knowledge Rating

Create a **Vocabulary Knowledge Rating Chart** ***(Professional Development Guidebook***, p. 33) for this selection. Include the selection vocabulary and the Big Question words that appear in the Writing About the Big Question sentence starters on this page. (The Big Question vocabulary is introduced on pp. 222–223.)

Give students a copy of the chart. Read the words aloud, and have students mark their rating in the Before Reading column. Urge them to be alert to these words as they read and discuss the selection.

Tally how many students think they know a word to gauge how much instruction to provide. As students read and discuss the selection, point out the words and their context.

PHLit Online! **Vocabulary Central**, featuring tools, activities, and songs for studying vocabulary, is available at **www.PHLitOnline.com**

Meet Josephina Niggli

(1910–1983)

Author of The Street of the Cañon

Josephina Niggli was born in Monterrey, Mexico, but she grew up on both sides of the border between Mexico and the United States. When Niggli was fifteen, her parents sent her to San Antonio, Texas, to attend school.

Writing for Stage and Screen Niggli published her first book shortly after her high school graduation. Later, she wrote plays. She found theater thrilling, writing, "Once you have experienced the emotion of having a play produced, you are forever lost to the ordinary world."

Later, Niggli worked on movie scripts in Hollywood. In 1945, she published *Mexican Village*, a collection of ten stories that capture the rich local color of Mexico.

Did You Know?

While still in college, Niggli won several prizes for her writing.

❹ BACKGROUND FOR THE STORY

Courtship and Marriage in Old Mexico

Historically, in some parts of Mexico, a man had to ask a woman's family for permission to marry her. In others, the parents arranged the match. In the town in this story, a man and woman are considered engaged if they walk together in the plaza.

Daily Bellringer

For each class during which you teach this selection, have students complete one of the five Sentence Modeling activities for Week 8 in the ***Daily Bellringer Activities*** booklet.

❹ Background

Courtship and Marriage in Old Mexico

Loyalty to family is highly regarded within the Mexican culture. It is not uncommon for children to live with their parents until they get married, no matter how old they are when they marry. It is not uncommon to find extended family living together in the same house or the same neighborhood.

Multidraft Reading

This icon ● marks natural pauses in the selection. To assist struggling readers and to deepen reading for all, assign the text in "chunks," following the icons, and apply multidraft reading protocols. For each reading, have students set the purpose indicated:

- **First reading**—literal comprehension: answer the Reading Check questions.
- **Second reading**—application of skills: answering the Make Inferences and the Setting prompts.
- **Third reading**—interpretation: answering the end-of-selection questions.

For more guidance, refer to the ***Classroom Strategies and Teaching Routines*** card on multidraft reading.

Differentiated Instruction Additional Instruction

EL Extended Support—English Learners
Have students complete the **Reading and Vocabulary Warm-ups, *Unit 2 Resources*,** pp. 62–65, before they read. Assign the prereading pages and the adapted selection in the ***Reader's Notebook: English Learner's Version***. Then, have students listen to portions of the selection on the ***Hear It!* Audio CD**.

L1 L2 Extended Support—Struggling Readers
Have students complete the **Reading and Vocabulary Warm-ups, *Unit 2 Resources*,** pp. 62–65, before they read. Assign the prereading pages and the adapted selection in the ***Reader's Notebook: Adapted Version***. Then, have students listen to portions of the selection on the ***Hear It!* Audio CD** (adapted text).

Extended Support—Reluctant Readers
To build motivation and engagement before assigning the selection, have students read "Identity Theft," a thematically related selection in ***Reality Central***. Then, use the questions at the conclusion of the related selection to guide discussion.

PHLit Online!
For more about the author, practice with the selection vocabulary, and more background, go online at **www.PHLitOnline.com**

TEACH

❶ Activating Prior Knowledge

Use the **Vocab-o-Gram** strategy (***Professional Development Guidebook***, pp. 39–40) to help students make predictions about selection elements. Put the following words on the board or overhead: *celebrating, mountains, moonlight, dared, jauntily, guitar, lanterns, toast, chaperone, flirt, haters,* and *plaza.*

Then, give students the Vocab-o-Gram chart and have them work with partners or in groups to place the words in appropriate categories and to make predictions about the story. Have students discuss or explain their word placements, their reasons, and their predictions.

Concept Connector ⟶

Students will reexamine their ideas after reading the story.

Individual Activity

As students read, have them create a chart that relates key details to the manner in which they were revealed—through the narrator, dialogue, or a character's thoughts. Students can then present their charts to the class.

❷ About the Selection

In "The Street of the Cañon," a stranger makes his way to Sarita Calderón's eighteenth-birthday celebration, carrying a mysterious package. Through the narrator's comments, conversations between characters, and glimpses into the characters' thoughts, it gradually becomes clear that the stranger is Pepe Gonzalez, a notorious, daring young "devil" from a rival town. What remains intriguingly unclear, however, are Pepe's intentions toward Sarita.

❸ Critical Viewing

Answer: The people are dressed in colorful party clothes. Both dancers and observers seem to be having a good time. The painting also suggests that the setting is Caribbean or Latin American and that the period is before modern times.

❶ ❷ The Street of the Cañon

JOSEPHINA NIGGLI

❸ ▲ **Critical Viewing** What does this painting suggest about the setting of the story? **[Infer]**

It was May, the flowering thorn was sweet in the air, and the village of San Juan Iglesias in the Valley of the Three Marys was celebrating. The long dark streets were empty because all of the people, from the lowest-paid cowboy to the mayor, were helping Don Roméo Calderón celebrate his daughter's eighteenth birthday.

On the other side of the town, where the Cañon Road led across the mountains to the Sabinas Valley, a tall slender man, a package clutched tightly against his side, slipped from shadow to shadow.

Vocabulary Development

Thematic Vocabulary: The Big Question

As students are discussing "The Street of the Cañon," encourage them to use the thematic vocabulary presented in Introducing the Big Question, pp. 222–223. You might encourage them with sentence starters like these:

1. The stranger wants to avoid *confrontation* with residents of San Juan Iglesias because . . .
2. The stranger's *motive* for bringing the package to the party is to . . .
3. The attitudes of the San Juan Iglesias's townspeople toward Hidalgo that the stranger hopes to *change* are . . .
4. The stranger's presence and behavior at the birthday party may be considered *radical* because . . .

Once a dog barked, and the man's black suit merged into the blackness of a wall. But no voice called out, and after a moment he slid into the narrow, dirt-packed street again.

4 The moonlight touched his shoulder and spilled across his narrow hips. He was young, no more than twenty-five, and his black curly head was bare. He walked swiftly along, heading always for the distant sound of guitar and flute. If he met anyone now, who could say from which direction he had come? He might be a trader from Monterrey, or a buyer of cow's milk from farther north in the Valley of the Three Marys. Who would guess that an Hidalgo man dared to walk alone in the moonlit streets of San Juan Iglesias?

5 Carefully adjusting his flat package so that it was not too prominent, he squared his shoulders and walked jauntily across the street to the laughter-filled house. Little boys packed in the doorway made way for him, smiling and nodding to him. The long, narrow room with the orchestra at one end was filled with whirling dancers. Rigid-backed chaperones[1] were gossiping together, seated in their straight chairs against the plaster walls. Over the scene was the yellow glow of kerosene lanterns, and the air was hot with the too-sweet perfume of gardenias, tuberoses,[2] and the pungent scent of close-packed humanity.

The man in the doorway, while trying to appear at ease, was carefully examining every smiling face. If just one person recognized him, the room would turn on him like a den of snarling mountain cats, but so far all the laughter-dancing eyes were friendly.

Suddenly a plump, officious little man, his round cheeks glistening with perspiration, pushed his way through the crowd. His voice, many times too large for his small body, boomed at the man in the doorway. "Welcome, stranger, welcome to our house." Thrusting his arm through the stranger's, and almost dislodging the package, he started to lead the way through the maze of dancers. "Come and drink a toast to my daughter—to my beautiful Sarita. She is eighteen this night."

In the square patio the gentle breeze ruffled the pink and white oleander bushes. A long table set up on sawhorses held loaves of flaky crusted French bread, stacks of thin, delicate tortillas, plates of barbecued beef, and long red rolls of spicy sausages. But most of all there were cheeses, for the Three Marys was a cheese-eating valley. There were yellow cheese and white cheese and curded

1. **chaperones** (shap´ ər ōnz´) older or married women who accompany and supervise the behavior of a young person in public.
2. **gardenias** (gär dēn´ yəz), **tuberoses** (to͞ob´ rōz´ əs) two types of plant with especially sweet-smelling flowers.

Reading Skill
Make Inferences Make an inference about the towns of Hidalgo and San Juan Iglesias. What kinds of details might confirm your inference?

Literary Analysis
Setting To which senses does this description of the setting appeal?

6 **Reading Check**
What occasion is the village of San Juan Iglesias celebrating?

4 Reading Skill
Make Inferences

1. Remind students that making inferences involves using what students know from experience and what they already know from a story to assess what happens, how it happens, and why it happens.
2. Then, **ask** students the Reading Skill question: Make an inference about the towns of Hidalgo and San Juan Iglesias. What kinds of details might confirm your inference?
   Possible response: The two towns are in conflict because the narrator says that it is daring for the man from Hidalgo to walk alone on the streets of San Juan Iglesias. Confirming details would include the man's further efforts to conceal his identity.

5 Literary Analysis
Setting

1. Remind students that setting is the time and place of the action.
2. **Ask:** Does the setting in this case serves as a backdrop for the action or as a crucial element that will influence the outcome of the story.
   Answer: The setting includes the conflict between the two towns. It will play a crucial role.
3. Then, **ask** students the Literary Analysis question: To which senses does this description of the setting appeal?
   Possible responses: Sight: friendly little boys; **Sound:** laughter; **Smell:** kerosene from lanterns; **Touch:** hot air

6 Reading Check

Answer: The village is celebrating the eighteenth birthday of Sarita Calderón.

Differentiated Instruction for Universal Access

Strategy for Special Needs Students
Have students read "The Street of the Cañon" along with the *Hear It!* **Audio CD.** Doing so will help them read the text fluently for comprehension, rather than reading one word at a time.

Enrichment for Advanced Readers
Ask students to analyze Niggli's ability to re-create a region and its culture. Have students evaluate her folk sayings, setting details, food descriptions, and the other ways she re-creates life in a Mexican village. Suggest that students identify how Niggli's language appeals to each of the five senses. Then, challenge students to write sensory descriptions of one of their own family or cultural traditions. Invite students to share their descriptions with the class.

PHLit Online!
This selection is available in interactive format in the **Enriched Online Student Edition, www.PHLitOnline.com,** which includes a thematically related video with writing prompt and an interactive graphic organizer.

❼ Literature in Context

Language Connection Many words in English come directly from Spanish. Spanish words were introduced to American English through three primary sources: the Spanish conquest and the subsequent settling of the American Southwest; Caribbean trade routes; and Spanish and Latin American cuisine. These words include *patio* (Spanish), *fiesta* (Spanish), *canyon* (Spanish), *corral* (Spanish), *bonanza* (Spanish), *vigilante* (Spanish), *macho* (Spanish), *ranch* (Spanish), *barbecue* (Caribbean), *hammock* (Caribbean), *canoe* (Caribbean), *poncho* (Caribbean), *hurricane* (Caribbean), and *potato* (Caribbean).

Connect to the Literature After discussing Spanish words now commonly used in English, ask students the Connect to the Literature question: Why do you think Niggli included these terms in the story? **Possible response:** The use of Spanish terms anchors the story more firmly in a Mexican setting, making it more vivid and realistic.

❼ **LITERATURE IN CONTEXT**

Language Connection

Spanish Vocabulary

Set in Mexico, the story contains several Spanish words and terms, including

- **cañon** canyon; a narrow valley between high cliffs
- **tío** uncle
- **hola** Spanish exclamation meaning "hi"
- **don** title of respect meaning "sir"; often placed before a man's name
- **parada** literally, "parade"; a dance in which partners stride around together

Connect to the Literature

Why do you think Niggli included these terms in the story? **[Hypothesize]**

cheese from cow's milk. There was even a flat white cake of goat cheese from distant Linares, a delicacy too expensive for any but feast days.

To set off this feast were bottles of beer floating in ice-filled tin tubs, and another table was covered with bottles of mescal, of tequila, of maguey wine.

Don Roméo Calderón thrust a glass of tequila into the stranger's hand. "Drink, friend, to the prettiest girl in San Juan. As pretty as my fine fighting cocks, she is. On her wedding day she takes to her man, and may she find him soon, the best fighter in my flock. Drink deep, friend. Even the rivers flow with wine."

The Hidalgo man laughed and raised his glass high. "May the earth be always fertile beneath her feet."

Someone called to Don Roméo that more guests were arriving, and with a final delighted pat on the stranger's shoulder, the little man scurried away. As the young fellow smiled after his retreating host, his eyes caught and held another pair of eyes—laughing black eyes set in a young girl's face. The last time he had seen that face it had been white and tense with rage, and the lips clenched tight to prevent an outgushing stream of angry words. That had been in February, and she had worn a white lace shawl over her hair. Now it was May, and a gardenia was a splash of white in the glossy dark braids. The moonlight had mottled his face that February night, and he knew that she did not recognize him. He grinned impudently[3] back at her, and her eyes widened, then slid sideways to one of the chaperones. The fan in her small hand snapped shut. She tapped its parchment tip against her mouth and slipped away to join the dancing couples in the front room. The gestures of a fan translate into a coded language on the frontier. The stranger raised one eyebrow as he interpreted the signal. ❽

But he did not move toward her at once. Instead, he inched slowly back against the table. No one was behind him, and his hands quickly unfastened the package he had been guarding so long. Then he **nonchalantly** walked into the front room.

The girl was sitting close to a chaperone. As he came up to her he swerved slightly toward the bushy-browed old lady.

"Your servant, señora. I kiss your hands and feet."

The chaperone stared at him in astonishment. Such fine manners were not common to the town of San Juan Iglesias.

"Eh, you're a stranger," she said. "I thought so."

Vocabulary
nonchalantly (nän′ shə länt′ lē) *adv.* casually; indifferently

3. **impudently** (im′ pyo͞o dənt lē) *adv.* in a shamelessly bold or provocative way.

Think Aloud

Make Inferences

Draw students' attention to the sentence, "The stranger raised one eyebrow as he interpreted the signal." Use the following "think aloud" to model the skill of making an inference:

When I read the sentence, I realize it holds an important clue about the stranger's and Sarita's behavior. In the previous sentences, Sarita sees the stranger looking at her and makes a motion with her fan. I do not know what this motion means, but the stranger does, because he raises his eyebrow in acknowledgment of the signal—perhaps he is surprised by it.

The next sentence gives me a clue about what the signal means: "But he did not move toward her at once." The word *but* indicates that although the stranger understands the signal, he did not do the thing the signal indicates, which is to move toward her. I can infer that Sarita is signaling the stranger to approach her. I can also infer from the stranger's reaction that he is being cautious or that he does not want to appear over-eager: He does not approach her at once.

"But a stranger no longer, señora, now that I have met you." He bent over her, so close she could smell the faint fragrance of talcum on his freshly shaven cheek.

"Will you dance the *parada* with me?"

This request startled her eyes into popping open beneath the heavy brows. "So, my young rooster, would you flirt with me, and I old enough to be your grandmother?"

"Can you show me a prettier woman to flirt with in the Valley of the Three Marys?" he asked **audaciously**.

8 She grinned at him and turned toward the girl at her side. "This young fool wants to meet you, my child."

The girl blushed to the roots of her hair and shyly lowered her white lids. The old woman laughed aloud.

"Go out and dance, the two of you. A man clever enough to pat the sheep has a right to play with the lamb."

The next moment they had joined the circle of dancers and Sarita was trying to control her laughter.

"She is the worst dragon in San Juan. And how easily you won her!"

"What is a dragon," he asked **imperiously**, "when I longed to dance with you?"

"Ay," she retorted, "you have a quick tongue. I think you are a dangerous man."

10 In answer he drew her closer to him, and turned her toward the orchestra. As he reached the chief violinist he called out, "Play the Virgencita, 'The Shy Young Maiden.'"

The violinist's mouth opened in soundless surprise. The girl in his arms said sharply, "You heard him, the *Borachita*, 'The Little Drunken Girl.'"

Vocabulary

audaciously (ô dā′ shəs lē) *adv.* in a bold manner

imperiously (im pir′ ē əs lē) *adv.* arrogantly

9 **Reading Check**

Why does the stranger ask the girl's chaperone to dance?

Fluency

Distribute copies of page 275. Have students work in pairs. Direct partners to take turns reading aloud, starting with "This request startled her eyes . . ." and ending with the last paragraph on the page. Have the partner who is listening mark any words or phrases with which the reader has difficulty. Collect and review students' copies. Look for these problem spots:

- If students have difficulty with the word *retorted*, point out that the word has a common prefix *re-*. Explain that it means "to return or go back again." Have students cover up parts of the word with their thumb and sound out each syllable. Then, have them read the sentence again as you check for fluency.
- If students have difficulty with the word *talcum*, remind them to use context clues. Point out the words *smell* and *fragrance*. Instruct students to reread the sentence surrounding the word. Point out that the words *smell* and *fragrance* can help them recognize and understand the word *talcum*. Instruct students to reread the sentence, giving special attention to these word clues.

8 Connecting to the Big Question

1. Remind students that the Unit Big Question suggests that conflict may lead to progress.
2. Have students reread the bracketed passage. **Ask** students to list each of the conflicts indicated in the passage.
   Answer: The stranger's memory of the girl's face "white and tense with rage" suggests that the two of them might have been in conflict in the past. The stranger's request for a dance could have led to conflict with the chaperone if he were not so smooth. The girl's blush suggests an internal conflict between modesty and a wish to dance with the stranger. Her reference to her chaperone as a "dragon" suggests that she resents the chaperone. Her accusation that the stranger has a "quick tongue" suggests a flirtatious conflict.
3. **Ask** students to explain the connections between conflict and romance or flirtation suggested by the passage.
   Possible response: The conflict involving the stranger and the girl in the past might be an obstacle to romance between them, but it might also encourage the stranger to pursue her. The girl's interest in the stranger leads to an internal conflict, shown by her blushing. The stranger's flirtation with the aunt and with the girl causes playful conflicts when they resist his charm.
4. **Ask** students to name examples from movies or literature in which conflict—such as teasing, pretending to be outraged or hurt, and so on—is part of the progress of a romance.
   Possible response: Students may give examples of conflicts between men and women in romantic comedies or situation comedies.
5. Tell students to look for further connections between romance and conflict as they read.

9 Reading Check

Answer: The stranger thinks that he will create a good impression by being polite. He hopes to put her in a good mood by flirting with her. If she is suitably impressed, she may let him dance with her charge.

⑩ Reading Skill
Make Inferences

1. Point out to students the way the author slowly peels back layers of the mystery about the enmity between the two towns.
2. Then, **ask** students to make an inference about why Sarita directs the violinist to play a different song from the one suggested by the mystery man. Then, **ask** them to make an inference about the relationship between the two towns, given her request. What details support the inferences? **Possible response:** It seems as if playing the song from Hidalgo would cause an uproar. Sarita probably wants to avoid an overreaction from the crowd at the party. She pretends that the violinist did not hear the request accurately. The violinist reacts with surprise about the first song suggested and shows relief when he does not have to play it. Students may point out that there are such hard feelings between the two towns that even playing the rival's song could mean trouble.

With a relieved grin, the violinist tapped his music stand with his bow, and the music swung into the sad farewell of a man to his sweetheart:

Farewell, my little drunken one,
I must go to the capital
To serve the master
⑩ *Who makes me weep for my return.*

The stranger frowned down at her. "Is this a joke, señorita?" he asked coldly.

"No," she whispered, looking about her quickly to see if the incident had been observed. "But the Virgencita is the favorite song of Hidalgo, a village on the other side of the mountains in the next valley. The people of Hidalgo and San Juan Iglesias do not speak."

"That is a stupid thing," said the man from Hidalgo as he swung her around in a large turn. "Is not music free as air? Why should one town own the rights to a song?"

The girl shuddered slightly. "Those people from Hidalgo—they are wicked monsters. Can you guess what they did not six months since?"

The man started to point out that the space of time from February to May was three months, but he thought it better not to appear too wise. "Did these Hidalgo monsters frighten you, señorita? If they did, I personally will kill them all."

She moved closer against him and tilted her face until her mouth was close to his ear. "They attempted to steal the bones of Don Rómolo Balderas."

"Is it possible?" He made his eyes grow round and his lips purse up in **disdain.** "Surely not that! Why, all the world knows that Don Rómolo Balderas was the greatest historian in the entire Republic. Every school child reads his books. Wise men from Quintana Roo to the Río Bravo bow their heads in admiration to his name. What a wicked thing to do!" He hoped his virtuous tone was not too virtuous for **plausibility,** but she did not seem to notice.

"It is true! In the night they came. Three devils!"

"Young devils, I hope."

"Young or old, who cares? They were devils. The blacksmith surprised them even as they were opening the grave. He raised such a shout that all of San Juan rushed to his aid, for they were fighting, I can tell you. Especially one of them—their leader."

"And who was he?"

"You have heard of him doubtless. A proper wild one named Pepe Gonzalez."

Vocabulary
disdain (dis dān′) *n.* a feeling or a show of a lack of respect

plausibility (plô′ zə bil′ i tē) *n.* believability; seeming truth

Vocabulary Development

Word Form Chart

Expand students' vocabulary by helping them learn related forms of the selection vocabulary. Give students a blank **Word Forms Chart** (***Professional Development Guidebook***, p. 42), with *nonchalantly, imperiously,* and *plausibility* in their appropriate columns. Work with the class, or have students work with a partner, to determine the related forms. The final chart should look like the one shown.

Noun	Verb	Adjective	Adverb
nonchalance		nonchalant	**nonchalantly**
imperiousness		imperious	**imperiously**
plausibility		plausible	plausibly

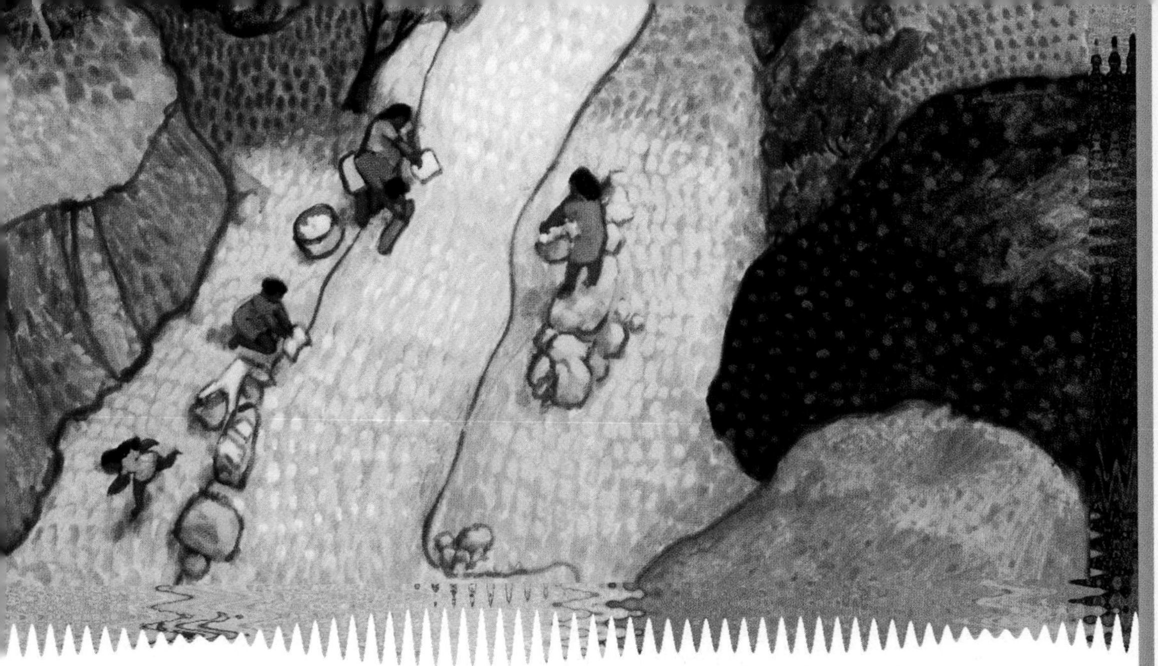

"And what happened to them?"

"They had horses and got away, but one, I think, was hurt."

12 The Hidalgo man twisted his mouth remembering how Rubén the candymaker had ridden across the whitewashed line high on the cañon trail that marked the division between the Three Marys' and the Sabinas' sides of the mountains, and then had fallen in a faint from his saddle because his left arm was broken. There was no candy in Hidalgo for six weeks, and the entire Sabinas Valley resented that broken arm as fiercely as did Rubén.

The stranger tightened his arm in reflexed anger about Sarita's waist as she said, "All the world knows that the men of Hidalgo are sons of the mountain witches."

"But even devils are shy of disturbing the honored dead," he said gravely.

"'Don Rómolo was born in our village,' Hidalgo says. 'His bones belong to us.' Well, anyone in the valley can tell you he died in San Juan Iglesias, and here his bones will stay! Is that not proper? Is that not right?"

To keep from answering, he guided her through an intricate dance pattern that led them past the patio door. Over her head he could see two men and a woman staring with amazement at the open package on the table.

11 ▲ **Critical Viewing**
Compare the mood of this painting with the mood of the story. **[Compare and Contrast]**

Reading Skill
Make Inferences
Make an inference about the stranger's connection to the men who tried to raid the grave.

13 **Reading Check**
What did three men from Hidalgo try to do six months earlier?

11 Critical Viewing

Possible response: The earth tones and the activity depicted (women washing at the river) create a calm feeling unlike the suspense and bitter rivalries of the story.

12 Reading Skill
Make Inferences

1. Remind students that the clues they encounter as they read are the basis of the inferences they make. Overlooking a detail or missing a clue may interfere with making predictions and understanding the story.
2. Then, **ask** students to respond to the Reading Skill prompt: Make an inference about the stranger's connection to the men who tried to raid the grave.
   Possible response: It is becoming increasingly clear that he is closely connected to the men and was probably involved in the grave-raiding incident. He knows too many details about the incident.

13 Reading Check

Answer: The three men attempted to raid the grave of Don Rómolo Balderas, the greatest historian of the Republic, and take his bones back to Hidalgo.

PROFESSIONAL DEVELOPMENT | **Jane Feber**

APPLY THE STRATEGY

After Reading Activity
During the course of "The Street of the Cañon," various characters are developed. The character of the stranger is a mysterious character throughout the story. To assist students understand the stranger and his motives, have students create a character chart with a column describing what he looks like, a column describing how he behaves, and a column describing what others think of him. Have them complete the chart after they read the selection. Encourage students to return to the story to locate details about the stranger.

For more of Jane Feber's strategies, see her Professional Development essay, pp. 222c–222d.

⓮ Reading Skill
Make Inferences

1. Remind students that they can make educated guesses about plot, character, and theme by reviewing details and information they have gleaned from the text.
2. Ask a volunteer to read the passage, and draw students' attention to the sentence, "Realizing that this might be the last moment of peace he would have that evening, he bent toward her."
3. Then, **ask** students to make inferences about why the stranger thinks this is the last moment of peace.
   Possible response: Once the townspeople realize what his package contains, there may be an uproar that will prevent him from talking further with Sarita.

⓯ Literary Analysis
Setting

1. Remind students that setting does not apply just to the physical background of the story. It also covers the time period and the daily manner of living of the characters.
2. Then, **ask** students the Literary Analysis question: How does the time and place of the story affect the way Sarita responds to the stranger?
   Possible response: During the time period, young girls in Mexico did not walk around the plaza with a young man unless they were engaged.

His eyes on the patio, he asked blandly, "You say the leader was one Pepe Gonzalez? The name seems to have a familiar sound."

"But naturally. He has a talent." She tossed her head and stepped away from him as the music stopped. It was a dance of two paradas. He slipped his hand through her arm and guided her into place in the large oval of parading couples. Twice around the room and the orchestra would play again.

"A talent?" he prompted.

"For doing the impossible. When all the world says a thing cannot be done, he does it to prove the world wrong. Why, he climbed to the top of the Prow, and not even the long vanished Joaquín Castillo had ever climbed that mountain before. And this same Pepe caught a mountain lion with nothing to aid him but a rope and his two bare hands."

"He doesn't sound such a bad friend," protested the stranger, slipping his arm around her waist as the music began to play the merry song of the soap bubbles:

Pretty bubbles of a thousand colors
That ride on the wind
And break as swiftly
As a lover's heart.

The events in the patio were claiming his attention. Little by little he edged her closer to the door. The group at the table had considerably enlarged. There was a low murmur of excitement from the crowd.

"What has happened?" asked Sarita, attracted by the noise.

⓮ "There seems to be something wrong at the table," he answered, while trying to peer over the heads of the people in front of him. Realizing that this might be the last moment of peace he would have that evening, he bent toward her.

"If I come back on Sunday, will you walk around the plaza with me?"

She was startled into exclaiming, "Ay, no!"

"Please. Just once around."

Literary Analysis ⓯
Setting How does the time and place of the story affect the way Sarita responds to the stranger?

"And you think I'd walk more than once with you, señor, even if you were no stranger? In San Juan Iglesias, to walk around the plaza with a girl means a wedding."

"Ha, and you think that is common to San Juan alone? Even the devils of Hidalgo respect that law," he added hastily at her puzzled upward glance. "And so they do in all the villages." To cover his lapse[4] he said softly, "I don't even know your name."

4. **lapse** (laps) *n.* slip; error.

Vocabulary Development

Vocabulary Knowledge Rating

When students have completed reading and discussing "The Street of the Cañon," have them take out their **Vocabulary Knowledge Rating Chart** for this selection. Read the words aloud once more and have students rate their knowledge of the words again in the After Reading column. Clarify any words that are still problematic. Have students write their own definition and example or sentence in the appropriate column. Then have students complete the Vocabulary Practice at the end of the selection. Encourage students to use the words in further discussion and written work about this selection. Remind them that they will be accountable for these words on the **Selection Test, *Unit 2 Resources,*** pp. 74–76 or 77–79.

A mischievous grin crinkled the corners of her eyes. "Nor do I know yours, señor. Strangers do not often walk the streets of San Juan."

Before he could answer, the chattering in the patio swelled to louder proportions. Don Roméo's voice lay on top, like thick cream on milk. "I tell you it is a jewel of a cheese. Such flavor, such texture, such whiteness. It is a jewel of a cheese."

"What has happened?" Sarita asked of a woman at her elbow.

"A fine goat's cheese appeared as if by magic on the table. No one knows where it came from."

"Probably an extra one from Linares," snorted a fat bald man on the right.

"Linares never made such a cheese as this," said the woman decisively.

"Silence!" roared Don Roméo. "Old Tío Daniel would speak a word to us."

A great hand of silence closed down over the mouths of the people. The girl was standing on tiptoe trying vainly to see what was happening. She was hardly aware of the stranger's whispering voice although she remembered the words that he said. "Sunday night—once around the plaza."

She did not realize that he had moved away, leaving a gap that was quickly filled by the blacksmith.

Old Tío Daniel's voice was a shrill squeak, and his thin, stringy neck jutted forth from his body like a turtle's from its shell. "This is no cheese from Linares," he said with authority, his mouth sucking in over his toothless gums between his sentences. "Years ago, when the great Don Rómolo Balderas was still alive, we had such cheese as this—ay, in those days we had it. But after he died and was buried in our own sainted ground, as was right and proper . . ."

"Yes, yes," muttered voices in the crowd. He glared at the interruption. As soon as there was silence again, he continued:

"After he died, we had it no more. Shall I tell you why?"

"Tell us, Tío Daniel," said the voices humbly.

"Because it is made in Hidalgo!"

The sound of a waterfall, the sound of a wind in a narrow cañon, and the sound of an angry crowd are much the same. There were no distinct words, but the sound was enough.

"Are you certain, Tío?" boomed Don Roméo.

18 "As certain as I am that a donkey has long ears. The people of Hidalgo have been famous for generations for making cheese like

16

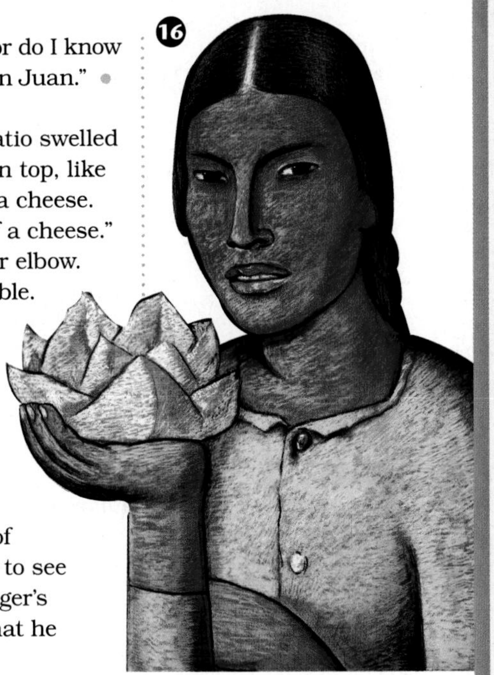

17 **Reading Check**

What has appeared on the table on the patio?

16 Humanities

Reina Xochtl (gouache on newspaper) by Alfredo Ramos Martinez (1872–1946)

Alfredo Ramos Martinez's artistic talent was realized early when, at age nine, he painted a portrait of a Mexican government official for a competition—and won first prize. Martinez went on to receive formal training in art at an academy in Mexico City; Martinez, however, found established techniques and subjects tedious and preferred to paint scenes from ordinary life. Martinez's medium, interestingly enough, was not canvas or plaster or clay but newspaper, which offered Martinez a unique texture on which to paint.

Martinez painted the subjects he loved: the varied Mexican landscape, poignant portraits of his fellow native people, both subjects of which he infused with religious themes. Use the following question for discussion:

In what ways does this painting reflect the events and mood of "The Streets of the Cañon?"

Possible response: The painting conveys the mood of mysteriousness, much like the stranger and Sarita do, who, at this point in the story, seems to know the stranger's identity, revealing this knowledge with a "mischievous grin [crinkling] the corners of her eyes." The woman in the painting, who could very well be Sarita, holds in her hand a beautiful object such as a flower or a "jewel of a cheese."

Concept Connector

Have students return to the **Vocab-o-Gram** they completed prior to reading the story. Review the words with them and clarify any word meanings by returning to the selection or using a dictionary. Then, have students determine whether their predictions about the story were accurate.

Writing About the Big Question

Have students compare their responses to the sentence starters they completed before reading the essay with their ideas afterwards. Ask them to explain whether their thoughts have changed.

Literary Analysis Graphic Organizer

Ask students to review the graphic organizer they completed with their inferences about setting. Show them the partially completed **Literary Analysis Graphic Organizer A** (*Graphic Organizer Transparencies,* p. 45) as an example. Then, have students share the graphic organizers they did and the inferences they made.

⓲ Reading Skill
Make Inferences

Read the passage aloud to students. Then, **ask** students the Reading Skill question: Do details here support your inference about the stranger's link with Hidalgo? Explain.
Possible response: Most students will confirm that the details support the inference that the stranger is from Hidalgo and was part of the grave-raiding group.

▶**Monitor Progress** Tell students to refer to their original inferences and share them with the class. Then, lead a discussion about how their inferences changed as they read.

▶**Reteach** If students have difficulty putting together the clues about the stranger's identity, have them make lists of the clues, such as the fact that the townspeople have not had this great goat cheese since Don Rómolo Balderas died, that the only place cheese of this quality is made is in Hidalgo, that the only way the cheese could have gotten to San Juan Iglesias is by the stranger.

ASSESS

Answers

Critical Thinking

1. **Possible response:** Students may want to read other stories in this colorful setting.
2. (a) **Possible response:** The man's *black* suit merges into the blackness of a wall. (b) The stranger does not want the townspeople to know who he is or where he comes from.
3. (a) He asks Sarita's chaperone. (b) He hopes that by flattering the chaperone he will get to dance with Sarita.
4. (a) The towns of San Juan Iglesias and Hidalgo quarrel over the bones of a famous historian. (b) **Possible response:** The villagers might have fought with the stranger if they had realized who he was.

Can progress be made without conflict?

The stranger may see the festivities as an opportunity to prove himself as a threat to his enemies and to romance Sarita. Students may point out that the conflict Pepe risks will contribute to the "progress," or growth, of his legend.

Reading Skill
Make Inferences Do details here support your inference about the stranger's link with Hidalgo? Explain. ⓲

this—especially that wicked one, that owner of a cheese factory, Timotéo Gonzalez, father to Pepe, the wild one, whom we have good cause to remember."

"We do, we do," came the sigh of assurance.

"But on the whole northern frontier there are no vats like his to produce so fine a product. Ask the people of Chihuahua, of Sonora. Ask the man on the bridge at Laredo, or the man in his boat at Tampico, 'Hola, friend, who makes the finest goat cheese?' And the answer will always be the same, 'Don Timotéo of Hidalgo.'"

It was the blacksmith who asked the great question. "Then where did that cheese come from, and we haters of Hidalgo these ten long years?"

No voice said, "The stranger," but with one fluid movement every head in the patio turned toward the girl in the doorway. She also turned, her eyes wide with something that she realized to her own amazement was more **apprehension** than anger.

Vocabulary
apprehension (ap′ rē hen′ shən) *n.* anxious feeling; fear

But the stranger was not in the room. When the angry, muttering men pushed through to the street, the stranger was not on the plaza. He was not anywhere in sight. A few of the more religious crossed themselves for fear that the Devil had walked in their midst. "Who was he?" one voice asked another. But Sarita, who was meekly listening to a lecture from Don Roméo on the propriety of dancing with strangers, did not have to ask. She had a strong suspicion that she had danced that night within the circling arm of Pepe Gonzalez.

Critical Thinking

1. **Respond:** Would you like to read some of the other stories in Niggli's book *Mexican Village*? Why or why not?
2. **(a)** What adjectives does the author use to describe the way the Hidalgo man walks into the village? **(b) Infer:** What does the man wish to prevent others from learning?
3. **(a)** Whom does the Hidalgo man first ask to dance? **(b) Infer:** Why does he ask her?
4. **(a) Summarize:** Why are the towns quarreling? **(b) Hypothesize:** What might the villagers have done to the stranger if they had known his identity? Support your answer.

Can progress be made without conflict?
Why does the stranger risk danger to dance with Sarita and leave the gift? Explain your answer using details from the story.

Assessment Resources

Unit 2 Resources

L1 L2 EL **Selection Test A**, pp. 74–76. Administer Test A to less advanced readers and English Learners.

L3 L4 **Selection Test B**, pp. 77–79. Administer Test B to on-level and more advanced students.

L3 L4 **Open-Book Test**, pp. 71–73. As an alternative, give the Open-Book Test.

All **Customizable Test Bank**

All **Self-tests**
Students may prepare for the **Selection Test** by taking the **Self-test** online.

PHLit Online! All assessment resources are available at **www.PHLitOnline.com**

After You Read — The Street of the Cañon

Literary Analysis: Setting

1. **(a)** Identify these aspects of the **setting** in "The Street of the Cañon": the country, the town, and the historical period in which the action occurs. **(b)** For each aspect, give an example of a **description** that helps make the setting vivid for readers.
2. Explain why the specific dangers the man from Hidalgo faces might not apply in a story set in a different town or historic time period.

Reading Skill: Make Inferences

3. **(a)** Based on the information in the first three paragraphs of the story, what two **inferences** could you make about the stranger's plans? **(b)** For each inference, note at least one detail later in the story that either proves it or disproves it. Record your answers in a chart like the one shown.

Inference	Confirming Details	Disproving Details

4. Make an inference concerning Sarita's feelings about the stranger at the end of the story. Give three details to support your response.

Vocabulary

Practice Match each statement with a word from the vocabulary list for "The Street of the Cañon" on page 270. Explain each choice.

1. Some say that a good story should have this quality.
2. A conceited individual might act in this way.
3. A nervous person may have difficulty behaving this way.
4. People with many fears often feel a sense of this.
5. A captain who treats his officers with this attitude would be disliked.
6. Extreme situations call for people to act in this way.

Word Study Use the context of the sentences and what you know about the **Latin suffix *-ity*** to explain your answer to each question.

1. Could you read a letter that lacked *legibility*?
2. Is a movie that is known for its *complexity* easy to understand?

Word Study

The **Latin suffix *-ity*** means "the quality of or state of being."

Challenge Explain how the suffix *-ity* contributes to the meanings of these words. Consult a dictionary if necessary.

accessibility
activity
responsibility

ASSESS/EXTEND

Answers

Literary Analysis

1. (a) and (b)The story takes place in a locale characterized by Hispanic names (Valley of the Three Marys, Cañon Road, Sabinas Valley); the setting may be Mexico. The story also takes place in a small village. The time period is before the modern era, shown by the fact that a chaperone figures prominently in the action and girls can only walk around the plaza with the men whom they are going to marry.
2. In a modern setting, the man would be protected by law enforcement if he went to a strange town; rivalries between towns would be regulated by higher authorities.

Reading Skill

3. (a) The stranger intends to create some mischief in a rival town. He will use his package in this mission. (b) He leaves his package on the food table, which causes an uproar when it is discovered to be the signature cheese of Hidalgo—a sign that a Hidalgo man was able to fool all the townspeople.

   For other sample answers, see ***Graphic Organizer Transparencies*, Reading Skill Graphic Organizer A**, p. 48, and the **Additional Answers** section.
4. **Possible response:** Sarita seems as interested in the stranger as he is in her. She shows that she is adventurous by dancing and flirting with him. She "rescues" him by preventing the violinist from playing the song he names.

Vocabulary

Practice

Sample answers:

1. *Plausibility:* If a story was not believable, it would not entertain.
2. *Imperiously:* A conceited person is likely to be arrogant.
3. *Nonchalantly:* A nervous person would be too uncomfortable to act casually or indifferently.
4. *Apprehension:* A person with many fears is likely to feel anxious.

Answers continued

5. *Disdain:* A captain who did not respect his officers would be disliked by them.
6. *Audaciously:* Extreme situations require people to act boldly and without apprehension.

Word Study

Sample answers:

1. No, the suffix *-ity* means "the quality of being," so *legibility* means "the quality of being readable." A letter lacking legibility cannot be read.
2. No, the suffix *-ity* means "the quality of being," so *complexity* means "the quality of being complex." A complex movie would be difficult to understand.

Word Study: Challenge

Sample answers: *Accessibility* is the quality of being accessible. *Activity* is the quality of being active. *Responsibility* is the quality of being responsible.

PRETEACH

Skills instruction for the ***Reading Skill*** *and* ***Literary Analysis*** *concept appears on p. 269.*

1 Writing About the Big Question

1. Review the assignment with the class.
2. Have students list three benefits of technology. Then, have them list three drawbacks. (**Possible response:** Convenience, medical progress, and efficient communication are advantages. Pollution, social withdrawal, and loss of self-reliance are drawbacks.)
3. Have students complete the sentence starters. Review responses as a class. (**Possible responses:** A benefit of technological progress is increased efficiency and convenience in everyday living. A possible downside of new technology is an overreliance on actions or services that can easily be performed by humans.)

While You Read

Tell students that as they read, they should notice what technology allows the house to do.

2 Vocabulary

1. Have students preview the selection vocabulary.
2. For each word, have students say the word aloud.
3. Then, use the word in a sentence that defines the word.
4. Finally, repeat your definitional sentence or a similar sentence with the word missing, and have the class "fill in the blank" chorally. Here are some examples:

   Something titanic is powerful or of great size. If a ship carries a thousand passengers and has a swimming pool on board, its size is [students say "titanic"].

3 Word Study

1. Introduce the skill, using the instruction in the box.
2. Have students explain how the suffix contributes to the meaning of these words: *sarcastic, sonic,* and *atomic.* (**Answer:** having the quality of sarcasm; pertaining to sound; pertaining to the atom)

Making Connections | There Will Come Soft Rains

Can progress be made without conflict?

1 Writing About the Big Question

In this story, the human race has achieved a high level of technology, but at a terrible cost. Use these sentence starters to develop your ideas about the Big Question:

A benefit of technological **progress** is ______.

A possible downside of new technology is ______.

While You Read Notice what technology allows the house to do during the course of one day. Then, determine if these advances are positive or negative.

2 Vocabulary

Read each word and its definition. Decide whether you know the word well, know it a little bit, or do not know it at all. After you read, see how your knowledge of each word has increased.

- **titanic** (tī tan′ ik) *adj.* powerful; of great size (p. 287) ***A single titanic wave sank the ship.*** *titan n.*
- **paranoia** (par′ ə noi′ ə) *n.* mental disorder characterized by delusions (p. 287) ***His irrational fear of crowded places could be a sign of paranoia.*** *paranoid adj.*
- **fluttered** (flut′ ərd) *v.* flapped or vibrated rapidly (p. 288) ***The papers fluttered in the wind and then blew away.*** *flutter n.*
- **manipulated** (mə nip′ yo͞o lāt′ id) *v.* managed or controlled through clever moves (p. 288) ***The sculptor molded and manipulated the clay into different shapes.*** *manipulative adj. manipulation n.*
- **tremulous** (trem′ yo͞o ləs) *adj.* trembling; quivering; timid; fearful (p. 289) ***The cup shook in his tremulous hands.*** *tremulously adv.*
- **oblivious** (ə bliv′ ē əs) *adj.* unaware (p. 291) ***Oblivious to the shark that was quickly approaching, the turtle swam peacefully.*** *oblivion n. obliviously adv.*

3 Word Study

The **Greek suffix *-ic*** means "having the characteristic of" or "pertaining to."

In this story, an event of **titanic** proportions, pertaining to giant consequences, has occurred.

Vocabulary Development

Vocabulary Knowledge Rating

Create a **Vocabulary Knowledge Rating Chart** (***Professional Development Guidebook***, p. 33) for this selection. Include the selection vocabulary and the Big Question word that appears in the Writing About the Big Question sentence starters on this page. (The Big Question vocabulary is introduced on pp. 222–223.)

Give students a copy of the chart. Read the words aloud, and have students mark their rating in the Before Reading column. Urge them to be alert to these words as they read and discuss the selection.

Tally how many students think they know a word to gauge how much instruction to provide. As students read and discuss the selection, point out the words and their context.

PHLit Online! **Vocabulary Central,** featuring tools, activities, and songs for studying vocabulary, is available online at **www.PHLitOnline.com.**

Meet Ray Bradbury (b. 1920)

Author of There Will Come Soft Rains

Ray Bradbury, one of the world's most celebrated science-fiction and fantasy writers, was born in Waukegan, Illinois, and grew up near Lake Michigan. As a child, he was influenced by the stories of Edgar Allan Poe and developed a fascination with horror movies and futuristic fantasy.

Dreaming the Impossible Bradbury considers most of his work fantasy rather than science fiction, explaining, "Science fiction is the art of the possible. Fantasy is the art of the impossible." One of his dreams remains an impossible fantasy, at least for now—he wants to go to Mars. "But since it's not going to happen," he explains, "I don't worry about it."

Did You Know?

In 2002, Bradbury was commemorated with a star on the Hollywood Walk of Fame.

4 BACKGROUND FOR THE STORY

The Atomic Age

Ray Bradbury published this story in 1950. Five years earlier, the United States had dropped the first atomic bombs on Japan. One year before the story was published, the Soviet Union had tested its own atomic device. This story reflects the fear at that time that these rival nations might unleash their deadly technology and destroy humanity.

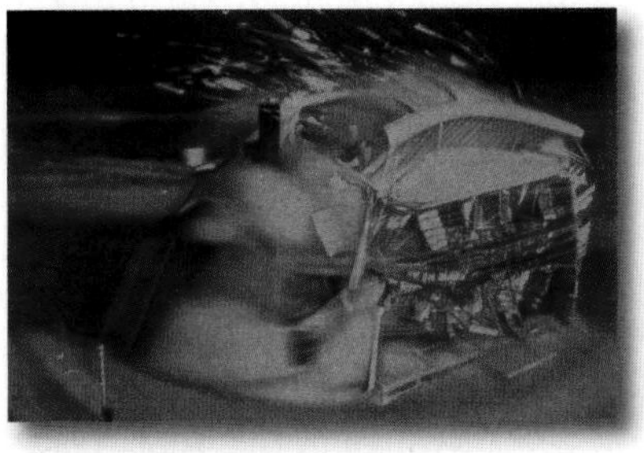

Daily Bellringer

For each class during which you will teach this selection, have students complete one of the five Sentence Modeling activities for Week 8 in the ***Daily Bellringer Activities*** booklet.

4 Background

The Atomic Age

Although the United States emerged from World War II victorious and powerful, it was not long before the Soviet Union developed its own stockpile of atomic bombs. The use of the first nuclear weapons at Hiroshima and Nagasaki initiated the Atomic Age, Cold War, and decades of fear.

Multidraft Reading

This icon ● marks natural pauses in the selection. To assist struggling readers and to deepen reading for all, assign the text in "chunks," following the icons, and apply multidraft reading protocols. For each reading, have students set the purpose indicated:

- **First reading**—literal comprehension: answering the Reading Check questions.
- **Second reading**—application of skills: answering the Make Inferences and Setting prompts.
- **Third reading**—interpretation: answering the end-of-selection questions.

For more guidance, refer to the ***Classroom Strategies and Teaching Routines*** card on multidraft reading.

Differentiated Instruction Additional Instruction

EL Extended Support—English Learners
Have students complete the **Reading and Vocabulary Warm-ups, *Unit 2 Resources,*** pp. 80–83, before they read. Assign the prereading pages for the selection in the ***Reader's Notebook: English Learner's Version.*** Then, have students listen to portions of the selection on the ***Hear It!* Audio CD.**

L1 L2 Extended Support—Struggling Readers
Have students complete the **Reading and Vocabulary Warm-ups, *Unit 2 Resources,*** pp. 80–83, before they read. Assign the prereading pages in the ***Reader's Notebook: Adapted Version.*** Then, have students listen to portions of the selection on the ***Hear It!* Audio CD** (adapted text).

Extended Support—Reluctant Readers
To build motivation and engagement before assigning the selection, have students read "Tracking Teen Drivers," a thematically related selection in ***Reality Central.*** Then, use the questions at the conclusion of the related selection to guide discussion.

PHLit Online!

For more about the author, practice with the selection vocabulary, or more background, go online at **www.PHLitOnline.com.**

❶ Activating Prior Knowledge

Use the **Vocab-o-Gram** strategy (***Professional Development Guidebook***, pp. 39–40) to help students make predictions about selection elements. Put the following words and phrases on the board or overhead: *tick, tock, seven o'clock, electric eyes, house, password, dog, nursery, fire, ritual,* and *paranoia.* Then give students the Vocab-o-Gram chart and have them work with partners or in groups to place the words in appropriate categories and to make predictions about the story.

Concept Connector →

Students will reexamine their ideas after reading the story.

Small-Group Activity

Ask students to work in small groups to design a futuristic dream house in which technology takes over many of the jobs typically done by family members. Once students have read "There Will Come Soft Rains," have them compare their designs to the house in the story.

❷ About the Selection

With no human characters, "There Will Come Soft Rains" is an ironic reflection on the strengths and weaknesses of human nature. It is also a warning about the limits and dangers of technology. The same technical wizardry that enables people of the future to create a fully automated house is also responsible for the creation of nuclear weapons that destroy the human race.

❶ ❷ There Will Come Soft Rains

Ray Bradbury

The Body of a House, #1 of 8. © Robert Beckmann 1993. Collection: Nevada Museum of Art, Reno.

In the living room the voice-clock sang, Tick-tock, seven o'clock, time to get up, time to get up, seven o'clock! as if it were afraid that nobody would. The morning house lay empty. The clock ticked on, repeating and repeating its sounds into the emptiness. *Seven-nine, breakfast time, seven-nine*!

In the kitchen the breakfast stove gave a hissing sigh and ejected from its warm interior eight pieces of perfectly browned toast, eight eggs sunnyside up, sixteen slices of bacon, two coffees, and two cool glasses of milk.

"Today is August 4, 2026," said a second voice from the kitchen ceiling, "in the city of Allendale, California." It repeated the date three times for memory's sake. "Today is Mr. Featherstone's birthday. Today is the anniversary of Tilita's marriage. Insurance is payable, as are the water, gas, and light bills."

Somewhere in the walls, relays clicked, memory tapes glided under electric eyes.

Eight-one, tick-tock, eight-one o'clock, off to school, off to work, run, run, eight one! But no doors slammed, no carpets took the soft tread of rubber heels. It was raining outside.

Vocabulary Development

Thematic Vocabulary: The Big Question

As students are discussing "There Will Come Soft Rains," encourage them to use the thematic vocabulary presented in Introducing the Big Question, pp. 222–223. You might encourage them with sentence starters like these:

1. One might not consider the house and its functions an example of *progress*, because . . .
2. Signs that the dog has faced much *adversity* are . . .
3. Throughout the day, things in the house *change*, such as . . .
4. It is ironic that the house must *struggle* to put out the fire, because . . .

❸ ◀ **Critical Viewing**
What does this painting suggest about the mood of the story? **[Predict]**

❹

❸ Critical Viewing

Answer: The red glow of the painting suggests an ominous mood; the house appears to be completely isolated.

❹ Humanities

***The Body of a House,* #1 of 8,** by Robert Beckmann

This painting is the first in a series of eight large oil paintings depicting the successive stages of destruction of a house during a nuclear explosion. (Paintings 2, 4, and 5 are on pp. 286, 289, and 291, respectively.) The paintings are based on actual film footage shot during a test of a nuclear weapon in Nevada in 1953. The original paintings are 8 feet long and nearly 6 feet high. Use the following question for discussion:

What effect might the size and style of the original paintings have?
Possible response: The monumental size and stark realism of the paintings dramatize the destructiveness of a nuclear explosion.

Differentiated Instruction for Universal Access

Strategy for Special Needs Students
To help students understand the unfamiliar elements of the story's setting, have them draw a picture of the house and the yard. Make sure they include details from the story, such as the breakfast stove and the silhouettes on the house's charred walls.

Strategy for Less Proficient Readers
As they read, have students make a list of the unfamiliar elements of the setting, such as the voice-clock and the breakfast stove. Discuss each element with students to make sure they understand its function.

PHLit Online!

This selection is available in interactive format in the **Enriched Online Student Edition, www.PHLitOnline.com**, which includes a thematically related video with writing prompt and an interactive graphic organizer.

❺ Critical Viewing

Answer: The house in the story is still functioning properly even though its inhabitants are not there to receive its services. In contrast, the house in the painting has begun to burn. In both the story and the painting, the house is the only thing left standing in a desolate landscape.

❻ Reading Skill

Make Inferences

1. Remind students that authors rarely state directly everything that readers need to understand in a piece of literature. Instead, they expect readers to read between the lines and think critically.
2. Tell students that a good way to make inferences is by asking themselves *how* and *why* questions as they read.
3. Then, **ask** students the Reading Skill question: Make an inference about the inhabitants of the house. What kinds of confirming details will you look for as you read on?
   Possible response: The inhabitants seem to have disappeared. They appear to have been people who were well-off, living a typical or ordinary lifestyle. I will look for details that might explain what happened to them.

The Body of a House, #2 of 8. © Robert Be
Nevada Museum of Art

❺ ▶ **Critical Viewing** Compare and contrast the house in this painting with the house at this point in the story. **[Compare and Contrast]**

❻ **Reading Skill**
Make Inferences
Make an inference about the inhabitants of the house. What kinds of confirming details will you look for as you read on?

The weather box
on the front door sang quietly: "Rain, rain,
go away; rubbers, raincoats for today . . ." And the rain tapped on the empty house, echoing.

Outside, the garage chimed and lifted its door to reveal the waiting car. After a long wait the door swung down again.

At eight-thirty the eggs were shriveled and the toast was like stone. An aluminum wedge scraped them into the sink, where hot water whirled them down a metal throat which digested and flushed them away to the distant sea. The dirty dishes were dropped into a hot washer and emerged twinkling dry.

Nine-fifteen, sang the clock, *time to clean*.

Out of warrens in the wall, tiny robot mice darted. The rooms were acrawl with the small cleaning animals, all rubber and metal. They thudded against chairs, whirling their mustached runners, kneading the rug nap, sucking gently at hidden dust. Then, like mysterious invaders, they popped into their burrows. Their pink electric eyes faded. The house was clean.

Ten o'clock. The sun came out from behind the rain. The house stood alone in a city of rubble and ashes. This was the one house left standing. At night the ruined city gave off a radioactive glow which could be seen for miles.

Ten-fifteen. The garden sprinklers whirled up in golden founts, filling the soft morning air with scatterings of brightness. The

Think Aloud

Vocabulary: Using Context

Direct students' attention to the word *warrens* on this page. Using the following "think aloud," model how to use context to infer the meaning of an unknown word.

In this sentence, *warrens* is being used to describe places in the walls from which the robot mice come. I know that walls are often divided into sections by wooden boards to form a foundation for wallboard. I also know that these sections of walls are often crowded with electrical wiring and plumbing. I think, therefore, that the robot mice live in these small, crowded sections within the walls. Since the mice return to these places when they are through cleaning, I can conclude that *warrens* is a synonym for *burrows*, a word that appears several sentences later.

water pelted windowpanes, running down the charred west side where the house had been burned evenly free of its white paint. The entire west face of the house was black, save for five places. Here the silhouette[1] in paint of a man mowing a lawn. Here, as in a photograph, a woman bent to pick flowers. Still farther over, their images burned on wood in one **titanic** instant, a small boy, hands flung into the air; higher up, the image of a thrown ball, and opposite him a girl, hands raised to catch a ball which never came down.

The five spots of paint—the man, the woman, the children, the ball—remained. The rest was a thin charcoaled layer.

The gentle-sprinkler rain filled the garden with falling light.

8 Until this day, how well the house had kept its peace. How carefully it had inquired, "Who goes there? What's the password?" and, getting no answer from lonely foxes and whining cats, it had shut up its windows and drawn shades in an old-maidenly preoccupation with self-protection which bordered on a mechanical **paranoia**.

It quivered at each sound, the house did. If a sparrow brushed a window, the shade snapped up. The bird, startled, flew off! No, not even a bird must touch the house!

The house was an altar with ten thousand attendants, big, small, servicing, attending, in choirs. But the gods had gone away, and the ritual of the religion continued senselessly, uselessly.

Twelve noon.

A dog whined, shivering, on the front porch.

The front door recognized the dog voice and opened. The dog, once huge and fleshy, but now gone to bone and covered with sores, moved in and through the house, tracking mud. Behind it whirred angry mice, angry at having to pick up mud, angry at inconvenience.

For not a leaf fragment blew under the door but what the wall panels flipped open and the copper scrap rats flashed swiftly out. The offending dust, hair, or paper, seized in miniature steel jaws, was raced back to the burrows. There, down tubes which fed into the cellar, it was dropped into the sighing vent of an incinerator which sat like evil Baal[2] in a dark corner.

The dog ran upstairs, hysterically yelping to each door, at last realizing, as the house realized, that only silence was here.

It sniffed the air and scratched the kitchen door. Behind the door, the stove was making pancakes which filled the house with a rich baked odor and the scent of maple syrup.

1. **silhouette** (sil′ ə wet′) *n.* outline of a figure, filled in with a solid color.
2. **Baal** (bā′ əl) *n.* ancient Near Eastern deity, later associated with evil.

Vocabulary
titanic (tī tan′ ik) *adj.* powerful; of great size

Literary Analysis
Setting What new information have you learned about the setting of the story?

Vocabulary
paranoia (par′ ə noi′ ə) *n.* mental disorder characterized by delusions

9 **Reading Check**
What has happened to the rest of the city?

7 Connecting to the Big Question

1. Remind students that, although people often view conflict negatively, conflict has the ability to create opportunities for progress.
2. Have students read the bracketed passage. **Ask** students: What does technology allow the house to do during the course of the day?
   Answer: Technology allows the house to attend to its occupants' needs. Technology also allows the house to protect itself and its inhabitants from intruders and stray animals.
3. **Ask** students to determine if the house's technology is an example of progress, having them explain why or why not.
   Possible response: In the past of the story, humans used technology to make their lives easier and convenient, which can be considered progress. However, technology in the form of a nuclear bomb caused the humans' demise.
4. Have students explain how progress in the story appears to involve a conflict.
   Possible response: The story dramatizes the conflict between the helpful and the harmful aspects of technology.

8 Literary Analysis
Setting

1. Remind students that the term *setting* applies to all the emotional, political, moral, technological, and psychological aspects of a place and a time, not merely the physical characteristics.
2. Then, **ask** students the Literary Analysis question: What new information have you learned about the setting of the story?
   Answer: Animals are still alive even though people are not. The family dog has not been fed for quite a while. The house has taken on a defensive "attitude."

9 Reading Check

Answer: Other than the house, the rest of the city has been destroyed, probably by an atomic bomb.

Differentiated Instruction for Universal Access

EL Pronunciation for English Learners

Some students might have difficulty pronouncing words with the short "i" sound, as in *its*, *pick*, and *did* on this page, replacing it with the "ee" sound. The following strategies can help students to pronounce the short "i" sound.

- Write the words *its/eats*, *pick/peek*, and *did/deed* on the board. Explain the meaning of each word. Then, pronounce each word in turn, having students repeat each. Next, call out the words at random, having student volunteers circle the called words on the board. Discuss the results with the class, noting what might have led to incorrect choices.
- Then, call out the words and have students write out each one. Have students compare and discuss results, noting what might have led to any discrepancies in their spellings.

❿ Literary Analysis
Setting

1. Ask a volunteer to read aloud the bracketed passage.
2. Have students comment on what is happening, such as the card party in the garden and the jungle scene in the nursery to amuse the children.
3. Then, **ask** students the Literary Analysis question: How does this description show that the story is set in a time different from the present?
   Answer: The house has futuristic technological devices that allow it to perform unusual functions, such as setting up a card party and creating "living" art on the walls of the nursery.

The dog frothed at the mouth, lying at the door, sniffing, its eyes turned to fire. It ran wildly in circles, biting at its tail, spun in a frenzy, and died. It lay in the parlor for an hour.

Two o'clock, sang a voice.

Delicately sensing decay at last, the regiments of mice hummed out as softly as blown gray leaves in an electrical wind.

Two-fifteen.

The dog was gone.

In the cellar, the incinerator glowed suddenly and a whirl of sparks leaped up the chimney.

Two thirty-five.

Vocabulary
fluttered (flut′ ərd) *v.* flapped or vibrated rapidly

Bridge tables sprouted from patio walls. Playing cards **fluttered** onto pads in a shower of pips. Glasses manifested on an oaken bench with egg-salad sandwiches. Music played.

But the tables were silent and the cards untouched.

At four o'clock the tables folded like great butterflies back through the paneled walls.

Four-thirty.

The nursery walls glowed.

❿ Animals took shape: yellow giraffes, blue lions, pink antelopes, lilac panthers cavorting in crystal substance. The walls were glass. They looked out upon color and fantasy. Hidden films clocked through well-oiled sprockets, and the walls lived. The nursery floor was woven to resemble a crisp, cereal meadow. Over this ran aluminum roaches and iron crickets, and in the hot still air butterflies of delicate red tissue wavered among the sharp aroma of animal spoors![3] There was the sound like a great matted yellow hive of bees within a dark bellows, the lazy bumble of a purring lion. And there was the patter of okapi[4] feet and the murmur of a fresh jungle rain, like other hoofs, falling upon the summer-starched grass. Now the walls dissolved into distances of parched weed, mile on mile, and warm endless sky. The animals drew away into thorn brakes and water holes.

Literary Analysis
Setting How does this description show that the story is set in a time different from the present?

It was the children's hour.

Five o'clock. The bath filled with clear hot water.

Vocabulary
manipulated (mə nip′ yo͞o lāt′ id) *v.* managed or controlled through clever moves

Six, seven, eight o'clock. The dinner dishes **manipulated** like magic tricks, and in the study a *click*. In the hearth a fire now blazed up warmly.

Nine o'clock. The beds warmed their hidden circuits, for nights were cool here.

Nine-five. A voice spoke from the study ceiling:

3. **spoors** (spo͝orz) *n.* droppings of wild animals.
4. **okapi** (ō kä′ pē) *n.* African animal related to the giraffe but with a much shorter neck.

Vocabulary Development

Expressive Vocabulary

To help students broaden their expressive vocabulary, encourage them to use the following words as they discuss the selection: *minimize, maximizing, display, challenge*, and *maintain*. Have them complete these sentence starters:

1. Technology in the home helped the family *minimize* . . .
2. By *maximizing* their free time, technology enabled people to . . .
3. A *display* on the walls of the children's room showed . . .
4. A life empty of *challenge* could be one effect of . . .
5. The house tried to *maintain* its routines long after . . .

11

The Body of a House, #4 of 8. © Robert Beckmann 1993. Collection: Nevada Museum of Art, Reno.

10 "Mrs. McClellan, which poem would you like this evening?"

The house was silent.

The voice said at last, "Since you express no preference, I shall select a poem at random." Quiet music rose to back the voice. "Sara Teasdale. As I recall, your favorite. . . .

13

There will come soft rains and the smell of the ground,
And swallows circling with their shimmering sound;

And frogs in the pools singing at night,
And wild plum trees in **tremulous** *white;*

Robins will wear their feathery fire,
Whistling their whims on a low fence-wire;

And not one will know of the war, not one
Will care at last when it is done.

Not one would mind, neither bird nor tree,
If mankind perished utterly;

12 **▲ Critical Viewing**

What does this painting suggest about the future of the house in the story? **[Predict]**

Vocabulary

tremulous (trem′ yo͞o ləs) *adj.* trembling; quivering; timid; fearful

14 **Reading Check**

What happens to the dog?

Differentiated Instruction for Universal Access

Culturally Responsive Instruction

Culture Connection Students may lack the background knowledge or context-building experiences necessary to fully comprehend the selection. Before students read, build background knowledge about the first Cold War. Discuss the tensions between the United States and the then Soviet Union, and how those tensions and the advancement in nuclear technology almost led to nuclear war. Invite students to discuss the ways in which citizens might react to the fear of knowing that nuclear war might occur. Then, have them consider ways in which technology has changed the way they live their lives.

11 Humanities

The Body of a House, #4 of 8, by Robert Beckmann

Robert Beckmann was born in Philadelphia and educated there and in Iowa. He taught art at Northern Illinois University until he began painting full time in 1971. Use this question for discussion:

What do you see happening in this painting?

Possible response: The house seems as if it is being stripped by a powerful wind.

12 Critical Viewing

Possible response: This house has no future. No longer does it look like a house. Instead, it seems caught in the moment before it is swept away.

13 Reading Skill

Make Inferences

1. Read the Teasdale poem aloud to students.
2. Have students list details from the poem that remind them of the setting of the story.
   Possible responses: There will come soft rains; not one will know of the war, not one will care at last when it is done; not one would mind if mankind perished utterly.
3. **Ask** students to comment on the "soft rains" in the poem and those in the story.
   Possible response: The soft rains of the poem are the life-giving rains of springtime. The soft rains of the story are deadly radioactive fallout from an atomic bomb.
4. Then, **ask** students to infer why Bradbury might have chosen to include this poem in the story.
   Possible response: The poem is about the destruction of civilization, which parallels the destruction in the story. In both cases, only nature is left to witness the destruction.

14 Reading Check

Answer: The front door opens to allow the starving dog to come in. The dog is nearly hysterical, running around the house looking for its owners, until it smells pancakes cooking on the stove, but the dog cannot get into the kitchen. Finally, the dog becomes frantic with hunger and dies in the parlor.

⓯ Literary Analysis
Setting

1. Invite a volunteer to read the passage in which the fire devours the house.
2. Then, **ask** students to define personification and identify what is being personified.
   Answer: Personification is a type of figurative language in which a nonhuman subject is given human characteristics. In this passage, both the house and the fire are personified. The fire is described as angry, and the house pump sighs.
3. **Ask** students why Bradbury uses personification and what effect it has on the setting.
   Possible responses: By giving the fire and the house human characteristics, the author emphasizes the absence of human beings. The personification also has the effect of creating a battle scene between two living beings. The personification also shows that the automated setting is not as perfect as its creators might have thought.

13 *And Spring herself, when she woke at dawn*
Would scarcely know that we were gone."

The fire burned on the stone hearth. The empty chairs faced each other between the silent walls, and the music played.

At ten o'clock the house began to die.

The wind blew. A falling tree bough crashed through the kitchen window. Cleaning solvent, bottled, shattered over the stove. The room was ablaze in an instant!

"Fire!" screamed a voice. The house lights flashed, water pumps shot water from the ceilings. But the solvent spread on the linoleum, licking, eating, under the kitchen door, while the voices took it up in chorus: "Fire, fire, fire!"

The house tried to save itself. Doors sprang tightly shut, but the windows were broken by the heat and the wind blew and sucked upon the fire.

The house gave ground as the fire in ten billion angry sparks moved with flaming ease from room to room and then up the stairs. While scurrying water rats squeaked from the walls, pistoled their water, and ran for more. And the wall sprays let down showers of mechanical rain.

15 But too late. Somewhere, sighing, a pump shrugged to a stop. The quenching rain ceased. The reserve water supply which had filled baths and washed dishes for many quiet days was gone.

The fire crackled up the stairs. It fed upon Picassos and Matisses[5] in the upper halls, like delicacies, baking off the oily flesh, tenderly crisping the canvases into black shavings.

Now the fire lay in beds, stood in windows, changed the colors of drapes!

And then, reinforcements.

From attic trapdoors, blind robot faces peered down with faucet mouths gushing green chemical.

The fire backed off, as even an elephant must at the sight of a dead snake. Now there were twenty snakes whipping over the floor, killing the fire with a clear cold venom of green froth.

But the fire was clever. It had sent flame outside the house, up through the attic to the pumps there. An explosion! The attic brain which directed the pumps was shattered into bronze shrapnel on the beams.

5. **Picassos** (pi kä′ sōz) **and Matisses** (mä tēs′ əz) paintings by the celebrated modern painters Pablo Picasso (1881–1973) and Henri Matisse (1869–1954).

Vocabulary Development

Vocabulary Knowledge Rating

When students have completed reading and discussing "There Will Come Soft Rains," have them take out their **Vocabulary Knowledge Rating Chart** for this selection. Read the words aloud once more and have students rate their knowledge of the words again in the After Reading column. Clarify any words that are still problematic. Have students write their own definitions and examples or sentences in the appropriate column. Then have students complete the Vocabulary Practice at the end of the selection. Encourage students to use the words in further discussion and written work about this selection. Remind them that they will be accountable for these words on the **Selection Test, *Unit 2 Resources*,** pp. 95–97 or 98–100.

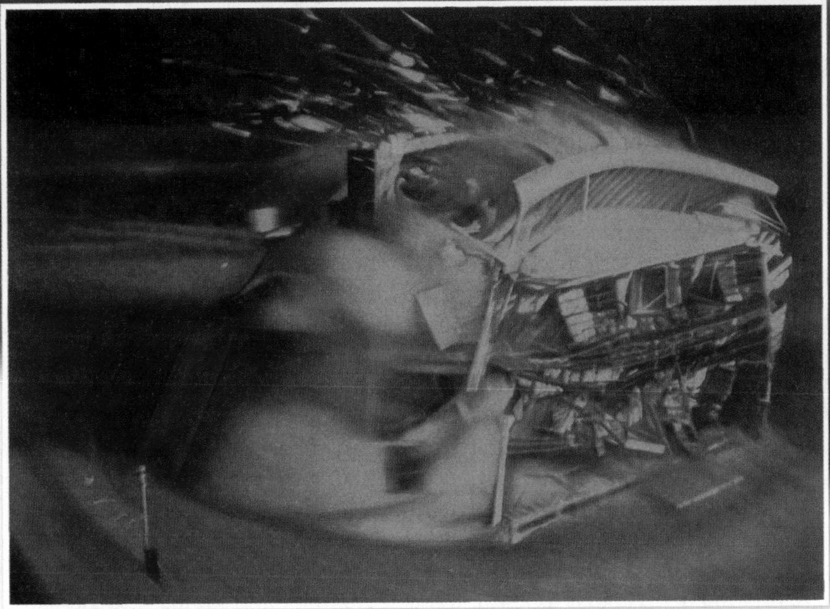

Collection: Nevada Museum of Art, Reno.

The fire rushed back into every closet and felt of the clothes hung there.

The house shuddered, oak bone on bone, its bared skeleton cringing from the heat, its wire, its nerves revealed as if a surgeon had torn the skin off to let the red veins and capillaries quiver in the scalded air. Help, help! Fire! Run, run! Heat snapped mirrors
16 like the first brittle winter ice. And the voices wailed Fire, fire, run, run, like a tragic nursery rhyme, a dozen voices, high, low, like children dying in a forest, alone, alone. And the voices fading as the wires popped their sheathings like hot chestnuts. One, two, three, four, five voices died.

In the nursery the jungle burned. Blue lions roared, purple giraffes bounded off. The panthers ran in circles, changing color, and ten million animals, running before the fire, vanished off toward a distant steaming river. . . .

Ten more voices died. In the last instant under the fire avalanche, other choruses, **oblivious**, could be heard announcing the time, playing music, cutting the lawn by remote-control mower, or setting an umbrella frantically out and in the slamming and opening front door, a thousand things happening, like a clock shop when each clock strikes the hour insanely before or after the other, a scene of maniac confusion, yet unity; singing, screaming, a few last cleaning mice darting bravely out to carry the horrid ashes away! And one voice, with sublime disregard for the situation, read poetry aloud in

Reading Skill
Make Inferences
Based on the details in this paragraph, what do you infer is happening?

Vocabulary
oblivious (ə bliv′ ē əs) *adj.* unaware

17 **Reading Check**
What starts the fire in the house?

16 Reading Skill
Making Inferences

1. Have a volunteer read the passage aloud.
2. **Ask** students the Reading Skill question: Based on the details in this paragraph, what do you infer is happening?
   Answer: The house is dying.

Monitor Progress Ask students to list details from the story that support their inferences.
Possible responses: The house shudders; it has been reduced to a bare skeleton; the systems are all breaking down.

Reteach To give students additional practice in finding details to support their inferences, have them continue their search in the second, third, and fourth paragraphs on p. 291. In addition, have them examine the effect of the numerous similes, such as "its nerves revealed as if a surgeon had torn the skin off to let the red veins and capillaries quiver in the scalded air" and "like children dying in a forest, alone, alone."

3. Then, **ask** students to compare the dying house to a dying person.
   Possible response: The house's life seems to flash before its eyes as each system catches fire and collapses. The process of dying may also be violent, noisy, and fearsome.

17 Reading Check

Answer: A gust of wind causes a tree bough to crash through the kitchen, knocking over a bottle of cleaning solvent, which breaks over the stove and ignites.

Concept Connector

Have students return to the **Vocab-o-Gram** they completed prior to reading the story. Review the words with them, and clarify any word meanings by returning to the selection or using a dictionary. Then have students determine whether their predictions about the story were accurate.

Writing About the Big Question
Have students compare their responses to the sentence starters they completed before reading the story with their ideas afterwards. Ask them to explain whether their thoughts have changed.

Literary Analysis Graphic Organizer
Ask students to review the graphic organizers they completed to make inferences about setting while reading. Show them the partially completed **Literary Analysis Graphic Organizer A** (*Graphic Organizer Transparencies,* p. 46) as an example. Then, have students share the graphic organizers they completed.

ASSESS

Answers

Critical Thinking

1. Some students will enjoy Bradbury's description and his imaginative use of technology. Others will find his view of the world too pessimistic.
2. **Possible responses:** (a) The house announces each hour of the day; it opens and closes doors; it self-cleans with robot mice; it sets tables; it prepares food. (b) The house performs routine activities for its inhabitants, but there are no people. (c) **Possible response:** The people must have died as a result of a nuclear explosion. Surrounded by rubble and ash, the house is the only thing left standing. The ruined city gives off a radioactive glow.
3. (a) It has been programmed to do so. (b) **Possible response:** Machines lack intelligence and feeling; they cannot self-regulate unless they are programmed.
4. (a) **Possible response:** Some students may find Bradbury's vision of future technology exaggerated. Other students may believe that because technology develops so quickly, automated houses like the one in the story are possible. (b) and (c) Students should specify how their discussions altered their views.

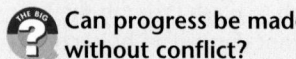

Can progress be made without conflict?

Possible response: The technological advances are more negative than positive. It was technology that created the nuclear bomb, which later flattened the land and killed the people. The house, with all its programmed action, inadvertently sets fire to itself, and because it has wasted its resources on mundane activities such as self-cleaning, it is not able to quench the fire. Advances in technology, then, lead it its own destruction.

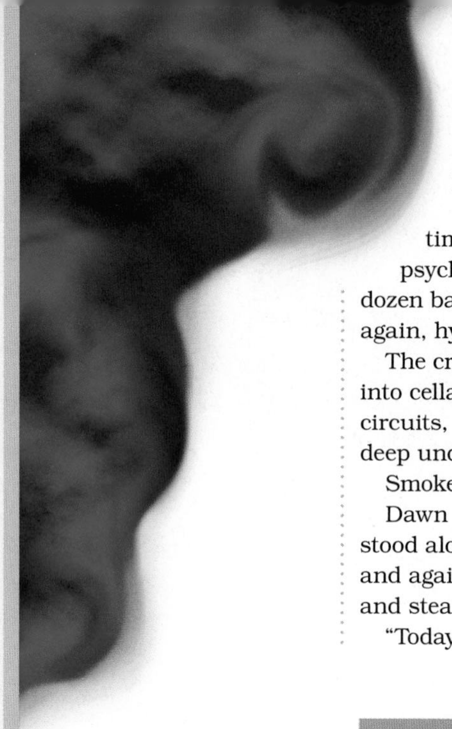

the fiery study, until all the film spools burned, until all the wires withered and the circuits cracked.

The fire burst the house and let it slam flat down, puffing out skirts of spark and smoke.

In the kitchen, an instant before the rain of fire and timber, the stove could be seen making breakfasts at a psychopathic rate, ten dozen eggs, six loaves of toast, twenty dozen bacon strips, which, eaten by fire, started the stove working again, hysterically hissing!

The crash. The attic smashing into kitchen and parlor. The parlor into cellar, cellar into subcellar. Deep freeze, armchair, film tapes, circuits, beds, and all like skeletons thrown in a cluttered mound deep under.

Smoke and silence. A great quantity of smoke.

Dawn showed faintly in the east. Among the ruins, one wall stood alone. Within the wall, a last voice said, over and over again and again, even as the sun rose to shine upon the heaped rubble and steam:

"Today is August 5, 2026, today is August 5, 2026, today is . . ."

Critical Thinking

1. **Respond:** Would you like to read other works by Ray Bradbury? Why or why not?
2. **(a)** List five automated functions the house performs. **(b) Infer:** What is missing in the routine of activity that the house performs? **(c) Interpret:** What is a likely reason for this absence? Give details in support of your answer.
3. **(a) Infer:** Why does the house continue its activity even when it no longer makes sense? **(b) Analyze:** What does this fact indicate about the human qualities the house does not have?
4. **(a) Make a Judgment:** Do you think Bradbury gives a realistic view of the future of technology? Explain. **(b) Discuss:** Trade answers with a partner. After you have read your partner's response, discuss your answers. **(c) Reflect:** Afterward, write a sentence or two explaining whether your partner's views have influenced your own.

Can progress be made without conflict?
Are the technological advances described in the story more positive or negative? Explain.

Assessment Resources

Unit 2 Resources

L1 L2 EL **Selection Test A**, pp. 95–97. Administer Test A to less advanced readers and English learners.

L3 L4 **Selection Test B**, pp. 98–100. Administer Test B to on-level and more advanced students.

L3 L4 **Open-Book Test**, pp. 92–94. As an alternative, give the Open-Book Test.

All **Customizable Test Bank**

All **Self-tests**
Students may prepare for the **Selection Test** by taking the **Self-test** online.

PHLit Online! All assessment resources are available at **www.PHLitOnline.com**

After You Read

There Will Come Soft Rains

There Will Come Soft Rains

Ray Bradbury

In the living room the voice-clock sang, *Tick-tock, seven o'clock, time to get up, time to get up, seven o'clock!* as if it were afraid that nobody would. The morning house lay empty. The clock ticked on, repeating and repeating its sounds into the emptiness. *Seven-nine, breakfast time, seven-nine!*

In the kitchen the breakfast stove gave a hissing sigh and ejected from its warm interior eight pieces of perfectly browned toast, eight eggs sunnyside up, sixteen slices of bacon, two coffees, and two cool glasses of milk.

"Today is August 4, 2026," said a second voice from the kitchen ceiling, "in the city of Allendale, California." It repeated the date three times for memory's sake. "Today is Mr. Featherstone's birthday. Today is the anniversary of Tilita's marriage. Insurance is payable, as are the water, gas, and light bills."

Somewhere in the walls, relays clicked, memory tapes glided under electric eyes.

Eight-one, tick-tock, eight-one o'clock, off to school, off to work, run, run, eight one! But no doors slammed, no carpets took the soft tread of rubber heels. It was raining outside.

284 Short Stories

Literary Analysis: Setting

1. (a) Identify these aspects of the **setting** in "There Will Come Soft Rains": the specific place in which events occur; the historical period. **(b)** For each aspect, give an example of a **description** that helps make this setting vivid for readers.

2. Explain why the setting of this story is also its main character.

Reading Skill: Make Inferences

3. (a) Based on information in the first two pages of the story, what two **inferences** could you make about events that occurred before the story opens? **(b)** For each inference, note at least one detail later in the story that either proves it or disproves it. Record your answers in a chart like the one shown.

Inference	Confirming Details	Disproving Details

4. (a) What can you infer about the future of the house when the fire starts in the kitchen? **(b)** What information can you learn by reading on to confirm this inference?

Vocabulary

Practice Match each statement with a word from the vocabulary list for "There Will Come Soft Rains" on page 282. Then, explain each choice.

1. This word might be used to describe a nervous person.
2. The flag did this in the breeze.
3. If you make an effort like this, you are working hard.
4. People who do not notice things can be described with this word.
5. People who see danger everywhere can be said to suffer from this.
6. If you adjusted a picture to make it brighter, you did this to it.

Word Study Use the context of the sentences and what you know about the **Greek suffix *-ic*** to explain your answer to each question.

1. Would a person be *emphatic* if he or she had a strong belief?
2. How might a person react to a *comedic* movie?

Word Study

The **Greek suffix *-ic*** means "having the characteristic of" or "pertaining to."

Challenge Explain how the suffix *-ic* contributes to the meanings of these words. Consult a dictionary if necessary.

dramatic
metallic
organic

Answers

Literary Analysis

1. (a) The events occur in a California city that has been destroyed by a nuclear blast. The time period is August 4 and 5, 2026. (b) **Possible response:** "At night the ruined city gave off a radioactive glow which could be seen for miles." "Out of warrens in the wall, tiny robot mice darted."
2. The house is given human qualities. It "began to die" and "tried to save itself." The voices that react to the fire are machines, but they sound human: they scream and sigh. The entire story concerns the fate of the house, just as if it were the main character.

Reading Skill

3. (a) **Possible response:** Inferences: The occupants of the house are gone and are not returning. No one has adjusted the programming of the house. (b) Confirmations: The house's occupants have left silhouettes of ash on the exterior of the house, indicating that they have been killed, along with everyone else in the city, in some kind of nuclear disaster. The house continues to function as if people are there.
4. **Possible response:** (a) Students will probably infer that the fire will destroy the house. (b) Reading ahead confirms that the house is destroyed.

   For other sample answers, see ***Graphic Organizer Transparencies*, Reading Skill Graphic Organizer** A, p. 49, and the **Additional Answers** section.

Vocabulary

Practice

1. *tremulous.* A nervous person might show signs of anxiety or fear through physical trembling or quaking.
2. *fluttered.* A flag is made of thin fabric, so the slightest wind will make it flap rapidly.
3. *titanic.* If you are working hard, then you must be putting in great effort.

Answers continued

4. *oblivious.* Someone who is unaware of his or her surroundings is oblivious.
5. *paranoia.* While there might not be danger everywhere, the person believing there is might be suffering from delusions.
6. *manipulated.* If you adjust a picture to the way you want it to look, you are controlling it.

Word Study

1. Yes, the suffix *-ic* means "having the characteristic of," so *emphatic* means "having the characteristic of emphasis or insistence on something." An emphatic person would strongly defend that belief.
2. The suffix *-ic* means "having the characteristic of," so *comedic* means "having the characteristic of humor." A person who sees a comedic movie might laugh.

Word Study: Challenge

Someone who is *dramatic* has the quality of drama. When something is *metallic* it has the quality of metal. Something *organic* has the quality of organisms, or life.

EXTEND/ASSESS

Answers

Grammar

1. Introduce the skill, using the instruction on the student page.
2. Discuss the definition and the principal parts in the chart.

Think Aloud: Model the Skill

Model the skill of identifying irregular verbs, using the following "think aloud":

> It can be tricky trying to determine the principal parts of an irregular verb. Take the verb *drink*, for instance. I can apply the rules for a regular verb. The past participle is created by adding *-ed*, so *drink* would be *drinked*. This formation is wrong, so *drink* must be an irregular verb. I know from memory that the past participle of *drink* is *drunk*. I realize that the only way to learn the principal parts is to memorize them. Fortunately, I know that many irregular verbs follow similar patterns: *drink, drinking, drank, drunk* follows the same pattern as *sing, singing, sang, sung*.

Writing and Grammar, Grade 10

Students will find further instruction and practice with irregular verbs in Chapter 22, Section 1.

Practice A

1. past
2. present participle
3. past participle
4. past

Challenge

Sample answer: ". . . after a moment, he slid into the narrow, dirt-packed street again." (*slide*; past); "'On her wedding day, she takes to her man . . .'" (*take*; present); ". . . she had worn a white lace shawl over her hair." (*wear*; past participle).

Practice B

1. *sang; had sung*
2. *swung; had swung*
3. *began; had begun*
4. *sat; had sat*

Challenge

Sample answer: Students' paragraph should contain at least four different irregular verbs.

Integrated Language Skills

The Street of the Cañon • There Will Come Soft Rains

Grammar: Irregular Verbs

An **irregular verb** is a verb whose tenses are not formed according to the standard rules.

Unlike regular verbs, the past and the past participle of an irregular verb are not formed by adding *-ed* or *-d* to the present form. Some common irregular verbs are shown in the following chart.

The Four Principal Parts of Irregular Verbs

Present	Present Participle	Past	Past Participle
lend	is lending	lent	(have) lent
fly	is flying	flew	(have) flown
spin	is spinning	spun	(have) spun
begin	is beginning	began	(have) begun

Practice A Identify which principal part each italicized verb represents.

1. The town church bells *rang* to announce the beginning of the party.
2. She *is eating* her birthday cake.
3. The guests *had begun* to dance.
4. People *ran* to see what the package contained.

Challenge Find three sentences in "The Street of the Cañon" that contain irregular verbs. Write the irregular verbs and identify which of the principal parts the verbs represent.

Practice B Rewrite each sentence twice: once with the past and once with the past participle form of the verb in parentheses.

1. The voice-clock ______ for the last time. (sing)
2. The garage door ______ up and down. (swing)
3. When the house _______ to die, it screamed "fire, fire." (begin)
4. The house ________ in its yard like a smoldering pile of trash. (sit)

Challenge Write a paragraph about an automated machine such as a car alarm or an ATM. In your writing, use at least four different irregular verbs.

Writing and Grammar Connection: Chapter 22, Section 1

Extend the Lesson

Sentence Modeling

Choose the sentence given from the selection students have read:

The last time he had seen that face it had been white and tense with rage, and the lips clenched tight to prevent an outgushing stream of angry words. ("The Street of the Cañon")

The morning house lay empty. ("There Will Come Soft Rains")

Elicit from students that the main verb(s) is irregular. Then, ask what else they notice. ("The Street of the Cañon": multiple verb phrases are used to describe the face, giving it a strong presence in the sentence; "There Will Come Soft Rains": the simple sentence is terse but its idea sharp and loud, like an echo in the empty house to which it refers; it uses an adjective in a surprising way.)

Have students imitate the sentence in a sentence on a topic of their own choosing, matching each grammatical and stylistic feature discussed. Collect the sentences, and share them with the class.

Writing

Write a brief **letter to a friend** summarizing either "The Street of the Cañon" or "There Will Come Soft Rains." Then, rewrite the summary as part of a **book review** for newspaper readers.

- As you transfer your ideas into a new format, exclude information and arguments that are irrelevant to your book review.
- Change your language as needed for your new audience, replacing informal words with formal ones.
- Add information that a newspaper audience would expect to find in a review, such as information about the author.
- State your opinion on the story and support your statement with descriptions and specific examples.

Writing Workshop: *Work in Progress*

Prewriting for Narration: Short Story Using the Character Descriptions in your writing portfolio, make a chart of potential conflicts that the protagonist and antagonist could have. Choose one of these conflicts and add notes about how the two characters could resolve this conflict during the course of the story. Save your Potential Conflict chart in your writing portfolio.

Use this prewriting activity to prepare for the Writing Workshop on page 328.

Listening and Speaking

Each of these stories can be compared to a well-known poem: Niggli's story bears similarity to Alfred Noyes's "The Highwayman"; Bradbury's story shares many similarities to the poem for which it was named, "There Will Come Soft Rains" by Sara Teasdale. Give an **oral reading** of the poem "The Highwayman" or the poem "There Will Come Soft Rains."

- **Use a dictionary to look up the definitions and pronunciations** of any words you do not know.
- Vary your **tone** of voice to reflect the poem's meaning. In addition, try different pacing to best capture the emotion and rhythm of the poetry.
- **Use gestures** as appropriate.
- Spend time practicing the reading before a mirror, or ask friends or family members to listen to your reading and offer you suggestions.

After reading the poem to the class, lead a class discussion in a comparison of the poem and the story.

PHLit Online!
www.PHLitOnline.com
- Interactive graphic organizers
- Grammar tutorial
- Interactive journals

EXTEND/ASSESS

Answers

Writing

1. Review the assignment, using the instruction on the student page.
2. To give students guidance for writing their summaries, give them the **Support for Writing**, p. 90 in ***Unit 2 Resources***.
3. To evaluate students' letter to a friend and book review, use the Letter and Response to Literature rubrics, pp. 224–225 and 236–237 in ***Professional Development Guidebook***.

Six Traits Focus

✔	Ideas	✔	Word Choice
✔	Organization		Sentence Fluency
✔	Voice		Conventions

Writing Workshop
Work in Progress

Have students save their completed Character Descriptions in their portfolios. They will use them later as they complete the Writing Workshop assignment (see pp. 328–333)

Listening and Speaking

1. Review the assignment, using the instruction on the student page.
2. Have students complete the **Support for Extend Your Learning** page (***Unit 2 Resources***, p. 91).

Teaching Resources

All *Unit 2 Resources*
L3 L4 **Integrated Language Skills: Grammar,** p. 89
L3 L4 **Support for Writing,** p. 90
L3 L4 **Support for Extend Your Learning,** p. 91
L4 **Enrichment,** pp. 70, 88

All **Enriched Online Student Edition**
Available under After You Read for this selection:
All **Interactive Grammar Tutorial**
L3 L4 **Internet Research Activity**

Professional Development Guidebook
Rubrics for Response to Literature and Letter, pp. 224–225 and 236–237

PHLit Online! All print and digital resources are available online at **www.PHLitOnline.com.** Online resources accessible to students are noted on the student page.

MONITORING PROGRESS

Using the Test Practice

In this two-page Test Practice, students apply the reading skill for the first half of Unit 2 to a passage of fiction and a passage of nonfiction.

Review this skill, making inferences, and then administer the test. For more guidance, consult the ***Classroom Strategies and Teaching Routines*** card, **Administering Timed Tests.**

ASSESS

Answers

Answers With Explanations

1. A—"Teacher", the sky gym, and anti-grav sneakers suggest the future. *Incorrect answers:* B—Technology in the story did not exist in the twentieth century. C—Technology is a recent development that did not exist long ago. D—Technology in the story does not exist today.
2. B—Anti-grav sneakers are for sports (hoops) in the sky gym. *Incorrect answers:* A—A live phone video of a friend does not suggest anything about sports. C—Studying with "Teacher" suggests the influence of technology on education, not sports. D—Postponing a class for sports has nothing to do with technology.
3. B—David uses "Teacher" technology for classes and testing. *Incorrect answers:* A—Nothing says that Jake is David's only Spanish study partner. C— David seems content with using "Teacher" rather than a classroom. D—David is learning Spanish on "Teacher," but it doesn't says whether he is fluent.
4. C—David is reviewing math, about to take a test, and planning to review Spanish, all with "Teacher." *Incorrect answers:* A—The story doesn't say whether he excels in athletics. B— Contacting friends would not improve his education. D— The story mentions math and Spanish, not all subjects.

Test Practice: Reading

Make Inferences

Fiction Selection

Directions: *Read the selection. Then, answer the questions.*

David pulled Teacher from his backpack. "Review math lesson," he said into the device. David curled up on his bed as he listened to Teacher's smooth, mechanical voice. "Give the test," David said. As test questions appeared on the small screen, David used a stylus to record his answers. A light on his device blinked, and he touched the *pause* button.

"What's up, Jake?" he said, as the image of his best friend appeared.

"Meet me in the sky gym for some hoops."

"I've got a Spanish class," David answered.

"Bring Teacher. We can do the class together later," said Jake.

"Good idea," answered David. "See you at the gym." David pushed a button, and Jake's face was replaced on the screen with David's test.

David touched the *send* button without hesitation. Pushing Teacher into his pocket, he slipped on his anti-grav sneakers and left for the gym.

1. What inference can you make about the setting of this selection?

A. It takes place in the future.
B. It takes place in the twentieth century.
C. It takes place long, long ago.
D. It takes place in the present.

2. What detail helps you infer that sports activities are influenced by technology?

A. having live video of a friend on the phone
B. wearing "anti-grav sneakers"
C. studying with an electronic "Teacher"
D. postponing a class to play sports

3. Based on details in this passage, what inference can you make about David's education?

A. He only reviews Spanish with Jake.
B. Technology plays a role in his education.
C. He wants to attend class in a school room.
D. Teacher has taught him to speak Spanish fluently.

4. What can you infer about how technology enhances David's education?

A. Technology helps him excel in athletics.
B. He can contact his friends from school using technology.
C. He can review material and take tests at his own pace.
D. Teacher can answer all of David's questions about any subject.

Writing for Assessment

Using your own knowledge and details from this passage, what inferences can you make about how other areas of David's life besides his education might be affected by technology? Write a paragraph in which you explain your ideas.

Writing for Assessment

Have students first identify different aspects of a young person's life, such as travel, shopping, news, money, and work. Then they should reflect on how technology might affect each aspect of David's life.

Strategies for Test Taking

Many test items are set up as sentence completions, such as those on page 297. Remind students that they have to find the best way to finish the sentence based on the stem. They might start by restating the item as a question and developing an idea of what the correct answer would be before looking at the choices.

Nonfiction Selection

Directions: *Read the selection. Then, answer the questions.*

Let's explore the implications of technological advancement on our students' lives now and on the lives of students in the future. The use of computers, the Internet, wireless systems, and hand-held mobile devices already impact our students' daily routines and some aspects of how we teach them. Information that once took hours or even days of library research to find can be retrieved in milliseconds. Research tools such as primary source documents and specialized reference books—previously found only in select libraries—can now be accessed easily. Along with the ease of accessibility, however, comes dangers. For example, some material found on the Internet contains misinformation. The act of using technology itself may cause unforeseen changes. I predict that both the dangers of technology and the advances in education due to technology will only increase.

1. Using the details in this text, you can infer that the writer is—

A. a student.
B. a teacher.
C. a salesperson.
D. an inventor.

2. You can infer that the remainder of this essay will elaborate on—

A. positive and negative aspects of technology.
B. positive aspects of technology.
C. negative aspects of technology.
D. the removal of technology from education.

3. Using your own knowledge, you can infer from the second sentence that the author—

A. is aware of the ways in which students currently use technology.
B. has limited knowledge about students.
C. is confused about students' use of technology.
D. is angry about students' use of technology.

4. After reading the last sentence, you can reasonably infer that the author—

A. is in favor of increasing use of technology.
B. is opposed to increasing use of technology.
C. is ignorant about technology.
D. has an open mind about technology.

Writing for Assessment

Connecting Across Texts

The author of this passage maintains that technology can have both positive and negative effects on students. Based on details from these two passages, what inferences can you make about the positive and negative effects of technology on David's education? Describe your conclusions in a paragraph.

PHLit Online!
www.PHLitOnline.com
- Online practice
- Instant feedback

Differentiated Instruction for Universal Access

Strategy for Less Proficient Readers
Help students to work through at least one sentence completion item on page 297. Ask a volunteer to read item 1 on page 297, including all the answer choices. Then encourage them to restate the item as a question, such as "What occupation does the writer have?" Then go over each choice. Help them to see that the passage only contains details which support the occupation of teaching. (The writer repeats the phrase "our students" several times in the opening to make this point.)

Strategy for English Learners
Before students read the selections ask them to complete a vocabulary scan of both passages and list types of technology, including "Teacher", anti-grav sneakers, sky gym, computers, Internet, wireless systems, etc. Then have them circle kinds of technology which actually exist today. This activity could lead to a review of characteristics of the science fiction genre.

ASSESS

Answers

Answers With Explanations

1. B—The opening sentences mention "our students," suggesting that the writer has students. *Incorrect answers:* A—The mention of "our students" suggests that the writer is not a student himself. C—The selection leads to a prediction, not a persuasive sales pitch. D—The writer mentions inventions but never hints at a part in creating them.
2. A—The last sentence suggests the essay will follow this direction. *Incorrect answers:* B—The last sentence suggests the essay will discuss both positive and negative aspects. C—same explanation as for B. D—All details suggest the opposite, that technology in education will only increase.
3. A—Sentences two and three include many examples of this technology. *Incorrect answers:* B—The opening sentences mention "our students," suggesting direct knowledge of students. C—Sentences two through six show the opposite, a clear understanding of how students use technology. D—The author makes a prediction, not an angry judgment, about students' use of technology.
4. D—The last sentence shows a recognition of the positive and negative potential of technology. *Incorrect answers:* A—The last sentence contains a prediction, not an opinion, about student's future use of technology. B—same explanation as for A. C—Sentences two through six show the opposite, knowledge of technology.

Writing for Assessment

Students should use at least two details from each selection to support their inferences. Suggest that they begin by setting up a two-column chart with examples of positive effects in one column and negative effects in the other.

PHLit Online!
Students may take the test in interactive format with instant feedback online at www.PHLitOnline.com.

PRETEACH

Meeting Your Standards

Students will

1. analyze texts to extend ideas.
2. understand and analyze charts and graphs in a technical article.
3. read a technical article and a news release.

Log on as a teacher at ***www.PHLitOnline.com*** *for a detailed lesson plan for Informational Texts.*

Reading Skill

1. Introduce the skill, using the instruction on the student page.
2. Review the chart.
3. Tell students that they will analyze texts to extend ideas.

Think Aloud: Model the Skill

Model the skill of analyzing texts to extend ideas, using the following "think aloud." Say to students:

> When I read a variety of sources, I like to provide myself with a solid understanding of the topic. To do so, I ask questions about the text to build on the information it presents. Let's say I am considering purchasing a new car and decide to read a review in a car magazine. As I read, I analyze the text to ensure that it presents the details that I need. If the review states that the car has great gas mileage, I evaluate how well the review supports this claim. When I finish reading, I think about ways that I can enhance my understanding of the review.

THE BIG ? Can progress be made without conflict?

Have students look for details about natural conflicts as they read the article.

Multidraft Reading

Have students follow a multidraft reading protocol after they read.

- **First reading**—Have students read for general understanding.
- **Second reading**—Have students compare the text's perspectives and features.
- **Third reading**—Have students read for details about conflicts.

Informational Texts

Real-Life Reading

Technical Article
Tides

News Release
Black Water Turns the Tide on Florida Coral

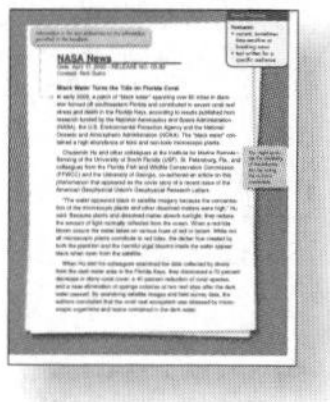

Reading Skill: Analyze Texts to Extend Ideas

When you **extend ideas** presented in informational texts, you consider, judge, and build on those ideas. You do this through **analysis, evaluation,** and **elaboration.** To extend ideas, consider these questions:

Extending Ideas	Questions to Ask
Analysis	• What is the text about? • What kinds of details are presented? • What characteristics—text features and structures—are used to present information?
Evaluation	• How well are the main ideas presented and supported? • Is the text suited for its audience? Does it achieve its purpose?
Elaboration	• What connections can I make with the text? • What additional ideas and questions do I have about this topic?

THE BIG ? Can progress be made without *conflict?*

Nature is constantly in conflict. These clashes perpetuate cycles that living things need to survive. As you read, consider the perspective each author has on "tidal battles"—the natural forces that cause and affect tides.

Differentiated Instruction for Universal Access

Reading Support
Give students reading support with the appropriate version of the *Reader's Notebooks:*

L2 L3 *Reader's Notebook*

L1 *Reader's Notebook: Adapted Version*

EL *Reader's Notebook: English Learner's Version*

PHLit Online! All student resources are available online at **www.PHLitOnline.com.**

Tides

Joseph D. Exline, Ed.D., Jay M. Pasachott, Ph.D., et al.

You're standing on a riverbank in the town of Saint John, Canada. In the distance there's a loud roaring sound, like a train approaching. Suddenly a wall of water twice your height thunders past. The surge of water rushes up the river channel so fast that it almost looks as if the river is flowing backward.

This thundering wall of water is an everyday event at Saint John. The town is located where the Saint John River enters the Bay of Fundy, an arm of the Atlantic Ocean. The Bay of Fundy is famous for its dramatic daily tides. When the tide comes in fishing boats float on the water near the piers, as shown in Figure 1A. But once the tide goes out, so much water flows back to sea that the boats are stranded on the muddy harbor bottom (Figure 1B).

Figure 1 The Bay of Fundy in Canada is noted for its great differences in water level at high and low tide. **A.** Near the mouth of the bay, boats float in the Saint John River at high tide. **B.** At low tide, the boats are grounded.

Technical Article

Features:

- main heads and subheads that organize the article into sections
- boldfaced words, phrases, or sentences that contain key ideas
- diagrams or charts that illustrate or summarize information
- text written for a specific audience

Photographs, as well as diagrams and other graphics, are used to extend ideas presented in the text.

TEACH

About Technical Articles

1. Review the features listed in the Technical Article box on this page. Explain that technical articles provide an abundance of information about a specific subject and that they are written for an audience that wants to learn about the subject.
2. **Ask** students to discuss technical articles they have read. Have them explain how the article presented information in a helpful way.
   Possible response: I read an article about the negative long-term effects that global warming might have on the agricultural industry. The article incorporated quotes, headings and subheadings, and insightful graphics that made for an informative read.
3. Remind students that it is important to consider the perspective of the text as well as the features that it offers.

Analyze Texts to Extend Ideas

1. Have students read "Tides."
2. Direct students' attention to the images in Figure 1, and discuss examples of the impact the tide has on the area, such as restricted times when boating can take place. **Ask** students why the authors might have chosen to use these images.
   Possible response: The images show how dramatic the change in tide is. It would be hard to describe in words what the area actually looks like at high and low tides.
3. Have students read the first paragraph again. **Ask** students to describe the writing style in the first paragraph and to give a reason why the authors chose to begin a technical article this way.
   Possible response: The first paragraph's style seems more like an opening scene in a movie or fictional story, rather than a technical article. The authors probably did this to get readers interested in the topic of tides.

Differentiated Instruction for Universal Access

Culturally Responsive Instruction

Culture Focus Students may lack the background knowledge or context-building experiences necessary to fully comprehend the selection. Before students read, build background knowledge about cultures that live near, and rely on, the ocean. Point out how living on the coast might be different from living inland. Locate the Bay of Fundy on a map as well as coastal cities and countries across the world. Then, discuss the different economic and recreational advantages that living on the coast would provide.

Analyze Texts to Extend Ideas

1. As a group, read the callout notes that explain the text features. Then, have students read the page. Tell them to read the text first, and then to study the diagram.
2. **Ask** students how the heading, boldfaced type, and diagram helped them locate essential information.
   Answer: The heading and boldfaced type show that this section is about the cause of tides. The diagram shows how the moon causes tides.
3. Have students review Figure 2. **Ask** how the diagram helps make the cause of tides more evident, and what it provides that text cannot do as well.
   Possible response: The diagram shows the position of the moon and the tidal bulges. It helps illustrate that the moon causes the tides. Combined with the information from the text, it is clear that when the water and Earth are pulled in one direction, the water bulges at the two opposite points. The diagram makes the spatial information more clear than text alone could.

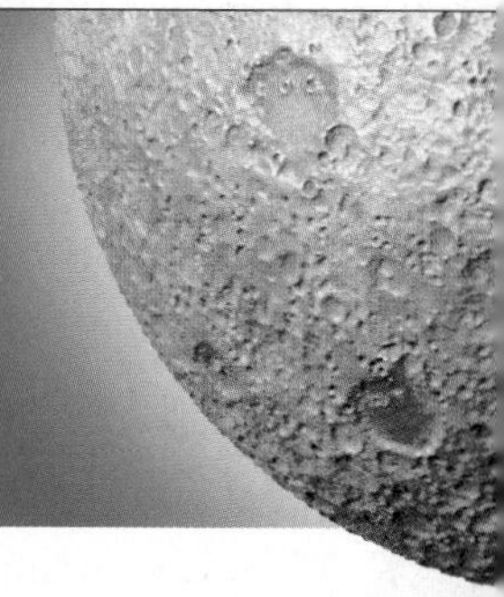

Headings such as this one allow you to identify and analyze the ideas being discussed.

What Causes Tides?

The daily rise and fall of Earth's waters on its coastlines are called tides. As the tide comes in, the level of the water on the beach rises gradually. When the water reaches its highest point, it is high tide. Then the tide goes out, flowing back toward the sea. When the water reaches its lowest point, it is low tide. **Tides are caused by the interaction of Earth, the moon, and the sun.**

Figure 2 shows the effect of the moon's gravity on the water on Earth's surface. The moon pulls on the water on the side closest to it (point A) more strongly than it pulls on the center of the Earth. This pull creates a bulge of water, called a tidal bulge, on the side of Earth facing the moon. The water at point C is pulled toward the moon less strongly than is Earth as a whole. This water is "left behind," forming a second bulge.

In the places in Figure 2 where there are tidal bulges (points A and C), high tide is occurring along the coastlines. In the places between the bulges (points B and D), low tide is occurring. As Earth rotates, different places on the planet's surface pass through the areas of the tidal bulges and experience the change in water levels.

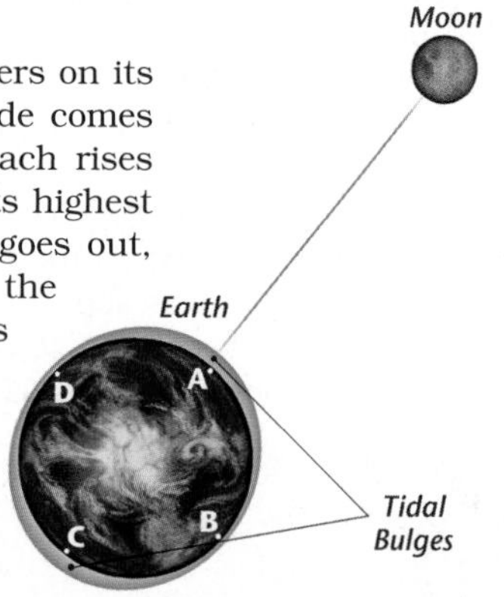

Figure 2
The moon's pull on Earth's water causes tidal bulges to form on the side closest to the moon and the side farthest from the moon.

Captions elaborate on information provided in the photos or graphics in a text.

Vocabulary Development

Vocabulary for Tides

Point out that technical articles often use vocabulary that is specific to a particular subject, in this case tides. Guide students to understand the meaning of the following words that are used in the technical article "Tides":

pier: a structure extending into water for use as a walkway or landing place, or to protect a harbor

gravity: the pull of the mass of the Earth and its moon

neap tide: the minimum range of a tide

spring tide: the maximum range of a tide

right angle: 90 degree angle, two lines at a perpendicular

PHLit Online! **Vocabulary Central**, featuring tools, activities, and songs for studying vocabulary, is available online at **www.PHLitOnline.com**.

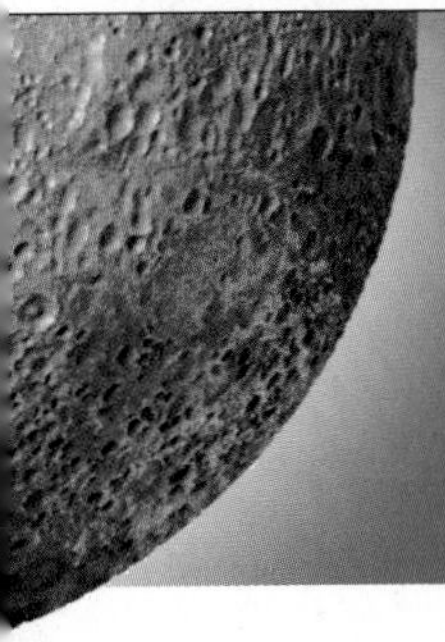

Day	Highest High Tide (m)	Lowest Low Tide (m)
1	1.9	0.2
2	2.1	0.1
3	2.3	0.0
4	2.4	-0.2
5	2.5	-0.2
6	2.6	-0.3
7	1.9	0.3

Figure 3
This table lists the highest high tides and lowest low tides at the mouth of the Savannah River at the Atlantic Ocean in Georgia for one week.

Tables present numerical data for you to analyze and evaluate.

The Daily Tide Cycle

As Earth turns completely around once each day, people on or near the shore observe the rise and fall of the tides as they reach the area of each tidal bulge. The high tides occur about 12 hours and 25 minutes apart in each location. As Earth rotates, eastern-most points pass through the area of the tidal bulge before points farther to the west. Therefore, high tide occurs later the farther west you go along a coastline.

The Monthly Tide Cycle

Even though the sun is 150 million kilometers from Earth, it is so massive that its gravity also affects the tides. The sun pulls the water on Earth's surface toward it. In Figure 4 (next page), you can follow the positions of the Earth, moon, and sun at different times during a month.

Spring Tides Twice a month, at the new moon and the full moon, the sun and moon are lined up. Their combined gravitational pull produces the greatest range between high and low tide, called a spring tide. These tides get their name not because they occur during the spring season, but from an Old English word, *springen*, which means "to jump."

Analyze Texts to Extend Ideas

1. Remind students to read the text first, and then review the chart.
2. Direct students to study the chart in Figure 3. **Ask** a volunteer to make a statement describing the relationship between days with higher tides and days with lower tides.
   Possible response: The days with the highest tides also seem to be the days with the lowest tides.
3. Point out that looking back at the text sometimes helps to clarify the meaning of a chart. **Ask** a volunteer for a statement in the text that helps to make the chart clearer.
   Possible response: The text makes it clear that the high tides occur about twice a day. The high tide numbers on the chart are for only one of the two tides on any given day unless the two tides happen to measure exactly the same.

Differentiated Instruction for Universal Access

Support for Special Needs Students
Divide the class into small groups of about five students each. Challenge each group to use three-dimensional models or other symbols to represent the Earth, moon, and sun positions and movements that explain tides. Provide time for student demonstrations.

Strategy for Less Proficient Readers
Remind students that the headings highlight the main ideas, so a good way to preview an article is to glance at the headings before starting to read. Ask students to read each heading and explain the idea in their own words. For example, for the heading "What Causes Tides?" students should state that the section tells why we have tides on Earth. Have students practice this procedure with each heading.

Analyze Texts to Extend Ideas

1. Remind students to read the information in the text first, and then to review the charts and diagrams for more information.
2. **Ask** students to explain the main ideas presented by the text on this page.
   Answer: The text explains neap tides and that the position of the moon and sun cause the least amount of disparity between low and high tides.
3. Have students review Figure 4. **Ask** what information the diagram provides and how it is different from what is presented in the text.
   Possible response: The diagram shows the position of the sun and the moon at spring and neap tides. Combined with the information from the text, it shows that when the sun, moon, and Earth are aligned, the pull is stronger, so a spring tide occurs. The diagram makes the textual information more clear.

ASSESS/EXTEND

Answers

Can progress be made without conflict?

(a) The gravitational force of both the moon and sun are constantly pulling Earth and creating tides.

(b) Tides on Earth are influenced by the conflict of the sun and moon resulting in either spring tides or neap tides.

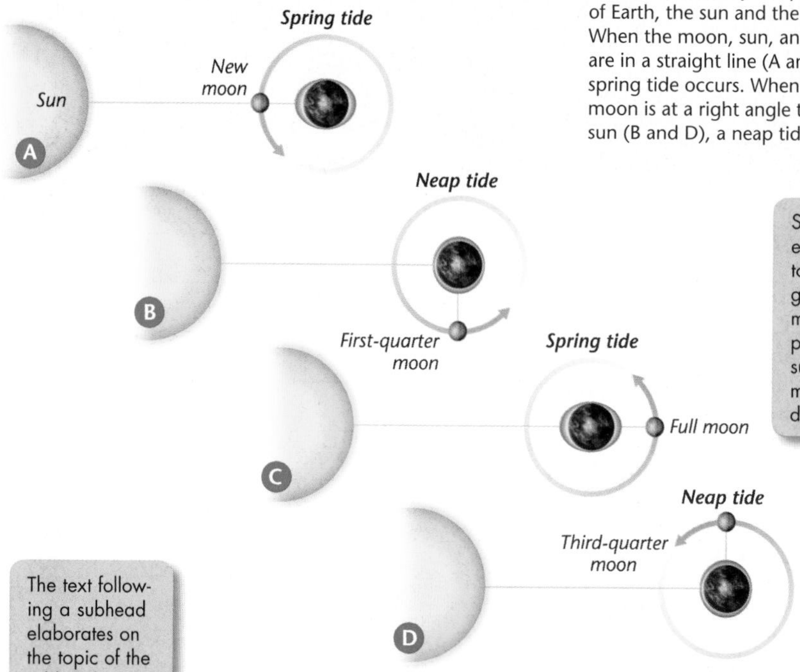

Figure 4 Spring tides and neap tides are caused by the positions of Earth, the sun and the moon. When the moon, sun, and Earth are in a straight line (A and C), a spring tide occurs. When the moon is at a right angle to the sun (B and D), a neap tide occurs.

Some captions explain how to read or use graphic information on the page. This one summarizes the main ideas in the diagram.

The text following a subhead elaborates on the topic of the subhead.

Neap Tides In between spring tides, at the first and third quarters of the moon, the sun and moon pull at right angles to each other. This line-up produces a neap tide, a tide with the least difference between low and high tide. During a neap tide, the sun's gravity pulls some of the water away from the tidal bulge facing the moon. This acts to "even out" the water level over Earth's surface, reducing the difference between high and low tides.

Can progress be made without conflict?
(a) According to this article, what natural conflict exists between the forces of the moon and the sun?
(b) What is the result of this conflict?

Vocabulary Development

Word Forms
Expand students' vocabulary by helping them learn related forms of key words. Review the following variations of the word *tide*.

tide (noun): periodic variation in Earth's surface water
tidal (adjective): related to or resembling tides
tidally (adverb): like a tide
tide (verb): to rise and fall like a tide

News Release

Features:
- current, sometimes time-sensitive or breaking news
- text written for a specific audience

Information in the text elaborates on the information provided in the headline.

NASA News

Date: April 17, 2003 - RELEASE NO: 03-39
Contact: Rob Gutro

Black Water Turns the Tide on Florida Coral

In early 2002, a patch of "black water" spanning over 60 miles in diameter formed off southwestern Florida and contributed to severe coral reef stress and death in the Florida Keys, according to results published from research funded by the National Aeronautics and Space Administration (NASA), the U.S. Environmental Protection Agency and the National Oceanic and Atmospheric Administration (NOAA). The "black water" contained a high abundance of toxic and non-toxic microscopic plants.

Chuanmin Hu and other colleagues at the Institute for Marine Remote Sensing of the University of South Florida (USF), St. Petersburg, Fla., and colleagues from the Florida Fish and Wildlife Conservation Commission (FFWCC) and the University of Georgia, co-authored an article on this phenomenon that appeared as the cover story of a recent issue of the American Geophysical Union's Geophysical Research Letters.

You might evaluate the credibility of this information by noting the author's credentials.

"The water appeared black in satellite imagery because the concentration of the microscopic plants and other dissolved matters were high," Hu said. Because plants and dissolved matter absorb sunlight, they reduce the amount of light normally reflected from the ocean. When a red-tide bloom occurs the water takes on various hues of red or brown. While not all microscopic plants contribute to red tides, the darker hue created by both the plankton and the harmful algal blooms made the water appear black when seen from the satellite.

When Hu and his colleagues examined the data collected by divers from the dark water area in the Florida Keys, they discovered a 70 percent decrease in stony coral cover, a 40 percent reduction of coral species, and a near-elimination of sponge colonies at two reef sites after the dark water passed. By examining satellite images and field survey data, the authors concluded that the coral reef ecosystem was stressed by microscopic organisms and toxins contained in the dark water.

Differentiated Instruction for Universal Access

Enrichment for Advanced Readers

Challenge students to learn more about NASA's involvement in Earth-focused activities. Ask students to choose an area of research, such as climate, atmosphere, or weather, and learn more about the discoveries that NASA has made about the ever-changing planet we live on. Allow time for students to share what they learn.

Enrichment for Gifted/Talented Students

Have students create a mixed-media art piece depicting the conditions off the Florida coast. Encourage them to use descriptions from the news release while incorporating their own interpretations. Have them display their completed art projects in the classroom.

About News Releases

1. Review the features listed in the News Release box on this page. Explain to students that a news release is a piece of writing that announces newsworthy information. Point out that it is typically issued by an organization to members of the media.
2. **Ask** students to offer topics that might appear in a news release. Then, **ask** them to discuss why news releases might be beneficial on such occasions. **Possible response:** Students may say that scientific discoveries, lucrative business transactions, and public apologies could be issued to the media in the form of a news release. Due to the time-sensitive nature of the topic, news releases can provide media outlets and industry professionals with appropriate up-to-date information.

Analyze Texts to Extend Ideas

1. Point out to students that news releases follow a particular format for presenting information. Explain that in order to read a news release effectively, it is important to pay attention to all the text features, such as text structure, headline, and quotations.
2. Have students read "Black Water Turns the Tide on Florida Coral" and the side notes. Then, **ask** students to identify the features used on this page. **Answer:** The news release uses a head, including a dateline and contact information, a headline, and a quotation.
3. Remind students that quotations are the precise words spoken by an individual. **Ask** students how quotations from experts help them to extend ideas. **Possible response:** By providing quotations from such individuals, the main idea of the news release is further supported and confirmed.
4. Remind students that they can evaluate ideas presented in the text by determining how well ideas are supported. **Ask** them to evaluate the use of supporting information in the text. **Possible response:** The authors use quotations from experts as well as statistics and satellite imagery that reinforce the main idea of the news release.

Analyze Texts to Extend Ideas

1. **Ask** students what questions they have about the topic.
Possible response: Students may say that they are curious about the impact that the black water has on the local community. Others may want to know what can be done to prevent black water from occurring in the future.
2. **Ask** them how they would elaborate on the ideas presented.
Possible response: Some students may say that they would research the accuracy at which the instruments perform. Others may say that they would read about the existence of such organisms in other costal waters to determine if the issue off Florida is an isolated case.

Reflecting on the Skill

After students have read both selections, ask them to consider what was most useful to them in applying the skill. **Ask** students to explain which selection allowed them to extend ideas more fully.
Possible response: Some students may say "Tides" provides a better understanding due to the use of visual features. Other students may say "Black Water Turns the Tide on Florida Coral" allows them to gain a better understanding because of the numerous reputable sources referenced throughout the release.

ASSESS/EXTEND

Answers

Can progress be made without conflict?

(a) Scientists addressed the stress and death of coral reef in the Florida Keys. **(b)** Scientists discovered that a large number of toxic plant-life existed in the water off the coast of Florida. These plants migrated to the Keys in red tides, causing the water to darken in color.

The "black water" event caused alarm among local fishermen, divers, and the public, as the color of the water was unusual and fish seemed to avoid this large area of dark water. Satellite instruments such as the Sea-viewing Wide Field-of-view Sensor (SeaWiFS) aboard Orbimage's SeaStar satellite and the Moderate Resolution Imaging Spectroradiometer (MODIS) aboard NASA's Terra and Aqua satellites provide information on ocean color that allows scientists to monitor the health of the water and the shallow benthic (ocean bottom) environment. The SeaWiFS and MODIS measurements of the dark water led to a number of investigations to help clarify the issues and to provide answers to the public's concerns.

You can evaluate how well the data and statistics support the main idea of the article.

During January 2002, SeaWiFS detected the dark-colored water in the Florida Bight, just southwest of the Everglades. In fall 2001, the SeaWiFS images showed an extensive red tide off Florida's central west coast, near Charlotte Harbor.

Red tides occur every year off Florida and are known to cause fish kills, coral stress and mortality, and skin and respiratory problems in humans. They are caused by high concentration of microscopic plants called dinoflagellates. Other microorganisms called cyanobacteria can also cause harmful algal blooms. The waters containing this red tide migrated to the south along the coast. Winter storms caused large amounts of fresh water to drain from the Everglades into Florida Bight (the curve in the shoreline from the Keys north to Everglades National Park on the mainland), carrying high levels of nutrients such as silicate, phosphorus, and nitrogen to the sea. These caused a bloom of the microscopic marine plants known as diatoms in the same patch. The bloom turned the water dark and the "black water" patch re-circulated for several months in a slow clockwise motion off southwest Florida in the Florida Bight. Slowly, the dark water drifted farther south and toward the Florida Keys. By May 2002, the "black water" had moved through passages in the Florida Keys, dispersing into the Atlantic and the Gulf Stream. . . .

To elaborate on these ideas, you might consult a resource on recent incidents of red tides.

NASA funded part of this research as part of its Earth Science mission to understand and protect our home planet. NASA's Earth Science Enterprise is dedicated to understanding the Earth as an integrated system and applying Earth System Science to improve prediction of climate, weather, and natural hazards using the unique vantage point of space.

Can progress be made without conflict?
(a) What conflict did the scientists in this news release address? **(b)** What did the scientists discover as a result of their studies?

Vocabulary Development

Vocabulary from the Natural Sciences

Students may benefit from identifying words in the selection that are associated with the natural sciences. Have students work with a partner to compile a list of unfamiliar technical vocabulary that appears in the selection. After students have compiled their lists, have them locate the definition of each word by using a dictionary. Possible words that students may be unfamiliar with are *plankton, algal, dinoflagellates, cyanobacteria, silicate, phosphorous,* and *diatoms.*

Test Practice: Informational Texts

Comparing Informational Texts

(a) Extend ideas presented in the technical article and news release by **analyzing** and comparing the two texts. What different kinds of details do the two texts present? **(b) Evaluate** how well those details support the main ideas of each text. Which text offers better support? Explain your response. **(c) Elaborate** by describing how the text you found to have weaker support could be improved.

Timed Writing

Write an Essay

Format
The prompt instructs you to write a brief essay. Therefore, your essay should be no longer than three to five paragraphs.

Both the technical article and the news release discuss tides, but from different perspectives. In a brief essay, identify each author's point of view and how it affects the tone and content of the text. Also, consider the combined information of the two sources and explain whether the authors' different perspectives cause discrepancies in the information presented. Support your response with details from the texts. (25 minutes)

Academic Vocabulary
When you *identify* something, you recognize and bring attention to it.

5-Minute Planner

Complete these steps before you begin to write:

1. Read the prompt carefully and completely.
2. Quickly review the two texts to compare the **perspectives,** tone, and content. Consider the effect each author's perspective has on his or her writing. Make notes about your observations. **TIP** Consider the purpose of each text—the author's reason for writing. Doing so will help you better understand the author's perspective.
3. **Synthesize,** or combine, the information in both texts by thinking about all the facts and details presented. Note any **discrepancies**—differences or conflicts—in the combined information.
4. Refer to your notes as you write your essay.

Extend the Lesson

Connecting to the Students' World

To help students enhance their understanding of technical articles and news releases and to help them apply the lesson to their own world, divide students into small groups. Have each group choose an organization in the community and research the organization. Then, have each group write and present a brief news release about recent news related to the organization. When all groups have finished presenting their reports, discuss with students how the information presented would have been different if they had been writing a technical article.

ASSESS/EXTEND

Answers

Comparing Informational Texts

(a) Technical articles present information with the help of a variety of text features. Heads and subheads separate articles into distinct sections while diagrams and images support the text. A news release does not include as many text features. It begins with a headline and the main idea is supported throughout the release. **(b)** Some students may say that the headings, boldfaced words, and graphics of the technical article provide better support because they explain the material more thoroughly. Other students may say that the data, statistics, and quotations from experts in the news release offer better support because they provide more in-depth information. **(c)** The technical article could include quotations from experts to support its main ideas. The news release could include graphics or boldfaced terms to explain its main ideas more thoroughly.

Timed Writing

1. Before students complete the activity, guide them in identifying and analyzing key words and phrases in the prompt, highlighted on the student page.
2. Work with students to draw up guidelines for their responses based on the key words in the prompt:
   - **Focus** The essay should clearly identify each author's perspective and its affect on the tone and content of the text.
   - **Organization** The essay should introduce the authors' perspectives, and then explain their affects and any discrepancies in the text.
   - **Elaboration** The essay should support its points with specific details from the text.
   - **Style** The audience is not specified, so a formal style is suitable.
3. Have students use the 5-Minute Planner to structure their time.
4. Allow students 25 minutes to complete the assignment. Evaluate their work using the guidelines they have developed.

PRETEACH

Meeting Your Standards

Students will

1. analyze and respond to point of view in fiction.
2. compare the effect of point of view in two works of fiction.
3. write a comparison of points of view.

*Log on at **www.PHLitOnline.com** for a detailed lesson plan for Comparing Literary Works.*

❶ Comparing Points of View

1. Introduce the skill, using the instruction on the student page.
2. Give students **Comparing Points of View Graphic Organizer B** (***Graphic Organizer Transparencies***, p. 52) to fill in.

Think Aloud: Model the Skill

Say to students:

To help me understand first-person point of view, I think of conversations I have with friends. When I talk to a friend, I use first-person pronouns such as *I, me,* and *my.* When writers use these pronouns to make it seem like a character is telling a story, the story is told from the first-person point of view.

To understand third-person point of view, I think about television shows. Instead of seeing events from one character's perspective, I can see all the characters and events as they occur. When writers use third-person point of view, they use pronouns such as *he, him, she, her, they,* and *them.*

❷ Vocabulary

1. Have students say each word aloud.
2. Then, use the word in a sentence that defines the word. Repeat the sentence, now with the word missing, and have the class "fill in the blank" orally.

For more guidance, see the ***Classroom Strategies and Teaching Routines*** card, **Introducing Selection Vocabulary**.

Comparing Literary Works

One Thousand Dollars • By the Waters of Babylon

❶ Comparing Points of View

The author's choice of a narrator can affect the credibility, or believability, of a story. **Point of view** is the perspective from which a story is told. Most stories are told from one of the following perspectives:

- **First-person point of view:** The narrator is one of the characters and refers to himself or herself with the pronouns *I* and *me.* One kind of first-person narrator is the **naïve first-person narrator.** This narrator understands less about events in the story than the readers do.
- **Third-person point of view:** The narrator does not participate in the action. Characters are referred to by the third-person pronouns *he, she, him, her, they,* and *them.* The narrator's point of view may be **omniscient** (all-knowing), or it may be **limited** (restricted).

By giving readers more information than the narrator or character has, writers can create **dramatic irony**—a contrast between what the readers know and what the narrator or character believes. Compare the use of point of view in these stories by using a chart like this one.

Story	Point of View	What Reader Knows	What Character Knows	Effect of Contrast in Knowledge	Impact of Story

❷ Vocabulary

- **stipulates** (stip´ yə lāts´) *v.* includes specifically as part of an agreement (p. 308) ***In the contract, he stipulates a May deadline.*** *stipulation n. stipulator n. stipulating v.*
- **prudent** (pro͞o´ dənt) *adj.* exercising sound judgment; cautious (p. 313) ***It is not prudent to go out in the cold without a jacket.*** *prudence n. prudential adj.*
- **purified** (pyo͝or´ ə fīd´) *v.* rid of impurities or pollution; made pure (p. 315) ***Using a filter, he purified the water.*** *purify v. pure adj. purification n. purity n.*
- **nevertheless** (nev´ ər thə les´) *adv.* in spite of that; however (p. 315) ***He expressed regret; nevertheless, the judge ruled harshly.***

PHLit Online! www.PHLitOnline.com

- Vocabulary flashcards
- Interactive journals
- More about the authors
- Selection audio
- Interactive graphic organizers

Vocabulary Development

Vocabulary Knowledge Rating

Create a **Vocabulary Knowledge Rating Chart** (***Professional Development Guidebook***, pp. 32–33) for this selection. Include the selection vocabulary and the Big Question words that appear in the Writing About the Big Question sentence starters on the next page. (The Big Question vocabulary is introduced on pp. 222–223.)

Give students a copy of the chart. Read the words aloud, and have students mark their rating in the Before Reading column. Urge them to be alert to these words as they read and discuss the selection. Tally how many students think they know a word to gauge how much instruction to provide. As students read and discuss the selection, point out the words and their context.

PHLit Online! **Vocabulary Central**, featuring tools, activities, and songs for studying vocabulary, is available at **www.PHLitOnline.com.**

Can progress be made without conflict?

❸ Writing About the Big Question

In each of these stories, the main character finds himself challenged by unusual circumstances. Both of these characters use conflict as a springboard toward **progress.** Use these sentence starters to develop your ideas about the Big Question.

Facing **adversity** could teach someone ________.
After a disagreement is **resolved**, a person may be able to ________.

Meet the Authors

O. Henry (1862–1910)

Author of "One Thousand Dollars"

A native of North Carolina, William Sydney Porter dropped out of school at age fifteen and by his twenties had made his way to Texas. After working for more than a decade as a bank teller, he was convicted—perhaps unjustly—of embezzling bank funds. In prison, he began to write short stories and took on the pen name O. Henry.

Hundreds of Stories Later Upon his release from jail, O. Henry settled in New York City, where he became a full-time and hugely successful short-story writer. He turned out nearly 300 tales, most of them featuring ironic twists of fate.

Stephen Vincent Benét (1898–1843)

Author of "By the Waters of Babylon"

Born in Bethlehem, Pennsylvania, Stephen Vincent Benét grew up listening to his father read poetry in the evenings. During World War I, Benét was barred from active army duty because of poor eyesight. Still, he took time off from his studies at Yale University to serve in the State Department during the war.

Touch of the Poet Benét considered himself a poet first and foremost. Much of his work centers on American history and the quest for American ideals. His interest in American history and folklore influenced his epic poem *John Brown's Body,* which won a Pulitzer Prize in 1929.

Daily Bellringer

For each class during which you will teach this selection, have students complete one of the five vocabulary activities for Week 9 in the *Daily Bellringer Activities* booklet.

❸ Writing About the Big Question

1. Review the assignment with the class.
2. Remind students that progress is a movement toward a goal.
3. Have students complete the sentence starters. Review responses as a class. **Possible response:** Facing adversity could teach someone the inherent ability to overcome something. After a disagreement is resolved, a person may be able to step back and see a different path toward reaching a goal.
4. Remind students that their answers will help them think about the Big Question, "Can progress be made without conflict?" Tell students that as they read, they should look for instances where a character encounters a challenge that he or she overcomes.

Concept Connector →

Students will return to their sentence starters after reading.

Multidraft Reading

For each reading, have students set the purpose indicated:

- **First reading**—literal comprehension: answering the Reading Check questions
- **Second reading**—application of skills: responding to the side-column notes
- **Third reading**—interpretation: answering the end-of-selection questions

For more guidance, refer to the **Classroom Strategies and Teaching Routines** card on multidraft reading.

eaching Resources

e following resources can be used to enrich, extend, or differentiate the instruction.

- *Unit 2 Resources,* pp. 100–117
- *Graphic Organizers Transparencies,* pp. 51, 52
- **Enriched Online Student Edition**

PHLit Online! All resources, including print and audio, are available online at **www.PHLitOnline.com.**

PHLit Online!
For more about the authors, practice with the selection vocabulary, and more background, go online at **www.PHLitOnline.com.**

❶ Background

O. Henry O. Henry thrived on the glamour of New York City. At the height of his popularity, he could afford to eat at the fanciest restaurants and attended parties with the cream of society. But even at the peak of his success, O. Henry was sensitive to the plight of the city's poor and working class. He wrote about New York's "four million" less fortunate souls who were typically ignored by other writers. His stories often juxtaposed the rich and the poor as well as those who came into or lost fortunes easily. O. Henry was wealthy for many years, but he died in poverty with just twenty-three cents in his pocket.

❷ Activating Prior Knowledge

Explain to students that in this selection, they will watch a young man of high society consider the value of one thousand dollars, which he calls an "awkward amount." Explain that from 1900 to 1925, today's dollar was worth $11.38, which means $1,000 was worth $11,380 and $50,000 had the purchasing power of $569,000 in today's money. **Ask** students if they would pick up a penny in the street. A nickel? A dime? A quarter? Have students explain their answers. Discuss what students would consider to be a significant amount of money today.

Concept Connector →

Students will return to the above questions once they have read the selection.

❸ About the Selection

In "One Thousand Dollars," a young New Yorker inherits a small fortune from his uncle and chooses to give it to his uncle's ward, the woman he loves, even though his love is unrequited.

❶ ❷ ❸ ❹

One Thousand Dollars

O. Henry

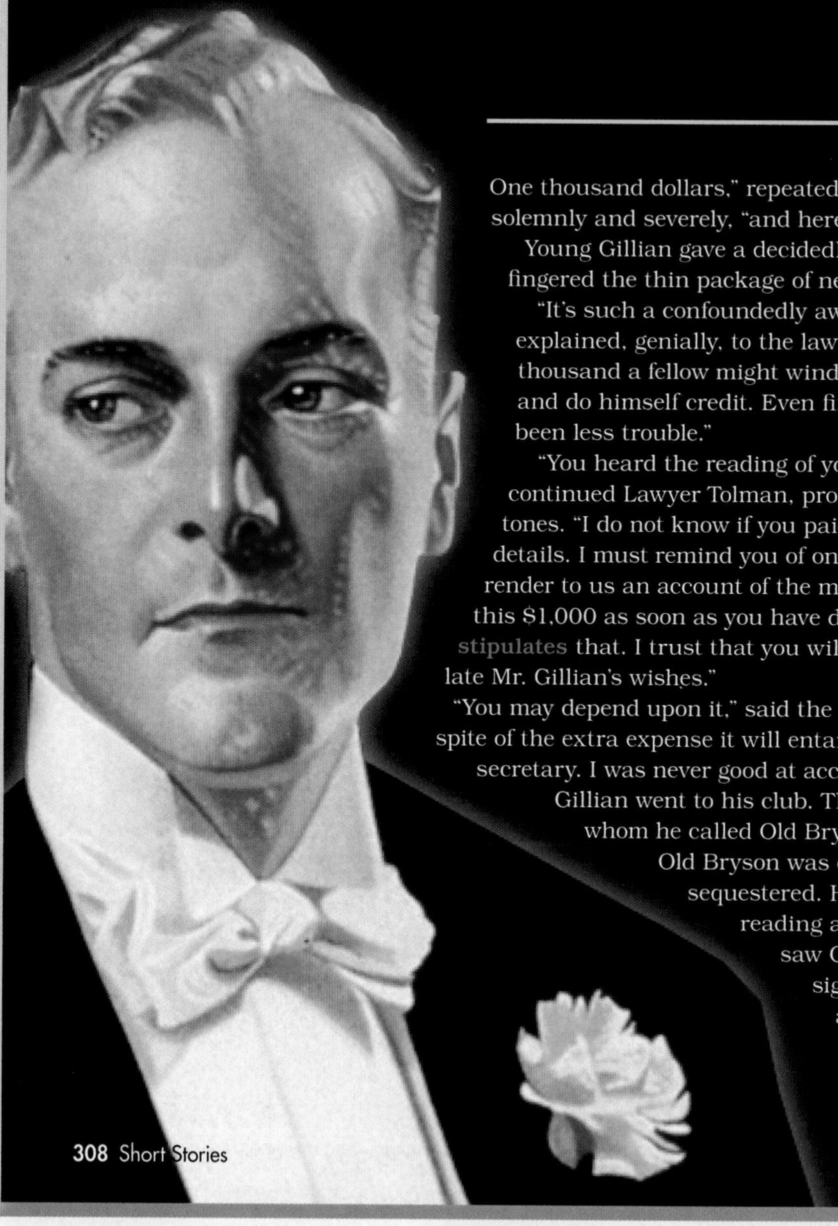

One thousand dollars," repeated Lawyer Tolman, solemnly and severely, "and here is the money."

Young Gillian gave a decidedly amused laugh as he fingered the thin package of new fifty-dollar notes.

"It's such a confoundedly awkward amount," he explained, genially, to the lawyer. "If it had been ten thousand a fellow might wind up with a lot of fireworks and do himself credit. Even fifty dollars would have been less trouble."

"You heard the reading of your uncle's will," continued Lawyer Tolman, professionally dry in his tones. "I do not know if you paid much attention to its details. I must remind you of one. You are required to render to us an account of the manner of expenditure of this $1,000 as soon as you have disposed of it. The will **stipulates** that. I trust that you will so far comply with the late Mr. Gillian's wishes."

"You may depend upon it," said the young man, politely, "in spite of the extra expense it will entail. I may have to engage a secretary. I was never good at accounts."

Gillian went to his club. There he hunted out one whom he called Old Bryson.

Old Bryson was calm and forty and sequestered. He was in a corner reading a book, and when he saw Gillian approaching he sighed, laid down his book and took off his glasses.

"Old Bryson, wake up," said Gillian. "I've a funny story to tell you."

Vocabulary Development

Word Form Chart

Expand students' vocabulary by helping them learn related forms of the Vocabulary words. Give students a blank **Word Form Chart** (***Professional Development Guidebook***, pp. 41–42), with *stipulates* and *prudent* in their appropriate columns. Work with the class, or have students work with a partner, to determine the related forms. The final chart should look like the one shown.

Noun	Verb	Adjective	Adverb
stipulation	**stipulates**	stipulatory	
prudence		**prudent**	prudently

"I wish you would tell it to someone in the billiard room," said Old Bryson. "You know how I hate your stories."

"This is a better one than usual," said Gillian . . . ; "and I'm glad to tell it to you. It's too sad and funny to go with the rattling of billiard balls. I've just come from my late uncle's firm of legal corsairs. He leaves me an even thousand dollars. Now, what can a man possibly do with a thousand dollars?"

"I thought," said Old Bryson, showing as much interest as a bee shows in a vinegar cruet, "that the late Septimus Gillian was worth something like half a million."

"He was," assented Gillian, joyously, "and that's where the joke comes in. He's left his whole cargo of doubloons[1] to a microbe. That is, part of it goes to the man who invents a new bacillus and the rest to establish a hospital for doing away with it again. There are one or two trifling bequests on the side. The butler and the housekeeper get a seal ring and $10 each. His nephew gets $1,000."

"You've always had plenty of money to spend," observed Old Bryson.

"Tons," said Gillian. "Uncle was the fairy godmother as far as an allowance was concerned."

"Any other heirs?" asked Old Bryson.

"None." Gillian frowned . . . and kicked the upholstered leather of a divan uneasily. "There is a Miss Hayden, a ward of my uncle, who lived in his house. She's a quiet thing—musical—the daughter of somebody who was unlucky enough to be his friend. I forgot to say that she was in on the seal ring and $10 joke, too. I wish I had been. Then I could have had two bottles of brut, tipped the waiter with the ring, and had the whole business off my hands. Don't be superior and insulting, Old Bryson—tell me what a fellow can do with a thousand dollars."

6 Old Bryson rubbed his glasses and smiled. And when Old Bryson smiled, Gillian knew that he intended to be more offensive than ever.

"A thousand dollars," he said, "means much or little. One man may buy a happy home with it and laugh at Rockefeller.[2] Another could send his wife South with it and save her life. A thousand dollars would buy pure milk for one hundred babies during June, July, and August and save fifty of their lives. You could count upon a half hour's diversion with it at faro in one of the fortified art galleries. It would furnish an education to an ambitious boy.

1. **doubloons** (də blo͞onz′) *n.* old gold coins of Spanish or Spanish American origin, often associated with pirates.
2. **Rockefeller** John D. Rockefeller (1839–1937), a businessman who became the first American billionaire.

5 ◀ **Critical Viewing** Based on the details in this illustration, what might you speculate about this man? **[Infer]**

Vocabulary
stipulates (stip′ yə lāts′) *v.* includes specifically as part of an agreement

Literary Analysis
Point of View Whose thoughts are revealed in this short paragraph? Who reveals them?

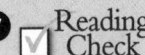

7 **Reading Check**
What problem does young Gillian face?

4 Humanities

Arrow Collars and Shirts—Advertising Poster by Joseph Christian Leyendecer
While studying art in Paris in the 1890s, Joseph Christian Leyendecer realized he could make a living at creating commercial art for posters, magazines, and other advertising media. Leyendecer's first advertising assignment for the Arrow Shirt Company brought him fame. The Arrow Collar Man became one of the most successful advertising images in history. The well-dressed, dignified man defined the fashionable American male. Leyendecer's distinctive brush technique and unique use of highlights and shadows in his images also helped turn Arrow into the largest collar and shirt company in America.

5 Critical Viewing

Possible response: Based on the clothing and the look on the man's face, he is a young, dignified, wealthy aristocrat.

6 Literary Analysis
Point of View

1. Explain that in the third-person point of view, the narrator can reveal the thoughts and emotions of all the characters, although he or she may choose not to do so.
2. Have students read the bracketed passage, paying attention to point of view. **Ask** the Literary Analysis question: Whose thoughts are revealed in this short paragraph? Who reveals them?
   Possible response: This passage reflects Gillian's point of view. The narrator reveals them.

7 Reading Check

Answer: Gillian has to decide how to expend one thousand dollars so that he can report back on the manner of the expenditure to his deceased uncle's lawyers.

Differentiated Instruction for Universal Access

Accessibility at a Glance
Use this information to guide your teaching of "One Thousand Dollars."

Context	Short story of a man who inherits a small fortune.	
Language/Vocabulary	• Conversational • Grade-appropriate vocabulary	
Concept Level	Accessible	
Literary Merit	Noted author	
Lexile/Length	Lexile: 850L	Word Count: 2,133

PHLit Online!
This selection is available in interactive format in the **Enriched Online Student Edition**, online at **www.PHLitOnline.com**, which includes an interactive graphic organizer.

❽ Literary Analysis
Point of View

1. Remind students that in the third-person point of view, the author allows the reader to know things that some characters do not know.
2. Point out that the author does not explain Miss Lotta Lauriere's thoughts. However, she does not seem enthusiastic about a thousand-dollar pendant. Her remark, "Oh, just as you say," suggests that she would accept the pendant, although accepting and valuing would be different ways of receiving Gillian's gift. The fact that he walks out and does not buy the pendant suggests that he assumes she would not value the gift.
3. **Ask** students the first part of the Literary Analysis question: Which details in the scene with Miss Lotta Lauriere would Gillian know firsthand?
   Answer: He would know what transpired when he was in the room with her. He would know that she called him "Bobby," that she was in a hurry to go on stage, and that when he asked if she would like a pendant worth one thousand dollars, she remarked that her friend had one worth more than twice as much.
4. Next, **ask** the second part of the Literary Analysis question: Which details might he not know?
   Answer: He would not know that she had said, "Let *it* in" instead of "Let *him* in." He wouldn't know if she would value a pendant worth one thousand dollars.

I am told that a genuine Corot[3] was secured for that amount in an auction room yesterday. You could move to a New Hampshire town and live respectably two years on it. You could rent Madison Square Garden for one evening with it, and lecture your audience, if you should have one, on the precariousness of the profession of heir presumptive."

"People might like you, Old Bryson," said Gillian, almost unruffled, "if you wouldn't moralize. I asked you to tell me what I could do with a thousand dollars."

"You?" said Bryson, with a gentle laugh. "Why, Bobby Gillian, there's only one logical thing you could do. You can go buy Miss Lotta Lauriere a diamond pendant with the money, and then take yourself off to Idaho and inflict your presence upon a ranch. I advise a sheep ranch, as I have a particular dislike for sheep."

"Thanks," said Gillian, rising. "I thought I could depend upon you, Old Bryson. You've hit on the very scheme. I wanted to chuck the money in a lump, for I've got to turn in an account for it, and I hate itemizing."

Gillian phoned for a cab and said to the driver:

"The stage entrance of the Columbine Theatre."

Literary Analysis
Point of View Which details in the scene with Miss Lotta Lauriere would Gillian know firsthand? Which might he not know?

Miss Lotta Lauriere was assisting nature with a powder puff, almost ready for her call at a crowded matinée, when her dresser mentioned the name of Mr. Gillian.

"Let it in," said Miss Lauriere. "Now, what is it, Bobby? I'm going on in two minutes."

"Rabbit-foot your right ear a little," suggested Gillian, critically. "That's better. It won't take two minutes for me. What do you say to ❽ a little thing in the pendant line? I can stand three ciphers[4] with a figure one in front of 'em."

"Oh, just as you say," carolled Miss Lauriere. "My right glove, Adams. Say, Bobby, did you see that necklace Della Stacey had on the other night? Twenty-two hundred dollars it cost at Tiffany's. But, of course—pull my sash a little to the left, Adams."

"Miss Lauriere for the opening chorus!" cried the call boy without.

Gillian strolled out to where his cab was waiting.

"What would you do with a thousand dollars if you had it?" he asked the driver.

"Open a s'loon," said the cabby promptly and huskily. "I know a place I could take money in with both hands. It's a four-story brick on a corner. I've got it figured out. Second story— . . . chop

---

3. **Corot** (kə rō´) a painting by Jean (zhän) Baptiste (bá tēst´) Camille (ká mē´y´) Corot (1796–1875), a famous French painter.
4. **ciphers** (sī´ fərz) *n.* zeroes.

Vocabulary Development

Thematic Vocabulary: The Big Question

As students are discussing "One Thousand Dollars," ask them to use the thematic vocabulary presented in Introducing the Big Question, pp. 222–223. You might encourage them with sentence starters like these:

1. The internal *struggle* Gillian encountered when he inherited the $1000 was . . .
2. Gillian approached Old Bryson so he could help him *resolve* his situation by . . .
3. Gillian's *motive* in giving Miss Hayden the $1000 might have been . . .
4. The *change* that occurs in Gillian after he learned he was due a far greater inheritance was . . .

suey; third floor—manicures and foreign missions; fourth floor—poolroom. If you was thinking of putting up the cap—"

"Oh, no," said Gillian, "I merely asked from curiosity. I take you by the hour. Drive till I tell you to stop."

Eight blocks down Broadway Gillian poked up the trap[5] with his cane and got out. A blind man sat upon a stool on the sidewalk selling pencils. Gillian went out and stood before him.

"Excuse me," he said, "but would you mind telling me what you would do if you had a thousand dollars?"

"You got out of that cab that just drove up, didn't you?" asked the blind man.

"I did," said Gillian.

"I guess you are all right," said the pencil dealer, "to ride in a cab by daylight. Take a look at that, if you like."

He drew a small book from his coat pocket and held it out. Gillian opened it and saw that it was a bank deposit book. It showed a balance of $1,785 to the blind man's credit.

Gillian returned the book and got into the cab.

"I forgot something," he said. "You may drive to the law offices of Tolman & Sharp, at —— Broadway."

Lawyer Tolman looked at him hostilely and inquiringly through his gold-rimmed glasses.

"I beg your pardon," said Gillian, cheerfully, "but may I ask you a question? It is not an impertinent one, I hope. Was Miss Hayden left anything by my uncle's will besides the ring and the $10?"

"Nothing," said Mr. Tolman.

"I thank you very much, sir," said Gillian, and out he went to his cab. He gave the driver the address of his late uncle's home.

9 Miss Hayden was writing letters in the library. She was small and slender and clothed in black. But you would have noticed her eyes. Gillian drifted in with his air of regarding the world as inconsequent.

"I've just come from old Tolman's," he explained. "They've been going over the papers down there. They found a"—Gillian searched his memory for a legal term—"they found an amendment or a postscript or something to the will. It seemed that the old boy loosened up a little on second thoughts and willed you a thousand dollars. I was driving up this way and Tolman asked me to bring you the money. Here it is. You'd better count it to see if it's right." Gillian laid the money beside her hand on the desk.

Miss Hayden turned white. "Oh!" she said, and again "Oh!"

5. **poked up the trap** pushed open the roof door of the cab so that the driver would know that he wanted to get out.

10 **Reading Check**

What are three ways other characters suggest Gillian spend the thousand dollars?

9 Connecting to the Big Question

1. Explain that when a person faces a challenge, he or she can benefit from what is experienced.
2. Have students read the bracketed text. **Ask:** What challenge has Gillian been faced with to this point in the story? **Answer:** He has to determine how to spend one thousand dollars.
3. **Ask:** Through the gesture that Gillian makes to Miss Hayden, what growth do we see in Gillian? **Possible response:** Gillian has learned he can do something good for another person without looking for recognition for his efforts.

10 Reading Check

Answer: Bryson tells Gillian to buy Lotta Lauriere a pendant; the cab driver tells him to open a saloon; the blind man implies he should save it.

Differentiated Instruction for Universal Access

Strategy for Less Proficient Readers

Some students may have difficulty in understanding Gillian's behavior as he considers how to dispose of the thousand dollars. Discuss as a class his conversations with Miss Lauriere, the cabby, and the blind man. Why does Gillian decide not to give the money to these individuals? Students may speculate that Miss Lauriere was seeking a more expensive gift, that the cabby was ambitious or greedy, and that the blind man already owned more than a thousand dollars.

Enrichment for Advanced Readers

Discuss the changes that might occur if this story were written in first person instead of third person. Ask students to choose one episode from the story. Choose a character to be the narrator, and then rewrite the episode from the first-person point of view. For example, a student may decide to write the library scene in the late uncle's den from Miss Hayden's point of view. Ask volunteers to read their rewritten story aloud.

⓫ Literary Analysis
Point of View

1. Remind students that in the third-person point of view, the reader learns things that remain hidden from other characters in the story.
2. **Ask** the Literary Analysis question: How does the use of a limited third-person narrator help readers see what Gillian is doing in secret?
   Possible response: He writes a letter; only he knows its contents. The reader knows what he has written, but Miss Hayden and the lawyers do not.

Gillian half turned and looked out of the window.

"I suppose, of course," he said, in a low voice, "that you know I love you."

"I am sorry," said Miss Hayden, taking up her money.

"There is no use?" asked Gillian, almost light-heartedly.

"I am sorry," she said again.

"May I write a note?" asked Gillian, with a smile. He seated himself at the big library table. She supplied him with paper and pen, and then went back to her secrétaire.

Literary Analysis
Point of View How does the use of a limited third-person narrator help readers see what Gillian is doing in secret? ⓫

Gillian made out his account of his expenditure of the thousand dollars in these words:

"Paid by the black sheep, Robert Gillian, $1,000 on account of the eternal happiness, owed by Heaven to the best and dearest woman on earth."

Gillian slipped his writing into an envelope, bowed and went his way.

His cab stopped again at the offices of Tolman & Sharp.

"I have expended the thousand dollars," he said, cheerily, to Tolman of the gold glasses, "and I have come to render account of it, as I agreed. There is quite a feeling of summer in the air—do you not think so, Mr. Tolman?" He tossed a white envelope on the lawyer's table. "You will find there a memorandum, sir, of the modus operandi of the vanishing of the dollars."

"I have expended the thousand dollars," he said, cheerily, to Tolman of the gold glasses. . .

Without touching the envelope, Mr. Tolman went to a door and called his partner, Sharp. Together they explored the caverns of an immense safe. Forth they dragged as trophy of their search a big envelope sealed with wax. This they forcibly invaded, and wagged their venerable heads together over its contents. Then Tolman became spokesman.

"Mr. Gillian," he said, formally, "there was a codicil[6] to your uncle's will. It was intrusted to us privately, with instructions that it be not opened until you had furnished us with a full account of your handling of the $1,000 bequest in the will. As you have fulfilled the conditions, my partner and I have read the codicil. I do not wish to encumber your understanding with its legal phraseology, but I will acquaint you with the spirit of its contents.

"In the event that your disposition of the $1,000 demonstrates that you possess any of the qualifications that deserve reward, much benefit will accrue to you. Mr. Sharp and I are named as the judges, and I assure you that we will do our duty strictly according to justice—with liberality. We are not at all unfavorably disposed toward you, Mr. Gillian. But let us return to the letter of the codicil.

6. **codicil** (käd′ i səl) *n.* an addition to a will changing or explaining the instructions it gives.

Vocabulary Development

Financial Vocabulary

Point out to students that the story "One Thousand Dollars" is filled with words particular to the world of finance and the law. Students will be familiar with these words from hearing them on television, reading them in the newspaper, or hearing them in class. Reinforce their comprehension by having groups of students write brief legal or banking dialogue using as many of the following words in any of their forms as appropriate to their dialogue: *expenditure, accounts, doubloons, bequests, heir, Rockefeller, scheme, itemize, ciphers, amendment, expended, render, memorandum, modus operandi, codicil, disposition, accrue, ward.*

Have volunteers perform the dialogues for the class.

If your disposal of the money in question has been **prudent**, wise, or unselfish, it is in our power to hand you over bonds to the value of $50,000, which have been placed in our hands for that purpose. But if—as our client, the late Mr. Gillian, explicitly provides—you have used this money as you have used money in the past—I quote the late Mr. Gillian—in reprehensible dissipation among disreputable associates—the $50,000 is to be paid to Miriam Hayden, ward of the late Mr. Gillian, without delay. Now, Mr. Gillian, Mr. Sharp and I will examine your account in regard to the $1,000. You submit it in writing, I believe. I hope you will repose confidence in our decision."

Mr. Tolman reached for the envelope. Gillian was a little the quicker in taking it up. He tore the account and its cover leisurely into strips and dropped them into his pocket.

"It's all right," he said, smilingly. "There isn't a bit of need to
2 bother you with this. I don't suppose you'd understand these itemized bets anyway. I lost the thousand dollars on the races. Good day to you, gentlemen."

Tolman & Sharp shook their heads mournfully at each other when Gillian left, for they heard him whistling gayly in the hallway as he started for the elevator.

Vocabulary
prudent (pro͞o′ dənt)
adj. exercising sound judgment; cautious

Literary Analysis
Point of View How does the use of a limited third-person narrator help readers know more about what is in the envelope than Mr. Tolman knows?

Critical Thinking

1. **Respond:** What would you have done with the thousand dollars if you had been in Bobby Gillian's place?
2. **(a)** According to his uncle's will, what must Bobby Gillian do after spending the thousand dollars? **(b) Infer:** What are Gillian's feelings about inheriting this amount?
3. **(a) Infer:** Why does Gillian decide to give Miss Hayden the money but not tell the lawyers? **(b) Draw Conclusions:** What do these decisions tell you about his character? **(c) Compare and Contrast:** Compare what these decisions indicate about his character with your first impressions of him.
4. **(a) Analyze:** Why do you think Gillian lets Miss Hayden think that the money was willed to her by his uncle? **(b) Interpret:** What do you think Gillian hopes to gain by doing this?

Can progress be made without conflict?
In this story, Bobby Gillian deals with the conflict of being in love with Miss Hayden, who does not return his affection. **(a)** How does Gillian address this conflict? **(b)** Does dealing with this conflict help him to grow as a person? Explain.

12 Literary Analysis
Point of View

Ask students the Literary Analysis question on this page.
Possible response: The use of this point of view has already provided the reader with the contents of the envelope. However, Mr. Tolman has not opened or read the account.

Concept Connector

Have students compare their Writing About the Big Question responses with their ideas after reading the selection.

ASSESS

Answers

1. Some students may save for college or want to buy a car.
2. (a) Gillian must record how he disposed of the money. (b) He seems almost irritated by it.
3. (a) If he were to tell the lawyers, he would inherit the bonds. As it stands, Miss Hayden will never know that he is her true benefactor. (b) They show that Gillian cares deeply about Miss Hayden's welfare. (c) At first, he seems to be spoiled and irresponsible. By the end of the story, he seems to be a generous man.
4. (a) He does not want her to feel obligated to him. (b) The knowledge that Miss Hayden will be financially stable.

Can progress be made without conflict?
(a) He secretly provides lifelong support for her by giving her the one thousand dollars. (b) Yes. It allows him to act unselfishly.

Differentiated Instruction for Universal Access

EL Pronunciation for English Learners

Some students might have difficulty pronouncing words with the letter "p", as in *power*, *paid*, and *pocket*, replacing the "p" with a "b" sound. The following strategies can help students to pronounce the letter "p."

1. Pair English learners with fluent speakers. Have partners take turns reading from the passage containing the words *power*, *paid*, and *pocket*. Ask fluent speakers to assist English learners when they have difficulty by pronouncing carefully each problem word, guiding the English learners to the correct sound.
2. Pronounce *power*, *paid*, and *pocket* with students. Then, call out words with the same vowel sounds but with different endings. Have students pronounce those, listening for the correct initial "p" sound.

PHLit Online!

This selection is available in interactive format in the **Enriched Online Student Edition**, online at **www.PHLitOnline.com**, which includes an interactive graphic organizer.

13 Background

History The ancient city of Babylon was located on the east bank of the River Euphrates, about thirty miles south of Baghdad, Iraq. Babylon was the site of one of the legendary Seven Wonders of the World, the Hanging Gardens. The Roman historian Diodorus Siculus described the gardens:

> *The approach to the Garden sloped like a hillside and the several parts of the structure rose from one another tier on tier. . . . On all this, the earth had been piled . . . and was thickly planted with trees of every kind that, by their great size and other charm, gave pleasure to the beholder. . . .*

Archaeologists continue to study the Babylonian ruins for the secrets of this once magnificent city.

14 Activating Prior Knowledge

Ask students to imagine that they are exploring an empty building and come on the following scene: "He was sitting in his chair, by the window . . . and, for the first moment, I thought that he was alive. Then I saw the skin on the back of his hand—it was like dry leather."

Discuss how students would react to this discovery.

Concept Connector

Students will compare their responses to the above scene with John's reaction after reading.

15 About the Selection

"By the Waters of Babylon" is set in a time long after our own civilization has been destroyed in a war. The descendants of survivors know little of the destroyed civilization and call its ruins "Places of the Gods." John's hunger for knowledge drives him to enter the forbidden ruins and learn the secrets of the "gods." John, the son of a priest, will reveal what he has learned. Will his people embark on a path toward their own destruction, or will they avoid the mistakes of the past? The story warns that unless we use technology wisely, we may destroy civilization.

13 14 15

BY THE WATERS OF BABYLON

STEVEN VINCENT BENÉT

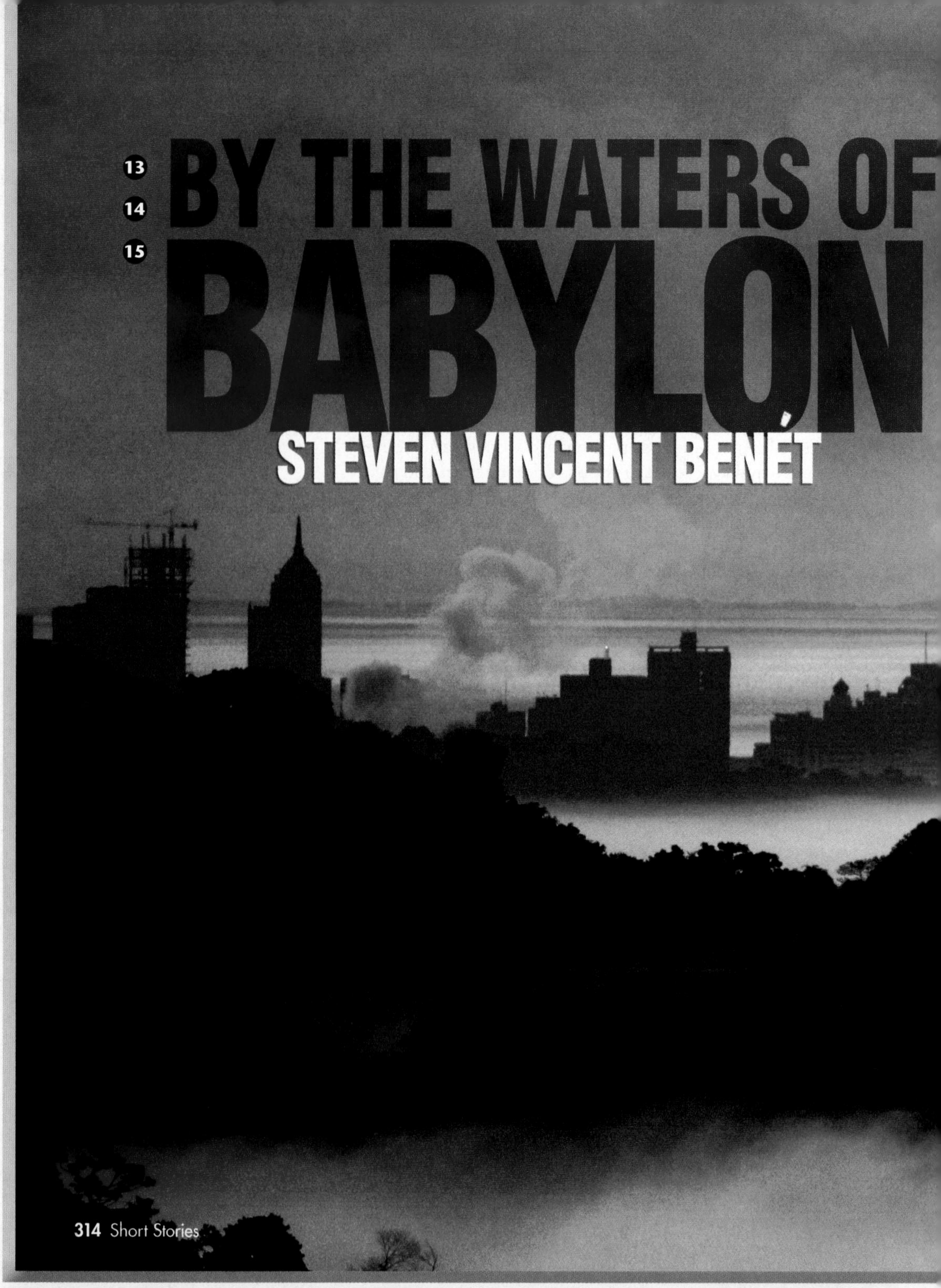

Vocabulary Development

Spiritual Vocabulary

Direct students' attention to words and phrases in the first paragraph that establish the mood, the sense of religion, and the rules of the society. Write the words on the board, including the following: *good hunting ground, forbidden, Dead Places, he who touches, must be, priest, look upon the place, Place of the Gods, purified, most strictly forbidden, do not even say its name, spirits live and demons, it is there, ashes, forbidden since the beginning of time.*

Ask students to summarize what they can tell about the civilization from these words. Elicit the understanding that the religion is primitive and the rules are absolute. The people may sound superstitious and fearful.

The north and the west and the south are good hunting ground, but it is forbidden to go east. It is forbidden to go to any of the Dead Places except to search for metal, and then he who touches the metal must be a priest or the son of a priest. Afterwards, both the man and the metal must be **purified**! These are the rules and the laws: they are well made. It is forbidden to cross the great river and look upon the place that was the Place of the Gods—this is most strictly forbidden. We do not even say its name though we know its name. It is there that spirits live, and demons—it is there that there
16 are the ashes of the Great Burning. These things are forbidden—they have been forbidden since the beginning of time.

My father is a priest; I am the son of a priest. I have been in the Dead Places near us, with my father—at first, I was afraid. When my father went into the house to search for the metal, I stood by the door and my heart felt small and weak. It was a dead man's house, a spirit house. It did not have the smell of man, though there were old bones in a corner. But it is not fitting that a priest's son should show fear. I looked at the bones in the shadow and kept my voice still.

Then my father came out with the metal—a good, strong piece. He looked at me with both eyes but I had not run away. He gave me the metal to hold—I took it and did not die. So he knew that I was truly his son and would be a priest in my time. That was when I was very young—**nevertheless**, my brothers would not have done it, though they are good hunters. After that, they gave me the good piece of meat and the warm corner by the fire. My father watched over me—he was glad that I should be a priest. But when I boasted or wept without a reason, he punished me more strictly than my brothers. That was right.

After a time, I myself was allowed to go into the dead houses and search for metal. So I learned the ways of those houses—and if I saw bones, I was no longer afraid. The bones are light and old—sometimes they will fall into dust if you touch them. But that is a great sin.

I was taught the chants and the spells—I was taught how to stop the running of blood from a wound and many secrets. A priest must know many secrets—that was what my father said. If the hunters think we do all things by chants and spells, they may believe so—it does not hurt them. I was taught how to read in the old books and 17
how to make the old writings—that was hard and took a long time. My knowledge made me happy—it was like a fire in my heart. Most of all, I liked to hear of the Old Days and the stories of the gods. I asked myself many questions that I could not answer, but it was good to ask them. At night, I would lie awake and listen to the

Vocabulary
purified (pyoor´ ə fīd´) *v.* rid of impurities or pollution; made pure

Literary Analysis
Point of View Which words in the first paragraph on this page tell you that the story is written from the first-person point of view?

Vocabulary
nevertheless (nev´ ər *th*ə les´) *adv.* in spite of that; however

Reading Check
Why are the narrator and his father allowed to bring back metal from the "Dead Places"?

16 Literary Analysis
Point of View

1. Have students name some of the signal words they would expect to find in a story told from the first-person point of view.
2. **Ask** students the Literary Analysis question: Which words in the first paragraph on this page tell you that the story is written from the first-person point of view?
   Answer: The narrator uses the words, *I*, *we*, and *my* throughout the paragraph—it is clear that he is telling his own story.

17 Reading Check

Answer: The father is a priest; the narrator is his son. "He who touches metal must be a priest or the son of a priest." And when they return, both the priests and the metal have to be purified.

Differentiated Instruction for Universal Access

Accessibility at a Glance
Use this information to guide your teaching of "By the Waters of Babylon."

Context	In a primitive future, a young priest journeys to the decaying remains of New York City
Language/ Vocabulary	• Long sentences, simple language • Grade-appropriate vocabulary
Concept Level	Challenging
Literary Merit	Noted author
Lexile/Length	Lexile: 810L Word Count: 906

PHLit Online!
This selection is available in interactive format in the **Enriched Online Student Edition**, online at **www.PHLitOnline.com**, which includes an interactive graphic organizer.

18 Literary Analysis
Point of View

1. Acknowledge that determining the credibility of a narrator is challenging. The narrator can present details in any way he or she wants, so it is important for a reader to be conscious of how sincere the narrator is.
2. Have students read the bracketed passage. Instruct them to pay attention to the point of view from which the story is told. **Ask** the Literary Analysis question: What details give the narrator credibility? Do you trust him? Why or why not?
3. **Possible response:** The narrator is forthcoming with his thoughts. Although he recounts what he said to his father, he informs the reader that these words differ from his true feelings. The narrator is honest with the reader, therefore he seems to be trustworthy.

19 Critical Viewing

Possible response: Some students may note that the city is large and developed. Others may note that the gods may have utilized their knowledge of technology to create massive buildings and "god-roads."

wind—it seemed to me that it was the voice of the gods as they flew through the air.

We are not ignorant like the Forest People—our women spin wool on the wheel, our priests wear a white robe. We do not eat grubs from the tree, we have not forgotten the old writings, although they are hard to understand. Nevertheless, my knowledge and my lack of knowledge burned in me—I wished to know more. When I was a man at last, I came to my father and said, "It is time for me to go on my journey. Give me your leave."

He looked at me for a long time, stroking his beard, then he said at last, "Yes. It is time." That night, in the house of the priesthood, I asked for and received purification. My body hurt but my spirit was a cool stone. It was my father himself who questioned me about my dreams.

He bade me look into the smoke of the fire and see—I saw and told what I saw. It was what I have always seen—a river, and, beyond it, a great Dead Place and in it the gods walking. I have always thought about that. His eyes were stern when I told him —he was no longer my father but a priest. He said, "This is a strong dream."

"It is mine," I said, while the smoke waved and my head felt light. They were singing the Star song in the outer chamber and it was like the buzzing of bees in my head.

He asked me how the gods were dressed and I told him how they were dressed. We know how they were dressed from the book, but I saw them as if they were before me. When I had finished, he threw

18 the sticks three times and studied them as they fell.

"This is a very strong dream," he said. "It may eat you up."

"I am not afraid," I said and looked at him with both eyes. My voice sounded thin in my ears but that was because of the smoke.

He touched me on the breast and the forehead. He gave me the bow and the three arrows.

"Take them," he said. "It is forbidden to travel east. It is forbidden to cross the river. It is forbidden to go to the Place of the Gods. All these things are forbidden."

"All these things are forbidden," I said, but it was my voice that spoke and not my spirit. He looked at me again.

"My son," he said. "Once I had young dreams. If your dreams do not eat you up, you may be a great priest. If they eat you, you are still my son. Now go on your journey."

I went fasting, as is the law. My body hurt but not my heart. When the dawn came, I was out of sight of the village. I prayed and purified myself, waiting for a sign. The sign was an eagle. It flew east.

Literary Analysis
Point of View What details give the narrator credibility? Do you trust him? Why or why not?

▶ **Critical Viewing**
Why do you think the tribes in the story refer to a city like the one in this image as "the Place of the Gods?" **[Infer]**

Vocabulary Development

Evolution of Language

Direct students' attention to the word *Ou-dis-sun,*" on the bottom of p. 317. This is the name of a "very long, very wide" sacred river. **Ask** students to name rivers in New York with which they are familiar. When pronounced quickly, do the names of any of these rivers sound similar to *Ou-dis-sun?*
Sample response: It is probably the Hudson, the great river that flows past Manhattan.

Discuss with students that our language is always evolving and that pronunciation changes over time. Write the words *palm* and *calm* on the board, and ask a volunteer to pronounce them. Then, ask if anyone pronounces the words differently. Many students will sound the letter "l" in the words; others may not. Explain that in 1900, few if any people would have sounded the "l." These words are evolving. Explain that the change in the pronunciation of the river's name may indicate how long it has been since the city was destroyed.

Sometimes signs are sent by bad spirits. I waited again on the flat rock, fasting, taking no food. I was very still—I could feel the sky above me and the earth beneath. I waited till the sun was beginning to sink. Then three deer passed in the valley, going east—they did not wind me or see me. There was a white fawn with them—a very great sign.

I followed them, at a distance, waiting for what would happen. My heart was troubled about going east, yet I knew that I must go. My head hummed with my fasting—I did not even see the panther spring upon the white fawn. But, before I knew it, the bow was in my hand. I shouted and the panther lifted his head from the fawn. It is not easy to kill a panther with one arrow but the arrow went through his eye and into his brain. He died as he tried to spring—he rolled over, tearing at the ground. Then I knew I was meant to go east—I knew that was my journey. When the night came, I made my fire and roasted meat.

It is eight suns' journey to the east and a man passes by many Dead Places. The Forest People are afraid of them but I am not. Once I made my fire on the edge of a Dead Place at night and, next morning, in the dead house, I found a good knife, little rusted. That was small to what came afterward, but it made my heart feel big. Always when I looked for game, it was in front of my arrow, and twice I passed hunting parties of the Forest People without their knowing. So I knew my magic was strong and my journey clean, in spite of the law.

Toward the setting of the eighth sun, I came to the banks of the great river. It was half-a-day's journey after I had left the god-road—we do not use the god-roads now for they are falling apart into great blocks of stone, and the forest is safer going. A long way off, I
21 had seen the water through trees but the trees were thick. At last, I came out upon an open place at the top of a cliff. There was the great river below, like a giant in the sun. It is very long, very wide. It could eat all the streams we know and still be thirsty. Its name is Ou-dis-sun, the Sacred, the Long. No man of my tribe had seen it, not even my father, the priest. It was magic and I prayed.

Literary Analysis
Point of View What might the reader understand about the Dead Places that John does not?

22 **Reading Check**

Where is the narrator journeying?

20 Humanities

Sydney Harbour Bridge, 1995 (oil on canvas) by Ted Blackall

The Sydney Harbour Bridge is the world's largest steel arch bridge. It is one of Australia's most popular landmarks, and it has become internationally known as a famous symbol of Australia. In 1815, the first proposal was submitted to build a bridge connecting the north and south sides of the Sydney Harbour. More than one hundred years later, the project was underway. In 1932, the engineering triumph was officially opened after 96 locomotives were lined up to test the strength and capacity of the structure. Today, the bridge links the economic city center in the south with the residential neighborhoods of the north.

21 Literary Analysis

Point of View

1. Help students recognize that the description is of our own decayed civilization. Ask students to share details in the story that lead them to suspect that John explores ruins of our own past.
2. **Ask** students the Literary Analysis question: What might the reader understand about the "Dead Places" that John does not?
   Possible response: The reader knows more than John does because the reader knows the history, geography, and important buildings of our current civilization. The reader would recognize the "god-roads" as the streets and highways leading to a city.

22 Reading Check

Answer: He is journeying to the Place of the Gods in the East.

Fluency

Students may have difficulty reading unfamiliar phrases on page 316. Distribute copies of this page. Read the passage aloud clearly and with expression. Have students mark areas they have difficulty with. Allow students to read the page back to you. Look for these problem spots:

- If students have difficulty with the phrase "hummed with my fasting," direct their attention to the use of the word "fasting" in the first paragraph. Note it is followed by "taking no food." Mention how not eating can make a person feel lightheaded. Reread the sentence, and ask students if the sentence makes sense. Have partners reread the page aloud. Monitor for fluency.
- If students have difficulty with the phrase "eight suns." Remind students about the daily patterns of the sun: It sets and rises each day, so "eight suns" would be eight days. Reread the sentence. Ask students if it makes sense. If so, have them reread the entire passage until they read it fluently.

㉓ Connecting to the Big Question

1. Remind students that change often occurs with the presence of struggle or resistance.
2. Have students read the bracketed passage. Then **ask** students: What challenge does John face at this point in the story?
   Possible response: John has to decide whether he should return to his home or continue on his journey to the Place of the Gods.
3. **Ask** students: Does John benefit from the decision he makes? Have them explain their response.
   Possible response: John benefits from his decision to continue his journey to the Place of the Gods, because he has chosen the prospect of knowledge over the risk of fear.
4. Tell students to look for other challenges John faces as they continue to read.

㉔ Literary Analysis
Point of View

1. Help students to see that the use of a naive first-person point of view allows the reader to know more about the events in the story than the character who is narrating the story.
2. Point out that John is viewing the ruins of Manhattan for the first time.
3. **Ask** the Literary Analysis question: How does the use of a first-person narrator help readers appreciate John's thoughts and actions in this passage?
   Possible response: When John begins to cross the river, he shares his fear. Through the first-person point of view, we feel his anxiety about the ruined city.

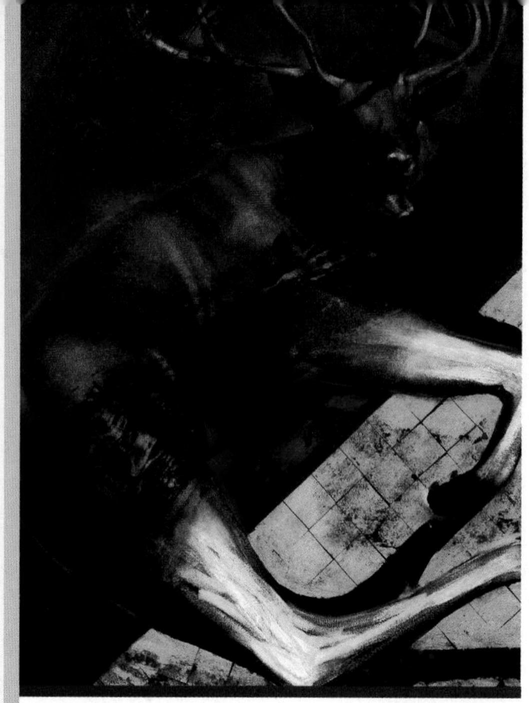

Then I raised my eyes and looked south. It was there, the Place of the Gods.

How can I tell what it was like—you do not know. It was there, in the red light, and they were too big to be houses. It was there with the red light upon it, mighty and ruined. I knew that in another moment the gods would see me. I covered my eyes with my hands and crept back into the forest.

Surely, that was enough to do, and live. Surely it was enough to spend the night upon the cliff. The Forest People themselves do not come near. Yet, all through the night, I knew that I should have to cross the river and walk in the places of the gods, although the gods ate me up. My magic did not help me at all and yet there was a fire in
my bowels, a fire in my mind. When the sun rose, I 2
thought, "My journey has been clean. Now I will go home from my journey." But, even as I thought so, I knew I could not. If I went to the place of the gods, I would surely die, but, if I did not go, I could never be at peace with my spirit again. It is better to lose one's life than one's spirit, if one is a priest and the son of a priest.

Literary Analysis
Point of View How does the use of a first-person narrator help readers appreciate John's thoughts and actions in this passage?

Nevertheless, as I made the raft, the tears ran out of my eyes. The Forest People could have killed me without fight, if they had come upon me then, but they did not come. When the raft was
made, I said the sayings for the dead and painted myself for death. 24
My heart was cold as a frog and my knees like water, but the burning in my mind would not let me have peace. As I pushed the raft from the shore, I began my death song—I had the right. It was a fine song.

"I am John, son of John," I sang. "My people are the Hill People.
They are the men.
I go into the Dead Places but I am not slain.
I take the metal from the Dead Places but I am not blasted.
I travel upon the god-roads and am not afraid. E-yah! I have killed the panther, I have killed the fawn!
E-yah! I have come to the great river. No man has come there before.
It is forbidden to go east, but I have gone, forbidden to go on the great river, but I am there.
Open your hearts, you spirits, and hear my song.
Now I go to the Place of the Gods, I shall not return.
My body is painted for death and my limbs weak, but my heart is big as I go to the Place of the Gods!"

Vocabulary Development

Thematic Vocabulary: The Big Question
As students are discussing "By the Waters of Babylon," ask them to use the thematic vocabulary presented in Introducing the Big Question, pp. 222–223. You might encourage them with sentence starters like these:

1. Father was afraid of the *confrontation* John might encounter when he told the people . . .
2. After telling Father what he saw, John made a *compromise* with himself to . . .
3. John understood that in order for his people to *progress*, he would . . .
4. John learned of the *adversity* that the "gods" faced by . . .

All the same, when I came to the Place of the Gods, I was afraid, afraid. The current of the great river is very strong—it gripped my raft with its hands. That was magic, for the river itself is wide and calm. I could feel evil spirits about me, in the bright morning; I could feel their breath on my neck as I was swept down the stream. Never have I been so much alone—I tried to think of my knowledge, but it was a squirrel's heap of winter nuts. There was no strength in my knowledge any more, and I felt small and naked as a new-hatched bird—alone upon the great river, the servant of the gods.

Yet, after a while, my eyes were opened and I saw. I saw both banks of the river—I saw that once there had been god-roads across it, though now they were broken and fallen like broken vines. Very great they were, and wonderful and broken—broken in the time of the Great Burning when the fire fell out of the sky. And always the current took me nearer to the Place of the Gods, and the huge ruins rose before my eyes.

I do not know the customs of rivers—we are the People of the Hills. I tried to guide my raft with the pole but it spun around. I thought the river meant to take me past the Place of the Gods and out into the Bitter Water of the legends. I grew angry then—my heart felt strong. I said aloud, "I am a priest and the son of a priest!" The gods heard me—they showed me how to paddle with the pole on one side of the raft. The current changed itself—I drew near to the Place of the Gods.

When I was very near, my raft struck and turned over. I can swim in our lakes—I swam to the shore. There was a great spike of rusted metal sticking out into the river—I hauled myself up upon it and sat there, panting. I had saved my bow and two arrows and the knife I found in the Dead Place but that was all. My raft went whirling downstream toward the Bitter Water. I looked after it, and thought if it had trod me under, at least I would be safely dead. Nevertheless, when I had dried my bow-string and restrung it, I walked forward to the Place of the Gods.

It felt like ground underfoot; it did not burn me. It is not true what some of the tales say, that the ground there burns forever, for I have been there. Here and there were the marks and stains of the Great Burning, on the ruins, that is true. But they were old marks and old stains. It is not true either, what some of our priests say, that it is an island covered with fogs and enchantments. It is not. 27 It is a great Dead Place—greater than any Dead Place we know. Everywhere in it there are god-roads, though most are cracked and broken. Everywhere there are the ruins of the high towers of the gods.

25 ◀ Critical Viewing

How does this image represent the natural dangers John has to overcome to get to the Place of the Gods? **[Infer]**

26 Reading Check

How does John feel as he approaches the Place of the Gods?

25 Critical Viewing

Possible response: Some students may note that the deer represents the natural world and the animals that exist within it. Although a deer is not a domesticated animal, wild animals that are domesticated have adapted a ferocious demeanor in order to survive. John will encounter such dangerous creatures.

26 Reading Check

Possible response: John experiences feelings of fear, awe, dread, insignificance, and loneliness.

Differentiated Instruction for Universal Access

Strategy for Less Proficient Readers
Invite students to write a song of their accomplishments. Have them model sections of John's song, "I am ________, son (or daughter) of ________. My people are the _______ people.
I have ________________________.
I have ________________________.
I have ________________________.
(Exclamation) I have
________________________."

Ask them to further model the song or to add lines of their own. Have students share their songs with partners when they are finished.

Enrichment for Gifted/Talented Students.
Invite students to write a song for their graduating class, citing the accomplishments of the class. Have them model sections of John's song, changing the "I" to "We." Have students share their songs with the class and create a composite song of the accomplishments of the class and individuals or groups within the class.

27 Literary Analysis
Point of View

1. Write the following details on the board, and **ask** students to identify the part of New York to which they refer.
   a. Everywhere in it there are god-roads, though most are cracked and broken. (bridges and highways)
   b. Everywhere there are the ruins of the high towers of the gods. (skyscrapers)
   c. The stone with the letters UBTREAS (the Subtreasury Building)
   d. The letters ASHING to describe a man who "wore his hair tied back like a woman's." (George Washington)
2. **Ask** the Literary Analysis question: Which details here suggest that John is a naive narrator—that the reader knows more about what John sees than John does?
3. **Possible response:** The reader recognizes the blind towers as skyscrapers with broken or empty windows. Where John sees strange artifacts, the reader sees the familiar features of a city.

28 Critical Viewing

Possible response: Students may note that the cat is large and muscular. Others may note that the cat is carrying food in its mouth as it runs.

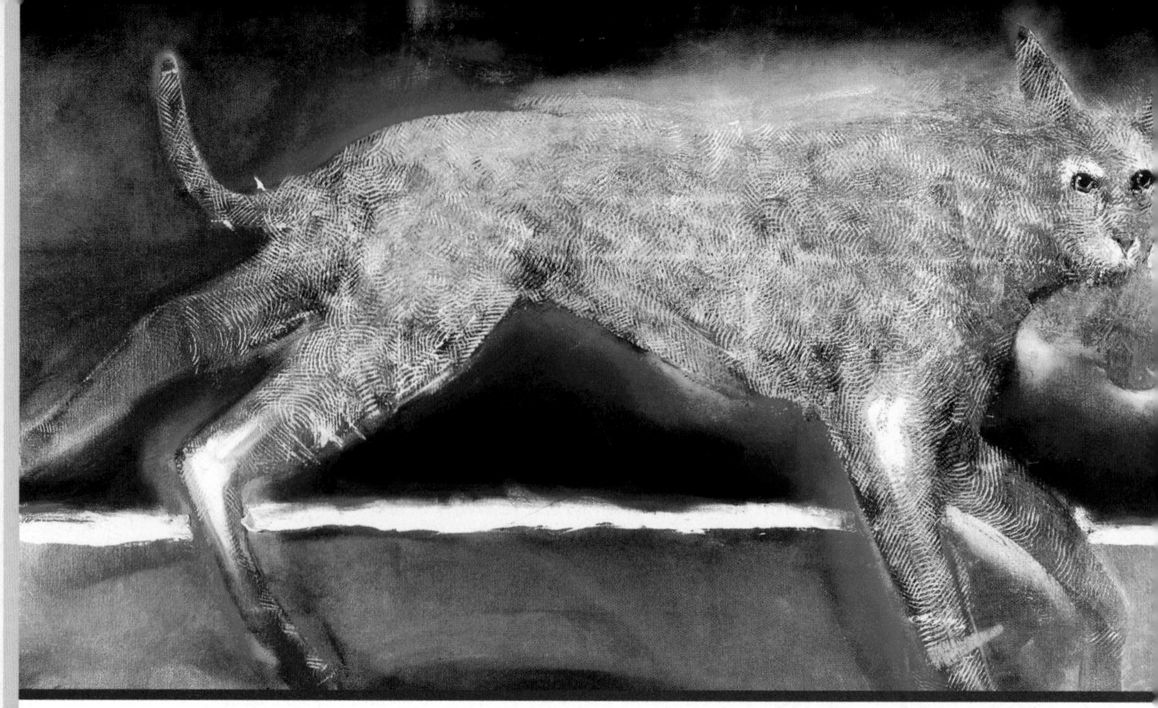

28 ▲ **Critical Viewing** Which details in this image suggest that this cat might be "wild" and "unafraid of men?" **[Infer]**

Literary Analysis Point of View Which details here suggest that John is a naive narrator—that the reader knows more about what John sees than John does?

How shall I tell what I saw? I went carefully, my strung bow in my hand, my skin ready for danger. There should have been the wailings of spirits and the shrieks of demons, but there were not. It was very silent and sunny where I had landed—the wind and the rain and the birds that drop seeds had done their work—the grass grew in the cracks of the broken stone. It is a fair island—no wonder the gods built there. If I had come there, a god, I also would have built.

How shall I tell what I saw? The towers are not all broken—here and there one still stands, like a great tree in a forest, and the birds nest high. But the towers themselves look blind, for the gods are gone. I saw a fish-hawk, catching fish in the river. I saw a little dance of white butterflies over a great heap of broken stones and columns. I went there and looked about me—there was a carved stone with cut-letters, broken in half. I can read letters but I could not understand these. They said UBTREAS. There was also the shattered image of a man or a god. It had been made of white stone and he wore his hair tied back like a woman's. His name was ASHING, as I read on the cracked half of a stone. I thought it wise to pray to ASHING, though I do not know that god. 27

How shall I tell what I saw? There was no smell of man left, on stone or metal. Nor were there many trees in that wilderness of stone. There are many pigeons, nesting and dropping in the

Vocabulary Development

Selection Vocabulary Reinforcement

Students will benefit from additional examples and practice with the selection vocabulary. Reinforce their comprehension with "show-you-know" sentences. The first part of the sentence uses the vocabulary word in an appropriate context. The second part of the sentence—the "show-you-know" part—clarifies the first. Model the strategy with this example for *purified*:

Boiling the water ensured that it was *purified*; we could safely use it for drinking and cooking.

Then give students these sentence prompts, and coach them in creating the clarification part:

1. At a special ceremony after his return, John was *purified*; ___________.
   Sample answer: His people believed that those who went to the Dead Places could be infected by evil.
2. Though fearful, John *nevertheless* proceeded on his journey; ___________.
   Sample answer: His curiosity was greater than his fear.

towers—the gods must have loved them, or, perhaps, they used them for sacrifices. There are wild cats that roam the god-roads, green-eyed, unafraid of man. At night they wail like demons, but they are not demons. The wild dogs are more dangerous, for they hunt in a pack, but them I did not meet till later. Everywhere there are the carved stones carved with magical numbers or words.

I went North—I did not try to hide myself. When a god or a demon saw me, then I would die, but meanwhile I was no longer afraid. My hunger for knowledge burned in me—there was so much that I could not understand. After a while, I knew that my belly was hungry. I could have hunted for my meat, but I did not hunt. It is known that the gods did not hunt as we do—they got their food from enchanted boxes and jars. Sometimes these are still found in the Dead Places—once, when I was a child and foolish, I opened such a jar and tasted it and found the food sweet. But my father found out and punished me for it strictly, for, often, that food is death. Now, though, I had long gone past what was forbidden, and I entered the likeliest towers, looking for the food of the gods.

30 I found it at last in the ruins of a great temple in the mid-city. A mighty temple it must have been, for the roof was painted like the sky at night with its stars—that much I could see, though the colors were faint and dim. It went down into great caves and tunnels—perhaps they kept their slaves there. But when I started to climb down, I heard the squeaking of rats, so I did not go—rats are unclean, and there must have been many tribes of them, from the squeaking. But near there, I found food, in the heart of a ruin, behind a door that still opened. I ate only the fruits from the jars—they had a very sweet taste. There was drink, too, in bottles of glass—the drink of the gods was strong and made my head swim. After I had eaten and drunk, I slept on the top of a stone, my bow at my side.

When I woke, the sun was low. Looking down from where I lay, I saw a dog sitting on his haunches. His tongue was hanging out of his mouth; he looked as if he were laughing. He was a big dog, with a gray-brown coat, as big as a wolf. I sprang up and shouted at him but he did not move—he just sat there as if he were laughing. I did not like that. When I reached for a stone to throw, he moved swiftly out of the way of the stone. He was not afraid of me; he looked at me as if I were meat. No doubt I could have killed him with an arrow, but I did not know if there were others. Moreover, night was falling.

29 LITERATURE IN CONTEXT

History Connection

The Babylonian Captivity

The title of this story, "By the Waters of Babylon," is an **allusion,** or reference, to Psalm 137 in the Bible. In 586 B.C., King Nebuchadnezzar (neb′ yə kəd nez′ ər) destroyed Jerusalem and exiled the Israelites to Babylon. The Babylonian Captivity, as this period is known, ended in 538 B.C. when King Cyrus of Persia formally freed the Israelites. In Psalm 137, the captive Israelites weep over their lost homeland, Zion, in lines such as this one: "By the rivers of Babylon, there we sat down, yea, we wept, when we remembered Zion."

Connect to the Literature

In what sense are John and his tribe in exile from the home where their ancestors lived?

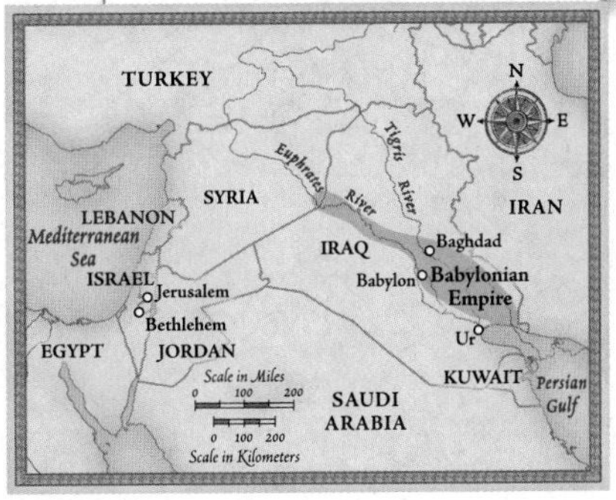

31 Reading Check

What are two things John sees in the Place of the Gods?

29 Literature in Context

History Connection At the time the Israelites were exiled to Babylon, Babylon was one of the most beautiful cities in the world, filled with luxurious gardens and beautiful palaces. Even Alexander the Great and his soldiers sang its praises. Yet, even amidst all the splendor of this great city, the Israelites wept when they remembered their home in Zion.

Connect to the Literature After discussing the Babylonian Captivity with students, **ask** the Connect to the Literature question: In what sense are John and his tribe in exile from the home where their ancestors lived?

Answer: The tribe members keep themselves exiled through the fear of confronting what once was.

30 Literary Analysis

Point of View

1. Have students describe the temple that John enters, and ask them to guess what the temple had been.
   Answer: John has found Grand Central Station, the transportation hub of the city, with its famous ceiling. The caves and tunnels would lead down to the trains. John finds a bar or restaurant in the station and eats canned food and drinks bottled beverages.
2. **Ask** students how this description of the "temple" and the "fruits from the jars" might be different if told from a point of view other than John's.
3. **Possible response:** An omniscient narrator would tell the reader that this was Grand Central Station instead of letting the reader explore the place through John's eyes. A third-person narrator would describe John drinking and eating without the sensations that John himself is able to describe of the drink being "strong" and his head "swimming."

31 Reading Check

Answer: He sees a dog as big as a wolf and a broken god-road leading north toward more towers that are not as tall as the ones in Lower Manhattan.

Differentiated Instruction for Universal Access

EL Strategy for English Learners

Point out that in this story, the main character uses language that is neither standard English nor modern spoken English. In particular, his language lacks nouns for the strange things he encounters on his journey and in his dreams; some descriptions may be unclear to readers. Encourage students to take notes as they read, listing phrases or references—*god-roads, towers, chariots, enchanted boxes*—that need clarification. Students might work in small groups to prepare simple glossaries of these terms.

Strategy for Less Proficient Readers

Point out that John leaves his home to explore a far land. Ask volunteers to share whether they or anyone in their family had ever left the place they considered to be their home. Elicit from students the different ways that people honor the memories of their home, such as posting photographs, telling stories or writing letters. Create a Venn diagram in which students describe the similarities and differences between their home and John's home.

32 Critical Thinking
Analyze

Ask students to discuss how John's being stalked by dogs as he approaches the city reflects the current and previous societies.
Answer: The dogs, which probably evolved from once-loved pets, are tracking John like an animal, sure of their kill. John uses a simple device from the society, a door, to save himself by entering the door and shutting them out. Even though the society is in ruins, the reader sees evidence of how society had once protected man.

33 Literary Analysis
Point of View

1. Remind students that a narrator's point of view can be directly related to the understanding that he or she has about a particular place or time.
2. Have a volunteer read the bracketed passage, keeping in mind the narrator's description of his surroundings.
3. **Ask** the Literary Analysis question: In what ways does John's perception of the "gods" influence his beliefs about his surroundings?
Possible responses: John believes that the gods were wise, magical beings who possessed the ability to enchant objects such as the bronze door. Also, John equates positions with power.
He believes the god who inhabited this home was powerful because he or she possessed many personal belongings. John's lack of knowledge causes him to make incorrect assumptions.

Literary Analysis
Point of View In what ways does John's perception of the "gods" influence his beliefs about his surroundings?

I looked about me—not far away there was a great, broken god-road, leading North. The towers were high enough, but not so high, and while many of the dead-houses were wrecked, there were some that stood. I went toward this god-road, keeping to the heights of the ruins, while the dog followed. When I had reached the god-road, I saw that there were others behind him. If I had slept later, they would have come upon me asleep and torn out my throat. As it was, they were sure enough of me; they did not hurry. When I went into the dead-house, they kept watch at the entrance—doubtless they thought they would have a fine hunt. But a dog cannot open a door and I knew, from the books, that the gods did not like to live on the ground but on high.

I had just found a door I could open when the dogs decided to rush. Ha! They were surprised when I shut the door in their faces—it was a good door, of strong metal. I could hear their foolish baying beyond it, but I did not stop to answer them. I was in darkness—I found stairs and climbed. There were many stairs, 32
turning around till my head was dizzy. At the top was another door—I found the knob and opened it. I was in a long small chamber—on one side of it was a bronze door that could not be opened, for it had no handle. Perhaps there was a magic word to open it, but I did not have the word. I turned to the door in the opposite side of the wall. The lock of it was broken and I opened it and went in

Within, there was a place of great riches. The god who lived there must have been a powerful god. The first room was a small anteroom—I waited there for some time, telling the spirits of the place that I came 33
in peace and not as a robber. When it seemed to me that they had had time to hear me, I went on. Ah, what riches! Few, even, of the windows had been broken—it was all as it had been. The great windows that looked over the city had not been broken at all though they were dusty and streaked with many years. There were coverings on the floors, the colors not greatly faded, and the chairs were soft and deep. There were pictures upon the walls, very strange, very wonderful—I remember one of a bunch of flowers in a jar—if you came close to it, you could see nothing but

Think Aloud

Vocabulary: Using Context
Direct students' attention to the word *anteroom* in the third paragraph. Using a think-aloud process, model how to use context to infer the meaning of an unknown word. Say to the students:

I'm going to think aloud to show you how I would figure out the meaning of *anteroom* from its context.

In this sentence, *anteroom* is being used to describe the first room John enters. It is described as small, and John waited there for some time, which suggests that he had several options of where to move from this room before he went on. I know the word *room*. I know that the prefix *ante* means "before" or "in front of." The *anteroom* must be the foyer or waiting room that leads to other, more important, rooms.

33 bits of color, but if you stood away from it, the flowers might have been picked yesterday. It made my heart feel strange to look at this picture—and to look at the figure of a bird, in some hard clay, on a table and see it so like our birds. Everywhere there were books and writings, many in tongues that I could not read. The god who lived there must have been a wise god and full of knowledge. I felt I had right there, as I sought knowledge also.

34 Nevertheless, it was strange. There was a washing-place but no water—perhaps the gods washed in air. There was a cooking-place but no wood, and though there was a machine to cook food, there was no place to put fire in it. Nor were there candles or lamps—there were things that looked like lamps but they had neither oil nor wick. All these things were magic, but I touched them and lived—the magic had gone out of them. Let me tell one thing to show. In the washing-place, a thing said "Hot" but it was not hot to the touch—another thing said "Cold" but it was not cold. This must have been a strong magic but the magic was gone. I do not understand—they had ways—I wish that I knew.

It was close and dry and dusty in their house of the gods. I have said the magic was gone but that is not true—it had gone from the magic things but it had not gone from the place. I felt the spirits about me, weighing upon me. Nor had I ever slept in a Dead Place before—and yet, tonight, I must sleep there. When I thought of it, my tongue felt dry in my throat, in spite of my wish for knowledge. Almost I would have gone down again and faced the dogs, but I did not.

I had not gone through all the rooms when the darkness fell. When it fell, I went back to the big room looking over the city and made fire. There was a place to make fire and a box with wood in it, though I do not think they cooked there. I wrapped myself in a floor-covering and slept in front of the fire—I was very tired.

Now I tell what is very strong magic. I woke in the midst of the night. When I woke, the fire had gone out and I was cold. It seemed to me that all around me there were whisperings and voices. I closed my eyes to shut them out. Some will say that I slept again, but I do not think that I slept. I could feel the spirits drawing my spirit out of my body as a fish is drawn on a line.

Why should I lie about it? I am a priest and the son of a priest. If there are spirits, as they say, in the small Dead Places near us, what spirits must there not be in that great Place of the Gods? And would not they wish to speak? After such long years? I know that I felt myself drawn as a fish is drawn on a line. I had stepped out of my body—I could see my body asleep in front of the cold fire, but it was not I. I was drawn to look out upon the city of the gods.

Literary Analysis
Point of View What might the reader know about the "thing that said 'Cold'" that John does not know?

35 **Reading Check**
In what way was the life of the gods different from the life John's tribe leads?

34 Literary Analysis
Point of View

1. Remind students of the difference between omniscient third-person and naive third-person. Ask a volunteer to explain the distinction.
2. Explain that the episode in the washroom is an example of naive first-person, since the reader knows what a bathroom looks like and John does not.
3. **Ask** the Literary Analysis question: What might the reader know about the "thing that said 'Cold'" that John does not know?
Possible response: John knows that he is in a "washing place," but he does not know that he is touching the tap for the cold water. The reader knows that only the water that comes from the tap should be cold, not the tap itself.

35 Reading Check

Answer: John's tribe cooks with wood; the New Yorkers would have used gas or electricity. John's tribe uses candles or oil lamps; the New Yorkers would have used electric lights. John's tribe does not have the artwork of flowers and animals, the rugs, the food in jars, or books in other languages.

Differentiated Instruction for Universal Access

Strategy for Less Proficient Students
Students may have difficulty understanding what John is describing. To help them visualize the ruined city, first show them several photographs of modern New York, pointing out skyscrapers, bridges, and highways. Then ask them to imagine these elements in ruins, using John's specific language. For example, the bridges were "broken and fallen like broken vines." Students might find it useful to draw simple sketches of broken bridges, buildings, and highways to help them understand John's descriptions.

Enrichment for Gifted/Talented Students
Challenge your students to make a map of John's journey. They will need to consult a general map of the New York area and a more detailed map of Manhattan. Note that John walks east eight days before viewing the Hudson from a cliff (the Palisades). He rafts south on the river, lands on Manhattan, and finds the ruins of Washington's statue at the U.S. Subtreasury (now the Federal Hall National Memorial at Broad and Wall Street). Students may work in groups, and then compare and discuss their different versions.

㊱ Literary Analysis
Point of View

1. For some readers, this dream scene will be the first time they understand where John is. **Ask** a volunteer to explain what John sees in his dream.
   Answer: John sees lights, gods on foot and in chariots, bridges, tunnels, and tools that allow the gods to fly.
2. Discuss the author's use of the dream to make the setting clear for the reader. Have students consider whether the dream is meant to develop John's character or to simply describe the real setting.
3. **Ask** students the Literary Analysis question: In what way is John's perception of these scenes different from what yours would be?
   Possible response: John does not understand the cars, planes, and trains that he sees in his dreams. He does not know the roaring is the rush of traffic. He does not know the lights were the lights of Broadway. He does not understand that New York City was alive day and night.

㊲ Critical Viewing

Possible response: John describes a city that is filled with the sounds and sights of life. People crammed the streets, on foot and in automobiles, and moved impatiently as blinding lights illuminated the sky around them. The picture mimics John's description, but it does not provide as much insight as his description does.

㊳ Humanities

Tudor City at Night, Overlooking East River, 1998 (oil on canvas) by Nicholas Gibbs

Tudor City was built in Midtown Manhattan overlooking the East River during the 1920s. It consisted of 12 apartment buildings that contained 3,000 housing units and 600 hotel rooms. The brickwork and fine intricate stonework used in the building were known as the Tudor style, and so the community was named Tudor City. Today, the exclusive area is a historic district that houses about 5,000 people and covers an area from 40th Street to 43rd Street between First and Second Avenue.

It should have been dark, for it was night, but it was not dark. Everywhere there were lights—lines of light—circles and blurs of light—ten thousand torches would not have been the same. The sky itself was alight—you could barely see the stars for the glow in the sky. I thought to myself "This is strong magic" and trembled. There was a roaring in my ears like the rushing of rivers. Then my eyes grew used to the light and my ears to the sound. I knew that I was seeing the city as it had been when the gods were alive.

That was a sight indeed—yes, that was a sight: I could not have seen it in the body—my body would have died. Everywhere went the gods, on foot and in chariots—there were gods beyond number and counting and their chariots blocked the streets. They had turned night to day for their pleasure—they did not sleep with the sun. The noise of their coming and going was the noise of many waters. It was magic what they could do—it was magic what they did.

㊱ **Literary Analysis**
Point of View
In what way is John's perception of these scenes different from what yours would be?

I looked out of another window—the great vines of their bridges were mended and the god-roads went East and West. Restless, restless, were the gods and always in motion! They burrowed tunnels under rivers—they flew in the air. With unbelievable tools they did giant works—no part of the earth was safe from them, for, if they wished for a thing, they summoned it from the other side of the world. And always, as they labored and rested, as they feasted and made love, there was a drum in their ears—the pulse of the giant city, beating and beating like a man's heart.

Were they happy? What is happiness to the gods? They were great, they were mighty, they were wonderful and terrible. As I looked upon them and their magic, I felt like a child—but a little more, it seemed to me, and they would pull down the moon from the sky. I saw them with wisdom beyond wisdom and knowledge beyond knowledge. And yet not all they did was well done—even I

㊲ ▼ **Critical Viewing**
Compare this picture with John's descriptions of the Place of the Gods. **[Compare and Contrast]**
㊳

Vocabulary Development

Selection Vocabulary: Reinforcement

To reinforce and assess students' comprehension of selection vocabulary words, give them sentences using the words in which the word may or may not be used correctly. Students must tell whether the use is correct and explain their answer. Use these sentences:

1. The worker's new contract *stipulates* the increase in wages and improved health care coverage.
   Answer: Yes, *stipulates* means "specifies in an agreement." A contract is something that is agreed upon.
2. Ana *stipulates* that she's the prettiest girl.
   Answer: No, Ana's statement is an opinion not an agreement.
3. Mason is a *prudent* man who always makes careless decisions.
   Answer: No, *prudent* is not used correctly. It means "cautious," but making a careless decision is not cautious.
4. *Prudent* people save part of their income.
   Answer: Yes, *prudent* is used correctly here. Saving one's wages is a sensible thing to do.

36 could see that—and yet their wisdom could not but grow until all was peace.

Then I saw their fate come upon them and that was terrible past speech. It came upon them as they walked the streets of their city. I have been in the fights with the Forest People—I have seen men die. But this was not like that. When gods war with gods, they use weapons we do not know. It was fire falling out of the sky and a mist that poisoned. It was the time of the Great Burning and
39 the Destruction. They ran about like ants in the streets of their city—poor gods, poor gods! Then the towers began to fall. A few escaped—yes, a few. The legends tell it. But, even after the city had become a Dead Place, for many years the poison was still in the ground. I saw it happen, I saw the last of them die. It was darkness over the broken city, and I wept.

Literary Analysis
Point of View In what way has John's view of the gods changed?

All this, I saw. I saw it as I have told it, though not in the body. When I woke in the morning, I was hungry, but I did not think first of my hunger, for my heart was perplexed and confused. I knew the reason for the Dead Places but I did not see why it had happened. It seemed to me it should not have happened, with all the magic they had. I went through the house looking for an answer. There was so much in the house I could not understand—and yet I am a priest and the son of a priest. It was like being on one side of the great river, at night, with no light to show the way.

Then I saw the dead god. He was sitting in his chair, by the window, in a room I had not entered before and, for the first moment, I thought that he was alive. Then I saw the skin on the back of his hand—it was like dry leather. The room was shut, hot and dry—no doubt that had kept him as he was. At first I was afraid to approach him—then the fear left me. He was sitting looking out over the city—he was dressed in the clothes of the gods. His age was neither young nor old—I could not tell his age. But there was wisdom in his face and great sadness. You could see that he would have not run away. He had sat at his window, watching his city die—then he himself had died. But it is better to lose one's life than one's spirit—and you could see from the face that his spirit had not been lost. I knew that, if I touched him, he would fall into dust—and yet, there was something unconquered in the face.

That is all of my story, for then I knew he was a man—I knew then that they had been men, neither gods nor demons. It is a great knowledge, hard to tell and believe. They were men—they went a
41 dark road, but they were men. I had no fear after that—I had no fear going home, though twice I fought off the dogs and once I was hunted for two days by the Forest People. When I saw my father again, I prayed and was purified. He touched my lips and my

40 **Reading Check**
What event does John see in his vision?

39 Literary Analysis
Point of View

1. Discuss John's perception of the gods up to this point. Have students make a list of words that John might use to describe the gods, such as *powerful, technological, builders*, and so on.
2. **Ask** students to evaluate why John assigns supernatural powers to the civilization that has passed.
   Possible response: John does not understand the technological advances that people took advantage of in the past. The only way he can make sense of everything is by attributing it all to supernatural powers.
   Ask a volunteer to explain why we assign magical powers to situations we do not understand.
   Possible response: Some students may explain that people have a difficult time leaving things unanswered. In response, some people assign magical powers to these situations in order to answer the unknown.
3. **Ask** the Literary Analysis question: In what way has John's view of the gods changed?
   Possible response: John pities them. He sees the gods running around like ants as the fire and poison fall from the sky. He says, "poor gods, poor gods." He sees the last of them die and he weeps.

40 Reading Check

Answer: He sees the war that destroys the city and all the people in it.

Differentiated Instruction for Universal Access

Strategy for Special Needs Students
Some students may need extra help understanding point of view. When a story is told from first-person point of view, readers know only details that the narrator knows. Ask students to make a Venn diagram. Together, list details in one circle that only John, the narrator, knows. This includes how he feels and what he thinks. In the second circle, list details that only a viewer watching the action from outside might know. In the center, list details that would be known by both.

Enrichment for Advanced Readers
Ask students to analyze Benét's decision to use a naive first-person point of view in this story. Point out that this choice produces both dramatic irony and tension. From early in the story, the reader knows far more about what John is seeing than he himself does. Much of the pleasure of reading the story derives from making discoveries based on the fragments of John's understanding. To consider alternate choices, ask students to mentally "replay" the story as if it were told from an omniscient third-person point of view. What effects would the story gain or lose?

Literary Analysis
Point of View

Ask the Literary Analysis question on the student page.
Answer: Yes, both John and the reader understand that John has encountered a lost city of men who were neither gods nor demons.

Concept Connector

Have students compare the Writing About the Big Question responses they had before reading the story to their ideas after reading.

ASSESS

Answers

1. **Possible responses:** Yes, because people don't often have time to process all the information they have in order to make a good decision. No, because having information at our fingertips is critical to maintaining and improving society.
2. The Dead Places are American homes before the last war. New York City is the Place of the Gods. (b) John's tribe is terrified of the Dead Places.
3. **Possible responses:** (a) From John's description of the horrific deaths, it seems as though the story is set in a time after the creation of the atom bomb. (b) A nuclear holocaust destroyed the city. The narrator recounts seeing fire that fell from the sky and poisonous gaseous materials.
4. (a) John's father wants the truth to be revealed gradually. He does not want his people to acquire knowledge before they have the wisdom to use it safely. (b) **Possible responses:** Some students may agree that man cannot control the power he has. Others may make a case that there are wise people who can handle the knowledge.

Can progress be made without conflict?

(a) John learns that the gods are actually people and that they died as the result of a great fire that fell from the sky. (b) No, because if John had not gone on the journey, he would not have learned the information that he did.

41 breast, he said, "You went away a boy. You come back a man and a priest." I said, "Father, they were men! I have been in the Place of the Gods and seen it! Now slay me, if it is the law—but still I know they were men."

He looked at me out of both eyes. He said, "The law is not always the same shape—you have done what you have done. I could not have done it in my time but you come after me. Tell!"

I told and he listened. After that, I wished to tell all the people but he showed me otherwise. He said, "Truth is a hard deer to hunt. If you eat too much truth at once, you may die of the truth. It was not idly that our fathers forbade the Dead Places." He was right—it is better the truth should come little by little. I have learned that, being a priest. Perhaps, in the old days, they ate knowledge too fast.

Literary Analysis
Point of View Does John's new understanding of the gods now match the reader's? Explain.

Nevertheless, we make a beginning. It is not for the metal alone we go to the Dead Places now—there are the books and the writings. They are hard to learn. And the magic tools are broken—but we can look at them and wonder. At least, we make a beginning. And, when I am chief priest we shall go beyond the great river. We shall go to the Place of the Gods—the place newyork—not one man but a company. We shall look for the images of the gods and find the god ASHING and the others—the gods Lincoln and Biltmore[1] and Moses.[2] But they were men who built the city, not gods or demons. They were men. I remember the dead man's face. They were men who were here before us. We must build again.

1. **Biltmore** hotel in New York City.
2. **Moses** Robert Moses, former New York City municipal official who oversaw many large construction projects.

Critical Thinking

1. **Respond:** After returning from the Dead Place, John thinks, "Perhaps, in the old days, they ate knowledge too fast." Do you think our society eats "knowledge too fast"? Explain.
2. **(a) Infer:** What are the Dead Places and the Place of the Gods? **(b) Synthesize:** How does John's tribe view the Dead Places?
3. **(a) Draw Conclusions:** When is this story set? Explain what led you to this conclusion. **(b) Infer:** What destroyed the city? Explain.
4. **(a) Speculate:** Why does John's father want to keep John's experience secret? **(b) Evaluate**: Do you agree with John's father?

Can progress be made without conflict?
(a) What progress does John make as a result of dealing with conflict? Explain. **(b)** Do you think he could have made this progress without facing conflict? Why or why not?

Vocabulary Development

Vocabulary Knowledge Rating

When students have completed reading and discussing "One Thousand Dollars" and "By the Waters of Babylon," have them take out their **Vocabulary Knowledge Rating Chart.** Read the words aloud once more and have students rate their knowledge of the words again in the After Reading column. Clarify any words that are still problematic. Have students write their own definition and example or sentence in the appropriate column. Then, have students complete the Vocabulary Practice activities on the next page. Encourage students to use the words in further discussion and written work about this selection. Remind them that they will be accountable for these words in the **Selection Test** (*Unit 2 Resources*, pp. 112–114 or 115–117).

After You Read

One Thousand Dollars • By the Waters of Babylon

Comparing Points of View

1. Using a chart like the one shown, compare the way the authors use **point of view** in "One Thousand Dollars" and "By the Waters of Babylon" to control the information the reader receives.

Story	Point of View	What Reader Knows	What Character Knows	Effect of Contrast in Knowledge	Impact of Story

2. **(a)** Compare the ways in which the ending of each story surprises the reader. **(b)** For each story, explain how the author's choice of narrator helps prepare for this surprise.
3. **(a)** The reader may find Gillian's final gesture moving because the reader sees that no one knows what he has done. Explain how point of view makes this effect possible. **(b)** Compare this feeling with the one the ending of "By the Waters of Babylon" creates. Why might a modern reader feel humbled by the end of Benét's story?

Writing to Compare Points of View

Both stories use **dramatic irony.** In an essay, compare and contrast how the irony is achieved in these stories. First, consider these questions:

- What is the point of view from which the story is told?
- What is the character or persona of the narrator?
- How much do you trust the narrator to tell you the truth?
- What is the nature of the truth that is revealed in the ending?

Finally, explain which use of irony you found more effective.

Vocabulary

Practice Answer each of the following sentences. Then, using your knowledge of the underlined word, explain your response.

1. Is it dangerous to drink water that has been purified?
2. If you are not hungry, might you nevertheless want to eat?
3. If you sell your bicycle, is it fair if the buyer stipulates the price?
4. Would it be prudent to stay up all night before a big test?

Assessment Resources

Unit 2 Resources

L1 L2 EL **Selection Test A,** pp. 112–114.
L3 L4 **Selection Test B,** pp. 115–117.
L3 L4 **Open-Book Test,** pp. 109–111.

PHLit Online! All assessment resources are available at **www.PHLitOnline.com.**

ASSESS

Answers

Comparing Points of View

1. **Sample answer:** "One Thousand Dollars": third-person limited; reader knows some, not all, of Gillian's thoughts; characters know only what Gillian says and does; contrast emphasizes Gillian's nobility; leads to surprise ending.
2. (a) By giving away a fortune, Gillian shows surprising depth of character. John shows that he has overcome his fears. (b) In "One Thousand Dollars," the reader cannot know Gillian's motives. In "By the Waters of Babylon," the reader shares John's perceptions and is more prepared for the surprise.
3. (a) The point of view allows only the reader to know about Gillian's generous act. (b) The reader is humbled that great knowledge does not prevent destruction.

Writing to Compare Points of View

1. Review the assignment criteria with students.
2. Instruct students to determine the use of dramatic irony in each selection. Then, as they draft, encourage students to refer to the information in the chart they completed for question 1.

Six Traits Focus

✓	Ideas	✓	Word Choice
✓	Organization		Sentence Fluency
	Voice		Conventions

Vocabulary

Sample answers:

1. No, it is not dangerous because purified water is clean.
2. You might have just eaten, but nevertheless, you might eat a cookie in spite of not being hungry.
3. No, it is not fair that a buyer stipulates the price, it should be up to the seller to decide on a price.
4. No, it would not be prudent because you may impair sound thinking.

PRETEACH

Meeting Your Standards

Students will

1. write a short story.
2. use writing strategies to generate ideas and to plan, organize, evaluate, and revise a short story.
3. use imagination to shape the story.
4. apply grammar skills.

Introducing the Writing Assignment

Review the assignment and the criteria, using the instruction on the student page.

Connecting to Real-Life Writing

Point out to students that short-story elements are often incorporated into other types of writing, such as travel writing and persuasive writing

Writing Workshop *Work in Progress*

If students have done the Work-in-Progress assignments on pp. 267 and 295, suggest that they examine their recorded ideas as they begin prewriting. They may wish to develop these ideas in a short story.

Prewriting

1. Introduce the prewriting strategies, using the instruction on the student page.
2. Have students apply the strategies to gather character details.

Six Traits Focus

✔	Ideas		Word Choice
✔	Organization		Sentence Fluency
	Voice		Conventions

Writing and Grammar Interactive Textbook Online

Students can use the following tools at **www.pearsonsuccessnet.com** as they complete their short stories:

- Character Trait Word Bin
- Story Wheels

Writing Workshop

Narration: Short Story

Defining the Form **Short stories** are a form of fiction that can take readers to exciting and unusual settings, or they can explore the conflicts and struggles of ordinary life. You might use elements of the short story in anecdotes, scripts, and reflective essays.

Assignment Write a short story in which you tell about a main character who undergoes a change or learns something. Include these elements:

✔ a clear *setting*—the time and place of the story

✔ a *plot,* or series of events, that builds to a dramatic climax

✔ effective descriptions using *sensory details*

✔ a *theme* that is revealed by the story's end

✔ error-free grammar, including use of *consistent verb tense*

To preview the criteria on which your short story may be judged, see the rubric on page 333.

Reading Writing Connection
To get a feel for short stories, read "A Problem" by Anton Chekhov, on p. 256.

Writing Workshop: *Work in Progress*

Review the work you did on pages 267 and 295.

Prewriting Strategy

Gather details about characters. Before you begin your draft, get to know the characters you will develop. Create a character chart describing your characters' unique dreams, fears, habits, and quirks.

Apply It!

Character Chart	
Name	Kei
Appearance	Small frame, dark hair, intense brown eyes
Three Key Adjectives	smart, clumsy, ambitious
Goals	to be a great trumpet player
Habits or Quirks	taps his fingers
Likes	jazz, football, reading
Dislikes	TV, his boss at his after school job

Teaching Resources

The following resources can be used to enrich, extend, or differentiate the instruction.

All *Unit 2 Resources*
Writing Workshop, pp. 118, 119

All *Professional Development Guidebook*
Rubric for Self Assesment: Short Story, pp. 226–227

All *Graphic Organizer Transparencies*
Rubric for Self-Assessment: Short Story, p. 55

PHLit Online! All resources are available online at **www.PHLitOnline.com.**

WRITER'S TOOLBOX

Ideas | Conventions | Sentence Fluency | Voice | Organization | Word Choice

Using Your Imagination

Ideas are building blocks of your story. They shape the plot, setting, and characters. As you search for ideas, begin with any one element—plot, setting, or characters—and develop the other two elements from there. Use these tips to engage your imagination and develop story ideas.

Imagining the Setting Create a setting you would choose if you could live anywhere or at any historical time. You can adapt most universal themes to any setting. For example, Shakespeare's play *Romeo and Juliet* is set in medieval Italy. The musical *West Side Story*, based loosely on the same plot, is set in 1950s New York City. Consider the setting before starting plot and character development. Often, the setting suggests the plot and characters. For example, a setting of a colony on a distant planet might suggest a struggle for survival.

Imagining the Plot Think about a dramatic moment in your life or the life of someone you know, or use the newspaper or TV news to find an intriguing story. Turn the outlines of the personal event or news story into a short story. Remember that a short story is fiction, so you can add details or change the facts in order to make the story more interesting.

You might also use one of the "universal themes" of stories that can be adapted to any time or place. Examples include

- a couple whose love is doomed, such as in *Romeo and Juliet*
- a hero who leads a desperate fight of good against evil
- a young person on a quest to save his family, his tribe, or his world

Imagining the Characters Think about the kind of character who would live in the setting or fit the plot you have chosen. As you develop your ideas, use a chart like the one shown to jot down notes.

	Plot	Setting	Character
Idea 1	a young boy struggles for survival in the wilderness	a remote area of the Rocky Mountains	a young boy scout who has wandered away during a camping trip
Idea 2			
Idea 3			

WG

Prentice Hall Writing and Grammar Connection: Chapter 5

Differentiated Instruction for Universal Access

Support for Less Proficient Readers

While students might be able to picture a place for the setting or a certain character for their short stories, some students might have difficulty organizing their ideas into a coherent plot.

Work with students to create a large chart like the one shown on the bottom of p. 329. Have students first describe and record the setting. Next, have students describe and record their characters, considering each character's age, appearances, and traits. Encourage students to brainstorm for ideas about what might happen to their characters in their chosen settings. Finally, work with students to lay out frameworks for their plots, including exposition, rising action, climax, and denouement.

Using Your Imagination

1. Introduce the writing skill, using the instruction on the student page.
2. Discuss the tips and strategies for imagining the setting, plot, and characters.

Teaching the Writing Skill

1. Explain to students that we have at least two lenses through which we can perceive the world: our senses and our imagination. Our senses allow us to note and understand what we see, hear, feel, taste, and smell. Often, we do not question what we experience through our senses, because we perceive these experiences as real. Our imagination, however, allows us to think and feel beyond what we experience through our senses.
2. Remind students that although short stories are fictional, a skillful writer can use his or her imagination to create a very realistic story. Sometimes a fictional story can seem more real than a nonfiction one. Ask students to name short stories or novels they have read that seemed real.
3. Encourage students to consider what our imaginations allow us to do as we read and write literature. **Ask:** Suppose imagination did not exist. How would writing and reading fiction be different? How would the value of writing and reading fiction change?
Possible response: Because we would not be able to picture the action, dialogue, setting, and character, fiction would be insipid and boring. As a result, fiction would not serve any worthwhile purpose.
4. Explain to students that the more vividly they picture the setting, plot, and characters in their story, the easier it will be to describe and, later, develop these short-story elements.

OES Online Essay Scorer

A writing prompt for this mode of writing can be found on the *PH Essay Scorer* at **www.PHLitOnline.com.**

Drafting Strategies

1. Introduce the drafting strategies, using the instruction on the student page.
2. Have students apply the strategies as they draft.

Teaching the Strategies

Tell students to record the events of their stories in plot charts. Below each event, students should explain how the event contributes to the characterization or conflict.

Think Aloud: Model Flashback

Model the strategy, using the following "think aloud":

> In my short story, Reuben is about to meet his twin sister, whom he hasn't seen in ten years. To add suspense, I can delay the meeting by preceding it with a flashback showing Reuben's memory of his sister and his anxiety. This flashback creates suspense, reveals Reuben's feelings, and provides information about him and his sister.

Six Traits Focus

✓	Ideas		Word Choice
✓	Organization		Sentence Fluency
✓	Voice		Conventions

Revising Strategies

1. Introduce the revision strategies, using the instruction on the student page.
2. Have students apply the strategies as they review their drafts.

Teaching the Strategies

Write this sentence on the board:

Lina and Ming argue.

Explain why this sentence *tells* rather than *shows.* Invite students to revise the "telling" sentence into "showing" paragraphs.

Six Traits Focus

	Ideas	✓	Word Choice
	Organization		Sentence Fluency
✓	Voice		Conventions

WG Writing and Grammar, Grade 10

Students will find additional instruction on drafting and revising a short story in Chapter 5, Sections 3 and 4.

Drafting Strategies

Make a plot diagram. The plot of your story should include exposition to set up the characters, setting, and conflict. Rising action will build to a climax, or point of highest tension. Then, the falling action leads to the resolution. Create a plot diagram like the one here and jot down your major story events to keep your writing on track.

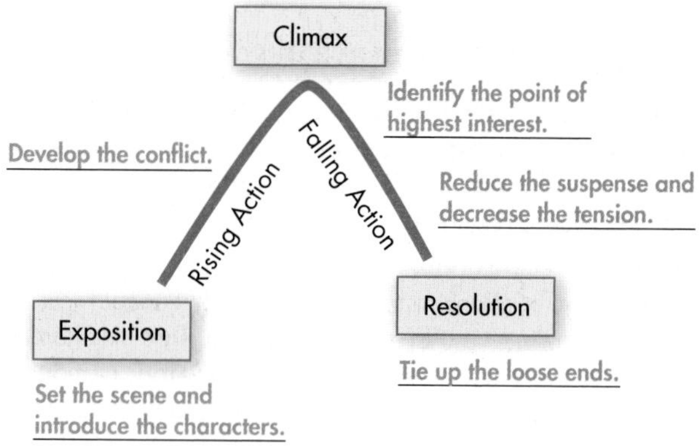
Climax
Identify the point of highest interest.
Develop the conflict.
Rising Action
Falling Action
Reduce the suspense and decrease the tension.
Exposition
Set the scene and introduce the characters.
Resolution
Tie up the loose ends.

Keep pacing in mind. To keep your story moving, consider introducing the problem early in the story. Then, add details that intensify the problem. Using *flashbacks*—or material that occurred earlier than the present time of the narrative—is one way to add intensity. Flashbacks can be in the form of a character's memories, dreams, or accounts of past events, or simply a shift in the narrative back to an earlier time. You might also delay the climax to create more suspense. After the climax, wrap things up quickly to hold your readers' interest.

Revising Strategies

Add dialogue to develop characters. Look for points where you can develop characters through dialogue and action. If your characters are from a specific region or background, including their dialect will help readers hear how they sound. Review your draft to identify direct statements that could be replaced with the characters' own words.

Revise to use active voice. Active voice is livelier and more engaging than the passive voice. In the passive voice, the action is done to the subject. In the active voice, the subject of the sentence performs the action.

Passive Voice: The deadline was met by Krista and Rachel.

Active Voice: Krista and Rachel met their deadline.

Add sensory details. Add sensory details to your writing to enable the reader to experience what you are describing. Sensory details are words that appeal to the senses: sight, smell, taste, touch, and hearing. Instead of writing, *The pie smelled good,* you might say, *The pie filled the house with the aroma of apples and cinnamon.* This allows the reader to partake in your description.

Understanding by Design

Clarifying Expected Outcomes: Using Rubrics

- Before students begin working on this assignment, have them preview the Rubric for Self-Assessment (p. 333) to learn what qualities their short story must have. A copy of this rubric appears in ***Graphic Organizer Transparencies***, p. 55.
- Review the criteria in the rubric with the class. Before students use the rubric to assess their writing, work with them to rate the Student Model (p. 332) using the rubric.
- If you wish to assess students' short story with either a 4-point or a 6-point scoring rubric, see ***Professional Development Guidebook***, pp. 226–227.

WRITER'S TOOLBOX

Conventions | Sentence Fluency | Voice | Organization | Word Choice | Ideas

Revising to Apply Consistent Verb Tense

Correct use of verb tenses indicates when an event occurred. It is best to stay with a single tense. Mixing tenses unnecessarily can confuse the reader.

Six Basic Verb Tenses	
Present	He *arrives* today.
Past	He *arrived* yesterday.
Future	He *will arrive* tomorrow.
Present Perfect	He *has arrived* already.
Past Perfect	He *had arrived* earlier than expected.
Future Perfect	He *will have arrived* by next week.

Identifying Mixed Tenses To identify mixed tenses, first recognize the verb tenses you use. Compare these examples:

Mixed Tenses: Kei *has knocked* and *was waiting* patiently at the door. Nothing *happens*. Kei *had decided* to leave.

Consistent Tense: Kei *knocked* and *waited* patiently at the door. Nothing *happened*. Kei *decided* to leave.

Mixing tenses is necessary when your work refers to two different times.

Past Perfect — Past

Kei had waited for ten minutes before the door opened.

Prentice Hall Writing and Grammar Connection: Chapter 11, Section 4

Fixing Errors To make sure that your verb tenses are consistent, find each verb in your writing.

1. **Identify your overall verb tense as past, present, or future.**
2. **Review the verbs in your writing, circling each one.**
3. **If you find a verb that is not in your basic verb tense, make sure the tense shift is necessary.**
4. **Revise the verb if the shift is unnecessary.**

Grammar in Your Writing

Review two paragraphs of your draft. Underline every verb and identify its tense. Use the steps you have just learned to fix confusing mixed tenses.

Differentiated Instruction for Universal Access

Support for Less Proficient Readers
Students may understand verb tense but have difficulty maintaining consistent tense or recognizing changes in tense. Emphasize that most stories are told in the past tense. Encourage students to use the past tense exclusively in their stories. Review drafts with students to check for events that occur in different time periods, requiring changes in tense.

Enrichment for Advanced Readers
Tell students that various verb tenses can be employed because of the effects and meanings they produce. Suggest that students experiment with tense by rewriting a paragraph or two of their stories in different tenses and noting the different impressions that are produced.

Revising to Apply Consistent Verb Tense

1. Introduce the grammar skill, using the instruction on the student page.
2. Discuss the examples and the strategies for fixing incorrect usage.
3. Have students follow the instruction under Grammar in Your Writing to correct errors in their drafts.

Teaching the Grammar Skill

1. To help students maintain consistent verb tense, ask them to identify when their narrators are telling their stories: as the events are happening or after all the events described have happened.
2. Have students practice using consistent verb tense with these examples. Tell them to choose one tense for each passage:
   a. *I'm going to the store, but I didn't want to buy too many things. I haven't had much money lately.*
   Sample answer: I'm going to the store, but I don't want to buy too many things. I haven't had much money lately.
   b. *She wants to see a movie. But when she called Carolyn, she has learned there will be something better to do downtown.*
   Sample answer: She wanted to see a movie. But when she called Carolyn, she learned that there was something better to do downtown.
   c. *I run up the stairs as fast as I could, but I will be too late. The cat already knocked everything off the table.*
   Sample answer: I ran up the stairs as fast I could, but I was too late. The cat had already knocked everything off the table.

Writing and Grammar, Grade 10

Students will find additional instruction on applying consistent verb tense in Chapter 22, Section 1.

Student Model

Review the Student Model with the class, using the annotations to analyze the writer's use of the elements of a short story.

Teaching From the Student Model

1. Point out that only the beginning of Aubrey's story is shown in the Student Model. Explain that the ellipsis at the end means that the rest of the text has been omitted.
2. **Ask** students to identify what the beginning of a short story is called.
   Answer: The opening of a short story is called the *exposition*.
3. Read the description of the setting aloud to students. **Ask** them to identify the sense to which each detail appeals.
   Answer: Hearing: dull rumble; Sight: flicker of light illuminated; Touch: cool breeze rustled her long skirt
4. **Ask** students to identify the type of conflict that the writer reveals through dialogue.
   Answer: The dialogue reveals an external conflict between two characters.

Connecting to Real-Life Writing

Explain to students that short stories can be found in many different media, such as magazines and journals. Point out that many of the stories students read in collections such as *Prentice Hall Literature* were first published in magazines or journals. The short-story structure also has a life beyond the printed page. Most television dramas and situation comedies are, in effect, dramatized short stories. Each episode has a setting, characters, and a clearly defined plot with a conflict building to a climax. Many films share these same elements.

Student Model: Aubrey Weatherford, Broken Arrow, OK

And Then the Rain Came

"Is it wrong for us to have a voice in our lives? We have to fight!" said the woman speaking to the crowd. Scarlett flashed instantly to the night of the fire. She could feel the young man holding her back; she could hear the child screaming in the burning building. She struggled to free herself, tears running down her face. Shaking herself back into reality, Scarlett walked slowly away from the park, the speaker's words fading as she went. There was a dull rumble in the distance, and a flicker of light illuminated the city around her. The cool breeze rustled her long skirt, and she began to quicken her pace for fear of being caught in the storm. Scarlett's mind was spinning, the speaker's words stirring her thoughts. The thought of speaking her opinion and of being able to choose whomever she wanted for public office, though she had never learned exactly what their jobs were—just the thought of having the choice was enough to excite her.

"Little Lady, you had better hurry on home now. There's a gonna be quite a storm a comin'." An old, wrinkled man had approached Scarlett from the shadows, seemingly trying to help. She was looking at him patiently.

"Hey you, crazy man, leave the lady alone. You go on home now, you worthless old fool!" A middle-aged businessman had approached the two.

"Don't talk to him that way! He wasn't bothering me!" Scarlett said. "You don't need to associate with street people like him. Go on home!"

"You have no right to speak to me in that fashion, good sir. I may associate with whomever I choose."

The businessman turned on his heel and left. "Thank yer for standing up for me, little lady. Mighty appreciative."

"It was nothing. You remind me so much of, oh, never mind," Scarlett replied.

"I am sure I will walk by here again sometime. I will look for you. Good day, sir." Though Scarlett did not see it, the old man began to come out of the shadows as she made her way down the crowded street, though his appearance had greatly changed. He was no longer a wrinkled, old man but a tall, young man with sandy hair and piercing eyes. Carefully, he watched as Scarlett hurried along the sidewalk. Tiny drops of rain began to fall from the ashen sky as Scarlett disappeared into the crowd. . . .

Aubrey introduces the main character in the first paragraph.

Sensory details describe the setting.

Aubrey develops the conflict through dialogue.

These details reveal an interesting twist in the plot.

Strategies for Using Technology in Writing

If students are using word processors to draft and revise their short stories, suggest that they create separate files for each of the major characters, settings, and events. In each of these files, students can create dialogue and details associated with these particular elements of their stories. Students may freewrite to create this material. As they draft and revise, students can copy and paste this material into their stories as appropriate. Students can also use the organizing tools available on the **Writing and Grammar Interactive Textbook Online.**

Editing and Proofreading

Reread your story to correct errors in grammar, usage, and mechanics.

Focus on Complete Sentences and Spelling: Check that all sentences in your draft contain a subject and a verb and express a complete thought. Words with double letters, such as *dilemma*, and words with two sets of double letters, such as *embarrass*, are often spelled incorrectly. Make up clues to help yourself remember any word that you often misspell.

Publishing and Presenting

Consider one of the following ways to share your writing:

Give a dramatic reading. Practice reading your story aloud, experimenting with pace, emphasis, and tone. Then, read your story to a group of classmates. After the presentation, discuss which of your story's elements were especially effective when presented dramatically.

Compile an anthology. Join with your classmates to create a class story anthology. Organize the stories by theme and illustrate them with suitable photographs or drawings. Place the collection in your class, school, or community library.

WG *Prentice Hall Writing and Grammar Connection: Chapter 5*

Reflecting on Your Writing

Writer's Journal Jot down your answers to this question:

How did writing about the work help you to understand it?

Rubric for Self-Assessment

Find evidence in your writing to address each category. Then, use the rating scale to grade your work.

Criteria	Rating Scale (not very — very)
Focus: How clear is the story's theme or message?	1 2 3 4 5
Organization: How effectively does the plot build to a climax?	1 2 3 4 5
Support/Elaboration: How effective is your choice of details?	1 2 3 4 5
Style: How well do you describe the characters and setting?	1 2 3 4 5
Conventions: How correct is your grammar, especially your use of verb tense?	1 2 3 4 5
Ideas: How effective and interesting are your ideas for plot, setting and characters?	1 2 3 4 5

Strategies for Test Taking

Some tests, including state assessments, require students to respond to narrative writing prompts. Make sure that students understand what a narrative writing prompt requires of them. Students should recognize that they are being asked to write a story, and they should pay close attention to specific elements they are required to incorporate. Instruct students to read the prompt carefully, looking for questions or topics they need to address. Students should also refer to the prompt as they prewrite, making sure that they are addressing every aspect of the prompt.

When students have completed the Writing Workshop, ask them to consider how their stories changed throughout the writing process. Remind them that even in a test-taking situation, the writing process will change their stories. After incorporating all the required elements of the prompt in the prewriting stage, students need to make sure their stories retain these elements in their final drafts.

Editing and Proofreading

1. Introduce the editing and proofreading focus, using the instruction on the student page.
2. Have students edit and proofread their short stories, correcting grammar, spelling, punctuation, and word choice. Make sure they check for errors of the type noted on the student page.

Teaching the Editing Focus

Explain that no sentence is complete unless it contains a subject and verb. Make sure students recognize that even sentence fragments can include both subjects and verbs.

Six Traits Focus

	Ideas		Word Choice
	Organization		Sentence Fluency
	Voice	✔	Conventions

ASSESS

Publishing and Presenting

1. Lead students in a discussion about whether readers need to read their stories to really understand them or whether hearing them read aloud with expression would better convey their messages.
2. Before students present their stories to the class, encourage them to practice reading them aloud. Have students practice in pairs or small groups.

Reflecting on Your Writing

As students prepare to reflect, have them look back at their prewriting notes. Ask students if the most important elements of their stories have changed. If so, how have they changed and why?

WG **Writing and Grammar, Grade 10**

Students will find additional guidance on editing and proofreading, publishing and presenting, and reflecting on a short story in Chapter 5, Section 6.

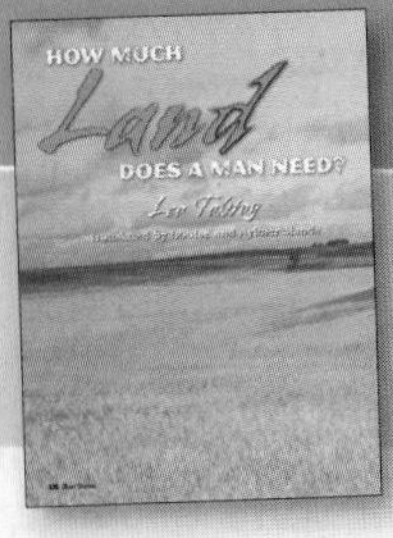

TIME AND RESOURCE MANAGER

How Much Land Does a Man Need? • Civil Peace

Lesson Pacing Guide

DAY 1 Preteach

- Administer the Reading and Vocabulary Warm-ups (*Unit 2 Resources*, pp. 127–130 or 145–148) as necessary.
- Introduce the Reading Skill: Draw Conclusions FT
- Introduce the Literary Analysis concept: Theme FT
- Distribute copies of the appropriate graphic organizer for the Reading Skill (*Graphic Organizer Transparencies*, pp. 56–58). CRI
- Distribute copies of the appropriate graphic organizer for Literary Analysis (*Graphic Organizer Transparencies*, pp. 59–61). CRI
- Teach the selection vocabulary. FT CRI
- Introduce the Word Study skill.

DAYS 2–3 Preteach/Teach

- Build background with the Background feature. CRI
- Develop thematic vocabulary and thematic thinking with Writing About the Big Question.
- Prepare students to read with the Activating Prior Knowledge activities (TE). CRI
- Informally monitor comprehension while students read. FT
- Use the Reading Check questions to confirm comprehension.
- Develop students' ability to draw a conclusion using the Reading Skill questions. CRI
- Develop students' understanding of theme using the Literary Analysis questions. CRI
- Reinforce vocabulary with the Vocabulary notes. CRI

DAY 4 Assess

- Assess students' comprehension and mastery of the skills by having them answer the Critical Thinking, Reading Skill, and Literary Analysis questions. FT
- Have students complete the Vocabulary Practice activities. FT
- Have students complete the Word Study activities.

DAY 5 Extend/Assess

- Have students complete the Grammar lesson. CRI
- Have students complete the Writing activity and write a character analysis. (You may assign as homework.) FT
- Extend learning by having students complete the Listening and Speaking activity, a theme. As an alternative, assign them "The Greed Game" or "Learning from Crime Victims" in *Reality Central*. CRI
- Administer Selection Test A or B (*Unit 2 Resources*, pp. 139–144 or 160–165). FT

"How Much Land Does a Man Need?" is a short story edited for English-language translation purposes. "Civil Peace" is a short story presented unedited and in its entirety.

Meeting Your Standards

Students will
1. analyze and respond to literary elements.
   - Literary Analysis: Theme
2. read, comprehend, and analyze short stories.
   - Reading Skill: Draw Conclusions
   - Reading Check questions
   - Apply the Skills questions
   - Assessment Practice
3. develop vocabulary.
   - Vocabulary
   - Word Study
4. apply grammar skills.
   - Action and Linking Verbs
5. Develop writing proficiency.
   - Work in Progress: Problem-and-Solution Essay
6. strengthen listening and speaking skills.
   - group discussion

CRI For a full explanation of Culturally Responsive Instruction opportunities in this lesson, see p. T86–T87.

FT For an accelerated lesson, use the Fast Track strategies and activities.

Managing Differentiated Instruction
This leveled selection pairing groups a more accessible with a more challenging selection. Choose either one to teach the lesson skills. For classroom management suggestions for using the pairing in a mixed-ability class, see pp. T68–T69.

Daily Block Scheduling
Each day in this Lesson Pacing Guide represents a 40–50 minute period. Teachers using block scheduling may combine days to revise pacing. In addition, teachers may differentiate and support core instruction by integrating components for extended and intensive support as students require. See the Guide to Selected Leveled Resources (facing page).

Guide to Selected Leveled Resources

EL English Learners

			How Much Land Does a Man Need?	Civil Peace
CORE COURSE	*Unit 2 Resources*	Selection Test A	pp. 139–141	pp. 160–162
	Graphic Organizer Transparencies	Reading Skill Graphic Organizer A	p. 56	p. 57
		Literary Analysis Graphic Organizer A	p. 59	p. 60
EXTENDED SUPPORT (Level 2)	*Unit 2 Resources*	Reading and Vocabulary Warm-ups A or B	pp. 127–130	pp. 145–148
	Reader's Notebook: English Learner's Version		adapted instruction and adapted selection	adapted instruction and summary
	Hear It! Audio CD		selection and summaries	selection and summaries
	Hear It! Audio CD (adapted text)		adapted selection and summaries	—
INTENSIVE SUPPORT (Level 1)	*Reality Central*		"The Greed Game"	"Learning from Crime Victims"
	Real-World Writing Journal		Lesson 5, pp. 52–55	Lesson 6, pp. 56–59

L2 Below-Level Students

			How Much Land Does a Man Need?	Civil Peace
CORE COURSE	*Unit 2 Resources*	Selection Test A	pp. 139–141	pp. 160–162
	Graphic Organizer Transparencies	Reading Skill Graphic Organizer A	p. 56	p. 57
		Literary Analysis Graphic Organizer A	p. 59	p. 60
EXTENDED SUPPORT (Level 2)	*Unit 2 Resources*	Reading and Vocabulary Warm-ups A or B	pp. 127–130	pp. 145–148
	Reader's Notebook		adapted instruction and full selection	adapted instruction and summary
	Hear It! Audio CD		selection and summaries	selection and summaries
INTENSIVE SUPPORT (Level 1)	*Reality Central*		"The Greed Game"	"Learning from Crime Victims"
	Real-World Writing Journal		Lesson 5, pp. 52–55	Lesson 6, pp. 56–59
	Reading Kit		Reteaching worksheets	Reteaching worksheets

L1 Special Needs Students

			How Much Land Does a Man Need?	Civil Peace
CORE COURSE	*Unit 2 Resources*	Selection Test A	pp. 139–141	pp. 160–162
	Graphic Organizer Transparencies	Reading Skill Graphic Organizer A	p. 56	p. 57
		Literary Analysis Graphic Organizer A	p. 59	p. 60
EXTENDED SUPPORT (Level 2)	*Unit 2 Resources*	Reading and Vocabulary Warm-ups A or B	pp. 127–130	pp. 145–148
	Reader's Notebook: Adapted Version		adapted instruction and adapted selection	adapted instruction and summary
	Hear It! Audio CD (adapted text)		adapted selection and summaries	—
INTENSIVE SUPPORT (Level 1)	*Reality Central*		"The Greed Game"	"Learning from Crime Victims"
	Real-World Writing Journal		Lesson 5, pp. 52–55	Lesson 6, pp. 56–59
	Reading Kit		Reteaching worksheets	Reteaching worksheets

The program includes resources for these students: L3 On-Level L4 Advanced All All
For a complete guide to selection support, see pp. T106–T108.

NOTE: All print materials are also available online at *www.PHLitOnline.com.*

VISUAL GUIDE to Featured Selection Resources

• How Much Land Does a Man Need?
• Civil Peace

RESOURCES FOR:

- EL English Learners
- L1 Special Needs Students
- L2 Below-Level Students
- L3 On-Level Students
- L4 Advanced Students
- All All Students

Vocabulary/Fluency/Prior Knowledge

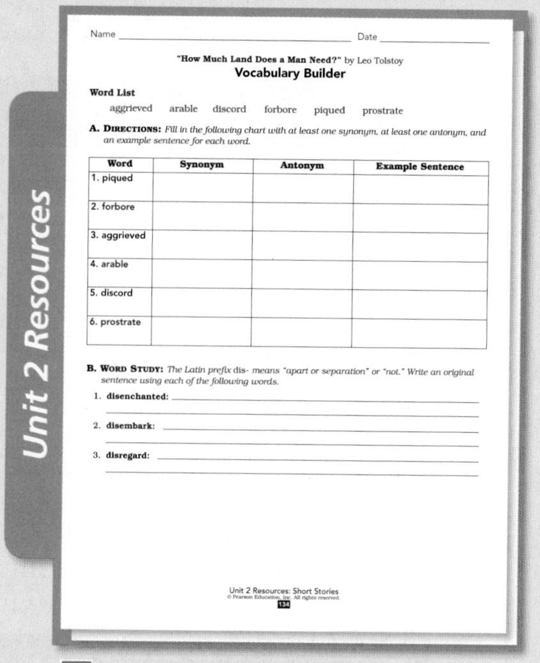

Unit 2 Resources

Name ______________________ Date ____________

"How Much Land Does a Man Need?" by Leo Tolstoy

Vocabulary Builder

Word List

aggrieved arable discord forbore piqued prostrate

A. Directions: *Fill in the following chart with at least one synonym, at least one antonym, and an example sentence for each word.*

Word	Synonym	Antonym	Example Sentence
1. piqued			
2. forbore			
3. aggrieved			
4. arable			
5. discord			
6. prostrate			

B. Word Study: *The Latin prefix* dis- *means "apart or separation" or "not." Write an original sentence using each of the following words.*

1. **disenchanted:** ____________
2. **disembark:** ____________
3. **disregard:** ____________

Unit 2 Resources: Short Stories
© Pearson Education, Inc. All rights reserved.
134

All **Vocabulary Builder,** pp. 134, 152

Also available for these selections:

EL L1 L2 Reading Warm-ups A and B, pp. 129–130, 147–148

EL L1 L2 Vocabulary Warm-ups A and B, pp. 127–128, 145–146

All Writing About the Big Question, pp. 131, 149

L2 L3 ***Reader's Notebook***

L1 ***Reader's Notebook: Adapted Version***

EL ***Reader's Notebook: English Learner's Version***

Reader's Notebooks

Pre- and postreading pages for both selections, as well as "How Much Land Does a Man Need?" appear in an interactive format in the *Reader's Notebooks.* Each *Notebook* is differentiated for a different group of learners.

The selections in the Adapted and English Learner's versions are abridged.

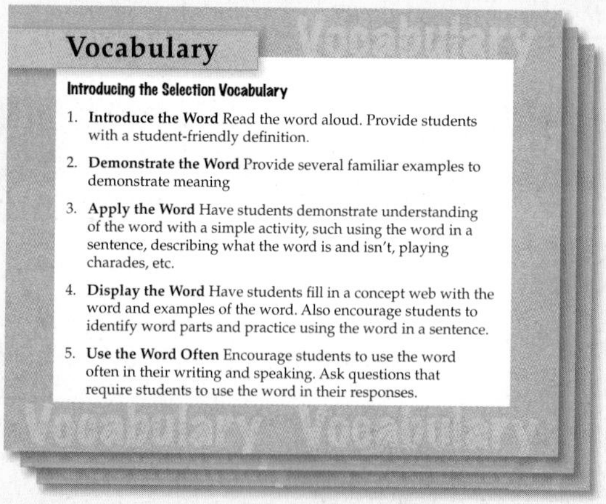

Vocabulary

Introducing the Selection Vocabulary

1. **Introduce the Word** Read the word aloud. Provide students with a student-friendly definition.
2. **Demonstrate the Word** Provide several familiar examples to demonstrate meaning
3. **Apply the Word** Have students demonstrate understanding of the word with a simple activity, such using the word in a sentence, describing what the word is and isn't, playing charades, etc.
4. **Display the Word** Have students fill in a concept web with the word and examples of the word. Also encourage students to identify word parts and practice using the word in a sentence.
5. **Use the Word Often** Encourage students to use the word often in their writing and speaking. Ask questions that require students to use the word in their responses.

Classroom Strategies and Teaching Routines

- core classroom routines outlined step-by-step
- convenient format for easy reference while teaching

Selection Support

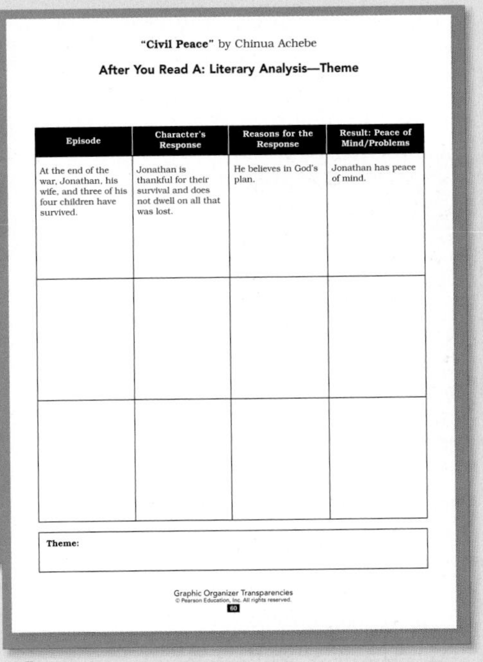
"Civil Peace" by Chinua Achebe

After You Read A: Literary Analysis—Theme

Episode	Character's Response	Reasons for the Response	Result: Peace of Mind/Problems
At the end of the war, Jonathan, his wife, and three of his four children have survived.	Jonathan is thankful for their survival and does not dwell on all that was lost.	He believes in God's plan.	Jonathan has peace of mind.

Theme:

Graphic Organizer Transparencies
© Pearson Education, Inc. All rights reserved.
60

EL L1 L2 **Literary Analysis: Graphic Organizer A,** pp. 59, 60 (partially filled in)

Also available for these selections:

EL L1 L2 Reading: Graphic Organizer A, pp. 56, 57 (partially filled in)

L3 Reading: Graphic Organizer B, p. 58

L3 Literary Analysis: Graphic Organizer B, p. 61

Skills Development/Extension

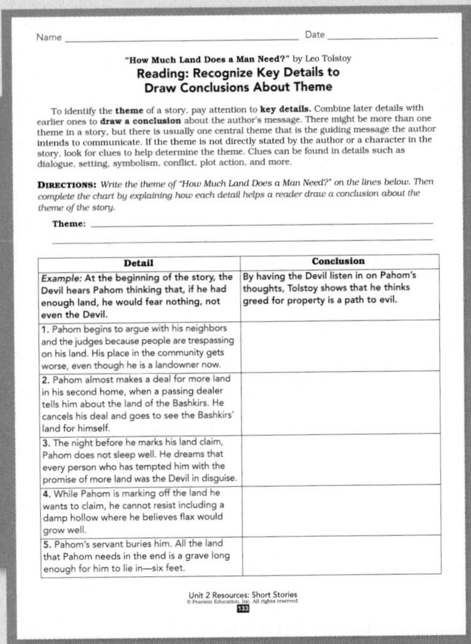
Name ______________ Date ______________

"How Much Land Does a Man Need?" by Leo Tolstoy

Reading: Recognize Key Details to Draw Conclusions About Theme

To identify the **theme** of a story, pay attention to **key details.** Combine later details with earlier ones to **draw a conclusion** about the author's message. There might be more than one theme in a story, but there is usually one central theme that is the guiding message the author intends to communicate. If the theme is not directly stated by the author or a character in the story, look for clues to help determine the theme. Clues can be found in details such as dialogue, setting, symbolism, conflict, plot action, and more.

Directions: *Write the theme of "How Much Land Does a Man Need?" on the lines below. Then complete the chart by explaining how each detail helps a reader draw a conclusion about the theme of the story.*

Theme: ______________

Detail	Conclusion
Example: At the beginning of the story, the Devil hears Pahom thinking that, if he had enough land, he would fear nothing, not even the Devil.	By having the Devil listen in on Pahom's thoughts, Tolstoy shows that he thinks greed for property is a path to evil.
1. Pahom begins to argue with his neighbors and the judges because people are trespassing on his land. His place in the community gets worse, even though he is a landowner now.	
2. Pahom almost makes a deal for more land in his second home, when a passing dealer tells him about the land of the Bashkirs. He cancels his deal and goes to see the Bashkirs' land for himself.	
3. The night before he marks his land claim, Pahom does not sleep well. He dreams that every person who has tempted him with the promise of more land was the Devil in disguise.	
4. While Pahom is marking off the land he wants to claim, he cannot resist including a damp hollow where he believes flax would grow well.	
5. Pahom's servant buries him. All the land that Pahom needs in the end is a grave long enough for him to lie in—six feet.	

Unit 2 Resources: Short Stories
© Pearson Education, Inc. All rights reserved.
133

Unit 2 Resources

All **Reading: Draw Conclusions,** pp. 133, 151

Also available for these selections:

All Literary Analysis: Theme, pp. 132, 150

L4 Enrichment, pp. 135, 153

L3 L4 Grammar, p. 154

L3 L4 Support for Writing, p. 155

L3 L4 Support for Extend Your Learning, p. 156

Assessment

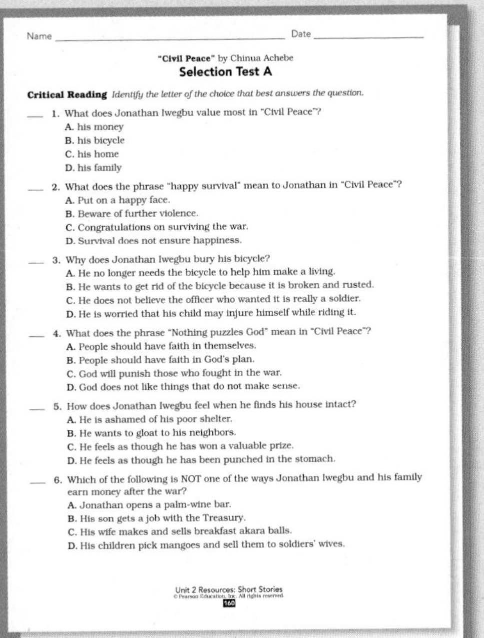
Name ______________ Date ______________

"Civil Peace" by Chinua Achebe

Selection Test A

Critical Reading *Identify the letter of the choice that best answers the question.*

___ 1. What does Jonathan Iwegbu value most in "Civil Peace"?
A. his money
B. his bicycle
C. his home
D. his family

___ 2. What does the phrase "happy survival" mean to Jonathan in "Civil Peace"?
A. Put on a happy face.
B. Beware of further violence.
C. Congratulations on surviving the war.
D. Survival does not ensure happiness.

___ 3. Why does Jonathan Iwegbu bury his bicycle?
A. He no longer needs the bicycle to help him make a living.
B. He wants to get rid of the bicycle because it is broken and rusted.
C. He does not believe the officer who wanted it is really a soldier.
D. He is worried that his child may injure himself while riding it.

___ 4. What does the phrase "Nothing puzzles God" mean in "Civil Peace"?
A. People should have faith in themselves.
B. People should have faith in God's plan.
C. God will punish those who fought in the war.
D. God does not like things that do not make sense.

___ 5. How does Jonathan Iwegbu feel when he finds his house intact?
A. He is ashamed of his poor shelter.
B. He wants to gloat to his neighbors.
C. He feels as though he has won a valuable prize.
D. He feels as though he has been punched in the stomach.

___ 6. Which of the following is NOT one of the ways Jonathan Iwegbu and his family earn money after the war?
A. Jonathan opens a palm-wine bar.
B. His son gets a job with the Treasury.
C. His wife makes and sells breakfast akara balls.
D. His children pick mangoes and sell them to soldiers' wives.

Unit 2 Resources: Short Stories
© Pearson Education, Inc. All rights reserved.
160

EL L1 L2 **Selection Test A,** pp. 139–141, 160–162

Also available for these selections:

L3 L4 Selection Test B, pp. 142–144, 163–165

L3 L4 Open-Book Test, pp. 136–138, 157–159

Transparencies

PHLit Online!

www.PHLitOnline.com

- complete narrated selection text
- a thematically related video with writing prompt
- an interactive graphic organizer
- highlighting feature
- access to all student print resources, adapted to individual student needs
- Spanish and English summaries

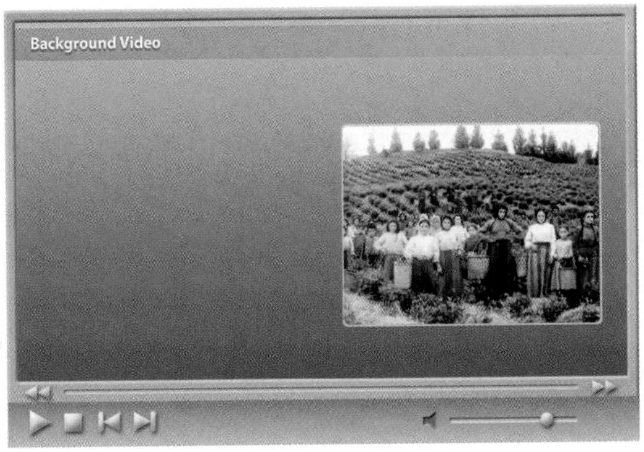

Background Video

Background video

Also available:

Get Connected! (thematic video with writing prompt)

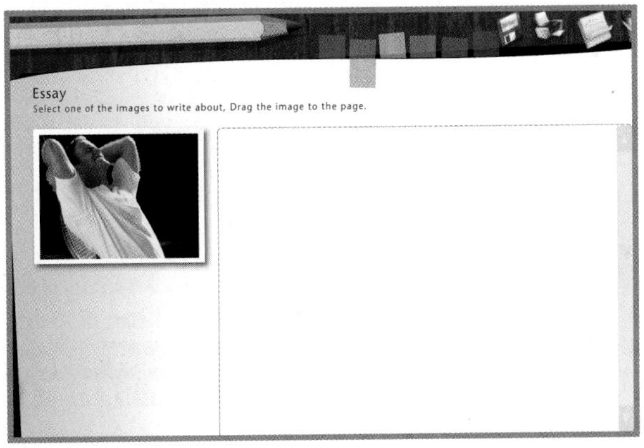

Essay
Select one of the images to write about. Drag the image to the page.

Writer's Journal (with graphics feature)

Also available:

Vocabulary Central (tools, activities, and songs for studying vocabulary)

DIFFERENTIATE/PRETEACH

❶ Selection Choices

You may use either "How Much Land Does a Man Need?" or "Civil Peace" to meet the lesson standards. Skills instruction for both selections appears on p. 335. Choose one selection to teach (or choose to teach both). The Accessibility at a Glance chart at the bottom of this page will help you determine which of the two selections is more appropriate for your students.

❷ Selection Skills

1. With the class, preview the selection skills. (The lesson meets the lesson objectives given on p. 334a.)
2. Explain that students will learn to use the skill of drawing conclusions (introduced on p. 335). By examining the theme as they read, they will gain deeper insight into short stories.
3. To introduce the Writing and Listening and Speaking activities (p. 367) tell students that when they have finished reading the selection, they will write a character analysis and hold a group discussion related to the selection.
4. Tell students that they will also study a grammar concept: action and linking verbs. By mastering this concept, they will improve their reading fluency and the quality of their own writing.

Before You Read

How Much Land Does a Man Need? • Civil Peace

❶ Selection Choices

HOW MUCH
Land
DOES A MAN NEED?
Leo Tolstoy
Translated by Louise and Aylmer Maude

▲ Read **"How Much Land Does a Man Need?"** to find out what happens when a man is never satisfied with what he has.

▲ Read **"Civil Peace"** to find out what happens when a man chooses to make the most of what he has.

❷ Selection Skills Guide

Practice these skills with either the selection **"How Much Land Does a Man Need?"** (p. 338) or **"Civil Peace"** (p. 358).

- Identify theme
- Understand philosophical assumption and historical context
- Draw conclusions
- Recognize key details
- Identify action and linking verbs
- Write a character analysis
- Hold a group discussion

Differentiated Instruction for Universal Access

Accessibility at a Glance: Selection Choices

	How Much Land Does a Man Need?	Civil Peace
Context	Nineteenth-century Russia; pre-Russian Revolution	Aftermath of civil war between the Republic of Biafra and Nigeria
Language/ Vocabulary	• Some difficult vocabulary • Complicated sentence structure	• Some difficult vocabulary • Complicated sentence structure • Dialect
Concept Level	Accessible (greed; materialism)	Challenging (response to adversity)
Literary Merit	Noted author	Cross-cultural experience
Lexile/Length	Lexile: 890L Word Count: 6,124	Lexile: 820L Word Count: 1,977
Other	Political and economic issues concerning class and land ownership	Survival in chaotic, lawless, post–civil war society
Overall Rating	**More accessible**	**More challenging**

Because a number of factors determine the relative accessibility of paired selections, in some cases the Lexile rating of the more challenging selection will be lower than that of the more accessible selection.

❸ Literary Analysis: Theme

The **theme** of a literary work is the central idea it communicates about life. For example, a simple story might convey the theme, "Honesty is the best policy." Another work might show that "Human suffering cannot be justified or explained." Frequently, writers' themes spring from the *historical context* of a selection, the social and cultural background of a story. The author's diction and use of figurative language contribute to the interpretation of the theme. To express a theme, a writer may take one of these approaches:

- Directly state the theme of the work, or have a character directly state it.
- Create patterns of story elements to suggest a larger meaning—for instance, by using language patterns or repeated phrases. In addition, a writer might contrast a generous man and his selfish brother to convey an idea about generosity.

In many cases, a theme reflects a **philosophical assumption**—the writer's basic beliefs about life. For instance, a writer may make the assumption that being generous leads to happiness and may explore that idea in his or her writing.

PHLit Online!
www.PHLitOnline.com

Hear It!
- Selection summary audio
- Selection audio

See It!
- Get Connected video
- Background video
- More about the author
- Vocabulary flashcards

Do It!
- Interactive journals
- Interactive graphic organizers
- Self-test
- Internet activity
- Grammar tutorial
- Interactive vocabulary games

❹ Reading Skill: Draw Conclusions

When you **draw a conclusion,** you reach a decision or form an opinion based on information in a text. To draw a conclusion identifying the theme of a work, **recognize key details.** Also, think about the characters' experiences and what they learn about life in the course of the story. Use that information to draw conclusions about theme.

❺ Using the Strategy: Key Details Diagram

Use a **key details diagram** to help draw a conclusion about a selection.

Story Detail		Story Detail		Pattern
Greedy Joe invests in a crooked scheme. He loses his money.	+	Generous John tricks the crooks and saves Joe.	→	Being greedy causes harm. Being generous leads to solutions.

Differentiated Instruction for Universal Access

Preparing Students for the More Challenging Selection

If you wish to prepare lower-level readers to read "Civil Peace," the more challenging selection, follow these steps:

- Discuss the cultural background of the story. Invite students to explain how the culture and history of a story's setting can influence the behavior of its characters. Explain how war leaves many people without everyday necessities.
- Discuss how people can go through the same tragedy, such as war, yet experience it differently. Prompt students to tell of a situation that they have been through in which they felt differently about it than someone else. Have them discuss whether they were able to see the brighter or darker side of the situation.
- Point out that certain repeated sayings in a story could indicate a special significance for a character. Draw students' attention to the phrase "Nothing puzzles God" throughout the story. Discuss why Jonathan utters this so many times and why it is the phrase that ends the story. Ask students if they have ever uttered something repeatedly to help them get through a situation.

PRETEACH

❸ Literary Analysis

Theme

1. Introduce the skill, using the instruction on the student page.
2. Tell students that they will examine the theme of the selection as they read.

Think Aloud: Model the Skill

Model the skill of identifying the theme, using the following "think aloud":

> To determine a story's theme, I can look at the events and ask myself what they suggest.
>
> Suppose I read a story about a man who finds a large sum of money. He assumes the money will make him happy. After buying many things, he still feels miserable. These events suggest that money does not buy happiness. I realize that this is what the author wants to teach us—it is the theme of the story.

❹ Reading Skill

1. Introduce the skill, using the instruction on the student page.
2. Tell students that they will practice drawing conclusions as they read.

Think Aloud: Model the Skill

Model the skill of drawing conclusions, using the following "think aloud":

> To draw a conclusion about a character I look at his or her actions and attitudes and identify patterns. If a character spends hours choosing an outfit, I might conclude that she is vain.
>
> As I continue to read, I might learn that she is getting ready for an important interview. I conclude that she is not vain but instead concerned about making a good impression. I should always be prepared to modify my conclusion based on new or overlooked facts.

❺ Using the Strategy

Give students a copy of either **Reading Skill Graphic Organizer A** or **B** (*Graphic Organizer Transparencies,* pp. 56 and 58) to record details about theme as they read. Use the examples in **Reading Skill Graphic Organizer A,** which is partially filled in, to model the process of completing the organizer.

PRETEACH

❶ Writing About the Big Question

1. Review the assignment with the class.
2. Ask students to think about the following ways in which people change their lives in order to achieve happiness: earning money, raising a family, or getting an education. Which of the three is the most important for their own happiness? Which is the most achievable?
3. Have students complete the sentence starters. Review responses as a class. (**Possible response:** Making a <u>change</u> can improve the quality of your life as long as you are open-minded. A person may <u>struggle</u> with finding happiness if he or she has unachievable goals and standards.)
4. Remind students that their answers will help them think about the Big Question, "Can progress be made without conflict?"

While You Read

Tell students that as they read, they should note signs of the main character's success as a farmer and signs of discontent with his life.

❷ Vocabulary

1. Have students preview the selection vocabulary.
2. For each word, have students say the word aloud.
3. Then, use the word in a sentence that defines the word.
4. Finally, repeat your definitional sentence or a similar sentence with the word missing and have the class "fill in the blank" chorally. Here is an example:

    <u>Discord</u> is conflict or disagreement. When two politicians who have opposing views debate, there is bound to be [students say "discord"].

❸ Word Study

1. Introduce the skill, using the instruction in the box.
2. Ask students to think of a word that means "untidy, such as in the appearance of one's hair or clothes." (**Answer:** *disheveled*)

Making Connections

How Much Land Does a Man Need?

Can progress be made without *conflict?*

❶ Writing About the Big Question

In "How Much Land Does a Man Need?", a man struggles to satisfy his desire for more land and prosperity. Use these sentence starters to help develop your ideas about the Big Question:

Making a **change** can improve the quality of your life as long as ______________ .

A person may **struggle** with finding happiness if ______________ .

While You Read Note signs of the main character's discontent with his life. Then, decide whether he faces the biggest conflict with others or within himself.

❷ Vocabulary

Read each word and its definition. Decide whether you know the word well, know it a little bit, or do not know it at all. After you read, see how your knowledge of each word has increased.

- **piqued** (pēkt) *adj.* annoyed or upset (p. 339) ***I am <u>piqued</u> by the fact that you did not tell me that you would be late.*** *pique n. piqued v. piquant adj.*
- **discord** (dis´ kôrd´) *n.* conflict; disagreement (p. 340) ***The new referee's questionable call caused <u>discord</u> between the teams.*** *discordant adj. concord n. cordial adj.*
- **forbore** (fôr bôr´) *v.* prevented oneself from doing something; refrained from (p. 342) ***The quarterback <u>forbore</u> responding to the linebackers' taunts.*** *forbearance n. forbearingly adv.*
- **aggrieved** (ə grēvd´) *adj.* wronged; suffering grief or injury (p. 343) ***The tenants were <u>aggrieved</u> by the landlord's delay in fixing the hot-water tank.*** *aggrieve v. grievance n.*
- **arable** (ar´ ə bəl) *adj.* suitable for growing crops (p. 344) ***After two years of poor crops, the farmer was forced to seek out more <u>arable</u> land.*** *arability adj.*
- **prostrate** (präs´ trāt´) *adj.* lying flat (p. 350) ***After a tiring day, Randall lay <u>prostrate</u> on the couch.*** *prostration n.*

❸ Word Study

The **Latin prefix *dis-*** means "wrong," "bad," or "not."

In this story, **discord** arises when the peasants are not in accord, or agreement, with one another. They pursue individual interests instead of a common goal.

Vocabulary Development

Vocabulary Knowledge Rating

Create a **Vocabulary Knowledge Rating Chart** (***Professional Development Guidebook***, p. 33) for this selection. Include the selection vocabulary and the Big Question words that appear in the Writing About the Big Question sentence starters on this page. (The Big Question vocabulary is introduced on pp. 222–223.)

Give students a copy of the chart. Read the words aloud, and have students mark their rating in the Before Reading column. Urge them to be alert to these words as they read and discuss the selection.

Tally how many students think they know a word to gauge how much instruction to provide. As students read and discuss the selection, point out the words and their context.

PHLit Online! **Vocabulary Central**, featuring tools, activities, and songs for studying vocabulary, is available at **www.PHLitOnline.com**.

Meet Leo Tolstoy

(1828–1910)

Author of HOW MUCH *Land* DOES A MAN NEED?

Leo Tolstoy is remembered almost as much for his unusual life as for his work. Born into a rich family, he inherited his family estate at age nineteen. He soon set about trying to improve the lives of the peasants who lived on his land.

Crisis and Renewal After the publication of two major masterpieces, the novels *War and Peace* (1865–1869) and *Anna Karenina* (1875–1877), Tolstoy fell into deep despair, questioning the value of his life and all his previous works. He found salvation and renewal in a mystical spirituality. He gave up small luxuries and worked in the fields. Tolstoy's beliefs about overcoming evil helped to inspire later activists such as Dr. Martin Luther King, Jr.

DID YOU KNOW?

Although the young Tolstoy volunteered for the army, he later came to believe that all forms of violence were wrong.

4 BACKGROUND FOR THE STORY

Landless in Russia

In Russia, from the sixteenth century to the mid-nineteenth century, peasants were serfs, bound by law to work land they could rent but not own. At the time of the story, peasants were allowed to own property. The memory of earlier times, however, kept peasants, like Pahom in this story, hungry for land.

Daily Bellringer

For each class during which you will teach this selection, have students complete one of the five Revision activities for Week 10 in the *Daily Bellringer Activities* booklet.

4 Background
Landless in Russia

When Czar Alexander II finally freed the serfs in 1861, many of the peasants were no better off than they had been. Many were too poor to buy the land they had worked on. Also, the lands they were allotted were too small to farm efficiently or to support a family. Tolstoy's "How Much Land Does a Man Need?" is set after the 1861 emancipation when peasants did all they could to pull themselves out of poverty.

Multidraft Reading

This icon ● marks natural pauses in the selection. To assist struggling readers and to deepen reading for all, assign the text in "chunks," following the icons, and apply multidraft reading protocols. For each reading, have students set the purpose indicated:

- **First reading**—literal comprehension: answering the Reading Check questions.
- **Second reading**—application of skills: answering the Draw Conclusions and Theme prompts.
- **Third reading**—interpretation: answering the end-of-selection questions.

For more guidance, refer to the ***Classroom Strategies and Teaching Routines*** card on multidraft reading.

Differentiated Instruction — Additional Instruction

EL Extended Support—English Learners
Have students complete the **Reading and Vocabulary Warm-ups, *Unit 2 Resources*,** pp. 127–130, before they read. Assign the prereading pages for the selection in the ***Reader's Notebook: English Learner's Version***. Then, have students listen to portions of the selection on the ***Hear It!* Audio CD.**

L1 L2 Extended Support—Struggling Readers
Have students complete the **Reading and Vocabulary Warm-ups, *Unit 2 Resources*,** pp. 127–130, before they read. Assign the prereading pages for the selection in the ***Reader's Notebook: Adapted Version***. Then, have students listen to portions of the selection on the ***Hear It!* Audio CD** (adapted text).

Extended Support—Reluctant Readers
To build motivation and engagement before assigning the selection, have students read "The Greed Game," a thematically related selection in ***Reality Central***. Then, use the questions at the conclusion of the related selection to guide discussion.

PHLit Online!
For more about the author, practice with the selection vocabulary, and more background, go online at **www.PHLitOnline.com**.

❶ Activating Prior Knowledge

1. Prepare an **Anticipation Guide** (see *Professional Development Guidebook*, pp. 36–38) with the following statements:
   - Greed is the root of evil.
   - A material life is a good life.
   - The land cannot be owned; it belongs to everyone.
   - To get ahead in life, one must take what he or she can from others.
2. Give students a copy of the prepared **Anticipation Guide** and have them mark their responses in the Me column. Have students discuss the statements in pairs or groups and mark the Guide again in the Group column.
3. For further guidance, use the **Classroom Strategies and Teaching Routines** card for Anticipation Guides.

Concept Connector →

Students will return to the **Anticipation Guide** after completing the story.

Individual Activity

During the course of the story, Pahom's land grows by leaps and bounds. Have students create a diagram or line graph showing how his holdings increase as the story progresses.

❷ About the Selection

"How Much Land Does a Man Need?" illuminates Tolstoy's sentiments about the perils of private ownership. A peasant named Pahom seeks to acquire more and more land. He rejects the advantages of cooperative ownership and finds fault with each new land acquisition until, far from his home, he at last dies in a final, desperate grab for even more land.

Tolstoy would have approved of the peasants owning the land jointly. Private property, this story tells us, encourages individual greed.

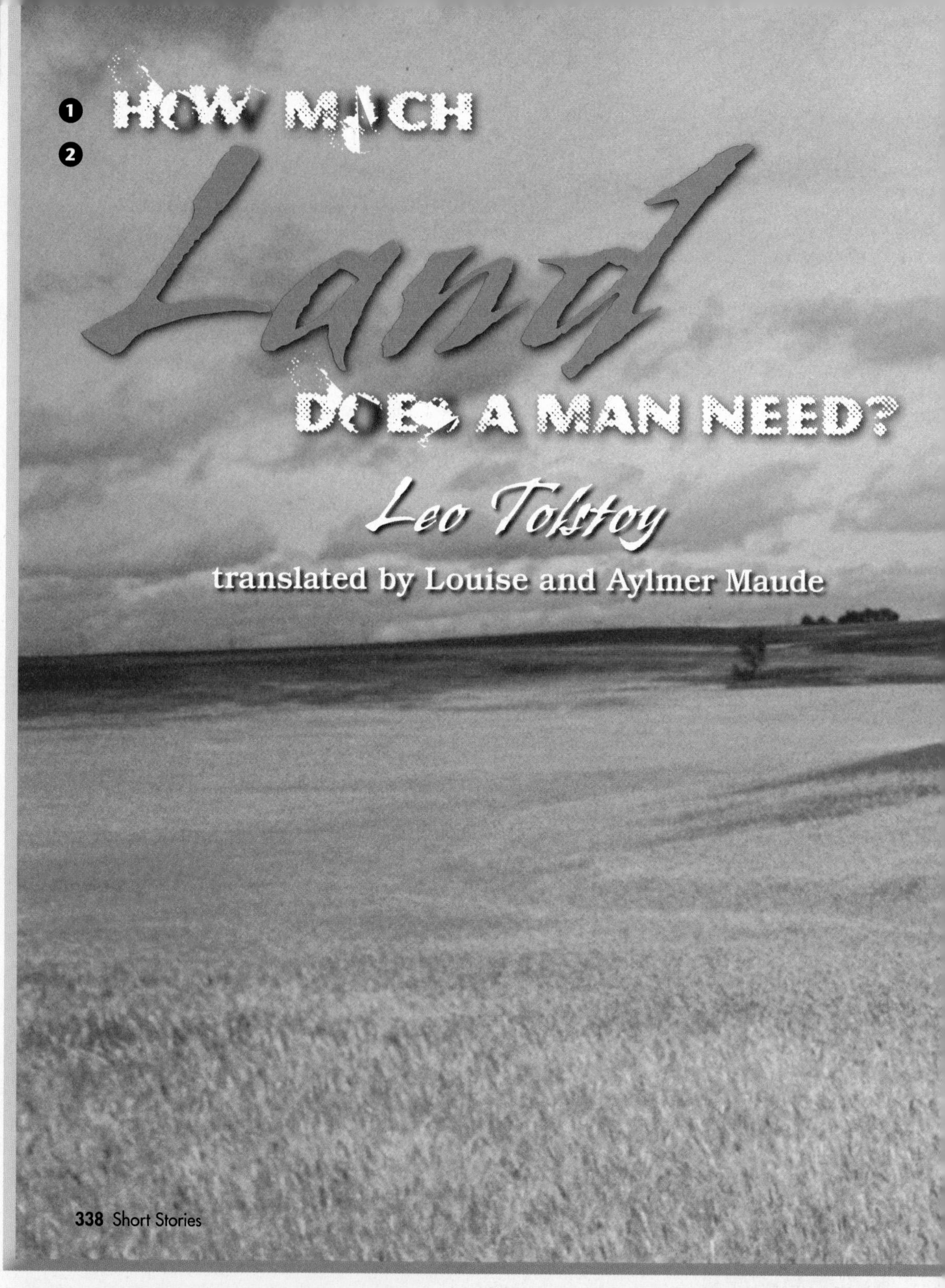

❶ ❷

How Much Land Does a Man Need?

Leo Tolstoy

translated by Louise and Aylmer Maude

Vocabulary Development

Word Form Chart

Expand students' vocabulary by helping them learn related forms of the Vocabulary Builder words. Give students a blank **Word Form Chart** (*Professional Development Guidebook*, pp. 41–42), with *piqued, forbore* in the verb column and *aggrieved* in the adjective column. Work with the class, or have students work with a partner, to determine the related forms. The final chart should look like the one shown.

Noun	Verb	Adjective	Adverb
pique	**piqued**		
forbearance	**forbore**		
aggrievedness	aggrieve	**aggrieved**	aggrievedly

1

An elder sister came to visit her younger sister in the country. The elder was married to a shopkeeper in town, the younger to a peasant in the village. As the sisters sat over their tea talking, the elder began to boast of the advantages of town life, saying how comfortably they lived there, how well they dressed, what fine clothes her children wore, what good things they ate and drank, and how she went to the theater, promenades, and entertainments.

❸ The younger sister was **piqued,** and in turn disparaged the life of a shopkeeper, and stood up for that of a peasant.

"I wouldn't change my way of life for yours," said she. "We may live roughly, but at least we're free from worry. You live in better style than we do, but though you often earn more than you need, you're very likely to lose all you have. You know the proverb, 'Loss and gain are brothers twain.' It often happens that people who're wealthy one day are begging their bread the next. Our way is safer. Though a peasant's life is not a rich one, it's long. We'll never grow rich, but we'll always have enough to eat."

The elder sister said sneeringly:

"Enough? Yes, if you like to share with the pigs and the calves! What do you know of elegance or manners! However much your good man may slave, you'll die as you live—in a dung heap—and your children the same."

❹ "Well, what of that?" replied the younger sister. "Of course our work is rough and hard. But on the other hand, it's sure, and we need not bow to anyone. But you, in your towns, are surrounded by temptations; today all may be right, but tomorrow the Evil One may tempt your husband with cards, wine, or women, and all will go to ruin. Don't such things happen often enough?"

Pahom, the master of the house, was lying on the top of the stove and he listened to the women's chatter.

"It is perfectly true," thought he. "Busy as we are from childhood tilling mother earth, we peasants have no time to let any nonsense settle in our heads. Our only trouble is that we haven't land enough. If I had plenty of land, I shouldn't fear the Devil himself!"

The women finished their tea, chatted a while about dress, and then cleared away the tea things and lay down to sleep.

But the Devil had been sitting behind the stove and had heard all that had been said. He was pleased that the peasant's wife had led her husband into boasting and that he had said that if he had plenty of land he would not fear the Devil himself.

"All right," thought the Devil. "We'll have a tussle. I'll give you land enough; and by means of the land I'll get you into my power."

Vocabulary
piqued (pēkt) *adj.* annoyed or upset

Literary Analysis
Theme What theme about work do the younger sister's remarks suggest?

Reading Check ❺
For what does Pahom wish?

❸ Critical Thinking
Relate

1. Read aloud the bracketed text. **Ask** students to identify the sentiments expressed here.
   Possible response: The two sisters express a sense of competition. Although she defends her life, the younger sister may feel some jealousy. Each appreciates and advocates her own lifestyle.
2. **Ask** students to identify other works in which a character expresses sentiments like these.
   Possible response: Students may refer to "The Town Mouse and the Country Mouse" or works with a similar theme.

❹ Literary Analysis
Theme

1. Remind students that the theme is the central message or insight revealed through a literary work. It is communicated through the plot, characters, and setting.
2. Tell students, too, that the theme may be stated directly or implied. When the theme is implied, readers must use clues in the work and to make inferences.
3. Have a volunteer read aloud the bracketed passage.
   Then, **ask** students the Literary Analysis question: What theme about work do the young sister's remarks suggest?
   Possible response: Although the life of peasants is difficult, they are not subject to temptation or to reversals of fortune. She believes that the more you have, the more you stand to lose.

❺ Reading Check

Answer: Pahom wishes to own as much land as possible.

PROFESSIONAL DEVELOPMENT | **Jane Feber**

APPLY THE STRATEGY

Prereading Activity

Explain to students that the story, "Civil Peace" takes place in Nigeria after a civil war. Instruct students to preview the illustrations that appear in the selection and have them think what challenges a family who has just experienced a civil war might face. Then, have students create a list of items and ideas that are important for surviving a civil war.

Give students sufficient time to prepare their lists individually. Then, discuss students' lists as a class.

For more of Jane Feber's strategies, see her Professional Development essay, pp. 222c–222d.

PHLit Online!

This selection is available in interactive format in the **Enriched Online Student Edition, www.PHLitOnline.com,** which includes a thematically related video and writing prompt and an interactive graphic organizer.

6 Humanities

The Toast by G. K. Totybadse

The act of raising a glass and drinking in honor of or to the health of a person has a long history. Toasting served a practical purpose in early Greece. Poisoning was a common method of resolving disputes or getting rid of enemies. Therefore, from about the sixth century B.C., the host of a party would pour a glass from a pitcher and drink it before serving his guests. If he survived, he raised his glass to his dinner guests as a signal that it was safe to drink. Use these questions for discussion:

- Why might this man be toasting with a bowl rather than with a cup?
  Possible response: Peasants may have used pottery or wooden drinking vessels instead of glassware.
- Does this painting better illustrate Pahom or the Bashkir chief? Explain.
  Possible response: The portrait appears to be Pahom because the man looks fierce, proud, and protective.

7 Critical Viewing

Possible response: The peasant in the picture probably does lead a life similar to Pahom's. He looks as if he has worked hard and is proud of what he has accomplished. He looks like the type of man who would challenge the devil as Pahom does.

8 Critical Thinking

Predict

1. Have a volunteer read aloud the bracketed text. Then, have another volunteer summarize the information.
2. **Ask** students to predict what Pahom will do about buying more land.
   Possible response: Pahom has expressed a clear desire for more land. He will want to buy some of the available land.
3. Then, **ask** students to predict whether they think Pahom will be happier now.
   Possible responses: Some students will observe that Pahom is ambitious and discontented, and they will predict that owning more land will not make him happy. Other students may believe that he will be satisfied.

2

Vocabulary
discord (dis′ kôrd′) *n.* conflict; disagreement

7 ▼ **Critical Viewing**
Based on details of his appearance, does the peasant in this portrait lead a life similar to Pahom's? Explain. **[Infer]**

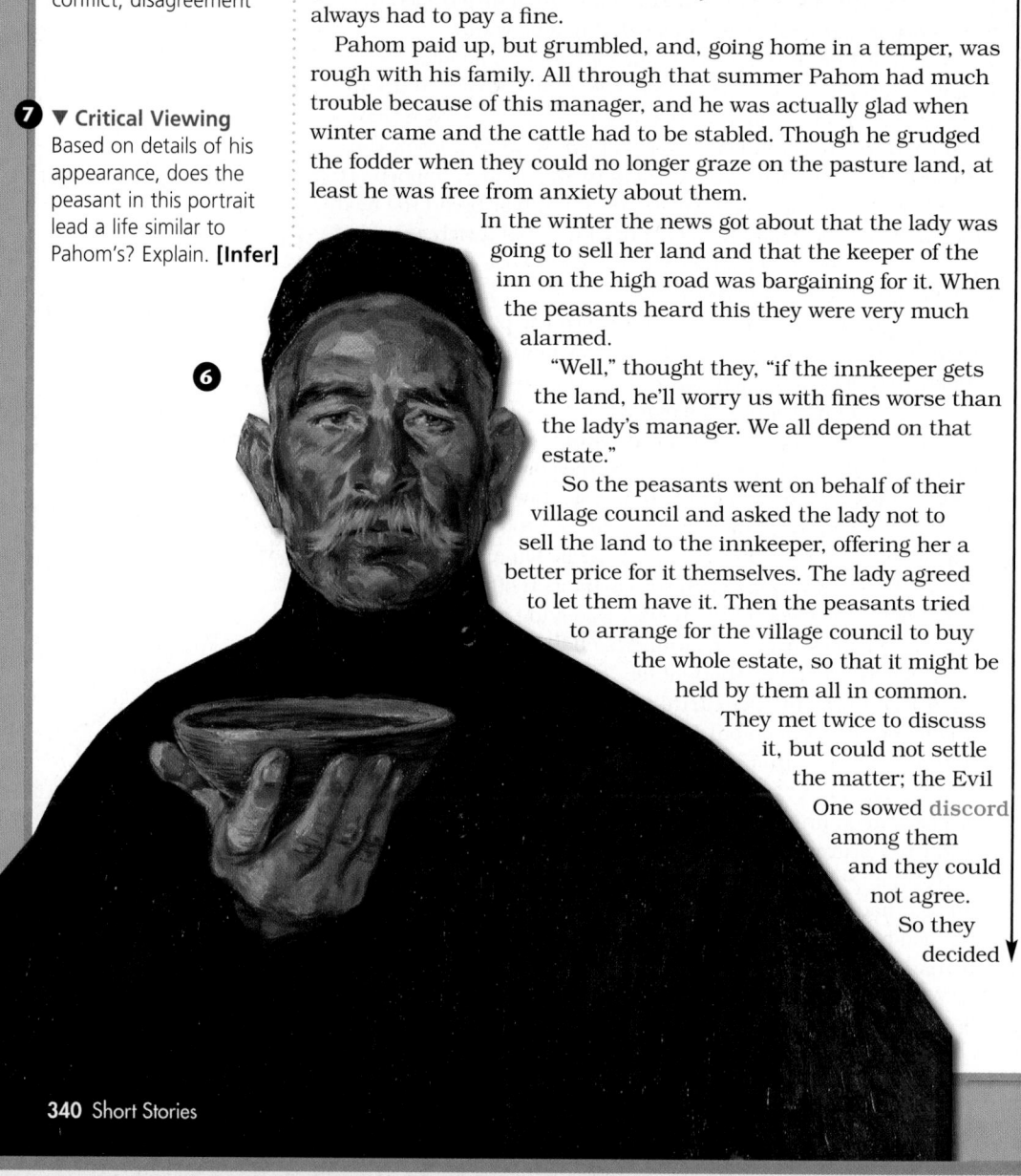

Close to the village there lived a lady, a small landowner who had an estate of about three hundred acres. She had always lived on good terms with the peasants until she engaged as her manager an old soldier, who took to burdening the people with fines. However careful Pahom tried to be, it happened again and again that now a horse of his got among the lady's oats, now a cow strayed into her garden, now his calves found their way into her meadows—and he always had to pay a fine.

Pahom paid up, but grumbled, and, going home in a temper, was rough with his family. All through that summer Pahom had much trouble because of this manager, and he was actually glad when winter came and the cattle had to be stabled. Though he grudged the fodder when they could no longer graze on the pasture land, at least he was free from anxiety about them.

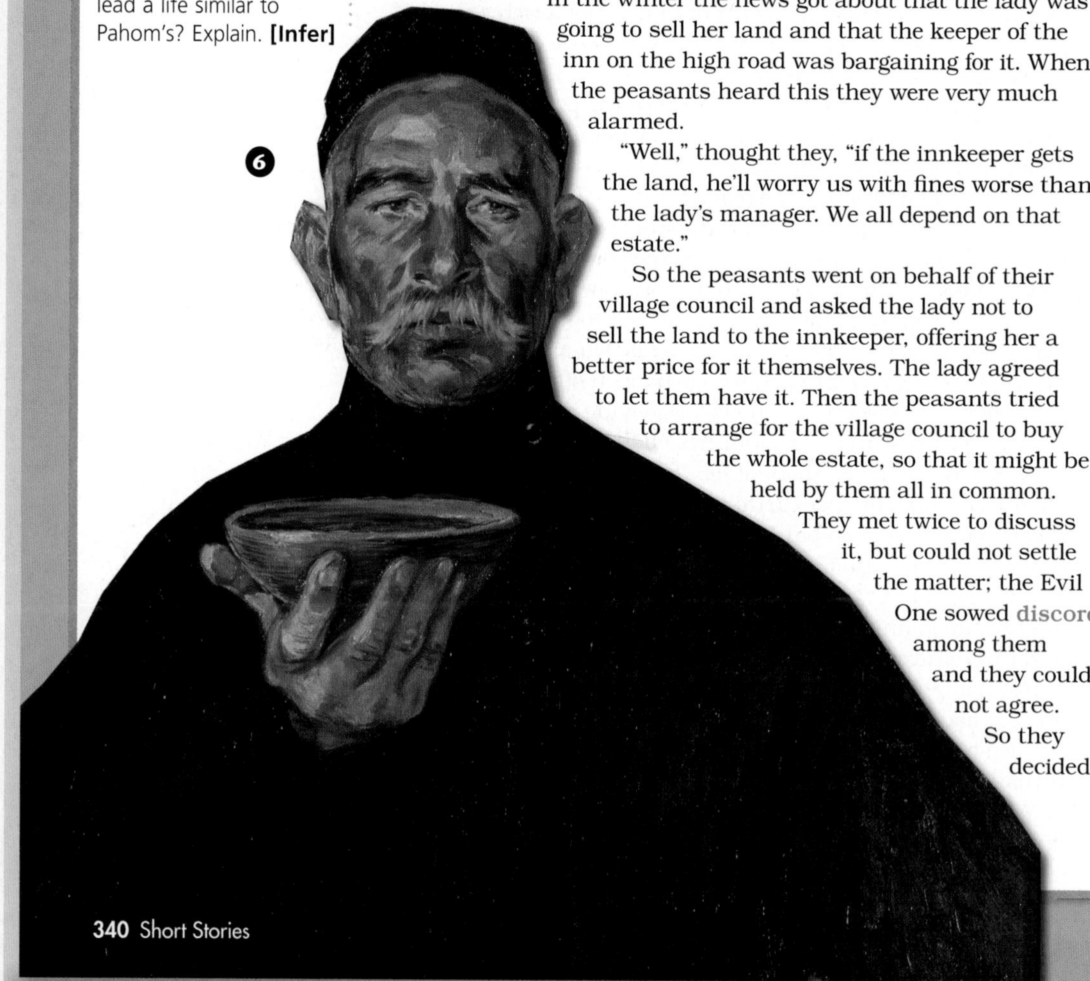

6

In the winter the news got about that the lady was going to sell her land and that the keeper of the inn on the high road was bargaining for it. When the peasants heard this they were very much alarmed.

"Well," thought they, "if the innkeeper gets the land, he'll worry us with fines worse than the lady's manager. We all depend on that estate." 8

So the peasants went on behalf of their village council and asked the lady not to sell the land to the innkeeper, offering her a better price for it themselves. The lady agreed to let them have it. Then the peasants tried to arrange for the village council to buy the whole estate, so that it might be held by them all in common. They met twice to discuss it, but could not settle the matter; the Evil One sowed **discord** among them and they could not agree. So they decided

Vocabulary Development

Thematic Vocabulary: The Big Question
As students are discussing "How Much Land Does a Man Need?" encourage them to use the thematic vocabulary presented in Introducing the Big Question, pp. 222–223. You might encourage them with sentence starters like these:

1. Pahom feels forced into a *confrontation* with his neighbors because . . .
2. Pahom's *motive* for acquiring more land is . . .
3. Pahom's neighbors begin to *oppose* his tactics because . . .
4. Rather than *negotiate* with his neighbors, Pahom decides to . . .

8 to buy the land individually, each according to his means; and the lady agreed to this plan as she had to the other.

Presently Pahom heard that a neighbor of his was buying fifty acres, and that the lady had consented to accept one half in cash and to wait a year for the other half. Pahom felt envious.

9 "Look at that," thought he, "the land is all being sold, and I'll get none of it." So he spoke to his wife.

"Other people are buying," said he, "and we must also buy twenty acres or so. Life is becoming impossible. That manager is simply crushing us with his fines."

So they put their heads together and considered how they could manage to buy it. They had one hundred rubles[1] laid by. They sold a colt and one half of their bees, hired out one of their sons as a farmhand and took his wages in advance, borrowed the rest from a brother-in-law, and so scraped together half the purchase money.

Having done this, Pahom chose a farm of forty acres, some of it wooded, and went to the lady to bargain for it. They came to an agreement, and he shook hands with her upon it and paid her a deposit in advance. Then they went to town and signed the deeds, he paying half the price down, and undertaking to pay the remainder within two years.

So now Pahom had land of his own. He borrowed seed and sowed it on the land he had bought. The harvest was a good one, and within a year he had managed to pay off his debts both to the lady and to his brother-in-law. So he became a landowner, plowing and sowing his own land, making hay on his own land, cutting his own trees, and feeding his cattle on his own pasture. When he went out to plow his fields, or to look at his growing corn, or at his grass meadows, his heart would fill with joy. The grass that grew and the flowers that bloomed there seemed to him unlike any that grew elsewhere. Formerly, when he had passed by that land, it had appeared the same as any other land, but now it seemed quite different.

Literary Analysis
Theme What do these details about Pahom's motives suggest about his "need" for land?

3

10 So Pahom was well contented, and everything would have been right if the neighboring peasants would only not have trespassed on his wheatfields and meadows. He appealed to them most civilly, but they still went on: now the herdsmen would let the village cows stray into his meadows, then horses from the night pasture would get among his corn. Pahom turned them out again and again, and

11 **Reading Check**
After acquiring his own land, how does Pahom feel at first?

1. **rubles** (ro͞o´ bəlz) *n.* A ruble is the basic unit of Russian currency.

9 Literary Analysis
Theme

1. Have students read the bracketed text. **Ask** students to identify what Pahom feels, thinks, and says about the sale of land.
   Answer: Pahom feels envy and thinks he might miss out on the land. In talking to his wife, however, he cites only the manager's fines as a reason for buying.
2. Then, **ask** the Literary Analysis question: What do these details about Pahom's motives suggest about his "need" for land?
   Possible response: Though Pahom complains to his wife about costly fines, his thoughts reveal that envy and competitiveness are important motives for him.

10 Connecting to the Big Question

1. Explain that sometimes people will do things in the name of progress that they normally wouldn't do.
2. Have students read the bracketed text. **Ask:** What evidence supports the idea that Pahom is discontented even though he appears successful?
   Possible response: Instead of appreciating the land he has acquired, Pahom almost immediately begins to suspect his neighbors of encroaching on it.
3. Remind students of the Big Question, "Can progress be made without conflict?" Invite students to discuss whether Pahom's "progress" of acquiring more land could be made without conflict with his neighbors.
   Possible responses: No, the moment he tries to acquire more land he is setting himself in conflict with his neighbors; Yes, he could peacefully acquire land if he was more forgiving.

11 Reading Check

Answer: He is proud and contented.

Differentiated Instruction for Universal Access

Strategy for Less Proficient Readers
Have students discuss the role the Devil, or the Evil One, plays in the story. Ask students what they expect will happen. Have them collect evidence from the story to support their predictions, such as Pahom's claim that if he had plenty of land, he would not fear the Devil himself.

Strategy for Advanced Readers
Have students discuss why they think Tolstoy divides the story into nine sections. Have them summarize what happens in Sections 1 and 2. Then, have them predict what will happen in Section 3. At this point, students may be able to draw the conclusion that the sections reinforce the passage of time and seem to suggest the progressive downfall of Pahom. Have students test their conclusions as they continue to read.

⓬ Reading Skill
Draw Conclusions

1. Remind students that when they draw conclusions, they form an opinion based on information from the story. In order to formulate a conclusion that is valid, they need to combine facts and details.
2. Remind them, too, that if they reach a conclusion based on too little information, they are "leaping to a conclusion." Tell them to ask themselves whether they have all the facts and whether there are other conclusions possible.
3. Then, **ask** students the Reading Skill question: Which key details in this passage show that the desire for land leads to discord among the peasants?
Possible response: Having become a landlord, Pahom becomes possessive, imposing fines on his neighbors, who retaliate with vandalism.

⓭ Literary Analysis
Theme

1. Read the passage aloud to students.
2. Then, **ask** why Pahom accuses Simon of cutting down his trees.
Possible response: It seems as if Pahom must blame someone for the sake of his prestige and his role as a landowner.
3. **Ask** students the Literary Analysis question: In what way does this episode reinforce the idea that the desire for land leads to division and unhappiness?
Possible response: Pahom's position in the community is much worse than it was before he owned land. He has become suspicious, mean, and greedy and has begun to act on these emotions.

Vocabulary
forbore (fôr bôr′) *v.* prevented oneself from doing something; refrained from

Reading Skill
Draw Conclusions ⓬ Which key details in this passage show that the desire for land leads to discord among the peasants?

Literary Analysis
Theme In what way does this episode reinforce the idea that the desire for land leads to division and unhappiness? ⓭

⓾ forgave their owners, and for a long time he forbore to prosecute anyone. But at last he lost patience and complained to the District Court. He knew it was the peasants' want of land, and no evil intent on their part, that caused the trouble, but he thought:

"I can't go on overlooking it, or they'll destroy all I have. They must be taught a lesson."

So he had them up, gave them one lesson, and then another, and two or three of the peasants were fined. After a time Pahom's neighbors began to bear him a grudge for this, and would now and then let their cattle onto his land on purpose. One peasant even got into Pahom's wood at night and cut down five young lime trees for their bark. Pahom, passing through the wood one day, noticed something white. He came nearer and saw the stripped trunks lying on the ground, and close by stood the stumps where the trees had been. Pahom was furious.

"If he'd only cut one here and there it would have been bad enough," thought Pahom, "but the rascal has actually cut down a whole clump. If I could only find out who did this, I'd get even with him."

He racked his brains as to who it could be. Finally he decided: "It must be Simon—no one else could have done it." So he went to Simon's homestead to have a look around, but he found nothing and only had an angry scene. However, he now felt more certain than ever that Simon had done it, and he lodged a complaint. Simon was summoned. The case was tried, and retried, and at the end of it all Simon was acquitted, there being no evidence against him. Pahom

Think Aloud

Vocabulary: Using Context
Direct students' attention to the word *acquitted* on this page. Using a think-aloud process, model how to use context to infer the meaning of an unknown word. Say to students:

> I'm going to think aloud to show you how to figure out the meaning of *acquitted* from its context.
>
> In this sentence, *acquitted* is being used to describe the outcome of Pahom's legal accusation against Simon. In this paragraph I have already learned that Pahom suspected Simon of cutting the trees and had lodged a complaint. Simon was summoned, or brought to trial, twice. Later I read that Simon was *acquitted* because there was no evidence against him, a result that angered his accuser, Pahom. I think that *acquitted* means "to be found free of blame or guilt."

felt still more aggrieved, and let his anger loose upon the Elders and the Judges.

13 "You let thieves grease your palms," said he. "If you were honest folk yourselves you wouldn't let a thief go free."

So Pahom quarreled with the judges and with his neighbors. Threats to burn his hut began to be uttered. So though Pahom had more land, his place in the community was much worse than before.

About this time a rumor got about that many people were moving to new parts.

"There's no need for me to leave my land," thought Pahom. "But some of the others may leave our village and then there'd be more room for us. I'd take over their land myself and make my estates somewhat bigger. I could then live more at ease. As it is, I'm still too cramped to be comfortable."

One day Pahom was sitting at home when a peasant, passing through the village, happened to drop in. He was allowed to stay the night, and supper was given him. Pahom had a talk with this peasant and asked him where he came from. The stranger answered that he came from beyond the Volga,[2] where he had been working. One word led to another, and the man went on to say that many people were settling in those parts. He told how some people from his village had settled there. They had joined the community there and had had twenty-five acres per man granted them. The land was so good, he said, that the rye sown on it grew as high as a horse, and so thick that five cuts of a sickle made a sheaf.[3] One peasant, he said, had brought nothing with him but his bare hands, and now he had six horses and two cows of his own.

Pahom's heart kindled with desire.

"Why should I suffer in this narrow hole, if one can live so well elsewhere?" he thought. "I'll sell my land and my homestead here, and with the money I'll start afresh over there and get everything new. In this crowded place one is always having trouble. But I must first go and find out all about it myself."

14 Toward summer he got ready and started out. He went down the Volga on a steamer to Samara, then walked another three hundred miles on foot, and at last reached the place. It was just as the stranger had said. The peasants had plenty of land: every man had twenty-five acres of communal land given him for his use, and anyone who had money could buy, besides, at a ruble and a half an acre, as much good freehold land[4] as he wanted.

Having found out all he wished to know, Pahom returned home as

2. **Volga** (väl′ gə) the major river in western Russia.
3. **sheaf** (shēf) *n.* bundle of grain.
4. **freehold land** privately owned land that the owner can lease to others for a fee.

Vocabulary
aggrieved (ə grēvd′) *adj.* wronged; suffering grief or injury

Reading Skill
Draw Conclusions
Based on the story so far, draw a conclusion about the amount of land Pahom will need before he is satisfied.

15 **Reading Check**
After quarreling with his neighbors, what does Pahom decide to do?

14 Reading Skill
Draw Conclusions

1. Have a volunteer read the passage aloud.
2. **Ask** students to discuss the pros and cons of the system of communal land.
   Possible response: Pros: The system is equitable. It allows everyone to be productive, and it fosters self-esteem. Cons: The system is rigid and does not allow people to get ahead on their own or to be independent.
3. Then, **ask** students the Reading Skill question: Based on the story so far, draw a conclusion about the amount of land Pahom will need before he is satisfied.
   Possible response: Pahom does not seem satisfied with an equitable distribution of land or with simply being productive. He wants more land than anyone else. There probably is no amount of land that will satisfy him.

15 Reading Check

Answer: Pahom decides to sell everything, buy land in Samara, and move there.

Differentiated Instruction for Universal Access

Strategy for Less Proficient Readers
Students may have difficulty distinguishing between the land Pahom now holds and freehold land. Help them to understand that freehold land is privately owned land that the owner can lease to others for a fee. Point out that, once again, Pahom thinks others are doing better than he is, which leads him to want even more land.

EL Strategy for English Learners
Use simpler language to explain the passage about communal land. Define the words *sowing* (planting), *fallow* (unplanted), and *arable* (fertile), and use a schematic map on the chalkboard to illustrate the uses of communal and freehold land.

⓰ Literary Analysis
Theme

1. Have a volunteer read the passage aloud.
2. **Ask** students to comment on how this incident is similar to and different from the land-buying episodes that have come before it.
   Answer: Once again, Pahom buys land and makes money. As has happened in the past, he gets into a conflict with other peasants, and a legal dispute ensues. This time, though, Pahom realizes he does not like to rent other people's land because he has to compete with others for it.
3. Finally, **ask** students the Literary Analysis question: What common idea comes across in each of the episodes in which Pahom acquires land?
   Possible response: Pahom is never satisfied with the amount of land he has and will do whatever it takes to get more.

autumn came on, and began selling off his belongings. He sold his land at a profit, sold his homestead and all his cattle, and withdrew from membership in the village. He only waited till the spring, and then started with his family for the new settlement.

4

As soon as Pahom and his family reached their new abode, he applied for admission into the council of a large village. He stood treat to the Elders and obtained the necessary documents. Five shares of communal land were given him for his own and his sons' use: that is to say—125 acres (not all together, but in different fields) besides the use of the communal pasture. Pahom put up the buildings he needed and bought cattle. Of the communal land alone he had three times as much as at his former home, and the land was good wheat land. He was ten times better off than he had been. He had plenty of **arable** land and pasturage, and could keep as many head of cattle as he liked.

Vocabulary
arable (ar´ ə bəl) *adj.* suitable for growing crops

At first, in the bustle of building and settling down, Pahom was pleased with it all, but when he got used to it he began to think that even here he hadn't enough land. The first year he sowed wheat on his share of the communal land and had a good crop. He wanted to go on sowing wheat, but had not enough communal land for the purpose, and what he had already used was not available, for in those parts wheat is sown only on virgin soil or on fallow land. It is sown for one or two years, and then the land lies fallow till it is again overgrown with steppe grass. There were many who wanted such land, and there was not enough for all, so that people quarreled about it. Those who were better off wanted it for growing wheat, and those who were poor wanted it to let to dealers, so that they might raise money to pay their taxes. Pahom wanted to sow more wheat, so he rented land from a dealer for a year. He sowed much wheat and had a fine crop, but the land was too far from the village—the wheat had to be carted more than ten miles. After a time Pahom noticed that some peasant dealers were living on separate farms and were growing wealthy, and he thought:

"If I were to buy some freehold land and have a homestead on it, it would be a different thing altogether. Then it would all be fine and close together."

Literary Analysis
Theme What common idea comes across in each of the episodes in which Pahom acquires land?

The question of buying freehold land recurred to him again and again.

⓰ He went on in the same way for three years, renting land and sowing wheat. The seasons turned out well and the crops were good, so that he began to lay by money. He might have gone on living contentedly, but he grew tired of having to rent other people's land every year and having to scramble for it. Wherever there was good

land to be had, the peasants would rush for it and it was taken up at once, so that unless you were sharp about it, you got none. It happened in the third year that he and a dealer together rented a piece of pasture land from some peasants, and they had already plowed it up, when there was some dispute and the peasants went to law about it, and things fell out so that the labor was all lost.

16 "If it were my own land," thought Pahom, "I should be independent, and there wouldn't be all this unpleasantness."

So Pahom began looking out for land which he could buy, and he came across a peasant who had bought thirteen hundred acres, but having got into difficulties was willing to sell again cheap. Pahom bargained and haggled with him, and at last they settled the price at fifteen hundred rubles, part in cash and part to be paid later. They had all but clinched the matter when a passing dealer happened to stop at Pahom's one day to get feed for his horses. He drank tea with Pahom, and they had a talk. The dealer said that he was just returning from the land of the Bashkirs,[5] far away, where he had bought thirteen thousand acres of land, all for a thousand rubles. Pahom questioned him further, and the dealer said:

5. **Bashkirs** (bash kirz´) *n.* originally nomadic people who live in the plains of southwestern Russia.

18 ▲ **Critical Viewing**
What assumptions could you make about the lifestyle of a peasant based on the details in this painting? **[Interpret]**

19 **Reading Check**
What information does the stranger who comes to visit give Pahom?

17 Humanities

Rest During the Harvest by Alexander Morozov (1835–1904)

Alexander Morozov was born in Russia. While he was a portrait painter, Morozov also painted pictures of everyday life. Use these questions for discussion:

- What are some of the people doing in the painting?
  Possible response: There is a man on a horse who appears to be coming in from the field. Another man drinks from a bucket, while another sleeps on a cart. A woman tends to her child.
- What do you think the artist was trying to accomplish in this painting?
  Possible response: He was trying to give viewers a glimpse into what everyday life was like for peasants in Russia at the time.

18 Critical Viewing

Possible response: I could assume that life as a peasant was difficult but bearable because people worked together.

19 Reading Check

Answer: The stranger tells Pahom about a faraway place where land can be gotten very cheaply.

Differentiated Instruction for Universal Access

Strategy for Less Proficient Readers
Students may need help comparing Pahom's two opportunities for land. Suggest that they use a Venn diagram to compare and contrast the opportunities. Direct them to compare the prices of the land and to consider the debt involved with the first opportunity. Then, ask them to explain why the second opportunity is better.

Enrichment for Gifted/Talented Students
Ask students to create calculations to demonstrate that Pahom's second opportunity for land is better than his first. Have them discuss their calculations and the factors that Pahom has to consider. Then, have students write paragraphs describing Pahom's choices with regard to the two land deals. Remind them to include explanations regarding his decision.

20 Critical Viewing

Possible response: The colors suggest that the painter sees nature as lush and vibrant. The painter seems to suggest that working on the land is desirable.

21 Reading Skill

Draw Conclusions

1. Read aloud the passage to students. **Ask** them to summarize what they know about the Bashkirs.
   Answer: The Bashkirs live in a distant land. Their chiefs are accepting of gifts (or bribes), and they are easily persuaded to sell unlimited amounts of land. The dealer suggests that the Bashkirs are easy to take advantage of.
2. **Ask** students to draw conclusions about the coincidental arrival of the passing dealer.
   Possible response: Students may speculate that there is so much temptation involved in buying land from the Bashkirs that the passing dealer could be the Devil. The idea of getting ten times as much land for his money is something that Pahom will never be able to resist.

20 ▶ **Critical Viewing** What do the vivid colors in this painting suggest about the painter's attitude toward nature and the land? **[Interpret]**

"All one has to do is to make friends with the chiefs. I gave away about one hundred rubles' worth of silk robes and carpets, besides a case of tea, and I gave wine to those who would drink it; and I got the land for less than three kopecks[6] an acre." And he showed Pahom the title deed, saying:

"The land lies near a river, and the whole steppe[7] is virgin soil."

Pahom plied him with questions, and the dealer said:

"There's more land there than you could cover if you walked a year, and it all belongs to the Bashkirs. They're as simple as sheep, and land can be got almost for nothing."

21 "There, now," thought Pahom, "with my one thousand rubles, why should I get only thirteen hundred acres, and saddle myself with a debt besides? If I take it out there, I can get more than ten times as much for my money."

5

Pahom inquired how to get to the place, and as soon as the grain dealer had left him, he prepared to go there himself. He left his wife to look after the homestead, and started on his journey, taking his hired man with him. They stopped at a town on their way and bought a case of tea, some wine, and other presents, as the grain dealer had advised.

6. **kopecks** (kō´ peks´) *n.* units of Russian money, each equal to one hundredth of a ruble.
7. **steppe** (step) *n.* high grassland plains stretching from Hungary through Russia into central Asia.

Vocabulary Development

Expressive Vocabulary

To help students broaden their expressive vocabulary, encourage them to use the following words as they discuss the selection: *deficient, inferior, avarice, gratification, discord.* Have them complete these sentence starters:

1. To Pahom, every land deal is *deficient* because . . .
2. Although Pahom sees the Bashkirs as being *inferior* to Russian peasants, . . .
3. Pahom originally wanted twenty acres of land, but his *avarice* is so consuming . . .
4. Pahom gets no *gratification* from . . .
5. *Discord* seems to follow Pahom as he . . .

22 On and on they went until they had gone more than three hundred miles, and on the seventh day they came to a place where the Bashkirs had pitched their round tents. It was all just as the dealer had said. The people lived on the steppe, by a river, in felt-covered tents. They neither tilled the ground nor ate bread. Their cattle and horses grazed in herds on the steppe. The colts were tethered behind the tents, and the mares were driven to them twice a day. The mares were milked, and from the milk kumiss[8] was made. It was the women who prepared the kumiss, and they also made cheese. As far as the men were concerned, drinking kumiss and tea, eating mutton, and playing on their pipes was all they cared about. They were all stout and merry, and all the summer long they never thought of doing any work. They were quite ignorant, and knew no Russian, but were good-natured enough.

As soon as they saw Pahom, they came out of their tents and gathered around the visitor. An interpreter was found, and Pahom told them he had come about some land. The Bashkirs seemed very glad; they took Pahom and led him into one of the best tents, where they made him sit on some down cushions placed on a carpet, while they sat around him. They gave him some tea and kumiss, and had a sheep killed, and gave him mutton to eat. Pahom took presents out of his cart and distributed them among the Bashkirs, and divided the tea amongst them. The Bashkirs were delighted. They talked a great deal among themselves and then told the interpreter what to say.

"They wish to tell you," said the interpreter, "that they like you and that it's our custom to do all we can to please a guest and to repay him for his gifts. You have given us presents, now tell us which of the things we possess please you best, that we may present them to you."

"What pleases me best here," answered Pahom, "is your land. Our land is crowded and the soil is worn out, but you have plenty of land, and it is good land. I never saw the likes of it."

The interpreter told the Bashkirs what Pahom had said. They talked among themselves for a while. Pahom could not understand what they were saying, but saw that they were much amused and heard them shout and laugh. Then they were silent and looked at Pahom while the interpreter said:

"They wish me to tell you that in return for your presents they will gladly give you as much land as you want. You have only to point it out with your hand and it is yours."

8. **kumiss** (ko͞o′ mis) *n.* fermented mare's or camel's milk that is used as a drink.

Reading Skill
Draw Conclusions
What details in this passage suggest that the Bashkirs have different priorities than Pahom?

23 **Reading Check**
Where does Pahom decide to go next?

22 Reading Skill
Draw Conclusions

1. Have a volunteer read aloud the bracketed text.
2. **Ask** students: What are the differences between the Bashkirs and Pahom and the peasants?
   Answer: Unlike Pahom, the Bashkirs do not care about work or investments. They are interested only in food and friendship. Unlike the peasants, they do not plow or plant the land, but they do live off it.
3. Then, **ask** students the Reading Skill question: What details in this passage suggest that the Bashkirs have different priorities than Pahom?
   Possible response: Instead of large houses, the Bashkirs prefer to live in tents. The Bashkirs only use and eat what is necessary. Rather than work all day to make money, they fill their free time with recreational activities. These details suggest that the Bashkirs represent attitudes of contentment and generosity. In contrast, Pahom is never satisfied with the amount of money he has or the amount of land he owns.

23 Reading Check

Answer: Pahom decides to travel to the land of the Bashkirs.

Differentiated Instruction for Universal Access

Enrichment for Advanced Readers
Tolstoy's story is part of a long tradition of "Devil's bargain" and "three wishes" literature that includes Goethe's *Faust* and W. W. Jacobs's "The Monkey's Paw" (pp. 32–42). Have students name other works they have read that have the premise of supernatural wish fulfillment. As a class, discuss the common features of these stories. What motivates the protagonist to make the bargain or wish? What is the usual outcome? What moral or lesson is taught or implied?

Enrichment for Gifted/Talented Students
Tolstoy's depiction of homesteading and the vast expanse of the Russian steppes may remind students of stories of pioneering in the American wilderness. Ask students to imagine that Pahom's story were to take place in America. Give Pahom an American name and place him in a specific region. Work as a class to briefly outline the basic story as it might have happened on the American frontier. What elements of the plot, if any, would have to be changed?

24 Reading Skill
Draw Conclusions

1. Invite a volunteer to read the passage.
2. **Ask** students why the Bashkirs are so generous with their land. **Answer:** They have a seemingly unlimited amount of land, much more than they need. Since they do not farm the land like the Russians, they do not focus on ownership of particular parcels of land.
3. **Ask** students why Pahom insists that the Bashkirs give him a deed to the land. What does this request reveal about him? **Possible response:** Since the dealer who told him about the Bashkirs and their land got a deed, Pahom wants one as well. He is distrustful and suspicious, fearing that someone will try to take away his land.
4. Then, **ask** students the Reading Skill question: What details suggest that the Bashkirs view the land differently from Pahom? **Possible response:** They live in tents, suggesting that they move around on their land; they neither till the land nor eat bread; they use the land for grazing; they repay guests and their gifts with anything the guest chooses, including land.

The Bashkirs talked again for a while and began to dispute. Pahom asked what they were disputing about, and the interpreter told him that some of them thought they ought to ask their chief about the land and not act in his absence, while others thought there was no need to wait for his return.

6

While the Bashkirs were disputing, a man in a large fox-fur cap appeared on the scene. They all became silent and rose to their feet. The interpreter said: "This is our chief himself."

Pahom immediately fetched the best dressing gown and five pounds of tea, and offered these to the chief. The chief accepted them and seated himself in the place of honor. The Bashkirs at once began telling him something. The chief listened for a while, then made a sign with his head for them to be silent, and addressing himself to Pahom, said in Russian:

Reading Skill
Draw Conclusions
What details suggest that the Bashkirs view the land differently from Pahom?

"Well, so be it. Choose whatever piece of land you like; we have plenty of it."

"How can I take as much as I like?" thought Pahom. "I must get a deed to make it secure, or else they may say: 'It is yours,' and afterward may take it away again."

"Thank you for your kind words," he said aloud. "You have much land, and I only want a little. But I should like to be sure which portion is mine. Could it not be measured and made over to me? Life and death are in God's hands. You good people give it to me, but your children might wish to take it back again."

"You are quite right," said the chief. "We will make it over to you."

"I heard that a dealer had been here," continued Pahom, "and that you gave him a little land, too, and signed title deeds to that effect. I should like to have it done in the same way."

The chief understood.

"Yes," replied he, "that can be done quite easily. We have a scribe, and we will go to town with you and have the deed properly sealed."

"And what will be the price?" asked Pahom.

"Our price is always the same: one thousand rubles a day."

Pahom did not understand.

"A day? What measure is that? How many acres would that be?"

"We do not know how to reckon it out," said the chief. "We sell it by the day. As much as you can go around on your feet in a day is yours, and the price is one thousand rubles a day."

Pahom was surprised.

"But in a day you can get around a large tract of land," he said.

The chief laughed.

Think Aloud

Predicting

Draw students' attention to this sentence beginning at the bottom of page 349: "Then he saw that it was not the peasant either, but the Devil himself with hoofs and horns, sitting there and chuckling, and before him lay a man prostrate on the ground, barefooted, with only trousers and a shirt on." Use the following "think aloud" to model the process of making a prediction:

When I read this sentence, I realize that it holds an important clue about what will happen next. I know that a reference to the Devil has to do with something bad or evil. I realize that this passage is foreshadowing an ominous event. Since Pahom is the person having this dream, I predict that something horrible is going to happen to him. I will read further to see if my prediction is correct or not.

"It will all be yours!" said he. "But there is one condition: If you don't return on the same day to the spot whence you started, your money is lost."

"But how am I to mark the way that I have gone?"

"Why, we shall go to any spot you like and stay there. You must start from that spot and make your round, taking a spade with you. Wherever you think necessary, make a mark. At every turning, dig a hole and pile up the turf; then afterward we will go around with a plow from hole to hole. You may make as large a circuit as you please, but before the sun sets you must return to the place you started from. All the land you cover will be yours."

"But there is one condition: If you don't return on the same day to the spot whence you started, your money is lost."

Pahom was delighted. It was decided to start early next morning. They talked a while, and after drinking some more kumiss and eating some more mutton, they had tea again, and then the night came on. They gave Pahom a featherbed to sleep on, and the Bashkirs dispersed for the night, promising to assemble the next morning at daybreak and ride out before sunrise to the appointed spot.

7

Pahom lay on the featherbed, but could not sleep. He kept thinking about the land.

25 "What a large tract I'll mark off!" thought he. "I can easily do thirty-five miles in a day. The days are long now, and within a circuit of thirty-five miles what a lot of land there will be! I'll sell the poorer land or let it to peasants, but I'll pick out the best and farm it myself. I'll buy two ox teams and hire two more laborers. About a hundred and fifty acres shall be plowland, and I'll pasture cattle on the rest."

Pahom lay awake all night and dozed off only just before dawn. Hardly were his eyes closed when he had a dream. He thought he was lying in that same tent and heard somebody chuckling outside. He wondered who it could be, and rose and went out, and he saw the Bashkir chief sitting in front of the tent holding his sides and rolling about with laughter. Going nearer to the chief, Pahom asked: "What are you laughing at?" But he saw that it was no longer the chief but the grain dealer who had recently stopped at his house and had told him about the land. Just as Pahom was going to ask: "Have you been here long?" he saw that it was not the dealer, but the peasant who had come up from the Volga long ago, to Pahom's old home. Then he saw that it was not the peasant either, but the Devil himself with hoofs and horns, sitting there and chuckling, and before him

26 **Reading Check**

How large a tract of land does Pahom decide he will mark off?

25 Reading Skill

Conclusions

1. Remind students that to draw a conclusion they must refer to knowledge they have gained through what they already have read.
2. **Ask:** Think of someone you know who always takes on more than he or she can handle. How does knowing this person help you to understand Pahom's actions?
   Possible response: I know someone who always takes on more than he can do, which causes him to overstretch himself. Pahom, in charting out such a wide swath of land, does the same. He tries to take on more land than he can reasonably cultivate.

26 Reading Check

Answer: Pahom is planning on doing a circuit of thirty-five miles.

Differentiated Instruction for Universal Access

Strategy for Less Proficient Readers

As students begin reading Section 8, have them note when Pahom turns the three corners to form the sides of his new property. Breaking down the story in this way will help them track the character's progress and make predictions about events in the story.

EL Strategy for English Learners

A few idioms in this selection may need clarification. Have native English speakers assist their classmates by restating these idioms in their own words:

It's high time (the time has come)

Dawn was breaking (the sun was beginning to rise)

㉗ Literature in Context

History Connection The reforms created by Czar Alexander II in the Edict of Emancipation worked better in theory than in practice. On paper, serfs were freed and given land. In reality, however, the state government advanced the money to the landlords and then collected it from the peasants in forty-nine yearly payments known as "redemption payments." These redemptions could stretch out for longer periods, resulting in peasants paying far more for the land than it was worth. Some former serfs chose "beggarly allotments." While these consisted of only a quarter of the amount of land, they carried with them no monetary obligations. In either case, the peasants did not control their land. It was under the supervision of the village commune, which was responsible for the redemption payments and redistributing the land to meet the changing needs of the community.

Connect to the Literature After reviewing the details of emancipation, **ask** the Connect to the Literature question: Based on Pahom's story, what do you think Tolstoy thought of land reform in Russia? Explain.

Possible response: Tolstoy would not have approved of the peasants owning the land individually because, as the story tells us, private property encourages individual greed.

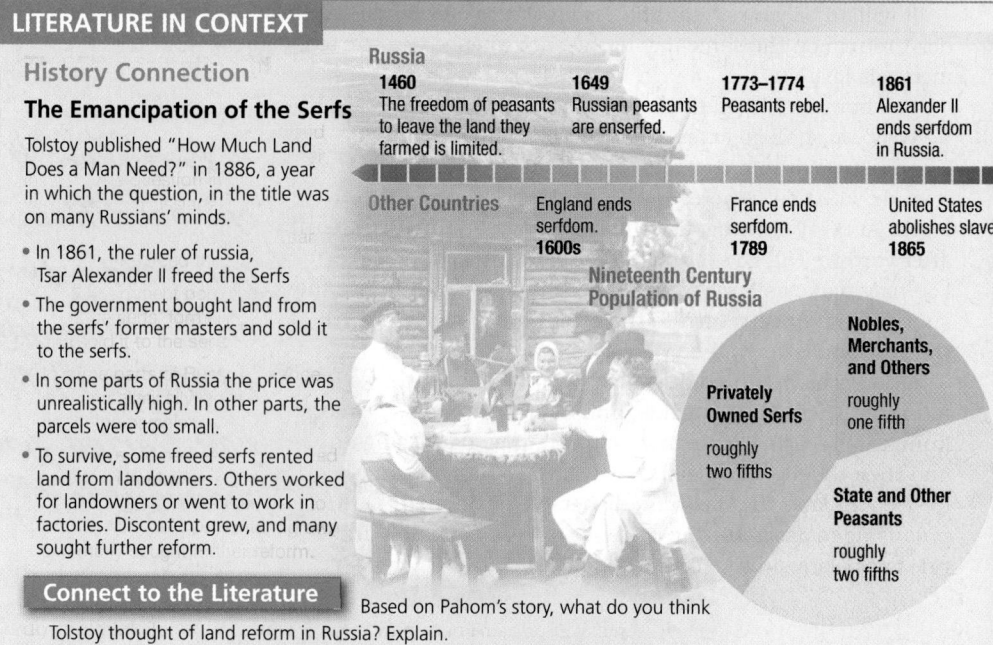

㉗ LITERATURE IN CONTEXT

History Connection

The Emancipation of the Serfs

Tolstoy published "How Much Land Does a Man Need?" in 1886, a year in which the question, in the title was on many Russians' minds.

- In 1861, the ruler of russia, Tsar Alexander II freed the Serfs
- The government bought land from the serfs' former masters and sold it to the serfs.
- In some parts of Russia the price was unrealistically high. In other parts, the parcels were too small.
- To survive, some freed serfs rented land from landowners. Others worked for landowners or went to work in factories. Discontent grew, and many sought further reform.

Russia

1460 The freedom of peasants to leave the land they farmed is limited.

1649 Russian peasants are enserfed.

1773–1774 Peasants rebel.

1861 Alexander II ends serfdom in Russia.

Other Countries

England ends serfdom. **1600s**

France ends serfdom. **1789**

United States abolishes slave **1865**

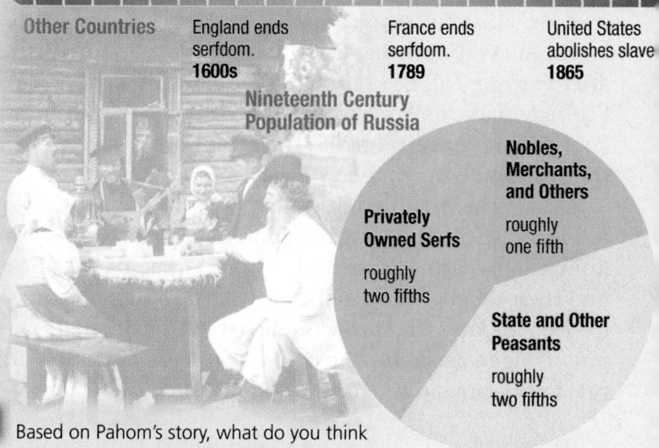

Connect to the Literature Based on Pahom's story, what do you think Tolstoy thought of land reform in Russia? Explain.

Vocabulary
prostrate (präs′ trāt′) *adj.* lying flat

lay a man, **prostrate** on the ground, barefooted, with only trousers and a shirt on. And Pahom dreamed that he looked more attentively to see what sort of man it was lying there, and he saw that the man was dead, and that it was himself. Horror-struck, he awoke.

"What things one dreams about!" thought he.

Looking around he saw through the open door that the dawn was breaking.

"It's time to wake them up," thought he. "We ought to be starting."

He got up, roused his man (who was sleeping in his cart), bade him harness, and went to call the Bashkirs.

"It's time to go to the steppe to measure the land," he said.

The Bashkirs rose and assembled, and the chief came, too. Then they began drinking kumiss again, and offered Pahom some tea, but he would not wait.

"If we are to go, let's go. It's high time," said he.

8

The Bashkirs got ready and they all started; some mounted on horses and some in carts. Pahom drove in his own small cart with his servant and took a spade with him. When they reached the

Vocabulary Development

Vocabulary Reinforcement

To reinforce and assess students' comprehension of selection vocabulary words, give them sentences using the words in which the word may or may not be used correctly. Students must tell whether the use is correct and explain their answer. Use these sentences.

1. Pahom *disparaged* Simon's acquittal because he was sure that Simon had cut down the trees.
   Answer: Yes, *disparaged* is used correctly here. Pahom would belittle a decision with which he disagreed.
2. Pahom was *piqued* at the low price the Bashkirs set for the land and happily accepted their conditions.
   Answer: No, *piqued* is not used correctly. Pahom was delighted, not angered, by the apparent good deal he was offered.

steppe, the red dawn was beginning to kindle. They ascended a hillock (called by the Bashkirs a *shikhan*) and, dismounting from their carts and their horses, gathered in one spot. The chief came up to Pahom and, stretching out his arm toward the plain:

"See," said he, "all this, as far as your eye can reach, is ours. You may have any part of it you like."

Pahom's eyes glistened: it was all virgin soil, as flat as the palm of your hand, as black as the seed of a poppy, and in the hollows different kinds of grasses grew breast-high.

The chief took off his fox-fur cap, placed it on the ground, and said:

"This will be the mark. Start from here, and return here again. All the land you go around shall be yours."

Pahom took out his money and put it on the cap. Then he took off his outer coat, remaining in his sleeveless undercoat. He unfastened his girdle[9] and tied it tight below his stomach, put a little bag of bread into the breast of his coat, and, tying a flask of water to his girdle, he drew up the tops of his boots, took the spade from his man, and stood ready to start. He considered for some moments which way he had better go—it was tempting everywhere.

"No matter," he concluded, "I'll go toward the rising sun."

He turned his face to the east, stretched himself, and waited for the sun to appear above the rim.

28 "I must lose no time," he thought, "and it's easier walking while it's still cool."

The sun's rays had hardly flashed above the horizon when Pahom, carrying the spade over his shoulder, went down into the steppe.

Pahom started walking neither slowly nor quickly. After having gone a thousand yards he stopped, dug a hole, and placed pieces of turf one on another to make it more visible. Then he went on; and now that he had walked off his stiffness he quickened his pace. After a while he dug another hole.

Pahom looked back. The hillock could be distinctly seen in the sunlight, with the people on it, and the glittering iron rims of the cartwheels. At a rough guess Pahom concluded that he had walked three miles. It was growing warmer; he took off his undercoat, slung it across his shoulder, and went on again. It had grown quite warm now; he looked at the sun—it was time to think of breakfast.

"The first shift is done, but there are four in a day, and it's too soon yet to turn. But I'll just take off my boots," said he to himself.

He sat down, took off his boots, stuck them into his girdle, and went on. It was easy walking now.

"I'll go on for another three miles," thought he, "and then turn

9. **girdle** (gurd′'l) *n.* old term for a belt or sash for the waist.

Literary Analysis
Theme How do Pahom's thoughts and actions now reflect his earlier attitude toward acquiring land?

29 **Reading Check**
At what sort of pace does Pahom set out?

28 Literary Analysis
Theme

1. Have a volunteer read the passage aloud.
2. **Ask** students what details in the passage show that Pahom is having a difficult time?
   Answer: Pahom is uncomfortable in the heat and takes off both his overcoat and his boots.
3. Then, **ask** the Literary Analysis question: How do Pahom's thoughts and actions now reflect his earlier attitude toward acquiring land?
   Possible response: Pahom's thoughts and actions continue to show his greediness. Earlier in the story, each acquisition only made Pahom want more. Here, each leg of his walk makes Pahom want to walk further.

29 Reading Check

Answer: Pahom begins his journey at a pace that is neither fast nor slow.

Differentiated Instruction for Universal Access

Strategy for Special Needs Students
Ask students to identify with Pahom's emotional and physical states as the story draws to a close. Ask them to role-play a scene with Pahom and the Bashkirs to understand Pahom's conflict and suffering.

EL Strategy for English Learners
Have students suggest words that describe Pahom's situation at the end of the story. Write their words on the board. Ask students to draw pictures of Pahom as he tries to make it back to the Bashkirs and close the border of his land. Using the words on the chalkboard, have them write captions for the drawings.

30 Critical Thinking
Infer

1. Read aloud the sentence to students.
2. **Ask** students to discuss how Pahom's observation may foreshadow the outcome of the story.
Possible response: The comment "a lifetime to live" is an ironic foreshadowing because Pahom may not live to enjoy the land.

31 Reading Skill
Draw Conclusions

1. Have a volunteer read aloud the bracketed text.
2. **Ask** students whether they think Pahom has learned a lesson about his greed. Have them point out details in the passage that support their conclusions.
Possible response: On one level, he has learned his lesson because he says, "Oh, Lord, if only I have not blundered trying for too much!" and "I've grasped too much and ruined the whole affair." On another level, he has not learned anything because he does not stop to rest or give up his attempts to get back in time.
3. Finally, **ask** students the Reading Skill question: Based on details here and earlier, what conclusions can you draw about the chances for Pahom's success?
Possible response: Once it becomes clear that Pahom had essentially challenged the Devil, the chance of him "winning" is negated. He does not stop to rest because he does not want to look like a fool to the Bashkirs.

to the left. This spot is so fine that it would be a pity to lose it. The further one goes, the better the land seems."

28 He went straight on for a while, and when he looked around, the hillock was scarcely visible and the people on it looked like black ants, and he could just see something glistening there in the sun.

"Ah," thought Pahom, "I have gone far enough in this direction; it's time to turn. Besides, I'm in a regular sweat, and very thirsty."

He stopped, dug a large hole, and heaped up pieces of turf. Next he untied his flask, had a drink, and then turned sharply to the left. He went on and on; the grass was high, and it was very hot.

Pahom began to grow tired: he looked at the sun and saw that it was noon.

"Well," he thought, "I must have a rest."

He sat down, and ate some bread and drank some water; but he did not lie down, thinking that if he did he might fall asleep. After sitting a little while, he went on again. At first he walked easily; the food had strengthened him; but it had become terribly hot and he felt sleepy. Still he went on, thinking: 30 "An hour to suffer, a lifetime to live."

He went a long way in this direction also, and was about to turn to the left again, when he perceived a damp hollow: "It would be a pity to leave that out," he thought. "Flax would do well there." So he went on past the hollow and dug a hole on the other side of it before he made a sharp turn. Pahom looked toward the hillock. The heat made the air hazy: it seemed to be quivering, and through the haze the people on the hillock could scarcely be seen.

"Ah," thought Pahom, "I have made the sides too long; I must make this one shorter." And he went along the third side, stepping faster. He looked at the sun: it was nearly halfway to the horizon, and he had not yet done two miles of the third side of the square. He was still ten miles from the goal.

"No," he thought, "though it will make my land lopsided, I must hurry back in a straight line now. I might go too far, and as it is I have a great deal of land."

So Pahom hurriedly dug a hole and turned straight toward the hillock.

9

Reading Skill
Draw Conclusions
Based on details here and earlier, what conclusion can you draw about the chances for Pahom's success?

31 Pahom went straight toward the hillock, but he now walked with difficulty. He was exhausted from the heat, his bare feet were cut and bruised, and his legs began to fail. He longed to rest, but it was impossible if he meant to get back before sunset. The sun waits for no man, and it was sinking lower and lower.

"Oh, Lord," he thought, "if only I have not blundered trying for

Vocabulary Development

Vocabulary Knowledge Rating

When students have completed reading and discussing "How Much Land Does a Man Need?" have them take out their **Vocabulary Knowledge Rating Chart** for this selection. Read the words aloud once more and have students rate their knowledge of the words again in the After Reading column. Clarify any words that are still problematic. Have students write their own definition and an example sentence in the appropriate column. Then, have students complete the Vocabulary Practice at the end of the selection. Encourage students to use the words in further discussion and written work about this selection. Remind them that they will be accountable for these words on the **Selection Test, *Unit 2 Resources*,** pp. 139–141 or 142–144.

too much! What if I am too late?"

He looked toward the hillock and at the sun. He was still far from his goal, and the sun was already near the rim of the sky.

31 Pahom walked on and on; it was very hard walking, but he went quicker and quicker. He pressed on, but was still far from the place. He began running, threw away his coat, his boots, his flask, and his cap, and kept only the spade which he used as a support.

"What am I to do?" he thought again. "I've grasped too much and ruined the whole affair. I can't get there before the sun sets."

32

And this fear made him still more breathless. Pahom kept on running; his soaking shirt and trousers stuck to him, and his mouth was parched. His breast was working like a blacksmith's bellows, his heart was beating like a hammer, and his legs were giving way as if they did not belong to him. Pahom was seized with terror lest he should die of the strain.

Though afraid of death, he could not stop.

"After having run all that way they will call me a fool if I stop now," thought he.

And he ran on and on, and drew near and heard the Bashkirs yelling and shouting to him, and their cries inflamed his heart still more. He gathered his last strength and ran on.

The sun was close to the rim of the sky and, cloaked in mist, looked large, and red as blood. Now, yes, now, it was about to set! The sun was quite low, but he was also quite near his goal. Pahom could already see the people on the hillock waving their arms to make him hurry. He could see the fox-fur cap on the ground and the money in it, and the chief sitting on the ground holding his sides. And Pahom remembered his dream.

33 "There's plenty of land," thought he, "but will God let me live on it? I have lost my life, I have lost my life! Never will I reach that spot!"

Pahom looked at the sun, which had reached the earth: one side of it had already disappeared. With all his remaining strength he rushed on, bending his body forward so that his legs could hardly follow fast enough to keep him from falling. Just as he reached the hillock it suddenly grew dark. He looked up—the sun had already set!

"I can't get there before the sun sets."

Literary Analysis
Theme Rephrase Pahom's words as a statement of a theme in the story.

34 **Reading Check**
What are Pahom's fears as the sun begins to set?

32 Humanities

Enclosed Field With Rising Sun by Vincent Van Gogh (1853–1890)

Van Gogh, a Dutch painter, never achieved fame in his lifetime. This painting represents one of more than two thousand works of Van Gogh's. Van Gogh committed suicide in 1890.

33 Literary Analysis

Theme

1. Read these sentences aloud to students.
2. Then, direct students to **respond** to the Literary Analysis prompt: Rephrase Pahom's words as a statement of a theme in the story.
   Possible answer: There is plenty of land for someone who has moderate desires.

▶ **Monitor Progress** Although Pahom learns a valuable lesson, he dies without being able to apply the lesson. **Ask** students to comment on how Pahom's death contributes to or modifies Tolstoy's theme.
Possible response: Pahom's death suggests to readers that greed breeds dire consequences.

▶ **Reteach** If students have difficulty identifying the story's theme, have them make lists of Pahom's good and bad character traits. For each of Pahom's bad character traits, such as being greedy, ask students to record any consequences that result from the traits. Once students have identified that Pahom ultimately loses his life due to his greed, ask students whether greed is a human trait that exists outside the story. Invite students to share examples of greedy behavior in themselves or people they know. Tell students to include any consequences of which they are aware for each of the examples that they share. Help students make connections between Pahom's greed and its consequences and their real life examples.

34 Reading Check

Answer: Pahom fears that he will not reach the spot from which he left and thus lose the land he wants.

Concept Connector

Anticipation Guide

Have students return to their **Anticipation Guides** and respond to the statements again in the After Reading column. They may do this individually or in their original groups. Then, lead a class discussion, probing for what students have learned that confirms or invalidates each statement. Encourage students to cite specific details, quotations, or other evidence from the text to support their responses to each statement.

Writing About the Big Question

Have students compare their responses to the sentence starters they completed before reading the story with their ideas afterwards. Ask them to explain whether their thoughts have changed.

Reading Skill Graphic Organizer

Ask students to review the graphic organizer they completed with their conclusions. Show them the partially completed **Reading Skill Graphic Organizer A** (*Graphic Organizer Transparencies,* p. 56) as an example. Then, have students share the graphic organizers they did and the conclusions they drew.

ASSESS

Answers

Critical Thinking

1. **Possible response:** Some students may not sympathize with Pahom because his greed is a very unattractive trait. Other students may say Pahom does not deserve to die simply because he is foolish.
2. (a) A local landowner is selling her property. (b) He is tired of having to pay fines; he is also envious of those who own land.
3. (a) Pahom starts to fine the peasants when he becomes a landowner. (b) **Possible response:** Owning land alienates him from his neighbors, and it stimulates his greed.
4. **Possible response:** (a) Some students will say that Pahom would have no choice but to be content with the amount of land that he had. (b) In discussion, some students may doubt Pahom could ever be content. (c) Tolstoy seems to believe that too much ambition is destructive.
5. (a) On the last day of his life, Pahom walks too far in order to get more land and dies of exhaustion. (b) A man needs only six feet for burial.

Can progress be made without conflict?

Possible response: (a) Pahom's main source of conflict is with himself. He thinks he must have more land, even though he can make a decent living with the amount of land he owns. (b) No, it should not. With each increase in the amount of land he owns, Pahom becomes greedier.

He gave a cry: "All my labor has been in vain," thought he, and was about to stop, but he heard the Bashkirs still shouting and remembered that though to him, from below, the sun seemed to have set, they on the hillock could still see it. He took a long breath and ran up the hillock. It was still light there. He reached the top and saw the cap. Before it sat the chief, laughing and holding his sides. Again Pahom remembered his dream, and he uttered a cry: his legs gave way beneath him, he fell forward and reached the cap with his hands.

"Ah, that's a fine fellow!" exclaimed the chief. "He has gained much land!"

Pahom's servant came running up and tried to raise him, but he saw that blood was flowing from his mouth. Pahom was dead.

The Bashkirs clicked their tongues to show their pity.

His servant picked up the spade and dug a grave long enough for Pahom to lie in, and buried him in it.

Six feet from his head to his toes was all he needed.

Critical Thinking

1. **Respond:** Do you sympathize with Pahom? Explain.
2. **(a)** What event allows Pahom to buy his first parcel of land? **(b) Interpret:** What is his main reason for wanting this land? Support your answer with details from the story.
3. **(a) Summarize:** Explain the events that change Pahom's relations with his neighbors. **(b) Analyze Cause and Effect:** What effect does owning land have on his life?
4. **(a) Hypothesize:** If Pahom had no chances to acquire more land, do you think he could find happiness with what he already has? Explain. **(b) Discuss:** Share and discuss answers with a partner. **(c) Apply:** Based on your discussion, write a sentence explaining the author's attitude toward ambition.
5. **(a) Summarize:** What events take place on the last day of Pahom's life? **(b) Interpret:** Explain the meaning of the story's last sentence both as a description of Pahom's fate and as an answer to the title of the story.

Can progress be made without conflict?
(a) Is Pahom's main source of conflict with others or with himself? Explain. **(b)** Should Pahom's acquisition of increasingly large parcels of land be considered progress? Why or why not?

Assessment Resources

Unit 2 Resources

L1 L2 EL **Selection Test A,** pp. 139–140. Administer Test A to less advanced readers and English learners.

L3 L4 **Selection Test B,** pp. 143–144. Administer Test B to on-level and more advanced students.

L3 L4 **Open-Book Test,** pp. 136–138. As an alternative, give the Open-Book Test.

All **Customizable Test Bank**

All **Self-tests**

Students may prepare for the **Selection Test** by taking the **Self-test** online.

PHLit Online! All assessment resources are available at **www.PHLitOnline.com.**

After You Read

How Much Land Does a Man Need?

Literary Analysis: Theme

1. **(a)** Using a chart like the one shown, analyze the episodes in which Pahom is given the chance to acquire property. **(b)** How are these episodes related? Are they similar or different? Explain.

Episode	Character's Response	Reasons for the Response	Result: Peace of Mind/Problems

   (c) State the **theme** of the story, explaining how each event helps convey it.

2. Tolstoy makes the **philosophical assumption** that people should not waste their lives on material things. How might Pahom's life have changed if he had applied this belief?

Reading Skill: Draw Conclusions

3. **(a) Draw a conclusion** about the Bashkirs' values based on their attitude toward land. **(b)** Which details in Tolstoy's depiction of the tribe contribute to the story's theme? Explain.

Vocabulary

Practice In vocabulary study, **antonyms** are words with opposite meanings. Rewrite each of the following sentences by replacing the word or phrase in italics with its antonym from the vocabulary list on page 336. Then, explain which version of the sentence makes more sense.

1. He *indulged* and ate half the cake.
2. After he took my bicycle, I was *forgiving* and lent him my radio.
3. I was *not hurt* by his insults, and I found his company enjoyable.
4. The *harmony* between the siblings made family dinners peaceful.
5. His land was *desert*, so he had no success with his crops.
6. Her body was *upright* and at attention as she received her medal.

Word Study Use the context of the sentences and what you know about the **Latin prefix *dis-*** to explain your answer to each question.

1. Are people living in *disharmony* good at working together?
2. What happens when a person is *disabled* in some way?

Word Study

The **Latin prefix *dis-*** means "wrong," "bad," or "not."

Challenge Explain how the prefix *dis-* contributes to the meanings of these words. Consult a dictionary if necessary.

disconnect
disembody
disregard

ASSESS/EXTEND

Answers

Literary Analysis

1. (a) Pahom first buys land from his landlady. Next, he leaves his home to buy land beyond the Volga River. Finally, he tries to buy land from the Bashkirs. (b) In every instance, Pahom desires to increase the amount of land he owns. He does not want to rent land; he wants to own it himself. (c) Tolstoy's theme is that a man only needs as much land as he can reasonably cultivate and work productively. Anything beyond this point is excessive and unnecessary. Indeed, at the end of life, as Tolstoy shows, a person only needs enough land to be buried in.

   For other sample answers, see ***Graphic Organizer Transparencies*, Literary Analysis Graphic Organizer A**, p. 59, and the **Additional Answers** section.

2. **Possible response:** Pahom might not have been led into his disastrous schemes to buy more land. He might have been contented with his situation and simply tried to cultivate and improve the land he owned.

Reading Skill

3. (a) **Possible response:** The Bashkirs respect nature and believe that man cannot have, as Pahom desires, unlimited domain over it. (b) Since the Bashkirs will not give Pahom any more land than he can circuit in a day, it is reasonable to assume that they insist that the owner of land must be able to responsibly cultivate all of it. Thus, the Bashkirs recognize the principle that labor, not money, is what gives a person ownership of the land.

Vocabulary

Practice

Sample answers:

1. He *forbore* and ate half the cake. The original makes more sense.
2. After he took my bicycle, I was *piqued* and lent him my radio. The original makes more sense.
3. I was *aggrieved* by his insults, and I found his company enjoyable. The original makes more sense.

Answers continued

4. The *discord* between the siblings made family dinners peaceful. The original makes more sense.
5. His land was *arable*, so he had no success with his crops. The original makes more sense.
6. Her body was *prostrate* and at attention as she received her medal. The original makes more sense.

Word Study

Sample answers:

1. No, the prefix *dis-* means "not" and *disharmony* means "lack of or not in harmony." Workers who are not in harmony will not work well together.
2. The prefix *dis-* means "not" and *disabled* means "not able or incapacitated." When a person is disabled, he or she is not able to make full use of his or her limbs and body.

Word Study: Challenge

Sample answers: When you are *disconnected*, you are not connected. When something is *disembodied*, it does not have a body or substance. When you *disregard* something, you do not regard or pay attention to it.

PRETEACH

Skills instruction for the ***Reading Skill*** *and* ***Literary Analysis*** *concepts appears on p. 335.*

❶ Writing About the Big Question

1. Review the assignment with the class.
2. Ask students to think of either someone they know or a character from a book who overcame a challenge. Ask them to compare the individual before and after the challenge. How did he or she grow as an individual?
3. Have students complete the sample sentence starter. Review responses as a class. (**Possible response:** Understanding what things are truly important in life can help a person overcome <u>adversity</u> because they will not be intimidated by minor obstacles.)

While You Read

Tell students that they should look for things that Jonathan appreciates after the war ends.

❷ Vocabulary

1. Have students preview the selection vocabulary.
2. Have students say each word aloud.
3. Then, use each word in a sentence that defines the word.
4. Finally, repeat your definitional sentence or a similar sentence with the word missing, and have the class "fill in the blank" chorally. Here is an example:

   To be <u>destitute</u> is to lack the basic necessities of life. A man who has no job, no money, and nowhere to live is [students say "destitute"].

❸ Word Study

1. Introduce the skill, using the instruction in the box.
2. Ask students to explain how the prefix *com-* in the word *community* contributes to its meaning. (**Answer:** *Com-* means "together." *Community* means "a group of people living or acting together.")

Making Connections | Civil Peace

Can progress be made without *conflict?*

❶ Writing About the Big Question

In "Civil Peace," a man and most of his family survive a civil war only to face new conflicts during peacetime. Use this sentence starter to develop your ideas about the Big Question.

Understanding what things are truly important in life can help a person overcome **adversity** because ________________.

While You Read Look for things Jonathan, the story's main character, counts as blessings after the conflict of war ends.

❷ Vocabulary

Read each word and its definition. Decide whether you know the word well, know it a little bit, or do not know it at all. After you read, see how your knowledge of each word has increased.

- **disreputable** (dis rep´ yo͞o tə bəl) *adj.* not respectable; having or deserving a bad reputation (p. 359) ***The travel guide warned against <u>disreputable</u> street vendors.*** *disreputably adv. disrepute n.*
- **amenable** (ə mē´ nə bəl) *adj.* responsive; open (p. 359) ***The plans are not set, so I will be <u>amenable</u> to your suggestions.*** *amenability n. amenably adv.*
- **destitute** (des´ tə to͞ot´) *adj.* lacking the basic necessities of life; poverty-stricken (p. 360) ***The city provided housing for families left <u>destitute</u> by the flood.*** *destitution n.*
- **inaudibly** (in ô´ də blē) *adv.* in a way that cannot be heard (p. 362) ***No one can understand what Lydia says when she mumbles <u>inaudibly</u>.*** *audible adj. inaudible adj. audio n.*
- **dissent** (di sent´) *n.* disagreement; refusal to accept a common opinion (p. 363) ***The dictator would not tolerate <u>dissent</u> from his subjects.*** *dissent v. dissenter n. assent v.*
- **commiserate** (kə miz´ ər āt´) *v.* sympathize with or show sorrow for (p. 364) ***The coach will usually <u>commiserate</u> with his team after a tough loss.*** *commiseration n. commiserative adj.*

❸ Word Study

The **Latin prefix** ***com-*** means "together" or "with."

In this story, a character and his neighbors **commiserate,** or feel sorrow together, after he and his family are robbed.

Vocabulary Development

Vocabulary Knowledge Rating

Create a **Vocabulary Knowledge Rating Chart** (***Professional Development Guidebook***, p. 33) for this selection. Include the selection vocabulary and the Big Question words that appear in the Writing About the Big Question sentence starter on this page. (The Big Question vocabulary is introduced on pp. 222–223.)

Give students a copy of the chart. Read the words aloud, and have students mark their rating in the Before Reading column. Urge them to be alert to these words as they read and discuss the selection.

Tally how many students think they know a word to gauge how much instruction to provide. As students read and discuss the selection, point out the words and their context.

PHLit Online! **Vocabulary Central**, featuring tools, activities, and songs for studying vocabulary, is available online at **www.PHLitOnline.com**.

Meet Chinua Achebe
(b. 1930)

Author of Civil Peace

Chinua (chin´ wä) Achebe (ä chā´ bā) is renowned for novels and stories that explore the conflicts of modern Africans. Achebe was born into the Ibo tribe of Nigeria. He grew up to pursue a varied career as a university teacher and as a director for the Nigerian Broadcasting Corporation. According to one critic, "In the English language, he is the founding father of modern African literature."

Africans Face the West Achebe wrote his first and most celebrated novel, *Things Fall Apart* (1958), in an effort to accurately portray the disruption of Ibo tribal society by Western colonial rule.

4 BACKGROUND FOR THE STORY

The Nigerian Civil War

In 1960, the West African nation of Nigeria finally won independence from Britain. The Ibo (also spelled *Igbo*), one people of Nigeria, seceded from the new country, setting up the independent Republic of Biafra. A brutal civil war followed. In 1970, a defeated Biafra rejoined Nigeria. "Civil Peace" unfolds in the aftermath of this war.

DID YOU KNOW?

During the civil war in Nigeria, Achebe's house was bombed. He fled, leaving behind a book of his that he had nearly finished printing. When he returned, a single copy of the book remained.

Daily Bellringer

For each class during which you will teach this selection, have students complete one of the five Revision activities for Week 10 in the ***Daily Bellringer Activities*** booklet.

4 Background

The Nigerian Civil War

Nigeria's borders, established during colonial times, held almost 300 ethnic and tribal groups. The country gained independence from Great Britain in 1960. However, self-government did not work well. The Muslim Hausa dominated the government, and ethnic and religious rivalries increased. During the 1960s, massacres of the largely Christian Ibo triggered a bloody civil war. When they were threatened by being cut off from both the sea and the rest of Nigeria's oil-rich areas, Ibo leaders declared their region the independent state of Biafra. Defeated, Biafra surrendered two and a half years later in January 1970.

Multidraft Reading

This icon ● marks natural pauses in the selection. To assist struggling readers and to deepen reading for all, assign the text in "chunks," following the icons, and apply multidraft reading protocols. For each reading, have students set the purpose indicated:

- **First reading**—literal comprehension: answering the Reading Check questions.
- **Second reading**—application of skills: answering the Theme and Draw Conclusions prompts.
- **Third reading**—interpretation: answering the end-of-selection questions.

For more guidance, refer to the ***Classroom Strategies and Teaching Routines*** card on multidraft reading.

Differentiated Instruction — Additional Instruction

EL Extended Support—English Learners

Have students complete the **Reading and Vocabulary Warm-ups, *Unit 2 Resources*,** pp. 145–148, before they read. Assign the prereading pages for the selection in the ***Reader's Notebook: English Learner's Version***. Then, have students listen to portions of the selection on the ***Hear It!* Audio CD.**

L1 L2 Extended Support—Struggling Readers

Have students complete the **Reading and Vocabulary Warm-ups, *Unit 2 Resources*,** pp. 145–148, before they read. Assign the prereading pages and the adapted selection in the ***Reader's Notebook: Adapted Version***. Then, have students listen to portions of the selection on the ***Hear It!* Audio CD** (adapted text).

Extended Support—Reluctant Readers

To build motivation and engagement before assigning the selection, have students read "Learning from Crime Victims," a thematically related selection in ***Reality Central***. Then, use the questions at the conclusion of the related selection to guide discussion.

PHLit Online!

For more about the author, practice with the selection vocabulary, and more background, go online at **www.PHLitOnline.com.**

TEACH

❶ Activating Prior Knowledge

1. Prepare an **Anticipation Guide** (see ***Professional Development Guidebook,*** pp. 36–38) with the following statements:
   - The way people cope with loss is highly individual.
   - "War is not friendly to children and other living things."
   - Optimists enjoy life more than pessimists do.
   - Everything happens for the best.
2. Give students a copy of the prepared **Anticipation Guide** and have them mark their responses in the Me column. Have students discuss the statements in pairs or groups and mark the Guide again in the Group column.
3. For further guidance, use the ***Classroom Strategies and Teaching Routines*** card: **Using an Anticipation Guide.**

Concept Connector ⟶

Students will return to the **Anticipation Guide** after completing the story.

Individual Activity

Have students keep reflective journals as they read "Civil Peace." Encourage them to write their thoughts and feelings each time Jonathan Iwegbu states, "Nothing puzzles God."

❷ About the Selection

"If life gives you lemons, make lemonade." In "Civil Peace," this expression sums up the main character's ability to make the best of the difficult situations thrust upon him by a chaotic, lawless post-civil war society. Having survived with most of his family intact, Jonathan Iwegbu realizes that flexibility is the key to success. If one business does not work, another one might. Even when thieves threaten his family and steal his money, Jonathan shows that a positive mental attitude helps one to adapt to change and loss.

❶ ❷

Civi
Peace

Chinua Ache

Jonathan Iwegbu counted himself extraordinarily lucky. "Happy survival!" meant so much more to him than just a current fashion of greeting old friends in the first hazy days of peace. It went deep to his heart. He had come out of the war with five inestimable blessings—his head, his

Vocabulary Development

Word Analysis

- Draw students' attention to the word *disreputable* and its definition, "not respectable."
- Explain that the Latin root *-reput-* means "to think" or "to consider." Therefore, you "think badly of" someone who is disreputable.
- Encourage students to think of other words that contain this root, such as *reputation* and *reputed.* Using their knowledge of the root, ask students to define each word.

wife Maria's head and the heads of three out of their four children. As a bonus he also had his old bicycle—a miracle too but naturally not to be compared to the safety of five human heads.

The bicycle had a little history of its own. One day at the height of the war it was commandeered "for urgent military action." Hard as its loss would have been to him he would still have let it go without a thought had he not had some doubts about the genuineness of the officer. It wasn't his **disreputable** rags, nor the toes peeping out of one blue and one brown canvas shoe, nor yet the two stars of his rank done obviously in a hurry in biro,[1] that troubled Jonathan; many good and heroic soldiers looked the same or worse. It was rather a certain lack of grip and firmness in his manner. So Jonathan, suspecting he might be **amenable** to influence, rummaged in his raffia bag and produced the two pounds with which he had been going to buy firewood which his wife, Maria, retailed to camp officials for extra stock-fish and corn meal, and got his bicycle back. That night he buried it in the little clearing in the bush where the dead of the camp, including his own youngest son, were buried. When he dug it up again a year later after the surrender all it needed was a little palm-oil greasing. "Nothing
3 puzzles God," he said in wonder.

He put it to immediate use as a taxi and accumulated a small pile of Biafran[2] money ferrying camp officials and their families across the four-mile stretch to the nearest tarred road. His standard charge per trip was six pounds and those who had the money were only glad to be rid of some of it in this way. At the end of a fortnight[3] he had made a small fortune of one hundred and fifteen pounds.

Then he made the journey to Enugu and found another miracle waiting for him. It was unbelievable. He rubbed his eyes and looked again and it was still standing there before him. But, needless to say, even that monumental blessing must be accounted also totally inferior to the five heads in the family. This newest miracle was his little house in Ogui Overside. Indeed nothing puzzles God! Only two houses away a huge concrete edifice some wealthy contractor had put up just before the war was a mountain of rubble. And here was Jonathan's little zinc house of no regrets built with mud blocks quite intact! Of course the doors and windows were missing 4
and five sheets off the roof. But what was that? And anyhow he had returned to Enugu early enough to pick up bits of old zinc and wood and soggy sheets of cardboard lying around the neighborhood before thousands more came out of their forest holes looking for

1. **biro** (bī´ rō) *n.* British expression for "ballpoint pen."
2. **Biafran** (bē äf´ rən) *adj.* of the rebellious southeastern region of Nigeria, which declared itself the independent Republic of Biafra in the civil war of 1967.
3. **fortnight** (fôrt´ nīt´) *n.* British English for "two weeks."

Vocabulary
disreputable (dis rep´ yo͞o tə bəl) *adj.* not respectable; having or deserving a bad reputation

amenable (ə mē´ nə bəl) *adj.* responsive; open

Literary Analysis
Theme What do these stories of Jonathan's "blessings" have in common?

Reading Check
What are the five blessings for which Jonathan is grateful?

3 Literary Analysis
Theme

1. Ask a volunteer to read the bracketed text.
2. Then, **ask** students the Literary Analysis question: What do these stories of Jonathan's "blessings" have in common?
   Possible response: The blessings all represent Jonathan's optimistic view of life. He feels he has been lucky to escape the devastation experienced by those around him.

4 Reading Check

Answer: Jonathan is grateful that he, his wife, and three of his four children survived the war.

Differentiated Instruction for Universal Access

Strategy for Special Needs Students
Students might have a difficult time understanding the story's dialect and unfamiliar vocabulary. Have them read the story in the **Adapted Reader's Notebook** to develop a basic understanding of the plot. Then, have them listen to the recording of the selection on the ***Hear It!* Audio CD** while they follow along in the text.

EL Strategy for English Learners
This story contains unfamiliar vocabulary, unexpected phrasing, and difficult dialect. Students will benefit from following along in their text as they listen to the recording of the selection on the ***Hear It!* Audio CD**. Pause the recording to discuss particularly difficult passages written in dialect.

PHLit Online!
This selection is available in interactive format in the **Enriched Online Student Edition, www.PHLitOnline.com**, which includes a thematically related video and writing prompt and an interactive graphic organizer.

❺ Critical Viewing

Possible response: Students may say that the man in the photograph could be Jonathan Iwegbu. He looks as if he has suffered, but his eyes and mouth show the hint of a smile.

❻ Connecting to the Big Question

1. Explain that sometimes to move forward after a crisis, we must count our blessings rather than focus on what has been lost or taken.
2. Have students read the bracketed text. **Ask:** What evidence supports the idea that Jonathan and his family continue to work hard despite the destruction left by the war? **Answer:** Jonathan has opened a bar to serve soldiers. His wife has started making breakfast akara balls for her neighbors. Jonathan's children have begun picking mangoes and selling them to soldier's wives.
3. **Ask:** How could Jonathan's response to the war, if universally adopted, quickly bring about peace and stability?
Possible response: If everyone behaved like Jonathan, people would focus on what is good in their lives rather than what is not. In so doing, everyone would find creative ways to better their situation and help their fellow citizens.

❺ ▲ **Critical Viewing**
Does the expression on this man's face suggest he has a personality similar to Jonathan's? Explain. **[Connect]**

Vocabulary
destitute (des′ tə to͞ot′) *adj.* lacking the basic necessities of life; poverty-stricken

the same things. He got a destitute carpenter with one old hammer, a blunt plane and a few bent and rusty nails in his tool bag to turn this assortment of wood, paper and metal into door and window shutters for five Nigerian shillings or fifty Biafran pounds. He paid the pounds, and moved in with his overjoyed family carrying five heads on their shoulders.

His children picked mangoes near the military cemetery and sold them to soldiers' wives for a few pennies—real pennies this time—and his wife started making breakfast akara balls[4] for neighbors in a hurry to start life again. With his family earnings he took his bicycle to the villages around and bought fresh palm-wine which he mixed generously in his ❻
rooms with the water which had recently started running again in the public tap down the road, and opened up a bar for soldiers and other lucky people with good money.

At first he went daily, then every other day and finally once a week, to the offices of the Coal Corporation where he used to be a miner, to find out what was what. The only thing he did find out in the end was that that little house of his was even a greater blessing than he had thought. Some of his fellow ex-miners who had nowhere to return at the end of the day's waiting just slept outside the doors of the offices and cooked what meal they could scrounge together in Bournvita tins. As the weeks lengthened and still nobody could say what was what Jonathan discontinued his weekly visits altogether and faced his palm-wine bar.

But nothing puzzles God. Came the day of the windfall when ❼

4. **akara** (ə kär′ ə) **balls** *n.* deep-fried balls of ground beans.

Vocabulary Development

Thematic Vocabulary: The Big Question
As students are discussing "Civil Peace," encourage them to use the thematic vocabulary presented in Introducing the Big Question, pp. 222–223. You might encourage them with sentence starters like these:

1. Jonathan's life is a constant *struggle* because . . .
2. One way Jonathan deals with *adversity* is to . . .
3. One *radical* change in Jonathan's village is . . .
4. Jonathan deals with a *confrontation* with the robbers by . . .

7 after five days of endless scuffles in queues[5] and counterqueues in the sun outside the Treasury he had twenty pounds counted into his palms as ex-gratia[6] award for the rebel money he had turned in. It was like Christmas for him and for many others like him when the payments began. They called it (since few could manage its proper official name) *egg-rasher*.

As soon as the pound notes were placed in his palm Jonathan simply closed it tight over them and buried fist and money inside his trouser pocket. He had to be extra careful because he had seen a man a couple of days earlier collapse into near-madness in an instant before that oceanic crowd because no sooner had he got his twenty pounds than some heartless ruffian picked it off him. Though it was not right that a man in such an extremity of agony should be blamed yet many in the queues that day were able to remark quietly at the victim's carelessness, especially after he pulled out the innards of his pocket and revealed a hole in it big enough to pass a thief's head. But of course he had insisted that the money had been in the other pocket, pulling it out too to show

5. **queues** (kyo͞oz) *n.* British English for "lines."
6. **ex-gratia** (eks grä′ shē ə) as a favor (Latin).

Reading Skill
Draw Conclusions
What conclusion can you draw about Jonathan's attitude toward good and bad events? Explain.

8 **Reading Check**
What does Jonathan get in exchange for the rebel money he has saved?

7 Reading Skill
Draw Conclusions

1. Ask a volunteer to read the bracketed passage.
2. Then, **ask** students the Reading Skill question: What conclusion can you draw about Jonathan's attitude toward good and bad events? Explain.
   Possible response: Jonathan is philosophical. He treasures the good things that happen and takes precautions to avoid bad events, such as not looking into approaching faces so that he does not have to withdraw his hand from his pocket in order to shake hands. He believes that all is for good, even if human beings cannot see the reasons.

8 Reading Check

Answer: He gets an egg-rasher in exchange for the money he has saved.

Differentiated Instruction for Universal Access

Strategy for Less Proficient Readers
Encourage students to explain the key phrase "Nothing puzzles God." Engage them in a discussion about the phrase's possible meanings as well as how it relates to Jonathan Iwegbu's attitude toward life. Have them consider the reasons the writer repeats the phrase several times throughout the story.

Enrichment for Advanced Readers
Have students brainstorm for other proverbs and sayings that have a similar meaning to "Nothing puzzles God," such as "Every cloud has a silver lining," "Everything happens for the best," "Fear not tomorrow, for God is already there," and "C'est la vie" (That's life!). Then, have students compose their own proverbs or sayings that echo the thought behind "Nothing puzzles God." Encourage students to share their sayings with the class.

9 Literature in Context

Geography Connection Close to one million people became casualties of the civil war in Nigeria. Many of these people were Biafrans (mostly Ibos). The Biafran government claimed that the Nigerians damaged farmland and engaged in genocide to win the war. International relief efforts were only partly successful because the Nigerian government accused the Biafran government of engaging foreign mercenaries to prolong the war.

Connect to the Literature Point out to students that collecting details is the first step to drawing conclusions. Then, **ask** students the Connect to Literature question: Which of Jonathan's experiences can you connect to events of the Nigerian Civil War? Explain.
Answer: Jonathan's bicycle is almost commandeered by the military; there is so little transportation that the bicycle comes in handy to ferry other people; his house is still standing when those around it are in rubble; he gets pounds for turning in rebel money.

- Direct students to complete their list of experiences that come about as a result of the civil war as they finish reading the story.

9 LITERATURE IN CONTEXT

Geography Connection

Nigerian Civil War
Jonathan is delighted that his home in Enugu still stands—and for good reason. Enugu was at the center of the civil war that broke out in Nigeria in 1967. The war began when the eastern region of Nigeria declared itself the independent Republic of Biafra, with Enugu as its capital. The city was invaded by Nigerian federal troops just five months after independence. The war resulted in horrific famine as well as violence. It ended in 1970 with the defeat of Biafra and the reunification of Nigeria.

Connect to the Literature

Which of Jonathan's experiences can you connect to events of the Nigerian Civil War? Explain.

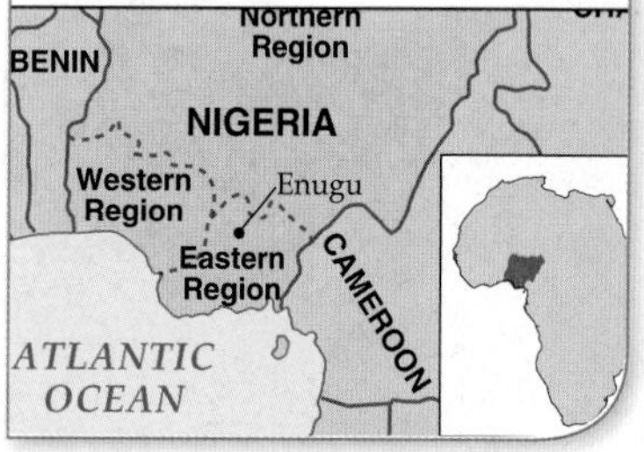

its comparative wholeness. So one had to be careful. 7

Jonathan soon transferred the money to his left hand and pocket so as to leave his right free for shaking hands should the need arise, though by fixing his gaze at such an elevation as to miss all approaching human faces he made sure that the need did not arise, until he got home.

He was normally a heavy sleeper but that night he heard all the neighborhood noises die down one after another. Even the night watchman who knocked the hour on some metal somewhere in the distance had fallen silent after knocking one o'clock. That must have been the last thought in Jonathan's mind before he was finally carried away himself. He couldn't have been gone for long, though, when he was violently awakened again.

"Who is knocking?" whispered his wife lying beside him on the floor.

"I don't know," he whispered back breathlessly.

The second time the knocking came it was so loud and imperious that the rickety old door could have fallen down.

"Who is knocking?" he asked them, his voice parched and trembling.

"Na tief-man and him people," came the cool reply. "Make you hopen de door."[7] This was followed by the heaviest knocking of all.

Maria was the first to raise the alarm, then he followed and all their children.

"Police-o! Thieves-o! Neighbors-o! Police-o! We are lost! We are dead! Neighbors, are you asleep? Wake up! Police-o!"

This went on for a long time and then stopped suddenly. Perhaps they had scared the thief away. There was total silence. But only for a short while.

"You done finish?" asked the voice outside. "Make we help you small. Oya, everybody!"

"Police-o! Tief-man-so! Neighbors-o! we done loss-o! Police-o! . . ."

There were at least five other voices besides the leader's.

Jonathan and his family were now completely paralyzed by terror. Maria and the children sobbed **inaudibly** like lost souls. Jonathan groaned continuously.

The silence that followed the thieves' alarm vibrated horribly. Jonathan all but begged their leader to speak again and be done with it.

Vocabulary
inaudibly (in ô´ də blē) *adv.* in a way that cannot be heard

7. **"Na tief-man . . . hopen de door"** (dialect) "I am a thief with my accomplices. Open the door."

Vocabulary Development

Vocabulary Knowledge Rating

When students have completed reading and discussing "Civil Peace," have them take out their **Vocabulary Knowledge Rating Chart** for this selection. Read the words aloud once more and have students rate their knowledge of the words again in the After Reading column. Clarify any words that are still problematic. Have students write their own definition and example or sentence in the appropriate column. Then, have students complete the Vocabulary Practice at the end of the selection. Encourage students to use the words in further discussion and written work about this selection. Remind them that they will be accountable for these words on the **Selection Test**, ***Unit 2 Resources,*** pp. 160–162 or 163–165.

"My frien," said he at long last, "we don try our best for call dem but I tink say dem all done sleep-o . . . So wetin we go do now? Sometaim you wan call soja? Or you wan make we call dem for you? Soja better pass police. No be so?"

"Na so!" replied his men. Jonathan thought he heard even more voices now than before and groaned heavily. His legs were sagging under him and his throat felt like sandpaper.

"My frien, why you no de talk again. I de ask you say you wan make we call soja?"

"No."

10 "Awrighto. Now make we talk business. We no be bad tief. We no like for make trouble. Trouble done finish. War done finish and all the katakata wey de for inside. No Civil War again. This time na Civil Peace. No be so?"

"Na so!" answered the horrible chorus.

"What do you want from me? I am a poor man. Everything I had went with this war. Why do you come to me? You know people who have money. We . . ."

"Awright! We know say you no get plenty money. But we sef no get even anini. So derefore make you open dis window and give us one hundred pound and we go commot. Orderwise we de come for inside now to show you guitar-boy like dis . . ."

A volley of automatic fire rang through the sky. Maria and the children began to weep aloud again.

"Ah, missisi de cry again. No need for dat. We done talk say we na good tief. We just take our small money and go nwayorly. No molest. Abi we de molest?"

"At all!" sang the chorus.

"My friends," began Jonathan hoarsely. "I hear what you say and I thank you. If I had one hundred pounds . . ."

"Lookia my frien, no be play we come play for your house. If we make mistake and step for inside you no go like am-o. So derefore . . ."

"To God who made me; if you come inside and find one hundred pounds, take it and shoot me and shoot my wife and children. I swear to God. The only money I have in this life is this twenty-pounds *egg-rasher* they gave me today . . ."

"Ok. Time de go. Make you open dis window and bring the twenty pound. We go manage am like dat."

There were now loud murmurs of **dissent** among the chorus: "Na lie de man de lie; e get plenty money . . . Make we go inside and search properly well . . . Wetin be twenty pound? . . ." 11

"Shurrup!" rang the leader's voice like a lone shot in the sky and silenced the murmuring at once. "Are you dere? Bring the money quick!"

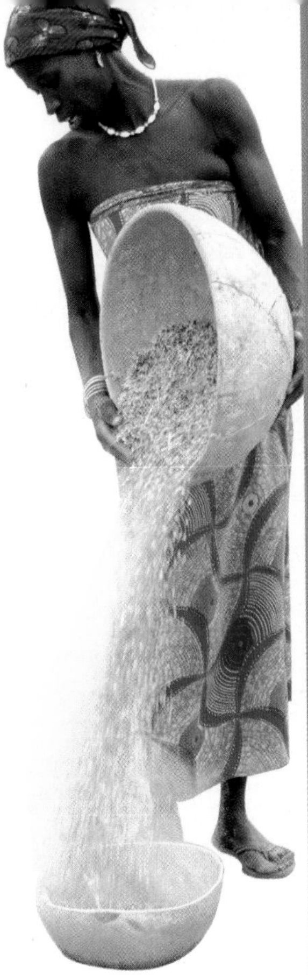

Vocabulary
dissent (di sent´) *n.* disagreement; refusal to accept a common opinion

Reading Check
Who are the people at Jonathan's door, and what do they want?

10 Reading Skill
Draw Conclusions

1. Have students read the bracketed text.
2. Then, **ask** them to discuss why the situation between the thieves and Jonathan is strange.
   Possible response: It is not normal for thieves to have so little apprehension about being caught that they would actually make fun of a threat to call the police. Students should understand that chaos and lawlessness often follow war. In a peaceful society, an active police force is a deterrent to crime.
3. **Ask:** Do Jonathan's experiences lead you to agree with the thief that "trouble done finish" in Nigeria? Explain.
   Possible response: Students may point out that a brazen robbery is proof that troubles are not over in Nigeria. Some may note, however, that the thief is being "civil" and moderate in his demands. He, too, knows how to survive.

11 Reading Check

Answer: They are robbers, and they want his money.

Concept Connector

Anticipation Guide
Have students return to their **Anticipation Guides** and respond to the statements again in the After Reading column. They may do this individually or in their original groups. Then, lead a class discussion, probing for what students have learned that confirms or invalidates each statement. Encourage students to cite specific details, quotations, or other evidence from the text to support their responses to each statement.

Writing About the Big Question
Have students compare their responses to the sentence starter they completed before reading the story with their ideas afterwards. Ask them to explain whether their thoughts have changed.

Reading Skill Graphic Organizer
Ask students to review the graphic organizer they completed with their conclusions. Show them the partially completed **Reading Skill Graphic Organizer A** (*Graphic Organizer Transparencies,* p. 57) as an example. Then, have students share the graphic organizers they did and the conclusions they drew.

ASSESS

Answers

Critical Thinking

1. **Possible response:** Some students may sympathize with Jonathan's difficulties. Others may find his dialogue with the thief to be almost comical.
2. (a) He is thankful that five of his family have survived the war. (b) **Possible response:** The war has made him realize that the safety of his family is the most important thing in his life.
3. (a) He is amazed that the house is still standing. (b) **Possible response:** Jonathan sensibly does not worry about material things.
4. He wants to avoid any further trouble, particularly any danger to his family.
5. (a) He is philosophical and treats it as just another incident. (b) His response is much like his reaction to finding his house still standing.

THE BIG ? Can progress be made without conflict?

Possible response: (a) Jonathan becomes a stronger, more resilient person as he faces the adversity of the postwar period. (b) He would not have been forced to develop many of the skills he needed to survive the war.

"I am coming," said Jonathan fumbling in the darkness with the key of the small wooden box he kept by his side on the mat.

Vocabulary
commiserate (kə miz´ ər āt´) *v.* sympathize with or show sorrow for

At the first sign of light as neighbors and others assembled to **commiserate** with him he was already strapping his five-gallon demijohn[8] to his bicycle carrier and his wife, sweating in the open fire, was turning over akara balls in a wide clay bowl of boiling oil. In the corner his eldest son was rinsing out dregs of yesterday's palm-wine from old beer bottles.

"I count it as nothing," he told his sympathizers, his eyes on the rope he was tying. "What is *egg-rasher*? Did I depend on it last week? Or is it greater than other things that went with the war? I say, let *egg-rasher* perish in the flames! Let it go where everything else has gone. Nothing puzzles God."

8. **demijohn** (dem´ i jän´) *n.* large glass or earthenware bottle with a wicker cover.

Critical Thinking

1. **Respond:** How did you react to the description of Jonathan's encounter with the thieves?
2. **(a)** What are the "five inestimable blessings" for which Jonathan is grateful? **(b) Infer:** In what sense has the war enhanced Jonathan's appreciation for his life?
3. **(a) Analyze:** Explain how Jonathan reacts to the damage to his house. **(b) Connect:** Considering the other damage the war has brought about, why might his reaction make sense?
4. **Infer:** By turning over the "egg-rasher" to the thieves, what does Jonathan hope to prevent from happening? Explain.
5. **(a) Infer:** What is Jonathan's reaction to the theft after it has occurred? Explain how you know. **(b) Connect:** In what way is Jonathan's response consistent with his other responses to loss?

THE BIG ? Can progress be made without conflict?
(a) How does Jonathan change as he experiences the conflicts in his life? **(b)** How might his life have changed without the conflict?

Assessment Resources

Unit 2 Resources

L1 L2 EL **Selection Test A,** pp. 160–162. Administer Test A to less advanced readers and English learners.

L3 L4 **Selection Test B,** pp. 163–165. Administer Test B to on-level and more advanced students.

L3 L4 **Open-Book Test,** pp. 157–159. As an alternative, give the Open-Book Test.

All **Customizable Test Bank**

All **Self-tests**
Students may prepare for the **Selection Test** by taking the **Self-test** online.

PHLit Online! All assessment resources are available at **www.PHLitOnline.com.**

After You Read | Civil Peace

Literary Analysis: Theme

1. **(a)** Using a chart like the one shown, analyze the episodes that spark a response in Jonathan. **(b)** How are these episodes related? Are they similar or different? Explain.

Episode	Character's Response	Reasons for the Response	Result: Peace of Mind/Problems

   (c) State the **theme** of the story, explaining how each event helps convey it.

2. Achebe makes the **philosophical assumption** that in order to survive, we must be able to let go of what we have lost. Explain what Jonathan might have done about the theft of the "egg-rasher" if he had refused to let go.

Reading Skill: Draw Conclusions

3. **(a) Draw a conclusion** about the thieves' response to the losses of war based on what they say and do. **(b)** Which details in Achebe's story contribute to its theme?

Vocabulary

Practice In vocabulary study, **antonyms** are words with opposite meanings. For each sentence, replace the word in italics with its antonym from the list on page 356. Explain which version makes more sense.

1. We should not give charity to the most *wealthy.*
2. People go to this bank because it is *respectable.*
3. In times of joy, people may get together to *celebrate.*
4. Ellen is *resistant* to trading bicycles with me because she likes hers.
5. His dog howled *audibly*, and the loud noise scared the cats away.
6. If there is *agreement* about going to the concert, I will buy a ticket.

Word Study Use the context of the sentences and what you know about the **Latin prefix *com-*** to explain your answer to each question.

1. What would happen to an egg under *compression?*
2. What effect would a *compromise* have on warring factions?

Word Study

The **Latin prefix *com-*** means "together" or "with."

Challenge Explain how the prefix *com-* contributes to the meanings of these words. Consult a dictionary if necessary.

compassion
compare
comfort

ASSESS/EXTEND

Answers

Literary Analysis

1. (a) Jonathan is very glad that his family and bicycle have made it through the war. When he discovers that his house still stands when others have been destroyed, he is amazed. At the end of the story, when he gives twenty pounds to thieves who threaten to kill him and his family, he refuses to get angry. (b) All of Jonathan's responses are related in that each time he shows his generous and forgiving nature. (c) In a postwar society, the best way to move on is not to dwell in the past, but to live with an appreciation of one's gifts and blessings.

   For other sample answers, see ***Graphic Organizer Transparencies*, Literary Analysis Graphic Organizer A**, p. 60, and the **Additional Answers** section.

2. **Possible response:** Jonathan might have acted vindictively and sought retribution.

Reading Skill

3. (a) **Possible response:** With the war over, the thieves still seek an outlet for violence. They would rather steal than work.
   (b) **Possible response:** Jonathan's willingness to resume a normal life and provide for his family demonstrates how one continues living after extreme loss and destruction. Instead of taking advantage of others, one should simply work hard and do one's duty.

Vocabulary

Practice

1. We should not give charity to the most *destitute.* The original sentence makes more sense because the wealthy don't need charity.
2. People go to this bank because it is *disreputable.* The original sentence makes more sense because people would not go to a bank with a bad reputation.
3. In times of joy, people may get together to *commiserate.* The original sentence makes more sense because people celebrate joyful occasions.
4. Ellen is *amenable* to trading bicycles with me because she likes hers. The original sentence makes more sense because someone who likes her bike will not likely trade it.

Answers continued

5. His dog howled *inaudibly*, and the loud noise scared the cats away. The original sentence makes more sense because the cats would be scared away by the dog's howling.
6. If there is *dissent* about going to the concert, I will buy a ticket. The original sentence makes more sense because when people agree about something, they act together.

Word Study

Sample answers:

1. The prefix *com-* means "with" and *compression* means "with pressure." The egg would break because it would be unable to withstand the pressure.
2. The prefix *com-* means "together" and *compromise* means "an agreement made together." If warring factions compromised, they would stop fighting with each other.

Word Study: Challenge

Sample answers: To show people *compassion* is to share feelings with them. To *compare* two items is to bring them together to see similarities between them. To *comfort* someone is to come together to show sympathy.

Answers

Grammar

1. Introduce the skill, using the instruction on the student page.
2. Discuss the definitions and examples on the page.

Think Aloud: Model the Skill

Model the skill of identifying action and linking verbs, using the following "think aloud." Say to students:

> Some verbs are always action verbs and some are always linking verbs. However, some verbs can be both, such as the verb *to taste*. Consider the sentences, "John *tastes* vanilla" and "The coffee *tastes* delicious." In the first, *taste* describes John's physical action and is an action verb. In the second, *taste* describes the coffee and is a linking verb.
>
> Linking verbs can be replaced with the verb *to be*. To make sure I have correctly identified the verb, I can replace it with *to be*. The second sentence, "The coffee *is* delicious," makes sense, so I can confirm that here *taste* is a linking verb.

WG Writing and Grammar, Grade 10

Students will find further instruction and practice with action and linking verbs in Chapter 16, Section 3.

Practice A

1. grows—action verb
2. is—linking verb
3. tastes—linking verb
4. grows—action verb

Challenge

Sample answer: Action verb: An elder sister *came* to visit her younger sister in the country. Linking verb: However, he now *felt* more certain than ever that Simon had done it, and he lodged a complaint.

Practice B

Sample answers:

1. The tomato looked green. He looked at the stars.
2. She grew silent. Al grows tomatoes.
3. The fish smelled awful. He smelled fish cooking.
4. John feels angry. John feels the basketball between his hands.

Challenge

Sample answer: Matthew learned that his aunt was a chef. Betsy discovered that her tooth was loose.

Integrated Language Skills

How Much Land Does a Man Need? • Civil Peace

Grammar: Action and Linking Verbs

An **action verb** is a verb that shows physical or mental action. A **linking verb** expresses state of being or tells what the subject is by linking it to one or more words in the predicate.

Examples:

Action Verb: Li *worries* about her grades. (shows mental action)

Linking Verb: She *is* a good student. (links *She* to *good student*)

The most common linking verb is *be* in one of its forms—*is, are, was, were,* and so on. Other linking verbs include *feel* when used in a sentence such as "I feel ill" and *grew* when used in a sentence such as "He grew tall." To tell whether a verb is functioning as a linking verb, replace it with the appropriate form of *be*. If the sentence still makes sense, then the verb is a linking verb.

Testing Verbs to See if They Are Linking Verbs:

Action Verb: I *smelled* a rose. (cannot replace with a form of *be*)

Linking Verb: The rose *smelled* fragrant. (can replace with *was*)

Practice A Identify the verb in each sentence, and tell whether it is an action verb or a linking verb.

1. Pahom grows wheat on his land.
2. The land on the steppe is rich and fertile.
3. Pahom's tea tastes delicious.
4. Each year Pahom's parcel of land grows larger.

Challenge In "How Much Land Does a Man Need?," find two sentences with action verbs and two sentences with linking verbs.

Practice B For each word, write a sentence using the word as a linking verb and another sentence using the verb as an action verb.

1. look
2. grow
3. smell
4. feel

Challenge Use this sentence as a model to write two sentences that contain both action and linking verbs: *Jonathan <u>realizes</u> that his family <u>is</u> more valuable than any possession.*

WG Writing and Grammar Connection: Chapter 16, Section 3

Extend the Lesson

Choose the sentence given from the selection students have read:

> An elder sister came to visit her younger sister in the country. ("How Much Land Does a Man Need?")
>
> This newest miracle was his little house in Ogui Overside. ("Civil Peace")

Ask students what they notice about the sentence. "How Much Land Does a Man Need?": Elicit from them that the verb is in the simple past tense. Ask what else they notice: the sentence is simple, but says a lot in a few words.

"Civil Peace": Elicit from students that "was" is a linking verb linking "miracle" to "house." Ask what else they notice: author's use of the word "newest" to modify "miracles" makes clear that there were other miracles; the use of the passive voice makes it uncertain as to who or what is responsible for the "newest miracle."

Have students imitate the sentence in a sentence on a topic of their own choosing, matching each grammatical and stylistic feature discussed. Collect the sentences and share them with the class.

Writing

The fate of the characters in these selections is determined in large part by their personalities. Write a brief **character analysis** of Pahom or Jonathan. In your analysis, identify the character's main character traits including strengths and weaknesses.

- Review the text to analyze the character. Using a two-column chart, list strengths and weaknesses.
- As you draft, introduce the ideas you will convey. Elaborate on these strengths and weaknesses by providing examples of incidents and descriptions in the story that show these traits.
- Use phrases such as *for example* to link supporting details to your main idea. Include transitional words such as *instead* to connect ideas.

Writing Workshop: *Work in Progress*

Prewriting for Problem and Solution Essay For an essay you may write, define a problem that you see in your school. Use this problem as the central circle of a web. Fill in spokes of the web with all the possible solutions. Put this Problem/Solution Web in your writing portfolio.

Use this prewriting activity to prepare for the **Writing Workshop** on page 420.

Listening and Speaking

In each of these stories, the author conveys a **theme,** or central idea about life. Hold a **group discussion** about the theme in Tolstoy's or Achebe's story. Begin by proposing and agreeing on a statement of the author's message. With your group, discuss ways in which the theme applies to your life or the lives of people today. Use persuasive techniques to support your ideas. To aid the discussion, follow these tips:

- Express your ideas in understandable and inoffensive ways.
- Add to others' ideas and **support your own viewpoints** by providing references to the text. Include quotations that help to prove your ideas.
- Allow your position to be challenged by the contributions of others.
- **Clarify, illustrate, or expand on a response** when asked to do so.
- Make sure all members of the group are given a chance to contribute to the discussion.
- As a group decide on a single idea to share with the class.

PHLit Online!
www.PHLitOnline.com
- Interactive graphic organizers
- Grammar tutorial
- Interactive journals

EXTEND/ASSESS

Writing

1. Review the assignment, using the instruction on the student page.
2. To give students guidance for writing a character analysis, give them the **Support for Writing,** p. 155 in ***Unit 2 Resources.***
3. To evaluate students' analyses, use the Problem-Solution Essay rubrics, pp. 244–245 in *Professional Development Guidebook.*

Six Traits Focus

✔	Ideas		Word Choice
✔	Organization	✔	Sentence Fluency
	Voice		Conventions

Writing and Grammar, Grade 10

Students will find additional instruction on character analysis writing in Chapter 5.

Writing Workshop
Work in Progress

Have students save their completed problem-and-solution notes in their portfolios. They will use them later as they continue this Work-in-Progress assignment (see p. 399). These assignments prepare them to complete the Writing Workshop assignment (see pp. 420–427).

Listening and Speaking

1. Review the assignment, using the instruction on the student page.
2. Have students complete the **Support for Extend Your Learning** page (***Unit 2 Resources,*** p. 156).

Teaching Resources

Unit 2 Resources

- L3 L4 **Integrated Language Skills: Grammar,** p. 154
- L3 L4 **Support for Writing,** p. 155
- L3 L4 **Support for Extend Your Learning,** p. 156
- L4 **Enrichment,** pp. 135, 153

Enriched Online Student Edition

Available under After You Read for this selection:

- All **Interactive Grammar Tutorial**
- L3 L4 **Internet Research Activity**

Professional Development Guidebook

Rubrics for Problem-Solution Essay, pp. 244–245

PHLit Online! All print and digital resources are available online at **www.PHLitOnline.com.** Online resources accessible by students are noted on the student page.

TIME AND RESOURCE MANAGER

The Masque of the Red Death • The Garden of Stubborn Cats

Lesson Pacing Guide

DAY 1 Preteach

- Administer the Reading and Vocabulary Warm-ups (*Unit 2 Resources*, pp. 166–169 or 184–189) as necessary.
- Introduce the Reading Skill: Draw Conclusions FT
- Introduce the Literary Analysis concept: Symbolism and Allegory FT
- Distribute copies of the appropriate graphic organizer for the Reading Skill (*Graphic Organizer Transparencies*, pp. 65–67). CRI
- Distribute copies of the appropriate graphic organizer for Literary Analysis (*Graphic Organizer Transparencies*, pp. 62–64). CRI
- Teach the selection vocabulary. FT CRI
- Introduce the Word Study skill.

DAYS 2–3 Preteach/Teach

- Build background with the Background feature. CRI
- Develop thematic vocabulary and thematic thinking with Writing About the Big Question.
- Prepare students to read with the Activating Prior Knowledge activities (TE). CRI
- Informally monitor comprehension while students read. FT
- Use the Reading Check questions to confirm comprehension.
- Develop students' ability to draw a conclusion using the Reading Skill questions. CRI
- Develop students' understanding of symbolism and allegory using the Literary Analysis questions. CRI
- Reinforce vocabulary with the Vocabulary notes. CRI

DAY 4 Assess

- Assess students' comprehension and mastery of the skills by having them answer the Critical Thinking, Reading Skill, and Literary Analysis questions. FT
- Have students complete the Vocabulary Practice activities. FT
- Have students complete the Word Study activities.

DAY 5 Extend/Assess

- Have students complete the Grammar lesson. CRI
- Have students complete the Writing activity and write a narrative. (You may assign as homework.) FT
- Extend learning by having students complete the Research and Technology activity, a research summary. (You may assign as homework.) As an alternative, assign them "Preparing for the Flu" or "The Development Debate" in *Reality Central*. CRI
- Administer Selection Test A or B (*Unit 2 Resources*, pp. 178–183 or 199–204). FT

"The Masque of the Red Death" is a short story presented unedited and in its entirety. "The Garden of Stubborn Cats" is an unedited episode from the novel *Marcovaldo, or the Seasons in the City*.

Meeting Your Standards

Students will

1. analyze and respond to literary elements.
   - Literary Analysis: Symbolism and Allegory
2. read, comprehend, and analyze short stories.
   - Reading Skill: Draw Conclusions
   - Reading Check questions
   - Apply the Skills questions
   - Assessment Practice
3. develop vocabulary.
   - Vocabulary
   - Word Study
4. apply grammar skills.
   - Active and Passive Voice
5. Develop writing proficiency.
   - Work in Progress: Problem-and-Solution Essay
   - narrative
6. strengthen research and technology skills.
   - research summary

CRI For a full explanation of Culturally Responsive Instruction opportunities in this lesson, see p. T86–T87.

FT For an accelerated lesson, use the Fast Track strategies and activities.

Managing Differentiated Instruction
This leveled selection pairing groups a more accessible with a more challenging selection. Choose either one to teach the lesson skills. For classroom management suggestions for using the pairing in a mixed-ability class, see pp. T68–T69.

Daily Block Scheduling
Each day in this Lesson Pacing Guide represents a 40–50 minute period. Teachers using block scheduling may combine days to revise pacing. In addition, teachers may differentiate and support core instruction by integrating components for extended and intensive support as students require. See the Guide to Selected Leveled Resources (facing page).

Guide to Selected Leveled Resources

EL English Learners

			The Masque of the Red Death	The Garden of Stubborn Cats
CORE COURSE	*Unit 2 Resources*	Selection Test A	pp. 178–180	pp. 199–201
	Graphic Organizer Transparencies	Reading Skill Graphic Organizer A	p. 65	p. 66
		Literary Analysis Graphic Organizer A	p. 62	p. 63
EXTENDED SUPPORT (Level 2)	*Unit 2 Resources*	Reading and Vocabulary Warm-ups A or B	pp. 166–169	pp. 184–187
	Reader's Notebook: English Learner's Version		adapted instruction and adapted selection	adapted instruction and summary
	Hear It! Audio CD		selection and summaries	selection and summaries
	Hear It! Audio CD (adapted text)		adapted selection and summaries	—
INTENSIVE SUPPORT (Level 1)	*Reality Central*		"Preparing for the Flu"	"The Development Debate"
	Real-World Writing Journal		Lesson 7, pp. 60–63	Lesson 8, pp. 64–67

L2 Below-Level Students

			The Masque of the Red Death	The Garden of Stubborn Cats
CORE COURSE	*Unit 2 Resources*	Selection Test A	pp. 178–180	pp. 199–201
	Graphic Organizer Transparencies	Reading Skill Graphic Organizer A	p. 65	p. 66
		Literary Analysis Graphic Organizer A	p. 62	p. 63
EXTENDED SUPPORT (Level 2)	*Unit 2 Resources*	Reading and Vocabulary Warm-ups A or B	pp. 166–169	pp. 184–187
	Reader's Notebook		adapted instruction and full selection	adapted instruction and summary
	Hear It! Audio CD		selection and summaries	selection and summaries
INTENSIVE SUPPORT (Level 1)	*Reality Central*		"Preparing for the Flu"	"The Development Debate"
	Real-World Writing Journal		Lesson 7, pp. 60–63	Lesson 8, pp. 64–67
	Reading Kit		Reteaching worksheets	Reteaching worksheets

L1 Special Needs Students

			The Masque of the Red Death	The Garden of Stubborn Cats
CORE COURSE	*Unit 2 Resources*	Selection Test A	pp. 178–180	pp. 199–201
	Graphic Organizer Transparencies	Reading Skill Graphic Organizer A	p. 65	p. 66
		Literary Analysis Graphic Organizer A	p. 62	p. 63
EXTENDED SUPPORT (Level 2)	*Unit 2 Resources*	Reading and Vocabulary Warm-ups A or B	pp. 166–169	pp. 184–187
	Reader's Notebook: Adapted Version		adapted instruction and adapted selection	adapted instruction and summary
	Hear It! Audio CD (adapted text)		adapted selection and summaries	—
INTENSIVE SUPPORT (Level 1)	*Reality Central*		"Preparing for the Flu"	"The Development Debate"
	Real-World Writing Journal		Lesson 7, pp. 60–63	Lesson 8, pp. 64–67
	Reading Kit		Reteaching worksheets	Reteaching worksheets

The program includes resources for these students: L3 On-Level L4 Advanced All All
For a complete guide to selection support, see pp. T106–T108.

NOTE: All print materials are also available online at *www.PHLitOnline.com.*

VISUAL GUIDE to Featured Selection Resources

• The Masque of the Red Death
• The Garden of Stubborn Cats

THE MASQUE of the RED DEATH
Edgar Allan Poe
372 Short Stories
THE GARDEN of STUBBORN CATS
Italo Calvino
Translated by William Weaver
384 Short Stories

RESOURCES FOR:

- EL English Learners
- L1 Special Needs Students
- L2 Below-Level Students
- L3 On-Level Students
- L4 Advanced Students
- All All Students

Vocabulary/Fluency/Prior Knowledge

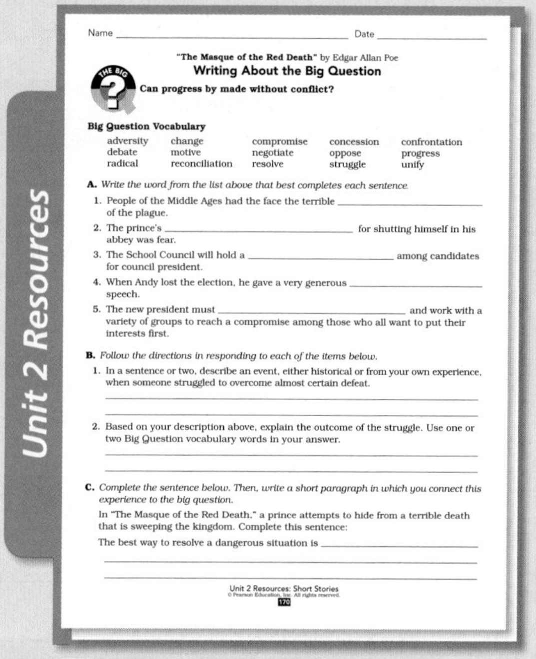

Name ______________ Date ______________

"The Masque of the Red Death" by Edgar Allan Poe

Writing About the Big Question

THE BIG ? **Can progress by made without conflict?**

Big Question Vocabulary

adversity	change	compromise	concession	confrontation
debate	motive	negotiate	oppose	progress
radical	reconciliation	resolve	struggle	unify

A. *Write the word from the list above that best completes each sentence.*

1. People of the Middle Ages had the face the terrible ______________ of the plague.
2. The prince's ______________ for shutting himself in his abbey was fear.
3. The School Council will hold a ______________ among candidates for council president.
4. When Andy lost the election, he gave a very generous ______________ speech.
5. The new president must ______________ and work with a variety of groups to reach a compromise among those who all want to put their interests first.

B. *Follow the directions in responding to each of the items below.*

1. In a sentence or two, describe an event, either historical or from your own experience, when someone struggled to overcome almost certain defeat.
2. Based on your description above, explain the outcome of the struggle. Use one or two Big Question vocabulary words in your answer.

C. *Complete the sentence below. Then, write a short paragraph in which you connect this experience to the big question.*

In "The Masque of the Red Death," a prince attempts to hide from a terrible death that is sweeping the kingdom. Complete this sentence:

The best way to resolve a dangerous situation is ______________

Unit 2 Resources: Short Stories

170

All **Writing About the Big Question, pp. 170, 188**

Also available for these selections:

EL L1 L2 **Reading Warm-ups A and B, pp. 168–169, 186–187**

All **Vocabulary Builder, pp. 173, 191**

EL L1 L2 **Vocabulary Warm-ups A and B, pp. 166–167, 184–185**

L2 L3 ***Reader's Notebook***

L1 ***Reader's Notebook: Adapted Version***

EL ***Reader's Notebook: English Learner's Version***

Reader's Notebooks

Pre- and postreading pages for both selections, as well as "The Masque of the Red Death" appear in an interactive format in the *Reader's Notebooks.* Each *Notebook* is differentiated for a different group of learners.

The selections in the Adapted and English Learner's versions are abridged.

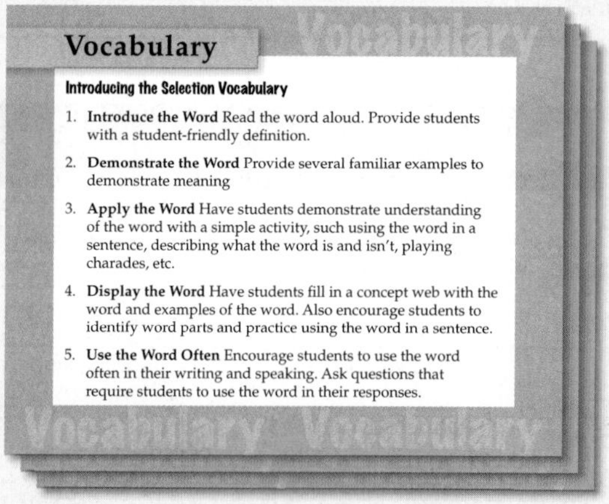

Vocabulary

Introducing the Selection Vocabulary

1. **Introduce the Word** Read the word aloud. Provide students with a student-friendly definition.
2. **Demonstrate the Word** Provide several familiar examples to demonstrate meaning
3. **Apply the Word** Have students demonstrate understanding of the word with a simple activity, such using the word in a sentence, describing what the word is and isn't, playing charades, etc.
4. **Display the Word** Have students fill in a concept web with the word and examples of the word. Also encourage students to identify word parts and practice using the word in a sentence.
5. **Use the Word Often** Encourage students to use the word often in their writing and speaking. Ask questions that require students to use the word in their responses.

Classroom Strategies and Teaching Routines

- core classroom routines outlined step-by-step
- convenient format for easy reference while teaching

Selection Support

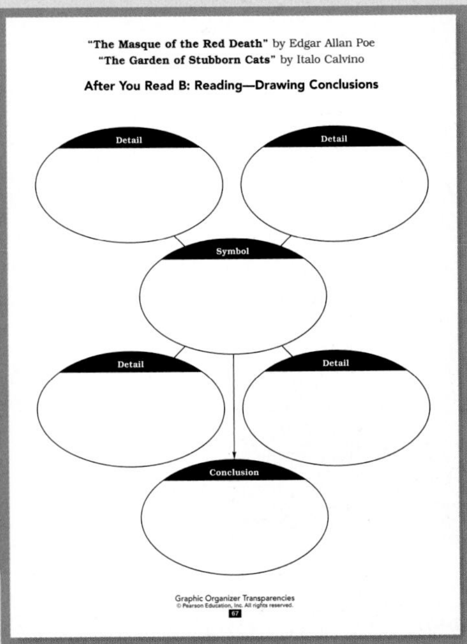

Graphic Organizer Transparencies

L3 **Reading: Graphic Organizer B, p. 67**

Also available for these selections:

- EL L1 L2 Reading: Graphic Organizer A, pp. 65, 66 (partially filled in)
- EL L1 L2 Literary Analysis: Graphic Organizer A, pp. 62, 63 (partially filled in)
- L3 Literary Analysis: Graphic Organizer B, p. 64

Skills Development/Extension

Unit 2 Resources

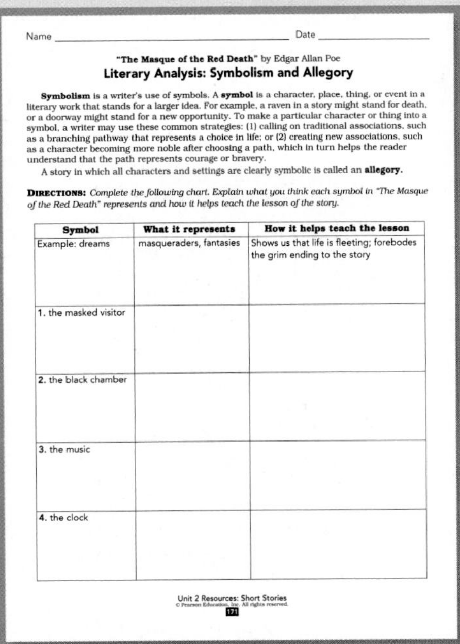

Name ____________________ Date ____________

"The Masque of the Red Death" by Edgar Allan Poe

Literary Analysis: Symbolism and Allegory

Symbolism is a writer's use of symbols. A **symbol** is a character, place, thing, or event in a literary work that stands for a larger idea. For example, a raven in a story might stand for death, or a doorway might stand for a new opportunity. To make a particular character or thing into a symbol, a writer may use these common strategies: (1) calling on traditional associations, such as a branching pathway that represents a choice in life; or (2) creating new associations, such as a character becoming more noble after choosing a path, which in turn helps the reader understand that the path represents courage or bravery.

A story in which all characters and settings are clearly symbolic is called an **allegory.**

Directions: *Complete the following chart. Explain what you think each symbol in "The Masque of the Red Death" represents and how it helps teach the lesson of the story.*

Symbol	What it represents	How it helps teach the lesson
Example: dreams	masqueraders, fantasies	Shows us that life is fleeting; forebodes the grim ending to the story
1. the masked visitor		
2. the black chamber		
3. the music		
4. the clock		

Unit 2 Resources: Short Stories
© Pearson Education, Inc. All rights reserved.
171

All **Literary Analysis: Symbolism and Allegory, pp. 171, 189**

Also available for these selections:

- All Reading: Draw Conclusions, pp. 172, 190
- L4 Enrichment, pp. 174, 192
- L3 L4 Grammar, p. 193
- L3 L4 Support for Writing, p. 194
- L3 L4 Support for Extend Your Learning, p. 195

Assessment

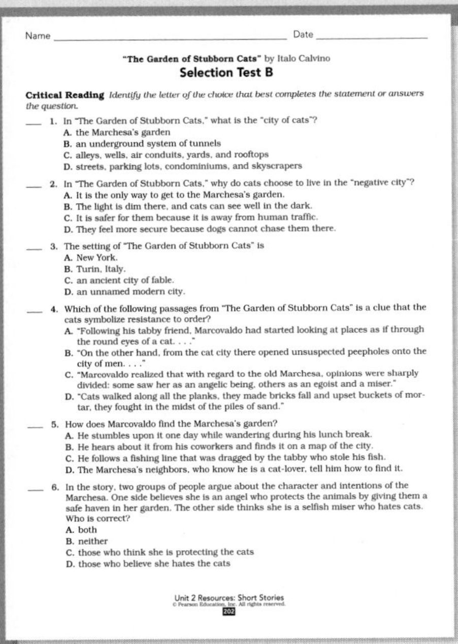

Name ____________________ Date ____________

"The Garden of Stubborn Cats" by Italo Calvino

Selection Test B

Critical Reading *Identify the letter of the choice that best completes the statement or answers the question.*

___ 1. In "The Garden of Stubborn Cats," what is the "city of cats"?
A. the Marchesa's garden
B. an underground system of tunnels
C. alleys, wells, air conduits, yards, and rooftops
D. streets, parking lots, condominiums, and skyscrapers

___ 2. In "The Garden of Stubborn Cats," why do cats choose to live in the "negative city"?
A. It is the only way to get to the Marchesa's garden.
B. The light is dim there, and cats can see well in the dark.
C. It is safer for them because it is away from human traffic.
D. They feel more secure because dogs cannot chase them there.

___ 3. The setting of "The Garden of Stubborn Cats" is
A. New York.
B. Turin, Italy.
C. an ancient city of fable.
D. an unnamed modern city.

___ 4. Which of the following passages from "The Garden of Stubborn Cats" is a clue that the cats symbolize resistance to order?
A. "Following his tabby friend, Marcovaldo had started looking at places as if through the round eyes of a cat. . . ."
B. "On the other hand, from the cat city there opened unsuspected peepholes onto the city of men. . . ."
C. "Marcovaldo realized that with regard to the old Marchesa, opinions were sharply divided: some saw her as an angelic being, others as an egoist and a miser."
D. "Cats walked along all the planks, they made bricks fall and upset buckets of mortar, they fought in the midst of the piles of sand."

___ 5. How does Marcovaldo find the Marchesa's garden?
A. He stumbles upon it one day while wandering during his lunch break.
B. He hears about it from his coworkers and finds it on a map of the city.
C. He follows a fishing line that was dragged by the tabby who stole his fish.
D. The Marchesa's neighbors, who know he is a cat-lover, tell him how to find it.

___ 6. In the story, two groups of people argue about the character and intentions of the Marchesa. One side believes she is an angel who protects the animals by giving them a safe haven in her garden. The other side thinks she is a selfish miser who hates cats. Who is correct?
A. both
B. neither
C. those who think she is protecting the cats
D. those who believe she hates the cats

Unit 2 Resources: Short Stories
© Pearson Education, Inc. All rights reserved.
202

L3 L4 **Selection Test B, pp. 181–183, 202–204**

Also available for these selections:

- EL L1 L2 Selection Test A, pp. 178–180, 199–201
- L3 L4 Open-Book Test, pp. 175–177, 196–198

PHLit Online!

www.PHLitOnline.com

- complete narrated selection text
- a thematically related video with writing prompt
- an interactive graphic organizer
- highlighting feature
- access to all student print resources, adapted to individual student needs
- Spanish and English summaries

Get Connected! (thematic video with writing prompt)

Also available:

Background video

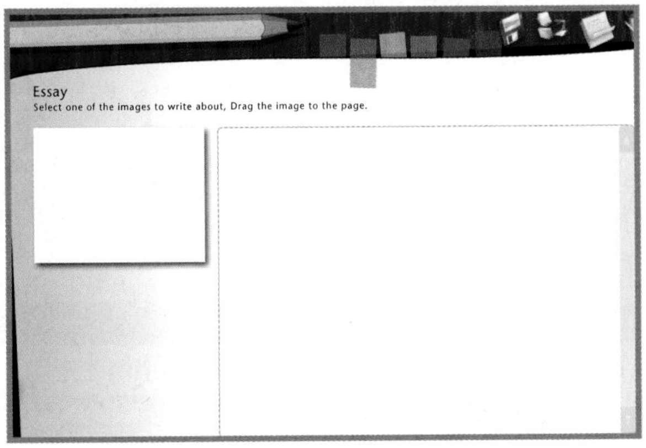

Writer's Journal (with graphics feature)

Also available:

Vocabulary Central (tools, activities, and songs for studying vocabulary)

DIFFERENTIATE/PRETEACH

❶ Selection Choices

You may use either "The Masque of the Red Death" or "The Garden of Stubborn Cats" to meet the lesson standards. Skills instruction for both selections appears on p. 369. Choose one selection to teach (or choose to teach both). The Accessibility at a Glance chart at the bottom of this page will help you determine which of the two selections is more appropriate for your students.

❷ Selection Skills

1. With the class, preview the selection skills. (The lesson meets the lesson objectives given on p. 368a.)
2. Explain that students will develop the skill of drawing conclusions (introduced on p. 335) as they read to better understand and enjoy the selection you choose. By examining symbolism as they read, they will gain deeper insight into short stories.
3. To introduce the Writing and Research and Technology activities (p. 399), tell students that when they have finished reading the selection, they will write a narrative and a research summary related to the selection.
4. Tell students that they will also study a grammar concept: active and passive voice. By mastering this concept, they will improve their reading fluency and the quality of their own writing.

Before You Read

The Masque of the Red Death • The Garden of Stubborn Cats

❶ Selection Choices

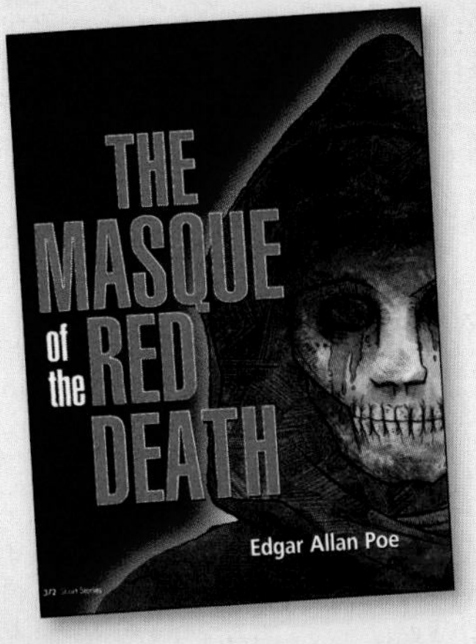

▲ Read **"The Masque of the Red Death"** to see how a prince tries to use his power to evade death.

▲ Read **"The Garden of Stubborn Cats"** to discover how the unexpected can spring up in the most ordinary places.

❷ Selection Skills Guide

Practice these skills with either **"The Masque of the Red Death"** (p. 372) or **"The Garden of Stubborn Cats"** (p. 384).

- Understand symbolism
- Understand allegory
- Draw conclusions
- Identify patterns
- Identify active and passive voice
- Write a narrative
- Present a research summary

Differentiated Instruction for Universal Access

Accessibility at a Glance: Selection Choices

	The Masque of the Red Death	The Garden of Stubborn Cats
Context	Medieval Europe; 1300s; Black Death	Nature versus development; set in Italy
Language/ Vocabulary	• Difficult vocabulary • Complicated sentence structure	• Difficult vocabulary • Complicated sentence structure
Concept Level	Accessible (mortality and trying to escape fate)	Challenging (progress and development versus nature)
Literary Merit	Noted author	Contemporary Theme
Lexile/Length	Lexile: 1140L Word Count: 2,395	Lexile: 930L Word Count: 3,688
Other	Allegory	
Overall Rating	**More accessible**	**More challenging**

Because a number of factors determine the relative accessibility of paired selections, in some cases the Lexile rating of the more challenging selection will be lower than that of the more accessible selection.

❸ Literary Analysis: Symbolism and Allegory

Symbolism is a writer's use of symbols. A **symbol** is a character, a place, a thing, or an event in a literary work that stands for a larger idea. For example, a dog in a story may stand for loyalty. To create symbols, a writer may use these strategies:

- Call on traditional associations—a dog is a symbol of loyalty because dogs are often praised for that virtue.
- Create new associations—if a story character cherishes an object because it had been his grandfather's, the object may come to symbolize family ties.

In most stories, the use of symbolism is subtle and open to interpretation. A story in which all characters, settings, events and actions are clearly symbolic is called an **allegory.**

PHLit Online!
www.PHLitOnline.com

Hear It!
- Selection summary audio
- Selection audio

See It!
- Get Connected video
- Background video
- More about the author
- Vocabulary flashcards

Do It!
- Interactive journals
- Interactive graphic organizers
- Self-test
- Internet activity
- Grammar tutorial
- Interactive vocabulary games

❹ Using the Strategy: Symbol Diagram

Use a **symbol diagram** like this one to identify details that show that an object or a character symbolizes a larger meaning.

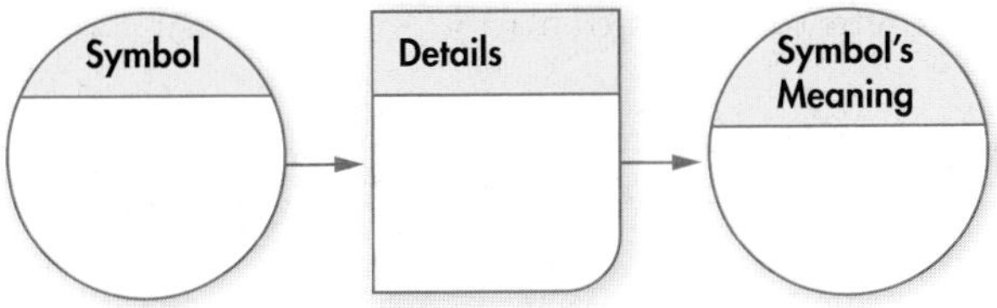

❺ Reading Skill: Draw Conclusions

When you **draw a conclusion,** you make a decision or develop an opinion based on facts and details in a text. To draw a conclusion about the meaning of a symbol, **identify patterns** that suggest its larger meaning.

- Consider the repeated actions, qualities, and other details that the work associates with the symbol.
- Use any background knowledge you have to help you identify symbols.
- Develop an idea about the meaning of the symbol—the meaning that best explains its role in the work.

Differentiated Instruction for Universal Access

Preparing Students for the More Challenging Selection

If you wish to prepare lower-level readers to read "The Garden of Stubborn Cats," the more challenging selection, follow these steps:

- Have students describe the characteristics of developed land and the natural environment. Then, in a two-column chart, discuss the advantages and disadvantages of living in each type of environment. Elicit from students the type of environment they would prefer to live in and why.
- Calvino describes the city in two ways on p. 385: as filled and as empty. To help students understand the setting as Calvino describes it, explain that filled space is *positive* space; empty space is *negative* space. Illustrate this concept by drawing colored buildings on a sheet of paper. Emphasize to students that the buildings take up positive space, whereas the unused space around it is negative space.
- Practice strategies for reading long sentences. Select several sentences to use as examples. Have students identify the main action(s), then break down the smaller parts for interpretation.

PRETEACH

❸ Literary Analysis

1. Introduce the skill, using the instruction on the student page.
2. Tell students that they will examine symbolism as they read.

Think Aloud: Model the Skill

Model the skill of identifying symbolism. Say to students:

> When I read a story, I know that a place, object, or event could be a symbol. To know for sure, I ask myself questions: *Is the detail a traditional symbol?* For example, doves are a common symbol for peace. *Does the detail have special associations in the story?* For example, a character that loses her mother is left only with her mother's ring. This particular ring, then, comes to symbolize the mother. My prior knowledge and the story's context can help me answer these questions.

❹ Using the Strategy

Give students a copy of **Literary Analysis Graphic Organizer A** or **B** (*Graphic Organizer Transparencies*, pp. 62 and 64) to record symbolism as they read. Use the examples in **Literary Analysis Graphic Organizer A**, which is partially filled in, to model the process of completing the organizer.

❺ Reading Skill

1. Introduce the skill, using the instruction on the student page.
2. Tell students that they will practice drawing conclusions as they read.

Think Aloud: Model the Skill

Model the skill of drawing conclusions. Say to students:

> To draw conclusions about the meaning of a symbol in a story, I look at the details and patterns in the text. For example, imagine I'm reading a story about a man who has beautiful tree in his yard. When the man gets sick, the tree begins to wilt. At the end of the story, the man dies and the tree withers completely. From this information, I can conclude that the tree symbolizes the man's life.

PRETEACH

❶ Writing About the Big Question

1. Review the assignment with the class.
2. Elicit from students the definition of *inevitable*, "unavoidable." Ask students what in life is unavoidable.
3. Have students complete the sentence starters. Review responses as a class. (**Possible responses:** People may struggle against the inevitable when they fear getting hurt. Sometimes a confrontation is necessary in order to resolve a conflict because the two sides won't agree on anything.
4. Remind students that their answers will help them think about the Big Question, "Can progress be made without conflict?"

While You Read

Tell students to look for descriptions as they read of how the partygoers behave.

❷ Vocabulary

1. Have students preview the selection vocabulary.
2. For each word, have students say the word aloud.
3. Then, use the word in a sentence that defines the word.
4. Finally, repeat your definitional sentence or a similar sentence with the word missing and have the class "fill in the blank" chorally. Here are some examples:

   If something is profuse, it comes forth freely. When John showed his parents the five As on his report card, their praise was [students say "profuse"].

   Decorum is behavior that is appropriate for an occasion. When Tom arrived for the interview in jeans and a tee shirt, it was clear that he lacked [students say "decorum"].

❸ Word Study

1. Introduce the skill, using the instruction in the box.
2. Given that *-tion* means "the act or quality of," have them define *exaltation*. (**Answer:** "the act of exalting")

Making Connections

The Masque of the Red Death

Can progress be made without *conflict?*

❶ Writing About the Big Question

In "The Masque of the Red Death," a prince attempts to hide from a terrible death that is sweeping the kingdom. Use these sentence starters to develop your ideas about the Big Question.

People may **struggle** against the inevitable when ________________.
Sometimes a **confrontation** is necessary in order to **resolve** a conflict because ________________.

While You Read Look for descriptions of how the people behave at the masque, the grand ball that the prince hosts. Then, decide whether you think the writer believes people can avoid conflict.

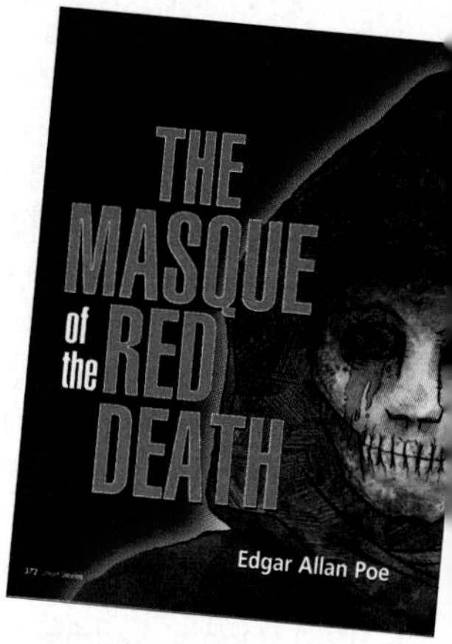

❷ Vocabulary

Read each word and its definition. Decide whether you know the word well, know it a little bit, or do not know it at all. After you read, see how your knowledge of each word has increased.

- **profuse** (prō fyo͞os´) *adj.* giving or pouring forth freely, often to excess (p. 373) ***Sheri offered her mother profuse apologies for forgetting her birthday.*** *profusely adv. profusion n.*
- **august** (ô gust´) *adj.* impressive; majestic (p. 373) ***The king was an august figure when he sat on his throne.*** *augustly adv. augustness n.*
- **impeded** (im pēd´ əd) *v.* blocked; obstructed (p. 373) ***The pillar I sat behind impeded my ability to see the stage.*** *impediment n.*
- **cessation** (se sā´ shən) *n.* halt; stopping (p. 377) ***After the sudden cessation of the car alarm, the silence seemed deep.*** *cease v.*
- **decorum** (di kôr´ əm) *n.* behavior that is polite and correct for an occasion (p. 378) ***The best man, lacking any decorum, showed up an hour late to the wedding.***
- **tangible** (tan´ jə bəl) *adj.* real and able to be touched (p. 380) ***The dream was so vivid, that it almost seemed tangible.*** *tangibly adv. tangibility n.*

❸ Word Study

The **Latin suffix *-tion*** means "the act or quality of."

In this selection, there is a **cessation** of activity when the clock chimes the hour of midnight. All activity stops.

Vocabulary Development

Vocabulary Knowledge Rating Chart

Create a **Vocabulary Knowledge Rating Chart** (***Professional Development Guidebook***, p. 33) for this selection. Include the selection vocabulary and the Big Question words that appear in the Writing About the Big Question sentence starters on this page. (The Big Question vocabulary is introduced on pp. 222–223.)

Give students a copy of the chart. Read the words aloud, and have students mark their rating in the Before Reading column. Urge them to be alert to these words as they read and discuss the selection.

Tally how many students think they know a word to gauge how much instruction to provide. As students read and discuss the selection, point out the words and their context.

PHLit Online! **Vocabulary Central**, featuring tools, activities, and songs for studying vocabulary, is available at **www.PHLitOnline.com**.

Meet
Edgar Allan Poe
(1809–1849)

Author of
The Masque of the Red Death

The son of traveling actors, Edgar Poe lost his mother at an early age. He was then raised by a wealthy Virginia family named Allan, from whom he took his middle name. After winning a writing contest with his story "MS. in a Bottle," Poe became a literary success, winning fame but not fortune. He died in poverty at the age of forty. Today, Poe is recognized as a master of the short story.

A Single Effect Poe believed that a work of fiction has the most impact if it can be read in one sitting and if all the elements work together to create a "single effect." He is best known for tales in which the single effect is horror. Poe also pioneered detective stories and science fiction.

DID YOU KNOW?

The Mystery Writers of America call their annual awards "Edgars" in Poe's honor.

4 **BACKGROUND FOR THE STORY**

The Black Death

In the 1300s, a plague called the Black Death swept across Europe, killing as many as 25 million people. Most of those who caught the disease died within three to five days after their symptoms appeared. Subsequent oubreaks of plague continued in Europe until recent times. Poe invented the "Red Death" for this story, but his tale plays on an age-old fear.

Daily Bellringer

For each class during which you will teach this selection, have students complete one of the five Research activities for Week 11 in the ***Daily Bellringer Activities*** booklet.

4 Background

The Black Death

The Black Death is another name for the bubonic plague, an epidemic disease that infects rats and other rodents and is transmitted to humans by flea bites. An attack of plague is characterized by sudden onset. The patient may seem well one moment and seriously ill the next. Symptoms are fever and body pains, followed by swelling of the lymph glands. These swellings, called buboes, give the disease its name.

Multidraft Reading

This icon ● marks natural pauses in the selection. To assist struggling readers and to deepen reading for all, assign the text in "chunks," following the icons, and apply multidraft reading protocols. For each reading, have students set the purpose indicated:

- **First reading**—literal comprehension: answering the Reading Check questions.
- **Second reading**—application of skills: answering the Draw Conclusions and Symbolism prompts.
- **Third reading**—interpretation: answering the end-of-selection questions.

For more guidance, refer to the ***Classroom Strategies and Teaching Routines*** card on multidraft reading.

Differentiated Instruction — Additional Instruction

EL Extended Support—English Learners

Have students complete the **Reading and Vocabulary Warm-ups, *Unit 2 Resources*,** pp. 166–169, before they read. Assign the prereading pages for the selection in the ***Reader's Notebook: English Learner's Version.*** Then, have students listen to portions of the selection on the ***Hear It!* Audio CD.**

L1 L2 Extended Support—Struggling Readers

Have students complete the **Reading and Vocabulary Warm-ups, *Unit 2 Resources*,** pp. 166–169, before they read. Assign the prereading pages for the selection in the ***Reader's Notebook: Adapted Version.*** Then, have students listen to portions of the selection on the ***Hear It!* Audio CD** (adapted text).

Extended Support—Reluctant Readers

To build motivation and engagement before assigning the selection, have students read "Preparing for the Flu," a thematically related selection in ***Reality Central.*** Then, use the questions at the conclusion of the related selection to guide discussion.

PHLit Online!

For more about the author, practice with the selection vocabulary, and more background, go online at **www.PHLitOnline.com.**

❶ Activating Prior Knowledge

Ask students to discuss ways that people today protect themselves from diseases. They might mention inoculations, good hygiene, nutrition, exercise, and donations to medical research. Others strategies might include holistic methods and home remedies. Ask students whether they believe that it is possible to avoid sickness entirely. Then, explain that the main character in "The Masque of the Red Death" uses extreme measures to try to protect himself from a fatal disease.

Concept Connector →

Students will return to these points of discussion after reading "The Masque of the Red Death."

Individual Activity

To help students understand the setting of the story, encourage them to draw a blueprint or floor plan of the rooms in which Prince Prospero receives his guests. Have students label each room with its predominant color, as described in the text, and the manner in which no room is visible to the next. Have students share their drawings with the class and discuss the effect these rooms might have on the people in them.

❷ About the Selection

In addition to being a chilling horror story, "The Masque of the Red Death" is a brilliant portrayal of the vanity of the rich and powerful and their illusions of invulnerability. Prince Prospero, the main character, believes he can save himself and a select few from the plague that menaces the country. In the story's climax, Prospero learns that wealth and privilege will not shield him from death.

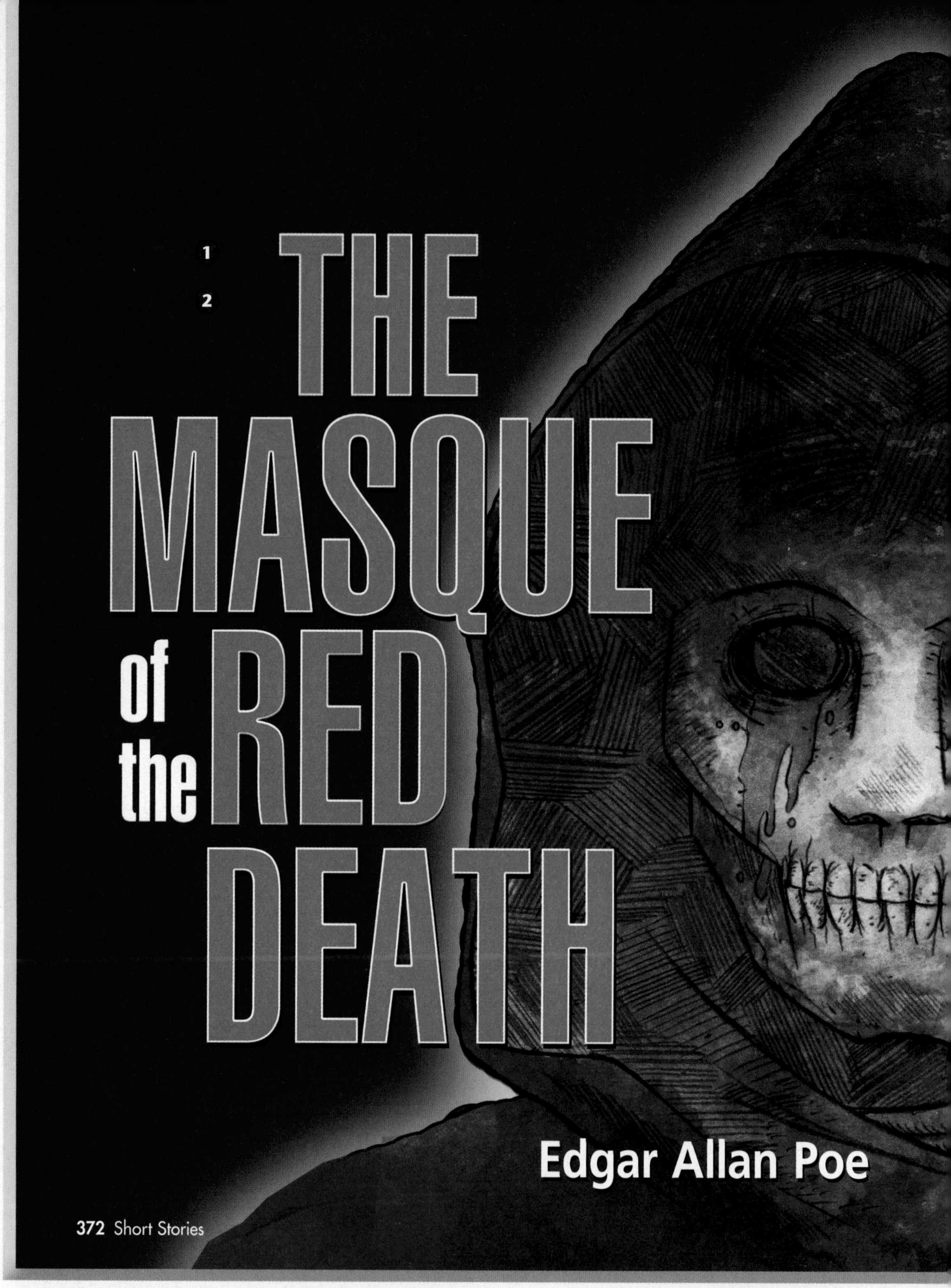

1
2
THE MASQUE of the RED DEATH
Edgar Allan Poe
372 Short Stories

The "Red Death" had long devastated the country. No pestilence had ever been so fatal, or so hideous. Blood was its Avatar[1] and its seal—the redness and the horror of blood. There were sharp pains, and sudden dizziness, and then **profuse** bleeding at the pores, with dissolution. The scarlet stains upon the body and especially upon the face of the victim, were the pest ban which shut him out from the aid and from the sympathy of his fellow men. And the whole seizure, progress and termination of the disease, were the incidents of half an hour.

But the Prince Prospero was happy and dauntless and sagacious. When his dominions were half depopulated, he summoned to his presence a thousand hale and lighthearted friends from among the knights and dames of his court, and with these retired to the deep seclusion of one of his castellated abbeys.[2] This was an extensive and magnificent structure, the creation of the prince's own eccentric
3 yet **august** taste. A strong and lofty wall girdled it in. This wall had gates of iron. The courtiers, having entered, brought furnaces and massy hammers and welded the bolts. They resolved to leave means neither of ingress or egress[3] to the sudden impulses of despair or frenzy from within. The abbey was amply provisioned. With such precautions the courtiers might bid defiance to contagion. The external world could take care of itself. In the meantime it was folly to grieve, or to think. The prince had provided all the appliances
4 of pleasure. There were buffoons, there were improvisatori, there were ballet dancers, there were musicians, there was Beauty, there was wine. All these and security were within. Without was the "Red Death."

It was toward the close of the fifth or sixth month of his seclusion, and while the pestilence raged most furiously abroad, that the Prince Prospero entertained his thousand friends at a masked ball of the most unusual magnificence.

It was a voluptuous scene, that masquerade. But first let me tell of the rooms in which it was held. There were seven—an imperial suite. In many palaces, however, such suites form a long and straight vista, while the folding doors slide back nearly to the walls on either hand, so that the view of the whole extent is scarcely **impeded**. Here the case was very different; as might have been expected from the duke's love of the bizarre. The apartments were so irregularly disposed that the vision embraced but little more than one at a time. There was a sharp turn at every twenty or thirty yards, and at each turn a novel effect. To the right and left, in the middle of each wall,

Vocabulary
profuse (prō fyo͞os´) *adj.* giving or pouring forth freely, often to excess

august (ô gust´) *adj.* impressive; majestic

Reading Skill
Draw Conclusions
What details here support the conclusion that the prince thinks he can escape the plague?

Vocabulary
impeded (im pēd´ əd) *v.* blocked; obstructed

Reading Check 5
Why has Prince Prospero locked himself and his guests in his castle?

1. **Avatar** (av´ ə tär´) *n.* sign; outward manifestation of an unseen force.
2. **castellated abbeys** (kas´ tə lāt´ əd ab´ ēz) monasteries or convents (religious retreats) with towers like those of a castle.
3. **ingress** (in´ gres´) or egress (è» gres«) entry or exit.

3 Reading Skill
Draw Conclusions

1. **Ask** students to comment on the significance of Prince Prospero's name.
   Possible response: The prince's name may come from *prosperous*, meaning "successful or thriving," or from *prospect*, meaning "something foreseen."
2. Have a volunteer read the bracketed passage.
3. Then, **ask** students the Reading Skill question: What details here support the conclusion that the prince thinks he can escape the plague?
   Answer: His abbey was surrounded by a strong wall, and everyone was sealed inside with plenty of provisions and entertainment. No one could come in or go out.

4 Connecting to the Big Question

1. Ask students what conflict the country in the story is facing.
   Possible response: The "Red Death" is devastating the country.
2. Have students read the bracketed text. **Ask:** How are Prince Prospero and the courtiers dealing with this conflict?
   Possible response: They are taking precautions by locking themselves away and letting the external world "take care of itself."
3. Invite students to discuss what drawbacks there might be to attempting to hide from a conflict rather than facing it directly. Guide students to think of this strategy in light of the Big Question, "Can progress be made without conflict?" as they read the story.

5 Reading Check

Answer: The prince wants to escape the "Red Death."

Differentiated Instruction for Universal Access

Enrichment for Gifted/Talented Students
Students may wish to write short radio scripts for this story. Remind them that listeners can only hear the action, not see it, so along with dialogue, sound effects must be inserted into the scripts. Ask students the following questions to help them plan their scripts: Where will you insert sound effects? How might you create the sound effects? Suggest that students tape record their radio scripts and play them for the class.

Enrichment for Advanced Readers
In an allegorical story, the characters, setting, and events are intended to have a meaning independent of the surface story and may be understood symbolically as well as literally. Challenge students as they read to determine the symbolic lessons about life being taught in this tale. Suggest that they depict these lessons in writing—poetry, fiction, or essay.

PHLit Online!
This selection is available in interactive format in the **Enriched Online Student Edition, www.PHLitOnline.com**, which includes a thematically related video and writing prompt and an interactive graphic organizer.

6 Literary Analysis
Symbolism

1. Have a volunteer read the bracketed text aloud.
2. Then, have students discuss their understanding of the symbolism of the colors red, blue, green, purple, orange, violet, and black. In their discussion, students can include everything from their personal associations with the colors to their understanding of different cultural interpretations of colors.
   Possible responses: purple: royalty and spirituality; **orange:** energy, warmth, autumn, good health; **green:** life, growth, renewal, balance, harmony, stability, health, jealousy, inexperience; **white:** purity, cleanliness, innocence; **violet:** grace, elegance, delicacy, femininity; **blue:** peace, intelligence, stability, unity, conservatism, depression; **black:** mourning, mystery, rebellion, evil; **red:** anger, blood, heat, love, power, danger, emergency
3. Then, **ask** students why Prince Prospero might have chosen the colors of purple, orange, green, white, violet, and blue for the apartments.
   Possible response: All of these colors have something positive about them. Perhaps he is trying to fight death with the energy of different environments, believing that sickness might not intrude on purity, peace, life, or energy.

7 Reading Skill
Draw Conclusions

1. Read the passage aloud to students.
2. Then, **ask** students to consider the previous discussion on the symbolism of color: Why do you think Prospero confined black and red to the one room?
   Possible response: Perhaps Prospero realizes that he cannot eliminate death, but he tries to isolate it.
3. Then, **ask** students the Reading Skill question: Judging from the title of the story and the colors of the seventh room, what might the room represent?
   Answer: The room probably represents death, illness, blood, danger, and evil.

Reading Skill
Draw Conclusions
Judging from the title of the story and the colors of the seventh room, what might the room represent?

a tall and narrow Gothic window looked out upon a closed corridor which pursued the windings of the suite. These windows were of stained glass whose color varied in accordance with the prevailing hue of the decorations of the chamber into which it opened. That at the eastern extremity was hung, for example, in blue—and 6 vividly blue were its windows. The second chamber was purple in its ornaments and tapestries, and here the panes were purple. The third was green throughout, and so were the casements. The fourth was furnished and lighted with orange—the fifth with white—the sixth with violet. The seventh apartment was closely shrouded in black velvet tapestries that hung all over the ceiling and down the walls, falling in heavy folds upon a carpet of the same material and hue. But in this chamber only, the color of the windows failed to correspond with the decorations. The panes here were scarlet—a deep blood color. Now in no one of the seven apartments was there any lamp or candelabrum amid the profusion of golden ornaments that lay scattered to and fro or depended from the roof. There was no light of any kind emanating from lamp or candle within the 7 suite of chambers. But in the corridors that followed the suite, there stood, opposite to each window, a heavy tripod, bearing a brazier[4] of fire that projected its rays through the tinted glass and so glaringly illumined the room. And thus were produced a multitude of gaudy and fantastic appearances. But in the western or black chamber the effect of the firelight that streamed upon the dark hangings through the blood-tinted panes, was ghastly in the extreme, and produced so wild a look upon the countenances of those who entered, that there were few of the company bold enough to set foot within its precincts at all.

It was in this apartment, also, that there stood against the western wall a gigantic clock of ebony.[5] Its pendulum swung to and fro with a dull, heavy, monotonous clang; and when the minute-hand made the circuit of the face, and the hour was to be stricken, there came from the brazen lungs of the clock a sound which was clear and loud and deep and exceedingly musical, but of so peculiar a note and emphasis that, at each lapse of an hour, the musicians 9 of the orchestra were constrained to pause, momentarily, in their performance, to hearken to the sound; and thus the waltzers perforce ceased their evolutions; and there was a brief disconcert[6] of the whole gay company; and, while the chimes of the clock yet rang, it was observed that the giddiest grew pale, and the more aged and sedate passed their hands over their brows as if in confused reverie or meditation. But when the echoes had fully ceased, a light laughter at once pervaded the assembly; the musicians looked at

4. **brazier** (brā′ zhər) *n.* metal pan or bowl used to hold burning coals.
5. **ebony** (eb′ ə nē) *n.* the black or dark wood of certain trees.
6. **disconcert** (dis kän′ sʉrt) *n.* embarrassment; confusion.

Vocabulary Development

Thematic Vocabulary: The Big Question

As students are discussing "The Masque of the Red Death," encourage them to use the thematic vocabulary presented in Introducing the Big Question, pp. 222–223. You might encourage them with sentence starters like these:

1. Prince Prospero's *motive* for decorating the rooms so unusually was to . . .
2. One effect of the *change* in the colors from room to room was . . .
3. The room I would most associate with *adversity* is . . .
4. The clanging of the clock creates a *radical* change in the room's atmosphere because . . .

9 each other and smiled as if at their own nervousness and folly, and made whispering vows, each to the other, that the next chiming of the clock should produce in them no similar emotion; and then, after the lapse of sixty minutes, (which embrace three thousand and six hundred seconds of the Time that flies), there came yet another chiming of the clock, and then were the same disconcert and tremulousness and meditation as before.

But, in spite of these things, it was a gay and magnificent revel. The tastes of the duke were peculiar. He had a fine eye for colors and effects. He disregarded the decora of mere fashion. His plans were bold and fiery, and his conceptions glowed with barbaric luster. There are some who would have thought him mad. His followers felt that he was not. It was necessary to hear and see and touch him to be sure that he was not.

He had directed, in great part, the movable embellishments of the seven chambers, upon occasion of this great fête; and it was his own guiding taste which had given character to the masqueraders. Be sure they were grotesque.[7] There were much glare and glitter and piquancy and phantasm—much of what has been since seen in Hernani.[8] There were arabesque figures with unsuited limbs and

8 ▲ **Critical Viewing**
What details does this scene share with the masque in the story? What differences can you find? **[Compare and Contrast]**

Reading Check 10
How do the partygoers and musicians react when the clock strikes?

7. **grotesque** (grō tesk′) *adj.* fantastic; distorted; bizarre; marked by strange mismatches of characteristics.
8. ***Hernani*** (hur nä′ nē) extravagant drama by the French author Victor Hugo.

8 Critical Viewing

Answer: The room shown is the seventh, indicated by its muted atmosphere. Revelers are shown glancing at the "gigantic clock of ebony," their expressions revealing their "disconcert and tremulousness." This scene, however, does not show the ghastly effect of the scarlet light streaming through the tinted panes.

9 Literary Analysis
Symbolism

1. Have a volunteer read the bracketed text that begins on the previous page.
2. **Ask** students to describe the clock, paying close attention to Poe's description including the clock's effect on the guests.
3. Then, **ask** students what the clock may symbolize.
Answer: The clock symbolizes the passage of time. It also symbolizes impending death for the dancers because each time it strikes, their end is closer.

10 Reading Check

Answer: The musicians pause, and the dancers stop dancing, growing pale. Some pass their hands over their brows as if they might be dreaming.

Differentiated Instruction for Universal Access

Strategy for Less Proficient Students

To help students visualize the action of the story, draw a diagram of the seven rooms in which the masquerade is held. If possible, use colors to correspond to the color theme of each room, and add as many visual details as possible. Have students copy the diagram in their notebooks. As they reread the story, have them write notes on the diagram recounting what occurs in each room.

EL Strategy for English Learners

"The Masque of the Red Death" contains challenging vocabulary and intricate diction. Students will benefit from following along in their text as they listen to the recording of the selection on the ***Hear It!* Audio CD**. Pause the recording as necessary to clarify particular words and phrases.

⓫ Humanities

Gothic Window by Stefan Grambart

Stefan Grambart's illustration of the seventh room shows the room in a deep monotone red with decorations from the period. The empty chairs, the lack of people in the room, and the presence of likenesses, such as the painting on the wall and the bust on the mantelpiece, create a sense of the stillness of death. The use of a single color gives the room a dream-like quality that seems almost unreal.

Use this question for discussion: How would you feel walking into a room such as this?
Possible response: I would feel nervous, because the decorations in the room and the deep red color give it a spooky feeling.

Vocabulary Development

Words from French

The Norman conquest of Great Britain in 1066 brought great changes to the English language. Thousands of French words became part of English vocabulary, initially in law, government, and the military. Today, we can appreciate French influences in the language of food, the arts, history, and fashion. In the paragraph that ends on p. 375 and continues to p. 377, Poe uses four words borrowed from French to add color to his writing.

grotesque: outlandish; incongruously distorted (from the French word for a fanciful style of decorative art)
arabesque: a complex or ornate design of flowers and leaves intertwined with geometric figures (from the French word meaning "in Arabic fashion")
fête: a festival or feast; an elaborate party (from the French word meaning "feast")
bizarre: strikingly unconventional in style or appearance; odd (from the French word meaning "brave")

appointments. There were delirious fancies such as the madman fashions. There was much of the beautiful, much of the wanton, much of the bizarre, something of the terrible, and not a little of that which might have excited disgust. To and fro in the seven chambers there stalked, in fact, a multitude of dreams. And these—the dreams—writhed in and about, taking hue from the rooms, and causing the wild music of the orchestra to seem as the echo of their steps. And, anon, there strikes the ebony clock which stands in the hall of the velvet. And then, for a moment, all is still, and all is silent save the voice of the clock. The dreams are stiff-frozen as they stand. But the echoes of the chime die away—they have endured
13 but an instant—and a light, half-subdued laughter floats after them as they depart. And now again the music swells, and the dreams live, and writhe to and fro more merrily than ever, taking hue from the many-tinted windows through which stream the rays from the tripods. But to the chamber which lies most westwardly of the seven, there are now none of the maskers who venture; for the night is waning away; and there flows a ruddier light through the blood-colored panes; and the blackness of the sable[9] drapery appalls; and to him whose foot falls upon the sable carpet, there comes from the near clock of ebony a muffled peal more solemnly emphatic than any which reaches *their* ears who indulge in the more remote gaieties of the other apartments.

But these other apartments were densely crowded, and in them beat feverishly the heart of life. And the revel went whirlingly on, until at length there commenced the sounding of midnight upon the clock. And then the music ceased, as I have told; and the evolutions of the waltzers were quieted; and there was an uneasy **cessation** of all things as before. But now there were twelve strokes to be sounded by the bell of the clock; and thus it happened, perhaps, that more of thought crept, with more of time, into the meditations of the thoughtful among those who reveled. And thus, too, it happened, perhaps, that before the last echoes of the last chime had utterly sunk into silence, there were many individuals in the crowd who had found leisure to become aware of the presence of a masked figure which had arrested the attention of no single individual before. And the rumor of this new presence having spread itself whisperingly around, there arose at length from the whole company a buzz, or murmur, expressive of disapprobation and surprise—then, finally, of terror, of horror, and of disgust.

In an assembly of phantasms such as I have painted, it may well be supposed that no ordinary appearance could have excited such

9. **sable** (sā´ bəl) *adj.* black; made of the black fur of the marten, an animal in the weasel family.

12 ◀ Critical Viewing
Does this illustration capture the mood of the seventh room as Poe describes it? Support your answer. **[Interpret]**

Reading Skill
Draw Conclusions
What does the contrast between activities in the first six rooms and the last one suggest about the symbolic meaning of this room?

Vocabulary
cessation (se sā´ shən) *n.* halt; stopping

Reading Check 14
Who draws the attention of the revelers?

12 Critical Viewing

Possible response: Yes, the room matches Poe's description because it is an eerie blood red color that produces a mysterious effect. Also, there is nobody in the room.

13 Reading Skill
Draw Conclusions

1. **Ask** students to summarize the activities that take place in the six colored rooms.
   Answer: People dance and the orchestra plays wild music in an atmosphere that is more like a nightmare than a party. The partygoers move freely from one room to the next.
2. Have a volunteer read the bracketed passage.
3. Then, **ask** students the Reading Skill question: What does the contrast between activities in the first six rooms and the last one suggest about the symbolic meaning of this room?
   Answer: People stay out of the seventh room. The six colored rooms are filled with life; the seventh is empty, and sound is muffled. This contrast emphasizes the symbolic meaning of the seventh room as representing death.

14 Reading Check

Answer: A masked figure who has gone unnoticed draws the attention of the partygoers as the clock strikes midnight.

Differentiated Instruction for Universal Access

Strategy for Special Needs Students
Help students understand the story's symbolism by using a graphic organizer. Draw a T-chart on the chalkboard with the heading "Poe's Use of Symbols." In the left-hand column, list elements of the story, such as the abbey, the revelers, and the clock. In the right-hand column, help students record what the elements symbolize.

Enrichment for Advanced Readers
Suggest that students read additional works by Edgar Allan Poe, such as "The Purloined Letter" and "The Tell-Tale Heart." After students have read these or other works, have them form discussion groups in which they compare and contrast the selections they have read. Suggest criteria for comparison, such as theme, setting, and symbolism.

⓯ Literary Analysis
Symbolism

1. Have students read the bracketed text to themselves. Tell them to pay close attention to the description of the new guest.
2. **Ask** students to describe the revelers' response to the new guest.
Answer: They are horrified and affronted.
3. Then, **ask** students what details in the description of the new guest help them understand the symbolism of this character.
Answer: He wears a shroud, and his face and costume are dabbled with blood. He is dressed as the Red Death.

▶**Monitor Progress** Have students think of what a symbol is: a character, place, or thing that stands for another important idea in the story.

▶**Reteach** If students have difficulty using the symbolic elements to draw conclusions, list some familiar symbols on the board: the flag of the United States, the dove, and the rose. **Ask** students to identify what each item commonly represents to people.
Answer: The items commonly represent freedom, peace, and love, respectively.
Ask students to identify what the new guest's face and costume represent to the guests at the party.
Answer: They represent death.

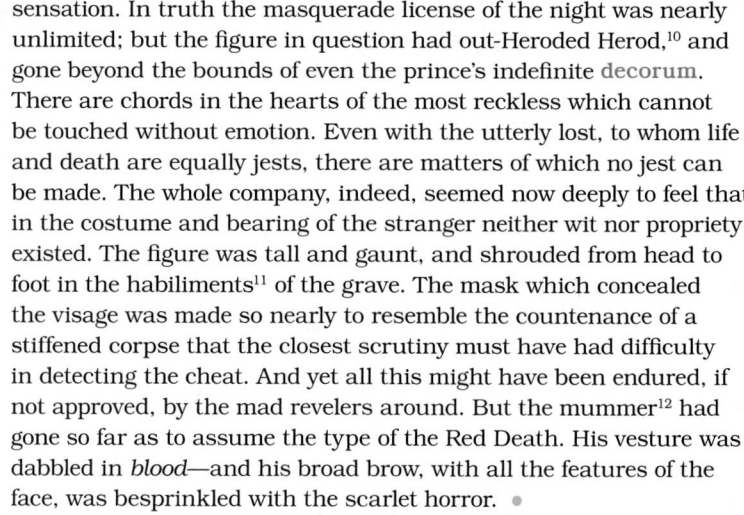

Vocabulary
decorum (di kôr′ əm) *n.* behavior that is polite and is correct for an occasion

sensation. In truth the masquerade license of the night was nearly unlimited; but the figure in question had out-Heroded Herod,[10] and gone beyond the bounds of even the prince's indefinite **decorum**. There are chords in the hearts of the most reckless which cannot be touched without emotion. Even with the utterly lost, to whom life and death are equally jests, there are matters of which no jest can be made. The whole company, indeed, seemed now deeply to feel that in the costume and bearing of the stranger neither wit nor propriety existed. The figure was tall and gaunt, and shrouded from head to foot in the habiliments[11] of the grave. The mask which concealed the visage was made so nearly to resemble the countenance of a stiffened corpse that the closest scrutiny must have had difficulty ⓯ in detecting the cheat. And yet all this might have been endured, if not approved, by the mad revelers around. But the mummer[12] had gone so far as to assume the type of the Red Death. His vesture was dabbled in *blood*—and his broad brow, with all the features of the face, was besprinkled with the scarlet horror.

When the eyes of Prince Prospero fell upon this spectral image (which with a slow and solemn movement, as if more fully to sustain its role, stalked to and fro among the waltzers) he was seen to be convulsed, in the first moment with a strong shudder either of terror or distaste; but, in the next, his brow reddened with rage.

"Who dares?" he demanded hoarsely of the courtiers who stood near him—"who dares insult us with this blasphemous mockery? Seize him and unmask him—that we may know whom we have to hang at sunrise, from the battlements!"

It was in the eastern or blue chamber in which stood the Prince Prospero as he uttered these words. They rang throughout the seven rooms loudly and clearly—for the prince was a bold and robust man, and the music had become hushed at the waving of his hand.

It was in the blue room where stood the prince, with a group of pale courtiers by his side. At first, as he spoke, there was a slight rushing movement of this group in the direction of the intruder, who at the moment was also near at hand, and now, with deliberate and stately step, made closer approach to the speaker. But from ⓰ a certain nameless awe with which the mad assumptions of the mummer had inspired the whole party, there were found none who put forth hand to seize him; so that, unimpeded, he passed within a yard of the prince's person; and, while the vast assembly, as if with one impulse, shrank from the centers of the rooms to

10. **out-Heroded Herod** (her′ əd) behaved even more excessively than Herod, a Biblical figure noted for his shocking acts.
11. **habiliments** (hə bil′ ə mənts) *n.* clothing.
12. **mummer** (mum′ ər) *n.* masked and costumed person.

Vocabulary Development

Vocabulary Knowledge Rating

When students have competed reading and discussing "The Masque of the Red Death," have them take out their **Vocabulary Knowledge Rating Chart** for this selection. Read the words aloud once more and have students rate their knowledge of the words again in the After Reading column. Clarify any words that are still problematic. Have students write their own definition and example or sentence in the appropriate column. Then have students complete the Vocabulary Practice at the end of the selection. Encourage students to use the words in further discussion and written work about this selection. Remind them that they will be accountable for these words on the **Selection Test**, ***Unit 2 Resources***, pp. 178–180 or 181–183.

16 the walls, he made his way uninterruptedly, but with the same solemn and measured step which had distinguished him from the first, through the blue chamber to the purple—through the purple to the green—through the green to the orange—through this again to the white—and even thence to the violet, ere a decided movement had been made to arrest him. It was then, however, that the Prince Prospero, maddening with rage and the shame of his own momentary cowardice, rushed hurriedly through the six chambers, while none followed him on account of a deadly terror that had seized upon all. He bore aloft a drawn dagger, and had approached, in rapid impetuosity, to within three or four feet of the retreating figure, when the latter, having attained the extremity of the velvet apartment, turned suddenly and confronted his pursuer. There was a sharp cry—and the dagger dropped gleaming upon the sable carpet, upon which, instantly afterwards, fell prostrate in death the Prince Prospero. Then, summoning the wild courage

17 **Reading Check**

How does Prince Prospero react to the stranger?

18 ◀ **Critical Viewing**

In what way does this image express the fears of the revelers? **[Connect]**

16 Critical Thinking

Interpret

1. Read aloud the bracketed text, and remind students that Prince Prospero has constructed a palace that people can neither enter nor leave.
2. **Ask** students how this fact and the details in the passage contribute to the symbolism of the character of the guest.
   Answer: If no one can get in or out, then the uninvited guest must not be human. This adds to the impression that the character symbolizes Death.

17 Reading Check

Answer: He reacts at first with shock and fear, and then with rage, to the presence of the uninvited guest.

18 Critical Viewing

Answer: The revelers fear death from the plague that is afflicting the country, and this image illustrates that death has come to the prince and will soon infect the guests.

Concept Connector

Activating Prior Knowledge

Have students return to the points they raised in their discussion about disease prevention and avoidance of the inevitable. Ask students to re-evaluate their perspective after reading "The Masque of the Red Death." Encourage students to cite specific details, quotations, or other evidence from the text to support how the story maintains or changes their points of view.

Writing About the Big Question

Have students compare their responses to the sentence starters they completed before reading "The Masque of the Red Death" with their ideas afterwards. Ask them to explain whether their thoughts have changed.

Literary Analysis Graphic Organizer

Ask students to review the graphic organizers they completed to draw conclusions about symbolism while reading. Show them **Literary Analysis Graphic Organizer A** (*Graphic Organizer Transparencies*, p. 62) as an example. Then, have students share the graphic organizers they completed.

⑲ Literary Analysis
Symbolism

Ask students the Literary Analysis question: How does the use of a number of symbols—the black room, the clock, the uninvited guest—show that the story is an allegory?

Possible response: The symbols, taken together, represent the inevitability of death. At midnight in the black room, the prince and his guests run out of time. In spite of the prince's best efforts, he has been unable to keep the uninvited guest out of his castle.

ASSESS
Answers

Critical Thinking

1. Some students might want Prospero as a friend because he is rich and likes to have fun. Others might suggest that his friendship is not worth the price they would have to pay.
2. (a) He hides to escape the Red Death. (b) Outside the abbey there is death and despair. Inside there is life and merriment.
3. (a) Each is decorated in a single color with matching stained-glass windows. Instead of leading into each other, each is a distinct entity. (b) **Possible response:** He has a love of the bizarre, and he is willing to spare no expense to create an atmosphere of beauty and comfort.
4. (a) Prospero decides to hold the masquerade as a celebration of five or six months of survival. (b) **Possible response:** He believes that he can control all aspects of his life and that his money and planning will enable him to escape death.

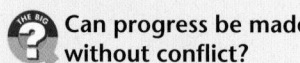

Can progress be made without conflict?

Possible response: We may try to avoid conflict, but some conflicts arise from the inevitable, such as illness, death, and aging. In these cases, we cannot escape conflict no matter how hard we try.

Vocabulary
tangible (tan′ jə bəl) *adj.* real and able to be touched

Literary Analysis
Symbolism How does the use of a number of symbols—the black room, the clock, the uninvited guest—show that the story is an allegory? ⑲

of despair, a throng of the revelers at once threw themselves into the black apartment, and, seizing the mummer, whose tall figure stood erect and motionless within the shadow of the ebony clock, gasped in unutterable horror at finding the grave cerements[13] and corpselike mask which they handled with so violent a rudeness, untenanted by any **tangible** form.

And now was acknowledged the presence of the Red Death. He had come like a thief in the night. And one by one dropped the revelers in the blood-bedewed halls of their revel, and died each in the despairing posture of his fall. And the life of the ebony clock went out with that of the last of the gay. And the flames of the tripods expired. And Darkness and Decay and the Red Death held illimitable dominion over all.

13. **cerements** (ser′ ə mənts) *n.* burial wrapping for a corpse; shroud.

Critical Thinking

1. **Respond:** Would you like the prince as a friend? Explain.
2. **(a)** Why does Prince Prospero hide in his palace? **(b) Contrast:** Contrast life outside the palace with life inside it.
3. **(a)** Use details from the story to briefly describe the rooms in which the masquerade is held. **(b) Infer:** What does the design of the rooms suggest about the prince's tastes and values?
4. **(a) Interpret:** Why does the prince decide to hold the masquerade? **(b) Evaluate:** What does the prince's response to the Red Death suggest about the kind of person he is? Explain.

Can progress be made without conflict? What message does Poe convey about attempting to avoid conflict? Explain your answer.

Assessment Resources

Unit 2 Resources

L1 L2 EL **Selection Test A,** pp. 178–180. Administer Test A to less advanced readers and English learners.

L3 L4 **Selection Test B,** pp. 181–183. Administer Test B to on-level and more advanced students.

L3 L4 **Open-Book Test,** pp. 175–177. As an alternative, give the Open-Book Test.

All **Customizable Test Bank**

All **Self-tests**
Students may prepare for the **Selection Test** by taking the **Self-test** online.

PHLit Online! All assessment resources are available at **www.PHLitOnline.com.**

After You Read | The Masque of the Red Death

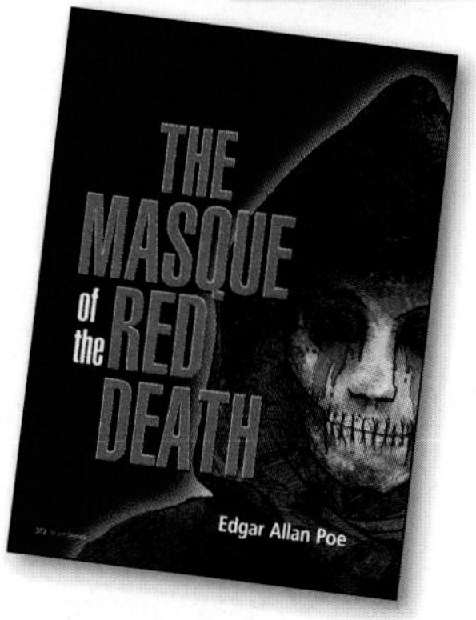

Literary Analysis: Symbolism and Allegory

1. In the story, the uninvited guest might be interpreted as a **symbol** of death. **(a)** Describe two responses of the partygoers to the stranger. **(b)** Explain how these responses are similar to ones associated with death. **(c)** Identify two other details supporting this interpretation of the stranger.
2. This story can be read as an **allegory.** Explain what the ability of the uninvited guest to enter a fortified palace might symbolize.

Reading Skill: Draw Conclusions

3. **(a)** In a chart like the one shown, identify the pattern of details that shows the importance of the clock. **(b)** Based on your chart, **draw a conclusion** about what the clock symbolizes.

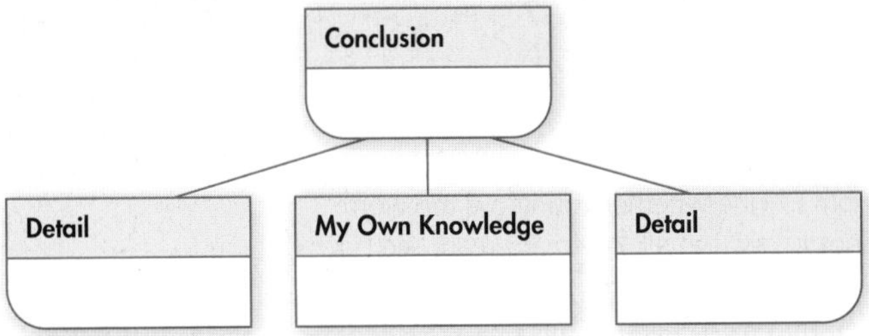

Vocabulary

Practice Words with similar meanings are called **synonyms.** For each set, choose the word that is *not* a synonym for the other two words. Explain.

1. plentiful; efficient; profuse
2. august; dignified; anguished
3. aided; hindered; impeded
4. end; cessation; hesitation
5. propriety; decisiveness; decorum
6. tangible; touchable; flavorful

Word Study Use the context of the sentences and what you know about the **Latin suffix *-tion*** to explain your answer to each question.

1. How would a positive job *evaluation* make you feel?
2. If you received a letter of *rejection,* would you be pleased?

Word Study

The **Latin suffix *-tion*** means "the act or quality of."

Challenge Explain how the suffix *-tion* contributes to the meanings of these words. Consult a dictionary, if necessary.

justification
protection
participation

ASSESS/EXTEND

Answers

Literary Analysis

1. **Possible responses:** (a) At first, the partygoers express surprise. Their attitude then changes to one of terror and horror. (b) One's attitude toward death can go through various stages, ranging from surprise to disgust and horror. (c) Poe describes the stranger as "tall and gaunt" and "shrouded from head to foot in the habiliments of the grave."
2. **Possible response:** Despite the partygoers' belief that they are insulated from the plague, they are clearly not. One may read this story, therefore, as a reminder that death and disease cannot be prevented or forestalled, even with the most elaborate precautions.

Reading Skill

3. **Possible responses:** (a) *Details:* Whenever the new hour comes, the clock strikes with a "heavy, monotonous clang," which makes all of the revelers temporarily stop what they are doing. The clock's clang has the effect of making the revelers become pale and worried. It is at the end of the story, when the clock strikes twelve times for midnight, that the revelers discover the stranger in the seventh room. (b) The clock is perhaps to announce death, or it is when the clock strikes twelve times that the revelers discover the stranger, who is death.

   For other sample answers, see ***Graphic Organizer Transparencies,* Reading Skill Graphic Organizer A**, p. 65, and the **Additional Answers** section.

Vocabulary

Practice

Sample answers:

1. *Efficient; Profuse* and *plentiful* both refer to abundance, while to be *efficient* is to be quick and accurate.
2. *Anguished; August* and *dignified* both refer to a person's standing in society or amongst his peers, while *anguished* refers to a particular emotional state.
3. *Aided;* To *aid* someone is to help them, which is the opposite of *impeding* or *hindering* them.

Answers continued

4. *Hesitation; End* and *cessation* are synonyms because both suggest a stop or termination, while *hesitation* suggests only delay.
5. *Decisiveness; Propriety* and *decorum* are synonyms because both suggest adhering to a set of rules or manners. *Decisiveness*, however, is quickness in decision and action.
6. *Flavorful; Tangible* and *touchable* have to do with the sense of touch. *Flavorful* has to do with the sense of taste.

Word Study

Sample answers:

1. A positive evaluation from a supervisor would make an employee feel happy and satisfied.
2. A letter of rejection from a college would make a student unhappy.

Word Study: Challenge

Sample answers: A *justification* for something involves the act of justifying. To offer *protection* to a person is to act to protect them. *Participation* is the act of participating.

*Skills instruction for the **Reading Skill** and **Literary Analysis** concepts appears on p. 369.*

❶ Writing About the Big Question

1. Review the assignment with the class.
2. Remind students that progress often doesn't come without considerable opposition.
3. Have students complete the sample sentence starters. Review responses as a class. (**Possible response:** A person may oppose change because he or she likes things the way they are. Progress can sometimes create conflict when people are afraid of being left behind.)

While You Read

Tell students that as they read, they should look for differences between the world of cats and the world of humans.

❷ Vocabulary

1. Have students preview the selection vocabulary.
2. For each word, have students say the word aloud.
3. Then, use the word in a sentence that defines the word.
4. Finally, repeat your definitional sentence or a similar sentence with the word missing, and have the class "fill in the blank" chorally. Here are some examples:

   An itinerary is a travel plan. Rufus discovered that there was more to do in Rome than he had planned, so he decided not to follow his strict [students say "itinerary"].

   Something futile is useless. Because she did not get promoted, Cindy thought all her hard work was [students say "futile"].

❸ Word Study

1. Introduce the skill, using the instruction in the box.
2. Write the suffix *-id* on the boards. Tell students it means "the body of" or "connected with." Have students write a list of words that end with this suffix. (**Sample answers:** *fervid, humid, pallid, fetid*)

Can progress be made without conflict?

❶ Writing About the Big Question

In this story, stubborn cats fight to preserve their space. Use these sentence starters to develop your ideas about the Big Question.

A person may **oppose change** because ______________________.

Progress can sometimes create conflict when ______________________.

While You Read Note the differences between the world of cats and the world of humans. Then, decide whether nature and people must be in conflict.

❷ Vocabulary

Read each word and its definition. Decide whether you know the word well, know it a little bit, or do not know it at all. After you read, see how your knowledge of each word has increased.

- **itinerary** (ī tin′ ər er′ ē) *n.* route; travel plan (p. 385) ***As part of our itinerary, we will be in Cleveland on Sunday.*** *itinerant adj.*
- **intrigues** (in′ trēgz) *n.* plots; schemes (p. 386) ***The twins whispered together and laughed, cooking up one of their intrigues.*** *intrigue v. intriguing adj.*
- **squalid** (skwäl′ id) *adj.* foul or unclean (p. 387) ***The restaurant was so squalid that the health board shut it down.*** *squalor n. squalidly adv.*
- **futile** (fyo͞ot′ l) *adj.* not successful; useless (p. 390) ***After a futile attempt to climb the steep and icy incline, the hikers had to seek another path.*** *futilely adv. futility n.*
- **indigence** (in′ di jəns) *n.* poverty (p. 393) ***Many lost their jobs, and the number of people living in indigence grew.*** *indigent adj.*
- **consigned** (kən sīnd′) *v.* handed over; gave up or delivered (p. 395) ***Thankfully, the stolen car was found and consigned to the owners.*** *consignable adj. consignment n.*

❸ Word Study

The **Latin suffix *-id*** means "the body of" or "connected with."

In this story, the cats lead Marcovaldo through **squalid** passageways, those that are filled with squalor, or dirt and grime.

Vocabulary Development

Vocabulary Knowledge Rating

Create a **Vocabulary Knowledge Rating Chart** (***Professional Development Guidebook***, p. 33) for this selection. Include the selection vocabulary and the Big Question words that appear in the Writing About the Big Question sentence starters on this page. (The Big Question vocabulary is introduced on pp. 222–223.)

Give students a copy of the chart. Read the words aloud, and have students mark their rating in the Before Reading column. Urge them to be alert to these words as they read and discuss the selection.

Tally how many students think they know a word to gauge how much instruction to provide. As students read and discuss the selection, point out the words and their context.

PHLit Online! **Vocabulary Central**, featuring tools, activities, and songs for studying vocabulary, is available at **www.PHLitOnline.com**.

Meet Italo Calvino

(1923–1985)

Author of *The Garden of Stubborn Cats*

The son of two Italian botanists, Italo Calvino was born in Cuba. He grew up in San Remo on the Italian Riviera and began his literary career in the Italian city of Turin.

A Writer of Fables According to Calvino, "A classic is a book that has never finished saying what it has to say." In this sense, Calvino's own works are classics. They say much more than appears on the page.

Though his ideas are complex, Calvino conveys them using events and characters as simple as those in a fable or fairy tale. Like a good fable, his stories blend reality and fantasy.

DID YOU KNOW?

During World War II, Calvino joined the Italian Resistance to fight Italy's fascist dictatorship.

❹ BACKGROUND FOR THE STORY

Marcovaldo

This story is one of the interrelated short stories in Italo Calvino's *Marcovaldo: or The Seasons in the City.* Set in a grim Italian industrial city in the 1950s and 1960s, the collection presents the adventures of Marcovaldo, an ordinary working man, as he uses his imagination to escape his surroundings.

Daily Bellringer

For each class during which you will teach this selection, have students complete one of the five Research activities for Week 11 in the *Daily Bellringer Activities* booklet.

❹ Background

Cats

Because of their mysterious nature, their sensitivity to light and sound, and their skill as nighttime hunters, cats have been credited with supernatural powers in many cultures and have even been worshipped as gods. The ancient Egyptians, for example, produced many statues of cats in honor of their cat-goddess, Bastet. Later, cats were associated with witches in European cultures. Today, the old wives' tale still lingers that cats will suck the breath of infants and kill them. Images of cats continue to show our mixed feelings about these creatures. They are sometimes depicted as cute, cuddly balls of fluff and sometimes as mysterious, predatory hunters.

Multidraft Reading

This icon ● marks natural pauses in the selection. To assist struggling readers and to deepen reading for all, assign the text in "chunks," following the icons, and apply multidraft reading protocols. For each reading, have students set the purpose indicated:

- **First reading**—literal comprehension: answering the Reading Check questions.
- **Second reading**—application of skills: answering the Draw Conclusions and Symbolism prompts.
- **Third reading**—interpretation: answering the end-of-selection questions.

For more guidance, refer to the ***Classroom Strategies and Teaching Routines*** card on multidraft reading.

Differentiated Instruction — Additional Instruction

EL Extended Support—English Learners
Have students complete the **Reading and Vocabulary Warm-ups,** ***Unit 2 Resources,*** pp. 184–187, before they read. Assign the prereading pages and the adapted selection in the ***Reader's Notebook: English Learner's Version.*** Then, have students listen to portions of the selection on the ***Hear It!*** **Audio CD.**

L1 L2 Extended Support—Struggling Readers
Have students complete the **Reading and Vocabulary Warm-ups,** ***Unit 2 Resources,*** pp. 184–187, before they read. Assign the prereading pages and the adapted selection in the ***Reader's Notebook: Adapted Version.*** Then, have students listen to portions of the selection on the ***Hear It!*** **Audio CD** (adapted text).

Extended Support—Reluctant Readers
To build motivation and engagement before assigning the selection, have students read "The Development Debate," a thematically related selection in ***Reality Central.*** Then, use the questions at the conclusion of the related selection to guide discussion.

PHLit Online!

For more about the author, practice with the selection vocabulary, and more background, go online at **www.PHLitOnline.com.**

❶ Activating Prior Knowledge

Write the following two lists on the board: List 1: malls, movie theaters, grocery stores, housing, hospitals, libraries, office buildings; List 2: forests, oceans, rivers, mountains, valleys, meadows, deserts. Lead students in a discussion about which list contains the items that are most important to each of them. Students should offer explanations and examples to support their statements.

Concept Connector →

Students will return to these discussion points after completing the story.

Individual Activity

To make sure that students understand the difference between the "city of men" and the "city of cats," have them create quick sketches of each. The drawings should contain details from the selection, such as the skyscrapers and the "mortal" traffic.

❷ About the Selection

In "The Garden of Stubborn Cats," an Italian worker named Marcovaldo becomes aware of cats and their pathways through a city. He discovers an old villa in a dilapidated garden where they congregate and resist the efforts of construction workers to build a new structure. For Calvino, cats symbolize nature's mysterious, persistent presence even in a big city. They also symbolize nature's resistance to human aims and designs.

❶
❷

THE GARDEN of STUBBORN CATS

Italo Calvino

translated by William Weaver

Vocabulary Development

Thematic Vocabulary: The Big Question

As students are discussing "The Garden of Stubborn Cats," encourage them use the thematic vocabulary presented in Introducing the Big Question, pp. 222–223. You might encourage them with sentence starters like these:

1. The cats faced *adversity* in their surroundings when . . .
2. *Progress* for men and cats is different because . . .
3. The Marchesa *struggles* against the cats because . . .
4. The city's *motive* for wanting to buy the land is . . .

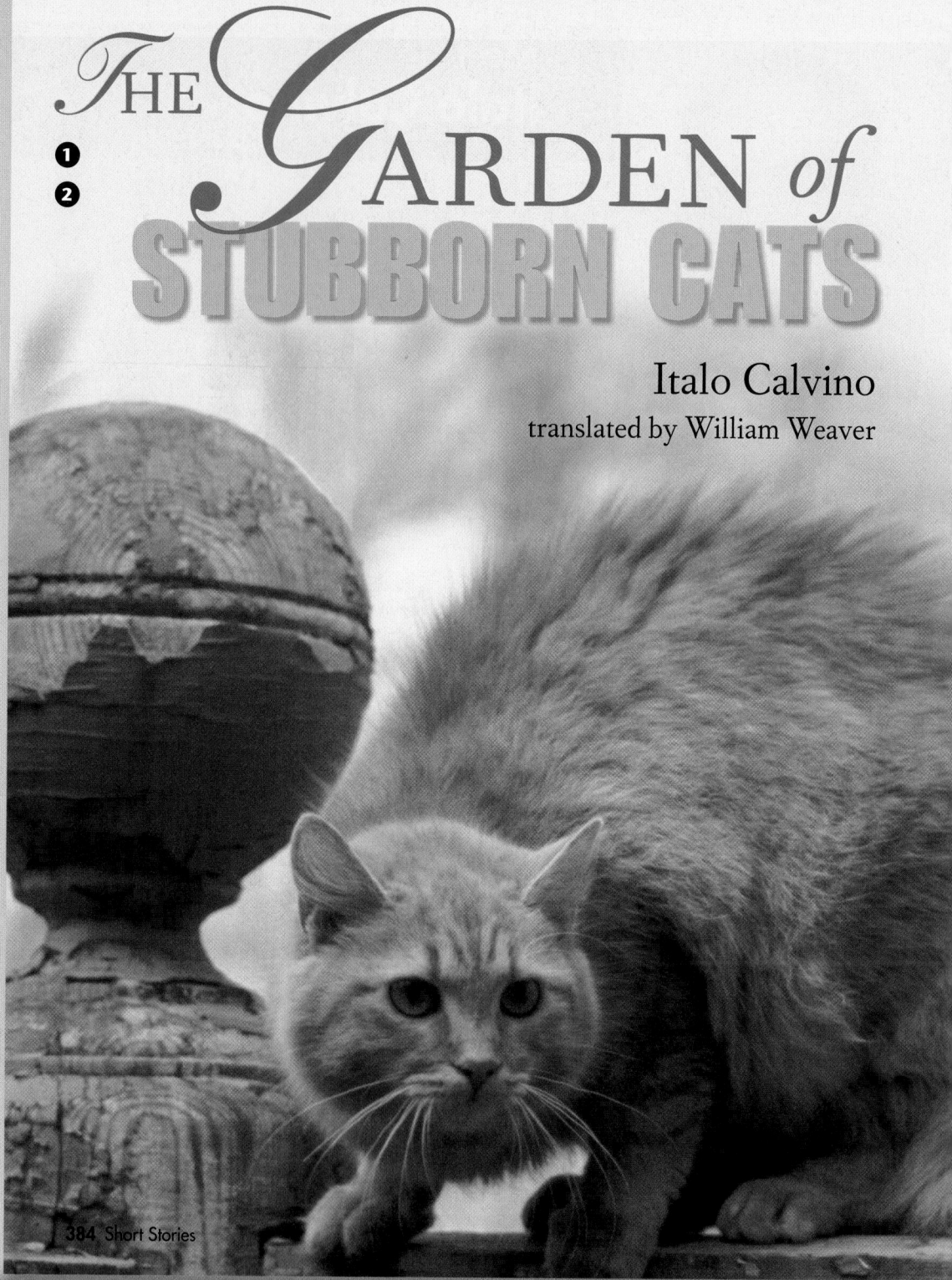

The city of cats and the city of men exist one inside the other, but they are not the same city.

Few cats recall the time when there was no distinction: the streets and squares of men were also streets and squares of cats, and the lawns, courtyards, balconies, and fountains: you lived in a broad and various space. But for several generations now domestic felines have been prisoners of an uninhabitable city: the streets are uninterruptedly overrun by the mortal traffic of cat-crushing automobiles; in every square foot of terrain where once a garden extended or a vacant lot or the ruins of an old demolition, now condominiums loom up, welfare housing, brand-new skyscrapers; every entrance is crammed with parked cars; the courtyards, one by one, have been roofed by reinforced concrete and transformed into garages or movie houses or storerooms or workshops. And where a rolling plateau of low roofs once extended, copings, terraces, water tanks, balconies, skylights, corrugated-iron sheds, now one general superstructure rises wherever structures can rise; the intermediate differences in height, between the low ground of the street and the supernal[1] heaven of the penthouses, disappear; the cat of a recent litter seeks in vain the itinerary of its fathers, the point from which to make the soft leap from balustrade to cornice to drainpipe, or for the quick climb on the roof-tiles. **3**

But in this vertical city, in this compressed city where all voids tend to fill up and every block of cement tends to mingle with other blocks of cement, a kind of counter-city opens, a negative city, that consists of empty slices between wall and wall, of the minimal distances ordained by the **5**

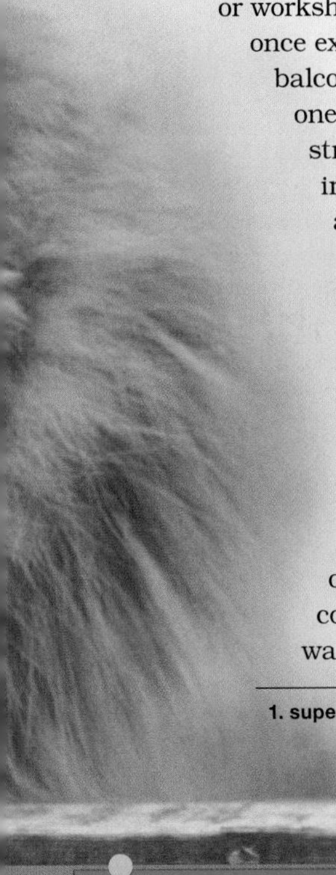

Literary Analysis
Symbolism What associations with cats is the author creating?

Vocabulary
itinerary (ī tin´ ər er´ ē) *n.* route; travel plan

Reading Check **4**
Why is the city uninhabitable for cats?

1. **supernal** (so͞o pʉr´ nəl) *adj.* of the heavens; divine.

3 Literary Analysis
Symbolism

1. Have students read the bracketed passage.
2. Then, **ask** them the Literary Analysis question: What associations with cats is the author creating?
   Answer: The cats may symbolize what has happened to nature as a result of progress. They may also represent the passage of time when there was no distinction between the city of men and the city of cats. They were able to live side-by-side.

4 Reading Check

Answer: The city is uninhabitable for cats because people have built huge structures and machines that are dangerous to cats.

Differentiated Instruction for Universal Access

Strategy for Less Proficient Readers
Based on the picture of the cat on page 384 and students' own knowledge of cats, ask them to describe the type of environment that would be ideally suited for cats. Ask students to give reasons for their answers. It may benefit them to sketch their ideas for an ideal environment before the discussion.

Enrichment for Gifted/Talented Students
Have students write real estate advertisements for a city that would be equally accommodating to people and cats. What passageways and green spaces would they include that would provide for cats' needs? How might people and cats coexist peacefully?

PHLit Online!

This selection is available in interactive format in the **Enriched Online Student Edition, www.PHLitOnline.com,** which includes a thematically related video and writing prompt and an interactive graphic organizer.

5 Reading Skill
Draw Conclusions

1. Have students read the passage that begins on the previous page.
2. Remind students that drawing conclusions involves using hints, clues, and details in the story to form logical opinions based on the information. Remind them, too, that people can draw different conclusions from the same information.
3. Then, **ask** students the Reading Skill question: Which details here support the conclusion that cats are not fully at home in the city? **Answer:** The city is crowded, and there are not many open spaces; there are only minimal distances between buildings. The city is filled with cavities, wells, air conduits, driveways, inner yards, and basements. These are places cats have been forced to inhabit.

Reading Skill
Draw Conclusions
Which details here support the conclusion that cats are not fully at home in the city? 5

building regulations between two constructions, between the rear of one construction and the rear of the next; it is a city of cavities, wells, air conduits, driveways, inner yards, accesses to basements, like a network of dry canals on a planet of stucco and tar, and it is through this network, grazing the walls, that the ancient cat population still scurries.

On occasion, to pass the time, Marcovaldo would follow a cat. It was during the work-break, between noon and three, when all the personnel except Marcovaldo went home to eat, and he—who brought his lunch in his bag—laid his place among the packing-cases in the warehouse, chewed his snack, smoked a half-cigar, and wandered around, alone and idle, waiting for work to resume. In those hours, a cat that peeped in at a window was always welcome company, and a guide for new explorations. He had made friends with a tabby, well fed, a blue ribbon around its neck, surely living with some well-to-do family. This tabby shared with Marcovaldo the habit of an afternoon stroll right after lunch; and naturally a friendship sprang up.

Following his tabby friend, Marcovaldo had started looking at places as if through the round eyes of a cat and even if these places were the usual environs of his firm he saw them in a different light, as settings for cattish stories, with connections practicable only by light, velvety paws. Though from the outside the neighborhood seemed poor in cats, every day on his rounds Marcovaldo made the acquaintance of some new face, and a miau, a hiss, a stiffening of fur on an arched back was enough for him to sense ties and **intrigues** and rivalries among them. At those moments he thought he had already penetrated the secrecy of the felines' society: and then he felt himself scrutinized by pupils that became slits, under the surveillance of the antennae of taut whiskers, and all the cats around him sat impassive as sphinxes, the pink triangles of their noses convergent on the black triangles of their

Vocabulary
intrigues (in´ trēgz) *n.* plots; schemes

Vocabulary Development

Idiomatic Expressions
The number of idioms and colloquialisms about cats that exist in English reflects the popularity of the animal in the United States. While not all of these expressions are positive, they do show that cats play an important role in the culture. Give students these expressions and their meanings. Challenge students to determine the original connection to the feline.

catcall: Human noises (primarily whistles) that express disapproval
curiosity killed the cat: It's best to mind one's own business.
fat cat: A wealthy and privileged person
grin like a Cheshire cat: Smile broadly in a self-satisfied way.
let the cat out of the bag: Give away a secret
look like something the cat dragged in: Appear completely bedraggled

lips, and the only things that moved were the tips of the ears, with a vibrant jerk like radar. They reached the end of a narrow passage, between **squalid** blank walls; and, looking around, Marcovaldo saw that the cats that had led him this far had vanished, all of them together, no telling in which direction, even his tabby friend, and they had left him alone. Their realm had territories, ceremonies, customs that it was not yet granted to him to discover.

On the other hand, from the cat city there opened unsuspected peepholes onto the city of men: and one day the same tabby led him to discover the great Biarritz Restaurant. ●

Anyone wishing to see the Biarritz Restaurant had only to assume the posture of a cat, that is, proceed on all fours. Cat and man, in this fashion, walked around a kind of dome, at whose foot some low, rectangular little windows opened. Following the tabby's example, Marcovaldo looked down. They were transoms through which the luxurious hall received air and light. To the sound of gypsy violins, partridges and quails swirled by on silver dishes balanced by the white-gloved fingers of waiters in tailcoats. Or, more precisely, above the partridges and quails the dishes whirled, and above the dishes the white gloves, and poised on the waiters' patent-leather shoes, the gleaming parquet floor, from which hung dwarf potted palms and tablecloths and crystal and buckets like bells with the champagne bottle for their clapper: everything was turned upside-down because Marcovaldo, for fear of being seen, wouldn't stick his head inside the window and confined himself to looking at the reversed reflection of the room in the tilted pane.

But it was not so much the windows of the dining-room as those of the kitchens that interested the cat: looking through the former you saw, distant and somehow transfigured, what in the

Vocabulary
squalid (skwäl′ id)
adj. foul or unclean

6

M.C. Escher's Relativity.

7 ▲ **Critical Viewing**
In what way does this picture, like the story, express the idea of multiple perspectives on the world? **[Interpret]**

8 **Reading Check**
To what place does Marcovaldo follow the tabby?

Differentiated Instruction for Universal Access

EL Pronunciation for English Learners

Some students might have difficulty pronouncing words with the short "u" sound on this page, as in *customs*, *buckets*, and *hung*, replacing it with the short "o" sound, as in *kŏsstoms*, *bŏkkets*, and *hŏng*. The following strategies can help students to pronounce the short "u" sound.

1. Write the words *customs*, *buckets*, and *hung* on the board. Model the pronunciation of each word in turn, with students repeating them. Then, isolate the short "u" sound in the two-syllable words *customs* and *buckets*, by calling out single-syllable words that feature the sound. Write these (such as *bus* and *luck*) on the board, and have students repeat them as well.
2. Play a game of "telephone" with the class, for each of the words written on the board, passing (saying) it to one student, who then pronounces it to another, and so on.

6 Humanities

Relativity by M. C. Escher (1898–1972)

Maurits Cornelius Escher is one of the world's most famous graphic artists. In addition to producing huge numbers of woodcuts, engravings, lithographs, and drawings, he also illustrated books, painted murals, and designed tapestries and postage stamps.

Escher was born in the Netherlands. Fascinated with mathematics and perspective, he went to architecture school but soon shifted his focus to drawing and printmaking. He created his own system of geometry that he called "mental imagery," which includes complex mazes and metamorphoses where one shape or object becomes something completely different. *Relativity* is one of a series of "impossible drawings" Escher made in 1953.

Use these questions for discussion:

a. Why do you think Escher called this lithograph *Relativity*?
Possible response: Escher suggests that in the space he creates, the existence of one entity is dependent on that of another. The people seem to live in different worlds that are both linked and separated.

b. Would you like to have a reproduction of this lithograph hanging in your room? Why or why not?
Possible response: Some students may find the drawing a fascinating source of discovery, seeing something new each time they look. Others may be disturbed by the perspective changes, the conflicting vantage points, and the figures that seem to live in different worlds.

7 Critical Viewing

Answer: The picture shows the distorted, disjointed angles and corners human beings have created for their own living spaces. It also shows their attempts to bring nature into a world of brick and steel. In addition, the picture shows the multiple perspectives that people and animals have of living conditions.

8 Reading Check

Answer: Marcovaldo discovers the places where cats live, the passageways by which they get around the city, and the Biarritz Restaurant.

❾ Literature in Context

Architectural Connection Other building terminology from the story that students may want to investigate includes *trestles, dome, conduits, stucco, parapet,* and *parquet*.

Connect to the Literature After discussing architectural features with students, **ask** them to respond to the Connect to the Literature prompt: Compare and contrast the purposes for which a cat and a person would use each of these features.

Answer: In most cases, the architectural features are either decorative or protective for humans. For cats, on the other hand, most are means of access, observation, or escape.

❿ Critical Thinking

Interpret

1. Ask a volunteer to read aloud the bracketed passage.
2. **Ask** students whether anything strikes them as humorous about this passage.
   Possible response: Students may point out the physical position of Marcovaldo looking at the fish tank reflected upside down in the window in a place where a human ordinarily would not be. Also, he is contemplating raiding the fish tank of the restaurant much like a cat would raid an aquarium. These notions, coupled with the fanciness of the restaurant and its patrons, are ludicrous.
3. **Ask** students how the author uses humor to reinforce the theme of the story.
   Possible response: Calvino seems to be saying that overbuilt cities have pushed both man and beast into behaviors foreign to them.

❾ **LITERATURE IN CONTEXT**

Architecture Connection

Architectural Features

The following building features are mentioned in the narrative:

- **balustrade** railing suported by posts
- **belvedere** long balcony with a roof
- **capitals** tops of columns
- **copings** top layer of a stone or brick wall, sloped to carry off water
- **cornice** overhanging part of a roof
- **transom** small window or shutter over a door or window

Connect to the Literature

Compare and contrast the purposes for which a cat and a person would use each of these features.

kitchens presented itself—quite concrete and within paw's reach—as a plucked bird or a fresh fish. And it was toward the kitchens, in fact, that the tabby wanted to lead Marcovaldo, either through a gesture of altruistic friendship or else because it counted on the man's help for one of its raids. Marcovaldo, however, was reluctant to leave his belvedere over the main room: first as he was fascinated by the luxury of the place, and then because something down there had riveted his attention. To such an extent that, overcoming his fear of being seen, he kept peeking in, with his head in the transom.

In the midst of the room, directly under that pane, there was a little glass fish tank, a kind of aquarium, where some fat trout were swimming. A special customer approached, a man with a shiny bald pate, black suit, black beard. An old waiter in tailcoat followed him, carrying a little net as if he were going to catch butterflies. The gentleman in black looked at the trout with a grave, intent air; then he raised one hand and with a slow, solemn gesture singled out a fish. The waiter dipped the net into the tank, pursued the appointed trout, captured it, headed for the kitchens, holding out in front of him, like a lance, the net in which the fish wriggled. The gentleman in black, solemn as a magistrate[2] who has handed down a capital sentence, went to take his seat and wait for the return of the trout, sautéed "à la meunière."[3] ❿

If I found a way to drop a line from up here and make one of those trout bite, Marcovaldo thought, I couldn't be accused of theft; at worst, of fishing in an unauthorized place. And ignoring the miaus that called him toward the kitchens, he went to collect his fishing tackle.

Nobody in the crowded dining room of the Biarritz saw the long, fine line, armed with hook and bait, as it slowly dropped into the tank. The fish saw the bait, and flung themselves on it. In the fray one trout managed to bite the worm: and immediately it began to rise, rise, emerge from the water, a silvery flash, it darted up high, over the laid tables and the trolleys of hors d'oeuvres, over the blue flames of the crêpes Suzette, until it vanished into the heavens of the transom.

Marcovaldo had yanked the rod with the brisk snap of the expert fisherman, so the fish landed behind his back. The trout had barely ⓫ touched the ground when the cat sprang. What little life the trout

2. **magistrate** (maj′ is trāt′) *n.* judge.
3. **sautéed "à la meunière"** (sô tād′ ä lä mə nyer′) rolled in flour, fried in butter, and sprinkled with lemon juice and chopped parsley.

still had was lost between the tabby's teeth. Marcovaldo, who had abandoned his line at that moment to run and grab the fish, saw it snatched from under his nose, hook and all. He was quick to put one foot on the rod, but the snatch had been so strong that the rod was all the man had left, while the tabby ran off with the fish, pulling the line after it. Treacherous kitty! It had vanished.

But this time it wouldn't escape him: there was that long line trailing after him and showing the way he had taken. Though he had lost sight of the cat, Marcovaldo followed the end of the line: there it was, running along a wall; it climbed a parapet,
11 wound through a doorway, was swallowed up by a basement . . . Marcovaldo, venturing into more and more cattish places, climbed roofs, straddled railings, always managed to catch a glimpse—perhaps only a second before it disappeared—of that moving trace that indicated the thief's path.

Literary Analysis
Symbolism Which details reinforce the contrast between a cat's view of the city and a human's view?

Now the line played out down a sidewalk, in the midst of the traffic, and Marcovaldo, running after it, almost managed to grab it. He flung himself down on his belly: there, he grabbed it! He managed
12 to seize one end of the line before it slipped between the bars of a gate.

Beyond a half-rusted gate and two bits of wall buried under climbing plants, there was a little rank[4] garden, with a small, abandoned-looking building at the far end of it. A carpet of dry leaves covered the path, and dry leaves lay everywhere under the boughs of the two plane-trees, forming actually some little mounds in the yard. A

13 **Reading Check**
Where does the tabby finally lead Marcovaldo?

4. **rank** (raŋk) *adj.* growing vigorously and coarsely.

11 Literary Analysis
Symbolism

1. Ask a volunteer to read the bracketed text aloud.
2. Then, **ask** the Literary Analysis question: Which details reinforce the contrast between a cat's view of the city and a human's view?
   Answer: Marcovaldo follows the fishing line along a wall, up a parapet, through a doorway, into a basement, on a roof, and across a railing. He is exposed to places that humans rarely go; in fact, he is functioning as a cat as he pursues the fishing line.

12 Reading Skill
Draw Conclusions

1. Have a volunteer read the bracketed text aloud.
2. **Ask** students to contrast the description of the garden with the description of the surrounding skyscrapers.
   Answer: The skyscrapers appear brand new and well cared for, although they are hard edged and crowded. Their windows look down like eyes on the garden below. The garden, in contrast, is old, seemingly abandoned by humans, and uncared for.
3. Then, **ask** students how the garden is symbolic.
   Answer: Surrounded by buildings on all sides, it is the one undeveloped space where the wildlife can congregate. Therefore, the garden symbolizes nature.

13 Reading Check

Answer: The cat leads Marcovaldo into a garden.

Differentiated Instruction for Universal Access

Enrichment for Gifted/Talented Students
To help all readers visualize the architectural details of this story, ask students to prepare an illustrated dictionary of the terms listed in the Architecture Connection on p. 388. Students may use photographs, diagrams, or their own drawings to show the details. Encourage them to elaborate on the original definitions provided. They may wish to include other building terms that appear in the story: *trestle, dome, conduits, stucco, parapet,* and *parquet.*

Enrichment for Advanced Readers
Suggest that students search city or state government Web sites to locate information about the guidelines for urban planning in their cities or states. In small groups, have students review their findings. Ask students to draw conclusions about the priorities for urban planning in their cities or states. Then, ask students to make lists of responsibilities for urban planners. Challenge students to brainstorm urban planning strategies that balance a community's need for a healthy environment that respects the natural world with meeting the needs of its human inhabitants.

⓮ Reading Skill
Draw Conclusions

1. Have a volunteer read the passage aloud.
2. **Ask** students why the strange rain comes at this moment in the story. What does it indicate about Marcovaldo's idea that he has discovered the secret world of the cats?
   Answer: The strange rain of fishbones, heads, tails, and lungs suggests that others know of the garden and the cats.
3. Then, **ask** students the Reading Skill question: Based on details of this event, what conclusion can you draw about whether the tabby has brought fish here before?
   Possible response: It would seem that those two yellow hands have gone through the same procedure before. However, it is difficult to tell whether the cat has brought the fish or the people feeding the cats have also contributed to the Marchesa's food supply.

⓬ layer of leaves was yellowing in the green water of a pool. Enormous buildings rose all around, skyscrapers with thousands of windows, like so many eyes trained disapprovingly on that little square patch with two trees, a few tiles, and all those yellow leaves, surviving right in the middle of an area of great traffic.

And in this garden, perched on the capitals and balustrades, lying on the dry leaves of the flowerbeds, climbing on the trunks of the trees or on the drainpipes, motionless on their four paws, their tails making a question-mark, seated to wash their faces, there were tiger cats, black cats, white cats, calico cats, tabbies, angoras, Persians, house cats and stray cats, perfumed cats and mangy cats. Marcovaldo realized he had finally reached the heart of the cats' realm, their secret island. And, in his emotion, he almost forgot his fish.

It had remained, that fish, hanging by the line from the branch of a tree, out of reach of the cats' leaps; it must have dropped from its kidnapper's mouth at some clumsy movement, perhaps as it was defended from the others, or perhaps displayed as an extraordinary prize. The line had got tangled, and Marcovaldo, tug as he would, couldn't manage to yank it loose. A furious battle had meanwhile been joined among the cats, to reach that unreachable fish, or rather, to win the right to try and reach it. Each wanted to prevent the others from leaping: they hurled themselves on one another, they tangled in midair, they rolled around clutching each other, and finally a general war broke out in a whirl of dry, crackling leaves.

Vocabulary
futile (fyo͞ot′ l) *adj.* not successful; useless

After many **futile** yanks, Marcovaldo now felt the line was free, but he took care not to pull it: the trout would have fallen right in the midst of that infuriated scrimmage of felines.

Reading Skill
Draw Conclusions
Based on details of this event, what conclusion can you draw about whether the tabby has brought fish here before? ⓮

It was at this moment that, from the top of the walls of the gardens, a strange rain began to fall: fish-bones, heads, tails, even bits of lung and lights.[5] Immediately the cats' attention was distracted from the suspended trout and they flung themselves on the new delicacies. To Marcovaldo, this seemed the right moment to pull the line and regain his fish. But, before he had time to act, from a blind of the little villa, two yellow, skinny hands darted out: one was brandishing scissors; the other, a frying pan. The hand with the scissors was raised above the trout, the hand with the frying pan was thrust under it. The scissors cut the line, the trout fell into the pan; hands, scissors and pan withdrew, the blind closed: all in the space of a second. Marcovaldo was totally bewildered.

5. **lights** term for animal organs used for catfood.

Think Aloud

Vocabulary: Using Context
Direct students' attention to the word *intimidation* on p. 391. Using a think-aloud process, model how to use context to infer the meaning of an unknown word. Say to students:

I am going to think aloud to show you how I would figure out the meaning of *intimidation* from its context.

In this sentence, *intimidation* is one of the techniques the contractors used to get the Marchesa to sell her house. In preceding sentences we are told that the contractors have offered "millions" for the property, but that they have also used negative strategies. *Intimidation* appears in a negative list that includes "threats" and "persecution." People in the crowd clearly disapprove of the contractors' strategies. I think *intimidation* refers to an attempt to influence actions in a negative way by playing on fears or by threatening force.

"Are you also a cat lover?" A voice at his back made him turn round. He was surrounded by little old women, some of them ancient, wearing old-fashioned hats on their heads; others, younger, but with the look of spinsters; and all were carrying in their hands or their bags packages of leftover meat or fish, and some even had little pans of milk. "Will you help me throw this package over the fence, for those poor creatures?"

All the ladies, cat lovers, gathered at this hour around the garden of dry leaves to take the food to their protégés.[6]

"Can you tell me why they are all here, these cats?" Marcovaldo inquired.

15 "Where else could they go? This garden is all they have left! Cats come here from other neighborhoods, too, from miles and miles around . . ."

"And birds, as well," another lady added. "They're forced to live by the hundreds and hundreds on these few trees . . ."

"And the frogs, they're all in that pool, and at night they never stop croaking . . . You can hear them even on the eighth floor of the buildings around here."

> Marcovaldo realized he had finally reached the heart of the cats' realm, their secret island.

"Who does this villa belong to anyway?" Marcovaldo asked. Now, outside the gate, there weren't just the cat-loving ladies but also other people: the man from the gas pump opposite, the apprentices from a mechanic's shop, the postman, the grocer, some passers-by. And none of them, men and women, had to be asked twice: all wanted to have their say, as always when a mysterious and controversial subject comes up.

"It belongs to a Marchesa.[7] She lives there, but you never see her . . ."

17 "She's been offered millions and millions, by developers, for this little patch of land, but she won't sell . . ."

"What would she do with millions, an old woman all alone in the world? She wants to hold on to her house, even if it's falling to pieces, rather than be forced to move . . ."

"It's the only undeveloped bit of land in the downtown area . . . Its value goes up every year . . . They've made her offers—"

"Offers! That's not all. Threats, intimidation, persecution . . . You don't know the half of it! Those contractors!"

"But she holds out. She's held out for years . . ."

"She's a saint. Without her, where would those poor animals go?"

16 **Reading Check**

What happens to Marcovaldo's trout?

6. **protégés** (prōt´ ə zhāz´) *n.* those guided and helped by another.
7. **Marchesa** (mär kā´ zä) *n.* title of an Italian noblewoman.

15 Connecting to the Big Question

1. Explain that what some might view as progress may not be seen as progress by others.
2. **Ask:** What "progress" has taken place in the time since the cats roamed freely?
   Possible response: The city has been built up with tall buildings, cars, and machines.
3. Have students read the bracketed text. **Ask:** What has been the result of this "progress" for the cats, birds, and frogs?
   Possible response: They have been relegated to a tiny patch of land.
4. **Ask** students if this progress could have occurred without creating the conflict that the animals face.
   Possible responses: No, any new development would have had an impact on the animals. Yes, they could have kept the animals in mind while developing and created a more animal-friendly city.

16 Reading Check

Answer: After the cat steals the fish and carries it off, the Marchesa, in turn, steals the trout and cooks it.

Differentiated Instruction for Universal Access

Culturally Responsive Instruction

Culture Connection Point out that the cats in the story can be seen to symbolize groups that are marginalized when society "advances" to meet the needs of one group. Invite students to discuss ways that urban development and other societal and technological changes can leave some people behind.

Discuss with students ways society can accommodate groups who have different interests or who share different cultural backgrounds. How do neighborhoods vary within a city to meet different peoples' cultural interests? How can society accommodate people who do not use technology such as cars or computers, or those who do not speak the dominant language? In what ways does the homogenization of a city detract from people's experiences?

17 Literary Analysis
Symbolism

1. Have a student read the bracketed passage aloud.
2. **Ask** students to summarize why some people think the Marchesa is an "angelic being" and others think she is an "egoist and a miser."
   Possible response: Some people think she is the cats' savior because she prevents the developers from destroying the house and garden. Others think she mistreats them and refuses to feed them.
3. **Ask** students to predict which analysis is more accurate and explain the basis of their prediction.
   Possible response: Based on the Marchesa's behavior of stealing the fish from the cats, some students will say that she probably does not care about the animals. On the other hand, she does not have enough food as she tries to hold on to her property.
4. Then, **ask** students the Literary Analysis question: What relationship with the city do the Marchesa and her property represent?
   Answer: The Marchesa and her property represent obstacles to the city's progress and development.

17

"A lot she cares about the animals, the old miser! Have you ever seen her give them anything to eat?"

"How can she feed the cats when she doesn't have food for herself? She's the last descendant of a ruined family!"

"She hates cats. I've seen her chasing them and hitting them with an umbrella!"

"Because they were tearing up her flowerbeds!"

"What flowerbeds? I've never seen anything in this garden but a great crop of weeds!"

Marcovaldo realized that with regard to the old Marchesa opinions were sharply divided: some saw her as an angelic being, others as an egoist and a miser.

Literary Analysis
Symbolism What relationship with the city do the Marchesa and her property represent?

"It's the same with the birds; she never gives them a crumb!"

"She gives them hospitality. Isn't that plenty?"

"Like she gives the mosquitoes, you mean. They all come from here, from that pool. In the summertime the mosquitoes eat us alive, and it's all the fault of that Marchesa!"

"And the mice? This villa is a mine of mice. Under the dead leaves they have their burrows, and at night they come out . . ."

"As far as the mice go, the cats take care of them . . ."

"Oh, you and your cats! If we had to rely on them . . ."

"Why? Have you got something to say against cats?"

Here the discussion degenerated into a general quarrel.

"The authorities should do something: confiscate the villa!" one man cried.

"What gives them the right?" another protested.

"In a modern neighborhood like ours, a mouse-nest like this . . . it should be forbidden . . ."

"Why, I picked my apartment precisely because it overlooked this little bit of green . . ."

"Green, hell! Think of the fine skyscraper they could build here!"

Marcovaldo would have liked to add something of his own, but he couldn't get a word in. Finally, all in one breath, he exclaimed: "The Marchesa stole a trout from me!"

The unexpected news supplied fresh ammunition to the old woman's enemies, but her defenders exploited it as proof of the indigence to which the unfortunate noblewoman was reduced. Both sides agreed that Marcovaldo should go and knock at her door to demand an explanation.

Vocabulary
indigence (in′ di jəns) *n.* poverty

It wasn't clear whether the gate was locked or unlocked; in any case, it opened, after a push, with a mournful creak. Marcovaldo picked his way among the leaves and cats, climbed the steps to the porch, knocked hard at the entrance.

"She hates cats. I've seen her chasing them and hitting them with an umbrella!"

At a window (the very one where the frying pan had appeared), the blind was raised slightly and in one corner a round, pale blue eye was seen, and a clump of hair dyed an undefinable color, and a dry skinny hand. A voice was heard, asking: "Who is it? Who's at the door?", the words accompanied by a cloud smelling of fried oil.

18 "It's me, Marchesa. The trout man," Marcovaldo explained. "I don't mean to trouble you. I only wanted to tell you, in case you didn't know, that the trout was stolen from me, by that cat, and I'm the one who caught it. In fact the line . . ."

Reading Check 19
Who owns the garden where the cats gather?

18 Reading Skill
Draw Conclusions

1. Have students read the bracketed passage that continues to the next page.
2. **Ask** them to explain the comic effect of Marcovaldo calling himself "the trout man" and the Marchesa referring to herself as a "prisoner" of the cats.
Answer: It is humorous that Marcovaldo, who stole the trout from the restaurant, still sees it as his even though the cat has carried it through the city. The Marchesa's comments about being a prisoner are ironic since she is the cause of her imprisonment as she tries to preserve her villa; the cats enjoy the open space that she tries to guard.
3. Then, **ask** students whether they believe that either character is a victim of the cats.
Possible response: Marcovaldo is an accomplice of the cats. He has had the chance to follow them and to see the world through their eyes. The Marchesa is a victim of her own greed and that of the developers who want her land. The cats have done little to change her life.

19 Reading Check
Answer: The Marchesa owns the garden where the cats gather.

Differentiated Instruction for Universal Access

Enrichment for Gifted/Talented Students
Students who prefer preserving the natural world over progress and development may cheer the cats, whereas students who believe progress and development are important may feel the cats should be removed. Have students write continuations of the story that reflect their beliefs about what the fate of the cats should be.

Enrichment for Advanced Readers
Have students conduct a debate on preserving the natural world versus encouraging progress and development. Have students devise a premise for the debate and then choose sides. Direct them to do online and library research to develop their arguments and rebuttals. Then, allow class time for the two sides to debate their premise. Have the class vote on which side is more convincing.

⑳ Reading Skill
Draw Conclusions

1. Have a volunteer read aloud the bracketed passage.
2. **Ask** a volunteer to paraphrase what the Marchesa says here.
   Answer: The Marchesa feels that her life is at the mercy of the cats; they keep her prisoner and have destroyed her life.
3. Then, **ask** students the Reading Skill question: Which details help you draw the conclusion that the Marchesa and the cats stand for similar ideas?
   Answer: Just as the cats need the open space of the garden to congregate in, the Marchesa needs to preserve her past and her possessions. The Marchesa even looks like a cat.

18 "Those cats! It's always those cats . . ." the Marchesa said, from behind the shutter, with a shrill, somewhat nasal voice. "All my troubles come from the cats! Nobody knows what I go through! Prisoner night and day of those horrid beasts! And with all the refuse people throw over the walls, to spite me!"

"But my trout . . ."

"Your trout! What am I supposed to know about your trout!" The Marchesa's voice became almost a scream, as if she wanted to drown out the sizzle of oil in the pan, which came through the window along with the aroma of fried fish. "How can I make sense of anything, with all the stuff that rains into my house?"

"I understand, but did you take the trout or didn't you?"

"When I think of all the damage I suffer because of the cats! Ah, fine state of affairs! I'm not responsible for anything! I can't tell you what I've lost! Thanks to those cats, who've occupied house and garden for years! My life at the mercy of those animals! Go and find the owners! Make them pay damages! Damages? A whole life destroyed! A prisoner here, unable to move a step!"

Reading Skill
Draw Conclusions
Which details help you draw the conclusion that the Marchesa and the cats stand for similar ideas?

"Excuse me for asking: but who's forcing you to stay?"

From the crack in the blind there appeared sometimes a round, pale blue eye, sometimes a mouth with two protruding teeth; for a moment the whole face was visible, and to Marcovaldo it seemed, bewilderingly, the face of a cat.

"They keep me prisoner, they do, those cats! Oh, I'd be glad to leave! What wouldn't I give for a little apartment all my own, in a nice clean modern building! But I can't go out . . . They follow me, they block my path, they trip me up!" The voice became a whisper, as if to confide a secret. "They're afraid I'll sell the lot . . . They won't leave me . . . won't allow me . . . When the builders come to offer me a contract, you should see them, those cats! They get in the way, pull out their claws; they even chased a lawyer off! Once I had the contract right here, I was about to sign it, and they dived in through the window, knocked over the inkwell, tore up all the pages . . ." ⑳

"All my troubles come from the cats! Nobody knows what I go through!"

All of a sudden Marcovaldo remembered the time, the shipping department, the boss. He tiptoed off over the dried leaves, as the voice continued to come through the slats of the blind, enfolded in that cloud apparently from the oil of a frying pan. "They even scratched me . . . I still have the scar . . . All alone here at the mercy of these demons . . ."

Winter came. A blossoming of white flakes

Vocabulary Development

Vocabulary Knowledge Rating

When students have completed reading and discussing "The Garden of Stubborn Cats," have them take out their **Vocabulary Knowledge Rating Chart** for this selection. Read the words aloud once more and have students rate their knowledge of the words again in the After Reading column. Clarify any words that are still problematic. Have students write their own definition and example or sentence in the appropriate column. Then have students complete the Vocabulary Practice at the end of the selection. Encourage students to use the words in further discussion and written work about this selection. Remind them that they will be accountable for these words on the **Selection Test**, ***Unit 2 Resources***, pp. 199–201 or 202–204.

decked the branches and capitals and the cats' tails. Under the snow, the dry leaves dissolved into mush. The cats were rarely seen, the cat lovers even less; the packages of fish-bones were consigned only to cats who came to the door. Nobody, for quite a while, had seen anything of the Marchesa. No smoke came now from the chimneypot of the villa.

One snowy day, the garden was again full of cats, who had returned as if it were spring, and they were miauing as if on a moonlight night. The neighbors realized that something had happened: they went and knocked at the Marchesa's door. She didn't answer: she was dead.

22 In the spring, instead of the garden, there was a huge building site that a contractor had set up. The steam shovels dug down to great depths to make room for the foundations, cement poured into the iron armatures, a very high crane passed beams to the workmen who were making the scaffoldings. But how could they get on with their work? Cats walked along all the planks, they made bricks fall and upset buckets of mortar, they fought in the midst of the piles of sand. When you started to raise an armature, you found a cat perched on top of it, hissing fiercely. More treacherous

21 ▲ **Critical Viewing** Compare this image with the garden in the story. **[Compare and Contrast]**

Vocabulary
consigned (kən sīnd′) *v.* handed over; gave up or delivered

Reading Check 23
How does the Marchesa feel about the cats?

21 Critical Viewing

Answer: This garden might be considered overgrown, like the one in the story, but the garden in the story has weeds instead of flowers.

22 Literary Analysis
Symbolism

Read aloud the bracketed passage.

▶ **Monitor Progress Ask** students to define *symbolism.*
Answer: *Symbolism* is the use of an item to represent an idea or quality.

Then, **ask** students how these details confirm the association of the cats with forces resisting to the modern city.
Possible response: Once again, the cats are squeezed into the uninhabited, leftover spaces, yet they will not give up. They and the other animals make their homes in the construction site.

▶ **Reteach** If students have difficulty understanding what the cats represent, draw or create a visual image for them of the cats trapped within the confines of an ever expanding city.

1. **Ask** students to explain what is happening to the cats.
   Answer: They are losing their homes to development.
2. Then, **ask** students whether the cats are part of the human world or the natural world.
   Answer: The cats are part of the natural world.
3. Help students make the connection between the cats as representatives of the natural world and the threat posed by urban development.

23 Reading Check

Answer: The Marchesa considers the cats to be a great nuisance and wishes she could be free of them.

Concept Connector

Activating Prior Knowledge

Have students return to the discussion points raised before reading the story regarding the two lists. Ask students to review these discussion points. Do they feel the same about the two lists after reading the story as they did before reading it? Why? During this post-story discussion, tell students to cite examples from the story to support their ideas regarding each list.

Writing About the Big Question

Have students compare their responses to the sentence starters they completed before reading the story with their ideas afterwards. Ask them to explain whether their thoughts have changed.

Literary Analysis Graphic Organizer

Ask students to review the graphic organizers they completed to draw conclusions about symbolism while reading. Show them **Literary Analysis Graphic Organizer A** (*Graphic Organizer Transparencies,* p. 63) as an example. Then, have students share their graphic organizers.

ASSESS

Answers

Critical Thinking

1. Some students may find Marcovaldo the most sympathetic because he shows the most interest in and care toward the cats. Other students may find the cats the most sympathetic. The cats appear to be the focus of the author's sympathy.
2. (a) The "negative city" is the in-between spaces that the cats inhabit. (b) Nearly all of the open spaces have been taken over by development.
3. (a) Marcovaldo follows the tabby into the secret garden. (b) **Possible response:** The city is described as a vertical city where all voids tend to fill up and every block of cement is part of every other block.
4. (a) Some students will support progress; other students will advocate protecting open spaces. (b) and (c) Students should explain why they selected particular opinions.

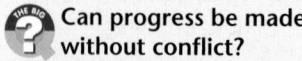

Can progress be made without conflict?

(a) **Possible response:** The development of the city has left the cats with no place to live. It has uprooted and displaced them, except for one small plot of undeveloped land that the Marchesa owns. The cats and the Marchesa struggle to keep their valuable piece of nature. (b) **Possible response:** It is very difficult to develop land and respect nature at the same time. However, with careful planning and making rules limiting the amount of development allowed, a balance between the two can be created.

22 pusses climbed onto the masons' backs as if to purr, and there was no getting rid of them. And the birds continued making their nests in all the trestles, the cab of the crane looked like an aviary[8] . . . And you couldn't dip up a bucket of water that wasn't full of frogs, croaking and hopping . . .

8. **aviary** (ā′ vē er′ ē) *n.* building or large cage for housing many birds.

Critical Thinking

1. **Respond:** In the story, whom did you find the most sympathetic—Marcovaldo, the Marchesa, or the cats? Why?
2. **(a)** What is the "negative city"? **(b) Infer:** How have changes in the city altered the way cats live?
3. **(a) Summarize:** How does Marcovaldo find the secret garden of the cats? **(b) Analyze:** List two details from Calvino's descriptions that suggest that such a garden is rare in the city.
4. **(a) Take a Position:** Should the garden of cats remain as it is, or should developers be free to build over it? Support your position. **(b) Discuss:** Share and discuss your opinions with a small group. **(c) Evaluate:** Choose the two best-supported opinions and share them with the class.

THE BIG ?

Can progress be made without conflict?
(a) How are nature and development at war with one another in this story? **(b)** Do you think the two can ever peacefully coexist? Explain.

Assessment Resources

Unit 2 Resources

L1 L2 EL **Selection Test A,** pp. 199–201. Administer Test A to less advanced readers and English learners.

L3 L4 **Selection Test B,** pp. 202–204. Administer Test B to on-level and more advanced students.

L3 L4 **Open-Book Test,** pp. 196–198. As an alternative, give the Open-Book Test.

All **Customizable Test Bank**

All **Self-tests**
Students may prepare for the **Selection Test** by taking the **Self-test** online.

PHLit Online! All assessment resources are available at **www.PHLitOnline.com.**

After You Read | The Garden of Stubborn Cats

Literary Analysis: Symbolism and Allegory

1. In the story, the cats might be interpreted as a force challenging order—they resist human attempts to define and control the city. **(a)** List two other forces in life—natural or human—that resist people's attempts to control space and life in a city. **(b)** Using your answer, explain the meaning of the cats as a **symbol.**

2. This story can be read as an **allegory.** Explain what the final conflict between cats and humans symbolizes.

Reading Skill: Draw Conclusions

3. (a) In a chart like the one shown, list two details showing the pattern in the Marchesa's relationship to other people in the city.

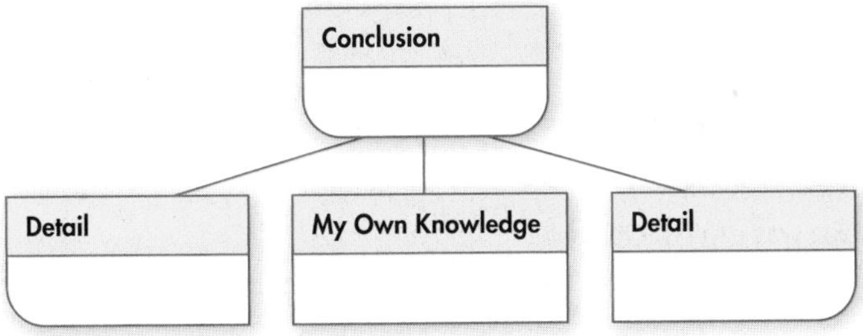

(b) Use your chart to **draw a conclusion** about what she may symbolize.

Vocabulary

Practice Words with similar meanings are called **synonyms**. For each set, choose the word that is *not* a synonym for the other two words. Explain.

1. schedule; itinerary; decision
2. intrigues; impulses; plots
3. dirty; nauseated; squalid
4. useless; futile; angry
5. indigence; poverty; laziness
6. delivered; agreed; consigned

Word Study Use the context of the sentences and what you know about the **Latin suffix *-id*** to explain your answer to each question.

1. If a deadline is *rigid*, can it be extended?
2. Should a mediator be *candid* in his or her judgments?

Word Study

The **Latin suffix *-id*** means "the body of" or "connected with."

Challenge Explain how the suffix *-id* contributes to the meanings of these words. Consult a dictionary if necessary.

valid
pallid
lucid

ASSESS/EXTEND

Answers

Literary Analysis

1. (a) **Possible response:** Nature itself limits how much people can control the life of a city. Environmentalists may also limit the degree to which a city may be controlled, as they seek to preserve the natural environment.
(b) **Possible response:** The cats may symbolize the opposition that many people have to the overdevelopment of cities.
2. **Possible response:** The final conflict between cats and humans may symbolize the death of nature and the natural world, as the cats run out of places in which they can thrive.

Reading Skill

3. **Possible response:**
(a) The Marchesa's relationship to the people of the city is somewhat complicated. Some see her as a hero because she refuses to sell her property to developers. Others view her as someone standing in the way of progress and modernization. For them, she represents a dying and obsolete way of life.
For other sample answers, see ***Graphic Organizer Transparencies,* Reading Skill Graphic Organizer** A, p. 65, and the **Additional Answers** section.
(b) **Possible response:** The Marchesa may represent the conflicted view that many have toward development and nature. She seems to want to preserve nature, but she also recognizes the advantages of modernization.

Vocabulary

Practice

1. *Decision; Schedule* and *itinerary* both suggest a plan. *Decision,* however, refers to making a choice among options.
2. *Impulses; Intrigues* and *plots* refer to secret plans. *Impulses* are sudden, spontaneous inclinations that are not planned.
3. *Nauseated; Squalid* describes extreme dirtiness often associated with poverty. *Nauseated* has to with sickness or an upset stomach.
4. *Angry; Useless* and *futile* both suggest ineffectiveness. *Angry* describes an emotional state.

Answers continued

5. *Laziness; Indigence* is an extreme form of *poverty,* whereas *laziness* has to do with a lack of effort or initiative.
6. *Agreed; Consigned* describes the way something is given or *delivered. Agreed* describes the outcome of a decision.

Word Study

Sample answers:

1. A rigid deadline cannot be adjusted because something rigid is firm.
2. A mediator should be candid because someone who is candid is honest and truthful.

Word Study: Challenge

The suffix *-id* suggests a connection with something. Something *valid* has a connection to the truth; Something *pallid* has a connection to paleness; Something *lucid* has a connection to clarity.

EXTEND/ASSESS

Answers

Grammar

1. Introduce the skill, using the instruction on the student page.
2. Discuss the examples on the page.

Think Aloud: Model the Skill

Model the skill of identifying active voice and passive voice. Say to students:

> To identify whether an author is using the passive or active voice, I ask myself, *Is the subject doing the action or receiving the action?*
>
> In the sentence "The boy threw the ball," the subject, *boy*, is doing the action: *threw the ball.* I know the sentence is active.
>
> In the sentence "The ball was thrown by the boy," the subject, *ball*, is receiving the action, so I know the sentence is passive.

WG Writing and Grammar, Grade 10

Students will find further instruction and practice with active and passive voice in Chapter 23, Section 2.

Practice A

1. active voice
2. passive voice
3. passive voice
4. active voice
5. passive voice

Challenge

Sample answer:

Active Sentence: He disregarded the decora of mere fashion.

Passive Rewrite: The decora of mere fashion was disregarded by the prince.

Practice B

1. The cat leads Marcovaldo through the alleys.
2. The Marchesa takes Marcovaldo's trout.
3. The cats eat the fish bones.
4. A building destroys and covers the garden.
5. The cats kept the Marchesa prisoner in her own apartment.

Challenge

Students' first paragraphs should employ the passive voice. The rewrite should use active voice. Students may say that the rewrites are more interesting to read.

Integrated Language Skills

The Masque of the Red Death • The Garden of Stubborn Cats

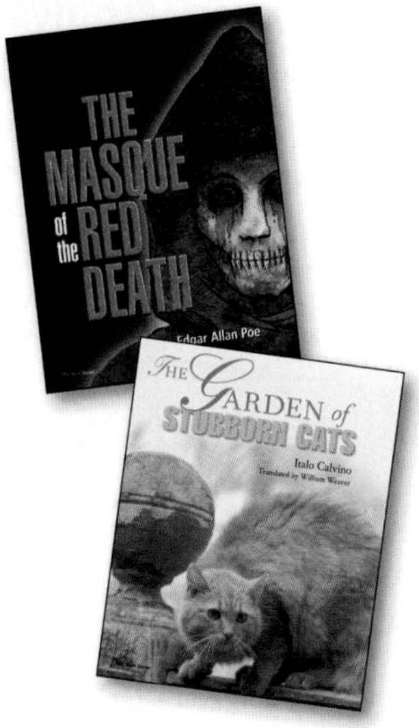

Grammar: Active and Passive Voice

A verb is in the **active voice** when the subject performs the action. A verb is in the **passive voice** when the action is performed on the subject.

Verbs in the passive voice consist of a form of *be* followed by the past participle of the main verb. Usually, active voice is stronger. However, passive voice is used when the writer wants to emphasize the recipient of the action. Passive voice is also used when the subject performing the action is unknown.

Active Voice: The student *answered* the question.
Passive Voice: The question *was answered.*

Active Voice: Jeremy ate the last cookie.
Passive Voice: The last cookie was eaten by Jeremy.

Practice A Identify each verb or verb phrase as active or passive.

1. The costumes *produced* gaudy and fantastic appearances.
2. Thousands of friends *were invited* to the ball.
3. The clock's heavy clang *was heard* throughout the rooms.
4. The prince *stood* in the blue room.
5. The intruder *was* not *stopped* as he walked through the rooms.

Challenge Choose four sentences from "The Masque of the Red Death," two in the active voice and two in the passive voice. Rewrite each sentence in the opposite voice.

Practice B Change the following sentences from passive voice to active voice. You may need to add words to indicate who performed the action.

1. Marcovaldo is led through alleys by the cat.
2. Marcovaldo's trout is taken by the Marchesa.
3. The fish bones are eaten by the cats.
4. The garden is destroyed and covered with a building.
5. The Marchesa was kept prisoner in her own apartment.

Challenge Write a brief paragraph in the passive voice describing a cat you have seen. Then, rewrite the paragraph in the active voice. Discuss the overall effect of each paragraph on a reader.

WG Writing and Grammar Connection: Chapter 22, Section 2

Extend the Lesson

Sentence Modeling

Choose the sentence given from the selection students have read:

> It was in this apartment, also, that there stood against the western wall a gigantic clock of ebony. ("The Masque of the Red Death")
>
> The fish saw the bait, and flung themselves on it. ("The Garden of Stubborn Cats")

Ask students what they notice about the sentence. ("The Masque of the Red Death": The main verbs "was" and "stood" are in the passive voice. The most important object in the sentence, the clock, is at the end of the sentence, which the descriptive words build up to. "The Garden of Stubborn Cats": The main verbs "saw" and "flung" are in the active voice. Two actions are fit into a short sentence, stressing and propelling the action.)

Have students imitate the sentence in a sentence on a topic of their own choosing, matching each grammatical and stylistic feature discussed. Collect the sentences, and share them with the class.

Writing

The authors of both of these selections use symbols to help convey important messages in the stories. Poe turns a simple clock into a symbol of doom. Calvino turns cats into a symbol of mischief and mystery. Write a brief **narrative** using another object or animal as a symbol. To show what the symbol stands for, follow these steps:

- In your narrative, develop an interesting, engaging plot.
- Describe your symbol using precise and vivid adjectives that suggest the qualities it represents. Provide information about its location or situation and its actions.
- Link your symbol to important events or give it a name that hints at what it symbolizes.

Writing Workshop: *Work in Progress*

Prewriting for Problem-and-Solution Essay Take the Problem/Solution Web from your portfolio and highlight one solution. Write additional details clarifying the solution. This additional evidence may include facts, logical reasoning, or expressions of commonly accepted beliefs. Save this Solution Support List in your portfolio.

Use this prewriting activity to prepare for the **Writing Workshop** on page 420.

Research and Technology

Conduct library and Internet research to find out more about a topic from the selections that interests you. You might learn more about how Poe influenced mysteries and detective fiction. You might study the historic architecture of a European city, focusing on one or two famous structures. Then, present your findings to classmates in a **research summary.** Use the following suggestions when you deliver your summary:

- Be sure to use words suited to your audience's knowledge level. Explain **technical terms** such as *whodunit* and *ratiocination* or *balustrade* and *gargoyle.*
- **Anticipate and address** listener's potential **misunderstandings and expectations.** Add information to help make your ideas easy to understand.
- At the end of your presentation, **ask for questions and comments** from the class.

After delivering your summary, revise it based on the feedback from the class.

PHLit Online!
www.PHLitOnline.com
- Interactive graphic organizers
- Grammar tutorial
- Interactive journals

EXTEND/ASSESS

Writing

1. Review the assignment, using the instruction on the student page.
2. To guide students in writing a narrative, give them the **Support for Writing**, p. 194 in ***Unit 2 Resources.***
3. To evaluate students' narratives, use the Narrative rubrics, pp. 226–227 in ***Professional Development Guidebook.***

Six Traits Focus

✔	Ideas	✔	Word Choice
	Organization	✔	Sentence Fluency
✔	Voice		Conventions

Writing and Grammar, Grade 10

Students will find additional instruction on narrative writing in Chapter 5.

Writing Workshop
Work in Progress

Have students save their completed Solution Support List in their portfolios. They will use them later as they complete the Writing Workshop assignment (see pp. 328–333).

Research and Technology

1. Review the assignment, using the instruction on the student page.
2. Have students complete the **Support for Extend Your Learning** page (*Unit 2 Resources,* p. 195).

Teaching Resources

All *Unit 2 Resources*
L3 L4 **Integrated Language Skills: Grammar,** p. 193
L3 L4 **Support for Writing,** p. 194
L3 L4 **Support for Extend Your Learning,** p. 195
L4 **Enrichment,** pp. 174 and 192

All **Enriched Online Student Edition**
Available under After You Read for this selection:
All **Interactive Grammar Tutorial**
L3 L4 **Internet Research Activity**

Professional Development Guidebook
Rubrics for Narratives, pp. 226–227

PHLit Online! All print and digital resources are available at **www.PHLitOnline.com.** Online resources accessible by students are noted on the student page.

MONITORING PROGRESS

Using the Test Practice

In this two-page Test Practice, students apply the reading skill for the first half of Unit 2 to a passage of fiction and a passage of nonfiction.

Review this skill, drawing conclusions, and then administer the test. For more guidance, consult the ***Classroom Strategies and Teaching Routines*** card, ***Administering Timed Tests.***

ASSESS

Answers

Answers With Explanations

1. A—The second sentence states that Cassandra has experienced the upheaval of frequent moves. *Incorrect answers:* B—It doesn't say whether frequent changes have made her life exciting or not. C—The passage suggests the opposite, that her life has been unsettled. D—The passage suggests that frequent change has made her life difficult, not happy.
2. C—Tiger, who has been a constant source of love in Cassandra's life, represents stability. *Incorrect answers:* A—Tiger's constant presence suggests loyalty, but not honesty or dishonesty. B—Tiger may have required some level of responsibility, but this is not something Cassandra focused on. D—Tiger is like many cats, loving and curious, but not mysterious.
3. B—The time she spends looking and then longing for Tiger show her feelings of deep loss. *Incorrect answers:* A—The opposite seems true; she gets consolation and support from her mother. C—The opposite seems true; her last thought is hope that Tiger will return. D—She thinks about Tiger returning, not about getting a new cat.
4. D—Tiger was always there, offering affection during years of upheaval. *Incorrect answers:* A—Though this statement is true, the story's focus is not on responsibility. B—The story's focus is on loss of a pet, rather than on true friends. C—Tiger was lost after many years of providing comfort and stability.

Test Practice: Reading

Draw Conclusions

Fiction Selection

Directions: *Read the selection. Then, answer the questions.*

Tiger had been Cassandra's cat since Cassandra was eight years old. Cassandra's father was in the army, and over the years her family moved from state to state, leaving behind friends, classmates, and favorite places. Then, Cassandra's father was sent overseas. Now, it was just Cassandra, her mom, and—until last weekend—Tiger. She and her mom had gone camping and had brought Tiger with them. He had enjoyed the trip, exploring the woods around the campground and snuggling up by Cassandra at night. As they packed to leave, they realized Tiger was gone. Cassandra and her mother spent hours searching for Tiger. Finally, they had to give up. Now at home, Cassandra lay on her bed, her mother sitting beside her. "You know, Sweetie," she said, "cats have amazing powers. We may yet see Tiger again." And somehow, Cassandra knew Tiger—and her dad—would come home someday.

1. Based on the passage, what can you conclude about Cassandra's life so far?

A. It has been a life of upheaval and change.
B. It has been exciting.
C. It has been a life of stability and security.
D. It has been happy.

2. What might Tiger symbolize to Cassandra?

A. honesty and loyalty
B. responsibility
C. love and stability
D. mystery

3. Based on details in this passage, what conclusion can you draw about how Cassandra probably feels about losing Tiger?

A. She blames her mother for losing Tiger.
B. She feels she has lost something important.
C. She is glad to be relieved of the responsibility.
D. She is excited about getting a new cat.

4. Which of the following is the *best* statement of this passage's theme?

A. Pets are a great responsibility that most teenagers are not ready to handle.
B. Pets can never replace a true friend.
C. Cats are unpredictable and easily lost.
D. Pets can be a source of comfort and stability in life.

Writing for Assessment

Consider the details in this passage. What conclusion can you draw about how Cassandra's mother feels about Tiger? Write a paragraph to explain your conclusion.

Writing for Assessment

Student responses should reflect an understanding that the mother's words and actions reflect her feelings about the cat, as well as her concern for Cassandra.

Strategies for Test Taking

Point out that many of the questions in this lesson start with the phrase "Based on the passage." In other words, students should be able to point out one or more sentences from the passage to support an answer choice.

Nonfiction Selection

Directions: *Read the selection. Then, answer the questions.*

The ancestors of the domestic cat appeared in Egypt nearly 3,500 years ago. Ancient Egyptians considered the cat sacred and worshipped a cat-headed goddess called Bast. Egyptians often mummified cats, and even mummified mice, presumably as a source of food for the cats.

Cats first appeared in the art and literature of other cultures several thousand years ago: in Greece 2,600 years ago, in China 2,500 years ago, and in India 2,100 years ago. The cat appears in Arabia, Japan, and Britain by A.D. 900.

The cat is noted for its independence, frequent aloofness, and cleanliness, as well as its uncanny ability to find its way home over long distances. Over the centuries, it has been associated with superstitions. Black cats in particular have been associated with supernatural powers. Whatever the reason is, cats continue to fascinate many people. There are 37.7 million cat-owning households in the United States today.

1. Based on this passage, what can you conclude about humans' attitudes toward cats?

A. All humans generally revere cats.
B. Humans throughout the world have long been fascinated with cats.
C. Humans generally dislike cats.
D. Humans around the world find cats useful for removing pests from homes.

2. What can you conclude about the Egyptians' attitude toward cats?

A. Egyptians believed cats live on in the afterworld just as they believed humans do.
B. Egyptians believed that cats should be treated just like humans.
C. Egyptians grieved over the death of a cat.
D. Egyptians were afraid of cats.

3. Based on the details in this passage about cats, what could you reasonably conclude?

A. Most cats are very clingy pets and cannot be left alone.
B. The average cat has a good sense of direction.
C. Few people keep cats as pets.
D. Cats are not loyal to humans.

4. Based on details in the passage, the cat would make a good symbol for—

A. affection.
B. loyalty.
C. the mysterious.
D. justice.

Writing for Assessment

Connecting Across Texts
Based on details from these two passages, what can you conclude about the chances of Cassandra recovering Tiger? Explain your answer in a paragraph.

PHLit Online!
www.PHLitOnline.com
- Online practice
- Instant feedback

Differentiated Instruction for Universal Access

Strategy for Special Needs Students

Show students how to find passage information to support an answer choice or eliminate incorrect choices, using item 3 on page 400 as an example. Ask a volunteer to identify the topic of the question. (Cassandra's loss of her cat.) Guide them to locate and read the part of the text that describes the loss of Tiger. Model using the text as the basis for asking questions which eliminate wrong choices and lead to the correct answer. A—How does Cassandra behave with her mother in this part of the reading? (comfortable and cared for, not angry) B—How is Cassandra feeling in this part of the reading? (sad, worried, and concerned) Why? (she has lost her dear cat) C—Does Cassandra seem glad, or relieved, about anything in this part of the reading? (no; her only comfort is the idea of getting Tiger back) D—Does the story say anything about a new cat after Tiger was lost? (no; it only mentions her feelings about losing Tiger)

ASSESS

Answers

Answers With Explanations

1. B—The selection gives examples from many countries of this fascination. *Incorrect answers:* A—The selection only mentions Egyptians, as actually worshiping cats. C—The selection illustrates the opposite. D—Cats can be useful, but the selection doesn't give details about this topic.
2. A—The third sentence mentions mummified cats and mice for their food in the afterlife which shows a respect for cats. *Incorrect answers:* B—The passage does not mention a belief in equal treatment. C—The passage isn't clear about whether their cats were pets whose loss families might have grieved. D—The passage suggests the opposite.
3. B—The mention of the cats' "uncanny ability to find its way home" supports this conclusion. *Incorrect answers:* A—The passage suggests the opposite, points out cats' "independence and frequent aloofness." C—The passage indicates the opposite, mentioning "37.7 million cat-owning households" in this country. D—Cats' ability to find their way home suggests loyalty.
4. C—Egyptian worship, superstition, and supernatural powers suggest the mysterious. *Incorrect answers:* A—The passage mentions independence and aloofness, not affection. B—Only one detail—ability to find its way home—suggests loyalty. D—No details link cats with justice here.

Writing for Assessment

Student responses should focus on information in the nonfiction selection that elucidates Tiger's disappearance and gives hope for his return, specifically a cat's ability to find its way home over long distances. Their responses should also recognize Tiger's attachment to Cassandra.

PHLit Online!
Students may take the test in interactive format with instant feedback online at **www.PHLitOnline.com**.

Meeting Your Standards

Students will

1. paraphrase.
2. read and analyze a newspaper editorial and a primary source.

Log on at ***www.PHLitOnline.com*** *as a teacher for a detailed lesson plan for Informational Texts.*

Reading Skill

1. Introduce the skill, using the instruction on the student page.
2. Tell students that they will paraphrase to connect ideas as they read.

Think Aloud: Model the Skill

Model the skill of paraphrasing to connect ideas, using the following "think aloud." Say to students:

> Paraphrasing can help me better understand a tricky idea. Say I read a paragraph about black holes that I'm not sure I understand. If I'm able to restate it in my own words, then I know I understood it pretty well. My paraphrase of the paragraph will also include the main idea.

THE BIG ? Can progress be made without conflict?

As students read, have them look for instances where opposing sides work toward a resolution.

Multidraft Reading

Have students follow a multidraft reading protocol after they scan the text:

- **First reading**—Have students read for general understanding.
- **Second reading**—Have students paraphrase the ideas and information they read.
- **Third reading**—Have students look for ways in which progress is achieved in prolonged conflicts.

Informational Texts

Real-Life Reading

Newspaper Editorial
Editorial on the Anniversary of the Fall of the Berlin Wall

Primary Source
Voices from the Wall

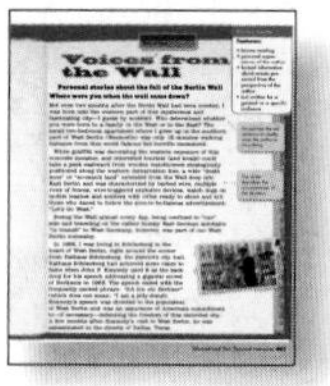

Reading Skills: Paraphrase to Connect Ideas

When you **paraphrase,** you use your own words to restate ideas presented in a text. Paraphrasing helps you to clarify meaning in a text so that you can determine the main idea and identify relevant details. By paraphrasing ideas in a text, you can more easily **connect** them to ideas in another text and **synthesize** content from the two sources. Use the following chart to guide your reading.

Guidelines for Paraphrasing and Connecting Ideas

- Paraphrase to identify the main ideas in source one.
- Look for similar or related ideas in source two.
- Synthesize the content from the sources by drawing a conclusion about the topic, based on your analysis of the main ideas.

THE BIG ? Can progress be made without conflict?

The editorial and the primary source both reflect on progress made between the conflicting countries and allies of Eastern and Western Europe during the Cold War. As you read, take note of the improvements.

Differentiated Instruction for Universal Access

Reading Support

Give students reading support with the appropriate version of the ***Reader's Notebooks***:

L2 L3 *Reader's Notebook*

L1 *Reader's Notebook: Adapted Version*

EL *Reader's Notebook: English Learner's Version*

PHLit Online! All student resources are available online at **www.PHLitOnline.com.**

Newspaper Editorial

Features:

- leisure reading
- author's opinion about a current or a historical event
- opinion, background information, and supporting arguments
- text written for a general or a specific audience

The New York Times

Editorial, November 10, 1999

The editorial begins with a statement of a main idea it will support: Gorbachev should be celebrated for his role in the fall of communism.

The Berlin Wall was bound to fall eventually. But that it came down as bloodlessly as it did 10 years ago this week is largely a tribute to one leader. Today Mikhail Gorbachev is a political pariah in Russia and increasingly forgotten in the West. But history will remember him generously for his crucial role in ending the cold war and pulling back the Iron Curtain that Stalin drew across Europe in 1945.[1]

Liquidating the Soviet empire was not what Mr. Gorbachev had in mind when he came to power in 1985. He was shrewd enough to recognize that radical changes were urgently needed to stave off economic and political bankruptcy in Russia and its European satellites.[2] [. . .]

Once Mr. Gorbachev lifted the lid with the openness of glasnost and the attempted economic restructuring of perestroika,[3] change took on a dynamic of its own. Similar energies were unleashed in the once-captive nations of Eastern Europe as it became clear that he would not send Soviet tanks to bail out the unpopular client regimes that had held sway there since World War II.

As political pressures began to build in the late 1980s, Mr. Gorbachev was left with two options. He could hurtle ahead toward full political and economic freedom. Or he could reverse course and crack down, as so many previous Soviet leaders had done. He chose to do neither. He was too much a creature of his Soviet Communist upbringing to subject his own power to the test of electoral democracy. But he was too enlightened to unleash the kind of thorough repression that might have preserved the Soviet empire for a few more years.

1. **Iron Curtain . . . 1945** At the end of the Second World War, in 1945, Europe was split between western countries, allied with the United States, and eastern countries, dominated by its rival, the Soviet Union, then led by Josef Stalin. West and East were said to be divided by an "iron curtain."
2. **European satellites** Eastern European countries dominated by the Soviet Union.
3. **glasnost** (glaz´ nōst) . . . **perestroika** (per´ ə stroi´ kə) policies of Gorbachev's designed to reform the Soviet Union. Glasnost involved lifting restrictions on free speech; perestroika referred to attempts to reform the government and economy.

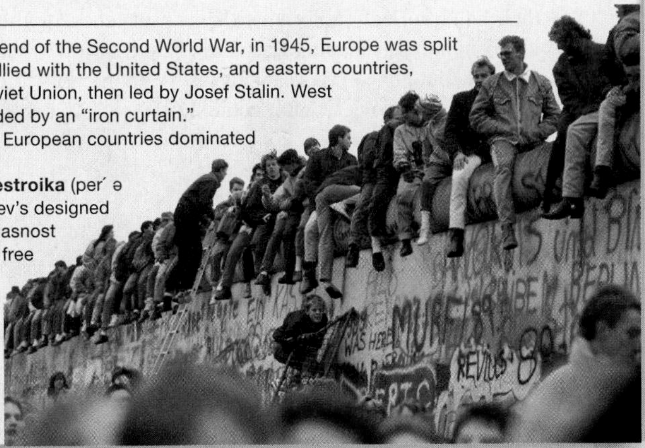

Although *glasnost* and *perestroika* are footnoted in the text, paraphrasing these definitions will help you understand them better.

TEACH

About Newspaper Editorials

1. Have students read about Newspaper Editorials in the box on the student page. **Ask:** What does *leisure reading* mean?
   Possible response: Reading someone does for enjoyment.
2. Explain to students that editorials are similar to other persuasive writings, but that they appear in newspapers, magazines, and on television as part of newscasts. Point out that it is important to consider the logic behind the arguments used in editorials, because editorials are meant to be persuasive and therefore should not be blindly accepted.
3. Read an editorial from the school paper or a local area paper. Choose a topic with which students can relate. **Ask** volunteers to identify the arguments that are used and to offer counter-arguments.

Paraphrase to Connect Ideas

1. Inform students that paraphrasing can help them better understand a text when writing or doing research.
2. Explain that they should examine the text before reading. **Ask:** How does paraphrasing help you understand a main idea?
   Possible response: Paraphrasing allows me to simplify a main idea by restating the information in my own words.
3. Read this sentence aloud:
   Once it was thought that global warming would work to increase crop yields, but today scientists are finding evidence to prove the opposite effect is taking place.
   Ask a volunteer to paraphrase the sentence.
   Possible response: Scientists now believe that global warming is hurting crop growth.
4. Explain that both sentences have the same information, only the paraphrased one is simpler.

Differentiated Instruction for Universal Access

Strategy for Special Needs Students

Point out to students that some people have difficulty reading newspapers because the columns and lines are so close together. Suggest that they try using strips of paper to cover columns they are not reading to make it easier to focus on the column they are reading.

Enrichment for Gifted/Talented Students

Have students work in groups to research and learn more about people's individual reactions to the fall of the Berlin Wall. Encourage students to conduct interviews, search library archives, or use Internet resources to locate individual reactions to this historical event. Instruct them to create a visual project, such as a book, collage, or video. Invite students to present their projects to the class.

Paraphrase to Connect Ideas

1. Explain that sometimes you have to read parts of a text over and over again before understanding it. Remind students that paraphrasing can help them clarify a difficult text by rewriting it in their own words.
2. Tell students that sometimes you need to look up the definition of a word in order to understand an idea. Direct students' attention to the first paragraph on this page. Read it aloud. **Ask:** How can you paraphrase this idea?
   Possible response: First, I need to look up the word *accelerate.* Then, I will simplify the idea in the text and rewrite it in my own words like this: *Others quickly carried out the changes Mr. Gorbachev began and the familiar empire began to crumble.*
3. Remind students to reread their work after they paraphrase to make sure they haven't left out any important details and to confirm that their information is accurate.

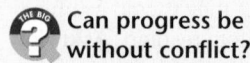

ASSESS/EXTEND

Answers

Can progress be made without conflict?

Possible response: Two examples of progress instituted by Mr. Gorbachev are: 1) restrictions on free speech were lifted; 2) East and West Germany were open to each other.

Others stepped in to accelerate the transformations Mr. Gorbachev had begun, and in 1989 fixtures of the Soviet empire began to crumble. . . .

Through it all, Mr. Gorbachev and his like-minded foreign minister, Eduard Shevardnadze, stayed their hand, reflecting not only their idealism about reshaping East-West relations but also a pragmatic calculation that the Soviet Union could no longer afford an empire. For permitting its dissolution, Mr. Gorbachev paid a high price. Within two years he had been pushed from power in Moscow. . . .

History has passed Mr. Gorbachev by. But this week, especially, he deserves to be remembered for what he did and, perhaps more important, what he refused to do. With a wisdom and decency that is sadly rare in international power politics, he chose not to defend a dying system with a final, futile spasm of murderous force.

The writer concludes the editorial with a statement that reinforces the main idea introduced in the first paragraph.

Can progress be made without conflict?
What are two examples of progress instituted by Mr. Gorbachev in the Soviet Union that helped soften the East-West conflict discussed in this editorial?

Vocabulary Development

Vocabulary from Social Studies

Point out that editorials often use vocabulary that is specific to one particular situation, in this case the politics surrounding the fall of the Berlin Wall. Guide students to understand the meaning of the following words that are used in *The New York Times* editorial:

stave off: to fend off

regimes: current social systems or patterns

Communist: one who believes in the elimination of private property; one who believes that goods are owned communally and available to all as needed

electoral: consisting of electors

futile: serving no useful purpose

PHLit Online! **Vocabulary Central**, featuring tools, activities, and songs for studying vocabulary, is available online at **www.PHLitOnline.com**.

Voices from the Wall

Personal stories about the fall of the Berlin Wall

Where were you when the wall came down?

Not even two months after the Berlin Wall had been erected, I was born into the western part of this mysterious and fascinating city—I guess by accident. Who determined whether you were born to a family in the West or in the East? The small two-bedroom apartment where I grew up in the southern part of West Berlin (Neukoelln) was only 15 minutes walking distance from this world famous but horrific monument.

While graffiti was decorating the western exposure of this concrete monster, and interested tourists (and locals) could take a peek eastward from wooden watchtowers strategically positioned along the western demarcation line, a wide "death zone" or "no-man's land" extended from the Wall deep into East Berlin and was characterized by barbed wire, multiple rows of fences, wire-triggered explosive devices, watch dogs on mobile leashes and soldiers with rifles ready to shoot and kill those who dared to follow the soon-to-be-famous advertisement: "Let's Go West."

Seeing the Wall almost every day, being confined to "our" side and traveling on the rather bumpy East German autobahn "in transit" to West Germany, however, was part of our West Berlin normalcy.

In 1989, I was living in Schöneberg in the heart of West Berlin, right around the corner from Rathaus Schöneberg, the district's city hall. Rathaus Schöneberg had achieved some claim to fame when John F. Kennedy used it as the backdrop for his speech addressing a gigantic crowd of Berliners in 1963. The speech ended with the frequently quoted phrase: *"Ich bin ein Berliner"* (which does not mean: "I am a jelly-donut"). Kennedy's speech was directed to the population of West Berlin and was an assurance of America's commitment to—if necessary—defending the freedom of this encircled city. A few months after Kennedy's visit to West Berlin, he was assassinated in the streets of Dallas, Texas.

Primary Source

Features:

- leisure reading
- personal experiences of the author
- factual information about events presented from the perspective of the author
- text written for a general or a specific audience

Paraphrasing the question the author poses will help clarify his main idea.

Paraphrasing this paragraph will ensure that you understand the situation described.

About Primary Sources

1. Direct students' attention to the box about Primary Sources. Explain that a primary source is a record of personal events experienced by an author and told in the first-person point of view.
2. **Ask** students to offer instances in which they would use primary sources.
   Possible response: Students may use primary sources when they are researching a specific subject or writing a report.
3. **Ask** students to discuss the benefits of using primary sources.
   Possible response: Primary sources offer readers an intimate perspective of an occurrence. An author may want to relay factual information about an event or personally reflect on an event that took place.

Paraphrase to Connect Ideas

1. Review the strategies for paraphrasing and connecting ideas on page 402.
2. Have students scan the primary source for main ideas. **Ask** students to restate one main idea in their own words.
   Possible response: East and West Germany were divided by a huge, concrete wall called the Berlin Wall.
3. Read the opening paragraph aloud. Then, encourage students to think about the question posed by the author. **Ask** students to discuss the idea behind the question.
   Possible response: The author is commenting on the existence of the Berlin Wall and questioning the need for it.

Differentiated Instruction for Universal Access

Culturally Responsive Instruction

Culture Focus Students may lack the background knowledge or context-building experiences necessary to fully comprehend the selection. Before students read, build background knowledge about the Berlin Wall. Provide information on the two main reasons for building the wall in 1961. (1) Economics: Many professionals educated in the East (where education was free) moved to the West to work because they were able to make more money there. (2) Politics: The western side interfered with the eastern side by using Berlin as a spy center.

To help students visually clarify the information, display a map and point out the areas of East and West Germany. You might also provide images of the Wall, both as it stood and while it was being torn down.

Paraphrase to Connect Ideas

1. After students have finished reading the selection, ask them to look back at the third paragraph on this page. Have a volunteer read it aloud.
2. **Ask** them to restate the main idea of this paragraph in their own words.
   Possible response: The author was shocked. He knew this was a politically historic moment.
3. Remind students that connecting ideas between sources allows them to come to a conclusion about a topic. **Ask:** What was the significance of the fall of the Berlin Wall?
   Possible response: Not only did the fall of the Berlin Wall signify the end of the Cold War, it also allowed a country to reunite.

ASSESS/EXTEND

Answers

Can progress be made without conflict?

(a) **Possible response:** The author witnessed the separation of Germany by the Berlin Wall.
(b) **Possible response:** The author witnessed East and West Berliners traveling freely and interacting with one another.

Reflecting on the Reading Skill

After students have finished reading the selections, **ask** them why paraphrasing to connect ideas between numerous sources might be useful to them when they research a historical event.
Possible response: Paraphrasing makes me break down a complex idea and put it into smaller, simpler parts. When I find similar ideas in another source, it allows me to grasp the idea better so I can write with a more knowledgeable understanding of the concept.

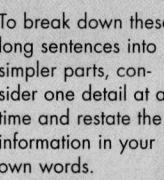

On November 9, 1989 late in the evening, I was watching the news on television in my cozy Schöneberg apartment. Gunter Schabowski, representative of the still-in-power East German government, was reading a declaration that surprisingly proclaimed East German citizens could—from now on—easily obtain travel permits to the West. It was apparently no longer required to provide unequivocal proof of a family emergency or similar hardship that would sometimes be accepted by East German authorities as justification for a "blitz-trip" to the golden West. Even in cases when a travel permit was granted, which was a rare event, the East German traveler's family had to stay behind to ensure his timely return to his beloved socialist fatherland. [. . .]

To break down these long sentences into simpler parts, consider one detail at a time and restate the information in your own words.

West Berliners lived in West Berlin and East Berliners were condemned to staying in East Berlin—that's the way it is. During the 28 years of my life that I had lived in this city, East Berliners traveling freely to West Berlin would be like running into polar bears in the Sahara desert. Thus, I did not pay too much attention to Schabowski's announcement and went to bed because I had to get up early the next day to go to work.

When I left my house the next morning I was stunned. Thousands of East German visitors had "arrived" and were hustling through the western part of the city. Visitors were waiting in long lines on sidewalks to receive their "Begrüssungsgeld" (welcome money), issued by the West German federal government through private banks. This was an unbelievable sight and the beginning of the probably most impressive political experience of my lifetime. The continuation of the story is well known.

I spent many days and nights in wintry Berlin witnessing pieces of the Wall being dismantled by East German soldiers and meeting people from the East. It was also the beginning of a period during which the West Berliners began to explore the other side of the iron curtain. Despite the physical proximity of East Berlin, this part of our city was largely unknown to us.

Four years after the fall of the Berlin Wall, in 1993, I moved to Seattle in the United States for job-related reasons. My wife is American. I am still captured by the events in November 1989 and will always remember them as a once-in-a-lifetime experience. [. . .]

Ich bin ein Berliner! And I will always be.

From Marco Mielcare
Seattle, Washington

Can progress be made without conflict?
(a) What conflicts did the author witness as a result of the Berlin Wall? **(b)** What progress did the author witness after the Berlin Wall came down?

Think Aloud

Vocabulary: Using Context

Direct students' attention to the word *justification* in the first paragraph on this page. Use the following "think aloud" to model how to use context to infer the meaning of an unknown word. Say to students:

> In the sentence above, the word *justification* is being used to help explain the difficulties of traveling from East Germany to West Germany prior to 1989. Some people were allowed to travel to the West, but the words *unequivocal proof*, *emergency*, and *hardship* are clues that tell me that people had to have a solid reason for their travel, so *justification* refers to convincing the authorities of this reason. The next sentence states that this was a "rare event," so I think *justification* refers to validating a reason, in this case for travel.

Test Practice: Informational Texts

Comparing Informational Texts

(a) Paraphrase the first paragraphs of both the newspaper editorial and the primary source. **(b)** State the **main idea** of each paraphrase. **(c)** In what ways does the main idea in the editorial paraphrase **connect** with the main idea of the primary source paraphrase? Explain your answer.

Timed Writing

Write a Response to Literature

Format
The prompt directs you to write a response to literature. Therefore, you must discuss your thoughts about a text you have read.

Each of these texts presents a different perspective on the same historical event, the fall of the Berlin Wall in 1989. Choose one of the texts and write a response to literature in which you describe what you found compelling about the text. Explain what effect the author's writing had on you, citing and paraphrasing sections of text to support your response. (40 minutes)

Academic Vocabulary
When you *cite* a section or passage from a text, you quote it as support for the argument or ideas you are presenting.

5-Minute Planner

Complete these steps before you begin to write:

1. Read the prompt carefully and completely. Look for key words that will help you understand the assignment.
2. Review the editorial and primary source. Think about the authors' perspectives and opinions. Consider your response to the texts when you first read them. Decide which article is more compelling. **TIP** Paraphrase any sections of text that are unclear to gain a better understanding of the information and locate main ideas.
3. Skim the text you have chosen and take notes about details and information you will include as support in your response.
4. Use your notes to draft an outline. Then use your outline and notes to draft your response.

Extend the Lesson

Connecting to the Students' World
To give students further practice with the editorial persuasive form, have students choose a community issue, such as an improved playground for younger children or a much-needed park clean-up. Have them form opinions about the issues they choose and then write letters to the editor of a local paper expressing their pro or con arguments. Encourage students to use logical assumptions and to support their arguments.

ASSESS/EXTEND

Answers

Comparing Informational Texts

(a) Possible response: Newspaper editorial: Despite Mikhail Gorbachev's fading popularity, he will be remembered for his significant role in ending the cold war and eliminating the Berlin Wall. Primary source: The author describes his experience of being born into the divided city of Berlin and questions the segregation caused by the city's infamous wall.
(b) Possible response: Newspaper editorial: Mikhail Gorbachev is acclaimed for his role in the fall of the Berlin Wall. Primary source: The Berlin Wall created unnecessary segregation. **(c) Possible response:** Mikhail Gorbachev's acclaim for his role in the fall of the Berlin Wall, discussed in the newspaper editorial, connects to the segregation that was caused by the Berlin Wall, which was discussed in the primary source. The Berlin Wall caused unfair separation of the city's citizens; therefore, Mikhail Gorbachev is celebrated for helping to eliminate the wall.

Timed Writing

1. Before students complete the activity, guide them in identifying and analyzing key words and phrases in the prompt, highlighted on the student page.
2. Work with students to draw up guidelines for their responses based on key words in the prompt:
   - Focus The response should clearly analyze the point of view, or perspective, of the author.
   - Organization The response should examine the author's perspective and then analyze the information that he chose to include.
   - Elaboration The response should provide sufficient details to support the author's perspective.
   - Style The audience is not specified, so a formal style is appropriate.
3. Have students use the 5-Minute Planner to structure their time.
4. Allow students 40 minutes to complete the assignment. Evaluate their work using the guidelines they have developed.

PRETEACH

Meeting Your Standards

Students will

1. analyze and respond to tone in fiction and nonfiction.
2. compare the authors' tone in fiction and nonfiction.
3. write a comparison of the authors' tone.

*Log on at **www.PHLitOnline.com** for a detailed lesson plan for Comparing Literary Works.*

❶ Comparing Tone

1. Introduce the skill to students, using the instruction on the student page.
2. Discuss the bulleted items.
3. Give students a copy of **Comparing Tone Graphic Organizer B** (***Graphic Organizer Transparencies,*** p. 69). Tell them they will fill it in to compare points of view as they read.

Think Aloud: Model the Skill

Model a way of understanding tone. Say to students:

When I read, I keep in mind that an author, like a reader, has personal attitudes toward subjects, and that these attitudes are often illustrated in the tone of his or her writing. After I read a text, the way I feel about the piece often reflects the tone of the author's writing.

A selection's tone can range from being objective, as in a news story, to being emotional and opinionated, as in a political speech. I try to keep in mind while comparing works, that although the content may be similar in each work, the tone can have can be very different.

Vocabulary

1. Have students say each word aloud.
2. Then, use the word in a sentence that defines the word. Repeat the sentence, now with the word missing, and have the class "fill in the blank" chorally.

For more guidance, see the ***Classroom Strategies and Teaching Routines*** card, **Introducing Selection Vocabulary.**

Comparing Literary Works

The Censors • The Leader in the Mirror

Comparing Tone in Fiction and Nonfiction

The **tone** of a work is the writer's attitude toward his or her subject and audience. A writer may treat a subject seriously or playfully, with anger or sadness, or in an objective tone that shows no emotion.

Tone is closely related to **voice** and **persona**—the personality that a writer shows to readers. Tone may be conveyed by the details the writer chooses to include. It can also be developed in the **diction,** or word choice, that the writer uses. Finally, tone may be revealed in direct statements of the writers feelings.

In these two selections, "The Censors" and "The Leader in the Mirror," Luisa Valenzuela and Pat Mora look at perceptions and values created by society. However, each writer takes a different tone. Use a chart like the one shown to note elements in each essay that create its distinctive tone.

Element of Tone
Striking Detail:
Diction:
Direct Statements:

→

Tone
Attitude Toward Subject:
Attitude Toward Reader:

Vocabulary

- **irreproachable** (ir′ i prō′ chə bəl) *adj.* above criticism (p. 411) ***His irreproachable record made him the ideal candidate.*** *reproach v.*
- **ulterior** (ul tir′ ē ər) *adj.* further; beyond what is openly stated or implied (p. 411) ***She had an ulterior motive for being extra nice to you.*** *ulteriorly adv.*
- **staidness** (stād′ nəs) *n.* state of being settled; calm (p. 412) ***His staidness is a contrast to his wild youth.*** *staid adj.*
- **aspirations** (as′ pə rā′ shənz) *n.* strong ambitions (p. 415) ***I have aspirations to run a marathon.*** *aspire v. aspiring v. aspirer n.*
- **catalyst** (kat′ ə list′) *n.* person or thing that triggers an event or action (p. 416) ***Slipping on the walk was the catalyst for shoveling the snow.*** *catalytic adj.*
- **inheritance** (in her′ i təns) *n.* gift handed down to a later generation (p. 417) ***The pin was her inheritance from her aunt.***

PHLit Online! www.PHLitOnline.com

- Vocabulary flashcards
- Interactive journals
- More about the authors
- Selection audio
- Interactive graphic organizers

Vocabulary Development

Vocabulary Knowledge Rating

Create a **Vocabulary Knowledge Rating Chart** (***Professional Development Guidebook,*** p. 33) for this selection. Include the selection vocabulary and the Big Question words that appear in the Writing About the Big Question sentence starter on the next page. (The Big Question vocabulary is introduced on pp. 222–223.)

Give students a copy of the chart. Read the words aloud, and have students mark their rating in the Before Reading column. Urge them to be alert to these words as they read and discuss the selection. Tally how many students think they know a word to gauge how much instruction to provide. As students read and discuss the selection, point out the words and their context.

PHLit Online! **Vocabulary Central,** featuring tools, activities, and songs for studying vocabulary, is available at **www.PHLitOnline.com.**

Can progress be made without *conflict?*

Writing About the Big Question

In these selections, authors present the idea that facing **adversity** in everyday life can change a person. Consider how dealing with challenges could help someone grow. Use these sentence starters to develop your ideas about the Big Question.

Because I have **struggled** with________, I know ________.

If someone asked me for advice on handling **conflict**, I would say ____.

Meet the Authors

Luisa Valenzuela (b. 1938)

Author of "The Censors"

Born in Buenos Aires, the capital of Argentina, Luisa Valenzuela has lived in places ranging from bustling New York City to Tepoztlán, Mexico, a little village where people still speak the ancient Aztec language. Valenzuela brings the same sense of adventure to her writing by changing spellings, creating new words, and using puns.

Politics and Writing Having lived under a repressive regime, Valenzuela is a strong defender of human rights. In "The Censors," she explores the dilemmas that life in a repressive society poses.

Pat Mora (b. 1942)

Author of "The Leader in the Mirror"

Pat Mora was born in El Paso, Texas, just across the United States border from Juarez, Mexico. A graduate of the University of Texas, she taught school and served as a museum director before becoming a full-time writer.

Celebrating Heritage As a young girl, Mora spoke Spanish at home but did not want her friends at school to know. Now, she celebrates her Mexican American background. "I write in part because Hispanic perspectives need to be part of our literary heritage," she explains.

Teaching Resources

The following resources can be used to enrich, extend, or differentiate the instruction.

- All *Unit 2 Resources,* pp. 205–212
- All *Graphic Organizer Transparencies,* pp. 68–71
- All **Enriched Online Student Edition**

PHLit Online! All resources, including print and audio, are available at **www.PHLitOnline.com.**

Daily Bellringer

For each class during which you will teach this selection, have students complete one of the five Sentence combining activities for Week 12 in the *Daily Bellringer Activities* booklet.

Writing About the Big Question

1. Review the assignment.
2. Ask students to describe a time they learned something from a challenging experience.
3. Have students complete the sentence starter. Review responses as a class. **Possible responses:** Because I have struggled with self-control, I know how to control my emotions. If someone asked me for advice on handling conflict, I would say try not to get angry and talk it out.
4. Remind students that their answers will help them think about the Big Question, **"Can progress be made without conflict?"** Tell students that as they read, they should look for growth that results from hardship.

Concept Connector →

Students will return to their sentence starters after they have finished reading.

Multidraft Reading

For each reading, have students set the purpose intended:

- **First reading**—literal comprehension: answering the Reading Check questions
- **Second reading**—application of skills: responding to the side-column notes
- **Third reading**—interpretation: answering the end-of-selection questions

For more guidance, refer to the **Classroom Strategies and Teaching Routines** card on multidraft reading.

PHLit Online!

For more about the authors, practice with the selection vocabulary, and more background, go online at **www.PHLitOnline.com.**

TEACH

❶ Background

Censorship in Argentina Juan Domingo Perón was first elected president of Argentina in 1946. Once in power, he became increasingly authoritarian, jailing opponents, controlling education, and stifling the press. Support for Perón fell in the early 1950s as the economy weakened and his popular wife, Eva, passed away. Perón was supplanted by a military government that ruled Argentina until 1982, instituting one of the bloodiest regimes in South American history.

❷ Activating Prior Knowledge

Have students think of examples of paradoxical situations in the history of the United States or the world. Offer examples of citizens willingly giving up freedoms that others have secured for them, such as neglecting to vote in a country that has fought for universal suffrage.

Concept Connector →

Students will follow up on this activity after completing the selection.

❸ About the Selection

In "The Censors," the main character becomes a censor to reclaim a letter he has written, but in the process he becomes obsessed with censorship. In his obsession, he seals his own fate in a way he never imagined.

❹ Critical Viewing

1. Direct students' attention to the image. Inform them that it is titled ***Screen*** and is an oil painting created in 1996 by Roberto Gil de Montes.
2. **Ask** students the Critical Viewing question on this page.
   Possible response: Some students may note that the appearance of the screen suggests that the main character is held back by something or has his view obstructed. Others may note that his expression conveys anger or focus.

The Censors

Luisa Valenzuela *translated by* David Unger ❶ ❷ ❸

❹ ▲ **Critical Viewing** What might this image suggest about the main character in the story? **[Preview]**

Background Like many other Latin American writers, Luisa Valenzuela often addresses political issues in her writing. Her native country, Argentina, now a democracy, has had an unfortunate history of censorship and other human rights violations. In the 1970s, a military regime took power, brutally hunting down suspected political foes and censoring news and mail. In "The Censors," Valenzuela explores the absurd aspects of such oppression.

Poor Juan! One day they caught him with his guard down before he could even realize that what he had taken as a stroke of luck was really one of fate's dirty tricks. These things happen the minute you're careless, as one often is. Juancito let happiness—a feeling you can't trust—get the better of him when he received from a confidential source Mariana's new address in Paris and knew

Vocabulary Development

Selection Vocabulary Reinforcement

Students will benefit from additional examples and practice with selection vocabulary words. Reinforce their comprehension with "show-you-know" sentences. The first part of the sentence uses the vocabulary word in an appropriate context. The second part of the sentence—the "show-you-know" part—clarifies the first. Model the strategy with this example for *aspirations*:

The woman had *aspirations* to become star tennis player; she practiced everyday and never once missed a lesson.

Then, give students these sentence prompts, and coach them in the clarification part:

1. I couldn't help but suspect that she had *ulterior* motives; ________.
   Sample answer: she was extra friendly to me after I won free concert tickets.
2. His *staidness* helped the members of his group feel calm; ________.
   Sample answer: they mirrored his behavior and sat quietly.

that she hadn't forgotten him. Without thinking twice, he sat down at his table and wrote her a letter. The letter that now keeps his mind off his job during the day and won't let him sleep at night (what had he scrawled, what had he put on that sheet of paper he sent to Mariana?).

Juan knows there won't be a problem with the letter's contents, that it's **irreproachable**, harmless. But what about the rest? He knows that they examine, sniff, feel, and read between the lines of each and every letter, and check its tiniest comma and most accidental stain. He knows that all letters pass from hand to hand and go through all sorts of tests in the huge censorship offices and that, in the end, very few continue on their way. Usually it takes months, even years, if there aren't any snags; all this time the freedom, maybe even the life, of both sender and receiver is in jeopardy. And that's why Juan's so troubled: thinking that something might happen to Mariana because of his letters. Of all people, Mariana, who must finally feel safe there where she always dreamt she'd live. But he knows that the *Censor's Secret Command* operates all over the world and cashes in on the discount in air fares; there's nothing to stop them from going as far as that hidden Paris neighborhood, kidnapping Mariana, and returning to their cozy homes, certain of having fulfilled their noble mission.

❻ Well, you've got to beat them to the punch, do what everyone tries to do: sabotage the machinery, throw sand in its gears, get to the bottom of the problem so as to stop it.

This was Juan's sound plan when he, like many others, applied for a censor's job—not because he had a calling or needed a job: no, he applied simply to intercept his own letter, a consoling albeit unoriginal idea. He was hired immediately, for each day more and more censors are needed and no one would bother to check on his references.

Ulterior motives couldn't be overlooked by the *Censorship Division*, but they needn't be too strict with those who applied. They knew how hard it would be for the poor guys to find the letter they wanted and even if they did, what's a letter or two when the new censor would snap up so many others? That's how Juan managed

Vocabulary
irreproachable (ir′ i prō′ chə bəl) *adj.* above criticism

ulterior (ul tir′ ē ər) *adj.* further; beyond what is openly stated or implied

Literary Analysis
Tone What does the author's use of phrases such as "beat them to the punch" and "throw sand in its gears" show you about her tone?

❼ **Reading Check**
What does Juan fear may happen as a result of his letter?

❺ Humanities

Man Writing (2004) by Ruth Addinall

Ruth Addinall is a self-taught artist who began painting in her late twenties. Her art focuses on the rituals of everyday activities and the mood set in these moments. As in *Man Writing,* Addinall captures the concentration and composure of carrying out the mundane ritual of writing a letter.

❻ Literary Analysis

Tone

1. Remind students that an author's tone is a direct result of the way that he or she feels about a particular subject.
2. Invite a student to name a current event that he or she feels passionately about—either positively or negatively. Discuss this topic with the class and encourage others to offer responses. Remind students to be conscious of the use of tone during the discussion.
3. Have students read the bracketed passage. **Ask** the Literary Analysis question: What does the author's use of phrases such as "beat them to the punch" and "throw sand in its gears" show you about her tone?
   Possible response: The author is opposed to censorship. She believes that it is the responsibility of the people to stand up for their rights and fight back.

❼ Reading Check

Answer: Juan is worried that Mariana may be kidnapped because of the words in his letter.

Differentiated Instruction for Universal Access

Accessibility at a Glance

Use this information to guide your teaching of "The Censors."

Context	A tale of censorship gone mad
Language/Vocabulary	• Accessible vocabulary • Complicated sentences • Subject-specific vocabulary
Concept Level	Challenging (censorship)
Literary Merit	Noted author
Lexile/Length	Lexile: 1,170L Word Count: 1,067

PHLit Online!

This selection is available in interactive format in the **Enriched Online Student Edition**, online at **www.PHLitOnline.com**, which includes an interactive graphic organizer.

❽ Critical Viewing

Possible response: The painting portrays a building that is festive-looking on the exterior. It is painted in bright colors and people are passing by on the sidewalk. A number of darkened windows give it a feeling of being closed or somber, similar to the air of staidness that encompasses the building in which Juan works.

❾ Literary Analysis

Tone

1. Read the bracketed passage aloud. Point out that Juan's "noble mission" has been compromised due to his enthusiasm for his job.
2. Explain to students that censorship is a form of information control that goes on in many nations even today.
3. **Ask** the Literary Analysis question: Based on the details in this paragraph, what do you think is the author's attitude about Juan and his hard work as a censor?
Possible response: The author is critical of Juan and his approach to his duties. Although Juan applied for a position as a censor in the attempt to destroy the censorship machine and save Mariana, he has forgotten his reason for applying, and has become the type of person he initially intended to overthrow.

❽ ▲ **Critical Viewing** What similarities and differences exist between the building represented in this painting and the building in which Juan works? **[Connect]**

Vocabulary
staidness (stād′ nəs) *n.* state of being settled; calm

Literary Analysis
Tone Based on the details in this paragraph, what do you think is the author's attitude about Juan and his hard work as a censor? ❾

to join the *Post Office's Censorship Division*, with a certain goal in mind.

The building had a festive air on the outside that contrasted with its inner **staidness**. Little by little, Juan was absorbed by his job, and he felt at peace since he was doing everything he could to get his letter for Mariana. He didn't even worry when, in his first month, he was sent to *Section K* where envelopes are very carefully screened for explosives.

It's true that on the third day, a fellow worker had his right hand blown off by a letter, but the division chief claimed it was sheer negligence on the victim's part. Juan and the other employees were allowed to go back to their work, though feeling less secure. After work, one of them tried to organize a strike to demand higher wages for unhealthy work, but Juan didn't join in; after thinking it over, he reported the man to his superiors and thus got promoted.

You don't form a habit by doing something once, he told himself as he left his boss's office. And when he was transferred to Section F, where letters are carefully checked for poison dust, he felt he had climbed a rung in the ladder.

By working hard, he quickly reached *Section E* where the job became more interesting, for he could now read and analyze the letters' contents. Here he could even hope to get hold of his letter, which, judging by the time that had elapsed, had gone through the other sections and was probably floating around in this one.

Soon his work became so absorbing that his noble mission blurred in his mind. Day after day he crossed out whole paragraphs in red ink, pitilessly chucking many letters into the censored basket. These were horrible days when he was shocked by the subtle and conniving ways employed by people to pass on subversive messages; his instincts were so sharp that he found behind a simple "the weather's unsettled" or "prices continue to soar" the wavering hand of someone secretly scheming to overthrow the Government.

Think Aloud

Vocabulary: Using Context
Direct students' attention to the word *zeal* on the next page. Using the following "think aloud," model how to use context to infer the meaning of an unknown word.

In this sentence, Juan's zeal brings him a swift promotion. I know that the government promotes him for turning in a fellow worker for arranging a strike. I know that he is now crossing out entire paragraphs. The next few sentences show him using an electronic microscope to look for clues in the letters. I think that *zeal* refers to Juan's extreme enthusiasm for his job.

His zeal brought him swift promotion. We don't know if this made him happy. Very few letters reached him in *Section B*—only a handful passed the other hurdles—so he read them over and over again, passed them under a magnifying glass, searched for microprint with an electronic microscope, and tuned his sense of smell so that he was beat by the time he made it home. He'd barely manage to warm up his soup, eat some fruit, and fall into bed, satisfied with having done his duty. Only his darling mother worried, but she couldn't get him back on the right track. She'd say, though it wasn't always true: Lola called, she's at the bar with the girls, they miss you, they're waiting for you. Or else she'd leave a bottle of red wine on the table. But Juan wouldn't overdo it: any distraction could make him lose his edge, and the perfect censor had to be alert, keen, attentive, and sharp to nab cheats. He had a truly patriotic task, both self-denying and uplifting.

His basket for censored letters became the best fed as well as the most cunning basket in the whole Censorship Division. He was about to congratulate himself for having finally discovered his true
10 mission, when his letter to Mariana reached his hands. Naturally, he censored it without regret. And just as naturally, he couldn't stop them from executing him the following morning, another victim of his devotion to his work.

Literary Analysis
Tone What does the last line of this selection contribute to the author's tone?

Critical Thinking

1. **Respond:** Do you think it was a good idea for Juan to become a censor? Why or why not?
2. **(a)** What worries Juan at the beginning of the story? **(b) Infer:** Judging from this concern, what can you tell about the situation in Juan's country?
3. **(a)** Why does Juan apply for the job in the censor's office? **(b) Analyze:** What character traits make Juan a good censor?
4. **(a) Summarize:** How does Juan's career as a censor progress? **(b) Draw Conclusions:** Why does Juan's attitude about censorship change?

Can progress be made without conflict?
(a) What advice would you give Juan on handling the conflicts he faces? **(b)** What details from the story would help you convince Juan to follow your advice? **(c)** Do you think this story suggests a positive outcome of the conflict? Why or why not?

10 Literary Analysis

Tone

Ask the question on the page.
Answer: The author continues to depict Juan's government as a hostile regime that forces those they govern to play a role in persecution.

Concept Connector

Have students discuss their previous examples of paradoxical situations in U.S. history and compare their Writing About the Big Question responses with their ideas after reading the selection.

ASSESS

Answers

1. **Possible response:** Some students may think that it is a good idea that goes awry; others may think that a scheme based on deception is bound to fail.
2. (a) Juan worries that Mariana is endangered because of the letter he sent. (b) The government of Juan's country is repressive.
3. (a) Juan applies to intercept his own letter. (b) Juan's obsession makes him an effective censor.
4. (a) Because of his zealousness, Juan receives many promotions. (b) Juan becomes so obsessed that he sees evil intent in the most innocent messages.

Can progress be made without conflict?
(a) **Possible response:** Some students may suggest that Juan not write a letter to Mariana. (b) **Possible response:** Some students may note the brutal behavior of Juan's government. (c) **Possible response:** Some students may suggest that the outcome is not positive because Juan is executed.

Differentiated Instruction for Universal Access

Strategy for Less Proficient Readers
Tell students to prepare a three-column chart to follow Juan's progress in the Censorship Division. In the first column, have students list the departments or sections where he worked. In the second column, they should describe his duties in each section. In the third column, students can record how Juan's attitude changes with each promotion.

Enrichment for Gifted/Talented Students
To give students hands-on experience with censorship, ask them to censor an article or an editorial from a local newspaper. Have students copy the article so that readers can see both the original and censored versions. They might censor a sports story to conceal the fact that the home team lost, or they might censor an editorial to subtract all the writer's opinions. Have them use a dark pen to cross out material; they may not rewrite or add words to the article. Have them share and discuss the original and censored material with a partner.

PHLit Online!
This selection is available in interactive format in the **Enriched Online Student Edition**, online at **www.PHLitOnline.com**, which includes an interactive graphic organizer.

⓫ Background

Pat Mora

Mexican American author Pat Mora grew up in the border city of El Paso, Texas. Her parents were native Mexicans who moved to the United States. Mora experienced the difficulties of learning English in school, and many of her writings reflect that conflict. She includes Spanish phrases in her work, an indication of her support for multiculturalism. As this selection reveals, Mora is an advocate of confronting our differences as well as honoring them.

⓬ Activating Prior Knowledge

Read the Background note on this page to the students. Then, **ask** whether any students have spent time in another country. If so, have them share their experience. How were the students able to get around in the country? Did they improve their knowledge of the language? If the students did speak the language and were with people who could not, what did they do to help the other people?

Concept Connector →

Students will follow up on this activity after completing the selection.

⓭ About the Selection

In "The Leader in the Mirror," Pat Mora uses the writing of a speech to high-achieving students as the catalyst for contemplating the challenges and opportunities in a multicultural community. Because she is a poet, Mora understands the force of symbols, so she gives the students imaginary gifts—confetti, tape recorders, photographs, and mirrors—to act as metaphors in their lives. She includes one of her poems to make a point about immigrant life, and she concludes the essay with a persuasive call to the students to embrace their differences and act toward unity.

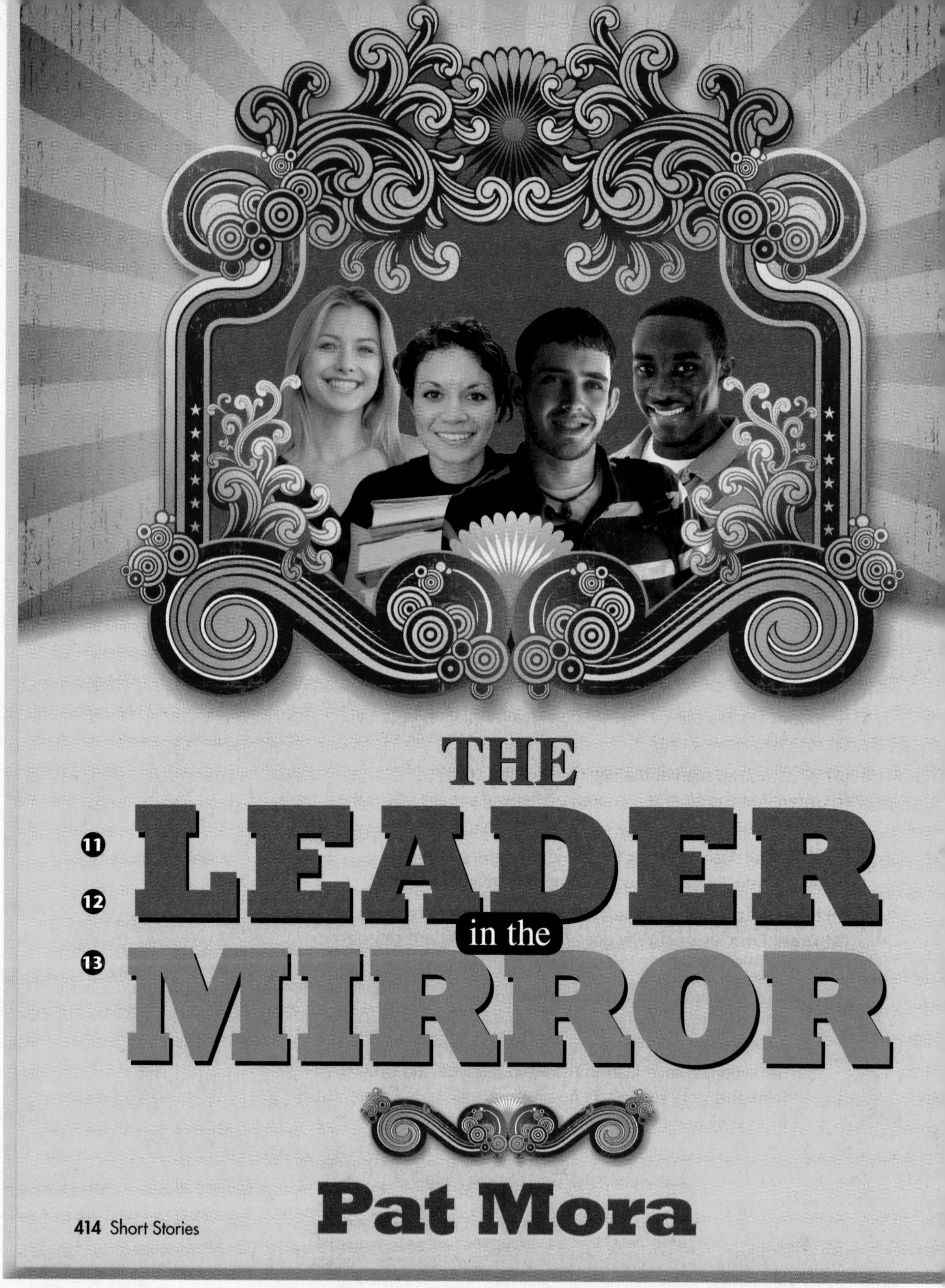

Vocabulary Development

Word Forms

Expand students' vocabulary by helping them learn related forms of the selection vocabulary. Give students a blank **Word Form Chart** (***Professional Development Guidebook***, p. 42), with *aspirations, catalyst,* and *inheritance* in the correct columns. Work with the class, or have students work with a partner, to determine the related forms. The final chart should look like the one shown.

Noun	Verb	Adjective	Adverb
aspirations	aspire	aspiring	
catalyst	catalyze	catalytic	
inheritance	inherit	inheritable	

Each year, the newspaper in my hometown of El Paso, Texas, honors the top five academic achievers from the local high schools at an annual banquet. Last year when I addressed the group, the room at the fancy hotel was full of proud students and their relatives.

The aspirations of the students were like a dose of powerful vitamins, filling parents, educators and guests with energy.

I began by congratulating the family members and teachers for being steady beacons[1] for those young people. In a society that undervalues families and educators, they had truly lived their commitments.

As I was planning the talk I would give to this group, I wondered how best to create an occasion for reflection. What could I say to the audience about the daily struggle to create a meaningful life?

I remembered planning parties for my children when they were young: the careful selection of party favors, the mementos for the guests to carry away. Since this banquet was to be a party of sorts, an academic celebration, I asked myself what favors I would choose for each place at the table.

I knew I would be very popular with the students if I could give them keys to a new red car or tickets to an island vacation. But I
14 am a writer, not a millionaire. So I decided to give them imaginary gifts: Each student would receive confetti, a tape recorder, a photograph and a mirror—symbols and metaphors to take with them through life.

I hoped that most of the students were going to enroll in college. The confetti would be for their private celebrations, those solitary moments when they had passed a test that worried them, finished a difficult paper at 2 a.m., found a summer internship.[2] Sometimes, even when no one else is around, it's important to celebrate when we have struggled and succeeded—to sprinkle a little confetti on our own heads.

Why a tape recorder? I read them my poem "Immigrants."

1. **beacons** (bē´ kənz) *n.* guiding lights; shining examples.
2. **internship** (in´ tʉrn´ ship´) *n.* temporary job providing training for an inexperienced young person.

Vocabulary
aspirations (as´ pə rā´ shənz) *n.* strong ambitions

Literary Analysis
Tone Which details here show you that the writer might be amused by students' values?

15 **Reading Check**
What does Mora say she used to do when planning parties for her children?

14 Literary Analysis
Tone

1. To help students identify tone, remind them that one of the elements of tone is the use of direct statements by the writer. **Ask** them to read the bracketed paragraph and identify a direct statement by the writer. Then, ask them to explain what the direct statement says about the writer.
Answer: *I am a writer, not a millionaire.* This statement tells readers that Mora is straightforward about her life; she does not pretend to be something she is not, and she wants her audience to know the truth about her life as an author.
2. Now **ask** the Literary Analysis question: Which details here show you that the writer might be amused by students' values?
Answer: The writer notes that she would be popular if she gave students cars or island vacations, a humorous assessment of students' self-centered values.

15 Reading Check

Answer: She would carefully select party favors for the guests.

Differentiated Instruction for Universal Access

Accessibility at a Glance
Use this information to guide your teaching of "The Leader in the Mirror."

Context	Speech to students before they go to college
Language/Vocabulary	• Accessible; some poetry • Grade-appropriate vocabulary
Concept Level	Accessible
Literary Merit	Cross-cultural experience
Lexile/Length	Lexile: 1210L Word Count: 906

PHLit Online!
This selection is available in interactive format in the **Enriched Online Student Edition**, at **www.PHLitOnline.com**, which includes an interactive graphic organizer.

16 Critical Thinking

1. Discuss with students what it might have been like for Mora and her family to immigrate to the border city of El Paso, Texas. **Ask:** What are some things you might be afraid of losing if you had to immigrate to another country?
   Possible responses: Students might show concern over losing their language, their cultural traditions and holidays, their friends, and their memories of the land they came from.
2. Have students read the poem on this page. **Ask:** According to the poem, what are some of the changes an immigrant to the United States might feel compelled to make in order to be accepted?
   Possible response: Students might state eating American food, giving American names to their children, following the American sport traditions, and speaking English.
3. **Ask** students whether the author agrees that these changes have to be made.
   Possible response: Students may say that the author does not agree, and she realizes the importance of keeping, and being proud of, one's past and traditions.

17 Critical Viewing

Possible response: Based on the photograph, Mora's audience might lead an urban, middle-class life.

Immigrants
wrap their babies in the American flag,
feed them mashed hot dogs and apple pie,
name them Bill and Daisy,
buy them blonde dolls that blink blue
eyes or a football and tiny cleats
before the baby can even walk,
16 *speak to them in thick English,*
hallo, babee, hallo,
whisper in Spanish or Polish
when the baby sleeps, whisper
in a dark parent bed, that dark
parent fear, "Will they like
our boy, our girl, our fine american
boy, our fine american girl?"

As a writer, I understand the value and necessity of knowing my past, of keeping that door open. My family stories are my catalyst for creativity. All of us have people in our lives whose voices merit saving if we'll only take the time.

Vocabulary
catalyst (kat´ ə list´) *n.* person or thing that triggers an event or action

17 ▶ **Critical Viewing** Drawing on the details in this photograph of El Paso, explain what sort of life Mora's audience might lead. **[Speculate]**

Vocabulary Development

Selection Vocabulary Reinforcement

Students will benefit from additional examples and practice with the selection vocabulary words. Reinforce their comprehension with "show-you-know" sentences. The first part of the sentence uses the vocabulary word in an appropriate context. The second part of the sentence—the "show-you-know" part—clarifies the first. Model the strategy with this example for the word *inheritance*:

His *inheritance* made him a wealthy man; his grandfather left him an exorbitant amount of money.

Then, give students these sentence prompts, and coach them in creating the clarification part:

1. Michael was the *catalyst* for social change; ______.
   Sample answer: his powerful speeches united our community.
2. His *irreproachable* conduct earned him the top award at the ceremony; ______.
   Sample answer: there wasn't a person who could find blame in his actions.

My own father was once a paper boy for the newspaper hosting the banquet. I might not have known that fact, nor his long history of hard work, had I not been listening to him with my tape recorder a few years ago. I did not want the students to wait as long as I had to begin preserving the rich **inheritance** of their family voices. The strength of their heritage would give them the courage to face the future.

My third gift was a photograph of the El Paso/Juarez border: the Chihuahua Desert. the Rio Grande,[3] a stern mountain, two sprawling border cities. Like our families, our geography is part of who we are.

18 When I was growing up on the U.S. side of that border, the society around me tried in subtle and not-so-subtle ways to convince me that my Mexican heritage was inferior to that of Anglo-Americans. I hope that today's educators on the border and throughout this nation are now committed to multiculturalism, to motivating the next generation to draw on their heritage as a resource for learning. The U.S. has been described as the first international country: Our varied cultures are our common wealth.

19 Borders—and if we're attentive, we realize we all live on borders, whether they are national or not—are sites of tension and sites for learning. Borders invite us to confront differences, inequities and stereotypes. They invite us to work for multicultural cooperation and to celebrate multilingual richness.

3. **El Paso** (el pas´ ō) / **Juárez** (hwä´ res) . . . **Chihuahua** (chi wä´ wä) . . . **Rio Grande** (rē´ ō grand´) El Paso is a city in Texas on the Rio Grande, the river forming the border between Texas and Mexico. Juárez, in the Mexican state of Chihuahua, is directly across the river.

Vocabulary
inheritance (in her´ i tәns) *n.* gift handed down to a later generation

Literary Analysis
Tone What tone do the details and diction in this paragraph help to create?

20 **Reading Check**
What aspects of life does the writer intend the second and third gifts to reflect?

18 Literary Analysis
Tone

1. Remind students that an author carefully selects words and details to convey a certain tone.
2. Have a volunteer read the bracketed passage.
3. **Ask** the Literary Analysis question: What tone do the details and diction in this paragraph help to create?
   Possible response: Words such as *hope*, *heritage*, *committed*, *multiculturalism*, and *motivating* contribute to an uplifting, inspirational tone.

19 Connecting to the Big Question

1. Explain that pressure from society can teach a person how to value himself or herself.
2. Have a volunteer read the bracketed passage. **Ask:** What hardship is Mora faced with at this point in the story? **Answer:** She must decide whether or not she agrees with society's beliefs about her heritage.
3. **Ask:** Does Mora benefit from her decision? Explain. **Possible response:** Yes. Mora understands that her heritage is important to her. She knows that groups will have differences, but she urges such groups to welcome diversity.

20 Reading Check

Answer: The tape recorder represents the preservation of the past because it can be used to record voices, and the photograph reflects honoring the geography of a people's homeland.

Differentiated Instruction for Universal Access

Strategy for Special Needs Students
Mora's essay describes a speech that is structured around four gifts. To help students visualize her points, bring (or have student volunteers bring) confetti, a tape recorder, a picture of a geographical border, and a mirror. Have students listen to the recording of the selection on the ***Hear It!*** **Audio CD.** Pause the recording after the author describes each gift. Display the "gift" to the class, and make sure students understand why Mora was offering it to her audience.

Strategy for Less Proficient Readers
Students may have trouble relating certain words the author uses to her tone in the piece. Explain to students that how they feel when they read—whether they are happy, sad, angry, or excited—is inspired by the tone the author uses. To help illustrate this concept for students, have them complete the chart on **Comparing Tones Transparency A** (***Graphic Organizer Transparencies***, p. 68) by rereading the selection and focusing on their emotions and reactions to the author's words.

Concept Connector

Have students compare their Writing About the Big Question responses before reading "The Censors" with their ideas afterwards.

ASSESS

Answers

1. **Possible response:** Students may appreciate the gifts for what they represent.
2. (a) Mora gives her speech at an awards banquet. (b) **Possible response:** This invitation shows that she is recognized for her achievements as a writer.
3. (a) Mora gives each student symbolic confetti, a tape recorder, a photograph, and a mirror. (b) The confetti is to celebrate personal victories. The students can use the tape recorders to record family stories. The photograph is to remind the students that "geography is part of who we are." The mirror is for the students to use to understand themselves.
4. **Possible responses:** Students may value the tape recorder the most because it would allow them to preserve family stories.

Can progress be made without conflict?

(a) **Possible response:** Mora faced tension when she was growing up in the United States because society made her feel like her Mexican heritage was inferior. Facing this adversity taught her to appreciate and celebrate her own heritage as well as the multicultural composition of the United States. (b) **Possible response:** Students may say that dealing with tenuous circumstances could teach a person the importance of inner strength.

"Am I satisfied with this world? If not, what will I do to improve it?"

The final gift of the evening, a mirror, was for serious gazing. I asked the students if they saw a leader when they looked into their mirrors. My guess is that too many of our young people do not see themselves as leaders because they don't look, dress or sound like the images of leaders presented to us. But leaders come in all colors, shapes and sizes. Some are talkative while others are quiet, but they all share a determination to contribute to the society of the future.

I urged the students to look often in their mirrors and to ask themselves these questions: "Am I satisfied with this world? If not, what will I do to improve it?" For if we are shaped by our surroundings, we in turn shape them. We deceive ourselves if we believe that we can live neutral[4] lives.

One-third of this nation now traces its heritage to regions other than Western Europe. We will continue to squander[5] our talent if our leaders—in politics, science, business, education and the arts—do not reflect our grand variety. I urged the students (and all of us) to ponder the strength of the mountains around us, to rise to the challenges.

---

4. **neutral** (no͞o´ trəl) *adj.* not taking a position; lacking vivid color.
5. **squander** (skwän´ dər) *v.* spend or use wastefully or extravagantly.

Critical Thinking

1. **Respond:** How would you have reacted to Mora's speech if you had been a student present when she gave it? Why?
2. **(a)** On what occasion does Mora give her speech? **(b) Infer:** What does the invitation to give this speech show about Mora's achievements?
3. **(a)** What "gifts" does Mora give the students? **(b) Interpret:** Explain the meaning or purpose of each. **(c) Connect:** In what way is each gift connected to the idea of respect for one's own heritage?
4. **Evaluate:** Which of Mora's gifts would you value the most? Explain your choice.

Can progress be made without conflict?
In this speech, Pat Mora mentions that borders are "sites of tension and sites of learning." **(a)** In what ways have tension and adversity affected Mora's life? Use examples from the speech to explain your answer. **(b)** How might tension lead to learning?

Vocabulary Development

Vocabulary Knowledge Rating

When students have completed reading and discussing "The Censors" and "The Leader in the Mirror," have them take out their **Vocabulary Knowledge Rating Chart**. Read the words aloud once more and have students rate their knowledge of the words again in the After Reading column. Clarify any words that are still problematic. Have students write their own definition and example or sentence in the appropriate column. Then, have students complete the Vocabulary Practice activities on the next page. Encourage students to use the words in further discussion and written work about these selections. Remind them that they will be accountable for these words on the **Selection Test** (*Unit 2 Resources*, pp. 216–218 or 219–221).

After You Read

The Censors • The Leader in the Mirror

Comparing Tones

1. Describe the author's attitude toward each of the following items. Support each answer with two details from the text.
   Valenzuela: (a) censorship **(b)** governments that censor
   Mora: (c) heritage **(d)** consumer goods
2. **(a)** Use a chart like the one shown to record words and phrases that express each writer's **tone**. Analyze the attitude each writer takes in discussing the perceptions created by a society. **(b)** Based on your chart, write a sentence comparing the mixture of tones in each piece.

	Inspirational	Sarcastic	Analytical	Other
Diction				
Direct Statements				
Other Details				

3. Based on the mix of tones in each piece, describe the **voice,** or "personality on the page," of each writer.

Writing to Compare Tone

In an essay, compare your reactions to the tone in each selection.

- First, discuss the details, diction, and statements that convey the tones.
- Then, explain how the tone affects your reactions to each selection.
- Finally, explain which tone you found more effective and why.

Vocabulary

Practice Rewrite the following sentences using words from the vocabulary list on page 408. Make any changes needed so that the new sentences are grammatically correct. Then, explain why your chosen word makes sense.

1. A good trainer encourages athletes' dreams.
2. She was careful so that she could not be blamed for any problems.
3. Jared's calmness makes him reliable and predictable.
4. My pocketwatch is one of the gifts I got from my grandfather.
5. This fertilizer is supposed to be a trigger for plant growth.
6. We knew he had underlying reasons for doing what he did.

Teaching Resources

Unit 2 Resources

L1 L2 EL **Selection Test A,** pp. 216–218.
L3 L4 **Selection Test B,** pp. 219–221.
L3 L4 **Open-Book Test,** pp. 213–215.

PHLit Online! All assessment resources are available at **www.PHLitOnline.com.**

ASSESS

Answers

Comparing Tones

1. **Possible responses:** Valenzuela: (a) dislikes censorship, as seen in her description of the process (b) views such governments as unjust, as seen by Juan's execution. Mora: (c) values heritage, as seen in her support of multiculturalism (d) distrusts consumer goods, as seen in her gift choices.
2. **Possible response:** Valenzuela uses "sabotage the machine"; Tone: anger over how people's freedom of speech has been taken away. Mora uses "squander our talent"; Tone: frustration over society's view of education.
   (b) Sentences should convey the tones revealed in student charts.
   Other sample answers appear in **Graphic Organizer Transparencies, Comparing Tones Graphic Organizer A (After You Read),** p. 70, and in the **Additional Answers** section.
3. **Possible response:** Valenzuela: angered; Mora: philosophical and upbeat.

Writing to Compare Tone

Review the assignment criteria. Have students organize their essays by describing the tone of each through a combination of details or by examining each element individually.

Six Traits Focus

✔	Ideas		Word Choice
✔	Organization		Sentence Fluency
✔	Voice		Conventions

Vocabulary

1. aspirations
2. irreproachable
3. staidness
4. inheritance
5. catalyst
6. ulterior

PREVIEW

PRETEACH

Meeting Your Standards

Students will

1. write a problem-and-solution essay.
2. use writing strategies to generate ideas and to plan, organize, evaluate, and revise a problem-and-solution essay.
3. apply grammar skills.

Introducing the Writing Assignment

Review the assignment and the criteria, using the instruction on the student page.

Connecting to Real-Life Writing

Point out to students that elements of a problem-and-solution essay are often incorporated into other types of writing. Point out these examples:

- A history paper may focus on a problem people faced in the past and how it was solved.
- Articles on health may describe specific problems and suggest solutions.
- Editorials frequently identify problems and compare and contrast possible solutions.

C. J. Cherryh on Problem-and-Solution Essays

Show students Segment 3 with C. J. Cherryh on the ***See It!*** **DVD** or from this page in the **Enriched Online Student Edition**, at **www.PHLitOnline.com.** Discuss the author's suggestions about dealing with obstacles to writing and her "rolling rewrite" method of revising.

Writing Workshop *Work in Progress*

If students have done the Work-in-Progress assignments on pp. 367 and 399, suggest that they examine their recorded ideas as they begin prewriting. They may wish to develop these ideas in a problem-and-solution essay.

Online Essay Scorer

A writing prompt for this mode of writing can be found on the *PH Essay Scorer* at **www.PHLitOnline.com.**

Writing Workshop

Exposition: Problem-and-Solution Essay

Individuals, schools, communities, and even entire nations face problems every day. **Problem-and-solution writing** helps identify the problems and then offers reasonable remedies. In this workshop, you will write a problem-and-solution essay on a subject of your choice.

Assignment: Write a problem-and-solution essay to identify a problem in your school or community and present one or more solutions.

What to Include Your problem-and-solution essay should feature the following elements:

- ✔ *a clear description* of a specific, real-life problem
- ✔ an *analysis* of the most important parts of the problem
- ✔ *proof, such as facts, anecdotes, or examples,* that shows the significance of the problem
- ✔ *a complete explanation* of one or more possible solutions
- ✔ *your personal evaluation* of any solutions you discuss
- ✔ error-free grammar, *including correct subject-verb agreement*

To preview the criteria on which your problem-and-solution essay may be assessed, see the rubric on page 427.

Writing Workshop: *Work in Progress*

If you have completed the Work-in-Progress assignments on pages 367 and 399, you already have ideas in your portfolio to use in your problem-and-solution essay. You may continue to develop these ideas or explore a new idea as you complete the Writing Workshop.

Reading Writing Connection

To get a feel for problem-and-solution essays, read "Nobel Lecture" by Alexander Solzhenitsyn on p. 548.

Teaching Resources

The following resources can be used to enrich or extend the instruction.

All *Unit 2 Resources*
Writing Workshop, pp. 224–225

All *Professional Development Guidebook*
Rubric for Self-Assessment: Problem-and-Solution Essay, pp. 244–245

All *Graphic Organizer Transparencies*
Rubric for Self-Assessment: Problem-and-Solution Essay, p. 72

All *See It!* **DVD**
C. J. Cherryh, Segments 3 and 4

PHLit Online! All resources, including print and video, are available at **www.PHLitOnline.com.**

Prewriting Strategies

Browse media sources. Look through newspapers, magazines, and Internet sites for recent stories that discuss a problem. Jot down problems for which you think you can offer solutions. Choose a topic from among these ideas.

Analyze your audience. Decide which people you want to reach—community members, students, or others. Consider that group's interests and needs. Conduct brief interviews to identify a problem that troubles your audience, and then choose a topic to pursue.

Categorize to narrow your topic. Some problems may be too large for your essay. Focus on manageable, local aspects of an issue.

- Write these categories: World, Nation, State, Town, and School. Identify one aspect of the problem for each category.
- Focus your essay on the aspect that you wrote under the local categories, such as "Town" or "School." For example, you cannot solve the problem of war in a few pages. However, you can write about the problem of bullies at school.

Evaluate possible solutions. Before you draft, use a chart to evaluate potential solutions. Look for specific details and consider the advantages and disadvantages of each solution. As you get ready to write, plan to offer the best solutions in your essay.

PHLit Online!
www.PHLitOnline.com
- Author video: Writing Process
- Author video: Rewards of Writing

Apply It!

Problem
Overcrowded computer lab
Details: students have the same deadlines; all need the lab at the same times

Solutions	Pros	Cons
1. teachers split classes into three parts, each with separate deadlines	Students won't need the lab at the same time.	Teachers will have to manage a lot of deadlines.
2. students sign up for lab time one week in advance	Students will have to plan their work.	Some students may not sign up.

Understanding by Design

Clarifying Expected Outcomes: Using Rubrics

- Before students begin work on this assignment, have them preview the Rubric for Self-Assessment on p. 427 to learn what qualities their problem-and-solution essay must have. A copy of this rubric appears in ***Graphic Organizer Transparencies***, p. 36.
- Review the criteria in the rubric with the class. Before students use the rubric to assess their own writing, work with them to rate the Student Model (p. 426) using the rubric.
- If you wish to assess students' problem-and-solution essays with a 4-point or a 6-point scoring rubric, see ***Professional Development Guidebook***, pp. 244–245.

TEACH

Prewriting Strategies

1. Introduce the Prewriting Strategies, using the instruction on the student page.
2. Have students apply the strategies to choose a topic.

Teaching Strategies

1. Have students bring newspapers and magazines to class.
2. Have students work in small groups to brainstorm for problems relevant to different audiences. For example, people living in the city might experiences a problem with air quality that people living in rural areas would not experience.

Think Aloud: Model Evaluating a Solution

Model the strategy, using this "think aloud." Say to students:

A problem can have several possible solutions, but some might be better than others. Suppose there aren't enough parking spaces at school for every student to park. One solution is to hold a lottery, but not every student would get a spot. Another solution is to enlarge the parking lot but this would cost the town money. Both solutions have advantages and disadvantages to consider.

Six Traits Focus

✔	Ideas		Word Choice
✔	Organization		Sentence Fluency
	Voice		Conventions

WG Writing and Grammar, Grade 10

Students will find additional instruction on prewriting for a problem-and-solution essay in Chapter 11, Section 2.

Writing and Grammar, Interactive Textbook Online

Students can use the following tools at **www.pearsonsuccessnet.com** as they complete their problem-and-solution essays:

- Talk With a Peer (Chapter 11, Section 2)
- Use Sentence Starters (Chapter 11, Section 2)

Drafting Strategies

1. Introduce the Drafting Strategies, using the instruction on the student page.
2. Have students apply the strategies as they draft.

Teaching the Strategies

1. Have each student choose one of the two outline formats shown. Students who wish to promote single solutions to problems should use Outline A. Students who wish to compare and contrast two or more solutions to problems should follow Outline B.
2. Direct students to open their essays with descriptions of their problems. Students should then clearly state and explain their problems. Tell students to introduce each solution in one or two sentences and then explain it in more detail.
3. Tell students to identify the audiences for their essays and to select appropriate tones before they begin writing.

Think Aloud: Model Identifying Evidence

Model identifying evidence, using this "think aloud." Say to students:

My readers are more likely to take my ideas and suggestions seriously when they are supported by information that can be proven. There are four different types of evidence I can use: facts, examples, statistics, and expert testimony.

As I gather information I organize my details on note cards. Then, I identify each detail as one of these types of evidence by writing on the note card *F* (fact), *E* (example), *S* (statistic), or *ET* (expert testimony). By labeling each detail, I can avoid inserting my personal opinion.

Six Traits Focus

✔	Ideas	✔	Word Choice
✔	Organization		Sentence Fluency
✔	Voice		Conventions

Writing and Grammar, Grade 10

Students will find additional instruction on drafting short stories in Chapter 11, Section 3.

Drafting Strategies

Create an essay map. For additional support during drafting, write each important idea on an index card. Then, write each supporting detail, such as a fact or an example, on an index card. Using the index cards, arrange the ideas and details in different orders. Once you have determined the best order, number the cards and use them as a map for your writing.

Write an outline. An outline gives you a quick overview of all your points. It also lets you figure out how best to structure, or order, the information and reasoning you want to present. The outlines here show two possible organizations for a problem-and-solution essay.

Outline A
I. Description of Problem
A. One aspect
B. Another aspect
II. Explanation of Solution
A. How it solves the first aspect
B. How it solves the second aspect
III. Personal Evaluation

Outline B
I. Description of Problem
A. One aspect
B. Another aspect
II. Explanation of First Solution
A. Advantages
B. Disadvantages
III. Explanation of Second Solution
A. Advantages
B. Disadvantages
IV. Personal Evaluation

Address your audience. Some audiences, such as your friends or young readers, might respond best to informal language. Other audiences will respect your thinking more if you use formal language.

Informal: Face it—lots of us like to eat junk food for lunch.

Formal: When choosing their own meals, many students select foods with little nutritional value.

Stick to the facts. To convince your readers that the problem you have identified is genuine, you must explain it clearly using solid evidence. This means presenting factual information rather than personal opinions. Reserve your opinions for your personal evaluation at the end of the essay.

Strategies for Using Technology in Writing

If students are using word-processing software to draft their essays, suggest that they use outline templates to organize the information they plan to include in their essays. When their outlines are complete, students may cut and paste the information from their outlines into their draft documents, and then flesh out their ideas in full sentences and elaborate them with details.

Students can also use features of the **Writing and Grammar Interactive Textbook Online** to draft or revise their essays.

C. J. Cherryh

On Revising to Tighten Sentences

Knowing what to delete is as important as knowing what to write in the first place. The value of that advice is illustrated both by "The Threads of Time" and by the passage below, which I have written especially for this workshop. The last few sentences of "Threads" relate to the novel that the story originally introduced. Now that the story exists on its own, I'd like to strike that final passage. It's too late for that, but in the passage below, I show how the timely deletion of unnecessary words can tighten a narrative.

"Perfect sentences are created by good editing."
—C. J. Cherryh

Professional Model:

Original writing by C. J. Cherryh

"Well," I said, ~~taking a moment to look out at the sunset~~ gazing over the porch railing at the gathering dark, ~~of the porch which my grandfather had built, "I really think, well,~~ "it was about this time of evening, yes—back ~~sometime~~ in June. ~~when~~ I saw ~~a truly~~ something terrible ~~thing over there~~ in the garden, right over there by the rose bushes."

I really want the reader to hear the word "June." I set it off with a long dash. Then, I cut out the choppy, chattery little words, and set the rhythms of the sentence to land on "something terrible in the garden."

~~The little girl who was standing next to me on the porch looked~~ Eight-year-old Susan glanced up at me, wide-eyed. ~~She had blue eyes. She was my sister's daughter. She was about eight. She looked very scared at first.~~

"Look" is a neutral word. "Glance" is sharp and fast. Choosing that word for "look" changes the impression in the reader's mind.

~~It wasn't fair to scare the girl. She was just like her mother. I used to tell her mother stories, too, when we were both kids in this house.~~ Then those eyes narrowed: "Mama said you~~'re~~ were a liar." ~~," she said.~~

Was I surprised? No. I knew my sister. ~~Her mother Louise never believed me, either.~~ Louise hated imagination: ~~and she missed a lot of~~ ever so many true things sat ~~that were~~ right under her nose, but she never believed ~~simply because she wouldn't believe~~ she saw them.

Do I need to spell out specifically who Louise is? Once the little girl talks about "mama" and I talk about "my sister," I trust my readers to figure it out.

C. J. Cherryh on Revising to Tighten Sentences

Review the passage on the student page with the class. Then, direct students' attention to C. J. Cherryh's comments to deepen the process of writing a problem-and-solution essay.

Teaching From the Professional Model

1. Show students Segment 3 on C. J. Cherryh on ***See It!*** **DVD** or from this page in the **Enriched Online Student Edition** at **www.PHLitOnline.com.**
2. Invite students to agree or disagree with Cherryh's statement about editing and to explain why they agree or disagree.
3. **Ask** students to consider why Cherryh juxtaposes the word *June* with "something terrible in the garden."
   Possible response: The word *June* suggests sunny images of spring. Cherryh elicits cheerful images from the reader and immediately undercuts these images by stating that there is "something terrible in the garden."
4. **Ask** students to explain how the words *look* and *glance* differ.
   Answer: The word *glance* suggests a quick movement of the head, while the word *look* does not give the reader any information about the character's body language.

Differentiated Instruction for Universal Access

Strategy for Special Needs Students
Students might not understand the purpose and importance of C. J. Cherryh's revisions and might fail to incorporate similar methods of revision into their own essays. Follow these steps to guide students in understanding Cherryh's revision process:

1. Write out the first paragraph of the Professional Model on a separate sheet of paper. Include all strikethrough text and omit the colored text. The paragraph should represent Cherryh's work before she made revisions.
2. On another sheet of paper, omit all strikethrough text and insert the colored text. This paragraph should represent Cherryh's work after she made revisions.
3. Have students compare the two paragraphs. Have them note obvious differences, such as paragraph length. Then, work with students to determine why Cherryh changed a particular phrase or word.

PHLit Online!

Enriched Online Student Edition
Show or assign the video online at **www.PHLitOnline.com.**

Revising Strategies

1. Introduce the Revising Strategies, using the instruction on the student page.
2. Have students apply the strategies as they revise.

Teaching the Strategies

1. Have students reread their drafts and jot down responses to the questions listed in the text. Then, have students use their answers to revise their essays.
2. Have students exchange essays with partners and evaluate the effectiveness of each other's essays. Direct students to respond to the same questions about their partners' essays and to evaluate their partners' use of tone and style. Ask them to make recommendations for improvements.

Think Aloud: Model Using Vivid Words

Model using vivid words, using the following "think aloud." Say to students:

> One way to make my ideas strong and convincing is to use vivid words. As I revise my writing, I can look for sentences that sound dull, such as, "The Highway Department was given little money by the state, so construction stopped at the intersection." Dull verbs, such as "given" and "stopped," dilute the potency of the sentence's message. The sentence can be changed this way: "The state stripped funding from the Highway Department, which, in turn, halted construction on the intersection." The weight of the sentence falls on the verbs "stripped" and "halted," alerting the reader to the severity of the problem.

Six Traits Focus

✔	Ideas	✔	Word Choice
✔	Organization		Sentence Fluency
✔	Voice		Conventions

WG Writing and Grammar, Grade 10

Students will find additional instruction on revising a problem-and-solution essay in Chapter 11, Section 4.

Revising Strategies

Ask questions to consider effectiveness. Review your draft to uncover illogical connections, weakly supported examples, or missing information. Ask yourself the following questions. If you have difficulty providing clear answers, adjust your writing.

- Is there a logical flow to my ideas?
- Did I provide enough details to support my ideas? Are there more facts, anecdotes, or examples that would be useful to include?
- Did I provide more details than I really need?
- Does every statement make sense? If not, what did I mean to say?
- Is this statement a fact or an opinion? If it is an opinion, am I sure I want to include it?
- Have I evaluated the solution I proposed?

Evaluate tone and style. The words you choose establish your **tone**—your attitude toward your subject and audience. To help your audience understand how you feel, you might want to present an optimistic or a pessimistic tone regarding a particular problem or solution.

Optimistic: Our challenge is to discover an effective solution.

Pessimistic: The difficulty will be in finding a workable solution.

Replace dull words. Word choice is also a key part of your writing style. To make your style more interesting, replace any dull words and phrases with vivid, expressive writing.

Flat: The board will make the final decision about the program.

Vivid: The fate of the program lies in the hands of the board.

Apply It!

Model: Revising to Replace Dull Words

The proposal is ~~good~~ convincing and should be ~~used soon~~ implemented immediately.

The writer replaced dull, lifeless words with more precise and vivid choices.

Peer Review

Ask a partner to read your draft and then conduct a conference about your work. Your reader can ask about the overall structure as well as specific details. Use your discussion to guide your revisions.

Strategies for Subject-Verb Agreement

Give students these additional rules for subject-verb agreement:

- Intervening expressions that include the words *along with, together with, including, in addition to,* and *as well as* do not affect the agreement of the subject and verb.
  The students, as well as their teacher, were excited about the field trip.
- Appositives—nouns or noun phrases explaining a noun or pronoun—do not change subject-verb agreement.
  The Red Sox, my favorite team, were the winners of the World Series.
- A subject that follows its verb must agree with the verb.
  Where are the dog and cat?

WRITER'S TOOLBOX

Conventions | Sentence Fluency | Voice | Organization | Word Choice | Ideas

Subject-Verb Agreement

For a subject and verb to agree, both must be singular or plural.

Identifying Errors Errors in agreement can occur when the subject and verb are separated by other words, phrases, or clauses. In the examples below, subjects are underlined, and verbs are set in italic type.

Singular Subject and Verb

Incorrect: The decision of the board members *are* final.

Correct: The decision of the board members *is* final.

Plural Subject and Verb

Incorrect: Students who park here seldom *follows* the rules.

Correct: Students who park here seldom *follow* the rules.

Agreement errors also occur with compound subjects and with indefinite pronouns serving as subjects.

Identifying Indefinite Pronouns These are the most common indefinite pronouns categorized by number:

Singular:	anybody, anyone, each, either, every, everybody, neither, nobody, nothing, somebody, something
Plural:	both, few, many, others, several
Singular or Plural:	all, any, more, most, none, some

Fixing Errors To correct mismatched subjects and verbs, follow these steps:

1. **Identify the subject and determine whether it is singular or plural.**
2. **Select the verb that matches the subject.**
   - For compound subjects joined by *and*, use the plural form.
   - For singular subjects joined by *or* or *nor*, use the singular form.
   - When the subject is an indefinite pronoun, use the appropriate form of the verb.

Grammar in Your Writing

Circle all the subjects in two paragraphs of your draft. For each subject, draw an arrow to the verb that tells what it does. Make sure that you have used the form of the verb that agrees with the subject.

WG

Prentice Hall Writing and Grammar Connection: Chapter 24, Section 1

Differentiated Instruction for Universal Access

Strategy for Special Needs Students

Have students exchange essays with partners. As they read each other's essays, have them use self-sticking notes to identify problem areas that need revision. Suggest that students write a very brief comment on each note to indicate the problem, such as "Don't Understand," "Need More Detail," "Opinion, Not Fact."

EL Strategy for English Learners

On the board, write a sentence with an error in subject-verb agreement. Have students copy the sentence. Then, guide them to circle the subject and verb, identifying each as singular or plural and checking whether they agree. Repeat this process for several sentences with different types of errors and for one sentence that is correct. Then, write five more sentences on the board and have students copy and correct them on their own.

Subject-Verb Agreement

1. Introduce the grammar skill, using the instruction on the student page.
2. Discuss the rules, the examples, and the strategies for fixing agreement errors.
3. Have students follow the instruction under Grammar in Your Writing to correct errors in their drafts.

Teaching the Grammar Skill

1. Provide the following example sentences for students to correct. Then, have volunteers share and explain the answers:
   - *Either Chung or Jamal are going to throw a party.*
     Answer: Either Chung or Jamal is going to throw a party.
   - *Nobody sing like Tony.*
     Answer: Nobody sings like Tony.
   - *In this group, none likes beef.*
     Answer: The sentence is correct whether the verb is singular or plural.
2. Discuss the last example with students. To show how *none* can be singular or plural, demonstrate that it can be replaced by either *no person* or by *no people*.
3. Have students work in pairs. Have each pair write ten sentences, some of which have errors in subject-verb agreement. Then, have pairs exchange papers with other pairs to correct the sentences.
4. When students apply this skill to their own editing, suggest that they use colored pens to identify the subjects of their sentences and the corresponding verbs. Tell students to correct any errors that they find.

WG Writing and Grammar, Grade 10

Students will find additional instruction on revising subject-verb agreement in Chapter 24, Section 1.

Student Model

Review the Student Model with the class, using the annotations to analyze the writer's use of the elements of a problem-and-solution essay.

Teaching From the Student Model

1. Explain that the Student Model is a sample and that students' problem-and-solution essays may be longer.
2. **Discuss** with students why it is a good practice to introduce the problem early in the essay.
   Answer: The purpose of an essay is generally to inform or to persuade. With this purpose in mind, it is important that a writer organize his or her essays so that readers are able to easily identify the topic and the supporting details.
3. **Ask** students why the writer may have chosen to break the problem into its elements.
   Answer: It is easier for readers to understand a complex problem if the writer discusses each of its elements separately.
4. **Ask** students to discuss what else is effective about the writer's conclusion.
   Possible response: In the first sentence of the conclusion, the writer leaves the reader with an important thought to consider.
5. Tell students that the conclusion is the part of the essay that readers will remember. Ask students to consider what it is that they want their readers to think about at the end of their essays.

Connecting to Real-Life Writing

Explain that the ability to describe problems and identify and analyze possible solutions is useful in many situations. Many jobs in industry and government involve problem solving. Officials at the local, state, and national levels of government, for example, focus on problems and offer solutions in the form of laws and other actions. People who work in construction, engineering, home decoration, and automobile repair and technical repair often identify problems and suggest solutions as they prepare job bids and provide explanations to customers.

Student Model: Jacquelyn Simone, Endicott, NY

Brand Names

A great majority of youth today have become walking advertisements. A person's worth is not based on the content of their character, but on the contents of their wallets. Labels have become the measure of merit, and the right clothing can lead to success and popularity. Society has forgotten the value of self-expression. Individuality has been dissolved in a world full of expensive brand names and styles. The problem has several main parts:

In her introduction, Jacquelyn clearly explains the problem she will discuss.

Expense: Students experience great pressure to purchase brand name clothes. However, these articles cost more than regular clothes, making it a challenge for many people to afford them. Despite these realities, those teens who do not own a popular brand are often shunned or ridiculed.

Sameness: Clothes should be a reflection of who you are, not an imitation of what you wish you were. For many teens, clothes no longer express their individuality. Instead, brand names express someone else's idea of who teens are supposed to be.

The writer breaks the problem down into its elements.

Poor Self-Esteem: We have a certain image of the ideal body, which has been fed to us by magazines, television, and movies. Girls are expected to be thin and tall, while boys should be muscular. However, everyone has a different body, and few fit these unrealistic images. The clothes that we are told to buy often suit only that one uncommon body type. The rest of the population is left to try to squeeze into stylish clothes or feel inferior. For many teens, self-esteem drops with every outfit they cannot wear.

The problem is complex, but there are some solutions:

Jacquelyn organizes her solutions into two main categories.

Change the media: Magazines should feature models with more common body types wearing flattering clothing. Fewer television programs should be dedicated to fashion, and more should focus on human character. Department stores should offer a greater selection of sizes, styles, and prices. Clothing manufacturers might be able to make attractive but inexpensive clothes, so that costly brands do not have a fashion monopoly.

Change values: Adults should try to build children's identities so that teens are able to express themselves instead of copying whatever they are told is stylish. Schools could offer seminars on celebrating our personal distinctiveness.

Diversity is beautiful, yet it is far too often hidden beneath layers of conformity. Making more affordable and unique styles could lessen the problem of people being judged based on the brand of their clothes. Clothing can be a wonderful medium of self-expression, but only if we eliminate the pressure of dressing the same as everyone else.

In her conclusion, the writer restates her key points.

Strategies for Test Taking

Tell students that time management is key to responding successfully to writing prompts on standardized tests. Suggest that students spend a quarter of their time prewriting, half their time drafting, and the remaining quarter of their time revising and editing. Proofreading should be left for the last few minutes. In the prewriting stage, encourage students to use simple outlines to organize their ideas for problem-and-solution writing prompts. Tell students that the outlines will help keep them focused during the drafting stage.

Editing and Proofreading

Check your draft for errors in grammar, spelling, and punctuation.

Focus on Clear References: Make sure you have used *that* and *which* correctly. Use *that* to introduce adjective clauses that are essential to the meaning of the noun and *which* to introduce clauses that are not essential to the meaning of the noun.

Publishing and Presenting

Consider one of the following ways to share your essay with others.

Launch a discussion. Use your essay to launch a class discussion about the problem you have analyzed. Read your essay to your classmates. Then, allow your audience members to ask questions and propose their own solutions.

Submit your essay. If your essay focused on a matter of local interest, send it to your school or community newspaper. If your school or town has its own Web site, consider posting your essay. First, make sure your essay meets the site's criteria for publication, then follow the steps to transfer your work to the new platform.

Reflecting on Your Writing

Writer's Journal Jot down your answers to these questions:

How did writing about the work help you understand it?

Which strategy would you use again? Why?

WG *Prentice Hall Writing and Grammar Connection: Chapter 11*

Rubric for Self-Assessment

Find evidence in your writing to address each category. Then, use the rating scale to grade your work.

Criteria	Rating Scale (not very — very)
Focus: How well do you explain a problem?	1 2 3 4 5
Organization: How logically do you present one or more solutions?	1 2 3 4 5
Support/Elaboration: How effective do you use facts, anecdotes, or examples to support your ideas?	1 2 3 4 5
Style: How confidently do you state your evaluations of the solutions?	1 2 3 4 5
Conventions: How correct is your grammar, especially your use of subject-verb agreement?	1 2 3 4 5

Differentiated Instruction for Universal Access

Support for Special Needs Students

Provide additional support to help students fully understand the concept discussed in Step 3 of Teaching From the Student Model on p. 426.

1. Read the Student Model aloud with students. Elicit from students that the essay's organization is composed of an introduction, description of the problem, solutions, and a conclusion.
2. Prompt students to identify other methods the writer has used to organize her essay. Emphasize that text features, such as titles and headings, often make a complex idea easier to understand. Encourage students to use the Student Model as a guide for their own essays.

Editing and Proofreading

1. Introduce the Editing and Proofreading focus, using the instruction on the student page.
2. Have students edit and proofread their problem-and-solution essays, correcting grammar, spelling, punctuation, and word choice. Make sure they check for errors of the type noted on the student page.

Teaching the Editing Focus

Use these examples to contrast the use of *that* and *which*:

The book that I took out of the library is due on Monday.

Great Expectations, *which was written by Dickens, is my favorite book.*

Point out that commas are used to set off clauses introduced by *which*.

Six Traits Focus

	Ideas	✓	Word Choice
	Organization		Sentence Fluency
	Voice	✓	Conventions

ASSESS

Publishing and Presenting

1. Have students form small groups to discuss the problems they analyzed in their essays. Direct students to read their essays aloud and discuss the problems they addressed.
2. If students choose to submit their essays to newspapers, guide them in writing cover letters.

Reflecting on Your Writing

Have each student identify another problem for a problem-and-solution essay. Tell students to describe how they would write it, focusing on what they would do differently this time.

WG **Writing and Grammar, Grade 10**

Students will find additional guidelines on editing, proofreading, publishing and presenting, and reflecting on a problem-and-solution essay in Chapter 11, Sections 5 and 6.

MONITORING PROGRESS

Think About It

1. Remind students that the Unit Big Question is "Can progress be made without conflict?"
2. Point out that students have read selections in Unit 2 that may help them answer the Big Question. **Ask** them for examples from the selections that show how progress is made.
   Possible response: John in "By the Waters of Babylon" went to the Place of the Gods so he could gain knowledge that would help people progress; Gillian in "One Thousand Dollars" had to resolve his conflict with the money he inherited before he could change.
3. Explain to students that the Big Question applies in many other areas besides literature. For example, students may learn in science class about a conflict between scientists researching a disease and animal rights activists who do not believe in using animals for research.
4. Point out that reaching a compromise or resolving this conflict can be critical to people suffering from the disease. **Ask** what might be a result if the two sides reach a compromise.
   Possible response: The scientists could continue their research toward a cure; animal activists might agree to a more humane use of animals in the research.
5. Review the headings on the chart. Emphasize that many types of conflict can lead to progress, but in some cases, conflict does not result in progress.
6. Have students copy and complete the chart on the student page. If they have difficulty finding examples from social studies, suggest the following starting points:
   - Did the conflict between the North and South in the Civil War result in change for the better?
   - Did conflict contribute to the progress made during the Women's Rights Movement in the early 1900s?
7. Have students discuss their answers in groups and present their examples to the class.

Applying the Big Question

THE BIG Q

Can progress be made without conflict?

Think About It

To consider the relationship between conflict and progress, think about what you have read in this unit and what you know from your other classes and from your own experiences. Copy and complete the chart below to apply what you have learned about how progress is made. One row has been completed for you.

Example	Type of conflict	Who won or lost?	Is progress made?	Did conflict contribute to progress?	What I learned
From Literature	Ivan Markovitch's fight with the uncles over Sasha in "A Problem"	Ivan won because Sasha will not have a trial . . . or did he?	Ivan makes progress with the uncles but not with Sasha.	Because of the long, intense argument, the uncles change their minds about Sasha.	Sometimes a conflict can lead to progress for some but not for others.
From Literature					
From Science					
From Social Studies					
From Real Life					

Teaching Resources

Unit 2 Resources

All **Applying the Big Question**, p. 5

PHLit Online! All print resources are also available online at **www.PHLitOnline.com.**

Talk About It

Working in a group, choose an example in your progress chart as the basis for a **discussion.** First, discuss the conflict, making sure that everyone offers and supports an opinion about the struggle. Next, decide whether progress was made. Use these questions to guide your discussion:

- Which people or characters made progress?
- Does progress always involve change for the better?

As group members consider the role of conflict in making progress, you should also discuss whether progress could have been made in ways other than those listed in the chart. Write a brief statement summarizing the group's major points of agreement. Share your statement with the class.

Write About It

At the beginning of Unit 2, you wrote a response to the Big Question. Now that you have completed the unit, see how your understanding has deepened. Write a new response in which you discuss whether your ideas have changed or been validated.

- ❑ Progress can be made without conflict.
- ❑ Progress cannot be made without conflict.
- ❑ My own response:____________.

Support your response with at least one example from literature and one example from an additional subject area or your own life. You may complete these sentences to help you gather ideas and organize your response.

- In this unit, I read a story in which there was conflict over ________, which led to progress that occurred when ________.
- One example of how conflict led to progress in Social Studies is ________.
- One example of progress being made without conflict in Science is ________.
- I have made progress in _________, but I first had to struggle with _____________.
- I made progress without conflict when ___________.
- In the world today, I see progress being made in _________.

Challenge What issues does this question still raise for you? How could you continue your exploration?

☆ shows an **Academic Vocabulary** word.

Big Question Vocabulary

adversity
change
compromise
concession
confrontation
☆ debate
☆ motive
negotiate
☆ oppose
progress
☆ radical
reconciliation
☆ resolve
struggle
☆ unify

Strategies for Listening and Speaking

Remind students to follow these rules for participating in a group discussion.

- Do not interrupt while someone is speaking. Instead, wait until he or she is finished.
- Offer criticism, but do it in a helpful, constructive way.
- Build on others' contributions whenever possible.

MONITORING PROGRESS

Talk About It

1. Have students complete the assignment, following the instruction on the student page.
2. Have students review all the different conflicts in their charts before choosing ones for small-group discussion. Encourage students to choose conflicts that they find interesting.

Write About It

1. Introduce the assignment, using the instruction on the student page.
2. Review the thematic vocabulary with the class (see pp. 222–223).

Teaching Prewriting

1. Point out that students may have read a selection in Unit 2 that expanded or changed their answers to the Big Question.
2. Encourage students to reflect on their new outlooks. Inform students that they will write new responses explaining what caused their thinking to change or to be reinforced.
3. Have students complete the sentence frames on the student page. Guide them to use the prompts in Introducing the Big Question, pp. 222–223, to help them compare their previous responses with their new ones.

Teaching Drafting

1. Remind students that every response should be concise and include a clear introduction, body, and conclusion.
2. Have students begin their drafts by writing statements that define their original ideas and state whether they have changed or been reinforced. Advise students to include details and examples.

Teaching Revising/Editing

1. Have students revise their responses. Encourage them to check their organization and word choice.
2. Have students work with partners for peer review. Encourage partners to point to areas that could use improvement.

Guiding Student Publishing

Students might share their responses by reading them aloud to the class.

Meeting Your Standards

Students will

1. understand etymology.
2. use a dictionary to discover the etymology of a word.

Word Origins

1. Introduce the skill, using the instruction on the student page.
2. Review the chart.

Think Aloud: Model the Skill

Model researching origins for words. Say to students:

If I see an unfamiliar word when I'm reading, it is helpful to know the word's etymology to clarify its meaning. Let's say I come across the word *narcissistic.* Because I know the Greek myth about Narcissus, a man who falls in love with his own reflection, I assume *narcissistic* comes from the Greek language. To be sure, I go to a dictionary and find the word. I see that I am correct—*narcissistic* comes from Greek. So, the word refers to someone who shows excessive interest in his or her own appearance.

Practice A (p. 431)
Sample answers:

1. **psyche** *n.* the mind regarded as an entity [Latin, *psȳchē,* from Greek *psukhē,* breath, soul]
2. **algebra** *n.* a mathematical system using symbols to generalize operations [Arabic, *al jabara,* to reunite]
3. **Saturday** *n.* a day of the week [Old English, *Sæterdæg,* Saturn's day]
4. **anger** *n.* displeasure and hostility [Old Norse, *angr,* distress]
5. **sleuth** *n.* a detective [Old Norse, *slóth,* a trail]
6. **theater** *n.* a place for plays and other presentations [Greek, *theasthai,* to view]

Vocabulary Workshop

Word Origins

Words come into the English language from many sources. A word's **origin,** or source, is shown in its **etymology.** A word's etymology identifies the language in which the word first appeared and tells how its spelling and meaning have changed over time.

English as a language dates back to about the year 500 when Germanic tribes including Angles, Saxons, and Jutes settled in England. This first English language is known as Old English. In the years following 1066, English changed dramatically as a result of the Norman invasion, which brought Old French to England and produced what we now call Middle English. During a period known as the Renaissance, roughly between 1300 and 1500, there was a renewed interest in the classical languages of Greek and Latin that greatly influenced the English language. As a result, grammar, spelling, and pronunciation changed and Modern English emerged.

This chart shows how a few words first entered the English language.

Word	Definition	Origin
Thursday	the fifth day of the week	Old Norse word *Thorsdagr,* which means "Thor's day," a reference to the god of thunder in Norse mythology
martial	of or suitable for war	Latin word *martialis,* which means "of Mars," a reference to the god of war in Roman mythology
narcissistic	showing excessive self-love	reference to Narcissus, a young man in Greek mythology who falls in love with his own reflection

Teaching Resources

Unit 2 Resources
Word Origins, pp. 222–223

PHLit Online! **Vocabulary Central,** featuring definitions, audio pronunciations, Word Families, and activities, is online at **www.PHLitOnline.com.**

Practice A Find each of the following words in a dictionary. Define each word and explain its origin.

1. psyche **2.** algebra **3.** Saturday
4. anger **5.** sleuth **6.** theater

Practice B Each numbered question contains a word that has come into the English language from the Greek, Latin, or Old Norse language or mythology. Use a dictionary to find each italicized word's origin and meaning. Then, use that information to answer the question.

1. How did the word *tantalizing* come to mean "tempting" or "enticing"?
2. What qualities does something *titanic* share with the Titans in Greek mythology?
3. What kind of days was the word *dismal* originally used to describe?
4. For which Norse god is *Wednesday* named?
5. What kind of journey is an *odyssey*, and which hero of Greek mythology took this kind of journey?
6. Why is the word *mercurial* used to describe someone who is lively and quick-witted?

PHLit Online!
www.PHLitOnline.com
- Illustrated vocabulary words
- Interactive vocabulary games
- Vocabulary flashcards

Activity Identify the source of each of the following English words. Then, use a graphic organizer like the one shown to explain how the English word and the source word are related. The first item has been completed as an example.

1. consequence **2.** agony **3.** detour **4.** thespian **5.** pendant

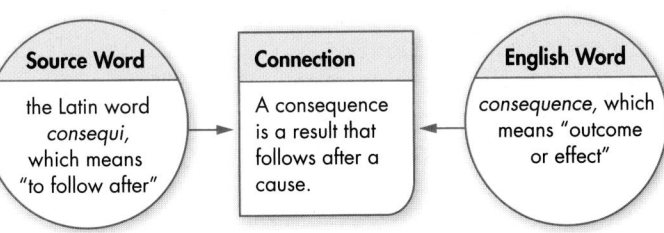

Source Word	Connection	English Word
the Latin word *consequi,* which means "to follow after" →	A consequence is a result that follows after a cause.	← *consequence,* which means "outcome or effect"

Challenge
With a partner, research the following words, which are all derived from ancient Greek theater. Then, write an explanation of how each word's theatrical meaning relates to its everyday meaning.
catastrophe
antagonist
chorus

Differentiated Instruction for Universal Access

EL Support for English Learners

Inform students that their knowledge of their native languages may help them identify many English words. Explain that some English words are cognate words, or words that have nearly identical sounds to the language from which they originated. For example, *echo* originated from the Greek word *ēchō*. Work with students to make a list of cognate words from their native languages. Point out that the words may come directly from their languages or the English word and their native word may share a common ancestor, such as Latin.

Enrichment for Gifted/Talented Students

Explain to students that many science words have roots originating in Greece. Tell students they will create a visual science dictionary. Give them the following roots and have them build a familiar word from it. Encourage students to use the Internet to find other roots.

aero-, air, wind; *astro-,* star; *bio-,* life; *eco-,* house; *geo-,* earth, world; *helio-,* sun; *hydro-,* water.

Display the dictionary in the classroom for student reference.

ASSESS/EXTEND

Answers

Practice B
Sample answers:

1. **Tantalizing** is from the Greek myth of Tantalus, who was doomed to stand in water that *tempted* him, receding as he bent to drink.
2. The Greek Titans were giants. Something **titanic** is of great size, strength, or power.
3. **Dismal** comes from the Middle Latin word, *dies mali,* which means "evil days."
4. **Wednesday** was named for the Norse god Woden.
5. The word **odyssey** comes from the Greek mythological hero Odysseus who took a long, difficult journey back home to Greece after the Trojan War.
6. **Mercurial** comes from Mercury, a Roman messenger god who moved very quickly.

Activity

To prepare students for this activity, have them use a dictionary or an online etymology site as you model how to identify the origin of the word *consequence.*

1. **agony** *n.* Greek, *agōn,* "a (mental) struggle for victory in games"; mental suffering; "extreme physical or mental suffering"
2. **detour** *n.* French, *détourner,* "turn away"; turn away from a route to avoid something; "an alternative route for traffic"
3. **thespian** *n.* Greek, ancient poet Thespis, "relating to drama and theater"; an actor in the theatre; "an actor"
4. **pendant** *n.* Latin, *pendere,* "hang"; decoration hanging downward; "a piece of jewelry worn around the neck hanging from a chain"

Challenge

Students should find that *catastrophe* comes from the conclusion of a tragedy, which relates to calamity. The *antagonist* is the main opponent in a drama; now it refers to a hostile person. The *chorus* was the group who recited parts of a play; now it refers to a group who sings together.

Meeting Your Standards

Students will

1. evaluate the content of a speech by identifying the purpose, assessing the arguments, and thinking about logic and accuracy
2. evaluate the speaker's communication skills, including word choice and nonverbal communication.

Introducing Viewing and Evaluating a Speech

Introduce the assignment and the strategies, using the instruction on the student page.

Evaluate the Content

1. Explain that there are different strategies that can be used to focus on content. First, the speaker's purpose must be identified. Why is the person talking? What is his or her goal in making this speech?
2. Next, explain that students should assess the arguments that a speaker makes. What supporting details, or proof, does the speaker use to support his or her claim?

Evaluate the Speaker's Communication Skills

1. Explain that another important consideration in the evaluation of a speech is the way in which it is delivered.
2. Point out the nonverbal cues are also important. Ask students to consider how they react when someone smiles at them. How do their reactions change if the same person rolls his or her eyes after smiling?

Assess the Activity

To evaluate students' delivery, use the **Listening: Evaluating a Media Presentation** rubric, p. 270 and **Listening: Evaluating a Media Presentation**, p. 267 in ***Professional Development Guidebook.***

Communications Workshop

Viewing and Evaluating a Speech

Do not believe everything you hear in a speech, regardless of who presents it. Analyze the presenter's message and speaking skills as you listen.

Evaluate the Content

Identify the purpose. The purpose of a speech may be to pay tribute to someone, inform, entertain, or persuade. The speaker's purpose will help you decide whether or not the speech is effective.

Assess the arguments. A speaker should present and support clear arguments, or ideas. Analyze the type of argument used by the speaker. The types of argument are *causation,* making a connection between a cause and an effect; *analogy,* comparing two situations to prove a point; and *authority,* using an expert's credibility to support an argument. Consider how details given by the speaker support the argument. A speech should include facts or quotations from reliable sources.

Consider logic and accuracy. Review the logic that holds statements in a speech together. Make sure that supporting details connect to the speaker's argument. Use your knowledge and experience to check the accuracy of statements and test those that seem exaggerated.

Evaluate the Speaker's Communication Skills

Think about how well the speaker communicates.

Check language level. A good speaker chooses language suited to the audience. For example, if members of the audience are scientists, then the speaker may use technical terms freely. When speaking to the general public, the speaker may use common terms instead.

Note word choice and style. A speaker may use formal or informal language. Speakers also may use emotionally charged wording. Charged words with powerful connotations, or associations, can make a statement memorable or make opinions appear to be facts. Words with negative connotations can obscure facts. Speakers may also use allusions, references to cultural figures or events, that evoke emotion.

Look at nonverbal communication. A speaker communicates with far more than words. The speaker's body language, eye contact, gestures, vocal tone, and pacing affect the audience's reaction.

Speech Evaluation		
Content	+	−
Purpose	+	−
Argument	+	−
Support	+	−
Language Level	+	−
Word Choice	+	−
Body Language	+	−
Eye Contact	+	−

Activity: Analyze a Media Presentation

Evaluate a speech presented in class or via media. Use the Speech Evaluation Checklist to help you focus on all the aspects of the speech.

Differentiated Instruction for Universal Access

Strategy for Gifted and Talented Students

The importance of nonverbal communication is easier to understand through live presentations. Invite volunteers to demonstrate several nonverbal gestures and expressions to the class.

Form two student groups. Ask students in one group to model good nonverbal communication. The other group will model bad nonverbal communication. Next, assign a paragraph from the student book to each student. Students in the first group should read the paragraphs loudly, making occasional eye contact with the audience. Students in the other group should mumble, fidget, and otherwise perform badly.

Afterward, lead a discussion about the differences among the performances and how the audience was affected by the differing performances.

Independent Reading

THE BIG ? Can progress be made without *conflict?*

Up From Slavery
Booker T. Washington
Signet

During his life, Booker T. Washington was a slave, an educator, an orator, and the founder of the Tuskegee University. In this autobiography, Washington tells the story of his struggles as he rose from houseboy to activist for social change.

Roughing It
Mark Twain
New American Library

When a twenty-six-year-old writer set out for the West with a suitcase and a plan for adventure, he discovered people and places enmeshed in conflict and change. In this book, Mark Twain recounts his six years in the volatile American West at a time when vigilantes ruled the land, gold prospecting was the rage, and women holstered guns beneath their petticoats.

The Collected Short Fiction of C. J. Cherryh
C. J. Cherryh
Daw Books

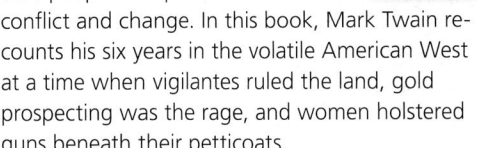

From stories of a turbulent world plagued by a cooling sun to a tale of a woman cursed with unbelievable visions, this collection introduces readers to Cherryh's boundless imagination. As enemies, friends, and worlds clash, readers will find themselves lost in these magical, exotic landscapes.

The Joy Luck Club
Amy Tan
Putnam

Four mothers and their Chinese American daughters strive to bridge generational and cultural differences. Inspired by Amy Tan's own relationship with her mother, this novel introduces readers to realistic characters who discover and rediscover themselves as they cling to hope and love of family.

Anton Chekov: Selected Stories
Anton Chekov
Signet

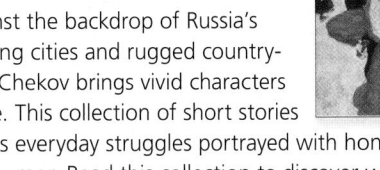

Against the backdrop of Russia's bustling cities and rugged countryside, Chekov brings vivid characters to life. This collection of short stories shows everyday struggles portrayed with honesty and humor. Read this collection to discover why Chekov is one of the world's most renowned short story writers.

Ancient Rome: Voyages Through Time
Peter Ackroyd
Dorling Kindersley

Spanning centuries of war and conquest, Ackroyd's book brings the reader face to face with famous and infamous Roman rulers, along with the architectural marvels of their age—aqueducts, amphitheaters, spectacular temples, and the Circus Maximus.

Consult your teacher before choosing one of these titles.

Planning Students' Further Reading

Have students choose a book for independent reading from those listed on the student page. Before recommending a work to students, preview it, taking into account the values of your community as well as the maturity of your students. The following notes offer some guidance for the titles on the student page. Because a variety of factors play a role in determining the accessibility of a work, a book with a higher readability rating may be deemed more accessible than a book with a lower rating.

L3 ***Up From Slavery*** Some students may be offended by the realities of racism portrayed in the book.
Lexile: 1320

L3 ***Roughing It*** Students may react to some of Twain's disparaging comment about Native Americans, African Americans, and Asians.
Fountas and Pinell: IL9+

L2 ***The Collected Short Stories of C.J. Cherryh*** The stories in this collection include references to violence, murder, suicide, torture, supernatural occurrences, imaginary creatures, ghosts, time travel, and shape-shifting.
Level suitable for high school students

L3 ***The Joy Luck Club*** Hardships of a war-torn country, including death and abandonment of children, may be distressing to some students. Divorce and the death of a parent might be uncomfortable subjects for sensitive readers.
Level suitable for high school students

L3 ***Anton Chekhov: Selected Stories*** In some of these stories, students will encounter drunkenness and acts of physical violence against women and children. Some sexual situations portrayed may be offensive.
Level suitable for high school students

L1 ***Ancient Rome: Voyages Through Time*** The book deals with the Roman's belief in gods and goddesses, and mentions the various assassinations and wars of Roman history.
Level suitable for high school students

Connecting to the Big Question

Have students form literature circles in which to discuss the books they read independently. See *Professional Development Guidebook,* pp. 47–49, for guidance in running literature circles.

Suggest that students discuss these questions:

- How do the characters in these novels respond to the conflicts they encounter?
- Do the character's responses lead them to learn or to change?
- If so, do these changes benefit others?

Challenge

The following titles for advanced readers are available in the Penguin Literature Library.

***The War of the Worlds* by H.G.Wells** This novel contains some graphic descriptions of violence and warfare; weaponry suggestive of germ and chemical warfare; thoughts of suicide; and an unsympathetic depiction of a clergyman.

***The Adventures of Ulysses* by Bernard Evslin** Students may be offended by Ulysses' sexual relations with many of the demigoddesses, phallic imagery, brutality, and descriptions of gruesome deaths.

MONITORING PROGRESS

Using the Unit Review

In this Test Practice workshop (pp. 434–439), students apply the skills in Unit 2. The practice is divided into four sections.

1. Before assigning each section, review the relevant Unit skills with students.
2. Set a time limit for the multiple choice items in each section, allowing a little over one minute per question. Allow ten to fifteen minutes for any Writing for Assessment questions.
3. Administer each section. Have students write the starting time at the top of their papers. When half the time for the multiple choice items has run out, ask students to write the time next to an answer on which they are working. Have them do the same when time is three quarters through and again when time is up. Have them note the start and end times for any Writing for Assessment questions as well.
4. Review with students the pacing reflected in their notes.

Reteaching Skills

1. For each practice, use the Reteach chart on the same page as the answers to determine which skills require reteaching, based on which items students answered incorrectly.
2. Reteach these skills prior to assigning the **Benchmark Test** for the second half of Unit 2 (***Unit 2 Resources***, pp. 226–231).

Test Practice: Unit 2 Review

I. Literary Skills

Directions: *Read the passage. Then, answer each question that follows.*

Futbol

Alex clutched the football under his arm and rubbed its rough surface. The plane was taking off. As he watched from his window seat, the cars on the freeway grew smaller and smaller, until they looked like toys. He gazed out over the city, trying to spot the football field at his old high school. He knew he would not see it again for a long time. Alex and his family were moving to Mexico City, Mexico. His dad had taken a job there.

"It will be an adventure, Alex," his dad had said when he announced the move. "You'll learn a new language and make new friends."

"But I'll have to leave my old friends—and football!" Alex had argued.

"They have football in Mexico—just not your kind."

"Very funny, dad! They call it *futbol*—we call it *soccer.* And I've never really played soccer." All during the conversation, Alex had tossed his football in the air, trying to imagine life without the game.

As soon as the family was settled in Mexico City, Alex enrolled in school. Although there were many English-speaking students, Alex still felt he didn't belong, like a <u>misfit.</u> He kept his football in his locker during the day and set it on the table by his bed at night.

One evening, a few months after the move, Alex's dad entered his room. "Alex, this is enough. You can't sit at home each night. I've enrolled you in a Saturday soccer league with kids from the neighborhood."

"You can't do that! I'm not going," Alex protested. "Those kids have played soccer all their lives!"

"Not all of them, Alex. Some are new to *futbol.*"

"Futbol. Soccer. I've never played it. I'll look stupid."

"You were a wide receiver on the football team, and you know how to move. You'll do fine."

Saturday after Saturday, Alex went to the field, but he always watched on the sidelines as the boys played. Alex was an outsider. Afterwards, he would go home and toss his football in the air for hours. One Saturday, the ball came flying towards his spot on the sidelines, high over the heads of the players. Without thinking, Alex stepped forward and butted it back into play with his head. "Bueno! Bueno!" a dark haired boy shouted at Alex with a grin. That afternoon, Alex picked up his football, gave it a pat, and put it on the top shelf in his closet.

Strategies for Test Taking

Remind students that they benefit by having adequate rest before taking a long standardized test. Suggest that they be sure to get enough sleep the night before the test. They should have at least 8 hours of sleep. This rest will make them more alert and more focused. They will also be able to think more clearly. Having a healthy breakfast will help with alertness and energy as well.

1. Which of the following sentences is an example of direct characterization?

   A. Alex was an outsider.
   B. "It will be an adventure, Alex."
   C. Alex's dad entered his room.
   D. "Some are new to *futbol*."

2. Which statement best describes the **theme?**

   A. Change can be painful, but it opens doors to new experiences.
   B. People around the world are very similar.
   C. Moving to a different country is an exciting adventure.
   D. Not everyone is good at sports.

3. From which **point of view** is the story told?

   A. first person
   B. second person
   C. third person
   D. limited

4. **Vocabulary in Context** What is the best definition of the underlined word *misfit?*

   A. someone who is not intelligent
   B. someone who feels out of place
   C. someone who feels superior
   D. someone who is disgusted

5. Which sentence best represents the **character development** that happens during the story?

   A. "Bueno! Bueno!" a dark haired boy shouted at Alex with a grin.
   B. That afternoon, Alex picked up his football, gave it a pat, and put it on the top shelf in his closet.
   C. He gazed out over the city, trying to spot the football field at his old high school.
   D. One Saturday, the ball came flying towards his spot on the sidelines, high over the heads of the players.

6. Which of the following statements includes the most **description?**

   A. He kept his football in his locker during the day and set it on the table by his bed at night.
   B. "And I've never really played soccer."
   C. He knew he would not see it again for a long time.
   D. As he watched from his window seat, the cars on the freeway grew smaller and smaller, until they looked like toys.

7. Which of the following best describes the **symbolic meaning** of Alex's football?

   A. his anger at his father for the move
   B. the family's move
   C. his source of comfort in new surroundings
   D. the football team's dedication

8. Which of the following does *not* describe the story's **setting?**

   A. an airplane
   B. a *futbol* field in Mexico City
   C. Alex's bedroom in Mexico
   D. a football field in the United States

9. The **dialogue** reveals that Alex's father—

   A. wants to leave Mexico City.
   B. believes Alex will adjust to *futbol.*
   C. has a high-paying job.
   D. knows how to play football.

Writing for Assessment

10. Write a literary analysis essay in which you **describe** the character of Alex and **explain** how his character develops. Use details from the passage to **support** your response.

GO ON

Answers With Explanations

1. **A**—The sentence directly states how Alex felt. *Incorrect answers:* B—This statement reflects Alex's father's attempt to encourage him. C—This statement is an element of the plot. D—This statement directly describes unnamed people and therefore is not characterization.
2. **A**—The story shows how Alex overcomes resistance to change. *Incorrect answers:* B—The focus is on Alex's adjustment to change, not to how he feels about the people he meets in Mexico. C—Alex experiences no excitement. D—Alex apparently is a skilled athlete.
3. **C**—Characters are described using third-person pronouns. *Incorrect answers:* A—The narrator is not in the story. B—You do not tell the story. D—While the narrator sees Alex's thoughts, his father's thoughts are not revealed.
4. **B**—Alex's loneliness shows that he feels he does not belong. *Incorrect answers:* A—Intelligence does not play a role in the story. C—Alex feels that he does not belong, not that he is better. D—Alex is not revolted by *futbol,* merely uninterested.
5. **B**—This action shows Alex has changed. *Incorrect answers:* A—This sentence is part of the falling action. C—This sentence is part of the rising action. D—This sentence sets up the climax.
6. **D**—The sentence uses several sense words to show what Alex saw. *Incorrect answers:* A—The sentence describes action, but has less description than answer D. B—This is dialogue, not description. C—This relates Alex's thoughts, but does not describe setting or action.
7. **B**—The football symbolizes what Alex feels he has lost through the move. *Incorrect answers:* A—The narrator does not reveal anger in Alex. C—While focusing on the football, Alex is not feeling comfortable. D—The team does not appear in the narrative.
8. **D**—None of the action takes place in this location. *Incorrect answers:* A—This location does appear in the story. B—same explanation as for A. C—same explanation as for A.

Answers continued

9. **B**—Alex's father is confident he will be able to play. *Incorrect answers:* A—The father expresses no regret over the move. C—The father's salary is not mentioned. D—The father's skill at football is not discussed.

Writing for Assessment

Students' analyses should describe Alex's journey from a familiar life to a new place with new people and a new sport. Students should discuss his mindset through the changes, citing details from the passage for support.

Reteach

Question	Instructional Pages to Reteach
1	239
2	335
3	306
4	—
5	239
6	269
7	239
8	369
9	269
10	239

Answers

Answers With Explanations

1. **C**—The story reveals how exciting a game can be. *Incorrect answers:* A—The story does not explain why players act as they do. B—The story assumes the reader knows or can infer relevant rules. D—The passage focuses on one game, not the sport in general.
2. **D**—The passage describes basic soccer rules. *Incorrect answers:* A—The passage does not describe soccer fans. B—The passage does not address the issue of stress. C—The passage does not discuss player's feelings.
3. **A**—This nonfiction piece is most likely to include statistics. *Incorrect answers:* B—The story focuses on the narrator's experience as a player, not on fans. C—Only the nonfiction piece is likely to include this information. D—While the story is unlikely to include this information, the nonfiction passage might.
4. **A**—All players want to achieve this particular aim. *Incorrect answers:* A—This goal is not necessarily the first aim. B—This goal is not necessarily the last one. D—This goal is not the lowest, but the highest.
5. **B**—The statement expresses the gist of the original using different words. *Incorrect answers:* A—The narrator's teammates do not appear in the original; the attempted paraphrase does not describe the fan's actions. C—The original does not describe the fans' clothing. D—The size of the crowd is not the issues; its appearance and behavior is.
6. **A**—This reflects the point of the sentence. *Incorrect answers:* B—The original calls the day appropriate for any soccer game. C—The sentence discusses the appropriateness of the weather for soccer only. D—This sentence does not describe the weather of that particular day.

II. Informational Reading Skills

Directions: *Read the passages. Then, answer each question that follows.*

Association Football

In the United States, tens of thousands of kids play a game called *soccer.* Elsewhere the same ball game is called *association football,* or, in some countries, *futbol.* Around the world, about 40 million players are registered, plus there are thousands of others who play pickup games in streets, parks, school yards, vacant lots, and even on beaches.

The game is played with two teams of eleven players each. The ultimate goal is to move the ball into the opposing team's goal net, without using the hands or arms. Players may bump the ball with their heads, hips, knees, or they may kick the ball, but only the goalie, who stands in front of the goal, can touch the ball with his or her hands. The rules are simple, and the game can be played almost anywhere, which makes it the most popular game in the world, not only for players but for spectators as well.

Champions!

It was a brisk, overcast Sunday morning—the best kind for soccer. I walked on to the field and was greeted by high fives from my ten excited teammates. It was championship game day. Proud spectators with painted faces colored the stands, wildly waving striped flags and banners. "Today is the day," I thought to myself. "Nothing gets by these hands today." I put my gloves on and clapped my hands three times for good luck, a ritual I started years before on the streets in my neighborhood. The whistle sounded. I protected the goal, throwing my body in front of every shot. With 30 seconds of play left, the score was 1–0, our favor. Suddenly, I saw two fast and furious feet dribbling the ball toward my goal. I glanced at the clock—22 seconds left and counting down. I took a deep breath and put my hands up to block the shot I knew was coming. The fans roared. Teammates cheered. I did it! I shut the other team down. We had won the championship!

1. Both of these articles are about soccer. The article "Champions" would be more useful for—
   A. learning how the game is played.
   B. understanding the rules for playing soccer.
   C. appreciating the excitement of watching a soccer game.
   D. learning about the popularity of the game.
2. "Association Football" would be more useful for—
   A. appreciating the fans.
   B. understanding the stress on soccer players.
   C. learning how soccer players feel.
   D. learning the rules of soccer.
3. If these two articles were to continue, in which of them would you likely find statistics about soccer fans?
   A. "Association Football"
   B. "Champions"
   C. Both articles
   D. Neither article
4. **Vocabulary in Context** What is the *best* definition of the underlined word *ultimate*?
   A. most important
   B. first
   C. rule
   D. lowest

Reteach

Question	Instructional Pages to Reteach
1	335
2	335
3	—
4	402
5	402
6	402

5. Which is the *best* paraphrase of these lines? *Proud spectators with painted faces colored the stands, wildly waving striped flags and banners.*

   A. My teammates and the spectators were excited about the game.
   B. Fans painted their faces and waved their flags and banners.
   C. People dressed up and cheered.
   D. Soccer brings out big crowds.

6. What is the *best* way to paraphrase the first line of "Champions"?

   A. It was a cold cloudy morning—perfect for soccer.
   B. This Sunday was an especially good morning for the championship game.
   C. The cool weather was good for sports.
   D. I have always enjoyed playing soccer in cool weather.

III. Vocabulary

Directions: *Read each question. Then, choose the best answer.*

1. Which pair of words are **synonyms?**

   A. motive, reason
   B. reconciliation, argument
   C. compromise, disagree
   D. oppose, settle

2. Which sentence uses a **synonym** of *resolved*?

   A. Julie is *determined* to make the team.
   B. He has *progressed* at an amazing rate.
   C. Andrew *struggled* to finish his history test.
   D. They *debated* the issue of climate change.

3. Which sentence uses a **synonym** of *adversity*?

   A. The leaders reached a *compromise*.
   B. Emma has faced a lot of *hardship* in her life.
   C. The tragedy helped our school build *unity*.
   D. We opposed Tim's *decision* to quit the team.

4. Which word below is the *best* **synonym** for the word *motive?*

   A. consequence
   B. purpose
   C. obstacle
   D. indifference

5. Which pair of words are **antonyms?**

   A. progress, retreat
   B. struggle, fight
   C. debate, decide
   D. resolve, anger

6. Which sentence uses an **antonym** of *unify*?

   A. Juan will *coordinate* the plans for the party.
   B. Lisa plans to *divide* us into two teams.
   C. Sandra will *oppose* the change in the rules.
   D. We will *compromise* about splitting the bill.

7. Which sentence uses an **antonym** of *radical*?

   A. The company's *generous* concessions ended the strike.
   B. Coach Li was a *competent* leader.
   C. The *lucrative* offer was too good to refuse.
   D. Amy is the *conservative* candidate for office.

8. Which word below is the *best* **antonym** of the word *confrontation*?

   A. clash
   B. dispute
   C. hostility
   D. agreement

GO ON

Reteach

Question	Instructional Pages to Reteach
1	222–223
2	222–223
3	222–223
4	222–223
5	222–223
6	222–223
7	222–223
8	222–223

Answers

Answers With Explanations

1. A—A *motive* is a reason for doing something. *Incorrect answers:* B—A reconciliation can end an argument;. C—To *compromise* is to settle a dispute; to *disagree* is to have one. D—To *oppose* is to stand against something; to *settle* is to end a dispute.
2. A—*Determination* and *resolve* both refer to the will to achieve something. *Incorrect answers:* B—To *progress* is to move forward, not to determine to do something. C—Andrew's *struggle* reflects the difficulty he is having, not his determination to persevere. D—To *debate* is to discuss; *resolved* refers to someone's drive to persevere.
3. B—*Adversity* and *hardship* both refer to difficulties a person faces. *Incorrect answers:* A—The word does not refer to a difficulty. C—same explanation as for A. D—same explanation as for A.
4. B—Like a *motive*, a *purpose* drives a person's actions. *Incorrect answers:* A—A *motive* is not a result. C—A *motive* is not a barrier. D—A *motive* is not lack of concern about an outcome.
5. A—To *progress* is to move forward; to *retreat* is to move backwards. *Incorrect answers:* B—This words are synonyms, not opposites. C—To *decide* is to reach a conclusion; to *debate* is to discuss. D—The words bear no relationship to each other.
6. B—To *divide* is to split apart; to *unify* is to bring together. *Incorrect answers:* A—To *coordinate* is to have different parts work together, which is not the opposite of *unify*. C—The opposite of *unify* must include more than one individual. D—A *compromise* might unity, so it is not an antonym.
7. D—*Conservatives*, unlike *radicals*, oppose great change. *Incorrect answers:* A—The word bears no relationship to *radical*. B—same explanation as for A. C—same explanation as for A.
8. D—An *agreement* can end a *confrontation*. *Incorrect answers:* A—The words are synonyms, not antonyms. B—A *dispute* can produce a confrontation. C—*Hostility* can lead to a *confrontation*.

ASSESS

Answers

Answers With Explanations

1. C—The contrast of the black sky and the red glow of the sun is vivid. *Incorrect answers:* A—The sentence has no vivid description words. B—The sentence has no vivid description words and gets into mood. D— same explanation as for B.
2. A—This substitution would describe the feeling of the air. *Incorrect answers:* B—The substitution provides no sensory details. C—same explanation as for B. D—same explanation as for B.
3. C—The substitution would clarify the meaning of *him* for any confused reader. *Incorrect answers:* A—The word *old* emphasizes Mark's distance from that life. B—The addition might intensify the sense of Mark's feelings, but would not add clarity. D—This substitution would create a fragment.
4. C—The action is described using the past tense. *Incorrect answers:* A—same explanation as for C. B—same explanation as for C. D—*Is saying* is incorrect; the past tense is needed.
5. D—"Doors opened" is an active construction. *Incorrect answers:* A—This version uses the passive voice. B—While this sentence uses the active voice, it suggests that Joey hissed, not the doors. D—same explanation as for A.
6. A—The past tense *moved* solves the tense problem in the original. *Incorrect answers:* B—The present *moves* is incorrect. C—The verb *brings* is incorrect. D—The verbs *is* and *will move* are both incorrect.

Reteach

Question	Instructional Pages to Reteach
1	269
2	330
3	—
4	331
5	330
6	331

IV. Writing and Language Conventions

Narration: Short Story

Directions: *Read the passage. Then, answer each question that follows.*

(1) The air lock doors were opened with a hiss. (2) As Mark stepped outside, he could feel the air, even through his protective suit. (3) Mark saw the sky as the sun set on Mars.

(4) "This is it, Joey," he is saying, looking down at the limp, furry, black body in his arms.

(5) He walked swiftly—bounced, really, in the thin gravity—away from the glowing glass dome of the city. (6) Carefully, Mark placed Joey's body in a shallow hole, kicking dirt back over it and mounding the grave with rocks. (7) Mark felt tears in his eyes, tears he couldn't wipe through his helmet. (8) Joey had been his first pet, brought to Mars when Mark's family moves there years earlier. (9) Losing him meant that his last tie to his old life on Earth was gone. (10) Mark was now completely Martian.

1. Which revision of sentence 3 most vividly describes the **setting** of the story?

A. Mark could see the sun setting on Mars.
B. Mark felt sadness as he watched the sun setting on Mars.
C. The blackness of the sky was broken by the glow at the horizon—the sun setting on Mars.
D. Mark watched the sun dip low in Mars's sky as he mourned the loss of his first pet, Joey.

2. What is the best way to incorporate **sensory details** in sentence 2?

A. Replace "air" with "icy winds."
B. Replace "he" with "Mark."
C. Replace "suit" with "gear."
D. Replace "protective" with "protecting."

3. Which revision would *best* clarify sentence 9?

A. Remove "old."
B. Add "suddenly" before "meant."
C. Replace "him" with "Joey."
D. Begin the sentence with "By."

4. How should the phrase "is saying" in sentence 4 be revised so that the **verb tense** is consistent in the story?

A. says
B. has said
C. said
D. keep as is

5. Which of the following is the *best* way to rewrite sentence 1 in the **active voice?**

A. Hissing, the air lock doors were opened.
B. Joey opened the air lock doors with a hiss.
C. With a hiss, the air lock doors were opened.
D. The air lock doors opened with a hiss.

6. How should sentence 8 be revised so that the **verb tense** in the sentence is consistent?

A. Joey was his first pet, brought to Mars when Mark's family moved there.
B. Joey was his first pet, brought to Mars when Mark's family moves there.
C. Joey had been his first pet, brings to Mars when Mark's family had moved there.
D. Joey is his first pet, brought to Mars when Mark's family will move there.

Differentiated Instruction for Universal Access

Strategy for Less Proficient Readers

Review skills and warm up for the test by walking students through item 1. Ask a volunteer to read item 1 aloud. Call on students to state the key requirements for a correct answer. (The answer should describe the setting and use vivid language.) Next, guide students in eliminating incorrect choices.

- **A**—The sentence describes the setting, but the language is not vivid. (Eliminate.)
- **B**—The sentence identifies the setting, but the language is not vivid. (Eliminate.)
- **C**—This sentence describes the setting using vivid words (*blackness, star-speckled sky, broken,* and *red glow*).
- **D**—While the sentence has some vivid words, it does not have as many as option C. (Eliminate.)

Guide students in seeing that **C** is the best choice. Have them complete the remaining items, encouraging them to apply a similar strategy to each. First, define key terms in the prompt and then eliminate incorrect choices.

Exposition: Problem-and-Solution Essay

Directions: *Read the passage. Then, answer each question that follows.*

(1) The bleachers in our stadium at Fairview High needs to be replaced. (2) The wood benches are badly weathered, even though they have been painted every few years. (3) I propose that we, the student body, raise the money to buy new bleachers for our field.

(4) Holding car washes and selling fund-raising items are ways we could start. (5) Another source of funds would be charging admission to varsity games, with a discounted rate for students. (6) We could charge students less. (7) We should also get permission from the school to operate concession stands at games and at other school events. (8) Raising money for new bleachers will be difficult, but I wonder if we can do it.

1. What is the correct way to revise sentence 1 so that the **subject** and the **verb agree?**

A. Change "replaced" to "replace."
B. Change "stadium" to "stadium's."
C. Change "bleachers" to "bleacher's."
D. Change "needs" to "need."

2. Which of the following sentences could be added to the first paragraph to support the claim that a **problem** exists?

A. The metal frames of the bleachers are worn and rusty.
B. Last year's football team went to the state championship.
C. Sports are popular at Fairview High.
D. I do not like the color of the bleachers.

3. How could you revise sentence 4 to make it stronger by using the **active voice?**

A. To wash cars and to sell fundraising items would help us start raising money.
B. Students raising money would be helped by washing cars and selling fundraising items.
C. We could hold car washes and sell fund raising items to start.
D. Holding car washes and selling fundraising items would be good ways to start.

4. Which sentence should be removed to eliminate redundancy?

A. sentence 2
B. sentence 3
C. sentence 6
D. sentence 7

5. Which of the following words should replace "wonder if" in sentence 8 to give this passage a positive **tone?**

A. doubt
B. wish
C. know
D. fear

Writing for Assessment

6. In a brief problem and solution essay, identify a problem in your school or community. Describe the problem and identify a solution. Include facts and details to support your ideas.

STOP

ASSESS

Answers

Answers With Explanations

1. D—The plural subject *bleachers* requires the plural verb *needs. Incorrect answers:* A—The tense of *replaced* is correct. B—The noun *stadium* is correct. C—The noun *bleachers* is correct.

2. A—The additional detail would support the idea that the bleachers are in bad shape. *Incorrect answers:* B—The addition is not relevant to the paragraph. C—same explanation as for B. D—same explanation as for B.

3. C—The new version correctly uses the active voice. *Incorrect answers:* A—This version uses the active voice but is wordy and unclear. B—This version does not use the active voice. D—same explanation as for B.

4. C—The sentence restates the meaning of the prepositional phrase in the prior sentence. *Incorrect answers:* A—The sentence provides details supporting the first sentence. B—The sentence first states the position the author advocates. D—The sentence introduces a new idea.

5. C—*Know* would be more forceful and positive. *Incorrect answers:* A—The replacement word would not create a positive tone. B—same explanation as for A. D—same explanation as for A.

Writing for Assessment

Students' short stories should identify a problem, describe how the protagonist solves it, and use descriptive details and the active voice.

Reteach

Question	Instructional Pages to Reteach
1	425
2	420
3	330
4	—
5	424
6	328–330

Benchmark

Reteach skills as indicated by students' performance, following the Reteach charts on pp. 435–439 administer the end-of-unit **Benchmark Test** (*Unit 2 Resources*, pp. 226–231). Follow the **Interpretation Guide** for the test (*Unit 2 Resources*, pp. 235–240) to assign reteaching pages as necessary in the *Reading Kit*. Use **Success Tracker** online to automatically assign these pages.

PHLit Online!

The **Benchmark Tests** and **Success Tracker** are available online at **www.PHLitOnline.com**.

Unit 3 Overview

Unit Genre and Unit Big Question

Explain to students that throughout this unit, they will read and analyze types of nonfiction. As they read, they will think about and discuss answers to the Unit Big Question: What kind of knowledge changes our lives?

Students will learn more about the Big Question on pp. 442–443. Then, on pp. 444–459, Erik Weihenmayer introduces the unit literary genre, types of nonfiction, and presents a model narrative essay of his own.

Using the Unit Selections

Teach Skills Instructional selections are presented in leveled pairs. To teach the skills and meet the objectives, you need to complete only one selection in each pairing.

Differentiate and Reinforce Choose the selection in a pairing that is best suited for your students. The selections are listed by accessibility in the Differentiated Instruction box on the next page. You may use the other selection in the pairing to reinforce comprehension and skills or to provide enrichment.

Integrate Skills Each selection pairing presents students with a reading strategy, a literary analysis concept, and a vocabulary skill, as well as vocabulary development opportunities and grammar instruction. In addition, students have opportunities to extend learning in the Writing and extension (Research and Technology or Listening and Speaking) activities.

Unit Features

Informational Texts Students learn to use and evaluate various types of informational texts.

Comparing Literary Works Students compare the use of a literary element in two or more works.

To help you plan your use of the unit, see the Unit Overview and Pacing Plan on pp. 442a–442b and the Time and Resource Manager preceding each selection pairing.

Types of Nonfiction
THE BIG ?
What kind of knowledge changes our lives?
440 Types of NonFiction

PHLit Online!
www.PHLitOnline.com

Teaching From Technology

Enriched Online Student Edition
- full narration of selections
- interactive graphic organizers
- linked Get Connected! and Background videos
- all worksheets and other student resources

Professional Development
- the *Professional Development Guidebook* online
- additional professional development articles by program authors

Planning, Assigning, and Monitoring
- software for online assignment of work to students, individually or to the whole class
- a system for tracking and grading students' work

UNIT 3

PHLit Online!
www.PHLitOnline.com

Hear It!
- Selection summary audio
- Selection audio
- BQ Tunes

See It!
- Penguin author video
- Big Question video
- Get Connected videos
- Background videos
- More about the authors
- Illustrated vocabulary words
- Vocabulary flashcards

Do It!
- Interactive journals
- Interactive graphic organizers
- Grammar tutorials
- Interactive vocabulary games
- Test practice

441

Instructional Resources

Unit 3 Resources supports unit skills with pages of the following types:

- **Benchmark Tests** assess and monitor students' progress at mid-unit and at unit's end.
- **Vocabulary and Reading Warm-ups** provide additional vocabulary support, based on Lexile rankings of words, for each selection. "A" Warm-ups are for students reading two grades below level. "B" Warm-ups are for students reading one grade below level.
- **Selection Support** These practice pages are available for each selection:
  - **Reading Skill**
  - **Literary Analysis**
  - **Writing About the Big Question**
  - **Vocabulary**
  - **Support for Writing**
  - **Support for Extend Your Learning**
  - **Enrichment**

PHLit Online!
All worksheets and other student resources are also available at **www.PHLitOnline.com.**

Differentiated Instruction for Universal Access

Accessibility for Various Ability Levels
This chart gives a general accessibility rating to help you decide which selection in each leveled pair is more appropriate for your students. **Choose one selection in each pair or choose to teach both.** You will meet the objectives for the pair when you teach either of the two selections. For additional guidance on factors that affect the accessibility of each selection, see the Selection Choices page for each selection set.

Accessibility for English Learners
EL This icon indicates support for English learners at point of use in this Teacher's Edition.

	More Accessible	More Challenging
Pair 1	The Spider and the Wasp	*from* Longitude
Pair 2	The Sun Parlor	*from* In Commemoration: One Million Volumes
Pair 3	Keep Memory Alive	*from* Nobel Lecture
Pair 4	The American Idea	What Makes a Degas a Degas?

UNIT OVERVIEW AND PACING PLAN

Meeting Your Standards

Students will

1. rrecognize and appreciate nonfiction as a literary form.
2. read and analyze a variety of essays and speeches.
3. apply reading skills.
   - Analyze main idea and supporting details
   - Ask questions to determine main idea
   - Evaluate the writer's argument
   - Evaluate persuasion and distinguish between fact and opinion
4. analyze literary elements.
   - Expository essay
   - Reflective essay
   - Persuasive writing and rhetorical devices
   - Analytic and interpretive essays
5. build vocabulary and vocabulary concepts.
   - Roots
   - Prefixes
   - Words with multiple meanings
6. learn elements of grammar, mechanics, and usage.
   - Direct and indirect objects
   - Subject complements
   - Combining short sentences
   - Degrees of adverbs
   - Degrees of adjectives
   - Parallelism
7. use a recursive writing process to write in a variety of forms.
   - Letter to the editor
   - Persuasive essay
8. read informational materials.
   - Follow and critique technical directions
   - Analyze text structures in a research source and a course catalog
9. compare literary works.
   - Compare humorous writing
   - Compare author's purpose
10. develop research and technology skills.
    - Cover letter and résumé
11. develop listening and speaking skills.
    - Interview
    - Humorous persuasive speech
    - Oral recollection
    - Debate
    - Deliver a persuasive speech

	Week 1					Week 2					Week 3				
	1	2	3	4	5	1	2	3	4	5	1	2	3	4	5
Introduce the Unit Big Question (pp. 442–443).	●														
Introduce the Unit author and the Unit genre, nonfiction (pp 444–447).	●														
Teach the Model selections (pp. 448–459).	●	●													
Teach one selection from Pairing 1 (pp. 460–485).		●	●	●	●	●									
Teach one selection from Pairing 2 (pp. 486–509).						●	●	●	●						
Complete the Test Practice: Reading (pp. 510–511).									●						
Teach Informational Texts (pp. 512–517).										●					
Teach Comparing Literary Works (pp. 518–531).											●	●			
Have students complete the Writing Workshop (pp. 532–537).										●	●	●	●	●	
Administer **Benchmark Test 5** (***Unit 3 Resources,*** pp. 120–125).														●	
Reteach skills, judging which skills to reteach by evaluating students' performance on **Benchmark Test 5**.															●

	Week 4					Week 5					Week 6				
	1	2	3	4	5	1	2	3	4	5	1	2	3	4	5
Teach one selection from Pairing 3 (pp. 538–555).	●	●	●	●											
Teach one selection from Pairing 4 (pp. 556–575).					●	●	●	●							
Complete the Test-Practice: Reading (pp. 576–577).								●							
Teach Informational Texts (pp. 578–583).									●						
Teach Comparing Literary Works (pp. 584–603).										●	●				
Have students complete the Writing Workshop (pp. 604–611).									●	●	●	●	●		
Have students complete Applying the Big Question (pp. 612–613).												●			
Have students complete the Vocabulary and Communications Workshops (pp. 614–615, 616).													●		
Complete the Test Practice: Unit 3 Review (pp. 618–623).													●		
Administer **Benchmark Test 6** (***Unit 3 Resources***, pp. 227–235).														●	
Reteach skills, judging which skills to reteach by evaluating students' performance on **Benchmark Test 6**.															●

Block and Daily Scheduling

The assignments and activities in this Unit planner are organized by week. You may adjust them to your daily or block schedule. The Time and Resource Manager for each selection set gives specific pacing suggestions, or you may use the comprehensive lesson planning support online at **www.PHLitOnline.com.**

Monitoring Progress

Diagnose Each main selection pairing in the Unit contains a more accessible and a more challenging selection. To determine which selection in each pairing to assign, refer to students' results on **Benchmark Test 4, *Unit 2 Resources,*** pp. 227–235 (administered at the end of the previous Unit). Use the **Interpretation Guide** to interpret the results of the diagnostic portion of the test. **Note:** For the most accurate diagnosis of students who score in the middle range, administer the additional diagnostic questions online at **www.PHLitOnline.com.**

Preteach and Prepare As indicated by the diagnostic, prepare students for reading by assigning the **Vocabulary** and **Reading Warm-ups** for the selections you assign.

Teach Follow this Pacing Plan and use the resources to teach the skills and selections. For specific pacing suggestions and a list of resources, see the Time and Resource Manager and the Visual Guide to Featured Selection Resources preceding each selection pairing.

Assess After students have completed the first half of the Unit, administer **Benchmark Test 5**. Administer **Benchmark Test 6** at the end of the Unit.

Intervention and Reteach After administering each test, use the **Interpretation Guide** for the tests to determine which reteaching pages, if any, you should assign from the ***Reading Kit.*** The appropriate pages are also available through the online Progress Monitoring software.

Independent Reading

To differentiate, reinforce, and extend your instruction, have students choose a full-length work from the Independent Reading page, page 617, and read it while working on this Unit. Consult the Sensitivity Issues notes for the page to guide students' choices.

CLASSROOM STRATEGIES

Expanding Academic Vocabulary Using Home Language

Sharroky Hollie

“In working with SELS, teachers should assume that the students have a comprehensive conceptual knowledge base that is rooted in their culture, community, and life experiences.”

Did your high school vocabulary exercises involve one or all of the following: a list of twenty words connected to upcoming text in a certain content area, looking up the words in the dictionary, attempting to use those words in a sentence or a story, and a quiz on Friday. On the surface, this traditional approach to vocabulary learning makes sense. Students are exposed to words weekly, practice and reinforcement are provided through a variety of formats, and a weekly assessment is conducted for monitoring and support. However, research has told us that this traditional approach is ineffective.

Principles of Effective Vocabulary Instruction

A survey of the research indicates that the following principles of vocabulary instruction should be included in any program or approach (Beck & McKewon, 2001)

- Providing definitional and contextual information about the word's meaning
- Actively involving students in word learning through talking about comparing, analyzing, and using the target words
- Provide multiple exposures to meaningful information about each word
- Teaching word analysis

When working with underachieving Standard English learners (SELs), teachers must consider the following time-proven strategies: Activating prior knowledge, making schematic connections, and building on the linguistic capital of the students.

Building on linguistic capital In working with SELS, teachers should assume that the students have a comprehensive conceptual knowledge base that is rooted in their culture, community, and life experiences. Through these experiences, the students have a multitude of thoughts, opinions, and concepts about the world they live in and the world around them. More importantly, they have given these concepts their own labels, names, and words. Teachers need to build and to bridge on the linguistic capital by providing students with Standard English and academic language labels.

Steps to Expanding Academic Vocabulary of Standard English Learners

Teaching context clues as a primary strategy. The use of context clues to guess the meaning of words that the students do not know is important. Create sentences or a brief paragraph with the vocabulary words embedded. Have students guess at the meanings conceptually, using context clues. Since the teacher is more interested in the conceptual meanings rather than the technical meanings, the students are going to initially provide words that they own from their vocabularies. Keep in mind that the meanings will not be exact matches at this point.

Create a Personal Thesaurus Creating a personal thesaurus activates student's prior knowledge, builds on schema, and teaches synonym development. Steps to creating a personal thesaurus:

1. Have students brainstorm synonymous concepts/words for the target vocabulary that they already have in their own vocabulary. Their words should indicate that they understand the concepts of the words, not the technical meaning.
2. Have students make a list of synonyms for the target word, with their words highlighted at the top of the chart, the target word follows on the next line and any other academic synonyms follow on the lines after.

Students may now continue to add to this list and utilize it as their own personal thesaurus during writing.

Tried and True Vocabulary Strategies

Use of the following vocabulary strategies is important for reinforcement and continued practice with the new words that the students are learning. The following sample strategies have stood the test of time:

Vocabulary Prediction Chart Make a table with the following titles: vocabulary word, my guess before reading, my guess after reading, and clue words. Have students guess at the meaning of the word prior to reading. After reading the selection containing the vocabulary words, have them try to define them again. Have them identify key words that helped them with their definition.

Cubing Give students a pattern for a cube. Have them do the following in each panel:

1. Write the vocabulary word
2. Define it
3. Write something personal it reminds them of
4. Write a synonym
5. Write an antonym and
6. Illustrate it. Hang the various vocabulary cubes in a mobile form.

Supporting Research

Beck, I.L., & McKeown, M.G. (2002). *Bringing words to life: Robust vocabulary instruction.* New York: Guilford.

Modeled Strategy

See pp. 476 and 502 for point-of-use notes modeling these strategies.

Teacher Resources

- ***Professional Development Guidebook***
- ***Classroom Strategies and Teaching Routines* cards**

PHLit Online!

Log on as a teacher at **www.PHLitOnline.com** to access a library of all Professional Development articles by the Contributing Authors of Pearson Prentice Hall *Literature*.

Sharroky Hollie

Sharroky Hollie is a Professor in Teacher Education at Cal State Dominguez Hills. He is also the co-Founder and co-director of a laboratory school in culturally and linguistically responsive teaching. Dr. Hollie's research interests are the language and literacy development for Standard English Learners, culturally responsive teaching, professional development design, and teacher development. He consults nationally on the topic of culturally responsive instruction.

INTRODUCE

Introducing the Big Question

1. Read the introductory paragraph on the student page. Give this example of knowledge that changed a person's life: Ann thought Jim was irresponsible because he was often late to school. She changed her opinion when she found out that he helped out at his parents' restaurant three mornings a week.
2. **Ask,** How might this knowledge change both of their lives? **Possible response:** Ann might respect Jim more. She might decide to help Jim. Jim might not be late to school as often. They might become friends.
3. **Ask** students the Big Question, "What kind of knowledge changes our lives? **Possible response:** Learning about a person can change your relationship with that person.
4. Tell students that the stories in this unit involve knowledge that has changed lives. As they read, ask them to think about what knowledge has changed their own lives.

Introducing the Big Question Vocabulary

1. Point out the Big Question Vocabulary on the facing page. Explain that these words are useful in discussing the Big Question.
2. Review the meaning of each word. (Definitions appear on the teacher edition on p. 443.)
3. Have students complete the **Big Question Vocabulary** worksheets, ***Unit 3 Resources***, pp. 1–3.

Write What You Know

1. Review the assignment with students, using the instruction on the student page.
2. Have students share their lists with partners and discuss what kinds of knowledge change people's lives the most.

PHLit Online!

Show the Big Question video, available at **www.PHLitOnline.com.**

Introducing the Big Question

THE BIG Q: What kind of *knowledge* changes our lives?

Knowledge is a mastering of a body of facts or a range of information about a topic. As you learn, you may also develop **insight** into a problem or arrive at a deeper **awareness** and **understanding** of the world around you. You gain knowledge when you leave **ignorance** behind, **question** old attitudes, and **revise** ideas that are outdated or wrong. While not all information may cause a noticeable difference in your life, some knowledge—such as information that makes you think about people and important issues—can change your life and **influence** your actions.

Start thinking about the Big Question by considering the different types of knowledge people gain throughout their lives.

Discuss It

Write What You Know

List the people, ideas, and subjects about which you have gained important knowledge. Describe one specific example of each of the following categories:

- discovering something new about a person that caused you to view that person differently
- a time you put a new skill to use
- an incident in **history** you studied that changed the way people live
- an essay or a book that **modified** how you view the world
- a problem or conflict that made you take action

Share your examples with a partner. Talk about how knowledge of these issues, ideas, and people has the potential to change lives.

PHLit Online!
www.PHLitOnline.com
- Big Question video
- Illustrated vocabulary words
- Interactive vocabulary games
- BQ Tunes

Understanding by Design

The Big Question

Explain to students that they will continue to consider the Big Question as they work through Unit 3.

- At the beginning of each selection, they will write a response to a Writing About the Big Question sentence frame.
- As they read the selection, they will look for details related to the Big Question.
- At the end of the selection, they will answer a Critical Thinking question that is related to the Big Question.
- At the end of Unit 3, they will complete an Applying the Big Question workshop (pp. 612–613). In the workshop, they will review literature in the unit and think about real-world examples that shed light on the Big Question. They will also have a chance to reflect on their first answers, thinking about how their ideas have changed.
- Tell students that their goal will be to gain a deeper understanding of literature and a more sophisticated way of discussing the Big Question.

Discuss It

Explain What You Know

Use the examples and ideas you discussed with your partner to help you complete these sentences about knowledge.

- Gaining **empathy** or compassion for a person may make you see him or her differently because ___________.
- Learning a new skill such as ____________ will change a person's life by ___________.
- Being aware of world events is important because _______.

Share your responses with a partner.

Write About It

Tell What You Think

Based on the discussions you have had, decide what you think right now. Your answer may change as you read the selections in this unit.

We can change our lives with knowledge about _____________.

Use one or more of these sentences, or your own ideas, to write a brief support of your response.

- Different ways people gain knowledge include ____________ and ____________.
- Reflecting on yourself and your life can lead to personal **growth** because ____________.
- Knowledge about ____________ can change your life because ____________.
- One reason a person may choose to remain ignorant about an issue or a person is ____________.

Discuss your response with a partner or a small group.

Connecting to the Literature

The readings in this unit will help you think about different types of knowledge and the effects that knowledge can have on people's lives. Each reading will give you an insight into the Big Question. At the end of the unit, you will see how your ideas have grown and changed.

☆ shows an **Academic Vocabulary** word.

Big Question Vocabulary

- ☆ adapt
- ☆ awareness
- empathy
- enlighten
- ☆ evolve
- growth
- history
- ignorance
- influence
- ☆ insight
- ☆ modified
- question
- reflect
- ☆ revise
- understanding

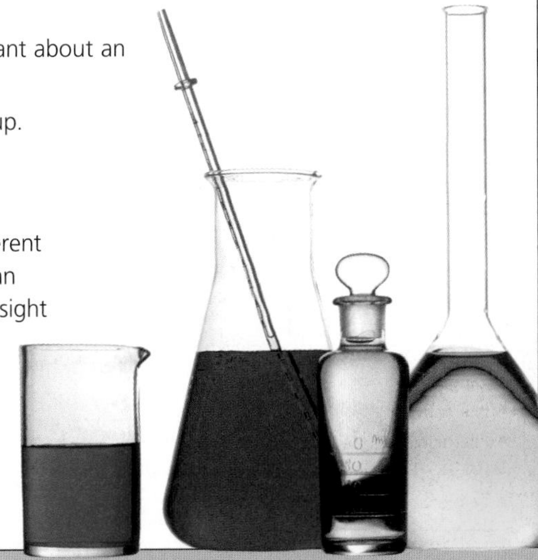

Explain What You Know

1. Introduce the assignment, using the instruction on the student page.
2. Have students work with partners and use the ideas and examples they discussed to consider how knowledge changes people's lives. Give definitions to the Big Question Vocabulary words as needed. (See the definitions below in the Big Question Vocabulary box.)
3. Guide students to complete the sentence starters and share their responses with a partner.

Tell What You Think

1. Introduce the assignment. Ask students to review their examples of knowledge that changed people's lives on their lists.
2. Have them review their "Explain What You Know" sentences as they consider what kinds of knowledge would change their lives.
3. Direct students to complete the sentence starters. Then have them choose one of the sentences to help them write brief paragraphs in support of their responses to what they think right now. Encourage them to base their responses on their previous work.
3. As they draft their paragraphs, tell students to support their decisions by including ideas and examples from previous activities.
4. Instruct students to discuss their writing in small groups.

Connecting to the Literature

Explain the structure of the Big Question strand in the unit, referring to the Understanding by Design box on the previous page.

Big Question Vocabulary

adapt (ə dapt′*) *v.* to change or adjust
awareness (ə wer′ nis*) *n.* having knowledge
empathy (em′pə thē) *n.* sharing in another person's feelings
enlighten (en līt′'n) *v.* to make clear through knowledge
evolve (ē välv, -vôlv*) *v.* to develop through gradual changes
growth (grōth) *n.* the process of developing
history (his′tə rē) *n.* an account of what has happened
ignorance (ig′nə rəns) *n.* lack of knowledge or education
influence (in′flo͞o əns) *n.* the power of people to change others
insight (in′sīt′) *n.* a clear idea of the nature of things
modified (mäd′ə fīd′) *v.* changed or altered slightly
question (kwes′chən) *v.* to express uncertainty about
reflect (ri flekt′) *v.* to think seriously about something
revise (ri vīz′) *v.* to reconsider and modify
understanding (un′dər stand iŋ) *n.* the power to comprehend and discern

PRETEACH

Meeting Your Standards

Students will

1. understand the characteristics, types, and purposes of essays and speeches.
2. learn about author Erik Weihenmayer.
3. read and analyze an example of an autobiographical essay.
4. relate visuals to types of nonfiction.

❶ What kind of knowledge changes our lives?

Remind students that they will think more about the Unit Big Question as they read and discuss the nonfiction essays and speeches in this unit.

❷ What Is Nonfiction?

Introduce Erik Weihenmayer

1. Erik Weihenmayer taught English in middle school and plans to write more books. His autobiography demonstrates that he is a man determined to overcome obstacles.
2. Use the *See It!* DVD to introduce the author and the genre. Show Segment 4 to provide insight into the way Weihenmayer meets challenges. After students have watched the segment, **ask:** What drives the author to write about his experiences?
   Answer: Weihenmayer hopes to be an inspiration and a role model to both blind and sighted people.
3. Interested students might enjoy reading Erik Weihenmayer's exciting memoir, *Touch the Top of the World: A Blind Man's Journey to Climb Farther Than the Eye Can See.*

Introduce Nonfiction

Point out to students that nonfiction includes many types of writing, including essays, autobiographies, and articles. Invite volunteers to discuss how an article in a newspaper might be different from an article in a textbook or an encyclopedia.

Introduction: Nonfiction

THE BIG ?

❶ **What kind of *knowledge* changes our lives?**

New information can alter perceptions and change lives.

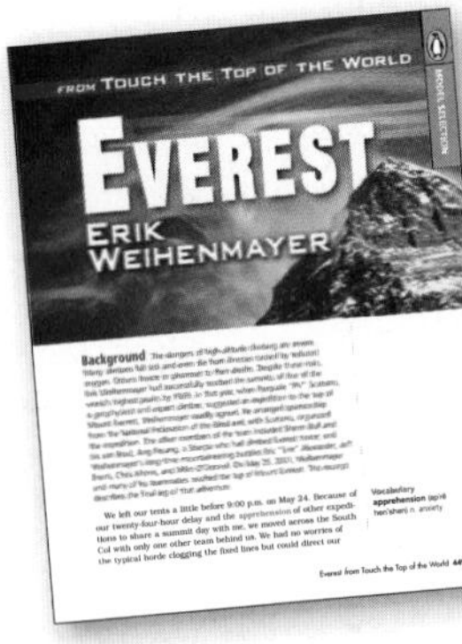

What Is Nonfiction? ❷

by Erik Weihenmayer

An **article** is a short nonfiction piece, often found in newspapers, magazines, textbooks, and encyclopedias. It presents facts, explains concepts, or tells about events. A **newspaper article,** for example, explores an event or an issue and fairly presents different points of view.

❸ The Informal Essay

In contrast to an article, an **essay** is usually longer and has more literary value. An **informal essay** gives writers the freedom to bring their own thoughts, feelings, and reflections into the discussion. For example, I have published informal essays on all sorts of topics, from why a blind person would ever enjoy climbing mountains to a comparison of my Everest climb with Sir Edmund Hillary's first ascent of that mountain over fifty years ago.

Although I start with a topic in mind, I never first write the beginning or end of the essay; that's too much pressure. I start with the content I know best or believe in most strongly. Later I mold the beginning and end around the middle.

❹ Autobiographical Essay to Autobiography

When I write an **autobiographical essay,** it takes self-reflection to chisel out the **themes** that give meaning to my life. A life can be rambling, fragmented, and ambiguous, not tidy like those of some fictional characters.

As I combined such essays to create my book-length **autobiography,** I faced the same challenge as I did when writing individual essays: how to tell my life as a unified story. I didn't want the book to seem like a series of short, isolated **vignettes,** or brief narratives. How could I find the sinuous strands of my life and weave them together so that they constantly built upon each other and strengthened the overall impact?

My editor had great advice. "Think of an autobiography as a tree trunk. Your characters, plots, and themes should flow together and stay connected. Branches or tangents may be interesting, but ultimately lead to dead ends." So, after some coercion, I cut two beloved chapters—autobiographical essays—which I came to realize were branches.

PHLit Online!
www.PHLitOnline.com

- Penguin author video
- Interactive journals
- Interactive graphic organizers
- Selection audio
- Self-test

Teaching Resources

The following resources can be used to enrich, extend, or differentiate the instruction.

- All *Unit 3 Resources,* pp. 1–13
- All *Professional Development Guidebook,* p. 33
- All *Graphic Organizer Transparency,* pp. 73–74
- All *See It!* DVD
  Erik Weihenmayer, Segment 4
- All **Enriched Online Student Edition**
- L2 L3 ***Reader's Notebook***
- L1 ***Reader's Notebook: Adapted Version***
- EL ***Reader's Notebook: English Learner's Version***
- L2 EL ***Hear It!* Audio CD**
- L1 EL ***Hear It!* Audio CD**

PHLit Online! All resources, including print and video, are available at **www.PHLitOnline.com.**

I also learned to weave together the threads of my life by reading *The World According to Garp*. In this novel, the "disharmonious parts" of a character's life can form a complete whole.

When she began with that sentence, an aura was cast over her autobiography that bound the disharmonious parts of her life's story together, the way fog shrouds an uneven landscape, the way heat reaches through a rambling house into every room.

from *The World According to Garp*

—John Irving

Meet
Erik Weihenmayer (b. 1968)

Author of *Touch the Top of the World*

Erik Weihenmayer has not allowed blindness to keep him from paragliding, biking, skiing, and climbing. He made the cover of *Time* magazine in 2001 after he had reached the summit of Mount Everest. He has said, "I truly believe that we will change what it means to be blind, and we'll do it one mountain at a time." In 2002, he completed his quest to climb the highest peak on each of the seven continents by climbing to the summit of Mount Kosciuszko in Australia.

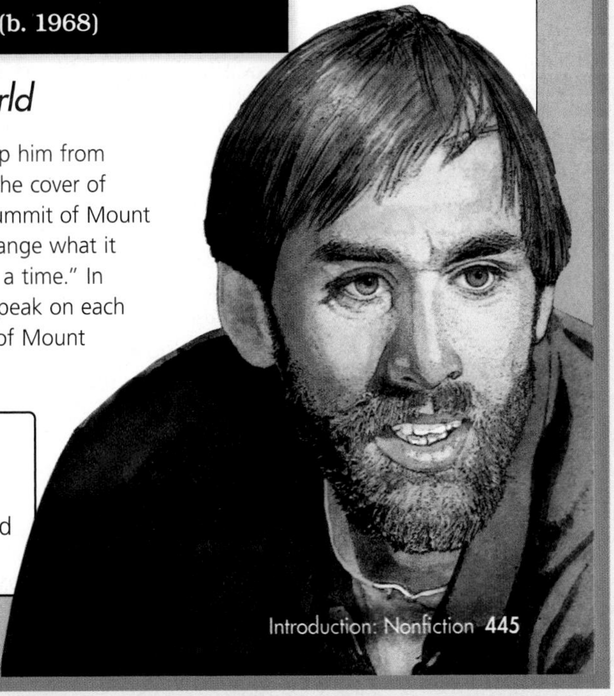

Did You Know?

Weihenmayer began mountain climbing at age 16. He uses sound and touch to guide him when he climbs.

❸ The Informal Essay (p. 444)

1. Explain to students that the word *essay* comes from the French word *essais,* meaning "attempts."
2. **Ask** students to think of examples of articles on the essay topics that Weihenmayer mentions. **Possible response:** Instead of an essay on why a blind person would enjoy climbing a mountain, an article might report facts of the climb.

❹ Autobiographical Essay to Autobiography (pp. 444–445)

1. **Ask:** What does Weihenmayer mean when he says he needs to "chisel out the themes" in his life? **Possible response:** He wants to focus on the things that are important enough in his life to pass on to his readers.
2. **Ask** students to comment on the connection between Weihenmayer's writing process and the self-reflection necessary in autobiographical essays.
3. **Possible response:** Weihenmayer writes first about the things he knows best—events or incidents of his life. In introductions and conclusions, he can make clear the importance or theme of those events.
4. Explain that *The World According to Garp* by John Irving concerns a man and his mother who are both writers. When Garp finally publishes his first novel after a long struggle, his mother publishes an instantly successful autobiography. In this quotation, Garp describes his mother's writing process. **Ask** students how the quotation captures Weihenmayer's view of autobiographical writing. **Possible response:** The images in the quotation, like Weihenmayer's image of weaving together the strands of his life, talk about combining separate parts into a whole.

Differentiated Instruction for Universal Access

EL Pronunciation for English Learners

Some students might find it difficult to pronounce words with the terminal consonant "ng" sound, as in *beginning* and *meaning,* and instead replace it with the "n" sound. The following strategies can help students to pronounce the "ng" sound.

- Pronounce each of the following words in turn: *interesting, according, biking, skiing,* and *climbing*. Have students follow by repeating each word. Then, call out verbs at random, and have students say the word, adding an *-ing* at the end. Discuss the results with the class, examining what might have led to discrepancies between spellings.
- Pair English learners with fluent speakers. Have the pair individually read the section entitled "Meet Erik Weihenmayer." Then, have each student draw a rendering of each word that is pronounced with the terminal consonant sound "ng." Have the pairs exchange their results, determining what might have led to differences between drawings.

PHLit Online!

Show or assign the Penguin author video segments for these pages, available at **www.PHLitOnline.com**

TEACH

5 Characteristics of Essays and Speeches

1. Tell students that essays can weave together everything from private thoughts and memories to anecdotes, research, and philosophy.
2. Explain that speeches have basically the same characteristics as essays and other forms of nonfiction. Speeches and essays both display style, tone, perspective, and purpose.
3. Discuss the concepts of *style* and *tone* with students. Tell students that a writer's style is often described by words such as *formal, informal, conversational, direct,* or *ornate*. These words describe how the writer uses language. Tone is often described using words such as *amused, angry, sincere,* or *sarcastic*. These words suggest the writer's attitude or approach to the subject.
4. Tell students that when reading essays, it can be helpful first to determine the writer's purpose. Suggest that after reading an essay, students ask themselves how well the author accomplished his or her purpose.

Exploring Types of Nonfiction

5 Characteristics of Essays and Speeches

Essays are short works of nonfiction. Their authors are usually named and are always real people. Speeches are nonfiction literary works that a speaker delivers to an audience.

- An **essay** examines and discusses a topic, often presenting the writer's personal viewpoints. Essays typically explore ideas and opinions.
- A **speech** presents a topic and often marks a specific occasion. There are many types of speeches, ranging from informal talks to formal lectures.

Peanuts, reprinted by permission of United Features Syndicate, Inc.

Essays or speeches offer more than ideas and facts; they also express a writer's style, tone, perspective, and purpose.

- **Style** is the distinctive way an author uses language. Many factors contribute to an author's style, including level of formality, use of figurative language, word choice, sentence patterns, and methods of organization.
- **Tone** is the author's attitude toward both the subject and the audience. When you listen to a speech, you can hear the speaker's tone just as you do when you engage in conversations. Authors of written works convey tone through word choice and details. Tone is often described with a single adjective: *formal, ironic, amused, angry,* and so on.
- **Perspective** is the viewpoint or opinion an author expresses. Bias occurs when the presentation of a viewpoint is one-sided and the writer distorts facts or uses emotional language to manipulate the audience.
- **Purpose** is the author's reason for writing or speaking. Common purposes include the following: to inform, to entertain, to persuade, to praise, to celebrate, to warn.

Understanding by Design

Clarifying Expected Outcomes

Explain to students that pages 446–447 set out their goals in this unit. By the end of Unit 3, they will understand the characteristics of nonfiction speeches and essays, including style, tone, perspective, and purpose. They will be able to identify and discuss these elements in specific types of nonfiction writing. They will also be able to use some of these elements in writing their own letter to the editor in the Writing Workshop on pp. 532–537 and in writing their own persuasive essay in the Writing Workshop on pp. 604–611.

Remind students that in addition, they will explore the impact of different types of knowledge as they work toward an answer to the Unit Big Question, "What kind of knowledge changes our lives?" They will also add words to their vocabulary that will help them when discussing knowledge/change. (See Introducing the Big Question, pp. 442-443.)

❻ Types of Essays

Essays can be categorized by the mode of composition or author's purpose.

- A **narrative essay** tells the story of real events or experiences.
- A **descriptive essay** creates an impression about a person, an object, or an experience.
- An **expository essay** provides information, explores ideas, or explains a process.
- A **persuasive essay** attempts to convince readers to take a course of action or adopt the writer's position on an issue.
- A **reflective essay** conveys the writer's thoughts and feelings about a personal experience or an idea.

❼ Types of Speeches

Speeches can be categorized by their levels of formality, which are determined by the speaker, occasion, and purpose.

- An **address** is a formal, prepared speech that is usually delivered by someone of importance.
- A **talk** is an informal speech delivered in a conversational style.
- An **oration** is an eloquent speech given on a formal occasion.
- A **lecture** is a prepared speech that informs or instructs an audience.

Put Yourself in the Picture

Use these sentence starters to connect this picture to nonfiction.

- The **purpose** of an essay based on this picture might be to ________.
- An **expository essay** would be more likely to talk about ______, but a **reflective essay** based on this picture could discuss ________.
- The **tone** of a nonfiction piece that I could write about this picture might be ________________ because ______________________.

Challenge Suppose you were one of the people in this picture. From a first-person perspective, write a brief **descriptive essay** explaining what you see, hear, smell, and touch as you learn how this car works.

Differentiated Instruction for Universal Access

Support for Special Needs Students

Have students read the **Exploring Essays and Speeches** page in the *Reader's Notebook: Adapted Version.* This version provides a basic-level introduction to the essay and the speech.

Support for Less Proficient Readers

Have students read the **Exploring Essays and Speeches** page in the *Reader's Notebook.* This version provides a basic-level introduction to the essay and the speech.

EL Support for English Learners

Have students read the **Exploring Essays and Speeches** page in the *Reader's Notebook: English Learner's Version.* This version provides a basic-level introduction to the essay and the speech.

❻ Types of Essays

1. Point out that the different modes of composition can be used within a single essay. A writer might combine narration with description, or exposition with persuasion. **Ask** students to think of topics that might require a combination of writing modes.
   Possible response: An essay might describe a place and include reflection about its history.
2. **Ask:** For what purposes might each of the listed kinds of writing be used?
   Possible responses: Narrative: entertain, inform, introduce a subject; Descriptive: re-create an experience, inform, celebrate, praise; Expository: inform; Persuasive: persuade, warn; Reflective: inform, celebrate

❼ Types of Speeches

Have students think of a topic and a situation for each type of speech.
Possible responses: Address: An author's discussion of his or her latest book at a library opening; Talk: A student's report to the Spanish Club on a recent trip to Mexico; Oration: Dr. Martin Luther King, Jr.'s "I Have a Dream" speech; Lecture: A teacher's introduction to Shakespeare

ASSESS

Answers

Put Yourself in the Picture

Sample response: The purpose of an essay based on this picture might be to explain how to fix a car engine. An **expository essay** would be more likely to talk about specific engine parts, but a **reflective essay** based on this picture could discuss the benefits of teamwork. The tone of a nonfiction piece that I could write about this picture might be serious because fixing an engine requires one to be very careful.

Challenge

Students' essays should contain relevant sensory details expressed in the first-person point of view.

PRETEACH

❶ Introducing the Selection

1. Invite students to read Erik Weihenmayer's introduction to "Everest."
2. **Ask:** What did the author hope to achieve by being so honest with his readers? **Possible response:** Weihenmayer wants his readers to understand that despite his disability, he has the same emotions and frustrations that any person has while trying to achieve a difficult goal.
3. Call students' attention to the terms used in discussing the essay: *autobiography, reflection,* and *theme*. Have them identify the terms as they read the essay.

❷ Background

Mount Everest As the highest point on Earth at 29,035 feet, Mount Everest has long been a challenge to climbers. Sir Edmund Hillary and his Sherpa guide Tenzing Norgay are credited with the first successful Everest climb. Since their 1953 ascent, about 4,000 others have made the attempt.

❷ Connecting to the Big Question

1. Prepare students to apply the Big Question, "What kind of knowledge changes our lives?" to the Model Selection.
2. Explain to students that in "Everest," Weihenmayer joins an expedition to climb Mt. Everest.
3. Have students complete this sentence starter, featuring thematic vocabulary from pp. 442–443:

   A mountain climber's awareness of the dangers involved in attaining a goal can influence his or her _____.

   Possible response: decision to proceed or turn back in a compromising situation.
4. Discuss students' responses. Then, as they read the essay, have students look for examples of situations where knowledge helped influence a decision.

Concept Connector →

Students will discuss the situations when they have concluded reading.

Model Selection: Types of Nonfiction

❶ Erik Weihenmayer

❷ Introduces "Everest"

❸ When I first considered writing an **autobiography,** people around me said, "It should be an 'inspirational book,'" but I had always been uncomfortable with that word. All a blind person has to do is to cross a road independently and people say, "How inspirational!" Whether a word is used to raise someone onto a pedestal, or to minimize someone through low expectations, it serves to separate that person from everyone else.

The Fears as Well as the Victories

I started by asking myself, "What books do I like?" They were books like *Dove* by Robin Lee Graham and Derek Gill: an **autobiography** describing the 16-year-old Graham's sailing trip around the world. The authors envelop you in so much **description** and **reflection** that you feel Graham's disappointments, his yearning, and you celebrate when he ultimately pushes through his human frailties.

So I decided to write a book that was honest: not a flattering tale of a hero conquering mountains or a stereotyped version of a blind person, but one that revealed moments when I was crushed by sadness, paralyzed by fear, clouded by doubt, and even when I was shallow or just plain mean. If there was inspiration to be found, I wanted it to come from the book's unexpected humor, its intensity of passion, and its gritty, sometimes unpleasant reality.

My Purpose: Connecting With You

By being honest and sharing deeply, I hoped to find connection points with my **audience,** those archetypal ways which make us human, so my life didn't seem remote from theirs. For me, the best compliment would be for a reader to say, "Although he's blind, in many ways we're the same, and goals that I feared were impossible to attain are within my reach."

The "Everest" chapter you are about to read is called an "Afterword." I compiled it from my journals soon after I returned from climbing Mt. Everest, and my publisher included it when the paperback edition came out. Although it is a self-contained adventure, it continues the intersecting **themes** of the book: relying on friends, reaching into the darkness, and pushing past the nay-sayers to breathe in as much joy, fulfillment, and accomplishment as humanly possible.

Vocabulary Development

Vocabulary Knowledge Rating

Create a **Vocabulary Knowledge Rating Chart** (***Professional Development Guidebook***, p. 33) with these words from the selection:

sparse *ambient* *arduously*

Give students a copy of the chart. Read the words aloud, and have students mark their rating in the Before Reading column. Urge them to be alert to these words as they read and discuss "Everest," because they will rate their knowledge of the words after they finish.

Tally how many students think they know a word to gauge how much instruction to provide. As students read, point out the words and their context.

PHLit Online! **Vocabulary Central,** featuring tools, activities, and songs for studying vocabulary, is available at **www.PHLitOnline.com.**

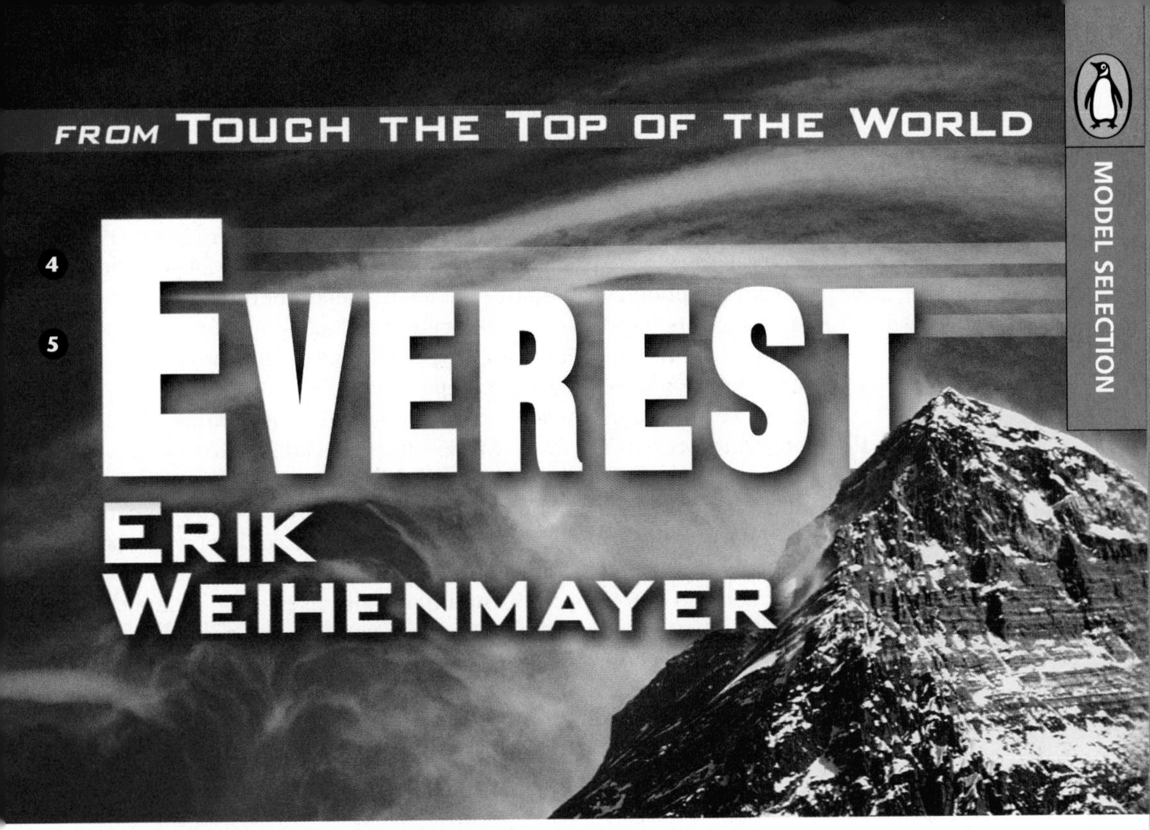

MODEL SELECTION

FROM TOUCH THE TOP OF THE WORLD

4

5

EVEREST

ERIK WEIHENMAYER

6 Background The dangers of high-altitude climbing are severe. Many climbers fall sick and even die from illnesses caused by reduced oxygen. Others freeze or plummet to their deaths. Despite these risks, Erik Weihenmayer had successfully reached the summits of five of the world's highest peaks by 1999. In that year, when Pasquale "PV" Scaturro, a geophysicist and expert climber, suggested an expedition to the top of Mount Everest, Weihenmayer readily agreed. He arranged sponsorship from the National Federation of the Blind and, with Scaturro, organized the expedition. The other members of the team included Sherm Bull and his son Brad; Ang Pasang, a Sherpa who had climbed Everest twice; and Weihenmayer's long-time mountaineering buddies Eric "Erie" Alexander, Jeff Evans, Chris Morris, and Mike O'Donnell. On May 25, 2001, Weihenmayer and many of his teammates reached the top of Mount Everest. This excerpt describes the final leg of that adventure.

We left our tents a little before 9:00 p.m. on May 24. Because of our twenty-four-hour delay and the apprehension of other expeditions to share a summit day with me, we moved across the South Col with only one other team behind us. We had no worries of the typical horde clogging the fixed lines but could direct our

Vocabulary
apprehension (ap´ rē hen´ shən) *n.* anxiety

Differentiated Instruction for Universal Access

Support for Special Needs Students
Have students read the adapted version of "Everest" in the ***Reader's Notebook: Adapted Version.*** They may also listen to the adapted version on the ***Hear It!* Audio CD** (adapted).

Support for Less Proficient Readers
Have students read "Everest" in the ***Reader's Notebook.*** After students finish the selection in the ***Reader's Notebook,*** have them complete the questions and activities in the student edition.

EL Support for English Learners
Have students read "Everest" in the ***Reader's Notebook: English Learner's Version.*** English learners may also read the selection as they listen to the recorded version on the ***Hear It!* Audio CD.**

TEACH

4 Activating Prior Knowledge

Ask students to consider whether they would undertake something as difficult as mountain climbing. Make a list on the board of their reasons for and against taking the physical, mental, and emotional risks.

Concept Connector →
Students will return to these discussion points when they have finished reading "Everest."

5 About the Selection

This excerpt from *Touch the Top of the World* follows Erik Weihenmayer for 24 hours as he navigates a perilous course to the summit of Mount Everest. The narrative reveals the character of the man who became the first blind person to climb Everest.

6 Background

Mount Everest Climbing Mount Everest demands high-level climbing and survival skills, enormous physical and emotional energy, and a seemingly endless well of motivation. Avalanches, hidden crevasses, and mountain storms are constant threats. Whiteout from snowstorms, severe exhaustion or dehydration, frostbite, and pulmonary or cerebral edema (collection of fluid in the lungs or brain) add to the danger and unpredictability.

The average climb on Everest takes two to three months. Supplies have to be carried up the mountain in multiple trips, and climbers need extra time at each higher level to adapt to the thinner air. Oxygen deprivation can lead to depression, irritability, confusion, and hallucinations. The descent is just as treacherous as the ascent.

PHLit Online!

Enriched Online Student Edition
To have students read the selection in interactive format, with narration and point-of-use interactive graphic organizers, go to **www.PHLitOnline.com.**

❼ Critical Thinking

Interpret

1. Have a volunteer read the bracketed passage aloud.
2. **Ask** students why the author might have felt maintaining an internal balance was more important than being concerned about where he stepped.
   Possible response: Students may point out that Weihenmayer was an experienced climber and trained to understand the patterns of the mountain, but keeping his emotions and internal reactions balanced and calm in such treacherous, changing conditions might prove to be more difficult.

❽ Critical Viewing

Possible response: Balancing on this ladder that appears to bridge a crevasse has to be difficult even for a sighted person. The rope handholds look insubstantial, and the ladder probably wobbles.

Vocabulary
sparse (spärs) *adj.* thinly spread; not plentiful

❽ ▼ **Critical Viewing** How does this photograph of Brad Bull help you appreciate the skills needed to climb Everest? Explain. **[Connect]**

full focus toward the mountain. The wind was blowing so loudly through the col that I couldn't hear the bells jingling from Chris's ice axe. Chris and I expected this, so for the first two hours he clanked his metal axe against rocks he passed. Finally, we worked our way around to the mountain's leeward[1] side, where Everest itself protected us from the wind. Chris had lost his voice, so his verbal directions were sparse. At each anchor, he'd hold the new line with his hand, so I could locate it and clip in. Chris was moving in front of me at his usual rock-solid pace, and I was right on his heels. We were making unbelievable time.

❼ As we got higher up the mountain, four distinct changes had begun to work in my favor. Earlier, in the icefall, each step was very specific, but the terrain above the South Col consisted of steep forty-five-degree snow faces a hundred yards wide, intermingled with ten-to-fifty-foot crumbly rock steps. I could stay in the kicked boot holes of Chris or kick my own steps. Where I stepped had become less important than maintaining internal balance. I could breathe, scan my ice axe, and count on the next step. The slope was often so steep that I could lean forward and feel

1. **leeward** (lē´ wərd´) *adj.* away from the wind.

Vocabulary Development

Thematic Vocabulary: The Big Question

As students are discussing "Everest," encourage them to use the thematic vocabulary presented in Introducing the Big Question, pp. 442–443. You might encourage them with sentence starters like these:

1. Erik could feel *empathy* for Jeff when he decided to turn back because . . .
2. Knowing the *history* of climbers who previously made it to the summit made Erik and the team feel . . .
3. During the climb, the climbers had to constantly *adjust* to . . .
4. A person would show great *ignorance* of climbing if he or she . . .

7 the rock or snow steps with my gloved hands, and I had trained myself long ago to save energy by landing my feet in the same holds my hands had just left. Finally, when I needed it most, the mountain had given me a pattern.

The thin oxygen of extreme altitude reduced us to a crawl. It was like moving through a bizarre atmosphere of syrup mixed with a narcotic. My team, struggling just to put one foot in front of the other, moved so slowly, it gave me more time to scan my axe across the snow and feel my way forward. The third equalizer was the darkness. With just a trickle of light produced by headlamps,
9 my sighted team could only see a few feet in front of them. Bulky goggles blocked their side vision, and oxygen masks covered much of their visual field. Also, the pure oxygen trickling through their masks would flow up and freeze the lenses of their goggles so that they constantly had to remove them to wipe the lenses clean. Those brief moments when eyes are exposed to the elements, corneas will freeze, and the intense rays of the sun reflecting off the snow cause instant snow blindness. Not once did I ever have to worry about these complications.

In addition, my teammates had chosen smaller masks that rode low and tight across their cheeks and hung mostly below their chins. This allowed climbers to see better and prevented pure oxygen from seeping into their lenses, but also allowed plenty of pure oxygen to escape into the wind. I, on the other hand, had the luxury of choosing the largest mask I could find and wore it high on my face, getting the most benefit from the oxygen flow and the

Narrative Essay
Tone The author matter-of-factly notes the irony that his blindness helped him avoid some problems experienced by the other climbers.

10 **Reading Check**
What condition reduces the party's progress "to a crawl"?

MODEL SELECTION

9 Narrative Essay

Tone

1. Point out that Weihenmayer uses understatement, a statement that says less than what is meant, to create a gap between his words and their real meaning.
2. **Ask** students to explain the irony of Weihenmayer's statement, "Not once did I ever have to worry about these complications."
   Possible response: Weihenmayer lists some of the difficulties that other climbers experienced: the inability to see far ahead because of poor lighting, the restriction of their field of vision by bulky goggles and oxygen masks, snow blindness, and so forth. Naturally, these would not have been inconveniences to the author because he is blind.
3. **Ask** students why the author describes the hardships of the climb in this ironic way.
   Possible response: He shows that he does not take himself too seriously, although he is conscious of the way others see him. He also makes a point about circumstances being great equalizers.

10 Reading Check

Answer: The thin oxygen at a high altitude makes it hard for the climbers to breathe and therefore move.

Differentiated Instruction for Universal Access

Culturally Responsive Instruction

Culture Connection Explain to students that, like most expeditions to the summit of Mount Everest, Erik Weihenmayer's team included a Sherpa guide, a native of the extreme terrain of the Himalayas well adapted to high altitudes.

From 1922, when the first climbers took to the treacherous slopes of Mount Everest, to the many expeditions today, the strength, positive attitude, and incredible endurance of the Sherpas have helped to make the ascent to the summit a repeated success.

Emphasize that native peoples such as the Sherpas of the Himalayas, the Inuit of the Arctic, and the San of the Kalahari have had to adapt to harsh environments. Then, have students choose a native people to research. Have students focus on the physical characteristics that have helped the people to thrive in this environment. Then, have students present their findings to the class.

⓫ Critical Viewing

Possible response: Climbers might face avalanches and serious falls.

⓬ Narrative Essay

Narration and Exposition

1. Point out the use of the phrase "Death Zone." Tell students that the phrase describes the highest levels of Mount Everest. Above this altitude, the human body can keep functioning only with great difficulty and often only with extensive support such as bottled oxygen. Human beings can remain in the Death Zone for short amounts of time, but their physical and mental functions deteriorate rapidly while they are there.
2. **Ask** students why Weihenmayer might have thought this exposition or background was necessary. **Possible response:** In addition to providing information so that readers understand why someone was available to help PV, it highlights how climbers must constantly balance their ambition to reach the top against their physical limitations and responsibility to others.

⓫ ▶ **Critical Viewing** What two challenges does this photograph suggest mountaineers face in surviving at high altitudes? **[Analyze]**

Vocabulary

ambient (am′ bē ənt) *adj.* surrounding; on all sides

arduously (är′ jo͞o əs lē) *adv.* with great difficulty; laboriously

Narrative Essay ⓬ **Narration and Exposition** The author provides the information readers need to understand the narrative by including some background details about Dr. Gipe.

ambient air around the mask. I'm sure I made a freakish sight with my gigantic mask covering my goggles, like a day long ago in wrestling practice when I had put my sweatshirt on backward, with the hood covering my face, and chased the terrified freshmen around the mat. The consistent terrain, the altitude, the mask, and the darkness were great equalizers. I wouldn't go so far as to claim these gave me an advantage, but it was a matter of perspective. The mountain had gotten desperately harder for everyone else, while it had gotten slightly easier for me.

For two and a half months, all the decisions, the logistics, the backup safety plans had been implemented and executed by PV, and now, somewhere below the Balcony, the exhausting burden of leadership finally took its toll. Suddenly feeling listless and unable to catch his breath even with his oxygen bottle at full flow, PV had arduously turned back. He managed to convince Brad and Sherm, next to him, that he was strong enough to descend alone, in retrospect, a ploy that might have turned deadly, but PV's weary brain had never stopped calculating the big picture. He had refused to divert any energy from the team's summit effort. Through periodic radio checks as PV dropped altitude, I could hear his characteristically hyper voice growing flat, and just below a steep ice bulge, only an hour from Camp Four, PV sat down in the snow. "I'm very tired," he said. "I don't know if I can make it. I might need some assistance." PV's one warning before we left the tent was "If you sit down, you'll stay there." So, beginning to panic, I ripped my radio out of my pocket. "Is anyone near PV who can help him down?" I asked. "Is anyone reading me?" I repeated myself several times to empty static.

A few weeks earlier, Dr. Gipe had received the sad news that a close family friend had been killed in a skiing accident; a three-thousand-foot day in the Death Zone just didn't seem fair to his family, so that night, he had never left his tent. His decision was a tough one to make, but extremely fortunate for PV's sake. "This is Gipe at the South Col," finally came over the radio. "I'm strapping on my crampons right now. I'm going out to get PV." Dr. Gipe met PV about a half an hour from camp, up again and staggering slowly toward the tents.

With the first crisis of the night averted, Chris and I plodded up a steep gully, which led us to the Balcony, a flat snow platform, ten feet wide. Michael Brown arrived first at about 2:00 a.m., with Chris and me right behind. All night, the weather had remained clear, with high clouds to the southeast and distant lightning flashes illuminating the sky, but at the Balcony, our luck suddenly ran out. We walked into a blasting storm. Wind and horizontal snow raked our down suits and covered us with a layer of ice. The

lightning strikes were now on top of us, exploding like a pyrotechnic[2] show. Chris later said he couldn't see his feet through the blowing snow, which stopped us short, since the southeast ridge above narrowed to fifteen feet wide. Mike O.'s and Didrik's headlamps had simultaneously flickered out, and one of Didrik's crampons had popped off. "Someone come and help us," Mike yelled over the radio. Charley headed back and found them sitting in the snow only twenty feet away.

MODEL SELECTION

13 Chris and I huddled together in the wind, waiting for the others to arrive. "What do you think, Big E?" he asked. "It's lookin' pretty grim." When the others trickled in, Sherm wanted to go on; Charley wanted to turn back, and Erie thought we should wait. For forty-five minutes, we waited, periodic arguments breaking out whether to go on or descend. I was beginning to shiver and forced myself to bounce up and down, and to windmill my arms. We were so close, and I was feeling strong. Turning back was a crushing proposition, but I also wasn't willing to go bullheadedly forward and throw my life away. My mind was starting to settle on the possibility of turning back, when Kevin's voice from Base Camp crackled over my radio. Throughout the expedition, Kevin had been learning to read the satellite weather reports we received every few days over the Internet. From the weather map, it appeared the storm was moving rapidly to the northeast toward Bhutan, and where we stood on the Balcony, we were directly northeast of Base Camp. "Hey you guys, don't quit yet," his voice sounded urgent. "The storm's cleared down here. It just might pass over you."

"Weather is also clearing here," Kami said from Camp Two below.

Chris glanced over at me. Beyond my right hip, shining through the storm clouds, he could see a star. "Let's see if this thing breaks up," he said. Sherm must have felt good tidings, too, because he pushed on. Chris and I followed. 14

Following the narrow exposed southeast shoulder, I felt the first warmth of the sun about 4:00 a.m.; so high up, no other mountain blocked the sunrise. The weather had thankfully turned spectacular.

Erik Weihenmayer
Author's Insight
Kevin's courageous advice represents the idea that leadership isn't only reserved for those who stand on the summit. We're all capable of contributing to something extraordinary.

Reading Check
How does the weather change when the party reaches the Balcony?

2. **pyrotechnic** (pī´ rə tek´ nik) *adj.* of or pertaining to fireworks; here, brilliant; dazzling.

13 Author's Insight
Erik Weihenmayer
1. Have a volunteer read the bracketed passage aloud.
2. **Ask:** In addition to suggesting that leadership is not reserved strictly for those on the summit, what else does this passage suggest about mountain climbing and Weihenmayer's attitude toward it?
Possible response: Making a successful climb is not only a matter of putting together a superior climbing team; it is also about being able to rely on people on the ground to make important contributions, including contributions to decision-making and morale.

14 Reading Check
Possible response: At the Balcony, the team walks into a snow and ice storm.

Differentiated Instruction for Universal Access

Strategy for Special Needs Students
To help students understand the demands of the climb as well as the chronology of the events in the narrative, suggest that they construct a timeline that covers several days. Have them include the time of day and location where possible.

Strategy for Less Proficient Readers
Students who have trouble making the connection between the events on the mountain and what they mean for Weihenmayer may benefit from formulating questions as they read. Encourage students to create a two-column chart. On the left side, they can write questions about ideas that are hard to understand. As they continue to read, they can look for answers to their questions and jot them in the right-hand column.

⑮ Background

Sherpas Ang Pasang, shown in the photograph on this page, is a Sherpa, an ethnic minority in Nepal. By 2002, Ang Pasang had climbed Everest sixteen times and reached the top three times.

Sherpas are essential to any climb. In most expeditions, there is at least one Sherpa for every foreign climber. Because most Sherpas are raised at high altitudes, they require little in the way of adaptation. They make numerous trips up and down, fixing the ropes, breaking up the ice to set the trail, carrying thousands of pounds of supplies, setting up camp, and accompanying the climbers up and down.

Skilled Sherpa climbing guides are widely respected and well paid compared to much of the population of Nepal. Sherpas have become so closely associated with climbing Mount Everest that many foreigners use the word *Sherpa* as a synonym for *guide*.

⑯ Critical Viewing

Possible response: Given that all the mountains in the background are much lower, Weihenmayer and Ang Pasang are probably at the summit of Mount Everest.

⑮

⑯ ▲ **Critical Viewing** What stage of the climb do you think is depicted in this photograph of Weihenmayer and Ang Pasang? Explain. **[Interpret]**

Still hours below the South Summit, we were stalled out again. The fixed lines, running up the steepest slope yet, had been frozen over by a hard windswept crust of snow. Jeff and Brad moved ahead, pulling the lines free, an exhausting job at twenty-eight thousand feet. The job was quickly wearing Jeff down, but he said later that with each gasping breath as he heaved the rope free, he envisioned the two of us standing on top together. Soon he was beginning to feel faint and dizzy. As he knelt in the snow, Brad, behind him, examined his oxygen equipment and assessed that his regulator, connecting the long tube of his mask to his bottle, had malfunctioned. The internal valves responsible for regulating flow were notoriously prone to freezing shut. "Who's got an extra regulator?" Brad called out over the radio, but tired bodies and brains could not recall who had thrown in the extras in the pre-summit shuffle. "My day's finished if I can't find the extra," Jeff yelled testily.

It may not have been PV's time to summit, but he wasn't through benefiting the team. "Calm down," he advised, lying weakly on his back in his tent. "Everyone take a deep breath. Ang Pasang and Sherm are carrying the extra regulators." Luckily, Ang Pasang was only a hundred feet behind. Together, Brad and Ang Pasang screwed on Jeff's new regulator.

Vocabulary Development

Climbing Vocabulary

Like any sport or pastime, climbing has a vocabulary all its own. You might wish to clarify with students terms related to climbing.

- *fixed lines:* ropes set up before a climb to establish a route and guide climbers
- *ice axe:* a special tool with a sharp point or spike at the bottom, used by mountain climbers to maintain balance, cut steps, or halt a slide
- *icefall:* A part of a glacier resembling a frozen waterfall that flows down a steep slope; an avalanche of ice
- *crampons:* Spiked iron or steel frameworks attached to the bottom of shoes or boots to prevent slipping when walking or climbing on ice and snow
- *crevasse:* A deep fissure or chasm in a glacier
- *short-roped:* connected to a guide by a short length of rope and dragged along or carried by that person

MODEL SELECTION

By 8:00 a.m., we had struggled on to the South Summit, 28,700 feet. After a short rest, Chris took off for the summit, cranking it into "Morris gear," and Luis took over in front of me. From the South Summit, the true summit is still at least two hours away across the three-hundred-foot-long knife-edge ridge, up the fifty-foot vertical Hillary Step, and finally traversing up a long slightly broader ridge to the summit.

Jeff, exhausted from his two-hour struggle pulling lines, stopped short in front of me. "I'm wasted. I've gotta go down," he said reluctantly. "This'll have to be my summit."

17 For a moment I wanted to goad him on the way we had done each other on winter training climbs of Colorado fourteeners. "If you wanna turn back, just say the word," we'd jab. "Of course, I'll have to tell everyone you were a whiney little crybaby." But 28,700 feet above sea level wasn't the place to motivate with bravado or ego, so assessing that he was strong enough to get down, I rested a hand on Jeff's shoulder and wished him a safe descent. Jeff had been with me from the beginning, practically introducing me to the mountains. He had shown extraordinary patience as I stumbled along experimenting with brand-new trekking poles. We had even stood together on the summit of Denali[3] and El Capitan,[4] so I knew that reaching the summit of Mt. Everest without him wouldn't feel complete. Suddenly, a wave of heavy exhaustion passed over me, and I felt weary and crumpled. "Maybe I'll go down too," I readied my lips to say, but then Luis was crunching through the snow in front of me, and I forced myself to revive.

18 Down-climbing the twenty-foot vertical snow face on the backside of the South Summit leading onto the knife-edge ridge went against my survival instinct. The ridge is the width of a picnic table and always heavily corniced[5] with snow. To the left is an eight- thousand-foot drop into Nepal, and on the right, a twelve-thousand-foot drop into Tibet. PV had told me that while crossing the ridge on his 1998 attempt, he had driven his ice axe into the snow and, after withdrawing it, had stared through the small hole into the early morning light of Tibet. In 1995, on Brad's second attempt, a climber in front of him had taken his first step onto the ridge just before the entire right half of it dropped away. The climber jumped back to safety, but a second later he would have ridden the cornice into Tibet. This year, the ridge was drier and more stable. Frozen boot steps traversed along the lefthand side.

Erik Weihenmayer
Author's Insight
If I hadn't maintained a journal on the mini-tape recorder I kept in my tent, I would have forgotten the intensity and emotion of moments like this.

Narrative Essay
Narration and Exposition These details about other expeditions help the author establish the true danger he faces.

19 Reading Check
At the South Summit, which member of the expedition turns back?

3. **Denali** (di nä´ lē) name of the National Park in which Mt. McKinley is located.
4. **El Capitan** (el´ ka´ pē tan´) a peak in the Sierra Nevada mountain range in the Yosemite Valley of central California.
5. **corniced** (kôr´ nist) *adj.* in architecture, a projecting decorative strip atop a wall or building; here, characterized by overhanging masses of snow or ice.

17 Author's Insight
Erik Weihenmayer

1. Have a volunteer read the passage aloud.
2. **Ask** students why the author might have forgotten the intensity and emotion of moments like the one he describes here.
Possible response: Students may point out that it is typical of human nature to forget the bad times and remember just the good times.
3. **Ask** students how they might use Weihenmayer's comment as advice for their own writing.
Possible response: He points out one of the benefits of keeping a journal. Not only can writers track events, but they can also preserve the thoughts and emotions triggered by those events.

18 Narrative Essay
Narration and Exposition

1. **Ask** students what near-disasters challenged the 1998 and 1995 expeditions.
Answer: Someone on each of those expeditions almost broke through or stepped on a dangerous patch of unstable snow that would have caused a fatal fall.
2. Then, **ask:** In what way is this passage exposition? What does it add to the essay?
Answer: The passage explains difficulties that sighted climbers have experienced. By telling these stories, Weihenmayer puts the dangers he as a blind person experiences into context. All expeditions on Everest are difficult and dangerous.

19 Reading Check
Answer: At the South Summit, Jeff decides he is too tired to continue.

Fluency

Distribute a copy of page 455, and pair students. Have partners take turns reading paragraphs aloud. While one partner reads, the other should mark any words with which the one reading has difficulty. Circulate to monitor the fluency of students' reading. Collect students' marked up copies of the story, and review difficult words and passages with the class. Look for these problem spots:

- If students have difficulty with the word *summit,* remind them to use context clues. Point out that they can use context clues in the sentence, such as *took off* and *cranking.*
- If students have difficulty with the word *ego,* point out words that begin with *ego,* such as *egomaniac* and *egotistical.* Then, explain that *ego* always refers to the self.
- If students have difficulty with the word *extraordinary,* practice oral clues with the sentence. First, read the sentence with the word *extraordinary* omitted. Then, reread the sentence, asking students to "fill in the blank" with the word that makes the most sense.

⑳ Essay

Purpose

1. Have students follow along as you read the bracketed passage aloud.
2. **Ask:** What language does Weihenmayer use to help the reader understand how difficult it was traversing the last slope to the summit? **Sample answer:** Weihenmayer says his "sluggish muscles felt as if they were pushing through wet cement."
3. Point out how Weihenmayer tells himself to hold back on thinking about standing on top of the summit at this point in the climb. **Ask:** Why was it dangerous for Erik to give in to believing that he would actually reach the top of the summit? **Possible response:** Students might respond that Erik knew the dangers of climbing and how things change instantly on the mountain; therefore, he needed to keep himself focused on each step of the climb rather than on what he hoped would be the climax of the climb—standing on top of the summit.

㉑ Critical Viewing

Possible response: This photograph shows Weihenmayer using his trekking poles and senses and operating independently on very rough terrain.

Erik Weihenmayer
Author's Insight
Writers describe the world around them in the way they best understand it: I used the senses of touch and hearing.

⑳

㉑ ▼ **Critical Viewing**
Some critics claimed Weihenmayer did not climb Everest under his own power. How does this photograph, showing Weihenmayer (center) disprove that claim? **[Support]**

I'd scan my pole until it dropped into a boot mark, then cautiously lower my foot. I knew I couldn't make a mistake here: six hard steady breaths, another solid step, and a relaxed, focused mind like clear water.

Climbing the Hillary Step, I felt I was in my element, feeling the rock under my gloves. I stuck the crampon points of my right foot tenuously into a tiny crack and the left points into a cornice of snow, slid my ascender as high as it would go on the rope, and stood up and quickly reached for the next knob of rock. At the top, I awkwardly belly-flopped onto a flat ledge, slowly pulled myself to my feet, and began traversing the last slope to the summit. For forty minutes I trudged upward. My heavy sluggish muscles felt as if they were pushing through wet cement. With each step closer, the real possibility of standing on top began to trickle through my focused brain. I had speculated success in a conceptual way and as a way to motivate myself when I was down, but it was dangerous to believe it as a fact. A team could be turned back for so many reasons at any time. Just keep moving, I thought. You're not there yet.

Then a body moved down the slope toward me and I felt thin wiry arms beneath a puffy down suit wrapping around me. "Big E!" The voice rasped, so hollow and wispy, I had trouble recogniz-

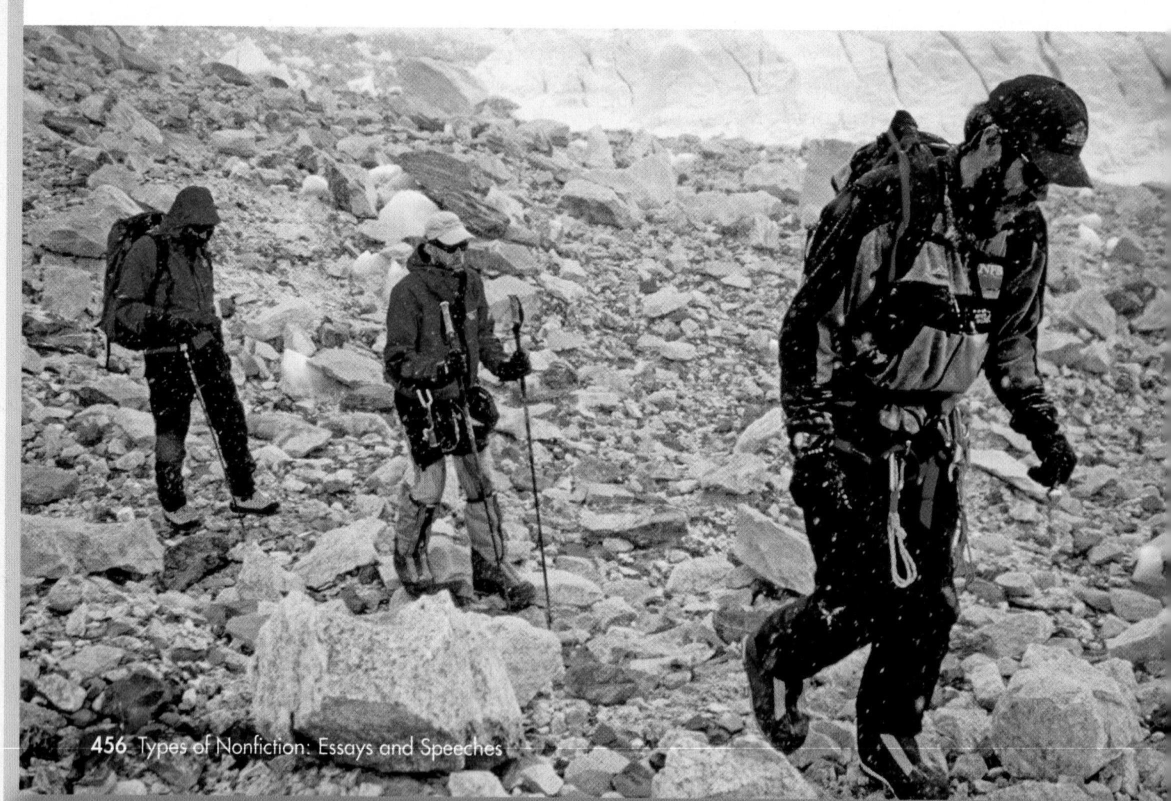

Think Aloud

Vocabulary: Using Context
Model the use of context clues for students. Direct students' attention to the word *tenuously* on this page. Say to students:

> I am going to think aloud to show you how I can use context to discover the meaning of an unfamiliar word.

The word *tenuously* appears in the sentence beginning "I stuck the crampon points of my right foot tenuously into a tiny crack . . ." I am not sure of the word's meaning, but I can look to its context to help me. I know Weihenmayer is climbing, and to help him climb, he is wearing crampons so he does not slip in the snow and ice. He says that he puts his right foot *tenuously* into a tiny crack. *Tenuously* is being used to describe the way he puts his foot in the crack. Because he has only a tiny crack to put his foot, he must have a weak or slight hold, even with the crampons on. From this context, then, I think *tenuously* means "weakly" or "slightly."

ing it as Chris. His voice tried to say more, but his quaking words dissipated in the wind. Then he leaned in against my ear. "Big E"—his voice gave way to tears, then struggled out in an immense effort—"you're about to stand on top of the world." Then he quickly let go and hurriedly moved down the slope.

22 Luis and I linked our arms, and in a few steps, the earth flattened and the massive sky closed around me on all sides. "This is Erik, Luis, and Ang Pasang," I said over the radio. "We're on the top. I can't believe it; we're on the top."

"You're the best, Big E!" Kevin yelled from Base Camp. "I love you guys." I could hear the entire Base Camp crew cheering behind him.

"You're the strongest man in the world," PV said.

I turned around, surprised to hear more crampons moving up behind me. "I wasn't gonna let you stand on top and hear about it the rest of my life," Jeff said, with a little pep left in his voice. One of the greatest joys of my summit was that Jeff hadn't turned back at all. From the South Summit, he had watched us down-climb onto the knife-edge ridge and move toward the Hillary Step. Later he told me, "I simply had to follow." Behind Jeff came Erie, Michael B., Didrik, Charley, and Mike O. Sherm had been the first on the team to summit, becoming the oldest man in history to stand on the top of the world, but better than his record was the fact that his son, Brad, had stepped onto the summit right behind him. Nineteen team members made it to the summit: eleven Westerners and eight Sherpas, the most from one team to reach the top in a single day. So it was a crowded summit as we all stood together, hugging and crying on a snow platform the size of a single-car garage.

23 Another storm was rolling in from the north. "Weather's changing fast," PV called up on the radio. "You guys need to go down immediately." I turned to head down with Erie, when Jeff said, "Wait a second, Big E. You'll only be here once in your life. Look around. Think about where you are and what you've done." So I suspended my nerves for a moment, reached down and touched the snow through my gloved hand, listened to the Sherpa prayer flags flapping in the wind, and heard the infinite sound of space around me, as on my first rock climb. After I had gone blind almost twenty years ago, I would have been proud to find the bathroom, so I said a quick prayer and thanked God for giving me so much. Then it was time to go down. 24

We descended through heavy snowfall but, thankfully, little wind. Erie took over guiding me, down the Hillary Step, across the knife edge, and contrary to his fears that he wouldn't be strong enough to make the top, he was stronger and more lucid on the way

Narrative Essay
Perspective While savoring his historic moment, the author honors achievements of other individuals and of the team.

Erik Weihenmayer
Author's Insight
I wanted to connect the end of my autobiography to the earliest chapters, which describe how I struggled after going blind.

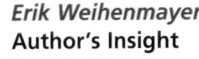

Reading Check
Who surprises Weihenmayer by arriving up at Everest's summit?

MODEL SELECTION

Differentiated Instruction for Universal Access

Enrichment for Advanced Readers
In reporting world reaction to his successful climb of Mount Everest, Erik Weihenmayer includes some comments representing negative opinions of his achievement. Have students write a letter of response to these detractors, either those whom Weihenmayer quotes or others who published their criticisms in print or on the Internet. Whether students agree or disagree with the detractor, they should support their responses with evidence gleaned from a careful review of Weihenmayer's account.

Enrichment for Gifted/Talented Students
Weihenmayer's exploits on Mount Everest drew worldwide media coverage; for example, his photo appeared on the cover of *Time* magazine. Have students use Internet and library resources to collect copies of articles, magazine covers, and photographs that appeared after the historic climb. Challenge students to work in groups to arrange these media materials on a poster that celebrates Weihenmayer's achievement. Be sure students give an appropriate title or headline to their posters.

22 Narrative Essay

Perspective

1. Direct students' attention to the passage in which Weihenmayer announces his completion of the climb.
2. **Ask** what the significance is of Weihenmayer's use of the word "we're."
   Possible response: Saying "we" reveals that Weihenmayer knows that the accomplishment is significant for all of the team, not just for himself.
3. Point out that Weihenmayer names all of the climbers who made it to the summit. **Ask** students why they think Weihenmayer includes the achievements of others in his autobiographical essay.
   Possible response: Weihenmayer knows that climbing Everest is a great accomplishment for anyone. Although this is his story, he does not ignore the accomplishments of others in order to make his own achievement seem more spectacular.

23 Author's Insight

Erik Weihenmayer

1. **Ask** students what this passage shows about Weihenmayer's personality.
   Possible response: Weihenmayer takes nothing for granted and appreciates every success—from finding the bathroom to finding the top of Everest. He also puts his accomplishment into perspective, because he finds it as satisfying as something he did twenty years ago.
2. Discuss with students why a writer would want to connect the beginning and end of a piece of nonfiction as Weihenmayer describes.
   Possible responses: Connecting the beginning and ending adds a sense of completion to a piece of writing. The writer can use both the beginning and the ending to emphasize the theme of the work.

24 Reading Check

Answer: Jeff overcomes his exhaustion and surprises Weihenmayer at the summit of Everest.

25 Narrative Essay

Style

1. Have students list the criticisms that were leveled against Weihenmayer after his climb. **Answer:** People said that Weihenmayer's climb was not a "big deal" because his teammates did all the work and that his success would encourage others to take foolish risks.
2. **Ask** students why Weihenmayer might have chosen to use direct quotations of the criticisms instead of summarizing them **Possible response:** Direct quotations add authenticity to the narrative. The reader knows that Weihenmayer really heard these criticisms and is not just speaking hypothetically. It also gives Weihenmayer another opportunity to praise his teammates for defending him.

Concept Connector →

Have students return to the discussion points about whether or not they would undertake a task as difficult as mountain climbing. Lead a class discussion, probing for what students have learned that confirms or invalidates the ideas they had before reading the essay. Encourage students to cite specific evidence from the text to support their responses.

Connecting to the Big Question

Ask: What might someone learn from Erik Weihenmayer's essay that could change a path in his or her life? **Possible response:** The knowledge that people can do amazing things, regardless of their differences, might help other people with disabilities accomplish something they never before thought possible.

---

down from Everest's summit than most were on the top of a peak in Colorado. Reaching our tents at about 3:00 p.m., I hugged Erie. "Today," I said, "you were my guardian angel. I'm glad you're here."

That night, Kevin radioed up to report that he had called Ellie on the sat phone with the news. "She screamed loud enough to break the neighbors' windows." He laughed. The next days were exhausting as we fought our way through the screaming wind of the South Col, down the Lhotse Face—where my rubbery legs refused to obey my brain—and finally one last trip through the icefall. At the bottom, in Superman's Palace, of course, the whole team was waiting, and the party lasted long after the sun had sunk below Pumori.

Vocabulary
detractors (dē trak′ tors) *n.* those who discredit someone's accomplishments

Despite our success, plenty of detractors voiced their opinions on Internet chat rooms and in letters to the editor. I've heard all the ridiculous assumptions.

25 "Now that a blind guy's climbed it, everyone's going to want to climb it. They're going to think it's easy. People will probably get hurt."

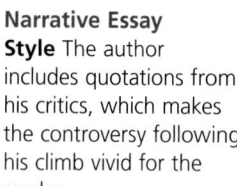

Narrative Essay
Style The author includes quotations from his critics, which makes the controversy following his climb vivid for the reader.

"Why are people thinking this is such a big deal? Anyone can be short-roped to the top by nineteen seeing-eye guides."

My teammates constantly come to my rescue with carefully crafted comebacks like "Before you start spouting a bunch of lies over a public forum, get your facts straight, dude!"

"Don't let 'em get to you," Chris Morris said after I shared with him their comments. "You climbed every inch of that mountain, and then some."

I knew he was right. There were some who would never be convinced, others who still had no idea what to think, but many others for whom the climb forced a higher expectation of their own possibilities. I don't climb mountains to prove to anyone that blind people can do this or that. I climb for the same reason an artist paints a picture: because it brings me great joy. But I'd be lying if I didn't admit my secret satisfaction in facing those cynics and blowing through their doubts, destroying their negative stereotypes, taking their very narrow parameters of what's possible and what's not, and shattering them into a million pieces.

Vocabulary
parameters (pə ram′ ət ərz) *n.* boundaries or limits

When those parameters are rebuilt, thousands and thousands of people will live with fewer barriers placed before them, and if my climbs can play a small role in opening doors of opportunity and hope for those who will come after us, then I am very proud of what we were able to achieve. . . .

Vocabulary Development

Vocabulary Knowledge Rating

When students have completed reading and discussing "Everest," have them take out their **Vocabulary Knowledge Rating Chart** for this selection. Read the words aloud once more, and have students rate their knowledge of the words again in the After Reading column. Clarify any words that are still problematic. Have students write their own definitions or examples in the appropriate column. Encourage students to use the words in further discussion and written work about this selection. Remind them that they will be accountable for these words on the **Selection Test, *Unit 3 Resources,*** pp. 8–10 and 11–13.

After You Read

Everest *from* Touch the Top of the World

Critical Thinking

1. **Respond:** Why does it matter to people around the world that a blind man climbed Everest?
2. **(a)** Identify two challenges that the altitude presents to the climbers. **(b) Connect:** In what ways is Weihenmayer's blindness a benefit as he meets these challenges? **(c) Generalize:** Based on his experience, what statement can you make about turning negatives into positives?
3. **(a)** How do some critics respond to Weihenmayer's success in reaching the summit of Mount Everest? **(b) Analyze:** Based on the details of Weihenmayer's climb, how would you answer those critics?
4. **Analyze:** Use a chart like the one shown to analyze decisions made by individuals or the team on Mount Everest.

Decision	Results of Decision	Importance to the Team's Success

What kind of knowledge changes our lives?
(a) What new insights and skills did Erik develop because he lost his sight? **(b)** In what ways could learning about Erik's climbing experiences change someone else's life?

Essay Review

1. **(a)** Identify three points where Weihenmayer delays the forward flow of his **narrative essay** to introduce information. **(b)** What information does he share in these moments of **exposition? (c)** How does this exposition clarify your understanding of the climbers' experience?
2. In what ways does Weihenmayer balance his own **perspective** with the views of others? Explain.

Research the Author

Using the Internet and library resources, write a **report** on Erik Weihenmayer's accomplishments as an athlete. Follow these steps:

- Research Weihenmayer's successes in scuba diving, distance running, ice climbing, mountain climbing, and skiing.
- Explain the techniques he developed to compete.
- Present your report to your class.

Research the Author

Students may complete this report for homework. Tell them that they can find information about Erik Weihenmayer in a library or online. Students can find more about the author at **www.PHLitOnline.com.**

Assessment Resources

The following resources can be used to assess students' knowledge and skills.

Unit 3 Resources

L1 L2 EL **Selection Test A,** pp. 8–10

L3 L4 **Selection Test B,** pp. 11–13

L3 L4 **Open-Book Test,** pp. 14–16

PHLit Online! Students may use the **Self-test,** available at **www.PHLitOnline.com,** to prepare for **Selection Test A** or **Selection Test B.**

ASSESS/EXTEND

Answers

Critical Thinking

1. Some students may say that the world needs more role models to provide examples of what people can achieve.
2. (a) The altitude poses challenges of severe cold and lack of oxygen. (b) The author can ignore vision problems his fellow climbers experience. (c) **Possible response:** It is more helpful to think about your resources than about your limitations.
3. (a) They say that his teammates pulled him up the mountain or that he was foolish to try. (b) **Possible response:** The critics are basing their statements on their preconceptions, not on what actually happened.
4. (a) **Possible response:** Decision: Dr. Gipe decides to stop at Camp Four. Result: Gipe is able to assist PV. Importance: PV's life is saved.

What kind of knowledge changes our lives?

(a) Erik learned the skills of mountain climbing by using his senses of touch and sound. He realized that trusting his knowledge and instinct while relying on friends helped push him to attain a very difficult goal, and he thinks others can do the same.
(b) Erik's accomplishments might make another person without sight realize that he or she can do many things once thought impossible.

Essay Review

1. (a) He stops the narrative to tell about the freshmen wrestlers; to give background about Dr. Gipe; and to tell about his earlier climbs with Jeff. (b) He gives information about other people on the expedition and about his past. (c) The information gives context that helps readers understand the motivations of the people involved.
2. Weihenmayer includes comments from his critics and relates failures and doubts as well as successes.

TIME AND RESOURCE MANAGER

The Spider and the Wasp • *from* Longitude

Lesson Pacing Guide

DAY 1 Preteach

- Administer the Reading and Vocabulary Warm-ups (*Unit 3 Resources*, pp. 23–26 or 41–44) as necessary.
- Introduce the Reading Skill: Main Idea FT
- Introduce the Literary Analysis concept: Expository Essay FT
- Distribute copies of the appropriate graphic organizer for the Reading Skill (*Graphic Organizer Transparencies*, pp. 78–81). CRI
- Distribute copies of the appropriate graphic organizer for Literary Analysis (*Graphic Organizer Transparencies*, pp. 75–77). CRI
- Teach the selection vocabulary. FT CRI
- Introduce the Word Study skill.

DAYS 2–3 Preteach/Teach

- Build background with the Background feature. CRI
- Develop thematic vocabulary and thematic thinking with Writing About the Big Question.
- Prepare students to read with the Activating Prior Knowledge activities (TE). CRI
- Informally monitor comprehension while students read. FT
- Use the Reading Check questions to confirm comprehension.
- Develop students' ability to analyze main ideas and supporting details using the Reading Skill questions. CRI
- Develop students' understanding of expository essay using the Literary Analysis questions. CRI
- Reinforce vocabulary with the Vocabulary notes. CRI

DAY 4 Assess

- Assess students' comprehension and mastery of the skills by having them answer the Critical Thinking, Reading Skill, and Literary Analysis questions. FT
- Have students complete the Vocabulary Practice activities. FT
- Have students complete the Word Study activities.

DAY 5 Extend/Assess

- Have students complete the Grammar lesson. CRI
- Have students complete the Writing activity and write a business letter. (You may assign as homework.) FT
- Extend learning by having students complete the Listening and Speaking activity, a humorous persuasive speech. As an alternative, assign them "Sixth Sense Survival" or "Looking over Your Shoulder" in *Reality Central*. CRI
- Administer Selection Test A or B (*Unit 3 Resources*, pp. 35–40 or 56–61). FT

"The Spider and the Wasp" is an essay presented unedited and in its entirety.
The excerpt from the nonfiction book *Longitude* appears unedited.

Meeting Your Standards

Students will

1. analyze and respond to literary elements.
   - Literary Analysis: Expository Essay
2. read, comprehend, and analyze short stories.
   - Reading Skill: Main Idea
   - Reading Check questions
   - Apply the Skills questions
   - Assessment Practice
3. develop vocabulary.
   - Vocabulary
   - Word Study
4. apply grammar skills.
   - Direct and Indirect Objects
5. Develop writing proficiency.
   - Work in Progress: Letter to the Editor
   - business letter
6. strengthen listening and speaking skills.
   - humorous persuasive speech

CRI For a full explanation of Culturally Responsive Instruction opportunities in this lesson, see p. T86–T87.

FT For an accelerated lesson, use the Fast Track strategies and activities.

Managing Differentiated Instruction
This leveled selection pairing groups a more accessible with a more challenging selection. Choose either one to teach the lesson skills. For classroom management suggestions for using the pairing in a mixed-ability class, see pp. T68–T69.

Daily Block Scheduling
Each day in this Lesson Pacing Guide represents a 40–50 minute period. Teachers using block scheduling may combine days to revise pacing. In addition, teachers may differentiate and support core instruction by integrating components for extended and intensive support as students require. See the Guide to Selected Leveled Resources (facing page).

Guide to Selected Leveled Resources

EL English Learners

			The Spider and the Wasp	*from* Longitude
CORE COURSE	*Unit 3 Resources*	Selection Test A	pp. 35–37	pp. 56–58
	Graphic Organizer Transparencies	Reading Skill Graphic Organizer A	p. 78	p. 80
		Literary Analysis Graphic Organizer A	p. 75	p. 76
EXTENDED SUPPORT (Level 2)	*Unit 3 Resources*	Reading and Vocabulary Warm-ups A or B	pp. 23–26	pp. 41–44
	Reader's Notebook: English Learner's Version		adapted instruction and adapted selection	adapted instruction and summary
	Hear It! Audio CD		selection and summaries	selection and summaries
	Hear It! Audio CD (adapted text)		adapted selection and summaries	—
INTENSIVE SUPPORT (Level 1)	*Reality Central*		"Sixth Sense Survival"	"Looking over Your Shoulder"
	Real-World Writing Journal		Lesson 1, pp. 70–73	Lesson 2, pp. 74–77

L2 Below-Level Students

			The Spider and the Wasp	*from* Longitude
CORE COURSE	*Unit 3 Resources*	Selection Test A	pp. 35–37	pp. 56–58
	Graphic Organizer Transparencies	Reading Skill Graphic Organizer A	p. 78	p. 80
		Literary Analysis Graphic Organizer A	p. 75	p. 76
EXTENDED SUPPORT (Level 2)	*Unit 3 Resources*	Reading and Vocabulary Warm-ups A or B	pp. 23–26	pp. 41–44
	Reader's Notebook		adapted instruction and full selection	adapted instruction and summary
	Hear It! Audio CD		selection and summaries	selection and summaries
INTENSIVE SUPPORT (Level 1)	*Reality Central*		"Sixth Sense Survival"	"Looking over Your Shoulder"
	Real-World Writing Journal		Lesson 1, pp. 70–73	Lesson 2, pp. 74–77
	Reading Kit		Reteaching worksheets	Reteaching worksheets

L1 Special Needs Students

			The Spider and the Wasp	*from* Longitude
CORE COURSE	*Unit 3 Resources*	Selection Test A	pp. 35–37	pp. 56–58
	Graphic Organizer Transparencies	Reading Skill Graphic Organizer A	p. 78	p. 80
		Literary Analysis Graphic Organizer A	p. 75	p. 76
EXTENDED SUPPORT (Level 2)	*Unit 3 Resources*	Reading and Vocabulary Warm-ups A or B	pp. 23–26	pp. 41–44
	Reader's Notebook: Adapted Version		adapted instruction and adapted selection	adapted instruction and summary
	Hear It! Audio CD (adapted text)		adapted selection and summaries	—
INTENSIVE SUPPORT (Level 1)	*Reality Central*		"Sixth Sense Survival"	"Looking over Your Shoulder"
	Real-World Writing Journal		Lesson 1, pp. 70–73	Lesson 2, pp. 74–77
	Reading Kit		Reteaching worksheets	Reteaching worksheets

The program includes resources for these students: L3 On-Level L4 Advanced All All
For a complete guide to selection support, see pp. T106–T108.

NOTE: All print materials are also available online at *www.PHLitOnline.com.*

VISUAL GUIDE to Featured Selection Resources

• The Spider and the Wasp
• *from* Longitude

The Spider and the Wasp

Alexander Petrunkevitch

To hold its own in the struggle for existence, every species of animal must have a regular source of food, and if it happens to live on other animals, its survival may be very delicately balanced. The hunter cannot exist without the hunted; if the latter should perish from the earth, the former would, too. When the hunted also prey on some of the hunters, the matter may become complicated.

This is nowhere better illustrated than in the insect world. Think of the complexity of a situation such as the following: There is a certain wasp, *Pimpla inquisitor*, whose larvae feed on the larvae of the tussock moth. *Pimpla*

from Longitude

Dava Sobel

474 Types of Nonfiction: Essays and Speeches

RESOURCES FOR:

- EL English Learners
- L1 Special Needs Students
- L2 Below-Level Students
- L3 On-Level Students
- L4 Advanced Students
- All All Students

Vocabulary/Fluency/Prior Knowledge

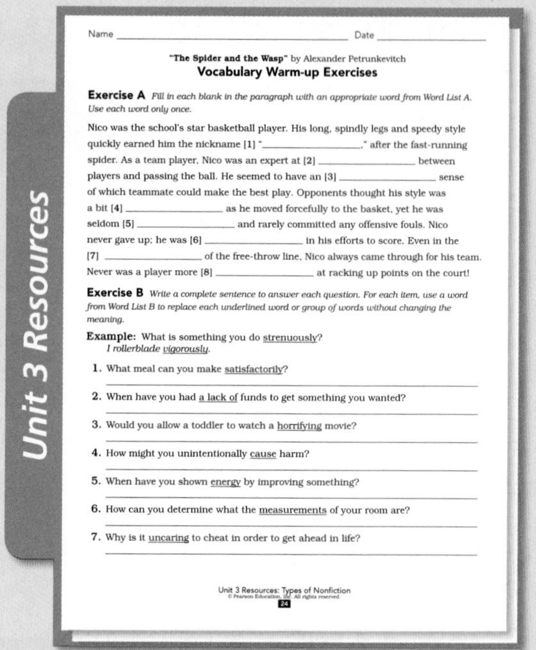

Name ______________________ Date ____________

"The Spider and the Wasp" by Alexander Petrunkevitch
Vocabulary Warm-up Exercises

Exercise A *Fill in each blank in the paragraph with an appropriate word from Word List A. Use each word only once.*

Nico was the school's star basketball player. His long, spindly legs and speedy style quickly earned him the nickname [1] "__________," after the fast-running spider. As a team player, Nico was an expert at [2] __________ between players and passing the ball. He seemed to have an [3] __________ sense of which teammate could make the best play. Opponents thought his style was a bit [4] __________ as he moved forcefully to the basket, yet he was seldom [5] __________ and rarely committed any offensive fouls. Nico never gave up; he was [6] __________ in his efforts to score. Even in the [7] __________ of the free-throw line, Nico always came through for his team. Never was a player more [8] __________ at racking up points on the court!

Exercise B *Write a complete sentence to answer each question. For each item, use a word from Word List B to replace each underlined word or group of words without changing the meaning.*

Example: What is something you do strenuously?
I rollerblade vigorously.

1. What meal can you make satisfactorily?
2. When have you had a lack of funds to get something you wanted?
3. Would you allow a toddler to watch a horrifying movie?
4. How might you unintentionally cause harm?
5. When have you shown energy by improving something?
6. How can you determine what the measurements of your room are?
7. Why is it uncaring to cheat in order to get ahead in life?

Unit 3 Resources: Types of Nonfiction
© Pearson Education, Inc. All rights reserved.
24

EL L1 L2 Vocabulary Warm-ups A and B, pp. 23–24, 41–42

Also available for these selections:

- **EL L1 L2 Reading Warm-ups A and B, pp. 25–26, 43–44**
- **All Vocabulary Builder, pp. 30, 48**
- **All Writing About the Big Question, pp. 27, 45**

Reader's Notebooks

Pre- and postreading pages for both selections, as well as "The Spider and the Wasp," appear in an interactive format in the *Reader's Notebooks*. Each *Notebook* is differentiated for a different group of learners.
The selections in the Adapted and English Learner's versions are abridged.

L2 L3 ***Reader's Notebook***

L1 ***Reader's Notebook: Adapted Version***

EL ***Reader's Notebook: English Learner's Version***

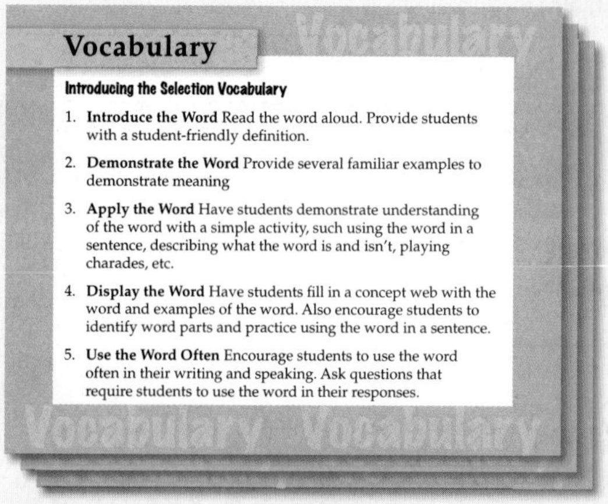
Vocabulary

Introducing the Selection Vocabulary

1. **Introduce the Word** Read the word aloud. Provide students with a student-friendly definition.
2. **Demonstrate the Word** Provide several familiar examples to demonstrate meaning
3. **Apply the Word** Have students demonstrate understanding of the word with a simple activity, such using the word in a sentence, describing what the word is and isn't, playing charades, etc.
4. **Display the Word** Have students fill in a concept web with the word and examples of the word. Also encourage students to identify word parts and practice using the word in a sentence.
5. **Use the Word Often** Encourage students to use the word often in their writing and speaking. Ask questions that require students to use the word in their responses.

Classroom Strategies and Teaching Routines

- core classroom routines outlined step-by-step
- convenient format for easy reference while teaching

Graphic Organizer Transparencies

Selection Support

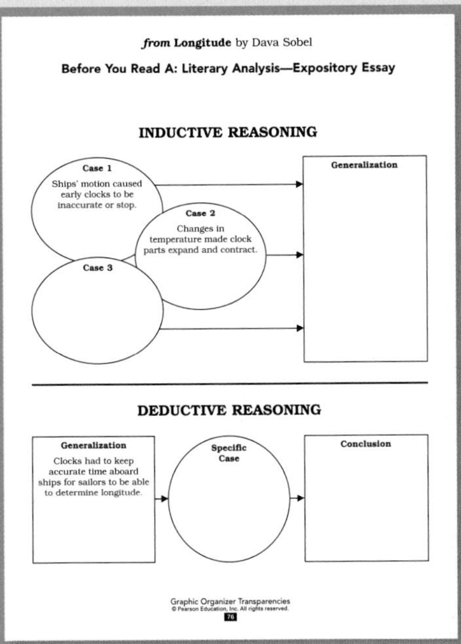
from **Longitude** by Dava Sobel

Before You Read A: Literary Analysis—Expository Essay

INDUCTIVE REASONING

Case 1
Ships' motion caused early clocks to be inaccurate or stop.
Case 2
Changes in temperature made clock parts expand and contract.
Case 3
Generalization

DEDUCTIVE REASONING

Generalization
Clocks had to keep accurate time aboard ships for sailors to be able to determine longitude.
Specific Case
Conclusion

Graphic Organizer Transparencies

76

EL L1 L2 **Literary Analysis: Graphic Organizer A,** pp. 75, 76 (partially filled in)

Also available for these selections:

EL L1 L2 Reading: Graphic Organizer A, pp. 78, 80 (partially filled in)

L3 Reading: Graphic Organizer B, p. 79, 81

L3 Literary Analysis: Graphic Organizer B, p. 77

Skills Development/Extension

Unit 3 Resources

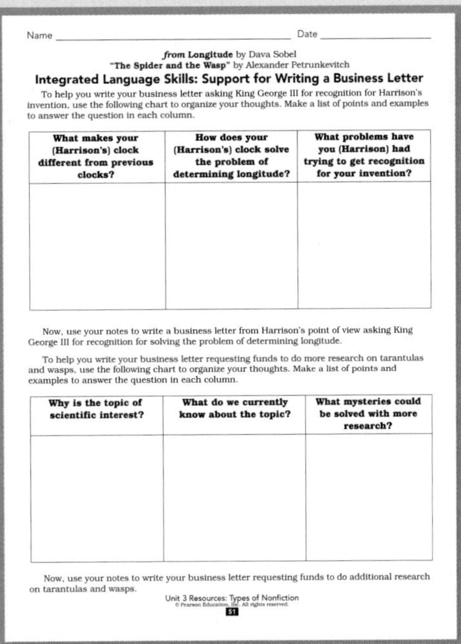
Name ______________________ Date ____________

from **Longitude** by Dava Sobel
"The Spider and the Wasp" by Alexander Petrunkevitch

Integrated Language Skills: Support for Writing a Business Letter

To help you write your business letter asking King George III for recognition for Harrison's invention, use the following chart to organize your thoughts. Make a list of points and examples to answer the question in each column.

What makes your (Harrison's) clock different from previous clocks?	How does your (Harrison's) clock solve the problem of determining longitude?	What problems have you (Harrison) had trying to get recognition for your invention?

Now, use your notes to write a business letter from Harrison's point of view asking King George III for recognition for solving the problem of determining longitude.

To help you write your business letter requesting funds to do more research on tarantulas and wasps, use the following chart to organize your thoughts. Make a list of points and examples to answer the question in each column.

Why is the topic of scientific interest?	What do we currently know about the topic?	What mysteries could be solved with more research?

Now, use your notes to write your business letter requesting funds to do additional research on tarantulas and wasps.

Unit 3 Resources: Types of Nonfiction

51

L3 L4 **Support for Writing,** p. 51

Also available for these selections:

All Literary Analysis: Expository Essay pp. 28, 46

All Reading: Main Idea, pp. 29, 47

L4 Enrichment, pp. 31, 49

L3 L4 Grammar, p. 50

L3 L4 Support for Extend Your Learning, p. 52

Assessment

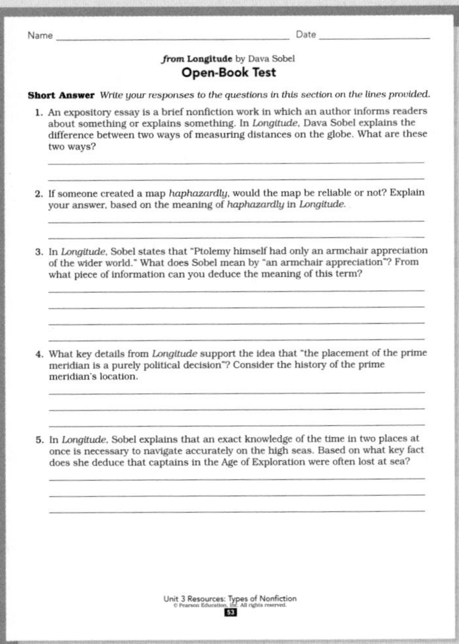
Name ______________________ Date ____________

from **Longitude** by Dava Sobel

Open-Book Test

Short Answer *Write your responses to the questions in this section on the lines provided.*

1. An expository essay is a brief nonfiction work in which an author informs readers about something or explains something. In *Longitude*, Dava Sobel explains the difference between two ways of measuring distances on the globe. What are these two ways?
2. If someone created a map *haphazardly*, would the map be reliable or not? Explain your answer, based on the meaning of *haphazardly* in *Longitude*.
3. In *Longitude*, Sobel states that "Ptolemy himself had only an armchair appreciation of the wider world." What does Sobel mean by "an armchair appreciation"? From what piece of information can you deduce the meaning of this term?
4. What key details from *Longitude* support the idea that "the placement of the prime meridian is a purely political decision"? Consider the history of the prime meridian's location.
5. In *Longitude*, Sobel explains that an exact knowledge of the time in two places at once is necessary to navigate accurately on the high seas. Based on what key fact does she deduce that captains in the Age of Exploration were often lost at sea?

Unit 3 Resources: Types of Nonfiction

53

L3 L4 **Open-Book Test,** pp. 32–34, 53–55

Also available for these selections:

EL L1 L2 Selection Test A, pp. 35–37, 56–58

L3 L4 Selection Test B, pp. 38–40, 59–61

PHLit Online!
www.PHLitOnline.com

- complete narrated selection text
- a thematically related video with writing prompt
- an interactive graphic organizer
- highlighting feature
- access to all student print resources, adapted to individual student needs
- Spanish and English summaries

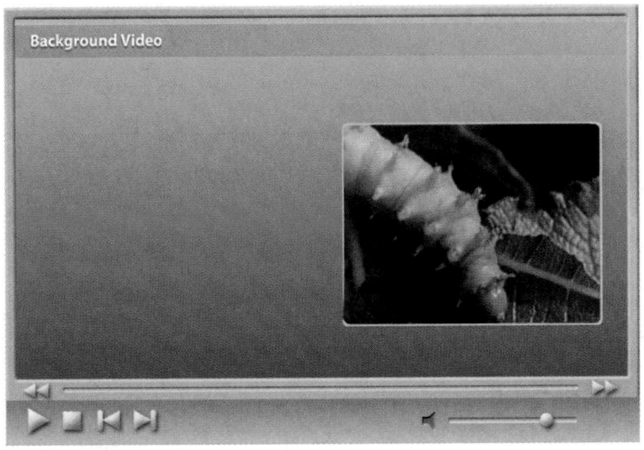
Background Video

Background video

Also available:

Get Connected! (thematic video with writing prompt)

Vocabulary Central

Vocabulary Central (tools, activities, and songs for studying vocabulary)

Also available:

Writer's Journal (with graphics feature)

DIFFERENTIATE/PRETEACH

❶ Selection Choices

You may use either "The Spider and the Wasp" or the selection from *Longitude* to meet the lesson standards. Skills instruction for both selections appears on p. 461. Choose one selection to teach (or choose to teach both). The Accessibility at a Glance chart at the bottom of this page will help you determine which of the two selections is more appropriate for your students.

❷ Selection Skills

1. With the class, preview the selection skills. (The lesson meets the lesson objectives given on p. 460a.)
2. Explain that students will learn to use the skill of analyzing the main idea as they read to better understand and enjoy the selection you choose. By examining elements of an expository essay as they read, they will gain deeper insight into nonfiction: speeches and essays.
3. To introduce the Writing and Listening and Speaking activities (p. 485), tell students that when they have finished reading the selection, they will write a business letter and a humorous persuasive speech related to the selection.
4. Tell students that they will also study a grammar concept: direct and indirect objects. By mastering this concept, they will improve their reading fluency and the quality of their own writing.

Before You Read

The Spider and the Wasp • *from* Longitude

❶ Selection Choices

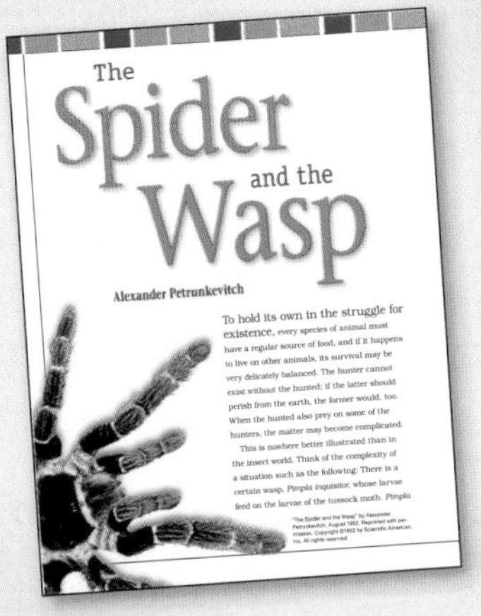

▲ Read **"The Spider and the Wasp"** to find out how a wasp ensures the survival of its young by conquering a large and potentially deadly spider.

▲ Read the excerpt from ***Longitude*** to learn how the demands of computing longitude have challenged people for hundreds of years.

❷ Selection Skills Guide

Practice these skills with either **"The Spider and the Wasp"** (p. 464) or the excerpt from ***Longitude*** (p. 474).

- Understand expository essays
- Recognize diction and tone
- Analyze main ideas and supporting details
- Summarize
- Identify direct and indirect objects
- Write a business letter
- Deliver a humorous persuasive speech

Differentiated Instruction for Universal Access

Accessibility at a Glance: Selection Choices

	The Spider and the Wasp	*from* Longitude	
Context	Biological	Historical and geographical	Because a number of factors determine the relative accessibility of paired selections, in some cases the Lexile rating of the more challenging selection will be lower than that of the more accessible selection.
Language/ Vocabulary	• Some subject-specific vocabulary • On-level vocabulary	• Some subject-specific vocabulary • Above-level vocabulary	
Concept Level	Accessible (nature-based; spiders and wasps)	Challenging (geography; latitude and longitude)	
Literary Merit	Cross-curricular	Cross-curricular	
Lexile/Length	Lexile: 1170L Word Count: 2,380	Lexile: 1430L Word Count: 1,982	
Overall Rating	**More accessible**	**More challenging**	

❸ Literary Analysis: Expository Essay

An **expository essay** is a brief nonfiction work in which an author informs by explaining, defining, or interpreting an idea. Often, the writer reaches a conclusion through reasoning, or logic.

An element that sets one expository essay off from another is **diction**, or the author's word choice. Diction may be formal, informal, sophisticated, or slangy. The writer's word choice and sentence structure help set a **tone** for the piece. The tone reflects the author's attitude towards his or her subject and affects the reader's perception.

PHLit Online!
www.PHLitOnline.com

Hear It!
- Selection summary audio
- Selection audio

See It!
- Get Connected video
- Background video
- More about the author
- Vocabulary flashcards

Do It!
- Interactive journals
- Interactive graphic organizers
- Self-test
- Internet activity
- Grammar tutorial
- Interactive vocabulary games

❹ Using the Strategy: Diction and Tone Chart

As you read, use a diction and tone chart like this one to find examples of the author's diction and to describe the tone it creates.

	Example of Diction	Description of Diction	Tone
The Spider and the Wasp	The hunter cannot exist without the hunted; if the latter should perish from the earth, the former would, too.	**Formal:** latter, former **Old-fashioned:** perish	scholarly philosophical
Longitude	Any sailor worth his salt can gauge his latitude well enough by the length of the day…	**Technical language:** gauge his latitude **Idiomatic expression:** worth his salt	not too formal friendly informative

❺ Reading Skill: Main Idea

To fully understand an essay, **analyze main ideas and supporting details**—recognize each main point the writer makes and identify its relation to the ideas or facts that explain or illustrate it. To help you organize your thoughts, pause occasionally to summarize what you have read. When you **summarize,** you briefly restate the main ideas and key details from the text.

Differentiated Instruction for Universal Access

Preparing Students for the More Challenging Selection

If you wish to prepare lower-level readers to read the selection from *Longitude,* the more challenging selection, follow these steps:

- Students might have difficulty remembering the difference between *latitude* and *longitude.* Provide mnemonics to help them. Latitude lines go across Earth, like the rungs of a *ladder.* Longitude lines are *long,* stretching from pole to pole.
- Define key terms that appear in the selection, such as *Prime Meridian* and *Equator.* Help students identify these lines on a globe or atlas.

For additional support, have students draw a simple diagram of Earth and its imaginary lines to use as a reference as they read the selection.

- The concept of measuring longitude on pp. 477–478 may be difficult for students to comprehend. Work with students to diagram the paragraphs by identifying the main idea(s) and listing the supporting details. Read each supporting detail aloud, using a globe or atlas to model the idea.

PRETEACH

❸ Literary Analysis

1. Introduce the skill, using the instruction on the student page.
2. Tell students that they will look for examples of diction and tone as they read.

Think Aloud: Model the Skill

Model the skill of identifying diction and tone. Say to students:

By examining the author's word choice, I can see his or her attitude toward a subject. An author can use formal words to create a serious tone: "At 3 o'clock, members convened in the lower court of the West Wing." Also, an author can use informal diction and a lighthearted tone: "People got together in the basement court."

❹ Using the Strategy

Give students a copy of either **Literary Analysis Graphic Organizer A** or **B** (***Graphic Organizer Transparencies,*** pp. 75–77) to record details about diction and tone as they read. Use the examples in **Literary Analysis Graphic Organizer A,** which is partially filled in, to model the process of completing the organizer.

❺ Reading Skill

1. Introduce the skill, using the instruction on the student page.
2. Tell students that they will practice finding the main idea as they read.

Think Aloud: Model the Skill

Model the skill of finding the main idea. Say to students:

I can read any well-written paragraph and identify the main idea.

I can look to the paragraph's first sentence, which often contains the main idea, because this sentence usually tells me what the paragraph is about. If the main idea is not stated, I can ask myself: *What is the paragraph about? What is the purpose of this paragraph?* I can also look to the supporting details—facts, reasons, and examples—to identify the main idea.

PRETEACH

❶ Writing About the Big Question

1. Review the assignment with the class.
2. Discuss with students the difference between knowledge, information acquired through experience or study, and instinct, a biologically determined way of behaving. Elicit from students examples in which instinct helps us to survive.
3. Have students complete the sentence starter. Review responses as a class. (**Possible response:** An example of a situation in which it would be important to adapt or revise a behavior based on instinct and gut reaction is running into a burning building to save people.)
4. Remind students that their answers will help them think about the Big Question, "What kind of knowledge changes our lives?"

While You Read

Tell students to look as they read at how the spider uses information provided by its body to protect itself.

❷ Vocabulary

1. Have students preview the selection vocabulary.
2. For each word, have students say the word aloud.
3. Then, use the word in a sentence that defines the word.
4. Finally, repeat your definitional sentence or a similar sentence with the word missing and have the class "fill in the bank" chorally. For example:

   Something distinct is clearly different or separate. It is nearly impossible to confuse a maple leaf with an oak leaf because each shape is [students say "distinct"].

❸ Word Study

1. Introduce the skill, using the instruction in the box.
2. Have students think of a word that means "not able to be touched." (**Answer:** *intangible*)

Making Connections | The Spider and the Wasp

What kind of *knowledge* changes our lives?

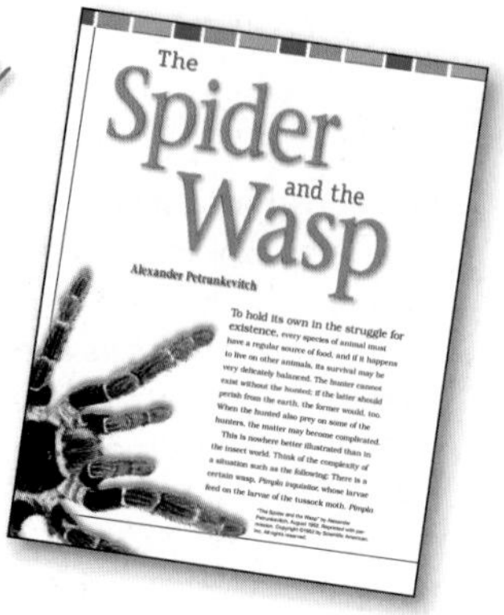

❶ Writing About the Big Question

In "The Spider and the Wasp," a spider's instinctive responses leave it vulnerable to attack by a wasp. Use this sentence starter to develop your ideas about the Big Question.

An example of a situation in which it would be important to **adapt** or **revise** a behavior based on instinct and gut reaction is ____________.

While You Read Look for examples of how the spider uses information provided by its body to protect itself under normal circumstances.

❷ Vocabulary

Read each word and its definition. Decide whether you know the word well, know it a little bit, or do not know it at all. After you read, see how your knowledge of each word has increased.

- **instinct** (in′ stiŋkt′) *n.* an inborn pattern of behavior, as opposed to a learned skill (p. 465) ***As soon as they hatch, sea turtles use instinct to find their way to the sea.*** *instinctive adj. instinctual adj.*
- **customarily** (kus′ tə mer′ ə lē) *adv.* usually; by habit or tradition (p. 465) ***Senior citizens customarily receive discounts.*** *custom n. customary adj.*
- **distinct** (di stiŋkt′) *adj.* clearly different; separate (p. 466) ***There are two distinct sides to the issue.*** *distinction n. distinctive adj.*
- **tactile** (tak′ təl) *adj.* related to the sense of touch (p. 467) ***I enjoy the tactile sensations of stroking a rabbit's fluffy fur.*** *tactility n. intact adj.*
- **formidable** (fôr′ mə də bəl) *adj.* causing fear or dread (p. 467) ***He is such a formidable enemy, that few dare to cross him.*** *formidably adv.*
- **evoking** (ē vōk′ iŋ) *v.* drawing forth emotions or responses (p. 468) ***His experimental plays are known for evoking mixed responses from the audience.*** *evocation n. evocative adj.*

❸ Word Study

The **Latin roots *-tact-*** and ***-tang-*** mean "touch" or "feel."

This essay describes a particular kind of tarantula that has three **tactile** responses that cause it to react when touched.

Vocabulary Development

Vocabulary Knowledge Rating

Create a **Vocabulary Knowledge Rating Chart** (***Professional Development Guidebook***, p. 33) for this selection. Include the selection vocabulary and the Big Question words that appear in the Writing About the Big Question sentence starter. (The Big Question vocabulary is introduced on pp. 442–443.)

Give students a copy of the chart. Read the words aloud, and have students mark their rating in the Before Reading column. Urge them to be alert to these words as they read and discuss the selection.

Tally how many students think they know a word to gauge how much instruction to provide. As students read and discuss the selection, point out the words and their context.

PHLit Online! **Vocabulary Central,** featuring tools, activities, and songs for studying vocabulary, is available at **www.PHLitOnline.com.**

Meet Alexander Petrunkevitch (1875–1964)

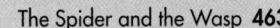

Author of *The Spider and the Wasp*

The Russian thinker Alexander Petrunkevitch (pə tro͞on′ kə vich) was one of the first scientists to explore the secret world of spiders. He classified at least 274 species.

From Politics to Poetry Although Petrunkevitch spent countless hours observing spiders, he did not bury himself away from the world in science. Inspired by his father, who had been jailed for supporting democratic reforms in the Russian government, the younger Petrunkevitch was politically active. He also translated many English poems into Russian.

❹

BACKGROUND FOR THE ESSAY

Instinct vs. Intelligence

Petrunkevitch's essay helps readers understand the distinction between instinct and intelligence. An animal's instincts cannot change, even when they lead to harm. Some animals, however, show intelligence: They learn and adjust their behavior to fit their experience.

Did You Know?

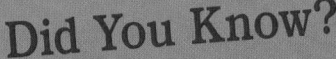

The scientific names for several spider species are based on Petrunkevitch's name.

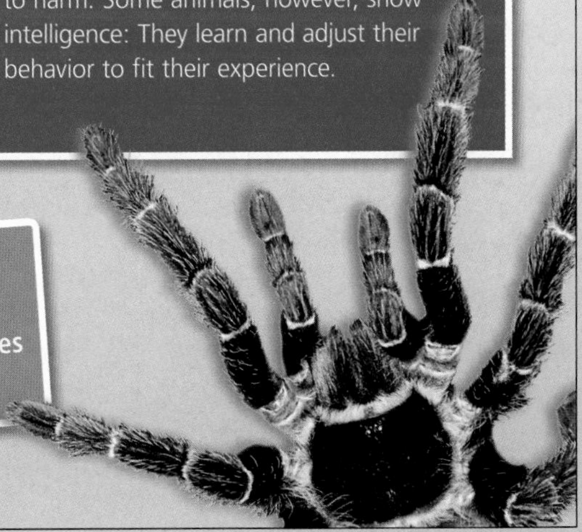

Daily Bellringer

For each class during which you will teach this selection, have students complete one of the five Quick Write activities for Week 13 in the *Daily Bellringer Activities* booklet.

❹ Background

Instinct vs. Intelligence

Instinct in animals produces a natural, unreasoned response to a situation, while intelligence produces a reaction based on experience and learning. To understand instinctual behavior, scientists usually study animals in their natural surroundings. There they can observe animals going about their normal activities without human interference. A laboratory, however, can be a better setting for observing intelligent, or learned, behavior. In the lab, scientists may conduct experiments that focus on how animals learn and the effects of learning on their behavior.

Multidraft Reading

This icon ● marks natural pauses in the selection. To assist struggling readers and to deepen reading for all, assign the text in "chunks," following the icons, and apply multidraft reading protocols. For each reading, have students set the purpose indicated:

- **First reading**—literal comprehension: answering the Reading Check questions.
- **Second reading**—application of skills: answering the Main Idea and Expository Essay prompts.
- **Third reading**—interpretation: answering the end-of-selection questions.

For more guidance, refer to the ***Classroom Strategies and Teaching Routines*** card on multidraft reading.

Differentiated Instruction — Additional Instruction

EL Extended Support—English Learners

Have students complete the **Reading and Vocabulary Warm-ups, *Unit 3 Resources,*** pp. 23–26, before they read. Assign the prereading pages and the adapted selection in the ***Reader's Notebook: English Learner's Version.*** Then, have students listen to portions of the selection on the ***Hear It!* Audio CD.**

L1 L2 Extended Support—Struggling Readers

Have students complete the **Reading and Vocabulary Warm-ups, *Unit 3 Resources,*** pp. 23–26, before they read. Assign the prereading pages and the adapted selection in the ***Reader's Notebook: Adapted Version.*** Then, have students listen to portions of the selection on the ***Hear It!* Audio CD** (adapted text).

Extended Support—Reluctant Readers

To build motivation and engagement before assigning the selection, have students read "Sixth Sense Survival" a thematically related selection in ***Reality Central.*** Then, use the questions at the conclusion of the related selection to guide discussion.

PHLit Online!

For more about the author, practice with the selection vocabulary, and more background, go online at **www.PHLitOnline.com.**

TEACH

❶ Activating Prior Knowledge

Have students work with partners. Give each student pair a copy of a **K-W-L Chart** (see ***Professional Development Guidebook,*** p. 75). Tell students that the topic is animal behavior. Have partners work together to complete the first two columns. Tell students to brainstorm for what they already know about the topic and write it in the Know column. In the Want to Know column, they should write questions they have about the topic.

Concept Connector →

Students will assess what they have learned after completing "The Spider and the Wasp."

Whole-Class Activity

Have students organize a panel discussion regarding animal behavior. Students on the panel can share anecdotes about animal behavior from their own experiences, discuss information from the selection or other sources, and field questions and comments from the rest of the class. One student can act as moderator to keep the panel interesting and promote interaction with the audience.

❷ About the Selection

In "The Spider and the Wasp," Petrunkevitch uses the example of the tarantula and the digger wasp to discuss the function of instinct and intelligence in animal behavior. While Petrunkevitch provides abundant and fascinating detail about the behaviors of the spider and the wasp and their unique interaction, his essay ends with several questions for which he readily admits there are no simple answers. Thus, Petrunkevitch underscores the mystery that envelops much animal behavior and makes it such a popular subject for study.

The Spider and the Wasp

❶ ❷

Alexander Petrunkevitch

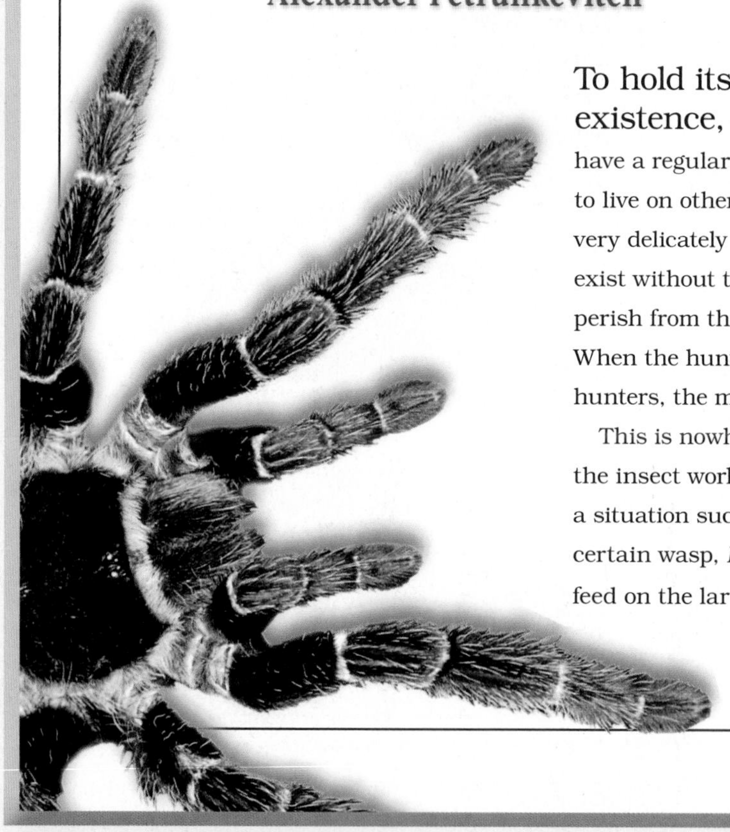

To hold its own in the struggle for existence, every species of animal must have a regular source of food, and if it happens to live on other animals, its survival may be very delicately balanced. The hunter cannot exist without the hunted; if the latter should perish from the earth, the former would, too. When the hunted also prey on some of the hunters, the matter may become complicated.

This is nowhere better illustrated than in the insect world. Think of the complexity of a situation such as the following: There is a certain wasp, *Pimpla inquisitor,* whose larvae feed on the larvae of the tussock moth. *Pimpla*

Vocabulary Development

Thematic Vocabulary: The Big Question

As students are discussing "The Spider and the Wasp," encourage them to use the thematic vocabulary presented in Introducing the Big Question, pp. 442–443. You might encourage them with sentence starters like these:

1. The digger wasp is able to *adapt* its strategy when the tarantula . . .
2. The trichobothria provides the tarantula with the highest level of tactile *awareness* by . . .
3. The tarantula's instinct makes it *ignorant* of the digger wasp's intentions because . . .
4. The example Petrunkevitch gives to describe how the moth-wasp larvae food chain can be *modified* again and again illustrates the idea that . . .

larvae in turn serve as food for the larvae of a second wasp, and the latter in their turn nourish still a third wasp. What subtle balance between fertility and mortality must exist in the case of each of these four species to prevent the extinction of all of them! An excess of mortality over fertility in a single member of the group would ultimately wipe out all four.

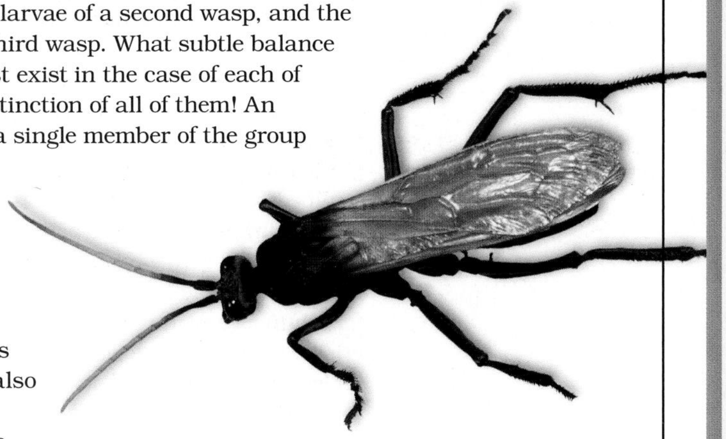

This is not a unique case. The two great orders of insects, Hymenoptera and Diptera, are full of such examples of interrelationship. And the spiders (which are not insects but members of a separate order of arthropods) also are killers and victims of insects.

The picture is complicated by the fact that those species which are carnivorous in the larval stage have to be provided with animal food by a vegetarian mother. The survival of the young depends on the mother's correct choice of a food which she does not eat herself.

In the feeding and safeguarding of their progeny[1] the insects and spiders exhibit some interesting analogies to reasoning and some crass examples of blind **instinct**. The case I propose to describe here is that of the tarantula spiders and their arch-enemy, the digger wasps of the genus Pepsis. It is a classic example of what looks like intelligence pitted against instinct—a strange situation in which the victim, though fully able to defend itself, submits unwittingly to its destruction.

Most tarantulas live in the tropics, but several species occur in the temperate zone and a few are common in the southern U.S. Some varieties are large and have powerful fangs with which they can inflict a deep wound. These formidable-looking spiders do not, however, attack man; you can hold one in your hand, if you are gentle, without being bitten. Their bite is dangerous only to insects and small mammals such as mice; for a man it is no worse than a hornet's sting.

Tarantulas **customarily** live in deep cylindrical burrows, from which they emerge at dusk and into which they retire at dawn. Mature males wander about after dark in search of females and occasionally stray into houses. After mating, the male dies in a few weeks, but a female lives much longer and can mate several years in succession. In a Paris museum is a tropical specimen which is said to have been living in captivity for 25 years.

1. **progeny** (präj´ ə nē) *n.* offspring; young.

Literary Analysis
Expository Essay
What does the writer's choice of words tell you about his attitude toward the subject?

Vocabulary
instinct (in´ stiŋkt´) *n.* an inborn pattern of behavior, as opposed to a learned skill

customarily (kus´ tə mer´ ə lē) *adv.* usually; by habit or tradition

4 **Reading Check**
What two concepts will the writer explore in this essay?

3 Literary Analysis
Expository Essay

1. Remind students that the author's attitude toward his subject is the tone. Diction, or choice of words, helps to set that tone.
2. **Ask** students the Literary Analysis question: What does the writer's choice of words tell you about his attitude toward the subject?
Possible response: The writer's choice of words, such as "interesting analogies" and "strange situation," reveals that the writer, also a scientist, is not accustomed to observing phenomena that cannot be explained. He is, therefore, bewildered by but respectful of the organisms' behavior.

4 Reading Check

Answer: The writer will explore how intelligence allows one insect to take advantage of another organism's weakness—its reliance on instinct to survive.

Differentiated Instruction for Universal Access

EL Support for English Learners
English learners will benefit from an increased use of visual aids. Provide students with maps and pictures to illustrate some of the details in the selection. In the fourth paragraph on this page, for instance, students may need visual references for terms such as *tropics, temperate zone, fangs, wound, mammals,* and *hornet*. Encourage students to create reading picture dictionaries for each selection.

Enrichment for Advanced Readers
Point out that sometimes the main idea of a paragraph or passage is not directly stated in the text, but implied. Explain that to identify an implied main idea, readers must carefully consider all the details in a paragraph or passage and then state what they are about. Have students examine the paragraph beginning "Most tarantulas live . . ." and state its main idea in one sentence. (Possible main idea statement: *There are similarities and differences among tarantulas.*)

PHLit Online!
This selection is available in interactive format in the **Enriched Online Student Edition, www.PHLitOnline.com,** which includes a thematically related video with writing prompt and an interactive graphic organizer.

5 Reading Skill
Main Idea

1. Tell students that the main idea of a paragraph or passage is often stated directly.
2. **Ask** students to respond to the Reading Skill question: Which sentence in this paragraph states the main idea?
   Answer: The third sentence in the paragraph states the main idea.
3. To check students' understanding of supporting details, **ask:** What example does the writer provide to illustrate the main idea?
   Answer: The writer provides the example of the tarantula and its reaction to the touch of a cricket.

6 Connecting to the Big Question

1. Emphasize to students that an organism's ability to use information from its environment determines its success at survival.
2. **Ask** students: How does the spider use information provided by its body to protect itself under normal circumstances?
   Answer: The spider has sensitive sensory organs that inform it of potential threat. For example, the trichobothria, fine hairs on the spider's body, are very sensitive to air movement. When something disturbs the air, thus triggering its hair, the spider reacts defensively, jerking its four front legs. If all its legs are stimulated, the spider jumps, scaring off any threats.
3. **Ask** students: How useful do you think the spider's method of receiving information is in ensuring its survival?
   Possible response: Under normal circumstances, this method works well. The spider's method, however, might not work well under different circumstances.

A fertilized female tarantula lays from 200 to 400 eggs at a time; thus it is possible for a single tarantula to produce several thousand young. She takes no care of them beyond weaving a cocoon of silk to enclose the eggs. After they hatch, the young walk away, find convenient places in which to dig their burrows and spend the rest of their lives in solitude. Tarantulas feed mostly on insects and millipedes. Once their appetite is appeased, they digest the food for several days before eating again. Their sight is poor, being limited to sensing a change in the intensity of light and to the perception of moving objects. They apparently have little or no sense of hearing, for a hungry tarantula will pay no attention to a loudly chirping cricket placed in its cage unless the insect happens to touch one of its legs.

But all spiders, and especially hairy ones, have an extremely delicate sense of touch. Laboratory experiments prove that tarantulas can distinguish three types of touch: pressure against the body wall, stroking of the body hair, and riffling of certain very fine hairs on the legs called trichobothria.[2] Pressure against the body, by a finger or the end of a pencil, causes the tarantula to move off slowly for a short distance. The touch excites no defensive response unless the approach is from above where the spider can see the motion, in which case it rises on its hind legs, lifts its front legs, opens its fangs and holds this threatening posture as long as the object continues to move. When the motion stops, the spider drops back to the ground, remains quiet for a few seconds and then moves slowly away.

But all spiders, and especially hairy ones, have an extremely delicate sense of touch.

Vocabulary
distinct (di stiŋkt′) *adj.* clearly different; separate

The entire body of a tarantula, especially its legs, is thickly clothed with hair. Some of it is short and woolly, some long and stiff. Touching this body hair produces one of two distinct reactions. When the spider is hungry, it responds with an immediate and swift attack. At the touch of a cricket's antennae the tarantula seizes the insect so swiftly that a motion picture taken at the rate of 64 frames per second shows only the result and not the process of capture. But when the spider is not hungry, the stimulation of its hairs merely causes it to shake the touched limb. An insect can walk under its hairy belly unharmed.

Reading Skill
Main Idea Which sentence in this paragraph states the main idea?

The trichobothria, very fine hairs growing from disklike membranes on the legs, were once thought to be the spider's hearing organs, but we now know that they have nothing to do with sound.

2. **trichobothria** (trik′ ə bäth′ rē ə)

Think Aloud

Vocabulary: Using Context
Direct students' attention to the word *gargantuan* on p. 467. Using a think-aloud process, model how to use context to infer the meaning of an unknown word. Say to students:

In this sentence *gargantuan* is used to describe the meal that the wasp larva makes of the spider. The surrounding sentences tell me that the wasp attaches its egg to a paralyzed tarantula to provide food for the larva when it hatches. The larva eats no other food than the spider. When it is finished eating, all that is left of the tarantula is its skeleton. We also learn from the context that the larva is many hundreds of times smaller than its victim. The spider, then, is many times larger than the larva. This information suggests that *gargantuan* means "giant or huge."

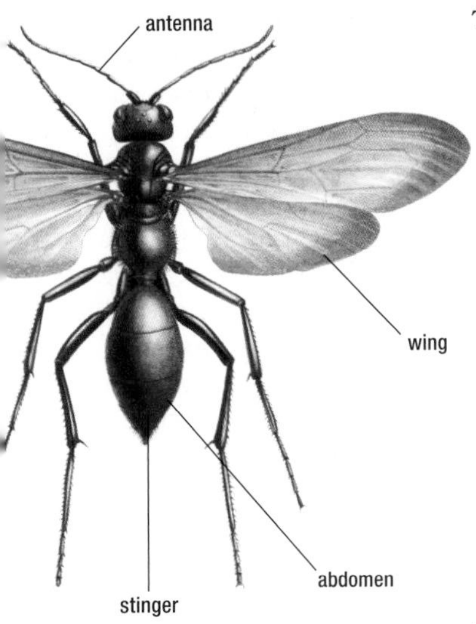

6 They are sensitive only to air movement. A light breeze makes them vibrate slowly, without disturbing the common hair. When one blows gently on the trichobothria, the tarantula reacts with a quick jerk of its four front legs. If the front and hind legs are stimulated at the same time, the spider makes a sudden jump. This reaction is quite independent of the state of its appetite.

These three **tactile** responses—to pressure on the body wall, to moving of the common hair, and to flexing of the trichobothria—are so different from one another that there is no possibility of confusing them. They serve the tarantula adequately for most of its needs and enable it to avoid most annoyances and dangers. But they fail the spider completely when it meets its deadly enemy, the digger wasp Pepsis. ●

Vocabulary

tactile (tak′ təl) *adj.* related to the sense of touch

formidable (fôr′ mə də bəl) *adj.* causing fear or dread

7 These solitary wasps are beautiful and **formidable** creatures. Most species are either a deep shiny blue all over, or deep blue with rusty wings. The largest have a wing span of about four inches. They live on nectar. When excited, they give off a pungent odor—a warning that they are ready to attack. The sting is much worse than that of a bee or common wasp, and the pain and swelling last longer. In the adult stage the wasp lives only a few months. 8 The female produces but a few eggs, one at a time at intervals of two or three days. For each egg the mother must provide one adult tarantula, alive but paralyzed. The tarantula must be of the correct species to nourish the larva. The mother wasp attaches the egg to the paralyzed spider's abdomen. Upon hatching from the egg, the larva is many hundreds of times smaller than its living but helpless victim. It eats no other food and drinks no water. By the time it has finished its single gargantuan meal and become ready for wasphood, nothing remains of the tarantula but its indigestible chitinous skeleton.[3]

The mother wasp goes tarantula-hunting when the egg in her ovary is almost ready to be laid. Flying low over the ground late on

Reading Check 9

What three tactile responses do spiders have?

3. **chitinous** (kī′ tin əs) **skeleton** tough outer covering of an insect's body. The external skeleton gives an insect's body its structure, as an insect has no internal skeleton.

7 Literary Analysis

Expository Essay

1. Have students read the bracketed text.
2. **Ask:** What does the author's choice of words in the first sentence reveal about his attitude toward the digger wasp?
   Possible response: The author uses the words "beautiful" and "formidable" to describe the digger wasp. Because these are adjectives with a positive connotation, their use reveals that the author respects and admires the digger wasp.

8 Reading Skill

Main Idea

1. Remind students that, in expository essays, supporting details usually consist of information that can be proved, such as facts, observations, and statistics.
2. **Ask** students to find and describe at least two details supporting the author's claim that digger wasps are formidable creatures.
   Possible response: The digger wasp's sting is more painful than that of a bee or common wasp. The mother wasp is able to paralyze a tarantula to provide food for her offspring.

➤ **Monitor Progress:** Review students' answers to make sure they are correctly identifying the appropriate supporting details.

➤ **Reteach:** If students have difficulty identifying supporting details, first discuss what it means for something to be *formidable.* If necessary, review the definition of *formidable,* using the word in context. Then, work with students to underline the relevant supporting details in the paragraph. On a separate sheet of paper, have students diagram the main idea and its supporting details by listing each detail below the main idea.

9 Reading Check

Answer: Spiders respond to pressure on the body wall, movement of the body hair, and movement of the trichobothria.

Fluency

Students may have difficulty reading the paragraph beginning with "These solitary wasps . . . " on this page because it contains several adjectives with which students may not be familiar. To model fluent reading, read the passage to students with expression as students track, or follow along by pointing at each word in the text, as you read. Then, have students read the passage aloud. Look for these problem spots:

- Students may stumble over the phrase "formidable creatures." Point out that *formidable,* meaning "strong," is an adjective that describes *creatures.* Remind students that this adjective, as well as *beautiful,* helps the reader to visualize what the wasps look like. Encourage students to sound the phrase "formidable creatures," repeating it until they can read the paragraph smoothly.
- Students may have trouble pronouncing *pungent.* Have students cover up parts of the word with their thumbs. First, have them pronounce *pun-* and then *-gent.* Then, have students blend the two syllables together to pronounce the word.

⑩ Literature in Context

Science Connection Although people have been studying animal behavior for centuries, Konrad Lorenz and Nikolaas Tinbergen are credited with founding the modern field of ethology in the 1920s. Ethology is linked with other scientific fields, including ecology, evolution, and physiology. Ethologists combine field studies and laboratory experiments to observe and analyze how animals behave. They focus not on particular animals but on certain behaviors that can be observed in a variety of animals.

Connect to the Literature After discussing the field of ethology, **ask** students the Connect to the Literature question: Judging from Petrunkevitch's essay, what two concepts are a key concern for ethologists?
Answer: Petrunkevitch's essay suggests that instinct and intelligence are a key concern for ethologists.

⑩ LITERATURE IN CONTEXT

Science Connection

Studying Animal Behavior
Ethology—the scientific study of animal behavior in the wild—has helped scientists better understand the role of instinct in animal interactions. For instance, Konrad Lorenz (lōr′ ens′), shown below, discovered that instinct causes a baby bird to imprint on, or become attached to, the first moving creature it sees after hatching—even if that creature is a human scientist, not the bird's mother!

Connect to the Literature

Judging from Petrunkevitch's essay, what two concepts are a key concern for ethologists?

a sunny afternoon, the wasp looks for its victim or for the mouth of a tarantula burrow, a round hole edged by a bit of silk. The sex of the spider makes no difference, but the mother is highly discriminating as to species. Each species of Pepsis requires a certain species of tarantula, and the wasp will not attack the wrong species. In a cage with a tarantula which is not its normal prey, the wasp avoids the spider, and is usually killed by it in the night.

Yet when a wasp finds the correct species, it is the other way about. To identify the species the wasp apparently must explore the spider with her antennae. The tarantula shows an amazing tolerance to this exploration. The wasp crawls under it and walks over it without **evoking** any hostile response. The molestation is so great and so persistent that the tarantula often rises on all eight legs, as if it were on stilts. It may stand this way for several minutes. Meanwhile the wasp, having satisfied itself that the victim is of the right species, moves off a few inches to dig the spider's grave. Working vigorously with legs and jaws, it excavates a hole 8 to 10 inches deep with a diameter slightly larger than the spider's girth. Now and again the wasp pops out of the hole to make sure that the spider is still there.

When the grave is finished, the wasp returns to the tarantula to complete her ghastly enterprise. First she feels it all over once more with her antennae. Then her behavior becomes more aggressive. She bends her abdomen, protruding her sting, and searches for the soft membrane at the point where the spider's leg joins its body—the only spot where she can penetrate the horny skeleton. From time to time, as the exasperated spider slowly shifts ground, the wasp turns on her back and slides along with the aid of her wings, trying to get under the tarantula for a shot at the vital spot. During all this maneuvering, which can last for several minutes, the tarantula makes no move to save itself. Finally the wasp corners it against some obstruction and grasps one of its legs in her powerful jaws. Now at last the harassed spider tries a desperate but vain defense. The two contestants roll over and over on the ground. It is a terrifying sight and the outcome is always the same. The wasp finally manages to thrust her sting into the soft spot and holds it there for a few seconds while she pumps in the poison. Almost immediately the tarantula falls paralyzed on its back. Its legs stop twitching; its heart stops beating. Yet it is not dead, as is shown by the fact that if taken from the wasp it can be restored to some sensitivity

Vocabulary
evoking (ē vōk′ iŋ) *v.* drawing forth emotions or responses

Vocabulary Development

Vocabulary Knowledge Rating
When students have completed reading and discussing "The Spider and the Wasp," have them take out their **Vocabulary Knowledge Rating Chart** for this selection. Read the words aloud once more and have students rate their knowledge of the words again in the After Reading column. Clarify any words that are still problematic. Have students write their own definition and example or sentence in the appropriate column. Then, have students complete the Vocabulary Practice at the end of the selection. Encourage students to use the words in further discussion and written work about this selection. Remind them that they will be accountable for these words on the **Selection Test, *Unit 3 Resources,*** pp. 35–37 or 38–40.

by being kept in a moist chamber for several months.

After paralyzing the tarantula, the wasp cleans herself by dragging her body along the ground and rubbing her feet, sucks the drop of blood oozing from the wound in the spider's abdomen, then grabs a leg of the flabby, helpless animal in her jaws and drags it down to the bottom of the grave. She stays there for many minutes, sometimes for several hours, and what she does all that time in the dark we do not know. Eventually she lays her egg and attaches it to the side of the spider's abdomen with a sticky secretion. Then she emerges, fills the grave with soil carried bit by bit in her jaws, and finally tramples the ground all around to hide any trace of the grave from prowlers. Then she flies away, leaving her descendant safely started in life.

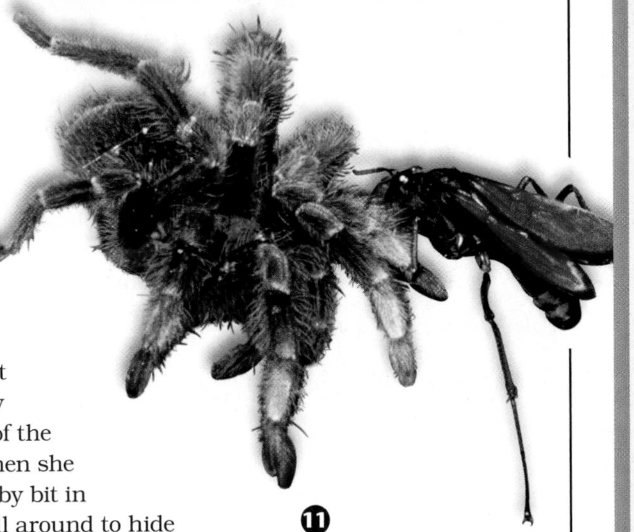

11 ▲ **Critical Viewing** Does the spider appear to be responding to the wasp as Petrunkevitch describes? Explain. **[Connect]**

In all this the behavior of the wasp evidently is qualitatively different from that of the spider. The wasp acts like an intelligent animal. This is not to say that instinct plays no part or that she reasons as man does. But her actions are to the point; they are not automatic and can be modified to fit the situation. We do not know for certain how she identifies the tarantula—probably it is by some olfactory or chemotactile sense[4]—but she does it purposefully and does not blindly tackle a wrong species.

12 On the other hand, the tarantula's behavior shows only confusion. Evidently the wasp's pawing gives it no pleasure, for it tries to move away. That the wasp is not simulating sexual stimulation is certain, because male and female tarantulas react in the same way to its advances. That the spider is not anesthetized by some odorless secretion is easily shown by blowing lightly at the tarantula and making it jump suddenly. What, then, makes the tarantula behave as stupidly as it does?

14 No clear, simple answer is available. Possibly the stimulation by the wasp's antennae is masked by a heavier pressure on the spider's body, so that it reacts as when prodded by a pencil. But the explanation may be much more complex. Initiative in attack is not in the nature of tarantulas; most species fight only when

Literary Analysis
Expository Essay How does the writer link his descriptions of behavior to the concepts identified at the beginning of the essay?

13 **Reading Check**
What does the wasp do to the tarantula?

4. **olfactory** (äl fak´ tə rē) . . . **chemotactile** (kē´ mō tak´ təl) **sense** An olfactory sense is a sense of smell. A chemotactile sense involves sensitivity by touch to the presence of specific chemicals.

11 Critical Viewing

Possible response: Yes, the spider appears to be responding to the wasp as Petrunkevitch describes because the spider does not seem to be attacking the wasp but is merely tolerating it.

12 Literary Analysis
Expository Essay

1. Have students recall the two concepts the writer proposed at the beginning of the essay.
   Answer: The writer planned to discuss the relationship and differences between intelligence and instinct, using the digger wasp and the tarantula as an example.
2. Have students read the bracketed text.
3. **Ask** students the Literary Analysis question: How does the writer link his descriptions of behavior to the concepts identified at the beginning of the essay?
   Possible response: The writer uses his descriptions of the wasp's and spider's behavior to support his idea that intelligence has the advantage over instinct.

13 Reading Check

Answer: The wasp finds the vulnerable spot on the tarantula where she can sting and paralyze it. Once the tarantula is immobilized, the wasp drags the spider into the hole she has dug and then lays her egg, attaching it to the side of the spider's abdomen, where the larvae will hatch and eat the tarantula. Finally, the wasp covers the hole and flies away.

Concept Connector

K-W-L Chart
Have students complete the last column of their **K-W-L Charts.** Ask students to evaluate what they have learned in relation to the questions they had before reading.

Writing About the Big Question
Have students compare their responses to the sentence starter they completed before reading the essay with their ideas afterwards. Ask them to explain whether their thoughts have changed.

Literary Analysis Graphic Organizer
Ask students to review the graphic organizers they completed to identify the writer's diction and tone while reading. Show them **Literary Analysis Graphic Organizer A** (*Graphic Organizer Transparencies,* p. 75) as an example. Then, have students use the graphic organizers they completed to make observations about the writer's diction and tone.

⓮ Reading Skill
Main Idea

Ask students to respond to the Reading Skill question.
Answer: When a tarantula is unable to create a three-dimensional web, it chooses to leave rather than to adapt to a single-plane web. Spiders consistently choose escape over problem solving.

ASSESS
Answers

Critical Thinking

1. Students may be surprised at the tarantula's lack of defense toward the wasp.
2. (a) Newly hatched digger wasps feed on the paralyzed body of a tarantula. (b) Tarantulas weave a cocoon around their eggs but, unlike wasps, they do not provide food for their young.
3. (a) The wasp's behavior seems to be one of the "interesting analogies to reasoning."
(b) Petrunkevitch classifies the wasp as intelligent because its actions can be modified to fit the situation. (c) Most students will agree with Petrunkevitch's point.
4. (a) Instinctive behavior: the spider's three tactile responses; intelligent behavior: the wasp's identification of a specific tarantula species. (b) The spider's tactile responses allow it to defend itself from danger and to feed itself; however, the responses do not protect the spider against the wasp; the wasp's identification of a specific tarantula species allows the wasp to feed its young; the need for one tarantula per egg limits reproduction.

What kind of knowledge changes our lives?

Possible response: Intelligence provides a greater advantage. In the example of the spider and the wasp, the wasp is able to modify its strategy in response to the spider's defense mechanisms. Even though the spider has the ability to defend itself before the wasp stings it, its instinct inhibits any lifesaving reaction.

Reading Skill
Main Idea In what way do the details about web-weaving support the idea that spiders cannot act creatively?

cornered so that escape is impossible. Their inherited patterns of behavior apparently prompt them to avoid problems rather than attack them. For example, spiders always weave their webs in three dimensions, and when a spider finds that there is insufficient space to attach certain threads in the third dimension, it leaves the place and seeks another, instead of finishing the web in a single plane. This urge to escape seems to arise under all circumstances, in all phases of life, and to take the place of reasoning. For a spider to change the pattern of its web is as impossible as for an inexperienced man to build a bridge across a chasm obstructing his way. ⓮

In a way the instinctive urge to escape is not only easier but often more efficient than reasoning. The tarantula does exactly what is most efficient in all cases except in an encounter with a ruthless and determined attacker dependent for the existence of her own species on killing as many tarantulas as she can lay eggs. Perhaps in this case the spider follows its usual pattern of trying to escape, instead of seizing and killing the wasp, because it is not aware of its danger. In any case, the survival of the tarantula species as a whole is protected by the fact that the spider is much more fertile than the wasp.

Critical Thinking

1. **Respond:** What fact in the essay surprised you most? Why?
2. **(a)** What do newly hatched digger wasps feed on? **(b) Compare and Contrast:** Using examples from the essay, compare the ways in which the wasp and the tarantula each provide for their young.
3. **(a) Classify:** According to Petrunkevitch, is the wasp's behavior closer to reasoning or instinct? **(b) Analyze:** Explain his reasons for the classification. **(c) Make a Judgment:** Do you agree with his idea? Explain.
4. **(a) Classify:** In a two-column chart, collect examples of instinctive behavior and intelligent behavior from the essay.
(b) Analyze: Identify the positive and the negative consequences of each behavior you list.

What kind of knowledge changes our lives?
For an animal in a conflict, does instinct or intelligence provide a greater advantage? Support your answer with details from the essay.

Assessment Resources

The following resources can be used to assess students' knowledge and skills.

Unit 3 Resources

L1 L2 EL **Selection Test A,** pp. 35–37
L3 L4 **Selection Test B,** pp. 38–40
L3 L4 **Open-Book Test,** pp. 32–34

PHLit Online! Students may use the **Self-test,** online at **www.PHLitOnline.com,** to prepare for the **Selection Test A** or **Selection Test B.**

After You Read | The Spider and the Wasp

Literary Analysis: Expository Essay

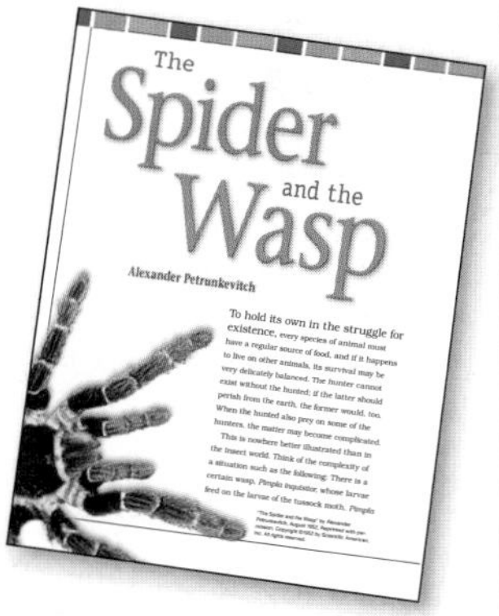

1. **(a)** What natural phenomenon does Petrunkevitch explain in this **expository essay? (b)** Explain how the essay helps readers understand the difference between instinct and intelligence.
2. Describe Petrunkevitch's attitude toward wasps and spiders based on his diction and the tone of the essay.

Reading Skill: Main Idea

3. Make a chart like the one shown to identify the **main ideas** and the **supporting details** in the essay. In each box, write the author's main idea about the topic in your own words. Then, find and record supporting details for each main idea.

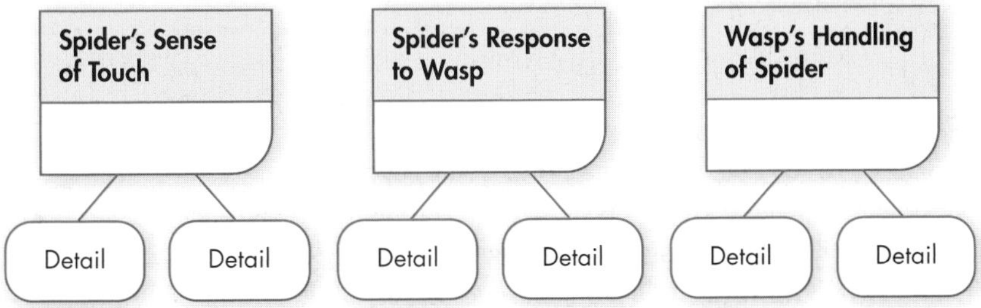

4. In your own words, **summarize** the essay.

Vocabulary

Practice Write a one-sentence answer to each question. Then, explain how the meaning of the underlined word helped you.

1. What is one <u>instinct</u> that all dogs have?
2. At what time do you <u>customarily</u> wake up?
3. How do scientists decide if two spiders belong to <u>distinct</u> species?
4. What fabric do you think has a lot of <u>tactile</u> appeal?
5. What traits make a grizzly bear a <u>formidable</u> creature?
6. Would a surprise party be effective in <u>evoking</u> a positive response?

Word Study Use the context of the sentences and what you know about the **Latin roots *-tact-*** and ***-tang-*** to explain your answers.

1. Why is it important for scientists to have *tangible* evidence?
2. Is someone who has *tact* in touch with the feelings of others?

Word Study

The **Latin roots *-tact-*** and ***-tang-*** mean "touch" or "feel."

Challenge Explain how the roots contribute to the meanings of these words. Consult a dictionary if necessary.

contact
intact
tangent

Answers

Literary Analysis

1. (a) Petrunkevitch explains how the digger wasp uses a tarantula to feed its young. (b) The essay presents the spider as an example of instinct and the wasp as an example of intelligence.
2. **Possible response:** Petrunkevitch has a respectful attitude toward the wasps and spiders. To describe spiders, he uses words such as "powerful," "formidable-looking," and "amazing." He seems in awe of the wasp, which he describes as "beautiful" and "formidable." He describes her done deed as a successful one, "leaving her descendant safely started in life."

Reading Skill

3. **Possible response:** Touch
   Detail 1: The tarantula can sense pressure against the body wall, stroking of the body hair, and riffling of very fine hairs on its legs.
   Detail 2: Touch excites a defensive response in the spider.
   For other sample answers, see *Graphic Organizer Transparencies,* **Reading Skill Graphic Organizer A,** p. 78, and the **Additional Answers** section.
4. **Possible response:** The behavior of the spider is driven by instinct, while the behavior of the wasp is driven by intelligence.

Vocabulary

Practice

Sample answers:

1. All dogs bark when they are afraid or challenged. An <u>instinct</u> is an inborn behavior.
2. I usually wake up at 7 in the morning. <u>Customarily</u> means "usually."
3. Scientists compare and contrast certain features of the spider. For something to be <u>distinct</u>, it has to be different.
4. Something <u>tactile</u> appeals to the sense of touch, so velvet, which is very soft, would have tactile appeal.

Answers continued

5. The bear's size and speed made the grizzly bear a <u>formidable</u> creature. <u>Formidable</u> means "strong."
6. Yes, it would, because surprise parties tend to draw forth positive emotions. Surprise parties usually <u>evoke</u> powerful responses.

Word Study

Sample answers:

1. The Latin root *-tact-* means "touch" or "feel" and *tangible* means "able to be physically felt or touched." It is important for scientists to have solid evidence so that they can make definitive conclusions.
2. Yes, the Latin root *-tact-* means "touch" or "feel" and *tact* means "a feel for what to say or do." Someone who has tact is in touch with others' feelings.

Word Study: Challenge

Sample answers: When two things make *contact,* they literally <u>touch</u> each other. When something is *intact,* it can be <u>felt</u> as a whole. To go off on a *tangent* is to <u>touch</u> upon something different.

PRETEACH

Skills instruction for the ***Reading Skill*** *and* ***Literary Analysis*** *concept for this selection appears on p. 461.*

❶ Writing About the Big Question

1. Review the assignment with the class.
2. Have students discuss specific inventions and how they have contributed to the advancement of our society and to the world in general.
3. Have students complete the sentence starter. Review responses as a class. (**Possible response:** New discoveries and inventions allow for growth in a person's understanding of the world because they make one see things and ideas that were previously thought impossible.
4. Remind students that their answers will help them think about the Big Question.

While You Read

Tell students they should look for steps that people have taken to understand longitude.

❷ Vocabulary

1. Have students preview the selection vocabulary.
2. For each word, have students say the word aloud.
3. Then, use the word in a sentence that defines the word.
4. Finally, repeat your definitional sentence or a similar sentence with the word missing and have the class "fill in the blank" chorally. For example:

   To do something haphazardly is to do it in an unplanned or a disorganized way. Because Shawna packed her clothes at the very last minute, she tossed her garments in the suitcase [students say "haphazardly"].

❸ Word Study

1. Introduce the skill, using the instruction in the box.
2. Instruct students to use the word *configuration* in a sentence. (**Sample answer:** At the archaeological site, the original configuration of the buildings could still be seen.)

Making Connections | *from* Longitude

What kind of *knowledge* changes our lives?

Writing About the Big Question

In the excerpt from *Longitude*, the author presents a history of the search for information about longitude. Use this sentence starter to develop your ideas about the Big Question.

New discoveries and inventions allow for **growth** in a person's **understanding** of the world because ______________________.

While You Read Look for steps taken throughout history to reach an understanding of longitude.

Vocabulary

Read each word and its definition. Decide whether you know the word well, know it a little bit, or do not know it at all. After you read, see how your knowledge of each word has increased.

- **haphazardly** (hap´ haz´ ərd lē) *adv.* in an unplanned or a disorganized way (p. 476) ***Dirty clothes lay haphazardly thrown about the messy room.*** *haphazard adj. haphazardness n.*
- **configuration** (kən fig´ yə rā´ shən) *n.* arrangement of parts; pattern (p. 476) ***We stood in a circular configuration.*** *configurative adj. configure v. figure n.*
- **converge** (kən vʉrj´) *v.* to come together (p. 476) ***Relatives from across the country will converge at the reunion.*** *convergence n.*
- **derived** (di rīvd´) *v.* reached by reasoning (p. 477) ***We derived the answer by solving the equation.*** *derivation n. derivative n.*
- **contested** (kən test´ əd) *v.* tried to disprove or invalidate something; disputed (p. 481) ***She contested the false charges with the credit card company.*** *contest n. contestant n.*
- **impervious** (im pʉr´ vē əs) *adj.* not affected by (used with *to*) (p. 481) ***In my new parka, I am impervious to cold weather.*** *imperviously adv. imperviousness n.*

Word Study

The **Latin root *-fig-*** means "form" or "shape."

In this essay, the author explains that although the world changes its **configuration,** its contours and how boundaries are formed, the lines of latitude and longitude stay fixed.

Vocabulary Development

Vocabulary Knowledge Rating

Create a **Vocabulary Knowledge Rating Chart** (***Professional Development Guidebook***, p. 33) for this selection. Include the selection vocabulary and the Big Question words that appear in the Writing About the Big Question sentence starter. (The Big Question vocabulary is introduced on pp. 442–443.)

Give students a copy of the chart. Read the words aloud, and have students mark their rating in the Before Reading column. Urge them to be alert to these words as they read and discuss the selection.

Tally how many students think they know a word to gauge how much instruction to provide. As students read and discuss the selection, point out the words and their context.

PHLit Online! **Vocabulary Central,** featuring tools, activities, and songs for studying vocabulary, is available online at **www.PHLitOnline.com.**

Meet Dava Sobel

(b. 1937)

Author of *Longitude*

As a child in the Bronx, New York, Dava Sobel enjoyed trips on her family's sailboat, navigated by one of her parents. Years later, she would transform a chapter of navigation history into her first bestseller, *Longitude*.

Curiosity and Inspiration Sobel attended the Bronx High School of Science and went on to become an award-winning science reporter for *The New York Times* and various magazines. In November 1993, she attended a conference about navigation. She became fascinated by the historic contributions of clockmaker John Harrison.

While researching the history of longitude, Sobel stumbled onto the topic of her next book: Italian Renaissance astronomer Galileo and his daughter. She wrote about their relationship in *Galileo's Daughter*.

BACKGROUND FOR THE ESSAY

Navigation

Navigation is the science of finding the position and direction of a craft such as a ship or plane. Since ancient times, mapmakers and sailors have used a system of imaginary lines—longitude and latitude—to identify positions on the Earth's surface.

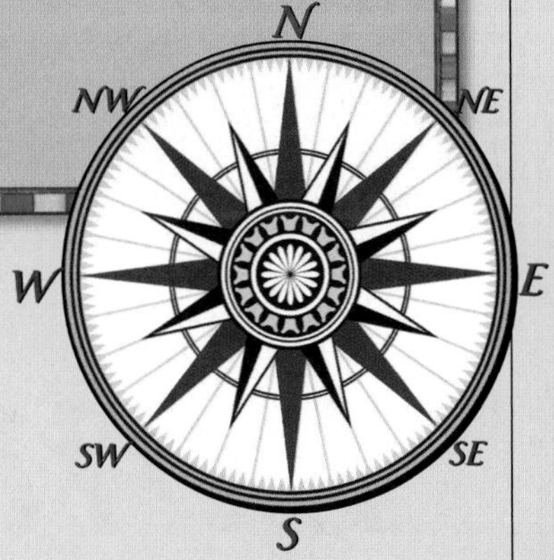

Did You Know?

While researching *Longitude*, Sobel traveled to London for research and to stand directly on the prime meridian.

Daily Bellringer

For each class during which you will teach this selection, have students complete one of the five Quick Write activities for Week 13 in the ***Daily Bellringer Activities*** booklet.

4 Background

Navigation

Travel by water helped ancient civilizations expand and develop contacts with other peoples. Skill in navigation was essential. At first ancient mariners, or sea travelers, stayed close to the coast, tracking their position by various landmarks. Soon they were traveling far from land. They then looked to the sun and stars for direction, made charts of their course, and calculated distances. In time, people developed instruments to help them find their way, including the magnetic compass and astrolabe. As European explorers set out across the oceans, however, these tools proved inadequate. By the 17th and 18th centuries, Britain, France, and other countries with a stake in travel on the seas had begun to support the development of new navigational aids. It was at this time that John Harrison developed the chronometers that solved the problem of determining longitude.

Multidraft Reading

This icon ● marks natural pauses in the selection. To assist struggling readers and to deepen reading for all, assign the text in "chunks," following the icons, and apply multidraft reading protocols. For each reading, have students set the purpose indicated:

- **First reading**—literal comprehension: answering the Reading Check questions.
- **Second reading**—application of skills: answering the Main Idea and Expository Essay prompts.
- **Third reading**—interpretation: answering the end-of-selection questions.

For more guidance, refer to the ***Classroom Strategies and Teaching Routines*** card on multidraft reading.

Differentiated Instruction — Additional Instruction

EL Extended Support—English Learners

Have students complete the **Reading and Vocabulary Warm-ups, *Unit 3 Resources*,** pp. 41–44, before they read. Assign the prereading pages for the selection in the ***Reader's Notebook: English Learner's Version.*** Then, have students listen to portions of the selection on the ***Hear It!* Audio CD.**

L1 L2 Extended Support—Struggling Readers

Have students complete the **Reading and Vocabulary Warm-ups, *Unit 3 Resources*,** pp. 41–44, before they read. Assign the prereading pages for the selection in the ***Reader's Notebook: Adapted Version.*** Then, have students listen to portions of the selection on the ***Hear It!* Audio CD** (adapted text).

Extended Support—Reluctant Readers

To build motivation and engagement before assigning the selection, have students read "Looking Over Your Shoulder," a thematically related selection in ***Reality Central.*** Then, use the questions at the conclusion of the related selection to guide discussion.

PHLit Online!

For more about the author, practice with the selection vocabulary, and more background, go online at **www.PHLitOnline.com.**

TEACH

❶ Activating Prior Knowledge

Have students work with partners. Give each student pair a copy of a **K-W-L Chart** (see ***Professional Development Guidebook***, p. 75). Tell students that the topic is longitude. Have partners work together to complete the first two columns. Tell students to brainstorm for what they already know about the topic and write it in the Know column. In the Want to Know column, they should write questions they have about the topic.

Concept Connector

Students will assess what they have learned after completing the passage from *Longitude.*

Small-Group Activity

Have small groups of students gather information about the clocks that John Harrison invented to help determine longitude. Have groups create posters that show how Harrison's clocks solved the problem of fixing longitude. Invite groups to use their posters to explain to the rest of the class how Harrison's invention worked.

❷ About the Selection

Dava Sobel begins this passage from *Longitude* with a brief history of her own fascination with parallels and meridians. To open her discussion of the challenge presented by longitude, she points out a key distinction between parallels and meridians. While the laws of nature set latitude, longitude would shift, at least until the prime meridian was fixed outside of London and Harrison invented his clocks. Sobel's comprehensive survey of the quest for a solution to the problem of longitude emphasizes the significance of Harrison's achievement.

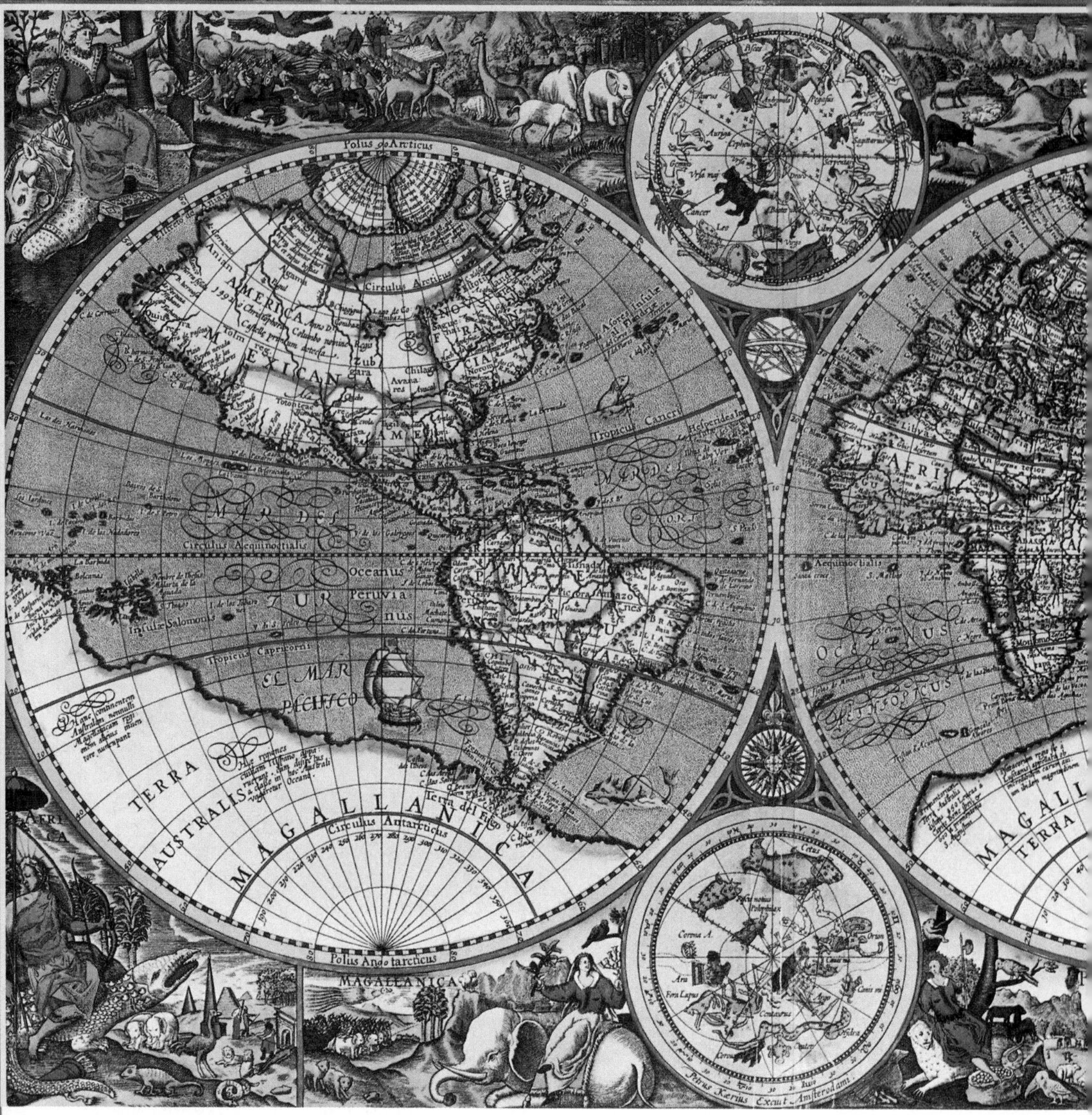

from Longitude

❶ ❷

Dava Sobel

474 Types of Nonfiction: Essays and Speeches

Vocabulary Development

Thematic Vocabulary: The Big Question

As students are discussing the passage from *Longitude,* encourage them to use the thematic vocabulary presented in Introducing the Big Question, pp. 442–443. You might encourage them with sentence starters like these:

1. In this excerpt from *Longitude,* Sobel provides a brief *history* of . . .
2. An *awareness* of both latitude and longitude would help sailors . . .
3. Seafarers' *ignorance* of how to calculate longitude caused . . .
4. The *influence* of John Harrison on navigation was . . .

When I'm playful
I use the meridians
of longitude and parallels
of latitude for a seine, and
drag the Atlantic Ocean
for whales.

—Mark Twain
Life on the Mississippi

3 Once on a Wednesday excursion when I was a little girl, my father bought me a beaded wire ball that I loved. At a touch, I could collapse the toy into a flat coil between my palms, or pop it open to make a hollow sphere. Rounded out, it resembled a tiny Earth, because its hinged wires traced the same pattern

3 Critical Thinking
Analyze

1. Read aloud the first several paragraphs of the selection. **Ask** students to summarize the content of the paragraphs.
   Answer: The paragraphs tell about experiences that interested the author in longitude.
2. **Ask:** Why do you think the author begins her essay with this information?
   Possible response: She wants the subject of longitude to grab readers' interest just as it grabbed her own interest.

Differentiated Instruction for Universal Access

EL Pronunciation for English Learners

Some students might find it difficult to pronounce words with the terminal consonant "t" sound, as in *bought,* and drop it entirely or replace it with the "tuh" sound. The following strategies can help students to pronounce the "t" sound.

- Write the words *fought, sought,* and *taught* on the board, pronouncing each in turn. Have the students repeat each. Then, call out each word at random and have volunteers circle the word on the board. Discuss the results, determining what led to incorrect choices.
- Have students form a circle around the classroom. Using the words *caught, knot,* and *pot,* play a game of "telephone" with each. Pass one word to one student, who in turn passes it to another, and so on. Have the final student write the word on the board. Discuss as a class what exactly led to any changes of the word.

PHLit Online!

This selection is available in interactive format in the **Enriched Online Student Edition, www.PHLitOnline.com,** which includes a thematically related video with writing prompt and an interactive graphic organizer.

❹ Critical Viewing

Possible response: The image of the sculpture of Atlas supporting a globe against the backdrop of a modern building in New York City suggests the endurance of latitude and longitude in modern times. The huge circles suggest not only the globe, but also lines of longitude. The metal construction suggests endurance.

Vocabulary

haphazardly (hap´ haz´ ərd lē) *adv.* in an unplanned or a disorganized way

configuration (kən fig´ yə rā´ shən) *n.* arrangement of parts; pattern

converge (kən vʉrj´) *v.* to come together

❹
▼ Critical Viewing
How does this image convey the endurance of the system of longitude and latitude? **[Interpret]**

❸ of intersecting circles that I had seen on the globe in my schoolroom—the thin black lines of latitude and longitude. The few colored beads slid along the wire paths haphazardly, like ships on the high seas.

My father strode up Fifth Avenue to Rockefeller Center with me on his shoulders, and we stopped to stare at the statue of Atlas,[1] carrying Heaven and Earth on his.

The bronze orb that Atlas held aloft, like the wire toy in my hands, was a see-through world, defined by imaginary lines. The Equator. The Ecliptic. The Tropic of Cancer. The Tropic of Capricorn. The Arctic Circle. The prime meridian. Even then I could recognize, in the graph-paper grid imposed on the globe, a powerful symbol of all the real lands and waters on the planet.

Today, the latitude and longitude lines govern with more authority than I could have imagined forty-odd years ago, for they stay fixed as the world changes its configuration underneath them—with continents adrift across a widening sea, and national boundaries repeatedly redrawn by war or peace.

As a child, I learned the trick for remembering the difference between latitude and longitude. The latitude lines, the *parallels*, really do stay parallel to each other as they girdle the globe from the Equator to the poles in a series of shrinking concentric[2] rings. The meridians of longitude go the other way: They loop from the North Pole to the South and back again in great circles of the same size, so they all converge at the ends of the Earth.

Lines of latitude and longitude began crisscrossing our worldview in ancient times, at least three centuries before the birth of Christ. By A.D. 150, the cartographer and astronomer Ptolemy had plotted them on the twenty-seven maps of his first world atlas. Also for this landmark volume, Ptolemy listed all the place names in an index, in alphabetical order, with the latitude and longitude of each—as well as he could gauge them from travelers' reports. Ptolemy himself had only an armchair appreciation of the wider world. A common misconception of

1. **Fifth Avenue . . . Rockefeller Center . . . Atlas** landmarks in the borough of Manhattan of New York City. Rockefeller Center features a statue of Atlas, the Greek giant condemned to carry the heavens on his shoulders.
2. **concentric** (kən sen´ trik) *adj.* having a center in common.

PROFESSIONAL DEVELOPMENT | **Dr. Hollie**

APPLY THE STRATEGY

Practicing Tiering Words
In her book *Bringing Words To Life,* Isabel Beck suggests "tiering," or separating words into three levels. The first level consists of words the students already know, the second level consists of words that mature readers should know, and the third level consists of uncommon words and content-specific vocabulary.

Tier the selection vocabulary words (p. 472) and create a chart for the students. Tell students that the second-level, or Tier 2 words, should become a part of students' personal thesaurus.

Focus on only 5–7 words per week for long-term retention and ownership.

For more of Dr. Hollie's strategies, see the Professional Development essay, pp. 442c–442d.

his day held that anyone living below the Equator would melt into deformity from the horrible heat.

The Equator marked the zero-degree parallel of latitude for Ptolemy. He did not choose it arbitrarily but took it on higher authority from his predecessors, who had **derived** it from nature while observing the motions of the heavenly bodies. The sun, moon, and planets pass almost directly overhead at the Equator. Likewise the Tropic of Cancer and the Tropic of Capricorn, two other famous parallels, assume their positions at the sun's command. They mark the northern and southern boundaries of the sun's apparent motion over the course of the year.

Vocabulary
derived (di rīvd′) *v.* reached by reasoning

5 Ptolemy was free, however, to lay his prime meridian, the zero-degree longitude line, wherever he liked. He chose to run it through the Fortunate Islands (now called the Canary and Madeira Islands) off the northwest coast of Africa. Later mapmakers moved the prime meridian to the Azores and to the Cape Verde Islands,[3] as well as to Rome, Copenhagen, Jerusalem, St. Petersburg, Pisa, Paris, and Philadelphia, among other places, before it settled down at last in London. As the world turns, any line drawn from pole to pole may serve as well as any other for a starting line of reference. The placement of the prime meridian is a purely political decision.

Reading Skill
Main Idea What main idea does the writer support using examples like Rome and Copenhagen?

Here lies the real, hard-core difference between latitude and longitude—beyond the superficial difference in line direction that any child can see: The zero-degree parallel of latitude is fixed by the laws of nature, while the zero-degree meridian of longitude shifts like the sands of time. This difference makes finding latitude child's play, and turns the determination of longitude, especially at sea, into an adult dilemma—one that stumped the wisest minds of the world for the better part of human history.

A common misconception of his day held that anyone living below the Equator would melt into deformity from the horrible heat.

Any sailor worth his salt can gauge his latitude well enough by the length of the day, or by the height of the sun or known guide stars above the horizon. Christopher Columbus followed a straight path across the Atlantic when he "sailed the parallel" on his 1492 journey, and the technique would doubtless have carried him to the Indies had not the Americas intervened.

6 **Reading Check**
Name an important contribution made to science or navigation by Ptolemy.

The measurement of longitude meridians, in comparison, is tempered by time. To learn one's longitude at sea, one needs to know what time it is aboard ship and also the time at the home

3. **Azores** (ā′ zôrz′) . . . **Cape Verde** (vurd) **Islands** two island groups in the Atlantic Ocean; the Azores are off Portugal and the Cape Verde Islands are off the westernmost point of Africa.

5 Reading Skill
Main Idea

1. Tell students that the main idea of a paragraph is often stated in a topic sentence. Lead students to identify the sentence *The Equator marked the zero-degree parallel of latitude for Ptolemy* as the main idea of the paragraph it begins.
2. Have students identify details in the paragraph that support the main idea.
   Answer: Supporting details include the facts that Ptolemy did not choose the Equator himself; he got the idea to make the Equator the zero-degree parallel of latitude from his predecessors, and his predecessors got the idea by observing that the sun, the moon, and the planets passed directly overhead at the Equator.
3. **Ask** students to respond to the Reading Skill question: What main idea does the writer support using examples like Rome and Copenhagen?
   Answer: The writer supports the idea that the placement of the prime meridian is political.

6 Reading Check

Answer: Ptolemy assembled a world atlas that included maps on which places had been plotted by latitude and longitude and an index that provided the latitude and longitude of places.

Differentiated Instruction for Universal Access

EL Strategy for English Learners

Pair English learners with students who are proficient in English. Have pairs read the selection together. Instruct students to proceed as follows: the student with English proficiency reads each paragraph aloud and provides an oral synopsis of its content, and the English learner reads the paragraph aloud and summarizes it. Encourage students who are proficient in English to help English learners pronounce words correctly, understand new vocabulary, and articulate main ideas.

Enrichment for Advanced Readers

Have students read Dava Sobel's *Longitude* in its entirety. When students have finished reading the book, ask them to summarize its key points in a brief book review. Students may share their reviews with the rest of the class orally.

7 Literature in Context

Science Connection The grid system of latitude and longitude uses the North Pole and the South Pole as points of reference. The Equator circles the Earth and lies halfway between the two poles, dividing the Earth into two halves, or hemispheres. Lines of latitude, also known as parallels, are parallel to the Equator and to each other.

Lines of longitude, or meridians, run only halfway around the Earth, from pole to pole. Each has a twin, or matching line, on the other side of the Earth. Each pair of meridians forms a circle that cuts the Earth into hemispheres. The circle formed by each meridian and its twin is known as a great circle. The only parallel that forms a great circle is the Equator.

Connect to the Literature After students have reviewed the information about latitude and longitude, **ask** the Connect to the Literature question: What does this information indicate about how sailors determine latitude by the sun?
Answer: Sailors can measure the height or angle of the sun at noon to determine latitude.

8 Reading Skill
Main Idea

1. Emphasize the importance of timekeeping in determining longitude at sea. Ask students to explain exactly what sailors or explorers needed to know to be able to measure longitude.
Answer: They needed to know what time it was in two different places.
2. **Ask** students: Which details in this paragraph support Sobel's idea that accurate timekeeping at sea was difficult?
Answer: Details that support the idea that accurate timekeeping was difficult at sea include the rolling ship's effect on how clocks ran, how changes in temperature affected the oil and metal parts of clocks, and how changes in barometric pressure caused clocks to gain or lose time.

---

7 **LITERATURE IN CONTEXT**

Science Connection

Longitude and Latitude
The lines of longitude and latitude form an imaginary grid that can be used to name the exact location of any place on Earth.

- The **equator** is the line of latitude on which all points are the same distance from the North and South poles. The sun appears directly overhead at the equator on March 21 and September 21 of each year.
- The **Tropic of Cancer** is 23° 27′ north of the equator. It marks the northernmost latitude at which the sun can appear directly overhead—an event that occurs at noon on June 20 or 21.
- The **Tropic of Capricorn,** at 23° 27′ south, is the southernmost latitude at which the sun can appear directly overhead. The sun reaches its highest position at this tropic at noon on December 20 or 21.
- The **prime meridian** is the line of longitude chosen as the 0° line.

Connect to the Literature

What does this information indicate about how sailors determine latitude by the sun?

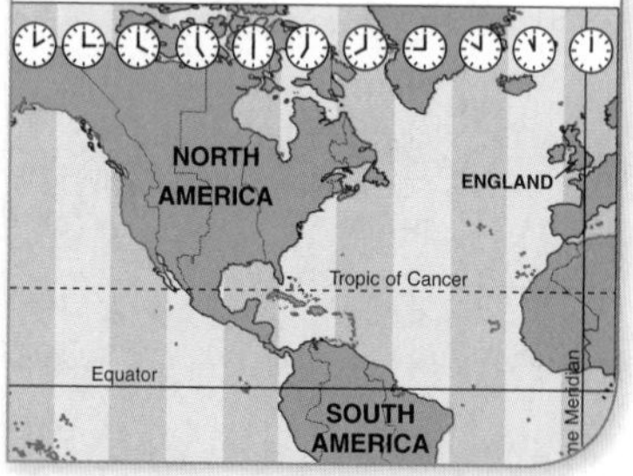

port or another place of known longitude—at that very same moment. The two clock times enable the navigator[4] to convert the hour difference into a geographical separation. Since the Earth takes twenty-four hours to complete one full revolution of three hundred sixty degrees, one hour marks one twenty-fourth of a spin, or fifteen degrees. And so each hour's time difference between the ship and the starting point marks a progress of fifteen degrees of longitude to the east or west. Every day at sea, when the navigator resets his ship's clock to local noon when the sun reaches its highest point in the sky, and then consults the home-port clock, every hour's discrepancy between them translates into another fifteen degrees of longitude.

Those same fifteen degrees of longitude also correspond to a distance traveled. At the Equator, where the girth of the Earth is greatest, fifteen degrees stretch fully one thousand miles. North or south of that line, however, the mileage value of each degree decreases. One degree of longitude equals four minutes of time the world over, but in terms of distance, one degree shrinks from sixty-eight miles at the Equator to virtually nothing at the poles.

Precise knowledge of the hour in two different places at once—a longitude prerequisite so easily accessible today from any pair of cheap wristwatches—was utterly unattainable up to and including the era of pendulum clocks.[5] On the deck of a rolling ship, such clocks would slow down, or speed up, or stop running altogether. Normal changes in temperature encountered en route 8
from a cold country of origin to a tropical trade zone thinned or thickened a clock's lubricating oil and made its metal parts expand or contract with equally disastrous results. A rise or fall in barometric pressure, or the subtle variations in the Earth's gravity from one latitude to another, could also cause a clock to gain or lose time.

For lack of a practical method of determining longitude, every great captain in the Age of Exploration[6]

4. **navigator** (nav′ ə gāt′ ər) *n.* a person skilled in locating the position and plotting the course of a ship or an aircraft.
5. **pendulum** (pen′ dyo͞o ləm) **clocks** clocks whose timekeeping movement is regulated by a pendulum, a weight swinging freely from a fixed point.
6. **Age of Exploration** the period from about 1450 to about 1700, when European navigators sailed to new territories and founded colonies in Africa, the Americas, and Asia.

Think Aloud

Expository Essay
Draw students' attention to the paragraph in the middle of p. 478 beginning with "Those same fifteen degrees . . ." Use the following "think aloud" to model the process of identifying the writer's diction and tone:

When I read this paragraph, I realize that the writer is explaining an important and complex idea about longitude. The writer uses specific details to explain that, depending on the distance from the Equator, fifteen degrees match a certain distance traveled on the Earth. To explain this idea, the writer uses scientific and mathematical terms such as "degrees," "girth," and "miles." The writer uses additional details to specify distances, such as "one thousand miles," "four minutes," and "sixty-eight miles."

I know that when writers explain scientific or mathematical processes, they use precise and subject-specific vocabulary. These choices of words create an objective tone—the writer does not feel a particular emotion toward the subject but is simply informing the reader.

became lost at sea despite the best available charts and compasses. From Vasco da Gama to Vasco Núñez de Balboa, from Ferdinand Magellan to Sir Francis Drake[7]—they all got where they were going willy-nilly, by forces attributed to good luck or the grace of God.

10 As more and more sailing vessels set out to conquer or explore new territories, to wage war, or to ferry gold and commodities between foreign lands, the wealth of nations floated upon the oceans. And still no ship owned a reliable means for establishing her whereabouts. In consequence, untold numbers of sailors died when their destinations suddenly loomed out of the sea and took them by surprise. In a single such accident, on October 22, 1707, at the Scilly Isles near the southwestern tip of England, four home-bound British warships ran aground and nearly two thousand men lost their lives.

7. **Vasco da Gama** (väs´ kô də gä´ mə) . . . **Vasco Núñez de Balboa** (väs´ kô no͞o´ nyeth *the* bal bō´ ə) . . . **Ferdinand Magellan** (mə jel´ ən) . . . **Sir Francis Drake** famous explorers of the fifteenth and sixteenth centuries.

Reading Skill
Main Idea Which detail in this paragraph supports Sobel's idea that not knowing one's longitude was dangerous?

11 **Reading Check**
What key technical problem prevented sailors from measuring longitude accurately?

9 Humanities

As for Resolution by Robin Brooks

Robin Brooks is a renowned marine artist in the United Kingdom. This painting features Captain James Cook's ship, the *Resolution,* in Antarctic waters during his 1772–1775 voyage.

10 Reading Skill

Main Idea

1. Have students read the bracketed passage.
2. **Ask** students to respond to the Reading Skill question: Which detail in this paragraph supports Sobel's idea that not knowing one's longitude was dangerous?
   Answer: In October 1707, four British warships ran aground, killing nearly two thousand sailors.

11 Reading Check

Answer: The key technical problem was that sailors could not keep time accurately so that they could know the exact time in two different places.

Differentiated Instruction for Universal Access

Culturally Responsive Instruction

Culture Focus Explain to students that advances in navigation and cartography (map-making) between the fifteenth and seventeenth centuries made what was previously impossible an achievable reality: global exploration. In this era, known as the Age of Exploration, European explorers embarked on the seas to acquire spices, to find trade routes, and to discover new lands.

Provide students with a list of explorers and the countries from which they came. Include notable personages, such as Vasco de Gama (Portugal), Vasco Nunez de Balboa (Spain), Sir Francis Drake (England), John Cabot (Italy), and Jacques Cartier (France). Have students choose an explorer from their native country to research. If students prefer, have them research their native country's involvement in the Age of Exploration. Invite students to present their findings to the class.

⓬ Literary Analysis

Expository Essay

1. Remind students that a writer can set a specific tone based on his or her diction. The tone may be formal or informal, playful, serious, and so on.
2. Have students read the bracketed text. Then **ask** the Literary Analysis question: How do the details in this paragraph contribute to the author's tone?
   Possible response: Details such as the names of kings and explorers and their historical actions lend Sobel's essay an informative and objective tone, because these details can be proven.

⓭ Connecting to the Big Question

1. Explain to students that often it takes small but necessary breakthroughs to initiate discoveries that alter or replace previously-held notions of the world.
2. Have students identify steps taken throughout history to reach an understanding of longitude.
   Possible response: For the purpose of studying longitude, great minds such as Galileo, Newton, and Haley made important discoveries in astronomy. Other individuals tried less reliable methods, such as cannon blasts of signal ships, to navigate.
3. **Ask** students: How did the quest for this knowledge change the lives of people in the early 1700s?
   Possible response: Knowledge acquired by astronomers changed people's perception of the world. For instance, astronomers calculated the distance of the Earth to the stars, which changed people's perception of the vastness of their world.

⓮ Critical Viewing

Possible response: No; it seems small and simple when one considers how it changed navigation.

⓯ Humanities

Portrait of George III (1738–1820) in his Coronation Robes by Allan Ramsay

This painting shows King George in 1760, when he was only twenty-two years old.

Literary Analysis Expository Essay
How do the details in this paragraph contribute to the author's tone? ⓬

⓮ ▶ **Critical Viewing**
Does the appearance of Harrison's marine watch reflect its world-altering importance? Explain. **[Support]** ⓭

The active quest for a solution to the problem of longitude persisted over four centuries and across the whole continent of Europe. Most crowned heads of state eventually played a part in the longitude story, notably King George III of England and King Louis XIV of France. Seafaring men such as Captain William Bligh of the Bounty and the great circumnavigator Captain James Cook, who made three long voyages of exploration and experimentation before his violent death in Hawaii, took the more promising methods to sea to test their accuracy and practicability.

Renowned astronomers approached the longitude challenge by appealing to the clockwork universe: Galileo Galilei, Jean Dominique Cassini, Christiaan Huygens, Sir Isaac Newton, and Edmond Halley,[8] of comet fame, all entreated the moon and stars for help. Palatial observatories were founded at Paris, London, and Berlin for the express purpose of determining longitude by the heavens. Meanwhile, lesser minds devised schemes that depended on the yelps of wounded dogs, or the cannon blasts of signal ships strategically anchored—somehow—on the open ocean.

In the course of their struggle to find longitude, scientists struck upon other discoveries that changed their view of the universe. These include the first accurate determinations of the weight of the Earth, the distance to the stars, and the speed of light.

⓯ ▲ King George III

As time passed and no method proved successful, the search for a solution to the longitude problem assumed legendary proportions, on a par with discovering the Fountain of Youth, the secret of perpetual motion, or the formula for transforming lead into gold.[9] The governments of the great maritime nations—including Spain, the Netherlands, and certain city-states of Italy—periodically roiled the fervor by offering jackpot purses for a workable method. The British Parliament, in its famed Longitude Act of 1714, set the highest bounty of all, naming a prize equal to a king's ransom (several million dollars in today's currency) for a "Practicable and Useful" means of determining longitude.

8. **Galileo Galilei** (gal´ ə lā´ ō gal´ ə lā ē) . . . **Jean-Dominique Cassini** (zhän dō mi nēk´ kä sē´ nē) . . . **Christiaan Huygens** (hī´ gənz) . . . **Sir Isaac Newton . . . Edmond Halley** (hal´ ē) pioneering astronomers and scientists of the sixteenth through the eighteenth centuries. Their work redefined people's picture of the universe, replacing traditional views with modern ones.

Vocabulary Development

Vocabulary Knowledge Rating

When students have completed reading and discussing the excerpt from *Longitude,* have them take out their **Vocabulary Knowledge Rating Chart** for this selection. Read the words aloud once more and have students rate their knowledge of the words again in the After Reading column. Clarify any words that are still problematic. Have students write their own definition and example or sentence in the appropriate column. Then, have students complete the Vocabulary Practice at the end of the selection. Encourage students to use the words in further discussion and written work about this selection. Remind them that they will be accountable for these words on the **Selection Test, *Unit 3 Resources*,** pp. 56–58 or 59–61.

English clockmaker John Harrison, a mechanical genius who pioneered the science of portable precision timekeeping, devoted his life to this quest. He accomplished what Newton had feared was impossible: He invented a clock that would carry the true time from the home port, like an eternal flame, to any remote corner of the world.

Harrison, a man of simple birth and high intelligence, crossed swords with the leading lights of his day. He made a special enemy of the Reverend Nevil Maskelyne, the fifth astronomer royal, who **contested** his claim to the coveted prize money, and whose tactics
16 at certain junctures can only be described as foul play.

With no formal education or apprenticeship to any watchmaker, Harrison nevertheless constructed a series of virtually friction-free clocks that required no lubrication and no cleaning, that were made from materials **impervious** to rust, and that kept their moving parts perfectly balanced in relation to one another, regardless of how the world pitched or tossed about them. He did away with the pendulum, and he combined different metals inside his works in such a way that when one component expanded or contracted with changes in temperature, the other counteracted the change and kept the clock's rate constant.

9. **Fountain of Youth . . . lead into gold** three imaginary goals seriously pursued by inquirers. The Fountain of Youth was supposed to restore youth. Perpetual motion would allow people to generate power endlessly without consuming fuel. A formula to turn the cheap metal lead into the precious metal gold was sought for centuries by alchemists.

Vocabulary

contested (kən test´ əd) *v.* tried to disprove or invalidate something; disputed

impervious (im pʉr´ vē əs) *adj.* not affected by

17 Reading Check

What important device did Harrison invent?

16 Reading Skill
Main Idea

1. Emphasize that sometimes the main idea is not stated but implied, which can be true of a passage when several paragraphs discuss the same topic.
2. Have students read the bracketed text.
3. **Ask** students: What is the main idea of this passage? What supporting details help you to know?
Possible response: Clockmaker John Harrison created the first portable clock that could show the true time on the sea, an invention that finally allowed navigators to calculate longitude. The first paragraph of the passage introduces his contribution; the third paragraph describes how Harrison, with no formal training by a master watchmaker, created clocks that would not be disturbed by ocean conditions and would thus keep the time constant.

Monitor Progress: Check students' answers to make sure that they are correctly identifying the main idea and supporting details.

Reteach: If students are having difficulty identifying the main idea and supporting details, diagram the passage on the board. For each paragraph, elicit from students the main idea, stated or implied. Then, ask students to list supporting details for each. Direct students' attention to each main idea, and have them summarize the main ideas in one sentence. Explain to students that main ideas can drive single paragraphs, passages, and entire essays. Thus, an essay can have one overarching main idea and several minor ones contained within it.

17 Reading Check

Answer: Harrison invented the first accurate portable clock.

Concept Connector

K-W-L Chart
Have students complete the last column of their **K-W-L Charts**. Ask students to evaluate what they have learned in relation to the questions they had before reading.

Writing About the Big Question
Have students compare their responses to the sentence starter they completed before reading the essay with their ideas afterwards. Ask them to explain whether their thoughts have changed.

Literary Analysis Graphic Organizer
Ask students to review the charts they completed to identify the writer's diction and tone while reading. Show them **Literary Analysis Graphic Organizer A** (*Graphic Organizer Transparencies*, p. 76) as an example. Then, have students use the graphic organizers they completed to make observations about the writer's diction and tone.

ASSESS

Answers

Critical Thinking

1. Students may be interested in meeting Harrison because of the impact of his work.
2. (a) Sailors can estimate latitude by the length of the day or by the height of the sun or known guide stars above the horizon. (b) Someone is at the Equator if the sun is overhead at noon. (c) Natural laws and landmarks can be used to determine latitude, while special instruments and calculations are needed to determine longitude.
3. To determine longitude, one needs to know the exact time in two different places.
4. Conflicts arose between astronomers and those using mechanical methods; judges favored astronomers.

What kind of knowledge changes our lives?

(a) Students should provide two examples of how a delay in accurate calculation of longitude would have affected people's lives and world events, such as difficulties with travel. (b) Students might say that longitude is a life-changing development because it made travel by sea safer, more dependable, and more efficient than it had been before.

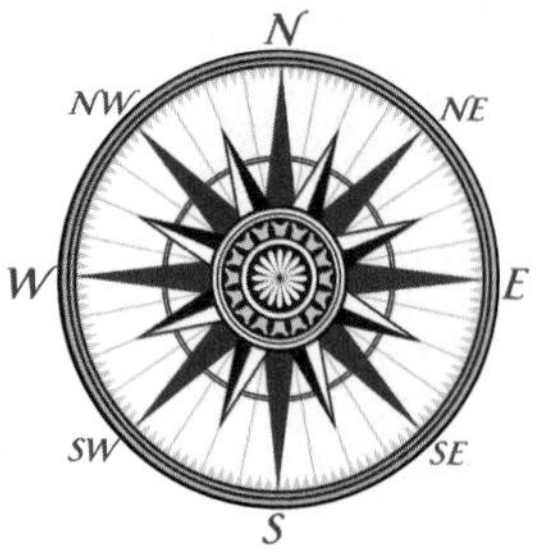

His every success, however, was parried by members of the scientific elite, who distrusted Harrison's magic box. The commissioners charged with awarding the longitude prize—Nevil Maskelyne among them—changed the contest rules whenever they saw fit, so as to favor the chances of astronomers over the likes of Harrison and his fellow "mechanics."[10] But the utility and accuracy of Harrison's approach triumphed in the end. His followers shepherded Harrison's intricate, exquisite invention through the design modifications that enabled it to be mass produced and enjoy wide use.

An aged, exhausted Harrison, taken under the wing of King George III, ultimately claimed his rightful monetary reward in 1773—after forty struggling years of political intrigue, international warfare, academic backbiting, scientific revolution, and economic upheaval.

All these threads, and more, entwine in the lines of longitude. To unravel them now—to retrace their story in an age when a network of orbiting satellites can nail down a ship's position within a few feet in just a moment or two—is to see the globe anew.

10. **"mechanics"** skilled workers and tradesmen, of a lower class than merchants or aristocrats.

Critical Thinking

1. **Respond:** If you could go back in time, which of the historic figures mentioned in this article would you like to meet? Why?
2. **(a)** According to Sobel, what two methods can sailors use to estimate their latitude? **(b) Apply:** Using one of these methods, how could you tell whether you were at the equator—the zero-degree latitude? **(c) Compare and Contrast:** Why is determining latitude easier than determining longitude?
3. **Analyze:** Briefly explain why the invention of an accurate clock was crucial to solving the problem of determining longitude.
4. **Analyze Cause and Effect:** Why did Harrison have difficulties getting his solution to the problem of longitude recognized?

What kind of knowledge changes our lives?
(a) The new type of clock invented by John Harrison had a profound impact on the world. Identify two ways in which the world would be different without Harrison's clocks. **(b)** Would you say longitude is a life-changing development? Explain.

Assessment Resources

The following resources can be used to assess students' knowledge and skills.

Unit 3 Resources

L1 L2 EL **Selection Test A,** pp. 56–58

L3 L4 **Selection Test B,** pp. 59–61

L3 L4 **Open-Book Test,** pp. 53–55

PHLit Online! Students may use the **Self-test**, online at **www.PHLitOnline.com**, to prepare for the **Selection Test A** or **Selection Test B.**

After You Read *from* Longitude

Literary Analysis: Expository Essay

1. **(a)** What event does Sobel explain in this **expository essay**? **(b)** Briefly explain how she uses facts about astronomy and navigation to help readers understand the significance of this event.
2. Describe Sobel's attitude about longitude and navigation based on her **diction** and the **tone** of the essay.

Reading Skill: Main Idea

3. Using a chart like the one shown, identify the **main ideas** and the **supporting details** in the essay.

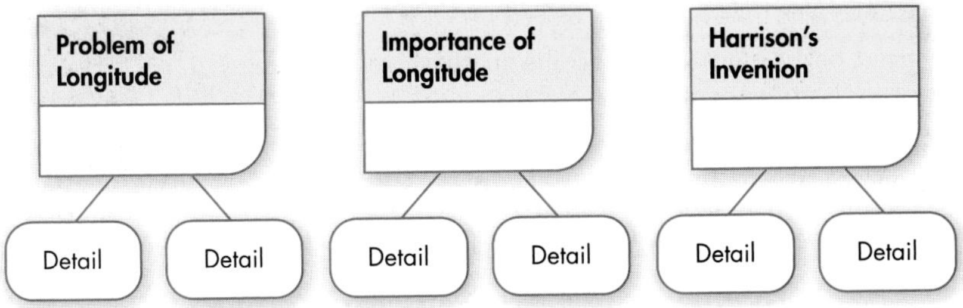

4. In your own words, **summarize** the essay.

Vocabulary

Practice Write a one-sentence answer to each question. Then, explain how the meaning of the underlined word helped you.

1. What might a room look like if it is haphazardly decorated?
2. Has he derived a correct conclusion if he was missing information?
3. What is the configuration of the desks in your classroom?
4. Do you think anyone is truly impervious to criticism?
5. How could you determine if two streets converge?
6. What tone would you find at a debate over a contested election?

Word Study Use the context of the sentences and what you know about the **Latin root *-fig-*** to explain your answer to each question.

1. If a room becomes *transfigured,* will it look different?
2. What are you doing if you *reconfigure* a chart?

Word Study

The **Latin root *-fig-*** means "form" or "shape."

Challenge Explain how the root *-fig-* contributes to the meanings of these words. Consult a dictionary if necessary.

effigy
figment
figurine

ASSESS/EXTEND

Answers

Literary Analysis

1. (a) Sobel explains how John Harrison's invention of accurate clocks solved the problem of determining longitude. (b) Sobel uses facts about astronomy and navigation to emphasize the difficulties people encountered in navigation without an accurate way of determining longitude.
2. Throughout her essay, Sobel uses navigation-specific terms, as well as sophisticated phrases and transitions such as *likewise, however,* and *in comparison,* which contribute to her matter-of-fact, or objective, tone.

Reading Skill

3. **Possible response: Problem of Determining Longitude: Detail 1:** The zero degree meridian of longitude is not fixed. **Detail 2:** Determination is tempered by time. **Detail 3:** At sea, a person needs to know what time it is aboard ship and also the time at the home port at the very same moment.
   For other sample answers, see ***Graphic Organizer Transparencies,*** **Reading Skill Graphic Organizer** A, p. 80, and the **Additional Answers** section.
4. Determining longitude was a problem for navigators for hundreds of years. It required knowing the exact time in two different places. The problem was finally solved when John Harrison invented a clock that could keep accurate time at sea.

Vocabulary

Practice

Sample answers:

1. It would look disordered or messy. Something done haphazardly would be done in an unplanned way.
2. No, his conclusion would probably be incorrect. A derived conclusion is reached by reasoning.
3. The desks are arranged in a circle. The configuration is way the desks are arranged.
4. No, everyone is affected by criticism. No one is unaffected by it.

Answers continued

5. You could look at a map to see if they meet. To converge is to come together.
6. The tone would be argumentative. Something contested is disputed.

Word Study

Sample answers:

1. Yes, the root *-fig-* means "form" or "shape" and *transfigured* means "changed shape." A room with a changed shape will look different.
2. The root *-fig-* means "form" or "shape" and *reconfigure* means "to reshape." If you reconfigure a chart, you are reshaping it.

Word Study: Challenge

Sample answers: *Effigy* means a representation of or form of, especially of a person. A *figment* is something formed in one's mind. A *figurine* is a small sculptured or shaped figure.

Answers

Grammar

1. Introduce the skill, using the instruction on the student page.
2. Discuss the definitions and the examples.

Think Aloud: Model the Skill

Model the skill using the following "think aloud." On the board, write *Carl bought him a bike.* Say to students:

> I know that a direct object always answers the question *Whom or what received the action?* Thus, to identify the direct object, I first identify the action—*bought.* Then I ask *What did Carl buy? A bike* is the direct object.
>
> An indirect object answers the question *To or for whom or what is the action done?* Thus, I ask *For whom did Carl buy? Him* is the indirect object.

WG Writing and Grammar, Grade 10

Students will find further instruction and practice on direct and indirect objects in Chapter 19, Section 3.

Practice A

1. attack, verb; insects, direct object
2. give, V; sting, DO; tarantulas, IO
3. throws, V; impulses, DO; brain, IO
4. attaches, V; egg, DO; spider, IO
5. told, V; story, DO; us, IO

Challenge

Sample answer: "The mother wasp attaches the egg to the paralyzed spider's abdomen." Attaches: V; egg: DO; abdomen: IO

Practice B

1. bought, verb; ball, direct object. The author's father bought his son a ball.
2. showed, V; ball, DO. The sailors showed the curious boy the compass.
3. presented, V; clock, DO. Harrison presented the British Parliament the clock.
4. granted, V; money, DO. The king granted his money to his subjects.
5. gave, V; results; DO. Astronomers gave the panel the results of their long research.

Challenge

Sample answer: The cartographer gave the captain a map.

Integrated Language Skills

The Spider and the Wasp • *from* Longitude

Grammar: Direct and Indirect Objects

A **direct object** is a noun or pronoun that receives the action of an action verb. An **indirect object** is used with a direct object and names the person or thing that something is given to or done for.

To find the direct object of a verb, answer the question "[verb] *whom?*" or "[verb] *what?*"

Example: Sam threw Fred the ball.

Threw what? ANSWER : the ball (direct object)

To find the indirect object of a verb, answer the question "[verb] *to or for whom?*" or "[verb] *to or for what?*"

Example: Sam threw Fred the ball.

Threw to whom? ANSWER : Fred (indirect object)

Indirect objects may appear only between verbs and direct objects in sentences.

Practice A Identify the verb and objects in each sentence. Then, tell whether the object is a direct object or an indirect object

1. Tarantulas attack insects.
2. Digger wasps give tarantulas a sting.
3. A spider's hair throws the brain impulses.
4. The wasp attaches her egg to the spider.
5. The writer told us the story of the spider and the wasp.

Challenge In "The Spider and the Wasp," find two sentences that have both direct and indirect objects. Identify and label the verb and the objects in each sentence.

Practice B Identify the action verb and direct object in each sentence below. Then, rewrite each sentence adding an indirect object, if possible.

1. The author's father bought a ball.
2. The sailors showed the compass.
3. Harrison presented a clock.
4. The king granted the prize money.
5. Astronomers gave the results of their long research study.

Challenge Write two sentences about using maps using the following grammatic order: subject, action verb, indirect object, direct object.

WG Writing and Grammar Connection: Chapter 19, Section 3

Extend the Lesson

Sentence Modeling

Choose the sentence given from the selection students have read:

For each egg the mother must provide one adult tarantula, alive but paralyzed. ("The Spider and the Wasp")

Once on a Wednesday excursion when I was a little girl, my father bought me a beaded wire ball that I loved. (from *Longitude*)

Ask students what they notice about the sentence. Elicit from them the direct and indirect objects. Then, ask what else they notice. ("The Spider and the Wasp": The indirect object is at the beginning of the sentence, putting emphasis on the direct object, the tarantula, the subject of the essay. From *Longitude:* This sentence's rhythm and simple language mirror Sobel's joy and curiosity as a little girl.)

Have students imitate the sentence in a sentence on a topic of their own choosing, matching each grammatical and stylistic feature discussed. Collect the sentences and share them with the class.

riting

h of these essays discuss important scientific discoveries. Write a **iness letter** in which you imagine that you are either a scientist uesting funds to do more research on tarantulas and wasps, or John rison explaining your invention to King George III. (For the format of a iness letter, see page 532.) Make sure to address your intended audi-e with the appropriate tone and language in your letter.

f you read "The Spider and the Wasp," use these ideas to help you te your letter.

- Explain why tarantulas and wasps are of scientific interest, and summarize what we currently know, as reported by Petrunkevitch.
- Tell what mysteries could be solved with additional research.

f you read the excerpt from *Longitude,* use these ideas to help you te your letter.

- Briefly describe your clock and explain how it determines longitude.
- Mention the resistance you have met from the Royal Society.

iting Workshop: *Work in Progress*

ewriting for a Letter to the Editor To prepare for a letter to the tor you may write, think of several issues in the news that spark your erest. Make a list of these issues and write down two important facts examples for each issue. Then, choose one issue about which to write ır letter. Put this Issues List in your writing portfolio.

Use this prewriting activity to prepare for the **Writing Workshop** on page 532.

stening and Speaking

.iver a **humorous persuasive speech** in which you encourage your lience to view wasps and tarantulas as pets, or propose moving the me meridian to your hometown.

- Plan humorous approaches to meet your audience's interests.
- Formulate a clear **thesis**—the main idea you want to get across.
- Support your ideas with facts, examples, and reasons.
- Address specific concerns your audience may have, anticipating and answering any objections.
- Choose effective language. Slang might seem contemporary, but formal language might command respect. Use **figurative language** such as similes, metaphors, or imagery to make your message more vivid and powerful.

PHLit Online!
www.PHLitOnline.com
- Interactive graphic organizers
- Grammar tutorial
- Interactive journals

EXTEND/ASSESS

Writing

1. Review the assignment, using the instruction on the student page.
2. To guide students in writing their business letters, give them **Support for Writing**, p. 51 in ***Unit 3 Resources.***
3. To evaluate students' business letters, use the Business Letter rubric, pp. 236–237 in ***Professional Development Guidebook.*** Also make sure students' letters reflect the bulleted items.

Six Traits Focus

✔	Ideas		Word Choice
✔	Organization		Sentence Fluency
✔	Voice		Conventions

Writing Workshop
Work in Progress

Have students save their completed Issues List in their portfolios. They will use their list later as they continue this Work-in-Progress assignment (see p. 509). These assignments prepare them to complete the Writing Workshop assignment (see pp. 532–537).

Listening and Speaking

1. Review the assignment, using the instruction on the student page.
2. Have students complete the **Support for Extend Your Learning** page (***Unit 3 Resources,*** p. 52).

Teaching Resources

All *Unit 3 Resources*
L3 L4 **Integrated Language Skills: Grammar,** p. 50
L3 L4 **Support for Writing,** p. 51
L3 L4 **Support for Extend Your Learning,** p. 52
L4 **Enrichment,** pp. 31 and 49

All **Enriched Online Student Edition**
Available under After You Read for this selection:
All **Interactive Grammar Tutorial**
L3 L4 **Internet Research Activity**

Professional Development Guidebook
Rubrics for Letters to the Editor, pp. 236–237

PHLit Online! All print and digital resources are available online at **www.PHLitOnline.com.** Online resources accessible by students are noted on the student page.

TIME AND RESOURCE MANAGER

The Sun Parlor • *from* In Commemoration: One Million Volumes

Lesson Pacing Guide

DAY 1 Preteach

- Administer the Reading and Vocabulary Warm-ups (*Unit 3 Resources*, pp. 62–65 or 80–83) as necessary.
- Introduce the Reading Skill: Main Idea FT
- Introduce the Literary Analysis concept: Reflective Essay FT
- Distribute copies of the appropriate graphic organizer for the Reading Skill (*Graphic Organizer Transparencies*, pp. 82–84). CRI
- Distribute copies of the appropriate graphic organizer for Literary Analysis (*Graphic Organizer Transparencies*, pp. 85–87). CRI
- Teach the selection vocabulary. FT CRI
- Introduce the Word Study skill.

DAYS 2–3 Preteach/Teach

- Build background with the Background feature. CRI
- Develop thematic vocabulary and thematic thinking with Writing About the Big Question.
- Prepare students to read with the Activating Prior Knowledge activities (TE). CRI
- Informally monitor comprehension while students read. FT
- Use the Reading Check questions to confirm comprehension.
- Develop students' ability to analyze main ideas and supporting details using the Reading Skill questions. CRI
- Develop students' understanding of reflective essay using the Literary Analysis questions. CRI
- Reinforce vocabulary with the Vocabulary notes. CRI

DAY 4 Assess

- Assess students' comprehension and mastery of the skills by having them answer the Critical Thinking, Reading Skill, and Literary Analysis questions. FT
- Have students complete the Vocabulary Practice activities. FT
- Have students complete the Word Study activities.

DAY 5 Extend/Assess

- Have students complete the Grammar lesson. CRI
- Have students complete the Writing activity and write a memoir. (You may assign as homework.) FT
- Extend learning by having students complete the Listening and Speaking activity, an oral recollection. As an alternative, assign them "Dressing by the Book" or "Textbook Technoloby" in *Reality Central*. CRI
- Administer Selection Test A or B (*Unit 3 Resources*, pp. 74–79 or 95–100). FT

"The Sun Parlor" is an unedited memoir. "In Commemoration: One Million Volumes" is an essay edited for length

Meeting Your Standards

Students will

1. analyze and respond to literary elements.
   - Literary Analysis: Reflective Essay
2. read, comprehend, and analyze short stories.
   - Reading Skill: Main Idea
   - Reading Check questions
   - Apply the Skills questions
   - Assessment Practice
3. develop vocabulary.
   - Vocabulary
   - Word Study
4. apply grammar skills.
   - Subject Complements
5. Develop writing proficiency.
   - Work in Progress: Letter to the Editor
   - memoir
6. strengthen research and technology skills.
   - oral recollection

CRI For a full explanation of Culturally Responsive Instruction opportunities in this lesson, see p. T86–T87.

FT For an accelerated lesson, use the Fast Track strategies and activities.

Managing Differentiated Instruction
This leveled selection pairing groups a more accessible with a more challenging selection. Choose either one to teach the lesson skills. For classroom management suggestions for using the pairing in a mixed-ability class, see pp. T68–T69.

Daily Block Scheduling
Each day in this Lesson Pacing Guide represents a 40–50 minute period. Teachers using block scheduling may combine days to revise pacing. In addition, teachers may differentiate and support core instruction by integrating components for extended and intensive support as students require. See the Guide to Selected Leveled Resources (facing page).

Guide to Selected Leveled Resources

EL English Learners

			The Sun Parlor	*from* In Commemoration: One Million Volumes
CORE COURSE	*Unit 3 Resources*	Selection Test A	pp. 74–76	pp. 95–97
	Graphic Organizer Transparencies	Reading Skill Graphic Organizer A	p. 82	p. 83
		Literary Analysis Graphic Organizer A	p. 85	p. 86
EXTENDED SUPPORT (Level 2)	*Unit 3 Resources*	Reading and Vocabulary Warm-ups A or B	pp. 62–65	pp. 80–83
	Reader's Notebook: English Learner's Version		adapted instruction and adapted selection	adapted instruction and summary
	Hear It! Audio CD		selection and summaries	selection and summaries
	Hear It! Audio CD (adapted text)		adapted selection and summaries	—
INTENSIVE SUPPORT (Level 1)	*Reality Central*		"Dressing by the Book"	"Textbook Technology"
	Real-World Writing Journal		Lesson 3, pp. 78–81	Lesson 4, pp. 82–85

L2 Below-Level Students

			The Sun Parlor	*from* In Commemoration: One Million Volumes
CORE COURSE	*Unit 3 Resources*	Selection Test A	pp. 74–76	pp. 95–97
	Graphic Organizer Transparencies	Reading Skill Graphic Organizer A	p. 82	p. 83
		Literary Analysis Graphic Organizer A	p. 85	p. 86
EXTENDED SUPPORT (Level 2)	*Unit 3 Resources*	Reading and Vocabulary Warm-ups A or B	pp. 62–65	pp. 80–83
	Reader's Notebook		adapted instruction and full selection	adapted instruction and summary
	Hear It! Audio CD		selection and summaries	selection and summaries
INTENSIVE SUPPORT (Level 1)	*Reality Central*		"Dressing by the Book"	"Textbook Technology"
	Real-World Writing Journal		Lesson 3, pp. 78–81	Lesson 4, pp. 82–85
	Reading Kit		Reteaching worksheets	Reteaching worksheets

L1 Special Needs Students

			The Sun Parlor	*from* In Commemoration: One Million Volumes
CORE COURSE	*Unit 3 Resources*	Selection Test A	pp. 74–76	pp. 95–97
	Graphic Organizer Transparencies	Reading Skill Graphic Organizer A	p. 82	p. 83
		Literary Analysis Graphic Organizer A	p. 85	p. 86
EXTENDED SUPPORT (Level 2)	*Unit 3 Resources*	Reading and Vocabulary Warm-ups A or B	pp. 62–65	pp. 80–83
	Reader's Notebook: Adapted Version		adapted instruction and adapted selection	adapted instruction and summary
	Hear It! Audio CD (adapted text)		adapted selection and summaries	—
INTENSIVE SUPPORT (Level 1)	*Reality Central*		"Dressing by the Book"	"Textbook Technology"
	Real-World Writing Journal		Lesson 3, pp. 78–81	Lesson 4, pp. 82–85
	Reading Kit		Reteaching worksheets	Reteaching worksheets

The program includes resources for these students: L3 On-Level L4 Advanced All All
For a complete guide to selection support, see pp. T106–T108.

NOTE: All print materials are also available online at *www.PHLitOnline.com.*

VISUAL GUIDE to Featured Selection Resources

- **The Sun Parlor**
- ***from* In Commemoration: One Million Volumes**

RESOURCES FOR:

- EL English Learners
- L1 Special Needs Students
- L2 Below-Level Students
- L3 On-Level Students
- L4 Advanced Students
- All All Students

Vocabulary/Fluency/Prior Knowledge

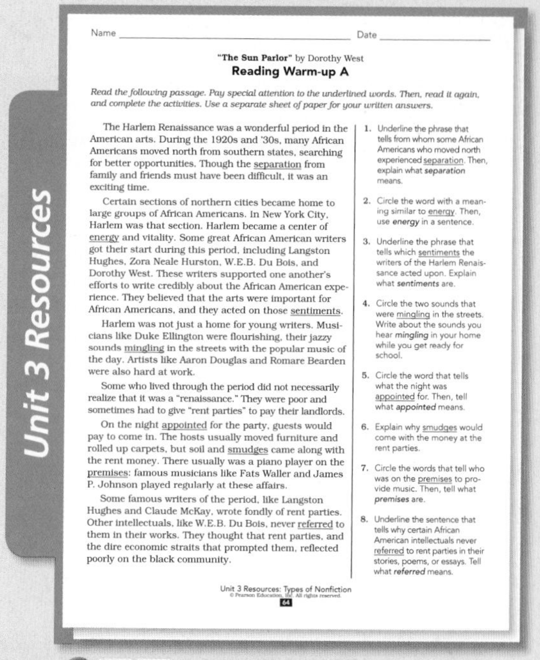

Name ____________ Date ____________

"The Sun Parlor" by Dorothy West

Reading Warm-up A

Read the following passage. Pay special attention to the underlined words. Then, read it again, and complete the activities. Use a separate sheet of paper for your written answers.

The Harlem Renaissance was a wonderful period in the American arts. During the 1920s and '30s, many African Americans moved north from southern states, searching for better opportunities. Though the separation from family and friends must have been difficult, it was an exciting time.

Certain sections of northern cities became home to large groups of African Americans. In New York City, Harlem was that section. Harlem became a center of energy and vitality. Some great African American writers got their start during this period, including Langston Hughes, Zora Neale Hurston, W.E.B. Du Bois, and Dorothy West. These writers supported one another's efforts to write credibly about the African American experience. They believed that the arts were important for African Americans, and they acted on those sentiments.

Harlem was not just a home for young writers. Musicians like Duke Ellington were flourishing, their jazzy sounds mingling in the streets with the popular music of the day. Artists like Aaron Douglas and Romare Bearden were also hard at work.

Some who lived through the period did not necessarily realize that it was a "renaissance." They were poor and sometimes had to give "rent parties" to pay their landlords.

On the night appointed for the party, guests would pay to come in. The hosts usually moved furniture and rolled up carpets, but soil and smudges came along with the rent money. There usually was a piano player on the premises: famous musicians like Fats Waller and James P. Johnson played regularly at these affairs.

Some famous writers of the period, like Langston Hughes and Claude McKay, wrote fondly of rent parties. Other intellectuals, like W.E.B. Du Bois, never referred to them in their works. They thought that rent parties, and the dire economic straits that prompted them, reflected poorly on the black community.

1. Underline the phrase that tells from whom some African Americans who moved north experienced separation. Then, explain what ***separation*** means.
2. Circle the word with a meaning similar to energy. Then, use ***energy*** in a sentence.
3. Underline the phrase that tells which sentiments the writers of the Harlem Renaissance acted upon. Explain what ***sentiments*** are.
4. Circle the two sounds that were mingling in the streets. Write about the sounds you hear ***mingling*** in your home while you get ready for school.
5. Circle the word that tells what the night was appointed for. Then, tell what ***appointed*** means.
6. Explain why smudges would come with the money at the rent parties.
7. Circle the words that tell who was on the premises to provide music. Then, tell what ***premises*** are.
8. Underline the sentence that tells why certain African American intellectuals never referred to rent parties in their stories, poems, or essays. Tell what ***referred*** means.

Unit 3 Resources: Types of Nonfiction
© Pearson Education, Inc. All rights reserved.
64

EL L1 L2 **Reading Warm-ups A and B, pp. 64–65, 82–83**

Also available for these selections:

EL L1 L2 Vocabulary Warm-ups A and B, pp. 62–63, 80–81

All Vocabulary Builder, pp. 69, 87

All Writing About the Big Question, pp. 66, 84

Reader's Notebooks

Pre- and postreading pages for both selections, as well as "The Sun Parlor" appear in an interactive format in the *Reader's Notebooks*. Each *Notebook* is differentiated for a different group of learners. The selections in the Adapted and English Learner's versions are abridged.

L2 L3 ***Reader's Notebook***

L1 ***Reader's Notebook: Adapted Version***

EL ***Reader's Notebook: English Learner's Version***

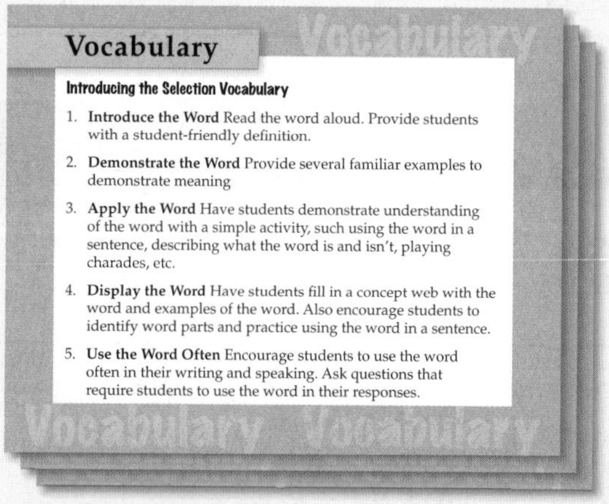

Vocabulary

Introducing the Selection Vocabulary

1. **Introduce the Word** Read the word aloud. Provide students with a student-friendly definition.
2. **Demonstrate the Word** Provide several familiar examples to demonstrate meaning
3. **Apply the Word** Have students demonstrate understanding of the word with a simple activity, such using the word in a sentence, describing what the word is and isn't, playing charades, etc.
4. **Display the Word** Have students fill in a concept web with the word and examples of the word. Also encourage students to identify word parts and practice using the word in a sentence.
5. **Use the Word Often** Encourage students to use the word often in their writing and speaking. Ask questions that require students to use the word in their responses.

Classroom Strategies and Teaching Routines

- core classroom routines outlined step-by-step
- convenient format for easy reference while teaching

Selection Support

Graphic Organizer Transparencies

"The Sun Parlor" by Dorothy West
from **In Commemoration: One Million Volumes** by Rudolfo A. Anaya

Before You Read B: Reading—Analyzing Main Ideas and Supporting Details

Question: ______________________

Main Idea

Supporting Detail | **Supporting Detail**

Question: ______________________

Main Idea

Supporting Detail | **Supporting Detail**

Graphic Organizer Transparencies

84

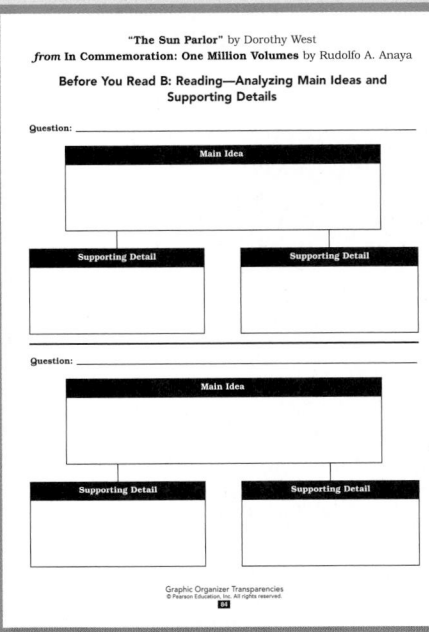

L3 Reading: Graphic Organizer B, p. 84

Also available for these selections:

- EL L1 L2 Reading: Graphic Organizer A, pp. 82, 83 (partially filled in)
- EL L1 L2 Literary Analysis: Graphic Organizer A, pp. 85, 86 (partially filled in)
- L3 Literary Analysis: Graphic Organizer B, p. 87

Skills Development/Extension

Unit 3 Resources

Name ______________________ Date ____________

"The Sun Parlor" by Dorothy West
from **In Commemoration: One Million Volumes** by Rudolfo A. Anaya
Integrated Language Skills: Grammar

Subject Complements: Predicate Nominatives and Predicate Adjectives

Predicate nominatives and predicate adjectives are subject complements. They appear after a linking verb and tell something about the subject of the sentence. A **predicate nominative** is a noun or pronoun that appears with a linking verb and renames, identifies, or explains the subject of the sentence. A subject and a predicate nominative are two different words for the same person, place, or thing. The linking verb joins them and equates them. A **predicate adjective** is an adjective that appears with a linking verb and describes the subject of the sentence.

Examples: Dorothy West's special room is her sun parlor. (*Parlor* is a predicate nominative, which renames the subject, *room*.)
Books are fascinating to Rudolfo Anaya. (*Fascinating* is a predicate adjective, which describes the subject, *books*.)

A. Practice: *The following sentences are based on "The Sun Parlor" or the excerpt from* In Commemoration: One Million Volumes. *Underline each predicate nominative or predicate adjective and write* PN *or* PA *on the line before each sentence.*

___ 1. Sis was a young girl who wanted to play in West's sun parlor.
___ 2. West seemed sad and regretful that she did not allow Sis to play in the room.
___ 3. The author and her brothers and sisters were obedient children.
___ 4. Libraries are Anaya's refuge.
___ 5. To Anaya, books are exciting and uplifting.
___ 6. Anaya, a writer, is an intelligent and thoughtful man.

B. Writing Application: *On the lines below, write a paragraph responding to either "The Sun Parlor" or the excerpt from* In Commemoration: One Million Volumes. *Use at least five subject complements in your paragraph. Underline each predicate nominative once and each predicate adjective twice.*

Unit 3 Resources: Types of Nonfiction

89

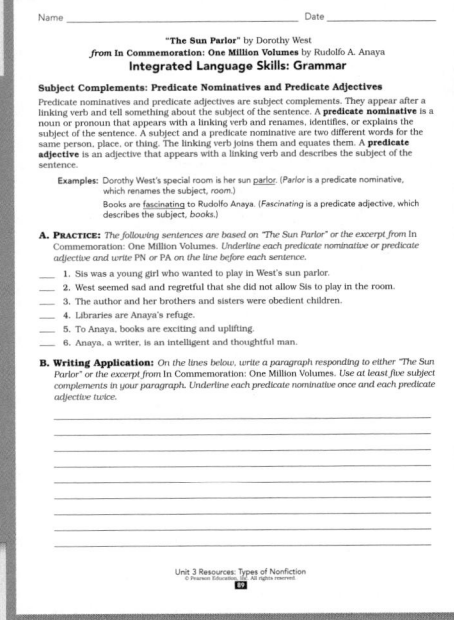

L3 L4 Grammar, p. 89

Also available for these selections:

- All Literary Analysis: Reflective Essay, pp. 67, 85
- All Reading: Main Idea, pp. 68, 86
- L4 Enrichment, pp. 70, 88
- L3 L4 Support for Writing, p. 90
- L3 L4 Support for Extend Your Learning, p. 91

Assessment

Name ______________________ Date ____________

from **In Commemoration: One Million Volumes** by Rudolfo A. Anaya
Selection Test A

Critical Reading *Identify the letter of the choice that best answers the question.*

___ 1. What is the focus of Anaya's reflective essay from *In Commemoration: One Million Volumes*?
A. stars
B. libraries
C. the author's childhood
D. the author's grandfather

___ 2. What was Anaya's first language?
A. English
B. Creole
C. Spanish
D. Navajo

___ 3. Which of the following is NOT among those who contributed to Anaya's interest in words and learning?
A. his mother
B. his grandfather
C. his childhood friends
D. Miss Pansy, the librarian

___ 4. What did Anaya learn from his grandfather?
A. to love words and learning
B. to speak only the Spanish language
C. to go to libraries and discuss issues with others
D. to value the spoken word over the written word

___ 5. What is the main idea of the following passage from *In Commemoration: One Million Volumes*?
I was fortunate to have had those old and wise *viejitos* as guides into the world of nature and knowledge. They taught me with their stories; they taught me the magic of words. Now the words lie captured in ink, but the magic is still there, the power inherent in each volume.
A. The stories *los viejitos* told focused on nature and knowledge.
B. Anaya listened to *los viejitos* tell magical stories on summer evenings.
C. The stories told by *los viejitos* inspired Anaya's love of words and books.
D. *Los viejitos* employed an oral tradition; now their stories are told in books.

Unit 3 Resources: Types of Nonfiction

95

EL L1 L2 Selection Test A, pp. 74–76, 95–97

Also available for these selections:

- L3 L4 Selection Test B, pp. 77–79, 98–100
- L3 L4 Open-Book Test, pp. 71–73, 92–94

PHLit Online!

www.PHLitOnline.com

- complete narrated selection text
- a thematically related video with writing prompt
- an interactive graphic organizer
- highlighting feature
- access to all student print resources, adapted to individual student needs
- Spanish and English summaries

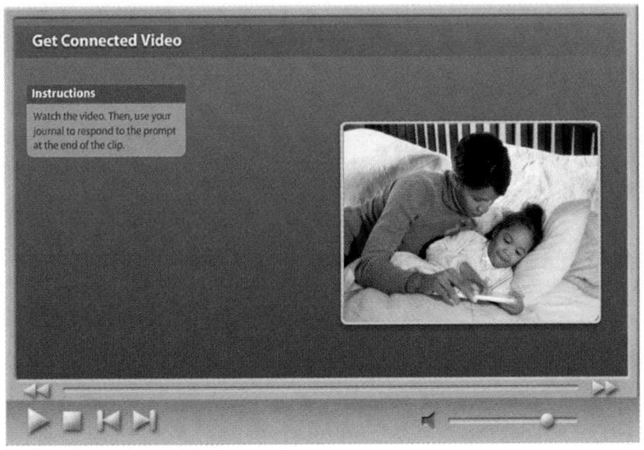

Get Connected! (thematic video with writing prompt)

Also available:

Background video

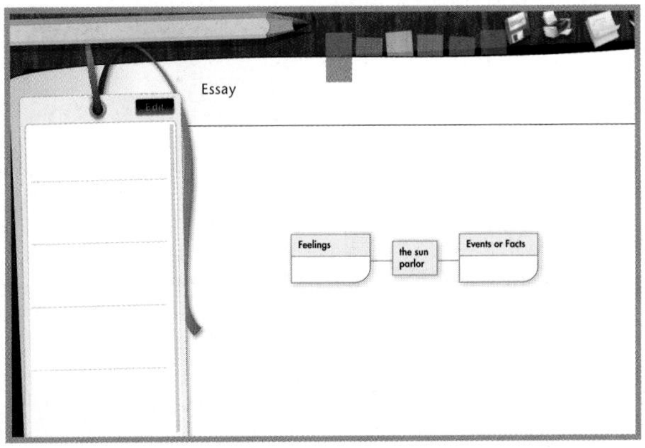

Writer's Journal (with graphics feature)

Also available:

Vocabulary Central (tools, activities, and songs for studying vocabulary)

❶ Selection Choices

You may use either "The Sun Parlor" or the excerpt from *In Commemoration: One Million Volumes* to meet the lesson standards. Skills instruction for both selections appears on p. 487. Choose one selection to teach (or choose to teach both). The Accessibility at a Glance chart at the bottom of this page will help you determine which of the two selections is more appropriate for your students.

❷ Selection Skills

1. With the class, preview the selection skills. (The lesson meets the lesson objectives given on p. 486a.)
2. Explain that students will develop the skill of analyzing main ideas introduced on p. 461 as they read to better understand and enjoy the selection. By examining reflective essays as they read, they will gain deeper insight into nonfiction: essays and speeches.
3. To introduce the Writing and Listening and Speaking activities (p. 509), tell students that when they have finished reading the selection, they will write a memoir and prepare an oral recollection.
4. Tell students that they will also study a grammar concept: subject complements. By mastering this concept, they will improve their reading fluency and the quality of their own writing.

Before You Read

The Sun Parlor • *from* In Commemoration: One Million Volumes

❶ Selection Choices

▲ Read **"The Sun Parlor"** to learn what happens when a woman puts her pride in a room ahead of her respect for a child.

▲ Read the excerpt from ***In Commemoration: One Million Volumes*** to see how a boy cultivates his love of books throughout his life.

❷ Selection Skills Guide

Practice these skills with either **"The Sun Parlor"** (p. 490) or the excerpt from ***In Commemmoration: One Million Volumes*** (p. 500).

- Understand reflective essays
- Analyze main ideas and supporting details
- Ask questions
- Identify predicate nominatives and predicate adjectives
- Write a memoir
- Prepare an oral recollection

Differentiated Instruction for Universal Access

Accessibility at a Glance: Selection Choices

	The Sun Parlor	*from* In Commemoration: One Million Volumes	
Context	Adult reflection on mistaken values	Commemorating the acquisition of the one-millionth book to the University of New Mexico library	Because a number of factors determine the relative accessibility of paired selections, in some cases the Lexile rating of the more challenging selection will be lower than that of the more accessible selection.
Language/ Vocabulary	• Fairly simple sentence structure • Grade-appropriate vocabulary	Some Spanish vocabulary	
Concept Level	Accessible (relationships between adults and children)	Challenging (connection among words, stories, and history)	
Literary Merit	Cross-generational	Noted author	
Lexile/Length	Lexile: 980L Word Count: 1,775	Lexile: 1060L Word Count: 2,039	
Overall Rating	**More accessible**	**More challenging**	

3 Literary Analysis: Reflective Essay

A **reflective essay** is a brief nonfiction work in which a writer presents the experiences that shaped or inspired his or her thoughts on a topic. In a reflective essay, a writer

- draws on an event, a time period, or an idea from his or her own life and experience.
- weaves a connection between personal experience and a point of general interest, such as a lesson about life.
- reflects on a specific object, scene, occasion, place, or idea.

Look for these characteristics of a reflective essay as you read.

4 Reading Skill: Main Idea

To fully understand an essay, **analyze main ideas and supporting details**—recognize each main point that the writer makes and identify the ideas or facts that explain or illustrate it. To help you analyze, **ask questions** like these as you read:

- What is the topic of this passage?
- What is the main point being made?
- Which details support this point?

5 Using the Strategy: Main Ideas and Supporting Details Chart

As you read, record details on a **main ideas and supporting details chart** like this one. After you have read, consider what you know about the issue the writer develops and identify other questions you may have.

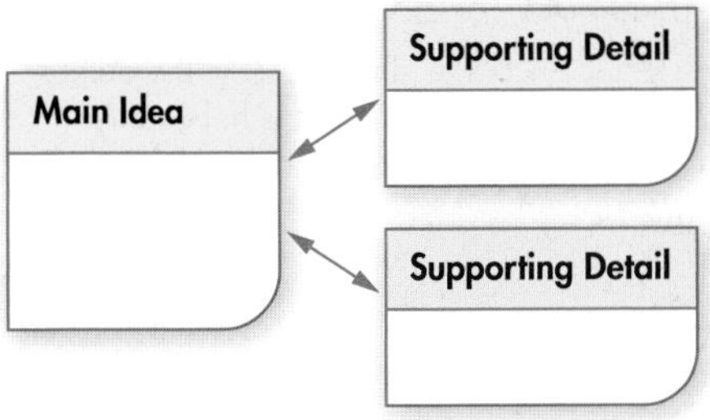

PHLit Online!
www.PHLitOnline.com

Hear It!
- Selection summary audio
- Selection audio

See It!
- Get Connected video
- Background video
- More about the author
- Vocabulary flashcards

Do It!
- Interactive journals
- Interactive graphic organizers
- Self-test
- Internet activity
- Grammar tutorial
- Interactive vocabulary games

Differentiated Instruction for Universal Access

Preparing Students for the More Challenging Selection

If you wish to prepare lower level readers to read the excerpt from *In Commemoration: One Million Volumes,* the more challenging selection, follow these steps:

- Prompt students to think of ways different cultures share or pass along stories. In this essay, for example, Anaya describes the *cuentos,* or stories of the Mexican people. Encourage students to think about their own cultural heritage and the way in which stories are communicated. Have students discuss ways they could find out more about their cultural history, such as talking to older family members or researching it in the library.
- Ask students how many books they think the school library has. Have them discuss the different types of books and how each type of book promotes learning and knowledge.
- This excerpt contains many Spanish words. To promote students' fluency, post a chart that lists the words, along with their definitions.

PRETEACH

3 Literary Analysis

Reflective Essay

1. Introduce the skill, using the instruction on the student page.
2. Tell students that they will analyze reflective essays as they read.

Think Aloud: Model the Skill

Model the skill of interpreting a reflective essay, using the following "think aloud":

> Suppose I read an essay written by an Olympic athlete. The athlete describes the type of training she had. Judging only from this detail, I would consider this a descriptive essay. As I continue to read, however, I learn how the strenuous training schedule made the athlete emotionally stronger. She talks about how it taught her to never give up and to always try her hardest. Because she includes this personal reflection on her experiences, I know this is a reflective essay.

4 Reading Skill

1. Introduce the skill, using the instruction on the student page.
2. Tell students that they will analyze main ideas and supporting details as they read.

Think Aloud: Model the Skill

Model the process of identifying main ideas, using the following "think aloud":

> Let's say I am reading a passage about trains, but the main idea is not stated. To find the main idea, I look at the details. The passage states that trains are less convenient than airplanes, slower than planes, and less profitable. From these details, I can infer that the main idea is "Travel on trains is inferior to airplane travel." All the details relate to this idea.

5 Using the Strategy

Give students a copy of either **Reading Skill Graphic Organizer A** or **B** (***Graphic Organizer Transparencies,*** pp. 82–84) to record main ideas as they read. Use the examples in **Reading Skill Graphic Organizer A,** which is partially filled in, to model the process of completing the organizer.

PRETEACH

1 Writing About the Big Question

1. Review the assignment with the class.
2. Guide students to consider experiences that can lead people to change their behavior.
3. Have students complete the sentence starters. Review responses as a class. (**Possible response:** Understanding what is truly important in life is valuable because people are more likely to make the most of their lives. Learning from past mistakes can lead to personal growth when a person avoids the same mistake and instead improves himself or herself.)
4. Remind students that their answers will help them think about the Big Question.

While You Read

Tell students that as they read, they should notice the author's attitude toward the sun room and compare it with the way she feels about her niece.

2 Vocabulary

1. Have students preview the selection vocabulary.
2. For each word, have students say the word aloud.
3. Then, use the word in a sentence that defines the word.
4. Finally, repeat your definitional sentence or a similar sentence with the word missing and have the class "fill in the blank" chorally. Here is an example:

   Someone cajoling another is attempting to persuade using flattery. Matt always knew when his brother Zack needed to borrow his car, because Zack would begin his [students say "cajoling"].

3 Word Study

1. Introduce the skill, using the instruction in the box.
2. Have students explain how the prefix *sub-* contributes to the meaning of *submerge.* (**Answer:** to put underwater)

Making Connections — The Sun Parlor

What kind of *knowledge* changes our lives?

1 Writing About the Big Question

In "The Sun Parlor," a woman learns an important lesson about values. Use these sentence starters to develop your ideas about the Big Question.

Understanding what is truly important in life is valuable because ____________________.

Learning from past mistakes can lead to personal **growth** when ____________________.

While You Read Notice the author's attitude toward the sun room, and compare it with the way she seems to feel about her niece.

2 Vocabulary

Read each word and its definition. Decide whether you know the word well, know it a little bit, or do not know it at all. After you read, see how your knowledge of each word has increased.

- **lavished** (lav′ isht) *v.* gave with extreme generosity (p. 491) ***She lavished candy on us, and we had to borrow a bag to carry it home.*** *lavish adj. lavishly adv. lavishness n.*
- **subordinate** (sə bôrd′ ’n it) *adj.* below another in importance or rank (p. 491) ***A private is subordinate to a general.*** *subordinate n. subordinately adv. subordination n.*
- **rejuvenation** (ri jo͞o′ və nā′ shən) *n.* the act of making new, youthful, or energetic again (p. 492) ***A warm bath is a good method for rejuvenation.*** *rejuvenate v. rejuvenator n. juvenile n.*
- **convalesce** (kän′ və les′) *v.* regain strength and health (p. 494) ***A few days at home will give you time to convalesce after the accident.*** *convalescence n. convalescent adj.*
- **cajoling** (kə jōl′ iŋ) *n.* coaxing with flattery (p. 494) ***I resisted her cajoling and did not sign up for the play.*** *cajole v. cajoler n. cajolingly adv.*
- **succinct** (sək siŋkt′) *adj.* clearly and briefly stated (p. 494) ***If your essay is too wordy, revise to make it more succinct.*** *succinctly adv. succinctness n.*

3 Word Study

The **Latin prefix *suc-*** is another spelling of the prefix ***sub-***, meaning "under," "less or lower than," or "following after."

In this essay, the author imagines how something could be said in a more **succinct** way, using fewer words.

Vocabulary Development

Vocabulary Knowledge Rating

Create a **Vocabulary Knowledge Rating Chart** (***Professional Development Guidebook,*** p. 33) for this selection. Include the selection vocabulary from this page and the Big Question words that appear in the Writing About the Big Question sentence starter on this page. (The Big Question vocabulary is introduced on pp. 442–443.)

Give students a copy of the chart. Read the words aloud, and have students mark their rating in the Before Reading column. Urge them to be alert to these words as they read and discuss the selection.

Tally how many students think they know a word to gauge how much instruction to provide. As students read and discuss the selection, point out the words and their context.

PHLit Online! **Vocabulary Central**, featuring tools, activities, and songs for studying vocabulary, is available at **www.PHLitOnline.com.**

Meet
Dorothy West
(1907–1998)

Author of
The Sun Parlor

Dorothy West enjoyed a comfortable childhood—one made possible by her family's fiery ambition and hard work. Her father, a former slave, came north and built a successful business in Boston.

A Lifetime of Writing By the age of fourteen, West was winning local writing competitions in Boston. A few years later, in 1926, she moved to New York City and contributed to the Harlem Renaissance, an outpouring of African American creativity in the 1920s.

West wrote short stories, novels, and essays. She spent the last half of her life in Oak Bluffs, the village in Martha's Vineyard that is the setting for "The Sun Parlor."

4 BACKGROUND FOR THE ESSAY

Parlors and Sun Parlors

In past eras, many houses, like the one described in "The Sun Parlor," included a room called the parlor. An early version of the modern living room, the parlor was a place for family members to visit with guests or with each other. A sun parlor, or solarium, enclosed mostly by glass, was intended for enjoying the sun and for reading and talking.

Did You Know?

Oprah Winfrey made West's second novel, *The Wedding,* into a television movie.

Daily Bellringer

For each class during which you teach this selection, have students complete one of the five Sentence Modeling activities for Week 14 in the ***Daily Bellringer Activities*** booklet.

4 Background

Parlors and Sun Parlors

The English word *parlor* derives from the Old French *parler,* meaning "to talk." The parlor was a room used for conversation with guests or family members. A typical colonial house had a large chimney in the center of the first floor with a room known as a hall on one side and the parlor on the other. The hall was where the family gathered for everyday activities. The parlor was where they entertained guests. The best furniture was often reserved for the parlor. The term *sunroom* or *sun parlor* refers to an extra living room or porch enclosed in glass with exposure to the sun. It is a later coinage dating to about 1902 and is probably descriptive of homes in that period.

Multidraft Reading

This icon ● marks natural pauses in the selection. To assist struggling readers and to deepen reading for all, assign the text in "chunks," following the icons, and apply multidraft reading protocols. For each reading, have students set the purpose indicated:

- **First reading**—literal comprehension: answer the Reading Check questions.
- **Second reading**—application of skills: answering the Main Idea and Reflective Essay prompts.
- **Third reading**—interpretation: answering the end-of-selection questions.

For more guidance, refer to the ***Classroom Strategies and Teaching Routines*** card on multidraft reading.

Differentiated Instruction Additional Instruction

EL Extended Support—English Learners

Have students complete the **Reading and Vocabulary Warm-ups, *Unit 3 Resources,*** pp. 62–65, before they read. Assign the prereading pages and the adapted selection in the ***Reader's Notebook: English Learner's Version.*** Then, have students listen to portions of the selection on the ***Hear It! Audio CD*** (adapted text).

L1 L2 Extended Support—Struggling Readers

Have students complete the **Reading and Vocabulary Warm-ups, *Unit 3 Resources,*** pp. 62–65, before they read. Assign the prereading pages and the adapted selection in the ***Reader's Notebook: Adapted Version.*** Then, have students listen to portions of the selection on the ***Hear It! Audio CD*** (adapted text).

Extended Support—Reluctant Readers

To build motivation and engagement before assigning the selection, have students read "Dressing by the Book" a thematically related selection in ***Reality Central.*** Then, use the questions at the conclusion of the related selection to guide discussion.

PHLit Online!

For more about the author, practice with the selection vocabulary, and more background, go to **www.PHLitOnline.com.**

❶ Activating Prior Knowledge

1. Prepare an Anticipation Guide (***Professional Development Guidebook,*** pp. 36–38) with the following statements:
   - Rooms in a house should be open to everyone.
   - Being a perfectionist has its drawbacks.
   - Regrets last a lifetime.
   - Nothing can be the same after it has been different.
2. Give students a copy of the prepared **Anticipation Guide** and have students mark their responses in the Me column. Have students discuss the statements in pairs or groups and mark the guides again in the Group column.
3. For further guidance, use the ***Classroom Strategies and Teaching Routines*** card: **Using an Anticipation Guide.**

Concept Connector →

Students will return to the **Anticipation Guide** after completing the story.

Small-Group Activity

Have students work in small groups, writing down their thoughts and feelings about the selection. Tell students to comment on whether they feel a personal connection to the author or story. Suggest that students answer these questions: Have you ever had a similar experience? Do you share the author's emotions and ideas? What insights do you gain by reading the story? Have students share their responses to these questions and to the selection in general with members of their group.

❷ About the Selection

West makes it clear at the outset that "The Sun Parlor" has a moral. In fact, the experience that West relates includes many small lessons in addition to its overarching moral. The sun parlor, and what happens there, ultimately will have greater meaning for West than she imagines on the summer day when she finishes painting it.

The Sun Parlor

❶ ❷

Dorothy West

Vocabulary Development

Thematic Vocabulary: The Big Question

As students are discussing "The Sun Parlor," encourage them to use the thematic vocabulary presented in Introducing the Big Question, pp. 442–443. You might encourage them with sentence starters like these:

1. When guests were horrified that the West children were allowed everywhere in the house, West's mother responded with *empathy* for her children, because . . .
2. The fact that West did not allow Sis in the sun parlor reveals that she was *ignorant* of . . .
3. West's relationship to the sun parlor reveals this *insight* about the importance of space in a home: . . .
4. At the end of her essay, West feels she needs to *question* Sis because . . .

This is a tale with a moral. I will try not to tax your attention too long. But I have to go way back to begin because it begins with my childhood. It is about houses and children, and which came first.

There were four of us children, well-schooled in good manners, well-behaved almost all of the time, and obedient to the commands of grown-ups, the power people who could make or break us.

We lived in a beautiful house. The reason I knew that is because all my mother's friends said so, and brought their other friends to see it. On the day appointed for the tour, which included inspection of every room on every floor, my mother would gather us around her and say in her gentlest voice, "I'm sorry, children, but Mrs. So-and-so is coming today and bringing a friend to see our house. You children keep clean and play quietly while they're here. It's not a real visit. They won't stay long. It'll be over before you can say Jack Robinson."

Most often a first-time caller, having **lavished** praise on everything she saw, including us, proceeded out without any further remarks. But there were others who, when they saw four children good as gold, did not see beyond their size, and asked my mother in outspoken horror, "How can you bear to let children loose in a lovely house like this?"

Every time it happened we were terrified. What would happen to us if my mother decided her house was too good for us and she hated the sight of us? What would we do, where would we go, would we starve?

My mother looked at our stricken faces, and her own face softened and her eyes filled with love. Then she would say to her inquisitor, though she did not say it rudely, "The children don't belong to the house. The house belongs to the children. No room says, *Do not enter.*"

I did not know I could ever forget those sentiments. But once, to my lasting regret, I did. With the passage of years I took my place with grown-ups, and there was another generation, among them the little girl, Sis, who was my mother's treasure. The summer she was eight was the one time I forgot that a child is not **subordinate** to a house.

We had a cottage in the Highlands of Oak Bluffs of unimpressive size and appearance. My mother loved it for its easy care. It couldn't even stand in the shade of our city house, and there certainly were no special rules for children. No one had ever looked aghast at a child on its premises.

4 Except me, the summer I painted the sun parlor. I am not a painter, but I am a perfectionist. I threw my whole soul into the project, and worked with such diligence and

3 ◀ Critical Viewing
Based on this painting, what feelings do you think will be described in the essay? **[Connect]**

Vocabulary
lavished (lav′ isht) *v.* gave with extreme generosity

subordinate (sə bôrd′ 'n it) *adj.* below another in importance or rank

5 Reading Check
What does the author say she regrets forgetting?

3 Critical Viewing

Possible response: The browns, black, and shades of blue in this painting suggest that feelings of sadness and regret will be described in this essay.

4 Connecting to the Big Question

1. Emphasize to students that our experiences, especially our mistakes, allow us to reflect on what we could have done differently. This opportunity for reflection allows us to learn from our experiences and to use this knowledge to change our lives.
2. Have students explain the author's attitude toward the sun parlor.
   Possible response: West is devoted to making the sun parlor a beautiful room, which makes her feel proud of her work.
3. **Ask** students: How does her attitude toward the room compare with her feelings toward her niece?
   Possible response: West's attitude toward the sun parlor is different from her feelings toward her niece. She admires the room, seeing it as a special space, but she perceives Sis as a trespasser—unpredictable and perhaps even unappreciative of the room.
4. **Ask** students: Why might West react this way to Sis, despite her own experiences as a child in this beautiful house?
   Possible response: West might feel strong ownership of the room, something she never had felt before, so her pride might block any empathy she might feel for Sis.

5 Reading Check

Answer: The author says that she regrets forgetting that children are more important than a house.

Differentiated Instruction for Universal Access

EL Strategy for English Learners

To enhance students' comprehension of the selection, preteach the selection vocabulary words and additional critical vocabulary from the selection. Reinforce students' awareness and understanding of the words by making a chart of the words on a large sheet of paper to post it in the classroom. Encourage students to add other key words from the selection to the chart as they encounter them.

Enrichment for Gifted/Talented Students

Invite pairs of students to dramatize the scenes between the author and Sis at the beginning and end of the selection. Instruct students to use the text of the selection as a script. Tell them to pay close attention to "stage directions" in the selection text. Students may perform their dramatization of the scenes for the rest of the class.

PHLit Online!

This selection is available in interactive format in the **Enriched Online Student Edition, www.PHLitOnline.com,** which includes a thematically related video with writing prompt and an interactive graphic organizer.

❻ Reading Skill
Main Idea

1. Have a student summarize Sis's reaction to the sun parlor.
Answer: She becomes very emotional when she sees the sun parlor and says that it is the most beautiful room she has ever seen.
2. Then **ask** students to respond to the Reading Skill question: Which details support the idea that Sis's reaction is exceptional?
Possible response: The author describes Sis as someone who is always in motion and who never pays anything much attention, so that "her first awareness of something outside herself," with "her face filled with the joy of her discovery" and her "voice on the edge of tears" indicates that Sis's reaction to the sun parlor is exceptional.

❼ Literary Analysis
Reflective Essay

1. Ask a volunteer to read the two paragraphs that describe how the author reacts to Sis. **Ask** why the author does not really hear what Sis says about the sun parlor.
Answer: The author does not hear what Sis says because she is completely focused on not having Sis enter the sun parlor.
2. Then have students consider what the author says to Sis. Lead students to observe that the author tells Sis not only to stay out of the sun parlor but also to go outside and play.
3. **Ask** students to respond to the Literary Analysis question: How is this experience connected to the lesson that the author learned from her mother?
Answer: The author's personal experience has to do with telling a child that a room in the house is off-limits to her; what the author tells Sis goes against the lesson the author learned from her mother that the house belongs to the children and that no room says *Do not enter.*

painstaking care that when the uncounted hours ended I felt that I had painted the Sistine Chapel.[1]

❺ School vacation began, and Sis arrived for the long holiday, the car pulling up at the edge of the brick walk, and Sis streaking into the house for a round of hugs, then turning to tear upstairs to take off her travel clothes and put on her play clothes, and suddenly her flying feet braking to a stop in front of the sun parlor, its open door inviting inspection.

❻ She who was always in motion, she who never took time for a second look at anything, or cared whether her bed was smooth or crumpled, or noticed what was on her plate as long as it was something to eat—she, in the awakening that came when she was eight, in her first awareness of something outside herself, stood in the doorway of the sun parlor, her face filled with the joy of her discovery, and said in a voice on the edge of tears, "It's the most beautiful room I ever saw in my whole life."

Reading Skill
Main Idea Which details support the idea that Sis's reaction is exceptional?

❼ I did not hear her. I did not really hear her. I did not recognize the magnitude of that moment. I let it sink to some low level of my subconscious. All I saw was that her foot was poised to cross the threshold of my chapel.

I let out a little cry of pain. "Sis," I said, "please don't go in the sun parlor. There's nothing in there to interest a child. It's not a place for children to play in. It's a place for grown-ups to sit in. Go and change. Summer is outside waiting for you to come and play wherever you please."

Literary Analysis
Reflective Essay How is this experience connected to the lesson that the author learned from her mother?

In a little while the sounds of Sis's soaring laughter were mingling with the happy sounds of other vacationing children. They kept any doubt I might have had from surfacing. Sis was surely more herself running free than squirming on a chair in the sun parlor.

All the same I monitored that room, looking for smudges and streaks, scanning the floor for signs of scuffing. The room bore no scars, and Sis showed no trace of frustration.

The summer flowed. My friends admired the room, though they did it without superlatives. To them it was a room I had talked about redoing for a long time. Now I had done it. So much for that.

The summer waned, and Sis went home for school's reopening, as did the other summer children, taking so much life and laughter with them that the ensuing days recovered slowly.

Then my mother's sister, my favorite aunt, arrived from New York for her usual stay at summer's end. She looked ten years younger than her actual years. She seemed to bounce with energy, as if she had gone through some process of **rejuvenation**. We asked her for the secret.

Vocabulary
rejuvenation (ri jo͞o′ və nā′ shən) *n.* the act of making new, youthful, or energetic again

1. **the Sistine Chapel** (sis′ tēn′ chap′ əl) place of worship in the Vatican, Rome, the Pope's residence. The chapel is famed for scenes painted on its walls and ceiling by Michelangelo.

Think Aloud

Vocabulary: Using Context
Direct students' attention to the word *superlatives* on this page. Using a think-aloud process, model how to use context to infer the meaning of an unknown word. Say to students:

> In this sentence, *superlatives* is being used to describe what people do or do not say about sun parlor. I know West is very proud of her room; she has spent hours making it perfect. Its beauty is confirmed by Sis, who says it's ". . . the most beautiful room. . . ." Later, when West's friends see the room, they admire it, too. West, however, follows this statement with the word *though,* which indicates a contrast in what West expected them to do: admire the room *with* superlatives. *Superlatives,* therefore, must mean a form of compliment beyond admiration. West continues to say that to her friends, the room was just one of West's projects. To West, however, the room is much, much more, deserving of the best praise, so *superlatives* must mean "of the highest or greatest kind."

I did not hear her. I did not really hear her.

There was no way for us to know in the brimful days that followed that there really was a secret she was keeping from us. She had had a heart attack some months before, and she had been ordered to follow a strict set of rules: plenty of rest during the day, early to bed at night, take her medicine faithfully, carefully watch her diet.

She was my mother's younger sister. My mother had been her babysitter. She didn't want my mother to know that she was back to being a baby again, needing to be watched over, having to be put down for a nap, having to be spoon-fed pap. She kept herself busy around the clock, walking, lifting, sitting up late, eating her favorite foods and forgetting her medicine.

9 ▲ **Critical Viewing**
Do you think this painting reflects the author's description of the summer children? Why or why not?
[Connect]

10 Reading Check
What is the matter with West's aunt?

8 Humanities

Follow Me, 1995, by Colin Bootman

A native of Trinidad, Colin Bootman immigrated to the United States and quickly discovered that art could help him adjust to and temporarily escape from this different land. So inspired by art, Bootman pursued an education in the visual arts, which gave him the opportunity to express himself through different mediums.

Bootman is best known as an illustrator of notable children's books, such as *Follow the Leader* and *In Mama's Kitchen,* for which he has received numerous awards. In 2006, Bootman published his first written and illustrated book *Fish for the Grand Lady.* Use these questions for discussion:

- Which of the children shown would you identify as Sis? Why?
  Possible response: The girl leading the line, because she seems excited and full of energy.
- What does the painting suggest about the children?
  Possible response: They have fun playing together outside in the sunshine.

9 Critical Viewing

Answer: Yes, the painting does reflect the author's description of the summer children because it shows children outside, happy and having fun, just as the author characterizes them.

10 Reading Check

Answer: West's aunt has had a heart attack and is supposed to follow a strict medical routine.

Fluency

Distribute copies of page 493, and have students work in small groups. Have group members take turns reading with expression as students track, or follow along by pointing at each word in the text. Have students then read the passage back. Look for these problem spots:

- If students have difficulty with the word *brimful,* which in this context means "happy and carefree," remind them to use context clues in the sentence. Point out that they can guess the word's meaning because "brimful" is contrasted with "secret," which appears later in the sentence and carries a negative meaning.
- If students have difficulty with the length of the sentence that begins "She kept herself busy . . . ," instruct them that the commas in the sentence separate the activities with which she keeps herself busy. Have students write their own sentences in which they use commas to separate activities.

⓫ Critical Viewing

Answer: The room seems to be a room apart from the rest of the house in this painting, because the view of it is from another room through a doorway.

⓬ Reading Skill

Main Idea

1. Tell students that sometimes the author does not state the main idea directly in the text. Point out that when this happens, the reader must use details in the text to determine the main idea.
2. Give students a copy of the **Reading Skill Graphic Organizer B** (p. 84 in ***Graphic Organizer Transparencies***). Have students list specific details about the aunt's stay in the sun parlor on the chart, and then use them to identify the implied main idea.
3. **Ask** students to respond to the Reading Skill question: What main idea do these details about the aunt's stay in the sun parlor suggest?
   Possible response: The details about the aunt feeling uncomfortable, lonely, abandoned, and even afraid in the sun parlor suggest that the sun parlor has changed and is no longer a warm, welcoming place.

➤ **Monitor Progress:** Review students' graphic organizers to make sure they are correctly identifying the main ideas and supporting details.

➤ **Reteach:** If students have difficulty identifying specific details and inferring the main idea from them, model the process using **Reading Skill Graphic Organizer A** (p. 82 in ***Graphic Organizer Transparencies***).

⓫ ▶ **Critical Viewing**
In what way does this painting suggest a room apart from the rest of the house, like the sun parlor? **[Connect]**

Reading Skill ⓬
Main Idea What main idea do these details about the aunt's stay in the sun parlor suggest?

Vocabulary
convalesce (kän′ və les′) *v.* regain strength and health
cajoling (kə jōl′ iŋ) *n.* coaxing with flattery
succinct (sək siŋkt′) *adj.* clearly and briefly stated

And then one day standing over the stove involved in the making of a meal that a master chef might envy, she collapsed, and the doctor was called, and the doctor called the ambulance.

She was in the hospital ten days. When she was ready to come home to **convalesce**, we turned the sun parlor into a sickroom, for the stairs to the upper story were forbidden to her. At night we who, when she slept upstairs, would talk family talk back and forth from our beds far into the night, without her we were now quiet, not wanting our voices to wake her if she was asleep, knowing her recovery depended on rest and quiet.

But at night she slept fitfully. The sleeping house and separation from the flock were unbearable. She was afraid of the sun parlor, seeing it as an abnormal offshoot from the main part of the house, its seven long windows giving access to so many imagined terrors. She did not know if we would hear her if she called. She did not know if she would ever get well.

She did not get well. She went back to the hospital, and for our sakes was brave in her last days, comforting us more than we comforted her.

When it was over, we took the sickbed away and restored the sun parlor to its natural look. But it did not look natural. The sadness resisted the sun's **cajoling**. It had settled in every corner. The seven long windows streaming light did not help. I closed the door and locked it.

My mother saw the closed door and the key in my hand. She said as a simple statement of fact, "A little girl wanted to love that room, and you wouldn't let her. We learn so many lessons as we go through life."

> "We learn so many lessons as we go through life."

"I know that now," I said. "I wish I had known it then."

Another summer came, and with it Sis. The sun parlor door was open again, the room full of light with the sadness trying to hide itself whenever she passed. I did not know how to say to her, "You can go in the sun parlor if you want to." I did not know whether she knew it had been a sickroom, and might say, "Take your sun parlor and you-know-what," though in less **succinct** phrasing. I did not know if she yet knew that nothing can be the same once it has been different.

Other summers passed, older family members died, and mine became the oldest generation. I was living on the Island year-round in the winterized cottage. The sun parlor was just another everyday room, its seven long windows reduced to three of standard size, most of the furniture replaced for sturdier sitting.

Vocabulary Development

Vocabulary Knowledge Rating

When students have completed reading and discussing "The Sun Parlor," have them take out their **Vocabulary Knowledge Rating Chart** for this selection. Read the words aloud once more, and have students rate their knowledge of the words again in the After Reading column. Clarify any words that are still problematic. Have students write their own definition and example or sentence in the appropriate column. Then have students complete the Vocabulary Practice at the end of the selection. Encourage students to use the words in further discussion and written work about this selection. Remind them that they will be accountable for these words on the **Selection Test, *Unit 3 Resources***, pp. 74–76 or 77–79.

13

13 Humanities

Quiet Chair by Connie Hayes

Connie Hayes is an accomplished artist from Maine. Her paintings of small seaside villages, elegant cityscapes, and serene wilderness areas show her talent for capturing the mood of a place. Hayes's characteristic style uses vibrant, rich colors to emphasize the sky, a building, and even a chair.

Concept Connector

Anticipation Guide

Have students return to their **Anticipation Guides** and respond to the statements again in the After Reading column. They may do this individually or in their original pairs or groups. Then lead a class discussion, probing for what students have learned that confirms or invalidates each statement. Encourage students to cite specific details and other evidence from the text to support their responses to each statement.

Writing About the Big Question

Have students compare their responses to the sentence starters they completed before reading the essay with their ideas afterwards. Ask them to explain whether their thoughts have changed.

Reading Skill Graphic Organizer

Ask students to review the graphic organizers they completed to identify main ideas and supporting details while reading. Show them the partially completed **Reading Skill Graphic Organizer A** (*Graphic Organizer Transparencies,* p. 82) as an example. Then have students use the graphic organizers they completed to make observations about main ideas in the selection.

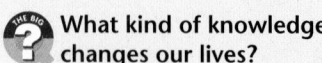

⓮ Literary Analysis
Reflective Essay

Ask students to respond to the Literary Analysis question: What lesson about life has the author learned?

Answer: The author has learned that people are more important than things.

ASSESS

Answers

Critical Thinking

1. Students may say that West's unwillingness to allow Sis into the sun parlor is typical of adults who have forgotten what it is to be children.
2. (a) She paints the sun parlor. **Possible response:** (b) She does not want Sis to ruin her work. (c) No, West acts as if the room is more important than Sis.
3. (a) Sis is usually in constant motion and pays little attention to anything, but she comes to an abrupt stop in front of the parlor and declares that it is the most beautiful room she has ever seen. (b) She means that Sis is growing up.
4. (a) West's aunt is ill and cannot go upstairs. (b) The sun parlor becomes lonely and uncomfortable for West's aunt and a sad place for the rest of the family. (c) The aunt's stay and her death make the point that the room has changed from a place of joy to one of sadness.

What kind of knowledge changes our lives?

Possible responses: (a) West means that she is relieved to have admitted that she was wrong. (b) The essay allows her to show she has learned a lesson from the experience. (c) Groups may discuss that West feels that listening is important because her regret about how she treated Sis was due to her not listening to her mother's moral lesson. West's idea of listening does not mean "hearing"; it means "understanding."

Sis was married, a mother, coming to visit when she could—coming, I think, to look for bits and pieces of my mother in me, wanting to see her ways, hear her words through me.

It was a year ago that I asked her the question that had been on my mind, it seems, forever. A dozen times I had bitten it off my tongue because I did not know what she might answer.

⓮ "Sis," I said, "do you remember the summer I painted the sun parlor and acted as if I thought more of it than I thought of you? I'm not asking you to forgive me. All I want to know is if sometimes my mother said to you when I went out, 'She's gone.'" My mother always referred to me as "she" when she was annoyed with me. "'She said she'd be gone awhile. You go play in that sun parlor if you want to. There's nothing in there you can hurt. Nothing in that room is worth as much as a child.'"

I saw her lips beginning to part. And I felt my heart trembling.

"I don't want to know the answer. Please don't tell me the answer. I had to ask the question. It's enough for me that you listened."

She smiled.

Literary Analysis
Reflective Essay What lesson about life has the author learned?

Critical Thinking

1. **Respond:** How did you react when West asks Sis not to go into the parlor?
2. **(a)** What project does West take on to improve the sun parlor? **(b) Infer:** Why does she tell Sis not to go into the room? **(c) Connect:** Does West's response to Sis reflect what her mother taught her about respect for children? Explain.
3. **(a) Compare and Contrast:** Using details from the selection, contrast Sis's first reaction to the parlor with her reactions to other things. **(b) Interpret:** What does West mean by calling Sis's reaction part of an "awakening"?
4. **(a) Infer:** Why does the family turn the parlor into a bedroom? **(b) Analyze:** How does this arrangement affect the aunt and the rest of the family? **(c) Interpret:** What point about the room is made by the story of the aunt's stay and her death?

What kind of knowledge changes our lives? **(a)** What does West mean when she says to Sis, "It's enough for me that you listened"? **(b)** Explain how the statement could also indicate the reason West wrote this essay. **(c)** In a group, discuss why it is important to West that people "listen." As a group, develop an explanation and present it to the class.

Assessment Resources

The following resources can be used to assess students' knowledge and skills.

Unit 3 Resources

L1 L2 EL **Selection Test A,** pp. 74–76

L3 L4 **Selection Test B,** pp. 77–79

L3 L4 **Open-Book Test,** pp. 71–73

PHLit Online! Students may use the **Self-test,** online at **www.PHLitOnline.com,** to prepare for the **Selection Test A** or **Selection Test B.**

After You Read | The Sun Parlor

Literary Analysis: Reflective Essay

1. Using a chart like the one shown, analyze West's use of the sun parlor as a focus for the elements of her **reflective essay.** For each detail you list, explain its connection to the sun parlor.

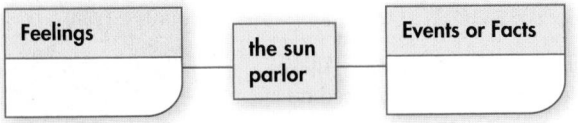

Feelings — the sun parlor — Events or Facts

2. Explain what point the author makes through the feelings and events she associates with the sun parlor.

Reading Skill: Main Idea

3. **(a)** Reread the first six paragraphs. What is the topic of this section? **(b)** What is the **main idea? (c)** What details support it?
4. **(a)** What is the next main idea you find in the essay? **(b)** Identify three **supporting details** that develop this idea.
5. **(a)** After reading the essay, identify one further question you have. **(b)** Where could you look to find the answer?

Vocabulary

Practice For each of these sentences, write a new sentence with the same meaning by using a word from the list on page 488.

1. I gave in to my brother's wheedling and lent him my new game.
2. The lesser-known actors must share a dressing room.
3. They showered praise on us for our successful fund drive.
4. The complete recovery of her knee after surgery was a wonder.
5. After she broke her leg, my sister had to stay home for a month to regain her strength and health.
6. He is a good debater because his responses are clear and brief.

Word Study Use the context of the sentences and what you know about the **Latin prefix *suc-*** to explain your answer to each question.

1. If books you requested from the library arrive in *succession*, will you receive them all at the same time?
2. Will a person with strong willpower easily *succumb* to others?

Word Study

The **Latin prefix *suc-*** is another spelling of the prefix ***sub-***, meaning "under," "less or lower than," or "following after."

Challenge Explain how the prefix *-suc-* contributes to the meanings of these words. Consult a dictionary if necessary.

succeed
successor
succor

ASSESS/EXTEND

Answers

Literary Analysis

1. **Events** include the exclusion of Sis from the sun parlor as well as the aunt's illness, her stay in the sun parlor, and her death. **Feelings** include sadness, shame, regret, and guilt.

   For other sample answers, see ***Graphic Organizer Transparencies,* Literary Analysis Graphic Organizer A**, p. 85, and the **Additional Answers** section.
2. **Possible response:** West makes the point that past events and feelings often cause guilt and hurt feelings among family members.

Reading Skill

3. **Possible responses:** (a) The topic of the opening section is the family's beautiful home. (b) The family's home is beautiful, but it is not more important than any of the people who live there. (c) Supporting details include the mother's several statements about the importance of children.
4. **Possible responses:** (a) West forgot the lesson her mother taught her about children and houses. (b) West did not share her mother's feeling that Sis was a treasure, she was overly protective of the sun parlor, and she told Sis not to go in the room.
5. **Possible answers:** (a) If West could go back in time and take back her words to Sis, would she do just that? (b) I would look in the section on page 496 for the conversation between West and Sis.

Vocabulary

Practice

Sample answers:

1. I gave into her <u>cajoling</u> and let her borrow some money.
2. The captain of the team gets to play every quarter while the <u>subordinate</u> members have to sit out parts of the game.
3. They <u>lavished</u> gifts on us for no reason at all.
4. The <u>rejuvenation</u> of the tree after the brush fire was surprising.

Answers continued

5. After the athlete's grueling triathlon, he didn't train for a week but instead <u>convalesced</u> at home.
6. I prefer listening to a <u>succinct</u> speaker rather than a long-winded one.

Word Study

Sample answers:

1. No, they will follow one after another.
2. No, a person with strong willpower will not easily bend under another's will.

Word Study: Challenge

Sample answers:

To *succeed* is to "come or <u>follow after</u>." A *successor* is someone who <u>follows</u> another. To *succor* is to "give someone <u>less</u> fortunate some relief or aid."

PRETEACH

Skills instruction for the ***Reading Skill*** *and* ***Literary Analysis*** *concept appears on p. 487.*

❶ Writing About the Big Question

1. Review the assignment with the class.
2. Have students list examples of people or things that spark their interests and of which they are familiar. Ask them how they might share their knowledge with others.
3. Have students complete the sample sentence starters. Review responses as a class. (**Possible responses:** In addition to books and libraries, a teacher may influence a person's desire to learn new things because the teacher may share his or her enthusiasm for a subject. One way to enlighten a person about new experiences and information is to share your knowledge about these experiences and information.
4. Remind students that their answers will help them think about the Big Question.

While You Read

Tell students that as they read, they should look for the different ways Anaya has gained knowledge throughout his life.

❷ Vocabulary

1. Have students preview the selection vocabulary.
2. For each word, have students say the word aloud.
3. Then, use the word in a sentence that defines the word.
4. Finally, repeat your definitional sentence or a similar sentence with the word missing, and have the class "fill in the blank" chorally. Here are some examples:

   For something to be inherent means it is a characteristic part of a person or thing. Anthropologists state that people's ability to use language to communicate is a feature [students say "inherent"] *to humans.*

❸ Word Study

1. Introduce the skill, using the instruction in the box.
2. Have students explain how the prefix *para-* contributes to the meaning of the word *paranormal.* (**Sample answer:** beyond normal)

Making Connections

from In Commemoration: One Million Volumes

THE BIG ? What kind of *knowledge* changes our lives?

❶ Writing About the Big Question

In the excerpt from *In Commemoration: One Million Volumes,* Anaya reflects on how a devotion to words and knowledge has shaped his life. Use these sentence starters to develop your ideas about the Big Question.

In addition to books and libraries, ______________ may **influence** a person's desire to learn new things because ______________.

One way to **enlighten** a person about new experiences and information is to ______________.

While You Read Look for the different ways Anaya has gained knowledge throughout his life.

❷ Vocabulary

Read each word and its definition. Decide whether you know the word well, know it a little bit, or do not know it at all. After you read, see how your knowledge of each word has increased.

- **infinite** (in´ fə nit) *adj.* beyond measure or comprehension; endless (p. 501) ***The number of stars in the sky seems infinite.*** *infinitely adv. infinity n. finite adj.*
- **inherent** (in hir´ ənt) *adj.* inborn; natural; characteristic (p. 502) ***Her inherent sweetness makes it hard for her to get angry.*** *inherently adv.*
- **paradox** (par´ ə däks´) *n.* a statement or situation that seems contradictory (p. 503) ***What a paradox it is for him to confess that he never tells the truth!*** *paradoxical adj. paradoxically adv.*
- **dilapidated** (də lap´ ə dāt´ id) *adj.* shabby; broken down (p. 503) ***The dilapidated chair broke when I sat on it.*** *dilapidate v. dilapidation n.*
- **enthralls** (en thrôlz´) *v.* captivates; fascinates (p. 505) ***This book enthralls me, and I cannot wait to read more.*** *enthrallment n.*
- **poignant** (poin´ yənt) *adj.* emotionally moving; piercing (p. 506) ***The poignant scene with the abandoned puppies always makes me cry.*** *poignancy n. poignantly adv.*

❸ Word Study

The **Greek prefix *para-*** means "beside" or "beyond."

In this essay, the author explains that books are a **paradox** because they provide answers to questions but also make the reader want to go beyond that information in order to learn more.

Vocabulary Development

Vocabulary Knowledge Rating

Create a **Vocabulary Knowledge Rating Chart** (***Professional Development Guidebook,*** p. 33) for this selection. Include the selection vocabulary from this page and the Big Question words that appear in the Writing About the Big Question sentence frame on this page. (The Big Question vocabulary is introduced on pp. 442–443.)

Give students a copy of the chart. Read the words aloud, and have students mark their rating in the Before Reading column. Urge them to be alert to these words as they read and discuss the selection.

Tally how many students think they know a word to gauge how much instruction to provide. As students read and discuss the selection, point out the words and their context.

PHLit Online! **Vocabulary Central,** featuring tools, activities, and songs for studying vocabulary, is available at **www.PHLitOnline.com.**

Meet Rudolfo A. Anaya

(b. 1937)

Author of In Commemoration: ONE MILLION VOLUMES

Rudolfo A. Anaya was born and raised in the rural village of Pastura in New Mexico. As a child, Anaya's imagination was nourished by *cuentos*—stories that Mexican Americans passed down from one generation to the next.

Teaching and Learning While teaching high school English, Anaya wrote *Bless Me, Ultima,* a highly praised novel about a young boy growing up in New Mexico. The novel was published in 1972. A strong voice of the Mexican American experience, Anaya is considered a founder of Chicano literature. He went on to teach at the University of New Mexico until his retirement in 1993. In his writing, though, he plays the student as much as the teacher. He explains, "Writing novels seems to be the medium which allows me to bring together all the questions I ask about life."

4 **BACKGROUND FOR THE ESSAY**

Libraries

In this essay, Anaya is astounded by the size of the University of New Mexico's library. Libraries perform a variety of functions. For example, a neighborhood library may preserve local history. A university library supports the research of scholars in a variety of subject areas. The Library of Congress guards the historical and cultural records of the United States.

DID YOU KNOW?

In 2002, Anaya was awarded a National Medal of the Arts; he has also received the Mexican Medal of Friendship.

Daily Bellringer

For each class during which you will teach this selection, have students complete one of the five Sentence Modeling activities for Week 14 in the ***Daily Bellringer Activities*** booklet.

4 Background

Libraries

Libraries are far more than collections of "millions of books." As Anaya himself points out, they are places not only for research and reading but also for the public to gather and exchange ideas as well as for the preservation of culture. Since the middle of the twentieth century, libraries have provided vast and varied information, resources, and services. The Internet and electronic devices that offer and access information from sources all over the world have made the virtual library a reality in the twenty-first century.

Multidraft Reading

This icon ● marks natural pauses in the selection. To assist struggling readers and to deepen reading for all, assign the text in "chunks," following the icons, and apply multidraft reading protocols. For each reading, have students set the purpose indicated:

- **First reading**—literal comprehension: answering the Reading Check questions.
- **Second reading**—application of skills: answering the Main Idea and Reflective Essay prompts.
- **Third reading**—interpretation: answering the end-of-selection questions.

For more guidance, refer to the ***Classroom Strategies and Teaching Resources*** card on multidraft reading.

Differentiated Instruction — Additional Instruction

EL Extended Support—English Learners

Have students complete the **Reading and Vocabulary Warm-ups, *Unit 3 Resources,*** pp. 80–83, before they read. Assign the prereading pages for the selection in the ***Reader's Notebook: English Learner's Version.*** Then, have students listen to portions of the selection on the ***Hear It!* Audio CD.**

L1 L2 Extended Support—Struggling Readers

Have students complete the **Reading and Vocabulary Warm-ups, *Unit 3 Resources,*** pp. 80–83, before they read Assign the Preview and Build Skills pages in the ***Reader's Notebook: Adapted Edition.*** Then, have students listen to portions of the selection on the ***Hear It!* Audio CD** (adapted text).

Extended Support—Reluctant Readers

To build motivation and engagement before assigning the selection, have students read "Textbook Technology" a thematically related selection in ***Reality Central.*** Then, use the questions at the conclusion of the related selection to guide discussion.

PHLit Online!

For more about the author, practice with the selection vocabulary, or more background, go to **www.PHLitOnline.com.**

TEACH

❶ Activating Prior Knowledge

1. Prepare an **Anticipation Guide** (***Professional Development Guidebook***, pp. 36–38) with the following statements:
   - Older people have a lot of wisdom to share with others.
   - Words are magic.
   - Growing up means moving into the knowledge of the world.
   - Words hold both joy and deadly power.
2. Give students a copy of the prepared **Anticipation Guide,** and have students mark their responses in the Me column. Have students discuss the statements in pairs or groups and mark the guides again in the Group column.
3. For further guidance, use the ***Classroom Strategies and Teaching Routines*** card: **Using an Anticipation Guide.**

Concept Connector →

Students will return to the **Anticipation Guide** after completing the story.

Whole-Class Activity

On the board, write the numerals for one million (1,000,000), one hundred million (100,000,000), and one billion (1,000,000,000). Have students think of items that might best illustrate these numbers, such as a million books, a hundred million people, and a billion stars. Have students make bar graphs comparing other collections of great magnitude.

❷ About the Selection

When the University of New Mexico library acquires its one-millionth book, Rudolfo Anaya uses the occasion to reflect on the great importance of libraries as places that stimulate and nurture free thought. What makes this excerpt from *In Commemoration: One Million Volumes* unique is that Anaya draws a connection between books and the many people and stories that opened up his childhood mind to the natural and intellectual world.

from In Commemoration: ONE MILLION VOLUMES

❶ ❷

Rudolfo A. Anaya

Vocabulary Development

Thematic Vocabulary: The Big Question

As students are discussing the excerpt from *In Commemoration: One Million Volumes,* encourage them to use the thematic vocabulary presented in Introducing the Big Question, pp. 442–443. You might encourage them with sentence starters like these:

1. Anaya reveals his grandfather's stories and *history* to . . .
2. Anaya had difficulty *adapting* his words to English because . . .
3. The teachings of the old ones gave Anaya an *awareness* of . . .
4. It is obvious that knowledge has been a significant *influence* in Anaya's life because . . .

❸ A MILLION VOLUMES.
A MAGIC NUMBER.
A MILLION BOOKS TO READ, TO LOOK AT, TO HOLD IN ONE'S HAND, TO LEARN, TO DREAM. . . .

I have always known there were at least a million stars. In the summer evenings when I was a child, we, all the children of the neighborhood, sat outside under the stars and listened to the stories of the old ones, los viejitos.[1] The stories of the old people taught us to wonder and imagine. Their adivinanzas[2] induced the stirring of our first questioning, our early learning.

I remember my grandfather raising his hand and pointing to the swirl of the Milky Way which swept over us. Then he would whisper his favorite riddle:

Hay un hombre con tanto dinero
Que no lo puede contar
Una mujer con una sábana tan grande
Que no la puede doblar.

There is a man with so much money
He cannot count it
A woman with a bedspread so large
She cannot fold it

❺ We knew the million stars were the coins of the Lord, and the heavens were the bedspread of his mother, and in our minds the sky was a million miles wide. A hundred million. **Infinite**. Stuff for the imagination. And what was more important, the teachings of the old ones made us see that we were bound to the infinity of that cosmic dance of life which swept around us. Their teachings created in us a thirst for knowledge. Can this library with its million volumes bestow that same inspiration?

I was fortunate to have had those old and wise viejitos as guides into the world of nature and knowledge. They taught me with their stories; they taught me the magic of words. Now

1. **los viejitos** (lôs byā hē´ tôs) *n.* Spanish for "the old ones."
2. **adivinanzas** (a *th*ē vē nan´ sas) *n.* Spanish for "riddles."

❹ ◄ **Critical Viewing**
How does this painting convey a sense of wonder and imagination? **[Connect]**

Vocabulary
infinite (in´ fə nit) *adj.* beyond measure or comprehension; endless

❻ **Reading Check**
What does Anaya learn to appreciate from the *viejitos*?

❸ Literary Analysis
Reflective Essay

1. Have students read the first three sentences of the selection aloud in unison.
2. Invite students to predict the subject of the personal experience the author will describe in this essay.
Possible response: The author will describe his experience of reading.

❹ Critical Viewing

Possible response: The painting shows people standing on the edge of the world, looking up at the stars. They seem to be in awe of the sky, for they are smiling and in rapt attention.

❺ Critical Thinking
Analyze

1. **Ask:** To what does the author compare the millions of stars in the universe?
Answer: He compares the millions of books in the library to the millions of stars in the universe.
2. Point out that by drawing this comparison, the author suggests the stars in the universe and the books in the library are similar in other ways than just their huge numbers. **Ask:** From the author's point of view, how are the millions of books and millions of stars the same?
Possible answer: They both inspire a thirst for knowledge.

❻ Reading Check

Answer: Anaya learns to appreciate his grandfather and the other *viejitos* who taught him about the magic of words.

Differentiated Instruction for Universal Access

Culturally Responsive Instruction: Culture Focus

Culture Focus Students may have difficulty understanding Anaya's purpose for including the riddle in his essay. Emphasize that Anaya's purpose is twofold: to illustrate the vastness of the universe and to reveal the significance of his Mexican heritage.

Emphasize the second point by asking students what they notice about the riddle. Elicit that the riddle is written in Spanish first and then in English. Explain to students that because Anaya identifies himself as a Mexican American, his Mexican ancestry and American ancestry are equally important, so it is possible to have connections to multiple cultures. Encourage students to consider how they have both an American identity and a native cultural identity. Discuss with students the advantages of having this "double" identity.

PHLit Online!

This selection is available in interactive format in the **Enriched Online Student Edition, www.PHLitOnline.com,** which includes a thematically related video with writing prompt and an interactive graphic organizer.

❼ Literary Analysis
Reflective Essay

1. Remind students that a reflective essay often draws on a specific period of time in the author's life.
2. **Ask** students to respond to the Literary Analysis question: Which period in his life is the writer describing?
   Answer: The writer is describing the beginning of his career in school.
3. Point out that the author has vivid memories of this period in his life.
   Ask: What made this period in the author's life both exciting and challenging?
   Answer: He was learning English and was looking forward to being able to read English books.

❽ Reading Skill
Main Idea

1. Direct students' attention to the grandfather's stories about the winter of the big snow and the spring that followed. **Ask** students to share their reaction to the stories.
   Possible response: The stories are so vivid that readers may feel as if they were there.
2. **Ask** students to respond to the Reading Skill question: What main idea do details about his grandfather's stories support?
   Answer: The details about the grandfather's stories support the idea of the magic of words.

Vocabulary
inherent (in hir´ ənt) *adj.* inborn; natural; characteristic

Literary Analysis
Reflective Essay Which period in his life is the writer describing?

Reading Skill
Main Idea What main idea do details about his grandfather's stories support?

the words lie captured in ink, but the magic is still there, the power **inherent** in each volume. Now with book in hand we can participate in the wisdom of mankind.

❼ Each person moves from innocence through rites of passage into the knowledge of the world, and so I entered the world of school in search of the magic in the words. The sounds were no longer the soft sounds of Spanish which my grandfather spoke; the words were in English, and with each new awareness came my first steps toward a million volumes. I, who was used to reading my oraciones en español[3] while I sat in the kitchen and answered the litany to the slap of my mother's tortillas,[4] I now stumbled from sound to word to groups of words, head throbbing, painfully aware that each new sound took me deeper into the maze of the new language. Oh, how I clutched the hands of my new guides then!

Learn, my mother encouraged me, learn. Be as wise as your grandfather. He could speak many languages. He could speak to the birds and the animals of the field.

❽ Yes, I remember the cuentos[5] of my grandfather, the stories of the people. Words are a way, he said, they hold joy, and they are a deadly power if misused. I clung to each syllable which lisped from his tobacco-stained lips. That was the winter the snow came, he would say, it piled high and we lost many sheep and cattle, and the trees groaned and broke with its weight. I looked across the llano[6] and saw the raging blizzard, the awful destruction of that winter which was imbedded in our people's mind.

And the following summer, he would say, the grass of the llano grew so high we couldn't see the top of the sheep. And I would look and see what was once clean and pure and green. I could see a million sheep and the pastores[7] caring for them, as I now care for the million words that pasture in my mind.

But a million books? How can we see a million books? I don't mean just the books lining the shelves here at the University of New Mexico Library, not just the fine worn covers, the intriguing titles; how can we see the worlds that lie waiting in each book? A million worlds. A million million worlds. And the beauty of it is that each world is related to the next, as was taught to us by the old ones. Perhaps it is easier for a child to see. Perhaps it is easier for a child to ask: How many stars are there in the sky? How many leaves in the trees of the river? How many blades of grass in the llano? How many dreams in a night of dreams?

---

3. **oraciones en español** (ô ra syôn´ ās en es pa nyōl´) prayers in Spanish.
4. **tortillas** (tôr tē´ yəs) *n.* thin, flat, round cakes of unleavened cornmeal.
5. **cuentos** (kwen´ tôs) *n.* Spanish for "stories."
6. **llano** (ya´ nō) *n.* Spanish for "plain."
7. **pastores** (pas tô´ rās) *n.* Spanish for "shepherds."

PROFESSIONAL DEVELOPMENT | **Dr. Hollie**

APPLY THE STRATEGY

"Academizing" Slang Terms
Slang is vocabulary largely associated with youth. These colorful words offer a chance for a meaningful vocabulary exercise called academization.

Choose 5 to 7 slang terms that your students frequently use. Next, discuss with students what these words mean. Then, ask the students to "academize" the word by choosing a synonym that is appropriate for academia. Assist students and allow them to use a dictionary or thesaurus. Finally, have students enter the slang words and their corresponding academic synonyms into their personal thesaurus.

For more of Dr. Hollie's strategies, see the Professional Development essay, pp. 442c–442d.

LITERATURE IN CONTEXT 9

Cultural Connection

Mexican American Pride
Anaya's celebration of his grandfather's cuentos shares in the spirit of the Chicano movement of the 1960s.

- Participants in the movement cultivated pride in their Mexican American heritage.
- Leaders included Cesar Chavez (shown in the mural), who unionized grape pickers in California.
- Chicano artists use the symbol of the eagle (seen in the mural) and serpent to reflect their connection with the Aztecs, founders of a great civilization in Mexico.

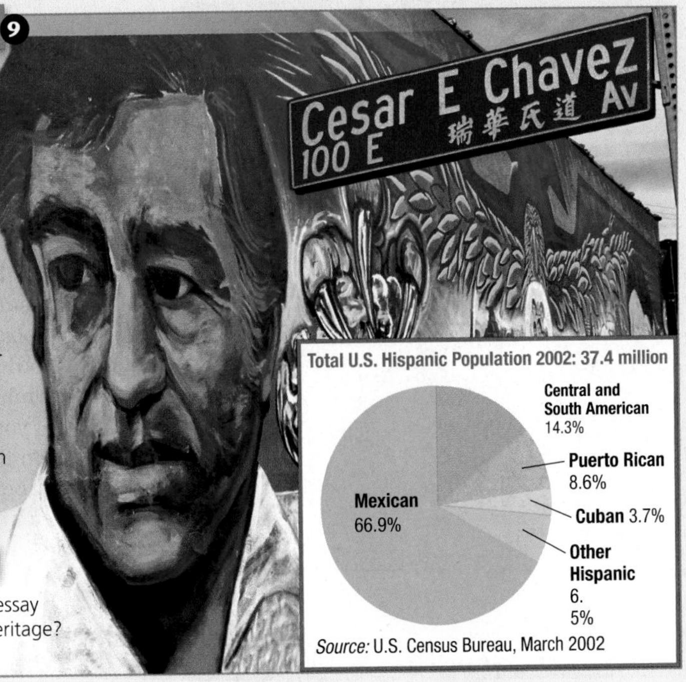

Connect to the Literature

What is one way in which Anaya's essay celebrates his Mexican American heritage? Explain your answer.

So I worked my way into the world of books, but here is the **paradox**, a book at once quenches the thirst of the imagination and ignites new fires. I learned that as I visited the library of my childhood, the Santa Rosa Library. It was only a dusty room in those days, a room sitting atop the town's fire department, which was comprised of one **dilapidated** fire truck used by the town's volunteers only in the direst emergencies. But in that small room I found my shelter and retreat. If there were a hundred books there we were fortunate, but to me there were a million volumes. I trembled in awe when I first entered that library, because I realized that if the books held as much magic as the words of the old ones, then indeed this was a room full of power.

10 Miss Pansy, the librarian, became my new guide. She fed me books as any mother would nurture her child. She brought me book after book, and I consumed them all. Saturday afternoons disappeared as the time of day dissolved into the time of distant worlds. In a world that occupied most of my other schoolmates with games, I took the time to read. I was a librarian's dream. My tattered library card was my ticket into the same worlds my grandfather had known, worlds of magic that fed the imagination. 11

Late in the afternoon, when I was satiated with reading, when I could no longer hold in my soul the characters that crowded there,

Vocabulary
paradox (par′ ə däks′) *n.* a statement or situation that seems contradictory
dilapidated (də lap′ ə dāt′ id) *adj.* shabby; broken down

Literary Analysis
Reflective Essay What general idea connects this new experience to those Anaya has already narrated?

Reading Check
How does Anaya pursue his love of words?

9 Literature in Context

Culture Connection Anaya's own writing has helped focus attention on the Mexican American experience. Anaya created his own *cuentos* in several works of fiction. His trilogy of novels—*Bless Me, Ultima* (1972), *Heart of Aztlán* (1976), and *Tortuga* (1979)—offers a perspective on the experiences of Mexican American children in the United States.

Connect to the Literature After discussing the Chicano movement, **ask** the Connect to the Literature question: What is one way in which Anaya's essay celebrates his Mexican American heritage? Explain your answer.
Possible response: In celebrating books, Anaya also honors his grandfather and other old ones whose stories made Anaya aware of his rich cultural heritage.

10 Literary Analysis
Reflective Essay

1. Remind students that the author of a reflective essay carefully selects experiences to support a general point or insight.
2. **Ask** students to respond to the Literary Analysis question: What general idea connects this new experience to those Anaya has already narrated?
   Answer: Reading allows Anaya to enter the same "worlds of magic" his grandfather had known.
3. **Ask** students to identify the new experience and the experiences the author describes.
   Answer: Having access to books in a library is the new experience. Listening to the stories of the old ones is the experience the author has already described.

11 Reading Check

Possible response: Anaya pursues his love of words by spending most of his Saturday afternoons in the library reading the books there.

Differentiated Instruction for Universal Access

EL Pronunciation for English Learners

Some students might have difficulty pronouncing words with the initial "sh" sound, as in *she* and *sheet,* replacing it with the "s" sound. The following strategies can help students to pronounce the "sh" sound.

- Write the words *she, sheet,* and *shop* on the board. Pronounce each word in turn, having students repeat each. Then, call out the words at random, having student volunteers circle the called word on the board. Discuss the results with the class, noting what might have led to incorrect choices.
- Pronounce *she, sheet,* and *shop* with students. Then, call out a word and have students write out the word. Have students compare and discuss results, noting what might have led to any discrepancies between writing.

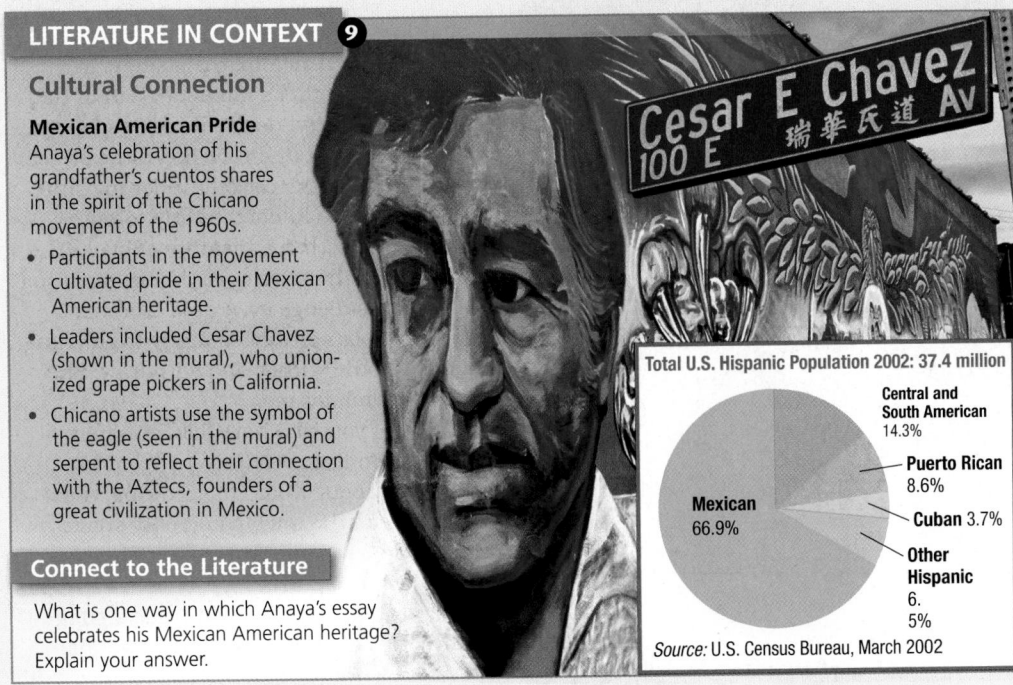

⓬ Critical Viewing

Possible response: Anaya might feel that the painting accurately reflects his feelings about the volume of books and the knowledge contained within them—that both seem to be infinite.

⓭ Reading Skill

Main Idea

1. **Ask:** Where did the author get his first writing contracts, and what were they for?
   Answer: He got his first writing contracts in the Albuquerque High School Library; his contracts were to write love notes for other students.
2. **Ask** students to respond to the Reading Skill question: Which details illustrate the main idea stated in the last sentence of this paragraph?
   Answer: The details about the library being the place where budding lovers wrote notes to each other illustrates the idea that a library is a place where love begins.

▶ Monitor Progress: To evaluate students' understanding of the skill, **ask:** What details does the author provide to support the idea that a library may be a cultural center in a city?
Answer: The author notes that not only scholars but also ordinary people come to libraries to do research, read, and think.

▶ Reteach: If students have difficulty analyzing main ideas and details, model the process with **Reading Skill Graphic Organizer** A (p. 83 in *Graphic Organizer Transparencies*).

⓬ ▲ **Critical Viewing** How might Anaya feel about a painting such as this one? How do you know? **[Connect]**

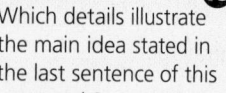

I heard the call of the llano, the real world of my father's ranchito, the solid, warm world of my mother's kitchen. Then to the surprise and bewilderment of Miss Pansy, I would rush out and race down the streets of our town, books tucked under my shirt, in my pockets, clutched tightly to my breast. Mad with the insanity of books, I would cross the river to get home, shouting my crazy challenge even at la Llorona,[8] and that poor spirit of so many frightening cuentos would wither and withdraw. She was no match for me.

Those of you who have felt the same exhilaration from reading—or from love—will know about what I'm speaking. Alas, the people of the town could only shake their heads and pity my mother. At least one of her sons was a bit touched. Perhaps they were right, for few will trade a snug reality to float on words to other worlds.

And now there are a million volumes for us to read here at the University of New Mexico Library. Books on every imaginable subject, in every field, a history of the thought of the world which we must keep free of censorship, because we treasure our freedoms. It is the word *freedom* which eventually must reflect what this collection, or the collection of any library, is all about. We know that as we preserve and use the literature of all cultures, we preserve and regenerate our own. The old ones knew and taught me this. They eagerly read the few newspapers that were available. They kept their diaries, they wrote décimas[9] and cuentos, and they survived on their oral stories and traditions.

Reading Skill
Main Idea ⓭
Which details illustrate the main idea stated in the last sentence of this paragraph?

Another time, another library. I entered Albuquerque[10] High School Library prepared to study, because that's where we spent our study time. For better or for worse, I received my first contracts as a writer there. It was a place where budding lovers spent most of their time writing notes to each other, and when my friends who didn't have the gift of words found out I could turn a phrase I quickly had all the business I could do. I wrote poetic love notes for a dime apiece and thus worked my way through high school.

8. **la Llorona** (la yô rô´ na) *n.* spirit of many Spanish stories, famous for shouting and crying for her lost love.
9. **décimas** (dā´ sē mas) *n.* Spanish for "ten-line stanzas."
10. **Albuquerque** (al´ bə kər´ kē) *n.* city in central New Mexico.

Vocabulary Development

Vocabulary Knowledge Rating

When students have completed reading and discussing the excerpt, have them take out their **Vocabulary Knowledge Rating Chart** for this selection. Read the words aloud once more, and have students rate their knowledge of the words again in the After Reading column. Clarify any words that are still problematic. Have students write their own definition and example or sentence in the appropriate column. Then have students complete the Vocabulary Practice at the end of the selection. Encourage students to use the words in further discussion and written work about this selection. Remind them that they will be accountable for these words on the **Selection Test,** ***Unit 3 Resources***, pp. 95–97 or 98–100.

And there were fringe benefits, because the young women knew very well who was writing the sweet words, and many a heart I was supposed to capture fell in love with me. And so, a library is also a place where love begins.

A library should be the heart of a city. With its storehouse of knowledge, it liberates, informs, teaches, and **enthralls**. A library indeed should be the cultural center of any city. Amidst the bustle of work and commerce, the great libraries of the world have provided a sanctuary where scholars and common man alike come to enlarge and clarify knowledge, to read and reflect in quiet solitude.

I knew a place like this. I spent many hours in the old library on Central Avenue and Edith Street. But my world was growing, and quite by accident I wandered up the hill to enroll in the University of New Mexico. And what a surprise lay in store for me. The libraries of my childhood paled in comparison to this new wealth of books housed in Zimmerman Library. Here there were stack after stack of books, and ample space and time to wander aimlessly in this labyrinth of new frontiers.

I had known the communal memory of my
4 people through the newspapers and few books my grandfather read to me and through the
5 rich oral tradition handed down by the old ones; now I discovered the collective memory of all mankind at my fingertips. I had only to reach for the books that laid all history bare. Here I could converse with the writers from every culture on earth, old and new, and at the same time I began my personal odyssey, which would add a few books to the collection which in 1981 would come to house a million volumes.

> **A LIBRARY INDEED SHOULD BE THE CULTURAL CENTER OF ANY CITY.**

Those were exciting times. Around me swirled the busy world of the university, in many respects an alien world. Like many fellow undergraduates, I sought refuge in the library. My haven during those student university years was the reading room of the west wing of the old library. There I found peace. The carved vigas[11] decorating the ceiling, the solid wooden tables and chairs and the warm adobe color of the stucco were things with which I was familiar. There I felt comfortable. With books scattered around me, I could read and doze and dream. I took my breaks in the warm sun of the portal, where I ate my tortilla sandwiches, which I carried in my brown paper bag. There, with friends, I sipped coffee as we talked of changing the world and exchanged idealistic dreams.

11. **vigas** (bē´ gas) *n.* Spanish for "roof beams."

Vocabulary
enthralls (en thrôlz´) *v.* captivates; fascinates

Literary Analysis
Reflective Essay What general idea does Anaya use to relate this new period in his life to previous ones?

16 **Reading Check**
What vital services do libraries provide to cities?

14 Literary Analysis
Reflective Essay

1. **Ask** students to respond to the Literary Analysis question: What general idea does Anaya use to relate this new period in his life to previous ones?
   Answer: Anaya finds that books are a way of preserving the collective memory of humankind, just as the rich oral tradition of his grandfather and the "old ones" preserves the communal memory of his people.
2. **Ask:** How will this new period in the author's life differ from previous ones?
   Answer: The author is going to write books that will become part of the library's collection and the collective memory of humankind.

15 Connecting to the Big Question

1. Explain to students that, just as a library is full of books containing immeasurable amounts of knowledge, people, too, can be receptacles for knowledge. Have students discuss how having this knowledge can impact their lives.
2. **Ask** students: What different ways has Anaya gained knowledge throughout his life?
   Answer: He has acquired knowledge from the printed word, such as from newspapers and books. He has also gained knowledge by talking and listening to his elders, especially his grandfather.
3. **Ask** students: Which way of acquiring knowledge—through the printed word or through oral storytelling—has influenced Anaya's life more?
   Possible response: Oral storytelling has influenced Anaya's life more, because he had been listening to the stories his elders told before he could even read. He was so inspired by his elders' words and the pictures they formed in his imagination that he grew to love words. This love of words led him to read books.

16 Reading Check

Answer: Libraries provide a wide realm of information that teaches and liberates through knowledge. They offer a safe place for one to read, think, and reflect.

Concept Connector

Anticipation Guide

Have students return to their **Anticipation Guides** and respond to the statements again in the After Reading column. They may do this individually or in their original pairs or groups. Then lead a class discussion, probing for what students have learned that confirms or invalidates each statement. Encourage students to cite specific details and other evidence from the text to support their responses to each statement.

Writing About the Big Question

Have students compare their responses to the sentence starters they completed before reading the essay with their ideas afterwards. Ask them to explain whether their thoughts have changed.

Reading Skill Graphic Organizer

Ask students to review the graphic organizers they completed to identify main ideas and supporting details while reading. Show them **Reading Skill Graphic Organizer A** (*Graphic Organizer Transparencies,* p. 83) as an example. Then have students use the graphic organizers they completed to make observations about main ideas in the selection.

ASSESS

Answers

Critical Thinking

1. Students who enjoy reading will probably agree with Anaya.
2. (a) The stories of *los viejitos* taught him and other children to wonder and imagine. **Possible response:** (b) The riddles and *cuentos* were like the books the author later read in inspiring a thirst for knowledge. They were different because they reflected one people's culture, while books gave access to the cultures of all humankind.
3. **Possible responses:** (a) Reading satisfies a desire for knowledge and also inspires questions.
(b) The riddles and *cuentos* also captivated Anaya, making him not only wonder and imagine but also to ask questions and form ideas.
4. **Possible response:** Anaya associates libraries with freedom, because it is there that people can open any book to learn what is contained within, and it is there that they can freely discuss ideas with others.

What kind of knowledge changes our lives?

Possible responses: (a) Libraries encourage individuals to learn and to seek more knowledge, to form ties among other like-minded individuals, and to create peace and sanctuary for deep thought.
(b) Older and wiser members of a community can inspire younger individuals to learn by sharing their unique and vivid stories.

Vocabulary
poignant (poin′ yənt) *adj.* emotionally moving; piercing

That is a rich and pleasant time in my memory. No matter how far across the world I find myself in the future, how deep in the creation of worlds with words, I shall keep the simple and poignant memories of those days. The sun set golden on the ocher walls, and the green pine trees and the blue spruce, sacred trees to our people, whispered in the breeze. I remembered my grandfather meeting with the old men of the village in the resolana[12] of one of the men's homes, or against the wall of the church on Sundays, and I remembered the things they said. Later, alone, dreaming against the sun-warmed wall of the library, I continued that discourse in my mind.

Yes, the library is a place where people should gather. It is a place for research, reading, and for the quiet fomentation of ideas, but because it houses the collective memory of our race, it should also be a place where present issues are discussed and debated and researched in order for us to gain the knowledge and insight to create a better future. The library should be a warm place that reflects the needs and aspirations of the people.

12. resolana (rā sô la′ na) *n.* Spanish for "place for enjoying the sun."

Critical Thinking

1. **Respond:** Do you share Anaya's feeling that a library is a place of comfort? Explain.
2. **(a)** According to Anaya, what did the stories of *los viejitos* teach him and other children? **(b) Compare and Contrast:** Identify a difference and a similarity between the riddles and *cuentos* Anaya learned in childhood and the books he later read.
3. **(a) Interpret:** What does Anaya mean when he writes that "a book at once quenches the thirst of the imagination and ignites new fires"? **(b) Connect:** How is this power of books similar to the power of the riddles and *cuentos* of Anaya's childhood?
4. **Interpret:** Why does Anaya associate libraries with freedom?

What kind of knowledge changes our lives?
(a) In what ways do libraries make an impact on individuals? **(b)** In today's world, what do you think is the best way to awaken wonder and imagination in people and inspire them to learn?

Assessment Resources

The following resources can be used to assess students' knowledge and skills.

Unit 3 Resources

L1 L2 EL **Selection Test A,** pp. 95–97
L3 L4 **Selection Test B,** pp. 98–100
L3 L4 **Open-Book Test,** pp. 92–94

PHLit Online! Students may use the **Self-test,** online at **www.PHLitOnline.com,** to prepare for the **Selection Test A** or **Selection Test B.**

After You Read | *from* In Commemoration: One Million Volumes

Literary Analysis: Reflective Essay

1. Using a chart like the one shown, analyze Anaya's use of libraries as a focus for his **reflective essay.** For each detail you list, explain its connection to libraries.

2. Choose an item from your chart, and explain how it is associated with something endless—an uncountable number, for example. What general truth about imagination does the item illustrate?

Reading Skill: Main Idea

3. **(a)** Reread up to the paragraph that begins, "But a million books?" What is the topic of this section? **(b)** What is the **main idea? (c)** What details support it?
4. **(a)** What is the next main idea you find in the essay? **(b)** Identify three **supporting details** for the idea.
5. **(a)** After reading the essay, identify one further question you have. **(b)** Where could you look to find the answer?

Vocabulary

Practice For each of these sentences, write a new sentence with the same meaning by using a word from the list on page 498.

1. Getting wet is a risk that is a built-in part of boating.
2. Their reunion was very emotional and touching.
3. My broken-down old bike is dangerous to ride.
4. That comic book is wildly interesting to him.
5. When she takes care of her little brother, her patience is endless.
6. It seemed like a contradiction that she loved to grow vegetables but did not like to eat them.

Word Study Use the context of the sentences and what you know about the **Greek prefix *para-*** to explain your answer to each question.

1. Would two *parallel* boards be crossing or touching each other?
2. Should you postpone a task of *paramount* importance?

Word Study

The **Greek prefix *para-*** means "beside" or "beyond."

Challenge Explain how the prefix *para-* contributes to the meanings of these words. Consult a dictionary if necessary.

paramedic
parameter
paraphrase

ASSESS/EXTEND

Answers

Literary Analysis

1. Students may cite any of Anaya's experiences in libraries as specific events or facts. Specific feelings associated with libraries include awe, excitement, inspiration, comfort, peacefulness, and community. Anaya felt awe the first time he went to his local library, he felt excitement as he read library books as a child, and he was inspired with a thirst for knowledge on various library visits as a child and a student.

   For other sample answers, see ***Graphic Organizer Transparencies,*** **Literary Analysis Graphic Organizer A,** p. 86, and the **Additional Answers** section.
2. Students may cite any of the author's library experiences as well as the feelings of inspiration and community as examples of things associated with a desire for ideas and knowledge. Students may observe that the more one feeds one's imagination, the hungrier it becomes.

Reading Skill

3. **Possible responses:** (a) The topic of the opening section is the magic of words. (b) Words have the power to capture the imagination and to inspire a thirst for knowledge. (c) The teachings and stories of the old ones support this point.
4. **Possible responses:** (a) Books also have the power to capture the imagination and inspire a thirst for knowledge. (b) Three supporting details from the text: *I found my shelter and retreat; I trembled in awe; a room full of power*

Vocabulary

Practice

1. Developing endurance is an inherent benefit of running long distances.
2. The speech the donor gave was memorable and poignant.
3. The old, neglected house is too dilapidated to be sold.
4. The movie reviewer promises to all audiences that the upcoming blockbuster will enthrall them.

Answers continued

5. The sage's compassion is as infinite as the sky.
6. That some types of trees and shrubs need to be damaged by fire in order to survive seems a paradox.

Word Study

Sample answers:

1. Two parallel boards would be side by side, or beside, one another.
2. No, a task of paramount importance has importance beyond all other tasks.

Word Study: Challenge

Sample answers:

A *paramedic* works beside a physician to provide medical assistance. *Parameter* means something that sets the boundary beside which something else is measured. To *paraphrase* is to phrase alongside or beside a statement or idea, so that the meanings are the same.

EXTEND/ASSESS

Answers

Grammar

1. Introduce the skill, using the instruction on the student page.
2. Discuss the examples on the page.

Think Aloud: Model the Skill

Model the skill of identifying subject complements, using the following "think aloud":

> To look for subject complements, I look for linking verbs. I know that they always come after linking verbs.
>
> In the sentence "Sacha is a writer," *is* is the linking verb and *writer* is the subject complement. Because *writer* renames the subject, *Sacha,* I know that this is a predicate nominative.
>
> In the sentence "Sacha seems tired," *seems* is the linking verb and *tired* is the subject complement. *Tired* describes Sacha, so I know that *tired* is a predicate adjective.

WG Writing and Grammar, Grade 10

Students will find further instruction and practice on predicate nominatives and predicative adjectives in Chapter 19, Section 4.

Practice A

1. narrator; predicate nominative
2. beautiful; predicate adjective
3. healthy; predicate adjective
4. treasures; predicate nominative
5. remorseful; predicate adjective

Challenge

Sample answer: She was my mother's younger sister. Subject: She; verb: was; predicate nominative: sister.

Practice B

Sample answers:

1. a writer
2. successful
3. mythical
4. their books
5. wonderful

Challenge

Sample answer: A library is a gateway to knowledge. (pred. nom.) Most libraries are large. (pred. adj.) A library seems like a world of ideas. (pred. nom.) Some books at the library are educational. (pred. adj.)

Integrated Language Skills

The Sun Parlor • *from* In Commemoration: One Million Volumes

Grammar: Subject Complements

Predicate nominatives and **predicate adjectives** are subject complements. They appear after a linking verb such as *be, is,* or *seem,* and they rename, identify, or describe the subject of the sentence.

A subject and a predicate nominative both name the same person, place, or thing. The linking verb joins them and makes them equal.

Examples: Their first choice was you.
Our vacation destination is the beach.

A predicate adjective appears with the linking verb and describes the subject of the sentence.

Examples: Roses are red.
Soccer equipment is expensive.

Practice A Identify the subject complement in each sentence and and label it predicate nominative or predicate adjective.

1. The author is the narrator.
2. The sun parlor was beautiful.
3. West's aunt seemed healthy.
4. Children are our greatest treasures.
5. West felt remorseful.

Challenge In "The Sun Parlor," find and copy one sentence that has a predicate nominative and one sentence that has a predicate adjective. For each sentence, label the complements, and underline the subject once and the linking verb twice.

Practice B Add a predicate nominative or predicate adjective, as indicated, to complete each sentence.

1. Anaya is (predicate nominative).
2. Anaya is (predicate adjective).
3. The stories of Anaya's youth seemed (predicate adjective).
4. One feature of libraries is (predicate nominative).
5. Books are (predicate adjective).

Challenge Write a brief paragraph about a library. At least two sentences should have predicate adjectives, and at least two sentences should have predicate nominatives. After you draft, identify the subject complements you have included.

WG **Writing and Grammar Connection:** Chapter 19, Section 4

Extend the Lesson

Sentence Modeling

Choose the sentence given from the selection students have read:

But it did not look natural. ("The Sun Parlor")

We knew the million stars were the coins of the Lord, and the heavens were the bedspread of his mother, and in our minds the sky was a million miles wide. (from *In Commemoration: One Million Volumes*)

Ask students what they notice about the sentence. Elicit from them the subject complement(s) used. Then, ask what else they notice. ("The Sun Parlor": the sentence uses context, terseness, and an emphasis on the predicate adjective to carry with it a strong feeling. From *In Commemoration: One Million Volumes:* the predicate nominatives serve as vivid metaphors and the predicate adjective as imagery.)

Have students imitate the sentence in a sentence on a topic of their own choosing, matching each grammatical and stylistic feature discussed. Collect the sentences, and share them with the class.

riting

authors of both of these essays reflect on an earlier time in their lives. e a brief **memoir,** or recollection based on your personal experience, room or a building that holds meaning for you.

Memoirs are autobiographical; write in the first person, using the pronoun *I* to refer to yourself.

Choose *precise words* to paint a vivid picture of the space or place you are recalling.

Use concrete *sensory details* to describe the sights, sounds, and smells of the scene.

Share your insights with readers, revealing why the room or building has special meaning for you.

iting Workshop: *Work in Progress*

writing for a Letter to the Editor Using the Issues List in your writ- portfolio, write an opening sentence for each item. This sentence uld identify the main point you want to accomplish in your letter. Save Main Idea List in your writing portfolio.

Use this prewriting activity to prepare for the **Writing Workshop** on page 532.

stening and Speaking

pare an **oral recollection.** You may choose to focus on someone you w who is interesting and important to you *or* on an organization or itution with which you have been involved, such as a team, a club, or nmunity group.

- Provide key details that will bring the person to life or will help others understand the spirit of the organization.
- Make sure to clearly **establish your point of view and relationship** with the subject of your recollection.
- Include **sensory details and concrete images.** Consider adding interest by **shifting perspectives** or views.
- First, present your recollection to a classmate. Then, **revise your draft based on feedback** from your partner.
- When you are ready, **present a revised version** of your recollection to the class.

PHLit Online!
www.PHLitOnline.com

- Interactive graphic organizers
- Grammar tutorial
- Interactive journals

EXTEND/ASSESS

Answers

Writing

1. Review the assignment, using the instruction on the student page.
2. To guide students in writing a memoir, give them **Support for Writing,** p. 90 in ***Unit 3 Resources.***
3. To evaluate students' memoirs, use one of the generic writing rubrics, pp. 256–257 in ***Professional Development Guidebook.*** Also, make sure that students use precise, vivid language to describe the building and clearly explain the power of the memory of the place.

Six Traits Focus

✔	Ideas	✔	Word Choice
	Organization		Sentence Fluency
	Voice		Conventions

Writing and Grammar, Grade 10

Students will find guidance on writing a memoir in Chapter 4.

Writing Workshop
Work in Progress

Have students save their completed Main Idea List in their portfolios. They will use the letter to the editor later as they complete the Writing Workshop assignment (see pp. 532–537).

Listening and Speaking

1. Review the assignment, using the instruction on the student page.
2. Have students complete the **Support for Extend Your Learning** page (***Unit 3 Resources,*** p. 91).

Teaching Resources

All *Unit 3 Resources*
L3 L4 **Integrated Language Skills: Grammar,** p. 89
L3 L4 **Support for Writing,** p. 90
L3 L4 **Support for Extend Your Learning,** p. 91
L4 **Enrichment,** pp. 70, 78

All **Enriched Online Student Edition**
Available under After You Read for this selection:
All **Interactive Grammar Tutorial**
L3 L4 **Internet Research Activity**

Professional Development Guidebook
Rubic for Writing, pp. 256–257

PHLit Online! All print and digital resources are available at **www.PHLitOnline.com.** Online resources accessible by students are noted on the student page.

MONITORING PROGRESS

Using the Test Practice

In this two-page Test Practice, students apply the reading skill for the first half of Unit 3 to a passage of fiction and a passage of nonfiction.

Review this skill, main idea, and then administer the test. For more guidance, consult the ***Classroom Strategies and Teaching Routines*** card, ***Administering Timed Tests.***

ASSESS

Answers

Answers With Explanations

1. **B**—The passage focuses on the cultivation of many types of food to sustain the city. *Incorrect answers:* A—The passage does not mention Aztec people being warriors. C—Though the passage suggests that the city of Tenochtitlan might be beautiful, this is not the main idea. D—The Aztec people cultivate the raised lake gardens, they do not live on them.
2. **D**—This detail proves that he appreciated the gardens. *Incorrect answers:* A—This detail does not tell us about his appreciation of the gardens. B—Working alongside his father was probably an obligation of his and does not necessarily show appreciation. C—Same explanation as for A.
3. **D**—This detail does not relate to how the Aztec people lives. *Incorrect answers:* A—This statement defines the chinampas, an important part of Aztec life. B—This statement tells us what foods the Aztecs grew. C—This statement suggests how the Aztecs moved around the lake gardens.
4. **C**—Researching this topic would provide insight into an important aspect of Aztec life. *Incorrect answers:* A—While it would be interesting to find out what happens in the story, this topic would not help us understand the Aztec way of life. B—Though this would reveal how hard it was for Aztecs to grow tomatoes, it does not help us understand their way of life. D—This topic would not tell us anything about the Aztec way of life.

Test Practice: Reading

Main Idea

Fiction Selection

Directions: *Read the selection. Then, answer the questions.*

Nahuaca's family were cultivators of the *chinampas,* the raised lake gardens of the Aztecs. Nahuaca worked beside his father, placing rows of long poles to form the sides of the chinampas in the shallow lake surrounding the great city of Tenochtitlán. He paddled the canoe, scooping mud and plants from the lake bottom to build the chinampas several feet above the lake. He transplanted the tiny tomato plants in the garden. As he worked, he marveled at the garden's beauty.

One day his father spoke to him. "Nahuaca, someday you will choose your own path, but know that if you choose to farm with your family, you will be contributing to your people. Growing these tomatoes, maize, and chilies allows us all to thrive. Without us, the people in our city would have no food. Food is not all we get from the lake gardens, though; they are an important part of our culture as well."

1. Which of the following *best* states the main idea of this passage?

A. Aztec people were great warriors.
B. Aztec people grew a variety of food in lake gardens.
C. Tenochtitlán was a beautiful city.
D. Aztec people lived on gardens in lakes and worked very hard.

2. Which detail supports the idea that Nahuaca appreciated the gardens?

A. His family were cultivators of the chinampas.
B. He worked alongside his father.
C. His father told Nahuaca he would choose his own path someday.
D. He marveled at the gardens' beauty.

3. Which of the following details *does not* tell how the Aztec people lived?

A. Chinampas were raised lake gardens.
B. "We grow tomatoes, maize, beans, and chilies."
C. Nahuaca paddled a flat-bottom canoe.
D. One day his father spoke to him.

4. To understand the Aztec way of life better, what question might you ask?

A. Did Nahuaca continue to grow food?
B. Is it difficult to grow tomatoes?
C. What did Aztecs do for recreation?
D. Why should people build lake gardens?

Writing for Assessment

Consider the main idea and details in this passage. Then write an appropriate title for it. In a paragraph, explain why your title makes sense.

Writing for Assessment

Student's should choose a title that reflects the main idea of the passage, which is the history of cultivation of a large variety of food in the lake gardens by the Aztecs. They should explain why their title is appropriate by using at least three supporting details from the passage.

Strategies for Test Taking

Remind students to read the questions carefully. Suggest that they pay special attention to key words such as *best and DOES NOT.* Remind students that when questions ask for the best answer, it usually means that more than one answer may seem correct. Have students eliminate the weaker answer choices one at a time to arrive at the best possible answer. Remind students that when a question contains the words *DOES NOT,* they will want to think of the opposite to find the correct answer.

Nonfiction Selection

Directions: *Read the selection. Then, answer the questions.*

You may not be able to imagine pizza without tomato sauce, but tomatoes have not always been such a popular food. Tomatoes began as a wild species in what is now Peru and Ecuador. The plant was probably domesticated in Mexico centuries before Europeans arrived. Its name is from the Náhuatl (Aztec) word *tomati.* In the early 1500s, the Spanish brought the tomato to Europe, where it was used as food by the Spanish and Italians. In England, France, and Northern Europe, however, the tomato was believed to be poisonous. The English used the plant simply for its beauty.

From Europe, the tomato was introduced to North America, where it was used as food in the early 1800s. By the early twentieth century, the tomato was widely popular as food, and by the late twentieth century, the United States led the world in tomato production.

1. Which of the following *best* states the main idea of the passage?

- **A.** Tomatoes originated in South America, probably in Ecuador and Peru, and were probably domesticated in Mexico.
- **B.** At one time, tomatoes were considered poisonous and planted for their beauty.
- **C.** The tomato has a long history that spans the world, but it did not become widely popular as a food until the 1900s.
- **D.** The Aztecs were the first to cultivate tomatoes.

2. Which of the following details *does not* support the main idea of the passage?

- **A.** Some believed tomatoes were poisonous.
- **B.** *Tomato* originated from a Náhautl word.
- **C.** Tomatoes originated in Ecuador and Peru.
- **D.** The Spanish brought the tomato to Europe.

3. The author's purpose is most likely to—

- **A.** entertain readers with a humorous story about pizza.
- **B.** describe what it is like to eat a tomato.
- **C.** inform readers about how the tomato became a popular food.
- **D.** explain the process of growing tomatoes.

4. To learn more about the popularity of tomatoes in the United States today, what question might you research?

- **A.** What caused people to believe that tomatoes might be poisonous?
- **B.** How many tomatoes were sold in the United States last year?
- **C.** Do Europeans still plant tomatoes for their beauty?
- **D.** Do wild tomatoes grow in the U.S.?

Writing for Assessment

Connecting Across Texts
What details from the nonfiction passage might be used to support the fiction passage? In a paragraph, explain your answer.

PHLit Online!
www.PHLitOnline.com
- Online practice
- Instant feedback

Differentiated Instruction for Universal Access

Strategy for Less Proficient Readers
Review with students how to determine the main idea of a passage. Remind them that the *main idea* is the central message, thought, or opinion found in the passage. Encourage students to take notes as they read each passage so they will be able to identify the various details and the main idea. You may also wish to provide students with copies of pages 510 and 511 so they can underline, circle, or highlight words. Tell them that focusing on details can help them identify the main idea, and once the main idea is identified, these details can help support and solidify it. Read each passage aloud, helping students to summarize them and identify the main ideas using key details. Suggest paraphrasing as a way to make certain ideas clearer.

ASSESS

Answers

Answers With Explanations

1. C—The passage details the history of the tomato. *Incorrect answers:* A—Though this is mentioned in the passage, it is not the main idea. B—Same explanation as for A. D—This is not stated in the passage.
2. A—The main idea of the passage is the history of the tomato and people's beliefs about the tomato tell us nothing about its history. *Incorrect answers:* B—This statement is part of the history of the tomato. C—Same explanation as for B. D—Same explanation as for B.
3. C—The passage tells us about the history of the tomato and how it became a popular food. *Incorrect answers:* A—This is not a humorous story and there are no details about eating pizza presented in this passage. B—The passage does not describe eating a tomato. D—The passage does not explain how tomatoes are grown.
4. B—Knowing how many tomatoes were sold in the United States last year would give us information about their popularity in the United States. *Incorrect answers:* A—While it might be interesting to know more about this, it would not give us insight into the popularity of tomatoes in the U.S. today. C—Same explanation as for A. D—Same explanation as for A.

Writing for Assessment

Students should use details from the nonfiction passage to support the fiction passage by drawing parallels between the two. Students might focus on the dates and cultural origins presented in the nonfiction passage, as well as the origin of the word.

PHLit Online!
Students may take the test in interactive format with instant feedback online at www.PHLitOnline.com.

Meeting Your Standards

Students will

1. follow and critique technical directions.
2. read and understand technical directions and a user's guide.

*Log on at **www.PHLitOnline.com** for a detailed lesson plan for Informational Texts.*

Reading Skill

1. Introduce the skill, using the instruction on the student page.
2. Tell students that they will follow and critique technical directions as they read.

Think Aloud: Model the Skill

Model the skill of following and critiquing technical directions. Say:

> When I read the heading "How to Use a Compass," I know that the directions will tell about using a compass. The illustration of a compass with its labeled parts and the subhead *Easy as 1-2-3* tell me that I can read this section to follow the directions for using a compass.

What kind of knowledge changes our lives?

Have students think about how technical directions and user's guides help them manage in today's world.

Multidraft Reading

Have students follow a multidraft reading protocol.

- **First reading**—Have students read for general understanding.
- **Second reading**—Have students read to follow the directions and to examine their sequence.
- **Third reading**—Have students think about how a product's directions affect day-to-day life.

Informational Texts

Real-Life Reading

Technical Directions
Compass Instructions and Warranty

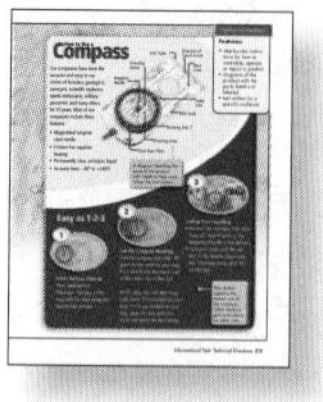

User's Guide
GPS Quick-Start Guide

Reading Skill: Follow and Critique Technical Directions

You can better understand technical directions if you first analyze the format of the text to get a sense of the information provided. Then, **critique the logic of the document by examining the sequence,** or structure, of information and procedures. Are the directions clear? Could anything be misunderstood by the reader?

Once you have analyzed the text, be sure you can answer the following questions before **following the technical directions.**

Questions for Technical Directions

- What does the device do?
- What tools or materials are needed?
- What steps or directions are provided?
- What information is given in charts, diagrams, and illustrations?
- What are the safety warnings?
- What should you do if something goes wrong?

THE BIG ? What kind of *knowledge* changes our lives?

Technical directions and user's guides provide guidance for using a specific product or device. Without this knowledge, it would be difficult or impossible to assemble or operate the item. Having this knowledge can save time, reduce or eliminate frustration, and keep the item from being damaged by misuse.

Differentiated Instruction for Universal Access

Reading Support

Give students reading support with the appropriate version of the ***Reader's Notebooks***:

- L2 L3 *Reader's Notebook*
- L1 *Reader's Notebook: Adapted Version*
- EL *Reader's Notebook: English Learner's Version*

PHLit Online! All student resources are available online at **www.PHLitOnline.com.**

How to Use a Compass

Our compasses have been the accurate and easy-to-use choice of foresters, geologists, surveyors, scientific explorers, sports enthusiasts, military personnel, and many others for 50 years. Most of our compasses include these features:

- Magnetized tungsten steel needle
- Friction-free sapphire bearing
- Permanently clear, antistatic liquid
- Accurate from – 40° to +140°F

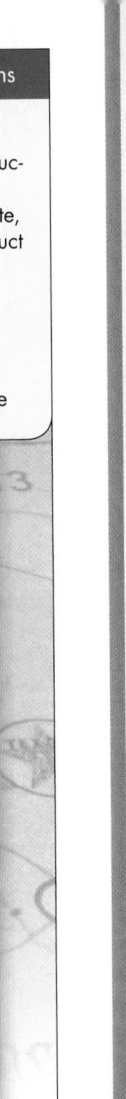

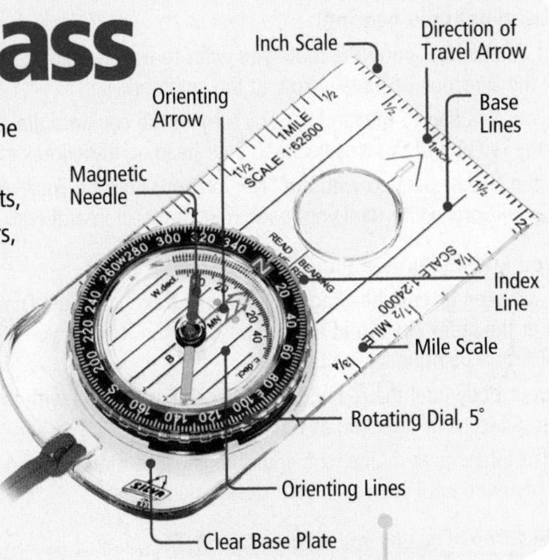

A diagram identifies the parts of the product with labels to help users follow the instructions.

Technical Directions

Features:

- step-by-step instructions for how to assemble, operate, or repair a product
- diagrams of the product with the parts listed and labeled
- text written for a specific audience

Easy as 1-2-3

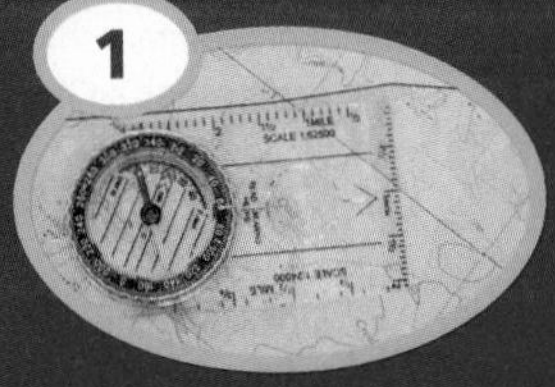

Point the Base Plate to Your Destination:
Place your compass on the map with the edge along the desired line of travel.

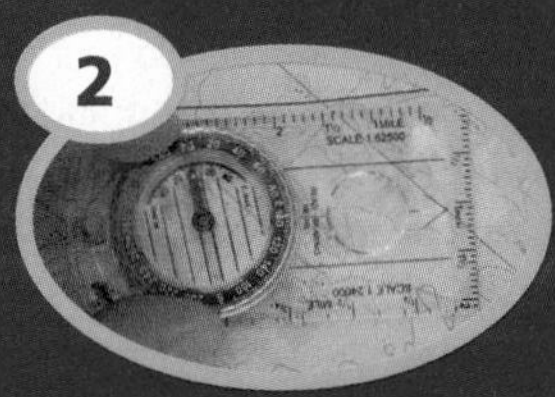

Set the Compass Heading:
Turn the compass Dial until "N" points to the north on your map. Your direction in degrees is read at the Index Line on the Dial.

NOTE: Align the Dial with magnetic north if it is marked on your map. If it is not marked on your map, align the Dial with true north and adjust for declination.

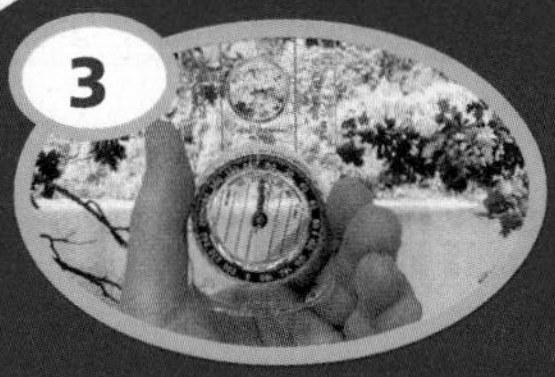

Follow Your Heading:

- Remove the compass from your map and hold it level, so the Magnetic Needle is free to turn.
- Turn your body until the red end of the Needle aligns with the Orienting Arrow and "N" on the Dial.

This section explains the easiest use of the compass. Other sections give instructions for other uses.

TEACH

About Technical Directions

1. Review the list of features of Technical Directions shown in the box on the student page.
2. Invite students to describe technical directions they have used. Ask them to share what they wanted to learn by reading the technical directions. Have them tell whether or not the directions met their needs.
3. Point out to students that they will likely encounter technical directions when they are learning to use a new piece of equipment, such as a calculator or cell phone.

Follow and Critique Technical Directions

1. Have students read "How to Use a Compass." Point out the note that explains the purpose of the diagram. **Ask:** How does showing a diagram of a compass with its labeled parts help users?
   Possible response: Users can look at the diagram as they read the instructions to help them understand the parts of the compass to which the instructions refer.
2. **Ask** students to identify specific features of this compass.
   Answer: Specific features of this compass include a magnetized tungsten steel needle, a friction-free sapphire bearing, and clear anti-static liquid, accurate from 240 to 140 degrees F.
3. Direct students' attention to the *Easy as 1-2-3* section. **Ask:** What other item in addition to a compass do you need in order to follow the instructions?
   Answer: You need a map.
4. **Ask** students what they should do after they have aligned the compass with their line of travel on the map.
   Answer: Turn the compass Dial until "N" points to the north on the map. Then, read their direction in degrees at the Index Line on the Dial.
5. Point out to students that the direction in degrees is called the "compass heading." **Ask:** What is the final step in the instructions?
   Answer: The final step is to follow your compass heading.

Differentiated Instruction for Universal Access

Strategy for Less Proficient Readers

To emphasize the importance of reading all directions before starting an activity, write these numbered directions on the board when the students are not in the room:

1. Write your name on the top left corner.
2. Write your birth date on the bottom right corner.
3. Write your favorite color on the top right corner.
4. Write your favorite movie on the bottom left corner.
5. Complete steps 2–4 only if you want additional homework.

Cover the directions with something such as paper, so that students cannot read them ahead of time. Ask students to take out a separate sheet of paper. Then, uncover the directions and ask students to follow them. After students are finished writing, ask students who have indicated they would like extra homework to raise their hands.

Follow and Critique Technical Directions

1. Remind students to read the headings to find out where to look for specific information. **Ask** a volunteer to identify the main headings on p. 514.
   Answer: The main headings are "Find Your Way Without a Map" and "Compass Warranty."
2. Have volunteers read aloud the section "Find Your Way Without a Map." **Ask:** What two ways of using a compass does this section explain?
   Answer: It explains how to use a compass to find a heading when you know the route you want to travel and how to use a compass to follow a given heading to reach your destination.
3. Tell students to assume that they are on a nature walk without a map and do not know their compass heading. **Ask** students what they should do after pointing the Direction of Travel Arrow at a chosen landmark.
   Answer: Turn the compass dial until the "N" aligns with the red end of the Needle.
4. **Ask** students why they should carefully read the warranty information before using the compass.
   Possible response: It is important to read the warranty information before using the compass to avoid doing anything that would void the warranty, such as taking the compass apart.

Find Your Way Without a Map:

Find a heading (field bearing):

1. Select a landmark along the route you want to travel. Hold the compass level and point the Direction of Travel Arrow at the landmark.
2. Find your heading to the landmark by turning the compass dial until the "N" aligns with the red end of the Needle. Read your heading in degrees to the Index Line.
3. Keep the Needle aligned with the "N"; look up; sight on your landmark and walk to it. Repeat this procedure until you reach your destination and walk to it.

Two ways of using the compass are explained, each in its own set of numbered steps.

When you know your heading:

1. If you've been given a heading in degrees to travel, turn the Dial so that the heading is set at the Index Line. Hold the compass level in front of you with the Direction of Travel Arrow pointing straight ahead.
2. Turn your body until the red end of the Needle is aligned with the "N" on the dial. You now face your direction of travel.
3. Pick out a landmark in line with your heading and move toward it. Repeat this procedure until you reach your destination.

NOTE: Be aware of nearby iron or steel objects. They may attract the Magnetic Needle if too close to the compass. Even a hidden nail can deflect the needle.

Compass Warranty

What Is Covered?
We warrant your compass to be free from defects in materials or workmanship, and we guarantee its accuracy, for the life of the compass.

Headings help users quickly locate answers to frequently-asked warranty questions.

What Is Not Covered?
Normal wear, abrasion, melting, misuse, alteration, abuse, or taking apart the compass is not covered by this warranty.

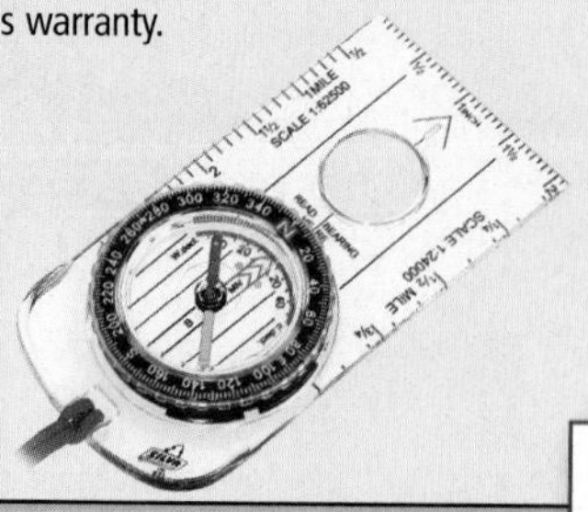

How to Obtain Warranty Service or Repair of Your Compass
Should your compass become defective under the terms of this warranty, call the Customer Satisfaction Department toll free at 1 (800) 123-4567 for return authorization. If, after our inspection, we find that the product was defective in material or workmanship, we shall, at our option, either repair or replace it without charge. If repairs not covered under this warranty are required, we will contact you for approval to proceed. You will be charged for the components repaired or replaced, plus a nominal charge for labor.

There are no other express warranties beyond the terms of this limited warranty. In no event shall our company be liable for incidental or consequential damages arising from using our compasses.

What kind of knowledge changes our lives?
(a) What problem is solved by using a compass?
(b) In what situation might a compass be useful?

ASSESS/EXTEND

Answers

What kind of knowledge changes our lives?

Possible responses:
(a) Using a compass solves the problem of not knowing which direction to go.

(b) A compass might be useful when you are lost on a hike through the woods.

Vocabulary Development

Vocabulary from Science

Point out that technical directions often use vocabulary that is specific to one particular task, in this case operating a compass. Guide students to understand the meaning of the following terms in "How to Use a Compass":

declination: the angle by which the needle on a compass deviates from true north

heading: the direction a traveler is going

magnetic needle: a magnetized rod in a compass that swings freely to indicate the position of north

magnetic north: the northerly direction in the Earth's magnetic field, slightly different from geographic, or true, north

PHLit Online!
Vocabulary Central, featuring tools, activities, and songs for studying vocabulary, is available online at **www.PHLitOnline.com.**

GPS[1] Quick-Start Guide

User's Guide

Features:
- instructions for how to operate a device
- explanations of the different functions and features of the device and how to access them
- diagrams, illustrations, or photographs of the device
- text written for a specific audience

The features of the Map Page are defined and explained. Instructions are provided for how to utilize them.

Using the Find Feature:

1. Tap the **Find** icon on the Map Page tool bar to display the Find Menu.
2. Then select a category icon and tap it to open the search list. To narrow the elist of items, tap the second field to display the list of search options. Choose "Near Current Location".
3. To shorten the list even more, tap the category field to display a list of sub-categories to refine the type of map item you are searching for.
4. Select the desired destination and tap to highlight it. Then tap the **Routes** icon at bottom of the page to begin route calculation. From the pop-up options window, select the calculation preference and then tap **OK** to complete route calculation.
5. When complete the route will be displayed on the Map Page along with navigation instructions and voice prompts.

Two sets of instructions are provided. The steps are numbered, and icons highlight key actions.

Managing a Route

Once you have selected a destination and calculated a route, you can modify the route, preview turns, and save it for later reuse.

1. Tap the **Routes** icon on the Map Page tool bar to display the Routes Page. Then tap the desired **Routes Options** icon.
2. Tap the **Turns Page** to view a list of turns for the route. Tape a turn entry to preview the turn on the map.
3. Tap **Recalculate** if you have left the route and want to calculate from your current location.
4. Tap the **Detour** icon if you want to detour the route around a traffic jam or road construction.
5. Tap the **Stop Navigation** icon if you want to quit the route.
6. Tap the **Route Preferences** icon if you want to change the way a route is managed in order to meet your personal requirements.
7. Tap **Edit Vias** if you want to add some new points to alter your route.
8. Tap **Saved Routes** if you want to save the current route or view a previously saved route.
9. Tap **Speak** if you want to listen to current route status voice prompts.

1. **GPS** An abbreviation that stands for Global Positioning System, a navigational system based on receiving signals from satellites orbiting earth.

Differentiated Instruction for Universal Access

Background for Special Needs Students

Before students read the GPS Quick-Start Guide, build background knowledge about the Global Positioning System. Explain that GPS units can tell you to within a few feet where you are currently located and can also tell how to get from your current location to another place. Tell students that GPS units are often found in vehicles but are also available as handheld units. Provide an explanation of how the GPS works:

- A GPS unit sends radio signals to satellites in orbit around the Earth.
- The unit determines current location by analyzing the radio signals sent back from the satellites.
- The GPS unit then marks the location on electronic maps that have been pre-stored in the unit.

About User's Guides

1. Have students read the features of User's guides shown in the box on the student page.
2. Then, **ask** students to name some items that come with user's guides.
   Possible responses: Students may name videogame players, cell phones, digital music players, or other electronic devices.
3. Tell students that this user's guide describes how to use a GPS, a Global Positioning System, to find your way from one location to another.

Follow and Critique Technical Directions

1. Point out that two sets of instructions are given below the headings, "Using the Find Feature" and "Managing a Route." Have a volunteer read aloud the note that calls attention to the numbered steps and highlighted icons in each set of instructions.
   Ask: Why do you think key actions in the instructions are highlighted with icons?
   Possible response: The instructions use the same icons that are shown on the GPS unit itself so users will know which icon to touch on the GPS screen.
2. Have students read the set of instructions below "Using the Find Feature." Tell them that some categories likely to be shown on the Find Menu are restaurants, shopping centers, hotels, businesses, hospitals, tourist attractions, and airports.
   Ask: Once you choose a destination, which icon do you tap to get directions to that destination?
   Answer: Tap the Routes icon.
3. Have students read the set of instructions below "Managing a Route." **Ask:** What are some options users have once they have chosen a route?
   Answer: Users can see a list of turns for the route, recalculate the route, detour the route, stop using the route, add new places to the route, save the route, and listen to spoken voice prompts for the route.
4. Discuss the meaning of *via*, "by way of." Point out that the "Edit Vias" icon allows users to include places that they can go "by way of" on the route to their destination.

Follow and Critique Technical Directions

1. Point out the graphic at the top of the page. Explain that graphics help users understand how to use the unit by showing them what they will see on the unit's screen.
2. Discuss the information given on this page. **Ask:** What do you learn about using the GPS unit from reading this page?
Answer: You learn how to navigate using the Map Page, how to navigate to a destination, and how to use the Map Pointer.
3. Have students finish reading the GPS user's guide. **Ask:** Do you think a user might be confused when reading the instructions for using the map pointer? Why?
Possible responses: Yes, because step 4 mentions a pop-up window with preferences, but the instructions don't describe the preferences; No, because the instructions are numbered so you can follow them step by step.

Reflecting on the Reading Skill

Have students think about the format and structure of each document. **Ask** them how analyzing the format and structure helped them critique the logic of the documents and understand how to follow the instructions.
Possible response: Students should indicate that the title, illustration, and section headings helped them understand where information could be found in the technical directions. Students should indicate that the headings, numbered steps, highlighted icons, and graphics helped them understand how the user's guide is organized.

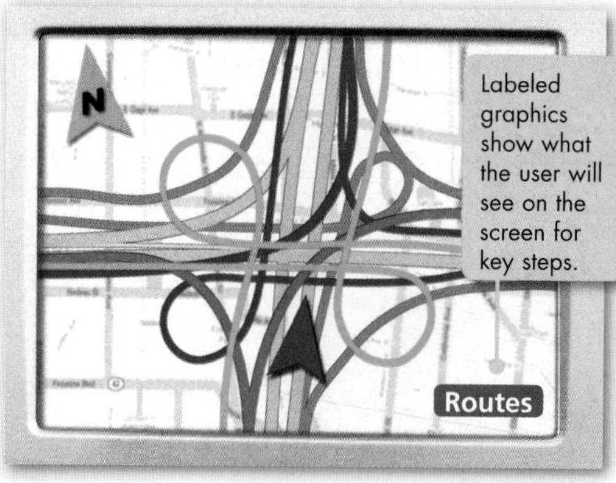

Labeled graphics show what the user will see on the screen for key steps.

Navigation Using the Map Page

Navigation is the process of going from your current location to another, and the Map Page has features to help you do that.

Data Fields—Provide GPS Status when not moving, Direction of Travel or Next Street Ahead, Compass Direction, Speed and Current Location

Map Detail—With downloaded detailed maps: Residential Streets, Rivers, Lakes, Points of Interest and Individual Addresses. Oriented with North Up unless in Track Up mode.

The Position Arrow—Indicates your current location. Tap to center it on the map page. Points in the direction of travel.

The Map Pointer—Marks map locations using the stylus. Displays information for a location if available.

The Map Scale—Tapping the Map Scale Box in the lower left corner of the map displays the moving Map Scale. Tap the arrows to move up or down the scale. Tap the desired scale to close.

Navigating to a Destination

A destination can be determined in two ways: you use the Map Pointer to mark a point on the map and then tap the Routes icon . . . or use the Find Feature to search for a destination form the map database and then, when found and highlighted, choose the "Route To It" option from the Find Options Menu.

Using the Map Pointer:

1. Tap the point on the Map Page that you want to navigate to. If there is information about that point in the map database, it will display next to the point.
2. Then tap the **Routes** con to display the Routes Page.
3. Tap the "Route To" field and the route will begin to calculate.
4. A pop-up window will offer three preferences for calculating the route. Select an option and tap **OK** to return to the Map Page to complete calculation.
5. When the calculation is complete, the route will display as a purple overlay on top of the map.
6. The first maneuver on your route is displayed at the top of the map page and is complemented by a voice prompt.
7. To view all of the turns on the route, open the Routes Page and tap the **Turns Page** icon. A list of turns will display and a preview page for each turn will display when the turn on the list is tapped.

What kind of knowledge changes our lives?
(a) What problem is solved by using a GPS unit? **(b)** Do you think GPS units can improve our lives? Explain.

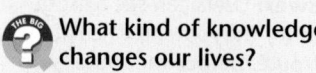

ASSESS/EXTEND

Answers

What kind of knowledge changes our lives?

Possible responses:
(a) The unit helps to figure out which route to take when traveling.
(b) GPS units can help us save time by mapping and recalculating travel routes.

Vocabulary Development

Vocabulary from Computer Science

Tell students that user's guides may contain words specific to the type of device being described. This GPS user's guide contains words that are used to describe electronic devices. Many features of electronic devices are also found on computer software applications. Specialized terms are used to describe these features. To clarify these terms, review these words and phrases and their meanings with students:

database: an organized collection of electronic data that can be easily searched

downloaded: moved a file or document from a Web site to a personal computer or other electronic device

pop-up window: a small window that appears on top of a computer screen's main window and offers options or menu choices for a user to select

stylus: a pointed instrument used for input on a touch-sensitive screen

Test Practice: Informational Texts

Comparing Informational Texts

(a) Critique the logic of the **technical directions** and user's guide by describing elements you think might be confusing for readers to follow.
(b) When you compare the format and **sequence of information** in the two documents, which one do you find has the more logical structure? Explain your response.

Timed Writing

Write a Persuasive Letter

Format and Audience
The prompt gives instructions to write a letter. Because the letter will be addressed to a business, the tone should be formal.

Write a letter in which you request a repair under warranty for your compass. In your letter, describe a specific problem with the compass. Then, cite details from the warranty to explain the reasons you believe that the repair is covered. (20 minutes)

Academic Vocabulary
When you *describe* something, you use precise words to create a vivid picture in your reader's mind.

5-Minute Planner

Complete these steps before you begin to write:

1. Read the prompt carefully and completely.
2. Reread the technical directions to identify a problem that might occur with the compass. Then, decide on the repair that you will request the manufacturer to perform, and make notes about how you will describe the problem.
3. Reread the compass warranty to be sure that the repair you are requesting is covered. Then, note passages that show why the company is obligated to make the repair.
4. Decide how you will structure your letter. For example, you might include a brief introductory paragraph before presenting the reasons why the company should repair your compass. **TIP** Remember that your letter will be more convincing if you present information in a logical order.
5. Use your notes to prepare a quick outline, based on the structure you have chosen. Refer to your outline as you draft your letter.

Extend the Lesson

Connecting to the Students' World

To give students more practice with technical directions and user's guides and to help them apply the lesson to their own world, divide students into small groups. Have each group choose a type of technical equipment or an electronic device with which they are very familiar. Have group members write precise technical directions for using the equipment or create a user's guide for the device. Tell students to include step-by-step instructions and information about the important features. Encourage students to include hand-drawn or computer-generated illustrations. Have group members give a class presentation, using their written directions or guides to demonstrate how to use the device. Have classmates critique the group's technical directions or user's guide, noting any elements that are confusing and that may be misunderstood.

ASSESS/EXTEND

Answers

Comparing Informational Texts

(a) Possible response: Readers might be confused by the Easy as 1-2-3 section in the technical directions. After a person reads his or her direction in degrees in step 2, step 3 gives no further mention of the direction in degrees and what to do with it. It seems like a step is missing. In the user's guide, the Navigation Using the Map Page section may confuse readers. It lists and describes features of the Map Page, but it does not show the features in the graphic. The reader might not be sure where to find or how to use these features.

(b) Some students may say that the user's guide has the more logical structure because it breaks the instructions into many clear steps, which define every point. Other students may say the structure of the technical directions is more logical because it includes pictures of each instruction in the first section; the user's guide only includes icons and a graphic of the GPS screen.

Timed Writing

1. Before students complete the activity, guide them in identifying and analyzing key words and phrases in the prompt, highlighted on the student page.
2. Work with students to draw up guidelines for their letters based on the key words:
   - Focus The letter should clearly describe a specific problem with the compass and request a repair.
   - Organization The letter should present, in a logical order, the problem with the compass, the requested repair, and the reasons that the writer believes the repair is covered under warranty.
   - Support The letter should cite details from the warranty to explain the belief that the repair is covered.
   - Style The letter will be addressed to a business, so it should be written in a formal style.
3. Have students use the 5-Minute Planner to structure their time.
4. Allow students 20 minutes to complete the assignment. Evaluate their work using the guidelines they have developed.

PRETEACH

Meeting Your Standards

Students will

1. analyze and respond to humorous writing.
2. compare a humorous essay and a humorous speech of two authors.
3. write a comparison of humorous writing.

Log on at ***www.PHLitOnline.com*** *for a detailed lesson plan for Comparing Literary Works.*

❶ Comparing Humorous Writing

1. Introduce the skill using the instruction on the student page.
2. Give students a copy of **Comparing Humorous Writing Graphic Organizer B,** ***Graphic Organizer Transparencies,*** p. 89. Tell them they will fill it in as they read.

Think Aloud: Model the Skill

Model a way of recognizing techniques for creating humor in writing. Say to students:

If a character says, "I can stretch my arms out and touch the next town," the author is using *hyperbole* to exaggerate the size of the town. If a character says, "That pyramid looks like it took a while to build," the author is using *understatement.* When I recognize the techniques used in humorous writing, it helps me understand how the author feels about a subject.

❷ Vocabulary

1. Have students say each word aloud.
2. Then, use the word in a sentence that defines the word. Repeat the sentence, now with the word missing, and have the class "fill in the blank" chorally.

For more guidance, see the ***Classroom Strategies and Teaching Routines*** card, **Introducing Selection Vocabulary.**

Comparing Literary Works

A Toast to the Oldest Inhabitant • The Dog That Bit People

❶ Comparing Humorous Writing

In a **humorous essay** or **speech**, a writer presents a subject in an unexpected, amusing way. The writer may treat a serious situation lightly or a ridiculous situation seriously. Techniques for creating humor include the following.

- Using **hyperbole,** or exaggeration, a writer describes people, things, or events as if they were much more important than they are—for instance, calling the discovery of a missing sock a "joyous reunion."
- Using **understatement,** a writer speaks of people, things, or events as if they were less important than they are—for instance, saying that "the weather was not ideal" after a tornado carries off picnic tables.

When a writer uses humor to point out the foolishness of a particular type of human behavior or of a particular institution, the result is called **satire.**

Mark Twain's speech "A Toast to the Oldest Inhabitant . . ." and James Thurber's essay "The Dog That Bit People" use humor, but their comic techniques are different. Use a chart like the one shown to compare the elements that make these selections humorous.

As you read, consider the way the selection of genre—whether story or speech—shapes the way the ideas are presented.

	Hyperbole	Understatement	Satire
Twain			
Thurber			

❷ Vocabulary

- **sumptuous** (sump´ cho͞o əs) *adj.* lavish (p. 521) ***The committee held a sumptuous dinner for the winners.*** *sumptuously adv.*
- **vagaries** (vā´ gər ēz) *n.* erratic or unpredictable actions (p. 524) ***A kite follows the vagaries of the wind.*** *vague adj.*
- **incredulity** (in´ krə do͞o´ lə tē) *n.* unwillingness to believe (p. 525) ***Experts responded to his wild ideas with incredulity.*** *incredulous adj. credulous adj*
- **irascible** (i ras´ ə bəl) *adj.* quick tempered (p. 527) ***Frustration made me irascible.***

PHLit Online! www.PHLitOnline.com

- Vocabulary flashcards
- Interactive journals
- More about the authors
- Selection audio
- Interactive graphic organizers

Vocabulary Development

Vocabulary Knowledge Rating

Create a **Vocabulary Knowledge Rating Chart** (***Professional Development Guidebook,*** p. 33) for this selection. Include the selection vocabulary and the Big Question word that appears in the Writing About the Big Question sentence starter on the next page. (The Big Question vocabulary is introduced on pp. 442–443.)

Give students a copy of the chart. Read the words aloud, and have students mark their rating in the Before Reading column. Urge them to be alert to these words as they read and discuss the selection. Tally how many students think they know a word to gauge how much instruction to provide. As students read and discuss the selection, point out the words and their context.

PHLit Online! **Vocabulary Central,** featuring tools, activities, and songs for studying vocabulary, is available online at **www.PHLitOnline.com.**

What kind of *knowledge* changes our lives?

Writing About the Big Question

In each story, the narrator tolerates something that would otherwise be intolerable—terrible weather or an exceptionally bad dog—by treating it with good humor. Think about a bad situation that you or someone else might typically experience. What knowledge might change your attitude? Use this sentence starter to develop your ideas about the Big Question.

When I need to **adapt** to a bad situation, I try to remember _________.

Meet the Authors

Mark Twain (1835–1910)

Author of "A Toast to the Oldest Inhabitant"

Mark Twain is the pen name of Samuel Langhorne Clemens, one of America's greatest writers. He is most famous for two classic novels: *The Adventures of Tom Sawyer* (1876) and *The Adventures of Huckleberry Finn* (1884).

A Standup Comic Mark Twain became a sought-after, highly paid public speaker. He delivered "A Toast to the Oldest Inhabitant . . ." at the annual dinner of the New England Society on December 22, 1876.

James Thurber (1894–1961)

Author of "The Dog That Bit People"

A native of Columbus, Ohio, James Thurber went to work for the U.S. State Department after college. Soon afterward, however, he found his true calling—he became a humorist, writing essays and drawing cartoons for *The New Yorker,* a famous magazine.

Growing Fame, Failing Vision Thurber won fame for his whimsical depictions of human (and animal) silliness. By the 1940s, though, his failing eyesight forced him to reduce the number of cartoon drawings he created. By 1952, Thurber was almost totally blind, but he still wrote stories and articles for the magazine. His collections, including *The Thurber Carnival* (1945), are considered classics of humor writing.

Daily Bellringer

For each class during which you will teach this selection, have students complete one of the five Vocabulary activities for Week 15 in the ***Daily Bellringer Activities*** booklet.

Writing About the Big Question

1. Review the assignment with the class.
2. Have students imagine that they locked themselves out of their homes. What would be the best attitude to have in this situation?
3. Have students complete the sentence starter. Review responses as a class. (**Possible response:** When I need to adapt to a bad situation, I try to remember positive ways that I have changed similar situations that I have been in.)
4. Remind students that their answers will help them think about the Big Question. Tell students that as they read, they should look for ways that knowledge helps a character deal with a challenging situation.

Concept Connector

Students will return to their sentence starter they completed before reading.

Multidraft Reading

To assist struggling readers and to deepen reading for all, apply multidraft reading protocols. For each reading, have students set the purpose indicated:

- **First reading**—literal comprehension: answering the Reading Check questions
- **Second reading**—application of skills: responding to the side-column notes
- **Third reading**—interpretation: answering the end-of-selection questions

For more guidance, refer to the ***Classroom Strategies and Teaching Routines*** card on multidraft reading.

Teaching Resources

The following resources can be used to enrich, extend, or differentiate the instruction.

- All *Unit 3 Resources,* pp. 101–117
- All *Graphic Organizer Transparencies,* pp. 88–89
- All Enriched Online Student Edition

PHLit Online! All resources, including print and audio, are available at **www.PHLitOnline.com.**

PHLit Online!

For more about the authors, practice with the selection vocabulary, and more background, go online at **www.PHLitOnline.com.**

TEACH

❶ Background

Mark Twain Born in Hannibal, Missouri, along the banks of the Mississippi River, Samuel Clemens (1835–1910) took the pen name Mark Twain. He was an apprentice printer and a steamboat pilot before he found a talent for writing humorous travel articles for various newspapers. Everywhere he went, he found humor and oddity in situations, events, and people to use as sources for his articles. Twain lived in New England for almost thirty years, during which time he endured the eccentricities of New England weather.

❷ Activating Prior Knowledge

Using the following questions as prompts, lead students in a discussion about humor in everyday life: What situations in your life have made you laugh? Why did these situations inspire laughter? How does humor make life easier to bear?

Concept Connector →

Students will return to the above discussion after they have read the selection.

❸ About the Selection

"A Toast to the Oldest Inhabitant: The Weather of New England" was first delivered as a speech to an audience intimately familiar with the patterns of New England weather. Employing mainly exaggeration, personification, and satire, Twain intertwines imaginary anecdotes about the vagaries of New England's climate to support his thesis that nowhere in the world is there daily weather as varied, bizarre, or magnificent.

❹ Critical Viewing

Possible response: Twain will tell how fierce the weather can be.

❶ A Toast to the Oldest Inhabitant: ❷ ❸ The WEATHER of New England

Mark Twain

❹ ▲ **Critical Viewing** Based on this scene, what comments do you think Twain makes about New England weather? **[Preview]**

Who can lose it and forget it?
Who can have it and regret it?
Be interposer 'twixt us Twain.[1]
—The Merchant of Venice, William Shakespeare

Gentlemen: I reverently believe that the Maker who made us all, makes everything in New England[2]—but the weather. I don't know who makes that, but I think it must be raw apprentices in the Weather Clerk's factory, who experiment and learn how in New England, for board and clothes, and then are promoted to make

1. **Twain** archaic word for "two" (and a pun on Twain's name).
2. **New England** the states of the northeastern United States: Maine, Vermont, New Hampshire, Massachusetts, Rhode Island, and Connecticut.

Vocabulary Development

Thematic Vocabulary: The Big Question

As students are discussing "A Toast to the Oldest Inhabitant: The Weather of New England," ask them to use the thematic vocabulary presented in Introducing the Big Question, pp. 442–443. You might encourage them with sentence starters like these:

1. Twain shows the *ignorance* of non-New Englanders by . . .
2. The unpredictable New England weather can *influence* . . .
3. Twain *reflects* on the beauty of . . .
4. Twain's *insight* into life in New England comes from . . .

weather for countries that require a good article, and will take their custom elsewhere if they don't get it. There is a **sumptuous** variety about the New England weather that compels the stranger's admiration—and regret. The weather is always doing something there; always attending strictly to business; always getting up new designs and trying them on the people to see how they will go. But it gets through more business in spring than in any other season. In the spring I have counted one hundred and thirty-six different kinds of weather inside of four and twenty hours. It was I that made the fame and fortune of that man that had that marvelous collection of weather on exhibition at the Centennial[3] that so astounded the foreigners. He was going to travel all over the world and get specimens from all the climes. I said, "Don't you do it; you come to New England on a favorable spring day." I told him what we could do, in the way of style, variety, and quantity. Well, he came, and he made his collection in four days. As to variety—why, he confessed that he got hundreds of kinds of weather that he had never heard of before. And as to quantity—well, after he had picked out and discarded all that was blemished in any way, he not only had weather enough, but weather to spare; weather to hire out; weather to sell; to deposit; weather to invest; weather to give to the poor.

3. **Centennial** international trade fair held in 1876 in Philadelphia to mark the hundredth anniversary of the Declaration of Independence. The fair featured scientific and technological marvels of the day.

Vocabulary
sumptuous (sump´ cho͞o əs) *adj.* lavish

Literary Analysis
Humorous Writing
What hyperbole does Twain use here to make his point about New England weather?

6 **Reading Check**
What is the main characteristic of New England weather according to Twain?

5 Literary Analysis
Humorous Writing

1. Have students discuss situations in their lives in which they would typically exaggerate when telling about them. Students may suggest how much food they eat at a meal; the amount of homework they have to do; or how hot or cold it is outside.
2. Have students read the bracketed passage. Write the word *hyperbole* on the board, and remind students that hyperbole is the use of exaggeration.
3. **Ask** the Literary Analysis question: What hyperbole does Twain use here to make his point about New England weather?
   Answer: Twain exaggerates the types of weather that occur in a single day.

6 Reading Check

Answer: New England has more varieties of weather than any other place of which Twain is aware.

Differentiated Instruction for Universal Access

Accessibility at a Glance
Use this information to guide your teaching of Twain's essay.

Context	Speech on New England weather
Language/Vocabulary	• Conversational, old-fashioned • Grade-appropriate vocabulary
Concept Level	Accessible (weather changes)
Literary Merit	Noted author
Lexile/Length	Lexile: 1030L Word Count: 1,223

PHLit Online!
This selection is available in interactive format in the **Enriched Online Student Edition,** online at **www.PHLitOnline.com,** which includes an interactive graphic organizer.

❼ Critical Viewing

Possible response: Yes, I am surprised about the variety of weather in New England, considering most areas in the United States have more reliable, stable weather patterns.

❽ Connecting to the Big Question

1. Explain to students that springtime in New England is a topic that many poets have praised in their poems.
2. Have a volunteer read the bracketed passage. **Ask:** Why would New Englanders get upset with poets who write about springtime in New England?
   Possible response: New Englanders have the knowledge of living through the harsh winter that precedes the springtime, and, therefore, they can appreciate the season in ways others cannot.
3. **Ask:** If an outsider had the knowledge of a New Englander, would his or her attitude toward springtime in New England change? Explain.
   Possible response: Yes, an outsider would be able to understand what it means to endure a New England winter and, therefore, be able to truly admire the oncoming spring.

❾ Critical Thinking

Compare and Contrast

1. Have students read the bracketed passage. Explain to them that "Old Probabilities" is the weather forecaster.
2. **Ask** them to tell how the forecaster appears when he reports the weather in the rest of the country. Explain how it is different when he reports the weather for New England.
   Answer: Old Probabilities is crisp and confident when predicting the weather in other parts of the country, but he is compared with a shame-faced dog when predicting the weather in New England.
3. **Ask** students to explain why this passage is humorous.
   Answer: The passage is humorous because Twain uses hyperbole to exaggerate the confidence of the weather forecaster.

▼ **Critical Viewing**
❼ Are you surprised there is such a wide variety of weather in such a small area of the United States? Why or why not?. **[Make a Judgment]**

❽ The people of New England are by nature patient and forbearing; but there are some things which they will not stand. Every year they kill a lot of poets for writing about "Beautiful Spring." These are generally casual visitors, who bring their notions of spring from somewhere else, and cannot, of course, know how the natives feel about spring. And so, the first thing they know, the opportunity to inquire how they feel has permanently gone by.

❾ Old Probabilities has a mighty reputation for accurate prophecy, and thoroughly well deserves it. You take up the papers and observe how crisply and confidently he checks off what today's weather is going to be on the Pacific, down South, in the Middle States, in the Wisconsin region; see him sail along in the joy and pride of his power till he gets to New England, and then—see his tail drop. He doesn't know what the weather is going to be like in New England. He can't any more tell than he can tell how many Presidents of the United States there's going to be next year.[4] Well, he mulls over it, and by and by he gets out something about like this: Probable nor'-east to sou'-west winds, varying to the southard and westard and eastard and points between; high and low barometer, swapping around from place to place; probable

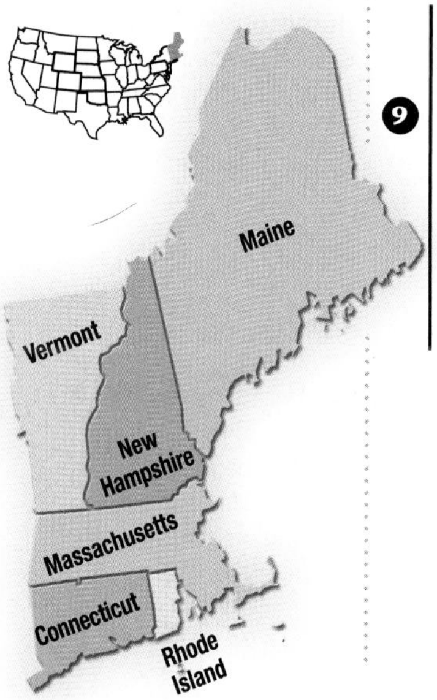

4. **how many Presidents of the United States there's going to be next year** The United States presidential election of 1876 was one of the most disputed, with two declared "winners" when Twain gave this speech. Rutherford B. Hayes was declared the final victor on March 2, 1877.

Think Aloud

Vocabulary: Using Context

Direct students' attention to the word *prophecy* on this page. Using the following "think aloud," model how to use context to infer the meaning of an unknown word. Say to students:

> I'm going to think aloud to show you how I would figure out the meaning of *prophecy* from its context.
>
> In this sentence, *prophecy* is a noun that is modified by the adjective *accurate*. The word is also associated with Twain's satirical name of a weather forecaster, "Old Probabilities." I know that a weather forecaster tries to accurately predict the weather. In the next sentence, Twain indicates that the forecaster can predict the weather accurately in all parts of the nation except New England. From this evidence, I think that the word *prophecy* means "a forecast or prediction."

areas of rain, snow, hail, and drought, succeeded or preceded by earthquakes, with thunder and lightning. Then he jots down this postscript from his wandering mind, to cover accidents: "But it is possible that the program may be wholly changed in the meantime."

Yes, one of the brightest gems in the New England weather is the dazzling uncertainty of it. There is only one thing certain about it, you are certain there is going to be plenty of weather—a perfect grand review; but you never can tell which end of the procession is going to move first. You fix up for the drought; you leave your umbrella in the house and sally out with your sprinkling pot, and ten to one you get drowned. You make up your mind that the earthquake is due; you stand from under, and take hold of something to steady yourself, and the first thing you know, you get struck by lightning. These are great disappointments. But they can't be helped. The lightning there is peculiar; it is so convincing! When it strikes a thing, it doesn't leave enough of that thing behind for you to tell whether—well, you'd think it was something valuable, and a Congressman had been there.

And the thunder. When the thunder commences to merely tune up, and scrape, and saw, and key up the instruments for the performance, strangers say, "Why, what awful thunder you have here!" But when the baton is raised and the real concert begins, you'll find that stranger down in the cellar, with his head in the ash barrel.

Now, as to the size of the weather in New England—lengthways, I mean. It is utterly disproportioned to the size of that little country. Half the time, when it is packed as full as it can stick, you will see that New England weather sticking out beyond the edges and projecting around hundreds and hundreds of miles over the neighboring states. She can't hold a tenth part of her weather. You can see cracks all about, where she has strained herself trying to do it.

I could speak volumes about the inhuman perversity of the New England weather, but I will give but a single specimen. I like to hear rain on a tin roof, so I covered part of my roof with tin, with an eye to that luxury. Well, sir, do you think it ever rains on the tin? No, sir; skips it every time.

Mind, in this speech I have been trying merely to do honor to the New England weather—no language could do it justice. But, after all, there are at least one or two things about that weather (or, if you please, effects produced by it) which we residents would not like to part with. If we hadn't our bewitching autumn foliage, we should still have to credit the weather with one

Literary Analysis
Humorous Writing
How does Twain use understatement here to add humor?

Literary Analysis
Humorous Writing
What does Twain satirically imply about congressmen in this paragraph?

Yes, one of the brightest gems in the New England weather is the dazzling uncertainty of it.

12 **Reading Check**
According to Twain, how easy is it to predict New England weather?

Fluency

Distribute a copy of page 523, and pair students. Read selected passages with expression as students track, or follow along by pointing at each word in the text. Have students then read the passage back. Look for these problem spots:

- If students have difficulty with the long sentences, have them break up the sentence into two parts. For example, explain that semicolons are used to break up two independent clauses.
- If students have difficulty with the word *specimen,* remind them to use context clues. Point out that they can look for context clues in the sentence, such as *single.*
- If students have difficulty pronouncing the word *bewitching,* have them cover up parts of the word with their thumbs. First, have them pronounce *be-*, then *-witch,* and finally *-ing.* Now, have students blend all the syllables together to pronounce the word.

10 Literary Analysis
Humorous Writing

1. Remind students that the opposite of *hyperbole,* or exaggeration, is *understatement,* or the presentation of an event, a situation, or a person as if it were less than it actually is.
2. Have a volunteer explain how understatement produces humor. Point out that the reader knows more than what is written and, thus, is in on the joke with the writer.
3. Have a student read the bracketed passage aloud while other students read along.
4. **Ask** the first Literary Analysis question: How does Twain use understatement here to add humor?
   Answer: Twain uses understatement to describe reactions to errant forecasts. To be drowned rather than parched or to be struck by lightning rather than shaken by an earthquake are described as "great disappointments."

11 Literary Analysis
Humorous Writing

1. Write the word *satire* on the board and have a volunteer define the term (the use of humor to show that the writer considers the behaviors of a person or an institution foolish and ridiculous).
2. Have students read the bracketed passage. **Ask:** What does Twain point out about lightning in New England?
   Answer: Lightning in New England is so damaging that it leaves no trace of what it strikes.
3. **Ask** the second Literary Analysis question: What does Twain satirically imply about congressmen in this paragraph?
   Answer: Twain implies that congressmen do not have any value.

12 Reading Check

Answer: According to Twain, predicting New England weather is impossible.

⓭ Literary Analysis
Humorous Writing

Ask the Literary Analysis question: What makes this paragraph different from the rest of the essay?
Answer: After insisting that New England weather is harsh, ugly, and unpredictable, Twain now glorifies it by describing the beauty of the ice storm.

Concept Connector

Have students compare the Writing About the Big Question responses and their responses to the class discussion they had before reading the speech with their ideas after reading.

ASSESS

Answers

Critical Thinking

1. Students may cite the description of the weather as a product of apprentices at the Weather Clerk's factory; or how the rain never falls on Twain's tin roof.
2. (a) The lavish, extensive variety of New England weather produces admiration. (b) New England can produce every type of weather in a short period of time.
3. (a) Old Probabilities is an imaginary weather forecaster.
(b) Twain satirizes forecasters who approximate the next day's weather, even though they make their predictions sound as if they are accurate.
4. Yes, the magnificence and glory of the ice storm overwhelms all Twain's previous complaints.

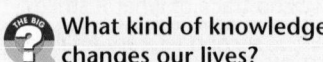

What kind of knowledge changes our lives?

Possible response: The narrator knows that the ever-changing environment will provide beautiful, unpredictable scenes.

PHLit Online!

This selection is available in interactive format in the **Enriched Online Student Edition**, online at **www.PHLitOnline.com**, which includes an interactive graphic organizer.

Vocabulary
vagaries (vā′ gər ēz) *n.* erratic or unpredictable actions

Literary Analysis
Humorous Writing
What makes this paragraph different from the rest of the essay?

feature which compensates for all its bullying vagaries—the ice storm—when a leafless tree is clothed with ice from the bottom to the top—ice that is as bright and clear as crystal; when every bough and twig is strung with ice beads, frozen dewdrops, and the whole tree sparkles, cold and white, like the Shah[5] of Persia's diamond plume. Then the wind waves the branches, and the sun comes out and turns all those myriads of beads and drops to prisms, that glow and burn and flash with all manner of colored fires, which change and change again, with inconceivable rapidity, from blue to red, from red to green, and green to gold—the tree becomes a spraying fountain, a very explosion of dazzling jewels; and it stands there the acme, the climax, the supremest possibility in art or nature, of bewildering, intoxicating, intolerable magnificence! One cannot make the words too strong.

Month after month I lay up my hate and grudge against the New England weather; but when the ice storm comes at last, I say: "There—I forgive you, now—the books are square between us, you don't owe me a cent; go, and sin no more; your little faults and foibles count for nothing—you are the most enchanting weather in the world!"

5. **Shah** (shä) *n.* formerly, the title of the ruler of Persia (now Iran).

Critical Thinking

1. **Respond:** Which part of Twain's essay did you find most clever or amusing? Explain.
2. **(a)** According to Twain, what quality or feature of New England weather "compels the stranger's admiration"? **(b) Connect:** What point does Twain support with the story of the man who collected and exhibited weather?
3. **(a) Infer:** What is the profession of "Old Probabilities"?
(b) Interpret: What point is Twain making in the anecdote about this character?
4. **Interpret:** For Twain, does the ice storm make up for the rest of New England weather? Explain.

What kind of knowledge changes our lives?
In this selection, the narrator is able to tolerate the unpredictable weather of New England, despite his proclaimed hatred of it. What knowledge allows him to appreciate New England's tumultuous weather?

Vocabulary Development

Latin Word Origins

Call students' attention to the word *vagaries* and its definition, "erratic or unpredictable actions." Explain that the word comes from the Latin word *vagari,* which means "to wander."

Invite students to brainstorm a list of English words that derive from the Latin word *vagary,* such as *vagrant, vagabond, vague,* and *vagility.* Have students discuss what the words have in common and make educated guesses about each word's meaning. Finally, have them check the dictionary for the definition of each word.

The Dog (14) That (15) Bit (16) People

Nobody Knew Exactly What Was the Matter with Him, James Thurber

James Thurber

Probably no one man should have as many dogs in his life as I have had, but there was more pleasure than distress in them for me except in the case of an Airedale named Muggs. He gave me more trouble than all the other fifty-four or -five put together, although my moment of keenest embarrassment was the time a Scotch terrier named Jeannie, who had just had six puppies in the clothes closet of a fourth floor apartment in New York, had the unexpected seventh and last at the corner of Eleventh Street and Fifth Avenue during a walk she had insisted on taking. Then, too, there was the prize winning French poodle, a great big black poodle—none of your little, untroublesome white miniatures—who got sick riding in the rumble seat[1] of a car with me on her way to the Greenwich Dog Show. She had a red rubber bib tucked around her throat and, since a rain storm came up when we were halfway through the Bronx, I had to hold over her a small green umbrella, really more of a parasol. The rain beat down fearfully and suddenly the driver of the car drove into a big garage, filled with mechanics. It happened so quickly that I forgot to put the umbrella down and I will always remember, with sickening distress, the look of incredulity mixed with hatred that came over the face of the particular hardened garage man that came over to see what we

(17) ▲ **Critical Viewing**
Which elements of this drawing by Thurber suggest that Muggs has a difficult personality? **[Analyze]**

Vocabulary
incredulity
(in′ krə do͞o′ lə tē) *n.* unwillingness to believe

(18) **Reading Check**
What does Thurber say was his most embarrassing moment?

1. **rumble seat** *n.* in some early automobiles, an open seat in the rear, behind the roofed seat, which could be folded shut when not in use.

Differentiated Instruction for Universal Access

Accessibility at a Glance
Use this information to guide your teaching of "The Dog That Bit People."

Context	Essay on a family dog
Language/Vocabulary	• Conversational • Grade-appropriate vocabulary
Concept Level	Accessible
Literary Merit	Noted humorist
Lexile/Length	Lexile: 1,180L Word Count: 2,287

(14) Background

James Thurber Thurber loved the English language and was constantly at war with those who sought to reduce it to nonsensical babble, jingles, and slang. To his mind, "automation"(a neologism) and "spectacular"(as a noun) were some of the signs of the End of the World. Today, he is well known for his sketches of sad-faced animals and frustrated humans trying to deal with zany situations. The cartoon of Muggs is typical of his cartoon style.

(15) Activating Prior Knowledge

Thurber once wrote, "The dog has seldom been successful in pulling man up to its level of sagacity, but man has frequently dragged the dog down to his." Write Thurber's quotation on the board and lead students in a discussion of what Thurber meant. Then, invite students to share stories about pets from their own lives. Ask students what human traits they would assign to their pets, such as *humorous, annoying, lovable,* or *silly*. Have students explain why humorous pet behaviors or habits are funny.

Concept Connector →

Students will return to the above discussion after they have read the selection.

(16) About the Selection

In "The Dog That Bit People," Thurber uses exaggeration and contrast to achieve humor. He also uses understatement, irony, absurdity, and digression to keep readers chuckling. Thurber demonstrates that humor is a combination of the keen observation of details and a unique style of reporting these details.

(17) Critical Viewing

Answer: Muggs's eyes, frown, and posture suggest a difficult personality.

(18) Reading Check

Answer: Thurber was most embarrassed when Jeannie, his Scotch terrier, gave birth to a puppy, while he was walking her.

⓳ Literary Analysis
Humorous Writing

1. Remind students that one humorous technique is *understatement.*
2. Have a volunteer read the bracketed passage aloud.
3. **Ask** students to respond to the first Literary Analysis prompt: Explain how Thurber uses understatement when comparing Muggs's treatment of family and strangers.
   Answer: Although Thurber says that Muggs bites everyone except Mother, he cites the "advantage" that the dog bites family members less often.

⓴ Literary Analysis
Humorous Writing

1. Remind students that writers often use hyperbole, or exaggeration, for humorous effect.
2. Have students read the bracketed passage and fill in their graphic organizers.
3. Then, **ask** the second Literary Analysis question: Which details in this paragraph seem to be hyperboles?
   Answer: Thurber seems to be using hyperbole when he claims his mother sent a box of candy to forty or more people whom their dog bit that year; when several people try to poison Muggs; when Major Moberly takes a shot at Muggs in the middle of New York City; and when the congressman returned the candy because he suspected it was trick candy.

PHLit Online!

This selection is available in interactive format in the **Enriched Online Student Edition**, online at **www.PHLitOnline.com,** which includes an interactive graphic organizer.

wanted, when he took a look at me and the poodle. All garage men, and people of that intolerant stripe, hate poodles with their curious hair cut, especially the pom-poms that you got to leave on their hips if you expect the dogs to win a prize.

But the Airedale, as I have said, was the worst of all my dogs. He really wasn't my dog, as a matter of fact: I came home from a vacation one summer to find that my brother Roy had bought him while I was away. A big, burly, choleric dog, he always acted as if he thought I wasn't one of the family. There was a slight advantage in being one of the family, for he didn't bite the family as often as he bit strangers. Still, in the years that we had him he bit everybody but mother, and he made a pass at her once but missed. That was during the month when we suddenly had mice, and Muggs refused to do anything about them. Nobody ever had mice exactly like the mice we had that month. They acted like pet mice, almost like mice somebody had trained. They were so friendly that one night when mother entertained at dinner the Friraliras, a club she and my father had belonged to for twenty years, she put down a lot of little dishes with food in them on the pantry floor so that the mice would be satisfied with that and wouldn't come into the dining room. Muggs stayed out in the pantry with the mice, lying on the floor, growling to himself—not at the mice, but about all the people in the next room that he would have liked to get at. Mother slipped out into the pantry once to see how everything was going. Everything was going fine. It made her so mad to see Muggs lying there, oblivious of the mice—they came running up to her—that she slapped him and he slashed at her, but didn't make it. He was sorry immediately, mother said. He was always sorry, she said, after he bit someone, but we could not understand how she figured this out. He didn't act sorry.

Literary Analysis
Humorous Writing
Explain how Thurber uses understatement when comparing Muggs's treatment of family and strangers. ⓳

Mother used to send a box of candy every Christmas to the people the Airedale bit. The list finally contained forty or more names. Nobody could understand why we didn't get rid of the dog. I didn't understand it very well myself, but we didn't get rid of him. I think that one or two people tried to poison Muggs—he acted poisoned once in a while—and old Major Moberly fired at him once with his service revolver near the Seneca Hotel in East Broad Street—but Muggs lived to be almost eleven years old and even when he could hardly get around he bit a Congressman who had called to see my father on business. My mother had never liked the Congressman—she said the signs of his horoscope showed he couldn't be trusted (he was Saturn with the moon in Virgo)—but she sent him a box of candy that Christmas. He sent it right back, probably because he suspected it was trick candy. Mother

⓴

Literary Analysis
Humorous Writing
Which details in this paragraph seem to be hyperboles?

Vocabulary Development

Selection Vocabulary Reinforcement

Students will benefit from additional examples and practice with the selection vocabulary words. Reinforce their comprehension with "show-you-know" sentences. The first part of the sentence uses the vocabulary word in an appropriate context. The second part of the sentence—the "show-you-know" part—clarifies the first. Model the strategy with this example for *incredulity*:

The bank teller had a look of *incredulity* on his face as the woman made a deposit; he couldn't believe she handed him a paper bag full of one-thousand dollar bills.

1. The five-star meal was the most sumptuous he had ever experienced; ____________.
   Sample answer: he felt like a prince eating dinner in a grand palace.
2. The elderly man had an *irascible* manner; ____________.
   Sample answer: he was easily irritated.

20 persuaded herself it was all for the best that the dog had bitten him, even though father lost an important business association because of it. "I wouldn't be associated with such a man," mother said, "Muggs could read him like a book."

We used to take turns feeding Muggs to be on his good side, but that didn't always work. He was never in a very good humor, even after a meal. Nobody knew exactly what was the matter with him, but whatever it was it made him irascible, especially in the mornings. Roy never felt very well in the morning, either, especially before breakfast, and once when he came downstairs and found that Muggs had moodily chewed up the morning paper he hit him in the face with a grapefruit and then jumped up on the dining room table, scattering dishes and silverware and spilling the coffee. Muggs' first free leap carried him all the way across the table and into a brass fire screen in front of the gas grate but he was back on his feet in a moment and in the end he got Roy and gave him a pretty vicious bite in the leg. Then he was all over it; he never bit anyone more than once at a time. Mother always mentioned that as an argument in his favor; she said he had a quick temper but that he didn't hold a grudge. She was forever defending him. I think she liked him because he wasn't well. "He's not strong," she would say, pityingly, but that was inaccurate; he may not have been well but he was terribly strong.

21 One time my mother went to the Chittenden Hotel to call on a woman mental healer who was lecturing in Columbus on the subject of "Harmonious Vibrations." She wanted to find out if it was possible to get harmonious vibrations into a dog. "He's a large tan-colored Airedale," mother explained. The woman said that she had never treated a dog but she advised my mother to hold the thought that he did not bite and would not bite. Mother was holding the thought the very next morning when Muggs got the iceman but she blamed that slip-up on the iceman. "If you didn't think he would bite you, he wouldn't," mother told him. He stomped out of the house in a terrible jangle of vibrations.

23 One morning when Muggs bit me slightly, more or less in passing, I reached down and grabbed his short stumpy tail and hoisted him into the air. It was a foolhardy thing to do and the last time I saw my mother, about six months ago, she said she didn't know what possessed me. I don't either, except that I was pretty mad. As long as I held the dog off the floor by his tail he couldn't get at me, but he twisted and jerked so, snarling all the time, that I realized I couldn't hold him that way very long. I carried him to the kitchen and flung him onto the floor and shut the door on him just as he crashed against it. But I forgot about the backstairs.

Vocabulary
irascible (i ras´ ə bəl) *adj.* quick tempered

22 **Reading Check**
How does Muggs generally respond to people?

21 Critical Thinking
Draw Conclusions

1. Have students recall that Thurber's mother, more than anyone else in the family, loves Muggs.
2. Have students read the bracketed passage.
3. **Ask:** Using evidence from the essay, what conclusions can be drawn from Mother's decision to seek the help of a mental healer? **Possible response:** Mother thinks that Muggs is special, and she does not trust that a veterinarian or doctor will recognize Muggs's special features. She is afraid a vet will recommend that the dog be tied up, sent to dog-training school, or sent away.

22 Reading Check

Answer: Muggs generally bites, or tries to bite, every person he encounters.

Differentiated Instruction for Universal Access

Strategy for Special Needs Students
Encourage students to skim through the first two pages of the selection, listing Thurber's descriptive, colorful words. For example, they may list "white miniatures," "red rubber bib," or "parasol." Make sure students can define each word. Then, discuss how each word adds humor to the essay.

Enrichment for Gifted/Talented Students
Have each student choose a passage that contains a colorful and humorous description. Then, ask each student to draw a cartoon that illustrates the passage. The cartoon should contain specific details from the passage and a humorous caption. When students finish, have volunteers share their cartoons with the class. Display the cartoons in the classroom.

㉓ Critical Thinking

Support

1. Write the word *personification* on the board. Have a volunteer define the word (human traits assigned to an inanimate object or animal).
2. Have a volunteer read the bracketed passage.
3. **Ask** students to offer examples of human traits Muggs displays. **Answer:** Muggs is personified with the human trait of anger or vengefulness. We see this when he bites Thurber as well as when he reacts with vengeful rage to being picked up by the tail. Muggs also attacks Mrs. Detweiler when she is seated in the living room.

㉔ Critical Viewing

Possible response: Muggs's behavior and his intimidating expression agree with Thurber's description of the dog. However, Muggs appears to be neatly positioned, with each paw carefully placed on either side of the plate, in contrast to the wild behavior described by Thurber.

Muggs at His Meals Was an Unusual Sight, James Thurber

㉔ ▲ **Critical Viewing** How does this drawing of Muggs compare and contrast with the behavior described in the essay? **[Compare and Contrast]**

㉓ Muggs went up the backstairs and down the frontstairs and had me cornered in the living room. I managed to get up onto the mantelpiece above the fireplace, but it gave way and came down with a tremendous crash throwing a large marble clock, several vases, and myself heavily to the floor. Muggs was so alarmed by the racket that when I picked myself up he had disappeared. We couldn't find him anywhere, although we whistled and shouted, until old Mrs. Detweiler called after dinner that night. Muggs had bitten her once, in the leg, and she came into the living room only after we assured her that Muggs had run away. She had just seated herself when, with a great growling and scratching of claws, Muggs emerged from under a davenport where he had been quietly hiding

Vocabulary Development

Selection Vocabulary Reinforcement

Give students sentences in which the italicized word may or may not be used correctly. Students must tell whether the use is correct and explain their answers.

1. Visitors to the Thurber household responded with *incredulity* at how Muggs was treated by Mother.
   Answer: Yes, *incredulity* means "an inability to believe," and visitors couldn't believe that Muggs was not punished for biting them.
2. When Muggs bit Thurber, his *choleric* response was to grab the dog by the tail.
   Answer: Yes, Thurber lashed out in anger at Muggs right away, and *choleric* means "having a quick temper."
3. Thurber's *irascible* mother babied her Airedale pet.
   Answer: No, *irascible* means "irritable or quick-tempered," and Thurber's mother was patient and never angry at the dog.

all the time, and bit her again. Mother examined the bite and put arnica[2] on it and told Mrs. Detweiler that it was only a bruise. "He just bumped you," she said. But Mrs. Detweiler left the house in a nasty state of mind.

Lots of people reported our Airedale to the police but my father held a municipal office at the time and was on friendly terms with the police. Even so, the cops had been out a couple of times—once
25 when Muggs bit Mrs. Rufus Sturtevant and again when he bit Lieutenant-Governor Malloy—but mother told them that it hadn't been Muggs' fault but the fault of the people who were bitten. "When he starts for them, they scream," she explained, "and that excites him." The cops suggested that it might be a good idea to tie the dog up, but mother said that it mortified him to be tied up and that he wouldn't eat when he was tied up.

Literary Analysis
Humorous Writing Which details here suggest that Thurber is satirizing pet owners?

Muggs at his meals was an unusual sight. Because of the fact that if you reached toward the floor he would bite you, we usually put his food plate on top of an old kitchen table with a bench alongside the table. Muggs would stand on the bench and eat. I remember that my mother's Uncle Horatio, who boasted that he was the third man up Missionary Ridge,[3] was splutteringly indignant when he found out that we fed the dog on a table because we were
26 afraid to put his plate on the floor. He said he wasn't afraid of any dog that ever lived and that he would put the dog's plate on the floor if we would give it to him. Roy said that if Uncle Horatio had fed Muggs on the ground just before the battle he would have been the first man up Missionary Ridge. Uncle Horatio was furious. "Bring him in! Bring him in now!" he shouted. "I'll feed the — on the floor!" Roy was all for giving him a chance, but my father wouldn't hear of it. He said that Muggs had already been fed. "I'll feed him again!" bawled Uncle Horatio. We had quite a time quieting him.

In his last year Muggs used to spend practically all of his time outdoors. He didn't like to stay in the house for some reason or other—perhaps it held too many unpleasant memories for him. Anyway, it was hard to get him to come in and as a result the garbage man, the iceman, and the laundryman wouldn't come near the house. We had to haul the garbage down to the corner, take the laundry out and bring it back, and meet the iceman a block from home. After this had gone on for some time we hit on an ingenious arrangement for getting the dog in the house so that we could lock him up while the gas meter was read, and so on. Muggs was afraid of only one thing, an electrical storm. Thunder and lightning frightened him out of his senses (I think he thought a storm had broken the day the mantelpiece fell). He would rush into the house and hide under

27 **Reading Check**
Why does Uncle Horatio get angry?

2. **arnica** (är´ ni kə) *n.* preparation once used for treating bruises.
3. **Missionary Ridge** hill near Chattanooga, Tennessee, that was the site of a Civil War battle.

Differentiated Instruction for Universal Access

Strategy for Less Proficient Readers
The nonlinear pattern of this essay may be difficult for students to follow, rendering the humor hard to understand. Suggest that students create a timeline of events in the essay. Once students understand the plot of the essay, help them understand its humor.

Enrichment for Advanced Readers
James Thurber wrote many humorous essays about his family. Suggest that students read other essays by Thurber and write reports that summarize the essays, excerpt several humorous passages, and identify the humorous techniques that Thurber employs. Have volunteers share their reports.

25 Literary Analysis
Humorous Writing
1. Remind students that one technique that a writer may use in a humorous essay is *satire.*
2. Have students read the bracketed passage and explain how the police get involved in the problem with Muggs.
3. **Ask** students whether they think that the suggestion to have Muggs tied up is reasonable and why.
Answer: Yes; what the police suggest is probably what they have told other people who own dogs that bite people.
4. Now **ask** the Literary Analysis question: Which details here suggest that Thurber is satirizing pet owners?
Answer: Thurber mocks the foolishness of pet owners when his mother insists that the people bitten are at fault rather than the dog.

26 Connecting to the Big Question
1. Remind students that knowledge often dictates the actions a person will take when in a situation.
2. Have a volunteer read the bracketed passage to the class.
3. Remind students that the family alters their home life to accommodate Muggs's violent nature. Then, **ask** students why the family allows Muggs to eat at the kitchen table.
Answer: The family knows that Muggs will not bite them if the food is placed on the table.
4. **Ask:** Would Uncle Horatio's desire to feed Muggs change if he had the same knowledge as the family? Explain.
Possible response: Yes, if Uncle Horatio had the knowledge that the family does he wouldn't try to feed Muggs. He would know that any attempt to alter Muggs's feeding habits would result in being bitten.

27 Reading Check
Answer: Uncle Horatio gets angry because he does not believe that a dog should be fed at the table, and he thinks that the family's fear of the dog is foolish.

28 Literary Analysis
Humorous Writing

1. **Ask** students to list the three humorous techniques they have discovered in Thurber's essay.
   Answer: Thurber uses understatement, hyperbole, and satire.
2. Read the bracketed passage aloud.
3. **Ask** the Literary Analysis question: Why is this anecdote about the thunder machine an example of both hyperbole and of understatement?
   Answer: Thurber exaggerates when he says, "it was the most roundabout system for running a household that was ever devised." He uses understatement when he writes, "It took a lot out of mother."

Concept Connector

Have students compare the Writing About the Big Question responses and their responses to the class discussion they had before reading the essay to their ideas after reading.

ASSESS
Answers

Critical Thinking

1. Students may point to Muggs's: attack on Roy; manner of eating; or attack on Thurber.
2. (a) Thurber picks Muggs up by the tail after the dog bites him. After letting him go, he is cornered by the dog, and he breaks the mantelpiece trying to escape. (b) Several of the family members might applaud Thurber for his bravery; his mother might punish her son for hurting the dog and breaking the mantelpiece; his father might laugh at the humor of the situation.
3. (a) **Possible response:** People do not understand the family's tolerance. (b) **Possible response:** The characters outside the family react differently to Muggs's behavior.

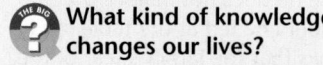

What kind of knowledge changes our lives?

Possible response: The family does not get rid of Muggs because they know how much Mother loves him.

Literary Analysis
Humorous Writing
28 Why is this anecdote about the thunder machine an example both of hyperbole and of understatement?

a bed or in a clothes closet. So we fixed up a thunder machine out of a long narrow piece of sheet iron with a wooden handle on one end. Mother would shake this vigorously when she wanted to get Muggs into the house. It made an excellent imitation of thunder, but I suppose it was the most roundabout system for running a household that was ever devised. It took a lot out of mother.

A few months before Muggs died, he got to "seeing things." He would rise slowly from the floor, growling low, and stalk stiff-legged and menacing toward nothing at all. Sometimes the Thing would be just a little to the right or left of a visitor. Once a Fuller Brush salesman[4] got hysterics. Muggs came wandering into the room like Hamlet[5] following his father's ghost. His eyes were fixed on a spot just to the left of the Fuller Brush man, who stood it until Muggs was about three slow, creeping paces from him. Then he shouted. Muggs wavered on past him into the hallway grumbling to himself but the Fuller man went on shouting. I think mother had to throw a pan of cold water on him before he stopped. That was the way she used to stop us boys when we got into fights.

Muggs died quite suddenly one night. Mother wanted to bury him in the family lot under a marble stone with some such inscription as "Flights of angels sing thee to thy rest" but we persuaded her it was against the law. In the end we just put up a smooth board above his grave along a lonely road. On the board I wrote with an indelible pencil "Cave Canem."[6] Mother was quite pleased with the simple classic dignity of the old Latin epitaph.

---

4. **Fuller Brush salesman** salesman for the Fuller Brush Company who went door-to-door demonstrating cleaning equipment; a figure celebrated in comic strips and movies of the 1920s through the 1940s.
5. **Hamlet** the main character of William Shakespeare's play *Hamlet*; in the play, he is visited by the ghost of his murdered father.
6 **"Cave Canem"** (kă′ vā kā′ nem′) Latin for "Beware of the dog."

Critical Thinking

1. **Respond:** Which story about Muggs amused you the most?
2. **(a)** Which event was Thurber's "foolhardy" experience with Muggs? **(b) Analyze:** List reactions you expect the family to have to this experience, and explain which are missing in the essay.
3. **(a) Infer:** What do other people think of the family's tolerance for Muggs's behavior? **(b) Support:** How do you know?

What kind of knowledge changes our lives?
Why do you think the family kept Muggs despite their knowledge of his bad nature?

Vocabulary Development

Vocabulary Knowledge Rating

When students have completed reading and discussing "A Toast to the Oldest Inhabitant: The New England Weather" and "The Dog That Bit People," have them take out their **Vocabulary Knowledge Rating Chart.** Read the words aloud once more, and have students rate their knowledge of the words again in the After Reading column. Clarify any words that are still problematic. Have students write their own definition and example or sentence in the appropriate column. Then, have students complete the Vocabulary Practice activities on the next page. Encourage students to use the words in further discussion and written work about these selections. Remind them that they will be accountable for these words in the **Selection Test** (*Unit 3 Resources,* pp. 112–114 or 115–117).

After You Read

A Toast to the Oldest Inhabitant • The Dog That Bit People

Comparing Humorous Writing

1. **(a)** Find an example of **hyperbole** in each work. **(b)** Find an example of **understatement** in each work. **(c)** Compare Twain's and Thurber's use of these devices, explaining which device each writer uses most.
2. **(a)** Which of the two authors treats a potentially serious subject lightly? **(b)** Which one treats an ordinary subject with exaggerated seriousness? **(c)** How do the forms—essay and speech—shape the way ideas are presented? Support your answers with examples.
3. **(a)** Find an example of **satire** in each essay. **(b)** Identify the type of person that is satirized in each example and explain whether you think satirizing such people is fair or justified.

Writing to Compare Humorous Writing

In an essay, explain how Twain and Thurber use **conflict** to develop their humorous writing. Before you write, complete a chart like the one shown. Identify the conflict and the comic details the writers use to depict it.

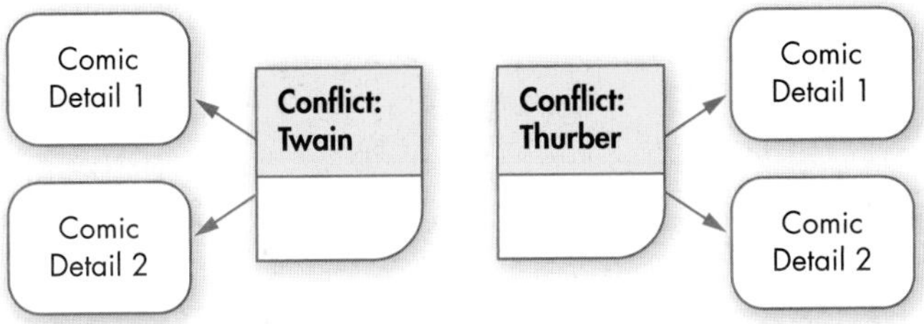

Vocabulary

Practice Complete each of the following sentences in a way that makes sense. Explain your answers.

1. If the décor in a room is *sumptuous,* it is likely to have ______.
2. Sailors who follow the *vagaries* of the wind may end up ______.
3. When told that all the ice cream in the freezer section has melted, an *irascible* shopkeeper might ______.
4. A coach may respond with *incredulity* if an athlete says ______.

Assessment Resources

Unit 3 Resources

L1 L2 EL **Selection Test A,** pp. 112–114.
L3 L4 **Selection Test B,** pp. 115–117.
L3 L4 **Open-Book Test,** pp. 109–111.

PHLit Online! All assessment resources are available at **www.PHLitOnline.com.**

ASSESS

Answers

Comparing Humorous Writing

1. (a) Twain's claim of one hundred thirty-six different types of weather in one day and Thurber's description of the mice invasion.
   (b) Twain describes New England people as patient and forbearing; Thurber's mother checks on the mice. (c) Twain uses hyperbole more often, and Thurber uses understatement more often.
2. (a) Thurber treats a serious subject lightly. Thurber's mother acknowledges Muggs's habit of biting people only once. (b) Twain exaggerates the seriousness of the weather. (c) Thurber's essay supports each idea with evidence. Twain's speech is less formal and presents the ideas in a conversational tone.
3. (a) **Possible response:** Twain satirizes the weather forecaster, Old Probabilities. Thurber satirizes dog owners. (b) Twain is justified in mocking inaccurate forecasters. Thurber is justified in making fun of indulgent pet owners.

Other sample answers appear in ***Graphic Organizer Transparencies,*** **Comparing Humorous Writing Graphic Organizer A (After You Read),** p. 90, and in the **Additional Answers** section.

Writing to Compare Humorous Writing

1. Review the assignment criteria with students.
2. As they draft, have students refer to the chart they completed (p. 518).

Six Traits Focus

✔	Ideas	Word Choice
✔	Organization	Sentence Fluency
	Voice	Conventions

Vocabulary

1. . . . lavish furnishings.
2. . . . getting lost.
3. . . . yell at the clerk.
4. . . . something the coach can't believe.

PRETEACH

Meeting Your Standards

Students will

1. write a letter to the editor.
2. use writing strategies to generate ideas and to plan, organize, evaluate, and revise the letter.
3. choose effective words to find their voice.
4. apply grammar skills.

Introducing the Writing Assignment

Review the assignment and the criteria, using the instruction on the student page.

Connecting to Real-Life Writing

Point out to students that elements of a letter to the editor are often incorporated into other types of writing.

- A position paper often contains the writer's viewpoint on an issue.
- A proposal is often presented in the format of a formal business letter.

Writing Workshop *Work in Progress*

If students have done the Work-in-Progress assignments on pp. 485 and 509, suggest that they examine their recorded ideas as they begin prewriting. They may wish to develop these ideas in a letter to the editor.

OES Online Essay Scorer

A writing prompt for this mode of writing can be found on the *PH Essay Scorer* at **www.PHLitOnline.com.**

Writing Workshop

Persuasion: Letter to the Editor

Defining the Form A **letter to the editor** is a formal business letter that presents the writer's viewpoints about important issues and is addressed to the opinion page of a newspaper or magazine. You might use elements of this form in position papers, speeches, and proposals.

Assignment Write a letter to the editor of a magazine, a newspaper, or an Internet site to share your opinion about a current event. Include these elements:

✔ *standard business letter format*, including a heading, an inside address, a greeting, a body, a closing, and a signature

✔ *formal, polite language*

✔ *a clear statement of opinion* supported by relevant facts, examples, or personal experiences

✔ use of *persuasive techniques* designed to convince readers of the point you make

✔ error-free grammar, including *well-combined sentences*

To preview the criteria on which your letter to the editor may be judged, see the rubric on page 537.

Writing Workshop: *Work in Progress*

Review the work you did on pages 485 and 509.

Prewriting Strategy

Find a hot topic. Watch television, scan newspapers, and listen to neighborhood discussions to identify topics that concern you. List these issues and note differing opinions about each one. Determine which issue and which opinion prompt your strongest feelings.

Apply It!

Pro	Hot Topic	Con
Professional athletes have a responsibility to the public.	**Sports heroes as role models**	Excellent athletes are not models for behavior outside the court or off the field.
Restrictions can protect our youngest citizens.	**Laws restricting the Internet**	Freedom of speech is denied by restrictions.

TEACH

Prewriting Strategies

1. Introduce the Prewriting Strategy, using the instruction on the student page.
2. Have students apply the strategy to choose a topic.

Six Traits Focus

✔	Ideas		Word Choice
✔	Organization		Sentence Fluency
	Voice		Conventions

Writing and Grammar, **Interactive Textbook Online**

Students can use the following tools at **www.pearsonsuccessnet.com** as they complete their letters to the editor:

- Scan Newspapers (Chapter 7, Section 2)
- Make a Quicklist (Chapter 7, Section 2)

Teaching Resources

The following resources can be used to enrich or extend the instruction.

All *Unit 3 Resources,* pp. 118–119

All *Professional Development Guidebook* **Rubric for Self-Assessment: Business Letter,** pp. 265–266

All *Graphic Organizer Transparencies* **Rubric for Self-Assessment: Letter to the Editor,** p. 92

PHLit Online! All resources are available at **www.PHLitOnline.com.**

WRITER'S TOOLBOX

Voice | Organization | Word Choice | Ideas | Conventions | Sentence Fluency

Finding Your Voice

Voice is the writer's distinctive "sound" or way of "speaking" on the page. It is created through elements such as word choice, sentence structure, and tone. Voice, in its written form, is related to the writer's speech style and can be described in the same way the spoken word is described—fast, slow, blunt, and so on. Use the following tips to help you find the appropriate voice for your letter.

Choose effective words. Before you begin your letter, think about how you want to sound: for example, impassioned, concerned, reasoned, or detached. Your choice of words and the structure of your sentences communicate your voice. Try saying a few sentences aloud. You might tape-record your voice, or have a friend listen to you speak. Then, decide whether the sound of your voice is what you wish to convey on paper. Use a chart like the following to record words or phrases that reflect your voice.

Prentice Hall Writing and Grammar Connection: Chapter 7, Section 4

Apply It!

Voice and/or Tone	Words and Phrases
impassioned	*We urgently need . . . ; So much is at stake . . .*
concerned	*I am concerned . . . ; The problem is serious . . .*
reasoned	*We all will benefit from . . . ; We have the resources to . . . ; Some people may disagree with me . . .*

Consider your audience and tone. Your voice in writing should reflect your audience. Your letter will address the general public, so include information that is essential to your case. Be respectful to your audience. Even if you are voicing a complaint, maintain a calm and reasonable tone. Your goal is to persuade, not to insult.

Revise to create appropriate formality. Check that your tone is polite and your style is formal. Replace casual language with formal language.

Casual: The park's a big old mess.
Formal: The park is littered with trash.

Finding Your Voice

1. Introduce the writing skill, using the instruction on the student page.
2. Discuss the strategies and examples for finding and developing voice.

Teaching the Writing Skill

1. Explain to students that the purpose of persuasive writing is to change the reader's mind about an opinion or a course of action. Emphasize that a reader is more likely to be persuaded if the writer's ideas are organized, well supported, and written in an effective and appropriate way. One way the writer can make his or her writing effective and appropriate is to adopt a clear, unique voice that the reader will remember.
2. Distinguish the literary elements *tone* and *voice,* two ideas that are closely related. *Tone* is a writer's attitude toward his or her subject and audience. *Voice* is the way the writer "speaks" through his or her words. A writer's voice is like a fingerprint—voice gives every piece of an author's writing a uniquely identifiable sound.
3. Model different voices with students. On the board, write, "You must stop global warming. Now." Have a student read it aloud. Then, elicit from students the way this statement "sounds"—immediate and commanding. Contrast the voice with this example: "The polar bears are hopping from one ice floe to another as though they were on hot coals, looking for a stable place to rest, to eat, to survive. Please stop global warming before the bears' home melts entirely away." Discuss the tender, more eloquent voice of this passage. Challenge students to determine which voice might be more effective in persuading readers to stop global warming.

Differentiated Instruction for Universal Access

Support for Special Needs Students

The concept of *voice* can be difficult for many students to comprehend. To help students "hear" the voice in their writing, follow these steps:

1. Assign partners and give each pair a topic to discuss. Tell students they will attempt to persuade each other using their "voices."
2. Have students write down ideas and describe their feelings about the topic, considering answers to questions such as these: *How might this topic be of interest to others? Why should people know about this?*
3. Have partners try to persuade each other with their ideas. While one speaks, instruct the other to observe "voice": how quickly the partner speaks, how long the sentences are, and so on. Then, have partners switch roles.
4. Have partners describe each other's voices. Prompt students to characterize the voices as impassioned, concerned, timid, unassuming, and so on.

Drafting Strategies

1. Introduce the Drafting Strategies, using the instruction on the student page.
2. Have students apply the strategies as they draft.

Teaching the Strategies

Use page R36 to review business letter format.

Think Aloud: Model Persuasive Techniques

Use this "think aloud" to model the strategy. Say to students:

> I want to persuade people to eat whole grain bread instead of white bread, but I won't be convincing if I just tell them what to do. Instead, I'll use persuasive techniques, such as an appeal to logic: "Studies have shown that a diet high in whole grains helps prevent certain cancers." I can also ask a rhetorical question: "Don't you want to be healthier?" These techniques can help me to convince my readers.

Six Traits Focus

	Ideas		Word Choice
✔	Organization		Sentence Fluency
✔	Voice		Conventions

Revising Strategies

1. Introduce the Revising Strategies, using the instruction on the student page.
2. Have students apply the strategies as they review their drafts.

Teaching the Strategies

Have students work in pairs to evaluate each other's papers and to explain what is convincing and what is not.

Six Traits Focus

✔	Ideas	✔	Word Choice
✔	Organization		Sentence Fluency
✔	Voice		Conventions

WG Writing and Grammar, Grade 10

Students will find additional instruction on drafting and revising a letter to the editor in Chapter 7, Sections 3 and 4.

Drafting Strategies

Use the proper format. Your letter to the editor must follow a standard business letter format. Here are two commonly accepted conventions:

- **Block format:** each part of the letter begins at the left margin
- **Modified block format:** the heading, closing, and signature are indented to the center of the page

Use a checklist to ensure that you include all six elements of a formal business letter—heading, inside address, salutation, body, closing, and signature. (For more on business letters, see page R36.) When using modified block format, be sure to use a tab to indent the elements. Make sure that all the tabbed elements align under one another on the page.

Use persuasive techniques. As you draft your letter, include persuasive techniques and rhetorical devices to convince your readers to adopt your opinion or take a course of action. Use this chart to help develop your own persuasive words and phrases to make your letter effective.

Persuasive Techniques	Rhetorical Devices
Appeal to Emotion Abandoned animals are suffering needlessly. **Appeal to Logic** Taking care of these animals will help eliminate sources of diseases to our pets.	**Parallelism** Homeless animals deserve our compassion. Homeless animals deserve a home. **Rhetorical Question** Can we allow this situation to continue?

Revising Strategy

Evaluate support. As you review your draft, highlight your main ideas to check that they are supported with evidence. If a point is not sufficiently important, omit it. If it is important, add evidence to support it.

Select a variety of types of evidence to make your letter both convincing and interesting for readers. Plan to include evidence in these categories:

- facts and statistics
- real-life examples
- personal experiences
- expert opinions

Model: Highlighting to Add Supporting Details

Many pets in this city have been abandoned, left homeless by uncaring owners. These animals roam the city streets. Most are hungry, and many are sick and diseased. ^I personally rescued a puppy who was scavenging in our trash can for food. My vet said he had heartworms and fleas.

The writer adds support in the form of personal experience.

Understanding by Design

Clarifying Expected Outcomes: Using Rubrics

- Before students begin working on this assignment, have them preview the Rubric for Self-Assessment (p. 537) to learn what qualities their letter to the editor must have. A copy of this rubric appears in ***Graphic Organizer Transparencies,*** p. 92.
- Review the criteria in the Rubric with the class. Before students use the Rubric to assess their writing, work with them to rate the Student Model (p. 536) using the Rubric.
- If you wish to assess students' letters to the editor with either a 4-point or a 6-point scoring rubric, see ***Professional Development Guidebook,*** pp. 265–266.

WRITER'S TOOLBOX

Sentence Fluency | Voice | Organization | Word Choice | Ideas | Conventions

Revising to Combine Short Sentences

If you use too many short sentences, your work can seem as if it was written for very young readers rather than a mature audience. To avoid this problem, combine short sentences that express related ideas.

Methods of Sentence Combining Use compound verbs to combine two short sentences:

Choppy: I *cancelled* my service. I *turned* my phone in for a refund.

Combined: I *cancelled* my service and *turned* my phone in for a refund.

You may use **compound objects:**

Choppy: I ate *a sandwich.* I ate *an ice cream cone.*

Combined: I ate *a sandwich* and *an ice cream cone.*

Use **compound predicate nominatives** or **predicate adjectives.**

predicate nominative	predicate adjective
a noun or pronoun that appears with a linking verb and identifies or explains the subject Example: Parakeets are birds.	an adjective that appears with a linking verb and describes the subject Example: Parakeets are colorful.

Choppy: My favorite celebrity *is* a *singer.* She is also *an actress.*

Combined: My favorite celebrity is *a singer and actress.*

Choppy: The bicycle is *very lightweight.* It is *extremely fast.*

Combined: The bicycle is *very lightweight and extremely fast.*

Fixing Choppy Sentences Follow these steps to fix short sentences:

1. **Read your draft aloud,** listening for choppy sentences.
2. **Identify sentences to combine.** Determine which sentences share a common subject or a common predicate.
3. **Try a variety of sentence-combining techniques.** Use the methods above to create a variety of fluid sentences.

Grammar in Your Writing

Reread two paragraphs in your letter. Look for places where a single sentence would express related ideas better than a series of shorter sentences. Combine these sentences using one of the methods above.

WG *Prentice Hall Writing and Grammar Connection: Chapter 3, Section 1*

Revising to Combine Short Sentences

1. Introduce the grammar skill, using the instruction on the student page.
2. Discuss the examples and the strategies for fixing incorrect usage.
3. Have students follow the instruction under Grammar in Your Writing to correct errors in their drafts.

Teaching the Grammar Skill

1. Students' writing may display strings of short sentences. A series of short sentences produces a choppy style. Give this example: *I walk to school. I get a ride home.* Explain that combining related ideas in a single sentence is one way to write more mature, less choppy sentences.
2. Draw students' attention to the four methods of combining sentences described on this page: compound verbs, compound objects, compound predicate nominatives, and compound predicate adjectives.
3. Have students correct these choppy sentences using one of the methods explained on this page.
   a. *He rode his bike. He went to the park.*
   Answer: He rode his bike to the park.
   b. *I can make spaghetti. I can make sauce.*
   Answer: I can make spaghetti and sauce.
   c. *She is class president. She is captain of the swimming team.*
   Answer: She is class president and captain of the swimming team.
   d. *Her bedroom is small. It is warm. It is cozy.*
   Answer: Her bedroom is small, warm, and cozy.
4. As students apply the skill to their letters, check that they have identified sentences with common subjects or predicates and combined them.

WG Writing and Grammar, Grade 10

Students will find additional instruction on revising choppy sentences in Chapter 21, Sections 2 and 3.

Strategies for Using Technology in Writing

If students are using word-processing software, suggest that they use the *cut, copy,* and *paste* features or commands to combine sentences. After they have combined choppy sentences, advise students to check each new sentence they have created to make sure it reads properly and has appropriate punctuation, including additional commas as needed, and a period.

Students can also use features of the **Writing and Grammar Interactive Textbook Online** to revise choppy sentences.

Student Model

Review the Student Model with the class, using the annotations to analyze the writer's use of the elements of a letter to the editor.

Teaching From the Student Model

1. Explain that the Student Model is a sample and that students' own letters to the editor may be longer or shorter depending on their topics and what they want to convey.
2. Direct students' attention to elements of the business letter format. Emphasize the importance of the correct return address, date, internal address, and proper salutation.
3. Point out that in the first sentence of the letter, the writer clearly and succinctly states his reason for writing. In this way, he catches the editor's interest.
4. Observe that the personal experiences the writer offers provide appropriate evidence for the letter to the editor.
5. **Ask** students to identify how the writer supports his proposal. **Answer:** He provides evidence in the form of personal observations that the current band program is inadequate. He also notes that his proposal will cost less than an alternative solution.
6. Finally, **ask** students what the purpose of the final paragraph is. **Possible response:** Its purpose is to refer to the reason for writing the letter and to strengthen the proposal.

Connecting to Real-Life Writing

Tell students that they will often encounter situations and issues about which they want to share an opinion. A letter to the editor is a good vehicle for that purpose. In class, discuss situations and issues that might generate letters to the editor, such as local elections or community problems.

Student Model: Clay Creamans, Independence, KY

Clay Creamans
2351 Any Drive
Independence, Kentucky 41051

September 25, 2005

Editor-in-Chief
The Daily Independent
552 Downtown Street
Ashland, Kentucky 41000

Clay uses a correct modified block format.

Dear Editor-in-Chief:

I am writing in response to the letter you published from Mr. Jones, who complained about our band's playing at the last football game.

Formal language shows that Clay takes both his opinion and his readers seriously.

The point of high school band programs is to train students to play together, to produce one stirring, harmonious sound. Because of a lack of instruction, education, and familiarity with music and instruments, this is difficult for some students. Band programs all over the country have inspired many students to go into the field of music, but many do not meet the requirements students need to compete after high school. I personally know students who have been denied scholarships and have had scholarships revoked because they have not been properly trained. The Kenton County School District needs to devise a class that will alleviate these problems.

Clay supports his argument with personal experiences.

This new music class should have a staff composed of teachers who can play and teach all of the band instruments. Students need one-on-one, as well as group, instruction. Of course, hiring a full staff of musicians for every school would cost a lot. Instead, full band directors could be hired for all the schools to share. This would allow students to gain a greater knowledge of music from a larger group of musicians. These teachers would offer more insight into the history and theory of music.

Clay points out an opposing argument and suggests an alternative plan.

With so many young people interested in fine arts, band directors cannot offer everyone the instruction that is needed. For the band to improve as a whole, everyone has to grow. Many of today's band directors try hard to develop better musicians, yet, because of a lack of time and staffing, they feel disappointed and discouraged.

With adequate time and staffing, students will be able to make music together and demonstrate their talents. With an experienced music staff and better classes, I believe that Mr. Jones will be happier with our band's performance.

The conclusion reinforces Clay's ideas.

Sincerely,

Clay Creamans

Clay Creamans

Strategies for Test Taking

A writing prompt on a standardized test may assess a student's ability to develop a point of view on an issue. Advise students to allow enough time for each step of the writing process. Emphasize that although a prompt or an excerpt is likely to be provided on the test, the prewriting stage is still important because students will need to identify and organize evidence to support their points of view. Suggest that students use two-column pro-and-con charts to jot down what they know about their issues. Each student should choose the point of view for which he or she has the most supporting evidence, whether or not the student really believes in the point of view.

Editing and Proofreading

Check your draft for errors in format, grammar, and punctuation.

Focus on Accuracy: Make sure that the names of individuals, periodicals, and any quoted experts are spelled correctly. Make sure that any statistics or numerical data are accurately stated, and double-check street addresses.

Publishing and Presenting

Consider one of the following ways to share your writing:

Submit your letter. Send your letter to the editor of the media source you have addressed. When the letter is published, share the newspaper, periodical, or Web site with classmates.

Hold a speaker's corner. Conduct a speaker's corner in which you and your classmates read your letters aloud and discuss the topics presented. To help maintain the flow of the discussion, set time limits for each speaker.

Reflecting on Your Writing

Writer's Journal Jot down your answers to this question:

How did writing about the issue you chose help you to understand it?

Rubric for Self-Assessment

Find evidence in your writing to address each category. Then, use the rating scale to grade your work.

Criteria	Rating Scale (not very — very)
Focus: How clearly do you state your opinion?	1 2 3 4 5
Organization: How accurately do you use standard business letter format?	1 2 3 4 5
Support/Elaboration: How relevant are the facts, examples, or experiences you use to support your opinion?	1 2 3 4 5
Style: How formal and polite is your use of language?	1 2 3 4 5
Conventions: How correct is your grammar, especially your use of well-combined sentences?	1 2 3 4 5
Voice: How well do your word choice and sentence structure reflect your voice?	1 2 3 4 5

Editing and Proofreading

1. Introduce the editing and proofreading focus, using the instruction on the student page.
2. Have students edit and proofread their letters to the editor, correcting grammar, spelling, punctuation, and word choice. Make sure they check for errors of the type noted on the student page.

Teaching the Editing Focus

Explain that inaccuracies will undercut the arguments of students' letters. Urge students to use reliable sources to confirm the spelling of proper nouns, to verify data, and to double-check addresses.

Six Traits Focus

	Ideas		Word Choice
	Organization		Sentence Fluency
	Voice	✔	Conventions

ASSESS

Publishing and Presenting

1. Review with students the proper way to address an envelope for a business letter. Remind students to include a return address and to use correct postage for letters sent through the mail.
2. Direct students sending letters to a Web site to follow guidelines posted there for submissions.
3. In the speaker's corner, tell students to say something positive about each letter before offering criticism. Remind them that a diplomatic tone and careful word choice are as important in offering criticism as in writing a letter to the editor.

Reflecting on Your Writing

1. Ask students to consider what elements of a letter to the editor might apply to another writing assignment.
2. Tell students to discuss how the writing process affected their views of their topics. Students may note that the process helped them organize their ideas and express them clearly, ultimately making them feel more strongly about their topics.

Differentiated Instruction for Universal Access

Strategy for Less Proficient Readers

Provide several good models of letters to the editor from magazines or newspapers. Have students follow the text of each letter as you read it aloud. Help students identify the topic of each letter and the details the writer provides to support important points. Tell students to use these examples as models for their own letters.

WG Writing and Grammar, Grade 10

Students will find additional guidance on editing and proofreading, publishing and presenting, and reflecting on the letters to the editor in Chapter 7, Section 5.

TIME AND RESOURCE MANAGER

Keep Memory Alive • *from* Nobel Lecture

Lesson Pacing Guide

DAY 1 Preteach

- Administer the Reading and Vocabulary Warm-ups (*Unit 3 Resources*, pp. 127–130 or 145–148) as necessary.
- Introduce the Reading Skill: Evaluate Persuasion FT
- Introduce the Literary Analysis concept: Persuasive Writing and Rhetorical Devices FT
- Distribute copies of the appropriate graphic organizer for the Reading Skill (*Graphic Organizer Transparencies*, pp. 93–95). CRI
- Distribute copies of the appropriate graphic organizer for Literary Analysis (*Graphic Organizer Transparencies*, pp. 96–98). CRI
- Teach the selection vocabulary. FT CRI
- Introduce the Word Study skill.

DAYS 2–3 Preteach/Teach

- Build background with the Background feature. CRI
- Develop thematic vocabulary and thematic thinking with Writing About the Big Question.
- Prepare students to read with the Activating Prior Knowledge activities (TE). CRI
- Informally monitor comprehension while students read. FT
- Use the Reading Check questions to confirm comprehension.
- Develop students' ability to evaluate the writer's argument using the Reading Skill questions. CRI
- Develop students' understanding of persuasive writing and rhetorical devices using the Literary Analysis questions. CRI
- Reinforce vocabulary with the Vocabulary notes. CRI

DAY 4 Assess

- Assess students' comprehension and mastery of the skills by having them answer the Critical Thinking, Reading Skill, and Literary Analysis questions. FT
- Have students complete the Vocabulary Practice activities. FT
- Have students complete the Word Study activities.

DAY 5 Extend/Assess

- Have students complete the Grammar lesson. CRI
- Have students complete the Writing activity and write a letter. (You may assign as homework.) FT
- Extend learning by having students complete the Listening and Speaking activity, a debate. As an alternative, assign them "The Witness Dilemma" or "Instant Friends" in *Reality Central*. CRI
- Administer Selection Test A or B (*Unit 3 Resources*, pp. 139–144 or 160–165). FT

The excerpt from *Elie Wiesel's Nobel Prize Acceptance Speech* is unedited.
The excerpt from Nobel Lecture speech has been edited for length and level.

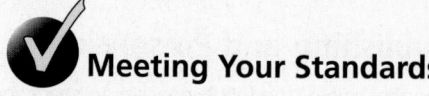

Meeting Your Standards

Students will

1. **analyze and respond to literary elements.**
   - **Literary Analysis: Persuasive Writing and Rhetorical Devices**
2. **read, comprehend, and analyze short stories.**
   - **Reading Skill: Evaluate Persuasion**
   - **Reading Check questions**
   - **Apply the Skills questions**
   - **Assessment Practice**
3. **develop vocabulary.**
   - **Vocabulary**
   - **Word Study**
4. **apply grammar skills.**
   - **Degrees of Adverbs**
5. **Develop writing proficiency.**
   - **Work in Progress: Persuasive Essay**
   - **letter**
6. **strengthen listening and speaking skills.**
   - **debate**

CRI For a full explanation of Culturally Responsive Instruction opportunities in this lesson, see p. T86–T87.

FT For an accelerated lesson, use the Fast Track strategies and activities.

Managing Differentiated Instruction
This leveled selection pairing groups a more accessible with a more challenging selection. Choose either one to teach the lesson skills. For classroom management suggestions for using the pairing in a mixed-ability class, see pp. T68–T69.

Daily Block Scheduling
Each day in this Lesson Pacing Guide represents a 40–50 minute period. Teachers using block scheduling may combine days to revise pacing. In addition, teachers may differentiate and support core instruction by integrating components for extended and intensive support as students require. See the Guide to Selected Leveled Resources (facing page).

Guide to Selected Leveled Resources

EL English Learners

			Keep Memory Alive	*from* Nobel Lecture
CORE COURSE	*Unit 3 Resources*	Selection Test A	pp. 139–141	pp. 160–162
	Graphic Organizer Transparencies	Reading Skill Graphic Organizer A	p. 93	p. 94
		Literary Analysis Graphic Organizer A	p. 96	p. 97
EXTENDED SUPPORT (Level 2)	*Unit 3 Resources*	Reading and Vocabulary Warm-ups A or B	pp. 127–130	pp. 145–148
	Reader's Notebook: English Learner's Version		adapted instruction and adapted selection	adapted instruction and summary
	Hear It! Audio CD		selection and summaries	selection and summaries
	Hear It! Audio CD (adapted text)		adapted selection and summaries	—
INTENSIVE SUPPORT (Level 1)	*Reality Central*		"The Witness Dilemma"	"Instant Friends"
	Real-World Writing Journal		Lesson 5, pp. 86–89	Lesson 6, pp. 90–93

L2 Below-Level Students

			Keep Memory Alive	*from* Nobel Lecture
CORE COURSE	*Unit 3 Resources*	Selection Test A	pp. 139–141	pp. 160–162
	Graphic Organizer Transparencies	Reading Skill Graphic Organizer A	p. 93	p. 94
		Literary Analysis Graphic Organizer A	p. 96	p. 97
EXTENDED SUPPORT (Level 2)	*Unit 3 Resources*	Reading and Vocabulary Warm-ups A or B	pp. 127–130	pp. 145–148
	Reader's Notebook		adapted instruction and full selection	adapted instruction and summary
	Hear It! Audio CD		selection and summaries	selection and summaries
INTENSIVE SUPPORT (Level 1)	*Reality Central*		"The Witness Dilemma"	"Instant Friends"
	Real-World Writing Journal		Lesson 5, pp. 86–89	Lesson 6, pp. 90–93
	Reading Kit		Reteaching worksheets	Reteaching worksheets

L1 Special Needs Students

			Keep Memory Alive	*from* Nobel Lecture
CORE COURSE	*Unit 3 Resources*	Selection Test A	pp. 139–141	pp. 160–162
	Graphic Organizer Transparencies	Reading Skill Graphic Organizer A	p. 93	p. 94
		Literary Analysis Graphic Organizer A	p. 96	p. 97
EXTENDED SUPPORT (Level 2)	*Unit 3 Resources*	Reading and Vocabulary Warm-ups A or B	pp. 127–130	pp. 145–148
	Reader's Notebook: Adapted Version		adapted instruction and adapted selection	adapted instruction and summary
	Hear It! Audio CD (adapted text)		adapted selection and summaries	—
INTENSIVE SUPPORT (Level 1)	*Reality Central*		"The Witness Dilemma"	"Instant Friends"
	Real-World Writing Journal		Lesson 5, pp. 86–89	Lesson 6, pp. 90–93
	Reading Kit		Reteaching worksheets	Reteaching worksheets

The program includes resources for these students: L3 On-Level L4 Advanced All All
For a complete guide to selection support, see pp. T106–T108.

NOTE: All print materials are also available online at *www.PHLitOnline.com.*

VISUAL GUIDE to Featured Selection Resources

• Keep Memory Alive
• *from* Nobel Lecture

Keep Memory Alive
Elie Wiesel
from
Nobel Lecture
Alexander Solzhenitsyn
translated by F.D. Reeve
▲ Critical Viewing
Why is it surprising that Solzhenitsyn was sent to a prison camp, like this one, for writing letters?
[Connect]
I am, however, encouraged by a keen sense of WORLD LITERATURE as the one great heart that beats for the cares and misfortunes of our world, even though each corner sees and experiences them in a different way.
In past times, also, besides age-old national literatures there existed a concept of world literature as the link between the

RESOURCES FOR:

- EL English Learners
- L1 Special Needs Students
- L2 Below-Level Students
- L3 On-Level Students
- L4 Advanced Students
- All All Students

Vocabulary/Fluency/Prior Knowledge

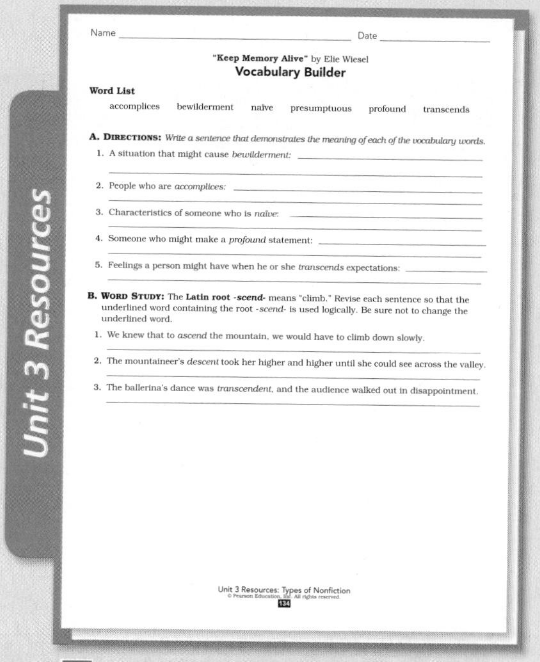

Unit 3 Resources

Name ______ Date ______

"Keep Memory Alive" by Elie Wiesel
Vocabulary Builder

Word List
accomplices bewilderment naive presumptuous profound transcends

A. DIRECTIONS: *Write a sentence that demonstrates the meaning of each of the vocabulary words.*

1. A situation that might cause *bewilderment*:
2. People who are *accomplices*:
3. Characteristics of someone who is *naive*:
4. Someone who might make a *profound* statement:
5. Feelings a person might have when he or she *transcends* expectations:

B. WORD STUDY: The **Latin root** ***-scend-*** means "climb." Revise each sentence so that the underlined word containing the root *-scend-* is used logically. Be sure not to change the underlined word.

1. We knew that to *ascend* the mountain, we would have to climb down slowly.
2. The mountaineer's *descent* took her higher and higher until she could see across the valley.
3. The ballerina's dance was *transcendent*, and the audience walked out in disappointment.

Unit 3 Resources: Types of Nonfiction
© Pearson Education, Inc. All rights reserved.
134

All **Vocabulary Builder, pp. 134, 152**

Also available for these selections:

EL L1 L2 **Vocabulary Warm-ups A and B, pp. 127–128, 145–146**

EL L1 L2 **Reading Warm-ups A and B, pp. 129–130, 147–148**

All **Writing About the Big Question, pp. 131, 149**

Prentice Hall LITERATURE
Reader's Notebook
Differentiated Instruction
GRADE TEN

L2 L3 ***Reader's Notebook***

L1 ***Reader's Notebook: Adapted Version***

EL ***Reader's Notebook: English Learner's Version***

Reader's Notebooks

Pre- and postreading pages for both selections, as well as "Keep Memory Alive," appear in an interactive format in the *Reader's Notebooks*. Each *Notebook* is differentiated for a different group of learners. The selections in the Adapted and English Learner's versions are abridged.

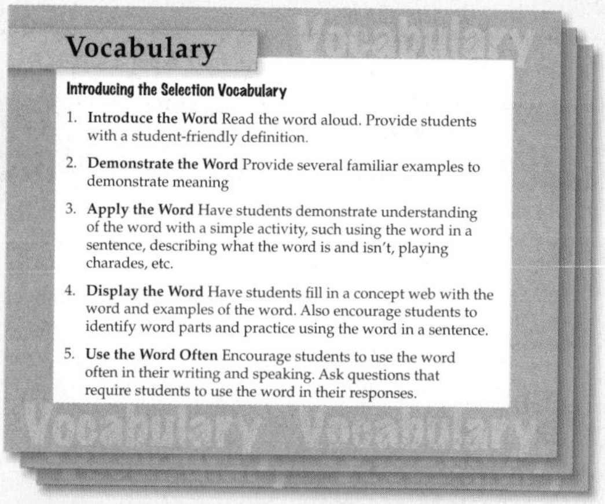

Vocabulary

Introducing the Selection Vocabulary

1. **Introduce the Word** Read the word aloud. Provide students with a student-friendly definition.
2. **Demonstrate the Word** Provide several familiar examples to demonstrate meaning
3. **Apply the Word** Have students demonstrate understanding of the word with a simple activity, such using the word in a sentence, describing what the word is and isn't, playing charades, etc.
4. **Display the Word** Have students fill in a concept web with the word and examples of the word. Also encourage students to identify word parts and practice using the word in a sentence.
5. **Use the Word Often** Encourage students to use the word often in their writing and speaking. Ask questions that require students to use the word in their responses.

Classroom Strategies and Teaching Routines

- core classroom routines outlined step-by-step
- convenient format for easy reference while teaching

Selection Support

Graphic Organizer Transparencies

from **Nobel Lecture** by Alexander Solzhenitsyn

After You Read A: Reading—Persuasive Speech

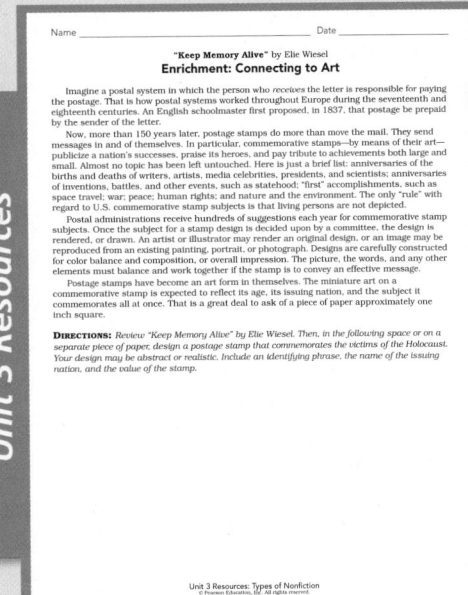

	Example	Effect
Repetition	the words *lies* and *truth*	emphasizes the central argument of truth defeating lies and violence
Parallelism		
Slogans or Saws		
Rhetorical Questions		

Graphic Organizer Transparencies

EL L1 L2 **Literary Analysis: Graphic Organizer A,** pp. 96, 97 (partially filled in)

Also available for these selections:

- EL L1 L2 Reading: Graphic Organizer A, pp. 93, 94 (partially filled in)
- L3 Reading: Graphic Organizer B, p. 95
- L3 Literary Analysis: Graphic Organizer B, p. 98

Skills Development/Extension

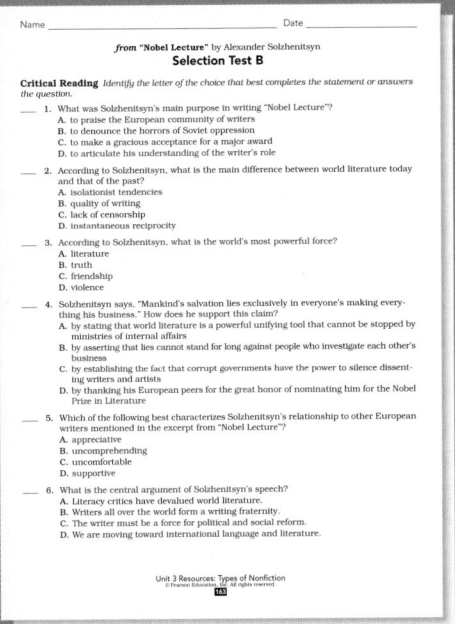

Unit 3 Resources

Name ________________ Date ________

"Keep Memory Alive" by Elie Wiesel

Enrichment: Connecting to Art

Imagine a postal system in which the person who *receives* the letter is responsible for paying the postage. That is how postal systems worked throughout Europe during the seventeenth and eighteenth centuries. An English schoolmaster first proposed, in 1837, that postage be prepaid by the sender of the letter.

Now, more than 150 years later, postage stamps do more than move the mail. They send messages in and of themselves. In particular, commemorative stamps—by means of their art—publicize a nation's successes, praise its heroes, and pay tribute to achievements both large and small. Almost no topic has been left untouched. Here is just a brief list: anniversaries of the births and deaths of writers, artists, media celebrities, presidents, and scientists; anniversaries of inventions, battles, and other events, such as statehood; "first" accomplishments, such as space travel; war; peace; human rights; and nature and the environment. The only "rule" with regard to U.S. commemorative stamp subjects is that living persons are not depicted.

Postal administrations receive hundreds of suggestions each year for commemorative stamp subjects. Once the subject for a stamp design is decided upon by a committee, the design is rendered, or drawn. An artist or illustrator may render an original design, or an image may be reproduced from an existing painting, portrait, or photograph. Designs are carefully constructed for color balance and composition, or overall impression. The picture, the words, and any other elements must balance and work together if the stamp is to convey an effective message.

Postage stamps have become an art form in themselves. The miniature art on a commemorative stamp is expected to reflect its age, its issuing nation, and the subject it commemorates all at once. That is a great deal to ask of a piece of paper approximately one inch square.

Directions: *Review "Keep Memory Alive" by Elie Wiesel. Then, in the following space or on a separate piece of paper, design a postage stamp that commemorates the victims of the Holocaust. Your design may be abstract or realistic. Include an identifying phrase, the name of the issuing nation, and the value of the stamp.*

Unit 3 Resources: Types of Nonfiction

L4 **Enrichment,** pp. 135, 153

Also available for these selections:

- All Literary Analysis: Persuasive Writing and Rhetorical Devices, pp. 132, 150
- All Reading: Evaluate Persuasion, pp. 133, 151
- L3 L4 Grammar, p. 154
- L3 L4 Support for Writing, p. 155
- L3 L4 Support for Extend Your Learning, p. 156

Assessment

Name ________________ Date ________

from **"Nobel Lecture"** by Alexander Solzhenitsyn

Selection Test B

Critical Reading *Identify the letter of the choice that best completes the statement or answers the question.*

___ 1. What was Solzhenitsyn's main purpose in writing "Nobel Lecture"?
A. to praise the European community of writers
B. to denounce the horrors of Soviet oppression
C. to make a gracious acceptance for a major award
D. to articulate his understanding of the writer's role

___ 2. According to Solzhenitsyn, what is the main difference between world literature today and that of the past?
A. isolationist tendencies
B. quality of writing
C. lack of censorship
D. instantaneous reciprocity

___ 3. According to Solzhenitsyn, what is the world's most powerful force?
A. literature
B. truth
C. friendship
D. violence

___ 4. Solzhenitsyn says, "Mankind's salvation lies exclusively in everyone's making everything his business." How does he support this claim?
A. by stating that world literature is a powerful unifying tool that cannot be stopped by ministries of internal affairs
B. by asserting that lies cannot stand for long against people who investigate each other's business
C. by establishing the fact that corrupt governments have the power to silence dissenting writers and artists
D. by thanking his European peers for the great honor of nominating him for the Nobel Prize in Literature

___ 5. Which of the following best characterizes Solzhenitsyn's relationship to other European writers mentioned in the excerpt from "Nobel Lecture"?
A. appreciative
B. uncomprehending
C. uncomfortable
D. supportive

___ 6. What is the central argument of Solzhenitsyn's speech?
A. Literacy critics have devalued world literature.
B. Writers all over the world form a writing fraternity.
C. The writer must be a force for political and social reform.
D. We are moving toward international language and literature.

Unit 3 Resources: Types of Nonfiction

L3 L4 **Selection Test B,** pp. 142–144, 163–165

Also available for these selections:

- EL L1 L2 Selection Test A, pp. 139–141, 160–162
- L3 L4 Open-Book Test, pp. 136–138, 157–159

PHLit Online!
www.PHLitOnline.com

- complete narrated selection text
- a thematically related video with writing prompt
- an interactive graphic organizer
- highlighting feature
- access to all student print resources, adapted to individual student needs
- Spanish and English summaries

Background Video

Background video

Also available:

Get Connected! (thematic video with writing prompt)

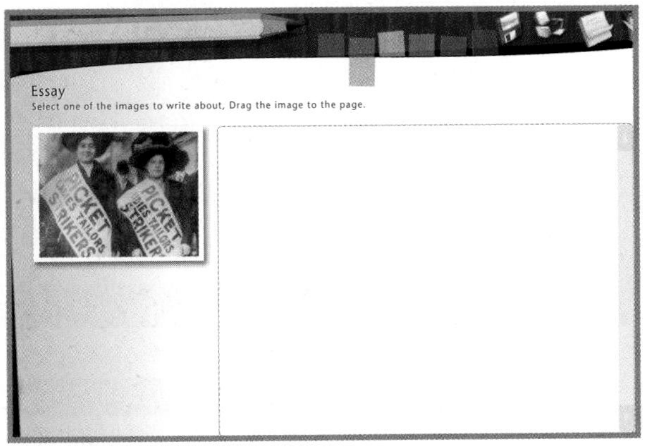
Essay
Select one of the images to write about. Drag the image to the page.

Writer's Journal (with graphics feature)

Also available:

Vocabulary Central (tools, activities, and songs for studying vocabulary)

DIFFERENTIATE/PRETEACH

❶ Selection Choices

You may use either "Keep Memory Alive" or the selection from "Nobel Lecture" to meet the lesson standards. Skills instruction for both selections appears on p. 539. Choose one selection to teach (or choose to teach both). The Accessibility at a Glance chart at the bottom of this page will help you determine which of the two selections is more appropriate for your students.

❷ Selection Skills

1. With the class, preview the selection skills. (The lesson meets the lesson objectives given on p. 538a.)
2. Explain that students will learn to use the skill of evaluating persuasive appeals as they read to better understand and enjoy the selection you choose. By examining persuasive writing and rhetorical devices as they read, they will gain deeper insight into the genre.
3. To introduce the Writing and Listening and Speaking activities (p. 555), tell students that when they have finished reading the selection, they will write letters and hold a group debate.
4. Tell students that they will also study a grammar concept: degrees of adverbs. By mastering this concept, they will improve their reading fluency and the quality of their own writing.

Before You Read

Keep Memory Alive • *from* Nobel Lecture

❶ Selection Choices

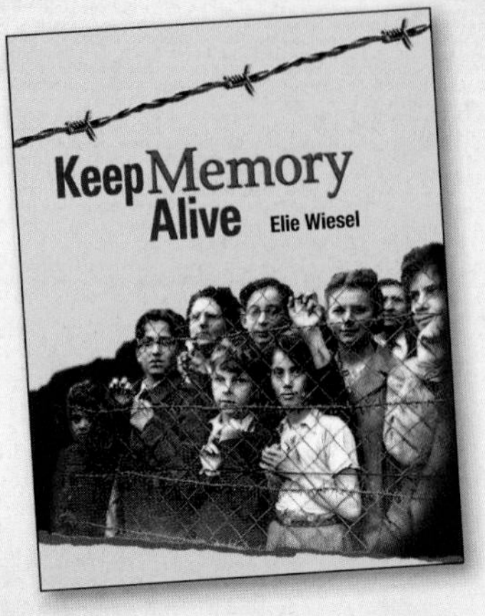

▲ Read **"Keep Memory Alive"** to learn why a man has devoted his life to ensuring that the horrors of the Holocaust are not forgotten.

▲ Read the excerpt from ***Nobel Lecture*** to find out how one author uses literature to fight against global forces of injustice.

❷ Selection Skills Guide

Practice these skills with either **"Keep Memory Alive"** (p. 542) or the excerpt from ***Nobel Lecture*** (p. 548).

- Understand persuasive writing
- Recognize rhetorical devices
- Evaluate the writer's argument
- Identify degrees of adverbs
- Write a letter
- Hold a group debate

Differentiated Instruction for Universal Access

Accessibility at a Glance: Selection Choices

	Keep Memory Alive		*from* Nobel Lecture	
Context	Historical: importance of keeping the memory of the Holocaust alive		Historical: importance of world literature to link people around the world	
Language/ Vocabulary	Subject-specific vocabulary		Grade-appropriate vocabulary	
Concept Level	Accessible (concepts are familiar; language direct and simple)		Challenging (concepts are abstract; sentence structure is complex)	
Literary Merit	Noted author, philosopher, and death camp survivor		Noted author and dissident	
Lexile/Length	Lexile: 480L	Word Count: 327	Lexile: 1230L	Word Count: 1,138
Overall Rating	**More accessible**		**More challenging**	

Because a number of factors determine the relative accessibility of paired selections, in some cases the Lexile rating of the more challenging selection will be lower than that of the more accessible selection.

PREVIEW

❸ Literary Analysis: Persuasive Writing and Rhetorical Devices

Persuasive writing, including **speeches,** is intended to convince people to take a particular action or position. Persuasive writers present **arguments** or positions using reason to support and defend their ideas. They also use **rhetorical devices,** or verbal techniques that create emphasis and appeal to emotions. Here are some common rhetorical devices:

- **repetition:** the reuse of a key word or idea for emphasis
- **parallelism:** similar grammatical structures expressing related ideas
- **slogans and saws:** short, catchy phrases
- **rhetorical questions:** questions that are intended to have obvious answers; asked for effect

❹ Reading Skill: Evaluate Persuasion

When reading persuasive writing, **evaluate the writer's argument.** Consider whether the writer supports claims with sound evidence and logical reasoning.

Determine when **persuasive techniques** are effectively used to enhance the impact of the supporting evidence and reasoning, and recognize when they are used to cover up a lack of logical support.

❺ Using the Strategy: Argument Chart

Use an **argument chart** like the one shown to take notes as you read.

Claim	Support	Persuasive Technique
Local businesses will suffer.	Prices at malls are lower.	Rhetorical question: Do you want your neighbor to lose his business?

PHLit Online!
www.PHLitOnline.com

Hear It!
- Selection summary audio
- Selection audio

See It!
- Get Connected video
- Background video
- More about the author
- Vocabulary flashcards

Do It!
- Interactive journals
- Interactive graphic organizers
- Self-test
- Internet activity
- Grammar tutorial
- Interactive vocabulary games

Differentiated Instruction for Universal Access

Preparing Students for the More Challenging Selection

If you wish to prepare lower-level readers to read the excerpt from "Nobel Lecture," the more challenging selection, follow these steps:

- Have students discuss the meaning of "literature" and give some examples. Ask them if they have ever read any pieces of literature that had an impact on their lives.
- Guide students to use context clues and their understanding of word roots to define difficult words such as *befogging* (p. 551), *complicity* (p. 551), and *conspicuously* (p. 552).
- Students may have difficulty with complex sentence constructions such as the sentence found on p. 549 that begins "As I have understood it . . ." Guide students to break down the sentence into simpler sentences. Have them identify a good "breaking point" for the sentence. Explain that certain ideas need to be kept together to maintain the author's message. Model breaking the sentence at the "but" conjunction to form two sentences.

PRETEACH

❸ Literary Analysis

1. Introduce the skill, using the instruction on the student page.
2. Tell students that they will identify persuasive writing and rhetorical devices as they read.

Think Aloud: Model the Skill

Model the skill of identifying persuasive writing and rhetorical devices. Say to students:

> Say I want to use persuasive and rhetorical devices to convince students to vote for me for class president. I can use arguments in my speeches, such as telling them what I would do to improve the school. I can use slogans like "Change is good!" and ask rhetorical questions like "Do you want better food in the cafeteria?"
>
> I also pay attention to these devices as I read so I can identify the author's position on a topic and the author's purpose for writing.

❹ Reading Skill

1. Introduce the skill, using the instruction on the student page.
2. Tell students that they will practice evaluating persuasive appeals as they read.

Think Aloud: Model the Skill

Model the skill of persuasive appeal using the following "think aloud."

> Sometimes arguments appeal to both my emotions and my intellect. For example, a group of artists might appeal to me for funding to repair a theater by saying that it would keep local children out of trouble. This appeals to my emotions. If the group tells me that free educational movies will be shown every week, I might be convinced, because the artists are appealing to my intellect and emotions.

❺ Using the Strategy

Give students a copy of either **Reading Skill Graphic Organizer A** or **B** (*Graphic Organizer Transparencies*, pp. 93–94) to record their evaluations of persuasive appeals as they read. Use the examples in **Reading Skill Graphic Organizer A**, which is partially filled in, to model the process of completing the organizer.

PRETEACH

❶ Writing About the Big Question

1. Review the assignment with the class.
2. Discuss with students the many kinds of knowledge. List them on the board.
3. Have students complete the sentence starters. Review responses as a class. (**Possible responses:** The kinds of facts we learn through studying <u>history</u> include important dates, people, movements, and eras. From these facts, we can learn important lessons such as how other people lived. Living in <u>ignorance</u> of problems of the past and present can be dangerous because we might repeat the same mistakes of the past.
4. Remind students that their answers will help them think about the Big Question, "What kind of knowledge changes our lives?"

While You Read

Tell students that as they read, they should look for childhood lessons that the author carries with him as an adult.

❷ Vocabulary

1. Have students preview the selection vocabulary.
2. For each word, have students say the word aloud.
3. Then, use the word in a sentence that defines the word.
4. Finally, repeat your definitional sentence or a similar sentence with the word missing and have the class "fill in the blank" chorally. For example:

   To be <u>presumptuous</u> is to be too bold. Susan thought Steven's rude response to her friend was too [students say "presumptuous"] *of him.*

❸ Word Study

1. Introduce the skill, using the instruction in the box.
2. Have students think of a *-scend* word that means "a person related to someone who lived in the past." (**Answer:** descendant)

Making Connections | Keep Memory Alive

What kind of *knowledge* changes our lives?

❶ Writing About the Big Question

In "Keep Memory Alive," Wiesel shows that testifying to the evils of the past can be a difficult but important duty. He argues that studying history is important not just for the facts and information it teaches us, but for the important lessons it reveals. Use these sentence starters to develop your ideas about the Big Question.

The kinds of facts we may learn through studying **history** include ________, and ________.

From these facts, we can learn important lessons such as ________.

Living in **ignorance** of problems of the past and present can be dangerous because ________.

While You Read Look for lessons the author learns in childhood that he carries with him as an adult.

❷ Vocabulary

Read each word and its definition. Decide whether you know the word well, know it a little bit, or do not know it at all. After you read, see how your knowledge of each word has increased.

- **transcends** (tran sendz´) *v.* goes beyond the limits of; exceeds (p. 543) ***The indescribable beauty of the Grand Canyon <u>transcends</u> the words used to describe it.*** *transcendent adj. transcendence n.*
- **presumptuous** (prē zump´ cho͞o əs) *adj.* overstepping appropriate bounds; too bold (p. 543) ***It would be <u>presumptuous</u> of me to give medical advice, because I am not a doctor.*** *presume v. presumption n. presumptuously adv.*
- **accomplices** (ə käm´ plis iz) *n.* people who help another person commit a crime (p. 544) ***His <u>accomplices</u> kept a lookout while he robbed the bank.***

❸ Word Study

The **Latin root *-scend-*** means "climb."

In this speech, the author talks about receiving an honor that **transcends**, or climbs and goes beyond, him as just one person.

Vocabulary Development

Vocabulary Knowledge Rating

Create a **Vocabulary Knowledge Rating Chart** (***Professional Development Guidebook***, p. 33) for this selection. Include the selection vocabulary and the Big Question words that appear in the Writing About the Big Question sentence starter. (The Big Question vocabulary is introduced on pp. 442–443.)

Give students a copy of the chart. Read the words aloud, and have students mark their rating in the Before Reading column. Urge them to be alert to these words as they read and discuss the selection.

Tally how many students think they know a word to gauge how much instruction to provide. As students read and discuss the selection, point out the words and their context.

PHLit Online! **Vocabulary Central**, featuring tools, activities, and songs for studying vocabulary, is available at **www.PHLitOnline.com**.

Meet Elie Wiesel (b. 1928)

Author of Keep Memory Alive

The Romanian-born teacher, philosopher, and writer Elie Wiesel was deported to the Nazi death camp at Auschwitz at age fifteen. His parents and sister all perished at the hands of the Nazis.

Survivor and Witness After surviving the war, Wiesel did not write a single word about his wartime experiences for ten years. Finally, in 1955, he wrote an account of his experiences, *And the World Kept Silent.* His English adaptation of the work, *Night,* was published in 1960. He says, "I wrote it for the other survivors who found it difficult to speak. And I wanted really to tell them, 'Look, you must speak . . . we must try.'"

4 BACKGROUND FOR THE SPEECH

The Holocaust

The Holocaust was the systematic persecution and murder of Jews and others deemed "unfit" by Germany's Nazi Party. The Nazis came to power in Germany in 1933. During World War II (1939–1945), Nazi forces killed Jews throughout German-occupied lands or sent them to concentration camps. There, prisoners like Elie Wiesel were worked to death, starved to death, or killed outright.

Did You Know?

Wiesel was perhaps the first to use the term *Holocaust* to describe the Nazis' brutal program of persecution.

Daily Bellringer

For each class during which you will teach this selection, have students complete one of the five Revision activities for Week 13 in the ***Daily Bellringer Activities*** booklet.

4 Background

The Holocaust

Elie Wiesel and other survivors of the Holocaust have taken on a double responsibility to those who perished at the hands of the Nazis during World War II: to make sure that the world never forgets the evil that destroyed so many millions and that such evil never happens again to any people. The tireless efforts of Holocaust survivors to "keep memory alive" have led to annual events across the world in remembrance of the Holocaust and an increased awareness of the history of the Holocaust through museums, films, lectures, and educational programs.

Multidraft Reading

To assist struggling readers and to deepen reading for all, assign the text in "chunks" and apply multidraft reading protocols. For each reading, have students set the purpose indicated:

- **First reading**—literal comprehension: answering the Reading Check questions.
- **Second reading**—application of skills: answering the Persuasive Writing and Evaluate Persuasion prompts.
- **Third reading**—interpretation: answering the end-of-selection questions.

For more guidance, refer to the ***Classroom Strategies and Teaching Routines*** card on multidraft reading.

Differentiated Instruction — Additional Instruction

EL Extended Support—English Learners
Have students complete the **Reading and Vocabulary Warm-ups, *Unit 3 Resources,*** pp. 127–130 before they read. Assign the prereading and the adapted selection pages for the selection in the ***Reader's Notebook: English Learner's Version***. Then, have students listen to portions of the selection on the ***Hear It!* Audio CD.**

L1 L2 Extended Support—Struggling Readers
Have students complete the **Reading and Vocabulary Warm-ups, *Unit 3 Resources,*** pp. 127–130, before they read. Assign the prereading pages and the adapted selection in the ***Reader's Notebook: Adapted Version***. Then, have students listen to portions of the selection on the ***Hear It!* Audio CD** (adapted text).

Extended Support—Reluctant Readers
To build motivation and engagement before assigning the selection, have students read "The Witness Dilemma," a thematically related selection in ***Reality Central.*** Then, use the questions at the conclusion of the related selection to guide discussion.

PHLit Online!
For more about the author, practice with the selection vocabulary, and more background, go to **www.PHLitOnline.com.**

❶ Activating Prior Knowledge

Have students form small groups. Give each group a copy of a **K-W-L Chart** (see ***Professional Development Guidebook*** p. 75), with the topic identified as the Holocaust. Ask group members to work together to complete the first two columns. In the Know column, they can write what they know about the Holocaust. In the Want to Know column, they should write questions they have about the topic.

Concept Connector ⟶

Students will return to the **K-W-L Chart** after completing "Keep Memory Alive."

Individual Activity

Point out to students that several museums have opened in the United States to bear witness to the Holocaust. Have these students locate and explore the Web site of one of these museums on the Internet and then write a personal response that expresses their feelings and thoughts about the Holocaust based on what they learned.

❷ About the Selection

In "Keep Memory Alive," Elie Wiesel reminds us of the urgent importance of remembering the Holocaust and the evil that drove it. Wiesel casts those who would remain silent in the role of perpetrators. To support his ideas, Wiesel shares vivid memories, images, and questions from his own experience at a concentration camp as a child.

❶ ❷ Keep Memory Alive

Elie Wiesel

Vocabulary Development

Vocabulary Knowledge Rating

When students have completed reading and discussing "Keep Memory Alive," have them take out their **Vocabulary Knowledge Rating Chart** for this selection. Read the words aloud once more, and have students rate their knowledge of the words again in the After Reading column. Clarify any words that are still problematic. Have students write their own definition and example or sentence in the appropriate column. Then have students complete the Vocabulary Practice at the end of the selection. Encourage students to use the words in further discussion and written work about this selection. Remind them that they will be accountable for these words on the **Selection Test**, ***Unit 3 Resources***, pp. 139–141 or 142–144.

It is with a profound sense of humility that I accept the honor you have chosen to bestow upon me. I know: your choice transcends me. This both frightens and pleases me.

3 It frightens me because I wonder: do I have the right to represent the multitudes who have perished? Do I have the right to accept this great honor on their behalf? I do not. That would be presumptuous. No one may speak for the dead, no one may interpret their mutilated dreams and visions.

It pleases me because I may say that this honor belongs to all the survivors and their children, and through us, to the Jewish people with whose destiny I have always identified.

I remember: it happened yesterday or eternities ago. A young Jewish boy discovered the kingdom of night. I remember his bewilderment, I remember his anguish. It all happened so fast. The ghetto.[1] The deportation. The sealed cattle car. The fiery altar upon which the history of our people and the future of mankind were meant to be sacrificed.

Literary Analysis
Persuasive Writing
Identify two examples of parallelism in the second paragraph.

Vocabulary
transcends (tran sendz´) *v.* goes beyond the limits of; exceeds

presumptuous (prē zump´ cho͞o əs) *adj.* overstepping appropriate bounds; too bold

1. **The ghetto** (get´ ō) During the Second World War, the Nazis forced Jews in European cities to live in crowded, restricted neighborhoods, or ghettos.

4 ◀ **Critical Viewing** How does this image of children being sent to a Nazi concentration camp add force to Wiesel's point about the necessity of remembering? Explain. **[Support]**

3 Literary Analysis
Persuasive Writing

1. Have students name rhetorical devices persuasive writers use to reinforce their point of view.
2. **Ask** students to respond to the Literary Analysis prompt: Identify two examples of parallelism in the second paragraph.
   Possible responses: Students may identify the repeated clauses "do I have the right" and "no one may" as examples of parallelism.

4 Critical Viewing

Possible response: Most students will respond that the photograph definitely adds force to Wiesel's point. Wiesel emphasizes that the evil of the Holocaust must be remembered because the evil was so great that it spared no one, not even children. It should never be allowed to happen again.

Concept Connector

K-W-L Chart
Have students complete the last column of their **K-W-L Charts.** As a class, discuss what questions have been answered and what new questions have emerged.

Writing About the Big Question
Have students compare their responses to the sentence starters they completed before reading the essay with their ideas afterwards. Ask them to explain whether their thoughts have changed.

Reading Skill Graphic Organizer
Ask students to review the charts they completed to evaluate the writer's persuasive appeals. Show them **Reading Skill Graphic Organizer A** (*Graphic Organizer Transparencies,* p. 96) as an example. Then, have students share the charts they made and their evaluations of the writer's logic.

PHLit Online!
This selection is available in interactive format in the **Enriched Online Student Edition, www.PHLitOnline.com,** which includes a thematically related video and writing prompt and an interactive graphic organizer.

5 Connecting to the Big Question

1. Remind students that knowledge can be a valuable tool toward change.
2. Have students read the bracketed text.
3. **Ask:** How is Wiesel using his knowledge of the Holocaust to bring about change in others?
Possible response: He is using his knowledge to educate others about what happened and also to encourage others to speak out and to never remain silent.

ASSESS
Answers

Critical Thinking

1. Students may share Wiesel's shock and explain that they would expect everyone to speak out against human suffering.
2. (a) He accepts the prize on behalf of those who died in the Holocaust. (b) **Possible response:** He believes the award belongs to them because they made the ultimate sacrifice.
(c) **Possible response:** It frightens him because he worries that he cannot represent those who died. It pleases him because he knows that he shares the honor with all survivors.
3. (a) The boy Wiesel asks what the adult Wiesel has done with the boy's future (his own life).
(b) **Possible response:** The boy's questions imply that Wiesel has a responsibility to keep the memory of the Holocaust alive.
(c) **Possible response:** Wiesel believes that forgetfulness and silence are complicit with evil.
4. **Possible response:** If someone saw that another person was about to trip over something but decided to remain silent instead of warning that person, it would be harmful.

What kind of knowledge changes our lives?
Possible response: Wiesel's knowledge of his experiences of the Holocaust helps others make changes so the same mistakes are not made in the present or the future.

I remember: he asked his father: "Can this be true? This is the 20th century, not the Middle Ages. Who would allow such crimes to be committed? How could the world remain silent?"

And now the boy is turning to me: "Tell me," he asks. "What have you done with my future? What have you done with your life?"

And I tell him that I have tried. That I have 5
tried to keep memory alive, that I have tried to fight those who would forget. Because if we forget, we are guilty, we are accomplices.

And then I explained to him how naive we were, that the world did know and remain silent. And that is why I swore never to be silent whenever and wherever human beings endure suffering and humiliation. We must always take sides. Neutrality[2] helps the oppressor, never the victim. Silence encourages the tormentor, never the tormented.

Vocabulary
accomplices (ə käm′ plis iz) *n.* people who help another person commit a crime

2. **Neutrality** (no͞o tral′ ə tē) *n.* state of not taking sides in a conflict; quality of being unbiased.

Critical Thinking

1. **Respond:** Do you share the young Wiesel's shock that the world did not prevent the Holocaust? Why or why not?
2. **(a)** On whose behalf does Wiesel accept the Nobel Prize?
(b) Draw Conclusions: Why does he believe the award belongs to those people? **(c) Interpret:** Why does he say that receiving the award both "frightens and pleases" him?
3. **(a)** What does the boy Wiesel ask the adult Wiesel?
(b) Interpret: What do his questions imply about Wiesel's adult responsibilities? **(c) Draw Conclusions:** Why does Wiesel believe we have a moral duty to remember?
4. **Extend:** Describe a situation in which silence might do harm.

What kind of knowledge changes our lives?
In this speech, the author uses the lessons he learned in a Nazi concentration camp to guide his actions as an adult. What are some of these lessons?

Assessment Resources

Unit 3 Resources
L1 L2 EL **Selection Test A,** pp. 139–141
L3 L4 **Selection Test B,** pp. 141–143
L3 L4 **Open-Book Test,** pp. 136–138

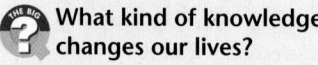

PHLit Online! All assessment resources are available at **www.PHLitOnline.com.**

After You Read — Keep Memory Alive

Literary Analysis: Persuasive Writing and Rhetorical Devices

1. Identify the central **argument** in Wiesel's **persuasive speech.**
2. What **rhetorical devices** does Wiesel use in his speech? Use a chart like the one shown to analyze examples.

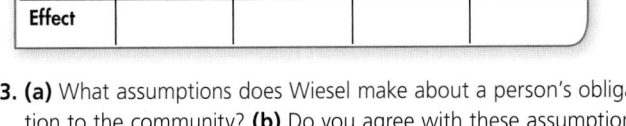

	Repetition	Parallelism	Slogans or Saws	Rhetorical Questions
Example				
Effect				

3. **(a)** What assumptions does Wiesel make about a person's obligation to the community? **(b)** Do you agree with these assumptions? **(c)** Share your response with a small group.

Reading Skill: Evaluate Persuasion

4. **(a)** Wiesel says, "Because if we forget, we are guilty, we are accomplices." What are his reasons for making the claim? **(b)** Explain whether there are any important facts he has not taken into account. **(c)** Is the claim logical? Why or why not?
5. Use your answers to **evaluate** this claim. Consider the rhetorical power of Wiesel's statement as well as the support he gives.

Vocabulary

Practice Words that have similar meanings are called **synonyms**. Words that have opposite meanings are called **antonyms.** Explain whether each word pair contains synonyms or antonyms. Then, write a sentence using both words.

1. presumptuous, modest
2. transcends, exceeds
3. accomplices, collaborators

Word Study Use the context of the sentences and what you know about the **Latin root *-scend-*** to explain your answer to each question.

1. Are you going uphill or downhill as you *ascend* a mountain?
2. If a person is a *descendant* of a mayor, are the two related?

Word Study

The **Latin root *-scend-*** means "climb."

Challenge Explain how the root *-scend-* contributes to the meanings of these words. Consult a dictionary if necessary.

condescend
descend
ascend

ASSESS/EXTEND

Answers

Literary Analysis

1. Wiesel's central argument is that we must keep the memory of the Holocaust alive by retelling the events and speaking up whenever we see injustice.
2. **Possible responses: Repetition: Example:** "I remember" **Effect:** Bears witness to the atrocities of the Holocaust. **Parallelism: Example:** "Neutrality helps the oppressor, never the tormented." **Effect:** Strengthens Wiesel's argument. **Slogans: Example:** "If we forget, we are guilty." **Effect:** Drives home Wiesel's message. **Rhetorical Questions: Example:** Do I have the right. . . ? **Effect:** The reader can only reply, "Of course, you have the right."

   For other sample answers, see ***Graphic Organizer Transparencies*, Literary Analysis Graphic Organizer A**, p. 96, and the **Additional Answers** section.
3. (a) Wiesel assumes that each individual has a duty to protect the rights of others. (b) Students should support their response. (c) Students should share their findings with a small group.

Reading Skill

4. (a) The world remained silent, allowing the Holocaust to continue. (b) **Possible response:** Wiesel might not be taking into account the fact that some people who "forgot" the Holocaust were not born at the time and, therefore, cannot be "accomplices." (c) **Possible response:** Students may say part of the claim is logical. It is true that forgetting such a horrific crime makes it seem as though the crime doesn't matter. But, the claim is not logical because there is a difference between a real accomplice and someone who does not understand how important the crime is.
5. **Possible response:** Wiesel's claim may not be entirely logical because he uses the word *accomplices* to mean more than it usually does. However, his claim is phrased in a powerful, persuasive way.

Vocabulary

Practice

Sample answers:

1. *Presumptuous* and *modest* are antonyms. Billy's presumptuous behavior offended the more modest Marc.
2. *Transcends* and *exceeds* are synonyms. John's novel transcends explanation and exceeds the reader's expectations.
3. *Accomplices* and *collaborators* are synonyms. The accomplices to the crime preferred to call themselves collaborators.

Word Study

Sample answers:

1. You are going uphill, because to ascend is to go up.
2. Yes, they are related, because the mayor is the person's ancestor.

Word Study: Challenge

Sample answers:

To *condescend* is to climb down to a less dignified level. To *descend* is to climb down to a lower level. To *ascend* is to climb up to a higher level.

PRETEACH

Skills instruction for the ***Reading Skill*** *and* ***Literary Analysis*** *concept appears on p. 539.*

❶ Writing About the Big Question

1. Review the assignment with the class.
2. Point out to students that for knowledge to expand, people must know the truth. Have students discuss the importance of free speech in their lives. Ask students to explain how society benefits from truths told through free speech and a free press.
3. Have students complete the sentence starter. Review responses as a class. (**Possible response:** In order to develop a better awareness of and insight into issues such as free speech, one can become better informed about what is going on in the world.)
4. Remind students that their answers will help them think about the Big Question.

While You Read

Tell students that as they read, they should look for Solzhenitsyn's suggestions about how writers can be the voice of truth.

❷ Vocabulary

1. Have students preview the selection vocabulary.
2. For each word, have students say the word aloud.
3. Then, use the word in a sentence that defines the word.
4. Finally, repeat your definitional sentence or a similar sentence with the word missing and have the class "fill in the blank" chorally. For example:

   To condemn something is to disapprove of it. The protestors are marching to show that they [students say "condemn"] *the company's actions.*

❸ Word Study

1. Introduce the skill, using the instruction in the box.
2. Have students explain how the root *-jur-* contributes to the meaning of the word *perjury.* (**Answer:** *Perjury* is "the telling of a lie while under oath to tell the truth," which is against the law.)

Making Connections *from* Nobel Lecture

What kind of *knowledge* changes our lives?

❶ Writing About the Big Question

In the excerpt from Nobel Lecture, the author insists that writers should be the voices of truth against the lies and oppression of corrupt governments. Use this sentence starter to develop your ideas about the Big Question.

In order to develop a better **awareness** of and **insight** into issues such as free speech, one can ________________.

While You Read Look for ways Solzhenitsyn suggests that writers can help one another to be the voice of truth.

❷ Vocabulary

Read each word and its definition. Decide whether you know the word well, know it a little bit, or do not know it at all. After you read, see how your knowledge of each word has increased.

- **aggregate** (ag´ rə git) *n.* a group of distinct things gathered into a whole; a sum (p. 549) ***The aggregate of ants worked together to rebuild their colony.*** *aggregate adj. aggregate v. aggregation n.*
- **reciprocity** (res´ ə präs´ ə tē) *n.* relations of exchange; interdependence (p. 549) ***Reciprocity between nations means helping each other out during difficult times.*** *reciprocal adj. reciprocate v.*
- **jurisdiction** (jo͝or´ is dik´ shən) *n.* sphere of authority or power (p. 549) ***The mayor's jurisdiction does not extend beyond this town.*** *jurisdictional adj. jury n.*
- **condemn** (kən dem´) *v.* disapprove of; pass unfavorable judgment on (p. 551) ***The court is certain to condemn the traitor for his crimes.*** *condemnable adj. condemnation n. condemned adj.*
- **inexorably** (in eks´ ə rə blē) *adv.* without the possibility of being delayed or stopped (p. 551) ***The hurricane moved inexorably up the coast.*** *inexorable adj. inexorability n.*
- **oratory** (ôr´ ə tôr´ ē) *n.* act of public speaking; strategies used in such speaking (p. 551) ***The speaker's oratory fired up the crowd.*** *orate v. orator n. oration n.*

❸ Word Study

The **Latin root *-jur-*** means "law" or "right."

In this speech, the author asserts that a nation's government should not have **jurisdiction,** or the right to make laws, over the literature produced there.

Vocabulary Development

Vocabulary Knowledge Rating

Create a **Vocabulary Knowledge Rating Chart** (***Professional Development Guidebook***, p. 33) for this selection. Include the selection vocabulary and the Big Question words that appear in the Writing About the Big Question sentence starter. (The Big Question vocabulary is introduced on pp. 442–443.)

Give students a copy of the chart. Read the words aloud, and have students mark their rating in the Before Reading column. Urge them to be alert to these words as they read and discuss the selection.

Tally how many students think they know a word to gauge how much instruction to provide. As students read and discuss the selection, point out the words and their context.

PHLit Online! **Vocabulary Central**, featuring tools, activities, and songs for studying vocabulary, is available at **www.PHLitOnline.com**.

Meet
Alexander Solzhenitsyn
(b. 1918)

Author of
Nobel Lecture

Russian writer Alexander Solzhenitsyn spent years in prison camps because of his political views. Yet he was never intimidated into silence. He experienced the hardship of being a dissident—someone who publicly disagrees with an established system.

A Powerful Voice During the Second World War, Solzhenitsyn was imprisoned for writing letters to a friend that were critical of the Soviet leader, Joseph Stalin. In his first novel, *A Day in the Life of Ivan Denisovich,* he described the harsh climate, backbreaking work, and poor diet at the camp in which he was imprisoned. In 1974, after the publication in Paris of parts of *The Gulag Archipelago,* Solzhenitsyn was tried for treason and exiled. In 1994, three years after the fall of the Soviet Union, he returned to his homeland.

4 BACKGROUND FOR THE SPEECH
A Writer in Exile

By writing critically about the U.S.S.R. (now Russia and other nations), Alexander Solzhenitsyn faced punishment and censorship. As he explains in his Nobel Lecture, writers and publishers around the world offered their support. When Solzhenitsyn was exiled in 1974, he was first welcomed by fellow author and Nobel Prize winner Heinrich Böll.

Did You Know?
Solzhenitsyn won the Nobel Prize in Literature in 1970.

Daily Bellringer
For each class during which you will teach this selection, have students complete one of the five Revision activities for Week 13 in the *Daily Bellringer Activities* booklet.

4 Background
A Writer in Exile

After two years of exile in Europe, Alexander Solzhenitsyn moved to the United States, where he continued his pursuit of the truth from a farm in Cavendish, Vermont. Solzhenitsyn was a critical voice in the 1970s and 1980s, taking aim not only at the Soviet Union, but also at America and Western culture. In a speech at Harvard University in 1978, Solzhenitsyn warned of a dangerous split in the world and an even more threatening moral and spiritual decline. In 1994, three years after the breakup of the USSR and the end of communism, the writer in exile returned to his homeland. Under the new umbrella of free speech, Solzhenitsyn was outspoken in his criticism of the new Russia.

Multidraft Reading
To assist struggling readers and to deepen reading for all, assign the text in "chunks" and apply multidraft reading protocols. For each reading, have students set the purpose indicated:

- **First reading**—literal comprehension: answering the Reading Check questions.
- **Second reading**—application of skills: answering the Evaluating Persuasive Appeals and Evaluate Persuasion prompts.
- **Third reading**—interpretation: answering the end-of-selection questions.

For more guidance, refer to the ***Classroom Strategies and Teaching Routines*** card on multidraft reading.

Differentiated Instruction — Additional Instruction

EL Extended Support—English Learners
Have students complete the **Reading and Vocabulary Warm-ups, *Unit 3 Resources,*** pp. 145–148, before they read. Assign the prereading pages for the selection in the ***Reader's Notebook: English Learner's Version.*** Then, have students listen to portions of the selection on the ***Hear It!* Audio CD.**

L1 L2 Extended Support—Struggling Readers
Have students complete the **Reading and Vocabulary Warm-ups, *Unit 3 Resources,*** pp. 145–148, before they read. Assign the prereading pages for the selection in the ***Reader's Notebook: Adapted Version.*** Then, have students listen to portions of the selection on the ***Hear It!* Audio CD** (adapted text).

Extended Support—Reluctant Readers
To build motivation and engagement before assigning the selection, have students read "Instant Friends," a thematically related selection in ***Reality Central.*** Then, use the questions at the conclusion of the related selection to guide discussion.

PHLit Online!
For more about the author, practice with the selection vocabulary, and more background, go to **www.PHLitOnline.com.**

TEACH

❶ Activating Prior Knowledge

Have students form small groups. Give each group a copy of a **K-W-L Chart** (see ***Professional Development Guidebook*** p. 75), with the topic identified as *repression*. Ask group members to work together to complete the first two columns. In the Know column, they can write what they know about ideas or people who have been repressed. In the Want to Know column, they will write questions about the repression of ideas in the former Soviet Union.

Concept Connector →

Students will review their ideas after reading from "Nobel Lecture."

Small-Group Activity

Have students work in small groups. Ask each group to select a passage they find most persuasive and identify the persuasive techniques Solzhenitsyn uses. Have one student from each group read their passage to the class and explain why it was selected.

❷ About the Selection

In this portion of his Nobel Prize lecture, Solzhenitsyn reflects upon the importance of literature that bears witness—writers whose voices override lies and the readers who respond to and align with them.

❸ Critical Viewing

Possible response: Students may observe that the conditions at this prison camp seem extremely harsh for someone guilty of merely "writing letters" criticizing Stalin.

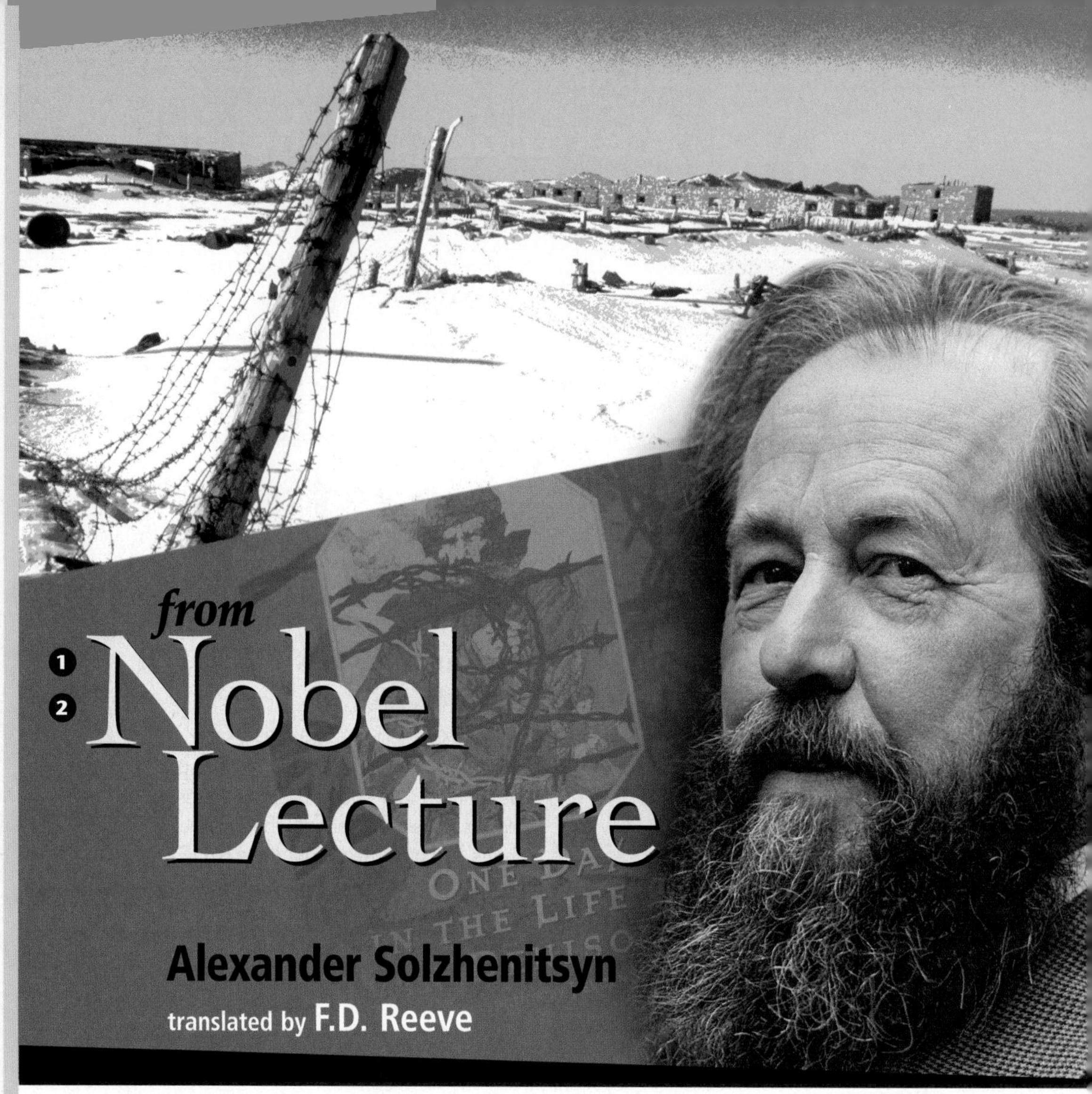

from ❶ ❷ Nobel Lecture

Alexander Solzhenitsyn

translated by F.D. Reeve

❸ ▲ **Critical Viewing** Why is it surprising that Solzhenitsyn was sent to a prison camp, like this one, for writing letters? **[Connect]**

I am, however, encouraged by a keen sense of WORLD LITERATURE as the one great heart that beats for the cares and misfortunes of our world, even though each corner sees and experiences them in a different way.

In past times, also, besides age-old national literatures there existed a concept of world literature as the link between the

Vocabulary Development

Thematic Vocabulary: The Big Question

As students are discussing the excerpt from "Nobel Lecture," encourage them to use the thematic vocabulary presented in Introducing the Big Question, pp. 442–443. You might encourage them with sentence starters like these:

1. Solzhenitsyn believes the truth will *enlighten* people because . . .
2. In this essay, Solzhenitsyn maintains that *understanding* world literature is . . .
3. Solzhenitsyn believes that knowing the *history* of other peoples . . .
4. Solzhenitsyn thinks writers should use their *influence* to spread . . .

summits of national literatures and as the aggregate of reciprocal literary influences. But there was a time lag: readers and writers came to know foreign writers only belatedly, sometimes centuries later, so that mutual influences were delayed and the network of national literary high points was visible not to contemporaries but to later generations.

Today, between writers of one country and the readers and writers of another, there is an almost instantaneous reciprocity, as I myself know. My books, unpublished, alas, in my own country, despite hasty and often bad translations have quickly found a responsive world readership. Critical analysis of them has been undertaken by such leading Western writers as Heinrich Böll.[1] During all these recent years, when both my work and my freedom did not collapse, when against the laws of gravity they held on seemingly in thin air, seemingly on nothing, on the invisible, mute surface tension of sympathetic people, with warm gratitude I learned, to my complete surprise, of the support of the world's writing fraternity. On my fiftieth birthday I was astounded to receive greetings from well-known European writers. No pressure put on me now passed unnoticed. During the dangerous weeks when I was being expelled from the Writers' Union,[2] THE PROTECTIVE WALL put forward by prominent writers of the world saved me from worse persecution, and Norwegian writers and artists hospitably prepared shelter for me in the event that I was exiled from my country. Finally, my being nominated for a Nobel Prize was originated not in the land where I live and write but by François Mauriac[3] and his colleagues. Afterward, national writers' organizations expressed unanimous support for me.

4 As I have understood it and experienced it myself, world literature is no longer an abstraction or a generalized concept invented by literary critics, but a common body and common spirit, a living, heartfelt unity reflecting the growing spiritual unity of mankind. State borders still turn crimson, heated red-hot by electric fences and machine-gun fire; some ministries of internal affairs still suppose that literature is "an internal affair" of the countries under their jurisdiction; and newspaper headlines still herald, "They have no right to interfere in our internal affairs!" Meanwhile, no such thing as INTERNAL AFFAIRS remains on our crowded Earth. Mankind's salvation lies exclusively in everyone's making everything his business, in the people of the East being anything but indifferent to what is thought in the West, and in the

1. **Heinrich** (hīn´ riH) **Böll** (böl) (1917–1985) German novelist and winner of the Nobel Prize in Literature.
2. **Writers' Union** official Soviet writers' organization, which enforced government policies on literature and gave privileges to writers. In addition to being expelled from this union, Solzhenitsyn was forbidden to live in Moscow.
3. **François** (frän swá´) **Mauriac** (mô´ rē ak´) (1885–1970) French novelist and essayist.

Vocabulary

aggregate (ag´ rə git) *n.* a group of distinct things gathered into a whole; a sum

reciprocity (res´ ə präs´ ə tē) *n.* relations of exchange; interdependence

jurisdiction (jo͝or´ is dik´ shən) *n.* sphere of authority or power

Literary Analysis
Persuasive Writing How does repetition of the words *common, unity, West,* and *East* add to the power of this paragraph?

5 **Reading Check**
Name one way in which writers in other countries helped Solzhenitsyn.

4 Literary Analysis
Persuasive Writing

1. Remind students that word patterns such as repetition can make persuasive writing more powerful and effective.
2. **Ask** students to respond to the Literary Analysis question: How does repetition of the words *common, unity, West,* and *East* add to the power of this paragraph?
Possible responses: The repetition helps make the point that people in the East and the West are not separate from each other but are part of one world and have the same concerns and goals.

5 Reading Check

Answer: Some writers translated and published Solzhenitsyn's works for readers in other countries. Other writers prepared a place for him to live if he was exiled.

Differentiated Instruction for Universal Access

Strategy for Less Proficient Readers
Students may need more contextual information to help them approach Solzhenitsyn's lecture. Tell students that the Nobel Prizes, which are given every year in a number of categories, were established by a financial gift from Alfred Nobel, the Swedish inventor of dynamite. Each winner of the prize receives a medal, a large sum of money, and, for a time, much attention. The prize in literature gives a writer an equally precious gift—the opportunity to speak to and be heard by a world audience.

Enrichment for Advanced Readers
Encourage interested students to compare Solzhenitsyn's lecture with the remarks of at least two other writers who have won the Nobel Prize in Literature. What topics do these writers choose to address? What assertions, if any, do they make about the power of the written word to affect change? What role do they say the writer plays in the world? Ask students to report their findings to the class.

PHLit Online!
This selection is available in interactive format in the Enriched Online Student Edition, **www.PHLitOnline.com**, which includes a thematically related video with writing prompt and an interactive graphic organizer.

❻ Literature in Context

World Events Connection
Literature became a tool of repression of the Soviet state soon after the Russian Revolution. All writing in the Soviet Union was expected to serve the aims of the Communist party. The only kind of literature that could be published was writing officially approved by the government. Writers who dared criticize the state or who tried to maintain some level of objectivity were censored, terrorized, or sent to prison camps. Nevertheless, dissident writers circumvented the system and continued to create unofficial literature.

Connect to the Literature Have students read the Literature in Context feature. **Ask** students the Connect to the Literature question.
Possible response: Solzhenitsyn probably welcomed the greater toleration of freedom of expression.

❼ Connecting to the Big Question

1. Remind students that an author can use knowledge to transmit truths to others.
2. **Ask** students how they use knowledge to transmit truths and change the lives of others.
Possible response: I use my knowledge about the dangers of not wearing a seat belt to convince my friends and family to wear their seat belts.
3. Have students read the bracketed text. **Ask:** What does Solzhenitsyn suggest is the power world literature holds in these times?
Possible response: Solzhenitsyn suggests that world literature has the power to transmit concise and accurate past histories and current values of regions so people can see themselves as they are in the world.
4. Have students explain how having an accurate view and knowledge of the world might help human beings advance?
Possible response: By having an awareness about what happened in the past and what is happening in the present, people can make better judgments and avoid repeating the mistakes as we move forward.

❻ **LITERATURE IN CONTEXT**

World Events Connection

Repression in the Soviet Union

◀ Many of Solzhenitsyn's difficulties with the Soviet authorities stemmed from his works exposing the evils of the Soviet Gulag.

The Gulag consisted of prison camps such as the one shown. Many were located in Siberia, where harsh weather, poor diet, and intensive labor led to much suffering among inmates. ▶

1929–1953	1956–1964	mid-1960s–mid-1980s	1985–1991
Dictatorship of Josef Stalin Millions are imprisoned for allegedly opposing the government.	**The "Thaw"** New freedoms are permitted.	Renewed Repression	**Glasnost ("openness")** Mikhail Gorbachev introduces policies tolerating freedom of expression.

Connect to the Literature

Judging from Solzhenitsyn's Nobel Lecture, how might he have responded to news of Gorbachev's policies from 1985 to 1991?

❹ people of the West being anything but indifferent to what happens in the East. Literature, one of the most sensitive and responsive tools of human existence, has been the first to pick up, adopt, and assimilate this sense of the growing unity of mankind. I therefore confidently turn to the world literature of the present, to hundreds of friends whom I have not met face to face and perhaps never will see.

My friends! Let us try to be helpful, if we are worth anything. In our own countries, torn by differences among parties, movements, castes, and groups, who for ages past has been not the dividing but the uniting force? This, essentially, is the position of writers, spokesmen of a national language, of the chief tie binding the nation, the very soil which the people inhabit, and, in fortunate circumstances, the nation's spirit too.

❼ I think that world literature has the power in these frightening times to help mankind see itself accurately despite what is advocated by partisans and by parties. It has the power to transmit the condensed experience of one region to another, so that different scales of values are combined, and so that one people accurately and concisely knows the true history of another with a power of recognition and acute awareness as if it had lived through that history itself—and could thus be spared repeating old mistakes. At

Vocabulary Development

Vocabulary Knowledge Rating
When students have completed reading and discussing the excerpt from "Nobel Lecture," have them take out their **Vocabulary Knowledge Rating Chart** for this selection. Read the words aloud once more, and have students rate their knowledge of the words again in the After Reading column. Clarify any words that are still problematic. Have students write their own definition and example or sentence in the appropriate column. Then, have students complete the Vocabulary Practice at the end of the selection. Encourage students to use the words in further discussion and written work about this selection. Remind them that they will be accountable for these words on the **Selection Test**, ***Unit 3 Resources***, pp. 160–162 or 163–165.

7 the same time, perhaps we ourselves may succeed in developing our own WORLDWIDE VIEW, like any man, with the center of the eye seeing what is nearby but the periphery of vision taking in what is happening in the rest of the world. We will make correlations and maintain worldwide standards.

Who, if not writers, are to condemn their own unsuccessful governments (in some states this is the easiest way to make a living; everyone who is not too lazy does it) as well as society itself, whether for its cowardly humiliation or for its self-satisfied weakness, or the lightheaded escapades of the young, or the youthful pirates brandishing knives?

We will be told: What can literature do against the pitiless onslaught of naked violence? Let us not forget that violence does not and cannot flourish by itself; it is inevitably intertwined with LYING. Between them there is the closest, the most profound and natural bond: nothing screens violence except lies, and the only way lies can hold out is by violence. Whoever has once announced violence as his METHOD must inexorably choose lying as his PRINCIPLE. At birth, violence behaves openly and even proudly. But as soon as it becomes stronger and firmly established, it senses the thinning of the air around it and cannot go on without befogging itself in lies, coating itself with lying's sugary oratory. It does not always or necessarily go straight for the gullet; usually it demands of its victims only allegiance to the lie, only complicity in the lie.

Vocabulary

condemn (kən dem′) *v.* disapprove of; pass unfavorable judgment on

inexorably (in eks′ ə rə blē) *adv.* without the possibility of being delayed or stopped

oratory (ôr′ ə tôr′ ē) *n.* act of public speaking; strategies used in such speaking

8 **Reading Check**

According to Solzhenitsyn, what does world literature have the power to do?

YOU ARE LEAVING
THE AMERICAN SECTOR
ВЫ ВЫЕЗЖАЕТЕ ИЗ
АМЕРИКАНСКОЙ ЗО
VOUS SORTEZ
DU SECTEUR A AIN
DER TAGESSPIEGEL
DER TAG

9 ◀ **Critical Viewing** The Berlin Wall once separated East and West Berlin. How does this scene of newspaper readers by the wall support what the author says about truth? **[Connect]**

8 Reading Check

Answer: World literature can help give people an accurate view of the experiences and histories of other regions around the world.

9 Critical Viewing

Possible response: Government obstacles cannot stifle people's desire for free communication. People will find a way and even take risks to overcome obstacles to free communication.

Concept Connector

K-W-L Chart

Have students complete the last column of their **K-W-L Charts.** As a class, discuss what questions have been answered about repression and what new questions have emerged.

Writing About the Big Question

Have students compare their responses to the sentence starter they completed before reading the essay with their ideas afterwards. Ask them to explain whether their thoughts have changed.

Reading Skill Graphic Organizer

Ask students to review the charts they completed to evaluate the writer's persuasive appeals. Show them **Reading Skill Graphic Organizer A** (*Graphic Organizer Transparencies,* p. 94) as an example. Then, have students share the charts they made and their evaluations of the writer's logic.

⑩ Reading Skill
Evaluate Persuasion

Ask students the Reading Skill question: Does Solzhenitsyn support his claim that "art has always won and always will"? Explain.
Possible response: Students may note that Solzhenitsyn repeats his original assertion in other words but offers no historical evidence.

ASSESS

Answers

Critical Thinking

1. Most students will respond that they find the celebration of truth stirring.
2. (a) In the past, a time lag prevented readers and writers from getting to know world literature. (b) He calls world literature "one great heart" because it concerns itself with the cares and misfortunes of all people.
3. (a) They publicized his persecution and offered him sanctuary. (b) This confirms his view of world literature as a community.
4. He believes that the role of artists is to conquer lies and tell the truth.
5. Students might cite a situation in which a lie was told about another person. Solzhenitsyn might tell others to reveal the truth so the person will not be wrongfully accused.

What kind of knowledge changes our lives?

Possible responses:
(a) Solzhenitsyn thinks that the role of violence in society must be examined. Also, he thinks writers should examine corruption and lying. (b) Yes, Solzhenitsyn thinks that knowing the truth about certain issues will help bring people together and also ensure that the mistakes of the past will not be repeated. Solzhenitsyn is using his own knowledge to spread truths and in turn to change people's lives for the better.

Reading Skill
Evaluate Persuasion
Does Solzhenitsyn support his claim that "art has always won and always will"? Explain. ⑩

The simple act of an ordinary courageous man is not to take part, not to support lies! Let *that* come into the world and even reign over it, but not through me. Writers and artists can do more: they can VANQUISH LIES! In the struggle against lies, art has always won and always will. Conspicuously, incontestably for everyone. Lies can stand up against much in the world, but not against art.

Once lies have been dispelled, the repulsive nakedness of violence will be exposed—and hollow violence will collapse.

That, my friends, is why I think we can help the world in its red-hot hour: not by the nay-saying of having no armaments,[4] not by abandoning oneself to the carefree life, but by going into battle!

In Russian, proverbs about TRUTH are favorites. They persistently express the considerable, bitter, grim experience of the people, often astonishingly:

ONE WORD OF TRUTH OUTWEIGHS THE WORLD.

On such a seemingly fantastic violation of the law of the conservation of mass and energy are based both my own activities and my appeal to the writers of the whole world.

ONE WORD OF TRUTH OUTWEIGHS THE WORLD.

4. **the nay-saying of having no armaments** Solzhenitsyn is referring to the idea that nations should limit the number or kind of weapons that they hold ready for war.

Critical Thinking

1. **Respond:** Were you stirred by the conclusion? Why or why not?
2. **(a)** According to Solzhenitsyn, what is a key difference between world literature today and in the past? **(b) Interpret:** Why does he call world literature "one great heart"?
3. **(a)** According to Solzhenitsyn, what were two ways in which European writers showed support for him? **(b) Connect:** How does this support confirm his view of world literature?
4. **Analyze:** What role does Solzhenitsyn believe artists have in the struggle against injustice?
5. **Apply:** Identify a situation in which it matters whether people speak up. Explain what Solzhenitsyn might say about it.

What kind of knowledge changes our lives? Solzhenitsyn wants writers to write about "the truth." **(a)** What issues would he think are most in need of this truthful examination? **(b)** Does he want the truth about these issues to change people? Explain.

Assessment Resources

Unit 3 Resources
L1 L2 EL **Selection Test A**, pp. 160–162
L3 L4 **Selection Test B**, pp. 163–165
L3 L4 **Open-Book Test**, pp. 157–159

PHLit Online! All assessment resources are available at www.PHLitOnline.com.

After You Read *from* Nobel Lecture

Literary Analysis: Persuasive Writing and Rhetorical Devices

1. Identify the central argument in Solzhenitsyn's **persuasive speech.**
2. What **rhetorical devices** does Solzhenitsyn use to emphasize his message? Use a chart like the one shown to analyze examples.

	Repetition	Parallelism	Slogans or Saws	Rhetorical Questions
Example				
Effect				

3. **(a)** What assumptions does Solzhenitsyn make about the rights of individuals as opposed to the dictates of the state? **(b)** Do you agree with his assumptions? **(c)** Discuss your responses in a group.

Reading Skill: Evaluate Persuasion

4. **(a)** Solzhenitsyn writes, "Once lies have been dispelled . . . hollow violence will collapse." Explain his reasons for making the claim. **(b)** Explain whether there are any important facts he has not taken into account. **(c)** Explain whether the claim is logical.
5. Evaluate Solzhenitsyn's claim. In your answer, consider the rhetorical power of the statement as well as the support he gives.

Vocabulary

Practice Words with the same or similar meanings are **synonyms.** Words with opposite meanings are **antonyms.** Explain whether each item contains synonyms or antonyms. Then, write a sentence using both words.

1. reciprocity, independence
2. inexorably, avoidably
3. oratory, rhetoric
4. aggregate, total
5. jurisdiction, authority
6. condemn, approve

Word Study Use the context of the sentences and what you know about the **Latin root *-jur-*** to explain your answer to each question.

1. Would you expect to see a *jury* in a courtroom or in a gymnasium?
2. Why would it be a bad idea to commit *perjury* during a trial?

Word Study

The **Latin root *-jur-*** means "law" or "right."

Challenge Explain how the root *-jur-* contributes to the meanings of these words. Consult a dictionary if necessary.

abjure
injury
jurisprudence

ASSESS/EXTEND

Answers

Literary Analysis

1. Writers and artists must tell the truth to overcome government lies and repression.
2. **Possible responses: Repetition: Examples:** *world literature, unity* **Effect:** Emphasizes the unifying strength of world literature. **Parallelism: Example:** "with the center of the eye seeing what is nearby . . . what is happening in the rest of the world." **Effect:** Moves the reader from an egocentric view to a global one. **Slogans or Saws: Example:** "One Word of Truth Outweighs the World." **Effect:** This phrase uses exaggeration for effect. **Rhetorical Questions: Example:** "What can literature do against the pitiless onslaught of naked violence?" **Effect:** "Pitiless" and "naked violence" add drama.

   For other sample answers, see ***Graphic Organizer Transparencies,*** **Literary Analysis Graphic Organizer A**, p. 97, and the **Additional Answers** section.
3. (a) He assumes the rights of individuals are higher than the dictates of the state. (b) Students should support their response. (c) Students discuss in groups.

Reading Skill

4. **Possible responses:** (a) He believes that lies and violence cannot stand up against the truth. (b) He might not have taken into account the fact that people in power could use brute force to rule. (c) It is logical to think that if people stop respecting the government, it will lose power. However, words are not enough. People have to take action.
5. **Possible response:** His claim exaggerates the power of words and does not say enough about the importance of people's actions. However, he phrases the claim in a persuasive way that gives people faith in the power of truth.

Vocabulary

Practice

1. Antonyms. In a relationship based on reciprocity, neither party has independence.
2. Antonyms. It seemed the country was headed inexorably toward war, though avoidably.
3. Synonyms. The art of oratory involves a lot of rhetoric.
4. Synonyms. To take an aggregate of a set of numbers is to take their total.
5. Synonyms. When the courts assert their jurisdiction over a matter, they are exercising their authority.
6. Antonyms. When you condemn an action, you do not approve of it.

Word Study

1. You would find a jury in a courtroom, because juries decide court cases.
2. It would be a bad idea, because if you commit perjury, you are lying.

Word Study: Challenge

Sample answers: If you *abjure* your beliefs, you give them up, usually under threat of the law. If you cause *injury* to someone, you're violating their rights. *Jurisprudence* is the study of the law.

EXTEND/ASSESS

Answers

Grammar

1. Introduce the skill, using the instruction on the student page.
2. Discuss the degrees of adverbs chart.

Think Aloud: Model the Skill

Model the skill of identifying the degrees of adverbs: Say to students:

> In the sentence *John did well in the race,* I know the adverb *well* is positive since it does not compare John to anyone else. In the sentence *John did better than Billy in the race,* I know the adverb *better* is comparative since it compares John's performance to Billy's. In the sentence *Out of the whole team, John had the best time in the race,* I know the adverb *best* is superlative because John's time is compared to all the others on the team.

WG Writing and Grammar, Grade 10

Students will find further instruction on practice with degrees of adverbs Chapter 25, Section 1.

Practice A

1. most convincingly, superlative
2. powerfully, positive
3. painfully, positive
4. stronger, comparative

Challenge

Sample answers: *It all happened so fast; fast* is positive. *We must always take sides; always* is superlative.

Practice B

Sample answers:

1. Solzhenitsyn wrote more passionately than other writers.
2. The Russian government searched more than once for dissenting voices.
3. A courageous author writes more truthfully than others.
4. Dedicated writers work most diligently at uniting people.

Challenge

Sample answer: Freedom of speech is one of America's most important [superlative] rights. Each person can speak freely [positive] about issues. This makes us likelier [comparative] to speak than the person who is forced to suppress his or her views.

Integrated Language Skills

Keep Memory Alive • *from* Nobel Lecture

Grammar: Degrees of Adverbs

An **adverb** is a word that modifies a verb, an adjective, or another adverb.

Most adverbs have three different forms, called degrees of comparison—the *positive,* the *comparative,* and the *superlative.* Use the positive form to describe a single action or quality. Use the comparative to compare two items. Use the superlative to compare more than two items.

There are several ways to indicate these degrees. For single syllable words, add *-er* or *-est.* For longer words, use *more* or *most.* Some adverbs take on a completely different form. Look at these examples:

Positive	Comparative	Superlative
soon	sooner	soonest
impressively	more impressively	most impressively
well	better	best

Practice A Underline the adverb in each sentence. Tell whether its form is positive, comparative, or superlative.

1. Of all the writers, Wiesel spoke most convincingly.
2. He wrote powerfully about the concentration camps.
3. Wiesel painfully recalled his experiences during World War II.
4. We must be stronger than the person who wants to hurt us.

Challenge In "Keep Memory Alive," find at least one example of a positive and a superlative adverb.

Practice B Rewrite each sentence, replacing each positive adverb with either a comparative or a superlative adverb. You may need to add words to the sentences.

1. Solzhenitsyn wrote passionately.
2. The Russian government searched often for dissenting voices.
3. A courageous author writes truthfully.
4. Dedicated writers work diligently at uniting people.

Challenge Write a brief paragraph about the importance of free speech. Make sure to include at least one example of a positive, a comparative, and a superlative adverb in your writing.

WG Writing and Grammar Connection: Chapter 25, Section 1

Extend the Lesson

Sentence Modeling

Choose the sentence given from the selections students have read:

We must always take sides. ("Keep Memory Alive")

I therefore confidently turn to the world literature of the present, to the hundreds of friends whom I have not met face to face and perhaps never will see. ("Nobel Lecture")

Ask students what they notice about the sentence. Elicit from them that each sentence contains adverbs. Then, ask what else they notice. ("Keep Memory Alive": *Always* is in the superlative degree because it compares more than two items. "Nobel Lecture": *Confidently* is in the positive degree because it describes a single quality, while *never* is in the superlative degree.

Have students imitate the sentence using a sentence on a topic of their own choosing, matching each grammatical feature discussed. Collect the sentences, and share them with the class.

Writing

Wiesel and Solzhenitsyn both discuss the importance of speaking out against oppression. Write a **letter** either to Elie Wiesel in which you take a position on his claim that silence makes us accomplices *or* to Solzhenitsyn in which you evaluate his idea that telling the truth can change the world.

If you are writing to Wiesel follow these tips:

- Identify and state the general definition of "accomplice."
- Describe the specific results of silence that Wiesel points out.
- Use *rhetorical devices* that create emphasis and appeal to emotions.

If you are writing to Solzhenitsyn follow these tips:

- State a general definition of "changing the world."
- Describe the effects of truth that Solzhenitsyn identifies.
- Use *rhetorical devices* to create emphasis and appeal to emotions.

In your letter, use formal language appropriate to your audience.

Writing Workshop: *Work in Progress*

Prewriting for Persuasive Essay For a persuasive essay you may write, jot down five local or national practices that you would like to see changed or modified. Prioritize your list, numbering the items 1 through 5. Save this Topic List in your writing portfolio.

Use this prewriting activity to prepare for the Writing Workshop on page 604.

Listening and Speaking

Hold a group **debate** about one of the following paraphrased claims.

Wiesel: *People who do not speak up against injustice are accomplices.*

Solzhenitsyn: *Telling the truth will bring down an unjust government.*

Choose a notetaker and moderator, and divide the group into teams to argue for and against the statement.

- Present an **engaging introduction** with **quotations** or **anecdotes.**
- During the debate, listen to the arguments presented and prepare to respond. Clarify what you hear by paraphrasing their points.
- Explain how your points relate to what has been said, and provide evidence for your position.
- **Conclude** your argument by summarizing your position.

After the debate, review the notes to identify the best ideas.

PHLit Online!
www.PHLitOnline.com
- Interactive graphic organizers
- Grammar tutorial
- Interactive journals

EXTEND/ASSESS

Writing

1. Review the assignment, using the instruction on the student page.
2. To guide students in writing their letters to Wiesel or Solzhenitsyn, give them **Support for Writing,** p. 155 in ***Unit 3 Resources.***
3. To evaluate students' letters, use the **Persuasive Essay** rubrics, pp. 230–231 in ***Professional Development Guidebook.*** You might also evaluate students' letters based on the evidence and reasoning they provide in support of their position.

Six Traits Focus

✔	Ideas	✔	Word Choice
✔	Organization		Sentence Fluency
✔	Voice		Conventions

Writing and Grammar, Grade 10

Students will find additional instruction on letter writing in Chapter 15.

Writing Workshop
Work in Progress

Have students save their completed Topic Lists in their portfolios. They will use these as they continue this Work-in-Progress assignment (see p. 575). These assignments prepare them to complete the Writing Workshop assignment (see pp. 604–611).

Listening and Speaking

1. Review the assignment, using the instruction on the student page.
2. Have students complete the **Support for Extend Your Learning** page (***Unit 3 Resources,*** p. 156).

Teaching Resources

Unit 3 Resources
- L3 L4 **Integrated Language Skills: Grammar,** p. 154
- L3 L4 **Support for Writing,** p. 155
- L3 L4 **Support for Extend Your Learning,** p. 156
- L4 **Enrichment,** pp. 135, 153

Enriched Online Student Edition
Available under After You Read for this selection:
- All **Interactive Grammar Tutorial**
- L3 L4 **Internet Research Activity**

Professional Development Guidebook
Rubrics for Persuasive Essay, pp. 230–231

PHLit Online! All print and digital resources are available at **www.PHLitOnline.com.** Online resources accessible by students are noted on the student page.

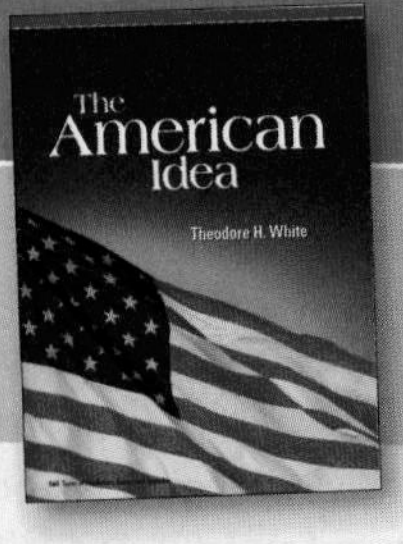

TIME AND RESOURCE MANAGER

The American Idea • What Makes a Degas a Degas?

Lesson Pacing Guide

DAY 1 Preteach

- Administer the Reading and Vocabulary Warm-ups (*Unit 3 Resources*, pp. 166–169 or 184–187) as necessary.
- Introduce the Reading Skill: Evaluate Persuasion FT
- Introduce the Literary Analysis concept: Analytic and Interpretive Essays FT
- Distribute copies of the appropriate graphic organizer for the Reading Skill (*Graphic Organizer Transparencies*, pp. 99–101). CRI
- Distribute copies of the appropriate graphic organizer for Literary Analysis (*Graphic Organizer Transparencies*, pp. 102–104). CRI
- Teach the selection vocabulary. FT CRI
- Introduce the Word Study skill.

DAYS 2–3 Preteach/Teach

- Build background with the Background feature. CRI
- Develop thematic vocabulary and thematic thinking with Writing About the Big Question.
- Prepare students to read with the Activating Prior Knowledge activities (TE). CRI
- Informally monitor comprehension while students read. FT
- Use the Reading Check questions to confirm comprehension.
- Develop students' ability to evaluate a writer's appeals using the Reading Skill questions. CRI
- Develop students' understanding of analytic and interpretive essays using the Literary Analysis questions. CRI
- Reinforce vocabulary with the Vocabulary notes. CRI

DAY 4 Assess

- Assess students' comprehension and mastery of the skills by having them answer the Critical Thinking, Reading Skill, and Literary Analysis questions. FT
- Have students complete the Vocabulary Practice activities. FT
- Have students complete the Word Study activities.

DAY 5 Extend/Assess

- Have students complete the Grammar lesson. CRI
- Have students complete the Writing activity and write a critique. (You may assign as homework.) FT
- Extend learning by having students complete the Research and Technology activity, a cover letter and résumé. (You may assign as homework.) As an alternative, assign them "The Newest Newcomers" or "Hip-Hop: Keeping It Real" in *Reality Central*. CRI
- Administer Selection Test A or B (*Unit 3 Resources*, pp. 178–183 or 199–204). FT

The essay "The American Idea" is presented unedited and in its entirety. The excerpt from the nonfiction book *What Makes a Degas a Degas?* is presented unedited.

Meeting Your Standards

Students will

1. analyze and respond to literary elements.
   - Literary Analysis: Analytic and Interpretive Essays
2. read, comprehend, and analyze short stories.
   - Reading Skill: Evaluate Persuasion
   - Reading Check questions
   - Apply the Skills questions
   - Assessment Practice
3. develop vocabulary.
   - Vocabulary
   - Word Study
4. apply grammar skills.
   - Degrees of Adjectives
5. Develop writing proficiency.
   - Work in Progress: Persuasive Essay
   - critique
6. strengthen research and technology skills.
   - cover letter and résumé

CRI For a full explanation of Culturally Responsive Instruction opportunities in this lesson, see p. T86–T87.

FT For an accelerated lesson, use the Fast Track strategies and activities.

Managing Differentiated Instruction
This leveled selection pairing groups a more accessible with a more challenging selection. Choose either one to teach the lesson skills. For classroom management suggestions for using the pairing in a mixed-ability class, see pp. T68–T69.

Daily Block Scheduling
Each day in this Lesson Pacing Guide represents a 40–50 minute period. Teachers using block scheduling may combine days to revise pacing. In addition, teachers may differentiate and support core instruction by integrating components for extended and intensive support as students require. See the Guide to Selected Leveled Resources (facing page).

Guide to Selected Leveled Resources

EL English Learners

			The American Idea	What Makes a Degas a Degas?
CORE COURSE	*Unit 3 Resources*	Selection Test A	pp. 178–180	pp. 199–201
	Graphic Organizer Transparencies	Reading Skill Graphic Organizer A	p. 99	p. 100
		Literary Analysis Graphic Organizer A	p. 102	p. 103
EXTENDED SUPPORT (Level 2)	*Unit 3 Resources*	Reading and Vocabulary Warm-ups A or B	pp. 166–169	pp. 184–187
	Reader's Notebook: English Learner's Version		adapted instruction and adapted selection	adapted instruction and summary
	Hear It! Audio CD		selection and summaries	selection and summaries
	Hear It! Audio CD (adapted text)		adapted selection and summaries	—
INTENSIVE SUPPORT (Level 1)	*Reality Central*		"The Newest Newcomers"	"Hip-Hop: Keeping It Real"
	Real-World Writing Journal		Lesson 7, pp. 94–97	Lesson 8, pp. 98–101

L2 Below-Level Students

			The American Idea	What Makes a Degas a Degas?
CORE COURSE	*Unit 3 Resources*	Selection Test A	pp. 178–180	pp. 199–201
	Graphic Organizer Transparencies	Reading Skill Graphic Organizer A	p. 99	p. 100
		Literary Analysis Graphic Organizer A	p. 102	p. 103
EXTENDED SUPPORT (Level 2)	*Unit 3 Resources*	Reading and Vocabulary Warm-ups A or B	pp. 166–169	pp. 184–187
	Reader's Notebook		adapted instruction and full selection	adapted instruction and summary
	Hear It! Audio CD		selection and summaries	selection and summaries
INTENSIVE SUPPORT (Level 1)	*Reality Central*		"The Newest Newcomers"	"Hip-Hop: Keeping It Real"
	Real-World Writing Journal		Lesson 7, pp. 94–97	Lesson 8, pp. 98–101
	Reading Kit		Reteaching worksheets	Reteaching worksheets

L1 Special Needs Students

			The American Idea	What Makes a Degas a Degas?
CORE COURSE	*Unit 3 Resources*	Selection Test A	pp. 178–180	pp. 199–201
	Graphic Organizer Transparencies	Reading Skill Graphic Organizer A	p. 99	p. 100
		Literary Analysis Graphic Organizer A	p. 102	p. 103
EXTENDED SUPPORT (Level 2)	*Unit 3 Resources*	Reading and Vocabulary Warm-ups A or B	pp. 166–169	pp. 184–187
	Reader's Notebook: Adapted Version		adapted instruction and adapted selection	adapted instruction and summary
	Hear It! Audio CD (adapted text)		adapted selection and summaries	—
INTENSIVE SUPPORT (Level 1)	*Reality Central*		"The Newest Newcomers"	"Hip-Hop: Keeping It Real"
	Real-World Writing Journal		Lesson 7, pp. 94–97	Lesson 8, pp. 98–101
	Reading Kit		Reteaching worksheets	Reteaching worksheets

The program includes resources for these students: L3 On-Level L4 Advanced All All
For a complete guide to selection support, see pp. T106–T108.

NOTE: All print materials are also available online at *www.PHLitOnline.com*.

VISUAL GUIDE to Featured Selection Resources

• The American Idea
• What Makes a Degas a Degas?

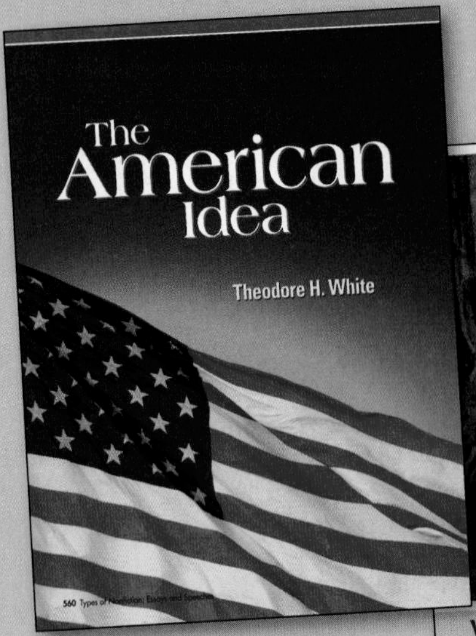

RESOURCES FOR:

- EL English Learners
- L1 Special Needs Students
- L2 Below-Level Students
- L3 On-Level Students
- L4 Advanced Students
- All All Students

Vocabulary/Fluency/Prior Knowledge

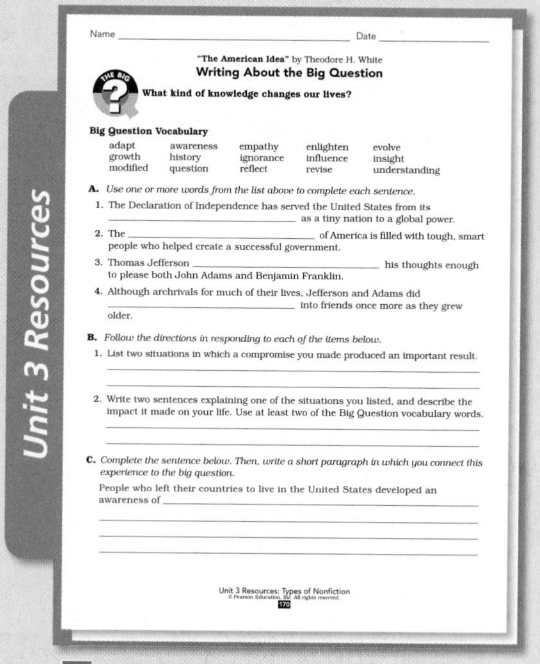

Name ______________________ Date ____________

"The American Idea" by Theodore H. White
Writing About the Big Question

What kind of knowledge changes our lives?

Big Question Vocabulary

adapt	awareness	empathy	enlighten	evolve
growth	history	ignorance	influence	insight
modified	question	reflect	revise	understanding

A. *Use one or more words from the list above to complete each sentence.*

1. The Declaration of Independence has served the United States from its ______________ as a tiny nation to a global power.
2. The ______________ of America is filled with tough, smart people who helped create a successful government.
3. Thomas Jefferson ______________ his thoughts enough to please both John Adams and Benjamin Franklin.
4. Although archrivals for much of their lives, Jefferson and Adams did ______________ into friends once more as they grew older.

B. *Follow the directions in responding to each of the items below.*

1. List two situations in which a compromise you made produced an important result.
2. Write two sentences explaining one of the situations you listed, and describe the impact it made on your life. Use at least two of the Big Question vocabulary words.

C. *Complete the sentence below. Then, write a short paragraph in which you connect this experience to the big question.*

People who left their countries to live in the United States developed an awareness of ______________

Unit 3 Resources: Types of Nonfiction
170

All Writing About the Big Question, pp. 170, 188

Also available for these selections:

- EL L1 L2 Vocabulary Warm-ups A and B, pp. 166–167, 184–185
- EL L1 L2 Reading Warm-ups A and B, pp. 168–169, 186–187
- All Vocabulary Builder, pp. 173, 191

Reader's Notebooks

Pre- and postreading pages for both selections, as well as "The American Idea" appear in an interactive format in the *Reader's Notebooks*. Each *Notebook* is differentiated for a different group of learners. The selections in the Adapted and English Learner's versions are abridged.

- L2 L3 ***Reader's Notebook***
- L1 ***Reader's Notebook: Adapted Version***
- EL ***Reader's Notebook: English Learner's Version***

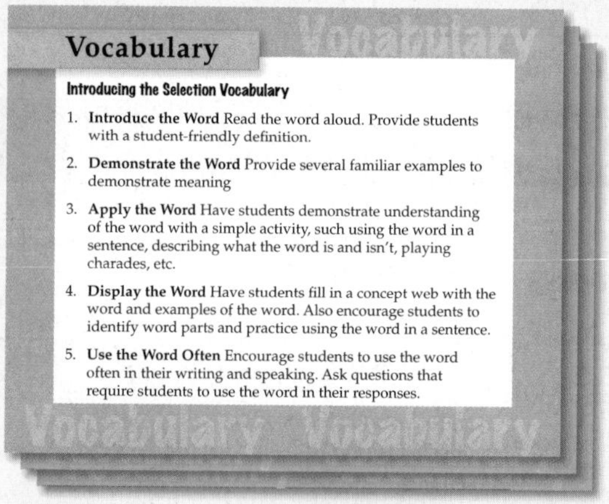

Vocabulary

Introducing the Selection Vocabulary

1. **Introduce the Word** Read the word aloud. Provide students with a student-friendly definition.
2. **Demonstrate the Word** Provide several familiar examples to demonstrate meaning
3. **Apply the Word** Have students demonstrate understanding of the word with a simple activity, such using the word in a sentence, describing what the word is and isn't, playing charades, etc.
4. **Display the Word** Have students fill in a concept web with the word and examples of the word. Also encourage students to identify word parts and practice using the word in a sentence.
5. **Use the Word Often** Encourage students to use the word often in their writing and speaking. Ask questions that require students to use the word in their responses.

Classroom Strategies and Teaching Routines

- core classroom routines outlined step-by-step
- convenient format for easy reference while teaching

Graphic Organizer Transparencies

Selection Support

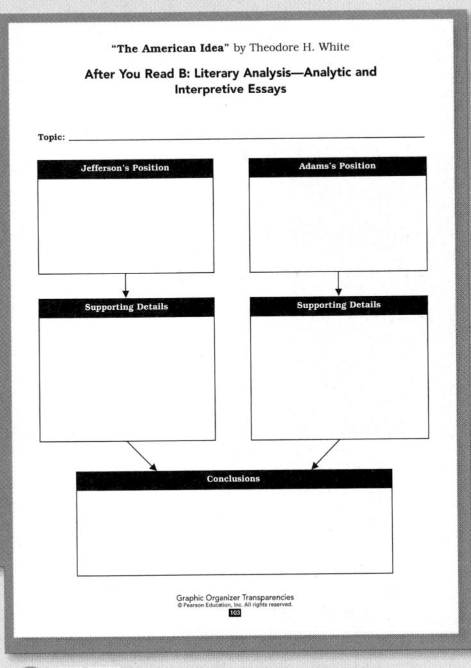
"The American Idea" by Theodore H. White

After You Read B: Literary Analysis—Analytic and Interpretive Essays

Topic: ______

Jefferson's Position	Adams's Position

Supporting Details	Supporting Details

Conclusions

Graphic Organizer Transparencies
© Pearson Education, Inc. All rights reserved.
103

EL L1 L2 **Literary Analysis: Graphic Organizer A,** pp. 102, 103 (partially filled in)

Also available for these selections:

- EL L1 L2 Reading: Graphic Organizer A, pp. 99, 100 (partially filled in)
- L3 Reading: Graphic Organizer B, p. 101
- L3 Literary Analysis: Graphic Organizer B, p. 104

Skills Development/Extension

Unit 3 Resources

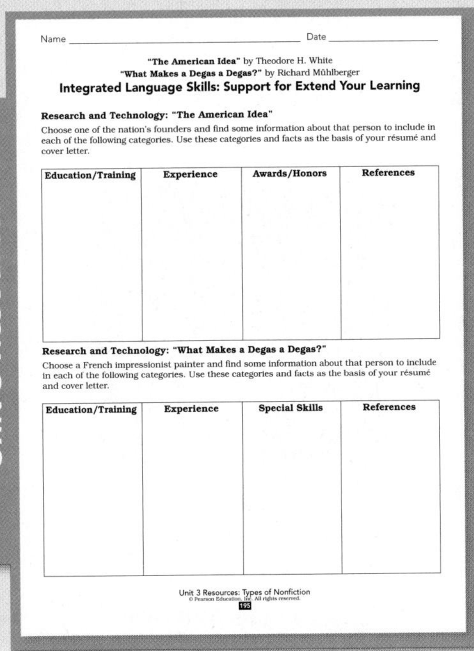
Name ______ Date ______

"The American Idea" by Theodore H. White
"What Makes a Degas a Degas?" by Richard Mühlberger

Integrated Language Skills: Support for Extend Your Learning

Research and Technology: "The American Idea"

Choose one of the nation's founders and find some information about that person to include in each of the following categories. Use these categories and facts as the basis of your résumé and cover letter.

Education/Training	Experience	Awards/Honors	References

Research and Technology: "What Makes a Degas a Degas?"

Choose a French impressionist painter and find some information about that person to include in each of the following categories. Use these categories and facts as the basis of your résumé and cover letter.

Education/Training	Experience	Special Skills	References

Unit 3 Resources: Types of Nonfiction
© Pearson Education, Inc. All rights reserved.
195

L3 L4 **Support for Extend Your Learning,** p. 195

Also available for these selections:

- All Literary Analysis: Analytic and Interpretive Essays, pp. 171, 189
- L4 Enrichment, pp. 174, 192
- All Reading: Evaluate Persuasion, pp. 172, 190
- L3 L4 Grammar, p. 193
- L3 L4 Support for Writing, p. 194

Assessment

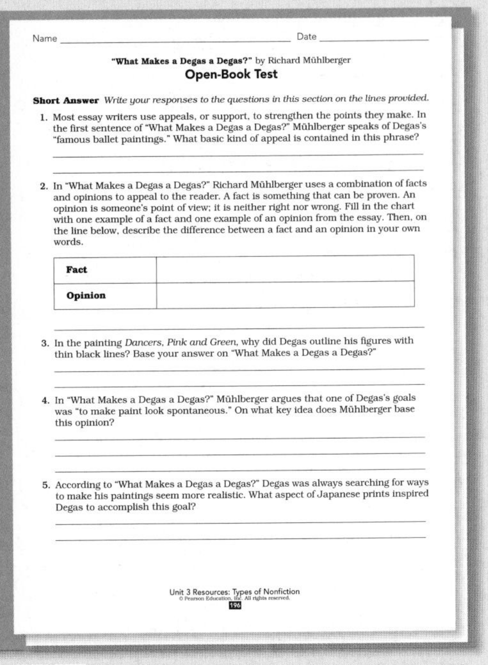
Name ______ Date ______

"What Makes a Degas a Degas?" by Richard Mühlberger

Open-Book Test

Short Answer *Write your responses to the questions in this section on the lines provided.*

1. Most essay writers use appeals, or support, to strengthen the points they make. In the first sentence of "What Makes a Degas a Degas?" Mühlberger speaks of Degas's "famous ballet paintings." What basic kind of appeal is contained in this phrase?

2. In "What Makes a Degas a Degas?" Richard Mühlberger uses a combination of facts and opinions to appeal to the reader. A fact is something that can be proven. An opinion is someone's point of view; it is neither right nor wrong. Fill in the chart with one example of a fact and one example of an opinion from the essay. Then, on the line below, describe the difference between a fact and an opinion in your own words.

Fact	
Opinion	

3. In the painting *Dancers, Pink and Green,* why did Degas outline his figures with thin black lines? Base your answer on "What Makes a Degas a Degas?"

4. In "What Makes a Degas a Degas?" Mühlberger argues that one of Degas's goals was "to make paint look spontaneous." On what key idea does Mühlberger base this opinion?

5. According to "What Makes a Degas a Degas?" Degas was always searching for ways to make his paintings seem more realistic. What aspect of Japanese prints inspired Degas to accomplish this goal?

Unit 3 Resources: Types of Nonfiction
© Pearson Education, Inc. All rights reserved.
196

L3 L4 **Open-Book Test,** pp. 175–177, 196–198

Also available for these selections:

- EL L1 L2 Selection Test A, pp. 178–180, 199–201
- L3 L4 Selection Test B, pp. 181–183, 202–204

PHLit Online!
www.PHLitOnline.com

- complete narrated selection text
- a thematically related video with writing prompt
- an interactive graphic organizer
- highlighting feature
- access to all student print resources, adapted to individual student needs
- Spanish and English summaries

Get Connected Video
Instructions
Watch the video. Then, use your journal to respond to the prompt at the end of the clip.

Get Connected! (thematic video with writing prompt)

Also available:

Background video

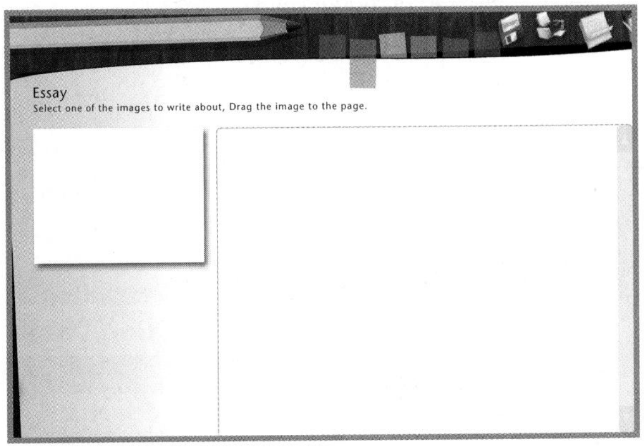
Essay
Select one of the images to write about. Drag the image to the page.

Writer's Journal (with graphics feature)

Also available:

Vocabulary Central (tools, activities, and songs for studying vocabulary)

DIFFERENTIATE/PRETEACH

❶ Selection Choices

You may use either "The American Idea" or "What Makes a Degas a Degas?" to meet the lesson standards. Skills instruction for both selections appears on p. 557. Choose one selection to teach (or choose to teach both). The Accessibility at a Glance chart at the bottom of this page will help you determine which of the two selections is more appropriate for your students.

❷ Selection Skills

1. With the class, preview the selection skills. (The lesson meets the lesson objectives given on p. 556a.)
2. Explain that students will develop the skill of evaluating persuasion (introduced on p. 539) they read to better understand and enjoy the selection. By examining analytic and interpretive essays as they read, they will gain deeper insight into nonfiction: essays and speeches.
3. To introduce the Writing and Research and Technology activities (p. 575), tell students that when they have finished reading the selection, they will write a critique, a cover letter, and a résumé related to the selection.
4. Tell students that they will also study a grammar concept: degrees of adjectives. By mastering this concept, they will improve their reading fluency and the quality of their own writing.

Before You Read

The American Idea • What Makes a Degas a Degas?

❶ Selection Choices

▲ Read **"The American Idea"** to learn about the ideas that influenced the founding of the United States.

▲ Read **"What Makes a Degas a Degas?"** to learn about a famous artist's life and work.

❷ Selection Skills Guide

Practice these skills with either **"The American Idea"** (p. 560) or **"What Makes a Degas a Degas?"** (p. 568).

- Understand analytical essays and interpretive essays
- Recognize appeals
- Evaluate a writer's appeals
- Distinguish between fact and opinions
- Identify degrees of adjectives
- Write a critique
- Write a cover letter and résumé

Differentiated Instruction for Universal Access

Accessibility at a Glance: Selection Choices

	The American Idea	What Makes a Degas a Degas?
Context	Interpretive essay on democracy	Analytic essay of fine art
Language/ Vocabulary	• Accessible vocabulary • Complex sentences and clauses	• Some subject-related vocabulary • Numerous complex sentences • On-level vocabulary
Concept Level	Accessible (the principle of democracy)	Challenging (viewing and interpreting two works by Degas)
Literary Merit	Cross curricular; noted author and political reporter	Cross curricular; noted author
Lexile/Length	Lexile: 1270L Word Count: 983	Lexile: 1060L Word Count: 906
Overall Rating	**More accessible**	**More challenging**

Because a number of factors determine the relative accessibility of paired selections, in some cases the Lexile rating of the more challenging selection will be lower than that of the more accessible selection.

❸ Literary Analysis: Analytic and Interpretive Essays

An **analytic essay** is a brief work of nonfiction in which a writer explores a subject by breaking it into parts. In an **interpretive essay,** a writer offers a view of the meaning or significance of an issue of general interest. A single essay may combine features of both types of essay.

To bring readers to accept an analysis or interpretation, a writer may build in **appeals** of the following types:

- *appeals to authority,* or calls upon the opinions of experts or other respected people
- *appeals to reason,* or calls upon logic
- *emotional appeals,* or calls upon feelings like fear, sympathy, or pride
- *appeals to shared values,* or calls upon beliefs shared by many about what is good, right, or fair

PHLit Online!
www.PHLitOnline.com

Hear It!
- Selection summary audio
- Selection audio

See It!
- Get Connected video
- Background video
- More about the author
- Vocabulary flashcards

Do It!
- Interactive journals
- Interactive graphic organizers
- Self-test
- Internet activity
- Grammar tutorial
- Interactive vocabulary games

❹ Reading Skill: Evaluate Persuasion

To **evaluate a writer's appeals,** decide whether the writer balances logic with emotional appeals. **Distinguish between fact and opinion.**

- A statement of **fact** can be proved true.
- A statement of **opinion** expresses a belief or a viewpoint and should be supported by facts or reason.

In presenting an argument, a weak essay may rely too much on persuasive appeal and opinion and not enough on fact.

❺ Using the Strategy: Fact and Opinion Chart

Record details on a **fact and opinion chart** like this one to help you decide if the writer has made a strong argument for a position.

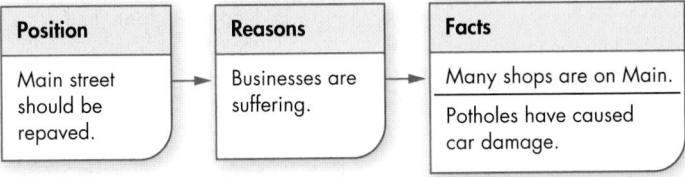

Position	→	Reasons	→	Facts
Main street should be repaved.	→	Businesses are suffering.	→	Many shops are on Main.
				Potholes have caused car damage.

Differentiated Instruction for Universal Access

Preparing Students for the More Challenging Selection

If you wish to prepare lower-level readers to read "What Makes a Degas a Degas?"—the more challenging selection—follow these steps:

- Build background before students read, using the Background note on p. 567. Then, show samples of well-known Impressionists, such as Claude Monet, Mary Cassatt, or Auguste Renoir. Have volunteers discuss their responses to the art.
- Identify several art terms students will encounter in the selection, such as *canvas, composition, silhouette,* and *matte.* Discuss the meanings of these terms with students.
- Discuss with students why someone would want to analyze two different paintings by the same artist. Suggest that we might learn something about the artist as well as the era in which he or she lived.

PRETEACH

❸ Literary Analysis

1. Introduce the skill, using the instruction on the student page.
2. Tell students that they will identify elements of analytic and interpretive essays as they read.

Think Aloud: Model the Skill

Model the skill of identifying analytic and interpretive essays, using the following "think aloud":

> Suppose I am writing a report on a stock-market crash. I can *analyze* the crash by explaining what caused the crash and how it affected the economy. I can also *interpret* it by looking at the impact it had on the economy.
>
> To make my ideas more persuasive, I can use appeals. I might use an *appeal to authority,* which is a reference to experts' opinions or an *appeal to logic* to show the logical progression of events leading up to the crash.

❹ Reading Skill

1. Introduce the skill, using the instruction on the student page.
2. Tell students that they will distinguish fact from opinion as they read.

Think Aloud: Model the Skill

Model the skill of distinguishing fact from opinion, using the following "think aloud":

> Suppose I want to argue that Main Street should be repaved. I can give my opinion—the newly paved street will look better—but it cannot be proved.
>
> Facts will make my argument stronger. I might say that people have reported damage to their cars from potholes. I can prove these arguments by checking public records, so I know that these are facts.

❺ Using the Strategy

Give students a copy of either **Reading Skill Graphic Organizer A** or B (*Graphic Organizer Transparencies,* pp. 99–101) to record their ideas about fact and opinion as they read. Use the examples in **Reading Skill Graphic Organizer A,** which is partially filled in, to model the process of completing the organizer.

PRETEACH

1 Writing About the Big Question

1. Review the assignment with the class.
2. Have students list reasons why they might move to another country. Then, ask students what challenges they might experience as they adjust to life in a new land.
3. Have students complete the sentence starters. Review responses as a class. (**Possible responses:** The kind of knowledge that may influence a person's decision to move to another country is information about a promising new job. Having friends who are knowledgeable about the area can make it easier to adapt to life in a new land.)
4. Remind students that their answers will help them think about the Big Question, "What kind of knowledge changes our lives?"

While You Read

Tell students that as they read, they should look for the statement that White believes was most important to those who drafted the idea of American freedom.

2 Vocabulary

1. Have students preview the selection vocabulary.
2. For each word, have students say the word aloud.
3. Then, use the word in a sentence that defines the word.
4. Finally, repeat your definitional sentence or a similar sentence with the word missing and have the class "fill in the blank" chorally. Here are some examples:

   Subversion is an attempt to overthrow authority. People who want to overthrow the government often participate in acts of [students say "subversion"].

3 Word Study

1. Introduce the skill, using the instruction in the box.
2. Ask students to define the words *embryo* and *employ* using their knowledge of the prefix *em-*. (**Answers:** *embryo*: early stage of offspring in the womb; *employ*: to hire to work in a company.)

What kind of *knowledge* changes our lives?

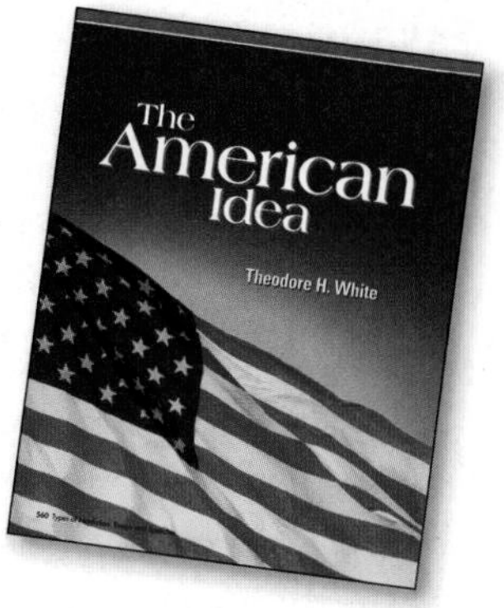

1 Writing About the Big Question

In "The American Idea," the author explores the concept of America as a nation tied together by an idea of freedom. Use these sentence starters to develop your ideas about the Big Question.

The kind of knowledge that may **influence** a person's decision to move to another country is ________________.

__________ can make it easier to **adapt** to life in a new land.

While You Read Look for the statement that White believes was most important to those who drafted the idea of American freedom. Then, consider White's proposal that this idea meant different things to different people.

2 Vocabulary

Read each word and its definition. Decide whether you know the word well, know it a little bit, or do not know it at all. After you read, see how your knowledge of each word has increased.

- **embodied** (em bäd´ ēd) *v.* gave form to; made concrete (p. 561) *The poem embodied her most hidden hopes and dreams.* *body n. embodiment n.*
- **emigrants** (em´ i grənts) *n.* people who leave their country or region to settle elsewhere (p. 561) *Many emigrants left Ireland in the 1840s and moved to other countries.* *emigrate v. emigration n. migrant adj.*
- **successive** (sək ses´ iv) *adj.* following one after another in sequence (p. 563) *Phil received an award after winning all five successive tennis matches.* *succeed v. succession n.*
- **subversion** (səb vʉr´ zhən) *n.* activity meant to overthrow something established (p. 564) *Disobedience is a subversion of authority.* *subversive adj. subversively adv. subvert v.*

3 Word Study

The **Greek prefix *em-*** means "in" or "into."

In this essay, the author explains that Jefferson's ideas about liberty are **embodied,** or put into concrete form, in the Statue of Liberty.

Vocabulary Development

Vocabulary Knowledge Rating

Create a **Vocabulary Knowledge Rating Chart** (***Professional Development Guidebook***, p. 33) for this selection. Include the selection vocabulary and the Big Question words that appear in the Writing About the Big Question sentence starters. (The Big Question vocabulary is introduced on pp. 442–443.)

Give students a copy of the chart. Read the words aloud, and have students mark their rating in the Before Reading column. Urge them to be alert to these words as they read and discuss the selection.

Tally how many students think they know a word to gauge how much instruction to provide. As students read and discuss the selection, point out the words and their context.

PHLit Online! **Vocabulary Central**, featuring tools, activities, and songs for studying vocabulary, is available at **www.PHLitOnline.com**.

Meet Theodore H. White
(1915–1986)

Author of The American Idea

A Boston native, Theodore H. White worked as a newsboy for the *Boston Globe* to help pay for his education at Harvard University. At Harvard, he studied Chinese history and Asian languages. After he graduated, Henry Luce, founder of *Time* magazine, made him *Time*'s correspondent in eastern Asia.

The Making of a Reporter White earned fame writing about the election of John F. Kennedy in *The Making of the President, 1960*. "There is no excitement anywhere in the world, short of war, to match the excitement of the American presidential campaign," White observed. Today, he is viewed as one of the finest political reporters of the twentieth century.

Did You Know?

President Kennedy's widow, Jacqueline Kennedy, chose White to write a magazine essay honoring her husband.

4 BACKGROUND FOR THE ESSAY

Coming to America

In his essay, Theodore H. White asserts that immigration is key to the idea of America. Since its founding, the United States has welcomed more immigrants than any other nation. From 1820 to 1930, about 60 percent of all immigration worldwide was to the United States. From 1905 to 1914, more than a million people immigrated to the United States each year, seeking opportunity or fleeing oppression.

Daily Bellringer

For each class during which you will teach this selection, have students complete one of the five Research activities for Week 17 in the *Daily Bellringer Activities* booklet.

4 Background
Coming to America

The democratic values of liberty and equality and the opportunity to pursue dreams still draw people to the United States to live and work. Large numbers of today's immigrants come from Mexico, Central America, and Asia. Many choose to make the United States their permanent home and become naturalized citizens. The naturalization process involves a period of residence as well as knowledge of English and U.S. history and government, including an understanding of the Constitution. On fulfilling the naturalization requirements, United States citizens-to-be take an oath of allegiance to their new country at a special ceremony.

Multidraft Reading

This icon ● marks natural pauses in the selection. To assist struggling readers and to deepen reading for all, assign the text in "chunks," following the icons, and apply multidraft reading protocols. For each reading, have students set the purpose indicated:

- **First reading**—literal comprehension: answering the Reading Check questions.
- **Second reading**—application of skills: answering the Evaluate Persuasion and Analytic and Interpretive Essays prompts.
- **Third reading**—interpretation: answering the end-of-selection questions.

For more guidance, refer to the *Classroom Strategies and Teaching Routines* card on multidraft reading.

Differentiated Instruction — Additional Instruction

EL Extended Support—English Learners
Have students complete the **Reading and Vocabulary Warm-ups, *Unit 3 Resources,*** pp. 166–169, before they read. Assign the prereading pages and the adapted selection in the ***Reader's Notebook: English Learner's Version.*** Then, have students listen to portions of the selection on the ***Hear It!* Audio CD.**

L1 L2 Extended Support—Struggling Readers
Have students complete the **Reading and Vocabulary Warm-ups, *Unit 3 Resources,*** pp. 166–169, before they read. Assign the prereading pages and the adapted selection in the ***Reader's Notebook: Adapted Version.*** Then, have students listen to portions of the selection on the ***Hear It!* Audio CD** (adapted text).

Extended Support—Reluctant Readers
To build motivation and engagement before assigning the selection, have students read "The Newest Newcomers," a thematically related selection in ***Reality Central.*** Then, use the questions at the conclusion of the related selection to guide discussion.

PHLit Online!
For more about the author, practice with the selection vocabulary, and more background, go to **www.PHLitOnline.com.**

TEACH

❶ Activating Prior Knowledge

1. Prepare an **Anticipation Guide** (***Professional Development Guidebook,*** pp. 36–38) with the following statements:
   - Immigrants have made the United States the unique nation it is.
   - The leaders of the American colonies took a risk when they signed the Declaration of Independence.
   - The American idea means different things to different people.
   - No other nation in the world is like the United States.
2. Give students a copy of the prepared **Anticipation Guide**, and have students mark their responses in the Me column. Have students discuss the statements in pairs or groups and mark the guides again in the Group column.
3. For further guidance, use the ***Classroom Strategies and Teaching Routines*** card: Using an **Anticipation Guide.**

Concept Connector ⟶

Students will return to the **Anticipation Guide** after completing "The American Idea."

Individual Activity

Have students work individually to brainstorm for phrases that tell what the American idea means to them. Then, have them share their phrases with the class.

❷ About the Selection

In "The American Idea," Theodore H. White traces the development of the American idea and considers its powerful appeal to people across the world.

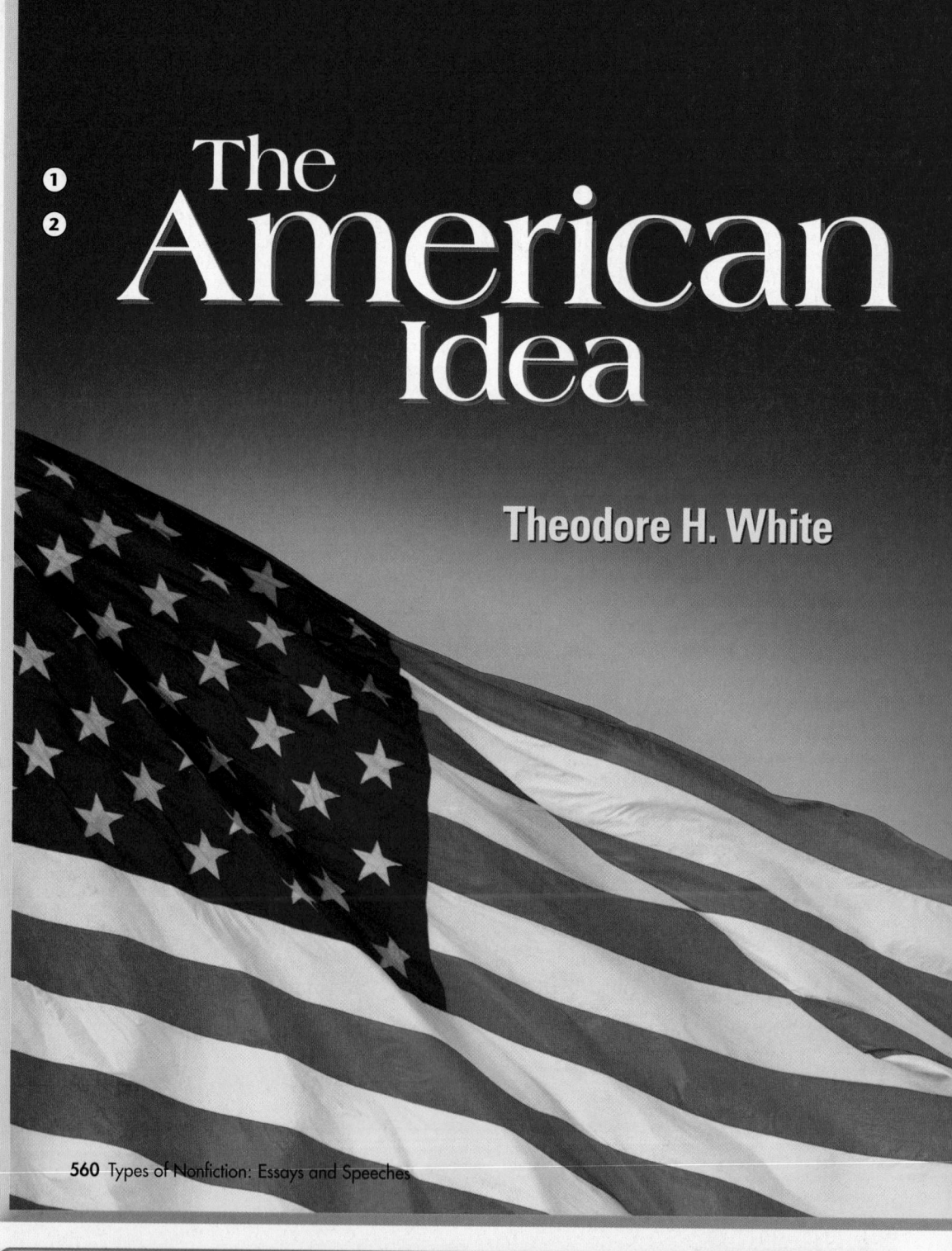

①
②

The American Idea

Theodore H. White

Vocabulary Development

Thematic Vocabulary: The Big Question

As students are discussing "The American Idea," encourage them to use the thematic vocabulary presented in Introducing the Big Question, pp. 442–443. You might encourage them with sentence starters like these:

1. With the help of John Adams and Benjamin Franklin, Jefferson's Declaration of Independence started to *evolve* from a rough draft into a . . .
2. Jefferson's *empathy* for people of the world was the basis for . . .
3. In this essay, the main idea that White tries to *reflect* is . . .
4. Although America provided opportunities for immigrants, it required them to *adapt* to . . .

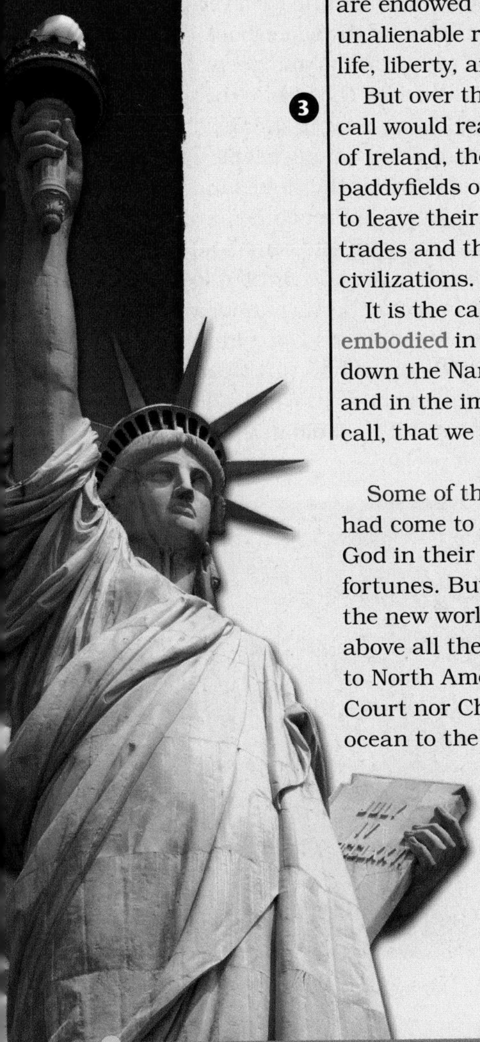

The idea was there at the very beginning, well before Thomas Jefferson put it into words—and the idea rang the call.

Jefferson himself could not have imagined the reach of his call across the world in time to come when he wrote:

"We hold these truths to be self-evident, that all men are created equal, that they are endowed by their Creator with certain unalienable rights, that among these are life, liberty, and the pursuit of happiness."

3 But over the next two centuries the call would reach the potato patches of Ireland, the ghettoes of Europe, the paddyfields of China, stirring farmers to leave their lands and townsmen their trades and thus unsettling all traditional civilizations.

It is the call from Thomas Jefferson, **embodied** in the great statue that looks down the Narrows of New York Harbor,[1] and in the immigrants who answered the call, that we now celebrate.

Some of the first European Americans had come to the new continent to worship God in their own way, others to seek their fortunes. But, over a century-and-a-half, the new world changed those Europeans, above all the Englishmen who had come to North America. Neither King nor Court nor Church could stretch over the ocean to the wild continent. To survive, the first **emigrants** had to learn to govern themselves.

1. **the great statue that looks down the Narrows of New York Harbor** Statue of Liberty.

Literary Analysis
Analytic and Interpretive Essays
What emotional appeals does White use in the opening paragraphs of this essay?

Vocabulary
embodied (em bäd′ ēd) *v.* gave form to; made concrete

emigrants (em′ i grənts) *n.* people who leave their country or region to settle elsewhere

4 **Reading Check**
According to Thomas Jefferson, what three rights do all men have?

3 Literary Analysis
Analytic and Interpretive Essays

1. Remind students that the author of an analytic essay breaks a subject into parts to examine it.
2. **Ask** students to respond to the Literary Analysis question: What emotional appeals does White use in the opening paragraphs of this essay?
   Answer: He uses the image of a call that was heard by people in various places across the world: in potato patches, ghettoes, paddyfields, farms, and towns.

5 Reading Check

Answer: According to Jefferson, all men have the right to life, liberty, and the pursuit of happiness.

Differentiated Instruction for Universal Access

Strategy for Less Proficient Readers
"The American Idea" contains challenging vocabulary, abstract ideas, and many historical references. Students will benefit from following along in their text as they listen to the recording of the selection on the ***Hear It!* Audio CD** (adapted text). Be sure students are able to distill "the American idea" into its purest form: "all people are created equal."

Enrichment for Gifted/Talented Students
White states that Adams believed the idea that "all men are created equal" should be supported within the United States, while Jefferson thought the idea should be promoted throughout the world. Ask students to consider whether their "great debate" continues in the present day. How would Adams and Jefferson use events in recent history to support their positions? Students might role-play a debate between the two men using current events to discuss the implications of the American idea.

PHLit Online!
This selection is available in interactive format in the **Enriched Online Student Edition, www.PHLitOnline.com**, which includes a thematically related video and writing prompt and an interactive graphic organizer.

❺ Reading Skill
Evaluate Persuasion

1. Point out that an essay combining features of both an analytic and an interpretive essay will contain both facts and opinions.
2. **Ask** students the Reading Skill question: Identify one fact and one opinion expressed in the essay so far.
   Possible response: Fact: Some of the first European Americans came to North America to be able to worship God in their own way. Opinion: Only something worth dying for could unite the American colonists.

▶**Monitor Progress** Assess students' answers to the Reading Skill question to make sure that they are correctly distinguishing fact from opinion.

▶**Reteach** Remind students that facts can be proved, but opinions cannot. Illustrate by explaining that facts such as why European Americans came to North America can be verified in encyclopedias and other references. Opinions such as "only something worth dying for could unite Americans" cannot be checked in a source.

❻ Connecting to the Big Question

1. Remind students that a person's knowledge of something can include facts, opinions, ideas, and experiences.
2. Have students look for the statement that White believes was most important to those who drafted the idea of American freedom. **Possible response:** White believes the statement asserting the three unalienable rights, "life, liberty, and the pursuit of happiness," is the most important.
3. Discuss with students the different ideas Jefferson and Adams had of this statement.
4. **Ask** students: How has this idea of certain unalienable rights changed the lives of people who immigrated to America?
   Possible response: People who were not granted the same rights in their homeland had more freedoms in America, which probably improved the quality of their lives.

But the freedom of the wilderness whetted their appetites for more freedoms. By the time Jefferson drafted his call, men were in the field fighting for those new-learned freedoms, killing and being killed by English soldiers, the best-trained troops in the world, supplied by the world's greatest navy. Only something worth dying for could unite American volunteers and keep them in the field—a stated cause, a flag, a nation they could call their own.

When, on the Fourth of July, 1776, the colonial leaders who had been meeting as a Continental Congress in Philadelphia voted to approve Jefferson's Declaration of Independence, it was not puffed-up rhetoric for them to pledge to each other "our lives, our fortunes and our sacred honor." Unless their new "United States of America" won the war, the Congressmen would be judged traitors as relentlessly as would the irregulars-under-arms in the field. . . .

The new Americans were tough men fighting for a very tough idea. How they won their battles is a story for the schoolbooks, studied by scholars, wrapped in myths by historians and poets. But what is most important is the story of the idea that made them into a
❺ nation, the idea that had an explosive power undreamed of in 1776.

All other nations had come into being among people whose families had lived for time out of mind on the same land where they were born. Englishmen are English, Frenchmen are French, Chinese are Chinese, while their governments come and go; their national states can be torn apart and remade without losing their nationhood. But Americans are a nation born of an idea; not the place, but the idea, created the United States Government.

The story we celebrate . . . is the story of how this idea worked itself out, how it stretched and changed and how the call for "life, liberty and the pursuit of happiness" does still, as it did in the beginning, mean different things to different people.

Reading Skill
Evaluate Persuasion ❻
Identify one fact and one opinion expressed in the essay so far.

The new Americans were tough men fighting for a very tough idea.

Vocabulary Development

Vocabulary Knowledge Rating

When students have completed reading and discussing "The American Idea," have them take out their **Vocabulary Knowledge Rating Chart** for this selection. Read the words aloud once more, and have students rate their knowledge of the words again in the After Reading column. Clarify any words that are still problematic. Have students write their own definition and example or sentence in the appropriate column. Then have students complete the Vocabulary Practice at the end of the selection. Encourage students to use the words in further discussion and written work about this selection. Remind them that they will be accountable for these words on the **Selection Test,** ***Unit 3 Resources***, pp. 178–180 or 181–183.

▲ Thomas Jefferson

▲ John Adams

6 The debate began with the drafting of the Declaration of Independence. That task was left to Jefferson of Virginia, who spent two weeks in an upstairs room in a Philadelphia boarding house penning a draft, while John Adams and Benjamin Franklin questioned, edited, hardened his phrases. By the end of that hot and muggy June, the three had reached agreement: the Declaration contained the ringing universal theme Jefferson strove for and, at the same time, voiced American grievances toughly enough to please the feisty Adams and the pragmatic Franklin. After brief debate, Congress passed it.

As the years wore on, the great debate expanded between Jefferson and Adams. The young nation flourished and Jefferson chose to think of America's promise as a call to all the world, its promises universal. A few weeks before he died, he wrote, "May it be to the world, what I believe it will be (to some parts sooner, to others later, but finally to all), the signal of arousing men to burst their chains." To Adams, the call meant something else—it was the call for American independence, the cornerstone of an American state.

Their argument ran through their **successive** Administrations. Adams, the second President, suspected the French Revolutionaries; Alien and Sedition Acts[2] were passed during his term of office to protect the American state and its liberties

2. **Alien and Sedition Acts** laws passed by Congress in 1798 restricting immigration and regulating the expression of criticism of the government.

7 LITERATURE IN CONTEXT

History Connection

The American Revolution
White makes a number of references to the era of the American Revolution.

- **The Declaration of Independence** Written by Thomas Jefferson, the Declaration announced the colonies' decision in 1776 to break away from Great Britain. In the opening paragraph, Jefferson refers to the phrase *unalienable* (un āl´ yən ə bəl) rights—those rights that cannot be taken or given away.
- **Irregulars-Under-Arms** The colonists who fought the British in the Revolution could be considered irregulars-under-arms. As rebels, they did not belong to a regularly established army.

Connect to the Literature

What contrasting views of the American idea are represented by Jefferson's "unalienable rights" and by Adams's views on immigration?

Vocabulary
successive (sək ses´ iv) *adj.* following one after another in sequence

8 Reading Check
What document did the Founders draft to present their ideals?

7 Literature in Context

History Connection The American Revolution was already well underway when the Declaration of Independence was adopted on July 4, 1776. War had broken out in April 1775 when British troops fired on American soldiers in Lexington, Massachusetts. The conflict between American colonists and the British began as a fight for rights but soon became a war for independence.

By the spring of 1776, the colonies were moving toward declaring their independence. A committee made up of John Adams, Benjamin Franklin, Thomas Jefferson, Robert R. Livingston, and Roger Sherman was chosen to frame a statement. Jefferson drafted the document, which began with a proclamation of the natural rights of all human beings. The Declaration of Independence set forth these fundamental ideas: (a) all people are created equal, with the right to life, liberty, and the pursuit of happiness, (b) the purpose of government is to protect these rights, and (c) if government does not uphold these rights, the people are free to revolt and establish a new government.

Connect to the Literature Review the information on the Declaration of Independence, then **ask** students the Connect to the Literature question: What contrasting views of the American idea are represented by Jefferson's "unalienable rights" and by Adams's views on immigration?
Possible response: Jefferson's "unalienable rights" represents the view that the American idea is open to interpretation by all people; Adams's views on immigration suggest that the American idea should be protected from outside influences.

8 Reading Check

Answer: The Founders drafted the Declaration of Independence to present their ideals.

Concept Connector

Anticipation Guide
Have students return to their **Anticipation Guides** and respond to the statements again in the After Reading column. They may do this individually or in their original pairs or groups. Then lead a class discussion, probing for what students have learned that confirms or invalidates each statement. Encourage students to cite specific details, quotations, or other evidence from the text to support their responses to each statement.

Writing About the Big Question
Have students compare their responses to the sentence starters they completed before reading the essay with their ideas afterwards. Ask them to explain whether their thoughts have changed.

Reading Skill Graphic Organizer
Ask students to review the charts they completed to differentiate between facts and opinions. Show them the partially completed **Reading Skill Graphic Organizer A** (*Graphic Organizer Transparencies*, p. 104) as an example. Then have students share the charts they made.

ASSESS

Answers

Critical Thinking

1. **Possible response:** "The new Americans were tough men fighting for a very tough idea," because it emphasizes that the struggle for freedom was not an easy one.
2. (a) Irish, Europeans, and Chinese heard the call of the American idea. (b) The American idea persuaded them to leave their homelands.
3. "The freedom of the wilderness" inspired settlers with a desire for other freedoms. American settlers were willing to fight for freedom and a new government while people living in other places were content with conditions as they had been.
4. (a) He means that an idea, not a place, unites Americans as a nation. (b) **Possible response:** To be "American" refers to a person or thing that exemplifies the American ideals of life, liberty, and the pursuit of happiness.

THE BIG ? **What kind of knowledge changes our lives?**

Possible responses: (a) Yes, I agree with White that "life, liberty, and the pursuit of happiness" means different things to different people because these are only ideas, and I know that, depending on where and how people live, they will have different interpretations of the same idea. (b) If a person knows that he has the right to liberty and the right to find happiness, then that person is more likely to feel entitled to certain things in life; should those things be at risk, he is more likely to fight for them.

Vocabulary
subversion (səb vʉr′ zhən) *n.* activity meant to overthrow something established

against French **subversion**. But Jefferson, the third President, welcomed the French. The two men, once close friends, became archrivals. Still, as they grew old, their rivalry faded; there was glory enough to share in what they had made; in 1812, they began a correspondence that has since become classic, remembering and taking comfort in the triumphs of their youth.

Adams and Jefferson lived long lives and died on the same day—the Fourth of July, 1826, 50 years to the day from the Continental Congress's approval of the Declaration. Legend has it that Adams breathed on his death bed, "Thomas Jefferson still survives." As couriers set out from Braintree[3] carrying the news of Adams's death, couriers were riding north from Virginia with the news of Jefferson's death. The couriers met in Philadelphia. Horace Greeley,[4] then a youth in Vermont, later remembered: ". . . When we learned . . . that Thomas Jefferson and John Adams, the author and the great champion, respectively, of the Declaration, had both died on that day, and that the messengers bearing South and North, respectively, the tidings of their decease, had met in Philadelphia, under the shadow of that Hall in which our independence was declared, it seemed that a Divine attestation had solemnly hallowed and sanctified the great anniversary by the impressive ministration of Death."

3. **Braintree** town in Massachusetts (now called Quincy) where John Adams lived and died.
4. **Horace Greeley** famous American newspaper publisher.

Critical Thinking

1. **Respond:** Which idea about America meant the most to you? Why?
2. **(a)** Identify three groups that White says heard the call of the American idea. **(b) Infer:** How did it affect each of them?
3. **Compare and Contrast:** What differences does White see between early American settlers and people living elsewhere?
4. **(a) Interpret:** What does White mean when he writes, "Americans are a nation born of an idea"? **(b) Extend:** What might White say defines somebody or something as American?

THE BIG ? **What kind of knowledge changes our lives?**
(a) Do you agree with White that "life, liberty, and the pursuit of happiness" means different things to different people? Why or why not? **(b)** How might these ideals shape a person's life?

Assessment Resources

Unit 3 Resources

L1 L2 EL **Selection Test A,** pp. 160–162
L3 L4 **Selection Test B,** pp. 163–165
L3 L4 **Open-Book Test,** pp. 175–177

PHLit Online! All assessment resources are available at www.PHLitOnline.com.

After You Read The American Idea

Literary Analysis: Analytic and Interpretive Essays

1. The author of this **interpretive essay** focuses on the "American idea." Briefly summarize White's view.
2. **(a)** Use a chart like this one to organize details of the **analytic** sections of White's essay. **(b)** Explain how White uses the story about Adams and Jefferson along with other details and **persuasive appeals** to strengthen his presentation of an "American idea."

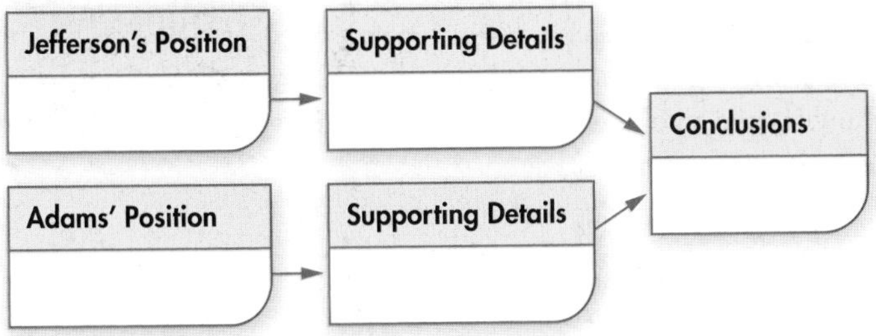

Reading Skill: Evaluate Persuasion

3. **(a)** List two **opinions** that White includes about people or events. **(b)** Which **facts** does he use to support each opinion?
4. Based on an analysis of his persuasive appeals and the facts and opinions presented, evaluate the validity of White's argument.

Vocabulary

Practice Word **analogies** match the relationship in one pair of words with that in another. For each item, choose the word that will make the relationships in the first and second pair of words most similar.

1. immigrants : enter :: emigrants : **(a)** leave, **(b)** stay, **(c)** build
2. entertainment : comedian :: subversion : **(a)** film, **(b)** spy, **(c)** ship
3. build : construct :: embodied : **(a)** formed, **(b)** chosen, **(c)** broke
4. many : few :: successive : **(a)** logical, **(b)** interrupted, **(c)** finished

Word Study Use the context of the sentences and what you know about the **Greek prefix *em-*** to explain your answer to each question.

1. Would a person feel *embittered* after winning the lottery?
2. Is someone who is *emboldened* courageous or fearful?

Word Study

The **Greek prefix *em-*** means "in" or "into."

Challenge Explain how the prefix *em-* contributes to the meanings of these words. Consult a dictionary if necessary.

empathy
emphasize
empower

ASSESS/EXTEND

Answers

Literary Analysis

1. The idea of freedom unites Americans as a nation.
2. (a) **Possible response: Jefferson's Position:** America's call is universal. Supporting Detail: America supports all people who yearn for freedom. **Adam's Position:** America's call is only for America. Supporting Detail: America should protect itself and its liberties, such as through the Alien and Sedition Acts. **Conclusion:** America means different things to different people.

   For other sample answers, see ***Graphic Organizer Transparencies*, Literary Analysis Graphic Organizer A**, p. 104, and the **Additional Answers** section.

   (b) **Possible response:** White portrays Jefferson and Adams as strong American voices and representatives of the "American idea." At the end, he appeals to the readers' emotions and describes how they became friends and supported each other as fellow Americans. Also, he explains that they both died on Independence Day, and that Adams's last words refer to Jefferson.

Reading Skill

3. (a) 1. The freedom of the wilderness increased the desire of settlers for more freedom. 2. The new Americans were tough men. (b) 1. White provides the fact that colonists fought the British to hold onto their new freedoms. 2. White provides the fact that the new Americans won many battles and fought until their Declaration of Independence was written.
4. **Possible response:** White presents a contradictory argument that proposes America unites its people in its promise of freedom, yet he claims the ideas on which America and freedom are based mean different things to different people. White takes this difference into account with his contrastive analysis of Jefferson's and Adams's ideas of freedom, but he seems to side more with Jefferson, the author of the call "that we now celebrate."

This bias leads me to believe that White agrees more with Jefferson's idea of freedom, which comes across as the correct or more acceptable idea.

Vocabulary

Practice

1. (a) leave
2. (b) spy
3. (a) formed
4. (b) interrupted

Word Study

1. No, *embittered* means "in a state of feeling bitter." A person who won the lottery would not feel bitter but elated.
2. *Emboldened* means "instilled with boldness." Someone who is filled with boldness is courageous, not fearful.

Word Study: Challenge

Empathy is another's feelings taken into oneself. To *emphasize* is "to put stress into." To *empower* is "to put energy or strength into something."

PRETEACH

Skills instruction for the ***Reading Skill*** *and* ***Literary Analysis*** *concept appears on p. 557.*

❶ Writing About the Big Question

1. Review the assignment with the class.
2. Discuss students' favorite works of art. Ask them if they prefer art that is realistic or interpretive.
3. Have students complete the sample sentence starters. Review responses as a class. (**Possible responses:** Understanding how to interpret art is valuable because you gain insight into how the artist perceives the world. Artists can influence our understanding of the world by revealing insights we had not considered before and showing ordinary things in a new way.)
4. Remind students that their answers will help them think about the Big Question, "What kind of knowledge changes our lives?"

While You Read

Tell students that as they read, they should consider the types of knowledge that interested Degas and influenced his work.

❷ Vocabulary

1. Have students preview the selection vocabulary.
2. For each word, have students say the word aloud.
3. Then, use the word in a sentence that defines the word.
4. Finally, repeat your definitional sentence or a similar sentence with the word missing and have the class "fill in the blank" chorally. Here are some examples:

   Something that is immaterial *is not made of anything. Travelers crossing the desert often think they see a lake in the distance, but it is just an illusion and is* [students say "immaterial"].

❸ Word Study

1. Introduce the skill, using the instruction in the box.
2. Ask students to think of a word beginning with the prefix *im-* that means "lacking growth or development." (**Answer:** *immature*)

What kind of *knowledge* changes our lives?

❶ Writing About the Big Question

In "What Makes a Degas a Degas?," the author "reads" two Degas paintings by combining his own knowledge of art with his knowledge about Degas's life. Use these sentence starters to develop your ideas about the Big Question.

Understanding how to interpret art is valuable because you gain **insight** into _______________.

Artists can **influence** our understanding of the world by _________ and _________.

While You Read Consider the types of knowledge that interested Degas and influenced his work.

❷ Vocabulary

Read each word and its definition. Decide whether you know the word well, know it a little bit, or do not know it at all. After you read, see how your knowledge of each word has increased.

- **immaterial** (im´ ə tir´ ē əl) *adj.* not consisting of matter (p. 569) *The baby does not understand that his shadow is immaterial and cannot be touched.* *immaterialize v. immaterially adv. material adj.*
- **silhouette** (sil´ ə wet´) *n.* an outline drawing filled in with a solid color (p. 569) *He drew a solid black silhouette of Emily's profile.* *silhouette v.*
- **simulating** (sim´ yo͞o lāt´ iŋ) *v.* giving the appearance of (p. 569) *The machine trained new pilots by simulating a realistic crash.* *simulation n. simulator n.*
- **lacquered** (lak´ ərd) *adj.* covered in tough, sticky varnish (p. 570) *The artist combined charcoal and sap to coat this lacquered music box.* *lacquer n. lacquer v.*

❸ Word Study

The **Latin prefix** ***im-*** means "not" or "opposite of."

In this essay, the author explains that a painted landscape has an **immaterial** quality, which makes the picture seem as though it is not made of physical materials.

Vocabulary Development

Vocabulary Knowledge Rating

Create a **Vocabulary Knowledge Rating Chart** (***Professional Development Guidebook***, p. 33) for this selection. Include the selection vocabulary and the Big Question words that appear in the Writing About the Big Question sentence starters. (The Big Question vocabulary is introduced on pp. 442–443.)

Give students a copy of the chart. Read the words aloud, and have students mark their rating in the Before Reading column. Urge them to be alert to these words as they read and discuss the selection.

Tally how many students think they know a word to gauge how much instruction to provide. As students read and discuss the selection, point out the words and their context.

PHLit Online! **Vocabulary Central**, featuring tools, activities, and songs for studying vocabulary, is available at **www.PHLitOnline.com**.

Meet Richard Mühlberger (b. 1938)

Author of What Makes a Degas a *Degas?*

Born in New Jersey, Richard Mühlberger has spent more than thirty-five years as an art critic and museum administrator. During the 1990s, he was vice-director in charge of education at the Metropolitan Museum of Art in New York City, one of the foremost art museums in the world.

Aiding in Art Appreciation While at the Metropolitan Museum of Art, Mühlberger began producing a series of books that make the works of famous artists accessible to the average viewer. The series includes *What Makes a Degas a Degas?*, from which this selection is taken, and similarly titled books on Van Gogh, Monet, and others.

4 BACKGROUND FOR THE ESSAY

Degas and Impressionism

In the 1860s, a group of French painters known as the Impressionists shocked the art world. Abandoning strict forms, they used short, dabbed brushstrokes to capture fleeting impressions of color and light. Their work had a great impact on Edgar Degas (**ed gär′ də gä′**; 1834–1917). At the same time, as Richard Mühlberger explains in his essay, Degas introduced his own innovative style.

Did You Know?

Mühlberger served as director of the Museum of Fine Art in Springfield, Massachusetts.

Daily Bellringer

For each class during which you will teach this selection, have students complete one of the five Research activities for Week 17 in the ***Daily Bellringer Activities*** booklet.

4 Background
Degas and Impressionism

Humans have a natural inclination to create art. Works of art date back to the Upper Paleolithic period (38,000 B.C.–10,000 B.C.), which marked the beginning of the human species. The art of each historical period gives us insight into the people who lived at that time—we learn about aspects of their culture, beliefs, and society. Paintings and other works of art provide our only visual records of what life was like in the centuries before photography was invented in the 1830s.

Multidraft Reading

To assist struggling readers and to deepen reading for all, assign the text in "chunks" and apply multidraft reading protocols. For each reading, have students set the purpose indicated:

- **First reading**—literal comprehension: answering the Reading Check questions.
- **Second reading**—application of skills: answering the Evaluate Persuasion and Analytic and Interpretive Essays prompts.
- **Third reading**—interpretation: answering the end-of-selection questions.

For more guidance, refer to the ***Classroom Strategies and Teaching Routines*** card on multidraft reading.

Differentiated Instruction — Additional Instruction

EL Extended Support—English Learners
Have students complete the **Reading and Vocabulary Warm-ups, *Unit 3 Resources*,** pp. 184–187, before they read. Assign the prereading pages for the selection in the ***Reader's Notebook: English Learner's Version***. Then, have students listen to portions of the selection on the ***Hear It!* Audio CD**.

L1 L2 Extended Support—Struggling Readers
Have students complete the **Reading and Vocabulary Warm-ups, *Unit 3 Resources*,** pp. 184–187, before they read. Assign the prereading pages for the selection in the ***Reader's Notebook: Adapted Version***. Then, have students listen to portions of the selection on the ***Hear It!* Audio CD** (adapted text).

Extended Support—Reluctant Readers
To build motivation and engagement before assigning the selection, have students read "Hip-Hop: Keeping It Real," a thematically related selection in ***Reality Central***. Then, use the questions at the conclusion of the related selection to guide discussion.

PHLit Online!
For more about the author, practice with the selection vocabulary, and more background, go to **www.PHLitOnline.com**.

1 Activating Prior Knowledge

1. Prepare an **Anticipation Guide** (***Professional Development Guidebook,*** pp. 36–38) with the following statements:
   - People's expectations affect their perceptions.
   - People bring different perceptions when they view fine art.
   - Look for details as well as overall impressions when viewing fine art.
   - The artist's technique and the historical period are part of viewing fine art.
2. Give students a copy of the prepared **Anticipation Guide** and have students mark their responses in the Me column. Have students discuss the statements in pairs or groups and mark the Guides again in the Group column.
3. For further guidance, use the ***Classroom Strategies and Teaching Routines*** card: Using an **Anticipation Guide.**

Concept Connector →

Students will follow up on this activity after reading "What Makes a Degas a Degas?"

Small-Group Activity

This essay requires readers to move between pictures and text. Assign small groups a paragraph from the selection. Have groups use the details from their paragraph to give a short presentation on an important aspect of the piece of art they are assigned.

2 About the Selection

In "What Makes a Degas a Degas?" Richard Mühlberger analyzes the painting style of Edgar Degas and points out the techniques he used to bring immediacy and the illusion of reality to his work.

3 Humanities

Dancers, Pink and Green, by Edgar Degas

This piece of art is one of the many paintings of ballet dancers composed by Degas. Degas tried to capture the idea that ballet is work; the dancers in his paintings sometimes look tired or bored. In this painting, the body positions of the dancers reflect strength and energy as well as grace and delicacy.

3

1 2 What Makes a Degas a *Degas?*

Richard Mühlberger

Vocabulary Development

Thematic Vocabulary: The Big Question

As students are discussing "What Makes a Degas a Degas?" encourage them to use the thematic vocabulary presented in Introducing the Big Question, pp. 442–443. You might encourage them with sentence starters like these:

1. Photography had a strong *influence* on Degas's work, which is evident in *Carriage at the Races,* through . . .
2. Degas was able to *adapt* oil paint to match . . .
3. Degas hoped to *enlighten* his viewers through his art by . . .
4. Degas's *insight* about ballet helped him to . . .

Dancers, Pink and Green

5 Degas's famous ballet paintings witness his enthusiasm for dance and his intimacy with the private backstage areas of the Paris Opéra, the huge complex where the ballet made its home. He was equally familiar with the theater's more public boxes and stalls, where he watched many performances. During his lifetime, he produced about fifteen hundred drawings, prints, pastels, and oil paintings with ballet themes.

In *Dancers, Pink and Green* [left], each ballerina is caught in a characteristic pose as she waits to go on the stage. One stretches and flexes her foot. Another secures her hair, while a third is almost hidden. The fourth dancer, who looks at her shoulder strap as she adjusts it, holds a pose that was a favorite of the artist and one he used in many paintings. An upright beam separates her from the fifth ballerina, who also turns her head but in the opposite direction, full of anticipation. Above her in the distance are the box seats, which Degas simplified into a stack of six red and orange rectangles along the edge of the canvas. The vertical beam the ballerina is touching extends to the top and the bottom of the painting. The multicolored vertical shapes behind the dancers represent a large, painted landscape used as a backdrop for one of the dances. It will provide an **immaterial**, dreamworld quality to the performance, as it does to the painting.

Subscribers to the Opéra were allowed backstage in the theater, and some took advantage of this access to pester dancers. On the far side of the tall wood column is the partial **silhouette** of a large man in a top hat. He seems to be trying to keep out of the way, but his protruding profile overlaps a ballerina. None of the dancers pay attention to him. They also ignore one another, for this scene represents the tense moments just before the curtain rises.

Degas discovered that with oil paints he could achieve the same fresh feeling conveyed with pastels. Although this painting took the same amount of time to finish as many of his others and was designed and executed in his studio, Degas wanted to make it look as though it had been executed quickly, backstage. To do this, he
6 imitated the marks of a charcoal pencil with his brush, making narrow black lines that edge the dancers' bodies and costumes. Next, he used his own innovation of **simulating** the matte[1] finish of pastels by taking the sheen out of oil paint, then filling in the sketchy "charcoal" outlines of his figures with a limited range of colors. The colors he used for the dancers extend to the floor and

4 ◀ **Critical Viewing**
Do you agree with Mühlberger that this painting looks as if Degas painted it hastily, on the spot? Why? **[Support]**

Vocabulary

immaterial (im′ ə tir′ ē əl) *adj.* not consisting of matter

silhouette (sil′ ə wet′) *n.* an outline drawing filled in with a solid color

simulating (sim′ yo͞o lāt′ iŋ) *v.* giving the appearance of

Literary Analysis
Analytic and Interpretive Essays
What is analytic about this essay?

7 **Reading Check**
What materials did Degas use to execute *Dancers, Pink and Green?*

1. **matte** (mat) *adj.* dull; not shiny.

4 Critical Viewing

Answer: Students may agree that the painting looks as if it had been painted hastily and on the spot, explaining that the limited colors and the black outlining give the painting an unfinished, sketchy quality.

5 Connecting to the Big Question

1. Explain to students that our preferences for and dislikes of certain things often determine the knowledge we choose to acquire.
2. Prompt students to consider the types of knowledge that interested Degas and influenced his work. **Possible response:** Degas had a fondness for ballet.
3. **Ask** students: How did knowledge of ballet help to make Degas famous? **Possible response:** Degas was so enthusiastic about and familiar with ballet that he completed about 1500 pieces of art in different mediums with ballet themes.
4. Tell students to look for other types of knowledge that interested Degas and influenced his work.

6 Literary Analysis
Analytic and Interpretive Essays

1. Remind students that writers of analytic and interpretive essays use a variety of appeals to support their views.
2. **Ask** students the Literary Analysis question: What is analytic about this essay?
   Answer: The writer points to techniques used in the painting to support his interpretation that the artist wanted to make the painting look as if it had been executed quickly.

7 Reading Check

Answer: Degas used oil paints and a brush.

Differentiated Instruction for Universal Access

Strategy for Special Needs Students
Students may have difficulty going back and forth between text and pictures. You may want to have students look at the pictures while listening to a recording of the selection. Use the ***Hear It!* Audio CD.** Pause the recording after passages that contain many details referring to the picture, and give students time to locate each detail.

Strategy for Less Proficient Readers
To help students make connections between Mühlberger's description and the art, have students match each detail in the passage with a detail in the painting. Have students locate the dancer in the painting whom Mühlberger describes as stretching and flexing her foot, the one securing her hair, and so on. Ask students whether they would describe the painting in the same way or differently. Continue with questions that encourage students to think about the writer's interpretation of the painting.

PHLit Online!
This selection is available in interactive format in the **Enriched Online Student Edition, www.PHLitOnline.com**, which includes a thematically related video and writing prompt and an interactive graphic organizer.

8 Reading Skill
Evaluate Persuasion

1. **Ask** students to state the basic difference between a fact and an opinion
   Answer: A fact is provable; an opinion is not.
2. **Ask** students to identify two examples of fact from this page.
   Possible responses: Degas was a friend of Paul Valpinçon from their school days; he visited Valpinçon at his country house in Normandy in 1869; Normandy is in northwestern France.
3. **Ask** students to identify two examples of opinion from this page.
   Possible responses: Normandy is exactly like England; the composition of Degas's painting *Carriage at the Races* seems lopsided.
4. Point out that facts often include dates, statistics, and other information that can be checked in a source. Note that opinions frequently contain adjectives and descriptive phrases.

▶**Monitor Progress:** Review students' graphic organizers to make sure they are correctly identifying facts and opinions in the essay.

▶**Reteach:** If students have difficulty distinguishing fact from opinion, point out that statements of opinion often contain signal words such as *think, believe, seem,* and *suggest.*

9 Critical Viewing

Answer: Students may agree that the "cropping" of the horses makes the painting seem more like a snapshot.

---

6 the background. The technique gives the impression that he applied the colors hastily while standing in the wings watching the dancers get ready.

The results of Degas's experiments could have been executed much more quickly had he used pastels instead of oils. What Degas wanted, however, was to make paint look spontaneous. This was part of his lifelong quest: to make viewers feel that they were right there, beside him.

Carriage at the Races

8 Paul Valpinçon was Degas's best friend in school and remained close to the artist all his life. Degas was a frequent visitor to his country house in Normandy, the northwest region of France, a long journey from Paris. Degas thought that the Normandy countryside was "exactly like England," and the beautiful horse farms there inspired him to paint equestrian subjects. During a visit in 1869, however, Degas found horses secondary to Paul Valpinçon's infant son, Henri. This becomes apparent by looking at the painting *Carriage at the Races* [right].

At first, Degas's composition seems lopsided. In one corner are the largest and darkest objects, a pair of horses and a carriage. Against the lacquered body of the carriage, the creamy white tones of the passengers stand out. They are framed by the dark colors rather than overwhelmed by them.

Vocabulary
lacquered (lak´ ərd) *adj.* covered in tough, sticky varnish

Degas placed a cream-colored umbrella in the middle of the painting above some of the figures in the carriage. Near it, balanced on the back of the driver's seat, is a black bulldog. Paul Valpinçon himself is the driver. Both Paul and the dog are gazing at the baby, who lies in the shade of the umbrella. With pink, dimpled knees, Henri, not yet a year old, sprawls on the lap of his nurse while his mother looks on.

9 ▶ **Critical Viewing** Does the way in which the horses "are cut off" make the picture seem like a photograph, as the essay suggests? **[Assess]**

Vocabulary Development

Vocabulary Knowledge Rating
When students have completed reading and discussing "What Makes a Degas a Degas?" have them take out their **Vocabulary Knowledge Rating Chart** for this selection. Read the words aloud once more, and have students rate their knowledge of the words again in the After Reading column. Clarify any words that are still problematic. Have students write their own definition and example or sentence in the appropriate column. Then have students complete the Vocabulary Practice at the end of the selection. Encourage students to use the words in further discussion and written work about this selection. Remind them that they will be accountable for these words on the **Selection Test**, ***Unit 3 Resources***, pp. 199–201 or 202–204.

This was part of his lifelong quest: to make viewers feel that they were right there, beside him.

10 Humanities

Carriage at the Races
by Edgar Degas

In this painting, Degas provides a snapshot of what was likely a familiar scene from his frequent visits to his friend Paul Valpinçon's home in the French countryside. The realism of the painting is suggestive of photography, a new visual medium that captured Degas's interest. Use these questions for discussion:

- Where is your eye first drawn when you look at this painting?
  Possible response: Students will probably mention an element of the family in the carriage in the painting's foreground.
- In what ways is this painting similar to a photograph?
  Possible response: The detail of the family group is very vivid and realistic, as a photograph would show it; the painting captures a specific moment, as a photograph would.

Concept Connector

Anticipation Guide

Have students return to their **Anticipation Guides** and respond to the statements again in the After Reading column. They may do this individually or in their original pairs or groups. Then lead a class discussion, probing for what students have learned that confirms or invalidates each statement. Encourage students to cite specific details, quotations, or other evidence from the text to support their responses to each statement.

Writing About the Big Question

Have students compare their responses to the sentence starters they completed before reading the essay with their ideas afterwards. Ask them to explain whether their thoughts have changed.

Reading Skill Graphic Organizer

Ask students to review the graphic organizers they completed to identify facts and opinions while reading. Show them the partially completed **Reading Skill Graphic Organizer A** (*Graphic Organizer Transparencies*, p. 99) as an example. Then have students share their graphic organizers.

ASSESS

Answers

Critical Thinking

1. **Possible responses:** Students may say yes because they like the interplay of light and dark in a Degas painting.
2. (a) Degas wants to make the painting look as if it had been executed quickly backstage. (b) His simulation of the matte finish of pastels and his use of a limited range of colors also contribute to this effect.
3. (a) The dominant image is the family in the carriage. (b) Degas focuses attention on the family scene by making the family and carriage the largest images.
4. **Possible response:** The realism and immediacy of Degas's paintings suggest that he might have been a good photographer.
5. (a) **Possible response:** Many television shows portray people in everyday situations, and some print advertisements use vivid color and other eye-catching elements.
(b) and (c) After discussion, groups should present their ideas.

What kind of knowledge changes our lives?

Students are likely to list the following as subjects and areas of interest that influenced Degas and his painting: Degas had an intimate relationship with the world of dance and he made about 1500 pieces of art with ballet themes. Degas also found inspiration from his close friends, particularly Paul Valpinçon, who lived in Normandy. Upon a visit, Degas was struck by the countryside but more so by his friend's infant son. The composition of *Carriage at the Races* hints at another one of Degas's influences: photography. Other interests were the masterpieces in the Louvre and Japanese prints.

Ideas From the Exotic, Old, and New

▲ Degas self-portrait

Degas always enjoyed looking at art. One of the thrills of his school years was being allowed to inspect the great paintings in the collection of Paul Valpinçon's father. Throughout his life, the artist drew inspiration from the masterpieces in the Louvre in Paris, one of the greatest museums in the world. He also found ideas in Japanese prints. They were considered cheap, disposable souvenirs in Japan, but were treasured by artists and others in the West as highly original, fascinating works of art. Photographs, then newly invented, also suggested to Degas ways of varying his paintings. He eventually became an enthusiastic photographer himself.

In *Carriage at the Races*, the way in which the horses and carriage are cut off recalls figures in photographs and Japanese prints. For Degas, showing only part of a subject made his paintings more intimate, immediate, and realistic. He wanted viewers to see the scene as if they were actually there.

Critical Thinking

1. **Respond:** Would you like to see more work by Degas? Explain.
2. **(a)** Use details from the essay to describe the effect Degas seeks by outlining the dancers in black lines in *Dancers, Pink and Green.* **(b) Analyze:** What other elements contribute to this effect?
3. **(a)** What is the dominant image in *Carriage at the Races?* **(b) Analyze:** How does Degas focus attention on this image?
4. **Connect:** What qualities in Degas's paintings suggest that he might have been a good photographer when he took up that hobby? Explain.
5. **(a) Extend:** Identify a way in which television shows or print advertisements create an impression of immediacy and spontaneity, as Degas did. **(b) Discuss:** Share your ideas in a small group. **(c) Evaluate:** Decide on the three most relevant or interesting ideas and present them to the whole class.

What kind of knowledge changes our lives? Degas and his art developed and changed based on knowledge he acquired throughout his life. Based on this essay, what subjects and areas of interest do you think influenced Degas and his painting?

Assessment Resources

Unit 3 Resources

L1 L2 EL **Selection Test A,** pp. 199–201
L3 L4 **Selection Test B,** pp. 202–204
L3 L4 **Open-Book Test,** pp. 196–198

PHLit Online! All assessment resources are available at www.PHLitOnline.com.

After You Read | What Makes a Degas a Degas?

Literary Analysis: Analytic and Interpretive Essays

1. This **interpretive essay** focuses on Degas's achievement. Briefly summarize Mühlberger's view of Degas's "lifelong quest."
2. **(a)** Use a chart like the one shown to organize details of the **analytic** sections of Mühlberger's essay. **(b)** Explain how Mühlberger uses **persuasive appeals** to reason to strengthen his presentation of the idea that Degas intentionally incorporated qualities that might make his paintings seem incomplete.

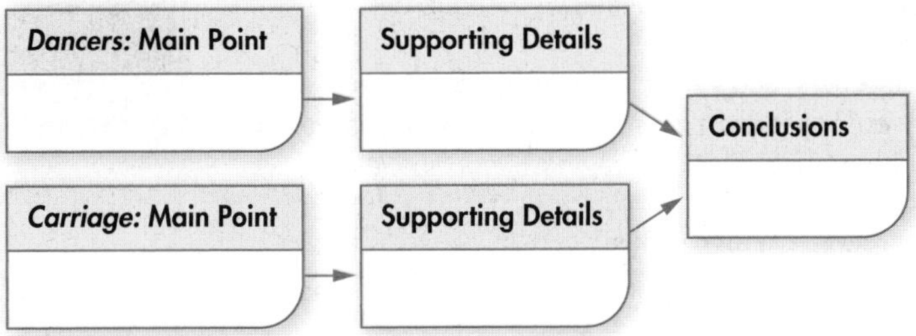

Reading Skill: Evaluate Persuasion

3. **(a)** List two **opinions** that Mühlberger includes about Degas. **(b)** What **facts** does he use to support each opinion?
4. Based on an analysis of his persuasive appeals and the facts and opinions presented, evaluate the validity of Mühlberger's argument.

Vocabulary

Practice Word **analogies** match relationships between two pairs of words. For each item, choose the word that will make the relationships in the first and second pair of words most similar.

1. hatchback : car :: silhouette : **(a)** bracelet, **(b)** portrait, **(c)** carving
2. performing : do :: simulating : **(a)** pretend, **(b)** be, **(c)** own
3. chaotic : still :: immaterial : **(a)** dreamy, **(b)** personal, **(c)** solid
4. upholstered : chair :: lacquered : **(a)** table, **(b)** clean, **(c)** discolor

Word Study Use the context of the sentences and what you know about the **Latin prefix *im-*** to explain your answer to each question.

1. Would you be able to cross an *impassable* river?
2. Is it easy to solve a problem of *immeasurable* difficulty?

Word Study

The **Latin prefix *im-*** means "not" or "opposite of."

Challenge Explain how the prefix *im-* contributes to the meanings of these words. Consult a dictionary if necessary.

imbalance
immoderate
impudent

ASSESS/EXTEND

Answers

Literary Analysis

1. Mühlberger holds that it was Degas's "lifelong quest" to make his paintings look spontaneous so viewers see a scene he painted as if they were actually there.
2. **Possible response:** (a) **Topic:** *Dancers, Pink and Green* **Main Point:** The painting has a sense of immediacy, of being backstage before the performance. **Supporting Details:** 1. Degas imitated the marks of a charcoal drawing with his brush. 2. He simulated a matte finish by taking the sheen out of oil paint. **Conclusion:** The painting gives the impression that the viewer is right there, beside Degas.

   For other sample answers, see ***Graphic Organizer Transparencies*, Literary Analysis Graphic Organizer A**, p.102, and the **Additional Answers** section.

   (b) **Possible response:** Mühlberger explains that by limiting the range of colors, he makes *Dancers, Pink and Green* seem as if it had been done on the spot. In *Carriage*, he explains that Degas cuts off the figures to recall Japanese prints and to make the painting seem more intimate, immediate, and realistic.

Reading Skill

3. (a) Mühlberger believes that Degas was enthusiastic about dance and that he was inspired by photography. (b) Degas's 1500 pieces of art with ballet themes support the first opinion; the invention of photography during Degas's lifetime and his eventually becoming a photographer himself are facts that support the second opinion.
4. **Possible response:** Though an interpretive essay is likely to contain bias, Mühlberger's experience as an art critic makes his judgments credible. Mühlberger takes care to analyze each painting, and his points are supported by his own knowledge of art. Coupled with his knowledge of Degas's life, Mühlberger's argument is valid.

Vocabulary

Practice

1. (b) portrait
2. (a) pretend
3. (c) solid
4. (a) table

Word Study

1. No, the prefix *im-* means "not," so *impassable* means "not capable of being passed." An impassable river cannot be passed or crossed.
2. No, the prefix *im-* means "not," so *immeasurable* means "not measurable or quantifiable." A problem of immeasurable difficulty would be extremely difficult to solve.

Word Study: Challenge

An *imbalance* is the opposite of a balance. To be *immoderate* is to not be moderate. To be *impudent* means to not be modest or ashamed.

EXTEND/ASSESS

Answers

Grammar

1. Introduce the skill, using the instruction on the student page.
2. Discuss the definitions and the examples in the chart.

Think Aloud: Model the Skill

Model the skill of identifying degrees of adjectives, using the following "think aloud." Say to students:

> To choose the correct form of the adjective—positive, comparative, or superlative—I must think about what I am comparing. Suppose I want to compare Mike and Sean's bravery. Here, I am comparing two people, so I use the comparative form and write, "Sean is *braver* than Mike." If I want to compare Sean's bravery with everyone's bravery, I use the superlative and write, "Sean is the *bravest* of everyone." I use the superlative form because I am comparing more than two people.

WG Writing and Grammar, Grade 10

Students will find further instruction on practice with degrees of adjectives in Chapter 25, Section 1.

Practice A

1. positive
2. superlative
3. positive
4. comparative

Challenge

Sample answers: The new Americans were *tough* men fighting for a very tough idea; positive. But what is *most important* is the story of the idea that made them into a nation; superlative.

Practice B

Sample answers:

1. No, the positive form should be used, since there is no comparison.
2. No, *shiniest* is in the superlative form. The comparative form is needed.
3. Correct.
4. No, the superlative form should be used, since the ballerina is being compared to the entire group.

Challenge

Sample answer: James's criticism was good, his short stories were better, and his novels were best.

Integrated Language Skills

The American Idea • What Makes a Degas a Degas?

Grammar: Degrees of Adjectives

An **adjective** is a word that describes a noun or a pronoun.

Most adjectives have three different forms, called degrees—the *positive degree*, the *comparative degree*, and the *superlative degree*. The positive is used to describe one item, group, or person. The comparative is used to describe two items, groups, or people. The superlative is used to describe three or more items, groups, or people.

For most two-syllable adjectives, add *–er* or use *more* or *less* to form the comparative and add *–est* or use *most* or *least* to form the superlative. For adjectives of three or more syllables, use *more*, *most*, *less*, and *least*.

Positive	Comparative	Superlative
brave	braver	bravest
alert	more alert	most alert
good	better	best
talented	less talented	least talented

Practice A Identify the degree of each italicized modifier.

1. Thomas Jefferson was a *brilliant* statesman.
2. Freedom is the *best* idea on which to build a nation.
3. The Declaration of Independence is an *important* document.
4. Some feel that Benjamin Franklin was *more pragmatic* than Thomas Jefferson.

Challenge In "The American Idea," find an example of a positive, a comparative, and a superlative adjective.

Practice B Determine if the italicized modifier is used correctly. Explain your answer.

1. Degas's ballerina painting is *prettier.*
2. Oil paints are *shiniest* than pastels.
3. In *Carriage at the Races*, the baby is *more important* than the carriage.
4. The center ballerina is the *taller* dancer in the entire group.

Challenge Write about a style of art or music you enjoy. Use this sentence as a model to write a new sentence that incorporates the three degrees of adjectives. *Degas's oil paintings were quick, his pastels were quicker, and his drawings were quickest.*

WG **Writing and Grammar Connection:** Chapter 25, Section 1

Extend the Lesson

Sentence Modeling

Choose the sentence given from the selection students have read:

The new Americans were tough men fighting for a very tough idea. ("The American Idea")

For Degas, showing only part of a subject made his paintings more intimate, immediate, and realistic. ("What Makes a Degas a Degas?")

Ask students what they notice about the sentence. Elicit from them that they use adjectives of different degrees; then, elicit the degree of adjectives used. Ask what else they notice. ("The American Idea": "tough" is used twice, once preceded by the intensifier "very," which adds degree to the adjective's double usage. "What Makes a Degas a Degas?": three adjectives, all preceded by "more," come at the end of the sentence, lending weight to their importance.)

Have students imitate the sentence in a sentence on a topic of their own choosing, matching each grammatical and stylistic feature discussed. Collect the sentences, and share them with the class.

Writing

Write a **critique,** or critical evaluation, of White's or Mühlberger's essay. Identify one of the central claims in the essay, and weigh the evidence the writer uses to support it.

- Before you draft, gather examples of the writer's *evidence.*
- For each piece of evidence, note your ideas about its effectiveness. In one sentence, state whether the writer's evidence is strong.
- Consider discussing each piece of evidence in a separate paragraph.
- Identify and assess ambiguities, nuances, and complexities within the text by looking for sections that were confusing to you. Decide whether the writer clarified the information for you, or determine the effect of the ambiguity.
- Conclude with a statement that evaluates the overall strength of White's or Mühlberger's evidence.
- Present your evaluation to the class.

Writing Workshop: *Work in Progress*

Prewriting for Persuasive Essay Make a flowchart for the first choice on your Topic List. In each supporting box, write a detail that shows why the change is needed or what positive result it would have. Save this Topic Defense List in your writing portfolio.

Use this prewriting activity to prepare for the **Writing Workshop** on page 604.

Research and Technology

Research one of the people associated with the essay you read. You might learn more about the nation's founders, such as Thomas Jefferson or Benjamin Franklin. Instead, you may study an artist associated with French Impressionism, such as Pierre Auguste Renoir or Mary Cassatt. Then, write a **cover letter** and **résumé** that he or she might have submitted for either the job of "Founder of the Republic" or "French Impressionist."

- Identify the education and experience that make your subject suitable for the job.
- Consult reference works to find a suitable **format** for cover letters and résumés. Use **action verbs** and vivid descriptions to make your writing engaging.
- Use appropriate **principles of design,** such as correct margins, tabs, columns, and use of white space, to create a visually interesting document.
- Proofread carefully to ensure that you follow the format and use language accurately.

PHLit Online!
www.PHLitOnline.com
- Interactive graphic organizers
- Grammar tutorial
- Interactive journals

Writing

1. Review the assignment, using the instruction on the student page.
2. To guide students in writing their critiques, give them **Support for Writing**, p. 90 in ***Unit 3 Resources.***
3. To evaluate students' critiques, use one of the Critique rubrics, pp. 250–251 in ***Professional Development Guidebook.*** Look for the following: a clear statement of a claim made by the author, identification of several pieces of evidence from the essay in support of the claim, and discussion of the effectiveness of each piece of evidence cited.

Six Traits Focus

✔	Ideas		Word Choice
✔	Organization		Sentence Fluency
	Voice		Conventions

Writing and Grammar, Grade 10

Students will find guidance on writing a critique in Chapter 31, Section 3.

Writing Workshop
Work in Progress

Have students save their completed Topic Defense List in their portfolios. They will use this later as they complete the Writing Workshop assignment (see pp. 604–611).

Research and Technology

1. Review the assignment, using the instruction on the student page.
2. Have students complete the **Support for Extend Your Learning** page (*Unit 3 Resources,* p. 195).

Teaching Resources

Unit 3 Resources
- L3 L4 **Integrated Language Skills: Grammar,** p. 193
- L3 L4 **Support for Writing,** p. 194
- L3 L4 **Support for Extend Your Learning,** p. 195
- L4 **Enrichment,** pp. 174, 192

Enriched Online Student Edition
Available under After You Read for this selection:
- All **Interactive Grammar Tutorial**
- L3 L4 **Internet Research Activity**

Professional Development Guidebook
Rubrics for Persuasive Essay, pp. 230–231

PHLit Online! All print and digital resources are available at **www.PHLitOnline.com.** Online resources accessible by students are noted on the student page.

MONITORING PROGRESS

Using the Test Practice

In this two-page Test Practice, students apply the reading skill for the second half of Unit 3 to a passage of fiction and a passage of nonfiction.

Review this skill, persuasive appeals, and then administer the test. For more guidance, consult the ***Classroom Strategies and Teaching Routines*** card, ***Administering Timed Tests.***

ASSESS

Answers

Answers With Explanations

1. B—Aaron suggests that the conditions at the city pound are inhumane. *Incorrect answers:* A—The passage does not mention how many stray dogs there are. C—This detail may be true, but it is not Aaron's main claim. D—Same explanation as for C.
2. B—If the city council gives the pound more money they will be able to improve the conditions there. *Incorrect answers:* A—Though this statement may be true, it does not represent Aaron's position. C—Same explanation as A. D—Same explanation as A.
3. D—This statement appeals to a sense of ethics or moral conviction. *Incorrect answers:* A—Though this statement may be logical, it is not intended to appeal to logic or reason. B—This statement does not appeal to economics or financial considerations. C—This statement is not humorous.
4. C—Aaron did not use statistics or numerical data in this passage. *Incorrect answers:* A—The statement "if the pound were cleaner and the animals better cared for, more people would adopt pets from there" is an appeal to logic or reasoning. B—The statement "Some of them look sick" appeals to the emotions and feelings. D—The statement "we should treat animals more humanely" appeals to a sense of ethics or moral conviction.

Test Practice: Reading

Evaluate Persuasion

Fiction Selection

Directions: *Read the selection. Then, answer the questions.*

Aaron called his best friend, Danny. "I just came from the city pound, looking for Jake. He got lost again," he told Danny. "You should see that place—crowded and smelly, no room for the dogs to run, not enough people to care for the animals. We need to do something."

"Like what?" asked Danny.

"We need to convince our city council to give more funds to the pound. We should treat animals humanely. These dogs are locked in small cages, with no place to exercise. Some of them look sick. They need better medical care. Also, if the pound were cleaner and the animals better cared for, more people would adopt pets from there. That would save the city money."

"Okay," said Danny. "Count me in. By the way, did you find Jake?"

"Yeah. He came home by himself!"

1. Which of the following *best* states the claim made by Aaron?
   A. There are too many stray dogs.
   B. The city pound is not a humane place for animals.
   C. The city pound is dirty.
   D. The city council is negligent.
2. What is Aaron's position?
   A. People should be convinced to adopt more animals from the pound.
   B. The city council should give the pound more money.
   C. Dogs should be taken for walks.
   D. People should be more humane.
3. The statement "We should treat animals humanely" appeals to—
   A. logic.
   B. economics.
   C. a sense of humor.
   D. a sense of ethics.
4. Which of the following persuasive techniques is *not* found in Aaron's appeal?
   A. logic
   B. emotion
   C. statistics
   D. a sense of ethics

Writing for Assessment

Which of Aaron's appeals do you find most persuasive? Explain your answer in three or four sentences, using details from the passage.

Writing for Assessment

Students should choose the persuasive technique used in the passage that they find most convincing. They should consider whether an appeal is made to reason or to emotion, using details from the passage to support their choices.

Strategies for Test Taking

Students should recognize that being asked to give the "best answer" may mean that even an answer that seems correct may be wrong if it is not the *best* answer. Model identifying the best answer for item 1. Point out that answer choices A and D are not directly stated or suggested by Aaron in the passage and should be eliminated. Guide students to then eliminate choice C, which serves only as a detail in support of Aaron's main claim that the city pound is not humane (choice B).

Nonfiction Selection

Directions: *Read the selection. Then, answer the questions.*

Adopting a family dog is a long-term commitment, so it is important to choose a dog wisely. The Labrador retriever is the most popular dog in the United States. More Labs are registered to owners than any other breed—for good reason.

Labs are affectionate and playful. They love the company of humans, and they always welcome attention. Labs also love any kind of active play. They love to play fetch, especially in the water. Toss a stick into the lake or pool, and you can be sure the Lab will never tire of retrieving it. Labs love to be part of a family, and they are patient and gentle with children. Labs are also easy to train, an important characteristic in a puppy. So when looking for a family pet, choose a Lab. You will not be sorry.

1. Which of the following is the *best* summary of the author's opinion?
- **A.** You should choose a pet carefully.
- **B.** Labrador retrievers are superior to other dogs.
- **C.** A dog's temperament is important.
- **D.** A Labrador retriever is the best family dog.

2. Repeated use of the word *love* serves to—
- **A.** help the reader identify with the writer's statements.
- **B.** emphasize the Lab's enthusiasm and good nature.
- **C.** show the writer's knowledge.
- **D.** show the superiority of Labs.

3. Which of the following persuasive techniques is found in the sentence *"More Labs are registered to owners than any other breed"*?
- **A.** fact
- **B.** repetition
- **C.** example
- **D.** humor

4. Which of the following statements can be verified?
- **A.** Labs love to be part of a family.
- **B.** More Labs are registered to owners than any other breed.
- **C.** You will not be sorry.
- **D.** Toss a stick in a pool, and you can be sure the Lab will never tire of retrieving it.

Writing for Assessment

Connecting Across Texts

What general attitude toward dogs is expressed in these two passages? In a well-developed paragraph, use details from the two passages to support your answer.

PHLit Online!
www.PHLitOnline.com
- Online practice
- Instant feedback

Differentiated Instruction for Universal Access

EL Strategy for Special Needs Students

Review with students what a persuasive essay is. Remind them that *persuasive appeals* can be an appeal to reason and logic, an appeal to emotion and feelings, or both. While reading the passage, students should ask themselves questions concerning whether the author's point is based of evidence that can be proved, or whether it is based on emotion. Remind students to take notes while reading the passage to help them determine the type of appeal that is being made. You may also encourage students to think about possible opposing arguments when reading a persuasive essay. This will help them to better identify the strength and purpose of the persuasive appeals. For example, students might pretend they are members of the city council referenced in the fiction selection. Encourage them to argue for and against getting more funding for the city pound, even if they don't agree with opposition.

ASSESS

Answers

Answers With Explanations

1. D—The passage persuasively discusses why the best family dog is a Labrador retriever. *Incorrect answers:* A—Though mentioned in the first paragraph, this is not the best summary of this passage. B—This is suggested but not stated in the passage. C—Same explanation as for B.
2. B—The Lab's enthusiasm and good nature are highlighted by the repeated use of the word love. *Incorrect answers:* A—Repeated use of the word love does not help the reader identify with the writer's statements. C—Though the writer may be knowledgeable about Labs, the word love does not strengthen that knowledge. D—The word love is not used to compare Labs to other dogs.
3. A—The persuasive technique of presenting evidence is clear and strengthens the author's opinion. *Incorrect answers:* B—This fact was not repeated. C—A particular example or instance was not identified. D—This sentence was intended to be factual, not humorous.
4. B—This statement is presented as a supporting fact and can be proved or disproved. *Incorrect answers:* A—This is a general statement in the form of an opinion and may not pertain to all Labs. C—This is an opinion and may not be shared by all future Lab owners. D—Same explanation as for A.

Writing for Assessment

Students' should focus on the attitude toward dogs expressed in the two passages, using details from each to discuss the similarities and differences. Students may focus on the general feeling of love expressed for dogs, noting that the fiction passage suggests love and a strong concern for all dogs, while the nonfiction does not express concern and focuses on why people should own Labs.

PHLit Online!

Students may take the test in interactive format with instant feedback online at **www.PHLitOnline.com**.

PREETEACH

Meeting Your Standards

Students will

1. analyze text structures.
2. read a research source and a course catalog.

*Log on at **www.PHLitOnline.com** for a detailed lesson plan.*

Reading Skill

1. Introduce the skill, using the instruction on the student page.
2. Tell students that they will analyze text structures as they read.

Think Aloud: Model the Skill

Model the skill of analyzing text structures, using the following "think aloud." Say to students:

Let's say I read an article about baseball. The title and headings indicate that the author's purpose is to describe the history of baseball. I then skim the text to critique how the author orders information. If the text presents baseball from inception to today, I know that this order supports the author's purpose.

What kind of knowledge changes our lives?

As they read, have students look for ways that text structures help present information.

Multidraft Reading

Have students follow a multidraft reading protocol after they preview.

- **First reading**—Have students read for general understanding.
- **Second reading**—Have students analyze text structures to determine if they support the author's purpose.
- **Third reading**—Have students look for ways that text structures are used to present information.

Informational Texts

Real-Life Reading

Research Source
The History of the Guitar

Course Catalog
California State University at Fullerton Course Catalog

Reading Skill: Analyze Text Structures

Authors **structure and format** their texts in order to help achieve their purposes. **Scan,** or glance over titles, headings, and subheadings, to **analyze how these features support the author's purpose.** Also, **critique the document** by **skimming,** or quickly reading key parts of the text, to determine the **sequence,** or order, of information. Then, decide whether that sequence is logical. This chart lists some common text structures.

Common Text Structures	
Cause and Effect	action followed by consequences
Chronological Order	in order of occurrence
Comparison and Contrast	according to the similarities and differences
List	connected items stated consecutively or sorted into categories
Order of Importance	in a logical progression
Spatial Order	according to location

What kind of *knowledge* changes our lives?

These two selections provide information for different purposes: the article for learning something, and the catalog for doing something.

Differentiated Instruction for Universal Access

Reading Support

Give students reading support with the appropriate version of the *Reader's Notebooks:*

L2 L3 *Reader's Notebook*
L1 *Reader's Notebook: Adapted Version*
EL *Reader's Notebook: English Learner's Version*

PHLit Online! All student resources are available online at **www.PHLitOnline.com.**

The History of the Guitar

Thomas A. Hill

Research Source

Features:

- authoritative information about a specific subject
- "navigational" text aids, such as index, table of contents, or alphabetical arrangement of entries
- formatting text aids, such as boldface heads or color-coded features
- text written for a specific audience

When we attempt to pinpoint the origins of deliberately produced, carefully designed instruments, we run into problems, because the very first instrument makers were not very concerned with posterity. They did not leave written records. One approach we might try, in an effort to find out where the guitar came from, would be an examination of languages.

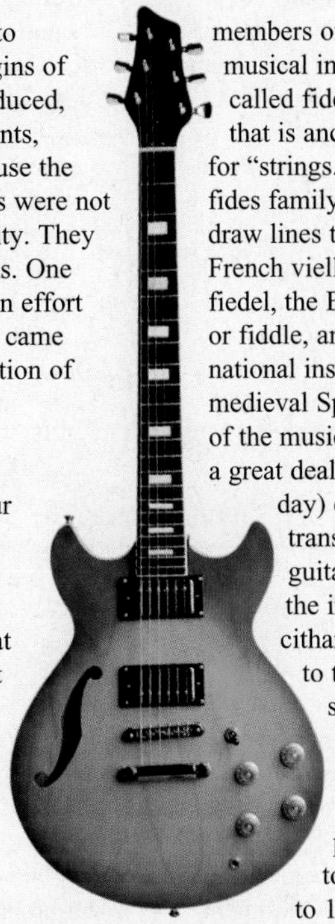

This paragraph is organized using a cause-and-effect structure.

Ancient Beginnings

The ancient Assyrians,[1] four thousand years ago, had an instrument that they called a chetarah. We know little more about it other than that it was a stringed instrument with a sound-box, but the name is intriguing. The ancient Hebrews had their kinnura, the Chaldeans[2] their qitra, and the Greeks their cithara and citharis—which Greek writers of the day were careful to emphasize were not the same instrument. It is with the Greeks, in fact, that the first clear history of the evolution of an instrument begins; some of this history can again be traced with purely linguistic devices. The cithara and citharis were members of a family of musical instruments called fides—a word that is ancient Greek for "strings." From the fides family it is easy to draw lines to the medieval French vielle, the German fiedel, the English fithele or fiddle, and the vihuela, national instrument of medieval Spain. Significantly, much of the music for the vihuela (of which a great deal survives to the present day) can easily be transcribed[3] for the guitar. In England, the influences of the cithara and citharis led to the evolution of such instruments as the cither, zither, cittern, and gittern, with which instrument the linguistic parallel we seek is fairly easy to draw. Gitterns dating back to 1330 can be seen in the British Museum. In Spain, there is music for the vihuela that dates back at least that far. What did these instruments look like? Superficially, they bore a substantial resemblance to the guitar as we know it today, although the sides seldom curved in as far as do the sides of the modern

The author gives information in spatial order, according to the regions in which the events took place.

1. **Assyrians** (ə sir′ ē ənz) founders of an ancient empire in the Middle East, flourishing in the seventh century B.C.
2. **Chaldeans** (kal dē′ ənz) a people that rose to power in Babylon, an ancient empire of the Middle East, during the sixth century B.C.
3. **transcribed** (tran skrībd′) *v.* adapted piece of music for an instrument other than the one for which it was originally written.

TEACH

About Research Sources

1. Review the features listed in the Research Sources box on this page. Remind students that they use these sources when they are researching topics for school or to learn about a new topic.
2. Invite students to share different research sources they have used. **Sample answers:** Encyclopedias, nonfiction books, periodicals
3. **Ask** students how the reader benefits from reading a well-organized research source. **Possible response:** The reader will know where to locate information that is important to his or her research.

Analyze Text Structures

1. Remind students that when they scan a text, they examine text features to help them understand the organization of the text.
2. **Ask** a volunteer what the subheadings tell readers about the sequence of the article. **Possible response:** The first subheading, "Ancient Beginnings," indicates that the history of the guitar is going to begin in ancient times. The second subheading, "The African Link," indicates that a parallel sequence is going to be presented beginning again in ancient times.
3. Have students read "The History of the Guitar" and the side notes. Tell them to watch for common text structures, such as chronological and spatial order.
4. **Ask** students to describe the organization of the facts under the heading "Ancient Beginnings." **Possible response:** The facts under the heading "Ancient Beginnings" are arranged mainly in a chronological order. Some parts, however, are also in a spatial order, so that they can be presented with other details from the same location.

Differentiated Instruction for Universal Access

Strategy for Special Needs Students
Students may have an easier time keeping track of information they are looking for in an article if they can mark the locations while they are reading. Give these students thin self-sticking notes or arrows to mark details they find while reading.

Enrichment for Advanced Readers
Challenge students to learn more about a musician known for his or her guitar-playing abilities. Ask them to discover how the musician became interested in the guitar and what led to his or her mastery of the instrument. Allow time for students to present their research. Encourage students to provide audio of the musician playing the guitar.

Analyze Text Structures

1. Draw students' attention to the heading "The African Link." Remind students that text features, such as headings, can signal a change in organization of the text's facts.
2. **Ask** students to identify new information that was added by "The African Link."
   Possible response: The section describes the *al-ud* and how it became known as the *lute*. The lute's main contribution to the evolution of the guitar was the fret. The section explains that when the Moors left Africa for Spain, they took the lute with them resulting in both the sharing of the fret and a creative artistic climate.
3. **Ask** students to discuss whether the sequence of the section is logical.
   Possible response: Some students may say that the sequence is logical because the section shows how the lute influenced what we know as a guitar. Others may say that there are definite gaps in the sequence of details.

A new pattern of organization—comparison and contrast—helps readers grasp details about instruments of the past.

guitar. They were usually strung with pairs of strings, or courses, much like a modern twelve-string guitar. The two strings of each course were tuned either in unison or an octave[4] apart. For a while, there seemed to be no standard for the number of courses an instrument should have; there are both vihuelas and gitterns with as few as four courses and as many as seven. By the fifteenth century, the vihuela seems to have settled on six as the standard number of courses. . . In England, the gittern settled down to four courses. . . . Historians of this period do note the existence in Spain of an instrument called the guitarra. . . . But no music was being written for this instrument, and nobody seems to have been paying much attention to it.

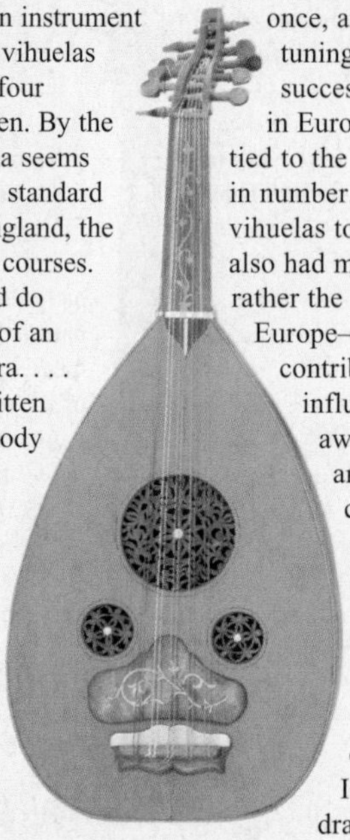

The African Link

Meanwhile, in Africa, the Arabs had been playing an instrument that they called al-ud, or "the wood," for centuries. When the Moors crossed the Straits of Gibraltar[5] in the twelfth century to conquer Spain, they brought this instrument with them. It quickly became popular, and by the time anybody who spoke English was talking about it, al-ud had become lute. The lute's main contribution to the evolution of the guitar as we know it today seems to have been the fret, a metal bar on the fingerboard. Until the arrival of the lute, the European forerunners of the guitar had no frets at all. Since the fret made it a little easier to play the same tune the same way more than once, and helped to standardize tunings, it was a resounding success. The first Arabic lutes in Europe had movable frets, tied to the neck, usually about eight in number. Consequently, the first vihuelas to which frets were added also had movable ones. The lute—or rather the people who brought it to Europe—made another important contribution. The Moorish artistic influence, blowing the cobwebs away from stodgy Spanish art and society, created an artistic climate that encouraged music to flourish. And so the instruments on which the music was played flourished as well, and continued to evolve and improve. This is a contribution that cannot be overestimated.

If any general lines can be drawn, perhaps it can be said that descendants of the original al-ud, crossing the Straits of Gibraltar, collided in Spain with the descendants of the Greek cithara and citharis. Sprinkled with a little bit of gittern influence from England, the result led ultimately to what we know today as the guitar.

This paragraph uses a cause-and-effect structure to explain the evolution of the first fret.

4. **unison** (yo͞on´ e sen) . . . octave (äk´ tiv) A unison consists of two tones of the same pitch. An octave consists of two tones that are eight notes apart in the scale. The pitches in an octave sound "the same" and are named by the same note.
5. **Moors** (mo͝orz) . . . Gibraltar (ji brôl´ tər) Groups of Moors, an Arab people of North Africa, invaded Spain at various times, beginning the in the eight century A.D. The Straits of Gibraltar are waters dividing Spain from Africa.

Vocabulary Development

Vocabulary From Historical Articles

Point out that research sources often use vocabulary that is specific to one particular setting, in this case the history of guitars. Guide students to understand the meaning of the following words that are used in "The History of the Guitar":

linguistic: pertaining to human speech
evolution: a process of continuous change from one form to another
superficially: in a manner that is obvious or apparent
standardize: to bring into conformity with a standard

PHLit Online! **Vocabulary Central,** featuring tools, activities, and songs for studying vocabulary, is available at **www.PHLitOnline.com.**

CALIFORNIA STATE UNIVERSITY AT FULLERTON

Course Catalog

Course Catalog

Features:

- functional reading
- descriptions of programs of study within each of the school's departments
- explanations of the requirements for completing programs and attaining certificates or degrees
- lists of the courses offered within each department and information about their value
- text written for a specific audience

PROGRAMS OFFERED

The text is organized by order of importance. The information becomes more specific through the document. This section lists all of the music programs offered.

Bachelor of Arts in Music

- Liberal Arts
- Music Education
- Music History and Theory

Bachelor of Music

- Composition
- Voice
- Instrumental
- Accompanying
- Keyboard
- Jazz and Commercial Music

Minor in Music

Master of Arts in Music

- Music History and Literature
- Music Education

Piano Pedagogy

Master of Music

- Performance
- Theory—Composition

Single Subject *(Secondary)* Credential

INTRODUCTION

An introduction provides an overview of the university's music program.

Music is one of the most rewarding of all human endeavors, and the faculty and students in the Department of Music share a deep love for their art and a common desire to achieve excellence in it. The department offers a wide spectrum of degree programs and options with an overall emphasis in the area of performance. The curriculum provides basic preparation for careers in music, music education, or further graduate study, and is designed to provide a balanced education in the many facets of musical experience. Artist-teachers offer instruction in all areas of performance; practicing composers and theorists teach courses in theory and composition; active musicologists provide instruction in history and literature; and specialists in music education teach the courses in that area. It is the goal of the department to develop each student's musical and intellectual potential to the highest level of individual capability. California State University at Fullerton is fully accredited by the National Association of Schools of Music and the Western Association of Schools and Colleges.

About Course Catalogs

1. Review the features listed in the Course Catalog box on the student page. **Ask** the class to define the term *functional reading* in their own words.
   Possible response: Functional reading is reading a person does to achieve a specific result.
2. Invite students to discuss experiences they have had with course catalogs.
   Possible response: Students may say that they have referenced course catalogs to help them determine what field they would like to study in college.
3. Review with students the way in which information is organized in a course catalog. Explain that course catalogs begin with an overview of the programs that are offered and then become more focused as the text progresses.

Analyze Text Structures

1. Review the analyzing strategies and common text structures that students learned on page 578.
2. Have students read the course catalog. Then, have them scan the text to identify text features and structures used by the author.
   Sample answer: The author uses title, headings, and subheadings, as well as list and order of importance.
3. **Ask** students to discuss how well the text features support the author's purpose.
   Possible response: The text features help separate the catalog into sections that are easily recognizable. The reader does not have to spend a long time looking for a particular section. The text structures allow the reader to understand the progression of the music program and what each degree requires.

Differentiated Instruction for Universal Access

Culturally Responsive Instruction

Culture Connection Point out to students that music exists in every culture. The music varies as widely as the regions it hails from and the instruments used to play it. Explain that many cultures have an instrument, or group of instruments, that define the culture's traditional music. For instance, a well-known percussion instrument in traditional Japanese music is a large drum called the ōdaiko. Encourage students to share their knowledge and experience of musical instruments in their home culture or family's country of origin.

Analyze Text Structures

1. After students have finished reading the selection, have them return to the section that outlines requirements for obtaining a bachelor's degree.
2. Invite students to skim the information. Then, **ask** them to explain whether the sequence of information is logical. **Possible response:** Yes, the sequence is logical because it shows that the student will begin by learning about the mechanics of music and finish by performing music.

Reflecting on the Skill

After students have read both selections, ask them to look at the structure and format of each selection. **Ask** students to explain which selection's structure and format was more effective in achieving the author's purpose.

Possible response: Some students may say that the structure and format of "The History of the Guitar" allowed them to easily understand what led to the creation of the guitar. Others may say that the Course Catalog gave them a solid understanding of the music program requirements through the use of various headings, lists, and the logical progression of information.

ASSESS/EXTEND

Answers

THE BIG ? What kind of knowledge changes our lives?

Possible response: After reading the catalog, a reader may decide to enroll in a different degree program than previously intended because the new course of study sounds more appealing.

MUSIC DEGREE PROGRAMS

The Department of Music offers a variety of courses that lead to baccalaureate and graduate degrees. The baccalaureate degree may be earned in either of two degree programs (Bachelor of Arts or Bachelor of Music). Within these programs, a student will pursue a concentration in Liberal Arts, Music History and Theory, Music Education, Performance, Composition, Accompanying, or Jazz and Commercial Music.

This section provides more specific information about one music degree program.

BACHELOR OF MUSIC

This degree program is designed to provide training for highly gifted students who show promise and capability of becoming professional performers and composers.

The degree consists of 132 semester units. A minimum of 70 semester units in music are required, at least 32 of which must be upper-division.

Core Requirements for the Bachelor of Music (38 units)

Music theory *(Music 109, 111, 112, 121, 122, 211, 221, 319, 320)* (16 units)
Music history and literature *(Music 151; 351A,B,C)* (11 units)
Principal performance area *(applied music)* (6 units)
Major performance ensemble *(Music 406)* (4 units)
Recital *(Music 498)* (1 unit)

KEYBOARD CONCENTRATION (70 units)

Second Language Graduation Requirement

You can skim the information provided here to determine if it is logically presented.

Since the Keyboard Concentration within the Bachelor of Music is a high-unit program, majors in this concentration are exempt from the Second Language Graduation Requirement.

Core Requirements for the Bachelor of Music (38 units)

Music theory *(Music 109, 111, 112, 121, 122, 211, 221, 319, 320)* (16 units)
Music history and literature *(Music 151; 351A, B, C)* (11 units)
Principal performance area *(applied music)* (6 units)
Major performance ensemble *(Music 406)* (4 units)
Recital *(Music 498)* (1 unit)

Additional Requirements (32 units)

Music theory *(two courses from Music 418, 420, 422)* (4–5 units)
Music history and literature *(Music 454A, B)* (4 units)
Conducting *(Music 382A or 383A)* (2 units)
Recital *(Music 398)* (1 unit)
Principal performance area *(applied music)* (6 units)
Chamber music *(Music 407D, E, M, Y and/or 408B, G, K, S, W, X)* (3 units)
Piano-Vocal Collaboration *(Music 386)* (1 unit)
Pedagogy *(Music 467A, B, C)* (6 units)
Harpsichord or organ class *(Music 372 or 373)* (1 unit)
Electives in music (3–4 units)

THE BIG ? What kind of knowledge changes our lives? Think about the circumstances under which someone might read this catalog. How might the information in the catalog change a reader's mind or intentions?

Test Practice: Informational Texts

Comparing Informational Texts

(a) Compare and contrast the **structures** and **formats** of each text, including the way these features are used to achieve the authors' purposes. **(b)** How do those similarities and differences affect how readers use each text?

Timed Writing

Write a Letter

Format and Audience
The prompt directs you to write a letter to an author. Therefore, be sure you use letter formatting, formal language, and a respectful tone.

Write a letter to the author of the research source in which you comment on "The History of the Guitar" and the sequence of the information presented. Mention whether the order made it easier or more difficult to understand the text. Explain and support your comments with relevant details from the text. (25 minutes)

Academic Vocabulary
When you *explain* something, you describe it in terms that will help someone understand it more clearly.

5-Minute Planner

Complete these steps before you begin to write:

1. Read the prompt carefully and completely. Look for key words, like the ones highlighted in color, that will help you understand the assignment.
2. Scan the features and skim the text of the research source.
3. As you skim and scan, consider and make notes about how the **sequence of information** helps you, the reader, better understand the text. Also note any areas where the order of information might confuse a reader.
4. Make a quick outline of your letter. Plan the order of the points you will make. Sequence your points in a way that will help the reader, the author, understand your ideas.
5. Refer to your outline and notes as you draft your letter to the author, Thomas A. Hill.

Answers

Comparing Informational Texts

(a) The title of the article informs the reader of its topic. The subheadings tell the main points discussed in each section of the article. Comparing and contrasting, cause-and-effect, and spatial order are used in the selection to explain the material more thoroughly. The Course Catalog has a title, headings, and subheadings. The information is arranged in labeled sections and follows a logical progression. This allows readers to skim the material and easily find the information they need.

(b) Readers will read "The History of the Guitar" fully in order to understand how the guitar evolved. Conversely, readers are more likely to scan or skim the course catalog to find information in which they are interested.

Timed Writing

1. Before students complete the activity, guide them in identifying and analyzing key words and phrases in the prompt, highlighted on the student page.
2. Work with students to draw up guidelines for their responses based on the key words in the prompt:
   - **Focus** The response should clearly analyze the sequence of information presented in the research source.
   - **Organization** The response should include comments about the research source and then provide an analysis of the sequence of information.
   - **Elaboration** The response should provide sufficient details to support the comments and analysis.
   - **Style** The audience is an author, so a formal style and respectful tone is suitable.
3. Have students use the 5-Minute Planner to structure their time.
4. Allow students 25 minutes to complete the assignment. Evaluate their work using the guidelines they have developed.

Extend the Lesson

Connecting to the Students' World

To help students enhance their understanding of research sources and course catalogs and to help them apply the lesson to their own world, divide students into small groups. Have each group conduct research to create a course catalog or a research source about their favorite genre of music. Instruct them to use a variety of text features and structures, such as headings and sequence, which would be helpful to musicians of the future interested in learning about the genre. Have each group present their original text to the class. When all groups have finished presenting, have students discuss which structures and formats were most helpful in presenting the information.

PREACH

Meeting Your Standards

Students will

1. analyze and respond to author's purpose.
2. compare the author's purpose in nonfiction.
3. write a comparison of authors' purposes.

*Log on at **www.PHLitOnline.com** for a detailed lesson plan for Comparing Literary Works.*

❶ Comparing Author's Purpose

1. Introduce the skill using the instruction on the student page.
2. Give students a copy of **Comparing Author's Purpose Graphic Organizer B** ***Graphic Organizer Transparencies,*** p. 107. Tell them they will fill it in to compare author's purpose and supporting details as they read.

Think Aloud: Model the Skill

Model a way to compare author's purpose. Say to students:

Let's say two authors are writing about Miami, Florida. One gives details about when the city was founded and its population. This author's purpose is to inform. Another might give details about the beautiful weather and beaches. This author's purpose is to persuade me to visit the city.

❷ Vocabulary

1. Have students say each word aloud.
2. Then, use the word in a sentence that defines the word. Repeat the sentence, now with the word missing, and have the class "fill in the blank" chorally.

For more guidance, see the ***Classroom Strategies and Teaching Routines*** card, **Introducing Selection Vocabulary.**

Comparing Literary Works

from **Desert Exile** • *from* **The Way to Rainy Mountain**

❶ Comparing Author's Purpose

An **author's purpose** is his or her main reason for writing. The following examples illustrate common purposes for nonfiction writers:

- A journalist might write to inform readers about a recent event.
- A humorist might write to entertain with a comical anecdote.
- An essayist might write to pay tribute to a person whom he or she thinks deserves honor.

A writer may have more than one purpose for writing. Generally, however, one purpose is the most important. Both Yoshiko Uchida and N. Scott Momaday write about their personal connections to historic events. Both authors intend to inform readers about the past. However, writers who write about the past often have another, deeper purpose than informing: They may write to heal old wounds, to bear witness to past injustice, or to better understand themselves. The author's purpose often influences the tone and structure of the text. As you read, use a chart like the one shown to compare Momaday's and Uchida's purposes and the details, or evidence, that they use for support.

	Uchida	Momaday
Details		
Purposes		

❷ Vocabulary

- **adept** (ə dept′) *adj.* expert; highly skilled (p. 588) *The lawyer was adept at arguing a case.* *adeptly adv. adeptness n.*
- **unwieldy** (un wēl′ dē) *adj.* hard to manage because of shape or weight (p. 589) *The tuba is an unwieldy instrument to carry.* *unwieldiness n. wield v. wieldable adj.*
- **nomadic** (nō mad′ ik) *adj.* moving from place to place; without a permanent home (p. 597) *The nomadic shepherds sought pastures for the flocks.* *nomad n. nomadism n.*
- **tenuous** (ten′ yo͞o əs) *adj.* flimsy; not strong (p. 599) *My memory is tenuous; can you remind me?* *tenuously adv. tenuousness n.*

PHLit Online! www.PHLitOnline.com

- Vocabulary flashcards
- Interactive journals
- More about the authors
- Selection audio
- Interactive graphic organizers

Vocabulary Development

Vocabulary Knowledge Rating

Create a **Vocabulary Knowledge Rating Chart** (***Professional Development Guidebook,*** p. 33) for this selection. Include the selection vocabulary and the form of the Big Question word that appears in the Writing About the Big Question sentence starter on the next page. (The Big Question vocabulary is introduced on pp. 442–443.)

Give students a copy of the chart. Read the words aloud, and have students mark their rating in the Before Reading column. Urge them to be alert to these words as they read and discuss the selection. Tally how many students think they know a word to gauge how much instruction to provide. As students read and discuss the selection, point out the words and their context.

PHLit Online! **Vocabulary Central,** featuring tools, activities, and songs for studying vocabulary, is available online at **www.PHLitOnline.com.**

What kind of *knowledge* changes our lives?

❸ Writing About the Big Question

Both Yoshiko Uchida and N. Scott Momaday write to record a vanishing past with a belief that passing down history is critical. Use this sentence starter to develop your ideas about the Big Question.

Reflecting on the past is important because ________.

Meet the Authors

Yoshiko Uchida (1921–1992)

Author of *Desert Exile*

Yoshiko Uchida's childhood was fairly uneventful—until history struck. In 1942, the United States and Japan went to war, and the United States government forced Japanese American families like Uchida's into relocation camps. Uchida and her family were sent to Tanforan Racetrack near San Francisco, where they lived in a stable. Later, they were relocated to a camp in Utah.

Supporting Awareness After the war, Uchida attended Smith College in Massachusetts. She became a teacher and an award-winning author who wrote more than thirty fiction and nonfiction books. Her ultimate goal, she said, was "to write of meaningful relationships between human beings, to celebrate our common humanity."

N. Scott Momaday (b. 1934)

Author of *The Way to Rainy Mountain*

Growing up on the Native American reservations where his parents taught, N. Scott Momaday learned the traditions of his father's Kiowa culture, as well as those of the Navajo, Apache, and Pueblo Indians. At the same time, he received a modern education. "I grew up in two worlds and straddle both those worlds even now," he says. "It has made for confusion and a richness in my life."

A Creative Heritage Momaday has made much of this "richness," celebrating Native American traditions in novels, poetry, and essays. His first novel, *House Made of Dawn*, received a Pulitzer Prize.

Daily Bellringer

For each class during which you will teach this selection, have students complete one of the five Sentence Combining activities for Week 18 in the ***Daily Bellringer Activities*** booklet.

❸ Writing About the Big Question

1. Review the assignment with the class.
2. Invite students to think about a time when a memory helped them to make a decision in the present.
3. Have students complete the sentence starter. Review responses as a class. (**Possible response:** Reflecting on the past is important because it can explain why certain changes took place or continue to take place.)
4. Remind students that their answers will help them think about the Big Question.

Tell students that as they read, they should look for changes that occur as a result of obtaining knowledge.

Concept Connector

Students will return to their responses to the sentence starter after they have completed reading.

Multidraft Reading

To assist struggling readers and to deepen reading for all, apply multidraft reading protocols. For each reading, have students set the purpose indicated:

- **First reading**—literal comprehension: answering the Reading Check questions
- **Second reading**—application of skills: responding to the side-column notes
- **Third reading**—interpretation: answering the end-of-selection questions

For more guidance, refer to the ***Classroom Strategies and Teaching Routines*** card on multidraft reading.

PHLit Online!

For more about the authors, practice with the selection vocabulary, and more background, go online at **www.PHLitOnline.com.**

Teaching Resources

The following resources can be used to enrich, extend, or differentiate the instruction.

- All *Unit 3 Resources,* pp. 106–109
- All *Graphic Organizer Transparencies,* pp. 106–107
- All **Enriched Online Student Edition**

PHLit Online! All resources, including print and audio, are available online at **www.PHLitOnline.com.**

TEACH

❶ Background

Relocation Camps in America

The forced relocation and confinement of people of Japanese descent reflected anti-Japanese sentiment on the West Coast during the 1940s that came from economic rivalry, racial prejudice, and fear of sabotage after the attack on Pearl Harbor. Japanese workers had been immigrating to California since the 1890s and had always struggled with discrimination, as had the Chinese who preceded them. In 1944, the United States Supreme Court ruled that the evacuation and internment was constitutional, despite the facts that about two-thirds of the internees were American citizens and half of them were children. As part of President Ford's apology in 1988, 60,000 surviving internees received $20,000 each as compensation for the ordeal.

❷ Activating Prior Knowledge

In this selection, students will learn about relocation camps and how the author's family and friends coped with injustice and harsh conditions. Lead students in a discussion about why Uchida's story is important for the well-being of all American citizens, not only those of Japanese descent. Use these questions to prompt critical thinking: How is the cross-cultural experience an American experience? How was the internment of Japanese Americans something in which all Americans participated either directly or indirectly? What lessons come from the study of Japanese internment? Are these lessons that Americans have mastered?

Concept Connector

Tell students they will return to their discussion responses after they read the selection.

❸ About the Selection

Author Yoshiko Uchida was twenty-one years old when the federal government ordered her family into a relocation camp. Throughout the excerpt from "Desert Exile," she closely details daily routines and challenges of the camp.

from

Desert Exile:

❶

The Uprooting of a Japanese-American Family

❷

❸

Yoshiko Uchida

Vocabulary Development

Word Analysis

Call students' attention to the word *cursory* in the second paragraph on the next page. Tell students that the word contains the Latin root *-curs-*, which means "to run." Have students suggest other words that contain the root *-curs-* and list them on the board. Possible responses may include *current, course, recur,* and *currency.*

Next, using a dictionary, have students identify the meanings of these words. Make sure that they check whether the word contains the root *-curs-*. Finally, ask students to use each word in a sentence. Invite volunteers to read their sentences aloud.

Background On December 7, 1941, Japan attacked the American naval base at Pearl Harbor, Hawaii. Two months later, under strong political pressure, President Franklin D. Roosevelt ordered more than 100,000 Japanese Americans from their homes and into government-run relocation camps. More than thirty years after the war, President Gerald Ford officially apologized to Japanese Americans and signed a proclamation officially ending the old order.

Yoshiko Uchida tells of her own family's experience of wartime internment. In 1942, her father was arrested and taken to Montana by the Federal Bureau of Investigation. A few months later, the rest of the family was ordered to report to the assembly camp at Tanforan.

As the bus pulled up to the grandstand, I could see hundreds of Japanese Americans jammed along the fence that lined the track. These people had arrived a few days earlier and were now watching for the arrival of friends or had come to while away the empty hours that had suddenly been thrust upon them. 4

As soon as we got off the bus, we were directed to an area beneath the grandstand where we registered and filled out a series of forms. Our baggage was inspected for contraband,[1] a cursory medical check made, and our living quarters assigned. We were to be housed in Barrack 16, Apartment 40. Fortunately, some friends who had
5 arrived earlier found us and offered to help us locate our quarters.

It had rained the day before and the hundreds of people who had trampled on the track had turned it into a miserable mass of slippery mud. We made our way on it carefully, helping my mother who was dressed just as she would have been to go to church. She wore a hat, gloves, her good coat, and her Sunday shoes, because she would not have thought of venturing outside our house dressed in any other way.

Everywhere there were black tar-papered barracks[2] that had been hastily erected to house the 8,000 Japanese Americans of the area who had been uprooted from their homes. Barrack 16, however, was not among them, and we couldn't find it until we had traveled half the length of the track and gone beyond it to the northern rim of the racetrack compound.

Finally one of our friends called out, "There it is, beyond that row of eucalyptus trees." Barrack 16 was not a barrack at all, but a long stable raised a few feet off the ground with a broad ramp the horses 6 had used to reach their stalls. Each stall was now numbered, and ours was number 40. That the stalls should have been called "apartments" was a euphemism so ludicrous it was comical.

1. **contraband** (kän´ trə band´) *n.* prohibited goods.
2. **barracks** (bar´ əks) *n.* large, plain, often temporary housing.

4 ◄ **Critical Viewing**
Which details suggest that the family in this photograph is being forced to move to a relocation camp?

Literary Analysis
Author's Purpose
Which details here show that part of the author's purpose is to pay tribute, or honor the people she describes?

6 **Reading Check**
What kind of building was Barrack 16 before it was turned into housing?

4 Critical Viewing

Answer: Students may say the family has only a few pieces of luggage among them; the children wear what appear to be identification tags; the children have sad expressions on their faces.

5 Literary Analysis

Author's Purpose

1. Remind students that one way to identify the purpose of an essay is to determine what the details have in common.
2. **Ask** the Literary Analysis question: Which details here show that part of the author's purpose is to pay tribute, or honor the people she describes?
   Answer: People seek out friends and help them get settled. Despite miserable conditions, the author's mother shows pride and strength by insisting on wearing her best clothes.

6 Reading Check

Answer: Barrack 16 had been a horse stable.

Differentiated Instruction for Universal Access

Accessibility at a Glance

Use this information to guide your teaching of the excerpt from "Desert Exile."

Context	Essay on life in a World War II relocation camp
Language/Vocabulary	• Descriptive • Grade-appropriate vocabulary
Concept Level	Accessible (camp life)
Literary Merit	Noted author
Lexile/Length	Lexile: 1270L Word Count: 3,041

PHLit Online!

This selection is available in interactive format in the **Enriched Online Student Edition**, online at **www.PHLitOnline.com**, which includes an interactive graphic organizer.

❼ Literary Analysis
Author's Purpose

1. Review with students some of the reasons that an author writes an essay: to inform, to persuade, to entertain, to pay tribute, or to express an opinion. Have students refer to their graphic organizers to review the purposes they have identified so far.
2. **Ask** the first Literary Analysis question: In addition to informing, what purpose might details about dust and dirt serve?
   Possible response: The description of the conditions fulfills the purpose of persuading readers that internment was unfair and unjust.

❽ Critical Thinking
Infer

1. Review with students that to make an inference is to use details and personal experience to think critically about an essay.
2. Have a volunteer read the bracketed passage aloud.
3. **Ask:** What fact in the paragraph prompts the author to comment on the nation's security?
   Answer: The camp is half-finished.
4. Now **ask** students to make an inference based on the camp's preparedness.
   Possible response: The decision to intern Japanese Americans was hastily made.

❾ Literary Analysis
Author's Purpose

1. Have students read the bracketed passage.
2. **Ask** the second Literary Analysis question: What might the author's purpose be in sharing such painful memories?
   Answer: The author wants the reader to fully understand the physical and emotional suffering endured by people in the camps.

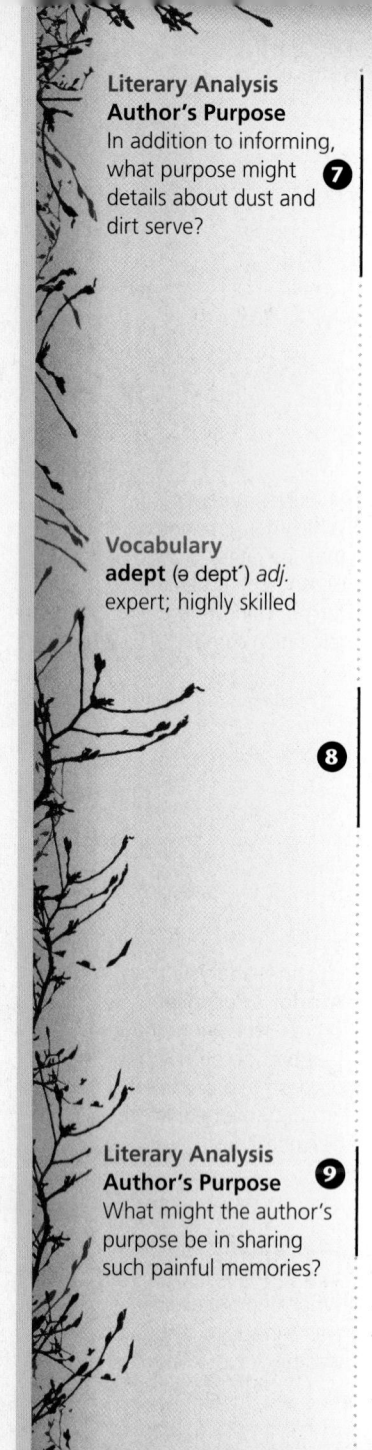

Literary Analysis
Author's Purpose
In addition to informing, what purpose might details about dust and dirt serve? ❼

Vocabulary
adept (ə dept′) *adj.* expert; highly skilled

Literary Analysis
Author's Purpose ❾
What might the author's purpose be in sharing such painful memories?

When we reached stall number 40, we pushed open the narrow door and looked uneasily into the vacant darkness. The stall was about ten by twenty feet and empty except for three folded Army cots lying on the floor. Dust, dirt, and wood shavings covered the linoleum that had been laid over manure-covered boards, the smell of horses hung in the air, and the whitened corpses of many insects still clung to the hastily white-washed walls.

High on either side of the entrance were two small windows which were our only source of daylight. The stall was divided into two sections by Dutch doors[3] worn down by teeth marks, and each stall in the stable was separated from the adjoining one only by rough partitions that stopped a foot short of the sloping roof. That space, while perhaps a good source of ventilation for the horses, deprived us of all but visual privacy, and we couldn't even be sure of that because of the crevices and knotholes in the dividing walls.

Because our friends had already spent a day as residents of Tanforan, they had become adept at scrounging for necessities. One found a broom and swept the floor for us. Two of the boys went to the barracks where mattresses were being issued, stuffed the ticking with straw themselves, and came back with three for our cots.

❽ Nothing in the camp was ready. Everything was only half-finished. I wondered how much the nation's security would have been threatened had the Army permitted us to remain in our homes a few more days until the camps were adequately prepared for occupancy by families.

By the time we had cleaned out the stall and set up the cots, it was time for supper. Somehow, in all the confusion, we had not had lunch, so I was eager to get to the main mess hall, which was located beneath the grandstand.

The sun was going down as we started along the muddy track, and a cold, piercing wind swept in from the bay. When we arrived, there were six long weaving lines of people waiting to get into the mess hall. We took our place at the end of one of them, each of us clutching a plate and silverware borrowed from friends who had already received their baggage.

Shivering in the cold, we pressed close together trying to shield Mama from the wind. As we stood in what seemed a breadline for the destitute, I felt degraded, humiliated, and overwhelmed with a longing for home. And I saw the unutterable sadness on my mother's face.

This was only the first of many lines we were to endure, and we soon discovered that waiting in line was as inevitable a part of Tanforan as the north wind that swept in from the bay stirring up all the dust and litter of the camp.

3. **Dutch doors** two-part door in which the top half and the bottom half can be opened separately.

Vocabulary Development

Thematic Vocabulary: The Big Question
As students are discussing the excerpt from "Desert Exile," ask them to use the thematic vocabulary presented in Introducing the Big Question, pp. 442–443. You might encourage them with sentence starters like these:

1. Uchida gives the reader *insight* into . . .
2. Living together in tight, dirty quarters forced many people to *adapt* to . . .
3. Friends at the camp showed *empathy* toward the Uchida family by . . .
4. Injustice often prompts people to promote *awareness* of . . .

Once we got inside the gloomy cavernous mess hall, I saw hundreds of people eating at wooden picnic tables, while those who had already eaten were shuffling aimlessly over the wet cement (10) floor. When I reached the serving table and held out my plate, a cook reached into a dishpan full of canned sausages and dropped two onto my plate with his fingers. Another man gave me a boiled potato and a piece of butterless bread.

With 5,000 people to be fed, there were few unoccupied tables, so we separated from our friends and shared a table with an elderly man and a young family with two crying babies. No one at the table spoke to us, and even Mama could seem to find no friendly word to offer as she normally would have done. We tried to eat, but the food wouldn't go down.

"Let's get out of here," my sister suggested.

We decided it would be better to go back to our barrack than to linger in the depressing confusion of the mess hall. It had grown dark by now and since Tanforan had no lights for nighttime occupancy, we had to pick our way carefully down the slippery track.

Once back in our stall, we found it no less depressing, for there was only a single electric light bulb dangling from the ceiling, and a one-inch crevice at the top of the north wall admitted a steady draft of the cold night air. We sat huddled on our cots, bundled in our coats, too cold and miserable even to talk. My sister and I worried about Mama, for she wasn't strong and had recently been troubled with neuralgia,[4] which could easily be aggravated by the cold. She in turn was worrying about us, and of course we all worried and wondered about Papa.

Suddenly we heard the sound of a truck stopping outside.

"Hey, Uchida! Apartment 40!" a boy shouted.

I rushed to the door and found the baggage boys trying to heave our enormous "camp bundle" over the railing that fronted our stall.

"What ya got in here anyway?" they shouted good-naturedly as (11) they struggled with the **unwieldy** bundle. "It's the biggest thing we got on our truck!"

I grinned, embarrassed, but I could hardly wait to get out our belongings. My sister and I fumbled to undo all the

4. **neuralgia** (nōō ral′ jə) *n.* severe pain along the path of a nerve.

Literary Analysis
Author's Purpose
How might these details affect the reader's opinion of the government relocation program?

Vocabulary
unwieldy (un wēl′ dē) *adj.* hard to manage because of shape or weight

Reading Check
Identify three details showing that the family's first day in the camp is miserable.

(10) Literary Analysis
Author's Purpose

1. Point out that the events described in this essay occurred more than fifty years ago. Explain that people often re-evaluate events of the past after time has passed. **Ask:** Why might one's opinion of an event or situation change over time?
   Possible responses: Perhaps laws have been passed or rewritten; attitudes may have changed; new information or discoveries may create a new way of evaluating the event or situation.
2. Remind students that details provide hints as to the author's purpose in an essay.
3. Recall that one purpose of an essay is to persuade readers to see the author's point of view about an event or situation.
4. **Ask** the Literary Analysis question: How might these details affect the reader's opinion of the government relocation program?
   Answer: These details describe circumstances so horrible and humiliating that the reader is likely to understand the program to be inhumane and unjust.

(11) Reading Check

Possible response: The servings of food are small; the ground is muddy; the stall is cold, smelly, and drafty.

Differentiated Instruction for Universal Access

Strategy for Less Proficient Readers
Students may have difficulty understanding the behavior of the people in the camp. Lead students in a discussion about why the elderly man, the young family, and Uchida's family do not speak to each other during the meal. Help students understand that the usual small talk in which one might engage with strangers is out of place in this situation. Students may also consider that the purpose of relocation camps is to strip people of their humanity.

⓬ Literary Analysis
Author's Purpose

1. Read the bracketed passage.
2. Have a volunteer explain why the mood of the family changes when their belongings arrive.
   Answer: Their belongings will make their lives somewhat more comfortable. Also, the personal belongings may restore some sense of home and humanity.
3. **Ask** the first Literary Analysis question: What do these details show readers about the family?
   Answer: The family is close, orderly, and enjoys spending time together.
4. **Ask** what the importance of the hot plate shows readers about the family.
   Answer: The hot plate comes to symbolize the importance of being together.

⓭ Connecting to the Big Question

1. Point out to students that the Uchidas gained knowledge about how to survive in the camp as they lived through it.
2. Read the bracketed passage aloud. **Ask:** Why were the prunes such a welcomed gift?
   Possible response: Outside of the camp, food was plentiful and the Uchidas could choose what to eat, but in the relocation camp there was very little food, so even prunes were special.
3. **Ask:** Now that the Uchidas know that food is scarce, what changes might they make while in the camp?
   Possible response: Students may state that they could eat as much as possible at meals; they could try to send messages to friends outside the camp to send nonperishable food.

⓮ Literary Analysis
Author's Purpose

1. Explain that authors sometimes employ humor to make a point or to lighten the tone of the essay.
2. **Ask** the second Literary Analysis question.
   Answer: Amusing details include the parents shouting and banging on the door without success; calling the son stupid; and the author poking at the boy with a broom.

---

knots we had tied into the rope around our bundle that morning and eagerly pulled out the familiar objects from home.

Literary Analysis
Author's Purpose
What do these details show readers about the family? ⓬

We unpacked our blankets, pillows, sheets, tea kettle, and, most welcome of all, our electric hot plate. I ran to the nearest washroom to fill the kettle with water, while Mama and Kay made up the Army cots with our bedding. Once we hooked up the hot plate and put the kettle on to boil, we felt better. We sat close to its warmth, holding our hands toward it as though it were our fireplace at home.

Before long some friends came by to see us, bringing with them the only gift they had—a box of dried prunes. Even the day before, we wouldn't have given the prunes a second glance, but now they were as welcome as the boxes of Maskey's chocolate my father used to bring home from San Francisco. ⓭

Mama managed to make some tea for our friends, and we sat around our steaming kettle, munching gratefully on our prunes. We spent much of the evening talking about food and the lack of it, a concern that grew obsessive over the next few weeks, when we were constantly hungry.

Our stable consisted of twenty-five stalls facing north which were back to back with an equal number facing south, so we were surrounded on three sides. Living in our stable were an assortment of people—mostly small family units—that included an artist, my father's barber and his wife, a dentist and his wife, an elderly retired couple, a group of Kibei[5] bachelors (Japanese born in the United States but educated in Japan), an insurance salesman and his wife, and a widow with two daughters. To say that we all became intimately acquainted would be an understatement. It was, in fact, communal living, with semi-private cubicles provided only for sleeping.

Our neighbors on one side spent much of their time playing cards, and at all hours of the day we could hear the sound of cards being shuffled and money changing hands. Our other neighbors had a teenage son who spent most of the day with his friends, coming home to his stall at night only after his parents were asleep. Family life began to show signs of strain almost immediately, not only in the next stall but throughout the entire camp.

Literary Analysis
Author's Purpose
Which details suggest that the author relates this incident to amuse readers? ⓮

One Sunday our neighbor's son fell asleep in the rear of his stall with the door bolted from inside. When his parents came home from church, no amount of shouting or banging on the door could awaken the boy.

"Our stupid son has locked us out," they explained, coming to us for help.

I climbed up on my cot and considered pouring water on him over the partition, for I knew he slept just on the other side of it. Instead

5. **Kibei** (kē′ bā′)

Vocabulary Development

Word Forms

Expand students' vocabulary by helping them learn related forms of the selection vocabulary words. Two of the selection vocabulary words for the excerpt from "Desert Exile" have related forms. Give students a blank **Word Form Chart** (*Professional Development Guidebook*, p. 42), with *adept* and *tenuous* in the adjective column. Work with the class, or have students work with partners, to determine the related forms. The final chart should look like the one shown. Hold students accountable for integrating the related forms of the words into their speaking and writing.

Adjective	Noun	Adverb
adept	adeptness	adeptly
tenuous	tenuousness	tenuously

14 I dangled a broom over the partition and poked and prodded with it, shouting, "Wake up! Wake up!" until the boy finally bestirred himself and let his parents in. We became good friends with our neighbors after that.

About one hundred feet from our stable were two latrines and two washrooms for our section of camp, one each for men and women. The latrines were crude wooden structures containing eight toilets, separated by partitions, but having no doors. The washrooms were divided into two sections. In the front section was a long tin trough spaced with spigots of hot and cold water where we washed our faces and brushed our teeth. To the rear were eight showers, also separated by partitions but lacking doors or curtains. The showers were difficult to adjust and we either got scalded by torrents of hot water or shocked by an icy blast of cold. Most of the Issei[6] were unaccustomed to showers, having known the luxury of soaking in deep pine-scented tubs during their years in Japan, and found the showers virtually impossible to use.

Once we hooked up the hot plate and put the kettle on to boil, we felt better.

Our card-playing neighbor scoured the camp for a container that might serve as a tub, and eventually found a large wooden barrel. She rolled it to the showers, filled it with warm water, and then climbed in for a pleasant and leisurely soak. The greatest compliment she could offer anyone was the use of her private tub.

15 The lack of privacy in the latrines and showers was an embarrassing hardship especially for the older women, and many would take newspapers to hold over their faces or squares of cloth to tack up for their own private curtain. The Army, obviously ill-equipped to build living quarters for women and children, had made no attempt to introduce even the most common of life's civilities into these camps for us.

During the first few weeks of camp life everything was erratic and in short supply. Hot water appeared only sporadically, and the minute it was available, everyone ran for the showers or the laundry. We had to be clever and quick just to keep clean, and my

16 **Reading Check**

Name two major problems Uchida and other residents of the camp face.

6. **Issei** (ē´ sā´) *n.* Japanese immigrants to North America, especially those who came after 1907 and were ineligible until 1952 to become U.S. citizens.

15 Literary Analysis

Author's Purpose

1. Clarify that an author's purpose is not always apparent at the beginning of an essay.
2. **Ask** students to suggest Uchida's purpose for writing an essay about her family's experience in the relocation camp.
   Answer: Uchida wants to demonstrate the injustice and absurdity of discrimination.
3. Read the bracketed passage.
4. **Ask** students to explain how the lack of privacy in the latrines and showers supports Uchida's purpose.
   Answer: The author points out that the Army did nothing to provide privacy, which demonstrates that the government did not respect the rights or customs of the people in the camps.

16 Reading Check

Answer: Staying clean and having enough food are two major problems in the camp.

Differentiated Instruction for Universal Access

Enrichment for Advanced Readers

Have students form small groups to discuss the following question: To what degree are people who live through historical events obligated to record them? Have students conduct library searches for other memoirs and compile lists of personal accounts of other historical events. Ask a volunteer from each group to give an account of the research and to highlight several memoirs that appear to be worth reading. Compile the lists into a single list and distribute it to advanced readers. Tell students to select one title from the list to read. Help students establish a schedule for memoir discussion groups.

17 Critical Thinking

Speculate

1. Remind students that challenging circumstances can cause people to act in ways they normally would not.
2. Have a volunteer read the bracketed passage. Then, **ask** students what Uchida means by "baser instincts."
   Possible response: Uchida is referring to a person's innate survival instincts.
3. **Ask:** Do you think that the internees will continue to act this way? Explain.
   Possible response: No, the last line of the paragraph makes it sound as if the internees change. The internees will realize that it is better to work together than to horde supplies.

18 Critical Viewing

Answer: People in both camps had to stand in long lines waiting for food and other necessities; the faces in the photo seem to have the same sadness Uchida describes; the weather in the photo does not show the weather to be as piercingly cold as Uchida described at Tanforan.

---

sister and I often walked a mile to the other end of the camp where hot water was in better supply, in order to boost our morale with a hot shower.

17 Even toilet paper was at a premium, for new rolls would disappear as soon as they were placed in the latrines. The shock of the evacuation compounded by the short supply of every necessity brought out the baser instincts of the internees,[7] and there was little inclination for anyone to feel responsible for anyone else. In the early days, at least, it was everyone for himself or herself.

One morning I saw some women emptying bed pans into the troughs where we washed our faces. The sight was enough to turn my stomach, and my mother quickly made several large signs in Japanese cautioning people against such unsanitary practices. We posted them in conspicuous spots in the washroom and hoped for the best.

Across from the latrines was a double barrack, one containing laundry tubs and the other equipped with clotheslines and ironing boards. Because there were so many families with young children, the laundry tubs were in constant use. The hot water was often gone by 9:00 a.m., and many women got up at 3:00 and 4:00 in the morning to do their wash, all of which, including sheets, had to be done entirely by hand.

We found it difficult to get to the laundry by 9:00 a.m., and by then every tub was taken and there were long lines of people with bags of dirty laundry waiting behind each one. When we finally got to a tub, there was no more hot water. Then we would leave my mother to hold the tub while my sister and I rushed to

7. **internees** (in´ turn´ ēz´) *n.* people detained or confined as prisoners of war or enemy aliens.

18 ▼ **Critical Viewing**
This photograph shows the Manzanar Relocation Center. Compare this camp with Tanforan. **[Compare and Contrast]**

Vocabulary Development

Selection Vocabulary Reinforcement

Students will benefit from additional examples and practice with the selection vocabulary. Reinforce their comprehension with "show-you-know" sentences. The first part of the sentence uses the vocabulary word in an appropriate context. The second part of the sentence—the "show-you-know" part—clarifies the first. Model the strategy with this example for *adept*:

> The landscape painting displayed the artist's *adept* skills; every detail was exactly as it should be.

Then, give students these sentence prompts, and coach them in creating the clarification process.

1. He had a *tenuous* excuse for being late; ______.
   Sample answer: he knew his parents would be upset with him.
2. His father found the new television set *unwieldy;* ______.
   Sample answer: he had to get his brother to help him carry it up the stairs.

the washroom where there was a better supply and carried back bucketfuls of hot water as everyone else learned to do. By the time we had finally hung our laundry on lines outside our stall, we were too exhausted to do much else for the rest of the day.

19 For four days after our arrival we continued to go to the main mess hall for all our meals. My sister and I usually missed breakfast because we were assigned to the early shift and we simply couldn't get there by 7:00 a.m. Dinner was at 4:45 p.m., which was a terrible hour, but not a major problem, as we were always hungry. Meals were uniformly bad and skimpy, with an abundance of starches such as beans and bread. I wrote to my non-Japanese friends in Berkeley shamelessly asking them to send us food, and they obliged with large cartons of cookies, nuts, dried fruit, and jams.

We looked forward with much anticipation to the opening of a half dozen smaller mess halls located throughout the camp. But when ours finally opened, we discovered that the preparation of smaller quantities had absolutely no effect on the quality of the food. We went eagerly to our new mess hall only to be confronted at our first meal with chili con carne, corn, and butterless bread. To assuage our disappointment, a friend and I went to the main mess hall which was still in operation, to see if it had anything better. Much to our amazement and delight, we found small lettuce salads, the first fresh vegetables we had seen in many days. We ate ravenously and exercised enormous self-control not to go back for second and third helpings.

The food improved gradually, and by the time we left Tanforan five months later, we had fried chicken and ice cream for Sunday dinner. By July tubs of soapy water were installed at the mess hall exits so we could wash our plates and utensils on the way out. Being slow eaters, however, we usually found the dishwater tepid and dirty by the time we reached the tubs, and we often rewashed our dishes in the washroom.

Most internees got into the habit of rushing for everything. They ran to the mess halls to be first in line, they dashed inside for the best tables and then rushed through their meals to get to the washtubs before the suds ran out. The three of us, however, seemed to be at the end of every line that formed and somehow never managed to be first for anything.

Literary Analysis
Author's Purpose
Which details here reveal something about Uchida's personality?

20 **Reading Check**
Name two necessities that were in short supply at the camp.

19 Literary Analysis
Author's Purpose

1. Remind students that the author is writing this essay based on memories.
2. **Ask:** Why does Uchida remember so much about the experience in the relocation camp?
   Answer: The experience is dramatic, unique, and significant in her life.
3. **Ask** the Literary Analysis question: Which details here reveal something about Uchida's personality?
   Possible responses: Uchida works hard for the family; she is able to write; and she is well-liked by friends in Berkeley because they are willing to help her.

20 Reading Check

Answer: Fresh foods and hot water for washing were in short supply.

Differentiated Instruction for Universal Access

Strategy for Special Needs Students
Students who have difficulty following the sequence of events may benefit from pausing two or three times on a page to discuss what is happening in the story. Have volunteers read a paragraph aloud, and then ask students to summarize what they have just read or heard.

Enrichment for Gifted/Talented Students
Remind students that people in the camp community help the Uchidas by making furniture and putting up shelves. Explain that in many camps, inmates organized schools, and worked on committees and in social clubs, in order to create a network of support and camaraderie. Have students do independent research on Japanese American relocation camps and gather details about some of the creative efforts people took part in. Using details from their research, have students present a visual report about camp organization.

㉑ Literary Analysis
Author's Purpose

1. **Ask** students to recall the reactions of most internees on the first day they arrive at the camp.
Answer: They are frightened.
2. Have students read the bracketed passage.
3. **Ask** the Literary Analysis question.
Answer: They have adapted to the harsh living conditions.

Concept Connector

Have students compare the Writing About the Big Question responses and their responses to the class discussion they had before reading the story to their ideas after reading.

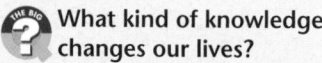

ASSESS

Answers

Critical Thinking

1. **Possible response:** Students may choose limited, small meals that cause hunger.
2. (a) The stall is small, dark, cold, dirty, smells of horses, and has a door and three cots. (b) The word *apartment* indicates a home for people, not horses.
3. Some people become selfish, while others act generously.
4. The government does not view Japanese Americans as citizens.

What kind of knowledge changes our lives?

(a) **Possible response:** Uchida learns to adapt to challenging situations. She walks more than one mile to take hot showers.
(b) **Possible response:** Readers will gain an understanding of the crude conditions and discrimination endured by Japanese Americans.

PHLit Online!

This selection is available in interactive format in the **Enriched Online Student Edition**, online at **www.PHLitOnline.com**, which includes an interactive graphic organizer.

Literary Analysis
Author's Purpose
What do the details in these two paragraphs show about how the camp experience has changed the prisoners?

One of the first things we all did at Tanforan was to make our living quarters as comfortable as possible. A pile of scrap lumber in one corner of camp melted away like snow on a hot day as residents salvaged whatever they could to make shelves and crude pieces of furniture to supplement the Army cots. They also made ingenious containers for carrying their dishes to the mess halls, with handles and lids that grew more and more elaborate in a sort of unspoken competition.

㉑ Because of my father's absence, our friends helped us in camp, just as they had in Berkeley, and we relied on them to put up shelves and build a crude table and two benches for us. We put our new camp furniture in the front half of our stall, which was our "living room," and put our three cots in the dark windowless rear section, which we promptly dubbed "the dungeon." We ordered some print fabric by mail and sewed curtains by hand to hang at our windows and to cover our shelves. Each new addition to our stall made it seem a little more like home.

One afternoon about a week after we had arrived at Tanforan, a messenger from the administration building appeared with a telegram for us. It was from my father, telling us he had been released on parole from Montana and would be able to join us soon in camp. Papa was coming home. The wonderful news had come like an unexpected gift, but even as we hugged each other in joy, we didn't quite dare believe it until we actually saw him. . . .

Critical Thinking

1. **Respond:** Which part of life in the camps would you have disliked the most? Why?
2. **(a)** Describe stall number 40. **(b) Analyze:** Why does Uchida feel that calling it an "apartment" was "ludicrous"?
3. **Analyze Cause and Effect:** How do the shortages at the camp affect people's attitudes and behavior? Support your answer.
4. **Draw Conclusions:** What do the conditions at the camp suggest about the government's attitude toward Japanese Americans?

What kind of knowledge changes our lives?
(a) In what ways did Uchida's experiences at the relocation camp change her? Support your answer with details from the selection. **(b)** What impact do you think Uchida hopes her narrative will have on readers? Explain.

from

The Way to Rainy Mountain

N. Scott Momaday

Background Like other Great Plains tribes, the Kiowa were buffalo hunters. When white settlers came to the Plains, the Kiowa fought them. By the late 1800s, however, United States troops had broken Kiowa resistance and white hunters had all but exterminated the buffalo. Traditional Kiowa life came to an end. In 1868, the Kiowas went to live on a reservation in southwestern Oklahoma.

A single knoll rises out of the plain in Oklahoma, north and west of the Wichita Range.[1] For my people, the Kiowas, it is an old landmark, and they gave it the name Rainy Mountain. The hardest weather in the world is there. Winter brings blizzards, hot tornadic winds arise in the spring, and in summer the prairie

1. **Wichita** (wich´ ə tô´) **Range** mountain range in southwestern Oklahoma.

Differentiated Instruction for Universal Access

Accessibility at a Glance
Use this information to guide your teaching of the excerpt from "The Way to Rainy Mountain."

Context	Essay on a Native American heritage
Language/Vocabulary	• Complicated sentence structure • Grade-appropriate vocabulary
Concept Level	Accessible (family relationships)
Literary Merit	Noted author
Lexile/Length	Lexile: 1020L Word Count: 2,664

22 Background

The Kiowa In the nineteenth century, the Kiowa adhered to a kinship system where relatives were grouped by generation and gender. Family groups, called kindreds, formed the basis of Kiowa society. Led by the oldest of a group of brothers, a kindred differentiated itself from other kindreds through a class system that was defined by wealth. By mid-century, ten to twenty kindreds dominated the Kiowa population, which numbered only about one thousand members. These kindreds ranged between Kansas and the Texas Panhandle.

23 Activating Prior Knowledge

Lead students in a discussion about the importance of preserving the memories of family and community. Invite students to contrast what they know about Native American family and tribal relationships with their own experiences of family.

Concept Connector

Students will return to the above discussion after they have completed reading.

24 About the Selection

The excerpt from "The Way to Rainy Mountain" focuses on the importance of memory in understanding the lessons of the past. In this essay, N. Scott Momaday interweaves his love for tradition, nature, and community to communicate the spiritual essence of the Kiowa of the Great Plains. Momaday returns to his homeland to mourn the death of his grandmother, his last link to the free-roaming Kiowa of the nineteenth century. Through his memories, Momaday concludes that the spirit of his grandmother and the Kiowa will never die as long as the glory of the land, symbolized by Rainy Mountain, remains.

25 Critical Viewing

Answer: Students may respond that the person's eyes reflect both pride and sadness, indicating that he may have been forced to give up something he cherished.

26 Critical Thinking

Infer

1. Remind students that the tone an author uses can help indicate his or her attitude toward a subject.
2. Have a volunteer read the bracketed passage.
3. **Ask:** What tone is reflected in the author's choice of such phrases as "the prairie is an anvil's edge" and "loneliness is an aspect of the land"?
   Possible response: Momaday's tone is serious as he confides in the reader his feelings about the land.
4. Then, **ask** students why they think Momaday chose to begin the story this way.
   Possible response: By beginning the story in such a way, Momaday lets the reader know that his people endured a long, hard journey.

▶ Chief Sa-tan-ta of the Kiowas

25 ▲ **Critical Viewing** Judging from Momaday's account, what hardships might this Kiowa person have experienced? **[Speculate]**

is an anvil's edge. The grass turns brittle and brown, and it cracks beneath your feet. There are green belts along the rivers and creeks, linear groves of hickory and pecan, willow and witch hazel. At a distance in July or August the steaming foliage seems almost to writhe in fire. Great green and yellow grasshoppers are everywhere in the tall grass, popping up like corn to sting the flesh,
26 and tortoises crawl about on the red earth, going nowhere in the plenty of time. Loneliness is an aspect of the land. All things in the plain are isolate; there is no confusion of objects in the eye, but one hill or one tree or one man. To look upon that landscape in the early morning, with the sun at your back, is to lose the sense of proportion. Your imagination comes to life, and this, you think, is where Creation was begun.

I returned to Rainy Mountain in July. My grandmother had died in the spring, and I wanted to be at her grave. She had lived to be very old and at last infirm. Her only living daughter was with her when she died, and I was told that in death her face was that of a child.

I like to think of her as a child. When she was born, the Kiowas
27 were living the last great moment of their history. For more than a hundred years they had controlled the open range from the

Vocabulary Development

Thematic Vocabulary: The Big Question

As students are discussing the excerpt from "The Way to Rainy Mountain," ask them to use the thematic vocabulary presented in Introducing the Big Question, pp. 442–443. You might encourage them with sentence starters like these:

1. The *history* of the Kiowa provides the reader with . . .
2. The author wants to *reflect* on his grandmother's memory as a way of . . .
3. From his pilgrimage, Momaday hopes to gain an *understanding* of . . .
4. Preserving the story of a group of people will *enlighten* . . .

PHLit Online!

This selection is available in interactive format in the **Enriched Online Student Edition**, online at **www.PHLitOnline.com**, which includes an interactive graphic organizer.

Smoky Hill River to the Red, from the headwaters of the Canadian to the fork of the Arkansas and Cimarron.[2] In alliance with the Comanches,[3] they had ruled the whole of the southern Plains. War was their sacred business, and they were among the finest horsemen the world has ever known. But warfare for the Kiowas was preeminently a matter of disposition rather than of survival, and they never understood the grim, unrelenting advance of the U.S. Cavalry. When at last, divided and ill-provisioned, they were
27 driven onto the Staked Plains in the cold rains of autumn, they fell into panic. In Palo Duro Canyon they abandoned their crucial stores to pillage and had nothing then but their lives. In order to save themselves, they surrendered to the soldiers at Fort Sill[4] and were imprisoned in the old stone corral that now stands as a military museum. My grandmother was spared the humiliation of those high gray walls by eight or ten years, but she must have known from birth the affliction of defeat, the dark brooding of old warriors.

Her name was Aho, and she belonged to the last culture to evolve in North America. Her forebears came down from the high country in western Montana nearly three centuries ago. They were a mountain people, a mysterious tribe of hunters whose language has never been positively classified in any major group. In the late seventeenth century they began a long migration to the south and east.

It was a journey toward the dawn, and it led to a golden age. Along the way the Kiowas were befriended by the Crows,[5] who
28 gave them the culture and religion of the Plains. They acquired horses, and their ancient **nomadic** spirit was suddenly free of the ground. They acquired Tai-me, the sacred Sun Dance doll, from that moment the object and symbol of their worship, and so shared in the divinity of the sun. Not least, they acquired the sense of destiny, therefore courage and pride. When they entered upon the southern Plains they had been transformed. No longer were they slaves to the simple necessity of survival; they were a lordly and dangerous society of fighters and thieves, hunters and priests of the sun. According to their origin myth, they entered the world through a hollow log. From one point of view, their migration was the fruit of an old prophecy, for indeed they emerged from a sunless world.

2. **Smoky Hill River . . . Cimarron** (sim´ ə rän´) these rivers all run through or near Oklahoma. The area Momaday is defining stretches from central Kansas south through Oklahoma and from the Texas panhandle east to Tulsa, Oklahoma.
3. **Comanches** (kə man´ chēz) *n.* formerly warlike Native American people of the southern Great Plains, famed for their horsemanship.
4. **Fort Sill** fort established by the United States government in 1869 to guard against Kiowa and Comanche attacks.
5. **Crows** members of a Native American tribe of the northern Plains; like other Plains tribes, they hunted buffalo.

Literary Analysis
Author's Purpose
In this paragraph focusing on history, which details reveal something about Momaday?

Vocabulary
nomadic (nō mad´ ik) *adj.* moving from place to place; without a permanent home

29 **Reading Check**
Who gave the Kiowa the culture and religion of the Plains?

27 Literary Analysis
Author's Purpose

1. Review the purposes for essay writing: to inform, to entertain, to persuade, or to pay tribute to or commemorate.
2. Remind students that an author may have more than a single purpose for writing an essay; but, in most essays, the author has a main purpose and that purpose is eventually revealed by the details the author chooses to include.
3. Read the bracketed passage aloud.
4. **Ask** the Literary Analysis question: In this paragraph focusing on history, which details reveal something about Momaday?
Answer: The numerous details regarding the influence, horsemanship, and nobility of the Kiowa indicate how much Momaday respects his people. His description of the fall of the Kiowa, including details about their surrender and his grandmother's feelings, reveal his sadness for his people's fate.

28 Critical Thinking
Analyze

1. Read the bracketed passage aloud.
2. Write the following phrases on the board: "toward the dawn," "a golden age," and "free of the ground."
3. **Ask** students to put the expressions in their own words: toward the dawn—eastward; a golden age—a time of great power; free of the ground—on horseback.
4. **Ask** students why the author chooses to use the words that he does instead of plainer language.
Answer: The author's descriptive language is more poetic. By evoking the language of poetry, Momaday elevates the Kiowa to an epic level.

29 Reading Check

Answer: The Crows gave the Kiowa the culture and religion of the Plains.

Differentiated Instruction for Universal Access

Strategy for Special Needs Students
Students may have difficulty following the narrative in this essay. Explain that the author has a reason for writing this essay. Have them listen to each paragraph on ***Hear It!* Audio CD** while they read along. Have them pause after each paragraph so they can write the details they hear or read in their graphic organizers. For reinforcement, show them the partially completed **Comparing Literary Works Graphic Organizer A** (*Graphic Organizer Transparencies,* p. 106).

Enrichment for Advanced Readers
Explain to students that Momaday is well known for his Native American poetry. Have students conduct a poetry reading of Momaday's poetry. Tell students to begin by conducting research in the library or on the Internet to locate one or more of Momaday's poems. Have each student select a poem that exemplifies Momaday's interest, respect, and concern for the fate of his Native American heritage. Allow class time for students to read their chosen poems aloud.

30 Literary Analysis
Author's Purpose

1. Discuss with students the reasons that people may be interested in researching their family's heritage or history: to record it so that others can learn about it; to keep it from getting lost; to learn about their ancestors and, in the process, about themselves.
2. **Ask:** What does this paragraph suggest about Momaday's purpose in writing about the Kiowa?
   Answer: The author wants to inform himself and his readers about the history and homelands of the Kiowa.

31 Critical Viewing

Possible response: The arduous journey from Wyoming to Oklahoma takes the Kiowa through four states comprised of undeveloped terrain and unknown inhabitants. Although such challenges test their resolve, the Kiowas emerge as a fierce, self-reliant group with a strong belief in the sun and the natural gifts of the Great Plains.

32 THE BIG ? Connecting to the Big Question

1. Explain to students that knowledge is an understanding of a subject that is gained through education and experience.
2. Read the bracketed passage to the class. Then, **ask** a volunteer to describe what the Kiowas see.
   Possible response: The Kiowas see a large, open expanse filled with lush, colorful vegetation. Animals graze beneath billowing clouds as sunshine spreads across the plain.
3. **Ask** students how the Kiowas know that this is where they should change their lives.
   Possible response: They feel free in the open expanse of the Plains and they feel the sun is at home here, so this is where their place in the world should be.

Literary Analysis
Author's Purpose 30
What does this paragraph suggest about Momaday's purpose in writing about the Kiowa?

Although my grandmother lived out her long life in the shadow of Rainy Mountain, the immense landscape of the continental interior lay like memory in her blood. She could tell of the Crows, whom she had never seen, and of the Black Hills,[6] where she had never been. I wanted to see in reality what she had seen more perfectly in the mind's eye, and traveled fifteen hundred miles to begin my pilgrimage.

Yellowstone,[7] it seemed to me, was the top of the world, a region of deep lakes and dark timber, canyons and waterfalls. But, beautiful as it is, one might have the sense of confinement there. The skyline in all directions is close at hand, the high wall of the woods and deep cleavages of shade. There is a perfect freedom in the mountains, but it belongs to the eagle and the elk, the badger and the bear. The Kiowas reckoned their stature by the distance they could see, and they were bent and blind in the wilderness.

Descending eastward, the highland meadows are a stairway to the plain. In July the inland slope of the Rockies is luxuriant with flax and buckwheat, stonecrop and larkspur.[8] The earth unfolds and the limit of the land recedes. Clusters of trees, and animals grazing far in the distance, cause the vision to reach away and wonder to build upon the mind. The sun follows a longer course in the day, and the sky is immense beyond all comparison. The great billowing clouds that sail upon it are shadows that move upon the brain like water, dividing light. Farther down, in the land of the Crows and Blackfeet,[9] the plain is yellow. Sweet clover takes hold of the hills and bends upon itself to cover and seal the soil. There the Kiowas paused on their way; they had come to the place where they must change their lives. The sun is at home on the plains. Precisely there does it have the certain character of a god. When the Kiowas came to the land of the Crows, they could see the dark lees of the hills at dawn across the Bighorn River, the profusion of light on the grain shelves, the oldest deity ranging after the solstices. Not yet would they veer southward to the caldron[10] of the land that lay below; they must wean their blood from the northern winter and hold the mountains a while longer in their view. They bore Tai-me in procession to the east. 32

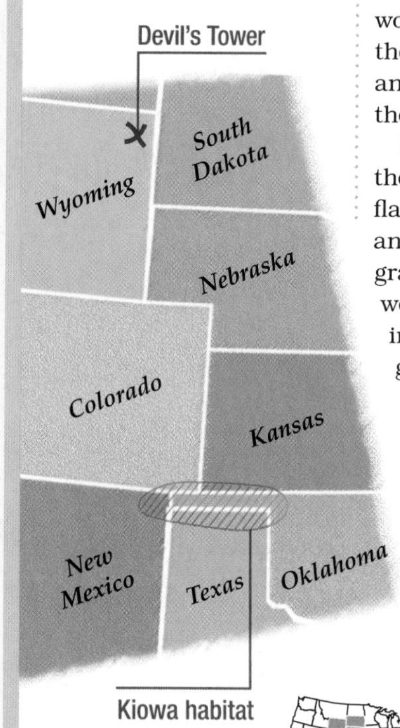

31 ▲ **Critical Viewing**
Based on this map and the details in the text, why might the Kiowa journey from Wyoming to Oklahoma have been challenging and rewarding at the same time? **[Connect]**

6. **Black Hills** mountain range running from southwestern South Dakota to northeastern Wyoming.
7. **Yellowstone** Yellowstone National Park, lying mostly in Wyoming but including strips in southern Montana and eastern Idaho.
8. **flax and buckwheat, stonecrop and larkspur** various types of plants.
9. **Blackfeet** Native American tribe of the region that includes present-day Montana and parts of Canada.
10. **caldron** (kôl′ drən) *n.* pot for boiling liquids; large kettle.

Vocabulary Development

Vocabulary Selection Reinforcement

To reinforce and assess students' comprehension of selection vocabulary words, give them sentences using the words in which the word may or may not be used correctly. Students must tell whether the use is correct and explain their answers.

1. The *infirm* band of warriors could ride for miles without feeling any pain.
   Answer: No, *infirm* means weak or feeble, and the men had to be strong to ride that far.
2. The *nomadic* people never moved from their original homeland.
   Answer: No, the people stayed in one place, and *nomadic* people migrate.
3. The mountain climber found a small, *tenuous* hold in a tiny crack but didn't stay there long.
   Answer: Yes, a *tenuous* hold would not be strong or substantial, and a climber might lose the hold by staying there too long.

A dark mist lay over the Black Hills, and the land was like iron. At the top of a ridge I caught sight of Devil's Tower upthrust against the gray sky as if in the birth of time the core of the earth had broken through its crust and the motion of the world was begun. There are things in nature that engender an awful quiet in the heart of man; Devil's Tower is one of them. Two centuries ago, because they could not do otherwise, the Kiowas made a legend at the base of the rock. My grandmother said:

Eight children were there at play, seven sisters and their brother. Suddenly the boy was struck dumb; he trembled and began to run upon his hands and feet. His fingers became claws, and his body was covered with fur. Directly there was a bear where the boy had been. The sisters were terrified; they ran, and the bear after them. They came to the stump of a great tree, and the tree spoke to them. It bade them climb upon it, and as they did so it began to rise in the air. The bear came to kill them, but they were just beyond its reach. It reared against the tree and scored the bark all around with its claws. The seven sisters were borne into the sky, and they became the stars of the Big Dipper.

From that moment, and so long as the legend lives, the Kiowas have kinsmen in the night sky. Whatever they were in the mountains, they could be no more. However tenuous their well-being, however much they had suffered and would suffer again, they had found a way out of the wilderness.

34 ▲ **Critical Viewing** Judging from this photograph of Devil's Tower, why might the landmark inspire Kiowa legends? **[Connect]**

Vocabulary
tenuous (ten′ yo͞o əs) *adj.* flimsy; not strong

35 **Reading Check**
What change did the Kiowa's beliefs undergo after they left the mountains?

33 Background
Devil's Tower

Devil's Tower is a National Monument that features a 1,267 foot tower of rock. Probably the remnant of an ancient volcano, the tower has fluted, striated sides and a flat top. It is considered a sacred place to more than twenty Native American Plains tribes. In addition to the Sun Dance ceremony, Devil's Tower is the site of prayer offerings, sweatlodge ceremonies, and vision quests.

The tower is also a major rock climbing destination, drawing expert climbers from all over the nation. This tourism has clashed with Native American groups who wish to set the tower off limits to climbers during their sacred month of June. Although the courts have not supported their claim, the National Parks Service has asked climbers to voluntarily abstain from climbing during the month of June to show respect for the native sacred traditions.

34 Critical Viewing

Possible response: Students may say the tower is unusual in shape; it appears to rise from the ground and has unusual scratch-like markings.

35 Reading Check

Answer: The Kiowa recognized the power of the sun and the majesty of the Great Plains.

Differentiated Instruction for Universal Access

Culturally Responsive Instruction

Culture Focus Review the legend the Kiowa people created about Devil's Tower. Legends were a way for Native American people to keep their culture alive. These legends tell of their beliefs, their traditions, and their lives. There are many different Native American tribes, and they all have different traditions and cultures. One common belief among the tribes is that they believe all things are bound together by spirits of natural life and, therefore, many of their legends are about animals, plants, the sky, land formations, and the Earth.

Many cultures around the world have legends that explain the mysteries of the Earth. Like the Native Americans, the land was very important to the aboriginal, or native, people of Australia. The sandstone rock known as Uluru was the focus of many legends about the beginning of time.

Invite students to share their knowledge and experience of similar stories from their home culture or their family's country of origin.

36 Literary Analysis
Author's Purpose

1. **Ask:** Why is the Sun Dance an integral part of Kiowa tradition? **Answer:** The Kiowa lived on the Great Plains where the sun has a dominating presence.
2. Have students read the bracketed passage, paying close attention to mention of the Sun Dance.
3. Have a volunteer summarize the scene at the last Sun Dance. Discuss how the Kiowa probably feel when the soldiers arrive to disperse the tribe.
4. **Ask** the Literary Analysis question: In this section, how does Momaday link his grandmother's life to the history of the Kiowa? **Answer:** His grandmother's life spans the period of final power and ultimate decline of the Kiowa people. By connecting her experiences with the revered Sun Dance, Momaday traces the last years of this tribe's freedom through his grandmother's memories and her conclusion that the gods die during the last Sun Dance.

37 Critical Viewing

Possible response: Students may expect to see individuals wearing colorful outfits made from natural materials such as animal hides and feathers; the angle of the dancer's head may indicate that the people bow their heads to honor the sun.

Literary Analysis
Author's Purpose
In this section, how does Momaday link his grandmother's life to the history of the Kiowa? 36

37 ▼ **Critical Viewing**
Based on the attire of this Kiowa dancer, what would you expect to see at a Kiowa Sun Dance? **[Infer]**

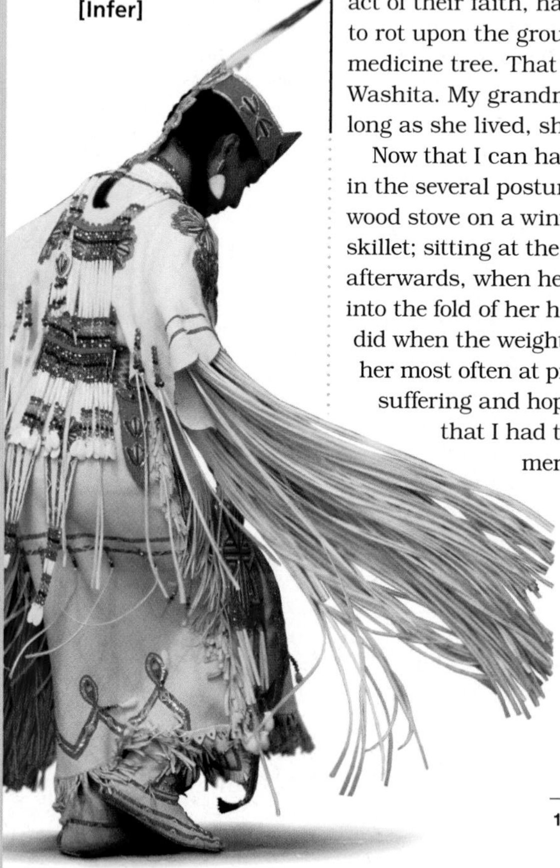

My grandmother had a reverence for the sun, a holy regard that now is all but gone out of mankind. There was a wariness in her, and an ancient awe. She was a Christian in her later years, but she had come a long way about, and she never forgot her birthright. As a child she had been to the Sun Dances; she had taken part in those annual rites, and by them she had learned the restoration of her people in the presence of Tai-me. She was about seven when the last Kiowa Sun Dance was held in 1887 on the Washita River above Rainy Mountain Creek. The buffalo were gone. In order to consummate the ancient sacrifice—to impale the head of a buffalo bull upon the medicine tree—a delegation of old men journeyed into Texas, there to beg and barter for an animal from the Goodnight herd. She was ten when the Kiowas came together for the last time as a living Sun Dance culture. They could find no buffalo; they had to hang an old hide from the sacred tree. Before the dance could begin, a company of soldiers rode out from Fort Sill under orders to disperse the tribe. Forbidden without cause the essential act of their faith, having seen the wild herds slaughtered and left to rot upon the ground, the Kiowas backed away forever from the medicine tree. That was July 20, 1890, at the great bend of the Washita. My grandmother was there. Without bitterness, and for as long as she lived, she bore a vision of deicide.[11]

Now that I can have her only in memory, I see my grandmother in the several postures that were peculiar to her: standing at the wood stove on a winter morning and turning meat in a great iron skillet; sitting at the south window, bent above her beadwork, and afterwards, when her vision failed, looking down for a long time into the fold of her hands; going out upon a cane, very slowly as she did when the weight of age came upon her; praying. I remember her most often at prayer. She made long, rambling prayers out of suffering and hope, having seen many things. I was never sure that I had the right to hear, so exclusive were they of all mere custom and company. The last time I saw her she prayed standing by the side of her bed at night, naked to the waist, the light of a kerosene lamp moving upon her dark skin. Her long, black hair, always drawn and braided in the day, lay upon her shoulders and against her breasts like a shawl. I do not speak Kiowa, and I never understood her prayers, but there was something inherently sad in the sound, some merest hesitation upon the syllables of sorrow. She began in a high and 38

11. **deicide** (dē´ ə sīd´) *n.* killing of a god.

Think Aloud

Vocabulary: Using Context
Direct students' attention to the word *consummate* in the first paragraph on this page. Using the following "think aloud," model how to use context to infer the meaning of an unknown word. Say to students:

> The word *consummate* is used as a verb that describes something that the Kiowa have to do. From the previous sentences, I understand that the word relates to a ceremony, the Sun Dance, that the people would like to perform. From the surrounding information, I understand that the ceremony requires the head of a buffalo and that a group has to go to Texas to look for one in order for the ceremony to occur.
>
> From this context, I think that the word *consummate* means "to complete or accomplish."

descending pitch, exhausting her breath to silence; then again and again—and always the same intensity of effort, of something that is, and is not, like urgency in the human voice. Transported so in the dancing light among the shadows of her room, she seemed beyond the reach of time. But that was illusion; I think I knew then that I should not see her again.

Houses are like sentinels in the plain, old keepers of the weather watch. There, in a very little while, wood takes on the appearance of great age. All colors wear soon away in the wind and rain, and then the wood is burned gray and the grain appears and the nails turn red with rust. The windowpanes are black and opaque; you imagine there is nothing within, and indeed there are many ghosts, bones given up to the land. They stand here and there against the sky, and you approach them for a longer time than you expect. They belong in the distance; it is their domain.

Once there was a lot of sound in my grandmother's house, a lot of coming and going, feasting and talk. The summers there were full of excitement and reunion. The Kiowas are a summer people; they abide the cold and keep to themselves, but when the season turns and the land becomes warm and vital they cannot hold still; an old love of going returns upon them. The aged visitors who came to my grandmother's house when I was a child were made of lean and leather, and they bore themselves upright. They wore great black hats and bright ample shirts that shook in the wind. They rubbed fat upon their hair and wound their braids with strips of colored cloth. Some of them painted their faces and carried the scars of old and cherished enmities. They were an old council of warlords, come to remind and be reminded of who they were. Their wives and daughters served them well. The women might indulge themselves; gossip was at once the mark and compensation of their servitude. They made loud and elaborate talk among themselves, full of jest and gesture, fright and false alarm. They went abroad in fringed and flowered shawls, bright beadwork and German silver. They were at home in the kitchen, and they prepared meals that were banquets.

There were frequent prayer meetings, and great nocturnal feasts. When I was a child I played with my cousins outside, where the lamplight fell upon the ground and the singing of the old people rose up around us and carried away into the darkness. There were a lot of good things to eat, a lot of laughter and surprise. And afterwards, when the quiet returned, I lay down with my grandmother and could hear the frogs away by the river and feel the motion of the air.

Now there is a funeral silence in the rooms, the endless wake of some final word. The walls have closed in upon my grandmother's

Literary Analysis
Author's Purpose
Which details here suggest Momaday writes to better understand his memories? Which details suggest he wants to pay tribute to his grandmother?

I do not speak Kiowa, and I never understood her prayers, but there was something inherently sad in the sound . . .

39 **Reading Check**
Who comes to visit Momaday's grandmother's house in the summer?

38 Literary Analysis
Author's Purpose

1. Remind students that the author may have more than one purpose for writing an essay.
2. Have students brainstorm for three purposes Momaday may have for writing this essay, such as to inform readers about the Kiowa; to pay tribute to his grandmother; to persuade readers that the Kiowa were unfairly treated.
3. Now **ask** the Literary Analysis question: Which details here suggest Momaday writes to better understand his memories? Which details suggest he wants to pay tribute to his grandmother?
Answer: To understand his memories, Momaday describes the tone, pitch, emotions, and secrecy of his grandmother's prayers to connect with the spirit of his heritage. Momaday describes the beauty of his grandmother, her devotion to prayer, and her transcendant appearance as tributes to her personality and character.

39 Reading Check

Answer: Kiowa elders come to visit the house.

Differentiated Instruction for Universal Access

EL Pronunciation for English Learners

Some students might find it difficult to pronounce words with the initial "th" sound, as in *think* and *them,* and replace it with the "d" sound. The following strategies can help students to pronounce the "th" sound.

- Write the words *their, themselves, they,* and *that* on the board. Pronounce each word, having students repeat each one. Then, call out the words at random and have student volunteers circle the word on the board. Discuss the results with the class, offering what might have led to incorrect choices.
- Pair English learners with fluent speakers. Have partners take turns reading from the paragraph beginning with "Once there was. . . ". If an English learner gets stuck on a "th" word, ask his or her partner to pronounce the word and then allow the English learner to continue.

40 Literary Analysis
Author's Purpose

- **Ask** the Literary Analysis question. **Answer:** The author describes Rainy Mountain from his grandmother's grave, which suggests that he better understands his sadness and his connection with the people and homeland of his ancestors.

Concept Connector

Have students compare the Writing About the Big Question responses and their responses to the class discussion they had before reading the story to their ideas after reading.

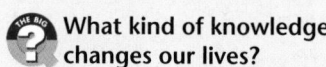

ASSESS

Answers

Critical Thinking

1. Students may be interested in exploring their cultural roots so that they can discover more about their personal identities.
2. (a) Students may say: feasting, talking, cooking, praying, or playing. (b) The house in which these activities take place is now empty, and the people are gone.
3. (a) The grandmother witnessed the last Sun Dance; she maintained the language and beliefs of the Kiowa. (b) Momaday laments the loss of Kiowa culture but seems comforted by his memories.
4. (a) The cricket symbolizes the unity of all things in the universe and the spiritual connection between them. (b) Momaday will always remember his grandmother as wise, practical, and religious.

What kind of knowledge changes our lives?

(a) Momaday's grandmother helped him understand what his people endured and the strength they drew from it. (b) Momaday respected her strength and solid beliefs.
(c) Momaday is proud of his connection with his Kiowa ancestors.

Literary Analysis
Author's Purpose
Which details here suggest that Momaday writes to understand himself?

40

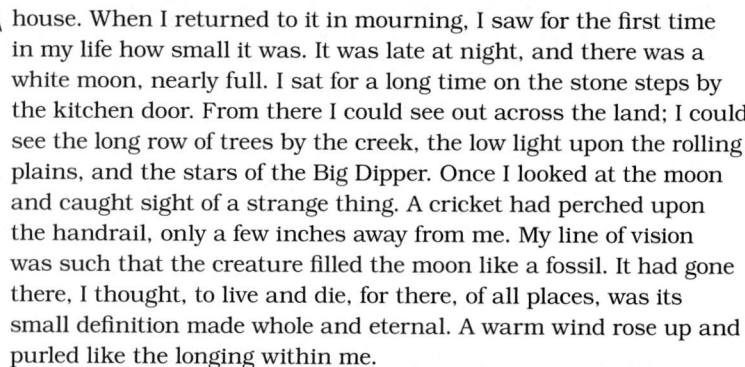

house. When I returned to it in mourning, I saw for the first time in my life how small it was. It was late at night, and there was a white moon, nearly full. I sat for a long time on the stone steps by the kitchen door. From there I could see out across the land; I could see the long row of trees by the creek, the low light upon the rolling plains, and the stars of the Big Dipper. Once I looked at the moon and caught sight of a strange thing. A cricket had perched upon the handrail, only a few inches away from me. My line of vision was such that the creature filled the moon like a fossil. It had gone there, I thought, to live and die, for there, of all places, was its small definition made whole and eternal. A warm wind rose up and purled like the longing within me.

The next morning I awoke at dawn and went out on the dirt road to Rainy Mountain. It was already hot, and the grasshoppers began to fill the air. Still, it was early in the morning, and the birds sang out of the shadows. The long yellow grass on the mountain shone in the bright light, and a scissortail hied above the land. There, where it ought to be, at the end of a long and legendary way, was my grandmother's grave. Here and there on the dark stones were ancestral names. Looking back once, I saw the mountain and came away.

Critical Thinking

1. **Respond:** Would you be interested in investigating your own cultural roots the way Momaday does? Explain.
2. **(a)** Describe two activities at Momaday's grandmother's house in summer. **(b) Connect:** In what ways are these activities connected to a vanishing way of life?
3. **(a) Support:** In what sense is Momaday's grandmother one of the last representatives of traditional Kiowa culture?
   (b) Draw Conclusions: How does Momaday seem to feel about the disappearance of this way of life? Support your answer with details from the selection.
4. **(a) Interpret:** When Momaday imagines the cricket on the moon, why does he say "there . . . was its small definition made whole and eternal"? **(b) Draw Conclusions:** In what sense is Momaday's memory of his grandmother similar to his vision of the cricket?

What kind of knowledge changes our lives?
(a) In what ways did Momaday's relationship with his grandmother shape his appreciation of Kiowa culture?
(b) How did his knowledge of Kiowa history impact his view of his grandmother? **(c)** How has the experience Momaday narrates in this essay changed his life?

Vocabulary Development

Vocabulary Knowledge Rating

When students have completed reading and discussing the excerpt from "Desert Exile" and the excerpt from "The Way to Rainy Mountain," have them take out their **Vocabulary Knowledge Rating Chart** for these essays. Read the words aloud once more, and have students rate their knowledge of the words again in the After Reading column. Clarify any words that are still problematic. Have students write their own definition and example or sentence in the appropriate column. Then, have students complete the Vocabulary Practice activities on the next page. Encourage students to use the words in further discussion and written work about this selection. Remind them that they will be accountable for these words on the **Selection Test** (*Unit 3 Resources,* pp. 186–188 or 189–191).

After You Read

from **Desert Exile** • *from* **The Way to Rainy Mountain**

Comparing Authors' Purposes

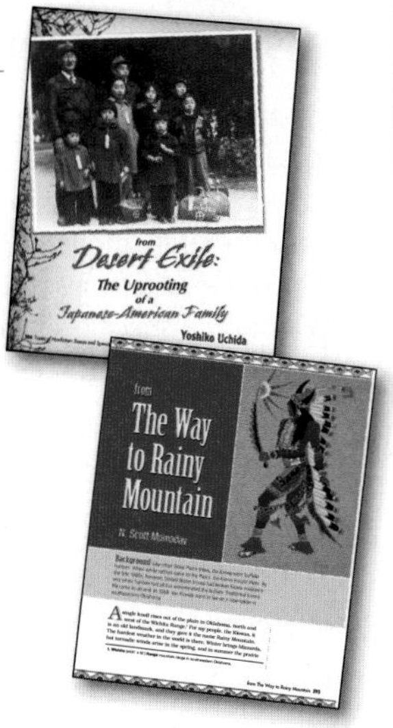

1. (a) Choose two powerful details from each selection. Using a chart like the one shown, analyze the writer's use of these details. **(b)** In a statement, identify the writer's purpose in sharing the details you have chosen. Explain your reasoning.

	Detail	Writer's Response to Detail	What Detail Adds to Meaning
Uchida			
Momaday			

2. (a) What general purpose for writing do Momaday and Uchida share? **(b)** Identify one major difference in their views of the events and scenes they describe.

Writing to Compare Authors' Purposes

Considering each author's purpose, write an essay to compare the effectiveness of the two selections. Use these questions to get started:

- Which passages best convey the author's purpose?
- How is the tone of each passage influenced by the writer's purpose?
- In these passages, are the details comprehensive enough to make the writing convincing or moving?
- Which writer generated more sympathy from you? How?

Vocabulary

Practice For each word pair, write a sentence that uses the words correctly. Explain why each sentence makes sense.

1. nomadic; desert

2. unwieldy; struggle

3. adept; clumsy

4. tenuous; relationship

ASSESS/EXTEND

Answers

Comparing Authors' Purposes

1. (a) **Possible response:** The hot plate shows the resilience of the Uchida family. The Devil's Tower symbolizes the Kiowa's connection with their spirits. (b) Uchida chooses details that pay tribute to her family and other Japanese Americans in captivity. Momaday chooses details that inform readers about the traditions and history of the Kiowa people.
2. (a) Both Momaday and Uchida pay tribute to the spirits of their relatives in the face of unjust situations. (b) Uchida shows how her family maintains their heritage despite the conditions imposed by the government. On the other hand, Momaday realizes his ancestral traditions cannot long survive.

Other sample answers appear in ***Graphic Organizer Transparencies*, Comparing Author's Purpose Graphic Organizer A (After You Read)**, p. 108, and the **Additional Answers** section.

Writing to Compare Authors' Purposes

1. Review the assignment criteria with students.
2. As they draft, have students refer to the chart they completed (p. 584).

Six Traits Focus

✔	Ideas		Word Choice
✔	Organization		Sentence Fluency
	Voice		Conventions

Vocabulary

1. The nomadic tribe scoured the dry desert for a resting place.
2. The unwieldy parcel caused the postman to struggle.
3. A good surgeon is adept at his work and is not clumsy.
4. The friends' tenuous relationship survived the argument.

Assessment Resources

Unit 3 Resources

L1 L2 EL **Selection Test A,** pp. 216–218

L3 L4 **Selection Test B,** pp. 219–221

L3 L4 **Open-Book Test,** pp. 213–215

PHLit Online! All assessment resources are available at **www.PHLitOnline.com.**

PREACH

Meeting Your Standards

Students will
1. write a persuasive essay.
2. learn the elements of a persuasive essay.
3. use writing strategies to generate ideas and to plan, organize, evaluate, and revise a persuasive essay.
4. apply grammar and revision skills.

Introducing the Writing Assignment

Review the assignment and the criteria, using the instruction on the student page.

Connecting to Real-Life Writing

Explain to students that elements of a persuasive essay are often incorporated into other types of writing. Point out these examples:

- An editorial often describes an issue and offers a point of view on it.
- A proposal uses specific details or examples to support an idea.

Erik Weihenmayer on Persuasive Essays

Show students Segment 3 on Eric Weihenmayer from ***See It!*** **DVD** or from this page in the **Enriched Online Student Edition**, at **www.PHLitOnline.com.** Discuss the use of personal anecdotes in writing.

Writing Workshop
Work in Progress

If students have done the Work-in-Progress assignments on pp. 555 and 575, suggest that they examine their recorded ideas as they begin prewriting. They may wish to develop these ideas in a persuasive essay.

OES Online Essay Scorer

A writing prompt for this mode of writing can be found on the *PH Essay Scorer* at **www.PHLitOnline.com.**

Writing Workshop

Persuasion: Persuasive Essay

Defining the Form Persuasion is a part of daily life. Friends or acquaintances may use persuasive techniques to convince you to try an exotic food, audition for a play, or volunteer for a cause. Persuasion is also an important literary mode. A **persuasive essay** is a nonfiction literary work, in which the writer tries to convince readers to accept a particular point of view or take a specific action. You might use elements of the persuasive essay in editorials, position papers, letters to the editor, and proposals.

Assignment Write a persuasive essay supporting your opinion about an issue that matters to you. Include these elements:

✔ a clear *description of the issue* and a clear *statement of your opinion*

✔ reliable and varied *evidence* that supports your opinion

✔ *arguments* that acknowledge and refute opposing opinions

✔ vivid, *persuasive language* that appeals to your audience

✔ a logical *organization*

✔ error-free grammar, including *correct use of parallel structures*

To preview the criteria on which your persuasive essay may be judged, see the rubric on page 611.

Writing Workshop: *Work in Progress*

If you have completed the Work in Progress assignments on pages 555 and 575, you already have many ideas to use in your persuasive essay. Work with these ideas, or explore a new idea, as you complete the Writing Workshop.

Reading Writing Connection

To get a feel for persuasive writing, read the excerpt from Alexander Solzhenitsyn's Nobel Lecture on page 548.

Teaching Resources

The following resources can be used to enrich or extend the instruction.

All *Unit 3 Resources*
Writing Workshop, pp. 224, 225

All *Professional Development Guidebook*
Rubric for Self-Assessment: Persuasive Essay, pp. 230–231

All *Graphic Organizer Transparencies*
Rubric for Self-Assessment: Persuasive Essay, p. 110

All *See It!* DVD
Erik Weihenmayer, Segments 3 and 4

PHLit Online! All resources, including print and video, are available at **www.PHLitOnline.com.**

Prewriting Strategies

Brainstorm and freewrite. Think about topics that cause you and others to argue. Using a chart like the one shown, make a list of the subjects and issues that have prompted emotional reactions and circle the one that most intrigues you. Then, freewrite for three minutes about that topic. Review what you have written and circle any statements of opinion that have emerged. Select the subject with the clearest statement and use it as the starting point for your essay.

PHLit Online!
www.PHLitOnline.com
- Author video: Writing Process
- Author video: Rewards of Writing

List of subjects and issues	→	Topic of interest	→	Freewrite	→	List of opinions

Apply It!

Conduct research. You may not have enough details about your topic to sufficiently focus your ideas. More information can help you break the topic into meaningful parts. For example, the concept of freedom of speech is far too broad to discuss in a brief essay. However, after you learn more about it, you may choose to write about balanced reporting in television news. Conduct research to identify an aspect of the topic that is manageable in the space of your essay.

Look at both sides of the issue. An effective persuasive essay anticipates and addresses differing opinions. It considers the concerns of readers and addresses their expectations. Use a pro-and-con chart like the one shown to identify counterarguments. In the left-hand column, list arguments that support your opinion. In the right-hand column, list opposing arguments. Use the chart to brainstorm for ideas that counter the opposing claims.

Apply It!

Pro-and-Con Chart

Topic: Honor Students Should Be Rewarded

Supporting	Opposing
• Honor roll students are responsible and dedicated. • They know the material.	• It is unfair to other students. • There would be inequality.

Understanding by Design

Clarifying Expected Outcomes: Using Rubrics

- Before students begin work on this assignment, have them preview the Rubric for Self-Assessment on p. 611 to learn what qualities their persuasive essay must have. A copy of this rubric appears in ***Graphic Organizer Transparencies***, p. 110.
- Review the criteria in the rubric with the class. Before students use the rubric to assess their own writing, work with them to rate the Student Model (p. 610) using the rubric.
- If you wish to assess students' persuasive essays with a 4-point or a 6-point scoring rubric, see ***Professional Development Guidebook***, pp. 230–231.

TEACH

Prewriting Strategies

Introduce the Prewriting Strategies, using the instruction on the student page. Have students apply the strategies to choose a topic.

Teaching the Strategies

1. Provide students with current newspapers, magazines, and Internet access to help them choose topics.
2. To help students narrow their topics, suggest that they use their general topics as keywords for Internet searches.

Think Aloud: Model Taking a Position

Model the strategy, using the following "think aloud":

When I write a persuasive essay, I must take a position. First I need to consider all the arguments.

Suppose my town wants to start a new waste program to help reduce the amount of trash. The current program allows residents to put out an unlimited number of bags on trash day. The new program would require residents to pay for special bags and only these bags would be picked up. As a bonus, residents could put out as many recyclables for free. Supporters believe that if people know they have to pay for each bag, they will throw out less. However, opponents argue that their taxes already pay for trash pickup; they would be unfairly charged for the same service.

People can be wasteful, but if there are controls on how much garbage they throw out and encouragement for recycling, then I think the new program is a good one.

Six Traits Focus

✔	Ideas		Word Choice
✔	Organization		Sentence Fluency
	Voice		Conventions

WG Writing and Grammar, Grade 10

Students will find additional instruction on prewriting for a persuasive essay in Chapter 7, Section 2.

Writing and Grammar, Interactive Textbook Online

Students can use the following tool at **www.pearsonsuccessnet.com** as they complete their persuasive essays:

- Persuasive Words Word Bin

Drafting Strategies

1. Introduce the Drafting Strategies, using the instruction on the student page.
2. Have students apply the strategies as they draft.

Teaching the Strategies

1. Students should arrange their notecards in the order that the information presented is the most persuasive. They can then number the notecards and use them as working outlines for their essays.
2. Tell students to address the concerns, biases, and expectations of their audiences. Explain that the audiences will determine not only what supporting information they include, but also what tones they use. For example, a piece on the benefits of school uniforms to be read by students will differ in content and tone from one written for parents.

Think Aloud: Model Evaluating Arguments

Model the strategy, using the following "think aloud":

Let's say I want to persuade the school board to ban student cell phone use. One of my reasons for writing is that I find the constant ringing in class very irritating. However, I cannot simply write in my essay that cell phones bother me—this is a weak argument not backed up by strong evidence. Instead, I can conduct interviews with other teachers to gather anecdotal evidence. I can also determine the percentage of teachers I interviewed who agreed with my view and use this statistic as authoritative evidence.

Six Traits Focus

✔	Ideas		Word Choice
✔	Organization		Sentence Fluency
	Voice		Conventions

WG Writing and Grammar, Grade 10

Students will find additional instruction on drafting persuasive essays in Chapter 7, Section 3.

Drafting Strategies

Evaluate your arguments. Write all of your ideas on separate notecards. Then, consider the impact each idea will have on your *intended audience.* Delete any cards that contain ideas that may not help you persuade readers. Then, organize the notecards in order of persuasiveness.

Emphasize your strongest argument. Introduce your topic and state your opinion in a clearly worded *thesis statement.* In the body of your essay, build your arguments to support your thesis. Finish with a conclusion that urges your readers to act. Consider the organization in the box shown here.

Offer evidence. While your own opinions form the basis for your writing, you need *authoritative evidence* to convince readers to accept your viewpoint. For each point you make, provide convincing *support.* Include a variety of types of evidence, including the following:

- **Facts:** information that can be proved true
- **Statistics:** numerical evidence
- **Expert opinion:** information or quotations from experts
- **Case studies:** analyses of examples that illustrate your opinions
- **Anecdotes:** relevant experiences, either your own or those of others

Organizing a Persuasive Essay

- Begin with a statement of your opinion.
- Explain your second-best argument.
- Argue against an opposing view.
- Organize the rest of your arguments in order of persuasiveness.
- Conclude with your best argument.

Model: Supporting Opinion With Evidence

Final exams are meant to test students' overall grasp of the course material. However, honor roll students have already shown that they have mastered the course. According to school records, over 95% of honor roll students have a straight "A" average.

Convincing statistical evidence supports the writer's opinion.

Identify your sources. The inclusion of *reliable sources* strengthens your arguments. For example, convincing statistical evidence offers proven support for your opinion. Whenever you present a fact or detail gathered from your research, attribute, or provide, the *source of the information.* If you are quoting someone, use quotation marks. When you quote or use information from an expert, tell your readers who the expert is and explain his or her qualifications. In addition, make sure to build a strong link between the quotation and your argument.

Erik Weihenmayer

On Persuasive Techniques

"Writing enables me to climb the mountain again."
—Erik Weihenmayer

Atop Mt. Kilimanjaro, a sign reads, "You Are Now at the Uhuru Peak. . . ." Sitting on the summit, feeling exhausted, nauseated, and dizzy, I asked my guide, Baltazar, what "Uhuru" meant. He replied, "Freedom." In this passage, I try to persuade you to accept the conclusion about freedom I reached.

Professional Model:

from *"Touch the Top of the World"*

Freedom. It was a word I didn't understand. Freedom from what? Freedom from the limits of my body? From pain? From disappointment? What did it mean? I wanted to believe that by standing atop mountains around the world, I was achieving this kind of freedom, . . . but when standing in these high places, the immense power of the mountains only served to magnify my own fragility, my human need for food, for oxygen, for the help that I received from my team. . . .

← First, I ask you a series of difficult questions, which lead you to ponder whether freedom is obtainable.

← Second, I try to shatter your traditional definition of freedom by emphasizing the obvious limits of our minds and bodies.

Then it came to me . . . Perhaps it was the freedom to make of my life what I wanted it to be, or at least the freedom to try, or to fail in the trying. Perhaps freedom itself was unobtainable and the goal was only to reach for it, strive for it, knowing all along that I would fall well short. Perhaps the importance was in the reaching out, and in the impossibility of it all, and in the reaching out through the impossibility, my body planted heavily on the earth but my spirit soaring up and coming impossibly close to its goal.

← Lastly, I find the answer and suggest, without insisting on, a surprising new understanding of what freedom means.

Erik Weihenmayer on Persuasive Techniques

Review the passage on the student page with the class, using Erik Weihenmayer's comments to deepen students' understanding of the process of writing a persuasive essay.

Teaching From the Professional Model

1. Show students Segment 3 on Erik Weihenmayer on ***See It!* DVD** or from this page in the **Enriched Online Student Edition** at **www.PHLitOnline.com**. Discuss how Weihenmayer documents his thinking process as part of his persuasive essay.
2. Invite students to consider the effect on the reader of Weihenmayer's rhetorical questions.
   Possible response: The questions force the reader to consider his or her own ideas about freedom before reading about the author's ideas.
3. Point out that Weihenmayer asks the reader, if only mentally, to offer his or her ideas about freedom to the essay; then, he immediately shatters these preconceptions by offering a nontraditional definition of his own.
   Ask students to consider the effectiveness of this technique.
   Possible response: By creating a sense of imbalance in the reader, Weihenmayer enables the reader to consider freedom in a new light.

Differentiated Instruction for Universal Access

EL Strategy for English Learners

Encourage students to focus on their experiences of other cultures to help them generate topics for their persuasive essays. Students may also address issues from their native cultures, but make sure to remind them to include enough details to enable their audiences in the United States to understand the issues well.

Enrichment for Advanced Readers

Encourage students to select issues about which they feel strongly but are not experts. Challenge students to research both sides of their issues fully and to incorporate their findings into their essays. You may also encourage each student to argue in favor of the side of the argument that he or she does not personally support.

PHLit Online!

Enriched Online Student Edition
Show or assign the video online at **www.pearsonsuccessnet.com.**

Revising Strategies

1. Introduce the Revising Strategies, using the instruction on the student page.
2. Have students apply the strategies as they revise.

Teaching the Strategies

1. Supply students with red pens or pencils, and have them follow the instructions in the text.
2. Tell students that in addition to evaluating the amount of support they have provided for each point, they should check the types of support they used. For example, if they used only anecdotes, they should consider adding other types of evidence, such as statistics or quotations from experts.
3. Encourage students to make certain that each detail in a paragraph supports the main idea of that paragraph. Irrelevant details will distract their audience and should be omitted.

Think Aloud: Model Using Vivid Words

Model the strategy, using the following "think aloud":

> As I revise my writing, I can look for weak words and phrases. For example, the sentence "Governor Hilson should be reelected because he has done a lot for this city" is weak. Instead of simply saying the governor has done a lot, I can replace the verb with one that has a positive connotation, such as "saved." I can also say exactly what the governor has accomplished, so that the new sentence reads, "Governor Hilson saved our beloved city of Norwell from an abject budgetary debt. Rather than just giving him praise, give him your vote." This sentence is more likely to persuade the reader because it uses strong words and appeals directly to the reader.

Six Traits Focus

✔	Ideas	✔	Word Choice
✔	Organization		Sentence Fluency
	Voice		Conventions

WG Writing and Grammar, Grade 10

Students will find additional instruction on revising a persuasive essay in Chapter 7, Section 4.

Revising Strategies

Test your support. Every paragraph in your essay should play a clear role in *supporting your argument*. Use these steps to test each paragraph:

- Underline the sentence that states the main idea of the paragraph. If a topic sentence is missing, consider adding one.
- Put a star next to each sentence that supports the main idea. If a sentence is not starred, consider modifying or deleting it.
- If a topic sentence has fewer than two supporting details, add more evidence or reconsider whether the point is worth including.

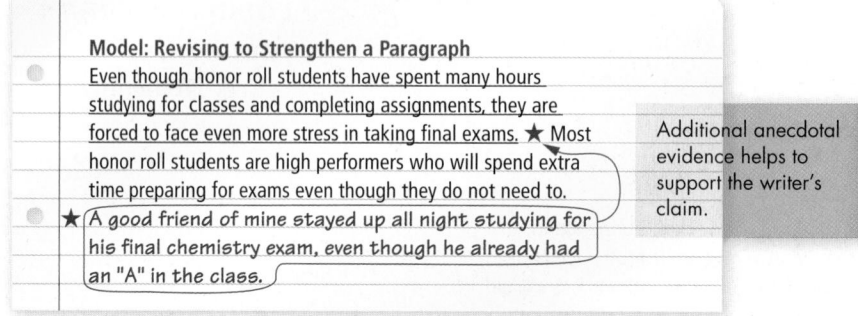

Model: Revising to Strengthen a Paragraph

Even though honor roll students have spent many hours studying for classes and completing assignments, they are forced to face even more stress in taking final exams. ★ Most honor roll students are high performers who will spend extra time preparing for exams even though they do not need to. ★ A good friend of mine stayed up all night studying for his final chemistry exam, even though he already had an "A" in the class.

Additional anecdotal evidence helps to support the writer's claim.

Choose powerful words. Clear, strong language will help make your ideas memorable. Consider these options:

- **Comparatives and Superlatives** Comparative adjectives, such as *sharper* and *bolder*, clarify your ideas. Avoid overuse of predictable or hard to prove superlatives, such as *best, smartest, strongest* or *bravest.*
- **Action Verbs** Strong verbs make your ideas more compelling.
  Linking verb: The policy *is* unfair. (weak)
  Action verb: The policy *cheats* us all. (strong)
- **Connotation** Be aware of **connotations**, the emotions a word sparks. Positive connotations can support your ideas. Negative connotations can emphasize the drawbacks of opposing arguments.
  Neutral: We can look into this problem.
  Positive: We can rise to meet this challenge.
  Negative: We can attempt to approach this impossible task.

Peer Review

Exchange drafts with a partner. Review each other's work, circling ten words in your partner's essay that are weak. In a peer conference, share ideas about possible replacements.

Strategies for Using Technology in Writing

If students are using word-processing software to draft and revise their persuasive compositions, suggest that they print out a copy of each draft before making any changes. Students will then have a record of the progress they have made throughout the writing process.

Students can also use features of the **Writing and Grammar Interactive Textbook Online** to draft or revise their essays.

SIX TRAITS WRITER'S TOOLBOX SIX TRAITS

Sentence Fluency | Voice | Organization | Word Choice | Ideas | Conventions

Revising to Create Parallelism

Parallelism is the use of similar grammatical forms or patterns to express similar ideas. Effective use of parallelism can connect your ideas and make them memorable.

Identifying Faulty Parallelism Parallel constructions place equal ideas in words, phrases, or clauses of similar types. Ideas are not parallel if the grammatical structure shifts.

Apply It!

	Nonparallel	Parallel
use of verbs	We want to be learning, growing, and to succeed.	We want to learn, to grow, and to succeed.
use of direct objects	Students benefit from limits that are respectful, reasonable freedoms, and being inspired by classes.	Students benefit from respectful limits, reasonable freedoms, and inspiring classes.

Fixing Errors Follow these steps to revise nonparallel constructions:

1. **Identify similar or equivalent ideas within a sentence.**
2. **Identify the form in which the ideas are expressed.** Then, read the sentence aloud to hear changes in rhythm or pattern.
3. **Rewrite the sentence so that all the elements match the stronger pattern.** Choose forms that produce the smoothest rhythm or require the fewest words. Look at these examples:

   Nouns: hand, heart, and mind

   Verbs: to seek, to question, and to learn

   Phrases: defining the borders, preserving our resources, securing the future

   Adverb clauses: wherever we go, whatever we do

   Adjective clauses: she who commits, who practices, who focuses
4. **Punctuate correctly.** Use commas to separate three or more words, phrases, or clauses in a parallel series.

Grammar in Your Writing

Review three paragraphs in your essay, circling sentences that present a series of equivalent ideas. If they have varying grammatical structures, revise them to build parallelism.

WG

Prentice Hall Writing and Grammar Connection: Chapter 7, Section 4

Revising to Create Parallelism

1. Introduce the grammar skill, using the instruction on the student page.
2. Discuss the rules, the examples, and the strategies for fixing agreement errors.
3. Have students follow the instruction under Grammar in Your Writing to correct errors in their drafts.

Teaching the Grammar Skill

1. Explain that when used successfully, parallelism—repeated grammatical structures—contributes to an argument's impact on an audience.
2. Write a nonparallel example on the board. Then, work with the class to make it parallel. Lead students in a discussion about why the parallel version is better.
3. Have students review their essays, looking for places where they might create parallel structures to add power to their messages. Tell students to rewrite such sentences to make all the elements match the predominant or suggested grammatical form or pattern. Remind students to punctuate correctly, using serial commas as appropriate.

WG Writing and Grammar, Grade 10

Students will find additional instruction on revising to create parallelism in Chapter 7, Section 4.

Differentiated Instruction for Universal Access

Support for Special Needs Students

Students may have difficulty "seeing" parallel structure in writing. On the board, write this sentence: *These skills will aid us in school, on the job, and aid us in our personal lives.* Point out that this sentence contains a list in the form of three phrases. Have students identify the three phrases (*in school, on the job,* and *aid us in our personal lives*). Write each phrase separately on the board. Have students identify the phrase that does not have the same syntactic structure as the others.

To provide a visual aid, circle *in school* and *on the job,* and box *aid us in our personal lives,* both in the sentence and in the separate phrases. Ask a volunteer to revise the boxed item so it has the same structure as the others (*in our personal lives*). Rewrite the new sentence below the old one, circling each phrase. Read the new sentence aloud. Point out how the parallel construction emphasizes the list.

Student Model

Review the Student Model with the class, using the annotations to analyze the writer's use of the elements of a persuasive essay.

Teaching From the Student Model

1. Explain that the Student Model is a sample and that students' persuasive essays may be longer.
2. Have students list the arguments in the Student Model and the types of evidence used to support each. Discuss how well each argument is supported.
3. Have students identify vivid words in the essay and discuss their effects on readers. Then, have students locate places where the writer used the connotations of words to strengthen her argument. Have students rephrase these sentences with the opposite connotations or with neutral connotations. Discuss how the technique of using connotations has strengthened this essay.
4. **Ask** students why it is a good idea to address opposing arguments in a persuasive essay. **Possible response:** Addressing opposing arguments gives the writer credibility by illustrating that the writer has considered all sides of an issue.

Connecting to Real-Life Writing

Explain to students that persuasive writing is not limited to nonfiction literary works and English class compositions but has real-world applications. Students may be called on to use persuasion in college or job applications, or interviews. Prompt students to identify types of evidence they might use to convince schools to admit them or employers to give them jobs. Also, discuss how persuasive writing and speaking are used in careers such as law, politics, activism, medicine, teaching, and advertising.

Student Model: Esther Herrera, Hialeah, FL

True Reward for Our Achievements

Straight-A students have been rewarded in different ways for their hard work. They have been given the chance to eat breakfast with the principal, they have received gifts and certificates, and they have been publicly acknowledged. Schools hope that these policies will not only serve as a reward to students but also as an inspiration to others to do well in their classes. However, these honor-roll students show little interest in the awards; they want something else. These students should be exempt from taking the final exam because they have demonstrated responsibility and dedication, they know the material, and most importantly they feel that other students will likely be inspired to achieve the ultimate honor-roll goal.

Esther clearly states her opinion on the issue.

Primarily, honor-roll students should be exempt from taking the final exam because they are responsible and dedicated. These students have stayed on task throughout the year, going out of their way to turn in a job well done. Sometimes, they sacrificed by staying up late to finish homework assignments. As one honor student recalled, "One time, I stayed up, literally, all night so that I could finish a project. The problem was not finishing it but making sure that it would come out perfect; it did."

The writer states the argument and then supports it with valid evidence.

In addition, teachers should not have to give these students the final examination. Because they got A's in the first, second, third, and fourth quarters, it is clear that the students know the material very well. Furthermore, the final exam is added stress, because students worry and get nervous taking tests.

On the other hand, eleven out of twenty-five students whom I interviewed believe that such an exemption policy would not be fair to the other students. However, all students were given the same opportunity to get A's. The striking thing about this survey is that many students who were in favor of an exemption policy were not honor students. Instead, they were students who might work harder to earn the privilege of not taking the final exam. What I say to the first eleven students is: Accept the challenge.

By referring to a survey she conducted, Esther shows her research and writes with authority.

Here, the writer addresses those who oppose her ideas.

In conclusion, honor-roll students should be exempt from taking the final exam because they have already proved themselves. These students deserve a true reward: the knowledge that their efforts have been recognized.

Esther restates her opinion in her conclusion.

Editing and Proofreading

Review your draft to correct errors in grammar, spelling, and punctuation.

Focus on Spelling: Some vowel sounds in words are silent, which can make correct spelling difficult. Generally, two vowels are used to spell a sound that usually takes only one vowel, as in the final syllable of *porcelain*. If a word gives you problems, make up a mnemonic device, or memory aid, to help you remember the spelling. For example, you may say *"u* hides in *camouflage."*

Publishing and Presenting

Consider one of the following ways to share your writing:

Publish for an audience. If your topic relates to a school or community issue, submit your essay to the school newspaper, the local newspaper, or post it on a local website. If it appeals to a larger audience, consider submitting it to a national publication.

Deliver a speech. Use your persuasive essay as the basis for an in-class speech followed by a question-and-answer session. Survey your audience before and after your speech to see if you have changed their minds about your topic. Encourage the entire class to join in the question-and-answer period.

WG *Prentice Hall Writing and Grammar Connection: Chapter 7*

Reflecting on Your Writing

Writer's Journal Jot down your answers to this question:
How did writing about an issue help you understand it?

Rubric for Self-Assessment

Find evidence in your writing to address each category. Then, use the rating scale to grade your work.

Criteria	Rating Scale (not very – very)				
Focus: How clearly do you explain both the issue and your opinion?	1	2	3	4	5
Organization: How well do you organize the elements of your arguments?	1	2	3	4	5
Support/Elaboration: How reliable and varied is your evidence?	1	2	3	4	5
Style: How vivid and persuasive is your language?	1	2	3	4	5
Conventions: How correct is your grammar, especially your use of parallel structures?	1	2	3	4	5

Editing and Proofreading

1. Introduce the editing and proofreading focus, using the instruction on the student page.
2. Have students edit and proofread their persuasive essays, correcting grammar, spelling, punctuation, and word choice. Make sure they check for errors of the type noted on the student page.

Teaching the Editing Focus

Encourage students to use dictionaries to check spellings of which they are uncertain.

Six Traits Focus

	Ideas		Word Choice
	Organization		Sentence Fluency
	Voice	✔	Conventions

ASSESS

Publishing and Presenting

1. Before submitting their essays to publications, tell students to review the publications' guidelines for submission.
2. If students are preparing to deliver their essays as speeches, have them practice in pairs.
3. Have students identify the strongest statement of each main point in their essay. As they practice their speeches, they should use pacing and expression to emphasize each of these statements.

Reflecting on Your Writing

1. Have students assess the process of writing a persuasive essay.
2. Have students comment on how writing their essays affected their views of their topics.

WG **Writing and Grammar, Grade 10**

Students will find additional guidance on editing and proofreading, publishing and presenting, and reflecting on persuasive essays in Chapter 7, Sections 5 and 6.

Strategies for Test Taking

Tell students that if they are required to respond to persuasive writing prompts on standardized tests, they should pace themselves as they work, allowing time for each stage of the writing process. For example, if they spend a few minutes organizing at the very beginning, they may save time during the drafting stage.

Suggest that students use a pro-and-con chart to jot down what they know about an assigned topic. If students are asked to choose between two topics, the chart may also be used to help them identify the topic and position for which they have the most evidence.

MONITORING PROGRESS

Think About It

1. Reiterate the Unit Big Question, "What kind of knowledge changes our lives?"
2. Tell students that some of the selections they have read in Unit 3 may help them answer the Big Question. **Ask** students for examples in the selections that show how having knowledge helped change, or could have helped change, a person's life. **Possible response:** In "The Sun Parlor," if Dorothy's family had known of her aunt's failing health, they would have helped her aunt do what she needed in order to stay healthy.
3. Explain to students that the Big Question applies in many other areas besides literature. For example, students may learn in social studies about marginalized groups that had to fight for basic rights in society.
4. Point out that people might fight for change in society if they have knowledge of the impact the change will make. Have students think of examples in which knowledge of poor conditions in cities, homes, or the workplace have compelled people to fight for better conditions. **Possible response:** Students may cite the formation of labor unions, and their hard-won successes such as getting the 8-hour workday, as an example in improving living conditions.
5. Review the headings on the chart. Emphasize that there are different kinds of knowledge that can change a person's life.
6. Have students copy and complete the chart on the student page. If they have difficulty finding examples from science, suggest these starting points:
   - How can having knowledge of a person's DNA help change his or her life?
   - What knowledge can help a scientist gather and process research toward finding a cure for a disease?
7. Have students discuss their answers in small groups and then present their examples to the class.

Applying the Big Question

What kind of *knowledge* changes our lives?

Think About It

Think about what you have read in this unit and what you know about the effects of knowledge from your other classes and from your own experiences. Copy and complete the chart below to apply what you have learned about how knowledge can change lives. One row has been completed for you.

Example	Source of knowledge	What was learned?	Were lives changed? How?	What I learned
From Literature	"Keep Memory Alive"	Silence about evils of the past and present harms everyone.	Yes, Wiesel speaks about his own experiences so that others will not suffer.	It is important to remember and learn from the past.
From Literature				
From Science				
From Social Studies				
From Real Life				

Teaching Resources

Unit 3 Resources

All **Applying the Big Question**, p. 5

PHLit Online! All print resources are also available at **www.PHLitOnline.com.**

Talk About It

Choose one of the examples in your progress chart as the basis for a **short speech.** On note cards, jot down the main points you want to address. Note the type of information that was learned and how someone's life was changed because of that knowledge. Make sure to prepare an engaging introduction and conclusion in order to reinforce the main message you want to deliver about how knowledge can changes lives. Present your speech to the class after you have practiced a few times. Afterwards, invite other students to share their own examples of how knowledge has changed their lives.

For tips on organizing and delivering a speech, see the Communications Workshop on page 616.

Write About It

At the beginning of Unit 3, you wrote a response to the Big Question. Now that you have completed the unit, see how your understanding of the question has deepened. Write a new response in which you discuss whether your ideas have changed or been reinforced. Support your response with at least one example from literature and one example from an additional subject area or your own life, drawing on your chart for examples. You may complete these sentences—or write one of your own—to help you organize your response.

- We can change our lives with knowledge about ________.
- In this unit, I read an essay in which a person's life was changed by acquiring knowledge about ____________.
- One example of a scientific discovery that changed people's lives is ____________.
- Learning about historical or world events in social studies can change people because ______________.
- Knowledge I have gained about ________ has made a deep impact on my life. It changed my life by ______________ .

Challenge What issues does this question still raise for you? How could you continue your exploration?

Big Question Vocabulary

- ☆ adapt
- ☆ awareness
- empathy
- enlighten
- ☆ evolve
- growth
- history
- ignorance
- influence
- ☆ insight
- ☆ modified
- question
- reflect
- ☆ revise
- understanding

☆ shows an **Academic Vocabulary** word.

Strategies for Listening and Speaking

Remind students to follow these rules for composing a short speech.

- Use terms and language that are suited to your audience.
- Use language that evokes emotion in your audience.
- Use nonverbal communication such as eye contact and vocal tone while speaking.

MONITORING PROGRESS

Talk About It

1. Have students complete the assignment, following the instruction on the student page.
2. Suggest that students review their charts and choose the examples that they find most powerful or interesting. Encourage them to discuss their examples in depth and to conclude their speeches with ways in which listeners can learn from each example—and gain knowledge that will change their lives.

Write About It

1. Introduce the assignment, using the instruction on the student page.
2. Review the thematic vocabulary with the class (pp. 442–443).

Teaching Prewriting

1. Remind students that they may have read a selection in Unit 3 that changed the way they now look at the Big Question.
2. Direct students to write new responses explaining how their thinking has changed or been reinforced.
3. Have students complete the sentence starters on the student page. Guide them to use the prompts in Introducing the Big Question, pp. 442–443, to help them compare their previous responses with their new ones.

Teaching Drafting

1. Remind students that every speech should include a clear purpose and details that logically support it.
2. Suggest that students begin their drafts by defining their original ideas and stating whether or not they have changed.

Teaching Revising/Editing

1. Remind students that both essays and speeches should be clear and concise. Have them revise by deleting extra and repetitive words.
2. Direct students to recite their work to partners for peer review.

Guiding Student Publishing

Students can present their speeches to the class.

EXTEND/ASSESS

Answers

Meeting Your Standards

Students will

1. determine the correct meaning of words with multiple meanings in context.
2. determine the correct meaning of words with multiple meanings in context.

Words With Multiple Meanings

1. Introduce the skill, using the instruction on the student page.
2. Review the example.

Think Aloud: Model the Skill

Model how to use context clues to determine the meaning of a word with multiple meanings. Say to students:

> Sometimes when I'm reading, I come across words that have more than one meaning. I can often find the meaning of a word by looking at the context clues, or the information surrounding the word. For example, the word *coast* has many meanings. Let's say I read the sentence "The houses along the coast got hit hardest by the storm because of the huge waves it created." If I look at the information surrounding the word *coast*, I can see that it is used as a noun. I can also see that a coast is near the ocean because the writer tells me there were huge waves created by a storm. Finally, I know houses are along the coast. From all this evidence, I can determine that the word *coast* used in this sentence means "land alongside the seashore."

Practice A

Sample Answers:

1. (a) negative, (b) negative
2. (a) vacuum, (b) vacuum
3. (a) police (b) police
4. (a) break, (b) break

Vocabulary Workshop

Words With Multiple Meanings

Many words in English have **multiple meanings**. Look at this dictionary entry for *coast*:

Dictionary

The first part of the entry gives meanings for the noun *coast*.

The second part of the entry gives meanings for the verb *coast*.

coast (kōst) ***n.*** [ME *coste*, coast < OFr, a rib, hill, shore, coast < L *costa*, a rib, side] **1.** land alongside the sea; seashore **2.** [Obs] frontier borderland **3.** a slide or ride, as on a sled going down an incline by the force of gravity— ***vi.*** **1.** to sail along or near a coast, esp. from port to port **2.** to go down an incline, as on a sled **3.** to continue in motion on momentum or by the force of gravity after propelling power has stopped **4.** to continue without serious effort, letting one's past efforts carry one along

This means "obsolete," or no longer useful.

To determine which meaning a writer is using in a sentence, look at the **context clues.** Context clues are in the information surrounding a word and can be used to determine the word's meaning. Look at the following sentence to identify context clues that help you determine the meaning used here:

My brother *coasted* through law school without opening a book.

One context clue is that *coast* is used as a verb. Another clue is *without opening a book,* which suggests "without much effort." Try each of the four definitions for verbs in the sentence. The definition that fits is 4— "to continue without serious effort, letting one's past efforts carry one along."

Practice A Read each sentence. Choose the multiple-meaning word that makes sense in each sentence pair: *vacuum, break, negative, police.*

1. (a) His _____ attitude kept him from succeeding in school.
(b) The _____ of a picture shows light and dark in reverse.

2. (a) I need to _____ the rug before company arrives.
(b) The absence of air creates a _____.

3. (a) We must _____ the campus for litter.
(b) My older sister went to the _____ academy when she was twenty.

4. (a) We definitely wanted to _____ free of our routine.
(b) The sun shone through a _____ in the clouds.

Teaching Resources

Unit 3 Resources

Words With Multiple Meanings, pp. 614–615

PHLit Online! **Vocabulary Central,** featuring definitions, audio pronunciations, Word Families, and activities, is available at **www.PHLitOnline.com.**

Practice B Using context clues, write your own definition for the underlined word in each sentence. With a partner discuss which context clues helped you to determine the meaning of the word. Then, look up the word in a dictionary to confirm or correct your definition.

1. The map didn't show the cardinal directions!
2. A cold draft came in under the door and through cracks around the window.
3. She didn't seem to harbor any hard feelings over what I'd said.
4. The launch sped across the choppy bay.
5. How can you gauge someone's interest in the drama?
6. To prepare for the long Alaskan winter, Andrew stocked his cabin with flour, cereal, potatoes, and other staples.
7. The truck bounced its way across the sandy wash.
8. Their plot to avoid the extra work failed completely.
9. Don't force the lock or you may break the key off.
10. The sailor could hardly stay on his feet as he walked across the heaving deck of the ship.

PHLit Online!
www.PHLitOnline.com
- Illustrated vocabulary words
- Interactive vocabulary games
- Vocabulary flashcards

Activity Look in a dictionary to find the multiple definitions of these words: *litter, fan, coat, pump,* and *contract.* Write each word on a separate notecard like the one shown. Fill in the left column of the notecard according to one of the word's meanings. Fill in the right-hand column according to another of the word's meanings. Then, trade note cards with a partner, and discuss the different meanings and uses of the words that each of you found.

Word	First Meaning	Second Meaning

Challenge
Find each of these words in a dictionary: *craft, switch, exhaust.* Select one of the meanings for each and write a sentence in which the context clearly illustrates the meaning. Trade sentences with a partner. Identify the definition of the word in each of your partner's sentences.

Differentiated Instruction for Universal Access

Strategy for Less Proficient Readers
Pair less proficient learners. Give each pair five notecards with a multiple-meaning word on each card. Have each pair use a dictionary to list the meanings of each word on its notecard. Then, have them write two sentences for each word, using the two different meanings.

Have pairs trade sentences. Taking turns, each student should choose a sentence, read it aloud, and give the definition of the word as it is used in the sentence. Partners can check each other's answers by using the definitions written on the notecards.

Strategy for Gifted and Talented Students
Have students work in a group to create a classroom "multiple-meaning" dictionary. Collect the notecards students created while completing the Activity. Encourage students to create a visually appealing book using all the words and their various meanings. Tell students the book should be easily accessible and the information must be accurate. Encourage them to use markers, colored papers, photographs, or any other medium that will make it a book students will want to use when looking up words with multiple meanings.

ASSESS/EXTEND

Answers

Practice B
Sample Answers

1. Cardinal means "important." The writer used the word as an adjective to define the kind of directions that were missing.
2. Draft means "air." It is used as a noun. The context clues *cold, under the door,* and *through cracks* helped me figure out it must be air that was getting in.
3. Harbor is used as a verb, meaning "to keep in one's mind." The context clue *any hard feelings* helped me realize the meaning.
4. Launch is used as a noun. It means "a new ship set afloat." *Across the choppy bay* helped me determine its meaning.
5. Gauge is used as a verb. *Someone's interest* helped me figure out it means "to form a judgment or estimate of something."
6. Staples is used as a noun. The context clues *prepare, long winter,* and *stocked with other* helped me determine it means "important, or main, items."
7. Wash is used as a noun. *Truck* and *sandy* helped me determine that wash in this context means "a piece of ground washed by a sea or river."
8. Plot is used as a noun. *Avoid the extra work* and *failed completely* helped me determine the meaning of the word: "a plan of action made in secret by a group."
9. Force is a verb that means to "break open by physical strength." The context clue *may break the key off* helped me realize the meaning of the word.
10. Deck is a wooden floor of a ship. The context clues are *sailor, walked across,* and of *the ship.*

Activity
To prepare students for the Activity, distribute notecards and dictionaries. Use the word *slip* to guide students in using a dictionary. Allow time for students to discuss their words.

Challenge
Provide dictionaries for students. Guide them in identifying the many uses of one word along with its definitions.

Meeting Your Standards

Students will
1. plan the content of a persuasive speech.
2. practice the delivery of a persuasive speech.

Introducing Delivering a Persuasive Speech

Introduce the assignment and the strategies, using the instruction on the student page.

Plan Your Content

1. Explain that the first goal in developing content is to support the main idea of the speech.
2. Tell students that rhetorical devices are important in speeches. A reader can review a paragraph that he or she did not understand. Listeners have no opportunity for review a live speech. Tell students that they should make sure to repeat important points for emphasis.
3. Explain that students should carefully develop their opening and closing. The opening grabs the audience's attention, and the closing is the part the audience will remember.

Prepare Your Delivery

1. Tell students that they should read their script aloud several times.
2. Explain that eye contact is an important strategy used by good speakers. Tell students to shift their focus to different points in the room in the course of the speech.

Assess the Activity

To evaluate students' delivery, use the **Speaking: Organizing and Delivering an Oral Summary** rubric, p. 267 in ***Professional Development Guidebook.***

Communications Workshop

Delivering a Persuasive Speech

A convincing **persuasive speech** depends on two key elements: strong writing and a powerful delivery. Your words and presentation style must connect with your audience, so use standard grammar and language.

Plan Your Content

After deciding your stance on an issue, choose a logical organization for your speech. Consider building to your strongest point.

Support your opinion. Your persuasive speech will define and support a position. Gather supporting evidence, such as facts, expert opinions, expressions of commonly accepted beliefs, and relevant anecdotes. Evaluate your evidence from your audience's point of view.

Use rhetorical devices. Strengthen the argument by using rhetorical devices, such as repetition, questions, or parallel structure. Choose words carefully, paying attention to both their sound and connotations. Work to appeal to your audience's emotions and beliefs.

Focus on your opening and closing. Your introduction needs to grab your audience's attention. Your conclusion should summarize your points in a memorable way. Use techniques such as quotations and anecdotes to develop your introduction and conclusion.

Prepare Your Delivery

Once you have written your speech, plan how you will present it.

Prepare a reader's script. Look at the sample and mark a copy of your speech to show words you will emphasize and places you will pause. Slow down to stress key statements; speed up to emphasize emotion. Use a casual tone when telling a personal anecdote. Use a serious tone when quoting an expert.

SAMPLE READER'S SCRIPT

start gradually
The plans for the new park at Elm Street call for a baseball field, ‖ a playground, ‖ and a big lawn. It sounds great, but it could be *energetic* better.

There is one thing missing: ‖ dogs! ‖ We need a dog run. We do not have a *slower* single public dog run in our city.

‖ = pause

Establish eye contact. Keep your audience interested by making eye contact as often as possible. Practice reading your speech so that the words are familiar to you.

Activity: Deliver a Persuasive Speech

Choose a topic that has two sides. Organize a presentation in which you take a stand. Practice your speech in front of a classmate. Revise your presentation and then deliver the speech for your class.

Differentiated Instruction for Universal Access

Strategy for Special Needs Students
Students may have difficulty with the delivery of a speech. After students have developed their readers' scripts, have them practice with partners. Instruct them to mark places in their speeches where they stumble. Explain that this portion of the speech may need to be revised if additional practice does not make it easier. As they work, circulate to offer advice and additional instruction.

Strategy for Advanced Readers
Tell students that the best public speakers do not read from scripts. Instead, they use them as guides. To discourage script reading, help students develop note cards for their presentations. First, ask students to create outlines of their presentations. The outline should include main ideas, as well as any details that may be difficult to remember. Next, have students transfer the outline onto note cards. Each index card should focus on one point.

Independent Reading

What kind of *knowledge* changes our lives?

Night
Elie Wiesel
Prentice Hall, 2000

For ten years after the Holocaust, Elie Wiesel was too tormented by what he had seen and experienced to tell his story. *Night* is the true story of what happened to him as a fifteen year old boy who was sent to a concentration camp. As the young Elie's knowledge of despair and survival evolves, so will yours.

One Day in the Life of Ivan Denisovich
Alexander Solzhenitsyn
Signet, 1974

Alexander Solzhenitsyn was imprisoned for eight years for allegedly making a disrespectful remark about Stalin. This fictional story, based on the author's own days in Soviet prison, presents a vivid picture of one day in the life of a wrongfully convicted man. Ivan Denisovich's struggle to survive shows readers the great potential of the human spirit.

Immigrant Voices
Twenty-four Narratives on Becoming an American
Edited by Gordon Hutner
Signet, 1999

This compelling collection of real-life stories of immigrants shows America through many different lenses. See the experience of becoming American through the eyes of a female doctor from Germany forbidden to practice or a man from India struggling to become a writer. Their stories, among others, redefine what it means to be an American.

Touch the Top of the World
Erik Weihenmayer
Plume, 2002

Reaching the summit of Everest was Erik Weihenmayer's dream. Read this true story of a blind man's quest to climb the highest mountain peaks in the world, and find out what can happen when you understand your true potential.

Narrative of the Life of Frederick Douglass
Frederick Douglass
Signet, 1968

If learning to read and write was a crime punishable by death, would you do it? Frederick Douglass, born into a life of slavery, took this terrifying risk. This is the autobiographical story of a man who survived the inhumanity of slavery and courageously beat the odds to become a writer and a leader.

Today's Nonfiction
Prentice Hall, 1999

This collection of real-life stories brings together different styles and different cultures to share real-world knowledge and insight. From Ernesto Galarza's story of learning English in school to Joan Didion's description of her visit to Pearl Harbor, each piece of writing vividly captures a moment in life as unique as it is universal.

Consult your teacher before choosing a title.

Planning Students' Further Reading

Have students choose a book for independent reading from those listed. Before recommending a work, preview it, taking into account the values of your community as well as the maturity of your students. The following notes offer some guidance. Because a variety of factors play a role in determining the accessibility of a work, a book with a higher readability rating may be deemed more accessible than a book with a lower rating.

L1 ***Night*** The book chronicles anti-Semitism and the enslavement, oppression, and genocide of European Jews during World War II, as well as the author's temporary loss of faith. Sexual abuse is also touched on, and offensive language is used.
Lexile: 590

L2 ***One Day in the Life of Ivan Denisovich*** Throughout this novel, Solzhenitsyn graphically portrays life at a Soviet labor camp in the 1950s. Some readers might be offended by the profanity used by the characters and by the inhumane, unsanitary conditions they live in. Also, the prisoners frequently mention tobacco and smoking.
Lexile: 900

L3 ***Immigrant Voices: Twenty-four Narratives on Becoming an American*** No sensitivity issues.
Level suitable for high school students

L2 ***Touch the Top of the World*** The book includes strong language and brief descriptions of gambling and spouse abuse. Some students may be upset by the sudden death of a parent and by the author's onset of blindness.
Level suitable for high school students

L4 ***Narrative of the Life of Frederick Douglass*** The narrative contains many disturbing images of slavery and language that is racially offensive.
Lexile: 1080L

L3 ***Today's Nonfiction*** Students may be disturbed by issues of racism and prejudice toward people with disabilities in *I Know Why the Caged Bird Sings*. In *Survival in Auschwitz*, sensitive issues include hatred, torture, and genocide.
Level suitable for high school students

Connecting to the Big Question

Have students form literature circles in which to discuss the books they read independently. See *Professional Development Guidebook*, pp. 47–49, for guidance in running literature circles.

Suggest that students discuss these questions:

- Do the characters acquire knowledge themselves or pass it on to others?
- Is it necessary just to receive knowledge for it to change our lives or must that knowledge be acted upon?

Challenge

The following titles for advanced readers are available in the Penguin Literature Library.

***The Awakening and Selected Stories* by Kate Chopin** The book's stories deal with adultery, derogatory racial references and the rejection of a baby because of its color.

***Silent Spring* by Rachel Carson** The depiction of environmental devastation may disturb some students.

MONITORING PROGRESS

Using the Unit Review

In this Test Practice workshop (pp. 618–623), students apply the skills in Unit 3. The practice is divided into four sections.

1. Before assigning each section, review the relevant Unit skills with students.
2. Set a time limit for the multiple choice items in each section, allowing a little over one minute per question. Allow ten to fifteen minutes for any Writing for Assessment questions.
3. Administer each section. Have students write the starting time at the top of their papers. When half the time for the multiple choice items has run out, ask students to write the time next to an answer on which they are working. Have them do the same when time is three quarters through and again when time is up. Have them note the start and end times for any Writing for Assessment questions as well.
4. Review with students the pacing reflected in their notes.

Reteaching Skills

1. For each practice, use the Reteach chart on the same page as the answers to determine which skills require reteaching, based on which items students answered incorrectly.
2. Reteach these skills prior to assigning the **Benchmark Test** for the second half of Unit 3 (***Unit 3 Resources***, pp. 226–231).

Test Practice: Unit 3 Review

I. Literary Skills

Directions: *Read the passage. Then, answer each question that follows.*

Playing the Piano

You have heard it before: practice, practice, practice! Whether it is kicking a soccer ball, shooting hoops, or playing the piano, practice makes perfect. My parents sincerely believed that.

When I was nine years old, they bought a second-hand piano, hoping that my older sister would become the musical genius of our family. Unfortunately (or fortunately) she had about as much musical talent as I had athletic talent—in other words, zilch. On the other hand, I thought the piano wasn't the worst thing ever. I was intrigued that simply by pressing the right "buttons," you could make a song. I begged my parents for piano lessons. They agreed, on the condition that I vow to practice every day. I promised. I was excited. My music teacher told me I had "promise."

At first, I practiced every day. My parents marveled at my budding genius. My practice filled the house with heavenly music every day. Everyone but my sister thought I was wonderful. Gradually, the novelty of the piano and the praise grew stale. I still loved the piano, and I still loved to play—when I was in the mood. When spring came, I would rather be out riding my bike. When summer came, I would rather go to the beach. When fall came, I would rather be downloading music online.

So it went. Gradually, the praise stopped and the nagging started: "Have you practiced piano today?" Finally, the piano lessons were stopped. I didn't mind. I enjoyed the free time, and I still played the piano when I felt like it.

There is a moral to this story, of course: practice. Why? There are many reasons, but becoming a superstar is not necessarily one of them. With a physical skill, remember that muscles have "memories." Once you master a skill, such as biking, you never lose it. Even if the skill is more complex, such as playing a musical instrument, which requires both physical motor skills and mental skills, you never lose it. I have not played the piano for years, but I can still pick out a tune, and I can still read music. I still love the piano—and I love to bike-ride, too. So if there is something you enjoy doing, practice until you have mastered it. Then you will always have it. You may get rusty, but the skills will remain with you to enrich, expand, and enhance the rest of your life.

Strategies for Test Taking

Remind students to use their time wisely. Careful time management is especially important when taking long tests such as this unit review. Caution them that, if they cannot answer a question after spending a reasonable amount of time on it, they should skip the question and move on to the next one. They can always return to troublesome questions after they have completed all the others, assuming time remains. Point out that they must be sure to leave blank the answer space for the question that they skipped. Doing so ensures that they place other answers in the correct spots.

1. The second paragraph of this passage is an example of which type of **essay** writing?
   A. narrative
   B. persuasive
   C. humorous
   D. expository

2. The following passage is an example of which **persuasive** or **rhetorical device**?
   When spring came, I would rather be out riding my bike. When summer came, I would rather go to the beach. When fall came, I would rather be downloading music online.
   A. rhetorical question
   B. appeal to logic
   C. parallelism
   D. appeal to emotion

3. What best describes the **author's purpose**?
   A. to persuade readers to practice to become superstars
   B. to describe how it feels to practice
   C. to analyze the effect of practice
   D. to persuade readers to practice something they enjoy

4. Which sentence from the passage contains an example of **understatement**?
   A. My parents sincerely believed that.
   B. On the other hand, I thought the piano wasn't the worst thing ever.
   C. My parents marveled at my budding genius.
   D. There is a moral to this story of course: practice.

5. Which paragraph contains a **rhetorical question**?
   A. paragraph 2
   B. paragraph 3
   C. paragraph 4
   D. paragraph 5

6. Which of the following sentences from the passage contains **hyperbole**?
   A. I begged my parents for piano lessons.
   B. My practice filled the house with heavenly music every day.
   C. Gradually, the novelty of the piano and the praise grew stale.
   D. Finally, the piano lessons were stopped.

7. This passage reflects elements of which types of **essays**?
   A. analytic, persuasive
   B. reflective, humorous
   C. persuasive, humorous
   D. expository, reflective

8. **Vocabulary in Context** Which is the closest definition of the underlined word *intrigued*?
   A. confused by
   B. frightened by
   C. attracted by
   D. angered by

9. With which of the following statements might the author agree?
   A. You should practice until you are perfect.
   B. An athlete should always strive to be the best in the world.
   C. Becoming skilled in a wide variety of activities is better than being perfect in one.
   D. Practicing daily makes you a better person.

Writing for Assessment

10. Write a brief essay to explain whether you agree or disagree with the author's "moral." Use **details** from the passage to **support** your argument.

GO ON

ASSESS

Answers

Answers With Explanations

1. C—Use of understatement and hyperbole provide humor. *Incorrect answers:* A—While the paragraph has narration, the overall effect is humorous. B—In this paragraph, the author is not trying to convince the reader. D—The author humorously recounts past experiences.
2. C—Each sentence has a similarly worded introductory phrase and independent clause. *Incorrect answers:* A—The author asks no questions in this passage. B—The author does not appeal to reason here. D—The author does not appeal to emotion here.
3. D—The persuasive purpose appears at the end. *Incorrect answers:* A—The author does not see stardom as the aim of practice. B—The author spends much space talking about not practicing. C—While the author discusses personal gains from practicing the piano, the essay's thrust is its moral.
4. B—The phrase downplays the interest the author took in the piano. *Incorrect answers:* A—This phrase seems to honestly depict the parents' beliefs. C—This sentence uses hyperbole. D—This sentence states the essay's message.
5. D—The rhetorical question is "Why?" *Incorrect answers:* A—The paragraph has no questions. B—same explanation as for A. C—same explanation as for A.
6. B—Calling the music "heavenly" is exaggeration. *Incorrect answers:* A—Begged seems accurate rather than exaggerated. C—Stale seems accurate rather than exaggerated. D—Stopped seems accurate rather than exaggerated.
7. C—The humorous tone helps support the persuasive purpose. *Incorrect answers:* A—The author does not analyze an issue deeply. B—While the author does reflect on past experience, the purpose is to persuade. D—The author's purpose is to move the reader to act.
8. C—The author was attracted by the sound of the piano. *Incorrect answers:* A—The author was clear in his or her desire to play. B—The author was drawn to the piano,

Answers continued

not away from it. D—The author found the piano appealing.

9. C—The author would probably agree that having many interests would be valuable. *Incorrect answers:* A—The author rejects the importance of attaining perfection. B—same explanation as for A. D—The author does not insist on practicing every day.

Writing for Assessment

10. Students' essays should agree or disagree with the author, using details from the essay in support. Students may suggest that practice is important in all areas of their lives or they may think that practicing at something that you won't use regularly is a waste of effort and time.

Reteach

Question	Instructional Pages to Reteach
1	518
2	539
3	584
4	518
5	539
6	518
7	447, 518
9	—
10	555

ASSESS

Answers

Answers With Explanations

1. **A**—To make a smoothie, you must first place the base on the counter. *Incorrect answers:* B—The suction cups are placed on the base only before the machine is used for the first time. C—The machine is readied before the ingredients are. D—The machine is plugged in only after it is fully assembled.
2. **C**—The direction states that careful handling is needed "to avoid injury." *Incorrect answers:* A—The cost of the blade is not mentioned. B—This is not a reason to handle it carefully. D—The text says nothing about contamination.
3. **B**—Skimming would reveal the steps. *Incorrect answers:* A—It would be better to read the article carefully to learn these facts. C—same explanation as for A. D—same explanation as for A.
4. **B**—Other parts are put together with the blade. *Incorrect answers:* A—The *assembly* is an object, not a condition. C—The whole smoothie maker is a machine. D—This term is synonymous with *machine*, not *assembly*.
5. **C**—This is the correct sequence, according to the third set of steps. *Incorrect answers:* A—This action occurs before the machine is plugged in. C—The blade assembly is unscrewed after the smoothie is made, and after the machine is plugged in. D—same explanation as for A.
6. **B**—A scan would show that the passage follows a step-by-step approach. *Incorrect answers:* A—The author is not trying to persuade the reader to adopt a point of view. C—The passage is nonfiction, not fiction. D—The passage does not analyze the effects of the process.

Reteach

Question	Instructional Pages to Reteach
1	512
2	512
3	578
5	512
6	578

II. Informational Reading Skills

Directions: *Read the passage. Then, answer each question that follows.*

Using the Easy Smoothie Maker

Now create a nutritious, energy-packed smoothie in just a few seconds.

Read Safety Precautions Before Operation

- Do not immerse cord or base in water.
- Operate only on a clean, flat surface.
- Handle the cutting blade carefully to avoid injury.

Before beginning—

- Wash blade assembly and the cup in warm soapy water before using.
- Firmly place the four rubber suction cups on the feet of the base.

To create your own delicious smoothie–

1) Place the base on the counter, pressing firmly to secure the suction cups.

- Make sure the counter is free of water or grease.
- Do NOT plug in the Easy Smoothie until it is completely assembled.

2) Place ingredients in Smoothie Cup and screw on cutting blade.

- Place the solid ingredients in the cup, and then add milk or yogurt.
- Screw the cutting blade <u>assembly</u> on top of the filled Smoothie Cup.

3) Set the filled Smoothie Cup on base and engage the motor.

- Turn the cup over and place on the base, clicking it into place.
- Plug in the Smoothie base and press the "on" button for 10 seconds.
- Remove the cup from the base, unscrew the blade assembly, and enjoy!

1. Which of the following parts should you handle first when making a smoothie?

A. the base assembly
B. the suction cups
C. milk or yogurt
D. the plug

2. Why should you handle the blade carefully?

A. It is worth a lot of money.
B. It can be difficult to replace if you lose it.
C. It is very sharp and can cause injuries.
D. It can contaminate the cup's ingredients.

3. By **skimming** the article, one could learn—

A. the dangers of improper appliance use.
B. the steps for making a smoothie.
C. how to care for the appliance.
D. recipes for smoothies.

4. Vocabulary in Context The word *assembly* most nearly means—

A. the condition of being put together.
B. a set of parts that have been put together.
C. a machine.
D. an appliance.

Differentiated Instruction for Universal Access

Strategy for Less Proficient Readers
Review skills and warm up for the test by walking students through item 1. Ask a volunteer to read item 1 aloud. Call on students to state the key requirements for a correct answer. (The answer should be the first part of the machine a person touches when making a smoothie.) Next, guide students in eliminating incorrect choices.

- A—Step 1 clearly states that placing the base on a counter is the first action.
- B—The suction cups are placed on the base only once; after they are in position, they need not be touched again. (Eliminate.)
- C—The question asks for "which parts" you handle; milk or yogurt are ingredients, not parts. (Eliminate.)
- D—The plug appears later in the process. (Eliminate.)

Guide students in seeing that **A** is the best choice. Have them complete the remaining items, encouraging them to apply a similar strategy to each. First, define key terms in the prompt and then eliminate incorrect choices.

5. According to the directions, when should the Smoothie Maker be plugged in?

A. before adding the ingredients
B. after unscrewing the blade assembly
C. before screwing on the cutting blade
D. after placing the filled cup on the base

6. **Scanning** this passage reveals that this is what type of writing?

A. persuasive essay
B. technical directions
C. narrative short story
D. cause-and-effect essay

III. Vocabulary

Directions: *Read each question. Then, choose the best answer.*

1. Which pair of words are **synonyms**?

A. evolve, adapt
B. reflect, deflect
C. modify, maintain
D. growth, healthiness

2. Which of the following is the closest **synonym** of *understanding*?

A. accepting
B. mistaken
C. ignorant
D. discordant

3. Which sentence uses a **synonym** of the word *empathy*?

A. His pride in his sister's victory was clear.
B. All the children valued the nurse's patience.
C. I felt compassion for Jon when he was hurt.
D. My bravery was tested when I had surgery.

4. Which of the following is the closest **synonym** of *adapt*?

A. adjust
B. revise
C. restore
D. disturb

5. Which pair of words are **antonyms**?

A. growth, change
B. history, past
C. awareness, obliviousness
D. misunderstanding, confusion

6. Which pair of words are **antonyms**?

A. supported, helped
B. altered, changed
C. modified, preserved
D. enlightened, inspired

7. Which sentence uses an **antonym** of the word *ignorance*?

A. Sarah is known for her empathy.
B. Paolo prides himself on his enlightenment.
C. It can be difficult to achieve insight.
D. Anton is willing to reach a compromise.

8. Which of the following is an **antonym** of the word *growth*?

A. change
B. development
C. decrease
D. advancement

GO ON

Reteach

Question	Instructional Pages to Reteach
1	442–443
2	442–443
3	442–443
4	442–443
5	442–443
6	442–443
7	442–443
8	442–443

ASSESS

Answers

Answers with Explanations

1. **A**—Something that evolves will be adapting to changing circumstances. *Incorrect answers:* B—The two words are antonyms, not synonyms. C—same explanation as for B. D—Growth can be the result of unhealthiness as well as healthiness. For instance, a cancer can grow.
2. **A**—Someone who understands something accepts it as true. *IIncorrect answers:* B—To understand is to comprehend or see the truth; mistaken means "to be incorrect." C—Being ignorant means being without understanding. D—Being discordant means being out of tune with others, not understanding them.
3. **C**—*Compassion* and *empathy* are synonyms. *Incorrect answers:* A—*Pride* means "a feeling of satisfaction," which is not the same as *empathy*. B—*Valued* means "treasured" or "saw the merit in," which is not the same as *empathy*. D—*Bravery* means "courage," which is not the same as *empathy*.
4. **A**—Something that adapts is adjusting to changing circumstances. *Incorrect answers:* B—Revising can be carried out by another agent separate from the thing being revised; a living thing adapts on its own. C—*Adapting* refers to changing to fit new circumstances, not returning to an original state. D—Something adapting might have cause a disturbance, but that is not the meaning of *adapt* itself.
5. **C**—*Awareness* means "cognizance of something"; *obliviousness* means "ignoring something." *Incorrect answers:* A—Growth is a kind of change. B—History is the record of the past. D—These words are synonyms confusion.
6. **C**—Something modified is changed; something preserved is unchanged. *Incorrect answers:* A—These words are synonyms. B—same explanation as for A. D—These words are unrelated to each other.
7. **B**—Enlightenment is the opposite of ignorance. *Incorrect answers:* A—Ignorance has to do with knowledge, and empathy with

Answers continued

feelings. C—Ignorance has to do with knowledge, often of facts; insight has to do with understanding. D—A compromise is a settlement to a disagreement, which has no relation to ignorance.

8. **C**—*Grow* means "to get larger"; decrease means "to get smaller." *Incorrect answers:* A—Growth is a kind of change. B—Growth can take place along with development. D—Growth can take place along with advancement.

ASSESS

Answers

Answers With Explanations

1. **C**—The author of the letter does not give his own address, so the editor-in-chief would not know where to send a response. *Incorrect answers:* A—Item 3 is the greeting. C—Item 13 is the closing. D—Item 1 is the date.
2. **B**—The author calmly and reasonably lays out the problem and the proposed solution. *Incorrect answers:* A—The author may be angry, but that tone does not appear. C—The author does not reveal fears, but frustration. D—The tone does not show these deep negative emotions.
3. **D**—Combining these two sentences would make the ending less choppy. *Incorrect answers:* A—These two long sentences are best left separate. B—These two sentences express distinct ideas that are better left separate. D—same explanation as for B.
4. **A**—Such words as *protest, citizens, options,* and *alternative* show a formal tone. *Incorrect answers:* B—The author avoids informal language. C—The author does not write sarcastically, but in a straightforward way. D—The author does not use emotionally charged language.
5. **D**—Given the imperative purpose of the sentence, the verb *write* should come near the beginning. *Incorrect answers:* A—This inverted sentence structure is awkward. B—This use of the passive voice is awkward. C—This version lacks a verb, making it a sentence fragment.

Reteach

Question	Instructional Pages to Reteach
1	536
2	533
3	535
4	533
5	—

IV. Writing and Language Conventions

Persuasion: Letter to the Editor

Directions: *Read the passage. Then, answer each question that follows.*

(1) October 9, 2008

(2) Editor-in-Chief
The Sentinel Dispatch
700 Viewmont Street
Sentinel, South Dakota 96501

(3) Dear Editor-in-Chief:

(4) The school board of Sentinel High School has cut funds for after-school music programs. (5) I am writing to protest this action and to ask citizens of Sentinel to write to the school board to protest this as well.

(6) Students need options. (7) Music programs should receive as much funding as sports programs. (8) For students who are not athletic, music is an alternative to athletics. (9) All students should receive opportunities. (10) Please to the school board write. (11) Ask them not to cut funds.

(13) Sincerely,
Damon Fitzgerald

1. What section needs to be added to this letter?

A. greeting
B. closing
C. return address
D. date

2. The author's **tone** can best be described as—

A. angry and disappointed.
B. calm and reasonable.
C. fearful and anxious.
D. enraged and bitter.

3. Which sentences should be **combined**?

A. sentences 4 and 5
B. sentences 6 and 7
C. sentences 8 and 9
D. sentences 11 and 12

4. The author of this letter uses ____ language.

A. formal
B. informal
C. sarcastic
D. emotional

5. What is the correct way to revise sentence 10?

A. To the school board write please.
B. The school board please be written to.
C. Writing to the school board please.
D. Please write to the school board.

Differentiated Instruction for Universal Access

Strategy for for English Learners
Review skills and warm up for the test by walking students through item 1 on p. 623. Call on students to define fact and opinion. (A fact is a statement that can be proven true or false. An opinion expresses a belief or position.) Next, guide students in eliminating incorrect choices based on key words.

- **A**—The word *should* signals that this statement is an opinion. (Eliminate.)
- **B**—The sentence takes a position on the length of the school year. (Eliminate.)
- **C**—This sentence makes an assertion that can be proven true or false.
- **D**—The sentence takes a position on the length of the school year. (Eliminate.)

Guide students in seeing that **C** is the best choice. Have them complete the remaining items, encouraging them to apply a similar strategy to each. First, define key terms in the prompt and then eliminate incorrect choices. Suggest that students create a study list of important terms that might appear on future tests.

Persuasion: Persuasive Essay

Directions: *Read the passage. Then, answer each question that follows.*

(1) Our school district is considering instituting a twelve-month school year. (2) I believe this would create a greatest hardship for many students. (3) I believe this would create a great hardship for their families as well. (4) Many high school students have full-time summer jobs, which they count on for spent money throughout the school year and savings for college. (5) Without full-time summer work, some students may not be able to attend college. (6) While students may work part time during the school year, it is difficult to keep up with work, studies, and what they are obligated to their families for. (7) To do so year-round without a break could be damaging, physically and mentally. (8) Furthermore, many families count on their summer vacation time together. (9) It is true that more material could be covered over a twelve-month period than currently. (10) However, the twelve-month school year could severely harm both students and families.

1. Which of the following is NOT a **statement of opinion**?
   - **A.** Students should work full time in the summer.
   - **B.** A nine-month school year is much too long already.
   - **C.** Without full-time summer work, some students may not be able to attend college.
   - **D.** A twelve-month school year would be a hardship on many students.

2. What should replace "greatest" to correct the **adjective degree** in sentence 2?
   - **A.** great
   - **B.** greater
   - **C.** most great
   - **D.** leave as is

3. What is the correct way to **combine** sentence 2 and sentence 3?
   - **A.** Hardship created for students and families.
   - **B.** I believe this would create a great hardship for many students and their families as well.
   - **C.** I believe this would create student hardships and for their families as well.
   - **D.** Student and family hardships would create.

4. How should sentence 6 be revised to use **parallel** construction?
   - **A.** Delete "studies."
   - **B.** Replace "While students may work part time" with "If students work part time."
   - **C.** Change "what they are obligated to their families for" to "obligations."
   - **D.** Add "and more."

5. What is the most effective subsitution for *spent* in sentence 4?
   - **A.** spending
   - **B.** spend
   - **C.** has spent
   - **D.** spends

Writing for Assessment

6. Choose one selection from Unit 3. **Explain** the persuasive techniques used by the author in the selection. **Support** your answer with **details** from the text.

STOP

ASSESS

Answers

Answers With Explanations

1. C—The statement reflects a reasoned conclusion from stated facts, which could be proven true or false. *Incorrect answers:* A—The sentence states an opinion. B—same explanation as for A. D—same explanation as for A.
2. A—Since the hardship is not being compared to anything else, the simple adjective great suffices. I*Incorrect answers:* B—The hardship is not being compared to anything else; the comparative form does not belong. C—*Most great* is not the correct superlative, and the superlative form does not belong in the sentence. D—The original, using the superlative *greatest* is incorrect.
3. B—This version effectively uses compound objects of the preposition for. *Incorrect answers:* A—The statement is a sentence fragment. C—The phrase *student hardships* is unclear. D—The hardships are the result of the problem, not the subjects; in addition this version lacks an object.
4. C—This change would produce parallel structure in the compound objects of preposition and more concise writing. *Incorrect answers:* A—The problem is with the phrase "what they are obligated to their families for." B—same explanation as for A. D—same explanation as for A.
5. A—The participle form is needed for the adjective here. *Incorrect answers:* B—same explanation as for A. C—same explanation as for A. D—same explanation as for A.

Writing for Assessment

6. Students should scan the Unit 3 selections for review and write essays that analyze the persuasive techniques from the chosen selection. They should look for examples of persuasive language and use these details as support.

Benchmark

Reteach skills as indicated by students' performance, following the Reteach charts on pp. 619–623 to administer the end-of-unit **Benchmark Test** (*Unit 3 Resources,* pp. 226–231). Follow the **Interpretation Guide** for the test (*Unit 3 Resources,* pp. 235–240) to assign reteaching pages as necessary in the *Reading Kit.* Use **Success Tracker** online to automatically assign these pages.

Reteach

Question	Instructional Pages to Reteach
1	606
2	574
3	535
4	609
5	—
6	604–606, 607

PHLit Online!

The **Benchmark Tests** and **Success Tracker** are available online at **www.PHLitOnline.com**

Unit 4 Overview

Unit Genre and Unit Big Question

Explain to students that throughout this unit, they will read and analyze poetry. As they read, they will think about and discuss answers to the Unit Big Question: Does all communication serve a positive purpose?

Students will learn more about the Big Question on pp. 626–627. Then, on pp. 628–637, Cornelius Eady introduces the unit literary genre, poetry, and presents a model poem of his own.

Using the Unit Selections

Teach Skills Instructional selections are presented in leveled pairs. To teach the skills and meet the objectives, you need to complete only one selection in each pairing.

Differentiate and Reinforce Choose the selection in a pairing that is best suited for your students. The selections are listed by accessibility in the Differentiated Instruction box on the next page. You may use the other selection in the pairing to reinforce comprehension and skills or to provide enrichment.

Integrate Skills Each selection pairing presents students with a reading strategy, a literary analysis concept, and a vocabulary skill, as well as vocabulary development opportunities and grammar instruction. In addition, students have opportunities to extend learning in the Writing and extension (Research and Technology or Listening and Speaking) activities.

Unit Features

Informational Texts Students learn to use and evaluate various types of informational texts.

Comparing Literary Works Students compare the use of a literary element in two or more works.

To help you plan your use of the unit, see the Unit Overview and Pacing Plan on pp. 626a–626b and the Time and Resource Manager preceding each selection pairing.

Poetry

THE BIG ?

Does all communication serve a positive purpose?

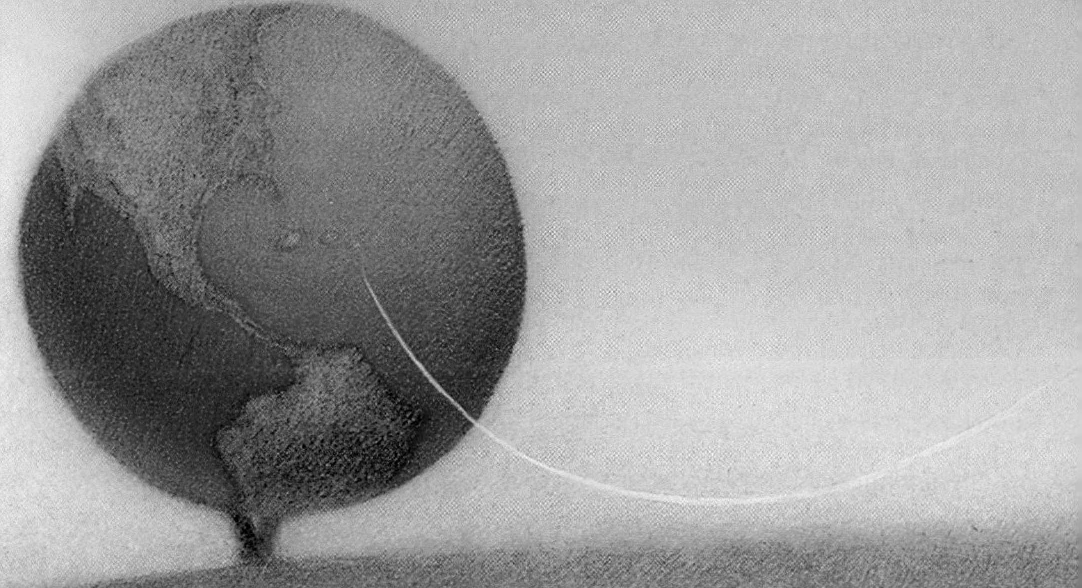

624 Poetry

PHLit Online!

www.PHLitOnline.com

Teaching From Technology

Enriched Online Student Edition
- full narration of selections
- interactive graphic organizers
- linked Get Connected! and Background videos
- all worksheets and other student resources

Professional Development
- the *Professional Development Guidebook* online
- additional professional development articles by program authors

Planning, Assigning, and Monitoring
- software for online assignment of work to students, individually or to the whole class
- a system for tracking and grading students' work

UNIT OVERVIEW AND PACING PLAN

Meeting Your Standards

Students will
1. recognize and appreciate poetry as a literary genre.
2. read and analyze a variety of poems.
3. apply reading skills.
   - Read fluently and adjust reading rate
   - Use punctuation to read fluently
   - Paraphrase by picturing the imagery
   - Break down long sentences to paraphrase
4. analyze literary elements.
   - The speaker in poetry
   - Poetic forms
   - Figurative language
   - Sound devices
5. build vocabulary and vocabulary concepts.
   - Prefixes
   - Roots
   - Suffixes
   - Connotation and denotation
6. learn elements of grammar, mechanics, and usage.
   - Prepositions and prepositional phrases
   - Direct objects
   - Varying sentence patterns
   - Prepositional phrases
   - Infinitives
   - Correcting common usage problems
7. use a recursive writing process to write in a variety of forms.
   - Descriptive essay
   - Analytic response to literature
8. read informational materials.
   - Predict the purpose of a sign and a Web site
   - Synthesize and make generalizations in an atlas and a magazine article
9. compare literary works.
   - Compare tone and mood
   - Compare theme
10. develop research and technology skills.
    - Literary history report
    - Visual arts presentation
11. develop listening and speaking skills.
    - Oral interpretation
    - Poetry reading discussion
    - Deliver an oral interpretation of a literary work

	Week 1					Week 2					Week 3				
	1	2	3	4	5	1	2	3	4	5	1	2	3	4	5
Introduce the Unit Big Question (pp. 626–627).	●														
Introduce the Unit author and the Unit genre, poetry (pp 628–631).	●														
Teach the Model selections (pp. 632–637).	●	●													
Teach one selection from Pairing 1 (pp. 638–669).		●	●	●	●	●									
Teach one selection from Pairing 2 (pp. 670–691).						●	●	●	●						
Complete the Test Practice: Reading (pp. 692–693).									●						
Teach Informational Texts (pp. 694–699).										●					
Teach Comparing Literary Works (pp. 700–707).											●	●			
Have students complete the Writing Workshop (pp. 708–713).										●	●	●	●	●	
Administer **Benchmark Test 7** (***Unit 4 Resources,*** pp. 120–125).														●	
Reteach skills, judging which skills to reteach by evaluating students' performance on **Benchmark Test 7**.															●

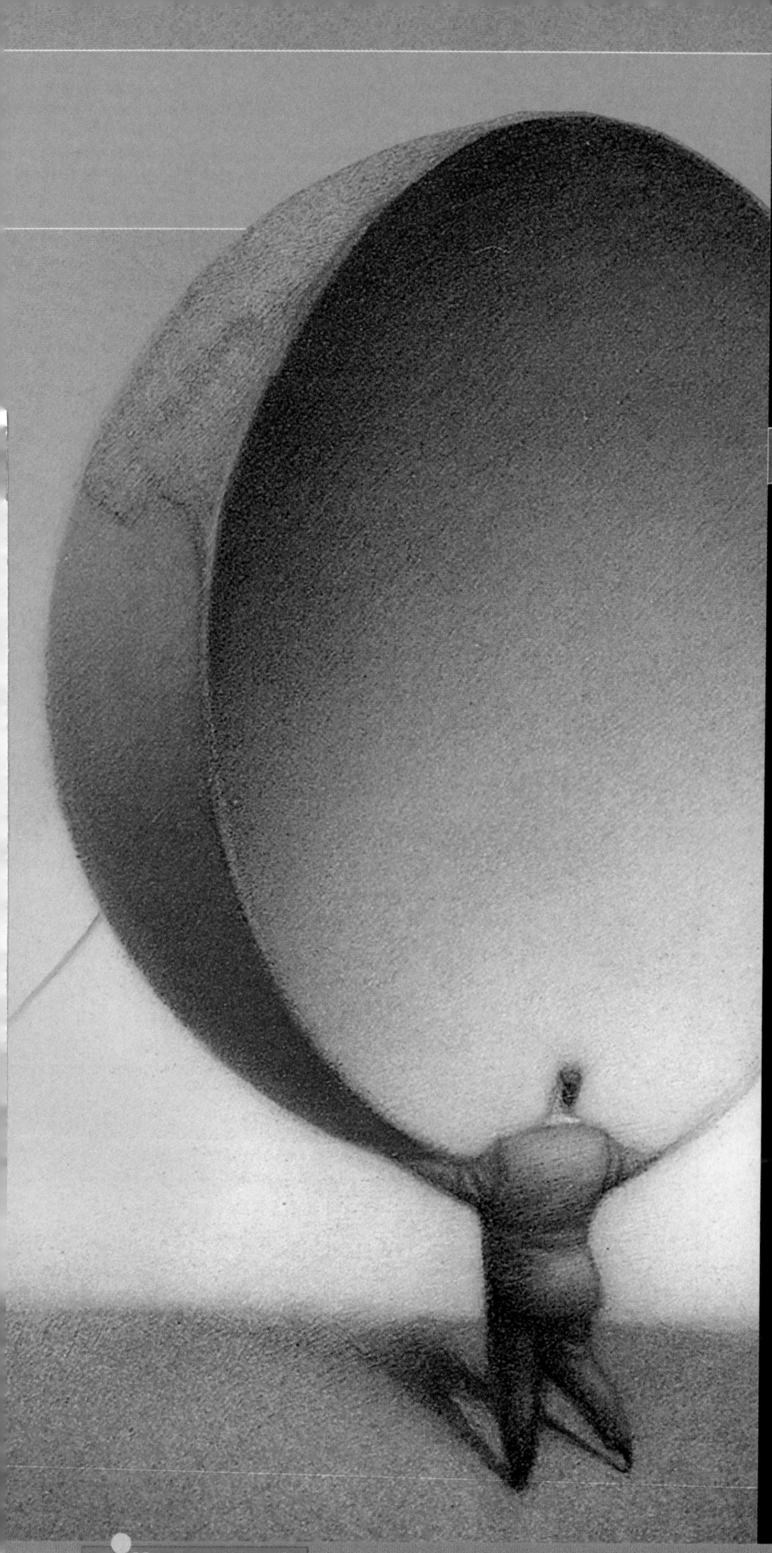

UNIT 4

PHLit Online!

www.PHLitOnline.com

Hear It!
- Selection summary audio
- Selection audio
- BQ Tunes

See It!
- Penguin author video
- Big Question video
- Get Connected videos
- Background videos
- More about the authors
- Illustrated vocabulary words
- Vocabulary flashcards

Do It!
- Interactive journals
- Interactive graphic organizers
- Grammar tutorials
- Interactive vocabulary games
- Test practice

625

Instructional Resources

Unit 4 Resources supports unit skills with pages of the following types:

- **Benchmark Tests** assess and monitor students' progress at mid-unit and at unit's end.
- **Vocabulary and Reading Warm-ups** provide additional vocabulary support, based on Lexile rankings of words, for each selection. **"A" Warm-ups** are for students reading two grades below level. **"B" Warm-ups** are for students reading one grade below level.
- **Selection Support** These practice pages are available for each selection:
  - **Reading Skill**
  - **Literary Analysis**
  - **Writing About the Big Question**
  - **Vocabulary**
  - **Support for Writing**
  - **Support for Extend Your Learning**
  - **Enrichment**

PHLit Online!

All worksheets and other student resources are also available at www.PHLitOnline.com.

Differentiated Instruction for Universal Access

Accessibility for Various Ability Levels

This chart gives a general accessibility rating to help you decide which selection in each leveled pair is more appropriate for your students. **Choose one selection in each pair or choose to teach both.** You will meet the objectives for the pair when you teach either of the two selections. For additional guidance on factors that affect the accessibility of each selection, see the Selection Choices page for each selection set.

	More Accessible	More Challenging
Pair 1	Collection 1	Collection 2
Pair 2	Collection 3	Collection 4
Pair 3	Collection 5	Collection 6
Pair 4	Collection 7	Collection 8

Accessibility for English Learners

EL This icon indicates support for English learners at point of use in this Teacher's Edition.

	Week 4					Week 5					Week 6				
	1	2	3	4	5	1	2	3	4	5	1	2	3	4	5
Teach one selection from Pairing 3 (pp. 714–731).	●	●	●	●											
Teach one selection from Pairing 4 (pp. 732–749).					●	●	●	●							
Complete the Test-Practice: Reading (pp. 750–751).								●							
Teach Informational Texts (pp. 752–757).									●						
Teach Comparing Literary Works (pp. 758–767).										●	●				
Have students complete the Writing Workshop (pp. 768–775).									●	●	●	●	●		
Have students complete Applying the Big Question (pp. 776–777).												●			
Have students complete the Vocabulary and Communications Workshops (pp. 778–779, 780).													●		
Complete the Test Practice: Unit 3 Review (pp. 782–787).													●		
Administer **Benchmark Test 8** (***Unit 4 Resources***, pp. 227–235).														●	
Reteach skills, judging which skills to reteach by evaluating students' performance on **Benchmark Test 8**.															●

Block and Daily Scheduling

The assignments and activities in this Unit planner are organized by week. You may adjust them to your daily or block schedule. The Time and Resource Manager for each selection set gives specific pacing suggestions, or you may use the comprehensive lesson planning support online at **www.PHLitOnline.com.**

Monitoring Progress

Diagnose Each main selection pairing in the Unit contains a more accessible and a more challenging selection. To determine which selection in each pairing to assign, refer to students' results on **Benchmark Test 6, *Unit 3 Resources*,** pp. 227–235 (administered at the end of the previous Unit). Use the **Interpretation Guide** to interpret the results of the diagnostic portion of the test. **Note:** For the most accurate diagnosis of students who score in the middle range, administer the additional diagnostic questions online at **www.PHLitOnline.com.**

Preteach and Prepare As indicated by the diagnostic, prepare students for reading by assigning the **Vocabulary** and **Reading Warm-ups** for the selections you assign.

Teach Follow this Pacing Plan and use the resources to teach the skills and selections. For specific pacing suggestions and a list of resources, see the Time and Resource Manager and the Visual Guide to Featured Selection Resources preceding each selection pairing.

Assess After students have completed the first half of the Unit, administer **Benchmark Test 7**. Administer **Benchmark Test 8** at the end of the Unit.

Intervention and Reteach After administering each test, use the **Interpretation Guide** for the tests to determine which reteaching pages, if any, you should assign from the ***Reading Kit.*** The appropriate pages are also available through the online Progress Monitoring software.

Independent Reading

To differentiate, reinforce, and extend your instruction, have students choose a full-length work from the Independent Reading page, page 781, and read it while working on this Unit. Consult the Sensitivity Issues notes for the page to guide students' choices.

CLASSROOM STRATEGIES

Teaching Online Reading Comprehension **Donald Leu**

> With Internet Reciprocal Teaching, students and teachers teach one another useful strategies to use while reading on the Internet.

Reading comprehension is something we can not see. It happens in the recesses of our mind, hidden from view. How do we make the invisible, visible to our students? This is the central challenge of reading comprehension instruction. The most effective teaching methods make invisible strategies visible (Hacker & Tenent, 2002; Rosenshine & Meister, 1994). Think alouds are one example.

We now face an additional challenge. Continuously new online reading comprehension skills emerge from continuously new technologies. How do we teach something that is so new we are also still learning about it? In this challenge lies an opportunity.

Internet Reciprocal Teaching (IRT)

Internet Reciprocal Teaching (IRT) is based on Reciprocal Teaching principles (See Leu, et. al., in press). With IRT, students and teachers teach one another useful strategies to use while reading on the Internet.

How To Teach? IRT is a three-phase instructional model:

1. Direct instruction of basic computer and Internet use skills (when necessary);
2. Exchange of effective online reading strategies in small groups or whole class contexts;
3. Independent inquiry with the exchange of effective online reading strategies.

What Online Reading Comprehension Skills and Strategies Do We Teach?

- *Which search engine do I use? Why?*
- *How do I read search engine results?*
- *How do I critically evaluate the reliability of a site like* Save the Pacific Northwest Tree Octopus?

The skills and strategies necessary to answer these questions are the new literacy skills of online reading comprehension need to be taught if we want our students to be fully prepared for the 21st century. These skills and strategies include the following: Generating Important Questions; Locating Information; Critically Evaluating Information; Synthesizing Information and Communicating Information. (For a complete description of these skills see Leu, et. al., in press).

Using IRT: Two Examples of Strategy Exchange

Reading Search Engines Results Most students never read search engine results. Instead, they use a "click and look" strategy, clicking on the top result, and looking quickly to see if the site looks promising. Gradually they work their way down the results page, clicking and looking, without reading a single word from the search engine results.

This impedes their ability to quickly locate the information they require.

Here is an IRT strategy to help students learn about reading the results page of a search engine:

1. Select an author you are reading (e.g. John Phillip Santos).
2. Enter that author's name in a search engine and obtain the results page.
3. Print out copies of this search engine results page and distribute it to your class.
4. Have groups or the entire class use the results page to answer these questions: "Which link would you select:
   - to hear John Phillip Santos reading from his works?
   - to hear an interview with John Phillip Santos?
   - to read an essay by John Phillip Santos?"
5. After students provide each correct answer, make certain they explain the strategy they used. Ask, "Tell us how you figured that out?" ("I read the paragraph under each entry and this one said it had audio files of him reading aloud. That probably means he will be reading his work.")
6. Now have the students ask new questions about other items on the same page, e.g., "Which link would you select if you wanted to read about . . . ?" Invite other students to answer these questions and explain their strategies.

The Critical Evaluation of Web Sites We want students to be "healthy skeptics" when they read online. Most are not. Here is an activity that will encourage students to be more critical readers:

1. Locate a spoof site, a site that looks reliable but provides completely false information. Use a search engine and search for "spoof sites." Locate sites such as *Dog Island* (http://www.thedogisland.com/) or *Save the Guinea Worm Foundation* (http://www.deadlysins.com/guineaworm/index.htm).
   Ask students, "Is this site: a) very reliable; b) sort of reliable; or c) not at all reliable? Why do you think so?
2. Have your students work in small groups or work with the whole class to discuss their evaluation of each site. Ask them to also share the reading strategies they used to reach this evaluation. Did they use a search engine to see what others said about this site? Did they go to www.snopes.com to see if it was rated as a bogus site? Develop a list of useful evaluation strategies and post this in your room.

Modeled Strategy

See pp. 629 and 677 for point-of-use notes modeling these strategies.

Teacher Resources

- ***Professional Development Guidebook***
- ***Classroom Strategies and Teaching Routines* cards**

PHLit Online!

Log on as a teacher at **www.PHLitOnline.com** to access a library of all Professional Development articles by the Contributing Authors of Pearson Prentice Hall *Literature*.

Donald J. Leu, Ph.D.

Donald J. Leu, Ph.D. is the Neag Endowed Chair in Literacy and Technology at the University of Connecticut and co-directs the New Literacies Research Lab. He is a member of the Reading Hall of Fame, former President of the National Reading Conference, and a member of the International Reading Association Board of Directors.

Supporting Research

Hacker, D. J., Tenent, A. (2002). Implementing reciprocal teaching in the classroom: Overcoming obstacles and making modifications. *Journal of Educational Psychology*, 94, 699–718.

International Reading Association. (2001). *Integrating literacy and technology in the curriculum: A position statement of the International Reading Association*. Newark, DE: Author.

Leu, D. J., Coiro, J., Castek, J., Hartman, D., Henry, L.A., & Reinking, D. (in press). Research on instruction and assessment in the new literacies of online reading comprehension. In Cathy Collins Block, Sherri Parris, & Peter Afflerbach (Eds.). *Comprehension instruction: Research-based best practices*. New York: Guilford Press.

Rosenshine, B., & Meister, C. (1994). Reciprocal teaching: A review of the research. *Review of Educational Research*, 64, 479–530.

INTRODUCE

Introducing the Big Question

1. Give examples of both positive and negative communication, such as a love letter or "Dear John" letter enumerating the reasons for breaking up with someone.
2. Call on students to give their own examples of different forms of communication.
3. **Ask** students the Big Question: "Does all communication serve a positive purpose?" **Possible responses:** Yes. Even criticism is positive because it conveys someone's honest opinion. No. Gossip and slander are only meant to hurt people.
4. Tell students that the readings in this unit explore different purposes of communication. As they read, have students consider the insights they gain about communication.

Introducing the Big Question Vocabulary

1. Point out the Big Question Vocabulary on the facing page. Explain that these words are useful in discussing the Big Question.
2. Review the meaning of each word. (Definitions appear in the teacher edition on p. 627.)
3. Have students complete the **Big Question Vocabulary** worksheets, *Unit 5 Resources,* pp. 1–3.

Write What You Know

1. Review the assignment with students, using the instruction on the student page.
2. Emphasize that communication shared for positive purposes may, in fact, produce negative effects. The opposite is also true.
3. Have students discuss reasons people have for communicating and whether all communication is intended to be positive.

PHLit Online!

Show the Big Question video, at **www.PHLitOnline.com.**

Introducing the Big Question

Does all *communication* serve a positive purpose?

Communication, the act of exchanging information, can take on many forms: it can be **verbal,** visual, or auditory. For example, people may **convey** ideas and **emotion** using **language,** creating a painting, or playing music. People communicate for various reasons. If a person feels as though he or she is in **isolation,** communicating can help him or her make a **connection** or **interact** with others. Communication allows you to provide an **explanation** about an issue or can help clarify a source of **confusion.** Communication is not always positive, however, and can lead to problems when words are taken out of **context** or are misinterpreted. Words can also be used as weapons to hurt other people.

Start thinking about the Big Question by identifying why people communicate with each other.

Discuss It

Write What You Know

Make a list of the different reasons for communicating that you have experienced, heard about, or read about. Describe one specific example of each of the following categories.

- Informing people of a problem or an important issue
- Using art or music as a form of **self-expression**
- Clearing up a misunderstanding
- Understanding the feelings and experiences of others
- Telling a new story or present an old story in a new way
- Passing along the latest gossip to a friend

Share your examples with a partner. Talk about the reasons that someone would communicate in each of these situations and whether the communication would have a positive or negative effect.

PHLit Online!
www.PHLitOnline.com
- Big Question video
- Illustrated vocabulary words
- Interactive vocabulary games
- BQ Tunes

Understanding by Design

The Big Question

Explain to students that they will continue to consider the Big Question as they work through the unit.

- At the beginning of each selection, they will write a response to a Writing About the Big Question sentence starter.
- As they read the selection, they will look for details related to the Big Question.
- At the end of the selection, they will answer a Critical Thinking question that is related to the Big Question.
- At the end of Unit 4, they will complete an Applying the Big Question workshop (pp. 776–777). In the workshop, they will review literature in the unit and think about real-world examples that shed light on the Big Question. They will also have a chance to reflect on their first answers, thinking about how their ideas have changed.
- Tell students that their goal will be to gain a deeper understanding of literature and a more sophisticated way of discussing the Big Question.

Explain What You Know

Use the examples and ideas you discussed with your partner to help you complete these sentences about communication.

- Communicating about your feelings can make an impact on people because ________________. Responses might be positive when ________________ or negative when ________________.
- When two people are in a disagreement, communication might help because ________________. It could also make the situation worse when ________________.
- Telling stories, orally or in writing, is an important form of communication because ________________.

Share your responses with a partner.

Tell What You Think

Based on the discussions you have had, decide what you think right now. Your answer may change as you read the selections in this unit. Choose one of these responses to the Big Question or write one of your own:

- ❑ All communication serves a positive purpose.
- ❑ All communication does not serve a positive purpose.

Use one or more of these sentences, or your own ideas, to write a brief support of your response.

- Communicating about ________________ can reach many people and prompt them to think about ________________.
- People communicate harmful information when ________________.
- We depend on communication to help us ________________.

Discuss your response with a partner or a small group.

Connecting to the Literature

The readings in this unit will help you think about communication and the different purposes it can serve. Each reading will give you an insight into the Big Question. At the end of the unit, you will see how your ideas have grown and changed.

☆ shows an **Academic Vocabulary** word.

Big Question Vocabulary

confusion
connection
☆ context
☆ convey
☆ discourse
emotion
☆ explanation
☆ interact
☆ isolation
language
☆ meaning
☆ misinterpret
☆ respond
self-expression
verbal

Explain What You Know

1. Introduce the assignment, using the instruction on the student page.
2. Have students review their answers to the sentence starters. As needed, review definitions of Big Question Vocabulary and clarify meanings.
3. Guide students to complete the sentence starters by thinking of relevant examples of each point they make. Have students share and compare their responses with partners.

Tell What You Think

1. Introduce the assignment. Have students review the discussions they had with their partners and to consider the ideas that were expressed. Then ask whether or not they believe that all communication serves a positive purpose. Have students mark their page with their answers.
2. Tell students to write a paragraph to support their opinions. Encourage them to complete the sentence starters to help them write their opinions.
3. As students write, remind them to give examples from previous discussions or activities that support their points of view.
4. Call on volunteers to share their responses with the class.

Connecting to the Literature

Explain the structure of the Big Question strand in the unit, referring to the Understanding by Design box on the previous page.

Big Question Vocabulary

confusion (kən fyo͞o zhən) *n.* a state of disorder or distraction
connection (kə nek′ shən) *n.* a relationship between things
context* (kän′ tekst′) *n.* the circumstances that form the setting of an event
convey* (kən vā′) *v.* to communicate or make known
discourse* (dis′ kors) *n.* an ongoing communication of ideas and information
emotion (ē mō′ shən) *n.* a strong feeling, such as love
explanation* (eks′plə nā′ shən) *n.* something that makes clear
interact* (in′tər akt′) *v.* to act on one another
isolation* (ī′sə lā′ shən) *n.* being alone or set apart
language (laŋ′gwij) *n.* a system used for expressing or communicating
meaning* (mē niŋ) *n.* the significance of something
misinterpret* (mis in tʉr′ prət) *v.* to not understand correctly
respond* (ri spänd′) *v.* to answer
self-expression (self ek spresh′ ən) *n.* sharing one's personality or emotions
verbal (vʉr′bəl) *adj.* relating to words

Meeting Your Standards

Students will

1. understand the characteristics and types of poetry.
2. learn about poet Cornelius Eady.
3. read and analyze two poems.
4. relate visuals to poetry.

❶ THE BIG ? **Does all communication serve a positive purpose?**

Remind students that they will think more about the Unit Big Question as they read and discuss the poetry in Unit 4.

❷ What Is Poetry?

Introduce Cornelius Eady

1. Eady's poems are emotional and experiential. He has won many prizes, including an Obie award for best musical score.
2. Use the *See It!* DVD to introduce the author and the genre. Show Segments 1 and 2 to provide insights into why Cornelius Eady became a poet. After students have watched the segments, **ask:** How have music and drama influenced Eady?
   Answer: Both have made him aware of the force and rhythm of language.
3. Interested students might enjoy *Autobiography of a Jukebox*, more than forty poems by Cornelius Eady. (We recommend that you preview it before recommending it to students.)

Introduce Poetry

1. Explore students' prior knowledge of the elements of poetry. Prompt them to recognize that poetry differs from other types of writing in its appearance, use of language, and sound.
2. Have students read Cornelius Eady's discussion of poetry.

Introduction: Poetry

THE BIG ?

❶ **Does all *communication* serve a positive purpose?**

Poetry can communicate to a broad audience.

PHLit Online!
www.PHLitOnline.com

- Penguin author video
- Interactive journals
- Interactive graphic organizers
- Selection audio
- Self-test

What Is Poetry? ❷

by Cornelius Eady

When I was in high school, the first poets whose work I encountered were the ones I was assigned to read: Robert Frost, Gwendolyn Brooks, William Carlos Williams, and Langston Hughes.

In the **poetry** I wrote myself, I imitated some of these poets and songs I heard on the radio by using regular rhythms and rhymes.

❸ Jazz Helped Me Understand Poetry

Then, when I was in my late teens or maybe my early twenties, I had a great epiphany, or sudden insight, that helped me understand what poetry could express.

I had been lucky enough to get a scholarship to a summer poetry workshop in Rochester, New York, run by the well-known black poet Michael S. Harper. One day, Harper read his poem "Brother John" while also playing a tape of saxophonist John Coltrane's *A Love Supreme.*

Suddenly, I understood what Harper was getting at—that jazz is a language, that when a musician is doing a solo, he is telling you a story. He's telling you where he is from and what he knows. It took me a few more years to work out the implications of that idea for my own poetry. But, eventually, I was able to write poems like jazz riffs, poems that told stories about myself and others, culture and history.

❹ Poetry and Music

Poetry and music are alike in so many ways—the term *lyric poetry* reminds us that poetry was once read to the accompaniment of the stringed instrument known as a lyre.

In the quotation shown here, Michael S. Harper compares the progression of a sentence in a poem with the development of a musical solo. And I've always believed that like a saxophone solo or a song, poetry is concerned with breath. A poem is human breath measured out in stanzas and lines.

When I write, I always listen for the music of the lines. There's always a point in the writing process when I start reading passages aloud. And I do that because for my money, a poem should work both on the page and in the air. Hearing the lines is the only way I can test them lyrically, and know for sure that they sing.

Teaching Resources

The following resources can be used to enrich, extend, or differentiate the instruction.

- All *Unit 4 Resources,* pp. 6–22
- All *Professional Development Guidebook,* p. 33
- All *See It!* DVD Cornelius Eady, Segments 1 and 2
- All *Graphic Organizer Transparencies,* pp. 111–112
- All **Enriched Online Student Edition**
- L2 L3 *Reader's Notebook*
- L1 *Reader's Notebook: Adapted Version*
- EL *Reader's Notebook: English Learner's Version*
- L2 EL *Hear It!* Audio CD
- L1 EL *Adapted Reader's Notebook* Online Audio

PHLit Online! All resources, including print and video, are available at **www.PHLitOnline.com.**

A . . . sentence . . . that waits until the end to give you the [meaning] . . . is like a solo that gives you a certain kind of suspense but is also building towards something.

Interview with Graham Lock
—Michael S. Harper

Meet Cornelius Eady (b. 1954)

Author of "The Poetic Interpretation of the Twist" and "The Empty Dance Shoes"

Cornelius Eady has received numerous awards for his poetry, and his work is widely anthologized. The traditions of jazz, blues, and gospel music have influenced his writing. When he listens to jazz, Eady says he hears a story: "I try to find a way to translate or interpret what I hear in music." He has adapted some of his poems as theater pieces. He has also collaborated with jazz musician Diedre Murray on what they call a "jazz opera."

Did You Know?

Eady is a co-founder of Cave Canem, a summer workshop and retreat for African American poets. Its title—Latin for "Beware of the Dog"—signifies a safe space in which to dream and work.

❸ Jazz Helped Me Understand Poetry (p. 628)

1. Point out that Cornelius Eady understood the language of jazz music, but it took him a few years to realize how that music would influence his own writing.
2. Have students read Cornelius Eady's discussion of jazz and poetry. **Ask** students what Eady's epiphany was and how it influenced his writing.
   Answer: Eady discovered the "story" within jazz and realized that poetry could likewise express what its author knows, feels, and thinks.

❹ Poetry and Music (p. 628)

1. **Ask** students to brainstorm for ways in which poetry and music are similar.
   Possible response: Students may mention elements such as sound effects, rhythm/beat/tempo, and the expression of emotion. They may note that musical lyrics often *are* poems.
2. A professor of English at Brown University, Michael S. Harper, like Eady, deals with themes of music, race, family, and history. Direct students' attention to the quotation. **Ask** students to paraphrase the poet's words.
   Possible response: A long, complex sentence is like a musical solo because both carry you along until their meaning becomes clear.

PROFESSIONAL DEVELOPMENT | **Don Leu**

APPLY THE STRATEGY

Use Internet Reciprocal Teaching to increase students' ability to read and infer. Using Google, conduct a search for the term "poetry" and another for "Cornelius Eady". Print out enough copies of the first page of the search results for the class. Distribute the page for "poetry" and ask the students a few questions about the results. For example, *Which site will let you publish your own poetry?* After each answer, ask students, "How do you know?"

Then, distribute the "Cornelius Eady" page. Have students work in groups, ask each other similar questions about the search results, and explain their answers.

For more of Don Leu's strategies, see his Professional Development essay, pp. 626c–626d.

PHLit Online!

Show or assign the Penguin author video segments for these pages at **www.PHLitOnline.com.**

TEACH

❺ Characteristics of Poetry

1. Explain to students that the purpose of figurative language is to help readers recognize relationships and similarities among different things. When poets compare the world to a stage or they compare fog to little cat feet, they are not stating things that are literally true. Instead, they nudge the reader to think of ways in which the comparison may be imaginatively true.
2. Have students think of examples for simile, metaphor, and personification. Some students will provide examples from poems they remember, but others will cite idioms, advertising, and popular culture. Help students to see that figurative language is part of their daily lives.
3. Explain that poets increase their readers' involvement by using imagery. Poets typically use visual images, but they can also make us hear the click of a dog's tread on a wooden floor or feel the relief of a cool glass windowpane on one's forehead.
4. Connect the use of rhythm, rhyme, alliteration, consonance, and assonance with the discussion of music and poetry you had earlier. Point out that in choosing their words, poets consider musical quality as well as meaning. In addition, they often use sound to reinforce meaning.

Exploring Poetry

❺ Characteristics of Poetry

Poetry is literature in verse form, a controlled arrangement of lines and stanzas. Poems use concise, musical, and emotionally charged language to express multiple layers of meaning.

- **Figurative language** is language that is used imaginatively, rather than literally, to express ideas or feelings in new ways.
- These **figures of speech** make comparisons between dissimilar things:
  Similes use *like* or *as* to compare two essentially unlike things, as in *"She runs like the wind."*
  Metaphors speak of one thing in terms of another, as in *"All the world's a stage."*
  Personification gives human traits to nonhuman things, as in *"The ocean snarled and pounded against the shore."*
- **Imagery** is descriptive language that creates vivid impressions. These impressions, or **images,** are developed through **sensory language**, which provides details related to sight, sound, taste, touch, smell, and movement.

CALVIN AND HOBBES ©1999 Watterson Reprinted with permission of UNIVERSAL PRESS.

Poets use a number of **sound devices** to achieve a musical quality.

- **Rhythm** is the pattern created by stressed and unstressed syllables of words in sequence. A pattern of rhythm is called **meter.**
- **Rhyme** is the repetition of identical sounds in the last syllables of words. A pattern of rhyme at the ends of lines is a **rhyme scheme.**
- **Alliteration,** or initial rhyme, is the repetition of the initial consonant sounds of words, as in the words *light* and *lemon*. **Assonance,** or vowel rhyme, is the repetition of vowel sounds in nearby words, as in the words *date* and *fade*. **Consonance** is the repetition of consonants within nearby words in which the preceding vowels differ, as in the words *milk* and *walk*.

Understanding by Design

Clarifying Expected Outcomes

Explain to students that pages 630–631 set out their goals in Unit 4. By the end of the unit, they will understand the characteristics of poetry, including figurative language, figures of speech, and imagery. They will be able to identify and discuss these elements in specific types of poetry. They will also be able to use some of these elements in writing a descriptive essay in the Writing Workshop on pp. 708–713.

Remind students that, in addition, they will explore different purposes for communicating as they work toward an answer to the Unit Big Question, "Does all communication serve a positive purpose?" They will also add words to their vocabulary that will help them to discuss communication and its purposes. (See Introducing the Big Question, pp. 626–627.)

6 Types of Poetry

There are three main types of poetry.

- **Narrative** poetry tells a story and has a plot, characters, and a setting. An **epic** is a long narrative poem about the feats of gods or heroes. A **ballad** is a songlike narrative that has short stanzas and a refrain.
- **Dramatic** poetry tells a story using a character's own thoughts or spoken statements.
- **Lyric** poems express the feelings of a single speaker. Lyrics are the most common type of poem in modern literature.

Poems can also be categorized by form. Poetic forms are defined by specific organizations of line and stanza length, rhythm, and rhyme.

- A **haiku** is a verse form with three unrhymed lines of five, seven, and five syllables. A **tanka** is a verse form with five unrhymed lines of five, seven, five, seven, and seven syllables. Both forms use imagery to convey a single vivid emotion.
- Some poems, described as **free verse,** have neither a set pattern of rhythm nor rhyme.
- A **sonnet** is a fourteen-line lyric poem with formal patterns of rhyme, rhythm, and line structure.

Put Yourself in the Picture

Use these sentence starters to connect this picture to poetry.

- A **lyric poem** based on this picture might reveal that the girl in the background is thinking ____________________.
- **Sensory language** such as ___________ could describe the expression on the face of _______.
- In a **narrative poem** about this picture, a writer might say_______.

Challenge Which type of poetry do you think would best fit this picture? Explain your choice.

6 Types of Poetry

1. To help students understand the different forms poets use, point out that narrative, dramatic, and lyric poems are like styles of music. Each style has its own conventions. A dramatic poem is like an opera, with a dramatic situation and emotional conflict. A tanka, though, could be compared to a song verse, compressed and formalized.
2. If time permits, you may want to give students a Shakespearean sonnet and have them rewrite it as a tanka or some other form (or vice versa). This kind of activity helps students see that there are many ways to express the same idea.

ASSESS

Answers

Put Yourself in the Picture

Possible response: A lyric poem based on this picture might reveal that the girl in the background is thinking about how awful it is that the two girls are talking about her. Sensory language such as the blurred face of sadness could describe the expression on the face of the girl. In a narrative poem about this picture, a writer might say why the two girls are talking about the girl in the background and how they resolve their conflict.

Challenge

Possible response: Students may respond that a lyric poem would allow the poet to express fully and imaginatively his or her feelings about rumors, gossip, and alienation.

Differentiated Instruction for Universal Access

Support for Special Needs Students
Have students read the **Exploring Poetry** page in the ***Reader's Notebook: Adapted Version.*** This version provides a basic-level introduction to the essay and the speech.

Support for Less Proficient Readers
Have students read the **Exploring Poetry** page in the ***Reader's Notebook.*** This version provides a basic-level introduction to the essay and the speech.

EL Support for English Learners
Have students read the **Exploring Poetry** page in the ***Reader's Notebook: English Learner's Version.*** This version provides a basic-level introduction to the essay and the speech.

PREETEACH

❶ Introducing the Selection

1. Invite students to read Cornelius Eady's introduction to his poems.
2. **Ask** students to explain how the poet's introduction prepare them to read the poems. Students might say that because they expect to feel a rhythm in the poem as they read, they might read it more smoothly.
3. Call students' attention to the terms: *theme, rhythm, imagery,* and *speaker.* **Ask** students to identify these elements as they read the poems.

❷ Background

The Twist The top tune of 1960 was "The Twist," performed by Chubby Checker. The twist revolutionized social dancing. No longer did partners need to touch each other or learn steps or patterns. Doing the twist involved moving the feet in a left-to-right fashion as if crushing a hard bug, combined with swinging the arms and hips as if the dancer were drying his or her back with an imaginary towel.

❸ Connecting to the Big Question

1. Prepare students to apply the Big Question to the Model Selections.
2. Explain to students that in "The Poetic Interpretation of the Twist," Eady uses the dance as a focus for communicating what his life was like when the twist was popular.
3. Have students complete this sentence frame, featuring thematic vocabulary from pp. 626–627:

   Poets use self-expression as a way to convey a message to their audience by ______.

   Possible response: allowing their personality or emotions to come out in their words.
4. Discuss students' responses as a class. Then, have students look for examples of different purposes for communicating as they read the poems.

Concept Connector

Students will discuss the purposes for communicating in poetry when they have concluded reading.

Model Selection: Poetry

❶ Cornelius Eady ❷ ❸ Introduces His Poems

I grew up in a small, African American neighborhood in the city of Rochester, New York, and some of my strongest memories are of the street where I lived, the tall weeds along the railroad tracks, the bricks on the streets, the way my family and neighbors thought and spoke. Much of this helped to shape the writer I was to become.

Using Images From My Old Neighborhood

At the time I wrote "The Poetic Interpretation of the Twist," I was at work on a group of poems that were all connected by the **theme** of dance and dancing. I was discovering the way a poem sounds and moves was close to what happens when we dance.

All poems have a **rhythm,** a beat to which we write and read. I wanted to find a way to make the elements of my old neighborhood, the **imagery** in my head, "dance" as a poem.

One day I read that "The Twist" was the step that marked the end of couples holding each other on the dance floor! This started me thinking about how we danced that step where I grew up. So I began to write, or "interpret," what I remembered.

A Rhythm That Pulls the Reader

I made the **speaker** in the poem recall the strongest images of that time for me: the way my sister ran, the strange behavior of my father, the smell of the barbershop. That listing begins a rhythm that I hoped would pull the reader across and down the page.

"The Empty Dance Shoes," another poem from this group, is about the lack of movement. But even in a poem about not dancing, repeated phrases like "empty pair of dance shoes" help me "dance" around the idea of stillness.

So, as you read these poems, I hope the movement of the lines and the beat of the words will allow you to dance to what you find there.

Vocabulary Development

Vocabulary Knowledge Rating

Create a **Vocabulary Knowledge Rating Chart** (***Professional Development Guidebook,*** p. 33) with these words from the selection:

slight *application*

Give students a copy of the chart. Read the words aloud, and have students mark their rating in the Before Reading column. Urge them to be alert to these words as they read and discuss "The Poetic Interpretation of the Twist," because they will rate their knowledge of the words again after they finish.

Tally how many students think they know a word to gauge how much instruction to provide. As students read, point out the words and their context.

PHLit Online! **Vocabulary Central,** featuring tools, activities, and songs for studying vocabulary, is available at **www.PHLitOnline.com.**

The Poetic Interpretation of the Twist

Cornelius Eady

I know what you're expecting to hear.
You think to yourself: Here's a guy who must understand
what the twist was all about.
Look at the knuckles of his hands,
Look at his plain, blue shirt hanging out of the back
of his trousers.
The twist must have been the equivalent of
the high sign
In a secret cult.

I know
I know
I know

But listen: I am still confused by the mini-skirt
As well as the deep meaning of vinyl on everything.
The twist was just a children's game to us.
I know you expect there ought to be more to this,
The reason the whole world decided to uncouple,

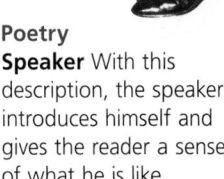

Poetry
Speaker With this description, the speaker introduces himself and gives the reader a sense of what he is like.

Reading Check
What does the speaker say the reader is expecting to hear?

MODEL SELECTION

TEACH

4 Activating Prior Knowledge

Ask students to think about which popular song or dance best epitomizes their generation. Discuss why it is difficult to capture so many experiences with one piece of music. See if students can reach some consensus on the music and the different themes it could be used to represent.

Concept Connector →

Students will return to these discussion points when they have completed their reading of "The Poetic Interpretation of the Twist" and "The Empty Dancing Shoes."

5 About the Selections

In these two poems, Cornelius Eady uses dancing as a vehicle to record memories and to explain inertia. In "The Poetic Interpretation of the Twist," the poet presents a vision of his life growing up in the early 1960s. In "The Empty Dance Shoes," Eady gives a "scientific" interpretation of what happens when there is no one to fill the dancing shoes.

6 Poetry
Speaker

Tell students that the speaker in a poem, like the narrator in a novel, may represent the poet or may be a fictional creation that the poet invents.

7 Reading Check

Answer: The speaker thinks the reader is expecting to hear about some special historical or cultural significance of the twist.

Differentiated Instruction for Universal Access

Support for Special Needs Students
Have students read the adapted version of these selections in the ***Reader's Notebook: Adapted Version***. They may also listen to the adapted version on the **Reader's Notebook: *Hear It!* Audio CD** (adapted text).

Support for Less Proficient Readers
Have students read these selections in the ***Reader's Notebook***. After students finish the selection in the ***Reader's Notebook***, have them complete the questions and activities in the student edition.

EL Support for English Learners
Have students read these selections in the ***Reader's Notebook: English Learner's Version***. English learners may also read the selection as they listen to the recorded version on the ***Hear It!* Audio CD**.

PHLit Online!

Enriched Online Student Edition
To have students read the selection in interactive format, with narration and point-of-use interactive graphic organizers, go to **www.PHLitOnline.com.**

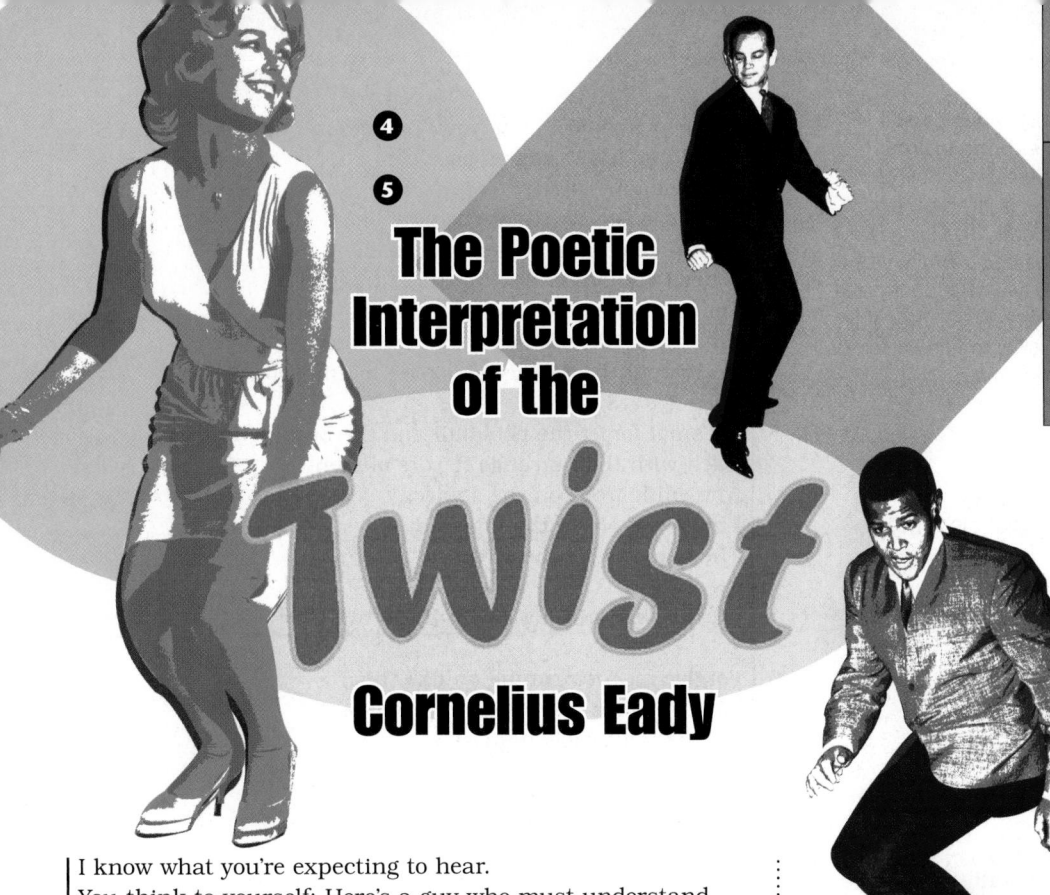

❽ Author's Insight
Cornelius Eady

1. Have a volunteer read the bracketed stanzas aloud.
2. **Ask** students what the speaker is telling you about his or her world.
   Possible response: The speaker's world is fairly ordinary. He or she lives in a neighborhood that probably looks like any other, has a sister who runs and a father who bicycles and does the grocery shopping. The speaker also sees beauty even in the ordinary.
3. **Ask:** If this were a short story instead of a poem, what information would these stanzas provide?
   Answer: These stanzas would establish the setting of a story.

❾ Poetry
Figurative Language

1. Direct students' attention to the three bracketed lines and to the explanation in the margin.
2. **Ask** students to offer another interpretation of these images and how they suggest the theme of the poem.
   Possible response: Speaking of the twist as the foundation of a bridge gives it strength and substance. The poet seems to be saying that the dance provided the underpinnings of what came after it.

Cornelius Eady
Author's Insight
Here, I'm telling you about my past, my world. One thing I have learned over the years is that each of us has a story. We all have this ability to find ourselves in writing.

Vocabulary
slight (slīt) *v.* treat with disrespect or indifference

Poetry
Figurative Language
The metaphor of the twist as a missing bridge emphasizes the speaker's inability to explain the meaning of the dance.

But why should I lie to you? Let me pull up a chair
And in as few words as possible,
Re-create my sister,
Who was renowned for running like a giraffe.
Let me re-create my neighborhood,
A dead-end street next to the railroad tracks.
Let me re-create
My father, who would escape the house by bicycle
And do all the grocery shopping by himself.

Let's not forget the pool hall and the barbershop,
Each with their strange flavors of men,
And while we're on the subject,
I must not **slight** the ragweed,
The true rose of the street.

All this will still not give you the twist.

Forgive me for running on like this.
Your question has set an expectation
That is impossible to meet

Your question has put on my shoulders
A troublesome responsibility

Because the twist is gone.
It is the foundation of a bridge
That has made way for a housing project

And I am sorry to admit
You have come to the wrong person.
I recall the twist
The way we recall meeting a distant aunt as a baby
Or the afternoons spent in homeroom
Waiting for the last bell.

My head hurts.
I am tired of remembering.
Perhaps you can refresh my memory
And tell me
How we got on this topic?
As a favor to me,
Let's not talk anymore about old dances.

I have an entire world on the tip of my tongue.

Think Aloud

Figures of Speech

Use lines 20–31 on p. 634 to show how to identify figures of speech. Say to students:

> When I read lines 20–31, I come across some language that shows a comparison between two dissimilar things. For example, in lines 20–21, the speaker describes his sister "running like a giraffe." Because the speaker compares two different things—his sister and a giraffe—using the word *like*, I know that these lines contain a simile. This simile allows me to picture vividly a girl running gracefully and quickly like a giraffe.
>
> Lines 30–31 contain a different figure of speech. The poet speaks of the common ragweed plant as a "true rose of the street." This is a metaphor, because the speaker identifies one thing, ragweed, in terms of another thing, a rose. This metaphor allows me to understand that beauty can be found in the ordinary things in the speaker's neighborhood. By identifying figures of speech, I can appreciate and imagine images in poems more fully.

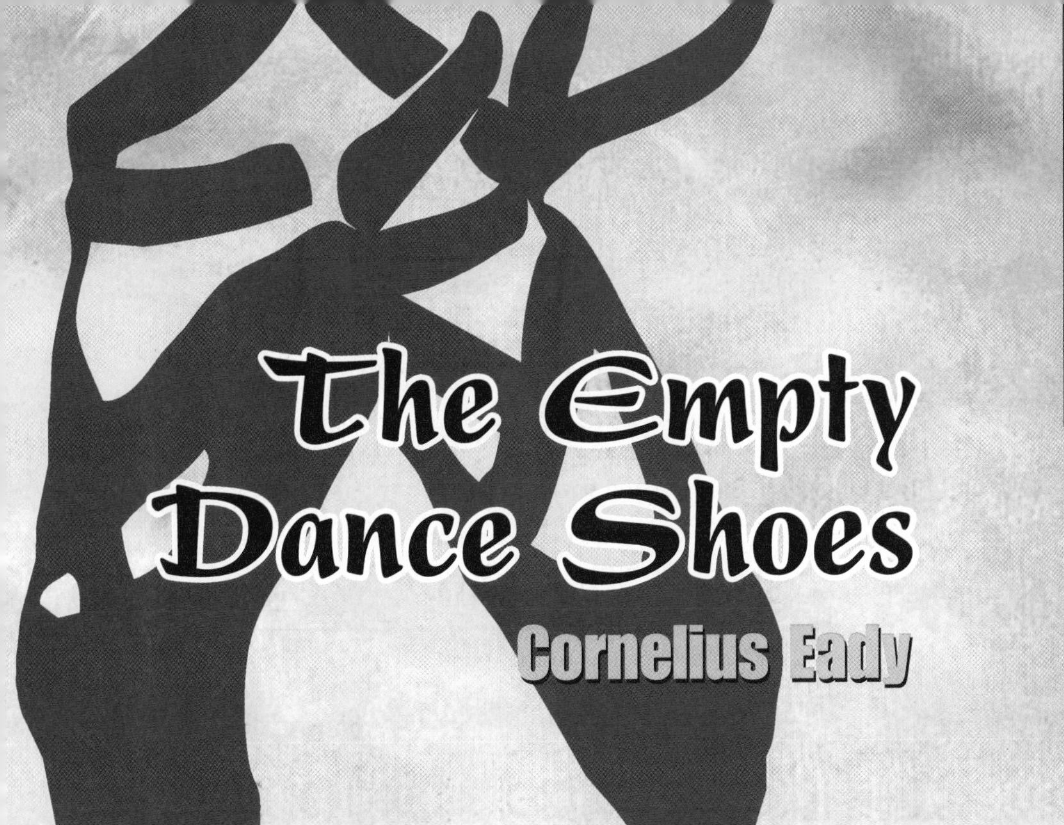

MODEL SELECTION

The Empty Dance Shoes

Cornelius Eady

My friends,
As it has been proven in the laboratory,
An empty pair of dance shoes
Will sit on the floor like a wart
Until it is given a reason to move.

Those of us who study inertia[1]
(Those of us covered with wild hair and sleep)
Can state this without fear:
The energy in a pair of shoes at rest
Is about the same as that of a clown

Knocked flat by a sandbag.
10 This you can tell your friends with certainty:
A clown, flat on his back,
Is a lot like an empty pair of
dancing shoes.

1. **inertia** (in ʉr′ shə) *n.* in physics, the tendency of matter at rest to remain at rest or, if moving, to keep doing so in the same direction unless affected by an outside force.

Cornelius Eady
Author's Insight Even though the image of the clown shows lack of movement, the short words with a lot of energy reinforce a sense of movement.

10 Author's Insight
Cornelius Eady

1. Read the bracketed passage aloud to students.
2. **Ask** students to close their eyes and picture the clown knocked flat on his back by a sandbag. What do they see?
Possible response: Although the clown's body would be prone, there is a good chance that his head, arms, and legs would still be moving.
3. Then, **ask** students what the images of a prone clown and empty dancing shoes suggest.
Possible response: Both the clown and the dancing shoes are things that are usually in motion but now are not.
4. Have students list the "short words with a lot of energy" that the poet mentions in his comment.
Answer: *Knocked, flat,* and *back* are all short words. *Knocked* and *back*, with their "k" sounds, sound like punches.

Differentiated Instruction for Universal Access

Culturally Responsive Instruction

Culture Connection Provide background information on the contributions African Americans have made to the development of musical genres, such as rock-and-roll. Explain to students that in the early 1950s, the catchy groundbreaking sound of rock legends Elvis Presley and Chuck Berry quickly attracted fervent listeners. Emphasize rock-and-roll's roots in African American musical forms: blues, rhythm and blues, and jazz.

Have students think about a musical genre—such as Latin, folk, reggae, or hip hop—that they feel contributes to their own cultural identity. Then, have students research the origins, development, or characteristics of that genre. Have students share their findings with the class. Encourage students to bring in samples of this music to share with the class.

⓫ Poetry
Repetition

1. Call students' attention to the repeated phrase "An empty pair of dancing shoes/Is also a lot like . . ." Point out that the phrase "an empty pair of dance (or dancing) shoes" appears in the poem six times.
2. **Ask** students to comment on the effect of the repetition.
   Possible response: The repetition suggests that the empty pair of dancing shoes is an important image. The series of examples helps create the portrait of the dancing shoes, each comparison building on the last while adding a new dimension.
3. **Ask** students why they think Eady chose a leaf pressed in a book of poems as a comparison for empty dancing shoes.
   Possible response: A leaf pressed in a book is static and lifeless, but both the leaf and the poems can bring to mind memories if the book is opened. Empty dancing shoes are static until someone gives them life.

⓬ Poetry
Theme

Ask students how the last three lines of the poem shift its meaning.
Possible response: The empty dance shoes as they exist are not any good to anyone, except when they inspire change.

Concept Connector

Have students return to the discussion points about the song or dance that best captures the spirit of their generation. Lead a class discussion, probing for what students have learned that confirms or invalidates their ideas before reading the poems.

Connecting to the Big Question

Ask: Does Eady communicate something positive about a pair of empty dance shoes? Explain.
Possible response: Yes; although empty dance shoes are inert, they carry with them the potential to inspire and motivate.

Poetry
Repetition Repeating the phrase "an empty pair of dancing shoes" creates a sense of unity in the poem. ⓫

Vocabulary
application (ap′ li kā′ shən) *n.* act of putting something to use

An empty pair of dancing shoes
Is also a lot like a leaf
Pressed in a book.
And now you know a simple truth:
A leaf pressed in, say, *The Colossus*
by Sylvia Plath,[2]
Is no different from an empty pair of dance shoes

Even if those shoes are in the middle of the Stardust Ballroom
With all the lights on, and hot music shakes the windows
up and down the block.

This is the secret of inertia:
The shoes run on their own sense of the world.
They are in sympathy with the rock the kid skips
over the lake
After it settles to the mud.
Not with the ripples,
But with the rock.

A practical and personal application of inertia
Can be found in the question:
Whose Turn Is It
To Take Out the Garbage?
An empty pair of dance shoes
Is a lot like the answer to this question,
As well as book-length poems
Set in the Midwest.

To sum up:
An empty pair of dance shoes
Is a lot like the sand the 98-pound weakling
brushes from his cheeks
As the bully tows away his girlfriend.
Later,

⓬
When he spies the coupon at the back of the comic book,
He is about to act upon a different set of scientific principles.
He is ready to dance.

2. ***The Colossus* by Sylvia Plath** volume of poetry by American poet Sylvia Plath (1932–1963).

Vocabulary Development

Vocabulary Knowledge Rating

When students have completed reading and discussing "The Poetic Interpretation of the Twist" and "The Empty Dance Shoes," have them take out their **Vocabulary Rating Chart** for these poems. Read the words aloud once more, and have students rate their knowledge of the words again in the After Reading column. Clarify any words that are still problematic.

Have students write their own definitions or examples in the appropriate column. Encourage students to use the words in further discussion and written work about this selection. Remind them that they will be accountable for these words on the **Selection Test, *Unit 4 Resources,*** pp. 8–10 or 11–13.

After You Read

The Poetic Interpretation of the Twist • The Empty Dance Shoes

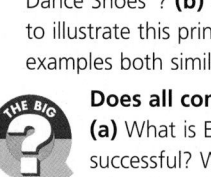

Critical Thinking

1. **Respond:** Which poem did you find more intriguing? Explain.
2. **(a)** In "The Poetic Interpretation of the Twist," what memories does the speaker mention as he tries to remember the dance? **(b) Analyze Cause and Effect:** How is the speaker affected by these memories? **(c) Speculate:** Why do you think the speaker wants to change the subject at the end of the poem?
3. **(a)** What scientific concept is repeatedly mentioned in "The Empty Dance Shoes"? **(b) Connect:** Note three examples the speaker uses to illustrate this principle. **(c) Compare and Contrast:** How are these examples both similar and different?

Does all communication serve a positive purpose?
(a) What is Eady trying to say about the twist? Was he successful? Why or why not? **(b)** In "The Empty Dance Shoes," what do you think Eady was trying to tell readers? Explain.

Poetry Review

1. Compare the **speakers** in the two poems. In which poem does the speaker's personal life play a more significant role? Explain.
2. **(a)** In the first column of a chart like the one shown, list examples of **figurative language** from "The Empty Dance Shoes" that compare the shoes to other things. In the second column, describe the effect of each example. In the third column, write one sentence to explain the meaning of the shoes in that example. **(b)** Discuss your chart with a partner, and use the feedback to revise your statements.

What It Says	Feeling It Creates	What It Means

Research the Author

Create an **annotated poster** that displays the music or dance imagery in poems by Cornelius Eady. Follow these steps:

- Use the library and Internet to identify six Eady poems that emphasize music or dance. Briefly describe each one.
- Find images that relate to music, dance, or performers as described in the poems. Use them to illustrate your writing. Display your poster.

Research the Author

Students may complete this poster for homework. Tell them that they can find information in a library or online.

PHLit Online!
Students can find more about the author at **www.PHLitOnline.com.**

Assessment Resources

The following resources can be used to assess students' knowledge and skills.

Unit 4 Resources

L1 L2 EL **Selection Test A,** pp. 8–10
L3 L4 **Selection Test B,** pp. 11–13
L3 L4 **Open-Book Test,** pp. 14–16

PHLit Online! Students may use the **Self-test,** online at **www.PHLitOnline.com,** to prepare for **Selection Test A** or **Selection Test B.**

ASSESS/EXTEND

Answers

Critical Thinking

1. **Possible response:** Students may be intrigued by the connection Eady makes between empty dancing shoes and inertia. Others may be surprised by the memories triggered by the twist.
2. (a) The speaker recalls his sister, father, and neighborhood. (b) He recalls them with fondness. (c) **Possible response:** Perhaps his memories are too intense or jumbled to be easily shared with others.
3. (a) Inertia is the scientific concept. (b) Three examples are the sandbagged clown, a leaf pressed in a book, and a skipped rock that settles into the mud. (c) All three have been removed from their normal state of operation. The leaf and the rock will be inert unless someone moves them. The clown has the ability to move.

Does all communication serve a positive purpose?

(a) **Possible response:** Eady is showing that, to him, the twist is not a dance but a series of childhood memories. He was successful because the figures of speech and imagery he uses to describe his family and neighborhood are clear and strong.
(b) **Possible response:** Eady uses the empty shoes to show that many objects that seem static in life are just waiting for someone to bring them to life.

Poetry Review

1. The speaker in "The Poetic Interpretation of the Twist" is more personal because of the examples he provides of his father, sister, and neighborhood. The speaker of "The Empty Dance Shoes" seems more impersonal and is stepping back from his subject to analyze it in a scientific way. However, both speakers approach readers in a direct manner with a lighthearted tone.
2. **Possible response:** (a) **Column 1:** shoes and wart; **Column 2:** silliness; **Column 3:** Neither the empty shoes nor the wart will move under its own power. (b) Students discuss their responses.

TIME AND RESOURCE MANAGER

Poetry Collection 1 • Poetry Collection 2

Lesson Pacing Guide

DAY 1 Preteach

- Administer the Reading and Vocabulary Warm-ups (*Unit 4 Resources*, pp. 23–26 or 41–44) as necessary.
- Introduce the Reading Skill: Read Fluently FT
- Introduce the Literary Analysis concept: The Speaker in Poetry FT
- Distribute copies of the appropriate graphic organizer for the Reading Skill (*Graphic Organizer Transparencies*, pp. 113–115). CRI
- Distribute copies of the appropriate graphic organizer for Literary Analysis (*Graphic Organizer Transparencies*, pp. 116–119). CRI
- Teach the selection vocabulary. FT CRI
- Introduce the Word Study skill.

DAYS 2–3 Preteach/Teach

- Build background with the Background feature. CRI
- Develop thematic vocabulary and thematic thinking with Writing About the Big Question.
- Prepare students to read with the Activating Prior Knowledge activities (TE). CRI
- Informally monitor comprehension while students read. FT
- Use the Reading Check questions to confirm comprehension.
- Develop students' ability to read fluently and adjust their reading rate using the Reading Skill questions. CRI
- Develop students' understanding of the speaker in poetry using the Literary Analysis questions. CRI
- Reinforce vocabulary with the Vocabulary notes. CRI

DAY 4 Assess

- Assess students' comprehension and mastery of the skills by having them answer the Critical Thinking, Reading Skill, and Literary Analysis questions. FT
- Have students complete the Vocabulary Practice activities. FT
- Have students complete the Word Study activities.

DAY 5 Extend/Assess

- Have students complete the Grammar lesson. CRI
- Have students complete the Writing activity and write a lyric poem. (You may assign as homework.) FT
- Extend learning by having students complete the Listening and Speaking activity, an oral interpretation. As an alternative, assign them "Ooooh, Scary!" or "Up a Tree" in *Reality Central*. CRI
- Administer Selection Test A or B (*Unit 4 Resources*, pp. 35–40 or 56–61). FT

The poems in Poetry Collections 1 and 2 appear unedited and in their entirety.

Meeting Your Standards

Students will

1. **analyze and respond to literary elements.**
   - **Literary Analysis: The Speaker in Poetry**
2. **read, comprehend, and analyze poetry.**
   - **Reading Skill: Read Fluently**
   - **Reading Check questions**
   - **Apply the Skills questions**
   - **Assessment Practice**
3. **develop vocabulary.**
   - **Vocabulary**
   - **Word Study**
4. **apply grammar skills.**
   - **Prepositions and Prepositional Phrases**
5. **Develop writing proficiency.**
   - **Work in Progress: Descriptive Essay**
   - **lyric poem**
6. **strengthen listening and speaking skills.**
   - **oral interpretation**

CRI For a full explanation of Culturally Responsive Instruction opportunities in this lesson, see p. T86–T87.

FT For an accelerated lesson, use the Fast Track strategies and activities.

Managing Differentiated Instruction

This leveled selection pairing groups a more accessible with a more challenging selection. Choose either one to teach the lesson skills. For classroom management suggestions for using the pairing in a mixed-ability class, see pp. T68–T69.

Daily Block Scheduling

Each day in this Lesson Pacing Guide represents a 40–50 minute period. Teachers using block scheduling may combine days to revise pacing. In addition, teachers may differentiate and support core instruction by integrating components for extended and intensive support as students require. See the Guide to Selected Leveled Resources (facing page).

Guide to Selected Leveled Resources

EL English Learners

			Poetry Collection 1	Poetry Collection 2
CORE COURSE	*Unit 4 Resources*	Selection Test A	pp. 35–37	pp. 56–58
	Graphic Organizer Transparencies	Reading Skill Graphic Organizer A	p. 113	p. 114
		Literary Analysis Graphic Organizer A	p. 116	p. 118
EXTENDED SUPPORT (Level 2)	*Unit 4 Resources*	Reading and Vocabulary Warm-ups A or B	pp. 23–26	pp. 41–44
	Reader's Notebook: English Learner's Version		adapted instruction and adapted selection	adapted instruction and summary
	Hear It! Audio CD		selection and summaries	selection and summaries
	Hear It! Audio CD (adapted text)		adapted selection and summaries	—
INTENSIVE SUPPORT (Level 1)	*Reality Central*		"Ooooh, Scary!"	"Up a Tree"
	Real-World Writing Journal		Lesson 1, pp. 104–107	Lesson 2, pp. 108–111

L2 Below-Level Students

			Poetry Collection 1	Poetry Collection 2
CORE COURSE	*Unit 4 Resources*	Selection Test A	pp. 35–37	pp. 56–58
	Graphic Organizer Transparencies	Reading Skill Graphic Organizer A	p. 113	p. 114
		Literary Analysis Graphic Organizer A	p. 116	p. 118
EXTENDED SUPPORT (Level 2)	*Unit 4 Resources*	Reading and Vocabulary Warm-ups A or B	pp. 23–26	pp. 41–44
	Reader's Notebook		adapted instruction and full selection	adapted instruction and summary
	Hear It! Audio CD		selection and summaries	selection and summaries
INTENSIVE SUPPORT (Level 1)	*Reality Central*		"Ooooh, Scary!"	"Up a Tree"
	Real-World Writing Journal		Lesson 1, pp. 104–107	Lesson 2, pp. 108–111
	Reading Kit		Reteaching worksheets	Reteaching worksheets

L1 Special Needs Students

			Poetry Collection 1	Poetry Collection 2
CORE COURSE	*Unit 4 Resources*	Selection Test A	pp. 35–37	pp. 56–58
	Graphic Organizer Transparencies	Reading Skill Graphic Organizer A	p. 113	p. 114
		Literary Analysis Graphic Organizer A	p. 116	p. 118
EXTENDED SUPPORT (Level 2)	*Unit 4 Resources*	Reading and Vocabulary Warm-ups A or B	pp. 23–26	pp. 41–44
	Reader's Notebook: Adapted Version		adapted instruction and adapted selection	adapted instruction and summary
	Hear It! Audio CD (adapted text)		adapted selection and summaries	—
INTENSIVE SUPPORT (Level 1)	*Reality Central*		"Ooooh, Scary!"	"Up a Tree"
	Real-World Writing Journal		Lesson 1, pp. 104–107	Lesson 2, pp. 108–111
	Reading Kit		Reteaching worksheets	Reteaching worksheets

The program includes resources for these students: L3 On-Level L4 Advanced All All
For a complete guide to selection support, see pp. T106–T108.

NOTE: All print materials are also available online at *www.PHLitOnline.com.*

• Poetry Collection 1
• Poetry Collection 2

RESOURCES FOR:

- EL English Learners
- L1 Special Needs Students
- L2 Below-Level Students
- L3 On-Level Students
- L4 Advanced Students
- All All Students

Vocabulary/Fluency/Prior Knowledge

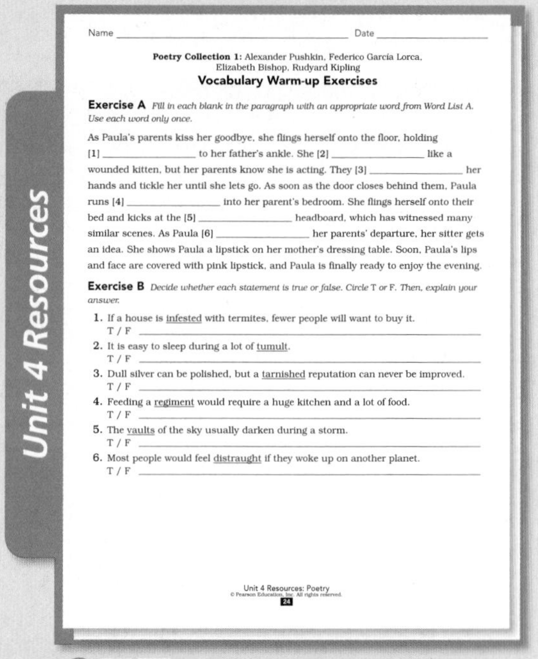

Unit 4 Resources

Name ______________ Date ______________

Poetry Collection 1: Alexander Pushkin, Federico García Lorca, Elizabeth Bishop, Rudyard Kipling

Vocabulary Warm-up Exercises

Exercise A *Fill in each blank in the paragraph with an appropriate word from Word List A. Use each word only once.*

As Paula's parents kiss her goodbye, she flings herself onto the floor, holding [1] ______________ to her father's ankle. She [2] ______________ like a wounded kitten, but her parents know she is acting. They [3] ______________ her hands and tickle her until she lets go. As soon as the door closes behind them, Paula runs [4] ______________ into her parent's bedroom. She flings herself onto their bed and kicks at the [5] ______________ headboard, which has witnessed many similar scenes. As Paula [6] ______________ her parents' departure, her sitter gets an idea. She shows Paula a lipstick on her mother's dressing table. Soon, Paula's lips and face are covered with pink lipstick, and Paula is finally ready to enjoy the evening.

Exercise B *Decide whether each statement is true or false. Circle* T *or* F. *Then, explain your answer.*

1. If a house is infested with termites, fewer people will want to buy it.
   T / F ______________
2. It is easy to sleep during a lot of tumult.
   T / F ______________
3. Dull silver can be polished, but a tarnished reputation can never be improved.
   T / F ______________
4. Feeding a regiment would require a huge kitchen and a lot of food.
   T / F ______________
5. The vaults of the sky usually darken during a storm.
   T / F ______________
6. Most people would feel distraught if they woke up on another planet.
   T / F ______________

Unit 4 Resources: Poetry
© Pearson Education, Inc. All rights reserved.
24

EL L1 L2 **Vocabulary Warm-ups A and B, pp. 23–24, 41–42**

Also available for these selections:

- EL L1 L2 **Reading Warm-ups A and B, pp. 25–26, 43–44**
- All **Writing About the Big Question, pp. 27, 45**
- All **Vocabulary Builder, pp. 30, 48**

Reader's Notebooks

Pre- and postreading pages, as well as the selections in Poetry Collection 1, appear in an interactive format in the *Reader's Notebooks*. Each *Notebook* is differentiated for a different group of learners.
The selections in the Adapted and English Learner's versions are abridged.

L2 L3 ***Reader's Notebook***

L1 ***Reader's Notebook: Adapted Version***

EL ***Reader's Notebook: English Learner's Version***

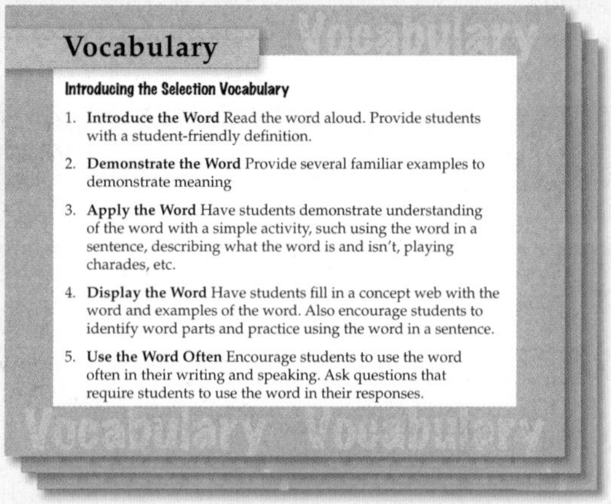

Vocabulary

Introducing the Selection Vocabulary

1. **Introduce the Word** Read the word aloud. Provide students with a student-friendly definition.
2. **Demonstrate the Word** Provide several familiar examples to demonstrate meaning
3. **Apply the Word** Have students demonstrate understanding of the word with a simple activity, such using the word in a sentence, describing what the word is and isn't, playing charades, etc.
4. **Display the Word** Have students fill in a concept web with the word and examples of the word. Also encourage students to identify word parts and practice using the word in a sentence.
5. **Use the Word Often** Encourage students to use the word often in their writing and speaking. Ask questions that require students to use the word in their responses.

Classroom Strategies and Teaching Routines

- core classroom routines outlined step-by-step
- convenient format for easy reference while teaching

Selection Support

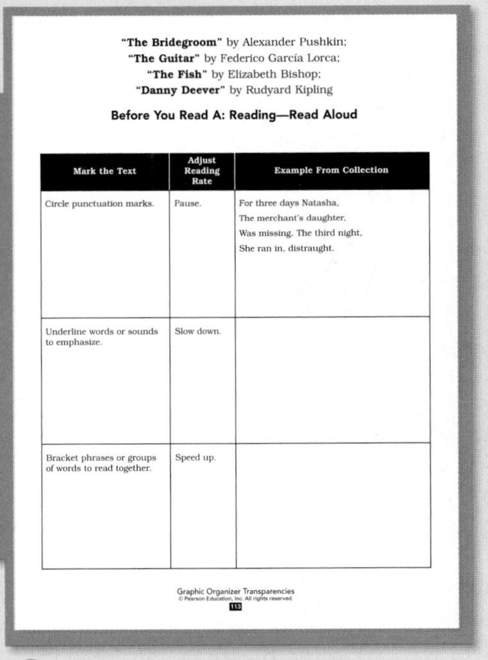

"The Bridegroom" by Alexander Pushkin;
"The Guitar" by Federico García Lorca;
"The Fish" by Elizabeth Bishop;
"Danny Deever" by Rudyard Kipling

Before You Read A: Reading—Read Aloud

Mark the Text	Adjust Reading Rate	Example From Collection
Circle punctuation marks.	Pause.	For three days Natasha, The merchant's daughter, Was missing. The third night, She ran in, distraught.
Underline words or sounds to emphasize.	Slow down.	
Bracket phrases or groups of words to read together.	Speed up.	

Graphic Organizer Transparencies
© Pearson Education, Inc. All rights reserved.
113

Graphic Organizer Transparencies

EL L1 L2 **Reading: Graphic Organizer A,** pp. 113, 114 (partially filled in)

Also available for these selections:

EL L1 L2 Literary Analysis: Graphic Organizer A, pp. 116, 118 (partially filled in)

L3 Literary Analysis: Graphic Organizer B, pp. 117, 119

L3 Reading: Graphic Organizer B, p. 115

Skills Development/Extension

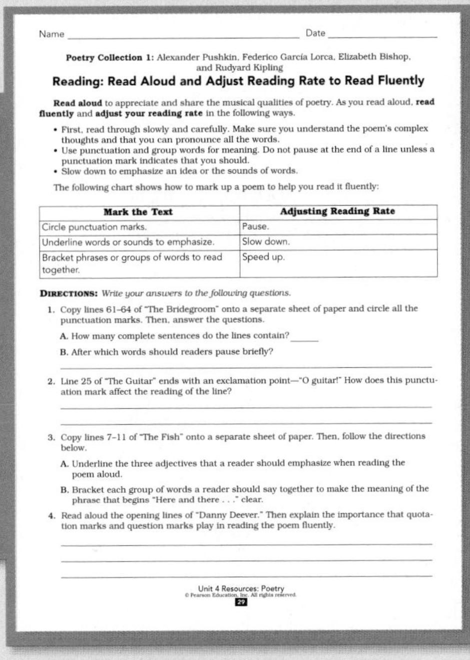

Name ______ Date ______

Poetry Collection 1: Alexander Pushkin, Federico García Lorca, Elizabeth Bishop, and Rudyard Kipling

Reading: Read Aloud and Adjust Reading Rate to Read Fluently

Read aloud to appreciate and share the musical qualities of poetry. As you read aloud, **read fluently** and **adjust your reading rate** in the following ways.

- First, read through slowly and carefully. Make sure you understand the poem's complex thoughts and that you can pronounce all the words.
- Use punctuation and group words for meaning. Do not pause at the end of a line unless a punctuation mark indicates that you should.
- Slow down to emphasize an idea or the sounds of words.

The following chart shows how to mark up a poem to help you read it fluently:

Mark the Text	Adjusting Reading Rate
Circle punctuation marks.	Pause.
Underline words or sounds to emphasize.	Slow down.
Bracket phrases or groups of words to read together.	Speed up.

Directions: *Write your answers to the following questions.*

1. Copy lines 61–64 of "The Bridegroom" onto a separate sheet of paper and circle all the punctuation marks. Then, answer the questions.
   A. How many complete sentences do the lines contain? ______
   B. After which words should readers pause briefly?
2. Line 25 of "The Guitar" ends with an exclamation point—"O guitar!" How does this punctuation mark affect the reading of the line?
3. Copy lines 7–11 of "The Fish" onto a separate sheet of paper. Then, follow the directions below.
   A. Underline the three adjectives that a reader should emphasize when reading the poem aloud.
   B. Bracket each group of words a reader should say together to make the meaning of the phrase that begins "Here and there . . ." clear.
4. Read aloud the opening lines of "Danny Deever." Then explain the importance that quotation marks and question marks play in reading the poem fluently.

Unit 4 Resources: Poetry
© Pearson Education, Inc. All rights reserved.
29

Unit 4 Resources

All **Reading: Read Fluently,** pp. 29, 47

Also available for these selections:

All Literary Analysis: The Speaker in Poetry, pp. 28, 46

L4 Enrichment, pp. 31, 49

L3 L4 Grammar, p. 50

L3 L4 Support for Writing, p. 51

L3 L4 Support for Extend Your Learning, p. 52

Assessment

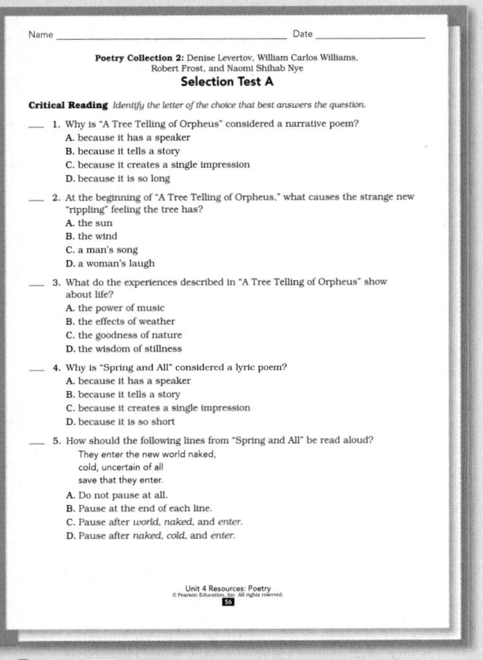

Name ______ Date ______

Poetry Collection 2: Denise Levertov, William Carlos Williams, Robert Frost, and Naomi Shihab Nye

Selection Test A

Critical Reading *Identify the letter of the choice that best answers the question.*

___ 1. Why is "A Tree Telling of Orpheus" considered a narrative poem?
A. because it has a speaker
B. because it tells a story
C. because it creates a single impression
D. because it is so long

___ 2. At the beginning of "A Tree Telling of Orpheus," what causes the strange new "rippling" feeling the tree has?
A. the sun
B. the wind
C. a man's song
D. a woman's laugh

___ 3. What do the experiences described in "A Tree Telling of Orpheus" show about life?
A. the power of music
B. the effects of weather
C. the goodness of nature
D. the wisdom of stillness

___ 4. Why is "Spring and All" considered a lyric poem?
A. because it has a speaker
B. because it tells a story
C. because it creates a single impression
D. because it is so short

___ 5. How should the following lines from "Spring and All" be read aloud?
They enter the new world naked,
cold, uncertain of all
save that they enter.
A. Do not pause at all.
B. Pause at the end of each line.
C. Pause after *world, naked,* and *enter.*
D. Pause after *naked, cold,* and *enter.*

Unit 4 Resources: Poetry
© Pearson Education, Inc. All rights reserved.
56

EL L1 L2 **Selection Test A,** pp. 35–37, 56–58

Also available for these selections:

L3 L4 Selection Test B, pp. 38–40, 59–61

L3 L4 Open-Book Test, pp. 32–34, 53–55

PHLit Online!
www.PHLitOnline.com

- complete narrated selection text
- a thematically related video with writing prompt
- an interactive graphic organizer
- highlighting feature
- access to all student print resources, adapted to individual student needs
- Spanish and English summaries

Get Connected Video
Instructions
Watch the video. Then, use your journal to respond to the prompt at the end of the clip.

Get Connected! (thematic video with writing prompt)

Also available:

Background video

Vocabulary Central

Vocabulary Central (tools, activities, and songs for studying vocabulary)

Also available:

Writer's Journal (with graphics feature)

DIFFERENTIATE/PRETEACH

❶ Collection Choices

You may use either Poetry Collection 1 or Poetry Collection 2 to meet the lesson standards. Skills instruction for both selections appears on p. 639. Choose one selection to teach (or choose to teach both). The Accessibility at a Glance chart at the bottom of this page will help you determine which of the two selections is more appropriate for your students.

❷ Selection Skills

1. With the class, preview the selection skills. (The lesson meets the lesson objectives given on p. 638a.)
2. Explain that students will learn to use the skill of reading fluently as they read to better understand and enjoy the selection you choose. By examining the speaker as they read, they will gain deeper insight into the poems.
3. To introduce the Writing and Listening and Speaking activities (p. 669), tell students that when they have finished reading the selection, they will write a lyric poem and present an oral interpretation related to the selection.
4. Tell students that they will also study a grammar concept: prepositions and prepositional phrases. By mastering this concept, they will improve their reading fluency and the quality of their own writing.

Before You Read | Poetry Collection 1 • Poetry Collection 2

❶ Collection Choices

▲ The artistic works in **Poetry Collection 1** explore conflicts, choices, and challenges.

▲ In **Poetry Collection 2** each poem shows something—an ancient story, a road, people mowing, a fist—from a fresh perspective.

❷ Collection Skills Guide

Practice these skills with either **Poetry Collection 1** (p. 642) or **Poetry Collection 2** (p. 658).

- Analyze the speaker in narrative and lyric poetry
- Understand figurative language
- Read fluently
- Adjust reading rate
- Identify prepositions and prepositional phrases
- Write a lyric poem
- Present an oral interpretation

Differentiated Instruction for Universal Access

Accessibility at a Glance: Selection Choices

	Collection 1	Collection 2	
Context	Collection is mostly narrative (marriage, fishing, military)	Collection suggests connections between nature and human experience	Because a number of factors determine the relative accessibility of paired selections, in some cases the Lexile rating of the more challenging selection will be lower than that of the more accessible selection.
Language/ Vocabulary	Difficult vocabulary and sentence structure	Difficult vocabulary and sentence structure	
Concept Level	Accessible	Challenging	
Literary Merit	Noted poets	Noted poets	
Lexile/Length	NP Word Count: 856; 83; 373; 322	NP Word Count: 130; 998; 133; 141	
Overall Rating	**More accessible**	**More challenging**	

❸ Literary Analysis: The Speaker in Poetry

In poetry, the **speaker** is the voice that says the words of the poem. The speaker may be the poet, or the speaker may be a character the poet invents to give the poem a particular viewpoint. All poems have a speaker, but some poems have qualities that set them apart as a distinct form.

- In **narrative poetry,** the speaker tells a story from a particular point of view.
- In **lyric poetry,** the speaker shares thoughts, feelings, and insights to create a single, unified impression.

Both lyric and narrative poems include deliberate word choice, including the use of types of **figurative language** such as imagery, or language that appeals to the senses.

❹ Reading Skill: Read Fluently

Read aloud to appreciate and share the musical qualities of poetry. As you read aloud, **read fluently**—with expression and understanding. To achieve reading fluency, **adjust your reading rate.**

- First, read the poem slowly and carefully. Make sure that you understand it and that you can pronounce all the words.
- Pay attention to punctuation, and group words for meaning. Do not pause at line ends unless punctuation indicates that you should.
- Slow down to emphasize an idea or the sounds of words.
- Read the poem more than once. Listen for the **tone** that the words give to the poem.

❺ Using the Strategy: Reading Rate Chart

To prepare to read aloud, mark a copy of the poem to indicate adjustments to your reading rate. Use a **reading rate chart** like this one:

Mark the Text	Adjust Reading Rate
Circle punctuation marks.	Pause.
Underline words or sounds to emphasize.	Slow down.
Bracket phrases or groups of words to read together.	Speed up.

PHLit Online!
www.PHLitOnline.com

Hear It!
- Selection summary audio
- Selection audio

See It!
- Get Connected video
- Background video
- More about the author
- Vocabulary flashcards

Do It!
- Interactive journals
- Interactive graphic organizers
- Self-test
- Internet activity
- Grammar tutorial
- Interactive vocabulary games

Differentiated Instruction for Universal Access

Preparing Students for the More Challenging Selection

If you wish to prepare lower-level readers to read Poetry Collection 2, the more challenging selection, follow these steps:

- Guide students to use context clues to define difficult words such as *scythe* (p. 658), *akin* (p. 661), *asunder* (p. 662), and *mottled* (p. 665).
- Review strategies for interpreting difficult language. Suggest that when students encounter a sentence or a phrase that they do not understand, they should attempt to rephrase it in their own words. For example, the line "I knew not well myself;" can be rephrased as "I did not know"(p. 658).
- Students may have difficulty with fluency when reading "A Tree Telling of Orpheus." Point out that even though the positions of lines vary widely, the lines still follow basic grammar and punctuation rules. Guide students to read each sentence with the normal pauses after commas, briefly stopping after periods, and reading as a continuous thought when there is no punctuation.

PRETEACH

❸ Literary Analysis

1. Introduce the skill, using the instruction on the student page.
2. Tell students that they will identify the speaker as they read.

Think Aloud: Model the Skill

Model the skill of analyzing the speaker. Say to students:

I know that the speaker in a poem, just like a narrator in fiction, is the voice I hear when I read. Knowing the type of poem I am reading can help me to determine the identity of the speaker. For instance, a narrative poem told from the perspective of an old woman would be "spoken" by the old woman. The speaker in a lyric poem, however, might be the actual poet, because a lyric poem reveals the speaker's personal thoughts and feelings.

❹ Reading Skill

1. Introduce the skill, using the instruction on the student page.
2. Tell students that they will learn to read fluently and adjust their reading rate as they read.

Think Aloud: Model the Skill

Model the skill of reading fluently. Say to students:

Reading a poem aloud can help me to hear the music in the lines. I need to know how to pronounce all the words and pay attention to punctuation. For example, if a period falls in the middle of a line, I need to come to a full stop. By reading fluently, I can appreciate the rhythms of the poem and understand its meanings.

❺ Using the Strategy

Give students a copy of either **Reading Skill Graphic Organizer A** or **B** (*Graphic Organizer Transparencies,* pp. 113–115) to record their reading rate as they read. Use the examples in **Reading Skill Graphic Organizer A,** which is partially filled in, to model the process of completing the organizer.

PRETEACH

1 Writing About the Big Question

1. Review the assignment with the class.
2. Elicit from students synonyms for *convey*. (**Sample answers:** *communicate, reveal, express, tell*) Then, invite students to think of ways that people communicate their feelings to others.
3. Have students complete the sentence starters. Review responses as a class. (**Possible response:** One way to convey an emotion or communicate how you feel about something is to have an open and honest conversation with someone about it. Another method might be to write a letter.)
4. Remind students that their answers will help them think about the Big Question.

While You Read

Tell students that as they read, they should pay attention to their emotional reactions to the poems.

2 Vocabulary

1. Have students preview the selection vocabulary.
2. For each word, have students say the word aloud.
3. Then, use the word in a sentence that defines the word.
4. Finally, repeat your definitional sentence or a similar sentence with the word missing and have the class "fill in the blank" chorally. Here is an example:

   To feel foreboding is to have anticipation that something bad will happen. This month's eerie, full moon, tinged a dark, cloudy red, gave Daphne a feeling of [students say "foreboding"].

3 Word Study

1. Introduce the skill, using the instruction in the box.
2. Have students explain how the prefix *fore-* contributes to the meaning of these words: *foreground, foresee,* and *foremost.* (**Sample answers:** "front" of a scene; to know "beforehand"; "before" all else)

Does all communication serve a positive purpose?

1 Writing About the Big Question

The poems in Poetry Collection 1 conjure up complicated feelings such as suspense, wonder, and melancholy. Use these sentence starters to develop your ideas about the Big Question.

One way to **convey** an **emotion** or communicate how you feel about something is to __________. Another method might be __________.

While You Read Notice the different feelings that arise in you as you read these poems.

2 Vocabulary

Read each word and its definition. Decide whether you know the word well, know it a little bit, or do not know it at all. After you read, see how your knowledge of each word has increased.

- **foreboding** (fôr bōd′ iŋ) *n.* a feeling that something bad will happen (p. 643) *Alone in the spooky house, I was filled with foreboding. forebode v.*
- **tumult** (to͞o′ mult) *n.* noisy commotion (p. 645) *The tumult from the crowd at the parade in the street below kept me awake for most of the night. tumultuous adj. tumultuously adv.*
- **monotonously** (mə nät′ 'n əs lē) *adv.* in a dull, unvarying way (p. 649) *The official's boring speech continued monotonously. monotonous adj. monotony n.*
- **venerable** (ven′ ər ə bəl) *adj.* worthy of respect because of age or character (p. 650) *He asked for the wise advice of his venerable elders. venerability n. venerate v.*
- **sullen** (sul′ ən) *adj.* gloomy and showing resentment (p. 651) *The children were sullen when they had to leave the playground. sullenly adv. sullenness n.*
- **comrade** (käm′ rad′) *n.* a close companion (p. 653) *A soldier and his comrade share many experiences during a battle. comradeship n. comradery n.*

3 Word Study

The **Old English prefix *fore-*** means "before," "in front," or "beforehand."

In "The Bridegroom," when a young girl arrives home distraught, her parents are filled with **foreboding,** sensing something bad before it actually happens.

Vocabulary Development

Vocabulary Knowledge Rating

Create a **Vocabulary Knowledge Rating Chart** (***Professional Development Guidebook***, p. 33) for this selection. Include the selection vocabulary and the Big Question words that appear in the Writing About the Big Question sentence starters on this page. (The Big Question vocabulary is introduced on pp. 626–627.

Give students a copy of the chart. Read the words aloud, and have students mark their rating in the Before Reading column. Urge them to be alert to these words as they read and discuss the selection.

Tally how many students think they know a word to gauge how much instruction to provide. As students read and discuss the selection, point out the words and their context.

PHLit Online! **Vocabulary Central**, featuring tools, activities, and songs for studying vocabulary, is available at **www.PHLitOnline.com.**

Meet the Authors

Alexander Pushkin

(1799–1837)

Author of "The Bridegroom" (p. 642)

Alexander Pushkin is considered the father of modern Russian literature. Though a nobleman, he had great sympathy for poor Russian peasants. In literature, too, he was a rebel, drawing on folklore to express his democratic ideas.

Federico García Lorca

(1898–1936)

Author of "The Guitar" (p. 648)

Poet and playwright Federico García Lorca is considered one of the greatest Spanish writers. A native of rural Andulasia, García Lorca wrote many of his poems shortly after World War I.

Elizabeth Bishop

(1911–1979)

Author of "The Fish" (p. 650)

In 1945, Elizabeth Bishop won a poetry contest, leading to the publication of her first poetry collection, *North and South,* which included "The Fish." Her work is noted for its powerful images.

Rudyard Kipling

(1865–1936)

Author of "Danny Deever" (p. 652)

Rudyard Kipling was born in India to English parents. He worked as a journalist in India, eventually moving to England. In 1907, he was awarded the Nobel Prize in Literature.

Daily Bellringer

For each class during which you will teach this selection, have students complete one of the five Quick Write activities for Week 19 in the *Daily Bellringer Activities* booklet.

Multidraft Reading

This icon ● marks natural pauses in the selection. To assist struggling readers and to deepen reading for all, assign the text in "chunks," following the icons, and apply multidraft reading protocols. For each reading, have students set the purpose indicated:

- **First reading**—literal comprehension: answering the Reading Check questions.
- **Second reading**—application of skills: answering the Read Fluently and The Speaker in Poetry prompts.
- **Third reading**—interpretation: answering the end-of-selection questions.

For more guidance, see the ***Classroom Strategies and Teaching Routines*** card on multidraft reading.

Differentiated Instruction — Additional Instruction

EL Extended Support—English Learners

Have students complete the **Reading and Vocabulary Warm-ups, *Unit 4 Resources,*** pp. 23–26, before they read. Assign the prereading pages for the selection and the adapted selection in the ***Reader's Notebook: English Learner's Version.*** Then, have students listen to portions of the selection on the ***Hear It!* Audio CD** (adapted text).

L1 L2 Extended Support—Struggling Readers

Have students complete the **Reading and Vocabulary Warm-ups, *Unit 4 Resources,*** pp. 23–26, before they read. Assign the prereading pages for the selection and the adapted selection in the ***Reader's Notebook: Adapted Version.*** Then, have students listen to portions of the selection on the ***Hear It!* Audio CD** (adapted text).

Extended Support—Reluctant Readers

To build motivation and engagement before assigning the selection, have students read "Ooooh, Scary!" a thematically related selection in ***Reality Central.*** Then, use the questions at the conclusion of the related selection to guide discussion.

PHLit Online!

For more about the author, practice with the selection vocabulary, and more background, go to **www.PHLitOnline.com.**

TEACH

❶ Activating Prior Knowledge

Use the resources in your local library to obtain cassettes or CDs with the following musical pieces: (1) a rendition of "The Wedding March"; (2) George Harrison's "While My Guitar Gently Weeps"; (3) something from the soundtrack for the movie *Big Fish;* and (4) a military anthem such as "The Battle Hymn of the Republic." Lead students in a discussion about the tone, mood, and message of each song. Have students comment on the connections between life and music. Extend these connections to illustrate the relationship between music and poetry.

Concept Connector →

Students will return to these discussion points after completing the poems.

Whole-Class Activity

Students will find the narrative poems in this collection easier to follow if they are not slowed down by the frequent line and stanza breaks. Play the ***Hear It!* Audio CD** and have students follow along in their books.

❷ About the Selections

"The Bridegroom" is a variation on the folk motif of a worthy young person declaring independence. In "The Guitar," the speaker compares the mournful notes of a guitar to a wounded heart. At the opening of "The Fish," the conflict seems to be resolved—the fish is caught—but an internal conflict leads to an unexpected outcome. In "Danny Deever," young soldiers are about to witness the hanging of one of their ranks.

❸ Critical Viewing

Possible response: The world seems to be drawn to the couple from the flying figure with a trumpet to the musicians, people, and animals.

❹ Background

Allusion Allusions to literature, history, religion, myth, politics, sports, science, and popular culture are common in poetry because they call to mind a whole series of associations and feelings.

1 2 The Bridegroom

Alexander Pushkin *translated by D.M. Thomas*

5

The Lights of Marriage (detail), Marc Chagall, Kunsthaus, Zurich. © 1998 Artists Rights Society (ARS), New York/ADAGP, Paris.

3 ▲ **Critical Viewing** Which details in this painting suggest that a single marriage is significant to the whole world? **[Interpret]**

4 **Background** An **allusion** is a reference to a person, event, place, or artistic work (often, to one that is well known). Pushkin's poem is an extended allusion to a folk tale, "The Robber Bridegroom." From the opening lines, Pushkin's Russian readers would have recognized the story, in which a woman witnesses a horrible crime—and nearly marries the person who committed it.

Vocabulary Development

Word Form Chart

Expand students' vocabulary by helping them learn related forms of the selection vocabulary words. Give students a blank **Word Form Chart** (***Professional Development Guidebook***, pp. 41–42), with *foreboding, monotonously,* and *venerable* in their appropriate columns. Have students work with partners to determine the related forms. The final chart should look like the one shown.

Noun	Verb	Adjective	Adverb
foreboding	forebode	foreboding	forebodingly
monotony		monotonous	**monotonously**
venerability, or venerableness		**venerable**	venerably

For three days Natasha,
The merchant's daughter,
Was missing. The third night,
She ran in, distraught.
Her father and mother
Plied her with questions.
She did not hear them,
She could hardly breathe.

Stricken with foreboding
They pleaded, got angry,
But still she was silent;
At last they gave up.
Natasha's cheeks regained
Their rosy color.
And cheerfully again
She sat with her sisters.

Once at the shingle-gate
She sat with her friends
—And a swift troika[1]
Flashed by before them;
A handsome young man
Stood driving the horses;
Snow and mud went flying,
Splashing the girls.

He gazed as he flew past,
And Natasha gazed.
He flew on. Natasha froze.
6 Headlong she ran home.
"It was he! It was he!"
She cried. "I know it!
I recognized him! Papa,
Mama, save me from him!"

Full of grief and fear,
They shake their heads, sighing.
Her father says: "My child,
Tell me everything.
If someone has harmed you,
Tell us . . . even a hint."
She weeps again and
Her lips remain sealed.

Vocabulary
foreboding (fôr bōd′ iŋ) *n.* a feeling that something bad will happen

Literary Analysis
The Speaker in Poetry
Which details in this stanza does the speaker use to tell a story?

7 **Reading Check**
Why do Natasha's mother and father question her?

1. **troika** (troi′ kə) *n.* Russian carriage or sleigh drawn by a team of three horses.

5 Humanities

The Lights of Marriage by Marc Chagall (1887–1985) depicts a wedding scene that is suggestive of the wedding scene described in "The Bridegroom."

Chagall was born in Russia, where he studied painting under Leon Bakst in St. Petersburg. His paintings are distinguished by deeply colored landscapes in which people, objects, and animals fly and float in dreamlike fantasy. Use this question for discussion:

- How is the mood of the painting similar to the mood of Natasha's wedding?
  Possible response: Just as the painting creates a mysterious tension with its unexplained flying human and animal figures, so Natasha's wedding is unsettling with its vivid description of a violent dream and its melodramatic conclusion.

6 Literary Analysis
The Speaker in Poetry

1. Have a volunteer read the bracketed text.
2. Then, **ask** students the Literary Analysis question: Which details in this stanza does the speaker use to tell a story?
   Answer: Natasha is obviously frightened by something that she cannot or will not discuss with her concerned parents. The story has conflict, character development, and dialogue.

7 Reading Check

Answer: Natasha disappears for three days and returns home visibly upset. They want to know what is wrong.

Differentiated Instruction for Universal Access

Strategy for Less Proficient Readers
To help students follow the story that Pushkin presents, instruct them to read the poem in sentences, rather than pausing at the end of each line. In addition, have students pause at the end of each stanza to summarize the events and details that it presents.

EL Strategy for English Learners
Idioms can be difficult for English learners because familiar words often take on different meanings. To help students follow the story, assist them in understanding the idioms the writer uses. For example, English learners may have trouble with the expressions "sings the girl's praises" (commend someone, especially to others) and "talks in riddles" (makes no sense).

PHLit Online!
This selection is available in interactive format in the **Enriched Online Student Edition, www.PHLitOnline.com,** which includes a thematically related video and writing prompt and an interactive graphic organizer.

8 Reading Skill
Read Fluently

1. Point out to students that different end marks require slight differences in pauses. The comma requires a brief pause so that the reader does not run together words and phrases. A semicolon or a colon signals a pause that is longer than a comma's pause but shorter than a period's.
2. Ask a volunteer to read aloud the bracketed stanza, paying attention to punctuation at the ends of lines.
3. Then, **ask** students the Reading Skill question: How many sentences are there in this stanza of eight lines?
   Answer: There are two sentences in the eight-line stanza.

The next morning, the old
Matchmaking woman
Unexpectedly calls and
Sings the girl's praises;
Says to the father: "You
Have the goods and I
A buyer for them:
A handsome young man.

"He bows low to no one,
He lives like a lord
With no debts nor worries;
He's rich and he's generous,
Says he will give his bride,
On their wedding-day,
A fox-fur coat, a pearl,
Gold rings, brocaded[2] dresses,

Reading Skill
Read Fluently How many sentences are there in this stanza of eight lines? **8**

"Yesterday, out driving,
He saw your Natasha;
Shall we shake hands
And get her to church?"
The woman starts to eat
A pie, and talks in riddles,
While the poor girl
Does not know where to look.

"Agreed," says her father;
"Go in happiness
To the altar, Natasha;
It's dull for you here;
A swallow should not spend
All its time singing,
It's time for you to build
A nest for your children."

Natasha leaned against
The wall and tried
To speak—but found herself
Sobbing; she was shuddering
And laughing. The matchmaker
Poured out a cup of water,
Gave her some to drink,
Splashed some in her face.

2. **brocaded** (brō kād′ əd) *adj.* with raised designs woven into the cloth.

Vocabulary Development

Thematic Vocabulary: The Big Question

As students are discussing Poetry Collection 1, encourage them to use the thematic vocabulary presented in Introducing the Big Question, pp. 626–627. You might encourage them with sentence starters like these:

1. Natasha does not use *verbal* communication to tell how she's feeling at first because . . .
2. Natasha explains the *context* of her dream in order to . . .
3. Bishop gives *meaning* to the fish's life by . . .
4. The dialect, a distinct form of *language,* plays an important role in "Danny Deever" because . . .

Her parents are distressed.
Then Natasha recovered,
And calmly she said:
"Your will be done. Call
My bridegroom to the feast,
Bake loaves for the whole world,
Brew sweet mead[3] and call
The law to the feast."

"Of course, Natasha, angel!
You know we'd give our lives
To make you happy!"
They bake and they brew;
The worthy guests come,
The bride is led to the feast,
Her maids sing and weep;
Then horses and a sledge[4]

With the groom—and all sit.
The glasses ring and clatter,
The toasting-cup is passed
From hand to hand in **tumult**,
The guests are drunk.

BRIDEGROOM
"Friends, why is my fair bride
Sad, why is she not
Feasting and serving?"

10
The bride answers the groom:
"I will tell you why
As best I can. My soul
Knows no rest, day and night
I weep; an evil dream
Oppresses me." Her father
Says: "My dear child, tell us
What your dream is."

"I dreamed," she says, "that I
Went into a forest,
It was late and dark;

3. **mead** (mēd) *n.* drink made of fermented honey and water.
4. **sledge** (slej) *n.* sleigh.

Vocabulary
tumult (to͞o′ mult) *n.* noisy commotion

9

11 **Reading Check**
What plans does Natasha's father make for her?

9 Humanities

The Fiancés by Marc Chagall (1887–1985)

Though Chagall was influenced by contemporary developments in art, he remained for the most part an independent artist who did not fit into the mainstream. He created surreal, dreamlike works of art that were often inspired by his personal life and stories from folklore. His talent as a poet was often reflected in his work, creating colorful, vivid stories with recurring images such as lovers and angels.

1. Have students discuss the feeling created by the images in *The Fiancés.*
2. **Ask** students: How does this painting reflect the relationship between Natasha and the bridegroom?
   Possible response: The groom in the picture seems infatuated with the bride and possessive of her, just as the bridegroom in the poem. As she is in the poem, the bride in the painting seems frightened and reluctant to be with the man, for she is leaning away from the groom's tight embrace.

10 Literary Analysis
The Speaker in Poetry

1. Have students read the bracketed stanza silently to themselves.
2. Then, **ask** students: Who are the speakers in this stanza?
   Answer: Natasha speaks first. Then her father speaks.

11 Reading Check

Answer: Natasha's father arranges her marriage through a matchmaker.

Fluency

Distribute copies of page 645. Explain that many of the sentences in this poem are spread over multiple lines and contain punctuation that signals to the reader where to pause or speed up. Emphasize the importance of continuous and fluid reading at the ends of lines that do not contain any punctuation. For an example, point out that the end of line 96 should flow smoothly into line 97, even though each belong to different stanzas. Read lines 81–101 aloud once, having the students follow along. Model appropriate pauses and stops, particularly those followed by exclamation points, such as "angel" in line 89. Read the lines aloud once more, this time encouraging students to mark up their copies with notes. Then, reread the lines one full sentence at a time, having the students echo what you are reading. Pay attention for trouble spots, repeating those phrases or sentences to build fluency.

(12) Critical Viewing

Possible response: This woman seems as timid and sad as Natasha is. Her bowed head, closed eyes, and solemn mouth all contribute to her resigned demeanor.

(13) THE BIG ? Connecting to the Big Question

1. **Ask** students to describe their reactions to the details of Natasha's dream.
   Possible response: I feel tense from the suspense that the speaker creates by unfolding details of the dream slowly.
2. Have students read the bracketed text.
3. **Ask** students: How does using this dream to tell the story about the bridegroom create suspense?
   Possible response: A dream, though not real, usually reflects a person's worries and fears. The bride's dream does just this, but she uses powerful language and action verbs to describe her reaction. She uses words such as "shout," "clatter," and "slammed," which suggest something out of the ordinary is happening. The bride's reaction—she slams the door and hides—reveals that she feels she should not be there. All these clues from the dream reveal to the reader that something is amiss.

▲ **Critical Viewing**
(12) What traits does this young woman seem to share with Natasha? Explain which details in the painting support your answer. **[Interpret]**

The moon was faintly
Shining behind a cloud;
I strayed from the path;
Nothing stirred except
The tops of the pine-trees.

"And suddenly, as if
I was awake, I saw
A hut. I approach the hut
And knock at the door
—Silence. A prayer on my lips
I open the door and enter.
A candle burns. All
Is silver and gold."

BRIDEGROOM
"What is bad about that?
It promises wealth."

BRIDE
"Wait, sir, I've not finished.
Silently I gazed
On the silver and gold,
The cloths, the rugs, the silks
From Novgorod,[5] and I
Was lost in wonder.

"Then I heard a shout
(13) And a clatter of hoofs . . .
Someone has driven up
To the porch. Quickly
I slammed the door and hid
Behind the stove. Now
I hear many voices . . .
Twelve young men come in,

"And with them is a girl,
Pure and beautiful.
They've taken no notice
Of the ikons,[6] they sit
To the table without
Praying or taking off

5. **Novgorod** (näv´ gə räd´) city in northwestern Russia.
6. **ikons** (ī´ känz´) *n.* sacred religious images.

646 Poetry

Think Aloud

Vocabulary: Using Context

Direct students' attention to the word *clamor* in line 155 of the poem. Using a think-aloud process, model how to use context to infer the meaning of an unknown word. Say to students:

> I'm going to think aloud to show you how to figure out the meaning of *clamor* from its context.
>
> In this stanza, *clamor* occurs in a description of what the speaker hidden in the hut, hears when twelve men enter. Earlier, in line 143, the speaker mentions "many voices." Because clamor is preceded by "shouts" and "laughs," I think it must refer to sound in some way. In line 158, the speaker repeats the word "drunken" but now says "din" that "goes on." This suggests that *clamor* is similar to *din*—a loud, continuing noise. The words "grows louder still," in line 159, confirm my inference.

Their hats. At the head,
The eldest brother,
At his right, the youngest;
At his left, the girl.
Shouts, laughs, drunken clamor . . . "

BRIDEGROOM
"That betokens merriment."

BRIDE
"Wait, sir, I've not finished.
The drunken din goes on
And grows louder still.
Only the girl is sad.

"She sits silent, neither
Eating nor drinking;
(14) But sheds tears in plenty;
The eldest brother
Takes his knife and, whistling,
Sharpens it; seizing her by
The hair he kills her
And cuts off her right hand."

"Why," says the groom, "this
Is nonsense! Believe me,
My love, your dream is not evil."
She looks him in the eyes.
"And from whose hand
Does this ring come?"
The bride said. The whole throng
Rose in the silence.

With a clatter the ring
(15) Falls, and rolls along
The floor. The groom blanches,
Trembles. Confusion . . .
"Seize him!" the law commands.
He's bound, judged, put to death.
Natasha is famous!
Our song at an end.

Literary Analysis
The Speaker in Poetry
What details help the bride's narrative grow in excitement?

(14) Literary Analysis
The Speaker in Poetry

1. Have a volunteer read aloud the bracketed passage.
2. Then, **ask** students the Literary Analysis question: What details help the bride's narrative grow in excitement?
   Answer: The details—*takes his knife, sharpens it, seizing her,* and *kills her*—help build excitement in the narrative.

(15) Reading Skill
Read Aloud

1. Ask several different students to read the bracketed text aloud to lend different interpretations to the lines by speeding up or slowing down their reading rates.
2. Then, **ask** students to describe the effect of these different interpretations on the message of the poem and on the reader.
   Possible response: The first four lines of the stanza, which are choppy due to frequent punctuation, bring the poem to a rapid close. Because of their tempo, the reader experiences surprise when the bridegroom is discovered, tried, and put to death all at once.

▶**Monitor Progress** If students have difficulty reading the passage aloud effectively, choose another group of lines and have them continue practicing.

▶**Reteach** Remind students that a poet's punctuation choices are important. Briefly review the different types of punctuation that students will encounter and the actions they signal.

Differentiated Instruction for Universal Access

Enrichment for Gifted/Talented Students
Invite students to stage a dramatic performance of Pushkin's "The Bridegroom." In addition to the speaking parts for Natasha, her parents, and the bridegroom, suggest that students add sound effects, props, and costumes to enliven the show. Give students plenty of time to rehearse their performance. Invite other classes studying the same work to view the performance. Also, ask students to be prepared to lead a discussion following the performance regarding the interpretations they made within the performance and why they made them.

⓰ Humanities

The Old Guitarist by Pablo Picasso (1881–1973)

Spanish-born Pablo Picasso is one of the most important visual artists of the twentieth century. During his career, Picasso went through numerous stylistic periods. In his Blue Period, epitomized by *The Old Guitarist,* he painted figures in a dark, sorrowful, and pessimistic mood.

Picasso was one of the most widely known, controversial, and influential art figures of his time. His enormous volume of work is unparalleled. Use this question to discuss the painting:

- How do you think Federico Garcia Lorca would have responded to Picasso's painting?
  Possible response: Lorca would probably have liked the painting, because it expresses in a visual medium much of what Lorca is expressing in words.

⓱ Critical Viewing

Possible response: The man's bent posture suggests weariness, submission, and defeat.

16

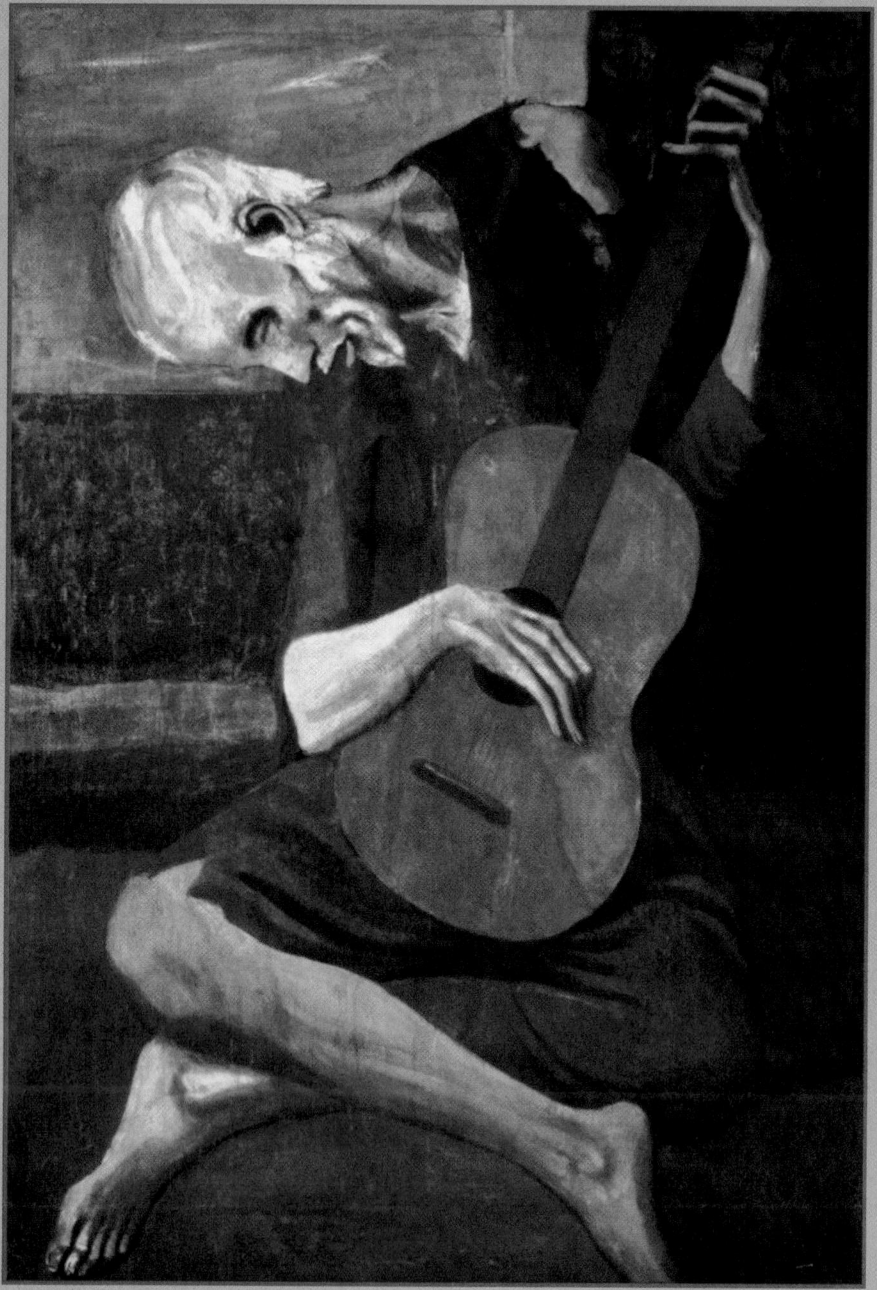

The Old Guitarist, 1903, Pablo Picasso. The Art Institute of Chicago. ©2004 Estate of Pablo Picasso/Artists Rights Society (ARS), New York.

17 ▲ **Critical Viewing** How does the man's pose add to the sad mood of this image? **[Analyze]**

Vocabulary Development

Translations

Draw students' attention to the fact that Lorca's poem has been translated into English. Discuss the problems of translation with students, including the fact that no word may exist in English with the exact same meaning and connotation as each of the original Spanish words. Translators must choose the English word that is closest to the meaning of the original Spanish word. This process changes the meaning of the original poem, however subtly. If you have students who are literate in Spanish or know a willing Spanish teacher in your school, invite them to read Lorca's poem in the original Spanish. Ask them to prepare an informal presentation for the class regarding the accuracy of this translation. Ask them to identify problems that the translator likely faced and how she chose to solve them.

The GUITAR

Federico García Lorca
translated by Elizabeth du Gué Trapier

Now begins the cry
Of the guitar,
Breaking the vaults
Of dawn.
Now begins the cry
Of the guitar.
Useless
[18] To still it.
Impossible
To still it.
It weeps monotonously
As weeps the water,
As weeps the wind
Over snow.
Impossible
To still it.
It weeps
For distant things,
Warm southern sands
Desiring white camellias.
[19] It mourns the arrow without a target,
The evening without morning.
And the first bird dead
Upon a branch.
O guitar!
A wounded heart,
Wounded by five swords.

Vocabulary
monotonously (mə nät′ 'n əs lē) *adv.* in a dull, unvarying way

Literary Analysis
The Speaker in Poetry
What feelings do the speaker's use of images in lines 19–24 convey?

18 Reading Skill
Read Aloud

1. Remind students that repetition is used for musical effect and for emphasis.
2. Have a volunteer read aloud the bracketed lines.
3. Then, **ask** students to comment on how Lorca uses repetition in the poem. What effects does he achieve?
   Answer: The repetition nearly forms a refrain of the lines "Now begins the cry/Of the guitar" and "Impossible/To still it." These lines set up the structure of the poem on which the poet adds images and emotional content that describe music as a metaphor of both life and death.

19 Literary Analysis
The Speaker in Poetry

1. **Ask** students to identify the poem as a narrative or a lyric poem. Have them discuss the reasons for their choice.
   Answer: It is a lyric poem that concentrates on expressing hope amidst sorrow.
2. Have a volunteer read the bracketed lines.
3. Then, **ask** students the Literary Analysis question: What feelings do the speaker's use of images in lines 19–24 convey?
   Possible response: The images—bleak, stark, and unsettling—are of death, and the emotion expressed is sorrow. Yet, in the midst of tragedy and despair, there is still hope—there is still life as long as there is music and someone to play it.

Differentiated Instruction for Universal Access

EL Pronunciation for English Learners

Some students might have difficulty with consonant clusters at the ends of words, especially when the final consonant is "s." Students may omit the "s" sound from the ends of words such as *begins, vaults, weeps,* and *sands.* The following strategies can help students to pronounce terminal consonant clusters that end in "s."

- Write the words *begins, vaults, weeps,* and *sands* on the board, pronouncing each word as it is written. Then, have students repeat each word multiple times. Invite students to discuss the importance of the "s" at the end of these words.
- Since "The Guitar" contains many pronunciation challenges, pair English learners with fluent speakers. Have English learners read the poem aloud to their partners. Ask fluent speakers to assist their partners with these difficult words by guiding them to the correct sound.

⓴ Literary Analysis
The Speaker in Poetry

1. Have students read the first six lines of the poem to themselves.
2. Then, **ask** students what event triggers the speaker's thought in this poem?
   Answer: The fact that the fish never fights triggers the speaker's thoughts about the creature.

㉑ Reading Skill
Read Fluently

1. Have a volunteer read aloud the bracketed passage that continues to the next page.
2. Then, **ask** students the Reading Skill prompt: Identify the pauses signaled by punctuation marks in lines 34–40.
   Answer: There are only two brief pauses, before and after "and yellowed."

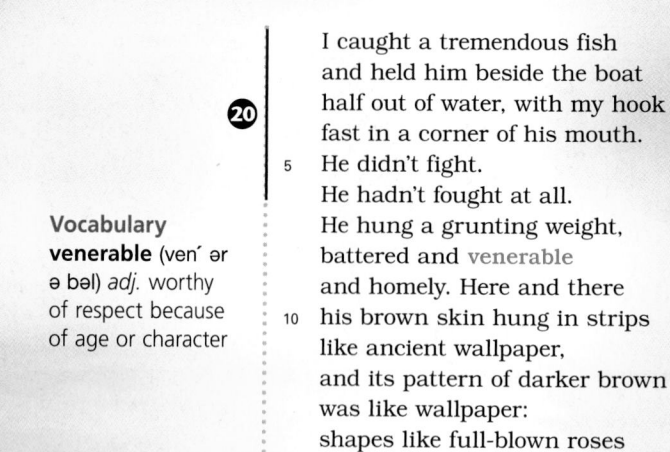

The Fish

Elizabeth Bishop

I caught a tremendous fish
and held him beside the boat
half out of water, with my hook
fast in a corner of his mouth.
He didn't fight.
He hadn't fought at all.
He hung a grunting weight,
battered and venerable
and homely. Here and there
his brown skin hung in strips
like ancient wallpaper,
and its pattern of darker brown
was like wallpaper:
shapes like full-blown roses
stained and lost through age.
He was speckled with barnacles,
fine rosettes of lime,
and infested
with tiny white sea-lice,
and underneath two or three
rags of green weed hung down.
While his gills were breathing in
the terrible oxygen
—the frightening gills,
fresh and crisp with blood,
that can cut so badly—
I thought of the coarse white flesh
packed in like feathers,
the big bones and the little bones,
the dramatic reds and blacks
of his shiny entrails,
and the pink swim-bladder
like a big peony.
I looked into his eyes
which were far larger than mine
but shallower, and yellowed,
the irises backed and packed
with tarnished tinfoil

Vocabulary
venerable (ven′ ər ə bəl) *adj.* worthy of respect because of age or character

Reading Skill
Read Fluently
Identify the pauses signaled by punctuation marks in lines 34–40.

Vocabulary Development

Mythological Words
Three words in "The Fish" derive from Greek and Roman mythology. *Venerable* comes from the Roman goddess of love, Venus. *Peony* comes from the Greek word for healing. *Iris* comes from Iris, the Greek goddess of the rainbow and messenger of the gods. Have students connect the definitions of these words with their word histories.

seen through the lenses
of old scratched isinglass.[1]
They shifted a little, but not
to return my stare.
—It was more like the tipping
of an object toward the light.
I admired his **sullen** face,
the mechanism of his jaw,
and then I saw
that from his lower lip
—if you could call it a lip—
grim, wet, and weaponlike,
hung five old pieces of fish-line,
or four and a wire leader
with the swivel still attached,
with all their five big hooks
grown firmly in his mouth.
A green line, frayed at the end
where he broke it, two heavier lines,
and a fine black thread
still crimped from the strain and snap
when it broke and he got away.
Like medals with their ribbons
frayed and wavering,
a five-haired beard of wisdom
trailing from his aching jaw.
I stared and stared
and victory filled up
the little rented boat,
from the pool of bilge
where oil had spread a rainbow
around the rusted engine
to the bailer rusted orange,
the sun-cracked thwarts[2]
the oarlocks on their strings,
the gunnels[3] —until everything
was rainbow, rainbow, rainbow!
And I let the fish go.

1. **isinglass** (ī´ zin glas´) *n.* transparent material once used in windows.
2. **thwarts** (*th*wôrtz) *n.* seats in a boat for rowers.
3. **gunnels** (gun´ əlz) *n.* upper edges of the sides of a ship or boat.

Vocabulary
sullen (sul´ ən) *adj.* gloomy and showing resentment

◀ Critical Viewing
Does this fish look like the "venerable" old warrior described in the poem? Explain. **[Analyze]**

Literary Analysis
The Speaker in Poetry
What details in the speaker's conclusion provide a dramatic insight and a surprising action?

22 Critical Viewing

Possible response: This fish does look like the venerable old warrior described in the poem. It is large, homely, and strong; it looks capable of having escaped capture many times.

23 Literary Analysis
The Speaker in Poetry

1. Have students read the bracketed text.
2. Then, **ask** the Literary Analysis question: What details in the speaker's conclusion provide a dramatic insight and a surprising action?
   Possible response: In a moment of insight, the speaker recognizes that the fish is a tough, experienced, and wise old fighter. This recognition leads the speaker to release the fish.

Differentiated Instruction for Universal Access

Strategy for Special Needs Students
To help students find their way into this poem, ask students who have been fishing to describe the first fish they ever caught or the largest fish they ever caught. Encourage them to provide specific details about the *when, where,* and *how* of the experience. As you read the poem as a class, ask students with fishing experience to comment on the details that the speaker includes.

Enrichment for Gifted/Talented Students
Bishop provides more than a dozen precise details of the fish's appearance, creating a poetic photograph. Students with artistic talent might use these physical details to create their own impressions of the fish's appearance. Give students their choice of art medium, but challenge them to carefully approximate the details of color, shape, and size that Bishop presents in "The Fish."

㉔ Visual Connections

Whole-Class Activity

1. Have students describe what they see in the picture.
   Possible response: A man stands on the steps to a platform. He looks sad and resigned, staring off into the distance. There is also another solider who looks like a guard standing among some spectators at the bottom of the picture.
2. Then, **ask** students: Who might this man be? Explain.
   Possible response: The man might be Danny Deever, since the title of the poem is a man's name.
3. Have students discuss what the poem might be about by analyzing the depicted scene.
   Possible response: The poem might be about a man, Danny Deever, who is to be put to death. The man looks sorrowful and hopeless, as if he knows his fate. Also, his arms are tied behind his back with rope, so he must be a prisoner. The background contains buildings with spherical, gold tops, so it may take place somewhere in India.

Small-Group Activity

1. Have students work in small groups. Tell them to write a short poem, no more than eight lines, that is based on their understanding of the image. Remind them that any interpretation is correct as long as it is supported by examples.
2. Ask a volunteer from each group to read the poem aloud.

Individual Activity

1. Have students write a paragraph describing their reactions to the picture. Prompt students to interpret the mood of the poem based on what this image suggests.
2. Display students' work in the room. Have students compare and contrast their reactions and interpretations.

Vocabulary Development

Understanding British Dialect

The dialect Kipling uses in "Danny Deever" reflects the British working class, especially the residents of London. (Cockney is a distinctive form of this dialect common to London's East End.) Several of the hallmarks of this dialect are evident in the poem:

Dropping final consonant sounds. Many American dialects share this tendency to drop final *g*'s and *d*'s: *and* becomes *an'*; *marching* becomes *marchin.'*

Dropping of initial "h" sounds. Hollow becomes *'ollow; hundred* becomes *'undred*. There are exceptions, however, in "Danny Deever": the *h* in *hangin'* is pronounced distinctly every time. The Color-Sergeant says *hear* in line 5 but *'ear* in line 29.

Distinctive pronunciations. One example of this occurs in line 15, where *half* is pronounced *'arf*.

25 **Background** In this poem, Kipling writes in **dialect,** a distinct form of a language, spoken by people living in a particular region or belonging to a particular group. The characters' dialect reflects their working-class British origins.

"What are the bugles blowin' for?" said Files-on-Parade.[1]
"To turn you out, to turn you out," the Color-Sergeant[2] said.
"What makes you look so white, so white?" said Files-on-Parade.
"I'm dreadin' what I've got to watch," the Color-Sergeant said.
For they're hangin' Danny Deever, you can hear the Dead March play,
The regiment's in 'ollow square[3] —they're hangin' him today;
They've taken of his buttons off an' cut his stripes away,
An' they're hangin' Danny Deever in the mornin'.

"What makes the rear-rank breathe so 'ard?" said Files-on-Parade.
"It's bitter cold, it's bitter cold," the Color-Sergeant said.
"What makes that front-rank man fall down?" says Files-on-Parade.
"A touch o' sun, a touch o' sun," the Color-Sergeant said.
26 They are hangin' Danny Deever, they are marchin' of 'im round,
They 'ave 'alted Danny Deever by 'is coffin on the ground;
An' 'e'll swing in 'arf a minute for a sneakin' shootin' hound—
O they're hangin' Danny Deever in the mornin'!

27 "'Is cot was right-'and cot to mine," said Files-on-Parade.
"'E's sleepin' out an' far tonight," the Color-Sergeant said.
"I've drunk 'is beer a score o' times," said Files-on-Parade.
"'E's drinkin' bitter beer alone," the Color-Sergeant said.
They are hangin' Danny Deever, you must mark 'im to 'is place,
For 'e shot a comrade sleepin'—you must look 'im in the face;
Nine 'undred of 'is county an' the regiment's disgrace,
While they're hangin' Danny Deever in the mornin'.

1. **Files-on-Parade** soldier who directs marching formations.
2. **Color-Sergeant** flag-bearer.
3. **'ollow square** At a hanging, soldiers standing in ranks form three sides of a square; the gallows occupies the fourth side.

Reading Skill
Read Fluently How should the punctuation in lines 13–16 affect your reading rate and pace?

Vocabulary
comrade (käm´ rad´) *n.* a close companion

25 Background
Dialect
Point out to students that writers use dialect to make their characters sound realistic and to create the local color of language. Pronunciation, vocabulary, and sentence structure reflect dialect.

26 Reading Skill
Read Fluently
1. Have students read the bracketed passage aloud.
2. Then, **ask** students the Reading Skill question: How should the punctuation in lines 13–16 affect your reading rate and pace?
   Possible response: The punctuation barely slows the pace of the lines, which is regular and swift because of the rhythm and rhyme scheme.

27 Literary Analysis
The Speaker in Poetry
1. Point out to students that in dramatic poems, one or more characters speaks. By using the words of these speakers to tell the story, the poet creates the illusion that the reader is actually witnessing the event.
2. Have a volunteer read the bracketed passage aloud.
3. Then, **ask** students how this passage helps them to feel that they are witnessing the events in the poem.
   Possible response: The conversation creates a sense of immediacy, as if the reader is standing near the speakers, overhearing the conversation.

Concept Connector
Activating Prior Knowledge
Have students return to the discussion points they raised before reading the selection. Lead a class discussion, focusing on what students have learned that confirms or invalidates their ideas about the role music plays in human lives and the connection between music and poetry. Encourage students to cite specific details, quotations, or other evidence from the texts to support their responses.

Writing About the Big Question
Have students compare their responses to the sentence starters they completed before reading the story with their ideas afterwards. Ask them to explain whether their thoughts have changed.

Reading Skill Graphic Organizer
Ask students to review the graphic organizers they completed while reading. Show them **Reading Skill Graphic Organizer A** (*Graphic Organizer Transparencies,* page 113) as an example. Then have students share their graphic organizers.

Answers

Critical Thinking

1. **Possible response:** Images: Warm southern sands; Heart wounded by five swords; rainbow. Listening to another reader's response to a poem is likely to create a deeper appreciation of the poem for the listener.
2. (a) Natasha is horrified by the matchmaker's visit. She has seen the man murder someone the night before, but she says nothing. She sobs, shudders, and laughs. (b) Her dream reveals that she knows her bridegroom is a murderer.
3. (a) The guitar weeps for an arrow without a target, an evening without a morning, and the first bird dead upon a branch.
(b) **Possible response:** These things represent unfulfilled potential or promise. An arrow without a target cannot have a purpose. An evening without a morning seems to indicate that life has been cut off.
4. (a) The speaker decides to return the fish to the water.
(b) **Possible response:** The fact that the fish has successfully survived so many battles motivates the speaker to let it go.
5. (a) The Color-Sergeant and Files-on-Parade are the two characters who speak in "Danny Deever."
(b) **Possible response:** The Color-Sergeant seems wiser and more hardened to the ways of the military; Files-on-Parade seems more naive and inexperienced.

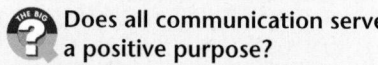

Does all communication serve a positive purpose?

Possible response: In "The Bridegroom," many feelings and emotions are conveyed. For example, Natasha's silence indicates foreboding; her refusal to speak reveals her anger; and when she sits with her sisters, she is cheerful. Natasha experiences a range of feelings that are a result of events described in her dream and in conversations with others. Her capacity for feeling makes her character more convincing, so the reader is more likely to empathize with her in her distress.

"What's that so black agin the sun?" said Files-on-Parade.
"It's Danny fightin' 'ard for life," the Color-Sergeant said.
"What's that that whimpers over'ead?" said Files-on-Parade.
It's Danny's soul that's passin' now," the Color-Sergeant said.
For they're done with Danny Deever, you can 'ear the
quick-step play,
The regiment's in column, an' they're marchin' us away;
Ho! the young recruits are shakin', an' they'll want their
beer to-day,
After hangin' Danny Deever in the mornin'.

Critical Thinking

1. **Respond:** Identify the images you find most vivid in these poems. Then, discuss them with a partner, noting the choices you share. Finally, explain how your appreciation of the poems has or has not changed as a result of your discussion.
2. **(a)** In "The Bridegroom," how does Natasha react during the matchmaker's visit? **(b) Connect:** Explain what her "dream" reveals about the reasons for her reaction.
3. **(a)** List three things in "The Guitar" for which the guitar weeps. **(b) Connect:** Explain how each of these things expresses an unfulfilled desire or something incomplete.
4. **(a)** What decision does the speaker of "The Fish" make at the end of the poem? **(b) Analyze:** What realization about the fish motivates this decision? Support your answer with details.
5. **(a)** Who are the two characters who speak in "Danny Deever"? **(b)** Contrast: How are these two characters different?

Does all communication serve a positive purpose? Choose one of the poems and describe the feelings and emotions that it conveys. Would you say the poem serves a positive purpose? Explain.

Assessment Resources

Unit 4 Resources

L1 L2 EL **Selection Test A**, pp. 35–37. Administer Test A to less advanced students and English learners.

L3 L4 **Selection Test B**, pp. 38–40. Administer Test B to on-level and more advanced students.

L3 L4 **Open-Book Test**, pp. 32–34. As an alternative, give the Open-Book Test.

All **Customizable Test Bank**

All **Self-tests**
Students may prepare for the **Selection Test** by taking the **Self-test** online.

PHLit Online! All assessment resources are available at **www.PHLitOnline.com.**

After You Read
Poetry Collection 1

The Bridegroom • The Guitar • The Fish • Danny Deever

Literary Analysis: The Speaker in Poetry

1. Identify the best example of **narrative poetry** from among the poems in Poetry Collection 1. Explain your choice.
2. Use this chart to list an example of visual **imagery**—a passage that appeals to sight. Add the sensory language that the poet uses to build the image. Finally, note the effect that these details generate.

Image	Sensory Language	Effect

3. Compare the **speakers** in "The Guitar" and "The Fish." In your response, consider how much or how little you know about the speaker and whether the speaker is the poet or a character taking part in the action of the poem.

Reading Skill: Read Fluently

4. Choose one of the poems and use your notes from the **reading rate chart** on page 639. Then, practice reading the poem aloud until you can **read** it fluently.

Vocabulary

Practice For each of the following items, write a sentence about the situation described. In each of your sentences, use a word from the vocabulary list for Poetry Collection 1, on page 640.

1. a visit with an elderly, much-admired jazz drummer
2. a terrible feeling about whether you lost something important
3. a dripping faucet
4. a loud and crowded city council meeting
5. a camping trip with a close friend
6. a rainy day causes someone to feel gloomy and sad

Word Study Use the context of the sentences and what you know about the **Old English prefix *fore-*** to explain your answers.

1. Why should you check the weather *forecast* before going outside?
2. Would you *forewarn* a friend if you thought he was in danger?

Word Study

The **Old English prefix *fore-*** means "before," "in front," or "beforehand."

Challenge Explain how the prefix *fore-* contributes to the meanings of these words. Consult a dictionary if necessary.

forerunner
foreshadow
foretell

Answers

Literary Analysis

1. Many students will suggest "The Bridegroom" as a good example of a narrative poem because it presents realistic characters, contains a well-developed plot, and creates suspense.
2. **Possible response: Example:** ". . . its pattern of darker brown was like wallpaper:" **Sensory Language:** "shapes like full-blown roses stained . . . through age"; "speckled with barnacles . . ." **Effect:** They paint a vivid picture of the way the fish looks.
3. **Possible response:** The speaker of "The Guitar" uses highly condensed, repetitive language to mirror the effect of guitar music. The speaker of "The Fish" uses direct language and vivid imagery to explain the reasons for returning the huge fish to the water. In neither case do readers know very much about the speaker, nor can the reader determine whether the speaker is the poet or an invented character.

Reading Skill

4. Check students' marks for accuracy. Reading rates should be correctly adjusted wherever there is any punctuation, important words or sounds, and groups of words that express a single thought.

   For other sample answers, see ***Graphic Organizer Transparencies,* Reading Skills Graphic Organizer A, p. 116,** and the **Additional Answers** section.

Vocabulary
Practice
Possible responses:

1. The venerable Charlie Bird not only played for his visitors, but he also spoke lovingly of his friendships with some of jazz's finest musicians.
2. One hour into our drive, Mom was overcome with the foreboding that she had misplaced her wallet.

Answers continued

3. The monotonous dripping of the faucet in the chemistry lab did nothing to enliven the tired students.
4. The controversial topic to be discussed, in addition to the packed room, served only to excite the council members to a general tumult.
5. Carlos and his comrade, David, experienced an unexpected rain shower while they were pitching their tent.
6. Patrice spent the entire day sullen in her room while she listened to the rain clink against the window.

Word Study
Sample answers:

1. You should check the forecast so you know beforehand what to wear.
2. Yes, I would forewarn a friend to prevent him or her from getting hurt.

Word Study: Challenge
Sample answers: *Forerunner* means "someone who goes before or in front of others." *Foreshadow* means "to suggest that something might happen before it does." *Foretell* means "to guess what will happen beforehand."

PRETEACH

Skills instruction for the ***Reading Skill*** *and* ***Literary Analysis*** *concept for this selection appears on p. 639.*

❶ Writing About the Big Question

1. Review the assignment with the class.
2. Hold up a pencil. Ask students to give their feeling about this familiar object. (Students may not feel anything for it.) Ask why someone might want to portray it in a different way.
   (**Possible response:** It can make a dull object more interesting.
3. Have students complete the sentence starter. Review responses as a class.
   (**Possible response:** Looking at a familiar object or situation in a different way can give it a new <u>meaning</u> because *it changes your feelings about it.*)
4. Remind students that their answers will help them think about the Big Question.

While You Read

Tell students that as they read, they should pay attention to ideas, things, or people that unexpectedly change.

❷ Vocabulary

1. Have students preview the selection vocabulary.
2. For each word, have students say the word aloud.
3. Then, use the word in a sentence that defines the word.
4. Finally, repeat your definitional sentence or a similar sentence with the word missing, and have the class "fill in the blank" chorally. Here is an example:

   Something <u>stark</u> is bare or harsh. The lush forest, ravaged by the brush fire, was now lifeless and [students say "stark"].

❸ Word Study

1. Introduce the skill, using the instruction in the box.
2. Ask students how the prefix *re-* contributes to the meaning of the word: *reiterate.* (**Sample answer:** to say "again")

Does all *communication* serve a positive purpose?

❶ Writing About the Big Question

In Poetry Collection 2, the speakers in the poems communicate unusual perspectives about a variety of things, many of them found in nature. Use this sentence starter to develop your ideas about the Big Question.

Looking at a familiar object or situation in a different way can give it a new **meaning** because ______________.

While You Read As you read these poems, look for items, stories, or people that change in surprising ways.

❷ Vocabulary

Read each word and its definition. Decide whether you know the word well, know it a little bit, or do not know it at all. After you read, see how your knowledge of each word has increased.

- **idle** (īd´ 'l) *adj.* useless; not busy (p. 658) ***<u>Idle</u> hands are not helping hands.*** *idle v. idleness n. idly adv.*
- **earnest** (ʉr´ nist) *adj.* serious and intense; not joking (p. 658) ***The <u>earnest</u> effort of the farmer saved the crops from the drought.*** *earnestly adv. earnestness n.*
- **rejoiced** (ri joist´) *v.* showed happiness (p. 661) ***The team members <u>rejoiced</u> when they won the tournament.*** *rejoicingly adv. joy n.*
- **anguish** (aŋ´ gwish) *n.* extreme suffering, as from grief or pain (p. 662) ***Her <u>anguish</u> at the funeral was obvious.*** *anguish v. anguished adj.*
- **clenching** (klench´ iŋ) *v.* closing or holding tightly (p. 664) ***The child was <u>clenching</u> her fist in anger.*** *clench n. clenched adj.*
- **stark** (stärk) *adj.* bare; harsh (p. 666) ***The <u>stark</u> room contained only a table and chair.*** *starkly adv. starkness n.*

❸ Word Study

The **Latin prefix *re-*** means "again" or "anew."

In "A Tree Telling of Orpheus," a tree **rejoiced**, or experienced new happiness, when it heard Orpheus' music.

Vocabulary Development

Vocabulary Knowledge Rating

Create a **Vocabulary Knowledge Rating Chart** (***Professional Development Guidebook***, p. 33) for this selection. Include the selection vocabulary and the Big Question word in the Writing About the Big Question sentence starter on this page. (The Big Question vocabulary is introduced on pp. 626–627.

Give students a copy of the chart. Read the words aloud, and have students mark their rating in the Before Reading column. Urge them to be alert to these words as they read and discuss the selection.

Tally how many students think they know a word to gauge how much instruction to provide. As students read and discuss the selection, point out the words and their context.

PHLit Online! **Vocabulary Central**, featuring tools, activities, and songs for studying vocabulary, is available at **www.PHLitOnline.com.**

Meet the Authors

Robert Frost

(1874–1963)

Author of "Mowing" (p. 658)

Robert Frost worked as a farmer, an editor, and a schoolteacher, absorbing the ebb and flow of New England life. He went on to become one of America's most successful poets, winning many awards, including four Pulitzer Prizes.

Denise Levertov

(1923–1997)

Author of "A Tree Telling of Orpheus" (p. 659)

When Denise Levertov moved to the United States from England in 1948, she became associated with an experimental community of writers. She said that the freewheeling "open forms" she used allowed her to "explore chaos."

Naomi Shihab Nye

(b. 1952)

Author of "Making a Fist" (p. 664)

Naomi Shihab Nye began publishing poetry in magazines when she was in high school. Her poetry often draws inspiration from the places where she has lived—St. Louis, Missouri, and Jerusalem, in Israel, as well as her current home, San Antonio, Texas.

William Carlos Williams

(1883–1963)

Author of "Spring and All" (p. 665)

William Carlos Williams was both a doctor and a poet. When asked how he managed his double career, he replied that he treated his patients like poems and his poems like patients. Williams also said that a poet should listen "to the language of his locality."

Daily Bellringer

For each class during which you will teach this selection, have students complete one of the five Quick Write activities for Week 19 in the ***Daily Bellringer Activities*** booklet.

Multidraft Reading

To assist struggling readers and to deepen reading for all, apply multidraft reading protocols. For each reading, have students set the purpose indicated:

- **First reading**—literal comprehension: answering the Reading Check questions.
- **Second reading**—application of skills: answering the Read Fluently and The Speaker in Poetry prompts.
- **Third reading**—interpretation: answering the end-of-selection questions.

For more guidance, refer to the ***Classroom Strategies and Teaching Routines*** card on multidraft reading.

Differentiated Instruction

Additional Instruction

EL Extended Support—English Learners

Have students complete the **Reading and Vocabulary Warm-ups, *Unit 4 Resources*,** pp. 23–26, before they read. Assign the prereading pages for the selection in the ***Reader's Notebook: English Learner's Version.*** Then, have students listen to portions of the selection on the ***Hear It!* Audio CD.**

L1 L2 Extended Support—Struggling Readers

Have students complete the **Reading and Vocabulary Warm-ups, *Unit 4 Resources*,** pp. 23–26, before they read. Assign the prereading pages for the selection in the ***Reader's Notebook: Adapted Version.*** Then, have students listen to portions of the selection on the ***Hear It!* Audio CD** (adapted text).

Extended Support—Reluctant Readers

To build motivation and engagement before assigning the selection, have students read "Up a Tree," a thematically related selection in ***Reality Central.*** Then, use the questions at the conclusion of the related selection to guide discussion.

PHLit Online!

For more about the author, practice with the selection vocabulary, or more background, go to **www.PHLitOnline.com.**

TEACH

❶ Activating Prior Knowledge

Use the resources in your local library to obtain cassettes or CDs with the following natural sounds: (1) woodland sounds; (2) wind sounds; and (3) sea, ocean, or water sounds. Lead students in a discussion about the connections. Extend these connections to illustrate the relationships among nature, music, and poetry.

Concept Connector →

Students will return to these discussion points after completing the poems.

Individual Activity

After students read the poems, have them choose pieces of music that would provide appropriate backgrounds for "A Tree Telling of Orpheus," "Mowing," "Spring and All," or "Making a Fist." Have students play their choices for the class as they read the poems aloud.

❷ About the Selections

In "Mowing," Frost celebrates the physicality of mowing. In "A Tree Telling of Orpheus," Denise Levertov uses the point of view of a tree to describe the stirrings of the emotions created by the music of nature. A fist becomes the central image in Nye's "Making a Fist." In "Spring and All," the speaker realizes that birth and renewal can be both joyous and difficult.

❸ Critical Viewing

Answer: A *scythe* is present in both the painting and the poem.

❹ Background
Dialect

One way Robert Frost captures the flavor of life in New England is by using dialect, a manner of speaking that is common to a particular region or group. Dialect affects pronunciation, word choice, and grammatical structure. Dialect is a cultural phenomenon found in many parts of the world; it should not be associated with illiteracy or the lack of intelligence.

Mowing

❶

❷

❸ ▶ **Critical Viewing** Which word in the poem names one of the tools shown in the painting? Explain how you know. **[Integrate Vocabulary]**

ROBERT FROST

❹ **Background** A **dialect** is the distinct form of a language spoken by people in a particular region or group. The speaker of this poem uses New England dialect words such as *swale*, referring to a marshland, and *make*, referring to the process of drying out hay. He also uses the outdated word *fay*, meaning "fairy" or "elf." Through these words, Frost creates a speaker who is a man of the land, a traditional New England farmer.

There was never a sound beside the wood but one,
And that was my long scythe whispering to the ground.
What was it it whispered? I knew not well myself;
Perhaps it was something about the heat of the sun,
Something, perhaps, about the lack of sound—
And that was why it whispered and did not speak.
It was no dream of the gift of idle hours,
Or easy gold at the hand of fay or elf:
Anything more than the truth would have seemed too weak
To the earnest love that laid the swale in rows,
Not without feeble-pointed spikes of flowers
(Pale orchises), and scared a bright green snake.
The fact is the sweetest dream that labor knows.
My long scythe whispered and left the hay to make.

Vocabulary
idle (īd´ 'l) *adj.* useless; not busy
earnest (ʉr´ nist) *adj.* serious and intense; not joking

Vocabulary Development

Thematic Vocabulary: The Big Question

As students are discussing Poetry Collection 2, encourage them to use the thematic vocabulary presented in Introducing the Big Question, pp. 626–627. You might encourage them with sentence starters like these:

1. Frost wrote "Mowing" in a *language* specific to a certain group of people because . . .
2. The tree in Levertov's poem communicates its *connection* to the music by . . .
3. The message that the speaker in "Making a Fist" is trying to *convey* is . . .
4. In "Spring & All," Williams creates a feeling of *isolation* when he describes . . .

A Tree Telling of Orpheus

Denise Levertov

5 Background An **allusion** is a reference to a person, event, place, or artistic work. Levertov's poem is an extended allusion to the classic Greek myth of Orpheus. Orpheus' skill on the lyre, an ancient stringed instrument, was so great and his voice so beautiful that trees were said to uproot themselves to follow him. In the end, he was torn limb from limb by his frenzied followers, the Maenads (mē´ nadz ´). Flung into a nearby river, his head was said to continue singing as it floated downstream.

6

White dawn. Stillness.   When the rippling began
    I took it for sea-wind, coming to our valley with rumors
    of salt, of treeless horizons. But the white fog
didn't stir; the leaves of my brothers remained outstretched,
unmoving.
        Yet the rippling drew nearer—and then
my own outermost branches began to tingle, almost as if
fire had been lit below them, too close, and their twig-tips
were drying and curling.
                Yet I was not afraid, only
                deeply alert.

Literary Analysis
The Speaker in Poetry What clue to the speaker's identity appears in line 4?

5 Background
Orpheus

After the death of his wife Eurydice, Orpheus descended into the underworld; charmed Hades, lord of the dead, with his enchanting music; and convinced him to let Eurydice return to the land of the living. Hades set one condition: Orpheus could not look upon his wife until they were both back in the land of the living. Orpheus was so eager to be sure that his wife was behind him that he looked back at her an instant too soon. She was lost forever. Grief-stricken, Orpheus wandered through the country of Thrace, lamenting his loss in song.

6 Literary Analysis
The Speaker in Poetry

1. Remind students that it is safest to treat the voice in a poem as that of an invented character.
2. Then, **ask** them the Literary Analysis question: What clue to the speaker's identity appears in line 4?
   Answer: The speaker is a tree, because it refers to the other trees as "my brothers."

Differentiated Instruction for Universal Access

Strategy for Special Needs Students
Poems often pose a challenge to readers. Form small student groups, and have each group use passages from the poem to practice such reading strategies as paraphrasing, breaking down long passages, and forming mental images. Suggest that students use tools such as note-cards for breaking down long passage, or markers and drawing paper for forming mental images. Students can write individual words or phrases on note cards so that they can view the poem in smaller parts and arrange the words or phrases for understanding. Students can draw the images that the words in the poem evoke to emphasize the skill of forming mental images while reading.

PHLit Online!
This selection is available in interactive format in the **Enriched Online Student Edition, www.PHLitOnline.com,** which includes a thematically related video and writing prompt and an interactive graphic organizer.

❼ Literary Analysis
The Speaker in Poetry

1. Have students read the bracketed text.
2. Then, **ask** them the Literary Analysis question: What do lines 14–20 tell you about the speaker who provides the description?
   Answer: The speaker is the first tree to see Orpheus.
3. **Ask** students to comment on the way in which the tree describes Orpheus.
   Answer: Although the tree knows that Orpheus is a man, it describes him in terms of a tree—he has "moving stems" for legs, a "short trunk" for a body, "two arm-branches" each with "five leafless twigs at their ends," grass for hair, and a face like a flower.

❽ Critical Viewing

Possible response: Such details as the lyre and the Grecian clothing may match students' mental images.

❾ Humanities

This piece of Greek pottery shows Orpheus and a lyre. The repeated geometric design along the border is referred to as the Greek key, a symbol of eternity.

Literary Analysis
The Speaker in Poetry What do lines 14–20 tell you about the speaker who provides the description?

❽ ▼ **Critical Viewing** This ancient Greek vessel depicts Orpheus. Which details match the picture of Orpheus you form as you read the poem? Which do not? **[Compare and Contrast]**

❾

I was the first to see him, for I grew
❼ out on the pasture slope, beyond the forest.
He was a man, it seemed: the two
moving stems, the short trunk, the two
arm-branches, flexible, each with five leafless
twigs at their ends,
and the head that's crowned by brown or gold grass,
bearing a face not like the beaked face of a bird,
more like a flower's.
He carried a burden made of
some cut branch bent while it was green,
strands of a vine tight-stretched across it. From this,
when he touched it, and from his voice
which unlike the wind's voice had no need of our
leaves and branches to complete its sound,
came the ripple,
But it was now no longer a ripple (he had come near and
stopped in my first shadow) it was a wave that bathed me
as if rain
rose from below and around me
instead of falling.
And what I felt was no longer a dry tingling:

I seemed to be singing as he sang, I seemed to know
what the lark knows; all my sap
was mounting towards the sun that by now
had risen, the mist was rising, the grass
was drying, yet my roots felt music moisten them
deep under earth.
He came still closer, leaned on my trunk:
the bark thrilled like a leaf still-folded.
Music! There was no twig of me not
trembling with joy and fear.

Then as he sang
it was no longer sounds only that made the music:
he spoke, and as no tree listens I listened, and language
came into my roots
❿ out of the earth,
into my bark
out of the air,
into the pores of my greenest shoots
gently as dew

Think Aloud

Figurative Language
Draw students' attention to lines 34–43. Use the following "think aloud" to model how to interpret figurative language in these lines:

When I read these lines, I notice many vivid details, such as "my sap/was mounting towards the sun" and "no twig of me not/trembling with joy and fear." These examples are imagery because they help me to picture what is being described. They also help me to "see" what the speaker, the tree, is experiencing. From the first example, I can picture the tree's sap rising in excitement, as a person's blood pressure might rise when he or she is excited. The second example allows me to picture the entire tree, shaking from the intensity of its emotions. These images make the tree's reactions so real and tangible that I can almost feel the tree's excitement. Imagery, then, helps me, the reader, to connect to the emotion in the poem.

and there was no word he sang but I knew its meaning.
He told of journeys,
of where sun and moon go while we stand in dark,
of an earth-journey he dreamed he would take some day
deeper than roots . . .
He told of the dreams of man, wars, passions, griefs,
and I, a tree, understood words—ah, it seemed
my thick bark would split like a sapling's that
grew too fast in the spring
when a late frost wounds it.

(10)

Vocabulary
rejoiced (ri joist′) *v.* showed happiness

Fire he sang,
that trees fear, and I, a tree, rejoiced in its flames.
New buds broke forth from me though it was full summer.
As though his lyre (now I knew its name)
(11) were both frost and fire, its chords flamed
up to the crown of me.
I was seed again.
I was fern in the swamp.
I was coal.

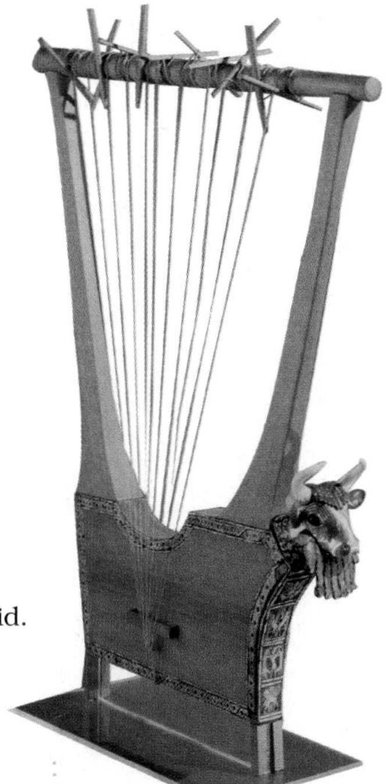

And at the heart of my wood
(so close I was to becoming man or a god)
there was a kind of silence, a kind of sickness,
something akin to what men call boredom,
something

(the poem descended a scale, a stream over stones)
that gives to a candle a coldness
in the midst of its burning, he said.

It was then,
when in the blaze of his power that
reached me and changed me
I thought I should fall my length,
that the singer began
to leave me. Slowly
moved from my noon shadow
to open light,
(14) words leaping and dancing over his shoulders
back to me
rivery sweep of lyre-tones becoming

Reading Check (13)
What does Orpheus do to cause the tree to respond so powerfully to him?

(10) Reading Skill
Read Fluently

1. Ask a volunteer to read the bracketed passage aloud.
2. Then, **ask** students the Reading Skill question: What does the poet's grouping of words in lines 44–52 indicate about the way to read the lines?
Possible response: The way that lines are shortened and staggered seems to indicate that each phrase is to be read with a distinct emphasis, set off with pauses.

(11) Connecting to the Big Question

1. Explain to students that by using a tree to relate firsthand the irresistible effects of Orpheus' music, the poet conveys this mythological story from a unique and novel perspective.
2. Have students reread the bracketed text. Then, **ask** students: What details in these lines indicate that the tree has been changed in some way by Orpheus' music?
Possible response: Trees are highly flammable, and the tree knows this danger, for it says, "Fire he sang,/that trees fear," yet the tree is so overcome by the music that it invites the fire. Then, the tree explains that, when the fire engulfed it, the tree changed from seed to fern to coal—an entire life cycle.
3. **Ask** students: Does the speaker convey this change in a positive way? Explain.
Possible response: Yes, the tree says it "rejoiced in its flames," as if it wanted to be changed.

(12) Humanities

This reconstruction of the Queen's Lyre was made nearly 5,000 years ago in Ur (present-day Iraq.)

(13) Reading Check

Answer: Orpheus sings and plays his lyre, transforming the tree's experience.

Differentiated Instruction for Universal Access

Strategy for Less Proficient Readers
Have students make a list of words that describe the tree's feelings as they are revealed in the poem. Then have them organize these words in a flow chart to indicate the changes the trees go through in the poem.

⓮ Literary Analysis
The Speaker in Poetry

1. Ask a volunteer to read aloud the bracketed text that begins on the previous page.
2. **Ask** students to choose images and emotions in the passage.
Possible responses: Students may suggest the words "leaping and dancing over his shoulders"; the tree feeling anguish and terror at being left behind by Orpheus; references to pain, wrenching, tearing, and pulling of tree roots as they are cut off from the music.
3. Then, **ask** students the Literary Analysis question: Why might lines 85–92 be said to have a lyrical quality?
Possible response: These lines incorporate the thoughts and feelings of the tree into the story that it is telling, using vivid, evocative language.

Literary Analysis ⓮
The Speaker in Poetry
Why might lines 85–92 be said to have a lyrical quality?

Vocabulary
anguish (aŋ´ gwish) *n.* extreme suffering, as from grief or pain

slowly again
ripple.
And I
in terror
but not in doubt of
what I must do
in **anguish**, in haste,
wrenched from the earth root after root,
the soil heaving and cracking, the moss tearing asunder—
and behind me the others: my brothers
forgotten since dawn. In the forest
they too had heard,
and were pulling their roots in pain
out of a thousand years' layers of dead leaves,
rolling the rocks away,
breaking themselves
out of
their depths.
You would have thought we would lose the sound of the lyre,
of the singing
so dreadful the storm-sounds were, where there was no storm,
no wind but the rush of our
branches moving, our trunks breasting the air.
But the music!
The music reached us.

Clumsily,
stumbling over our own roots,
rustling our leaves
in answer,
we moved, we followed.
All day we followed, up hill and down.
We learned to dance,
for he would stop, where the ground was flat,
and words he said
taught us to leap and to wind in and out
around one another in figures the lyre's measure designed.
The singer
laughed till he wept to see us, he was so glad.
At sunset
we came to this place I stand in, this knoll[1]
with its ancient grove that was bare grass then.
In the last light of the day his song became
farewell.
He stilled our longing.

⓯

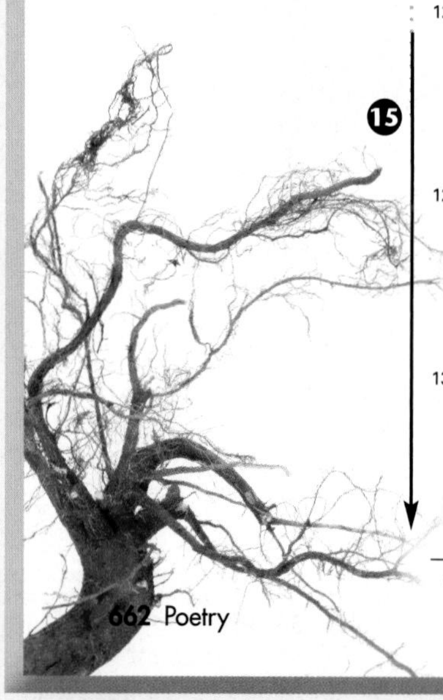

1. **knoll** (nōl) *n.* small hill.

Vocabulary Development

Word Form Chart
Expand students' vocabulary by helping them learn related forms of the selection vocabulary words. Give students a blank **Word Form Chart** (***Professional Development Guidebook***, p. 42), with *anguish, stark,* and *clenching* in their appropriate columns. Work with the class, or have students work with partners, to determine the related forms. The final chart should look like the one shown.

Noun	Verb	Adjective	Adverb
anguish	anguish	anguished	
starkness		**stark**	starkly
clencher	**clenching**	clenched	

He sang our sun-dried roots back into earth,
watered them: all-night rain of music so quiet
we could almost
not hear it in the
moonless dark.
By dawn he was gone.
We have stood here since,
in our new life.
We have waited.
He does not return.
It is said he made his earth-journey, and lost
what he sought.
It is said they felled him
and cut up his limbs for firewood.
And it is said
his head still sang and was swept out to sea singing.
Perhaps he will not return.
But what we have lived
comes back to us.
We see more.
We feel, as our rings increase,
something that lifts our branches, that stretches our furthest
leaf-tips
further.
The wind, the birds,
do not sound poorer but clearer,
recalling our agony, and the way we danced.
The music!

Literary Analysis
The Speaker in Poetry What key event does the narrative relate?

◀ **Critical Viewing** How does the tree pictured here suggest the images in the poem? **[Analyze]**

15 Literary Analysis
The Speaker in Poetry

1. Ask students to read aloud the bracketed text that begins on the previous page.
2. Then, **ask** students the Literary Analysis question: What key event does the narrative relate?
Answer: The trees uproot themselves and follow Orpheus so that they are not separated from his music. The trees stop and plant themselves in the ground when the music stops.

▶**Monitor Progress** Ask students to predict what will happen in the resolution of this narrative poem.
Answer: Students should point out that based on the mythic quality of this poem, the trees will have to take root elsewhere; otherwise, the trees would still be following music today.

▶**Reteach** Remind students that narrative poems share many characteristics with fictional stories. They have plot, character, conflict, setting, and theme. If students have difficulty predicting the resolution of the narrative, have them find details that support or refute their predictions, such as "his song became farewell," "He stilled our longing," "He sang our sun-dried roots back into earth," and "We have stood here since, in our new life."

16 Critical Viewing

Possible response: The features of the tree reflects both movement and grace. Similar, too, are the interplay of light and shadow and contrasting textures. The viewer can almost see branches and twigs trembling with joy as the music pours over them.

Differentiated Instruction for Universal Access

Enrichment for Advanced Readers
Have students investigate other poems based on the Orpheus myth, such as Margaret Atwood's "Orpheus (1)" and "Orpheus (2)" and Rainer Maria Rilke's "Sonnets to Orpheus." Have students compare and contrast the poems. Which poem contributes best to students' understanding of the myth?

Enrichment for Gifted/Talented Students
Have students locate and play a cantata for soprano, flute, clarinet, violin, viola, and cello written by David Lumsdaine and based on the Levertov poem "A Tree Telling of Orpheus." Have them write an essay comparing the music of the cantata with the music of the poem.

17 Literary Analysis
The Speaker in Poetry

1. Have a volunteer read aloud the bracketed stanza.
2. Then, **ask** students to respond to the Literary Analysis prompt: Identify one detail the poet uses to tell a story and one she uses to present an image or convey a feeling.
   Answer: A narrative detail is that the speaker is on a car trip north of Tampico. A lyric detail is that the speaker expresses an emotion—the fear that he or she is going to die.

18 Literary Analysis
The Speaker in Poetry

1. Remind students that since this is primarily a lyric poem, the observations and feelings of a single speaker are expressed.
2. Read aloud the bracketed lines to students.
3. **Ask** students to summarize the speaker's feelings in these lines.
   Answer: As an adult, the speaker is still like a child with a painful curiosity about (and fear of) death.

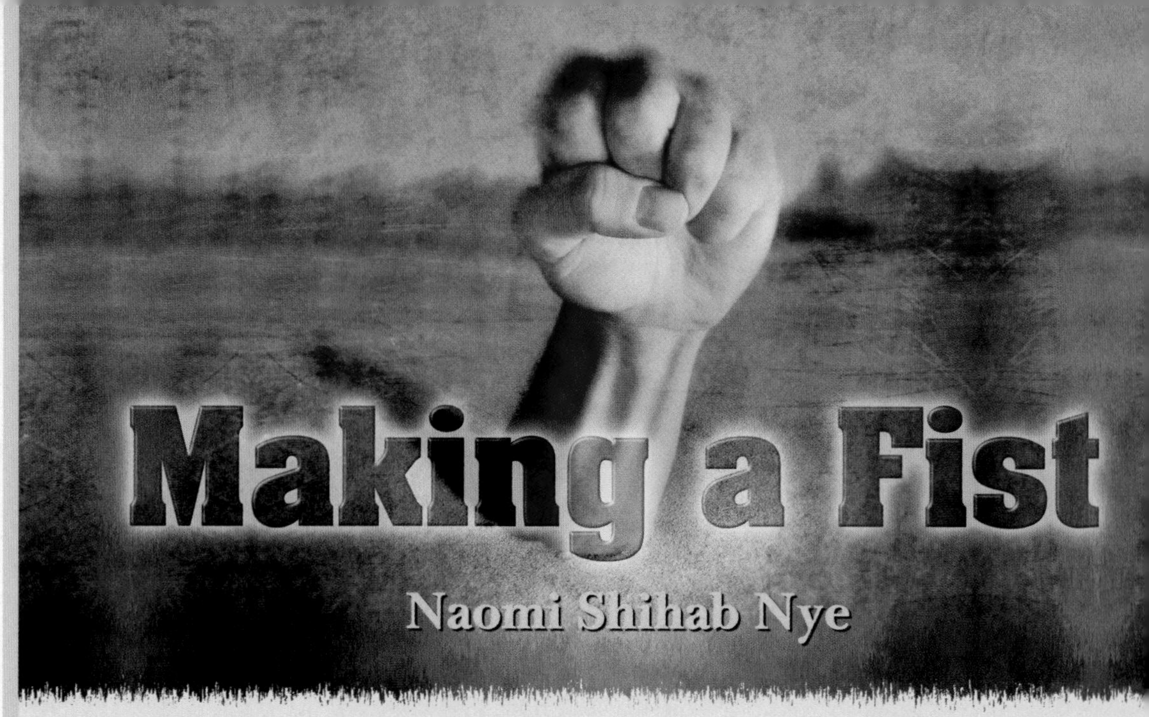

Making a Fist

Naomi Shihab Nye

Literary Analysis
The Speaker in Poetry
Identify one detail the poet uses to tell a story and one she uses to present an image or convey a feeling.

For the first time, on the road north of Tampico,[1]
I felt the life sliding out of me,
(17) a drum in the desert, harder and harder to hear.
I was seven, I lay in the car
watching palm trees swirl a sickening pattern
past the glass.
My stomach was a melon split wide inside my skin.

"How do you know if you are going to die?"
I begged my mother.
We had been traveling for days.
With strange confidence she answered,
"When you can no longer make a fist."

Years later I smile to think of that journey,
the borders we must cross separately,
stamped with our unanswerable woes.
I who did not die, who am still living,
(18) still lying in the backseat behind all my questions,
clenching and opening one small hand.

Vocabulary
clenching (klench′ iŋ) *v.* closing or holding tightly

1. **Tampico** (täm pē′ kō) seaport in eastern Mexico.

Vocabulary Development

Vocabulary Knowledge Rating
When students have completed reading and discussing the four poems, have them take out their **Vocabulary Knowledge Rating Chart** for this selection. Read the words aloud once more, and have students rate their knowledge of the words again in the After Reading column. Clarify any words that are still problematic. Have students write their own definition and example or sentence in the appropriate column. Then have students complete the Vocabulary Practice at the end of the selection. Encourage students to use the words in further discussion and written work about this selection. Remind them that they will be accountable for these words on the **Selection Test,** ***Unit 4 Resources,*** pp. 56–58 or 59–61.

Spring & All

William Carlos Williams

By the road to the contagious hospital
under the surge of the blue
19 mottled clouds driven from the
northeast—a cold wind. Beyond, the
waste of broad, muddy fields
brown with dried weeds, standing
and fallen

patches of standing water
the scattering of tall trees

All along the road the reddish
purplish, forked, upstanding, twiggy
stuff of bushes and small trees
20 with dead, brown leaves under them
leafless vines—

Literary Analysis
The Speaker in Poetry To what senses do the images in these stanzas appeal?

Reading Skill
Read Fluently What punctuation mark indicates a pause at the end of the third stanza?

19 Literary Analysis
The Speaker in Poetry

1. Have a volunteer read the bracketed passage aloud.
2. Then, **ask** students the Literary Analysis question: To what senses do the images in these stanzas appeal?
   Answer: The following images appeal to the sense of sight: "blue mottled clouds"; "broad muddy fields"; "dried weeds"; "patches of standing water"; and "tall trees." The "cold wind" appeals to the sense of touch.
3. **Ask** students to comment on the image of the "contagious hospital." What do they think it means?
   Possible response: The image seems strange and surprising in a poem about spring. However, the images in the first stanza are confined mostly to the death of winter. The poet may use the "contagious hospital" as a metaphor for recovery from winter/disease.

20 Reading Skill
Read Fluently

1. Have a volunteer read aloud the bracketed text.
2. Then, **ask** students the Reading Skill question: What punctuation mark indicates a pause at the end of the third stanza?
   Answer: The dash indicates that the reader should pause.

Concept Connector

Activating Prior Knowledge
Have students return to the discussion points they raised before reading the selection. Lead a class discussion, focusing on what students have learned that confirms or invalidates their ideas about the connections among music, nature, and poetry. Encourage students to cite specific details, quotations, or other evidence from the texts to support their responses. Ask students to comment on how these connections among music, nature, and poetry are further connected to the experience of being human.

Writing About the Big Question
Have students compare their responses to the sentence starter they completed before reading the selections with their ideas afterwards. Ask them to explain whether their thoughts have changed.

Reading Skill Graphic Organizer
Ask students to review the graphic organizers they completed while reading. Show them **Reading Skill Graphic Organizer A** (*Graphic Organizer Transparencies,* p. 114) as an example. Then have students share their graphic organizers.

ASSESS

Answers

Critical Thinking

1. **Possible response:** Images: the trees following Orpheus; the fist; Listening to another reader's response to a poem is likely to create a deeper appreciation of the poem for the listener.
2. (a) The speaker is cutting hay with a scythe. (b) **Possible response:** The speaker loves his work, finding satisfaction in accomplishment.
3. (a) The trees uproot themselves to follow Orpheus. (b) The trees are inspired by the beauty of the music and feel more alive than they felt.
4. (a) **Possible response:** Images in the poem include "muddy fields," "dried weeds," and "patches of standing water." (b) It is bleak, cold, and dead.

Does all communication serve a positive purpose?

Possible responses: (a) In "Spring & All," the poet presents the idea of spring in a unique way, for he creates a feeling of coldness and struggle that the plants, trees, and flowers must face when spring begins, as if they must do everything to survive and grow. This perspective contradicts what I know about spring—that it is about renewal, growth, and the blossoming of beauty. This poem expands my understanding because it allows me to see spring in a different but still truthful way. (b) Because the poem expands my understanding, it serves a positive purpose.

Lifeless in appearance, sluggish
dazed spring approaches—

20 They enter the new world naked,
cold, uncertain of all
save that they enter. All about them
the cold, familiar wind—

Now the grass, tomorrow
the stiff curl of wildcarrot leaf
One by one objects are defined—
It quickens: clarity, outline of leaf

But now the stark dignity of
entrance—Still, the profound change
has come upon them: rooted, they
grip down and begin to awaken

Vocabulary
stark (stärk) *adj.* bare; harsh

Critical Thinking

1. **Respond:** Identify the images you find most vivid in these poems. Discuss them with a partner, noting the choices you share. Finally, explain how your appreciation of the poems has or has not altered based on your discussion.
2. **(a) Infer:** What is the speaker doing in "Mowing"? **(b) Interpret:** What does the speaker imply about accomplishing a task when he says that "The fact is the sweetest dream that labor knows"?
3. **(a)** In "A Tree Telling of Orpheus," how do the trees respond when Orpheus begins to leave them? **(b) Analyze:** Why do they react this way?
4. **(a)** List three details of the landscape in "Spring and All." **(b) Synthesize:** What is the general quality of the landscape?

Does all communication serve a positive purpose? **(a)** Choose one of the poems and describe how the poet presents the subject in a unique way. Explain what this fresh perspective adds to your understanding of the subject. **(b)** Would you say the poem serves a positive purpose? Why or why not?

Assessment Resources

Unit 4 Resources

L1 L2 EL **Selection Test A**, pp. 56–58. Administer Test A to less advanced readers and English learners.

L3 L4 **Selection Test B**, pp. 59–61. Administer Test B to on-level or more advanced students.

L3 L4 **Open-Book Test**, pp. 53–55. As an alternative, give the Open-Book Test.

All **Customizable Test Bank**

All **Self-tests**
Students may prepare for the **Selection Test** by taking the **Self-test** online.

PHLit Online! All assessment resources are available at **www.PHLitOnline.com.**

After You Read
Poetry Collection 2

Mowing • A Tree Telling of Orpheus • Making a Fist • Spring and All

Literary Analysis: The Speaker in Poetry

1. Identify the best example of **narrative poetry** from among the poems in Poetry Collection 2. Explain your choice.
2. Use this chart to list an example of visual **imagery**—a passage that appeals to sight. Add the sensory language that the poet uses to build the image. Finally, note the effect that these details generate.

Image	Sensory Language	Effect

3. Compare the **speakers** in "Spring and All" and "Making a Fist." In your response, consider how much you know about the speaker and whether the speaker is the poet or a character taking part in the action of the poem.

Reading Skill: Read Fluently

4. Choose one of the poems and use your notes from the reading rate chart on page 639. Then, practice reading the poem aloud until you can **read** it **fluently.**

Vocabulary

Practice For each of the following items, write a sentence about the situation described. In each of your sentences, use a word from the vocabulary list for Poetry Collection 2, on page 656.

1. watching a race while holding something tightly
2. getting a cavity filled
3. a prison cell
4. waiting for the bus with nothing to do
5. receiving news that creates great happiness
6. delivering an important and serious speech

Word Study Use the context of the sentences and what you know about the **Latin prefix *re-*** to explain your answer to each question.

1. If you *recount* a story, are you telling it for the first time?
2. When someone is thirsty, should you *replenish* his or her glass?

Word Study

The **Latin prefix *re-*** means "again" or "anew."

Challenge Explain how the prefix *re-* contributes to the meanings of these words. Consult a dictionary if necessary.

reaccustom
reassurance
rejuvenate

ASSESS/EXTEND

Answers

Literary Analysis

1. Many students will say that "A Tree Telling of Orpheus" is a good example of narrative poetry because it tells a story with a strong beginning, middle, and end, and it has a conflict and characters.
2. **Possible response:** Image: a tree dancing and walking, tripping, and shaking its leaves. **Sensory Language:** "Clumsily, stumbling, rustling"; **Effect:** They create a vivid picture of the action.
3. **Possible response:** The speakers of the two poems both notice minute details in the world around them and are both concerned about the boundaries between life and death. It is best to assume that the poems' speakers are invented characters.

Reading Skill

4. Check students' marks for accuracy. Reading rates should be correctly adjusted wherever there is any punctuation, important words or sounds, and groups of words that express a single thought.

For other sample answers, see ***Graphic Organizer Transparencies,*** **Reading Skills Graphic Organizer A**, p. 118, and the **Additional Answers** section.

Vocabulary
Practice

1. Clenching the school banner in her hand, Hannah cheered for Liam as he approached the finish line.
2. For two weeks before a dental appointment, I am plagued with nightmares and anguish about my fate.

Answers continued

3. With only a seatless toilet bowl and a metal shelf for a bed, the stark prison cell welcomed its newest inhabitant.
4. I sit on the bench, idle, watching the cars buzz by.
5. When I found out that my essay had won first prize, I rejoiced in my success.
6. He spoke slowly and clearly in order to accurately communicate the important ideas in his earnest speech.

Word Study
Sample answers:

1. No, a story that has been recounted has been told before.
2. Yes, a thirsty person would want his or her glass filled again.

Word Study: Challenge
Sample answers:

To *reaccustom* is to "become familiar with again."
To have *reassurance* is to "feel confident again."
To *rejuvenate* is to "make someone feel young again."

EXTEND/ASSESS

Answers

Grammar

1. Introduce the skill, using the instruction on the student page.
2. Discuss the examples.

Think Aloud: Model the Skill

Model the skill of identifying prepositions and prepositional phrases. Say to students:

To help me identify prepositions and prepositional phrases in my reading, I can look at how the parts of a sentence relate to each other. For example, in the sentence "Dan spotted a raccoon in the tree," *Dan* is the subject, *spotted* is the verb, and *raccoon* is the object. I know that the word *in* is a preposition; *tree* is a noun. These parts make up a prepositional phrase.

Writing and Grammar, Grade 10

Students will find further instruction on and practice with prepositions in Chapter 18, Section 1.

Practice A

Answers:

1. behind, in, preposition; stove, house, objects of prepositions
2. into, P; distance, OP
3. through, P; fish's lip, OP
4. without, from, in, of, P; Danny Deever, gallows, middle, square, OP
5. by, P; Rudyard Kipling, OP

Challenge

Sample answer: The bride is led to the *feast;* It mourns the arrow without a *target* . . .

Practice B

Sample answers:

1. *Away from* changes Orpheus' direction.
2. *Walks with* indicates that trees can walk.
3. *Behind* reveals that he is hidden or in the background.
4. *Through* creates a magical effect.

Challenge

Sample answer:

(1) Julie walked into the room before her friends. (2) The man ran across the street so he could get on the train. (3) The star player stood beside the coach to pose for pictures.

Integrated Language Skills

Poetry Collections 1 and 2

Poetry Collection 1

Poetry Collection 2

Grammar: Prepositions and Prepositional Phrases

A **preposition** is a word that relates the noun or pronoun that appears with it to another word in the sentence.

The choice of preposition affects the way the other words in a sentence relate to one another. Common prepositions are *on, at, of, across, to, under,* and *with.*

In English, a preposition comes at the beginning of a **prepositional phrase.** This is a group of words that includes a preposition and a noun or pronoun, which is called the **object of the preposition.**

In each of these examples, the preposition is underlined and the object of the preposition is in boldface.

Examples:

on the **couch**	under the **couch**	beside the **couch**
in the **backpack**	near the **backpack**	behind the **backpack**
in my **lifetime**	after the **rainstorm**	before the **party**

Practice A Write each of the following sentences, underlining the prepositions and circling all the objects of the prepositions.

1. The girl hid behind the stove in the house.
2. The guitar sings into the distance.
3. A hook stuck through the fish's lip.
4. The soldiers marched without Danny Deever away from the gallows in the middle of the square.
5. The poem was written by Rudyard Kipling.

Challenge Find two examples of prepositional phrases in Poetry Collection 1. Identify the preposition and the object of the preposition.

Practice B Rewrite the sentence, substituting the numbered prepositions for the preposition *to.* Then, write a brief explanation of how the change in preposition changes the sentence.

Orpheus walks to the trees.

1. away from
2. with
3. behind
4. through

Challenge Write three different sentences based on the model. Use different prepositions and prepositional phrases in each sentence.

Sam showed up in the morning without his coat.

Writing and Grammar Connection: Chapter 18, Section 1

Extend the Lesson

Sentence Modeling

Choose the sentence given from the selection students have read:

The moon was faintly/Shining behind a cloud;/I strayed from the path; Nothing stirred except/The tops of the pine-trees. ("The Bridegroom")

he spoke, and as no tree listens I listened, and language/came into my roots/out of the earth,/into my bark/ out of the air,/into the pores of my greenest shoots ("A Tree Telling of Orpheus")

Ask students what they notice about the sentence. Elicit that it has prepositional phrases. Ask what else they notice. ("The Bridegroom": the "s" sound lends a sense of silence. "A Tree Telling of Orpheus": the prepositions "into" and "out of" are used repeatedly, adding emphasis to the image described.")

Have students imitate the sentence in a sentence on a topic of their own choosing, matching each grammatical and stylistic feature discussed. Collect the sentences, and share them with the class.

Writing

Write your own **lyric poem** in response to any of the poems in Poetry Collection 1 or Poetry Collection 2.

- Analyze the language techniques used by the authors of these poems and make a list of *figurative language* you find in the poems. Refer to these examples as you create your own poetic style.
- Collect ideas for imagery in a chart with columns labeled *sight, hearing, taste, touch,* and *smell.*
- Review your draft to ensure that your writing communicates a feeling or an emotion. Note ideas in your poem that might be clarified by the use of an allusion to another classic or contemporary work, and add an allusion to the original poem if appropriate.
- Read your draft aloud to a partner. Ask your partner whether any ideas or images in the poem are unclear. Use your partner's answers to guide you in revising your poem.

Writing Workshop: *Work in Progress*

Prewriting for Descriptive Essay For a descriptive essay you might write, fold a piece of paper into three columns: label one *spatial organization*, one *chronological organization,* and one *casual organization.* In each column, note two things, events, or actions that could be described using that structure. Put this Organization Chart in your portfolio.

Use this prewriting activity to prepare for the **Writing Workshop** on page 708.

Listening and Speaking

Present an **oral interpretation** of another Kipling poem or another Frost poem that uses dialect. Go online or use library resources to find and study poetry by the author. Then, choose a single poem and answer these questions to help aid your understanding of the poem:

- Is the poet's use of language different from that of other poets?
- Does the poet's language reflect a specific region or group?
- What is the main emotion that the poem communicates?

Research the meaning of any unfamiliar words. Practice reading the poem aloud with fluency, making sure to pay attention to the punctuation marks within the poem. As you practice, work to be sure your reading conveys the poem's emotion and main idea. After your presentation, lead a group discussion about whether the dialect helps create a believable speaker.

PHLit Online!
www.PHLitOnline.com
- Interactive graphic organizers
- Grammar tutorial
- Interactive journals

EXTEND/ASSESS

Answers

Writing

1. Review the assignment, using the instruction on the student page.
2. To guide students in writing lyric poems, give them **Support for Writing**, p. 51 in ***Unit 4 Resources.***
3. To evaluate students' lyric poems, use the Poem rubrics on pp. 248–249 in ***Professional Development Guidebook.*** In addition, evaluate how well students use images and the voice of the speaker to communicate ideas.

Six Traits Focus

✔	Ideas	✔	Word Choice
	Organization		Sentence Fluency
✔	Voice		Conventions

Writing Workshop
Work in Progress

Have students save their completed Organization Chart in their portfolios. They will use the Organization Chart later as they continue this Work-in-Progress assignment (see p. 691). These assignments prepare them to complete the Writing Workshop assignment (see pp. 708–713).

Listening and Speaking

1. Review the assignment, using the instruction on the student page.
2. Have students complete the **Support for Extend Your Learning** page (***Unit 4 Resources,*** p. 52).

Teaching Resources

Unit 4 Resources

- L3 L4 **Integrated Language Skills: Grammar,** p. 50
- L3 L4 **Support for Writing,** p. 51
- L3 L4 **Support for Extend Your Learning,** p. 52
- L4 **Enrichment,** pp. 31, 49

Enriched Online Student Edition
Available under After You Read for this selection:

- All **Interactive Grammar Tutorial**
- L3 L4 **Internet Research Activity**

Professional Development Guidebook
Rubrics for Poems, pp. 248–249

PHLit Online! All print and digital resources are available at **www.PHLitOnline.com.** Online resources accessible by students are noted on the student page.

TIME AND RESOURCE MANAGER

Poetry Collection 3 • Poetry Collection 4

Lesson Pacing Guide

DAY 1 Preteach

- Administer the Reading and Vocabulary Warm-ups (*Unit 4 Resources*, pp. 62–65 or 80–83) as necessary.
- Introduce the Reading Skill: Read Fluently FT
- Introduce the Literary Analysis concept: Poetic Forms FT
- Distribute copies of the appropriate graphic organizer for the Reading Skill (*Graphic Organizer Transparencies*, pp. 120–122). CRI
- Distribute copies of the appropriate graphic organizer for Literary Analysis (*Graphic Organizer Transparencies*, pp. 123–126). CRI
- Teach the selection vocabulary. FT CRI
- Introduce the Word Study skill.

DAYS 2–3 Preteach/Teach

- Build background with the Background feature. CRI
- Develop thematic vocabulary and thematic thinking with Writing About the Big Question.
- Prepare students to read with the Activating Prior Knowledge activities (TE). CRI
- Informally monitor comprehension while students read. FT
- Use the Reading Check questions to confirm comprehension.
- Develop students' ability to read fluently using the Reading Skill questions. CRI
- Develop students' understanding of poetic forms using the Literary Analysis questions. CRI
- Reinforce vocabulary with the Vocabulary notes. CRI

DAY 4 Assess

- Assess students' comprehension and mastery of the skills by having them answer the Critical Thinking, Reading Skill, and Literary Analysis questions. FT
- Have students complete the Vocabulary Practice activities. FT
- Have students complete the Word Study activities.

DAY 5 Extend/Assess

- Have students complete the Grammar lesson. CRI
- Have students complete the Writing activity and write a tanka. (You may assign as homework.) FT
- Extend learning by having students complete the Listening and Speaking activity, a poetry reading discussion. As an alternative, assign them "As Big As All Outdoors" or "Put Me In, Coach!" in *Reality Central*. CRI
- Administer Selection Test A or B (*Unit 4 Resources*, pp. 74–79 or 95–100). FT

The poems in Poetry Collections 3 and 4 appear unedited and in their entirety.

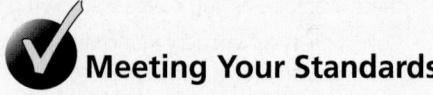

Meeting Your Standards

Students will

1. analyze and respond to literary elements.
   - Literary Analysis: Poetic Forms
2. read, comprehend, and analyze poetry.
   - Reading Skill: Read Fluently
   - Reading Check questions
   - Apply the Skills questions
   - Assessment Practice
3. develop vocabulary.
   - Vocabulary
   - Word Study
4. apply grammar skills.
   - Direct Objects
5. Develop writing proficiency.
   - Work in Progress: Descriptive Essay
   - tanka
6. strengthen research and technology skills.
   - poetry reading discussion

CRI For a full explanation of Culturally Responsive Instruction opportunities in this lesson, see p. T86–T87.

FT For an accelerated lesson, use the Fast Track strategies and activities.

Managing Differentiated Instruction
This leveled selection pairing groups a more accessible with a more challenging selection. Choose either one to teach the lesson skills. For classroom management suggestions for using the pairing in a mixed-ability class, see pp. T68–T69.

Daily Block Scheduling
Each day in this Lesson Pacing Guide represents a 40–50 minute period. Teachers using block scheduling may combine days to revise pacing. In addition, teachers may differentiate and support core instruction by integrating components for extended and intensive support as students require. See the Guide to Selected Leveled Resources (facing page).

Guide to Selected Leveled Resources

EL English Learners

			Poetry Collection 3	Poetry Collection 4
CORE COURSE	*Unit 4 Resources*	Selection Test A	pp. 74–76	pp. 95–97
	Graphic Organizer Transparencies	Reading Skill Graphic Organizer A	p. 120	p. 121
		Literary Analysis Graphic Organizer A	p. 123	p. 125
EXTENDED SUPPORT (Level 2)	*Unit 4 Resources*	Reading and Vocabulary Warm-ups A or B	pp. 62–65	pp. 80–83
	Reader's Notebook: English Learner's Version		adapted instruction and adapted selection	adapted instruction and summary
	Hear It! Audio CD		selection and summaries	selection and summaries
	Hear It! Audio CD (adapted text)		adapted selection and summaries	—
INTENSIVE SUPPORT (Level 1)	*Reality Central*		"As Big As All Outdoors"	"Put Me In, Coach!"
	Real-World Writing Journal		Lesson 3, pp. 112–115	Lesson 4, pp. 116–119

L2 Below-Level Students

			Poetry Collection 3	Poetry Collection 4
CORE COURSE	*Unit 4 Resources*	Selection Test A	pp. 74–76	pp. 95–97
	Graphic Organizer Transparencies	Reading Skill Graphic Organizer A	p. 120	p. 121
		Literary Analysis Graphic Organizer A	p. 123	p. 125
EXTENDED SUPPORT (Level 2)	*Unit 4 Resources*	Reading and Vocabulary Warm-ups A or B	pp. 62–65	pp. 80–83
	Reader's Notebook		adapted instruction and full selection	adapted instruction and summary
	Hear It! Audio CD		selection and summaries	selection and summaries
INTENSIVE SUPPORT (Level 1)	*Reality Central*		"As Big As All Outdoors"	"Put Me In, Coach!"
	Real-World Writing Journal		Lesson 3, pp. 112–115	Lesson 4, pp. 116–119
	Reading Kit		Reteaching worksheets	Reteaching worksheets

L1 Special Needs Students

			Poetry Collection 3	Poetry Collection 4
CORE COURSE	*Unit 4 Resources*	Selection Test A	pp. 74–76	pp. 95–97
	Graphic Organizer Transparencies	Reading Skill Graphic Organizer A	p. 120	p. 121
		Literary Analysis Graphic Organizer A	p. 123	p. 125
EXTENDED SUPPORT (Level 2)	*Unit 4 Resources*	Reading and Vocabulary Warm-ups A or B	pp. 62–65	pp. 80–83
	Reader's Notebook: Adapted Version		adapted instruction and adapted selection	adapted instruction and summary
	Hear It! Audio CD (adapted text)		adapted selection and summaries	—
INTENSIVE SUPPORT (Level 1)	*Reality Central*		"As Big As All Outdoors"	"Put Me In, Coach!"
	Real-World Writing Journal		Lesson 3, pp. 112–115	Lesson 4, pp. 116–119
	Reading Kit		Reteaching worksheets	Reteaching worksheets

The program includes resources for these students: L3 On-Level L4 Advanced All All
For a complete guide to selection support, see pp. T106–T108.

NOTE: All print materials are also available online at *www.PHLitOnline.com.*

VISUAL GUIDE to Featured Selection Resources

- **Poetry Collection 3**
- **Poetry Collection 4**

RESOURCES FOR:

- EL English Learners
- L1 Special Needs Students
- L2 Below-Level Students
- L3 On-Level Students
- L4 Advanced Students
- All All Students

Vocabulary/Fluency/Prior Knowledge

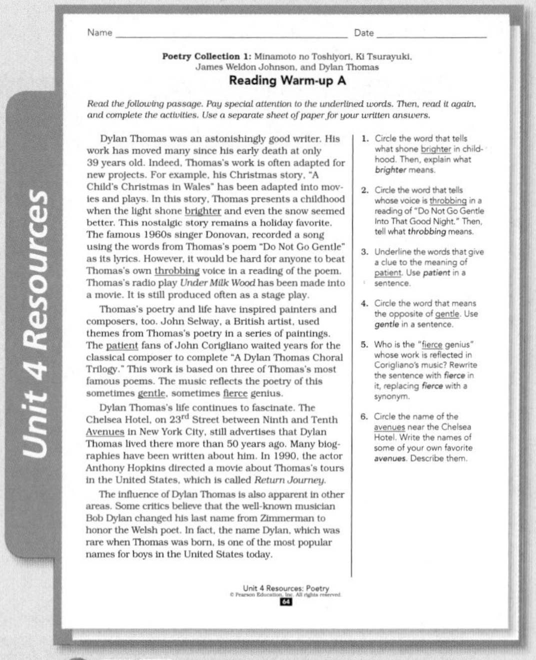

Name ____________________ Date ____________

Poetry Collection 1: Minamoto no Toshiyori, Ki Tsurayuki, James Weldon Johnson, and Dylan Thomas

Reading Warm-up A

Read the following passage. Pay special attention to the underlined words. Then, read it again, and complete the activities. Use a separate sheet of paper for your written answers.

Dylan Thomas was an astonishingly good writer. His work has moved many since his early death at only 39 years old. Indeed, Thomas's work is often adapted for new projects. For example, his Christmas story, "A Child's Christmas in Wales" has been adapted into movies and plays. In this story, Thomas presents a childhood when the light shone brighter and even the snow seemed better. This nostalgic story remains a holiday favorite. The famous 1960s singer Donovan, recorded a song using the words from Thomas's poem "Do Not Go Gentle" as its lyrics. However, it would be hard for anyone to beat Thomas's own throbbing voice in a reading of the poem. Thomas's radio play *Under Milk Wood* has been made into a movie. It is still produced often as a stage play.

Thomas's poetry and life have inspired painters and composers, too. John Selway, a British artist, used themes from Thomas's poetry in a series of paintings. The patient fans of John Corigliano waited years for the classical composer to complete "A Dylan Thomas Choral Trilogy." This work is based on three of Thomas's most famous poems. The music reflects the poetry of this sometimes gentle, sometimes fierce genius.

Dylan Thomas's life continues to fascinate. The Chelsea Hotel, on 23rd Street between Ninth and Tenth Avenues in New York City, still advertises that Dylan Thomas lived there more than 50 years ago. Many biographies have been written about him. In 1990, the actor Anthony Hopkins directed a movie about Thomas's tours in the United States, which is called *Return Journey*.

The influence of Dylan Thomas is also apparent in other areas. Some critics believe that the well-known musician Bob Dylan changed his last name from Zimmerman to honor the Welsh poet. In fact, the name Dylan, which was rare when Thomas was born, is one of the most popular names for boys in the United States today.

1. Circle the word that tells what shone brighter in childhood. Then, explain what *brighter* means.
2. Circle the word that tells whose voice is throbbing in a reading of "Do Not Go Gentle Into That Good Night." Then, tell what *throbbing* means.
3. Underline the words that give a clue to the meaning of patient. Use *patient* in a sentence.
4. Circle the word that means the opposite of gentle. Use *gentle* in a sentence.
5. Who is the "fierce genius" whose work is reflected in Corigliano's music? Rewrite the sentence with *fierce* in it, replacing *fierce* with a synonym.
6. Circle the name of the avenues near the Chelsea Hotel. Write the names of some of your own favorite *avenues*. Describe them.

Unit 4 Resources: Poetry

64

EL L1 L2 Reading Warm-ups A and B, pp. 64–65, 82–83

Also available for these selections:

- **EL L1 L2 Vocabulary Warm-ups A and B, pp. 62–63, 80–81**
- **All Writing About the Big Question, pp. 66, 84**
- **All Vocabulary Builder, pp. 69, 87**

L2 L3 *Reader's Notebook*

L1 *Reader's Notebook: Adapted Version*

EL *Reader's Notebook: English Learner's Version*

Reader's Notebooks

Pre- and postreading pages, as well as the selections in Poetry Collection 3, appear in an interactive format in the *Reader's Notebooks*. Each *Notebook* is differentiated for a different group of learners.
The selections in the Adapted and English Learner's versions are abridged.

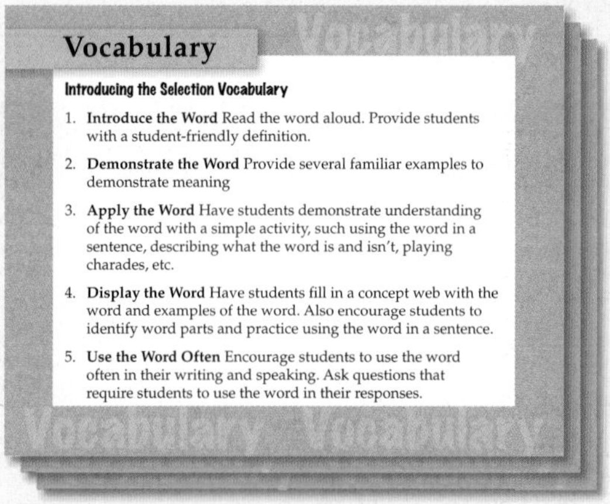

Vocabulary

Introducing the Selection Vocabulary

1. **Introduce the Word** Read the word aloud. Provide students with a student-friendly definition.
2. **Demonstrate the Word** Provide several familiar examples to demonstrate meaning
3. **Apply the Word** Have students demonstrate understanding of the word with a simple activity, such using the word in a sentence, describing what the word is and isn't, playing charades, etc.
4. **Display the Word** Have students fill in a concept web with the word and examples of the word. Also encourage students to identify word parts and practice using the word in a sentence.
5. **Use the Word Often** Encourage students to use the word often in their writing and speaking. Ask questions that require students to use the word in their responses.

Classroom Strategies and Teaching Routines

- core classroom routines outlined step-by-step
- convenient format for easy reference while teaching

Selection Support

Graphic Organizer Transparencies

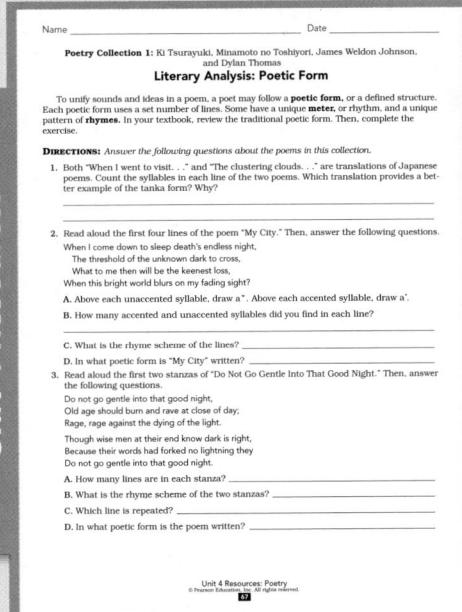

"The clustering clouds" by Minamoto no Toshiyori; **"When I went to visit"** by Ki Tsurayuki; **"My City"** by James Weldon Johnson; **"Do Not Go Gentle into That Good Night"** by Dylan Thomas; **"One cannot ask loneliness"** by Priest Jakuren; **"Was it that I went to sleep"** by Ono Komachi; **"The Waking"** by Theodore Roethke; **"Sonnet 18"** by William Shakespeare

Before You Read B: Literary Analysis—Poetic Forms

Poem:

Number of lines:	Number of syllables in each line:	Pattern of accented and unaccented syllables in each line:	Rhyme scheme:
Form:			

Poem:

Number of lines:	Number of syllables in each line:	Pattern of accented and unaccented syllables in each line:	Rhyme scheme:
Form:			

Poem:

Number of lines:	Number of syllables in each line:	Pattern of accented and unaccented syllables in each line:	Rhyme scheme:
Form:			

Poem:

Number of lines:	Number of syllables in each line:	Pattern of accented and unaccented syllables in each line:	Rhyme scheme:
Form:			

Graphic Organizer Transparencies

122

EL L1 L2 **Literary Analysis: Graphic Organizer A,** pp. 123, 125 (partially filled in)

Also available for these selections:

L3 Literary Analysis: Graphic Organizer B, pp. 124, 126

EL L1 L2 Reading: Graphic Organizer A, pp. 120, 121 (partially filled in)

L3 Reading: Graphic Organizer B, p. 122

Skills Development/Extension

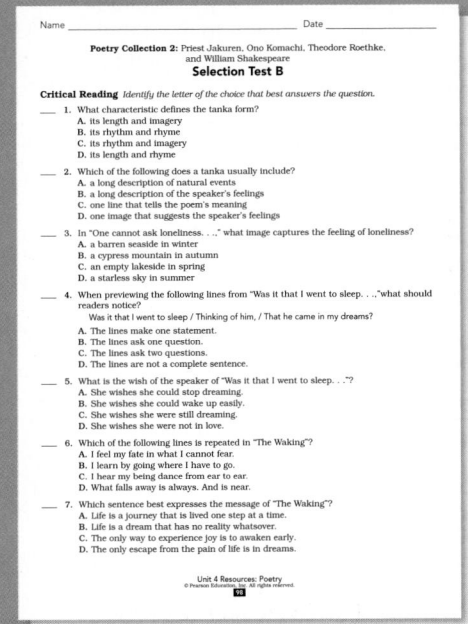

Unit 4 Resources

Name ______________________ Date ______________

Poetry Collection 1: Ki Tsurayuki, Minamoto no Toshiyori, James Weldon Johnson, and Dylan Thomas

Literary Analysis: Poetic Form

To unify sounds and ideas in a poem, a poet may follow a **poetic form,** or a defined structure. Each poetic form uses a set number of lines. Some have a unique **meter,** or rhythm, and a unique pattern of **rhymes.** In your textbook, review the traditional poetic form. Then, complete the exercise.

Directions: *Answer the following questions about the poems in this collection.*

1. Both "When I went to visit. . ." and "The clustering clouds. . ." are translations of Japanese poems. Count the syllables in each line of the two poems. Which translation provides a better example of the tanka form? Why?

____

____

2. Read aloud the first four lines of the poem "My City." Then, answer the following questions.

When I come down to sleep death's endless night,
The threshold of the unknown dark to cross,
What to me then will be the keenest loss,
When this bright world blurs on my fading sight?

A. Above each unaccented syllable, draw a ˘. Above each accented syllable, draw a ´.

B. How many accented and unaccented syllables did you find in each line?

____

C. What is the rhyme scheme of the lines? ______________

D. In what poetic form is "My City" written? ______________

3. Read aloud the first two stanzas of "Do Not Go Gentle Into That Good Night." Then, answer the following questions.

Do not go gentle into that good night,
Old age should burn and rave at close of day;
Rage, rage against the dying of the light.

Though wise men at their end know dark is right,
Because their words had forked no lightning they
Do not go gentle into that good night.

A. How many lines are in each stanza? ______________

B. What is the rhyme scheme of the two stanzas? ______________

C. Which line is repeated? ______________

D. In what poetic form is the poem written? ______________

Unit 4 Resources: Poetry

67

All **Literary Analysis: Poetic Forms,** pp. 67, 85

Also available for these selections:

All Reading: Read Fluently, pp. 68, 86

L4 Enrichment, pp. 70, 88

L3 L4 Grammar, p. 89

L3 L4 Support for Writing, p. 90

L3 L4 Support for Extend Your Learning, p. 91

Assessment

Name ______________________ Date ______________

Poetry Collection 2: Priest Jakuren, Ono Komachi, Theodore Roethke, and William Shakespeare

Selection Test B

Critical Reading *Identify the letter of the choice that best answers the question.*

___ 1. What characteristic defines the tanka form?
A. its length and imagery
B. its rhythm and rhyme
C. its rhythm and imagery
D. its length and rhyme

___ 2. Which of the following does a tanka usually include?
A. a long description of natural events
B. a long description of the speaker's feelings
C. one line that tells the poem's meaning
D. one image that suggests the speaker's feelings

___ 3. In "One cannot ask loneliness. . .," what image captures the feeling of loneliness?
A. a barren seaside in winter
B. a cypress mountain in autumn
C. an empty lakeside in spring
D. a starless sky in summer

___ 4. When previewing the following lines from "Was it that I went to sleep. . .,"what should readers notice?
Was it that I went to sleep / Thinking of him, / That he came in my dreams?
A. The lines make one statement.
B. The lines ask one question.
C. The lines ask two questions.
D. The lines are not a complete sentence.

___ 5. What is the wish of the speaker of "Was it that I went to sleep. . ."?
A. She wishes she could stop dreaming.
B. She wishes she could wake up easily.
C. She wishes she were still dreaming.
D. She wishes she were not in love.

___ 6. Which of the following lines is repeated in "The Waking"?
A. I feel my fate in what I cannot fear.
B. I learn by going where I have to go.
C. I hear my being dance from ear to ear.
D. What falls away is always. And is near.

___ 7. Which sentence best expresses the message of "The Waking"?
A. Life is a journey that is lived one step at a time.
B. Life is a dream that has no reality whatsover.
C. The only way to experience joy is to awaken early.
D. The only escape from the pain of life is in dreams.

Unit 4 Resources: Poetry

98

L3 L4 **Selection Test B,** pp. 77–79, 98–100

Also available for these selections:

EL L1 L2 Selection Test A, pp. 74–76, 95–97

L3 L4 Open-Book Test, pp. 71–73, 92–94

PHLit Online!
www.PHLitOnline.com

- complete narrated selection text
- a thematically related video with writing prompt
- an interactive graphic organizer
- highlighting feature
- access to all student print resources, adapted to individual student needs
- Spanish and English summaries

Get Connected! (thematic video with writing prompt)

Also available:

Background video

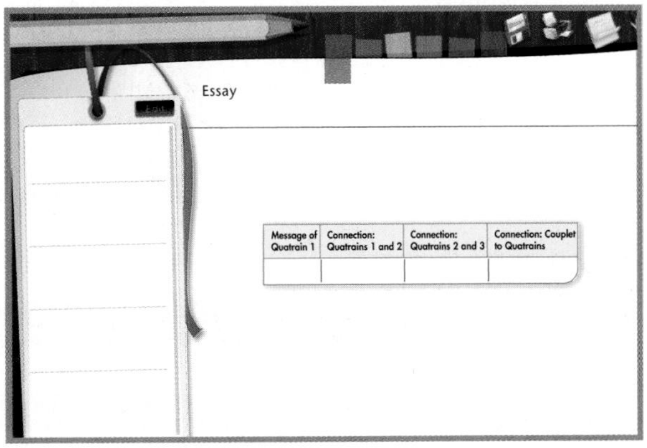

Writer's Journal (with graphics feature)

Also available:

Vocabulary Central (tools, activities, and songs for studying vocabulary)

DIFFERENTIATE/PRETEACH

❶ Collection Choices

You may use either Poetry Collection 3 or Poetry Collection 4 to meet the lesson standards. Skills instruction for both selections appears on pp. 671–673. Choose one selection to teach (or choose to teach both). The Accessibility at a Glance chart at the bottom of this page will help you determine which of the two selections is more appropriate for your students.

❷ Selection Skills

1. With the class, preview the selection skills. (The lesson meets the lesson objectives given on p. 670a.)
2. Explain that students will develop the skill of reading fluently (introduced on p. 639) as they read to better understand and enjoy the selection you choose. By examining poetic forms as they read, they will gain deeper insight into poetry.
3. To introduce the Writing and Listening and Speaking activities (p. 691), tell students that when they have finished reading the selection, they will write a tanka and hold a poetry reading discussion related to the selection.
4. Tell students that they will also study a grammar concept: direct objects. By mastering this concept, they will improve their reading fluency and the quality of their own writing.

Before You Read

Poetry Collection 3 • Poetry Collection 4

❶ Collection Choices

▲ The poems in **Poetry Collection 3** include vivid images of landscapes, both real and imagined.

▲ In **Poetry Collection 4**, the speaker of each poem shares insight gained in moments of solitary reflection.

❷ Collection Skills Guide

Practice these skills with either **Poetry Collection 3** (p. 676) or **Poetry Collection 4** (p. 684).

- Analyze poetic forms
- Understand meter and rhyme
- Read fluently
- Preview
- Identify direct objects
- Write a tanka
- Hold a poetry reading discussion

Differentiated Instruction for Universal Access

Accessibility at a Glance: Selection Choices

	Collection 3	Collection 4
Context	Cross-cultural collection of poems about death, literal and figurative	Cross-cultural collection of poems about relationship between humans and nature
Language/ Vocabulary	• Some difficult vocabulary • On-level vocabulary	• Difficult vocabulary and sentence structure • Above-level vocabulary
Concept Level	Challenging (abstract ideas such as nostalgia, despair, and loneliness)	Challenging (reveal insights about life using abstract language)
Literary Merit	Cross-cultural experience; noted poets	Cross-cultural experience; noted poets
Lexile/Length	NP Word Count: 121; 168; 23; 24	NP Word Count: 159; 114; 15; 27
Overall Rating	**More accessible**	**More challenging**

Because a number of factors determine the relative accessibility of paired selections, in some cases the Lexile rating of the more challenging selection will be lower than that of the more accessible selection.

❸ Literary Analysis: Poetic Forms

To unify sounds and ideas in a poem, a poet may follow a **poetic form,** or defined structure. Each poetic form uses a set number of lines and a distinctive **meter** and pattern of **rhymes.** (For more on these elements, see pages 630–631.) Traditional poetic forms include the following:

Tanka is a five-line, unrhymed Japanese form.

- The first and third lines of tanka contain five syllables. The second, fourth, and fifth lines have seven syllables. (The number of syllables can vary when a tanka is translated into English.) Thus, the syllable pattern is 5-7-5-7-7.

Example: The flowing river (5)
Twists and turns and runs away (7)
Thinking of the sea (5)
Through the forests light and dark (7)
At last kissing salty waves. (7)

- The briefness of the tanka helps poets focus on a single strong image or idea. In this example, the poet concentrates on a river's journey through varied landscapes as it flows toward and empties into the ocean.

A sonnet is a fourteen-line form with a specific line count, rhyme scheme, and rhythmic pattern. In a **Shakespearean sonnet,** the lines are grouped into three **quatrains** (groups of four lines) and a **couplet,** a pair of rhymed lines. The rhyme scheme is *abab, cdcd, efef, gg.* This form is so common in English poetry and was so identified with William Shakespeare, and the time period during which he lived, that these sonnets are also called *English sonnets* or *Elizabethan sonnets.*

Another common sonnet form is the *Italian,* or *Petrarchan sonnet,* which breaks into an octet of eight lines with a rhyme scheme of *abba abba*, and a sestet of six lines, with a variety of rhyme schemes.

- In a Shakespearean sonnet the first quatrain introduces a situation or a topic to be considered, identifies a problem, or presents a question.
- The second and third quatrains develop the issue introduced in the first quatrain.
- Often at the beginning of the third quatrain or in the couplet, the writer presents a turning point in which the situation is explained, the problem is solved, or the question is answered.
- The couplet often provides a final commentary on or summary of the ideas explored in the first twelve lines.

PHLit Online!
www.PHLitOnline.com

Hear It!
- Selection summary audio
- Selection audio

See It!
- Get Connected video
- Background video
- More about the author
- Vocabulary flashcards

Do It!
- Interactive journals
- Interactive graphic organizers
- Self-test
- Internet activity
- Grammar tutorial
- Interactive vocabulary games

PRETEACH

❸ Literary Analysis

1. Introduce the skill, using the instruction on the student page.
2. Tell students that they will practice identifying poetic forms.

Think Aloud: Model the Skill

Model the skill of identifying poetic forms, using the following "think aloud." Say to students:

To determine the poetic form of a poem, I can consider its length and number of syllables. For example, if I see that a poem has only five lines, I know that it could be a tanka. To check my assumption, I can use what I know about the structure of a tanka to see if each line includes the correct number of syllables.

I can use other clues to help me, too. Suppose I am reading a fourteen-line poem. I know that a sonnet has fourteen lines, but to be sure, I need to check the poem's rhyme scheme. Suppose the rhyme scheme does not match the rhyme scheme of a sonnet. I know, then, that this poem is not a sonnet.

Teach the Skill

1. Read the sample tanka slowly with students, making a mark each time a syllable is read. Then, count up the syllables in each line to confirm that the poem is a tanka.
2. Have students look ahead to Shakespeare's Sonnet 18. Write the last word of each line on the board, and demonstrate the rhyme scheme, writing the letters *abab cdcd efef gg* beside each appropriate line.

Differentiated Instruction for Universal Access

Preparing Students for the More Challenging Selection

If you wish to prepare lower-level readers to read Poetry Collection 4, the more challenging selection, follow these steps:

- Students might have difficulty relating to poetry about nature. Discuss with students the aspects of nature that make it a good topic for poetry, such as its beauty and peacefulness.
- Remind students that the sentence structure of poetry differs from the sentence structure of prose. Although in poetry it is appropriate to have incomplete sentences, in prose this is not usually the case.
- Students might have difficulty with the vocabulary used in some of the poems, such as in Shakespeare's Sonnet 18. Go over such words as *lease* and *complexion.* Also, remind students that certain words that Shakespeare uses, such as *hath* and *wander'st,* might be read as *have* and *wanders.*

Think Aloud: Model the Skill

Model the skill of identifying a villanelle, using the following "think aloud." Say to students:

If I want to determine whether a poem is a villanelle, I should first make sure that the poem has nineteen lines. Next, I should check the arrangement of the stanzas to see whether they are grouped into five three-line stanzas and one four-line stanza. Finally, I should see whether certain lines are repeated. For example, if the poem is a villanelle, line 1 will be repeated in lines 6, 12, and 18.

❹ Using the Strategy

Model the Strategy

Give students a copy of either **Reading Skill Graphic Organizer A** or **B** (*Graphic Organizer Transparencies,* pp. 120–122) to record their ideas about reading fluently as they read. Use the examples in **Reading Skill Graphic Organizer A,** which is partially filled in, to model the process of completing the organizer.

Before You Read — Poetry Collection 3 • Poetry Collection 4

Literary Analysis: Poetic Forms (continued)

- Beyond their specific rhyme scheme and formula for content, sonnets also follow a strict rhythmic pattern called *iambic pentameter.* An *iamb* is a poetic foot with one unstressed syllable followed by a stressed syllable, as in the word *again. Pentameter* is verse written in five-foot lines. In a sonnet, each line contains five unaccented and five accented syllables in the pattern "da-DUM, da-DUM, da-DUM, da-DUM, da-DUM."

Another common sonnet form is known as the **Italian sonnet,** or the **Petrarchan sonnet,** named for the Italian poet Petrarch who lived from 1304 to 1374. In this format, the sonnet's 14 lines are split into an *octet,* or a group of eight lines, and a *sestet,* or a group of six lines. The octet follows a set rhyme scheme of *abba abba,* but the sestet may vary in its rhyme scheme. For example, it might have a pattern of *cdecde,* or *ccddee,* or *cddcdd.*

A **villanelle** is a nineteen-line form with a pattern of repeated lines and a specific rhyme scheme.

- The lines of a villanelle are grouped into five three-line stanzas and one four-line stanza. The lines rhyme *aba, aba, aba, aba, aba, abaa.*
- Line 1 is repeated in lines 6, 12, and 18. Line 3 is repeated in lines 9, 15, and 19.
- This deliberate repetition can create a chanting effect—such as "I wake to sleep, and take my waking slow" in "The Waking"—or suggest intense passion.

❹ Using the Strategy: Analyze Poetic Form Chart

Use a **Poetic Form Chart** like the one shown to analyze poetic forms as you read.

Analyzing the Form of a Poem			
Number of Lines?	Number of syllables in each line?	Pattern of accented and unaccented syllables in each line?	Which lines rhyme?

❺ Reading Skill: Read Fluently

When you **read fluently,** you read smoothly and with understanding, placing emphasis appropriately and pausing where necessary. To increase your fluency when reading a poem, **preview** the work, looking over the text in advance.

- Use footnotes and other text aids to learn unfamiliar words. Practice saying each unfamiliar word by following the pronunciation given, and learn each word's definition. Pay special attention to which syllables are accented.
- Determine where each sentence in the poem begins and ends. If you notice that a sentence stretches over more than one line, prepare to read it "through" the end of each line, pausing only when the punctuation indicates you should. Try not to stop at the end of a line if there is no punctuation there. Refer to the diagram here for the type of pause associated with common marks.

Punctuation	Type of Pause
. Period	Full stop
: Colon	Almost as strong as a period. End with your voice raised just enough so that a listener knows to expect more.
; Semicolon	Less strong than a colon. Pause briefly, with your voice raised.
, Comma	A slight pause

- Form a rough idea of the *topic* and *mood* of the work. A quick look at the type of words and images used in the poem may show you whether the mood of the poem is sad or happy, serious or humorous. For example, a poem about a robin that "chirps" on a "sunny" day is probably a happy poem.
- Read the poem with its *mood* in mind. You might change the *tone of your voice*, whispering or speaking loudly. You may read at a quicker pace if the action is exciting, or at a slower pace if the mood is suspenseful.

❺ Reading Skill

1. Introduce the skill, using the instruction on the student page.
2. Tell students that they will practice reading fluently as they read.

Think Aloud: Model the Skill

Model the skill of reading fluently, using the following "think aloud." Say to students:

In order to read a poem fluently, I need to pay attention to the poem's mood and to the punctuation used throughout.

For example, if I am reading a poem that praises nature, my voice should reflect this celebratory mood. I might raise my voice but speak firmly and slowly. In contrast, if a poem describes loneliness, I might speak softly and without much emotion. I also should make sure that I do not read too slowly or too quickly; my speed should adjust itself to the rhythm of the poem.

Punctuation also gives me clues about how to read a poem. For example, when I see a comma, I should pause slightly. A period demands that I come to a full stop. If I pay close attention to the mood and the punctuation in a poem, I will be able to read it fluently, with control and with the appropriate emotion.

❶ Writing About the Big Question

1. Review the assignment with the class.
2. Discuss with students the reasons why people might feel compelled to communicate their thoughts and feelings about nature.
3. Have students complete the sentence starters. Review responses as a class. (**Possible responses:** When people interact and respond to nature, they might feel closer to it. Poets, in particular, might feel a connection to nature because they are close observers of nature.)
4. Remind students that their answers will help them think about the Big Question, "Does all communication serve a positive purpose?"

While You Read

Tell students that as they read, they should note the different elements of nature in the poems.

❷ Vocabulary

1. Have students preview the selection vocabulary.
2. For each word, have students say the word aloud.
3. Then, use the word in a sentence that defines the word.
4. Finally, repeat your definitional sentence or a similar sentence with the word missing and have the class "fill in the blank" chorally. Here is an example:

   Someone on the threshold is at the entrance or at the beginning. Before stepping into the darkened house, he paused nervously at the [students say "threshold"].

❸ Word Study

1. Introduce the skill, using the instruction in the box.
2. Challenge students to identify a *-lun-* word by providing its etymology: "a person who experiences periodic bouts of insanity in response to the changing of the moon's phases." (**Answer:** *lunatic*)

Making Connections
Poetry Collection 3

My City • Do Not Go Gentle into That Good Night • The clustering clouds . . . • When I went to visit . . .

Does all *communication* serve a positive purpose?

❶ Writing About the Big Question

In Poetry Collection 3, the authors present their messages using images from a variety of landscapes. Use these sentence starters to develop your ideas about the Big Question:

When people **interact** and **respond** to nature they might feel _______________.

Poets, in particular, might feel a **connection** to nature because _______________.

While You Read Look for different elements of nature as you read these poems. Consider what the poet communicates to you about nature.

❷ Vocabulary

Read each word and its definition. Decide whether you know the word well, know it a little bit, or do not know it at all. After you read, see how your knowledge of each word has increased.

- **threshold** (thresh´ ōld´) *n.* the bottom of a doorway; entrance or a point of beginning (p. 677) ***She opened the door and stepped across the threshold.***
- **keenest** (kēn´ ist) *adj.* sharpest; most cutting (p. 677) ***The keenest disappointment was losing the last game.*** *keen adj. keenly adv. keenness n.*
- **clustering** (klus´ tər iŋ) *adj.* gathering; forming in a group (p. 680) ***I knew from the clustering wasps that their hive had been disturbed.*** *cluster n. cluster v.*
- **lunar** (lo͞o´ nər) *adj.* of the moon (p. 680) ***Neil Armstrong was the first person to set foot on the lunar surface.***

❸ Word Study

The **Latin root *-lun-*** means "moon."

In the tanka by Minamoto no Toshiyori, the speaker refers to **lunar** shadows, or shadows made by the light of the moon.

Vocabulary Development

Vocabulary Knowledge Rating

Create a **Vocabulary Knowledge Rating Chart** (*Professional Development Guidebook*, p. 33) for this selection. Include the selection vocabulary and the Big Question words that appear in the Writing About the Big Question sentence starters on this page. (The Big Question vocabulary is introduced on pp. 626–627.)

Give students a copy of the chart. Read the words aloud, and have students mark their rating in the Before Reading column. Urge them to be alert to these words as they read and discuss the selection.

Tally how many students think they know a word to gauge how much instruction to provide. As students read and discuss the selection, point out the words and their context.

PHLitOnline! **Vocabulary Central,** featuring tools, activities, and songs for studying vocabulary, is available at **www.PHLitOnline.com.**

Meet the Authors

James Weldon Johnson

(1871–1938)

Author of "My City" (p. 677)

Born in Jacksonville, Florida, James Weldon Johnson became the first African American allowed to practice law in Florida. Johnson also published a newspaper and was a leader in civil rights work.

Dylan Thomas

(1914–1953)

Author of "Do Not Go Gentle into That Goodnight" (p. 679)

Born in Wales, in Great Britain, Dylan Thomas fell in love with words early in life. Poems poured out of him, and by the age of twenty, he had written most of the poems for which he is famous today.

Minamoto no Toshiyori

(1055?–1129?)

Author of "The clustering clouds . . ." (p. 680)

Japanese poet and critic Minamoto no Toshiyori (mi′ nä′ mō′ tō′ nō′ tō′ shē′ yō′ rē′) rebelled against tradition and helped forge a new style. In addition to writing poetry, Toshiyori judged poetry contests.

Ki no Tsurayuki

(ca. 872–945)

Author of "When I went to visit . . ." (p. 680)

Ki no Tsurayuki (kē′ nō tso͞or′ ī′ o͞o′ kē′) was one of the leading Japanese poets, critics, and diarists of his time. In his preface to a major literary anthology, he said that "The poetry of Japan . . . springs from the heart of man."

Daily Bellringer

For each class during which you will teach this selection, have students complete one of the five Sentence Modeling activities for Week 20 in the *Daily Bellringer Activities* booklet.

Multidraft Reading

To assist struggling readers and to deepen reading for all, apply multidraft reading protocols. For each reading, have students set the purpose indicated:

- **First reading**—literal comprehension: answering the Reading Check questions.
- **Second reading**—application of skills: answering the Read Fluently and Poetic Forms prompts.
- **Third reading**—interpretation: answering the end-of-selection questions.

For more guidance, refer to the *Classroom Strategies and Teaching Routines* card on multidraft reading.

Differentiated Instruction — Additional Instruction

EL Extended Support—English Learners

Have students complete the **Reading and Vocabulary Warm-ups,** ***Unit 4 Resources,*** pp. 62–65, before they read. Assign the prereading pages and the adapted selection in the ***Reader's Notebook: English Learner's Version.*** Then, have students listen to portions of the selection on the ***Hear It!*** **Audio CD**.

L1 L2 Extended Support—Struggling Readers

Have students complete the **Reading and Vocabulary Warm-ups,** ***Unit 4 Resources,*** pp. 62–65, before they read. Assign the prereading pages and the adapted selection in the ***Reader's Notebook: Adapted Version.*** Then, have students listen to portions of the selection on the ***Hear It!*** **Audio CD** (adapted text).

Extended Support—Reluctant Readers

To build motivation and engagement before assigning the selection, have students read "As Big As All Outdoors," a thematically related selection in ***Reality Central.*** Then, use the questions at the conclusion of the related selection to guide discussion.

PHLit Online!

For more about the author, practice with the selection vocabulary, and more background, go to **www.PHLitOnline.com.**

❶ Activating Prior Knowledge

1. Prepare an **Anticipation Guide** (***Professional Development Guidebook,*** pp. 36–38) with the following statements:
   - Nature is the path to wisdom.
   - No one knows what to expect in death.
   - People should fight against dying.
   - People should welcome death as a part of the process of living.
2. Give students a copy of the prepared **Anticipation Guide** and have students mark their responses in the Me column. Have students discuss the statements in pairs or groups and mark the guides again in the Group column.
3. For further guidance, use the ***Classroom Strategies and Teaching Routines*** card, **Anticipation Guides.**

Concept Connector →

Students will return to the **Anticipation Guide** after completing the poems.

Individual Activity

Have students find examples of music that would enhance the mood and atmosphere of one of the poems.

❷ About the Selections

Unlike poets whose inspiration comes from nature, James Weldon Johnson is imaginatively stimulated by the city. In Dylan Thomas's poem, the speaker offers his father advice about meeting the challenge of death. The two Japanese poems reflect a traditional emphasis on the contemplation of nature as a path to wisdom.

❸ Humanities

Racing Taxis by Patti Mollica

Mollica, an American painter, focuses her work on everyday life, believing that everyday objects have as much interest and beauty as things found in nature. Her work reflects her interest in subjects that artists often overlook, such as soaring buildings and racing taxis in New York City at night.

Vocabulary Development

Thematic Vocabulary: The Big Question

As students are discussing Poetry Collection 3, encourage them to use the thematic vocabulary presented in Introducing the Big Question, pp. 626–627. You might encourage them with sentence starters like these:

1. Upon contemplating his death, the speaker in "My City" provides the *explanation* that he will miss Manhattan because . . .
2. The *emotion* the speaker in Dylan Thomas's "Do Not Go Gentle into That Good Night" conveys toward his father is . . .
3. The simple *language* in Minamoto no Toshiyori's tanka serves to . . .
4. Clues that hint at the speaker's feeling of *isolation* in Ki Tsurayuki's tanka are . . .

MY CITY

JAMES WELDON JOHNSON

❹ **Background** Contemporary poets who write Shakespearean sonnets may slightly modify the rhyme scheme. In this sonnet, Johnson uses a modified scheme in the first two quatrains, or groups of four lines. In the rest of the poem, however, he follows classic Shakespearean form.

When I come down to sleep death's endless night,
The **threshold** of the unknown dark to cross,
What to me then will be the **keenest** loss,
When this bright world blurs on my fading sight?
Will it be that no more I shall see the trees
Or smell the flowers or hear the singing birds
Or watch the flashing streams or patient herds?
No, I am sure it will be none of these.
❺ But, ah! Manhattan's sights and sounds, her smells,
Her crowds, her throbbing force, the thrill that comes
❻ From being of her a part, her subtile spells,
Her shining towers, her avenues, her slums—
O God! the stark, unutterable pity,
To be dead, and never again behold my city!

Vocabulary
threshold (thresh´ ōld´) *n.* the bottom of a doorway; entrance or a point of beginning
keenest (kēn´ ist) *adj.* sharpest; most cutting

Literary Analysis
Poetic Forms Which syllables are stressed in the iambic pentameter of line 9?

❼ ◄ **Critical Viewing** Which lines in the poem does this painting best illustrate? Explain. **[Connect]**

❹ Background
Sonnets

Remind students that the quatrains in a Shakespearean sonnet typically have a rhyme scheme of *abab, cdcd, efef.* Johnson's scheme is *abba, cddc, efef.*

❺ Literary Analysis
Poetic Forms

1. Have several volunteers read aloud line 9 of the poem, experimenting with different readings and emphases.
2. Then, **ask** students the Literary Analysis question: Which syllables are stressed in the iambic pentameter of line 9?
   Answer: *Ah, hat, sights, sounds,* and *smells* are all stressed.
3. **Ask** students to comment on the effect of this pattern of stresses.
   Possible response: The pattern of stresses in iambic pentameter imitates ordinary speech.

❻ Reading Skill
Read Fluently

1. Have students read the final four lines of the poem.
2. **Ask** students: Which punctuation marks show that the last two lines should receive special emphasis?
   Answer: The line that ends with *slums* ends with a dash, suggesting a fading out or substantial pause. Then the next line barely gets started before the first two words are followed by an explanation point. The last line also ends with an explanation point.
3. Then, **ask** students how these last two lines stand out aside from the special emphasis of the punctuation.
   Answer: The last words of these lines rhyme with each other but not with the other end rhymes. The last two lines also contain the poet's central message.

❼ Critical Viewing

Answer: The painting best illustrates line 12, where the poet speaks about Manhattan's "shining towers." However, the painting may also illustrate the more general notion of Manhattan's "throbbing force."

PROFESSIONAL DEVELOPMENT | **Don Leu**

APPLY THE STRATEGY

Use Internet Reciprocal Teaching to increase students' ability to search for and evaluate information. Reserve your school's computer lab in advance or use classroom laptops.

Put students in small groups and instruct each group to select two poets from "Poetry Collection 3." Have each group locate three interesting facts on the Internet about the poets they selected. Then, have them write down and evaluate each fact. Ask, "How reliable do you think each fact is: completely reliable, somewhat reliable, or not at all reliable? Why?" Then, as a class, discuss the results and reading strategies the students used.

For more of Don Leu's strategies, see his Professional Development essay, pp. 626c–626d.

❽ Humanities

Old Man in Sorrow by Vincent Van Gogh (1853–1890)

Vincent Van Gogh was a Dutch painter of the post-Impressionist school. Though van Gogh committed suicide at the age of thirty-seven, in his lifetime he produced more than two thousand paintings. In this painting, an old man appears to be suffering greatly.

Use these questions for discussion:

- What details of the man's expression and posture tell you about his mood and attitude?
  Possible response: The old man seems tired and weak. He is slumped in his chair, and he has to support his head in his hands.
- Do you think Dylan Thomas would have chosen this portrait to illustrate his poem? Why or why not?
  Possible response: Yes, because the portrait seems to represent a man who needs Thomas's advice. The old man in the painting seems to have given up and does not seem to be raging against the dying of the light.

❽

Vocabulary Development

Vocabulary Knowledge Rating

When students have competed reading and discussing the poems, have them take out their **Vocabulary Knowledge Rating Chart** for this selection. Read the words aloud once more, and have students rate their knowledge of the words again in the After Reading column. Clarify any words that are still problematic. Have students write their own definition and example or sentence in the appropriate column. Then have students complete the Vocabulary Practice activities at the end of the selection. Encourage students to use the words in further discussion and written work about this selection. Remind them that they will be accountable for these words on the **Selection Test, *Unit 4 Resources*,** pp. 74–76 or 77–79.

PHLit Online!

This selection is available in interactive format in the **Enriched Online Student Edition, www.PHLitOnline.com,** which includes a thematically related video with writing prompt and an interactive graphic organizer.

Do Not Go Gentle into That Good Night

Dylan Thomas

Do not go gentle into that good night,
Old age should burn and rave at close of day;
9 Rage, rage against the dying of the light.

Though wise men at their end know dark is right,
Because their words had forked no lightning they
Do not go gentle into that good night.

Good men, the last wave by, crying how bright
Their frail deeds might have danced in a green bay,
Rage, rage against the dying of the light.

Wild men who caught and sang the sun in flight,
And learn, too late, they grieved it on its way,
Do not go gentle into that good night.

Grave men, near death, who see with blinding sight
Blind eyes could blaze like meteors and be gay,
Rage, rage against the dying of the light.

And you, my father, there on the sad height,
10 Curse, bless, me now with your fierce tears, I pray.
Do not go gentle into that good night.
Rage, rage against the dying of the light.

Literary Analysis
Poetic Forms Where are the first and third lines of the first stanza repeated in this villanelle?

Reading Skill
Read Fluently Where will you pause when reading lines 16–19? What punctuation indicates each pause?

11 ◀ **Critical Viewing** Which of the four types of men do you think is represented in this painting? Explain. **[Interpret]**

9 Literary Analysis

Poetic Forms

1. Read the poem aloud for students.
2. Then, **ask** them the Literary Analysis question: Where are the first and third lines of the first stanza repeated in this villanelle?
Answer: "Do not go gentle into that good night" is repeated at the end of the second and fourth stanzas and is the penultimate line in the sixth stanza. "Rage, rage against the dying of the light" is repeated at the end of the third, fifth, and sixth stanzas.

10 Reading Skill

Read Fluently

1. Have a volunteer read the poem aloud.
2. Then, **ask** students the Reading Skill question: Where will you pause when reading lines 16–19?
Answer: Although there are brief comma pauses in lines 16, 17, and 19, the longest pauses come at the end of lines 17, 18, and 19 because of the periods.

11 Critical Viewing

Possible response: The man in the picture could be any of these men or none of them. He seems defeated as he sits in the chair, but he may be wise (he knows that death is in some way good); good (he cries about his weak deeds); wild (he has learned too late); or grave (he sees and understands too late). This man could also be the speaker's father, to whom he addresses the poem.

Concept Connector

Anticipation Guide

Have students return to their Anticipation Guides and respond to the statements again in the After Reading column. They may do this individually or in their original pairs or groups. Then, lead a class discussion, focusing on what students have learned that confirms or invalidates each statement. Encourage students to cite specific details, quotations, or other evidence from the text to support their responses to each statement.

Writing About the Big Question

Have students compare their responses to the sentence starters they completed before reading the essay with their ideas afterwards. Ask them to explain whether their thoughts have changed.

Literary Analysis Graphic Organizer

Ask students to review the graphic organizers they completed while reading. Show them the **Literary Analysis Graphic Organizer A** (*Graphic Organizer Transparencies,* p. 123) as an example. Then have students share their graphic organizers.

12 Connecting to the Big Question

1. Have students read the bracketed text. **Ask:** What elements of nature do you notice in this poem?
   Possible response: The poet mentions the "clustering clouds."
2. **Ask:** How do "the clustering clouds" contribute to the feeling the poet communicates about nature?
   Possible response: We can see nature more clearly when our vision is not obstructed.

ASSESS

Answers

Critical Thinking

1. Students who live in cities may respond strongly to Johnson's image of Manhattan. Students who live in rural areas may appreciate the tanka.
2. (a) The speaker contrasts the "smell of flowers," "sound of singing birds," and the sight of "flashing streams" or "patient herds" with the sights and sounds of Manhattan. (b) **Possible response:** Yes, the speaker successfully communicates his or her preference.
3. (a) The speaker believes that people should fight to live.
   (b) Students should explain why they agree or disagree.
4. (a) The weather is bitterly cold.
   (b) His willingness to endure the bitter cold suggests great love.
5. (a) The clouds obscure the moonlight, while the speaker infuses the event with meaning.
   (b) **Possible response:** Contrasts help us to perceive the similarities and differences more clearly.

Does all communication serve a positive purpose?

Possible response: In "My City," the speaker claims that the city has more meaning for him than nature. In "Do Not Go Gentle into That Good Night," the speaker thinks that nature attracts us and increases our desire to live.

TANKA

Vocabulary 12

clustering (klus′ tər iŋ) *adj.* gathering; forming in a group

lunar (lo͞o′ nər) *adj.* of the moon

The clustering clouds—
Can it be they wipe away
The lunar shadows?
Every time they clear a bit
The moonlight shines the brighter.
— Minamoto no Toshiyori
translated by Donald Keene

When I went to visit
The girl I love so much,
That winter night
The river blew so cold
That the plovers[1] were crying.
— Ki Tsurayuki
translated by Geoffrey Bownas

1. **plovers** (pluv′ ərz) *n.* shorebirds with short tails and long, pointed wings.

Critical Thinking

1. **Respond:** Which image from the poems in Poetry Collection 3 made the strongest impression on you? Why?
2. **(a) Contrast:** Contrast the landscape the speaker prefers in "My City" with the one he first describes. **(b) Evaluate:** Did the contrast help you appreciate his perspective? Explain.
3. **(a) Interpret:** In "Do Not Go Gentle . . . ," what does the speaker mean when he says, "Old age should burn and rave at close of day"? **(b) Evaluate:** Do you agree? Why or why not?
4. **(a)** What is the weather like when the speaker goes visiting in "When I went to visit . . ."? **(b) Infer:** What does his reaction to such weather indicate about his love? Explain.
5. **(a) Contrast:** Contrast the events actually taking place in "The clustering clouds . . ." with the speaker's interpretation of those events. **(b) Interpret:** What does the poem suggest about the effect of contrasts on our perceptions?

Does all communication serve a positive purpose? Select two of the poems from this collection and describe what message or feeling about nature the speaker in each poem conveys.

Assessment Resources

Unit 4 Resources

L1 L2 EL **Selection Test A,** pp. 74–76. Administer Test A to less advanced readers and English learners.

L3 L4 **Selection Test B,** pp. 77–79. Administer Test B to on-level and more advanced students.

L3 L4 **Open-Book Test,** pp. 71–73. As an alternative, give the Open-Book Test.

All **Customizable Test Bank**

All **Self-tests**
Students may prepare for the **Selection Test** by taking the **Self-test** online.

PHLit Online! All assessment resources are available at **www.PHLitOnline.com.**

After You Read
Poetry Collection 3

My City • Do Not Go Gentle into That Good Night • The clustering clouds . . . • When I went to visit . . .

Literary Analysis: Poetic Forms

1. Which features of **tanka** appear in the translations of "The clustering clouds . . ." and "When I went to visit . . ."?
2. Using a chart like the one shown, analyze the meaning of the three quatrains and the couplet in the **sonnet** "My City."

Message of Quatrain 1	Connection: Quatrains 1 and 2	Connection: Quatrains 2 and 3	Connection: Couplet to Quatrains

3. **(a)** Identify the repeated lines in the **villanelle** "Do Not Go Gentle into That Good Night." **(b)** What feeling does the repetition of these lines help create? **(c)** Discuss your answers with a partner. Explain how your discussion affected your thoughts and your understanding of the poem.

Reading Skill: Read Fluently

4. **(a)** Preview the first eight lines of "My City." What information about vocabulary and sentence structure can you learn? **(b)** Explain how this information might help you **read fluently.**

Vocabulary

Practice Identify the word that does not belong in each group and explain why.

1. clustering, crowding, repairing
2. lunar, rectangular, earthly
3. threshold, doorway, harvest
4. keenest, sharpest, silliest

Word Study Use the context of the sentences and what you know about the **Latin root *-lun-*** to explain your answer to each question.

1. If someone displays *lunatic* behavior, is that person behaving rationally?
2. If the emblem over a door is a *lune,* is the emblem in the shape of a square?

Word Study

The **Latin root *-lun-*** means "moon."

Challenge Explain how the root *-lun-* contributes to the meanings of these words. Consult a dictionary if necessary.

lunate
lunette
lunacy

ASSESS/EXTEND

Answers

Literary Analysis

1. Each tanka has five lines of unrhymed verse. The language is simple and direct, and the emotional attitude of the speaker is connected to the image from nature.
2. **Possible response: Message of quatrain 1:** The speaker asks what will be missed most when he or she dies. **Message of quatrain 2:** In the eighth line, the speaker answers these questions. **Message of quatrain 3:** The speaker gives sensory descriptions of Manhattan. **Message of couplet:** The speaker laments that he will miss his city when he is dead.

   For other sample answers, see ***Graphic Organizer Transparencies,*** **Literary Analysis Graphic Organizer A,** p. 120, and the **Additional Answers** section.
3. (a) Lines 1 and 3 are repeated. (b) **Possible response:** The repetition creates a feeling of urgency. (c) Students should report specific reasons for any change.

Reading Skill

4. (a) Students might note the question/answer format in these first lines. By recognizing the questions, readers will know to expect answers. (b) Previewing these challenging elements of the poem will help students know where to place the emphasis when reading.

Vocabulary

Practice

Sample answers:

1. *Repairing* does not fit because it has nothing to do with crowds.
2. *Rectangular* does not fit because it is not related to celestial bodies.
3. *Harvest* does not fit because it has nothing to do with entrances.
4. *Silliest* does not fit because it refers to one's sense of humor.

Word Study

Sample answers:

1. A person who displays lunatic behavior is not behaving rationally but wildly.
2. The emblem would not be in the shape of a square because a lune is something circular, like the moon.

Word Study: Challenge

Sample answers: Something *lunate* is shaped like a moon. A *lunette* has the shape of a half-moon. *Lunacy* is a state of madness that was once associated with phases of the moon.

PREREACH

Skills instruction for the ***Reading Skill*** *and* ***Literary Analysis*** *concept for this selection appear on p. 639.*

❶ Writing About the Big Question

1. Review the assignment with the class.
2. Explain to students that effective communication requires a careful and clear articulation of ideas and reflection on what is to be communicated. Writers must first think about what they want to say.
3. Have students complete the sample sentence starters. Review responses as a class. (**Possible responses:** Isolation and thinking something through on your own can be useful when you want to work completely through an idea. It is also important at times to interact and communicate with others because they will help you to develop your ideas.
4. Remind students that their answers will help them think about the Big Question.

While You Read

Tell students that as they read, they should look for the conclusions that each speaker reaches.

❷ Vocabulary

1. Have students preview the selection vocabulary.
2. For each word, have students say the word aloud.
3. Then, use the word in a sentence that defines the word.
4. Finally, repeat your definitional sentence or a similar sentence with the word missing, and have the class "fill in the blank" chorally. Here is an example:

   Something temperate is mild. People who can no longer endure bitter New England winters often move to Florida for the [students say "temperate"] *weather.*

❸ Word Study

1. Introduce the skill, using the instruction in the box.
2. Instruct students to use the word *tempest* in a sentence. (**Sample answer:** The tempest that swept through the village destroyed the crops.)

Making Connections
Poetry Collection 4

The Waking • Sonnet 18 • One cannot ask loneliness . . . • Was it that I went to sleep . . .

THE BIG ? Does all *communication* serve a positive purpose?

❶ Writing About the Big Question

In Poetry Collection 4, the speakers communicate insights they have gained through solitary reflection. Use these sentence starters to develop your ideas about the Big Question:

Isolation and thinking something through on your own can be useful when ________________.

It is also important at times to **interact** and communicate with others because ________________.

While You Read As you read these poems, look for the insights reached by each of the speakers about the relationship between isolation and communication.

❷ Vocabulary

Read each word and its definition. Decide whether you know the word well, know it a little bit, or do not know it at all. After you read, see how your knowledge of each word has increased.

- **fate** (fāt) *n.* destiny; what happens to a person or thing; final outcome (p. 685) ***The judge decided the defendant's fate.*** *fated adj. fateful adj. fatefully adv.*
- **lowly** (lō´ lē) *adj.* humble; of low rank (p. 685) ***Starting as a lowly stable boy, he worked hard to become a top trainer.*** *lowliness n.*
- **temperate** (tem´ pər it) *adj.* mild; kept within limits (p. 687) ***I prefer temperate weather much more than the snow.*** *temper v. temperately adv. temperateness n.*
- **eternal** (ē tʉr´ nəl) *adj.* without beginning or end; everlasting (p. 687) ***Our friendship is eternal and will last forever.*** *eternally adv. eternalness n. eternity n.*

❸ Word Study

The **Latin root *-temp-*** means "regulate," "moderate," or "time."

In Sonnet 18 by Shakespeare, the speaker explains that his beloved is more **temperate,** or moderate and less extreme, than the weather on a summer's day.

Vocabulary Development

Vocabulary Knowledge Rating

Create a **Vocabulary Knowledge Rating Chart** (***Professional Development Guidebook,*** p. 33) for this selection. Include the selection vocabulary and the Big Question words that appear in the Writing About the Big Question sentence starter. (The Big Question vocabulary is introduced on pp. 626–627.)

Give students a copy of the chart. Read the words aloud, and have students mark their rating in the Before Reading column. Urge them to be alert to these words as they read and discuss the selection.

Tally how many students think they know a word to gauge how much instruction to provide. As students read and discuss the selection, point out the words and their context.

PHLit Online! **Vocabulary Central,** featuring tools, activities, and songs for studying vocabulary, is available at **www.PHLitOnline.com.**

Meet the Authors

Theodore Roethke

(1908–1963)

Author of "The Waking" (p. 685)

Born in Michigan, Theodore Roethke developed his great love of nature from observing the plants in his family's commercial greenhouses. This love is often reflected in his poetry. In 1954, Roethke received a Pulitzer Prize for his poetry.

William Shakespeare

(1564–1616)

Author of Sonnet 18 (p. 687)

Even though he is most famous as a playwright, Shakespeare also wrote brilliant sonnets. Today, the English sonnet, which he perfected, is also known as the Shakespearean sonnet. (For more about Shakespeare and his career, see pages 890–891.)

Priest Jakuren

(1139–1202)

Author of "One cannot ask loneliness . . " (p. 688)

Priest Jakuren (jä′ ko͞o′ rən′) was a Buddhist priest whose poems are filled with beautiful yet melancholy imagery. After entering the priesthood at the age of twenty-three, he traveled the Japanese countryside.

Ono Komachi

(active ca. 833–857)

Author of "Was it that I went to sleep . . ." (p. 688)

A beautiful woman with a strong personality, Ono Komachi (ō′ nō′ kō′ mä′ chē′) was an early Japanese tanka poet. Her poems are marked by passion and energy. The few details known about her life have inspired many legends.

Daily Bellringer

For each class during which you will teach this selection, have students complete one of the five Sentence Modeling activities for Week 20 in the ***Daily Bellringer Activities*** booklet.

Multidraft Reading

To assist struggling readers and to deepen reading for all, assign the text in "chunks," following the icons, and apply multidraft reading protocols. For each reading, have students set the purpose indicated:

- **First reading**—literal comprehension: answering the Reading Check questions.
- **Second reading**—application of skills: answering the Read Fluently and Poetic Forms prompts.
- **Third reading**—interpretation: answering the end-of-selection questions.

For more guidance, refer to the ***Classroom Strategies and Teaching Routines*** card on multidraft reading.

Differentiated Instruction

Additional Instruction

EL Extended Support—English Learners

Have students complete the **Reading and Vocabulary Warm-ups, *Unit 4 Resources*,** pp. 80–83, before they read. Assign the prereading pages for the selection in the ***Reader's Notebook: English Learner's Version.*** Then, have students listen to portions of the selection on the ***Hear It!*** **Audio CD.**

L1 L2 Extended Support—Struggling Readers

Have students complete the **Reading and Vocabulary Warm-ups, *Unit 3 Resources*,** pp. 80–83, before they read. Assign the prereading pages in the ***Reader's Notebook: Adapted Version.*** Then, have students listen to portions of the selection on the ***Hear It!*** **Audio CD.**

Extended Support—Reluctant Readers

To build motivation and engagement before assigning the selection, have students read "Put Me In, Coach!" a thematically related selection in ***Reality Central.*** Then, use the questions at the conclusion of the related selection to guide discussion.

PHLit Online!

For more about the author, practice with the selection vocabulary, and more background, go to **www.PHLitOnline.com.**

❶ Activating Prior Knowledge

1. Prepare an **Anticipation Guide** (***Professional Development Guidebook,*** pp. 36–38) with the following statements:
   - Loneliness has no beginning and no ending.
   - The life of dreams is rich with opportunity.
   - Writing about something or someone grants immortality.
2. Give students a copy of the prepared **Anticipation Guide,** and have students mark their responses in the Me column. Have students discuss the statements in pairs or groups and mark the guides again in the Group column.
3. For further guidance, use the ***Classroom Strategies and Teaching Routines*** card: Using **Anticipation Guide.**

Concept Connector ⟶

Students will return to the **Anticipation Guide** after completing the poems.

Individual Activity

Encourage students to use a dictionary to find precise meanings of unfamiliar words within the contexts of the poems. Have students write down the words and their meanings for reference.

❷ About the Selections

"The Waking" reflects upon the daily process of waking up—literally and figuratively. Shakespeare's famous sonnet praises the beauty of his beloved as surpassing that of a summer day. Two Japanese tanka evoke impressions of love and loneliness.

❸ Humanities

Cumberland Hills by Winifred Nicholson (1893–1981)

Winifred Nicholson was an English painter who often painted domestic objects and landscapes. In this painting, she combined both focusing on the vase with flowers (the domestic object) and the hills outside the window (the landscape).

Vocabulary Development

Thematic Vocabulary: The Big Question

As students are discussing Poetry Collection 4, encourage them to use the thematic vocabulary presented in Introducing the Big Question, pp. 626–627. You might encourage them with sentence starters like these:

1. In "The Waking", the poet shows the *connection* between . . .
2. Shakespeare uses the sonnet form to *convey* . . .
3. In Sonnet 18, Shakespeare's formal *language* . . .
4. In Jakuren's tanka, the speaker relates *isolation* to . . .

The Waking

Theodore Roethke

I wake to sleep, and take my waking slow.
I feel my fate in what I cannot fear.
I learn by going where I have to go.

We think by feeling. What is there to know?
I hear my being dance from ear to ear.
I wake to sleep, and take my waking slow.

4 Of those so close beside me, which are you?
God bless the Ground! I shall walk softly there,
And learn by going where I have to go.

Light takes the Tree; but who can tell us how?
The lowly worm climbs up a winding stair;
I wake to sleep, and take my waking slow.

Great Nature has another thing to do
To you and me; so take the lively air,
And, lovely, learn by going where to go.

This shaking keeps me steady. I should know.
What falls away is always. And is near.
5 I wake to sleep, and take my waking slow.
I learn by going where I have to go.

Vocabulary
fate (fāt) *n.* destiny; what happens to a person or thing; final outcome

lowly (lō´ lē) *adj.* humble; of low rank

Literary Analysis
Poetic Forms How has the repetition of lines 1 and 3 changed their significance or associated feelings by the end of the villanelle?

6 ◀ **Critical Viewing** Which stanza of the poem might this painting illustrate best? **[Connect]**

4 Reading Skill
Read Fluently

1. Have several volunteers read the poem.
2. Remind students that punctuation helps slow down the reading of poetry and often aids the reader in knowing where emphasis should fall.
3. Then, **ask** them what way the punctuation in lines 7–9 should affect the pace and emphasis of their reading.
   Answer: This stanza has four pauses: one short pause after *there* and three long pauses after each of the end marks. The pace of the reading will be slowed by the multiple pauses.

5 Literary Analysis
Poetic Forms

1. Have a volunteer read the last quatrain two or three times.
2. Then, **ask** students the Literary Analysis question: How has the repetition of lines 1 and 3 changed their significance or associated feelings by the end of the villanelle?
   Answer: The repetition expresses the central meaning of the poem that is reinforced in each stanza—that waking up to life and learning about life represent a gradual process that cannot be rushed or planned.

6 Critical Viewing
Possible response: It might best illustrate the fifth stanza, where the poet mentions "Great Nature" and taking the "lively air."

Differentiated Instruction for Universal Access

EL Strategy for English Learners
To help students understand the rhyme scheme of the villanelle, have them fill out charts as they read. Under the left-hand heading *Rhyming Words,* tell them to write the words that occur at the ends of lines, such as *slow/go/know* and *fear/ear/there/stair/air*. Explain that the rhyme scheme of a poem is designated by letters, with matching letters representing matching sounds. In the right-hand column, entitled *Rhyme Scheme,* have them write the matching letters for the sounds, such as *aba*.

Enrichment for Advanced Readers
Because of the format restrictions of the villanelle, the words of the poem often carry multiple meanings to set forth and reinforce ideas. Have students identify words, phrases, and images that are ambiguous and then explain possible meanings. Examples may include "The lowly worm climbs up a winding stair" and "What falls away is always."

❼ Humanities

Frances Howard by Isaac Oliver (1568–1617)

Lady Frances Howard was one of the great beauties of her day and the center of a court scandal. She was married at the age of thirteen to Robert Devereux, Earl of Essex, but the marriage was dissolved so that she could marry a favorite of King James I, Robert Carr, Earl of Somerset. Husband and wife were imprisoned in the Tower of London after being found guilty of poisoning Sir Thomas Overbury, a man who had insulted Lady Frances in his letters and who was against her remarriage.

The portrait was done by a famous French miniaturist of the day, who studied and worked in England. In addition to portraits, Isaac Oliver also painted religious and classical scenes. His patrons included Queen Anne of Denmark and Henry, Prince of Wales. Use this question for discussion:

Ask: Are the portrait and the sonnet greater testaments to the beauty of the women or to the skills of the artists?

Possible response: The portrait and the sonnet are greater testaments to the skills of the artists than the beauty of the women. The art probably would not have survived the ages unless the artists were skilled.

PHLit Online!

This selection is available in interactive format in the **Enriched Online Student Edition, www.PHLitOnline.com,** which includes a thematically related video with writing prompt and an interactive graphic organizer.

Vocabulary Development

Vocabulary Knowledge Rating

When students have completed reading and discussing the four poems, have them take out their **Vocabulary Knowledge Rating Chart** for these selections. Read the words aloud once more, and have students rate their knowledge of the words again in the After Reading column. Clarify any words that are still problematic. Have students write their own definition and example or sentence in the appropriate column. Then have students complete the Vocabulary Practice at the end of the selection. Encourage students to use the words in further discussion and written work about these selections. Remind them that they will be accountable for these words on the **Selection Test, *Unit 4 Resources,*** pp. 95–97 or 98–100.

Sonnet 18

William Shakespeare

8 **Background** The Italian poet Petrarch (pē´ trärk´) wrote during the 14th century. His sonnets, overflowing with enthusiastic, exaggerated comparisons in praise of his beloved Laura, inspired Shakespeare and other poets living in 17th century England. In Sonnet 18, Shakespeare offers a unique perspective on the comparisons that were popular in the sonnets of the time.

9
Shall I compare thee to a summer's day?
Thou art more lovely and more temperate:
Rough winds do shake the darling buds of May,
And summer's lease hath all too short a date:
Sometime too hot the eye of heaven shines,
And often is his gold complexion dimmed;
And every fair from fair sometime declines,
By chance or nature's changing course untrimmed;[1]
But thy eternal summer shall not fade,
Nor lose possession of that fair thou owest;[2]
Nor shall Death brag thou wander'st in his shade,
When in eternal lines to time thou grow'st:

10
So long as men can breathe, or eyes can see,
So long lives this, and this gives life to thee.

Vocabulary

temperate (tem´ pər it) *adj.* mild; kept within limits

eternal (ē tʉr´ nəl) *adj.* without beginning or end; everlasting

Literary Analysis
Poetic Forms In what way does the couplet at the conclusion summarize the main idea of the poem?

1. **untrimmed** *adj.* stripped of ornaments or beautiful features.
2. **owest** (ō´ ist) *v.* own.

11 ◄ **Critical Viewing** Which characteristics of the woman in the sonnet does this woman seem to share? Explain. **[Connect]**

Concept Connector

Anticipation Guide

Have students return to their **Anticipation Guides** and respond to the statements again in the After Reading column. They may do this individually or in their original pairs or groups. Then, lead a class discussion, focusing on what students have learned that confirms or invalidates each statement. Encourage students to cite specific details, quotations, or other evidence from the text to support their responses to each statement.

Writing About the Big Question

Have students compare their responses to the sentence starters they completed before reading the poems with their ideas afterwards. Ask them to explain whether their thoughts have changed.

Literary Analysis Graphic Organizer

Ask students to review the graphic organizers they completed while reading. Show them **Literary Analysis Graphic Organizer A** (*Graphic Organizer Transparencies,* p. 125) as an example. Then have students share their graphic organizers.

8 Background
Sonnets

The Petrarchan sonnet consists of an octave (an eight-line stanza) and a sestet (a six-line stanza). The octave states a theme or asks a question. The sestet comments on the theme or answers the question.

In contrast, the English, or Shakespearean, sonnet consists of three quatrains (four-line stanzas) and a couplet (two lines). The couplet comments on the ideas contained in the preceding twelve lines.

9 Connecting to the Big Question

1. Explain to students that a writer can use comparisons to communicate effectively two different things or ideas.
2. Have students read the bracketed text. **Ask:** How does the speaker compare the beauty in nature to the beauty of the individual of whom he speaks?
   Possible response: The speaker claims that his beloved is more beautiful than a summer's day because her beauty lasts, whereas nature's does not.
3. **Ask:** Why might the speaker use the beauty in nature to communicate his insights about his beloved?
   Possible response: There are many beautiful things found in nature, but they do not last forever. In expressing these sentiments about his beloved's beauty, he immortalizes her and her fairness, something nature can never achieve.

10 Literary Analysis
Poetic Forms

1. Read the couplet aloud to students.
2. **Ask** them the Literary Analysis question: In what way does the couplet at the conclusion summarize the main idea of the poem?
   Answer: The power of poetry immortalizes the beloved.

11 Critical Viewing

Possible response: Like the woman in the sonnet, the woman in the portrait seems both fair and mild.

⓬ Reading Skill
Read Fluently

Ask students the Reading Skill question: How might the mood, or general feeling, of each poem affect the way that you read it?

Possible response: Students may suggest that somber moods might slow down a reading while joyful moods might quicken the pace.

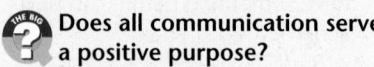

ASSESS
Answers

Critical Thinking

1. Students may respond to the romance in the works of Ono Komachi or William Shakespeare.
2. The speaker advises us to appreciate life and nature during the daily course of events.
3. (a) A summer's day may be marred by rough winds, hot sun, or overcast skies. (b) The beloved's beauty does not fade as the season does.
4. (a) One cannot ask loneliness how or where it starts. (b) **Possible response:** Loneliness can feel constant and enduring, much like the cypress trees on the mountain that do not change.
5. (a) She thinks that she may have gone to sleep thinking of the man. (b) **Possible response:** The comments suggest that she cares deeply for him.

Does all communication serve a positive purpose?

(a) **Possible response:** If a person wants to communicate effectively, it often helps to reflect on ideas before communicating them. Often, people wish to be alone when they think deeply, or reflect, about things.
(b) **Possible response:** The poet, though thinking and writing in isolation, communicates to the reader through the poem.

Tanka

Reading Skill
Read Fluently How might the mood, or general feeling, of each poem affect the way that you read it? ⓬

One cannot ask loneliness
How or where it starts.
On the cypress-mountain,[1]
Autumn evening.
— Priest Jakuren
translated by Geoffrey Bownas

Was it that I went to sleep
Thinking of him,
That he came in my dreams?
Had I known it a dream
I should not have wakened.
— Ono Komachi
translated by Geoffrey Bownas

1. **cypress-mountain** Cypress trees are cone-bearing evergreen trees native to North America, Europe, and Asia.

Critical Thinking

1. **Respond:** Which poem made the greatest impact on you? Why?
2. **Interpret:** What advice about life is implied in line 19 of "The Waking"?
3. **(a) Analyze:** Identify three ways in which, according to the speaker in Sonnet 18, a summer day may become less than perfect. **(b) Infer:** What is the main reason the speaker gives for claiming that the woman is superior to a summer's day?
4. **(a)** What question cannot be asked in "One cannot ask loneliness . . ."? **(b) Connect:** How does the image of the mountain relate to the speaker's thoughts about loneliness?
5. **(a)** What reason does the speaker in "Was it that I went to sleep . . ." give for dreaming about the man? **(b) Infer:** What do the speaker's comments reveal about her feelings for the man?

Does all communication serve a positive purpose?
(a) "Isolation" and "communication" seem to be opposite ideas. How can they be connected to each other?
(b) How are the ideas of isolation and communication connected in each poem?

Assessment Resources

Unit 4 Resources

L1 L2 EL **Selection Test A,** pp. 95–97. Administer Test A to less advanced readers and English learners.

L3 L4 **Selection Test B,** pp. 98–100. Administer Test B to on-level and more advanced students.

L3 L4 **Open-Book Test,** pp. 92–94. As an alternative, give the Open-Book Test.

All **Customizable Test Bank**

All **Self-tests**
Students may prepare for the **Selection Test** by taking the **Self-test** online.

PHLit Online! All assessment resources are available at **www.PHLitOnline.com.**

After You Read
Poetry Collection 4

The Waking • Sonnet 18 • One cannot ask loneliness . . . • Was it that I went to sleep . . .

Literary Analysis: Poetic Forms

1. Which features of **tanka** appear in the translations of "One cannot ask loneliness . . ." and "Was it that I went to sleep . . ."?
2. Using a chart like the one shown, analyze the meaning of the three quatrains and the couplet in Sonnet 18.

Message of Quatrain 1	Connection: Quatrains 1 and 2	Connection: Quatrains 2 and 3	Connection: Couplet to Quatrains

3. **(a)** Identify the repeated lines in the **villanelle** "The Waking." **(b)** What feeling does the repetition of these lines help create?

Reading Skill: Read Fluently

4. **(a)** Preview the first eight lines of Sonnet 18. What information about vocabulary and sentence structure can you learn? **(b)** Explain how this information might help you **read fluently.**

Vocabulary

Practice For each item, identify the word that does not belong in the group and explain why.

1. fate, destiny, loneliness
2. temperate, experienced, extreme
3. lowly, humble, clever
4. eternal, everlasting, terminal

Word Study Use the context of the sentences and what you know about the **Latin root *-temp-*** to explain your answer to each question.

1. If you describe the *temporal* aspect of a plan, are you talking about time, space, or rules?
2. Is a *temporary* building characterized by how long it will last or how tall it is?

Word Study

The **Latin root *-temp-*** means "regulate," "moderate," or "time."

Explain how the root *-temp-* contributes to the meanings of these words. Consult a dictionary if necessary.

contemporary
extemporaneous
tempo

ASSESS/EXTEND
Answers

Literary Analysis

1. These tanka each have five unrhymed lines. The poets use imagery of nature to capture feelings.
2. **Possible response: Quatrain 1:** The beloved is far better than a summer's day. **Quatrain 2:** These lines elaborate on summer's shortcomings. **Quatrain 3:** These lines explain why the beloved's beauty is superior.
   For other sample answers, see ***Graphic Organizer Transparencies,* Literary Analysis Graphic Organizer A,** p. 121, and the **Additional Answers** section.
3. (a) Lines 1 and 3 are repeated. (b) **Possible response:** The repetition expresses the central meaning of the poem—that waking up to life is a gradual, unplanned process.

Reading Skill

4. (a) Responses will vary, but students may cite unfamiliar words. (b) Students might explain that by previewing the poem, they grow accustomed to unfamiliar words and inverted sentence structure that would ordinarily slow down their reading pace.

Vocabulary
Practice
Sample answers:

1. *Loneliness* does not belong because it refers to a feeling.
2. *Experienced* does not belong because it has nothing to do with variations or climate.
3. *Clever* does not fit because it is a type of intelligence, whereas *lowly* and *humble* describe one's status.
4. *Terminal* does not fit because something terminal does not last forever.

Word Study
Sample answers:

1. You are talking about the aspects of the plan related to time.
2. A temporary building is characterized by how long it will last.

Word Study: Challenge

Sample answers: Something *contemporary* is of this time. An *extemporaneous* speech is given without preparation but at just that time. To keep the *tempo* is to keep time.

EXTEND

Grammar

1. Introduce the skill, using the instruction on the student page.
2. Discuss the definitions and the examples in the chart.

Think Aloud: Model the Skill

Model the skill of identifying direct objects, using the following "think aloud." Say to students:

To find the direct object in a sentence, I first look to the verb and ask myself what or whom receives the action. In the sentence "John threw the ball to his father," the verb "throw" is an action verb, so I know that it can take a direct object. Then, I ask myself a question about what or whom receives the action: *What* did John throw? The answer to this question is the "ball."

WG Writing and Grammar, Grade 10

Students will find further instruction and practice on direct objects in Chapter 19, Section 3.

Practice A

1. describes, action verb; clouds, direct object
2. heard, action verb; plovers, direct object
3. contains, action verb; lines, direct object
4. celebrates, action verb; city, direct object
5. implores, action verb; father, direct object

Challenge

Sample answer: "And learn, too late, they grieved it on its way." grieved, action verb; it, direct object. "Every time they clear a bit." clear, action verb; bit, direct object.

Practice B

Sample answers:

1. Priest Jakuren created beautiful images.
2. Ono Komachi wrote poems.
3. Hikers navigate mountains.
4. A beautiful woman inspired a sonnet.

Challenge

Sample answers: Priest Jakuren *bought* beautiful <u>flowers</u>. Ono Komachi *created* <u>tanka</u>. Hikers *carry* <u>backpacks</u>. A beautiful woman *wrote* a <u>poem</u>.

Integrated Language Skills

Poetry Collections 3 and 4

Poetry Collection 3

Poetry Collection 4

Grammar: Direct Objects

A **direct object** is a noun or pronoun that receives the action of a verb. (Action verbs that take a direct object are called *transitive verbs.*)

A direct object's function in a sentence is to add specific information. A direct object answers the question formed by putting *what* or *whom* after an action verb, as in the following examples. Verbs such as *am, is, are, was,* and *were* are linking verbs. They do not take direct objects.

Examples:

<u>Tyrell</u> **steers** the (car.)[DO] (Tyrell **steers** *what?* Answer: the car)

<u>Erin</u> **admires** her (friend.)[DO] (Erin **admires** *whom?* Answer: her friend)

<u>The twins</u> **were** happy. (**Were** is a linking verb, so there is no direct object.)

Practice A Copy each sentence. Underline the action verb and circle the direct object in each sentence.

1. The poet describes the clouds.
2. Ki no Tsurayuki heard the plovers.
3. The sonnet contains fourteen lines.
4. Johnson celebrates his city.
5. The poet implores his father to fight death.

Challenge Find and label two examples of action verbs with direct objects in any of the poems in Poetry Collection 3.

Practice B The following phrases require a direct object to complete the thought. Copy each phrase and complete it by adding a direct object.

1. Priest Jakuren created beautiful ______________.
2. Ono Komachi wrote ______________.
3. Hikers navigate ______________.
4. A beautiful woman inspired ______________.

Challenge Rewrite each sentence by keeping the subject and choosing a new action verb and direct object.

WG Writing and Grammar Connection: Chapter 19, Section 3

Extend the Lesson

Sentence Modeling

Choose the sentence given from the selection students have read:

Wild men who caught and sang the sun in flight, ("Do Not Go Gentle into That Good Night")

God bless the Ground! ("The Waking")

Ask students what they notice about the sentence. Elicit from them the action verb(s) and the direct object. Then, ask what else they notice. ("Do Not Go Gentle into That Good Night": the most important words in the line, including the two action verbs, *caught* and *sang,* and the direct object *sun,* are stressed in iambic pentameter; "The Waking": the brevity of the sentence, the alliteration in *God* and *Ground,* and the "b" sound in *bless* make this sentence a very powerful one that conveys the speaker's awe of nature.)

Have students imitate the sentence in a sentence on a topic of their own choosing, matching each grammatical and stylistic feature discussed. Collect the sentences, and share them with the class.

Writing

Write your own **tanka,** following the traditional Japanese form. Follow these steps:

- Think of a subject for your poem. Keep in mind that a tanka usually focuses on a single strong image or idea.
- Review the definition of a tanka on page 671.
- As you draft, choose words that will allow you to follow the prescribed syllable pattern for each line.
- After you draft, read your tanka aloud. Jot down ideas and then rephrase them to fit the form.

To help follow the form, *invert* normal word order as long as your meaning is clear. For example, you might write, "To the store did he run."

Writing Workshop: *Work in Progress*

Prewriting for Descriptive Essay Using the Organization Chart from your writing portfolio, choose one item to describe. Outline your description using the corresponding organizational structure. Then, using the outline, add the sensory details that would best convey each item. Cross out items that do not add to your description. Put this Outline in your writing portfolio.

Use this prewriting activity to prepare for the **Writing Workshop** on page 708.

Listening and Speaking

In a small group, listen several times to a recording of either Dylan Thomas reading "Do Not Go Gentle into That Good Night" or someone reading Shakespeare's Sonnet 18. Afterward, hold a **poetry reading discussion** in which you explore what the reading added to your understanding and appreciation of the poem.

Answer the following questions as you hold your discussion:

- Does the reader speed up at certain parts of the poem? Does he or she slow down at other parts?
- Does the reader put emphasis on certain words? Are there similarities in the words that the reader emphasizes?
- Does the reader stress the rhythm?
- Does the reader emphasize the rhyme?
- Does the reader convey a specific emotion or mood?
- Did hearing the poem aloud help your understanding of it?

After your discussion, have several people in your group read the poem aloud. Assess how the different readings **impact the audience.**

PHLit Online!
www.PHLitOnline.com
- Interactive graphic organizers
- Grammar tutorial
- Interactive journals

EXTEND/ASSESS

Writing

1. Review the assignment, using the instruction on the student page.
2. To guide students in writing a tanka, give them **Support for Writing,** p. 90 in ***Unit 4 Resources.***
3. To evaluate students' tankas, use the Poem rubrics on pages 248–249 in ***Professional Development Guidebook.*** In addition, evaluate how well students use images and the voice of the speaker to communicate ideas.

Six Traits Focus

✔	Ideas	✔	Word Choice
	Organization		Sentence Fluency
	Voice		Conventions

Writing Workshop
Work in Progress

Have students save their completed Outline in their portfolios. They will use them later as they complete the Writing Workshop assignment (see pp. 708–713).

Listening and Speaking

1. Review the assignment, using the instruction on the student page.
2. Have students complete the **Support for Extend Your Learning** page (***Unit 4 Resources,*** p. 91).

Teaching Resources

Unit 4 Resources

L3 L4 **Integrated Language Skills: Grammar,** p. 89

L3 L4 **Support for Writing,** p. 90

L3 L4 **Support for Extend Your Learning,** p. 91

L4 **Enrichment,** pp. 70 and 88

Enriched Online Student Edition
Available under After You Read for this selection:

All **Interactive Grammar Tutorial**

L3 L4 **Internet Research Activity**

Professional Development Guidebook
Rubrics for Poems, pp. 224–225

PHLit Online! All print and digital resources are available at **www.PHLitOnline.com.** Online resources accessible by students are noted on the student page.

MONITORING PROGRESS

Using the Test Practice

In this two-page Test Practice, students apply the reading skill for the first half of Unit 4 to a passage of fiction and a passage of nonfiction.

Review this skill, reading fluently, and then administer the test. For more guidance, consult the ***Classroom Strategies and Teaching Routines*** card, **Administering Timed Tests.**

ASSESS

Answers

Answers With Explanations

1. **C**—Building a radio is a complex, difficult task, requiring a slower reading than this short poem. *Incorrect answers:* A—The opposite is true; a grocery list can be read quickly, as it is simple and straightforward, unlike a poem. B—Scientific theory requires extraordinarily slow, careful reading. D—Song lyrics have form and content similar to poetry and require a similar reading.
2. **C**—The verbs *flies* (line 3) and *found* (line 5) are both actions of the "invisible worm" (line 2). *Incorrect answers:* A—Lines 3 and 5 both describe actions, not subjects. B—same explanation as for A. D—The actions describe in line 3 (flies) and line 5 (found) have nothing to do with the subject of line 6 (joy).
3. **D**—The lack of punctuation after *worm* shows that these words should be grouped when reading. *Incorrect answers:* A—The comma after *joy* shows that these words should not be grouped. B—The period after *sick* shows that these words should not be grouped. C—The comma after *storm* shows that these words should not be grouped.
4. **C**—The punctuation (two periods) shows that the first line contains one sentence and the rest of the lines a second sentence. *Incorrect answers:* A—The poem has eight lines, but every line is not a sentence. B—The punctuation (two periods) shows that there are not four sentences. D—same explanation as for B.

Test Practice: Reading

Read Fluently

Fiction Selection

Directions: *Read the selection. Then, answer the questions.*

O Rose, thou art sick.
The invisible worm
That flies in the night,
In the howling storm,

Has found out thy bed
Of crimson joy,
And his dark secret love
Does thy life destroy.

—"The Sick Rose" by William Blake

1. How many sentences does this poem consist of?
A. 8
B. 4
C. 2
D. 1

2. The reader should expect to read this poem—
A. faster than a grocery list.
B. slower than a science text.
C. faster than directions for building a radio.
D. at the same pace as than song lyrics.

3. Which lines should you read without pausing?
A. Of crimson joy, - And his dark secret love
B. thou art sick. - The invisible worm
C. the howling storm, - has found out thy bed
D. the invisible worm - that flies in the night

4. Which statement best conveys the basic meaning of the poem?
A. A rose befriends a worm.
B. A rain storm causes the destruction of a rose.
C. A rose's petals are soft and inviting.
D. A worm has a secret love for the rose.

Writing for Assessment

Explain how the mood and tone of this poem affect the way it should be read aloud. In a brief paragraph, use details from the passage to support your answer.

Writing for Assessment

In their responses, students should use at least two details to support their answer. They should pay attention to specific words such as *sick*, *worm*, *night*, *dark*, and *destroy* to help them identify the sad mood and brooding tone.

Strategies for Test Taking

Remind students to reread each line of the poem referred to in the question prompts. Suggest that they number each line to help them locate each reference quickly. Students may also find it helpful to take the time to briefly summarize or paraphrase poems that appear on tests to ensure that they understand the meaning before answering the questions.

Nonfiction Selection

Directions: *Read the selection. Then, answer the questions.*

Introduction to Black Spot

(1) A common disease that affects roses is Black Spot. (2) The disease can be identified by round black spots on the upper surface of the leaves. (3) Each spot has a yellow halo around it. (4) Over time, the blemishes grow and join, until the entire leaf becomes yellow and drops from the plant.

Black Spot: Preventing the Spread of the Disease

(5) The cause of Black Spot is a fungus that thrives in humid and rainy conditions. (6) There is no simple chemical treatment. (7) The best remedy is to prune infected stems in early spring and apply an anti-fungal spray before the leaves open. (8) Wet leaves provide a hospitable environment for germinating fungus spores; thus, to avoid Black Spot, do not water rose plants from above. (9) Instead, soak the soil around the plants. (10) If a plant is infected, remove yellowed leaves from the plant and the ground around it. (11) Spray nearby plants with a fungicide to prevent the disease from spreading.

1. Based on the first few lines, at what speed should the reader read this passage?
- **A.** The reader should read as fast as he or she would read a shopping list.
- **B.** The reader should read as fast as he or she would read a magazine article.
- **C.** The reader should read as fast as he or she would read a textbook.
- **D.** The reader should read as fast as he or she would read poetry.

2. What should the reader do before reading this passage?
- **A.** Preview the headings.
- **B.** Scan to find any unfamiliar words.
- **C.** Read the last sentence.
- **D.** Research the background of this topic.

3. When reading this passage aloud, which of the following would be appropriate?
- **A.** Read paragraph 1 more quickly than paragraph 2.
- **B.** Stop at the end of sentence 7.
- **C.** Reread sentence 5 aloud.
- **D.** Pause at the end of sentence 4.

4. Which sentence requires the reader to pause in three places?
- **A.** sentence 2
- **B.** sentence 7
- **C.** sentence 8
- **D.** sentence 10

Writing for Assessment

Connecting Across Texts

How would your purpose for reading affect the rate at which you would read the two passages aloud? In a paragraph, use details from the passages to support your answer.

PHLit Online!
www.PHLitOnline.com
- Online practice
- Instant feedback

Differentiated Instruction for Universal Access

EL Strategy for English Learners

Preview difficult vocabulary in the nonfiction selection to ensure understanding: *fungus* (a leafless plant that lives off other plants); *chemical treatment* (a kind of spray or powder that stops a disease); remedy (cure); *infected* (sick); *germinating* (growing); *spores* (cells that grow into new fungi); *fungicide* (a spray that kills fungi). Have students create a chart containing these words and their definitions for quick reference when reading the passage.

Strategy for Less Proficient Readers

Students may have difficulty with the Writing for Assessment assignment provided on page 692. Make sure that they understand the terms *mood* and *tone*: Mood is the feeling of a literary selection. Mood can be sad, light-hearted, strange, or thoughtful. Tone is the writer's attitude toward the topic. It can be respectful, concerned, brooding, humorous or scornful.

Answers With Explanations

1. C—A science text would have similar form and content, requiring a similar reading. *Incorrect answers:* A—The opposite is true; a list can be read quickly, unlike a demanding text. B—Science text requires a slower, more careful reading. D—Song lyrics can generally be read faster than a demanding text.
2. A—Previewing gives insight into content and makes reading more effective. *Incorrect answers:* B—Scanning to find unfamiliar words will not increase understanding. C—Reading the last sentence will not give insight into general content or increase understanding. D—While it may be interesting to gain additional knowledge about this topic, this would not be helpful before reading the passage.
3. D—A pause makes sense, as it emphases the end of one section and start of another. *Incorrect answers:* A—The paragraphs hold equal importance and should be read at equal speeds. B—There is no reason for a stop, as this sentence is in the middle of paragraph 2. C—Re-reading would stop the flow while reading aloud.
4. B—Lack of punctuation shows that these phrases should be read together. *Incorrect answers:* A—The period after *open* means these words should not be grouped. C—The period after *it* means these words should not be grouped. D—The period after *plants* means these words should not be grouped.

Writing for Assessment

Students should first identify two specific purposes for reading each selection. Then they should respond to the prompt, using two details from each selection to support their ideas.

PHLit Online!

Students may take the test in interactive format with instant feedback online at **www.PHLitOnline.com**

PRETEACH

Meeting Your Standards

Students will

1. predict the purpose of informational material.
2. understand and use information from signs and Web sites.

Log on at ***www.PHLitOnline.com*** *for a detailed lesson plan for Informational Texts.*

Reading Skill

1. Introduce the skill, using the instruction on the student page and review the chart.
2. Tell students that as they read, they will make and confirm predictions about the author's purpose.

Think Aloud: Model the Skill

Model the skill of making predictions about the author's purpose. Say:

> When I look at the museum sign on page 695, I notice the large letters, the basic information, and arrows. These clues suggest that the purpose is to give basic facts and directions for the library.

Does all communication serve a positive purpose?

Have students think about how the Web site information is helpful.

Multidraft Reading

Have students follow a multidraft reading protocol.

- **First reading**—Have students read for general understanding.
- **Second reading**—Have students confirm predictions they made about the author's purpose.
- **Third reading**—Have students consider the favorable effects that the information provides.

Informational Texts

Real-Life Reading

Signs
Folger Shakespeare Library Hours and Exhibit Placards

Web Site
Atlanta-Fulton Public Library System Web Site

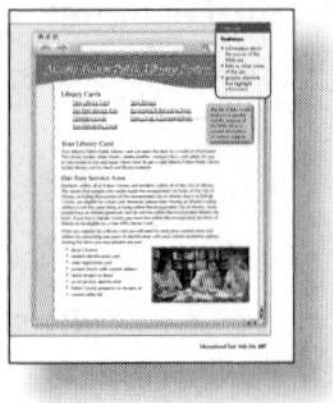

Reading Skill: Make Predictions: Purpose

Along with precise wording, authors use many techniques and elements to achieve their purposes. Previewing a document—**analyzing the structure, format, and features** of a text—allows you to **make predictions,** or educated guesses, about the **purpose** of that text. Before reading, look at the document and use a chart like this one to record your predictions about the author's purpose. Then, after you have read the text confirm whether your predictions were correct.

Previewing Observation	Prediction About Purpose	Confirmation
large, colorful graphics	grab readers' attention	
headings that categorize text	present several key ideas about a subject	
bulleted lists	provide examples	

THE BIG ? Does all communication serve a positive purpose?

The museum signs and library Web site communicate information to visitors and patrons. Consider how each positively benefits its readers.

Differentiated Instruction for Universal Access

Reading Support
Give students reading support with the appropriate version of the *Reader's Notebooks:*

- L2 L3 *Reader's Notebook*
- L1 *Reader's Notebook: Adapted Version*
- EL *Reader's Notebook: English Learner's Version*

PHLit Online! All student resources are also available at **www.PHLitOnline.com.**

Sign

Features:

- large, clear type
- information about rules, hours, and warnings
- directional arrows and/or maps
- key points and concise background information

FOLGER
SHAKESPEARE LIBRARY
VISITOR ENTRANCE
ELIZABETHAN THEATRE
BOX OFFICE OPENS
ONE HOUR BEFORE EVENTS
EXHIBITIONS
◀ELIZABETHAN GARDEN
MONDAY–SATURDAY
10:00 A.M. – 4:00 P.M.
RESEARCH ENTRANCE▶
READING ROOM • MUSEUM SHOP
ADMINISTRATIVE OFFICES
CLOSED ALL FEDERAL HOLIDAYS

The purpose behind large, bold letters is usually to draw the reader's attention.

Because the text is presented simply and in short lines, you can predict that the writer is trying to convey short, simple ideas.

Differentiated Instruction for Universal Access

Enrichment for Advanced Readers
Challenge students to learn more about Shakespeare and his plays. Tell them to consider ideas such as his personal life, his writing style, the era in which he lived, and topics of his plays. Allow time for students to share what they learn.

TEACH

About Signs

1. Review the list of sign features.
2. Invite students to tell about signs they have seen. Have them describe the signs' features. Then **ask** what they learned by reading the signs.
   Possible responses: Students may say they learned a store's return policy, a national park's campsite rules, or a subway station's hours of operation.
3. Remind students that signs are public displays of information. Tell them that the signs on pages 695–696 are displayed at the Folger Shakespeare Library, a museum in Washington, D.C.

Make Predictions: Purpose

1. Have students create a chart like the one shown on page 694, leaving the rows blank. Tell them they will fill in their own observations.
2. Tell students to preview the sign, paying attention to features such as how the words are arranged, the letters' sizes, and the type of graphics and their placement. Have students record their observations in their charts.
3. Draw students' attention to the notes. Point out that you can use each observation to make a prediction about the author's purpose. *(simple text, short lines; convey short, simple ideas) (large, bold letters; draw reader's attention)*
4. Tell students to use the observations in their charts to make predictions about the author's purpose. Have them record their predictions in their charts. **Ask** volunteers to share their observations and predictions.
   Possible responses: Students may notice that small text is shown beneath large text and predict that its purpose is to give details about the topic of the large text. Students may notice the lines separating sections of text and predict their purpose is to organize different kinds of information for the reader.
5. Have students read the sign and then record in their charts whether their predictions were correct.

Make Predictions: Purpose

1. Have students preview the sign and make predictions about the author's purpose. Have students either use charts to record their observations and predictions or have a class discussion.
2. Remind students to look at the format and structure of the sign to help them make predictions.
3. **Ask:** What is most noticeable about this sign?
   Possible response: Readers will notice the large heading "Elizabeth I" and the portrait.
4. **Ask** students to predict why the author included these features.
   Possible response: The author is going to give information about Elizabeth I.
5. Have a volunteer read aloud the note beside the portrait. Discuss the details in the illustration that indicate the stature and wealth of Elizabeth I. *(well-dressed; elegant clothing with intricate details)* Guide students to understand that thinking about the type of information conveyed by an illustration can lead them to make a prediction about the type of information the text will provide.
6. Have students read the sign to confirm whether their predictions were correct.

Elizabeth I

This illustration conveys information about Elizabeth I (her stature and wealth). You could predict that the article will do the same.

"TO BE A KING AND WEAR A CROWN IS a thing more glorious to them that see it than it is pleasant to them that bear it." These words, spoken by Elizabeth I to her Parliament in1601, might just as well be echoed by any head of state today. All the perks of office—the fine clothes, jewels, servants, and now, private planes and media attention—are there to be enjoyed, but they come with the high price of responsibility to the people and the nation. Elizabeth was not elected, she inherited this responsibility from her father, Henry VIII, But she took it seriously and was educated to be a prince. In 1558 after the death of her Catholic sister Mary, Elizabeth came to the throne and reigned for forty-four years. Though she restored the Protestant church to England, she resisted extremes in religion as well as policy. She also resisted pressure by her male council and Parliament to marry, turning the many offers for her hand into a game of political chess. She was a true "career woman" long before the term was coined; her job was her life.

Now, four hundred years after Elizabeth's death in March of 1603, the Folger Library honors her memory and her reign. Because Emily and Henry Folger focused their collecting on the age of Shakespeare, when Elizabeth was queen, the Folger Library has the largest collection of artifacts relating to Elizabeth in America. She has never really gone out of style. Every generation has re-read her through their own ideas of womanhood, and today perhaps we can appreciate her political skills more than did any other era. In her "Golden Speech" quoted above, she also said: "though you have had and may have many princes more mighty and wise sitting in this seat, yet you never had or shall have any that will be more careful and loving."

Major support for this exhibition comes from the Winton and Carolyn Blount Exhibition Fund of the Folger Shakespeare Library.

THE BIG ? Does all communication serve a positive purpose?
(a) What positive influence do libraries and museum exhibitions have on the general public? (b) Why might the supporters of the Elizabeth I exhibition have thought it important to communicate information about the Queen?

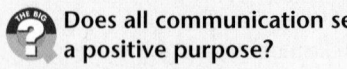

ASSESS/EXTEND

Answers

THE BIG ? Does all communication serve a positive purpose?

Possible responses:

(a) Libraries and museum exhibitions educate the general public. They provide ideas and historical information that can help the public better understand modern-day culture and society.

(b) Elizabeth I faced difficult challenges, yet ruled wisely and responsibly. Exhibition supporters might have wanted visitors to understand her reign so that they could compare her with today's political rulers.

Vocabulary Development

Cross-Curricular Vocabulary: Social Studies

Students may benefit from additional instruction for words displayed on the sign that relate to social studies. Review with students the meaning of the following words and phrases:

artifacts: objects made by people that are of historical or cultural interest
head of state: the chief representative of a country, usually also the head of government
Parliament: the section of the English government concerned with making laws
perks: privileges or benefits arising from being in a certain situation
prince: a person of noble rank
reign: *v.* to rule over; *n.* the time period during which a monarch or leader rules

PHLit Online! **Vocabulary Central**, featuring tools, activities, and songs for studying vocabulary, is available at **www.PHLitOnline.com.**

Atlanta-Fulton Public Library System

Web Site

Features:

- information about the source of the Web site
- links to other areas of the site
- graphic elements that highlight information

Library Cards

[Your Library Card](#) [Your Privacy](#)
[Our Free Service Area](#) [Borrowing & Returning Items](#)
[Children's Cards](#) [Fines / Lost & Damaged Items](#)
[Non-Residents' Cards](#)

This list of links could lead you to predict that the purpose of the Web site is to present information on various subjects.

Your Library Card

Your Atlanta-Fulton Public Library card can open the door to a world of information. The Library System offers books, audiocassettes, compact discs, and videos for you to take home to use and enjoy. Here's how to get a valid Atlanta-Fulton Public Library System library card to check out library materials.

Our Free Service Area

Residents within all of Fulton County and residents within all of the City of Atlanta. This means that people who reside inside the incorporated city limits of the City of Atlanta, including that portion of the incorporated city of Atlanta that is in DeKalb County, are eligible for a free card. However, please note: Having an Atlanta mailing address is not the same thing as living within the incorporated City of Atlanta. Many people have an Atlanta postmark, but do not live within the incorporated Atlanta city limits. If you live in Dekalb County you must live within the incorporated city limits of Atlanta to be eligible for a free AFPL Library Card.

When you register for a library card you will need to verify your current name and address by presenting one piece of identification with your current residential address. Among the items you may present are your

- driver's license
- student identification card
- voter registration card
- printed checks with current address
- rental receipts or lease
- social services identification
- Fulton County property tax receipts or
- current utility bill.

About Web Sites

1. Review with the class the features of Web sites shown on the student page.
2. **Ask** students to list occasions when they use Web sites. Then, ask them to explain why Web sites are helpful on these occasions.
   Possible responses: Some students may say that they use Web sites when they write research papers because information can be easily found. Others may say that they use Web sites to find information about potential purchases because they provide details about products.
3. Remind students to keep in mind a Web site's source when they are reading information given on a Web site.

Make Predictions: Purpose

1. Review with students the predicting strategies used for the sign.
2. Have students preview the Web site on the student page, noting its structure, format, and features.
   Ask: What is the purpose of this Web site?
   Answer: Its purpose is to tell about a public library system.
3. **Ask** students to describe the features of the Web site that helped them recognize this.
   Possible responses: The title "Atlanta-Fulton Public Library System" is set in large type across the top of the page. The headings "Library Cards," "Your Library Card," and "Our Free Service Area" suggest that the text will describe library policies. The photo of students reading suggests that the Web site has something to do with books.
4. Draw students' attention to the list of bulleted items at the bottom of the Web site.
   Ask: Why do you think the author of the Web site placed these items here?
   Answer: The list lets readers know what forms of identification are accepted to obtain a library card.

Differentiated Instruction for Universal Access

Enrichment for Gifted and Talented Students

Challenge students to design and create their own Web sites. Suggest ideas for Web site topics, such as a school club Web site, a sports information Web site, or other topics that students are interested in. Tell students to narrow their topic so that their Web site will have a specific purpose. Remind them to consider what they would like readers to learn from the site. Encourage students to use formatting techniques, graphical elements, and structural arrangements in their Web site design. When Web sites are completed, allow time for students to demonstrate their sites to the class. Have the class preview each Web site and predict what its purpose is. Then, have volunteers read aloud the information on the Web site to confirm whether the class's prediction was correct.

Make Predictions: Purpose

1. Have students preview this page of the Web site. **Ask** them to make observations about how it is structured.
   Possible responses: The page has headings that appear above the main sections of text.
2. **Ask:** What do you predict this page of the Web site will tell about? Explain.
   Answer: Based on the boldfaced heads, the page will tell about rules and procedures for borrowing books from the library.
3. Have students read the Web site page to confirm whether their predictions were correct.

Reflecting on the Reading Skill

Have students think about the different observations they made about a document's structure, format, and features. **Ask** them what they found most interesting about using those features to help them make predictions about a document's purpose.

Possible response: Students may say that although they had always noticed different text structures and elements, they had not realized that they could use them to make predictions about what the document would be about.

ASSESS/EXTEND

Answers

Does all communication serve a positive purpose?

Possible response: Libraries, like other public institutions, exist for the benefit of the people. By communicating their policies, libraries keep the public informed about the requirements and expectations for using the services they provide.

Children's Cards

Children under the age of 13 who want to register for a library card must have the library card application signed by a parent or legal guardian. The parent or guardian must supply identification that shows the current residential address. By signing the child's application, the parent or guardian accepts the responsibility for all items borrowed on the child's library card.

Non-residents' cards

Non-residents may apply for a library card by paying a non-refundable fee of $25.00 per person per year.

Your Privacy

The Library System will keep confidential all records relating to your library card registration and the materials you borrow.

Borrowing & Returning Items

The text in the section headings indicates that this Web site is intended to provide patrons with information about library policies and procedures.

Loan Periods: You may borrow items for the following time periods:

Popular or "Browse" Materials............14 days *(no renewals)*
CDs..28 days *(10 per card, two renewals)*
DVDs and VHS.......................................7 days *(5 per card, two renewals)*
All other materials................................28 days

Renewals: You may renew MOST materials one time. Popular or "Browse" materials, books on hold can NOT be renewed. You may renew materials over the phone by using our TeleLibrarian Service or Go Online.

We strongly encourage you to return materials by the due date. Overdue materials will impact your borrowing privileges.

Fines/Lost & Damaged Items

Fines for overdue materials are as follows:

Adult Books and other materials.........10 cents a day, *maximum $5.00 per item.*
Adult Videos..$1.00 per day, *maximum $5.00 per item.*
Children's books....................................5 cents a day, *maximum $3.00 per item.*
Children's VHS and DVD's....................$1.00 per day, *maximum $3.00 per item.*
Lost library cards:.................................Replacement cards cost $1.00 each.

Lost & Damaged Materials: Replacement cost for lost or damaged materials is based on the library's average cost charts. Please save your receipt when you pay for lost or damaged material. If you find library material that you have paid for within 30 days of the payment date, bring the material and your receipt to your branch to receive a refund.

Theft: Anyone caught stealing or damaging material with intent to steal will be prosecuted in accordance with the law.

Does all communication serve a positive purpose?
Why is it important for public institutions, such as libraries, to communicate their rules and policies?

Think Aloud

Scanning the Text
Remind students that scanning the text allows them to find important information without reading the entire document. Direct students' attention to the section labeled "Borrowing & Returning Items." Say to students:

> ISuppose I want to borrow a CD from the library. I will first check the library's Web site to determine the length of time I am allowed to borrow the CD. As I look at the Web site on the student page, I will scan the headings until I see "Borrowing & Returning Items." After I read the information in that section, I learn that I can borrow a CD for 28 days. By scanning the text I have learned about the contents of the document without having to read all of it.

Test Practice: Informational Texts

Comparing Informational Texts

(a) Compare and contrast the **structures and formats** of the signs and Web site. **(b)** Explain how these elements help you **make predictions about the purpose** of each text.

Timed Writing

Write an Evaluation

Format
The prompt directs you to write an evaluation. Therefore, your response should include observations and judgments about the elements mentioned in the prompt.

Write an evaluation of either the signs or the Web site. Assess the usefulness of the text structures and formatting in helping the reader to understand the content and make predictions. Suggest improvements to features, such as graphics and headings, which will help better achieve the author's purpose. (30 minutes)

Academic Vocabulary
When you *assess*, you make a determination about something's value.

5-Minute Planner

Complete these steps before you begin to write:

1. Read the prompt carefully and completely. Look for key words, like the ones highlighted, that will help you understand the assignment.
2. Quickly look back at the signs and Web site. Decide which you will evaluate.
3. Review the text you chose. Make notes about the text structures and formatting you find helpful.
4. Consider the author's purpose and improvements that could be made to better achieve that purpose. **TIP** Think about when you first read the text. Did you have to reread any sections in order to fully understand them? Consider improvements that would have made those sections clearer to you when you first read them.
5. Create an outline for your evaluation. Then, refer to your notes and outline as you write.

Extend the Lesson

Connecting to the Students' World

To give students more practice with Web sites and maps and to help them apply the lesson to their own world, divide students into small groups. Have each group select a local site around the school or in the neighborhood to research. Have group members create signs to inform readers about their site. Tell students to use formatting and structural elements to set off the information in their signs. Remind them that color and graphic elements can convey important information as well. Allow time for groups to present their signs to the class.

ASSESS/EXTEND

Answers

Comparing Informational Texts

(a) **Possible response:** Both the sign and the Web site use large text in their titles. They both use structural elements, such as lines separating sections of text, to set off one section of text from another. Both use a graphic element, either an illustration or a photo. The sign provides all its information for the reader to see. The Web site offers links for the reader to quickly access information.

(b) **Possible response:** The arrows and times given on the sign, along with the photo of Elizabeth I, help you predict that the sign tells about the museum's resources, hours of operation, and a particular exhibit about Elizabeth I. The headings on the Web site help you predict that it tells about the way the Atlanta-Fulton Public Library operates.

Timed Writing

1. Before students complete the activity, guide them in identifying and analyzing key words and phrases in the prompt, highlighted on the student page.
2. Work with students to draw up guidelines for their Short Responses based on the key words:
   - **Focus** The evaluation should clearly examine either the sign or the Web site.
   - **Organization** The evaluation should assess the value of the text structures and formatting in helping the reader make predictions.
   - **Elaboration** The evaluation should suggest improvements to elements that will help better achieve the author's purpose.
   - **Style** The audience is not specified, so a formal style is appropriate.
3. Have students use the 5-Minute Planner to structure their time.
4. Allow students 30 minutes to complete the assignment. Evaluate their work using the guidelines they have developed.

PRETEACH

Meeting Your Standards

Students will

1. analyze and respond to tone and mood in poetry.
2. compare the effect of tone and mood in two poems and an essay.
3. write a comparison of tone and mood.

Log on at ***www.PHLitOnline.com*** *for a detailed lesson plan for Comparing Literary Works.*

❶ Comparing Tone and Mood

1. Introduce the skill, using the instruction on the student page.
2. Give students a copy of **Comparing Tone and Mood Graphic Organizer B,** ***Graphic Organizer Transparencies,*** p. 128. Have them fill in details and words that describe tone and mood as they read.

Think Aloud: Model the Skill

Model a way to identify tone and mood. Say to students:

Details and word choice can help to identify the tone and mood of a piece of writing. If an author writes "My momma always told me never to talk to strangers, and boy was she right," the author's tone is casual. If the author states that "the storm clouds loomed overhead," she is setting a somber mood.

❷ Vocabulary

1. Have students say each word.
2. Then, use the word in a sentence that defines the word. Repeat the sentence, now with the word missing, and have the class "fill in the blank" chorally.

For more guidance, see the ***Classroom Strategies and Teaching Routines*** card: **Introducing Selection Vocabulary.**

Comparing Literary Works

Fear • The Bean Eaters • How to React to Familiar Faces

❶ Comparing Tone and Mood

The overall feeling or impression conveyed by a literary work can be affected by two elements: **tone** and **mood.**

- **Tone** is the author's attitude toward the reader or the subject of the work. It can be described with adjectives such as *formal* or *informal, scolding* or *encouraging*, or *humorous* or *serious*.
- **Mood,** or atmosphere, is a general, unified feeling conveyed by the details of a literary work. The mood of a work may be described with adjectives such as *gloomy* or *joyous, menacing* or *cozy.*

Writers create tone and mood through their use of descriptive details and figurative language. A writer's choice of subject and setting can also help to define a mood.

In the selections presented here, the authors create unique worlds, defined by tone, mood, and the characters and events in the works. For example, the mood of "Fear" captures the emotional world of a mother. In contrast, the tone of "How to React to Familiar Faces" is mostly analytical, revealing a hint of humor and mild accusation. As you read, compare the moods and tones of the selections. Consider how specific words and details influence tone and mood. Use a diagram like this to help you.

Details Suggesting Attitude → **Tone**

Details Suggesting Feelings → **Mood**

❷ Vocabulary

- **twinges** (twinj´ əz) *n.* sharp pains, either physical or mental (p. 703) *After a strenuous practice, I feel twinges in my sore muscles.*
- **context** (kän´ tekst´) *n.* situation in which something is found (p. 704) *I explained my question by establishing its context.* text *n.*
- **expound** (ek spound´) *v.* explain in detail (p. 705) *He loves to expound on the subject of history, but today he kept it brief.*
- **amiably** (ā´ mē ə blē) *adv.* in a friendly way (p. 706) *The hostess smiled amiably and led us to our table.* amiable *adj.*

PHLit Online! www.PHLitOnline.com

- Vocabulary flashcards
- Interactive journals
- More about the authors
- Selection audio
- Interactive graphic organizers

Vocabulary Development

Vocabulary Knowledge Rating

Create a **Vocabulary Knowledge Rating Chart** (***Professional Development Guidebook,*** p. 33) for this selection. Include the selection vocabulary and the form of the Big Question word that appears in the Writing About the Big Question sentence starter on the next page. (The Big Question vocabulary is introduced on pp. 626–627.)

Give students a copy of the chart. Read the words aloud, and have students mark their rating in the Before Reading column. Urge them to be alert to these words as they read and discuss the selection.

Tally how many students think they know a word to gauge how much instruction to provide. As students read and discuss the selection, point out the words and their context.

PHLit Online! **Vocabulary Central,** featuring tools, activities, and songs for studying vocabulary, is available at **www.PHLitOnline.com.**

Does all *communication* serve a positive purpose?

❸ Writing About the Big Question

In these selections, the writer describes human interactions. Think about how people you know communicate with each other. Use this sentence starter to develop your ideas.

When one person **misinterprets** what another has said, it can lead to ______.

Meet the Authors

Gabriela Mistral (1889–1957)

Author of "Fear" (p. 702)

At fifteen, Gabriela Mistral (gä brē ä′ lä mē sträl′) was already a full-time grade-school teacher in her native Chile. Mistral, born Lucila Godoy y Alcayaga (lo͞o sē′ lə gō doi′ ē äl kī ä′ gə), published her poetry under a variety of pen names before she settled on Gabriela Mistral. In 1945, she became the first Latin American to receive the Nobel Prize in Literature.

Gwendolyn Brooks (1917–2000)

Author of "The Bean Eaters" (p. 703)

Gwendolyn Brooks began writing poetry at the age of seven. Encouraged by her family, she published her first poem at thirteen. In 1950, Brooks became the first African American writer to win a Pulitzer Prize. She is one of the most admired American poets of the twentieth century.

Umberto Eco (b. 1932)

Author of "How to React to Familiar Faces" (p. 704)

Italian author Umberto Eco has a personal library of more than 30,000 volumes—larger than many school libraries! He is interested in communication of every kind. At the University of Bologna, he teaches semiotics, the study of communication through signs and symbols. He also follows the information revolution with great interest.

Daily Bellringer

For each class during which you will teach this selection, have students complete one of the five Vocabulary activities for Week 21 in the *Daily Bellringer Activities* booklet.

Writing About the Big Question

1. Review the assignment with the class.
2. Discuss with students the advantages and disadvantages of various methods of communication, such as telephone calls, emails, and face-to-face contact.
3. Have students complete the sentence starter. Review responses as a class. (**Possible response:** When one person misinterprets what another has said, it can lead to confusion and misunderstanding.)
4. Remind students that their answers will help them think about the Big Question.

Concept Connector →

Students will return to their responses to the sentence starter they complete before reading.

Multidraft Reading

To assist struggling readers and to deepen reading for all, apply multidraft reading protocols. For each reading, have students set the purpose intended:

- **First reading**—literal comprehension: answering the Reading Check questions
- **Second reading**—application of skills: responding to the side-column notes
- **Third reading**—interpretation: answering the end-of-selection questions

For more guidance, refer to the **Classroom Strategies and Teaching Routines** card on multidraft reading.

Teaching Resources

The following resources can be used to enrich, extend, or differentiate the instruction.

- All *Unit 4 Resources,* pp. 101–117
- All **Graphic Organizer Transparencies,** pp. 127–130
- All **Enriched Online Student Edition**

PHLit Online! All resources, including print and audio, are available at **www.PHLitOnline.com.**

PHLit Online! For more about the authors, practice with the selection vocabulary, and more background, go to **www.PHLitOnline.com.**

1 Background

Two poets Published in 1924, Mistral's second major volume of poetry, which includes "Fear," addresses themes relating to children. While Brooks had explored socioeconomic themes in the past, the volume containing "The Bean Eaters" was criticized for expressing too much social consciousness.

2 Activating Prior Knowledge

Ask each student to select a strong emotion such as anger or sorrow and write a sentence that conveys the emotion without stating it directly. For instance, a student might write, "I could feel my cheeks flush as the rage boiled inside of me."

Concept Connector →

Students will follow up on this activity after completing the selections.

3 About the Selections

"Fear," explores the anxiety and uncertainty that parents face. Brooks evokes the texture of everyday life in "The Bean Eaters."

4 Critical Viewing

Possible response: Students may say that the mother looks worried, and her close hold on the child indicates that she wants to protect the child.

5 Literary Analysis

Tone and Mood

1. Remind students that tone is how the author feels about the subject of a piece.
2. **Ask** the Literary Analysis question: In what tone of voice do you imagine the mother uttering lines 9–12? Why?
   Possible response: The mother is probably speaking in a soft, protective tone of voice.

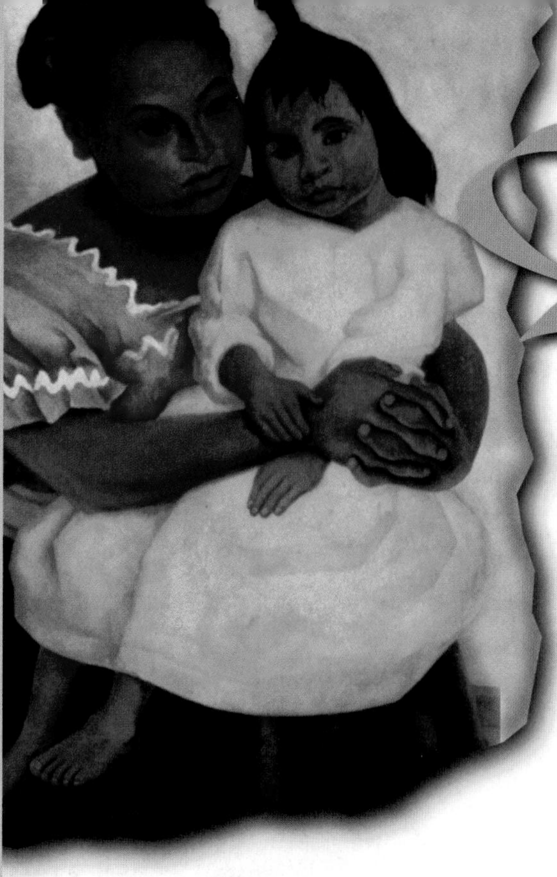

Fear

1 2 3

Gabriela Mistral

translated by Doris Dana

I don't want them to turn
my little girl into a swallow.
She would fly far away into the sky
and never fly again to my straw bed,
or she would nest in the eaves[1]
where I could not comb her hair.
I don't want them to turn
my little girl into a swallow.

I don't want them to make
5 my little girl a princess.
In tiny golden slippers
how could she play on the meadow?
And when night came, no longer
would she sleep at my side.
I don't want them to make
my little girl a princess.

And even less do I want them
one day to make her queen.
They would put her on a throne
where I could not go to see her.
And when nighttime came
I could never rock her . . .
I don't want them to make
my little girl a queen!

4 ▲ **Critical Viewing** Does the mother's expression in this painting express the fears described in the poem? Explain. **[Interpret]**

Literary Analysis
Tone and Mood In what tone of voice do you imagine the mother uttering lines 9–12? Why?

1. **eaves** (ēvz) *n.* lower edges of a roof.

Vocabulary Development

Vocabulary: Using Context

Direct students' attention to the word *swallow* on this page. Use the following "think aloud" to model how to use context to infer the meaning of an unknown word. Say to students:

> I'm to going to think aloud to show you how I would figure out the meaning of the word *swallow* from its context.

In the first sentence, the word *swallow* describes something that the speaker does not want her daughter to turn into. As I read, I see that if the daughter turned into a *swallow,* she would fly away. Also, she would create a nest. I know that flying and creating a nest are things that birds do. Therefore, I conclude that a *swallow* is a type of bird.

PHLit Online! **Vocabulary Central,** featuring tools, activities, and songs for studying vocabulary, is available online at **www.PHLitOnline.com.**

The Bean Eaters

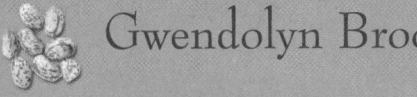

Gwendolyn Brooks

They eat beans mostly, this old yellow pair.
6 Dinner is a casual affair.
Plain chipware on a plain and creaking wood,
Tin flatware.

Two who are Mostly Good.
Two who have lived their day,
But keep on putting on their clothes
And putting things away.

And remembering . . .
Remembering, with twinklings and twinges,
7 As they lean over the beans in their rented back room
    that is full of beads and receipts and dolls and cloths,
    tobacco crumbs, vases and fringes.

Literary Analysis
Tone and Mood What attitude toward her subject does the speaker show in her repetition of *plain*?

Vocabulary
twinges [twinj′ əz] *n.* sharp pains, either physical or mental

Critical Thinking

1. **Respond:** Which poem did you enjoy reading more? Explain.
2. **(a)** Describe the three fears expressed by the speaker of "Fear." **(b) Apply:** What insight does the poem give into the relationship between mothers and their growing daughters?
3. **(a)** What does the couple in "The Bean Eaters" do as they eat their beans? **(b) Draw Conclusions:** In what way are their lives rich even though they are poor?

Does all communication serve a positive purpose?
(a) If you were the daughter of the speaker of "Fear," would you see the poem as a positive or negative expression of love? Explain. **(b)** Which poem do you think paints a truer picture of an attachment between people? Explain.

6 Literary Analysis

Tone and Mood

1. Remind students that the author's word choice creates tone.
2. **Ask** the Literary Analysis question.
   Answer: The speaker shows a sympathetic attitude.

7 Connecting to the Big Question

1. Explain that writers often use description to communicate their feelings about people or places.
2. Have students read the bracketed text. **Ask:** How does Brooks's description show the poverty of the "old yellow pair"?
   Possible response: She describes the common things they possess, such as vases and cloths.
3. **Ask:** Do these descriptions communicate a positive idea about the couple?
   Possible response: Brooks seems to have affection for them.

Concept Connector

Have students compare the Writing About the Big Question responses and sentences they wrote before reading the selections with their ideas afterwards.

ASSESS

Answers

1. **Possible response:** Students may say that they enjoyed "Fear" because it expresses an unusual point of view.
2. (a) Her daughter will be turned into a swallow, a princess, or a queen. (b) Mothers are anxious about their daughters becoming older.
3. (a) They remember their past. (b) They have each other and many memories.

Does all communication serve a positive purpose?

Possible responses: (a) Positive; the mother wants to hold onto her child. (b) "Fear"; it shows the fear that all people have when they anticipate the breaking of a bond.

Differentiated Instruction for Universal Access

Accessibility at a Glance

Use this information to guide your teaching of the two poems.

Language/ Vocabulary	• Difficult or historic vocabulary defined • Subject-specific vocabulary
Concept Level	Accessible
Literary Merit	Award-winning poets
Lexile/Length	NP

PHLit Online!

This selection is available in interactive format in the **Enriched Online Student Edition,** online at **www.PHLitOnline.com,** which includes an interactive graphic organizer.

TEACH

❶ Background

1. Anthony Quinn (1915–2001) was born in Mexico but was best known for his portrayal of Zorba in the stage and film versions of *Zorba the Greek.*
2. Charlton Heston (1924–present) is best known for the movie roles he played in the fifties and sixties. Though he won an Oscar for *Ben-Hur* in 1956, students might recognize him from his starring role in *Planet of the Apes* (1967).
3. Johnny Carson (1925–2005) won six Emmy awards for his work as the host of *The Tonight Show.*
4. In addition to running and hosting *The Oprah Winfrey Show* for twenty years, Oprah Winfrey has also acted in films, such as *The Color Purple* (1985).

❷ Activating Prior Knowledge

Read to students the Background note on this page. Then, ask students whether they have seen or met a local, national, or an international celebrity. Perhaps students have seen a local news celebrity in a grocery store or spotted a famous athlete at an airport. If so, ask each student how he or she reacted to the situation. Was it a surprise? If so, why? Did the student talk to the celebrity? Why or why not?

Concept Connector →

Tell students they will return to their discussion responses after they read the selection.

❸ About the Selection

In "How to React to Familiar Faces," Umberto Eco humorously reflects on how, in a media-dominated society, it is often difficult to ascertain the effects that media have on how we interpret the world.

❹ Critical Viewing

Possible response: Eco argues that because of the expanding influence of the mass media, people can be confused as to what is real and what is imaginary. Warhol's images suggest that it is acceptable to manipulate a famous person's face because she has become an image. Marilyn Monroe is no longer seen as a real person.

HOW TO REACT TO FAMILIAR FACES ❷

❸ UMBERTO ECO

Marilyn Monroe, Andy Warhol. © Andy Warhol Foundation.

❹ ▲ **Critical Viewing** Artist Andy Warhol made these prints repeating movie star Marilyn Monroe's face. Which of Eco's points do the prints help illustrate? **[Connect]**

❶ **Background** In this essay, Umberto Eco mentions several celebrities with whom you may not be familiar:

- Anthony Quinn was a film actor who won two Academy Awards.
- Charlton Heston, another film actor, won an Academy Award for his role in the film *Ben-Hur.*
- Johnny Carson was the host of the nighttime talk show *The Tonight Show* for thirty years.
- Oprah Winfrey is a successful talk-show host. She produces her show, publishes a magazine, and has a significant influence on public opinion.

A few months ago, as I was strolling in New York, I saw, at a distance, a man I knew very well heading in my direction. The trouble was that I couldn't remember his name or where I had met him. This is one of those sensations you encounter especially when, in a foreign city, you run into someone you met back home, or vice versa. A face out of **context** creates confusion. Still, that face was so familiar that, I felt, I should certainly stop, greet him, converse; perhaps he would immediately respond, "My dear Umberto, how are you?" or "Were you able to do that thing you were telling me about?" And I would be at a total loss. It was too late to flee. He was still looking at the opposite side of the street, but now he was beginning to turn his eyes towards me. I might as well make the first move; I would wave and then, from his voice, his first remarks, I would try to guess his identity.

Vocabulary
context (kän′ tekst′) *n.* situation in which something is found

We were now only a few feet from each other, I was just about to break into a broad, radiant smile, when suddenly I recognized him.

It was Anthony Quinn. Naturally, I had never met him in my life, nor he me. In a thousandth of a second I was able to check myself, and I walked past him, my eyes staring into space.

Vocabulary Development

Word Forms

Expand students' vocabulary by helping them learn related forms of the selection vocabulary words. Give students a blank **Word Form Chart** (***Professional Development Guidebook***, p. 42), with *confusion, context,* and *respond* in the correct columns. Work with the class, or have students work with a partner, to determine the related forms. The final chart should look like the one shown.

Noun	Verb	Adjective	Adverb
confusion	confuse	confusing	confusingly
context		contextual	contextually
response	**respond**		

PHLit Online! **Vocabulary Central,** featuring tools, activities, and songs for studying vocabulary, is available at **www.PHLitOnline.com.**

5 

Afterwards, reflecting on this incident, I realized how totally normal it was. Once before, in a restaurant, I had glimpsed Charlton Heston and had felt an impulse to say hello. These faces inhabit our memory; watching the screen, we spend so many hours with them that they are as familiar to us as our relatives', even more so. You can be a student of mass communication, debate the effects of reality, or the confusion between the real and the imagined, and **expound** the way some people fall permanently into this confusion; but still you are not immune to the syndrome.[1] And there is worse.

6 I have received confidences from people who, appearing fairly frequently on TV, have been subjected to the mass media over a certain period of time. I'm not talking about Johnny Carson or Oprah Winfrey, but public figures, experts who have participated in panel discussions often enough to become recognizable. All of them complain of the same disagreeable experience. Now, as a rule, when we see someone we don't know personally, we don't stare into his or her face at length, we don't point out the person to the friend at our side, we don't speak of this person in a loud voice when he
7 or she can overhear. Such behavior would be rude, even—if carried too far—aggressive. But the same people who would never point to a customer at a counter and remark to a friend that the man is wearing a smart[2] tie behave quite differently with famous faces.

My guinea pigs[3] insist that, at a newsstand, in the tobacconist's, as they are boarding a train or entering a restaurant toilet, they

1. **syndrome** (sin´ drōm´) *n.* set of symptoms or characteristics occurring together and defining a disease or condition.
2. **smart** *adj.* stylish; fashionable.
3. **guinea** (gin´ ē) **pigs** subjects of an experiment (so-called because of the use of guinea pigs in laboratory experiments).

Vocabulary
expound (ek spound´) *v.* explain in detail

Literary Analysis
Tone and Mood What does the writer's choice of the verb *subjected* tell you about his attitude toward mass media?

Reading Check
How does the writer react at first when he sees Anthony Quinn?

5 Humanities

Marilyn Monroe by Andy Warhol (1928?–1987)

Born in Pittsburgh, Pennsylvania, Andy Warhol gained fame in the 1960s as the leader of the pop-art movement, which is famous for depicting images from popular culture.

6 Literary Analysis

Tone and Mood

1. Before students read the bracketed text, remind them that the author's tone is influenced by diction, or word choice.
2. Now **ask** the Literary Analysis question.
   Answer: *Subjected* means that something is being forced on a person or group. Eco suggests that people are being forced to see and hear mass media.

7 Connecting to the Big Question

1. Remind students that the author is referring to the mass communication of the media and person-to-person communication.
2. Have students read the bracketed text. **Ask:** How does Eco believe the media's mass communication affects our personal communication in public?
   Answer: It changes the way we communicate when we see people from the mass media, because we don't realize that they are real.
3. Discuss how this problem could be alleviated. (**Possible response:** People could read Eco's essay to recognize the problem.)

8 Reading Check

Answer: Eco stops himself from speaking to Quinn, stops looking at him, and walks past.

Differentiated Instruction for Universal Access

Accessibility at a Glance

Use this information to guide your teaching of "How to React to Familiar Faces."

Context	Investigating mass media's influence
Language/Vocabulary	• Conversational; difficult vocabulary defined • Above-level vocabulary
Concept Level	Abstract
Literary Merit	Investigative, award-winning author
Lexile/Length	Lexile: 1110L Word Count: xxxxx
Other	Contemporary

PHLit Online!

This selection is available in interactive format in the **Enriched Online Student Edition**, at **www.PHLitOnline.com**, which includes an interactive graphic organizer.

❾ Literary Analysis

Tone and Mood

1. Before students read the bracketed text, remind them that the details in a piece can help them identify an author's tone.
2. Now **ask** the Literary Analysis question.
   Answer: The details contribute to Eco's critical, ironic tone.

Concept Connector

Have students compare the Writing About the Big Question responses and their responses to the class discussion they had before reading the selections with their ideas afterwards.

ASSESS

Answers

1. **Possible response:** Students may say that they would not react to a celebrity in the same way as Eco did. They might explain that they would stare and then try to get close enough to eavesdrop.
2. (a) Anthony Quinn (b) The author plans to wave because he thinks Quinn is someone he knows, but then he realizes that he only recognizes Quinn from television. (c) He realizes that Quinn's face is out of context. Seeing Quinn in real life rather than on television confuses the author.
3. (a) People often talk about the celebrity as if he or she is not there. (b) Eco suggests that because most people have only seen celebrities in movies or on television, celebrities are not perceived as real, leading them to treat celebrities differently.
4. (a) Mass media creates an image of celebrities, an image that does not exist in the everyday world. (b) Eco suggests that mass media is blurring the boundary between real and imaginary worlds.

Does all communication serve a positive purpose?

Possible response: No. It treats the celebrity without the consideration usually given to a real person.

Vocabulary
amiably (ā′ mē ə blē) *adv.* in a friendly way

Literary Analysis
Tone and Mood What do the details in this paragraph contribute to the author's tone?

❼ encounter others who, among themselves, say aloud, "Look there's X." "Are you sure?" "Of course I'm sure. It's X, I tell you." And they continue their conversation **amiably**, while X hears them, and they don't care if he hears them: it's as if he didn't exist.

Such people are confused by the fact that a protagonist of the mass media's imaginary world should abruptly enter real life, but at the same time they behave in the presence of the real person as if he still belonged to the world of images, as if he were on a screen, or in a weekly picture magazine. As if they were speaking in his absence.

❾ I might as well have grabbed Anthony Quinn by the lapel, dragged him to a phone booth, and called a friend to say, "Talk about coincidence! I've run into Anthony Quinn. And you know something? He seems real!" (After which I would throw Quinn aside and go on about my business.)

The mass media first convinced us that the imaginary was real, and now they are convincing us that the real is imaginary; and the more reality the TV screen shows us, the more cinematic[4] our everyday world becomes.

4. **cinematic** (sin′ ə mat′ ik) *adj.* of or like movies.

Critical Thinking

1. **Respond:** Do you think you would react to a celebrity in the way Eco describes? Explain.
2. **(a)** Whom does the author see while strolling in New York City? **(b) Summarize:** Why does he plan to wave and then change his mind? **(c) Analyze Cause and Effect:** How does Eco explain his reaction to this familiar face?
3. **Summarize:** According to Eco, how do many people behave when they run into a celebrity? **(b) Infer:** What does Eco suggest is the reason for their behavior?
4. **(a) Analyze:** Explain Eco's understanding of the role that media plays in our attitude toward reality. **(b) Generalize:** According to Eco, what changes in society may the media be causing?

Does all communication serve a positive purpose? In this story, the speaker describes how some people will talk about a celebrity—in his or her presence—as if the celebrity were not even there. Does this kind of communication serve a positive purpose? Why or why not?

Vocabulary Development

Vocabulary Knowledge Rating

When students have completed reading and discussing "Fear," "The Bean Eaters," and "How to React to Familiar Faces," have them take out their **Vocabulary Knowledge Rating Chart.** Read the words aloud once more, and have students rate their knowledge of the words again in the After Reading column. Clarify any words that are still problematic. Have students write their own definition and example or sentence in the appropriate column. Then, have students complete the Vocabulary Practice activities at the end of the selections. Encourage them to use the words in further discussion and written work about these selections. Remind students that they will be accountable for these words on the **Selection Test,** ***Unit 4 Resources,*** pp. 112–114 or pp. 115–117.

PHLit Online! **Vocabulary Central,** featuring tools, activities, and songs for studying vocabulary, is available at **www.PHLitOnline.com.**

After You Read

Fear • The Bean Eaters • How to React to Familiar Faces

Comparing Tone and Mood

1. **(a)** Identify two details in "Fear" and two in "The Bean Eaters" that give each poem a dreamlike feeling. **(b)** Explain the differences in mood between the two poems.
2. **(a)** In "The Bean Eaters," what is the speaker's attitude toward the couple? **(b)** Give two examples of descriptive words and details in the poem that convey this attitude.
3. Explain in what way the use of high-level vocabulary and formal language creates a scholarly and analytical tone in "How to React to Familiar Faces." Support your answer with examples.
4. At times, Eco departs from his serious tone. Give one example of this.
5. **(a)** Using a chart like the one shown, compare the tone and mood in the selections. **(b)** Use your chart to compare each speaker's emotional connection with his or her subject. Explain which is most direct and which is most distant.

Tone	Similarities/ Differences	Mood	Similarities/ Differences

Writing to Compare Tone and Mood

In an essay, analyze the way the author generates a mood in each selection. Use these questions to get started:

- How is the mood of the selection linked to the speaker's emotions?
- How is the mood conveyed by descriptive details or figurative language?
- How is the mood connected to the scenes and objects described?

Draw a conclusion about the world of each selection. Is it the inner world of a person, the outer world of everyday experience, or a special world in which outer things reflect an inward state?

Vocabulary Builder

Practice Write a sentence about each of the following people. For each, correctly use a word from the vocabulary list on page 700.

1. a person feeling sharp pains
2. a person explaining something in detail
3. a person acting in a cheerful way
4. a person providing background information

Assessment Resources

Unit 4 Resources

L1 L2 EL **Selection Test A**, pp. 112–114

L3 L4 **Selection Test B**, pp. 115–117

L3 L4 **Open Book Test**, pp. 109–111

PHLit Online! All assessment resources are available at **www.PHLitOnline.com.**

ASSESS

Answers

Comparing Tone and Mood

1. (a) The speaker's thoughts in "Fear" are dreamlike. The speaker in "The Bean Eaters" talks about "remembering." (b) "Fear": sorrowful; "The Bean Trees": contemplative.
2. (a) The speaker is sympathetic. (b) "Two who are Mostly Good" and "Two who have lived their day"
3. Technical words such as "expound" and "syndrome" create a scholarly tone.
4. Eco uses an ironic tone when he writes, " 'I might as well have grabbed Anthony Quinn by the lapel . . ."
5. (a) "Fear": tone—protective; mood—anxious; "The Bean Eaters": tone—sympathetic; mood— melancholic; "How to React to Familiar Faces": tone—analytical; mood—lighthearted (b) "How to React to Familiar Faces" is the most direct; it provides matter-of-fact descriptions; "The Bean Eaters" is the most distant; it does not state emotions.

   Other sample answers appear in ***Graphic Organizer Transparencies,*** **Comparing Tone and Mood Graphic Organizer A,** p. 129, and in the **Additional Answers** section.

Writing to Compare Tone and Mood

Review the assignment criteria with students and remind them to use specific details from the selections.

Six Traits Focus

✓	Ideas	✓	Word Choice
	Organization		Sentence Fluency
	Voice		Conventions

Vocabulary

1. twinges
2. expound
3. amiably
4. context

PRETEACH

Meeting Your Standards

Students will

1. write a descriptive essay.
2. use writing strategies to generate ideas and to plan, organize, evaluate, and revise the essay.
3. choose words to create a memorable image.
4. apply grammar skills.

Introducing the Writing Assignment

Review the assignment and the criteria, using the instruction on the student page.

Connecting to Real-Life Writing

Tell students that elements of description are often incorporated into other types of writing. Point out these examples:

- Writing an analysis of fine art or architecture requires accurate description.
- Book reviews often require descriptive details about setting.

Writing Workshop

Work in Progress

If students have done the Work-in-Progress assignments on pp. 669 and 691, suggest that they examine their recorded ideas as they begin prewriting. They may wish to develop these ideas in a descriptive essay.

Prewriting Strategies

1. Introduce the Prewriting Strategies, using the instruction on the student page.
2. Have students apply the strategy to develop figurative language.

Six Traits Focus

✔	Ideas		Word Choice
✔	Organization		Sentence Fluency
	Voice		Conventions

Writing Workshop

Description: Descriptive Essay

Defining the Form **Descriptive writing** portrays people, places, objects, experiences, or ideas in vivid detail so that the reader can create a mental picture of the subject. You might use elements of descriptive writing in short stories, reflective essays, character sketches, and scientific observations.

Assignment Write a descriptive essay about someone or something that is important to you or that you find interesting. Include these elements:

- ✔ *precise word choices* that create a strong impression
- ✔ *sensory details* of sight, sound, smell, taste, texture, and movements
- ✔ *figurative language*, such as personification, simile, and metaphor
- ✔ a logical *organization*
- ✔ error-free grammar, including correct use of *prepositional phrases*

To preview the criteria on which your descriptive essay may be judged, see the rubric on page 713.

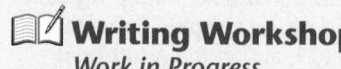

Writing Workshop: *Work in Progress*

Review the work you did on pages 669 and 691.

Prewriting Strategy

Gather details to develop figurative language. After you have found a topic that interests you, list key details in a chart like the one shown. Create figurative language by comparing these details with something that is familiar to your readers.

Apply It!

Detail	Reminds Me of...	Figure of Speech
a star pitcher's fastball	a knife slicing through the air	Metaphor: His fastball is a knife slicing through the air.
	a runaway train	Simile: His fastball is like a runaway train that stops for nothing.
	an emotion, such as anger	Personification: His angry fastball makes batters want to run!

Teaching Resources

The following resources can be used to enrich or extend the instruction.

All *Unit 4 Resources*
Writing Workshop, pp. 118–119

All *Professional Development Guidebook*
Rubric for Self-Assessment: Descriptive Essay, pp. 220–221

All *Graphic Organizer Transparencies*
Rubric for Self-Assessment: Descriptive Essay, p. 127

PHLit Online! All resources, including print and video, are available at **www.PHLitOnline.com.**

SIX TRAITS WRITER'S TOOLBOX SIX TRAITS

Word Choice | Ideas | Conventions | Sentence Fluency | Voice | Organization

Creating a Memorable Image

Word choice refers to the specific words or figures of speech that a writer chooses to create a memorable impression in the reader's mind. To create vivid and memorable images, writers of descriptive essays choose words that appeal to the five senses of sight, sound, smell, taste, and touch. Use these tips to create descriptions that will move your readers and make your essay memorable:

Choosing Appropriate Images Before you begin your essay, think about what impression you wish to create about the person or object you are describing. For example, if you are describing a favorite uncle, tell what is most memorable about him—his sense of humor, his quiet wisdom, or his kindness and generosity. Use a chart like this one to help you choose the appropriate images and words that appeal to the senses.

Apply It!

Characteristic	Words and Phrases
humor	*His soft blue eyes, edged with tiny laugh wrinkles, always had a smile behind them. When he laughed his whole body shook; just watching him made others laugh along with him.*

WG *Prentice Hall Writing and Grammar Connection: Chapter 6, Section 3*

Reviewing Word Choice Think about not only the meaning, or *denotation* of the words you choose, but also their *connotation*—the set of ideas and emotions associated with the word. For example, consider the following:

His jaw was set in firm *lines*

His jaw was set in hard *lines.*

Even though the words *firm* and *hard* have similar denotations, *firm* has a more positive connotation. It implies that the person has a strong character. In contrast, the word *hard* implies that the person is unbending or lacking in compassion for others.

Personalize Voice To create a genuine voice that "sounds" like you, choose words that both create vivid descriptions and reflect your personality. Review your essay, circling words or phrases that sound forced. Consider revising your essay with words that are truer to your voice.

Forced: *Father always sported a fedora of unobtrusive green.*

Genuine: *Dad always wore a hat that was a soft, faded green.*

Differentiated Instruction for Universal Access

EL Strategy for English Learners

English learners may have difficulty choosing the right word to express a particular meaning. Pair them with native speakers who can suggest descriptive words that might convey the desired meaning. Native speakers should explain the connotation of every word suggested by either partner. Pairs should write down each word and work together to form a sentence that contains clues to its denotation and connotation. English learners can keep these lists of words and sentences as a reference for later use.

Strategy for Gifted and Talented Students

Working with small groups or partners, have students choose an object in the classroom and write a description of it using vivid details and at least four of the five senses. Descriptions should not include the name of the object but should include metaphors and similes. Have groups trade descriptions and try to guess one another's objects.

Creating a Memorable Image

1. Introduce the writing skill, using the instruction on the student page.
2. Discuss the tips and strategies for creating a memorable image, and review the chart.

Teaching the Writing Skill

1. Remind students that sensory language creates vivid impressions using details related to the five senses. Emphasize that sensory language is not restricted to the genre of poetry. Any writer of poetry or prose can use sensory language to enrich descriptions.
2. Prompt students to consider why it is important to use most or all five of the senses in a description. **Possible response:** Using numerous senses helps readers place themselves inside the scene and imagine just how they would perceive it.
3. Remind students that they do not have to describe every detail at length. They should describe only the most interesting and relevant details.
4. Choose a movie or television character with which most students are familiar. Have students use sensory language to describe that person. Make sure they use all five senses. Write their responses in a chart on the board. Then, ask students to explain the connotation for each word or phrase, and write the connotation beside each. Ask volunteers for words or phrases that have the same denotations but different connotations. Write these on the board beside their counterparts.

OES Online Essay Scorer

A writing prompt for this mode of writing can be found on the *PH Essay Scorer* at www.PHLitOnline.com.

Writing and Grammar Interactive Textbook Online

Students can use the following tools at **www.pearsonsuccessnet.com** as they complete their descriptive pieces:

- Vague Adjectives Revising Tool
- Sensory Words Word Bin

TEACH

Drafting Strategies

1. Introduce the Drafting Strategies, using the instruction on the student page.
2. Have students apply the strategies as they draft.

Teaching the Strategy

Explain that the central idea is like a thesis statement; the rest of the essay should support it with details.

Think Aloud: Model Elaborating

Use the following "think-aloud" to model how to elaborate on ideas. Say to students:

> My central idea is "My cat is my best friend." To elaborate, I ask myself why. One answer is "She comforts me when I'm upset." Then I ask "How?" "She touches her nose to mine." I ask "How?" again, and describe how her wet nose feels. I keep questioning myself about why she's my best friend, and I use vivid details for each answer.

Six Traits Focus

	Ideas		Word Choice
✔	Organization		Sentence Fluency
✔	Voice		Conventions

Revising Strategies

1. Introduce the Revising Strategies, using the instruction on the student page.
2. Have students apply the strategies as they draft.

Teaching the Strategies

Have students read their essays aloud to partners and work together to determine where they need to add or revise details.

Six Traits Focus

✔	Ideas	✔	Word Choice
✔	Organization		Sentence Fluency
✔	Voice		Conventions

WG Writing and Grammar, Grade 10

Students will find additional instruction on drafting and revising their descriptive essays in Chapter 6, Sections 3 and 4.

Drafting Strategies

Present a controlling idea. All the details in your essay should build toward conveying a single main impression. Write one sentence that captures the main idea you want to express. Present this sentence in your introduction. Then, develop that idea in the rest of your essay.

Organize to describe. Choose an organization that showcases the details you will feature. These plans are useful when drafting descriptive writing:

- **General to specific** Use this structure when describing a person, thing or idea.
- **Chronological organization** Use time order to bring events to life for reader.
- **Spatial Organization** Use this plan to show where things are locating in relation to each other; for example, a place, a building, or an object.

Fully develop your ideas. Begin each paragraph with a statement that conveys the main idea. Next, extend that idea by restating or explaining the first sentence. Then, elaborate by providing supporting details.

Statement: At track meets, my coach shows few of her reactions.

Extension: She watches quietly from the sidelines.

Elaboration: She offers a smile and an encouraging word before we compete, but she rarely explodes with emotion.

Revising Strategies

Frame your description. Review the opening and closing paragraphs of your essay to be sure they frame your work. Circle details in your introduction that vividly establish your topic. Circle details in your conclusion that add insight. If too few details are circled, consider adding some.

Apply It!

Model: Revising to Add Detail

Barney's fur was ragged-looking, *filled with burrs and bits of leaves. A deep bloody gash on his left hind leg* ~~He moved~~ *caused him to move* slowly, with a severe limp.

The addition of vivid details clearly establishes the topic.

Choose vivid words. Review your essay, circling vague or dull word choices. Consider replacements that appeal to the senses.

Dull: The blanket felt good.

Vivid: The soft flannel blanket felt smooth, warm, and cozy.

Understanding by Design

Clarifying Expected Outcomes: Using Rubrics

- Before students begin working on this assignment, have them preview the Rubric for Self-Assessment (p. 713) to learn what qualities their descriptive essays must have. A copy of this rubric appears in ***Graphic Organizer Transparencies,*** p. 127.
- Review the criteria in the rubric with the class. Before students use the rubric to assess their writing, work with them to rate the Student Model (p. 712) using the rubric.
- If you wish to assess students' descriptive essays with either a 4-point or a 6-point scoring rubric, see ***Professional Development Guidebook,*** pp. 220–221.

WRITER'S TOOLBOX

Sentence Fluency | Voice | Organization | Word Choice | Ideas | Conventions

Revising to Vary Sentence Patterns

To make your writing more fluid and engaging, vary your style by beginning some sentences with prepositional phrases.

Identifying Prepositional Phrases A preposition and its object—the accompanying noun or pronoun—is called a prepositional phrase. Some prepositional phrases act as adjectives and some act as adverbs.

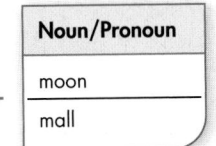

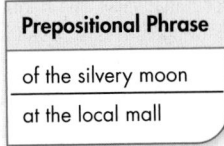

Preposition	+	Noun/Pronoun	=	Prepositional Phrase
of		moon		of the silvery moon
at		mall		at the local mall

Many prepositions express spatial or time-order relationships, which make them useful tools when writing a description.

Time: after the game; before dinner; at two o'clock; for a day

Space: under the table; near the river; in school; in my hand

Varying Sentences With Prepositional Phrases In these examples, subjects are italicized, verbs are underlined, and prepositional phrases appear in parentheses:

Repeated subject-verb pattern: *She* <u>wakes</u> up early. *She* <u>makes</u> breakfast. *She* <u>makes</u> lunch (after that).

Revision: *She* <u>wakes</u> up early. *She* <u>makes</u> breakfast. (After that), *she* <u>makes</u> lunch.

Follow these steps to vary your sentences in your own writing.

1. **Read your draft aloud.** Listen for overuse of the subject-verb sentence pattern.
2. **Identify sentences that contain a prepositional phrase.**
3. **Rewrite the sentence, starting with the prepositional phrase.** Be sure the phrase is close to the word it modifies.
4. **If the prepositional phrase contains four or more words, set it off from the words that follow with a comma.**

Grammar in Your Writing

Reread the first two paragraphs of your descriptive essay, looking for overuse of the subject-verb sentence pattern. Rewrite some sentences by beginning them with prepositional phrases.

WG *Prentice Hall Writing and Grammar Connection: Chapter 21, Section 3*

Writing Workshop 711

Revising to Vary Sentence Patterns

1. Introduce the writing skill, using the instruction on the student page.
2. Discuss the examples and the strategies for varying sentence patterns.
3. Have students follow the instruction under Grammar in Your Writing to correct errors in their drafts.

Teaching the Writing Skill

1. Ask for prepositions related to time and space. Write them in two separate lists on the board.
2. Ask volunteers to write sentences with prepositional phrases on the board. Have other volunteers draw arrows from the prepositional phrases to the words they modify and identify the phrases as either adjectives or adverbs.
3. Assign partners and have them read each other's essays aloud, listening for the subject-verb pattern. Ask them to note where the pattern feels repetitive.
4. Have students underline the prepositional phrases in their own papers. Ask them to experiment with moving these phrases to the beginnings of sentences, reminding them to revise only when the revision improves the essay. Suggest that they read paragraphs aloud both with and without the revisions and decide which sounds better.
5. Remind students to check that they have correctly used commas in their sentences with prepositional phrases.

WG Writing and Grammar, Grade 10

Students will find additional instruction on combining sentences in Chapter 21, Section 2.

Differentiated Instruction for Universal Access

Strategy for Less Proficient Readers

Have students read through their drafts and circle any passages that seem dull or incomplete. Then, have them add descriptive details that answer the questions *who? what? where? when? why?* and *how?* Students might find it helpful to make six-column charts, with one of the six questions in each column. They can then fill in the chart with modifiers that answer each question.

EL Strategy for English Learners

Remind students that sensory details can be words, phrases, or clauses that engage the readers' senses. Ask for examples of all three, and write them on the board. Suggest that students experiment with all three in their essays. Encourage students to keep a list of vivid sensory details they encounter while reading, and to consider using some of these details in their writing when appropriate.

Student Model

Review the Student Model with the class, using the annotations to analyze the writer's use of the elements of a descriptive essay.

Teaching From the Student Model

1. Explain that the Student Model is a sample and that the students' own descriptive essays may be longer or shorter depending on their topics.
2. **Ask** students to identify the central impression established by the details of the opening sentences.
   Possible response: *Ragged* suggests the cuts, blisters, and unkempt hands of a worker, a doer. The words *messy, clammy,* and *bitten* show the writer's honesty in her portrayal; she is not afraid of pointing out her own flaws.
3. Observe that Jordan continues to build upon an image of self-effacing immaturity with phrases such as: *my hands in my mouth* and *socially awkward moment*.
4. Have students discuss whether they think the author's description is intended to be funny. Ask for examples of humor in the description.
5. By writing the description, Jordan has come to terms with the *ragged* hands she describes in her first sentence. **Ask** students to give examples of pride in her hands.
   Possible response: She is proud she does not have *lady's hands.* She says her hands are *strong, capable,* and *tough* even though they are *callused, bony,* and *cold.*

Connecting to Real-Life Writing

Tell students that description will become a part of written responses in all content areas in college. Description reflects careful observation, which is a skill in many professions, including medicine, research, science, law, education, and law enforcement.

Student Model: Jordan Kurtzman, Brookline, MA

Hands

My hands are ragged. They look like the hands of a messy toddler in a way, with bitten cuticles and visibly clammy palms. But they are also covered in small scars, tiny and white or larger and more raw-looking red marks. They were unmarked when I was a baby, but not anymore. I scar easily.

> Jordan establishes her topic with vivid details

We had an assignment in drawing class to draw our hands holding an object. The teacher didn't tell us that the object had to be important in our lives until we'd already brought them in, so apparently handcuffs are important to me. The drawing wasn't terrible, but I never spent that much time staring at my hands before. My usual attention span for drawing is, at most, a half an hour, and I usually tend to give up once the shading gets complicated and careful attention must be paid to detail. I'm not a detail person. But in this assignment, I was forced to look at all the craggy grossness of my hands. I tried to stop biting my nails so that I wouldn't have to attempt the stubby, oddly textured things that pass for my fingernails, but it's a habit. I didn't start biting my nails until high school; whenever I have a lot of stress in my life, my nails look like they have been through a shredder.

I often find myself with my hands in my mouth when talking to someone, making for an extremely socially awkward moment. I never know if I should finish the nail-biting process or stop in mid-bite, leaving a partially severed nail.

> Jordan discusses what her topic means, not just what it looks like.

I can't leave my hands alone. An unpicked cuticle is an incomplete cuticle; a long, unbitten nail is not a true nail. I also have calluses on my fingertips from playing bass, guitar, and violin, and those provide endless fodder for fidgeting. Other people choose to stare off into space; I choose, or am compelled, to endlessly pick at my hands.

My hands are also extremely cold. They are the long-fingered, clammy hands of the Grim Reaper, un-holdable hands. Even my mother has told me that they are cold and clammy. Cold, clammy hands are things that cannot possibly be put in a good light. There is no bright side. I can imagine a palm reader, one who has seen countless hands, recoiling in horror from my hands, pointing at my life line from a distance instead of mapping it out on the skin.

> Jordan's genuine voice comes through here. Her sense of humor is evident.

Novels from a certain era always take care to point out the condition of a lady's hands. Long, white, glove-enclosed fingers are lady's hands. Cracked red hands are scullery maid hands. My hands place me squarely in the pot-scrubbing set.

But I'm not sure that I'd want lady's hands. I have a friend who has uncallused, soft and feminine hands. Her fingers are faintly chubby in an extremely cute, cherubic way. They don't look strong or capable, just soft and helpless as those of a baby. My hands, callused, bony, and cold, look strong and capable, not dainty, lily-white, and frail, but tough.

> Jordan draws a clear and interesting conclusion in her essay.

Strategies for Using Technology in Writing

If students are using word-processing software, suggest that they use the *Cut, Copy,* and *Paste* features or commands to move or insert prepositional phrases. After they have revised their sentences, advise students to use the grammar function to check that each new sentence reads properly and has appropriate punctuation, including additional commas as needed, and a period. Caution students that not all grammar suggestions are accurate on most word-processing software packages.

Students can also use features of the **Writing and Grammar Interactive Textbook Online** to revise repetitious sentence structure.

Editing and Proofreading

Check your draft for errors in grammar, punctuation, and capitalization.

Focus on Spelling: Remember to check your spelling even if you use a word processor's spelling software. Spell-checkers cannot tell if you have spelled a word correctly but have used the wrong word. For example, you might have used a *homophone*—a word that sounds like another but is spelled differently, such as *site* and *sight* or *role* and *roll*.

Publishing and Presenting

Consider one of the following ways to share your writing:

Organize a display. Work with classmates to create a display of your essays. Select an appropriate title and organization. For example, you might use one area of the display for essays that describe people. Add artwork or photographs to complement the essays. Consider posting the collection online.

Prepare an oral reading. Select music or sound effects to accompany your essay in an oral reading. Practice until you are confident. Then, deliver your reading for the class. When you are done, gracefully accept applause and express your thanks. If possible, record the reading on audiotape.

WG *Prentice Hall Writing and Grammar Connection: Chapter 6*

Reflecting on Your Writing

Jot down your answers to this question:

How did writing to describe your subject help you understand it?

Rubric for Self-Assessment

Find evidence in your writing to address each category. Then, use the rating scale to grade your work.

Criteria	Rating Scale (not very — very)				
Focus: How clear is the impression you create of your subject?	1	2	3	4	5
Organization: How logical is your organization?	1	2	3	4	5
Support/Elaboration: How well do you use sensory details?	1	2	3	4	5
Style: How effective is your use of figurative language?	1	2	3	4	5
Conventions: How correct is your grammar, especially your use of prepositional phrases?	1	2	3	4	5
Word Choice: How effective are the words and images you have chosen?	1	2	3	4	5

Editing and Proofreading

1. Introduce the editing and proofreading focus, using the instruction on the student page.
2. Have students edit and proofread their descriptive essays, correcting grammar, spelling, punctuation, and word choice. Make sure they check for errors of the type noted on the student page.

Teaching the Editing Focus

Assign partners to proofread each other's essays. Ask them to look for homophones and use dictionaries to make sure the correct word is used.

Six Traits Focus

	Ideas		Word Choice
	Organization	✔	Sentence Fluency
	Voice	✔	Conventions

ASSESS

Publishing and Presenting

1. Guide students to plan their display. Encourage creativity.
2. Tell students to work in pairs to practice their oral readings. Partners should give constructive feedback.

Reflecting on Your Writing

Ask students to record in their journals details they would not have remembered without writing their descriptions.

WG **Writing and Grammar, Grade 10**

Students will find additional guidelines for editing and proofreading, publishing and presenting, and reflecting on their essays in Chapter 6, Sections 5 and 6.

Strategies for Test Taking

A writing prompt on a standardized test may assess a student's ability to use sensory details to create a vivid experience for the reader. Suggest that students use charts to jot down sensory details about their topics. Some of the senses will prompt many details, especially sight and hearing. Point out that smell is the sense that evokes the most memories and therefore can sometimes make the strongest connection with the reader.

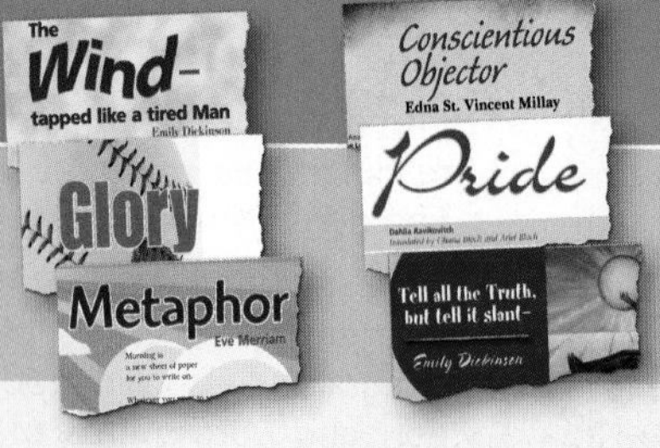

TIME AND RESOURCE MANAGER

Poetry Collection 5 • Poetry Collection 6

Lesson Pacing Guide

DAY 1 Preteach

- Administer the Reading and Vocabulary Warm-ups (*Unit 4 Resources*, pp. 127–130 or 145–148) as necessary.
- Introduce the Reading Skill: Paraphrase FT
- Introduce the Literary Analysis concept: Figurative Language FT
- Distribute copies of the appropriate graphic organizer for the Reading Skill (*Graphic Organizer Transparencies*, pp. 132–134). CRI
- Distribute copies of the appropriate graphic organizer for Literary Analysis (*Graphic Organizer Transparencies*, pp. 135–138). CRI
- Teach the selection vocabulary. FT CRI
- Introduce the Word Study skill.

DAYS 2–3 Preteach/Teach

- Build background with the Background feature. CRI
- Develop thematic vocabulary and thematic thinking with Writing About the Big Question.
- Prepare students to read with the Activating Prior Knowledge activities (TE). CRI
- Informally monitor comprehension while students read. FT
- Use the Reading Check questions to confirm comprehension.
- Develop students' ability to paraphrase a poem using the Reading Skill questions. CRI
- Develop students' understanding of figurative language using the Literary Analysis questions. CRI
- Reinforce vocabulary with the Vocabulary notes. CRI

DAY 4 Assess

- Assess students' comprehension and mastery of the skills by having them answer the Critical Thinking, Reading Skill, and Literary Analysis questions. FT
- Have students complete the Vocabulary Practice activities. FT
- Have students complete the Word Study activities.

DAY 5 Extend/Assess

- Have students complete the Grammar lesson. CRI
- Have students complete the Writing activity and write a critical essay. (You may assign as homework.) FT
- Extend learning by having students complete the Research and Technology activity, a literary history report. (You may assign as homework.) As an alternative, assign them "Longing to Be Like Mike" or "Time to Serve" in *Reality Central*. CRI
- Administer Selection Test A or B (*Unit 4 Resources*, pp. 139–144 or 160–165). FT

The poems in Poetry Collections 5 and 6 appear unedited and in their entirety.

Meeting Your Standards

Students will

1. **analyze and respond to literary elements.**
   - **Literary Analysis: Figurative Language**
2. **read, comprehend, and analyze poetry.**
   - **Reading Skill: Paraphrase**
   - **Reading Check questions**
   - **Apply the Skills questions**
   - **Assessment Practice**
3. **develop vocabulary.**
   - **Vocabulary**
   - **Word Study**
4. **apply grammar skills.**
   - **Prepositional Phrases**
5. **Develop writing proficiency.**
   - **Work in Progress: Analytical Response to Literature**
   - **critical essay**
6. **strengthen research and technology skills.**
   - **literary history report**

CRI For a full explanation of Culturally Responsive Instruction opportunities in this lesson, see p. T86–T87.

FT For an accelerated lesson, use the Fast Track strategies and activities.

Managing Differentiated Instruction

This leveled selection pairing groups a more accessible with a more challenging selection. Choose either one to teach the lesson skills. For classroom management suggestions for using the pairing in a mixed-ability class, see pp. T68–T69.

Daily Block Scheduling

Each day in this Lesson Pacing Guide represents a 40–50 minute period. Teachers using block scheduling may combine days to revise pacing. In addition, teachers may differentiate and support core instruction by integrating components for extended and intensive support as students require. See the Guide to Selected Leveled Resources (facing page).

Guide to Selected Leveled Resources

EL English Learners

			Poetry Collection 5	Poetry Collection 6
CORE COURSE	*Unit 4 Resources*	Selection Test A	pp. 139–141	pp. 160–162
	Graphic Organizer Transparencies	Reading Skill Graphic Organizer A	p. 132	p. 133
		Literary Analysis Graphic Organizer A	p. 135	p. 137
EXTENDED SUPPORT (Level 2)	*Unit 4 Resources*	Reading and Vocabulary Warm-ups A or B	pp. 127–130	pp. 145–148
	Reader's Notebook: English Learner's Version		adapted instruction and adapted selection	adapted instruction and summary
	Hear It! Audio CD		selection and summaries	selection and summaries
	Hear It! Audio CD (adapted text)		adapted selection and summaries	—
INTENSIVE SUPPORT (Level 1)	*Reality Central*		"Longing to Be Like Mike"	"Time to Serve"
	Real-World Writing Journal		Lesson 5, pp. 120–123	Lesson 6, pp. 124–127

L2 Below-Level Students

			Poetry Collection 5	Poetry Collection 6
CORE COURSE	*Unit 4 Resources*	Selection Test A	pp. 139–141	pp. 160–162
	Graphic Organizer Transparencies	Reading Skill Graphic Organizer A	p. 132	p. 133
		Literary Analysis Graphic Organizer A	p. 135	p. 137
EXTENDED SUPPORT (Level 2)	*Unit 4 Resources*	Reading and Vocabulary Warm-ups A or B	pp. 127–130	pp. 145–148
	Reader's Notebook		adapted instruction and full selection	adapted instruction and summary
	Hear It! Audio CD		selection and summaries	selection and summaries
INTENSIVE SUPPORT (Level 1)	*Reality Central*		"Longing to Be Like Mike"	"Time to Serve"
	Real-World Writing Journal		Lesson 5, pp. 120–123	Lesson 6, pp. 124–127
	Reading Kit		Reteaching worksheets	Reteaching worksheets

L1 Special Needs Students

			Poetry Collection 5	Poetry Collection 6
CORE COURSE	*Unit 4 Resources*	Selection Test A	pp. 139–141	pp. 160–162
	Graphic Organizer Transparencies	Reading Skill Graphic Organizer A	p. 132	p. 133
		Literary Analysis Graphic Organizer A	p. 135	p. 137
EXTENDED SUPPORT (Level 2)	*Unit 4 Resources*	Reading and Vocabulary Warm-ups A or B	pp. 127–130	pp. 145–148
	Reader's Notebook: Adapted Version		adapted instruction and adapted selection	adapted instruction and summary
	Hear It! Audio CD (adapted text)		adapted selection and summaries	—
INTENSIVE SUPPORT (Level 1)	*Reality Central*		"Longing to Be Like Mike"	"Time to Serve"
	Real-World Writing Journal		Lesson 5, pp. 120–123	Lesson 6, pp. 124–127
	Reading Kit		Reteaching worksheets	Reteaching worksheets

The program includes resources for these students: L3 On-Level L4 Advanced All All
For a complete guide to selection support, see pp. T106–T108.

NOTE: All print materials are also available online at *www.PHLitOnline.com.*

VISUAL GUIDE to Featured Selection Resources

- **Poetry Collection 5**
- **Poetry Collection 6**

The Wind—
tapped like a tired Man
Emily Dickinson
Glory
Metaphor
Eve Merriam
Morning is
a new sheet of paper
for you to write on.
Conscientious Objector
Edna St. Vincent Millay
Pride
Dahlia Ravikovitch
translated by Chana Bloch and Ariel Bloch
Tell all the Truth, but tell it slant—
Emily Dickinson

RESOURCES FOR:

- EL English Learners
- L1 Special Needs Students
- L2 Below-Level Students
- L3 On-Level Students
- L4 Advanced Students
- All All Students

Vocabulary/Fluency/Prior Knowledge

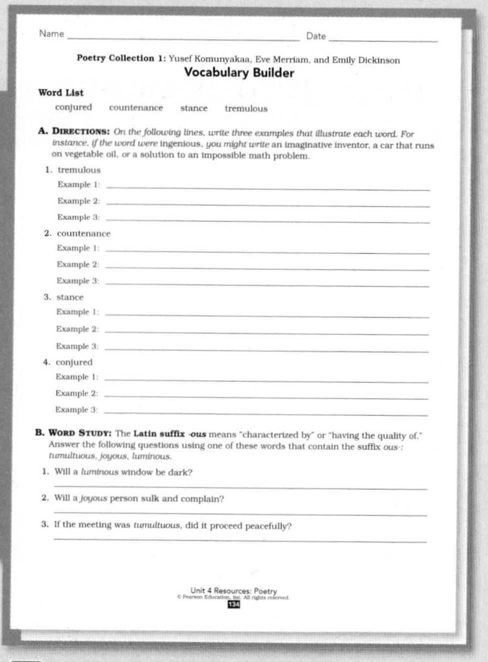

Unit 4 Resources

Name ______________________ Date ______________

Poetry Collection 1: Yusef Komunyakaa, Eve Merriam, and Emily Dickinson

Vocabulary Builder

Word List

conjured countenance stance tremulous

A. Directions: *On the following lines, write three examples that illustrate each word. For instance, if the word were* ingenious, *you might write* an imaginative inventor, a car that runs on vegetable oil, *or* a solution to an impossible math problem.

1. tremulous
   Example 1: ______
   Example 2: ______
   Example 3: ______
2. countenance
   Example 1: ______
   Example 2: ______
   Example 3: ______
3. stance
   Example 1: ______
   Example 2: ______
   Example 3: ______
4. conjured
   Example 1: ______
   Example 2: ______
   Example 3: ______

B. Word Study: The **Latin suffix -ous** means "characterized by" or "having the quality of." Answer the following questions using one of these words that contain the suffix *-ous*: *tumultuous, joyous, luminous.*

1. Will a *luminous* window be dark?
2. Will a *joyous* person sulk and complain?
3. If the meeting was *tumultuous*, did it proceed peacefully?

Unit 4 Resources: Poetry
© Pearson Education, Inc. All rights reserved.
134

All Vocabulary Builder, pp. 134, 152

Also available for these selections:

EL L1 L2 Vocabulary Warm-ups A and B, pp. 127–128, 145–146

EL L1 L2 Reading Warm-ups A and B, pp. 129–130, 147–148

All Writing About the Big Question, pp. 131, 149

Reader's Notebooks

Pre- and postreading pages, as well as the selections in Poetry Collection 5, appear in an interactive format in the *Reader's Notebooks.* Each *Notebook* is differentiated for a different group of learners.

The selections in the Adapted and English Learner's versions are abridged.

L2 L3 ***Reader's Notebook***

L1 ***Reader's Notebook: Adapted Version***

EL ***Reader's Notebook: English Learner's Version***

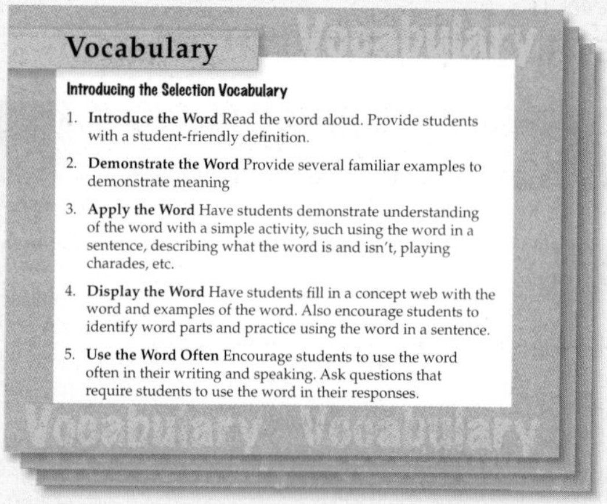

Vocabulary

Introducing the Selection Vocabulary

1. **Introduce the Word** Read the word aloud. Provide students with a student-friendly definition.
2. **Demonstrate the Word** Provide several familiar examples to demonstrate meaning
3. **Apply the Word** Have students demonstrate understanding of the word with a simple activity, such using the word in a sentence, describing what the word is and isn't, playing charades, etc.
4. **Display the Word** Have students fill in a concept web with the word and examples of the word. Also encourage students to identify word parts and practice using the word in a sentence.
5. **Use the Word Often** Encourage students to use the word often in their writing and speaking. Ask questions that require students to use the word in their responses.

Classroom Strategies and Teaching Routines

- core classroom routines outlined step-by-step
- convenient format for easy reference while teaching

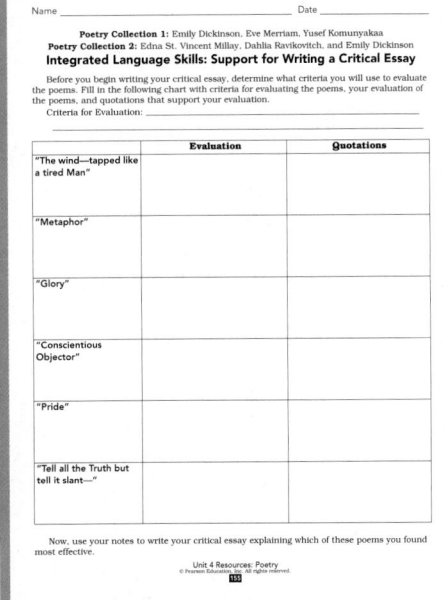

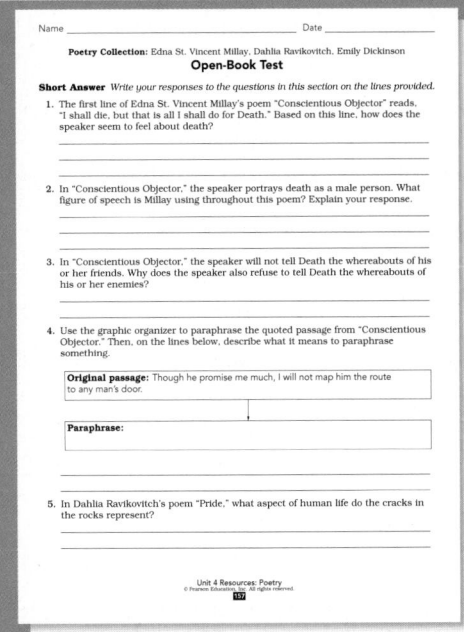

Selection Support

Transparencies

"**Conscientious Objector**" by Edna St. Vincent Millay;
"**Pride**" by Dahlia Ravikovich;
"**Tell all the Truth, but tell it slant**" by Emily Dickinson

After You Read A: Literary Analysis—Figurative Language

Poem	**"Conscientious Objector"**	**"Pride"**	**"Tell all the Truth, but tell it slant"**
Device(s)	Personification/ Metaphor: "I hear him (Death) leading his horse"		
Explanation	Imagines Death as a person who comes to take people's lives		
First Evaluation	Helps show how the speaker tries to understand death		
Final Evaluation	Makes Death even more frightening to imagine it as a person with dark or evil intentions		

Graphic Organizer Transparencies

137

EL L1 L2 **Literary Analysis: Graphic Organizer A,** pp. 135, 137 (partially filled in)

Also available for these selections:

- L3 Literary Analysis: Graphic Organizer B, pp. 136, 138
- EL L1 L2 Reading: Graphic Organizer A, pp. 132, 133 (partially filled in)
- L3 Reading: Graphic Organizer B, p. 134

Skills Development/Extension

Unit 4 Resources

Name ______________________ Date ____________

Poetry Collection 1: Emily Dickinson, Eve Merriam, Yusef Komunyakaa
Poetry Collection 2: Edna St. Vincent Millay, Dahlia Ravikovitch, and Emily Dickinson

Integrated Language Skills: Support for Writing a Critical Essay

Before you begin writing your critical essay, determine what criteria you will use to evaluate the poems. Fill in the following chart with criteria for evaluating the poems, your evaluation of the poems, and quotations that support your evaluation.

Criteria for Evaluation: ______________________

	Evaluation	**Quotations**
"The wind—tapped like a tired Man"		
"Metaphor"		
"Glory"		
"Conscientious Objector"		
"Pride"		
"Tell all the Truth but tell it slant—"		

Now, use your notes to write your critical essay explaining which of these poems you found most effective.

Unit 4 Resources: Poetry

155

L3 L4 **Support for Writing,** p. 155

Also available for these selections:

- All Literary Analysis: Figurative Language, pp. 132, 150
- L4 Enrichment, pp. 135, 153
- L3 L4 Grammar, p. 154
- All Reading: Paraphrase, pp. 133, 151
- L3 L4 Support for Extend Your Learning, p. 156

Assessment

Name ______________________ Date ____________

Poetry Collection: Edna St. Vincent Millay, Dahlia Ravikovitch, Emily Dickinson

Open-Book Test

Short Answer *Write your responses to the questions in this section on the lines provided.*

1. The first line of Edna St. Vincent Millay's poem "Conscientious Objector" reads, "I shall die, but that is all I shall do for Death." Based on this line, how does the speaker seem to feel about death?
2. In "Conscientious Objector," the speaker portrays death as a male person. What figure of speech is Millay using throughout this poem? Explain your response.
3. In "Conscientious Objector," the speaker will not tell Death the whereabouts of his or her friends. Why does the speaker also refuse to tell Death the whereabouts of his or her enemies?
4. Use the graphic organizer to paraphrase the quoted passage from "Conscientious Objector." Then, on the lines below, describe what it means to paraphrase something.

Original passage: Though he promise me much, I will not map him the route to any man's door.

Paraphrase:

5. In Dahlia Ravikovitch's poem "Pride," what aspect of human life do the cracks in the rocks represent?

Unit 4 Resources: Poetry

157

L3 L4 **Open-Book Test,** pp. 136–138, 157–159

Also available for these selections:

- EL L1 L2 Selection Test A, pp. 139–141, 160–162
- L3 L4 Selection Test B, pp. 142–144, 163–165

PHLit Online!

www.PHLitOnline.com

- complete narrated selection text
- a thematically related video with writing prompt
- an interactive graphic organizer
- highlighting feature
- access to all student print resources, adapted to individual student needs
- Spanish and English summaries

Get Connected Video
Instructions
Watch the video. Then, use your journal to respond to the prompt at the end of the clip.

Get Connected! (thematic video with writing prompt)

Also available:

Background video

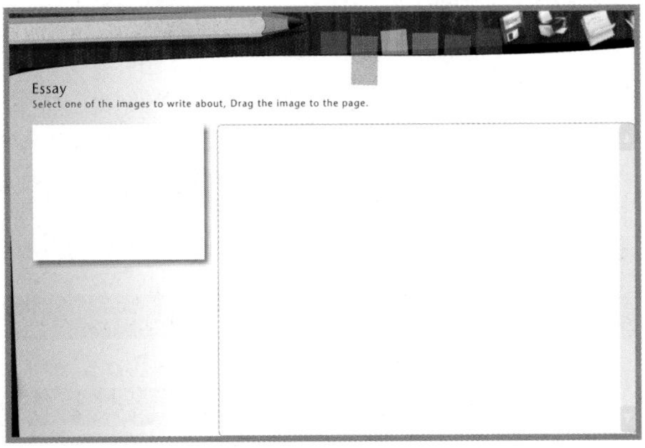
Essay
Select one of the images to write about. Drag the image to the page.

Writer's Journal (with graphics feature)

Also available:

Vocabulary Central (tools, activities, and songs for studying vocabulary)

DIFFERENTIATE/PRETEACH

❶ Collection Choices

You may use either Poetry Collection 5 or Poetry Collection 6 to meet the lesson standards. Skills instruction for both selections appears on p. 715. Choose one selection to teach (or choose to teach both). The Accessibility at a Glance chart at the bottom of this page will help you determine which of the two selections is more appropriate for your students.

❷ Selection Skills

1. With the class, preview the selection skills. (The lesson meets the lesson objectives given on p. 714a.)
2. Explain that students will learn to use the skill of paraphrasing as they read to better understand and enjoy the selection you choose. By examining figurative language as they read, they will gain deeper insight into the selection.
3. To introduce the Writing and Research and Technology activities (p. 731), tell students that when they have finished reading the selection, they will write a critical essay and a literary history report related to the selection.
4. Tell students that they will also study a grammar concept: prepositional phrases. By mastering this concept, they will improve their reading fluency and the quality of their own writing.

Before You Read

Poetry Collection 5 • Poetry Collection 6

❶ Collection Choices

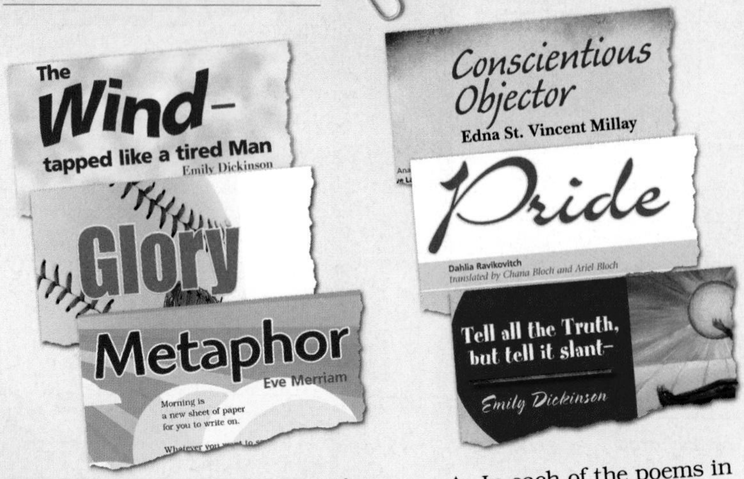

▲ The poets in **Poetry Collection 5** remind us that even ordinary events contain a little bit of the extraordinary.

▲ In each of the poems in **Poetry Collection 6,** the poet confronts life's limitations.

❷ Collection Skills Guide

Practice these skills with either **Poetry Collection 5** (p. 718) or **Poetry Collection 6** (p. 726).

- Understand figurative language including simile, metaphor, and personification
- Paraphrase
- Picture the imagery
- Identify prepositional phrases
- Write a critical essay
- Present a literary history report

Differentiated Instruction for Universal Access

Accessibility at a Glance: Selection Choices

	Collection 5	Collection 6
Context	Revelations in life	Profound human issues
Language/ Vocabulary	• Complex sentence structure • Grade-level vocabulary	• Complex sentence structure • Grade-level vocabulary
Concept Level	Accessible (concrete images: baseball, paper, wind)	Challenging (abstract concepts: death, pride, and truth)
Literary Merit	Noted poets	Noted poets
Lexile/Length	Lexile: NP Word Count: 101, 163, 46	Lexile: NP Word Count: 197, 111, 41
Overall Rating	**More accessible**	**More challenging**

Because a number of factors determine the relative accessibility of paired selections, in some cases the Lexile rating of the more challenging selection will be lower than that of the more accessible selection.

❸ Literary Analysis: Figurative Language

Figurative language is language that is not meant to be taken literally. Poets often use the following **figures of speech,** or specific types of figurative language, to convey their ideas in fresh and innovative ways.

Each of these figures of speech is a type of **analogy,** a comparison of two things that are alike in certain respects but not in others.

- A **simile** is a comparison of unlike things using the word *like* or *as.* *Example:* He runs *like* a cheetah. A simile is an expressed analogy.
- In a **metaphor,** one thing is spoken about as if it were something else. *Example:* During the holidays, the stores *are* zoos. A metaphor is an implied analogy.
- In **personification,** an object, animal, or idea is spoken of as if it were human. *Example:* Our cow was queen of the fair.

Because figurative language is often used to express meaning in concrete pictures, it is an important source of **imagery,** or word-pictures, in poetry.

PHLit Online!
www.PHLitOnline.com

Hear It!
- Selection summary audio
- Selection audio

See It!
- Get Connected video
- Background video
- More about the author
- Vocabulary flashcards

Do It!
- Interactive journals
- Interactive graphic organizers
- Self-test
- Internet activity
- Grammar tutorial
- Interactive vocabulary games

❹ Reading Skill: Paraphrase

To understand a poem's main message, **paraphrase** it, or restate the meaning of lines in your own words.

- Begin by **picturing the imagery,** forming clear pictures of the descriptive details in the poem.
- Then, consider how ideas in the lines you paraphrase are related to these pictures.

❺ Using the Strategy: Paraphrase Chart

Use a chart like the one shown to paraphrase passages as you read.

Descriptive Details	→	What I Picture	→	My Paraphrase
"A snapshot in the radiant flood, / Raccoon glares, as any outlaw should. / His craft lies knotted in his paws; / His canny forest ways undo suburban laws."	→	a raccoon caught in the light when someone opens the back door	→	The raccoon freezes in the light of an open door. He is clever with his paws and can outsmart the person whose yard he is visiting.

Differentiated Instruction for Universal Access

Preparing Students for the More Challenging Selection

If you wish to prepare lower level readers to read Poetry Collection 6, the more challenging selection, follow these steps:

- Discuss the cultural context of Millay's poem "Conscientious Objector." Emphasize that Millay lived during both World Wars, experiences that could have influenced Millay to write this poem. Discuss the concept of war, prompting students to explain why one person might support a war, whereas another might oppose it.
- Before students read "Tell all the Truth but tell it slant—" elicit from students their definitions of *truth.* Explain that some truths are very difficult to bear—the death of a loved one, for example. Discuss with students why someone might use much care to tell another person the truth.

PRETEACH

❸ Literary Analysis

1. Introduce the skill, using the instruction on the student page.
2. Tell students that they will identify figurative language as they read.

Think Aloud: Model the Skill

Model the skill of identifying figurative language. Say to students:

Sometimes in my reading I come across a phrase or a sentence that expresses an idea that is logically impossible. For example, in the sentence, "Don's eyes shone like stars," I know it is impossible for Don's eyes to shine as brightly as stars. If I picture the image, however, I understand that the writer wants to emphasize how brightly Don's eyes shine. Because the word *like* connects *eyes* and *stars,* two different things, I know this sentence is a simile.

❹ Reading Skill

1. Introduce the skill, using the instruction on the student page.
2. Tell students that they will practice paraphrasing as they read.

Think Aloud: Model the Skill

Model the skill of paraphrasing. Say to students:

When someone is explaining a complicated process or idea to me, I find it helpful to periodically paraphrase what he or she is saying to make sure I understand it.

For example, let's say a doctor is explaining to me the intricate process of how bones heal. Throughout her explanation, the doctor uses scientific terms. To make sure I understand the concept of how bones heal, I rephrase the doctor's words, using simpler language.

❺ Using the Strategy

Give students a copy of either **Reading Skill Graphic Organizer A** or **B** (***Graphic Organizer Transparencies,*** pp. 132–134) to record their ideas about paraphrasing as they read. Use the examples in **Reading Skill Graphic Organizer A,** which is partially filled in, to model the process of completing the organizer.

PREACH

❶ Writing About the Big Question

1. Review the assignment with the class.
2. Prompt students to think about why it is important for people to make emotional connections to people, places, or things. Then, discuss why people find meaning in the most mundane things.
3. Have students complete the sentence starters. Review responses as a class. **Possible responses:** People can make a deeper connection to everyday experiences by appreciating every moment. Meaning can be found in ordinary things or events when we think about their significance in our lives.)
4. Remind students that their answers will help them think about the Big Question.

While You Read

Tell students that as they read, they should look for interesting or unusual descriptions of ordinary people, actions, or things.

❷ Vocabulary

1. Have students preview the selection vocabulary.
2. For each word, have students say the word aloud.
3. Then, use the word in a sentence that defines the word.
4. Finally, repeat your definitional sentence or a similar sentence with the word missing, and have the class "fill in the blank" chorally. For example:

   Someone's countenance is the appearance of his or her face. I could tell Mark was embarrassed just from looking at his blushing [students say "countenance"].

❸ Word Study

1. Introduce the skill, using the instruction in the box.
2. Have students explain the definitions of the word *fallacious,* using "characterized by" or "having the quality of." (**Answer:** "having the quality of falseness")

Making Connections
Poetry Collection 5

The Wind—tapped like a tired Man • Glory • Metaphor

Does all *communication* serve a positive purpose?

The
Wind-
tapped like a tired Man
Emily Dickinson
Glory
Metaphor
Eve Merriam
Morning is
a new sheet of paper
for you to write on.

❶ Writing About the Big Question

In Poetry Collection 5, the poets communicate their reflections about details associated with ordinary events. Use these sentence starters to develop your ideas about the Big Question.

People can make a deeper **connection** to everyday experiences by ______________.

Meaning can be found in ordinary things or events when ______________.

While You Read Look for interesting, unusual, or positive descriptions of ordinary people, actions, or things.

❷ Vocabulary

Read each word and its definition. Decide whether you know the word well, know it a little bit, or do not know it at all. After you read, see how your knowledge of each word has increased.

- **countenance** (kount´ 'n əns) *n.* a person's face or expression (p. 718) *Danielle's countenance showed the calm she felt.*
- **tremulous** (trem´ yo͞o ləs) *adj.* trembling; quivering (p. 718) *I could tell the speaker was nervous by his tremulous voice.* *tremulously adv. tremulousness n.*
- **stance** (stans) *n.* the way one stands, especially the placement of the feet (p. 721) *The hockey player's stance was relaxed and upright as he swung. stand n. stand v.*
- **conjured** (kän´ jərd) *v.* performed tricks in which things seem to appear, disappear, or change as if by magic (p. 721) *As a child, I believed my mother conjured perfect weather for my party.* *conjurer n.*

❸ Word Study

The **Latin suffix *-ous*** means "characterized by" or "having the quality of."

In "The Wind—tapped like a tired Man," the wind makes a **tremulous** sound, like the sound glass makes when it shakes or quivers.

Vocabulary Development

Vocabulary Knowledge Rating

Create a **Vocabulary Knowledge Rating Chart** (***Professional Development Guidebook***, p. 33) for this selection. Include the selection vocabulary and the Big Question words that appear in the Writing About the Big Question sentence starters on this page. (The Big Question vocabulary is introduced on pp. 626–627.)

Give students a copy of the chart. Read the words aloud, and have students mark their rating in the Before Reading column. Urge them to be alert to these words as they read and discuss the selection.

Tally how many students think they know a word to gauge how much instruction to provide. As students read and discuss the selection, point out the words and their context.

PHLit Online! **Vocabulary Central,** featuring tools, activities, and songs for studying vocabulary, is available at **www.PHLitOnline.com.**

Meet the Authors

Emily Dickinson

(1830–1886)

Author of "The Wind—tapped like a tired Man" (p. 718)

Now regarded as one of America's greatest poets, Emily Dickinson was scarcely known during her own time. She never married and spent almost her entire life in the home of her family. As she grew older, she rarely left her house. Although she wrote 1,775 poems, only seven were published during her life—and those were published anonymously.

4

Yusef Komunyakaa

(b. 1947)

Author of "Glory" (p. 720)

Poet Yusef Komunyakaa has come a long way in his life. Born in the small rural town of Bogalusa, Louisiana, he is now a creative writing professor at Princeton University in New Jersey. Komunyakaa's collection *Neon Vernacular* earned him a Pulitzer Prize in 1994. He has said that "the writer has to get down to the guts of the thing. . . . "

Eve Merriam

(1916–1992)

Author of "Metaphor" (p. 722)

Eve Merriam developed a fascination with poetry at an early age. She has written poetry for both children and adults. Merriam has called poetry the most immediate and richest form of communication.

Daily Bellringer

For each class during which you will teach this selection, have students complete one of the five Revision activities for Week 22 in the ***Daily Bellringer Activities*** booklet.

4 Background

"Glory" In this poem, Komunyakaa names four of the greatest African American baseball players: Jackie Robinson, Satchel Paige, Willie Mays, and Josh Gibson. All are now immortalized in the Baseball Hall of Fame.

Jackie Robinson broke the color barrier in the Major Leagues, segregated for fifty-eight years, when the Brooklyn Dodgers took him on in 1947.

A year later, Leroy "Satchel" Paige joined the Cleveland Indians as a pitcher, helping them win the pennant. He played in the Major Leagues for five decades.

In 1951, the New York Giants signed Willie Mays. He had one of the best throwing arms the Major Leagues had ever seen.

Though Josh Gibson never played in the Major Leagues, he was a power hitter in the Negro National League and was nicknamed the "black Babe Ruth."

Multidraft Reading

To assist struggling readers and to deepen reading for all, apply multidraft reading protocols. For each reading, have students set the purpose indicated:

- **First reading**—literal comprehension: answering the Reading Check questions.
- **Second reading**—application of skills: answering the Paraphrase and Figurative Language prompts.
- **Third reading**—interpretation: answering the end-of-selection questions.

For more guidance, refer to the ***Classroom Strategies and Teaching Routines*** card on multidraft reading.

Differentiated Instruction

Additional Instruction

EL Extended Support—English Learners

Have students complete the **Reading and Vocabulary Warm-ups, *Unit 4 Resources,*** pp. 127–130, before they read. Assign the prereading pages and the adapted selection in the ***Reader's Notebook: English Learner's Version.*** Then, have students listen to portions of the selection on the ***Hear It!* Audio CD.**

L1 L2 Extended Support—Struggling Readers

Have students complete the **Reading and Vocabulary Warm-ups, *Unit 4 Resources,*** pp. 127–130, before they read. Assign the prereading pages and the adapted selection in the ***Reader's Notebook: Adapted Version.*** Then, have students listen to portions of the selection on the ***Hear It!* Audio CD** (adapted text).

Extended Support—Reluctant Readers

To build motivation and engagement before assigning the selection, have students read "Put Me In, Coach!" a thematically related selection in ***Reality Central.*** Then, use the questions at the conclusion of the related selection to guide discussion.

PHLit Online!

For more about the author, practice with the selection vocabulary, and more background, go to **www.PHLitOnline.com.**

TEACH

❶ Activating Prior Knowledge

1. Prepare an **Anticipation Guide** (***Professional Development Guidebook,*** pp. 36–38) with the following statements:
   - Baseball is life.
   - Each new day is a clean slate.
   - Common, everyday events deserve attention.
2. Give students a copy of the prepared **Anticipation Guide,** and have students mark their responses in the Me column. Have students discuss the statements in pairs or groups and mark the guides again in the Group column.
3. For further guidance, use the ***Classroom Strategies and Teaching Routines*** card: **Using an Anticipation Guide.**

Concept Connector →

Students will return to the **Anticipation Guide** after completing the poems.

Small-Group Activity

Students may better understand figurative language by discussing common expressions. Have small groups think of examples for simile, metaphor, and personification. Have groups write fresh replacements.

❷ About the Selections

All the selections in this collection reveal something about life. By personifying a gentle wind, Emily Dickinson conveys a sense of connection with nature in "The Wind—tapped like a tired Man." In "Glory," a baseball game is more than recreational—it means survival.

The poet of "Metaphor" conveys an optimistic view of life: Each new day is important because it brings an opportunity for a fresh start.

❸ Reading Skill

Paraphrase

Ask students to respond to the Reading Skill prompt.

Possible response: The images are of a man without bones and a flight of hummingbirds. He was boneless, and his speech had the strength of tiny birds bursting from a shrub.

The *Wind*—tapped like a tired Man

❶ ❷

Emily Dickinson

Reading Skill
Paraphrase Describe two images that the third stanza suggests, and then paraphrase the stanza to understand its content.

Vocabulary
countenance (kount′'n əns) *n.* a person's face or expression

tremulous (trem′ yo͞o ləs) *adj.* trembling; quivering

The Wind—tapped like a tired Man—
And like a Host—"Come in"
I boldly answered—entered then
My Residence within

A Rapid—footless Guest—
To offer whom a Chair
Were as impossible as hand
A Sofa to the Air—

❸
No Bone had He to bind Him—
His Speech was like the Push
Of numerous Humming Birds at once
From a superior Bush—

His **Countenance**—a Billow—
His Fingers, as He passed
Let go a music—as of tunes
Blown **tremulous** in Glass—

He visited—still flitting—
Then like a timid Man
Again, He tapped—'twas flurriedly—
And I became alone—

Vocabulary Development

Thematic Vocabulary: The Big Question

As students are discussing "The Wind—tapped like a tired Man," encourage them to use the thematic vocabulary presented in Introducing the Big Question, pp. 626–627. You might encourage them with sentence starters like these:

1. The speaker makes a *connection* from a tired man to the wind by . . .
2. The speaker describes the wind's *language* as . . .
3. The way the speaker *interacts* with the wind reveals that she feels . . .
4. The message the speaker *conveys* through her poem about her intangible guest is . . .

4

❹ Visual Connections

Whole-Class Activity

1. **Ask** students to describe what they see in the picture.
   Possible response: Students may say that they see a man slumped beneath a wind-blown tree in a field.
2. Then, **ask** students: Does the picture of the man under the tree match the images of wind in Dickinson's poem? Explain.
   Possible response: Yes, the man seems like the wind in the poem, because he appears tired.
3. Now, **ask** students to compare the mood of the poem to the mood conveyed by the picture.
   Possible response: The mood of Dickinson's poem is friendly. The speaker is delighted by her guest's arrival. The mood of the picture is forlorn. The feeling of loneliness is accentuated by the bare tree and the monochromatic pallor.

Small-Group Activity

1. Have students work in small groups. Tell students to describe details in the picture using figurative language.
2. **Ask** a person from each group to read the examples of figurative language.
3. Create a three-column chart on the board to categorize students' examples as simile, metaphor, or personification. Discuss.

Individual Activity

1. Have students write a paragraph describing their reactions to the picture's depiction of wind. Prompt students to describe wind in their own words.
2. Post the paragraphs in the room. Have students note the many ways to describe one ordinary thing.

Differentiated Instruction for Universal Access

Strategy for Special Needs Students
Pair students with more advanced readers. Have the pairs work through the poems together, pausing to paraphrase each stanza and discussing what the poet means. Encourage students to listen to each other's ideas, carefully considering the different points of view. Remind students that there are no "wrong" or "right" answers when interpreting poetry as long as the interpretations can be supported by evidence in the text.

Strategy for Advanced Readers
As students read poetry, they will find it meaningful to study the various styles of writing. Poets use detail, rhythm, figurative language, punctuation, and word choice to create a mood, tell a story, or make an observation about life. Have students work together in groups to compare the writing styles of the poets in this collection. Suggest that they develop comparison charts to show the similarities and differences they detect in the poets' styles.

PHLit Online!
This selection is available in interactive format in the **Enriched Online Student Edition, www.PHLitOnline.com**, which includes a thematically related video and writing prompt and an interactive graphic organizer.

❺ Background

Baseball Leagues Although African Americans had been playing baseball since right after the Civil War, segregation barred them from organized leagues.

The first all-African American team was organized in 1885. As a result of the Great Migration, African American teams began to concentrate in northern cities. In 1920, eight teams joined the first Negro National League. With the Eastern Colored League, formed in 1923, the two leagues played their first World Series in 1924. By the 1940s, these games attracted a large number of fans.

Vocabulary Development

Vocabulary Knowledge Rating

When students have competed reading and discussing the poems, have them take out their **Vocabulary Knowledge Rating Chart** for these selections. Read the words aloud once more, and have students rate their knowledge of the words again in the After Reading column. Clarify any words that are still problematic. Have students write their own definition and example or sentence in the appropriate column. Then have students complete the Vocabulary Practice at the end of the selection. Encourage students to use the words in further discussion and written work about these poems. Remind them that they will be accountable for these words on the **Selection Test,** ***Unit 4 Resources***, pp. 139–141 and 142–144.

Vocabulary

stance (stans) *n.* the way one stands, especially the placement of the feet

conjured (kän´ jərd) *v.* performed tricks in which things seem to appear, disappear, or change as if by magic

Most were married teenagers
Working knockout shifts daybreak
To sunset six days a week—
Already old men playing ball
In a field between a row of shotgun houses
& the Magazine Lumber Company.
They were all Jackie Robinson
& Willie Mays, a touch of
Josh Gibson & Satchell Paige[1]
In each stance & swing, a promise
Like a hesitation pitch always
At the edge of their lives,
Arms sharp as rifles.
The Sunday afternoon heat
Flared like thin flowered skirts
As children & wives cheered.
The men were like cats
Running backwards to snag
Pop-ups & high-flies off
Fences, stealing each other's glory.
The old deacons & raconteurs[2]
Who umpired made an *Out* or *Safe*
Into a song & dance routine.
Runners hit the dirt
& slid into homeplate,
Cleats catching light,
As they conjured escapes, outfoxing
Double plays. In the few seconds
It took a man to eye a woman
Upon the makeshift bleachers,
A stolen base or homerun
Would help another man
Survive the new week.

1. **Jackie Robinson / & Willie Mays . . . / Josh Gibson & Satchell Paige** African American baseball stars of the 1920s through the 1970s.
2. **deacons & raconteurs** (rak´ än tʉrz´) assistant officers of a church and skilled storytellers.

6 Literary Analysis

Figurative Language

1. Tell students that Satchel Paige, one of the best African American baseball players, developed the hesitation pitch, which kept batters off balance.
2. **Ask** students to identify one figure of speech in these lines and to comment on why the poet may have used this comparison. **Possible response:** The figure of speech is a simile. The author compares a hesitation pitch to the promise that lurks at the edge of the lives of men who wish that they will be discovered as the next baseball great.

Monitor Progress Ask students to identify the other figure of speech and comment on why the poet may have used this comparison. **Possible response:** The figure of speech is a simile. The author compares the pitcher's arms to the sharpness of rifles to convey the precision of aim and the power of the pitch.

Reteach If students can identify the figure of speech but have difficulty explaining its purpose, have students describe a pitcher's throw. Then, have students explain why their descriptions might not work in a poem. Explain that a figure of speech works more efficiently than a description, allowing the reader to imagine a vivid idea while using fewer words.

7 Connecting to the Big Question

1. Explain to students that because people may perceive the same thing differently, the way they communicate their experiences may differ greatly from the way others do.
2. Have students read the bracketed text. **Ask** students: How does the simile in lines 13–15 describe an ordinary event in a different way? **Possible response:** The simile describes the summer heat, but instead of stating it directly, the simile conveys the idea that the summer heat is gentle and comfortable. Flared skirts made of thin material move easily, allowing air to circulate.
3. **Ask** students: Why might a poet choose to communicate his ideas in an unusual way? **Possible response:** A poet might want the reader to think about a subject in an innovative way that readers will remember.

Concept Connector

Anticipation Guide

Have students return to their **Anticipation Guides** and respond to the statements in the After Reading column. They may do this individually or in their original pairs or groups. Then, lead a class discussion, focusing on what students have learned that confirms or invalidates each statement. Encourage students to cite specific details, quotations, or other evidence from the text to support their responses to each statement.

Writing About the Big Question

Have students compare their responses to the sentence starters they completed before reading the essay with their ideas afterwards. Ask them to explain whether their thoughts have changed.

Reading Skill Graphic Organizer

Ask students to review the graphic organizer they completed while reading. Show them the **Reading Skill Graphic Organizer A** (*Graphic Organizer Transparencies,* p. 132) as an example. Then have students share their graphic organizers.

8 Literary Analysis

Figurative Language

Ask the Literary Analysis question.
Answer: The poet uses the image of a new sheet of paper. The metaphor implies that a new sheet of paper and a morning both offer new beginnings.

ASSESS

Answers

Critical Thinking

1. Students are likely to respond to "Glory," as many of them have probably played baseball.
2. (a) The wind is the guest. (b) The guest has no feet or bones and its face is a billow. (c) The speaker sees the wind as kind because he or she speaks of him as if he were a welcome guest who plays music.
3. (a) The men work daybreak to sunset six days a week. (b) They are worn down by long hours. (c) The sense of satisfaction would help the men survive their humdrum lives.
4. (a) The speaker compares morning to a new sheet of paper. (b) She compares a person's actions to bright or dark words put on the paper. (c) The poem suggests that it is never too late to start over.

Does all communication serve a positive purpose?

Possible response: (a) Dickinson describes the ordinary event of wind blowing through a room. She uses figurative language to present the wind not as a rush of air but as a timid old man. Komunyakaa describes people gathering to play baseball, but to them, the game is more than recreation—it is a source of hope and glory, something that will get a man through the week. Merriam compares an ordinary event, the course of a day, to writing on a new sheet of paper. Every day is a new day, like a fresh sheet of paper on which to write. (b) **Possible response:** These three poems are positive in tone. They each reflect hope and encourage the reader not to give up.

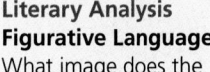

Metaphor

Eve Merriam

Morning is
a new sheet of paper
for you to write on.

Whatever you want to say,
all day,
until night
[8] folds it up
and files it away.

The bright words and the dark words
are gone
until dawn
and a new day
to write on.

Literary Analysis
Figurative Language
What image does the poet use to convey the idea that each morning is a new start?

Critical Thinking

1. **Respond:** Which poem spoke to you most directly? Why?
2. **(a)** Who is the guest in "The Wind—tapped like a tired Man"? **(b) Analyze:** Identify three ways in which the guest is unlike any other. **(c) Hypothesize:** Do you think the speaker sees the wind as menacing or kind? Use details from the poem to explain.
3. **(a)** What hours do the men in "Glory" work? **(b) Analyze Cause and Effect:** What does the phrase "already old men" suggest about the effect of this work schedule? **(c) Draw Conclusions:** In what way might a "stolen base or home run" help a man "survive the new week"?
4. **(a)** In "Metaphor," to what does the speaker compare the morning? **(b) Analyze:** To what does she compare a person's actions during the day? **(c) Apply:** What outlook or attitude toward a new day might this poem inspire in readers? Explain.

Does all communication serve a positive purpose?
(a) Identify the ordinary events described in these poems. Then, explain how the poets present these events in a new light. **(b)** Do you see these as positive poems? Explain?

Assessment Resources

Unit 4 Resources

L1 L2 EL **Selection Test A,** pp. 139–141
L3 L4 **Selection Test B,** pp. 142–144
L3 L4 **Open Book Test,** pp. 136–138

PHLit Online!
All assessment resources are available at **www.PHLitOnline.com.**

After You Read
Poetry Collection 5

The Wind—tapped like a tired Man • Glory • Metaphor

Literary Analysis: Figurative Language

The
Wind–
tapped like a tired Man
Emily Dickinson
Glory
Metaphor
Eve Merriam
Morning is
a new sheet of paper
for you to write on.

1. Among the three poems in Poetry Collection 1, find two examples of a **simile.**
2. Find an example of a **metaphor** in one of the three poems.
3. Identify an example of **personification** in one of the three poems.
4. **(a)** Using a chart like the one shown, explain and evaluate each of the devices you have identified. **(b)** Discuss your evaluations with a partner. **(c)** In the last column of the chart, explain whether or not your discussion changed your appreciation of the poems.

Poem	Device	Explanation	First Evaluation	Final Evaluation

Reading Skill: Paraphrase

5. **(a)** Describe the image you picture when reading the third stanza of "The Wind—tapped like a tired Man." **(b) Paraphrase** this stanza. **(c)** How does paraphrasing this stanza help you understand its content?
6. **(a)** Choose either "Glory" or "Metaphor" and paraphrase it. **(b)** Compare your paraphrase to the original. What qualities does the poem have that your paraphrase does not?

Vocabulary

Practice Use the following word pairs correctly in sentences.

1. countenance; mirror
2. tremulous; speech
3. stance; feet
4. conjured; thought

Word Study Use the context of the sentences and what you know about the **Latin suffix *-ous*** to explain your answer to each question.

1. Will a *joyous* person want to skip, jump, and laugh?
2. Could a *disastrous* situation be fixed quickly with little effort?

Word Study

The **Latin suffix *-ous*** means "characterized by" or "having the quality of."

Challenge Explain how the suffix *-ous* contributes to the meanings of these words. Consult a dictionary if necessary.

bilious
dexterous
garrulous

ASSESS/EXTEND

Answers

Literary Analysis

1. **Possible response:** Arms sharp as rifles; The men were like cats.
2. **Possible response:** His countenance—a Billow; Morning is/a new sheet of paper.
3. **Possible response:** His fingers, as He passed/Let go a music—as of tunes/Blown tremulous in Glass; until night/folds it up/and files it away.
4. (a) Students should express their opinions about the quality or value of the figurative language they chose. (b) and (c) Each opinion should be supported with specific facts, examples, and details from the poems. Finally, students should include ways in which their opinions were affected by the group discussion.

   For other sample answers, see ***Graphic Organizer Transparencies,*** **Literary Analysis Graphic Organizer A,** p. 135, and the **Additional Answers** section.

Reading Skill

5. **Possible response:** (a) I can see the quiet but rapid flutterings of a hummingbird's wings and imagine that the wind makes the same sound. (b) The wind has no structure, and his speech is like the air from the wing beats of many hummingbirds. (c) Paraphrasing helps to put an abstract idea into simpler words, making it easier to understand.
6. **Possible response:** (a) Each morning starts a new day for whatever a person wishes to do. Each nighttime means that the activities of the day, good or bad, are over and done. The next day brings the same promise of a new beginning. (b) The poem communicates the same thought but more indirectly and poetically, with vivid images and an extended metaphor.

Vocabulary
Practice
Sample answers:

1. The mirror was so cracked and dirty that none of the men could examine his <u>countenance</u>.
2. Although her voice was <u>tremulous</u> with emotion, the actress's speech was memorable.
3. Once the sergeant exited, the officer moved his feet to relax his rigid <u>stance</u>.
4. The writer's vivid description of blueberry pancakes <u>conjured</u> in the reader a thought of breakfast.

Word Study
Sample answers:

1. Yes, the suffix *-ous* means "having the quality of," so *joyous* means "having the quality of joy."
2. No, the suffix *-ous* means "characterized by," so *disastrous* means "characterized by disaster." Thus, the situation would need much effort to fix.

Word Study: Challenge
Sample answers:

Something *bilious* is <u>characterized by</u> bile. To be *dexterous* is to <u>have the quality</u> of being skillful. Someone who is *garrulous* is characterized by talk-

PRETEACH

Skills instruction for the ***Reading Skill*** *and* ***Literary Analysis*** *concept appears on p. 715.*

1 Writing About the Big Question

1. Review the assignment with the class.
2. Have students discuss any challenges they have experienced. Prompt students to share how they handled these challenges.
3. Have students complete the sentence starters. Review responses as a class. (**Possible response:** An example of a situation or challenge that a person may not completely understand or know how to respond to appropriately is becoming physically paralyzed. Our limitations as humans can lead to isolation if we become depressed by what we aren't able to do.
4. Remind students that their answers will help them think about the Big Question.

While You Read

Tell students that as they read, they should look for the ways the poets characterize concepts such as death, pride, and truth.

2 Vocabulary

1. Have students preview the selection vocabulary.
2. For each word, have students say the word aloud.
3. Then, use the word in a sentence that defines the word.
4. Finally, repeat your definitional sentence or a similar sentence with the word missing, and have the class "fill in the blank" chorally. For example:

   Someone infirm is frail and sickly. Even though Audrey was nearly eighty, her quick wit and high energy revealed that she was anything but [students say "infirm"].

3 Word Study

1. Introduce the skill, using the instruction in the box.
2. Tell students to think of a word that means "relating to honor." (**Answer:** *honorary*)

Making Connections
Poetry Collection 6

Conscientious Objector • Pride • Tell all the Truth but tell it slant—

Does all *communication* serve a positive purpose?

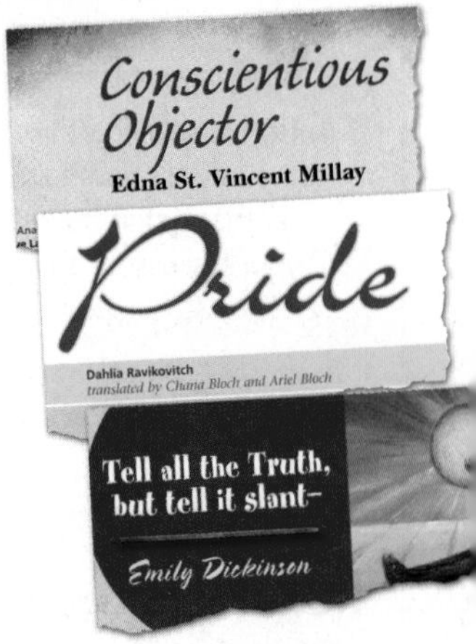

Conscientious Objector
Edna St. Vincent Millay
Pride
Dahlia Ravikovitch
translated by Chana Bloch and Ariel Bloch
Tell all the Truth, but tell it slant–
Emily Dickinson

1 Writing About the Big Question

In Poetry Collection 6, the poems' speakers present their plans for dealing with life's limitations and challenges. Use these sentence starters to develop your ideas about the Big Question.

An example of a situation or challenge that a person may not completely understand or know how to **respond** to appropriately is ______________.

Our limitations as humans can lead to **isolation** if ______________.

While You Read Look for the the ways the poets characterize complex concepts such as death, pride, and truth. Then, determine whether literature like this can help us get through difficult times.

2 Vocabulary

Read each word and its definition. Decide whether you know the word well, know it a little bit, or do not know it at all. After you read, see how your knowledge of each word has increased.

- **overcome** (ō′ vər kum′) *v.* to master or prevail over (p. 726) *I knew I could overcome my poor start and win the race.*
- **flourishes** (flʉr′ ish əs) *v.* grows vigorously; thrives (p. 727) *This plant flourishes in sunlight but has a hard time growing in shade. flourish n. flourishing adj.*
- **circuit** (sʉr′ kit) *n.* act of going around something (p. 728) *The moon makes a monthly circuit of Earth. circuit v. circuitous adj. circuitously adj.*
- **infirm** (in fʉrm′) *adj.* weak; feeble (p. 728) *Our infirm uncle had trouble walking up the stairs. infirmly adv. infirmity n. infirmary n.*

3 Word Study

The **Latin suffix *-ary*** means "relating to" or "like."

"Tell all the Truth but tell it slant," describes an **infirm** delight, or one that is "weak" or "frail." An **infirmary** is a place for people who are frail or sick.

Vocabulary Development

Vocabulary Knowledge Rating

Create a **Vocabulary Knowledge Rating Chart** (***Professional Development Guidebook***, p. 33) for this selection. Include the selection vocabulary and the Big Question word that appears in the Writing About the Big Question sentence starters on this page. (The Big Question vocabulary is introduced on pp. 626–627.

Give students a copy of the chart. Read the words aloud, and have students mark their rating in the Before Reading column. Urge them to be alert to these words as they read and discuss the selection.

Tally how many students think they know a word to gauge how much instruction to provide. As students read and discuss the selection, point out the words and their context.

PHLit Online! **Vocabulary Central**, featuring tools, activities, and songs for studying vocabulary, is available at **www.PHLitOnline.com**.

❹

Edna St. Vincent Millay

(1892–1950)

Author of "Conscientious Objector" (p. 726)

Edna St. Vincent Millay was not yet in college when she first won fame as a poet. After graduating from Vassar, in Poughkeepsie, New York, she moved to New York City, where she acted in plays and pursued her writing career. Beautiful and outspoken, she received both praise and scorn for her controversial opinions on issues such as women's rights.

Dahlia Ravikovitch

(1936–2005)

Author of "Pride" (p. 727)

The Israeli poet Dahlia Ravikovitch was born in a town near Tel Aviv and was raised on a kibbutz, a cooperative settlement. Her father's death in an accident when she was six was a powerful influence. Her intensely personal poems are charged with images from nature, history, and religion.

Emily Dickinson

(1830–1886)

Author of "Tell all the Truth but tell it slant—" (p. 728)

Although Emily Dickinson led a reclusive life—she rarely left her home and saw only seven of her poems published in her lifetime—today she shines as one of the brightest stars of American poetry. It was only in 1955 that a scholar, Thomas H. Johnson, was able to assemble her complete works in one book. Dickinson is widely considered a truly individual voice in poetry.

Differentiated Instruction — Additional Instruction

EL Extended Support—English Learners

Have students complete the **Reading and Vocabulary Warm-ups,** ***Unit 4 Resources,*** pp. 145–148, before they read. Assign the prereading pages for the selection in the ***Reader's Notebook: English Learner's Version.*** Then, have students listen to portions of the selection on the ***Hear It!*** **Audio CD.**

L1 L2 Extended Support—Struggling Readers

Have students complete the **Reading and Vocabulary Warm-ups,** ***Unit 4 Resources,*** pp. 145–148, before they read. Assign the prereading pages for the selection in the ***Reader's Notebook: Adapted Version.*** Then, have students listen to portions of the selection on the ***Hear It!*** **Audio CD** (adapted text).

Extended Support—Reluctant Readers

To build motivation and engagement before assigning the selection, have students read "Time To Serve," a thematically related selection in ***Reality Central.*** Then, use the questions at the conclusion of the related selection to guide discussion.

Daily Bellringer

For each class during which you will teach this selection, have students complete one of the five Revision activities for Week 22 in the ***Daily Bellringer Activities*** booklet.

❹ Background

"Conscientious Objector"

Conscientious objection—the right of individuals to refuse to enter military service for religious, moral, and ethical reasons—is an idea of historical significance. At the start of the Revolutionary War, George Washington issued a draft but exempted individuals with strong objections to the war.

As time passed, conscientious objection was not so acceptable. During the Civil War, the North offered its men the option to buy their way out of the draft. However, those who could not afford to pay were punished under military law.

The next draft came during World War I. Rules for conscientious objectors became harsher. Hundreds were sent to prison for their refusal to fight. Many Americans scorned conscientious objectors for their noncompliance during a time that called for a united purpose. Millay's poem is a response to this call.

Multidraft Reading

To assist struggling readers and to deepen reading for all, apply multidraft reading protocols. For each reading, have students set the purpose indicated:

- **First reading**—literal comprehension: answering the Reading Check questions.
- **Second reading**—application of skills: answering the Paraphrase and Figurative Language prompts.
- **Third reading**—interpretation: answering the end-of-selection questions.

For more guidance, refer to the ***Classroom Strategies and Teaching Routines*** card on multidraft reading.

PHLit Online!

For more about the author, practice with the selection vocabulary, and more background, go to **www.PHLitOnline.com.**

TEACH

❶ Activating Prior Knowledge

1. Prepare an **Anticipation Guide** (*Professonal Development Guidebook,* pp. 36–38) with the following statements:
   - People cannot fight death.
   - Everyone will break under pressure.
   - Always tell the truth.
2. Give students a copy of the prepared **Anticipation Guide,** and have students mark their responses in the Me column. Have students discuss the statements in pairs or groups and mark the guides again in the Group column.
3. For further guidance, use the *Classroom Strategies and Teaching Routines* card: **Using an Anticipation Guide.**

Concept Connector

Students will return to the **Anticipation Guide** after completing the poems.

Individual Activity

After students read each poem, have them decide what instrument would best express its rhythm, content, and tone. Have students explain their choices.

❷ About the Selections

In "Conscientious Objector," the proud, determined speaker refuses to cooperate in any way—passively or actively—with the forces of Death.

In "Pride," the poet uses a rock to represent a person, strong on the outside but capable of breaking under pressure.

Emily Dickinson suggests that the truth can be both illuminating and hurtful in "Tell all the Truth but tell it slant."

❸ Literary Analysis

Figurative Language

1. Have students read the bracketed passage to themselves.
2. Then, **ask** students to respond to the Literary Analysis prompt.
   Answer: Death has an arm that wields a whip, and he has hooves.

Conscientious Objector ❶ ❷

Edna St. Vincent Millay

I shall die, but that is all that I shall do for Death.

I hear him leading his horse out of the stall; I hear the clatter on the barn-floor.
He is in haste; he has business in Cuba, business in the Balkans, many calls to make this morning.
But I will not hold the bridle while he cinches the girth.[2]
And he may mount by himself: I will not give him a leg up.

Though he flick my shoulders with his whip, I will not tell him which way the fox ran.
With his hoof on my breast, I will not tell him where the black boy hides in the swamp.
I shall die, but that is all that I shall do for Death; I am not on his pay-roll.

I will not tell him the whereabouts of my friends nor of my enemies either.
Though he promise me much, I will not map him the route to any man's door.

Am I a spy in the land of the living, that I should deliver men to Death?
Brother, the password and the plans of our city are safe with me; never through me
Shall you be overcome.

Literary Analysis
Figurative Language Identify two details in ❸ this stanza that contribute to the personification of Death.

Vocabulary
overcome (ō′vər kum′) *v.* to master or prevail over

1. **conscientious** (kän′ shē en′ shəs) **objector** one who refuses to participate in warfare for religious or ethical reasons.
2. **cinches the girth** securely fastens the band that goes around a horse's belly to hold the saddle on.

Vocabulary Development

Vocabulary Knowledge Rating

When students have completed reading and discussing the three poems, have them take out their **Vocabulary Knowledge Rating Chart** for these selections. Read the words aloud once more, and have students rate their knowledge of the words again in the After Reading column. Clarify any words that are still problematic. Have students write their own definition and example or sentence in the appropriate column. Then have students complete the Vocabulary Practice at the end of the selection. Encourage students to use the words in further discussion and written work about these poems. Remind them that they will be accountable for these words on the **Selection Test,** ***Unit 4 Resources,*** pp. 160–162 or 163–165.

Pride

Dahlia Ravikovitch
translated by Chana Bloch and Ariel Bloch

I tell you, even rocks crack,
and not because of age.
❹ For years they lie on their backs
in the heat and the cold,
so many years,
it almost seems peaceful.
They don't move, so the cracks stay hidden.
A kind of pride.
Years pass over them, waiting.
Whoever is going to shatter them
❺ hasn't come yet.
And so the moss **flourishes**, the seaweed
whips around,
the sea pushes through and rolls back—
the rocks seem motionless.
Till a little seal comes to rub against them,
❻ comes and goes away.
And suddenly the rock has an open wound.
I told you, when rocks break, it happens by surprise.
And people, too.

Vocabulary
flourishes (flur′ ish əs) *v.* grows vigorously; thrives

▼ Critical Viewing
In what ways does this image show both the strength and the fragility identified in the poem? **[Analyze]**

❹ Literary Analysis

Figurative Language

1. **Ask** students to identify a line that contains personification.
   Answer: "They lie on their backs."
2. **Ask** students why the poet compares rocks to human beings.
   Possible response: With both, a crack that starts out small can turn into a complete break under pressure.

❺ Connecting to the Big Question

1. Explain that pride is an abstract idea that can be difficult to conceptualize. Emphasize that Ravikovitch uses figurative language to help make this abstract idea more concrete.
2. Have students define *pride.*
   Possible response: *Pride* is having a high opinion of one's self.
3. **Ask** students: How does Ravikovitch use figurative language to communicate ideas about pride?
   Possible response: Ravikovitch uses personification to convey that rocks can break under pressure, but when they do, they do not reveal the fissure, much like people who are too proud to show weakness.

❻ Reading Skill

Paraphrase

1. Have a volunteer paraphrase what the poet is saying.
   Possible response: When a seal rubs against a rock, it opens up a hidden crack.
2. **Ask:** What might the image represent?
   Possible response: The seal represents the last straw; it makes visible the crack that was there.

❼ Critical Viewing

Possible response: Massiveness of the rock shows strength; erosion by wave action shows vulnerability.

Concept Connector

Anticipation Guide

Have students return to their **Anticipation Guides** and respond to the statements in the After Reading column. They may do this individually or in their original pairs or groups. Then, lead a class discussion, focusing on what students have learned that confirms or invalidates each statement. Encourage students to cite specific details, quotations, or other evidence from the text to support their responses to each statement.

Writing About the Big Question

Have students compare their responses to the sentence starters they completed before reading the poems with their ideas afterwards. Ask them to explain whether their thoughts have changed.

Reading Skill Graphic Organizer

Ask students to review the graphic organizers they completed while reading. Show them **Reading Skill Graphic Organizers A** (*Graphic Organizer Transparencies,* p. 137) as an example. Then have students share the graphic organizers they did and the things they learned.

PHLit Online!

This selection is available in interactive format in the **Enriched Online Student Edition, www.PHLitOnline.com,** which includes a thematically related video with writing prompt and an interactive graphic organizer.

❽ Reading Skill

Paraphrase

Ask students to respond to the Reading Skill prompt.

Possible response: Tell the truth, but deliver it at an angle instead of directly, to ease the hurt.

ASSESS

Answers

Critical Thinking

1. Students may find themselves identifying with the poems by Ravikovitch or Dickinson.
2. (a) The speaker will not help Death locate or conquer its victims. (b) **Possible response:** The speaker also probably will not succumb easily to Death, because the speaker strongly objects to Death.
3. (a) Rocks hide their cracks from view. (b) **Possible response:** They may be embarrassed or ashamed of the cracks. (c) **Possible response:** People should allow themselves to experience stress or grief and work through these complex emotions.
4. (a) The speaker says to tell all the truth but not directly. (b) Truth should be told indirectly. (c) Some students may say it is a surprise because people tend to tell each other what they want to hear. Others will say it is an expectation, not a surprise.

Does all communication serve a positive purpose?

Possible responses:
(a) "Conscientious Objector" reflects the primary limitation posed by mortality—death. "Pride" reflects the limitation of pride: A rock or a person can hide a crack or a weakness only so long before it breaks. In "Tell all the Truth but tell it slant—" the speaker suggests that people cannot handle the full truth, so it must be told slowly and indirectly.
(b) People might choose to read it because poetry has the ability to present well-known ideas such as death, pride, and truth in novel ways.
(c) No, the poems enlighten us about problems but do not provide practical solutions.

Tell all the Truth but tell it slant—

Emily Dickinson

Reading Skill ❽
Paraphrase Restate the first line in your own words.

Vocabulary
circuit (sur′ kit) *n.* act of going around something

infirm (in furm′) *adj.* weak; feeble

Tell all the Truth but tell it slant—
Success in **Circuit** lies
Too bright for our **infirm** Delight
The Truth's superb surprise
As Lightning to the Children eased
With explanation kind
The Truth must dazzle gradually
Or every man be blind—

Critical Thinking

1. **Respond:** Which poem did you agree with the most? Why?
2. **(a)** What are two things the speaker in "Conscientious Objector" will not do? **(b) Apply:** Give your own example of a specific action the speaker would not take. Explain your choice.
3. **(a)** According to the speaker in "Pride," what may rocks hide from view? **(b) Interpret:** Why might "a kind of pride" lead them to hide this thing? **(c) Extend:** What advice would the speaker in "Pride" give to someone dealing with stress or grief?
4. **(a)** According to the speaker in "Tell all the Truth but tell it slant—," how much of the truth should be told? **(b) Interpret:** What does the speaker mean by the expression "tell it slant"? **(c) Make a Judgment:** Do you agree that truth often takes the form of a "surprise"? Explain.

Does all communication serve a positive purpose?
(a) In what ways does each poem reflect limitations that all people share? **(b)** Why might people choose to read poetry that reflects these common elements? **(c)** Do you think these poems present workable solutions to difficult problems? Explain.

Assessment Resources

Unit 4 Resources

L1 L2 EL **Selection Test A,** pp. 160–162
L3 L4 **Selection Test B,** pp. 163–165
L3 L4 **Open Book Test,** pp. 157–159

PHLit Online! All assessment resources are available at **www.PHLitOnline.com.**

After You Read
Poetry Collection 6

Conscientious Objector • Pride • Tell all the Truth but tell it slant—

Literary Analysis: Figurative Language

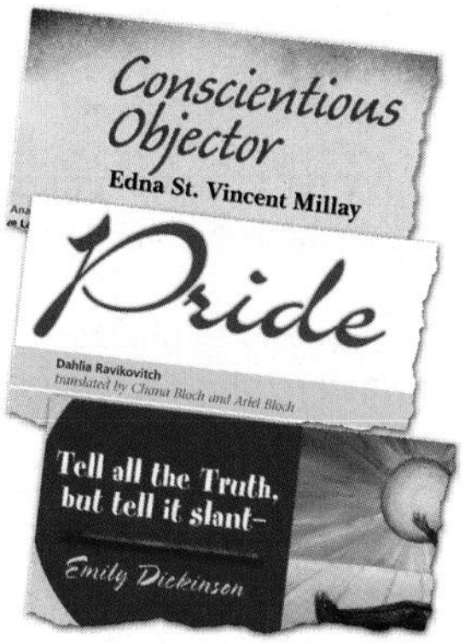

1. Among the three poems in Poetry Collection 6, find one example of a **simile.**
2. Find an example of a **metaphor** in one of the three poems.
3. Identify an example of **personification** in one of the three poems.
4. **(a)** Using a chart like the one shown, explain and evaluate each of the devices you have identified. **(b)** Discuss your evaluations with a partner. **(c)** In the last column of the chart, explain whether or not your discussion changed your appreciation of the poems.

Poem	Device	Explanation	First Evaluation	Final Evaluation

Reading Skill: Paraphrase

5. **(a) Paraphrase** the last two stanzas of "Conscientious Objector." **(b)** Compare your paraphrase to the original. What qualities does the poem have that your paraphrase does not? **(c)** Based on your paraphrase, what do you think is this poem's main message?
6. **(a)** Describe an image you pictured when reading "Tell all the Truth but tell it slant—" or "Pride." **(b)** Paraphrase one of these two poems.

Vocabulary

Practice Use the following word pairs correctly in sentences.

1. flourishes; talent
2. circuit; speed
3. overcome; adversity
4. infirm; recuperate

Word Study Use the context of the sentences and what you know about the **Latin suffix *-ary*** to explain your answer to each question.

1. Would a *mortuary* be a place to help people after an illness?
2. If your activities after school are *customary,* are you doing them for the first time?

Word Study

The **Latin suffix *-ary*** means "relating to" or "like."

Challenge Explain how the suffix *-ary* contributes to the meanings of these words. Consult a dictionary if necessary.

emissary
tributary
proprietary

ASSESS/EXTEND

Answers

Literary Analysis

1. **Simile:** "The Truth's superb surprise/As Lightning to the Children eased"
2. **Metaphor:** "I am not on his pay-roll."
3. **Personification:** "For years they lie on their backs/. . . They don't move, so the cracks stay hidden./ A kind of pride."
4. (a) Students' evaluations should be supported with specific facts, examples, and details from the poems. (b) and (c) Students should include ways in which their opinions were affected by the group discussion.

   For other sample answers, see ***Graphic Organizer Transparencies,*** **Literary Analysis Graphic Organizer A,** p. 137, and the **Additional Answers** section.

Reading Skill

5. **Possible responses:** (a) I will not help Death find any of his victims, no matter what rewards he promises. I am no traitor or spy; no one should fear death at my hands. (b) The paraphrase lacks the beauty, precision, and imagery in the poem. (c) The only death I am responsible for is my own.
6. **Possible responses:** (a) Students may say that they pictured a maze while reading "Tell all the Truth but tell it slant—". (b) Soften the truth with kindness so that people can accept it gradually.

Vocabulary
Practice
Sample answers:

1. Talent flourishes with practice and dedication.
2. As you complete the second circuit of the track, try to improve your speed.
3. You may find it difficult to overcome adversity, but when you do, you are a stronger person.
4. Someone who is infirm may need several days of good bed rest to recuperate.

Word Study
Sample answers:

1. No, *mortuary* means "a place relating to death," so only deceased people would be there.
2. No, activities that are *customary* are "related to custom," so they have been done many times.

Word Study: Challenge
Sample answers: An *emissary* is a person related to a mission. A *tributary* is a stream that relates to a larger body of water. *Proprietary* is related to holding property.

Answers

Grammar

1. Introduce the skill, using the instruction on the student page.
2. Discuss the definitions and examples given.

Think Aloud: Model the Skill

Model the skill of identifying prepositional phrases. Write the sentence on the board: *After the game, we met at Tamara's house.* Say to students:

> To decide which type of prepositional phrase is used in a sentence, I use the following strategies.
>
> First, I locate the prepositional phrase(s). I know from the two prepositions *after* and *at* that there are two prepositional phrases in the sentence: *after the game* and *at Tamara's house.* To decide what kinds of phrases they are, I ask myself: *What does the phrase tell me about the subject* we *or the verb* met? *After the game* tells me *when* we met, so the phrase modifies the verb. *At Tamara's house* tells me *where* we met, so this is also an adverb phrase.

Writing and Grammar, Grade 10

Students will find further instruction and practice on prepositional phrases in Chapter 19, Section 1.

Practice A

1. into second base; adverb
2. in the sky; adverb
3. in the bleachers; adjective
4. from the page; adverb

Challenge

Sample answer: "out of the stall"; "on their backs"

Practice B

Sample answers:

1. on air
2. in the water
3. on the surface
4. with her family

Challenge

Sample answer: "at the seashore," adjective phrase; "on the rock," adverb phrase. The lady at the market buys fruits from the seller.

Integrated Language Skills

Poetry Collections 5 and 6

Grammar: Prepositional Phrases

A **prepositional phrase** is a phrase that can modify other words by functioning either as an adjective or as an adverb within sentences.

A prepositional phrase that serves as an adjective is called an **adjective phrase.** It modifies a noun or pronoun and tells *what kind* or *which one.*

Example: Adjective Phrase: The woman *in the blue dress* is a singer.

The phrase *in the blue dress* modifies *woman,* a noun, by telling *which one:* Which woman? the one *in the blue dress*

A prepositional phrase that serves as an adverb is called an **adverb phrase.** It modifies a verb and tells *where, when, in what way,* or *to what extent.*

Example: Adverb Phrase: Her music group sings *at the folk festival.*

The phrase *at the folk festival* modifies *sings,* a verb, by telling *where:* Where does her music group sing? *at the folk festival*

Poetry Collection 5

Poetry Collection 6

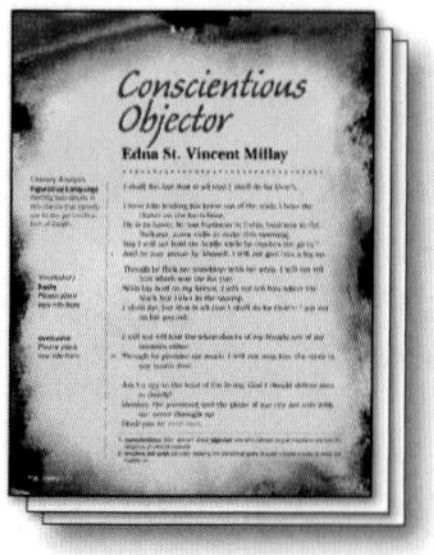

Practice A Identify the prepositional phrase in each sentence and tell whether it is an adjective phrase or an adverb phrase.

1. The runner slid into second base.
2. The sun rises in the sky.
3. Children in the bleachers cheered.
4. Dickinson's ideas leap from the page.

Challenge Find two examples of prepositional phrases, either adjective phrases or adverb phrases, in the poems in Poetry Collection 5.

Practice B Add a prepositional phrase in the blank. The phrase should act as an adjective or adverb phrase and give additional information.

1. Death walks ______________.
2. The rocks ______________ lie motionless.
3. The crack ______________ can open wide.
4. Emily Dickinson lived ______________.

Challenge Look at the model sentence and tell which prepositional phrase is an adjective and which is an adverb. Then, following the model, write three sentences of your own.

The seal at the seashore rubs its back on the rock.

Writing and Grammar Connection: Chapter 20, Section 1

Extend the Lesson

Sentence Modeling

Choose the sentence given from the selection students have read:

Runners hit the dirt/& slid into homeplate, ("Glory")

Brother, the password and the plans of our city are safe with/me; never through me/Shall you be overcome ("Conscientious Objector")

Elicit from them the type of prepositional phrases used. Then, ask what else they notice. ("Glory": important actions "hit" and "slid" are stressed by their rhythm in the lines; the ampersand adds an informality and ease to the action, the slide; "Conscientious Objector": the first line ends with the preposition "with," which places emphasis on "me" in the following line; the repetition of "me," strengthens the speaker's promise that she will never betray her fellow objectors.)

Have students write two related independent clauses. Then, have students combine the clauses using a semicolon. Collect the sentences, and share them with the class.

Writing

Write a **critical essay** in which you explain which of the **language techniques** in the poems you found most effective. Choose a poem from either Poetry Collection 5 or Poetry Collection 6.

- Decide on the criteria you will use in your evaluation. For example, you might rate the poems based on the strength of the feelings each inspired in you. Alternatively, you might judge each on the basis of how clever the use of language is.
- Review the poems carefully, using your criteria as a guide.
- Note any words, lines, or sections of the poem that still confuse you. To clarify the text, try finding the word in a dictionary, paraphrasing the lines, or describing the image. If you still do not understand part of the text, work with a partner to discuss possible interpretations.
- As you draft, present your evaluation concisely. Then, support each point with relevant quotations from the poems.

Writing Workshop: *Work in Progress*

Prewriting for an Analytical Response For an analytical response you might write, choose a story or poem that you like. Write five questions about the work's quality. Then, write five questions about how the work achieves its purpose. Put your Questions List in your writing portfolio.

Use this prewriting activity to prepare for the Writing Workshop on page 768.

Research and Technology

Write and present a brief **literary history report** explaining how Dickinson's poems were eventually published *or* describing Edna St. Vincent Millay's career. Follow these guidelines:

- Conduct research by using a **variety of sources,** including encyclopedias, biographical encyclopedias, and the Internet.
- Check the claims in one source against the claims in the others, considering the **reliability** of each source.
- Choose **information** to present that is **significant,** such as specific facts, dates, and ideas. Eliminate details that do not support your purpose.
- **Integrate the information** from your sources into an informational report.

Present your report to the class and invite discussion about the information you have gathered.

PHLit Online!
www.PHLitOnline.com
- Interactive graphic organizers
- Grammar tutorial
- Interactive journals

EXTEND/ASSESS

Writing

1. Review the assignment, using the instruction on the student page.
2. To guide students in writing a critical essay, give them **Support for Writing,** p. 155 in ***Unit 4 Resources.***
3. To evaluate students' critical essays, use the Response to Literature rubrics on pp. 224–225 in ***Professional Development Guidebook.*** In addition, you may want to evaluate how well students use images and the voice of the speaker to communicate ideas.

Six Traits Focus

✔	Ideas	Word Choice
✔	Organization	Sentence Fluency
	Voice	Conventions

Writing and Grammar, Grade 10

Students will find guidance on critical essays in Chapter 13, Response to Literature.

Writing Workshop
Work in Progress

Have students save their completed Questions List in their portfolios. They will use the Prewriting later as they continue this Work-in-Progress assignment (see p. 749). These assignments prepare them to complete the Writing Workshop assignment (see pp. 768–775).

Research and Technology

1. Review the assignment, using the instruction on the student page.
2. To support students' work on the assignment, have students complete the **Support for Extend Your Learning** page (***Unit 4 Resources,*** p. 156).

Teaching Resources

All *Unit 4 Resources*

L3 L4 **Integrated Language Skills: Grammar,** p. 154

L3 L4 **Support for Writing,** p. 155

L3 L4 **Support for Extend Your Learning,** p. 156

L4 **Enrichment,** pp. 135 and 153

All **Enriched Online Student Edition**
Available under After You Read for this selection:

All **Interactive Grammar Tutorial**

L3 L4 **Internet Research Activity**

Professional Development Guidebook
Rubrics for Response to Literature, pp. 224–225

PHLit Online! All print and digital resources are available at **www.PHLitOnline.com.** Online resources accessible by students are noted on the student page.

TIME AND RESOURCE MANAGER

Poetry Collection 7 • Poetry Collection 8

Lesson Pacing Guide

DAY 1 Preteach

- Administer the Reading and Vocabulary Warm-ups (*Unit 4 Resources*, pp. 166–169 or 184–187) as necessary.
- Introduce the Reading Skill: Paraphrase FT
- Introduce the Literary Analysis concept: Sound Devices FT
- Distribute copies of the appropriate graphic organizer for the Reading Skill (*Graphic Organizer Transparencies*, pp. 139–141). CRI
- Distribute copies of the appropriate graphic organizer for Literary Analysis (*Graphic Organizer Transparencies*, pp. 142–145). CRI
- Teach the selection vocabulary. FT CRI
- Introduce the Word Study skill.

DAYS 2–3 Preteach/Teach

- Build background with the Background feature. CRI
- Develop thematic vocabulary and thematic thinking with Writing About the Big Question.
- Prepare students to read with the Activating Prior Knowledge activities (TE). CRI
- Informally monitor comprehension while students read. FT
- Use the Reading Check questions to confirm comprehension.
- Develop students' ability to paraphrase using the Reading Skill questions. CRI
- Develop students' understanding of sound devices using the Literary Analysis questions. CRI
- Reinforce vocabulary with the Vocabulary notes. CRI

DAY 4 Assess

- Assess students' comprehension and mastery of the skills by having them answer the Critical Thinking, Reading Skill, and Literary Analysis questions. FT
- Have students complete the Vocabulary Practice activities. FT
- Have students complete the Word Study activities.

DAY 5 Extend/Assess

- Have students complete the Grammar lesson. CRI
- Have students complete the Writing activity and write a poem. (You may assign as homework.) FT
- Extend learning by having students complete the Research and Technology activity, a visual arts presentation. (You may assign as homework.) As an alternative, assign them "Hip-Hop into Hall of Fame" or "Texting on Trial" in *Reality Central*. CRI
- Administer Selection Test A or B (*Unit 4 Resources*, pp. 178–183 or 199–204). FT

The poems in Poetry Collections 7 and 8 appear unedited and in their entirety.

Meeting Your Standards

Students will
1. analyze and respond to literary elements.
   - Literary Analysis: Sound Devices
2. read, comprehend, and analyze poetry.
   - Reading Skill: Paraphrase
   - Reading Check questions
   - Apply the Skills questions
   - Assessment Practice
3. develop vocabulary.
   - Vocabulary
   - Word Study
4. apply grammar skills.
   - Infinitives
5. Develop writing proficiency.

•Work in Progress: Analytic Response to Literature

•poem

6. strengthen research and technology skills.
   - visual arts presentation

CRI For a full explanation of Culturally Responsive Instruction opportunities in this lesson, see p. T86–T87.

FT For an accelerated lesson, use the Fast Track strategies and activities.

Managing Differentiated Instruction
This leveled selection pairing groups a more accessible with a more challenging selection. Choose either one to teach the lesson skills. For classroom management suggestions for using the pairing in a mixed-ability class, see pp. T68–T69.

Daily Block Scheduling
Each day in this Lesson Pacing Guide represents a 40–50 minute period. Teachers using block scheduling may combine days to revise pacing. In addition, teachers may differentiate and support core instruction by integrating components for extended and intensive support as students require. See the Guide to Selected Leveled Resources (facing page).

Guide to Selected Leveled Resources

EL English Learners

			Poetry Collection 7	Poetry Collection 8
CORE COURSE	*Unit 4 Resources*	Selection Test A	pp. 178–180	pp. 199–201
	Graphic Organizer Transparencies	Reading Skill Graphic Organizer A	p. 139	p. 140
		Literary Analysis Graphic Organizer A	p. 142	p. 144
EXTENDED SUPPORT (Level 2)	*Unit 4 Resources*	Reading and Vocabulary Warm-ups A or B	pp. 166–169	pp. 184–187
	Reader's Notebook: English Learner's Version		adapted instruction and adapted selection	adapted instruction and summary
	Hear It! Audio CD		selection and summaries	selection and summaries
	Hear It! Audio CD (adapted text)		adapted selection and summaries	—
INTENSIVE SUPPORT (Level 1)	*Reality Central*		"Hip-Hop into Hall of Fame"	"Texting on Trial"
	Real-World Writing Journal		Lesson 7, pp. 128–131	Lesson 8, pp. 132–135

L2 Below-Level Students

			Poetry Collection 7	Poetry Collection 8
CORE COURSE	*Unit 4 Resources*	Selection Test A	pp. 178–180	pp. 199–201
	Graphic Organizer Transparencies	Reading Skill Graphic Organizer A	p. 139	p. 140
		Literary Analysis Graphic Organizer A	p. 142	p. 144
EXTENDED SUPPORT (Level 2)	*Unit 4 Resources*	Reading and Vocabulary Warm-ups A or B	pp. 166–169	pp. 184–187
	Reader's Notebook		adapted instruction and full selection	adapted instruction and summary
	Hear It! Audio CD		selection and summaries	selection and summaries
INTENSIVE SUPPORT (Level 1)	*Reality Central*		"Hip-Hop into Hall of Fame"	"Texting on Trial"
	Real-World Writing Journal		Lesson 7, pp. 128–131	Lesson 8, pp. 132–135
	Reading Kit		Reteaching worksheets	Reteaching worksheets

L1 Special Needs Students

			Poetry Collection 7	Poetry Collection 8
CORE COURSE	*Unit 4 Resources*	Selection Test A	pp. 178–180	pp. 199–201
	Graphic Organizer Transparencies	Reading Skill Graphic Organizer A	p. 139	p. 140
		Literary Analysis Graphic Organizer A	p. 142	p. 144
EXTENDED SUPPORT (Level 2)	*Unit 4 Resources*	Reading and Vocabulary Warm-ups A or B	pp. 166–169	pp. 184–187
	Reader's Notebook: Adapted Version		adapted instruction and adapted selection	adapted instruction and summary
	Hear It! Audio CD (adapted text)		adapted selection and summaries	—
INTENSIVE SUPPORT (Level 1)	*Reality Central*		"Hip-Hop into Hall of Fame"	"Texting on Trial"
	Real-World Writing Journal		Lesson 7, pp. 128–131	Lesson 8, pp. 132–135
	Reading Kit		Reteaching worksheets	Reteaching worksheets

The program includes resources for these students: L3 On-Level L4 Advanced All All
For a complete guide to selection support, see pp. T106–T108.

NOTE: All print materials are also available online at *www.PHLitOnline.com.*

VISUAL GUIDE to Featured Selection Resources

- Poetry Collection 7
- Poetry Collection 8

RESOURCES FOR:

EL English Learners
L1 Special Needs Students
L2 Below-Level Students
L3 On-Level Students
L4 Advanced Students
All All Students

Vocabulary/Fluency/Prior Knowledge

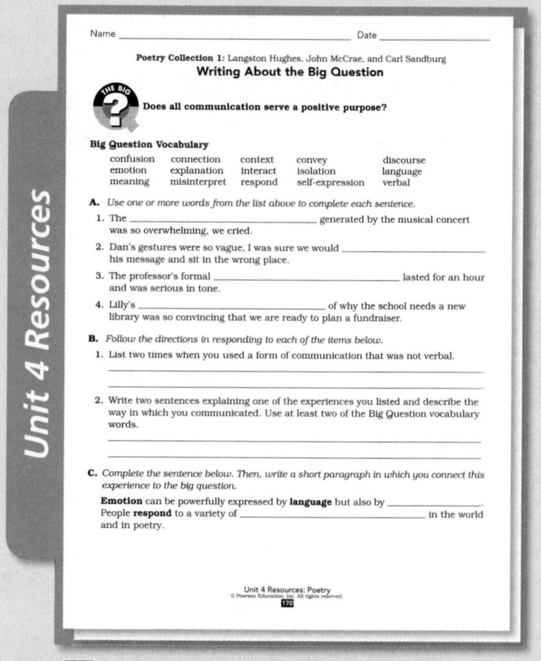

Name ______ Date ______

Poetry Collection 1: Langston Hughes, John McCrae, and Carl Sandburg

Writing About the Big Question

Does all communication serve a positive purpose?

Big Question Vocabulary

confusion	connection	context	convey	discourse
emotion	explanation	interact	isolation	language
meaning	misinterpret	respond	self-expression	verbal

A. *Use one or more words from the list above to complete each sentence.*

1. The ______ generated by the musical concert was so overwhelming, we cried.
2. Dan's gestures were so vague, I was sure we would ______ his message and sit in the wrong place.
3. The professor's formal ______ lasted for an hour and was serious in tone.
4. Lilly's ______ of why the school needs a new library was so convincing that we are ready to plan a fundraiser.

B. *Follow the directions in responding to each of the items below.*

1. List two times when you used a form of communication that was not verbal.
______.
______.
2. Write two sentences explaining one of the experiences you listed and describe the way in which you communicated. Use at least two of the Big Question vocabulary words.
______
______

C. *Complete the sentence below. Then, write a short paragraph in which you connect this experience to the big question.*

Emotion can be powerfully expressed by **language** but also by ______. People **respond** to a variety of ______ in the world and in poetry.

Unit 4 Resources: Poetry
© Pearson Education, Inc. All rights reserved.
170

All **Writing About the Big Question, pp. 170, 188**

Also available for these selections:

EL L1 L2 **Vocabulary Warm-ups A and B, pp. 166–167, 184–185**

EL L1 L2 **Reading Warm-ups A and B, pp. 168–169, 186–187**

All **Vocabulary Builder, pp. 173, 191**

L2 L3 ***Reader's Notebook***

L1 ***Reader's Notebook: Adapted Version***

EL ***Reader's Notebook: English Learner's Version***

Reader's Notebooks

Pre- and postreading pages, as well as the selections in Poetry Collection 7, appear in an interactive format in the *Reader's Notebooks*. Each *Notebook* is differentiated for a different group of learners.
The selections in the Adapted and English Learner's versions are abridged.

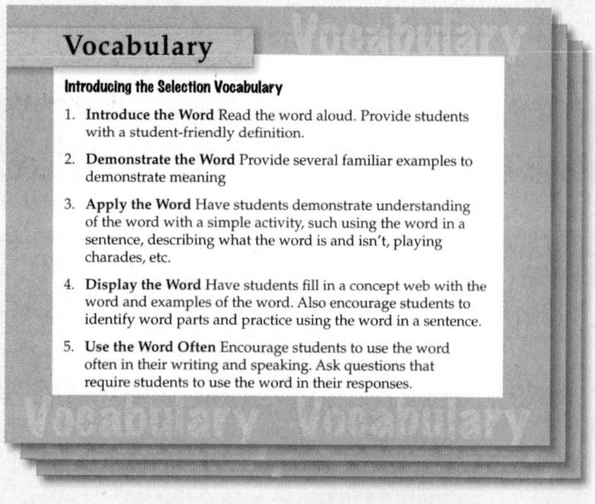

Vocabulary

Introducing the Selection Vocabulary

1. **Introduce the Word** Read the word aloud. Provide students with a student-friendly definition.
2. **Demonstrate the Word** Provide several familiar examples to demonstrate meaning
3. **Apply the Word** Have students demonstrate understanding of the word with a simple activity, such using the word in a sentence, describing what the word is and isn't, playing charades, etc.
4. **Display the Word** Have students fill in a concept web with the word and examples of the word. Also encourage students to identify word parts and practice using the word in a sentence.
5. **Use the Word Often** Encourage students to use the word often in their writing and speaking. Ask questions that require students to use the word in their responses.

Classroom Strategies and Teaching Routines

- core classroom routines outlined step-by-step
- convenient format for easy reference while teaching

Selection Support

Transparencies

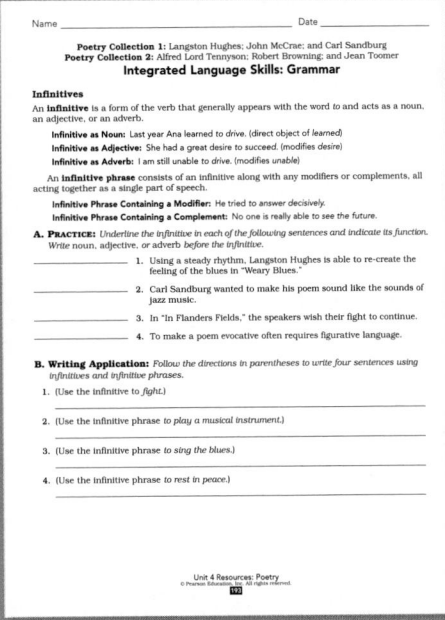

"**The Kraken**" by Alfred, Lord Tennyson;
"**Meeting at Night**" by Robert Browning;
"**Reapers**" by Jean Toomer

After You Read B: Literary Analysis—Sound Devices

Poem	Alliteration	Consonance	Assonance	Onomatopoeia
"The Kraken"				
"Meeting at Night"				
"Reapers"				

Graphic Organizer Transparencies

145

L3 **Literary Analysis: Graphic Organizer B, p. 143, 145**

Also available for these selections:

EL L1 L2 Literary Analysis: Graphic Organizer A, pp. 142, 144 (partially filled in)

EL L1 L2 Reading: Graphic Organizer A, pp. 139, 140 (partially filled in)

L3 Reading: Graphic Organizer B, p. 141

Skills Development/Extension

Unit 4 Resources

Name ______________________ Date ______________

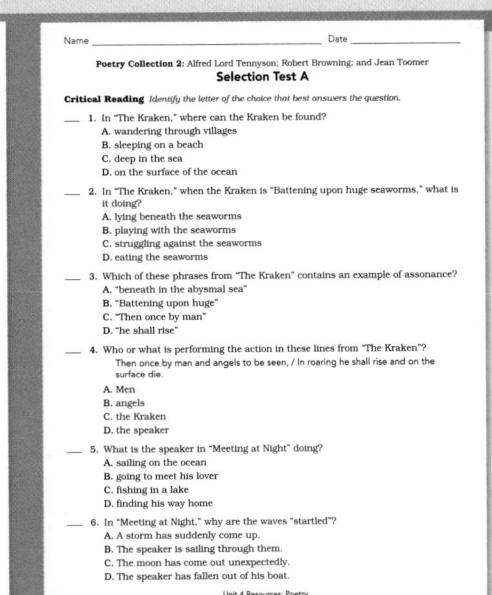

Poetry Collection 1: Langston Hughes; John McCrae; and Carl Sandburg
Poetry Collection 2: Alfred Lord Tennyson; Robert Browning; and Jean Toomer
Integrated Language Skills: Grammar

Infinitives

An **infinitive** is a form of the verb that generally appears with the word *to* and acts as a noun, an adjective, or an adverb.

Infinitive as Noun: Last year Ana learned to drive. (direct object of *learned*)
Infinitive as Adjective: She had a great desire to succeed. (modifies *desire*)
Infinitive as Adverb: I am still unable to drive. (modifies *unable*)

An **infinitive phrase** consists of an infinitive along with any modifiers or complements, all acting together as a single part of speech.

Infinitive Phrase Containing a Modifier: He tried to answer decisively.
Infinitive Phrase Containing a Complement: No one is really able to see the future.

A. PRACTICE: *Underline the infinitive in each of the following sentences and indicate its function. Write* noun, adjective, *or* adverb *before the infinitive.*

______ 1. Using a steady rhythm, Langston Hughes is able to re-create the feeling of the blues in "Weary Blues."
______ 2. Carl Sandburg wanted to make his poem sound like the sounds of jazz music.
______ 3. In "In Flanders Fields," the speakers wish their fight to continue.
______ 4. To make a poem evocative often requires figurative language.

B. Writing Application: *Follow the directions in parentheses to write four sentences using infinitives and infinitive phrases.*

1. (Use the infinitive *to fight*.)
2. (Use the infinitive phrase *to play a musical instrument*.)
3. (Use the infinitive phrase *to sing the blues*.)
4. (Use the infinitive phrase *to rest in peace*.)

Unit 4 Resources: Poetry

193

L3 L4 **Grammar, p. 193**

Also available for these selections:

All Literary Analysis: Sound Devices, pp. 171, 189

All Reading: Paraphrase, pp. 172, 190

L4 Enrichment, pp. 174, 192

L3 L4 Support for Writing, p. 194

L3 L4 Support for Extend Your Learning, p. 195

Assessment

Name ______________________ Date ______________

Poetry Collection 2: Alfred Lord Tennyson; Robert Browning; and Jean Toomer
Selection Test A

Critical Reading *Identify the letter of the choice that best answers the question.*

___ 1. In "The Kraken," where can the Kraken be found?
A. wandering through villages
B. sleeping on a beach
C. deep in the sea
D. on the surface of the ocean

___ 2. In "The Kraken," when the Kraken is "Battening upon huge seaworms," what is it doing?
A. lying beneath the seaworms
B. playing with the seaworms
C. struggling against the seaworms
D. eating the seaworms

___ 3. Which of these phrases from "The Kraken" contains an example of assonance?
A. "beneath in the abysmal sea"
B. "Battening upon huge"
C. "Then once by man"
D. "he shall rise"

___ 4. Who or what is performing the action in these lines from "The Kraken"?
Then once by man and angels to be seen, / In roaring he shall rise and on the surface die.
A. Men
B. angels
C. the Kraken
D. the speaker

___ 5. What is the speaker in "Meeting at Night" doing?
A. sailing on the ocean
B. going to meet his lover
C. fishing in a lake
D. finding his way home

___ 6. In "Meeting at Night," why are the waves "startled"?
A. A storm has suddenly come up.
B. The speaker is sailing through them.
C. The moon has come out unexpectedly.
D. The speaker has fallen out of his boat.

Unit 4 Resources: Poetry

199

EL L1 L2 **Selection Test A, pp. 178–180, 199–201**

Also available for these selections:

L3 L4 Selection Test B, pp. 181–183, 202–204

L3 L4 Open-Book Test, pp. 175–177, 196–198

PHLit Online!
www.PHLitOnline.com

- complete narrated selection text
- a thematically related video with writing prompt
- an interactive graphic organizer
- highlighting feature
- access to all student print resources, adapted to individual student needs
- Spanish and English summaries

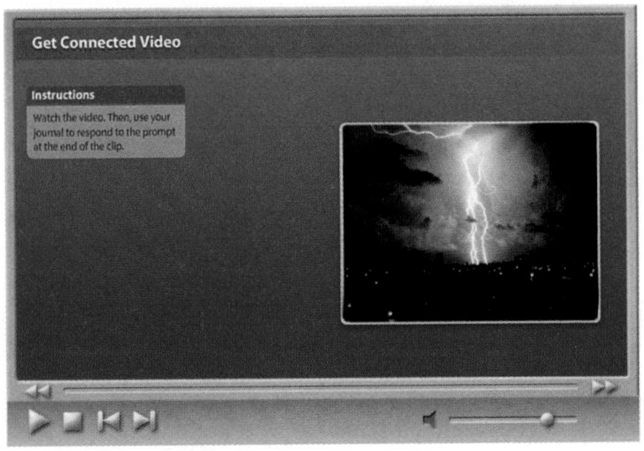
Get Connected Video
Instructions
Watch the video. Then, use your journal to respond to the prompt at the end of the clip.

Get Connected! (thematic video with writing prompt)

Also available:

Background video

Vocabulary Central

Vocabulary Central (tools, activities, and songs for studying vocabulary)

Also available:

Writer's Journal (with graphics feature)

DIFFERENTIATE/PRETEACH

❶ Collection Choices

You may use either Poetry Collection 7 or Poetry Collection 8 to meet the lesson standards. Skills instruction for both selections appears on p. 733. Choose one selection to teach (or choose to teach both). The Accessibility at a Glance chart at the bottom of this page will help you determine which of the two selections is more appropriate for your students.

❷ Selection Skills

1. With the class, preview the selection skills. (The lesson meets the lesson objectives given on p. 732a.)
2. Explain that students will develop the skill of paraphrasing as they read to better understand and enjoy the selection you choose. By examining sound devices as they read, they will gain deeper insight into poetry.
3. To introduce the Writing and Research and Technology activities (p. 749), tell students that when they have finished reading the selection, they will write a poem and prepare a visual arts presentation related to the selection.
4. Tell students that they will also study a grammar concept: infinitives. By mastering this concept, they will improve their reading fluency and the quality of their own writing.

Before You Read

Poetry Collection 7 • Poetry Collection 8

❶ Collection Choices

▲ The poems in **Poetry Collection 7** describe the beauty of sight and sound.

▲ Each poem in **Poetry Collection 8** uses descriptive language to capture a specific mood.

Collection Skills Guide

❷ Practice these skills with either **Poetry Collection 7** (p. 736) or **Poetry Collection 8** (p. 744).

- Identify sound devices including alliteration, assonance, consonance, and onomatopoeia
- Paraphrase
- Break down long sentences
- Identify infinitives and infinitive phrases
- Write a poem
- Prepare a visual arts presentation

Differentiated Instruction for Universal Access

Accessibility at a Glance: Selection Choices

	Collection 7	Collection 8
Context	Verbal representations of music	Ruminations about life and death
Language/ Vocabulary	• Complex sentence structure • Grade-level vocabulary	• Complex sentence structure • Above-level vocabulary
Concept Level	Accessible (musical language and references)	Accessible (life and death)
Literary Merit	Noted poets	Noted poets
Lexile/Length	NP Word Count: 242; 97; 159	Lexile: 1170L Word Count: 96; 109; 65
Overall Rating	**More accessible**	**More challenging**

❸ Literary Analysis: Sound Devices

To tap the music in words, poets use a variety of **sound devices,** or patterns of word-sounds. These include the following:

- **Alliteration:** repetition of consonant sounds at the beginnings of nearby words, as in "*silent song*"
- **Assonance:** repetition of vowel sounds in nearby stressed syllables, as in "*deep and dreamless.*" Unlike rhyming syllables, assonant syllables end in different consonants.
- **Consonance:** repetition of consonant sounds at the ends of nearby stressed syllables with different vowel sounds, as in the words "*heat* of *lightning*"
- **Onomatopoeia:** use of words to imitate actual sounds, such as *buzz, tap,* or *splash*

Sound devices can add to the mood of a poem, imitate the sound of events, or reflect a poem's meaning. As you read, note how poets use sound devices to create a mood or emphasize their ideas.

❹ Reading Skill: Paraphrase

To help you understand poetry and relate it to other reading and experience in your life, **paraphrase** the text, restating the ideas in your own words. First, **break down long sentences** into parts. Identify the main actions and who or what performs them. Next, identify details that show when, where, how, or why each action is performed. Then, write the paraphrase in your own words.

❺ Using the Strategy: Paraphrase Chart

As you read, use a paraphrase chart like this to break down sentences.

Breaking Down Long Sentences to Paraphrase
"When fighting for his country, he lost an arm and was suddenly afraid: 'From now on, I shall only be able to do things by halves. . . .'" from "A Man," by Nina Cassian
Who? he **Did what?** lost, was suddenly afraid
Paraphrase: He lost his arm fighting in a war and was afraid of what his life would be like.

PHLit Online!
www.PHLitOnline.com

Hear It!
- Selection summary audio
- Selection audio

See It!
- Get Connected video
- Background video
- More about the author
- Vocabulary flashcards

Do It!
- Interactive journals
- Interactive graphic organizers
- Self-test
- Internet activity
- Grammar tutorial
- Interactive vocabulary games

Differentiated Instruction for Universal Access

Preparing Students for the More Challenging Selection

If you wish to prepare lower-level readers to read Poetry Collection 8, the more challenging selection, follow these steps:

- Students may have difficulty decoding complex lines in these poems. After they read each line, have them ask themselves, *What is the purpose of this line? What information is it giving?* Then, have students use their answers to help them paraphrase the ideas. For example, direct students to "The Kraken" on p. 475. The first two lines tell where the Kraken lies; the third line describes his long sleep; the fourth line tells exactly what the Kraken is doing.
- To build students' background on the poem "The Kraken," read them the Background note on p. 743. Prompt students to discuss why a poet might want to write about a mythical creature like the Kraken. Discuss with students what poetry might reveal or add to a subject that prose might not.

PRETEACH

❸ Literary Analysis

1. Introduce the skill, using the instruction on the student page.
2. Tell students that they will practice identifying sound devices.

Think Aloud: Model the Skill

Model the skill of identifying sound devices, using the following "think aloud." Say to students:

> Suppose I see the phrase "daring to dream" in a poem. Because the beginning consonant sound "d" is repeated, I know this is alliteration.
> Suppose I see the phrase "black frock." The "k" sound is repeated at the end of each word, so I know this is an example of consonance.
> Repetition of vowel sounds, as in "true blue," is an example of assonance. I also know that any word that sounds like the noise it imitates is onomatopoeia. *Click, crash, meow,* and *bump* are examples.

❹ Reading Skill

1. Introduce the skill, using the instruction on the student page.
2. Tell students that they will practice paraphrasing as they read.

Think Aloud: Model the Skill

Model the skill of paraphrasing, using the following "think aloud." Say to students:

> Say I come across a long, complicated stanza of poetry. I first break it into parts and ask myself what the main actions are—perhaps it's about a man walking through the woods. I then look for details about this walk through the woods. Using these details, I can paraphrase the poem. When I read it again, I will better understand what it means.

❺ Using the Strategy

Give students a copy of either **Reading Skill Graphic Organizer A** or **B** (*Graphic Organizer Transparencies,* pp. 139–140) to record their paraphrases as they read. Use the examples in **Reading Skill Graphic Organizer A,** which is partially filled in, to model the process of completing the organizer.

❶ Writing About the Big Question

1. Review the assignment with the class.
2. **Ask** students how they prefer to express emotion. Emphasize that art, writing, and music, offer people such an outlet. Have volunteers share their responses.
3. Have students complete the sentence starters. Review responses as a class. (**Possible responses:** Photographs or stunning scenes can tap emotion without words because they have powerful images. One reason a person may feel a connection to a particular song or piece of music is that it reminds him or her of a memorable event.
4. Remind students that their answers will help them think about the Big Question, "Does all communication serve a positive purpose?"

While You Read

Tell students that as they read, they should look for how the poems convey emotion.

❷ Vocabulary

1. Have students preview the selection vocabulary.
2. For each word, have students say the word aloud.
3. Then, use the word in a sentence that defines the word.
4. Finally, repeat your definitional sentence or a similar sentence with the word missing and have the class "fill in the blank" chorally. For example:

   A foe is an enemy. Once the race was over, Linda hoped her competitor would be her friend, not her [students say "foe"].

❸ Word Study

1. Introduce the skill, using the instruction in the box.
2. Write the word *valor* on the board. Have students say the definition of the word, using "condition, quality, or property of something." (**Sample answer:** "having the qualities of a hero")

Making Connections
Poetry Collection 7

The Weary Blues • In Flanders Fields • Jazz Fantasia

THE BIG ? Does all communication serve a positive purpose?

❶ Writing About the Big Question

These poems show how music and a cemetery's striking visual scene can communicate and express human emotions. Use these sentence starters to develop your ideas.

Photographs or stunning scenes can tap **emotion** without words because _______________.

One reason a person may feel a **connection** to a particular song or piece of music is _______________.

While You Read Look for different ways the subjects of these poems convey emotion to readers.

❷ Vocabulary

Read each word and its definition. Decide whether you know the word well, know it a little bit, or do not know it at all. After you read, see how your knowledge of each word has increased.

- **pallor** (pal′ ər) *n.* lack of color; unnatural paleness (p. 737) ***When I saw the pallor of his face, I knew that he was frightened.*** *pale adj. pallid adj.*
- **ebony** (eb′ ə nē) *adj.* black (p. 737) ***The ebony floor contrasts with the white walls.*** *ebony n.*
- **melancholy** (mel′ ən käl′ ē) *adj.* sad (p. 737) ***The melancholy tone in her voice revealed how much she missed her best friend.*** *melancholy n.*
- **foe** (fō) *n.* enemy (p. 738) ***Judging by how kindly he treats everyone, I doubt he has a single foe.***

❸ Word Study

The **Latin suffix *-or*** means "one who takes part in" or "condition, quality, or property of something."

In "The Weary Blues," an old gaslight has the quality of being pale. Its **pallor** provides a backdrop for the blues-playing pianist.

Vocabulary Development

Vocabulary Knowledge Rating

Create a **Vocabulary Knowledge Rating Chart** (***Professional Development Guidebook***, p. 33) for this selection. Include the selection vocabulary and the Big Question words that appear in the Writing About the Big Question sentence starters. (The Big Question vocabulary is introduced on pp. 626–627.)

Give students a copy of the chart. Read the words aloud, and have students mark their rating in the Before Reading column. Urge them to be alert to these words as they read and discuss the selections.

Tally how many students think they know a word to gauge how much instruction to provide. As students read and discuss the selections, point out the words and their context.

PHLit Online! **Vocabulary Central,** featuring tools, activities, and songs for studying vocabulary, is available at **www.PHLitOnline.com.**

Meet the Authors

Langston Hughes

(1902–1967)

Author of "The Weary Blues" (p. 736)

As a young man, Langston Hughes moved from Missouri to Kansas to Illinois to Cleveland, Ohio, where he was voted class poet in high school. Later, he settled in the Harlem section of New York City. He contributed to the Harlem Renaissance, a flowering of African American artistic activity in the 1920s and 1930s. Hughes once defined poetry as "the human soul entire, squeezed like a lemon or lime, drop by drop, into atomic words."

John McCrae

(1872–1918)

Author of "In Flanders Fields" (p. 738)

Soldier, poet, doctor—John McCrae was a man of many talents. As a teenager in Ontario, Canada, McCrae joined the militia his father commanded. He also began writing poetry, and he published his first poems as a student at the University of Toronto. After earning a degree in medicine, McCrae fought in the Boer War in South Africa (1899–1902) and served as a medical officer in World War I (1914–1918). He died before the war ended.

Carl Sandburg

(1878–1967)

Author of "Jazz Fantasia" (p. 739)

Carl Sandburg once observed that some poetry was perfect only in form: "All dressed up with nowhere to go." In contrast, his own poetry dresses in blue jeans, going everywhere and speaking in the voices of everyday people. Born in Galesburg, Illinois, Sandburg settled for a time in Chicago. In addition to poetry, Sandburg is famous for his biography of Abraham Lincoln.

Daily Bellringer

For each class during which you will teach this selection, have students complete one of the five Research activities for Week 23 in the ***Daily Bellringer Activities*** booklet.

❹ Background

"The Weary Blues" The Great Migration, in which thousands of African Americans moved from the South to the North following the Civil War, created large African American urban communities in cities such as Chicago, Detroit, and New York. The speaker of "The Weary Blues" describes the mournful tunes he hears on Lenox Avenue, a street in Harlem, one such African American community. During the 1920s and 1930s, Harlem became the hub of a highly creative and culturally productive movement known as the Harlem Renaissance. During this movement, Langston Hughes, as well as such notable African Americans as Duke Ellington, Bessie Smith, and Zora Neale Hurston, helped to bring to the fore African American artistic expression.

Multidraft Reading

To assist struggling readers and to deepen reading for all, apply multidraft reading protocols. For each reading, have students set the purpose indicated:

- **First reading**—literal comprehension: answering the Reading Check questions.
- **Second reading**—application of skills: answering the Paraphrase and Sound Devices prompts.
- **Third reading**—interpretation: answering the end-of-selection questions.

For more guidance, refer to the ***Classroom Strategies and Teaching Routines*** card on multidraft reading.

Differentiated Instruction — Additional Instruction

EL Extended Support—English Learners

Have students complete the **Reading and Vocabulary Warm-ups, *Unit 4 Resources,*** pp. 166–169, before they read. Assign the prereading pages for the selection in the ***Reader's Notebook: English Learner's Version.*** Then, have students listen to portions of the selection on the ***Hear It!* Audio CD.**

L1 L2 Extended Support—Struggling Readers

Have students complete the **Reading and Vocabulary Warm-ups, *Unit 4 Resources,*** pp. 166–169, before they read. Assign the prereading pages for the selection in the ***Reader's Notebook: Adapted Version.*** Then, have students listen to portions of the selection on the ***Hear It!* Audio CD** (adapted text).

Extended Support—Reluctant Readers

To build motivation and engagement before assigning the selection, have students read "Hip-Hop into Hall of Fame," a thematically related selection in ***Reality Central.*** Then, use the questions at the conclusion of the related selection to guide discussion.

PHLit Online!

For more about the author, practice with the selection vocabulary, and more background, go to **www.PHLitOnline.com.**

❶ Activating Prior Knowledge

Play such songs as "J Mood," "Autumn Lamp," or "Laughin' and Talkin'" on the CD *Romare Bearden Revealed.* Have students freewrite as they listen, trying to capture mood, thoughts, and feelings about jazz and the blues in words. Then, have them share their ideas with the class.

Concept Connector →

Students will return to these associations after reading the poems.

Individual Activity

Have students draw freehand while listening to jazz or blues recordings as Romare Bearden did. Ask them to compare their drawings with the collage on this page and to the poems in this collection.

❷ About the Selections

In "The Weary Blues," Langston Hughes captures the languid repetition and syncopation of the blues. Using musical effects, "In Flanders Fields" calls on the living to acknowledge our debt to those who gave their lives. In "Jazz Fantasia," Carl Sandburg combines slang and musical expressions to create a unique, jumpy rhythm that echoes the energetic rhythms of jazz.

❸ Humanities

Autumn Lamp (Guitar Player)
by Romare Bearden (1911–1988)

Romare Bearden grew up in Harlem, in New York City, during the Harlem Renaissance. Both of his parents were active in the local arts scene, and such notables as Langston Hughes and Duke Ellington were frequent visitors to his home.

Bearden created a style all his own, constructing collages with anything available—fabric, sandpaper, foil, etc.—in addition to traditional oils and watercolors. Like jazz and blues musicians, he left his art open to interpretation. Use this question for discussion:

Based on the painting, what generalizations can you make about jazz and the blues?

Possible response: Both forms of music are colorful and many-layered. Both also seem animated and enthusiastic.

The Weary Blues

❶ ❷

Langston Hughes

❸

Autumn Lamp (Guitar Player, 1983), Romare Bearden. From the Mecklenburg Autumn Series. Private Collection.

Vocabulary Development

Thematic Vocabulary: The Big Question

As students are discussing Poetry Collection 7, encourage them to use the thematic vocabulary presented in Introducing the Big Question, pp. 626–627. You might encourage them with sentence starters like these:

1. In "The Weary Blues," Hughes uses sound devices to *convey* . . .
2. The *context* of "In Flanders Fields" is important because . . .
3. The mood, or *emotion,* McCrae creates in his poem is . . .
4. In the third stanza of "Jazz Fantasia," Sandburg captures the *confusion* of sounds by . . .

4 Droning a drowsy syncopated[1] tune,
Rocking back and forth to a mellow croon,
I heard a Negro play.
Down on Lenox Avenue[2] the other night
By the pale dull **pallor** of an old gas light
He did a lazy sway. . . .
He did a lazy sway. . . .
To the tune o' those Weary Blues.
With his **ebony** hands on each ivory key
He made that poor piano moan with melody.
O Blues!
Swaying to and fro on his rickety stool
He played that sad raggy tune like a musical fool.
Sweet Blues!
Coming from a black man's soul.
O Blues!
In a deep song voice with a **melancholy** tone
I heard that Negro sing, that old piano moan—
"Ain't got nobody in all this world,
Ain't got nobody but ma self.
I's gwine to quit ma frownin'
And put ma troubles on the shelf."
5 Thump, thump, thump, went his foot on the floor.
He played a few chords then he sang some more—
"I got the Weary Blues
And I can't be satisfied.
Got the Weary Blues
And can't be satisfied—
I ain't happy no mo'
And I wish that I had died."
And far into the night he crooned that tune.
The stars went out and so did the moon.
The singer stopped playing and went to bed
While the Weary Blues echoed through his head.
He slept like a rock or a man that's dead.

1. **syncopated** (siŋ′ kə pāt′ id) *adj.* with a catchy or an emphatic rhythm created by accenting beats that are usually unaccented.
2. **Lenox Avenue** street in Harlem, a historic African American neighborhood in New York City.

6 ◀ **Critical Viewing** Does this painting express the same mood as Hughes's poem? Explain. **[Interpret]**

Vocabulary
pallor (pal′ ər) *n.* lack of color; unnatural paleness
ebony (eb′ ə nē) *adj.* black
melancholy (mel′ ən käl′ ē) *adj.* sad

Literary Analysis
Sound Devices Why is "thump, thump, thump" an example of onomatopoeia?

4 Literary Analysis
Sound Devices
1. Have a volunteer read the first ten lines of the poem aloud.
2. Then, **ask** students to choose examples of alliteration and explain their effects.
Answer: Examples of alliteration include *droning/drowsy; pale/pallor; tune/those; poor/piano; moan/melody*. The effects are musical, as if a musician is repeating notes for emphasis.

5 Literary Analysis
Sound Devices
1. Read the bracketed lines aloud to students.
2. **Ask** a volunteer to review the definition of onomatopoeia.
Answer: Onomatopoeia is the use of words to imitate actual sounds.
3. Then, **ask** students the Literary Analysis question: Why is "thump, thump, thump" an example of onomatopoeia?
Answer: It imitates the sound of the musician's foot tapping on the floor.

6 Critical Viewing
Possible response: Some students may say that there does not seem to be a connection of mood between the poem and the painting. Although the musician sits beneath a gaslight, he does not seem to be melancholy. Instead, he seems pleased, calm, and self-assured. Others may think that the dark tones of the painting and the quiet, thoughtful demeanor of the musician echo the feeling of the poem.

Fluency
Students might have difficulty reading the dialect of "The Weary Blues." Have students read lines 19–22. To model fluent reading, read the passage to students with expression as students track, or follow along by pointing at each word in the text as you read. Then, have students read the passage back to you. Look for this problem spot:
- Students may stumble with the phrase *I's gwine.* Point out that the phrase is another rendering of *I am going.*

PHLit Online!
This selection is available in interactive format in the **Enriched Online Student Edition, www.PHLitOnline.com,** which includes a thematically related video with writing prompt and an interactive graphic organizer.

❼ Critical Viewing

Answer: Yes, it is a fitting tombstone because its simplicity gives it a degree of dignity that a more elaborate tombstone might not.

❽ Background

Remembrance John McCrae wrote "In Flanders Fields" not only in response to the war he witnessed firsthand, but also as a way of coping with his grief over the death of a close friend. According to soldiers who served with him, McCrae wrote the poem between treating groups of wounded soldiers. Dissatisfied with its meter, he threw the poem away, but his commanding officer retrieved it and sent the poem, originally entitled "We shall not sleep," to a magazine. The poem was first published on December 8, 1915.

❾ Literary Analysis

Sound Devices

Have volunteers each read a different stanza of the poem.

▶**Monitor Progress** Then, **ask** students to review the poem, identifying examples of consonance and alliteration.

Answer: Examples of alliteration include *F*landers/*f*ields, *s*till/*s*inging, *d*ead/*d*ays, *l*oved/*l*oved/*l*ie, *t*he/*t*orch, *h*old/*h*igh, *w*ith/*w*ho, and *s*hall/*s*leep. Examples of consonance include hear*d*/ami*d* and sa*w*/glo*w*.

Ask students what the effect of these sound devices is.

Possible response: Alliteration places the stress on the beginning of each word. Scattered throughout the poem as they are, the hard sounds of the *f*'s and *d*'s are offset by the softer sounds of *w*'s and *s*'s. The use of consonance almost makes the lines echo. The use of these two devices parallels the poem itself—the beauty of the poppies, crosses, and larks in a place of horrible destruction.

▶**Reteach** If students have difficulty identifying alliteration, assign the letters *F, S, D, L, T, H,* and *W* to different students. As you read the poem aloud, tell students to "jump in" and read any words that begin with their assigned letters.

In FLANDERS FIELDS

John McCrae

❼ ▲ **Critical Viewing** Do you think that this tombstone is a fitting memorial for a soldier who died during the war? Explain. **[Make a Judgment]**

❽ **Background** The devastation of the First World War (1914–1918) brought forth a sad beauty. In the torn-up battlegrounds of Flanders, a region of Belgium, thousands of poppies sprang up, flourishing in the fields cleared by war. McCrae turned these flowers into a symbol that generations have worn to honor the dead.

In Flanders fields the poppies blow
Between the crosses, row on row,
  That mark our place; and in the sky
  The larks, still bravely singing, fly
Scarce heard amid the guns below.

❾

We are the Dead. Short days ago
We lived, felt dawn, saw sunset glow,
  Loved and were loved, and now we lie
      In Flanders fields.

Take up our quarrel with the **foe**:
To you from failing hands we throw
  The torch; be yours to hold it high.
  If ye break faith with us who die
We shall not sleep, though poppies grow
      In Flanders fields.

Vocabulary
foe (fō) *n.* enemy

Vocabulary Development

Vocabulary Knowledge Rating

When students have completed reading and discussing the poems, have them take out their **Vocabulary Knowledge Rating Chart** for these poems. Read the words aloud once more, and have students rate their knowledge of the words again in the After Reading column. Clarify any words that are still problematic. Have students write their own definition and example or sentence in the appropriate column. Then, have students complete the Vocabulary Practice at the end of the selection. Encourage students to use the words in further discussion and written work about these poems. Remind them that they will be accountable for these words on the **Selection Test,** ***Unit 4 Resources,*** pp. 155–157 or 158–160.

Jazz Fantasia

Carl Sandburg

◀ **Critical Viewing** 10
What details in the painting suggest that the music being played is filled with energy and life? **[Analyze]**

Drum on your drums, batter on your banjoes,
sob on the long cool winding saxophones.
Go to it, O jazzmen.

Sling your knuckles on the bottoms of the happy
tin pans, let your trombones ooze, and go husha-
husha-hush with the slippery sand-paper.

Moan like an autumn wind high in the lonesome treetops,
11 moan soft like you wanted somebody terrible, cry like a
racing car slipping away from a motorcycle cop,
bang-bang! you jazzmen, bang altogether drums, traps,
banjoes, horns, tin cans—make two people fight on the
12 top of a stairway and scratch each other's eyes in a
clinch[1] tumbling down the stairs.

Reading Skill
Paraphrase Who or what performs the main action in this stanza?

1. **clinch** *n.* in boxing, the act of gripping the opponent's body with the arms.

10 Critical Viewing

Answer: The colors of the picture—a mixture of orange, blue, green, and red—in addition to the wavy and elaborate lines coming out of the instruments, all indicate the energy of the music.

11 Reading Skill

Paraphrase

1. Have a volunteer read the bracketed stanza aloud.
2. **Ask** students the Reading Skill question: Who or what performs the main action in this stanza?
   Answer: The speaker is talking directly to the musicians. He addresses them as the jazzmen.

12 Connecting to the Big Question

1. Remind students that artists can use different methods to evoke emotion, such as using particular words, vivid images, and poignant music.
2. Have students reread the third stanza. Then, **ask:** What emotion(s) does the speaker create in this stanza? How is this emotion conveyed?
   Possible response: The speaker creates different emotions through specific images and words. For example, the speaker creates a somber emotion using the line "like an autumn wind high in the lonesome treetops." The speaker also creates anger by using such phrases as "bang-bang!" and "scratch each other's eyes."
3. Then, **ask** students: Why might the speaker communicate these emotions about jazz?
   Possible response: The speaker might want to share with the reader the different feelings jazz evokes in people.

Concept Connector

Activating Prior Knowledge

Have students return to the discussion points about jazz and the blues. Lead a class discussion, probing for what students have learned that confirms or invalidates the ideas they had before reading the selections. Encourage students to cite specific details, quotations, or other evidence from the text to support their responses.

Writing About the Big Question

Have students compare their responses to the sentence starters they completed before reading the poems with their ideas afterwards. Ask them to explain whether their thoughts have changed.

Reading Skill Graphic Organizer

Ask students to review the graphic organizers they completed while reading. Show them the **Reading Skill Graphic Organizer A** (*Graphic Organizer Transparencies,* page 139) as an example. Then, have students share their graphic organizers.

ASSESS

Answers

Critical Thinking

1. Students may favor the two poems about music because the experiences described are more familiar to them.
2. (a) Possible words include *droning, drowsy, rocking, lazy, sad,* and *raggy*. (b) **Possible response:** The mood is tired and melancholy. (c) **Possible response:** He seems easygoing but tired and sad.
3. (a) The speakers are the dead. (b) The poet builds a contrast in both stanzas between life and death. (c) **Possible response:** Yes, because the speaker is saying that the living have a responsibility to carry on the cause of the dead.
4. (a) Jazz can be sad and soothing, rough and angry, or lonesome and gentle. (b) **Possible response:** The poet seems to suggest that jazz can and does capture all human emotions.

Does all communication serve a positive purpose?

Possible responses: (a) In "The Weary Blues," the speaker tries to convey the sadness and suffering of the blues player. In "In Flanders Field," the poet conveys the sorrow that is inevitable in war. In "Jazz Fantasia," the poet shows the versatility and vibrancy of jazz music. (b) All three poets use various poetic devices, such as onomatopoeia, assonance, and alliteration to contribute to the emotion of their poems. (c) It is a good thing to want to convey emotion in poetry because doing so helps to establish a powerful connection between the reader and the poet.

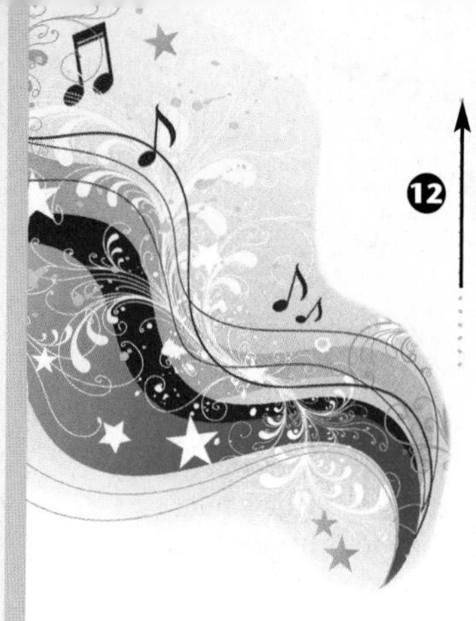

Can[2] the rough stuff . . . now a Mississippi steamboat
pushes up the night river with a hoo-hoo-hoo-oo . . . and
(12) the green lanterns calling to the high soft stars . . . a red
moon rides on the humps of the low river hills . . . go to it,
O jazzmen.

2. **Can** *v.* slang for "stop" or "cease."

Critical Thinking

1. **Respond:** Which poem affected you most strongly? Why?
2. **(a)** List four adjectives that Hughes uses to describe the music in "The Weary Blues." **(b) Infer:** What mood do these adjectives, together with the lyrics the man sings, create?
(c) Interpret: Do the descriptions of the piano player also support this mood? Explain.
3. **(a)** Who are the speakers of "In Flanders Fields"?
(b) Contrast: Explain the contrasts in the first stanza and the contrasts in the second stanza. **(c) Evaluate:** Do these contrasts help make the speaker's concluding warning effective? Explain.
4. **(a) Contrast:** Contrast three of the musical moods described in the third and fourth stanzas of "Jazz Fantasia."
(b) Draw Conclusions: What do these changing moods suggest about the power of jazz to capture human experience?

THE BIG ?

Does all communication serve a positive purpose?
(a) In each poem, what emotion do you think the writer wants to convey? **(b)** How does each poet's use of the style and sound of poetry support this goal? **(c)** Do you think the expression of emotion in poetry is a worthy goal? Why or why not?

Assessment Resources

Unit 4 Resources

L1 L2 EL **Selection Test A,** pp. 178–180. Administer Test A to less advanced readers and English learners.

L3 L4 **Selection Test B,** pp. 181–183. Administer Test B to on-level and more advanced students.

L3 L4 **Open-Book Test,** pp. 175–177. As an alternative, give the Open-Book Test.

All **Customizable Test Bank**

All **Self-tests**
Students may prepare for the **Selection Test** by taking the **Self-test** online.

PHLit Online! All assessment resources are available at **www.PHLitOnline.com.**

After You Read
Poetry Collection 7

The Weary Blues • In Flanders Fields • Jazz Fantasia

Literary Analysis: Sound Devices

1. **(a)** Using a chart like the one shown, identify examples of **sound devices** in "The Weary Blues" and "Jazz Fantasia." **(b)** For each device you list, explain what it adds to the poem.

Alliteration	Consonance	Assonance	Onomatopoeia

2. **(a)** Compare the effects of sound devices in "In Flanders Fields" with their effects in one of the other poems in Poetry Collection 7. **(b)** Discuss your answer with a partner. **(c)** Together, draw a conclusion about the ways that sound devices can be used in poetry. Present your conclusion to the class.

Reading Skill: Paraphrase

3. **(a)** Break down the sentence in the first stanza of "In Flanders Fields" by identifying the action and who or what is completing the action. **(b) Paraphrase** the stanza.
4. **(a)** Paraphrase the third stanza of "Jazz Fantasia." **(b)** How does this paraphrase help you understand the poem?

Vocabulary

Practice An **oxymoron** is a phrase combining contradictory or opposing ideas, often used as a figure of speech for poetic effect. Explain whether each phrase below is an oxymoron.

1. healthy pallor
2. dark ebony
3. melancholy celebration
4. friendly foe

Word Study Use the context of the sentences and what you know about the **Latin suffix *-or*** to explain your answer to each question.

1. Would you press an *accelerator* to make a car go slower?
2. Would you ever put a *conductor* in charge of anything?

Word Study

The **Latin suffix *-or*** means "one who takes part in" or "condition, quality, or property of something or someone."

Challenge Explain how the suffix *-or* contributes to the meanings of these words. Consult a dictionary if necessary.

candor
compactor
competitor

ASSESS/EXTEND

Answers

Literary Analysis

1. **Possible response:** (a) "The Weary Blues": **alliteration:** *dr*oning/*dr*owsy, *p*ale/*p*allor, *m*oan/*m*elody; **consonance:** roc*k*ing ba*ck*, pa*l*e du*ll* pa*ll*or, me*l*an*ch*o*l*y to*n*e; **assonance:** l*a*zy sw*a*y, s*a*d r*a*ggy; **onomatopoeia:** droning, croon, thump. (b) Hughes uses these sound devices to capture both the rhythm and mood of the blues. They help achieve an easygoing but somewhat sad, weary mood and an admiration for the blues.

   For other sample answers, see ***Graphic Organizer Transparencies,* Literary Analysis Graphic Organizer A**, p. 142, and the **Additional Answers** section.
2. (a) **Possible responses:** The sound devices, particularly the alliterative "s," in "In Flanders Fields" give the speaker a soft, sweeping disembodied voice like that of a spirit or of the wind. In contrast, the hard sounds of "Jazz Fantasia," such as the "k," "t," and "d" sounds, work to ground and make very tangible jazz and its effects on listeners. (b) and (c) After discussion, partners should present their conclusions.

Reading Skill

3. (a) The dead describe nature continuing, even as gunfire erupts, and as they lie beneath the crosses that mark their graves. (b) Poppies grow between the graves of the soldiers who died during a World War I battle in Belgium. The singing birds can barely be heard over the gunfire.
4. **Possible responses:** (a) Moan like the wind, moan like you miss someone, cry like a speeding car. Play so that the sounds of different instruments clash against each other like people fighting. (b) The paraphrase shows how Sandburg makes the moods and the energy of jazz vivid for readers by comparing the music to a few different scenes.

Vocabulary

Practice

Sample answers:

1. Healthy pallor is an oxymoron because one who is very pale is not healthy.
2. Dark ebony is not an oxymoron because something ebony is black.
3. Melancholy celebration is an oxymoron because *melancholy* means "sad," not "joyful."
4. Friendly foe is an oxymoron because a foe is an enemy, not one's friend.

Word Study

Sample answers:

1. No, an *accelerator* is "something that accelerates," so pressing it would make the car go faster.
2. Yes, a *conductor* is "one who conducts," so someone who conducts or guides would be a good leader.

Word Study: Challenge

Sample answers: Something said with *candor* has the quality of truth. A *compactor* is a machine that has the quality of compacting things. A *competitor* is one who takes part in a competition.

PRETEACH

*Skills instruction for the **Reading Skill** and **Literary Analysis** concept for this collection appears on p. 733.*

1 Writing About the Big Question

1. Review the assignment with the class.
2. Elicit from students which poetic device they find most effective at communicating ideas and emotion and why.
3. Have students complete the sentence starters. Review responses as a class. (**Possible response:** Poets use language to communicate meaning and mood in various ways, such as through metaphors and similes. Sometimes readers respond to the meaning of words and other times they react to the rhythm.
4. Remind students that their answers will help them think about the Big Question.

While You Read

Tell students that as they read, they should look for sound devices that create "special effects."

2 Vocabulary

1. Have students preview the selection vocabulary.
2. For each word, have students say the word aloud.
3. Then, use the word in a sentence that defines the word.
4. Finally, repeat your definitional sentence or a similar sentence with the word missing, and have the class "fill in the blank" chorally. For example:

   Something abysmal is very deep. The depth of the ocean varies from visible shallows to trenches that are [students say "abysmal"].

3 Word Study

1. Introduce the skill, using the instruction in the box.
2. Have students explain how the suffix *-ial* contributes to the meaning of the word *partial.* (**Answer:** "related to a part")

Making Connections
Poetry Collection 8

Meeting at Night • The Kraken • Reapers

Does all communication serve a positive purpose?

1 Writing About the Big Question

In Poetry Collection 8, these poets use sound devices to create a dreamlike mood in their poems. Use these sentence starters to develop your ideas about the Big Question:

Poets use **language** to communicate **meaning** and mood in various ways, such as ______________.

Sometimes readers **respond** to the **meaning** of the words and other times they react to the ______________.

While You Read Look for examples of sound devices that create "special effects" in the poems.

2 Vocabulary

Read each word and its definition. Decide whether you know the word well, know it a little bit, or do not know it at all. After you read, see how your knowledge of each word has increased.

- **quench** (kwench) *v.* satisfy; to fulfill a need (p. 744) ***I quench my thirst with cold water in the summer.*** *quenchable adj.*
- **abysmal** (ə biz′ məl) *adj.* immeasurably deep (p. 745) ***The canyon was so abysmal that they could not see the bottom of it.*** *abyss n. abysmally adv.*
- **millennial** (mi len′ ē əl) *adj.* of 1,000 years (p. 745) ***Built in 1023, the abbey will hold its millennial celebration in 2023.*** *millennium n.*
- **slumbering** (slum′ bər iŋ) *adj.* sleeping (p. 745) ***Do not wake a slumbering bear.*** *slumber v. slumber n.*

3 Word Study

The **Latin suffix *-ial*** means "relating to," "characterized," or "a function of."

In "The Kraken," the **millennial** growth of the huge sea sponges suggests that their size reflects their growth over a millennium, or a thousand years.

Vocabulary Development

Vocabulary Knowledge Rating

Create a **Vocabulary Knowledge Rating Chart** (***Professional Development Guidebook,*** p. 33) for this selection. Include the selection vocabulary and the Big Question words that appear in the Writing About the Big Question sentence starters. (The Big Question vocabulary is introduced on pp. 626–627)

Give students a copy of the chart. Read the words aloud, and have students mark their rating in the Before Reading column. Urge them to be alert to these words as they read and discuss the selection.

Tally how many students think they know a word to gauge how much instruction to provide. As students read and discuss the selection, point out the words and their context.

PHLit Online!

Vocabulary Central, featuring tools, activities, and songs for studying vocabulary, is available at **www.PHLitOnline.com.**

Meet the Authors

Robert Browning

(1812–1889)

Author of "Meeting at Night" (p. 744)

During his lifetime, Robert Browning was not as famous as his wife, poet Elizabeth Barrett Browning. Today, though, it is Robert who is considered the more innovative poet. He is admired especially for his dramatic monologues, poems in which characters speak directly to readers or other characters. Browning's eerie poem "Childe Roland to the Dark Tower Came" helped inspire Stephen King's *Dark Tower* series.

Alfred, Lord Tennyson

(1809–1892)

Author of "The Kraken" (p. 745)

In an age when poets were often celebrities, Alfred, Lord Tennyson was perhaps the most celebrated of all. Named Great Britain's poet laureate in 1850, Tennyson cut quite a figure, dressing in a dashing cape and large-brimmed felt hat. When not in London, he lived on the Isle of Wight in a large home that is now an inn. As laureate, he often wrote patriotic verse and poems drawn from history and legend.

Jean Toomer

(1894–1967)

Author of "Reapers" (p. 746)

"My position in America has been a curious one," Jean Toomer once observed. His maternal grandfather was the first African American ever to serve as a state governor (of Louisiana). Reflecting on his diverse ethnic background—French, Dutch, German, and Native American, as well as African American—Toomer called himself the "human race." He won early fame with the 1923 publication of his book *Cane*, an exploration of African American culture.

Daily Bellringer

For each class during which you will teach this selection, have students complete one of the five Research activities for Week 23 in the ***Daily Bellringer Activities*** booklet.

❷ Background

"The Kraken" Seafarers have regarded the Kraken, a legendary squidlike sea monster, as a menace to their safety for nearly a thousand years, when the beast was first described in Scandinavian stories. By the eighteenth century, the Kraken still carried a fearsome reputation, whose size the Bishop of Bergen, in *The Natural History of Norway,* compared to a "floating island." Indeed, the Kraken's immeasurable size—in addition its huge net of tentacles—was said to pull down ships in its wake when it surfaced and dived back down into the deep, where it fed on fish. This sea monster may not be just a product of sailors' imaginations, however—recently, scientists discovered the largest-known squid, the "colossal squid," which is even larger than the giant squid. Said to grow as long as forty feet, this secretive sea animal certainly could have been the inspiration for the mythical Kraken.

Multidraft Reading

To assist struggling readers and to deepen reading for all, apply multidraft reading protocols. For each reading, have students set the purpose indicated:

- **First reading**—literal comprehension: answering the Reading Check questions.
- **Second reading**—application of skills: answering the Paraphrase and Sound Devices prompts.
- **Third reading**—interpretation: answering the end-of-selection questions.

For more guidance, refer to the ***Classroom Strategies and Teaching Routines*** card on multidraft reading.

Differentiated Instruction — Additional Instruction

EL Extended Support—English Learners
Have students complete the **Reading and Vocabulary Warm-ups, *Unit 4 Resources,*** pp. 184–187, before they read. Assign the prereading pages and the adapted selection in the ***Reader's Notebook: English Learner's Version.*** Then, have students listen to portions of the selection on the ***Hear It!* Audio CD.**

L1 L2 Extended Support—Struggling Readers
Have students complete the **Reading and Vocabulary Warm-ups, *Unit 4 Resources,*** pp. 184–187, before they read. Assign the prereading pages and the adapted selection in the ***Reader's Notebook: Adapted Version.*** Then, have students listen to portions of the selection on the ***Hear It!* Audio CD** (adapted text).

Extended Support—Reluctant Readers
To build motivation and engagement before assigning the selection, have students read "Texting on Trial," a thematically related selection in ***Reality Central.*** Then, use the questions at the conclusion of the related selection to guide discussion.

PHLit Online!
For more about the author, practice with the selection vocabulary, and more background, go to **www.PHLitOnline.com.**

TEACH

❶ Activating Prior Knowledge

Play such CDs or sound tracks as Modest Mussorgsky's *Pictures at an Exhibition,* Alan Hovhaness's *And God Created Great Whales,* or Camille Saint-Saën's *Carnival of the Animals* for students. Have students freewrite as they listen, trying to capture mood, thoughts, and feelings about the animals depicted in the music. Then, have them share their ideas with the class as you record them on the board.

Concept Connector →

Students will return to these associations after reading the poems.

Individual Activity

Students will find that reading poetry provides an excellent opportunity for them to expand their vocabulary. Have students skim through the poems in the collection and make a list of new words they encounter.

❷ About the Selections

Lovers star in "Meeting of Night," where nature and love converge in a secret rendezvous. In "The Kraken," the poet's imagination is captured by the mythical sea monster. In "Reapers," the workers are too busy to notice the field rat injured by the blade of one of their mowers.

❸ Critical Viewing

Answer: The contrast of the dark night and the effect of moonlight on water creates a mysterious, haunting mood in both the painting and the poem.

❹ Literary Analysis

Sound Devices

1. Read the poem aloud to students.
2. Focus students' attention on line 7. **Ask** students the Literary Analysis question: Why is "sea-scented beach" an example of both alliteration and of assonance?
   Answer: The repetition of *s*'s in *sea-scented* is alliterative. The repetition of *ea* in *sea* and *beach* is assonant.

Meeting at Night

❶ ❷

Robert Browning

❸ ▲ **Critical Viewing** Compare the mood of this scene with the mood in the poem. **[Compare and Contrast]**

Vocabulary
quench (kwench) *v.* satisfy; to fulfill a need

1

The gray sea and the long black land;
And the yellow half-moon large and low;
And the startled little waves that leap
In fiery ringlets from their sleep,
As I gain the cove with pushing prow,
And quench its speed i' the slushy sand.

2

❹

Then a mile of warm sea-scented beach;
Three fields to cross till a farm appears;
A tap at the pane, the quick sharp scratch
And blue spurt of a lighted match,
And a voice less loud, through its joys and fears,
Than the two hearts beating each to each!

Literary Analysis
Sound Devices Why is "sea-scented beach" an example of both alliteration and of assonance?

Vocabulary Development

Vocabulary Knowledge Rating

When students have completed reading and discussing the three poems, have them take out their **Vocabulary Knowledge Rating Chart** for these selections. Read the words aloud once more, and have students rate their knowledge of the words again in the After Reading column. Clarify any words that are still problematic. Have students write their own definition and example or sentence in the appropriate column. Then, have students complete the Vocabulary Practice at the end of the selection. Encourage students to use the words in further discussion and written work about these poems. Remind them that they will be accountable for these words on the **Selection Test, *Unit 4 Resources*,** pp. 199–201 or 202–204.

The Kraken

Alfred, Lord Tennyson

Below the thunders of the upper deep;
5 Far, far beneath in the abysmal sea,
His ancient, dreamless, uninvaded sleep
The Kraken[1] sleepeth: faintest sunlights flee
About his shadowy sides: above him swell
Huge sponges of millennial growth and height;
And far away into the sickly light,
6 From many a wondrous grot[2] and secret cell
Unnumbered and enormous polypi[3]
Winnow[4] with giant arms the slumbering green.
There hath he lain for ages and will lie
Battening[5] upon huge seaworms in his sleep,
Until the latter fire[6] shall heat the deep;
Then once by man and angels to be seen,
In roaring he shall rise and on the surface die.

1. **Kraken** (krä′ kən) *n.* in Scandinavian folklore, a sea monster resembling a giant squid.
2. **grot** (grät) *n.* grotto; cave.
3. **polypi** (päl′ i pē) *n.* sea creatures with long, waving tentacles around the mouth, such as the sea anemone or hydra.
4. **Winnow** (win′ ō) *v.* fan; beat with wings or, here, tentacles.
5. **Battening** (bat′ 'n iŋ) *v.* feeding on; growing fat on.
6. **the latter fire** the apocalypse; the end of the world.

Vocabulary

abysmal (ə biz′ məl) *adj.* immeasurably deep

millennial (mi len′ ē əl) *adj.* of 1,000 years

slumbering (slum′ bər iŋ) *adj.* sleeping

Reading Skill

Paraphrase What is the main action in lines 7–10, and who or what performs that action?

5 Connecting to the Big Question

1. Remind students that poets can manipulate language in various ways to create specific effects. For instance, a poet might use a certain rhythm to imitate the sound of music.
2. Read the bracketed text aloud. Then, **ask:** What sound devices does Tennyson use in the first four lines of the poem and what effect do they create?
   Possible response: Tennyson uses alliteration and assonance. Examples of alliteration include *the*/*th*unders, *f*ar/*f*ar, *b*eneath/a*b*ysmal, and *f*aintest/*f*lee. Examples of assonance include B*e*low/d*ee*p, th*u*nders/*u*pper, ben*ea*th/s*ea*, and dr*ea*mless/sl*ee*p. The alliteration and assonance create a dreamlike storytelling quality.
3. **Ask:** Why might Tennyson have decided to communicate this dreamlike quality in his description of the Kraken?
   Possible response: The Kraken is a mythical beast and is therefore not real. Tennyson tells the story of the Kraken in a dreamlike way to make it more interesting and dramatic.
4. Tell students to look for more "special effects" as they continue to read the poems.

6 Reading Skill

Paraphrase

1. Read the bracketed lines aloud to students.
2. Then, **ask** students the Reading Skill question: What is the main action in lines 7–10, and who or what performs that action?
   Answer: Many sea creatures come out of their caves and beat the sleeping Kraken with their tentacles.

Concept Connector

Activating Prior Knowledge

Have students return to the freewriting and class discussion they did before reading these selections. Lead a class discussion, probing for what students have learned that confirms or invalidates the ideas they had before reading the selections.

Writing About the Big Question

Have students compare their responses to the sentence starters they completed before reading the poems with their ideas afterwards. Ask them to explain whether their thoughts have changed.

Reading Skill Graphic Organizer

Ask students to review the graphic organizer they completed while reading. Show them the **Reading Skill Graphic Organizer A** (*Graphic Organizer Transparencies,* p. 140) as an example. Then, have students share their graphic organizers.

PHLit Online!

This selection is available in interactive format in the **Enriched Online Student Edition, www.PHLitOnline.com,** which includes a thematically related video with writing prompt and an interactive graphic organizer.

❼ Critical Viewing

Answer: There is no mower and no field rat in the painting. However, the scythe cutting the weeds and the destruction of the shade from the poem are depicted.

ASSESS

Answers

Critical Thinking

1. Students may respond strongly to the images of the Kraken.
2. (a) Colors mentioned are gray, black, and yellow. The wave tips might be orange or yellow; the lighted match is a "blue spurt." (b) **Possible response:** The colors may mirror his journey from the sadness of separation (black and gray) to the excitement of meeting his love (yellow and orange).
3. (a) It has been sleeping an "ancient, dreamless, uninvaded sleep." (b) An apocalypse is the only thing that would change the Kraken's activity.
4. (a) It would seem that nothing will interrupt their work. (b) **Possible response:** The blade is a positive force because it removes weeds. At the same time, it's a negative force because it destroys shade and wildlife.

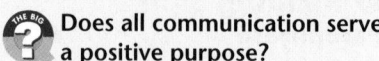

THE BIG ? Does all communication serve a positive purpose?

(a) **Possible response:** All three poems show the connections that people or things have to nature through vivid images such as farms and the ocean. (b) **Possible response:** The sensory language used by the poets gives the poems a quality of authenticity and uniqueness they otherwise might not have. For instance, Toomer's description of the rat that is killed by the mower works to convey the utter callousness people can have toward nature.

REAPERS

Jean Toomer

❼ ▲ **Critical Viewing** Identify one similarity and one difference between this scene and the scene in the poem. **[Compare and Contrast]**

Black reapers with the sound of steel on stones
Are sharpening scythes. I see them place the hones[1]
In their hip-pockets as a thing that's done,
And start their silent swinging, one by one.
Black horses drive a mower through the weeds,
And there, a field rat, startled, squealing bleeds,
His belly close to ground. I see the blade,
Blood-stained, continue cutting weeds and shade.

1. **scythes** (sīthz) **. . . hones** A scythe is a tool for cutting grain or grass, consisting of a sharp blade attached to a long handle. A hone is a hard stone used to sharpen a metal blade.

Critical Thinking

1. **Respond:** Which of the three poems left you with the picture you might remember longest? Why?
2. **(a) Analyze:** Identify the series of colors named or suggested in "Meeting at Night." **(b) Connect:** How might this series of colors reflect the speaker's emotional and physical journey?
3. **(a)** In "The Kraken," what has the Kraken been doing? **(b) Infer:** According to the poem, what is the only thing that could cause a change in the Kraken's activity?
4. **(a) Infer:** According to the poem, "Reapers," will the reapers stop their work before it is done? Explain. **(b) Analyze:** What two contrasting ideas are expressed in the final description of the blade?

THE BIG ? Does all communication serve a positive purpose?
(a) How does the poets' use of sensory language help convey the main message of each of these poems?
(b) What do you think was the purpose of each of these three poems?

Assessment Resources

Unit 4 Resources

L1 L2 EL **Selection Test A**, pp. 199–201. Administer Test A to less advanced readers and English learners.

L3 L4 **Selection Test B**, pp. 202–204. Administer Test B to on-level and more advanced students.

L3 L4 **Open-Book Test**, pp. 196–198. As an alternative, give the Open-Book Test.

All **Customizable Test Bank**

All **Self-tests**
Students may prepare for the **Selection Test** by taking the **Self-test** online.

PHLit Online! All assessment resources are available at **www.PHLitOnline.com.**

After You Read
Poetry Collection 8

Meeting at Night • The Kraken • Reapers

Literary Analysis: Sound Devices

1. **(a)** Using a chart like the one shown, identify examples of **sound devices** in "The Kraken" and "Reapers." **(b)** For each device you list, explain what it adds to the poem.

Alliteration	Consonance	Assonance	Onomatopoeia

2. **(a)** Compare the effects of sound devices in "Meeting at Night" with the effects of sound devices in one of the other poems. **(b)** With a partner, draw a conclusion about the use of sound devices in poetry. Present your conclusion to the class.

Reading Skill: Paraphrase

3. **(a)** Break down the first clause (ending on the colon) of "The Kraken" by identifying the action and who or what is completing the action. **(b) Paraphrase** the clause.
4. **(a)** Paraphrase the second stanza of "Meeting at Night." **(b)** How does this paraphrase help you understand the poem?

Vocabulary

Practice An **oxymoron** is a phrase combining contradictory or opposing ideas, often used as a figure of speech for poetic effect. Explain whether each phrase below is an oxymoron.

1. millennial instant
2. restful slumber
3. abysmally shallow
4. quenchable thirst

Word Study Use the context of the sentences and what you know about the **Latin suffix *-ial*** to explain your answer to each question.

1. If you have a *managerial* role, are you in charge of other people or is someone else in charge of you?
2. Will an *industrial* area of a city be filled with parks and wildlife?

Word Study

The **Latin suffix *-ial*** means "relating to," "characterized," or "a function of."

Challenge Explain how the suffix *-ial* contributes to the meanings of these words. Consult a dictionary if necessary.

celestial
financial
territorial

ASSESS/EXTEND

Answers

Literary Analysis

1. **Possible response:** (a) "The Kraken": **alliteration:** secret/cell, faintest/flee; sides/swell, roaring/rise; **consonance:** upper/deep, unnumbered/enormous; **assonance:** thunder/upper, dreamless/sleep, seaworms/sleep (b) These sound devices help achieve an eerie, dreamy mood.

   For other sample answers, see ***Graphic Organizer Transparencies,*** **Literary Analysis Graphic Organizer A,** p. 144, and the **Additional Answers** section.
2. **Possible response:** (a) The speaker of "Reapers" tells the reader that there is a sound "of steel on stones" but does not describe the sound. The alliterative "s," however, serves to imitate the swishing sound of the scythes. "Meeting at Night" uses onomatopoeia to convey sound directly, as in *tap, spurt,* and *scratch,* which makes the action more immediate and the meeting more tangible and real. (b) After discussion, partners should present their conclusions.

Reading Skill

3. (a) *Sleeping* is the action, and *the Kraken* performs the action. (b) The Kraken sleeps in the depths of the ocean.
4. (a) The speaker crosses a beach. He crosses three fields until a farm appears. He taps at the windowpane and hears a match being lit and a voice full of joy and fear. The voice is not as loud as the beating of two hearts. (b) **Possible response:** The paraphrase clarifies the action of the poem.

Vocabulary
Practice

1. Millennial instant is an oxymoron because *millennial* describes a long period of time.
2. Restful slumber is not an oxymoron because to *slumber* is to sleep.
3. Abysmally shallow is an oxymoron because something shallow is not deep.
4. Quenchable thirst is not an oxymoron because you can satisfy your thirst.

Word Study

1. *Managerial* means "relating to a manager," so if you have a managerial role, you are in charge of other people.
2. No, an *industrial* area is "characterized by industry," so it will not be full of parks and wildlife but by buildings and factories.

Word Study: Challenge

Something *celestial* is characterized by the heavens. A *financial* matter is related to money. A *territorial* dispute is related to land.

EXTEND/ASSESS

Answers

Grammar

1. Introduce the skill, using the instruction on the student page.
2. Discuss the definitions and the examples in the chart.

Think Aloud: Model the Skill

Model the skill of identifying infinitives. Say to students:

> To find an infinitive, look for the preposition *to.* If a verb comes after *to,* then I know it is an infinitive.
>
> I know that an infinitive can act as a noun, an adjective, or an adverb. For example, in the sentence, "Children often have a desire to eat sweets," *to eat* is the infinitive. Because *to eat sweets* modifies the noun *desire,* this infinitive acts as an adjective.

WG Writing and Grammar, Grade 10

Students will find further instruction and practice on infinitives in Chapter 20, Section 1.

Practice A

1. to hear; noun
2. to be; noun
3. to play; noun
4. to fill; adverb
5. to play; noun

Challenge

Sample answer: I's gwine to quit ma frownin'; be yours to hold it high.

Practice B

Sample answers:

1. to come; John plans to come home after the movie.
2. to hide; Susan likes to hide from Sally.
3. to see; Wally went to see his friend about a job.
4. to continue; After taking a course in Mark Twain, Sally plans to continue reading his works.

Challenge

Sample answer: The squid went to wrap its tentacles around the boat. The sailors began to jump overboard. The boat started to sink.

Integrated Language Skills

Poetry Collection 7 and 8

Grammar: Infinitives

An **infinitive** is a form of the verb that generally appears with the word *to* and acts as a noun, an adjective, or an adverb.

Example:
Infinitive (*noun*): Last year, my friend Ana learned *to drive.*
Infinitive (*adjective*): She was motivated by a desire *to succeed.*
Infinitive (*adverb*): Unfortunately. I am still unable *to drive.*

An **infinitive phrase** consists of an infinitive along with any modifiers or complements, all acting together as a single part of speech. In standard English, the word *to* should not be split or separated from its verb—its modifiers follow the verb.

Example:
Infinitive phrase: He tried *to answer decisively.* (*decisively* modifies the infinitive *to answer*)

Notice that an infinitive phrase always includes *to* and a verb, as in *to remember.* When *to* is used in a prepositional phrase, it is followed by a noun or pronoun and its modifier, as in *to the store.*

Practice A Identify the infinitive in each sentence and tell whether it acts as a noun, an adjective, or an adverb.

1. The speaker wants to hear the blues.
2. The dead have a longing to be remembered.
3. The band prepared to play their instruments.
4. The sound of music began to fill the air.
5. My goal in life is to play the saxophone.

Challenge Find and identify two lines from the poems in Poetry Collection 7 that include examples of infinitives.

Practice B Identify the infinitive or infinitive phrase in each sentence. Then, use the infinitive or infinitive phrase in an original sentence.

1. The Kraken's death is due to come later.
2. The sea is able to hide the squid.
3. The speaker is driven by his longing to see his beloved.
4. The reapers are able to continue their cutting.

Challenge Choose one illustration from Poetry Collection 8 and write three sentences about this image. In each sentence, include an infinitive or infinitive phrase that functions as a noun, an adjective, or an adverb.

WG **Writing and Grammar Connection:** Chapter 20, Section 1

Extend the Lesson

Sentence Modeling

Choose the quote given from the selection students have read:

I's gwine to quit ma frownin' ("The Weary Blues")

Three fields to cross till a farm appears ("Meeting at Night")

Ask students what they notice about the quote. Elicit from them that it contains an infinitive. Then, ask what else they notice. ("The Weary Blues": Hughes uses dialect to create a more authentic voice in his poem. "Meeting at Night": the subject is not mentioned, which makes the action seem yet another step to complete in a long journey.)

Have students imitate the quote in a sentence on a topic of their own choosing, matching each grammatical and stylistic feature discussed. Collect the sentences, and share them with the class.

Writing

Write a **poem,** like "The Weary Blues" or "Jazz Fantasia," that tells about your favorite kind of music *or* write a poem, like "The Kraken" or "Reapers," that tells about a collision between nature and the world of people. Use sound devices to help you create a mood, make your ideas memorable, or capture the sounds that you describe.

- Before you write, complete one of these prewriting activities: jot down the emotions and feelings your favorite type of music inspires in you *or* list details of a situation that pits nature against people or the developed world. Based on your list, determine the mood you want to convey.
- As you draft, work sound devices such as alliteration and onomatopoeia into your poem to bring out the energy of your ideas. Look to the language techniques used by the authors of the poems in this pairing to help you create your own personal style.
- Read your draft aloud. Then, revise your writing in order to achieve the sounds, tone, and controlling perspective you want to express. Review your word choice to delete weak words. Replace them with specific language that suits your purpose better.

Writing Workshop: *Work in Progress*

Prewriting for an Analytical Response Use the Questions List from your writing portfolio. Answer each question with both a statement of your opinion and a textual detail that supports that opinion. Put this Analysis Work in your writing portfolio.

Use this prewriting activity to prepare for the Writing Workshop on page 768.

Research and Technology

Learn more about the Harlem Renaissance, a movement Hughes and Toomer helped define. Choose a visual artist associated with the movement, and prepare a **visual arts presentation** about three of his or her works. Follow these tips:

- Research an artist to learn about his or her styles subject matter, and most famous work.
- In your presentation, compare the artwork to Hughes's or Toomer's poem.
- **Use props and visual aids to enhance the appeal** of your presentation.
- Afterward, lead a **discussion** about the artworks and how they reflect African American experience.
- Then, collect classmates' questions and report back with answers.

PHLit Online!
www.PHLitOnline.com
- Interactive graphic organizers
- Grammar tutorial
- Interactive journals

EXTEND/ASSESS

Writing

1. Review the assignment, using the instruction on the student page.
2. To guide students in writing their poems, give them **Support for Writing,** p. 194 in ***Unit 4 Resources.***
3. To evaluate students' poems, use the Poem rubric, pp. 248–249 in ***Professional Development Guidebook.*** In addition, evaluate how well students use images and the voice of the speaker to communicate ideas.

Six Traits Focus

✔	Ideas	✔	Word Choice
	Organization		Sentence Fluency
✔	Voice		Conventions

Writing Workshop
Work in Progress

Have students save their completed Analysis Work in their portfolios. They will use this later as they complete the Writing Workshop assignment (see pp. 768–775).

Research and Technology

1. Review the assignment, using the instruction on the student page.
2. Have students complete the **Support for Extend Your Learning** page (*Unit 4 Resources,* p. 52).

Teaching Resources

Unit 4 Resources

L3 L4 **Integrated Language Skills: Grammar,** p. 193

L3 L4 **Support for Writing,** p. 194

L3 L4 **Support for Extend Your Learning,** p. 195

L4 **Enrichment,** pp. 174 and 192

Enriched Online Student Edition
Available under After You Read for this selection:

All **Interactive Grammar Tutorial**

L3 L4 **Internet Research Activity**

Professional Development Guidebook
Rubrics for Poem, pp. 248–249

PHLit Online! All print and digital resources are available at **www.PHLitOnline.com.** Online resources accessible by students are noted on the student page.

MONITORING PROGRESS

Using the Test Practice

n this two-page Test Practice, students apply the reading skill for the second half of Unit 4 to a passage of fiction and a passage of nonfiction.

Review this skill, paraphrasing, and then administer the test. For more guidance, consult the ***Classroom Strategies and Teaching Routines*** card, **Administering Timed Tests.**

ASSESS

Answers

Answers With Explanations

1. C—The words *before* and *huge black engine* in sentence 1, paragraph 2, show that she is waiting for a train. *Incorrect answers:* A—She is waiting for a train, not watching a car, as the words *boxcar, before,* and *huge black engine* show. B—The train has not come into sight, as the word *before* in sentence 1, paragraph 2, shows. D—The story describes Marta's train watching, not riding.
2. D—The *vibrations of the train* paraphrases "the rumble in her chest"; *Before she could see it* paraphrases before it "roared into sight". *Incorrect answers:* A—This paraphrase is too vague. B—The phrase describes Marta's feelings, not the impact on the house. C—The phrase describes feeling, not predicting.
3. C—*Sleeping* is synonymous with "slumbering deeply." *Incorrect answers:* A—"Slumbering deeply" does not suggest snoring. B—"Slumbering deeply" does not suggest dreaming. D—"Slumbering deeply" suggests sleeping, but not covers or lack of covers.
4. A—The phrase, "the noise and shaking stopped suddenly," paraphrases the first sentence; the phrase with "when the last train went by" paraphrases the second sentence. *Incorrect answers:* B—The last two sentences don't say that the shaking got louder. C—The last two sentences don't say that the train slowed down. D—The last two sentences don't compare the train's front and back.

Test Practice: Reading

Paraphrase

Fiction Selection

Directions: *Read the selection. Then, answer the questions.*

Marta propped her elbows on the windowsill and rested her chin in her hands, watching the boxcars rumble by. She had to get up early the next morning and knew she should have been in bed slumbering deeply, but she'd never been able to resist.

She could feel the rumble in her chest, in her spine long before the huge black engine roared into sight. Each night at midnight, car after car thundered past. And every night for as long as she could remember, she played the same game in her head. *How many cars tonight?* She'd make a guess, sometimes realistic: *ninety.* Sometimes wildly improbable: *six hundred!* And then she'd count each one as it went by. *One, two, three, four, five, six . . .* It got harder with the large numbers; she couldn't say them as quickly as the cars raced by. *Sixtyonesixtytwosixtythree . . .* And then, after all the noise and shaking, suddenly it was over. It was as if all that sound and motion got chopped off as the last car whipped by her.

1. Which sentence would form the main idea of a paraphrase of this passage?
A. Marta is watching cars drive by her.
B. Marta is watching a train.
C. Marta is waiting for a train.
D. Marta is thinking about a train ride.

2. Which of the following *best* paraphrases this phrase: "feel the rumble in her chest, in her spine long before the huge black engine roared into sight"?
A. "imagine the train even when it wasn't there"
B. "feel the shaking of her house as the train went by"
C. "predict when the train would pass by each night"
D. "feel the vibrations of the train even before she could see it"

3. In a paraphrase, the words "slumbering deeply" would *best* be replaced with—
A. the word "snoring."
B. the phrase "dreaming of tomorrow."
C. the word "sleeping."
D. the phrase "asleep beneath the covers."

4. Which of the following statements *best* paraphrases the last two sentences?
A. When the last train car went by, the noise and shaking stopped suddenly.
B. The noise and shaking got louder as the last train car passed by.
C. The train slowed down as it went by.
D. The front of the train was louder than the back of the train.

Writing for Assessment

In a few sentences, describe the images that you would picture to help you paraphrase the first paragraph of this passage.

Writing for Assessment

Students should first reread the part of the story that describes the train passing and indicates what Marta was thinking. Then they should write what she thought in their own words.

Strategies for Test Taking

Many of these questions require careful reading of single sentences. Encourage students to stay focused as they reread a sentence from the story and then make sure that each word in the paraphrase is suggested by the original sentence.

Nonfiction Selection

Directions: *Read the selection. Then, answer the questions.*

More than 500 individual railroad systems span from coast to coast of the United States, but the seven largest rail carriers generate over 90% of the country's total rail revenue. Passenger rail service is only a small part of rail operations; the most important use of the country's railways is for the transportation of freight.

The Federal Railroad Administration (FRA), one of the many agencies of the U.S. Department of Transportation, is in charge of the railroads. The key mission of the FRA is to enforce rail safety, but its functions also include research, financial assistance, and technical assistance. Other government entities that participate in regulating, assisting, and ensuring the safety of freight carriers in the U.S. are the Surface Transportation Board, the Department of Homeland Security, the Transportation Security Agency, the Railroad-Shipper Transportation Advisory Council, the National Grain Car Council, and various offices and bureaus of the U.S. Department of the Treasury.

1. The phrase "span from coast to coast of the United States" could *best* be reworded as—
- **A.** "spread the broad width of the U.S."
- **B.** "are all over"
- **C.** "exist in the United States"
- **D.** "span wide tracks of land"

2. How would you paraphrase this phrase so that an elementary student could understand it? *"Other government entities that participate in . . ."*
- **A.** The entire government participates
- **B.** Other government groups that help with
- **C.** More than one government group takes part in
- **D.** Participation by other governments

3. What is the *best* paraphrase of the sentence, "The key mission of the FRA is to enforce rail safety, but its functions also include research, financial assistance, and technical assistance"?
- **A.** The FRA mainly enforces rail safety but performs other functions as well.
- **B.** The FRA performs many functions.
- **C.** In addition to enforcing rail safety, the FRA is involved in research, financial, and technical assistance.
- **D.** The FRA is very important for railroads.

4. To paraphrase this passage, you might do all of the following *except*—
- **A.** restate the meaning in your own words.
- **B.** break down long sentences into parts.
- **C.** identify main actions and crucial details.
- **D.** brainstorm for questions to ask.

Writing for Assessment

Connecting Across Texts
If you were making recommendations for reading, to whom would you suggest each passage? Write a paragraph to support your recommendations by explaining why each is a good choice for the readers you select.

PHLit Online!
www.PHLitOnline.com
- Online practice
- Instant feedback

Differentiated Instruction for Universal Access

Strategy for Special Needs Students
Make sure that students understand that the fiction selection is mostly written as a flashback or reflection on past experience (from the fourth sentence to the end). Reread the flashback together, and call on volunteers to summarize what happened.

Strategy for Less Proficient Readers
Students may have difficulty understanding the details of the FRA in the nonfiction selection. After they read the passage, help them to create a word web that shows the functions of the FRA (rail safety, research, financial assistance, technical assistance). Then have students list, in one column, the five other agencies and offices involved with railroads; in a second column, have them identify their functions (regulation, assistance, safety of freight carriers).

ASSESS

Answers

Answers With Explanations

1. A—"Spread" paraphrases *span*; "broad width of" paraphrases coast to coast, and "U.S." is an abbreviation of *United States*. *Incorrect answers:* B—This paraphrase is too vague. C—same explanation as for B. D—This paraphrase repeats, without explaining, the word *span* and is too vague.
2. C—This statement covers all the agencies and offices mentioned in the paragraph and describes their functions. *Incorrect answers:* A—This statement is too vague and unclear. B— This statement is not true; the government is involved in regulation. D—This statement is not true; the government has other functions, as well.
3. A—"The FRA Mainly enforces rail safety" paraphrases the first phrase; "but performs other functions as well" paraphrases the rest of the sentence. *Incorrect answers:* B—This statement only generalizes about the last part of the sentence. C—This statement restates the last part of the sentence. D—This statement is too vague.
4. D—Asking questions of the author would not help with restating the meaning in one's own words. *Incorrect answers:* A—This is exactly what a paraphrase involves. B—Breaking down long sentences is a necessary step for clarifying meaning in order to paraphrase. C—Identifying main actions and crucial details is a necessary step in paraphrasing.

Writing for Assessment

In their responses, students' recommendations should reflect an understanding of the purpose of each passage. Their responses should include at least two details from each passage.

PHLit Online!
Students may take the test in interactive format with instant feedback online at **www.PHLitOnline.com**

PRETEACH

Meeting Your Standards

Students will

1. make generalizations.
2. read and understand an atlas entry and a magazine article.

Log on at ***www.PHLitOnline.com*** *for a detailed lesson plan for Informational Texts.*

Reading Skill

1. Introduce the skill, using the instruction on the student page.
2. Tell students that they make generalizations about a topic.

Think Aloud: Model the Skill

Model the skill of synthesizing to make generalizations. Say to students:

> I can make connections between the facts in separate articles to come to a larger conclusion, or generalization, about the information in the articles. For example, in an article about colonial America, I read that only property-owning adult white males had the right to vote, but by 1830, all adult white males could vote. In another article, I read that the 15th Amendment to the Constitution paved the way for African Americans to vote in 1870. I can put together the information from the separate articles to make a generalization: democracy in the United States is a continually evolving process.

Does all communication serve a positive purpose?

Have students think about how the information given deepens their knowledge.

Multidraft Reading

Have students follow a multidraft reading protocol.

- **First reading**—Have students read for general understanding.
- **Second reading**—Have students make generalizations about the topic.
- **Third reading**—Have students consider the effects of consulting multiple sources.

Informational Texts

Real-Life Reading

Atlas Entry
Mali

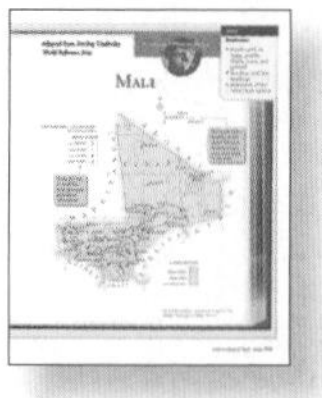

Magazine Article
Will All the Blue Men End Up in Timbuktu?

Reading Skill: Synthesize: Make Generalizations

When researching a topic, you often need to consult several sources. Compare and contrast the texts to see what types of information are presented in each. Then, **synthesize,** or bring together, the facts and ideas from the various sources so that you can **find connections** between them and make generalizations. When you **make generalizations,** you formulate broad statements that explain, connect, or sum up various facts, as in this example:

Fact		Fact		Generalization
Desertification in Mali is causing a scarcity of basic resources.	+	Poverty is a main political issue.	=	Many people in Mali struggle to make a living.

THE BIG ?

Does all communication serve a positive purpose?

The atlas entry and the magazine article each communicate different aspects of a region in Africa. As you read, consider why it might be helpful to consult more than one source on a topic.

Differentiated Instruction for Universal Access

Reading Support

Give students reading support with the appropriate version of the ***Reader's Notebooks***:

L2 L3 *Reader's Notebook*

L1 *Reader's Notebook: Adapted Version*

EL *Reader's Notebook: English Learner's Version*

PHLit Online!

All student resources are available online at **www.PHLitOnline.com.**

Atlas Entry

Features:

- visuals, such as maps, graphs, charts, icons, and symbols
- headings and sub-headings
- statements of fact rather than opinion

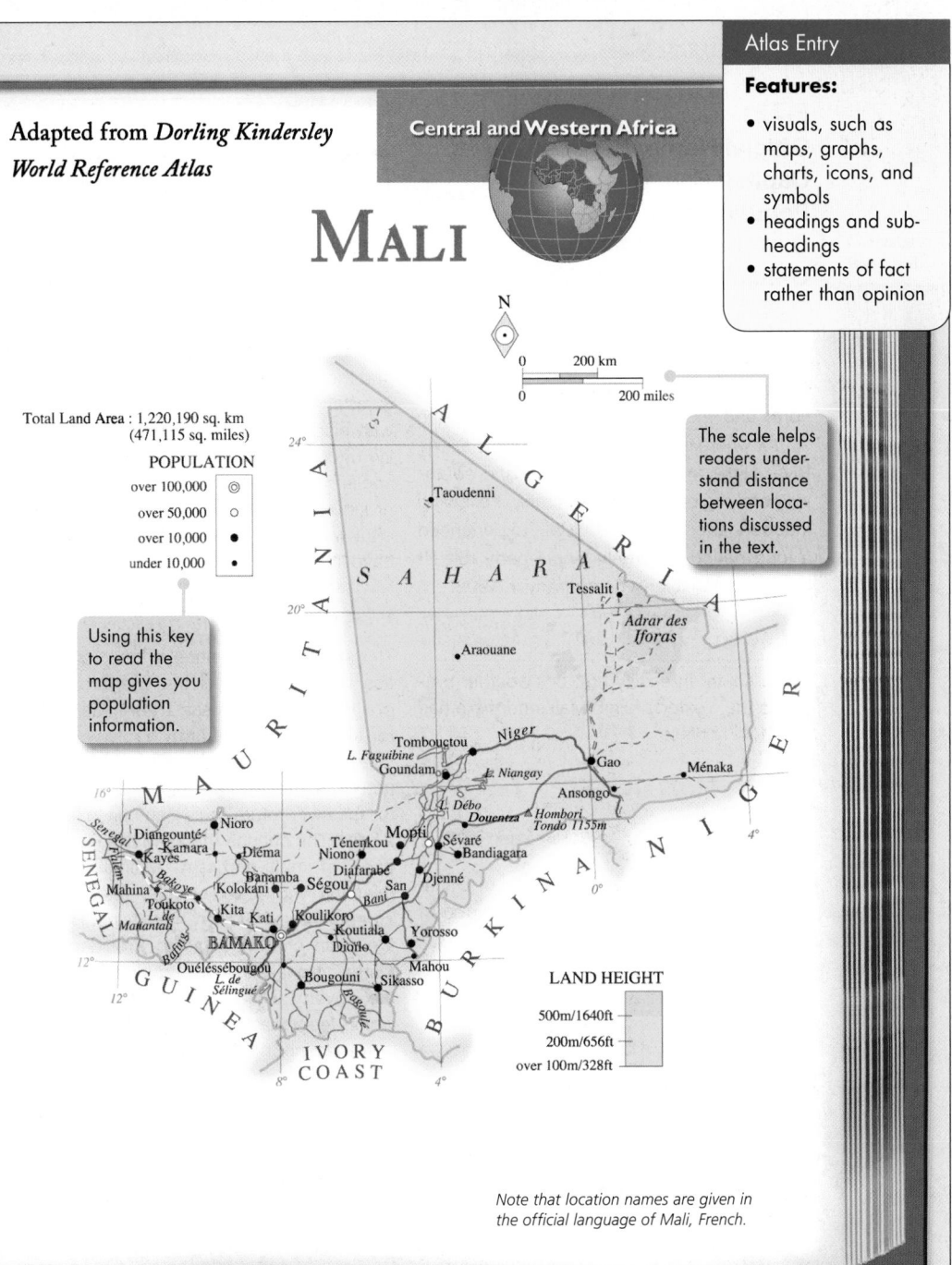

Adapted from *Dorling Kindersley World Reference Atlas*

Central and Western Africa

MALI

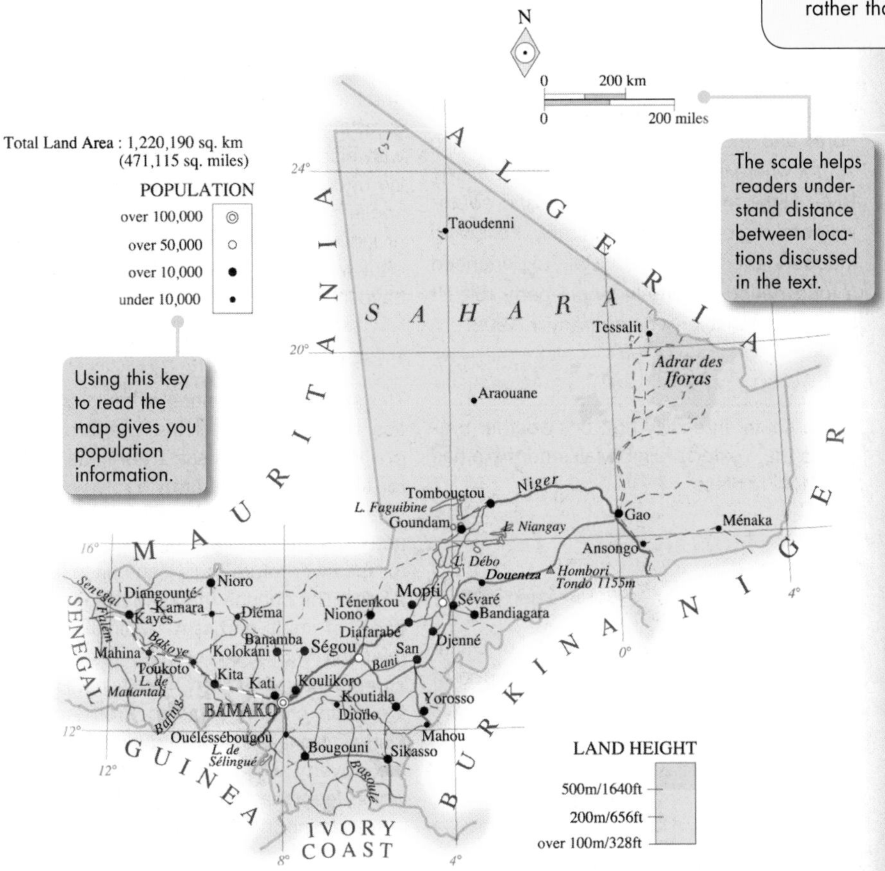

The scale helps readers understand distance between locations discussed in the text.

Using this key to read the map gives you population information.

Note that location names are given in the official language of Mali, French.

TEACH

About Atlas Entries

1. Review the features of atlas entries. Recall with students how facts differ from opinions. *(Facts are true statements. Opinions are statements expressing a belief or viewpoint.)*
2. Invite students to describe atlases they have used. **Ask** them to share what they learned by reading atlas entries.
   Possible responses: Students may say they learned the name of a country's capital, its land features, or where a country is located relative to another country.
3. Tell students that the atlas entry on pages 753–754 shows a map and gives facts about Mali, a country in Africa.

Synthesize: Make Generalizations

1. Have students look at the entry for Mali. Point out the inset map at the top. Tell students that the shaded section shows the area of central and western Africa where Mali is located.
2. Point out the map scale. **Ask:** What keys are shown on the map?
   Answer: The map has a population key and a land height key.
3. Have students use the land height key. **Ask:** What do you know about Mali from looking at the map and reading the land height key?
   Answer: Most of Mali has low elevation.
4. Direct students' attention to the cities and towns shown on the map. **Ask** them what they notice about the distribution of cities and towns across Mali.
   Answer: Most of the cities and towns are in southern Mali.
5. **Ask** students why they think there are few cities and towns in northern Mali.
   Answer: The Sahara desert is in northern Mali, and the desert is hot and dry.
6. Help students make a connection between these facts: few people live in northern Mali and the Sahara desert is in northern Mali. Guide students to make a generalization about deserts: the hot, dry conditions in deserts make them difficult places in which to live.

Differentiated Instruction for Universal Access

Support for Special Needs Students

Some students with special needs will have difficulty reading the print on the map, both because it is small and because the location names are in French. Make an outline drawing of the map and enlarge it on a copier. Then, ask students to plot the bordering countries and the larger cities so they can get a general sense of Mali. Also have them shade the non-rainy north a light tan and the south a light green on their maps.

Synthesize: Make Generalizations

1. Point out to students that the text in this atlas entry organizes the information into subtopics.
2. **Ask** students which heading they would look under to find information about Mali's weather patterns.
   Answer: They would look under the heading "Climate."
3. Discuss the information about northern Mali that is given in the "Climate" section. *(Northern Mali is almost rainless.)* Have students look back at the map on page 753. Guide them to make a connection between Mali's rainless northern half and the Sahara desert in the north of Mali.
4. Point out that the "People" section tells about Mali's different ethnic groups. **Ask:** What ethnic group lives in the north of Mali?
   Answer: The Tuareg nomads live in the north.
5. Discuss the meaning of the phrase *lingua franca,* "a common language used to communicate among people speaking different languages."
6. Tell students that they can make connections between facts given in the atlas entry and ideas they will read about in the magazine article.

ASSESS/EXTEND

Answers

Does all communication serve a positive purpose?

Possible responses: (a) A tourist might use the map to plan a safari or a trip to the historic cities along the River Niger.

(b) A business leader might use the map to help decide where to locate an industry. The population key on the map indicates where potential employees and customers might be found.

MALI

Official Name: *Republic of Mali*
Capital: *Bamako*
Population: *10.8 million*
Currency: *CFA franc*
Official Language: *French*

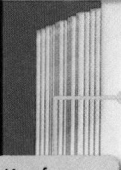

Key facts are summarized here.

Mali is landlocked in the heart of West Africa. Its mostly flat terrain comprises virtually uninhabited Saharan plains in the north and more fertile savanna land in the south, where most of the population live. The River Niger irrigates the central and southwestern regions of the country. Following independence in 1960, Mali experienced a long period of largely single-party rule. It became a multiparty democracy in 1992.

CLIMATE

Headings clearly state the types of information presented and help you find connections with other texts.

In the south, intensely hot, dry weather precedes the westerly rains. Mali's northern half is almost rainless.

TRANSPORTATION

Has no fleet

Bamako-Senou

Mali is linked by rail with the port of Dakar in Senegal, and by good roads to the port of Abidjan in Ivory Coast.

TOURISM

16,000 visitors

Down 33% in 1994

Tourism is largely safari-oriented, although the historic cities of Djénné, Gao and Mopti, lying on the banks of the River Niger, also attract visitors. A national domestic airline began operating in 1990.

PEOPLE

Bambara, Fulani, Senufo, Soninke, French

24 people per sq. mile

Mali's most significant ethnic group, the Bambara, is also politically dominant. The Bambara speak the lingua franca of the River Niger, which is shared with other groups including the Malinke. The relationship between the Bambara–Malinke majority and the Tuareg nomads of the Saharan north is often tense and sometimes violent. As with elsewhere in Africa, the extended family, often based around the village, is a vital social security system and a link between the urban and rural poor. There are a few powerful women in Mali but, in general, women have little status.

POLITICS

The successful transition to multi-party politics in 1992 followed the overthrow in the previous year of Moussa Traoré, Mali's dictator for 23 years. The army's role was crucial in leading the coup, while Colonel Touré, who acted as interim president, was responsible for the swift return to civilian rule in less than a year. The change marks Mali's first experience of multi-partyism. Maintaining good relations with the Tuaregs, after a peace agreement in 1991, is a key issue. However, the main challenge facing President Alpha Oumar Konaré's government is to alleviate poverty while placating the opposition, which feels that the luxury of multi-partyism is something that Mali cannot afford.

Does all communication serve a positive purpose?

(a) How might a tourist to Mali use the information communicated by the map? (b) Who else might find the map useful? Explain.

Vocabulary Development

Cross-Curricular Vocabulary: Social Studies

Atlases often contain vocabulary that is specific to geography and government. Review with students the meaning of the following terms:

Geography:

landlocked: enclosed or nearly enclosed by land

uninhabited: having no people living there

savanna: a tropical or subtropical grassland

Government:

single-party rule: a system of government in which only one political group has control

multi-party rule: a system of government in which multiple political groups exist, with any group having the capacity to govern

coup: a takeover of a government, often by force

civilian: related to ordinary citizens; non-military

PHLit Online!

Vocabulary Central, featuring tools, activities, and songs for studying vocabulary, is available online at **www.PHLitOnline.com.**

Magazine Article

Features:

- leisure reading
- specialized subject matter
- text written for a general or specific audience

Will All the Blue Men End Up in Timbuktu?

'Desertification' forces nomads into the city

BY STEFAN LOVGREN

Posted 11/29/98

TIMBUKTU, Mali—To most people, this outpost on the southern fringe of the Sahara suggests the end of the world. To the blue-turbaned nomads known as the Tuareg, Timbuktu is the opposite, a busy city that does not agree with their unhurried ways. In the solitude of the surrounding desert, there are no telephones, newspapers, schools, or government services. Fathers teach their sons to care for goats and camels, then spend a lifetime following rain clouds in search of water.

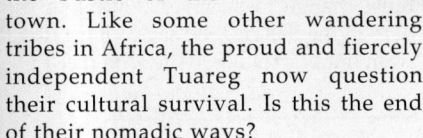

Here, the author discusses climate. These facts can be synthesized with other sources on climate.

But rains and the green pastures they yield have become increasingly scarce. Sweeping sand dunes now blanket what used to be fertile grazing lands. Tuaregs who once owned hundreds of animals are down to a dozen. Many have been forced to do the unthinkable and settle in the bustle of the town. Like some other wandering tribes in Africa, the proud and fiercely independent Tuareg now question their cultural survival. Is this the end of their nomadic ways?

The area around Timbuktu has suffered greatly from "desertification." Decades of overgrazing and drought have converted this land into a near desert. It is difficult to imagine that elephants and giraffes once roamed here; now, the only vegetation is an occasional thorn tree, and sandstorms flare up in seconds. Calling desertification "the biggest threat facing Africa," the presidents of Mali and neighboring Burkina Faso warned recently that the battle for shrinking resources will lead to civil wars and famines. The United Nations estimates the worldwide annual losses to desertification at $42 billion, much of it in Africa, where two thirds of the continent is desert or dry land. This week, representatives of some 150 countries will meet in Senegal to discuss how to involve local communities, like the Tuareg, in combating the problem.

About Magazine Articles

1. Review with the class the features of magazine articles.
2. **Ask** students what types of magazines they have read.
   Possible responses: Students may say they have read sports magazines or fitness magazines.
3. Tell students that this magazine article is about the Tuareg nomads of Mali and that students can synthesize information from this article and the atlas entry they have previously read in order to make generalizations.

Synthesize: Make Generalizations

1. Discuss the article's title, "Will All the Blue Men End Up in Timbuktu?" **Ask** students who they think the "blue men" might be and why they think so.
   Possible response: The "blue men" might be people who live in the desert because the photos show a person riding a camel in the desert and a person wearing blue desert garb.
2. Have students look back at the map of Mali on page 753 and locate Timbuktu. Remind students that the location names on the map are given in French.
   Ask: Which location name is likely to be Timbuktu?
   Answer: Tombouctou
3. Have students read the article. Tell them to note details about Mali's people and climate as they read. **Ask:** Why are the Tuareg people called "blue men"? What problem do the Tuareg face?
   Answer: Tuaregs are called "blue men" because they wear blue turbans. There is not enough land to graze their cattle.
4. Discuss the meaning of *desertification*, "a natural or human-caused process by which usable land turns into desert." Discuss how desertification affects the Tuareg people. *(Because Tuaregs are able to graze fewer cattle, they are settling in town.)*
5. Lead students to put together the information about Mali's climate that they read in the atlas entry *(Its northern half is almost rainless)* and the information given about Mali's climate in this article *(Rains have become increasingly scarce).*

Fluency

Distribute copies of pages 755–756 and pair students. Have partners take turns reading paragraphs aloud. While one partner reads, the other partner should mark words with which the reading partner has difficulty. Circulate to monitor the fluency of students' reading. Collect students' marked-up copies of the article and review difficult words and phrases with the class. Look for these problem areas:

- If students are reading slowly, word-by-word, or otherwise struggling with the text, engage students in "echo reading." Have students track the text as you read a passage fluently and with expression. Then, have students read the passage back.
- If students have difficulty with the word *desertification* (p. 755), remind them to use context clues. Point out that if they read the next sentence (*Decades of overgrazing and drought have converted this land into a near desert*), it describes what *desertification* is.

Synthesize: Make Generalizations

1. Remind students to synthesize information from the article and the atlas entry as they read.
2. **Ask:** Why did the Tuaregs revolt?
   Answer: The Tuaregs are a minority and felt that the government neglected them.
3. Tell students that the Paris-Dakar auto rally consists of cars racing from Europe to Dakar, the capital of Senegal. Competitors travel more than 5,700 miles in hot desert conditions, navigating over poor or nonexistent roads.
4. **Ask** students how Tuaregs are changing their ways of living.
   Answer: Some Tuaregs are moving from the desert to Timbuktu, while others are staying in the desert and moving back and forth between small villages.
5. Guide students to make a generalization about how climate affects people's way of life. *(When climate conditions change in a region, people adapt the way they live there.)*

Reflecting on the Reading Skill

Have students think about the information they learned about Mali. **Ask** them what was most helpful in enabling them to make generalizations.
Possible response: Students may say that the details in the article helped them use their knowledge of Mali from the atlas entry to make a generalization about the way cultural changes may occur based on changes in climate or living conditions.

Arab Berbers, ancestors of the Tuaregs, first arrived here 900 years ago. But with only 500,000 of Mali's 8.9 million people, the Tuareg have long felt neglected. In the early 1990s, they revolted against the government. The conflict ended in 1996 with the nomads earning greater representation in both the government and the army. Most of the 150,000 Tuaregs who fled to neighboring countries to escape the fighting are now back in Mali.

This information builds on information given about Tuaregs on p. 754.

Paris-Dakar. Abdou Ag Alhassane used to live in the desert, herding animals and making traditional swords for slaughtering camels. As camels dwindled in number, he moved to Timbuktu. He still makes swords but only to sell to tourists. Business is good when the Paris-Dakar auto rally passes through town, he says, but usually there are few travelers adventurous enough to make the eight-hour desert drive from the town of Douentza to Timbuktu. "If I had animals tonight, I would leave for the desert tomorrow," he says.

You can connect this text to the map on p. 753 by finding the locations mentioned (Douentza and Timbuktu (Tombouctou)) and tracing the route between them.

Other Tuaregs are determined to live out their days in the desert. In a dried-out creek at the foot of the Farach escarpment, 50 miles west of Timbuktu, a desert chieftain named Mohamed Aly Ag Moctar resides in a camp with his wife and two children. Seven other children have moved to towns. The heat in the camp reaches a staggering 120 degrees; flies are everywhere. But there are compensations. "Life here is simple," the 61-year-old chief says. "I don't need a watch."

As the traditional leader of 160,000 Tuaregs, Moctar mediates everything from family quarrels to political issues. These days, the most common dispute is over the use of pastoral wells—whose animals get to drink. "If we have animals, we can stay out here," the chief says. "If we have no animals, it is our obligation to go to town."

Instead of erecting ad-hoc camps every three months, some Tuaregs have begun rotating between a handful of semipermanent desert villages, all built around one well. The men may move their herds for up to a month before returning to one of the villages, where the women generally stay put. "This is a new tendency," says Sidebe Draman, an engineer with CARE, an American aid organization that helps rebuild pastoral wells in the region. Draman believes it could evolve into a new kind of nomadism.

Sipping tea in the sand of Farach, Chief Moctar says the Tuareg realize that they must change to survive. "I want to die here in the Sahara," he says. "But I don't want our way of life to die with me."

Does all communication serve a positive purpose?
What purpose might the author have in writing this article about the Tuaregs? Why do you think so?

ASSESS/EXTEND

Answers

Does all communication serve a positive purpose?

Possible response: The author might want to bring the world's attention to the Tuaregs' situation so that others can get involved and help. Students may say they think so because the author mentions that there will be wars and famines resulting from the scarcity of resources.

Vocabulary Development

Cross-Curricular Vocabulary: Social Studies

Guide students to understand the meaning of the following words that are used in "Will All the Blue Men End Up in Timbuktu?":

ad-hoc: set up for a particular purpose

compensations: things that make up for undesirable situations or losses

dwindled: became smaller or less numerous

escarpment: a steep cliff between two different levels of elevation

mediates: acts as a go-between in a dispute in order to bring about a solution

pastoral: having to do with shepherds or herdsmen

Test Practice: Informational Texts

Comparing Informational Texts

(a) Compare and contrast the types of details and information found in the atlas entry and the magazine article. **(b) Synthesize** the texts. Choose a specific topic and use details and information from both the atlas entry and the magazine article to **make a generalization** about that topic.

Timed Writing

Write a Comparison-and-Contrast Essay

Format
The prompt directs you to write an essay. Therefore, be sure your response includes an introduction, several supporting paragraphs, and a conclusion.

Write an essay comparing and contrasting the perspectives of the atlas entry and the magazine article. What effect does the perspective of each text have on the types of details included and the way information is presented? Support your response with examples from the texts. (35 minutes)

Academic Vocabulary
When you *support* your response, you use details and examples to show that your ideas are reasonable and correct.

5-Minute Planner

Complete these steps before you begin to write:

1. Read the prompt carefully and completely. Look for key words that will help you understand the assignment.
2. Review the atlas entry and the magazine article to identify each author's **perspective,** or point of view.
3. Synthesize the texts, by considering and making notes about the similarities and differences between the perspectives.
4. Consider and make notes about how the perspective of each text affects the content and the way information is presented. **TIP** Note any **discrepancies,** or inconsistencies, between the texts. Consider how different perspectives may explain discrepancies in information.
5. Refer to your notes as you draft your essay.

Extend the Lesson

Connecting to the Students' World

To give students more practice with atlases and magazine articles and to help them apply the lesson to their own world, divide students into small groups. Have each group choose a country. Have group members do research to find a magazine article about a subject that relates to their country. Then, have students make a plan for a two-page atlas entry. Tell students to include a map with a key on the first page. For the second page, tell them to be sure to choose subtopics that have a connection to the subject of their magazine article. Have them first plan the layout and the graphics. Then, tell them to write the information they will include in each subtopic. Suggest to students that they create their final versions on a computer so they can take advantage of graphics and text features. Allow time for students to share their atlas entries and magazine articles with the class.

Comparing Informational Texts

(a) Possible response: Both the atlas entry and the magazine article give facts about the climate, the terrain, the people, and the government of Mali. The atlas entry has a map and gives city and town names and population ranges. The magazine article gives details about how the Tuareg people live from day to day and gives examples from individual Tuaregs' lives.

(b) Possible response: The atlas shows the Sahara desert in northern Mali and explains that area is almost rainless. The article describes how the desert has spread into areas that were once grasslands, making it difficult for the nomadic Tuaregs to graze their herds and causing them to move into town. I can make a generalization that people adapt their way of life to changing climate and terrain.

Timed Writing

1. Before students complete the activity, guide them in identifying and analyzing key words and phrases in the prompt, highlighted on the student page.
2. Work with students to draw up guidelines for their essays based on the key words:
   - **Focus** The essay should compare and contrast the perspectives of the atlas entry and the magazine article.
   - **Organization** The essay should compare and contrast how the perspectives of the atlas entry and the magazine article present information. The essay should contain an introduction, several supporting paragraphs, and a conclusion.
   - **Support** The essay should cite specific details from the atlas entry and the magazine article.
   - **Style** The audience is not specified, so a formal style is appropriate.
3. Have students use the 5-Minute Planner to structure their time.
4. Allow students 35 minutes to complete the assignment. Evaluate their work using the guidelines they have developed.

Meeting Your Standards

Students will

1. analyze and respond to theme in poetry and speech.
2. compare the effects of theme in two poems and a speech.
3. write a comparison of themes.

*Log on at **www.PHLitOnline.com** for a detailed lesson plan for Comparing Literary Works.*

❶ Comparing Theme

1. Introduce the skill, using the instruction on the student page.
2. Give students a copy of **Comparing Theme Graphic Organizer B, *Graphic Organizer Transparencies,*** p. 147. Tell them they will fill it in to compare themes as they read.

Think Aloud: Model the Skill

Model a way to compare theme. Say to students:

Suppose I read two poems about love. If the first poem uses words such as *magical* and *thrilling,* this word choice lets me know that the poet's attitude towards love is optimistic, so the theme will reflect this optimistic tone. If the second poem uses words such as *despair* and *regret,* this shows me that the poet has a pessimistic attitude toward love. Although both poems discuss love, I know that the theme of each differs.

❷ Vocabulary

1. Have students say each word aloud.
2. Then, use the word in a sentence that defines the word. Repeat the sentence, now with the word missing, and have the class "fill in the blank" chorally. For more guidance, see the ***Classroom Strategies and Teaching Routines*** card, **Introducing Selection Vocabulary.**

Comparing Literary Works

Hold Fast Your Dreams—and Trust Your Mistakes • All • Also All

❶ Comparing Theme

A **theme** is the essential idea that the author of a literary work conveys. Paying attention to an author's diction, or choice of words, can help a reader grasp the main message that an author wants to convey. Authors use diction, among other aspects of style, to guide readers to their theme. Some authors present a theme by dramatizing the contradictions, conflicts, or complications of life, including the following:

- By having hopes and making plans, people make their lives meaningful—yet if their plans fail, their lives may seem empty.
- People strive for what they desire—yet they may long most intensely for what they have lost or can never have.

By presenting such contradictions or conflicts, writers remind us that life is not just what happens to us. It is also the desires, fears, and joys that define us—even in the face of failure. Each of the authors in this group writes, asks whether our actions add up to something, whether we should strive for success or find peace in ourselves.

Though their general topic is the same, each writer's theme, or insight into that topic, is different. In addition, a writer may use slang, formal language, or another specific choice of words to emphasize his or her particular theme. As you read, use a chart like the one shown to note which specific word choices help you understand the theme.

Key Word / Phrase / Detail	Relationship to Message / Theme

❷ Vocabulary

- **unorthodox** (un or´ thə daks´) *adj.* not traditional (p. 761) ***The detective's methods seem unorthodox, but he solves cases.***
- **idealistic** (ī´dē ə lis´ tik) *adj.* thinking or acting based on how things should be rather than how they are (p. 762) ***Kyle is easily upset with the world because he is idealistic.***
- **lamentation** (lam´ ən tā´ shən) *n.* act of crying out in grief; wailing (p. 764) ***We heard the widow's mournful lamentation.*** *lament v. lamentable adj. lamentably adv.*
- **wither** (with´ ər) *v.* shrivel from loss of moisture (p. 765) ***A tree's leaves will wither without water.*** *withering v. withered adj.*

PHLit Online! www.PHLitOnline.com

- Vocabulary flashcards
- Interactive journals
- More about the authors
- Selection audio
- Interactive graphic organizers

Vocabulary Development

Vocabulary Knowledge Rating

Create a **Vocabulary Knowledge Rating Chart** (***Professional Development Guidebook,*** p. 33) for this selection. Include the selection vocabulary and the Big Question word that appears in the Writing About the Big Question sentence starter on the next page. (The Big Question vocabulary is introduced on pp. 626–627.)

Give students a copy of the chart. Read the words aloud, and have students mark their rating in the Before Reading column. Urge them to be alert to these words as they read and discuss the selection.

Tally how many students think they know a word to gauge how much instruction to provide. As students read and discuss the selection, point out the words and their context.

PHLit Online! **Vocabulary Central,** featuring tools, activities, and songs for studying vocabulary, is available at **www.PHLitOnline.com.**

Does all *communication* serve a positive purpose?

❸ Writing About the Big Question

In these selections, the speaker communicates a positive or negative vision for the future. Use this sentence starter to develop your ideas.

I think it is (important / not important) to make a positive **connection** to the future because ____________.

Meet the Authors

Billy Joel (b. 1949)

Author of "Hold Fast Your Dreams—and Trust Your Mistakes" (p. 760)

Billy Joel grew up on Long Island, in the suburbs of New York City. He studied classical music as a child, but it was a performance by the Beatles that convinced him to become a professional musician. One of the most successful artists of his generation, Joel has sold more than 100 million records worldwide. He was inducted into the Rock and Roll Hall of Fame in 1999.

Bei Dao (b. 1949)

Author of "All" (p. 764)

In the 1970s, Bei Dao's poems became rallying cries for those Chinese who wanted their country to become more democratic. Since 1989, when government troops gunned down protesters in Tiananmen Square in Beijing, China's capital, Bei Dao has lived abroad.

Shu Ting (b. 1952)

Author of "Also All" (p. 765)

As a teenager, Shu Ting (the pen name of Gong Peiyu) was forced by political events in China to leave Beijing, the capital, and live in a small peasant village. She gained fame as a poet while still in her twenties, winning China's National Poetry Award in 1981 and 1983.

Teaching Resources

The following resources can be used to enrich, extend, or differentiate the instruction.

- All *Unit 4 Resources,* pp. 205–212
- All *Graphic Organizer Transparencies,* pp. 146–149
- All **Enriched Online Student Edition**

PHLit Online! All resources, including print and audio, are available at **www.PHLitOnline.com.**

Daily Bellringer

For each class during which you will teach this selection, have students complete one of the five Sentence Combining activities for Week 24 in the *Daily Bellringer Activities* booklet.

❸ Writing About the Big Question

1. Review the assignment with the class.
2. Guide students in a discussion about whether they believe the world will be a better or worse place in the future.
3. Have students complete the sentence starter. Review responses as a class. (**Possible response:** I think it is important to make a positive connection to the future because it gives people hope.)
4. Remind students that their answers will help them think about the Big Question, "Does all communication serve a positive purpose?"

Concept Connector

Students will return to the sentence starter after they have finished reading the selections.

Multidraft Reading

To assist struggling readers and to deepen reading for all, apply multidraft reading protocols. For each reading, have students set the purpose intended:

- **First reading**—literal comprehension: answering the Reading Check questions
- **Second reading**—application of skills: responding to the side-column notes
- **Third reading**—interpretation: answering the end-of-selection questions

For more guidance, refer to the *Classroom Strategies and Teaching Routines* card on multidraft reading.

PHLit Online!

For more about the authors, practice with the selection vocabulary, and more background, go online at **www.PHLitOnline.com.**

❶ Background

When a student graduates from high school or college, he or she participates in a ceremony called a *commencement,* which literally means "a beginning." Though graduation may not seem like a beginning, but rather, an end to years of studying, it is the threshold to the next step—whatever that step may be. During these ceremonies, a commencement speaker, often a notable person who has graduated from that particular institution, shares his or her experiences, advice, and vision of the world to help students grasp the significance of this step.

❷ Activating Prior Knowledge

Play one of Billy Joel's hit songs for the class. Ask students whether they have heard the song before and if they can identify the artist. Then, ask what kind of advice they would expect a musician to give young adults.

Concept Connector →

Students will return to their responses once they have read the selection.

❸ About the Selection

Professional musician Billy Joel made a commencement speech at Fairfield University in Connecticut in 1991. In his speech, Joel shared some life experiences and his thoughts about what it means to become an adult.

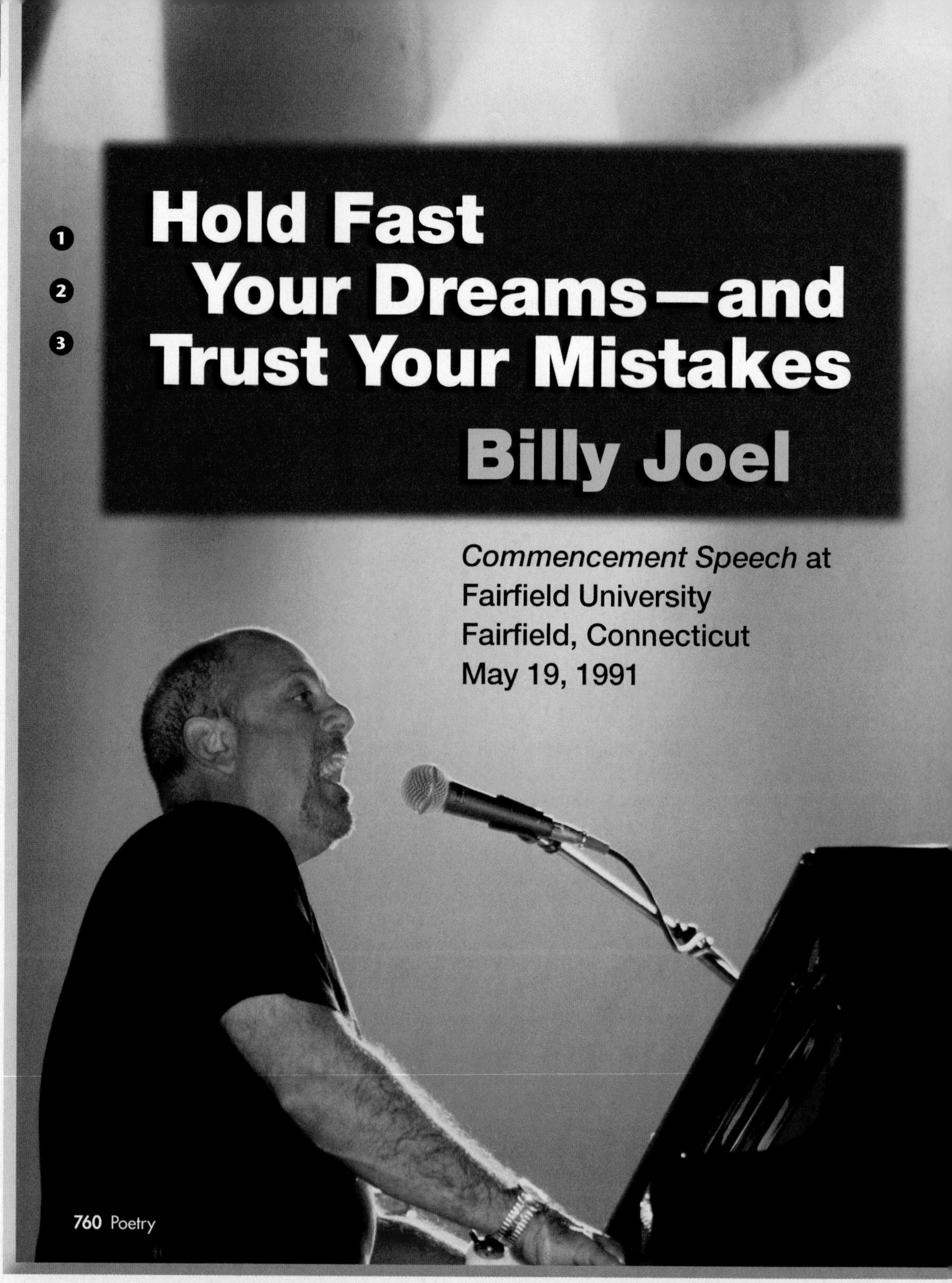

❶ ❷ ❸

Hold Fast Your Dreams—and Trust Your Mistakes

Billy Joel

Commencement Speech at
Fairfield University
Fairfield, Connecticut
May 19, 1991

Think Aloud

Author's Purpose

Model a way of determining the author's purpose, using this "think aloud." Say to students:

> When I want to identify an author's purpose in a selection, I first look at the type of writing it is. For example, "Hold Fast Your Dreams—and Trust Your Mistakes" is a commencement speech. I know that commencement speeches are usually given at graduation to motivate the graduates by having a successful person share his or her own experiences and lessons they have learned. So, based on my knowledge of the selection type, I think the author's purpose in this selection is to encourage and inspire graduating students.

4 When I was first asked to speak to the graduating class of Fairfield University, my initial reaction was not too dissimilar to a certain philosophy professor who is a member of the faculty here. I had to ask myself, What makes me qualified to do this? What relevance do I have to the future lives of these young people? After all, I did not even go to college, and I did write a song called "Only the Good Die Young." So, why me?

After meeting with a group of Fairfield students, I realized what I might be able to share with you from my perspective. I have lived what many would consider to be an unorthodox life, but it has always been an interesting one.

It is true that I did not graduate from high school; but like you, I did spend years majoring in my own area of study. I am a graduate of the University of Rock and Roll, Class of 1970. My diploma was a check—a week's worth of wages earned from playing long nights in smoky, crowded clubs in the New York area. Through the years, I have been given platinum albums, Grammys, keys to cities, and many other awards which are considered prestigious in my profession. But the greatest award I have ever received was that check—my diploma—made out to Billy Joel in 1970. This particular check was enough to cover my rent and my expenses. It was also enough to convince me that I no longer needed to work in a factory or be a short-order cook or pump gas or paint houses or do any of the other day jobs I had done in order to make ends meet. That check meant that I was now able to make a living solely by doing

Vocabulary
unorthodox (un or´ thə däks´) *adj.* not traditional

5 **Reading Check**
What does Joel say was his area of study?

4 Connecting to the Big Question

1. Remind students that communication is the conveying of ideas or opinions through speech or written word.
2. Have students read the bracketed passage. Then, **ask** them why Joel feels unqualified to speak to the graduates.
   Answer: Joel feels unqualified to speak to the graduates because he did not attend college.
3. **Ask** students to discuss whether Joel's lack of a college education will prevent him from communicating positively.
   Possible response: No, even though Joel has not attended college, he has learned important lessons through experiencing life.

5 Reading Check

Answer: Joel said his area of study was Rock and Roll.

Differentiated Instruction for Universal Access

Accessibility at a Glance
Use this information to guide your teaching of "Hold Fast Your Dreams—and Trust Your Mistakes."

Language/ Vocabulary	• Difficult vocabulary defined • Grade-appropriate vocabulary
Concept Level	Accessible (Speech offering advice on life.)
Literary Merit	Famous musician (Billy Joel)
Lexile/Length	NP Word Count: 932

PHLit Online!
This selection is available in interactive format in the **Enriched Online Student Edition**, online at **www.PHLitOnline.com**, which includes an interactive graphic organizer.

❻ Literary Analysis

Theme

1. Have students read the bracketed passage.
2. **Ask** students how Joel feels about his twenty-one-year-old self.
   Possible response: Joel thinks highly of his twenty-one-year-old self. He tries to make decisions and behave in ways that would not disappoint the person he was at twenty-one.
3. **Ask** students the first Literary Analysis question: What does Joel's imagined relationship with his twenty-one-year-old self reveal about his lifelong hopes and dreams?
   Possible response: The relationship reveals that Joel continues to strive toward achieving the hopes and dreams he set for himself when he was twenty-one.

❼ Literary Analysis

Theme

1. **Ask** students how the term "foul-up" might convey a different meaning from the word "mistake."
   Possible response: The word "mistake" has a negative connotation, so making a mistake might have a serious outcome. The word "foul-up" is informal, so making a foul-up isn't a big deal.
2. **Ask** students the second Literary Analysis question: What does the use of words "flubs" and "foul-ups" show about Joel's attitude towards mistakes?
   Possible response: Joel's use of informal language, such as "flubs" and "foul-ups", shows that he does not think that making mistakes is a serious matter.

the thing that I loved most—making music. It meant that I had become self-reliant as a musician. I will never forget that day. I consider it to be one of the most important days in my life.

I also remember the twenty-one-year-old Billy Joel and I often wonder what it would be like if we could, somehow, meet each other. Here I am, forty-two, exactly twice his age. What would I think of him? Would I find him to be naive, arrogant, simplistic, crude, noble, hopelessly **idealistic**? Perhaps all of these things. But more important, what would he think of me? Have I fulfilled his dream? Have I created the kind of music he would have wanted to have written? Have I compromised any of his ideals? Have I broken any of the promises I made to him? Have I lost the desire to be the best he could be? Would he be disappointed in me? Would he even like me?

Vocabulary
idealistic (ī´dē ə lis´ tik) *adj.* thinking or acting based on how things should be rather than how they are

Literary Analysis ❻
Theme What does Joel's imagined relationship with his 21-year-old self reveal about his lifelong hopes and dreams?

That twenty-one-year-old has been the biggest pain in the neck I have had to endure in my life. Yet he has had more influence on the work I have done than anyone else for the last twenty-one years. He has been my greatest teacher, my deepest conscience, my toughest editor, and my harshest critic. He has significantly shaped my life. I can say to you today that what you are at this moment in your lives you will always be in your hearts.

When I met with your fellow students, they asked me what is the most powerful lesson I have learned. After eleven years of classical training, I learned to play the piano, but I realized that I was not destined to be another Van Cliburn. I learned to write songs, although what I really wanted to write were symphonies like Beethoven. I have learned to perform, but somehow I knew I would never be able to move like Michael Jackson or sing like Ray Charles.

Literary Analysis ❼
Theme What does the use of words "flubs" and "foul-ups" show about Joel's attitude towards mistakes?"

Out of respect for things that I was never destined to do, I have learned that my strengths are a result of my weaknesses, my success is due to my failures, and my style is directly related to my limitations. You see, the only original things I have ever done have been accidents, mistakes, flubs, foul-ups, and their attendant solutions. I have an inherent talent for stumbling onto something. I am an expert at making bad choices and illogical decisions. I have discovered that after all those years of musical instruction, after all that practice to be perfect, after all that hard work trying to compose the right notes, I am gifted with the knack of hitting exactly the wrong notes at precisely the right time.

Vocabulary Development

Thematic Vocabulary: The Big Question
As students are discussing "Hold Fast Your Dreams—and Trust Your Mistakes," ask them to use the thematic vocabulary presented in Introducing the Big Question, pp. 626–627. You might encourage them with sentence starters like these:

1. The main message that Joel tries to *convey* is . . .
2. If I were asked to *respond* to Joel's message, I would say . . .
3. The *context* of Joel's speech is important because . . .
4. Music can be a form of *self-expression* because . . .

This is the secret of originality. Think about it. You may have learned all there is to know about reproducing the art of someone else, but only you can commit a colossal blunder in your own exquisite style. This is what makes you unique. But then you are faced with solving the problem. This is what makes you inventive. Commit enough blunders and you become an artist. Solve all the problems you have created and they will call you a genius.

I have learned that no matter how successful or proficient or accomplished I might think I am, I am always going to make mistakes. I will always have to face some difficulties. I am always going to have to deal with the possibility of failure, and I will
8 always be able to utilize these things in my work. So I am no longer afraid of becoming lost, because the journey back always reveals to me something new about my life and about my own humanity, and that is, ultimately, good for the artist.

Literary Analysis
Theme Why doesn't Joel fear "becoming lost"?

Critical Thinking

1. **Respond:** What do you think is the most surprising, interesting, or useful thing Joel said in his speech and why?
2. **(a)** What did Billy Joel receive that he felt was his "college diploma"? **(b) Infer:** How did getting it change his life? Explain.
3. **(a) Interpret:** Why do you think Joel says that his younger self has been "the biggest pain in [his] neck"? **(b) Deduce:** Which values do you think the young Joel may have held that his older self may have struggled to fulfill?
4. **(a) Analyze:** In what ways did making mistakes help Billy Joel? **(b) Connect:** Has making a mistake ever helped you? Explain.

THE BIG ?

Does all communication serve a positive purpose?
(a) What positive effects might Joel's speech have on his audience? Explain. **(b)** In what ways could giving this speech serve a positive purpose in Joel's life? Explain.

8 Literary Analysis

Theme

1. **Ask** the Literary Analysis question.
Possible response: Joel does not fear "becoming lost" because he learns from his mistakes. They help him to become a better artist.

Concept Connector

Have students compare their Writing About the Big Question and Activating Prior Knowledge responses with their ideas after reading the selection.

ASSESS

Answers

Critical Thinking

1. Students may say that the most useful thing Joel said was to not be afraid to make mistakes.
2. (a) Joel felt that the first check he received as a performer was his "college diploma." (b) **Possible response:** Getting the check made Joel realize that he could make a living doing what he loved.
3. (a) **Possible response:** He feels he has to meet the goals he set for himself when he was younger. (b) **Possible answer:** He might have valued his independence, which, as he grew older, might have been limited because of music contracts, engagements, and his popularity.
4. (a) **Possible response:** Making mistakes has allowed Joel to find solutions to his problems. (b) Students may say that their mistakes allowed them to strengthen their weaknesses.

THE BIG ? **Does all communication serve a positive purpose?**

(a) **Possible response:** Joel's speech tells his listeners to learn from their mistakes and not to fear them. Because of this listeners might become more self-aware and creative. (b) **Possible response:** Sharing what he has learned in life might motivate Joel to help people in other ways.

Fluency

Have partners take turns reading the first paragraph on page 763 aloud. Circulate to monitor the fluency of students' reading. Take note of the words with which students are having difficulty. Some possibilities are *originality, colossal, exquisite, unique,* and *genius.* Review the difficult words with students. Then, practice echo reading. Read the paragraph aloud fluently and with expression as the students track each word in the text. Have students read the passage back to you with fluency and expression.

PHLit Online!

This selection is available in interactive format in the **Enriched Online Student Edition**, online at **www.PHLitOnline.com**, which includes an interactive graphic organizer.

TEACH

9 Background

Cultural Revolution During China's Cultural Revolution, from 1966–1976, artists were persecuted. After the revolution ended, Chinese writers gained increased literary freedom. This freedom was short-lived, however. By 1989, many Chinese artists, such as Bei Dao, had to flee their homeland to avoid persecution for their democratic affiliations. That year, student-led demonstrations took place in Beijing's Tiananmen Square. On June 4, many demonstrators were killed by armed soldiers.

10 Activating Prior Knowledge

1. Prepare an **Anticipation Guide** (see *Professional Development Guidebook,* pp. 36–38) with the following statements:
   - Even if it seems that you cannot win, it is important to fight for what you believe in.
   - Every cloud has a silver lining.
   - Failure is not an option.
   - You're nobody if you're not famous.
2. Give students the prepared **Anticipation Guide,** and have them mark their responses in the Me column. Have students discuss the statements in groups and mark the guides in the Group column.

Concept Connector →

Students will return to the **Anticipation Guide** after completing the poems.

11 About the Selections

"All" and "Also All" offer contrasting insights into life's struggles and the fate of our future.

12 Literary Analysis
Theme

1. Remind students that theme is an insight about life that is conveyed through writing.
2. **Ask** the Literary Analysis question.
   Answer: Line 8 suggests that one person can never thoroughly know another, so no one can ever be fully trusted.

9 10 11

All

Bei Dao

translated by
Donald Finkel and Xueliang Chen

All is fated,
all cloudy,

all an endless beginning,
all a search for what vanishes,

all joys grave,
all griefs tearless,

every speech a repetition,
every meeting a first encounter,

all love buried in the heart,
all history prisoned in a dream,

all hope hedged with doubt,
all faith drowned in lamentation.

Every explosion heralds an instant of stillness,
every death reverberates forever.

Literary Analysis
Theme What doubt about people's ability to trust one another is implied in line 8? 12

Vocabulary
lamentation
(lam′ ən tā′ shən) *n.* act of crying out in grief; wailing

Vocabulary Development

Selection Vocabulary Reinforcement
To reinforce and assess students' comprehension of selection vocabulary words, give them the following sentences. For each item, have students tell whether the vocabulary word is used correctly and explain their answer.

1. Because of unseasonably heavy rains, our plants began to *wither,* and we feared we would lose the entire crop.
   Answer: No, *wither* is not used correctly. Heavy rain would not cause plants to dry out from loss of moisture.
2. As the flames raced across their ripening fields, the villagers broke into cries of woe and *lamentation.*
   Answer: Yes, *lamentation* is used correctly. Expressing grief is an appropriate response to a significant loss.

Also All

Shu Ting

In answer to Bei Dao's "All"

Background Bei Dao and Shu Ting both belonged to a group of Chinese writers known as the Misty Poets. Influenced by Western poets and breaking with Chinese tradition, the Misty Poets used vivid imagery and expressed strong personal emotions. By speaking up for individual feelings, they expressed a quiet opposition to the government of China. In "Also All," Shu Ting answers Bei Dao's poem "All."

Not all trees are felled by storms.
Not every seed finds barren soil.
14 Not all the wings of dream are broken,
nor is all affection doomed
to **wither** in a desolate heart.

13 ▲ **Critical Viewing**
This photograph shows a lone protester confronting a tank in China. Which poem do you think the image illustrates best? Explain. **[Apply]**

Vocabulary
wither (wi*th*′ər) *v.* shrivel from loss of moisture

13 Critical Viewing

Possible responses: Students may say that it belongs with "All" because the lone protester's efforts seem futile. Others may say that the protester is effective in stopping the tank and therefore represents the hope expressed in "Also All."

Explain to students that this famous photograph, titled "The Unknown Rebel" and taken by Associated Press photographer Jeff Widener, depicts an unarmed Tiananmen Square (1989) protester who temporarily stopped a column of tanks.

14 The Big Question: Connecting to the Big Question

1. Draw students' attention to the title "Also All" and to the first word in each line of the poem.
   Ask: With what word do many of the lines in "Also All" begin?
   Answer: In "Also All," many of the lines begin with the word *not*.
2. Then, **ask** students to explain whether the title "Also All" and the repetition of the word *not* seem contradictory.
   Possible response: The title "Also All" has a positive connotation. At first glance, the repetition of *not* may seem negative; however, the word *not* takes on a positive connotation when Shu Ting uses it to refute the negative situations she describes, further strengthening the positive impact of her poem, in contrast to Bei Dao's perspective.

Differentiated Instruction for Universal Access

Accessibility at a Glance
Use this information to guide your teaching of the two poems.

Language/Vocabulary	• Difficult vocabulary defined • Grade-appropriate vocabulary	
Concept Level	Challenging (abstract concepts: resignation, hope, success)	
Literary Merit	Cross-cultural experience (Bei Dao and Shu Ting)	
Lexile/Length	NP	Word Count: 63; 142

PHLit Online!
This selection is available in interactive format in the **Enriched Online Student Edition**, online at **www.PHLitOnline.com**, which includes an interactive graphic organizer.

Concept Connector

Have students compare their Writing About the Big Question and **Anticipation Guide** responses with their ideas after reading the selection.

ASSESS

Answers

Critical Thinking

1. Students may choose "Also All" because it is inspiring.
2. (a) The speaker says that all joys are "grave" and all hope is "hedged with doubt."
(b) **Possible response:** The statements suggest that the speaker has a negative view of life.
3. (a) She says, "Not all trees are felled by storms." (b) **Possible response:** Her viewpoint is optimistic because she believes there is reason to have hope for the future. (c) **Possible response:** The last two lines indicate that people must continue to hope, even when it seems difficult to do so.
4. (a) "Also All" replies with an optimistic worldview. Ting pointedly responds to Dao's repetition of "all" with "not all." (b) **Possible response:** The speaker of "All" might repeat the line that "all hope [is] hedged with doubt."

Does all communication serve a positive purpose?

(a) **Possible response:** Dao has a pessimistic and cynical attitude about life and what the future may bring. (b) **Possible response:** Ting is optimistic about the present and hopeful about the future. (c) **Possible response:** Bei Dao's poem served a positive purpose because it inspired Shu Ting to respond to it with a positive and hopeful poem.

No, not all is as you say.

Not all flames consume themselves,
14 shedding no light on other lives.
Not all stars announce the night
and never dawn. Not every song
will drift past every ear and heart.

No, not all is as you say.

Not every cry for help is silenced,
nor every loss beyond recall.
Not every chasm spells disaster.
Not only the weak will be brought to their knees,
nor every soul be trodden under.

It won't all end in tears and blood.
Today is heavy with tomorrow—
the future was planted yesterday.
Hope is a burden all of us shoulder
though we might stumble under the load.

Critical Thinking

1. **Respond:** Would you rather display "All" or "Also All" on a poster in your classroom? Why?
2. **(a)** What does the speaker in "All" say about "all joys" and about "all hope"? **(b) Infer:** What do these statements suggest about the speaker's view of life?
3. **(a)** What does the speaker in "Also All" point out about the effect of a storm on trees? **(b) Infer:** Is her viewpoint basically optimistic or pessimistic? Support your answer. **(c) Interpret:** According to the last two lines of "Also All," what responsibility do people have to others?
4. **(a) Connect:** In what way does "Also All" answer the speaker's points in "All"? **(b) Speculate:** How might the speaker in "All" answer the point in the last two lines of "Also All"?

Does all communication serve a positive purpose? **(a)** What is Bei Dao's attitude about life and what the future may bring? **(b)** What is Shu Ting's attitude about the present and the future? **(c)** Do both Bei Dao's and Shu Ting's poems serve a positive purpose? Explain.

Vocabulary Development

Vocabulary Knowledge Rating

When students have completed reading and discussing "Hold Fast Your Dreams—and Trust Your Mistakes," "All," and "Also All," have them take out their **Vocabulary Knowledge Rating Chart.** Read the words aloud once more, and have students rate their knowledge of words again in the After Reading column. Clarify any words that are still problematic. Have students write their own definition and example or sentence in the appropriate column. Then, have students complete the Vocabulary Practice activities on the next page. Encourage them to use the words in further discussion and written work about these selections. Remind students that they will be accountable for these words on the **Selection Test** (***Unit 4 Resources,*** pp. 216–218 or pp. 219–221).

After You Read

Hold Fast Your Dreams—and Trust Your Mistakes • All • Also All

Comparing Theme

1. **(a)** Summarize the central insights in "Hold Fast Your Dreams—and Trust Your Mistakes." **(b)** Would you view the central insights differently if Joel had used more formal diction? Why or why not?
2. **(a)** Summarize the insights into life expressed in "All" and "Also All." **(b)** List three phrases in each poem that help reveal these insights.
3. What reaction might the speaker in "All" have to Joel's graduation speech? Support your answer with details from the selections.
4. **(a)** The following diagram lists four possible responses to disappointment and failure. In your own copy of the diagram, list details from the selections that reflect these responses. **(b)** Use your analysis to compare the insights into success and failure in these selections.

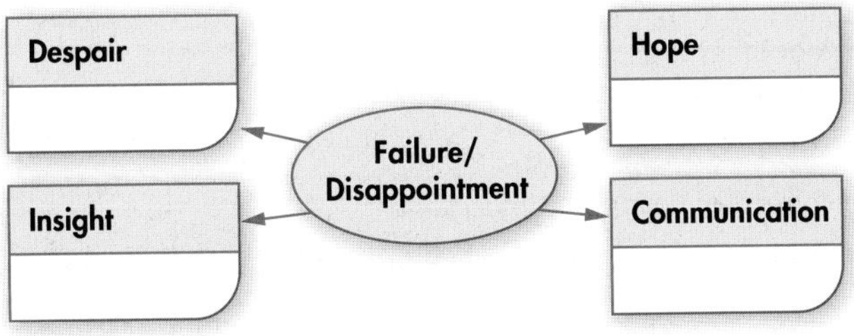

Writing to Compare Theme

In an essay, compare each writer's insights about success. Consider how each writer's style conveys this message. Use these questions:

- What is the attitude of each author toward hope and success?
- How does each writer's word choice help reveal this attitude?
- Which details in each selection support its theme most strongly?

To continue your response, write a poem that expresses your views about these issues.

Vocabulary

Practice In an **analogy,** the relationship between the second pair of words should be the same as the relationship between the first pair. Complete each analogy with a word from the vocabulary list on page 758.

1. build : destroy :: bloom : ______________
2. mature : youthful :: realistic : ______________
3. tasty : delicious :: nontraditional : ______________
4. parade : cheering :: funeral : ______________

Assessment Resources

Unit 4 Resources

L1 L2 EL **Selection Test A,** pp. 216–218. Administer **Selection Test A** to less advanced students and English learners.

L3 L4 **Selection Test B,** pp. 219–221. Administer **Selection Test B** to on-level and more advanced students.

L3 L4 **Open-Book Test,** pp. 213–215. As an alternative, give the **Open-Book Test.**

All **Customizable Test Bank**

All **Self-tests**
Students may prepare for the **Selection Test** by taking the **Self-test** online.

PHLit Online! All assessment resources are available at **www.PHLitOnline.com.**

ASSESS

Answers

Comparing Theme

1. (a) **Possible response:** Making mistakes is an integral part of becoming successful.
(b) **Possible response:** No, because his message would be the same.
2. (a) In "All," disappointment is inevitable and hope is futile. In "Also All," loss is uncertain and hope is vital to human life.
(b) **Possible responses:** "All": "All is fated," "all joys grave," and "all faith drowned in lamentation." "Also All": "Not all the wings of dream are broken," "Not every cry for help is silenced," and "It won't all end in tears and blood."
3. The speaker would disagree. The speaker has a fatalistic view about life and says "all faith drowned in lamentation."
4. (a) **Possible response: Despair:** "all joys grave" from "All." **Hope:** "Not every cry for help is silenced" from "Also All." **Insight:** "I am no longer afraid of becoming lost . . ." from "Hold Fast Your Dreams—and Trust Your Mistakes." **Communication:** "No, not all is as you say." (b) In Joel's speech, success is possible if you learn from your mistakes. In "All," success is impossible. In "Also All," success is possible, and failure is overcome only by trying again.

Other sample answers appear in ***Graphic Organizer Transparencies,*** **Comparing Theme Graphic Organizer A (After You Read),** p. 148, and in the **Additional Answers** section.

Writing to Compare Theme

1. Review the assignment criteria with students.
2. Encourage them to include the expressive vocabulary words.

Six Traits Focus

✔	Ideas	✔	Word Choice
✔	Organization		Sentence Fluency
	Voice		Conventions

Vocabulary

1. wither
2. idealistic
3. unorthodox
4. lamentation

PRETEACH

Meeting Your Standards

Students will

1. write a an analytic response to literature.
2. learn the elements of an analytic essay
3. use writing strategies to generate ideas and to plan, organize, evaluate, and revise the response.
4. apply grammar and revision skills.

Introducing the Writing Assignment

Review the assignment and the criteria, using the instruction on the student page.

Connecting to Real-Life Writing

Point out that elements of an analytic response to literature will be expected after almost any reading assignment. In college, many disciplines, including social work, psychology, communications, and business require analytical evaluation of field-specific literature.

Cornelius Eady on Analytic Responses to Literature

Show students Segment 3 on Cornelius Eady on ***See It!*** **DVD** or from this page in the **Enriched Online Student Edition**, at **www.PHLitOnline.com.**

Writing Workshop
Work in Progress

If students have done the Work-in-Progress assignments on pp. 731 and 749, suggest that they examine their recorded ideas as they begin prewriting. They may wish to develop these ideas in an analytic response to literature.

OES Online Essay Scorer

A writing prompt for this mode of writing can be found on the *PH Essay Scorer* at **www.PHLitOnline.com.**

Writing Workshop

Analytic Response to Literature

Defining the Form An analytic response to literature presents a reader's critical response to an entire literary work or focuses on a specific aspect. You might use elements of this type of writing in book reviews, annotated bibliographies, articles, and readers' journals.

Assignment Write an analytic response to a favorite piece of literature. You might analyze a poem, a play, a story, or a screenplay. Include these elements:

- ✔ a *thesis statement* that presents your personal response to the work being analyzed
- ✔ *references* to specific literary aspects of the work, such as theme or style
- ✔ *evidence* from the literary work or other texts, including accurate quotations, to support your opinions
- ✔ effective and logical *organization*
- ✔ error-free grammar, including *correct formation of comparisons*

To preview the criteria on which your analytic response to literature may be judged, see the rubric on page 775.

Writing Workshop: *Work in Progress*

If you have completed the Work in Progress assignments on pages 731 and 749, you already have many ideas to use in your analytic response to literature. Work with these ideas, or explore a new idea as you complete the Writing Workshop.

Teaching Resources

The following resources can be used to enrich or extend the instruction.

- All *Unit 4 Resources*
  Writing Workshop, pp. 222–223
- All *Professional Development Guidebook*
  Rubric for Self-Assessment: Analytic Response to Literature, pp. 224–225
- All *Graphic Organizer Transparencies*
  Rubric for Self-Assessment: Analytic Response to Literature, p. 150
- All *See It!* **DVD**
  Cornelius Eady, Segments 3 and 4

PHLit Online! All resources, including print and video, are available at **www.PHLitOnline.com.**

Prewriting Strategies

Use these strategies to find a topic:

Hold a group discussion. With a small group, list the literary works that have provoked strong feelings in you. For each item, briefly describe any memorable details about the work or your experience reading it. Review your ideas and choose one work as your topic.

Ask your own questions. Decide which aspects of the literary work interested you, bothered you, or raised questions. For example, the actions or personality of one character may have seemed ambiguous or confusing. The complexity of the plot and characters may cause you to wonder how each character's action affects the others and how the actions of a particular character affect the unfolding of the plot. Jot down two or three questions that you hope to answer by writing your analytical response.

PHLit Online!
www.PHLitOnline.com
- Author video: Writing Process
- Author video: Rewards of Writing

Example Questions
In *Julius Caesar*, why do Antony and Cassius meet different fates?
How does the death of Brutus's wife affect the plot?
Why does "Contents of the Dead Man's Pocket" end as it does?

Consider your audience. Identify your audience and assess their knowledge of your topic. If you need to cover subjects that are unfamiliar to your readers, plan to include details that will help them understand. Use a chart like the one shown to plan your response.

My Topic and Audience
Topic: Tennyson's Kraken and the giant squid
Audience: classmates
What they know: They are familiar with the poem "The Kraken" because we read it in class.
What they do not know: They may not be familiar with giant squid, the real sea creatures that might have inspired the legend.

Go back to the source. Find the information you need by skimming the work for details, examples, and passages that relate to your topic. Write each detail or quotation on a separate index card. Then, organize the cards into general categories. For example, you might group together all the cards containing details about one character.

Understanding by Design

Clarifying Expected Outcomes: Using Rubrics

- Before students begin work on this assignment, have them preview the Rubric for Self-Assessment (p. 775) to learn what qualities their analytic responses to literature must have. A copy of this rubric appears in ***Graphic Organizer Transparencies,*** p. 150.
- Review the criteria in the rubric with the class. Before students use the rubric to assess their writing, work with them to rate the Student Model (p. 774) using the rubric.
- If you wish to assess students' analytic responses to literature essays with either a 4-point or a 6-point scoring rubric, see ***Professional Development Guidebook,*** pp. 224–225.

TEACH

Prewriting Strategies

1. Introduce the Prewriting Strategies, using the instruction on the student page.
2. Have students apply the strategies to choose a topic.

Teaching the Strategies

1. Have volunteers suggest categories to analyze, such as characters, plot, dialogue, or theme.
2. Tell students to assume that the reader has read the work but provide details that will lead to a new understanding of it.
3. Have students record details, examples, and passages on separate index cards that can be used to organize their essays.

Think Aloud: Model Asking Your Own Questions

Model the strategy, using this "think aloud." Say to students:

I read *Romeo and Juliet,* and asked myself, *What would have happened if one lover had survived?* To answer, I need to consider the context of the play—the feud between the Montagues and Capulets—and the role of fate. As I gather evidence from the play, I can evaluate whether the tragedy was necessary.

Six Traits Focus

✔	Ideas		Word Choice
✔	Organization		Sentence Fluency
	Voice		Conventions

WG Writing and Grammar, Grade 10

Students will find additional instruction on prewriting for an analytic response to literature essay in Chapter 13, Section 2.

Writing and Grammar Online Interactive Textbook at www.pearsonsuccessnet.com.

Students can use the following tools as they complete their analytic response to literature essay:

Polish Your Paragraphs (Chapter 13, Section 4)

Drafting Strategies

1. Introduce the Drafting Strategies, using the instruction on the student page.
2. Have students apply the strategies as they draft.

Teaching the Strategies

1. Explain that an analytic essay is similar to a persuasive essay because the writer must convince the reader of a particular opinion.
2. In only one sentence, have students tell partners the main arguments of their essays. They can revise their sentences for use as thesis statements.
3. Remind students that each idea in an essay should relate to the thesis.
4. Tell students that the conclusion should not only summarize the thesis and main arguments but should also tell why they are important.
5. Remind students that using textual information in a variety of ways will make their essays more interesting to read.

Think Aloud: Model Using Precise Language

Use the following "think aloud" to model using strong, precise language in an essay. Say to students:

To convince readers of my analysis, I need to show that I am confident in my ideas. Consider my statement "I think maybe Rose is a bit paralyzed by fear." The phrase "I think" makes this statement an opinion. Without it, readers can focus more on my argument and evidence instead. "Maybe" and "a bit" show uncertainty about my argument, making it weaker. If I delete these words, my revised statement declares, "Rose is paralyzed by fear." Now I sound confident and convincing.

Six Traits Focus

✔	Ideas	✔	Word Choice
✔	Organization		Sentence Fluency
✔	Voice		Conventions

WG Writing and Grammar, Grade 10

Students will find additional instruction on drafting an analytic response to literature essay in Chapter 13, Section 3.

Drafting Strategies

Write a thesis statement. Review your notes and consider the main point you want to make about the literary work. Write a statement that expresses that point. Include this thesis in your introduction and use it to direct the rest of your essay.

Organize your response. A compelling response to literature can be organized into three parts: the introduction; the body, in which you analyze key elements and support with examples; and the conclusion, in which you summarize and tell readers why your ideas are important. Each part should relate directly to your thesis.

Use information from the text in various ways. For every major idea in your essay, provide evidence from the literary work or another relevant source. Consider these options:

- Use **exact quotations** to show a character's personality, a poet's use of imagery, or a writer's style. Identify all quotations clearly and use quotation marks.
- Use **paraphrases**—your own restatement of ideas—in the text to clarify a conflict, to present a writer's theme, or to include key concepts. Be sure your paraphrase accurately reflects the original text and that you cite sources for any ideas that are not your own.
- Use **summaries** to provide an overview of a writer's opinion or to explain a series of events. However, do not use summaries to fill up pages with material that is not relevant to your thesis.

Using Information From the Text

Exact quotation	"Brutus. Into what dangers would you lead me, Cassius, That you would have me seek into myself For that which is not in me?" *(Julius Caesar, Act I, sc. ii, ll. 63–65)*
Paraphrase	What dangerous situation are you leading me into, Cassius, by telling me I have greatness in me when I do not?
Summary	Brutus asks Cassius why Cassius is leading him into a dangerous situation by flattering him.

Whatever format you use for supporting your ideas, use transitional words and phrases to explain the link between the literature and your thesis.

Use strong, precise language. As you draft, choose vivid and exact language. Avoid the use of general or vague statements that will not illuminate your point of view.

Strategies for Test Taking

Tell students that when they respond to a test prompt on literary elements such as character and theme, they should read the question carefully, looking for words such as *analyze, discuss, draw conclusions, identify, compare,* and so on. Students should form their essays in direct response to such words.

Cornelius Eady

On Writing Poetry About Music

In my poem "Thelonious Monk"—named for the famous jazz composer and pianist—I was finding a way of duplicating the playfulness in Monk's music. I also wanted to capture another quality—his music is very rhythmic, but also very hard. It's as if you can hear body language—lots of elbows and knees. He forces you to pay attention to melody in a way you wouldn't ordinarily.

There's a link there in terms of the way poetry operates. Poetry makes you look at details or highlights within language that you wouldn't otherwise catch in other circumstances.

"Writing a poem about a certain song can yield some really wonderful results."
—Cornelius Eady

Professional Model:

from *"Thelonious Monk"*

I know what to do with this math.
Listen to this. It's
Arithmetic, a soundtrack. The motion

I was trying to get at the quality of Monk's form that's like broken-field running in football. Most of the lines are primarily monosyllabic, and I like to end them with hard percussive words like *It's*.

Frozen in these lampposts, it
Can be sung. I can lift away
Its logic, make it spin

These lines came out of a story someone told me about Monk. He said he'd seen Monk go up to a lamppost and listen to it, and then Monk went home and tried to play the sound he heard in the lamppost.

Like an orbital satellite, find
Gambling's true pitch.
It can be *played*:

Adventure, the trying of
Patience, holding back, holding
Up, laying out, stop-time, . . .

I imagined the poem could be Monk saying, "Look, *this* is what I'm up to." I wanted the poem to be representing Monk representing himself.

Cornelius Eady on Writing Poetry About Music

Review the passage on the student page with the class, using Cornelius Eady's comments to deepen students' understanding of the process of analyzing literature.

Teaching From the Professional Model

1. Show students Segment 3 on Cornelius Eady on ***See It!* DVD** or from this page in the **Enriched Online Student Edition** at **www.PHLitOnline.com.** Discuss how the form and language of Eady's poem fit his subject.
2. Play a recording of Monk's music. Explain that Monk was known for his alternating rhythms. Help students see how the line breaks fit the form of jazz. Have a volunteer explain the comparison to "broken-field running" in Eady's comments.
3. Have students experiment with breaking lines in more expected ways, and discuss how that alters the poem.
4. In his comment, Eady uses the word *percussive* to describe *It's* in line 2. Ask students to explain why ending the lines with hard percussive words is fitting.
   Possible response: Ending lines with hard percussive sounds mimics the music Monk plays. *It's,* for example, imitates the hiss of the cymbals in jazz.
5. Eady captures Monk listening to a lamppost for a "soundtrack" that "can be sung." Have students discuss the sounds that might be captured in other objects.
   Possible response: Anything might have its own music, such as metal objects that vibrate. Other objects make noise, such as clothing, leaves, machines, or wind.

Differentiated Instruction for Universal Access

EL Strategy for English Learners

Students may have difficulty interpreting the poem. Write the poem on the board and read it aloud. Use Eady's margin notes to discuss each stanza. Then, discuss the meaning of each line by guiding students to translate it into prose. Write the translation next to the line. Have a student read aloud the entire prose translation of the poem. Finally, have volunteers paraphrase what they think the poem means.

Strategy for Gifted and Talented Students

Challenge students to write their own analytic poems based on the music of their choice. Urge them to include sound devices, as well as rhythm and line breaks, to capture the unique sound of the music. Content, as long as it is appropriate, can be related to the music in any way. Have students read their poems to the class.

PHLit Online!

Enriched Online Student Edition
Show or assign the video at **www.pearsonsuccessnet.com.**

Revising Strategies

1. Introduce the Revising Strategies, using the instruction on the student page.
2. Have students apply the strategies as they revise.

Teaching the Strategies

1. Explain to students that the thesis should be clearly stated in the introduction and then restated in a different way in the conclusion. No other ideas, however, should be repeated.
2. Assign groups based upon the genre of students' analytic responses: poetry, drama, novel, and so on. Have them review the formal terminology of their genres.
3. Offer the following examples of changing nonspecific sentences to specific sentences.

   Nonspecific: The person telling the story sometimes tricks the reader.

   Specific: The narrator is unreliable.

   Nonspecific: Directions say that the bad guy picks up a knife.

   Specific: Stage directions indicate that the villain (or antagonist) picks up a knife.

Think Aloud: Model Relating Details to the Thesis

Model the strategy, using the following "think aloud":

My essay needs to be clearly organized so the reader can easily follow the reasoning that proves my thesis. Each paragraph should express one main idea that relates to my thesis. When I revise, I highlight the main idea in each paragraph. If the main idea doesn't relate to my thesis, I delete the paragraph or revise it. Next, I check each paragraph to make sure its supporting details relate to its main idea. If one doesn't, I delete it, move it to another paragraph, or use it to make a new paragraph. Then, I can organize my paragraphs in a logical order. Completing these steps helps me present a well-supported and logical thesis.

Six Traits Focus

✔	Ideas	✔	Word Choice
✔	Organization	✔	Sentence Fluency
✔	Voice		Conventions

Revising Strategies

Use specific terms. The correct use of formal or specialized terms can help you express shades of meaning and add a sense of serious scholarship to your work. Use a dictionary and/or a thesaurus to locate the words with the precise meaning you want to express. Formal terminology may include literary terms, the names of literary movements, references to periods in history, or place names. Review your use of such terms to make sure they are correct.

Nonspecific: the old system of government

Specific: the ancient Roman republic

Cut excess writing. When revising, one of your most important goals is to delete words, phrases, sentences, and even paragraphs that do not add meaning or depth to your essay. As you review your draft, look for these types of unnecessary material:

- **Repeated Ideas:** Extend important ideas with fresh information, but cut repetitions that add nothing new.
- **Unrelated Details:** Be sure that every detail relates directly to your thesis. Eliminate material that seems off target, or revise to show its relationship to your thesis.
- **Inconsistencies:** Make sure that every sentence and every paragraph clearly relates to those that precede and follow.

Peer Review

Exchange drafts with a partner. Highlight passages that include ineffective repetition, unrelated details, or inconsistent statements. Discuss whether to delete the highlighted material. Then, revise your draft, cutting unnecessary language.

Apply It!

Model: Eliminating Unnecessary Writing

In Act I, scene ii, Cassius shows his careful attention to others' moods and intentions. Cassius tells Brutus that he senses Brutus has something on his mind. ~~Cassius sees that something is bothering Brutus.~~ Brutus assures Cassius that what is troubling him has nothing to do with Cassius, who is one of his good friends. ~~He is not upset with Cassius.~~

This writer deletes repeated ideas to make this paragraph more effective.

Writing and Grammar, Grade 10

Students will find additional instruction on revising an analytic response to literature in Chapter 13, Section 4.

Strategies for Using Technology in Writing

Students with access to the Internet might wish to create Web literary pages to share their responses to literature with others. Most Web pages use a computer language called HTML. Students can learn the basic HTML codes fairly quickly, or they can use Web design software that writes the necessary codes for them. The following elements might be included on Web pages: images, book reviews, lists of favorite authors, and lists of book recommendations.

WRITER'S TOOLBOX

Conventions | Sentence Fluency | Voice | Organization | Word Choice | Ideas

Revising Common Usage Problems

Many students misuse certain words when making comparisons.

Identifying Usage Problems With *like*, *as*, and *as if* When it is not used as a verb (I *like* red), the word *like* is a preposition meaning "similar to" or "such as." The word *like* should not be used in place of *as*, *as if*, or *as though*, which are conjunctions that introduce clauses.

Incorrect: The sand felt *like* it was a warm slipper. (before a clause)
Correct: The sand felt *like* a warm slipper. (before a noun)
Correct: The sand felt *as if* it were a warm slipper. (before a clause)

Prepositional Phrase vs. Clause

A **prepositional phrase** includes a preposition and a noun or pronoun. It has no subject or verb.

like a feather   like a snoring elephant

A **clause** has a subject and a verb.

My friend looked [as if *she* (S) had overslept (V).] (clause)

Identifying Usage Problems With *among* and *between* Use *between* to compare two things. Use *among* to compare three or more things.

Incorrect: The cloud hovered *among* the horizon and infinity.
Correct: The cloud hovered *between* the horizon and infinity.

Incorrect: The sunlight danced *between* the many clouds.
Correct: The sunlight danced *among* the many clouds.

Fixing Usage Problems To revise usage problems with *like, as,* or *as if:*

If you have used *like* to introduce a clause, replace it with the conjunction *as*, *as if*, or *as though*.

To correct usage problems with *among* and *between*, follow these steps:

1. **Identify the number of elements involved in the sentence.**
2. **Use *between* with phrases involving two elements.**
3. **Use *among* with phrases involving three or more elements.**

Grammar in Your Writing
Review two paragraphs of your essay and circle uses of *like, as, as if, between,* or *among.* Revise any incorrect usage.

WG *Prentice Hall Writing and Grammar Connection: Chapter 26, Section 2*

Differentiated Instruction for Universal Access

Strategy for Less Proficient Readers

Tell students that *between* should be followed either by a plural (between classes, between the cushions) or by two elements joined by *and* (between study hall and algebra class, between the curb and the sidewalk).

Point out that when using *between* to present choices or options, writers often make the mistake of using *or* instead of *and.* Help students to see that this phrasing is illogical.

Incorrect: Mark had to choose between missing practice or finishing his paper.
Correct: Mark had to choose between missing practice and finishing his paper.

When using *between* to show a range of dates or time, writers sometimes make the mistake of using *to* instead of *and.*
Incorrect: I will be on vacation between July 1st to July 10th.
Correct: I will be on vacation between July 1st and July 10th.

Revising Common Usage Problems

1. Introduce the grammar skills, using the instruction on the student page.
2. Discuss the examples of common usage problems and the strategies for fixing them.
3. Have students follow the instruction under Grammar in Your Writing to correct errors in their drafts.

Teaching the Grammar Skills

1. Ask volunteers to write and revise sentences with usage problems on the board.
2. In the first set of sample sentences on the student page, have students circle the nouns and underline the clauses.
3. Explain that *between* should be used with more than two elements when all elements are considered individuals, rather than a group.
   - The money was divided *among* the children.
   - There was an agreement *between* the six heirs.
4. Help students see the difference in using *among* and *between* by having them create sentences in which either could be correct and sentences in which only one could be correct.

   Either: We kept the secret *among* us. We kept the secret *between* us.

   Only *between*: He ran *between* two trees.

   Only *among*: He swam *among* many dolphins.
5. Have students work in pairs to create dialogues in which *like, as, as if, as though, among,* and *between* are used incorrectly. Then, have them trade papers and revise. Have them read both versions to the class.

WG Writing and Grammar, Grade 10

Students will find additional instruction on revising common usage problems in Chapter 26, Section 2.

Student Model

Review the Student Model with the class, using the annotations to analyze the writer's successful use of the elements of an analytic response to literature essay.

Teaching From the Student Model

1. Explain to students that the Student Model is a sample, and their own analytic response to literature essays may be longer.
2. **Ask** students to identify the thesis statement.
   Answer: The thesis statement is "No exception to this rule, Shakespeare's Antony and Cassius of *The Tragedy of Julius Caesar* share many characteristics but come to very different ends."
3. Point out that Christopher uses quotes as supporting evidence. **Ask** students to explain how the quotes support the writer's evidence.
   Answer: The quotes reveal Cassius's personality by showing how he speaks and looks.
4. Have students identify the different topics in Christopher's consistent point-by-point organization.
5. Remind students that a good conclusion restates the thesis and may also go beyond the original analysis. **Ask** students what new insight Christopher offers in his conclusion.
   Answer: The differences between the characters determine their respective fates.

Connecting to Real-Life Writing

Explain to students that literary analysis is not limited to English class compositions but also has real-world applications. Many professions, including social work, psychology, science research, and communications, require workers to read articles or essays and analyze their strengths and weaknesses. For example, a scientist may need to write an analytic response to a colleague's essay about a new theory, or a politician may need to analyze an article written by a rival candidate.

Student Model: Christopher Rich, Omaha, Nebraska

Response to *The Tragedy of Julius Caesar*

In all tales, modern or ancient, characters at odds often differ in obvious ways. One may be likable and honest—a natural leader. The other may be unpleasant and sneaky. However, sometimes enemies are actually very similar. No exception to this rule, Shakespeare's Antony and Cassius of *The Tragedy of Julius Caesar* share many characteristics but come to very different ends.

> Christopher includes a clear thesis statement in his introduction.

Marcus Antonius and Caius Cassius, both patricians and warriors, are presented as two of Rome's most noble citizens. Both are seen by plebians as noble and honest, if humanly flawed, men. In truth, they are among the most manipulative characters in the play. Cassius is the first to exploit his power to manipulate, using it to coerce Brutus onto the side of the conspirators. Flattering Brutus, ("I know that virtue to be in you, Brutus, / As well as I do know your outward favor") (I, ii, 90–91) and challenging his honor as a Roman, Cassius wins the support of his brother-in-law. Antony, however, shows his ability in a far less conspicuous way. After the assassination of Caesar in Act III, Antony cleverly manipulates the commoners. His subtle and smooth way of controlling the crowd with a pause in his voice reflects his manipulative ability.

> Christopher accurately quotes significant passages from the text.

Despite their powers of persuasion, these two show great allegiance to their loved ones. Over Caesar's body, in Act III, Scene i, Antony says he is willing to throw his country into civil war. Later, Cassius kills himself when he thinks that his best friend has been killed, taking loyalty to the extreme.

Though people may have many similarities, it is the differences that separate warriors and politicians. Always at the beck and call of the dictator who would be king, Antony is known by the common folk to be a possible successor to the "coronet." Cassius, however, is opposed to Caesar, not only politically but also personally, and is one of Caesar's least favorite people: *"Yon Cassius has a lean and hungry look"* (I, ii, 194). Cassius himself admits to his own dislike of Caesar by telling a story from their youth, in Act I, Scene ii, lines 97–131. It is their differences that determine the eventual fate of the characters.

> A point-by-point plan of organization focuses first on similarities and then moves onto differences.

In the end, the obvious similarities of these characters are not as important as their differences. The fate that each meets—Cassius commits suicide and Antony becomes part of the triumvirate that rules Rome—is determined by how each uses his personality traits.

> In his conclusion, Christopher restates his thesis and provides an insight that takes the analysis further.

Strategies for Test Taking

Tell students that when writing for assessment, it is a good idea to write a brief outline before beginning work on the actual essay. Suggest to students that after reading the prompt, they should begin by formulating a thesis and listing the main arguments beneath it. Then they should make an outline, listing the main arguments in a logical order. To make sure their essays will be organized, they can follow their outlines as they write.

Editing and Proofreading

Review your draft to correct errors in grammar, spelling, and punctuation.

Focus on Spelling: Endings that sound the same or almost the same, such as *-ize*, *-ise*, and *-yze*, can be tricky to spell. Usually, *-ize* is added to another word to make a verb, such as *civilize* or *characterize*. For *-ise* and *-yze*, there are no dependable rules. Memorize the spellings or refer to a dictionary if you are unsure of the spelling.

Publishing and Presenting

Consider one of the following ways to share your writing:

Present your response to a book club. Share your response to literature with members of a book club. Invite a group of students, friends, or family members to read the work of literature you will address. Set a meeting time and give a brief introduction to the work. Then, read your essay aloud. Follow your reading with a general discussion to share ideas and responses. As you discuss the literature and your analysis, be open to the ideas of others rather than simply defending your own.

Publish an online review. Post a literary review on a student or bookstore Web site. Remember to check each site for specific submission requirements. Then, follow the correct procedures to retrieve and reproduce your document across platforms.

WG *Prentice Hall Writing and Grammar Connection: Chapter 13*

Reflecting on Your Writing

Writer's Journal Jot down your answers to this question:

How did writing about the work help you understand it?

Rubric for Self-Assessment

Find evidence in your writing to address each category. Then, use the rating scale to grade your work.

Criteria	Rating Scale (not very — very)
Focus: How clear is your thesis statement?	1 2 3 4 5
Organization: How logical is your organization?	1 2 3 4 5
Support/Elaboration: How effectively do you include evidence from the literary work to support your opinions?	1 2 3 4 5
Style: How precise and vivid is your use of language?	1 2 3 4 5
Conventions: How correct is your grammar, especially your formation of comparisons?	1 2 3 4 5

Differentiated Instruction for Universal Access

Strategy for Less Proficient Readers

Students who have difficulty with spelling and grammar will have varying strengths and weaknesses in these areas. For example, one student might have difficulty determining correct spelling, while another might struggle with correct punctuation. Have students trade papers and proofread for grammar and spelling errors. When they find mistakes, have them explain the correct spelling or usage to their partners.

Strategy for Advanced Students

Advanced students may gain a deeper understanding of spelling and grammar by helping less proficient readers or English language learners. Pair each advanced student with a student experiencing difficulty. Have them work together to proofread both papers. Have lower level readers slowly read each paper aloud while advanced students follow along. When an advanced student identifies an error, partners should stop reading and correct the error with guidance from the advanced student.

Editing and Proofreading

1. Introduce the editing and proofreading focus, using the instruction on the student page.
2. Have students edit and proofread their analytic response to literature essays, correcting grammar, spelling, punctuation, and word choice. Make sure they check for errors of the type noted on the student page.

Teaching the Editing Focus

Encourage students to review their essays a final time to make sure they have used proper terminology.

Six Traits Focus

	Ideas	✔	Word Choice
	Organization	✔	Sentence Fluency
	Voice	✔	Conventions

ASSESS

Publishing and Presenting

1. Help students coordinate a book club meeting by connecting students of similar interests in various classes.
2. If students are preparing to read their essays to a book club, have them practice in pairs. Partners should offer suggestions about delivery.
3. If students publish their work on Web sites, suggest that they share the links to the sites with family members and friends.

Reflecting on Your Writing

Ask students if their opinions of the work changed after analyzing it. Have them explain what changed their opinions.

WG Writing and Grammar, Grade 10

Students will find additional guidelines for editing and proofreading, publishing and presenting, and reflecting on analytic response to literature essays in Chapter 13, Sections 5 and 6.

MONITORING PROGRESS

Think About It

1. Remind students that the Unit Big Question is "Does all communication serve a positive purpose?"
2. Point out that students have read selections in this unit in which communication varied in form and in impact. Remind students to consider what they know about communication from their own experiences as well.
3. Point out that it is important to look at the intention behind communication in order to judge it. Review the Example from Literature shown in the chart. Point out that despite the inherent criticism of a war that takes lives, the poem inspires patriotism.
4. Explain that the Big Question is relevant not only in literature but in other areas as well. For example, Martin Luther King, Jr.'s oratory inspired many people to become involved in the civil rights movement. In contrast, a Ku Klux Klan speech promotes racism by preying on people's fears and prejudices.
5. Review the headings on the chart. Remind students of the importance not only of the "message" but also of the person delivering it. How can the same message delivered by different people have opposite effects? For example, compare the case of an elected official admitting a mistake to the case of his or her opponent calling attention to it.
6. Have students copy and complete the chart shown on the student page. If they have difficulty finding examples from science, suggest these starting points:
   - What scientific issues are controversial (i.e., stem cell research, cloning)?
   - How might an announcement of a "breakthrough" be perceived and communicated by people with different points of view?

   Have volunteers read aloud their completed charts. Invite the class to discuss their examples.

Applying the Big Question

THE BIG ? Does all *communication* serve a positive purpose?

Think About It

Think about what you have read in this unit, and what you know about communication from your other classes and from your own experiences. Copy and complete the chart below to apply what you have learned about the ways communication makes a positive or a negative impact on others. One row has been completed for you.

Example	Message communicated	Who communicates	Positive or negative purpose? Explain	What I learned
From Literature	Men fought and died "In Flanders Fields" during World War I.	Dead soldiers buried in Flanders Fields are the speakers.	Positive. The poem rallies patriotism and also tries to save lives.	Communication can be critical but still have a positive purpose.
From Literature				
From Science				
From Social Studies				
From Real Life				

Teaching Resources

Unit 4 Resources

All **Applying the Big Question,** p. 5

PHLit Online! All print resources are also available at **www.PHLitOnline.com.**

Talk About It

Working with a small group, choose one of the examples in your chart as the basis for a **debate.** Focus on the responses given in the fourth column about whether the purpose of the communication is positive or negative. Have half of the group endorse a positive purpose and the other half argue for a negative purpose. Each group should write a list of reasons supporting its position. Take turns presenting your points. When everyone has given his or her point of view and supporting claims, decide, as a class, which side was most convincing.

Write About It

At the beginning of Unit 4, you wrote a response to the Big Question. Now that you have completed the unit, see how your understanding of the question has deepened. Write a new response in which you discuss whether your initial ideas have changed or been validated.

- ❑ All communication serves a positive purpose.
- ❑ All communication does not serve a positive purpose.
- ❑ My own response: ___________________.

Support your response with at least one example from literature and one example from an additional subject area or your own life. You can draw on your chart for examples. You may complete these sentences to help you form your response.

- In this unit, I read a poem in which someone conveyed information about ___________________. The effect of this communication was ___________________.
- One example of how communication can serve a positive purpose in Science is ___________________.
- One example of how communication can serve a negative purpose in Social Studies is ___________________.
- My communication about ___________________ has had a positive effect because ___________________. My communication about ___________________ did not serve a positive purpose because ___________________.

Challenge What issues does this question still raise for you? How could you continue your exploration?

Big Question Vocabulary

- confusion
- connection
- ☆ context
- ☆ convey
- ☆ discourse
- emotion
- ☆ explanation
- ☆ interact
- ☆ isolation
- language
- ☆ meaning
- ☆ misinterpret
- ☆ respond
- self-expression
- verbal

☆ shows an **Academic Vocabulary** word.

Strategies for Listening and Speaking

Remind students how to organize and prepare for a debate.

For listeners:

- Tell students to be quiet and attentive during the debates and to note arguments that are particularly persuasive. They should be prepared to share these examples with the rest of the class.

For speakers:

- Remind students to prepare arguments that support their positions and persuade others to accept them. Students should also think of arguments that weaken the claims of the opposition.
- Speakers should be prepared to defend their positions. However, they should also note particularly good arguments from the opposing side.

MONITORING PROGRESS

Talk About It

1. Have students complete the assignment, following the instruction on the student page.
2. Review the format of a debate. Encourage students to think of convincing arguments to support their position and to anticipate the other side's arguments.

Write About It

1. Introduce the assignment, using the instruction on the student page.
2. Review the thematic vocabulary with the class (see pp. 2–3).

Teaching Prewriting

1. Suggest that students may have read a selection that changed their opinions of the Big Question.
2. Have students respond to the Big Question, completing the sentences on the student page to guide their thinking. Then refer students to their responses in Introducing the Big Question, pp. 626–627, to see how their thinking may have changed.

Teaching Drafting

1. Have students use their charts or their completed sentences for ideas.
2. Suggest the technique of beginning with an example that illustrates the main idea, stating the main idea, and then following up with supporting details and a conclusion.

Teaching Revising/Editing

1. Remind students to remove information that is not relevant and to add additional details to support their main ideas.
2. After students have revised their drafts, have them reread their edited versions.

Guiding Student Publishing

Students can create a bulletin board display with examples of both negative and positive purposes of communication. Students can add examples throughout the term.

EXTEND/ASSESS

Answers

Meeting Your Standards

Students will

1. understand negative and positive connotations of words.
2. distinguish denotative and connotative meanings of words.

Connotation and Denotation

1. Introduce the skill, using the instruction on the student page.
2. Review the chart.

Think Aloud: Model the Skill

Model how writers use connotation to persuade readers. Say to students:

Say I read of one apartment that is "tiny, bare, and inaccessible," and another that is "cozy, simple, and secluded." The apartments sound very different, but if I examine the denotations of the words, I find that both are small, minimal, and remote. The denotations show the characteristics of the apartments, while the connotations show how the writer feels about those characteristics. *Tiny, bare,* and *inaccessible* all have negative connotations. *Cozy, simple,* and *secluded* all have positive connotations, so I know that the writer dislikes the first apartment and likes the second.

It's important to be aware of both connotations and denotations. A realtor might make the second apartment sound great when it's just as bad as the first apartment!

Practice A

Sample answers:

1. shack
2. reckless
3. smirk
4. glared
5. feuding
6. stamped

Vocabulary Workshop

Connotation and Denotation

A word's **denotation** is its dictionary meaning, independent of other associations that the word may have. In contrast, a word's **connotations** are the ideas or emotions associated with the word in addition to its meaning. Often, words have positive, negative, or neutral connotations, which can affect how people respond to them when the words appear in writing.

For example, the denotations of *illustrious*, *famous*, and *notorious* all describe someone who is well-known. However, the connotation of *illustrious* is of someone who is admired, while *notorious* suggests someone who is well-known for something bad. *Famous* has a more neutral connotation. This chart shows other words that illustrate differences in the connotations of words.

Positive ⟶	Neutral ⟶	Negative
prudent	timid	cowardly
self-confident	proud	arrogant
thrifty	economical	miserly

Dictionaries can give clues to connotations. The entry for *miserly*, for instance, might read, "greedy and stingy" to suggest the negative connotations of the word. Some dictionaries will also give example phrases or sentences that show how the word is used and that suggest its connotations.

Practice A Choose the word that has the more negative connotation in each item.

1. My parents lived in that (shack, house) for twenty years.
2. Christy's uncle has always lived a/an (reckless, adventurous) life.
3. As she looked his way, the (smile, smirk) on Jarod's face disappeared.
4. When I stumbled against the stranger, he (gazed, glared) at me.
5. The two families had been (feuding, quarreling) for years.
6. The football player turned and (stomped, walked) off the field.

$500
REWARD
For the Arrest and Conviction of
JESSE JAMES
St. Louis Midland Railroad

Teaching Resources

Unit 4 Resources

Connotation and Denotation, pp. 224–225

PHLit Online! Vocabulary Central, featuring definitions, audio pronunciations, Word Families, and activities, is at **www.PHLitOnline.com.**

Practice B Make a chart like the one shown and classify each of the words below as *positive, neutral,* or *negative.* There is one word that will fit in each blank space. Use a dictionary or thesaurus if necessary.

dreamer	overwrought	skinny
strategy	new	pushy
persistent	laughable	drudgery
high-strung	slender	newfangled
visionary	save	employment
scheme	aggressive	stubborn

Positive →	Neutral →	Negative
1. persevering	______	______
2. ______	______	nervous
3. up-to-date	______	______
4. ______	______	inventor
5. ______	store	hoard
6. ______	______	thin
7. hilarious	______	ludicrous
8. assertive	______	______
9. ______	______	work
10. ______	plan	______

Challenge

Using neutral connotations, write an ad about a product. Then, trade ads with a classmate and rewrite each other's ads, using words with negative connotations. Trade ads with a third classmate. Rewrite the ad using positive connotations. Read your ad and talk about the changes in meaning.

Activity Make a note card for each of the following words: *bossy, daring, glamorous, scrawny.* Look up each word in a dictionary and write its denotation. Then, write its connotation. Finally, use the word in an original sentence that shows its connotative meaning.

Word:

Denotation:

Connotation:

Sentence:

PHLit Online!
www.PHLitOnline.com
- Illustrated vocabulary words
- Interactive vocabulary games
- Vocabulary flashcards

Differentiated Instruction for Universal Access

Strategy for Less Proficient Readers

Assign groups of three. Have each group choose a set of three words with the same denotation and different connotations. Groups can make posters with three images or perform skits with three scenes. Each image or scene should show the denotation and connotation of one word. Have groups perform their skits or display their posters and challenge the class to guess which words they chose.

Strategy for Special Needs Students

In magazines or on the Internet, find pictures showing the same denotation with different connotations. For example, find a picture of a flower and one of a weed. Show the pictures to special needs students and explain how they show different attitudes toward the same subjects. Then, explain the connotations for *fragrance, stench,* and *smell,* and have students go online and find pictures that show these connotations.

ASSESS/EXTEND

Answers

Practice B

Sample answers:

1. persevering; persistent; stubborn
2. overwrought; nervous; high-strung
3. up-to-date; new; newfangled
4. visionary; inventor; dreamer
5. save; store; hoard
6. slender; thin; skinny
7. hilarious; laughable; ludicrous
8. assertive; aggressive; pushy
9. employment; work; drudgery
10. strategy; plan; scheme

Activity

For this activity, provide each student with four note cards and a dictionary or a list of reliable dictionary Web sites.

Sample answers:

Word: *bossy*; **Denotation:** given to ordering people around; **Connotation:** inappropriately authoritative; **Sentence:** The bossy boy always wanted me to do things his way.

Word: *daring*; **Denotation:** willing to take risks; **Connotation:** courageous, adventurous; **Sentence:** A daring woman climbed Mount Everest alone.

Word: *glamorous*; **Denotation:** fascinatingly attractive; **Connotation:** rich and beautiful; **Sentence:** The glamorous actress sprinkled gold dust in her hair.

Word: *scrawny*; **Denotation:** very thin; **Connotation:** unattractively thin; **Sentence:** Scrawny stray dogs roam the dirty alleyways.

Challenge

Students should choose words for their ads that clearly show neutral, negative, or positive connotations. For the negative and positive ads, remind them to choose words with the same denotations as those in the original ads, but with different connotations. Allow time for volunteers to read aloud all three versions of a single ad. Discuss the differences as a class.

Meeting Your Standards

Students will

1. prepare an oral interpretation of a literary work by advancing a judgment, supporting ideas, and posing questions.
2. deliver a well-organized oral interpretation of a literary work with the effective use of voice and body language.

Introducing Delivering an Oral Interpretation

Introduce the assignment and the strategies, using the instruction on the student page.

Evaluate the Content

1. Ask students to write their thesis statements and check that their ideas support this thesis. Tell students to note possible support for their judgments as they review the works. This information will help them to support their positions.
2. Remind students that one of the important aspects of literature is to raise questions in the mind of the reader. Students need to encourage listeners to respond to what the author says and what the author implies or does not say.

Prepare Your Delivery

1. Remind students to create logical organizational patterns that lead the audience to understand their points.
2. Remind students that they must adjust their voices to account for the room size as well as uncontrollable noises. **Ask** the class: What types of uncontrollable problems may occur while you are speaking?
   Possible answers: The heater fan may turn on, traffic noises may come in from the street, hall noises or other classes such as the band may be nearby.
   Point out to students that if any of these interruptions interfere with their presentations, they need to adjust their volumes so that they can still be heard clearly.

Communications Workshop

Delivering an Oral Interpretation of a Literary Work

You can share your ideas about a poem—or anything else you read—by **delivering an oral interpretation** for an audience in which you combine a careful analysis of the work with your own response.

Prepare the Content

Advance a judgment about significant ideas. Clearly state the main ideas in the literature. Discuss ways in which the ideas are developed and why they are important. Formulate a thesis statement that clearly reflects your view of the literature.

Support ideas and viewpoints. Your views will carry more weight if you support them with details from the text. Read excerpts from the work to share the writer's style and tone with your audience. Choose sections that illustrate key ideas and are pleasing or powerful when read aloud.

Pose questions. Authors do not state all of their ideas directly. Introduce some of the unstated themes or complexities of a work by asking a question and then answering it using examples from the works.

Prepare Your Delivery

Preparation is the key to feeling relaxed in front of an audience. These techniques can help you deliver a confident and effective presentation:

Organize your ideas. Write each key idea on a separate notecard. As you rehearse, experiment with the order of the cards. Then, number the cards in the best order.

Communicate with your voice. Speak clearly and comfortably without rushing. Use the tone and pitch of your voice to add variety.

Use effective body language. Your gestures and posture send a signal to your audience. Energetic body language shows that you think your subject is important. Maintain eye contact to keep your audience's attention.

Activity: Deliver an Oral Interpretation

Select a poem, short story, or piece of nonfiction. Prepare a three-minute interpretation in which you respond to this work. Ask your listeners to use the Feedback Form to evaluate your presentation.

Feedback Form for Oral Intepretation

Rating System

Poor				Excellent
1	2	3	4	5

Content

___ Clear main idea
___ Effective support
___ Appropriate quotations from text
___ Analysis of subtleties in text

Presentation

___ Logical organization
___ Clear speaking voice
___ Varied delivery
___ Effective gestures and body language

Conclusions

- Is the presentation unified? Does each statement support the main idea?
- Is the speaker's personal response to the literary work clear?

Assess the Activity

To evaluate students' delivery, use the *Speaking: Organizing and Delivering an Oral Summery* rubric, p. 274 in ***Professional Development Guidebook.***

Independent Reading

Does all *communication* serve a positive purpose?

The Waste Land and Other Poems
T. S. Eliot
Signet, 1998

In this collection of poems, the poet explores the difficulty of communicating in a post-world war society without clear ideals and points of reference. Using allusions from great works of the past, he tries to forge a language to convey ideas.

Victims of the Latest Dance Craze
Cornelius Eady
Carnegie Mellon University Press, 1997

Eady's words invite readers to experience the world as a rhythmic place alive with sound and motion. The poems in this collection connect different aspects of life to the energy and elegance of dance.

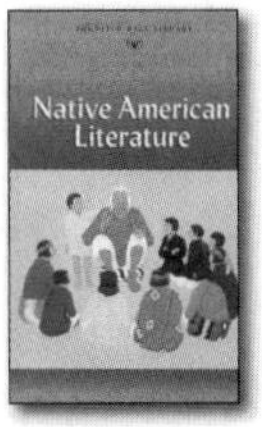

Native American Literature
Prentice Hall, 2000

This collection of myths, essays, poems, and more from Native American authors is just a small sampling of the vibrant literary tradition of North American tribes. These works communicate the spirit of the Native American cultures and invite readers to consider the purpose of telling stories and sharing ideas.

The Song of the Larks
Willa Cather
Signet, 1991

In the small Colorado town where she grows up, Thea Kronberg is not encouraged to follow her artistic passions. This novel tells the story of a girl who finds a way to communicate her passions through music, and how she struggles to fulfill her dreams.

The Complete Poetry of Edgar Allan Poe
Edgar Allan Poe
Signet, 1991

The poems that have delighted and frightened generations of readers are collected in this anthology. Poe is a master of communicating feelings of fear and horror, as well as despair over lost love.

Leaves of Grass
Walt Whitman
Signet, 2000

Driven by a passion for life and a reverence for nature, Walt Whitman expressed his views in this compelling volume of poetry still considered one of the best American collections ever. Get to know this famous thinker and idealist through his own words.

Consult your teacher before choosing one of these titles.

Connecting to the Big Question

Have students form literature circles in which to discuss the books they read independently. See *Professional Development Guidebook*, pp. 47–49, for guidance in running literature circles.

Suggest that students discuss these questions:

- In this work is the lack of communication a problem or is communication more of a problem? Explain.
- Is there communication or the illusion of communication?

Challenge

The following titles for advanced readers are available in the Penguin Literature Library.

***A Portrait of the Artist as a Young Man* by James Joyce** The book contains offensive language, a main character's obsession with sex, religious arguments and rejection of religion.

***The Hunchback of Notre Dame* by Victor Hugo** False accusations of witchcraft, defamation of gypsies, the suicide of Quasimodo, murder, physical torture, seduction and the inhumane treatment of the mentally ill might be disturbing.

Planning Students' Further Reading

Have students choose a book for independent reading from those listed on the student page. Before recommending a work to students, preview it, taking into account the values of your community as well as the maturity of your students. The following notes offer some guidance for the titles on the student page.

Because a variety of factors play a role in determining the accessibility of a work, a book with a higher readability rating may be deemed more accessible than a book with a lower rating.

L4 ***The Waste Land and Other Poems*** Eliot's poems question religious faith, love and other aspects of modern society. They occasionally mention sex, private parts, homosexuality, the theory of evolution and drinking; they contain coarse language, anti-Semitism, and other ethnic slurs.
Level suitable for high school students

L2 ***Victims of the Latest Dance Craze*** No sensitive issues.
Level suitable for high school students

L2 ***Native American Literature*** The selections depict violence, prejudice, and harsh living conditions and contain criticism of white Americans, missionaries, and the U.S. government.
Level suitable for high school students

L3 ***The Song of the Lark*** This story contains negative stereotypes of African Americans, Mexicans, Native Americans, and Jews; looting of sacred Native American burial grounds; alcoholism; sexism; extramarital affairs.
Lexile: 950L

L3 ***The Complete Poetry of Edgar Allan Poe*** Poe's poems often touch on the supernatural and on death, including the eerie and haunting deaths of young women. Some details of Poe's biography may also be problematic for some.
Level suitable for high school students

L1 ***Leaves of Grass*** Whitman's poems contain details about human sexuality, drinking, crime, slavery, the violence of war, suicide, prostitution, venereal disease, and various bodily functions. He occasionally uses dated ethnic, racial, and religious language and stereotypes that may be problematic.
Level suitable for high school students

MONITORING PROGRESS

Using the Unit Review

In this Test Pratice workshop (pp. 782–787), students apply the skills in Unit 4. The practice is divided into four sections.

1. Before assigning each section, review the relevant Unit skills with students.
2. Set a time limit for the multiple choice items in each section, allowing a little over one minute per question. Allow ten to fifteen minutes for any Writing for Assessment questions.
3. Administer each section. Have students write the starting time at the top of their papers. When half the time for the multiple choice items has run out, ask students to write the time next to an answer on which they are working. Have them do the same when time is three quarters through and again when time is up. Have them note the start and end times for any Writing for Assessment questions as well.
4. Review with students the pacing reflected in their notes.

Reteaching Skills

1. For each practice, use the Reteach chart on the same page as the answers to determine which skills require reteaching, based on which items students answered incorrectly.
2. Reteach these skills prior to assigning the **Benchmark Test** for the second half of Unit 4 (***Unit 4 Resources***, pp. 226–231).

Test Practice: Unit 4 Review

I. Literary Skills

Directions: *Read the passage. Then, answer each question that follows.*

TO AUTUMN

I

Season of mists and mellow fruitfulness,
Close bosom-friend of the maturing sun;
Conspiring with him how to load and bless
With fruit the vines that round the thatch-eves run;
To bend with apples the mossed cottage-trees,
And fill all fruit with ripeness to the core;
To swell the gourd, and plump the hazel shells
With a sweet kernel; to set budding more,
And still more, later flowers for the bees,
Until they think warm days will never cease,
For Summer has o'er-brimmed their clammy cells.

II

Who hath not seen thee oft amid thy store?
Sometimes whoever seeks abroad may find
Thee sitting careless on a granary floor,
Thy hair soft-lifted by the winnowing wind;
Or on a half-reaped furrow sound asleep,
Drowned with the fume of poppies, while thy hook
Spares the next swath and all its twinèd flowers:
And sometimes like a gleaner thou dost keep
Steady thy laden head across a brook;
Or by a cider-press, with patient look,
Thou watchest the last oozings hours by hours.

III

Where are the songs of Spring? Ay, where are they?
Think not of them, thou hast thy music too,—
While barrèd clouds bloom the soft-dying day,
And touch the stubble-plains with rosy hue;
Then in a wailful choir the small gnats mourn
Among the river sallows, borne aloft
Or sinking as the light wind lives or dies;
And full-grown lambs loud bleat from hilly bourn;
Hedge-crickets sing; and now with treble soft
The red-breast whistles from a garden-croft;
And gathering swallows twitter in the skies.

—*by John Keats*

Strategies for Test Taking

Remind students to use key words to determine how to respond to writing prompts, such as the Writing for Assessment question on p. 783. Tell them to break such assignments down into specific parts. That is, they must do the following:

- Product: a paragraph
- Purpose: describe the mood or feeling you think the poet is trying to express
- Elaboration: explain how the poet feels about autumn
- Support: use details from the passage

1. Which of the following best describes the **speaker** of the poem?
   - **A.** someone who prefers Spring
   - **B.** a farmer
   - **C.** someone who admires Autumn
   - **D.** a friend of the sun

2. When the speaker says, *Where are the songs of Spring? Ay, where are they? / Think not of them, thou has thy music too,—* he means—
   - **A.** there are more songs written about Autumn than Spring.
   - **B.** Spring is a beautiful season.
   - **C.** the birds sing lovely songs in Autumn.
   - **D.** Autumn is beautiful in its own way.

3. What is the dominant sensory **imagery** in stanza III?
   - **A.** sight/sound
   - **B.** smell/taste
   - **C.** touch/taste
   - **D.** sound/touch

4. **Vocabulary in Context** Which of the following is the closest definition of the underlined word *conspiring*?
   - **A.** secretly working together with
   - **B.** finding fault with
   - **C.** making an argument against
   - **D.** separating from by a great distance

5. Which **sound device** is represented in the following line?

   While barrèd clouds bloom the soft-dying day,
   - **A.** assonance
   - **B.** alliteration
   - **C.** rhyme
   - **D.** rhyme scheme

6. Which of the following **rhyme schemes** is represented in the first seven lines of the poem?
   - **A.** abbacdc
   - **B.** ababcdc
   - **C.** ababcde
   - **D.** aabbcde

7. Who or what is the speaker addressing in this poem?
   - **A.** a close friend
   - **B.** the sun
   - **C.** autumn
   - **D.** spring

8. Which best describes the **tone** of this poem?
   - **A.** reverent
   - **B.** playful
   - **C.** bitter
   - **D.** sad

9. Which of the following lines is an example of **personification**?
   - **A.** With a sweet kernel; to set budding more,
   - **B.** And full-grown lambs loud bleat from hilly bourn
   - **C.** Then in a wailful choir the small gnats mourn
   - **D.** Among the river sallows, borne aloft

Writing for Assessment

10. Write a paragraph in which you **describe** the **mood** or feeling that you think the poet is trying to express in this poem. **Explain** how you think the speaker feels about the subject of the poem. **Support** your answer with details from the passage.

GO ON

Answers

Answers With Explanations

1. C—The images of autumn causing fruit to ripen in the opening stanza set an admiring tone. *Incorrect answers:* A—The opening of stanza III show that the speaker does not treasure spring over autumn. B—It is the speaker's view of the season, not occupation, that matters. D—The speaker is writing about autumn.
2. D—This sentence aptly paraphrases the passage. Incorrect answers: A—The speaker does not compare the number of songs about the two seasons. B—The speaker does not describe the beauty of spring. C—The speaker also identifies insects as sources of song.
3. A—The speaker describes the colors of the season and the sounds made by different animals. *Incorrect answers:* B—The images appeal to neither sense. C—same explanation as for B. D—The stanza appeals to sound, but not to touch.
4. A—Autumn and the sun secretly work together to ripen fruit. *Incorrect answers:* B—Autumn does not criticize the sun. C—Autumn does not dispute the sun. D—The proximity of the two is not discussed.
5. B—The use of *barred* and *bloom* and *dying* and *day* shows alliteration. *Incorrect answers:* A—Vowel sounds are not repeated. C—The words do not rhyme. D—A rhyme scheme cannot be found in a single line.
6. C—Lines 1 and 3 rhyme, as do lines 2 and 4. The remaining lines do not repeat their sounds. *Incorrect answers:* A—Lines 2 and 3, 1 and 4, and 5 and 7 do not rhyme. C—While the first four lines are correct, lines 5 and 7 do not rhyme. D—Lines 1 and 2 do not rhyme; nor do lines 3 and 4.
7. C—The first word shows the poem is directed at the season. *Incorrect answers:* A—The poem is directed at the season, not a person. B—While the speaker refers to the sun, the objects of address is autumn. D—The poem celebrates autumn, not spring.
8. A—The formal diction and serious tone show reverence.

Reteach

Question	Pages to Reteach
1	639
2	715
3	715
5	733
6	671
7	—
8	700
9	715
10	731

Answers continued

Incorrect answers: B—The tone is serious. C—The speaker cherishes autumn, rather than harboring negative feelings. D—The speaker is not sad, but pleased that autumn provides so many pleasures.

9. C—The line gives human emotions to insects. *Incorrect answers:* A—The line describes ripening. B—Lambs do bleat, and they might be loud. D—The line describes the effect of wind on gnats.

Writing for Assessment

10. Students' paragraphs should express the speaker's mood and attitude toward autumn, using support from the poem.

ASSESS

Answers

Answers With Explanations

1. **B**—Since this passage only describes bees, you would need more information to learn about dangerous insects in general. *Incorrect answers:* A—Reading further in this article might tell you about the dangers posed by bee stings, but you would need other sources to learn about other dangerous insects. C—You could skim the article to find a section on bee stings, but you would still need to find other sources. D—Such a strategy would only tell you about the dangers of bees.
2. **D**—You need to read the sections on all three specialized types of bees. *Incorrect answers:* B—The introduction says nothing about reproduction. C—This section does not tell you about the role of two other types of bees in reproduction. D—same explanation as for C.
3. **C**—Since the queen bee is the only one that can reproduce, she is essential to a colony's survival. *Incorrect answers:* A—The passage does not describe the difficulties the queen might face. B—Not being human, bees cannot feel jealousy. D—The queen's role as producer of the future arguably makes her more important.
4. **B**—The eggs described by this word are unfertilized. *Incorrect answers:* A—The term refers to the birth of the drones, not their development. C—The term refers to drones of all types of bees. D—The term refers to the birth of drones, not mating.
5. **C**—The passage begins by speaking of bees in general and then examines the three specialized types. *Incorrect answers:* A—The passage begins with the general, not the specific. B—The passage does not move spatially through the hive. D—This description might fit the last three paragraphs, but not the selection as a whole.
6. **D**—The passage reveals the intricate interrelationships in a beehive. *Incorrect answers:* A—While the passage mentions the danger of bee stings, it does not examine

II. Informational Reading Skills

Directions: *Read the passage. Then, answer each question that follows.*

The Bees

Bees, known for their fearful sting and their delicious honey, are a common sight in flower gardens. The flowers provide bees with their food—pollen and nectar. Bees have specialized adaptations for collecting food. They have hairy bodies, pollen baskets, and special tongues for collecting nectar.

Honeybees

Honeybees, the most commonly known type of bee, are organized social insects. Honeybees live in complex colonies in which large numbers of individuals act together nearly as a single organism. The bee colony consists of specialized individuals: the queen bee, worker bees, and drones.

Queen bee. The queen bee is a fully developed female. Her only job is to lay eggs. When summer flowers begin blooming, the queen begins to lay her eggs, as many as a thousand or more per day.

Worker bees. Worker bees are undeveloped females. A colony can have up to 60,000 female bees. They collect nectar and pollen, convert it into honey, raise the young, and build their honeycomb. As they collect pollen, some clings to the hairs on their bodies. As they fly from blossom to blossom, they pollinate flowers, fruit trees, and vegetable plants.

Drones. The drones are male bees. Their only job is to mate with the queen. When fall arrives, drones are driven out of the hive to die. The queen can lay drone, or unfertilized eggs, which develop into adult drones. This process of producing life from unfertilized eggs is known as parthenogenesis.

1. If you wanted to learn about dangerous insects, after **scanning** this passage you would—

A. read the entire article
B. move on to another source
C. skim the article
D. look for more information on honeybees

2. To learn how insects reproduce, the section most useful to you would be—

A. the entire article
B. the introduction
C. "Drones"
D. "Queen bee"

3. What **generalization** can you make about the queen bee?

A. She has an easy life.
B. Her worker bees are jealous of her.
C. The colony would not survive without her.
D. The other bees are more important than she is.

4. Vocabulary in Context What is the best definition of the underlined word *parthenogenesis?*

A. growth of undeveloped bees
B. reproduction without fertilization
C. the creation of honeybees
D. mating with queen bees

Answers continued

them in detail. B—The passage does not consider the distribution of bees. C—The passage does not suggest that these adjectives are applicable to bees.

Reteach

Question	Pages to Reteach
1	694
2	694
3	694
5	750
6	694

5. Which of the following best describes the **pattern of organization** of the passage?

A. specific to general
B. spatial
C. general to specific
D. comparison-contrast

6. What **generalization** can you make about honeybees after reading the passage?

A. Honeybees are dangerous insects.
B. Honeybees can be found all over the world.
C. Honeybees are cruel and ruthless creatures.
D. Honeybees have a complex life cycle.

III. Vocabulary

Directions: *Choose the sentence in which each word best fits.*

1. misinterpreted

A. Ed _____ the data, so his answer was wrong.
B. I was grateful that Drew _____ the directions.
C. The two dogs _____ with hostility.
D. Heather _____ very quickly to the question.

2. confusion

A. In his _____, Barry suffered terribly from loneliness.
B. In the _____, none of us knew what the others were doing.
C. The _____ of the sentence clarified your idea.
D. The _____ led us directly to the exact answer.

3. interact

A. The two competing teams found it difficult to _____ in a friendly way.
B. Jake could not _____ to the question quickly.
C. They did not _____ the two events until it was too late.
D. My quick reflexes help me _____ the goal.

4. isolation

A. The hotel's _____ downtown made it pricey.
B. Brian's strong _____ kept him in the race.
C. The _____ of the situation led to many mistakes.
D. The _____ of the town meant that few people visited.

5. convey

A. Andrea did not want to _____ the situation further by adding her opinion.
B. Mr. Hahn tried to _____ struggling students.
C. Susan was able to _____ her ideas clearly.
D. I knew the difficult problem would _____ her.

6. connection

A. Scientists decided that _____ of the microbes was necessary despite previous studies.
B. Jeff's _____ was not accepted by his dad.
C. His _____ seemed argumentative at the time.
D. We did not understand the _____ between Randy's offense and his punishment.

7. respond

A. Jim would _____ his complaints to anyone.
B. Paramedics _____ to emergencies every day.
C. Reporters must accurately _____ to both sides.
D. When I _____ for a test, I need total silence.

8. discourse

A. The competitive _____ exhausted the soccer team.
B. Civil _____ requires courtesy from the participants.
C. Whatever the _____, we will work together.
D. We all face some _____ in our lives.

GO ON

Reteach

Question	Pages to Reteach
1	626–627
2	626–627
3	626–627
4	626–627
5	626–627
6	626–627
7	626–627
8	626–627

Answers With Explanations

1. A—Not understanding data can lead to incorrect conclusions. *Incorrect answers:* B—Misreading directions probably results in being lost, which is unlikely to cause pleasure. C—The dogs might bark, but they could not misinterpret. D—*Responded* would be more suitable here.
2. B—Confusion is likely to result in several people being unaware of others' actions. *Incorrect answers:* A—*Isolation* would be more appropriate here. C—Confusion does not lead to greater clarity. D—Confusion does not produce correct responses.
3. A—Teams that are competing can have a hard time working together. *Incorrect answers:* B—*Respond* is more appropriate here. C—*Connect* is more appropriate here. D—*Block* is more appropriate here.
4. D—A town far from any other community is, indeed, likely to have few visitors. *Incorrect answers:* A—*Location* is more appropriate here. B—*Determination* is more appropriate here. C—*Tension* is more appropriate here.
5. C—*Convey* means "to communicate," which would fit Susan's actions. *Incorrect answers:* A—*Confuse* is more appropriate here. B—*Help* is more appropriate here. D—same explanation as for A.
6. D—People often try to understand the relationship between an action and punishment for it. *Incorrect answers:* A—*Investigation* is more appropriate here. B—*Apology* is more appropriate here. C—*Explanation* or *response* is more appropriate here.
7. B—Paramedics' job is to react to emergencies. *Incorrect answers:* A—*Offer* or *utter* is more appropriate here. C—Reporters do not respond to individuals, individuals respond to reporters. D—*Study* is more appropriate here.
8. B—*Discourse* is communication. *Incorrect answers:* A—The soccer team would be more likely to be exhausted by play rather than a talk. C—*Disagreement* is more appropriate here. D—*Difficulties* is more appropriate here.

ASSESS

Answers

Answers With Explanations

1. **C**—The comparison of trees to skyscrapers is a simile. *Incorrect answers:* A—Since the comparison uses *as,* it is not a metaphor. B—The trees are not given human qualities. D—The trees are simply compared to skyscrapers, not used to represent an abstract quality.
2. **A**—This addition would clarify how the air felt. *Incorrect answers:* B—This addition would change the meaning, but make it no more sensory. C—The weak "very, very" would not appeal to the senses. D—The passage already gives a mental picture of the terrain.
3. **B**—The less formal "dad" and "appreciate its beauty" reflect the voice of the rest of the passage. *Incorrect answers:* A—The wordy sentence is inelegant, and "papa" does not fit with the rest of the essay. C—This substitute does not convey the full meaning of the original. D—This very informal version does not match the voice of the rest.
4. **A**—Placing the preposition first gives the sentence a varied structure. *Incorrect answers:* B—This version maintains the original sentence structure, and adds unnecessary commas. C—This version is a sentence fragment, not a sentence. D—This does not vary the sentence pattern.
5. **C**—The image of light dancing is personification. *Incorrect answers:* A—No human traits are given to nonhuman objects in this sentence. B—same explanation as for A. D—same explanation as for A.
6. **D**—This addition would clarify what is heard. *Incorrect answers:* A—This addition has nothing to do with the senses. B—same explanation as for A. C—same explanation as for A.

Reteach

Question	Pages to Reteach
1	709
2	709
3	709
4	709
5	709
6	709

IV. Writing and Language Conventions

Descriptive Essay

Directions: *Read the passage. Then, answer each question that follows.*

(1) I hear my dad's huge green hiking boots crunching on the leaves about ten feet ahead of me. (2) I struggle to keep up with him during our hike. (3) Although I was born and raised in the city, my dad is determined to make me appreciate what he calls "the great outdoors."

(4) Each November, he and I drive miles from the city to a state park. (5) When I was younger, I begged not to go, but he refused to listen. (6) Now, as I walk behind him up a steep hill, I take a deep breath of the air. (7) The trees around me are as tall as city skyscrapers, and just as impressive, in their own way. (8) Light is dancing across the floor of the forest, flickering here and there. (9) The forest is quiet; you can actually hear the breeze. (10) For the first time, I view the forest as my father does, and acknowledge its exquisiteness.

1. Which type of **figurative language** can be found in sentence 7?

A. metaphor
B. personification
C. simile
D. symbol

2. How could you incorporate more **sensory details** in sentence 6?

A. Add "crisp, clear" before "air."
B. Replace "deep" with "shallow."
C. Add "very, very" before "steep."
D. Replace "hill" with "mountain."

3. How should sentence 10 be revised to keep the **voice** consistent throughout the passage?

A. Now, for the first time, do I enjoy this beautiful scenery as my papa has for years.
B. For the first time, I see the forest as my dad does, and appreciate its beauty.
C. Suddenly, I enjoy nature's rustic beauty.
D. Like daddy said, the forest isn't bad.

4. How might you best revise sentence 2 to **vary the pattern** using a **prepositional phrase**?

A. During our hike, I struggle to keep up with him.
B. I struggle, to keep up, during our hike.
C. Keep up with him, I struggle, during our hike.
D. I struggle to keep up, during our hike, with him.

5. Which sentence uses **personification** to paint a picture in the reader's mind?

A. sentence 1
B. sentence 4
C. sentence 8
D. sentence 10

6. Which phrase would be *best* to add to the end of sentence 9 to appeal to the senses?

A. "which distracted me from my thoughts"
B. "coming out of the southeast"
C. "blowing around"
D. "rustling the leaves on the ground"

Differentiated Instruction for Universal Access

Strategy for Special Needs Students

Review skills and warm up for the test by walking students through item 5. Ask a volunteer to read item 5 aloud. Call on students to define personification. (Giving human qualities to something that is not human.) Next, guide students in eliminating incorrect choices.

- **A**—Boots can make a crunching noise, and making that noise is not exclusively human. (Eliminate.)
- **B**—It is humans who do the driving, not nonhuman objects. (Eliminate.)
- **C**—People can dance, light cannot.
- **D**—The narrator, who is human, is expressing his own thoughts. (Eliminate.)

Guide students in seeing that **D** is the best choice. Have them complete the remaining items, encouraging them to apply a similar strategy to each. First, define key terms in the prompt and then eliminate incorrect choices.

Analytic Response to Literature

Directions: *Read the passage. Then, answer each question that follows.*

(1) In his ode, "To Autumn," Keats uses sound devices conveys the softness of the harvest season. (2) The poem opens with the sounds of the soft consonants *m, f, w,* and *s*: "*S*easons of *m*ists and *m*ellow *f*ruitful-ness." (3) The poet starts with soft consonants. (4) The motif of "mellow fruitfulness" is further emphasized with the use of alliteration of the soft consonants: "fill all fruit," "warm days will never," "winnowing wind."

(5) Stanza III stresses that autumn has its own music and beauty. (6) Keats again uses sound devices for emphasis. (7) Stanza III opens with the repetition of "where are," and the repeated use of the soft *s* and *th* sounds. (8) Through the use of these sound devices, the poet emphasizes the beauty and softness of autumn.

1. Which of the following best *restates* the **thesis** of this passage?

A. The poet stresses the softness of autumn.
B. Autumn is a beautiful and fruitful season.
C. The poem focuses on the motif of "mellow fruitfulness."
D. The poet uses sound devices to emphasize the softness of autumn.

2. What is the primary **evidence** the writer uses to support the thesis?

A. paraphrases
B. organization
C. quotations
D. summaries

3. How does sentence 7 support the **thesis** of this passage?

A. It explains the poet's intention.
B. It gives examples of sound devices the poet uses.
C. It describes the motif of the poem.
D. It stresses the softness of consonants.

4. Which of the following revisions should be made to sentence 1?

A. Replace "conveys" with the infinitive "to convey."
B. Begin the passage with sentence 2.
C. Remove the words "of the harvest season."
D. Add the prepositional phrase "a poet" after "Keats."

5. Which sentence should be removed because it is redundant, or needlessly repeats an idea?

A. sentence 2
B. sentence 3
C. sentence 5
D. sentence 7

Writing for Assessment

6. Write a response to literature **analyzing** an aspect of "To Autumn" by John Keats which appears on p. 782. Formulate a **thesis** and **support** it using **details** from the text of the poem.

STOP

Benchmark

Reteach skills as indicated by students' performance, following the Reteach charts on pp. 783–787 to administer the end-of-unit **Benchmark Test** (*Unit 4 Resources,* pp. 226–231). Follow the **Interpretation Guide** for the test (*Unit 4 Resources,* pp. 235–240) to assign reteaching pages as necessary in the ***Reading Kit.*** Use **Success Tracker** online to automatically assign these pages.

Reteach

Question	Pages to Reteach
1	770
2	770
3	770
4	748
5	772
6	768–770, 772

Answers With Explanations

1. D—The point of the passage is the poet's use of sound techniques to describe the character of autumn. *Incorrect answers:* A—This restatement omits consideration of the poet's sound techniques. B—This restatement does not reflect the view or techniques of the poet. C—This restatement incorrectly focuses on one detail.

2. C—The passage is full of direct quotations from the poem. *Incorrect answers:* A—Since the focus is on the poet's language, the author must use quotations rather than paraphrases. B—The organization does not provide supporting evidence. D—The author uses direct quotations, not summaries.

3. B—The sentence refers to repeated words and sounds. *Incorrect answers:* A—The sentence describes the poet's techniques, not his intentions. C—The author focuses on the poet's language. D—This response ignores the fact that the author mentions the repetition of "where are."

4. A—The infinitive form is needed as the phrase is an adverb modifying uses. *Incorrect answers:* B—Sentence 1 introduces the thesis and needs to be retained. C—This phrase helps explain what softness is being described; it is needed. D—"A poet" is not a prepositional phrase, and its insertion would add nothing to the poem.

5. B—The sentence repeats an idea in sentence 2. *Incorrect answers:* A—Sentence 2 helps establish the use of sound techniques. C—Sentence 5 shifts focus to another section of the poem and is needed. D—Sentence 7 cites specific sound devices as evidence.

Writing for Assessment

6. Students' responses should have a clear thesis and have adequate support from the poem.

PHLit Online!

The **Benchmark Tests** and **Success Tracker** are available online at **www.PHLitOnline.com**

Unit 5 Overview

Unit Genre and Unit Big Question

Explain to students that throughout this unit, they will read and analyze drama. As they read, they will think about and discuss answers to the Unit Big Question: To what extent does experience determine what we perceive?

Students will learn more about the Big Question on pp. 790–791. Then, on pp. 792–807, David Henry Hwang introduces the unit literary form, drama, and presents a model play of his own.

Using the Unit Selections

Teach Skills To meet the standards, teach the reading skill, literary analysis concept, and vocabulary skill presented with each selection.

Differentiate and Reinforce Use the information in the Differentiated Instruction box on the next page to guide your teaching of the selections.

Integrate Skills In addition to the reading skill, literary analysis concept, and vocabulary skill, each lesson includes vocabulary development opportunities and grammar instruction. Students also have opportunities to extend learning in the Writing and extension (Research and Technology or Listening and Speaking) activities. Each supports or reinforces a standard.

Unit Features

Informational Texts Students learn to use and evaluate various types of informational texts.

Comparing Literary Works Students compare the use of a literary element in two or more works.

To help you plan your use of the unit, see the Unit Overview and Pacing Plan on pp. 790a–790b and the Time and Resource Manager preceding each selection pairing.

Drama

PHLit Online! www.PHLitOnline.com

Teaching from Technology

Enriched Online Student Edition
- full narration of selections
- interactive graphic organizers
- linked Get Connected! and Background videos
- all worksheets and other student resources

Professional Development
- the *Professional Development Guidebook* online
- additional professional development articles by program authors

Planning, Assigning, and Monitoring
- software for online assignment of work to students, individually or to the whole class
- a system for tracking and grading students' work

UNIT 5

PHLit Online!
www.PHLitOnline.com

Hear It!
- Selection summary audio
- Selection audio
- BQ Tunes

See It!
- Penguin author video
- Big Question video
- Get Connected videos
- Background videos
- More about the authors
- Illustrated vocabulary words
- Vocabulary flashcards

Do It!
- Interactive journals
- Interactive graphic organizers
- Grammar tutorials
- Interactive vocabulary games
- Test practice

789

Instructional Resources

Unit 5 Resources supports unit skills with pages of the following types:

- **Benchmark Tests** assess and monitor students' progress at mid-unit and at unit's end.
- **Vocabulary and Reading Warm-ups** provide additional vocabulary support, based on Lexile rankings of words, for each selection. "A" **Warm-ups** are for students reading two grades below level. "B" **Warm-ups** are for students reading one grade below level.
- **Selection Support** These practice pages are available for each selection:
  - **Reading Skill**
  - **Literary Analysis**
  - **Writing About the Big Question**
  - **Vocabulary**
  - **Support for Writing**
  - **Support for Extend Your Learning**
  - **Enrichment**

PHLit Online!
All worksheets and other student resources are also available at www.PHLitOnline.com.

Differentiated Instruction for Universal Access

Accessibility for Various Ability Levels

This chart gives a general accessibility rating to help you determine the depth of the prereading and reading support you will need to provide students for each selection. For additional guidance on factors that affect the accessibility of each selection, see the Before You Read page for each.

	More Accessible	More Challenging
Pair 1	Antigone	
Pair 2		The Tragedy of Julius Caesar

Accessibility for English Learners

EL This icon indicates support for English learners at point of use in this Teacher's Edition.

UNIT OVERVIEW AND PACING PLAN

Meeting Your Standards

Students will

1. recognize and appreciate drama as a literary genre.
2. read and analyze a variety of dramatic literature.
3. apply reading skills.
   - Summarize by identifying key details
   - Take notes to summarize
   - Use text aids
   - Paraphrase
   - Analyze imagery
   - Read between the lines
   - Compare and contrast characters
4. analyze literary elements.
   - Protagonist and antagonist
   - Greek tragedies
   - Shakespeare's tragedies
   - Blank verse
   - Dramatic speeches
   - External and internal conflict
   - Tragic heroes
5. build vocabulary and vocabulary concepts.
   - Roots
   - Suffixes
   - Prefixes
   - Borrowed and foreign words
6. learn elements of grammar, mechanics, and usage.
   - Participles and gerunds
   - Independent and subordinate clauses
   - Combining sentences with verbal phrases
   - Absolute and absolute phrases
   - Combining sentences using adverb clauses
7. use a recursive writing process to write in a variety of forms.
   - Reflective essay
   - Research report
8. read informational materials.
   - Synthesize to connect ideas in drama reviews
   - Analyze workplace documents
9. compare literary works.
   - Compare universal and culturally specific themes
   - Compare character motivation
10. develop research and technology skills.
    - Women's history report
    - Advertising poster
    - Multimedia presentatio
11. develop listening and speaking skills.
    - Oral report
    - Mock trial
    - Dramatic reading
    - Group screening
    - Deliver a multimedia presentation

	Week 1					Week 2					
	1	2	3	4	5	1	2	3	4	5	
Introduce the Unit Big Question (pp. 790–791).	●										Teach *The Tragedy of Julius Caesar* (pp. 886–1003).
Introduce the Unit author and the Unit genre, drama (pp. 792–795).	●										Complete the Test-Practice: Reading (pp. 1006–1007).
Teach the Model selections (pp. 796–807).	●	●									Teach Informational Texts (pp. 1008–1013).
Teach *Antigone* (pp. 810–861).		●	●	●	●						Teach Comparing Literary Works (pp. 1014–1019).
Complete the Test Practice: Reading (pp. 862–863).						●					Have students complete the Writing Workshop (pp. 1020–1031).
Teach Informational Texts (pp. 864–867).							●	●			Have students complete Applying the Big Question (pp. 1032–1033).
Teach Comparing Literary Works (pp. 868–876).							●	●	●	●	Have students complete the Vocabulary and Communications Workshops (pp. 1034–1035, 1036).
Have students complete the Writing Workshop (pp. 878–883).									●		Complete the Test Practice: Unit 5 Review (pp. 1038–1043).
Administer **Benchmark Test 9** (***Unit 5 Resources,*** pp. 84–89).										●	Administer **Benchmark Test 10** (***Unit 5 Resources,*** pp. 207–218).
Reteach skills, judging which skills to reteach by evaluating students' performance on **Benchmark Test 9**.											Reteach skills, judging which skills to reteach by evaluating students' performance on **Benchmark Test 10**.

Week 3					Week 4					Week 5					Week 6				
1	2	3	4	5	1	2	3	4	5	1	2	3	4	5	1	2	3	4	5
•	•	•	•	•	•	•	•	•	•	•									
										•									
											•								
											•	•							
												•	•	•	•				
															•				
																•			
																	•		
																		•	
																			•

Block and Daily Scheduling

The assignments and activities in this Unit planner are organized by week. You may adjust them to your daily or block schedule. The Time and Resource Manager for each selection set gives specific pacing suggestions, or you may use the comprehensive lesson planning support online at **www.PHLitOnline.com.**

Monitoring Progress

Diagnose Refer to students' results on **Benchmark Test 8,** ***Unit 4 Resources,*** pp. 227–235 (administered at the end of the previous Unit). Use the **Interpretation Guide** to interpret the results of the diagnostic portion of the test. **Note:** For the most accurate diagnosis of students who score in the middle range, administer the additional diagnostic questions online at **www.PHLitOnline.com.**

Preteach and Prepare As indicated by the diagnostic, prepare students for reading by assigning the **Vocabulary** and **Reading Warm-ups** for the selections you assign.

Teach Follow this Pacing Plan and use the resources to teach the skills and selections. For specific pacing suggestions and a list of resources, see the Time and Resource Manager and the Visual Guide to Featured Selection Resources preceding each selection pairing.

Assess After students have completed the first half of the Unit, administer **Benchmark Test 9**. Administer **Benchmark Test 10** at the end of the Unit.

Intervention and Reteach After administering each test, use the **Interpretation Guide** for the tests to determine which reteaching pages, if any, you should assign from the ***Reading Kit.*** The appropriate pages are also available through the online Progress Monitoring software.

Independent Reading

To differentiate, reinforce, and extend your instruction, have students choose a full-length work from the Independent Reading page, page 1037, and read it while working on this Unit. Consult the Sensitivity Issues notes for the page to guide students' choices.

CLASSROOM STRATEGIES

The Ups and Downs of Reading Drama **Kelly Gallagher**

> In over twenty years of teaching, I have yet to meet a single sophomore who can read a rich play once and completely understand it, even on a surface level.

When discussing the writing process, Anne Lamott talks about the differences between the "down" draft and the "up" draft. Simply, the purpose of the down draft—the first draft—is to get our thoughts down. The purpose of the up draft—the second draft—is to fix our writing up. Lamott uses these terms to illustrate the writing process, but these terms also work well when examining how we read. When reading challenging text for the first time, we try to get the main ideas down. When we re-read, we often move beneath the surface into a deeper appreciation of the text. Though this is true with all challenging texts, I have found these terms particularly helpful when I ask my students to read classic works of drama.

Getting it Down: Strategies For Literal Understanding

When reading a play, students must first develop a literal understanding if they are to have any chance of moving into deeper levels of comprehension. Unfortunately, in over twenty years of teaching, I have yet to meet a single sophomore who can read a rich play once and completely understand it, even on a surface level. With this in mind, I have found the following strategies useful in helping my students achieve a literal understanding of difficult text:

Text frames with gaps. Prior to reading, students are provided with outlines of chapters or scenes, consisting of 5–7 bullets. Before beginning Act 1, Scene I of *Julius Caesar*, for example, I hand students the following bulleted outline:

Act I Scene I

- Flavius and Murellus are walking down the street in anticipation of Caesar's procession.
-
-
-
- Murellus reminds Flavius of the good old days, when processions were held for victorious warriors.

As students read the scene, they try to determine the missing bullets. As the play progresses and students become more confident, I provide fewer bulleted plot points, thus requiring students to "take over" the reading.

Say What? In groups, students are assigned small chunks of the play and are asked to respond to the following prompts in a chart format:

- *What does the text say?*
- *How would this be said in modern English?*
- *How would this be said in modern slang?*

The prompts run as headings from left to right on the top of the paper. Completing this chart requires students to read, and re-read, the text closely to make sure they have achieved literal comprehension of the text.

How Should It Be Read? After multiple readings, ask students how a given passage should be read aloud. Sarcastically? Happily? Angrily? Ask students to give oral presentations of their interpretations of the scene. Students should be prepared to defend their interpretations; doing so will require them to read the scene many times.

Fixing It Up: Strategies For Deepening Reading Comprehension

Once students have a literal understanding of the play, it is time to revisit it in search of deeper comprehension. Here are four strategies proven to move students into deeper comprehension:

Close readings. Choose a "hot spot" in the play—a passage that prompts deeper thinking—and copy it for students to annotate. Students can highlight confusion, make connections, ask questions, or comment on the author's craft. This strategy works best when there is something in the text that is generally not detected in a first-draft reading (e.g. symbolism, sonnet form). Though we don't have time to re-read the entire play, we do have time for students to deepen their comprehension through re-reading *segments* of the play.

Sentence Starters. Eventually, we want students to determine their own "hot spots" in the play. The following sentence starters help nudge students into meaningful reflection:

I noticed...	If I were...
I wonder...	The central issue(s) is (are)...
I was reminded of...	I'm not sure...
I think...	If ____, then...
I'd like to know...	One consequence of ____ would be...
I'm surprised that...	Although it seems...
I realized...	I don't understand...

Yes/No Chart. Most major works of drama present a "yes/no" question. In *Antigone*, for example, students might be asked, "Is Creon correct to banish Antigone?" Students create t-charts and cite evidence on both sides—reasons found in the text to support a "yes" answer and reasons in the text that support a "no" answer. Each student is then asked to take a stand and defend it.

Literary Dominoes. Both of the major plays in this unit, *Antigone* and *Julius Caesar* end in tragedy. But tragedies in drama do not simply occur; they are preceded by a chain of events. Much like dominoes set up to knock each other over, one event leads to another, which leads to another, which leads to another, until the last "domino" falls. With this metaphor in mind, ask students to identify the "dominoes"—the key events—that lead to the tragic endings of these plays.

Supporting Research

Lamott, Anne. 1994. *Bird by Bird: Some Instructions on Writing and Life.* New York: Anchor.

Modeled Strategy

See pp. 845 and 951 for point-of-use notes modeling these strategies.

Teacher Resources

- ***Professional Development Guidebook***
- ***Classroom Strategies and Teaching Routines cards***

PHLit Online!

Log on as a teacher at **www.PHLitOnline.com** to access a library of all Professional Development articles by the Contributing Authors of Pearson Prentice Hall *Literature*.

Kelly Gallagher

Kelly Gallagher is a full-time English teacher at Magnolia High School in Anaheim, California, where he has taught twenty-two years. He is a former co-director of the South Basin Writing Project and is the author of *Reading Reasons: Motivational Mini-Lessons for the Middle and High School, Deeper Reading: Comprehending Challenging Texts,* and *Teaching Adolescent Writers.*

Introducing the Big Question

1. Give this example: An outgoing person might view moving as an opportunity for making new friends. A shy person may be nervous about moving and being with new people.
2. Invite students to give examples of how people's different outlooks can shape their perspectives.
3. Ask students the Big Question. **Possible response:** Experience greatly affects our perceptions because it leads us to make assumptions about what we perceive.
4. Tell students that the characters in this unit's stories act based on their perceptions about themselves and the world. As they read, have students consider the forces that shape each character's perspective.

Introducing the Big Question Vocabulary

1. Point out the Big Question Vocabulary on the facing page. Explain that these words are useful in discussing the Big Question.
2. Review the meaning of each word. (Definitions appear in the teacher edition on p. 791.)
3. Have students complete the **Big Question Vocabulary** worksheets, *Unit 5 Resources*, pp. 1–3.

Write What You Know

1. Review the assignment with students, using the instruction on the student page.
2. For each situation, guide students to think of one previous experience that might positively affect a person's perception of a situation and one experience that might negatively affect it.
3. Have students share and discuss their examples.

PHLit Online!

Show the Big Question video, online at **www.PHLitOnline.com.**

Introducing the Big Question

THE BIG ? To what extent does *experience* determine what we *perceive?*

A person's experience is everything one has lived through, seen, read, or heard about. It is the **background** information that shapes one's **perspective,** or point of view, about the world. Each **individual** uses his or her **knowledge** and **insight** to try to make sense of things that happen in life.

Universal experiences are those that most, if not all, people in a culture have known. Such experiences help people in a society share a sense of **identity.** Each person's life experiences are unique, however, and these experiences determine how one perceives the world. For example, a person who has always struggled with schoolwork might perceive a college entrance test as a frightening prospect, while a person who has always had positive educational experiences might look forward to the same test as an exciting challenge.

Start thinking about the Big Question by identifying situations that people with varying backgrounds might perceive very differently.

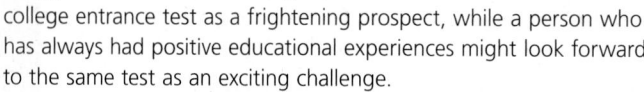

Discuss It

Write What You Know

For each of the following situations, describe how different background experiences might affect two people's perception of the same situation.

- Moving to a new school
- Meeting someone for the first time
- Deciding whether or not someone is being truthful about a situation
- Persuading someone to do the right thing
- Trying to get a person of another generation to understand your point of view

Share your examples with a partner. Talk about how each person's experiences would affect his or her point of view.

PHLit Online!
www.PHLitOnline.com
- Big Question video
- Illustrated vocabulary words
- Interactive vocabulary games
- BQ Tunes

Understanding by Design

The Big Question

Explain to students that they will continue to consider the Big Question as they work through the unit.

- At the beginning of each selection, they will write a response to a Writing About the Big Question sentence starter.
- As they read the selection, they will look for details related to the Big Question.
- At the end of the selection, they will answer a Critical Thinking question that is related to the Big Question.
- At the end of Unit 5, they will complete an Applying the Big Question workshop (pp. 1032–1033). In the workshop, they will review literature in the unit and think about real-world examples that shed light on the Big Question. They will also have a chance to reflect on their first answers, thinking about how their ideas have changed.
- Tell students that their goal will be to gain a deeper understanding of literature and a more sophisticated way of discussing the Big Question.

Discuss It

Explain What You Know

Use the examples and ideas you discussed with your partner to help you complete these sentences about how experiences influence perception.

- Making a good first **impression** is important because ___________.
- When people communicate, it helps to be aware of each other's background because ___________.
- The choices people make differ because ___________.
- Learning how to see something from another person's perspective is valuable because ___________.

Share your responses with a partner.

Write About It

Tell What You Think

Based in the discussions you have had, decide what you think right now. Your answer may change as you read the selections in this unit. Complete this sentence to respond to the Big Question or write one of your own:

The extent to which experience determines what we perceive is _____.

Use one or more of these sentences or your own ideas to write a brief support of your response.

- Life experiences such as ___________ or ___________ can influence a person's perception by ___________.
- Experience does not greatly matter when ___________. Experience matters more when ___________.
- Experience can have a positive influence on perception when _____. It can negatively influence a situation when _______.

Discuss your response with a partner or a small group.

Connecting to the Literature

The readings in this unit will help you think about the ways that people's unique life experiences can influence how they see the world and the decisions they make. Each reading will give you an insight into the Big Question. At the end of the unit, you will see how your ideas have grown or changed.

★ shows an **Academic Vocabulary** word.

Big Question Vocabulary

- ★ anticipate
- ★ background
- ★ bias
- ★ distortion
- expectations
- identity
- impression
- ★ individual
- ★ insight
- ★ interpretation
- knowledge
- ★ manipulate
- ★ perspective
- stereotype
- universal

Explain What You Know

1. Introduce the assignment, using the instruction on the student page.
2. Guide students to complete the sentence starters by thinking of relevant examples of each point they make.
3. Invite students to share their answers to the sentence starters. As needed, review definitions of Big Question Vocabulary and clarify meanings.

Tell What You Think

1. Introduce the assignment. Guide students to review the discussion they had with partners and to consider the different points of view expressed. Then, ask them whether they believe experience determines perception. Have students mark their pages with their answers.
2. Tell students to write a paragraph to support their opinions. Encourage them to complete the sentence starters to help them write their opinions.
3. As students write, remind them to give examples from previous discussions or activities that support their points of view.
4. Call on volunteers to share their responses with the class.

Connecting to the Literature

Explain the structure of the Big Question strand in the unit, referring to the Understanding by Design box on the previous page.

Big Question Vocabulary

anticipate* (an tis′ə pāt′) *v.* to look forward to
background* (bak ground) *n.* the conditions that surround or come before something
bias* (bī′ əs) *n.* a preference for one thing, person, or group, often in a way considered unfair
distortion* (di stôr shən) *n.* anything that shows something in an untrue way
expectations (ek′spec tā′shəns) *n.* something looked forward to
identity (ī den′ tə tē) *n.* the qualities of a person that make up who he or she is
impression (im presh′ ən) *n.* an effect produced on the mind
individual* (in də vij o͞o əl) *adj.* relating to a single person or thing
insight* (in′ sīt′) *n.* a clear idea of the nature of things
interpretation* (in tur prə tā shən) *n.* a person's idea of the meaning of something
knowledge (näl′ ij) *n.* awareness and understanding of information
manipulate* (mə nip′ yo͞o lāt′) *v.* to control by use of influence, often in an unfair way
perspective* (pər spek′ tiv) *n.* the way one sees things
stereotype (ster′ē ə tīp) *n.* an overly broad and often incorrect notion of a group
universal (yo͞o nə vur′ səl) *adj.* existing in all things

PRETEACH

Meeting Your Standards

Students will

1. understand some of the characteristics of drama.
2. learn about playwright David Henry Hwang.
3. read and analyze an excerpt of a play.
4. relate visuals to elements of drama.

❶ To what extent does experience determine what we perceive?

Remind students that they will think more about the Unit Big Question as they read and discuss drama in this unit.

❷ What Is Drama?

Introduce David Henry Hwang

1. David Henry Hwang's early off-Broadway plays explored the experiences of Asian immigrants and their families. In 1988, Hwang's play *M. Butterfly* played on Broadway and won him not only awards but critical and popular acclaim.
2. Use the ***See It!*** **DVD** to introduce the author and the genre. Show Segments 2 and 3 to provide insights into David Henry Hwang's writing process. **Ask** students what they think an adaptation is, based on Hwang's description.
   Possible response: An adaptation is the rewriting of a work from its original form to another form, as in reworking a novel into a play.
3. Interested students might enjoy the play *Trying to Find Chinatown: The Selected Plays* by David Henry Hwang. We recommend that you preview it before recommending it to students.

Introduce Drama

Explore students' prior knowledge of drama. Lead a class discussion about plays that students have read and those they have seen performed.

Introduction: Drama

❶ **To what extent does *experience* determine what we *perceive?***

Drama can show how different perceptions develop.

PHLit Online!
www.PHLitOnline.com

- Penguin author video
- Interactive journals
- Interactive graphic organizers
- Selection audio
- Self-test

❷ What Is Drama?

by David Henry Hwang

For many centuries, **drama** was not considered a literary form. Plays were entertainments performed on stages. Or plays were simply the words actors spoke, regarded much the way we regard scripts for movies and television shows today. William Shakespeare, probably the English language's greatest dramatist, did not even pay much attention to having his plays published during his lifetime.

❸ The Journey from Page to Stage: Discovering What "Works"

Though we do think of drama as literature today, plays are really written to be performed, not read from a book. For me, the two most critical moments in the journey from page to stage are the first time I hear my new play read by actors and the first time I see it performed in front of an audience.

On both occasions, I learn what parts of my drama do and don't "work." When an audience sits silent after a line I thought would be funny, or yawns during a speech I thought would be moving, then I know it's time to rewrite. There's a famous saying that plays are not written, they're rewritten.

❹ Dialogue: Writing the Way People Talk

When I first began to explore creative writing, I tried short stories, but didn't really enjoy the form. Plays, however, felt much more enjoyable to me: I was simply writing the way people talk, so my grammar didn't have to be perfect. I didn't even have to use complete sentences! And I loved collaborating with other artists—actors.

As you read a play, become the director yourself and imagine it being staged in your mind. Or gather a group of classmates together and read the lines to one another. Don't worry if your performance isn't perfect. Remember that the work before you was created through a process more chaotic than you might have imagined.

Teaching Resources

The following resources can be used to enrich, extend, or differentiate the instruction.

- All *Unit 5 Resources,* pp. 6–22
- All *Professional Development Guidebook,* pp. 33, 36–38, 42
- All *See It!* DVD
  David Henry Hwang, Segments 1 and 2
- All *Graphic Organizer Transparencies,* pp. 151–152
- All **Enriched Online Student Edition**
- L2 L3 *Reader's Notebook*
- L1 *Reader's Notebook: Adapted Version*
- EL *Reader's Notebook: English Learner's Version*
- L2 EL *Hear It!* **Audio CD**
- L1 EL *Hear It!* **Audio CD** (adapted text)

PHLit Online! All resources, including print and video, are available at **www.PHLitOnline.com.**

The reality of creating a drama was portrayed in the 1999 Academy Award Winning Best Picture, *Shakespeare In Love*, whose screenplay was co-written by the great British playwright Tom Stoppard. In the passage shown here, Shakespeare ("Will") is rehearsing his new play, "Romeo and Juliet," and gives direction to Viola, who's playing the part of Romeo. This brief scene shows that drama, which may be the liveliest art, is not always the tidiest.

> WILL (interfering): No, no, no, no, don't spend it all at once! (He jumps on the stage.)
>
> VIOLA (hesitantly): Yes, sir.
>
> WILL (to Viola): What will you do in Act Two, when he meets the love of his life?
>
> VIOLA (timidly): Ah, I am very sorry, sir, I have not seen Act Two.
>
> WILL (stopping short): Of course you have not. I have not written it. Go once more!
>
> from *Shakespeare in Love*
> —Marc Norman and Tom Stoppard

Meet David Henry Hwang (b. 1957)

Author of *Tibet Through the Red Box*

When he was young, David Henry Hwang considered his Chinese heritage "a minor detail, like having red hair." He became interested in his background, however, when he was in college. His first play was produced while he was still an undergraduate at Stanford. Later, the play *M. Butterfly* established him as a major talent in the world of theater. Hwang has produced texts for Broadway musicals, opera, and even a science-fiction music drama.

Did You Know?

Hwang wrote a screenplay that eventually became the movie *Seven Years in Tibet* starring Brad Pitt.

❸ The Journey From Page to Stage: Discovering What "Works" (p. 792)

Ask students what they think Hwang means by the statement, "plays are not written, they're rewritten."
Possible response: A play is not as "permanent" as a novel or short story because the playwright can watch a performance and determine what works with the audience and what does not and change it accordingly.

❹ Dialogue: Writing the Way People Talk (p. 792)

1. **Ask** students what Hwang prefers about playwriting to other forms of writing.
   Answer: He likes the looseness of the language and writing dialogue that sounds like the real speech of people. He also likes the collaboration.
2. Point out Hwang's suggestion that readers of a play should "become the director" and imagine the play staged in their minds. Recommend that students try this technique as they read the selection.
3. The popular film *Shakespeare in Love*, while not trying to be a historical account, captures the flavor and chaos of the Elizabethan era in the theater. Direct students' attention to the lines of dialogue. **Ask** students: What do these lines reveal about the play-writing process?
   Possible response: The dialogue reveals that plays do not begin with complete, fully written scripts. The author is constantly creating and revising.

PHLit Online!

Show or assign the Penguin author video segments for these pages at **www.PHLitOnline.com**

TEACH

❺ Elements of Drama

1. After students read the first paragraph, **ask** them to summarize the ways in which a play is similar to and different from a short story.
   Answer: A play contains the same elements of characters, plot, conflict, theme, and dialogue that are present in a fictional story. In a play, however, there is no narrator.
2. Tell students that the success of a play depends on the writer's skillful use of dialogue and action, since these are the sole means by which the playwright can portray character, advance theme, and develop plot.
3. Point out to students that stage directions include more than just information about lighting, music, sound effects, costumes, props, and set design. Stage directions can also provide information to actors and directors about facial expression, body language, tone of voice, and other details that help the cast understand the emotions they are supposed to portray.

Exploring Drama

❺ Elements of Drama

Like fiction, drama features **characters** facing a **conflict,** or struggle, that sparks a sequence of events called the **plot.** Sometimes, a drama includes **parallel plots**—two simultaneous sequences. The conflict reaches a **climax,** or point of greatest intensity, before being solved in the **resolution** at the end. Unlike fiction, however, a drama is a story written to be performed by actors speaking **dialogue,** the characters' words, rather than by a narrator.

- **Acts** and **scenes** are the basic divisions of drama. A drama may consist of one or more acts, divided into scenes.
- The **script,** or text, of a play contains dialogue and stage directions. **Dialogue** is the words the characters say. **Stage directions** are notes telling how the work is to be performed or staged. Directions are often printed in italics and set off in brackets. Some dramatists use abbreviations such as *OS* (offstage), *DS* (downstage, or close to the audience), or *US* (upstage, or near the rear of the stage).
- **Sets** represent or simulate the place where a scene is set. A set may include such items as painted backdrops and wooden frames.
- **Props** are movable objects, like a spear, that actors use onstage.

In performance, these various elements of drama combine to produce the illusion of reality known as **dramatic effect.** Through this effect, the dramatist explores a **theme,** or central message about life.

Understanding by Design

Clarifying Expected Outcomes

Explain to students that pages 794–795 set out their goals in this unit. By the end of Unit 5, they will understand the elements of drama, including dialogue, acts and scenes, script, stage directions, sets, props, and dramatic effects. They will be able to identify and discuss these elements in a specific drama.

Remind students that, in addition, they will explore the relationship between experience and perception as they work toward an answer to the Unit Big Question, "To what extent does experience determine what we perceive?" They will also add words to their vocabulary that will help them discuss communication and its purposes. (See Introducing the Big Question, pp. 790–791.)

❻ Types of Drama and Dramatic Speech

The ancient Greeks developed drama, creating two basic types of plays:

- A **tragedy** shows the downfall or death of the **tragic hero,** or main character. In ancient Greek drama, the hero was an outstanding person brought low by a **tragic flaw,** a mistaken action or defect in character. A **chorus,** or group of performers, sang, danced, and commented on events. The hero's downfall was meant to bring about a **catharsis,** or calming release of tension, in the audience.

  William Shakespeare's tragedies differ from Greek tragedies in several ways. In **Shakespearean tragedy,** the hero has greater free will, or power of choice, and reveals more of an inner life. There is no formal chorus. Shakespeare often uses a **foil,** or a character intended to provide a contrast to another character, to emphasize a hero's strengths or weaknesses. Patterns of **imagery,** or sensory language, in the character's dialogue reinforces themes.
- In contrast to tragedy, **a comedy** ends happily after an amusing series of predicaments. If tragedy stresses human greatness in facing inescapable fate, comedy emphasizes human faults and the weaknesses of society itself.

In addition to dialogue involving conversations between two or more characters, dramatists use these types of dramatic speech:

- In a **monologue,** a character speaks at length to silent listeners.
- In a **soliloquy,** a character alone on stage reveals private thoughts.
- In an **aside,** a character briefly expresses to the audience private thoughts that other characters on stage cannot hear.

Put Yourself in the Picture

Use these sentence starters to imagine a play based on the picture below.

- The **props** for the scene in this photograph might include ____________________.
- The actor in the center of the image may be delivering a **monologue** in which he describes __________.
- To create a **dramatic effect** in this scene, the other actors are __________.

Challenge Is it more likely that these people are performing in a comedy or a tragedy? What details led you to your conclusion?

Differentiated Instruction for Universal Access

Support for Special Needs Students
Have students read the **Exploring Drama** page in the ***Reader's Notebook: Adapted Version***. This version provides a basic-level introduction to the genre.

Support for Less Proficient Readers
Have students read the **Exploring Drama** page in the ***Reader's Notebook***. This version provides a basic-level introduction to the genre.

EL Support for English Learners
Have students read the **Exploring Drama** page in the ***Reader's Notebook: English Learner's Version***. This version provides a basic-level introduction to the genre.

❻ Types of Drama and Dramatic Speech

1. Point out to students that the ordinary definition of *tragedy*, "an unfortunate or disastrous occurrence," is not the same as the dramatic definition of *tragedy*—"the downfall of a hero caused by a flaw in the person's character or actions." **Ask** students: Why is the death of a person killed by an earthquake not a tragedy in the dramatic sense of the word?
   Possible answer: A person's death in an earthquake does not meet the dramatic definition of tragedy because the person killed did nothing to cause the earthquake or bring about his or her own demise.
2. **Ask** students to identify situations in which a playwright might want characters to speak a monologue, a soliloquy, or an aside.
   Possible responses: Playwrights might use a monologue when they want to reveal aspects of a character's personality or background. A soliloquy might be delivered by a character alone on stage so the audience will understand the character's motivations. An aside might be used when characters share secrets or formulate schemes.

ASSESS
Answers

Put Yourself in the Picture
Possible response: The props in this photograph include a bloody toga. The actor in the center of the image may be delivering a monologue in which he describes what happened. To create a dramatic effect in this scene, the other actors are expressing shock andd sorrow.

Challenge
Possible response: Students may respond that these young people are performing in a tragedy. They may note details such as the bloody toga and sorrowful looks of the populace as indicative of a tragedy.

PRETEACH

❶ Introducing the Selection

1. Invite students to read David Henry Hwang's introduction.
2. **Ask** students: Why might Hwang include in his introduction his conversation with the Dalai Lama?
   Possible response: Since the conflict between China and Tibet is an important part of the play, and Hwang is Chinese, he wants to show that, despite this conflict and his Chinese heritage, he can be Tibet's ally.
3. Call students' attention to the terms used in discussing the play: *adaptation, character, audience, parallel plots,* and *staging*. Ask students to identify these elements as they read the excerpt.

❷ Background

Tibet The conflict between China and Tibet intensified in 1949 when the Chinese Communists enforced their claim on Tibet. The spiritual leader of Tibet, the Dalai Lama, fled to exile in India.

❸ Connecting to the Big Question

1. Prepare students to apply the Big Question to the Model Selection.
2. Explain to students that people often build expectations of others based on what they have experienced in the past. These expectations, though derived from reasoning, can be faulty.
3. Have students complete this sentence starter, featuring thematic vocabulary from pp. 790–791:
   Our expectations of others often distort our perspective of ______.
   Possible response: who they really are.
4. Discuss students' responses as a class. Then, have students look for ways in which Peter's perception of his father changes.

Concept Connector →

Students will discuss to what extent experience determines what we perceive after they read.

Model Selection: Drama

❶ David Henry Hwang ❷ ❸ Introduces *Tibet Through the Red Box*

In 1985, I visited Tibet to research a screenplay I was writing, which would eventually became the movie *Seven Years In Tibet*, starring Brad Pitt. I then traveled to India to meet the Dalai Lama, exiled leader of the Tibetan people, who fled his country when Chinese troops invaded in 1959.

I apologized to him for the fact that my own ancestry was Chinese, like the invaders', yet I was writing a movie about his country. The Dalai Lama draped a prayer-shawl around my neck and said, "Tibet needs more good Chinese." I certainly felt I was in the presence of a profoundly good and spiritual being.

Adaptation: Turning a Story Into a Drama

Almost twenty years later, I was asked to write a play based on a wonderful book by Peter Sís, *Tibet Through the Red Box*. This book told how, when Sís was a boy in Czechoslovakia, his father was sent to Tibet to make a documentary film about the Chinese invasion.

My play would be an **adaptation** of this story, a dramatic version of it. The challenge of adaptation lies in a paradox: In order to preserve the essence of the original story, you must often change a good many of its details.

Parallel Plots and Spectacular Staging

Peter Sís's book focused on his father's adventures in Tibet. In order to keep the **character** of young Peter active, and therefore interesting to the **audience,** I had to find a stronger story for the boy. I constructed **parallel plots:** The action of the play shifts back and forth between the father in Tibet and Peter in Czechoslovakia.

Furthermore, since much of the magic of Sís's book lies in the brilliant and mysterious artwork with which he illustrates his tale, I tried to create a theatrical equivalent through opportunities for spectacular and beautiful **staging:** flying characters, abominable snowmen, martial arts sequences, and many-headed demons.

You can use your imagination to "see" that staging as you read this excerpt from my play.

Vocabulary Development

Vocabulary Knowledge Rating

Create a **Vocabulary Knowledge Rating Chart** (***Professional Development Guidebook***, p. 33) with these words from the selection:

priority *venture* *reprise*

Give students a copy of the chart. Read the words aloud, and have students mark their rating in the Before Reading column. Urge them to be alert to these words as they read and discuss the excerpt from *Tibet Through the Red Box,* because they will rate their knowledge again after they finish.

Tally how many students think they know a word to gauge how much instruction to provide. As students read, point out the words and their context.

PHLit Online! **Vocabulary Central,** featuring tools, activities and songs for studying vocabulary, is available at **www.PHLitOnline.com.**

from Tibet Through the Red Box

MODEL SELECTION

DAVID HENRY HWANG

CHARACTERS

Peter a boy

Alenka Peter's mother

The Boy Spirit A guiding spirit who assumes many forms including a cat and Jingle-Bell Boy

Vladimir Peter's father, a filmmaker

Yeti Abominable Snowman

Ensemble 1 & 2 Groups of characters who act as a chorus and serve different functions

4 Activating Prior Knowledge

1. Prepare an **Anticipation Guide** (see ***Professional Development Guidebook***, pp. 36–38) with the following statements:
   - People who are not feeling well may be irritable and impatient.
   - The creatures that visit you in your dreams may be symbolic.
   - Be careful what you wish for; you may get it.
   - It may be difficult to open your mind to accept ideas that are unfamiliar and uncomfortable.
2. Give students a copy of the prepared **Anticipation Guide** and have students mark their responses in the Me column. Have students discuss the statements in pairs or groups and mark the guide again in the Group column.
3. For further guidance, use the ***Classroom Strategies and Teaching Routines*** card: **Using an Anticipation Guide**.

Concept Connector →

Students will return to the **Anticipation Guide** after reading the selection.

5 About the Selection

In Act II of *Tibet Through the Red Box*, dream and reality combine to encourage Peter to read his father's letter from Tibet, to come to terms with his own fears, and to understand the importance of his father's work.

Differentiated Instruction for Universal Access

Strategy for Special Needs Students
Have students read the adapted version of *Tibet Through the Red Box* in the ***Reader's Notebook: Adapted Version***. They may also listen to the adapted version on the ***Hear It!* Audio CD** (adapted text).

Support for Less Proficient Readers
Have students read *Tibet Through the Red Box* in the ***Reader's Notebook***. After students finish the selection in the ***Reader's Notebook***, have them complete the questions and activities in the student edition.

EL Support for English Learners
Have students read *Tibet Through the Red Box* in the ***Reader's Notebook: English Learner's Version***. English learners may also read the selection as they listen to the recorded version on the ***Hear It!* Audio CD**.

PHLit Online!

Enriched Online Student Edition
To have students read the selection in interactive format, with narration and point-of-use interactive graphic organizers, go to **www.PHLitOnline.com**.

❻ Drama

Monologue

1. Have a volunteer read the bracketed passage.
2. **Ask** students why a playwright might use a monologue at this place in the play.
   Possible response: It allows him to give crucial information to another character as well as to the audience.
3. **Ask** students to summarize what both the audience and Peter learn from Alenka's monologue.
   Possible response: Alenka and her son have feared for Vladimir's safety; the fact that a letter has arrived is a comfort. She also sets the stage for the idea of magical adventures, mentioning castles, lamas, and an abominable snowman.

❼ Drama

Dialogue

1. Have two students read the roles of Peter and Alenka for the bracketed passage that continues on page 799.
2. **Ask** students what they can conclude about Peter's attitude toward his father as well as the community's attitude.
   Possible response: Peter questions whether his father had no choice about going to Tibet. Some members of the community call Peter's father a traitor, yet Alenka defends him. Peter perhaps feels as if his father has gone off on some whim and should be home now to console and entertain him.

BACKGROUND The play is set in Czechoslovakia and Tibet during the second half of the twentieth century. At that time, the Soviet Union, with Russia as its dominant state, occupied Czechoslovakia. It was also during this period that China, a rival of the Soviet Union, invaded Tibet.

In Act I, the Russian government has sent Peter's father, Vladimir, to Tibet to film preparations that the Chinese are making to invade. During his father's absence, Peter was injured while making trouble for the Russian troops. As a result, he is confined to bed. At the same time, an avalanche strands Vladimir in Tibet. Helped by various fantasy characters, including the Boy Spirit, father and son communicate through messages and dreams.

from Act II

ALENKA *(O.S.)* Peter, we received another letter — from your Father!

Lights reveal ALENKA *and* PETER, *in bed. She holds the same letter that the* JINGLE-BELL BOY *pinched from* VLADIMIR.

ALENKA All covered with a strange postmark, and these odd little stamps, and characters that can only be Chinese or maybe Japanese or — Peter, he's still alive!
(pause)
❻ I had to run down to the post office to sign for it, and on the way home, of course, I couldn't wait to read it. He is having the most amazing adventures. In a land so strange — lamas, castles, even an abominable snowman! Here — read it.

Drama
Monologue Alenka's short monologue provides the audience with information about the contents of Vladimir's letter.

PETER I read the last one.

ALENKA What is wrong with you?

PETER Everytime we get a letter, it's like we have a big party. If he really cares about us, how come he's not home yet?

ALENKA You are so brave, Peter. The hardest thing of all is not knowing. Where he is, or whether he's even still — whether he's all right. You don't know how strong you are.

❼ **PETER** Does Father know?

ALENKA Oh, I bet he does. And when he returns you'll be all better, running around like your old self.

PETER How can I get better unless he comes home?
(pause)
How much money does Father make?

ALENKA Why are you —? Enough to survive, like everyone else.

PETER How come, all of a sudden, we can afford paints?

Drama
Dialogue This conversation reveals Peter's fears about his father and the attitudes of others in his community.

Vocabulary Development

Thematic Vocabulary: The Big Question
As students are discussing the excerpt from *Tibet Through the Red Box*, encourage them to use the thematic vocabulary presented in Introducing the Big Question, pp. 790–791. You might encourage them with sentence starters like these:

1. The *background* of this play is important because . . .
2. When the Yeti appears, Peter does not *anticipate* that it . . .
3. Peter's *interpretation* of his father's letter is revealed through . . .
4. Sharing his father's *perspective* through the letter is important for Peter because . . .

ALENKA I make it a priority, what kind of —?

PETER Is Father a traitor?

ALENKA Who says such a —?

PETER It doesn't matter.

ALENKA Do your friends talk like that? The delinquents?

PETER Mother, they're not —

7 ALENKA He was sent away by the Russians. But he had no choice!

PETER You said he did.

ALENKA I never said any such —

PETER Before he left.

ALENKA Who are you? The secret police? You tell your friends, your Father loves his country, he's a man of peace. Then send them to me — and I'll cuff them on their pointed heads!

ALENKA *exits, leaving the letter behind.* THE BOY SPIRIT *enters, as the cat.*

THE BOY SPIRIT Meow. Spreading joy and happiness everywhere?

8 PETER Want me to pull your tail?

THE BOY SPIRIT *(re: the letter)* Oh, you got it.

PETER But I'm not gonna read it. That'll show him.

THE BOY SPIRIT Show him what?

PETER He can't soften me up with, "I miss you, I love you." Not when I know the truth about him.

THE BOY SPIRIT Does that mean you're not even curious about the Abominable Snowman?

The YETI, *an abominable snowman, enters. He is very tall.*

9 PETER "Abominable snowman."

The YETI *approaches* THE BOY SPIRIT, *who flees, running around the stage.*

PETER Who ever heard of such a stupid —?

The YETI *is tall enough to stand eye to eye with* PETER *in his bed.*

YETI Hello, there!

THE BOY SPIRIT Meow meow meow!

MODEL SELECTION

Vocabulary
priority (prī ôr′ ə tē) *n.* something given or meriting more attention than competing alternatives

David Henry Hwang
Author's Insight
I wanted to create a benevolent spirit to guide Peter towards greater insights into himself—like the Tibetan Boddhisattvas, who appear in many forms

Drama
Stage Directions The appearance of the Abominable Snowman onstage intensifies the fantasy and humor of the scene.

10 Reading Check
Where is Peter's father?

8 Author's Insight

David Henry Hwang

1. Explain to students that Bodhisattvas are Buddhist holy spirits that are somewhat like saints. They choose to remain in the endless cycle of birth, death, and rebirth so that they can help others on the path to enlightenment. Bodhisattvas represent virtues such as mercy, compassion, wisdom, and determination.
2. **Ask** students why they think Peter might need a guiding spirit. **Possible response:** He does not seem to have much faith in his father and cannot wholly trust his mother. The spirit may help him to see the truth about his father.

9 Drama

Stage Directions

1. Ask students what they already know about the Yeti, or abominable snowman. Tell them that the Yeti is a mythical creature much like the "bigfoot" or "Sasquatch" of North America. In Tibetan, *yeti* means "magical creature."
2. **Ask** students what the stage directions reveal about the Yeti. **Answer:** The stage directions say that the Yeti is very tall and stands eye-to-eye with Peter in his bed. The Yeti is frightening to the Boy Spirit, who runs away from it.
3. Then **ask** students what creates the humor in this situation. **Possible response:** A Boy Spirit dressed as a cat and a Yeti that does not realize he is an abominable snowman create a sense of comic irony.

10 Reading Check

Possible response: He is in a strange land, visiting castles and meeting lamas and an abominable snowman.

Differentiated Instruction for Universal Access

Support for Less Proficient Readers

Students may need more contextual help to understand this excerpt from the second act of an unusual play. Use a world map or globe to establish the locations of Czechoslovakia and Tibet. Make sure that students grasp the following:

- Peter's father was sent to Tibet to make a film. Now he is stranded in the Himalayan Mountains and cannot return home.
- Peter lives in Czechoslovakia. He has been injured by one of the Russian soldiers who occupy his city. Peter is angry at the Russians and at his father for being away.
- Yeti (or abominable snowmen) are legendary creatures thought to live in the Himalayas. In this play, they are creatures of fantasy from Peter's imagination. The Boy Spirit, who appears in several roles, is also a fantasy.
- Tell students that the play, for all its fantastic elements, is based on the real-life experiences of Peter Sis, who was born in Czechoslovakia and whose father was stranded in Tibet while making a film.

⓫ Critical Thinking

Evaluate

1. Have two volunteers read the bracketed parts of Peter and the Yeti. Then, **ask** students: Of which things does the Yeti seem ignorant?
   Possible response: He seems ignorant of what he is—an abominable snowman. He is also ignorant of Peter, who is precisely the boy for whom the Yeti is looking: "a boy, about twelve years old, who's stuck in a bed."
2. **Ask:** Is the Yeti's explanation of what he claims not to be a valid argument? Explain.
   Possible response: Yes, because he reasons that he is not made of snow but has fur instead, so he is not a snowman.
3. Remind students that irony is the contrast between what is expected to happen and what actually happens. Often, in comedy, irony creates humor. **Ask** students why the Yeti's response to Peter's assertion that he is an abominable snowman comical, and explain why.
   Possible response: The abominable snowman is supposed to be just that: a repulsive, intimidating creature. Instead, the Yeti seems naive, easygoing, and has common sense. That he is the opposite of what an abominable snowman should be makes his behavior comical.

⓬ Critical Viewing

Possible response: The bed is out of proportion with normal-sized things and people. Its surface is above Alenka's head but at the Yeti's eye level. The huge bed gives a sense of altered reality or fantasy.

PETER What the —?

YETI Could you help me?

PETER It's the abominable snowman!

YETI Oh my god! Where?

PETER "Where?" You are the abominable snowman!

⓫ **YETI** Snowmen are made of snow. This is fur. I am a yeti. I'm trying to find a city called Prague. In a country called Chicken-slovakia. A boy, about twelve years old, who's stuck in a bed, and can't get himself out. You know anyone like that?

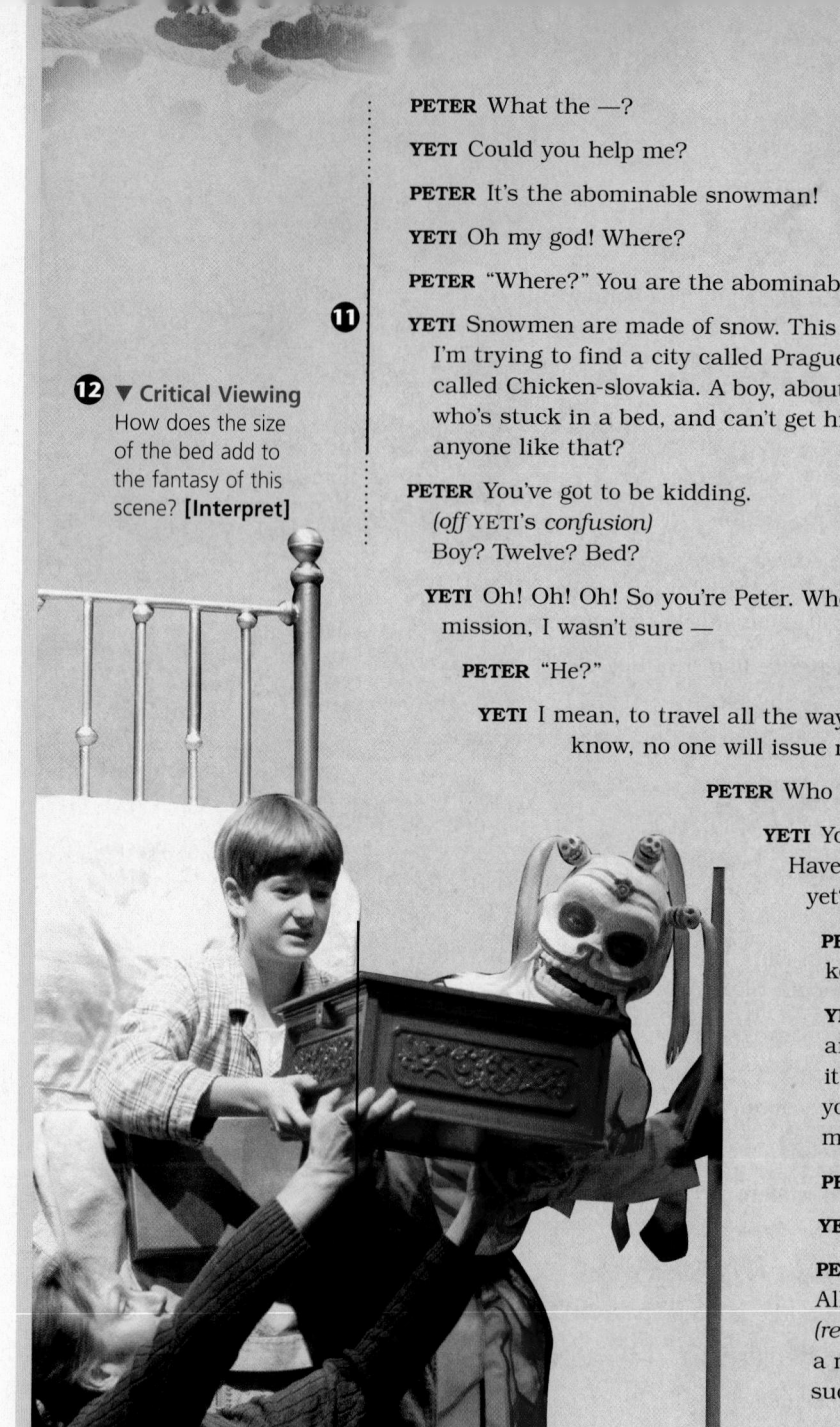

⓬ ▼ **Critical Viewing** How does the size of the bed add to the fantasy of this scene? **[Interpret]**

PETER You've got to be kidding.
(off YETI's *confusion)*
Boy? Twelve? Bed?

YETI Oh! Oh! Oh! So you're Peter. When he sent me on this mission, I wasn't sure —

PETER "He?"

YETI I mean, to travel all the way to Europe — and, you know, no one will issue me a passport.

PETER Who sent you?

YETI Your Father, of course. Haven't you read his letter yet?

PETER Why's everyone keep asking me that?

YETI Not to be boastful or anything, but . . . a lot of it is about me. *(pause)* If you read it, I'll grant you a magical wish.

PETER Anything?

YETI Anything.

PETER *(pulls out the letter)*
All right . . . sucker.
(reads:) "I was crossing a mountain pass when suddenly —"

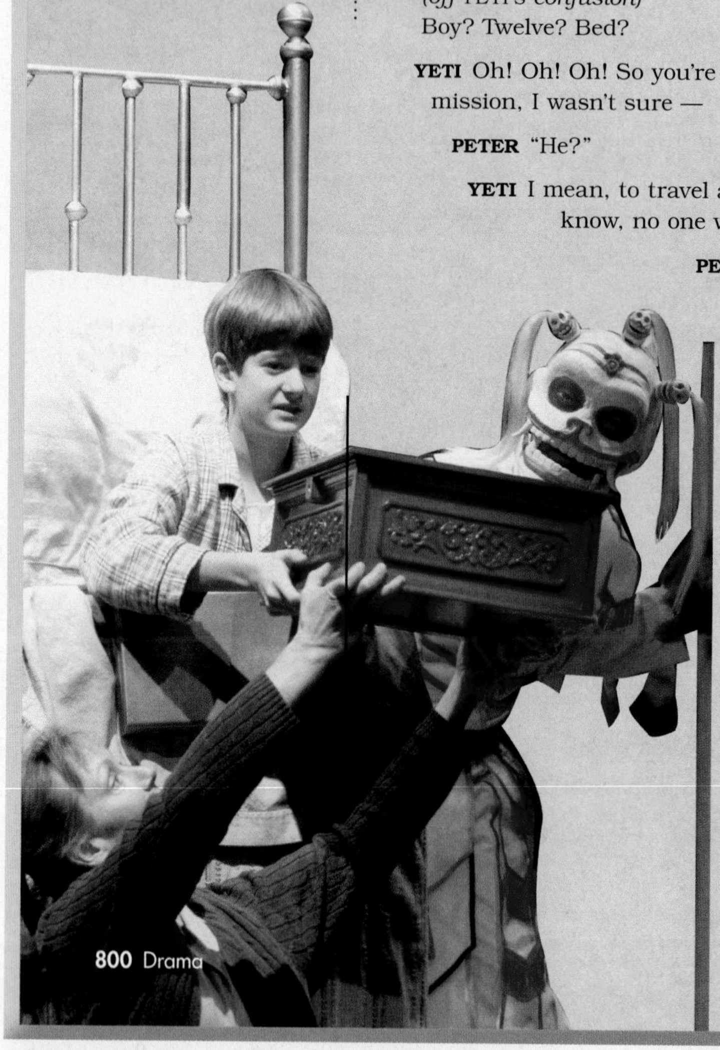

Vocabulary Development

Vocabulary Reinforcement

Give students' sentences using the words in which a word may or may not be used correctly. Students must tell whether the use is correct and explain their answer. Use these sentences:

1. The composer began the concerto with a full *reprise* of several chords.
   Answer: *Reprise* is not used correctly. A reprise is a repetition of a musical phrase or verse. A reprise would not be at the beginning of a concerto but would more likely appear later in the work.
2. Because of the rash of fatal car accidents, highway safety has become this mayor's highest *priority*.
   Answer: *Priority* is used correctly to mean something more important than other matters.
3. Although the cats have not yet *ventured* beyond the yard, the surrounding woods seem to be very tempting.
   Answer: *Ventured* is used correctly to mean "braved the dangers of."

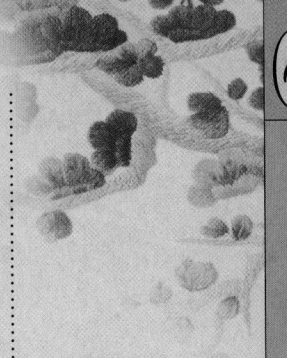

Paper cutouts of snowflakes are projected onto the U.S. wall, moving. MUSICIANS *enter with percussion, simulating the sounds of a snowstorm. U.S.,* VLADIMIR *enters, fighting his way against a blizzard.*

VLADIMIR "A snowstorm took me by surprise. I was looking for shelter, but the winds and snow pushed me to the ground."

U.S., VLADIMIR *is forced to the ground. He sits in a cross-legged meditation position for the rest of the scene.*

VLADIMIR "I probably lost consciousness, but have some vague memory — like a dream —"

PETER "Of being lifted up —" Hey!

The YETI *mimes lifting* PETER, *as he flies out of his bed.*

VLADIMIR "Lifted up and carried!"

PETER *flies across the stage, with the* YETI *beneath, "carrying" him. Together, they move O.S.*

PETER *(to* YETI:*)* What are you doing?

YETI Welcome to the Land of Magic.

13 YETI *releases* PETER. *He finds he can stand on his own two legs.*

VLADIMIR I awoke in a dark cave, on a bed of leaves. Beside me was a potion of honey and herbs. I drank this potion, and soon my strength began to return.

The projections of snowflakes become silhouettes of YETIS, *moving across the stage.*

VLADIMIR One day, I finally felt well-enough to venture out of my dark cave.

PETER *re-enters (having detached his wires), carried by the* YETI. *Dancers enter in Yeti-like costumes, begin to move through a series of warm-up rituals resembling Tai Chi.*

VLADIMIR After my eyes had adjusted to the light, I could see giant fairy beings moving gently in a kind of slow motion throughout the valley.

YETI *starts to put* PETER *down amidst the* DANCERS.

VLADIMIR They seemed to be working, gathering, tending to young ones, playing in the streams and waterfalls. Was this a lost civilization? I did not know. I crawled back into the cave, but this time I managed not to fall asleep. And I saw . . .

MODEL SELECTION

Drama
Dialogue and Stage Directions Both the dialogue and stage directions, including the use of visual images and sound effects, dramatize the reading of Vladimir's letter.

Vocabulary
venture (ven´ chər) *v.* to do or go at some risk

14 **Reading Check**
To what land does the Yeti carry Peter?

13 Drama

Dialogue and Stage Directions

1. Have volunteers read aloud the parts of Peter and Vladimir as you read aloud the stage directions in the long bracketed passage.
2. **Ask** students why they think the playwright decided to stage the scene in this way.
   Possible response: When Peter is finally persuaded to read the letter, its importance is underscored by the paper cutouts and the music. This is an effective way to dramatize the father's adventures, both for Peter and the audience. The staging also adds to the fantasy atmosphere.
3. **Ask** students what they think the purpose is of having Peter fly in this scene.
   Possible responses: It underscores the fantasy aspect of the scene. The adventure is not played out for Peter as he lies in bed; in fact, he recovers and is able to stand on his own when he reaches the Land of Magic. Also, by flying, Peter is sharing Vladimir's experience of being "lifted up and carried," possibly showing a deep connection between them.
4. Then, **ask** students to discuss how Vladimir perceives the Yeti. How does this perception differ from the way the Yeti has appeared in the play so far?
   Possible response: Vladimir sees the Yeti as "giant fairy beings" that move in slow motion through a lost civilization and nurse him back to health. The Yeti in the play has seemed frightening or comical, not gentle or fairylike.

14 Reading Check

Answer: The Yeti carries Peter to the Land of Magic.

Differentiated Instruction for Universal Access

Strategy for Less Proficient Readers

Help students understand the characters in the play and their reactions. Guide students through the play, pausing after each scene to discuss what the characters are doing and how they respond to each situation. Ask students how they would have felt in that same situation and how they would have responded. Discuss why the characters' reactions might differ from their own.

Culturally Responsive Instruction

Culture Focus The play is rich in research possibilities. Students may be interested in further investigating Tibet, in similarities and differences between the yeti and the bigfoot legend, in Tai Chi, or in the lamas and their Buddhist principles. Then, as part of a cultural fair on Tibet, have students present ten-minute informational talks on the topic of their choice.

15 Drama

Comedy

1. Have students read the bracketed passage to themselves.
2. **Ask** volunteers to summarize what is going on in this scene. **Possible response:** Peter watches the Yeti practice for battle and decides to use his wish to get them to help him fight the Russians in Czechoslovakia.
3. Then, **ask** students what is humorous about the passage. **Possible response:** The Yeti has already said it is a monster, yet in this passage it takes pride in its strength and excellent gums. These decidedly human reactions are particularly funny because the Yeti appears so nonhuman.
4. Introduce the idea of comic relief. Explain to students that playwrights sometimes include a lighthearted or humorous episode to give the audience a break between two very serious or violent scenes.

16 Drama

Stage Directions

Ask students why the playwright might use the repetition of drumbeats at this point in the play. **Possible responses:** The drumbeats remind the audience of past action quickly and without needing to use dialogue to cover the same material. Also, drumbeats suggest a military scene to come.

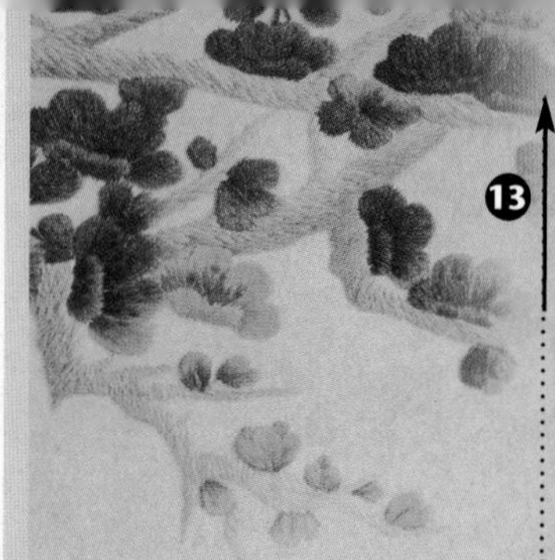

One of the YETIS *places food before* VLADIMIR.

13 **VLADIMIR** Slowly, these gentle giants nursed me to recovery.

The DANCERS *begin to assume the almost martial exercises lamas perform when practicing their theological dialectics.*

PETER *(to* YETI:*)* What are they doing now?

YETI Practicing for battle.

PETER How tough are you guys, anyway?

YETI Look at us — we're big, we're strong, and we love to work out.

PETER And you've got big teeth.

YETI With excellent gums.

PETER OK, I order you to help me fight the Russians. This is gonna be a heck of a lot better than stealing their lunches.

YETI Wait a second.

15 **PETER** You promised, remember? Want the whole world to learn Yetis are big liars?

YETI *(to other* YETIS:*)* Guys, we're being called to battle!

ENSEMBLE 1 Battle?

PETER We're gonna get the Russians.

ENSEMBLE 2 The who?

YETI I . . . granted the boy a wish.

ENSEMBLE 2 Oh. Great.

YETI It's a long story, but a wish is a wish!

ENSEMBLE 1 Where are we going?

PETER Prague. Czechoslovakia.

ENSEMBLE 2 Is the food any good?

Musicians ***reprise*** *the drumbeat which underscored the attack on the Russians in Act One.*

16 **PETER** All right. Let's go back to when everything went wrong. I threw the rock at the Russian soldier, then he followed me into the dead-end alley.

ENSEMBLE 1, ENSEMBLE 2, *and the* YETI *criss-cross the stage, recalling the sequence in Act I.*

PETER This time he's in for a surprise!

Drama
Comedy This interaction stresses the Yeti's human-like—and funny—sense of pride.

Drama
Stage Directions Music reminds the audience of an event that happened earlier.

Vocabulary
reprise (ri prīz´) *n.* repetition of a song, or part of a song, performed earlier

Think Aloud

Vocabulary: Word Roots

Using a "think aloud," model how to use roots and affixes to break down and define unfamiliar words. Apply the strategy to the term *theological dialectics* on this page. Say to students:

> To figure out the meaning of *theological dialectics*, I start by breaking each word into syllables. I know the suffixes *-ic* and *-cal* change a noun into an adjective, so *theological* is the adjective form of *theology*. I know the prefix *theo-* relates to religion. I look at the suffix *-logy*, which I know refers to "the study of something." When I put my knowledge of the word parts together, the meaning of *theological* is "relating to religious study."
>
> To find the meaning of *dialectics*, I look at the prefix *dia-*, which means "between," and *lect-*, which means "speak." I can infer from these that *dialectics* relates to a discussion between people.
>
> Putting all my knowledge of the words together, *theological dialectics* must mean "discussion related to religion."

MODEL SELECTION

THE BOY SPIRIT *enters, dressed as a Russian soldier.*

PETER And here comes the Rooskie!

THE BOY SPIRIT Nyet! Nyet!

PETER I climb up the wall — the exit's blocked!

THE BOY SPIRIT *(bad Russian accent)* Stop, you stupid kid-ski!

PETER He sees me!

THE BOY SPIRIT I say, stop!

PETER Only this time, I don't even try to escape.

THE BOY SPIRIT Nyet! We have you cornered!

PETER I just stand there, spitting down at them.

THE BOY SPIRIT I never again will lose another lunch to you!

PETER Doing my little victory dance.

THE BOY SPIRIT That's disgusting! Come down — else, I shoot!

PETER Suddenly, out of nowhere —

THE BOY SPIRIT One, two —

PETER The Yeti cavalry appears!

THE BOY SPIRIT What?

YETIS *rush* THE BOY SPIRIT.

17 **YETIS** Roar!

THE BOY SPIRIT Oh my god-ski!

PETER He's so scared, he can't even move!

THE BOY SPIRIT The Abominable Snowman?

YETI We're Yeti, why does everyone get that wrong?

PETER Tries to use his gun —

THE BOY SPIRIT N-n-nice snowman . . .

PETER — but his hands are shaking.

YETIS Roar!

THE BOY SPIRIT Bang, bang-ski!

YETI Bullets can't go through our fur.

THE BOY SPIRIT Mama!

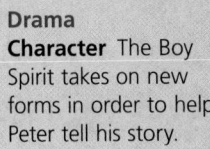

Drama
Character The Boy Spirit takes on new forms in order to help Peter tell his story.

18 **Reading Check**

What do the Yetis help Peter do?

17 Drama

Character

1. Have volunteers read aloud the roles of Peter, the Boy Spirit, the Yeti, and Ensemble 2 (on p. 804) for the bracketed passage.
2. **Ask** students to describe the roles the Boy Spirit has taken on in this act of the play.
   Answer: The Boy Spirit has appeared as a cat, as Peter's father, and now as a bad imitation of a Russian soldier.
3. Discuss with students why Hwang might have had the Boy Spirit take on so many different roles.
   Possible responses: People often change roles in dreams to help the dreamer work out problematic situations. The Boy Spirit may represent the part of Peter that is like his father and like the Russian soldier.
4. **Ask** students what they think the purpose of this scene is.
   Possible response: In Act I, Peter was injured when he confronted a Russian soldier. In his dream, he can turn the situation around and triumph.

18 Reading Check

Answer: The Yetis help Peter defeat the Boy Spirit playing the role of a Russian soldier.

Differentiated Instruction for Universal Access

EL Pronunciation for English Learners

Some students might have difficulty pronouncing words with the medial short "o" sound, as in *got*, *lot*, *blocked*, and *stopped*, replacing it with the long "o" sound, as in *goat*. The following strategies can help students pronounce the medial short "o" sound.

- Write these word pairs on the board: *bought/boat*; *caught/coat*; and *dot/dote*. Pronounce each word in the pair, emphasizing the difference in the short "o" and the long "o" sounds. Then, have students repeat after you.
- Pronounce *got*, *lot*, *blocked*, and *stopped* with students. Then, call out a word and have students write the word. Have students compare and discuss results, noting what might have led to any discrepancies in their spellings.

⓳ Author's Insight

David Henry Hwang

1. Have volunteers take the roles of Peter, the Boy Spirit, the Yeti, and the two Ensembles. Then, read the bracketed passage aloud.
2. **Ask** another volunteer to summarize what is being enacted in this passage.
   Possible response: The Boy Spirit represents Peter's father, who has been forced to travel to Tibet. Peter sees him as a monster for accepting his orders and leaving his family. The playwright puts the decision of what is to happen to his father in Peter's hands.
3. Discuss with students the irony of the Yeti's line, "Actually, *we're* the monsters here." Whom do students think are the monsters in the scene?
   Possible responses: The line is ironic because the Yeti is literally a monster, but Peter wants to believe that his father is a figurative monster who deserves to die. Students may say that Peter is a monster for saying that his father is not a real human being or for his magical wish to humiliate and kill his father.

⓱ **ENSEMBLE 2** They only make us angrier!

YETIS Roar, roar!

YETIS *duplicate their martial exercises, which buffet the "*SOLDIER*" without actually touching him.*

PETER They close in, clutching their paws around the soldier's throat —

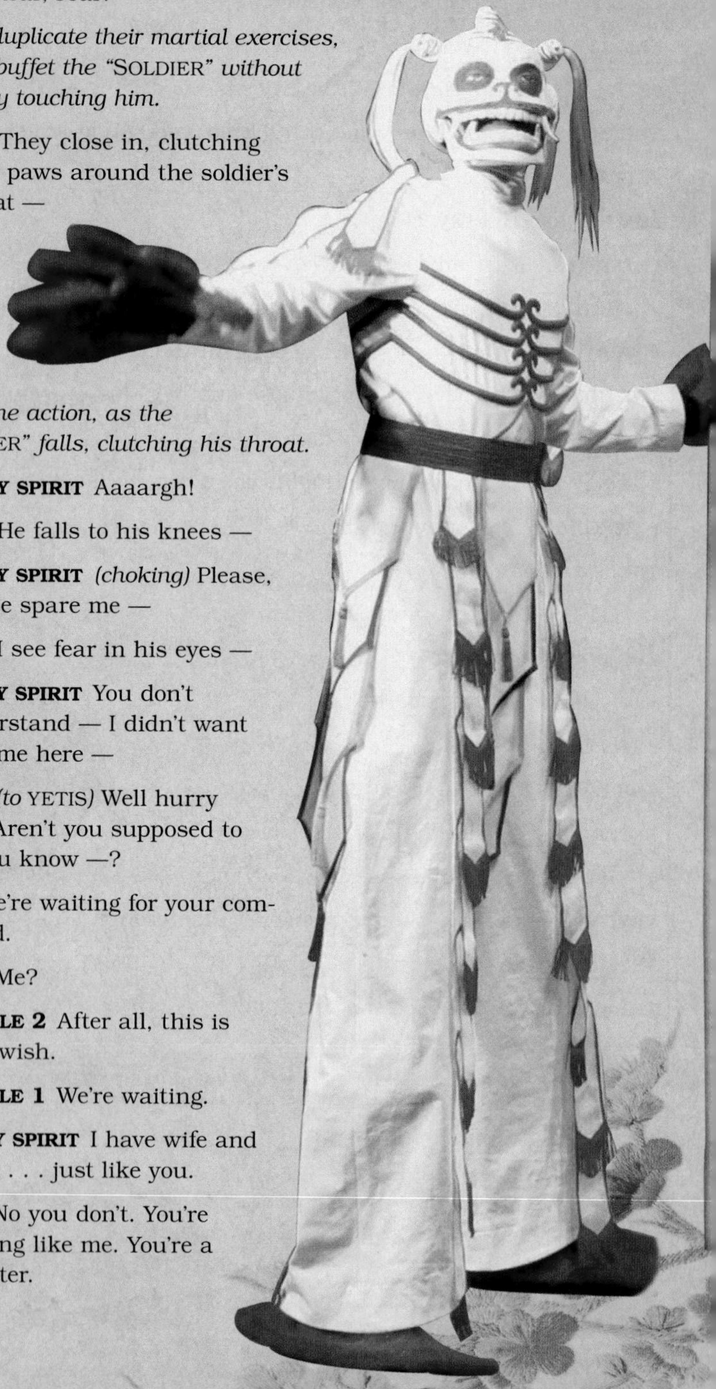

YETIS *mime the action, as the "*SOLDIER*" falls, clutching his throat.*

THE BOY SPIRIT Aaaargh!

PETER He falls to his knees —

THE BOY SPIRIT *(choking)* Please, please spare me —

PETER I see fear in his eyes —

THE BOY SPIRIT You don't understand — I didn't want to come here —

PETER *(to* YETIS*)* Well hurry up? Aren't you supposed to — you know —?

⓳ **YETI** We're waiting for your command.

PETER Me?

ENSEMBLE 2 After all, this is your wish.

ENSEMBLE 1 We're waiting.

THE BOY SPIRIT I have wife and a son . . . just like you.

PETER No you don't. You're nothing like me. You're a monster.

David Henry Hwang
Author's Insight In order for Peter to grow, he must first learn compassion, especially towards those he has long regarded as his enemies.

Vocabulary Development

Word Form Chart

Expand students' vocabulary by helping them learn related forms of the selection vocabulary words. Give students a **Word Form Chart** (***Professional Development Guidebook***, p. 42), with *priority, venture,* and *reprise* in their appropriate columns. Work with the class, or have students work in pairs, to determine the related forms of each word. The final chart should look like the one shown.

Noun	Verb	Adjective
priority	prioritize	
venture; venturer	**venture**	venturesome
reprise	reprise	

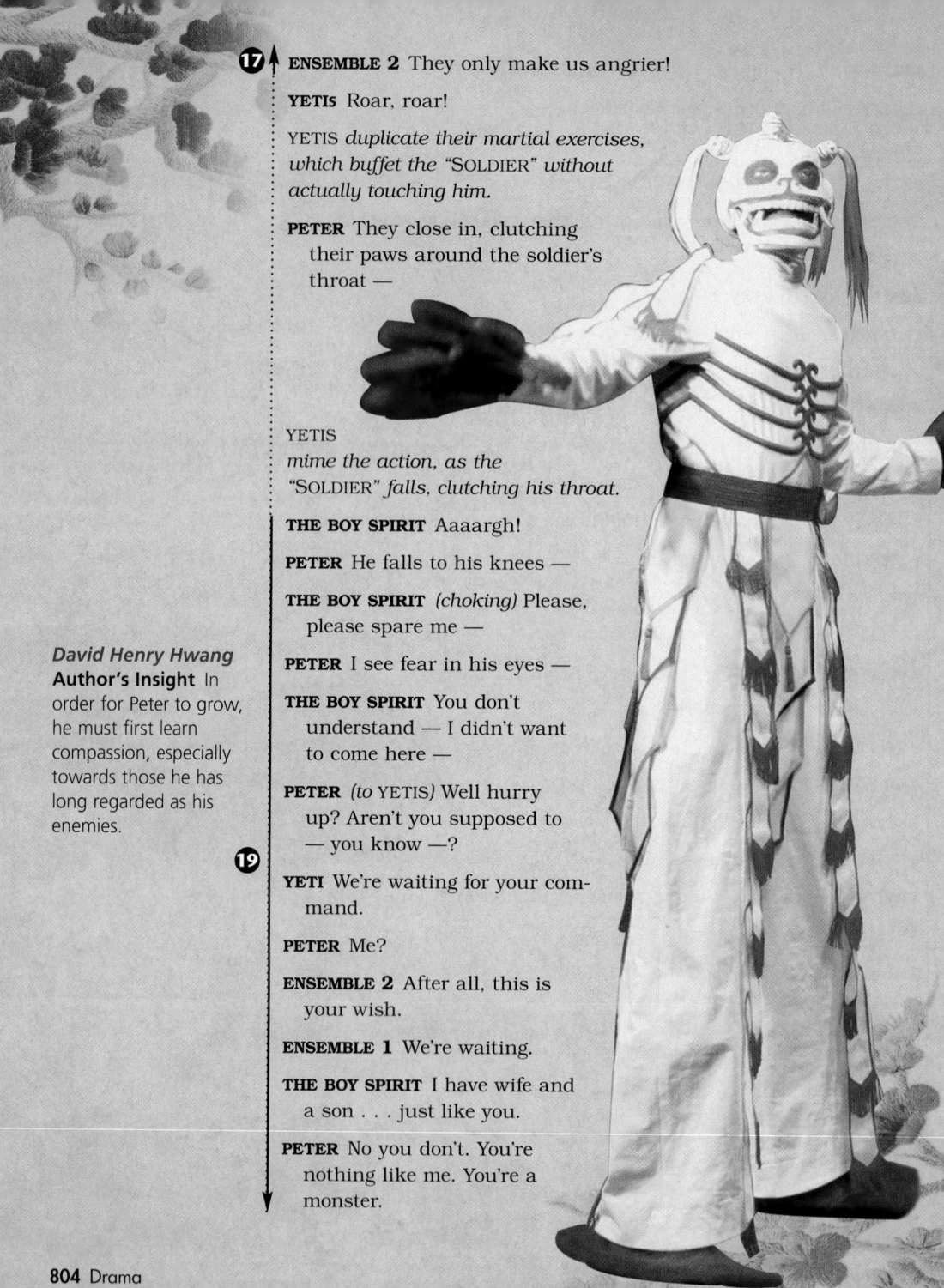

YETI Actually, we're the monsters here.

PETER *(to* YETI:*)* Shut up! *(to* THE BOY SPIRIT:*)* I mean you're not a human being.

THE BOY SPIRIT In my back pocket . . .

19 **PETER** Not a real one anyway.

THE BOY SPIRIT A letter . . .

PETER You're . . . you're . . .

THE BOY SPIRIT Send it to my son.

YETI Hey, um, Peter, it's hard to hold this position.

MODEL SELECTION

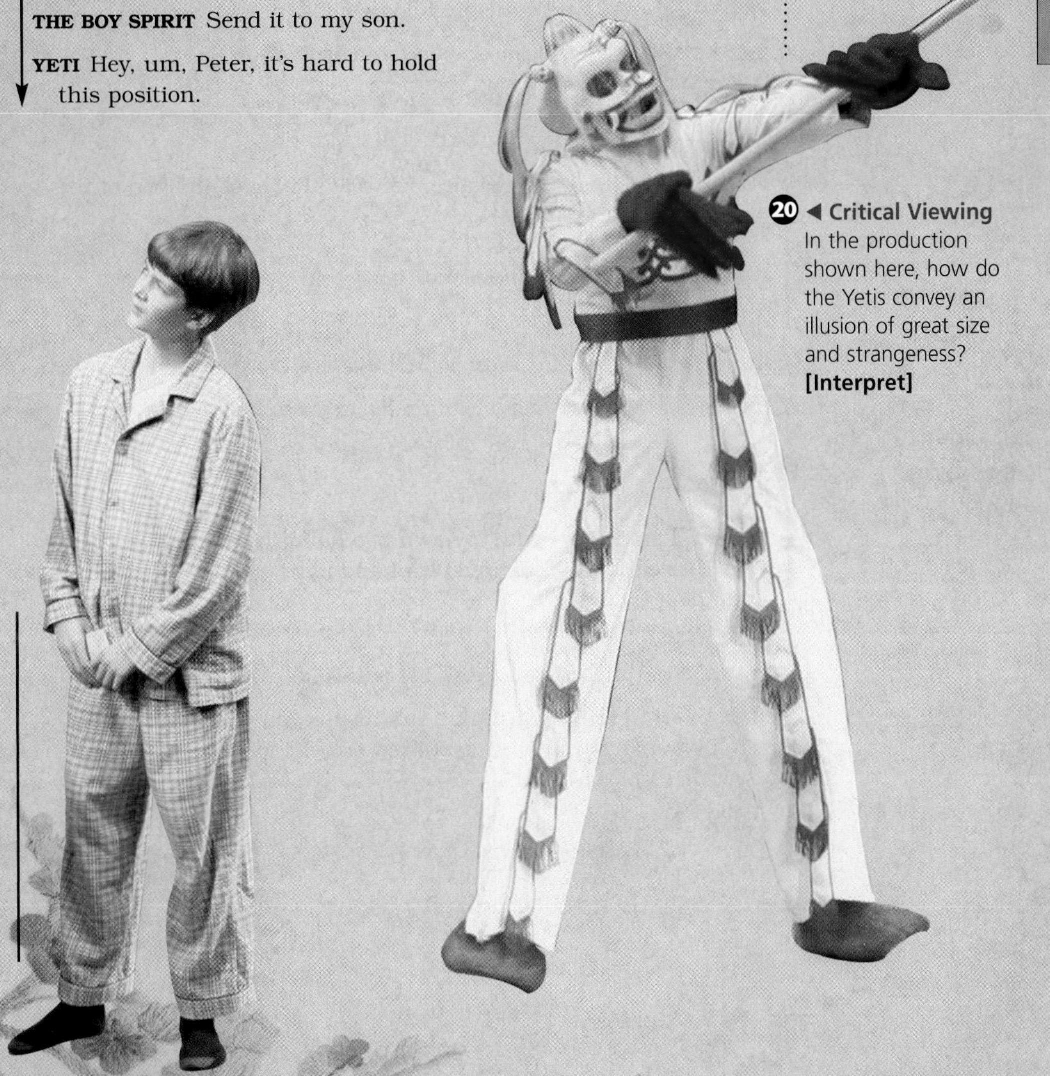

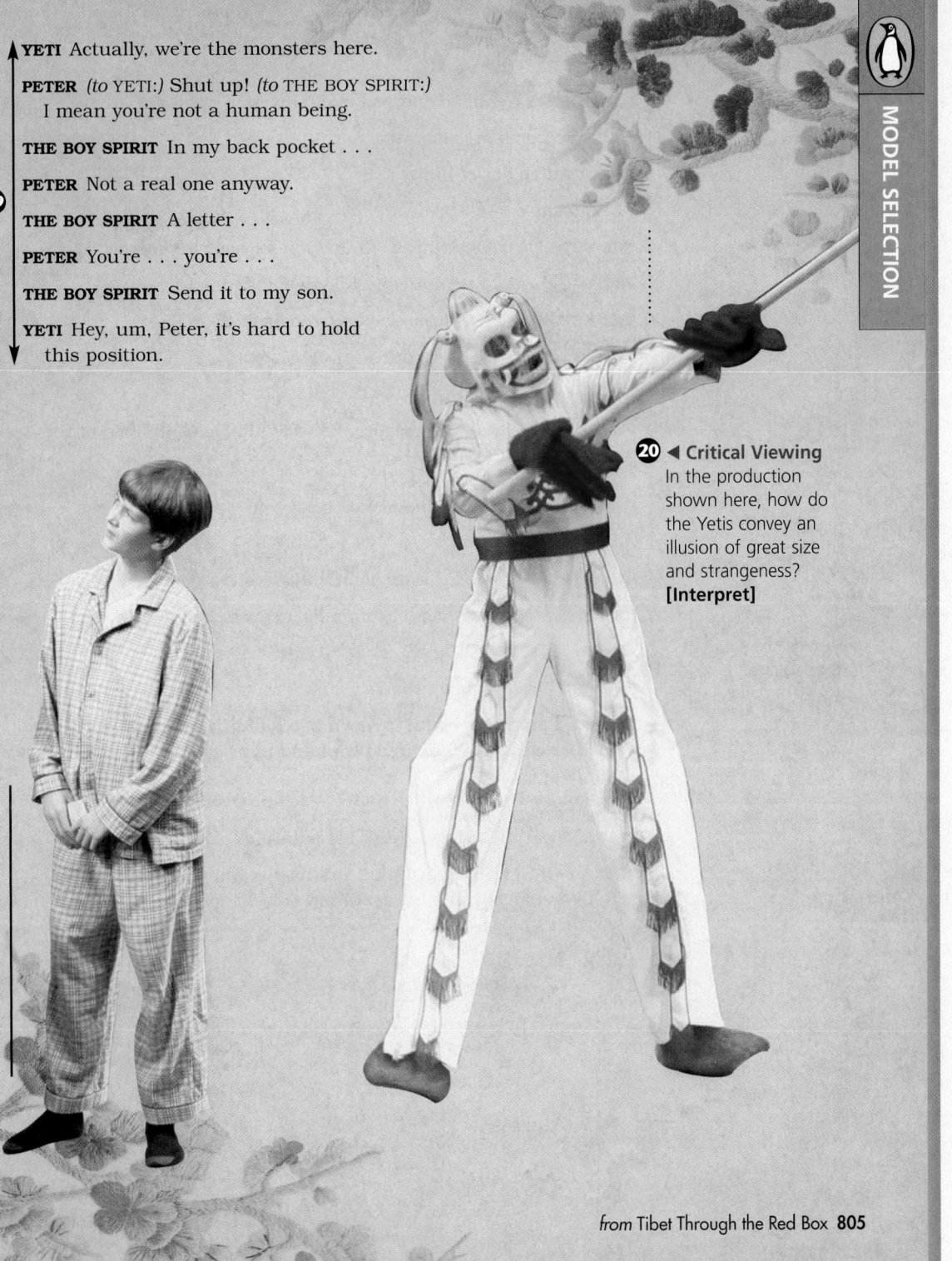

20 ◂ Critical Viewing
In the production shown here, how do the Yetis convey an illusion of great size and strangeness?
[Interpret]

20 Critical Viewing

Possible response: The Yeti are shown as larger than life. It is likely that they are on stilts, because they are so much taller than Peter. Their masks with enormous mouths make them look extremely fearsome, as do their large hands and weapons. The bright colors of their costumes seem strange next to Peter's dull, ordinary pajamas.

Differentiated Instruction for Universal Access

Strategy for Special Needs Students

As they read the selection, have students take time to study the photographs. Ask them to describe what they see and which lines of the play may be spoken at the moments the pictures illustrate. Point out aspects of the pictures that suggest the play is taking place in a culture other than the United States.

Strategy for Less Proficient Readers

To help students understand the notion of parallel plots and the difference between Peter's reality and his dreams, have them draw multiple timelines. The first should include all of the events that actually happened—Peter's father leaving, Peter's attempt to harass the Russian soldier and getting hurt as a result, and the arrival of the letter. The second timeline should include the dream sequences.

21 Drama

Character

Ask students to describe any changes they have seen in Peter's character since the beginning of this selection.

Possible response: Peter seems to have learned that things are not always the way they seem. He has learned compassion and how to look at things from other people's point of view.

22 Drama

Props

1. **Ask** students what they already know about Peter and painting. **Answer:** At the beginning of Act II, Peter has questioned his mother about how they can suddenly afford paints. She starts to tell him she has made the paints a priority.
2. Then, **ask** students why painting could be important to Peter. **Possible response:** Painting could be another way besides dreams that helps Peter cope with conflicting emotions.
3. The title of the play reveals that the red box is very important. **Ask** students: What might the red box represent? **Possible responses:** As a place for Peter to store his paintings, the red box may represent Peter's imagination, his memory, or the part of himself where his true feelings are hidden.

Concept Connector

Anticipation Guide

Have students return to the **Anticipation Guide** and respond to the statements again in the After Reading column.

Connecting to the Big Question

Ask students how the Boy Spirit and the Yeti allow Peter to "see" beyond his narrow perception of his father.

Possible response: The Boy Spirit and the Yeti whisk Peter into a fantastical world in which Peter sees and understands events, such as those relating to his father, as if he were there experiencing them firsthand.

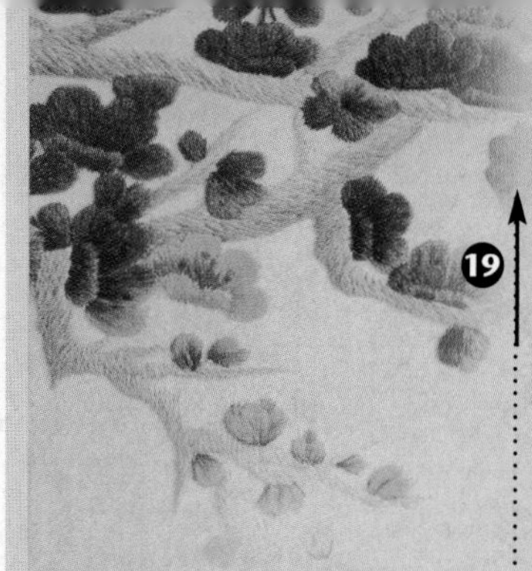

ENSEMBLE 2 Yeah, so will you make up your mind?

19 PETER *screams in frustration.*

PETER All right, let him go.

YETIS *release* THE BOY SPIRIT.

THE BOY SPIRIT Thank you, thank you for showing mercy.

PETER Get out of here. Before I change my mind.

THE BOY SPIRIT I will remember you always

PETER *(to* YETIS:*)* All of you!

YETI But your wish . . .

21 **PETER** I don't want any wishes, I'm sick of magic, of Tibet, of this whole stupid business!
(he flies back into his bed)
Everyone just leave me alone.

All exit.

ALENKA (*O.S.*) Peter? I have something to show you.

ALENKA *enters, carrying a beautifully lacquered red box.*

ALENKA Isn't it beautiful?

PETER Where'd you get this?

22 **ALENKA** I made it — with my own two hands. You think your old mother can only cook and clean and nag?
(pause)
I thought you might like a box — to store your paintings in.

PETER What makes you think I'm painting?

ALENKA Oh, I know you're not. But maybe you will someday. So I am giving you this beautiful red box . . . for all the paintings you have never made.

ALENKA *exits.*

Drama

Props The title of the play alerts the audience to the significance of the box Alenka brings.

Vocabulary Development

Vocabulary Knowledge Rating

When students have completed reading and discussing *Tibet Through the Red Box*, have them take out their **Vocabulary Rating Chart** for this play. Read the words aloud once more, and have students rate their knowledge of the words again in the After Reading column. Clarify any words that are still problematic.

Have students write their own definition and example sentence in the appropriate column. Encourage students to use the word in further discussion and written work about the selection. Remind them that they will be accountable for these words on the **Selection Test**, ***Unit 5 Resources***, pp. 17–19 or 20–22.

After You Read

from Tibet Through the Red Box

Critical Thinking

1. **Respond:** What was your favorite line of dialogue in the play? Why?
2. **(a)** Where is Vladimir, Peter's father? **(b) Infer:** What accusations have Peter's peers leveled at Vladimir? Explain how you know.
3. **(a)** What fantastic or unreal characters appear in this excerpt? **(b) Interpret:** What, if anything, is surprising about the ways in which these characters think and behave?
4. **(a) Analyze:** In what ways do the fantasy characters help Peter connect with his father? **(b) Extend:** How else do they help Peter?

To what extent does experience determine what we perceive? How does Peter's perception of his father change after he experiences his father's adventures? Use details from the story to explain.

Drama Review

5. **(a)** In a chart like the one shown, list the **conflicts** Peter experiences in this **drama. (b)** Then, note **dialogue** and **stage directions** that Hwang uses to dramatize each conflict. **(c)** In a small group, discuss your findings and select the most effective dramatization of conflict in the excerpt. Choose a point person to share your ideas with the class.

Peter's Conflicts	Stage Direction/Dialogue	What It Shows

6. In addition to Peter, which **character** is most essential in this excerpt from the play? Explain your choice.

Research the Author

Create a **poster** advertising a speaking appearance at your school by David Hwang. Your poster should highlight information about the author that would be of greatest interest to your classmates.

- Research details of Hwang's life and published works.
- Write a brief note introducing Hwang. Include descriptions of his best-known works and statements by critics.
- Display your poster in class.

Research the Author

Students may complete this research assignment for homework. Tell them that they can find information about David Henry Hwang's works in a library or online at **www.PHLitOnline.com.**

Assessment Resources

The following resources can be used to assess students' knowledge and skills.

Unit 5 Resources

L1 L2 EL **Selection Test A,** pp. 17–19

L3 L4 **Selection Test B,** pp. 20–22

L3 L4 **Open-Book Test,** pp. 14–16

PHLit Online! Students may use the **Self-test,** at **www.PHLitOnline.com,** to prepare for **Selection Test A** or **Selection Test B.**

ASSESS/EXTEND

Answers

Critical Thinking

1. Some students may choose comments made by the Yeti because of their humor.
2. (a) Vladimir is in Tibet. (b) Some of Peter's friends have suggested that his father is a traitor. This is revealed when Peter asks his mother whether his father chose to go or was forced.
3. (a) The Boy Spirit dressed as a cat and as a Russian soldier and the Yeti appear in the excerpt. (b) **Possible response:** All of the fantasy characters reveal profoundly human traits.
4. (a) The fantasy characters help Peter better understand his father and share in his father's experiences. (b) **Possible response:** The characters help Peter learn that truth is not a single or absolute interpretation of facts.

To what extent does experience determine what we perceive?

Possible response: Because Peter experiences his father's adventures through the Boy Spirit's and the Yeti's magical reenactment, he perceives what his father sees—and thus knows his father's true character. His expectations of his father as a traitorous and selfish man change to an understanding of his father as human, with strengths and weaknesses, and, most important of all, as someone whom Peter can forgive.

Drama Review

5. (a) **Possible response: Peter's Conflicts:** Conflict with father; **Stage Directions/Dialogue:** "Every time we get a letter, it's like we have a big party. If he really cares about us, how come he's not home yet?" **What It Shows:** Peter is angry and resentful. He misses his father and the comfort his presence would provide. (b) and (c) Students should explain their reasons for choosing one example as the best.
6. Students are likely to choose the Boy Spirit, the Yeti, or perhaps Vladimir. Students should support their choices with examples from the text.

Background

Greek Tragedy A Greek tragedy is usually centered on the suffering of a major character and ends in disaster. The origins of tragedy are obscure, but by the time Sophocles wrote, tragedy was a highly developed dramatic form, strongly linked with both religious ritual and artistic performance. It used poetic language as well as song and never completely abandoned its sacred origins.

Students living in secular societies may have some difficulty understanding the degree to which religion informed daily life in ancient Greece. The Greeks believed that the good will of the gods determined the city's welfare. Reverence, the fulfillment of religious duty, and patriotism were often synonymous.

Dramatic characters had human traits but were actually larger than life. Students accustomed to characters with personality and accustomed to seeing cameras focus on revealing muscular twitches on the faces of tragic characters will miss these aspects in Greek drama. Although characters have their assigned traits, these characteristics are so universal that the personages represent examples or types rather than unique personalities.

Finally, tragedies were usually presented as part of a trilogy. Much of the content was based on myths familiar to the ancient Greeks. This inherited and familiar cultural background made it possible for the playwright to include subtle allusions whose importance could be understood by ancient Greek audiences without the benefit of explanation.

Critical Viewing

Possible response: Some students may enjoy watching a performance in the fresh air. Others may express concern over whether the actors could be seen or heard.

THE GREEK THEATER

The Birth of Western Theater

From hit Broadway plays to popular television series, contemporary drama owes much to the ancient Greek dramatists. The Greek playwrights gave European culture its first dramatic characters—men and women confronting crises and the consequences of their own decisions. In their tragedies, the Greeks raised questions of fate, responsibility, and suffering that dramatists explore to this day.

From Ritual to Art

Theater in ancient Greece began as a celebration held in honor of Dionysos (dī´ ə nī´ səs), the god of wine. At his festivals, a chorus would chant songs in honor of the god. According to Greek legend, drama began when Thespis added to the chorus an actor who would take on the role of different characters and hold dialogues with the chorus.

Dramatic Competitions The city of Athens held its first annual dramatic festival in 534 B.C. Competitors each presented three tragedies accompanied by a bawdy, humorous satyr play. In the fifth century B.C., comedies were also produced and judged at the competitions.

Thousands of Athenians attended the annual festival. They viewed the plays in an amphitheater, an outdoor theater like the one shown below. The seats of the amphitheater rose in a semicircle from a level dancing floor, or orchestra area. Painted scenery could be hung at the back. There were no curtains to allow for changes of scenery between acts. The large

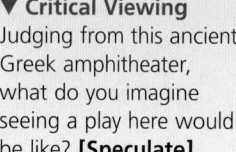

▼ **Critical Viewing** Judging from this ancient Greek amphitheater, what do you imagine seeing a play here would be like? **[Speculate]**

masks worn by the actors amplified their voices and helped even spectators in back rows identify characters and their emotions.

Dramatic Structure

The playwrights of ancient Greece followed a consistent format. Plays opened with a **prologue,** or exposition, that presented background on the conflict. The entering chorus then sang a **parodos** (par′ əd əs), or opening song. This was followed by the first scene. Additional songs by the chorus, called **odes,** divided scenes, as a curtain falling does in modern theater. At the conclusion of a tragedy, the chorus presented a **paean** (pē′ ən) of thanksgiving to Dionysos. The tragedy concluded with an **exodos** (eks′ ə dəs), or final scene.

▲ **Critical Viewing** Which of these photographs shows a modernized production of a Greek tragedy? Which shows a production that recreates the original staging? Explain how you know. **[Connect]**

The Chorus The chorus was central to the production. During the odes, the leader of the chorus, called the **choragos** (kō rā′ gəs), might exchange thoughts with the group in a dialogue. During the recital the group would rotate from right to left, singing the **strophe** (strō′ fē), or verse. Then, the chorus would move in the opposite direction during the **antistrophe,** a verse answering the strophe. An **epode,** or stanza that follows the strophe and antistrophe, was included in some odes.

The chorus is probably a survivor from the ritual in which tragedy originated. In the fully developed plays of the fifth century B.C., the chorus plays a number of roles, from a city crowd to a poetic commentator on events. Reacting to the story as it unfolds, the chorus helps direct the audience's responses.

Antigone

Antigone is part of a trilogy of plays by Sophocles. Like all Greek tragedies, the plays are based on a myth well known to the original audience. In the myth, Oedipus (ed′ i pəs), raised by adoptive parents, is king of Thebes. A plague strikes his city, and Oedipus discovers that the gods have sent the plague in punishment for his own crimes. A stranger whom he struck down in an argument was, he learns, his real father, Laios (lā′ yəs). His wife, Iocaste, is his mother. Ravaged by this knowledge, Oedipus blinds himself. After his death, his sons, Polyneices (päl′ i nī sēz′) and Eteocles (ē tē′ ə klēz′), battle for the throne, and both die. In *Antigone*, Oedipus' daughter Antigone struggles with the new king, her uncle Creon (krē′ än′), as she strives to do right by her dead brothers.

Background

The Big Three The main contenders for the tragedy prize at the dramatic competitions were Aeschylus, Euripides, and Sophocles. Our knowledge of Greek tragedy is based mainly on the work of these three playwrights of the fifth century.

The oldest, Aeschylus, was born to an aristocratic family. As a young man, he earned fame as a soldier fighting against the Persians. He won his first prize for tragedy at approximately forty years of age. (He had been writing for sixteen years.) He won his last prize for tragedy when he was past sixty, with the *Oresteia*, a trilogy considered by many to be his masterpiece. Although Aeschylus wrote ninety plays, only seven of them have survived to the present day.

At the age of twenty-seven, Sophocles defeated Aeschylus in the playwrights' contest with his first tragedy. Like Aeschylus, Sophocles had served in the military. He held political positions as well and was a priest of Asclepius, the Greek god of healing. He was the most conservative of the three great tragedians, both socially and religiously.

Euripides, the youngest of the three, had surprisingly modern attitudes. His characters had greater psychological depth and were more human than the characters of the other two tragedians. In addition, his language was simpler and more colloquial. He disapproved of the prevailing Greek attitudes that subordinated women and glorified war. Euripides' beliefs, embedded in the social criticism in his plays, may account for the limited popularity of his plays in ancient Greece. (He won only four prizes in his lifetime.) Today he is acknowledged as one of the most powerful dramatists in history.

Critical Viewing

Answer: The mask and costume of the photograph on the right indicates a traditional staging. The modern clothing shown in the other image is from a modern production.

TIME AND RESOURCE MANAGER

Antigone, Prologue through Scene 2

Lesson Pacing Guide

DAY 1 Preteach

- Administer the Reading and Vocabulary Warm-ups (*Unit 5 Resources*, pp. 23–26) as necessary.
- Introduce the Reading Skill: Summarize. FT
- Introduce the Literary Analysis concept: Protagonist and Antagonist. FT
- Distribute copies of the appropriate graphic organizer for the Reading Skill (*Graphic Organizer Transparencies*, pp. 153–154). CRI
- Distribute copies of the appropriate graphic organizer for Literary Analysis (*Graphic Organizer Transparencies*, pp. 155–156). CRI
- Teach the selection vocabulary. FT CRI
- Introduce the Word Study skill.

DAYS 2–3 Preteach/Teach

- Build background with the Background feature. CRI
- Develop thematic vocabulary and thematic thinking with Writing About the Big Question.
- Prepare students to read with the Activating Prior Knowledge activities (TE). CRI
- Informally monitor comprehension while students read. FT
- Use the Reading Check questions to confirm comprehension.
- Develop students' ability to summarize using the Reading Skill questions. CRI
- Develop students' understanding of Protagonist and Antagonist using the Literary Analysis questions. CRI
- Reinforce vocabulary with the Vocabulary notes. CRI

DAY 4 Assess

- Assess students' comprehension and mastery of the skills by having them answer the Critical Thinking, Reading Skill, and Literary Analysis questions. FT

DAY 5 Extend/Assess

- Have students complete the Grammar lesson. CRI
- Have students complete the Writing activity and write an essay. (You may assign as homework.) FT
- Extend learning by having students complete the Listening and Speaking activity, an oral report. As an alternative, assign them "Pros and Cons of Protest" in *Reality Central*. CRI
- Administer Selection Test A or B (*Unit 5 Resources*, pp. 28–33). FT

The play *Antigone* appears unedited and in its entirety.
Act I appears on pp. 814–832 and Act II appears on pp. 839–858.

Meeting Your Standards

Students will

1. **analyze and respond to literary elements.**
   - **Literary Analysis: Protagonist and Antagonist**
2. **read, comprehend, and analyze drama.**
   - **Reading Skill: Summarize**
   - **Reading Check questions**
   - **Apply the Skills questions**
   - **Assessment Practice**
3. **develop vocabulary.**
   - **Vocabulary**
   - **Word Study**

CRI For a full explanation of Culturally Responsive Instruction opportunities in this lesson, see p. T86–T87.

FT For an accelerated lesson, use the Fast Track strategies and activities.

Managing Differentiated Instruction
This leveled selection pairing groups a more accessible with a more challenging selection. Choose either one to teach the lesson skills. For classroom management suggestions for using the pairing in a mixed-ability class, see pp. T68–T69.

Daily Block Scheduling
Each day in this Lesson Pacing Guide represents a 40–50 minute period. Teachers using block scheduling may combine days to revise pacing. In addition, teachers may differentiate and support core instruction by integrating components for extended and intensive support as students require. See the Guide to Selected Leveled Resources (facing page).

Guide to Selected Leveled Resources

EL English Learners

			Antigone, Prologue through Scene 2
CORE COURSE	*Unit 5 Resources*	Selection Test A	pp. 38–40
	Graphic Organizer Transparencies	Reading Skill Graphic Organizer A	p. 153
		Literary Analysis Graphic Organizer A	p. 155
EXTENDED SUPPORT (Level 2)	*Unit 5 Resources*	Reading and Vocabulary Warm-ups A or B	pp. 23–26
	Reader's Notebook: English Learner's Version		adapted instruction and adapted selection
	Hear It! Audio CD		selection and summaries
	Hear It! Audio CD (adapted text)		adapted selection and summaries
INTENSIVE SUPPORT (Level 1)	*Reality Central*		"Pros and Cons of Protest"
	Real-World Writing Journal		Lesson 1, pp. 138–141

L2 Below-Level Students

			Antigone, Prologue through Scene 2
CORE COURSE	*Unit 5 Resources*	Selection Test A	pp. 38–40
	Graphic Organizer Transparencies	Reading Skill Graphic Organizer A	p. 153
		Literary Analysis Graphic Organizer A	p. 155
EXTENDED SUPPORT (Level 2)	*Unit 5 Resources*	Reading and Vocabulary Warm-ups A or B	pp. 23–26
	Reader's Notebook		adapted instruction and full selection
	Hear It! Audio CD		selection and summaries
INTENSIVE SUPPORT (Level 1)	*Reality Central*		"Pros and Cons of Protest"
	Real-World Writing Journal		Lesson 1, pp. 138–141
	Reading Kit		Reteaching worksheets

L1 Special Needs Students

			Antigone, Prologue through Scene 2
CORE COURSE	*Unit 5 Resources*	Selection Test A	pp. 38–40
	Graphic Organizer Transparencies	Reading Skill Graphic Organizer A	p. 153
		Literary Analysis Graphic Organizer A	p. 155
EXTENDED SUPPORT (Level 2)	*Unit 5 Resources*	Reading and Vocabulary Warm-ups A or B	pp. 23–26
	Reader's Notebook: Adapted Version		adapted instruction and adapted selection
	Hear It! Audio CD (adapted text)		adapted selection and summaries
INTENSIVE SUPPORT (Level 1)	*Reality Central*		"Pros and Cons of Protest"
	Real-World Writing Journal		Lesson 1, pp. 138–141
	Reading Kit		Reteaching worksheets

The program includes resources for these students: L3 On-Level L4 Advanced All All
For a complete guide to selection support, see pp. T106–T108.

NOTE: All print materials are also available online at *www.PHLitOnline.com.*

VISUAL GUIDE to Featured Selection Resources

Antigone, Prologue through Scene 2

RESOURCES FOR:

EL English Learners

L1 Special Needs Students

L2 Below-Level Students

L3 On-Level Students

L4 Advanced Students

All All Students

Vocabulary/Fluency/Prior Knowledge

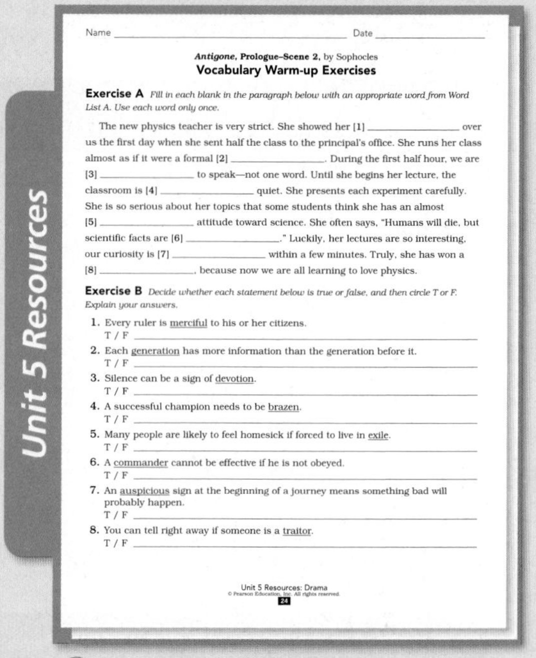

Unit 5 Resources

Name ____________________ Date ____________

Antigone, Prologue–Scene 2, by Sophocles
Vocabulary Warm-up Exercises

Exercise A *Fill in each blank in the paragraph below with an appropriate word from Word List A. Use each word only once.*

The new physics teacher is very strict. She showed her [1] ____________ over us the first day when she sent half the class to the principal's office. She runs her class almost as if it were a formal [2] ____________. During the first half hour, we are [3] ____________ to speak—not one word. Until she begins her lecture, the classroom is [4] ____________ quiet. She presents each experiment carefully. She is so serious about her topics that some students think she has an almost [5] ____________ attitude toward science. She often says, "Humans will die, but scientific facts are [6] ____________." Luckily, her lectures are so interesting, our curiosity is [7] ____________ within a few minutes. Truly, she has won a [8] ____________, because now we are all learning to love physics.

Exercise B *Decide whether each statement below is true or false, and then circle T or F. Explain your answers.*

1. Every ruler is merciful to his or her citizens.
   T / F ____________
2. Each generation has more information than the generation before it.
   T / F ____________
3. Silence can be a sign of devotion.
   T / F ____________
4. A successful champion needs to be brazen.
   T / F ____________
5. Many people are likely to feel homesick if forced to live in exile.
   T / F ____________
6. A commander cannot be effective if he is not obeyed.
   T / F ____________
7. An auspicious sign at the beginning of a journey means something bad will probably happen.
   T / F ____________
8. You can tell right away if someone is a traitor.
   T / F ____________

Unit 5 Resources: Drama
© Pearson Education, Inc. All rights reserved.
24

EL L1 L2 **Vocabulary Warm-ups A and B, pp. 23–24**

Also available for these selections:

EL L1 L2 **Reading Warm-ups A and B, pp. 25–26**

All **Vocabulary Builder, p. 30**

All **Writing About the Big Question, p. 27**

L2 L3 ***Reader's Notebook***

L1 ***Reader's Notebook: Adapted Version***

EL ***Reader's Notebook: English Learner's Version***

Reader's Notebooks

Pre- and postreading pages for both selections, as well as *Antigone, Prologue through Scene 2* appear in an interactive format in the *Reader's Notebooks.* Each *Notebook* is differentiated for a different group of learners.
The selections in the Adapted and English Learner's versions are abridged.

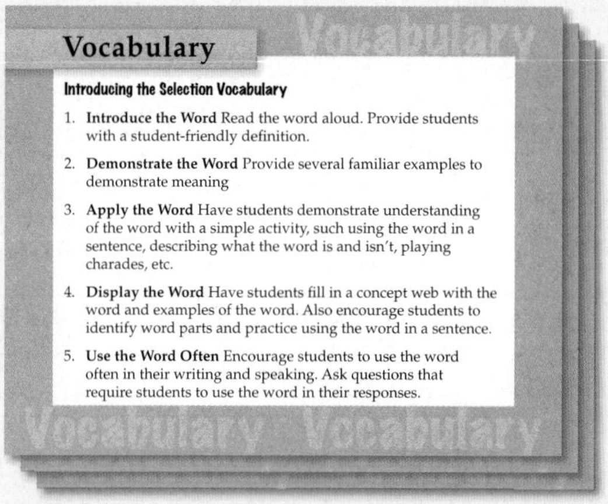

Vocabulary

Introducing the Selection Vocabulary

1. **Introduce the Word** Read the word aloud. Provide students with a student-friendly definition.
2. **Demonstrate the Word** Provide several familiar examples to demonstrate meaning
3. **Apply the Word** Have students demonstrate understanding of the word with a simple activity, such using the word in a sentence, describing what the word is and isn't, playing charades, etc.
4. **Display the Word** Have students fill in a concept web with the word and examples of the word. Also encourage students to identify word parts and practice using the word in a sentence.
5. **Use the Word Often** Encourage students to use the word often in their writing and speaking. Ask questions that require students to use the word in their responses.

Classroom Strategies and Teaching Routines

- core classroom routines outlined step-by-step
- convenient format for easy reference while teaching

Selection Support

Transparencies

Antigone, **Prologue through Scene 2** by Sophocles

Before You Read A: Reading—Summarizing

Who is the most important character?
Antigone
What does the character want?
Who or what gets in the character's way?
the sentry
What is the outcome?

Graphic Organizer Transparencies
© Pearson Education, Inc. All rights reserved.
153

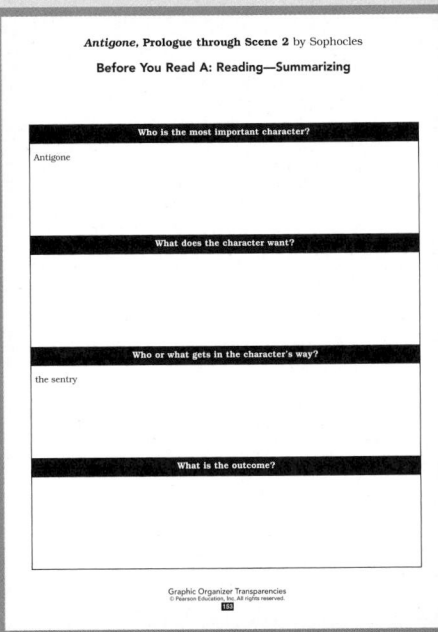

EL L1 L2 **Reading: Graphic Organizer A,** p. 153 (partially filled in)

Also available for these selections:

- L3 Reading: Graphic Organizer B, p. 154
- EL L1 L2 Literary Analysis: Graphic Organizer A, p. 155 (partially filled in)
- L3 Literary Analysis: Graphic Organizer B, p. 156

Skills Development/Extension

Unit 5 Resources

Name ______________________ Date ____________

Antigone, **Prologue–Scene 2,** by Sophocles

Enrichment: Drama, Spectacle, and the Olympics

The ancient Greeks presented plays during competitions held at popular festivals honoring the god Dionysos. They gave prizes and honors to the winners. Although such drama competitions are no longer held, the modern Olympic Games still treat audiences to music, entertainment, and cultural events along with the excitement of athletics. When the 2004 Olympic Games took place in Athens, Greece, the opening and closing ceremonies included parades and performances of actors, acrobats, and musicians that connected Greece's ancient heritage to its present-day world.

Use a library or the Internet to read about or find a picture of one of the spectacles (forms of entertainment) or cultural performances from the 2004 Olympic Games or the Games of any other year.

1. Describe the spectacle or cultural performance.

2. What message about culture or people's values did the spectacle convey?

Unit 5 Resources: Drama
© Pearson Education, Inc. All rights reserved.
31

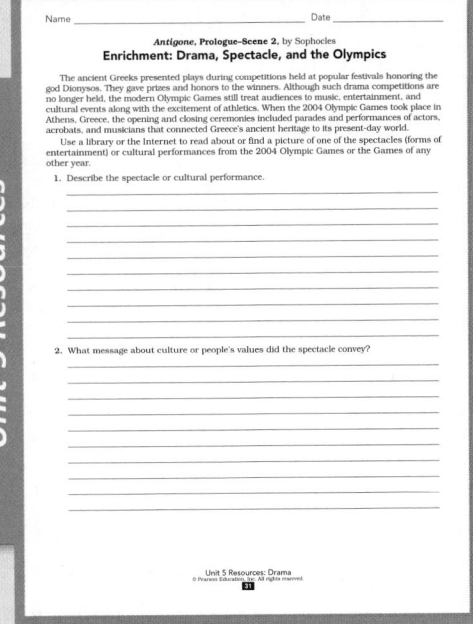

L4 **Enrichment,** p. 31

Also available for these selections:

- All Reading: Summarize, p. 29
- All Literary Analysis: Protagonist and Antagonist, p. 28
- L3 L4 Grammar, p. 32
- L3 L4 Support for Writing, p. 33
- L3 L4 Support for Extend Your Learning, p. 34

Assessment

Name ______________________ Date ____________

Antigone, **Prologue–Scene 2,** by Sophocles

Selection Test B

Critical Reading *Identify the letter of the choice that best completes the statement or answers the question.*

___ 1. Which of these events related to *Antigone* took place first?
A. the assault on Thebes
B. the death of the brothers
C. the decree of Creon
D. the crime of Oedipus

___ 2. Which of the following statements best summarizes the Prologue of *Antigone*?
A. Antigone asks her sister to help bury their brother.
B. Antigone says, "I will bury the brother I love."
C. The Chorus comments on Antigone's point of view.
D. Creon is Antigone's uncle and the king of Thebes.

___ 3. Why does Ismene plead with Antigone not to defy Creon?
A. She fears challenging authority.
B. She feels that Antigone is right.
C. She believes that Creon will punish her.
D. She must assert her will over others.

___ 4. Why does Antigone want to bury Polyneices?
A. She is basically stubborn.
B. She has too much pride.
C. She feels a sense of loyalty.
D. She is consumed by hatred.

___ 5. According to Antigone, why is she defying Creon?
A. She wants to overthrow him.
B. She wishes to join her dead brothers.
C. She would rather die than marry Haimon.
D. She believes in obedience to a higher law.

___ 6. Which one of the following is a conflict in *Antigone*?
A. conflict between the king and the chorus
B. conflict between Creon and Choragos
C. conflict between laws of humans and laws of gods
D. conflict between Antigone and Polyneices

___ 7. Who is the play's antagonist?
A. Antigone
B. Ismene
C. Creon
D. Choragos

Unit 5 Resources: Drama
© Pearson Education, Inc. All rights reserved.
41

L3 L4 **Selection Test B, pp. 41–43**

Also available for these selections:

- EL L1 L2 Selection Test A, pp. 38–40
- L3 L4 Open-Book Test, pp. 35–37

PHLit Online!

www.PHLitOnline.com

- complete narrated selection text
- a thematically related video with writing prompt
- an interactive graphic organizer
- highlighting feature
- access to all student print resources, adapted to individual student needs
- Spanish and English summaries

Background video

Also available:

Get Connected! (thematic video with writing prompt)

Vocabulary Central (tools, activities, and songs for studying vocabulary)

Also available:

Writer's Journal (with graphics feature)

DIFFERENTIATE/PRETEACH

❶ Selection Skills

1. With the class, preview the selection skills. (The lesson meets the lesson objectives given on p. 810a.)
2. Explain that students will learn to use the skill of summarizing as they read to better understand and enjoy the selection. By examining protagonists and antagonists as they read, they will gain deeper insight into drama.
3. To introduce the Writing and Listening and Speaking activities (p. 835), tell students that when they have finished reading the selection, they will write an essay and present an oral report related to the selection.
4. Tell students that they will also study a grammar concept: participles and gerunds. By mastering this concept, they will improve their reading fluency and the quality of their own writing.

Before You Read

Antigone, Prologue through Scene 2

Drama Selection

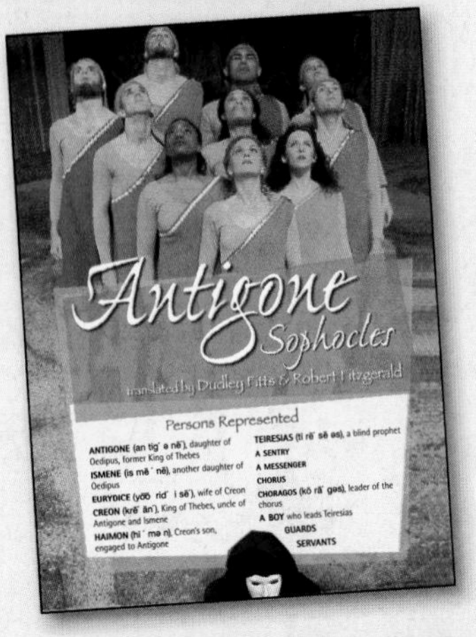

▲ Read ***Antigone*** to find out how members of a family battle each other over their different values.

❶

Selection Skills Guide

Practice these skills with ***Antigone*, Prologue through Scene 2** (p. 814).

- Identify protagonist and antagonist
- Summarize
- Retell
- Understand participles and gerunds
- Write an essay
- Present an oral report

Differentiated Instruction for Universal Access

Accessibility at a Glance: Selection

	Antigone, Part 1
Context	Historical: ancient Greece
Language/ Vocabulary	• Dialogue • Formal language and monologues
Concept Level	Challenging (individual against society)
Literary Merit	Noted author
Lexile/Length	NP Word Count: 4,439
Overall Rating	**Accessible**

❷ Literary Analysis: Protagonist and Antagonist

Greek tragedies, like many other plays and stories, typically focus on a **protagonist,** or main character, and an **antagonist,** the character who is in conflict with the protagonist. In fact, these two literary terms were first applied to Greek tragedies such as *Antigone*.

In a play, the struggle between a protagonist and an antagonist may take the form of a dramatic life-or-death conflict. At the same time, the two characters may stand for larger conflicting ideas or values. The characters' struggle may reflect deep questions of concern to people of all times and places. Here are some of the conflicting ideas in *Antigone*:

- Antigone, the protagonist, breaks the law because she believes that the laws of the gods are higher than human laws.
- Her antagonist, Creon, insists that everyone must obey the law. He believes that no one is above the law.

PHLit Online!
www.PHLitOnline.com

Hear It!
- Selection summary audio
- Selection audio

See It!
- Get Connected video
- Background video
- More about the author
- Vocabulary flashcards

Do It!
- Interactive journals
- Interactive graphic organizers
- Self-test
- Internet activity
- Grammar tutorial
- Interactive vocabulary games

❸ Reading Skill: Summarize

A **summary** is a short statement of the main ideas and events in a work. To summarize, pause occasionally to **retell** what you have read, using only the most important information. Summarizing improves your understanding of a work because it leads you to identify its key elements.

As you read *Antigone*, pause to summarize scenes and conversations.

❹ Using the Strategy: Summary Chart

Use a **summary chart** like this one to identify the key elements of this part of *Antigone*.

Who is the most important character?	What does the character want?	Who or what gets in the character's way?	What is the outcome?

Differentiated Instruction for Universal Access

Preparing Students for the Selection

If you wish to prepare lower level readers to read *Antigone*, Prologue through Scene 2, follow these steps:

- Students might have difficulty with the central concept of the play: an individual opposing society. Have students think of the reasons why an individual might fight against some aspect of society, such as the government. How would he or she feel? Encourage students to refer to examples from history or other stories they know.
- Ask students what they know about ancient Greece, its history, and its culture. Have students share their knowledge with each other.
- Students may find Sophocles' use of formal language challenging. Review strategies for paraphrasing and breaking down sentences. As they read, encourage students to rephrase difficult sentences in their own words.

PRETEACH

❷ Literary Analysis

1. Introduce the skill, using the instruction on the student page.
2. Tell students that they will practice identifying the protagonist and antagonist as they read.

Think Aloud: Model the Skill

Model the skill of identifying the protagonist and antagonist, using the following "think aloud":

> I know that every story focuses on a conflict. When the conflict is between two people, one person is the antagonist and one is the protagonist. To decide which is which, I examine the characters' roles. For example, in a story about a young man who struggles to escape wrongful capture by a cruel king, the young man is the main character with whom the reader sympathizes. The young man is the protagonist, whereas the king is the antagonist, the character who thwarts the young man's progress.

❸ Reading Skill

1. Introduce the skill, using the instruction on the student page.
2. Tell students that they will practice summarizing as they read.

Think Aloud: Model the Skill

Model the skill of summarizing, using the following "think aloud":

> Imagine I am reading a long play in which there is a complicated plot as well as many characters to remember. To help me keep track of all these details as I read, I can summarize, or retell in simple words, the main events of the story. For instance, I can summarize the events of each scene. Then, when I have finished the play, I can read my notes to help me summarize the play as a whole.

❹ Using the Strategy

Give students a copy of either **Reading Skill Graphic Organizer A** or **B** (*Graphic Organizer Transparencies,* pp. 153–154) to record main ideas as they read. Use the examples in **Reading Skill Graphic Organizer A,** which is partially filled in, to model the process of completing the organizer.

PRETEACH

❶ Writing About the Big Question

1. Review the assignment with the class.
2. Ask students to think about and discuss the following questions: Why do people disobey rules? Is it acceptable to break a rule you do not agree with? Explain.
3. Have students complete the sentence starters. Review responses as a class.
(**Possible response:** An individual may go against what others say when he or she disagrees with their ideas. The interpretation of an action or an event can differ between two people because they have different perspectives and beliefs.)
4. Remind students that their answers will help them think about the Big Question.

While You Read

Tell students that as they read, they should look for Antigone's and Creon's expressions of their points of view.

❷ Vocabulary

1. Have students preview the selection vocabulary.
2. For each word, have students say the word aloud.
3. Then, use the word in a sentence that defines the word.
4. Finally, repeat your definitional sentence or a similar sentence with the word missing, and have the class "fill in the blank" chorally. For example:

Something said sententiously is said in a preachy manner. I try to avoid my great-uncle, because I cannot bear to listen to the advice he gives so [students say "sententiously"].

❸ Word Study

1. Introduce the skill, using the instruction in the box.
2. Using their knowledge of the root *-dict-*, ask students for a word that means "to speak against or contrary to something."
(**Answer:** *contradict*)

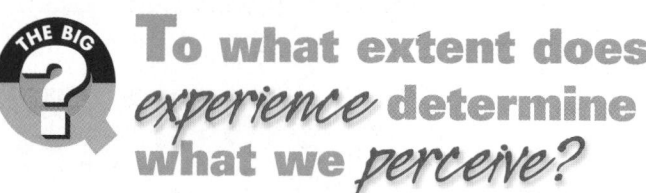

To what extent does *experience* determine what we *perceive?*

❶ Writing About the Big Question

In the first part of *Antigone*, a woman breaks the king's law in order to uphold her deeply felt beliefs. Use these sentence starters to develop your ideas about the Big Question.

An **individual** may go against what others say when _______________.

The **interpretation** of an action or an event can differ between two people because _______________.

While You Read Look for moments when Antigone and Creon express their own points of view about what is right and what is wrong.

❷ Vocabulary

Read each word and its definition. Decide whether you know the word well, know it a little bit, or do not know it at all. After you read, see how your knowledge of each word has increased.

- **sated** (sāt´ əd) *adj.* satisfied; provided with more than enough (p. 818) *We were sated after the big lunch.* sate *v.*
- **sententiously** (sen ten´ shəs lē) *adv.* in a way that shows excessive fondness for wise sayings; in lecturing tones (p. 822) *I told him I felt ill, and he answered sententiously, "An apple a day keeps the doctor away."* sententious *adj.* sententiousness *n.*
- **deflects** (dē flekts´) *v.* turns or makes go to one side (p. 824) *He deflects his opponent's blows by blocking with his forearm.* deflection *n.* deflective *adj.* deflector *n.*
- **edict** (ē´ dikt´) *n.* a public order; decree (p. 827) *At the press conference, the mayor gave his edict about stray animals.*
- **brazen** (brā´ zən) *adj.* shameless; bold (p. 828) *There was chocolate all over her mouth, but she told a brazen lie about the cookies.* brazenly *adv.* brazenness *n.*
- **waver** (wā´ vər) *v.* show indecision; fluctuate (p. 831) *He dipped his toe into the icy water and began to waver about diving in.* waveringly *adv.*

❸ Word Study

The **Latin root *-dict-*** means "speak" or "say."

In this play, a king issues an **edict,** publicly saying that no one is permitted to bury his enemy.

Vocabulary Development

Vocabulary Knowledge Rating

Create a **Vocabulary Knowledge Rating Chart** (***Professional Development Guidebook,*** p. 33) for this selection. Include the selection vocabulary from this page and the Big Question words that appear in the Writing About the Big Question sentence frame on this page. (The Big Question vocabulary is introduced on pp. 790–791.)

Give students a copy of the chart. Read the words aloud, and have students mark their rating in the Before Reading column. Urge them to be alert to these words as they read and discuss the selection.

Tally how many students think they know a word to gauge how much instruction to provide. As students read and discuss the selection,

PHLit Online! **Vocabulary Central,** featuring tools, activities, and songs for studying vocabulary, is available at **www.PHLitOnline.com.**

Meet Sophocles
(496–406 B.C.)

Author of *Antigone*

Born in Colonos, near Athens, the Greek dramatist Sophocles (säf´ ə klēz´) wrote 123 plays, of which only 7 still exist. His most famous plays, including *Antigone*, chronicle the lives of Oedipus and his children.

A Much Admired Man Sophocles served as a general in the wars Athens fought with neighboring city-states. Admired for his good looks and athleticism, he also excelled at music.

It was in the theater, however, that Sophocles truly shone. He won the prize for tragedy at the Greek dramatic competitions twenty-four times. Earlier plays had featured only two characters on stage at a time. Sophocles was the first to use a third actor in dramatic performance. This innovation changed the genre significantly.

DID YOU KNOW?
In drama competitions, Sophocles never placed below second.

4 BACKGROUND FOR THE PLAY
Family Feud

Antigone is one of the three children of Oedipus, the former king of Thebes. When Oedipus went into exile for his crimes, Antigone's brothers, Polyneices and Eteocles, fought over who would rule, and Polyneices attacked Thebes. Eventually, the two brothers killed each other, and their uncle Creon, who had supported Eteocles, became king. The play opens after the battle in which the two brothers are killed.

Daily Bellringer
For each class during which you will teach this selection, have students complete one of the five Sentence Modeling activities for Week 26 in the *Daily Bellringer Activities* booklet.

4 Background
Family Feud

In the prologue to *Antigone*, Sophocles provides details about the status of the conflict among members of the royal family of Thebes. The prologue in a Greek tragedy is an introductory scene that establishes the situation for the play. The prologue may be a monologue, a speech by one character, or a dialogue, a conversation between two characters. In this case, the prologue is a dialogue between Antigone and Ismene, the sisters of Eteocles and Polyneices. It alerts readers that the sisters have lost their brothers, who fought on opposite sides in a battle for Thebes. One brother has been buried with honors; the other has been left unburied by order of the king.

Multidraft Reading
This icon ● marks natural pauses in the selection. To assist struggling readers and to deepen reading for all, assign the text in "chunks," following the icons, and apply multidraft reading protocols. For each reading, have students set the purpose indicated:

- **First reading**—literal comprehension: answering the Reading Check questions.
- **Second reading**—application of skills: answering the Protagonist and Antagonist and Summarize prompts.
- **Third reading**—interpretation: answering the end-of-selection questions.

For more guidance, refer to the ***Classroom Strategies and Teaching Routines*** card on multidraft reading.

Differentiated Instruction
Additional Instruction

EL Extended Support—English Learners
Have students complete the **Reading and Vocabulary Warm-ups, *Unit 5 Resources*,** pp. 23–26, before they read. Assign the prereading pages and the adapted selection in the ***Reader's Notebook: English Learner's Version.*** Then, have students listen to portions of the selection on the ***Hear It! Audio* CD.**

L1 L2 Extended Support—Struggling Readers
Have students complete the **Reading and Vocabulary Warm-ups, *Unit 5 Resources*,** pp. 23–26, before they read. Assign the prereading pages and the adapted selection in the ***Reader's Notebook: Adapted Version.*** Then, have students listen to portions of the selection on the ***Hear It! Audio* CD** (adapted text).

Extended Support—Reluctant Readers
To build motivation and engagement before assigning the selection, have students read "Pros and Cons of Protest," a thematically related selection in ***Reality Central.*** Then, use the questions at the conclusion of the related selection to guide discussion.

PHLit Online!
For more about the author, practice with the selection vocabulary, and more background, go to **www.PHLitOnline.com.**

TEACH

❶ Activating Prior Knowledge

1. Prepare an **Anticipation Guide** (see ***Professional Development Guidebook***, pp. 36–38) with the following statements:
   - Family members should always support each other.
   - Following an order is sometimes more important than being true to a personal belief.
   - Strong leaders should not show compassion.
   - Courage is often foolhardy.
2. Give students a copy of the prepared **Anticipation Guide** and have them mark their responses in the Me column. Have students discuss the statements in pairs or groups and mark the guides again in the Group column.
3. For further guidance, use the ***Classroom Strategies and Teaching Routines*** card: **Using an Anticipation Guide.**

Concept Connector →

Students will return to the **Anticipation Guide** after completing the story.

Whole-Class Activity

As they would when reading poetry, students should pay attention to the punctuation cues in the play. Demonstrate by reading one of Antigone's speeches, showing how it should be read aloud in sentence form. Then have students practice reading aloud any speeches of their choosing from the selection.

❷ About the Selection

In the first part of the play, Sophocles establishes the main characters and the conflict. A proud and reckless princess of Thebes, Antigone breaks the law to bury her brother, who has been labeled a traitor by the king, her uncle. In so doing, she embarks on a course toward her own destruction and the destruction of those around her.

Antigone argues more than once with Creon, her uncle and king, that her actions honor the gods. These arguments firmly establish the conflict between human law, Creon's order, and divine law, the burial rites Antigone respects.

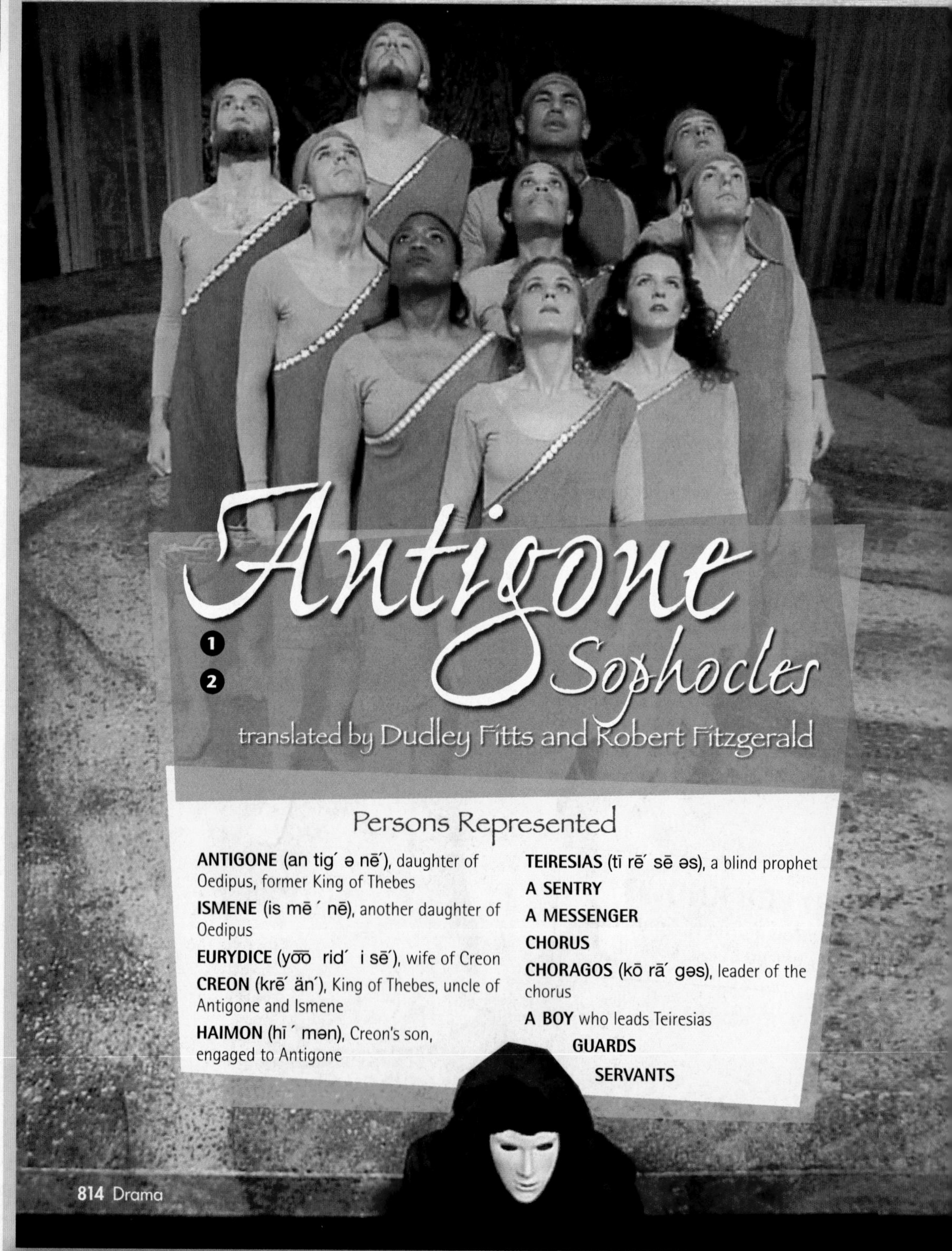

Antigone

❶ ❷

Sophocles

translated by Dudley Fitts and Robert Fitzgerald

Persons Represented

ANTIGONE (an tig′ ə nē′), daughter of Oedipus, former King of Thebes

ISMENE (is mē′ nē), another daughter of Oedipus

EURYDICE (yo͞o rid′ i sē′), wife of Creon

CREON (krē′ än′), King of Thebes, uncle of Antigone and Ismene

HAIMON (hī′ mən), Creon's son, engaged to Antigone

TEIRESIAS (tī rē′ sē əs), a blind prophet

A SENTRY

A MESSENGER

CHORUS

CHORAGOS (kō rā′ gəs), leader of the chorus

A BOY who leads Teiresias

GUARDS

SERVANTS

Vocabulary Development

Thematic Vocabulary: The Big Question

As students are discussing *Antigone*, encourage them to use the thematic vocabulary presented in Introducing the Big Question, pp. 790–791. You might encourage them with sentence starters like these:

1. The *background* that the Prologue provides serves to . . .
2. Creon tells his subjects what his *expectations* of their behavior are so that . . .
3. Antigone is not afraid to reveal her *identity* as the one who has buried Polyneices because she . . .
4. Creon considers Ismene's *knowledge* of Antigone's intentions a betrayal because . . .

Prologue–Scene 2

Scene. *Before the palace of* CREON, *King of Thebes. A central double door, and two lateral doors. A platform extends the length of the facade, and from this platform three steps lead down into the "orchestra," or chorus-ground.*

Time. *Dawn of the day after the repulse of the Argive*[1] *army from the assault on Thebes.*

Prologue

[ANTIGONE *and* ISMENE *enter from the central door of the Palace.*]

ANTIGONE. Ismene, dear sister,
You would think that we had already suffered enough
For the curse on Oedipus:[2]
I cannot imagine any grief
That you and I have not gone through. And now—
Have they told you of the new decree of our King Creon?

ISMENE. I have heard nothing: I know
That two sisters lost two brothers, a double death
In a single hour; and I know that the Argive army
Fled in the night; but beyond this, nothing.

ANTIGONE. I thought so. And that is why I wanted you
To come out here with me. There is something we must do.

ISMENE. Why do you speak so strangely?

3

ANTIGONE. Listen, Ismene:
Creon buried our brother Eteocles
With military honors, gave him a soldier's funeral,
And it was right that he should; but Polyneices,
Who fought as bravely and died as miserably,—
They say that Creon has sworn
No one shall bury him, no one mourn for him,
But his body must lie in the fields, a sweet treasure
For carrion birds[3] to find as they search for food.
That is what they say, and our good Creon is coming here
To announce it publicly; and the penalty—
Stoning to death in the public square!
There it is,

1. **Argive** (är′ giv′) from Argos, the capital of a section of ancient Greece.

2. **curse on Oedipus** reference to the fate of Oedipus, who was doomed by a decree of the gods to kill his father and marry his mother while ignorant of their true identities.

3. **carrion** (kar′ ē ən) **birds** scavenger birds, such as vultures.

Literary Analysis
Protagonist and Antagonist What conflict between Antigone and Creon does Antigone begin explaining here?

4

Reading Check
What order will Creon give about Polyneices' body?

◀ **Critical Viewing** What do you predict will be the mood of the play based on the actors' expressions? **[Predict]**

3 Literary Analysis

Protagonist and Antagonist

1. Tell students that protagonists are the main characters with whom audience members usually sympathize. Their actions and motivations are central to the plot.
2. Read the bracketed passage aloud. Remind students that Antigone is the protagonist of the play.
   Ask students to identify qualities that Antigone shows that help identify her as the protagonist.
   Possible response: She sets the action in motion and elicits the audience's sympathy through her determination to "do the right thing."
3. **Ask** students to respond to the Literary Analysis question: What conflict between Antigone and Creon does Antigone begin explaining here?
   Answer: Antigone begins to explain the conflict between herself and Creon about the burial of Polyneices. Antigone wants to honor her dead brother Polyneices by burying him, but Creon has issued an order that Polyneices is not to be buried or mourned.

4 Reading Check

Answer: Creon has ordered that Polyneices' body be left unburied and no one should mourn him.

Differentiated Instruction for Universal Access

Strategy for Special Needs Students

To increase understanding of the characters and conflict that form the centerpiece of this play, create a family tree for the royal family of Thebes. Reread the Prologue with students, and list the people in the royal family whom it mentions. Then elicit students' help in structuring a simple family tree that shows the relationships among the people listed. Suggest that students copy the family tree for reference as they read the rest of the play.

Strategy for Less Proficient Readers

Have students summarize what they have learned from the Prologue about the main characters and conflict of the play. (King Creon has ordered that Polyneices not be buried; Antigone is deeply upset with his order.) Then use the **Reading Skill Graphic Organizer B** (p. 154 in ***Graphic Organizer Transparencies***) to prompt students to predict what will happen as the play continues. Direct students to continue reading to confirm or revise their predictions.

PHLit Online!

This selection is available in interactive format in the **Enriched Online Student Edition, www.PHLitOnline.com,** which includes a thematically related video with writing prompt and an interactive graphic organizer.

❺ Reading Skill

Summarize

1. Have students reread the bracketed passage. Then have them write one sentence about how each of the following people is related to the others and what tragic event(s) happened to him or her: Oedipus, Iocaste, Eteocles, Polyneices, Antigone, and Ismene.
2. **Ask** students to respond to the Reading Skill prompt: Review Ismene's speech and then retell the tragic history of Antigone's family.
   Answer: The father of the family, Oedipus, blinded himself when he found out that he had married his own mother; he died hated by everyone; the mother of the family, Iocaste, killed herself; their sons killed each other in battle; the sisters, Antigone and Ismene, are the only members of the family left.
3. Invite students to summarize in two sentences what Ismene thinks they should do about Polyneices' body and why.
   Answer: Ismene thinks that they should leave Polyneices' body unburied. Creon has ordered it, and they must obey his law.

❻ Literary Analysis

Protagonist and Antagonist

1. Have students contrast Antigone and Ismene. **Ask:** What personality traits make Ismene unlike Antigone? What personality traits make Antigone the stronger character?
   Possible response: Ismene is fearful and passive. Antigone is determined, brave, and loyal.
2. **Ask** students to respond to the Literary Analysis question: What details in Antigone's speech give the reader reason to sympathize with Antigone?
   Possible response: Antigone refuses to abandon her brother, shows that she does not fear death, and indicates that she is going to follow the laws of the gods over the human law of her uncle.

And now you can prove what you are:
A true sister, or a traitor to your family.

ISMENE. Antigone, you are mad! What could I possibly do?

ANTIGONE. You must decide whether you will help me or not.

ISMENE. I do not understand you. Help you in what?

ANTIGONE. Ismene, I am going to bury him. Will you come?

ISMENE. Bury him! You have just said the new law forbids it.

ANTIGONE. He is my brother. And he is your brother, too.

ISMENE. But think of the danger! Think what Creon will do!

ANTIGONE. Creon is not strong enough to stand in my way.

ISMENE. Ah sister!
Oedipus died, everyone hating him
For what his own search brought to light, his eyes
Ripped out by his own hand; and Iocaste died,
His mother and wife at once: she twisted the cords
That strangled her life; and our two brothers died,
Each killed by the other's sword. And we are left:
But oh, Antigone,
Think how much more terrible than these
Our own death would be if we should go against Creon
And do what he has forbidden! We are only women,
We cannot fight with men, Antigone!
The law is strong, we must give in to the law
In this thing, and in worse. I beg the Dead
To forgive me, but I am helpless: I must yield
To those in authority. And I think it is dangerous business
To be always meddling.

❺ **Reading Skill**
Summarize Review Ismene's speech and then retell the tragic history of Antigone's family.

ANTIGONE. If that is what you think,
I should not want you, even if you asked to come.
You have made your choice, you can be what you want to be.
But I will bury him; and if I must die,
I say that this crime is holy: I shall lie down
With him in death, and I shall be as dear
To him as he to me.
It is the dead,
Not the living, who make the longest demands;
We die for ever . . .
You may do as you like,

❻ **Literary Analysis**
Protagonist and Antagonist What details in Antigone's speech give the reader reason to sympathize with Antigone?

Think Aloud

Vocabulary: Using Context

Direct students' attention to the word *meddling* at the end of Ismene's speech on this page. Then, use a think-aloud process to model how to infer the meaning of an unknown word using the context.

In this sentence, beginning in line 52, Ismene says that she thinks that *meddling* is dangerous. To get an idea of what *meddling* means, I am going to look at the sentences that come before this one. In one sentence, Ismene says it will be dangerous to go against Creon and what he has ordered. Then she says that she has to give in to the law. In another sentence, she explains that she is helpless and must yield to authority. It is clear that Ismene thinks it would be dangerous to go against the law by burying Polyneices. Since she says *meddling* is dangerous, I think *meddling* refers to getting involved in something in which one does not have a clear right to be involved.

Since apparently the laws of the gods mean nothing to you.

ISMENE. They mean a great deal to me; but I have no strength
To break laws that were made for the public good.

ANTIGONE. That must be your excuse, I suppose. But as for me,
I will bury the brother I love.

ISMENE. Antigone,
I am so afraid for you!

ANTIGONE. You need not be:
You have yourself to consider, after all.

ISMENE. But no one must hear of this, you must tell no one!
I will keep it a secret, I promise!

ANTIGONE. Oh tell it! Tell everyone!
Think how they'll hate you when it all comes out
If they learn that you knew about it all the time!

ISMENE. So fiery! You should be cold with fear.

ANTIGONE. Perhaps. But I am doing only what I must.

ISMENE. But can you do it? I say that you cannot.

ANTIGONE. Very well: when my strength gives out, I shall do no more.

ISMENE. Impossible things should not be tried at all.

ANTIGONE. Go away, Ismene:
I shall be hating you soon, and the dead will too,
For your words are hateful. Leave me my foolish plan:
I am not afraid of the danger; if it means death,
It will not be the worst of deaths—death without honor.

8 **ISMENE.** Go then, if you feel that you must.
You are unwise,
But a loyal friend indeed to those who love you.

[Exit into the Palace. ANTIGONE *goes off, left. Enter the* CHORUS.*]*

7 ▲ **Critical Viewing** Which details of this image convey the intense emotions of Antigone and Ismene's conversation? **[Analyze]**

9 **Reading Check**

What does Antigone ask Ismene to decide?

7 Critical Viewing

Answer: Ismene's furrowed brow, parted lips, and locked gaze, and Antigone's sharp profile and pursed lips all convey the intense emotion of the sisters' conversation.

8 Critical Thinking

Interpret

1. **Ask** students what they might say to Antigone about her decision to disobey Creon and risk death.
   Possible response: Some students may state that they would give the same advice as Ismene. Other students may say that they would support and help Antigone.
2. Have students read Ismene's remarks in lines 89–91 and consider how a person can be both unwise and a loyal friend at the same time.
   Possible response: Sometimes loyalty can turn into stubbornness and endanger the loyal person. In this situation, it may be unwise to continue being loyal.

9 Reading Check

Answer: Antigone asks Ismene to decide if she will follow the laws of the gods and help bury their dead brother Polyneices.

Differentiated Instruction for Universal Access

Strategy for Special Needs Students

To make this play and others more reader-friendly for students, explain some of the conventions used. Point out that speakers in a play are usually indicated by their names in capital letters on the left, followed by a period. Stage directions usually appear in brackets or parentheses. Have students identify these elements of the play in their books.

EL Strategy for English Learners

To enhance fluency, have students listen to Ismene's and Antigone's speeches and conversation in this scene on the ***Hear It!*** **Audio CD.** Suggest that students then practice reading aloud one of the speeches individually or reading the conversation between the two sisters with a partner. Give students suggestions for improved pronunciation and inflection.

⑩ Reading Skill

Summarize

1. Point out that the Chorus is an essential element of Greek drama. Explain to students that this group comments on and may explain the action of the play. In the opening song, or *Parodos,* the Chorus explains the central conflict of the play.
2. Remind students to pause after reading the Parodos and summarize the main ideas and events described. Emphasize that a summary of the Parodos will increase students' understanding of the conflict around which the play has been written.
3. **Ask** students to respond to the Reading Skill prompt: Reread the Parados, and summarize Polyneices' attack on Thebes. **Answer:** Polyneices and his troops attacked the seven gates of Thebes to seize control of the city. Eteocles and his forces fought back. The attack finally resulted in a fight between Polyneices and Eteocles, and the two brothers killed each other.

Parodos

CHORUS. [STROPHE 1]
Now the long blade of the sun, lying
Level east to west, touches with glory
Thebes of the Seven Gates.[4] Open, unlidded
Eye of golden day! O marching light
Across the eddy and rush of Dirce's stream,[5]
Striking the white shields of the enemy
Thrown headlong backward from the blaze of morning!

CHORAGOS. Polyneices their commander
Roused them with windy phrases,
He the wild eagle screaming
Insults above our land,
His wings their shields of snow,
His crest their marshalled helms.

CHORUS. [ANTISTROPHE 1]
Against our seven gates in a yawning ring
The famished spears came onward in the night;
But before his jaws were **sated** with our blood,
Or pinefire took the garland of our towers,
He was thrown back; and as he turned, great Thebes—
No tender victim for his noisy power—
Rose like a dragon behind him, shouting war. ⑩

CHORAGOS. For God hates utterly
The bray of bragging tongues;
And when he beheld their smiling,
Their swagger of golden helms,
The frown of his thunder blasted
Their first man from our walls.

CHORUS. [STROPHE 2]
We heard his shout of triumph high in the air
Turn to a scream; far out in a flaming arc
He fell with his windy torch, and the earth struck him.
And others storming in fury no less than his
Found shock of death in the dusty joy of battle.

CHORAGOS. Seven captains at seven gates
Yielded their clanging arms to the god
That bends the battle-line and breaks it.
These two only, brothers in blood,
Face to face in matchless rage,
Mirroring each the other's death,
Clashed in long combat.

4. **Seven Gates** The city of Thebes was defended by walls containing seven entrances.
5. **Dirce's** (dur′ sēz) **stream** small river near Thebes into which the body of Dirce, one of the city's early queens, was thrown after her murder.

Vocabulary
sated (sāt′ əd) *adj.* satisfied; provided with more than enough

Reading Skill
Summarize Reread the Parados, and summarize Polyneices' attack on Thebes.

Vocabulary Development

Recognizing Related Words: Homophones
Explain that words that sound alike but have different spellings and meanings are called *homophones*. Tell students that knowing which meanings match which spellings can help them use the correct words in writing. List these words from the selection: *plain, counsel,* and *principle.* Discuss their meanings in the context of the selection (a flat area of land; advice; an idea or belief). Then ask students to spell a homophone, or like-sounding word, for each word listed. List these words: *plane, council,* and *principal.* Define these words (an airplane; a meeting for discussion; the main or most important issue, object, etc.). Challenge students to use each of the six homophones in a sentence that shows an understanding of the word's meaning.

CHORUS. [ANTISTROPHE 2]

But now in the beautiful morning of victory
Let Thebes of the many chariots sing for joy!
With hearts for dancing we'll take leave of war:
Our temples shall be sweet with hymns of praise,
And the long night shall echo with our chorus.

Scene 1

CHORAGOS. But now at last our new King is coming:
Creon of Thebes, Menoikeus'[6] son.
In this auspicious dawn of his reign
What are the new complexities
That shifting Fate has woven for him?
What is his counsel? Why has he summoned
The old men to hear him?

[*Enter* CREON *from the Palace, center. He addresses the* CHORUS *from the top step.*]

CREON. Gentlemen: I have the honor to inform you that our Ship of State, which recent storms have threatened to destroy, has come safely to harbor at last, guided by the merciful wisdom of Heaven. I have summoned you here this morning because I know that I can depend upon you: your devotion to King Laïos was absolute; you never hesitated in your duty to our late ruler Oedipus; and when Oedipus died, your loyalty was transferred to his children. Unfortunately, as you know, his two sons, the princes Eteocles and Polyneices, have killed each other in battle; and I, as the next in blood, have suceeded to the full power of the throne.

11 I am aware, of course, that no Ruler can expect complete loyalty from his subjects until he has been tested in office. Nevertheless, I say to you at the very outset

6. **Menoikeus'** (me noi´ kē əs)

12 **Reading Check**

Why is Creon named king?

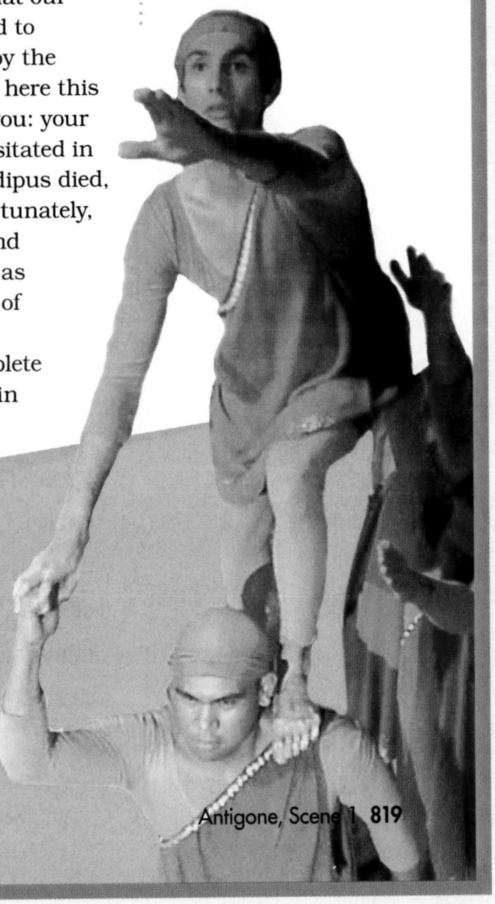

11 Connecting to the Big Question

1. Remind students that one person's point of view may not necessarily be the same as someone else's. Often, these differing points of view cause conflicts among people.
2. **Ask** students: What is the subject or idea of Creon's point of view in the bracketed passage? What is his point of view?
   Possible response: The subject of Creon's point of view is the traits a leader should and should not possess. He believes the interests of the State take priority over everything, even friendship.
3. **Ask** students: How might Creon's point of view be different if he were a subject, rather than a leader of the State?
   Possible response: If Creon were a subject, he might not feel that the State's priorities trump everything else. He might look out for his friends' best interests rather than the State's.

12 Reading Check

Answer: Creon is the next in line to inherit the throne, now that Eteocles and Polyneices, the late ruler's sons, are dead.

Differentiated Instruction for Universal Access

Enrichment for Gifted and Talented Students

Invite students to perform the *Parodos*, or entrance-song, of the Chorus. Explain that the Chorus comes on stage for the first time for the Parodos. Sometimes the Chorus speaks with a single voice as a group, sometimes in dialogue as two sections of the group, and sometimes with only one voice, that of the *Choragos*, or leader of the Chorus. Suggest that students choose one person to be the Choragos and then separate into two groups to recite the strophe and antistrophe parts of the Parodos. After practice, students may perform the Parodos for the rest of the class.

⓭ Literary Analysis

Protagonist and Antagonist

1. Review with students that the antagonist in a literary work is the character who is in conflict with the protagonist—the person with whom the audience most sympathizes.
2. **Ask** students the Literary Analysis question: How do Creon's words in lines 42–49 show that he is Antigone's antagonist?
   Possible response: Creon's cold words about Polyneices and his hard stance as king put him in opposition to Antigone, who shows love and loyalty toward her brother and puts the laws of the gods before Creon's laws.

⓮ Reading Skill

Summarize

1. Remind students that a summary should include only the main points, not every detail.
2. Suggest that students reread Creon's speech and pause to jot down the main points of the beginning, middle, and end of the speech.
3. **Ask** students to respond to the Reading Skill prompt: Summarize the main points in Creon's speech.
   Answer: Creon says that since Eteocles and Polyneices are dead, he has taken over the rule of Thebes. He explains that he will not place private friendship over the public welfare. He says that Eteocles will be buried as a hero, but Polyneices will remain unburied as a traitor. He states that he will always respect whoever is on the side of the State.

that I have nothing but contempt for the kind of Governor who is afraid, for whatever reason, to follow the course that he knows is best for the State; and as for the man who sets private friendship above the public welfare,—I have no use for him, either. I call God to witness that if I saw my country headed for ruin, I should not be afraid to speak out plainly; and I need hardly remind you that I would never have any dealings with an enemy of the people. No one values friendship more highly than I; but we must remember that friends made at the risk of wrecking our Ship are not real friends at all. ⓫

These are my principles, at any rate, and that is why I have made the following decision concerning the sons of Oedipus: Eteocles, who died as a man should die, fighting for his country, is to be buried with full military honors, with all the ceremony that is usual when the greatest heroes die; but his brother Polyneices, who broke his exile to come back with fire and sword against his native city and the shrines of his fathers' gods, whose one idea was to spill the blood of his blood and sell his own people into slavery—Polyneices, I say, is to have no burial: no man is to touch him or say the least prayer for him; he shall lie on the plain, unburied; and the birds and the scavenging dogs can do with him whatever they like. ⓮

This is my command, and you can see the wisdom behind it. As long as I am King, no traitor is going to be honored with the loyal man. But whoever shows by word and deed that he is on the side of the State,—he shall have my respect while he is living, and my reverence when he is dead.

Literary Analysis Protagonist and Antagonist How do Creon's words in lines 42–49 show that he is Antigone's antagonist? ⓭

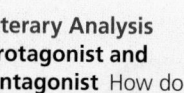

Reading Skill Summarize Summarize the main points in Creon's speech.

CHORAGOS. If that is your will, Creon son of Menoikeus,
You have the right to enforce it: we are yours.

CREON. That is my will. Take care that you do your part.

CHORAGOS. We are old men: let the younger ones carry it out.

CREON. I do not mean that: the sentries have been appointed.

CHORAGOS. Then what is it that you would have us do?

CREON. You will give no support to whoever breaks this law.

CHORAGOS. Only a crazy man is in love with death!

CREON. And death it is; yet money talks, and the wisest
Have sometimes been known to count a few coins too many.

Vocabulary Development

Word Origins

By the time Sophocles wrote *Antigone*, tragedy was a highly developed dramatic form, strongly linked with both religious and artistic performance. The word *tragedy* can be traced to the ancient Greek word *tragoidia*, which literally means "goat song." There are various theories about why Greek drama was originally characterized as a "goat song." According to Aristotle, tragedy originated as a performance by a chorus of satyrs, or singers in goat costumes. Satyrs were goatlike creatures. It has also been suggested that singers competed for the prize of a goat or at a goat sacrifice.

[*Enter* SENTRY *from left.*]

15 **SENTRY.** I'll not say that I'm out of breath from running, King, because every time I stopped to think about what I have to tell you, I felt like going back. And all the time a voice kept saying, "You fool, don't you know you're walking straight into trouble?"; and then another voice: "Yes, but if you let somebody else get the news to Creon first, it will be even worse than that for you!" But good sense won out, at least I hope it was good sense, and here I am with a story that makes no sense at all; but I'll tell it anyhow, because, as they say, what's going to happen's going to happen, and—

CREON. Come to the point. What have you to say?

SENTRY. I did not do it. I did not see who did it. You must not punish me for what someone else has done.

CREON. A comprehensive defense! More effective, perhaps,
If I knew its purpose. Come: what is it?

SENTRY. A dreadful thing . . . I don't know how to put it—

CREON. Out with it!

SENTRY. Well, then;
The dead man—
Polyneices—

[*Pause. The* SENTRY *is overcome, fumbles for words.* CREON *waits impassively.*]

out there—
someone,—
New dust on the slimy flesh!

[*Pause. No sign from* CREON.]

18 Someone has given it burial that way, and
Gone . . .

[*Long pause.* CREON *finally speaks with deadly control.*]

CREON. And the man who dared do this?

SENTRY. I swear I
Do not know! You must believe me!
Listen:
The ground was dry, not a sign of digging, no,
Not a wheeltrack in the dust, no trace of anyone.
It was when they relieved us this morning: and one of them,

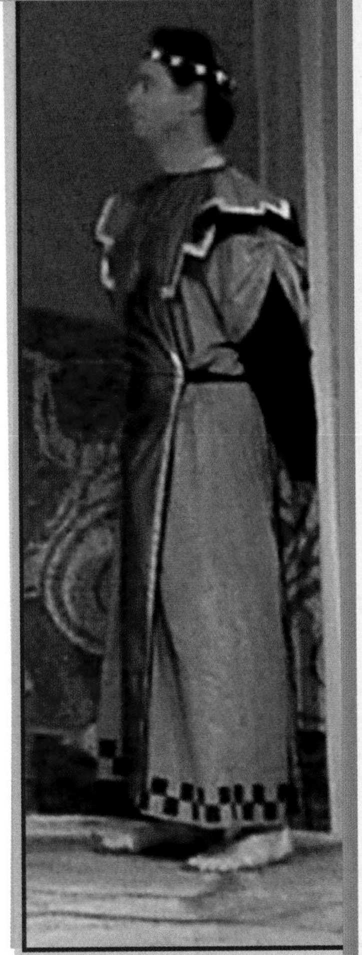

16 ▲ **Critical Viewing** What elements of this actor's appearance reflect Creon's status as king? **[Interpret]**

17 **Reading Check** What has happened to Polyneices' body?

15 Critical Thinking

Interpret

1. Remind students that they can interpret characters' thoughts by looking carefully at what they say.
2. Have students read the bracketed passage. Then, **ask** students to explain why the sentry hesitates when reporting to Creon.
   Possible response: The sentry hesitates because he fears Creon's wrath. The sentry does not want to be punished for bringing bad news to the king.

16 Critical Viewing

Answer: Creon's crown, luxurious clothing, and rigidly upright posture reflect the power and authority of a king.

17 Reading Check

Answer: Polyneices' body has been covered with dust.

Differentiated Instruction for Universal Access

Enrichment for Gifted and Talented Students

Challenge students to write the sentry's report about the body of Polyneices as a feature news article. Tell students to answer the questions *who, what, where, when, why,* and *how*. Invite students to read their articles aloud to the class.

Enrichment for Advanced Readers

Tell students to analyze each character and his or her motivations thus far in the play. Taking the character motivations into account, students should then predict what will happen in the second half of the play. Have students write summaries of their predictions and discuss them with partners.

⓲ Reading Skill

Summarize

1. Explain to students that another convention of ancient Greek theater is that much of a play's action is imagined to have occurred offstage and is reported to the audience through dialogue. Tell students that this leads to the extensive use of messengers, such as the sentry, in Greek drama. Although the sentry is a minor role, he plays an important function in the play by retelling or supplying information about events.
2. Read aloud the bracketed passage from the sentry's speech. Then **ask** students to respond to the Reading Skill prompt: Summarize the sentry's report through line 102.
   Answer: The sentry reports that light dust has been mounded over the dead body of Polyneices, but there is no sign of who might have done this.

⓳ Literary Analysis

Protagonist and Antagonist

1. Remind students that Antigone says that she will follow the laws of the gods, not the law of the State, in burying Polyneices. **Ask** students why Creon does not think the gods will favor burying Polyneices.
   Answer: Creon says that Polyneices looted the temples of the gods and burned their images.
2. Then **ask** students the Literary Analysis question: What does Creon's fear of people scheming against him show about his conflict with Antigone?
   Possible response: He is not aware yet that Antigone opposes him; at this time, he is concerned with establishing his authority and suspects many people.

The corporal, pointed to it.
There it was,
The strangest—
Look:
The body, just mounded over with light dust: you see?
Not buried really, but as if they'd covered it
Just enough for the ghost's peace. And no sign
Of dogs or any wild animal that had been there.

And then what a scene there was! Every man of us
Accusing the other: we all proved the other man did it,
We all had proof that we could not have done it.
We were ready to take hot iron in our hands,
Walk through fire, swear by all the gods,
It was not I!
I do not know who it was, but it was not I!

[CREON's *rage has been mounting steadily, but the* SENTRY *is too intent upon his story to notice it.*]

And then, when this came to nothing, someone said
A thing that silenced us and made us stare
Down at the ground: you had to be told the news,
And one of us had to do it! We threw the dice,
And the bad luck fell to me. So here I am,
No happier to be here than you are to have me:
Nobody likes the man who brings bad news.

CHORAGOS. I have been wondering, King: can it be that the gods have done this?

CREON. [*Furiously*] Stop!
Must you doddering wrecks
Go out of your heads entirely? "The gods!"
Intolerable!
The gods favor this corpse? Why? How had he served them?
Tried to loot their temples, burn their images,
Yes, and the whole State, and its laws with it!
Is it your senile opinion that the gods love to honor bad men?
A pious thought!—
No, from the very beginning
There have been those who have whispered together,
Stiff-necked anarchists, putting their heads together,
Scheming against me in alleys. These are the men,
And they have bribed my own guard to do this thing.
Money! [*Sententiously*]

⓲ **Reading Skill**
Summarize Summarize the sentry's report through line 102.

Literary Analysis
Protagonist and Antagonist What does Creon's fear of people scheming against him show about his conflict with Antigone? ⓳

Vocabulary
sententiously (sen ten′ shəs lē) *adv.* in a way that shows excessive fondness for wise sayings; in lecturing tones

Vocabulary Development

Vocabulary Reinforcement

Reinforce students' comprehension of the selection vocabulary words with "show-you-know" sentences. The first part of the sentence uses the vocabulary word in an appropriate context. The second part of the sentence—the "show-you-know" part—clarifies the first. Model the strategy with this example:

He always spoke so *sententiously,* as if he had some special wisdom to share.

Then give students a sentence prompt such as the following, and coach them in creating the clarification part:

When she responded *sententiously,* he felt that __________

Possible response: she was lecturing him, not listening to him.

There's nothing in the world so demoralizing as money.
Down go your cities,
Homes gone, men gone, honest hearts corrupted,
Crookedness of all kinds, and all for money!
[*To* SENTRY] But you—!
I swear by God and by the throne of God,
The man who has done this thing shall pay for it!
Find that man, bring him here to me, or your death
Will be the least of your problems: I'll string you up
Alive, and there will be certain ways to make you
20 Discover your employer before you die;
And the process may teach you a lesson you seem to have missed:
The dearest profit is sometimes all too dear:
That depends on the source. Do you understand me?
A fortune won is often misfortune.

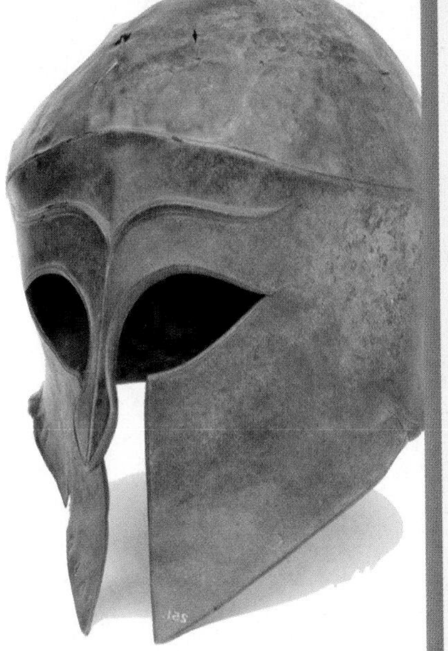

SENTRY. King, may I speak?

CREON. Your very voice distresses me.

SENTRY. Are you sure that it is my voice, and not your conscience?

CREON. By God, he wants to analyze me now!

SENTRY. It is not what I say, but what has been done, that hurts you.

CREON. You talk too much.

SENTRY. Maybe; but I've done nothing.

CREON. Sold your soul for some silver: that's all you've done.

SENTRY. How dreadful it is when the right judge judges wrong!

CREON. Your figures of speech
May entertain you now; but unless you bring me the man,
You will get little profit from them in the end.

[*Exit* CREON *into the Palace.*]

SENTRY. "Bring me the man"—!
I'd like nothing better than bringing him the man!
But bring him or not, you have seen the last of me here.
At any rate, I am safe!

[*Exit* SENTRY.]

21 ▲ Critical Viewing
What does this ancient Greek helmet indicate about the type of weapons against which the sentry was prepared to defend himself? **[Infer]**

22 Reading Check
What does Creon order the sentry to do?

20 Critical Thinking

Analyze

1. Remind students that a story's main character is its protagonist, who is in opposition with the story's antagonist.
2. **Ask** students what characteristics Antigone, the protagonist in this story, displays.
Possible response: Antigone is headstrong, determined, devoted, and caring.
3. Have students read the bracketed passage. Then **ask** students how Creon's threats to the sentry reinforce the king's antagonistic role.
Possible response: Creon seems to be abusing his role as an authoritative figure in being hostile to the sentry. While Antigone is loyal and caring as the protagonist, Creon reinforces his role as antagonist by being cold and unforgiving.

21 Critical Viewing

Answer: The helmet is metal and indicates that the sentry probably carried metal weapons or weapons with metal parts.

22 Reading Check

Answer: Creon orders the sentry to bring him the man who covered Polyneices' body with dust.

Fluency

Explain to students that reading with expression is an integral part of fluent reading. Have students identify the punctuation marks used in lines 99–148. Clarify that punctuation marks help readers interpret the author's intent. Explain that this is especially important in plays, which are written with the purpose of being read aloud. Point out that in plays, stage directions are an additional clue to how the text should be expressed.

- Model reading fluently and with expression by reading aloud lines 118–132. Use appropriate pausing, emphasis, and tone of voice for commas, periods, exclamation marks, and question marks.
- Have partners practice reading aloud lines 99–148 fluently and with expression. Circulate to monitor the fluency of students' reading.

23 Background

Choral Odes

Between scenes in the play, the Chorus recites an *ode*. During the ode, the group moves from right to left, singing the strophe. Then they move in the opposite direction during the antistrophe. The ode does not advance the action of the play. In this case, it is a celebration of humans' seeming superiority over the world of nature.

24 Critical Viewing

Answer: Her stiff posture makes her look determined, and she will probably continue to be proud and defiant.

Ode I

CHORUS. [STROPHE 1]

Numberless are the world's wonders, but none
More wonderful than man; the stormgray sea
Yields to his prows, the huge crests bear him high;
Earth, holy and inexhaustible, is graven
With shining furrows where his plows have gone
Year after year, the timeless labor of stallions.

[ANTISTROPHE 1]

The lightboned birds and beasts that cling to cover,
The lithe fish lighting their reaches of dim water,
All are taken, tamed in the net of his mind;
The lion on the hill, the wild horse windy-maned,
Resign to him; and his blunt yoke has broken
The sultry shoulders of the mountain bull.

[STROPHE 2]

Words also, and thought as rapid as air,
He fashions to his good use; statecraft is his,
And his the skill that **deflects** the arrows of snow,
The spears of winter rain: from every wind
He has made himself secure—from all but one:
In the late wind of death he cannot stand.

23

25

Vocabulary
deflects (dē flekts′) *v.* turns or makes go to one side

24 ▼ **Critical Viewing** Judging from this image, what is Antigone's reaction to her capture? **[Connect]**

Vocabulary Development

Word Analysis

Call students' attention to the Vocabulary Builder word *deflects* in line 15 of the choral ode. Tell students that the prefix *de-* means "down, away." Explain that in *deflect*, the prefix is added to the Latin root *-flect-*, meaning "bend, turn." Thus, *deflect* means "turn away, aside." Point out that the prefix *de-* is added to other Latin roots to form such words as *deduce, detract, descend,* and *depart*. Have students look up the meanings of these words in a dictionary and find three additional words that begin with the prefix *de-*. Students may share the words they have found with the rest of the class.

[ANTISTROPHE 2]

25

O clear intelligence, force beyond all measure!
O fate of man, working both good and evil!
When the laws are kept, how proudly his city stands!
When the laws are broken, what of his city then?
Never may the anarchic man find rest at my hearth,
Never be it said that my thoughts are his thoughts.

Reading Skill
Summarize Summarize the main ideas in lines 10–24 of the chorus's ode.

Scene 2

[*Re-enter* SENTRY *leading* ANTIGONE.]

CHORAGOS. What does this mean? Surely this captive woman
Is the Princess, Antigone. Why should she be taken?

SENTRY. Here is the one who did it! We caught her
In the very act of burying him.—Where is Creon?

CHORAGOS. Just coming from the house.

[*Enter* CREON, *center.*]

CREON. What has happened?
Why have you come back so soon?

SENTRY. [*Expansively*] O King,
A man should never be too sure of anything:
I would have sworn
That you'd not see me here again: your anger
Frightened me so, and the things you threatened me with;
But how could I tell then
That I'd be able to solve the case so soon?

No dice-throwing this time: I was only too glad to come!
Here is this woman. She is the guilty one:
We found her trying to bury him.
Take her, then; question her; judge her as you will.
I am through with the whole thing now, and glad of it.

27

CREON. But this is Antigone! Why have you brought her here?

SENTRY. She was burying him, I tell you!

CREON. [*Severely*] Is this the truth?

SENTRY. I saw her with my own eyes. Can I say more?

26 **Reading Check**
What has the sentry seen Antigone doing?

25 Reading Skill

Summarize

1. Remind students that a summary focuses on main ideas. Review the first strophe of the ode. Help students summarize its main idea.
   Answer: The main idea of the first strophe is that man is the greatest of the world's wonders.
2. Then **ask** students to respond to the Reading Skill prompt: Summarize the main ideas in lines 10–24 of the Chorus's ode.
   Answer: Man rules nature. Man uses language and rational thought to achieve many things, but man cannot protect himself from death. The man who breaks the law harms the city.

26 Reading Check

Answer: The sentry has seen Antigone mourning for Polyneices and trying to bury him.

Differentiated Instruction for Universal Access

Enrichment for Gifted and Talented Students
Students who excel at dance might like to choose a scene from the play to choreograph and perform (with or without words or music). Suggest that students research the costumes and masks that were often used for performances of ancient Greek drama and somehow incorporate their findings into their performances.

Enrichment for Advanced Readers
Tell students that all the characters they have met so far would have been played by only three actors (all men) in the original ancient Greek performances. Point out that in the play up to this point, except for the Chorus, there are usually only two characters on stage at a time. That means that the actor who plays Antigone cannot play Creon, and so on. Have students research the history of Greek drama and the rules for its performance in the school library.

㉗ Literary Analysis

Protagonist and Antagonist

1. **Ask:** How does Creon react when the sentry returns with Antigone?
   Answer: Creon is surprised and does not understand why the sentry has brought Antigone.
2. **Ask** the Literary Analysis question: Has Creon realized that he is Antigone's antagonist before this point? Explain.
   Answer: No; his surprise at seeing Antigone shows that he never suspects her to be someone who would bury Polyneices.
3. **Ask** students whom Creon expects the sentry to bring to him. Have students explain their reasoning.
   Possible responses: Creon does not expect the sentry to bring anyone, because he suspects that the sentry himself tried to bury Polyneices. Or, Creon expects the sentry to bring one of the people Creon believes are plotting against him.

Literary Analysis Protagonist and Antagonist Has Creon realized that he is Antigone's antagonist before this point? Explain.

CREON. The details: come, tell me quickly!

SENTRY. It was like this:
After those terrible threats of yours, King,
We went back and brushed the dust away from the body.
The flesh was soft by now, and stinking,
So we sat on a hill to windward and kept guard.
No napping this time! We kept each other awake.
But nothing happened until the white round sun
Whirled in the center of the round sky over us:
Then, suddenly,
A storm of dust roared up from the earth, and the sky
Went out, the plain vanished with all its trees
In the stinging dark. We closed our eyes and endured it.
The whirlwind lasted a long time, but it passed;
And then we looked, and there was Antigone!
I have seen
A mother bird come back to a stripped nest, heard
Her crying bitterly a broken note or two
For the young ones stolen. Just so, when this girl
Found the bare corpse, and all her love's work wasted,
She wept, and cried on heaven to damn the hands
That had done this thing.
And then she brought more dust
And sprinkled wine three times for her brother's ghost.

We ran and took her at once. She was not afraid,
Not even when we charged her with what she had done.
She denied nothing.
And this was a comfort to me,
And some uneasiness: for it is a good thing
To escape from death, but it is no great pleasure
To bring death to a friend.
Yet I always say
There is nothing so comfortable as your own safe skin!

CREON. [*Slowly, dangerously*] And you, Antigone,
You with your head hanging,—do you confess this thing?

ANTIGONE. I do. I deny nothing.

CREON. [*To* SENTRY] You may go.

[*Exit* SENTRY.]

[*To* ANTIGONE] Tell me, tell me briefly:
Had you heard my proclamation touching this matter?

Vocabulary Development

Recognizing Related Words: Synonyms
Write the words *proclamation, edict,* and *decree* on the board. Point out that all three words are used to describe Creon's order about the burial of Polyneices. Explain that all three words are *synonyms*, or words with similar meaning. All three refer to an official declaration. Challenge students to use a thesaurus or dictionary to find two synonyms for each of the following words from this scene: *immortal, insolence, boast, praise, reverence.* Then have students use each word or one of its synonyms in a sentence.

ANTIGONE. It was public. Could I help hearing it?

CREON. And yet you dared defy the law.

ANTIGONE. I dared.
It was not God's proclamation. That final Justice
That rules the world below makes no such laws.

Your edict, King, was strong,
But all your strength is weakness itself against
The immortal unrecorded laws of God.
They are not merely now: they were, and shall be,
Operative forever, beyond man utterly.

I knew I must die, even without your decree:
I am only mortal. And if I must die
Now, before it is my time to die,
Surely this is no hardship: can anyone
Living, as I live, with evil all about me,
Think Death less than a friend? This death of mine
Is of no importance; but if I had left my brother
Lying in death unburied, I should have suffered.
Now I do not.
You smile at me. Ah Creon,
Think me a fool, if you like; but it may well be
That a fool convicts me of folly.

CHORAGOS. Like father, like daughter: both headstrong, deaf to reason!
She has never learned to yield.

CREON. She has much to learn.
The inflexible heart breaks first, the toughest iron
Cracks first, and the wildest horses bend their necks
At the pull of the smallest curb.
Pride? In a slave?
This girl is guilty of a double insolence,
Breaking the given laws and boasting of it.
Who is the man here,
She or I, if this crime goes unpunished?
Sister's child, or more than sister's child,
Or closer yet in blood—she and her sister
Win bitter death for this!
[*To* SERVANTS] Go, some of you,
Arrest Ismene. I accuse her equally.
Bring her: you will find her sniffling in the house there.

Vocabulary
edict (ē′ dikt′) *n.* public order; decree

Literary Analysis
Protagonist and Antagonist Which details in this scene solidify Antigone's role as protagonist and Creon's role as antagonist?

29 **Reading Check**
What is Antigone's response to the charges?

28 Literary Analysis

Protagonist and Antagonist

1. Ask volunteers to read the parts of Creon and Antigone in the bracketed passage. Then have students compare and contrast the laws Antigone and Creon call to their defense. **Ask:** What laws does Antigone say she follows in burying Polyneices?
   Answer: Antigone says she follows the laws of God.
   Then **ask:** How has she broken the law, according to Creon?
   Answer: Creon says she has broken the law by not obeying his proclamation.
2. Remind students that the protagonist is the character who usually wins the sympathy of the audience in some way, and the antagonist is the character who comes into conflict with the protagonist.
3. **Ask** the Literary Analysis question: Which details in this scene solidify Antigone's role as protagonist and Creon's role as antagonist?
   Possible response: Antigone's allegiance to the higher laws of God, her willingness to risk death, and her loyalty to her brother make her the sympathetic character; Creon's harshness and his rigid application of the law bring him into conflict with Antigone and make him the less sympathetic character.

29 Reading Check

Answer: Antigone does not deny the charges. She stands by her decision to bury her brother and accepts death as a consequence of her actions.

Differentiated Instruction for Universal Access

Culturally Responsive Instruction

Culture Connection Point out that in this myth, the king is the one person who holds the power to punish people when they break the law. Explain that this power and responsibility falls on various people, depending on the culture being examined. Invite students to share their knowledge of the legal systems of different countries, including the United States. If students are recent immigrants, have them compare the legal systems of their home countries to that of the United States.

30 Literary Analysis
Protagonist and Antagonist

1. Read the bracketed passage aloud. **Ask** students what two crimes Creon accuses Antigone of committing.
   Answer: He accuses her of breaking the law and boasting about it.
2. Then **ask:** What additional motive beyond upholding the law does Creon reveal here?
   Possible response: He implies that if he does not punish Antigone, he will be perceived as a weak leader.
3. Have students consider Antigone's response to Creon. **Ask:** Why does Antigone beg Creon to kill her?
   Possible response: She says that she is tired of listening to him and finds what he says distasteful; she sees that he refuses to listen to her and probably will not change his mind about her death.
4. Finally, **ask** which attitudes of Creon and Antigone make a compromise unlikely.
   Possible response: Creon's determination to punish Antigone and Antigone's willingness to die make a compromise unlikely.

31 Critical Viewing

Answer: Creon's hand around Antigone's neck conveys anger and frustration. Antigone's pose conveys bravery and defiance.

Vocabulary
brazen (brā′ zən) *adj.* shameless; bold

Her mind's a traitor: crimes kept in the dark
Cry for light, and the guardian brain shudders;
But how much worse than this
Is **brazen** boasting of barefaced anarchy!

ANTIGONE. Creon, what more do you want than my death?

CREON. Nothing.
That gives me everything.

30

ANTIGONE. Then I beg you: kill me.
This talking is a great weariness: your words
Are distasteful to me, and I am sure that mine
Seem so to you. And yet they should not seem so:
I should have praise and honor for what I have done.
All these men here would praise me
Were their lips not frozen shut with fear of you.

[*Bitterly*]

Ah the good fortune of kings,
Licensed to say and do whatever they please!

CREON. You are alone here in that opinion.

ANTIGONE. No, they are with me. But they keep their tongues in leash.

31 ▼ **Critical Viewing** What feelings are conveyed in this photo of Antigone and Creon? **[Interpret]**

CREON. Maybe. But you are guilty, and they are not.

ANTIGONE. There is no guilt in reverence for the dead.

CREON. But Eteocles—was he not your brother too?

ANTIGONE. My brother too.

CREON. And you insult his memory?

32 **ANTIGONE.** [*Softly*] The dead man would not say that I insult it.

CREON. He would: for you honor a traitor as much as him.

ANTIGONE. His own brother, traitor or not, and equal in blood.

CREON. He made war on his country. Eteocles defended it.

ANTIGONE. Nevertheless, there are honors due all the dead.

CREON. But not the same for the wicked as for the just.

ANTIGONE. Ah Creon, Creon,
Which of us can say what the gods hold wicked?

CREON. An enemy is an enemy, even dead.

ANTIGONE. It is my nature to join in love, not hate.

CREON. [*Finally losing patience*] Go join them, then; if you must have your love,
Find it in hell!

CHORAGOS. But see, Ismene comes:

[*Enter* ISMENE, *guarded.*]

Those tears are sisterly, the cloud
That shadows her eyes rains down gentle sorrow.

CREON. You too, Ismene,
Snake in my ordered house, sucking my blood
Stealthily—and all the time I never knew
That these two sisters were aiming at my throne!
Ismene,
Do you confess your share in this crime, or deny it?
Answer me.

ISMENE. Yes, if she will let me say so. I am guilty.

34 **ANTIGONE.** [*Coldly*] No, Ismene. You have no right to say so.
You would not help me, and I will not have you help me.

ISMENE. But now I know what you meant; and I am here
To join you, to take my share of punishment.

Reading Skill
Summarize Summarize the argument in lines 120–130.

33 **Reading Check**
What does Creon decide will be done with Antigone?

32 Reading Skill

Summarize

1. Have two students read lines 128–134, taking the parts of Creon and Antigone. Then **ask** students to respond to the Reading Skill prompt: Summarize the argument in lines 120–130.
Answer: Creon thinks only the just should be honored in death. Antigone believes honors are due to all the dead.
2. **Ask** students to describe the flaw Antigone hears in Creon's argument.
Possible response: Creon says the wicked do not deserve honors, but Antigone points out that deciding who is wicked is up to the gods, not humans.

33 Reading Check

Answer: Creon sentences Antigone to death.

Differentiated Instruction for Universal Access

Strategy for Special Needs Students
Help students identify the events leading up to Antigone's arrest and sentencing by organizing the events in timelines. Remind students that even events that occur offstage should be included. Have students use their timelines as visual prompts to help them summarize the play.

Enrichment for Advanced Readers
Have students write character analyses of Antigone and Creon, highlighting the qualities of each that contribute to the conflict between them. Ask students also to describe a quality that, if either Creon or Antigone had possessed it, might have defused the conflict. Students may share their analyses with the class to shed further light on the roles of protagonist and antagonist in the play.

34 Literary Analysis

Protagonist and Antagonist

1. **Ask** students to recall Ismene's response earlier in the play when Antigone asked for her help in burying their brother.
   Answer: Ismene refused to break the law by helping Antigone.
2. Encourage students to **hypothesize** about why Ismene now wants to share the guilt for burying Polyneices.
   Possible response: Ismene may feel guilty for not obeying the laws of the gods.
3. **Ask** students to contrast Antigone with Ismene.
   Answer: Unlike Ismene, Antigone never wavers in her intent to bury Polyneices.
4. **Ask** the Literary Analysis question: How does the contrast between the sisters emphasize Antigone's role as the protagonist?
   Possible response: Antigone is a much stronger character than Ismene; Antigone holds to her beliefs and takes action based on them.

35 Literature in Context

Culture Connection Remind students that the Chorus accompanied its words with formal movements, rotating from right to left during the strophe and from left to right during the antistrophe.

Connect to Literature Point out that the role of the Greek Chorus has survived throughout the development of drama to modern times. Shakespeare used an individual actor as a Chorus in *The Tragedy of Romeo and Juliet*, for example. In Thornton Wilder's *Our Town*, the Stage Manager acts as a Chorus. Many modern teleplays and dramas use a voiceover to accomplish the same purposes as the Greek Chorus. **Ask** students to respond to the Connect to the Literature prompt: Identify a speech by the Chorus in Scene 2 that probably mirrored the thoughts and feelings of the audience. Explain your choice.

Possible response: Students may think that Choragos is speaking for the audience when he incredulously questions Creon's intent to kill his son's bride in line 180.

Literary Analysis Protagonist and Antagonist How does the contrast between the sisters emphasize Antigone's role as the protagonist?

ANTIGONE. The dead man and the gods who rule the dead
Know whose act this was. Words are not friends.

ISMENE. Do you refuse me, Antigone? I want to die with you:
I too have a duty that I must discharge to the dead.

ANTIGONE. You shall not lessen my death by sharing it.

ISMENE. What do I care for life when you are dead?

ANTIGONE. Ask Creon. You're always hanging on his opinions.

ISMENE. You are laughing at me. Why, Antigone?

34

ANTIGONE. It's a joyless laughter, Ismene.

ISMENE. But can I do nothing?

ANTIGONE. Yes. Save yourself. I shall not envy you.
There are those who will praise you; I shall have honor, too.

ISMENE. But we are equally guilty!

ANTIGONE. No more, Ismene.
You are alive, but I belong to Death.

CREON. [*To the* CHORUS] Gentlemen, I beg you to observe these girls:

35

LITERATURE IN CONTEXT

Humanities Connection

Greek Chorus

In ancient Greek theater, the chorus was central to both the production and the meaning of the play. The chorus helped to tell the story, commented on the action, and divided scenes with odes, or songs. The chorus's commentary often expressed the audience's feelings. For Sophocles, a member of the chorus was an Everyman, an average Athenian citizen. A Greek chorus consisted of 12 or 15 men who sang and danced while wearing large masks.

▲ Objects like this vase reveal the importance of music and dance to Greek culture.

◄ In a modern-day production, this chorus reacts to events taking place on stage.

Connect to the Literature Identify a speech by the chorus in Scene 2 that probably mirrored the thoughts and feelings of the audience. Explain your choice.

Vocabulary Development

Vocabulary Knowledge Rating

When students have completed reading and discussing *Antigone:* Prologue–Scene 2, have them take out their **Vocabulary Knowledge Rating Chart** for this part. Read the words aloud once more, and have students rate their knowledge of the words again in the After Reading column. Clarify any words that are still problematic. Have students write their own definition and example or sentence in the appropriate column. Then have students complete the Vocabulary Practice at the end of the selection. Encourage students to use the words in further discussion and written work about the play. Remind them that they will be accountable for these words on the **Selection Test**, ***Unit 5 Resources***, pp. 38–43.

One has just now lost her mind; the other,
It seems, has never had a mind at all.

ISMENE. Grief teaches the steadiest minds to waver, King.

CREON. Yours certainly did, when you assumed guilt with the guilty!

ISMENE. But how could I go on living without her?

CREON. You are.
She is already dead.

ISMENE. But your own son's bride!

CREON. There are places enough for him to push his plow.
I want no wicked women for my sons!

36 **ISMENE.** O dearest Haimon, how your father wrongs you!

CREON. I've had enough of your childish talk of marriage!

CHORAGOS. Do you really intend to steal this girl from your son?

CREON. No; Death will do that for me.

CHORAGOS. Then she must die?

CREON. [*Ironically*] You dazzle me.
—But enough of this talk!
[*To* GUARDS] You, there, take them away and guard them well:
For they are but women, and even brave men run
When they see Death coming.

[*Exit* ISMENE, ANTIGONE, *and* GUARDS.]

Vocabulary
waver (wā′ vər) *v.* show indecision; fluctuate

Literary Analysis Protagonist and Antagonist What fact may force Haimon to become involved in the conflict between Creon and Antigone?

Ode II

CHORUS. [STROPHE 1]
Fortunate is the man who has never tasted God's vengeance!
Where once the anger of heaven has struck, that house is shaken
For ever: damnation rises behind each child
38 Like a wave cresting out of the black northeast,
When the long darkness under sea roars up
And bursts drumming death upon the windwhipped sand.

[ANTISTROPHE 1]
I have seen this gathering sorrow from time long past
Loom upon Oedipus' children: generation from generation

37 **Reading Check**
What does Ismene say she wants to do?

36 Literary Analysis
Protagonist and Antagonist

1. Read the bracketed passage aloud, and have students follow along in their books. **Ask** students who Haimon is.
Answer: Haimon is Creon's son.
2. **Ask** the Literary Analysis question: What fact may force Haimon to become involved in the conflict between Creon and Antigone?
Answer: Haimon and Antigone are to be married.

37 Reading Check

Answer: Ismene wants to share the guilt for burying Polyneices and wishes to die with Antigone.

Concept Connector

Anticipation Guide
Have students return to their **Anticipation Guides** and respond to the statements again in the After Reading column. They may do this individually or in their original pairs or groups. Then, lead a class discussion, probing for what students have learned that confirms or invalidates each statement. Encourage students to cite specific details, quotations, or other evidence from the text to support their responses to each statement.

Writing About the Big Question
Have students compare their responses to the sentence starters they completed before reading *Antigone* with their ideas afterwards. Ask them to explain whether their thoughts have changed.

Reading Skill Graphic Organizer
Ask students to review the graphic organizers they completed to identify the key elements of the selection. Show them the partially completed **Reading Skill Graphic Organizer A** (*Graphic Organizer Transparencies,* p. 153) as an example. Then have students use the graphic organizers they completed to summarize the selection.

38 Reading Skill
Summarize

Ask students to respond to the Reading Skill prompt: Summarize the main ideas in the concluding ode.
Answer: The vengeance of Zeus is a terrible thing. Oedipus draws the vengeance of Zeus on himself and brings suffering to generations of his family, including his daughter Antigone. Human pride angers Zeus.

ASSESS
Answers

Critical Thinking

1. Students may sympathize with Antigone because she loves her brother.
2. (a) Antigone tells Ismene that she is going to bury Polyneices.
(b) Ismene tells Antigone that they are only powerless women.
(c) Students may find Ismene cowardly and passive and Antigone courageous and motivated. Students may cite Ismene's fear of Creon and her inclination to obey an unjust law. They may also cite Antigone's allegiance to the laws of God and her willingness to face death.
3. (a) Creon accuses Polyneices of attacking his native city and plotting to enslave the people of Thebes. (b) The State is more important than friends and family.
4. (a) Antigone means that the laws of God are more powerful than human laws. (b) Antigone believes she is obeying the laws of God. Creon believes that Polyneices does not deserve burial under any law.

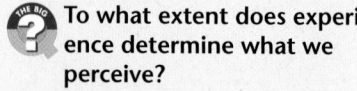

To what extent does experience determine what we perceive?

(a) **Possible response:** Antigone and Creon have opposing opinions in regard to who holds the ultimate power over the people. While Antigone believes God has absolute power, Creon believes the State does. A person whose religious beliefs place power in a higher being may perceive Antigone's views as "right." A person who believes that the government has ultimate power over the people, might see Creon's view as "right."

Takes the compulsive rage of the enemy god.
So lately this last flower of Oedipus' line
Drank the sunlight! but now a passionate word
And a handful of dust have closed up all its beauty.

[STROPHE 2]

What mortal arrogance
Transcends the wrath of Zeus?[7]
Sleep cannot lull him, nor the effortless long months
Of the timeless gods: but he is young for ever,
And his house is the shining day of high Olympos.[8]
All that is and shall be,
And all the past, is his.
No pride on earth is free of the curse of heaven.

[ANTISTROPHE 2]

The straying dreams of men
May bring them ghosts of joy:
But as they drowse, the waking embers burn them;
Or they walk with fixed eyes, as blind men walk.
But the ancient wisdom speaks for our own time:
Fate works most for woe
With Folly's fairest show.
Man's little pleasure is the spring of sorrow.

7. **Zeus** (zo͞os) King of all Greek gods, he was believed to throw lightning bolts when angry.

8. **Olympos** (ō lim′ pəs) mountain in Greece where the gods were believed to live in ease and splendor (also spelled "Olympus").

38

Reading Skill
Summarize Summarize the main ideas in the concluding ode.

Critical Thinking

1. **Respond:** Do you sympathize with Antigone? Explain.
2. **(a)** At the opening of the play, what does Antigone tell Ismene she plans to do? **(b) Analyze:** What reasons does Ismene give as she urges Antigone not to disobey Creon? **(c) Infer:** What does their argument reveal about the personality of each character? Support your answer with details.
3. **(a)** Identify two of the accusations Creon makes against Polyneices in his speech about "the Ship of State." **(b) Analyze:** What is the key belief or principle that he states in this speech?
4. **(a) Interpret:** What does Antigone mean when she says, "Your edict, King, was strong, / But all your strength is weakness itself against / The immortal unrecorded laws of God"? **(b) Compare and Contrast:** Compare Antigone's position with Creon's.

To what extent does experience determine what we perceive? How does each individual's view of "right" and "wrong" determine how a reader views the conflict between Antigone and Creon?

Assessment Resources

Unit 5 Resources

L1 L2 EL **Selection Test A**, pp. 38–40.
Administer Test A to less advanced readers and English learners.

L3 L4 **Selection Test B**, pp. 41–43.
Administer Test B to on-level and more advanced students.

L3 L4 **Open-Book Test**, pp. 35–37. As an alternative, give the Open-Book Test.

All **Customizable Test Bank**

All **Self-tests**
Students may prepare for the **Selection Test** by taking the **Self-test** online.

PHLit Online! All assessment resources are available at **www.PHLitOnline.com.**

After You Read | Antigone, Prologue through Scene 2

Literary Analysis: Protagonist and Antagonist

1. **(a)** Using a chart like the one shown, identify actions and language that present Antigone, the **protagonist,** in a sympathetic light. **(b)** Identify passages that show that Creon, the **antagonist,** is hostile to her.
2. **(a)** In Ode I, what powers does the Chorus say humanity possesses? **(b)** Against what force is humanity powerless? **(c)** Does the Chorus favor Creon or Antigone in this ode? Explain.

Reading Skill: Summarize

3. **(a) Summarize** the following conversations:
   - between Antigone and Ismene at the end of Scene 2
   - between Ismene and Creon at the end of Scene 2

   (b) How does summarizing aid your understanding of the work?

Vocabulary

Practice In each item, find the two words that make the most logical pair, and identify the word that does not belong. Explain your choices.

1. sated, full, standing
2. sententiously, pompously, randomly
3. deflects, reverses, admires
4. edict, law, forecast
5. brazen, shy, cooked
6. waver, decide, smooth

Word Study Use the context of the sentences and what you know about the **Latin root *-dict-*** to explain your answer to each question.

1. If someone *dictates* a letter, is she typing silently on the computer?
2. Is it useful to have good *diction* if you are an actor?

Word Study

The **Latin root *-dict-*** means "speak" or "say."

Challenge Explain how the root *-dict-* contributes to the meanings of these words. Consult a dictionary if necessary.

indict
predict
valediction

ASSESS/EXTEND

Answers

Literary Analysis

1. (a) Students may identify the following passages as presenting Antigone as a sympathetic character: Prologue: lines 34, 36, 54–65, 68–69; Scene 2: lines 65–80, 121. (b) The following passages show Creon's hostility to Antigone: Scene 2: lines 87–98, 167–169.

   For other sample answers, see ***Graphic Organizer Transparencies,* Literary Analysis Graphic Organizer A**, p. 155, and the **Additional Answers** section.
2. (a) The Chorus says humanity possesses the power to tame nature, the power of language, and the power of rational thought. (b) Humanity is powerless against death, fate, and the laws of the gods. (c) **Possible response:** The Chorus takes Antigone's side in this ode when it suggests that humanity is not all powerful and that higher laws have jurisdiction.

Reading Skill

3. (a) In the conversation with Antigone, Ismene wants to share in the guilt by dying with Antigone; Antigone rejects her request. In the conversation with Creon, Ismene reminds him that Antigone is going to marry his son, Haimon; Creon will not change his mind. (b) **Possible response:** Students may observe that summarizing requires them to identify main ideas or events.

Vocabulary

Practice

Sample answers:

1. standing; *sated* and *full* mean satisfied; *standing* does not
2. randomly; *sententiously* and *pompously* are synonyms; *randomly* is not
3. admires; *deflects* and *reverses* are synonyms; *admires* is not
4. forecast; *edict* and *law* are synonyms; *forecast* is not
5. cooked; *brazen* and *shy* are antonyms; *cooked* does not fit
6. smooth; *waver* and *decide* are antonyms; *smooth* does not fit

Word Study

Sample answers:

1. No. The root *-dict-* means "speak" or "say," so *dictates* means "says or reads aloud for another person to transcribe." If someone dictates a letter, she is speaking aloud.
2. Yes. The root *-dict-* means "speak" or "say," so *diction* means "enunciation or style of speaking." An actor should have good diction and enunciate well.

Word Study: Challenge

Sample answers: To *indict* is to "accuse or say that one has committed a crime." To *predict* is to "say or declare in advance." *Valediction* is "the act of saying goodbye."

EXTEND/ASSESS

Answers

Grammar

1. Introduce the skill, using the instruction on the student page.
2. Discuss the definitions and examples.

Think Aloud: Model the Skill

Model the skill of identifying participles and gerunds. Say to students:

Verbs have many forms. One form, participles, act as adjectives. Consider the sentence "The girl, tired of waiting, watched the movie." The participle phrase *tired of waiting* modifies the noun *girl*. Consider the sentence "Watching movies is fun." Here, *watching* is a gerund. *Watching movies* is the gerund phrase; it acts as the subject of the sentence, a noun.

WG Writing and Grammar, Grade 10

Students will find further instruction and practice on participles and gerunds in Chapter 20, Section 1.

Practice A

1. Fighting, gerund
2. expressed by Antigone, participial phrase
3. dried, participle
4. running, participle

Challenge

Sample answer: Participle: ". . . and the birds and the scavenging dogs can do with him whatever they like." Gerund: "And when he beheld their smiling . . ."

Practice B

Sample answers:

1. The plan hatched by Antigone shocked her family.
2. The Chorus sings, commenting on the action of the play.
3. Antigone debates, arguing with her uncle.
4. The punishment orchestrated by Creon was harsh.

Challenge

Answer: Determined to honor her brother, Antigone opposes Creon's edict. Dying for honor is something Antigone is willing to do.

Integrated Language Skills

Antigone, Prologue through Scene 2

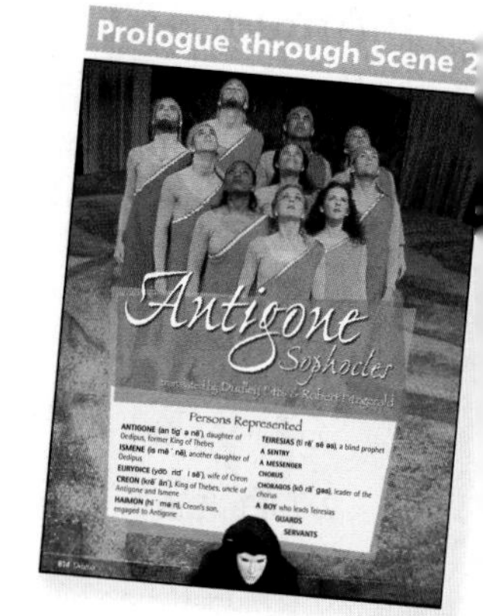

Grammar: Participles and Gerunds

A **participle** is a verb form used as an adjective to modify a noun or pronoun. A **gerund** is a verb form ending in *-ing* that acts as a noun.

Examples: *a creaking floor* (present participle)
a fried egg (past participle)
Dancing is my favorite pastime. (gerund—noun as subject)
I enjoy singing. (gerund—noun as direct object)

A **participial phrase** consists of a participle and its complements and modifiers. Participial phrases can add details to descriptions. A **gerund phrase** includes a gerund with its modifiers and complements.

Example: *a dress designed by her aunt* (participial phrase)
Limping badly, the hiker continued down the slope. (participial phrase)
David was incapable of reciting the poem. (gerund phrase—noun as object of a preposition)
Quickly gathering details is important (gerund phrase—noun as subject)

Practice A Underline and identify the participle, participial phrase, or gerund in each sentence.

1. Fighting was an important concern of the royal families of ancient Greece.
2. Ismene worries about the emotions expressed by Antigone.
3. Antigone used dried earth to cover the body of Polyneices.
4. A running messenger delivered the news to Creon.

Challenge Identify and label two participles and two gerunds in the Prologue, Scene 1, or Scene 2 of *Antigone.*

Practice B Combine each pair of sentences by using a participial or gerund phrase.

1. Antigone hatched a plan. The plan shocked her family.
2. The Chorus sings. The Chorus comments on the action of the play.
3. Antigone debates. She argues with her uncle.
4. Creon orchestrated a punishment. Creon's punishment was harsh.

Challenge Write a brief paragraph about events that happen in the first half of the play. Include at least one participial phrase and one gerund phrase in your paragraph.

Writing and Grammar Connection: Chapter 20, Section 1

Extend the Lesson

Sentence Modeling

Provide this sentence from the selection:
"A storm of dust roared up from the earth, and the sky/Went out, the plain vanished with all its trees/In the stinging dark."

Ask students what they notice about the sentence. Elicit from them that the sentence has a present participle that functions as an adjective. Then, ask what else they notice. (The participle Sophocles uses is an example of metaphor. He connects the word "dark" to the word "stinging," equating dark with something that delivers a sting, such as an insect or the extreme cold. Also, the intensity of this imagery is important, as it echoes the intensity of the moment in the play.)

Have students imitate the sentence in a sentence on a topic of their own choosing, matching each grammatical and stylistic feature discussed. Collect the sentences and share them with the class.

Writing

In *Antigone*, Sophocles explores the universal theme of conflict between the individual and society. Write an **essay** exploring this theme. Use these tips to make sure your essay follows a logical organization:

- Identify the message Sophocles communicates about this conflict in Scenes 1 and 2 of the play. Find details from the scenes to support your ideas.
- Explain what that message might mean to people today.
- Then, explain why that message is still important centuries after the play was written and performed. As you draft, provide relevant contemporary examples to help readers understand your thinking.

Writing Workshop: *Work in Progress*

Prewriting for a Reflective Essay For a reflective essay you may write, work in a small group to brainstorm for a list of ten small, everyday events. Then, for five of those events, note specific ways in which they affect people. Include these Event Notes in your writing portfolio.

Use this prewriting activity to prepare for the **Writing Workshop** on page 878.

Listening and Speaking

The myths that drive the story of Antigone continue to influence culture today. Present an **oral report** on the influence of Greek mythology on contemporary literature and language. Include at least three examples of English words, such as *titanic* or *narcissist*, that are related to figures in Greek myths. Follow these steps:

- Use a dictionary, thesaurus, and digital tools to **research the origins** of words.
- **Convey information and ideas** from the sources **accurately and coherently.**
- Use notes, if necessary, and make **eye contact** with audience members as you speak.
- Watch for confusion in your audience and **clarify points** as needed.
- Invite classmates to share their own examples of the Greek influences they have found.

PHLit Online!
www.PHLitOnline.com
- Interactive graphic organizers
- Grammar tutorial
- Interactive journals

EXTEND/ASSESS

Answers

Writing

1. Review the assignment, using the instruction on the student page.
2. To guide students in writing an essay, give them **Support for Writing**, p. 33 in ***Unit 5 Resources.***
3. To evaluate students' essays, use one of the Response to Literature rubrics on pp. 224–225 in ***Professional Development Guidebook.***

Six Traits Focus

✔	Ideas		Word Choice
✔	Organization		Sentence Fluency
	Voice		Conventions

Writing and Grammar, Grade 10

Students will find guidance on writing an essay in Chapter 13.

Writing Workshop
Work in Progress

Have students save their completed Event Notes in their portfolios. They will use the Event Notes later as they continue this Work-in-Progress assignment (see p. 835). These assignments prepare them to complete the Writing Workshop assignment (see pp. 1020–1031).

Listening and Speaking

1. Review the assignment, using the instruction on the student page.
2. To guide students in presenting an oral report, give them **Support for Extend Your Learning** page (***Unit 5 Resources***, p. 34).

Teaching Resources

All *Unit 5 Resources*
L3 L4 **Integrated Language Skills: Grammar,** p. 32
L3 L4 **Support for Writing,** p. 33
L3 L4 **Support for Extend Your Learning,** p. 34
L4 **Enrichment,** p. 31

All **Enriched Online Student Edition**
Available under After You Read for this selection:
All **Interactive Grammar Tutorial**
L3 L4 **Internet Research Activity**

Professional Development Guidebook
Rubrics for Response to Literature, pp. 224–225

PHLit Online! All print and digital resources are available at **www.PHLitOnline.com.** Online resources accessible by students are noted on the student page.

TIME AND RESOURCE MANAGER

Antigone, Scenes 3 through 5

Lesson Pacing Guide

DAY 1 Preteach

- Administer the Reading and Vocabulary Warm-ups (*Unit 5 Resources*, pp. 44–47) as necessary.
- Introduce the Reading Skill: Summarize. FT
- Introduce the Literary Analysis concept: Greek Tragedies. FT
- Distribute copies of the appropriate graphic organizer for the Reading Skill (*Graphic Organizer Transparencies*, pp. 157–158). CRI
- Distribute copies of the appropriate graphic organizer for Literary Analysis (*Graphic Organizer Transparencies*, pp. 159–160). CRI
- Teach the selection vocabulary. FT CRI
- Introduce the Word Study skill.

DAYS 2–3 Preteach/Teach

- Build background with the Background feature. CRI
- Develop thematic vocabulary and thematic thinking with Writing About the Big Question.
- Prepare students to read with the Activating Prior Knowledge activities (TE). CRI
- Informally monitor comprehension while students read. FT
- Use the Reading Check questions to confirm comprehension.
- Develop students' ability to summarize using the Reading Skill questions. CRI
- Develop students' understanding of Greek tragedies using the Literary Analysis questions. CRI
- Reinforce vocabulary with the Vocabulary notes. CRI

DAY 4 Assess

- Assess students' comprehension and mastery of the skills by having them answer the Critical Thinking, Reading Skill, and Literary Analysis questions. FT

DAY 5 Extend/Assess

- Have students complete the Grammar lesson. CRI
- Have students complete the Writing activity and write a reflective essay. (You may assign as homework.) FT
- Extend learning by having students complete the Listening and Speaking activity, a mock trial. As an alternative, assign them "Royal Rights to Privacy" in *Reality Central*. CRI
- Administer Selection Test A or B (*Unit 5 Resources*, pp. 59–64). FT

The play *Antigone* appears unedited and in its entirety.
Act I appears on pp. 814–832 and Act II appears on pp. 839–858.

Meeting Your Standards

Students will

1. **analyze and respond to literary elements.**
   - **Literary Analysis: Greek Tragedies**
2. **read, comprehend, and analyze drama.**
   - **Reading Skill: Summarize**
   - **Reading Check questions**
   - **Apply the Skills questions**
   - **Assessment Practice**
3. **develop vocabulary.**
   - **Vocabulary**
   - **Word Study**
4. **apply grammar skills.**
   - **Independent and Subordinate Clauses**
5. **Develop writing proficiency.**
   - **Work in Progress: Reflective Essay**
   - **reflective essay**
6. **strengthen listening and speaking skills.**
   - **mock trial**

CRI For a full explanation of Culturally Responsive Instruction opportunities in this lesson, see p. T86–T87.

FT For an accelerated lesson, use the Fast Track strategies and activities.

Managing Differentiated Instruction

This leveled selection pairing groups a more accessible with a more challenging selection. Choose either one to teach the lesson skills. For classroom management suggestions for using the pairing in a mixed-ability class, see pp. T68–T69.

Daily Block Scheduling

Each day in this Lesson Pacing Guide represents a 40–50 minute period. Teachers using block scheduling may combine days to revise pacing. In addition, teachers may differentiate and support core instruction by integrating components for extended and intensive support as students require. See the Guide to Selected Leveled Resources (facing page).

Guide to Selected Leveled Resources

EL English Learners

			Antigone, Scenes 3 through 5
CORE COURSE	*Unit 5 Resources*	Selection Test A	pp. 59–61
	Graphic Organizer Transparencies	Reading Skill Graphic Organizer A	p. 157
		Literary Analysis Graphic Organizer A	p. 159
EXTENDED SUPPORT (Level 2)	*Unit 5 Resources*	Reading and Vocabulary Warm-ups A or B	pp. 44–47
	Reader's Notebook: English Learner's Version		adapted instruction and selection
	Hear It! Audio CD		selection and summaries
	Hear It! Audio CD (adapted text)		adapted selection and summaries
INTENSIVE SUPPORT (Level 1)	*Reality Central*		"Royal Rights to Privacy"
	Real-World Writing Journal		Lessons 2, pp. 142–145

L2 Below-Level Students

			Antigone, Scenes 3 through 5
CORE COURSE	*Unit 5 Resources*	Selection Test A	pp. 59–61
	Graphic Organizer Transparencies	Reading Skill Graphic Organizer A	p. 157
		Literary Analysis Graphic Organizer A	p. 159
EXTENDED SUPPORT (Level 2)	*Unit 5 Resources*	Reading and Vocabulary Warm-ups A or B	pp. 44–47
	Reader's Notebook		adapted instruction and selection
	Hear It! Audio CD		selection and summaries
INTENSIVE SUPPORT (Level 1)	*Reality Central*		"Royal Rights to Privacy"
	Real-World Writing Journal		Lessons 2, pp. 142–145
	Reading Kit		Reteaching worksheets

L1

			Antigone, Scenes 3 through 5
CORE COURSE	*Unit 5 Resources*	Selection Test A	pp. 59–61
	Graphic Organizer Transparencies	Reading Skill Graphic Organizer A	p. 157
		Literary Analysis Graphic Organizer A	p. 159
EXTENDED SUPPORT (Level 2)	*Unit 5 Resources*	Reading and Vocabulary Warm-ups A or B	pp. 44–47
	Reader's Notebook: Adapted Version		adapted instruction and selection
	Hear It! Audio CD (adapted text)		adapted selection and summaries
INTENSIVE SUPPORT (Level 1)	*Reality Central*		"Royal Rights to Privacy"
	Real-World Writing Journal		Lessons 2, pp. 142–145
	Reading Kit		Reteaching worksheets

The program includes resources for these students: L3 On-Level L4 Advanced All All
For a complete guide to selection support, see pp. T106–T108.

NOTE: All print materials are also available online at *www.PHLitOnline.com.*

Antigone, Scenes 3 through 5

RESOURCES FOR:

- EL English Learners
- L1 Special Needs Students
- L2 Below-Level Students
- L3 On-Level Students
- L4 Advanced Students
- All All Students

Vocabulary/Fluency/Prior Knowledge

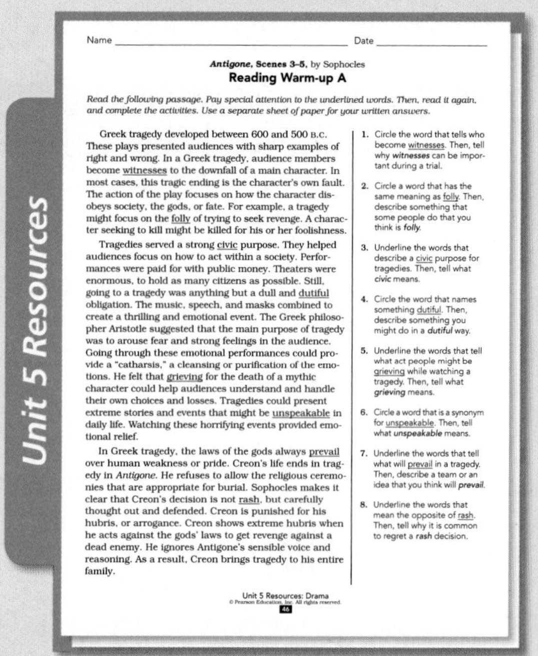

Name ______________________ Date ____________

***Antigone*, Scenes 3–5**, by Sophocles
Reading Warm-up A

Read the following passage. Pay special attention to the underlined words. Then, read it again, and complete the activities. Use a separate sheet of paper for your written answers.

Greek tragedy developed between 600 and 500 B.C. These plays presented audiences with sharp examples of right and wrong. In a Greek tragedy, audience members become witnesses to the downfall of a main character. In most cases, this tragic ending is the character's own fault. The action of the play focuses on how the character disobeys society, the gods, or fate. For example, a tragedy might focus on the folly of trying to seek revenge. A character seeking to kill might be killed for his or her foolishness.

Tragedies served a strong civic purpose. They helped audiences focus on how to act within a society. Performances were paid for with public money. Theaters were enormous, to hold as many citizens as possible. Still, going to a tragedy was anything but a dull and dutiful obligation. The music, speech, and masks combined to create a thrilling and emotional event. The Greek philosopher Aristotle suggested that the main purpose of tragedy was to arouse fear and strong feelings in the audience. Going through these emotional performances could provide a "catharsis," a cleansing or purification of the emotions. He felt that grieving for the death of a mythic character could help audiences understand and handle their own choices and losses. Tragedies could present extreme stories and events that might be unspeakable in daily life. Watching these horrifying events provided emotional relief.

In Greek tragedy, the laws of the gods always prevail over human weakness or pride. Creon's life ends in tragedy in *Antigone*. He refuses to allow the religious ceremonies that are appropriate for burial. Sophocles makes it clear that Creon's decision is not rash, but carefully thought out and defended. Creon is punished for his hubris, or arrogance. Creon shows extreme hubris when he acts against the gods' laws to get revenge against a dead enemy. He ignores Antigone's sensible voice and reasoning. As a result, Creon brings tragedy to his entire family.

1. Circle the word that tells who become witnesses. Then, tell why *witnesses* can be important during a trial.
2. Circle a word that has the same meaning as folly. Then, describe something that some people do that you think is *folly*.
3. Underline the words that describe a civic purpose for tragedies. Then, tell what *civic* means.
4. Circle the word that names something dutiful. Then, describe something you might do in a *dutiful* way.
5. Underline the words that tell what act people might be grieving while watching a tragedy. Then, tell what *grieving* means.
6. Circle a word that is a synonym for unspeakable. Then, tell what *unspeakable* means.
7. Underline the words that tell what will prevail in a tragedy. Then, describe a team or an idea that you think will *prevail*.
8. Underline the words that mean the opposite of rash. Then, tell why it is common to regret a *rash* decision.

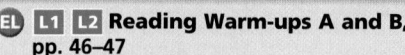

Unit 5 Resources: Drama
© Pearson Education, Inc. All rights reserved.
46

EL L1 L2 **Reading Warm-ups A and B, pp. 46–47**

Also available for these selections:

EL L1 L2 **Vocabulary Warm-ups A and B, pp. 44–45**

All **Vocabulary Builder, p. 51**

All **Writing About the Big Question, p. 48**

Reader's Notebooks

Pre- and postreading pages for both selections, as well as *Antigone, Scenes 3 through 5* appear in an interactive format in the *Reader's Notebooks*. Each *Notebook* is differentiated for a different group of learners.
The selections in the Adapted and English Learner's versions are abridged.

L2 L3 ***Reader's Notebook***

L1 ***Reader's Notebook: Adapted Version***

EL ***Reader's Notebook: English Learner's Version***

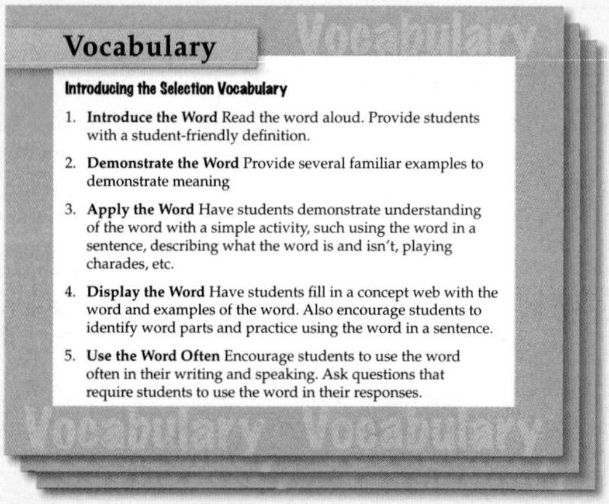

Vocabulary

Introducing the Selection Vocabulary

1. **Introduce the Word** Read the word aloud. Provide students with a student-friendly definition.
2. **Demonstrate the Word** Provide several familiar examples to demonstrate meaning
3. **Apply the Word** Have students demonstrate understanding of the word with a simple activity, such using the word in a sentence, describing what the word is and isn't, playing charades, etc.
4. **Display the Word** Have students fill in a concept web with the word and examples of the word. Also encourage students to identify word parts and practice using the word in a sentence.
5. **Use the Word Often** Encourage students to use the word often in their writing and speaking. Ask questions that require students to use the word in their responses.

Classroom Strategies and Teaching Routines

- core classroom routines outlined step-by-step
- convenient format for easy reference while teaching

Selection Support

Graphic Organizer Transparencies

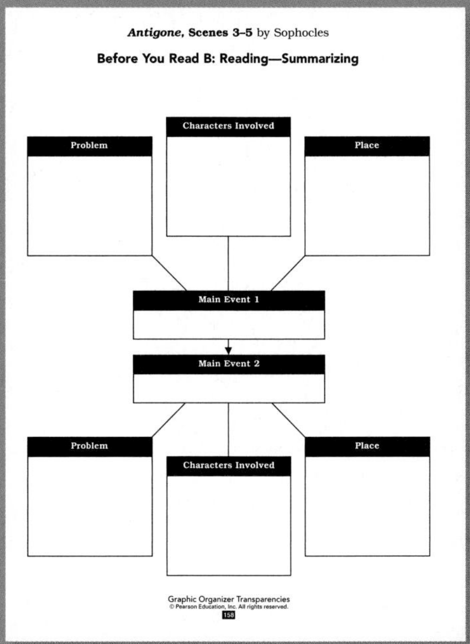
Antigone, Scenes 3–5 by Sophocles

Before You Read B: Reading—Summarizing

L3 Reading: Graphic Organizer B, p. 158

Also available for these selections:

- EL L1 L2 Reading: Graphic Organizer A, p. 157 (partially filled in)
- EL L1 L2 Literary Analysis: Graphic Organizer A, p. 159 (partially filled in)
- L3 Literary Analysis: Graphic Organizer B, p. 160

Skills Development/Extension

Unit 5 Resources

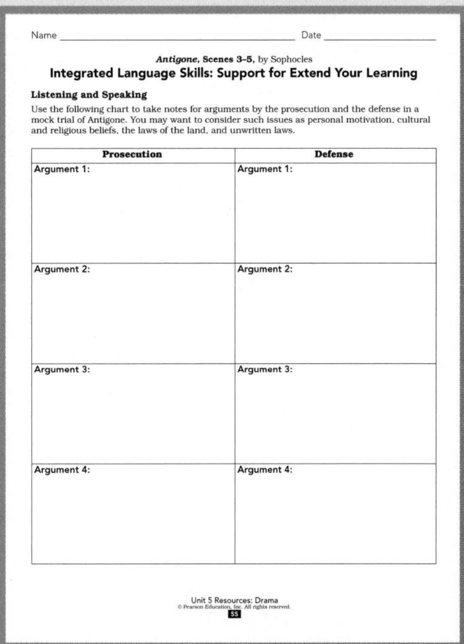
Name ______ Date ______

Antigone, Scenes 3–5, by Sophocles

Integrated Language Skills: Support for Extend Your Learning

Listening and Speaking

Use the following chart to take notes for arguments by the prosecution and the defense in a mock trial of Antigone. You may want to consider such issues as personal motivation, cultural and religious beliefs, the laws of the land, and unwritten laws.

Prosecution	Defense
Argument 1:	Argument 1:
Argument 2:	Argument 2:
Argument 3:	Argument 3:
Argument 4:	Argument 4:

L3 L4 Support for Extend Your Learning, p. 55

Also available for these selections:

- All Literary Analysis: Greek Tragedies, p. 49
- All Reading: Summarize, p. 50
- L4 Enrichment, p. 52
- L3 L4 Grammar, p. 53
- L3 L4 Support for Writing, p. 54

Assessment

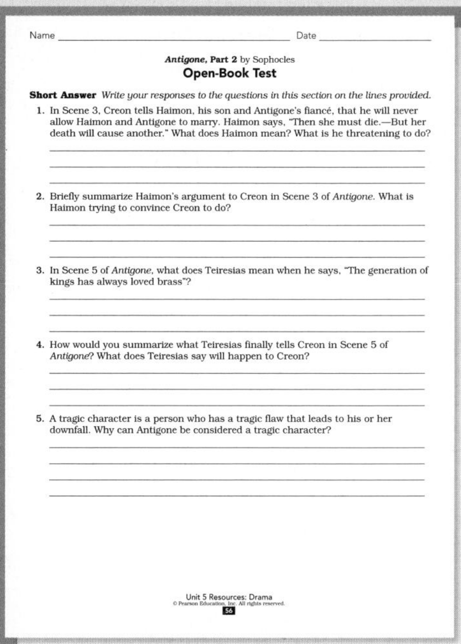
Name ______ Date ______

Antigone, Part 2 by Sophocles

Open-Book Test

Short Answer *Write your responses to the questions in this section on the lines provided.*

1. In Scene 3, Creon tells Haimon, his son and Antigone's fiancé, that he will never allow Haimon and Antigone to marry. Haimon says, "Then she must die.—But her death will cause another." What does Haimon mean? What is he threatening to do?
2. Briefly summarize Haimon's argument to Creon in Scene 3 of *Antigone*. What is Haimon trying to convince Creon to do?
3. In Scene 5 of *Antigone*, what does Teiresias mean when he says, "The generation of kings has always loved brass"?
4. How would you summarize what Teiresias finally tells Creon in Scene 5 of *Antigone*? What does Teiresias say will happen to Creon?
5. A tragic character is a person who has a tragic flaw that leads to his or her downfall. Why can Antigone be considered a tragic character?

L3 L4 Open-Book Test, pp. 56–58

Also available for these selections:

- EL L1 L2 Selection Test A, pp. 59–61
- L3 L4 Selection Test B, pp. 62–64

PHLit Online!

www.PHLitOnline.com

- complete narrated selection text
- a thematically related video with writing prompt
- an interactive graphic organizer
- highlighting feature
- access to all student print resources, adapted to individual student needs
- Spanish and English summaries

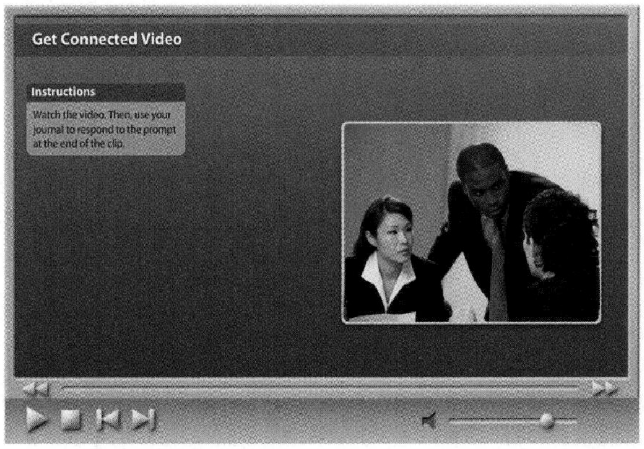

Get Connected! (thematic video with writing prompt)

Also available:

Background video

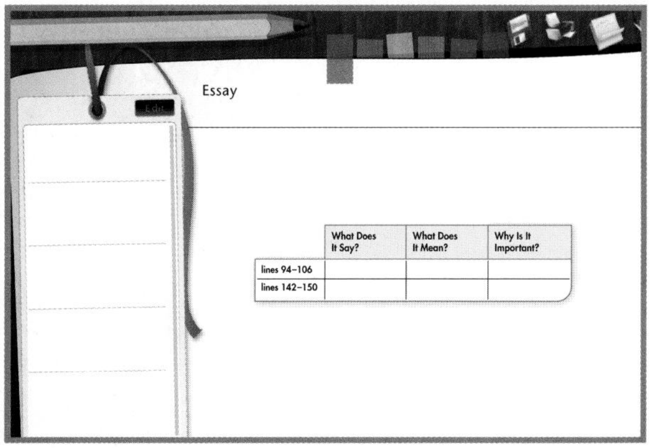

Writer's Journal (with graphics feature)

Also available:

Vocabulary Central (tools, activities, and songs for studying vocabulary)

DIFFERENTIATE/PRETEACH

❶ Selection Skills

1. With the class, preview the selection skills. (The lesson meets the lesson objectives given on p. 837a.)
2. Explain that students will develop the skill of summarizing (introduced on p. 811) as they read to better understand and enjoy the selection. By examining summarizing as they read, they will gain deeper insight into drama.
3. To introduce the Writing and Listening and Speaking activities (p. 861), tell students that when they have finished reading the selection, they will write a reflective essay and hold a mock trial related to the selection.
4. Tell students that they will also study a grammar concept: independent and subordinate clauses. By mastering this concept, they will improve their reading fluency and the quality of their own writing.

Before You Read

Antigone, Scenes 3 through 5

Drama Selection

Review and Anticipate
In Scenes 1 and 2, Antigone defies the order of her uncle, King Creon of Thebes, and symbolically buries her brother Polyneices. When Creon discovers her guilt, he sentences Antigone to death, refusing to pardon her just because she is his niece. As Scene 2 ends, the chorus sings, "*Fate works most for woe / With Folly's fairest show.*" The remaining scenes play out the truth of these words.

❶

Selection Skills Guide

Practice these skills with ***Antigone*****, Scenes 3 through 5** (p. 839).

- Understand Greek tragedies
- Identify theme
- Summarize
- Take notes
- Identify independent and subordinate clauses
- Write a reflective essay
- Hold a mock trial

Differentiated Instruction for Universal Access

Accessibility at a Glance

	Antigone, Part 2	
Context	Historical: Ancient Greece	
Language/Vocabulary	• Dialogue • Formal language • Monologues • Above-level vocabulary	
Concept Level	Challenging (individual against society)	
Literary Merit	Noted author	
Lexile/Length	Lexile: NP	Word Count: 4742
Other	**Accessible**	

Literary Analysis: Greek Tragedies

Greek tragedies are serious dramas that share certain characteristics:

- They are based on myths that were familiar to the original audience.
- They tell of a reversal of fortune, from good to bad, experienced by a man or woman of noble birth.
- The main character may have a *tragic flaw,* a characteristic that leads to his or her downfall.
- Tragedy often presents audiences with a dilemma about understanding the hero's demise. The character's downfall results from his or her own actions. At the same time, this doom is clearly destined; it is brought about by *fate,* a force beyond the character's control.

The **theme,** or central message, of a Greek tragedy is often a warning against excess, such as pride or passion. Tragedies demonstrate the limitations of human knowledge, sympathy, and foresight. They remind us that every decision involves choosing—and living with—the unforeseen consequences of these choices.

Reading Skill: Summarize

To **summarize** a play, briefly state the most important actions and ideas in your own words. To gather details for a summary, **take notes.** Write down the most important elements of what you read; for example, note the characters, the places, the problems, and the key events.

Using the Strategy: Summary Chart

Use a **summary chart** like this one to take notes that will help you summarize *Antigone.*

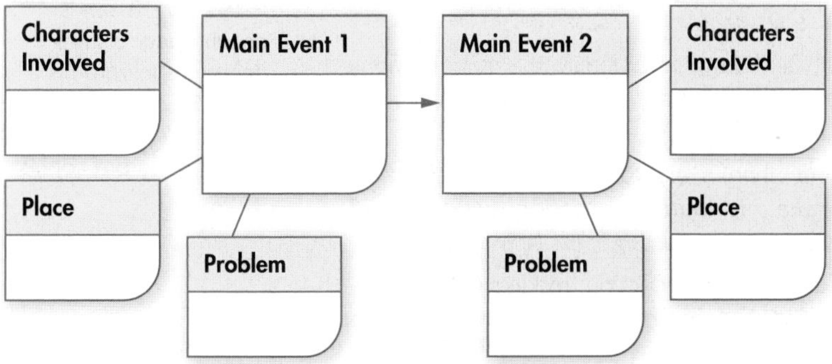

PHLit Online!
www.PHLitOnline.com

Hear It!
- Selection summary audio
- Selection audio

See It!
- Get Connected video
- Background video
- More about the author
- Vocabulary flashcards

Do It!
- Interactive journals
- Interactive graphic organizers
- Self-test
- Internet activity
- Grammar tutorial
- Interactive vocabulary games

Differentiated Instruction for Universal Access

Preparing Students for the Selection

If you wish to prepare lower-level readers to read *Antigone,* Scenes 3 through 5, follow these steps:

- Explain to students that Antigone's staunch beliefs help to create change in Creon's kingdom. Explain that one dedicated individual has the ability to spark necessary change in society. For example, Rosa Parks's pivotal refusal to give up her bus seat catalyzed the Civil Rights Movement, which, through the efforts of many impassioned activists, granted equal rights to African Americans. Prompt students to think of other activists and discuss how they have changed society.
- Students might have difficulty with the formality of the language. Encourage them to rephrase difficult sentences. For example, explain that the sentence "But if the guilt lies upon Creon who judged me, then, I pray, may his punishment equal my own" can be rephrased as "If Creon, who judged me, is guilty, then I hope his punishment is the same as mine."

❷ Literary Analysis

1. Introduce the skill, using the instruction on the student page.
2. Tell students that they will practice interpreting Greek tragedies as they read.

Think Aloud: Model the Skill

Model the skill of interpreting Greek tragedies. Say to students:

Imagine I am reading a Greek play about a queen whose son makes a mistake. She refuses to speak to him because she is very stubborn. A prophet warns her that this will lead to misery, but she won't listen. Because she ignores him, her son goes crazy—and she is never happy again. This play has the key elements of a Greek Tragedy: it is about a noble woman; she experiences a downfall due to her tragic flaw; the story is fueled by fate; and it has a theme of warning against excess.

❸ Reading Skill

1. Introduce the skill, using the instruction on the student page.
2. Tell students that they will practice summarizing as they read.

Think Aloud: Model the Skill

Model the skill of summarizing. Say to students:

Suppose I am reading the play *Romeo and Juliet.* In order to *summarize* it—state important actions and ideas in my own words—I take notes. I note its main characters: Romeo and Juliet; the places or setting: Verona, a balcony; the problems: dueling families, forbidden lovers; and the key events: Juliet fakes her death, Romeo commits suicide, and Juliet commits suicide. This helps me better understand the play.

❹ Using the Strategy

Give students a copy of either **Graphic Organizer A** or **B** (***Graphic Organizer Transparencies,*** pp. 157–158) to record their ideas about summarizing as they read. Use the examples in **Reading Skill Graphic Organizer A,** which is partially filled in, to model the process of completing the organizer by taking notes.

PRETEACH

❶ Writing About the Big Question

1. Review the assignment with the class.
2. Ask students to discuss if they agree or disagree with the following statement: *Sometimes it is okay to manipulate the truth.* Prompt them to explain their opinions.
3. Have students complete the sentence starters. Review responses as a class.
   Possible response: People try to manipulate the truth because they want to be seen in a positive way. Bias against others can distort a person's perception and lead to an incorrect assumption.
4. Remind students that their answers will help them think about the Big Question.

While You Read

Tell students that as they read, they should identify Creon's reasons for not pardoning Antigone.

❷ Vocabulary

1. Have students preview the selection vocabulary.
2. For each word, have students say the word aloud.
3. Then, use the word in a sentence that defines the word.
4. Finally, repeat your definitional sentence or a similar sentence with the word missing and have the class "fill in the blank" chorally. Here are some examples:
   To show deference to someone is to yield to the ideas and wishes of him or her. Because of her extensive knowledge and experience, the audience showed the visiting speaker great [students say "deference"].

❸ Word Study

1. Introduce the skill, using the instruction in the box.
2. Ask students to think of a word with the root *-fer-*. Then, using their knowledge of the root *-fer-*, have them define it.
   (**Sample answer:** *coniferous;* "belonging to a category of trees that bear cones")

To what extent does *experience* determine what we *perceive?*

❶ Writing About the Big Question

In the last three scenes of *Antigone*, Creon is unwilling and unable to accept anyone else's perception of events or anyone else's advice about what to do. Use these sentence starters to develop your ideas about the Big Question.

People try to **manipulate** the truth because ____________.

Bias against others can distort a person's perception and lead to ____________.

While You Read Look for the reasons Creon gives to explain why he will not pardon Antigone. Decide whether you agree or disagree with him.

❷ Vocabulary

Read each word and its definition. Decide whether you know the word well, know it a little bit, or do not know it at all. After you read, see how your knowledge of each word has increased.

- **deference** (def´ ər əns) *n.* a yielding to the ideas, wishes, and so on of another (p. 839) ***Out of deference to him, she gave up her seat.*** *defer v. deferential adj.*
- **contempt** (kən tempt´) *n.* scorn; the attitude of someone who looks down on something or someone else (p. 840) ***He expressed his contempt by ignoring his opponent.*** *contemptible adj.*
- **vile** (vīl) *adj.* evil; low; extremely disgusting (p. 843) ***The week-old food tasted vile.*** *vilely adv. vileness n.*
- **piety** (pī´ ə tē) *n.* loyalty and devotion to family, the divine, or some other object of respect (p. 844) ***Her elders were pleased by her piety.*** *pious adj. piously adv.*
- **lamentation** (lam´ ən tā´ shən) *n.* expression of grief; weeping (p. 847) ***The crowd broke into loud lamentation when the sad news of the death was announced.*** *lament v. lamentable adj.*
- **rash** (rash) *adj.* too hasty in speech or action; reckless (p. 858) ***It was rash to yell at the toddler before understanding what had happened.*** *rashly adv. rashness n.*

❸ Word Study

The **Latin root *-fer-*** means "to carry," "to bear," or "to bring."

In this play, a son is encouraged to show **deference** toward his father by carrying out his father's wishes—even if these are not his own.

Vocabulary Development

Vocabulary Knowledge Rating

Create a **Vocabulary Knowledge Rating Chart** (***Professional Development Guidebook***, p. 33) for the selection. Include the selection vocabulary and the Big Question words that appear in the Writing About the Big Question sentence starters on this page. (The Big Question vocabulary is introduced on pp. 790–791).

Give students a copy of the chart. Read the words aloud, and have students mark their rating in the Before Reading column. Urge them to be alert to these words as they read and discuss the selection.

Tally how many students think they know a word to gauge how much instruction to provide. As students read and discuss the selection, point out the words and their context.

PHLit Online! **Vocabulary Central,** featuring tools, activities, and songs for studying vocabulary, is available online at **www.PHLitOnline.com.**

Scenes 3–5

Scene 3

CHORAGOS. But here is Haimon, King, the last of all your sons.
Is it grief for Antigone that brings him here,
And bitterness at being robbed of his bride?

[*Enter* HAIMON.]

CREON. We shall soon see, and no need of diviners.[1]
—Son,
You have heard my final judgment on that girl:
Have you come here hating me, or have you come
With deference and with love, whatever I do?

HAIMON. I am your son, father. You are my guide.

1. **diviners** (də vin′ ərz) *n.* those who claim to forecast the future.

Vocabulary
deference (def′ ər əns) *n.* a yielding to the ideas, wishes, and so on of another

▼ Critical Viewing What details of this image suggest that the chorus is pleading? Explain. **[Analyze]**

Differentiated Instruction — Additional Instruction

EL Extended Support—English Learners
Have students complete the **Reading and Vocabulary Warm-ups, *Unit 5 Resources,*** pp. 44–47, before they read. Assign the prereading pages for the selection in the ***Reader's Notebook: English Learner's Version.*** Then, have students listen to portions of the selection on the ***Hear It!* Audio CD.**

L1 L2 Extended Support—Struggling Readers
Have students complete the **Reading and Vocabulary Warm-ups, *Unit 5 Resources,*** pp. 44–47, before they read. Assign the prereading pages for the selection in the ***Reader's Notebook: Adapted Version.*** Then, have students listen to portions of the selection on the ***Hear It!* Audio CD** (adapted text).

Extended Support—Reluctant Readers
To build motivation and engagement before assigning the selection, have students read "In or Out of the In Crowd," a thematically related selection in ***Reality Central.*** Then, use the questions at the conclusion of the related selection to guide discussion.

TEACH

1 Activating Prior Knowledge

1. Prepare an **Anticipation Guide** (see ***Professional Development Guidebook,*** pp. 36–38) with the following statements:
   - Being stubborn is the same as being dedicated.
   - Leaders who have a sense of pride will help their societies.
   - Only people with years of experience can show wisdom.
2. Give students a copy of the pre-pared **Anticipation Guide** and have students mark their responses in the Me column. Have students discuss the statements in pairs or groups and mark the guides again in the Group column.
3. For further guidance, use the ***Classroom Strategies and Teaching Routines*** card for **Anticipation Guides.**

Concept Connector
Students will reconsider their original ideas after reading the selection.

Small-Group Activity
Have groups summarize the main movements of the characters in Scene 5. Have groups analyze how the major gestures, and strong emotions match the plot.

2 About the Selection

As the events in the second part of *Antigone* unfold, Creon and Antigone move inexorably toward their respective fates. The events set in motion lead each character to his or her downfall.

3 Critical Viewing

Answer: The chorus reaches out with arms as if asking for something.

PHLit Online!
This selection is available in interactive format in the **Enriched Online Student Edition,** at **www.PHLitOnline.com,** which includes a thematically related video with writing prompt and an interactive graphic organizer.

❹ Reading Skill
Summarize

1. Read Creon's speech aloud, pausing after lines 20, 27, 35, 44, 47, and 51 for students to take brief notes on the most important information in the passage you have just finished reading.
2. **Ask** students to respond to the Reading Skill prompt: As you read Creon's speech in lines 12–51, take brief notes. Then, summarize the speech.
   Possible response: Creon tells Haimon that he is behaving properly by obeying his father. He says he is not going to change his mind about Antigone because she is a family member. She has broken the law and must be punished. If left unpunished, lawbreakers create anarchy in the state.

❺ Literary Analysis
Greek Tragedies

1. Remind students that Creon is one of the two main tragic characters in the play. Emphasize that these characters usually exhibit a tragic flaw, or a fault in their characters that will damage or destroy their lives.
2. **Ask** students the Literary Analysis question: What flaw in Creon's character do lines 28–29 reveal?
   Answer: Creon's words reveal his stubborn pride. He fears that he will appear weak if he softens his stance on Antigone's crime.
3. Then, **ask** students how Creon's rigidity might drive him into a conflict that cannot be resolved.
   Possible response: Creon could have a bitter conflict with anyone who challenges his will because he sees any deviation from submission to his will as anarchy and a threat to the state.

You make things clear for me, and I obey you.
No marriage means more to me than your continuing
wisdom.

CREON. Good. That is the way to behave: subordinate
Everything else, my son, to your father's will.
This is what a man prays for, that he may get
Sons attentive and dutiful in his house,
Each one hating his father's enemies,
Honoring his father's friends. But if his sons
Fail him, if they turn out unprofitably,
What has he fathered but trouble for himself
And amusement for the malicious?
So you are right
Not to lose your head over this woman.
Your pleasure with her would soon grow cold, Haimon,
And then you'd have a hellcat in bed and elsewhere.
Let her find her husband in Hell!
Of all the people in this city, only she
Has had contempt for my law and broken it.

Do you want me to show myself weak before the people?
Or to break my sworn word? No, and I will not.
The woman dies.
I suppose she'll plead "family ties." Well, let her.
If I permit my own family to rebel,
How shall I earn the world's obedience?
Show me the man who keeps his house in hand,
He's fit for public authority.
I'll have no dealings
With law-breakers, critics of the government:
Whoever is chosen to govern should be obeyed—
Must be obeyed, in all things, great and small,
Just and unjust! O Haimon,
The man who knows how to obey, and that man only,
Knows how to give commands when the time comes.
You can depend on him, no matter how fast
The spears come: he's a good soldier, he'll stick it out.

Anarchy, anarchy! Show me a greater evil!
This is why cities tumble and the great houses rain down,
This is what scatters armies!

No, no: good lives are made so by discipline.
We keep the laws then, and the lawmakers,

Reading Skill
Summarize ❹ As you read Creon's speech in lines 12–51, take brief notes. Then, summarize the speech.

Vocabulary
contempt (kən tempt′) *n.* scorn; the attitude of someone who looks down on something or someone else

Literary Analysis
Greek Tragedies ❺ What flaw in Creon's character do lines 28–29 reveal?

Vocabulary Development

Thematic Vocabulary: The Big Question
As students are discussing *Antigone,* Scenes 3 through 5, encourage them to use the thematic vocabulary presented in Introducing the Big Question, pp. 790–791. You might encourage them with sentence starters like these:

1. Haimon responded to Creon's question about *deference* by . . .
2. Because of Creon's *rash* decision, . . .
3. The *contempt* that Antigone has for Creon was expressed in . . .
4. According to Creon, "*Piety* shown the dead" is . . .

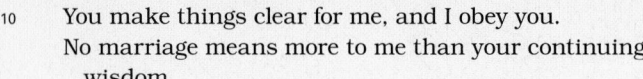

And no woman shall seduce us. If we must lose,
Let's lose to a man, at least! Is a woman stronger than we?

CHORAGOS. Unless time has rusted my wits,
What you say, King, is said with point and dignity.

HAIMON. [*Boyishly earnest*] Father:
Reason is God's crowning gift to man, and you are right
To warn me against losing mine. I cannot say—
I hope that I shall never want to say!—that you
Have reasoned badly. Yet there are other men
Who can reason, too; and their opinions might be helpful.
You are not in a position to know everything
That people say or do, or what they feel:
Your temper terrifies them—everyone
Will tell you only what you like to hear.
But I, at any rate, can listen; and I have heard them
Muttering and whispering in the dark about this girl.
They say no woman has ever, so unreasonably,
Died so shameful a death for a generous act:
"She covered her brother's body. Is this indecent?
She kept him from dogs and vultures. Is this a crime?
Death?—She should have all the honor that we can give her!"

This is the way they talk out there in the city.

You must believe me:
Nothing is closer to me than your happiness.
What could be closer? Must not any son
Value his father's fortune as his father does his?
I beg you, do not be unchangeable:
Do not believe that you alone can be right.
The man who thinks that,
The man who maintains that only he has the power
To reason correctly, the gift to speak, the soul—
A man like that, when you know him, turns out empty.

It is not reason never to yield to reason!

In flood time you can see how some trees bend,
And because they bend, even their twigs are safe,
While stubborn trees are torn up, roots and all.
And the same thing happens in sailing:
Make your sheet fast, never slacken,—and over you go,
Head over heels and under: and there's your voyage.
Forget you are angry! Let yourself be moved!
I know I am young; but please let me say this:
The ideal condition

Literary Analysis
Greek Tragedies What basic limitation of human beings does Haimon describe?

Reading Check
What does Haimon beg Creon to do?

6 Literary Analysis
Greek Tragedies

1. Assign sequences of lines from Haimon's speech to volunteers, and have them take turns reading the speech aloud.
2. Challenge students to name the focus of Haimon's speech in one word.
   Answer: The focus of Haimon's speech is reason.
3. Draw attention to Haimon's repetition of the word *reason* and related words in lines 55, 58, 59, 66, 80, and 82. Point out that Haimon uses the word *unreasonably* when he refers to Antigone's death sentence.
4. Then, **ask** students to respond to the Literary Analysis question: What basic limitation of human beings does Haimon describe?
   Possible response: Haimon describes humans' frequent self-centeredness and their inability to listen rationally to the opinions of others.

7 Reading Check

Answer: Haimon begs Creon to listen to what people are saying about the punishment of Antigone, and to change his mind about her death.

Differentiated Instruction for Universal Access

Support for Special Needs Students
Have students read along with the recording of this scene on the ***Hear It!* Audio CD.** Then, invite students to role-play the scene between Creon and Haimon for the class.

Support for Less Proficient Readers
Have students read along with the recording of this scene on the ***Hear It!* Audio CD.** Then, encourage students to draw parallels between one of their own experiences trying to change the mind of a person who refused to listen to reason and Haimon's experience. Suggest that students write their own impressions in their journals and describe what they think was keeping the person from listening or changing his or her mind.

8 Connecting to the Big Question

1. Explain that Creon's reaction to Antigone's rebellion is largely based on his understanding of what it means to be king.
2. Have students read the bracketed text. **Ask** students to explain Creon's reasoning for his refusal to pardon Antigone.
   Answer: He believes that it is wrong to stand up for an anarchist, and that it is wrong for the City to propose to teach him how to rule his own kingdom. He also believes that Haimon has "sold out to a woman."
3. **Ask** students to explain why Creon's experience might make him so rigid in his thinking.
   Possible answer: He is used to ruling the kingdom in his own way—putting the State above the personal or above the gods. To do otherwise might be to lose respect or show weakness.
4. As students continue reading, have them notice what kinds of experiences force Creon to change his outlook.

9 Critical Viewing

Answer: The physical closeness of the two in this image suggests that they are related; the way Haimon is looking up at Creon suggests that he is Creon's son; their relaxed stances, with arms behind their backs, is indicative of a father and son relationship.

6
Would be, I admit, that men should be right by instinct;
But since we are all too likely to go astray,
The reasonable thing is to learn from those who can teach.

CHORAGOS. You will do well to listen to him, King,
If what he says is sensible. And you, Haimon,
Must listen to your father.—Both speak well.

CREON. You consider it right for a man of my years and experience
To go to school to a boy?

HAIMON. It is not right
If I am wrong. But if I am young, and right,
What does my age matter?

8
CREON. You think it right to stand up for an anarchist?

HAIMON. Not at all. I pay no respect to criminals.

CREON. Then she is not a criminal?

HAIMON. The City would deny it, to a man.

CREON. And the City proposes to teach me how to rule?

HAIMON. Ah. Who is it that's talking like a boy now?

9 ▼ **Critical Viewing** Which details of this image from a production of *Antigone* show that Creon and Haimon are father and son? **[Analyze]**

Vocabulary Development

Vocabulary Reinforcement

To reinforce and assess students' comprehension of selection vocabulary words, instruct students to use the "yes/no—why" format to tell whether the words are used correctly and explain why. Use these sentences:

1. She sent a card expressing her *contempt* for his mother, who was in the hospital.
   Answer: No, *contempt* is not used correctly. It means "scorn" and probably would not describe the feelings of someone sending a card to a person who was ill.
2. Their *vile* behavior shocked the entire school.
   Answer: Yes, *vile* is used correctly here. It can mean "very disgusting" and would be an appropriate adjective to describe shocking behavior.

CREON. My voice is the one voice giving orders in this City!

HAIMON. It is no City if it takes orders from one voice.

CREON. The State is the King!

8

HAIMON. Yes, if the State is a desert.

[*Pause*]

CREON. This boy, it seems, has sold out to a woman.

HAIMON. If you are a woman: my concern is only for you.

CREON. So? Your "concern"! In a public brawl with your father!

HAIMON. How about you, in a public brawl with justice?

CREON. With justice, when all that I do is within my rights?

HAIMON. You have no right to trample on God's right.

CREON. [*Completely out of control*] Fool, adolescent fool! Taken in by a woman!

HAIMON. You'll never see me taken in by anything **vile**.

CREON. Every word you say is for her!

HAIMON. [*Quietly, darkly*] And for you. And for me. And for the gods under the earth.

CREON. You'll never marry her while she lives.

10

HAIMON. Then she must die.—But her death will cause another.

CREON. Another? Have you lost your senses? Is this an open threat?

HAIMON. There is no threat in speaking to emptiness.

CREON. I swear you'll regret this superior tone of yours! You are the empty one!

HAIMON. If you were not my father, I'd say you were perverse.

CREON. You girlstruck fool, don't play at words with me!

Vocabulary
vile (vīl) *adj.* evil; low; extremely disgusting

Literary Analysis
Greek Tragedies
How do Haimon's words in line 125 warn of the fateful consequences of Creon's decision?

11 **Reading Check**
How does Creon respond to Haimon's arguments?

10 Literary Analysis
Greek Tragedies

1. Ask a volunteer to read aloud the exchange between Creon and Haimon in lines 122–124.
2. **Ask** students what the message is behind Creon's words in line 124 and why he says it in this way.
   Possible response: Creon is saying that Antigone is going to be put to death very soon. He casts what he says in terms of Haimon's marriage to Antigone to make her death a more personal affront to Haimon.
3. Then, **ask** students to respond to the Literary Analysis question: How do Haimon's words in line 125 warn of the fateful consequences of Creon's decision?
   Possible response: In saying "Then she must die," Haimon shows his determination to marry Antigone; he implies that he will marry Antigone in death if he must. Thus, Haimon hints that by insisting upon Antigone's death, Creon will help bring about his own son's death.

11 Reading Check

Answer: Creon gets upset at Haimon's arguments and claims that Haimon is acting adolescent and girlstruck.

Differentiated Instruction for Universal Access

Enrichment for Gifted and Talented Students
Have students imagine that they write advice columns for a newspaper. They receive a letter from a young man whose father does not pay attention to his point of view or heed any opinions except those that agree with his own. What advice would students offer the young man? Have students write their responses in the form of a letter.

Enrichment for Advanced Readers
In one column of two-column charts, have students list the reasons they think Creon should change his mind about punishing Antigone for burying her brother against his orders. In a second column, have students list the reasons he should not change his mind. Which list has the stronger reasons? Have students write a few sentences giving advice to Creon about what they think he should do. Students should support their advice with the reasons they have listed.

⓬ Literature in Context

Culture Connection Covering the body of a dead person with earth, whether the body had already been burned or not, was an important step in handling the dead in ancient Greece. Several handfuls of dirt or even the thin coating of dust that Antigone cast over Polyneices' body was sufficient. A covering of earth hid the dead person from the sight of the gods and avoided offending them. It also allowed the dead person to be admitted to the underworld. Burying the dead or allowing the burial of the dead, whether friend or enemy, was considered an act of piety in ancient Greece. Instances of the dead, even criminals, being left unburied were rare. Creon's order concerning Polyneices in *Antigone* is a *locus classicus,* classic example, of this rare exception.

Connect to the Literature Have students read the Literature in Context feature and supplement the facts provided in the feature with the additional information above. Then, **ask** students the Connect to the Literature question: How do Creon's decisions about Polyneices and Antigone blur the boundaries between the dead and the living?

Possible response: Creon's decision to leave the dead Polyneices unburied makes it impossible for his soul to move on to the underworld, the world of the dead. Creon's decision to bury Antigone alive in a stone vault does not allow her to live among the living and will eventually cause her death.

⓬ LITERATURE IN CONTEXT

Culture Connection

Ancient Greek Funeral Rites

In ancient Greek funeral ritual, the body was washed and laid out. Mourners sang ritual songs of grief. A funeral procession followed. The body was in many cases burned, and its ashes were buried in a grave or tomb. Without rites such as these, the Greeks believed, the soul would remain trapped between the underworld and the world of the living.

Connect to the Literature

How do Creon's decisions about Polyneices and Antigone blur the boundaries between the dead and the living?

HAIMON. I am sorry. You prefer silence.

CREON. Now, by God—!
I swear, by all the gods in heaven above us,
You'll watch it, I swear you shall!
[*To the* SERVANTS] Bring her out!
Bring the woman out! Let her die before his eyes!
Here, this instant, with her bridegroom beside her!

HAIMON. Not here, no; she will not die here, King.
And you will never see my face again.
Go on raving as long as you've a friend to endure you.

[*Exit* HAIMON.]

CHORAGOS. Gone, gone.
Creon, a young man in a rage is dangerous!

CREON. Let him do, or dream to do, more than a man can.
He shall not save these girls from death.

CHORAGOS. These girls?
You have sentenced them both?

CREON. No, you are right.
I will not kill the one whose hands are clean.

CHORAGOS. But Antigone?

CREON. [*Somberly*] I will carry her far away
Out there in the wilderness, and lock her
Living in a vault of stone. She shall have food,
As the custom is, to absolve the State of her death.
And there let her pray to the gods of hell:
They are her only gods:
Perhaps they will show her an escape from death,
Or she may learn,
though late,
That piety shown the dead is pity in vain.

[*Exit* CREON.]

Vocabulary
piety (pī′ ə tē) *n.* loyalty and devotion to family, the divine, or some other object of respect

Ode III

CHORUS. Love, unconquerable [STROPHE 1]
Waster of rich men, keeper
Of warm lights and all-night vigil
In the soft face of a girl:
Sea-wanderer, forest-visitor!
Even the pure Immortals cannot escape you,
And mortal man, in his one day's dusk,
Trembles before your glory.

Vocabulary Development

Vocabulary Reinforcement

Students will benefit from additional examples and practice with the selection vocabulary words. Reinforce their comprehension with "show-you-know" sentences. The first part of the sentence uses the vocabulary word in an appropriate context. The second part of the sentence—the "show-you-know" part—clarifies the first. Model the strategy with this example for *piety:*

She was renowned for her *piety;* her faithful attendance at worship services is only one example.

Then, give students a sentence prompt such as the following and coach them in creating the clarification part:

He showed *piety* toward his parents by ______________

Sample answer: always respecting their ideas.

Surely you swerve upon ruin [ANTISTROPHE]
The just man's consenting heart,
As here you have made bright anger
Strike between father and son—
And none has conquered but Love!
A girl's glance working the will of heaven:
Pleasure to her alone who mocks us,
Merciless Aphrodite.[2]

Scene 4

CHORAGOS. [*As* ANTIGONE *enters guarded*] But I can no longer stand in awe of this,
Nor, seeing what I see, keep back my tears.
Here is Antigone, passing to that chamber
Where all find sleep at last.

ANTIGONE. Look upon me, friends, and pity me [STROPHE 1]
Turning back at the night's edge to say
Good-by to the sun that shines for me no longer;
Now sleepy Death
Summons me down to Acheron,[3] that cold shore:
There is no bridesong there, nor any music.

13

CHORUS. Yet not unpraised, not without a kind of honor,
You walk at last into the underworld;
Untouched by sickness, broken by no sword.
What woman has ever found your way to death?

ANTIGONE [ANTISTROPHE 1]
How often I have heard the story of Niobe,[4]
Tantalos'[5] wretched daughter, how the stone
Clung fast about her, ivy-close: and they say
The rain falls endlessly
And sifting soft snow; her tears are never done.
I feel the loneliness of her death in mine.

CHORUS. But she was born of heaven, and you
Are woman, woman-born. If her death is yours,
A mortal woman's, is this not for you
Glory in our world and in the world beyond?

ANTIGONE. [STROPHE 2]
You laugh at me. Ah, friends, friends,
Can you not wait until I am dead? O Thebes,
O men many-charioted, in love with Fortune,

2. **Aphrodite** (af′ rə dīt′ ē) goddess of beauty and love who is sometimes vengeful in her retaliation for offenses.
3. **Acheron** (ak′ ər än′) In Greek mythology, river in the underworld over which the dead are ferried.
4. **Niobe** (nī′ ō bē′) a queen of Thebes who was turned to stone while weeping for her slain children. Her seven sons and seven daughters were killed by Artemis and Apollo, the divine twins of Leto, after Leto complained that Niobe insulted her by bragging of maternal superiority. It was Zeus who turned the bereaved Niobe to stone, but her lament continued and her tears created a stream.
5. **Tantalos'** (tan′ tə ləs) Niobe's father, who was condemned to eternal frustration in the underworld because he revealed the secrets of the gods.

Reading Skill
Summarize
Summarize the conversation between Antigone and the chorus in lines 1–20.

14 **Reading Check**
What punishment for Antigone does Creon announce?

13 Reading Skill
Summarize

1. Remind students that taking notes while reading is an effective way to gather details for a summary.
2. Read aloud the conversation between Antigone and the chorus in lines 1–20 of Scene 4. Pause at five-line intervals to discuss each short passage and identify important information in it. Have students jot down notes on the key details that you identify.
3. **Ask** students to respond to the Reading Skill prompt: Summarize the conversation between Antigone and the chorus in lines 1–20.
Possible response: Antigone says farewell to the world of the living as she goes to her death. The chorus tells her she goes to her death with a kind of honor. Antigone compares herself to Niobe, who was also from a cursed family and was encased in stone in her death.

14 Reading Check
Answer: Antigone will be locked in a stone vault in the wilderness.

Differentiated Instruction for Universal Access

EL Support for English Learners
Preview the pronunciation of footnoted words in lines 5–36 at the start of Scene 4. Then, divide students into two groups and read aloud lines 5–36. Have one group read aloud Antigone's lines 5–10, 15–20, and 25–32. Have the other group answer with the chorus lines 11–14, 21–24, and 33–36. Ask each group to identify two sentences or examples of descriptive writing that the group finds confusing. As a class, discuss the sentence structure or literal meaning of each example.

Enrichment for Advanced Readers
Suggest that students read additional works by Sophocles. After students have read this selection and other works by Sophocles, have them form discussion groups in which they compare and contrast the tragic flaws of the tragic characters in each work. They might also discuss the role of fate in the plays.

⓯ Literary Analysis
Greek Tragedies

1. Ask a volunteer to read aloud lines 45–48.
2. Remind students that although Antigone has admirable qualities, she is a tragic character with a tragic flaw that will lead to her downfall. **Ask** students which of Antigone's virtues, or good qualities, is identified by the chorus.
   Answer: The chorus points out Antigone's reverence for the gods as a virtue.
3. Then, **ask** students what flaw in Antigone the chorus points out.
   Answer: The chorus points out her unwillingness to recognize human law.
4. Finally, **ask** students to respond to the Literary Analysis question: In lines 45–48, which does the chorus say is responsible for Antigone's doom—fate or her own choices?
   Answer: The chorus says that Antigone's own choices have led to her death.

⓰ Critical Viewing

Possible answer: Antigone seems distracted and dejected. Her back is to the chorus, and her pose indicates that she is thinking deeply about something.

Dear springs of Dirce, sacred Theban grove,
Be witnesses for me, denied all pity,
Unjustly judged! and think a word of love
For her whose path turns
Under dark earth, where there are no more tears.

CHORUS. You have passed beyond human daring and come
at last
Into a place of stone where Justice sits.
I cannot tell
What shape of your father's guilt appears in this.

ANTIGONE. [ANTISTROPHE 2]
You have touched it at last: that bridal bed
Unspeakable, horror of son and mother mingling:
Their crime, infection of all our family!
O Oedipus, father and brother!
Your marriage strikes from the grave to murder mine.
I have been a stranger here in my own land:
All my life
The blasphemy of my birth has followed me.

CHORUS. Reverence is a virtue, but strength
Lives in established law: that must prevail.
You have made your choice,
Your death is the doing of your conscious hand.

ANTIGONE. [EPODE]
Then let me go, since all your words are bitter,
And the very light of the sun is cold to me.

Literary Analysis
Greek Tragedies In lines 45–48, which does the chorus say is responsible for Antigone's doom—fate or her own choices? ⓯

⓰ **▼ Critical Viewing**
What does the actress's pose in this image suggest about Antigone's attitude toward her fate? Explain. **[Interpret]**

Vocabulary Development

Word Forms

Give students a blank **Word Form Chart** (***Professional Development Guidebook***, p. 42) with *deference, blasphemy,* and *lamentation* in the correct columns. Work with the class, or have students work with a partner, to determine the related forms. The final chart should look like the one shown.

Noun	Verb	Adjective	Adverb
deference	defer	deferential	deferentially
blasphemy	blaspheme	blasphemous	blasphemously
lamentation	lament	lamentable	lamentably

Lead me to my vigil, where I must have
Neither love nor lamentation: no song, but silence.

[CREON *interrupts impatiently.*]

CREON. If dirges and planned lamentations could put off death,
Men would be singing forever.
[*To the* SERVANTS] Take her, go!
You know your orders: take her to the vault
And leave her alone there. And if she lives or dies,
That's her affair, not ours: our hands are clean.

ANTIGONE. O tomb, vaulted bride-bed in eternal rock,
Soon I shall be with my own again
Where Persephone[6] welcomes the thin ghosts underground:
And I shall see my father again, and you, mother,
And dearest Polyneices—
dearest indeed
To me, since it was my hand
That washed him clean and poured the ritual wine:
And my reward is death before my time!

17 And yet, as men's hearts know, I have done no wrong,
I have not sinned before God. Or if I have,
I shall know the truth in death. But if the guilt
Lies upon Creon who judged me, then, I pray,
May his punishment equal my own.

CHORAGOS. O passionate heart,
Unyielding, tormented still by the same winds!

CREON. Her guards shall have good cause to regret their
delaying.

ANTIGONE. Ah! That voice is like the voice of death!

CREON. I can give you no reason to think you are mistaken.

ANTIGONE. Thebes, and you my fathers' gods,
And rulers of Thebes, you see me now, the last
Unhappy daughter of a line of kings,
Your kings, led away to death. You will remember
What things I suffer, and at what men's hands,
Because I would not transgress the laws of heaven.

[*To the* GUARDS, *simply*] 18

Come: let us wait no longer

[*Exit* ANTIGONE, *left, guarded.*]

Vocabulary
lamentation (lam′ ən tā′ shən) *n.* expression of grief; weeping

6. **Persephone** (pər sef′ ə nē) queen of the underworld.

Reading Check
Why does Antigone believe that she is not guilty of a crime?

17 Literary Analysis
Greek Tragedies

1. Emphasize that a tragic character's downfall is not recognizing a consequence of his or her actions. Explain that in Greek tragedies, fate's role is to ensure that the character's actions work with events to bring about the character's doom.
2. Have students read lines 68–72. Then, **ask** students why Antigone might say that her doom is a result of fate, rather than choice.
Answer: Antigone believes that the choice she made to bury Polyneices was right under the laws of the gods, and so her doom must be the result of fate, not of her choice.

18 Reading Check

Answer: Antigone does not believe she is guilty of a crime because her actions followed the laws of the gods.

Differentiated Instruction for Universal Access

Culturally Responsive Instruction

Culture Focus Read lines 59–67 aloud. Explain to students that these lines reveal Antigone's belief in an afterlife. As the ancient Greeks had a complex view of the afterlife, provide the following background to students.

Explain that, according to the ancient Greeks, once souls departed from their earthly bodies, they traveled down to the Underworld, where, depending on their behavior on Earth, they passed through one of several places: Erebus, where souls pass first once they die; Tartarus, the place of punishment; and the Elysian Fields, a beautiful abode for all virtuous souls. Before the souls could travel anywhere in the Underworld, however, they had to cross the river Acheron by means of a boat, ferried by old Charon. Charon would only ferry those souls whose bodies had been buried properly, including having coins placed on the eyes to pay for this important passage. Thus, the proper burial of an ancient Greek was essential to travel in the Underworld and to lead the soul to its judgment and final resting place.

19 Critical Thinking
Infer

1. Have students do a choral reading as a class of the first strophe of Ode IV, lines 1–9.
2. Then, **ask** why the chorus chooses to recount Danae's story at this point.
   Answer: Danae's story is similar to Antigone's. Both were princesses sealed away in a vault and left to die.
3. Then, **ask** students to explain how the cases of Danae and Antigone illustrate the strength of the power of fate.
   Possible response: Although both were of royal birth, Danae's and Antigone's high stations in human society did not protect them from ruin.

20 Background
Mythology

The chorus refers to the story of King Phineus of Salmydessus in Thrace. Phineus imprisoned his first wife, Cleopatra (not the Egyptian queen), after marrying a second wife, Idaea. Out of jealousy, Idaea made false accusations of treachery against Cleopatra's sons, Plesippus and Pandion, and put out their eyes with a weaver's shuttle. This last detail recalls the story of Oedipus, who put out his own eyes.

Ode IV

19

CHORUS. [STROPHE 1]

All Danae's beauty[7] was locked away
In a brazen cell where the sunlight could not come:
A small room, still as any grave, enclosed her.
Yet she was a princess too,
And Zeus in a rain of gold poured love upon her.
O child, child,
No power in wealth or war
Or tough sea-blackened ships
Can prevail against untiring Destiny!

[ANTISTROPHE 1]

And Dryas' son[8] also, that furious king,
Bore the god's prisoning anger for his pride:
Sealed up by Dionysos[9] in deaf stone,
His madness died among echoes.
So at the last he learned what dreadful power
His tongue had mocked:
For he had profaned the revels,
And fired the wrath of the nine
Implacable Sisters[10] that love the sound of the flute.

[STROPHE 2]

And old men tell a half-remembered tale
Of horror done where a dark ledge splits the sea
And a double surf beats on the gray shores:
How a king's new woman, sick
With hatred for the queen he had imprisoned,
Ripped out his two sons' eyes with her bloody hands
While grinning Ares[11] watched the shuttle plunge
Four times: four blind wounds crying for revenge,

[ANTISTROPHE 2]

Crying, tears and blood mingled.—Piteously born,
Those sons whose mother was of heavenly birth!
Her father was the god of the North Wind
And she was cradled by gales,
She raced with young colts on the glittering hills
And walked untrammeled in the open light:
But in her marriage deathless Fate found means
To build a tomb like yours for all her joy.

20

7. **Danae's** (dan′ ā ēz′) **beauty** Danae was imprisoned when it was foretold that she would mother a son who would kill her father, King Acrisios. Her beauty attracted Zeus, who visited her in the form of a shower of gold. Perseus was born of the union, and Danae was exiled with the child. Years later, as prophesied, the boy did kill Acrisios, whom he failed to recognize as his grandfather.
8. **Dryas'** (drī′ əs) **son** Lycorgos (lī kur′ gəs), whose opposition to the worship of Dionysos was severely punished by the gods. He drove the followers of Dionysos from Thrace and was driven insane. Lycorgos recovered from his madness while imprisoned in a cave, but he was later blinded by Zeus as additional punishment.
9. **Dionysos** (dī′ ə nī′ səs) god of wine, in whose honor the Greek plays were performed.
10. **nine / Implacable Sisters** nine Muses, or goddesses, of science and literature. Implacable (im plak′ ə bəl) means "unforgiving."
11. **Ares** (er′ ēz′) god of war.

Vocabulary Development

Terms from Classical Greek Theater

Share the following terms from classical Greek theater with students. Then, invite students to identify parts of *Antigone* to which they could be applied.

Catharsis: emotional relief or purification that an audience was supposed to experience upon watching a Greek tragedy

Exodus: the departure of the chorus from the stage at the end of a Greek tragedy

Hamartia: the tragic flaw that causes the downfall of a tragic hero or heroine

Hubris: excessive pride on the part of a character; a common form of *harmatia*

Orchestra: the circular space in front of the stage of a Greek theater where the chorus performed

Parodos: the initial entrance of the chorus; their entrance song

Scene 5

[Enter blind TEIRESIAS, *led by a boy. The opening speeches of* TEIRESIAS *should be in singsong contrast to the realistic lines of* CREON.]

TEIRESIAS. This is the way the blind man comes, Princes, Princes,
Lock-step, two heads lit by the eyes of one.

CREON. What new thing have you to tell us, old Teiresias?

TEIRESIAS. I have much to tell you: listen to the prophet, Creon.

CREON. I am not aware that I have ever failed to listen.

TEIRESIAS. Then you have done wisely, King, and ruled well.

CREON. I admit my debt to you.[12] But what have you to say?

TEIRESIAS. This, Creon: you stand once more on the edge of fate.

CREON. What do you mean? Your words are a kind of dread.

TEIRESIAS. Listen, Creon:
21 I was sitting in my chair of augury,[13] at the place
Where the birds gather about me. They were all a-chatter,
As is their habit, when suddenly I heard
A strange note in their jangling, a scream, a
Whirring fury; I knew that they were fighting,
Tearing each other, dying
23 In a whirlwind of wings clashing. And I was afraid.
I began the rites of burnt-offering at the altar,
But Hephaistos[14] failed me: instead of bright flame,

12. **my debt to you** Creon is admitting that he would not have acquired the throne if Teiresias had not moved the former king, Oedipus, to undertake an investigation that led eventually to his own downfall.

13. **chair of augury** the seat near the temple from which Teiresias would deliver his predictions about the future. Augury is the practice of reading the future from omens, such as the flight of birds.

22 ▼ **Critical Viewing**
Judging from this image of Teiresias, how does he feel about Creon? Explain. **[Infer]**

21 Reading Skill
Summarize

- Have students take brief notes on lines 10–32. Then, have them identify two details that would not be included in a brief summary of the speech.
  Possible response: Students should omit details about the sounds of the birds and specific details about Teiresias' offering to the gods.

22 Critical Viewing

Answer: Based on his stance and the expression on his face, Teiresias clearly feels dominant over Creon.

Differentiated Instruction for Universal Access

Support for Special Needs Students

Have students locate notes 7–11 that accompany Ode IV. Identify which notes elaborate on specific lines in the ode, and have students make the cross-reference by drawing an imaginary line from each note to the corresponding text with their fingers. Then, read the ode with students, stopping to use each note to clarify the content.

EL Support for English Learners

Help students with the difficult vocabulary and complex sentence structure in Ode IV. Have students skim the ode to find words with meanings that are unclear to them. List these words on the board and discuss their meanings. Then, read the ode with students, pausing to recast ideas in simple, declarative sentences.

㉓ Critical Thinking
Analyze

1. Have students reread Teiresias' speech in lines 10–36. Tell them to notice how Teiresias delivers his message to Creon.
2. **Ask** students why Teiresias tells Creon the story of the failed burnt-offering at the altar. **Possible response:** Teiresias wants Creon to see that his edict has already angered the gods and brought consequences not only to Antigone and her family but to all Greek citizens.
3. **Ask** students to identify the exact lines in which Teiresias tells Creon that his actions as king have affected all people of Greece. **Answer:** In lines 25–32, Teiresias blames Creon's actions for the gods' lack of response to people's rituals.

There was only the sputtering slime of the fat thigh-flesh
Melting: the entrails dissolved in gray smoke,
The bare bone burst from the welter. And no blaze!

This was a sign from heaven. My boy described it,
Seeing for me as I see for others.

㉑

I tell you, Creon, you yourself have brought
This new calamity upon us. Our hearths and altars
Are stained with the corruption of dogs and carrion birds
That glut themselves on the corpse of Oedipus' son.
The gods are deaf when we pray to them, their fire
Recoils from our offering, their birds of omen
Have no cry of comfort, for they are gorged
With the thick blood of the dead.
O my son,
These are no trifles! Think: all men make mistakes,
But a good man yields when he knows his course is wrong,
And repairs the evil. The only crime is pride.

㉓

Give in to the dead man, then: do not fight with a corpse—
What glory is it to kill a man who is dead?
Think, I beg you:
It is for your own good that I speak as I do.
You should be able to yield for your own good.

CREON. It seems that prophets have made me their
especial province.
All my life long
I have been a kind of butt for the dull arrows
Of doddering fortunetellers!
No, Teiresias:
If your birds—if the great eagles of God
himself
Should carry him stinking bit by bit to
heaven,
I would not yield. I am not afraid of
pollution:
No man can defile the gods.
Do what you will,
Go into business, make money,
speculate
In India gold or that synthetic gold from
Sardis,[15]
Get rich otherwise than by my consent to
bury him.

㉔

14. Hephaistos (hē fes′ təs) god of fire and the forge, who would be invoked, as he was by Teiresias, for aid in the starting of ceremonial fires.

15. Sardis (sär′ dis) capital of ancient Lydia, which produced the first coins made from an alloy of gold and silver.

Think Aloud

Vocabulary: Using Context

Direct students' attention to the term *carrion birds* in line 27. Use the following "think aloud" to model using context to determine the meaning of an unfamiliar term. Say to students:

Often a writer uses explanations that help me define an unfamiliar term. Look at lines 27 and 28. If I did not know the term *carrion birds,* I might figure it out by looking at the explanation that the writer presents. He refers to "carrion birds/That glut themselves on the corpse of Oedipus' son." The carrion birds are eating something that is dead. I can tell that a carrion bird would not be a robin or sparrow; it would be a crow or a vulture, or any kind of bird that eats dead flesh. By reading the explanation, I can learn enough about the term to have a good understanding of the sentence.

Teiresias, it is a sorry thing when a wise
man
Sells his wisdom, lets out his words for
hire!

TEIRESIAS. Ah Creon! Is there no man left in the
world—

CREON. To do what?—Come, let's have the aphorism![16]

TEIRESIAS. No man who knows that wisdom outweighs any
wealth?

CREON. As surely as bribes are baser than any baseness.

TEIRESIAS. You are sick, Creon! You are deathly sick!

CREON. As you say: it is not my place to challenge a prophet.

TEIRESIAS. Yet you have said my prophecy is for sale.

CREON. The generation of prophets has always loved gold.

TEIRESIAS. The generation of kings has always loved brass.

CREON. You forget yourself! You are speaking to your King.

TEIRESIAS. I know it. You are a king because of me.

CREON. You have a certain skill; but you have sold out.

TEIRESIAS. King, you will drive me to words that—

CREON. Say them, say them!
Only remember: I will not pay you for them.

TEIRESIAS. No, you will find them too costly.

CREON. No doubt. Speak:
Whatever you say, you will not change my will.

TEIRESIAS. Then take this, and take it to heart!
The time is not far off when you shall pay back
Corpse for corpse, flesh of your own flesh.
You have thrust the child of this world into living night,
You have kept from the gods below the child that is theirs:
The one in a grave before her death, the other,
Dead, denied the grave. This is your crime:
And the Furies[17] and the dark gods of Hell
Are swift with terrible punishment for you.

Do you want to buy me now, Creon?

Literary Analysis
Greek Tragedies What ideas in Creon's speech to Teiresias reflect the king's tragic flaw?

16. **aphorism** (af´ ə riz´ əm) *n.* brief saying. Creon is taunting the prophet and suggesting that the old man relies on profound-sounding expressions to make an impression.

17. **Furies** (fyoor´ ēz) goddesses of vengeance who punished those who committed crimes against their own families.

26 **Reading Check**
What does Teiresias come to tell Creon?

24 Literary Analysis
Greek Tragedies

1. Ask a volunteer to read Creon's speech. Then, **ask** students to describe Creon's tragic flaw.
Possible response: Students may observe that Creon's tragic flaw is excessive pride.
2. **Ask** students the Literary Analysis question: What ideas in Creon's speech to Teiresias reflect the king's tragic flaw?
Possible response: Creon's tragic flaw of excessive pride is reflected in his refusal to yield about burying Polyneices and his lack of fear about pollution.
3. Have students identify the part of his speech in which Creon seems to be placing himself above the gods.
Possible response: Creon seems to place himself above the gods when he says he would not yield even "if the great eagles of God himself" carried Polyneices to heaven.

25 Reading Skill
Summarize

1. Read aloud lines 55–68. Point out Creon's references to money at the end of the speech and in his exchange with Teiresias.
2. **Ask** students to summarize Creon's reason for rejecting Teiresias' advice.
Possible response: Creon rejects Teiresias' advice because he says Teiresias has taken bribes to give prophecies.

26 Reading Check

Answer: Teiresias has come to tell Creon to give in and bury Polyneices.

Differentiated Instruction for Universal Access

Support for Less Proficient Readers
Help students understand the exchange between Creon and Teiresias by dividing it into three parts. First, have students identify what Teiresias did and saw before he encountered Creon. Next, have students describe the conflict between Creon and Teiresias. Finally, have students summarize Teiresias' prophecy for Creon.

Enrichment for Advanced Readers
Have students relate historical figures or public figures in current events to Creon. Tell students to consider the following question: Can any of the figures be said to have tragic flaws that led or appear to be leading them to their downfall? Have students discuss the question as a group and then present their conclusions to the class for further discussion.

27 Humanities

Etruscan Amphora

Most of the ancient Greek painting that survives today is found on vases. Vase painters depicted the myths, legends, wars, athletic games, and domestic affairs of ancient Greece. One of the vessels that painters chose to paint was a two-handled jar called an *amphora,* such as the one shown here. The painting on this amphora shows warriors and a shield with a dove on it. Use the following question for discussion:

What events from *Antigone* might the scene on this vase portray?
Possible response: The scene could be showing the battle in which Antigone's two brothers were killed.

28 Critical Viewing

Possible response: Both the image on the vessel and the play itself seem to celebrate honorable combat, evidence that conflict played a significant role in Greek culture.

29 Literary Analysis

Greek Tragedies

1. Remind students that Creon's tragic flaw is his pride. Point out that until now he believed that his own rules superseded those of the gods.
2. Ask a volunteer to read the bracketed text. Then **ask:** What does Creon say that reveals that he recognizes his own tragic flaw?
Possible response: Creon admits the importance of serving the laws of the gods, rather than the laws of man.

27

28 ▲ **Critical Viewing** In what way do both the play and this vessel show the importance of conflict in Greek art? **[Synthesize]**

Not many days,
And your house will be full of men and women weeping,
And curses will be hurled at you from far
Cities grieving for sons unburied, left to rot
Before the walls of Thebes.

These are my arrows, Creon: they are all for you.

[*To* BOY] But come, child: lead me home.
Let him waste his fine anger upon younger men.
Maybe he will learn at last
To control a wiser tongue in a better head.

[*Exit* TEIRESIAS.]

CHORAGOS. The old man has gone, King, but his words
Remain to plague us. I am old, too,
But I cannot remember that he was ever false.

CREON. That is true. . . . It troubles me.
Oh it is hard to give in! but it is worse
To risk everything for stubborn pride.

CHORAGOS. Creon: take my advice.

CREON. What shall I do?

CHORAGOS. Go quickly: free Antigone from her vault
And build a tomb for the body of Polyneices.

CREON. You would have me do this?

CHORAGOS. Creon, yes!
And it must be done at once: God moves
Swiftly to cancel the folly of stubborn men.

CREON. It is hard to deny the heart! But I
Will do it: I will not fight with destiny.

CHORAGOS. You must go yourself, you cannot leave it to others.

CREON. I will go.
—Bring axes, servants:
Come with me to the tomb. I buried her, I
Will set her free.
Oh quickly!
My mind misgives—
29 The laws of the gods are mighty, and a man must serve them
To the last day of his life!

[*Exit* CREON.]

Vocabulary Development

Word Origin

Point out to students that the word *rapture* in line 32 on page 853 means "a powerful emotion, often delight or joy, that fills the mind." The word is derived from the Latin verb *rapere,* "to seize or carry off," and conveys the image of someone seized by strong feeling. Similarly, when people are *rapt,* they are "carried away" by their thoughts or emotions. *Rapere* is the root of several other English words: *raptor, rapacious, rapine,* and *rapid.*

Several other descendants of *rapere* come to English via a detour in France. Among them are *ravish, ravage, ravenous,* and *ravine.* You may wish to conclude exploration of this word family by asking students to discuss how each English word reflects the meaning of its Latin root.

Pæan

CHORAGOS.
God of many names [STROPHE 1]

30 **CHORUS.** O Iacchos[18]
son
of Kadmeian Semele[19]
O born of the Thunder!
Guardian of the West
Regent
of Eleusis' plain[20]
O Prince of maenad Thebes[21]
and the Dragon Field by rippling Ismenos:[22]

CHORAGOS. [ANTISTROPHE 1]
God of many names

CHORUS.
the flame of torches
flares on our hills
the nymphs of Iacchos
dance at the spring of Castalia:[23]

from the vine-close mountain
come ah come in ivy:
Evohe evohe! [24] sings through the streets of Thebes

CHORAGOS. [STROPHE 2]
God of many names

CHORUS. Iacchos of Thebes
heavenly Child
of Semele bride of the Thunderer!
The shadow of plague is upon us:
come
with clement[25] feet
oh come from Parnasos[26]
down the long slopes
across the lamenting water

CHORAGOS. [ANTISTROPHE 2]
Io [27] Fire! Chorister of the throbbing stars!
O purest among the voices of the night!
Thou son of God, blaze for us!

CHORUS. Come with choric rapture of circling Maenads
Who cry *Io Iacche!*[28]
God of many names!

18. Iacchos (ē´ ə kəs) one of several alternate names for Dionysos.

19. Kadmeian Semele (sem´ ə lē´) Semele was a mortal and the mother of Dionysos. She was the daughter of Thebes' founder, Kadmos.

20. Eleusis' (e lo͞o´ sis) **plain** Located north of Athens, this plain was a site of worship for Dionysos and Demeter.

21. maenad (mē´ nad´) **Thebes** The city is here compared to a maenad, one of Dionysos' female worshipers. Such a follower would be thought of as uncontrolled or disturbed.

22. Dragon Field . . . Ismenos (is mē´ nas) The Dragon Field was located by the banks of Ismenos, a river near Thebes. Kadmos created warriors by sowing in the Dragon Field the teeth of the dragon he killed there.

23. Castalia (kas tā´ lē ə) location of a site sacred to Apollo.

24. Evohe (ē vō´ ē) triumphant shout of affirmation.

25. clement kind; favorable

26. Parnasos (pär nas´ əs) mountain that was sacred to both Dionysos and Apollo, located in central Greece.

27. Io (ē´ ō´) Greek word for "behold" or "hail."

28. Io Iacche (ē´ ō´ ē´ ə ke) cry of celebration used by Dionysian worshipers.

31 **Reading Check**

In the Pæan, from whom does the chorus ask help?

30 Background

The Founding of Thebes

While on a quest to find his abducted sister Europa, Kadmos appealed to Apollo at Delphi to ask the god of truth where Europa had been taken. Instead of helping Kadmos to locate his sister, Apollo instructed Kadmos to found a city himself. Upon leaving Delphi, Apollo foretold, Kadmos would find a heifer, which Kadmos was to follow until she stopped to rest. The land upon which she lay to rest would become the city of Thebes.

Before Kadmos could begin building his city, however, he had to slay a dragon that guarded a spring and kill any man who dared come near it. Kadmos succeeded in killing the dragon, but all his companions had died in the process, leaving only Kadmos to build this prophesied city. Athena then appeared to Kadmos, instructing him to sow the earth with the dragon's teeth. Kadmos complied but became alarmed when soldiers sprouted from the earth, only to fight and kill each other. Kadmos managed to save five of these men, whose aid helped to build the great city of Thebes.

31 Reading Check

Answer: The chorus asks for help from Dionysos.

Fluency

The unusual placement of words on this page may present some students with difficulties in reading aloud. Ask individual students to read aloud lines 20–28. Listen for hesitancies and awkward pauses. If necessary, have students break down the meaning of the text before rereading it. Use these questions to help them do that:

Who is Iacchos' mother? (Semele)
Who is the bride of the Thunderer? (Semele)
Whom does the chorus want to "come/with clement feet"? (Iacchos)
What path will he follow when he comes? (He will come from Parnasos, heading down the long slopes and across the lamenting water.)

32 Literary Analysis
Greek Tragedies

1. Ask a volunteer to read the bracketed text aloud. Then, **ask** students whether the messenger brings bad news or good news.
Answer: He brings bad news.
2. **Ask** students to identify the words that signal what kind of news the messenger brings.
Answer: The messenger's words "Creon was happy once" signal bad news.
3. **Ask:** What reversal of fortune has the messenger come to announce?
Possible response: Creon has lost what is more valuable to him than any riches. Something has happened that will erase all of Creon's happiness.

33 Critical Viewing

Answer: Yes; the actress conveys tragic grief by showing sorrow and strength at the same time.

Exodus

29. **Kadmos** (kad′ məs) founder of the city of Thebes, whose daughter, Semele, gave birth to Dionysos.

30. **Amphion's** (am fī′ ənz) **citadel** Amphion was a king of Thebes credited with erecting the walls of the fortress, or citadel, by using a magic lyre.

31. **Pallas'** (pal′ əs) Pallas Athena, the goddess of wisdom.

33 ▼ **Critical Viewing**
Do you think the actress portraying Eurydice effectively conveys tragic grief? Explain. **[Evaluate]**

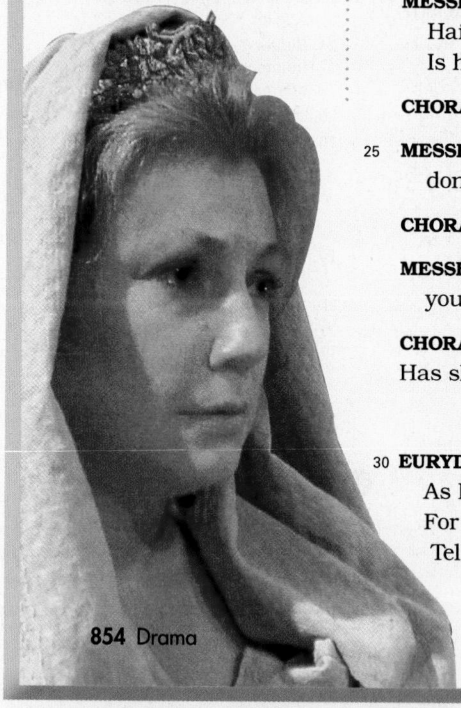

[*Enter* MESSENGER, *left.*]

32

MESSENGER. Men of the line of Kadmos,[29] you who live
Near Amphion's citadel:[30]
I cannot say
Of any condition of human life "This is fixed,
This is clearly good, or bad." Fate raises up,
And Fate casts down the happy and unhappy alike:
No man can foretell his Fate.
Take the case of Creon:
Creon was happy once, as I count happiness:
Victorious in battle, sole governor of the land,
Fortunate father of children nobly born.
And now it has all gone from him! Who can say
That a man is still alive when his life's joy fails?
He is a walking dead man. Grant him rich,
Let him live like a king in his great house:
If his pleasure is gone, I would not give
So much as the shadow of smoke for all he owns.

CHORAGOS. Your words hint at sorrow: what is your news for us?

MESSENGER. They are dead. The living are guilty of their death.

CHORAGOS. Who is guilty? Who is dead? Speak!

MESSENGER. Haimon.
Haimon is dead; and the hand that killed him
Is his own hand.

CHORAGOS. His father's? or his own?

MESSENGER. His own, driven mad by the murder his father had done.

CHORAGOS. Teiresias, Teiresias, how clearly you saw it all!

MESSENGER. This is my news: you must draw what conclusions you can from it.

CHORAGOS. But look: Eurydice, our Queen:
Has she overheard us?

[*Enter* EURYDICE *from the Palace, center.*]

EURYDICE. I have heard something, friends:
As I was unlocking the gate of Pallas'[31] shrine,
For I needed her help today, I heard a voice
Telling of some new sorrow. And I fainted

Think Aloud

Vocabulary: Using Context

Direct students' attention to the word *crevice* in line 62 of the messenger's speech on p. 855. Then, use a think-aloud process to model how to use context to infer the meaning of an unknown word. Say the following to students:

I'm going to think aloud to show you how I would figure out the meaning of *crevice* from its context.

In line 62, Creon orders his servants to look through a *crevice*. To get an idea of what *crevice* means, I am going to look at its context, or the words and sentences that surround *crevice*. I already know that Creon and his servants are at the stone vault where Antigone is imprisoned. If I read ahead, I find out that when the servants look through the *crevice* they can see Antigone lying in the corner of the vault, or cavern, as it is called here. Since I know the place where Antigone is imprisoned is stone, I think a *crevice* must be a crack or opening in the stone or rock.

There at the temple with all my maidens about me.
But speak again: whatever it is, I can bear it:
Grief and I are no strangers.

MESSENGER. Dearest Lady,
I will tell you plainly all that I have seen.
I shall not try to comfort you: what is the use,
Since comfort could lie only in what is not true?
The truth is always best.
I went with Creon
To the outer plain where Polyneices was lying,
No friend to pity him, his body shredded by dogs.
We made our prayers in that place to Hecate[32]
And Pluto,[33] that they would be merciful. And we bathed
The corpse with holy water, and we brought
Fresh-broken branches to burn what was left of it,
And upon the urn we heaped up a towering barrow
Of the earth of his own land.
When we were done, we ran
To the vault where Antigone lay on her couch of stone.
One of the servants had gone ahead,
And while he was yet far off he heard a voice
Grieving within the chamber, and he came back
And told Creon. And as the King went closer,
The air was full of wailing, the words lost,
And he begged us to make all haste. "Am I a prophet?"
He said, weeping, "And must I walk this road,
The saddest of all that I have gone before?
My son's voice calls me on. Oh quickly, quickly!
Look through the crevice there, and tell me
If it is Haimon, or some deception of the gods!"

We obeyed; and in the cavern's farthest corner
We saw her lying:
She had made a noose of her fine linen veil
And hanged herself. Haimon lay beside her,
His arms about her waist, lamenting her,
His love lost underground, crying out
That his father had stolen her away from him.

When Creon saw him the tears rushed to his eyes
And he called to him: "What have you done, child? Speak
to me.
What are you thinking that makes your eyes so strange?
O my son, my son, I come to you on my knees!"

Reading Skill
Summarize Identify three details in lines 37–50 that you would not include in summarizing the speech.

32. **Hecate** (hek´ ə tē) A goddess of the underworld, the resting place of dead souls in Greek mythology.

33. **Pluto** (plo͞o t´ ō) Chief god of the underworld, who ruled the souls of the dead in Greek mythology.

35 Reading Check
What has happened to Antigone and Haimon?

34 Reading Skill
Summarize

1. Remind students that a summary includes only the main ideas or events and the most important details. Have students reread the messenger's speech silently and take brief notes on the main events that he relates.
2. Then, **ask** students to respond to the Reading Skill prompt: Identify three details in lines 37–50 that you would not include in summarizing the speech.
   Possible responses: A summary would not need to include the fact that the messenger says he will not try to comfort Eurydice. It would also not need to include the specific details about burying Polyneices, such as where Polyneices was lying or to whom the messenger prayed.

Monitor Progress: Circulate among students to check their use of the **Reading Skill Graphic Organizer B** (*Graphic Organizer Transparencies,* p. 158) to take notes on this and other passages of the play.

Reteach Remind students that they should use their own words when taking notes on important information in a passage. Give students practice by pointing to key events and significant details in the messenger's speech and having students restate each in their own words. For example, lines 30–36 can be restated as, "Eurydice faints at the temple when she hears there is bad news."

35 Reading Check

Answer: Antigone has hanged herself. Haimon, attempting to kill Creon, stabs himself and dies.

Differentiated Instruction for Universal Access

Support for Special Needs Students
Help students organize the final events of the play in a sequence chart or timeline. Explain to students that a chart or timeline will help them understand the relationships among the many events that are revealed in quick succession. Students may then use the chart as an aid in summarizing these key events.

Enrichment for Gifted and Talented Students
Have students evaluate the play and decide what Creon could do that would be fairer and would bring about a happier ending. Suggest that students work together to compose a screenplay with an ending that makes *Antigone* a Greek comedy instead of a Greek tragedy. Students may then dramatize the different ending for the rest of the class.

36 Literary Analysis
Greek Tragedies

1. Remind students that while Creon's tragic flaw and own actions lead to his downfall, fate also plays a role. Point out that in Greek tragedies, it is fate that ensures a final outcome that fits a character's attitudes and actions.
2. Have students read lines 95–98. Then, **ask** them to respond to the Literary Analysis question: In what sense might Creon's loss of his son be fitting punishment for his misjudgment?
Possible response: With Haimon dead, Creon will experience the grief and loss that he refused to acknowledge or honor in Antigone, and it was his actions and attitude toward her that set in motion the events that led to his son's death.

But Haimon spat in his face. He said not a word,
Staring—
And suddenly drew his sword
And lunged. Creon shrank back, the blade missed; and the boy,
Desperate against himself, drove it half its length
Into his own side, and fell. And as he died
He gathered Antigone close in his arms again,
Choking, his blood bright red on her white cheek.
And now he lies dead with the dead, and she is his
At last, his bride in the houses of the dead.

[*Exit* EURYDICE *into the Palace.*]

CHORAGOS. She has left us without a word. What can this mean?

MESSENGER. It troubles me, too; yet she knows what is best,
Her grief is too great for public lamentation,
And doubtless she has gone to her chamber to weep
For her dead son, leading her maidens in his dirge.

CHORAGOS. It may be so: but I fear this deep silence.

[*Pause*]

MESSENGER. I will see what she is doing. I will go in.

[*Exit* MESSENGER *into the Palace.*]

[*Enter* CREON *with attendants, bearing* HAIMON'S *body.*]

CHORAGOS. But here is the King himself: oh look at him,
Bearing his own damnation in his arms.

Literary Analysis
Greek Tragedies
In what sense might Creon's loss of his son be fitting punishment for his misjudgment? 36

CREON. Nothing you say can touch me any more.
My own blind heart has brought me
From darkness to final darkness. Here you see
The father murdering, the murdered son—
And all my civic wisdom!

Haimon my son, so young, so young to die,
I was the fool, not you; and you died for me.

CHORAGOS. That is the truth; but you were late in learning it.

CREON. This truth is hard to bear. Surely a god
Has crushed me beneath the hugest weight of heaven,
And driven me headlong a barbaric way
To trample out the thing I held most dear.

The pains that men will take to come to pain!

Vocabulary Development

Vocabulary Knowledge Rating

When students have completed reading and discussing *Antigone,* Scenes 3–5, have them take out their **Vocabulary Knowledge Rating Chart** for this selection. Read the words aloud once more and have students rate their knowledge of the words again in the After Reading column. Clarify any words that are still problematic. Have students write their own definition or example in the appropriate column. Then, have students complete the Vocabulary Practice at the end of the selection. Encourage students to use the words in further discussion and written work about this selection. Remind them that they will be accountable for these words on the **Selection Test,** ***Unit 5 Resources,*** pp. 59–61 or 62–64.

[Enter MESSENGER *from the Palace.]*

MESSENGER. The burden you carry in your hands is heavy,
But it is not all: you will find more in your house.

CREON. What burden worse than this shall I find there?

MESSENGER. The Queen is dead.

CREON. O port of death, deaf world,
Is there no pity for me? And you, Angel of evil,
I was dead, and your words are death again.
Is it true, boy? Can it be true?
Is my wife dead? Has death bred death?

MESSENGER. You can see for yourself.

[The doors are opened, and the body of EURYDICE *is disclosed within.]*

CREON. Oh pity!
37 All true, all true, and more than I can bear!
O my wife, my son!

MESSENGER. She stood before the altar, and her heart
Welcomed the knife her own hand guided,
And a great cry burst from her lips for Megareus[34] dead,
And for Haimon dead, her sons; and her last breath
Was a curse for their father, the murderer of her sons.
And she fell, and the dark flowed in through her closing eyes.

CREON. O God, I am sick with fear.
Are there no swords here? Has no one a blow for me?

MESSENGER. Her curse is upon you for the deaths of both.

CREON. It is right that it should be. I alone am guilty.
I know it, and I say it. Lead me in,
Quickly, friends.
I have neither life nor substance. Lead me in.

CHORAGOS. You are right, if there can be right in
so much wrong.
The briefest way is best in a world of sorrow.

34. **Megareus** (mə gaʹ rē əs) oldest son of Creon and Eurydice, who was killed in the civil war by Argive forces invading Thebes.

38 **Reading Check**

What has happened to Eurydice?

37 Literary Analysis
Greek Tragedies

1. Remind students that a reversal of fortune for a person of noble birth is a key characteristic of Greek tragedy. Point out that although in the beginning of the play Creon has already lost one son, Megareus, in the battle for Thebes, Creon seems to be in a position of power as the new king of Thebes.
2. Have students compare and contrast Creon's situation now with his position at the beginning of the play.
   Possible response: Creon now seems to be a weak leader who shows excessive pride and a lack of wisdom. He also loses his other son, Haimon.
3. Ask a volunteer to read the messenger's account of the latest tragic event for Creon. Then, **ask** students: What reversal of fortune has Creon experienced?
   Answer: Creon has now lost all the members of his immediate family: his wife, Eurydice, and his two sons, Megareus and Haimon.

38 Reading Check

Answer: She has killed herself with a knife over the death of her sons and the cruelty of their father.

Concept Connector

Anticipation Guide

Have students return to their **Anticipation Guides** and respond to the statements again in the After Reading column. They may do this individually or in their original pairs or groups. Then, lead a class discussion, probing for what students have learned that confirms or invalidates each statement. Encourage students to cite specific details, quotations, or other evidence from the text to support their responses to each statement.

Writing About the Big Question

Have students compare their responses to the sentence starters they completed before reading the scenes with their ideas afterward. Ask them to explain whether their thoughts have changed.

Reading Skill Graphic Organizer

Ask students to review the graphic organizers they used to take notes while reading. Show them the partially completed **Reading Skill Graphic Organizer A** (*Graphic Organizer Transparencies*, p. 157) as an example. Then, have students use their graphic organizers to summarize the play.

ASSESS

Answers

Critical Thinking

1. Students may say that he was right to change his decision but should have done so earlier.
2. (a) Haimon advises his father to be reasonable. (b) Creon insists that he is right. (c) Haimon's main concerns are the laws of the gods and Antigone. Creon's main concerns are the law of the state and his own power.
3. (a) Creon has Antigone buried alive. (b) **Possible response:** Creon wants both to uphold the law and to appear strong. Details that support this include his claim that the state is king, and his refusal to change his mind.
4. (a) Creon's house will be full of grief. (b) Creon sets out to bury Polyneices and free Antigone. (c) Creon's entire family is dead.

To what extent does experience determine what we perceive?

Possible response: Antigone's sense of herself as Oedipus' daughter makes her brave enough to stand up to Creon and committed enough to insist upon what she believes is right. Creon's sense of himself as king means that he is unwilling to do anything that might look as though he is giving up power—especially to a woman.

CREON. Let it come,
Let death come quickly, and be kind to me.
I would not ever see the sun again.

CHORAGOS. All that will come when it will; but we, meanwhile,
Have much to do. Leave the future to itself.

CREON. All my heart was in that prayer!

CHORAGOS. Then do not pray any more: the sky is deaf.

CREON. Lead me away. I have been rash and foolish.
I have killed my son and my wife.
I look for comfort; my comfort lies here dead.
Whatever my hands have touched has come to nothing.
Fate has brought all my pride to a thought of dust.

Vocabulary
rash (rash) *adj.* too hasty in speech or action; reckless

[As CREON *is being led into the house, the* CHORAGOS *advances and speaks directly to the audience.]*

CHORAGOS. There is no happiness where there is no wisdom;
No wisdom but in submission to the gods.
Big words are always punished,
And proud men in old age learn to be wise.

Critical Thinking

1. **Respond:** Do you think Creon should have changed his decision regarding Antigone? Why or why not?
2. **(a)** In Scene 3, lines 55–94, what advice does Haimon give his father? **(b) Analyze:** Describe Creon's response to the advice. **(c) Contrast:** Contrast Haimon's main concerns with Creon's.
3. **(a)** What does Creon rule must be done to Antigone? **(b) Make a Judgment:** Is upholding the law Creon's only motive, or is he also guided by a desire to appear strong? Support your answer with details from the play.
4. **(a)** What prophecy does Teiresias make about Creon? **(b) Analyze Cause and Effect:** What action does Creon take because of the prophecy? **(c) Connect:** In what way is Teiresias' prophecy fulfilled?

To what extent does experience determine what we perceive? How does Antigone's sense of herself as Oedipus' daughter and Creon's sense of himself as king determine the paths they each take in the play?

Assessment Resources

Unit 5 Resources

L1 L2 EL **Selection Test A,** pp. 38–40. Administer Test A to less advanced readers and English learners.

L3 L4 **Selection Test B,** pp. 41–43. Administer Test B to on-level and more advanced students.

L3 L4 **Open-Book Test,** pp. 35–37. As an alternative, give the Open-Book Test.

All **Customizable Test Bank**

All **Self-tests**
Students may prepare for the **Selection Test** by taking the **Self-test** online.

PHLit Online! All assessment resources are available at **www.PHLitOnline.com.**

After You Read

Antigone, Scenes 3 through 5

Literary Analysis: Greek Tragedies

1. Identify three characteristics of a **Greek tragedy** that *Antigone* displays. Support your answer.
2. **(a)** What is Antigone's **tragic flaw?** Explain. **(b)** To what extent does this flaw lead to her downfall? To what extent is her downfall due to **fate?** Explain.
3. **(a)** What is Creon's tragic flaw? Explain. **(b)** To what extent does this flaw lead to his downfall? To what extent is his downfall due to fate? Explain.
4. Who is the true tragic hero of this play? Defend your response.
5. **(a)** Use a chart like this one to explore the play's **theme. (b)** Share and discuss answers with a partner. **(c)** Explain whether your discussion has changed your thoughts on the theme of the play.

Lines from Exodus	What Does It Say?	What Does It Mean?	Why Is It Important?
lines 94–106			
lines 142–150			

Reading Skill: Summarize

6. **Summarize** Scenes 3 through 5 scene by scene.

Vocabulary

Practice Replace each italicized word with its synonym from the vocabulary list on page 838. Then, use the phrase correctly in a sentence.

1. a great *wailing*
2. a *thoughtless* action
3. a *nasty* remark
4. show *meekness* before
5. given out of *reverence*
6. his *disdain* for

Word Study Use the context of the sentences and what you know about the **Latin root *-fer-*** to explain your answer to each question.

1. If an award has been *conferred* for a heroic act, has the award been taken away from someone?
2. Is *fertile* land good for farming?

Word Study

The **Latin root *-fer-*** means "to carry," "to bear," or "to bring."

Challenge Explain how the root *-fer-* contributes to the meanings of these words. Consult a dictionary if necessary.

circumference
ferry
transfer

ASSESS/EXTEND

Answers

Literary Analysis

1. **Possible response:** Antigone is based on myth; it depicts a reversal of fortune and its theme has to do with excessive pride and human limitations.
2. (a) Antigone is unwilling to compromise. (b) Her flaw causes her to defy the state. Fate prevents her rescue.
3. **Possible response:** (a) Creon's tragic flaw is his pride. He feels power as king, and he lets that power rule his choices. (b) Creon's flaw, his pride, causes him to make the choices that lead to his downfall. At the same time, Creon's downfall also can be viewed as a punishment from fate for his actions.
4. **Possible response:** Creon is the true tragic hero because he experiences a downfall because of his actions. Creon's dishonorable actions also position him to be punished by fate.
5. **Possible response:** (a) In lines 94–106, Creon expresses grief for his son's death. He realizes that by punishing Antigone, he has destroyed his entire family. In lines 142–150, Creon says that his own pride has caused his downfall. The Choragos states that humans must submit to the laws of the gods or be punished. (b) and (c) Partners should explain any change in ideas.

   For other sample answers, see ***Graphic Organizer Transparencies,* Literary Analysis Graphic Organizer A,** p. 159, and the **Additional Answers** section.

Reading Skill

6. Scene 3: Creon and Haimon argue about Creon's punishment of Antigone; Haimon urges Creon to listen to reason. Scene 4: Antigone goes to her death in the stone vault. Scene 5: Teiresias shares a prophecy with Creon, which later influences him to free Antigone, but he is too late.

Vocabulary

Practice

Sample answers:

1. lamentation; A great lamentation could be heard near Antigone's tomb.

Answers continued

2. rash; A rash action often has bad consequences.
3. vile; They were shocked by Creon's vile remarks.
4. deference; She showed deference to the king.
5. piety; The statue was given out of piety, as a sign of respect.
6. contempt; His contempt for politics was evident in his negative response.

Word Study

Sample answers:

1. No. The root *-fer-* means "to bring," so *conferred* means "brought by a position of superiority." If an award is conferred for a heroic act, it is given to someone.
2. Yes. The root *-fer-* means "to bear," so *fertile* means "able to bear fruit in great quantities." Fertile land is excellent for farming.

Word Study: Challenge

Sample answers: *Circumference* is the distance to bring something around a circle. A *ferry* is a boat that carries passengers or cargo across a body of water. To *transfer* is to bring or carry from one place to another.

EXTEND/ASSESS

Answers

Grammar

Introduce the skill and discuss the examples.

Think Aloud: Model the Skill

Model the skill of identifying subordinate clauses. Say:

In the sentence "We went to the beach that was near our house," the adjective clause *that was near our house* describes the beach. In the sentence "Although it was raining, we went to the beach," the adverb clause *Although it was raining* modifies the verb *went*. In the sentence "Whatever he brings will get sandy," the clause *Whatever he brings* acts as a noun.

Writing and Grammar, Grade 10

Students will find further instruction and practice in Chapter 20, Section 2.

Practice A

1. Although Creon was angry, adverb; he listened to Teiresias, independent
2. Antigone dies in the tomb, independent
3. Wherever Creon lives, noun
4. Haimon used the sword, independent; that he brought with him to the stone, adjective

Challenge
Sample answer:

Subordinate: And while he was yet far off; if dirges and lamentations could put off death; *Independent:* you will not change my will; your death is the doing of your conscious hand

Practice B

Sample answers:

1. Creon was troubled . . .
2. . . . who was the son of Creon.
3. Whatever they once had had . . .
4. . . . even though she didn't want to hear his message.

Challenge
Sample answer:

Students' responses should accurately represent events from *Antigone.*

Integrated Language Skills

Antigone, Scenes 3 through 5

Grammar: Independent and Subordinate Clauses

A **clause** is a group of words that has both a subject and a verb. An **independent clause** can stand by itself as a sentence. A **subordinate clause,** however, cannot stand by itself. There are three types of subordinate clauses: **adjective clauses, adverb clauses,** and **noun clauses.**

- **Independent clause:** *We visited the mountains.*
- **Adjective Clause:** Sam forgot to return the calculator *that he borrowed from Tito.* (modifies *calculator*)
- **Adverb Clause:** *Although it was cold out,* we jumped in the pool. (modifies *jumped*)
- **Noun Clause:** *Whatever you decide* is fine with me. (functions as the subject of the independent clause)

Practice A Identify the clause in each item. Then, state whether it is an independent or subordinate clause. Classify subordinate clauses as adjective, adverb, or noun clause.

1. Although Creon was angry, he listened to Teiresias.
2. Antigone dies in the tomb.
3. Wherever Creon lives will be filled with sorrow.
4. Haimon used the sword that he brought with him to the stone.

Challenge Identify two dependent clauses and two independent clauses in the second half of *Antigone.*

Practice B Complete each sentence by adding the type of clause named in parentheses.

1. (Independent clause) when Teiresias gave his prophecy.
2. Antigone was engaged to Haimon (adjective clause).
3. (Noun clause) was meaningless now.
4. The queen listened to the messenger (adverb clause).

Challenge Write a brief paragraph about the events that happen in the second half of *Antigone.* Your paragraph should include at least two independent and two subordinate clauses. Label your writing by identifing the types of subordinate clauses you used.

Writing and Grammar Connection: Chapter 20, Section 2

Extend the Lesson

Sentence Modeling

Have the students consider the following sentence from the selection:

"The gods are deaf when we pray to them, their fire recoils from our offering, their birds of omen have no cry of comfort, for they are gorged with the thick blood of the dead."

Ask students what they notice about the sentence. Elicit from them the independent and subordinate clauses. Then, ask what else they notice. (Sophocles links multiple independent clauses together in an unconventional way, emphasizing the forward motion of the language and the urgency in the speaker's message.)

Have students imitate the sentence in a sentence on a topic of their own choosing, matching each grammatical and stylistic feature discussed. Collect the sentences and share them with the class.

Writing

In *Antigone*, Creon puts the state above family loyalty—and loses his family. Write a brief **reflective essay** on Creon's fate. As you write, consider these questions:

- Is Creon's fate just punishment for his decisions?
- Was there a single right course of action for him to take?
- What does his fate suggest about human action in general?

To develop your ideas in a logical organization, write a clear statement of your opinion about Creon at the beginning of your essay. Outline your main points before expanding them in the body of your essay. Use quotations and details from the play to support and elaborate your ideas.

Writing Workshop: *Work in Progress*

Prewriting for a Reflective Essay Use the Event Notes from your writing portfolio. For each of the five events you chose, write a brief answer to this question: What might be different if this event had not taken place? Put the Answer File in your writing portfolio.

Use this prewriting activity to prepare for the Writing Workshop on page 878.

Listening and Speaking

Hold a **mock trial** in which both sides in the dispute between Antigone and Creon are presented before the class. Select students to play various roles: judge, several defense attorneys, several prosecuting attorneys, and witnesses. Have attorneys for both sides provide witnesses. As you prepare for the trial, consider these suggestions:

- Attorneys should develop points they will make supporting their client and choose a **logical organization** to inform and persuade the jury.
- Attorneys should identify points that could be argued against their client and develop counterarguments to those attacks.
- Attorneys and witnesses should use **rhetorical devices** such as appeals to logic or emotion to support their argument or testimony.
- One attorney on each side should be chosen to make closing remarks that summarize and present the strongest arguments before the jury.

The class should act as a jury to decide which argument is more convincing. During the deliberations, the jury should work to negotiate a unanimous decision.

PHLit Online!
www.PHLitOnline.com
- Interactive graphic organizers
- Grammar tutorial
- Interactive journals

EXTEND/ASSESS

Writing

1. Review the assignment, using the instructions on the student page.
2. To guide students in writing a reflective essay, give them **Support For Writing**, p. 54 in ***Unit 5 Resources.***
3. To evaluate students' reflective essays, use the general (holistic) writing rubrics, pp. 256–257 in ***Professional Development Guidebook.*** Also, make sure that students use the questions provided as a framework for their essays and that they supply quotations from the play to support their main points.

Six Traits Focus

✔	Ideas		Word Choice
✔	Organization		Sentence Fluency
	Voice		Conventions

Writing and Grammar, Grade 10

Students will find guidance on writing an essay in Chapter 11.

Writing Workshop
Work in Progress

Have students save their completed answers in their portfolios. They will use their answers later as they complete the Writing Workshop assignment (see pp. 878–883).

Listening and Speaking

1. Review the assignment, using the instruction on the student page.
2. Have students complete the **Support for Extend Your Learning** page (***Unit 5 Resources,*** p. 55).

Teaching Resources

Unit 5 Resources

- L3 L4 **Integrated Language Skills: Grammar,** p. 53
- L3 L4 **Support for Writing,** p. 54
- L3 L4 **Support for Extend Your Learning,** p. 55
- L4 **Enrichment,** p. 52

Enriched Online Student Edition

Available under After You Read for this selection:

- All **Interactive Grammar Tutorial**
- L3 L4 **Internet Research Activity**

Professional Development Guidebook
Rubrics for General (Holistic) Writing pp. 256–257

PHLit Online! All print and digital resources are available online at **www.PHLitOnline.com.** Online resources accessible by students are noted on the student page.

MONITORING PROGRESS

Using the Test Practice

In this two-page Test Practice, students apply the reading skill for the first half of Unit 5 to a passage of fiction and a passage of nonfiction.

Review this skill, summarizing, and then administer the test. For more guidance, consult the ***Classroom Strategies and Teaching Routines*** card, **Administering Timed Tests.**

ASSESS

Answers

Answers With Explanations

1. **B**—A stage direction (his name in capital letters) and the introduction show that Creon is speaking. *Incorrect answers:* A—Oedipus is the subject of the excerpt, not the speaker. C—Creon refers to Antigone (his kinsfolk), whom he is holding captive. D—Creon is addressing Theseus, son of Aegeus, in the excerpt.
2. **C**—Creon suggests that he can't believe that Athens would help a "parricide"; that he thought they had better judgment. *Incorrect answers:* A—Creon says the opposite, that Oedipus is a murderer and "polluted man". B—Creon questions Athens' decision to help Oedipus, not their honesty. D—same explanation as for A.
3. **B**—Creon is simply responding to Theseus, son of Aegeus, as the first sentence shows. *Incorrect answers:* A—This action has already taken place, as the introduction shows. C—Creon says that Oedipus is a murderer and "polluted man". D—He is contemplating action against Oedipus, but hasn't captured him.
4. **D**—Creon is feeling weak, but it isn't a significant detail that affects the excerpt's meaning or purpose. *Incorrect answers:* A—This information is significant for understanding the excerpt's meaning and purpose. B—same explanation as for A. C—He addresses the speech to Theseus, a detail of central importance

Test Practice: Reading

Summarize

Drama Selection

Directions: *Read the selection. Then, answer the questions.*

In Sophocles' Oedipus at Colonus, *Creon is holding Oedipus' daughters Antigone and Ismene against their will in order to capture Oedipus himself. Theseus, the king of Athens, intervenes on behalf of Oedipus. Creon's response to Theseus is retold in the following passage.*

CREON. It is not that I believe this city lacks courage, King Theseus, or wisdom . . . that I have sought to capture Oedipus . . . I knew that your people would not allow a murderer—a polluted man who married his own mother—to enter this great city. Knowing that outlaws are not permitted to live in your land, I came here to hunt for the former king of Thebes, Oedipus. . .

King Theseus, I know you will do what you think is right in this situation; although I believe my actions were right, the lack of support makes me weak: however, even though I feel old, I will not willingly give up my quest to destroy this man.

1. Who is speaking in the excerpt?

A. Oedipus
B. Creon
C. Antigone
D. Theseus

2. What is the main idea of the speech?

A. Oedipus should be forgiven.
B. The people of Athens are untrustworthy.
C. Athens should not welcome Oedipus.
D. I hope to reconcile with Oedipus.

3. What is Creon's most significant action in this excerpt?

A. He kidnaps Antigone and Ismene.
B. He answers Theseus.
C. He forgives Oedipus.
D. He kills Oedipus.

4. Which of the following details would be *least* important to include in a summary of this excerpt?

A. Creon has captured Antigone and Ismene.
B. Creon seeks to capture Oedipus.
C. Creon is speaking to Theseus.
D. Creon is feeling weak.

Writing for Assessment

Write a paragraph in which you summarize Creon's opinion of Oedipus. Include details from this excerpt in your summary.

Writing for Assessment

Students should first underline the sentence from the excerpt, where Creon gives his opinion of Oedipus (i.e., sentence 2). They can then use this as the basis for explaining Creon's feelings and intentions.

Strategies for Test Taking

Remind students to read each question carefully. They should pay attention to details which affect the point of each question. For example, question 1 asks for the speaker, not the subject or the person addressed. Question 3 asks for the "most" significant action; the answer choices may include other actions. Question 4 asks to find "the least important" detail.

Nonfiction Selection

Directions: *Read the selection. Then, answer the questions.*

All tragedies have a tragic hero, who is the protagonist. This character is usually of high or noble birth. The tragic hero is in a difficult situation for one of two reasons: Either he or she creates the situation because of a character flaw, or the situation itself is fated. Sometimes, the situation involves a combination of the two. For example, Oedipus is doomed by fate but makes his situation worse. The tragic hero ultimately experiences disaster.

Tragedies are timeless: The protagonist is a character with whom any audience will sympathize. The audience can identify with the hero's feelings of helplessness as he or she tries to fix past mistakes.

1. What is the *best* one-sentence summary of paragraph 1?

A. For a tragic hero, fate interferes and the main character experiences disaster.
B. The main character in a tragedy is a person of high status who faces a downfall due to fate or a character flaw.
C. A tragedy is a play about a character who cannot avoid fate no matter what.
D. Oedipus is a tragic hero because, no matter what he does, he cannot avoid the tragic fate that is waiting for him.

2. Which trait does *not* apply to a tragic hero?

A. experiences disaster
B. of high or noble birth
C. doomed by fate
D. sympathizes with the gods

3. What is the *best* paraphrase of the first sentence in paragraph 2?

A. A tragic hero appeals to readers in any period of time.
B. A tragic hero's feelings don't make sense to most readers.
C. Readers always want to see the protagonist fail.
D. Readers want to learn more about the protagonist.

4. Which of the following details could be left out of a summary of this selection?

A. The protagonist is a character for whom the audience feels sympathy.
B. The audience can identify with the main character's feelings of helplessness.
C. Oedipus makes his situation worse.
D. The tragic hero experiences disaster.

Writing for Assessment

Connecting Across Texts
Based on the passage on the left, in what ways does Oedipus fit the criteria of a tragic hero? Explain your answer in a paragraph. Support your response with details from both selections.

PHLit Online!
www.PHLitOnline.com
- Online practice
- Instant feedback

Differentiated Instruction for Universal Access

Strategy for Less Proficient Readers
The excerpt contains very difficult language and vocabulary, so students may require additional help for comprehension. First, make sure that they understand the introductory background. Next, read the excerpt orally to them. Finally, do a choral reading with them. Make sure that students understand the meaning of each phrase. Suggest the following summary: *I don't consider this city weak or unwise; that's not why I took this action; I thought Athens would never support my extended family [i.e., Oedipus' daughters were his nieces;] over me. Also I believed that Athens wouldn't take in Oedipus who murdered his father and married his mother. So, do as you must; but your lack of support of my just cause hurts me; even though I'm old I will try to give Oedipus what he deserves for his actions.)*

ASSESS

Answers

Answers With Explanations

1. B—This sentence covers all the important information: the tragic hero's status and the reasons for his downfall. *Incorrect answers:* A—This sentence is too vague and leaves out information about status. C—same explanation as for A. D—This sentence is too specific, focusing on one example, Oedipus.
2. D—This information refers to audience reaction, not the tragic hero. *Incorrect answers:* A—A tragic hero does experience disaster. B—A tragic hero is of high or noble birth. C—A tragic hero is doomed by fate or character flaw.
3. A—*In any period of time* paraphrases "Tragedies are timeless"; A tragic hero appeals to readers paraphrases the second part of the sentence. *Incorrect answers:* B—The sentence suggests the opposite; that readers "sympathize". C—same explanation as for B. D—The sentence doesn't say that they want to learn more, only that they sympathize.
4. C—This information is in the excerpt, but it isn't a significant detail that affects the meaning or purpose. *Incorrect answers:* A—This information is significant for understanding the excerpt's meaning and purpose. B—same explanation as for A. C—same explanation as for A.

Writing for Assessment

Students should list the criteria from the nonfiction selection for a tragic hero. In their paper, they should explain how Oedipus fits each criterion from this list, using details to support their responses

PHLit Online!
Students may take the test in interactive format with instant feedback online at **www.PHLitOnline.com**.

PREACH

Meeting Your Standards

Students will

1. synthesize to connect ideas.
2. understand and evaluate criticisms in drama reviews.
3. read drama reviews.

Log on at ***www.PHLitOnline.com*** *for a detailed lesson plan for Informational Texts.*

Reading Skill

1. Introduce the skill and review the steps described in the instruction.
2. Tell students that they will connect and synthesize ideas as they read.

Think Aloud: Model the Skill

Model the skill of connecting ideas to synthesize. Say to students:

By considering my friends' opinions about a movie, I can decide whether I want to watch it. I can connect and synthesize what they like, dislike, and disagree about to come up with a useful conclusion.

To what extent does experience determine what we perceive?

Have students look for connections between the reviewers' comments and their own impressions.

Multidraft Reading

Have students follow a multidraft reading protocol.

- **First reading:** Have students read for general understanding.
- **Second reading:** Have students identify similarities and differences.
- **Third reading:** Have students think about whether the similarities or differences are more important.

Informational Texts

Real-Life Reading

Drama Review
Santa Claus Meets Sophocles

Drama Review
A "Prequel" to Antigone

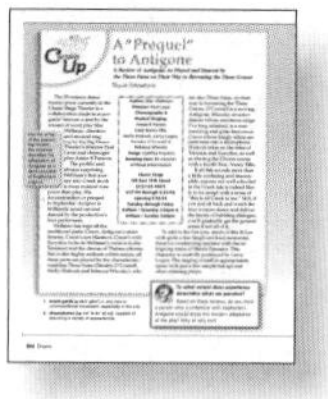

Reading Skill: Synthesize: Connect Ideas

When you read multiple texts dealing with a single issue, you will often find both agreement and disagreement among the texts. To draw your own conclusions about the issue, you must **synthesize** the content from those sources by **connecting ideas** presented in the texts.

Begin by **paraphrasing,** or restating, the key ideas in one text to be sure you comprehend them. Then, look for related ideas in another text. For example, when you read two reviews of a single theatrical production, you might look for what each review says about the play's staging, or overall appearance. Finally, you can synthesize the content of the two reviews by analyzing what each one says and drawing conclusions about the production, based on your analysis. This chart shows an example.

Idea in Text One	Idea in Text Two	Synthesis
The set design is plain, but it looks good and sometimes surprises.	Few props are used, but they are used in clever ways.	The staging of the production is simple but effective.

THE BIG ? To what extent does *experience* determine what we perceive?

The subject of these two reviews is a modern adaptation of Sophocles' play *Antigone*. As you read, consider how each reviewer's opinion might be influenced by his or her familiarity with the original play.

Differentiated Instruction for Universal Acce

Reading Support

Give students reading support with the appropriate version of the *Reader's Notebooks*:

- L2 L3 *Reader's Notebook*
- L1 *Reader's Notebook: Adapted Version*
- EL *Reader's Notebook: English Learner's Version*

PHLit Online! All student resources, are available at **www.PHLitOnline.com.**

Drama Review

Features:

- a summary of the play's plot
- a critique of the direction and acting
- support for opinions
- judgments about the staging

OFF BROADWAY...

Santa Claus Meets Sophocles

A Review of *Antigone:* As Played and Danced by the Three Fates on the Way to Becoming the Three Graces

Matthew Murray

If you're familiar with Sophocles' classic Greek tragedy and have a solid working knowledge of Greek mythology, you might well appreciate the opportunity to see Big Dance Theater's production of Wellman's interpretation of the story, which is playing at Classic Stage Company through May 23. If you don't know Sophocles' original, or you have only a casual familiarity with it, chances are you'll be utterly baffled by what you see onstage.

The full title of Wellman's play is *Antigone: As Played and Danced by the Three Fates on Their Way to Becoming the Three Graces.* That should give you an idea of what you're in for: a highly deconstructed[1] take on Sophocles' story.

As the Fates (one who spins the thread of life, one who weaves it into actions, and one who determines when it must be snipped) existed eons before Sophocles, this story bears only a perfunctory similarity to his. The story the Fates enact features a handful of characters from the play, and is overseen by a narrator (and disc jockey) named E Shriek, whom Wellman describes as "an unknown god of unknown origin."

As the play progresses, the Fates become the Three Graces, and pass along the story of the young Antigone and the steadfast uncle she defied to Sophocles himself. (Well, as represented by a hand puppet.) The story is told and retold until it reaches the version we currently know, at which point the play stops: what is is of no interest to Wellman. He's more concerned with what was and what might have been.

That idea, and the stagecraft used to present it, are the most engaging parts of this *Antigone*. Director Paul Lazar and choreographer[2] Annie-B Parson have done an excellent job of making the play visually appealing, providing almost constant movement onstage, and no shortage of surprises in the way the Fates' journeys are conveyed. (They employ microphones, dust busters, yellow slippers and toy pianos.)

Cynthia Hopkins has provided a few attractive songs for the production; Joanne Howard's set design is spartan[3], but handsome and occasionally surprising; Claudia Stephens's costumes provide nice definition for the characters; Jay Ryan's lights are colorful and inventive; and Jane Shaw's sound design is never overdone. Leroy Logan, as E Shriek, is a fine combination of paternal and frightening, Santa Claus by way of Socrates (and Sophocles).

> Paraphrasing these comments about the staging of the play can help you to connect the reviewer's ideas to related ideas in another review.

It's the lack of immediacy and freshness that hurts this *Antigone* more than anything else: the production never feels as crisp and well-defined as it needs to be. The theatrical concept on which Wellman and Lazar have collaborated is daring and intelligent, but it's currently missing the piquant[4] energy needed to really put it across.

1. **deconstructed** (dē kən strukt′ id) *adj.* (said of a text) having been broken into its elements in order to question its meaning.
2. **choreographer** (kôr′ ē äg′ rə fər) *n.* a person who creates and directs dances.
3. **spartan** (spärt′ n) *adj.* very plain; lacking ornament.
4. **piquant** (pē′ kənt) *adj.* exciting agreeable interest or curiosity.

Differentiated Instruction for Universal Access

Strategy for Special Needs Students

Direct students' attention to the chart on p. 864. Guide them to see how the different statements in column 1 and column 2 can be used to reach the synthesis in column 3. Then, have them prepare similar charts for other aspects of the play, such as the script, the direction, the acting, the costumes, and the lighting. Encourage students to share their syntheses with the rest of the class.

Enrichment for Advanced Readers

Challenge students to find conflicting reviews of the same performance, such as a television show, movie, play, or musical performance. Ask each student to synthesize his or her reviews using a chart with such headings as *Script, Acting, Direction, Sound and Lighting, Costuming, Scenery,* and *Overall Impression.* Allow time for students to share their charts and discuss the degree to which the two reviews agreed.

TEACH

About Drama Reviews

1. Review the features listed in the Drama Review box on p. 865 with students. **Ask** the class to define the term *critique* in their own words
   Possible response: A critique is an assessment of how interesting or affecting an artistic presentation is.
2. Discuss with students kinds of formal and informal reviews they have heard, seen, or given themselves. Point out that, in addition to plays and dances, reviews might apply to books, movies and television shows, concerts, albums or songs, restaurants, or countless other offerings to the public.
3. Speak to students about how to approach a review. Point out that reviewers state specific details about the participants in the performance, convey the goals or interpretation of the production, and give a sense of what the experience was like to view.

Synthesize: Connect Ideas

1. Remind students that reviews express the writer's opinion about a production. Explain that the two reviews they will read express two opinions about the same production.
2. Direct students' attention to the callout pointing to the play's staging. Remind them that a paraphrase expresses the sense of the original, using different words. **Ask** students to paraphrase the paragraph.
   Possible response: The new songs are appealing; the set is simple but well done; the costumes help differentiate each character; the lighting is clever and unusual; the sound is well balanced; and the performance by the narrator is varied and interesting.
3. Then, direct their attention to the following paragraph. **Ask** them to paraphrase Murray's overall impression of the play.
   Possible response: The concept of the play is intriguing and many aspects of it clever, but overall the production seemed lifeless and fuzzy.

Synthesize: Connect Ideas

1. Direct students' attention to the first callout. **Ask:** What does this similarity suggest?
   Possible response: Both reviews say the production takes a nontraditional look at *Antigone.*
2. Direct their attention to the paragraph that begins "Wellman has kept . . ." **Ask** what Sommers focuses on here and whether Murray covered the same issue.
   Answer: Sommers describes the functions of the Three Fates, mentions that there is a fourth, and evaluates the actors' performances. Murray did not address these issues.
3. Point to the paragraph that begins "If all this sounds . . ." **Ask** them how these comments are similar to and different from Murray's.
   Possible response: Sommers, like Murray, says that knowing Greek mythology helps in understanding the play but suggests that anyone could enjoy the show.
4. Finally, look at the last sentence in this review. **Ask** students how this analysis contrasts with Murray's review.
   Answer: Sommers sums up the staging in one sentence. Murray gives much more detail about aspects of the production.

Reflecting on the Reading Skill

After students have finished reading, **ask** them to explain which elements they found most useful for connecting and synthesizing.
Possible response: Students might respond that comments on the same elements were easier to synthesize than aspects of the production that received unequal coverage.

Curtain Up

A "Prequel" to Antigone

A Review of *Antigone: As Played and Danced by the Three Fates on Their Way to Becoming the Three Graces*

Elyse Sommers

The 55-minute dance theater piece currently at the Classic Stage Theater is a collaboration made in avant-garde[1] heaven: a text by the wizard of word play Mac Wellman, direction and musical staging by the Big Dance Theater's director Paul Lazar and choreographer Annie-B Parson.

Like the writer of the preceding review, this reviewer describes the adaptation of *Antigone* as a deconstruction of Sophocles' original.

The prolific and always surprising Wellman's first journey into Greek myth is more musical tone poem than play. His deconstruction or prequel to Sophocles' *Antigone* is brilliantly acted out and danced by the production's four performers.

Author: Mac Wellman
Director: Paul Lazar
Choreography & Musical Staging: Annie-B Parson
Cast: Nancy Ellis, Molly Hickock, Leroy Logan, Deirdre O'Connell & Rebecca Wisocky
Songs: Cynthia Hopkins
Running time: 60 minutes without intermission

Classic Stage
136 East 13th Street
(212/123-4567)
4/27/04 through 5/23/04; opening 5/02/04
Tuesday through Friday 8:00pm / Saturday 2:00pm & 8:00pm / Sunday 3:00pm

Wellman has kept all the traditional parts: Creon, Antigone's sister Ismene, Creon's son Haemon, Creon's wife Eurydice (who in Wellman's version is also Teiresias) and the chorus of Theban citizens. But in this highly stylized collaboration, all these parts are played by the chameleonic,[2] maskless Three Fates (Deirdre O'Connell, Molly Hickock and Rebecca Wisocky), who are also Three Fates, on their way to becoming the Three Graces. O'Connell is a moving Antigone. Wisocky, an actor-dancer whose enormous range I've long admired, is a mesmerizing and quite humorous Creon whose kingly edicts are delivered into a microphone. Hickock takes on the roles of Teiresias and Eurydice, as well as sharing the Chorus scenes with a fourth Fate, Nancy Ellis.

If all this sounds more than a little confusing and inaccessible, anyone not well schooled in the Greek tale is indeed likely to be swept with a sense of "this is all Greek to me." Still, if you just sit back and watch the four women dance and deliver the bursts of babbling dialogue, you'll gradually get the general sense if not all of it.

To add to the fun (yes, much of this IS fun with quite a few laugh-out-loud moments), there's a nondancing narrator with the intriguing name of Shriek Operator. This character is zestfully portrayed by Leroy Logan. The staging overall is appropriately spare with just a few simple but apt and often amusing props.

1. **avant-garde** (ə vänt′ gärd′) *n.* any new or unconventional movement, especially in the arts.
2. **chameleonic** (kə mē′ lē än′ ik) *adj.* capable of assuming a variety of appearances.

To what extent does experience determine what we perceive?
Based on these reviews, do you think a person who is unfamiliar with Sophocles' *Antigone* would enjoy this modern adaptation of the play? Why or why not?

ASSESS/EXTEND

Answers

To what extent does experience determine what we perceive?

Murray suggests that a person unfamiliar with Greek mythology would be confused, but Sommers says that "you'll gradually get the general sense if not all of it."

Vocabulary Development

Cross-Curricular Vocabulary: Drama

Point out that drama reviews often use vocabulary that is specific to one particular setting; in this case, a live performance of a play based on *Antigone*. Guide students to understand the meaning of the following words used in these drama reviews:

perfunctory: lacking in interest or enthusiasm
collaboration: to work jointly with others
prequel: a dramatic work with a story that takes place before that of an earlier work
stylized: to represent or design according to a style rather than according to nature or tradition
staging: the use of sets, costumes, and props along with sound and lighting

PHLit Online!

Vocabulary Central, featuring tools, activities, and songs for studying vocabulary, is available at **www.PHLitOnline.com.**

Test Practice: Informational Texts

Comparing Informational Texts

(a) In what ways are the two reviewers' critiques of the actors' performances similar? **(b)** In what ways are they different? **(c)** When you **synthesize** information from both reviews, what is one conclusion you can draw about the actors' performances? Explain your response.

Timed Writing

Write a Persuasive Essay

Format
The prompt directs you to write a persuasive essay. Therefore, you should use vivid, convincing language and support your ideas with strong evidence.

Your school will perform *Antigone: As Played. . . .* Write a persuasive essay offering suggestions for the performance. Combine criticism and praise from the reviews, synthesizing the ideas. Then, connect those ideas to your own ideas about drama to make suggestions. Cite details from the reviews as support. (35 minutes)

Academic Vocabulary
When you *connect* ideas, you find links between them, joining them together to draw conclusions and form new ideas.

5-Minute Planner

Complete these steps before you begin to write:

1. Read the prompt carefully and completely.
2. Skim the reviews to find criticisms and praise. Synthesize these ideas by combining them and making a quick list of points and details.
3. Think about what makes a good theatrical performance. Make a quick list of your ideas.
4. Review your lists and find connections between the items. Make notes about these connections.
5. Consider your lists and the connections you found. Formulate suggestions based on those ideas.
6. Consider in what order you will present your suggestions. **TIP** You may wish to place the ideas for which you have the strongest support at the beginning of your essay.
7. Create a rough outline for your persuasive essay. Then, refer to your notes and outline as you write.

Extend the Lesson

Connecting to the Students' World

Divide the class into groups, and tell each group to identify three movie reviewers and obtain reviews written by those reviewers of the same three movies. The groups should choose one movie that a majority of group members liked, one that a majority of them did not like, and one that none have seen. First, have the groups apply the skills in this unit to connect and synthesize the three reviews of each movie. Second, they should synthesize from the reviews of each reviewer the common set of concerns, tastes, or interests each reviewer brings to watching movies. Third, they should decide how much they agree with each reviewer's approach to movies. Finally, they should decide—based on their other findings—if the review of the movie they have not seen makes them want to see that third movie and why or why not. Have the groups present their findings to the rest of the class.

Answers

Comparing Informational Texts

Possible responses: (a) Both reviewers praise the performance of Leroy Logan. (b) Murray says little about the performances of the actors playing the Three Fates, and does not mention the existence of a fourth. Sommers gives far more detail about these actors. (c) **Possible response:** From both reviews, it is clear that Logan gave a good performance. From the greater detail in the second review, it seems that the other actors were very good also.

Timed Writing

1. Before students complete the activity, guide them in identifying and analyzing key words and phrases in the prompt, highlighted on the student page.
2. Work with students to draw up guidelines for their essays based on the key words:
   - **Focus** The writer should clearly synthesize ideas from the two reviews, and connect ideas to make suggestions.
   - **Organization** The writer should introduce ideas from the reviews. Then, the writer should make suggestions to incorporate his or her own ideas in connection to the reviews.
   - **Support** The writer must support statements about the reviews with details and quotations from them.
   - **Style** The writer should be evenhanded in evaluating the reviews while maintaining convincing language.
3. Have students use the 5-Minute Planner to structure their time.
4. Allow students 35 minutes to complete the assignment. Evaluate their work using the guidelines they have developed.

Meeting Your Standards

Students will

1. analyze and respond to universal and culturally specific themes.
2. compare the themes of two dramatic works.

*Log on at **www.PHLitOnline.com** for a detailed lesson plan.*

1 Comparing Universal and Culturally Specific Themes

1. Introduce the skill using the instruction on the student page.
2. Give students a copy of **Comparing Universal and Culturally Specific Themes Graphic Organizer B, *Graphic Organizer Transparencies*,** p. 162. Tell them they will fill it in with details as they read.

Think Aloud: Model the Skill

Model a way to compare themes. Say:

When comparing universal and culturally specific themes, I think of the play *Romeo and Juliet*. It reflects the culture of its time because it warns that overemphasis on familial honor can lead to tragedy. The play's universal theme is the idea that rigid thinking can lead to tragic results.

2 Vocabulary

1. Have students say each word.
2. Then, use the word in a sentence that defines the word. Repeat the sentence, now with the word missing, and have the class "fill in the blank" chorally.

For more guidance, see the ***Classroom Strategies and Teaching Routines*** card, **Introducing Selection Vocabulary.**

Comparing Literary Works

Antigone • *from* An Enemy of the People

1 Comparing Universal and Culturally Specific Themes

The **theme** of a literary work is its message. The theme may have aspects that are **culturally specific,** reflecting the circumstances and beliefs of the writer's culture. In contrast, the theme may also have aspects that are **universal,** or that are meaningful to people of all times and places.

For instance, an ancient poem might tell of an arrogant warrior who does not obey his people's traditions and who is punished by the gods.

- The poem's theme is culturally specific because it reflects the beliefs of the culture: "The gods punish those who do not obey our traditions."
- The poem also expresses a universal theme, one that people of all times and places can appreciate: "No one is above the law."

In the ancient Greek play *Antigone*, Antigone bravely defies a king. In the nineteenth-century European drama *An Enemy of the People,* a doctor bravely defies his brother and boss, the mayor. The "local" or culturally specific elements of each play are different. Yet both plays express an important universal theme: "People may be torn between duty to authority and some higher value." As you read, use a diagram like the one shown to compare the universal and the culturally specific aspects of the two plays.

Culturally Specific Element ← Situation or Motive → Universal Element

2 Vocabulary

- **exorbitant** (eg zôr′ bi tənt) *adj.* excessive (p. 871) *The price of the dress is exorbitant—it costs a week's salary!*
- **impending** (im pend′ iŋ) *adj.* about to happen (p. 873) *We evacuated when we heard of an impending storm.* pend *v.*
- **impetuosity** (im pech′ o͞o äs′ i tē) *n.* sudden action with little thought (p. 874) *Impetuosity led him to buy a car without taking a test drive.* impetuous *adj.*
- **adamant** (ad′ ə mənt) *adj.* firm (p. 875) *I want to compromise, but he is adamant.*

PHLit Online! www.PHLitOnline.com

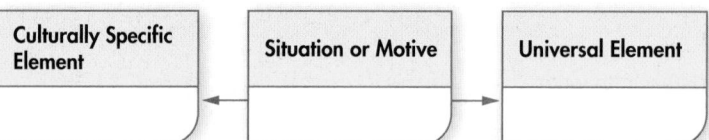

- Vocabulary flashcards
- Interactive journals
- More about the authors
- Selection audio
- Interactive graphic organizers

Vocabulary Development

Vocabulary Knowledge Rating

Create a **Vocabulary Knowledge Rating Chart** (***Professional Development Guidebook***, p. 33) for this selection. Include the selection vocabulary and the forms of the Big Question words that appear in the Writing About the Big Question sentence starters. (The Big Question vocabulary is introduced on pp. 790–791.)

Give students a copy of the chart. Read the words aloud, and have students mark their rating in the Before Reading column. Urge them to be alert to these words as they read and discuss the selection.

Tally how many students think they know a word to gauge how much instruction to provide. As students read and discuss the selection, point out the words and their context.

PHLit Online! **Vocabulary Central**, featuring tools, activities, and songs for studying vocabulary, is available online at **www.PHLitOnline.com**.

To what extent does *experience* determine what we *perceive?*

❸ Writing About the Big Question

In both *Antigone* and *An Enemy of the People,* characters must decide between following a person in power and following their own perception of what is morally right. Use these sentence starters to develop your ideas about the Big Question.

Individuals must balance respect for authority with _______________.

When people in power try to **distort** your views of right and wrong, thinking about your own experiences can help you _______________.

Meet the Author

Henrik Ibsen (1828–1906)

Author of *An Enemy of the People*

Born in Skien, Norway, Henrik Ibsen was a pioneer of modern realistic drama. The popular drama of his day specialized in idealized heroes, ridiculous buffoons, and happy endings. Breaking with convention, Ibsen showed ordinary people facing grimly realistic problems. Instead of developing perfect heroes and utter villains, he presented psychologically complex characters with a mix of good and bad motives.

Creating Controversy Ibsen also offered a brutally honest look at cutting-edge issues of his day. For instance, his play *A Doll House* concerns women's rights, a subject that was highly controversial in the nineteenth century. Outraged by such inflammatory subject matter, critics condemned him. In the end, though, Ibsen triumphed. Today, his plays are considered classics, and his realistic approach to character, plot, dialogue, and staging continues to influence drama.

Daily Bellringer

For each class during which you will teach this selection, have students complete one of the five Vocabulary activities for Week 27 in the ***Daily Bellringer Activities*** booklet.

❸ Writing About the Big Question

1. Review the assignment with the class.
2. Explain that people sometimes face tests in which their own beliefs are challenged by others.
3. Have students complete the sentence starters. Review responses as a class. (**Possible response:** Individuals must balance respect for authority with adherence to their own principles. When people in power try to distort your views of right and wrong, thinking about your own experiences can help you determine how to act.)
4. Remind students that their answers will help them think about the Big Question. Tell them that as they read, they should look for ways the characters are shaped by their experiences.

Concept Connector →

Tell students that they will return to their sentence starters after they have concluded reading.

Multidraft Reading

For each reading, have students set the purpose intended:

- **First reading**—literal comprehension: answering the Reading Check questions
- **Second reading**—application of skills: responding to the side-column notes
- **Third reading**—interpretation: answering the end-of-selection questions

For more guidance, refer to the ***Classroom Strategies and Teaching Routines*** card on multidraft reading.

Teaching Resources

The following resources can be used to enrich, extend, or differentiate the instruction.

- All *Unit 5 Resources,* pp. 65–81
- All *Professional Development Guidebook,* pp. 33, 36–38, 42
- All *Graphic Organizer Transparencies,* pp. 162, 164
- All **Enriched Online Student Edition**

PHLit Online! All resources, including print and video, are available online at **www.PHLitOnline.com.**

PHLit Online!

For more about the authors, practice with the selection vocabulary, and more background, go to **www.PHLitOnline.com.**

❶ Background

An Enemy of the People This social drama harshly criticizes the values of late-nineteenth-century Europe and explores the ethical relationships between people. Ibsen illustrates society's ills in plays such as *An Enemy of the People*, *Ghosts*, and *A Doll House* in an effort to cure these ills. The moral dilemma presented to the mayor—and the attacks his brother faces—mirror the complications of modern life that Ibsen invariably examines in his plays: the struggles between truth and profit, authority and reform, and morality and popular culture.

❷ Activating Prior Knowledge

1. Prepare an **Anticipation Guide** (see ***Professional Development Guidebook***, pp. 36–38) with the following statements:
   - Standing up for one's beliefs is not worth the loss of friends, money, or reputation.
   - Sometimes it is better to put one's beliefs aside and compromise.
   - Financial security is more important than a clear conscience.
2. Give students a copy of the prepared **Anticipation Guide**, and have them mark their responses in the Me column. Have students discuss the statements in pairs or groups and mark the guides again in the Group column.

Concept Connector →

Students will return to the **Anticipation Guide** after completing the scene from the play.

❸ About the Selection

This selection, excerpted from the second act of a four-act play, takes place at the home of Dr. Stockmann. The doctor's brother, Mayor Stockmann, has come to control the damage that the release of the report will have on business at the baths. He initially tries to cajole his brother, but, faced with the doctor's stubborn adherence to scientific truth, the mayor ends up threatening him with economic reprisals.

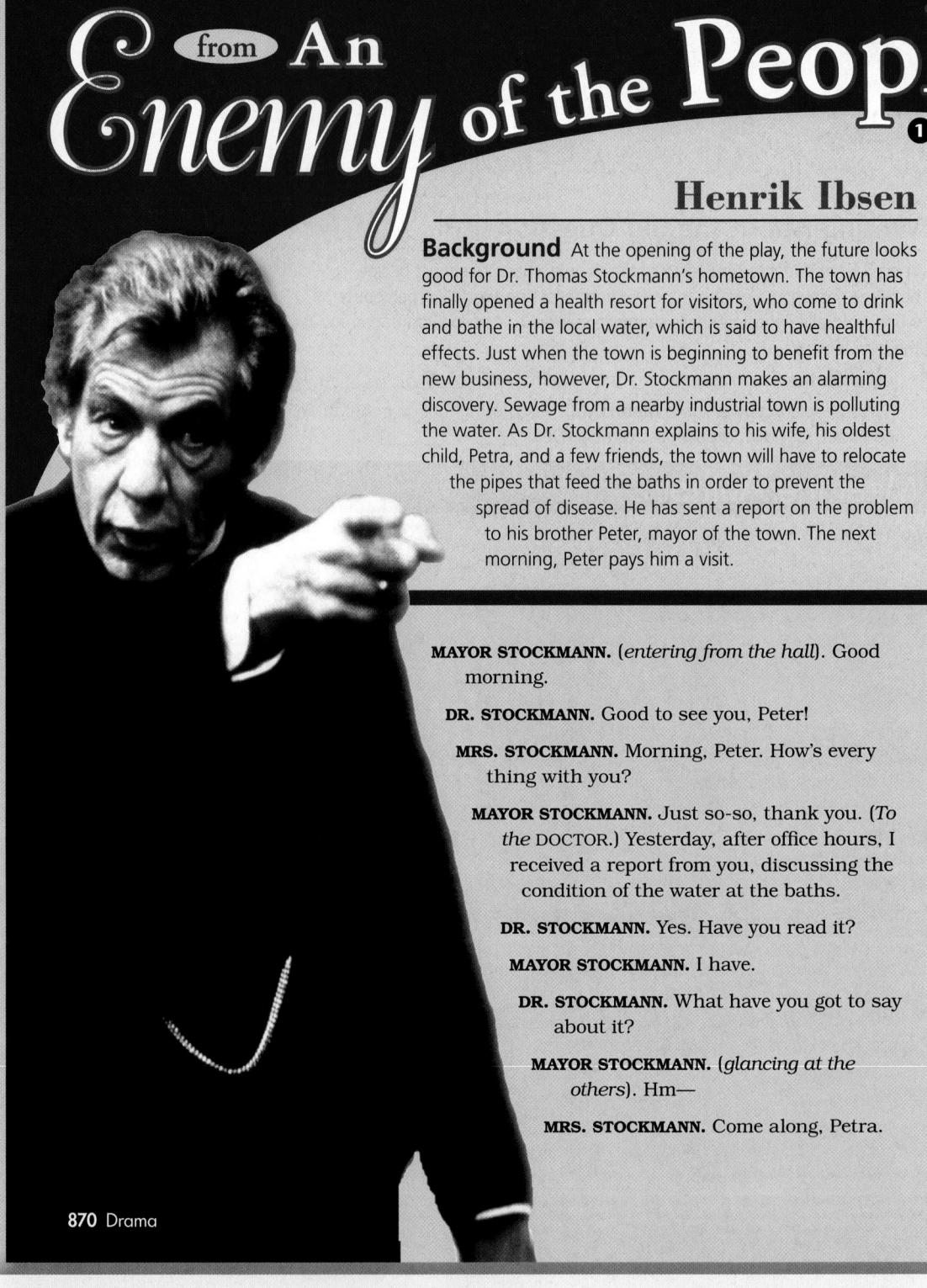

from An Enemy of the People ❶ ❷

Henrik Ibsen

Background At the opening of the play, the future looks good for Dr. Thomas Stockmann's hometown. The town has finally opened a health resort for visitors, who come to drink and bathe in the local water, which is said to have healthful effects. Just when the town is beginning to benefit from the new business, however, Dr. Stockmann makes an alarming discovery. Sewage from a nearby industrial town is polluting the water. As Dr. Stockmann explains to his wife, his oldest child, Petra, and a few friends, the town will have to relocate the pipes that feed the baths in order to prevent the spread of disease. He has sent a report on the problem to his brother Peter, mayor of the town. The next morning, Peter pays him a visit.

MAYOR STOCKMANN. (*entering from the hall*). Good morning.

DR. STOCKMANN. Good to see you, Peter!

MRS. STOCKMANN. Morning, Peter. How's every thing with you?

MAYOR STOCKMANN. Just so-so, thank you. (*To the* DOCTOR.) Yesterday, after office hours, I received a report from you, discussing the condition of the water at the baths.

DR. STOCKMANN. Yes. Have you read it?

MAYOR STOCKMANN. I have.

DR. STOCKMANN. What have you got to say about it?

MAYOR STOCKMANN. (*glancing at the others*). Hm—

MRS. STOCKMANN. Come along, Petra.

Vocabulary Development

Thematic Vocabulary: The Big Question

As students are discussing the excerpt from *An Enemy of the People*, ask them to use the thematic vocabulary presented in Introducing the Big Question, pp. 790–791. You might encourage them with sentence starters such as these:

1. Dr. Stockmann's *knowledge* of science led him to conclude that . . .
2. Dr. Stockmann's *expectation* in giving the mayor the report was that . . .
3. After reading the report, Mayor Stockmann can *anticipate* that . . .
4. In the scene, the brothers reveal *background* information about . . .
5. From the doctor's *perspective*, the town is in danger because . . .
6. The mayor's *interpretation* of the situation is that . . .

(She and PETRA *go into the room on the left.)*

MAYOR STOCKMANN. (*after a moment*). Was it necessary to press all these investigations behind my back?

DR. STOCKMANN. Well, as long as I didn't have absolute proof, then—

MAYOR STOCKMANN. And now you think you do?

DR. STOCKMANN. You must be convinced of that yourself.

MAYOR STOCKMANN. Is it your object to put this document before the board of directors by way of an official recommendation?

DR. STOCKMANN. Of course. Something has to be done about this. And fast.

MAYOR STOCKMANN. As usual, in your report you let your language get out of hand. You say, among other things, that what we're offering our summer visitors is guaranteed poison.

DR. STOCKMANN. But, Peter, how else can you describe it? You've got to realize—this water is poison for internal or external use! And it's foisted on poor, suffering creatures who turn to us in good faith and pay us exorbitant fees to gain their health back again!

5 **MAYOR STOCKMANN.** And then you arrive at the conclusion, by your line of reasoning, that we have to build a sewer to drain off these so-called impurities from Mølledal,[1] and that all the water mains have to be relaid.

DR. STOCKMANN. Well, do you see any other way out? I don't.

MAYOR STOCKMANN. I invented a little business this morning down at the town engineer's office. And in a half-joking way, I brought up these proposals as something we perhaps ought to take under advisement[2] at some time in the future.

DR. STOCKMANN. Some time in the future!

MAYOR STOCKMANN. He smiled at my whimsical extravagance—naturally. Have you gone to the trouble of estimating just what these proposed changes would cost? From the information I received, the expenditure would probably run up into several hundred thousand crowns.[3]

DR. STOCKMANN. As high as that?

MAYOR STOCKMANN. Yes. But that's not the worst. The work would extend over at least two years.

1. **Mølledal** (möl´ ə däl´) fictional Norwegian town.
2. **to take under advisement** to think over carefully.
3. **crowns** *n.* A crown is the Norwegian unit of currency; krone (krō´ nə).

4 ◀ **Critical Viewing**
Judging from Dr. Stockmann's expression in this film still, how might others respond to his discovery? **[Predict]**

Vocabulary
exorbitant (eg zôr´ bi tənt) *adj.* excessive

Literary Analysis
Themes What details of the issue raised by Dr. Stockmann are characteristic of life in modern, industrial times?

6 **Reading Check**
What problem does Dr. Stockmann's town face?

4 Critical Viewing

Possible response: The doctor's serious, threatening expression will likely cause others to take his findings seriously.

5 Literary Analysis

Themes

1. Remind students that this play is set in nineteenth-century Europe, a period of rapid industrial and economic growth. **Ask** students to explain whether this setting is a universal or culturally specific element.
   Answer: The setting is a culturally specific element because the play occurs during a particular time period.
2. **Ask** students to speculate on the impact such economic growth would have on the environment.
   Possible response: Industrialization can result in pollution as a result of burning fuels and using strong chemicals.
3. After students read the bracketed passage, **ask** the Literary Analysis question: What details of the issue raised by Dr. Stockmann are characteristic of life in modern, industrial times?
   Answer: Dr. Stockmann raises the issue of water pollution; this pollution, which can harm people internally and externally, is the result of industrialization.

6 Reading Check

Answer: The water in the public baths, a major source of income for the town, has become polluted.

Differentiated Instruction for Universal Access

Accessibility at a Glance

Use this information to guide your teaching of the excerpt from *An Enemy of the People*.

Context	Dramatic play set in nineteenth-century Scandinavia
Language/Vocabulary	• Dramatic, conversational • Above-grade vocabulary
Concept Level	Accessible (pollution; moral dilemma)
Literary Merit	Noted playwright
Lexile/Length	Lexile: NP — Word Count: 1,928

PHLit Online!

This selection is available in interactive format in the **Enriched Online Student Edition**, **www.PHLitOnline.com**, which includes an interactive graphic organizer.

7 Literary Analysis
Themes

1. Remind students that one key to determining the theme in a play is to look for the details in the characters' speeches.
2. Have one student take the part of Mayor Stockmann and read the bracketed passage aloud while other students read along.
3. **Ask:** What is the mayor describing?
   Answer: He is describing what will happen if the baths are closed.
4. **Ask** the Literary Analysis question: What ideas in the mayor's speech might provoke feelings of guilt in most people?
   Answer: For most people, being responsible for jeopardizing the town's future as a health resort and the economic welfare of its citizens would cause feelings of guilt.

8 Critical Thinking
Predict

1. Remind students that reasonable predictions of future events are based on evidence gathered prior to the event.
2. Have students read the bracketed passage. Then, **ask:** What evidence can be used to predict what the mayor will do about the contaminated baths?
   Possible responses: The mayor says that he is not persuaded by the doctor's findings; that the doctor is exaggerating; that the water system cannot be changed; and that no danger exists.
3. Finally, **ask:** From the evidence, what do you think the mayor will do about the contaminated baths?
   Possible response: Students may say that the mayor will do as little as possible. He disagrees with the doctor that the problem is dangerous to the health of the visitors, and he wants to protect the town's economic future.

DR. STOCKMANN. Two years? Two full years?

MAYOR STOCKMANN. At the least. And meanwhile what do we do with the baths? Shut them down? Yes, we'll have to. Do you really think anyone would make the effort to come all the distance here if the rumor got out that the water was contaminated?

DR. STOCKMANN. Yes, but Peter, that's what it is.

Literary Analysis Themes What ideas in the mayor's speech might provoke feelings of guilt in most people? 7

MAYOR STOCKMANN. And then all this happens now—just now, when the baths were being recognized. Other towns in this area have the same resources for development as health resorts. Don't you think they'll leap at the chance to attract the whole flow of tourists to them? No question of it. And there we are, left stranded. We'll most likely have to abandon the whole costly enterprise; and then you'll have ruined the town you were born in.

DR. STOCKMANN. I—ruined—!

MAYOR STOCKMANN. It's through the baths alone that this town has any future to speak of. You can see that just as plain as I can.

DR. STOCKMANN. But then what do you think ought to be done?

MAYOR STOCKMANN. From your report I'm unable to persuade myself that the condition of the baths is as critical as you claim.

DR. STOCKMANN. Look, if anything, it's worse! Or it'll be that by summer, when the warm weather comes.

8

MAYOR STOCKMANN. Once again. I think you're exaggerating considerably. A capable doctor must know the right steps to take—he should be able to control toxic[4] elements, and to treat them if they make their presence too obvious.

DR. STOCKMANN. And then—? What else—?

MAYOR STOCKMANN. The water system for the baths as it now stands is simply a fact and clearly has to be accepted as such. But in time the directors will more than likely agree to take under consideration to what extent—depending on the funds available—they can institute certain improvements.

DR. STOCKMANN. And you can think I'd play along with that kind of trickery!

MAYOR STOCKMANN. Trickery?

DR. STOCKMANN. Yes, it's a trick—a deception, a lie, an out-and-out crime against the public and society at large!

MAYOR STOCKMANN. As I've already observed, I've not yet persuaded

4. **toxic** (täk´ sik) *adj.* poisonous.

Vocabulary Development

Word Form Chart

Expand students' vocabulary by helping them learn related forms of the selection vocabulary words. Give students a **Word Form Chart** (***Professional Development Guidebook***, p. 42), with *exorbitant, impending, impetuosity,* and *adamant* in the appropriate columns. Work with the class or have students work in pairs to determine the related word forms. The final chart should look like the one shown.

Noun	Verb	Adjective	Adverb
exorbitance		**exorbitant**	exorbitantly
	impend	**impending**	
impetuosity		impetuous	impetuously
adamant		**adamant**	adamantly

myself that there's any real impending danger here.

DR. STOCKMANN. Yes, you have! There's no alternative. My report is perfectly accurate, I know that! And you're very much aware of it, Peter, but you won't admit it. You're the one who got the baths and the water system laid out where they are today; and it's this—it's this hellish miscalculation that you won't concede. Pah! You don't think I can see right through you?

9 **MAYOR STOCKMANN.** And even if it were true? Even if I seem a bit overanxious about my reputation, it's all for the good of the town. Without moral authority I could hardly guide and direct affairs in the way I believe serves the general welfare. For this reason—among many others—it strikes me as imperative[5] that your report not be submitted to the board of directors. It has to be withheld for the common good. Then, later, I'll bring the matter up for discussion, and we'll do the very best we can, as quietly as possible. But nothing—not the slightest word of this catastrophe must leak out to the public.

DR. STOCKMANN. My dear Peter, there's no stopping it now.

MAYOR STOCKMANN. It must and it will be stopped.

DR. STOCKMANN. I'm telling you, it's no use. Too many people know already.

MAYOR STOCKMANN. Know already! Who? Not those fellows from the *Courier*—?

DR. STOCKMANN. Why, of course they know. The independent liberal press is going to see that you do your duty.

10 **MAYOR STOCKMANN** (*after a short pause*). You're an exceptionally thoughtless man, Thomas. Haven't you considered the consequences that can follow for you?

DR. STOCKMANN. Consequences? For me?

MAYOR STOCKMANN. For you and your family as well.

DR. STOCKMANN. What the devil does *that* mean?

MAYOR STOCKMANN. I think, over the years, I've proved a helpful and accommodating brother to you.

DR. STOCKMANN. Yes, you have, and I'm thankful to you for that.

MAYOR STOCKMANN. I'm not after thanks. Because, in part, I was forced into it—for my own sake. I always hoped I could keep you in check somewhat if I helped better your economic status.

5. **imperative** (im per′ ə tiv) *adj.* absolutely necessary; urgent.

Vocabulary
impending (im pend′ iŋ) *adj.* about to happen

Literary Analysis
Themes What situations in modern life does Peter's suggestion call to mind?

Literary Analysis
Themes Which details of this scene emphasize the universal theme of "brother against brother"?

11 **Reading Check**
What does the mayor wish to do about Dr. Stockmann's discovery?

Differentiated Instruction for Universal Access

EL Pronunciation for English Learners

Some students might have difficulty with the /i/ sound that appears in the words *it's*, *impending*, *is*, and *direct*. To help them, write several other /i/ words on the board, such as *in*, *swim*, and *sit*. Then, pronounce each word in turn, calling on the students to repeat each pronunciation. Pair English learners with fluent speakers, and give the fluent speakers the task of assisting English learners in successfully discriminating the words given. If the English learner errs, ask the "peer tutor" to pronounce each word carefully, guiding the English learner to the correct answer.

9 Literary Analysis

Themes

1. Have a student read the bracketed passage aloud while others read along silently.
2. **Ask** students to describe the mayor's attitude toward the situation.
   Answer: The mayor is determined to keep the information a secret and to address the problem only in a hidden way later on.
3. **Ask** the first Literary Analysis question: What situations in modern life does Peter's suggestion call to mind?
   Possible responses: Students may cite politicians covering up damaging information, athletes denying that they have taken steroids, or government officials releasing only portions of records.

10 Literary Analysis

Themes

1. Have one student read the part of Dr. Stockmann and another student read the part of Mayor Stockmann while the rest of the class reads along silently.
2. Then, **ask** students why they think the playwright chooses to make the two characters brothers.
   Answer: Having two brothers disagreeing over a critical issue adds tension because brothers typically know each other well, and their roles in the family further complicate professional relationships outside the family.
3. **Ask** the second Literary Analysis question: Which details of this scene emphasize the universal theme of "brother against brother"?
   Answer: Details include the doctor calling his brother by an affectionate term; the mayor pointing out that there will be consequences for his brother's family; the mayor saying he has been helpful to the doctor; the doctor being shocked by his brother's suggestions; and the mayor talking down to the doctor.

11 Reading Check

Answer: The mayor wishes to keep the information a secret.

12 Connecting to the Big Question

1. Remind students that the doctor and the mayor are brothers, with long-standing knowledge of each other, as well as professionals with particular responsibilities.
   Ask: Why does Dr. Stockmann say he has acted to reveal the problem?
   Answer: The doctor says that he acted out of concern for public health.
2. **Ask** what the mayor says is the reason for his brother's actions.
   Answer: The mayor claims that his brother is raising a fuss simply because he acts impulsively.
3. Finally, **ask** students which explanation they think is closer to the truth.
   Possible responses: Students may say that the doctor seems more credible since he has scientific reasons for his position. Some may say that the mayor seems interested only in protecting his own position, which makes him less believable.

   Tell students to think about how the characters' personal and professional experiences have affected the situation they are now in.

13 Critical Viewing

Possible response: Students may say that the doctor would be concerned first about his children's health, but that the economic threat that the mayor raises would also cause him to worry about their economic future.

DR. STOCKMANN. What? Just for your own sake—!

MAYOR STOCKMANN. In part, I said. It's embarrassing for a public servant when his closest relative goes and compromises himself again and again.

DR. STOCKMANN. And that's what you think I do?

12 **MAYOR STOCKMANN.** Yes, unfortunately you do, without your knowing it. You have a restless, unruly, combative nature. And then this unhappy knack[6] of bursting into print on all kinds of likely and unlikely subjects. You're no sooner struck by an idea than right away you have to scribble a newspaper article on it, or a whole pamphlet even.

DR. STOCKMANN. Well, but isn't it a citizen's duty to inform the public if he comes on a new idea?

MAYOR STOCKMANN. Oh, the public doesn't need new ideas. The public is served best by the good, old, time-tested ideas it's always had.

DR. STOCKMANN. That's putting it plainly!

MAYOR STOCKMANN. I have to talk to you plainly for once. Up till now I've always tried to avoid that because I know how irritable you are; but now I'm telling you the truth, Thomas. You have no conception how much you injure yourself with your **impetuosity.** You complain about the authorities and, yes, the government; you rail against them—and insist you're being passed over and persecuted. But what can you expect—someone as troublesome as you.

DR. STOCKMANN. Ah—so I'm troublesome, too?

MAYOR STOCKMANN. Yes, Thomas, you're a very troublesome man to work with. I know from experience. You show no consideration at all. You seem to forget completely that I'm the one you can thank for your post here as staff physician at the baths—

DR. STOCKMANN. I was the inevitable[7] choice—I and nobody else! I was the

Vocabulary
impetuosity (im pech´ o͞o äs´ i tē) *n.* sudden action with little thought

13 ▼ **Critical Viewing** How might concern for his children, one of whom is shown here, affect Dr. Stockmann's handling of his conflict with the town? Why? **[Speculate]**

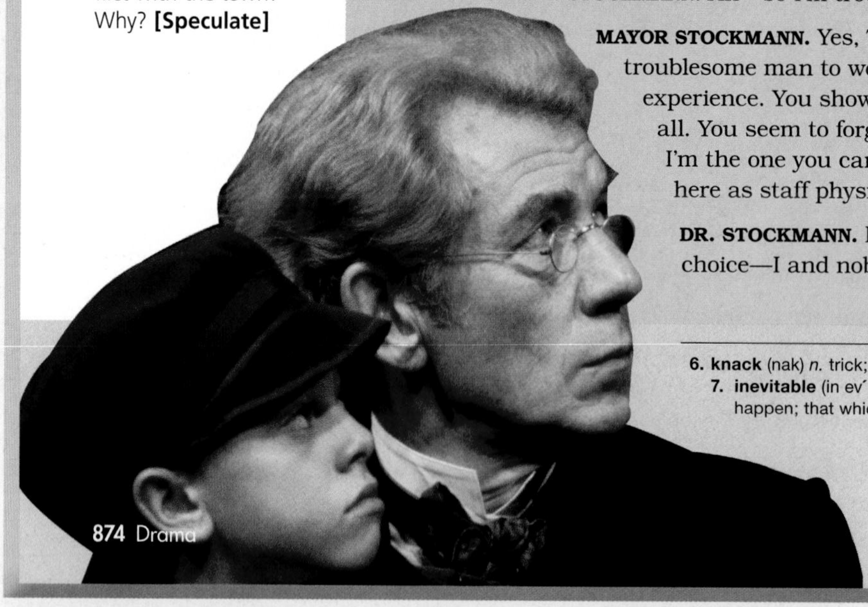

6. **knack** (nak) *n.* trick; particular skill.
7. **inevitable** (in ev´ i tə bəl) *adj.* certain to happen; that which cannot be avoided.

Think Aloud

Vocabulary: Using Context
Model the way to define unfamiliar words by using context with this "think aloud." Say to students:

> I'm going to show you how I use context to understand the meaning of the unfamiliar word *bungled* in the doctor's first full speech on p. 875. I know that the doctor thinks that the idea of building a spa is a good one, because he says in the speech at the top of this page that it was his idea. I know, too, that he thinks there is a serious problem with the spa now because of the water pollution. He clearly thinks that the *way* the spa plan was carried out is the source of the problem. From these clues, I can see that *bungled* means to "make mistakes when doing something." The mayor and his allies bungled because they made a plan that caused problems.

first to see that this town could become a flourishing spa;[8] and I was the *only* one who could see it then. I stood alone fighting for that idea for years; and I wrote and wrote—

MAYOR STOCKMANN. Unquestionably. But the right moment hadn't arrived yet. Of course you couldn't judge that from up there in the wilds. But when the opportune time came, and I—and a few others—took the matter in hand—

DR. STOCKMANN. Yes, and bungled the whole magnificent plan. Oh yes, it's really coming out now what a brilliant crew you've been!

MAYOR STOCKMANN. All that's coming out, to my mind, is your usual hunger for a good fight. You want to attack your superiors—it's your old pattern. You can't stand any authority over you; you resent anyone in a higher position and regard him as a personal enemy—and then one weapon's as good as another to use. But now I've acquainted you with the vital interests at stake here for this whole town—and, naturally, for me as well. And so I'm warning you, Thomas, I'll be adamant about the demand I am going to make of you.

Vocabulary
adamant (ad′ ə mənt) *adj.* firm

DR. STOCKMANN. What demand?

14 **MAYOR STOCKMANN.** Since you've been so indiscreet as to discuss this delicate issue with outsiders, even though it should have been kept secret among the directors, it of course can't be hushed up now. All kinds of rumors will go flying around, and the maliciously inclined will dress them up with trimmings of their own. It'll therefore be necessary that you publicly deny these rumors.

Literary Analysis
Themes What ideas about rumors lead to Dr. Stockmann's new predicament?

DR. STOCKMANN. I! How? I don't understand.

MAYOR STOCKMANN. We can expect that, after further investigation, you'll arrive at the conclusion that things are far from being as critical or dangerous as you'd first imagined.

DR. STOCKMANN. Ah—you expect that!

MAYOR STOCKMANN. Moreover, we expect that you'll support and publicly affirm your confidence in the present directors to take thorough and conscientious measures, as necessary, to remedy any possible defects.

15 **Reading Check**
What does the mayor tell Dr. Stockmann he must do?

DR. STOCKMANN. But that's utterly out of the question for me, as long as they try to get by with patchwork. I'm telling you that, Peter; and it's my unqualified opinion—!

---

8. **spa** (spä) *n.* health resort where people drink and bathe in mineral waters.

14 Literary Analysis

Themes

1. Have students read the bracketed passage. **Ask** them to define the word *rumor*.
   Answer: A rumor is information alleged to be true without supporting evidence.
2. **Ask** students how rumors change as they spread and what effect those changes have on people.
   Possible responses: The rumored information often becomes more and more exaggerated. The people about whom the rumors circulate are often viewed more negatively as the rumors get worse and worse.
3. Finally, **ask** students the Literary Analysis question: What ideas about rumors lead to Dr. Stockmann's new predicament?
   Possible responses: Students may say that if the rumors worsen, the public might panic about the spa. Alternatively, if rumors arise that the charges about the spa are false, the doctor might be singled out for attacks since he originated the charges.

15 Reading Check

Answer: The mayor tells the doctor he must deny that the baths are contaminated.

Differentiated Instruction for Universal Access

Strategy for Less Proficient Readers
Students may have an easier time understanding the scene if they read it aloud, either in small groups or with partners. If necessary, students can trade or alternate roles so that everyone has a chance to read and listen. At the end of each page, have students summarize what they have read, making sure they can explain the positions of the two brothers.

Enrichment for Gifted/Talented Students
Students may enjoy acting out this scene for their classmates. Have two students who are interested in acting choose which roles to play. Encourage students to use costumes and props to make their scenes more memorable.

MAYOR STOCKMANN. As a member of the staff, you're not entitled to any personal opinions.

DR. STOCKMANN. (*stunned*). Not entitled—?

MAYOR STOCKMANN. As a staff member, I said. As a private person—why, that's another matter. But as a subordinate official at the baths, you're not entitled to express any opinions that contradict your superiors.

Literary Analysis
Themes Why might the idea of obedience to authority be universal?

DR. STOCKMANN. That's going too far! I, as a doctor, a man of science, aren't entitled to—!

16 **MAYOR STOCKMANN.** What's involved here isn't a purely scientific problem. It's a mixture of both technical and economic considerations.

DR. STOCKMANN. I don't care what . . . it is! I want the freedom to express myself on any problem under the sun!

MAYOR STOCKMANN. Anything you like—except for the baths. We forbid you that.

DR. STOCKMANN (*shouting*). You forbid—! You! A crowd of—!

MAYOR STOCKMANN. *I* forbid it—*I*, your supervisor. And when I forbid you, then you obey.

Critical Thinking

1. **Respond:** Do you sympathize at all with Mayor Stockmann? Explain.
2. **(a)** What problem does Dr. Stockmann report to his brother? **(b) Connect:** What solution does he propose?
3. **(a)** What information does the mayor acquire from an engineer about the proposed solution? **(b) Infer:** What effect does this information have on his reaction?
4. **(a) Draw Conclusions:** What is the mayor's main goal with regard to the problem? Explain. **(b) Connect:** What is the mayor willing to sacrifice to achieve this goal? **(c) Make a Judgment:** Is he being realistic or immoral? Explain.

THE BIG ? **To what extent does experience determine what we perceive?** Do you think this conversation will change Dr. Stockmann's perception of the Mayor as both a brother and a leader? Explain your answer.

16 Literary Analysis

Themes

1. **Ask** the Literary Analysis question: Why might the idea of obedience to authority be universal?
   Possible response: Most cultures develop a system of authority in family, work, and government to solve problems and provide for the welfare of people. For such a system to work, some people must lead and others must follow.

Concept Connector

Have students compare their responses to Writing About the Big Question and the **Anticipation Guides** from before reading the selection to their ideas afterwards.

ASSESS

Answers

Critical Thinking

1. **Possible response:** Students may say no, because Mayor Stockmann is willing to jeopardize people's health in order to preserve the town's economic growth and his position as mayor.
2. (a) The health baths in the town are contaminated. (b) The doctor proposes to close down the baths and rebuild the sewer and water supply systems.
3. (a) He gets an estimate of its costs and construction time. (b) This information convinces the mayor not to reveal the problem because it would hurt the town economically.
4. (a) The mayor wants to keep the problem quiet because closing the baths will destroy the town's chances of competing with neighboring towns to become a major health resort. (b) He is willing to sacrifice the health of bathers. (c) Students may say he is immoral because he is placing personal gain above his responsibility for safeguarding the public's health.

THE BIG ? **To what extent does experience determine what we perceive?**

Possible response: Students may say that the doctor will leave the conversation ashamed at or appalled by his brother's views.

Vocabulary Development

Vocabulary Knowledge Rating

When students have completed reading and discussion of this excerpt from *An Enemy of the People*, have them take out their **Vocabulary Knowledge Rating Chart** for this selection. Read the words aloud once more, and have students rate their knowledge of the words again in the After Reading column. Clarify any words that are still problematic. Have students write their own definition and example or sentence in the appropriate column. Then, have students complete the Vocabulary Practice activities on the next page. Encourage students to use the words in further discussion and written work about this selection. Remind them that they will be accountable for these words on the **Selection Test** (*Unit 5 Resources*, pp. 76–78 or 79–81).

After You Read

Antigone • *from* An Enemy of the People

Comparing Universal and Culturally Specific Themes

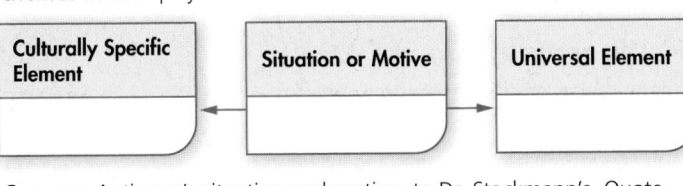

1. **(a)** Use a chart like the one shown to analyze both universal and culturally specific elements of Dr. Stockmann's situation in *An Enemy of the People.* **(b)** Complete another chart like the one shown, using details from Antigone's speech in *Antigone,* Scene 2, lines 65–84. **(c)** Referring to your charts, draw a conclusion about the universal **themes** in each play.

Culturally Specific Element	Situation or Motive	Universal Element

2. Compare Antigone's situation and motives to Dr. Stockmann's. Quote from both plays to support your ideas.
3. **(a)** Review Creon's speech in *Antigone,* Scene 1, lines 8–53, and describe his situation and attitude. **(b)** Compare Creon's reasoning with Mayor Stockmann's, quoting from both plays in support of your answer.
4. To what extent do you think Antigone and Dr. Stockmann act out of pride in their own virtue? Explain.

Writing to Compare Themes

In an essay, discuss whether or not *Antigone* and *An Enemy of the People* express the same universal theme. Use these questions to get started:

- What are the culturally specific elements in each work?
- What universal ideas does each play suggest?
- How would you state the general problem in each play?
- Which side are you on?

Vocabulary

Practice For each item, write a sentence in which you use the word pair correctly.

1. impending; worry
2. adamant; argue
3. exorbitant; budget
4. impetuosity; regret

ASSESS/EXTEND

Answers

Comparing Universal and Culturally Specific Themes

1. **Sample answers:** (a) *Specific:* the public's right to know; *Motive:* Mayor Stockmann wants to keep the pollution secret for economic reasons; *Universal:* public good versus individual desires (b) *Specific:* traitors remain unburied; *Motive:* Antigone must bury her brother for loyalty and religious reasons; *Universal:* divine law versus human law
(c) **Possible responses:** Students may say that both plays address the issue of the conflict between individual moral conscience and the demands of authority or the community as a whole.
Other sample answers appear in ***Graphic Organizer Transparencies,*** **Comparing Universal and Culturally Specific Themes Graphic Organizer A,** p. 163, and in the **Additional Answers** section.
2. Both Antigone and Dr. Stockmann struggle with a family member with greater legal authority. Both characters believe they are acting for a greater good.
3. (a) Creon decides to punish the betrayal of Polyneices by forbidding his burial. He believes he is acting in the best interest of the State. (b) Each man understands himself to be the moral and legal authority for his community.
4. Antigone's proud loyalty to her brother blinds her to consequences. Dr. Stockmann's pride in his scientific knowledge overrides any compromise.

Writing to Compare Themes

1. Review the assignment criteria with students.
2. As they draft, have students refer to their completed **Comparing Universal and Culturally Specific Themes Graphic Organizers** or to the chart in item 1, above.

Six Traits Focus

✓	Ideas		Word Choice
✓	Organization		Sentence Fluency
	Voice		Conventions

Assessment Resources

Unit 5 Resources

L1 L2 EL **Selection Test A,** pp. 76–78
L3 L4 **Selection Test B,** pp. 79–81
L3 L4 **Open-Book Test,** pp. 73–75

PHLit Online! All assessment resources are available at **www.PHLitOnline.com.**

Vocabulary

Sample answers:

1. The impending decision from the jury caused both sides to worry about how the outcome would affect them.
2. The senator was adamant when he argued that the bill was a bad idea.
3. An exorbitant rise in gas prices strained the family's budget.
4. Seeing his friend's sad face, he could only regret the impetuosity of his remark.

PREACH

Meeting Your Standards

Students will

1. write a reflective essay.
2. use writing strategies to generate ideas and to plan, organize, evaluate, and revise the essay.
3. find an effective idea for the essay.
4. apply grammar skills.

Introducing the Writing Assignment

Review the assignment and the criteria, using the instruction on the student page.

Connecting to Real-Life Writing

Point out to students that reflective essay writing is often incorporated into other types of writing. For example, an application to college or for a scholarship often requires reflective writing.

Writing Workshop

Work in Progress

If students have done the Work-in-Progress assignments on pp. 835 and 861, suggest that they examine their recorded ideas as they begin prewriting. They may wish to develop these ideas in a reflective essay.

Prewriting Strategies

1. Introduce the prewriting strategies, using the instruction on the student page.
2. Have students apply the strategies to generate sensory details.

Six Traits Focus

✔	Ideas	✔	Word Choice
	Organization		Sentence Fluency
	Voice		Conventions

Writing Workshop

Narration: Reflective Essay

Defining the Form A **reflective essay** describes a personal experience, memory, object, or idea and explains why and how it is significant. You might use elements of the reflective essay in journals, responses to literature, autobiographical narratives, and travel reports.

Assignment Write a reflective essay that describes a personal experience and explains its special meaning for you. Include these elements:

✔ an *insight* or *observation* about life based on your personal experience

✔ a *thorough explanation* of the events that inspire this insight

✔ a *logical organization* that balances past events and your present understanding

✔ use of *sensory details and images* to describe scenes and incidents

✔ error-free grammar, especially the use of *verbal phrases to vary sentence lengths*

To preview the criteria on which your reflective essay may be judged, see the rubric on page 883.

Writing Workshop: *Work in Progress*

Review the work you did on pages 835 and 861.

Prewriting Strategy

Gather sensory details. Create a list of words and phrases that both describe your experience and appeal to the senses of sight, hearing, touch, taste, and smell. Include words that spark clear, vivid pictures of the setting, people, and events. Identify a strong image that captures a key part of your central insight. Use a chart like this one to record sensory details.

Apply It!

	Detail	Detail
Sight:	snowy trails through dark trees	
Hearing:	lonesome sound of birds in woods	
Smell:	scent of pines	
Touch:	the velvety feel of wet snow falling on my face	
Taste:	the warm, rich taste of double hot chocolate	

Teaching Resources

The following resources can be used to enrich or extend the instruction.

All *Unit 5 Resources*
Writing Workshop, pp. 82–83

All *Professional Development Guidebook*
Rubric for Self-Assessment: Reflective Essay, pp. 222–223

All *Graphic Organizer Transparencies*
Rubric for Self-Assessment: Reflective Essay, p. 165

PHLit Online! All resources are available at **www.PHLitOnline.com.**

SIX TRAITS WRITER'S TOOLBOX SIX TRAITS

Ideas | Conventions | Sentence Fluency | Voice | Organization | Word Choice

Finding an Effective Idea

Finding the right **idea** for your reflective essay is the most important task. When searching for the right idea, remember that a reflective essay must include a dramatic incident from your past that influenced your beliefs or way of thinking, and/or your future behavior. Your essay must include a clear and vivid description of the event, as well as a reflection about the meaning of that event and how it influenced you.

Thinking About the Past Think about events or experiences from your past and ask yourself why you find them memorable. You might look in journals, scrapbooks, or photo albums to refresh your memories about your past. Choose an event from your early childhood that you still find vivid, or choose a more recent event. Whatever the time period in which the event occurred, it should have made a lasting impression on you.

Considering the Significance Not only must the idea or event you choose be significant, but you must have also learned an important lesson from it. The lesson should hold the reader's interest. For example, if you choose an event in which you and a friend were lost in the woods and later found by the authorities, you may have learned not to go into unfamiliar areas alone or without a guide. While this is an important lesson, it is one that almost anyone would take away from that experience. However, if you and your friend were lost in the woods, and the two of you worked together to escape, giving each other courage and hope, you might have learned not to go into unfamiliar areas as well as the value of friendship and the importance of working together.

Refining Your Idea As you consider events from your past, jot them down in a chart like the one below. Also, include the lessons you took from the event. Then, choose the event that has had the most significance and has taught you an uncommon lesson.

Apply It!

How Old Was I?	What Happened/Where?	What Did I Learn?

WG *Prentice Hall Writing and Grammar Connection: Chapter 4, Section 2*

Differentiated Instruction for Universal Access

Strategy for Special Needs Students

If students have difficulty thinking of topics, use the following questions to help them generate ideas:

- What are the greatest challenges you've faced?
- What have you done that you are truly proud of?
- What have you done or experienced that might inspire others?
- What events in your life have surprised you, changed you, or caused you to see the world differently?
- What are your most cherished memories?
- What anecdotes do you most enjoy telling people?

Finding an Effective Idea

1. Introduce the writing skill, using the instruction on the student page.
2. Discuss the examples and strategies for finding an effective idea.

Teaching the Writing Skill

1. Ask students to make three-column charts like the one in the student text, and brainstorm for some ideas on their own.
2. Assign students to small groups. Have them share and discuss ideas within their groups. Challenge them to think of new ideas together.
3. Once students have generated lists of ideas, have them advise each other on which idea is best. Students can choose whether or not to take their peers' advice.
4. Remind students to choose lessons that are not obvious. Point out that a reflective essay should give readers an opportunity to reflect on their own lives in a new way.
5. Have students work with partners and share the events they've chosen. Partners should ask questions that help clarify ideas.
6. After talking to their partners, have students write notes about the most important aspects of their reflections and the aspects most in need of clarification.
7. Have students switch partners and tell their stories and reflections again, trying to clarify the points that were unclear the first time. Partners should ask questions as before, and students should take notes after they are finished.

OES Online Essay Scorer

A writing prompt for this mode of writing can be found on the *PH Essay Scorer* at www.PHLitOnline.com.

Writing and Grammar Interactive Textbook Online

Students can use the following tools at **www.pearsonsuccessnet.com** as they complete their reflective essays:

- Sensory Word Bin
- Language Variety Revision Checker

Drafting Strategies

1. Introduce the drafting strategies, using the instruction on the student page.
2. Have students apply the strategies as they draft.

Teaching the Strategies

1. Have students make outlines using both types of organization; then, have them choose the one that works best.
2. Have students list similes, metaphors, and personification ideas to include in their essays.

Think Aloud: Model Adding Figurative Language

Model how to generate figurative language. Say to students:

> Let's say I have the sentence "The sun was bright." I need to revise for vividness, so I'll add personification. First, I ask myself, "How did the sun make me feel?" It made me happy. Then, I ask "Who makes me happy in a similar way?" I think of a smiling baby. I can write my personification as a simile: "The sun was as bright as a smiling baby."

Six Traits Focus

✔	Ideas	✔	Word Choice
✔	Organization		Sentence Fluency
	Voice		Conventions

Writing and Grammar, Grade 10

Students will find additional instruction on drafting for a reflective essay in Chapter 4, Section 3.

Revising Strategies

1. Introduce the revising strategies, using the instruction on the student page.
2. Have students apply the strategies as they review their drafts.

Teaching the Strategies

Have partners read each other's essays to identify vague words and superfluous details.

Six Traits Focus

✔	Ideas	✔	Word Choice
	Organization		Sentence Fluency
✔	Voice		Conventions

Writing and Grammar, Grade 10

Students will find additional instruction on revising for a reflective essay in Chapter 4, Section 4.

Drafting Strategies

Choose a logical organization. Balance the description of events from the past with your present thoughts. Consider using *chronological order* to describe the events in sequence. Alternatively, consider using *order of importance organization* to interweave descriptions of the most memorable parts of the event.

Chronological Order	Order of Importance
Introduction Setting and first event: what happened Next events: what happened **Conclusion:** Explanation of overall insight gained through this experience	**Introduction** Setting: why it is meaningful Each event: why each one is meaningful Most important moment: why it is critical **Conclusion:** Explanation of overall insight gained

Use effective imagery. Use sensory images to create word pictures.

- A **simile** compares two unlike things using the words *like* or *as*. (My eyes were as wide as saucers.)
- A **metaphor** compares two unlike things by stating that one thing *is* the other. (Suddenly, a herd of children stampeded down the stairs.)
- **Personification** applies human qualities or behavior to something nonhuman. (Disappointment grabbed me and would not let go.)

Revising Strategies

Revise for unity. Reread your draft and highlight any sentences that do not support your overall meaning. Cut or rewrite those sentences.

Revise to replace vague words. Review your essay, circling vague words. Consider more precise replacements that will reinforce your idea. Use a chart like this one to identify and replace vague words and phrases.

Apply It!

Vague	Precise
It was one of the *best things* I had ever seen.	It was one of the *most colorful packages* I had ever seen.
It was very cold.	My breath made frosty clouds in the bitter cold.

Understanding by Design

Clarifying Expected Outcomes: Using Rubrics

- Before students begin working on this assignment, have them preview the Rubric for Self-Assessment (p. 883) to learn what qualities their reflective essays must have. A copy of this rubric appears in ***Graphic Organizer Transparencies,*** p. 165.
- Review the criteria in the rubric with the class. Before students use the rubric to assess their writing, work with them to rate the Student Model (p. 882) using the rubric.
- If you wish to assess students' reflective essays with either a 4-point or a 6-point scoring rubric, see ***Professional Development Guidebook,*** pp. 222–223.

WRITER'S TOOLBOX

Sentence Fluency | Voice | Organization | Word Choice | Ideas | Conventions

Revising to Combine Sentences With Verbal Phrases

The repetition of too many sentences with the same structure can create choppy, uninteresting writing. Use verbal phrases to combine a series of short choppy sentences into longer, more flowing ones.

Identifying Verbal Phrases Verbal phrases use verbs and act as nouns, adjectives, or adverbs.

The Three Types of Verbal Phrases

Participial Phrase	Gerund Phrase	Infinitive Phrase
a participle — a form of a verb that can act as an **adjective** — and its modifiers	a gerund — a verb ending in *-ing* that functions as a **noun** — and its modifiers	an infinitive — a form of verb that appears with the word *to* and acts as a **noun, adjective,** or **adverb** — and its modifiers
Walking by *herself,* Sara felt peaceful. *(modifies Sara)*	*Speaking in public* is scary. *(acts as subject)*	Her advice was *to start small. (acts as predicate nominative)*

A verbal phrase should be close to the word it modifies.

Misplaced: *Eating fish,* the scientists saw a baby seal.

Correct: The scientists saw a baby seal *eating fish.*

WG *Prentice Hall Writing and Grammar Connection: Chapter 20, Section 1*

Combining Sentences Using Verbal Phrases Use verbal phrases to combine choppy sentences. Follow these steps:

1. **Express the ideas from a short sentence as a verbal phrase.**
2. **Insert the phrase into a new sentence, locating it near the word or words being modified.**
3. **Punctuate the new sentence correctly.** Look at this example:

   Choppy sentences: The cheetah moves silently. It stalks its prey.

   Combined sentence: Stalking its prey, the cheetah moves silently.

Grammar in Your Writing

Review the last four paragraphs of your essay. Look for short sentences that might be combined using participial, gerund, or infinitive phrases. Avoid misplaced modifiers by placing phrases in your combined sentences as close as possible to the words they modify.

Strategies for Using Technology in Writing

If students are using word-processing software, suggest that they use the comments feature to include notes about sentences that could be improved by adding figurative language, sentences that could be combined using verbal phrases, or sentences that should be eliminated. Students can highlight each sentence in question, then write a note about how it could be improved. This will allow students to think about improvements without altering the original sentences.

Revising to Combine Sentences With Verbal Phrases

1. Introduce the grammar skill, using the instruction on the student page.
2. Discuss the examples and strategies for combining sentences.
3. Have students follow the instruction under Grammar in Your Writing to correct errors in their drafts.

Teaching the Grammar Skill

1. Assign small groups. Give them a list of the following sentences and have them work together to identify the type of verbal phrase in each:
   - <u>Swimming in the ocean</u> is my favorite summer activity. **Answer:** gerund phrase
   - <u>Floating on my back</u>, I stare up at the sky. **Answer:** participial phrase
   - It's <u>fun to build sand castles</u>, too. **Answer:** infinitive phrase
2. Have each group write ten sentences using all three phrase types. Then, have groups exchange papers and identify one another's phrases.
3. Provide the following choppy sentences and have groups combine them using verbal phrases:
   - We walked to school. We jumped in puddles. **Possible response:** Walking to school, we jumped in puddles. (participial phrase)
   - I like to run. It is my favorite exercise. **Possible response:** Running is my favorite exercise. (gerund phrase)
   - I drink water. It's important. **Possible response:** It is important to drink water. (infinitive phrase)
4. Ask students to check their papers for sentences that can be combined using verbal phrases.

WG **Writing and Grammar, Grade 10**

Students will find additional instruction on sentence combining in Chapter 21, Section 2.

Student Model

Review the Student Model with the class, using the annotations to analyze the writer's effective use of the elements of a reflective essay.

Teaching From the Student Model

1. Explain that the student model is a sample and that students' own reflective essays may be longer.
2. Note that the writer presents the events in this essay in chronological order, starting with how she received the gift that led to her insight. **Ask** students to identify the wording the writer uses to signal readers that her perspective changes.
   Answer: "I began to look at the dollhouse in a new light."
3. Point out that the writer's insight is relevant to her readers, giving us an opportunity to reflect on it and apply it to our own lives. Ask a few volunteers to discuss their reactions to her insight.
4. Ask students to circle the details that bring the student model to life and engage readers.
5. Have students read the first paragraph and notice the verbal phrase used to combine two sentences ("glowing with pleasure"). **Ask** students to identify other passages where the writer uses verbal phrases to combine sentences.
   Possible response: In the fourth paragraph, the writer uses "hoping my eyes did not reveal . . ." as a verbal phrase combining two sentences.

Connecting to Real-Life Writing

Point out that journalists and writers create reflective pieces for newspapers, magazines, Web sites, and books. Artists also write reflective artist statements.

In addition, nearly everyone is required to do reflective writing when applying for colleges, scholarships, or jobs. Discuss with students why employers and admissions reviewers might require reflective writing in their applications. Have a few volunteers share what they might write about if they were applying to college now.

Student Model: Samantha Duffy, Santa Clarita, CA

The Dollhouse

I was sitting on my couch eating chocolate chip ice cream when the front door was flung open. Suddenly, a huge colorfully wrapped box with a giant red bow appeared. The only other thing I could see was the strong hands of a man gripping the box tightly. He placed it carefully on the table in front of me.

> The essay focuses on Samantha's personal experience.

My father, glowing with pleasure, emerged from behind the box and said, "My daughter deserves the best present that money can buy for her birthday, and here it is. Go on, open it. What are you waiting for?"

I stood up and ripped the shiny paper from the box, but I could not help but stare when I saw what the paper had been hiding.

"Thank you, Daddy, it's truly beautiful," I said, hoping my eyes did not reveal the confusion I felt as I looked at the item.

In front of me was a delicately handcrafted dollhouse, and inside was a family of tiny porcelain dolls. The furniture in the dollhouse looked real, except that it had no flaws. There were pretty paintings on the wall and little glass chandeliers. It was amazing how peaceful and perfect the family inside appeared.

> Samantha orders events sequentially.

It would have been a terrific birthday present except for one thing: The magical miniature world was enclosed in a glass case. My father brought it up to my bedroom and warned me never to touch the glass for fear I would destroy its perfection. The dollhouse was there for me to admire but never to touch or play with.

> She clearly sets events in a specific place and time of her life.

The dollhouse sat in the same place for many years. I obeyed my father and never touched it. At first, I was intrigued by this beautiful world and did as I was supposed to: I admired it. Time passed, though, and I started to find it boring and useless. I began to look at the dollhouse in a new light. Those pretty porcelain dolls had no expression. They would never experience life or feel the way real people do because in that perfect world there was no emotion.

> Samantha shares the insight she gained through reflection.

On my eighth birthday, I received a gift that taught me a lot about what I want out of life: Many times I had imagined myself in that house, never being able to interact with the outside world. I do not think I could stand to be so closed off. I would much rather be a part of the world and feel and see everything possible. The dollhouse made me realize that as long as I opened myself up to the world, I would never be lonely. But if I shut the world out of my life, like one of those porcelain perfections, then I would be completely by myself.

> Samantha includes a truth about life that she learned through personal experience.

882 Drama

Strategies for Test Taking

A writing prompt on a standardized test may assess students' ability to write an essay. Explain that one aspect of this assessment is staying focused on the topic. Recommend that students first identify their topics so that they can focus their planning and writing efforts around them. Remind students that when they review their drafts, they should consider eliminating details that do not directly contribute to their topics. Have students assess the student model with this in mind, checking each paragraph for its main idea.

Editing and Proofreading

Check your draft for errors in spelling, grammar, and punctuation.

Focus on Punctuation: Check that you have used commas correctly throughout your essay. Read the essay aloud and notice where you pause naturally. Consider whether or not these pauses need to be punctuated with commas.

Publishing and Presenting

Consider one of the following ways to share your writing with classmates:

Publish electronically. Share your essay by uploading it onto a classroom computer or Web site. Ask readers to post their reactions online. Then, share your favorite responses with the class.

Give a reading. Practice reading your essay aloud to yourself. Emphasize specific emotions or ideas by varying the speed and volume of your reading. Mark your draft to indicate these changes. Then, read your essay aloud to your class, making use of your notes.

WG *Prentice Hall Writing and Grammar Connection: Chapter 4*

Reflecting on Your Writing

Writer's Journal Jot down your answers to this question:

How did writing about the topic help you discover its importance?

Rubric for Self-Assessment

Find evidence in your writing to address each category. Then, use the rating scale to grade your work.

Criteria	Rating Scale (not very — very)
Focus: How clearly do you connect the events with your insight?	1 2 3 4 5
Organization: How easy is it for readers to follow your interweaving of past events with your present understanding?	1 2 3 4 5
Support/Elaboration: How thorough is your description of events and ideas?	1 2 3 4 5
Style: How effectively do you use details to describe scenes and incidents?	1 2 3 4 5
Conventions: How correct is your grammar, especially your use of verbals to vary sentence length?	1 2 3 4 5
Ideas: How significant is the event and the lesson you learned from it?	1 2 3 4 5

Editing and Proofreading

1. Introduce the editing and proofreading focus, using the instruction on the student page.
2. Have students edit and proofread their reflective essays, correcting grammar, spelling, punctuation, and word choice. Make sure they check for errors of the type noted on the student page.

Teaching the Editing Focus

1. Have students quietly read their essays aloud to themselves, noting pauses and checking if they require commas.
2. Assign partners to read each other's essays aloud. Listeners should note if their essays are not read as they intended, or if the readers become confused or out of breath.

Six Traits Focus

	Ideas		Word Choice
	Organization		Sentence Fluency
	Voice	✓	Conventions

ASSESS

Publishing and Presenting

1. Review how to give and receive constructive feedback. Ask students to give feedback on both content and execution.
2. Have students identify other audiences for a reading, such as friends or younger students, and discuss how they might alter their readings to match their audiences.

Reflecting on Your Writing

Have students consider what element of their writing required the most revision. Ask students what they could do differently next time to avoid major rewriting.

WG **Writing and Grammar, Grade 10**

Students will find additional guidance for editing and proofreading, publishing and presenting, and reflecting on a reflective essay in Chapter 4, Sections 5 and 6.

Background

Shakespeare's Globe Theater

Most of Shakespeare's plays were performed at the Globe theater, built by Richard and Cuthbert Burbage.

The Globe was small enough for actors' voices to reach the whole audience but large enough to hold several thousand people. The common people clamored to see actors perform at the Globe and other theaters. Actors enjoyed reputations somewhat like those of modern rock stars: not quite respectable but very much in demand. The elite looked down on actors but came to the theater hoping to be seen by the rest of the audience.

The experience of watching a play at the Globe was different in many ways from going to the theater today. Renaissance technology allowed only a limited number of homemade sound effects. Scenery was confined to the barest necessary pieces of furniture. The Globe could be lit only by daylight, as torches would have been dangerous in a wooden building with a thatched roof. Indications of light, sound, and setting were often written into the script. For example, at the beginning of a scene in *Macbeth*, a character looks around and remarks, "This castle hath a pleasant seat," thus informing the audience where the scene takes place.

The Globe burned to the ground in 1613, when a cannon fired during a performance of Shakespeare's *Henry VIII* set the theater's thatched roof on fire. A Londoner named Sir Henry Wooton wrote the following letter to his nephew, describing the fire that destroyed the Globe: "The King's players had a new play . . . representing some principal pieces of the reign of Henry VIII, which was set forth with many extraordinary circumstances of pomp and majesty. . . . Now, King Henry making a masque at the Cardinal Wolsey's house, and certain chambers being shot off at his entry, some of the paper . . . did light on the thatch . . . consuming within less than an hour the whole house to the very ground. . . . " The theater was rebuilt, and the foundations of the second Globe theater were discovered in 1990.

THE SHAKESPEAREAN THEATER

The Birth of Modern Theater

In Shakespeare's day, London was already a bustling city. Ships swept up and down the Thames River to dock in London and fuel the city with trade. Nearly 200,000 people crowded into London, making it the largest city in Europe. Reeking of garbage, ringing with street vendors' cries, Shakespeare's London was packed with danger and opportunity. In this stew of excitement, the first modern theaters were born.

The Globe Before the 1570s, Londoners had turned to traveling acting companies for entertainment. City officials, afraid of public unruliness, riots, and moral corruption, frequently cracked down on public performances. In 1576, an actor named James Burbage built the first public theater, north of the city. Other theaters followed. In 1599, Shakespeare's company built the Globe theater in Southwark, a neighorhood south of London.

Most of Shakespeare's plays were performed at the Globe, which was built around a roofless courtyard. The sun provided the only lighting; performances were given only during the day. Surrounding the courtyard were three levels of galleries with benches where wealthier playgoers sat. For only a penny, though, a person could stand in the courtyard, called the pit, and watch the performance.

Popcorn and Pickpockets Audiences were boisterous, cheering and booing loudly. Hazelnuts were Elizabethan "popcorn"; people munched on them all during a performance. Pickpockets were a constant danger, and fistfights occasionally broke out. Built to hold between 2,500 and 3,000 people, the theater drew the largest crowds on holidays.

The Stage The stage was a platform that extended into the pit. Actors entered and left the stage from doors located behind the platform. The galleries behind and above the stage were used primarily as dressing and storage rooms. The second-level gallery right above the stage, however, was used as an upper stage.

884 Drama

Vocabulary Development

Word Origins

The term *groundlings* refers to those who stood in the pit, and hence on the ground, to watch performances in Elizabethan theaters such as the Globe. The upper class and nobility paid two or three pennies to sit in raised galleries sheltered by a roof, but poorer groundlings paid only a penny for their admission and stood exposed to the elements. The first reference to these audience members as "groundlings" occurs in Shakespeare's *Hamlet*, Act III, Scene 2. Hamlet instructs a group of actors to avoid loud overacting, which will "split the ears of the groundlings. . . . " Hamlet goes on to note that groundlings "are capable of nothing but inexplicable dumb-shows and noise. . . . " Groundlings earned such criticism through their behavior during performances: Groundlings were known to talk, jeer the actors, and throw nut shells at the stage. It is from such behavior that the term "groundling" earned its negative connotation as "a person with inferior taste."

By modern standards, Elizabethan theater was hardly "realistic." No scenery was used: Settings were mentioned in the dialogue. The actors wore Elizabethan clothing, not costumes. Women were not allowed on stage: Young boys played the female roles. Shakespeare brought his world to life on stage at the Globe through imagination and words.

Reconstructing the Globe

In 1987, years of fundraising and effort resulted in a remarkable birthday present for the playwright. Work began on a faithful reconstruction of the Globe.

The design of the reconstruction is based on archaeological evidence and a drawing by Wenceslaus Hollar, an artist of the time. A contract drawn up in 1600 for the Fortune playhouse, a theater built by the same carpenter who built the Globe, provides additional details. In 1989, the foundation of the original Globe was uncovered, providing even more information about the theater.

The new Globe, like the original, is made of wood. Traditional sixteenth-century carpentry techniques were used for much of the construction. A thatched roof protects the stage and galleries, and lime plaster covers the walls. After long years of fundraising and construction, the theater opened to its first full season on June 8, 1997, with a production of *Henry V.*

▼ Critical Viewing
Judging from this reconstruction, what features did the Globe share with modern theaters? **[Compare and Contrast]**

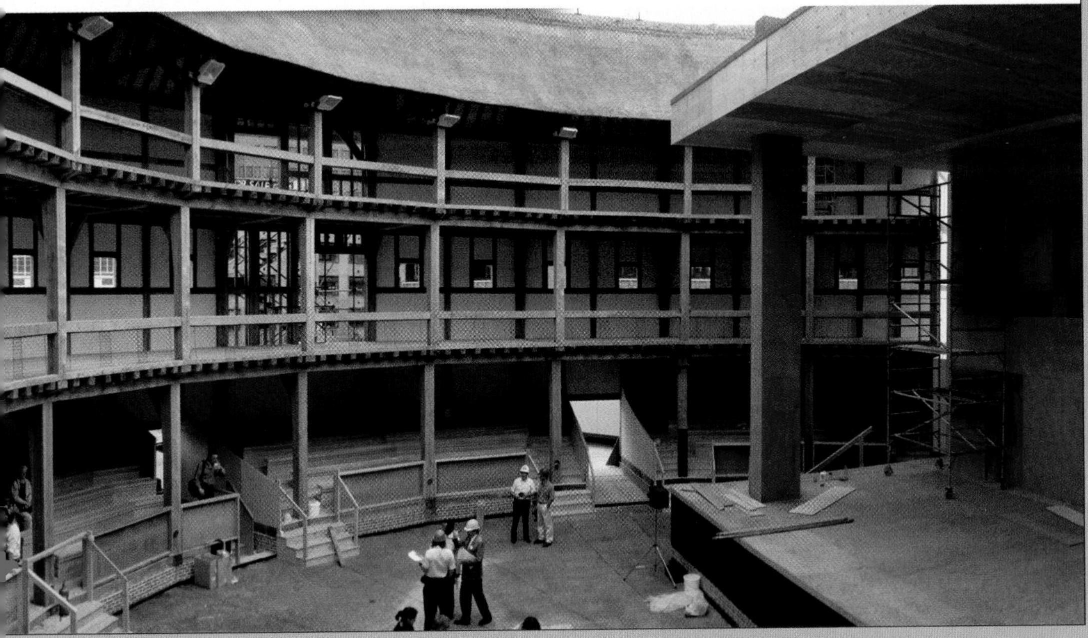

Background

The Globe Today London's new Globe theater is a remarkable replica of the original. The new Globe retains the circular shape, uncovered center, thatched roof, and bare bleacher-style seating of the original. The builders relied on surviving contracts for the Rose and Fortune theaters, which were built by the same carpenters who built the Globe, and on the existing foundations of the Rose, which were excavated in 1988. They used the same techniques and building materials as their predecessors 300 years earlier. The new Globe is held together by wooden pegs, not metal nails, and there are no bathrooms (these are in a museum building across the plaza from the theater). The only concessions made to modern times are the signs for fire exits.

The new Globe seats 1,000. The seats curve around the sides of the stage, giving everyone a view of the action. Some audience views are partly blocked by pillars, but no audience member is more than 50 feet from the stage. As in Elizabethan times, the audience tends to join in the proceedings, booing the French army in *Henry V* and tossing coins to Autolycus, the clown in *A Winter's Tale,* when he sings them a song.

The atmosphere at the Globe is much like it was in Shakespeare's day. Audience members move around as they please, and vendors circulate selling sandwiches and chocolate bars. Sets and sound effects are minimal; no microphones are used. The experience is a contrast to performances in modern theaters, which take place in darkened rooms with silent audiences who remain in their seats.

Critical Viewing

Answer: Students may note that the Globe, like modern theaters, has a stage, ground floor, and balconies.

Differentiated Instruction for Universal Access

Enrichment for Gifted and Talented Students

Have students reread each section of the text that describes the physical appearance of the Globe theater. As they read, students should take notes by listing the materials used to build the theater and sketching the layout of the theater. Then, provide students with paper, masking tape, and markers. Tell them to design a backdrop for part of one classroom wall that portrays the stage and galleries of the Globe as accurately as possible. Encourage students to consider the views that both "groundlings" and more affluent audience members see. Have students create the stage's platform by taping brown paper to the classroom floor. As the class reads *The Tragedy of Julius Caesar,* have students present scenes from the play and dramatic readings at the Globe theater they have built. Students can also use their stage when called on to read aloud from the play during class discussions and when they share any writing assignments related to the play.

TIME AND RESOURCE MANAGER

The Tragedy of Julius Caesar, Act I

Lesson Pacing Guide

DAY 1 Preteach

- Administer the Reading and Vocabulary Warm-ups (*Unit 5 Resources*, pp. 91–94) as necessary.
- Introduce the Reading Skill: Use Text Aids. FT
- Introduce the Literary Analysis concept: Shakespeare's Tragedies. FT
- Distribute copies of the appropriate graphic organizer for the Reading Skill (*Graphic Organizer Transparencies*, pp. 168–169). CRI
- Distribute copies of the appropriate graphic organizer for Literary Analysis (*Graphic Organizer Transparencies*, pp. 166–167). CRI
- Teach the selection vocabulary. FT CRI
- Introduce the Word Study skill.

DAYS 2–3 Preteach/Teach

- Build background with the Background feature. CRI
- Develop thematic vocabulary and thematic thinking with Writing About the Big Question.
- Prepare students to read with the Activating Prior Knowledge activities (TE). CRI
- Informally monitor comprehension while students read. FT
- Use the Reading Check questions to confirm comprehension.
- Develop students' ability to use text aids using the Reading Skill questions. CRI
- Develop students' understanding of Shakespeare's tragedies using the Literary Analysis questions. CRI
- Reinforce vocabulary with the Vocabulary notes. CRI

DAY 4 Assess

- Assess students' comprehension and mastery of the skills by having them answer the Critical Thinking, Reading Skill, and Literary Analysis questions. FT

DAY 5 Extend/Assess

- Extend learning by having students complete the Listening and Speaking activity, a dramatic reading, pp. 1004. (You may assign as homework.) As an alternative, assign them "In or Out of the In Crowd" or the Listening and Speaking and Research and Technology activities (pp. 1004–1005) in *Reality Central*. CRI
- Administer Selection Test A or B (*Unit 5 Resources*, pp. 103–108). FT

The play *The Tragedy of Julius Caesar* appears unedited and in its entirety. Act I appears on pp. 892–912, Act II appears on pp. 917–936, Act III appears on pp. 941–962, Act IV appears on pp. 967–982, and Act V appears on pp. 987–1000.

Meeting Your Standards

Students will
1. analyze and respond to literary elements.
   - Literary Analysis: Shakespeare's Tragedies
2. read, comprehend, and analyze drama.
   - Reading Skill: Use Text Aids
   - Reading Check questions
   - Apply the Skills questions
   - Assessment Practice
3. develop vocabulary.
   - Vocabulary
   - Word Study
4. strengthen listening and speaking skills.
   - dramatic reading

CRI For a full explanation of Culturally Responsive Instruction opportunities in this lesson, see p. T86–T87.

FT For an accelerated lesson, use the Fast Track strategies and activities.

Managing Differentiated Instruction
This leveled selection pairing groups a more accessible with a more challenging selection. Choose either one to teach the lesson skills. For classroom management suggestions for using the pairing in a mixed-ability class, see pp. T68–T69.

Daily Block Scheduling
Each day in this Lesson Pacing Guide represents a 40–50 minute period. Teachers using block scheduling may combine days to revise pacing. In addition, teachers may differentiate and support core instruction by integrating components for extended and intensive support as students require. See the Guide to Selected Leveled Resources (facing page).

Guide to Selected Leveled Resources

EL English Learners

			The Tragedy of Julius Caesar, Act I
CORE COURSE	*Unit 5 Resources*	Selection Test A	pp. 103–105
	Graphic Organizer Transparencies	Reading Skill Graphic Organizer A	p. 168
		Literary Analysis Graphic Organizer A	p. 166
EXTENDED SUPPORT (Level 2)	*Unit 5 Resources*	Reading and Vocabulary Warm-ups A or B	pp. 91–94
	Reader's Notebook: English Learner's Version		adapted instruction and adapted selection
	Hear It! Audio CD		selection and summaries
	Hear It! Audio CD (adapted text)		adapted selection and summaries
INTENSIVE SUPPORT (Level 1)	*Reality Central*		"In and Out of the In Crowd"
	Real-World Writing Journal		Lesson 3, pp. 146–149

L2 Below-Level Students

			The Tragedy of Julius Caesar, Act I
CORE COURSE	*Unit 5 Resources*	Selection Test A	pp. 103–105
	Graphic Organizer Transparencies	Reading Skill Graphic Organizer A	p. 168
		Literary Analysis Graphic Organizer A	p. 166
EXTENDED SUPPORT (Level 2)	*Unit 5 Resources*	Reading and Vocabulary Warm-ups A or B	pp. 91–94
	Reader's Notebook		adapted instruction and full selection
	Hear It! Audio CD		selection and summaries
INTENSIVE SUPPORT (Level 1)	*Reality Central*		"In and Out of the In Crowd"
	Real-World Writing Journal		Lesson 3, pp. 146–149
	Reading Kit		Reteaching worksheets

L1 Special Needs Students

			The Tragedy of Julius Caesar, Act I
CORE COURSE	*Unit 5 Resources*	Selection Test A	pp. 103–105
	Graphic Organizer Transparencies	Reading Skill Graphic Organizer A	p. 168
		Literary Analysis Graphic Organizer A	p. 166
EXTENDED SUPPORT (Level 2)	*Unit 5 Resources*	Reading and Vocabulary Warm-ups A or B	pp. 91–94
	Reader's Notebook: Adapted Version		adapted instruction and adapted selection
	Hear It! Audio CD (adapted text)		adapted selection and summaries
INTENSIVE SUPPORT (Level 1)	*Reality Central*		"In and Out of the In Crowd"
	Real-World Writing Journal		Lesson 3, pp. 146–149
	Reading Kit		Reteaching worksheets

The program includes resources for these students: L3 On-Level L4 Advanced All All
For a complete guide to selection support, see pp. T106–T108.

NOTE: All print materials are also available online at *www.PHLitOnline.com.*

The Tragedy of Julius Caesar, Act I

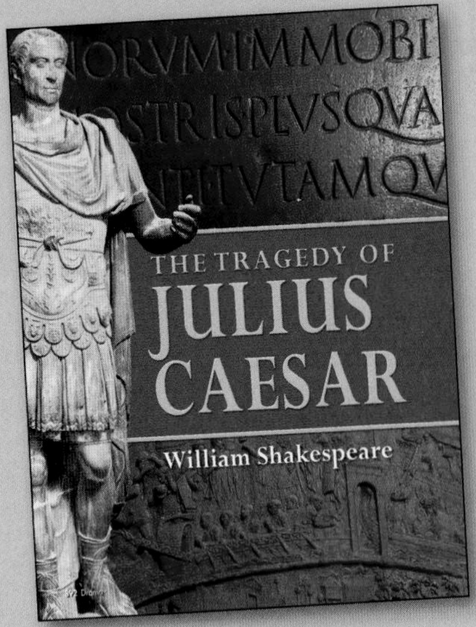

RESOURCES FOR:

- EL English Learners
- L1 Special Needs Students
- L2 Below-Level Students
- L3 On-Level Students
- L4 Advanced Students
- All All Students

Vocabulary/Fluency/Prior Knowledge

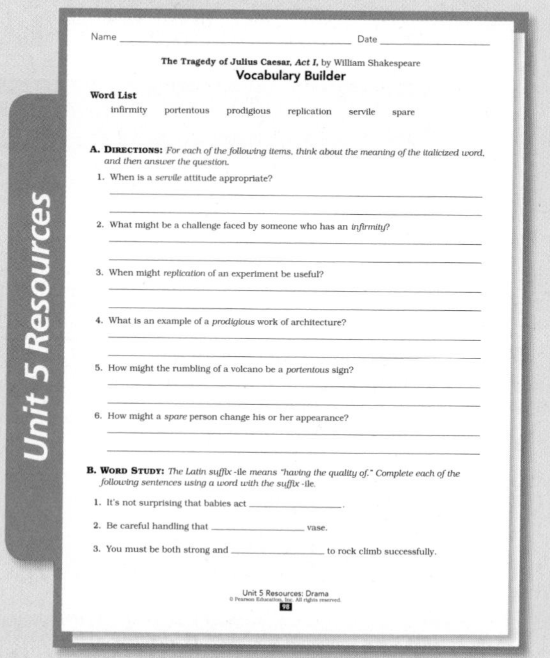

Name ______________ Date ______________

The Tragedy of Julius Caesar, Act I, by William Shakespeare

Vocabulary Builder

Word List

infirmity portentous prodigious replication servile spare

A. Directions: *For each of the following items, think about the meaning of the italicized word, and then answer the question.*

1. When is a *servile* attitude appropriate?
2. What might be a challenge faced by someone who has an *infirmity*?
3. When might *replication* of an experiment be useful?
4. What is an example of a *prodigious* work of architecture?
5. How might the rumbling of a volcano be a *portentous* sign?
6. How might a *spare* person change his or her appearance?

B. Word Study: *The Latin suffix -ile means "having the quality of." Complete each of the following sentences using a word with the suffix -ile.*

1. It's not surprising that babies act ______________.
2. Be careful handling that ______________ vase.
3. You must be both strong and ______________ to rock climb successfully.

Unit 5 Resources: Drama

© Pearson Education, Inc. All rights reserved.

98

All **Vocabulary Builder, p. 98**

Also available for these selections:

EL L1 L2 **Vocabulary Warm-ups A and B, pp. 91–92**

EL L1 L2 **Reading Warm-ups A and B, pp. 93–94**

All **Writing About the Big Question, p. 95**

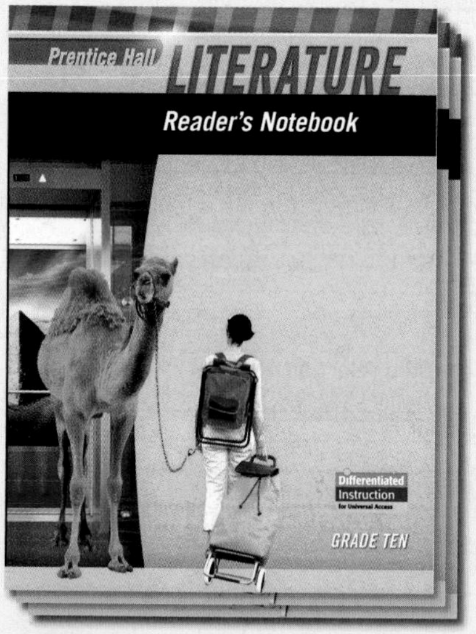

L2 L3 ***Reader's Notebook***

L1 ***Reader's Notebook: Adapted Version***

EL ***Reader's Notebook: English Learner's Version***

Reader's Notebooks

Pre- and postreading pages for both selections, as well as *The Tragedy of Julius Caesar,* Act I appear in an interactive format in the *Reader's Notebooks.* Each *Notebook* is differentiated for a different group of learners.

The selections in the Adapted and English Learner's versions are abridged.

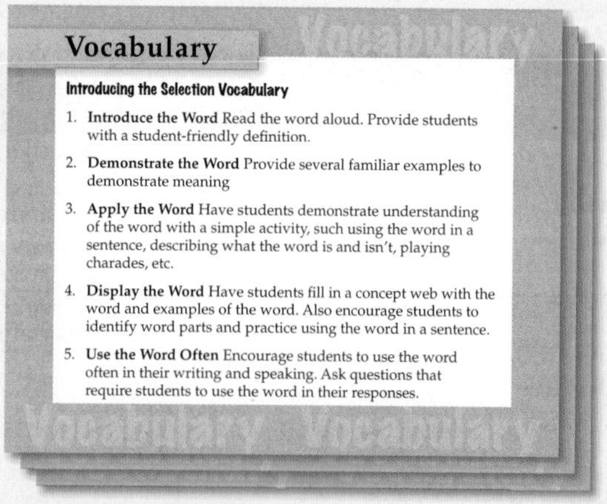

Vocabulary

Introducing the Selection Vocabulary

1. **Introduce the Word** Read the word aloud. Provide students with a student-friendly definition.
2. **Demonstrate the Word** Provide several familiar examples to demonstrate meaning
3. **Apply the Word** Have students demonstrate understanding of the word with a simple activity, such using the word in a sentence, describing what the word is and isn't, playing charades, etc.
4. **Display the Word** Have students fill in a concept web with the word and examples of the word. Also encourage students to identify word parts and practice using the word in a sentence.
5. **Use the Word Often** Encourage students to use the word often in their writing and speaking. Ask questions that require students to use the word in their responses.

Classroom Strategies and Teaching Routines

- core classroom routines outlined step-by-step
- convenient format for easy reference while teaching

Selection Support

Transparencies

The Tragedy of Julius Caesar, Act I by William Shakespeare

After You Read A: Reading—Using Text Aids

	Speech	What Does It Say?	What Does It Mean?	Why Is It Important?
Brutus	Scene ii, lines 82–89	When public welfare is at stake, I will show indifference to myself.	I love honor more than I fear death.	This speech displays Brutus' idealism—and shows Cassius how he might persuade Brutus to act.
Cassius	Scene ii, lines 135–161			

Graphic Organizer Transparencies

168

EL L1 L2 **Reading: Graphic Organizer A, p. 168 (partially filled in)**

Also available for these selections:

L3 Reading: Graphic Organizer B, p. 169

EL L1 L2 Literary Analysis: Graphic Organizer A, p. 166 (partially filled in)

L3 Literary Analysis: Graphic Organizer B, p. 167

Skills Development/Extension

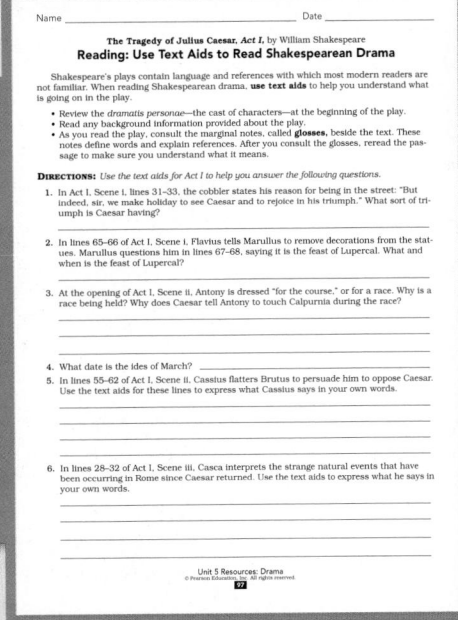

Unit 5 Resources

Name ____________________ Date __________

The Tragedy of Julius Caesar, *Act I*, by William Shakespeare

Reading: Use Text Aids to Read Shakespearean Drama

Shakespeare's plays contain language and references with which most modern readers are not familiar. When reading Shakespearean drama, **use text aids** to help you understand what is going on in the play.

- Review the *dramatis personae*—the cast of characters—at the beginning of the play.
- Read any background information provided about the play.
- As you read the play, consult the marginal notes, called **glosses,** beside the text. These notes define words and explain references. After you consult the glosses, reread the passage to make sure you understand what it means.

DIRECTIONS: *Use the text aids for Act I to help you answer the following questions.*

1. In Act I, Scene i, lines 31–33, the cobbler states his reason for being in the street: "But indeed, sir, we make holiday to see Caesar and to rejoice in his triumph." What sort of triumph is Caesar having?
2. In lines 65–66 of Act I, Scene i, Flavius tells Marullus to remove decorations from the statues. Marullus questions him in lines 67–68, saying it is the feast of Lupercal. What and when is the feast of Lupercal?
3. At the opening of Act I, Scene ii, Antony is dressed "for the course," or for a race. Why is a race being held? Why does Caesar tell Antony to touch Calpurnia during the race?
4. What date is the ides of March? __________
5. In lines 55–62 of Act I, Scene ii, Cassius flatters Brutus to persuade him to oppose Caesar. Use the text aids for these lines to express what Cassius says in your own words.
6. In lines 28–32 of Act I, Scene iii, Casca interprets the strange natural events that have been occurring in Rome since Caesar returned. Use the text aids to express what he says in your own words.

Unit 5 Resources: Drama

97

All **Reading: Use Text Aids,** p. 97

Also available for these selections:

All Literary Analysis: Shakespeare's Tragedies, p. 96

L4 Enrichment, pp. 171

L3 L4 Grammar, p. 172

L3 L4 Support for Writing, p. 173

L3 L4 Support for Extend Your Learning, p. 174

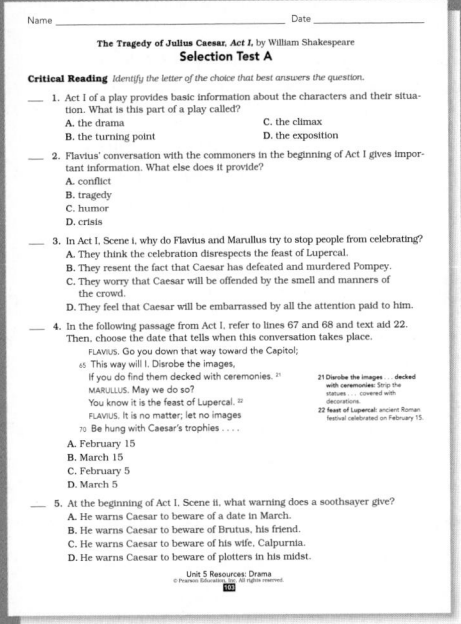

Assessment

Name ____________________ Date __________

The Tragedy of Julius Caesar, *Act I*, by William Shakespeare

Selection Test A

Critical Reading *Identify the letter of the choice that best answers the question.*

___ 1. Act I of a play provides basic information about the characters and their situation. What is this part of a play called?
A. the drama
B. the turning point
C. the climax
D. the exposition

___ 2. Flavius' conversation with the commoners in the beginning of Act I gives important information. What else does it provide?
A. conflict
B. tragedy
C. humor
D. crisis

___ 3. In Act I, Scene i, why do Flavius and Marullus try to stop people from celebrating?
A. They think the celebration disrespects the feast of Lupercal.
B. They resent the fact that Caesar has defeated and murdered Pompey.
C. They worry that Caesar will be offended by the smell and manners of the crowd.
D. They feel that Caesar will be embarrassed by all the attention paid to him.

___ 4. In the following passage from Act I, refer to lines 67 and 68 and text aid 22. Then, choose the date that tells when this conversation takes place.

FLAVIUS. Go you down that way toward the Capitol;
This way will I. Disrobe the images,
If you do find them decked with ceremonies. [21]
MARULLUS. May we do so?
You know it is the feast of Lupercal. [22]
FLAVIUS. It is no matter; let no images
Be hung with Caesar's trophies . . . .

21 **Disrobe the images . . . decked with ceremonies:** Strip the statues . . . covered with decorations.
22 **feast of Lupercal:** ancient Roman festival celebrated on February 15.

A. February 15
B. March 15
C. February 5
D. March 5

___ 5. At the beginning of Act I, Scene ii, what warning does a soothsayer give?
A. He warns Caesar to beware of a date in March.
B. He warns Caesar to beware of Brutus, his friend.
C. He warns Caesar to beware of his wife, Calpurnia.
D. He warns Caesar to beware of plotters in his midst.

Unit 5 Resources: Drama

103

EL L1 L2 **Selection Test A,** pp. 103–105

Also available for these selections:

L3 L4 Selection Test B, pp. 106–108

L3 L4 Open-Book Test, pp. 100–102

PHLit Online!
www.PHLitOnline.com

- complete narrated selection text
- a thematically related video with writing prompt
- an interactive graphic organizer
- highlighting feature
- access to all student print resources, adapted to individual student needs
- Spanish and English summaries

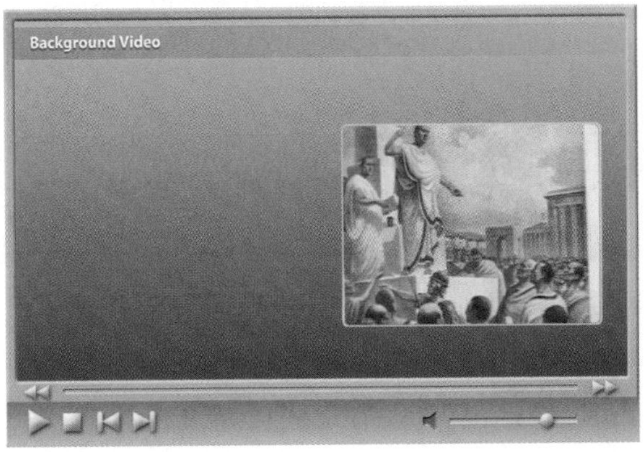

Background video

Also available:

Get Connected! (thematic video with writing prompt)

Vocabulary Central (tools, activities, and songs for studying vocabulary)

Also available:

Writer's Journal (with graphics feature)

DIFFERENTIATE/PRETEACH

❶ Selection Skills

1. With the class, preview the selection skills.
2. Explain that students will develop the skill of using text aids as they read to better understand and enjoy the selection. By examining elements of Shakespeare's tragedies as they read, they will gain deeper insight into drama.

❷ Literary Analysis

1. Introduce the skill, using the instruction on student page 887.
2. Tell students that they will practice identifying elements of Shakespeare's tragedies as they read.

Think Aloud: Model the Skill

Model the skill of identifying elements of Shakespeare's tragedies, using the following "think aloud":

> I know that Shakespeare's tragedies have distinctive features, such as being only five acts long, with each act developing the plot a certain way.
>
> For example, Act I of *Romeo and Juliet* gives background information—Romeo and Juliet come from feuding families. In Act II, the rising action occurs—Romeo and Juliet fall in love and marry. In Act III, the crisis or turning point occurs—Romeo commits murder and Juliet is being forced to marry another man. Act IV is the falling action—Juliet poisons herself. Act V is the catastrophe—Romeo and Juliet commit suicide.

Give students a copy of either **Literary Analysis Graphic Organizer A** or **B** (*Graphic Organizer Transparencies,* pp. 166–167) to record details of Shakespeare's tragedies as they read. Use the examples in **Literary Analysis Graphic Organizer A**, which is partially filled in, to model the process of completing the organizer by taking notes.

Before You Read | The Tragedy of Julius Caesar, Act I

Drama Selection

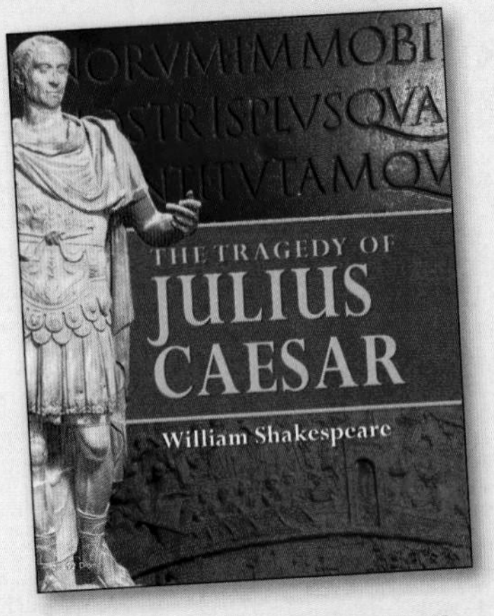

▲ Read ***The Tragedy of Julius Caesar*** to learn how acts of betrayal and loyalty shaped the history of ancient Rome.

❶ Selection Skills Guide

Practice these skills with ***The Tragedy of Julius Caesar,* Act I** (p. 892).

- Understand Shakespeare's tragedies
- Identify historical characters, heroes, tragic flaws, internal conflict, supporting roles, and comic relief
- Read Shakespearean drama
- Use text aids

Integrated Language Skills (Grammar; Listening and Speaking; Research and Technology; and Writing Activities) appear on pages 1002–1005.

Differentiated Instruction for Universal Access

Accessibility at a Glance: Selection

	***The Tragedy of Julius Caesar,* Act I**	
Context	Historical: ancient Rome	
Language/ Vocabulary	• Dialogue • Prose, verse, and soliloquies	
Concept Level	Challenging (internal conflicts within historical, political context	
Literary Merit	• Classic • Noted author	
Lexile/Length	Lexile: NP	Word Count: 4,692
Overall Rating	**Challenging**	

❷ Literary Analysis: Shakespeare's Tragedies

Like other tragedies, **Shakespeare's tragedies** are plays that tell of a reversal of fortune, from good to bad, experienced by a man or woman, usually of noble birth. Shakespeare's tragedies also have these distinctive features:

- They are sometimes based on **historical characters.**
- The **hero** often displays a **tragic flaw,** a characteristic that brings about his downfall.
- Shakespeare emphasizes the hero's **internal conflict.**
- Commoners often play key **supporting roles** and provide **comic relief** in humorous scenes that serve as a break from the intense emotions of the play.

Shakespeare's plays are structured in five acts. In his tragedies, the **crisis**—the turning point that determines how the play will end—occurs in Act III. The **climax,** or point of greatest emotional intensity, often occurs in Act V, when the **catastrophe,** or disaster, befalls the hero.

PHLit Online!
www.PHLitOnline.com

Hear It!
- Selection summary audio
- Selection audio

See It!
- Get Connected video
- Background video
- More about the author
- Vocabulary flashcards

Do It!
- Interactive journals
- Interactive graphic organizers
- Self-test
- Internet activity
- Grammar tutorial
- Interactive vocabulary games

Using the Strategy: Plot Diagram

Record the events of a play on a **plot diagram** such as this one.

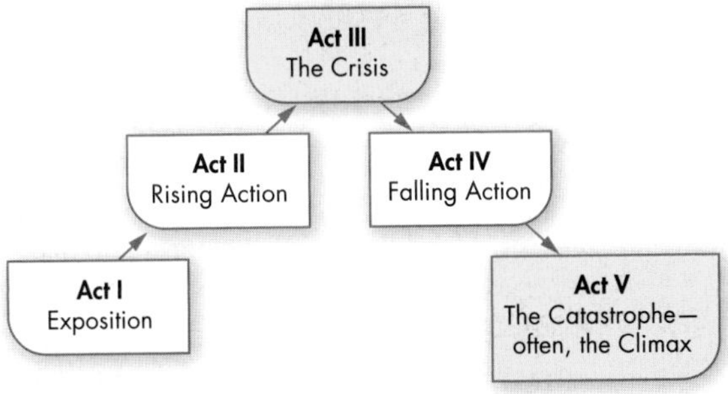

❸ Reading Skill: Use Text Aids

Because they were written in the 17th Century, Shakespeare's plays contain unfamiliar language and references. When **reading Shakespearean drama, use text aids:**

- Review the list of *dramatis personae* (the cast of characters).
- Read the background information provided (p. 889).
- As you read the play, consult the notes, called **glosses,** beside the text. These notes define words and explain references.

PRETEACH

❸ Reading Skill

1. Introduce the skill, using the instruction on the student page.
2. Tell students that they will practice using text aids as they read.

Think Aloud: Model the Skill

Model the skill of using text aids, using the following "think aloud:"

> If I find Shakespeare's wording and vocabulary confusing, I can use text aids. Before I read, I review the *dramatis personae*, which tells me about the characters. Then, when a character enters for the first time, I know who he or she is and the relationship to the other characters. The background information helps me learn more about the historical context.
>
> While I read, I look at the glosses, which help me understand the meaning of unfamiliar words and references and make the play easier to read.

Differentiated Instruction for Universal Access

Preparing Students for the Selection

If you wish to prepare lower level readers to read *The Tragedy of Julius Caesar*, Act 1, follow these steps:

- Students might have difficulty with the main concept: conflict within a historical, political context. Prompt students to think of examples of political conflict in United States history, such as the Civil War or the Red Scare and McCarthyism. Discuss why these events occurred and how they were resolved.
- Remind students that Shakespeare often uses blank verse—unrhymed iambic pentameter—which follows a regular pattern of stressed then unstressed syllables. Practice reading sections of the play aloud with students to focus on hearing the rhythm.
- Students might have difficulty with the lengthy speeches and soliloquies, such as the one on pp. 900–901. Review strategies of paraphrasing and breaking down complex sentences. Encourage them to phrase difficult parts of soliloquies in their own words.

PRETEACH

1 Writing About the Big Question

1. Review the assignment with the class.
2. Prompt a discussion about how much first impressions influence their opinions of people. Discuss whether they have ever changed their impression of someone after getting to know him or her better.
3. Have students complete the sentence starters. Review responses as a class.
(**Possible response:** A person might form an impression of someone based on his or her appearance. Our own values and beliefs may also affect the way we see others because we might compare them to ourselves and cast *judgement.*)
4. Remind students that their answers will help them think about the Big Question.

While You Read

Tell students that as they read they should look for characters' different opinions of Caesar.

2 Vocabulary

1. Have students preview the selection vocabulary.
2. For each word, have students say the word aloud.
3. Then, use the word in a sentence that defines the word.
4. Finally, repeat your definitional sentence or a similar sentence with the word missing, and have the class "fill in the blank" chorally. Here is an example:

   Something prodigious is of great size or power. We hope this year's bountiful rains and mild temperatures will produce a [students say "prodigious"] *crop.*

3 Word Study

1. Introduce the skill, using the instruction in the box.
2. Ask students to think of a word with the suffix *-ile*. Ask them to write the definition using their knowledge of the suffix. Then, have students form pairs and try to guess each other's word. (**Sample answer:** "capable of being touched" *tactile*)

Making Connections | The Tragedy of Julius Caesar, Act 1

To what extent does *experience* determine what we *perceive?*

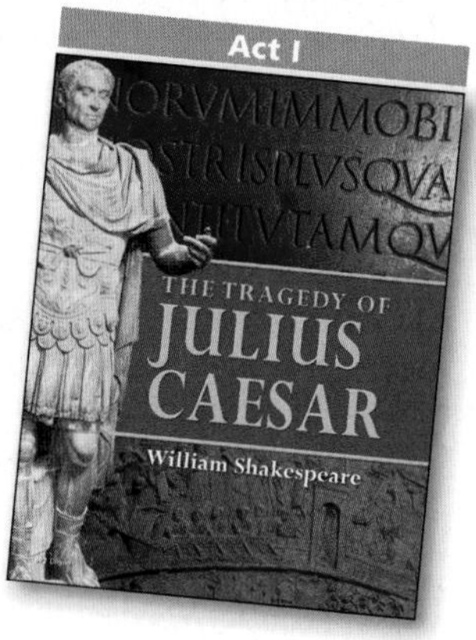

1 Writing About the Big Question

In *The Tragedy of Julius Caesar,* Shakespeare reveals the dangers of misinterpreting people and their intentions. Use these sentence starters to develop your ideas about the Big Question.

A person might form an **impression** of someone based on ________.
Our own values and beliefs may also affect the way we see others because ________.

While You Read Look for the opinions different characters have of Caesar, and look for signs that tell you why these characters' views of the leader differ.

2 Vocabulary

Read each word and its definition. Decide whether you know the word well, know it a little bit, or do not know it at all. After you read, see how your knowledge of each word has increased.

- **replication** (rep´ li kā´ shən) *n.* duplicate; reproduction (p. 894) *His house is an exact replication of mine.* *replica n. replicate v.*
- **servile** (sʉr´ vəl) *adj.* slavelike; humbly submissive to authority (p. 896) *The butler bowed in a servile manner.* *serve v. servility n. servitude n.*
- **spare** (sper) *adj.* lean; thin (p. 903) *She has a spare frame and is underweight.*
- **infirmity** (in fʉr´ mə tē) *n.* weakness; physical defect (p. 905) *A doctor cured his infirmity.* *infirm adj. infirmary n. infirmness n.*
- **portentous** (pôr ten´ təs) *adj.* ominous; giving signs of evil to come (p. 908) *The portentous clouds promised snow.* *portent n. portentously adv.*
- **prodigious** (prō dij´ əs) *adj.* of great size or power (p. 909) *The runner made a prodigious effort just before the finish line.* *prodigiously adv.*

3 Word Study

The **Latin suffix *-ile*** means "capable of" or "having the quality of."

In the play, a character is worried that he will become **servile** and take on the qualities of a slave if Caesar becomes king.

Vocabulary Development

Vocabulary Knowledge Rating

Create a **Vocabulary Knowledge Rating Chart** (***Professional Development Guidebook***, p. 33) for this selection. Include the selection vocabulary and the Big Question words that appear in the Writing About the Big Question sentence starters. (The Big Question vocabulary is introduced on pp. 790–791.)

Give students a copy of the chart. Read the words aloud, and have students mark their rating in the Before Reading column. Urge them to be alert to these words as they read and discuss the selection.

Tally how many students think they know a word to gauge how much instruction to provide. As students read and discuss the selection, point out the words and their context.

PHLit Online! **Vocabulary Central**, featuring tools, activities, and songs for studying vocabulary, is available at **www.PHLitOnline.com.**

❹ Background for the Play

Ancient Rome A republic since 509 B.C., Rome was ruled for decades by two public officials called *consuls* along with the senate, made up of high-born *patricians,* or aristocrats, and assemblies of *plebeians,* or lower-class citizens.

By the era of Julius Caesar (100–44 B.C.), Rome ruled an empire won by military expansion. Powerful generals arose, and the balance of power grew unstable. Civil war was common. When a general named Pompey tried to make himself sole consul, another popular general, Julius Caesar, defeated him. As Shakespeare's play opens, all of Rome wonders whether Caesar will become emperor, ending the Republic.

from SHAKESPEARE ALIVE!

Joseph Papp and Elizabeth Kirkland

Joseph Papp, the founder of the New York Shakespeare festival, devoted his life to making Shakespeare accessible to all. In Shakespeare Alive! he re-creates England in Shakespeare's day. As he explains, Shakespeare and his audience viewed nature and society as a unified whole.

In the heavenly kingdom . . . several levels of archangels and angels spread downwards from God's throne, and each level knew its place. . . . The universe was a hierarchy too, and each planet and star was assigned to a specific position. . . . The animal world was another very stratified society in which each species had its king: the eagle was the king of birds; the whale the king of fish; and the lion, of course, king of beasts.

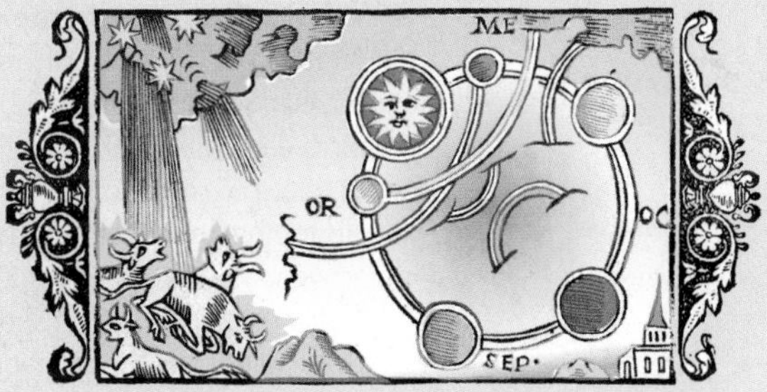

De circulis repentinis, & effectibus cometarum.

The Great Chain of Being, stretching from the lowliest creature in the natural world all the way up to God, connected these worlds to each other, and the hierarchy of one was mirrored in the others. . . .

Since all living things were linked by the Great Chain of Being, violations of order in society were thought to set off violent disturbances in the heavens or the world of nature. . . . In *Julius Caesar* [Act I, Scene iii], strange and terrible goings-on are reported in Rome as the conspirators hatch an assassination plot against the emperor. . . .

Differentiated Instruction — Additional Instruction

EL Extended Support—English Learners
Have students complete the **Reading and Vocabulary Warm-ups, *Unit 5 Resources,*** pp. 91–94 before they read. Assign the prereading pages for the selection in the ***Reader's Notebook: English Learner's Version***. Then, have students listen to portions of the selection on the ***Hear It!* Audio CD.**

L1 L2 Extended Support—Struggling Readers
Have students complete the **Reading and Vocabulary Warm-ups, *Unit 5 Resources,*** pp. 91–94, before they read. Assign the prereading pages for the selection in the ***Reader's Notebook: Adapted Version***. Then, have students listen to portions of the selection on the ***Hear It!* Audio CD** (adapted text).

Extended Support—Reluctant Readers
To build motivation and engagement before assigning the selection, have students read "In or Out of the In Crowd," a thematically related selection in ***Reality Central.*** Then, use the questions at the conclusion of the related selection to guide discussion.

Daily Bellringer

For each class during which you will teach this selection, have students complete one of the relevant activities for Weeks 27, 28, and 29 in the ***Daily Bellringer Activities*** booklet.

❹ Background

Roman Government

The Roman republic was founded in 509 B.C. when the harsh Etruscan king Tarquinius Superbus was overthrown. Rome then remained a Republic until 27 B.C. Rome's consuls were elected by the *Comita Centuriata* for one-year terms. Each consul had the right to veto the decisions of the others. In 509 B.C., the Roman Senate consisted of 300 senators appointed for life by the consuls. Because the *Comita Centuriata* was controlled by the patrician (noble) class, the plebeian (common) class set up its own assembly, called the *Concilium Plebis*. Other government officials at Rome included *praetors* (judicial officials), *quaestors* (financial officials), and *censors* (supervisors of public morals).

Multidraft Reading

This icon ● marks natural pauses in the selection. To assist struggling readers and to deepen reading for all, assign the text in "chunks," following the icons, and apply multidraft reading protocols. For each reading, have students set the purpose indicated:

- **First reading**—literal comprehension: answering the Reading Check questions.
- **Second reading**—application of skills: answering the Shakespeare's Tragedies and Use Text Aids prompts.
- **Third reading**—interpretation: answering the end-of-selection questions.

For more guidance, refer to the ***Classroom Strategies and Teaching Routines*** card on multidraft reading.

PHLit Online!
For more about the author, practice with the selection vocabulary, and more background, go to **www.PHLitOnline.com**.

Background

Elizabethan England Shakespeare lived in the intellectual world of the Renaissance, the religious world of the Reformation, and the widening geographic world of the Age of Exploration. Although Shakespeare and his contemporaries did not apply these labels to their time, they were profoundly influenced by the climate of change and adventure.

Ironically, the more that boundaries and traditions were challenged, the more fiercely Elizabethans clung to them. For this reason, rank, social status, and rules of propriety were extremely important to the people of Shakespeare's day. So fanatical were the Elizabethans about social order that Clothing Acts—laws that specified the clothing to be worn by different classes of people—were passed. Not surprisingly, the Clothing Acts were largely ignored, but they reflected the sentiment of the times. Students will notice at the opening of Act I of *The Tragedy of Julius Caesar* that members of the working class are chided for going about in public without the proper attire that indicates their status and function.

Meet William Shakespeare

(1564–1616)

Author of

THE TRAGEDY OF JULIUS CAESAR

His characters are known by name around the world. The phrases he coined still slip into people's conversations. Filmmakers, painters, and composers reuse his plots. Writers continue to sift through his thirty-seven plays and his poems, borrowing titles, stories, and insights into the human soul. Nearly 400 years after his death, William Shakespeare's plays are still read and produced internationally. He is regarded as the greatest writer in the English language.

What's Past Is Prologue Shakespeare was born in Stratford-on-Avon, northwest of London. Based on a baptism record for April 26, 1564, scholars estimate that his birth date was April 23 of the same year. Shakespeare's father, John, a successful glove maker and businessman, was a respected leader in the community. His mother, born Mary Arden, was the daughter of John's landlord.

No written evidence of Shakespeare's boyhood exists. Based on his father's status, though, scholars speculate that young Will attended the Stratford Grammar School. In addition to studying Latin grammar, Shakespeare and his classmates would have read the Roman playwrights Plautus and Terence and the Roman poets Ovid, Horace, and Virgil. They would also have studied logic, history, natural history, and some Greek. When Shakespeare left school, he would have had a solid foundation in classical literature.

Scholars pick up the written trail of Shakespeare's life in 1582. Records show that he married Anne Hathaway in late November or early December of that year. Anne was twenty-six; William was eighteen. They had a daughter, Susanna, in 1583, and twins, Judith and Hamnet, two years later.

Vocabulary Development

Familiar Expressions From Shakespeare
Emphasize that Shakespeare's plays have not only had a powerful impact on audiences over the centuries, they have also had a powerful impact on everyday contemporary English. Explain that Shakespeare invented dozens of familiar words and phrases, including *"Knock, knock! Who's there," "Too much of a good thing,"* and *"Something wicked this way comes."* Share with students the following observation of critic Christopher Morley: "Everyone is a Shakespeare scholar unconsciously. You yourself have probably quoted him today." Then have students choose partners and create a very brief skit that demonstrates how one of the expressions listed might be used in a contemporary context. Invite students to perform their skits for the class.

All the World's a Stage For a brief time, Shakespeare may have worked as a country schoolmaster. In the 1580s, however, he found his true calling—the theater. Some speculate that traveling performers, stopping off in Stratford on their way to London, introduced him to the magic of the stage. At the age of eighteen or nineteen, Shakespeare was probably already acting in plays in London. Friends in the city helped him financially and professionally, and he advanced quickly.

By 1594, Shakespeare was part owner of the Lord Chamberlain's Men, one of the most successful theater companies in London. More importantly, in view of his contributions to English literature, he was the company's chief playwright. Many of Shakespeare's enduring plays first took form as scripts he wrote for performances by the Lord Chamberlain's Men. In 1599, the company built the Globe theater, and it was at the Globe that audiences first saw the plays of Shakespeare.

In 1603, following the death of Elizabeth I, James I became king and took control of the Lord Chamberlain's Men. He renamed the company the King's Men. Shakespeare, a major stockholder in the company, continued to write for and act with the group.

Parting Is Such Sweet Sorrow Around 1610, Shakespeare, now a prosperous middle-class man enriched by his theatrical career, retired to Stratford. He lived in the second-largest house in the town, invested in grain and farmland, and continued to write plays.

Shakespeare wrote his will on March 25, 1616. He left the bulk of his property to his oldest daughter, Susanna, and a smaller sum to his other daughter, Judith. (Hamnet had died in 1596.) By law, his widow automatically received a lifetime income from the estate. On April 23, 1616 (his birthday, if scholars are correct), Shakespeare died.

FAMILIAR EXPRESSIONS TAKEN FROM SHAKESPEARE

You have probably quoted Shakespeare without even realizing it! Look for familiar expressions and phrases in the following list. You may be surprised at how many lines by Shakespeare you already know!

"Eaten out of house and home," *Henry IV*, Part 2, Act II, Scene i
"Cruel to be kind," *Hamlet*, Act III, Scene iv
"Knock, knock! Who's there . . .?" *Macbeth*, Act II, Scene iii
"Too much of a good thing," *As You Like It*, Act IV, Scene i
"Neither a borrower nor a lender be," *Hamlet*, Act I, Scene iii
"Something wicked this way comes," *Macbeth*, Act IV, Scene i
"To thine own self be true," *Hamlet*, Act I, Scene iii
"A tower of strength," *Richard III*, Act V, Scene iii

Background

***The Tragedy of Julius Caesar* in Performance** In 1988, Joseph Papp's New York Shakespeare Festival produced *The Tragedy of Julius Caesar.* The performance starred Al Pacino as Mark Antony and Martin Sheen as Brutus. This was not the first time popular actors played these prestigious roles. Marlon Brando played Mark Antony in Metro-Goldwyn-Mayer's 1953 movie production of the play. Both Papp's and MGM's productions were traditional interpretations, with classic settings and period costumes. Others, however, have used the political themes in the play as a comment on contemporary social and political issues. In 1937, Orson Welles staged a production in which Antony's "Friends, Romans, countrymen" funeral oration was delivered amidst searchlights and symbols suggesting a Nazi rally. A 1993 production portrayed Cassius as an ambitious businessman and Mark Antony as a contemporary military leader. One of the first plays to be performed at the newly constructed Globe theater in 1599, *The Tragedy of Julius Caesar* has remained a vital and relevant production piece for more than four centuries.

Differentiated Instruction for Universal Access

EL Strategy for English Learners

The expressions from Shakespeare are not likely to be familiar to English learners. Work through the list of Familiar Expressions Taken From Shakespeare with students, explaining the idioms and images. Brainstorm with students to generate some idiomatic expressions in their first languages, translated into English, that correspond to expressions from Shakespeare. Challenge students to use an expression from Shakespeare in a sentence to demonstrate their understanding of its meaning.

TEACH

❶ Activating Prior Knowledge

1. Prepare an **Anticipation Guide** (see ***Professional Development Guidebook***, pp. 36–38) with the following statements:
   - Power and manipulation go hand in hand.
   - Citizens do not have to monitor or participate in government.
   - Other people know a person better than he or she knows himself or herself.
   - Sympathy is a stronger emotion than envy.
2. Give students a copy of the prepared **Anticipation Guide**, and have students mark their responses in the Me column. Have students discuss the statements in pairs or groups and mark the guides again in the Group column.

Concept Connector →

Students will return to the **Anticipation Guide** after completing *The Tragedy of Julius Caesar,* Act I.

Small-Group Activity

Have students form discussion groups to analyze the conflicts introduced in this play. They can discuss external conflicts and internal conflicts. Suggest that students continue their discussions as the conflicts develop throughout the play.

❷ About the Selection

Caesar returns to Rome triumphant after his defeat of Pompey, but many citizens worry that he will use his popularity to declare himself king. Cassius is especially bitter and envious of Caesar. Brutus is worried about the future of the empire. The two friends discuss their concerns.

A soothsayer warns Caesar to beware the ides of March. Caesar dismisses the warning. Mark Antony offers Caesar a crown three times; he reluctantly refuses it.

Cassius recruits Casca into the party of conspirators against Caesar. They go together to speak to Brutus about their plans against the Roman leader.

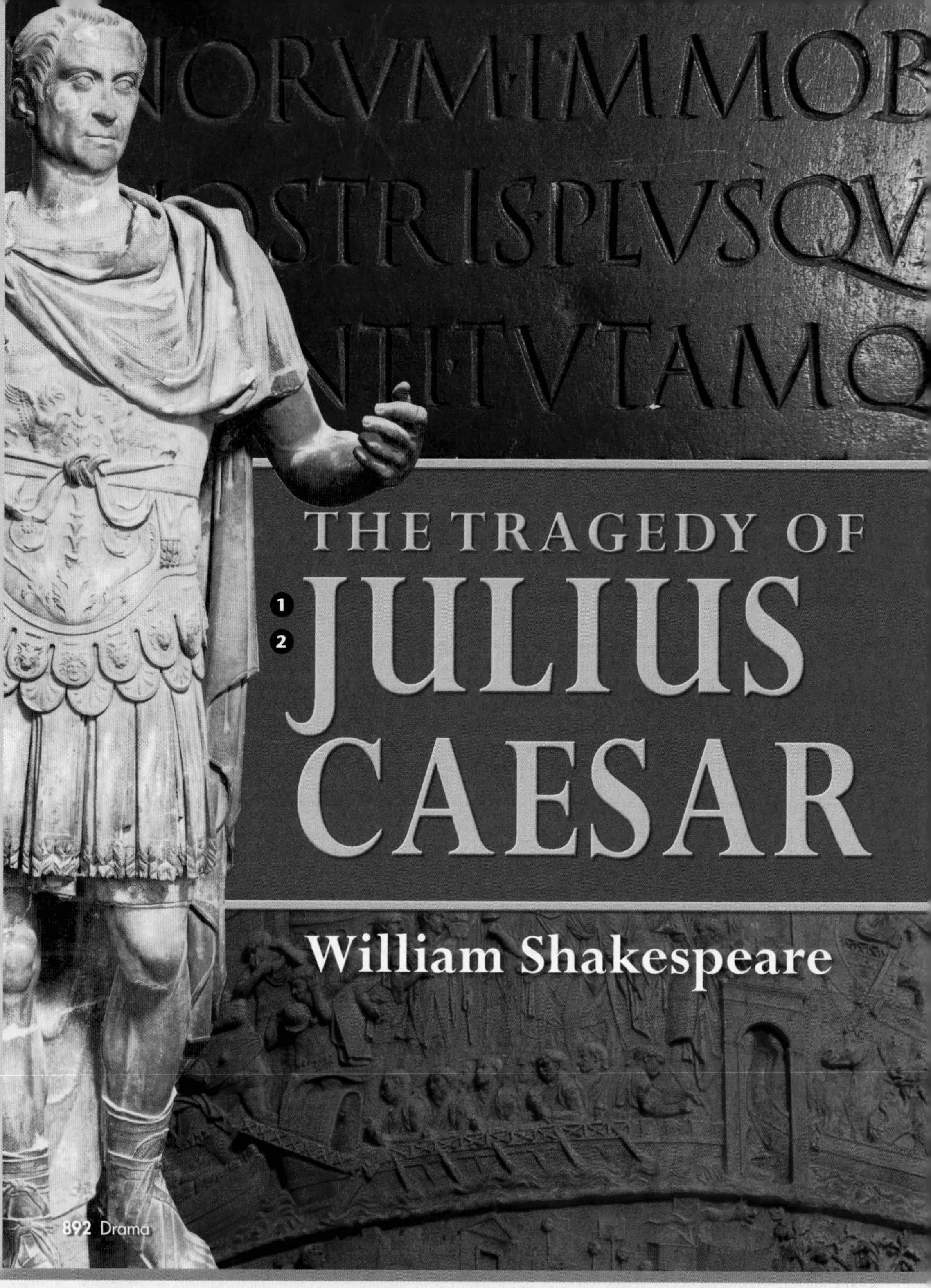

THE TRAGEDY OF ❶ ❷ JULIUS CAESAR

William Shakespeare

Vocabulary Development

Thematic Vocabulary: The Big Question

As students are discussing *The Tragedy of Julius Caesar*, Act I, encourage them to use the thematic vocabulary presented in Introducing the Big Question, pp. 790–791. You might encourage them with sentence starters like these:

1. Brutus does not share Cassius' *perspective* of Julius Caesar because . . .
2. Caesar ignores the soothsayer's *insight*, "Beware the ides of March," because . . .
3. In his soliloquy to Brutus (pp. 900–901), Cassius shares his *impression* of . . .
4. Cassius, Cinna, and Casca plan to *manipulate* Brutus and convince him to join their conspiracy by . . .

CHARACTERS

JULIUS CAESAR		CINNA, ANOTHER POET	Poets
OCTAVIUS CAESAR, MARCUS ANTONIUS, M. AEMILIUS LEPIDUS	Triumvirs* After the Death of Julius Caesar	LUCILIUS, TITINIUS, MESSALA, YOUNG CATO, VOLUMNIUS	Friends to Brutus and Cassius
CICERO, PUBLIUS, POPILIUS LENA	Senators	VARRO, CLITUS, CLAUDIUS, STRATO, LUCIUS, DARDANIUS	Servants to Brutus
MARCUS BRUTUS, CASSIUS, CASCA, TREBONIUS, LIGARIUS, DECIUS BRUTUS, METELLUS CIMBER, CINNA	Conspirators Against Julius Caesar	PINDARUS	Servant to Cassius
FLAVIUS, MARULLUS	Senators	CALPURNIA	Wife of Caesar
ARTEMIDORUS OF CNIDOS	Teacher of Rhetoric	PORTIA	Wife of Brutus
		SOOTHSAYER	
		SENATORS, CITIZENS, GUARDS, ATTENDANTS, and so on	

3

Scene: During most of the play, at Rome; afterwards near Sardis, and near Philippi.

***Triumvirs** (trī um′ virz) *n.* in ancient Rome, a group of three leaders who shared power equally.

ACT I

Scene i. Rome. A street.

[*Enter* FLAVIUS, MARULLUS, *and certain* COMMONERS[1] *over the stage.*]

FLAVIUS. Hence! Home, you idle creatures, get you home!
Is this a holiday? What, know you not,
Being mechanical,[2] you ought not walk
Upon a laboring day without the sign
Of your profession?[3] Speak, what trade art thou?

CARPENTER. Why, sir, a carpenter.

MARULLUS. Where is thy leather apron and thy rule?
What dost thou with thy best apparel on?
You, sir, what trade are you?

COBBLER. Truly, sir, in respect of a fine workman,[4] I am but, as you would say, a cobbler.[5]

1. **COMMONERS** (kam′ ən ərz) *n.* people not of the nobility or upper classes.
2. **mechanical** of the working class.
3. **sign/Of your profession** work clothes and tools.
4. **in respect of a fine workman** in relation to a skilled worker.
5. **cobbler** (a pun) "mender of shoes" or "a clumsy, bungling worker."

4 **Reading Check**

What fact about the commoners attracts Flavius' attention?

3 Reading Skill

Use Text Aids

1. Examine the list of characters with students. **Ask** students what they learn from the list.
Answer: The list tells the names of the characters and their relationships to one another.
2. **Ask** students how they might use the list while reading the play.
Possible response: While reading, readers can refer to the list when new characters are introduced or when they need a reminder of who someone is.
3. Point out that stage directions in the play are also a kind of text aid. Draw students' attention to the bracketed stage directions. Explain that stage directions in Shakespeare's plays are usually limited to indications of the characters' exits and entrances.

4 Reading Check

Answer: Flavius notices that although it is a workday, the commoners are wearing their best clothes.

Differentiated Instruction for Universal Access

EL Support for English Learners

Help students engage with Shakespearian language by putting students into four groups. Assign each group to read aloud the lines of Flavius, the Carpenter, Marullus, or the Cobbler. Stop after each group reads its part; discuss the meaning of the lines. Define words that students find difficult; invite students to list synonyms of challenging words in their first languages.

Enrichment for Advanced Readers

Explain that many of the stage directions in Shakespeare's plays were not written by him but supplied by editors. Contrast the use of stage directions in Shakespeare's plays with their use in many modern plays. Tell students that modern playwrights often provide detailed descriptions of settings and directions for actors. Challenge students to write more detailed stage directions for each scene. Direct them to use the stage directions already present and any clues in the dialogue to elaborate.

PHLit Online!

This selection is available in interactive format in the **Enriched Online Student Edition, www.PHLitOnline.com,** which includes a thematically related video with writing prompt and an interactive graphic organizer.

❺ Reading Skill

Use Text Aids

1. Point out the glosses, or side notes, on this page. Remind students that these notes, found throughout the text, can help readers understand the meaning of unfamiliar words and phrases and idioms, or expressions.
2. **Ask** students to respond to the Reading Skill prompt: Explain how glosses, or side notes, 7 and 8 help you to understand Marullus' reaction in lines 19–20.
Answer: The notes clarify that the language in lines 19–20 has a double meaning. The words and phrases apply to shoes, but they also have an idiomatic meaning. Marullus is irritated by the Cobbler's words and wants the Cobbler to mend, or improve, his mood. Marullus' reaction is to use the Cobbler's work language in an idiomatic sense.

❻ Critical Viewing

Answer: The painting suggests that they are wearing loose-fitting clothing appropriate for a warm climate and that they are wearing covering on their heads. The text suggests that clothing like this would be the commoners' "best" clothes, not their work clothes. For Flavius and Marullus, the clothing shown in the painting would probably be typical daily attire.

6. **knave** (nāv) *n.* tricky rascal; rogue.
7. **be not out . . . if you be out** be not angry . . . if you have worn-out shoes.
8. **mend you** (a pun) "mend your shoes" or "improve your disposition."

Reading Skill
Use Text Aids ❺
Explain how glosses, or sidenotes, 7 and 8 help you to understand Marullus' reaction in lines 19–20.

MARULLUS. But what trade art thou? Answer me directly.

COBBLER. A trade, sir, that, I hope, I may use with a safe conscience, which is indeed, sir, a mender of bad soles.

FLAVIUS. What trade, thou knave?[6] Thou naughty knave what trade?

COBBLER. Nay, I beseech you, sir, be not out with me: yet, if you be out,[7] sir, I can mend you.[8]

MARULLUS. What mean'st thou by that? Mend me, thou saucy fellow?

COBBLER. Why, sir, cobble you.

FLAVIUS. Thou art a cobbler, art thou?

COBBLER. Truly, sir, all that I live by is with the awl:[9] I meddle with no tradesman's matters, nor women's matters; but withal,[10] I am indeed, sir, a surgeon to old shoes: when they are in great danger, I recover them. As proper men as ever trod upon neat's leather[11] have gone upon my handiwork.

FLAVIUS. But wherefore art not in thy shop today?
Why dost thou lead these men about the streets?

COBBLER. Truly, sir, to wear out their shoes, to get myself into more work. But indeed, sir, we make holiday to see Caesar and to rejoice in his triumph.[12]

MARULLUS. Wherefore rejoice? What conquest brings he home?
What tributaries[13] follow him to Rome,
To grace in captive bonds his chariot wheels?
You blocks, you stones, you worse than senseless things!
O you hard hearts, you cruel men of Rome,
Knew you not Pompey?[14] Many a time and oft
Have you climbed up to walls and battlements,
To tow'rs and windows, yea, to chimney tops,
Your infants in your arms, and there have sat
The livelong day, with patient expectation,
To see great Pompey pass the streets of Rome.
And when you saw his chariot but appear,
Have you not made an universal shout,
That Tiber[15] trembled underneath her banks
To hear the replication of your sounds
Made in her concave shores?[16]
And do you now put on your best attire?
And do you now cull out[17] a holiday?

9. **awl** (ôl) *n.* small, pointed tool for making holes in leather.
10. **withal** (*with* ôl′) *adv.* nevertheless (also a pun on "with awl").
11. **neat's leather** leather made from the hides of cattle.
12. **triumph** (trī′ əmf) *n.* procession celebrating the return of a victorious general.
13. **tributaries** (trib′ yo͞o ter′ ēz) *n.* captives.
14. **Pompey** (päm′ pē) A Roman general and triumvir defeated by Caesar in 48 b.c. and later murdered.
15. **Tiber** (tī′ bər) river that flows through Rome.
16. **concave shores** hollowed-out banks; overhanging banks.
17. **cull out** pick out; select.

Vocabulary
replication (rep′ li kā′ sh ən) *n.* duplicate; reproduction

❻ ▶ **Critical Viewing**
Judging from this Roman painting, how might the characters be dressed? Explain. **[Connect]**

Vocabulary Development

Wordplay

Explain that much of Shakespeare's humor depends on wordplay. He makes frequent use of puns—that is, he uses words in a humorous way that plays on their multiple meanings or on the meanings of homophones. Help students understand the pun on *awl, all,* and *withal* (lines 23–25): the Cobbler literally lives by his awl, the tool of his trade. Shakespeare also plays with the word *recover* (line 26): a surgeon helps his patient recover, while a cobbler literally recovers old shoes by patching their holes. Have students read aloud these lines and others so that they understand the wordplay with sound and meaning.

7 And do you now strew flowers in his way
That comes in triumph over Pompey's blood?[18]
Be gone!
Run to your houses, fall upon your knees,
Pray to the gods to intermit the plague[19]
That needs must light on this ingratitude.

FLAVIUS. Go, go, good countrymen, and, for this fault,
Assemble all the poor men of your sort;
Draw them to Tiber banks and weep your tears
Into the channel, till the lowest stream
Do kiss the most exalted shores of all.[20]

[All the commoners exit.]

18. Pompey's blood Pompey's sons, whom Caesar has just defeated.

19. intermit the plague (plāg) stop the calamity or trouble.

20. the most exalted shores of all the highest banks.

9 **Reading Check**

What does Marullus think about the people celebrating in the streets?

8

Differentiated Instruction for Universal Access

EL Strategy for English Learners

The glosses, or side notes, throughout the play should be very helpful to students learning English. To interpret the text using the glosses provided, suggest that students use a simple chart like the one below. Model how to use the chart with the example shown:

Original lines	Words Explained in Side Notes	My Own Words
And do you now cull out a holiday?	cull out: pick out, select	Are you picking a holiday now?

7 Background

Pompey the Great

Pompey grew up in a wealthy Roman family during a time of war between followers of Gaius Marius and those of Lucius Sulla. When Pompey was in his twenties, he raised his own army, allied himself with Sulla, and defeated Marius. Pompey became a popular hero. In 60 B.C., Pompey, Julius Caesar, and Marcus Crassus formed a triumvirate—a group of three rulers—and took control of Rome.

Pompey grew more and more concerned with Caesar's growing popularity and decided to crush him. Violent civil war broke out between their followers. Eventually, Caesar defeated Pompey, who escaped to Egypt only to be put to death by the Egyptian government.

8 Humanities

Fresco

Fresco is a way of painting in which the artist applies water-based paint to fresh plaster. Thus, frescos often decorate plaster walls and have become a favorite technique of muralists.

The fresco on page 895 was found in Villa Boscoreale, an Italian home buried by ash during the eruption of Mt. Vesuvius. Excavations during the twentieth century revealed this and other frescos that decorated the homes of people in ancient Rome. Use this question for discussion:

- What details of the fresco seem to relate to civic life in Rome?
  Possible response: One person is holding a spear and has a shield; he could be a soldier.

9 Reading Check

Answer: Marullus thinks the people are wrong to celebrate Caesar's triumph and reminds them that they once also celebrated Pompey, whom Caesar defeated. Marullus thinks the people in the streets are ungrateful and should go home.

⑩ Background

Film

The photographs shown throughout this selection are from the 1953 Hollywood film *Julius Caesar,* in which Louis Calhern played the title role. The cast included many British actors: James Mason as Brutus, John Gielgud as Cassius, Deborah Kerr as Portia, and Greer Garson as Calpurnia. The American star Marlon Brando (pictured on this page center) stole the show as Mark Antony. Brando was nominated for an Academy Award for his stirring performance.

⑪ Critical Viewing

Answer: The actors' poses imply that they are friends and that Caesar has more power than Antony. Caesar has placed his hand on Antony's shoulder in a way that shows a friendly connection. Antony does not reciprocate with a gesture, which shows that Caesar is the dominant, or more powerful, of the two.

See, whe'r their basest mettle[21] be not moved,
They vanish tongue-tied in their guiltiness.
Go you down that way toward the Capitol;
This way will I. Disrobe the images,
If you do find them decked with ceremonies.[22]

MARULLUS. May we do so?
You know it is the feast of Lupercal.[23]

FLAVIUS. It is no matter; let no images
Be hung with Caesar's trophies. I'll about
And drive away the vulgar[24] from the streets;
So do you too, where you perceive them thick.
These growing feathers plucked from Caesar's wing
Will make him fly an ordinary pitch,[25]
Who else would soar above the view of men
And keep us all in servile fearfulness. [*Exit*]

21. whe'r their basest mettle whether the most inferior material of which they are made.

22. Disrobe the images . . . decked with ceremonies strip the statues . . . covered with decorations.

23. feast of Lupercal (lo͞o′ pər kal) ancient Roman festival celebrated on February 15.

24. vulgar (vul′ gər) *n.* common people.

25. pitch upward flight of a hawk.

Vocabulary
servile (sur′ vəl) *adj.* slavelike; humbly submissive to authority

⑪ ▼ **Critical Viewing** What do the actors' poses in this movie still imply about the relation between Caesar (left) and Antony (middle)? **[Infer]**

⑩

Vocabulary Development

Word Origins

Call students' attention to the selection vocabulary word *servile* in line 77. Review the definition of *servile* with students: "slavelike, submissive to authority." Explain that the adjective *servile* in English derives from the Latin word *servus*, meaning "slave." Challenge students to identify and define other English words that share the Latin root *serv-*. Students may name the following: *serve, servant, servitude, service.*

Scene ii. A public place.

12 [*Enter* CAESAR, ANTONY (*for the course*),[1] CALPURNIA, PORTIA, DECIUS, CICERO, BRUTUS, CASSIUS, CASCA, *a* SOOTHSAYER; *after them,* MARULLUS *and* FLAVIUS.]

CAESAR. Calpurnia!

CASCA. Peace, ho! Caesar speaks.

CAESAR. Calpurnia!

13 **CALPURNIA.** Here, my lord.

CAESAR. Stand you directly in Antonius' way
When he doth run his course. Antonius!

ANTONY. Caesar, my lord?

CAESAR. Forget not in your speed, Antonius,
To touch Calpurnia; for our elders say
The barren, touchèd in this holy chase,
Shake off their sterile curse.[2]

ANTONY. I shall remember:
When Caesar says "Do this," it is performed.

CAESAR. Set on, and leave no ceremony out.

SOOTHSAYER. Caesar!

CAESAR. Ha! Who calls?

CASCA. Bid every noise be still; peace yet again!

CAESAR. Who is it in the press[3] that calls on me?
I hear a tongue, shriller than all the music,
Cry "Caesar." Speak; Caesar is turned to hear.

14 **SOOTHSAYER.** Beware the ides of March.[4]

CAESAR. What man is that?

BRUTUS. A soothsayer bids you beware the ides of March.

CAESAR. Set him before me; let me see his face.

CASSIUS. Fellow, come from the throng; look upon Caesar.

CAESAR. What say'st thou to me now? Speak once again.

SOOTHSAYER. Beware the ides of March.

CAESAR. He is a dreamer, let us leave him. Pass.

[*A trumpet sounds. Exit all but* BRUTUS *and* CASSIUS.]

1. **for the course** ready for the foot race that was part of the Lupercal festivities.

Reading Skill
Use Text Aids
What information about the relationship between Caesar and Calpurnia do you find in the "Characters" list, on page 893?

Literary Analysis
Shakespeare's Tragedies What is Caesar's rank?

2. **barren . . . sterile curse** It was believed that women who were unable to bear children (such as Calpurnia), if touched by a runner during this race, would then be able to bear children.

3. **press** *n.* crowd.

4. **ides of March** in the ancient Roman calendar, March 15.

15 **Reading Check**
How does Caesar respond to the soothsayer's warning?

Differentiated Instruction for Universal Access

Enrichment for Gifted and Talented Students
Shakespeare's language was meant to be heard rather than read silently. Have students form a group to read the play aloud together. Readers can maintain the same roles or alternate so that everyone has a chance to read both major and minor characters' lines. Tell students to read with expression appropriate to the content of the lines. Have students discuss how hearing the language enriches their experience of the play.

12 Reading Skill
Use Text Aids

1. Draw students' attention to the stage direction at the beginning of Scene ii. **Ask:** What does the stage direction at the beginning of Scene ii tell you?
Answer: The stage direction tells which characters come on stage for Scene ii and the order in which they enter. It also says that Antony is ready for the foot race.
2. Remind students that they can refer to the list of characters at the beginning of the play for information about the characters' identities and relationships.
3. **Ask** students the Reading Skill question: What information about the relationship between Caesar and Calpurnia do you find in the "Characters" list, on page 893?
Answer: The list explains that Calpurnia is Caesar's wife.

13 Literary Analysis
Shakespeare's Tragedies

1. Ask four volunteers to read the parts of Caesar, Casca, Calpurnia, and Antony in lines 1–5. **Ask** students how people address Caesar.
Answer: They call him "my lord."
2. Check students' understanding of the title "lord."
3. **Ask** students to respond to the Literary Analysis question: What is Caesar's rank?
Answer: He is a person of noble birth and high status.

14 Background
The Ides of March

When the soothsayer mentions "the ides of March," he is referring to March 15. This term comes from the ancient Roman calendar, which did not number the days of each month.

15 Reading Check

Answer: Caesar is scornful of the soothsayer's warning and ignores it.

16 Literary Analysis

Shakespeare's Tragedies

1. Ask two volunteers to take the parts of Brutus and Cassius and read aloud their exchange in lines 32–47.
2. Remind students that in his tragedies, Shakespeare focuses on the hero's internal conflict, or his or her struggle with conflicting ideas, values, or beliefs. **Ask:** How do you know that Brutus is struggling with an internal conflict?
   Answer: In lines 39–47, Brutus explains that his behavior has been affected by "passions," or feelings, "of some difference" and "conceptions," or thoughts, that only concern him. He also says that he is "with himself at war."

17 Critical Thinking

Analyze

1. As a class, read aloud lines 48–65. Point out the repeated use of the words *see, sees,* and *eye* or *eyes* in lines 51, 52, 57, 58, and 62.
2. **Ask** students what Cassius wants Brutus to see.
3. **Answer:** Cassius wants Brutus to see that he is a respected nobleman whom others would support as their leader.
4. **Ask** students why Brutus suggests in line 63 that thinking of himself as a respected nobleman is dangerous.
   Answer: Brutus thinks that seeking power, or thinking of himself as entitled to power, could force him into a political conflict of some kind.

5. order of the course the race.

6. gamesome (gām´ səm) *adj.* having a liking for sports.

7. quick spirit lively disposition.

8. wont (wōnt) *adj.* accustomed.

9. bear . . . hand treat too harshly and too like a stranger.

16

10. if I . . . upon myself if I have been less open, it is because I am troubled with myself.

11. passions *n.* feelings; emotions.

12. of some difference in conflict.

13. Conceptions . . . myself thoughts that concern only me.

14. soil *n.* blemish.

15. By means . . . buried because of which I have kept to myself.

16. cogitations (käj ə tā´ shənz) *n.* thoughts.

17. 'Tis just it is true.

17

18. lamented (lə men´ təd) *v.* regretted.

19. turn . . . shadow reflect your hidden noble qualities so you could see their image.

20. the best respect the best reputation.

21. this age's yoke the tyranny of Caesar.

CASSIUS. Will you go see the order of the course?[5]

BRUTUS. Not I.

CASSIUS. I pray you do.

BRUTUS. I am not gamesome:[6] I do lack some part
Of that quick spirit[7] that is in Antony.
Let me not hinder, Cassius, your desires;
I'll leave you.

CASSIUS. Brutus, I do observe you now of late;
I have not from your eyes that gentleness
And show of love as I was wont[8] to have;
You bear too stubborn and too strange a hand[9]
Over your friend that loves you.

BRUTUS. Cassius,
Be not deceived: if I have veiled my look,
I turn the trouble of my countenance
Merely upon myself.[10] Vexèd I am
Of late with passions[11] of some difference,[12]
Conceptions only proper to myself,[13]
Which give some soil,[14] perhaps, to my behaviors;
But let not therefore my good friends be grieved
(Among which number, Cassius, be you one)
Nor construe any further my neglect
Than that poor Brutus, with himself at war,
Forgets the shows of love to other men.

CASSIUS. Then, Brutus, I have much mistook your passion;
By means whereof this breast of mine hath buried[15]
Thoughts of great value, worthy cogitations.[16]
Tell me, good Brutus, can you see your face?

BRUTUS. No, Cassius; for the eye sees not itself
But by reflection, by some other things.

CASSIUS. 'Tis just.[17]
And it is very much lamented,[18] Brutus,
That you have no such mirrors as will turn
Your hidden worthiness into your eye,
That you might see your shadow.[19] I have heard
Where many of the best respect[20] in Rome
(Except immortal Caesar), speaking of Brutus,
And groaning underneath this age's yoke,[21]
Have wished that noble Brutus had his eyes.

Think Aloud

Vocabulary: Using Context

Direct students' attention to the word *countenance* in line 38 of Brutus' speech. Then, use a think-aloud process to model how to use context to infer the meaning of an unknown word. Say the following to students:

> Brutus refers to the trouble of his countenance. To get an idea of what *countenance* means, I am going to look at other words in the same sentence and in surrounding lines. In the same sentence in which Brutus refers to his countenance, he talks about veiling his look. Just before this, in lines 32–34, Cassius says that he hasn't noticed the usual gentleness and show of love in Brutus' eyes lately. These references to the eyes, a certain expression, and a look in general could be clues to the meaning of *countenance.* In line 51, I see another clue: Cassius asks Brutus if he can see his face. I think *countenance* means "face."

17

BRUTUS. Into what dangers would you lead me, Cassius,
That you would have me seek into myself
For that which is not in me?

CASSIUS. Therefore, good Brutus, be prepared to hear;
And since you know you cannot see yourself
So well as by reflection, I, your glass
Will modestly discover to yourself
That of yourself which you yet know not of.[22]
And be not jealous on[23] me, gentle Brutus:
Were I a common laughter,[24] or did use
To stale with ordinary oaths my love
To every new protester;[25] if you know
That I do fawn on men and hug them hard,
And after scandal[26] them; or if you know
That I profess myself in banqueting
To all the rout,[27] then hold me dangerous.

[*Flourish of trumpets and shout*]

22. your glass . . . know not of your mirror will make known to you without exaggeration the qualities you have of which you are unaware.

23. be not jealous on do not be suspicious of.

24. common laughter object of ridicule.

25. To stale . . . new protester to cheapen my friendship by avowing it to anyone who promises to be my friend.

26. scandal *v.* slander; gossip about.

27. profess myself . . . rout declare my friendship to the common crowd.

19 **Reading Check**

According to Cassius, what does Brutus not realize about himself?

18

20 ◀ **Critical Viewing**

What does the expression of this actor in the role of Cassius convey about Cassius' intelligence? Explain. **[Infer]**

18 Humanities

Togas

The actor in the picture is wearing a togalike garment of draped material.

Romans adapted togas from a loosely draped garment worn by Etruscans. Togas were oval pieces of cloth folded carefully around a body. The art of folding or draping a toga could be so complex that households kept slaves who knew how to dress people in togas.

Togas did not allow fast, free movement. Women and working-class people gave up the toga first. As a result, togas became the garments worn by upper classes, and eventually, they became the prescribed uniforms of state officials.

19 Reading Check

Answer: According to Cassius, Brutus does not realize that he has several noble qualities and is respected by many.

20 Critical Viewing

Answer: The expression of the actor playing Cassius conveys that Cassius is serious and analytical. His furrowed, or wrinkled, forehead suggests that he is a thorough, thoughtful observer.

Differentiated Instruction for Universal Access

Strategy for Less Proficient Readers

To increase understanding of Brutus and Cassius, two of the main characters of *The Tragedy of Julius Caesar,* guide students in making a word web for each character. Write the character's name in the center of the web. Then reread the conversation of Brutus and Cassius in this scene to identify personality traits of each. Show these traits in the outer circles of each web. Note the line numbers of the text that support each trait on the ray that connects the center and outer circles of the web.

21 Literary Analysis

Shakespeare's Tragedies

1. Read aloud the exchange between Brutus and Cassius in lines 79–82.
2. Then **ask** students the Literary Analysis question: What internal conflict in Brutus do lines 79–82 reveal?
   Answer: Brutus loves Caesar but does not want Caesar to be king.
3. **Ask:** How does Cassius know that Brutus does not want Caesar to be king even before Brutus says so?
   Answer: Cassius notes that Brutus says he "fears" that the people have chosen Caesar to be their king.

22 Literature in Context

History Connection Tradition holds that the distinction between patricians and plebeians dates back to the founding of Rome, but many scholars today believe that the social orders arose gradually during the early Roman Republic. Originally, the patricians probably represented the most important families of Rome. Over the history of the Republic, the plebeians struggled for legal equality with the patricians. By the end of the Roman Empire, they were largely successful.

Connect to the Literature Review the three scenes in Act 1, and have students summarize them. Then **ask** students the Connect to the Literature question: Which scenes in Act I best reflect the division in Roman society? Explain.
Possible response: Students will probably respond that Scene i best represents the division in Roman society because it portrays an encounter between noblemen and commoners and illustrates their very different views of Caesar.

Literary Analysis Shakespeare's Tragedies 21 What internal conflict in Brutus do lines 79–82 reveal?

BRUTUS. What means this shouting? I do fear the people
Choose Caesar for their king.

CASSIUS. Ay, do you fear it?
Then must I think you would not have it so.

BRUTUS. I would not, Cassius, yet I love him well.
But wherefore do you hold me here so long?
What is it that you would impart to me?
If it be aught toward the general good,[28]
Set honor in one eye and death i' th' other,
And I will look on both indifferently;[29]
For let the gods so speed[30] me, as I love
The name of honor more than I fear death.

CASSIUS. I know that virtue to be in you, Brutus,
As well as I do know your outward favor.[31]
Well, honor is the subject of my story.
I cannot tell what you and other men
Think of this life, but for my single self,
I had as lief not be,[32] as live to be
In awe of such a thing as I myself.[33]
I was born free as Caesar; so were you:
We both have fed as well, and we can both
Endure the winter's cold as well as he:
For once, upon a raw and gusty day,
The troubled Tiber chafing with[34] her shores,

23

28. **aught . . . good** anything to do with the public welfare.
29. **indifferently** (in dif′ ər ənt lē) *adv.* without preference; impartially.
30. **speed** *v.* give good fortune to.
31. **favor** *n.* face; appearance.
32. **as lief not be** just as soon not exist.
33. **such a thing as I myself** another human being (Caesar).
34. **chafing with** raging against.

22 **LITERATURE IN CONTEXT**

History Connection

Roman Society

Brutus and Cassius fear that the common people will support Caesar in his bid to become emperor. Their fear reflects tensions in Roman society of the time.

- Poor *plebeians* (commoners), including farmers who could no longer compete with wealthy landowners, flooded Rome.
- They created a restless mass of unemployed poor.
- Some leaders took their side and won power with their support.
- Other leaders took the side of the *patricians* (aristocrats) and the wealthy plebeians.
- The conflict between rich and poor led to civil unrest, including riots and assassinations.

Connect to the Literature

Which scenes in Act I best reflect the division in Roman society? Explain.

Caesar said to me "Darest thou, Cassius, now
Leap in with me into this angry flood,
And swim to yonder point?" Upon the word,
Accout'red[35] as I was, I plungèd in
And bade him follow: so indeed he did.
The torrent roared, and we did buffet[36] it
With lusty sinews,[37] throwing it aside
And stemming it with hearts of controversy.[38]
But ere we could arrive the point proposed,
Caesar cried "Help me, Cassius, or I sink!"
I, as Aeneas,[39] our great ancestor,
Did from the flames of Troy upon his shoulder
The old Anchises bear, so from the waves of Tiber
Did I the tired Caesar. And this man
Is now become a god, and Cassius is
A wretched creature, and must bend his body
If Caesar carelessly but nod on him.
He had a fever when he was in Spain,
And when the fit was on him, I did mark
How he did shake: 'tis true, this god did shake.
His coward lips did from their color fly,[40]
And that same eye whose bend[41] doth awe the world
did lose his[42] luster: I did hear him groan;
Ay, and that tongue of his, that bade the Romans
Mark him and write his speeches in their books,
Alas, it cried, "Give me some drink, Titinius,"
As a sick girl. Ye gods! It doth amaze me,
A man of such a feeble temper[43] should
So get the start of[44] the majestic world,
And bear the palm[45] alone. [*Shout. Flourish of trumpets*]

BRUTUS. Another general shout?
I do believe that these applauses are
For some new honors that are heaped on Caesar.

CASSIUS. Why, man, he doth bestride the narrow world
Like a Colossus,[46] and we petty men
Walk under his huge legs and peep about
To find ourselves dishonorable[47] graves.
Men at some time are masters of their fates:
The fault, dear Brutus, is not in our stars,[48]
But in ourselves, that we are underlings.[49]
Brutus and Caesar: what should be in that "Caesar"?
Why should that name be sounded[50] more than yours?
Write them together, yours is as fair a name;

35. Accout'red (ə ko͞o′ trəd) *adj.* dressed in armor.
36. buffet (buf′ it) *v.* struggle against.
37. lusty sinews (sin′ yo͞oz) strong muscles.
38. stemming it . . . controversy making progress against it with our intense rivalry.
39. Aeneas (i nē′ əs) Trojan hero of the poet Virgil's epic poem *Aeneid*, who carried his old father, Anchises, from the burning city of Troy and later founded Rome.
40. His coward lips . . . fly color fled from his lips, which were like cowardly soldiers fleeing from a battle.
41. bend *n.* glance.
42. his *pron.* its.
43. feeble temper weak physical constitution.
44. get the start of outdistance.
45. palm *n.* leaf of a palm tree carried or worn as a symbol of victory; victor's prize.
46. Colossus (kə läs′ əs) *n.* gigantic ancient statue of Apollo, a Greek and Roman god, that was set at the entrance to the harbor of Rhodes; ships would sail under its legs.
47. dishonorable (dis än′ ər ə bəl) *adj.* shameful (because they will not be of free men).
48. stars *n.* destinies. The stars were thought to control people's lives.
49. underlings *n.* inferior people.
50. sounded *v.* spoken or announced by trumpets.

24 **Reading Check**
What has Cassius done to help Caesar in the past?

23 Connecting to the Big Question

1. Explain to students that our experiences, and the conclusions we draw from them, often color our perception of the world and the people in it.
2. Read aloud Cassius' speech. **Ask** students to determine Cassius' opinion of Caesar.
   Possible response: Cassius thinks he is a better, stronger person than Caesar, so he is furious at having to bow down to a person to whom he feels more worthy.
3. Have students contrast Cassius' feelings about Caesar with those of Brutus. **Ask:** Is Cassius feeling as conflicted about Caesar as Brutus is? Explain.
   Possible response: No; Cassius is not conflicted about Caesar. He relates Caesar's weaknesses, which shows that he does not love Caesar as Brutus does.
4. **Ask** students: Considering Cassius' past experiences with Caesar, is Cassius justified in feeling bitter about Caesar's quick rise to power? Explain.
   Possible response: Yes; Cassius saved Caesar's life because Caesar was not strong enough to swim. Cassius feels that, as the stronger man—and as Caesar's savior—he, or anyone, should not bow down to a man who does not deserve such power.
5. Tell students to continue to look for the characters' opinions of Caesar as they read.

24 Reading Check

Answer: Cassius saved Caesar from drowning in the Tiber River.

Differentiated Instruction for Universal Access

Enrichment for Advanced Readers

Have students identify and discuss the various conflicts described in Act I. Explain that some conflicts, such as a war between two countries, are external. Others, such as a conflict between duty and inclination, are internal. Ask students to consider which seems to be the central conflict in *The Tragedy of Julius Caesar* and to support their answers with specific details from the different acts in the play. Students can meet in discussion groups after reading each act and talk about new conflicts that have arisen, how conflicts introduced earlier have been resolved, and how various conflicts have developed.

25 Reading Skill

Use Text Aids

1. Remind students that, in addition to the side notes, they should refer to the Background features on page 889 for additional information that will enhance their understanding of the play.
2. Have students read lines 158–161. Then **ask** the Reading Skill question: How does the Background on page 889 along with note 55 help you understand Cassius' appeal to Brutus?
Possible response: The information in the feature and note help the reader understand that Cassius is using the example of Lucius Junius Brutus, who overthrew the last king of Rome and thus helped create the Republic, to appeal to Brutus to prevent Caesar from becoming king and ending the Republic.

26 Critical Thinking

Infer

1. Discuss with students the implications of Cassius' appeal to Brutus.
2. Have students infer what Cassius thinks Brutus and he should do to make sure that Caesar does not become king. Have students explain their reasoning.
Possible response: Cassius' intense dislike for Caesar and envy of him suggest that he thinks that they should use any means necessary to keep Caesar from becoming king.

27 Literary Analysis

Shakespeare's Tragedies

1. Read the bracketed passage aloud. Then **ask** students what Brutus means when he says he would rather be a villager than a son of Rome under the circumstances.
Answer: With these words, Brutus shows that he is concerned about developments in Rome and knows he has a responsibility to come to some decision about a course of action.
2. **Ask** students to respond to the Literary Analysis question: What tragic flaw in Brutus' character might lines 172–175 reveal?
Answer: These lines suggest that he may ignore his own instincts and go along with Cassius. His flaw might be an error in judgment.

Sound them, it doth become the mouth as well;
Weigh them, it is as heavy; conjure[51] with 'em,
"Brutus" will start[52] a spirit as soon as "Caesar."
Now, in the names of all the gods at once,
Upon what meat doth this our Caesar feed,
That he is grown so great? Age, thou art shamed!
Rome, thou hast lost the breed of noble bloods!
When went there by an age, since the great flood,[53]
But it was famed with[54] more than with one man?
When could they say (till now) that talked of Rome,
That her wide walks encompassed but one man?
Now is it Rome indeed, and room enough,
When there is in it but one only man.
O, you and I have heard our fathers say,
There was a Brutus[55] once that would have brooked[56]
Th' eternal devil to keep his state in Rome
As easily as a king.

BRUTUS. That you do love me, I am nothing jealous;[57]
What you would work me to,[58] I have some aim;[59]
How I have thought of this, and of these times,
I shall recount hereafter. For this present,
I would not so (with love I might entreat you)
Be any further moved. What you have said
I will consider; what you have to say
I will with patience hear, and find a time
Both meet[60] to hear and answer such high things.
Till then, my noble friend, chew upon[61] this:
Brutus had rather be a villager
Than to repute himself a son of Rome
Under these hard conditions as this time
Is like to lay upon us.

CASSIUS. I am glad
That my weak words have struck but thus much show
Of fire from Brutus.

[*Enter* CAESAR *and his* TRAIN.][62]

BRUTUS. The games are done, and Caesar is returning.

CASSIUS. As they pass by, pluck Casca by the sleeve,
And he will (after his sour fashion) tell you
What hath proceeded worthy note today.

BRUTUS. I will do so. But look you, Cassius,
The angry spot doth glow on Caesar's brow,
And all the rest look like a chidden train:[63]

51. **conjure** (kän′ jər) *v.* summon a spirit by a magic spell.
52. **start** *v.* raise.
53. **great flood** in Greek mythology, a flood that drowned everyone except Deucalion and his wife Pyrrha, who were saved by the god Zeus because of their virtue.
54. **But it was famed with** without the age being made famous by.
55. **Brutus** Lucius Junius Brutus had helped expel the last king of Rome and had helped found the Republic in 509 B.C.
56. **brooked** *v.* put up with.

Reading Skill 25
Use Text Aids 26
How does the Background on page 889 along with note 55 help you understand Cassius' appeal to Brutus?

57. **nothing jealous** not at all doubting.
58. **work me to** persuade me of.
59. **aim** *n.* idea.
60. **meet** *adj.* fit; suitable.
61. **chew upon** think about.

Literary Analysis
Shakespeare's Tragedies 27 What tragic flaw in Brutus' character might lines 172–175 reveal?

62. **train** *n.* attendants.

63. **chidden train** scolded attendants.

Vocabulary Development

Recognizing Related Words

Write the words *spare, lean,* and *thin* on the board. Explain that the three words are synonyms, or words with similar meaning. Point out that Caesar uses the first two words to describe Cassius. Explain that antonyms are words with opposite meanings. Ask students what antonym for *spare* Caesar uses *(fat)*. Have students brainstorm for other antonyms for *spare*. Then have students use a dictionary to find definitions for *spare* used as a noun and a verb. Explain that the adjective, noun, and verb *spare* are homographs—words that are spelled the same but have different meanings.

Calpurnia's cheek is pale, and Cicero
Looks with such ferret[64] and such fiery eyes
As we have seen him in the Capitol,
Being crossed in conference[65] by some senators.

CASSIUS. Casca will tell us what the matter is.

CAESAR. Antonius.

ANTONY. Caesar?

CAESAR. Let me have men about me that are fat,
Sleek-headed men, and such as sleep a-nights.
Yond Cassius has a lean and hungry look;
28 He thinks too much: such men are dangerous.

ANTONY. Fear him not, Caesar, he's not dangerous;
He is a noble Roman, and well given.[66]

CAESAR. Would he were fatter! But I fear him not.
Yet if my name were liable to fear,
I do not know the man I should avoid
So soon as that spare Cassius. He reads much,
He is a great observer, and he looks
quite through the deeds of men.[67] He loves no plays,
As thou dost, Antony; he hears no music;
Seldom he smiles, and smiles in such a sort[68]
29 As if he mocked himself, and scorned his spirit
That could be moved to smile at anything.
Such men as he be never at heart's ease
Whiles they behold a greater than themselves,
And therefore are they very dangerous.
I rather tell thee what is to be feared
Than what I fear; for always I am Caesar.
Come on my right hand, for this ear is deaf,
And tell me truly what thou think'st of him.

[*A trumpet sounds.* CAESAR *and his* TRAIN *exit.*]

CASCA. You pulled me by the cloak; would you speak with me?

BRUTUS. Ay, Casca; tell us what hath chanced[69] today,
That Caesar looks so sad.

CASCA. Why, you were with him, were you not?

BRUTUS. I should not then ask Casca what had chanced.

31 **CASCA.** Why, there was a crown offered him; and being offered him, he put it by[70] with the back of his hand, thus; and then the people fell a-shouting.

64. **ferret** (fer′ it) *n.* small animal, like a weasel, with reddish eyes.

65. **crossed in conference** opposed in debate.

66. **well given** well disposed.

67. **looks . . . deeds of men** sees through people's actions to their motives.

Vocabulary
spare (sper) *adj.* lean; thin

68. **sort** way.

69. **hath chanced** has happened.

70. **put it by** pushed it away.

30 **Reading Check**
Why does Cassius compare Brutus and Caesar?

28 Critical Thinking

Making Judgments

1. Read aloud lines 192–214. Then **ask** students to summarize Caesar's judgment of Cassius.
Possible response: Caesar thinks Cassius is dangerous because he thinks too much.
2. **Ask** students what judgment they can make about Caesar, based on his remarks about Cassius.
Possible response: Caesar is observant and shrewd. He accurately judges Cassius' enmity toward him. Even though he claims he is not afraid of Cassius, he remarks to Antony that Cassius is dangerous.

29 Background

Cassius and Caesar

According to Plutarch, the Greek biographer whose work was Shakespeare's major source for this play, Caesar had good reason to distrust Cassius. The following excerpt from Plutarch's life of Cassius tells why:

"Cassius, a man of fierce disposition, and one that out of private malice, rather than love of public, hated Caesar, not the tyrant, continually fired and stirred him up. Brutus felt the rule an oppression, but Cassius hated the ruler; and among other reasons on which he grounded his quarrel against Caesar, the loss of his lions which he had procured . . . Caesar, finding these, seized them for himself."

30 Reading Check

Answer: Cassius compares Brutus and Caesar to prove that Caesar is no greater than Brutus. Thus, Cassius makes the comparison to appeal to Brutus to prevent Caesar from becoming king.

Differentiated Instruction for Universal Access

EL Support for English Learners

Shakespeare's language can be a challenge for many students. Struggling with the language prevents many students from enjoying and appreciating the plays. Here is a strategy that helps students work out the meaning of key passages.

Pair fluent English speakers with English learners, and have them "translate" key sections of the play that are important to their overall understanding of the plot or characters.

Start by reading aloud the segment to be worked on, or play the segment on the ***Hear It!* Audio CD**. Explain what each line means after students have heard it aloud. Then, have students work in pairs to rewrite the segment in their own words. Students then form groups of four and share their "translations," combining them to come up with one good translation to present to the class.

❸❶ Reading Skill

Use Text Aids

1. Have a volunteer read aloud Casca's account in lines 220–232 of Antony's attempt to crown Caesar. **Ask:** What is the common people's reaction to Antony's gesture, and what does it mean?
   Answer: They shout. Their shout means that they want Caesar to be king.
2. Direct students to reread the Literature in Context background information on Roman society to understand more fully the crowd's response to Antony's attempt to crown Caesar.
3. **Ask** the Reading Skill question: According to the Literature in Context feature on page 900, why might the common people support Caesar?
   Possible response: A mass of poor people with no work, including many farmers who could no longer compete with wealthy landowners, have poured into Rome. These common people may believe that if Caesar became king, their situation would improve.

❸❷ Literary Analysis

Shakespeare's Tragedies

1. Have students discuss Casca's effect on this scene. Point out that Casca, like the commoners from Scene i, speaks in prose. Note that Shakespeare reserved verse for his aristocratic and tragic characters and prose for the lower class and broadly comic ones.
2. Explain that although he speaks in prose, Casca is not a commoner. **Ask:** How can you tell that Casca is not one of the common people?
   Answer: He refers to the common people in a negative way as "the rabblement" in line 243 and "the tag-rag people" in line 258.
3. Have students hypothesize about why Shakespeare chooses to have Casca speak in prose.
   Possible response: Shakespeare may have Casca speak in prose to make the scene he is recounting about the common people more vivid or even to poke fun at the commoners and their support of Caesar.

Reading Skill
Use Text Aids
According to the Literature in Context feature on page 900, why might the common people support Caesar? ❸❶

BRUTUS. What was the second noise for?

CASCA. Why, for that too.

CASSIUS. They shouted thrice; what was the last cry for?

CASCA. Why, for that too.

BRUTUS. Was the crown offered him thrice?

CASCA. Ay, marry,[71] was't, and he put it by thrice, every time gentler than other; and at every putting-by mine honest neighbors shouted.

CASSIUS. Who offered him the crown?

CASCA. Why, Antony.

BRUTUS. Tell us the manner of it, gentle Casca.

CASCA. I can as well be hanged as tell the manner of it: it was mere foolery; I did not mark it. I saw Mark Antony offer him a crown—yet 'twas not a crown neither, 'twas one of these coronets[72]—and, as I told you, he put it by once; but for all that, to my thinking, he would fain[73] have had it. Then he offered it to him again; then he put it by again; but to my thinking, he was very loath to lay his fingers off it. And then he offered it the third time. He put it the third time by; and still[74] as he refused it, the rabblement[75] hooted, and clapped their chopt[76] hands, and threw up their sweaty nightcaps,[77] and uttered such a deal of stinking breath because Caesar refused the crown, that it had, almost, choked Caesar; for he swounded[78] and fell down at it. And for mine own part, I durst not laugh, for fear of opening my lips and receiving the bad air.

CASSIUS. But, soft,[79] I pray you; what, did Caesar swound?

CASCA. He fell down in the market place, and foamed at mouth, and was speechless.

BRUTUS. 'Tis very like he hath the falling-sickness.[80]

CASSIUS. No, Caesar hath it not; but you, and I,
And honest Casca, we have the falling-sickness.[81]

CASCA. I know not what you mean by that, but I am sure Caesar fell down. If the tag-rag people[82] did not clap him and hiss him, according as he pleased and displeased them, as they use[83] to do the players in the theater, I am no true man.

71. **marry** *interjection* truly.
72. **coronets** (kôr′ ə nets′) *n.* ornamental bands used as crowns.
73. **fain** (fān) *adv.* gladly.
74. **still** *adv.* every time. ❸❷
75. **rabblement** (rab′ əl mənt) *n.* mob.
76. **chopt** (chäpt) *adj.* chapped.
77. **nightcaps** *n.* workers' caps.
78. **swounded** *v.* swooned; fainted.
79. **soft** *adv.* slowly.
80. **falling-sickness** *n.* epilepsy.
81. **we have the falling-sickness** We are losing power and falling in status under Caesar's rule. ❸❸
82. **tag-rag people** the rabble; lower-class people.
83. **use** *v.* are accustomed.

Vocabulary Development

Word Forms

Expand students' vocabulary by helping them learn related forms of two of the selection vocabulary words for *The Tragedy of Julius Caesar,* Act I. Give students a blank **Word Form Chart** (***Professional Development Guidebook,*** p. 42), with *replication* and *infirmity* in the correct columns. Work with the class, or have students work with a partner, to determine the related forms. The final chart should look like the one shown. Hold students accountable for integrating the related forms of the words into their speaking and writing.

Noun	Verb	Adjective	Adverb
replication, replica	replicate		
infirmity		infirm	infirmly

BRUTUS. What said he when he came unto himself?

CASCA. Marry, before he fell down, when he perceived the common herd was glad he refused the crown, he plucked me ope his doublet[84] and offered them his throat to cut. An I had been a man of any occupation,[85] if I would not have taken him at a word, I would I might go to hell among the rogues. And so he fell. When he came to himself again, he said, if he had done or said anything amiss, he desired their worships to think it was his **infirmity**.[86] Three or four wenches,[87] where I stood, cried "Alas, good soul!" and forgave him with all their hearts; but there's no heed to be taken of them; if Caesar had stabbed their mothers, they would have done no less.

33

BRUTUS. And after that, he came thus sad away?

CASCA. Ay.

CASSIUS. Did Cicero say anything?

CASCA. Ay, he spoke Greek.

CASSIUS. To what effect?

CASCA. Nay, an I tell you that, I'll ne'er look you i' th' face again. But those that understood him smiled at one another and shook their heads; but for mine own part, it was Greek to me. I could tell you more news too: Marullus and Flavius, for pulling scarfs off Caesar's images, are put to silence.[88] Fare you well. There was more foolery yet, if I could remember it.

CASSIUS. Will you sup with me tonight, Casca?

CASCA. No, I am promised forth.[89]

CASSIUS. Will you dine with me tomorrow?

CASCA. Ay, if I be alive, and your mind hold,[90] and your dinner worth the eating.

CASSIUS. Good; I will expect you.

CASCA. Do so. Farewell, both. [*Exit*]

BRUTUS. What a blunt[91] fellow is this grown to be!
He was quick mettle[92] when he went to school.

CASSIUS. So is he now in execution[93]
Of any bold or noble enterprise,
However he puts on this tardy form.[94]

84. **doublet** (dub′ lit) *n.* close-fitting jacket.

85. **An I . . . occupation** if I had been a workingman (or a man of action).

86. **infirmity** *n.* Caesar's illness is epilepsy.

87. **wenches** (wench′ əz) *n.* young women.

Vocabulary
infirmity (in fʉr′ mə tē) *n.* weakness; physical defect

88. **for pulling . . . silence** For taking decorations off statues of Caesar, they have been silenced (by being forbidden to take part in public affairs, exiled, or perhaps even executed).

89. **am promised forth** have a previous engagement.

90. **hold** *v.* does not change.

91. **blunt** *adj.* dull; not sharp.

92. **quick mettle** of a lively disposition.

93. **execution** *n.* carrying out; doing.

94. **tardy form** sluggish appearance.

34 **Reading Check**

How does Caesar respond when he is offered the crown?

33 Background

The Falling Sickness

Casca tells Brutus and Cassius that Caesar "swounded [fainted] and fell down . . . and foamed at the mouth, and was speechless." Brutus explains that Caesar "hath the falling-sickness." Historians believe that Caesar suffered from epilepsy, a general term used to cover a variety of chronic neurological disorders. Epileptics can suffer from seizures that involve muscle spasms and loss of consciousness. Some forms of epilepsy are known to be caused by injury or infection of the brain. Today, epileptic seizures like those Caesar suffered can usually be controlled by medications and diet.

34 Reading Check

Answer: Caesar refuses the crown when it is offered, but according to Casca, he seems to want to accept the crown.

Differentiated Instruction for Universal Access

Strategy for Special Needs Students

Have students read along with the adapted version of *The Tragedy of Julius Caesar:* Act I in the ***Reader's Notebook: Adapted Version*** as they listen to the ***Hear It!* Audio CD** (adapted text). This version provides basic-level instruction in an interactive format with questions and write-on lines. Working with the adapted version will support students as they read the selection in their textbooks.

Strategy for Less Proficient Readers

Have students read the selection in the ***Reader's Notebook.*** This version provides basic-level instruction in an interactive format with questions and write-on lines. After students finish the selection in the ***Reader's Notebook,*** have them complete the questions and activities in the student edition.

35 Reading Skill

Use Text Aids

1. Direct students' attention to the stage direction "Exit Brutus" just before line 308. Point out that when Brutus leaves, Cassius is left alone on stage.
2. Tell students that the stage direction indicates to readers that the speech Cassius gives here is a soliloquy. Explain that a soliloquy is a special category of monologue in which a character speaks his or her thoughts aloud. The character's thoughts are understood to be audible only to the audience, not to any other character. In a soliloquy, a character is generally understood to be completely honest.
3. Read Cassius' soliloquy aloud. Then have students examine the stage direction at the beginning of Scene iii. **Ask:** What prediction can you make based on Cassius' speech at the end of Scene ii and the stage direction at the beginning of Scene iii?
   Possible response: The last several lines of Cassius' speech and the violent weather at the beginning of Scene iii suggest that Cassius plans to use violence to make sure Caesar does not become king.

36 Critical Viewing

Answer: This scene reflects a calm, relaxed atmosphere, while the events taking place in the play are full of emotional turmoil and conflict.

This rudeness is a sauce to his good wit,[95]
Which gives men stomach to disgest[96] his words
With better appetite.

BRUTUS. And so it is. For this time I will leave you.
Tomorrow, if you please to speak with me,
I will come home to you; or if you will,
Come home to me, and I will wait for you.

CASSIUS. I will do so. Till then, think of the world.[97]

[*Exit* BRUTUS.]

Well, Brutus, thou art noble; yet I see
Thy honorable mettle may be wrought
From that it is disposed;[98] therefore it is meet
That noble minds keep ever with their likes;
For who so firm that cannot be seduced?

95. **wit** *n.* intelligence.
96. **disgest** *v.* digest.
97. **the world** present state of affairs.
98. **wrought . . . is disposed** shaped (like iron) in a way different from its usual form.

36 ▼ **Critical Viewing** How does this idyllic scene of Rome contrast with the events taking place in the play? **[Contrast]**

35

Vocabulary Development

Selection Vocabulary Reinforcement

To reinforce and assess students' comprehension of the selection vocabulary words, provide sentences in which the words may or may not be used correctly. Instruct students to use the "yes/no—why" format to tell whether the words are used correctly and explain why. Use these sentences:

1. He was *prodigious* about flying and always drove if he could.
   Answer: No, *prodigious* is not used correctly. It means "of great size or power" and does not have to do with being afraid.
2. His *infirmity* made it impossible for him to take part in sports.
   Answer: Yes, *infirmity* is used correctly here. It means "illness or weakness"; either condition might make it impossible for someone to participate in sports.

Caesar doth bear me hard,[99] but he loves Brutus.
If I were Brutus now, and he were Cassius,
He should not humor me.[100] I will this night,
In several hands,[101] in at his windows throw,
As if they came from several citizens,
Writings, all tending to the great opinion[102]
That Rome holds of his name; wherein obscurely
Caesar's ambition shall be glancèd at.[103]
And after this, let Caesar seat him sure;[104]
For we will shake him, or worse days endure. [*Exit*]

Scene iii. A street.

[*Thunder and lightning. Enter from opposite sides,* CASCA *and* CICERO.]

CICERO. Good even, Casca; brought you Caesar home?
Why are you breathless? And why stare you so?

CASCA. Are not you moved, when all the sway of earth[1]
Shakes like a thing unfirm? O Cicero,
I have seen tempests, when the scolding winds
Have rived[2] the knotty oaks, and I have seen
Th' ambitious ocean swell and rage and foam,
To be exalted with[3] the threat'ning clouds;
But never till tonight, never till now,
Did I go through a tempest dropping fire.
Either there is a civil strife in heaven,
Or else the world, too saucy[4] with the gods,
Incenses[5] them to send destruction.

CICERO. Why, saw you anything more wonderful?

CASCA. A common slave—you know him well by sight—
Held up his left hand, which did flame and burn
Like twenty torches joined, and yet his hand,
Not sensible of[6] fire, remained unscorched.
Besides—I ha' not since put up my sword—
Against[7] the Capitol I met a lion,
Who glazed[8] upon me and went surly by
Without annoying me. And there were drawn
Upon a heap[9] a hundred ghastly[10] women,
Transformèd with their fear, who swore they saw
Men, all in fire, walk up and down the streets.
And yesterday the bird of night[11] did sit
Even at noonday upon the market place,
Hooting and shrieking. When these prodigies[12]
Do so conjointly meet,[13] let not men say,
"These are their reasons, they are natural,"

99. **bear me hard** dislike me.
100. **humor me** win me over.
101. **several hands** different handwritings.
102. **tending to the great opinion** pointing out the great respect.
103. **glancèd at** hinted at.
104. **seat him sure** establish himself securely.

1. **all the sway of earth** the stable order of Earth.
2. **Have rived** have split.
3. **exalted with** lifted up to.
4. **saucy** *adj.* rude; impudent.
5. **Incenses** *v.* enrages.

Reading Skill
Use Text Aids
According to the information on page 889, why would Shakespeare's audience have connected these unnatural events with the political situation in the play?

6. **sensible of** sensitive to.
7. **Against** *prep.* opposite or near.
8. **glazed** *v.* stared.
9. **were drawn . . . heap** huddled together.
10. **ghastly** (gast´ lē) *adj.* ghostlike; pale.
11. **bird of night** owl.
12. **prodigies** (präd´ ə jēz) *n.* extraordinary happenings.
13. **conjointly meet** occur at the same time and place.

38 **Reading Check**
After his conversation with Brutus, what does Cassius say he will do?

Differentiated Instruction for Universal Access

Enrichment for Advanced Readers
Have students analyze the figurative language in Casca's speech (lines 15–32). Tell students to look for details that appeal to the senses. Ask students to write a brief essay on the effects of Casca's descriptive language. To help students begin, suggest that students respond to the following questions: Why does Shakespeare have Casca speak this way? What is the effect of his speech on the audience? How successfully does Shakespeare convey sensory impressions through words? Which images do students find especially vivid? Why do these images impress them?

37 Reading Skill

Use Text Aids

1. Read Casca's speech (lines 15–32) aloud. **Ask** students to identify text aids that might help them better understand the references in the speech.
   Answer: Glosses and background information might explain references in the speech.
2. Use the relevant side notes to elucidate the references. Then **ask** the Reading Skill question: According to the information on page 889, why would Shakespeare's audience have connected these unnatural events with the political situation in the play?
   Possible response: Shakespeare's audience believed that all living things were connected by The Great Chain of Being and thus that natural events mirrored human society and actions.

38 Reading Check

Answer: Cassius says that he will throw forged notes into Brutus' windows. The notes will praise Brutus and hint at Caesar's ambition—a cunning part of Cassius' plan to force Brutus to act.

39 Reading Skill

Use Text Aids

1. Challenge students to cover the side notes and read Cassius' speech (lines 57–78). Have students discuss what they think the speech means.
2. Then have students consult the side notes to explain what Cassius says in lines 57–71.
   Possible response: Cassius says that Casca lacks the Roman virtue of courage. He fears the omens without understanding them. If Casca thought about it, he would know that they are warnings about the present Roman government.

Monitor Progress Have students write a list of text aids that they have had access to while reading Act I. Next to each list entry, students should explain how the aid is helpful and cite the number of the page on which the aid can be found. Ask them to write a few sentences that explain which text aids have been most useful and why.

Reteach Have each student write a brief summary of a speech or conversation in the play after using side notes and other text aids to explain words and references. Then have each student compare his or her summary with another student's summary. Encourage student partners to discuss and help each other correct misconceptions about the meaning of the text in question.

Vocabulary
portentous (pôr ten´ təs) *adj.* ominous; giving signs of evil to come

37

For I believe they are portentous things
Unto the climate that they point upon.[14]

CICERO. Indeed, it is a strange-disposèd[15] time:
But men may construe things after their fashion,[16]
Clean from the purpose[17] of the things themselves.
Comes Caesar to the Capitol tomorrow?

CASCA. He doth; for he did bid Antonius
Send word to you he would be there tomorrow.

CICERO. Good night then, Casca; this disturbèd sky
Is not to walk in.

CASCA. Farewell, Cicero. [*Exit* CICERO.]

[*Enter* CASSIUS.]

CASSIUS. Who's there?

CASCA. A Roman.

CASSIUS. Casca, by your voice.

CASCA. Your ear is good. Cassius, what night is this?

CASSIUS. A very pleasing night to honest men.

CASCA. Who ever knew the heavens menace so?

CASSIUS. Those that have known the earth so full of faults.
For my part, I have walked about the streets,
Submitting me unto the perilous night,
And thus unbracèd,[18] Casca, as you see,
Have bared my bosom to the thunder-stone;[19]
And when the cross[20] blue lightning seemed to open
The breast of heaven, I did present myself
Even in the aim and very flash of it.

CASCA. But wherefore did you so much tempt the heavens?
It is the part[21] of men to fear and tremble
When the most mighty gods by tokens send
Such dreadful heralds to astonish[22] us.

CASSIUS. You are dull, Casca, and those sparks of life
That should be in a Roman you do want,[23]
Or else you use not. You look pale, and gaze,
And put on fear, and cast yourself in wonder,[24]
To see the strange impatience of the heavens;
But if you would consider the true cause
Why all these fires, why all these gliding ghosts,
Why birds and beasts from quality and kind,[25]
Why old men, fools, and children calculate,[26]

14. portentous (pôr ten´ təs) **. . . upon** bad omens for the country they point to.
15. strange-disposèd abnormal.
16. construe . . . fashion explain in their own way.
17. Clean from the purpose different from the real meaning.

18. unbracèd *adj.* with jacket open.
19. thunder-stone *n.* thunderbolt.
20. cross *adj.* zigzag.
21. part *n.* role.
22. by tokens . . . to astonish by portentous signs send such awful announcements to frighten and stun.
23. want *v.* lack.
24. put on . . . in wonder show fear and are amazed.
39
25. from quality and kind acting contrary to their nature.
26. calculate *v.* make predictions.

Think Aloud

Vocabulary: Using Context

Draw students' attention to the word *portentous* in line 31 of Scene iii. Using a think-aloud process, model how to use context to infer the meaning of an unknown word.

In this sentence, the word *portentous* is used to describe the unusual events that Casca witnesses. I know from lines 9–13 that Casca believes that this storm is one of the most terrible that he has ever experienced and he thinks it has been decreed by the gods. In lines 34–35, Cicero answers Casca by saying that men add meanings to events even if these events do not necessarily have meaning. *Portentous* must have something to do with negative connotations, or meanings; if I replace "portentous things" in line 31 with "ominous events," the line reads: "For I believe they are ominous events/Unto the climate that they point upon." I think that *portentous* means "ominous; foreshadowing sinister events."

39

Why all these things change from their ordinance,[27]
Their natures and preformèd faculties,
To monstrous quality,[28] why, you shall find
That heaven hath infused them with these spirits[29]
To make them instruments of fear and warning
Unto some monstrous state.[30]
Now could I, Casca, name to thee a man
Most like this dreadful night,
That thunders, lightens, opens graves, and roars
As doth the lion in the Capitol;
A man no mightier than thyself, or me,
In personal action, yet **prodigious** grown
And fearful,[31] as these strange eruptions are.

CASCA. 'Tis Caesar that you mean, is it not, Cassius?

CASSIUS. Let it be who it is; for Romans now
Have thews[32] and limbs like to their ancestors;
But, woe the while![33] Our fathers' minds are dead,
And we are governed with our mothers' spirits;
Our yoke and sufferance[34] show us womanish.

40

CASCA. Indeed, they say the senators tomorrow
Mean to establish Caesar as a king;
And he shall wear his crown by sea and land,
In every place save here in Italy.

CASSIUS. I know where I will wear this dagger then;
Cassius from bondage will deliver[35] Cassius.
Therein,[36] ye gods, you make the weak most strong;
Therein, ye gods, you tyrants do defeat.
Nor stony tower, nor walls of beaten brass,
Nor airless dungeon, nor strong links of iron,
Can be retentive to[37] the strength of spirit;
But life, being weary of these worldly bars,
Never lacks power to dismiss itself.
If I know this, know all the world besides,
That part of tyranny that I do bear
I can shake off at pleasure. *[Thunder still]*

CASCA. So can I;
So every bondman in his own hand bears
The power to cancel his captivity.

CASSIUS. And why should Caesar be a tyrant then?
Poor man, I know he would not be a wolf
But that he sees the Romans are but sheep;
He were no lion, were not Romans hinds.[38]

27. ordinance (ôrd´ 'n əns) *n.* regular behavior.

28. preformèd . . . quality established function to unnatural behavior.

29. infused . . . spirits filled them with supernatural powers.

30. monstrous state abnormal condition of government.

Vocabulary

prodigious (prō dij´ əs) *adj.* of great size or power

31. fearful *adj.* causing fear.

32. thews (*thy*o͞oz) *n.* muscles or sinews; strength.

33. woe the while alas for the times.

34. yoke and sufferance slavery and meek acceptance of it.

35. will deliver will set free.

36. Therein (*th*er in´) *adv.* in that way (that is, by giving the weak the power to end their own lives).

Literary Analysis Shakespeare's Tragedies What main conflict has Shakespeare established in Act I?

37. be retentive to confine.

38. hinds (hīndz) *n.* female deer; peasants; servants.

41 **Reading Check**

What connection does Cassius make between the night's strange events and Caesar's rise to power?

40 Literary Analysis

Shakespeare's Tragedies

1. Ask two volunteers to read the exchange between Casca and Cassius in lines 85–91. **Ask** students to explain what Casca has said he heard will happen the next day.
   Answer: Casca has heard that the senators will make Caesar king.
2. **Ask:** How does Cassius react?
   Answer: Cassius says he will take violent action if Caesar becomes king.
3. **Ask** students to respond to the Literary Analysis question: What main conflict has Shakespeare established in Act I?
   Answer: He has established a conflict between those who want Caesar to be king and those who do not.

41 Reading Check

Answer: Cassius suggests that the night's strange events indicate that Caesar's rise to power is not a good thing and will have terrible consequences.

Differentiated Instruction for Universal Access

EL Pronunciation for English Learners

Some students might have difficulty pronouncing words with the medial consonant "r" sound, as in *tomorrow*, and replace it with a rolled or trilled "r" sound. The following strategies can help students pronounce words with the medial consonant "r" sound.

- Write the words *farewell, perilous, wherefore,* and *sparks* on the board, pronouncing each word as it is written. Have students repeat after you. Then call out each word at random, and have volunteers circle the word on the board. Discuss the results, determining what led to incorrect choices.
- Pair English learners with fluent speakers. Have English learners practice saying the words on the board. Assign the fluent speakers the role of "peer tutor," guiding the English learners to correctly pronounce the words.

㊷ Critical Thinking

Infer

1. Have students read Cassius' lines 112–114. **Ask** students what Cassius worries about in these lines.
   Answer: Cassius worries that he has said too much about his political ideas in front of a possible enemy.
2. **Ask** students to infer why Cassius puts himself in this potentially dangerous situation.
   Possible response: Cassius is passionate about keeping Caesar from the throne, and he wants Casca to help him. Thus, Cassius risks speaking his true emotions.

㊸ Reading Skill

Use Text Aids

1. Read aloud lines 140–146. **Ask** students what Cinna's main concern is.
   Answer: Cinna is concerned about whether they can get Brutus to join them in their conspiracy.
2. Point out to students that Cassius responds to Cinna's concern by describing his plan for winning Brutus over. Then walk students through lines 142–146 to explain Cassius' plan. Pause to summarize after each action is described to make sure students are clear that Cinna is supposed to plant three letters calling for Brutus to lead. As you proceed, ask questions that will prompt students to consult the side notes.
3. Then **ask** students to respond to the Reading Skill question: Why might you need to consult glosses 56 and 57 to understand Cassius' plan?
   Answer: The side notes explain certain details in Cassius' plan, such as the fact that Brutus is the chief magistrate.

39. offal (ôf′ əl) *n.* refuse; waste.
40. base matter inferior or low material; foundation materials.
41. speak this . . . answer must be made say this before a willing servant of Caesar's; then I know I will have to answer for my words.
42. fleering tell-tale sneering tattletale.
43. factious (fak′ shəs) *adj.* active in forming a faction or a political party.
44. redress (ri dres′) of all these griefs setting right all these grievances.
45. undergo (un′ dər gō′) *v.* undertake.
46. consequence (kän′ sə kwens′) *n.* importance.
47. by this by this time.
48. Pompey's porch portico of Pompey's Theater.
49. complexion of the element condition of the sky; weather.
50. In favor's like in appearance is like.

Those that with haste will make a mighty fire
Begin it with weak straws. What trash is Rome,
What rubbish and what offal,[39] when it serves
For the base matter[40] to illuminate
So vile a thing as Caesar! But, O grief,
Where hast thou led me? I, perhaps, speak this
Before a willing bondman; then I know
My answer must be made.[41] But I am armed,
And dangers are to me indifferent.

CASCA. You speak to Casca, and to such a man
That is no fleering tell-tale.[42] Hold, my hand.
Be factious[43] for redress of all these griefs,[44]
And I will set this foot of mine as far
As who goes farthest. [*They clasp hands.*]

CASSIUS. There's a bargain made.
Now know you, Casca, I have moved already
Some certain of the noblest-minded Romans
To undergo[45] with me an enterprise
Of honorable dangerous consequence;[46]
And I do know, by this[47] they stay for me
In Pompey's porch;[48] for now, this fearful night,
There is no stir or walking in the streets,
And the complexion of the element[49]
In favor's like[50] the work we have in hand,
Most bloody, fiery, and most terrible.

[*Enter* CINNA.]

51. close *adj.* hidden.
52. gait (gāt) *n.* style of walking.
53. incorporate (in kôr′ pə rit) / **To our attempts** part of our efforts.
54. stayed for waited for.
55. on't (ônt) contraction of it.
56. praetor's (prē′ tərz) **chair** Roman magistrate's (or judge's) chair.

CASCA. Stand close[51] awhile, for here comes one in haste.

CASSIUS. 'Tis Cinna; I do know him by his gait;[52]
He is a friend. Cinna, where haste you so?

CINNA. To find out you. Who's that? Metellus Cimber?

CASSIUS. No, it is Casca, one incorporate
To our attempts.[53] Am I not stayed for,[54] Cinna?

CINNA. I am glad on't.[55] What a fearful night is this!
There's two or three of us have seen strange sights.

CASSIUS. Am I not stayed for? Tell me.

CINNA. Yes, you are.
O Cassius, if you could
But win the noble Brutus to our party—

CASSIUS. Be you content. Good Cinna, take this paper,
And look you lay it in the praetor's chair,[56]

Reading Skill
Use Text Aids Why might you need to consult glosses 56 and 57 to understand Cassius' plan? ㊸

Vocabulary Development

Vocabulary Knowledge Rating

When students have completed reading and discussing *The Tragedy of Julius Caesar,* Act I, have them take out their **Vocabulary Knowledge Rating Chart** for this selection. Read the words aloud once more, and have students rate their knowledge of the words again in the After Reading column. Clarify any words that are still problematic. Have students write their own definition or example in the appropriate column. Then have students complete the Vocabulary Practice at the end of the selection. Encourage students to use the words in further discussion and written work about this selection. Remind them that they will be accountable for these words on the **Selection Test,** ***Unit 5 Resources,*** pp. 139–141 or 142–144.

44

45 ▲ **Critical Viewing** Which details in this relief sculpture indicate the respect and awe with which Romans regarded their leaders? **[Interpret]**

44 Humanities

Relief Sculpture

The art on this page is a relief sculpture, from the Italian *relievare*, which means "to raise." There are high, low, and middle relief sculptures; a sculpture's category depends on how far from the background the objects and figures extend.

The ancient Egyptians showcased low-relief sculptures, and the ancient Greeks developed high-relief sculptures. During the second and third centuries A.D., relief sculptures on Roman sarcophagi, or stone coffins, were popular.

Sculpture in general has been used throughout history to commemorate a society's people and events. It is an art form that lends itself easily to formal, civic decoration in a town's streets, markets, and squares. This Roman relief probably displayed the significant political values of the Romans. Use this question for discussion:

- How does this relief sculpture symbolize the conspirators' fears?
  Answer: The sculpture shows that Romans value respect for their leaders; the conspirators fear that blind respect could turn Rome into a monarchy and threaten the Republic.

45 Critical Viewing

Answer: The look of awe on the face of the person on the left and the use of a trumpet by the person on the right to herald the arrival of the leader in the chariot are signs of the respect the Romans had for their leaders. Also, the angel above the leader links him to the Romans' divine beliefs.

Concept Connector

Activating Prior Knowledge

Have students return to their **Anticipation Guides** and respond to the statements again in the After Reading column. They may do this individually or in their original pairs or groups. Then, lead a class discussion, probing for what students have learned that confirms or invalidates each statement. Encourage students to cite specific details, quotations, or other evidence from the text to support their responses to each statement.

Writing About the Big Question

Have students compare their responses to the sentence starters they completed before reading *The Tragedy of Julius Caesar*, Act 1, with their ideas afterwards. Ask them to explain whether their thoughts have changed.

Literary Analysis Graphic Organizer

Ask students to review the graphic organizers they completed to identify the key elements of the selection. Show them the partially completed **Literary Analysis Graphic Organizer A** (*Graphic Organizer Transparencies*, p. 166) as an example. Then have students use the graphic organizers they completed to discuss the structure of the play.

ASSESS

Answers

Critical Thinking

1. Students may respond that Brutus interests them most because of his internal conflict.
2. (a) Commoners celebrate Caesar's return. (b) **Possible response:** Nobles resent Caesar's rise and fear his support among the commoners; Marullus remarks that Caesar "comes in triumph over Pompey's blood"; Cassius comments: "And this man is now become a god."
3. (a) The soothsayer tells Caesar to beware the ides of March. (b) **Possible response:** Caesar's reaction shows that he is neither superstitious nor fearful.
4. (b) Brutus is a friend of Caesar, holds high office, and is also highly respected.

To what extent does experience determine what we perceive?

Possible responses: (a) Brutus reveals that acting honorably is a very important value. He also reveals that he does not want Caesar to be king, despite the loyalty he feels to Caesar as a friend. (b) Cassius appeals to Brutus with flattery—Cassius assures Brutus he is just as good and noble as Caesar. He appeals to Brutus' commitment to loyalty by encouraging him to be loyal to and follow in the steps of his father, who helped to found and maintain the Republic. (c) The speech reveals some of Brutus' significant attributes and also that he is not easily swayed. Cassius' speech reveals that he is determined to win over Brutus using whatever flattery or cunning necessary.

Where Brutus may but find it;[57] and throw this
In at his window: set this up with wax
Upon old Brutus'[58] statue. All this done,
Repair[59] to Pompey's porch, where you shall find us.
Is Decius Brutus and Trebonius there?

CINNA. All but Metellus Cimber, and he's gone
To seek you at your house. Well, I will hie,[60]
And so bestow these papers as you bade me.

CASSIUS. That done, repair to Pompey's Theater. [*Exit* CINNA.]
Come, Casca, you and I will yet ere day
See Brutus at his house; three parts of him
Is ours already, and the man entire
Upon the next encounter yields him ours.

CASCA. O, he sits high in all the people's hearts;
And that which would appear offense[61] in us,
His countenance,[62] like richest alchemy,[63]
Will change to virtue and to worthiness.

CASSIUS. Him, and his worth, and our great need of him,
You have right well conceited.[64] Let us go,
For it is after midnight, and ere day
We will awake him and be sure of him. [*Exit*]

57. **Where . . . find it** where only Brutus (as the chief magistrate) will find it. **43**
58. **old Brutus'** Junius Brutus, the founder of the Roman Republic.
59. **Repair** *v.* go.
60. **hie** (hī) *v.* hurry.
61. **offense** (ə fens′) *n.* crime.
62. **countenance** (koun′ tə nəns) *n.* support.
63. **alchemy** (al′ kə mē) *n.* an early form of chemistry in which the goal was to change metals of little value into gold.
64. **conceited** (kən sēt′ id) *v.* understood.

Critical Thinking

1. **Respond:** Which character interests you most so far? Why?
2. **(a)** At the opening of the play, how do common Romans such as the Cobbler react to Caesar's return? **(b) Interpret:** What do noble Romans such as Flavius and Cassius fear or resent about Caesar's success? Support your answer with quotations.
3. **(a)** What warning does the soothsayer give Caesar? **(b) Infer:** What does Caesar's reaction show about him?
4. **Hypothesize:** Why is it important for Cassius and his co-conspirators to win Brutus' support for their plan against Caesar?

THE BIG ? **To what extent does experience determine what we perceive? (a)** Analyze Brutus' values as expressed in the speech in Scene ii, lines 82–89. **(b)** Then, analyze Cassius' speech appealing to those values in lines 135–161 of Scene ii. **(c)** How do these speeches help you understand how each character feels about Caesar?

Assessment Resources

Unit 5 Resources

L1 L2 EL **Selection Test A,** pp. 103–105. Administer Test A to less advanced readers and English learners.

L3 L4 **Selection Test B,** pp. 106–108. Administer Test B to on-level and more advanced students.

L3 L4 **Open-Book Test,** pp. 100–102. As an alternative, give the Open-Book Test.

All **Customizable Test Bank**

All **Self-tests**
Students may prepare for the **Selection Test** by taking the **Self-test** online.

PHLit Online! All assessment resources are available at **www.PHLitOnline.com.**

After You Read | The Tragedy of Julius Caesar, Act I

Literary Analysis: Shakespeare's Tragedies

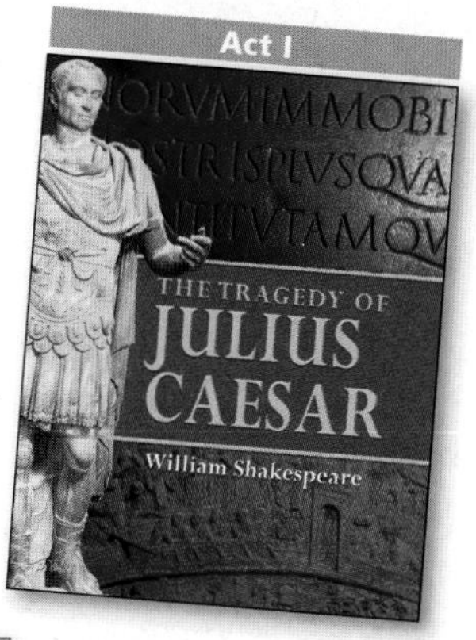

1. Summarize what you learned in Act I of this **Shakespearean tragedy.**
2. Given what you have read so far, explain what **tragic flaw** in Brutus' character might lead him to disaster.

Reading Skill: Use Text Aids

3. The **text aids** before the play include a background section on ancient Rome (p. 889). Using a chart like the one shown, identify two passages in Act I that are clarified by this background information. Explain your choices.

	Location of Passage	Text Aids	What text aids add to understanding
Passage 1			
Passage 2			

4. In Scene ii, how do glosses 73 and 74 help readers understand what happened in the marketplace?

Vocabulary

Practice Replace the italicized word with an **antonym,** a word that is opposite in meaning. Then decide which sentence makes better sense. Explain your answers.

1. The fine art collector bought a *replication.*
2. His *servile* behavior makes me uncomfortable.
3. This suit was not tailored for someone with a *spare* build.
4. His *infirmity* is due to chance, not to the way he lives.
5. I found the unlocked door *portentous.*
6. She has a *prodigious* appetite.

Word Study Use the context of the sentences and what you know about the **Latin suffix *-ile*** to explain your answer to each question.

1. If all efforts to find your missing keys are *futile,* should you keep looking?
2. If a person's behavior is *infantile,* is he or she acting like an adult?

Word Study

The **Latin suffix *-ile*** means "capable of" or "having the quality of."

Challenge Explain how the suffix *-ile* contributes to the meanings of these words. Consult a dictionary if necessary.

facile
mobile
projectile

ASSESS/EXTEND

Answers

Literary Analysis

1. **Possible response:** Caesar has returned home in triumph, but a group of nobles resent Caesar's rise and make plans to prevent him from ruling as king. Brutus is concerned about Caesar's ambition.
2. **Possible response:** Brutus can be too easily influenced by others, and he may make an error in judgment.

Reading Skill

3. **Sample answer:** Passage 1—*Location:* Scene ii, lines 158–161. *Text Aids:* Background for the play *What text aids add:* The background information clarifies Cassius' appeal using "another Brutus." **Passage 2**—*Location:* Scene iii. *Text Aids:* Background for the play *What text aids add:* The background information clarifies Casca's speech about the various omens that suggest that the situation in Rome and Caesar's rise to power are dangerous.

   For other sample answers, see ***Graphic Organizer Transparencies,* Reading Skill Graphic Organizer** A, p. 168, and the **Additional Answers** section.
4. **Possible response:** Gloss 73 explains that Caesar might *gladly* take the crown; 74 indicates that he refuses it *every* time.

Vocabulary

Practice

Sample answers:

1. original; <u>replication</u> is the opposite of *original.*
2. authoritarian; <u>servile</u> is the opposite of *authoritarian.*
3. heavy; <u>spare</u> is the opposite of *heavy.*
4. wellness; <u>infirmity</u> is the opposite of *wellness.*
5. welcoming; <u>portentous</u> is the opposite of *welcoming.*
6. tiny; <u>prodigious</u> is the opposite of *tiny.*

Word Study

Sample answers:

1. No, the suffix *-ile* means "capable of," so *futile* means "not capable of producing a result." If your

Answers continued

efforts to find your keys are futile, you should stop looking.

2. No, the suffix *-ile* means "having the quality of," so *infantile* means "having the quality of an infant or a child." Someone acting in an *infantile* manner is acting like a child.

Word Study: Challenge

Sample answers: To be *facile* is "to be <u>capable of</u> being done with ease." To be *mobile* is "to be <u>capable of</u> moving." A *projectile* is <u>capable of</u> being projected or impelled forward.

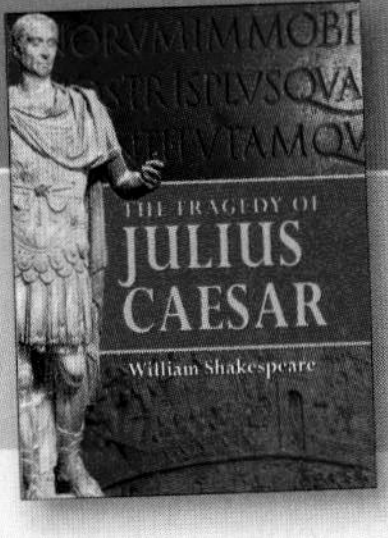

TIME AND RESOURCE MANAGER

The Tragedy of Julius Caesar, Act II

Lesson Pacing Guide

DAY 1 Preteach

- Administer the Reading and Vocabulary Warm-ups (*Unit 5 Resources*, pp. 109–112) as necessary.
- Introduce the Reading Skill: Paraphrase. FT
- Introduce the Literary Analysis concept: Blank Verse. FT
- Distribute copies of the appropriate graphic organizer for the Reading Skill (*Graphic Organizer Transparencies*, pp. 170–171). CRI
- Distribute copies of the appropriate graphic organizer for Literary Analysis (*Graphic Organizer Transparencies*, pp. 172–173). CRI
- Teach the selection vocabulary. FT CRI
- Introduce the Word Study skill.

DAYS 2–3 Preteach/Teach

- Build background with the Background feature. CRI
- Develop thematic vocabulary and thematic thinking with Writing About the Big Question.
- Prepare students to read with the Activating Prior Knowledge activities (TE). CRI
- Informally monitor comprehension while students read. FT
- Use the Reading Check questions to confirm comprehension.
- Develop students' ability to paraphrase using the Reading Skill questions. CRI
- Develop students' understanding of blank verse using the Literary Analysis questions. CRI
- Reinforce vocabulary with the Vocabulary notes. CRI

DAY 4 Assess

- Assess students' comprehension and mastery of the skills by having them answer the Critical Thinking, Reading Skill, and Literary Analysis questions. FT

DAY 5 Extend/Assess

- Extend learning by having students complete the Research and Technology activity, a women's history report. (You may assign as homework.) As an alternative, assign them "In and Out of the In Crowd" in *Reality Central*. CRI
- Administer Selection Test A or B (*Unit 5 Resources*, pp. 121–126). FT

The play *The Tragedy of Julius Caesar* appears unedited and in its entirety. Act I appears on pp. 892–912, Act II appears on pp. 917–936, Act III appears on pp. 941–962, Act IV appears on pp. 967–982, and Act V appears on pp. 987–1000.

Meeting Your Standards

Students will

1. **analyze and respond to literary elements.**
   - **Literary Analysis: Blank Verse**
2. **read, comprehend, and analyze drama.**
   - **Reading Skill: Paraphrase**
   - **Reading Check questions**
   - **Apply the Skills questions**
   - **Assessment Practice**
3. **develop vocabulary.**
   - **Vocabulary**
   - **Word Study**
4. **strengthen research and technology skills.**
   - **women's history report**

CRI For a full explanation of Culturally Responsive Instruction opportunities in this lesson, see p. T86–T87.

FT For an accelerated lesson, use the Fast Track strategies and activities.

Managing Differentiated Instruction

This leveled selection pairing groups a more accessible with a more challenging selection. Choose either one to teach the lesson skills. For classroom management suggestions for using the pairing in a mixed-ability class, see pp. T68–T69.

Daily Block Scheduling

Each day in this Lesson Pacing Guide represents a 40–50 minute period. Teachers using block scheduling may combine days to revise pacing. In addition, teachers may differentiate and support core instruction by integrating components for extended and intensive support as students require. See the Guide to Selected Leveled Resources (facing page).

Guide to Selected Leveled Resources

EL English Learners

			The Tragedy of Julius Caesar, Act II
CORE COURSE	*Unit 5 Resources*	Selection Test A	pp. 121–123
	Graphic Organizer Transparencies	Reading Skill Graphic Organizer A	p. 170
		Literary Analysis Graphic Organizer A	p. 172
EXTENDED SUPPORT (Level 2)	*Unit 5 Resources*	Reading and Vocabulary Warm-ups A or B	pp. 109–112
	Reader's Notebook: English Learner's Version		adapted instruction and adapted selection
	Hear It! Audio CD		selection and summaries
	Hear It! Audio CD (adapted text)		adapted selection and summaries
INTENSIVE SUPPORT (Level 1)	*Reality Central*		"In and Out of the In Crowd"
	Real-World Writing Journal		Lesson 3, pp. 146–149

L2 Below-Level Students

			The Tragedy of Julius Caesar, Act II
CORE COURSE	*Unit 5 Resources*	Selection Test A	pp. 121–123
	Graphic Organizer Transparencies	Reading Skill Graphic Organizer A	p. 170
		Literary Analysis Graphic Organizer A	p. 172
EXTENDED SUPPORT (Level 2)	*Unit 5 Resources*	Reading and Vocabulary Warm-ups A or B	pp. 109–112
	Reader's Notebook		adapted instruction and full selection
	Hear It! Audio CD		selection and summaries
INTENSIVE SUPPORT (Level 1)	*Reality Central*		"In and Out of the In Crowd"
	Real-World Writing Journal		Lesson 3, pp. 146–149
	Reading Kit		Reteaching worksheets

L1 Special Needs Students

			The Tragedy of Julius Caesar, Act II
CORE COURSE	*Unit 5 Resources*	Selection Test A	pp. 121–123
	Graphic Organizer Transparencies	Reading Skill Graphic Organizer A	p. 170
		Literary Analysis Graphic Organizer A	p. 172
EXTENDED SUPPORT (Level 2)	*Unit 5 Resources*	Reading and Vocabulary Warm-ups A or B	pp. 109–112
	Reader's Notebook: Adapted Version		adapted instruction and adapted selection
	Hear It! Audio CD (adapted text)		adapted selection and summaries
INTENSIVE SUPPORT (Level 1)	*Reality Central*		"In and Out of the In Crowd"
	Real-World Writing Journal		Lesson 3, pp. 146–149
	Reading Kit		Reteaching worksheets

The program includes resources for these students: L3 On-Level L4 Advanced All All
For a complete guide to selection support, see pp. T106–T108.

NOTE: All print materials are also available online at *www.PHLitOnline.com.*

VISUAL GUIDE to Featured Selection Resources

The Tragedy of Julius Caesar, Act II

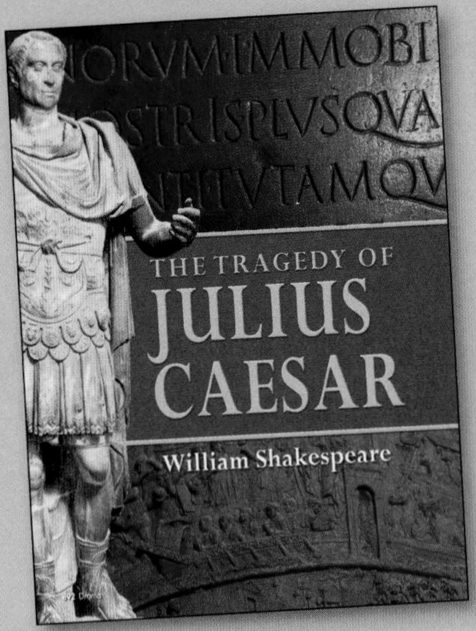

RESOURCES FOR:

- EL English Learners
- L1 Special Needs Students
- L2 Below-Level Students
- L3 On-Level Students
- L4 Advanced Students
- All All Students

Vocabulary/Fluency/Prior Knowledge

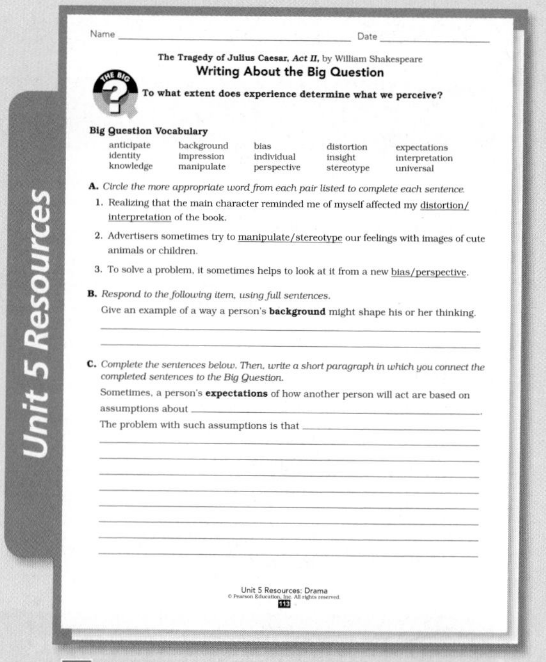
Unit 5 Resources

Name ______ Date ______

The Tragedy of Julius Caesar, *Act II*, by William Shakespeare

Writing About the Big Question

To what extent does experience determine what we perceive?

Big Question Vocabulary

anticipate	background	bias	distortion	expectations
identity	impression	individual	insight	interpretation
knowledge	manipulate	perspective	stereotype	universal

A. *Circle the more appropriate word from each pair listed to complete each sentence.*

1. Realizing that the main character reminded me of myself affected my distortion/interpretation of the book.
2. Advertisers sometimes try to manipulate/stereotype our feelings with images of cute animals or children.
3. To solve a problem, it sometimes helps to look at it from a new bias/perspective.

B. *Respond to the following item, using full sentences.*

Give an example of a way a person's **background** might shape his or her thinking.

C. *Complete the sentences below. Then, write a short paragraph in which you connect the completed sentences to the Big Question.*

Sometimes, a person's **expectations** of how another person will act are based on assumptions about ______.

The problem with such assumptions is that ______

Unit 5 Resources: Drama
© Pearson Education, Inc. All rights reserved.
113

All **Writing About the Big Question, p. 113**

Also available for these selections:

EL L1 L2 **Vocabulary Warm-ups A and B, pp. 109–110**

EL L1 L2 **Reading Warm-ups A and B, pp. 111–112**

All **Vocabulary Builder, p. 116**

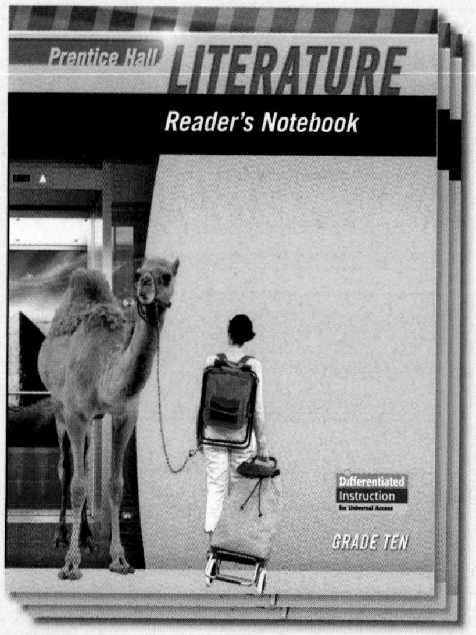

Reader's Notebooks

Pre- and postreading pages for both selections, as well as *The Tragedy of Julius Caesar, Act II* appear in an interactive format in the *Reader's Notebooks*. Each *Notebook* is differentiated for a different group of learners.

The selections in the Adapted and English Learner's versions are abridged.

L2 L3 ***Reader's Notebook***

L1 ***Reader's Notebook: Adapted Version***

EL ***Reader's Notebook: English Learner's Version***

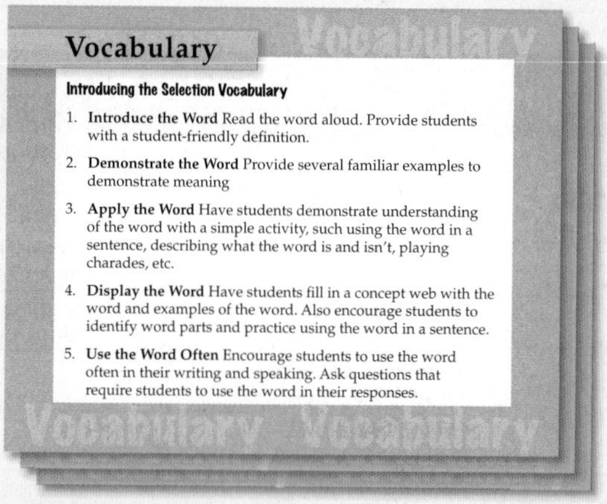
Vocabulary

Introducing the Selection Vocabulary

1. **Introduce the Word** Read the word aloud. Provide students with a student-friendly definition.
2. **Demonstrate the Word** Provide several familiar examples to demonstrate meaning
3. **Apply the Word** Have students demonstrate understanding of the word with a simple activity, such using the word in a sentence, describing what the word is and isn't, playing charades, etc.
4. **Display the Word** Have students fill in a concept web with the word and examples of the word. Also encourage students to identify word parts and practice using the word in a sentence.
5. **Use the Word Often** Encourage students to use the word often in their writing and speaking. Ask questions that require students to use the word in their responses.

Classroom Strategies and Teaching Routines

- core classroom routines outlined step-by-step
- convenient format for easy reference while teaching

Selection Support

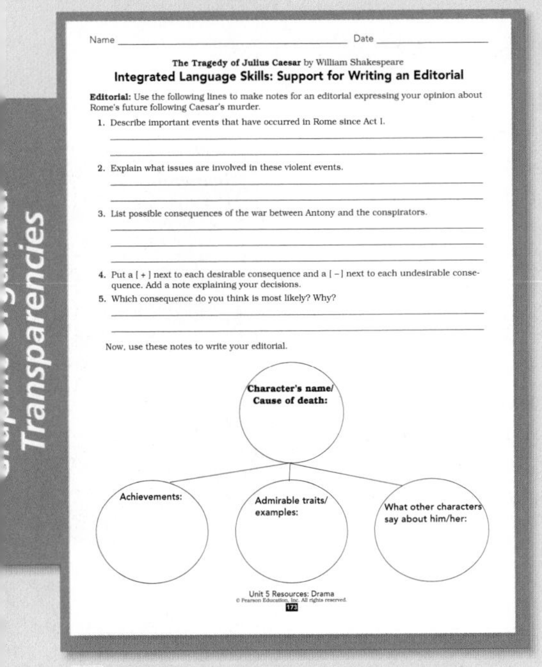
Name ______ Date ______

The Tragedy of Julius Caesar by William Shakespeare
Integrated Language Skills: Support for Writing an Editorial

Editorial: Use the following lines to make notes for an editorial expressing your opinion about Rome's future following Caesar's murder.

1. Describe important events that have occurred in Rome since Act I.
2. Explain what issues are involved in these violent events.
3. List possible consequences of the war between Antony and the conspirators.
4. Put a [+] next to each desirable consequence and a [–] next to each undesirable consequence. Add a note explaining your decisions.
5. Which consequence do you think is most likely? Why?

Now, use these notes to write your editorial.

Unit 5 Resources: Drama

173

L3 Literary Analysis: Graphic Organizer B, p. 173

Also available for these selections:

EL L1 L2 Reading: Graphic Organizer A, p. 170 (partially filled in)

L3 Reading: Graphic Organizer B, p. 171

EL L1 L2 Literary Analysis: Graphic Organizer A, p. 172 (partially filled in)

Skills Development/Extension

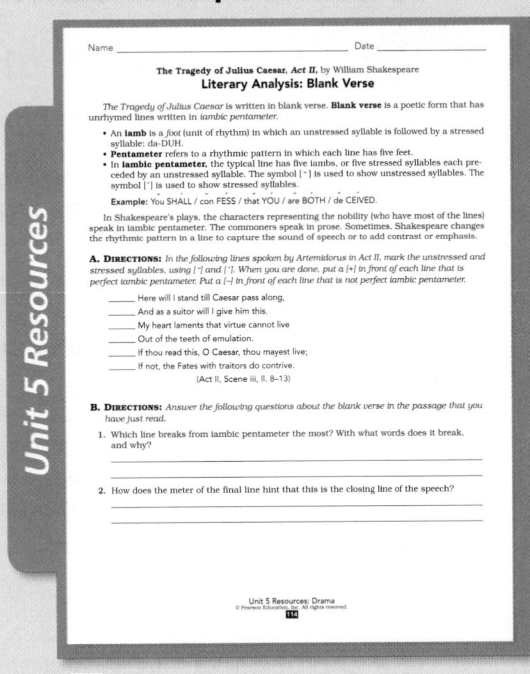
Name ______ Date ______

The Tragedy of Julius Caesar, Act II, by William Shakespeare
Literary Analysis: Blank Verse

The Tragedy of Julius Caesar is written in blank verse. **Blank verse** is a poetic form that has unrhymed lines written in *iambic pentameter.*

- An **iamb** is a *foot* (unit of rhythm) in which an unstressed syllable is followed by a stressed syllable: da-DUH.
- **Pentameter** refers to a rhythmic pattern in which each line has five feet.
- In **iambic pentameter**, the typical line has five iambs, or five stressed syllables each preceded by an unstressed syllable. The symbol [˘] is used to show unstressed syllables. The symbol [´] is used to show stressed syllables.

Example: You SHALL / con FESS / that YOU / are BOTH / de CEIVED.

In Shakespeare's plays, the characters representing the nobility (who have most of the lines) speak in iambic pentameter. The commoners speak in prose. Sometimes, Shakespeare changes the rhythmic pattern in a line to capture the sound of speech or to add contrast or emphasis.

A. Directions: *In the following lines spoken by Artemidorus in Act II, mark the unstressed and stressed syllables, using [˘] and [´]. When you are done, put a [+] in front of each line that is perfect iambic pentameter. Put a [–] in front of each line that is not perfect iambic pentameter.*

____ Here will I stand till Caesar pass along,
____ And as a suitor will I give him this.
____ My heart laments that virtue cannot live
____ Out of the teeth of emulation.
____ If thou read this, O Caesar, thou mayest live;
____ If not, the Fates with traitors do contrive.
(Act II, Scene iii, ll. 8–13)

B. Directions: *Answer the following questions about the blank verse in the passage that you have just read.*

1. Which line breaks from iambic pentameter the most? With what words does it break, and why?
2. How does the meter of the final line hint that this is the closing line of the speech?

Unit 5 Resources: Drama

114

All Literary Analysis: Blank Verse, p. 114

Also available for these selections:

All Reading: Paraphrase, p. 115

L4 Enrichment, p. 117

L3 L4 Grammar, p. 172

L3 L4 Support for Writing, p. 173

L3 L4 Support for Extend Your Learning, p. 175

Assessment

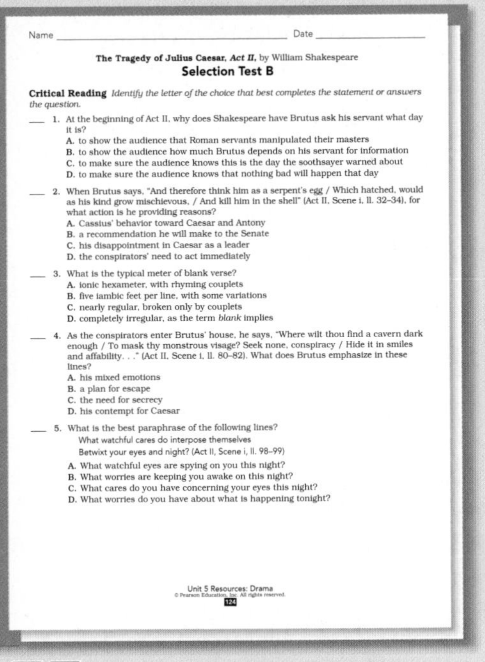
Name ______ Date ______

The Tragedy of Julius Caesar, Act II, by William Shakespeare
Selection Test B

Critical Reading *Identify the letter of the choice that best completes the statement or answers the question.*

____ 1. At the beginning of Act II, why does Shakespeare have Brutus ask his servant what day it is?
A. to show the audience that Roman servants manipulated their masters
B. to show the audience how much Brutus depends on his servant for information
C. to make sure the audience knows this is the day the soothsayer warned about
D. to make sure the audience knows that nothing bad will happen that day

____ 2. When Brutus says, "And therefore think him as a serpent's egg / Which hatched, would as his kind grow mischievous, / And kill him in the shell" (Act II, Scene i, ll. 32–34), for what action is he providing reasons?
A. Cassius' behavior toward Caesar and Antony
B. a recommendation he will make to the Senate
C. his disappointment in Caesar as a leader
D. the conspirators' need to act immediately

____ 3. What is the typical meter of blank verse?
A. ionic hexameter, with rhyming couplets
B. five iambic feet per line, with some variations
C. nearly regular, broken only by couplets
D. completely irregular, as the term *blank* implies

____ 4. As the conspirators enter Brutus' house, he says, "Where wilt thou find a cavern dark enough / To mask thy monstrous visage? Seek none, conspiracy / Hide it in smiles and affability. . ." (Act II, Scene i, ll. 80–82). What does Brutus emphasize in these lines?
A. his mixed emotions
B. a plan for escape
C. the need for secrecy
D. his contempt for Caesar

____ 5. What is the best paraphrase of the following lines?
What watchful cares do interpose themselves
Betwixt your eyes and night? (Act II, Scene i, ll. 98–99)
A. What watchful eyes are spying on you this night?
B. What worries are keeping you awake on this night?
C. What cares do you have concerning your eyes this night?
D. What worries do you have about what is happening tonight?

Unit 5 Resources: Drama

124

L3 L4 Selection Test B, pp. 124–126

Also available for these selections:

EL L1 L2 Selection Test A, pp. 121–123

L3 L4 Open-Book Test, pp. 118–120

PHLit Online!

www.PHLitOnline.com

- complete narrated selection text
- a thematically related video with writing prompt
- an interactive graphic organizer
- highlighting feature
- access to all student print resources, adapted to individual student needs
- Spanish and English summaries

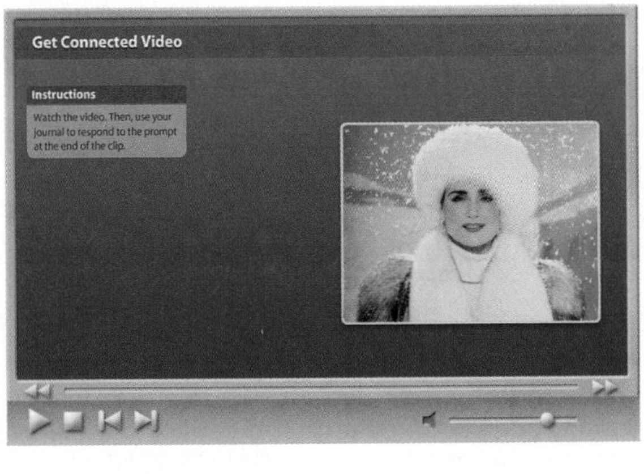

Get Connected! (thematic video with writing prompt)

Also available:

Background video

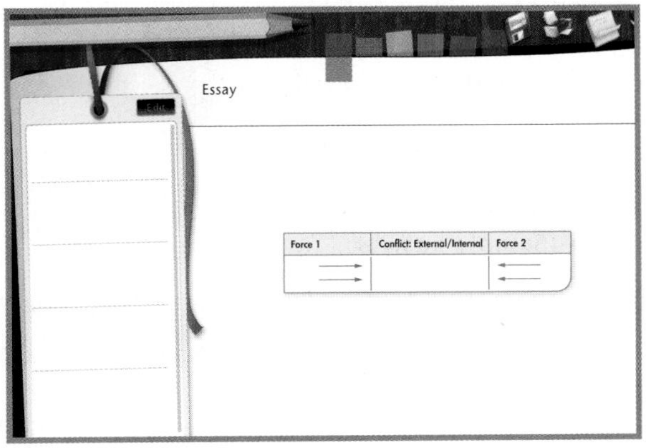

Writer's Journal (with graphics feature)

Also available:

Vocabulary Central (tools, activities, and songs for studying vocabulary)

DIFFERENTIATE/PRETEACH

❶ Selection Skills

1. With the class, preview the selection skills. (The lesson meets the lesson objectives given on p. 914a.)
2. Explain that students will learn to use the skill of paraphrasing as they read to better understand and enjoy the selection. By examining blank verse as they read, they will gain deeper insight into the selection.

❷ Vocabulary

1. Have students preview the selection vocabulary.
2. For each word, have students say the word aloud.
3. Then, use the word in a sentence that defines the word.
4. Finally, repeat your definitional sentence or a similar sentence with the word missing and have the class "fill in the blank" chorally. Here are some examples:

   Augmented means enhanced or made greater. After buying five new books at the bookstore, her book collection was [students say "augmented"].

   If something is imminent, it is about to happen. They knew from the dark, threatening rain clouds overhead that a storm was [students say "imminent"].

❸ Word Study

1. Introduce the skill, using the instruction in the box.
2. Choose a word beginning with the prefix *en-*. State the word's definition using your knowledge of the prefix. Then, have students identify the word from your definition. (**Sample answer:** "To wrap in a covering." *Enwrap*.)

Before You Read — The Tragedy of Julius Caesar, Act II

THE BIG ? To what extent does *experience* determine what we *perceive?*

While You Read In response to the state of unrest in Rome, Calpurnia has a cryptic dream. Look for different characters' perceptions of her dream.

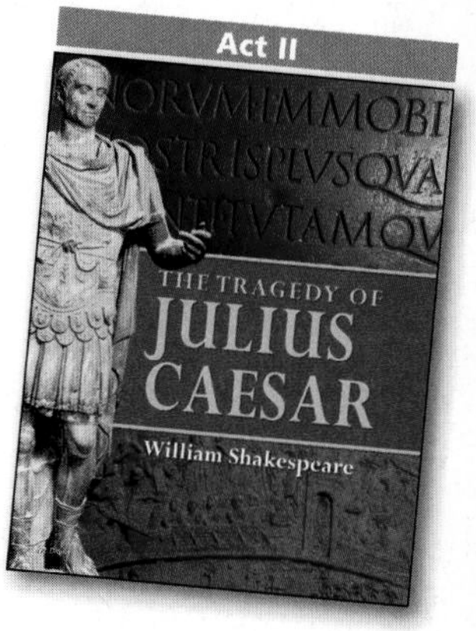

❶ Selection Skills Guide

Practice these skills with ***The Tragedy of Julius Caesar,* Act II** (p. 916).

- Understand blank verse
- Identify iambs, pentameter, and iambic pentameter
- Read Shakespearean drama
- Paraphrase

Integrated Language Skills (Grammar; Listening and Speaking; Research and Technology; and Writing Activities) appear on pages 1002–1005.

❷ Vocabulary

Read each word and its definition. Decide whether you know the word well, know it a little bit, or do not know it at all. After you read, see how your knowledge of each word has increased.

- **augmented** (ôg ment′ id) *adj.* made greater; enhanced (p. 917) ***Her augmented library has hundreds more books than mine.*** *augment v. augmentation n.*
- **entreated** (en trēt′ id) *v.* begged; pleaded with (p. 919) ***He entreated her for mercy.*** *entreatingly adv. entreaty n.*
- **insurrection** (in′ sə rek′ shən) *n.* rebellion (p. 919) ***The insurrection against the government started in the town square.*** *insurgence n. insurgent adj.*
- **resolution** (rez′ ə lo͞o′ shən) *n.* strong determination; a plan or decision (p. 920) ***Lou stuck to his plans with firm resolution.*** *resolute adj. resolutely adv. resolve n.*
- **wrathfully** (rath′ fəl lē) *adv.* with intense anger (p. 922) ***She shook her fist wrathfully at the tailgating driver.*** *wrath n. wrathful adj.*
- **imminent** (im′ ə nənt) *adj.* about to happen (p. 931) ***The lightning flash meant thunder was imminent.*** *imminence n. imminently adv.*

❸ Word Study

The **Latin prefix *-en*** means "in, into, or within."

In the play, a character wonders if he is being **entreated,** or asked in earnest, to act for the good of his country.

Vocabulary Development

Vocabulary Knowledge Rating

Create a **Vocabulary Knowledge Rating Chart** (***Professional Development Guidebook,*** p. 33) for this selection. Include the selection vocabulary that appears.

Give students a copy of the chart. Read the words aloud, and have students mark their rating in the Before Reading column. Urge them to be alert to these words as they read and discuss the selection.

Tally how many students think they know a word to gauge how much instruction to provide. As students read and discuss the selection, point out the words and their context.

PHLit Online! **Vocabulary Central,** featuring tools, activities, and songs for studying vocabulary, is available online at **www.PHLitOnline.com.**

❹ Literary Analysis: Blank Verse

The Tragedy of Julius Caesar is written in blank verse. **Blank verse** is a poetic form characterized by unrhymed lines written in iambic pentameter.

- An **iamb** is a *foot* (unit of rhythm) in which an unstressed syllable is followed by a stressed syllable: da-DUH.
- **Pentameter** refers to a rhythmic pattern in which each line has five feet.
- In **iambic pentameter,** the typical line has five iambs, or five stressed syllables each preceded by an unstressed syllable: And THERE | fore THINK | him AS | a SER | pent's EGG

Shakespeare's "upperclass" characters speak in iambic pentameter. Lower-born characters speak in prose. Sometimes, Shakespeare breaks the rhythmic pattern in a line to add contrast or emphasis.

❺ Reading Skill: Paraphrase

Paraphrasing a line or passage from a work means restating its meaning in your own words. To paraphrase when **reading Shakespearean drama,** follow these steps:

- Look for punctuation showing where sentences end.
- For each sentence, identify the subject and verb and put them into the usual order. You may also need to add helping verbs and use modern verb and pronoun forms.

❻ Using the Strategy: Paraphrase Diagram

As you read, record details on a **paraphrase diagram** like the one shown.

Original Lines	Paraphrase
Verb: Sham'st; Subj.: thou "O conspiracy, / Sham'st thou to show thy dang'rous brow by night, / When evils are most free?" —Scene i, lines 77–79	O conspiracy, are you not ashamed to show your dangerous face at night, when it is easiest to be evil?

PHLit Online!
www.PHLitOnline.com

Hear It!
- Selection summary audio
- Selection audio

See It!
- Get Connected video
- Background video
- More about the author
- Vocabulary flashcards

Do It!
- Interactive journals
- Interactive graphic organizers
- Self-test
- Internet activity
- Grammar tutorial
- Interactive vocabulary games

Differentiated Instruction for Universal Access

Preparing Students for the Selection

To prepare lower-level readers to read Act II of *Julius Caesar,* follow these steps:

- Remind students that the selection deals with a challenging concept: internal conflicts within a historical and political context. Ask students to think of examples of internal conflict or civil war from history. How do these conflicts differ from external conflicts? How were the conflicts resolved?
- Students may have difficulty with the archaic vocabulary Shakespeare uses in the selection (e.g., "wafter" on p. 924). Remind and encourage students to look up unfamiliar words.
- Students may have difficulty understanding the long monologues and soliloquies in the selection (e.g., pp. 922–923). Review strategies of summarizing passages. Encourage students to pause after reading difficult sections and recap the passages in their own words.

❹ Literary Analysis

1. Introduce the skill, using the instruction on the student page.
2. Tell students that they will analyze blank verse as they read.

Think Aloud: Model the Skill

Model the skill of analyzing blank verse. Say to students:

Sometimes I like to read blank verse aloud so I can hear the rhythmic pattern of the iambic pentameter. For example, if I read the line from *Julius Caesar,* "You SHALL conFESS that YOU are BOTH deCEIVED," I can hear the five pairs of stressed-unstressed syllables.

I know that sometimes Shakespeare breaks this rhythmic pattern to add contrast or emphasis. I read, "LET'S be SAcrificers, but not BUTchers, CAius." Here, I note extra syllables and an irregular rhythmic pattern. Thus, I assume that this line has particular importance.

❺ Reading Skill

1. Introduce the skill, using the instruction on the student page.
2. Tell students that they will use paraphrasing as they read.

Think Aloud: Model the Skill

Model the skill of paraphrasing. Say to students:

When I read Shakespeare, I paraphrase difficult lines by restating them in my own words. First I locate a difficult sentence. Then, I identify the subject and verb and put them in the correct order. For example, I rephrase, "Know I these men that come along with you?" as "Do I know these men that have come along with you?"

Paraphrasing in this way makes Shakespeare's complicated language easier for me to understand.

❻ Using the Strategy

Give students a copy of either **Reading Skill Graphic Organizer A** or **B** (*Graphic Organizer Transparencies,* pp. 170–171) to record details of paraphrasing as they read. Use the examples in **Reading Skill Graphic Organizer A,** which is partially filled in, to model the process of completing the organizer.

TEACH

❶ Activating Prior Knowledge

1. Prepare an **Anticipation Guide** (see ***Professional Development Guidebook***, pp. 36–38) with the following statements:
   - Friendship is only as important as one wants it to be.
   - Life gives each person what he or she deserves.
   - Fear serves no purpose.
   - Confidence can only carry a person so far.
2. Give students a copy of the prepared **Anticipation Guide** and have students mark their responses in the Me column. Have students discuss the statements in pairs or groups and mark the Guides again in the Group column.
3. For further guidance, use the *Classroom Strategies and Teaching Routines* card: **Using an Anticipation Guide.**

Concept Connector

Students will return to the **Anticipation Guide** after completing Act II of the play.

Small-Group Activity

Have students lead groups in tapping or clapping out the iambic pentameter of the poetry in this act.

❷ About the Selection

On the eve of the ides of March, Cassius and the other conspirators visit Brutus. All agree to kill Caesar the next day.

The next morning, Calpurnia, fearing danger, begs Caesar to stay home. He agrees at first, but Decius Brutus persuades him to go to the Senate.

❸ Critical Viewing

Answer: The painting depicts a distraught Caesar walking away from his wife who has nearly collapsed. He is shunning everyone around him, including his wife who is trying to prevent him from leaving by grabbing his robe. The woman crying on Portia's lap and the man who is holding her are trying to comfort her.

REVIEW AND ANTICIPATE

❶ ❷ In Act I, as Caesar returns victorious from war, the common people are calling for him to be crowned emperor. Fearful of Caesar's ambitions and unwilling to surrender their own power, Cassius and others conspire against Caesar. Cassius attempts to win the support of Brutus, a highly respected Roman. Although Brutus is a friend of Caesar's, he worries about Caesar's ambition. In the meantime, Caesar receives a warning to "beware the ides of March." Act II opens on the evening before that fateful day. As you read, note how Caesar's own pride leads him to ignore danger. Note also the contrasts that emerge between Brutus and the conspirators.

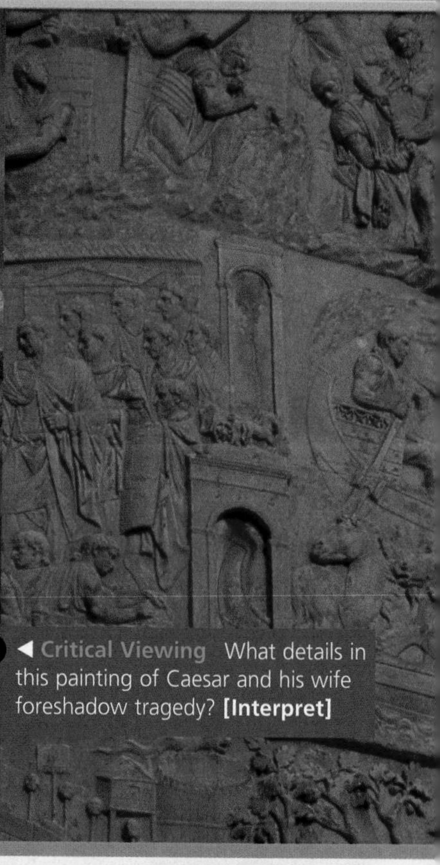

❸ ◀ **Critical Viewing** What details in this painting of Caesar and his wife foreshadow tragedy? **[Interpret]**

916 Drama

Differentiated Instruction for Universal Access

Accessibility at a Glance: Selection

	***The Tragedy of Julius Caesar*, Act II**
Context	Historical: Ancient Rome
Language/Vocabulary	• Dialogue • Prose, verse, and soliloquies
Concept Level	Challenging (internal conflicts within historical, political context)
Literary Merit	Classic; noted author
Lexile/Length	Lexile: NP Word Count: 4,410
Overall Rating	**Challenging**

ACT II

Scene i. Rome.

[*Enter* BRUTUS *in his orchard.*]

BRUTUS. What, Lucius, ho!
I cannot, by the progress of the stars,
Give guess how near to day. Lucius, I say!
I would it were my fault to sleep so soundly.
When, Lucius, when? Awake, I say! What, Lucius!

4 [*Enter* LUCIUS.]

LUCIUS. Called you, my lord?

BRUTUS. Get me a taper in my study, Lucius.
When it is lighted, come and call me here.

LUCIUS. I will, my lord. [*Exit*]

BRUTUS. It must be by his death; and for my part,
I know no personal cause to spurn at[1] him,
But for the general.[2] He would be crowned.
How that might change his nature, there's the question.
It is the bright day that brings forth the adder,[3]
And that craves[4] wary walking. Crown him that,
And then I grant we put a sting in him
That at his will he may do danger with.
Th' abuse of greatness is when it disjoins
Remorse from power;[5] and, to speak truth of Caesar,
I have not known when his affections swayed[6]
More than his reason. But 'tis a common proof[7]
That lowliness[8] is young ambition's ladder,
Whereto the climber upward turns his face;
5 But when he once attains the upmost round,
He then unto the ladder turns his back,
Looks in the clouds, scorning the base degrees[9]
By which he did ascend. So Caesar may;
Then lest he may, prevent.[10] And, since the quarrel
Will bear no color for the thing he is,[11]
Fashion it[12] thus: that what he is, augmented
Would run to these and these extremities;[13]
And therefore think him as a serpent's egg
Which hatched, would as his kind grow mischievous,
And kill him in the shell.

[*Enter* LUCIUS.]

Literary Analysis
Blank Verse Explain which character, Brutus or Lucius, speaks in blank verse and why.

1. **spurn at** kick against; rebel against.
2. **the general** the public good.
3. **adder** (ad´ ər) *n.* poisonous snake.
4. **craves** *v.* requires.
5. **disjoins . . . power** separates mercy from power.
6. **affections swayed** emotions ruled.
7. **proof** *n.* experience.
8. **lowliness** (lō´ lē nəs) *n.* humility.
9. **base degrees** low steps or people in lower positions.
10. **lest . . . prevent** in case he may, we must stop him.
11. **the quarrel . . . the thing he is** our complaint cannot be justified in terms of what he now is.
12. **Fashion it** state the case.
13. **extremities** (ek strem´ ə tēz) *n.* extremes (of tyranny).

Vocabulary
augmented (ôg ment´ id) *adj.* made greater; enhanced

6 **Reading Check**
What does Brutus fear may happen if Caesar is crowned?

4 Literary Analysis
Blank Verse

1. Have students read lines 1–9.
2. **Ask** students to respond to the Literary Analysis item: Explain which character, Brutus or Lucius, speaks in blank verse and why.
   Answer: Lucius' brief replies would scan if they were part of longer blank verse lines. (Later in the scene, Lucius does speak in blank verse. His use of it is unusual because he is a servant. It may show Lucius' respect for Brutus or that Lucius is well born.)

5 Reading Skill
Paraphrase

1. Have students paraphrase lines 21–27 in Brutus' speech.
   Sample answer: An ambitious man is humble when he begins his career. Once he is successful, however, he sneers at everyone and everything he knew on his way to the top.
2. **Ask** students: How do the semicolon and the period in lines 21–27 help you paraphrase the lines?
   Answer: Students can use the semicolon and period as cues to paraphrase lines 21–27 in two sentences.

6 Reading Check

Answer: Brutus fears that Caesar may abuse his power if crowned.

Differentiated Instruction — Additional Instruction

EL Extended Support—English Learners
Have students complete the **Reading and Vocabulary Warm-ups,** ***Unit 5 Resources,*** pp. 109–112, before they read. Assign the prereading pages for the selection in the ***Reader's Notebook: English Learner's Version.*** Then, have students listen to portions of the selection on the ***Hear It!*** **Audio CD.**

L1 L2 Extended Support—Struggling Readers
Have students complete the **Reading and Vocabulary Warm-ups,** ***Unit 5 Resources,*** pp. 109–112, before they read. Assign the prereading pages for the selection in the ***Reader's Notebook: Adapted Version.*** Then, have students listen to portions of the selection on the ***Hear It!*** **Audio CD** (adapted text).

Extended Support—Reluctant Readers
To build motivation and engagement before assigning the selection, have students read "In or Out of the In Crowd," a thematically related selection in ***Reality Central.*** Then, use the questions at the conclusion of the related selection to guide discussion.

PHLit Online!
This selection is available in interactive format in the **Enriched Online Student Edition, www.PHLitOnline.com,** which includes a thematically related video with writing prompt and an interactive graphic organizer.

7 Literature in Context

Language Connection The informal pronouns *thou, thee,* and *thy* have passed out of use in modern times. Close friends and family members once called one another *thou* instead of *you. You* was the pronoun used to show respect, formality, or politeness, while *thou* showed familiarity. Masters would call their servants *thou,* but servants would call their masters *you.*

Thou has its own verb forms, which usually end in *-st.* Examples on pages 918–919 include "thou sleep-'st" and "thou receivest." When the pronoun *thou* faded from use, its verb forms also disappeared.

Connect to the Literature Have students locate archaic words and word forms on pages 918–919. Guide students in paraphrasing the lines in which such words and forms occur. Then, **ask** students the Connect to the Literature question: What does this archaic language add to your experience of the play? What challenges does it pose?

Possible response: The formal, archaic language helps distinguish among upper- and lower-class characters and conveys the atmosphere of a different era.

LUCIUS. The taper burneth in your closet,[14] sir.
Searching the window for a flint,[15] I found
This paper thus sealed up, and I am sure
It did not lie there when I went to bed. [*Gives him the letter*]

BRUTUS. Get you to bed again; it is not day.
Is not tomorrow, boy, the ides of March?

LUCIUS. I know not, sir.

BRUTUS. Look in the calendar and bring me word.

LUCIUS. I will, sir. [*Exit*]

BRUTUS. The exhalations[16] whizzing in the air
Give so much light that I may read by them.
[*Opens the letter and reads*]

"Brutus, thou sleep'st; awake, and see thyself.
Shall Rome, &c.[17] Speak, strike, redress.
Brutus, thou sleep'st; awake."

Such instigations[18] have been often dropped
Where I have took them up.
"Shall Rome, &c." Thus must I piece it out:[19]
Shall Rome stand under one man's awe?[20] What, Rome?
My ancestors did from the streets of Rome
The Tarquin[21] drive, when he was called a king.

14. **closet** *n.* study; small, private room for reading, meditation, and so on.
15. **flint** *n.* hard stone which, when struck with steel, makes sparks.
16. **exhalations** (eks′ hə lā′ shənz) *n.* meteors.
17. **&c.** et cetera (et set′ ər ə); Latin for "and so forth."
18. **instigations** (in′ stə gā′ shənz) *n.* urgings, incitements, or spurs to act.
19. **piece it out** figure out the meaning.
20. **under one man's awe** in fearful reverence of one man.
21. **Tarquin** (tär′ kwin) king of Rome driven out by Lucius Junius Brutus, Brutus' ancestor.

7 LITERATURE IN CONTEXT

Language Connection

Archaic Word Forms

Shakespeare uses some word forms that are now archaic, or out of date. For modern readers, these words give his work a tone that is both more formal and more poetic than contemporary English. These archaic forms include the following:

thou *pron.* subjective case of a pronoun meaning "you" (the form used with family, friends, or the young)

thee *pron.* you (objective case of *thou*)

thy *pron.* your (possessive case of *thou*)

burneth *v.* third-person singular present tense of *burn*

'tis *contraction* it is

doth *v.* third-person singular present tense of *do*

dost *v.* second-person singular present tense of *do* (used with *thou*)

sham'st *v.* second-person singular present tense of *shame* (used with *thou*)

Connect to the Literature

What does this archaic language add to your experience of the play? What challenges does it pose?

Vocabulary Development

Thematic Vocabulary: The Big Question

As students are discussing *The Tragedy of Julius Caesar,* Act II, encourage them to use the thematic vocabulary presented in Introducing the Big Question, pp. 790–791. You might encourage them with sentence starters like these:

1. In his opening soliloquy, Brutus begins to *anticipate* . . .
2. Brutus' *perspective* about the murder of Caesar differs from the other conspirators' in that . . .
3. Portia uses her power of speech to *manipulate* Brutus to . . .
4. Decius' *interpretation* of Calpurnia's dream is . . .

"Speak, strike, redress." Am I entreated
To speak and strike? O Rome, I make thee promise,
If the redress will follow, thou receivest
Thy full petition at the hand of[22] Brutus!

[*Enter* LUCIUS.]

LUCIUS. Sir, March is wasted fifteen days. [*Knock within*]

BRUTUS. 'Tis good. Go to the gate; somebody knocks. [*Exit* LUCIUS.]

Since Cassius first did whet[23] me against Caesar,
I have not slept.
Between the acting of a dreadful thing
And the first motion,[24] all the interim is
Like a phantasma,[25] or a hideous dream.
The genius and the mortal instruments[26]
Are then in council, and the state of a man,
Like to a little kingdom, suffers then
The nature of an insurrection.

[*Enter* LUCIUS.]

LUCIUS. Sir, 'tis your brother[27] Cassius at the door,
Who doth desire to see you.

BRUTUS. Is he alone?

LUCIUS. No, sir, there are moe[28] with him.

BRUTUS. Do you know them?

LUCIUS. No, sir; their hats are plucked about their ears,
And half their faces buried in their cloaks,
That by no means I may discover them
By any mark of favor.[29]

8

BRUTUS. Let 'em enter. [*Exit* LUCIUS.]
They are the faction. O conspiracy,
Sham'st thou to show thy dang'rous brow by night,
When evils are most free? O, then by day
Where wilt thou find a cavern dark enough
To mask thy monstrous visage? Seek none, conspiracy;
Hide it in smiles and affability:
For if thou path, thy native semblance on,[30]
Not Erebus[31] itself were dim enough
To hide thee from prevention.[32]

[*Enter the conspirators,* CASSIUS, CASCA, DECIUS, CINNA, METELLUS CIMBER, *and* TREBONIUS.]

Vocabulary
entreated (en trēt′ id) *v.* begged; pleaded
insurrection (in′ sə rek′ shən) *n.* rebellion

22. **Thy full . . . hand of** all you ask from.
23. **whet** (hwet) *v.* sharpen; incite.
24. **motion** *n.* idea; suggestion.
25. **all the interim . . . a phantasma** (fan taz′ mə) all the time between seems like a hallucination.
26. **mortal instruments** bodily powers.

27. **brother** *n.* brother-in-law. (Cassius was married to Brutus' sister.)
28. **moe** *n.* more.
29. **discover . . . favor** identify them by any sign of their appearance.

Literary Analysis
Blank Verse Which interjection does Shakespeare use to maintain iambic pentameter in lines 77 and 79?

30. **path . . . semblance on** walk looking as you normally do.
31. **Erebus** (er′ ə bəs) in Greek mythology, a dark region under the earth through which the dead pass on their way to Hades, the afterworld.
32. **prevention** *n.* being discovered and stopped.

9 **Reading Check**
What is Brutus' state of mind?

8 Literary Analysis
Blank Verse

1. Ask two volunteers to take the parts of Lucius and Brutus and read aloud lines 70–76. **Ask** students what they notice about lines 71, 72, and 76.
   Answer: Each line is made up of dialogue spoken by more than one character.
2. Explain that blank verse often uses this technique, which is called shared meter. The way the lines are printed on the page, with the second part of the line indented to align with the end of the first, shows readers these lines are in blank verse rather than prose or some other verse meter.
3. Have students consider why Shakespeare uses shared meter. **Ask:** What effect does shared meter have on the actors speaking the lines, and on the listeners?
   Possible response: Shared meter suggests that there is no pause between lines; that actors speak almost on top of each other's lines. To listeners, this sounds like ordinary conversation, in which people often interrupt each other or answer without pausing for thought.
4. Read aloud Brutus' speech after Lucius exits (lines 77–85). Then, **ask** students to respond to the Literary Analysis question: Which interjection does Shakespeare use to maintain iambic pentameter in lines 77 and 79?
   Answer: Shakespeare uses the interjection *O*.

9 Reading Check

Answer: Brutus is still uncertain about what to do about Caesar.

Differentiated Instruction for Universal Access

Strategy for Special Needs Students
Have students listen to the ***Hear It!* Audio CD** of *The Tragedy of Julius Caesar* and follow along with the printed text. Have them pay careful attention to the way the actors speak their lines. Students should notice that actors speak Shakespeare's blank verse as if it were prose—they emphasize the sense of what they are saying, not the sound of the verse. Listening to the play read aloud will help students follow the story.

Strategy for Less Proficient Readers
The blank verse of some of the long speeches in this play may prove a barrier to students' understanding. Suggest that students write out the speeches as though they were paragraphs of prose and then read them aloud. Without the distraction of line breaks, students should find the speeches easier to understand.

⓾ Reading Skill
Paraphrase

1. Have two students read aloud the exchange between Cassius and Brutus in lines 86–94.
2. **Ask** students to respond to the Reading Skill prompt: Paraphrase Cassius' words in lines 90–93. **Sample answer:** You [Brutus] know everyone here, and they all respect you. They all wish you thought as highly of yourself as all noble Romans think of you.

⓫ Connecting to the Big Question

1. Point out that throughout the play, the key characters develop unique perceptions of situations and other characters based on their experiences.
2. Have students read the bracketed text. **Ask** them to discuss how Brutus' perception of swearing an oath is different from Cassius'. **Possible response:** Brutus feels that swearing an oath is meant for doubtful, weak, and uncertain men and that the strength of the cause that unites them should be enough to join them together. Cassius disagrees and feels it is necessary. Perhaps he does not trust the conspirators.
3. **Ask:** How do Cassius' and Brutus' different experiences in dealing with Cicero affect each one's perceptions of whether or not he should be a conspirator? **Possible response:** Cassius' experience with Cicero sets his focus on the fact that Cicero is powerful, and having him as a conspirator would improve public opinion of them and their plan. Brutus' experience with Cicero leads him to believe that joining forces with Cicero would have the opposite effect because Cicero is not the type of man to follow the plans or ideas of others.

CASSIUS. I think we are too bold upon[33] your rest.
Good morrow, Brutus; do we trouble you?

BRUTUS. I have been up this hour, awake all night.
Know I these men that come along with you?

CASSIUS. Yes, every man of them; and no man here
But honors you; and every one doth wish
You had but that opinion of yourself
Which every noble Roman bears of you.
This is Trebonius.

BRUTUS. He is welcome hither.

CASSIUS. This, Decius Brutus.

BRUTUS. He is welcome too.

CASSIUS. This, Casca; this, Cinna; and this, Metellus Cimber.

BRUTUS. They are all welcome.
What watchful cares do interpose themselves
Betwixt your eyes and night?[34]

CASSIUS. Shall I entreat a word?[35] [*They whisper.*]

DECIUS. Here lies the east; doth not the day break here?

CASCA. No.

CINNA. O, pardon, sir, it doth; and yon gray lines
That fret[36] the clouds are messengers of day.

CASCA. You shall confess that you are both deceived.
Here, as I point my sword, the sun arises,
Which is a great way growing on[37] the south,
Weighing[38] the youthful season of the year.
Some two months hence, up higher toward the north
He first presents his fire; and the high[39] east
Stands as the Capitol, directly here.

BRUTUS. Give me your hands all over, one by one.

CASSIUS. And let us swear our resolution.

BRUTUS. No, not an oath. If not the face of men,
The sufferance of our souls, the time's abuse[40]—
If these be motives weak, break off betimes,[41]
And every man hence to his idle bed.
So let high-sighted[42] tyranny range on
Till each man drop by lottery.[43] But if these
(As I am sure they do) bear fire enough
To kindle cowards and to steel with valor

33. upon *adv.* in interfering with.

Reading Skill
Paraphrase ⓾
Paraphrase Cassius' words in lines 90–93.

34. watchful . . . night worries keep you from sleep.
35. entreat (in trēt´) **a word** ask for a chance to speak with you.
36. fret (fret) *v.* decorate with a pattern.
37. growing on tending toward.
38. Weighing *v.* considering.
39. high *adj.* due.

Vocabulary
resolution (rez´ ə lo͞o´ shən) *n.* strong determination; a plan or decision

40. the face . . . time's abuse the sadness on men's faces, the patient endurance of our souls, the present abuses (that is, Caesar's abuses of power).
41. betimes (bē tīmz´) *adv.* quickly. ⓫
42. high-sighted *adj.* arrogant (a reference to a hawk about to swoop down on prey).
43. by lottery by chance or in his turn.

Vocabulary Development

Word Forms

Expand students' vocabulary by helping them learn related forms of two of the Selection Vocabulary words for *The Tragedy of Julius Caesar,* Act II. Give students a blank **Word Form Chart** (***Professional Development Guidebook,*** p. 42), with *entreated* and *resolution* in the correct columns. Work with the class, or have students work with a partner, to determine the related forms. The final chart should look like the one shown.

Noun	Verb	Adjective	Adverb
entreaty	**entreated**	entreating	entreatingly
resolution	resolve	resolute	resolutely

The melting spirits of women, then, countrymen,
What need we any spur but our own cause
To prick us to redress?[44] What other bond
Than secret Romans, that have spoke the word,
And will not palter?[45] And what other oath
Than honesty to honesty[46] engaged
That this shall be, or we will fall for it?
Swear priests and cowards and men cautelous,[47]
Old feeble carrions[48] and such suffering souls
That welcome wrongs; unto bad causes swear
Such creatures as men doubt; but do not stain
The even[49] virtue of our enterprise,
Nor th' insuppressive mettle[50] of our spirits,
To think that or our cause or[51] our performance
Did need an oath; when every drop of blood
That every Roman bears, and nobly bears,
Is guilty of a several bastardy[52]
If he do break the smallest particle
Of any promise that hath passed from him.

CASSIUS. But what of Cicero? Shall we sound him?[53]
I think he will stand very strong with us.

CASCA. Let us not leave him out.

CINNA. No, by no means.

METELLUS. O, let us have him, for his silver hairs
Will purchase us a good opinion,
And buy men's voices to commend our deeds.
It shall be said his judgment ruled our hands;
Our youths and wildness shall no whit[54] appear,
But all be buried in his gravity.

BRUTUS. O, name him not! Let us not break with him;[55]
For he will never follow anything
That other men begin.

CASSIUS. Then leave him out.

CASCA. Indeed, he is not fit.

DECIUS. Shall no man else be touched but only Caesar?

CASSIUS. Decius, well urged. I think it is not meet
Mark Antony, so well beloved of Caesar,
Should outlive Caesar; we shall find of[56] him
A shrewd contriver;[57] and you know, his means,
If he improve[58] them, may well stretch so far

44. **prick us to redress** goad or spur us on to correct these evils.
45. **palter** (pôl´ tər) *v.* talk insincerely.
46. **honesty** personal honor.
47. **cautelous** (kôt´ ə ləs) *adj.* deceitful.
48. **carrions** (kar´ ē ənz) *n.* men who are nearly corpses.
49. **even** *adj.* constant.
50. **insuppressive mettle** uncrushable courage.
51. **or . . . or** either our cause or.
52. **guilty . . . bastardy** is no true Roman.

53. **sound him** find out his opinion.

54. **no whit** (hwit) not the least bit.
55. **break with him** confide in him.

56. **of** *prep.* in.
57. **contriver** (kən trīv´ ər) *n.* schemer.
58. **improve** *v.* increase.

14 Reading Check

Why does Brutus think the conspirators should not swear an oath?

12 Critical Thinking

Analyze

1. Have students read lines 129–136 of Brutus' speech.
2. **Ask** students who Brutus says are people who swear oaths.
   Answer: Brutus says that priests, cowards, cautious men, and the dying swear oaths.
3. **Ask** students to paraphrase lines 132–136.
   Sample answer: Brutus thinks that swearing an oath would shame their courageous, noble plans and abilities.

13 Background

Cicero

In lines 141–153, the conspirators discuss inviting Cicero to join them. Marcus Tullius Cicero was one of the great speakers and writers of the age. His prose became the model for literary expression throughout Europe, and his orations are among the most commonly studied Latin works. Cicero studied philosophy and rhetoric in Greece. After returning to Rome in 66 B.C. he was elected praetor (administrator of civil justice). In 63 B.C., he was elected consul.

Cicero supported Pompey in his struggle with Caesar for control of Rome, and he approved of Caesar's assassination. In 43 B.C., when Octavius Caesar, Mark Antony, and Marcus Aemilius Lepidus assumed power as the Second Triumvirate (see Act IV, Scene i), Cicero was one of many whom they condemned to death. He was killed at his home in Tuscany.

14 Reading Check

Answer: Brutus does not think the conspirators need to swear an oath because they are honest and noble Romans who can trust one another.

Fluency

Distribute copies of pages 920 and 921. Explain that many of the sentences in this play are spread over multiple lines and contain punctuation that signifies to the reader when to pause or speed up. Guide students to read each sentence with the normal pauses after commas, briefly stopping after periods, and to read as a continuous thought when there is no punctuation.

For an example, point out that the end of line 118 should flow smoothly into line 119.

Have students follow along as you read Brutus' speech (lines 114 to 140) aloud once, modeling appropriate pauses and stops. Read the lines aloud once more, this time encouraging students to draw a slash mark (/) whenever you pause or stop and circle any words that they find difficult. Then, reread the lines one full sentence at a time, having the students echo what you are reading. Pay attention for trouble spots, repeating those words, phrases, or sentences to build fluency.

15 Critical Thinking

Analyze

1. Have students read Cassius' speech in lines 155–161, in which he proposes that Mark Antony also be killed.
2. **Ask** students what reasons Cassius offers to justify the killing of Antony.
   Answer: Cassius says that Antony is a "shrewd contriver" who might be able to damage the conspirators.
3. Point out that, in describing Mark Antony, Cassius could almost be describing himself. (Note, for example, how well Cassius has improved "his means" in his plot against Caesar.)

16 Critical Viewing

Possible response: Brutus is alone on one side, signifying his private conflict about the plan to murder Caesar. He looks serious but not rushed or pressured. The others stand opposite Brutus in a group, which signifies their unity of purpose. The dagger one is holding and the tense, determined looks on the men's faces show a firm commitment to their plan and suggest a feeling of urgency about carrying out the plan.

59. annoy *n.* harm.
60. Like . . . envy afterwards as if we were killing in anger with hatred afterward.
61. come by Caesar's spirit get hold of the principles of tyranny for which Caesar stands.
62. gentle *adj.* honorable; noble.

15

As to annoy[59] us all; which to prevent,
Let Antony and Caesar fall together.

BRUTUS. Our course will seem too bloody, Caius Cassius,
To cut the head off and then hack the limbs,
Like wrath in death and envy afterwards;[60]
For Antony is but a limb of Caesar.
Let's be sacrificers, but not butchers, Caius.
We all stand up against the spirit of Caesar,
And in the spirit of men there is no blood.
O, that we then could come by Caesar's spirit,[61]
And not dismember Caesar! But, alas,
Caesar must bleed for it. And, gentle[62] friends,
Let's kill him boldly, but not **wrathfully**;
Let's carve him as a dish fit for the gods,
Not hew him as a carcass fit for hounds.

17

Vocabulary
wrathfully (ra*th*´ fəl lē) *adv.* with intense anger

16 ▼ **Critical Viewing** What details of this image emphasize the differences between Brutus, on the left, and the other conspirators? **[Analyze]**

Vocabulary Development

Vocabulary Reinforcement

Students will benefit from additional examples and practice with the selection vocabulary words. Reinforce their comprehension with "show-you-know" sentences. The first part of the sentence uses the vocabulary word in an appropriate context. The second part of the sentence—the "show-you-know" part—clarifies the first. Model the strategy with this example for *wrathfully*:

She responded *wrathfully*, with anger flashing in her eyes.

Then, give students a sentence prompt such as the following, and coach them in writing the clarification part:

When he pounded the table *wrathfully*, they understood ____________

Sample answer: immediately that he was very angry.

And let our hearts, as subtle masters do,
Stir up their servants[63] to an act of rage,
And after seem to chide 'em.[64] This shall make
Our purpose necessary, and not envious;
Which so appearing to the common eyes,
We shall be called purgers,[65] not murderers.
And for Mark Antony, think not of him;
For he can do no more than Caesar's arm
When Caesar's head is off.

CASSIUS. Yet I fear him;
For in the ingrafted[66] love he bears to Caesar—

BRUTUS. Alas, good Cassius, do not think of him.
If he love Caesar, all that he can do
Is to himself—take thought[67] and die for Caesar.
And that were much he should,[68] for he is given
To sports, to wildness, and much company.

TREBONIUS. There is no fear in him; let him not die,
For he will live and laugh at this hereafter.

[*Clock strikes.*]

BRUTUS. Peace! Count the clock.

CASSIUS. The clock hath stricken three.

TREBONIUS. 'Tis time to part.

CASSIUS. But it is doubtful yet
Whether Caesar will come forth today or no;
For he is superstitious grown of late,
Quite from the main[69] opinion he held once
Of fantasy, of dreams, and ceremonies.[70]
It may be these apparent prodigies,[71]
The unaccustomed terror of this night,
And the persuasion of his augurers[72]
May hold him from the Capitol today.

DECIUS. Never fear that. If he be so resolved,
I can o'ersway him;[73] for he loves to hear
That unicorns may be betrayed with trees,[74]
And bears with glasses,[75] elephants with holes,[76]
Lions with toils,[77] and men with flatterers;
But when I tell him he hates flatterers
He says he does, being then most flatterèd.
Let me work;
For I can give his humor the true bent,[78]
And I will bring him to the Capitol.

63. **their servants** that is, the hands or the passions.
64. **chide 'em** scold them.
65. **purgers** (purj ərz) *n.* healers.
66. **ingrafted** (in graft′ id) *adj.* deeply rooted.
67. **take thought** become melancholy.
68. **that were much he should** It is unlikely he would do that.
69. **Quite from the main** quite changed from the strong.
70. **ceremonies** *n.* omens.
71. **apparent prodigies** obvious omens of disaster.
72. **augurers** (ô′ gər ərz) *n.* augurs; officials who interpreted omens to decide if they were favorable or unfavorable for an undertaking.
73. **I can o'ersway him** I can change his mind.
74. **unicorns . . . trees** reference to the belief that standing in front of a tree as a unicorn charges and then stepping aside at the last moment causes the unicorn to bury its horn in the tree and so allows it to be caught.
75. **glasses** *n.* mirrors.
76. **holes** *n.* pitfalls.
77. **toils** *n.* nets; snares.
78. **give his humor the true bent** bend his feelings in the right direction.

18 **Reading Check**
According to Brutus, why should Antony not be killed?

17 Literary Analysis
Blank Verse

1. Read aloud Brutus' speech in lines 162–183.
2. **Ask** students to explain how the iambic pentameter in lines 173–174 helps emphasize contrasting ideas.
   Possible response: The meter places stress on *bold* in *boldly* and on *wrath* in *wrathfully*, which draws the reader's or audience's attention to these contrasting ideas. The iambic pentameter of the second line stresses and concludes with "fit for the gods," which emphasizes that they should lend nobility to the act, not arrogance.
3. Draw students' attention to the last, short line of the speech.
   Ask: What is Shakespeare trying to achieve with such a short line?
   Answer: The short line ends the speech abruptly and echoes the image of an abrupt ending to Caesar's life.

18 Reading Check

Answer: Brutus argues that since Antony will have no power without Caesar, killing Antony would be a dishonorable act of anger and not in the interest of Rome.

Differentiated Instruction for Universal Access

Enrichment for Gifted and Talented Students
Challenge students to stage Act II, Scene i from the conspirators' entrance to their exit (lines 86–228). This scene has roles for seven actors; other students may take part in directing, staging, or costuming. Meet with participants to discuss the scene's challenges and to hear students' ideas about staging. Remind students that in Shakespeare's day all female roles were played by boys; encourage the girls in your class to take on some of the male roles and vice versa. Give students sufficient time to rehearse and learn their lines before performing the scene for the class.

19 Reading Skill
Paraphrase

1. Have students read Brutus' remarks to a sleeping Lucius in lines 229–233.
2. Then, **ask** students to respond to the Reading Skill prompt: Paraphrase Brutus' speech in lines 229–233 and explain which punctuation mark helps you identify the conclusion he draws.
   Possible response: Boy! Lucius! Are you sleeping? Never mind; enjoy your rest. You have none of the concerns that responsibility pulls into men's minds; that is why you sleep so well. The second semicolon sets off Brutus' conclusion.

20 Literary Analysis
Blank Verse

1. Remind students that changing the rhythmic pattern of a line is a way of emphasizing ideas.
2. Read aloud line 240, stressing the first and fourth syllables. **Ask** students to respond to the Literary Analysis question: How does shifting the accent to the first and fourth syllables in line 240 add dramatic energy to this speech?
   Possible response: It focuses attention on Brutus' mood by emphasizing the verbs *muse* and *sigh*.
3. Point out that Portia and Brutus use the formal pronoun *you* when speaking to each other. Given that they are husband and wife, **ask** students what effect this formality has.
   Possible response: The formality between Brutus and Portia echoes Lucius' formality in speaking to Brutus in blank verse. It suggests that Brutus is formal and somewhat distant with everyone, and that he doesn't show his emotions.

79. uttermost *adj.* latest.
80. doth bear Caesar hard has a grudge against Caesar.
81. rated *v.* berated; scolded forcefully.

CASSIUS. Nay, we will all of us be there to fetch him.

BRUTUS. By the eighth hour; is that the uttermost?[79]

CINNA. Be that the uttermost, and fail not then.

METELLUS. Caius Ligarius doth bear Caesar hard,[80]
Who rated[81] him for speaking well of Pompey.
I wonder none of you have thought of him.

BRUTUS. Now, good Metellus, go along by him.
He loves me well, and I have given him reasons;
Send him but hither, and I'll fashion[82] him.

82. fashion *v.* mold.
83. put on show.
84. bear it carry it off.
85. formal constancy consistent dignity.

CASSIUS. The morning comes upon 's; we'll leave you, Brutus.
And, friends, disperse yourselves; but all remember
What you have said, and show yourselves true Romans.

BRUTUS. Good gentlemen, look fresh and merrily.
Let not our looks put on[83] our purposes,
But bear it[84] as our Roman actors do,
With untired spirits and formal constancy.[85]
And so good morrow to you every one. [*Exit all but* BRUTUS.]
Boy! Lucius! Fast asleep? It is no matter;
Enjoy the honey-heavy dew of slumber.
Thou hast no figures nor no fantasies
Which busy care draws in the brains of men;
Therefore thou sleep'st so sound.

Reading Skill
Paraphrase Paraphrase Brutus' speech in lines 229–233 and explain which punctuation mark helps you identify the conclusion he draws. 19

[*Enter* PORTIA.]

PORTIA. Brutus, my lord.

BRUTUS. Portia, what mean you? Wherefore rise you now?
It is not for your health thus to commit
Your weak condition to the raw cold morning.

PORTIA. Nor for yours neither. Y'have ungently, Brutus,
Stole from my bed; and yesternight at supper
You suddenly arose and walked about,
Musing and sighing, with your arms across;
And when I asked you what the matter was,
You stared upon me with ungentle looks.
I urged you further; then you scratched your head,
And too impatiently stamped with your foot.
Yet I insisted, yet you answered not,
But with an angry wafter[86] of your hand
Gave sign for me to leave you. So I did,
Fearing to strengthen that impatience
Which seemed too much enkindled, and withal

Literary Analysis 20
Blank Verse How does shifting the accent to the first and fourth syllables in line 240 add dramatic energy to this speech?

86. wafter (wäf′ tər) *n.* wave.

Vocabulary Development

Contractions

Define a contraction as a word shortened by the removal of a letter or letters. Tell students that an apostrophe is inserted in a contraction to indicate that letters are missing. Have students brainstorm for examples of contractions. Write the examples on the chalkboard. Emphasize that contractions are informal in style; some are even considered slangy. The general rule is not to use contractions in formal speech or writing. Note, however, that Shakespeare uses contractions in blank verse. Direct students' attention to "upon's" in line 221, for example, which is a contraction of "upon us." Copy line 221 on the chalkboard, and scan its meter. Point out that the contraction "upon's" helps maintain the rhythm of the iambic pentameter.

Challenge students to locate additional examples of contractions used for the sake of meter. On pages 923–924, students can cite "o'ersway" in line 203, "sleep'st" in line 233, and "Y'have" in line 237.

Hoping it was but an effect of humor,
Which sometime hath his[87] hour with every man.
It will not let you eat, nor talk, nor sleep,
And could it work so much upon your shape
As it hath much prevailed on your condition,[88]
I should not know you[89] Brutus. Dear my lord,
Make me acquainted with your cause of grief.

BRUTUS. I am not well in health, and that is all.

PORTIA. Brutus is wise and, were he not in health,
He would embrace the means to come by it.

BRUTUS. Why, so I do. Good Portia, go to bed.

PORTIA. Is Brutus sick, and is it physical[90]
To walk unbracèd and suck up the humors[91]
Of the dank morning? What, is Brutus sick,
And will he steal out of his wholesome bed,
To dare the vile contagion of the night,
And tempt the rheumy and unpurgèd air[92]
To add unto his sickness? No, my Brutus:
You have some sick offense[93] within your mind,
Which by the right and virtue of my place
I ought to know of; and upon my knees
I charm[94] you, by my once commended[95] beauty,
By all your vows of love, and that great vow[96]
Which did incorporate and make us one,
That you unfold to me, your self, your half,
Why you are heavy,[97] and what men tonight
Have had resort to you; for here have been
Some six or seven, who did hide their faces
Even from darkness.

BRUTUS. Kneel not, gentle Portia.

PORTIA. I should not need, if you were gentle Brutus.
Within the bond of marriage, tell me, Brutus,
Is it excepted[98] I should know no secrets
That appertain[99] to you? Am I your self
But, as it were, in sort or limitation,[100]
To keep with you at meals, comfort your bed,
And talk to you sometimes? Dwell I but in the suburbs[101]
Of your good pleasure? If it be no more,
Portia is Brutus' harlot, not his wife.

87. **his** *pron.* its.
88. **condition** *n.* disposition; mood.
89. **I should not know you** I would not recognize you as.
90. **physical** *adj.* healthy.
91. **walk unbracèd . . . humors** walk with jacket unfastened and take in the dampness.
92. **tempt . . . air** risk exposing yourself to the night air, which is likely to cause rheumatism and has not been purified by the sun.
93. **sick offense** harmful sickness.
94. **charm** *v.* beg.
95. **commended** *adj.* praised.
96. **great vow** marriage vow.
97. **heavy** *adj.* sorrowful.
98. **excepted** *v.* made an exception that.
99. **appertain** (ap´ ər tān´) *v.* belong.
100. **in sort or limitation** in a limited way (legal terms).
101. **suburbs** *n.* outskirts.

23 Reading Check

What does Portia ask of Brutus?

21 Critical Thinking
Analyze

1. Have students read lines 268–274. **Ask** the class to list words and phrases from these lines that pertain to Portia's place in society.
   Answer: List may include: "right and virtue of my place" in line 269, "my once commended beauty" in line 271, "incorporate and make us one" in line 273, and "to me, your self, your half" in line 274.
2. **Ask:** In lines 268–274, what is Portia's main argument for encouraging Brutus to tell her what is troubling him?
   Answer: Portia states that her place in life and society is to be his wife, the woman with whom he chose to become one. She believes that part of her duty as a wife is to share Brutus' burdens.

22 Reading Skill
Paraphrase

1. Call on a volunteer to read Portia's appeal to Brutus in lines 280–286.
2. Note that she asks Brutus three questions. Then, **ask** students to paraphrase Portia's questions in lines 280–286.
   Answer: Don't most wives know their husband's secrets? Am I just your partner in a limited way, eating, sleeping, and talking with you only sometimes? Are you angry with me?

23 Reading Check

Answer: Portia asks Brutus to tell her what is troubling him.

Differentiated Instruction for Universal Access

Enrichment for Advanced Readers
Have students write brief essays on why Shakespeare chooses to include a speech by Portia in lines 237–256. Tell students to read this speech aloud with partners before they write their essays to gain a better understanding of the relationship between Brutus and Portia. Suggest that students consider what Portia reveals about Brutus, in what ways she contrasts with the conspirators, and how her speech affects the mood of the scene.

24 Critical Viewing

Possible response: Portia's pose with her hand on Brutus' arm and her serious look show the care and concern she feels for him. Brutus has turned his body and face away from Portia somewhat and is looking away, showing that he does not feel like sharing his thoughts with her.

25 Literary Analysis

Blank Verse

1. Remind students that variations in iambic pentameter occur. With students, scan the meter of lines 291–293.
2. Then, **ask** students to find one line that follows strict iambic pentameter and one that does not. **Answer:** Line 293 follows strict iambic pentameter. Line 292 does not.

24 ▲ **Critical Viewing**
What do the pose and expressions of Brutus and Portia in this film still reveal about their feelings? **[Interpret]**

BRUTUS. You are my true and honorable wife,
As dear to me as are the ruddy drops[102]
That visit my sad heart.

25

PORTIA. If this were true, then should I know this secret.
I grant I am a woman; but withal[103]
A woman that Lord Brutus took to wife.
I grant I am a woman; but withal
A woman well reputed, Cato's daughter.[104]
Think you I am no stronger than my sex,
Being so fathered and so husbanded?
Tell me your counsels,[105] I will not disclose 'em.
I have made strong proof of my constancy,
Giving myself a voluntary wound
Here in the thigh; can I bear that with patience,
And not my husband's secrets?

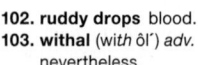

102. ruddy drops blood.
103. withal (wi*th* ôl′) *adv.* nevertheless.
104. Cato's daughter Marcus Porcius (pôr′ shəs) Cato (Cato the Younger; 95–46 B.C.) supported Pompey in his quarrel with Caesar and killed himself rather than allow himself to be captured by Caesar.
105. counsels *n.* secrets. make.

Think Aloud

Vocabulary: Using Context

Direct students' attention to the phrase "have had resort to" at the end of Portia's speech in line 276. Then, use a think-aloud process to model how to use context to infer the meaning of an unknown phrase.

Portia says that she wants to know what men have had resort to Brutus that night. To get an idea of what the phrase "have had resort to" means, I am going to look at words and phrases around it. In the same sentence, Portia says six or seven men have been there that night. She must be referring to Cassius and the other conspirators who came to visit Brutus. That makes me think that "have had resort to" means "have visited."

BRUTUS. O ye gods,
Render[106] me worthy of this noble wife! [*Knock*]
Hark, hark! One knocks. Portia, go in a while,
26 And by and by thy bosom shall partake
The secrets of my heart.
All my engagements[107] I will construe to thee,
All the charactery of my sad brows.[108]
Leave me with haste. [*Exit* PORTIA.]

[*Enter* LUCIUS *and* CAIUS LIGARIUS.]

Lucius, who's that knocks?

LUCIUS. Here is a sick man that would speak with you.

BRUTUS. Caius Ligarius, that Metellus spake of.
Boy, stand aside. Caius Ligarius! How?

CAIUS. Vouchsafe good morrow from a feeble tongue.

BRUTUS. O, what a time have you chose out,[109] brave Caius,
To wear a kerchief![110] Would you were not sick!

CAIUS. I am not sick, if Brutus have in hand
Any exploit worthy the name of honor.

BRUTUS. Such an exploit have I in hand, Ligarius,
Had you a healthful ear to hear of it.

CAIUS. By all the gods that Romans bow before,
I here discard my sickness! Soul of Rome,
Brave son, derived from honorable loins,[111]
Thou, like an exorcist,[112] hast conjured up
My mortifièd spirit.[113] Now bid me run,
And I will strive with things impossible.
Yea, get the better of them. What's to do?

BRUTUS. A piece of work that will make sick men whole.

CAIUS. But are not some whole that we must make sick?

BRUTUS. That must we also. What it is, my Caius,
I shall unfold[114] to thee, as we are going
To whom it must be done.

CAIUS. Set on[115] your foot,
And with a heart new-fired I follow you,
To do I know not what; but it sufficeth[116]
That Brutus leads me on. [*Thunder*]

BRUTUS. Follow me, then. [*Exit*]

106. **Render** (ren′ dər) *v.*

Literary Analysis
Blank Verse By breaking the pattern of iambic pentameter, which words are emphasized in lines 307 and 308?

107. **engagements** *n.* commitments.
108. **All the charactery of my sad brows** all that is written on my sad face.

109. **chose out** picked out.
110. **To wear a kerchief** Caius wears a scarf to protect himself from drafts because he is sick.

111. **derived from honorable loins** descended from Lucius (lo͞o′ shē əs) Junius Brutus, founder of the Roman Republic.
112. **exorcist** (ek′ sôr sist) *n.* one who calls up spirits.
113. **mortifièd** (môrt′ ə fī ed) *adj.* deadened.
114. **unfold** *v.* disclose.
115. **Set on** advance.
116. **sufficeth** (sə fis′ *eth*) *v.* is enough.

27 **Reading Check**
Why does Portia feel that Brutus should confide in her?

26 Literary Analysis
Blank Verse

1. Have students read Brutus' speech in lines 302–309. **Ask** students where they would pause in reading Brutus' speech aloud.
Answer: Readers should pause at the exclamation points and periods. An actor might also pause very slightly after the comma at the end of line 302.
2. Write the lines of Brutus' speech on the chalkboard and, with students' help, scan the meter of each line.
3. Then, **ask** students the Literary Analysis question: By breaking the pattern of iambic pentameter, which words are emphasized in lines 307 and 308?
Answer: The pattern break emphasizes the words "All" in both lines, "construe to thee," and "sad brows."

Monitor Progress Have students identify and list at least four other lines where the rhythmic pattern is broken. Have them describe the effect Shakespeare achieves in each instance by breaking away from his usual rhythms.

Reteach On the chalkboard write the metrical scheme for iambic pentameter. Tap out the rhythm for students, and then have students tap it out on their own. Have students, either individually or in pairs, choose a line from *The Tragedy of Julius Caesar* to tap. Challenge students to find perfect and imperfect examples of iambic pentameter to tap.

27 Reading Check

Answer: She is trustworthy and intelligent; she is deeply concerned about him; their marriage gives her the right to share his troubles.

Differentiated Instruction for Universal Access

Enrichment for Gifted and Talented Students
Have students write an additional scene for Act II, in which Brutus tells Portia what the conspirators are planning instead of sending her inside the house at line 304. Allow students to write their scenes in prose or blank verse. Have them try to maintain Shakespeare's style and diction. Students may want to choose partners with whom to read or perform their scenes.

Enrichment for Advanced Readers
Ask students to analyze the role of Lucius in the play. Suggest that students begin by reviewing all of the servant's lines, focusing particularly on how he responds to Brutus and how Brutus reacts to him. Students may choose to write a character sketch of Lucius, supporting each trait described with details from the play. Alternatively, students might write an essay analyzing how Shakespeare uses a relatively minor character (Lucius) to deepen and enrich a reader's understanding of a major character (Brutus).

28 Reading Skill
Paraphrase

1. **Ask** students to paraphrase Caesar's remarks in lines 1–3, rearranging the subject and verb in line 2.
   Possible response: Heaven and Earth are not at peace tonight: Calpurnia has cried out, "Help, they are killing Caesar" three times. Who is inside?
2. Have students discuss how they arrived at their paraphrases.

29 Literature in Context

Culture Connection Roman augurs, or diviners, interpreted signs, or *auguria*, to determine whether the gods favored an action or not. These signs might be watched for or just encountered. Birds were a main source of signs. To obtain signs before battle, Roman armies carried chickens with them on campaigns. The chickens were given feed and then carefully watched as they ate it. It was a highly favorable sign if some feed spilled from the chickens' beaks.

Connect to the Literature Read aloud Scene ii from Caesar's entrance through line 56 and the entrance of Decius, pausing to prompt students to identify references to omens. These include the stage direction, Calpurnia's dream, the sights reported by the watchman, and the reading of the entrails.

- **Ask** students the Connect to the Literature question: What does Caesar's own interpretation of his augurs' omen show about the straightforwardness of augury?
  Possible response: Caesar's interpretation of the omen differs from that of the augurs. They urge him not to go out. He thinks the entrails give a sign that he should not be a coward and stay in. Although the results of the augury are clear, they are open to interpretation.

Reading Skill
Paraphrase Paraphrase Caesar's remarks in lines 1–3, rearranging the subject and verb in line 2. 28

Scene ii. Caesar's house.

[*Thunder and lightning. Enter* JULIUS CAESAR *in his nightgown.*]

CAESAR. Nor heaven nor earth have been at peace tonight:
Thrice hath Calpurnia in her sleep cried out,
"Help, ho! They murder Caesar!" Who's within?

[*Enter a* SERVANT.]

SERVANT. My lord?

CAESAR. Go bid the priests do present[1] sacrifice,
And bring me their opinions of success.

SERVANT. I will, my lord. [*Exit*]

[*Enter* CALPURNIA.]

CALPURNIA. What mean you, Caesar? Think you to walk forth?
You shall not stir out of your house today.

CAESAR. Caesar shall forth. The things that threatened me
Ne'er looked but on my back; when they shall see
The face of Caesar, they are vanishèd.

1. **present** *adj.* immediate.

29 LITERATURE IN CONTEXT

Culture Connection

Roman Augurs

In Scene ii, Caesar orders his "priests," or augurs (ô´ gə rz), to make a sacrifice to determine whether he should go to the Senate.

▲ Another class of priest, the *haruspices* (hə rus´ pə sēs´), examined the patterns in the innards of a sacrificed animal.

- In ancient Rome, augurs were officials who examined signs to determine whether the gods would grant success to a particular venture or plan.
- After receiving a negative judgment from the augurs, a Roman leader might postpone an attack or cancel a meeting.
- By the first century A.D., there were sixteen official augurs.

Augurs watched for signs ▶ such as thunder and lightning and the flights of birds. They also observed the pecking of sacred chickens. Omens related to birds were called auspices.

Connect to the Literature What does Caesar's own interpretation of his augurs' omen show about the straightforwardness of augury?

CALPURNIA. Caesar, I never stood on ceremonies,[2]
Yet now they fright me. There is one within,
Besides the things that we have heard and seen,
Recounts most horrid sights seen by the watch.[3]
A lioness hath whelpèd[4] in the streets,
And graves have yawned, and yielded up their dead;
Fierce fiery warriors fought upon the clouds
In ranks and squadrons and right form of war,[5]
Which drizzled blood upon the Capitol;
The noise of battle hurtled[6] in the air,
Horses did neigh and dying men did groan,
And ghosts did shriek and squeal about the street.
O Caesar, these things are beyond all use,[7]
And I do fear them.

CAESAR. What can be avoided
Whose end is purposed[8] by the mighty gods?
Yet Caesar shall go forth; for these predictions
Are to the world in general as to Caesar.[9]

CALPURNIA. When beggars die, there are no comets seen;
The heavens themselves blaze forth[10] the death of princes.

CAESAR. Cowards die many times before their deaths;
The valiant never taste of death but once.
Of all the wonders that I yet have heard,
It seems to me most strange that men should fear,
Seeing that death, a necessary end,
Will come when it will come.

[*Enter a* SERVANT.]

What say the augurers?

SERVANT. They would not have you to stir forth today.
Plucking the entrails of an offering forth,[11]
They could not find a heart within the beast.

CAESAR. The gods do this in shame of[12] cowardice:
Caesar should be a beast without a heart
If he should stay at home today for fear.
No, Caesar shall not; Danger knows full well
That Caesar is more dangerous than he.
We are two lions littered[13] in one day,
And I the elder and more terrible,
And Caesar shall go forth.

CALPURNIA. Alas, my lord,
Your wisdom is consumed in confidence.[14]

2. **stood on ceremonies** paid attention to omens.
3. **Recounts . . . watch** tells about the awful sights seen by the watchman.
4. **whelpèd** *v.* given birth.
5. **right form of war** proper military formation of war.
6. **hurtled** (hurt′ əld) *v.* clashed.
7. **beyond all use** contrary to all experience.
8. **is purposed** is intended.
9. **for these . . . as to Caesar** because these predictions apply to the rest of the world as much as they apply to Caesar.
10. **blaze forth** proclaim with meteors and comets.
11. **Plucking . . . forth** pulling out the insides of a sacrificed animal (which were then "read" by augurs).
12. **in shame of** in order to shame.
13. **littered** *v.* born.
14. **confidence** *n.* overconfidence.

Reading Skill
Paraphrase
Paraphrase the ideas in lines 32–33.

32 **Reading Check**
Why does Calpurnia urge Caesar to stay home?

30 Critical Thinking
Connect

1. Have students read Calpurnia's lines 13–26. **Ask** students to identify at least two examples of unusual signs that she lists.
2. **Answer:** Calpurnia describes an unusual birth by a lioness, and she describes an unusually powerful storm as a terrible battle in the sky.

31 Reading Skill
Paraphrase

1. Ask a volunteer to read aloud lines 32–33. **Ask** students which two groups Caesar is contrasting here.
   Answer: Caesar is drawing a contrast between cowardly people and brave people.
2. Then, **ask** students to respond to the Reading Skill prompt: Paraphrase the ideas in lines 32–33.
   Sample answer: Cowards live in fear of everything, so are not truly living. Brave people live life courageously until their deaths.

32 Reading Check
Answer: Calpurnia urges Caesar to stay home because omens have made her worry for his safety.

Differentiated Instruction for Universal Access

Enrichment for Gifted and Talented Students
Have students read silently to themselves Calpurnia's speech at lines 13–26. Tell students to work with a partner to write new lines for Caesar to say in direct reply to each statement Calpurnia makes. For example, Caesar could explain that the "fiery warriors" of which Calpurnia speaks are simply lightning bolts, part of the storms that are normal at this time of year. Have students draft Caesar's responses in iambic pentameter.

Enrichment for Advanced Readers
It can be no accident that Shakespeare, in consecutive scenes, presents confrontations between husbands and wives. Ask students to compare and contrast these two scenes and the marriages that are glimpsed within them. What issues are Portia and Calpurnia concerned about? What feelings do they express to their husbands? What emotions do Brutus and Caesar reveal in response to their wives? What actions or decisions do they take? Have students report their findings in a comparison-and-contrast essay.

33 Critical Thinking

Make Judgments

1. Have students review Caesar's conversation with Calpurnia in lines 49–68.
2. **Ask** students if they think Caesar's decision to stay home is consistent with his remarks about courage.
   Possible response: Caesar chooses to remain home as a concession to his wife's fears, not his own. He also refuses to make a false excuse for his intended absence.

34 Literature in Context

History Connection Unlike the Senate of the United States, the Roman Senate did not pass laws. Its decrees, however, had a powerful influence on government, including the formation of armies and making war. Caesar's efforts to make the Senate more representative had the effect of weakening Senate influence. After his assassination, the role of the Senate diminished steeply, though it always remained a part of the political landscape.

Connect to the Literature After discussing the role of the Senate, **ask** students the Connect to the Literature question: How does this information help explain the motives of the conspirators, many of whom are senators?
Possible response: The senators probably blamed Caesar for their loss of power and prestige.

Do not go forth today. Call it my fear
That keeps you in the house and not your own.
We'll send Mark Antony to the Senate House,
And he shall say you are not well today.
Let me, upon my knee, prevail in this.

CAESAR. Mark Antony shall say I am not well,
And for thy humor,[15] I will stay at home.

[*Enter* DECIUS.]

33 Here's Decius Brutus, he shall tell them so.

DECIUS. Caesar, all hail! Good morrow, worthy Caesar;
I come to fetch you to the Senate House.

CAESAR. And you are come in very happy time[16]
To bear my greeting to the senators,
And tell them that I will not come today.
Cannot, is false; and that I dare not, falser:
I will not come today. Tell them so, Decius.

CALPURNIA. Say he is sick.

15. **humor** *n.* whim.

16. **in very happy time** at just the right moment.

34 LITERATURE IN CONTEXT

History Connection

The Roman Senate

Caesar is preparing to meet the Senate, the oldest Roman political institution. By this time, the Senate had evolved into the most powerful part of the Roman government:

- Before Caesar's rise to power, the Senate was made up of 500 to 600 members.
- The Senate met in the Curia in the Roman Forum (see page 942).
- Senators were appointed for life. Originally, all were from the *patrician*, or aristocratic, class.
- The Senate shaped policy through advice it issued to various officials, its powers to appoint officials, and its power to negotiate with foreign countries.
- After Caesar won his victory over Pompey, he eliminated his enemies in the Senate and packed it with supporters, including men of lower rank and people from outlying provinces.

Connect to the Literature How does this information help explain the motives of the conspirators, many of whom are senators?

Vocabulary Development

Vocabulary Reinforcement

To reinforce and assess students' comprehension of selection vocabulary words, provide sentences in which the words may or may not be used correctly. Instruct students to use the "yes/no—why" format to tell whether the words are used correctly and explain why. Use these sentences:

1. He made a *resolution* to run three miles every day.
   Answer: Yes, *resolution* is used correctly here. A resolution can be a plan or strong decision.
2. They had known each other all their lives and were *imminent* friends.
   Answer: No, *imminent* is not used correctly. It means "about to happen" and would not be used to describe friends.

33 **CAESAR.** Shall Caesar send a lie?
Have I in conquest stretched mine arm so far
To be afeard to tell graybeards[17] the truth?
Decius, go tell them Caesar will not come.

DECIUS. Most mighty Caesar, let me know some cause,
Lest I be laughed at when I tell them so.

CAESAR. The cause is in my will: I will not come.
That is enough to satisfy the Senate.
But for your private satisfaction,
Because I love you, I will let you know.
Calpurnia here, my wife, stays me at home.
She dreamt tonight she saw my statue,
Which, like a fountain with an hundred spouts,
Did run pure blood, and many lusty Romans
Came smiling and did bathe their hands in it.
And these does she apply for[18] warnings and portents
And evils **imminent**, and on her knee
Hath begged that I will stay at home today.

DECIUS. This dream is all amiss interpreted;
It was a vision fair and fortunate:
Your statue spouting blood in many pipes,
In which so many smiling Romans bathed,
Signifies that from you great Rome shall suck
Reviving blood, and that great men shall press
For tinctures, stains, relics, and cognizance.[19]
This by Calpurnia's dream is signified.

CAESAR. And this way have you well expounded[20] it.

35 **DECIUS.** I have, when you have heard what I can say;
And know it now, the Senate have concluded
36 To give this day a crown to mighty Caesar.
If you shall send them word you will not come,
Their minds may change. Besides, it were a mock
Apt to be rendered,[21] for someone to say
"Break up the Senate till another time,
When Caesar's wife shall meet with better dreams."
If Caesar hide himself, shall they not whisper
"Lo, Caesar is afraid"?
Pardon me, Caesar, for my dear dear love
To your proceeding[22] bids me tell you this,
And reason to my love is liable.[23]

17. **afeard to tell graybeards** afraid to tell old men (the senators).
18. **apply for** consider to be.

Vocabulary
imminent (im′ ə nənt) *adj.* about to happen

19. **shall press . . . cognizance** Decius interprets Calpurnia's dream with a double meaning. To Caesar he suggests that people will beg for badges to show they are Caesar's servants; to the audience, that people will seek remembrances of his death.
20. **expounded** (eks pound′ id) *v.* interpreted; explained.
21. **mock . . . rendered** jeering comment likely to be made.
22. **proceeding** *n.* advancing in your career.
23. **reason . . . liable** my judgment about what I should or should not say is not as strong as my affection for you is.

37 **Reading Check**
What does Decius say about the dream?

35 Critical Thinking
Analyze

1. Have students refer to Scene i, lines 202–211. **Ask** what Decius promises in these lines.
Answer: Decius promises to bring Caesar to the capitol by telling Caesar what he wants to hear.
2. Tell students to read lines 83–104 of Scene ii. **Ask** students how this passage exemplifies Decius' earlier promise.
Possible response: Decius interprets the omens in ways that flatter Caesar's pride and confidence.

36 Literary Analysis
Blank Verse

1. Remind students that the use of prose or verse by characters in Shakespeare's plays can indicate social rank.
2. **Ask** students: How does Shakespeare indicate that Decius is a noble character?
Answer: Shakespeare indicates that Decius is a noble character by having him speak in blank verse.
3. Enlist students' help in reading aloud the lines of Decius' speech at lines 83–90 in order to hear the rhythm of blank verse.

37 Reading Check

Answer: Decius says that it was a dream of good omens, not bad.

Differentiated Instruction for Universal Access

Strategy for Less Proficient Readers
Work with students to develop their paraphrasing skills. Use **Reading Skill Graphic Organizer A** (p. 170 in ***Graphic Organizer Transparencies***) to model the process of paraphrasing a line or passage. Then, give students a blank graphic organizer (**Reading Skill Graphic Organizer B** on p. 171 in ***Graphic Organizer Transparencies***) to use to paraphrase Caesar's speech in lines 71–82. Monitor students' work to make sure they are using their own words and taking the punctuation of the text into account.

EL Strategy for English Learners
Pair students with a partner to practice paraphrasing. Have student partners work on recasting the exchange between Decius and Caesar in their own words. Remind students to consult the side notes to understand difficult words, phrases, and references. Have students write out their paraphrases. Then, ask them to give a reading of the scene, taking the parts of Decius and Caesar and using their paraphrases as scripts.

38 Background
Julius Caesar

Although he speaks few lines in the play of which he is the title character, Gaius Julius Caesar was one of the most powerful men in history. He began his political career as a director of public works and games in 65 B.C., about twenty years before the events of the play. In 62, he became praetor, the office ranking just below consul. In 60, he joined forces with Marcus Licinius Crassus and Gaeus Pompey. They ruled Rome as the First Triumvirate. In 59, Caesar married Calpurnia (his third wife), and Pompey married Caesar's daughter, Julia. In 58, Caesar began a campaign to conquer Gaul (modern France). A military genius, Caesar drove the Germans out of Gaul and marched all the way to Britain, which he and his troops invaded in 55 and again in 54. By 49 B.C., Pompey had become alarmed at Caesar's tremendous success and popularity. He and a group of allies ordered Caesar to give up his army. Caesar's response was to attack Pompey's troops, thus starting a civil war. Pompey's army retreated from Rome to Greece and then to Egypt, where Pompey was executed.

39 Reading Skill
Paraphrase

1. Ask for volunteers to read aloud the parts of Publius, Caesar, Brutus, Antony, and Trebonius in lines 109–129.
2. Have students **summarize** the scene.
   Answer: Brutus and the other conspirators and Caesar's friend Antony arrive to escort Caesar to the Senate. They have refreshments together before leaving.
3. **Ask** to whom Caesar addresses lines 122–123.
   Answer: He is talking to Cinna, Metellus, and Trebonius.
4. Then, **ask** students to respond to the Reading Skill prompt: Paraphrase lines 124–125.
   Sample answer: Remember that you are my friends. Stay close to me, so that I will remember who you are if you act against me.

CAESAR. How foolish do your fears seem now, Calpurnia!
I am ashamèd I did yield to them.
Give me my robe,[24] for I will go.

[*Enter* BRUTUS, LIGARIUS, METELLUS CIMBER, CASCA, TREBONIUS, CINNA, *and* PUBLIUS.]

And look where Publius is come to fetch me.

PUBLIUS. Good morrow, Caesar.

CAESAR. Welcome, Publius.
What, Brutus, are you stirred so early too?
Good morrow, Casca. Caius Ligarius.
Caesar was ne'er so much your enemy[25]
As that same ague[26] which hath made you lean.
What is't o'clock?

BRUTUS. Caesar, 'tis strucken eight.

CAESAR. I thank you for your pains and courtesy.

[*Enter* ANTONY.]

See! Antony, that revels[27] long a-nights,
Is notwithstanding up. Good morrow, Antony.

ANTONY. So to most noble Caesar.

CAESAR. Bid them prepare[28] within.
I am to blame to be thus waited for.
Now, Cinna; now, Metellus; what Trebonius,
I have an hour's talk in store for you;
Remember that you call on me today;
Be near me, that I may remember you.

TREBONIUS. Caesar, I will [*aside*] and so near will I be,
That your best friends shall wish I had been further.

CAESAR. Good friends, go in and taste some wine with me,
And we (like friends) will straightway go together.

BRUTUS. [*Aside*] That every like is not the same,[29] O Caesar,
The heart of Brutus earns[30] to think upon. [*Exit*]

Scene iii. A street near the Capitol, close to Brutus' house.

[*Enter* ARTEMIDORUS, *reading a paper.*]

ARTEMIDORUS. "Caesar, beware of Brutus; take heed off Cassius; come not near Casca; have an eye to Cinna; trust not Trebonius; mark well Metellus Cimber; Decius Brutus loves

24. robe *n.* toga.

38

25. Caius Ligarius . . . your enemy Caesar had recently pardoned Ligarius for supporting Pompey during the civil war.

26. ague (ā´ gyo͞o) *n.* fever.

27. revels (rev´ əlz) *v.* makes merry.

28. prepare *v.* set out refreshments.

Reading Skill 39
Paraphrase Paraphrase lines 124–125.

29. That every like . . . the same that is, that everyone who seems *like* a friend may actually be an enemy.

30. earns *v.* sorrows.

Differentiated Instruction for Universal Access

Pronunciation for English Learners

Some students may have difficulty with the short "e" sound in words such as *them, fetch,* and *bent,* often replacing it with the "ei" sound. The following strategies can help students to pronounce words with the short "e" sound.

- Write the words *them, fetch,* and *bent* on the board, pronouncing each word as it is being written. Then, have students repeat each word multiple times.
- Call out the word pairs *men/main* and *pen/pain.* Have students write the words as you pronounce them. Then, have students repeat each word back to you, one word at a time, as you write it on the board based on their pronunciation. Invite students to discuss the differences in the ways their mouths move when they pronounce the short "e" sound and the "ei" sound.

thee not; thou hast wronged Caius Ligarius. There is but one mind in all these men, and it is bent against Caesar. If thou beest not immortal, look about you: security gives way to conspiracy.[1] The mighty gods defend thee!

Thy lover,[2] ARTEMIDORUS."

Here will I stand till Caesar pass along,
And as a suitor[3] will I give him this.
My heart laments that virtue cannot live
Out of the teeth of emulation.[4]
If thou read this, O Caesar, thou mayest live;
If not, the Fates with traitors do contrive.[5] [*Exit*]

1. **security . . . conspiracy** overconfident carelessness allows the conspiracy to proceed.
2. **lover** *n.* devoted friend.
3. **suitor** (so͞ot´ ər) *n.* person who requests, petitions, or entreats.
4. **Out of the teeth of emulation** beyond the reach of envy.
5. **contrive** *v.* conspire.

Scene iv. Another part of the street.

[*Enter* PORTIA *and* LUCIUS.]

43

PORTIA. I prithee,[1] boy, run to the Senate House;
Stay not to answer me, but get thee gone.
Why dost thou stay?

LUCIUS. To know my errand, madam.

PORTIA. I would have had thee there and here again
Ere I can tell thee what thou shouldst do there.

1. **prithee** (prith´ ē) "pray thee"; ask you please.

41 Reading Check

What does Artemidorus plan to do?

40 ◀ **Critical Viewing**

When might Caesar have participated in an event like the one depicted on this cup? Explain. **[Speculate]**

40 Critical Viewing

Possible response: Caesar might have taken part in an event like that depicted on the cup on his triumphant return to Rome, since the public welcomed him enthusiastically then and Antony tried to crown him, as the figure on the left is crowning the leader in the chariot.

41 Reading Check

Answer: Artemidorus plans to give Caesar a letter that reveals the conspiracy against him.

Differentiated Instruction for Universal Access

Strategy for Special Needs Students

The archaic and unfamiliar contractions Shakespeare uses in this scene and others may prove a barrier to students' paraphrasing of the text as well as scanning its meter. Help students use context clues to figure out the meaning of the contractions *ne'er, is't, 'tis*. Then, have students write each contraction out in full. Point out that in some cases, Shakespeare uses contractions because the full word or two words would add a syllable and make the line too long for iambic pentameter. Show how these contractions work in blank verse.

42 Visual Connections

Whole-Class Activity

1. Have students describe what they see in the picture.
   Possible response: An area that includes the ruins of old buildings. The buildings in front are in ruins, while the buildings in the back appear to still be in use.
2. Then, **ask** students: How does this image relate to the events described in Scene iv?
   Possible response: Scene iv takes place on the streets outside the Capitol building where Caesar is expected to appear. This picture may show the area from the scene as it appears now.

Small-Group Activity

1. Have students work in small groups. Ask them to write a short description of the feeling or mood that the image creates.
   Possible response: Students may describe the ominous and foreboding feeling that the colors, clouds, shadows, and lighting create.
2. Ask volunteers to read their group's description aloud. Invite groups to compare descriptions and discuss how they compare to the mood of the story.

Individual Activity

1. Invite volunteers to assume the roles of Lucius, Portia, and the Soothsayer and read aloud Scene iv, lines 10–46. Have students who are not reading look at the picture while they listen.
2. Have students discuss how looking at the picture changes the way they understand the scene.
   Possible response: Students may suggest that looking at the picture helps them imagine exactly where the characters may have been standing, where the Soothsayer will wait for Caesar, and where the Capitol was.

42

Vocabulary Development

Vocabulary Knowledge Rating

When students have completed reading and discussing Act II, have them take out their **Vocabulary Knowledge Rating Chart** for this selection. Read the words aloud once more and have students rate their knowledge of the words again in the After Reading column. Clarify any words that are still problematic. Have students write their own definition or example in the appropriate column. Then, have students complete the Vocabulary Practice at the end of the selection. Encourage students to use the words in further discussion and written work about this selection. Remind them that they will be accountable for these words on the **Selection Test,** ***Unit 5 Resources,*** pp. 121–123 or 124–126.

O constancy,[2] be strong upon my side;
Set a huge mountain 'tween my heart and tongue!
I have a man's mind, but a woman's might.[3]
How hard it is for women to keep counsel![4]
Art thou here yet?

LUCIUS. Madam, what should I do?
Run to the Capitol, and nothing else?
And so return to you, and nothing else?

PORTIA. Yes, bring me word, boy, if thy lord look well,
For he went sickly forth; and take good note
What Caesar doth, what suitors press to him.
Hark, boy, what noise is that?

LUCIUS. I hear none, madam.

PORTIA. Prithee, listen well.
I heard a bustling rumor like a fray,[5]
And the wind brings it from the Capitol.

LUCIUS. Sooth,[6] madam, I hear nothing.

[*Enter the* SOOTHSAYER.]

PORTIA. Come hither, fellow. Which way hast thou been?

SOOTHSAYER. At mine own house, good lady.

PORTIA. What is't o'clock?

SOOTHSAYER. About the ninth hour, lady.

PORTIA. Is Caesar yet gone to the Capitol?

SOOTHSAYER. Madam, not yet; I go to take my stand,
To see him pass on the Capitol.

PORTIA. Thou hast some suit[7] to Caesar, hast thou not?

SOOTHSAYER. That I have, lady; if it will please Caesar
To be so good to Caesar as to hear me,
I shall beseech him to befriend himself.

PORTIA. Why, know'st thou any harm's intended towards him?

SOOTHSAYER. None that I know will be, much that I fear may chance.
Good morrow to you. Here the street is narrow;
The throng that follows Caesar at the heels,
Of senators, of praetors,[8] common suitors,

44 ◀ **Critical Viewing** Judging from its ruins, how might the Forum in Rome have compared to a modern city center?

2. **constancy** (kän′ stən sē) *n.* firmness of mind or purpose; resoluteness.
3. **might** *n.* strength.
4. **keep counsel** keep secrets.

Literary Analysis
Blank Verse Why might Shakespeare present Lucius' lines in blank verse in this scene?

5. **fray** (frā) *n.* fight; brawl.
6. **Sooth** (sōōth) interjection truly.

7. **suit** (sōōt) *n.* petition.
8. **praetors** (prē′ tərz) *n.* Roman officials of the rank below consul.

45 **Reading Check**
What does Portia ask of Lucius?

43 Literary Analysis
Blank Verse

1. Have two volunteers read aloud the Scene iv exchange between Portia and Lucius in lines 1–20. **Ask** students what they notice about the lines of iambic pentameter in this scene and have them describe the effect.
   Answer: The scene has a few shared meter lines. Portia and Lucius finish each other's lines. The broken lines emphasize Portia's anxiety and both characters' sense of urgency and give the scene a breathless quality that adds to the suspense.
2. Point out that although Lucius is a servant, he speaks in blank verse. Then, **ask** students to respond to the Literary Analysis question: Why might Shakespeare present Lucius' lines in blank verse in this scene?
   Possible response: Shakespeare might present Lucius' lines in blank verse to show that Lucius shares Portia's concern and purpose.

44 Critical Viewing

Possible response: The Roman Forum was like a modern city center because it included a variety of buildings, open areas in which people could gather, walkways and streets, and monuments.

45 Reading Check

Answer: Portia asks Lucius to run to the Capitol and report back to her how Caesar is doing.

Concept Connector

Anticipation Guide

Have students return to their **Anticipation Guides** and respond to the statements again in the After Reading column. They may do this individually or in their original pairs or groups. Then, lead a class discussion, probing for what students have learned that confirms or invalidates each statement. Encourage students to cite specific details, quotations, or other evidence from the text to support their responses to each statement.

Reading Skill Graphic Organizer

Ask students to review the graphic organizers they completed to paraphrase lines and passages while reading. Show them **Reading Skill Graphic Organizer A** (***Graphic Organizer Transparencies,*** p. 170) as an example. Then, have students share their graphic organizers.

ASSESS

Answers

Critical Thinking

1. **Possible response:** Yes, because the republic must be saved. No, because Caesar has not yet tried to declare himself king.
2. (a) The upcoming crowning of Caesar disturbs Brutus. (b) Brutus believes that Caesar is potentially dangerous and should be killed. (c) **Possible response:** They are flawed because Brutus is allowing himself to be swayed by Cassius.
3. (a) The letter urges Brutus to wake up and look at what is happening to Rome. It asks him to take action and set things right. (b) **Possible response:** The writer probably leaves the gaps to create a feeling of mystery and desperation, thus sparking Brutus' interest and causing him to use his imagination. (c) **Possible response:** Brutus' interpretation suggests that he yearns to be honored and revered.
4. (a) Brutus feels that if crowned, Caesar will become dangerous and tyrannical. He believes that by killing Caesar, he will be protecting the Romans and the greater good. (b) **Possible response:** Brutus' desire to protect the people of Rome and fight for the greater good is the most honorable and convincing.

To what extent does experience determine what we perceive?

Possible responses: (a) Calpurnia believes her dream is a warning that Caesar will be harmed if he goes to the Senate. She dreams that Caesar's statue is dripping with blood. The Roman people are dipping their hands in the blood and smiling. (b) Decius says that Calpurnia's dream is not a bad omen but a good one. The bleeding statue symbolizes how Caesar will revive Rome with his blood and work. The smiling Romans are not rejoicing in his death, but rather seek a remembrance of him and his efforts. Decius' interpretation corresponds with his character's motives. He is a conspirator and therefore wants Caesar to go to the Senate so he will be killed.

Will crowd a feeble man almost to death.
I'll get me to a place more void,[9] and there
Speak to great Caesar as he comes along.

[*Exit*]

PORTIA. I must go in. Ay me, how weak a thing
The heart of woman is! O Brutus,
The heavens speed[10] thee in thine enterprise![11]
Sure, the boy heard me—Brutus hath a suit
That Caesar will not grant—O, I grow faint.
Run, Lucius, and commend me[12] to my lord;
Say I am merry; come to me again,
And bring me word what he doth say to thee.

[*Exit separately*]

9. **void** (void) *adj.* empty.

10. **speed** *v.* make successful.

11. **enterprise** (en′ tər prīz′) *n.* undertaking; project.

12. **command me** give my kind regard.

Critical Thinking

1. **Respond:** If you had been a Roman citizen, would you have sided with the conspirators? Why or why not?
2. **(a)** In Act II, Scene i, what coming event disturbs Brutus? **(b) Interpret:** In Scene i, lines 32–34, what point does Brutus make in comparing Caesar to a serpent's egg? **(c) Evaluate:** Are Brutus' reasons for joining the conspiracy convincing or flawed? Explain.
3. **(a)** What does the writer of the letter that Lucius finds urge Brutus to do? **(b)** Infer: Why do you think the writer leaves gaps in the letter? **(c)** Infer: What inferences can you draw from the way Brutus fills in these gaps?
4. **(a) Analyze:** Why does Brutus decide to join the conspirators? **(b) Assess:** Which of Brutus' reasons do you find most convincing? Explain.

THE BIG ?

To what extent does experience determine what we perceive? Calpurnia and Decius Brutus have different interpretations of Calpurnia's dream. **(a)** What is Calpurnia's perception of her dream? What information contributes to her point of view? **(b)** What is Decius Brutus' interpretation of her dream? What information underlies his explanation?

Assessment Resources

Unit 5 Resources

L1 L2 EL **Selection Test A**, pp. 121–123. Administer Test A to less advanced readers and English learners.

L3 L4 **Selection Test B**, pp. 124–126. Administer Test B to on-level and more advanced students.

L3 L4 **Open-Book Test**, pp. 118–120. As an alternative, give the Open-Book Test.

All **Customizable Test Bank**

All **Self-tests**
Students may prepare for the **Selection Test** by taking the **Self-test** online.

PHLit Online! All assessment resources are available at **www.PHLitOnline.com.**

After You Read | The Tragedy of Julius Caesar, Act II

Literary Analysis: Blank Verse

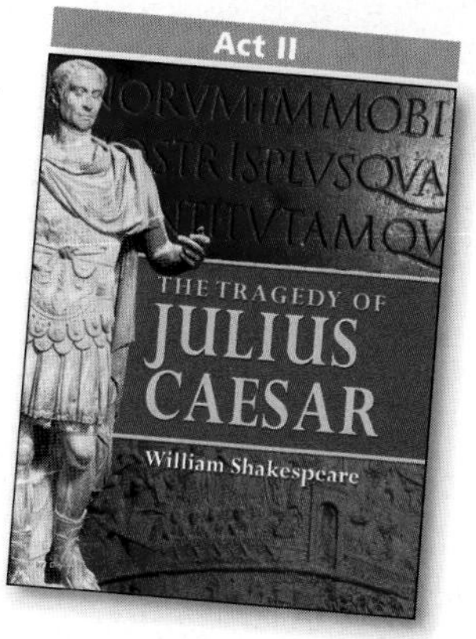

1. **(a)** Copy lines 42–43 of Scene ii and mark them to indicate the stressed (´) and unstressed (~) syllables. **(b)** Which line of **blank verse** illustrates perfect iambic pentameter? **(c)** Explain how the rhythm of the other line reinforces the importance of certain words.
2. Using a chart like the one shown, examine the dialogue of the characters in Acts I and II. **(a)** Indicate whether each typically speaks in blank verse or prose. **(b)** Identify each as an aristocrat or a commoner based on your findings.

Character	Blank Verse or Prose?	Aristocrat or Commoner?
Flavius		
the Cobbler		
Brutus		
Portia		

Reading Skill: Paraphrase

3. **Paraphrase** Brutus' two questions in line 234 of Scene i. Make your new sentences sound like modern English.
4. **(a)** List four words in Portia's final speech in Scene iv that are no longer used or no longer used in the same sense. For each, give a modern word that means the same thing. **(b)** **Paraphrase** the speech.

Vocabulary

Practice A **synonym** of a word is a word that has a similar meaning: for example, *start* is a synonym of *begin*. For each of the following items, explain whether or not the words are synonyms.

1. augmented, angered
2. entreated, appealed
3. insurrection, revolt
4. resolution, glory
5. wrathfully, furiously
6. imminent, enduring

Word Study Use the context of the sentences and what you know about the **Latin prefix *en-*** to explain your answer to each question.

1. Are children safe if the new toy *endangers* them?
2. If critics are *enthralled* by a movie, would they give it bad reviews?

Word Study

The **Latin prefix *en-*** means "in," "into," or "within."

Challenge Explain how the prefix *en-* contributes to the meanings of these words. Consult a dictionary if necessary.

enamor
encircle
enlighten

Answers

Literary Analysis

1. (a) CAEsar should BE a BEAST withOUT a HEART/if HE should STAY at HOME toDAY for FEAR. A sample answer can be found on **Literary Analysis Graphic Organizer A**, p. 172 in ***Graphic Organizer Transparencies.*** (b) Line 43 is perfect iambic pentameter. (c) "Caesar" scans as a trochee, a typical variation in blank verse. As a variation, it emphasizes that word; the rest of the line is regular iambic pentameter.
2. (a) Flavius, Brutus, and Portia speak in blank verse; the Cobbler speaks in prose. (b) Flavius, Brutus, and Portia are aristocrats, and the Cobbler is a commoner.

Reading Skill

3. **Possible response:** Why are you getting up so early, Portia?
4. (a) Students may cite *speed, thee, thine, hath, merry,* and *doth;* modern synonyms include *bring success, you, your, has, well,* and *does.* (b) **Possible response:** I must go in. A woman's heart is weak. O Brutus, I hope what you have set out to do is successful. I'm sure the boy heard me. Caesar will not grant Brutus' request. I feel faint. Run to Brutus, Lucius, and tell him I'm fine. Then come back and tell me what Brutus has to say.

Vocabulary

Practice

Sample answers:

1. not synonyms
2. synonyms
3. synonyms
4. not synonyms
5. synonyms
6. not synonyms

Word Study

Sample answers:

1. No. The prefix *en-* means "in, into, or within" and *endanger* means "to put in danger." Children are not safe if a new toy endangers them.
2. No. The prefix *en-* means "in, into, or within" and *enthralled* means "spellbound or interested in." Critics would not give a poor review if they were enthralled by a movie.

Word Study: Challenge

Sample answers: To *enamor* means "to fill or inspire with love." *Encircle* means "to put in a circle." To *enlighten* means "to give knowledge from within."

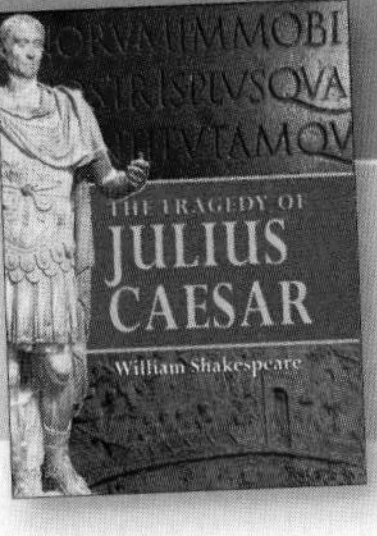

TIME AND RESOURCE MANAGER

The Tragedy of Julius Caesar, Act III

Lesson Pacing Guide

DAY 1 Preteach

- Administer the Reading and Vocabulary Warm-ups (*Unit 5 Resources*, pp. 127–130) as necessary.
- Introduce the Reading Skill: Analyze Imagery. FT
- Introduce the Literary Analysis concept: Dramatic Speeches. FT
- Distribute copies of the appropriate graphic organizer for the Reading Skill (*Graphic Organizer Transparencies*, pp. 174–175). CRI
- Distribute copies of the appropriate graphic organizer for Literary Analysis (*Graphic Organizer Transparencies*, pp. 176–177). CRI
- Teach the selection vocabulary. FT CRI
- Introduce the Word Study skill.

DAYS 2–3 Preteach/Teach

- Build background with the Background feature. CRI
- Develop thematic vocabulary and thematic thinking with Writing About the Big Question.
- Prepare students to read with the Activating Prior Knowledge activities (TE). CRI
- Informally monitor comprehension while students read. FT
- Use the Reading Check questions to confirm comprehension.
- Develop students' ability to analyze imagery using the Reading Skill questions. CRI
- Develop students' understanding of dramatic speeches using the Literary Analysis questions. CRI
- Reinforce vocabulary with the Vocabulary notes. CRI

DAY 4 Assess

- Assess students' comprehension and mastery of the skills by having them answer the Critical Thinking, Reading Skill, and Literary Analysis questions. FT

DAY 5 Extend/Assess

- Have students complete the Writing activity and write an editorial. (You may assign as homework.) FT
- Extend learning by having students complete the Research and Technology activity, an advertising poster. (You may assign as homework.) As an alternative, assign them "In and Out of the In Crowd" in *Reality Central*. CRI
- Administer Selection Test A or B (*Unit 5 Resources*, pp. 139–144). FT

The play *The Tragedy of Julius Caesar* appears unedited and in its entirety. Act I appears on pp. 892–912, Act II appears on pp. 917–936, Act III appears on pp. 941–962, Act IV appears on pp. 967–982, and Act V appears on pp. 987–1000.

Meeting Your Standards

Students will

1. analyze and respond to literary elements.
   - Literary Analysis: Dramatic Speeches
2. read, comprehend, and analyze drama.
   - Reading Skill: Analyze Imagery
   - Reading Check questions
   - Apply the Skills questions
   - Assessment Practice
3. develop vocabulary.
   - Vocabulary
   - Word Study
4. Develop writing proficiency.
   - editorial
5. strengthen research and technology skills.
   - advertising poster

CRI For a full explanation of Culturally Responsive Instruction opportunities in this lesson, see p. T86–T87.

FT For an accelerated lesson, use the Fast Track strategies and activities.

Managing Differentiated Instruction
This leveled selection pairing groups a more accessible with a more challenging selection. Choose either one to teach the lesson skills. For classroom management suggestions for using the pairing in a mixed-ability class, see pp. T68–T69.

Daily Block Scheduling
Each day in this Lesson Pacing Guide represents a 40–50 minute period. Teachers using block scheduling may combine days to revise pacing. In addition, teachers may differentiate and support core instruction by integrating components for extended and intensive support as students require. See the Guide to Selected Leveled Resources (facing page).

Guide to Selected Leveled Resources

EL English Learners

			The Tragedy of Julius Caesar, Act III
CORE COURSE	*Unit 5 Resources*	Selection Test A	pp. 139–141
	Graphic Organizer Transparencies	Reading Skill Graphic Organizer A	p. 174
		Literary Analysis Graphic Organizer A	p. 176
EXTENDED SUPPORT (Level 2)	*Unit 5 Resources*	Reading and Vocabulary Warm-ups A or B	pp. 127–130
	Reader's Notebook: English Learner's Version		adapted instruction and adapted selection
	Hear It! Audio CD		selection and summaries
	Hear It! Audio CD (adapted text)		adapted selection and summaries
INTENSIVE SUPPORT (Level 1)	*Reality Central*		"In and Out of the In Crowd"
	Real-World Writing Journal		Lesson 3, pp. 146–149

L2 Below-Level Students

			The Tragedy of Julius Caesar, Act III
CORE COURSE	*Unit 5 Resources*	Selection Test A	pp. 139–141
	Graphic Organizer Transparencies	Reading Skill Graphic Organizer A	p. 174
		Literary Analysis Graphic Organizer A	p. 176
EXTENDED SUPPORT (Level 2)	*Unit 5 Resources*	Reading and Vocabulary Warm-ups A or B	pp. 127–130
	Reader's Notebook		adapted instruction and full selection
	Hear It! Audio CD		selection and summaries
INTENSIVE SUPPORT (Level 1)	*Reality Central*		"In and Out of the In Crowd"
	Real-World Writing Journal		Lesson 3, pp. 146–149
	Reading Kit		Reteaching worksheets

L1 Special Needs Students

			The Tragedy of Julius Caesar, Act III
CORE COURSE	*Unit 5 Resources*	Selection Test A	pp. 139–141
	Graphic Organizer Transparencies	Reading Skill Graphic Organizer A	p. 174
		Literary Analysis Graphic Organizer A	p. 176
EXTENDED SUPPORT (Level 2)	*Unit 5 Resources*	Reading and Vocabulary Warm-ups A or B	pp. 127–130
	Reader's Notebook: Adapted Version		adapted instruction and adapted selection
	Hear It! Audio CD (adapted text)		adapted selection and summaries
INTENSIVE SUPPORT (Level 1)	*Reality Central*		"In and Out of the In Crowd"
	Real-World Writing Journal		Lesson 3, pp. 146–149
	Reading Kit		Reteaching worksheets

The program includes resources for these students: L3 On-Level L4 Advanced All All
For a complete guide to selection support, see pp. T106–T108.

NOTE: All print materials are also available online at *www.PHLitOnline.com.*

VISUAL GUIDE to Featured Selection Resources

The Tragedy of Julius Caesar, Act III

RESOURCES FOR:

- EL English Learners
- L1 Special Needs Students
- L2 Below-Level Students
- L3 On-Level Students
- L4 Advanced Students
- All All Students

Vocabulary/Fluency/Prior Knowledge

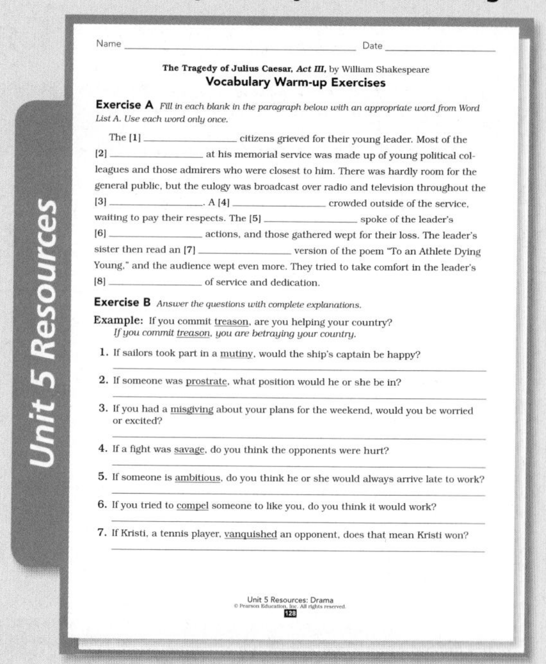

Name ______________ Date ______________

The Tragedy of Julius Caesar, *Act III*, by William Shakespeare
Vocabulary Warm-up Exercises

Exercise A *Fill in each blank in the paragraph below with an appropriate word from Word List A. Use each word only once.*

The [1] ______________ citizens grieved for their young leader. Most of the [2] ______________ at his memorial service was made up of young political colleagues and those admirers who were closest to him. There was hardly room for the general public, but the eulogy was broadcast over radio and television throughout the [3] ______________. A [4] ______________ crowded outside of the service, waiting to pay their respects. The [5] ______________ spoke of the leader's [6] ______________ actions, and those gathered wept for their loss. The leader's sister then read an [7] ______________ version of the poem "To an Athlete Dying Young," and the audience wept even more. They tried to take comfort in the leader's [8] ______________ of service and dedication.

Exercise B *Answer the questions with complete explanations.*

Example: If you commit treason, are you helping your country?
If you commit treason, you are betraying your country.

1. If sailors took part in a mutiny, would the ship's captain be happy?
2. If someone was prostrate, what position would he or she be in?
3. If you had a misgiving about your plans for the weekend, would you be worried or excited?
4. If a fight was savage, do you think the opponents were hurt?
5. If someone is ambitious, do you think he or she would always arrive late to work?
6. If you tried to compel someone to like you, do you think it would work?
7. If Kristi, a tennis player, vanquished an opponent, does that mean Kristi won?

Unit 5 Resources: Drama
© Pearson Education, Inc. All rights reserved.
128

EL L1 L2 **Vocabulary Warm-ups A and B, pp. 127–128**

Also available for these selections:

- EL L1 L2 **Reading Warm-ups A and B, pp. 129–130**
- All **Vocabulary Builder, p. 134**
- All **Writing About the Big Question, p. 131**

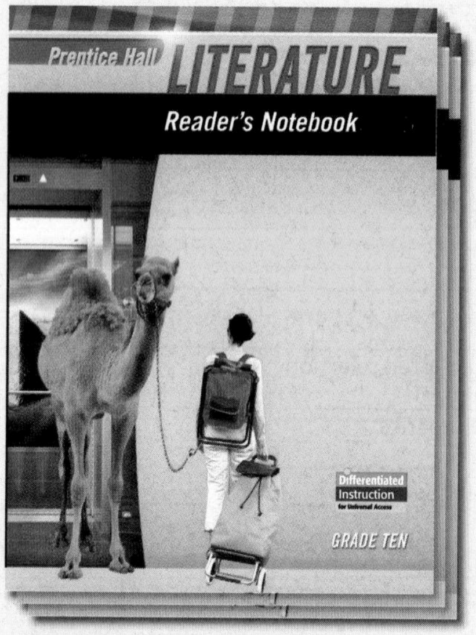

L2 L3 ***Reader's Notebook***

L1 ***Reader's Notebook: Adapted Version***

EL ***Reader's Notebook: English Learner's Version***

Reader's Notebooks

Pre- and postreading pages for both selections, as well as *The Tragedy of Julius Caesar, Act III* appear in an interactive format in the *Reader's Notebooks*. Each *Notebook* is differentiated for a different group of learners.

The selections in the Adapted and English Learner's versions are abridged.

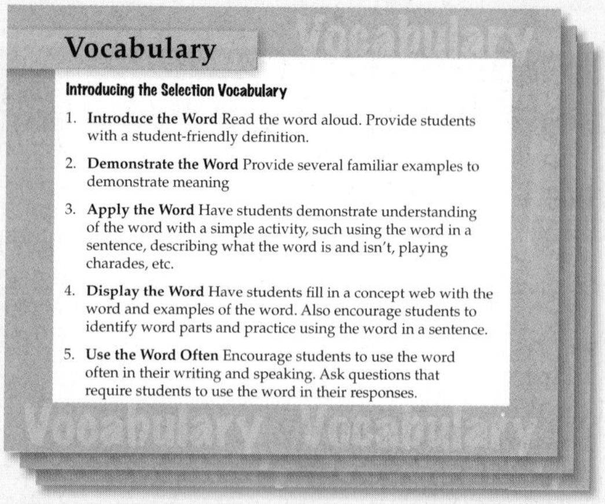

Vocabulary

Introducing the Selection Vocabulary

1. **Introduce the Word** Read the word aloud. Provide students with a student-friendly definition.
2. **Demonstrate the Word** Provide several familiar examples to demonstrate meaning
3. **Apply the Word** Have students demonstrate understanding of the word with a simple activity, such using the word in a sentence, describing what the word is and isn't, playing charades, etc.
4. **Display the Word** Have students fill in a concept web with the word and examples of the word. Also encourage students to identify word parts and practice using the word in a sentence.
5. **Use the Word Often** Encourage students to use the word often in their writing and speaking. Ask questions that require students to use the word in their responses.

Classroom Strategies and Teaching Routines

- core classroom routines outlined step-by-step
- convenient format for easy reference while teaching

Selection Support

Graphic Organizer Transparencies

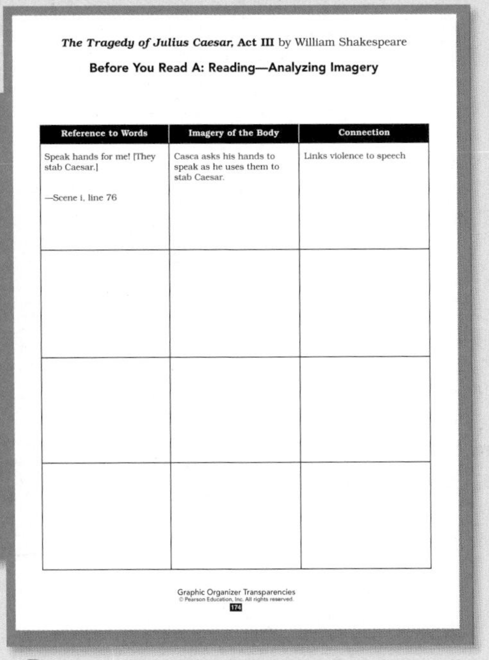
The Tragedy of Julius Caesar, Act III by William Shakespeare

Before You Read A: Reading—Analyzing Imagery

Reference to Words	Imagery of the Body	Connection
Speak hands for me! [They stab Caesar.] —Scene i, line 76	Casca asks his hands to speak as he uses them to stab Caesar.	Links violence to speech

Graphic Organizer Transparencies
© Pearson Education, Inc. All rights reserved.
174

EL L1 L2 **Reading: Graphic Organizer A,** p. 174 (partially filled in)

Also available for these selections:

- L3 Reading: Graphic Organizer B, p. 175
- EL L1 L2 Literary Analysis: Graphic Organizer A, p. 176 (partially filled in)
- L3 Literary Analysis: Graphic Organizer B, p. 177

Skills Development/Extension

Unit 5 Resources

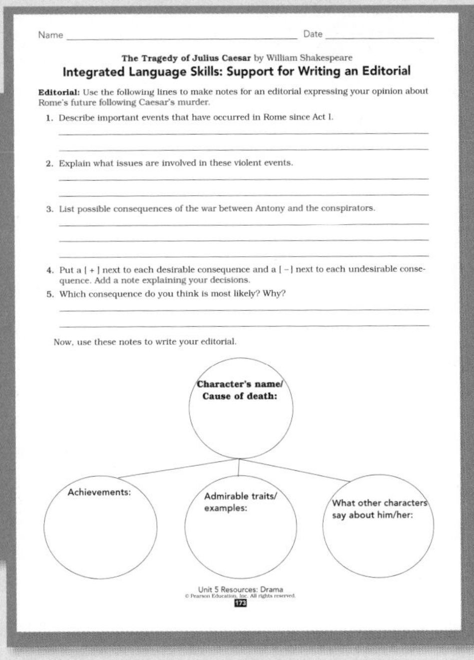
Name ______________ Date ______________

The Tragedy of Julius Caesar by William Shakespeare

Integrated Language Skills: Support for Writing an Editorial

Editorial: Use the following lines to make notes for an editorial expressing your opinion about Rome's future following Caesar's murder.

1. Describe important events that have occurred in Rome since Act I.
2. Explain what issues are involved in these violent events.
3. List possible consequences of the war between Antony and the conspirators.
4. Put a [+] next to each desirable consequence and a [−] next to each undesirable consequence. Add a note explaining your decisions.
5. Which consequence do you think is most likely? Why?

Now, use these notes to write your editorial.

Unit 5 Resources: Drama
© Pearson Education, Inc. All rights reserved.
173

L3 L4 **Support for Writing,** p. 173

Also available for these selections:

- All Reading: Analyze Imagery, p. 133
- All Literary Analysis: Dramatic Speeches, p. 132
- L4 Enrichment, p. 135
- L3 L4 Grammar, p. 172
- L3 L4 Support for Extend Your Learning, p. 175

Assessment

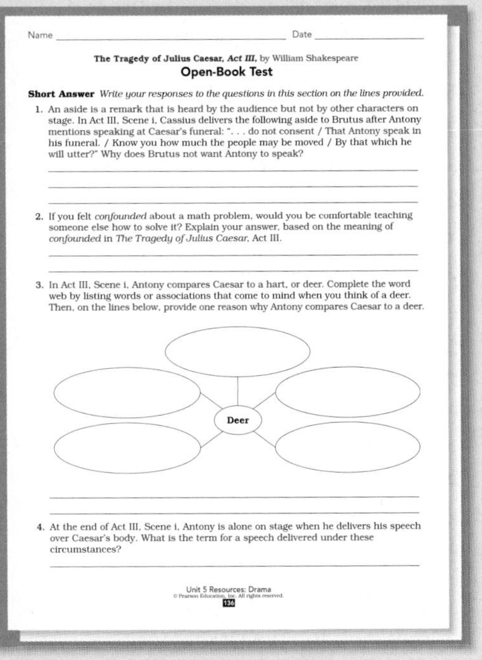
Name ______________ Date ______________

The Tragedy of Julius Caesar, *Act III,* by William Shakespeare

Open-Book Test

Short Answer *Write your responses to the questions in this section on the lines provided.*

1. An aside is a remark that is heard by the audience but not by other characters on stage. In Act III, Scene i, Cassius delivers the following aside to Brutus after Antony mentions speaking at Caesar's funeral: ". . . do not consent / That Antony speak in his funeral. / Know you how much the people may be moved / By that which he will utter?" Why does Brutus not want Antony to speak?
2. If you felt *confounded* about a math problem, would you be comfortable teaching someone else how to solve it? Explain your answer, based on the meaning of *confounded* in *The Tragedy of Julius Caesar,* Act III.
3. In Act III, Scene i, Antony compares Caesar to a hart, or deer. Complete the word web by listing words or associations that come to mind when you think of a deer. Then, on the lines below, provide one reason why Antony compares Caesar to a deer.

4. At the end of Act III, Scene i, Antony is alone on stage when he delivers his speech over Caesar's body. What is the term for a speech delivered under these circumstances?

Unit 5 Resources: Drama
© Pearson Education, Inc. All rights reserved.
136

L L4 **Open-Book Test,** pp. 136–138

Also available for these selections:

- EL L1 L2 Selection Test A, pp. 142–144
- L3 L4 Selection Test B, pp. 139–141

PHLit Online!
www.PHLitOnline.com

- complete narrated selection text
- a thematically related video with writing prompt
- an interactive graphic organizer
- highlighting feature
- access to all student print resources, adapted to individual student needs
- Spanish and English summaries

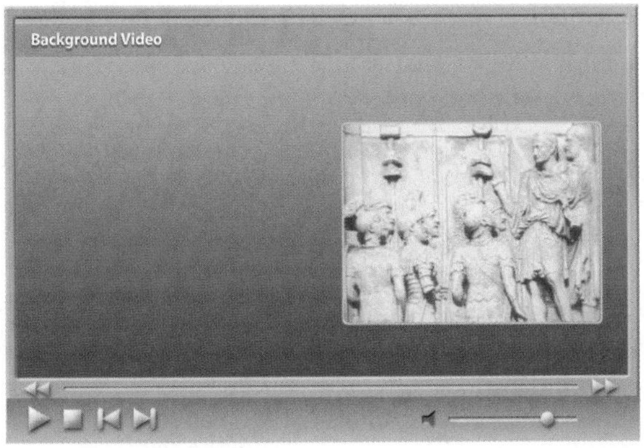

Background video

Also available:

Get Connected! (thematic video with writing prompt)

Vocabulary Central (tools, activities, and songs for studying vocabulary)

Also available:

Writer's Journal (with graphics feature)

DIFFERENTIATE/PRETEACH

❶ Selection Skills

1. With the class, preview the selection skills. (The lesson meets the lesson objectives given on p. 938a.)
2. Explain that students will learn to use the skill of analyzing imagery as they read to better understand and enjoy the selection. By examining dramatic speeches as they read, they will gain deeper insight into the selection.

❷ Vocabulary

1. Have students preview the selection vocabulary.
2. For each word, have students say the word aloud.
3. Then, use the word in a sentence that defines the word.
4. Finally, repeat your definitional sentence or a similar sentence with the word missing, and have the class "fill in the blank" chorally. Here are some examples:

   To be confounded is to be made to feel confused. The math teacher's explanations were always unclear and the students felt [students say "confounded"].

   Strife means "conflict." Someone who is of a peaceful nature will try his or her best to avoid [students say "strife"].

❸ Word Study

1. Introduce the skill, using the instruction in the box.
2. Ask students for a word with the root *-spec-* that is an antonym for "general." (**Answer:** specific)

Before You Read

The Tragedy of Julius Caesar, Act III

THE BIG ?

To what extent does *experience* determine what we *perceive?*

While You Read Act III features a key moment of the plot. Consider the way Brutus and Antony perceive the event and the way they try to sway others' perceptions.

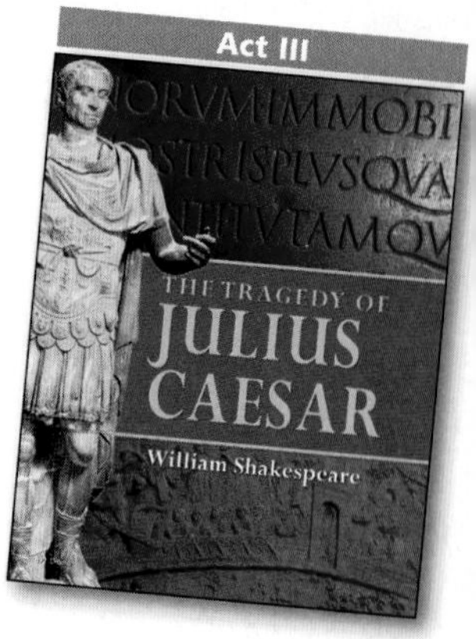

❶ Selection Skills Guide

Practice these skills with ***The Tragedy of Julius Caesar,* Act III** (p. 940).

- Understand dramatic speeches
- Identify dialogue, soliloquies, asides, and monologues
- Analyze imagery

Integrated Language Skills (Grammar; Listening and Speaking; Research and Technology; and Writing Activities) appear on pages 1002–1005.

❷ Vocabulary

Read each word and its definition. Decide whether you know the word well, know it a little bit, or do not know it at all. After you read, see how your knowledge of each word has increased.

- **confounded** (kən foun´ did) *adj.* made to feel confused (p. 945) ***Confounded by the difficult puzzle, he gave up.*** *confound v. confoundedly adv.*
- **spectacle** (spek´ tə kəl) *n.* strange or remarkable sight (p. 949) ***I was fascinated by the spectacle of ten acrobats performing.*** *spectacular adj.*
- **prophesy** (präf´ ə sī´) *v.* predict what will happen (p. 950) ***Who can truly prophesy the future?*** *prophecy n. prophet n. prophetic adj.*
- **strife** (strīf) *n.* struggle; conflict (p. 950) ***Afraid of causing strife, I did not take sides.***
- **discourse** (dis´ kôrs´) *v.* speak on a topic formally and at length (p. 951) ***He wanted to discourse on seashells.*** *discourse n.*
- **interred** (in turd´) *v.* buried (said of a dead body) (p. 955) ***They interred the body at the cemetery.*** *interment n.*

❸ Word Study

The **Latin root *-spect-*** means "to look at" or "behold."

In the play, a character refers to the **spectacle**, or remarkable sight, of Caesar's death and wonders how others will view it.

Vocabulary Development

Vocabulary Knowledge Rating

Create a **Vocabulary Knowledge Rating Chart** (***Professional Development Guidebook***, p. 33) for this selection. Include the selection vocabulary words that appear on this page.

Give students a copy of the chart. Read the words aloud, and have students mark their rating in the Before Reading column. Urge them to be alert to these words as they read and discuss the selection.

Tally how many students think they know a word to gauge how much instruction to provide. As students read and discuss the selection, point out the words and their context.

PHLit Online! **Vocabulary Central**, featuring tools, activities, and songs for studying vocabulary, is available at **www.PHLitOnline.com**.

❹ Literary Analysis: Dramatic Speeches

In plays, most of the information is expressed through characters' words and actions. Plays feature the following types of **dramatic speeches:**

- **Dialogue:** the conversations between characters
- **Soliloquy:** a long speech in which a character, usually alone on stage, speaks to himself or herself, unheard by any other character
- **Aside:** a remark a character makes, usually to the audience, that is not heard by other characters on stage
- **Monologue:** a long speech by one character usually heard by the other characters

As you read, notice characters traits that are revealed in dramatic speeches.

PHLit Online!
www.PHLitOnline.com

Hear It!
- Selection summary audio
- Selection audio

See It!
- Get Connected video
- Background video
- More about the author
- Vocabulary flashcards

Do It!
- Interactive journals
- Interactive graphic organizers
- Self-test
- Internet activity
- Grammar tutorial
- Interactive vocabulary games

❺ Reading Skill: Analyze Imagery

Writers sometimes use **imagery,** language that appeals to the senses, to make abstract ideas vivid and concrete. In Act III, Shakespeare uses many images that focus on words and the body including these:

- wounds that speak
- burying Caesar's body rather than speaking praise of him
- "plucking" a poet's name out of his heart

In each case, a reference to words—speech, praise, names—is coupled with an image of a person's physical body—a corpse, wounds, the heart. In this way, Shakespeare links physical violence in Rome with disrespect for laws—the words that bind society.

❻ Using the Strategy: Imagery Chart

Record details on an **imagery chart** like this one.

Reference to Words	Imagery of the Body	Connection
And waving our red weapons o'er our heads, Let's all cry **"Peace, freedom, and liberty!"**	Swords covered in **blood** from Caesar's body	The words name the ideals the conspirators use to justify killing Caesar.

PRETEACH

❹ Literary Analysis

1. Introduce the skill, using the instruction on the student page.
2. Tell students that they will practice identifying and interpreting dramatic speeches as they read.

Think Aloud: Model the Skill

Model the skill of identifying and interpreting dramatic speeches, using the following "think aloud." Say:

Imagine I am reading a play about a man who meets his long-lost sister. There are *asides*— jokes the man makes about the awkwardness of the meeting that only the audience can hear. There is a *monologue*—a speech in which the man tells his sister he has missed her. Also, there is a *soliloquy*—the man, alone on stage, reflects upon and exposes his emotions.

❺ Reading Skill

1. Introduce the skill, using the instruction on the student page.
2. Tell students that they will practice analyzing imagery as they read.

Think Aloud: Model the Skill

Model the skill of analyzing imagery, using the following "think aloud." Say:

Suppose I am reading a play about a boy who is writing the final paper for a class he is failing. I read, "As the boy typed, fear strangled him. Frustration clung to his fingers, and anxiety smothered his thoughts."

I see here that the author uses *imagery* to connect the boy's abstract feelings—frustration, fear, and anxiety—to concrete images of physical struggle—strangled, clung, smothered. The imagery helps me visualize the boys' feelings and shows me that the threat of failing is real and concrete.

❻ Using the Strategy

Give students a copy of either **Reading Skill Graphic Organizer A** or **B** (*Graphic Organizer Transparencies,* pp. 170–171) to record details of analyzing imagery as they read. Use the examples in Literary Analysis **Graphic Organizer A,** which is partially filled in, to model the process of completing the organizer.

Differentiated Instruction for Universal Access

Preparing Students for the Selection

To prepare lower level readers to read this act of *Julius Caesar,* follow these steps:

- Remind students that the language in plays is unique because it consists entirely of dialogue. As students read, encourage them not only to consider what is being said, but also what the dialogue reveals about the characters.
- Point out that Shakespeare often omits letters (p. 950, "ope" instead of "open") and words (p. 958, "as" instead of "as in") to make his writing more poetic. Practice identifying and decoding these omissions with students. Encourage them to look to the glosses for help.
- Students might have difficulty with the lengthy speeches and soliloquies, such as the one on pages 955–956. Review strategies of paraphrasing and breaking down complex sentences. Encourage them to rephrase difficult parts of soliloquies in their own words.

TEACH

❶ Activating Prior Knowledge

Prepare an **Anticipation Guide** (see ***Professional Development Guidebook***, pp. 36–38) with the following statements:

- Sometimes violence is necessary.
- People should always follow their instincts.
- Emotions often lead to chaos.

Give students a copy of the prepared **Anticipation Guide**, and have students mark their responses in the Me column. Have students discuss the statements in pairs or groups and mark the guides again in the Group column.

Concept Connector

Students will return to the **Anticipation Guide** after completing Act III.

Individual Activity

Have students read Brutus' and Antony's orations (Brutus: Scene ii, lines 12–34; Antony: Scene ii, lines 74–108). Direct them to examine the rhetorical devices that each man uses to achieve a certain effect. Then, have students memorize one of the orations and deliver it to the class.

❷ About the Selection

In the Senate chamber, the conspirators surround Caesar and stab him to death. Brutus speaks first at Caesar's funeral, but Antony's speech stirs the plebeians' desire for vengeance against the conspirators.

REVIEW AND ANTICIPATE ❶ ❷

Having ignored the warnings of the soothsayer in Act I and those of his wife, Calpurnia, in Act II, Caesar proceeds to the Capitol on the ides of March. Decius has told him that the Senate is ready to confer a crown upon him. Caesar is accompanied by the conspirators, led by Cassius and Brutus, as well as by his friend Mark Antony. Meanwhile, Artemidorus plans to reveal the conspiracy to Caesar. As Act III unfolds, Caesar approaches the Capitol, and events take a fateful, irreversible turn.

Differentiated Instruction for Universal Access

Accessibility at a Glance: Selection

	***The Tragedy of Julius Caesar*, Act III**
Context	Historical: ancient Rome
Language/ Vocabulary	• Dialogue • Prose, verse, and soliloquies
Concept Level	Challenging (internal conflicts within historical, political context
Literary Merit	• Classic • Noted author
Lexile/Length	Lexile: NP — Word Count: 4,754
Overall Rating	**Challenging**

ACT III

Scene i. Rome. Before the Capitol.

[*Flourish of trumpets. Enter* CAESAR, BRUTUS, CASSIUS, CASCA, DECIUS, METELLUS CIMBER, TREBONIUS, CINNA, ANTONY, LEPIDUS, ARTEMIDORUS, PUBLIUS, POPILIUS, *and the* SOOTHSAYER.]

CAESAR. The ides of March are come.

SOOTHSAYER. Ay, Caesar, but not gone.

ARTEMIDORUS. Hail, Caesar! Read this schedule.[1]

DECIUS. Trebonius doth desire you to o'er-read,
At your best leisure, this his humble suit.[2]

❸

ARTEMIDORUS. O Caesar, read mine first; for mine's a suit
That touches[3] Caesar nearer. Read it, great Caesar.

CAESAR. What touches us ourself shall be last served.

ARTEMIDORUS. Delay not, Caesar; read it instantly.

CAESAR. What, is the fellow mad?

PUBLIUS. Sirrah, give place.[4]

CASSIUS. What, urge you your petitions in the street?
Come to the Capitol.

[CAESAR *goes to the Capitol, the rest following.*]

POPILIUS. I wish your enterprise today may thrive.

CASSIUS. What enterprise, Popilius?

POPILIUS. Fare you well.

[*Advances to* CAESAR]

BRUTUS. What said Popilius Lena?

CASSIUS. He wished today our enterprise might thrive.
I fear our purpose is discoverèd.

BRUTUS. Look how he makes to[5] Caesar; mark him.

❹

CASSIUS. Casca, be sudden,[6] for we fear prevention.
Brutus, what shall be done? If this be known,
Cassius or Caesar never shall turn back,[7]
For I will slay myself.

1. **schedule** (ske´ jool) *n.* paper.
2. **suit** *n.* petition; plea.
3. **touches** *v.* concerns.
4. **give place** get out of the way.
5. **makes to** approaches.
6. **be sudden** be quick.
7. **Cassius . . . back** either Cassius or Caesar will not return alive.

Literary Analysis
Dramatic Speeches
How does the dialogue between Artemidorus and Caesar create suspense?

❺ **Reading Check**
What does Artemidorus want Caesar to do?

❸ Literary Analysis

Dramatic Speeches

1. Remind students of the definition of *suspense*: a state of anxious wondering about what might happen next.
2. **Ask** students to respond to the Literary Analysis question: How does the dialogue between Artemidorus and Caesar create suspense?
Answer: If Caesar does not read the warning letter, he will probably be killed.

❹ Critical Thinking

Draw Conclusions

1. Have students read Cassius' speech at lines 19–22. **Ask** students what Cassius says he will do if their plan to kill Caesar has been discovered.
Answer: Cassius says that he will kill himself.
2. Remind students that Cassius also suggests at the end of Act I (Scene iii, lines 89–92) that he may use his dagger on himself. **Ask** students to use what they know about Cassius, Caesar, and the situation in Rome to explain why Cassius would kill himself if the conspirators' plan fails and Caesar lives.
Possible responses: It is likely that if found out, the conspirators would be put to death as traitors; Cassius may feel it is better to die by his own hand. Cassius may be making the point that he will not live under a tyrant, especially Caesar.

❺ Reading Check

Answer: Artemidorus wants Caesar to read a letter warning him of the danger he is in.

Differentiated Instruction — Additional Instruction

EL Extended Support—English Learners
Have students complete the **Reading and Vocabulary Warm-ups, *Unit 5 Resources,*** pp. 127–130, before they read. Assign the prereading pages for the selection in the ***Reader's Notebook: English Learner's Version.*** Then, have students listen to portions of the selection on the ***Hear It!* Audio CD.**

L1 L2 Extended Support—Struggling Readers
Have students complete the **Reading and Vocabulary Warm-ups, *Unit 5 Resources,*** pp. 127–130, before they read. Assign the prereading pages for the selection in the ***Reader's Notebook: Adapted Version.*** Then, have students listen to portions of the selection on the ***Hear It!* Audio CD** (adapted text).

Extended Support—Reluctant Readers
To build motivation and engagement before assigning the selection, have students read "In or Out of the In Crowd," a thematically related selection in ***Reality Central.*** Then, use the questions at the conclusion of the related selection to guide discussion.

PHLit Online!
This selection is available in interactive format in the **Enriched Online Student Edition**, at **www.PHLitOnline.com**, which includes a thematically related video and writing prompt and an interactive graphic organizer.

❻ Literature in Context

History Connection Evidence suggests that the Forum was set up as the center of civic life in Rome in the sixth century B.C. This great public square was located in a low, swampy area between the Palatine, Oppian, Quirinal, and Capitoline hills. The Temple of Saturn was one of the earliest buildings in the Forum, dating to 497 B.C. The *rostra,* or speaker's platform, was an important feature of the Forum. Triumphal arches and other monuments were also built in the Forum.

Connect to the Literature Tell students that archaeologists have excavated much of the Forum. Today, people can visit the ruins and understand something of its significance and grandeur in ancient times. Then, **ask** the Connect to the Literature question.

Possible response: There are no walls around the Forum, and each building has wide-open access.

❼ Background

Caesar and the Forum

Julius Caesar had great plans for enlarging and refurbishing the Forum. He began construction of the Basilica Julia and ordered a new Rostra built, the remains of which can be seen today. More notable, perhaps, are Caesar's associations with the Forum after his death. It was from the new Rostra that Antony spoke after the murder of Caesar. Caesar's body lay in state in the Forum, and his corpse was burned on a pyre there. A column was erected on the site of his pyre. It was later replaced by an altar and temple dedicated to the deified leader, Divus Julius, or Divine Julius. These additions to the Forum marked a departure from earlier monuments and practices.

BRUTUS. Cassius, be constant.[8]
Popilius Lena speaks not of our purposes;
For look, he smiles, and Caesar doth not change.[9]

CASSIUS. Trebonius knows his time; for look you, Brutus,
He draws Mark Antony out of the way.

[*Exit* ANTONY *and* TREBONIUS.]

DECIUS. Where is Metellus Cimber? Let him go
And presently prefer his suit[10] to Caesar.

BRUTUS. He is addressed.[11] Press near and second[12] him.

CINNA. Casca, you are the first that rears your hand.

CAESAR. Are we all ready? What is now amiss
That Caesar and his Senate must redress?[13]

METELLUS. Most high, most mighty, and most puissant[14] Caesar,
Metellus Cimber throws before thy seat
An humble heart. [*Kneeling*]

8. **constant** *adj.* firm; calm.
9. **change** *v.* that is, change the expression on his face.
10. **presently prefer his suit** immediately present his petition.
11. **addressed** *adj.* ready.
12. **second** *v.* support.
13. **amiss . . . redress** wrong that Caesar and his Senate must correct.
14. **puissant** (pyōō´ i sənt) *adj.* powerful.

❻ LITERATURE IN CONTEXT

History Connection

❼ **The Roman Forum**

Caesar receives petitioners at the Senate House in the Roman Forum. Consisting of a plaza, or open space lined with buildings, the Forum (shown here) was the center of government and commercial activity in ancient Rome.

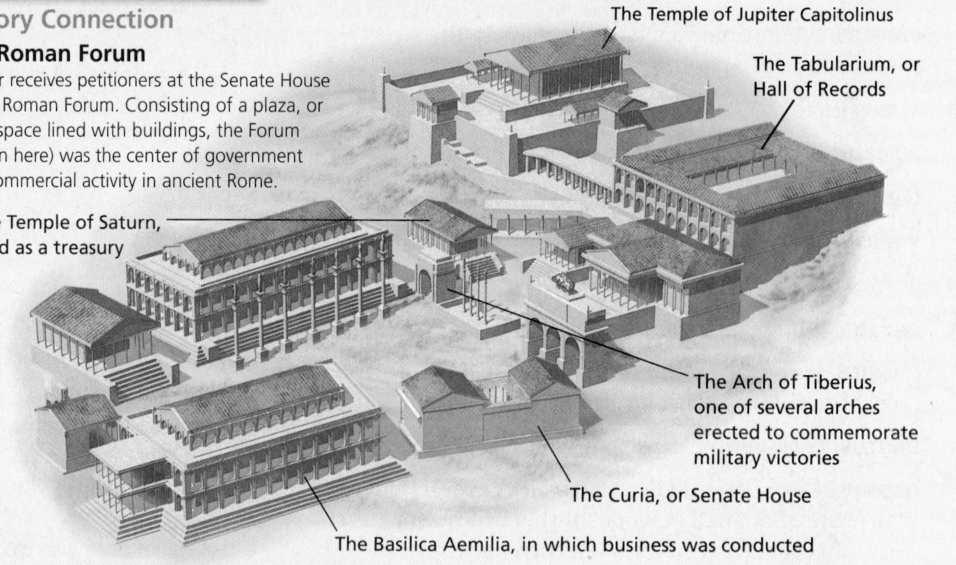

Connect to the Literature Why might the arrangement of the Roman Forum enable public attacks such as the one the conspirators have planned?

Vocabulary Development

Thematic Vocabulary: The Big Question

As students are discussing *The Tragedy of Julius Caesar*, Act III, encourage them to use the thematic vocabulary presented in Introducing the Big Question, pp. 790–791. You might encourage them with sentence starters like these:

1. After Caesar is killed, Antony manages to *manipulate* Brutus by . . .
2. At the funeral, Brutus does not *anticipate* . . .
3. The crowd's *perspective* of Caesar changes when . . .
4. In the final scene, the plebeians' *bias* leads them mistakenly to believe that . . .

CAESAR. I must prevent thee, Cimber.
These couchings and these lowly courtesies[15]
Might fire the blood of ordinary men,
And turn preordinance and first decree
Into the law of children.[16] Be not fond[17]
To think that Caesar bears such rebel blood
That will be thawed from the true quality[18]
With that which melteth fools—I mean sweet words,
Low-crookèd curtsies, and base spaniel fawning.[19]
Thy brother by decree is banishèd.
If thou dost bend and pray and fawn for him,
I spurn[20] thee like a cur out of my way.
Know, Caesar doth not wrong, nor without cause
Will he be satisfied.

METELLUS. Is there no voice more worthy than my own,
To sound more sweetly in great Caesar's ear
For the repealing[21] of my banished brother?

BRUTUS. I kiss thy hand, but not in flattery, Caesar,
Desiring thee that Publius Cimber may
Have an immediate freedom of repeal.[22]

CAESAR. What, Brutus?

15. **couchings . . . courtesies** low bowings and humble gestures of reverence.
16. **And turn . . . law of children** and change what has already been decided as children might change their minds.
17. **fond** *adj.* foolish (enough).
18. **rebel . . . quality** unstable disposition that will lose its firmness.
19. **base spaniel fawning** low doglike cringing.
20. **spurn** *v.* kick disdainfully.
21. **repealing** *n.* recalling; ending the banishment.
22. **freedom of repeal** permission to be recalled.

10 Reading Check
What worries Cassius?

8

9 ▼ **Critical Viewing**
Judging from these ruins of the Roman Forum, how large might the crowds around the Senate have been on the ides of March? Explain. **[Hypothesize]**

Differentiated Instruction for Universal Access

Strategy for Special Needs Students
Give students a plan of the Roman Forum, and help them locate structures shown in the photograph. Have students point to items in the photograph and then cross-reference with their fingers to the plan of the Forum. Draw parallels between the Forum and a civic or commercial center in students' local community or a location in a nearby or well-known big city to help students understand the setting of this act in the play.

Enrichment for Gifted and Talented Students
Invite students to work individually, in pairs, or in small groups to research and build models of the Roman Forum as it was at the time of Caesar. Students can use cardboard and construction paper to show buildings and monuments in the Forum before Caesar's murder. Suggest that they create an overlay for the plan to show the structures that honored Caesar after this death. Display students' models in the classroom for the rest of the class to use as reference.

8 Humanities

View of the Roman Forum
The columns in the foreground (left) are the Temple of Saturn. The Column of Phocas can be seen through these columns. Close by the Column of Phocas was the Rostra. Just beyond are the ruins of the Basilica Aemilia. To the right of the road are the ruins of the Basilica Julia. The three columns beyond it are what remain of the Temple of Castor and Pollux. Beyond and slightly to the left middle is the round Temple of Vesta. The Colosseum can also be glimpsed in the middle distance just over the top of the temple. Use this question for discussion:

- How would you describe the function of the Forum based on the buildings there and what you know about their uses?
  Answer: It was a government, commercial, and religious center.

9 Critical Viewing
Answer: The crowds would likely have been quite large. Even with buildings still standing, there would have been a great deal of open space where people could gather.

10 Reading Check
Answer: Cassius is worried that their plan to murder Caesar has been discovered.

11 Critical Thinking

Make Judgments

1. Have students summarize what Caesar says in this speech.
   Ask: How does what Caesar says affect your opinion of him?
   Possible response: Caesar says that he never changes his mind. Students may respond that they admire him for standing by his policies and ideas, or they may think he should be more flexible.
2. Remind students of Caesar's change of mind about going to the Senate in Act II, Scene ii.
   Ask: If Caesar desires to be seen as a man who always keeps his word, why might he have changed his mind in the earlier scene?
   Possible response: Caesar had always planned to go to the Senate, despite Calpurnia's worries. He responds to Decius' flattery not because it is flattery, but because it agrees with his own wishes.

12 Humanities

***Still Photograph, from the film* Julius Caesar (1953), written and directed by Joseph Mankiewicz and produced by John Houseman**

This still photograph from the film *Julius Caesar* depicts the moment of Caesar's assassination. The character in the center is Julius Caesar, played by Louis Calhern. The character with the raised dagger at the left is Casca, played by Edmond O'Brien. In the far right bottom corner, with arms outstretched to Caesar, is Cassius, played by John Gielgud. Brutus, played by James Mason, is in the foreground, kneeling and with his back to the camera. Use this question for discussion:

- How does this photograph capture the tension of the scene?
  Answer: Caesar is surrounded by assassins; a knife is poised to strike.

13 Critical Viewing

Answer: Caesar is completely unaware that he is about to be stabbed. His back is to the assassin, and others are distracting him.

CASSIUS. Pardon, Caesar; Caesar, pardon!
As low as to thy foot doth Cassius fall
To beg enfranchisement[23] for Publius Cimber.

CAESAR. I could be well moved, if I were as you;
If I could pray to move,[24] prayers would move me;
But I am constant as the Northern Star,
Of whose true-fixed and resting[25] quality
There is no fellow[26] in the firmament.[27]
The skies are painted with unnumb'red sparks,
They are all fire and every one doth shine;
But there's but one in all doth hold his[28] place.
So in the world; 'tis furnished well with men,
And men are flesh and blood, and apprehensive;[29]
Yet in the number I do know but one
That unassailable holds on his rank,[30]
Unshaked of motion;[31] and that I am he,

23. **enfranchisement** (en fran´ chīz mənt) *n.* freedom.
24. **pray to move** beg others to change their minds.
25. **resting** *adj.* immovable.
26. **fellow** *n.* equal.
27. **firmament** (fʉr´ mə mənt) *n.* sky.
28. **his** *pron.* its.
29. **apprehensive** (ap´ rə hen´ siv) *adj.* able to understand.
30. **one/That unassailable . . . rank** one who, unattackable, maintains his position.
31. **Unshaked of motion** unmoved by his own or others' impulses.

11

13 ▼ **Critical Viewing** Which details in this picture suggest Caesar's ignorance? **[Analyze]**

12

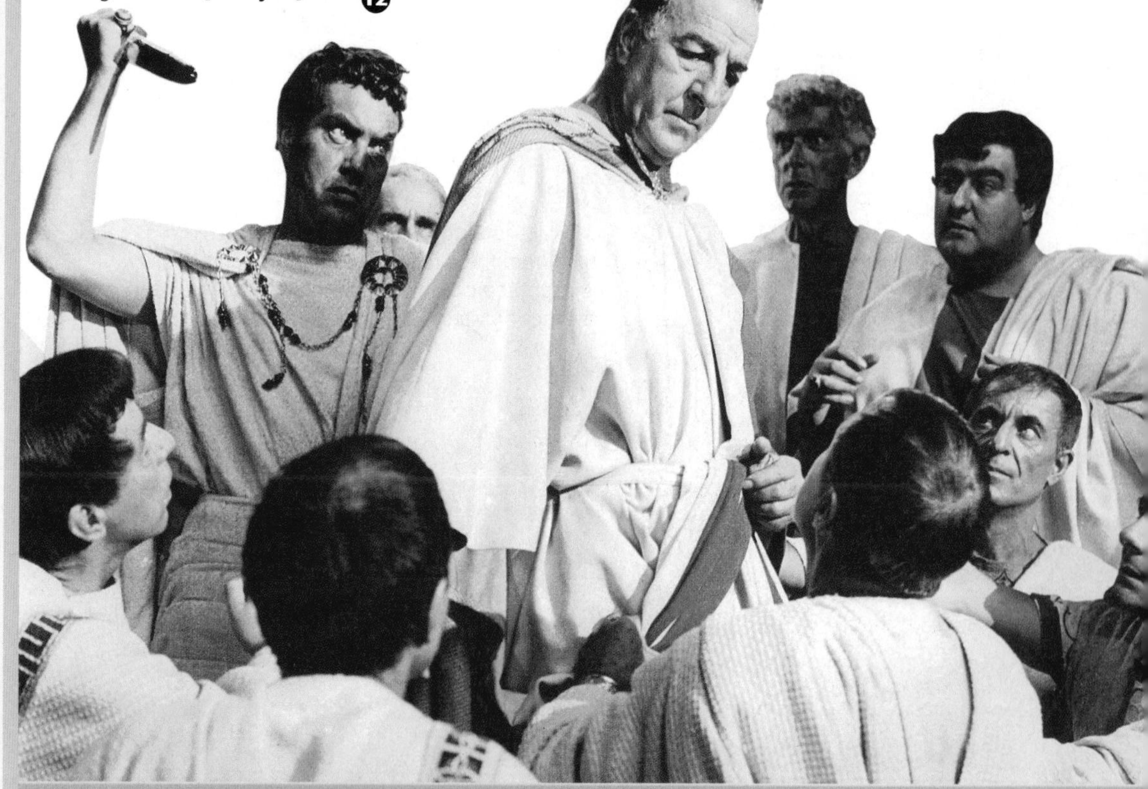

944 Drama

Vocabulary Development

Word Analysis

Call students' attention to the word *confounded* in line 86 and to its definition. Tell students that the adjective *confounded* is actually the past participle of the verb *confound*, which means "to confuse." *Confound* combines the prefix *con-*, meaning "together," and the base word *found*, which can be traced to the Latin root *-fund-*. The Latin root *-fund-* means "to pour." Thus the literal meaning of *confounded* is "poured together." Point out that the Latin prefix *con-* is used to form many other words. Have students brainstorm for words with the prefix. Then, separate the class into groups, and assign each group several of the words. Have the groups look up these words in a dictionary to find their meanings and understand their origins. Tell the groups to use each word in a sentence.

Let me a little show it, even in this—
That I was constant[32] Cimber should be banished,
And constant do remain to keep him so.

[14] **CINNA.** O Caesar—

CAESAR. Hence! Wilt thou lift up Olympus?[33]

DECIUS. Great Caesar—

CAESAR. Doth not Brutus bootless[34] kneel?

[15] **CASCA.** Speak hands for me! [*They stab* CAESAR.]

CAESAR. *Et tu, Brutè?*[35] Then fall, Caesar. [*Dies*]

CINNA. Liberty! Freedom! Tyranny is dead!
Run hence, proclaim, cry it about the streets.

CASSIUS. Some to the common pulpits,[36] and cry out
"Liberty, freedom, and enfranchisement!"

BRUTUS. People, and senators, be not affrighted.
Fly not; stand still; ambition's debt is paid.[37]

CASCA. Go to the pulpit, Brutus.

DECIUS. And Cassius too.

BRUTUS. Where's Publius?[38]

[16] **CINNA.** Here, quite confounded with this mutiny.[39]

METELLUS. Stand fast together, lest some friend of Caesar's
Should chance—

BRUTUS. Talk not of standing. Publius, good cheer;
There is no harm intended to your person,
Nor to no Roman else. So tell them, Publius.

CASSIUS. And leave us, Publius, lest that the people
Rushing on us should do your age some mischief.

BRUTUS. Do so; and let no man abide[40] this deed
But we the doers.

[*Enter* TREBONIUS.]

CASSIUS. Where is Antony?

TREBONIUS. Fled to his house amazed.[41]
Men, wives, and children stare, cry out and run,
As[42] it were doomsday.

BRUTUS. Fates, we will know your pleasures.

32. **constant** *adj.* determined.
33. **Olympus** (ō lim′ pəs) *n.* mountain in Greece on which the Greek gods were said to live.
34. **bootless** (bo͞ot′ lis) *adv.* uselessly.

Reading Skill
Analyze Imagery
In what way does line 76 combine ideas of words with images of violence?

35. ***Et tu, Brutè?*** Latin for "And you, too, Brutus?"
36. **pulpits** (pul′ pits) *n.* speakers' platforms.
37. **ambition's . . . paid** ambition received what it deserved.
38. **Publius** (po͞ob′ lē əs) an elderly senator.

Vocabulary
confounded (kən foun′ did) *adj.* made to feel confused

39. **mutiny** (myo͞ot′ ′n ē) *n.* revolt against authority, such as a rebellion of soldiers against their officers.
40. **let no man abide** let no man take responsibility for.
41. **amazed** *adj.* astounded.
42. **As** *conj.* as if.

[17] **Reading Check**
What do the conspirators do to Caesar?

Differentiated Instruction for Universal Access

Enrichment for Advanced Readers
Have students consider how Shakespeare uses imagery to foreshadow events in the play. Remind students that foreshadowing is suggesting events that have yet to occur. Have students recall Calpurnia's dream (Act II, Scene ii), in which she sees Romans bathing in the blood flowing from a statue of Caesar. Have students compare Calpurnia's dream with the violent murder of Caesar. Ask students to find other images from Acts I and II that foreshadow events and elements of Act III, Scene i. Direct students to write brief analyses of this use of foreshadowing by Shakespeare. Students should consider the following questions: Would the effect of seeing Caesar's murder be less horrifying without the foreshadowing? Why or why not?

14 Critical Thinking

Analyze

1. Have students analyze Caesar's remark in line 74. **Ask:** What does Caesar suggest in comparing himself to Olympus?
Answer: He suggests that he has the status of a god.
2. **Ask** students how Caesar's remark supports the action the conspirators are about to take.
Possible response: It indicates that Caesar sees himself as superior to other mortals and as having absolute power.

15 Reading Skill

Analyze Imagery

1. Guide students in using the **Reading Skill Graphic Organizer B** (p. 174 in *Graphic Organizer Transparencies*) to analyze the imagery in line 76.
2. **Ask** students to respond to the Reading Skill question: In what way does line 76 combine ideas of words with images of violence?
3. **Answer:** Casca asks his hands to speak as he uses them to stab Caesar. He and the other conspirators have chosen to use violence to express their concern about Caesar's rise to power and the threat it represents to the Republic.

16 Critical Thinking

Compare and Contrast

1. Choose six students to read the parts of the conspirators in lines 78–95 aloud. **Ask** students to compare and contrast the conspirators' reactions to the murder.
Answer: Cinna and Cassius seem excited and triumphant. Brutus is calm. Metellus fears retaliation.
2. **Ask** what their reactions suggest about their various motivations for the crime.
Answer: Brutus is calm because he believes that he did his duty. Cassius is triumphant because he envied Caesar and was bitter about his success. Metellus may be frightened because he feels guilty.

17 Reading Check

Answer: They stab him to death.

⓲ Reading Skill

Analyze Imagery

1. Have students read Brutus' speech.
2. **Ask** students to respond to the Reading Skill prompt: Find an example of an image linking blood and words in lines 103–110.
   Answer: Brutus urges Romans to bathe up to their elbows in Caesar's blood, to smear his blood on their swords, and then to wave their bloody weapons as they march in the Forum crying "Peace, freedom, and liberty!"
3. **Ask** students to **describe** why this image is jarring.
   Possible response: The image is vivid and jarring since it connects gory violence with the high ideals of peace, freedom, and liberty.
4. **Ask** what Shakespeare means to suggest with such an image.
   Possible response: Shakespeare may be suggesting that no lofty idea justifies a violent act or that idealism can lead to fanaticism.

⓳ Critical Thinking

Analyze

1. Ask two volunteers to read the parts of Cassius and Brutus in lines 111–116 on p. 946. Then, **ask** students to summarize the lines.
   Answer: Cassius wonders about the actors who in future centuries will play Caesar and the conspirators on stage. Brutus wonders how often an actor will pretend to die as Caesar.
2. **Ask** students to discuss the effect of these lines on the audience.
   Possible response: The lines may remind the audience that they are watching a play, not real events. [Students, too, may appreciate the irony that, thanks to Shakespeare, the assassination *has* been reenacted thousands of years after it occurred—though not for the reasons Cassius expects.]
3. **Ask** students to describe how the audience may react to the lines.
   Possible response: The conspirators believe that their literal bloodbath is a "lofty scene" that will be admired for ages to come—but Roman citizens and Shakespeare's audience may be horrified by the linkage of butchery with idealism.

43. 'tis but the time . . . upon It is only the time of death and the length of life that people care about.

Reading Skill
Analyze Imagery
Find an example of an image linking blood and words in lines 103–110. ⓲

44. market place the open area of the Roman Forum, the center of government, business, and public life in ancient Rome.

45. in sport for amusement; the deed will be acted out in plays.

46. on Pompey's basis lies along by the pedestal of Pompey's statue lies stretched out. ⓳

47. knot *n.* group.

48. grace his heels do honor to his heels; follow him.

49. Soft *interjection* wait

50. royal *adj.* showing noble generosity.

51. be resolved have it explained.

That we shall die, we know; 'tis but the time,
And drawing days out, that men stand upon.[43]

CASCA. Why, he that cuts off twenty years of life
Cuts off so many years of fearing death.

BRUTUS. Grant that, and then is death a benefit.
So are we Caesar's friends, that have abridged
His time of fearing death. Stoop, Romans, stoop,
And let us bathe our hands in Caesar's blood
Up to the elbows, and besmear our swords.
Then walk we forth, even to the market place,[44]
And waving our red weapons o'er our heads,
Let's all cry "Peace, freedom, and liberty!"

CASSIUS. Stoop then, and wash. How many ages hence
Shall this our lofty scene be acted over
In states unborn and accents yet unknown!

BRUTUS. How many times shall Caesar bleed in sport,[45]
That now on Pompey's basis lies along[46]
No worthier than the dust!

CASSIUS. So oft as that shall be,
So often shall the knot[47] of us be called
The men that gave their country liberty.

DECIUS. What, shall we forth?

CASSIUS. Ay, every man away.
Brutus shall lead, and we will grace his heels[48]
With the most boldest and best hearts of Rome.

[*Enter a* SERVANT.]

BRUTUS. Soft,[49] who comes here? A friend of Antony's.

SERVANT. Thus, Brutus, did my master bid me kneel;
Thus did Mark Antony bid me fall down;
And, being prostrate, thus he bade me say:
Brutus is noble, wise, valiant, and honest;
Caesar was mighty, bold, royal,[50] and loving.
Say I love Brutus and I honor him;
Say I feared Caesar, honored him, and loved him.
If Brutus will vouchsafe that Antony
May safely come to him and be resolved[51]
How Caesar hath deserved to lie in death,
Mark Antony shall not love Caesar dead
So well as Brutus living; but will follow
The fortunes and affairs of noble Brutus

Think Aloud

Vocabulary: Using Context

Direct students' attention to the word *abridged* in line 104 of Brutus' speech. Then, use the following "think aloud" to model how to use context to infer the meaning of an unknown word. Say to students:

I'm going to think aloud to show you how I would figure out the meaning of *abridged* from its context.

In this sentence, Brutus says that they have *abridged* the time of Caesar's fearing death. I see that Casca also talks about fearing death in lines 101–102. He says that the person who cuts off years of life cuts off years of fearing death. I think that *abridged* may mean "cut off." I'll substitute *cut off* in Brutus' lines: "So are we Caesar's friends, that have cut off/His time of fearing death." That seems to make sense. I think *abridged* means "cut off or shortened."

Thorough the hazards of this untrod state[52]
With all true faith. So says my master Antony.

BRUTUS. Thy master is a wise and valiant Roman;
I never thought him worse.
Tell him, so[53] please him come unto this place,
He shall be satisfied and, by my honor,
Depart untouched.

SERVANT. I'll fetch him presently.[54]

[*Exit* SERVANT]

BRUTUS. I know that we shall have him well to friend.[55]

CASSIUS. I wish we may. But yet have I a mind
That fears him much; and my misgiving still
20 Falls shrewdly to the purpose.[56]

[*Enter* ANTONY.]

BRUTUS. But here comes Antony. Welcome, Mark Antony.

ANTONY. O mighty Caesar! Dost thou lie so low?
Are all thy conquests, glories, triumphs, spoils,
Shrunk to this little measure? Fare thee well.
I know not, gentlemen, what you intend,
Who else must be let blood,[57] who else is rank.[58]
If I myself, there is no hour so fit
As Caesar's death's hour, nor no instrument
21 Of half that worth as those your swords, made rich
With the most noble blood of all this world.
I do beseech ye, if you bear me hard,[59]
Now, whilst your purpled hands[60] do reek and smoke,
Fulfill your pleasure. Live[61] a thousand years,
I shall not find myself so apt[62] to die;
No place will please me so, no mean of death,[63]
As here by Caesar, and by you cut off,
The choice and master spirits of this age.

BRUTUS. O Antony, beg not your death of us!
Though now we must appear bloody and cruel,
As by our hands and this our present act
You see we do, yet see you but our hands
And this the bleeding business they have done.
Our hearts you see not; they are pitiful;[64]
And pity to the general wrong of Rome—
As fire drives out fire, so pity pity[65]—
Hath done this deed on Caesar. For your part,
To you our swords have leaden[66] points, Mark Antony:

52. Thorough . . . state through the dangers of this new state of affairs.

53. so *conj.* if it should.

54. presently *adv.* immediately.

55. to friend as a friend.

56. my misgiving . . . to the purpose my doubts always turn out to be justified.

Literary Analysis
Dramatic Speeches
What is Antony's purpose in delivering this monologue?

57. be let blood (a pun) "be bled for medical purposes" or "be killed."

58. rank (a pun) "too powerful" or "swollen with disease and therefore in need of bloodletting."

59. bear me hard have a grudge against me.

60. purpled hands bloody hands.

61. Live if I live.

62. apt *adj.* ready.

63. mean of death way of dying.

64. pitiful *adj.* full of pity or compassion.

65. pity pity pity for Rome drove out pity for Caesar.

66. leaden *adj.* dull; blunt.

22 **Reading Check**
What does Antony ask of the conspirators?

Differentiated Instruction for Universal Access

Strategy for Less Proficient Readers

Have students read Act III, Scene i in the ***Reader's Notebook***. This version provides basic-level instruction in an interactive format with questions and write-on lines. After students finish the selection in ***Reader's Notebook***, have them complete the questions and activities in the student edition.

EL Strategy for English Learners

Have students read the version of Act III, Scene i in the ***Reader's Notebook: English Learner's Version***. Monitor students' comprehension of the adapted version, clarifying vocabulary and sentence structure as needed. The basic-level instruction and interactive format of this adapted version will prepare students to read the selection in the student edition.

20 Literary Analysis

Dramatic Speeches

1. Have two students read lines 143–146 aloud. **Ask** students whether they agree with Brutus or Cassius and to explain why.
Possible response: Students will probably agree with Cassius because Antony offers Caesar a crown in Act I and because Antony and Caesar had been close.
2. Have a volunteer to read Antony's monologue at lines 148–163. Then, **ask** students to respond to the Literary Analysis question: What is Antony's purpose in delivering this monologue?
Answer: Antony sincerely mourns Caesar and wants the conspirators to know his grief. His suggestion that they kill him, too, may be a test of their motives and intentions.

21 Connecting to the Big Question

1. Remind students that the conspirators have killed Caesar because they thought him a tyrant. Now Antony appears, asking to have the deed explained to him.
2. Have students read the bracketed soliloquy. **Ask** students to explain what Antony's speech tells about his opinion of Caesar.
Answer: Antony believes that Caesar's blood is the "most noble" in the world and that all of his "conquests, glories, triumphs, spoils" are now diminished by death. He even chooses to die next to Caesar, saying that "No place will please me so."
3. **Ask** students to explain how Antony's experience affects his view of Caesar.
Possible response: He has known Caesar as a friend and mentor.
4. As they continue reading, have students notice how Antony manages to change other characters' opinions about Caesar.

22 Reading Check

Answer: Antony asks the conspirators to kill him, too, right then, if that is their eventual intent.

㉓ Literary Analysis

Dramatic Speeches

1. Direct students' attention to Antony's speech at lines 183–210. Ask students to analyze the second half of the speech, in which Antony addresses Caesar's corpse. **Ask** students how they would characterize the speech.
   Answer: When he speaks to Caesar's corpse, Antony's language is emotional and exaggerated. His use of the pronoun *thou* emphasizes his emotional closeness and intimacy with Caesar.
2. **Ask** students to respond to the Literary Analysis question: In this monologue, what image of his state of mind does Antony create for the conspirators?
   Answer: Antony reveals how distraught and overwhelmed he is about the loss of Caesar; however, he also displays presence of mind by contemplating political consequences and his role in the state.

㉔ Reading Skill

Analyze Imagery

1. **Ask** students to respond to the Reading Skill question: What images of the body does Antony use to contrast his real grief with his words of friendship?
   Answer: The image of shaking "bloody fingers" represents Antony's feigned agreement with the conspirators. This contrasts with his true feeling, a grief represented by the image linking weeping eyes and bleeding wounds.
2. **Ask** students what point Antony makes with these images.
   Answer: Antony makes the point that grieving for his friend Caesar is what he should be doing, not making friends with his enemies.
3. **Ask** students to describe the imagery Antony uses at the end of his monologue, and explain why the conspirators might be concerned about it.
   Answer: Antony uses the image of a deer being killed by many noble hunters to allude to the violence of the murder of Caesar by the conspirators. The conspirators may be concerned because such images may shift the audience's sympathy from them to the victim, Caesar.

Our arms in strength of malice, and our hearts
Of brothers' temper,[67] do receive you in
With all kind love, good thoughts, and reverence.

CASSIUS. Your voice[68] shall be as strong as any man's
In the disposing of new dignities.[69]

BRUTUS. Only be patient till we have appeased
The multitude, beside themselves with fear,
And then we will deliver[70] you the cause
Why I, that did love Caesar when I struck him,
Have thus proceeded.

ANTONY. I doubt not of your wisdom.
Let each man render me his bloody hand.
First, Marcus Brutus, will I shake with you;
Next, Caius Cassius, do I take your hand;
Now, Decius Brutus, yours; now yours, Metellus;
Yours, Cinna; and, my valiant Casca, yours;
Though last, not least in love, yours, good Trebonius.
Gentlemen all—alas, what shall I say?
My credit[71] now stands on such slippery ground
That one of two bad ways you must conceit[72] me,
Either a coward or a flatterer.
That I did love thee, Caesar, O, 'tis true!
If then thy spirit look upon us now,
Shall it not grieve thee dearer[73] than thy death
To see thy Antony making his peace,
Shaking the bloody fingers of thy foes,
Most noble, in the presence of thy corse?[74]
Had I as many eyes as thou hast wounds,
Weeping as fast as they stream forth thy blood,
It would become me better than to close[75]
In terms of friendship with thine enemies.
Pardon me, Julius! Here wast thou bayed,[76] brave hart;[77]
Here didst thou fall, and here thy hunters stand,
Signed in thy spoil[78] and crimsoned in thy Lethe.[79]
O world, thou wast the forest to this hart;
And this indeed, O world, the heart of thee.
How like a deer, stroken[80] by many princes.
Dost thou here lie!

CASSIUS. Mark Antony—

---

67. **Our arms . . . / Of brothers' temper** our arms strengthened with the desire to do harm and our hearts filled with brotherly feelings.
68. **voice** *n.* vote.
69. **dignities** *n.* offices.
70. **deliver** *v.* tell to.

Literary Analysis
Dramatic Speeches
In this monologue, what image of his state of mind does Antony create for the conspirators? ㉓

71. **credit** *n.* reputation.
72. **conceit** (kən sē t′) *v.* think of.
73. **dearer** *adv.* more deeply.
74. **corse** *n.* corpse.
75. **close** (clōz) *v.* reach an agreement.
76. **bayed** *v.* cornered.
77. **hart** (härt) *n.* deer.

㉔ **Reading Skill**
Analyze Imagery
What images of the body does Antony use to contrast his real grief with his words of friendship?

78. **Signed in thy spoil** marked by signs of your slaughter.
79. **Lethe** (lē´ *thē*) river in Hades, the mythological Greek underworld inhabited by the dead; here, a river of blood.
80. **stroken** *v.* struck down.

Vocabulary Development

Selection Vocabulary Reinforcement

Students will benefit from additional examples and practice with the selection vocabulary words. Reinforce their comprehension with "show-you-know" sentences. The first part of the sentence uses the vocabulary word in an appropriate context. The second part of the sentence—the "show-you-know" part—clarifies the first. Model the strategy with this example for *spectacle*:

The opening ceremony was a real *spectacle*, with teams from around the world marching in special costumes and waving the flags of their countries.

Then, give students a sentence prompt such as the following, and coach them in creating the clarification part:

They created a *spectacle* when they arrived by ________

Sample answer: singing, shouting, and wildly honking the car's horn.

ANTONY. Pardon me, Caius Cassius.
The enemies of Caesar shall say this;
Then, in a friend, it is cold modesty.[81]

CASSIUS. I blame you not for praising Caesar so;
But what compact[82] mean you to have with us?
Will you be pricked[83] in number of our friends,
Or shall we on,[84] and not depend on you?

ANTONY. Therefore I took your hands, but was indeed
Swayed from the point by looking down on Caesar.
Friends am I with you all, and love you all,
Upon this hope, that you shall give me reasons
Why, and wherein, Caesar was dangerous.

BRUTUS. Or else were this a savage **spectacle**.
Our reasons are so full of good regard[85]
That were you, Antony, the son of Caesar,
You should be satisfied.

ANTONY. That's all I seek;
And am moreover suitor that I may
Produce[86] his body to the market place,
And in the pulpit, as becomes a friend,
Speak in the order[87] of his funeral.

BRUTUS. You shall, Mark Antony.

CASSIUS. Brutus, a word with you.
[*Aside to* BRUTUS] You know not what you do; do not consent
That Antony speak in his funeral.
Know you how much the people may be moved
By that which he will utter?

BRUTUS. By your pardon:
I will myself into the pulpit first,
And show the reason of our Caesar's death.
What Antony shall speak, I will protest[88]
He speaks by leave and by permission,
And that we are contented Caesar shall
Have all true rites and lawful ceremonies.
It shall advantage more than do us wrong.[89]

CASSIUS. I know not what may fall;[90] I like it not.

BRUTUS. Mark Antony, here, take you Caesar's body.
You shall not in your funeral speech blame us,
But speak all good you can devise of Caesar,

81. **cold modesty** calm, moderate speech.
82. **compact** (käm′ pakt) *n.* agreement.
83. **pricked** *v.* marked down; included.
84. **on** proceed.

Vocabulary
spectacle (spek′ tə kəl) *n.* strange or remarkable sight

85. **so full of good regard** so carefully considered.
86. **Produce** *v.* bring forth.
87. **order** *n.* course of the ceremonies.

Literary Analysis
Dramatic Speeches
Why does Cassius wish to prevent others from hearing what he says in this aside to Brutus?

88. **protest** *v.* declare.
89. **advantage . . . wrong** benefit us more than hurt us.
90. **what may fall** what may happen.

27 **Reading Check**
What rules must Antony follow in delivering his funeral speech for Caesar?

25 Reading Skill
Analyze Imagery

1. Have three volunteers read aloud the dialogue between Cassius, Antony, and Brutus in lines 214–226. **Ask:** What does Cassius want Antony to make clear?
Answer: Cassius wants to know whether Antony will ally himself with them.
2. **Ask:** Why does Antony hesitate?
Answer: He wants them to explain what made Caesar so dangerous that they had to kill him.
3. **Ask:** For Brutus, what difference will the right words, or "reasons," make to the "spectacle" of Caesar's bloody body?
Answer: For Brutus, the right words, or "reasons," will justify the "savage spectacle" of Caesar's bloody body even to those closest to Caesar—that is, to Antony.

26 Literary Analysis
Dramatic Speeches

1. Read aloud Brutus' response to Antony's request to speak at Caesar's funeral in line 231. Then, point out the shared meter of the line and how Cassius breaks in to speak to Brutus.
2. **Ask** students to respond to the Literary Analysis question: Why does Cassius wish to prevent others from hearing what he says in this aside to Brutus?
3. **Answer:** Cassius' main concern is probably to prevent Antony from hearing him. Cassius doesn't want Antony to know that he suspects Antony's intentions.
4. **Ask** students which character they think is right about Antony—Cassius or Brutus—and why.
Possible response: Cassius is right. Antony is obviously deeply upset about Caesar's murder and probably wants revenge of some kind.

27 Reading Check

Answer: Antony can praise Caesar but must say he does so with the conspirators' permission. He cannot blame the conspirators.

Differentiated Instruction for Universal Access

EL Strategy for English Learners
Work with students to restate in simpler English the formal, stylized language of Antony's monologue in lines 184–210 and the private remarks of Cassius and Brutus to each other in lines 232–243. Have students write paraphrases of the monologue and the other conversation. Then, invite pairs of students to perform a reading of the paraphrases for the class.

Enrichment for Gifted and Talented Students
Have small groups of students take the parts of Brutus, Antony, and Cassius and read or memorize and perform their parts in lines 214–243 for the rest of the class. Direct students to practice their brief scenes together several times, whether they have chosen to read from a script or to speak from memory. Encourage students to establish eye contact with each other and to use appropriate gestures as the text dictates.

28 Literary Analysis

Dramatic Speeches

1. **Ask** students to identify the type of dramatic speech that Antony makes in lines 254–275. Have them explain their answers.
Answer: It is a soliloquy. Antony is alone on stage and is sharing his thoughts with the audience.
2. **Ask** students to respond to the Literary Analysis question: What does Antony's soliloquy in lines 254–275 reveal to the audience that other characters do not know?
Answer: He reveals that his loyalty will always be to Caesar; he does not support the conspirators.

29 Reading Skill

Analyze Imagery

1. Have students focus on Antony's prediction about the effects of the murder of Caesar in lines 259–275. **Ask** students to summarize what Antony predicts will happen.
Answer: Civil war will break out all over Italy, causing death and destruction throughout Roman society.
2. Draw students' attention to the many images of violence and the body in Antony's prophecy.
Ask students to respond to the Reading Skill prompt: Identify two ways in which lines 259–262 combine ideas of words and bodies.
Answer: The ideas of words and bodies are combined in the image of wounds that are like open mouths with ruby lips that are begging Antony to speak; the image of a spoken curse landing on the limbs of men also combines words and the physical body.
3. **Ask** students to identify other images in the speech that combine words and the body and to explain their meaning.
Answer: The image of the mothers only smiling when they see their children slaughtered in war, not saying anything or uttering a cry, suggests that violence will overcome speech and civilized society. The image of Caesar calling for revenge suggests that language will be used to incite physical violence.

And say you do't by our permission;
Else shall you not have any hand at all
About his funeral. And you shall speak
In the same pulpit whereto I am going,
After my speech is ended.

ANTONY. Be it so;
I do desire no more.

BRUTUS. Prepare the body then, and follow us.

[*Exit all but* ANTONY.]

ANTONY. O pardon me, thou bleeding piece of earth,
That I am meek and gentle with these butchers!
Thou art the ruins of the noblest man
That ever livèd in the tide of times.[91]
Woe to the hand that shed this costly blood!
Over thy wounds now do I **prophesy**
(Which like dumb mouths do ope their ruby lips
To beg the voice and utterance of my tongue),
A curse shall light upon the limbs of men;
Domestic fury and fierce civil **strife**
Shall cumber[92] all the parts of Italy;
Blood and destruction shall be so in use,[93]
And dreadful objects so familiar,
That mothers shall but smile when they behold
Their infants quartered with the hands of war,
All pity choked with custom of fell deeds;[94]
And Caesar's spirit, ranging[95] for revenge,
With Atè[96] by his side come hot from hell,
Shall in these confines[97] with a monarch's voice
Cry "Havoc,"[98] and let slip[99] the dogs of war,
That this foul deed shall smell above the earth
With carrion[100] men, groaning for burial.

[*Enter* OCTAVIUS' SERVANT.]

You serve Octavius Caesar, do you not?

SERVANT. I do, Mark Antony.

ANTONY. Caesar did write for him to come to Rome.

SERVANT. He did receive his letters and is coming,
And bid me say to you by word of mouth—
O Caesar! [*Seeing the body*]

Literary Analysis
Dramatic Speeches
What does Antony's soliloquy in lines 254–275 reveal to the audience that other characters do not know? (28)

91. tide of times course of all history.
92. cumber (kum´ bər) *v.* distress; burden.

Reading Skill
Analyze Imagery
Identify two ways in which lines 259–262 combine ideas of words and bodies. (29)

Vocabulary
prophesy (präf´ ə sī´) *v.* predict what will happen
strife (strīf) *n.* struggle; conflict

93. in use customary.
94. custom of fell deeds being used to cruel acts.
95. ranging *adj.* roaming like a wild beast in search of prey.
96. Atè (ā´ tē) Greek goddess personifying criminal folly or reckless ambition in people.
97. confines (kän´ fī nz) *n.* boundaries.
98. Havoc Latin for "no quarter," a signal for general slaughter.
99. let slip release from a leash.
100. carrion (kar´ ē ən) *adj.* dead and rotting.

Vocabulary Development

Terms of Measurement
In line 286, the servant reports that Octavius is camped 7 leagues from Rome. A *league* is an ancient unit of measure that has not always represented the same distance. Today, a league is usually understood to equal 3 miles (4.8 km). In Roman times, however, a league equaled 1,500 paces, or steps. A pace was 5 feet (1.5 m), making a Roman league approximately 7,500 feet—not quite a mile and a half. So, 7 leagues was about 10 miles.

30 

31 ▲ **Critical Viewing** Which scene in the play might this image depict? Explain. **[Connect]**

ANTONY. Thy heart is big;[101] get thee apart and weep.
Passion, I see, is catching, for mine eyes,
Seeing those beads of sorrow stand in thine,
Began to water. Is thy master coming?

SERVANT. He lies tonight within seven leagues[102] of Rome.

ANTONY. Post[103] back with speed, and tell him what hath
chanced.[104]
Here is a mourning Rome, a dangerous Rome,
No Rome of safety for Octavius yet.
Hie hence and tell him so. Yet stay awhile;
Thou shalt not back till I have borne this corse
Into the market place; there shall I try[105]
In my oration[106] how the people take
The cruel issue[107] of these bloody men;
According to the which, thou shalt **discourse**
To young Octavius of the state of things.
Lend me your hand. [*Exit*]

101. big *adj.* swollen with grief.

102. leagues (lēgz) *n.* units of measure, each equivalent in Roman times to about a mile and a half.

103. Post *v.* hasten.

104. hath chanced has happened.

105. try *v.* test.

106. oration (ō rā´ shən) *n.* formal public speech.

107. cruel issue outcome of the cruelty.

Vocabulary
discourse (dis´ kôrs´) *v.* speak on a topic formally and at length

32 **Reading Check**
What is Antony's real response to Caesar's death?

30 Humanities

***Still Photograph, from* Julius Caesar (1953)**

This still photograph from the film version of *Julius Caesar* offers an opportunity to study Roman jewelry. Jewelry was popular in ancient Rome, and the city became known for its goldsmiths. Notice the large ring on each actor's left hand. At first, only ambassadors, noblemen, and senators wore gold rings. Slowly, people in each strata of society began owning rings. Large gold rings became a way for Romans to show the grandness of imperial Rome. Necklaces, arm bands, and bracelets were also worn. Roman men sometimes wore a *lacerna*, or open cloak, which was fastened at the shoulder with a brooch, or pin. Use these questions for discussion:

1. Which of the two characters is wearing a toga? How do you know?
Answer: Brutus is wearing a toga. It is draped over his left shoulder and arm.
2. Compare and contrast Cassius' clothing with that of Brutus.
Answer: Both are wearing tunics, but Cassius is wearing a lacerna, fastened with a brooch, instead of a toga, like Brutus.

31 Critical Viewing

Answer: This photograph probably depicts a scene after Caesar's murder, because both Brutus and Cassius have blood on their clothing and are holding their daggers; their serious expressions suggest that it may show the scene in which Cassius addresses Brutus in an aside and they discuss allowing Antony to speak at Caesar's funeral.

32 Reading Check

Answer: Antony plans to turn the people of Rome against the conspirators.

PROFESSIONAL DEVELOPMENT

APPLY THE STRATEGY

After students read *Julius Caesar,* Act III, Scene i, have them create a two-column chart centered on the question, "Was Caesar killed out of a genuine concern for the state of Rome?" Instruct them to label one column "Yes" and the other column "No".

Divide the class in half. Have one side represent "yes"—Caesar's murderers genuinely believed Caesar would bring Rome to ruin. Have the other side represent "no"—Caesar's murderers were more concerned with their own ambitions. Tell each side to look in previously read scenes for textual evidence to support their argument. Then, have students read the remainder of the play, inserting additional evidence in their charts.

For more of this author's strategies, see the Professional Development Essay, pp. 790c–790d.

33 Literary Analysis

Dramatic Speeches

1. Direct students' attention to Brutus' speech in lines 12–34. Point out that for the first time in the play, Brutus speaks in prose. **Ask** students why Shakespeare makes this choice.
   Answer: Brutus' motive for murder is reason, not emotion. The choice of prose reflects this motivation. Brutus has always insisted that he is an honest man who has nothing to hide from the crowd. The prose reflects his desire to be straightforward. A speech in verse would be more emotional. Verse and figurative language would give the people the idea that he is trying to conceal something.
2. **Ask** students to respond to the Literary Analysis question: What is Brutus' purpose in delivering this monologue?
   Answer: His purpose is to persuade the crowd that there is a logical explanation for the murder.

34 Background

Rhetoric

The speeches given by Brutus (lines 12–34) and Antony (lines 74–108) are examples of rhetoric. Rhetoric is the art of public speaking.

The word *rhetoric* comes from ancient Greek. The Greek word *rhetor* means "orator or public speaker" and derives from the verb *eirein*, meaning "to say or speak." The Latin verb *orare*, meaning "to pray, argue, or speak," is related to the Greek *eirein*.

Artemidorus, who tried to warn Caesar of danger at the beginning of Act III, is described in the list of characters at the beginning of the play (p. 893) as a teacher of rhetoric. Aristotle and Hermagoras wrote treatises about rhetoric. The famous Roman orator Cicero also wrote about rhetoric.

Rhetoric was a necessary skill for Roman youths embarking on careers in law or politics. Orators learned to speak loudly enough to be heard at a distance and clearly enough to be easily understood. Style was an important aspect of rhetoric. Rhetorical devices in Brutus' and Antony's speeches include parallelism and repetition.

Scene ii. The Forum

[*Enter* BRUTUS *and goes into the pulpit, and* CASSIUS, *with the* PLEBEIANS.[1]]

PLEBEIANS. We will be satisfied![2] Let us be satisfied!

BRUTUS. Then follow me, and give me audience, friends.
Cassius, go you into the other street
And part the numbers.[3]
Those that will hear me speak, let 'em stay here;
Those that will follow Cassius, go with him;
And public reasons shall be renderèd
Of Caesar's death.

FIRST PLEBEIAN. I will hear Brutus speak.

SECOND PLEBEIAN. I will hear Cassius, and compare their reasons,
When severally[4] we hear them renderèd.

[*Exit* CASSIUS, *with some of the* PLEBEIANS.]

THIRD PLEBEIAN. The noble Brutus is ascended. Silence!

BRUTUS. Be patient till the last.
Romans, countrymen, and lovers,[5] hear me for my cause, and be silent, that you may hear. Believe me for mine honor, and have respect to mine honor, that you may believe. Censure[6] me in your wisdom, and awake your senses,[7] that you may the better judge. If there be any in this assembly, any dear friend of Caesar's, to him I say that Brutus' love to Caesar was no less than his. If then that friend demand why Brutus rose against Caesar, this is my answer: Not that I loved Caesar less, but that I loved Rome more. Had you rather Caesar were living, and die all slaves, than that Caesar were dead, to live all free men? As Caesar loved me, I weep for him; as he was fortunate, I rejoice at it; as he was valiant, I honor him; but, as he was ambitious, I slew him. There is tears, for his love; joy, for his fortune; honor, for his valor; and death, for his ambition. Who is here so base,[8] that would be a bondman?[9] If any, speak; for him have I offended. Who is here so rude,[10] that would not be a Roman? If any, speak; for him have I offended. Who is here so vile,[11] that will not love his country? If any, speak; for him have I offended. I pause for a reply.

ALL. None, Brutus, none!

Literary Analysis
Dramatic Speeches
What is Brutus' purpose in delivering this monologue? 33

1. **Plebeians** (ple bē ´ənz) *n.* commoners; members of the lower class.
2. **be satisfied** get an explanation.
3. **part the numbers** divide the crowd.
4. **severally** (sev´ ər əl ē) *adv.* separately.
5. **lovers** *n.* dear friends.
6. **Censure** (sen´ shər) *v.* judge.
7. **senses** *n.* powers of reason.
8. **base** *adj.* low.
9. **bondman** *n.* slave.
10. **rude** *adj.* uncivilized.
11. **vile** (vil) *adj.* mean; lowborn; of low character.

Think Aloud

Dramatic Speeches

Help students see how language and sentence structure is used in dramatic speeches. Say:

> In his monologue, Brutus uses many skillful tricks to excite and involve his audience. He asks rhetorical questions, or questions not meant to be answered. For example, he asks: "Had you rather Caesar were living, and die all slaves, than that Caesar were dead, to live all free men?" In lines 29 through 33, he also asks questions. In this way, Brutus draws the listeners in and makes them part of a conversation.
>
> Brutus also uses parallel structure to build tension in his listeners. This means that he repeats the same phrases, changing a few words, as in lines 24 through 27. It's easy for me to imagine an actor saying these lines on stage, building to a crescendo as he says, "But, as he was ambitious, I slew him." These rhetorical tricks help Brutus engage his audience—and they help the actor playing Brutus engage the theater audience, too.

34 **BRUTUS.** Then none have I offended. I have done no more to Caesar than you shall do to Brutus. The question of his death is enrolled in the Capitol;[12] his glory not extenuated,[13] wherein he was worthy, nor his offenses enforced,[14] for which he suffered death.

[*Enter* MARK ANTONY, *with* CAESAR'*s body.*]

35 Here comes his body, mourned by Mark Antony, who, though he had no hand in his death, shall receive the benefit of his dying, a place in the commonwealth, as which of you shall not? With this I depart, that, as I slew my best lover for the good of Rome, I have the same dagger for myself, when it shall please my country to need my death.

ALL. Live, Brutus! Live, live!

FIRST PLEBEIAN. Bring him with triumph home unto his house.

SECOND PLEBEIAN. Give him a statue with his ancestors.

THIRD PLEBEIAN. Let him be Caesar.

FOURTH PLEBEIAN. Caesar's better parts[15]
Shall be crowned in Brutus.

36 **FIRST PLEBEIAN.** We'll bring him to his house with shouts and clamors.

BRUTUS. My countrymen—

SECOND PLEBEIAN. Peace! Silence! Brutus speaks.

FIRST PLEBEIAN. Peace, ho!

BRUTUS. Good countrymen, let me depart alone,
And, for my sake, stay here with Antony.
Do grace to Caesar's corpse, and grace his speech
Tending to Caesar's glories,[16] which Mark Antony
By our permission, is allowed to make.
I do entreat you, not a man depart,
Save I alone, till Antony have spoke. [*Exit*]

FIRST PLEBEIAN. Stay, ho! And let us hear Mark Antony.

THIRD PLEBEIAN. Let him go up into the public chair;
We'll hear him. Noble Antony, go up.

ANTONY. For Brutus' sake, I am beholding[17] to you.

FOURTH PLEBEIAN. What does he say of Brutus?

12. The question . . . in the Capitol The issues that led to his death are on record in the Capitol.

13. extenuated (ek sten´ yo͞o āt´ id) *adj.* undervalued; made less of.

14. enforced (en fôrs'd´) *adj.* exaggerated.

Literary Analysis
Dramatic Speeches
In this monologue, how does Brutus emphasize his sincerity?

15. parts *n.* qualities.

16. Do grace . . . glories Show respect for Caesar's body and for the speech telling of Caesar's achievements.

17. beholding *adj.* indebted.

37 **Reading Check**
What reason for killing Caesar does Brutus offer to the plebeians?

35 Literary Analysis

Dramatic Speeches

1. Have a volunteer to read Brutus' final lines (41–47). Then, **ask** students to answer the Literary Analysis question: In this monologue, how does Brutus emphasize his sincerity?
   Answer: He says he will kill himself if necessary for his country.
2. Prompt students to **speculate** about why Brutus leaves before Antony's speech.
   Answer: He may leave in fairness to Antony, since the crowd is still distracted by Brutus' presence. He clearly has no sense that Antony might be a threat, since he encourages everyone to remain for Antony's speech.

36 Critical Thinking

Analyze

1. **Ask** students how the crowd reacts to Brutus' speech.
   Answer: The plebeians seem to accept his explanation and absolve him of any blame.
2. Remind students that orators use a variety of rhetorical devices and other techniques to persuade, or win over, their audience. Discuss rhetorical devices such as parallelism, repetition, historical allusions, appeals to authority, rhetorical questions, anecdotes, examples, similes, and metaphors.
3. **Ask** students to analyze how Brutus is able to win the people's good opinion and support.
   Answer: Brutus uses parallelism and repetition to impress the plebeians and help them remember what he says. He also suggests that the murder will benefit the plebeians, so they support it.

37 Reading Check

Answer: Caesar was ambitious.

Differentiated Instruction for Universal Access

Strategy for Special Needs Students
Help students identify examples of the different types of dramatic speeches as they read Act III. Suggest that students use self-sticking notes to call out the speeches. Tell students to write the speaker and type of speech on each self-sticking note and attach it to the page in the margin next to the speech.

Strategy for Less Proficient Readers
To help students distinguish among the different types of dramatic speeches, have them make a three-column chart with the column heads *Aside, Soliloquy,* and *Monologue.* Encourage students to look for examples of each type of speech in this act. Students may complete the chart by identifying the scene and line numbers of each dramatic speech and naming the speaker.

38 Humanities

***Still Photograph, from* Julius Caesar (1953)**

This still from the film *Julius Caesar* shows Antony, played by Marlon Brando, giving his funeral speech for Caesar in the Forum. Antony is standing on the Rostra, or speaker's platform. Although redesigned and even relocated over the years, the Rostra was a fixture of the Forum from very early times. Use this question for discussion:

- In what ways does the Rostra help a speaker?
  Answer: It allows the speaker to be clearly seen and easily heard.

38

Vocabulary Development

Legal Language

Point out that Mark Antony uses the terms *testament* and *will* in referring to the document that expresses Caesar's final wishes.

A *will* is the legal declaration of what a person wants done after his or her death. The word is derived from the Old English *willen* and clearly relies on its ordinary meaning of "intention" or "purpose."

Testament is derived from *testis*, the Latin word for "witness" (and the root of another family of legal words, including *testify* and *testimony*). A *testament* can be said to be the legal "witness" of the wishes of a deceased person.

In law, a *will* and a *testament* are the same thing, a fact that has not prevented their redundant pairing in the phrase "last will and testament."

Point out that legal language as expressed in laws, contracts, warranties, and wills is filled with such redundant pairings of words ("cease and desist," for example).

THIRD PLEBEIAN. He says, for Brutus' sake,
He finds himself beholding to us all.

FOURTH PLEBEIAN. 'Twere best he speak no harm of Brutus here!

FIRST PLEBEIAN. This Caesar was a tyrant.

THIRD PLEBEIAN. Nay, that's certain.
We are blest that Rome is rid of him.

SECOND PLEBEIAN. Peace! Let us hear what Antony can say.

ANTONY. You gentle Romans—

ALL. Peace, ho! Let us hear him.

ANTONY. Friends, Romans, countrymen, lend me your ears;
I come to bury Caesar, not to praise him.
The evil that men do lives after them,
The good is oft interrèd with their bones;
So let it be with Caesar. The noble Brutus
Hath told you Caesar was ambitious.
If it were so, it was a grievous fault,
And grievously hath Caesar answered[18] it.
Here, under leave of Brutus and the rest
(For Brutus is an honorable man,
So are they all, all honorable men),
Come I to speak in Caesar's funeral.
40 He was my friend, faithful and just to me;
But Brutus says he was ambitious,
And Brutus is an honorable man.
He hath brought many captives home to Rome,
Whose ransoms did the general coffers[19] fill;
Did this in Caesar seem ambitious?
When that the poor have cried, Caesar hath wept;
Ambition should be made of sterner stuff.
Yet Brutus says he was ambitious;
And Brutus is an honorable man.
41 You all did see that on the Lupercal
I thrice presented him a kingly crown,
Which he did thrice refuse. Was this ambition?
Yet Brutus says he was ambitious;
And sure he is an honorable man.
I speak not to disprove what Brutus spoke,
But here I am to speak what I do know.
You all did love him once, not without cause;
What cause withholds you then to mourn for him?

39 ◀ **Critical Viewing**
What does this film still of Antony addressing the plebeians suggest about the power of his words? Explain. **[Interpret]**

Literary Analysis
Dramatic Speeches
How is Antony's monologue both similar to and different from Brutus' in lines 12–34?

Vocabulary
interred (in turd′) *v.* buried (said of a dead body)

18. **answered** *v.* paid the penalty for.

19. **general coffers** public treasury.

Literary Analysis
Dramatic Speeches
Contrast Antony's stated purpose in this monologue with the probable effect of lines 92–100 on his audience.

42 **Reading Check**
How does Antony describe Brutus' character?

39 Critical Viewing

Answer: The picture suggests that Antony's words are having an extremely powerful effect on the crowd. The attentive posture of people in the crowd suggests that they are entranced by what he is saying and that what he is saying is persuasive.

40 Literary Analysis

Dramatic Speeches

1. Remind students that Antony's and Brutus' purposes in addressing the people are different.
2. **Ask** students to answer the Literary Analysis question: How is Antony's monologue both similar to and different from Brutus' in lines 12–34?
   Answer: Both Antony and Brutus address the crowd in the same way as fellow Romans, countrymen, and friends, and both ask to be heard. Antony, however, uses verse, making his speech more emotional and affecting, whereas Brutus uses prose.

41 Literary Analysis

Dramatic Speeches

1. Have students focus on Antony's use of repetition and parallelism in this speech. **Ask:** What idea does Antony repeat in various forms?
   Answer: Brutus says Caesar was ambitious, and Brutus is an honorable man.
2. **Ask:** When does Antony repeat this idea?
   Answer: He repeats it after he praises Caesar for a good deed.
3. **Ask** students to respond to the Literary Analysis item: Contrast Antony's stated purpose in this monologue with the probable effect of lines 92–100 on his audience.
   Answer: Antony says he has come to bury Caesar, not to praise him, yet he goes on to describe various praiseworthy deeds of Caesar. By the time the audience hears lines 99–100, they will no longer agree that Caesar was ambitious and deserved to be killed.

42 Reading Check

Answer: Antony describes Brutus as "honorable," but his inclusion of examples that belie Brutus' words makes it clear that he is being ironic.

Differentiated Instruction for Universal Access

Enrichment for Gifted and Talented Students
Tell students that despite his saying that he will not praise Caesar, Antony's monologue on this page is a *eulogy*, an oral memorial that praises someone who has died. Challenge them to look online and to read and analyze a more modern eulogy; for example, Robert F. Kennedy's eulogy for Martin Luther King, Jr., or Edward Kennedy's eulogy for Robert F. Kennedy.

Strategy for Less Proficient Readers
Provide each student with a copy of Antony's monologue. Have students find and highlight each point where he repeats "Brutus is an honorable man." Discuss the lines that precede each of those lines to answer this question: Why does Antony think Brutus is wrong about Caesar's ambition?

43 Reading Skill
Analyze Imagery

1. Point out that Antony ends his speech on an emotional note by referring to his and the people's love for Caesar and by asking what keeps the people from mourning Caesar.
2. Tell students to use the **Reading Skill Graphic Organizer B** (p. 175 in ***Graphic Organizer Transparencies***) to analyze the references to words and the body in the last lines of the speech. Show students the completed organizer **Reading Skill Graphic Organizer A** (p. 174 in ***Graphic Organizer Transparencies***) and have them compare it to their own work.
3. Then, **ask** students the Reading Skill question: In lines 106–108, which images link Antony's heart and inability to continue speaking?
   Answer: In order to explain to the crowd that he is too overcome with grief to speak further, Antony says that his heart is in the coffin with Caesar.

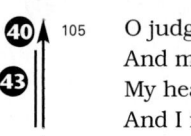

Reading Skill
Analyze Imagery In lines 106–108, which images link Antony's heart and inability to continue speaking? 40 43

O judgment, thou art fled to brutish beasts,
And men have lost their reason! Bear with me;
My heart is in the coffin there with Caesar,
And I must pause till it come back to me.

FIRST PLEBEIAN. Methinks there is much reason in his sayings.

SECOND PLEBEIAN. If thou consider rightly of the matter,
Caesar has had great wrong.

THIRD PLEBEIAN. Has he, masters?
I fear there will a worse come in his place.

FOURTH PLEBEIAN. Marked ye his words? He would not take the crown,
Therefore 'tis certain he was not ambitious.

FIRST PLEBEIAN. If it be found so, some will dear abide it.[20]

SECOND PLEBEIAN. Poor soul, his eyes are red as fire with weeping.

THIRD PLEBEIAN. There's not a nobler man in Rome than Antony.

FOURTH PLEBEIAN. Now mark him, he begins again to speak.

ANTONY. But yesterday the word of Caesar might
Have stood against the world; now lies he there,
And none so poor to[21] do him reverence.
O masters! If I were disposed to stir
Your hearts and minds to mutiny and rage,
I should do Brutus wrong and Cassius wrong,
Who, you all know, are honorable men.
I will not do them wrong; I rather choose
To wrong the dead, to wrong myself and you,
Than I will wrong such honorable men.
But here's a parchment with the seal of Caesar;
I found it in his closet; 'tis his will.
Let but the commons[22] hear this testament,
Which, pardon me, I do not mean to read,
And they would go and kiss dead Caesar's wounds,
And dip their napkins[23] in his sacred blood;
Yea, beg a hair of him for memory,
And dying, mention it within their wills,
Bequeathing it as a rich legacy
Unto their issue.[24]

FOURTH PLEBEIAN. We'll hear the will; read it, Mark Antony.

ALL. The will, the will! We will hear Caesar's will!

20. **dear abide it** pay dearly for it.
21. **so poor to** low enough in rank to.
22. **commons** *n.* plebeians; commoners.
23. **napkins** *n.* handkerchiefs.
24. **issue** *n.* children; offspring.

Vocabulary Development

Word Origins

Point out the word *leave* in line 161. Explain to students that this is not the most common use of the word today. Tell them that you are going to think aloud as you use a dictionary to find the exact definition of the word *leave*.

There are three separate entries for the word *leave* in the dictionary. Now I will note the part of speech listed for each entry and then read the first definition given for each entry. The first entry is for *leave* as a verb meaning "bequeath." The second entry is for *leave* as a noun meaning "permission to do something." The third entry is for *leave* again as a verb, "to leaf."

Antony asks if the plebeians will "give him leave." Most likely, since the word *leave* is the object of *give*, the entry in which *leave* is a noun is the correct one. I will substitute the second entry's definition: "And will you give me permission to do something?" This makes sense. Antony is asking for permission to descend.

ANTONY. Have patience, gentle friends, I must not read it.
It is not meet[25] you know how Caesar loved you.
You are not wood, you are not stones, but men;
And being men, hearing the will of Caesar,
(44) It will inflame you, it will make you mad.
'Tis good you know not that you are his heirs;
For if you should, O, what would come of it?

FOURTH PLEBEIAN. Read the will! We'll hear it, Antony!
You shall read us the will, Caesar's will!

ANTONY. Will you be patient? Will you stay awhile?
I have o'ershot myself[26] to tell you of it.
I fear I wrong the honorable men
Whose daggers have stabbed Caesar; I do fear it.

FOURTH PLEBEIAN. They were traitors. Honorable men!

ALL. The will! The testament!

SECOND PLEBEIAN. They were villains, murderers! The will!
Read the will!

ANTONY. You will compel me then to read the will?
(45) Then make a ring about the corpse of Caesar,
And let me show you him that made the will.
Shall I descend? And will you give me leave?

ALL. Come down.

SECOND PLEBEIAN. Descend. [ANTONY *comes down.*]

THIRD PLEBEIAN. You shall have leave.

FOURTH PLEBEIAN. A ring! Stand round.

FIRST PLEBEIAN. Stand from the hearse,[27] stand from the body!

SECOND PLEBEIAN. Room for Antony, most noble Antony!

ANTONY. Nay, press not so upon me; stand far[28] off.

ALL. Stand back! Room! Bear back.

ANTONY. If you have tears, prepare to shed them now.
You all do know this mantle;[29] I remember
The first time ever Caesar put it on:
'Twas on a summer's evening, in his tent,
That day he overcame the Nervii.[30]
Look, in this place ran Cassius' dagger through;
See what a rent[31] the envious[32] Casca made;
Through this the well-belovèd Brutus stabbed,
And as he plucked his cursèd steel away,

25. **meet** *adj.* fitting; suitable.

26. **o'ershot myself** gone further than I meant to.

Reading Skill
Analyze Imagery
In what way does the action on stage connect Caesar's body and the words in his will?

27. **hearse** (hurs) *n.* coffin.
28. **far** *adv.* farther.
29. **mantle** (man′ təl) *n.* cloak; toga.
30. **Nervii** (nur′ vē ī) *n.* warlike European tribe conquered by Caesar in 57 B.C.
31. **rent** *n.* hole; tear; rip.
32. **envious** (en′ vē əs) *adj.* spiteful.

(46) **Reading Check**
What effect does Antony's speech have on the crowd?

(44) Literary Analysis
Dramatic Speeches

1. **Ask** students which words and ideas in lines 143–147 of his monologue ensure Antony's audience's interest and attention.
   Answer: Antony reminds his audience that they are not wood or stone—that is, they are not unfeeling and incapable of speech or action; he tells them that the will shall inflame them, or make them mad enough to take action; he calls them the heirs of Caesar.
2. **Ask** students what the crowd's reaction suggests about Antony's decision to withhold the will temporarily.
   Answer: Their insistence on hearing the will suggests that he makes the right decision. His refusal to read the will whets their appetite to hear the will's contents.

(45) Reading Skill
Analyze Imagery

1. Ask a volunteer to read aloud lines 158–161. Then, **ask** students the Reading Skill question: In what way does the action on stage connect Caesar's body and the words in his will?
   Answer: The crowd follows Antony's direction to make a ring around Caesar's body to hear his will; in this way, the words are physically close to the body of the man who wrote them.
2. **Ask** students what Antony achieves by drawing the crowd around the corpse to hear the will.
   Answer: He promotes their sympathy for Caesar by allowing them to approach his corpse, and he strengthens his own bond with the crowd by joining them to read the will.

(46) Reading Check

Answer: They decide that Caesar may have been wrongly murdered.

Differentiated Instruction for Universal Access

Enrichment for Advanced Readers

Have students note that the plebeians of the crowd have no individual identity and there is not much variation among their reactions. Shakespeare makes them a collective character. Direct students to discuss these questions: Are real crowds usually as easily swayed as this crowd? Why does Shakespeare present the crowd of plebeians as he does? What does the crowd contribute to the play? Invite students to research crowd psychology, especially mob mentality. Tell students to rewrite the scene with plebeians who are more difficult to persuade.

47 Critical Viewing

Answer: Antony is no longer addressing the crowd from a platform but has descended to be among them. Once below, he stretches his arm out to keep the crowd back. Caesar's body lies at his feet.

48 Background

The Funeral of Julius Caesar

The Roman writer Suetonius' *Life of Julius Caesar* is a valuable source of information about Caesar's life and death. When the funeral of Caesar was announced, a shrine modeled after a temple of Venus was set up on the Rostra. Inside it was an ivory couch with purple and gold coverlets. The mantle Caesar wore when he was murdered was hung on a pillar at the head of the couch. Suetonius reported that instead of a eulogy, Antony had a herald read both the decree in which the Senate had voted to give Caesar both divine and human honors and the oath the senators had taken to protect Caesar's safety. Then, various officials carried Caesar's funeral bier from the Rostra down into the Forum. A funeral pyre had been set up nearby in the Campus Martius, and there was some discussion also that Caesar's body might be burned in the Temple of Jupiter on the Capitoline or elsewhere. However, two armed men appeared suddenly and set fire to it there in the Forum, and the crowd created a makeshift pyre on the spot by piling up branches, benches, and whatever they could offer, including their robes, weapons, and jewelry.

47 ▲ **Critical Viewing** Compare this image with the one on page 954. Which details here suggest Antony's growing bond with his audience? **[Contrast]**

Mark how the blood of Caesar followed it, 48
As[33] rushing out of doors, to be resolved[34]
If Brutus so unkindly[35] knocked, or no;
For Brutus, as you know, was Caesar's angel.
Judge, O you gods, how dearly Caesar loved him!
This was the most unkindest cut of all;
For when the noble Caesar saw him stab,
Ingratitude, more strong than traitors' arms,
Quite vanquished him. Then burst his mighty heart;
And, in his mantle muffling up his face,
Even at the base of Pompey's statue
(Which all the while ran blood) great Caesar fell.
O, what a fall was there, my countrymen!
Then I, and you, and all of us fell down,
Whilst bloody treason flourished[36] over us.
O, now you weep, and I perceive you feel
The dint[37] of pity; these are gracious drops.
Kind souls, what[38] weep you when you but behold
Our Caesar's vesture[39] wounded? Look you here,
Here is himself, marred as you see with[40] traitors.

FIRST PLEBEIAN. O piteous spectacle!

SECOND PLEBEIAN. O noble Caesar!

33. As *conj.* as if.
34. to be resolved to learn for certain.
35. unkindly *adj.* cruelly; also, unnaturally.
36. flourished (flʉr´ ish 'd) *v.* swaggered; waved a sword in triumph.
37. dint *n.* stroke; blow.
38. what *adv.* why.
39. vesture (ves´ chər) *n.* clothing.
40. with *prep.* by.

Think Aloud

Analyze Imagery

Help students analyze the imagery Antony uses in his monologue. Say to students:

> Antony is a strong speaker who uses imagery to excite his audience. Antony refers to Caesar's fall at the base of Pompey's statue. He gives enough detail that his audience can picture the scene. Then, he says, "O, what a fall was there, my countrymen!/Then I, and you, and all of us fell down." I know that he does not mean this literally; only Caesar *literally* fell down. Instead, Antony means to give his audience the feeling that all of them, and Rome itself, have been dragged down by Caesar's death. This image of all of them falling is stronger than if he had simply said, "This death has harmed us all." The strength of the image stimulates the plebeians to seek revenge.

THIRD PLEBEIAN. O woeful day!

FOURTH PLEBEIAN. O traitors, villains!

FIRST PLEBEIAN. O most bloody sight!

SECOND PLEBEIAN. We will be revenged.

ALL. Revenge! About![41] Seek! Burn! Fire! Kill! Slay!
Let not a traitor live!

ANTONY. Stay, countrymen.

FIRST PLEBEIAN. Peace there! Hear the noble Antony.

SECOND PLEBEIAN. We'll hear him, we'll follow him, we'll die
with him!

ANTONY. Good friends, sweet friends, let me not stir you up
To such a sudden flood of mutiny.
They that have done this deed are honorable.
What private griefs[42] they have, alas, I know not,
That made them do it. They are wise and honorable,
And will, no doubt, with reasons answer you.
I come not, friends, to steal away your hearts;
I am no orator, as Brutus is;
But (as you know me all) a plain blunt man
That love my friend, and that they know full well
That gave me public leave to speak[43] of him.
For I have neither writ, nor words, nor worth,
Action, or utterance,[44] nor the power of speech
49 To stir men's blood; I only speak right on.[45]
I tell you that which you yourselves do know,
Show you sweet Caesar's wounds, poor poor dumb mouths,
And bid them speak for me. But were I Brutus,
And Brutus Antony, there were an Antony
Would ruffle up your spirits, and put a tongue
In every wound of Caesar's that should move
The stones of Rome to rise and mutiny.

ALL. We'll mutiny.

FIRST PLEBEIAN. We'll burn the house of Brutus.

THIRD PLEBEIAN. Away, then! Come, seek the conspirators.

ANTONY. Yet hear me, countrymen. Yet hear me speak.

ALL. Peace, ho! Hear Antony, most noble Antony!

ANTONY. Why, friends, you go to do you know not what:
Wherein hath Caesar thus deserved your loves?

41. About let's go.

42. private griefs personal grievances.

43. public leave to speak permission to speak in public.

44. neither writ . . . utterance (ut′ ər əns) neither a written speech, nor fluency, nor reputation, nor gestures, nor style of speaking.

45. right on directly.

Reading Skill
Analyze Imagery
Which images in Antony's speech combine ideas of words, the body, and violence?

50 **Reading Check**
How does the crowd feel toward the conspirators after Antony's speech?

49 Reading Skill

Analyze Imagery

1. Have students recall the style and content of Brutus' speech and of Antony's various speeches to the crowd to this point. Then **ask:** What is ironic about the way Antony describes his own speech?
   Answer: Antony speaks to the crowd in high-flown, emotionally packed blank verse and has played on their feelings. Brutus spoke calmly in prose and appealed to the crowd's logic and reason. Antony pretends here that the opposite is true: that he is the "plain blunt man" and Brutus the charismatic speaker.
2. **Ask** students to respond to the Reading Skill question.
   Answer: Antony describes Caesar's wounds as having mouths that would speak; the wounds would probably speak of a violent way to mutiny against the conspirators.

Monitor Progress Check students' understanding of the imagery and ideas in the conclusion of the speech by having them paraphrase lines 227–231.
Answer: Antony says: If I were the orator that Brutus is, I would have the rhetorical ability to make the corpse of Caesar seem to speak to you and move even the most uninspired of you to rise up and revolt.

Reteach If students have trouble paraphrasing lines, present individual images from Antony's speech and have students explain them in their own words.

- "a sudden flood of mutiny"
  Possible response: A sudden flood is quick and violent. That is the kind of mutiny Antony hopes to achieve.
- "steal away your hearts"
  Possible response: Antony means that he will win the listeners to his side by stealthy means, as he in fact does.

50 Reading Check

Answer: They feel that the conspirators are traitors who should be killed.

Fluency

Tell students that the poetic structure of Shakespeare's lines helps an actor or reader know where to place emphasis. Readers must not drop their voices at the end of lines unless a period indicates that the end of the line is the end of a thought. In other cases, the thought continues from line to line, just as it does in poetry.

Duplicate Antony's speech on this page, and allow students to read it aloud. As they read, mark a copy to indicate any difficulties with long words or with sentence structure. If necessary, read the speech aloud in sections and have the students repeat it after you. Sections that contain complete thoughts might include lines 211–216, lines 217–221, lines 222–224, and lines 225–231.

51 Background

Caesar's Will

According to Suetonius, Caesar's will was actually unsealed and read at Antony's house before the funeral. From the time of his first consulship to the days of the civil wars, Caesar had specified Pompey as his heir. In his last will, however, he named several different heirs, including Gaius Octavius, whom he also adopted into his family, and who would later become the emperor Augustus. Caesar also listed several of his assassins as beneficiaries. To the Roman people, Caesar left his gardens by the Tiber River and 300 sesterces (referenced in the play as 75 drachmas) each.

52 Reading Skill

Analyze Imagery

1. Have students use the **Reading Skill Graphic Organizer B** (p. 175 in ***Graphic Organizer Transparencies***) to identify and analyze the combination of words (what Caesar's will says and what Antony says about the will and Caesar) and physical body (Caesar's corpse) in lines 236–260.
2. **Ask** students to respond to the Reading Skill question: Moved by news of Caesar's words, what action does the crowd take involving Caesar's body? **Answer:** They take the body to be burned.

---

46. several *adj.* individual.
47. royal *adj.* showing noble generosity.
48. walks . . . orchards parks, his private stands of trees, and newly planted gardens.
49. common pleasures public places of recreation.

Reading Skill
Analyze Imagery
Moved by news of Caesar's words, what action does the crowd take involving Caesar's body?

50. brands *n.* torches.
51. forms, windows benches and shutters.
52. work *v.* spread and expand, as yeast does; follow through to a conclusion.

53. thither *adv.* there.
54. upon a wish as I wished.
55. Are rid have ridden.

Alas, you know not; I must tell you then:
You have forgot the will I told you of.

ALL. Most true, the will! Let's stay and hear the will.

ANTONY. Here is the will, and under Caesar's seal.
To every Roman citizen he gives,
To every several[46] man, seventy-five drachmas.

SECOND PLEBEIAN. Most noble Caesar! We'll revenge his death!

THIRD PLEBEIAN. O royal[47] Caesar!

ANTONY. Hear me with patience.

ALL. Peace, ho!

ANTONY. Moreover, he hath left you all his walks,
His private arbors, and new-planted orchards,[48]
On this side Tiber; he hath left them you,
And to your heirs forever: common pleasures,[49]
To walk abroad and recreate yourselves.
Here was a Caesar! When comes such another?

FIRST PLEBEIAN. Never, never! Come, away, away!
We'll burn his body in the holy place,
And with the brands[50] fire the traitors' houses.
Take up the body.

SECOND PLEBEIAN. Go fetch fire.

THIRD PLEBEIAN. Pluck down benches.

FOURTH PLEBEIAN. Pluck down forms, windows,[51] anything!

[*Exit* PLEBEIANS *with the body.*]

ANTONY. Now let it work:[52] Mischief, thou art afoot,
Take thou what course thou wilt.

[*Enter* SERVANT.]

How now, fellow?

SERVANT. Sir, Octavius is already come to Rome.

ANTONY. Where is he?

SERVANT. He and Lepidus are at Caesar's house.

ANTONY. And thither[53] will I straight to visit him;
He comes upon a wish.[54] Fortune is merry,
And in this mood will give us anything.

SERVANT. I heard him say, Brutus and Cassius
Are rid[55] like madmen through the gates of Rome.

Vocabulary Development

Vocabulary Knowledge Rating

When students have completed reading and discussing *The Tragedy of Julius Caesar:* Act III, have them take out their **Vocabulary Knowledge Rating Chart**. Read the words aloud once more, and have students rate their knowledge of the words again in the After Reading column. Clarify any words that are still problematic. Have students write their own definition or example in the appropriate column. Then, have students complete the Vocabulary Practice activities at the end of the selection. Encourage students to use the words in further discussion and written work about the play. Remind them that they will be accountable for these words on the **Selection Test, Unit 5 Resources**, pp. 139–141 or 142–144.

53 **ANTONY.** Belike[56] they had some notice of the people,[57]
How I had moved them. Bring me to Octavius. [*Exit*]

Scene iii. A street.

[*Enter* CINNA THE POET, *and after him the* PLEBEIANS.]

54 **CINNA.** I dreamt tonight[1] that I did feast with Caesar,
And things unluckily charge my fantasy.[2]
I have no will to wander forth of doors,[3]
Yet something leads me forth.

FIRST PLEBEIAN. What is your name?

SECOND PLEBEIAN. Whither are you going?

THIRD PLEBEIAN. Where do you dwell?

FOURTH PLEBEIAN. Are you a married man or a bachelor?

SECOND PLEBEIAN. Answer every man directly.[4]

FIRST PLEBEIAN. Ay, and briefly.

FOURTH PLEBEIAN. Ay, and wisely.

THIRD PLEBEIAN. Ay, and truly, you were best.

CINNA. What is my name? Whither am I going? Where do I dwell? Am I a married man or a bachelor? Then, to answer every man directly and briefly, wisely and truly: wisely I say, I am a bachelor.

SECOND PLEBEIAN. That's as much as to say, they are fools that marry; you'll bear me a bang[5] for that, I fear. Proceed directly.

56. Belike *adv.* probably.
57. notice of the people word about the mood of the people.

Literary Analysis
Dramatic Speeches
To whom is Cinna's speech addressed?

1. tonight *adv.* last night.
2. things . . . fantasy the events that have happened give an unlucky meaning to my dream.
3. forth of doors outdoors.
4. directly *adv.* in a straightforward manner.
5. bear me a bang get a blow from me.

55 **Reading Check**
What has Caesar left the citizens of Rome in his will?

Extispicium relief (inspection of entrails) from the Forum of Trajan, Rome. Louvre, Paris, France.

53 Background

Octavius

Gaius Octavius, with whom Antony hopes to join forces, was born in 63 B.C. to Caesar's niece. Julius Caesar took Octavius under his wing after his father died in 59. He became pontifex and accompanied Caesar in his triumph in 46 B.C. Octavius was away from Rome with some friends when Caesar was assassinated. Caesar's will revealed that he was Caesar's main heir and had been adopted as Caesar's son.

In 27 B.C., after alliance and conflict with the leading men of Rome, including Antony, Octavius took the name Augustus and became the first emperor of Rome. Rome was then no longer a republic but a monarchy, as Brutus, Cassius, and the other conspirators had feared. Yet the reign of Augustus marked the beginning of the Pax Romana, a time of peace and prosperity at home and abroad, during which the arts flourished, commerce boomed, and the standard of living rose.

54 Literary Analysis

Dramatic Speeches

1. Draw students' attention to the stage direction. Point out that Cinna enters ahead of the plebeians, so his speech in lines 1–4 might be considered an aside.
2. **Ask** students to answer the Literary Analysis question: To whom is Cinna's speech addressed?
   Answer: Cinna is speaking to the audience.
3. **Ask** students to predict what is going to happen to Cinna and to support their prediction with details from Cinna's speech.
   Answer: Cinna is going to be killed by the angry crowd. He says that he dreamt that he dined with Caesar, who is dead. He also says that something strange leads him to go out in spite of his own feeling that he should have stayed in.

55 Reading Check

Answer: He leaves the citizens of Rome 75 drachmas each and his orchards, gardens, and walks as parks and common areas for their recreation.

Concept Connector

Activating Prior Knowledge

Have students return to their **Anticipation Guides** and respond to the statements again in the After Reading column. They may do this individually or in their original pairs or groups. Then, lead a class discussion, probing for what students have learned that confirms or invalidates each statement. Encourage students to cite specific details, quotations, or other evidence from the text to support their responses to each statement.

Reading Skill Graphic Organizer

Ask students to review the graphic organizers they completed to analyze imagery in Act III. Show them **Reading Skill Graphic Organizer A** (*Graphic Organizer Transparencies*, p. 174) as an example. Then, have students use the graphic organizers they completed to discuss the images used in Act III and their effect.

56 Reading Skill

Analyze Imagery

1. **Ask** students to answer the Reading Skill question: How does a confusion about Cinna's name place his body in danger?
   Answer: This Cinna is a poet, but because he has the same name as one of the conspirators, he is attacked by the crowd.
2. **Ask** students to identify the lines in this scene in which Shakespeare couples a reference to words with an image of a person's physical body.
   Answer: He makes this connection in lines 33–34, where one of the plebeians says that if they could take the name Cinna out of the man's heart, they could let him go unharmed.

ASSESS

Answers

Critical Thinking

1. Some students might applaud, because men who commit murder are not honorable.
2. (a) He says, "And you, too, Brutus?" (b) Caesar had thought that Brutus was his friend and would never betray him.
3. (a) Antony responds to the conspirators by saying that they are honorable men. He then turns on them, appealing to the crowd's emotions by telling them how much Caesar loved the people of Rome and how he had planned to share his wealth with them. (b) His motives are to convince the people of Rome to unite against the conspirators and avenge the unjust death of Caesar.
4. **Possible response:** Yes, because he ignores warnings.

To what extent does experience determine what we perceive?

Possible response: (a) Brutus explains that he sacrificed Caesar's life for the well-being of his country. His love of Rome outweighed his love of his friend. (b) Antony appeals to the crowd's emotions. He speaks dramatically and expresses his feelings of loss, creating pity in his listeners. He describes Caesar as honorable and provides evidence of his good character.

CINNA. Directly, I am going to Caesar's funeral.

FIRST PLEBEIAN. As a friend or an enemy?

CINNA. As a friend.

SECOND PLEBEIAN. That matter is answered directly.

FOURTH PLEBEIAN. For your dwelling, briefly.

CINNA. Briefly, I dwell by the Capitol.

THIRD PLEBEIAN. Your name, sir, truly.

CINNA. Truly, my name is Cinna.

FIRST PLEBEIAN. Tear him to pieces! He's a conspirator.

CINNA. I am Cinna the poet! I am Cinna the poet!

FOURTH PLEBEIAN. Tear him for his bad verses! Tear him for his bad verses!

CINNA. I am not Cinna the conspirator.

FOURTH PLEBEIAN. It is no matter, his name's Cinna; pluck but his name out of his heart, and turn him going.[6]

THIRD PLEBEIAN. Tear him, tear him! [*They attack him.*]
Come, brands, ho! Firebrands![7] To Brutus', to Cassius'!
Burn all! Some to Decius' house, and some to
Casca's; some to Ligarius'! Away, go!

[*Exit all the* PLEBEIANS *with* CINNA.]

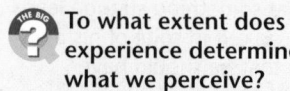

Reading Skill 56
Analyze Imagery
How does a confusion about Cinna's name place his body in danger?

6. **turn him going** send him on his way.
7. **Firebrands** *n.* burning pieces of wood; also, people who stir up others to revolt.

Critical Thinking

1. **Respond:** As a Roman, would you have applauded Antony's speech? Explain.
2. **(a)** What does Caesar say when he sees Brutus among the assassins? **(b) Infer:** What feelings do these words convey?
3. **(a)** How does Antony respond to the conspirators after the assassination? **(b) Analyze:** What are the motives for his actions?
4. **Make a Judgment:** Is Caesar responsible for his death? Explain.

To what extent does experience determine what we perceive? The crowd's perception of Caesar's death changes based on the different accounts given.
(a) Summarize: Explain how Brutus justifies the assassination in his speech to the crowd. **(b) Analyze:** Explain how Antony turns the crowd against the conspirators.

Assessment Resources

Unit 5 Resources

L1 L2 EL **Selection Test A,** pp. 139–141. Administer Test A to less advanced readers and English learners.

L3 L4 **Selection Test B,** pp. 142–144. Administer Test B to on-level and more advanced students.

L3 L4 **Open-Book Test,** pp. 136–138. As an alternative, give the Open-Book Test.

All **Customizable Test Bank**

All **Self-tests**
Students may prepare for the **Selection Test** by taking the **Self-test** online.

PHLit Online! All assessment resources are available at **www.PHLitOnline.com.**

After You Read | The Tragedy of Julius Caesar, Act III

Literary Analysis: Dramatic Speeches

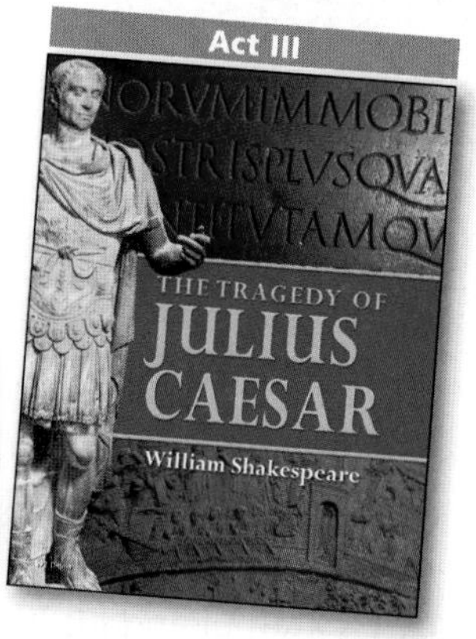

1. On a chart like the one shown, identify each speech as an **aside,** a **soliloquy,** or a **monologue.** Then, paraphrase the speech and identify who hears it.

Lines	Type of Speech	Paraphrase	Who Hears It?
Scene i, lines 218–222			
Scene i, lines 254–275			
Scene ii, lines 261–262			

2. **(a)** Contrast the style and purpose of Antony's and Brutus' funeral speeches. **(b)** Share your ideas with a partner. **(c)** Explain whether learning another person's responses changed your own and why.

Reading Skill: Analyze Imagery

3. **(a)** Give three examples of **imagery** in Act III related to the human body and to words. **(b) Analyze the imagery** by explaining how words and bodies are linked in each example.

Vocabulary

Practice In word study, **analogies** show relationships between pairs of words. In each item, match the relationship between the first two words by choosing the correct word to complete the second pair.

1. vague : definite :: confounded : **(a)** certain, **(b)** lost, **(c)** unclear
2. insult : offended :: spectacle: **(a)** learned, **(b)** fascinated, **(c)** tired
3. remember : past :: prophesy : **(a)** sky, **(b)** present, **(c)** future
4. tuxedo : T-shirt :: discourse : **(a)** jeans, **(b)** lecture, **(c)** chat
5. stored : attic :: interred : **(a)** museum, **(b)** cemetery, **(c)** exit
6. merriment : laughter :: strife : **(a)** yelling, **(b)** singing, **(c)** blushing

Word Study Use the context of the sentences and what you know about the **Latin root *-spect-*** to explain your answer to each question.

1. Why is it important to *inspect* a car before buying it?
2. If you *speculate* about how to build a bookcase, are you actively building it?

Word Study

The **Latin root *-spect-*** means "to look at" or "behold."

Challenge Explain how the root *-spect-* contributes to the meanings of these words. Consult a dictionary if necessary.

perspective
spectator
spectrum

ASSESS/EXTEND

Answers

Literary Analysis

1. **Sample answer:** (Scene i, lines 218–222) Because we are all friends, I hope you will explain to me why Caesar was so dangerous that you had to kill him. Brutus and the other conspirators hear the speech. (Scene i, lines 254–275) Soliloquy; Caesar was the noblest man who ever lived. I predict that Caesar's murder will bring civil war and more violence. Romans will become used to violence. Caesar will be avenged; the audience hears the speech. (Scene ii, lines 261–262) Aside; My speech has stirred up trouble. Let it take its course; the audience hears the speech.

   For other sample answers, see ***Graphic Organizer Transparencies,* Literary Analysis Graphic Organizer A**, p. 176, and the **Additional Answers** section.

2. (a) Brutus speaks in prose; Antony, in blank verse. Both use parallel structure and repetition. Brutus intends to justify the murder of Caesar; Antony intends to praise Caesar and undercut Brutus' rationale. (b) and (c) Students should report any changes in their thinking.

Reading Skill

3. (a) Scene i, lines 105–110; Scene i, lines 259–261; Scene ii, lines 106–108 (b) In Scene i, lines 105–110, Brutus urges conspirators to wash their hands with Caesar's blood. In Scene i, lines 259–261, Antony says that Caesar's wounds are like mouths that beg him to speak; in Scene ii, lines 106–108, Antony says he cannot speak because his heart is in the coffin with Caesar's body.

Vocabulary

Practice

1. certain; antonym
2. fascinated; action that belongs with the noun
3. future; time period associated with the verb
4. chat; antonym
5. cemetery; the place where the action occurs
6. yelling; behavior associated with the noun

Word Study

Sample answers:

1. The root *-spect-* means "to look at" or "behold," and *inspect* means "to look at or examine carefully." You should inspect a car before buying it to make sure everything works properly.
2. No. The root *-spect-* means "to look at" or "behold," and *speculate* means "to reflect upon, consider, or behold something." If you speculate about how to build a bookcase, you are thinking about it, not building it.

Word Study: Challenge

Sample answers: Your *perspective* is the way in which you view, or look at, things. A *spectator* is someone who looks at, or watches, something. A *spectrum* is the array of colors that you can see, or look at.

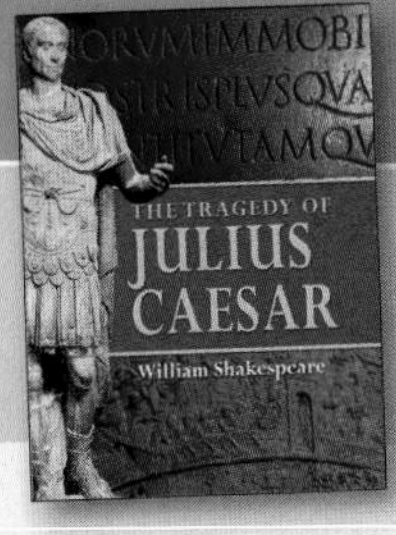

TIME AND RESOURCE MANAGER

The Tragedy of Julius Caesar, Act IV

Lesson Pacing Guide

DAY 1 Preteach

- Administer the Reading and Vocabulary Warm-ups (*Unit 5 Resources*, pp. 145–148) as necessary.
- Introduce the Reading Skill: Read Between the Lines. FT
- Introduce the Literary Analysis concept: External and Internal Conflict. FT
- Distribute copies of the appropriate graphic organizer for the Reading Skill (*Graphic Organizer Transparencies*, pp. 178–179). CRI
- Distribute copies of the appropriate graphic organizer for Literary Analysis (*Graphic Organizer Transparencies*, pp. 180–181). CRI
- Teach the selection vocabulary. FT CRI
- Introduce the Word Study skill.

DAYS 2–3 Preteach/Teach

- Build background with the Background feature. CRI
- Develop thematic vocabulary and thematic thinking with Writing About the Big Question.
- Prepare students to read with the Activating Prior Knowledge activities (TE). CRI
- Informally monitor comprehension while students read. FT
- Use the Reading Check questions to confirm comprehension.
- Develop students' ability to read between the lines using the Reading Skill questions. CRI
- Develop students' understanding of external and internal conflicts using the Literary Analysis questions. CRI
- Reinforce vocabulary with the Vocabulary notes. CRI

DAY 4 Assess

- Assess students' comprehension and mastery of the skills by having them answer the Critical Thinking, Reading Skill, and Literary Analysis questions. FT

DAY 5 Extend/Assess

- Extend learning by having students complete the Research and Technology activity, a multimedia presentation. (You may assign as homework.) As an alternative, assign them "The Titanic Tragedy" in *Reality Central*. CRI
- Administer Selection Test A or B (*Unit 5 Resources*, pp. 157–162). FT

The play *The Tragedy of Julius Caesar* appears unedited and in its entirety. Act I appears on pp. 892–912, Act II appears on pp. 917–936, Act III appears on pp. 941–962, Act IV appears on pp. 967–982, and Act V appears on pp. 987–1000.

Meeting Your Standards

Students will

1. analyze and respond to literary elements.
   - Literary Analysis: External and Internal Conflict
2. read, comprehend, and analyze drama.
   - Reading Skill: Read Between the Lines
   - Reading Check questions
   - Apply the Skills questions
   - Assessment Practice
3. develop vocabulary.
   - Vocabulary
   - Word Study
4. strengthen research and technology skills.
   - multimedia presentation

CRI For a full explanation of Culturally Responsive Instruction opportunities in this lesson, see p. T86–T87.

FT For an accelerated lesson, use the Fast Track strategies and activities.

Managing Differentiated Instruction
This leveled selection pairing groups a more accessible with a more challenging selection. Choose either one to teach the lesson skills. For classroom management suggestions for using the pairing in a mixed-ability class, see pp. T68–T69.

Daily Block Scheduling
Each day in this Lesson Pacing Guide represents a 40–50 minute period. Teachers using block scheduling may combine days to revise pacing. In addition, teachers may differentiate and support core instruction by integrating components for extended and intensive support as students require. See the Guide to Selected Leveled Resources (facing page).

Guide to Selected Leveled Resources

EL English Learners

			The Tragedy of Julius Caesar, Act IV
CORE COURSE	*Unit 5 Resources*	Selection Test A	pp. 157–159
	Graphic Organizer Transparencies	Reading Skill Graphic Organizer A	p. 178
		Literary Analysis Graphic Organizer A	p. 180
EXTENDED SUPPORT (Level 2)	*Unit 5 Resources*	Reading and Vocabulary Warm-ups A or B	pp. 145–148
	Reader's Notebook: English Learner's Version		adapted instruction and adapted selection
	Hear It! Audio CD		selection and summaries
	Hear It! Audio CD (adapted text)		adapted selection and summaries
INTENSIVE SUPPORT (Level 1)	*Reality Central*		"The Titanic Tragedy"
	Real-World Writing Journal		Lesson 4, pp. 150–153

L2 Below-Level Students

			The Tragedy of Julius Caesar, Act IV
CORE COURSE	*Unit 5 Resources*	Selection Test A	pp. 157–159
	Graphic Organizer Transparencies	Reading Skill Graphic Organizer A	p. 178
		Literary Analysis Graphic Organizer A	p. 180
EXTENDED SUPPORT (Level 2)	*Unit 5 Resources*	Reading and Vocabulary Warm-ups A or B	pp. 145–148
	Reader's Notebook		adapted instruction and full selection
	Hear It! Audio CD		selection and summaries
INTENSIVE SUPPORT (Level 1)	*Reality Central*		"The Titanic Tragedy"
	Real-World Writing Journal		Lesson 4, pp. 150–153
	Reading Kit		Reteaching worksheets

L1 Special Needs Students

			The Tragedy of Julius Caesar, Act IV
CORE COURSE	*Unit 5 Resources*	Selection Test A	pp. 157–159
	Graphic Organizer Transparencies	Reading Skill Graphic Organizer A	p. 178
		Literary Analysis Graphic Organizer A	p. 180
EXTENDED SUPPORT (Level 2)	*Unit 5 Resources*	Reading and Vocabulary Warm-ups A or B	pp. 145–148
	Reader's Notebook: Adapted Version		adapted instruction and adapted selection
	Hear It! Audio CD (adapted text)		adapted selection and summaries
INTENSIVE SUPPORT (Level 1)	*Reality Central*		"The Titanic Tragedy"
	Real-World Writing Journal		Lesson 4, pp. 150–153
	Reading Kit		Reteaching worksheets

The program includes resources for these students: L3 On-Level L4 Advanced All All
For a complete guide to selection support, see pp. T106–T108.

NOTE: All print materials are also available online at *www.PHLitOnline.com.*

VISUAL GUIDE to Featured Selection Resources

The Tragedy of Julius Caesar, Act IV

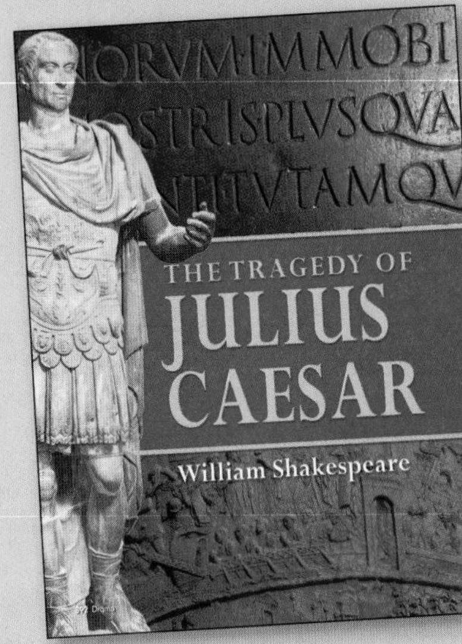

RESOURCES FOR:

- EL English Learners
- L1 Special Needs Students
- L2 Below-Level Students
- L3 On-Level Students
- L4 Advanced Students
- All All Students

Vocabulary/Fluency/Prior Knowledge

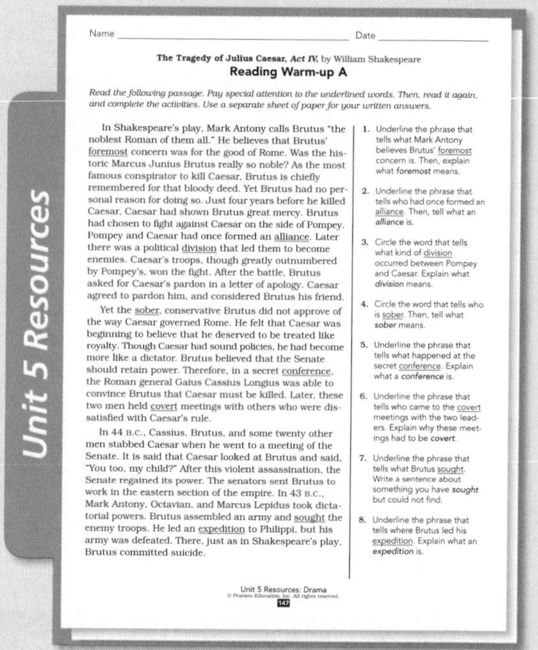
Unit 5 Resources

Name ______________________ Date ______________

The Tragedy of Julius Caesar, *Act IV,* by William Shakespeare

Reading Warm-up A

Read the following passage. Pay special attention to the underlined words. Then, read it again, and complete the activities. Use a separate sheet of paper for your written answers.

In Shakespeare's play, Mark Antony calls Brutus "the noblest Roman of them all." He believes that Brutus' foremost concern was for the good of Rome. Was the historic Marcus Junius Brutus really so noble? As the most famous conspirator to kill Caesar, Brutus is chiefly remembered for that bloody deed. Yet Brutus had no personal reason for doing so. Just four years before he killed Caesar, Caesar had shown Brutus great mercy. Brutus had chosen to fight against Caesar on the side of Pompey. Pompey and Caesar had once formed an alliance. Later there was a political division that led them to become enemies. Caesar's troops, though greatly outnumbered by Pompey's, won the fight. After the battle, Brutus asked for Caesar's pardon in a letter of apology. Caesar agreed to pardon him, and considered Brutus his friend.

Yet the sober, conservative Brutus did not approve of the way Caesar governed Rome. He felt that Caesar was beginning to believe that he deserved to be treated like royalty. Though Caesar had sound policies, he had become more like a dictator. Brutus believed that the Senate should retain power. Therefore, in a secret conference, the Roman general Gaius Cassius Longius was able to convince Brutus that Caesar must be killed. Later, these two men held covert meetings with others who were dissatisfied with Caesar's rule.

In 44 B.C., Cassius, Brutus, and some twenty other men stabbed Caesar when he went to a meeting of the Senate. It is said that Caesar looked at Brutus and said, "You too, my child?" After this violent assassination, the Senate regained its power. The senators sent Brutus to work in the eastern section of the empire. In 43 B.C., Mark Antony, Octavian, and Marcus Lepidus took dictatorial powers. Brutus assembled an army and sought the enemy troops. He led an expedition to Philippi, but his army was defeated. There, just as in Shakespeare's play, Brutus committed suicide.

1. Underline the phrase that tells what Mark Antony believes Brutus' foremost concern is. Then, explain what *foremost* means.
2. Underline the phrase that tells who had once formed an alliance. Then, tell what an *alliance* is.
3. Circle the word that tells what kind of division occurred between Pompey and Caesar. Explain what *division* means.
4. Circle the word that tells who is sober. Then, tell what *sober* means.
5. Underline the phrase that tells what happened at the secret conference. Explain what a *conference* is.
6. Underline the phrase that tells who came to the covert meetings with the two leaders. Explain why these meetings had to be *covert*.
7. Underline the phrase that tells what Brutus sought. Write a sentence about something you have *sought* but could not find.
8. Underline the phrase that tells where Brutus led his expedition. Explain what an *expedition* is.

Unit 5 Resources: Drama
© Pearson Education, Inc. All rights reserved.
147

EL L1 L2 **Reading Warm-ups A and B, pp. 147–148**

Also available for these selections:

- EL L1 L2 Vocabulary Warm-ups A and B, pp. 145–146
- All Vocabulary Builder, p. 152
- All Writing About the Big Question, p. 149

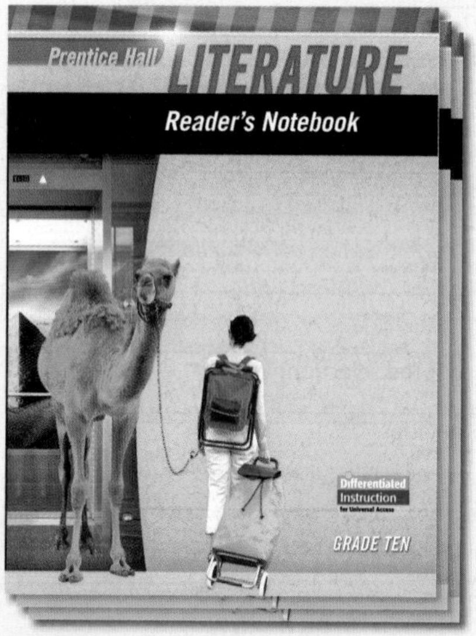

Reader's Notebooks

Pre- and postreading pages for both selections, as well as *The Tragedy of Julius Caesar, Act IV* appear in an interactive format in the *Reader's Notebooks*. Each *Notebook* is differentiated for a different group of learners.
The selections in the Adapted and English Learner's versions are abridged.

L2 L3 ***Reader's Notebook***

L1 ***Reader's Notebook: Adapted Version***

EL ***Reader's Notebook: English Learner's Version***

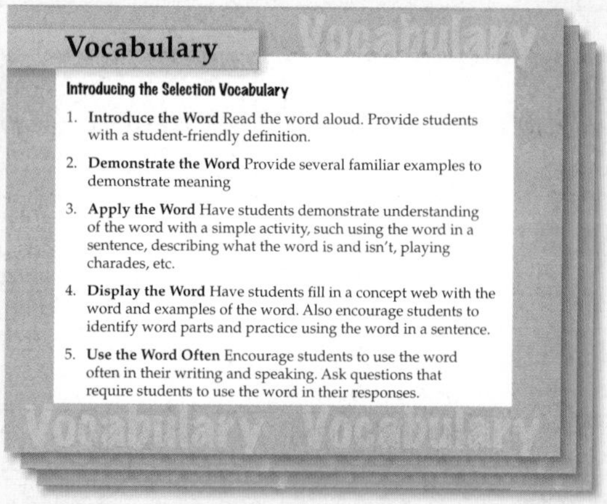
Vocabulary

Introducing the Selection Vocabulary

1. **Introduce the Word** Read the word aloud. Provide students with a student-friendly definition.
2. **Demonstrate the Word** Provide several familiar examples to demonstrate meaning
3. **Apply the Word** Have students demonstrate understanding of the word with a simple activity, such using the word in a sentence, describing what the word is and isn't, playing charades, etc.
4. **Display the Word** Have students fill in a concept web with the word and examples of the word. Also encourage students to identify word parts and practice using the word in a sentence.
5. **Use the Word Often** Encourage students to use the word often in their writing and speaking. Ask questions that require students to use the word in their responses.

Classroom Strategies and Teaching Routines

- core classroom routines outlined step-by-step
- convenient format for easy reference while teaching

Selection Support

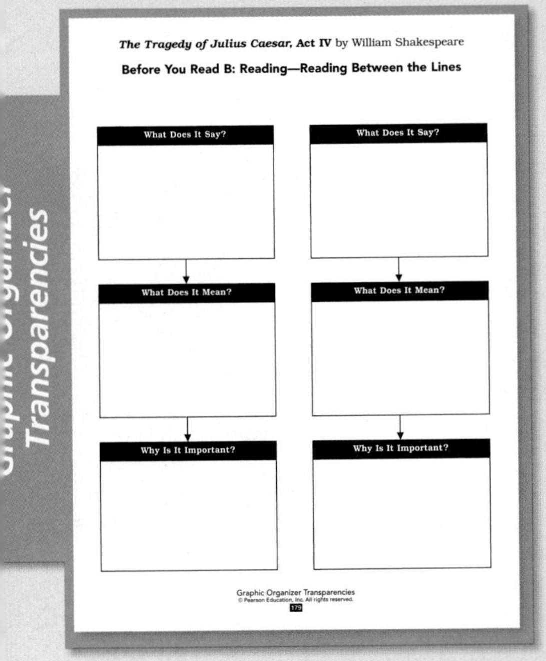
The Tragedy of Julius Caesar, Act IV by William Shakespeare

Before You Read B: Reading—Reading Between the Lines

What Does It Say?	What Does It Say?
What Does It Mean?	What Does It Mean?
Why Is It Important?	Why Is It Important?

Graphic Organizer Transparencies

179
Graphic Organizer Transparencies

L3 **Reading: Graphic Organizer B,** p. 179

Also available for these selections:

- EL L1 L2 Reading: Graphic Organizer A, p. 178 (partially filled in)
- EL L1 L2 Literary Analysis: Graphic Organizer A, p. 180 (partially filled in)
- L3 Literary Analysis: Graphic Organizer B, p. 181

Skills Development/Extension

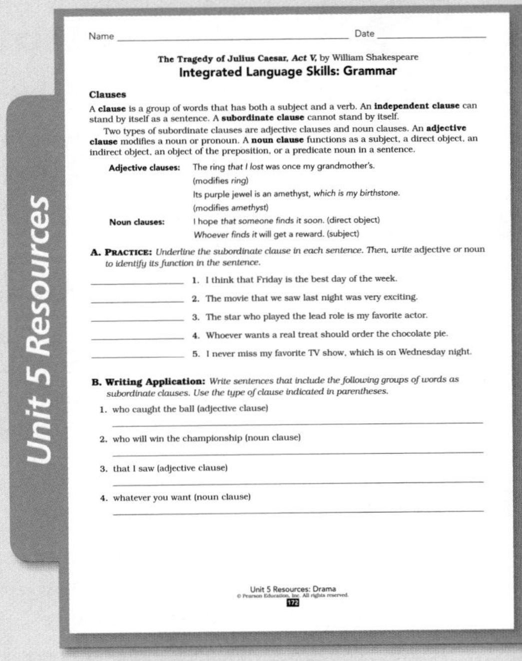
Name ______________________ Date ____________

The Tragedy of Julius Caesar, Act V, by William Shakespeare

Integrated Language Skills: Grammar

Clauses

A **clause** is a group of words that has both a subject and a verb. An **independent clause** can stand by itself as a sentence. A **subordinate clause** cannot stand by itself.

Two types of subordinate clauses are adjective clauses and noun clauses. An **adjective clause** modifies a noun or pronoun. A **noun clause** functions as a subject, a direct object, an indirect object, an object of the preposition, or a predicate noun in a sentence.

Adjective clauses: The ring *that I lost* was once my grandmother's. (modifies *ring*)
Its purple jewel is an amethyst, *which is my birthstone.* (modifies *amethyst*)

Noun clauses: I hope *that someone finds it soon.* (direct object)
Whoever finds it will get a reward. (subject)

A. Practice: *Underline the subordinate clause in each sentence. Then, write* adjective *or* noun *to identify its function in the sentence.*

______ 1. I think that Friday is the best day of the week.
______ 2. The movie that we saw last night was very exciting.
______ 3. The star who played the lead role is my favorite actor.
______ 4. Whoever wants a real treat should order the chocolate pie.
______ 5. I never miss my favorite TV show, which is on Wednesday night.

B. Writing Application: *Write sentences that include the following groups of words as subordinate clauses. Use the type of clause indicated in parentheses.*

1. who caught the ball (adjective clause)
2. who will win the championship (noun clause)
3. that I saw (adjective clause)
4. whatever you want (noun clause)

Unit 5 Resources: Drama

172
Unit 5 Resources

L3 L4 **Grammar,** p. 172

Also available for these selections:

- All Reading: Read Between the Lines, p. 151
- All Literary Analysis: External and Internal Conflicts, p. 150
- L4 Enrichment, p. 153
- L3 L4 Support for Writing, p. 173
- L3 L4 Support for Extend Your Learning, p. 174

Assessment

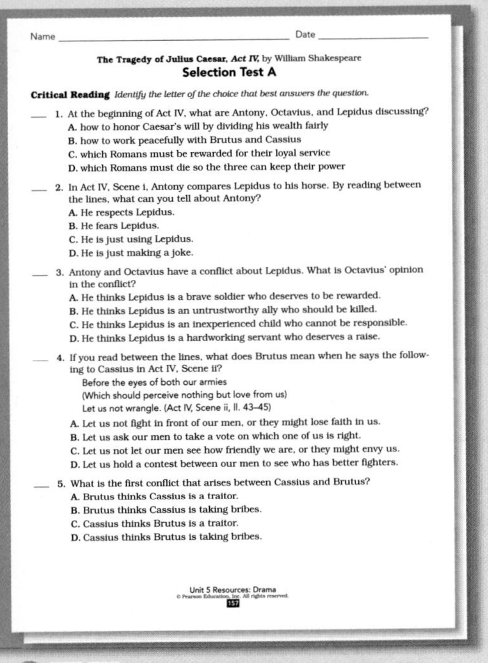
Name ______________________ Date ____________

The Tragedy of Julius Caesar, Act IV, by William Shakespeare

Selection Test A

Critical Reading *Identify the letter of the choice that best answers the question.*

____ 1. At the beginning of Act IV, what are Antony, Octavius, and Lepidus discussing?
A. how to honor Caesar's will by dividing his wealth fairly
B. how to work peacefully with Brutus and Cassius
C. which Romans must be rewarded for their loyal service
D. which Romans must die so the three can keep their power

____ 2. In Act IV, Scene i, Antony compares Lepidus to his horse. By reading between the lines, what can you tell about Antony?
A. He respects Lepidus.
B. He fears Lepidus.
C. He is just using Lepidus.
D. He is just making a joke.

____ 3. Antony and Octavius have a conflict about Lepidus. What is Octavius' opinion in the conflict?
A. He thinks Lepidus is a brave soldier who deserves to be rewarded.
B. He thinks Lepidus is an untrustworthy ally who should be killed.
C. He thinks Lepidus is an inexperienced child who cannot be responsible.
D. He thinks Lepidus is a hardworking servant who deserves a raise.

____ 4. If you read between the lines, what does Brutus mean when he says the following to Cassius in Act IV, Scene ii?
Before the eyes of both our armies
(Which should perceive nothing but love from us)
Let us not wrangle. (Act IV, Scene ii, ll. 43–45)
A. Let us not fight in front of our men, or they might lose faith in us.
B. Let us ask our men to take a vote on which one of us is right.
C. Let us not let our men see how friendly we are, or they might envy us.
D. Let us hold a contest between our men to see who has better fighters.

____ 5. What is the first conflict that arises between Cassius and Brutus?
A. Brutus thinks Cassius is a traitor.
B. Brutus thinks Cassius is taking bribes.
C. Cassius thinks Brutus is a traitor.
D. Cassius thinks Brutus is taking bribes.

Unit 5 Resources: Drama

157

EL L1 L2 **Selection Test A,** pp. 157–159

Also available for these selections:

- L3 L4 Selection Test B, pp. 160–162
- L3 L4 Open-Book Test, pp. 154–156

PHLit Online!
www.PHLitOnline.com

- complete narrated selection text
- a thematically related video with writing prompt
- an interactive graphic organizer
- highlighting feature
- access to all student print resources, adapted to individual student needs
- Spanish and English summaries

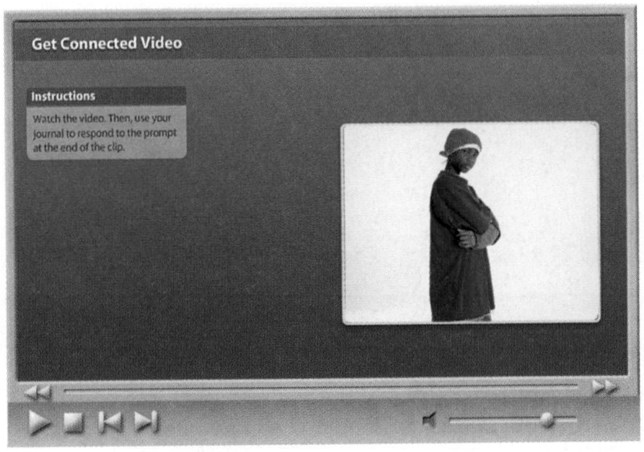
Get Connected Video
Instructions
Watch the video. Then, use your journal to respond to the prompt at the end of the clip.

Get Connected! (thematic video with writing prompt)

Also available:

Background video

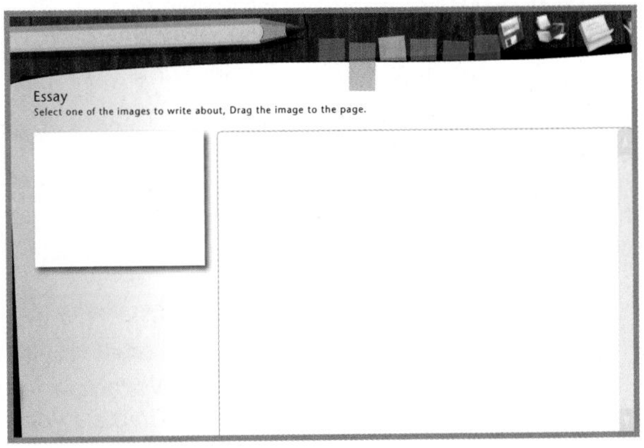
Essay
Select one of the images to write about. Drag the image to the page.

Writer's Journal (with graphics feature)

Also available:

Vocabulary Central (tools, activities, and songs for studying vocabulary)

DIFFERENTIATE/PRETEACH

❶ Selections Skills

1. With the class, preview the selection skills. (The lesson meets the lesson objectives given on p. 964a.)
2. Explain that students will learn to use the skill of reading between the lines as they read to better understand and enjoy the selection. By examining external and internal conflict as they read, they will gain deeper insight into drama.

❷ Vocabulary

1. Have students preview the selection vocabulary.
2. For each word, have students say the word aloud.
3. Then, use the word in a sentence that defines the word.
4. Finally, repeat your definitional sentence or a similar sentence with the word missing, and have the class "fill in the blank" chorally. Here are some examples:

   Someone who is rash acts without thinking. Though Henry had a habit of acting impulsively, he managed to be cautious, not [students say "rash"].

   Mirth is a state of joyfulness. The beautiful weather, smiling faces, and laughter at the summer festival filled everyone with [students say "mirth"].

❸ Word Study

1. Introduce the skill, using the instruction in the box.
2. Without naming the word, state this definition: "to take for granted or without proof." Then, have students identify the word. (**Answer:** *assume*)

Before You Read

The Tragedy of Julius Caesar, Act IV

THE BIG ?

To what extent does *experience* determine what we *perceive*?

While You Read Look for ways that his experiences in Act III affect Brutus in Act IV.

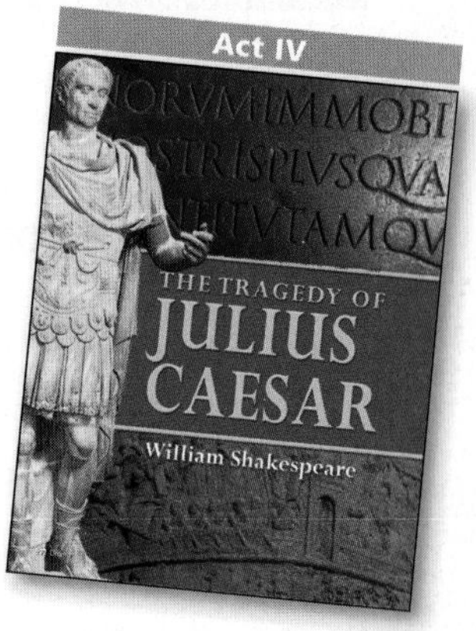

❶ Selection Skills Guide

Practice these skills with ***The Tragedy of Julius Caesar,* Act IV** (p. 966).

- Understand external and internal conflict
- Read Shakespearean drama
- Read between the lines

Integrated Language Skills (Grammar; Listening and Speaking; Research and Technology; and Writing Activities) appear on pages 1002–1005.

❷ Vocabulary

Read each word and its definition. Decide whether you know the word well, know it a little bit, or do not know it at all. After you read, see how your knowledge of each word has increased.

- **legacies** (leg´ ə sēz) *n.* money, property, or position left in a will to someone (p. 967) ***The legacies in his will included a gift to charity.*** *legacy n.*
- **condemned** (kən demd´) *v.* declared to be guilty of wrongdoings (p. 970) ***The reporter condemned the politician for failing to keep his promise.*** *condemnable adj. condemnation n. condemnatory adj.*
- **chastisement** (chas´ tiz mənt) *n.* severe criticism; punishment (p. 971) ***As chastisement, the child was sent to bed early.*** *chastise v. chastiser n.*
- **rash** (rash) *adj.* given to acting without thinking; impulsive (p. 971) ***Do not be so rash; think before you act.*** *rashly adv. rashness n.*
- **mirth** (murth) *n.* joyfulness; merriment (p. 972) ***The children were full of mirth and laughed joyfully.*** *mirthful adj. mirthfully adv.*
- **presume** (prē zo͞om´) *v.* rely too much on; take advantage of (p. 972) ***Do not presume on their good nature and expect them to pay for everything.*** *presumable adj. presumption n. presumptive adj.*

❸ Word Study

The **Latin root *-sum-*** means "to take" or "to use."

In the play, Cassius tells Brutus not to **presume** upon his friendship or take for granted his good will.

Vocabulary Development

Vocabulary Knowledge Rating

Create a **Vocabulary Knowledge Rating Chart** (***Professional Development Guidebook***, p. 33) for this selection. Include the selection vocabulary from this page.

Give students a copy of the chart. Read the words aloud, and have students mark their ratings in the Before Reading column. Urge them to be alert to these words as they read and discuss the selection.

Tally how many students think they know a word to gauge how much instruction to provide. As students read and discuss the selection, point out the words and their context.

PHLit Online! **Vocabulary Central**, featuring tools, activities, and songs for studying vocabulary, is available at **www.PHLitOnline.com.**

❹ Literary Analysis: External and Internal Conflict

Conflict, a struggle between opposing forces, creates drama:

- In an **external conflict,** a character struggles with an outside force, such as another character, or a force such as the weather.
- In an **internal conflict,** the character struggles with his or her own opposing beliefs, desires, or values.

The Tragedy of Julius Caesar involves a number of different conflicts both internal and external. In many cases, these types of conflict are directly related. For instance, earlier in the play, the external conflict between Brutus and Caesar creates an internal conflict for Brutus—he wishes to check Caesar's ambition, but he also considers Caesar a friend.

PHLit Online!
www.PHLitOnline.com

Hear It!
- Selection summary audio
- Selection audio

See It!
- Get Connected video
- Background video
- More about the author
- Vocabulary flashcards

Do It!
- Interactive journals
- Interactive graphic organizers
- Self-test
- Internet activity
- Grammar tutorial
- Interactive vocabulary games

❺ Reading Skill: Read Between the Lines

When **reading Shakespearean drama, read between the lines** or make inferences to find the deeper meaning of a character's words.

- Keep the larger situation in mind. For instance, early in Act IV, Antony describes Lepidus as "Meet to be sent on errands." Note that Antony has been deciding which of his political rivals will share power. Between the lines, he is saying, "Fit to run errands—and nothing else."
- Follow indirect references. For example, when Lucilius reports on Cassius, Brutus says, "Thou has described / A hot friend cooling." "A hot friend" refers to Cassius, whom Brutus worries is no longer his ally.
- Notice what details the author provides, and what he does not include.

❻ Using the Strategy: Inference Chart

Recording details on an **inference chart** will help you read between the lines.

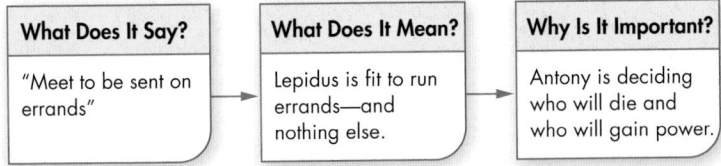

What Does It Say?	What Does It Mean?	Why Is It Important?
"Meet to be sent on errands"	Lepidus is fit to run errands—and nothing else.	Antony is deciding who will die and who will gain power.

PRETEACH

❹ Literary Analysis

1. Introduce the skill, using the instruction on the student page.
2. Tell students that they will practice identifying external and internal conflict as they read.

Think Aloud: Model the Skill

Model the skill of identifying and understanding external and internal conflict, using the following "think aloud":

Suppose I am reading about a woman who faces death because she defies the king's wishes. She would rather die, however, than give up her beliefs.

This woman experiences two types of conflict. Because she is struggling with an outside force, the king, she is experiencing an external conflict. She also experiences an internal conflict, a struggle within herself, for she needs to decide whether sticking to her beliefs is more important than avoiding an early death.

❺ Reading Skill

1. Introduce the skill, using the instruction on the student page.
2. Tell students that they will learn to read between the lines.

Think Aloud: Model the Skill

Model the skill of reading between the lines, using the following "think aloud":

To read between the lines, I must first read a sentence to get its literal meaning. For example, a soothsayer warns Caesar, "Beware the ides of March." I know that the ides of a month is the fifteenth, so the soothsayer is referring to a particular day. Because the soothsayer says "beware," I can infer that what will happen to Caesar on the fifteenth will not be good.

❻ Using the Strategy

Give students a copy of either **Reading Skill Graphic Organizer A** or **B** (*Graphic Organizer Transparencies,* pp. 178–179) to record inferences they make as they read. Use the examples in **Reading Skill Graphic Organizer A,** which is partially filled in, to model the process of completing the organizer.

Differentiated Instruction for Universal Access

Preparing Students for the Selection

If you wish to prepare lower level readers to read *The Tragedy of Julius Caesar:* Act IV, follow these steps:

- Students might have difficulty with the lengthy speeches and soliloquies, such as the one on pp. 967–968. Review strategies of paraphrasing and breaking down complex sentences. Encourage them to rephrase difficult parts of soliloquies in their own words.
- Encourage students to rephrase archaic phrases in contemporary English. For example, "This is a slight unmeritable man/Meet to be sent on errands," can be rephrased as "This is an unworthy man/Fit only to be sent on errands."
- Remind students that Shakespeare uses blank verse—unrhymed iambic pentameter—in his plays, which follows a regular pattern of five unstressed-stressed syllable pairs. Practice reading sections of the play aloud with students, focusing on hearing the rhythm of this language.

PRETEACH

❶ Activating Prior Knowledge

1. Prepare an **Anticipation Guide** (see *Professional Development Guidebook,* pp. 36–38) with the following statements:
   - Friends should discuss each other's faults.
   - A person can be simultaneously kind and cruel.
   - Taking action is always better than worrying.
   - No one can be truly noble.
2. Give students a copy of the prepared **Anticipation Guide,** and have students mark their responses in the Me column. Have students discuss the statements in pairs or groups and mark the guides again in the Group column.
3. For further guidance, use the *Classroom Strategies and Teaching Routines* card **Anticipation Guides.**

Concept Connector ➞

Students will return to the **Anticipation Guide** after completing the story.

Small-Group Activity

Have pairs and small groups of students stage the various scenes in Act IV. Assign each pair or group to a different scene. Give students time to learn their lines and determine how the characters will enter, exit, and move during the scenes. Invite students to perform their scenes for the class.

❷ About the Selection

Antony and Octavius prepare for battle against the conspirators and their troops. Tension between Brutus and Cassius explodes into anger, but they resolve their quarrel as Brutus tells Cassius that Portia has killed herself. The conspirators agree to march on Philippi. Later that night, Brutus is visited by Caesar's ghost, who tells him that they will meet again at Philippi.

❸ Critical Viewing

Possible response: Confidence, power, intelligence, and ambition are portrayed.

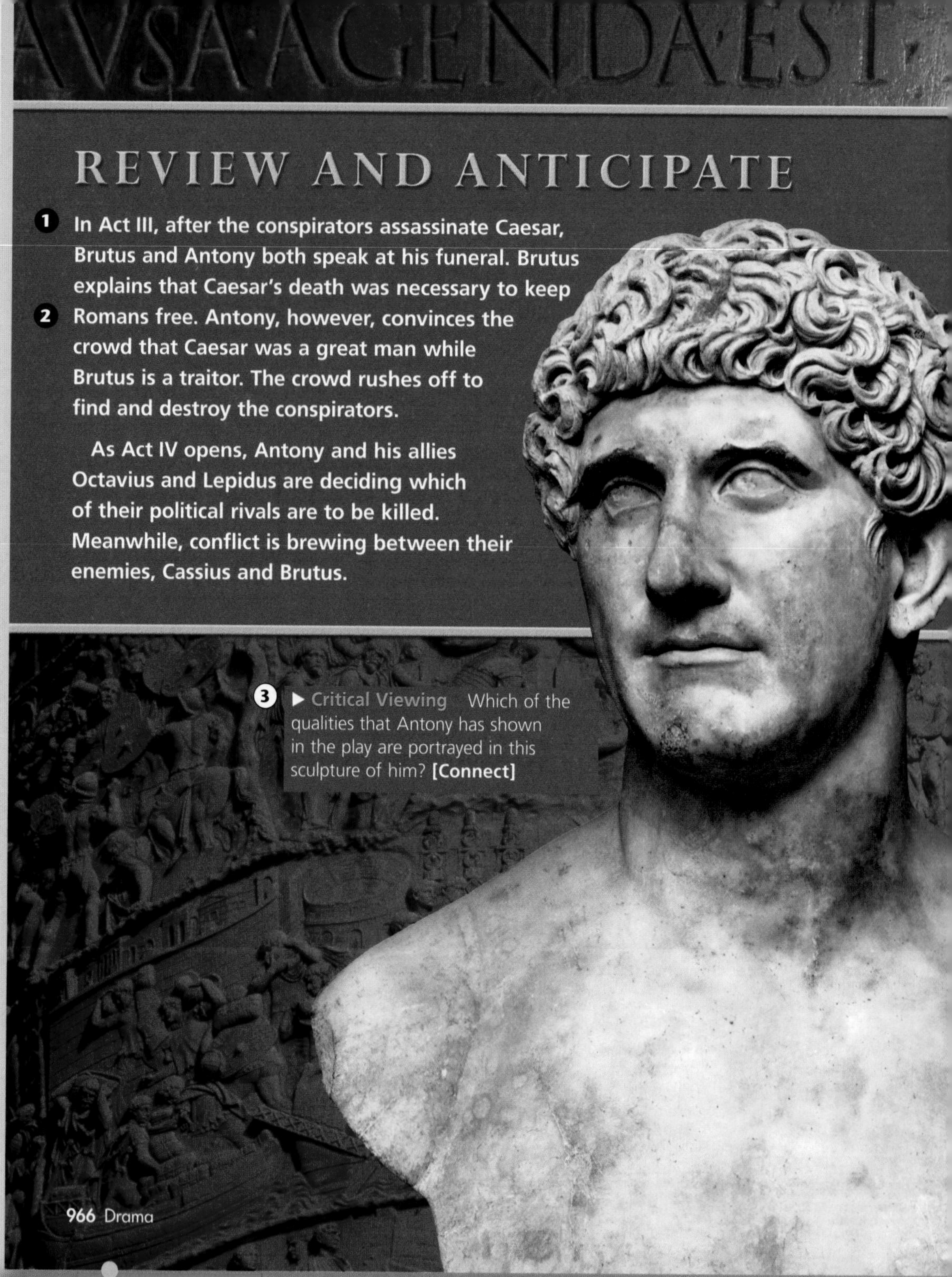

REVIEW AND ANTICIPATE

❶ In Act III, after the conspirators assassinate Caesar, Brutus and Antony both speak at his funeral. Brutus explains that Caesar's death was necessary to keep ❷ Romans free. Antony, however, convinces the crowd that Caesar was a great man while Brutus is a traitor. The crowd rushes off to find and destroy the conspirators.

As Act IV opens, Antony and his allies Octavius and Lepidus are deciding which of their political rivals are to be killed. Meanwhile, conflict is brewing between their enemies, Cassius and Brutus.

❸ ▶ Critical Viewing Which of the qualities that Antony has shown in the play are portrayed in this sculpture of him? **[Connect]**

Differentiated Instruction for Universal Access

Accessibility at a Glance: Selection Choices

	***The Tragedy of Julius Caesar*, Act IV**	
Context	Historical: ancient Rome	
Language/ Vocabulary	• Dialogue • Prose, verse, and soliloquies • Above-level vocabulary	
Concept Level	Challenging (internal conflicts within historical, political context)	
Literary Merit	Classic; noted author	
Lexile/Length	Lexile: NP	Word Count: 3,228
Overall Rating	**Challenging**	

ACT IV

Scene i. A house in Rome.

[*Enter* ANTONY, OCTAVIUS, *and* LEPIDUS.]

ANTONY. These many then shall die; their names are pricked.[1]

OCTAVIUS. Your brother too must die; consent you, Lepidus?

LEPIDUS. I do consent—

OCTAVIUS. Prick him down, Antony.

LEPIDUS. Upon condition Publius shall not live,
Who is your sister's son, Mark Antony.

ANTONY. He shall not live; look, with a spot I damn him.[2]
But, Lepidus, go you to Caesar's house;
Fetch the will hither, and we shall determine
How to cut off some charge in legacies.[3]

LEPIDUS. What, shall I find you here?

OCTAVIUS. Or[4] here or at the Capitol. [*Exit* LEPIDUS.]

ANTONY. This is a slight unmeritable[5] man,
Meet[6] to be sent on errands; is it fit,
The threefold world[7] divided, he should stand
One of the three to share it?

OCTAVIUS. So you thought him,
And took his voice[8] who should be pricked to die
In our black sentence and proscription.[9]

ANTONY. Octavius, I have seen more days[10] than you;
And though we lay these honors on this man,
To ease ourselves of divers sland'rous loads,[11]
He shall but bear them as the ass bears gold,
To groan and sweat under the business,
Either led or driven, as we point the way;
And having brought our treasure where we will,
Then take we down his load, and turn him off,
(Like to the empty ass) to shake his ears
And graze in commons.[12]

OCTAVIUS. You may do your will;
But he's a tried and valiant soldier.

ANTONY. So is my horse, Octavius, and for that
I do appoint him store of provender.[13]

1. **pricked** *v.* checked off.
2. **with a spot . . . him** with a mark on the tablet, I condemn him.
3. **cut off some charge in legacies** save costs by changing the amount of gifts left in the will.

Vocabulary
legacies (leg´ ə sēz) *n.* money, property, or position left in a will to someone

4. **Or** *conj.* either.
5. **slight unmeritable** insignificant and without merit.
6. **Meet** *adj.* suitable.
7. **threefold world** three areas of the Roman Empire—Europe, Asia, and Africa.
8. **voice** *n.* vote; opinion.
9. **black . . . proscription** list of those sentenced to death or exile.
10. **have seen more days** am older.
11. **divers sland'rous loads** various burdens of blame.
12. **in commons** on public pasture.
13. **appoint . . . provender** give him a supply of food.

5 **Reading Check**
What is the conflict between Antony and Octavius?

4 Literary Analysis

Conflict

1. Read aloud the conversation between Antony and Octavius in lines 12–39. Point out the reference to the triumvirate of Antony, Lepidus, and Octavius in lines 13–15. Explain that as one of the three, Lepidus shares power equally with Antony and Octavius. Note that Antony questions whether it is right or suitable ("fit") for Lepidus to have an equal share.
2. Have students focus on Antony's characterization of Lepidus.
   Ask: What words and images does Antony use to describe Lepidus?
   Answer: He uses the words *slight, unmeritable,* and *barren-spirited.* He compares Lepidus to an ass and a horse.
3. Then **ask** students: How does Octavius characterize Lepidus?
   Answer: Octavius says he is an experienced and brave soldier.

5 Reading Check

Answer: They have different opinions of Lepidus. Octavius thinks more highly of him than Antony does. Antony does not think Lepidus should have an equal share of power.

Differentiated Instruction — Additional Instruction

EL Extended Support—English Learners
Have students complete the **Reading and Vocabulary Warm-ups,** ***Unit 5 Resources,*** pp. 145–148, before they read. Assign the prereading pages for the selection in the ***Reader's Notebook: English Learner's Version.*** Then, have students listen to portions of the selection on the ***Hear It!*** **Audio CD.**

L1 L2 Extended Support—Struggling Readers
Have students complete the **Reading and Vocabulary Warm-ups,** ***Unit 5 Resources,*** pp. 145–148, before they read. Assign the prereading pages for the selection in the ***Reader's Notebook: Adapted Version.*** Then, have students listen to portions of the selection on the ***Hear It!*** **Audio CD.**

Extended Support—Reluctant Readers
To build motivation and engagement before assigning the selection, have students read "The *Titanic* Tragedy," a thematically related selection in ***Reality Central.*** Then, use the questions at the conclusion of the related selection to guide discussion.

PHLit Online!
This selection is available in interactive format in the **Enriched Online Student Edition, www.PHLitOnline.com,** which includes a thematically related video with writing prompt and an interactive graphic organizer.

6 Critical Thinking

Analyze

1. **Ask** students what Antony's speech (lines 29–47) reveals about him.
   Possible responses: Antony is decisive and even absolute; he takes charge of situations and will use Lepidus for his own purposes. He is deceptive; he will mislead Lepidus about how much power Lepidus will have.
2. Have students discuss what they think of Antony's character at this point in the play. **Ask:** What kind of person is he? Do you admire him? Why or why not?
   Possible responses: Students may respond that Antony is cool and calculating. They may admire his initial loyalty to Caesar but dislike his apparent ulterior motives for power regarding Lepidus.

7 Literary Analysis

Conflict

1. **Ask** students to identify whether the conflict being discussed in this conversation is external or internal.
   Answer: The conversation reveals a conflict between Brutus and Cassius. The conflict is external.
2. **Ask** students what details or remarks in the conversation suggest that tension is increasing in the conflict between Brutus and Cassius.
   Possible response: Lucilius says that Cassius seems less friendly than usual. Brutus suggests that Cassius will let them down in the coming battle.

---

14. **wind** (wīnd) *v.* turn.
15. **His . . . spirit** his bodily movements governed by my mind.
16. **taste** *n.* degree; measure.
17. **barren-spirited** without ideas of his own.
18. **feeds / On objects, arts, and imitations** enjoys curiosities, clever ways, and fashions.
19. **staled** *v.* cheapened.
20. **Begin his fashion** he begins to use. (He is hopelessly behind the times.)
21. **property** *n.* tool; object.
22. **levying powers** enlisting troops.
23. **straight make head** quickly gather soldiers.
24. **best friends made** closest allies chosen.
25. **stretched** *adj.* used to full advantage.
26. **presently** *adv.* immediately.
27. **How . . . answerèd** how hidden dangers may be discovered and known dangers met.
28. **at the stake . . . enemies** surrounded by enemies like a bear tied to a stake and set upon by many dogs. (Bear-baiting was a popular amusement in Elizabethan England.)
29. **mischiefs** *n.* plans to injure us.

It is a creature that I teach to fight,
To wind,[14] to stop, to run directly on,
His corporal motion governed by my spirit.[15]
And, in some taste,[16] is Lepidus but so.
He must be taught, and trained, and bid go forth.
A barren-spirited[17] fellow; one that feeds
On objects, arts, and imitations,[18]
Which, out of use and staled[19] by other men,
Begin his fashion.[20] Do not talk of him
But as a property.[21] And now, Octavius,
Listen great things. Brutus and Cassius
Are levying powers;[22] we must straight make head.[23]
Therefore let our alliance be combined,
Our best friends made,[24] our means stretched;[25]
And let us presently[26] go sit in council
How covert matters may be best disclosed,
And open perils surest answerèd.[27]

OCTAVIUS. Let us do so; for we are at the stake,
And bayed about with many enemies;[28]
And some that smile have in their hearts, I fear,
Millions of mischiefs.[29] [*Exit*]

Scene ii. Camp near Sardis.

[*Drum. Enter* BRUTUS, LUCILIUS, LUCIUS, *and the* ARMY. TITINIUS *and* PINDARUS *meet them.*]

BRUTUS. Stand ho!

LUCILIUS. Give the word, ho! and stand.

BRUTUS. What now, Lucilius, is Cassius near?

LUCILIUS. He is at hand, and Pindarus is come
To do you salutation[1] from his master.

BRUTUS. He greets me well. Your master, Pindarus,
In his own change, or by ill officers,
Hath given me some worthy cause to wish
Things done undone;[2] but if he be at hand,
I shall be satisfied.[3]

PINDARUS. I do not doubt
But that my noble master will appear
Such as he is, full of regard[4] and honor.

BRUTUS. He is not doubted. A word, Lucilius,
How he received you; let me be resolved.[5]

1. **To do you salutation** to bring you greetings.
2. **In his own . . . done undone** Whether his actions are due to a change in his feelings toward me or to bad advice from subordinates, he has made me wish we did not do what we did.
3. **be satisfied** obtain an explanation.
4. **full of regard** worthy of respect.
5. **resolved** *adj.* fully informed.

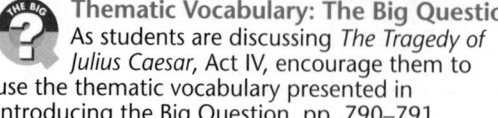

Vocabulary Development

Thematic Vocabulary: The Big Question

As students are discussing *The Tragedy of Julius Caesar*, Act IV, encourage them to use the thematic vocabulary presented in Introducing the Big Question, pp. 790–791. You might encourage them with sentence starters like these:

1. At the beginning of Act IV, Antony shows his *insight* into Lepidus by . . .
2. Antony plans to *manipulate* Lepidus by . . .
3. Antony has the *impression* that Brutus and Cassius . . .
4. One of the *universal* themes Shakespeare presents in this act is . . .

LUCILIUS. With courtesy and with respect enough,
But not with such familiar instances,[6]
Nor with such free and friendly conference[7]
As he hath used of old.

BRUTUS. Thou hast described
A hot friend cooling. Ever note, Lucilius,
When love begins to sicken and decay
It useth an enforcèd ceremony.[8]
There are no tricks in plain and simple faith;
8 But hollow[9] men, like horses hot at hand,[10]
Make gallant show and promise of their mettle;[11]

[*Low march within*]

But when they should endure the bloody spur,
They fall their crests, and like deceitful jades
Sink in the trial.[12] Comes his army on?

6. **familiar instances** marks of friendship.
7. **conference** *n.* conversation.
8. **enforcèd ceremony** forced formality.
9. **hollow** *adj.* insincere.
10. **hot at hand** full of spirit when reined in.
11. **mettle** *n.* spirit; high character; courage.
12. **They fall . . . the trial** They drop their necks, and like worn-out, worthless horses, fail the test.

11 **Reading Check**
What is Brutus' present attitude toward Cassius?

9 10 ▼ **Critical Viewing** Which details in this film still reflect the fact that Antony dominates over both Lepidus and Octavius? **[Interpret]**

Differentiated Instruction for Universal Access

Strategy for Special Needs Students
Explain to students that the discussion between Octavius and Antony in Scene i concerns the man who just left the room. Point out the stage direction "Exit Lepidus" on p. 967. Then, with students, make a survey of the stage directions throughout Act IV, beginning with the first stage directions for Scene ii, and explain their meaning as necessary. Remind students to use these text aids as they read the play.

EL Strategy for English Learners
Help students understand that Antony is comparing Lepidus to a horse in lines 29–39 of Scene i. Explain that Antony makes this comparison to highlight Lepidus' inability to think and act on his own, and thus his unsuitability as an equal partner in the triumvirate. Have students point out words and phrases in which Antony names specific qualities that Lepidus shares with a horse.

8 Background
Cassius
Between the assassination of Caesar and the battle at Philippi, Cassius traveled widely in the Roman world, arriving in Syria in 43 B.C. The governors of that province gave him use of their armies. Cassius picked up other troops throughout the eastern provinces and raised a considerable amount of money for their support. In the summer of 42, he and Brutus crossed to Thrace and met Antony and Octavius in battle at Philippi. Cassius' camp was captured in the first battle. He subsequently killed himself. Though practical-minded, especially in contrast to Brutus, Cassius did not enjoy the respect that Brutus garnered. His fierce temper, sarcasm, and ruthlessness were well known.

9 Humanities
Still Photograph from *Julius Caesar* (1953)
This still photograph from the film version of *Julius Caesar* shows (from left) Lepidus, Octavius, and Antony at table. Although the table setting here appears luxurious with abundant food, the meal shown is representative of the basic Roman diet, which was quite simple. The staples of the Roman diet were grain, oil, and wine. Bread was eaten with cheese or honey. Fish was also a common accompaniment for bread. Poultry, game, and eggs were other animal sources of protein. In general, however, the Roman diet was vegetarian. Legumes and onions, radishes, beets, and garlic were common vegetable offerings. Favorite fruits included figs, grapes, peaches, apricots, and cherries.

10 Critical Viewing
Answer: Both Lepidus and Octavius are looking intently at Antony. Their posture is more receptive than that of Antony, who is leaning forward in a more aggressive, commanding pose.

11 Reading Check
Answer: Brutus questions Cassius' commitment and is cautious about meeting him.

12 Reading Skill

Read Between the Lines

1. Ask five volunteers to read aloud the entrance of Cassius at lines 30–37. Ask students to describe the scene and atmosphere as Cassius arrives.
   Possible responses: The short, sharp words and exclamations—"Hark!" "Stand, ho!" "Stand!"—create a formal, intense atmosphere. With such a welcome, Cassius can be viewed as an enemy soldier coming to negotiate, rather than a commander on the same side as Brutus. Cassius' line "you have done me wrong" is a strong accusation and suggests deep-seated resentment and unresolved conflict.
2. **Ask** students to respond to the Reading Skill question: Brutus and Cassius are standing near their troops. Why does Brutus suggest meeting in his tent?
   Possibe response: Brutus understands that Cassius is upset with him, and he does not want their troops to see that there is conflict between them. He is concerned that if they do not present a united front, their troops might lose courage.

---

13. **quartered** *v.* provided with places to stay.
14. **horse in general** cavalry.
15. ***Powers*** *n.* forces; troops.

LUCILIUS. They mean this night in Sardis to be quartered;[13]
The greater part, the horse in general,[14]
Are come with Cassius.

[*Enter* CASSIUS *and his Powers.*[15]]

16. **gently** *adv.* slowly.

BRUTUS. Hark! He is arrived.
March gently[16] on to meet him.

CASSIUS. Stand, ho!

BRUTUS. Stand, ho! Speak the word along.

FIRST SOLDIER. Stand!

SECOND SOLDIER. Stand!

THIRD SOLDIER. Stand!

12

CASSIUS. Most noble brother, you have done me wrong.

BRUTUS. Judge me, you gods! Wrong I mine enemies?
And if not so, how should I wrong a brother?

17. **sober form** serious manner.

CASSIUS. Brutus, this sober form[17] of yours hides wrongs;
And when you do them—

18. **be content** be patient.

BRUTUS. Cassius, be content.[18]
Speak your griefs softly; I do know you well.
Before the eyes of both our armies here
(Which should perceive nothing but love from us)
Let us not wrangle. Bid them move away;
Then in my tent, Cassius, enlarge[19] your griefs,
And I will give you audience.

Reading Skill
Read Between the Lines Brutus and Cassius are standing near their troops. Why does Brutus suggest meeting in his tent?

19. **enlarge** *v.* freely express.
20. **charges** *n.* troops.

CASSIUS. Pindarus,
Bid our commanders lead their charges[20] off
A little from this ground.

BRUTUS. Lucilius, do you the like, and let no man
Come to our tent till we have done our conference.
Let Lucius and Titinius guard our door.

[*Exit all but* BRUTUS *and* CASSIUS]

Vocabulary
condemned (kən demd′) *v.* declared to be guilty of wrongdoings

Scene iii. Brutus' tent.

13

1. **noted** *v.* publicly denounced.
2. **praying on his side** pleading on his behalf.
3. **slighted off** disregarded.

CASSIUS. That you have wronged me doth appear in this:
You have condemned and noted[1] Lucius Pella
For taking bribes here of the Sardians;
Wherein my letters, praying on his side,[2]
Because I knew the man, was slighted off.[3]

BRUTUS. You wronged yourself to write in such a case.

Vocabulary Development

Vocabulary Reinforcement

Students will benefit from additional examples and practice with the selection vocabulary words. Reinforce their comprehension with "show-you-know" sentences. The first part of the sentence uses the vocabulary word in an appropriate context. The second part of the sentence—the "show-you-know" part—clarifies the first. Model the strategy with this example for *chastisement*:

The teacher's *chastisement* surprised him because he did not think he had done anything to deserve punishment.

Then, give students a sentence prompt such as the following, and coach them in creating the clarification part:

They knew they would face *chastisement* because ________.

Sample answer: there were penalties for breaking the rules.

CASSIUS. In such a time as this it is not meet
That every nice offense should bear his comment.[4]

BRUTUS. Let me tell you, Cassius, you yourself
Are much condemned to have an itching palm,[5]
To sell and mart[6] your offices for gold
To undeservers.

CASSIUS. I an itching palm?
You know that you are Brutus that speaks this,
Or, by the gods, this speech were else your last.

BRUTUS. The name of Cassius honors[7] this corruption,
And **chastisement** doth therefore hide his head.

CASSIUS. Chastisement!

BRUTUS. Remember March, the ides of March remember.
Did not great Julius bleed for justice' sake?
What villain touched his body, that did stab,
And not[8] for justice? What, shall one of us,
That struck the foremost man of all this world
But for supporting robbers,[9] shall we now
Contaminate our fingers with base bribes,
And sell the mighty space of our large honors[10]
For so much trash[11] as may be graspèd thus?
I had rather be a dog, and bay[12] the moon,
Than such a Roman.

CASSIUS. Brutus, bait[13] not me;
I'll not endure it. You forget yourself
To hedge me in.[14] I am a soldier, I,
Older in practice, abler than yourself
To make conditions.[15]

BRUTUS. Go to! You are not, Cassius.

CASSIUS. I am.

BRUTUS. I say you are not.

CASSIUS. Urge[16] me no more, I shall forget myself;
Have mind upon your health;[17] tempt me no farther.

BRUTUS. Away, slight[18] man!

CASSIUS. Is't possible?

BRUTUS. Hear me, for I will speak.
Must I give way and room to your **rash** choler?[19]
Shall I be frighted when a madman stares?

4. **every . . . comment** every petty fault should receive his criticism.
5. **condemned . . . palm** accused of having a hand eager to accept bribes.
6. **mart** *v.* trade.
7. **honors** *v.* gives respectability to.

Vocabulary
chastisement (chas´ tiz mənt) *n.* severe criticism; punishment
rash (rash) *adj.* given to acting without thinking; impulsive

Reading Skill
Read Between the Lines When Brutus asks who stabbed Caesar "not for justice," what is he suggesting about Cassius?

8. **And not** except.
9. **But . . . robbers** Here Brutus says, for the first time, that Caesar's officials were also involved in taking bribes and that this was a motive in his assassination.
10. **honors** *n.* reputations.
11. **trash** *n.* that is, money.
12. **bay** *v.* howl at.
13. **bait** harass (as a bear tied to a stake is harassed by dogs).
14. **hedge me in** restrict my actions.
15. **make conditions** manage affairs.
16. **Urge** *v.* drive onward.
17. **health** *n.* safety.
18. **slight** *adj.* insignificant.
19. **choler** (käl´ ə r) *n.* anger.

15 **Reading Check**
Of what does Brutus accuse Cassius?

Differentiated Instruction for Universal Access

Enrichment for Advanced Readers
Have students choose partners to find and read aloud the play's crucial conversations between Brutus and Cassius in Acts I, II, and III. Then have students participate in a panel discussion in which they analyze the causes and course of the conflict between the two friends up until the beginning of Scene iii in Act IV. The panel might discuss the following questions: What is the conflict between Brutus and Cassius in Act I? Is the conflict the same in Act III? How might their relationship have changed its course? What might have happened between them if Brutus had accepted any of Cassius' advice in Acts II and III? Is the conflict resolved in Act IV? If so, how? If not, do students think it will be resolved in Act V? How?

13 Reading Skill
Read Between the Lines
1. Ask two volunteers to take the parts of Brutus and Cassius and read aloud their conversation in lines 1–32.
2. **Ask:** What wrong has Brutus done to Cassius by condemning Lucius?
Answer: Brutus has shown disrespect toward Cassius by ignoring his pleas on Lucius' behalf.
3. Then have students consider Brutus' complaints against Cassius in lines 18–26. **Ask** students to answer the Reading Skill question: When Brutus asks who stabbed Caesar "not for justice," what is he suggesting about Cassius?
Possible response: Brutus is suggesting that Cassius had personal reasons for murdering Caesar.
4. Then **ask:** What contrast does Brutus suggest between himself and Cassius?
Possible response: Brutus suggests that in killing Caesar, he acted honorably for the sake of justice, while Cassius acted dishonorably for personal reasons. He also suggests that he is a better Roman than Cassius.

14 Background
Roman Names
Brutus sometimes calls Cassius "Caius Cassius" and sometimes refers to himself as "Marcus Brutus." Caesar's full name was Gaius Julius Caesar.

Romans had three names. All members of the same family had the same second and third names. The first name, or *praenomen*, distinguished a person from other members of his or her family; it was the equivalent of a modern given name, like Dolores, Richard, or José. The second name, or *nomen*, distinguished a particular clan. The third name, or *cognomen*, named the family within the larger clan.

The praenomen Gaius would be used only by those who knew Caesar intimately—his parents, aunts and uncles, brothers and sisters. Julius designated the Julian house to which the family of Caesar belonged.

15 Reading Check
Answer: Brutus accuses Cassius of killing Caesar because his officials were taking bribes and then of taking bribes himself.

16 Literary Analysis

Conflict

1. Ask students to read the dialogue between Brutus and Cassius in lines 33–64. Have students note the insults, taunts, and threats that Brutus and Cassius trade. Point out the many references that Brutus makes to Cassius' anger ("rash choler," "choleric," "test humor," "venom of your spleen," "waspish").
2. **Ask:** Which of Cassius' reactions show the building tension of the conflict in this scene?
   Answer: The building tension is evident in line 58 when Cassius refers to Caesar, pointedly making Brutus compare himself to his murdered friend. Also, Cassius' suggestion in line 64 that he might do something for which he will be sorry shows how heated the discussion has become.
3. **Ask** students what the dialogue suggests might happen.
   Possible response: The dialogue suggests that one of the two might attack or even kill the other.

17 Critical Thinking

Cause and Effect

1. Review previous encounters between Brutus and Cassius. Then, ask students to identify the real causes of the quarrel in this scene.
   Possible responses: Brutus may be angry because Cassius urged the conspiracy on him and now seems to lack the courage to fight to the end. Cassius may blame Brutus for showing mercy to Antony and thus causing the present trouble. Brutus now seems to doubt Cassius' motives in the murder of Caesar.
2. Invite students to speculate about the effects of this quarrel.
   Possible response: The alliance between Brutus and Cassius may break down, and they may be defeated by Antony and Octavius.

---

20. choleric (käl′ ə rik) *adj.* quick-tempered.
21. bondmen *n.* slaves.
22. budge *v.* flinch away from you.
23. observe you show reverence toward you.
24. crouch *v.* bow.
25. testy humor irritability.
26. digest . . . spleen eat the poison of your spleen. (The spleen was thought to be the source of anger.)

16

Vocabulary
mirth (mʉrth) *n.* joyfulness; merriment

CASSIUS. O ye gods, ye gods! Must I endure all this?

BRUTUS. All this? Ay, more: fret till your proud heart break.
Go show your slaves how choleric[20] you are,
And make your bondmen[21] tremble. Must I budge?[22]
Must I observe you?[23] Must I stand and crouch[24]
Under your testy humor?[25] By the gods,
You shall digest the venom of your spleen,[26]
Though it do split you; for, from this day forth,
I'll use you for my **mirth**, yea, for my laughter,
When you are waspish.[27]

CASSIUS. Is it come to this?

BRUTUS. You say you are a better soldier:
Let it appear so; make your vaunting[28] true,
And it shall please me well. For mine own part,
I shall be glad to learn of[29] noble men.

27. waspish *adj.* bad-tempered.
28. vaunting (vônt′ iŋ) *n.* boasting.
29. learn of hear about; learn from.
30. durst *v.* dared.
31. moved *v.* angered.

17

CASSIUS. You wrong me every way; you wrong me, Brutus;
I said, an elder soldier, not a better.
Did I say, better?

BRUTUS. If you did, I care not.

CASSIUS. When Caesar lived, he durst[30] not thus have moved[31] me.

BRUTUS. Peace, peace, you durst not so have tempted him.

CASSIUS. I durst not?

BRUTUS. No.

CASSIUS. What? Durst not tempt him?

BRUTUS. For your life you durst not.

Vocabulary
presume (prē zo͞om′) *v.* rely too much on; take advantage of

CASSIUS. Do not **presume** too much upon my love;
I may do that I shall be sorry for.

BRUTUS. You have done that you should be sorry for.
There is no terror, Cassius, in your threats;
For I am armed so strong in honesty
That they pass by me as the idle wind,
Which I respect not. I did send to you
For certain sums of gold, which you denied me;
For I can raise no money by vile means.
By heaven, I had rather coin my heart
And drop my blood for drachmas[32] than to wring
From the hard hands of peasants their vile trash
By any indirection.[33] I did send

20

32. drachmas (drak′ məz) *n.* silver coins of ancient Greece.
33. indirection *n.* irregular methods.

Vocabulary Development

Word Forms

Give students a blank **Word Form Chart** (***Professional Development Guidebook***, p. 42), with *covert, chastisement,* and *mirth* in the correct columns. Work with the class, or have students work with partners, to determine the related forms. The final chart should look like the one shown.

Noun	Verb	Adjective	Adverb
covertness		**covert**	covertly
chastisement	chastise	chastised	
mirth		mirthful	mirthfully

18 ◀ **Critical Viewing**
What does this ancient Roman sculpture suggest about the Roman attitude toward war? **[Interpret]**

19

20

To you for gold to pay my legions,[34]
Which you denied me. Was that done like Cassius?
Should I have answered Caius Cassius so?
When Marcus Brutus grows so covetous[35]
To lock such rascal counters[36] from his friends,
Be ready, gods, with all your thunderbolts,
Dash him to pieces!

CASSIUS. I denied you not.

BRUTUS. You did.

CASSIUS. I did not. He was but a fool
That brought my answer back. Brutus hath rived[37] my heart.

34. **legions** *n.* Roman military divisions of several thousand soldiers.
35. **covetous** (kuv′ ət əs) *adj.* greedy.
36. **rascal counters** worthless coins.
37. **rived** (rīvd) *v.* broken.

21 ☑ Reading Check
What is the second accusation Brutus makes against Cassius?

Differentiated Instruction for Universal Access

Strategy for Special Needs Students
Have students read lines 63–91in their textbooks while you play the ***Hear It!* Audio CD**. Pause the recording after each character's lines or after every five lines to discuss the conflict developments in the plot. Identify this exchange as an external conflict.

Strategy for Less Proficient Readers
Read Brutus' monologue aloud. With students, paraphrase his statements. Then, have students continue reading Scene iii aloud until line 122, either in small groups or with partners. If necessary, students can trade or alternate roles so that everyone has a chance to read and to listen. After each character's part, ask students to summarize what they have read.

18 Critical Viewing
Answer: The sculpture suggests that war was an integral, even familiar, part of Roman culture, and that victory and feats in battle were a demonstration of manhood and power.

19 Background
Latin Inscriptions
The Romans inscribed text on all kinds of objects. Latin inscriptions include epitaphs and official documents (laws, wills, treaties, and records of honors bestowed on individuals). They provide valuable information about events, policy, and elements of public and private life. Most inscriptions were incised, or carved into a surface, on stone or bronze. Letters were also often colored for better legibility—red on stone and white on bronze. Inscribers generally used one or the other of two styles of capital letters, one larger and more formal, the other smaller, yet still neat.

20 Critical Thinking
Interpret
1. Have two students take turns reading aloud Brutus' monologue from line 65–82.
2. **Ask** students to identify the main issue Brutus takes with Cassius in this speech.
   Answer: Brutus accuses Cassius of being corrupt and greedy when it comes to money.
3. **Ask** students to paraphrase how Brutus describes himself in his speech.
   Possible response: Brutus says that he is honest and incapable of stealing, coveting, or otherwise manipulating money.
4. Have students reread lines 79–82. Then **ask** students how these lines reaffirm Brutus' claim that he is noble.
   Possible response: In these lines, Brutus asks the gods to kill him if he ever lets monetary greed rule his actions; he is stating that he is so noble that he would die before being dishonest.

21 Reading Check
Answer: Brutus accuses Cassius of not providing the necessary funds for his army in lines 75–77.

22 Reading Skill

Reading Between the Lines

1. Have students look for the deeper meaning in the dialogue between Brutus and Cassius in lines 84–117. **Ask** students to read between the lines to explain why Cassius is so offended by what Brutus says.
   Possible response: Cassius' language and general demeanor throughout this scene and elsewhere show that he has great respect for Brutus. He is hurt by Brutus' accusations because he wants Brutus' good opinion.
2. Have students infer why Brutus drops the quarrel at line 106.
   Possible response: Brutus may understand that he has pushed Cassius too far. Cassius' suggestion that Brutus kill him may convince Brutus of Cassius' sincerity and commitment to Rome.

23 Critical Viewing

Possible response: Brutus and Cassius do not look as if they will be able to settle their conflict. Cassius is drawing his dagger, and Brutus' indignant stance and unyielding facial expression suggest anger.

24 Humanities

Still Photograph from *Julius Caesar* (1953)

In this film still, Cassius is at the left and Brutus at the right. Both are in military dress. Cassius carries arms.

The primary Roman weapon was the *pilum*, or throwing spear. The *gladius*, or two-edged thrusting sword, was used for close fighting. Roman soldiers were generally equipped with the armor they could afford. The richest had the most complete armor. Poorer soldiers wore a bronze plate, or *pectorale*, over a sleeveless leather jacket. The richest were protected by a coat of mail. Use these questions for discussion.

- How does Cassius' dress compare with that of Brutus?
  Answer: Both appear to be wearing leather, but Cassius' dress is slightly more decorated than Brutus' dress.
- Why do you think Cassius is carrying weapons, but Brutus is not?
  Possible response: Cassius has just arrived from the field, where he would have needed to carry arms, and Brutus has been in his camp.

A friend should bear his friend's infirmities;
But Brutus makes mine greater than they are.

BRUTUS. I do not, till you practice them on me.

CASSIUS. You love me not.

BRUTUS. I do not like your faults.

CASSIUS. A friendly eye could never see such faults.

BRUTUS. A flatterer's would not, though they do appear
As huge as high Olympus.

CASSIUS. Come, Antony, and young Octavius, come,
Revenge yourselves alone[38] on Cassius,
For Cassius is aweary of the world:
Hated by one he loves; braved[39] by his brother;
Checked like a bondman;[40] all his faults observed,
Set in a notebook, learned and conned by rote[41]
To cast into my teeth. O, I could weep
My spirit from mine eyes! There is my dagger,

38. **alone** *adv.* only.
39. **braved** *adj.* defied; challenged.
40. **Checked like a bondman** scolded like a slave.
41. **conned by rote** memorized.

23 ▼ **Critical Viewing** In this film still, do Brutus and Cassius look as if they will be able to settle their conflict? Explain. **[Hypothesize]**

24

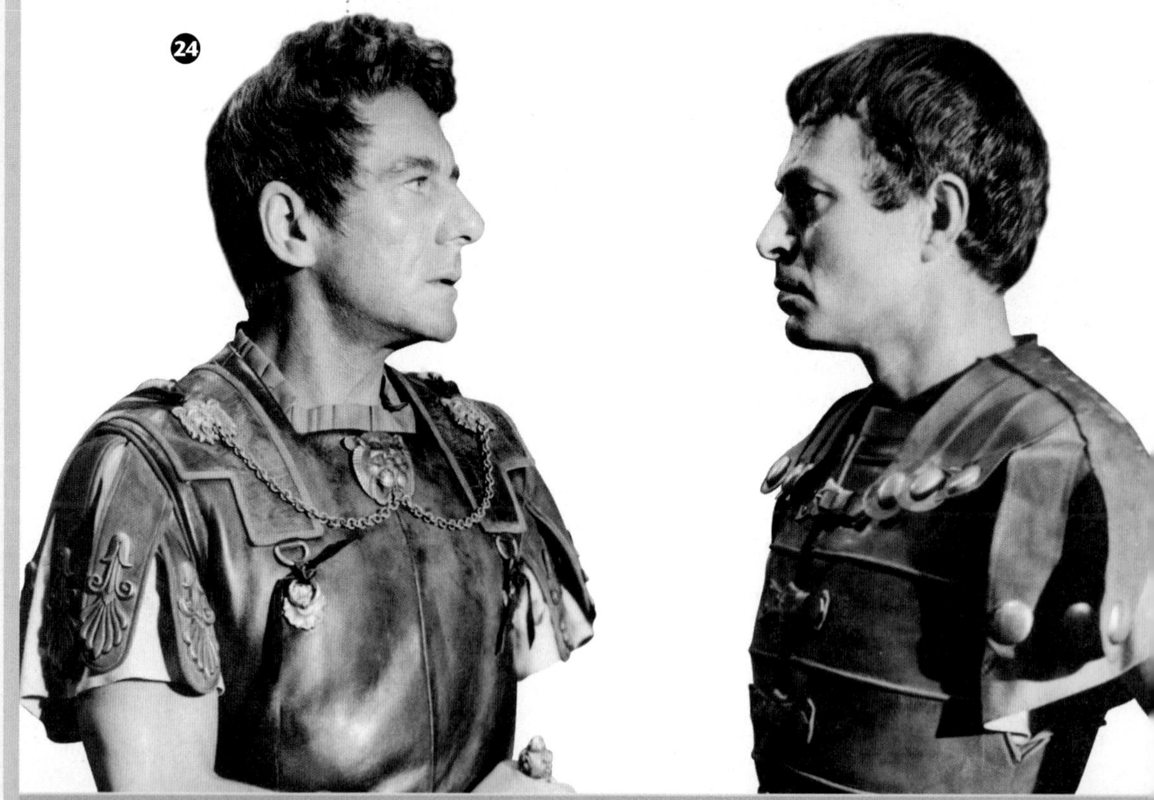

And here my naked breast; within, a heart
Dearer than Pluto's mine,[42] richer than gold;
If that thou be'st a Roman, take it forth.
I, that denied thee gold, will give my heart.
Strike as thou didst at Caesar; for I know,
(22) When thou didst hate him worst, thou lovedst him better
Than ever thou lovedst Cassius.

BRUTUS. Sheathe your dagger.
Be angry when you will, it shall have scope.[43]
Do what you will, dishonor shall be humor.[44]
O Cassius, you are yokèd[45] with a lamb
That carries anger as the flint[46] bears fire,
Who, much enforcèd,[47] shows a hasty spark,
And straight[48] is cold again.

(25) **CASSIUS.** Hath Cassius lived
To be but mirth and laughter to his Brutus
When grief and blood ill-tempered vexeth him?

BRUTUS. When I spoke that, I was ill-tempered too.

CASSIUS. Do you confess so much? Give me your hand.

BRUTUS. And my heart too.

CASSIUS. O Brutus!

BRUTUS. What's the matter?

CASSIUS. Have not you love enough to bear with me
When that rash humor[49] which my mother gave me
(26) Makes me forgetful?

BRUTUS. Yes, Cassius, and from henceforth,
When you are overearnest with your Brutus,
He'll think your mother chides, and leave you so.[50]

[*Enter a* POET, *followed by* LUCILIUS, TITINIUS, *and* LUCIUS.]

POET. Let me go in to see the generals;
There is some grudge between 'em; 'tis not meet
They be alone.

LUCILIUS. You shall not come to them.

(28) **POET.** Nothing but death shall stay me.

CASSIUS. How now? What's the matter?

POET. For shame, you generals! What do you mean?
Love, and be friends, as two such men should be;
For I have seen more years, I'm sure, than ye.

42. **Pluto's mine** all the riches in the Earth.
43. **scope** *n.* free play.
44. **dishonor . . . humor** I will consider any insults to be just the effect of your irritable disposition.
45. **yokèd** *adj.* in partnership.
46. **flint** *n.* hard mineral that, when struck by steel, makes sparks.
47. **enforcèd** *adj.* provoked.
48. **straight** *adv.* immediately.
49. **humor** *n.* temperament.
50. **your mother . . . so** it is just your inherited disposition and let it go at that.

Reading Skill
Read Between the Lines In this situation, what does Cassius' use of the phrase "his Brutus" suggest?

(27) **Reading Check**
What happens in the quarrel between Cassius and Brutus?

(25) Reading Skill

Read Between the Lines

1. Have students read lines 112–114.
2. **Ask** students the Reading Skill question: In this situation, what does Cassius' use of the phrase "his Brutus" suggest?
   Possible response: Cassius' use of the phrase here shows both friendship and subordination to Brutus. Cassius suggests that Brutus is worthy of deciding whether Cassius is a worthy friend, and Cassius is ready to do as Brutus wishes to earn that respect.
3. **Ask:** How do you think Brutus is affected by Cassius' use of the phrase?
   Possible response: The phrase seems to soften Brutus' reaction to Cassius, which allows Brutus to admit his own anger and to pledge Cassius his friendship.

(26) THE BIG ? Connecting to the Big Question

1. Explain to students that friends, family, and enemies influence the way we perceive ourselves and the world around us.
2. Have students read the bracketed text. **Ask:** What is Cassius' explanation for his rash behavior?
   Possible response: He maintains that he inherited his irritable disposition from his mother.
3. **Ask:** How does Cassius' explanation allow Brutus to perceive him differently?
   Possible response: Brutus accepts Cassius' explanation and says he will take Cassius' anger as the result of his inherited disposition.

(27) Reading Check

Answer: They blame their quarrel on their anger and reconfirm their friendship.

Differentiated Instruction for Universal Access

Enrichment for Gifted and Talented Students
Remind students that Act IV, Scene iii, marks the second time a poet wanders into a scene. The first occurs at the end of Act III, when Cinna the Poet is mistaken for a conspirator and is attacked. The poet in Act IV, Scene iii, tries to mend the quarrel between Brutus and Cassius, only to be insulted and told to leave. Ask students to hypothesize why Shakespeare includes poets in Acts III and IV. How do these two instances comment on poetry's place in ancient Rome or in Shakespeare's time?

Enrichment for Advanced Readers
Have students analyze the quarrel between Cassius and Brutus and assess whether it is realistic. Tell students to look at such details in the scene as line length, length of individual speeches, and the language and images that the characters use in speaking to each other. Then ask students to write brief essays presenting their analyses of the reality of the scene and hypothesizing about why Shakespeare presents the conflict in this way.

28 Literary Analysis

Conflict

1. Read aloud lines 123–143.
2. **Ask** students to respond to the Literary Analysis question: How does the arrival of the poet help end the conflict between Cassius and Brutus?
   Possible response: Cassius and Brutus have just settled their bitter quarrel. When the poet arrives, they can use him as a target for any remaining hostility.

29 Literary Analysis

Conflict

1. **Ask** students why Brutus' internal conflict would affect his earlier external conflict with Cassius.
   Possible response: Brutus may have been preoccupied with Portia's death, which may have affected his ability to listen to Cassius' complaints calmly and rationally.
2. Read aloud lines 149–155 after Brutus shares the news of Portia's death. Then **ask:** How does Cassius acknowledge the effect of Brutus' grief on their earlier conflict?
   Answer: Cassius says that he is surprised Brutus did not kill him.

30 Literature in Context

Humanities Connection The philosophical school of Stoicism took its name from the Stoa Poikile (which means "painted colonnade"), the public hall in Athens where Zeno taught. Panaetius, foremost teacher of Stoicism during its Middle Period (second and first centuries B.C.), is largely responsible for the adoption of Stoic philosophy by Brutus and other members of the Roman nobility.

Connect to the Literature After reviewing the information on Stoicism, **ask** the Connect to the Literature question: How do Brutus' Stoic beliefs affect his actions in Act IV?
Possible response: Brutus generally guards his emotions and does not allow the death of his wife, Portia, which is an event out of his control, to affect his immediate activities and concerns as a general.

---

51. cynic *n.* rude fellow.
52. Saucy *adj.* rude; insolent.
53. I'll know . . . time I'll accept his eccentricity when he chooses a proper time to exhibit it.
54. jigging *adj.* rhyming.
55. Companion *n.* fellow (used to show contempt).

28

Literary Analysis
Conflict How does the arrival of the poet help end the conflict between Cassius and Brutus?

CASSIUS. Ha, ha! How vilely doth this cynic[51] rhyme!

BRUTUS. Get you hence, sirrah! Saucy[52] fellow, hence!

CASSIUS. Bear with him, Brutus, 'tis his fashion.

BRUTUS. I'll know his humor when he knows his time.[53]
What should the wars do with these jigging[54] fools?
Companion,[55] hence!

CASSIUS. Away, away, be gone! [*Exit* POET.]

BRUTUS. Lucilius and Titinius, bid the commanders
Prepare to lodge their companies tonight.

CASSIUS. And come yourselves, and bring Messala with you
Immediately to us. [*Exit* LUCILIUS *and* TITINIUS.]

BRUTUS. Lucius, a bowl of wine. [*Exit* LUCIUS.]

CASSIUS. I did not think you could have been so angry.

BRUTUS. O Cassius, I am sick of many griefs.

CASSIUS. Of your philosophy you make no use,
If you give place to accidental evils.[56]

BRUTUS. No man bears sorrow better. Portia is dead.

CASSIUS. Ha? Portia?

BRUTUS. She is dead.

56. Of your philosophy . . . evils As a Stoic, Brutus believed that chance misfortunes should not disturb his peace of mind.

29

30

LITERATURE IN CONTEXT

Humanities Connection

Stoicism
Brutus follows a philosophy called Stoicism (stō´ i siz´ əm), a school of thought established by the ancient Greek thinker Zeno sometime after 312 B.C. Stoicism stresses the following ideas:

- The universe is ruled by unchanging natural laws.
- A wise person lives a virtuous life, using reason to understand natural laws and to act accordingly.
- A wise person is not ruled by his or her emotions.
- Using reason, a wise person distinguishes between what is truly in his or her power and what is not.
- A wise person does not allow events that he or she does not control—even the loss of a loved one—to affect him or her.

Connect to the Literature

How do Brutus' Stoic beliefs affect his actions in Act IV?

Vocabulary Development

Word Analysis

Call students' attention to the word *philosophy* in line 144. Tell students that the word derives from ancient Greek. It combines the Greek root *-phil-*, which means "love," with the Greek root *-soph-*, meaning "wisdom." Thus the literal meaning of *philosophy* is "love of wisdom." Point out that these roots are used to form many other words. Divide the class into groups and have the groups use dictionaries to identify as many words with either of these roots as they can. Have the groups also look up the meanings of the words they have identified and be prepared to use each word in a sentence.

CASSIUS. How scaped I killing when I crossed you so?[57]
29 O insupportable and touching[58] loss!
Upon[59] what sickness?

BRUTUS. Impatient of my absence,
And grief that young Octavius with Mark Antony
Have made themselves so strong—for with her death
That tidings[60] came—with this she fell distract,[61]
And (her attendants absent) swallowed fire.

CASSIUS. And died so?

31 **BRUTUS.** Even so.

CASSIUS. O ye immortal gods!

[*Enter* LUCIUS, *with wine and tapers.*]

BRUTUS. Speak no more of her. Give me a bowl of wine.
In this I bury all unkindness, Cassius. [*Drinks*]

CASSIUS. My heart is thirsty for that noble pledge.
Fill, Lucius, till the wine o'erswell the cup;
I cannot drink too much of Brutus' love.

[*Drinks. Exit* LUCIUS.]

[*Enter* TITINIUS *and* MESSALA.]

BRUTUS. Come in, Titinius! Welcome, good Messala.
Now sit we close about this taper here,
And call in question[62] our necessities.

CASSIUS. Portia, art thou gone?

BRUTUS. No more, I pray you.
Messala, I have here receivèd letters
That young Octavius and Mark Antony
Come down upon us with a mighty power,[63]
34 Bending their expedition toward Philippi.[64]

MESSALA. Myself have letters of the selfsame tenure.[65]

BRUTUS. With what addition?

MESSALA. That by proscription and bills of outlawry[66]
Octavius, Antony, and Lepidus
32 Have put to death an hundred senators.

BRUTUS. Therein our letters do not well agree.
Mine speak of seventy senators that died
By their proscriptions, Cicero being one.

CASSIUS. Cicero one?

57. **How scaped . . . you so?** How did I escape being killed when I opposed you so?
58. **touching** *adj.* deeply wounding.
59. **Upon** *prep.* as a result of.

Literary Analysis
Conflict With what internal conflict has Brutus been struggling?

60. **with . . . tidings came** That is, Brutus received two messages at the same time: news of Portia's death and news of Octavius and Antony's success.
61. **fell distract** became distraught.
62. **call in question** examine.
63. **power** *n.* army.
64. **Bending . . . Philippi** (fi lip´ ī) directing their rapid march toward Philippi, a city in Macedonia.
65. **selfsame tenure** same message.
66. **proscription . . . outlawry** proclamation of death sentences and lists of those condemned.

33 **Reading Check**
What has happened to Brutus' wife, Portia?

31 Literary Analysis
Conflict
Ask students the Literary Analysis question: With what internal conflict has Brutus been struggling?
Answer: Brutus is struggling with his grief over Portia's death.

32 Background
Death of Cicero
Antony, Octavius, and Lepidus used proscription to execute Cicero, among other senators. Under an order of proscription, they published a list of Roman citizens whom they designated as outlaws and seized their property. Then soldiers were dispatched to hunt down those on the list and execute them, wherever they were in Rome or in all of Italy. Family members, slaves, and the general public were rewarded or punished for their help or lack of it. Antony had Cicero put on the list, and he was caught trying to escape by sea. His slaves stood by him. He was executed on December 7, 43 B.C.

33 Reading Check
Answer: Portia killed herself.

Differentiated Instruction for Universal Access

EL Strategy for English Learners
With students, choose and write on the board six words from lines 162–188 challenging or that are used differently than in modern speech. For example, *taper, tenure, proscription, writ, aught*, and *manner* may be difficult for English learners in this context. Assign groups and give each group one of the words. Have students research the word using dictionaries and encyclopedias. They should report what they find to the class. Reread lines 162–188 after discussing the vocabulary together.

Enrichment for Advanced Readers
Have students research Stoicism and its principle of accepting death and other events beyond one's control without grief, fear, or other emotion, as presented in the play. Have them examine this scene and earlier passages in the play that reflect this idea, such as Act II, Scene ii, lines 35–37, and Act III, Scene i, lines 99–100. Have them note which characters seem not to fear death, what happens to these characters, and how they die (if they do). Then ask students to write paragraphs about what the Stoic motif adds to the play's impact.

34 Reading Skill

Read Between the Lines

1. **Ask** students to summarize the news that Brutus and Messala share in lines 165–179.
   Answer: Octavius and Antony are approaching Philippi with a huge army. The triumvirate has had as many as one hundred senators murdered, including Cicero.
2. **Ask** students the Reading Skill question: In this situation, why might Messala ask Brutus about news of Portia?
   Possible response: The murder of senators who supported Caesar's assassination suggests that the situation in Rome is unstable, and Messala may be concerned for the safety of senators' families.
3. Point out that although he has shared the news with Cassius, Brutus does not volunteer information about Portia's death to Messala. **Ask:** What does Brutus' concealment of Portia's death from Messala suggest about their relationship?
   Possible response: They are probably not close friends. Brutus may not trust Messala or want to confide in any but an intimate friend such as Cassius.

35 Background

Philippi

Located in eastern Macedonia, Philippi was known as Daton until it was claimed in 356 B.C. by Philip II of Macedon and renamed after him. Antony, Cassius, and Brutus met in battle there in 42 B.C. Afterward, Antony founded a veterans' colony in Philippi, and Octavian later sent additional veterans there.

Reading Skill 34
Read Between the Lines In this situation, why might Messala ask Brutus about news of Portia?

MESSALA. Cicero is dead,
And by that order of proscription.
Had you your letters from your wife, my lord?

BRUTUS. No, Messala.

MESSALA. Nor nothing in your letters writ of her?

BRUTUS. Nothing, Messala.

MESSALA. That methinks is strange.

BRUTUS. Why ask you? Hear you aught[67] of her in yours?

MESSALA. No, my lord.

BRUTUS. Now as you are a Roman, tell me true.

MESSALA. Then like a Roman bear the truth I tell,
For certain she is dead, and by strange manner.

BRUTUS. Why, farewell, Portia. We must die, Messala.
With meditating that she must die once,
I have the patience to endure it now.

MESSALA. Even so great men great losses should endure.

CASSIUS. I have as much of this in art[68] as you,
But yet my nature could not bear it so.

BRUTUS. Well, to our work alive.[69] What do you think
Of marching to Philippi presently?[70]

CASSIUS. I do not think it good.

BRUTUS. Your reason?

CASSIUS. This it is:
'Tis better that the enemy seek us;
So shall he waste his means, weary his soldiers,
Doing himself offense,[71] whilst we, lying still,
Are full of rest, defense, and nimbleness.

BRUTUS. Good reasons must of force[72] give place to better.
The people 'twixt Philippi and this ground
Do stand but in a forced affection;[73]
For they have grudged us contribution.[74]
The enemy, marching along by them,
By them shall make a fuller number up,[75]
Come on refreshed, new-added[76] and encouraged;
From which advantage shall we cut him off
If at Philippi we do face him there,
These people at our back.

35 36

67. **aught** (ôt) *n.* anything at all.
68. **have . . . art** have as much Stoicism in theory.
69. **to our work alive** Let us go about the work we have to do as living men.
70. **presently** *adv.* immediately.
71. **offense** *n.* harm.
72. **of force** of necessity.
73. **Do stand . . . affection** support us only out of fear of force.
74. **grudged us contribution** given us aid and supplies grudgingly.
75. **shall make . . . up** will add more to their numbers.
76. **new-added** reinforced.

Vocabulary Development

Vocabulary Reinforcement

To reinforce and assess students' comprehension of selection vocabulary, provide sentences in which the words may or may not be used correctly. Instruct students to use the "yes/no—why" format to tell whether the words are used correctly and explain why. Use these sentences:

1. She made a *rash* decision without considering the consequences.
   Answer: Yes, *rash* is used correctly here. A decision that did not take consequences into account could be described as impulsive.
2. He did not notice the *nimbleness* of his nose and ears until they turned red from the cold.
   Answer: No, *nimbleness* is not used correctly. It means "the ability to move quickly" and would not be used to describe a person's cold nose and ears.

CASSIUS. Hear me, good brother.

BRUTUS. Under your pardon.[77] You must note beside
That we have tried the utmost of our friends,
Our legions are brimful, our cause is ripe.
The enemy increaseth every day;
We, at the height, are ready to decline.
36 There is a tide in the affairs of men
Which, taken at the flood, leads on to fortune;
Omitted,[78] all the voyage of their life
Is bound[79] in shallows and in miseries.
On such a full sea are we now afloat,
And we must take the current when it serves,
Or lose our ventures.[80]

37 **CASSIUS.** Then, with your will,[81] go on;
We'll along ourselves and meet them at Philippi.

BRUTUS. The deep of night is crept upon our talk,
And nature must obey necessity,
Which we will niggard with a little rest.[82]
There is no more to say?

CASSIUS. No more. Good night.
Early tomorrow will we rise and hence.[83]

[*Enter* LUCIUS.]

BRUTUS. Lucius, my gown.[84] [*Exit* LUCIUS.]
Farewell, good Messala.
Good night, Titinius. Noble, noble Cassius,
Good night, and good repose.

CASSIUS. O my dear brother,
This was an ill beginning of the night.
Never come[85] such division 'tween our souls!
Let it not, Brutus.

[*Enter* LUCIUS, *with the gown.*]

BRUTUS. Everything is well.

CASSIUS. Good night, my lord.

BRUTUS. Good night, good brother.

TITINIUS, MESSALA. Good night, Lord Brutus.

BRUTUS. Farewell, every one. 38

[*Exit*]

Give me the gown. Where is thy instrument?[86]

77. **Under your pardon** excuse me.

Reading Skill
Read Between the Lines What does Brutus' speech indicate about the chances that he and Cassius will lose the war?

78. **Omitted** *adj.* neglected.
79. **bound** *adj.* confined.
80. **ventures** *n.* things put at risk in hope of profit—as a merchant risks goods in sending them by sea.
81. **with your will** as you wish.
82. **niggard . . . rest** satisfy stingily with a short sleep.

83. **hence** leave.

84. **gown** *n.* dressing gown; robe.

85. **Never come** may there never again come.

86. **instrument** *n.* lute (probably), a small stringed instrument related to the guitar.

Reading Check
What do Brutus and Cassius plan to do?

Fluency

Students might have difficulty reading lines 202–230 because they contain phrases with which students may be unfamiliar. To model fluent reading, read the passage to students with expression as students track, or follow along by pointing at each word in the text as you read. Then, have students read the passage back to you. Look for these problem spots:

- Students may stumble with the phrase "twixt Philippi and this ground." Point out that *twixt* means "between." Have students read the line again, substituting "between" for *twixt.*
- Encourage students to sound out the phrases, repeating them until students can read the paragraph smoothly.

36 Reading Skill

Read Between the Lines

1. Have students read Brutus' description in lines 202–211 of his and Cassius' situation as compared to that of Antony and Octavius.
   Ask: Are Brutus and Cassius at an advantage or a disadvantage? Explain.
   Answer: They are at a disadvantage. People in the region fear them but do not support them.
2. **Ask** students the Reading Skill question: What does Brutus' speech indicate about the chances that he and Cassius will lose the war?
   Possible response: Brutus' speech suggests that the chances he and Cassius will lose the war are greater than the chances that they will win.

37 Literary Analysis

Conflict

1. Point out that once again, as in Acts II and III, Cassius and Brutus disagree over the best course of action. **Ask** students to describe the course of action each recommends.
   Answer: Cassius thinks they should wait for the enemy to come to them. Brutus thinks they should march to Philippi.
2. **Ask:** How is this conflict resolved?
   Answer: Cassius once again gives in to Brutus.
3. Have students discuss why the resolution of the conflict adds to the suspense, or feeling of tension, about how the play will end.
   Possible response: Students should note that so far Cassius has been right and Brutus has been wrong. Students should suspect that once again Brutus' suggested course of action will end badly. The foreboding that events will go wrong adds to the suspense.

38 Reading Check

Answer: They plan to march to Philippi.

39 Reading Skill

Read Between the Lines

1. Call on a volunteer to read lines 239–242. **Ask:** What does this passage reveal about Brutus?
   Possible response: He is a thoughtful leader who is aware of his servant's and his men's weariness.
2. Point out that these lines reveal a glimpse of Brutus' complex personality.
3. **Ask** students to elaborate on the complexity of Brutus' personality as shown in this scene and the whole act. Tell them to cite specific details from Act IV to this point.
   Possible response: In Brutus' remarks to his servant, the audience understands the gentle, compassionate side of Brutus' personality. Only a short time ago, Brutus angrily critiqued his friend's personality and stoically put his wife's death out of his mind to discuss a cold, calculated battle plan.

Monitor Progress Circulate among students to check their use of the **Reading Skill Graphic Organizer B** in Act IV.

Reteach Select one of the Reading Skill questions from earlier in Act IV, and walk students through the three-step process of reading between the lines. As a class, consider what the passage says. Next, interpret the passage to determine what it means. Finally, determine why the passage is important, or how it works in the scene, act, or play as a whole. Repeating this process, have students work in pairs or small groups with a different Reading Skill question from earlier in Act IV. Students should write their interpretations for review.

LUCIUS. Here in the tent.

BRUTUS. What, thou speak'st drowsily?
Poor knave,[87] I blame thee not; thou art o'erwatched.[88]
Call Claudius and some other of my men;
I'll have them sleep on cushions in my tent.

LUCIUS. Varro and Claudius!

[*Enter* VARRO *and* CLAUDIUS.]

VARRO. Calls my lord?

BRUTUS. I pray you, sirs, lie in my tent and sleep.
It may be I shall raise[89] you by and by
On business to my brother Cassius.

VARRO. So please you, we will stand and watch your pleasure.[90]

BRUTUS. I will not have it so; lie down, good sirs;
It may be I shall otherwise bethink me.[91]

[VARRO *and* CLAUDIUS *lie down.*]

Look. Lucius, here's the book I sought for so;
I put it in the pocket of my gown.

LUCIUS. I was sure your lordship did not give it me.

BRUTUS. Bear with me, good boy, I am much forgetful.
Canst thou hold up thy heavy eyes awhile,
And touch thy instrument a strain or two?[92]

LUCIUS. Ay, my lord, an't[93] please you.

BRUTUS. It does, my boy.
I trouble thee too much, but thou art willing.

LUCIUS. It is my duty, sir.

BRUTUS. I should not urge thy duty past thy might;
I know young bloods[94] look for a time of rest.

LUCIUS. I have slept, my lord, already.

BRUTUS. It was well done, and thou shalt sleep again;
I will not hold thee long. If I do live,
I will be good to thee.

[*Music, and a song*]

This is a sleepy tune. O murd'rous[95] slumber!
Layest thou thy leaden mace[96] upon my boy,
That plays thee music? Gentle knave, good night;
I will not do thee so much wrong to wake thee.
If thou dost nod, thou break'st thy instrument;

87. **knave** (nāv) *n.* servant.
88. **o'erwatched** *adj.* weary with too much watchfulness.
89. **raise** *v.* wake.
90. **watch your pleasure** stay alert for your command.
91. **otherwise bethink me** change my mind.
92. **touch . . . a strain or two?** play a melody or two on your instrument.
93. **an't** if it.
94. **young bloods** young bodies.
95. **murd'rous** *adj.* deathlike.
96. **mace** (mās) *n.* staff of office (an allusion to the practice of tapping a person on the shoulder with a mace when arresting him).

Vocabulary Development

Vocabulary Knowledge Rating

When students have completed reading and discussing *The Tragedy of Julius Caesar,* Act IV, have them take out their **Vocabulary Knowledge Rating Chart** for this selection. Read the words aloud once more, and have students rate their knowledge of the words again in the After Reading column. Clarify any words that are still problematic. Have students write their own definition and example or sentence in the appropriate column. Then have students complete the Vocabulary Practice at the end of the selection. Encourage students to use the words in further discussion and written work about this selection. Remind them that they will be accountable for these words on the **Selection Test,** ***Unit 5 Resources,*** pp. 157–159 or 160–162.

I'll take it from thee; and, good boy, good night.
Let me see, let me see; is not the leaf[97] turned down
Where I left reading? Here it is, I think.

40 [*Enter the ghost of* CAESAR.]

How ill this taper burns. Ha! Who comes here?
I think it is the weakness of mine eyes
That shapes this monstrous apparition.[98]
It comes upon[99] me. Art thou anything?
Art thou some god, some angel, or some devil,
That mak'st my blood cold, and my hair to stare?[100]
Speak to me what thou art.

GHOST. Thy evil spirit, Brutus.

BRUTUS. Why com'st thou?

GHOST. To tell thee thou shalt see me at Philippi.

41 **BRUTUS.** Well; then I shall see thee again?

GHOST. Ay, at Philippi.

BRUTUS. Why, I will see thee at Philippi then.

[*Exit* GHOST.]

Now I have taken heart thou vanishest.
Ill spirit, I would hold more talk with thee.
Boy! Lucius! Varro! Claudius! Sirs, awake!
Claudius!

LUCIUS. The strings, my lord, are false.[101]

BRUTUS. He thinks he still is at his instrument.
Lucius, awake!

42 **LUCIUS.** My lord?

BRUTUS. Didst thou dream, Lucius, that thou so criedst out?

LUCIUS. My lord, I do not know that I did cry.

BRUTUS. Yes, that thou didst. Didst thou see anything?

LUCIUS. Nothing, my lord.

BRUTUS. Sleep again, Lucius. Sirrah Claudius!
[*To* VARRO] Fellow thou, awake!

VARRO. My lord?

CLAUDIUS. My lord?

BRUTUS. Why did you so cry out, sirs, in your sleep?

97. **leaf** *n.* page.
98. **monstrous apparition** ominous ghost.
99. **upon** *prep.* toward.
100. **stare** *n.* stand on end.

Reading Skill
Read Between the Lines Brutus is planning to march to battle at Philippi. In this situation, what might the ghost's warning mean?

101. **false** *adj.* out of tune.

Literary Analysis
Conflict What internal conflict might the ghost's warning create for Brutus?

Reading Check
What frightens Brutus in his sleep?

40 Background

Shakespeare's Ghosts

Several of Shakespeare's plays feature ghosts. In *Hamlet*, the ghost of King Hamlet appears to his son, urging him to avenge his murder. In *Macbeth*, the ghost of Banquo appears to Macbeth at a banquet, terrifying the man who earlier that day had ordered his murder.

On the Elizabethan stage, ghosts were assumed to be real, not figments of a character's imagination. The audience accepted the notion that a ghost had the power to make itself visible and heard at will.

41 Reading Skill

Read Between the Lines

1. **Ask** students the Reading Skill question: Brutus is planning to march to battle at Philippi. In this situation, what might the ghost's warning mean?
   Possible response: The ghost's warning may mean that Brutus will not see him again until he is a ghost himself; if so, the ghost means that Brutus will die at Philippi.
2. **Ask** students to speculate about why Brutus might want "to hold more talk with" the ghost.
   Possible response: Brutus may think the ghost can foretell the future. He may want the ghost to tell him what will happen at Philippi.

42 Literary Analysis

Conflict

1. Have a student read aloud line 285. **Ask** how this line develops the plot and prepares the audience for Act V.
   Possible response: In the statement, Brutus reinforces his decision to march to Philippi. The audience anticipates the meeting between Brutus and the ghost at Philippi.
2. **Ask** students the Literary Analysis question: What internal conflict might the ghost's warning create for Brutus?
   Possible response: He might question whether or not he should march to Philippi.

Concept Connector

Activating Prior Knowledge

Have students return to their **Anticipation Guides** and respond to the statements again in the After Reading column. They may do this individually or in their original pairs or groups. Then, lead a class discussion, probing for what students have learned that confirms or invalidates each statement. Encourage students to cite specific details, quotations, or other evidence from the text to support their responses to each statement.

Reading Skill Graphic Organizer

Ask students to review the graphic organizers they completed to help them read between the lines while reading. Show them the partially completed **Reading Skill Graphic Organizer A** (*Graphic Organizer Transparencies,* page 178) as an example. Then have students share the graphic organizers they completed.

43 Background

Roman Coins

Rome had its own mint, and *denarii* were the main currency. They were usually silver. On one side, they often featured the head of Roma; and on the reverse, they usually showed a god or goddess in a chariot drawn by horses. Below was the name *Roma*. Coins during the rule of Julius Caesar featured the portrait of a living man.

44 Critical Viewing

Answer: It suggests that Romans used chariots and horses in battle.

ASSESS

Answers

Critical Thinking

1. Students may sympathize with Brutus because Cassius is being difficult, or with Cassius because Brutus' standards are strict.
2. (a) Antony thinks Lepidus is not worthy of sharing power. (b) Octavius has interacted with Lepidus as if he will have an equal share of power with them. (c) **Possible response:** Antony plans to control and use Lepidus for his own purposes, as he did the crowd.
3. (a) Brutus accuses Cassius of taking bribes and of not supplying funds for Brutus' army. (b) **Possible response:** Brutus is more reasoned and controlled, and Cassius is more emotional.
4. (a) **Possible response:** Students may say Antony, because he is practical, decisive, and ruthless; or Brutus, because he is noble and loves his country. (b) Students should share their ideas in small groups. (c) Groups should present their choices to the class.

To what extent does experience determine what we perceive?

(a) **Possible response:** Brutus has killed Caesar. The appearance of Caesar's ghost indicates that retribution is in order. (b) **Possible response:** Caesar's ghost represents Brutus' evil spirit.

BOTH. Did we, my lord?

42

BRUTUS. Ay. Saw you anything?

VARRO. No, my lord, I saw nothing.

CLAUDIUS. Nor I, my lord.

BRUTUS. Go and commend me[102] to my brother Cassius;
Bid him set on his pow'rs betimes before,[103]
And we will follow.

BOTH. It shall be done, my lord. [*Exit*]

102. **commend me** carry my greetings.
103. **set on . . . before** advance his troops early, before me.

43

44

◀ **Critical Viewing**
What does this ancient Roman coin suggest about how war was fought at the time? **[Interpret]**

Critical Thinking

1. **Respond:** Do you sympathize with anyone in Act IV? Why?
2. **(a)** In Scene i, what opinion of Lepidus does Antony express? **(b) Infer:** Why is Octavius surprised to hear this opinion? **(c) Connect:** In what way is Antony's behavior toward Lepidus similar to his manipulation of the crowd at Caesar's funeral?
3. **(a)** What are two accusations Brutus makes against Cassius in Scene iii? **(b) Compare and Contrast:** What difference in their characters does their argument emphasize?
4. **(a) Make a Judgment:** Which character in Act IV do you think would make the best leader for Rome? Explain. **(b) Discuss:** Share your ideas and the reasons for them in a small group discussion. **(c) Evaluate:** As a group, choose the two best candidates and present the reasons for your choices to the class.

THE BIG ? **To what extent does experience determine what we perceive? (a)** How do Brutus' past actions contribute to the appearance of Caesar's ghost? **(b)** What does Caesar's ghost represent?

Assessment Resources

Unit 5 Resources

L1 L2 EL **Selection Test A,** pp. 157–159. Administer Test A to less advanced readers and English learners.

L3 L4 **Selection Test B,** pp. 160–162. Administer Test B to on-level and more advanced students.

L3 L4 **Open-Book Test,** pp. 154–156. As an alternative, give the Open-Book Test.

All **Customizable Test Bank**

All **Self-tests**
Students may prepare for the **Selection Test** by taking the **Self-test** online.

PHLit Online! All assessment resources are available at **www.PHLitOnline.com.**

After You Read

The Tragedy of Julius Caesar, Act IV

Literary Analysis: External and Internal Conflict

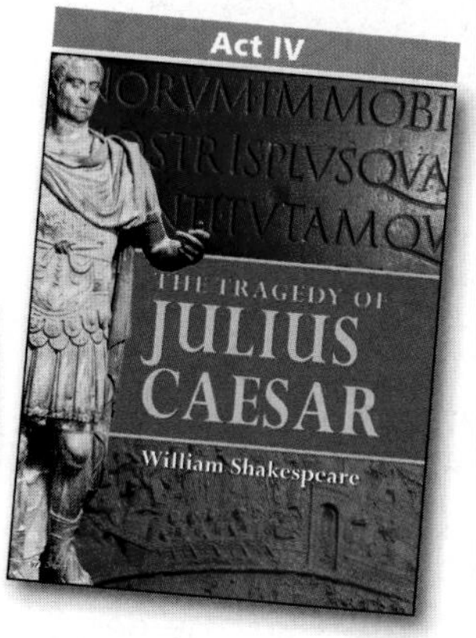

1. **(a)** Using a diagram like the one shown, identify two **external conflicts** shown or referred to in Act IV. **(b)** Describe two of the **internal conflicts** Brutus experiences in Act IV.

Force 1	Conflict: External/Internal	Force 2
→ →		← ←

2. **(a)** Explain the connection Brutus makes in Scene iii, lines 18–28 between his reasons for joining the conspirators and his conflict with Cassius. **(b)** Do you think Brutus will feel an internal conflict over his decision to join the conspirators? Explain.

Reading Skill: Read Between the Lines

3. **(a)** To whom is Brutus referring as "a brother" in Scene ii, lines 38–39? **(b)** What is the meaning of what he says?
4. **(a)** What does Cassius say in Scene iii, lines 92–98? **(b)** What is the situation? **(c) Read between the lines** to explain the unspoken significance of his words.

Vocabulary

Practice For each word from the vocabulary list on page 964, write a definition in your own words. Then, write a brief paragraph in which you use the words correctly to describe a profession or career.

1. legacies
2. chastisement
3. mirth
4. rash
5. condemned
6. presume

Word Study Use the context of the sentences and what you know about the **Latin root *-sum-*** to explain your answer to each question.

1. If Rafael *assumes* the role of class president, has he stepped down from the position?
2. Does her *presumptuous* remark reveal her modesty?

Word Study

The **Latin root *-sum-*** means "to take" or "to use."

Challenge Explain how the root *-sum-* contributes to the meanings of these words. Consult a dictionary if necessary.

consume
resume
sumptuous

ASSESS/EXTEND

Answers

Literary Analysis

1. (a) **Possible response:** External conflicts include the conflict between Antony and Octavius over Lepidus in Scene i, and the conflict between Brutus and Cassius concerning their alliance in Scene iii. (b) **Possible response:** Two internal conflicts experienced by Brutus are his grief over Portia's death and his guilt about Caesar's murder.
   For other sample answers, see *Graphic Organizer Transparencies,* **Literary Analysis Graphic Organizer A**, p. 180, and the **Additional Answers** section.
2. (a) Brutus joins the conspiracy for the betterment of Rome. He now suspects that Cassius acted for personal gain and questions his dedication. (b) **Possible response:** Students may state that he will not feel an internal conflict because of his idealism, which leads him to make the decision for the sake of Rome.

Reading Skill

3. (a) He is referring to Cassius. (b) His bond with Cassius is as close as family, and they are equals.
4. (a) Cassius wants Antony and Octavius to take their revenge for Caesar's murder by killing him. (b) Brutus has questioned Cassius' motives. (c) **Possible response:** Cassius is devastated by Brutus' criticism and no longer wants to live.

Vocabulary

Practice

Sample answers:

1. Legacies are the gifts someone leaves to others in a will.
2. Chastisement can be the same as a scolding.
3. To have mirth is to have happiness.
4. A rash decision is thoughtless.
5. If you are condemned, you are declared guilty.
6. If you presume, you take advantage of someone.

Check students' paragraphs for correct usage of the vocabulary words.

Word Study

Sample answers:

1. No. The root *-sum-* means "to take," so *assume* is "to take on (a position)." If Rafael assumes the role of class president, he is taking the position.
2. No. The root *-sum-* means "to take," so *presumptuous* means "taking liberties." A presumptuous remark does not reveal modesty.

Word Study: Challenge

Sample answers: If someone *consumes* something, he or she "uses it up." To *resume* something is "to take it up again." Something *sumptuous* "uses luxury."

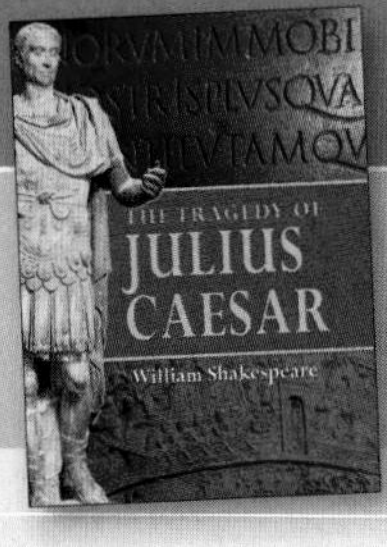

TIME AND RESOURCE MANAGER

The Tragedy of Julius Caesar, Act V

Lesson Pacing Guide

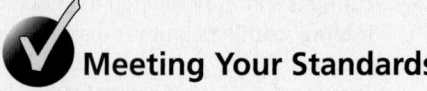

DAY 1 Preteach

- Administer the Reading and Vocabulary Warm-ups (*Unit 5 Resources*, pp. 163–166) as necessary.
- Introduce the Reading Skill: Compare and Contrast Characters. FT
- Introduce the Literary Analysis concept: Tragic Heroes. FT
- Distribute copies of the appropriate graphic organizer for the Reading Skill (*Graphic Organizer Transparencies*, pp. 182–183). CRI
- Distribute copies of the appropriate graphic organizer for Literary Analysis (*Graphic Organizer Transparencies*, pp. 184–185). CRI
- Teach the selection vocabulary. FT CRI
- Introduce the Word Study skill.

DAYS 2–3 Preteach/Teach

- Build background with the Background feature. CRI
- Develop thematic vocabulary and thematic thinking with Writing About the Big Question.
- Prepare students to read with the Activating Prior Knowledge activities (TE). CRI
- Informally monitor comprehension while students read. FT
- Use the Reading Check questions to confirm comprehension.
- Develop students' ability to compare and contrast characters using the Reading Skill questions. CRI
- Develop students' understanding of tragic heroes using the Literary Analysis questions. CRI
- Reinforce vocabulary with the Vocabulary notes. CRI

DAY 4 Assess

- Assess students' comprehension and mastery of the skills by having them answer the Critical Thinking, Reading Skill, and Literary Analysis questions. FT

DAY 5 Extend/Assess

- Have students complet the Grammar lesson (p. 1002). CRI
- Have students complete the Writing activity and write an obituary. (You may assign as homework.)
- Extend learning by having students complete the Listening and Speaking activity, a dramatic reading. (You may assign as homework.) As an alternative, assign them "The Titanic Tragedy" in *Reality Central*. CRI
- Administer Selection Test A or B (*Unit 5 Resources*, pp. 179–184). FT

The play *The Tragedy of Julius Caesar* appears unedited and in its entirety. Act I appears on pp. 892–912, Act II appears on pp. 917–936, Act III appears on pp. 941–962, Act IV appears on pp. 967–982, and Act V appears on pp. 987–1000.

Meeting Your Standards

Students will

1. analyze and respond to literary elements.
   - Literary Analysis: Tragic heroes
2. read, comprehend, and analyze drama.
   - Reading Skill: Compare and Contrast Characters
   - Reading Check questions
   - Apply the Skills questions
   - Assessment Practice
3. develop vocabulary.
   - Vocabulary
   - Word Study
4. apply grammar skills.
   - Absolutes and Absolute Phrases
5. Develop writing proficiency.
   - Work in Progress: Research Report
   - obituary
6. strengthen listening and speaking skills.
   - group screening

CRI For a full explanation of Culturally Responsive Instruction opportunities in this lesson, see p. T86–T87.

FT For an accelerated lesson, use the Fast Track strategies and activities.

Managing Differentiated Instruction
This leveled selection pairing groups a more accessible with a more challenging selection. Choose either one to teach the lesson skills. For classroom management suggestions for using the pairing in a mixed-ability class, see pp. T68–T69.

Daily Block Scheduling
Each day in this Lesson Pacing Guide represents a 40–50 minute period. Teachers using block scheduling may combine days to revise pacing. In addition, teachers may differentiate and support core instruction by integrating components for extended and intensive support as students require. See the Guide to Selected Leveled Resources (facing page).

Guide to Selected Leveled Resources

EL English Learners

			The Tragedy of Julius Caesar, Act V
CORE COURSE	*Unit 5 Resources*	Selection Test A	pp. 179–181
	Graphic Organizer Transparencies	Reading Skill Graphic Organizer A	p. 182
		Literary Analysis Graphic Organizer A	p. 184
EXTENDED SUPPORT (Level 2)	*Unit 5 Resources*	Reading and Vocabulary Warm-ups A or B	pp. 163–166
	Reader's Notebook: English Learner's Version		adapted instruction and adapted selection
	Hear It! Audio CD		selection and summaries
	Hear It! Audio CD (adapted text)		adapted selection and summaries
INTENSIVE SUPPORT (Level 1)	*Reality Central*		"The Titanic Tragedy"
	Real-World Writing Journal		Lesson 4, pp. 150–153

L2 Below-Level Students

			The Tragedy of Julius Caesar, Act V
CORE COURSE	*Unit 5 Resources*	Selection Test A	pp. 179–181
	Graphic Organizer Transparencies	Reading Skill Graphic Organizer A	p. 182
		Literary Analysis Graphic Organizer A	p. 184
EXTENDED SUPPORT (Level 2)	*Unit 5 Resources*	Reading and Vocabulary Warm-ups A or B	pp. 163–166
	Reader's Notebook		adapted instruction and full selection
	Hear It! Audio CD		selection and summaries
INTENSIVE SUPPORT (Level 1)	*Reality Central*		"The Titanic Tragedy"
	Real-World Writing Journal		Lesson 4, pp. 150–153
	Reading Kit		Reteaching worksheets

L1 Special Needs Students

			The Tragedy of Julius Caesar, Act V
CORE COURSE	*Unit 5 Resources*	Selection Test A	pp. 179–181
	Graphic Organizer Transparencies	Reading Skill Graphic Organizer A	p. 182
		Literary Analysis Graphic Organizer A	p. 184
EXTENDED SUPPORT (Level 2)	*Unit 5 Resources*	Reading and Vocabulary Warm-ups A or B	pp. 163–166
	Reader's Notebook: Adapted Version		adapted instruction and adapted selection
	Hear It! Audio CD (adapted text)		adapted selection and summaries
INTENSIVE SUPPORT (Level 1)	*Reality Central*		"The Titanic Tragedy"
	Real-World Writing Journal		Lesson 4, pp. 150–153
	Reading Kit		Reteaching worksheets

The program includes resources for these students: L3 On-Level L4 Advanced All All
For a complete guide to selection support, see pp. T106–T108.

NOTE: All print materials are also available online at *www.PHLitOnline.com.*

VISUAL GUIDE to Featured Selection Resources

The Tragedy of Julius Caesar, Act V

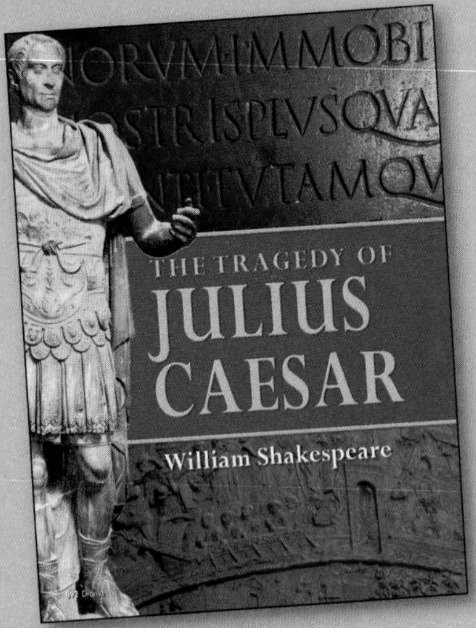

RESOURCES FOR:

- EL English Learners
- L1 Special Needs Students
- L2 Below-Level Students
- L3 On-Level Students
- L4 Advanced Students
- All All Students

Vocabulary/Fluency/Prior Knowledge

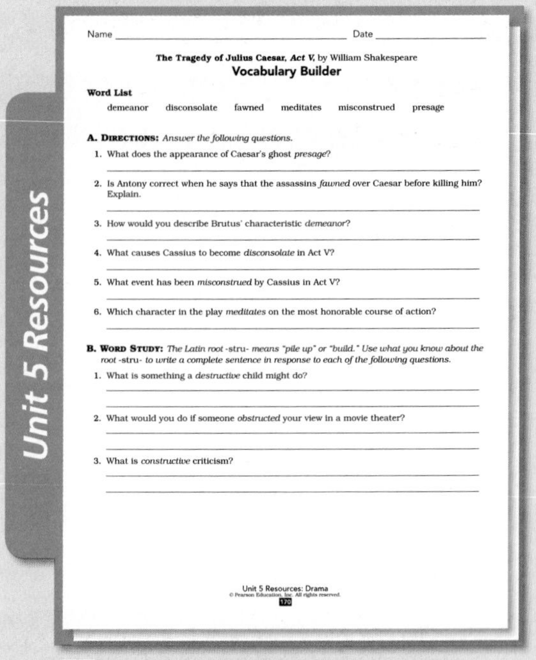

Name ______________________ Date ____________

The Tragedy of Julius Caesar, *Act V*, by William Shakespeare

Vocabulary Builder

Word List

demeanor disconsolate fawned meditates misconstrued presage

A. Directions: *Answer the following questions.*

1. What does the appearance of Caesar's ghost *presage*?
2. Is Antony correct when he says that the assassins *fawned* over Caesar before killing him? Explain.
3. How would you describe Brutus' characteristic *demeanor*?
4. What causes Cassius to become *disconsolate* in Act V?
5. What event has been *misconstrued* by Cassius in Act V?
6. Which character in the play *meditates* on the most honorable course of action?

B. Word Study: *The Latin root* -stru- *means "pile up" or "build." Use what you know about the root* -stru- *to write a complete sentence in response to each of the following questions.*

1. What is something a *destructive* child might do?
2. What would you do if someone *obstructed* your view in a movie theater?
3. What is *constructive* criticism?

Unit 5 Resources: Drama

170

All **Vocabulary Builder, p. 170**

Also available for these selections:

- EL L1 L2 **Vocabulary Warm-ups A and B, pp. 163–164**
- EL L1 L2 **Reading Warm-ups A and B, pp. 165–166**
- All **Writing About the Big Question, p. 167**

L2 L3 ***Reader's Notebook***

L1 ***Reader's Notebook: Adapted Version***

EL ***Reader's Notebook: English Learner's Version***

Reader's Notebooks

Pre- and postreading pages for both selections, as well as *The Tragedy of Julius Caesar, Act V* appear in an interactive format in the *Reader's Notebooks*. Each *Notebook* is differentiated for a different group of learners.

The selections in the Adapted and English Learner's versions are abridged.

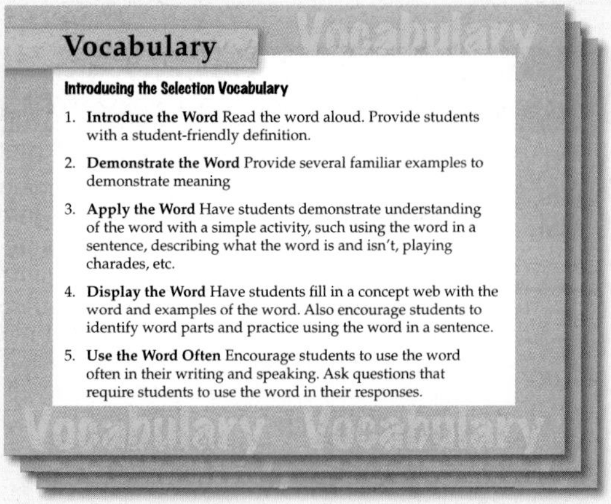

Vocabulary

Introducing the Selection Vocabulary

1. **Introduce the Word** Read the word aloud. Provide students with a student-friendly definition.
2. **Demonstrate the Word** Provide several familiar examples to demonstrate meaning
3. **Apply the Word** Have students demonstrate understanding of the word with a simple activity, such using the word in a sentence, describing what the word is and isn't, playing charades, etc.
4. **Display the Word** Have students fill in a concept web with the word and examples of the word. Also encourage students to identify word parts and practice using the word in a sentence.
5. **Use the Word Often** Encourage students to use the word often in their writing and speaking. Ask questions that require students to use the word in their responses.

Classroom Strategies and Teaching Routines

- core classroom routines outlined step-by-step
- convenient format for easy reference while teaching

Selection Support

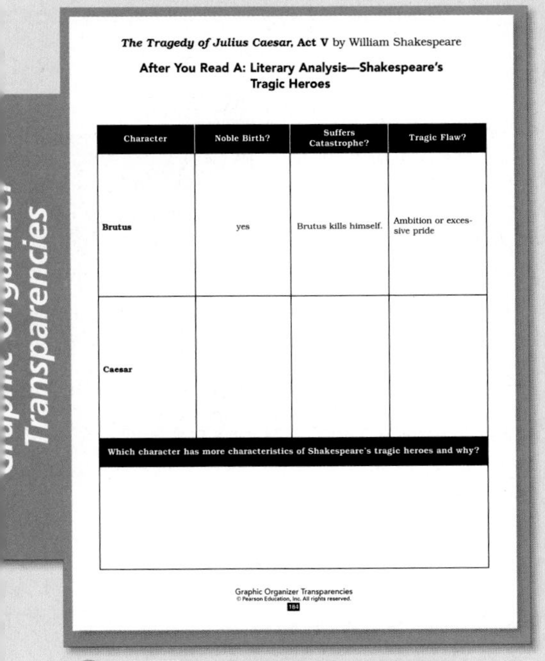

The Tragedy of Julius Caesar, Act V by William Shakespeare

After You Read A: Literary Analysis—Shakespeare's Tragic Heroes

Character	Noble Birth?	Suffers Catastrophe?	Tragic Flaw?
Brutus	yes	Brutus kills himself.	Ambition or excessive pride
Caesar			

Which character has more characteristics of Shakespeare's tragic heroes and why?

Graphic Organizer Transparencies
© Pearson Education, Inc. All rights reserved.
184

EL L1 L2 **Literary Analysis: Graphic Organizer A,** p. 184 (partially filled in)

Also available for these selections:

EL L1 L2 Reading: Graphic Organizer A, p. 182 (partially filled in)

L3 Reading: Graphic Organizer B, p. 185

L3 Literary Analysis: Graphic Organizer B, p. 185

Skills Development/Extension

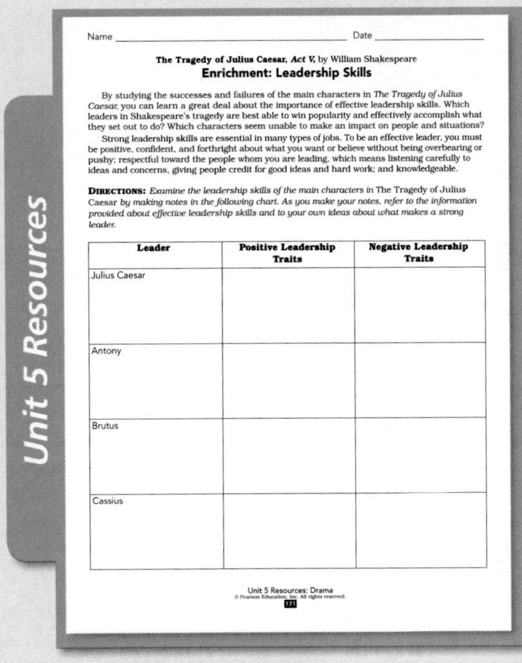

Name ______________________ Date ____________

The Tragedy of Julius Caesar, *Act V,* by William Shakespeare

Enrichment: Leadership Skills

By studying the successes and failures of the main characters in *The Tragedy of Julius Caesar,* you can learn a great deal about the importance of effective leadership skills. Which leaders in Shakespeare's tragedy are best able to win popularity and effectively accomplish what they set out to do? Which characters seem unable to make an impact on people and situations?

Strong leadership skills are essential in many types of jobs. To be an effective leader, you must be positive, confident, and forthright about what you want or believe without being overbearing or pushy; respectful toward the people whom you are leading, which means listening carefully to ideas and concerns, giving people credit for good ideas and hard work; and knowledgeable.

Directions: *Examine the leadership skills of the main characters in* The Tragedy of Julius Caesar *by making notes in the following chart. As you make your notes, refer to the information provided about effective leadership skills and to your own ideas about what makes a strong leader.*

Leader	Positive Leadership Traits	Negative Leadership Traits
Julius Caesar		
Antony		
Brutus		
Cassius		

Unit 5 Resources: Drama
© Pearson Education, Inc. All rights reserved.
171

L4 **Enrichment,** p. 171

Also available for these selections:

All Reading: Compare and Contrast Characters, p. 169

All Literary Analysis: Tragic Heroes, p. 168

L3 L4 Grammar, p. 172

L3 L4 Support for Writing, p. 173

L3 L4 Support for Extend Your Learning, p. 175

Assessment

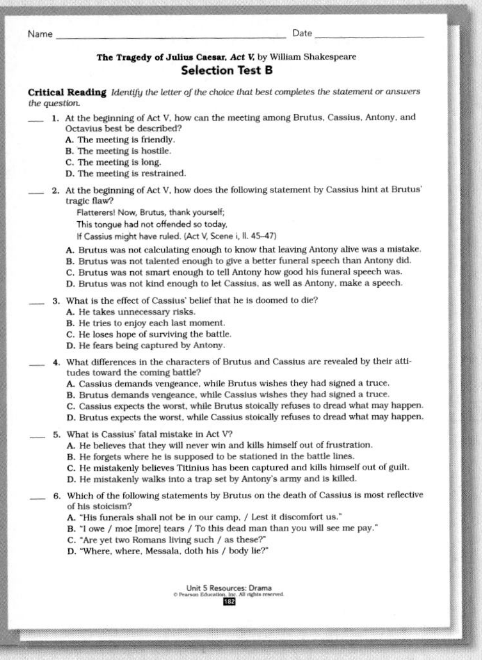

Name ______________________ Date ____________

The Tragedy of Julius Caesar, *Act V,* by William Shakespeare

Selection Test B

Critical Reading *Identify the letter of the choice that best completes the statement or answers the question.*

___ 1. At the beginning of Act V, how can the meeting among Brutus, Cassius, Antony, and Octavius best be described?
A. The meeting is friendly.
B. The meeting is hostile.
C. The meeting is long.
D. The meeting is restrained.

___ 2. At the beginning of Act V, how does the following statement by Cassius hint at Brutus' tragic flaw?
Flatterers! Now, Brutus, thank yourself;
This tongue had not offended so today,
If Cassius might have ruled. (Act V, Scene i, ll. 45–47)
A. Brutus was not calculating enough to know that leaving Antony alive was a mistake.
B. Brutus was not talented enough to give a better funeral speech than Antony did.
C. Brutus was not smart enough to tell Antony how good his funeral speech was.
D. Brutus was not kind enough to let Cassius, as well as Antony, make a speech.

___ 3. What is the effect of Cassius' belief that he is doomed to die?
A. He takes unnecessary risks.
B. He tries to enjoy each last moment.
C. He loses hope of surviving the battle.
D. He fears being captured by Antony.

___ 4. What differences in the characters of Brutus and Cassius are revealed by their attitudes toward the coming battle?
A. Cassius demands vengeance, while Brutus wishes they had signed a truce.
B. Brutus demands vengeance, while Cassius wishes they had signed a truce.
C. Cassius expects the worst, while Brutus stoically refuses to dread what may happen.
D. Brutus expects the worst, while Cassius stoically refuses to dread what may happen.

___ 5. What is Cassius' fatal mistake in Act V?
A. He believes that they will never win and kills himself out of frustration.
B. He forgets where he is supposed to be stationed in the battle lines.
C. He mistakenly believes Titinius has been captured and kills himself out of guilt.
D. He mistakenly walks into a trap set by Antony's army and is killed.

___ 6. Which of the following statements by Brutus on the death of Cassius is most reflective of his stoicism?
A. "His funerals shall not be in our camp, / Lest it discomfort us."
B. "I owe / moe [more] tears / To this dead man than you will see me pay."
C. "Are yet two Romans living such / as these?"
D. "Where, where, Messala, doth his / body lie?"

Unit 5 Resources: Drama
© Pearson Education, Inc. All rights reserved.
182

L3 L4 **Selection Test B,** pp. 182–184

Also available for these selections:

EL L1 L2 Selection Test A, pp. 179–181

L3 L4 Open-Book Test, pp. 176–178

PHLit Online!

www.PHLitOnline.com

- complete narrated selection text
- a thematically related video with writing prompt
- an interactive graphic organizer
- highlighting feature
- access to all student print resources, adapted to individual student needs
- Spanish and English summaries

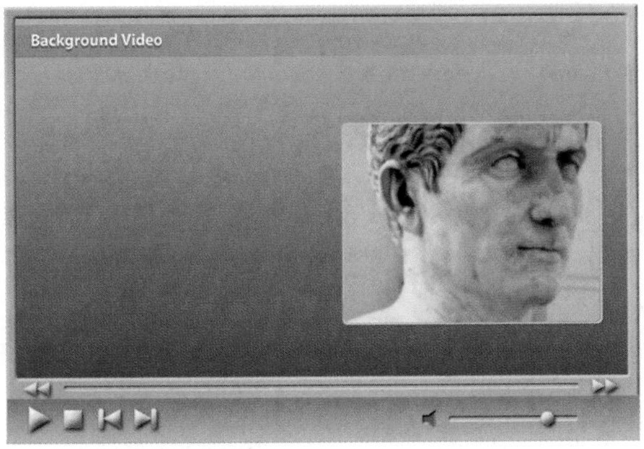

Background video

Also available:

Get Connected! (thematic video with writing prompt)

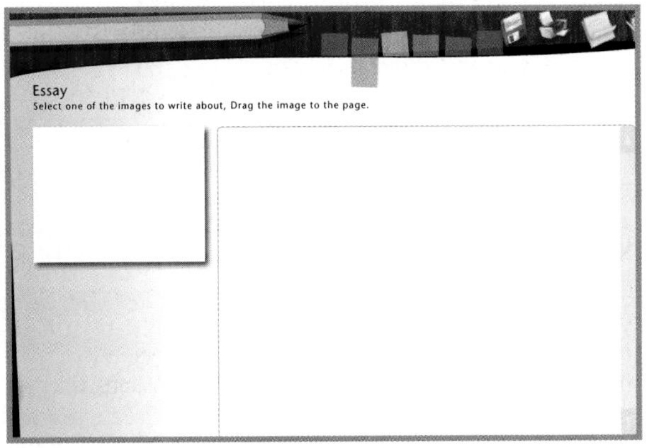

Writer's Journal (with graphics feature)

Also available:

Vocabulary Central (tools, activities, and songs for studying vocabulary)

DIFFERENTIATE/PRETEACH

❶ Selection Skills

1. With the class, preview the selection skills. (The lesson meets the lesson objectives given on p. 984a.)
2. Explain that students will learn to use the skill of comparing and contrasting characters as they read to better understand and enjoy the selection. By examining tragic heroes as they read, they will gain deeper insight into the selection.
3. Tell students that when they have finished reading the selection, they will complete a variety of Writing, Listening and Speaking, and Research and Technology activities related to the selection.
4. Tell students that they will also study a grammar concept: absolutes and absolute phrases. By mastering this concept, they will improve their reading fluency and the quality of their writing.

❷ Vocabulary

1. Have students preview the selection vocabulary.
2. For each word, have students say the word aloud.
3. Then, use the word in a sentence that defines the word.
4. Finally, repeat your definitional sentence or a similar sentence with the word missing, and have the class "fill in the blank" chorally. Here is an example:
   Demeanor is a way of conducting oneself or one's behavior. He was never in any arguments due to his quiet [students say "demeanor"].

❸ Word Study

1. Introduce the skill, using the instruction in the box.
2. Using their knowledge of the root, ask students which of the following means "the part of a building entirely above its foundation": superconductor, superstructure, supersystem. (**Answer:** superstructure)

Before You Read

The Tragedy of Julius Caesar, Act V

THE BIG ? To what extent does *experience* determine what we *perceive?*

While You Read Look for evidence that explains how Brutus perceives the world, and consider the way his ideas shape his actions.

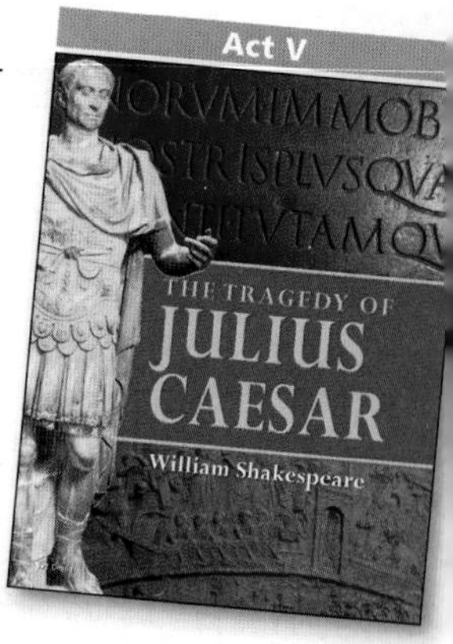

Selection Skills Guide

❶ Practice these skills with ***The Tragedy of Julius Caesar*, Act V** (p. 986).

- Understand tragic heroes and tragic flaws
- Compare and contrast characters
- Identify character foils
- Identify absolutes and absolute phrases
- Write an editorial
- Write an obituary
- Give a dramatic reading
- Hold a group screening
- Write a women's history report
- Create an advertising poster
- Produce a multimedia presentation

Integrated Language Skills (Grammar; Listening and Speaking; Research and Technology; and Writing Activities) appear on pages 1002–1005.

❷ Vocabulary

Read each word and its definition. Decide whether you know the word well, know it a little bit, or do not know it at all. After you read, see how your knowledge of each word has increased.

- **fawned** (fônd) *v.* flattered; acted with excessive concern for the wishes and moods of another, as a servant might (p. 988) *She fawned on her new boss as if he were a king.* fawner *n.* fawningly *adv.*
- **presage** (prē sāj′) *v.* give a warning sign about a future event (p. 989) *His frown seemed to presage a stern lecture.* presage *n.*
- **demeanor** (di mēn′ ər) *n.* way of conducting oneself; behavior (p. 990) *The child's good demeanor earned him a gold star.*
- **disconsolate** (dis kän′ sə lit) *adj.* so unhappy that nothing brings comfort (p. 994) *Disconsolate, he would not stop weeping for his loss.* console *v.* disconsolately *adv.*
- **misconstrued** (mis′ kən stro͞od′) *v.* misinterpreted (p. 994) *I misconstrued the directions and wound up lost.* construe *v.* misconstruction *n.*
- **meditates** (med′ ə tāts′) *v.* thinks deeply (p. 997) *The philosopher quietly meditates on a new idea.* meditation *n.* meditative *adj.*

❸ Word Study

The **Latin root *-stru-*** means "pile up" or "build."

In the play, a scene on the battlefield is **misconstrued**, or interpreted incorrectly.

Vocabulary Development

Vocabulary Knowledge Rating

Create a **Vocabulary Knowledge Rating Chart** (***Professional Development Guidebook***, p. 33) for this selection. Include the selection vocabulary from this page.

Give students a copy of the chart. Read the words aloud, and have students mark their rating in the Before Reading column. Urge them to be alert to these words as they read and discuss the selection.

Tally how many students think they know a word to gauge how much instruction to provide. As students read and discuss the selection, point out the words and their context.

PHLit Online! **Vocabulary Central**, featuring tools, activities, and songs for studying vocabulary, is available at **www.PHLitOnline.com.**

❹ Literary Analysis: Tragic Heroes

Traditionally, a **tragic hero** is a person, usually of noble birth, who suffers a catastrophe. The hero's choices leading to the catastrophe may reflect a personal shortcoming, such as pride, called a **tragic flaw.** While **Shakespeare's tragic heroes** incorporate these traditional elements, he develops them in new ways:

- He adds complexity to his heroes, who may have opposing desires and who may suffer hesitation and doubt before acting.
- He presents a character's inner turmoil directly, through devices like the *soliloquy,* a speech in which a character thinks aloud.
- He focuses on the choices characters make rather than on fate.
- His characters' problems often concern the difference between the reasons for an action and its outcome. For example, Brutus acts for reasons of honor—the right reasons—but in a world of men who are less than honorable, the results are disastrous.

❺ Reading Skill: Compare and Contrast Characters

Shakespeare often emphasizes the important qualities of one character by presenting another character with contrasting qualities. A **foil** is a character who sets off another character by providing a strong contrast. When **reading Shakespearean drama,** you can often gain understanding by **comparing and contrasting characters.** Look for similarities and differences in the characters' personalities, situations, behaviors, and attitudes.

❻ Using the Strategy: Character Chart

Record details on a **character chart** to compare and contrast characters' qualities.

Brutus	Cassius
nobleman	nobleman
idealistic	practical

PHLit Online!
www.PHLitOnline.com

Hear It!
- Selection summary audio
- Selection audio

See It!
- Get Connected video
- Background video
- More about the author
- Vocabulary flashcards

Do It!
- Interactive journals
- Interactive graphic organizers
- Self-test
- Internet activity
- Grammar tutorial
- Interactive vocabulary games

Differentiated Instruction for Universal Access

Preparing Students for the Selection

To prepare lower level readers to read this act of *Julius Caesar,* follow these steps:

- Review strategies for interpreting difficult language. Encourage students to rephrase sentences and phrases they do not understand in their own words. For example, the line "I prithee, Strato, stay thou by thy lord" (p. 998) can be paraphrased as "Please, Strato. Stay by me."
- Remind students that plays are unique because, unlike stories, they consist entirely of dialogue and are meant to be spoken. Suggest that students read difficult passages aloud, focusing on both content and tone, noting who is speaking to whom.
- Students may have difficulty keeping track of the fast-paced events in the selection. Review strategies for summarizing. Encourage students to pause after difficult passages and recap the events in their own words. Suggest that they take notes as they read.

PRETEACH

❹ Literary Analysis

1. Introduce the skill, using the instruction on the student page.
2. Tell students that they will identify tragic heroes as they read.

Think Aloud: Model the Skill

Model the skill of identifying and analyzing tragic heroes, using the following "think aloud." Say to students:

> I know that Shakespeare's tragic heroes are complex. For example, Brutus, in *Julius Caesar,* has conflicting desires. He is pulled between his friendship with Caesar and his devotion to the greater good. His character is driven by his decisions and actions, not by fate. Brutus expresses his inner turmoil through *soliloquies.*
>
> Recognizing these elements helps me fully understand Brutus and Shakespeare's tragic heroes.

❺ Reading Skill

1. Introduce the skill, using the instruction on the student page.
2. Tell students that they will compare and contrast characters as they read.

Think Aloud: Model the Skill

Model a way to compare and contrast characters, using the following "think aloud." Say to students:

> I know that authors often highlight important traits of one character by presenting a *foil* with contrasting traits. Thus, when I read, I like to compare and contrast characters.
>
> For example, imagine I'm reading a story about a firefighter who rescues a child from a burning building. I know he is brave, but only when I compare him to his timid and anxious wife, do I appreciate how courageous he is.

❻ Using the Strategy

Give students a copy of either **Reading Skill Graphic Organizer A** or **B** (***Graphic Organizer Transparencies,*** pp. 182–183) to record details of comparing and contrasting characters as they read. Use the examples in **Reading Skill Graphic Organizer A,** which is partially filled in, to model the process of completing the organizer.

❶ Activating Prior Knowledge

1. Prepare an **Anticipation Guide** (see *Professional Develpment Guidebook,* pp. 36–38) with the following statements:
   - Personal sacrifice is the best way to demonstrate honor.
   - People do not always have to take responsibility for their actions.
   - Respect is a key part of any relationship.
   - It is important for everyone to experience humiliation.
2. Give students a copy of the prepared **Anticipation Guide**, and have students mark their responses in the Me column. Have students discuss the statements in pairs or groups and mark the guides again in the Group column.
3. For further guidance, use the ***Classroom Strategies and Teaching Routines*** card for Anticipation Guides.

Concept Connector →

Students will return to the **Anticipation Guide** after completing the play.

Small-Group Activity

Invite students to choose and share pieces of music that capture the mood of the battle scene. Have the rest of the class analyze the musical choices and discuss its suitability to the scene.

❷ About the Selection

Antony and Octavius exchange insults with Brutus and Cassius at Philippi. Believing that his best friend Titinius has been captured, Cassius kills himself. Realizing that the battle is ending and Antony's side will win, Brutus kills himself.

❸ Critical Viewing

Answer: Yes, the personality that is suggested by this statue fits with Brutus' personality as the story's tragic hero. He is strong, determined, and loyal, willing to bravely do whatever it takes to protect Rome and its people.

REVIEW AND ANTICIPATE

① ② By the end of Act IV, Cassius and Brutus have patched up their quarrel. Brutus persuades Cassius to agree to his strategy—taking the battle to the enemy. He reasons that they should march to the city of Philippi and attack before Octavius and Antony swell their forces with new recruits. The act ends ominously as Brutus is visited by Caesar's ghost. Before disappearing, the ghost tells Brutus that they will meet again at Philippi. As Act V opens, the two armies are poised for battle on the plains of Philippi. Nothing less than the future of Rome is at stake.

③ ▶ **Critical Viewing** Does Brutus' personality, as suggested by this statue, fit with his personality in the story? Explain. **[Connect]**

Differentiated Instruction for Universal Access

Accessibility at a Glance

	***The Tragedy of Julius Caesar,* Act V**	
Context	Historical: ancient Rome	
Language/ Vocabulary	• Dialogue • Prose, verse, and soliloquies	
Concept Level	Challenging (internal conflicts within historical, political context)	
Literary Merit	Classic; noted author	
Lexile/Length	Lexile: NP	Word Count: 2,902
Overall Rating	**Challenging**	

ACT V

Scene i. The plains of Philippi.

[*Enter* OCTAVIUS, ANTONY, *and their Army.*]

OCTAVIUS. Now, Antony, our hopes are answerèd;
You said the enemy would not come down,
But keep the hills and upper regions.
It proves not so; their battles[1] are at hand;
They mean to warn[2] us at Philippi here,
Answering before we do demand of them.[3]

❹ **ANTONY.** Tut, I am in their bosoms,[4] and I know
Wherefore[5] they do it. They could be content
To visit other places, and come down
With fearful bravery,[6] thinking by this face[7]
To fasten in our thoughts[8] that they have courage;
But 'tis not so.

[*Enter a* MESSENGER.]

MESSENGER. Prepare you, generals,
The enemy comes on in gallant show;
Their bloody sign[9] of battle is hung out,
And something to be done immediately.

ANTONY. Octavius, lead your battle softly[10] on
Upon the left hand of the even[11] field.

OCTAVIUS. Upon the right hand I; keep thou the left.

ANTONY. Why do you cross me in this exigent?[12]

OCTAVIUS. I do not cross you; but I will do so. [*March*]

[*Drum. Enter* BRUTUS, CASSIUS, *and their Army;* LUCILIUS, TITINIUS, MESSALA, *and others.*]

BRUTUS. They stand, and would have parley.[13]

CASSIUS. Stand fast, Titinius, we must out and talk.

OCTAVIUS. Mark Antony, shall we give sign of battle?

ANTONY. No, Caesar, we will answer on their charge.[14]
Make forth;[15] the generals would have some words.

OCTAVIUS. Stir not until the signal.

BRUTUS. Words before blows; is it so, countrymen?

OCTAVIUS. Not that we love words better, as you do.

1. **battles** *n.* armies.
2. **warn** *v.* challenge.
3. **Answering . . . of them** appearing in opposition to us before we challenge them.
4. **am in their bosoms** know what they are thinking.
5. **Wherefore** *conj.* why.
6. **fearful bravery** show of magnificence and pretend courage concealing fear.
7. **face** *n.* appearance.
8. **fasten in our thoughts** convince us.

Reading Skill
Compare and Contrast Characters
What contrast between Octavius and Antony is suggested by their opening speeches?

9. **bloody sign** red flag.
10. **softly** *adv.* slowly.
11. **even** *adj.* level.
12. **exigent** *n.* critical situation.
13. **parley** *n.* conference between enemies.
14. **answer on their charge** meet them when they attack.
15. **Make forth** go forward.

❺ **Reading Check**
What news does the messenger bring Octavius and Antony?

❹ Reading Skill
Compare and Contrast Characters

- **Ask** students to respond to the Reading Skill question: What contrast between Octavius and Antony is suggested by their opening speeches?
  Answer: Octavius thinks Brutus and Cassius have come to Philippi to attack. Antony thinks they want to make a display. Octavius thinks more objectively about Brutus and Cassius than Antony does.

❺ Reading Check

Answer: The messenger reports to Octavius and Antony that the enemy is ready for battle and that they must act immediately.

Differentiated Instruction — Additional Instruction

EL Extended Support—English Learners
Have students complete the **Reading and Vocabulary Warm-ups, *Unit 5 Resources,*** pp. 163–166, before they read. Assign the prereading pages for the selection in the ***Reader's Notebook: English Learner's Version.*** Then, have students listen to portions of the selection on the ***Hear It!* Audio CD.**

L1 L2 Extended Support—Struggling Readers
Have students complete the **Reading and Vocabulary Warm-ups, *Unit 5 Resources,*** pp. 163–166, before they read. Assign the prereading pages for the selection in the ***Reader's Notebook: Adapted Version.*** Then, have students listen to portions of the selection on the ***Hear It!* Audio CD** (adapted text).

Extended Support—Reluctant Readers
To build motivation and engagement before assigning the selection, have students read "The *Titanic* Tragedy," a thematically related selection in ***Reality Central.*** Then, use the questions at the conclusion of the related selection to guide discussion.

PHLit Online!
This selection is available in interactive format in the **Enriched Online Student Edition, www.PHLitOnline.com,** which includes a thematically related video with writing prompt and an interactive graphic organizer.

6 Literary Analysis

Tragic Heroes

1. Note that Brutus and Antony contrast "good words" and "bad strokes" in their exchange at lines 29–32. Tell students that they may understand strokes as actions. Point out that while Brutus makes a very general statement about words and actions in line 29, Antony specifies Brutus' own words and deeds in lines 30–32.
2. Then, **ask** students: What flaw in Brutus' idealistic character does Antony describe?
   Answer: Brutus uses noble words to justify and carry out dishonorable actions.

7 Literary Analysis

Tragic Heroes

1. Have students read aloud lines 45–47. **Ask** to whom Cassius is referring in line 46.
   Answer: He is referring to Antony, who has just insulted them.
2. Then, **ask** students to explain what Cassius is referring to when he says "If Cassius might have ruled."
   Answer: He is referring to his advice that Brutus kill Antony as well as Caesar, which Brutus did not follow.
3. Then, **ask** the Literary Analysis question: Which of Brutus' earlier decisions would Cassius call tragic?
   Answer: Cassius would call the decision not to kill Antony tragic.
4. Challenge students to recall Brutus' reasons for not killing Antony.
   Ask whether they think Brutus was right or wrong and to explain their answers.
   Possible responses: Brutus is willing to kill only for noble reasons; Antony's murder would have been self-serving. Students may say that it is always right to refuse to kill. Others may say that Brutus was wrong because allowing Antony to live causes the present situation, as Cassius notes, and many soldiers may die.

BRUTUS. Good words are better than bad strokes, Octavius.

6

ANTONY. In your bad strokes, Brutus, you give good words;
Witness the hole you made in Caesar's heart,
Crying "Long live! Hail, Caesar!"

CASSIUS. Antony,
The posture[16] of your blows are yet unknown;
But for your words, they rob the Hybla bees,[17]
And leave them honeyless.

ANTONY. Not stingless too.

BRUTUS. O, yes, and soundless too;
For you have stol'n their buzzing, Antony,
And very wisely threat before you sting.

ANTONY. Villains! You did not so, when your vile daggers
Hacked one another in the sides of Caesar.
You showed your teeth[18] like apes, and **fawned** like hounds,
And bowed like bondmen,[19] kissing Caesar's feet;
Whilst damnèd Casca, like a cur,[20] behind
Struck Caesar on the neck. O you flatterers!

7

CASSIUS. Flatterers! Now, Brutus, thank yourself;
This tongue had not offended so today,
If Cassius might have ruled.[21]

OCTAVIUS. Come, come, the cause.[22] If arguing make us sweat,
The proof[23] of it will turn to redder drops.
Look,
I draw a sword against conspirators.
When think you that the sword goes up[24] again?
Never, till Caesar's three and thirty wounds
Be well avenged; or till another Caesar
Have added slaughter to the sword of traitors.[25]

BRUTUS. Caesar, thou canst not die by traitors' hands,
Unless thou bring'st them with thee.

OCTAVIUS. So I hope.
I was not born to die on Brutus' sword.

BRUTUS. O, if thou wert the noblest of thy strain,[26]
Young man, thou couldst not die more honorable.

CASSIUS. A peevish[27] schoolboy, worthless[28] of such honor,
Joined with a masker and a reveler.[29]

ANTONY. Old Cassius still!

OCTAVIUS. Come, Antony; away!

16. **posture** *n.* quality.
17. **Hybla bees** bees from the town of Hybla in Sicily, noted for their sweet honey.

Vocabulary
fawned (fônd) *v.* flattered; acted with excessive concern for the wishes and moods of another, as a servant might

18. **showed your teeth** grinned.
19. **bondmen** *n.* slaves.
20. **cur** *n.* dog.
21. **If Cassius might have ruled** if Cassius had had his way when he urged that Antony be killed.

Literary Analysis
Tragic Heroes Which of Brutus' earlier decisions would Cassius call tragic?

22. **cause** *n.* business at hand.
23. **proof** *n.* test.
24. **goes up** goes into its scabbard.
25. **till another Caesar . . . traitors** until I, another Caesar, have also been killed by you.
26. **noblest of thy strain** best of your family.
27. **peevish** silly.
28. **worthless** *adj.* unworthy.
29. **a masker and a reveler** one who attends masquerades and parties; Antony.

Vocabulary Development

Thematic Vocabulary: The Big Question

As students are discussing *The Tragedy of Julius Caesar:* Act 5, encourage them to use the thematic vocabulary presented in Introducing the Big Question, pp. 790–791. You might encourage them with sentence starters like these:

1. Cassius' *interpretation* of his enemies' shout for joy leads him to wrongly believe . . .
2. Though the Roman soldiers are under the *impression* that they have captured Brutus, in reality . . .
3. Even in his death, Brutus maintains his *universal* belief in . . .
4. At the end, Antony explains that Brutus' *individual* motive for killing Caesar was . . .

Defiance, traitors, hurl we in your teeth.
If you dare fight today, come to the field;
If not, when you have stomachs.[30]

[*Exit* OCTAVIUS, ANTONY, *and Army.*]

CASSIUS. Why, now blow wind, swell billow, and swim bark![31]
The storm is up, and all is on the hazard.[32]

BRUTUS. Ho, Lucilius, hark, a word with you.

[LUCILIUS *and* MESSALA *stand forth.*]

LUCILIUS. My lord?

[BRUTUS *and* LUCILIUS *converse apart.*]

CASSIUS. Messala.

MESSALA. What says my general?

CASSIUS. Messala,
This is my birthday; as this very day
Was Cassius born. Give me thy hand, Messala:
Be thou my witness that against my will
(As Pompey was)[33] am I compelled to set[34]
Upon one battle all our liberties.
You know that I held Epicurus strong,[35]
[8] And his opinion; now I change my mind.
And partly credit things that do **presage.**
Coming from Sardis, on our former ensign[36]
Two mighty eagles fell,[37] and there they perched,
Gorging and feeding from our soldiers' hands,
Who to Philippi here consorted[38] us.
[9] This morning are they fled away and gone,
And in their steads do ravens, crows, and kites[39]
Fly o'er our heads and downward look on us
As we were sickly prey; their shadows seem
A canopy most fatal,[40] under which
Our army lies, ready to give up the ghost.

MESSALA. Believe not so.

CASSIUS. I but believe it partly,
For I am fresh of spirit and resolved
To meet all perils very constantly.[41]

BRUTUS. Even so, Lucilius.

CASSIUS. Now, most noble Brutus,
[11] The gods today stand friendly, that we may,
Lovers[42] in peace, lead on our days to age!

30. stomachs appetites for battle.
31. bark ship.
32. on the hazard at stake.

33. As Pompey was Against his own judgment, Pompey was urged to do battle against Caesar. The battle resulted in Pompey's defeat and murder.
34. set stake.
35. held Epicurus strong believed in Epicurus' philosophy that the gods do not interest themselves in human affairs and that omens are merely superstitions.

Vocabulary
presage (prē sāj´) *v.* give a warning sign about a future event

36. former ensign (en´ sīn´) standard-bearer (soldier carrying a flag) farthest in front.
37. fell swooped down.
38. consorted *v.* accompanied.
39. ravens, crows, and kites scavenger birds, said to gather before a battle.
40. A canopy most fatal a rooflike covering foretelling death.
41. very constantly most resolutely.
42. Lovers *n.* true friends.

[10] **Reading Check**
What is Cassius' complaint about the battle they are about to fight?

Differentiated Instruction for Universal Access

Strategy for Special Needs Students
Help students review the structure and action of Scene i up to Cassius' monologue at line 70. Draw a chart on the board with a column for each of the following characters: Brutus, Cassius, Antony, and Octavius. With students, record adjectives to describe how each man behaves while talking before battle. Can the same adjectives be used to describe all four men? Do they seem more similar to or different from one another than in previous acts? Guide students to identify any tragic flaws that are revealed.

EL Strategy for English Learners
Before reading, have students skim each scene to identify unfamiliar words and expressions. As students read the scene, work with them to determine the meaning of these unknown words and expressions. Help students begin by walking through lines 21–66; note the words *stir, villains, avenged, peevish,* and *defiance.* Take a variety of approaches, including using side notes, context clues, and a dictionary. Check students' understanding after reading by having them paraphrase in writing or orally the lines containing the new vocabulary.

8 Critical Thinking
Analyze
1. Ask a volunteer to read the bracketed text. **Ask** students what the subject of the speech is.
Answer: The speech focuses on the upcoming battle and an omen Cassius sees regarding it.
2. Cassius states that he goes to battle against his will. **Ask:** Why might Cassius be cautious about going into battle on his birthday?
Answer: He may fear that he will die on the day he was born.
3. Observe that in lines 76–78, Cassius confesses that he has changed his mind about the validity of omens. Have students **speculate** about why Cassius begins to believe in omens.
Answer: He may sense that his defeat and death are near. He may also be discouraged that everything seems to be an omen.
4. With students, interpret the omen Cassius describes. **Ask** students to hypothesize about whom the two eagles in the omen might be, what it means that they feed from Cassius and Brutus' soldiers' hands, and what the ravens, crows, and kites signify.
Answer: The two eagles may be Antony and Octavius. Their feeding from the soldiers' hands may mean defeat for Brutus and Cassius. The ravens, crows, and kites feed on carrion, and they may thus foretell death for Brutus and Cassius.

9 Background
Omens
In observing the flight of eagles, ravens, crows, and kites, Cassius is interpreting omens—signs of good or bad luck—for the upcoming battle.

The Romans were very superstitious. For example, it was an omen of disaster for a black cat to enter the house or for a beam of the house to split. Many Romans would choose to spend the day at home on the basis of such a sign.

10 Reading Check
Answer: The battle occurs on Cassius' birthday.

11 Reading Skill

Compare and Contrast Characters

1. Have two volunteers read the exchange between Cassius and Brutus in lines 92–107.
2. Then, **ask** students to explain why Cassius says that it may be the last time that he and Brutus speak together.
   Answer: Cassius expects the worst, believing that they will lose the battle.
3. **Ask** students to respond to the Reading Skill prompt: Contrast the outlook Brutus expresses here with Cassius' misgivings in lines 70–88.
   Answer: In contrast to Cassius' concern and fear about the omens regarding the battle and what he thinks they mean, Brutus is a Stoic who prefers to not waste time fearing what might happen, since it is largely out of his control.

12 Literary Analysis

Tragic Heroes

1. **Ask:** What does Brutus mean in lines 110–112 when he says that he has too great a mind to be led as a captive through the streets of Rome?
   Answer: He means that it would be a humiliating experience that he will not endure.
2. **Ask** students to respond to the Literary Analysis question: What details of Brutus' preoccupation with honor, expressed here, reflect his decision to join the conspirators?
   Answer: The details "He bears too great a mind" and "Must end that work the ides of March begun" reveal how seriously and thoroughly Brutus considers honorable decisions; he joined the conspirators because he believed this action was honorable.
3. Remind students that in explaining their downfall, Shakespeare focuses on the choices his tragic heroes make, rather than their fates. Suggest that Brutus' choices have put him in the situation of having to engage in battle with Antony, while being fully aware that the outcome of the battle is outside his control.

---

43. **rests still incertain** always remain uncertain.
44. **reason . . . befall** reason about the worst that may happen.
45. **that philosophy** here, Stoicism.
46. **Cato** Marcus Porcius Cato (Cato the Younger) supported Pompey in his quarrel with Caesar and killed himself after Pompey's defeat.
47. **so to prevent . . . life** thus to anticipate the natural end of life.
48. **stay the providence** await the ordained fate.

But since the affairs of men rests still incertain,[43]
Let's reason with the worst that may befall.[44]
If we do lose this battle, then is this
The very last time we shall speak together.
What are you then determinèd to do? **11**

BRUTUS. Even by the rule of that philosophy[45]
By which I did blame Cato[46] for the death
Which he did give himself; I know not how,
But I do find it cowardly and vile,
For fear of what might fall, so to prevent
The time of life,[47] arming myself with patience
To stay the providence[48] of some high powers
That govern us below.

Reading Skill
Compare and Contrast Characters Contrast the outlook Brutus expresses here with Cassius' misgivings in lines 70–88. **12**

CASSIUS. Then, if we lose this battle,
You are contented to be led in triumph[49]
Thorough[50] the streets of Rome?

49. **in triumph** as a captive in the victor's procession.
50. **Thorough** *prep.* through.

BRUTUS. No, Cassius, no; think not, thou noble Roman,
That ever Brutus will go bound to Rome;
He bears too great a mind. But this same day
Must end that work the ides of March begun;
And whether we shall meet again I know not.
Therefore our everlasting farewell take.
Forever, and forever, farewell, Cassius!
If we do meet again, why, we shall smile;
If not, why then this parting was well made.

Literary Analysis
Tragic Heroes What details of Brutus' preoccupation with honor, expressed here, reflect his decision to join the conspirators?

CASSIUS. Forever, and forever, farewell, Brutus!
If we do meet again, we'll smile indeed;
If not, 'tis true this parting was well made.

BRUTUS. Why then, lead on. O, that a man might know
The end of this day's business ere it come!
But it sufficeth that the day will end,
And then the end is known. Come, ho! Away! [*Exit*]

Scene ii. The field of battle.

[*Call to arms sounds. Enter* BRUTUS *and* MESSALA.]

BRUTUS. Ride, ride, Messala, ride, and give these bills[1]
Unto the legions on the other side.[2]

[*Loud call to arms*]

Let them set on at once; for I perceive
But cold demeanor[3] in Octavius' wing,

1. **bills** written orders.
2. **other side** wing of the army commanded by Cassius.
3. **cold demeanor** (di mēn′ ər) lack of spirit in their conduct.

Vocabulary
demeanor (di mēn′ ər) *n.* way of conducting oneself; behavior

Think Aloud

Vocabulary: Using Context

Direct students' attention to the word *perils* in line 91. Then, use the following "think aloud" to model how to use context to infer the meaning of an unknown word.

In this sentence, Cassius says that he is resolved to meet all perils. To get an idea of what *perils* means, I am going to look at the sentences surrounding this one. I see that in his preceding speech Cassius talks about bad omens that he thinks have to do with the upcoming battle. In the speech that follows his use of the word *perils,* he also refers to the battle and whether they might lose it. Since in between these speeches Cassius says he is ready to meet all perils, I think the perils are connected with the *dangers* of battle. I'll substitute *dangers* in Cassius' lines: "I but believe it partly,/For I am fresh of spirit and resolved/To meet all *dangers* very constantly." I think that meaning makes sense. I think that *perils* are dangers.

LITERATURE IN CONTEXT

History Connection

Roman Triumphs

Brutus and Cassius reflect on the humiliation they will experience if they are defeated and brought in triumph to Rome. A *triumph,* held to celebrate a general's victory, included these events:

- Temples were decorated and sacrifices were held.
- The victorious general and his troops marched through the city to the Capitol, preceded by the Roman Senators and trumpeters.
- The triumphant general, dressed in a royal purple toga and holding a laurel branch, rode in a golden chariot drawn by four white horses.
- On display were the spoils of war, including carts full of treasure, and exotic animals.
- Captive enemy leaders—and even their children—were marched in front of the general.
- The people of Rome gathered to view and cheer the spectacle.

7

Connect to the Literature Why would Cassius and Brutus wish to escape at any cost being led as prisoners in a triumph?

And sudden push gives them the overthrow,[4]
Ride, ride, Messala! Let them all come down.[5] [*Exit*]

4. **sudden push . . . overthrow** sudden attack will defeat them.
5. **Let . . . down** attack all at once.

Scene iii. The field of battle.

[*Calls to arms sound. Enter* CASSIUS *and* TITINIUS.]

CASSIUS. O, look, Titinius, look, the villains[1] fly!
Myself have to mine own turned enemy.[2]
This ensign here of mine was turning back;
I slew the coward, and did take it[3] from him.

TITINIUS. O Cassius, Brutus gave the word too early,
Who, having some advantage on Octavius,
Took it too eagerly; his soldiers fell to spoil,[4]
Whilst we by Antony are all enclosed.

[*Enter* PINDARUS.]

PINDARUS. Fly further off, my lord, fly further off!
Mark Antony is in your tents, my lord.
Fly, therefore, noble Cassius, fly far off!

1. **villains** here, cowards among his own men.
2. **Myself . . . enemy** I have become an enemy to my own soldiers.
3. **it** here, the ensign's banner.
4. **fell to spoil** began to loot.

14 Reading Check

How well is the battle going for Cassius and his forces?

13 Literature in Context

History Connection Romans could watch a triumphal procession from various points in the city. The procession started in the Campus Martius and passed through the Circus Flaminius and Circus Maximus. It wound around the Palatine hill and then proceeded along the Via Sacra, or Sacred Way, ending at the Capitol above the Roman Forum. The victorious general was usually accompanied in the chariot by his family and a slave, who held a crown over the victor's head as he rode along.

Connect to the Literature After students have discussed the Roman triumph, **ask** the Connect to the Literature question: Why would Cassius and Brutus wish to escape at any cost being led as prisoners in a triumph?

Answer: As members of the conspiracy to murder Caesar, they would likely face a hostile crowd. It would be extremely humiliating to be paraded as the prisoners of other Romans (Antony and Octavius) when they, and especially Brutus, previously justified their action against Caesar as a noble deed for the sake of Rome.

14 Reading Check

Answer: Cassius' men are surrounded by Antony's troops, while Brutus' men are looting instead of coming to their aid.

Differentiated Instruction for Universal Access

Enrichment for Gifted and Talented Students

Invite students to research Roman triumphs further and then stage a triumph in class. Direct students to learn more about the different participants in the procession, the music (musicians, songs, and cheers), and art (banners, paintings, allegorical groups) that were part of the spectacle as well as the triumphant general's appearance with his personal entourage. Students may wish to appoint one or two commentators to share information about the history of triumphs and to identify and comment on elements of the triumph included in the performance. The rest of the class may participate as the Roman people in cheering on the victor.

15 Critical Thinking

Identify Cause and Effect

1. Ask two volunteers to take the parts of Pindarus and Cassius and read aloud lines 26–46.
2. Have students paraphrase the scene as Pindarus understands it.
   Answer: Titinius is surrounded by enemy soldiers on horseback who come toward him rapidly. Some dismount, as does Titinius. They take Titinius prisoner.
3. **Ask:** Why does Cassius ask Pindarus to kill him?
   Answer: Cassius believes he has acted as a coward by sending Titinius into danger where he is captured.
4. Encourage students to **speculate** about why Cassius reacts so strongly to Titinius' capture.
   Answer: He and Titinius are close friends; Cassius feels responsible for Titinius because Cassius is the one who insisted on killing Caesar.
5. **Ask** students to predict some effects of Cassius' death.
   Answer: His death may mean the beginning of defeat for the conspirators; his soldiers will be left without a commander.

16 Literary Analysis

Tragic Heroes

1. Have students reread Cassius' final speech (lines 36–46). Then **ask:** What is the relationship between Cassius and Pindarus?
   Answer: Pindarus is Cassius' slave. Cassius took Pindarus captive in Parthia.
2. **Ask:** What will Pindarus gain by killing Cassius?
   Answer: If Pindarus kills Cassius, he will gain his freedom.
3. **Ask:** How does Cassius describe his sword?
   Answer: Cassius asks Pindarus to kill him using the "good sword" that Cassius used to stab Caesar.
4. **Ask** students to respond to the Literary Analysis question: What heroic qualities does Cassius show?
   Answer: By choosing to die by the same sword he used to kill Caesar, Cassius makes his death a revenge for Caesar's death.

CASSIUS. This hill is far enough. Look, look, Titinius!
Are those my tents where I perceive the fire?

TITINIUS. They are, my lord.

CASSIUS. Titinius, if thou lovest me,
Mount thou my horse and hide[5] thy spurs in him
Till he have brought thee up to yonder troops
And here again, that I may rest assured
Whether yond troops are friend or enemy.

TITINIUS. I will be here again even with a thought.[6] [*Exit*]

CASSIUS. Go, Pindarus, get higher on that hill;
My sight was ever thick.[7] Regard[8] Titinius,
And tell me what thou not'st about the field.

[*Exit* PINDARUS.]

This day I breathèd first. Time is come round,
And where I did begin, there shall I end.
My life is run his compass.[9] Sirrah, what news?

PINDARUS. [*Above*] O my lord!

CASSIUS. What news?

PINDARUS. [*Above*] Titinius is enclosèd round about
With horsemen that make to him on the spur;[10]
Yet he spurs on. Now they are almost on him.
Now, Titinius! Now some light.[11] O, he lights too!
He's ta'en![12] [*Shout*] And, hark! They shout for joy.

15

CASSIUS. Come down; behold no more.
O, coward that I am, to live so long,
To see my best friend ta'en before my face!

[*Enter* PINDARUS.]

Come hither, sirrah.
In Parthia did I take thee prisoner;
And then I swore thee, saving of thy life,[13]
That whatsoever I did bid thee do,
Thou shouldst attempt it. Come now, keep thine oath.
Now be a freeman, and with this good sword,
That ran through Caesar's bowels, search[14] this bosom.
Stand not[15] to answer. Here, take thou the hilts,
And when my face is covered, as 'tis now,
Guide thou the sword—Caesar, thou art revenged,
Even with the sword that killed thee. [*Dies*]

5. **hide** sink.
6. **even with a thought** as quick as a thought.
7. **thick** dim.
8. **Regard** observe.
9. **his compass** its full course.
10. **make . . . spur** ride toward him at top speed.
11. **light** dismount from their horses.
12. **ta'en** taken; captured.
13. **swore thee . . . thy life** made you promise when I spared your life.
14. **search** penetrate.
15. **Stand not** do not wait.

16

Literary Analysis
Tragic Heroes What heroic qualities does Cassius show?

⑱ ▲ **Critical Viewing** Can you tell whether the horseman in this picture is the friend or enemy of the foot soldiers? Explain what your answer shows about the conclusions Cassius draws in battle. **[Connect]**

PINDARUS. So, I am free; yet would not so have been,
Durst[16] I have done my will. O Cassius!
Far from this country Pindarus shall run,
Where never Roman shall take note of him. [*Exit*]

[*Enter* TITINIUS *and* MESSALA.]

MESSALA. It is but change,[17] Titinius; for Octavius
Is overthrown by noble Brutus' power,
As Cassius' legions are by Antony.

TITINIUS. These tidings[18] will well comfort Cassius.

MESSALA. Where did you leave him?

16. **Durst** if I had dared.

17. **change** an exchange.

18. **these tidings** *n.* this news.

⑲ Reading Check

What does Cassius think has happened to Titinius?

Differentiated Instruction for Universal Access

Strategy for Less Proficient Readers

Students may find the battle scenes confusing because the characters on stage describe fighting that occurs offstage. Have students work together in small groups to reread the first half of Scene iii, lines 1–55, and then write a brief summary of the battle thus far. Meet with each group to check and correct their summaries and comprehension of the text before finishing Scene iii.

Enrichment for Advanced Readers

Have students assess the effectiveness of the battle scenes thus far in Scene iii. Note that because of space limitations, the fighting takes place offstage. Ask how well students think Shakespeare solves the problem of having to keep the battles offstage. Students can view the 1953 movie on DVD to compare and contrast the film's battle scenes to the play's battle scenes. Then, encourage students to research other film adaptations of Shakespeare's plays. Students may share their observations regarding the crossover of genres in brief oral or written reports.

⑰ Humanities

***Still Photograph, from* Julius Caesar (1953)**

No battle scene like that shown in the film still takes place in the play as it is written. Shakespeare's stage was not large enough to accommodate many actors at once, so most of the fighting took place offstage. In the film, of course, there were no space limitations, and it is dramatically appropriate to stage the battle scene. Use these questions for discussion.

- What details in the picture reflect details in Shakespeare's text?
  Answer: The land by the battlefield is hilly. Horses are involved in the battle.
- What details in the picture suggest that the battle at Philippi resulted in many casualties?
  Possible response: Although the foot soldiers are equipped with helmets, shields, and chest armor, parts of their bodies are not protected; they have both swords and spears but had to fight hand to hand, or in close contact with, enemy soldiers.

⑱ Critical Viewing

Possible response: It is difficult to tell whether the horseman is a friend or an enemy of the foot soldiers. The foot soldiers seem to be defending themselves against him, but they may just be protecting themselves from his rearing horse. The horseman also is wearing different, darker clothes from those worn by the foot soldiers, but that may indicate only a difference in rank and not that he is an enemy. In any case, this picture makes clear that there was considerable confusion on the battlefield, so Pindarus' description of what he sees and the conclusions Cassius draws may not have been accurate.

⑲ Reading Check

Answer: Cassius believes that Titinius has been captured by the enemy.

20 Literary Analysis

Tragic Heroes

1. Read aloud the speeches of Titinius and Messala (lines 59–71) on discovering that Cassius is dead.
2. Discuss Titinius' reaction to the death of Cassius and the imagery he uses. **Ask:** How does Titinius' speech reflect his close relationship with Cassius?
   Possible response: Titinius' speech is emotional. He shows how much he admires Cassius by comparing him to the sun and suggesting that his death is a dark day for Rome.
3. **Ask:** What is the cause of Cassius' death according to Titinius?
   Answer: Cassius feared that Titinius would not prevail in battle.
4. Point out that in line 66, Messala echoes Titinius' observation about the cause of Cassius' death, but with a small change. **Ask** students to respond to the Literary Analysis question: According to Messala, what flaw doomed Cassius?
   Answer: According to Messala, Cassius' fear that he acted as a coward by helping to start the war and then endangering Titinius dooms Cassius.

21 Critical Thinking

Identify Cause and Effect

1. Have students track the events in this scene up to line 90. **Ask:** What series of events does Pindarus' false report set into motion?
   Answer: Cassius kills himself. When Titinius discovers the body and the reason for Cassius' death, he also kills himself.
2. Challenge students to **predict** the effect Cassius' death is likely to have on Brutus.
   Possible response: Brutus may doubt that he can win the battle without Cassius. He may consider the choices he now has and decide to kill himself.
3. Have students read lines 94–96.
   Ask: How does Brutus account for the deaths of Cassius and Titinius?
   Answer: Cassius has himself killed with the sword he used to stab Caesar. Then, Titinius continues the chain of death by using Cassius' sword to kill himself. Brutus observes "that work the ides of March begun" causes both deaths.

Vocabulary
disconsolate (dis kän′ sə lit) *adj.* so unhappy that nothing brings comfort

19. dews *n.* in Shakespeare's day, dew was considered harmful to the health
20. Mistrust . . . success fear that I would not succeed.

Literary Analysis 20
Tragic Heroes According to Messala, what flaw doomed Cassius?

21. Melancholy's child one of gloomy temperament.
22. Why dost . . . are not? Why do you fill the receptive imagination of men with false ideas?
23. conceived *v.* created.
24. mother . . . thee Cassius (in this case), who conceived the error.
25. envenomèd poisoned.
26. Hie *v.* hurry.
27. brave *adj.* noble.

Vocabulary
misconstrued (mis′ kən stro͞od′) *v.* misinterpreted

28. hold thee wait a moment.
29. apace *adv.* quickly.
30. regarded *v.* honored.
31. By your leave with your permission.
32. part *n.* role; duty.

21

TITINIUS. All disconsolate,
With Pindarus his bondman, on this hill.

MESSALA. Is not that he that lies upon the ground?

TITINIUS. He lies not like the living. O my heart!

MESSALA. Is not that he?

TITINIUS. No, this was he, Messala,
But Cassius is no more. O setting sun,
As in thy red rays thou dost sink to night,
So in his red blood Cassius' day is set.
The sun of Rome is set. Our day is gone;
Clouds, dews,[19] and dangers come; our deeds are done!
Mistrust of my success[20] hath done this deed.

MESSALA. Mistrust of good success hath done this deed.
O hateful Error, Melancholy's child,[21]
Why dost thou show to the apt thoughts of men
The things that are not?[22] O Error, soon conceived,[23]
Thou never com'st unto a happy birth,
But kill'st the mother that engend'red thee![24]

TITINIUS. What, Pindarus! Where art thou, Pindarus?

MESSALA. Seek him, Titinius, whilst I go to meet
The noble Brutus, thrusting this report
Into his ears. I may say "thrusting" it;
For piercing steel and darts envenomèd[25]
Shall be as welcome to the ears of Brutus
As tidings of this sight.

TITINIUS. Hie[26] you, Messala,
And I will seek for Pindarus the while. [*Exit* MESSALA.]
Why didst thou send me forth, brave[27] Cassius?
Did I not meet thy friends, and did not they
Put on my brows this wreath of victory,
And bid me give it thee? Didst thou not hear their shouts?
Alas, thou hast misconstrued everything!
But hold thee,[28] take this garland on thy brow;
Thy Brutus bid me give it thee, and I
Will do his bidding. Brutus, come apace,[29]
And see how I regarded[30] Caius Cassius.
By your leave,[31] gods. This is a Roman's part:[32]
Come, Cassius' sword, and find Titinius' heart. [*Dies*]

[*Call to arms sounds. Enter* BRUTUS, MESSALA, YOUNG CATO, STRATO, VOLUMNIUS, *and* LUCILIUS.]

Vocabulary Development

Word Analysis

Call students' attention to the selection vocabulary word *disconsolate* in line 55 and to its definition. Tell students that the adjective *disconsolate* combines the prefix *dis-*, meaning "not," and the base word *consolat-*. *Consolat-* derives from the past participle *consolatus* of the Latin verb *consolari*, meaning "relieve grief or sorrow; comfort." The meaning of the past participle would be "comforted or relieved of grief or sorrow." Thus the literal meaning of *disconsolate* is "not relieved of grief or sorrow; not comforted." Point out that the Latin prefix dis-, meaning "not," is used to form many other words. Have students identify three additional words that include the prefix *dis-*. Have students look up the words in a dictionary to determine their meaning.

BRUTUS. Where, where, Messala, doth his body lie?

MESSALA. Lo, yonder, and Titinius mourning it.

BRUTUS. Titinius' face is upward.

CATO. He is slain.

BRUTUS. O Julius Caesar, thou art mighty yet!
Thy spirit walks abroad, and turns our swords
In our own proper entrails.[33] *[Low calls to arms]*

CATO. Brave Titinius!
Look, whe'r[34] he have not crowned dead Cassius.

BRUTUS. Are yet two Romans living such as these?
The last of all the Romans, fare thee well!
It is impossible that ever Rome
Should breed thy fellow.[35] Friends, I owe moe[36] tears
To this dead man than you shall see me pay.
I shall find time, Cassius; I shall find time.
(22) Come, therefore, and to Thasos[37] send his body;
His funerals shall not be in our camp,
(23) Lest it discomfort us.[38] Lucilius, come,
And come, young Cato; let us to the field.
Labeo and Flavius set our battles[39] on.
'Tis three o'clock; and, Romans, yet ere night
We shall try fortune in a second fight. *[Exit]*

33. **own proper entrails** very own inner organs.

34. **whe'r** whether.

Literary Analysis
Shakespeare's Tragic Heroes What noble or heroic qualities does Brutus display in his reactions to Cassius' death?

35. **fellow** equal.
36. **moe** *n.* more.
37. **Thasos** an island not far from Philippi.

38. **discomfort us** discourage our soldiers.
39. **battles** armies.

Scene iv. The field of battle.

[Call to arms sounds. Enter BRUTUS, MESSALA, YOUNG CATO, LUCILIUS, *and* FLAVIUS.*]*

BRUTUS. Yet, countrymen, O, yet hold up your heads!
[Exit, with followers]

CATO. What bastard[1] doth not? Who will go with me?
I will proclaim my name about the field.
I am the son of Marcus Cato,[2] ho!
A foe to tyrants, and my country's friend.
I am the son of Marcus Cato, ho!

[Enter SOLDIERS *and fight.]*

LUCILIUS. And I am Brutus, Marcus Brutus, I;
Brutus, my country's friend; know me for Brutus![3]
*[*YOUNG CATO *falls.]*

O young and noble Cato, art thou down?

1. **bastard** person who is not a true Roman.
2. **Marcus Cato** Brutus' wife's father.
3. **And I am Brutus** Lucilius impersonates Brutus in order to protect him and confuse the enemy.

(24) **Reading Check**
What error has led to Cassius' and Titinius' deaths?

Differentiated Instruction for Universal Access

Enrichment for Advanced Readers
Encourage students interested in learning more about Julius Caesar, Octavius, and other Roman emperors to read excerpts from *The Twelve Caesars*, a vivid account of Rome's first dozen absolute rulers by Roman historian Gaius Suetonius Tranquillus (A.D. 69–died after 122). Suetonius briefly practiced law but spent most of his career as a palace official, including serving as a secretary under the emperor Hadrian. Suetonius lived through nearly thirty years of the events he described. His sources include official imperial and senatorial records, memoirs, and various public documents. Have students read Suetonius' accounts of one or more of the Caesars and present their findings to the class.

(22) Literary Analysis

Tragic Heroes

1. Read aloud Brutus' speech in lines 98–110.
2. **Ask:** How does Brutus' reference to Titinius and Cassius as "the last of all Romans" reflect his feelings about the conspiracy?
   Answer: It suggests that the conspirators are true Romans who wanted to save Rome from absolute rule.
3. Then, have students consider Brutus' remarks about Cassius alone. **Ask** students to respond to the Literary Analysis question: What noble or heroic qualities does Brutus display in his reactions to Cassius' death?
   Possible response: He expresses grief for Cassius and orders the necessary arrangements to be made for Cassius. However, he remains focused on the battle, which continues the noble deed he believes the conspirators began with Caesar's death.

(23) Reading Skill

Compare and Contrast Characters

1. Remind students of Brutus' reaction to the death of Portia in Act IV. **Ask** them to compare and contrast his reactions to the two deaths.
   Answer: Brutus reacts in similar ways to both deaths. He expresses some grief but then turns to the business at hand.
2. **Ask** students how they would explain Brutus' rather restrained grief in both cases.
   Answer: As a follower of Stoicism, Brutus does not become overly concerned or emotional about events he cannot control.

(24) Reading Check

Answer: Pindarus' false report about Titinius' capture leads to Cassius' death, and Cassius' death led to Titinius' death.

25 Literary Analysis

Tragic Heroes

1. Remind students that tragic heroes are usually of noble birth. Clarify, however, that nobility can signify something more than a person's social station.
2. **Ask** students to describe a noble character.
   Answer: Being noble means being of high mind and excellent character, being idealistic and moral, being outstanding in one's thoughts and actions.
3. Have two students read aloud the dialogue between Lucilius and Antony in lines 20–32. Emphasize that Lucilius characterizes Brutus by saying: "the noble Brutus" and "He will be found like Brutus, like himself." **Ask:** Why might nobility be a tragic flaw?
   Possible response: A noble person such as Brutus may be idealistic and thoughtful but perhaps not practical. Also, a noble person may not be prepared to have relations with ignoble, manipulative people because he or she does not understand them.

26 Connecting to the Big Question

1. Have students suggest examples of how our experiences can change how we perceive things.
2. Have students read the bracketed passage. **Ask** students how Brutus' recent experiences have led him to the conclusion that he must die.
   Possible response: Brutus realizes that he has killed Caesar in vain and not for the good of Rome. After he dreams about Caesar visiting him, in which he states that it is Brutus' time to die, he feels that the only way to avenge Caesar's death is to kill himself.
3. Invite students to reflect on the actions of Brutus throughout the play, and while doing so, think about the Big Question: "To what extent does experience determine what we perceive?"

Why, now thou diest as bravely as Titinius,
And mayst be honored, being Cato's son.

FIRST SOLDIER. Yield, or thou diest.

LUCILIUS. Only I yield to die.[4]
There is so much that thou wilt kill me straight;[5]
Kill Brutus, and be honored in his death.

FIRST SOLDIER. We must not. A noble prisoner!

[*Enter* ANTONY.]

SECOND SOLDIER. Room, ho! Tell Antony, Brutus is ta'en.

FIRST SOLDIER. I'll tell thee news. Here comes the general.
Brutus is ta'en, Brutus is ta'en, my lord.

ANTONY. Where is he?

LUCILIUS. Safe, Antony; Brutus is safe enough.
I dare assure thee that no enemy
Shall ever take alive the noble Brutus.
The gods defend him from so great a shame!
When you do find him, or alive or dead,
He will be found like Brutus, like himself.[6]

ANTONY. This is not Brutus, friend, but, I assure you,
A prize no less in worth. Keep this man safe;
Give him all kindness. I had rather have
Such men my friends than enemies. Go on,
And see whe'r Brutus be alive or dead,
And bring us word unto[7] Octavius' tent
How everything is chanced.[8] [*Exit*]

4. **Only . . . die** I will surrender only to die.
5. **much . . . straight** much honor in it that you will kill me immediately.
6. **like himself** behaving in a noble way.
7. **unto** in.
8. **How everything is chanced** how everything has turned out; what has happened.

Scene v. The field of battle.

[*Enter* BRUTUS, DARDANIUS, CLITUS, STRATO, *and* VOLUMNIUS.]

BRUTUS. Come, poor remains[1] of friends, rest on this rock.

CLITUS. Statilius showed the torchlight,[2] but, my lord,
He came not back; he is or ta'en or slain.

BRUTUS. Sit thee down, Clitus. Slaying is the word;
It is a deed in fashion. Hark thee, Clitus. [*Whispers*]

CLITUS. What, I, my lord? No, not for all the world!

BRUTUS. Peace then, no words.

CLITUS. I'll rather kill myself.

BRUTUS. Hark thee, Dardanius. [*Whispers*]

1. **poor remains** pitiful survivors.
2. **showed the torchlight** signaled with a torch.

Vocabulary Development

Word Forms

Expand students' vocabulary by helping them learn related forms of two of the selection vocabulary words for Act V. Give students a blank **Word Form Chart** (*Professional Development Guidebook,* p. 42), with *misconstrue,* and *meditates* in the correct columns.

Work with the class, or have students work with a partner, to determine the related forms. The final chart should look like the one shown. Hold students accountable for integrating the related forms of the words into their speaking and writing.

Noun	Verb	Adjective	Adverb
misconstruction	misconstrue	**misconstrued**	
meditation	**meditates**	meditative	meditatively

DARDANIUS. Shall I do such a deed?

CLITUS. O Dardanius!

DARDANIUS. O Clitus!

26 **CLITUS.** What ill request did Brutus make to thee?

DARDANIUS. To kill him, Clitus. Look, he **meditates**.

27 **CLITUS.** Now is that noble vessel[3] full of grief,
That it runs over even at his eyes.

BRUTUS. Come hither, good Volumnius; list[4] a word.

VOLUMNIUS. What says my lord?

BRUTUS. Why, this, Volumnius:
The ghost of Caesar hath appeared to me
Two several[5] times by night; at Sardis once,
And this last night here in Philippi fields.
I know my hour is come.

VOLUMNIUS. Not so, my lord.

BRUTUS. Nay, I am sure it is, Volumnius.
Thou seest the world, Volumnius, how it goes;
Our enemies have beat us to the pit.[6]

[*Low calls to arms*]

It is more worthy to leap in ourselves
Than tarry till they push us.[7] Good Volumnius,
Thou know'st that we two went to school together;
Even for that our love of old, I prithee[8]
Hold thou my sword-hilts whilst I run on it.

VOLUMNIUS. That's not an office[9] for a friend, my lord.

[*Call to arms still*[10]]

CLITUS. Fly, fly, my lord, there is no tarrying here.

BRUTUS. Farewell to you; and you; and you, Volumnius.
Strato, thou hast been all this while asleep;
Farewell to thee too, Strato. Countrymen,
My heart doth joy that yet in all my life
I found no man but he was true to me.
I shall have glory by this losing day
28 More than Octavius and Mark Antony
By this vile conquest shall attain unto.[11]
So fare you well at once, for Brutus' tongue
Hath almost ended his life's history.

Vocabulary
meditates (med´ ə tāts´) *v.* thinks deeply

3. **vessel** container of liquid; here, a metaphor for Brutus.
4. **list** hear.
5. **several** separate.

Literary Analysis
Tragic Heroes Why does this scene of Brutus weeping add complexity or depth to his character?

6. **pit** trap or grave.
7. **tarry . . . us** wait until they kill us.
8. **prithee** (prith´ ē) *interjection* ask you, please; "pray thee."
9. **office** task.
10. **still** continuing.

Literary Analysis
Tragic Heroes What tragic flaw in Brutus is revealed in lines 33–35?

11. **By this . . . unto** by this evil victory shall gain. (Brutus sees the victory of Octavius and Antony as causing the downfall of Roman freedom.)

29 **Reading Check**
What does Brutus ask of his servants?

27 Literary Analysis

Tragic Heroes

1. Have students reread Clitus' observation in lines 13–14. Point out that "that noble vessel full of grief" is a reference to Brutus.
Ask: What does Clitus notice Brutus is doing?
Answer: He notices Brutus is weeping.
2. **Ask** students the first Literary Analysis question: Why does this scene of Brutus weeping add complexity or depth to his character?
Answer: To this point, Brutus has kept his emotions in check, adhering to Stoic principles. His weeping here shows a side of him that has not been revealed before.
3. Suggest that Brutus' weeping, his interpretation of the second appearance of Caesar's ghost, and his request to his friend Volumnius indicate that Brutus' downfall is complete.

28 Literary Analysis

Tragic Heroes

1. Ask a volunteer to read aloud lines 31–42. Discuss how these lines support the notion of Brutus as a tragic hero.
2. **Ask** students the second Literary Analysis question: What tragic flaw in Brutus is revealed in lines 33–35.
Answer: Brutus' tragic flaw is his error in judgment in trusting Cassius, Caesar, and Antony.
3. **Ask:** How are Cassius and Antony untrue to Brutus?
Answer: Cassius uses Brutus for his own purposes when he manipulates him into joining the conspiracy; Antony lies to Brutus and deliberately stirs the people of Rome against him

29 Reading Check

Answer: He asks them to kill him.

Fluency

Explain to students that a fundamental part of reading fluently is using appropriate expression and inflection. Have students take note of the punctuation marks used in Scene v, lines 1–16. Suggest that punctuation marks can often reveal the author's purpose for writing a particular sentence or line and can also help to build the plot through character dialogue. Discuss how this is especially crucial in plays, since they are intended to be read aloud or performed.

- Model reading lines 1–16 aloud fluently, emphasizing the correct pauses and inflection when reading sentences that end in periods, exclamation marks, and question marks.
- Have partners practice reading aloud lines 1–16 fluently, using appropriate expression. Circulate the room to monitor the fluency of the students' reading. If students continue to have difficulty anticipating what type of expression to use, hand out copies of pages 996 and 997, and model highlighting sentences that end in exclamation points in one color and those that end in question marks in another color.

30 Literary Analysis

Tragic Heroes

1. Have students read Brutus' final words in lines 44–51. **Ask:** How do Brutus' final words show his nobility?
   Answer: He shows kindness and respect toward his servant, Strato, and courage in taking responsibility for his own fate.
2. **Ask** students to explain their reactions to Brutus' decision.
   Possible responses: Students may admire Brutus and feel sorry for his death; some may say that since he is an assassin, he deserves to die; some may point out that he would have been executed by his enemies, and so it is better for him to die this way.

31 Reading Skill

Compare and Contrast Characters

- **Ask** students the Reading Skill question: What do the differences in the way in which Brutus and Cassius meet death show about their characters?
  Answer: Brutus' thoughtful, noble character shows when he acknowledges his bad judgment and says that he deserves to die more than Caesar did. Cassius' rash, emotional character shows when he mourns for his friend and then rushes to death based on faulty information that he himself has not checked.

▶ **Monitor Progress** Circulate among students to check their use of the Reading Skill charts to compare and contrast Brutus and Cassius. Make sure students include in their charts a comparison of the way in which the two characters meet death.

▶ **Reteach** Remind students that comparing involves identifying similarities, and contrasting is examining differences. With students, write character sketches on the board for each tragic hero in *The Tragedy of Julius Caesar.* Guide students to understand the similarities and differences between the characters. Then, have students label similarities in their Reading Skill charts with an *S* and differences with a *D* for review.

28

Night hangs upon mine eyes; my bones would rest,
That have but labored to attain this hour.[12]

[*Call to arms sounds. Cry within, "Fly, fly, fly!"*]

CLITUS. Fly, my lord, fly!

BRUTUS. Hence! I will follow.

[*Exit* CLITUS, DARDANIUS, *and* VOLUMNIUS.]

I prithee, Strato, stay thou by thy lord,
Thou art a fellow of a good respect.[13]
Thy life hath had some smatch[14] of honor in it;
Hold then my sword, and turn away thy face,
While I do run upon it. Wilt thou, Strato?

STRATO. Give me your hand first. Fare you well, my lord.

BRUTUS. Farewell, good Strato—Caesar, now be still;
I killed not thee with half so good a will.
[*Dies*]

[*Call to arms sounds. Retreat sounds. Enter* ANTONY, OCTAVIUS, MESSALA, LUCILIUS, *and the Army.*]

OCTAVIUS. What man is that?

MESSALA. My master's man.[15] Strato, where is thy master?

STRATO. Free from the bondage you are in, Messala;
The conquerors can but make a fire of him
For Brutus only overcame himself,[16]
And no man else hath honor[17] by his death.

LUCILIUS. So Brutus should be found. I thank thee, Brutus,
That thou hast proved Lucilius' saying[18] true.

OCTAVIUS. All that served Brutus, I will entertain them.[19]
Fellow, wilt thou bestow[20] thy time with me?

STRATO. Ay, if Messala will prefer[21] me to you.

OCTAVIUS. Do so, good Messala.

MESSALA. How died my master, Strato?

STRATO. I held the sword, and he did run on it.

MESSALA. Octavius, then take him to follow thee,
That did the latest service to my master.

ANTONY. This was the noblest Roman of them all.
All the conspirators save[22] only he
Did that[23] they did in envy of great Caesar;

12. **this hour** time of death.

13. **respect** reputation.

14. **smatch** smack or taste.

30 **Reading Skill**
Compare and Contrast Characters What do the differences in the way in which Brutus and Cassius meet death show about their characters? 31

15. **man** servant.

16. **Brutus only overcame himself** only Brutus, no one else, defeated Brutus.

17. **no man else hath honor** no other man gains honor.

18. **Lucilius' saying** See Act V, Scene iv, lines 21–22.

19. **entertain them** take them into my service.

20. **bestow** spend.

21. **prefer** recommend.

22. **save** except.

23. **that** what.

Vocabulary Development

Vocabulary Knowledge Rating

When students have completed reading and discussing *The Tragedy of Julius Caesar:* Act V, have them take out their **Vocabulary Knowledge Rating Chart** for Act V. Read the words aloud once more, and have students rate their knowledge of the words again in the After Reading column. Clarify any words that are still problematic. Have students write their own definition or example in the appropriate column. Then, have students complete the Vocabulary Practice at the end of the selection. Encourage students to use the words in further discussion and written work about this selection. Remind them that they will be accountable for these words on the Selection Test, ***Unit 5 Resources*** pp. 157–159 or 160–162.

32

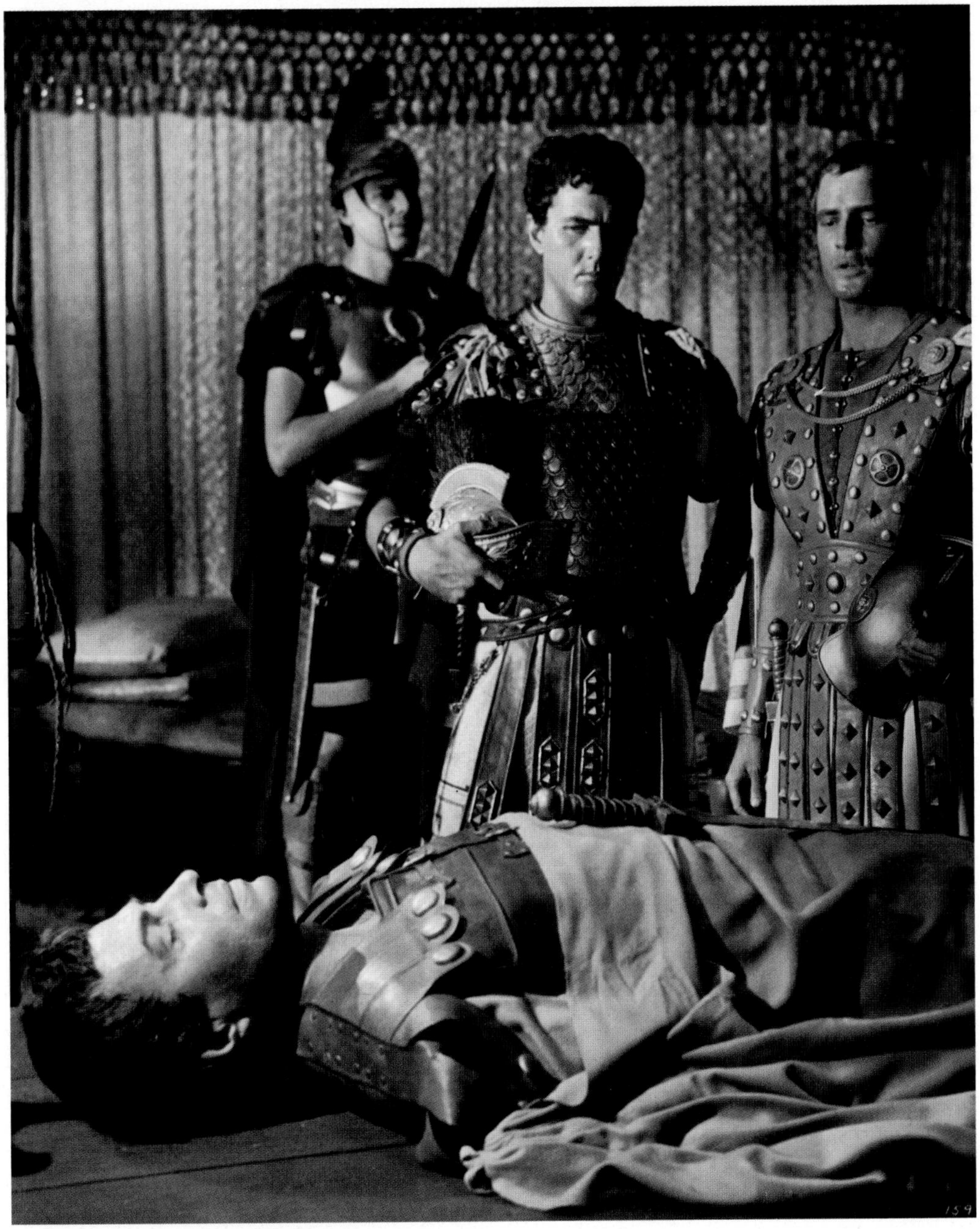

33 ▲ **Critical Viewing** Which details in this film still suggest the respect that Octavius and Antony have for Brutus, even in defeat? **[Analyze]**

32 Humanities

***Still Photograph, from* Julius Caesar (1953)**

A prominent leader such as Brutus would be given an elaborate funeral. Ritual wailing preceded the preparation of the corpse. Then the body was laid out in official dress on a bed in the atrium of the family's home. After the funeral, the body was escorted to the place where it would be buried or cremated. The procession included not only family members and Roman citizens but actors who impersonated the dead person's already deceased relatives. Musicians and professional mourners also came along. Use these questions for discussion:

- How has Brutus' body been prepared on the battlefield?
  Answer: Brutus' body has been covered with a cloth and his weapon has been placed on his chest.
- What will Brutus' funeral be like? How do you know?
  Answer: Brutus will have a funeral similar to that of any other prominent Roman because he is a public official. Octavius guarantees in lines 76–77 that he will be treated with respect and will receive the usual rites for a noble person.

33 Critical Viewing

Answer: A soldier stands at attention. Both Antony and Octavius are holding their helmets. The facial expressions of both are serious, respectful, and even sorrowful.

Concept Connector

Anticipation Guide

Have students return to their **Anticipation Guides** and respond to the statements again in the After Reading column. They may do this individually or in their original pairs or groups. Then, lead a class discussion, probing for what students have learned that confirms or invalidates each statement. Encourage students to cite specific details, quotations, or other evidence from the text to support their responses to each statement.

Reading Skill Graphic Organizer

Ask students to review the graphic organizers they completed in Act V. Show them **Reading Skill Graphic Organizer A** (*Graphic Organizer Transparencies,* page 182) as an example.

ASSESS

Answers

Critical Thinking

1. Students may respond that they understand why Brutus kills himself.
2. (a) They plan to kill themselves. (b) They hope to avoid the humiliation of being paraded as captives in the streets of Rome. (c) **Possible response:** Brutus' plan shows his concern for honor; Cassius' plan shows his fear of the future.
3. (a) He believes Titinius has been captured. (b) It leads him to kill himself. (c) **Possible response:** It is an impulsive, emotional decision that sets a series of other events in motion.
4. (a) Throughout the play, Antony manipulates and takes advantage of Brutus' naivete and honorable nature. He shows no respect for Brutus and is solely focused on defeating the conspirators and ruling Rome. (b) **Possible response:** At the end of the play, Antony publicly praises Brutus' noble, good, and honest nature, displaying respect for the fallen tragic hero. While Antony's change of opinion may have hints of sincerity, it is most likely an attempt to heal any remaining political wounds and win the hearts and support of the Roman people.

To what extent does experience determine what we perceive?

(a) Brutus believes that Cassius' motives in killing Caesar are honorable. He also trusts Antony to speak at Caesar's funeral. **(b)** Trusting Cassius leads to Caesar's death and civil war. Trusting Antony allows him to turn Romans against Brutus.
(c) They suggest that Brutus believes that he is always right and that his view of he world is idealistic and naive.

He, only in a general honest thought[24]
And common good to all, made one of them.[25]
His life was gentle,[26] and the elements
So mixed[27] in him that Nature might stand up
And say to all the world, "This was a man!"

OCTAVIUS. According to his virtue,[28] let us use[29] him
With all respect and rites of burial.
Within my tent his bones tonight shall lie,
Most like a soldier ordered honorably.[30]
So call the field[31] to rest, and let's away
To part[32] the glories of this happy day. [*Exit all.*]

24. **only in a general honest thought** with only public-minded motives.
25. **made one of them** became one of the conspirators.
26. **gentle** noble.
27. **So mixed** well balanced.
28. **virtue** excellence.
29. **use** treat.
30. **ordered honorably** treated with honor.
31. **field** army.
32. **part** share.

Critical Thinking

1. **Respond:** How did you respond to Brutus' death?
2. **(a)** What do Cassius and Brutus each plan to do if they lose the battle? **(b) Analyze Cause and Effect:** In making these plans, what do they hope to avoid? Support your answer. **(c) Draw Conclusions:** What do their plans show about their values?
3. **(a)** What does Cassius believe has happened to Titinius when Titinius rides to his tents? **(b) Analyze Cause and Effect:** What does his interpretation of events lead him to do? **(c) Connect:** In what way is this reaction like his reaction in Act I to signs that Caesar would become king?
4. **(a)** How has Antony felt toward Brutus throughout most of the play? **(b) Infer:** How and why does Antony's attitude toward Brutus change at the end?

To what extent does experience determine what we perceive? (a) Give two examples of situations in which Brutus expects others to act honorably and they fail to do so. **(b)** What is the outcome of each situation? **(c)** What do these situations suggest about Brutus' view of himself and the world?

Assessment Resources

Unit 5 Resources

L1 L2 EL **Selection Test A,** pp. 179–181. Administer Test A to less advanced readers and English learners.

L3 L4 **Selection Test B,** pp. 182–184. Administer Test B to on-level and more advanced students.

L3 L4 **Open-Book Test,** pp. 176–178. As an alternative, give the Open-Book Test.

All **Customizable Test Bank**

All **Self-tests**
Students may prepare for the **Selection Test** by taking the **Self-test** online.

PHLit Online! All assessment resources are available at **www.PHLitOnline.com.**

After You Read — The Tragedy of Julius Caesar, Act V

Literary Analysis: Tragic Heroes

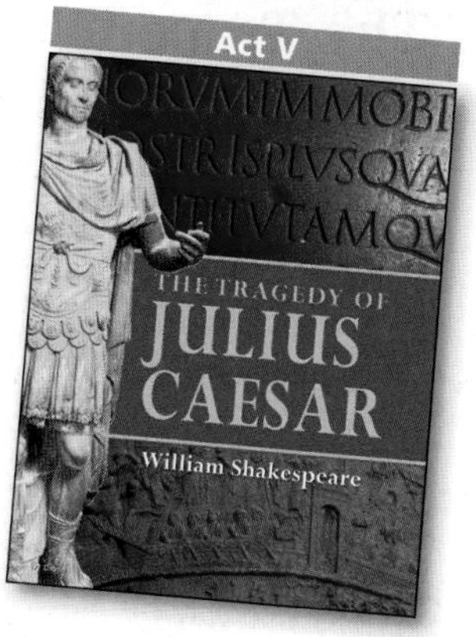

1. **(a)** Using a chart like the one shown, give examples showing that Brutus and Caesar have the qualities of traditional **tragic heroes.**

Noble Birth	Suffers Catastrophe	Tragic Flaw

(b) Which character has more characteristics of **Shakespeare's tragic heroes?** Support your answer with details from the text.

2. **(a) Interpret:** What does Brutus mean when he says, "My heart doth joy that yet in all my life / I found no man but he was true to me"? **(b) Make a Judgment:** Do these lines express a positive attitude or a blindness toward others? Explain. **(c) Discuss:** Discuss your interpretation with a partner. Then, explain whether or not the discussion changed your mind and why.

Reading Skill: Compare and Contrast Characters

3. **(a) Compare and contrast** Cassius and Brutus. Give specific examples in support of your points. **(b)** Find an example from the text to show that the two men are **foils. (c)** What do the differences between the two help to emphasize about Brutus' character?

Vocabulary

Practice Use a vocabulary word from the list on page 984 to write a complete sentence about each numbered item. Explain your choices.

1. being too eager to please
2. watching the sun set
3. learning a new language
4. losing a friend
5. hearing distant thunder
6. making a good impression

Word Study Use the context of the sentences and what you know about the **Latin root *-stru-*** to explain your answer to each question.

1. If someone *obstructs* a doorway, is he or she allowing you to pass through it?
2. If a mathematician breaks a challenging code, has he or she *construed* its meaning?

Word Study

The **Latin root *-stru-*** means "pile up" or "build."

Challenge Explain how the root *-stru-* contributes to the meanings of these words. Consult a dictionary if necessary.

construction
instruct
structural

Vocabulary

Practice

Sample answers:

1. When she fawned over her teacher, she was being too eager to please.
2. My father always meditates when he is watching the sun set.
3. When my best friend was learning a new language, he often misconstrued the grammar rules.
4. She was disconsolate after losing a friend.
5. The distant thunder seemed to presage the coming storm.
6. Having a good demeanor is essential to making a good impression.

Word Study

Sample answers:

1. No. The root *-stru-* means "pile up" or "build," and *obstructs* means "blocks with an obstacle, often something piled up."
2. Yes. The root *-stru-* means "pile up" or "build," and *construed* means "interpreted how something is structured or built."

Word Study: Challenge

Sample answers: *Construction* means "the act or art of building." *Instruct* means "to build or furnish knowledge." *Structural* means "relating to how something is structured or built."

ASSESS/EXTEND

Answers

Literary Analysis

1. (a) Both are of noble birth; both suffer a catastrophe: Caesar is murdered, and Brutus kills himself; Caesar's tragic flaw is ambition or excessive pride; Brutus' tragic flaw is poor judgment or excessive idealism. (b) Brutus has more characteristics of Shakespeare's tragic heroes: He is a complex character who struggles with his own values and beliefs in joining the conspiracy. Caesar's main deficiency as a Shakespearean tragic hero is his lack of complexity and internal conflict.

   For other sample answers, see ***Graphic Organizer Transparencies,*** **Literary Analysis Graphic Organizer A,** p. 184, and the **Additional Answers** section.

2. **Possible response:** (a) Brutus is happy to know that throughout his life, he only encountered people who were honest and true to him. (b) **Possible response:** These lines express a blindness toward others. In reality, many people throughout the play tricked, manipulated, and were untrue to Brutus. (c) Students should discuss their ideas with a partner. Students may say that their ideas changed after discussion.

Reading Skill

3. (a) Cassius is impulsive, liable to anger, envious of others, and fearful; Brutus is idealistic, calm, dedicated to the public good, and stoical. For example, Cassius rashly kills himself based on faulty information. Brutus kills himself in order to remain "worthy" and dedicated to the conspirators' original cause. (b) The differences between the two emphasize Brutus' nobility and idealism.

EXTEND

Grammar

1. Introduce the skill, using the instruction on the student page.
2. Discuss the definitions and examples.

Think Aloud: Model the Skill

Model the skill of identifying absolute adjectives and absolute phrases, using the following "think aloud." Say to students:

I know that an adjective is an absolute adjective when it cannot have a comparative or superlative form. Consider the adjective *dead.* I ask myself, "Can something be more dead or less dead?" Since the answer is no, I conclude that *dead* is an absolute adjective.

I know that an absolute phrase modifies a whole sentence, not just a word. When I consider the sentence, "Rain pouring, the girls ran into the house" I see that the phrase "Rain pouring" modifies the rest of the sentence. Thus, I conclude it is an absolute phrase.

ASSESS

Answers

Practice A

1. Given human nature
2. equal
3. dead

Challenge

Sample answer: "Our fathers' minds are dead/And we are governed with our mothers' spirits. . . ." (Act I, Scene iii). "Searching the window for a flint, I found/This paper thus sealed up. . . ." (Act II, Scene i)

Practice B

Sample answers:

1. complete
2. infinite
3. Honoring his character in a speech

Challenge

Possible response: Students' paragraphs should summarize the battle and include two absolute adjectives and two absolute phrases.

Integrated Language Skills

The Tragedy of Julius Caesar, Acts I–V

Grammar: Absolutes and Absolute Phrases

An **absolute adjective** is an adjective that has no comparative or superlative form: *complete, infinite, perfect, unique, dead, empty, full, definite,* or *equal.* Logically, one cannot be *less equal* or *more full.*

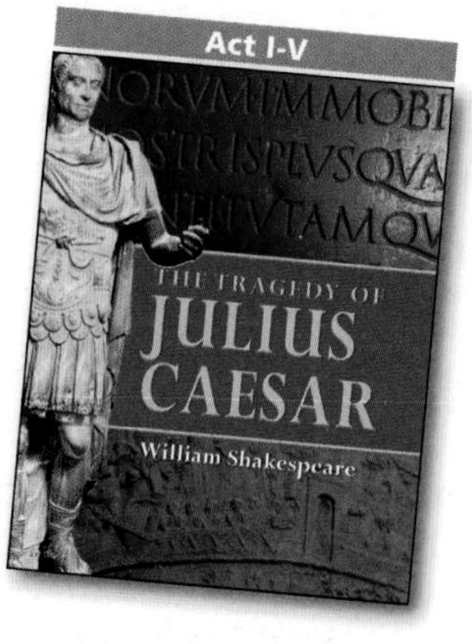

Examples

- Her dog is *bigger* than mine. (*non-absolute adjective:* The adjective *bigger* is the comparative form of *big.*)
- The bouquet of flowers is *perfect.* (*absolute adjective:* The flowers cannot be *more perfect.*)

An absolute phrase is a phrase that modifies an entire sentence, but does not modify any specific word in it. An absolute phrase usually acts as a comment on the main clause.

Example

All things considered, she decided that it was more important to help her brother than to attend the dance. (*absolute phrase*)

Practice A Identify the absolute adjective or absolute phrase in each sentence.

1. Given human nature, Caesar was bound to become too ambitious.
2. Brutus thinks that all Romans should be equal.
3. Cassius will be happy when Caesar is dead and no longer rules Rome.

Challenge Find an example of an absolute adjective and an absolute phrase in the first two acts of *Julius Caesar.*

Practice B Complete each sentence by adding the type of word or phrase in parenthesis.

1. The list of conspirators was (absolute adjective) when Brutus joined the group.
2. Caesar expressed (absolute adjective) sorrow when he saw that Brutus had betrayed him.
3. (Absolute phrase), Antony mourned Brutus' death.

Challenge Write a brief paragraph about the battle between the conspirators and Antony's forces using two absolute adjectives and two absolute phrases.

Extend the Lesson

Sentence Modeling

Have students consider the following sentence from the selection:

"Our day is gone;/Clouds, dews, and dangers come; our deeds are done."

Ask students what they notice about the sentence. Elicit from them that the sentence includes absolute adjectives: *gone* and *done.* Then, ask what else they notice. (Here, Shakespeare uses absolute adjectives to echo the finality of the moment. He describes the nouns *day* and *deeds* in absolute and unwavering terms, linking them to the irrevocable event that had just occurred: Cassius' death.)

Have students imitate the sentence in a sentence on a topic of their own choosing, matching each grammatical and stylistic feature discussed. Collect the sentences, and share them with the class.

Writing

Editorial Imagine that you are a journalist at the time of Caesar's murder. Write an editorial to express your opinion on Rome's future.

- Jot down notes on the major events and issues in the play.
- List consequences Rome faces because of the battle between the conspirators and Antony's allies.
- Mark each consequence as desirable or undesirable and add a note explaining why.
- As you draft your editorial, explain the consequences you foresee. Give reasons for each opinion you express.
- Anticipate your reader's concerns and biases. For each opinion you provide, add a sentence that deflects a counterargument someone might make against it.
- Include a concluding sentence that summarizes your overall opinion.

Obituary An obituary is a notice that someone has died. In addition to details about the death, an obituary often reports on the life and values of its subject. Write an obituary for a character who dies in *Julius Caesar.*

- Review the play for details about the character's life and personality.
- Choose an effective organization. For example, open with the circumstances of the character's death and provide brief background of the character's life.
- Use details from the text to construct a unified picture of the character's life.

Writing Workshop: *Work in Progress*

Prewriting for a Research Report For a research report you might write, brainstorm for topics by considering several different purposes. Fold a piece of paper in three and label the three sections as follows: "to persuade," "to make a recommendation," and "to inform." Under each label, write one or two topics on which you might write a report with the purpose described. Put these Purpose Notes in your portfolio.

Use this prewriting activity to prepare for the Writing Workshop on page 1020.

Writing

1. Review the assignments, using the instruction on the student page.
2. Guide students to select one of the Writing activities to complete.
3. To support students in writing an editorial and an obituary, give them **Support for Writing,** p. 173 in ***Unit 5 Resources.***
4. Provide the following tips for students:
   - When writing an editorial, there is no wrong opinion, as long as it can be supported with details from the text.
   - Obituaries should provide a well-rounded portrait of the individual that focuses on his or her positive qualities or contributions to society.

Six Traits Focus

✔	Ideas		Word Choice
✔	Organization		Sentence Fluency
	Voice		Conventions

Writing Workshop
Work in Progress

Have students save their completed research report notes in their portfolios. They will use the notes later as they complete the Writing Workshop assignment (see pp. 1020–1031).

Listening and Speaking

1. Review the assignments, using the instruction on the student page.
2. Guide students to select one of the Listening and Speaking activities to complete.
3. To support students' work on the assignments, have them complete the **Support for Extend Your Learning** page (***Unit 5 Resources***, p. 174).
4. Provide the following tips for students:
   - When preparing for a dramatic reading, highlight and practice challenging vocabulary to improve reading fluency during the performance.
   - Successful post-screening discussion should consist of equal contributions from each group member, keeping in mind that the questions provided elicit opinions.

Integrated Language Skills

Listening and Speaking

Dramatic Reading With a partner, give a **dramatic reading** of Cassius' discussion with Brutus in lines 132–177 of Act I, Scene ii. Review Act I for hints about the personality of each man. Let your knowledge of the character guide your **tone of voice** and **attitude**. Follow these suggestions:

- **Make notes** about how you want to pronounce certain lines: with contempt, with surprise, with suspicion, or with concern.
- Remember to **project your voice** strongly if you want to say a line loudly. Lower your voice if you want to convey a softer, quieter tone.
- Practice your parts and present your reading to the class.

Lead the class in a discussion to compare and contrast the experience of reading the scene silently to oneself with the experience of hearing it performed with different voices for the different roles.

Dramatic Reading With a small group of students, hold a **group screening** of a filmed production of *Julius Caesar.* Afterward, **discuss the production**, starting with these questions:

- How effective was each actor in a major role?
- How effective was the staging of the action?
- In what ways did the production surprise you, given your reading of the play and the way you "saw" the play in your mind as you read?
- **Identify and discuss the influence of the director** on the production using questions like these to guide you: How appropriate was the actors' performance style? Were the costumes effective? Did you agree with the director's overall interpretation of the story?
- During the discussion **listen to understand** and **evaluate** your classmate's ideas

Have two members of the group serve as notetakers. Afterward, review the discussion notes, and analyze the differences in members' responses. Make a chart showing the reactions to the film.

Research and Technology

Womans History Report Using books, reference articles, and reliable Internet sources, find out more about the life that married aristocratic women like Calpurnia and Portia led in ancient Rome. Then, write a women's history report. Follow these guidelines:

- Develop a **comprehensive search plan** to find and evalate information from primary and secondary sources.
- Compare these two characters with the typical upper-class woman of the time.
- Consider the role of each in political affairs and in relation to her husband.

Advertising Poster Create an advertising poster for a historically accurate performance of *Julius Caesar.* Include an illustration and appropriate text that capture the essence of the performance. **Conduct research** to find information about the following:

- the design of the ancient Roman theater
- the costumes
- the actors: were they men or women or both?

Include information to **attract spectators'** interest in the play, such as enticing details about the plot. As you develop your poster, be alert to the appeal of the payout you create. Choose a readable font or write legibly.

Multimedia Presentation Using computer software, produce a multimedia presentation on the philosophy of Stoicism. Conduct research to identify the main beliefs of the movement. Follow these research strategies:

- **Paraphrase** the information you find in your research sources. This step will let you know whether you fully understand the ideas you are using.
- Find visuals or music to accompany the information you will present.
- **Organize** the information you will use from most to least important. Put main ideas and evidence that supports your ideas at the top of the list. Add interesting but less relevant details at the bottom.
- Be sure to collect full information about each **source** you use: title, author, page number on which the information is found. Also note which ideas come from primary and which from secondary sources.

In your presentation, explain ways in which Brutus' behavior and attitudes reflect or do not reflect the ideas of Stoicism.

PHLit Online!
www.PHLitOnline.com
- Interactive graphic organizers
- Grammar tutorial
- Interactive journals

Research and Technology

1. Review the assignments, using the instruction on the student page.
2. Guide students to select one of the Research and Technology choices.
3. To support students' work on the assignments, have them complete the **Support for Extend Your Learning** page (***Unit 5 Resources,*** p. 175).
4. Provide the following tips for students:
   - When writing a women's history report, many different types of resources should be utilized to ensure that the analysis is comprehensive and accurate.
   - When deciding which details on an advertising poster would attract spectators, consider polling other students to find out which aspects of the play they found most alluring.
   - The multimedia slides are meant to *accompany* the oral presentation. Including too much text on the actual slides will overwhelm the audience and draw attention away from the presenter.

Teaching Resources

Unit 5 Resources
- L3 L4 **Integrated Language Skills: Grammar,** p. 172
- L3 L4 **Support for Writing,** p. 173
- L3 L4 **Support for Extend Your Learning,** pp. 174 and 175
- L4 **Enrichment,** pp. 99, 117, 135, 153, and 171

Enriched Online Student Edition
Available under After You Read for this selection:
- All **Interactive Grammar Tutorial**
- L3 L4 **Internet Research Activity**

Professional Development Guidebook
Rubrics for Research Report, pp. 242–243

PHLit Online! All print and digital resources are available at **www.PHLitOnline.com.** Online resources accessible by students are noted on the student page.

MONITORING PROGRESS

Using the Test Practice

In this two-page Test Practice, students apply the reading skill for the second half of Unit 5 to an excerpt from *The Tragedy of Macbeth*.

Review this skill, reading Shakespearean drama, and then administer the test. For more guidance, consult the ***Classroom Strategies and Teaching Routines*** card, **Administering Timed Tests**.

ASSESS

Answers

Answers With Explanations

1. C—Macbeth's castle is under attack and his wife has died; the mood is hopelessness. *Incorrect answers:* A—Macbeth's castle is under attack and his wife has died; there is no enthusiasm. B—Macbeth expresses anger for the siege; but the situation elicits mostly despair. D—The opposite is true, as Macbeth's castle is under attack and his wife has died.
2. B—*Let them lie here* paraphrases "here let them lie"; *until they die of hunger* paraphrases "Till famine and the ague eat them up." *Incorrect answers:* A—It says they should die of hunger, not that they will be hungry. C—It does not mention fighting. D—It is not talking about the problems of an invading army.
3. B—Line 11 states directly that he can no longer feel fear; the rest explains the reason: he has experienced too much horror. *Incorrect answers:* A—The subject of the queen doesn't come up until the announcement of her death (line 21). C—The lines never mention his ambition to be king at all. D—He says that hearing screams would no longer bother him.
4. A—Another word for *signifying* is "meaning"; so *signifying nothing* is "meaning nothing" or "meaningless." *Incorrect answers:* B—It means the opposite: "meaning nothing" or "insignificant". C—It is a near-antonym to amazing: "Meaning nothing." D—*Signifying nothing* is not directly related in meaning to the word before it, *fury*.

Test Practice: Reading

Reading Shakespearean Drama

Fiction Selection

Directions: *Read the selection. Then, answer the questions.*

Dunsinane. Within the castle.
[*Enter* MACBETH, SEYTON, *and* SOLDIERS, *with drum and colors.*]
MACBETH. Hang out our banners on the outward walls.
The cry is still "They come!" Our castle's strength
Will laugh a siege to scorn. Here let them lie
Till famine and the ague eat them up.
Were they not forced[1] with those that should be ours,
We might have met them dareful,[2] beard to beard,
And beat them backward home.
[*A cry within of women.*]
What is that noise?
SEYTON. It is the cry of women, my good lord. [*Exit.*]
MACBETH. I have almost forgot the taste of fears:
The time has been, my senses would have cooled
To hear a night-shriek; and my fell[3] of hair
Would at a dismal treatise[4] rouse and stir
As life were in't. I have supped full with horrors.
Direness,[5] familiar to my slaughterous thoughts,
Cannot once start[6] me.
[*Enter SEYTON.*]
Wherefore was that cry?
SEYTON. The queen, my lord, is dead.
MACBETH. She should have died hereafter;[7]
There would have been a time for such a word.[8]
Tomorrow, and tomorrow, and tomorrow
Creeps in this petty pace from day to day,
To the last syllable of recorded time;
And all our yesterdays have lighted fools
The way to dusty death. Out, out, brief candle!
Life's but a walking shadow, a poor player
That struts and frets his hour upon the stage
And then is heard no more. It is a tale
Told by an idiot, full of sound and fury
Signifying nothing.

—from *The Tragedy of Macbeth,* Act V, Scene v, by William Shakespeare

1. **forced** reinforced; **those that should be ours** deserters.
2. **dareful** boldly.
3. **fell** scalp.
4. **dismal treatise** horror.
5. **Direness** horror.
6. **start** startle.
7. **She should have died hereafter** She should have picked a more convenient time for her death.
8. **word** message.

Writing for Assessment

In response to the Writing for Assessment prompt on page 1007, students should underline examples of stage directions, including character identifications. Suggest that they circle the glosses on the right side of the excerpt. Students should look at each example and explain how it helps with understanding the text. Finally, they should be able to give a general opinion with examples.

Strategies for Test Taking

Suggest that students find and reread each line of the excerpt referred to in a question prompt, as well as connected lines. Remind them why this is necessary: because reading Shakespeare is like reading poetry and thus requires close and careful examination.

1. By reading lines 1–4, what inference can you make about Macbeth's state of mind?
   - **A.** He is enthusiastic.
   - **B.** He is angry.
   - **C.** He is full of despair.
   - **D.** He feels optimistic.

2. Which is the *best* paraphrase of "here let them lie / Till famine and the ague eat them up" in lines 3–5?
   - **A.** Our enemies will be very hungry.
   - **B.** Let them lie here until they die of hunger and illness.
   - **C.** They will lie here while we prepare to fight.
   - **D.** Invading armies are often plagued by a variety of illnesses.

3. When Macbeth speaks in lines 10 through 15, his words reveal that he no longer—
   - **A.** worries about the health of his wife.
   - **B.** finds anything frightening or shocking.
   - **C.** wants to be the king.
   - **D.** hears people shrieking at night.

4. Which word could replace "signifying nothing" (line 28) in a paraphrase?
   - **A.** meaningless
   - **B.** significant
   - **C.** amazing
   - **D.** furious

5. Which state of mind is conveyed by the image "Out, out, brief candle" (line 23)?
   - **A.** longing for death
   - **B.** wish for personal safety
   - **C.** curiosity about the future
   - **D.** sorrow over the cruelty of nature

6. Which of the following images appeals to the sense of hearing?
   - **A.** last syllable
   - **B.** dusty death
   - **C.** lighted fools
   - **D.** poor player

7. Which of the following is the *best* paraphrase of the phrase "sound and fury" in line 27?
   - **A.** delight and disappointment
   - **B.** pain and natural disasters
   - **C.** sensation and emotion
   - **D.** music and excitement

8. For what purpose are glosses, or annotations, provided?
   - **A.** to illustrate the imagery
   - **B.** to define the vocabulary
   - **C.** to depict the characters
   - **D.** to explain the setting

Writing for Assessment

Would Shakespearean drama be readable by the average student without glosses and stage directions? Explain your answer in a paragraph. Use examples from this selection to help support your response.

PHLit Online!
www.PHLitOnline.com
- Online practice
- Instant feedback

ASSESS

Answers

Answers With Explanations

5. A—"Brief candle" represents life; Macbeth is wishing that his life be extinguished. Incorrect answers: B—"Brief candle" represents life, not a safety hazard. C—The opposite is true; he wishes for the end, not for a future. D—He is wishing for the end of life, not bemoaning nature's cruelty.
6. D—In line 29, Macbeth uses this metaphor: "Life's but a [walking shadow,] a poor player." *Incorrect answers:* A—This phrase appears in line 26, where he is talking about time. B—This phrase appears in line 28, where he is talking about man's inevitable march toward death. C—same explanation as for B.
7. C—*Sound* is a sensation and *fury* is an emotion. *Incorrect answers:* A—"Delight" isn't an equivalent of *sound*, nor "disappointment" of *fury*. B—"Pain" isn't an equivalent of sound. D—Music is one of many sounds, but these words are not equivalents of "sound and fury."
8. B—The notations on the side explain the difficult, mostly obsolete vocabulary. *Incorrect answers:* A—They explain the vocabulary, not the imagery. C—They explain the vocabulary, not the characters. D—The stage notes, not the glosses, explain the setting.

Differentiated Instruction for Universal Access

Support for English Learners
Direct students to the margin glosses, and help them with additional difficult vocabulary: *scorn*: "mean laughter"; *famine*: "food shortage"; *ague*: "fever;" *rouse*: "awaken"; *supp'd*: "eaten"; *slaughterous*: "murderous"; *wherefore*: "for what purpose or reason"; *recorded time*: "history"; *struts*: "prances, parades"; *frets*: "fusses, worries"; *signifying*: "meaning".

Strategy for Less Proficient Readers
Ask students to listen carefully as you read the excerpt aloud. Then have partners reread the excerpt, with one student taking the stage directions and Seyton's lines and the other student reading Macbeth. Alternatively, you could match a strong reader with a less-proficient reader. When they finish their reading, partners should answer the questions together.

PHLit Online!
Students may take the test in interactive format with instant feedback online at **www.PHLitOnline.com**.

PREACHEACH

Meeting Your Standards

Students will

1. analyze workplace documents.
2. read and understand a job application and a public document.
3. prepare to complete a job application.

*Log on at **www.PHLitOnline.com** as a teacher for a detailed lesson plan for Informational Texts.*

Reading Skill

1. Introduce the skill, using the instruction on the student page.
2. Tell students that they will analyze structure and format for clues to the purpose of these documents as they read.

Think Aloud: Model the Skill

Model the skill of analyzing workplace documents. Say to students:

When analyzing workplace documents, use what I know a bout textbooks and reference books. These sources use larger type and boldface for headings to show the outline structure of the document. In the same way, workplace documents use such elements to divide the document into logical chunks.

THE BIG ? To what extent does experience determine what we perceive?

Have students look for sections of the documents that refer to experiece.

Multidraft Reading

Have students follow a multidraft reading protocol.

- **First reading:** Have students read for general understanding.
- **Second reading:** Have students determine the purpose of the documents.
- **Third reading:** Have students think about the role that experience plays in the workplace.

Informational Texts

Real-Life Reading

Job Application
County of Sonoma Volunteer Application

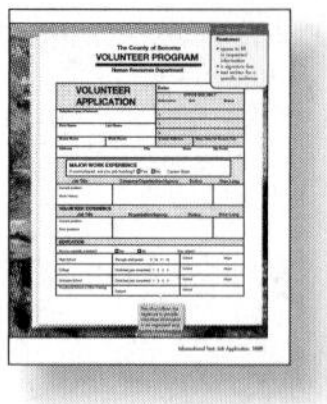

Public Document
BLS Career Information: Urban Planner

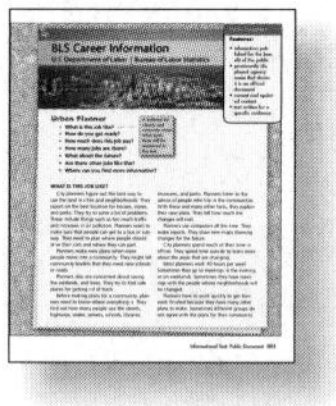

Reading Skill: Analyze Workplace Documents

Workplace documents often include bold or italic type, headers, and other structural features. Authors use these features to achieve their **purposes** and aid readers' understanding. These elements help organize the information presented, clarifying it and helping to convey an author's ideas. Use this chart to **analyze the structure and format** of a text.

Structural Feature	Purpose
title	states topic or main idea
heading or subheading	shows where to find categories of information
bulleted or numbered list	provides a quick way to reference essential information
diagram or graphic	provides additional or more specific information in a visual format
italic or boldface type	draws attention to key words
signature or write-on line	provides space for applicant to supply required information

THE BIG ? To what extent does *experience* determine what we perceive?

The job application asks applicants to state their experience in certain areas. The public document gives advice about the kinds of experience necessary to obtain particular jobs.

Differentiated Instruction for Universal Access

Reading Support
Give students reading support with the appropriate version of the *Reader's Notebooks*:

- L2 L3 ***Reader's Notebook***
- L1 ***Hear It!* Audio CD** (adapted text)
- EL ***Reader's Notebook: English Learner's Version***

PHLit Online! All student resources, are available online at **www.PHLitOnline.com.**

Job Application

Features:

- space to fill in requested information
- a signature line
- text written for a specific audience

The County of Sonoma
VOLUNTEER PROGRAM
Human Resources Department

VOLUNTEER APPLICATION			Date:	
			OFFICE USE ONLY Referred to: Job Status	
Volunteer area of interest			1.	
First Name	Last Name		2.	
			3.	
Home Phone	Work Phone		E-mail Address	Best Time to Reach You
Address	City		State	Zip Code

MAJOR WORK EXPERIENCE
If unemployed, are you job hunting? ☐ Yes ☐ No Career Goal:

Job Title	Company/Organization/Agency	Duties	How Long
Current position: Work History:			

VOLUNTEER EXPERIENCE

Job Title	Organization/Agency	Duties	How Long
Current position: Prior positions:			

EDUCATION

Are you currently a student?	☐ Yes ☐ No	If so, where?	
High School	Through what grade: 9 10 11 12	School	Major
College	Circle last year completed: 1 2 3 4	School	Major
Graduate School	Circle last year completed: 1 2 3 4	School	Major
Vocational School or Other Training	Subject:	School	

This chart allows the applicant to provide education information in an organized way.

TEACH

About Job Applications

1. Review the features listed in the Job Application box on this page with students. **Ask** the class to define the term *signature line* in their own words.
   Possible response: A signature line is the space on a form where the person filling out the form signs his or her name.
2. Have students describe experiences they have had in filling out job applications.
3. Talk to students about how to approach a job application. Remind them that job applications typically ask for specific names, addresses, phone numbers, and dates of employment in regards to previous jobs. Point out that students can simplify filling out applications by recording these details on a piece of paper and bringing it with them when they apply for jobs.

Analyze Workplace Documents

1. Direct students' attention to the top section of the application, through "Address." **Ask** students to summarize the kind of information requested here and name its purpose.
   Answer: This part asks for basic information so that the applicant can be identified and contacted.
2. Then, have them look at the section from "Major Work Experience" through "Volunteer Experience." **Ask** what kind of information is requested and the purpose of these questions.
   Answer: This section asks for an applicant's employment history and what skills he or she has. The purpose is to help determine what kind of volunteer work the applicant could perform.
3. Finally, have students look at the "Education" section. Explain that application sections are often in chart form to keep an applicant's information organized. **Ask** students to discuss reasons why an employer might use a chart for this section.
   Possible response: By organizing an applicant's educational background, an employer can scan the information to determine if an applicant has the required education.

Differentiated Instruction for Universal Access

Enrichment for Gifted and Talented Students
Challenge students to create an application for a profession in which they are interested. Have students use the library or the Internet to research the profession. Have them draft an application with sections that they think are important to the profession. Tell students that it is acceptable to include sections that are not typically seen on a standard application. Remind them to use other structural features. Allow time for students to present their applications to the class.

Strategy for Special Needs Students
Students sometimes have difficulty filling out job applications neatly or writing small enough to fit their answers on the lines provided. Photocopy this application page and give copies to students. Have them practice completing the form with their own information to gain confidence in filling out forms. Suggest that they use pencils so they can easily erase and begin a response again if necessary.

Analyze Workplace Documents

1. Explain that applications are usually divided into two parts; the first page asks for basic information while the second inquires about an applicant's personality and interests.
2. Direct students' attention to the "Goals," "Special Skills," and "Areas of Interest" sections. Then, **ask** them to infer why an employer would ask these questions.
   Possible response: By learning about the motivations, skills, and interests of an applicant, an employer can find out what other qualities an applicant can offer to a position.
3. Explain to students that it is important to consider the author's purpose when they read application questions, and to respond in a thoughtful, thorough manner.

ASSESS/EXTEND

Answers

To what extent does experience determine what we perceive?

(a) The application asks for information about the applicant's skills, relevant work or volunteer experience, and related education. (b) **Possible responses:** Students may say that this kind of information helps the employer determine what kind of work the applicant could perform. Others may say that this information reveals how experienced the applicant is and suggests what additional training might be required.

GOALS: What do you hope to gain through volunteering? (To help to contribute to our community, to gain work experience, to reenter the work world, to stay active, to test a new career field, etc.)

A column format is used here to organize and clarify options.

TIME AVAILABLE FOR VOLUNTEER WORK

Number of hours willing to give per week:	Availability:		Hours Preferred	Length of Assignment: (Some jobs may have minimum requirement.)	
	☐ Mon	☐ Fri	☐ Mornings	☐ Short Term	☐ 1 Year
	☐ Tues	☐ Sat	☐ Afternoons	☐ Months	☐ 2 Year
	☐ Wed	☐ Sun	☐ Evenings	☐ Months	☐ On going
	☐ Thurs				

SPECIAL SKILLS, CERTIFICATES OR LICENSES

Interpreter: Language(s)

In times of county-wide disaster, can we call you to assist in any of the above areas? ☐ Yes ☐ No

AREAS OF INTEREST OR HOBBIES (Tell us what you enjoy doing)

Headings organize questions about different topics into categories.

TRANSPORTATION

Do you drive? ☐ Yes ☐ No Do you have auto insurance? ☐ Yes ☐ No

If you don't drive, how will you reach your volunteer job?
Have you been put on probation or has your driver's license been suspended or revoked within the last five years? ☐ Yes ☐ No
If yes, please explain:

Some jobs may require a background check. Please fill this section in if you are applying for such a position.

Birth Date: CA Driver's License #: Social Security #:

I authorize the County to perform a background check as necessitated by the volunteer position I am applying for.

SIGNATURE ____________________

To what extent does experience determine what we perceive?
(a) What information about the applicant's experiences does the application require? (b) Why do you think the employer is interested in this information?

Vocabulary Development

Vocabulary from Law

Point out that the application has several terms or expressions from law, including *probation, suspended, revoked*, and *background check*. Explain that as students begin to take part in adult experiences such as applying for a job or getting a driver's license, they will be exposed to legal terminology. Have students work with a partner to infer the meanings of the unfamiliar words from their contexts. Then, have them use a dictionary or online legal reference to check whether their inferences are correct.

PHLit Online!
Vocabulary Central, featuring tools, activities, and songs for studying vocabulary, is available online at **www.PHLitOnline.com**.

Public Document

Features:

- information published for the benefit of the public
- prominently displayed agency name that shows it is an official document
- current and updated content
- text written for a specific audience

BLS Career Information

U.S. Department of Labor | Bureau of Labor Statistics

Urban Planner

- What is this job like?
- How do you get ready?
- How much does this job pay?
- How many jobs are there?
- What about the future?
- Are there other jobs like this?
- Where can you find more information?

A bulleted list clearly and concisely states what questions will be answered in the text.

WHAT IS THIS JOB LIKE?

City planners figure out the best way to use the land in cities and neighborhoods. They report on the best location for houses, stores, and parks. They try to solve a lot of problems. These include things such as too much traffic and increases in air pollution. Planners want to make sure that people can get to a bus or subway. They need to plan where people should drive their cars and where they can park.

Planners make new plans when more people move into a community. They might tell community leaders that they need new schools or roads.

Planners also are concerned about saving the wetlands, and trees. They try to find safe places for getting rid of trash.

Before making plans for a community, planners need to know where everything is. They find out how many people use the streets, highways, water, sewers, schools, libraries, museums, and parks. Planners listen to the advice of people who live in the communities. With these and many other facts, they explain their new plans. They tell how much the changes will cost.

Planners use computers all the time. They make reports. They draw new maps showing changes for the future.

City planners spend much of their time in offices. They spend time outside to learn more about the areas that are changing.

Most planners work 40 hours per week. Sometimes they go to meetings in the evening or on weekends. Sometimes they have meetings with the people whose neighborhoods will be changed.

Planners have to work quickly to get their work finished because they have many other plans to make. Sometimes different groups do not agree with the plans for their community.

About Public Documents

1. Review the features listed in the Public Document box on p. 1011 with students. **Ask** the class to define the term *public* in their own words.
   Possible response: The public is the people living in a community.
2. Discuss with students kinds of government notices with which they are familiar.
3. Talk to students about how to approach a public document. Point out that as workers, consumers, and voters, they will probably encounter many public documents that provide information and directions.

Evaluate Workplace Documents

1. Explain that the Bureau of Labor Statistics, part of the federal Department of Labor, has information on several dozen careers at its Web site. This profile of an urban planner is just one example.
2. Direct students' attention to the callout and the bulleted list at the top of the page. Then, have them look at the headings on this and the next page. **Ask** them how the list items and the headings are related. Have them explain the purpose of this relation.
   Possible responses: Each item in the list is a heading. Both the list and the headings give structure to the information, organizing it so it is easy to follow. Since the order of the list items and the headings is the same, users can look at the list and, if they wish to, go directly to a particular section rather than reading the whole document.
3. Have students review the list items. **Ask:** Based on these headings, what is the purpose of this document, and what audience they think it serves.
   Possible responses: The purpose is to describe the job and gave background employment information. The audience is people who might be considering this job as a potential career.

Differentiated Instruction for Universal Access

EL Pronunciation for English Learners

Some students might have difficulty with the /ng/ phoneme that appears in the words *things*, *saving*, *showing*, *changing*, and *meetings*. To help them, write the words on the board. Then, pronounce each word in turn, calling on the students to repeat each pronunciation. Next, call out the words at random. Have student volunteers circle the word on the board. Discuss the results with the class. Were there any incorrect choices? If so, what led to those errors?

Evaluate Workplace Documents

1. Remind students of the audience for this document: people who might be interested in the job. **Ask:** what kinds of information such a person would want to know. **Possible responses:** Students might give such responses as how someone prepares for the job, how much it pays, and how many people have the job.
2. **Ask** them to identify where they might find such information based on the headings on this page. **Answers:** How someone prepares for the job would be described in "How do you get ready?" Pay scales would appear in "How much does this job pay?" How many people have the job would be answered by "How many jobs are there?" Future prospects would appear in "What about the future?"
3. **Ask** students how the headings make reading this document easier. **Answer:** They organize the information into clearly identified pieces.

Reflecting on the Reading Skill

After students have finished reading, **ask** them to explain which elements in the selection they found most useful for determining the purpose of each document.
Possible response: Students might reply that the direction lines in the job application (such as "check all that apply" and "other than relatives") were helpful in clarifying how to fill out the form or what kind of information was desired. Some might say that the bulleted list and headings in the second document were very helpful because they organized the information effectively.

BLS Career Information

U.S. Department of Labor | Bureau of Labor Statistics

HOW DO YOU GET READY?

Employers want workers who have advanced training. Most employers seek persons who have a master's degree in city planning or urban design. Sometimes employers will hire persons who have worked as a planner for a long time, but do not have a master's degree. A bachelor's degree in planning and a master's degree in a related field are good to have when persons look for their first job. Persons who are interested in becoming a city planner should take courses in computer science and statistics.

Persons who are interested in becoming a city planner also should learn how to use a computer.

Local government planning offices often hire college students to work during the summer. Students can learn a lot before they get their first job after they graduate.

To become a certified planner, persons must take the right amount of classes. They must work in a planning office and pass a test. Planners must be able to speak and write well. They must be good at making things fit in place so that everyone can shop, work, and go to school.

HOW MUCH DOES THIS JOB PAY?

The middle half of all urban and regional planners earned between $41,950 and $67,530 a year in 2004. The lowest-paid 10 percent earned less than $33,840. The highest-paid 10 percent earned more than $82,610 a year.

HOW MANY JOBS ARE THERE?

Urban and regional planners held about 32,000 jobs in 2004. Most of them worked for local governments. Some planners work in private companies. Others work for State agencies. A small number of planners work for the Federal Government.

WHAT ABOUT THE FUTURE?

Bold subheadings allow readers to quickly locate information that interests them.

The number of jobs for planners is expected to grow about as fast as the average for all occupations through 2014. Most of their work will result from population growth. Most new jobs will be in rapidly expanding communities.

ARE THERE OTHER JOBS LIKE THIS?

- Architects
- City managers
- Civil engineers
- Community development directors
- Environmental engineers
- Landscape architects
- Social scientists *(geographers)*

WHERE CAN YOU FIND MORE INFORMATION?

More BLS information about urban and regional planners can be found in the Occupational Outlook Handbook. The Handbook also shows where to find out even more about this job.

To what extent does experience determine what we perceive?
What kinds of experience would help a person prepare for a job as an urban planner?

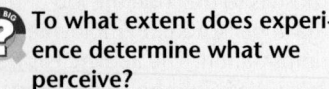

ASSESS/EXTEND

Answers

To what extent does experience determine what we perceive?

Possible responses: Based on the description, a person wanting to be an urban planner would need a master's degree. In addition, experience working in a planning office during the summers would help an applicant get such a job.

Think Aloud

Vocabulary: Using Context
Model the way to determine meanings from context with this "think aloud." Say to students:

I'm going to show you how I can use context to find the meaning of the term *advanced training*, in the first paragraph. Based on the description of the work urban planners do, I know that planners must take many people's needs and many factors into account. So, I think that *advanced training* means that urban planners must have lots of education—this is not the kind of job you can do with just a high school diploma. The next sentence confirms this inference. It says that urban planners must have a master's degree. I know that you get a bachelor's degree by graduating from college, which takes four years, and that a master's degree is the next step. I'm not sure how long it takes to earn a master's degree, but clearly *advanced training* means at least five years of education after high school.

Test Practice: Informational Texts

Comparing Informational Texts

(a) Analyze workplace documents by comparing and contrasting the **structures and formats** of the job application and the public document. **(b)** How does the structure and format of each text aid the reader's understanding?

Timed Writing

Write an Essay

Format
The prompt directs you to write an essay. Therefore, be sure your response includes an introduction, several supporting paragraphs, and a conclusion.

Using details and information from the texts, write an essay in which you discuss the authors' purposes in the job application and the public document. Explain how the structure and format of each text help the author achieve his or her purpose. Also, explain why you think the authors are or are not successful in achieving their purposes. (40 minutes)

Academic Vocabulary
When you *discuss* a subject, you write or speak about various aspects of that subject in detail.

5-Minute Planner

Complete these steps before you begin to write:

1. Read the prompt carefully and completely. Highlighting indicates key words and phrases. **TIP** The assignment contains several points you must address in your response. Be sure you understand all parts of the prompt.
2. Review the job application and public document. Consider the reason each text was written.
3. Analyze and make notes about the structures and formats and how those elements help achieve the purposes of the documents.
4. Consider whether each document achieves its purpose.
5. Create an outline for your essay and refer to your outline and notes as you write.

Extend the Lesson

Connecting to the Students' World

To give students more practice with job applications and public documents and to help them apply the lesson to their own world, divide the class into small groups. Give each group the task of contacting several businesses to obtain job applications. They might go to local businesses, such as supermarkets, stores, or service providers, or they could visit Web sites of national companies. Have the groups study the applications and prepare lists of the kinds of information found in all applications. Then, have the groups list the specific pieces of information found in one or a few applications but not in others. Call on the groups to present their findings to the class. Together, discuss what employers want to know about potential workers, and why they want to know it.

Answers

Comparing Informational Texts

Possible responses: (a) The job application is structured as a series of questions or statements and responses, which the applicant has to supply by writing in the spaces provided. The public document uses headings to organize the information it provides. (b) The prompts or directions in the job application tell the applicant what information to supply and, in some cases, how to supply it. The structure of the public document makes the information easy to follow and allows users who want to find only certain kinds of information the ability to locate that information quickly.

Timed Writing

1. Before students complete the activity, guide them in identifying and analyzing key words and phrases in the prompt, highlighted on the student page.
2. Work with students to draw up guidelines for their essays based on the key words:
   - **Thesis** The essay should explain how the structure and format of the document help its author achieve his or her purpose.
   - **Organization** The essay should discuss each structural element in turn.
   - **Support** The essay should cite specific details from the text and show how they help achieve the overall purpose.
   - **Voice** The essay should clearly present the evaluation.
3. Have students use the 5-Minute Planner to structure their time.
4. Allow students 40 minutes to complete the assignment. Evaluate their work using the guidelines they have developed.

PRETEACH

Meeting Your Standards

Students will

1. analyze and respond to character motivation.
2. compare character motivation in two plays.
3. write a comparison of the use of character motivations.

*Log on as a teacher at **www.PHLitOnline.com** for a detailed lesson plan.*

❶ Comparing Character Motivation

1. Introduce the skill using the instruction on the student page.
2. Give students a copy of **Comparing Character Motivation Graphic Organizer B,** ***Graphic Organizer Transparencies,*** p. 187. Tell them they will fill it in to compare characters as they read.

Think Aloud: Model the Skill

Model a way to determine a character's motivation. Say to students:

When I think about character motivation, I think about what drives a hero like Superman. He saves people who are in danger and catches criminals. I can see that his motivation is to help make the world a safer place. When I read, I use the same clues—the actions and words of each character—to try to determine their motivation.

❷ Vocabulary

1. Have students say each word aloud.
2. Then, use the word in a sentence that defines the word. Repeat the sentence, now with the word missing, and have the class "fill in the blank" chorally.

   For more guidance, see the ***Classroom Strategies and Teaching Routines*** card, **Introducing Selection Vocabulary.**

Comparing Literary Works

The Tragedy of Julius Caesar • *from* A Raisin in the Sun

❶ Comparing Character Motivation

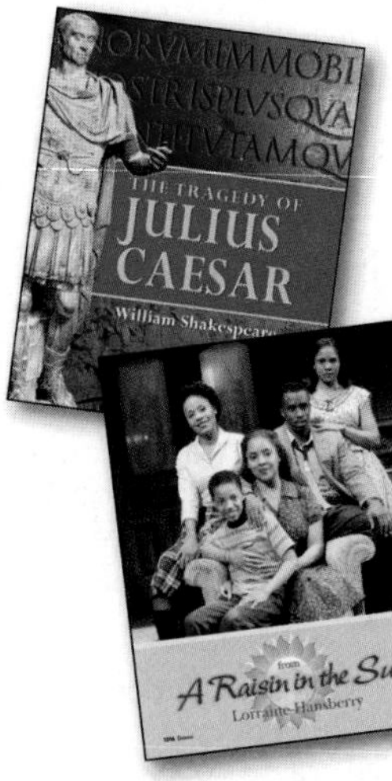

A **character's motivation** consists of the passions, convictions, ideas, and even illusions that guide his or her actions and shape his or her words. To develop your own understanding of a character's motivation, answer the following questions as you read:

- What does the character say in dramatic speeches that show what is important to him or her?
- What character traits and goals does the dialogue reveal?
- How does the character feel and behave toward other characters?
- What is the character's family and social background?
- Are there any striking similarities or differences between this character and others? If so, what are they?

Both William Shakespeare's *The Tragedy of Julius Caesar* and Lorraine Hansberry's *A Raisin in the Sun* feature characters motivated by a desire for dignity. As you read, compare the ideas of dignity that motivate Walter and Mama in *A Raisin in the Sun* with those motivating Cassius, Brutus, and Caesar in *Julius Caesar.* Use a diagram like the one shown to help track your comparison.

Character: ____________

Challenge to Character's Dignity	Character's Response	What Character Finds Essential

❷ Vocabulary

- **looming** (lo͞om′ iŋ) *adj.* appearing unclearly but in a threatening form; threatening to occur (p. 1017) ***I could not make out the name on the ship looming in the mist.*** *loom v. loomed v. loomingly adv.*
- **dignity** (dig′ nə tē) *n.* quality of deserving respect and honor; self-respect (p. 1018) ***Though the others lost our respect, she remained a figure of great dignity.*** *dignify v. dignified adj. dignitary n.*

PHLit Online! www.PHLitOnline.com

- Vocabulary flashcards
- Interactive journals
- More about the authors
- Selection audio
- Interactive graphic organizers

Vocabulary Development

Vocabulary Knowledge Rating

Create a **Vocabulary Knowledge Rating Chart** (***Professional Development Guidebook,*** p. 33) for this selection. Include the selection vocabulary and the forms of the Big Question words that appear in the Writing About the Big Question sentence starters. (The Big Question vocabulary is introduced on pp. 790–791.)

Give students a copy of the chart. Read the words aloud, and have students mark their rating in the Before Reading column. Urge them to be alert to these words as they read and discuss the selection.

Tally how many students think they know a word to gauge how much instruction to provide. As students read and discuss the selection, point out the words and their context.

PHLit Online! **Vocabulary Central,** featuring tools, activities, and songs for studying vocabulary, is available online at **www.PHLitOnline.com.**

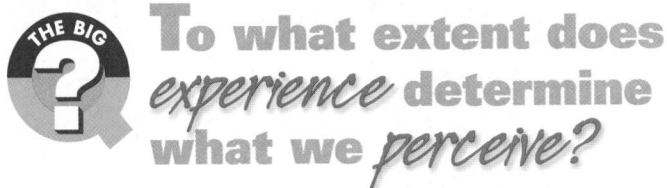

To what extent does *experience* determine what we *perceive?*

3 Writing About the Big Question

In both *Julius Caesar* and *A Raisin in the Sun,* characters experience conflicts between what they believe is right and what is actually happening around them. Consider how a person's background influences his or her expectations. Use these sentence starters to develop your ideas.

All people should **expect** to be treated ______________, but that is not everyone's experience.

Individual opinions about whether the world can be a just, fair place vary greatly because ________.

Meet the Author

Lorraine Hansberry (1930–1965)

Author of *A Raisin in the Sun*

An important voice of the civil rights era, Lorraine Hansberry grew up in Chicago. "Both of my parents were strong-minded, civic-minded, exceptionally race-minded people who made enormous sacrifices on behalf of the struggle for civil rights throughout their lifetimes," she once recalled.

Biographical Inspiration When Hansberry was about eight years old, her parents tried to move to a white neighborhood. Property owners in the neighborhood blocked African American families from purchasing homes there. Hansberry's father fought the restrictions all the way to the U.S. Supreme Court, where he eventually won his case. Years later, Hansberry used that experience as the basis of her award-winning play *A Raisin in the Sun*, which opened on Broadway in 1959.

Teaching Resources

The following resources can be used to enrich, extend, or differentiate the instruction.

- All *Unit 5 Resources,* pp. 185–201
- All *Professional Development Guidebook,* p. 33
- All *Graphic Organizer Transparencies,* pp. 187, 189
- All Enriched Online Student Edition

PHLit Online! All resources, including print and video, are available online at www.PHLitOnline.com.

Daily Bellringer

For each class during which you will teach this selection, have students complete one of the five Sentence Combining activities for Week 30 in the *Daily Bellringer Activities* booklet.

3 Writing About the Big Question

1. Review the assignment with the class.
2. Explain that people from different social classes or ethnic groups can experience the world differently in part because of how they are treated by others.
3. Have students complete the sentence starters. Review responses as a class. (**Possible response:** All people should expect to be treated fairly by others, but that is not everyone's experience. Individual opinions about whether the world can be a just, fair place vary greatly because some people are more fortunate than others.)
4. Remind students that their answers will help them think about the Big Question. Tell students that as they read, to look for what expectations the characters have about the world.

Concept Connector →

Tell students that they will return to their sentence starters after they have concluded reading.

Multidraft Reading

For each reading, have students set the purpose intended:

- **First reading**—literal comprehension: answering the Reading Check questions
- **Second reading**—application of skills: responding to the side-column notes
- **Third reading**—interpretation: answering the end-of-selection questions

For more guidance, refer to the ***Classroom Strategies and Teaching Routines*** card on multidraft reading.

PHLit Online!

For more about the authors, practice with the selection vocabulary, and more background, go to **www.PHLitOnline.com.**

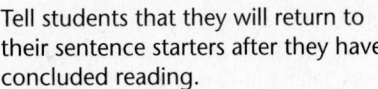

ASSESS

❶ Background

A Raisin in the Sun The name of the play comes from a stanza in "A Dream Deferred," a poem by Langston Hughes. Referring to a dream that has to be put on hold, Hughes wonders, "Does it dry up / Like a raisin in the sun? / Or fester like a sore—/ And then run?" The verse might have been on playwright Lorraine Hansberry's mind as the production struggled to find backing on Broadway because of its all-black cast. Finally opening on Broadway in 1959, the play gave theatergoers a realistic, uncompromising look at how urban-dwelling African Americans viewed their past, present, and future. The play ran in New York for two years and earned the New York Drama Critics Circle award for the best American play of 1959. The drama was produced as a film in 1961, starring most of the Broadway cast, including Sidney Poitier and Ruby Dee.

❷ Activating Prior Knowledge

In this excerpt, students will read a short scene between a mother and a son who have vastly different views of the value of money. Through the dialogue, Hansberry challenges both her characters and her readers to confront the issues of risk, dreams, success, failure, and dignity. Use these questions for discussion: How important is it to follow your dreams? What can stand in the way? How do you define success? How willing would you be to risk your own money on a promise of future wealth?

Concept Connector →

Tell students that they will return to these ideas after they have concluded reading.

❸ About the Selection

The scene centers on a conflict over what to do with Mama's insurance check. Walter yearns to quit his mundane chauffeur job and make his fortune. For his mother, the check represents security against poverty. As the scene closes, Mama muses on the changes for African Americans that have occurred in her lifetime, while Walter insists that she will never understand the modern world.

from *A Raisin in the Sun*

❶ ❷ ❸

Lorraine Hansberry

Vocabulary Development

Selection Vocabulary Reinforcement

Students will benefit from additional examples and practice with the selection vocabulary words. Reinforce their comprehension with "show-you-know" sentences. The first part of the sentence uses the vocabulary word in an appropriate context. The second part of the sentence—the "show-you-know" part—clarifies the first. Model the strategy with this example:

The whole family prepared for the *looming* move; they did everything they could to prepare for the arrival of the moving truck.

Then, give students these sentence prompts, and coach them in creating the clarification process.

1. The *looming* financial troubles worried the residents; ______________.
   Sample answer: they all began coming up with plans to make more money.
2. Her fellow teachers recalled her with *dignity;* ___________.
   Sample answer: they paid respect to her knowledge and love of her students.

from Act 1, Scene II

4 ◀ **Critical Viewing** This photograph is from the 2004 Broadway production of *A Raisin in the Sun.* Which details of the image suggest Mama's key role in running the family? **[Interpret]**

Background The Youngers are an African American family living in Chicago some time after World War II. During this period, African Americans faced a shortage of economic opportunities and were deprived of many civil rights. Walter Younger, his wife Ruth, and their son Travis live with Walter's mother and his younger sister, Beneatha. Walter's father has passed away. When the family learns that Walter's mother is to receive a check from the father's insurance, Walter pleads with his mother to give him money to invest in a store he wants to open with friends. She wants instead to purchase a new home and to pay for Beneatha's education.

WALTER. (*Picks up the check*) Do you know what this money means to me? Do you know what this money can do for us? *(Puts it back)* Mama—Mama—I want so many things . . .

MAMA. Yes, son—

WALTER. I want so many things that they are driving me kind of crazy . . . Mama—look at me.

MAMA. I'm looking at you. You a good-looking boy. You got a job, a nice wife, a fine boy and—

WALTER. A job. (*Looks at her*) Mama, a job? I open and close car doors all day long. I drive a man around in his limousine and I say, "Yes, sir; no, sir; very good, sir; shall I take the Drive, sir?" Mama, that ain't no kind of job . . . that ain't nothing at all. (*Very quietly*) Mama, I don't know if I can make you understand.

MAMA. Understand what, baby?

5 **WALTER.** (*Quietly*) Sometimes it's like I can see the future stretched out in front of me—just plain as day. The future, Mama. Hanging over there at the edge of my days. Just waiting for me—a big, looming blank space—full of nothing. Just waiting for me. But it don't have to be. *(Pause. Kneeling beside her chair)* Mama—sometimes when I'm downtown and I pass them cool, quiet-looking restaurants where them white boys are sitting back and talking 'bout things . . . sitting there turning deals worth millions of dollars . . . sometimes I see guys don't look much older than me—

Literary Analysis
Character Motivation
Explain what type of life Walter seems to desire.

Vocabulary
looming (lo͞om′ iŋ) *adj.* appearing unclearly but in a threatening form; threatening to occur

6 **Reading Check**
What good things does Mama see in Walter's life?

4 Critical Viewing

Possible response: The mother sits in the easy chair in the center of the photograph, while the rest of the family gathers around her. Her expression shows strength and compassion. Each member of the family is either directly or indirectly touching the mother.

5 Literary Analysis

Character Motivation

1. Point out that through passions, convictions, and illusions, people make choices in their lives. Reinforce that a character's motivation to act is shaped by a view of what he or she believes is desirable. Then, **ask** students to respond to the Literary Analysis prompt: Explain what type of life Walter seems to desire.
   Answer: Walter wants a life where he will not feel inferior to anyone and can make a lot of money.
2. **Ask** students to identify details in Walter's statements that support his motivations.
   Answer: He says the job he has now is not a real job. He says future success is waiting for him. He admires the white men making deals downtown.
3. **Ask** students to identify which type of motivation Walter exhibits.
   Possible response: Students may say that Walter acts from the passion of wanting to break through unfair barriers that held back African Americans. Others may say he follows an illusion because he has no guarantee that his life will be any better if he has a lot of money.

6 Reading Check

Mama sees that Walter is handsome, has a job, a wife, and a son.

Differentiated Instruction for Universal Access

Accessibility at a Glance
Use this information to guide your teaching of *A Raisin in the Sun.*

Context	Scene in play about African American family
Language/Vocabulary	• Colloquial • Grade-appropriate vocabulary
Concept Level	Accessible (family dynamics)
Literary Merit	Noted playwright
Lexile/Length	Lexile: NP Word Count: 456

PHLit Online!
This selection is available in interactive format in the **Enriched Online Student Edition**, **www.PHLitOnline.com**, which includes an interactive graphic organizer.

7 Connecting to the Big Question

1. Read the bracketed text aloud. Then, **ask:** What do Mama and Walter value in life?
   Answer: Mama values working and raising a family with dignity. Walter values money.
2. **Ask** how Mama thinks Walter views her values.
   Answer: She thinks he rejects them.

Concept Connector

Have students compare their responses to Writing About the Big Question and Activating Prior Knowledge ideas from before reading the selection with their ideas afterwards.

ASSESS

Answers

Critical Thinking

1. **Possible response:** Students may sympathize with Mama because she has a clearer view.
2. (a) Walter is a chauffer. (b) He feels that he does not have a chance for advancement: ". . . that ain't no kind of job . . . that ain't nothing at all," he tells his mother.
3. (a) Walter believes that money equals power. (b) **Possible responses:** Some students may agree that money can provide power. Others may argue that the ability to create and to love is a better source of power.
4. (a) Mama thinks Walter's passion for money may not remedy his problems. (b) Mama values a good family and a decent job. Walter values his family, but he believes that money will buy them dignity.

To what extent does experience determine what we perceive?

Possible response: (a) Mama faced prejudice and physical danger in the past and is grateful for her accomplishments. (b) Walter has not faced the same dangers, but he still sees barriers to having a better life.

MAMA. Son—how come you talk so much 'bout money?

WALTER. (*With immense passion*) Because it is life, Mama!

MAMA. (*Quietly*) Oh—(*Very quietly*) So now it's life. Money is life. Once upon a time freedom used to be life—now it's money. I guess the world really do change . . .

WALTER. No—it was always money, Mama. We just didn't know about it.

MAMA. No . . . something has changed. (*She looks at him*) You something new, boy. In my time we was worried about not being lynched and getting to the North if we could and how to stay alive and still have a pinch of dignity too . . . Now here come you and Beneatha—talking 'bout things we ain't never even thought about hardly, me and your daddy. You ain't satisfied or proud of nothing we done. I mean that you had a home; that we kept you out of trouble till you was grown; that you don't have to ride to work on the back of nobody's streetcar—You my children—but how different we done become.

WALTER. (*A long beat. He pats her hand and gets up*) You just don't understand, Mama, you just don't understand.

Vocabulary
dignity (dig′ nə tē) *n.* quality of deserving respect and honor; self-respect

Critical Thinking

1. **Respond:** Do you sympathize more with Walter or his mother? Explain.
2. **(a)** What does Walter do for a living? **(b) Infer:** How does this job make him feel about the future? Support your answer with a quotation from the selection.
3. **(a) Interpret:** Why does Walter think that money "is life"? **(b) Make a Judgment:** Do you agree with him? Explain why or why not.
4. **(a) Summarize:** What is Mama's reaction to Walter's complaint? **(b) Compare and Contrast:** Compare Mama's goals in life with Walter's.

To what extent does experience determine what we perceive? (a) In what ways do Mama's past experiences affect her perception of freedom and dignity? **(b)** How do Walter's past experiences influence his view of what it means to be free and have dignity? Explain your answer.

Vocabulary Development

Vocabulary Knowledge Rating

When students have completed reading and discussing *The Tragedy of Julius Caesar* and the excerpt from *A Raisin in the Sun,* have them take out their **Vocabulary Knowledge Rating Chart.** Read the words aloud once more, and have students rate their knowledge of the words again in the After Reading column. Clarify any words that are still problematic. Have students write their own definition and example or sentence in the appropriate column. Then, have students complete the Vocabulary Practice activities on the next page. Encourage students to use the words in further discussion and written work about this selection. Remind them that they will be accountable for these words in the **Selection Test** (***Unit 5 Resources***, pp. 196–198 or 199–201).

After You Read

The Tragedy of Julius Caesar • *from* A Raisin in the Sun

Comparing Characters' Motivations

1. **(a)** Using a chart like the one shown, analyze Walter's **motivation** in the scene from *A Raisin in the Sun.* **(b)** Complete a similar chart about Cassius' motivation in *The Tragedy of Julius Caesar,* Act I, Scene ii, lines 90–161. **(c)** What comparisons can you identify?

Social Background	Personality	Feelings	Values	Goals

2. **(a)** What ideals motivate Brutus' speech in Act II, Scene i, lines 114–140? **(b)** Compare these ideals to those described by Walter's mother. **(c)** What is one difference between Brutus' goal in joining the conspiracy and Walter's dream of having a business?
3. **(a)** Summarize Caesar's ideas about his own dignity, as expressed in *Julius Caesar,* Act III, Scene i, lines 58–73. **(b)** Is his notion of dignity more like that of Walter or of Walter's mother, or is it different from both? Explain.

Writing to Compare Characters' Motivations

Write a brief essay in which you compare the ideas of dignity that motivate characters in *The Tragedy of Julius Caesar* with those that motivate Walter and his mother in *A Raisin in the Sun.* Use these questions to get started:

- What are each character's beliefs, goals, and personality traits?
- Which statements reveal each character's view of dignity?
- What do each character's interactions with others show about his or her motivations?
- What are the merits and drawbacks of each character's ideals?
- Which character best represents your own ideals?

Vocabulary

Practice To complete these **analogies,** choose the word that will make the relationship between the second pair of words most like the relationship between the first pair.

1. looming : fading :: bored : **(a)** excited, **(b)** disinterested, **(c)** sad
2. dignity : insult :: property : **(a)** purchase. **(b)** vandalism, **(c)** loan

Assessment Resources

Unit 5 Resources

L1 L2 EL **Selection Test A,** pp. 196–198

L3 L4 **Selection Test B,** pp. 199–201

L3 L4 **Open-Book Test,** pp. 193–195

PHLit Online! All assessment resources are available at **www.PHLitOnline.com.**

Six Traits Focus

✔	Ideas		Word Choice
✔	Organization		Sentence Fluency
	Voice		Conventions

Vocabulary

1. excited
2. vandalism

ASSESS

Answers

Comparing Characters' Motivations

1. (a) *Background:* working-class African American; *Personality:* ambitious, forceful; *Feelings:* slighted, angry; *Values:* dignity, money, success; *Goals:* to make a lot of money, to be respected, to be envied (b) *Background:* military; *Personality:* shrewd, cunning; *Feelings:* underappreciated; scorned *Values:* stoicism, valor; *Goals:* to see Brutus come to power, to be recognized
   (c) Cassius shares Walter's feelings of oppression, injustice, and lack of opportunity.

   For other sample answers, see ***Graphic Organizer Transparencies,*** **Comparing Character Motivation Graphic Organizer A,** p. 188, and the **Additional Answers** section.
2. (a) The ideals of brotherhood and human dignity motivate Brutus' speech. (b) Walter's mother believes in the strength and dignity of her family. (c) Brutus joins the conspiracy to maintain the dignity of all Romans, while Walter dreams of owning a business for his own dignity.
3. (a) Caesar believes his status as ruler, determination, dedication, and destiny all define his dignity. (b) **Possible response:** Students may say that Caesar and Walter are similar because both of them believe in success and neither believes that others understand success as well as he does.

Writing to Compare Characters' Motivations

1. Review the assignment criteria with students.
2. As they draft, have students refer to their completed **Comparing Character Motivation Graphic Organizers** or to the chart in item 1, above.

PREACH

Meeting Your Standards

Students will

1. write a research report.
2. use writing strategies to generate ideas and to plan, organize, evaluate, and revise the report.
3. apply grammar skills.

Introducing the Writing Assignment

Review the assignment and the criteria, using the instruction on the student page.

Connecting to Real-Life Writing

Point out to students that research reporting is often incorporated into other types of writing. Provide these examples:

- Biographies are based on researched information.
- Historical fiction often includes well-researched facts.

David Henry Hwang on Using Research

Show students Segment 3 on David Henry Hwang on ***See It!* DVD** or from this page in the **Enriched Online Student Edition**, at **www.PHLitOnline.com.** Discuss the writing process and the impact of audience on Hwang's writing.

Writing Workshop

Work in Progress

If students have done the Work-in-Progress assignment on p. 1003, suggest that they examine their recorded ideas as they begin prewriting. They may have ideas in their portfolios that they wish to develop into research reports.

OES Online Essay Scorer

A writing prompt for this mode of writing can be found on the ***PH Essay Scorer*** at **www.PHLitOnline.com.**

Writing Workshop

Research Writing: Research Report

Defining the Form **Research writing** presents, interprets, and analyzes information gathered through comprehensive study of a subject. Writing a research report is a good way to learn about a topic that is outside your own experience. You might use elements of research writing in biographies, opinion papers, lab reports, and annotated bibliographies.

Assignment Write a research report on a topic that interests you and is substantial enough to merit an in-depth study. Include these elements:

✔ a *specific, narrow topic* that is summarized in a *thesis statement*

✔ relevant information from *primary and secondary sources*

✔ a *logical organization* of details and ideas

✔ *correct documentation of sources*, following an accepted format

✔ error-free grammar, including correct use of *adverb clauses*

To preview the criteria on which your research report may be judged, see the rubric on page 1031.

Writing Workshop: *Work in Progress*

If you have completed the Work in Progress assignment on page 1003, you already have ideas to use in your research report. Work with these ideas, or explore a new idea as you complete the Writing Workshop.

Teaching Resources

The following resources can be used to enrich or extend the instruction.

All *Unit 5 Resources*
Writing Workshop, pp. 202–203

All *Professional Development Guidebook*
Rubric for Self-Assessment: Research Report, pp. 242–243

All *Graphic Organizer Transparencies*
Rubric for Self-Assessment: Research Report, p. 190

All *See It!* DVD
David Henry Hwang, Segments 3 and 4

PHLit Online! All resources, including print and video, are available at **www.PHLitOnline.com.**

Prewriting Strategies

Scan your notebooks. Follow your instincts and interests when looking for a topic. Review the notes you have taken in any subject—from history to math to drama. Use a marker or self-sticking notes to highlight ideas that fascinate you. Then, choose one that you want to investigate further.

Review periodicals. Flip through newspaper and magazine articles for topics that you find intriguing. For example, you might consider researching the history behind a story that is currently in the news. Determine what you already know about the topic and what you would like to learn. Use a chart like the one shown to organize your thoughts.

What I Know	What I Want to Know

Apply It!

Develop a research plan. Generate questions to drive your study. After a brief overview of general information, plan to continue your research by developing a *working thesis statement.* This sentence will summarize the idea you intend to address in your report. Based on this statement, determine the types of sources you will need to consult. For example, you may need to gain a broad overview of a subject before investigating specific categories.

Working Thesis Statement: Dreams are important in a variety of ways.

My Research Plan	Possible Sources
Step 1: Get a solid overview about dreams and dream theory.	• Books on dream theory • Web sites (credible ones)
Step 2: Gather specific details and current information.	• Psychology journals (online and print) • Biographies of historical figures • Interviews with working psychologists

Apply It!

Your working thesis statement will guide your research—it should be flexible to help focus your study and you may need to change it to reflect what you have learned. As you gather information and refine your ideas, revise your thesis statement so that it is more precise. Include the final version of your thesis statement in the introduction of your report.

PHLit Online!
www.PHLitOnline.com
- Author video: Writing Process
- Author video: Rewards of Writing

Understanding by Design

Clarifying Expected Outcomes: Using Rubrics

- Before students begin working on this assignment, have them preview the Rubric for Self-Assessment (p. 1031) to learn what qualities their research reports must have. A copy of this rubric appears in ***Graphic Organizer Transparencies***, p. 190.
- Review the criteria in the rubric with the class. Before students use the rubric to assess their writing, work with them to rate the Student Model (p. 1028) using the rubric.
- If you wish to assess students' research reports with either a 4-point or a 6-point scoring rubric, see ***Professional Development Guidebook***, pp. 242–243.

TEACH

Prewriting Strategies

1. Introduce the Prewriting Strategies, using the instruction on the student page.
2. Have students apply the strategies to choose a topic.

Teaching the Strategies

1. Have students bring in magazines, newspapers, journals, notebooks, and textbooks. Have students form small groups to combine their resources. Then, encourage students to look through the group's materials and share their topic ideas with one another. Each student should make a list of possible topics, including interesting ideas generated by others.
2. Explain that a *working thesis* is a general statement that students can use to direct their research. Explain that as students acquire relevant information that supports their working theses, they will be able to narrow the scope of their theses.
3. Have students choose their top two topics and write working theses for them. Explain that the second topic is a backup in case the first is too difficult to research.

Think Aloud: Model Research Planning

Use the following "think aloud" to model how to narrow a topic and generate a working thesis. Say to students:

Suppose I want to research rainbows. I can narrow my topic by listing possible categories to research, such as the scientific causes of rainbows, the history of how humans have understood them, and their symbolism in myths and folk tales. The last topic interests me most, so I'll create a working thesis for it: "Rainbows are symbols in many myths and folk tales." Next, I'll do basic research and narrow my thesis to a specific culture, a specific meaning rainbows have across cultures, or even a specific myth. Then, I'll do more detailed research and finalize my thesis.

Prewriting (cont.)

4. Have students write two sets of research questions. The first set should contain all questions that will need to be answered in order to prove the thesis. The second set should contain nonessential questions that the student would like to answer, such as particular details the student would like to find. Remind students that these questions may need to be modified if the thesis is altered.
5. Have students brainstorm for possible primary sources for their research.
6. Explain that it is sometimes difficult to find unbiased information. **Ask:** What should you do if you find only biased information in your research?
   Possible response: You should try to separate the facts from the opinions and be aware that some pertinent facts may be missing. If possible, you should use sources from all sides of an issue. You should also verify facts by checking multiple sources.

Six Trait Focus

✔	Ideas		Word Choice
✔	Organization		Sentence Fluency
	Voice		Conventions

Writing and Grammar, Grade 10

Students will find additional instruction on prewriting for a research report in Chapter 12, Section 2.

Writing and Grammar, Interactive Textbook Online

Students can use the following tools at **www.pearsonsuccessnet.com** as they complete their research reports:

- Topic Bin
- Unity and Coherence
- Citing Sources/Preparing Manuscript

Make a list of open-ended research questions. Create a list of questions you would like to answer through research. The information you find may also inspire other ideas. Include new questions, but be sure that you continue to focus or narrow your topic rather than expand it.

Use a variety of primary and secondary sources. Consult *primary sources*—firsthand or original accounts of events. Primary sources include interview transcripts, journals, letters, eyewitness accounts, and speeches.

Also consult *secondary sources*, such as books, encyclopedia entries, magazine articles, and newspapers that present a report, a retelling, or an analysis of primary sources. Consider using specialized types of secondary sources as well, such as those listed in this chart.

Resource	Information
Almanacs	Social, political, and economic statistics
Atlases	Tables, charts, maps, and illustrations
Government publications	Information on laws, government programs, and topics such as agriculture and economics
Microfiche	Back issues of periodicals
Databases	Indexes to online and print sources

Evaluate sources. Be critical of your sources, looking for *bias* that may lead the writer to obscure or misrepresent the facts. Decide which of your sources are most reliable and objective.

Apply It!

Document sources and organize your notes. As you gather information, carefully record each key detail and its source.

- **Source Cards:** Write the identifying information—title, author, publisher, and date of publication—of every resource you consult. Use a separate notecard for each source. Label each card with a letter (A, B, C, and so on) or with a code word, such as the author's last name.
- **Notecards:** Record each relevant fact or idea on its own notecard. *Paraphrase,* or restate in your own words, the ideas of other authors. If you quote passages directly, use quotation marks and make sure your quotations are accurate. Include the letter or code word you have chosen to identify the source of the information.

Source Card

[A]

Kreisler, Kristin V. "Why We Dream What We Dream." Reader's Digest, Feb. 1995: 28, 30, 34–36,38.

Note Card

a dream helped Jack Nicklaus fix his golf swing

Source Card: A

Evaluate the validity of information and the bias of sources. As you gather information, evaluate its *validity,* or trustworthiness. Make sure the authors have the education, training, or personal experience to speak with authority. Notice any evidence of bias, or a tendency to make unfair judgments about certain topics. Bias includes the use of stereotypes, unsupported statements, or overly dramatic claims. Opinions should be based on factual evidence. Note your evaluations on your source notecards. Later, you can decide whether to use the information and how to present it.

Strategies for Taking Notes

Give students these suggestions for taking notes for research:

- Review your outline to make sure that you have at least one notecard addressing each topic in your outline.
- When you take notes from sources, record direct quotations. Then restate the main idea on the reverse of the card. This way, you have the exact wording and your interpretation on one card.
- Consider taking notes on some related subtopics in case your topic shifts focus due to a lack of information on one subtopic.

Drafting Strategies

Refine your thesis statement. Your working thesis statement should have evolved into a focused declaration as you gathered information. Now, make sure it can be proved using the facts and ideas you have compiled through research.

Final Thesis Statement: Dreams make a difference in people's lives—not only to the individuals who dream them, but to society.

Organize your information. Choose an organizational strategy that matches the content and purpose of your writing. Consider using one of the strategies described in this chart.

Apply It!

Organizational Strategy	Uses
Chronological Order offers information in the sequence in which it happened	historical topics; science experiments
Part-to-Whole Order examines how categories affect a larger subject	analysis of social issues; historical topics
Order of Importance presents information in order of increasing or decreasing importance	persuasive arguments; supporting a bold or challenging thesis
Comparison-and-Contrast presents similarities and differences	addressing two or more subjects

Synthesize ideas. Effective research writing does not merely present facts and details, but synthesizes—gathers, orders, and interprets—those elements. As you draft, synthesize information into a unified whole that is driven by your original thoughts.

Use and credit sources. You may choose any of the following methods to present the ideas, facts, and examples you discover in your research. In all cases, you must credit your source.

- **Direct Quotation:** Use the author's exact words when they are interesting or persuasive. Indicate any omissions with ellipsis points. Enclose direct quotations in quotation marks.
- **Paraphrase:** Restate an author's ideas in your own words.
- **Summary:** Compress a complex idea into a briefer version.
- **Facts:** If a fact is available only in one source, include documentation.

Incorporate graphic aids and visuals. Consider using illustrations, photographs, maps, graphs, or charts to clarify facts, highlight trends, or add dramatic impact. You may include visuals you discover in your research materials. If so, provide full citations for them.

Differentiated Instruction for Universal Access

Strategy for Less Proficient Readers
Once students have chosen topics, have them analyze the topics in terms of *who, what, when, where, why,* and *how*. Answers to these questions may form the outlines of their reports.

Enrichment for Gifted and Talented Students
Challenge students to research and write about historical figures whom they do not admire, controversial events, or events that had negative impacts on society. In their reports, students should address why their figures or events yielded negative impressions.

Drafting Strategies

1. Introduce the Drafting Strategies, using the instruction on the student page.
2. Have students apply the strategies as they draft.

Teaching the Strategies

1. Have students make multiple outlines. Then, instruct them to decide which type of organization will work best for their topics.
2. Assign partners to read each other's drafts to make sure that all ideas are clearly synthesized. Emphasize the importance of clearly showing the relationships between various details, rather than simply listing details.
3. Remind students that they must carefully credit any sources of information they use. It is also helpful to take notes with direct quotations so that students can verify whether they have used their own words or the author's.

Think Aloud: Model Choosing an Organizational Strategy

Use the following "think aloud" to model choosing an organizational method. Say to students:

I need to choose the organizational method that will best support my thesis. Let's say my thesis is "To stop global warming, we need to address each of its causes." Chronological order doesn't work because the causes occur simultaneously. Comparison-and-contrast doesn't fit since I'm not comparing the causes to one another. Part-to-whole can work—I can address each cause separately and discuss how it contributes to the problem. Order of importance can also work. I can even write a part-to-whole in which I address the different parts in the order of their importance. This combination seems to be the most effective method for my essay.

Six Traits

✔	Ideas		Word Choice
✔	Organization		Sentence Fluency
	Voice		Conventions

WG Writing and Grammar, Grade 10

Students will find additional instruction on drafting a research report in Chapter 12, Section 3.

David Henry Hwang on Using Research

Review the passage on the student page with the class, using David Henry Hwang's comments to deepen students' understanding of the process of writing a research report.

Teaching From the Professional Model

1. Show students Segment 4 on David Henry Hwang on the ***See It!*** **DVD** or from this page in the **Enriched Online Student Edition** at **www.PHLitOnline.com**
2. After the video, open a discussion using the following prompt: How are the rewards of being a writer different from the rewards of other professions?
3. Point out that David Henry Hwang states that even experts in their fields often have to look up information for accuracy.
4. **Ask:** What does the research contribute to Hwang's article?
   Possible response: The research makes Hwang sound knowledgeable about Broadway. It also makes the article more informative, providing readers with facts about New York, as well as reflections on a personal experience.
5. Review David Henry Hwang's comments about his last paragraph. **Ask** students how Hwang signals this "jump forward."
   Answer: He uses the transition word *now* and the phrase *more than 20 years later.*

   Then, **ask:** How does this transition help readers synthesize the information in these three paragraphs?
   Possible response: The transition tells readers that Hwang is comparing his current feelings about New York to his past feelings about it.

David Henry Hwang

On Using Research

As someone born and raised in California, I disliked New York very much. However, I have grown to love the city and now call it my home. The one aspect of New York I did enjoy was discovering Broadway. When I later wrote an article about Broadway, I relied on research as well as my own observations.

"My first Broadway producer . . . once told me that a success here is 'a shot fired round the world.'"
—David Henry Hwang

Professional Model:

from *"Place of a Lifetime . . ."*

Shows premiered here that helped a young nation define its identity: plays like *A Streetcar Named Desire* (at the Ethel Barrymore Theatre, on West 47th Street), musicals like *Guys and Dolls* (at the 46th Street Theatre, now renamed the Richard Rodgers).

I just don't know in my head which great plays were produced in which theatres; I had to look this information up.

Along with most theatre artists, I believe each of these theatres is home to at least one ghost; before leaving each evening, a stagehand will turn on the "ghost light," a single bulb that burns all night, to scare away bad spirits and attract good ones. Very little else about New York captured my imagination on that first visit; I only lasted four days before fleeing back to the West Coast, vowing never to return.

As with most legends, there are several different explanations for the origin of the "ghost light." Among the explanations I found in different books, this one seemed most common.

Now, more than 20 years later, I am a devoted New Yorker who has been privileged to see five of my shows performed on Broadway. I sometimes feel that my first hit, *M. Butterfly*, afflicted me with a Broadway virus: an unshakable affection for those aging theatres—roughly 40 in total—and the life that inhabits and surrounds them. . . .

Here, I jump forward in time to demonstrate how my views of New York have completely changed.

Strategies for Using Technology in Writing

If students are using word-processing software to draft and revise their research reports, suggest that they use the cut-and-paste functions to quickly move sentences and paragraphs to different places in their reports. Remind students that it is a good idea to save a copy of the first drafts and each revision with separate, distinct file names, so it will be easy to go back to previous versions.

Students can also use features of the **Writing and Grammar Interactive Textbook Online** to revise their reports.

Revising Strategies

Step back from your work. If time allows, leave yourself time between drafting and revising. Reading your work with new energy will allow you to see your work with more clarity.

Revise for conciseness. Your research report will be more effective if you avoid unnecessary complexity or wordiness. Reread your draft, circling any words that add clutter without meaning. Consider omitting those words or replacing them with better choices.

Apply It!

Model: Revising for Conciseness

In
~~Thus, in~~ conclusion, ~~one can see from careful observation that~~ political conflict often leads to economic change.

Revise to avoid plagiarism. To avoid plagiarism—the unethical presentation of someone else's ideas as if they were your own—you must cite sources for direct quotations, paraphrased information, or facts that are specific to a single source. Reread your draft, circling any words or ideas that are not your own. Follow the instructions on page 1026 and pages R40–R41 to correctly cite those passages.

Revise to strengthen coherence. Make sure that all of the elements in your draft follow your organizational strategy and appear in logical, or coherent, order.

- On a separate piece of paper, write the main idea of each paragraph.
- Review this list—an abbreviated version of your report—to decide whether your ideas flow logically from paragraph to paragraph.
- Check that the ideas in your introduction and conclusion match.
- Rearrange paragraphs or sections that do not build in a logical way. Consider eliminating any that stray from your thesis statement.
- Add transitional words or sentences to help readers see the connections you want to emphasize.

Peer Review

Share your draft and list of main ideas with a partner. Ask your partner to consider how well each main idea builds on the last in a logical flow. Consider moving paragraphs or sections to improve your report's coherence. Explain to your partner your reasons for specific revision choices.

Strategies for Research Report Style

Remind students that not all research writing should mimic the style of an encyclopedia. Students should consider their topics and audiences to decide which style will work best. Some topics, such as the history of animation, may benefit from some humor.

Revising Strategies

1. Introduce the Revising Strategies, using the instruction on the student page.
2. Have students apply the strategies as they revise.

Teaching the Strategies

1. Remind students that an essay should present ideas in a logical way, with each paragraph flowing into the next.
2. Have students work in pairs to read each other's research reports and identify any ideas or paragraphs that seem out of order. Have students discuss possible solutions to the organization of each other's reports.
3. Explain that even if ideas are sequenced logically, paragraphs without transitions might not flow smoothly into one another. Tell students that they may need to reorder ideas within paragraphs so the end of each paragraph leads to the beginning of the next. They may also need to add transition words.
4. Remind students that it is important that they give credit to others for ideas and words that are not their own. Any wording that does not sound natural is likely to be a copy of someone else's work. Students must indicate this by placing footnotes or endnotes after passages that should be credited to a source.

Think Aloud: Model Revising for Conciseness

Write this sentence on the board: *Way out in the middle of the Pacific Ocean, there is something called the Great Pacific Garbage Patch, which is a very large floating island of trash.* Use the following "think aloud" to model identifying and deleting extra words. Say to students:

As I check my essay for conciseness, I find this wordy sentence. I recognize the unnecessary words *way out*, *there is*, *something called*, *which is*, and *very*. I can delete these words so that the revised sentence reads, "In the middle of the Pacific Ocean lies the Great Pacific Garbage Patch, a floating island of trash." Notice how much clearer and to the point this sentence is now.

Revising (cont.)

5. Review with students the required information in a bibliography entry and the information required for footnotes and end-notes.
6. Have students turn to pages R40–R41 for information on cit-ing using the MLA style.

Six Traits Focus

	Ideas		Word Choice
✓	Organization		Sentence Fluency
	Voice		Conventions

WG Writing and Grammar, Grade 10

Students will find additional instruction on revising a research report in Chapter 12, Section 4.

Documenting Sources

Citing Sources in the Body of a Report When citing sources in your report, follow a specific format. Modern Language Association (MLA) style calls for parenthetical citations or references. For print works, the citation usually gives the author's or editor's name followed by a page number. If the work does not have an author, use a keyword or phrase from the title. For Web sources, use the author's name if it is available, the title of the article, if any, or the title of the site itself. Include a screen number if screens on the site are numbered.

Citing a Print Work: . . . men have more action-oriented dreams, while women imagine more emotional one-on-one struggles with loved ones (Van de Castle 45).

Citing a Web Source: Unsolvedmysteries.com shows how dreams can bring luck with the report of a lottery winner from Maine ("Winning the Lottery," screen 1).

Creating a Works-Cited List or Bibliography Publication information for each source you cite must appear at the end of your report. MLA style calls for a Works-Cited list, in which you list alphabetically the works you cite.

- For books, the Works-Cited entry usually takes the form of the author's name, last name first, followed by the title of the work. The entry gives full publication information, including the city of publication, the name of the publisher, and the year of publication.
- For articles in periodicals, the entry usually takes the form of the author's name, last name first, followed by the title of the article, then the name of the magazine. Publication information includes the date of the issue, the volume and issue number if any, and the pages on which the article appears. If the article is continued on a later, non-consecutive page, give the number of the first page, followed by a plus sign.
- For general Web sites, give any of the following information that is available, in the order indicated: author's name, the title of the page, the title of the site, the date of last update, and the name of the sponsoring organization. Give screen numbers, if any. Give the date that you consulted the site, and conclude with the full URL, or address, for the material.

For more information on MLA style, see pages R40–R41.

SIX TRAITS WRITER'S TOOLBOX SIX TRAITS

Sentence Fluency | Voice | Organization | Word Choice | Ideas | Conventions

Revising to Combine Sentences Using Adverb Clauses

Avoid choppy writing by combining some sentences using adverb clauses.

Two sentences: She had sent the letter. The mail was delayed.

Combined: Although the mail was delayed, she had sent the letter.

Identifying Adverb Clauses A clause is a group of words with a subject and a verb. An *independent clause* can stand alone as a complete sentence, but a *subordinate clause* cannot stand alone. An adverb clause is a subordinate clause that begins with a subordinating conjunction and tells *where, when, in what way, to what extent, under what condition,* or *why.*

When: *Before I got on the plane,* I was afraid of flying.

Condition: Dave will carry the box *if you will open the door.*

Why: I gave her my number *so she could call me later.*

In what way: The child swam *as if she had been born in the water.*

Combining Sentences When using adverb clauses to combine two shorter sentences, follow these steps.

1. **Identify the relationship between the ideas in the sentences.**
2. **Select a subordinate conjunction that clarifies that relationship.** Put the adverb clause at the beginning or end of the sentence.
3. **When a subordinate clause begins a sentence, use a comma to separate it from the rest of the sentence.**

Subordinating Conjunctions

after	although	as	as if
as long as	because	before	even though
if	since	so that	than
though	unless	until	when
whenever	where	wherever	while

Grammar in Your Writing

Review the introduction and conclusion of your report and highlight any short sentences. Look for a relationship between the ideas in the sentences that could be clarified with an adverb clause, and combine them using an appropriate subordinating conjunction.

WG

Prentice Hall Writing and Grammar Connection: Chapter 20, Section 2

Differentiated Instruction for Universal Access

Strategy for Less Proficient Readers
Guide students to find the subjects and verbs in the sample sentences. Show them that "I got on the plane" is an independent clause, but adding *before* makes it dependent on, or subordinate to, the clause "I was afraid of flying." Have students circle the subordinating conjunctions in the sample sentences, replacing them with other subordinating conjunctions. Discuss how the meanings of the sentences change.

Strategy for Advanced Students
Challenge students to write a few paragraphs in which they use all of the subordinating conjunctions listed in the student text. Next, have them rewrite their paragraphs, dividing the sentences and eliminating the subordinating conjunctions. Then, have them trade papers and try to combine their partners' sentences, using all of the subordinating conjunctions again.

Revising to Combine Sentences Using Adverb Clauses

1. Introduce the grammar skill, using the instruction on the student page.
2. Discuss the examples and the strategies for combining sentences using adverb clauses.
3. Have students follow the instruction under Grammar in Your Writing to correct errors in their drafts.

Teaching the Writing Skill

1. Explain that a subordinate clause can become an independent clause if the subordinating conjunction is deleted. Likewise, an independent clause can become a subordinate clause if a subordinating conjunction is added.
2. Have small groups work together to identify the subordinate clauses in the following sentences, stating whether the clauses answer *where, when, in what way, to what extent, under what condition,* or *why*:
   - <u>Unless I wear glass</u>, I can't see. **Answer:** condition
   - I'll go <u>whenever you want to go</u>. **Answer:** when
3. Have each group write ten sentences containing adverb clauses. Then, have groups trade papers and identify one another's clauses.
4. Ask groups to combine these sentences using adverb clauses:
   - He ate sushi. He was full. **Possible response:** He ate sushi even though he was full.
   - She jumped off the boat and splashed joyfully. She wasn't afraid of sharks. **Possible response:** Since she wasn't afraid of sharks, she jumped off the boat and splashed joyfully.
5. Have each group write ten pairs of sentences that can be combined using adverb clauses. Then, have groups trade papers and combine one another's sentences.

WG Writing and Grammar, Grade 10

Students will find additional instruction on adverb clauses in Chapter 20, Section 2.

Student Model

Review the Student Model with the class, using the annotations to analyze the writer's use of the elements of a research report.

Teaching From the Student Model

1. Explain that the Student Model is a sample and that students' research reports may be longer.
2. **Ask** students to identify the thesis statement in the writer's report.
   Answer: "Ever since humans have existed, dreams have made a difference in people's lives."
3. Draw students' attention to the adverb clause in the thesis statement. **Ask** students to identify other passages in which the writer uses adverb clauses to combine sentences.
   Possible response: In the fourth paragraph, the writer uses "even before it was diagnosed . . ." as an adverb clause to combine two sentences.
4. Point out to students the variety of ways the writer credits the sources of her information.

Connecting to Real-Life Writing

Explain to students that research writing is a highly useful skill. Students will most likely be required to produce research writing in college classes as well as in business situations. For example, they may be asked to find out more information about important topics and report their findings to people in their companies.

Student Model: Lisa Maiden, Phoenix, AZ

In Your Dreams

Ever since humans have existed, dreams have made a difference in people's lives. Julius Caesar's wife, Calpurnia, once dreamed that Caesar's statue spurted blood like a fountain while the Romans smiled and bathed in it. This nightmarish picture foreshadowed reality when Caesar was later assassinated. In 1793, Marie Antoinette had a dream of a red sun and pillar. After the sun rose, it suddenly set; this immediately preceded her beheading. Then, there is Robert Louis Stevenson, who believed his best stories came from dreams, including the infamous "Dr. Jekyll and Mr. Hyde." Neils Bohr dreamed of sitting on the sun with planets whizzing around him on small cords; he then developed the model of an atom. Even Genghis Khan claimed to receive his battle plans from his sleepy nights.

Who were the early interpreters of such dreams? Aristotle and Freud, of course, were among the scholars who labored over dream interpretation. Aristotle suggested that dreams were formed by disturbances in the body. Freud, however, believed that dreams were powerful tools for uncovering unconscious wishes. He said, "The purpose of dreams is to allow us to satisfy in fantasies the instinctual urges that society judges unacceptable" (Dreams: History, 2000).

Even today, creative people use their dreams in solving problems. A 1995 *Reader's Digest* article entitled "Why We Dream What We Dream" provides many examples. One such dreamer was the scientist Dmitri Ivanovich Mendeleev. He "saw" the periodic table of the elements in a dream and wrote it down the following day. Later, only one correction was needed. Screenwriter James Cameron dreamed of a robot with a red eye staring back at him. He woke up and wrote the script for *The Terminator.* Steve Allen's hit song "This Could Be the Start of Something Big" also began from a dream, as did the new way of swinging the club that allowed Jack Nicklaus to overcome his golfing problem (Kreisler, 28–38).

Besides being helpful in the creative aspect, dreams have, in many cases, foretold the future. In the weeks prior to his murder, Abraham Lincoln dreamed the White House was in mourning for an assassinated president. The video *The Secret World of Dreams* tells of a man whose dreams indicated a chronic illness even before it was diagnosed, as well as a man whose recurring nightmares of an explosion prepared him for the real thing and enabled him to save the life of a coworker. Unsolvedmysteries.com shows how dreams can bring luck with the report of a lottery winner from Maine whose dreams revealed a winning ticket (Unsolved Mysteries Home Page, screen 1). Given such cases as these, it is no mystery that modern psychology still believes in the prophetic power of dreams.

Lisa begins by introducing the topic in a concise sentence.

She correctly quotes and cites one of her sources.

Lisa incorporates the source of her information into the flow of her discussion.

Lisa demonstrates the wide variety of sources she consulted in her research.

Strategies for Test Taking

Point out that during in-class essay tests, it is especially important to make the first draft as polished as possible. To do this, prompt students to check each paragraph just after it is written, making sure that the paragraph clearly relates to the paragraph before it as well as to the thesis. If text needs to be added, it is much easier to add it before writing the next paragraph.

However, to understand one's dreams, one must uncover the meaning of dream symbols. Psychoanalyst Sigmund Freud said that the secret to the symbols in dreams lies within the dreamer (Bentley, p. 4). In other words, individuals can interpret dream symbols from their own lives and the imagery around them—not just by using a dream dictionary. Sleeps.com gives just a few examples of these symbols. For instance, to most dreamers, clothing symbolizes mood, attitude, or state of mind. One who wears a uniform in a dream may be influenced too much by society, while having clothes that are too short may suggest a longing for the pleasures of youth now gone. Death is also a recurring symbol. Whether the dreamer attends a funeral or is in a coffin, these pictures signify a change in one's attitude toward life or one's emotional balance. Finally, other people occur in dreams as reflections of the dreamer's own personality traits. For instance, if a dreamer is faced by the stares of others, that person may be worried about making a bad impression on other people (Dream Analysis and Interpretation, screens 6, 7).

While dreams can be interpreted according to symbols, the most common types of dreams vary throughout the human life cycle. People at different places in their lives tend to dream differently. Children's dreams reflect new impressions that they encounter each day. Bold geometric shapes are not just building blocks with which they play—they represent a fixation with family relationships. For example, a triangle would signify the relationship among the father, mother, and child. Dreams of giants indicate a child's impression of his or her own size and sense of self-worth. Naturally, everything is bigger to a child, but a child with giant proportions compared to the world around him may have an increasing self-awareness (Bentley, p. 25). Much like a scene from *The Nutcracker,* toys come to life as the child lives out fantasies, showing developments of the young person's persona. As children become teens, they dream more about romance. Among adults, men and women dream differently. "It's biology and social conditioning," says Milton Kramer, director of the Bethesda Oak Hospital's Sleep Center in Cincinnati. Research has shown that men dream twice as often of other men as they do of women, while women tend to have an equal number of dreams of both sexes (New Scientist, p. 2). A study by Robert Van de Castle, author of *Our Dreaming Mind*, analyzed 1,000 dreams and found that men have more action-oriented dreams, while women imagine more emotional one-on-one struggles with loved ones (Van de Castle, p. 45).

Studies are also beginning to show that a person's attitude can influence his or her dreams. University of Pennsylvania professor Aaron Beck found that angry

Each paragraph includes a topic sentence, which is then supported in the paragraph with details.

Teaching from the Student Model (cont.)

5. Have students review the topic sentence of each paragraph to gain a sense of the organization of this report. **Ask** students to describe the order of ideas in this report.
   Answer: The writer begins her report by discussing dreams in creative works. Then she discusses interpreters of dreams and instances of people using their dreams in problem solving and even in predicting the future. Finally, she discusses the use of symbols to interpret dreams and how dreams evolve through the life span.
6. Have students assess the writer's organization. Have them identify which organizational method she uses. **Ask:** Does the writer build a logical train of thought to support her thesis?
   Possible response: The writer does not use any of the organizational methods, nor is there clear logic to the order in which she presents her ideas.
7. Have students identify two supporting details for the topic sentence "However, to understand one's dreams, one must uncover the meaning of dream symbols."
   Possible response: Wearing a uniform in a dream can represent someone who is too influenced by society; a dreamer attending a funeral signifies a change in attitude toward life.

Differentiated Instruction for Universal Access

Strategy for Special Needs Students

A common mistake for students new to research papers is to choose topics that are too broad to cover within the given length constraints. Solve this problem by providing a list of several appropriately narrow topics from which students can choose. If students need further help, provide several well-written thesis statements. Have each student choose one thesis statement and do the research to support it, using the guidelines in the textbook.

Teaching from the Student Model (cont.)

8. Discuss whether the writer proved her thesis sufficiently. Guide them to see that she proved that dreams have made a difference in some people's lives, but she did not prove that dreams have influenced humans since they first existed, as there is no way to determine this. Warn students against stating absolutes that they cannot prove.
9. Direct students to the writer's Works Cited. Explain that although the writer mentions sources throughout her report, this listing of sources provides complete information so readers can locate the same source.
10. **Ask** students to skim the report and locate the information she used from the article "Why We Dream What We Dream." **Answer:** The writer cites this source on the first page, third paragraph, and on the third page, first full paragraph.
11. Ask students to identify whether each citation is for a book, a magazine article, a video, or an Internet site.

people are the ones throwing the punches in their dream, while depressed people often find themselves the victims of rejection. However, people who have a hard time standing up for themselves are the ones likely to suffer from restless nightmares (Kreisler, 36).

Through the fascinating history of dreams, the interpretation of some dream symbols, and the secret dreams of different sleepers, it is evident that dreams are important. They provide valuable insights, help solve problems, spark new thoughts and creations, and even foretell the future. Maybe people should pay more attention to their dreams. The hours one spends sleeping could be the key to a better life.

Works Cited

Bentley, Peter. *Book of Dream Symbols.* Chronicle Books, 1995.

"Dream Analysis and Interpretation, Doing It!" 9 March 2000: 6, 7. <http://www.sleeps.com/analysis.html>

"Dreams: History." 22 Mar. 2000. <http://library.thinkquest.org/11130/data/history/history.html>

"Get Real, Siggi." *New Scientist,* 26 April 1997: 2,5. 21 March 2000. <http://www.newscientist.com/ns/970426/siggi.html>

Great Moments in Dream History Home Page. 7 March 2000: 1–3. <http://www.dr-dream.com/hist.htm>

Kreisler, Kristin V. "Why We Dream What We Dream." *Reader's Digest,* Feb. 1995: 28, 30, 34–36, 38.

Kramer, Milton. Personal Interview. 10 March 2000.

The Secret World of Dreams. Videotape. Questar Video, 1997. 80 Min.

Bentley, Peter. *Book of Dream Symbols.* Chronicle Books, 1995.

Van de Castle, Robert L. *Our Dreaming Mind.* Ballantine, 1995.

"Winning the Lottery in Your dreams." Unsolved Mysteries Home Page. 11 11 March 2000: 1. <http://unsolvedmysteries.com/usm397.html>

Lisa lists, in a standard format, the sources from which her information was drawn.

Editing and Proofreading

Review your draft to correct errors in grammar, spelling, and punctuation.

Focus on Accuracy in Citations: Carefully check the spelling, punctuation, and format of title, including the use of quotation marks, underlining, and italics. Check the spelling of authors' names, and make sure that you have capitalized titles correctly. Be sure that your draft follows the proper manuscript format, including title page and correct page numbering.

Publishing and Presenting

Consider one of the following ways to share your writing:

Publish on the Internet. Post your research report on a Web site that publishes student writing, or send it to the Web site editors as an e-mail.

Share a multimedia presentation. Use your research report as the basis for a multimedia presentation, and include graphics, music, props, and other elements to engage your audience. If possible, rehearse your presentation with a live audience to coordinate the smooth combination of elements. Incorporate audience feedback to improve your report or presentation. Make sure you allow time for your audience to ask questions.

WG *Prentice Hall Writing and Grammar Connection: Chapter 12*

Reflecting on Your Writing

Writer's Journal Jot down your answers to this question:

How did writing a research report help you understand your topic?

Rubric for Self-Assessment

Find evidence in your writing to address each category. Then, use the rating scale to grade your work.

Criteria	Rating Scale (not very — very)
Focus: How specific is your thesis statement?	1 2 3 4 5
Organization: How logical and effective is your organization?	1 2 3 4 5
Support/Elaboration: How varied and reliable is your evidence?	1 2 3 4 5
Style: How concise is your phrasing of ideas?	1 2 3 4 5
Conventions: How accurately and thoroughly have you cited sources for ideas that are not your own?	1 2 3 4 5

Strategies for Using Technology in Writing

If students publish their reports online, suggest that they create links for their works cited. They can link directly to the Web sites used for their research, providing interested readers with an opportunity to continue learning.

Students can also link to reviews and summaries of the books they've cited or to Web sites selling the books. Additionally, they can add a Related Reading list of links to similar Web sites that might interest their readers.

Editing and Proofreading

1. Introduce the editing and proofreading focus, using the instruction on the student page.
2. Have students edit and proofread their research reports, correcting grammar, spelling, punctuation, and word choice. Make sure they check for errors of the type noted on the student page.
3. Explain to students that readers should be able to locate easily any source information. It is important that all titles, names, publications, dates, and page numbers are noted correctly. Tell students that it is best to double-check all information before proclaiming a draft final.

Six Traits Focus

	Ideas		Word Choice
	Organization		Sentence Fluency
	Voice	✔	Conventions

ASSESS

Publishing and Presenting

1. Have students identify other audiences for their essays in addition to their classmates. Discuss how students might reach these audiences.
2. Have students discuss how they would modify their reports if they choose to publish them electronically or to present them orally.

Reflecting on Your Writing

1. Have students consider the organization of their information. How easy was it for them to decide on final outlines?
2. **Ask** what they could do differently next time to avoid major rewriting.

WG Writing and Grammar, Grade 10

Students will find additional guidance on editing and proofreading, publishing and presenting, and reflecting on research reports in Chapter 12, Sections 5 and 6.

MONITORING PROGRESS

Think About It

1. Remind students that the Unit Big Question is "To what extent does experience determine what we perceive?"
2. Point out that students have read selections in this unit in which people's backgrounds and experiences affected their perceptions of situations. Remind students to draw on their own experiences about the topic as well.
3. Point out that it is important to look at different factors that affect perception. Review the Example From Literature shown in the chart. Point out that despite changing times, Mama maintains more modest goals than Walter.
4. Explain that experience can color perceptions not only in literature, but in other areas as well. For example, a president's policies might be considered controversial in his or her time but greatly admired years later because of the eventual results of his or her actions.
5. Review the headings on the chart. Remind students that people's priorities and expectations, which are influenced by past experience, can lead to disagreements. Encourage students to generate examples to support this, such as different opinions people might have about a controversial action.
6. Have students copy and complete the chart shown on the student page. If they have difficulty finding examples from real life, suggest these starting points:
   - Think of a time when you disagreed with someone about something you both witnessed. What was the reason for the disagreement?
   - Why are some topics controversial?

   Have volunteers read aloud their completed charts. Invite the class to discuss their examples.

Applying the Big Question

To what extent does *experience* determine what we *perceive?*

Think About It

Think about what you have read in this unit, and what you know about how experience determines people's perceptions from your other classes and your own experiences. Copy and complete the chart below to apply what you have learned. One row has been completed for you.

Example	Situation	One Person's Perception	Another Person's Perception	What I Learned
From Literature	In *A Raisin in the Sun,* Walter and Mama disagree about how to use some money they have inherited.	Walter wants to open a store so he can have better opportunities.	Mama wants to buy a house and pay for her daughter's education.	Walter comes from a time when equality and self-respect are his generation's goals, while Mama is simply grateful to have her freedom and her life.
From Literature				
From Science				
From Social Studies				
From Real Life				

Teaching Resources

Unit 5 Resources

All **Applying the Big Question**, p. 5

PHLit Online! All print resources are also available at **www.PHLitOnline.com.**

Talk About It

Choose one of the examples in your chart as the basis for a **short speech.** On note cards, write details about the example you chose. Explain how each person's or character's past experiences impact how he or she sees the world and the decisions he or she makes in your particular example. Then, present a short speech to the class in which you explain the situation, how two people respond to it, and how each person's background influences his or her interpretation of the situation. Conclude by stating to what extent you think experience influences what we perceive.

For tips on organizing and delivering a speech, see the Communications Workshop on page 616.

Write About It

At the beginning of Unit 5, you wrote a response to the Big Question. Now that you have completed the unit, see how your understanding has deepened or changed. Write a new response, discussing how your initial ideas have either been changed or reinforced.

The extent to which experience determines what we perceive is ______________.

Support your answer with two or more of the examples in your chart—one from literature, and one from another subject area or your own life. You may also complete these sentences to help you organize your response.

- In this unit, a selection that included a difference between how characters reacted to a situation based on their past experiences showed me ______________.
- One example from Social Studies of how experience affects perception is ______________.
- One real life situation in which people might have different perspectives based on differing experiences is ____________.
- A current issue in the news about which people have very different perceptions is ______________. Their life experiences influence their perceptions of this issue because ____________.
- When a friend and I make different decisions about the same problem, it is usually because ______________. When this happens, I feel ______________.

Challenge What issues does this question still raise for you? How could you continue your exploration?

☆ shows an **Academic Vocabulary** word.

Big Question Vocabulary

- ☆ anticipate
- ☆ background
- ☆ bias
- ☆ distortion
- expectations
- identity
- impression
- ☆ individual
- ☆ insight
- ☆ interpretation
- knowledge
- ☆ manipulate
- ☆ perspective
- stereotype
- universal

MONITORING PROGRESS

Talk About It

1. Have students complete the assignment, following the instruction on the student page.
2. Have students write quick notes for a diary entry or letter that each character might write about the event.
3. Have students practice their speeches with partners before presenting them to the class.

Write About It

1. Introduce the assignment, using the instruction on the student page.
2. Review the thematic vocabulary with the class (pp. 1046–1047).

Teaching Prewriting

1. Point out that students may have read a selection that changed their opinions of the Big Question.
2. Have students respond to the Big Question, completing the sentences on the student page to guide their thinking. Then refer students to their responses in Introducing the Big Question, pp. 790–791, to see how their thinking may have changed.

Teaching Drafting

1. Have students use examples from their chart or their completed sentences for ideas.
2. Remind students to begin with an example and to follow with details that expound on the idea.

Teaching Revising/Editing

1. After students have completed their drafts, have them revise them for organization.
2. Remind students to eliminate irrelevant information and to add additional details to support their examples.
3. After students have revised their drafts, have them reread their edited versions.

Guiding Student Publishing

Students might continue their exploration of the topic with journal entries of real-life situations they learn about in current events or examples from subject areas in school.

Strategies for Listening and Speaking

Remind students how to organize and prepare for a short speech.

For listeners:

- Tell students to be quiet and attentive during classmates' presentations and to take notes on issues they wish to question speakers about during the follow-up.
- After each speech, invite students to ask questions and express their views about the ideas presented.

For speakers:

- Encourage students to make eye contact as they deliver their speeches. Guide students to refer to notecards, but not to read from them directly.
- Remind students to speak slowly and loudly enough to be heard by classmates at the back of the room.
- Speakers should be prepared to answer questions at the end.

EXTEND/ASSESS

Answers

Meeting Your Standards

Students will

1. identify the meaning of words and phrases from other languages commonly used in English.
2. understand the origins of borrowed and foreign words.

Borrowed and Foreign Words

1. Introduce the skill, using the instruction on the student page.
2. Review the chart.

Think Aloud: Model the Skill

Use the following "think aloud" to model identifying and defining borrowed and foreign words. Say to students:

Sometimes context clues give a general understanding of a foreign or borrowed word, and I don't need to stop reading to look it up. Let's say I read "Sam is truly a *mensch*; he's the most honorable person I know." *Mensch* is italicized, so I know it's a foreign word, but I don't need to reach for a dictionary because there's a context clue: "honorable person." I can infer that *mensch* means "honorable person." If I check a dictionary, I find that *mensch* is Yiddish and means "a decent, responsible person with admirable characteristics."

Then I might read, "Sam is *gung-ho* about the project." *Gung-ho* is a borrowed word, and there aren't any context clues, so I need to use a dictionary to understand the sentence. When I look it up, I find that *gung-ho* is Chinese and means "wholeheartedly enthusiastic."

Practice A

Sample answers:

1. language: Latin; definition: an unwelcome person
2. language: Latin; definition: for the special purpose currently under consideration
3. language: French; definition: an

Vocabulary Workshop

Borrowed and Foreign Words

Many words in English have been taken directly from other languages. The meaning of these **borrowed words** may stay the same as in the original language, as in these examples: *pajamas* (Hindi), *sauna* (Finnish), and *plaza* (Spanish). In other cases, the meaning has changed. *Sleuth*, for example, comes from an Old Norse word meaning "trail." It has changed in English to mean "the person who follows a trail; a detective." Borrowed words include some of the most common words in English.

A **foreign word** is a borrowed word that is still treated as a foreign term in English. A foreign word or phrase is frequently set in italics. Some dictionaries indicate words that should be written in italics. Examples of foreign words that are frequently used in English include *mano a mano, mot juste, ex post facto,* and *quid pro quo.*

This chart shows some of the ways that new words enter a language.

Entry Point	Explanation	Examples
War	Conflict brings soldiers in contact with new people so new words enter the language.	*brigade, cavalry, infantry* (French); *arsenal* (Italian); *blitzkrieg* (German)
Immigration	When people settle in new countries, they bring their language with them.	*delicatessen* (German); *cappuccino, pasta, pizza* (Italian)
Travel and Trade	People who travel and do business in other countries bring words home with them.	*cruise, reef* (Dutch); *shampoo* (Hindi); *guitar, canyon* (Spanish)

Practice A Look up each word in a dictionary. Identify the language from which the word was borrowed and write the definition.

1. *persona non grata*
2. ad hoc
3. *je ne sais quoi*
4. hoi polloi
5. *verboten*
6. nom de guerre

Answers continued

indefinable, elusive quality

4. language: Greek; definition: the common people
5. language: German; definition: prohibited
6. language: French; definition: an assumed name

Teaching Resources

Unit 5 Resources

Borrowed and Foreign Words, pp. 204–205

PHLit Online! **Vocabulary Central,** featuring definitions, audio pronunciations, Word Families, and activities, is available at **www.PHLitOnline.com.**

Practice B Rewrite each sentence substituting the correct borrowed or foreign word from the box for the word or phrase in italics. Use context clues to determine the word's meaning. Use a dictionary if necessary.

niche	clique	ghetto	tempo	carte blanche
faux pas	prima facie	passé	grotesque	vis-à-vis

1. My brother had *the freedom* to visit the millionaire whenever he wanted to.
2. The ugly gargoyle sitting on the roof was *distorted and strange.*
3. After many years, Trudy found her *special place* as a fashion designer.
4. When they first immigrated to the United States, all of the Polish people lived in the *same neighborhood.*
5. The strangers fell in love *at first sight.*
6. The people on a soccer team have their own *exclusive group.*
7. Rafael had a discussion about his future *face to face* with his guidance counselor.
8. That style of skirt from the 1990s is *old-fashioned.*
9. Please, slow down the *speed* of that song or I will not be able to sing along with you.
10. By taking a bite of the salad before the hostess was served, Tiffany made a serious *social blunder.*

Challenge

Develop a vocabulary quiz based on Practice B. Following the model, write sentences with clues for these words: *cul-de-sac, ad nauseum, southpaw, ensemble, and sayonara.* Have a partner figure out which of the words fits in the sentence. If it is not clear, you may have to rewrite the sentence with better context clues.

Activity Prepare a note card like the following for each of these words: *arsenal, garage, précis, déjà vu, caveat, klutz.* Look up each word in a dictionary and write its pronunciation. Then, write the meaning of the word in its original language. Next, write the meaning of the word in English. Finally, write a sentence using the word correctly in English.

Word:

Pronunciation:

Definition in language of origin:

Definition in English:

Sentence:

PHLit Online!
www.PHLitOnline.com
- Illustrated vocabulary words
- Interactive vocabulary games
- Vocabulary flashcards

Differentiated Instruction for Universal Access

Enrichment for Advanced Students

Provide advanced students with etymology dictionaries and/or lists of reliable etymology Web sites. Have each student research the etymology of three words. At the top of a poster, students should write a sentence using all three words. Beneath the sentence, have students create timelines showing the words' etymology, with the origin of each word at the bottom and its current meaning at the top, beneath the sentence. Display students' posters in the classroom.

EL Strategy for English Learners

Have English language learners brainstorm for words in English that are borrowed from their native languages and words in their native languages that are borrowed from English. Have them create posters showing the meanings of the words in both languages, with sample sentences. Display students' posters in the classroom.

Answers

Practice B
Sample Answers

1. My brother had carte blanche to visit the millionaire whenever he wanted to.
2. The ugly gargoyle sitting on the roof was grotesque.
3. After many years, Trudy found her niche as a fashion designer.
4. When they first immigrated to the United States, all of the Polish people lived in the ghetto.
5. The strangers fell in love prima facie.
6. The people on a soccer team have their own clique.
7. Rafael had a discussion about his future vis-à-vis his guidance counselor.
8. That style of skirt from the 1990s is passé.
9. Please, slow down the tempo of that song or I will not be able to sing along with you.
10. By taking a bite of the salad before the hostess was served, Tiffany made a serious faux pas.

Activity

For this activity, you may wish to review pronunciation symbols with students. Then, provide each student with six cards and a dictionary and/or a list of reliable dictionary Web sites.

Sample answer:
Word: caveat
Pronunciation: kav-ee-aht
Definition in language of origin: "let him beware"
Definition in English: a caution
Sentence: My recommendation includes a caveat—he snores.

Challenge

Provide students with dictionaries and/or lists of reliable dictionary Web sites, and assign partners. Have students write their sentences and then trade papers with their partners and write the correct word beside each of their partners' sentences. If a sentence is unclear, students should ask their partners to revise it.

Sample answer:
Cul-de-sac: There isn't much traffic on my dead-end street.

Meeting Your Standards

Students will

1. prepare the content of a multimedia presentation of a research report.
2. prepare a multimedia presentation by rehearsing, double-checking equipment, and creating a backup plan.
3. present the multimedia presentation and receive feedback.

Introducing Multimedia Presentations

Introduce the assignment and the strategies, using the instruction on the student page.

Prepare the Content

1. Tell students that it is important to put themselves in the position of their audience when they are preparing a multimedia presentation. They need to identify what the audience needs and wants to know. Ask students to consider the following questions: What is the purpose of the presentation? What information addresses that purpose? How can the purpose best be accomplished?
2. Explain that students must assess the images they select. Are they clear? Do they help to explain or to clarify the presentation?

Preparing Your Delivery

1. Plan to have all media resources present in the classroom a day or so prior to the scheduled presentations. Allow students time to practice using the media within the classroom setting.
2. Do not plan too many presentations for the same day, as students will need preparation time before each presentation and clean-up time at the end of each presentation.
3. Suggest that students actually rehearse once using their backup plans. If the media fails, will the presentation continue? What alterations will they need to make in the presentation?

Assess the Activity

Use the Feedback Form for a Multimedia Presentation to evaluate the multimedia presentations.

Communications Workshop

Delivering a Multimedia Presentation

Transform your research report into a **multimedia presentation** by adding sounds and visuals that create drama and interest for an audience. A successful multimedia presentation offers clear ideas and information about a topic using a variety of supporting media such as images, music, charts, graphs, or video clips.

Prepare the Content

Consider your topic, audience, and available media and equipment when choosing which media to use.

- Using an outline of your report, decide which parts can be presented effectively using visuals or sounds throughout your presentation.
- Choose media that suits your topic. For example, you might play music of a time period appropriate to your report as a soundtrack.
- Make sure any media and technology you choose is used ethically. Identify persuasive techniques that are used. Consult copyright notices and cite your sources to avoid plagiarism.
- Verify that all visual images can be seen by the entire audience. Photocopy and enlarge small images to show them effectively.

Prepare Your Delivery

To smoothly integrate words, sounds, and images in your presentation, you must practice it.

- Double-check your equipment to make sure that everything is in working condition and properly connected.
- Have a backup plan in case your equipment fails. Prepare copies of illustrations or graphic organizers to hand out.
- Do not read your research report word for word. Instead, talk to your audience, articulating your ideas with energy. To make sure you stay on track, refer to your notes each time you shift to a new idea.

Activity: Share a Multimedia Presentation

Prepare and practice a media presentation to share research that you have done. Make sure that your media choices do not detract from your topic. Ask your listeners to use the Feedback Form to evaluate your presentation.

Feedback Form for a Multimedia Presentation

Rating System

Poor				Excellent
1	2	3	4	5

Content

___ Clearly expressed ideas
___ Media that illustrates ideas
___ Use of varied media
___ Effective pacing of media use

Presentation

___ Equipment functioning
___ Smooth delivery
___ Media visible and audible
___ Media supports topic without overwhelming it

Differentiated Instruction for Universal Access

EL Strategy for English Learners

For students who struggle with the English language, adding the element of media to their presentations may prove especially challenging. Meet with each student during the planning phase of the presentations to help the student limit the number of media he or she plans to include. Explain that the limited but effective use of media will help students deliver moving presentations.

Enrichment for Gifted and Talented Students

Students may wish to attempt a more challenging project. Suggest that if they have available equipment and materials, they could create presentations that include video clips or media presentations that incorporate text, music, sound, and pictures. Point out that their presentations must still meet the expectations outlined on the feedback form. Suggest before they begin planning their actual productions that they explain how they plan to meet these expectations.

Independent Reading

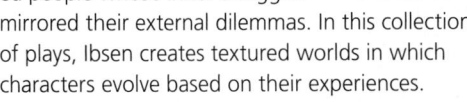

To what extent does *experience* determine what we *perceive?*

Ibsen: Four Major Plays

Henrik Ibsen
Signet, 1965

In a style that was innovative for its time, Ibsen's work showed men and women as they were: conflicted people whose inner struggles mirrored their external dilemmas. In this collection of plays, Ibsen creates textured worlds in which characters evolve based on their experiences.

The Prince and The Pauper

Mark Twain
Penguin Books, 1997

In this novel, a poor boy, Tom Canty, exchanges clothes and identities with Edward Tudor, the prince of England. The sixteenth-century royal court and the crowded boisterous London streets spring to life in this adventure story. As you read, determine whether people are able to perceive the differences between the two boys.

A Raisin in the Sun

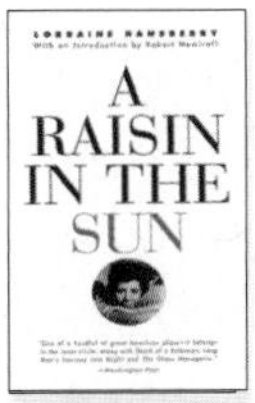

Lorraine Hansberry
Vintage Books, 1994

What would you do if you received a check for $10,000 in the mail? This is the challenge the Younger family must confront. In Hansberry's play, African American family members clash over their perceptions of success and what this $10,000 should mean for them.

Short Dramas and Teleplays

Prentice Hall, 2000

This collection of short plays entertains with a variety of tales from different authors and times. Whether you are in the mood for the classic story of *Oliver Twist*, or a modern play called *The Fast Food Fiasco,* you're sure to find something in this vast sampling of drama that reminds you of some of your own experiences.

Romeo and Juliet: An Adapted Classic

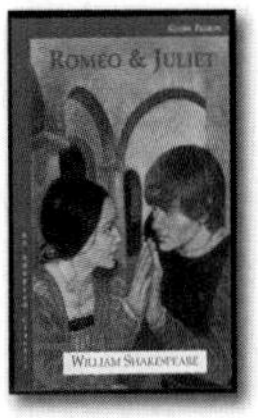

William Shakespeare
Globe Fearon, 1996

Two teenagers from feuding families discover love in this timeless tale. Swept up in a torrent of passion, the lovers make choices that change their own perceptions about life and love. Experience this classic play for yourself.

Consult your teacher before choosing a title.

Planning Students' Further Reading

Have students choose a book for independent reading from those listed on the student page. Before recommending a work to students, preview it, taking into account the values of your community as well as the maturity of your students. The following notes offer some guidance for the titles on the student page. Because a variety of factors play a role in determining the accessibility of a work, a book with a higher readability rating may be deemed more accessible than a book with a lower rating.

L4 ***Ibsen: Four Major Plays*** All of the plays contain marital situations that some may find offensive. In *A Doll House,* the wife walks out on the husband, leaving her children behind. In *The Wild Duck,* a past affair may have produced an illegitimate child. In *Hedda Gabler,* two of the characters seem to be carrying on an adulterous relationship. The main character kills herself at the end of the play. The main character in *The Master Builder,* who is married, seems to have an interest in two young women and may have had improper relations with one when she was underage. In addition, characters in *The Wild Duck* and *The Master Builder* drink excessively.

L3 ***The Prince and the Pauper*** The novel describes the violent behavior of Tom Canty's drunken father, who beats his children and physically attacks anyone who challenges him. **Lexile:** 1160L

L2 ***A Raisin in the Sun*** Students may take issue with Walter's drinking and his desire to own a liquor store. Mama's religion may offend some students. Some students may be upset at the suggestion that Ruth is considering an abortion. The play contains profanity and racial slurs.

L3 ***Short Dramas and Teleplays*** Students may be disturbed by the family conflict in *A Triumph of Wits,* the oppression of women in *M.D. in Petticoats,* the racism in *Barbara Jordan: Texas Treasure,* the violence of war in *The Red Badge of Courage,* and the terminal illness in *Brian's Song.*

L1 ***Romeo and Juliet*** *Romeo and Juliet* features a feud that leads to street violence, very young protagonists who marry without their families' knowledge, some sexual stereotyping, three killings, and two suicides.

Connecting to the Big Question

Have students form literature circles in which to discuss the books they read independently. See ***Professional Development Guidebook***, pp. 47–49, for guidance in running literature circles.

Suggest that students discuss these questions:

- What is the background, or experience, of the main character?
- How does the background of the main character differ from the reader's background?
- Does the reader perceive events differently than the main character? Why?

Challenge

The following titles for advanced readers are available in the Penguin Literature Library.

***The Portrait of a Lady* by James Joyce** This book contains offensive language, a main character's obsession with sex, religious arguments, and rejection of religion.

***The Bluest Eye* by Toni Morrison** The novel contains explicit sex, sexuality and profanity. Issues of incest, voyeurism, pedophilia, alcoholism, spousal abuse, prostitution, blasphemy, and racism are evident.

MONITORING PROGRESS

Using the Unit Review

In this Test Practice workshop (pp. 1038–1043), students apply the skills in Unit 5. The practice is divided into four sections.

1. Before assigning each section, review the relevant Unit skills with students.
2. Set a time limit for the multiple choice items in each section, allowing a little over one minute per question. Allow ten to fifteen minutes for any Writing for Assessment questions.
3. Administer each section. Have students write the starting time at the top of their papers. When half the time for the multiple choice items has run out, ask students to write the time next to an answer on which they are working. Have them do the same when time is three quarters through and again when time is up. Have them note the start and end times for any Writing for Assessment questions as well.
4. Review with students the pacing reflected in their notes.

Reteaching Skills

1. For each practice, use the Reteach chart on the same page as the answers to determine which skills require reteaching, based on which items students answered incorrectly.
2. Reteach these skills prior to assigning the **Benchmark Test** for the second half of Unit 5 (***Unit 5 Resources***, pp. 206–214).

Test Practice: Unit 5 Review

I. Literary Skills

Directions: *Read the passage. Then, answer each question that follows.*

Scene: The king's bedchamber. The king lies asleep in his bed.
[*Enter:* a ghost dressed in kingly robes]

[Ghost stands looking down on the sleeping king.]

Ghost. *[in a hoarse, rasping, heavy whisper]* Arise! Arise! The hour has struck
midnight. The new day is upon us.

[King awakens; looks at the Ghost with horror.]

King. What is this! What are you?
Ghost. You know me well.
King. No, I do not know you! *[The King turns away.]*
You are a figment of my mind, a black and horrible nightmare.
Ghost. Then look on this!

[The Ghost tears open his shirt, revealing a deep gash in his chest]

Know you now? This is your handiwork!
King. God save us! Is this Leopold?
Ghost. Ay. Your king, to whom you have sworn <u>fealty</u>,
And whose life and crown you robbed.
King. No, it was not I!
We have found the murderer and sent him to hell!
Ghost. You lie! Another bore the knife, but your gold was in his purse.
You bought my throne with murder and with gold!
Now you try to wash your hands of blood.

[The Ghost glides closer to the King and reaches out his bloody hand.

King. *[King recoils in horror.]* No! No! It was not I, I say!
Ghost. The time has come to answer for your lies.
The dawn is near, but you'll not see another sun arise.
King. No, no! *[King clutches his chest, falls to the floor dead.]*

[Ghost dissolves into mist, just as sunrise appears through the window.]

Strategies for Test Taking

Remind students to pace themselves when taking the test. Point out that they will need to ensure that they have adequate for writing questions, which take longer than multiple-choice items. Review the steps in responding to a writing question: analyze the prompt; develop their ideas; organize their response; write the assignment; and review their written response to fix any problems with spelling, grammar, or punctuation. Suggest that they double space their writing so they can use the additional line to make needed corrections or adjustments.

1. Which is the best statement of the **external conflict** between the King and the ghost of Leopold?
   - **A.** The Ghost is angry that he is no longer king and wants to destroy the King.
   - **B.** The new king had Leopold murdered, and the Ghost wants revenge.
   - **C.** The Ghost is angry because the new king does not fear him.
   - **D.** The King has been a poor leader, and the Ghost wants him replaced.

2. What is the Ghost's **motivation** for appearing to the King?
   - **A.** to announce his anger
   - **B.** to seek revenge
   - **C.** to regain his power
   - **D.** to frighten the King

3. The author has the Ghost speak in **blank verse** to show that—
   - **A.** the Ghost is from the upper class.
   - **B.** the King should not trust the Ghost.
   - **C.** the Ghost was murdered during his life.
   - **D.** the King might doubt what the Ghost says.

4. **Vocabulary in Context** Which of the following is the closest definition of the underlined word *fealty*?
   - **A.** jealousy
   - **B.** laughter
   - **C.** feudalism
   - **D.** faithfulness

5. Based on lines 15–16, what is the King's **internal conflict**?
   - **A.** He enjoys being the king too much.
   - **B.** He fears his kingdom will go to war.
   - **C.** He suffers guilt for having Leopold murdered.
   - **D.** He wants to have more power.

6. Which of the following **universal themes** is represented in this passage?
   - **A.** the loyalty of friends
   - **B.** the desire for power
   - **C.** the fear of death
   - **D.** the need for love

7. In a **Shakespearean tragedy,** the murdering King might represent which of the following?
   - **A.** the tragic hero
   - **B.** the antagonist
   - **C.** the foil
   - **D.** the supporting character

8. Which line represents the **climax** of the passage?
   - **A.** line 9
   - **B.** line 14
   - **C.** line 16
   - **D.** line 20

9. What is the *most important information* that the **dialogue** in lines 4–11 reveals?
   - **A.** The Ghost and the King are enemies.
   - **B.** The King murdered Leopold to gain power.
   - **C.** The King was the brother of Leopold.
   - **D.** The Ghost was King Leopold in life.

Writing for Assessment

10. In a developed paragraph, **describe** the character of the King. **Explain** what you think motivated him, and how he related to King Leopold before Leopold's murder. **Support** your answer with details from the passage.

GO ON

Answers

Answers With Explanations

1. **B**—The Ghost blames the new king for his murder and wants revenge. *Incorrect answers:* A—This summary leaves out the King's role in Leopold's murder. C—Revenge, not absence of fear, is the Ghost's motivation. D—The Ghost does not care about how effective the King has been.
2. **B**—The Ghost reveals his desire for revenge in line 18. *Incorrect answers:* A—The Ghost wants more than simply to tell the King of his anger. C—The Ghost knows that, since he is dead, he cannot rule again. D—The Ghost wants to punish the King with death.
3. **A**—Using blank verse for upper class speakers is a characteristic of Shakespearean drama. *Incorrect answers:* B—Verse form shows a character's station in life, not character. C—The King, not yet dead, also speaks in blank verse. D—same explanation as for B.
4. **D**—The Ghost complains that the King broke a debt of loyalty. *Incorrect answers:* A—Jealousy is not at issue in this passage. B—The scene has nothing comic. C—*Feudalism* was a social system, not the bond underlying it.
5. **C**—The King feels guilty. *Incorrect answers:* A—Enjoyment is not a conflict. B—The issue of war is never addressed. D—The King probably killed Leopold to gain power, but there is no suggestion of desire for further power.
6. **A**—The Ghost frames the King's crime as a failure of loyalty. *Incorrect answers:* B—The passage suggests that loyalty is the key issue. C—It is the King's actions in life that are the focus of the passage. D—Love has no role in this passage.
7. **A**—Shakespeare made his protagonists complex and gave them tragic flaws. *Incorrect answers:* B—The King would probably be the focus of the play. C—same explanation as for B. D—same explanation as for B.
8. **B**—This line brings the piece to its greatest emotional intensity. *Incorrect answers:* A—This recognition line is part of the crisis.

Answers continued

C—This line represents the falling action.
D—This line represents the catastrophe.

9. **B**—This passage reveals the murder. *Incorrect answers:* A—The point of the passage is why they now oppose each other. C—There was no family relationship. D—They are two separate individuals.

Writing for Assessment

10. Students' paragraphs should analyze the character of the king, reaching back into the time before the murder, and using evidence from the scene in support.

Reteach

Question	Instructional Pages to Reteach
1	965
2	1014
3	915
5	965
6	868
7	985
8	887
9	965
10	985

ASSESS

Answers

Answers With Explanations

1. **C**—The exhibit takes a broad view of both Asian and Western drama. *Incorrect answers:* A—The exhibit is about drama over time, not the Renaissance alone. C—The exhibit is unlikely to have much detail one playwright. D—The exhibit is not about architecture.
2. **C**—Items representing Japan's kabuki theater would be in the Asian hall. *Incorrect answers:* A—This issue would be covered in Hall Two, as part of western drama. C—same explanation as for A. D—same explanation as for A.
3. **A**—The sign would guide visitors to the halls. *Incorrect answers:* B—Such a graph would not be of interest to visitors. C—Images reflecting this medium do not belong on the sign. D—same explanation as for C.
4. **B**—The term is defined in the sentence in which it appears. *Incorrect answers:* A—The word does not refer to study of Chronos. C—Chronology refers to the proper sequencing of events. D—same explanation as for C.
5. **A**—The text establishes the importance of character to western drama and tradition to Asian drama. *Incorrect answers:* B—Both kinds of drama have ancient roots. C—Western drama, not Asian drama, developed out of mythology. D—Western drama does emphasize characters, but Asian drama does not use chronology.
6. **A**—Both kinds developed to promote values. *Incorrect answers:* B—The discussion of higher purposes to drama suggest that they did not aim for mere entertainment. C—The ruling class does not appear in either account. D—The sign pays no attention to performers.

Reteach

Question	Instructional Pages to Reteach
1	864
2	864
3	864
4	—
5	864
6	864

II. Informational Reading Skills

Directions: *Read the copy below from an informational sign. Then, answer each question that follows.*

Welcome to the Exhibit on the Origins of World Theater!
This **exhibit** presents the costumes, sets, staging, and music of some of the world's greatest drama from Asian and Western cultures. The **art of drama** ranges from the kabuki theater in Japan to the English plays of Shakespeare, from the Javanese puppet plays to the modern social drama. This sign can help you decide where to begin.

Hall One
Asian Drama Asian theater's roots are the classical theater of Hindu India, which influenced theater in Burma, Thailand, Java, Bali, Japan, and China. Asian theater does not focus on individual authors or on advancing drama as an art form, as in the West. Classical Asian theater is nonrealistic and does not emphasize chronology, or tell stories in time order. The actors used stylized performances that developed over time into formalized traditions of high sophistication and visual beauty. To learn more, visit Hall One.

Hall Two
Western Drama From its beginnings in ancient Greece, Western drama originated as community ritual meant to celebrate myth and affirm the moral beliefs of the time. Much of the aspect of the ritual was lost with Roman theater, with the development of individual characters. The idea of religious ritual resurfaced in the Middle Ages with the mystery plays, meant to impart values to the audience. Western drama became more realistic over the centuries and reached a high level of sophistication in character and plot by the Renaissance. To learn more, visit Hall Two.

1. Based on this informational sign, which research topics might be covered in this exhibit?
   A. how the Renaissance was a flowering of art
   B. the themes of Oscar Wilde's plays
   C. how Western drama developed
   D. the artistry of Roman architecture
2. In Hall One, you would most likely see—
   A. a display of a play about medieval values
   B. an actor giving a soliloquy
   C. a costume of a kabuki actor
   D. an image of a Roman amphitheater
3. What visual aid might you find on this sign?
   A. a map to help you locate the halls
   B. a graph reflecting the number of visitors
   C. an illustration of a soap opera star
   D. a timeline of early film history
4. **Vocabulary in Context** What is the best definition of the underlined word *chronology*?
   A. the study of the Greek god Chronos
   B. the sequence of events in time
   C. the study of time
   D. the history of events

Differentiated Instruction for Universal Access

Strategy for Less Proficient Readers
Review skills and warm up for the test by walking students through item 1. Ask a volunteer to read item 1 aloud. Call on students to state the key requirements for a correct answer. (The answer should fit into the topic and scope of the exhibit.) Next, guide students in eliminating incorrect choices.

- **A**—This option focuses on one period of western cultural history and does not address drama. (Eliminate.)
- **B**—This option focuses on one playwright, but the exhibit covers more than two thousand years. (Eliminate.)
- **C**—This option addresses the content of the exhibit—changes in western drama over time.
- **D**—This option addresses a completely separate art form. (Eliminate.)

Guide students in seeing that **C** is the best choice. Have them complete the remaining items, encouraging them to apply a similar strategy to each. First, define key terms in the prompt and then eliminate incorrect choices.

5. What is one major difference between Asian drama and Western drama?

A. Western drama focuses on characters, while Asian drama focuses on tradition.
B. Asian drama spans a much greater period of time than does Western drama.
C. Western theater developed out of rituals, but Asian theater developed out of mythology.
D. Asian drama is presented chronologically, while Western drama focuses on characters.

6. Which of the following might be considered the primary reason for the development of drama in both Asian and Western cultures?

A. to bind the community together and reaffirm common beliefs
B. as a source of entertainment for the people
C. to preserve the power of the ruling class
D. as a way to display the talents of the performers and serve as their source of income

III. Vocabulary

Directions: *Choose the word that best completes each sentence.*

1. Themes that are ____ connect to all people.

A. individual
B. stereotypical
C. universal
D. biased

2. Jean's ____ of the poem is right on target.

A. interpretation
B. distortion
C. perspective
D. anticipation

3. As Clare was raised in another country, she has a unique____ on life in America.

A. impression
B. perspective
C. stereotype
D. distortion

4. The new player on our team was even better than our ____ .

A. knowledge
B. expectations
C. background
D. bias

5. The judge's fair decision was free of ____ .

A. insights
B. stereotypes
C. bias
D. knowledge

6. We often hold a ____ view of distant cultures.

A. stereotyped
B. manipulated
C. individual
D. anticipated

7. The criminal tried to ____ the evidence to make him look innocent.

A. identify
B. manipulate
C. anticipate
D. stereotype

8. His deliberate ____ of the truth amounted to outright lying.

A. impression
B. stereotype
C. interpretation
D. distortion

GO ON

Reteach

Question	Instructional Pages to Reteach
1	790–791
2	790–791
3	790–791
5	790–791
6	790–791
7	790–791
8	790–791

Answers continued

7. **B**—A criminal would certainly try to present the evidence in a favorable way. *Incorrect answers:* A—Criminals tend to try to hide, rather than identify, evidence. C—In a trial, a criminal might anticipate the introduction of evidence, but not the evidence itself. D—A criminal might try to label evidence, but would not stereotype it.

8. **D**—Distorting the truth is lying. *Incorrect answers:* A—Having an impression of the truth would probably lead one to speak the truth. B—The truth cannot be stereotyped. C—Interpreting the truth is unlikely to lead to lying.

Answers

Answers With Explanations

1. **C**—Something universal applies to everyone. *Incorrect answers:* A—Individual themes would be idiosyncratic and not appeal to everyone. B—Stereotypes do not appeal to everyone. D—Many people would connect with something biased.

2. **A**—Since poems have indirect language, readers must interpret them. *Incorrect answers:* B—Something distorted is not on target. C—A perspective cannot be on or off target. D—Anticipation of reading or hearing a poem cannot be right or wrong.

3. **B**—The sentence refers to Clare's special point of view. *Incorrect answers:* A—Clare probably has more than one impression on America. C—. D—Clare might have a "stereotype of" America, but she would not have a stereotype "on" it.

4. **B**—The other players' prior ideas, or expectations, were shown incorrect by the new player's performance. *Incorrect answers:* A—The team had no knowledge of the new player beforehand. C—It is not the team's experience that were proven wrong, but what they expected from the new one. D—The sentence does not suggest that bias was involved.

5. **C**—Fair decisions are free of bias. *Incorrect answers:* A—That the decision was fair suggests a positive evaluation; being "free of insights" is a negative one. C—A decision does not have stereotypes, although a person might. D—A judge without knowledge is unlikely to make fair decisions.

6. **A**—People often have stereotypes about things they do not know. *Incorrect answers:* B—The context does not establish that anyone caused the view to be developed. C—With little information to go on, people viewing a different culture tend to think as others of do, not as individuals. D—People can hold views of other cultures without looking forward to contact with them.

ASSESS

Answers

Answers With Explanations

1. **A**—The author seems to be describing a day that awakened passion for the theater. *Incorrect answers:* B—As the passage is about theater, this sentence is inappropriate. C—The author clearly does enjoy the theater. D—Something expressing the author's own positive feelings is more appropriate.
2. **B**—The adverb is needed to fix the clause in time. *Incorrect answers:* A—The comma is acceptable after an introductory subordinate clause. C—As the sentence is set in the past, the tense is correct. D—A change is needed, as explained in the answer to B.
3. **D**—This version shows that the two actions took place at the same time. *Incorrect answers:* A—The dimming of the house lights was not conditional on the brightening of stage lights. B—The use of "Why" makes the sentence incoherent. C—The use of that to introduce an adjectival clause is incorrect; an adverbial clause is needed.
4. **C**—The author's affection for one type of film is irrelevant. *Incorrect answers:* A—Sentence 1 is needed to set the scene. B—Sentence 3 gives useful details. D—Sentence 15 describes the emotional impact of the event.
5. **B**—This addition would clarify what was smelled. *Incorrect answers:* A—This addition would simply be wordy. C—same explanation as for A. D—same explanation as for A.
6. **A**—The revised version clarifies who was doing what and in what sequence. *Incorrect answers:* B—The play did not stand. C—The play did not applaud. D—same explanations as for B and C.

Reteach

Question	Instructional Pages to Reteach
1	1027
2	860
3	860
4	880
5	880
6	880

V. Writing and Language Conventions

Narration: Reflective Essay

Directions: *Read the passage. Then, answer each question that follows.*

(1) But I was ten years old, my mother took me to a live theater performance for the first time. (2) I knew I would be bored. (3) As we filed into the theater and took our seats, I noticed no one was eating popcorn or candy. (4) This was not the movies or even TV! (5) I love horror movies! (6) The houselights dimmed. (7) The stage lights brightened at the same time. (8) Everyone became perfectly silent. (9) I was astonished as the characters began to speak. (10) I could have reached out and touched them. (11) I could see and almost *feel* the texture of their clothing, smell the stage. (12) This was real! (13) I could feel the sadness ripple through the audience when the hero died! (14) Applauding in unison, the play ended, everyone stood. (15) I felt part of it all.

1. Which statement should be added to the end of this passage to best express the writer's **main insight?**

A. To this day, I love live theater.
B. Horror movies are the best.
C. Some people enjoy live theater, but I do not.
D. Theater is not for everyone.

2. In what way should the **subordinate clause** in sentence 1 be revised?

A. Remove the comma.
B. Replace "but" with "when."
C. Replace "was" with "will be."
D. Leave as is.

3. Which of the following is the *best* use of **independent and subordinate clauses** to combine sentence 6 with sentence 7?

A. The houselights dimmed unless the stage lights brightened.
B. Why the houselights dimmed, the stage lights brightened.
C. The houselights dimmed that the stage lights brightened.
D. While the houselights dimmed, the stage lights brightened.

4. Which sentence should be removed so this passage has unity?

A. sentence 1
B. sentence 3
C. sentence 5
D. sentence 15

5. To incorporate more descriptive **sensory details** in sentence 11, add—

A. "touch and" before "texture."
B. "the faintly dusty odor of" after "smell."
C. "new costumes or" before "their clothing."
D. "and touch" after "I could see."

6. How should sentence 14 be revised for clarity?

A. As the play ended, everyone stood, applauding in unison.
B. Standing, the play ended, and everyone applauded in unison.
C. The play ended by applauding in unison, and everyone stood.
D. When the play stood and applauded, we ended the play.

Differentiated Instruction for Universal Access

Strategy for for English Learners

Students may benefit from practicing strategies of identifying the correct answer by eliminating incorrect ones. Ask a volunteer to read item 4 aloud. Call on students to define the term *unity*. (Every sentence in the passage belongs.) Next, guide students in eliminating incorrect choices.

- **A**—The sentence gives important information; it belongs in the passage and cannot be cut. (Eliminate.)
- **B**—The sentence describes an action that took place; it belongs in the passage and cannot be cut. (Eliminate.)
- **C**—The sentence does not describe what happened that day; it does not belong in the passage.
- **D**—The sentence describes how the experience affected the author; it cannot be cut. (Eliminate.)

Guide students in seeing that **C** is the best choice. Have them complete the remaining items, encouraging them to apply a similar strategy to each. Suggest that students physically cross off the incorrect choices as they are revealed.

Research Writing: Research Report

Directions: *Read the passage. Then, answer each question that follows.*

(1) After two thousand years, the name *Gaius Julius Caesar* is still famous for good reason. (2) Being famous could be fun. (3) Caesar was a man of extraordinary talents, accomplished in many areas. (4) Caesar's military genius is best known by his conquest of Gaul. (5) His military campaigns might be summed up in his own words: *Veni, vidi, vici* (I came, I saw, I conquered). (Suetonius, p. 88) (6) Caesar was a talented orator. (7) His speaking ability helped further his political career. (8) As his nobles assassinated him soon after this, we will never know what further greatness he could have achieved so we will always wonder. (9) Today, his family name *Caesar* has come to be a title indicating a ruler—*kaiser* in German, *tsar* in Russian. (10) We still organize our lives according to his (slightly modified) Julian calendar, and honor him with the month of July. (11) In 46 B.C., he became dictator of Rome and began a series of political and social reforms.

1. Which sentence should be removed because it does not support the writer's **thesis?**

A. sentence 1
B. sentence 2
C. sentence 4
D. sentence 9

2. Which **graphic aid** would be most appropriate for the writer to include with this brief essay?

A. a list of famous political assassinations
B. a map of Ancient Rome
C. a timeline of Caesar's achievements
D. a photograph of a Caesar salad

3. Which use of an **adverb clause** *best* combines sentences 5 and 6?

A. As Caesar was a talented orator, his speaking ability helped further his political career.
B. Though Caesar was a talented orator, his speaking ability helped further his career.
C. Caesar was a talented orator unless his speaking ability helped further his career.
D. Caesar was a talented orator, as long as his speaking ability helped forward his career.

4. What is the *best* way to revise sentence 8 for conciseness without changing its meaning?

A. Replace "nobles" with "men."
B. Remove "As his nobles assassinated him during this rule."
C. Remove "so we will always wonder."
D. Replace "assassinated" with "murdered."

5. Which change should be made to improve this passage's organization?

A. Reverse sentences 3 and 4.
B. Move sentence 7 before sentence 1.
C. Reverse sentences 8 and 9.
D. Move sentence 11 before sentence 8.

Writing for Assessment

6. Caesar's great abilities are known even today. Write a **reflective essay** describing one of your talents. Use **sensory details** to describe a moment in which your talents shone.

STOP

ASSESS

Answers

Answers With Explanations

1. **B**—The sentence is tangential to the passage. *Incorrect answers:* A—Sentence 1 is an effective introduction. C—Sentence 4 gives useful detail about Caesar. D—Sentence 9 adds useful detail about Caesar's fame.
2. **C**—The timeline is relevant. *Incorrect answers:* A—Such a list would stray beyond discussion of Caesar, which should be the focus. B—The map is not entirely useful because the passage focuses on Caesar, not Rome. D—This image would be completely tangential.
3. **A**—The subordinating conjunction as establishes the correct relationship between the two clauses. *Incorrect answers:* B—*Though* suggests "in spite of," but the appropriate relationship is "because of." C—His talent as a speaker contributed to his career. D—same explanation as for C.
4. **C**—These words give no additional meaning to the passage. *Incorrect answers:* A—The replacement does nothing for conciseness and sacrifices precision. B—The removal would lose important information. D—same explanation as for A.
5. **D**—This move would fix the chronology of the passage. Incorrect answers: A—The order of these sentences is logical. B—This movement would harm coherence. C—same explanation as for A.

Writing for Assessment

6. Students' essays should focus on one of their talents and employ sensory details. They might use an outline or web to organize their ideas.

Benchmark

Reteach skills as indicated by students' performance, following the Reteach charts on pp. 1039–1043 to administer the end-of-unit **Benchmark Test** (***Unit 5 Resources,*** pp. 206–214). Follow the **Interpretation Guide** for the test (***Unit 5 Resources,*** pp. 218–223) to assign reteaching pages as necessary in the ***Reading Kit.*** Use **Success Tracker** online to automatically assign these pages.

Reteach

Question	Instructional Pages to Reteach
1	1025
2	1023
3	1027
4	1025
5	1023
6	878–880

PHLit Online!

The **Benchmark Tests** and **Success Tracker** are available online at **www.PHLitOnline.com**

Unit 6 Overview

Unit Genre and Unit Big Question

Explain to students that throughout this unit, they will read and analyze themes in the oral tradition. As they read, they will think about and discuss answers to the Unit Big Question: Can anyone be a hero?

Students will learn more about the Big Question on pp. 1046–1047. Then, on pp. 1048–1061, John Phillip Santos introduces the unit literary form, themes in the oral tradition, and presents a model memoir of his own.

Using the Unit Selections

Teach Skills Instructional selections are presented in leveled pairs. To teach the skills and meet the objectives, you need to complete only one selection in each pairing.

Differentiate and Reinforce Choose the selection in a pairing that is best suited for your students. The selections are listed by accessibility in the Differentiated Instruction box on the next page. You may use the other selection in the pairing to reinforce comprehension and skills or to provide enrichment.

Integrate Skills Each selection pairing presents students with a reading strategy, a literary analysis concept, and a vocabulary skill, as well as vocabulary development opportunities and grammar instruction. In addition, students have opportunities to extend learning in the Writing and extension (Research and Technology or Listening and Speaking) activities.

Unit Features

Informational Texts Students learn to use and evaluate various types of informational texts.

Comparing Literary Works Students compare the use of a literary element in two or more works.

To help you plan your use of the unit, see the Unit Overview and Pacing Plan on pp. 1046a–1046b and the Time and Resource Manager preceding each selection pairing.

Themes in Literature: Heroes and

THE BIG ? Can anyone be a *hero?*

PHLit Online! www.PHLitOnline.com

Teaching from Technology

Enriched Online Student Edition
- full narration of selections
- interactive graphic organizers
- linked Get Connected! and Background videos
- all worksheets and other student resources

Professional Development
- the *Professional Development Guidebook* online
- additional professional development articles by program authors

Planning, Assigning, and Monitoring
- software for online assignment of work to students, individually or to the whole class
- a system for tracking and grading students' work

Dreamers

UNIT 6

PHLit Online!
www.PHLitOnline.com

Hear It!
- Selection summary audio
- Selection audio
- BQ Tunes

See It!
- Penguin author video
- Big Question video
- Get Connected videos
- Background videos
- More about the authors
- Illustrated vocabulary words
- Vocabulary flashcards

Do It!
- Interactive journals
- Interactive graphic organizers
- Grammar tutorials
- Interactive vocabulary games
- Test practice

1045

Instructional Resources

Unit 6 Resources supports unit skills with pages of the following types:

- **Benchmark Tests** assess and monitor students' progress at mid-unit and at unit's end.
- **Vocabulary and Reading Warm-ups** provide additional vocabulary support, based on Lexile rankings of words, for each selection. "A" **Warm-ups** are for students reading two grades below level. "B" **Warm-ups** are for students reading one grade below level.
- **Selection Support** These practice pages are available for each selection:
  - **Reading Skill**
  - **Literary Analysis**
  - **Writing About the Big Question**
  - **Vocabulary**
  - **Support for Writing**
  - **Support for Extend Your Learning**
  - **Enrichment**

PHLit Online!
All worksheets and other student resources are also available at **www.PHLitOnline.com**.

Differentiated Instruction for Universal Access

Accessibility for Various Ability Levels
This chart gives a general accessibility rating to help you decide which selection in each leveled pair is more appropriate for your students. **Choose one selection in each pair or choose to teach both.** You will meet the objectives for the pair when you teach either of the two selections. For additional guidance on factors that affect the accessibility of each selection, see the Selection Choices page for each selection set.

Accessibility for English Learners
EL This icon indicates support for English learners at point of use in this Teacher's Edition.

	More Accessible	More Challenging
Pair 1	Prometheus and the First People	The Orphan Boy and the Elk Dog
Pair 2	*from* Sundiata	*from the* Ramayana
Pair 3	Arthur Becomes King of Britain	Morte d'Arthur
Pair 4	*from* a Connecticut Yankee in King Arthur's Court	*from* Don Quixote

UNIT OVERVIEW AND PACING PLAN

Meeting Your Standards

Students will

1. recognize and appreciate oral tradition as a literary form.
2. read and analyze a variety of genres in the oral tradition.
3. apply reading skills.
   - Analyze cultural context
   - Acquire background knowledge to understand the cultural context
   - Compare and contrast worldviews
4. analyze literary elements.
   - Myths
   - Epic and epic hero
   - Legends and legendary heroes
   - Parody
5. build vocabulary and vocabulary concepts.
   - Roots
   - Suffixes
   - Prefixes
   - Idioms, jargon, and technical terms
6. learn elements of grammar, mechanics, and usage.
   - Simple and compound sentences
   - Complex and compound-complex sentences
   - Correcting fragments and run-on sentences
   - Commas and dashes
   - Semicolons, colons, and ellipsis points
   - Vary sentence structure and length
7. use a recursive writing process to write in a variety of forms.
   - Technical document
   - Comparison-and-contrast essay
8. read informational materials.
   - Generate questions about an interview and a public document
   - Critique generalizations and evidence in a book review and a movie review
9. compare literary works.
   - Compare archetypal narrative patterns
   - Compare themes and worldviews
10. develop research and technology skills.
    - "Influences" chart
    - Biographical brochure
11. develop listening and speaking skills.
    - Interview
    - Retelling
    - Improvised dialogue
    - Compare media coverage

	Week 1					Week 2					Week 3				
	1	2	3	4	5	1	2	3	4	5	1	2	3	4	5
Introduce the Unit Big Question (pp. 1046–1047).	●														
Introduce the Unit author and the Unit form, oral tradition (pp 1048–1051).	●														
Teach the Model selections (pp. 1052–1061).	●	●													
Teach one selection from Pairing 1 (pp. 1062–1089).		●	●	●	●	●									
Teach one selection from Pairing 2 (pp. 1090–1119).						●	●	●	●						
Complete the Test Practice: Reading (pp. 1120–1121).									●						
Teach Informational Texts (pp. 1122–1127).										●					
Teach Comparing Literary Works (pp. 1128–1145).											●	●			
Have students complete the Writing Workshop (pp. 1146–1151).										●	●	●	●	●	
Administer **Benchmark Test 11** (***Unit 6 Resources,*** pp. 120–125).														●	
Reteach skills, judging which skills to reteach by evaluating students' performance on **Benchmark Test 11**.															●

	Week 4					Week 5					Week 6				
	1	2	3	4	5	1	2	3	4	5	1	2	3	4	5
Teach one selection from Pairing 3 (pp. 1152–1187).	●	●	●	●											
Teach one selection from Pairing 4 (pp. 1188–1219).					●	●	●	●							
Complete the Test-Practice: Reading (pp. 1220–1221).								●							
Teach Informational Texts (pp. 1222–1227).									●						
Teach Comparing Literary Works (pp. 1228–1241).										●	●				
Have students complete the Writing Workshop (pp. 1242–1249).									●	●	●	●	●		
Have students complete Applying the Big Question (pp. 1250–1251).												●			
Have students complete the Vocabulary and Communications Workshops (pp. 1252–1253, 1254).													●		
Complete the Test Practice: Unit 6 Review (pp. 1256–1261).													●		
Administer **Benchmark Test 12** (*Unit 6 Resources*, pp. 227–235).														●	
Reteach skills, judging which skills to reteach by evaluating students' performance on **Benchmark Test 12.**															●

Block and Daily Scheduling

The assignments and activities in this Unit planner are organized by week. You may adjust them to your daily or block schedule. The Time and Resource Manager for each selection set gives specific pacing suggestions, or you may use the comprehensive lesson planning support online at **www.PHLitOnline.com.**

Monitoring Progress

Diagnose Each main selection pairing in the Unit contains a more accessible and a more challenging selection. To determine which selection in each pairing to assign, refer to students' results on **Benchmark Test 10, *Unit 5 Resources,*** pp. 207–220 (administered at the end of the previous Unit). Use the **Interpretation Guide** to interpret the results of the diagnostic portion of the test. **Note:** For the most accurate diagnosis of students who score in the middle range, administer the additional diagnostic questions online at **www.PHLitOnline.com.**

Preteach and Prepare As indicated by the diagnostic, prepare students for reading by assigning the **Vocabulary** and **Reading Warm-ups** for the selections you assign.

Teach Follow this Pacing Plan and use the resources to teach the skills and selections. For specific pacing suggestions and a list of resources, see the Time and Resource Manager and the Visual Guide to Featured Selection Resources preceding each selection pairing.

Assess After students have completed the first half of the Unit, administer **Benchmark Test 7**. Administer **Benchmark Test 8** at the end of the Unit.

Intervention and Reteach After administering each test, use the **Interpretation Guide** for the tests to determine which reteaching pages, if any, you should assign from the ***Reading Kit.*** The appropriate pages are also available through the online Progress Monitoring software.

Independent Reading

To differentiate, reinforce, and extend your instruction, have students choose a full-length work from the Independent Reading page, page 1255, and read it while working on this Unit. Consult the Sensitivity Issues notes for the page to guide students' choices.

CLASSROOM STRATEGIES

A Strategy for Eliciting Thoughtful Writing about Literature **Sheridan Blau**

"Notice what you notice" is the advice we need to give to inexperienced readers.

Strong readers seem highly aware of the state of their own understanding as they read. They possess what reading researchers call "metacognitive awareness." They take steps to make sense of confusing or unclear parts of a text. Weak readers, on the other hand, exhibit little metacognitive awareness and little capacity for the focused attention often required to overcome the difficulties of a challenging text. It's as if weak readers don't expect to understand difficult texts and therefore pay little attention to what questions they might have or what they might need to do to answer their questions. We can see this in the classroom: After reading a selection, strong readers tend to have the most questions while the weakest readers don't have any.

The Importance of Noticing

All readers become stronger when they pay attention to their questions, observations and responses as they read. "Notice what you notice" is the advice we need to give to inexperienced readers. It is a way of encouraging readers to trust their own thinking and to recognize that their thinking is proper material for writing and sharing in a classroom. When students notice what they notice, and most especially notice what puzzles or confuses them, they are exhibiting metacognitive awareness.

Literature Logs: A Strategy for Writing To Learn

In literature logs, students write about their observations, responses, and questions as they read assigned literary texts. Literature logs can highlight asking questions and exploring possible solutions—questions that represent the hard intellectual work of articulating a problem or confusion felt by the reader.

Lit Logs as Low Stakes Writing. Lit logs free students to express their responses, explore their thinking, and ask their questions without having to come up with correct answers. Writing in lit logs gets students thinking about their reading. The topics and questions that students generate in lit logs are an excellent reservoir of first draft writing that might be expanded and revised into a more formal academic paper.

Lit Logs as Participation in an Academic Community. When students share their lit logs in small groups, the logs become a vehicle for students to participate in a discourse about literature that makes them active members of an academic community. Through such participation they will learn from each other how to participate more effectively.

Teaching Strategies for Lit Logs

Introducing Lit Logs

- Invite students to make lit log entries as they read or when they finish reading individual selections.
- Use your own lit log entries to model what you notice and show how you ask questions about confusing or inconsistent parts of a story. Point out that your confusion does not make you a poor reader but a good one—a reader who is paying attention and noticing when something isn't clear.
- Show the value of writing in a lit log. Emphasize how the questions raised in lit logs, when shared in class, yield especially rich topics for discussion.
- Have students share their log entries in groups of three, and then answer the following questions: What is a lit log and how do you write one?. What, for example, would students tell a new student in the class about how to write a log entry? The answer should address questions about style (voice, formality, language) about content (topics, questions, focus) and conventions (length, format). Ask groups to report their findings, and the look for common practices that have emerged in the class.

Keeping Lit Logs Going

- Read exemplary entries aloud, and comment on useful observations or fruitful questions. Use these entries as questions to explore further in class.
- If teachers want to grade these logs, they should grade them not as finished writing, but as thinking in progress. The grade should reward participation and intellectual honesty, not right answers or stylistic correctness.
- Use lit logs for a threaded discussion. Have students make a legible copy of a literature log entry on a work being studied by the whole class. Put students in groups of four, where they will pass their lit log entries around for all members of the group to read. The first reader must reply to the entry. The next two readers may reply to the original entry and/or to the previous replies. Ask students in each group to share some entries and replies with the entire class. Collect all papers to check on student participation, and to select some exemplary and instructive discussions to read to the class.

Modeled Strategy

See pp. 1167 and 1201 for point-of-use notes modeling these strategies.

Teacher Resources

- ***Professional Development Guidebook***
- ***Classroom Strategies and Teaching Routines* cards**

PHLit Online!

Log on as a teacher at **www.PHLitOnline.com** to access a library of all Professional Development articles by the Contributing Authors of Pearson Prentice Hall *Literature*.

Sheridan Blau

Sheridan Blau is Professor of English and Education at the University of California, Santa Barbara, where he directs the South Coast Writing Project and the Literature Institute for Teachers. A former President of the National Council of Teachers of English, he has published widely in the fields of seventeenth century literature, composition theory, professional development for teachers, and the teaching of composition and literature. His book, The Literature Workshop: Teaching Texts and Their Readers (Heinemann, 2003), won the Richard Meade Award for outstanding research in English education.

Supporting Research

Blau, Sheridan. 2003. *The Literature Workshop: Teaching Texts and Their Readers*. Portsmouth NH. Heinemann

Fort, Keith. 1971. "Form, Authority, and the Critical Essay." *College English* 32 (6): 629-639.

Hammond, Lynn. 1991. "Using Focused Freewriting to Promote Critical Thinking." In *Nothing Begins with N: New Investigations of Freewriting*, edited by Pat Belanoff, Peter Elbow, and Sheryl Fontaine. Carbondale: Southern Illinois University Press.

Wilson, Nancy. 1989. "Learning from Confusion; Questions and Change in Reading Logs." *English Journal* (Nov.) 62–69.

Zeiger, William. 1985. "The Exploratory Essay: Enfranchising the Spirit of Inquiry in College Composition." *College English* 47 (September), 454–466.

INTRODUCE

Introducing the Big Question

1. Give examples of legendary heroes such as Martin Luther King, Jr., and everyday heroes, such as firefighters.
2. Call on students to give their own examples and explain what their choices have in common. On the board, list students' heroes and attributes.
3. **Ask** students the Big Question: "Can anyone be a hero?" **Possible responses:** No, only exceptional people can be heroes. Yes, any good person can be a hero in a difficult situation.
4. Tell students that the stories in this unit explore heroism and what it takes to be a hero. As they read, have students consider whether or not the people featured have much in common.

Introducing the Big Question Vocabulary

1. Point out the Big Question Vocabulary on the facing page. Explain that these words are useful in discussing the Big Question.
2. Review the meaning of each word. (Definitions appear in the teacher edition on p. 1047.)
3. Have students complete the **Big Question Vocabulary** worksheets, *Unit 6 Resources*, pp. 1–3.

Write What You Know

1. Review the assignment with students, using the instruction on the student page.
2. Tell students that they may list hypothetical situations if they have difficulty thinking of specific people or characters. For example, they could list organ donors as people who make sacrifices.
3. Have students discuss which attributes they consider to be most important in judging heroes.

PHLit Online!

Show the Big Question video, online at **www.PHLitOnline.com.**

Introducing the Big Question

THE BIG Q

Can anyone be a *hero?*

A hero is someone who displays **attributes** such as **selflessness** and **courage** in order to help others. You may think of a hero as a noble figure such as a **legendary** knight from days gone by, who goes on dangerous quests, and is dedicated to his king. On the other hand, you might imagine a hero as an everyday person whose **character** is defined by **integrity** and **principles.** Such a person may perform small, often unnoticed acts of heroism out of an **inherent** desire to do the right thing. Even though there are different kinds of heroes, they all strive to act with **honor.**

Start thinking about the Big Question by identifying people you think are heroes.

Discuss It

Write What You Know

Make a list of the different people you have known, heard about, or read about that can be considered heroes. Describe one specific example of each of the following types of heroes:

- a legendary or mythical person who performs great deeds
- someone who helps others on a daily basis
- a person who makes a personal **sacrifice** in order to help another person
- a courageous individual with a dangerous job
- a character in literature or a historical person whose **determination** led to great accomplishments

Share your responses with a partner. Talk about the heroic traits each example might demonstrate and decide which attributes are most important.

PHLit Online!

www.PHLitOnline.com

- Big Question video
- Illustrated vocabulary words
- Interactive vocabulary games
- BQ Tunes

Understanding by Design

The Big Question

Explain to students that they will continue to consider the Big Question as they work through the unit.

- At the beginning of each selection, they will write a response to a Writing About the Big Question sentence starter.
- As they read the selection, they will look for details related to the Big Question.
- At the end of the selection, they will answer a Critical Thinking question that is related to the Big Question.
- At the end of Unit 6, they will complete an Applying the Big Question workshop (pp. 1250–1251). In the workshop, they will review literature in the unit and think about real-world examples that shed light on the Big Question. They will also have a chance to reflect on their first answers, thinking about how their ideas have changed.
- Tell students that their goal will be to gain a deeper understanding of literature and a more sophisticated way of discussing the Big Question.

Discuss It

Explain What You Know

Use the examples and ideas you discussed with your partner to help you complete these sentences about heroes.

- Helping another person to __________ can be considered heroic because __________.
- One way a legendary hero may differ from an ordinary person who performs a heroic act is __________.
- Sometimes heroes reveal faults, such as __________. Heroes who show that they are human are interesting because __________.

Share your responses with a partner.

Write About It

Tell What You Think

Based on the discussions you have had, decide what you think right now. Your answer may change as you read the selections in this unit. Choose one of these responses to the Big Question or write one of your own:

- ❑ Anyone can be a hero.
- ❑ Not everyone can be a hero.

Use one or more of these sentences, or your own ideas, to write a brief support of your response.

- A person can be a hero if __________.
- Heroes usually possess the qualities of __________, __________, and __________.
- Sometimes an unlikely person becomes a hero when __________.
- Behavior such as __________ might prevent someone from being considered a hero because __________.

Discuss your response with a partner or a small group.

Connecting to the Literature

The readings in this unit will help you think about heroes and the different ways heroes are defined. Each reading will give you an insight into the Big Question. At the end of the unit, you will see how your ideas have grown and changed.

☆ shows an **Academic Vocabulary** word.

Big Question Vocabulary

attributes
☆ character
☆ conduct
courage
determination
honor
☆ inherent
☆ integrity
legendary
persevere
☆ principles
☆ resolute
☆ responsibility
sacrifice
selflessness

Explain What You Know

1. Introduce the assignment, using the instruction on the student page.
2. Have students review their lists of model heroes in each category. As needed, review definitions of Big Question Vocabulary and clarify meanings.
3. Guide students to complete the sentence starters by thinking of relevant examples of each point. Have students share and compare their responses with partners.

Tell What You Think

1. Introduce the assignment. Have students review the discussion they had with their partners and think of the different points of view expressed. Then, have them mark their pages with their answers to the Big Question.
2. Guide students to write a paragraph to support their decisions. Encourage them to complete the sentence starters to help them write their opinions.
3. As students write, remind them to give examples from previous discussions or activities that support their points of view.
4. Call on volunteers to share their responses with the class.

Connecting to the Literature

Explain the structure of the Big Question strand in the unit, referring to the Understanding by Design box on the previous page.

Big Question Vocabulary

attributes (a′trə byo͞ot′) *n.* characteristics of a person or thing
character (kar′ik tər) *n.* moral strength or discipline
conduct (kän′dukt′) *n.* the way a person acts
courage (kur′ij) *n.* willingness to deal with something dangerous
determination (dē tur′ mi nā′ shən) *n.* firmness of purpose
honor (än′ ər) *n.* a strong sense of right and wrong
inherent (in hir′ənt) *adj.* existing naturally in something
integrity (in teg′rə tē) *n.* willingness to stand by moral principles
legendary (lej′ən der′ē) *adj.* extraordinary or memorable
persevere (pur′sə vir′) *v.* to continue despite opposition
principles (prin′sə pəls) *n.* rules for right conduct

Meeting Your Standards

Students will

1. understand how the themes have been developed in the oral tradition.
2. learn about author John Phillip Santos.
3. read and analyze a memoir.
4. relate visuals to the oral tradition.

❶ Can anyone be a hero?

Remind students that they will think more about the Unit Big Question as they read and discuss the themes in this Unit.

❷ What Is the Oral Tradition?

Introduce John Phillip Santos

1. A student of philosophy and literature, Santos draws upon his Mexican American heritage as inspiration for his writing. Ask students whether they are familiar with John Phillip Santos and his writing.
2. Use the *See It!* DVD to introduce the author, the literary genre, and the themes. Show Segments 2 and 3 to introduce Santos's view of the memoir. After students have watched the segments, **ask** them why Santos believes that the genre of memoir is important. **Answer:** Santos says that memoir is important because it opens up history, making it real and accessible.
3. Interested students might enjoy the work *Songs Older Than Any Known Singer* by John Phillip Santos.

Introduce Oral Tradition

Ask students how Santos connects personal mythology with ancient literary forms of the oral tradition. **Possible response:** Santos says that personal and family stories address the same questions that were explored in myths, epics, and legends.

Introduction: Themes in Literature

❶ **Can anyone be a *hero?***

Stories from different cultures explore what it means to be a hero.

❷ What Is the Oral Tradition?

by John Phillip Santos

When you write about your **personal mythology**—blending stories of your own with **oral traditions** handed down by word of mouth in your family—you're writing autobiography, yes, but you're also writing about some of the oldest themes and mysteries known to humans: Who are we? Where did we come from? Where are we going? Where do I fit into the story?

Since humans could first use language, we have been seeking answers to these questions and recording them in **myths, epics,** and **legends** told around campfires. We have also recorded our answers in written form, **poetry** and **prose,** to share with others, now and into the future

❸ Stories of Ancestors

I began looking for answers to these questions in stories of the people and the lands where my family came from—South Texas, Mexico, and Spain.

How much of who we are was handed down from those ancestors? What happened to their old gods? When did we embrace new ones?

I found clues to these mysteries in unexpected places, in food, in seemingly insignificant objects, documents, and photographs left behind by my ancestors, and in the tales that many of my elders told me.

❹ Every Life Contains a Story

I began reading authors from all over the world—Cervantes and Edmund Spenser, Jorge Luis Borges, and the Ugandan poet Okot p'Bitek. As diverse as their voices and tales might be, one common theme was emerging. All of them offered us their personal stories so we would delve more deeply into the mystery of what it is to be human.

This is not about telling stories of important people. It doesn't matter who you are. As Laura (Riding) Jackson suggests, every life contains a story waiting to be told. You can tell your own story in conversations with friends and family, in poems, fiction, or in non-fiction, but we're all waiting to hear your story, which is unlike any other, ever.

We tell these stories to come to know ourselves, but don't expect answers. In the great human mystery, there are plenty of clues but few solutions. In many ways, the deeper you go, the greater the mystery will become. That's the fun part.

PHLit Online!
www.PHLitOnline.com

- Penguin author video
- Interactive journals
- Interactive graphic organizers
- Selection audio
- Self-test

Teaching Resources

The following resources can be used to enrich, extend, or differentiate the instruction.

- All *Unit 6 Resources,* pp. 6–22
- All *Professional Development Guidebook,* p. 33
- All *See It!* DVD
  John Phillip Santos, Segments 1 and 2
- All *Graphic Organizer Transparencies,* pp. 191–192
- All **Enriched Online Student Edition**
- L2 L3 ***Reader's Notebook***
- EL ***Reader's Notebook: English Learner's Version***
- L2 EL ***Hear It!* Audio CD**
- L1 EL ***Hear It!* Audio CD** (adapted text)

PHLit Online! All resources, including print and video, are available online at **www.PHLitOnline.com.**

> "There is something to be told about us for the telling of which we all wait. . . . We know we are explainable, and not explained. . . . Until the missing story of ourselves is told, nothing besides told can suffice us: we shall go on quietly craving it."
>
> from *The Telling*
> —Laura (Riding) Jackson

Meet **John Phillip Santos** (b. 1957)

Author of *Places Left Unfinished at the Time of Creation*

John Phillip Santos is a filmmaker and journalist. He began his memoir, *Places Left Unfinished at the Time of Creation,* in order to solve the mystery of his grandfather's death.

In his book, Santos explores his Mexican American roots by moving back through time to the land his ancestors knew, to find the "hidden light left behind in the past." His memoir combines personal memories with ancient history and literary sources, suggesting the great and mysterious influence of the past.

Did You Know?

Santos was the first Mexican American to win a Rhodes scholarship to Oxford University in England.

❸ Stories of Ancestors (p. 1048)

Discuss with students what motivates people of all times and places to tell stories and pass them on orally or in writing.
Possible response: People search for meaning in their lives and want to leave behind an account of what they learned and experienced.

❹ Every Life Contains a Story (p. 1048)

1. **Ask** students whether they agree with Santos that important literature can be about the lives of ordinary people.
   Possible response: Students may recognize that valuable insights can be gained from stories of everyday events as well as from stories of heroic deeds.
2. Direct students' attention to the quotation from ***The Telling.*** The poetry of Laura (Riding) Jackson (1901–1991) is not well known today because she stopped writing in 1938 and began exploring linguistics. **Ask** students to restate the comment in their own words.
   Possible response: All people want and need to hear stories about themselves that will help them better understand their lives.

Differentiated Instruction for Universal Access

Culturally Responsive Instruction

Culture Connection Explain to students that, like John Phillip Santos, every individual has a rich past, whether he or she is aware of it or not. Because of this unique ancestry, it does not matter who you are, Santos says—everyone has a story to tell.

As Santos draws his stories from his Mexican American heritage, an individual can recall and record those stories from his or her own cultural tradition that are passed from generation to generation. Have students delve into their own rich cultural histories to gather the pieces of *their* stories. Encourage students to interview family members such as grandparents or great-aunts and great-uncles. Suggest that students search through old photographs of family or of their native lands. Students may even look to traditional foods to help tell their stories.

Once students have gathered enough information, have them write their own story. Have volunteers share their stories with the class.

PHLit Online!

Show or assign the Penguin author video segments for these pages online at **www.PHLitOnline.com**.

TEACH

❺ Themes in the Oral Tradition

1. Explain that the oral tradition of passing on stories developed before literacy was widespread. Bards, minstrels, and storytellers memorized long poems or narratives and repeated them at social gatherings.
2. Tell students that examples of archetypes include the orphan, the warrior, the sage, the magician, and the fool. **Ask** students to match the archetypes with fairy tales, legends, myths, or films they know.
   Possible responses: Xena the Warrior Princess and Conan the Barbarian are examples of the warrior; Merlin is an example of the magician.
3. Point out that the existence of universal themes and archetypes reflects the common bonds that unite humanity, and the expressions of these ideas within historical context reveal the diversity of humanity.

Exploring Themes in Literature

❺ Themes in the Oral Tradition

Long before it was written down, literature was part of the **oral tradition,** the passing on of narratives and sayings by word of mouth. Stories lightened work and sweetened leisure, and people exchanged tales while doing chores or sitting around campfires. Storytellers, expressing what fascinated or moved them, explored **universal themes,** ideas about life shared by many cultures: for example, the value of friendship and the need for courage.

In telling their tales, people naturally used **archetypes,** the characters, situations, images, and symbols that appear in the narratives of many different cultures. Here are common **archetypical characters and ideas:**

- the **wise and virtuous king,** whose reign brings in a **golden age,** or time of peace and prosperity
- the **dreamer,** a character who imagines new possibilities and defies danger to bring an important gift to society
- the **hero,** who is an unpromising youth but who blossoms into a wise, strong, and courageous leader
- the struggle between the **protagonist,** the main character, and the **antagonist,** a person or force that opposes the protagonist

The presentation of these archetypes might vary depending on the **historical context,** the social and cultural background of the storyteller and the audience. Yet, the presence of archetypes in different times and places suggests that they arise from our common humanity. Some scholars even believe that archetypal patterns express truths about the human mind and unconscious.

Understanding by Design

Clarifying Expected Outcomes

Explain to students that pages 1050–1051 set out their goals in this Unit. By the end of the Unit, they will understand themes in oral tradition, including universal themes, archetypes, and historical context. They will be able to identify forms that express myths.

Remind students that, in addition, they will explore the qualities and behavior that make a hero as they work toward an answer to the Big Question, "Can anyone be a hero?" They will also add words to their vocabulary that will help them to discuss communication and its purposes. (See Introducing the Big Question, pp. 1046–1047.)

❻ Forms That Express Archetypes

Anonymous storytellers developed recognizable forms as they built narratives from archetypal patterns. At first, these narrative forms lived only in the memory and therefore might be recited in many different versions. Later, as stories were written, their content was fixed and the idea of an individual author emerged. These are the types of stories in which archetypes are often found.

- **Myths** explain the actions of gods and the humans who interact with them. They may also explain the causes of natural phenomena.
- **Legends** are traditional stories about the past that are usually based on historical fact.
- Epics are long narrative poems about a larger-than-life **epic hero.** The epic hero's career is important to the history of a group.
- **Folk tales** focus on human or animal heroes.
- **Fairy tales** are a kind of folk tale recounting the adventures of spirits who appear as very small humans.

Each of these forms expresses the **values,** or model behaviors, cherished by a society. Some ideas are **shared values,** which are held by many societies. Others are **culturally distinct values,** which are specific to a group. Similarly, **cultural details** in a narrative relate to the beliefs and customs that give a particular group its **identity,** or sense of self.

Modern fiction, though written by an individual rather than fashioned by a group, can express universal themes. It can also express a **parody,** or humorous mockery, of an archetypal pattern.

Put Yourself in the Picture

Use these sentence starters to connect this picture of a lawyer in court to the oral tradition.

- I think **values** such as ____________ are probably important to the man pictured because ____________.
- This man looks as though he could be an **archetypical hero** because ____________.
- ____________ is one **universal theme** that connects to this moment.

Challenge Are some people born to be heroes, or do situations make people heroes? Using the picture and your own insights, explain and support your response to this question.

Differentiated Instruction for Universal Access

Support for Special Needs Students
Have students read the **Exploring Themes in Literature** page in the ***Reader's Notebook: Adapted Version***. This version provides a basic-level introduction to the selection.

Support for Less Proficient Readers
Have students read the **Exploring Themes in Literature** page in the ***Reader's Notebook***. This version provides a basic-level introduction to the selection.

EL Support for English Learners
Have students read the **Exploring Themes in Literature** page in the ***Reader's Notebook: English Learner's Version***. This version provides a basic-level introduction to the selection.

❻ Forms That Express Archetypes

1. Review with students the list of story forms. Then, **ask** students for examples of each.
   Possible responses: Myths: the Minotaur; epics: the *Iliad*; folk tales: Aesop's fables; fairy tales: "The Shoemaker and the Elves."
2. Discuss with students how stories reveal what a society finds important or valuable. Tell students that one example of culturally distinct values is the way different societies view older people. In Asian and Native American cultures, for example, elders are respected as wise leaders and teachers. **Ask** students how this value might be expressed in stories.
   Possible response: Respect for elders might be expressed in stories that show elders in the role of sage, magician, or wise ruler.

ASSESS

Answers

Put Yourself in the Picture

Possible response: I think values such as <u>defending people in need</u> are probably important to the man pictured because <u>it his job as an attorney to fight for his clients' rights</u>. This man looks as though he could be an archetypical hero because <u>his purpose is to help those in need. Giving aid to people in unfortunate situations</u> is one universal theme that connects to this moment.

Challenge

Possible response: Students may respond that some people are born with certain qualities, such as leadership, loyalty, and fairness, that predispose them to being heroes. Students might say the man in the picture, for example, already had a strong sense of justice before he decided to go to school to become a lawyer. Other students might say that situations make people heroes. For instance, students might cite a situation in which a bystander witnesses an accident and saves the victim's life.

PRETEACH

❶ Introducing the Selection

1. Invite students to read John Phillip Santos's introduction.
2. Call students' attention to the terms used in discussing the memoir: *cultural context, theme,* and *mythology*.
3. **Ask** students to explain how the writer's introduction increases their interest in reading the selection. **Possible response:** Students might explain that because what prompted Santos to write his book was his grandfather's mysterious death, students are curious to know about Santos's mysterious heritage.

❷ Background

Texas and Mexico The battle of the Alamo and Texas's admission into the United States left many people feeling bitter and misunderstood. People of Mexican descent living in Texas became an increasingly impoverished working class relegated to unskilled farm or industrial labor. It was to this kind of environment that the Santos family came when they arrived in San Antonio in 1914.

❸ Connecting to the Big Question

1. Prepare students to apply the Big Question to the Model Selection.
2. Explain to students that challenging circumstances require individuals to brave adversity and adapt to change.
3. Have students complete this sentence frame, featuring thematic vocabulary from pp. 1046–1047:

   Courage and ________ are attributes that help people to persevere in challenging situations such as ________.

   Possible response: hope . . . devastating floods.
4. Discuss students' responses as a class. Then, have students look for examples of ways in which Santos's ancestors persevered in their struggles as they read.

Concept Connector →

Students will discuss what makes a hero when they have concluded reading.

Model Selection: Themes in Literature

❶

❷
John Phillip Santos
❸
Introduces His Work

My book, *Places Left Unfinished at the Time of Creation,* began in a curiosity about a family secret from the distant past: My grandfather Juan Jose's mysterious death in the San Antonio River on a cold January morning in 1939.

Even though I grew up in a very close family with two formidable grandmothers and lots of uncles, aunts, and cousins, I was already sixteen when I first learned of the strange circumstances of my abuelo's (ä bwə´ lōz)—grandfather's—death. Maybe I never asked.

Cultural Context: A Door Into the Past

But that mystery prompted me to learn more about the link between my family and the mythologies of the past. It set me on a quest for abuelo Juan Jose's story, and that story opened up another chain of stories, about the Mexicans of my hometown, old San Antonio, the landscapes of Texas and Mexico, the Conquest of Mexico by the Spanish that began the whole story, and tales of the indigenous civilizations that had preceded the arrival of the Spaniards. I discovered that my family story was a portal into an infinite past; my grandfather's story was part of a larger undiscovered myth of our ancestry.

The passages from my book that you will read, which begin on the next page, describe some of the ways I sought to recover that mythic story.

Family Stories and Powerful Objects

There are memories of time spent with the oldest members of my family, stories told to me by relatives like my Uncle Lico, who sought out genealogies and other knowledge of the family's remote past. Certain powerful objects remembered from childhood unlock troves of memories. And in the absence of written records of the family's history, journeys into the lands of our origins, north and south of the border, become an important part of my search.

I wanted to explore the **theme of my own identity** by telling my family's story and ended up finding a hidden mythology that connected us to the great human tale, the one that is incalculably old, but still being written.

Vocabulary Development

Vocabulary Knowledge Rating

Create a **Vocabulary Knowledge Rating Chart** (***Professional Development Guidebook***, p. 33) with these words from the selection:

facet *polarized* *inexorably*

Give students a copy of the chart. Read the words aloud, and have students mark their rating in the Before Reading column. Urge them to be alert to these words as they read and discuss the selection because they will rate their knowledge of the words again after they finish.

Tally how many students know the words to gauge how much instruction to provide. As students read, point out the words and their contexts.

PHLit Online! **Vocabulary Central**, featuring tools, activities, and songs for studying vocabulary, is available online at **www.PHLitOnline.com**.

MODEL SELECTION

from Places Left Unfinished at the Time of Creation

4
5

John Phillip Santos

. . . The past can be difficult to conjure again when so little has been left behind.

A few photographs, a golden medal, a pair of eyeglasses as delicate as eggshells, an old Bible, a letter or two. Some families in Mexico have troves of their ancestors' belongings, from pottery of the ancients and exquisite paintings of Mexico City in the eighteenth century to helmets and shields of the Spaniards, and even hundred-year-old parrots and maguey plants[1] that have been handed down, from the great-grandparents who first tended them.

1. **maguey** (mag′ wā′) **plants** *n.* fleshy-leaved plants common to Mexico, Central America and the southwestern U.S.; used for making rope and tequila.

TEACH

❹ Activating Prior Knowledge

Another Hispanic writer, Carlos Fuentes, has said this about the search for one's past: "Name and voice, memory and desire, they permit us to realize that we live surrounded by lost worlds, by vanished histories. These worlds and these histories are our responsibility: they were created by men and women. We can't forget them without condemning ourselves to be forgotten." Read this quotation to students and lead a discussion about their interest in the past. Do they agree or disagree with Fuentes and Santos? Is it the responsibility of the present generation to ensure that the past is not lost?

Concept Connector →

Students will return to these discussion points after they read the passage from *Places Left Unfinished at the Time of Creation.*

❺ About the Selection

John Phillip Santos uses mementos—from names on a Christmas card list to old photographs—as a way of capturing the subtle meaning in mundane events. In sometimes disjointed anecdotes, he explores the past and blends the story of his family with the spirit of his Mexican ancestors.

Differentiated Instruction for Universal Access

Support for Special Needs Students
Have students read the adapted version of the excerpt from *Places Left Unfinished at the Time of Creation* in the ***Reader's Notebook: Adapted Version***. They may also listen to the adapted version on the ***Hear It!* Audio CD** (adapted text).

Support for Less Proficient Readers
Have students read the excerpt from *Places Left Unfinished at the Time of Creation* in the ***Reader's Notebook***. After students finish the selection in the Reader's Notebook, have them complete the questions and activities in the Student Edition.

EL Support for English Learners
Have students read the excerpt from *Places Left Unfinished at the Time of Creation* in the ***Reader's Notebook: English Learner's Version***. English learners may also read the selection as they listen to the recorded version on the ***Hear It!* Audio CD**.

PHLit Online!

Enriched Online Student Edition
To have students read the selection in interactive format, with narration and point-of-use interactive graphic organizers, go online at **www.PHLitOnline.com**.

❻ Author's Insight

John Phillip Santos

1. Have a volunteer read aloud the bracketed passage.
2. **Ask** students why it may have appeared that no keepsakes had been handed down in Santos's family.
   Possible response: Perhaps Santos was looking for the wrong things, such as the treasures he mentions earlier (exquisite paintings, Spanish shields and helmets).
3. Have students watch for the kinds of keepsakes that Santos mentions as he pursues his family's history.

❼ Author's Insight

John Phillip Santos

1. Explain that in the past, scribes recorded important events and kept public records. Some scribes also wrote letters and other documents for those who could not do so themselves.
2. Then, **ask** students how Santos performed the role of a scribe for his grandmother.
   Possible response: By helping his grandmother with her Christmas cards, Santos helped record the passing of significant people in her life. He was also able to stimulate her memory and collect stories from her past.

John Phillip Santos
Author's Insight The idea there was nothing left behind was a part of our family myth. There were actually many keepsakes; it just didn't seem so at first. But looking for the stories of my ancestors set me on the path to write. ❻

John Phillip Santos
Author's Insight As your family's chief mythologist, you will always want to be useful to your elders when they need the services of a scribe. ❼

By comparison, the Santos are traveling light through time. In my family, virtually nothing has been handed down, not because there was nothing to give, but after leaving Mexico to come to Texas—so many loved ones left behind, cherished places and things abandoned—the antepasados[2] ceased to regard anything as a keepsake. Everything was given away. Or they may have secretly clung so closely to their treasured objects that they were never passed on.

Then they were lost.

My mother's mother, Leandra Lopez, whom we called simply "Grandmother," sat in her cluttered dark house on West Russell Street like an aged Tejana[3] sphinx during the last ten years of her life. Through the year, she filed away embossed death notices and patron saint prayer cards of departed family and friends in the black leather address book I consulted to write out her Christmas cards every year. In early December, I would sit down with her and first cross out the entries for all those who had "passed onward," as she used to say. By each name in the book, she had already scratched a cross with thick black pencil lines.

Memo Montalvo from Hebbronville, Texas. According to Grandmother, a good man. He had married a not-very-pretty cousin from Laredo.

Efraín Vela from Mier, Tamaulipas. Son of a cousin on her father's side whom she never spoke to. Supposedly, he was the keeper of the family coat of arms, awarded to the family by the Viceroy of Nueva España himself. What would happen to it now?

Socorro Mendiola, from Alice, Texas. She and Grandmother had taught school together in a one-room schoolhouse in Cotulla in 1910. Then Socorro became a Franciscan nun, breaking the heart of Grandmother's cousin, Emeterio Vela, whom, she noted with a sigh, had died just last year.

And every year, by the degrees of each ended life, as the world grew older, our addressing marathons grew

2. **antepasados** (än tā pä sä´ dōs) *n.* Spanish for "forebears, ancestors."
3. **Tejana** (tā jä´ nä) *adj.* Spanish for "Texan."

Think Aloud

Vocabulary: Using Context

Direct students' attention to the word *ferreted* on p. 1055. Using a think-aloud process, model how to use the context to infer the meaning of an unknown word.

In this sentence, *ferreted* is used to explain how Uncle Lico Lopez figures out the past to craft his genealogical charts. I know that a ferret is an animal that hunts rats and rabbits, digging its way into their burrows to track them down. Santos describes his uncle as pursuing the family genealogy for forty years. If he did it like a ferret, he probably searched intensively, never giving up until he got what he wanted. I think *ferreted* must mean "uncovered or brought to light by dedicated searching."

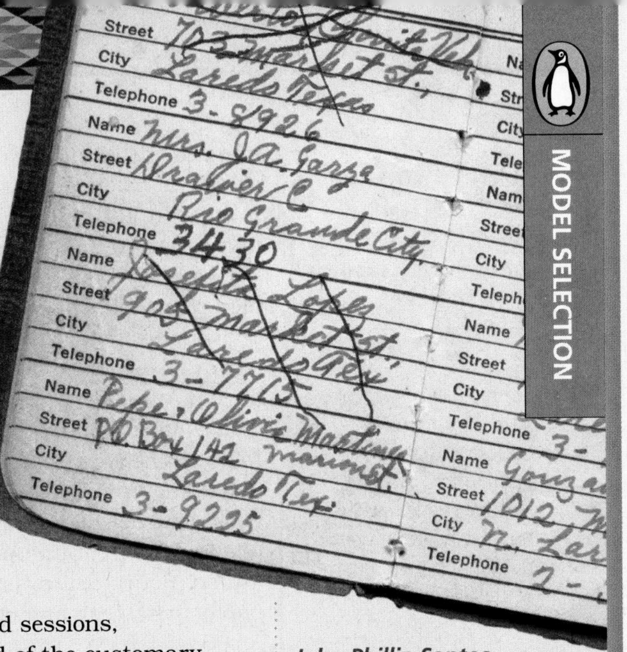

shorter—though Grandmother would change the subject if I pointed out this mortal ratio.

Inside her rolltop writing desk, she kept a mysterious wooden polygonal[4] star that had a different swatch of old Mexican fabrics glued on each facet. The multicolored curiosity smelled
8 like Mexico, all cumin, wild honey, and smoky rose, and when you shook it, a small solitary object rattled inside. A stone? A marble? A gem? To me, it seemed like some magician's puzzle, and locked inside were all of the secrets of old Mexico.

During one of our annual Christmas-card sessions, I asked her if I could have that star, instead of the customary reward of a box of animal crackers and five dollars in change, which she laboriously fished out of her zippered, yellowing plastic coin purse. Grandmother was almost completely blind by then, so I put her hand to the last of the Hallmark Christmas cards in the place for her to sign her name. She slowly scratched out Leandra Vela Lopez, and told me no, I could not have the star.

I never saw it again.

My uncle, Lico Lopez, her son, ferreted out the past as a passionate genealogist who used research, fantasy, and spells of breathless diabetic madness to craft his ancestral charts of the Lopez and Vela families. Some are elaborate discs, in which each outward concentric ring represents a new generation. In these, as you delve closer to the center, you also go deeper into the past. In others, quickly dashed off as notes to himself, ragged trees and
9 jagged lines are drawn between names like Evaristo, Viviano, Blas, and Hermenegilda. In one, going back to 1763, the capstone slot contains the cryptic entry,

"King of Spain,"

from whom, presumably, he believed we were descended. Subtle faculties and proclivities[5] were passed, speechlessly, through the flesh of successive generations. The ghosts of Spanish royalty

4. **polygonal** (pə lig´ ə nəl) *adj.* many-sided.
5. **proclivities** (prō kliv´ ə tēz) *n.* natural or habitual inclinations.

John Phillip Santos
Author's Insight
Sometimes the simplest object will open a door into many stories.

Vocabulary
facet (fas´ it) *n.* any of a number of sides or aspects

◀ **Critical Viewing** 10
Why might old photographs like these be important to the author? **[Connect]**

11 **Reading Check**
How did the author help his grandmother every year?

8 Author's Insight
John Phillip Santos

1. Point out that Santos provides a very detailed description of the wooden star. **Ask** how Santos makes this description vivid and real for readers.
   Answer: Santos's description appeals to the senses of sight, smell, and touch.
2. Discuss with students the associations that the star had for Santos.
   Possible response: Santos associated the star with mystery, magic, and his family's place of origin.
3. **Ask** students what they think Santos means when he says that the simplest object will open a door into many stories.
   Possible response: Santos is suggesting that an object such as the wooden star can trigger memories and associations that will inspire a writer or storyteller.

9 Themes in Literature
Tradition

1. Have a volunteer read the passage aloud.
2. **Ask** students why they think the author calls his uncle's work madness.
   Possible response: Uncle Lico seems to use a number of eclectic methods that did not necessarily depend on fact.

10 Critical Viewing
Possible response: Old photographs capture a time that the author was not there to observe, giving him information about what life was like for his ancestors.

11 Reading Check
Answer: Santos wrote out his grandmother's Christmas cards each year.

Fluency

Students may need additional help pronouncing vocabulary words from the selection. Help them skim or scan the memoir for unfamiliar words such as *conjure, troves, embossed, ferreted, concentric, delve, cryptic, capstone, manic, polarized, inexorably, filigreed, indelible, myriad, stigmatized, hoary,* and *primordial.* Encourage students to work with a partner to look up the words in a dictionary and pronounce each word correctly. Then, have pairs read each other a paragraph from the excerpt containing at least one of these words to monitor their fluency.

⓬ Author's Insight

John Phillip Santos

1. **Ask** students why they think that Santos is as interested in his grandfather's handwriting as in the document he wrote.
   Possible response: Santos may have realized that his grandfather's handwriting was an expression of his personality.
2. **Discuss** with students why the family might have preserved the receipt.
   Possible response: The receipt may have been a record of the first sale made at the family store.
3. **Ask** students what mysteries the receipt revealed.
   Possible response: The receipt revealed when the store was open, what was sold in the store, and how much money was earned.

Vocabulary

polarized (pō′ lə rīzd′) *adj.* divided into two opposing groups

inexorably (in eks′ ə rə blē) *adv.* unrelentingly

John Phillip Santos
Author's Insight
Your grandfather's handwriting always harbors many mysteries, not just what he wrote, but what his writing actually looked like.

mingled with Indios, Negros, and people from every part of the world—in Uncle Lico's secret genealogy of Mexico. Yet, despite the uninterest and ridicule of many, he managed to recover numerous family names and stories. ❾

Lico knew I had some of the same magnetic attraction to the past that fueled his manic genealogies, as if the molecules of our bodies were **polarized** in a way that drew us both back in time, back, **inexorably**, toward the ancestors. Before he died, suddenly, in San Antonio, of a heart attack, he sent me all of the notes and charts accumulated in his forty years of digging in the family root cellars. He also gave me a receipt, dated May 25, 1928, laminated and mounted on wood, from my grandfather's grocery store, Leonides Lopez Groceries, in Cotulla, Texas. In my grandfather's filigreed wrought iron pencil script, it details a sale on that day of *harina* (flour), *azúcar* (sugar), *fideos* (vermicelli), *manteca* (lard), *papas* (potatoes), and other assorted dry goods, for a total of \$5.05. ⓬

A relic like this is the exception, though. A trunkful of the Santos family photographs disappeared when Madrina moved out of the old house on Cincinnati Street. She swears she remembers seeing it fall off the truck near the corner of Zarzamora Street, where La Poblanita bakery was located. It was a pine box the size of a shipping trunk, stuffed with heirloom photographs. She can't remember why she said nothing at the time. It fell off a truck onto the dusty streets of old San Antonio de Bejar one day and was left behind, abandoned, lost.

In one photo that survived it is 1960, and the whole Santos tribe is standing on the porch of my grandmother's house, in early evening shadows. It must have been Easter because my many cousins and I are in church clothes, standing in the yard around the trunk of a great sycamore tree. My aunts and uncles are there, partly old Mexican, partly new American, looking handsome, hopeful, proud of the brood standing in front of them. In the very middle of the scene, *las Ancianas,* Grandmother Santos, whom we called "Uela," short for *abuela,* and Madrina, her sister, are standing regally in a perfect moment, radiating the indelible light of Mexico. On the porch, Mother and an aunt have my newborn twin brothers, George and Charles, wrapped in blankets in their arms. My father looks serious, with a distant gaze, in a dark suit and silky tie. To one side, standing apart from us, is one of my eldest cousins, René, who would be killed in Vietnam just seven years later. ⓭

These are the memento mori[6] of the Santos. There are a few photographs, rosary chains of half-remembered stories, carried out of another time by the old Mexicans I grew up with. In dreams, the ancestors who have passed on visit with me, in this world, and in a world that lies perhaps within, amidst, and still beyond this world—a mystical limbo dimension that the descendants of the Aztecs call *el Inframundo*. In the *Inframundo*, all that has been forgotten still lives. Nothing is lost. All remembrance is redeemed from oblivion.

John Phillip Santos
Author's Insight
Old family photographs and other newer media are treasure troves heaping with evidence from the past. Some of my earliest drafts are composed of collages of this "tribal media."

MODEL SELECTION

These ancestors, living and dead, have asked me the questions they were once asked: Where did our forebears come from and what have we amounted to in this world? Where have we come to in the span of all time, and where are we headed, like an arrow shot long ago into infinite empty space? What messages and markings of the ancient past do we carry in these handed-down bodies we live in today?

With these questions swirling inside me, I have rediscovered some stories of the family past in the landscapes of Texas and Mexico, in the timeless language of stone, river, wind, and trees. Tío Abrín, twin brother to my great-grandfather Jacobo, was a master of making charcoal. He lived in the hill country, where the cedars needed to make charcoal were planted a century ago to supply the industry. Today, long after he worked there, walking in that central Texas landscape crowded with deep green cedar, I feel old Abrán's presence, like the whisper of a tale still waiting to be told, wondering whether my intuition and the family's history are implicitly intertwined. Even if everything else had been lost—photographs, stories, rumors, and suspicions—if nothing at all from the past remained for us, the land remains, as the original book of the family.

It was always meant to be handed down. . . .

14 Reading Check
What happened to the box that contained the author's heirloom family photographs?

---

6. **memento mori** (mə men′ tō mōr′ ē) *n.* reminder of death.

13 Author's Insight
John Phillip Santos

1. Have students read the bracketed passage to themselves.
2. **Ask** students what Santos means by the phrase "tribal media."
Possible response: He is referring to family keepsakes that also represent the traditions of a culture.
3. **Ask** students why they think Santos goes into so much detail about tribal media such as the one photograph.
Possible response: The photograph captures his extended family from the old Mexican generation to the new American one, including some members who are now gone.

14 Reading Check

Answer: The trunkful of photographs disappeared when his aunt moved out of her house. The aunt thinks she remembers seeing it fall off the truck.

Differentiated Instruction for Universal Access

EL Pronunciation for English Learners

Some students find it difficult to pronounce words with the short medial vowel "i" sound in multisyllabic words, as in *living*, and replace it with the "ee" sound. The following strategies can help students to pronounce the "i" sound:

- Model the pronunciation of these words: *visit, within, amidst*, and *family*. Have students follow by repeating each.
- Then, as necessary, isolate the "i" sound in single syllable words featuring the sound. Give additional words with the same consonant sound, varying the vowel sound in the word, such as in *did* and *died* or *bit* and *beat*. Use these word pairs to help students differentiate between the "i" and "ee" sounds.
- Finally, return to the multisyllabic words from the selection and have students pronounce each again.

⓯ Humanities

Dream of a Sunday Afternoon in the Alameda Park by Diego Rivera (1886–1957)

Hailed as one of Mexico's greatest artists of his time, Diego Rivera spent his early life in Europe studying paintings of the masters, and later did commissioned work in the United States. While in Europe, he adopted the artistic style of cubism but never stopped searching for a new form of painting until he studied the Renaissance frescoes of Italy. Fresco painting, in which murals are painted on wet plaster, proved to be Rivera's trademark medium. He preferred to paint his murals on walls in public places—a perfect size and place for a large audience to glimpse his art and its sociopolitical messages.

What Rivera chose to depict in his murals, however, made him a controversial artist. He tended to paint scenes of daily life filled with historical significance, often related to Mexican culture. Some of the historical and political details he inserted in his murals were considered radical, particularly in the mural commissioned for the Rockefellers in New York City, and they caused uproars that forced Rivera to cease work on these murals.

⓰ Critical Viewing

Possible response: The muted colors of the townspeople, their heads drooping in sleep on park benches, and people crammed into one another convey a busy but despairing daily life for the people in the foreground of the painting, which reflects the "dusty streets, broken-down houses, and hunger." Also, important figures, evidenced by crowns and uniforms, stand crowded in the background, as if wanting to be noticed or heard. These figures could represent a country's forgotten or ignored history. This detail, then, reflects "loved ones left behind, cherished places and things abandoned."

⓯

⓰ ▲ **Critical Viewing** Which details in this painting of Mexico by Diego Rivera reflect the Santos's experience of "loved ones left behind, cherished places and things abandoned..." but also "dusty streets, broken-down houses, and hunger"? ⓱

Once they arrived in Texas during the revolution, maybe the Santos and Garcia families simply wanted to forget their past in Mexico—the dusty streets, broken-down houses, and hunger. They wanted to burn away the memory of when the families came north across the Rio Grande. Northern Mexico became one of the most violent and chaotic battlefields of *la Revolución* of 1910, a revolution that was to last eleven years. But for the first years, the revolution was only distant thunder, more of a concern to Mexicans well to the south of Coahuila in states such as Guerrero, Puebla, and Mexico City. The family's flight from Coahuila was in 1914, the year Pancho Villa, along with a myriad of other revolutionary bands, rose up to occupy the bare constellation of towns across the parched high Norteño desert where they had made their

Vocabulary Development

Expressive Vocabulary

To help students broaden their expressive vocabulary, encourage them to use the following words as they discuss the selection: *abandon*, *diverse*, *evaluate*, and *emphasis*. Have them complete these sentence starters:

1. When they left Mexico, the Santos family had to *abandon* . . .
2. The author provides *diverse* examples of . . .
3. Santos reflects on family stories to *evaluate* . . .
4. The family's *emphasis* on the value of _______ suggests . . .

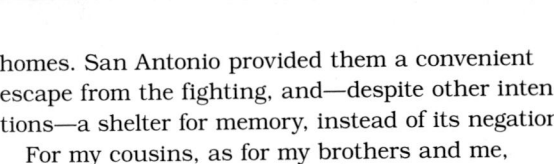

homes. San Antonio provided them a convenient escape from the fighting, and—despite other intentions—a shelter for memory, instead of its negation.

For my cousins, as for my brothers and me, the homes of *las Viejitas*[7] were sanctuaries where Coahuila was still alive, and places where the inhibitions and proprieties of the Gringo world of San Antonio, Texas, outside did not apply. Those were days when the taco and the tamal[8] were stigmatized in public, and Spanish was seldom heard on downtown streets. The old tíos[9] had to speak English, often haltingly, to get along in the working world. Most of *las Viejitas*, staying in their homes, spoke only Spanish, or at least pretended not to speak English. When Uela spoke Spanish, her sentences moved in one steady arc, like a bow across a violin, and her words were delicately pronounced, so that you could hear every tinkle of an old chandelier, every gust of a Coahuila wind falling to a hush, and the grain of a rustling squash blossom.

The migrations continued through the century. In the 1960s, my parents moved us from one of the old neighborhoods of the city to a new suburb at the city's northwestern edge, in order to get us into the better public schools in San Antonio. We were the first Mexicans in the neighborhood, in a two-floor house with a two-car garage, a built-in dishwasher, central air-conditioning, and intercom consoles in every room. We spoke English to each other, and Spanish to the old ones in the family. When the mariachis played in our backyard, the rapid plucking of the bajo sexto[10] and the shimmering trumpet lines echoed off the neighbors' houses and drew them out to listen. Out there in that virgin neighborhood, it always felt as if we were closer to the iridescent Texas sky, stripped of the protective canopy of sycamore, wisteria, china berry, and live oak that arched over so many of the streets of our old, secret Mexican city, San Antonio de Bejar.

7. **las Viejitas** (läs bē´ ā hē´ täs) *n.* Spanish for "little old ladies." Santos is using this as a term of endearment for his elderly women relatives.
8. **tamal** (tä´ mäl) *n.* tamale, a steamed corn husk filled with meat and cornmeal.
9. **tíos** (ti´ ōs) *n.* Spanish for "uncles."
10. **bajo sexto** (bä´ hō seks´ tō) *n.* Spanish for "six-string bass."

17
***John Phillip Santos* Author's Insight**
It's important to understand that family history happens inside of world history. The 1910 Revolución in Mexico caused my family, among many others, to flee Mexico for Texas.

18
Themes in Literature
Identity The author uses a flashback to show readers *las viejitas* he knew in his childhood.

19
Themes in Literature
Cultural Context
Details about the difficulties many Mexicans faced help make the author's experiences more meaningful.

20 **Reading Check**
Why did Santos's forebears flee Mexico in 1914?

Differentiated Instruction for Universal Access

Support for Less Proficient Readers
Point out Santos's use of modifiers to enliven his writing. Tell students that modifiers such as adjectives add more precise meaning to the words they modify. The writer's choice of modifiers can also reveal his or her attitudes. Point out the sentence in which Santos describes the Anglo neighborhood as "stripped of the protective canopy" of trees. **Ask** students what the use of the adjective *protective* reveals about the author's feelings.
Possible response: Santos felt safe and sheltered under the trees in his former residence.

Enrichment for Gifted/Talented Students
Invite students to write a memoir, concentrating on one event or situation. Suggest that they create a timeline of their lives and then select an event to serve as the basis of their reflection. Tell them that their goal is to explore the meaning of the event and to record it for generations to follow. Once students have completed their memoirs, have them discuss the process. Did they feel a responsibility in their writing? What connections to their past did they discover?

17 Author's Insight
John Phillip Santos

1. **Ask:** How do the events described affect the Santos family?
   Answer: The passage describes the revolution that began in 1910, which caused the Santos family to leave Mexico in 1914.
2. **Ask** students why they think Santos points out the relationship between family history and world history.
   Possible response: The interaction between family and world history is a matter of cause and effect. Had it not been for the violent revolution, the family might have stayed in Mexico.

18 Themes in Literature
Identity

Ask: What part of Santos's identity might the *las Viejitas* represent?
Possible response: Because they are from Coahuila, their native land, the *las Viejitas* are closest to the family's Mexican roots. The *las Viejitas,* then, represent Santos's Mexican roots.

19 Themes in Literature
Cultural Context

1. **Ask** students to discuss some of the reasons the family may have felt displaced.
   Possible response: Mexican food was looked down upon, Spanish was spoken only in the privacy of homes, and those who worked had to learn English to get along in the working world.
2. **Ask** students how these experiences affected the cultural context to which the family had to adjust.
   Possible response: They would have had to modify their behavior to a certain extent to fit in with the rest of the world. This might have meant that some traditions could no longer be practiced openly, and some might have been forgotten.

20 Reading Check

Possible response: Santos's family left Mexico because revolutionary bands brought the violence of the revolution to the towns where they lived.

21 Themes in Literature

Tradition

1. Have a volunteer read aloud the bracketed passage.
2. **Ask** students what they think Santos means by calling the stories of *las Viejitas* a promise but saying that they were never meant to be told.
   Possible response: The stories represent a continuation of the family tradition that should be passed from one generation to the next. The stories were never meant to be told because they might reveal personal information and powerful mysteries.

22 Critical Viewing

Possible response: This image suggests that in order to see the past, we must turn around and look behind us. The path from the past leads through the visible present and into an unknown future.

Concept Connector

Have students return to the discussion points raised before they read the selection. Lead a class discussion probing for what students have learned that confirms or invalidates the ideas they had before reading. Encourage students to cite specific details, quotations, or other evidence from the text to support their responses.

Connecting to the Big Question

Ask students describe the hardships Santos's family endured. How did the family handle these challenges?
Possible response: The family fled hostile and poor conditions in Mexico during the revolution and settled in Texas, where their ways of life were frowned upon. Members of the Santos family spoke Spanish at home but learned to speak enough English to acquire work.

That old San Antonio was part of the hoary earth of the ancestors. Out there in the suburb at the edge of the city, following the early Gemini and Apollo space missions, I read books about space and prepared for the day in the future, which would undoubtedly come, when I would leave this planet in a rocket of my own.

Today, in New York City, I live in a world *las Viejitas* never visited, very far from the land they knew well. I have been to places they never imagined, like England, Europe, Turkey, Peru, and the Sudan. Yet, wherever I go, there is a ribbon of primordial Mexican night, the color of obsidian,[11] snaking in a dream through the skies high over my head. Sometimes it is easily visible to me, like a burning galaxy, sometimes it is not. Sometimes it drizzles a fine rain of voices, images, and stories. And *las Viejitas* are here now, too, as they have always been, invisible yet abiding. (21) They are keeping a vigil over the stories they told to me as if they are a *compromiso*, a promise that has been handed on. I have always felt connected, oriented, and imparted to by them, but unsure how I fit into a story that was never meant to be told.

22 ▼ Critical Viewing In what ways does this photograph suggest a journey from the past into the future? **[Interpret]**

11. **obsidian** (əb sid′ ē ən) *n.* dark or black volcanic glass.

Vocabulary Development

Vocabulary Knowledge Rating

When students have completed reading and discussing the passage from *Places Left Unfinished at the Time of Creation*, have them take out their **Vocabulary Rating Chart** for this selection. Read the words aloud once more, and have students rate their knowledge of the words again in the After Reading column. Clarify any words that are still problematic. Have students write their own definition or example sentence in the appropriate column. Encourage students to use the words in further discussion and written work about this selection. Remind them that they will be accountable for the words on the **Selection Test**, *Unit 6 Resources*, pp. 17–19 or 20–22.

After You Read

from Places Left Unfinished at the Time of Creation

Critical Thinking

1. **Respond:** How important do you think it is for a family to actively preserve its history and traditions? Explain your answer.
2. **(a)** Why does the Santos family move to San Antonio? **(b) Analyze Cause and Effect:** Why might these circumstances have affected their desire to remember the past?
3. **(a) Interpret:** What does Santos mean when he says his family is "traveling light through time"? **(b) Generalize:** Do you think "traveling light" is common or unusual among families today? Explain.
4. **(a) Compare and Contrast:** In what specific ways is Santos's life different from the lives of his Mexican ancestors? **(b) Analyze:** How does Santos maintain a connection to his family's past?

THE BIG ? **Can anyone be a hero?**
(a) Do you think Santos sees his ancestors as heroes? Why or why not? **(b)** In what ways could Santos be seen as a hero?

Reviewing Themes in Literature

1. **(a)** Using a chart like the one shown, identify passages containing **cultural details** that help the Santos family maintain its **identity** over time. **(b)** Compare your findings with those of a classmate. Eliminate duplications and rewrite the list in order of importance. **(c)** Discuss the values each item represents to the Santos family.

Passage	Cultural Detail	Why It Is Important

2. What role does the **oral tradition** play in helping Santos understand his family's past?

Research the Author

Create an **annotated map** of the places where Santos and his family settled in Mexico and Texas. Follow these steps:

- Reread the selection and make a list of the places. Then, use library and Internet sources to study each place.
- Draw or adapt a poster-sized map showing these locations and note the major events that occurred while Santos or his family lived there.
- Display the map in class.

Answers

Critical Thinking

1. Students may say that it is important for a family to preserve its history and traditions because it connects the family to an otherwise empty past, giving it meaning and identity.
2. (a) They move to San Antonio to escape the violence of the revolution.
(b) **Possible response:** They had to leave raditions behind and adjust to a culture that in some ways did not accept what was familiar to them.
3. (a) **Possible response:** His family has few possessions that tie them to their past. (b) **Possible response:** Traveling light is common for some families and uncommon for others. Whether they carry their past with them depends on how much they value it.
4. (a) He lives in New York and travels around the world. (b) He cares enough about his past to record it in memoirs.

THE BIG ? **Can anyone be a hero?**
(a) Students may say that they think Santos sees his ancestors as heroes because they have imparted upon him his Mexican heritage, traditions, and stories, despite the hardships they have endured. (b) **Possible response:** Santos can be seen as a hero in that he has taken up the cause of preserving his family's history and rich culture.

Reviewing Themes in Literature

1. **Possible response:** Passage: Addressing Christmas cards; **Cultural Detail:** Wooden star; **Why It Is Important:** Represented the past for the author; (b) and (c) Students should discuss the values each item represents to the Santos family.
2. **Possible response:** Many of the stories were prompted by keepsakes, fleeting memories, or questions and were preserved by chance as one person told them to another.

Research the Author

Students may complete this research assignment for homework. Tell them that they can find information about Santos in the library or online.

PHLit Online!
Students can find more about the author at www.PHLitOnline.com.

Assessment Resources

Unit 6 Resources

L1 L2 EL **Selection Test A,** pp. 17–19
L3 L4 **Selection Test B,** pp. 20–22
L3 L4 **Open-Book Test,** pp. 14–16

PHLit Online! All assessment resources are available at **www.PHLitOnline.com.**

TIME AND RESOURCE MANAGER

Prometheus and the First People • The Orphan Boy and the Elk Dog

Lesson Pacing Guide

DAY 1 Preteach

- Administer the Reading and Vocabulary Warm-ups (*Unit 6 Resources*, pp. 23–26 or 41–44) as necessary.
- Introduce the Reading Skill: Analyze Cultural Context. FT
- Introduce the Literary Analysis concept: Myths. FT
- Distribute copies of the appropriate graphic organizer for the Reading Skill (*Graphic Organizer Transparencies*, pp. 193–195). CRI
- Distribute copies of the appropriate graphic organizer for Literary Analysis (*Graphic Organizer Transparencies*, pp. 196–198). CRI
- Teach the selection vocabulary. FT CRI
- Introduce the Word Study skill.

DAYS 2–3 Preteach/Teach

- Build background with the Background feature. CRI
- Develop thematic vocabulary and thematic thinking with Writing About the Big Question.
- Prepare students to read with the Activating Prior Knowledge activities (TE). CRI
- Informally monitor comprehension while students read. FT
- Use the Reading Check questions to confirm comprehension.
- Develop students' ability to analyze cultural context using the Reading Skill questions. CRI
- Develop students' understanding of myths using the Literary Analysis questions. CRI
- Reinforce vocabulary with the Vocabulary notes. CRI

DAY 4 Assess

- Assess students' comprehension and mastery of the skills by having them answer the Critical Thinking, Reading Skill, and Literary Analysis questions. FT
- Have students complete the Vocabulary Practice activities. FT
- Have students complete the Word Study activities.

DAY 5 Extend/Assess

- Have students complete the Grammar lesson. CRI
- Have students complete the Writing activity and write a myth. (You may assign as homework.) FT
- Extend learning by having students complete the Listening and Speaking activity, a retelling. As an alternative, assign them "Science's Double Edge Sword" or "Buffalo Battles" in *Reality Central*. CRI
- Administer Selection Test A or B (*Unit 6 Resources*, pp. 35–40 or 56–61). FT

"Prometheus and the First People" is an unedited excerpt from a retelling of a series of Greek myths. "The Orphan Boy and the Elk Dog" is a retelling of a myth presented unedited an in its entirety.

Meeting Your Standards

Students will
1. analyze and respond to literary elements.
   - Literary Analysis: Myths
2. read, comprehend, and analyze myths.
   - Reading Skill: Analyze Cultural Context
   - Reading Check questions
   - Apply the Skills questions
   - Assessment Practice
3. develop vocabulary.
   - Vocabulary
   - Word Study
4. apply grammar skills.
   - Simple and Compound Sentences
5. Develop writing proficiency.
   - Work in Progress: Technical Document
   - myth
6. strengthen listening and speaking skills.
   - retelling

CRI For a full explanation of Culturally Responsive Instruction opportunities in this lesson, see p. T86–T87.

FT For an accelerated lesson, use the Fast Track strategies and activities.

Managing Differentiated Instruction
This leveled selection pairing groups a more accessible with a more challenging selection. Choose either one to teach the lesson skills. For classroom management suggestions for using the pairing in a mixed-ability class, see pp. T68–T69.

Daily Block Scheduling
Each day in this Lesson Pacing Guide represents a 40–50 minute period. Teachers using block scheduling may combine days to revise pacing. In addition, teachers may differentiate and support core instruction by integrating components for extended and intensive support as students require. See the Guide to Selected Leveled Resources (facing page).

Guide to Selected Leveled Resources

EL English Learners

			Prometheus and the First People	The Orphan Boy and the Elk Dog
CORE COURSE	*Unit 6 Resources*	Selection Test A	pp. 35–37	pp. 56–58
	Graphic Organizer Transparencies	Reading Skill Graphic Organizer A	p. 193	p. 194
		Literary Analysis Graphic Organizer A	p. 196	p. 197
EXTENDED SUPPORT (Level 2)	*Unit 6 Resources*	Reading and Vocabulary Warm-ups A or B	pp. 23–26	pp. 41–44
	Reader's Notebook: English Learner's Version		adapted instruction and selection	adapted instruction and summary
	Hear It! Audio CD		selection and summaries	selection and summaries
	Hear It! Audio CD (adapted text)		adapted selection and summaries	—
INTENSIVE SUPPORT (Level 1)	*Reality Central*		"Science's Double Edge Sword"	"Buffalo Battles"
	Real-World Writing Journal		Lesson 1, pp. 156–159	Lesson 2, pp. 160–163

L2 Below-Level Students

			Prometheus and the First People	The Orphan Boy and the Elk Dog
CORE COURSE	*Unit 6 Resources*	Selection Test A	pp. 35–37	pp. 56–58
	Graphic Organizer Transparencies	Reading Skill Graphic Organizer A	p. 193	p. 194
		Literary Analysis Graphic Organizer A	p. 196	p. 197
EXTENDED SUPPORT (Level 2)	*Unit 6 Resources*	Reading and Vocabulary Warm-ups A or B	pp. 23–26	pp. 41–44
	Reader's Notebook		adapted instruction and selection	adapted instruction and summary
	Hear It! Audio CD		selection and summaries	selection and summaries
INTENSIVE SUPPORT (Level 1)	*Reality Central*		"Science's Double Edge Sword"	"Buffalo Battles"
	Real-World Writing Journal		Lesson 1, pp. 156–159	Lesson 2, pp. 160–163
	Reading Kit		Reteaching worksheets	Reteaching worksheets

L1 Special Needs Students

			Prometheus and the First People	The Orphan Boy and the Elk Dog
CORE COURSE	*Unit 6 Resources*	Selection Test A	pp. 35–37	pp. 56–58
	Graphic Organizer Transparencies	Reading Skill Graphic Organizer A	p. 193	p. 194
		Literary Analysis Graphic Organizer A	p. 196	p. 197
EXTENDED SUPPORT (Level 2)	*Unit 6 Resources*	Reading and Vocabulary Warm-ups A or B	pp. 23–26	pp. 41–44
	Reader's Notebook: Adapted Version		adapted instruction and selection	adapted instruction and summary
	Hear It! Audio CD (adapted text)		adapted selection and summaries	—
INTENSIVE SUPPORT (Level 1)	*Reality Central*		"Science's Double Edge Sword"	"Buffalo Battles"
	Real-World Writing Journal		Lesson 1, pp. 156–159	Lesson 2, pp. 160–163
	Reading Kit		Reteaching worksheets	Reteaching worksheets

The program includes resources for these students: L3 On-Level L4 Advanced All All
For a complete guide to selection support, see pp. T106–T108.

NOTE: All print materials are also available online at *www.PHLitOnline.com.*

• Prometheus and the First People
• The Orphan Boy and the Elk Dog

RESOURCES FOR:

- EL English Learners
- L Special Needs Students
- L2 Below-Level Students
- L3 On-Level Students
- L4 Advanced Students
- All All Students

Vocabulary/Fluency/Prior Knowledge

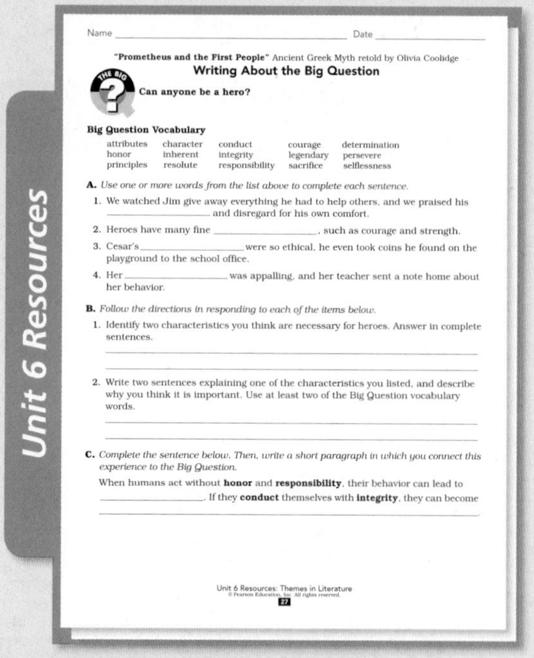
Unit 6 Resources

Name ______________________ Date ____________

"Prometheus and the First People" Ancient Greek Myth retold by Olivia Coolidge

Writing About the Big Question

THE BIG ?

Can anyone be a hero?

Big Question Vocabulary

attributes	character	conduct	courage	determination
honor	inherent	integrity	legendary	persevere
principles	resolute	responsibility	sacrifice	selflessness

A. *Use one or more words from the list above to complete each sentence.*

1. We watched Jim give away everything he had to help others, and we praised his ______________ and disregard for his own comfort.
2. Heroes have many fine ______________, such as courage and strength.
3. Cesar's ______________ were so ethical, he even took coins he found on the playground to the school office.
4. Her ______________ was appalling, and her teacher sent a note home about her behavior.

B. *Follow the directions in responding to each of the items below.*

1. Identify two characteristics you think are necessary for heroes. Answer in complete sentences.
2. Write two sentences explaining one of the characteristics you listed, and describe why you think it is important. Use at least two of the Big Question vocabulary words.

C. *Complete the sentence below. Then, write a short paragraph in which you connect this experience to the Big Question.*

When humans act without **honor** and **responsibility**, their behavior can lead to ______________. If they **conduct** themselves with **integrity**, they can become ______________.

Unit 6 Resources: Themes in Literature
© Pearson Education, Inc. All rights reserved.
27

All Writing About the Big Question, pp. 27, 45

Also available for these selections:

EL L1 L2 Vocabulary Warm-ups A and B, pp. 23–24, 41–42

EL L1 L2 Reading Warm-ups A and B, pp. 25–26, 43–44

All Vocabulary Builder, pp. 30, 48

Reader's Notebooks

Pre- and postreading pages for both selections, as well as "Prometheus and the First People," appear in an interactive format in the *Reader's Notebooks*. Each *Notebook* is differentiated for a different group of learners.

The selections in the Adapted and English Learner's versions are abridged.

L2 L3 *Reader's Notebook*

L1 *Reader's Notebook: Adapted Version*

EL *Reader's Notebook: English Learner's Version*

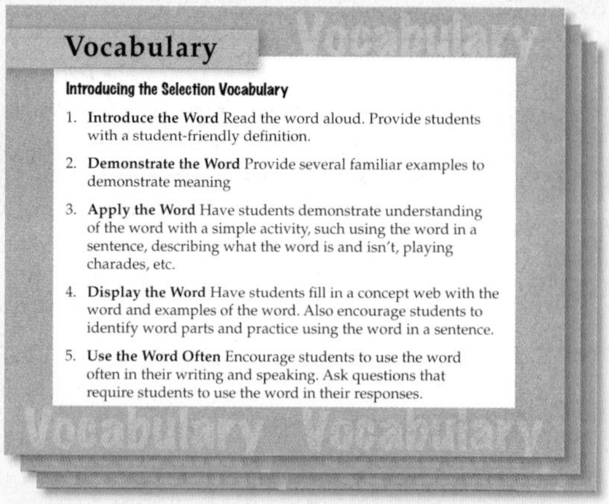
Vocabulary

Introducing the Selection Vocabulary

1. **Introduce the Word** Read the word aloud. Provide students with a student-friendly definition.
2. **Demonstrate the Word** Provide several familiar examples to demonstrate meaning
3. **Apply the Word** Have students demonstrate understanding of the word with a simple activity, such using the word in a sentence, describing what the word is and isn't, playing charades, etc.
4. **Display the Word** Have students fill in a concept web with the word and examples of the word. Also encourage students to identify word parts and practice using the word in a sentence.
5. **Use the Word Often** Encourage students to use the word often in their writing and speaking. Ask questions that require students to use the word in their responses.

Classroom Strategies and Teaching Routines

- core classroom routines outlined step-by-step
- convenient format for easy reference while teaching

Selection Support

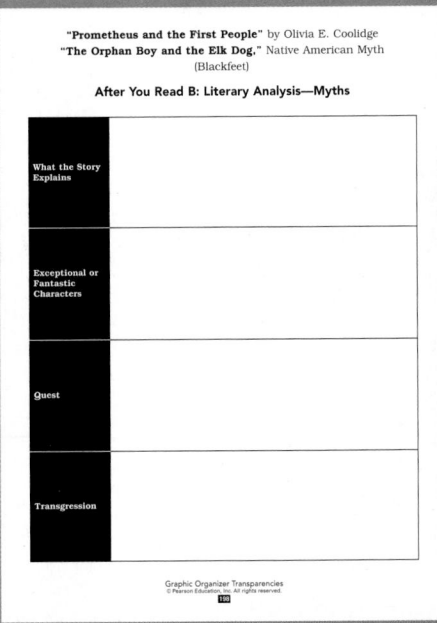

Transparencies

"**Prometheus and the First People**" by Olivia E. Coolidge
"**The Orphan Boy and the Elk Dog,**" Native American Myth (Blackfeet)

After You Read B: Literary Analysis—Myths

What the Story Explains	
Exceptional or Fantastic Characters	
Quest	
Transgression	

Graphic Organizer Transparencies

198

L3 Literary Analysis: Graphic Organizer B, p. 198

Also available for these selections:

- EL L1 L2 Literary Analysis: Graphic Organizer A, pp. 196, 197 (partially filled in)
- EL L1 L2 Reading: Graphic Organizer A, pp. 193, 194 (partially filled in)
- L3 Reading: Graphic Organizer B, p. 195

Skills Development/Extension

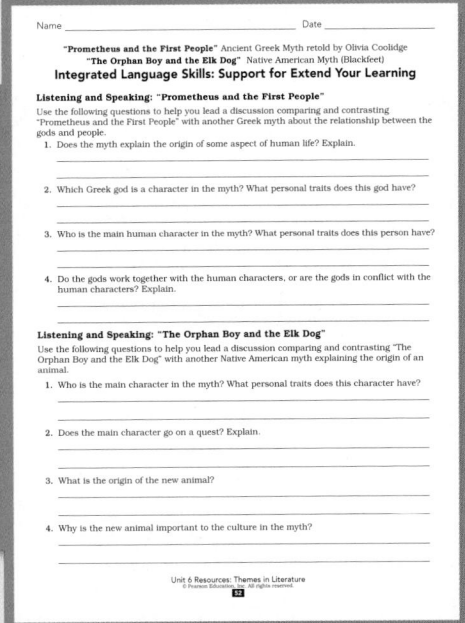

Unit 6 Resources

Name ______________________ Date ____________

"**Prometheus and the First People**" Ancient Greek Myth retold by Olivia Coolidge
"**The Orphan Boy and the Elk Dog**" Native American Myth (Blackfeet)

Integrated Language Skills: Support for Extend Your Learning

Listening and Speaking: "Prometheus and the First People"

Use the following questions to help you lead a discussion comparing and contrasting "Prometheus and the First People" with another Greek myth about the relationship between the gods and people.

1. Does the myth explain the origin of some aspect of human life? Explain.
2. Which Greek god is a character in the myth? What personal traits does this god have?
3. Who is the main human character in the myth? What personal traits does this person have?
4. Do the gods work together with the human characters, or are the gods in conflict with the human characters? Explain.

Listening and Speaking: "The Orphan Boy and the Elk Dog"

Use the following questions to help you lead a discussion comparing and contrasting "The Orphan Boy and the Elk Dog" with another Native American myth explaining the origin of an animal.

1. Who is the main character in the myth? What personal traits does this character have?
2. Does the main character go on a quest? Explain.
3. What is the origin of the new animal?
4. Why is the new animal important to the culture in the myth?

Unit 6 Resources: Themes in Literature

52

L3 L4 Support for Extend Your Learning, p. 52

Also available for these selections:

- All Literary Analysis: Myths, pp. 28, 46
- All Reading: Analyze Cultural Context, pp. 29, 47
- L4 Enrichment, pp. 31, 49
- L3 L4 Grammar, p. 50
- L3 L4 Support for Writing, p. 51

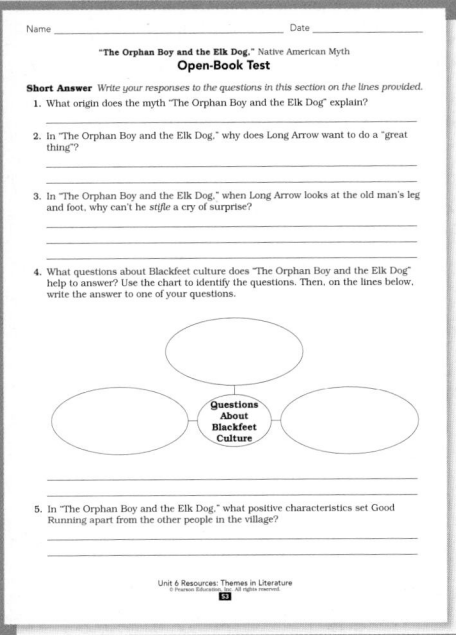

Assessment

Name ______________________ Date ____________

"**The Orphan Boy and the Elk Dog,**" Native American Myth

Open-Book Test

Short Answer *Write your responses to the questions in this section on the lines provided.*

1. What origin does the myth "The Orphan Boy and the Elk Dog" explain?
2. In "The Orphan Boy and the Elk Dog," why does Long Arrow want to do a "great thing"?
3. In "The Orphan Boy and the Elk Dog," when Long Arrow looks at the old man's leg and foot, why can't he *stifle* a cry of surprise?
4. What questions about Blackfeet culture does "The Orphan Boy and the Elk Dog" help to answer? Use the chart to identify the questions. Then, on the lines below, write the answer to one of your questions.

Questions About Blackfeet Culture

5. In "The Orphan Boy and the Elk Dog," what positive characteristics set Good Running apart from the other people in the village?

Unit 6 Resources: Themes in Literature

53

L3 L4 Open-Book Test, pp. 32–34, 53–55

Also available for these selections:

- EL L1 L2 Selection Test A, pp. 35–37, 56–58
- L3 L4 Selection Test B, pp. 38–40, 59–61

PHLit Online!

www.PHLitOnline.com

- complete narrated selection text
- a thematically related video with writing prompt
- an interactive graphic organizer
- highlighting feature
- access to all student print resources, adapted to individual student needs
- Spanish and English summaries

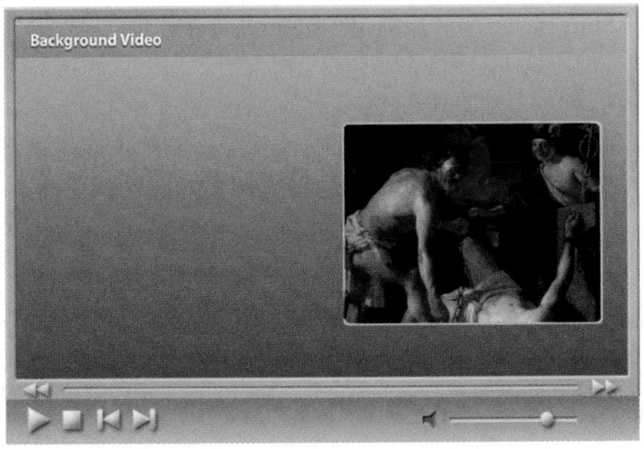

Background video

Also available:

Get Connected! (thematic video with writing prompt)

Vocabulary Central (tools, activities, and songs for studying vocabulary)

Also available:

Writer's Journal (with graphics feature)

DIFFERENTIATE/PRETEACH

❶ Selection Choices

You may use either "Prometheus and the First People" or "The Orphan Boy and the Elk Dog" to meet the lesson standards. Skills instruction for both selections appears on p. 1063. Choose one selection to teach (or choose to teach both). The Accessibility at a Glance chart at the bottom of this page will help you determine which of the two selections is more appropriate for your students.

❷ Selection Skills

1. With the class, preview the selection skills. (The lesson meets the lesson objectives given on p. 1062a.)
2. Explain that students will learn to use the skill of analyzing cultural context as they read to better understand and enjoy the selection you choose. By examining myths as they read, they will gain deeper insight into the selection.
3. To introduce the Writing and Listening and Speaking activities (p. 1089), tell students that when they have finished reading the selection, they will write a myth and present a retelling of another myth related to the selection.
4. Tell students that they will also study a grammar concept: simple and compound sentences. By mastering this concept, they will improve their reading fluency and the quality of their own writing.

Before You Read

Prometheus and the First People • The Orphan Boy and the Elk Dog

❶ Selection Choices

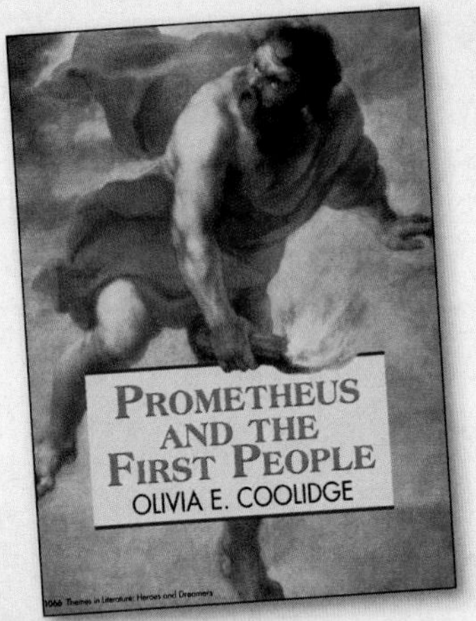

▲ Read **"Prometheus and the First People"** to discover what ancient Greeks believed and valued.

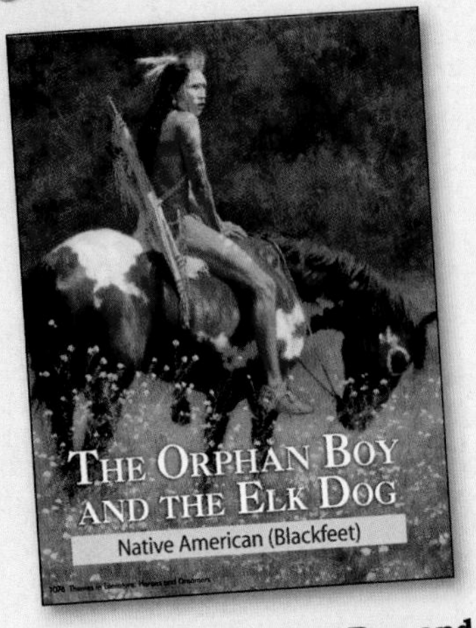

▲ Read **"The Orphan Boy and the Elk Dog"** to find out how the Blackfeet acquired horses.

❷ Selection Skills Guide

Practice these skills with either **"Prometheus and the First People"** (p. 1066) or **"The Orphan Boy and the Elk Dog"** (p. 1076).

- Understand myths
- Analyze cultural context
- Generate questions
- Identify simple and compound sentences
- Write a myth
- Present a retelling

Differentiated Instruction for Universal Access

Accessibility at a Glance: Selection Choices

	Prometheus and the First People	The Orphan Boy and the Elk Dog	
Context	Ancient Greece	Native Americans	Because a number of factors determine the relative accessibility of paired selections, in some cases the Lexile rating of the more challenging selection will be lower than that of the more accessible selection.
Language/ Vocabulary	• Formal • Follows myth conventions • Grade-level vocabulary	• Follows myth conventions • Some culture-specific vocabulary	
Concept Level	Accessible (three short myths that may be familiar to students)	Challenging (abstract fantasy elements)	
Literary Merit	Classic	Cross-cultural	
Lexile/Length	Lexile: 1090L Word Count: 1,933	Lexile: 960L Word Count: 3,564	
Overall Rating	**More accessible**	**More challenging**	

❸ Literary Analysis: Myths

Myths are stories that are part of an oral tradition: Before being written, they were told and retold from one generation to the next. Myths reflect the culture of the people who originated and shared them.

- Some myths explain a natural phenomenon or a specific custom by describing its **origins** or how it came to be. These myths reveal the beliefs of ancient cultures.
- Myths include characters with exceptional characteristics such as strength, bravery, or wisdom. These traits emphasize qualities that the culture admired or feared.
- Some myths tell of a **quest,** or search, for knowledge or a valued object. These myths reveal what was important to the culture.
- Other myths tell of a **transgression,** or the violation of a rule. By example, these myths teach the values of the culture.

❹ Reading Skill: Analyze Cultural Context

To understand a myth, **analyze cultural context,** or determine ways in which the myth reflects the lives and concerns of those who told it. Before you read, **generate questions** about cultural context. Ask yourself one question about each element shown in the chart.

❺ Using the Strategy: Cultural Context Chart

Use a **cultural context chart** to record the details in the myth that help you answer your questions.

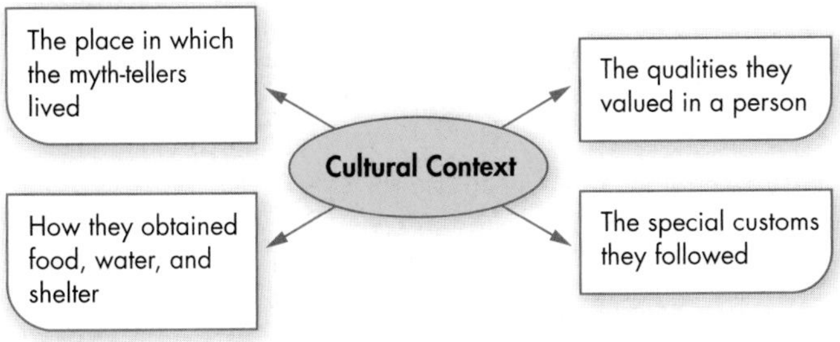

PHLit Online!
www.PHLitOnline.com

Hear It!
- Selection summary audio
- Selection audio

See It!
- Get Connected video
- Background video
- More about the author
- Vocabulary flashcards

Do It!
- Interactive journals
- Interactive graphic organizers
- Self-test
- Internet activity
- Grammar tutorial
- Interactive vocabulary games

Differentiated Instruction for Universal Access

Preparing Students for the More Challenging Selection

If you wish to prepare lower-level readers to read "The Orphan and the Elk Dog," the more challenging selection, follow these steps:

- Provide students with background on the Plains Indians, including their mode of travel, dwellings, and the foods they ate. For instance, explain that tipis suited the nomadic lifestyle: tipis consist of long poles and animal hide, allowing the dismantled structure to be carried easily. Prompt students to think about other characteristics that might have been influenced by a nomadic lifestyle.
- Explain to students that central to Native American belief is a reverence for and connection to the land and animals. Elements of nature are not only sacred but also infused with spirit and special abilities.
- Explain to students that this myth describes a rite of passage, a culturally significant event marking an individual's entrance into adulthood. Prompt students to think about the "rites of passage" they have experienced.

PRETEACH

❸ Literary Analysis

1. Introduce the skill, using the instruction on the student page.
2. Tell students that they will practice identifying and interpreting myths as they read.

Think Aloud: Model the Skill

Model the skill of identifying and interpreting myths. Say:

> I can use specific details to identify and interpret myths. If the myth is about the creation of the world, I know it is an *origin* myth—it reveals animals and physical features important to the culture. If the myth is about a search for a special object, I know it is a *quest*—it reveals objects and qualities valued by the culture. If the myth tells of how humans disobeyed the gods, I know it is a *transgression* myth—it reveals behavior that is acceptable or unacceptable in a culture.

❹ Reading Skill

1. Introduce the skill, using the instruction on the student page.
2. Tell students that they will practice analyzing cultural context as they read.

Think Aloud: Model the Skill

Model the skill of analyzing cultural context. Say:

> To help me understand a myth, I can ask myself questions about the myth's cultural context. If I am reading a myth about a boy who is shunned by his village because of his ugly appearance, I may ask myself, What physical characteristics do the myth-tellers consider to be attractive? How do the mythtellers treat social outcasts? These questions help guide my thoughts on the myth's cultural context as I read.

❺ Using the Strategy

Give students a copy of either **Reading Skill Graphic Organizer A** or **B** (*Graphic Organizer Transparencies,* pp. 193–195) to record details of cultural context as they read. Use the examples in **Reading Skill Graphic Organizer A,** which is partially filled in, to model the process.

PRETEACH

❶ Writing About the Big Question

1. Review the assignment with the class.
2. Have students define *honor* and *integrity* in their own words. Then, **ask** students why these qualities might be important to possess. (**Possible response:** People with a good sense of right and wrong make good judgments.)
3. Have students complete the sentence starters. Review responses as a class. (**Possible response:** One should always act with honor and responsibility because it is the correct and moral thing to do. Hope and integrity can help you persevere in difficult situations because they make you strong and inspire you to continue.)
4. Remind students that their answers will help them think about the Big Question, "Can anyone be a hero?"

While You Read

Tell students that as they read, they should look for examples of gods or people whose actions help others.

❷ Vocabulary

1. Have students preview the selection vocabulary.
2. For each word, have students say the word aloud.
3. Then, use the word in a sentence that defines the word.
4. Finally, repeat your definitional sentence or a similar sentence with the word missing and have the class "fill in the blank" chorally. Here is an example:

   To inhabit is to live in. It is a discomforting truth to know that whatever humans can live in, cockroaches can [students say "inhabit"], *too.*

❸ Word Study

1. Introduce the skill, using the instruction in the box.
2. Using their knowledge of the root *-dur-*, have students define the word *durable*. (**Answer:** "able to last")

Can anyone be a *hero?*

❶ Writing About the Big Question

In "Prometheus and the First People," a character helps out others, even though his actions put himself in danger. Use these sentence starters to develop your ideas about the Big Question:

One should always act with **honor** and **responsibility** because ________________.

Hope and **integrity** can help you **persevere** in difficult situations because ________________.

While You Read Look for examples of gods or people whose actions help others. Decide which characters act most heroically.

❷ Vocabulary

Read each word and its definition. Decide whether you know the word well, know it a little bit, or do not know it at all. After you read, see how your knowledge of each word has increased.

- **toil** (toil) *n.* hard, tiring work (p. 1067) *After much sweat and toil, I finally finished building the wall.* toil *v.* toiler *n.*
- **heedless** (hēd′ lis) *adj.* careless; thoughtless (p. 1067) *His heedless remark was hurtful.* heed *v.* heedlessly *adv.* heedlessness *n.*
- **inhabit** (in hab′ it) *v.* live in (p. 1067) *Many birds inhabit our yard because it has lots of trees.* inhabitable *adj.* inhabitation *n.* habitat *n.*
- **counsel** (koun′ səl) *n.* advice; discussion (p. 1069) *He sought his brother's counsel whenever he had to make a hard decision.* counsel *v.* counselor *n.*
- **disembarked** (dis′ im bärkt′) *v.* left a ship to go ashore (p. 1071) *They disembarked at the dock and waved goodbye to the ship's crew.* disembarkation *n.* embark *v.*
- **endure** (en do͝or′) *v.* hold up under pain or hardship (p. 1072) *They could endure anything after surviving the storm.* endurable *adj.* endurably *adv.* enduring *adj.*

❸ Word Study

The **Latin root *-dur-*** means "hard" or "to last."

In this story, humans learn to **endure** pain and sorrow, or to last through hardship and suffering without quitting.

Vocabulary Development

Vocabulary Knowledge Rating

Create a **Vocabulary Knowledge Rating Chart** (*Professional Development Guidebook*, p. 33) for this selection. Include the selection vocabulary and the Big Question words that appear in the Writing About the Big Question sentence starters. (The Big Question vocabulary is introduced on pp. 1046–1047.)

Give students a copy of the chart. Read the words aloud, and have students mark their rating in the Before Reading column. Urge them to be alert to these words as they read and discuss the selection.

Tally how many students think they know a word to gauge how much instruction to provide. As students read and discuss the selection, point out the words and their context.

Vocabulary Central, featuring tools, activities, and songs for studying vocabulary, is available online at **www.PHLitOnline.com**.

Meet The Ancient Greeks and Olivia E. Coolidge (b. 1908)

Author of the retelling of PROMETHEUS AND THE FIRST PEOPLE

Thousands of years ago in Greece, the Mycenaeans (mī´ sə nē´ ənz) told stories of a great sea god. Their civilization collapsed around 1200 B.C., but settlers from the north, the Dorians, blended the old myths with their own stories. Classical Greek mythology was born.

The ancient Greeks represented the Olympic gods as having human qualities. Just as the typical Greek household was dominated by the father, so Zeus dominates the Olympic gods.

Retelling the Tale Greek myths were a favorite of **Olivia E. Coolidge,** who retells the myth of Prometheus. Born in London, England, Coolidge studied Latin, Greek, and philosophy.

DID YOU KNOW?

Many traditions of Western civilization, including democracy, science, and philosophy, began with the ancient Greeks.

4 BACKGROUND FOR THE MYTH

The Greek Gods

Many of the characters in "Prometheus and the First People" are Olympians, the family of gods and goddesses ruled by Zeus and his wife Hera. Each god and goddess governs an aspect of nature or human life. For example, Ares (er´ ēz´) is the god of war.

Prometheus and the First People 1065

Daily Bellringer

For each class during which you will teach this selection, have students complete one of the five Quick Write activities for Week 31 in the ***Daily Bellringer Activities*** booklet.

4 Background

The Olympians are named for Mount Olympus, a mountain in Greece. More than 9,500 feet high, Olympus has snow cover year round and is often ringed by a low band of clouds from which its peak emerges. Perhaps because of this striking image, the mountain came to be regarded by the ancient Greeks as the home of Zeus and the rest of the Greek Pantheon, or collection of gods.

Each of the major Greek gods and goddesses had his or her domain. Zeus, the king of the gods, was the supreme deity. Most of the other major Greek gods were the offspring of Zeus by various consorts. Apollo, one of Zeus' sons, was the sun god and associated with the arts. Apollo's twin sister, Artemis, was the goddess of the moon and also of the hunt.

Prometheus and his brother Epimetheus were not Olympian gods or earthly men, but Titans, a race of giant gods overthrown by the gods of Olympus. The word *titanic,* meaning "tremendous," derives from these mythic origins.

Multidraft Reading

This icon ● marks natural pauses in the selection. To assist struggling readers and to deepen reading for all, assign the text in "chunks," following the icons, and apply multidraft reading protocols. For each reading, have students set the purpose indicated:

- **First reading**—literal comprehension: answering the Reading Check questions.
- **Second reading**—application of skills: answering the Myths and Analyze Cultural Context prompts.
- **Third reading**—interpretation: answering the end-of-selection questions.

For more guidance, refer to the ***Classroom Strategies and Teaching Routines*** card on multidraft reading.

Differentiated Instruction — Additional Instruction

EL Extended Support—English Learners

Have students complete the **Reading and Vocabulary Warm-ups,** ***Unit 6 Resources,*** pp. 23–26, before they read. Assign the prereading pages for the selection in the ***Reader's Notebook: English Learner's Version.*** Then, have students listen to portions of the selection on the ***Hear It!*** **Audio CD.**

L1 L2 Extended Support—Struggling Readers

Have students complete the **Reading and Vocabulary Warm-ups,** ***Unit 6 Resources,*** pp. 23–26, before they read. Assign the prereading pages and the adapted selection in the ***Reader's Notebook: Adapted Version.*** Then, have students listen to portions of the selection on the ***Hear It!*** **Audio CD** (adapted text).

Extended Support—Reluctant Readers

To build motivation and engagement before assigning the selection, have students read "Science's Double-Edged Swords," a thematically related selection in ***Reality Central.*** Then, use the questions at the conclusion of the related selection to guide discussion.

PHLit Online!

For more about the author, practice with the selection vocabulary, and more background, go online at **www.PHLitOnline.com.**

❶ Activating Prior Knowledge

1. Prepare an **Anticipation Guide** (see ***Professional Development Guidebook***, pp. 36–38) with the following statements:
   - The best way to learn is through experience.
   - In the end, virtue is always rewarded.
   - The purpose of a story is to entertain.
2. Give students a copy of the prepared **Anticipation Guide** and have students mark their responses in the Me column. Have students discuss the statements in pairs or groups and mark the guides again in the Group column.
3. For further guidance, use the ***Classroom Strategies and Teaching Routines*** card: **Using an Anticipation Guide**.

Concept Connector →

Students will return to the **Anticipation Guide** after completing the myth.

Small-Group Activity

Have students in small groups draw diagrams dividing the world into air, land, and sea. Groups should then list the various animals mentioned by Epimetheus, along with the special power given to each animal, in the appropriate section. Have students add human beings to the list after discussing where humans should be placed and what special powers they have.

❷ About the Selection

"Prometheus and the First People" provides explanations for humans' mental capacity and the source of humanity's miseries. Prometheus gives humans the gift of mental powers. Then he gives humans their first valuable tool by stealing fire from the gods, a transgression for which he is punished.

❸ Humanities

Prometheus Carrying Fire
by Jan Cossiers

Prometheus was such a compelling figure that he is featured in more than one myth. Also, his story became the focus of later works of literature and operas, as well as paintings such as the one shown here.

❶ ❷ ❸

Prometheus and the First People

OLIVIA E. COOLIDGE

Vocabulary Development

Thematic Vocabulary: The Big Question

As students are discussing "Prometheus and the First People," encourage them to use the thematic vocabulary presented in Introducing the Big Question, pp. 1046–1047. You might encourage them with sentence starters like these:

1. Epithemeus gave Prometheus the *responsibility* of . . .
2. Pandora's poor *conduct* caused . . .
3. Deucalion and Pyrrha *persevere* despite the flood because . . .
4. According to the myth, humans now have a stronger *character* because . . .

Humanity's Beginnings

The Greeks have several stories about how man came to be. One declares that he was created in the age of Kronos,[1] or Saturn, who ruled before Zeus [zo͞os]. At that time, the legend says, there was no sorrow, **toil**, sickness, or age. Men lived their lives in plenty and died as though they went to sleep. They tilled[2] no ground, built no
5 cities, killed no living thing, and among them war was unknown. The earth brought forth strawberries, cherries, and ears of wheat for them. Even on the bramble bushes grew berries good to eat. Milk and sweet nectar flowed in rivers for men to drink, and honey dripped from hollow trees. Men lived in caves and thickets, needing little shelter, for the season was always spring.

Another legend declares that Zeus conceived of animals first and he entrusted their creation to Prometheus [prō mē´ thē əs] and Epimetheus [ep ə mē´ thē əs], his brother. First, Epimetheus undertook to order all things, but he was a **heedless** person and soon got into trouble. Finally he was forced to appeal to Prometheus.

"What have you done?" asked Prometheus.

"Down on the earth," answered his brother, "there is a green, grassy clearing, ringed by tall oak trees and shaded by steep slopes from all but the midday sun. There I sat and the animals came to me, while I gave to each the gifts which should be his from this time forward. Air I gave to the birds, seas to the fishes, land to four-footed creatures and the creeping insects, and to some, like the moles, I gave burrows beneath the earth."

"That was well done," answered Prometheus. "What else did you do?"

"Strength," said Epimetheus, "I gave to lions and tigers, and the fierce animals of the woods. Size I gave to others like the great whales of the sea. The deer I made swift and timid, and the insects I made tiny that they might escape from sight. I gave warm fur to the
6 great bears and the little squirrels, keen eyes and sharp talons[3] to the birds of prey, tusks to the elephant, hide to the wild boar, sweet songs and bright feathers to the birds. To each I gave some special excellence, that whether large or small, kind or terrible, each might live in his own place, find food, escape enemies, and enjoy the wide world which is his to **inhabit**."

"All this is very good," said his brother, Prometheus. "You have done well. Wherein lies your trouble?"

1. **Kronos** (krō´ nəs) son of the sky and the earth; father of Zeus.
2. **tilled** *v.* cultivated; plowed or hoed.
3. **talons** (tal´ ənz) *n.* claws (of birds of prey).

4 ◄ **Critical Viewing** Which details in this painting of Prometheus suggest that he fears the gods' anger? **[Analyze]**

Vocabulary

toil (toil) *n.* hard, tiring work

heedless (hēd´ lis) *adj.* careless; thoughtless

inhabit (in hab´ it) *v.* live in

Literary Analysis
Myths Which details show you that this myth will explain the origins of something?

Reading Skill
Analyze Cultural Context What question does this paragraph suggest to you about the region where the Greeks lived?

7 **Reading Check**

What task does Zeus give to Prometheus and his brother?

4 Critical Viewing

Answer: Prometheus hides the torch with his body and looks back as if he is afraid that someone is following him or watching him. Also, the sky is stormy, which emphasizes the tense situation.

5 Literary Analysis
Myths

1. Have a student read aloud the first paragraph of "Prometheus and the First People."
2. **Ask** students to answer the Literary Analysis question: Which details show you that this myth will explain the origins of something?
   Answer: The myth opens by citing that the Greeks have several stories about how humans came to be. The myth then summarizes one such story.

6 Reading Skill
Analyze Cultural Context

1. Have a volunteer read the bracketed passage.
2. Then, **ask** students the Reading Skill question: What question does this paragraph suggest to you about the region where the Greeks lived?
   Answer: This paragraph suggests the question *What is the climate of Greece?* The paragraph also suggests questions such as *What kinds of animals are located in Greece? Where is Greece located?*
3. **Ask** students why the list includes animals from many different habitats.
   Answer: As an origin myth, the story must explain the origin of animals all over the planet, not just in Greece.

7 Reading Check

Answer: Zeus gives the responsibility of creating animals to Prometheus and Epimetheus.

Differentiated Instruction for Universal Access

Enrichment for Gifted/Talented Students
Encourage students to design a Greek mythology art exhibit. Students should illustrate "Humanity's Beginnings" using pencil, paint, chalk, collage, or another medium. Have each student write a brief note for his or her artwork that explains the element of the myth it captures. Display the artwork and lead a discussion about how myths in particular inspire works of art. Use students' creations and the painting of Prometheus on the previous page to prompt discussion.

Enrichment for Advanced Readers
Explain that Prometheus is a compelling figure in Western culture because his story combines advancement (the invention of fire) with consequences (punishment for overreaching). Discuss with students why this classic combination is still considered a prevalent theme in today's popular culture. Encourage students to research the origin myths of ancient Greece and other stories about Prometheus. Have them write essays that trace this theme from ancient Greece to contemporary American popular culture.

PHLit Online!
This selection is available in interactive format in the **Enriched Online Student Edition** at **www.PHLitOnline.com**, which includes a thematically related video and writing prompt and an interactive graphic organizer.

8 Literature in Context

Culture Connection The Olympian gods came into power after a fierce family struggle. Zeus overthrew his father, Cronos, who had overthrown his father, Uranus. To thwart a prophecy in which a child of his would drive him out of power, Cronos devoured several of his own children. His son Zeus, however, remained hidden and later overpowered his father. Zeus forced Cronos to disgorge the children he had eaten. Zeus's siblings include several other gods: Demeter, Hades, Hera, Hestia, and Poseidon. Zeus, in turn, became the father of Apollo, Ares, Artemis, Athena, and Hermes.

Connect to the Literature Briefly discuss with students any characteristics, associations, or stories they know about the Olympian gods. Then, **ask** the Connect to the Literature question: According to this myth, what is the relationship between the gods and humans like?
Answer: The myth about the great flood shows that the relationship between the gods and humans is far from equal. The gods hold much more power than humans and inflict destruction and misery on the humans at will. Humans submit to the gods and are helpless to check their power.

9 Literary Analysis
Myths

Ask students why Prometheus gives humans both intellectual and physical fire.
Answer: With the fire of intellect, men and women can invent ways to utilize physical fire for tools, food, industry, and so on.

10 Literary Analysis
Myths

1. **Ask** students why Prometheus' gift of fire is a transgression.
   Answer: The gift is a transgression because it is stolen. Fire is treasured by the gods, and Prometheus does not have permission to give it to humans.
2. **Ask** students why Zeus deems Prometheus' transgression worthy of such a cruel punishment.
   Possible response: When Prometheus gives away fire, he diminishes the gods' power. Zeus views the theft of fire as threatening to the gods' control of Earth.

8 **LITERATURE IN CONTEXT**

Culture Connection

The Twelve Olympian Gods
The ancient Greeks worshiped a family of gods said to have their home on Mount Olympus:

Zeus (zo͞os) ruler of the gods

Hera (hir′ ə) queen of the gods; goddess of marriage

Aphrodite (af′ rə dīt′ ē) goddess of love and beauty

Apollo (ə päl′ ō) god of music, poetry, and light

Ares (er′ ēz′) god of war

Artemis (är′ tə mis) goddess of the moon, wild animals, and hunting

Athene (ə thē′ nē) goddess of wisdom

Demeter (di mēt′ ər) goddess of grain and agriculture

Hephaestus (hē fes′ təs) god of fire; blacksmith of the gods

Hermes (hʉr′ mēz′) messenger of the gods; god of business, science, and speech

Hestia (hes′ tē ə) goddess of the hearth

Poseidon (pō sī′ dən) god of earthquakes, the sea, and horses

Connect to the Literature

According to this myth, what is the relationship between the gods and humans like?

"Because I did not think it out beforehand," said the heedless brother sadly, "I did not count how many animals there were to be before I started giving. Now when I have given all, there comes one last animal for whom I have neither skill nor shape, nor any place to dwell in. Everything has been given already."

"What is this animal," said Prometheus, "who has been forgotten?"

"His name," said Epimetheus, "is Man."

Thus it was that the future of man was left to Prometheus, who was forced to make man different from all other creatures. Therefore he gave him the shape of the gods themselves and the privilege of walking upright as they do. He gave him no special home, but made him ruler over the whole earth, and over the sea and air. Finally, he gave him no special strength or swiftness, but stole a spark from heaven and lighted a heavenly fire within his mind which 9
should teach him to understand, to count, to speak, to remember. Man learned from it how to build cities, tame animals, raise crops, build boats, and do all the things that animals cannot. Prometheus also kindled fire on earth that man might smelt[4] metals and make tools. In fact, from this heavenly fire of Prometheus all man's greatness comes.

Before this time fire was a divine thing and belonged only to the gods. It was one of their greatest treasures, and Zeus would never have given Prometheus permission to use it in the creation of man. Therefore when Prometheus stole it, Zeus was furious indeed. He chained Prometheus to a great, lofty rock, where the sun scorched him by day and the cruel frost tortured him by night. Not content 10
with that, he sent an eagle to tear him, so that, though he could not die, he lived in agony. For many centuries Prometheus hung in torment, but he was wiser than Zeus, and by reason of a secret he had, he forced Zeus in later ages to set him free. By then, also, Zeus had learned that there is more in ruling than power and cruelty. Thus, the two at last were friends.

4. **smelt** *v.* purify metal by melting it.

Vocabulary Development

Selection Vocabulary Reinforcement
Students will benefit from additional examples and practice with the selection vocabulary words. Reinforce their comprehension with "show-you-know" sentences. The first part of the sentence uses the vocabulary word in an appropriate context. The second part of the sentence—the "show-you-know" part—clarifies the first. Model the strategy with this example for *adapt:*

Even though moving was a big change, the puppy was able to *adapt* quickly to his new home because his new family made him feel comfortable.

Then, give students these sentence prompts, and coach them in creating the clarification part:

1. I needed *counsel*, so . . .
   Sample answer: I asked for my father's advice.
2. After everyone had *disembarked*, . . .
   Sample answer: the ship was empty.

The Coming of Evil

11 After the punishment of Prometheus, Zeus planned to take his revenge on man. He could not recall the gift of fire, since it had been given by one of the immortals,[5] but he was not content that man should possess this treasure in peace and become perhaps as great as were the gods themselves. He therefore took **counsel** with the other gods, and together they made for man a woman. All the gods gave gifts to this new creation. Aphrodite [af´ rə dīt´ ē] gave her fresh beauty like the spring itself. The goddess Athene [ə thē´ nē] dressed her and put on her a garland of flowers and green leaves. She had also a golden diadem[6] beautifully decorated with figures of animals. In her heart Hermes [hʉr´ mēz´] put cunning, deceit, and curiosity. She was named Pandora [pan dôr´ ə], which means All-Gifted, since each of the gods had given her something. The last gift was a chest in which there was supposed to be great treasure, but which Pandora was instructed never to open. Then Hermes, the Messenger, took the girl and brought her to Epimetheus.

Epimetheus had been warned by his brother to receive no gifts from Zeus, but he was a heedless person, as ever, and Pandora was very lovely. He accepted her, therefore, and for a while they lived together in happiness, for Pandora besides her beauty had been given both wit and charm. Eventually, however, her curiosity got the better of her, and she determined to see for herself what treasure it was that the gods had given her. One day when she was alone, she went over to the corner where her chest lay and cautiously lifted the lid for a peep. The lid flew up out of her hands and knocked her aside, while before her frightened eyes dreadful, shadowy shapes flew out of the box in an endless stream. There were hunger, disease, war, greed, anger, jealousy, toil, and all the griefs and hardships to which man from that day has been subject. Each was terrible in appearance, and as it passed, Pandora saw something of the misery that her thoughtless action had brought on her descendants. At last the stream slackened,[7] and Pandora, who had been paralyzed with fear and horror, found strength to shut her box. The only thing left in it now, however, was the one good gift the gods had put in among so many evil ones. This was hope, and since that time the hope that is in man's heart is the only thing which has made him able to bear the sorrows that Pandora brought upon him.

5. **immortals** (i môrt´ 'lz) *n.* those who do not die.
6. **diadem** (dī´ ə dem´) *n.* crown.
7. **slackened** (slak´ ənd) *v.* diminished; became less active.

12

Vocabulary
counsel (koun´ səl) *n.* advice; discussion

13 **Reading Check**
Why does Zeus punish Prometheus?

11 Reading Skill
Analyze Cultural Context

1. Have students read the description of Pandora. **Ask** students what gifts Pandora receives.
 Answer: Pandora receives beauty, clothes, a garland, a crown, a name, a box, and a heart full of cunning, deceit, and curiosity.
2. **Ask** students what questions they should ask about the ancient Greeks' view of women.
 Answer: Students may state questions such as the following: *What societal roles did women have? Did ancient Greek society hold unrealistic expectations for women regarding beauty? Were women in ancient Greece considered trustworthy?*

12 Humanities
Pandora by Dante Gabriel Rossetti

Born in London in 1828, Rossetti was an accomplished painter and poet. He was part of a group of painters who called themselves the Pre-Raphaelites. They focused on painting in the style of the medieval period. Not only did Rossetti create the artwork *Pandora*, but he also wrote a sonnet about it.

13 Reading Check
Answer: Zeus is threatened by the power that humans will gain with the stolen fire.

Differentiated Instruction for Universal Access

Strategy for Less Proficient Readers
Help students follow the transition between the first myth and the second. Draw a Venn diagram on the board, labeling one circle *Prometheus* and the other *Pandora*. Have students reread the last paragraph of the Prometheus myth and paraphrase it in their own words. Write the paraphrase in Prometheus' circle. Then, tell students to reread the first paragraph of the Pandora myth and paraphrase it in their own words. Write this paraphrase in Pandora's circle. Finally, ask students to identify the overlapping elements of the two paraphrases, such as the stolen fire and Prometheus' punishment. Guide students to note that because Prometheus steals fire, Zeus wants to punish both Prometheus who steals the fire and the humans who receive it.

⓮ Critical Viewing

Possible response: The rain and lightning from the sky suggest that the gods are the creators of the storm. The people stranded on the rock seem to raise their arms in fear and in supplication to the gods.

⓯ Connecting to the Big Question

1. Explain to students that heroes are prevalent in Greek myths. Explain that some of these heroes are mortals, such as Odysseus, while others, like Prometheus, are gods. Emphasize that there is a third kind of hero, the demi-god, who is half human and half god. For example, Hercules, the man of superhuman strength, is the son of Zeus and the mortal Alcmene.
2. Have a volunteer read the bracketed passage. **Ask:** Was Zeus justified in his decision to punish mankind? Explain.
   Possible response: Yes, because according to the gods' standards, everyone should possess heroic qualities such as selflessness, honor, and respect. The evil that was introduced to mankind caused people to act wickedly, thereby losing the heroic qualities they may have had.
3. **Ask:** Are Zeus' actions heroic? Why or why not?
   Possible response: No. By bringing death and destruction to mankind, Zeus does not embody any heroic qualities. Instead, he is cruel, shows a lack of compassion, and abuses his own power.

⓮ ▲ **Critical Viewing** Which details in this painting suggest that the gods are punishing man? **[Analyze]**

The Great Flood

When evil first came among mankind, people became very wicked. War, robbery, treachery, and murder prevailed throughout the world. Even the worship of the gods, the laws of truth and honor, reverence[8] for parents and brotherly love were neglected.

⓯ Finally, Zeus determined to destroy the race of men altogether, and the other gods agreed. All the winds were therefore shut up in a cave except the South Wind, the wet one. He raced over the earth with water streaming from his beard and long, white hair. Clouds gathered around his head, and dew dripped from his wings and the ends of his garments. With him went Iris, the rainbow goddess,

8. **reverence** (rev′ ə rəns) *n.* feeling or display of great respect.

Vocabulary Development

Vocabulary Knowledge Rating

When students have completed reading and discussing "Prometheus and the First People," have them take out their **Vocabulary Knowledge Rating Chart** for this selection. Read the words aloud once more and have students rate their knowledge of the words again in the After Reading column. Clarify any words that are still problematic. Have students write their own definition or example in the appropriate column. Then, have students complete the Vocabulary Practice at the end of the selection. Encourage students to use the words in further discussion and written work about this selection. Remind them that they will be accountable for these words on the **Selection Test, *Unit 6 Resources***, pp. 35–37 or 38–40.

while below Poseidon [pō sī´ dən] smote the earth with his trident until it shook and gaped open, so that the waters of the sea rushed up over the land. 15

Fields and farmhouses were buried. Fish swam in the tops of the trees. Sea beasts were quietly feeding where flocks and herds had grazed before. On the surface of the water, boars, stags, lions, and tigers struggled desperately to keep afloat. Wolves swam in the midst of flocks of sheep, but the sheep were not frightened by them, and the wolves never thought of their natural prey. Each fought for his own life and forgot the others. Over them wheeled countless birds, winging far and wide in the hope of finding something to rest upon. Eventually they too fell into the water and were drowned.

All over the water were men in small boats or makeshift rafts. Some even had oars which they tried to use, but the waters were fierce and stormy, and there was nowhere to go. In time all were drowned, until at last there was no one left but an old man and his wife, Deucalion [do͞o kāl´ ē ən] and Pyrrha [pir´ ə]. These two people had lived in truth and justice, unlike the rest of mankind. They had been warned of the coming of the flood and had built a boat and stocked it. For nine days and nights they floated until Zeus took pity on them and they came to the top of Mount Parnassus, the sacred home of the Muses.[9] There they found land and **disembarked** to wait while the gods recalled the water they had unloosed. 16

Vocabulary
disembarked (dis´ im bärkt´) *v.* left a ship to go ashore

When the waters fell, Deucalion and Pyrrha looked over the land, despairing. Mud and sea slime covered the earth; all living things had been swept away. Slowly and sadly they made their way down the mountain until they came to a temple where there had been an oracle.[10] Black seaweed dripped from the pillars now, and the mud was over all. Nevertheless the two knelt down and kissed the temple steps while Deucalion prayed to the goddess to tell them what they should do. All men were dead but themselves, and they were old. It was impossible that they should have children to people the earth again. Out of the temple a great voice was heard speaking strange words.

"Depart," it said, "with veiled heads and loosened robes, and throw behind you as you go the bones of your mother." 17

Reading Check
Why does Zeus punish man?

Pyrrha was in despair when she heard this saying. "The bones of our mother!" she cried. "How can we tell now where they lie? Even

9. **Muses** (myo͞oz´ əz) *n.* nine goddesses who rule over literature and the arts and sciences.
10. **oracle** (ôr´ ə kəl) *n.* person who, when consulted on a matter, is said to reveal the will of the gods.

16 Reading Skill
Analyze Cultural Context

1. Have students read the paragraph describing Deucalion and Pyrrha's experience during the flood.
2. **Ask** students what questions are suggested by the paragraph about the values of the ancient Greeks.
   Answer: Students may state questions such as *Why do the Greeks value honesty?* and *Do the Greeks value compassion and piety more than honesty?*
3. **Ask** students what questions are suggested by the paragraph about the land of Greece.
   Answer: Students may state questions such as *Where is Mount Parnassus?; Is the climate of the area largely dry, or does it include frequent flooding?;* and *Why would a flood be a particularly horrible catastrophe for people living in Greece?*

17 Reading Check

Answer: Zeus punishes humanity because people became evil and immoral. They also stopped showing respect for the gods.

Concept Connector

Anticipation Guide

Have students return to their ***Anticipation Guides*** and respond to the statements again in the After Reading column. They may do this individually or in their original pairs or groups. Then, lead a class discussion probing for what students have learned that confirms or invalidates each statement. Encourage students to cite specific details, quotations, or other evidence from the text to support their responses to each statement.

Writing About the Big Question

Have students compare their responses to the sentence starters they completed before reading "Prometheus and the First People" with their ideas afterward. Ask them to explain whether their thoughts have changed.

Reading Skill Graphic Organizer

Ask students to review the graphic organizers they completed to generate questions about cultural context in myths while reading. Show them the partially completed **Reading Skill Graphic Organizer A** (***Graphic Organizer Transparencies,*** page 193) as an example. Have students share their graphic organizers.

⓲ Literary Analysis
Myths

Ask students the Literary Analysis question: What fact of life is explained by the myth of Deucalion and Pyrrha?

Answer: The myth explains that life includes toil, sorrow, and pain, but that humans have the strength to endure each.

ASSESS
Answers

Critical Thinking

1. Some students might want to ask Zeus why he is so intent on punishing people.
2. (a) He believes he has run out of special qualities to give out. (b) Unlike the physical traits that Epimetheus gives the animals, mental powers are the gift that Prometheus gives human beings. (c) **Possible response:** Students may feel that the mental gifts given to human beings are the most valuable, because these gifts enable humans to control their environment.
3. (a) Prometheus steals divine fire and gives it to human beings. (b) Humans were not supposed to have the kind of power that fire would give them. (c) **Possible response:** Greeks seemed to view Zeus as a harsh, self-centered god.
4. (a) Pandora brings griefs and hardships such as illness, war, famine, and disaster. (b) Humans cannot become powerful enemies of Zeus because they fight one another and are weakened by illness and natural disasters.

Can anyone be a hero?

Possible response: Because they have remained virtuous and trustworthy throughout their lives—already a heroic achievement—Deucalion and Pyrrha are saved from the flood's destruction. Their world, however, is ruined; although despairing, they put their faith in the gods to aid them. Through the stones they cast on the ground, Deucalion and Pyrrha populate the land once again with the gods' blessing. In this way, then, Deucalion and Pyrrha are the model humans who have won the gods' favor, a difficult but heroic feat.

Literary Analysis
Myth What fact of life is explained by the myth of Deucalion and Pyrrha?

if we knew, we could never do such a dreadful thing as to disturb their resting place and scatter them over the earth like an armful of stones."

"Stones!" said Deucalion quickly. "That must be what the goddess means. After all Earth is our mother, and the other thing is too horrible for us to suppose that a goddess would ever command it."

⓲ Accordingly both picked up armfuls of stones, and as they went away from the temple with faces veiled, they cast the stones behind them. From each of those Deucalion cast sprang up a man, and from Pyrrha's stones sprang women. Thus the earth was repeopled, and in the course of time it brought forth again animals from itself, and all was as before. Only from that time men have been less sensitive and have found it easier to **endure** toil, and sorrow, and pain, since now they are descended from stones.

Vocabulary
endure (en do͝or′) *v.* hold up under pain or hardship

Critical Thinking

1. **Respond:** What questions would you like to ask Zeus? Explain.
2. **(a)** What problem does Epimetheus face when it is humanity's turn to receive a gift? **(b) Contrast:** Contrast the gifts Prometheus gives humanity with the gifts Epimetheus gives the animals. **(c) Evaluate:** Which gift is most valuable? Why?
3. **(a)** Which of Prometheus' actions angers Zeus? **(b) Infer:** Why does it anger him? **(c) Draw Conclusions:** How did the Greeks view Zeus? Support your answer with details from the text.
4. **(a) Analyze Cause and Effect:** What changes does Pandora bring to the world by opening the box? **(b) Connect:** How does her mistake solve the problem Prometheus caused for the gods?

Can anyone be a hero?
Which characters in these three myths make heroic efforts during trying circumstances? Explain their acts of heroism.

Assessment Resources

Unit 6 Resources

L1 L2 EL **Selection Test A,** pp. 35–37. Administer Test A to less advanced readers and English learners.

L3 L4 **Selection Test B,** pp. 38–40. Administer Test B to on-level and more advanced students.

L3 L4 **Open-Book Test,** pp. 32–34. As an alternative, give the Open-Book Test.

All **Customizable Test Bank**

All **Self-tests**
Students may prepare for the **Selection Test** by taking the **Self-test** online.

PHLit Online! All assessment resources are available at **www.PHLitOnline.com.**

After You Read

Prometheus and the First People

Literary Analysis: Myths

1. Using a chart like the one shown, identify which characteristics of **myths** are found in "Prometheus and the First People." Support your choices by supplying examples from the text.

What the Story Explains	Exceptional or Fantastic Characters	Quest	Transgression

2. **(a)** What do the myths suggest about the value the ancient Greeks placed on the human power to reason? Explain. **(b)** In what way does the story of Pandora show that the gift of intelligence is also a curse? **(c)** Working from your previous answer, draw a conclusion about the ancient Greek view of humanity.
3. **(a)** Why does Zeus save Deucalion and Pyrrha? **(b)** Draw a conclusion about ancient Greek values from their story.

Reading Skill: Analyze Cultural Context

4. **(a)** Give two examples of questions you might ask to **analyze the cultural context** of the myth. **(b)** Explain what answers the myth suggests, and support your answer with details from the text.

Vocabulary

Practice Copy each of the following word pairs. If the words have similar meanings, write *S* for **synonyms.** If the words have opposite meanings, write *A* for **antonyms.** Explain each of your choices.

1. toil, work
2. heedless, cautious
3. counsel, recommendation
4. disembarked, boarded
5. inhabit, abandon
6. endure, tolerate

Word Study Use the context of the sentences and what you know about the **Latin root *-dur-*** to explain your answer to each question.

1. Will a *durable* pair of jeans easily tear?
2. Does training for a marathon help to build up one's *endurance*?

Word Study

The **Latin root *-dur-*** means "hard" or "to last."

Challenge Explain how the root *-dur-* contributes to the meanings of these words. Consult a dictionary if necessary.

duration
duress
obdurate

ASSESS/EXTEND

Answers

Literary Analysis

1. **Possible response:** The Prometheus story explains how humans acquired their mental powers. Prometheus is a superhuman character, large in his ambition and his ability to suffer. Prometheus seeks to elevate humankind. Prometheus transgresses by stealing the gods' fire.

   For other sample answers, see ***Graphic Organizer Transparencies,* Literary Analysis Graphic Organizer A**, p. 196, and the **Additional Answers** section.
2. (a) Greeks saw the ability to reason as the most distinctive and important human trait. (b) Pandora's curiosity leads her to open the box and let evil into the world. (c) **Possible response:** The ancient Greeks seem to have a mixed view of human beings' gifts and flaws: that our greatest gift, intellect, can lead to ruin.
3. (a) Deucalion and Pyrrha are virtuous and devoted to the gods. (b) **Possible response:** The ancient Greeks greatly value virtue, restraint, and devotion to the gods.

Reading Skill

4. (a) **Possible response:** Students might ask what the flood reveals about the history of the society that produced the myth. They may also ask what the personal qualities of Deucalion and Pyrrha reveal about the values of the mythtellers' society. (b) **Possible response:** The myth of the flood suggests that the society valued the survivors' qualities of virtue, obedience, foresight, and intelligence.

Vocabulary

Practice

Sample answers:

1. S; Toil is difficult labor that causes pain and fatigue. *Work* is labor or toil.
2. A; Heedless means careless. *Cautious* means careful to avoid danger.
3. S; Both mean advice.
4. A; Disembarked means to have gotten off, or been removed from a ship or vessel. *Boarded* means to have gotten on board a ship or train.
5. A; Inhabit means to live in, while *abandon* means to leave.
6. S; Both mean to withstand or put up with.

Word Study

Sample answers:

1. No, the root *-dur-* means "to last," so *durable* means "able to last." A durable pair of jeans would not tear easily but would last a long time.
2. Yes, the root *-dur-* means "to last," so *endurance* means "the ability or strength to last." If you train for a marathon, you must run for long periods of time. This builds up your endurance.

Word Study: Challenge

Sample answers: *Duration* is the length of time something lasts. *Duress* is coercion by threat, hardness, or force. To be *obdurate* is to be hard or stubborn.

*Skills instruction for the **Reading Skill** and **Literary Analysis** concept for this selection appears on p. 1063.*

❶ Writing About the Big Question

1. Review the assignment with the class.
2. Prompt students to think about someone, either real or fictional, who experienced and overcame a time of hardship. Have them consider the personality characteristics or attributes that helped these people to overcome the hardship.
3. Have students complete the sentence starter. Review responses as a class. (**Possible response:** To persevere in times of hardship shows great character and reveals attributes such as courage, strength, and determination.)
4. Remind students that their answers will help them think about the Big Question, "Can anyone be a hero?"

While You Read

Tell students that as they read, they should look for examples of kind or brave behavior.

❷ Vocabulary

1. Have students preview the selection vocabulary.
2. For each word, have students say the word aloud.
3. Then, use the word in a sentence that defines the word.
4. Finally, repeat your definitional sentence or a similar sentence with the word missing and have the class "fill in the blank" chorally. Here are some examples:

   Relish means enjoyment. The hearty vegetable stew was so delicious, I ate slowly and with [students say "relish"].

   To be humble is to be modest. An actor who is extremely talented but is modest about his abilities can be described as [students say "humble"].

❸ Word Study

1. Introduce the skill, using the instruction in the box.
2. **Ask** students for a word containing the root *-fus-* that means "to put into." (**Answer:** *infuse*)

Can anyone be a *hero?*

❶ Writing About the Big Question

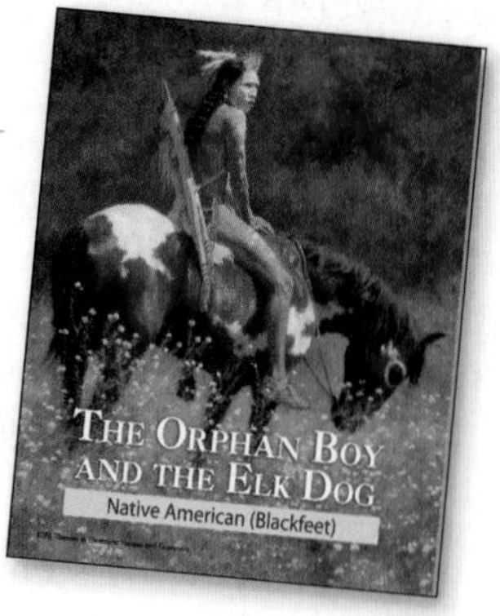

In "The Orphan Boy and the Elk Dog," a young man's bravery plays an important role in his quest to help his tribe and discover his own self worth. Use this sentence starter to develop your ideas about the Big Question.

To **persevere** in times of hardship shows great **character** and reveals **attributes** such as ______________ , and ______________.

While You Read Analyze the characteristics of Long Arrow and look for evidence to help you decide if he is capable of being a hero.

❷ Vocabulary

Read each word and its definition. Decide whether you know the word well, know it a little bit, or do not know it at all. After you read, see how your knowledge of each word has increased.

- **refuse** (ref′ yo͞os) *n.* waste; trash (p. 1077) ***We filled three trash cans in the park with refuse from the picnic.***
- **surpassed** (sər past′) *v.* went beyond; excelled (p. 1079) ***Her score was so high, it surpassed even her own expectations.*** *surpassable adj.*
- **emanating** (em′ ə nāt′ iŋ) *v.* coming forth, as from a source (p. 1082) ***We were curious about the light emanating from the basement window of the abandoned house.*** *emanation n.*
- **relish** (rel′ ish) *n.* enjoyment (p. 1082) ***Her vivid gestures show that she talks with relish.*** *relish v.*
- **stifle** (stī′ fəl) *v.* smother; hold back (p. 1084) ***She grew bored and could not stifle a yawn.*** *stifling adj. stiflingly adv.*
- **humble** (hum′ bəl) *adj.* showing an awareness of one's shortcomings; modest (p. 1085) ***She is humble and will not boast about her award.*** *humbleness n. humbly adv.*

❸ Word Study

The Latin root ***-fus-*** means "to pour."

In this story, a character is forced to survive on **refuse** material, or trash, that has been rejected and poured into the garbage.

Vocabulary Development

Vocabulary Knowledge Rating

Create a **Vocabulary Knowledge Rating Chart** (***Professional Development Guidebook***, p. 33) for this selection. Include the selection vocabulary and the Big Question words that appear in the Writing About the Big Question sentence starter on this page. (The Big Question vocabulary is introduced on pp. 1046–1047.)

Give students a copy of the chart. Read the words aloud, and have students mark their rating in the Before Reading column. Urge them to be alert to these words as they read and discuss the selection.

Tally how many students think they know a word to gauge how much instruction to provide. As students read and discuss the selection, point out the words and their context.

PHLit Online! **Vocabulary Central**, featuring tools, activities, and songs for studying vocabulary, is available online at **www.PHLitOnline.com**.

Meet The Blackfeet

Creators of THE ORPHAN BOY AND THE ELK DOG

The Blackfeet are one of the many Native American nations that have lived on the Great Plains of North America. At one time, most Plains Indians were farmers who lived in one place, grew their own food, and sometimes hunted buffalo on foot. Then, in the 1600s, many tribes captured and tamed wild horses.

New Way of Life In time, the Blackfeet became skillful riders, and horses transformed their way of life. A mounted hunter could search for game more efficiently. Hunting replaced farming, and the tribes followed the buffalo herds.

Today, the Blackfeet live on reservations in Montana and in Canada. Myths like "The Orphan Boy and the Elk Dog" reflect the importance of the horse in early Blackfeet culture.

4 BACKGROUND FOR THE MYTH

Horses in America

"The Orphan Boy and the Elk Dog" explains the origin of an important part of the North American Blackfeet culture—horses. Horses did not always exist in North America. Spanish explorer Hernando Cortés brought the first horses to Mexico in 1519, and they quickly spread northward. By the 1600s, many Native American tribes had captured and tamed wild horses.

DID YOU KNOW?

The name "Blackfeet" is a reference to the dark moccasins worn by early Blackfeet people.

Daily Bellringer

For each class during which you will teach this selection, have students complete one of the five Quick Write activities for Week 31 in the ***Daily Bellringer Activities*** booklet.

4 Background

Horses in America

The Blackfeet had no horses before the 1700s. The Shoshone (another group of Plains Indians) had herds of horses as early as 1680. One daring Blackfoot, who may have been the inspiration for the orphan boy in this myth, slipped into a Shoshone camp with his companions, untied four horses, and led them away.

Christopher Columbus brought horses to the New World on one of his voyages; however, most Native Americans never saw a horse until later, when Spanish explorer Hernan Cortés brought them to Mexico in 1519. At first, the native peoples thought that the Spaniards on horseback were actually half man, half beast. Most of the horses found in America today are descendants of those brought by the Spanish explorers.

Multidraft Reading

This icon ● marks natural pauses in the selection. To assist struggling readers and to deepen reading for all, assign the text in "chunks," following the icons, and apply multidraft reading protocols. For each reading, have students set the purpose indicated:

- **First reading**—literal comprehension: answering the Reading Check questions.
- **Second reading**—application of skills: answering the Myths and Analyze Cultural Context prompts.
- **Third reading**—interpretation: answering the end-of-selection questions.

For more guidance, refer to the ***Classroom Strategies and Teaching Routines*** card on multidraft reading.

Differentiated Instruction Additional Instruction

EL Extended Support—English Learners

Have students complete the **Reading and Vocabulary Warm-ups, *Unit 6 Resources,*** pp. 41–44, before they read. Assign the prereading pages for the selection in the ***Reader's Notebook: English Learner's Version.*** Then, have students listen to portions of the selection on the ***Hear It!* Audio CD.**

L1 L2 Extended Support—Struggling Readers

Have students complete the **Reading and Vocabulary Warm-ups, *Unit 6 Resources,*** pp. 41–44, before they read. Assign the prereading pages for the selection in the ***Reader's Notebook: Adapted Version.*** Then, have students listen to portions of the selection on the ***Hear It!* Audio CD** (adapted text).

L1 L2 Extended Support—Reluctant Readers

To build motivation and engagement before assigning the selection, have students read "Buffalo Battles," a thematically related selection in ***Reality Central.*** Then, use the questions at the conclusion of the related selection to guide discussion.

PHLit Online!

For more about the author, practice with the selection vocabulary, and more background, go online at **www.PHLitOnline.com**.

❶ Activating Prior Knowledge

1. Prepare an **Anticipation Guide** (see ***Professional Development Guidebook***, pp. 36–38) with the following statements:
   - Bravery is often another word for foolishness.
   - People do not need help from others to succeed.
   - People should be judged by their physical appearance.
2. Give students a copy of the pre-pared **Anticipation Guide** and have students mark their responses in the Me column. Have students discuss the statements in pairs or groups and mark the guides again in the Group column.
3. For further guidance, use the ***Classroom Strategies and Teaching Routines*** card: **Using an Anticipation Guide.**

Concept Connector →

Students will return to the **Anticipation Guide** after completing the story.

Individual Activity

Before students begin reading, have them view each piece of art in the selection. Tell students to note the color, composition, medium, and mood of each image. Ask students to predict elements of the story that the artwork suggests.

❷ About the Selection

According to this myth, an outcast young man goes on a dangerous quest to prove himself to his people and to prove his own self-worth.

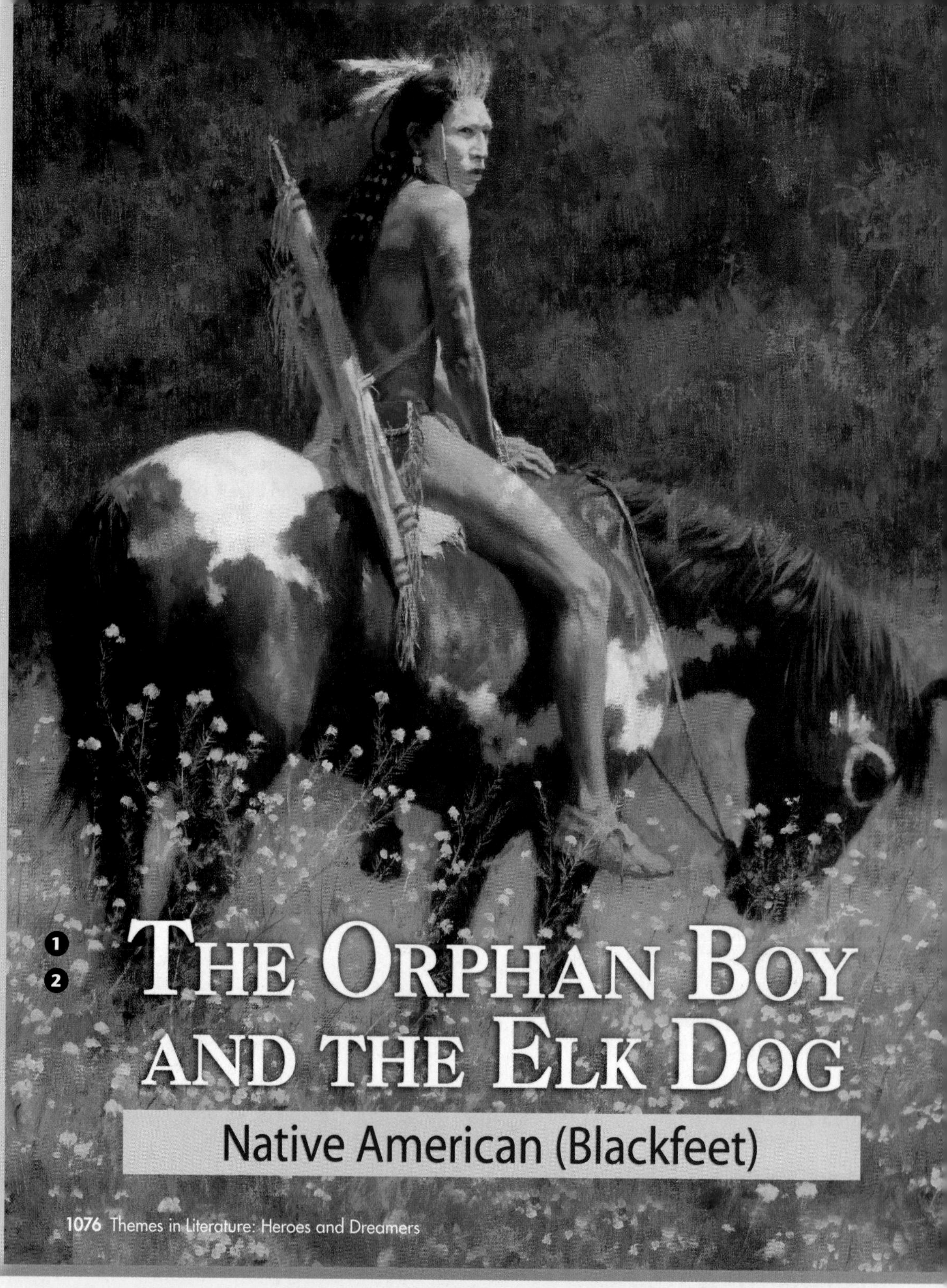

❶ ❷

The Orphan Boy and the Elk Dog

Native American (Blackfeet)

1076 Themes in Literature: Heroes and Dreamers

Vocabulary Development

Thematic Vocabulary: The Big Question

As students are discussing "The Orphan Boy and the Elk Dog," encourage them to use the thematic vocabulary presented in Introducing the Big Question, pp. 1046–1047. You might encourage them with sentence starters like these:

1. After the people in the camp leave him, Long Arrow must *persevere* to . . .
2. Long Arrow's *determination* to find the Elk Dogs shows that he is . . .
3. Long Arrow displays *courage* when he fol-lows the kingfisher to . . .
4. By describing Long Arrow's early hardships in life, the myth communicates the idea that *integrity* is . . .

4 In the days when people had only dogs to carry their bundles, two orphan children, a boy and his sister, were having a hard time. The boy was deaf, and because he could not understand what people said, they thought him foolish and dull-witted. Even his relatives wanted nothing to do with him. The name he had been given at birth, while his parents still lived, was Long Arrow. Now he was like a beaten, mangy dog, the kind who hungrily roams outside a camp, circling it from afar, smelling the good meat boiling in the kettles but never coming close for fear of being kicked. Only his sister, who was bright and beautiful, loved him.

Then the sister was adopted by a family from another camp, people who were attracted by her good looks and pleasing ways. Though they wanted her for a daughter, they certainly did not want the awkward, stupid boy. And so they took away the only person who cared about him, and the orphan boy was left to fend for himself. He lived on scraps thrown to the dogs and things he found on the **refuse** heaps. He dressed in remnants of skins and frayed robes discarded by the poorest people. At night he bedded down in a grass-lined dugout, like an animal in its den.

5 Eventually the game was hunted out near the camp that the boy regarded as his, and the people decided to move. The lodges were taken down, belongings were packed into rawhide bags and put on dog travois,[1] and the village departed. "Stay here," they told the boy. "We don't want your kind coming with us."

6 For two or three days the boy fed on scraps the people had left behind, but he knew he would starve if he stayed. He had to join his people, whether they liked it or not. He followed their tracks, frantic that he would lose them, and crying at the same time. Soon the sweat was running down his skinny body. As he was stumbling, running, panting, something suddenly snapped in his left ear with a sound like a small crack, and a wormlike substance came out of that ear. All at once on his left side he could hear birdsongs for the first time. He took this wormlike thing in his left hand and hurried on. Then there was a snap in his right ear and a wormlike thing came out of it, and on his right side he could hear the rushing waters of a stream. His hearing was restored! And it was razor-sharp—he could make out the rustling of a tiny mouse in dry leaves a good distance away. The orphan boy laughed and was happy for the first time in his life. With renewed courage he followed the trail his people had made.

In the meantime the village had settled into its new place. Men were already out hunting. Thus the boy came upon Good Running,

1. **travois** (trə voiˊ) *n.* sled with two poles and a net or platform in between, pulled along the ground by a person or an animal.

◀ **Critical Viewing** 3
Use the selection title and this painting to predict what this story is about. **[Predict]**

Reading Skill
Analyze Cultural Context What questions about Blackfeet culture does the first paragraph suggest?

Vocabulary
refuse (refˊ yo͞os) *n.* waste; trash

Reading Skill
Analyze Cultural Context In this paragraph, what do you learn about Blackfeet life?

7 **Reading Check**
What difficulties does Long Arrow face?

The Color of Sun, Howard Terpnin. Licensed by The Greenwich Workshop, Inc.

3 Critical Viewing

Answer: The painting suggests that the story will be about Native Americans and horses. The title suggests that the story focuses on an orphan.

4 Reading Skill
Analyze Cultural Context

Ask students the first Reading Skill question: What questions about Blackfeet culture does the first paragraph suggest?
Answer: Students may suggest such questions as *How does Blackfeet society provide for orphans or other dependents?* and *How do people move from place to place if they have only dogs?*

5 Reading Skill
Analyze Cultural Context

Ask students to respond to the second Reading Skill question: In this paragraph, what do you learn about Blackfeet life?
Answer: The Blackfeet are mobile, moving the camp from place to place in search of game. Their lodgings are portable; they use dogs to pull their belongings.

6 Critical Thinking
Analyze

Ask students how the worms leaving Long Arrow's ears might symbolize his assertive action.
Answer: Long Arrow thinks of himself the way his people think of him—awkward and unwanted. He decides to take control of his fate and assert his rights as a tribe member. The worms fall out of his ears when he decides to no longer be a victim.

7 Reading Check

Answer: Long Arrow is deaf, so he cannot easily communicate with other members of his tribe, who reject him.

Differentiated Instruction for Universal Access

Strategy for Less Proficient Readers
Have students read aloud the first paragraph of "The Orphan Boy and the Elk Dog" one or two sentences at a time. With students, write down the important information in each sentence; use **Reading Skill Graphic Organizer B,** p. 195 in ***Graphic Organizer Transparencies.*** Note characters, their names, and their characteristics. Also note details about the culture. When you finish reading the first paragraph, use the information that has been listed to discuss the foundation of the myth. Help students identify the story as a quest myth.

PHLit Online!

This selection is available in interactive format in the **Enriched Online Student Edition** at **www.PHLitOnline.com,** which includes a thematically related video and writing prompt and an interactive graphic organizer.

❽ Critical Viewing

Answer: The picture suggests that the Blackfeet live in large, well-constructed, decorated tipis; that they are skilled with bows and arrows; and that they are social people who live in close proximity to their neighbors.

❾ Critical Thinking

Analyze

1. Have students read the bracketed passage.
2. **Ask:** Why does Good Running like Long Arrow?
   Answer: Good Running notices a change in Long Arrow's manner after he acquires his hearing. Good Running can perceive through Long Arrow's behavior and disposition that he is quite alert—not stupid or crazy as once thought.
3. **Ask:** How does this passage reveal character traits that the Blackfeet value?
   Possible response: The Blackfeet value intelligence and strength. Good Running decides to adopt Long Arrow because he realizes Long Arrow is not stupid. Good Running also tells Long Arrow that he will make him into a good hunter and warrior.

❿ Critical Thinking

Compare and Contrast

1. **Ask:** How does Good Running's wife describe Long Arrow?
   Answer: She says he is a "burden" on her.
2. Remind students that in the Blackfeet society, men are hunters, warriors, and chiefs. **Ask** students to speculate about the work women do in Blackfeet society.
   Answer: The women are probably in charge of feeding and clothing their families.
3. **Ask:** Why might Good Running's wife view Long Arrow as a burden?
   Answer: She might view Long Arrow as an extra person to feed and clothe. Also, since she has not seen the change in him that the chief has, she probably thinks it will be difficult to teach and care for a boy who cannot hear.

❽ ▶ **Critical Viewing** Based on this painting, what can you tell about the life of the Blackfeet? Explain. **[Analyze]**

a kindly old chief, butchering a fat buffalo cow he had just killed. When the chief saw the boy, he said to himself, "Here comes that poor good-for-nothing boy. It was wrong to abandon him." To the boy Good Running said "Rest here, grandson, you're sweaty and covered with dust. Here, have some tripe."[2]

❾ The boy wolfed down the meat. He was not used to hearing and talking yet, but his eyes were alert and Good Running also noticed a change in his manner. "This boy," the chief said to himself, "is neither stupid nor crazy." He gave the orphan a piece of the hump meat, then a piece of liver, then a piece of raw kidney, and at last the very best kind of meat—a slice of tongue. The more the old man looked at the boy, the more he liked him. On the spur of the moment he said, "Grandson, I'm going to adopt you; there's a place for you in my tipi. And I'm going to make you into a good hunter and warrior." The boy wept, this time for joy. Good Running said, "They called you a stupid, crazy boy, but now that I think of it, the name you were given at birth is Long Arrow. I'll see that people call you by your right name. Now come along."

❿ The chief's wife was not pleased. "Why do you put this burden on me," she said, "bringing into our lodge this good-for-nothing, this slow-witted crazy boy? Maybe you're a little slow-witted and crazy yourself!"

---

2. **tripe** (trīp) *n.* walls of the stomach of a buffalo or other grazing animal, used as food.

Think Aloud

Vocabulary: Using Context

Direct students' attention to the phrase *ward off* in the last line of page 1079. Using the following "think aloud," model how to use context to infer the meaning of an unknown word or phrase:

In this sentence, Long Arrow is given a shield made especially for him by the tribe's holy men to "ward off danger." To get an idea of what *ward off* means, I am going to examine the sentences surrounding this one. In this and the previous sentences, Long Arrow, being purified, is prepared to meet dangerous situations while on his quest. These preparations include the gift of the shield, a tool for defense. Since these preparations are made to protect Long Arrow and to help him defend himself from danger, I think *ward off* must mean "turn away." I'll substitute *turn away* in the sentence: "The tribe's holy men gave him a medicine and made for him a shield with designs on it to turn away danger." I think that meaning makes sense. I think that to *ward* something *off* is to "deflect it," or "turn it away."

"Woman, keep talking like that and I'll beat you! This boy isn't slow or crazy; he's a good boy, and I have taken him for my grandson. Look—he's barefooted. Hurry up, and make a pair of moccasins for him, and if you don't do it well I'll take a stick to you."

Good Running's wife grumbled but did as she was told. Her husband was a kind man, but when aroused, his anger was great.

So a new life began for Long Arrow. He had to learn to speak and to understand well, and to catch up on all the things a boy should know. He was a fast learner and soon surpassed other boys his age in knowledge and skills. At last even Good Running's wife accepted him.

He grew up into a fine young hunter, tall and good-looking in the quilled buckskin outfit the chief's wife made for him. He helped his grandfather in everything and became a staff for Good Running to lean on. But he was lonely, for most people in the camp could not forget that Long Arrow had once been an outcast. "Grandfather," he said one day, "I want to do something to make you proud and show people that you were wise to adopt me. What can I do?"

Good Running answered, "Someday you will be a chief and do great things."

"But what's a great thing I could do now, Grandfather?"

The chief thought for a long time. "Maybe I shouldn't tell you this," he said. "I love you and don't want to lose you. But on winter nights, men talk of powerful spirit people living at the bottom of a faraway lake. Down in that lake the spirit people keep mystery
11 animals who do their work for them. These animals are larger than a great elk, but they carry the burdens of the spirit people like dogs. So they're called Pono-Kamita—Elk Dogs. They are said to be swift, strong, gentle, and beautiful beyond imagination. Every fourth generation, one of our young warriors has gone to find these spirit folk and bring back an Elk Dog for us. But none of our brave young men has ever returned."

"Grandfather, I'm not afraid. I'll go and find the Elk Dog."

"Grandson, first learn to be a man. Learn the right prayers and ceremonies. Be brave. Be generous and open-handed. Pity the old and the fatherless, and let the holy men of the tribe find a medicine for you which will protect you on your dangerous journey. We will begin by purifying you in the sweat bath."

So Long Arrow was purified with the white steam of the sweat lodge. He was taught how to use the pipe, and how to pray to the Great Mystery Power. The tribe's holy men gave him a medicine[3] and made for him a shield with designs on it to ward off danger.

Vocabulary
surpassed (sər past') *v.* went beyond; excelled

Literary Analysis
Myths What mythical qualities do the Elk Dogs have?

12 **Reading Check**
Identify two ways Long Arrow's life has improved.

3. **medicine** in Native American culture, an object, a ceremony, a song, and so on with religious or magical power.

11 Literary Analysis
Myths

1. Remind students that many myths involve animals or fictional beasts with remarkable appearances or qualities.
2. Have students read the bracketed passage.
3. Then, **ask** students the Literary Analysis question: What mythical qualities do the Elk Dogs have?
   Possible response: The Elk Dogs are mysterious animals that are kept by powerful spirit people. No one has ever seen or captured one, but the Elk Dogs are supposedly large, powerful, able to carry great burdens, fleet, strong, gentle, and beautiful.
4. **Ask** students what the description of Elk Dogs says about Blackfeet values.
   Possible response: The Elk Dogs are described as being strong, gentle, swift, and beautiful. These reflect the values that are important to the Blackfeet people. Since the Elk Dogs have always eluded capture, the Blackfeet people also value the bravery of those who attempt to catch one.

12 Reading Check
Answer: Long Arrow now has his hearing and a home.

Differentiated Instruction for Universal Access

Strategy for Special Needs Students
Help students draw charts to keep track of the various steps in Long Arrow's development as a hero. Suggest that the first entry is "Loses his family." Tell them to include his decision to follow his people and the restoration of his hearing. Encourage them to note what happens to him on each page of the myth as they continue reading. When they finish, students can compare lists with partners, adding any omissions or correcting discrepancies.

Enrichment for Advanced Readers
Encourage students to analyze Long Arrow's experience. How do his deafness and then his powerful hearing capabilities make him a typical hero? Have students research the heroes and heroines in other myths. Do heroes of myths often have hard lives or particular ailments or fears? Why? What typically happens to heroes? Students can report their findings to the class. Guide students in a discussion about the archetype of a quest myth hero.

⓭ Literary Analysis
Myths

1. Have a student read aloud the bracketed passage.
2. Then **ask** students to respond to the Literary Analysis question: What quest does Long Arrow undertake?
   Answer: He undertakes a quest to bring back an Elk Dog.
3. **Ask** students how this passage in particular identifies "The Orphan Boy and the Elk Dog" as a quest myth.
   Answer: Long Arrow wants to do something important; Good Running helps him prepare to go in search of an Elk Dog. A quest myth is often about a hero or heroine who goes in search of knowledge or an important object.

⓮ Critical Viewing

Answer: The landscape includes various elements such as mountains, a body of water, and dense forests that might make travel difficult or impossible. Having a means of transportation would make it easier to travel and to hunt.

Literary Analysis
Myths What quest does Long Arrow undertake?

Then one morning, without telling anybody, Good Running loaded his best travois dog with all the things Long Arrow would need for traveling. The chief gave him his medicine, his shield, and his own fine bow and, just as the sun came up, went with his grandson to the edge of the camp to purify him with sweet-smelling cedar smoke. Long Arrow left unheard and unseen by anyone else. ⓭ After a while some people noticed that he was gone, but no one except his grandfather knew where and for what purpose.

Following Good Running's advice, Long Arrow wandered southward. On the fourth day of his journey he came to a small pond, where a strange man was standing as if waiting for him. "Why have you come here?" the stranger asked.

"I have come to find the mysterious Elk Dog."

"Ah, there I cannot help you," said the man, who was the spirit of the pond. "But if you travel further south, four-times-four days, you might chance upon a bigger lake and there meet one of my uncles. Possibly he might talk to you; then again, he might not. That's all I can tell you."

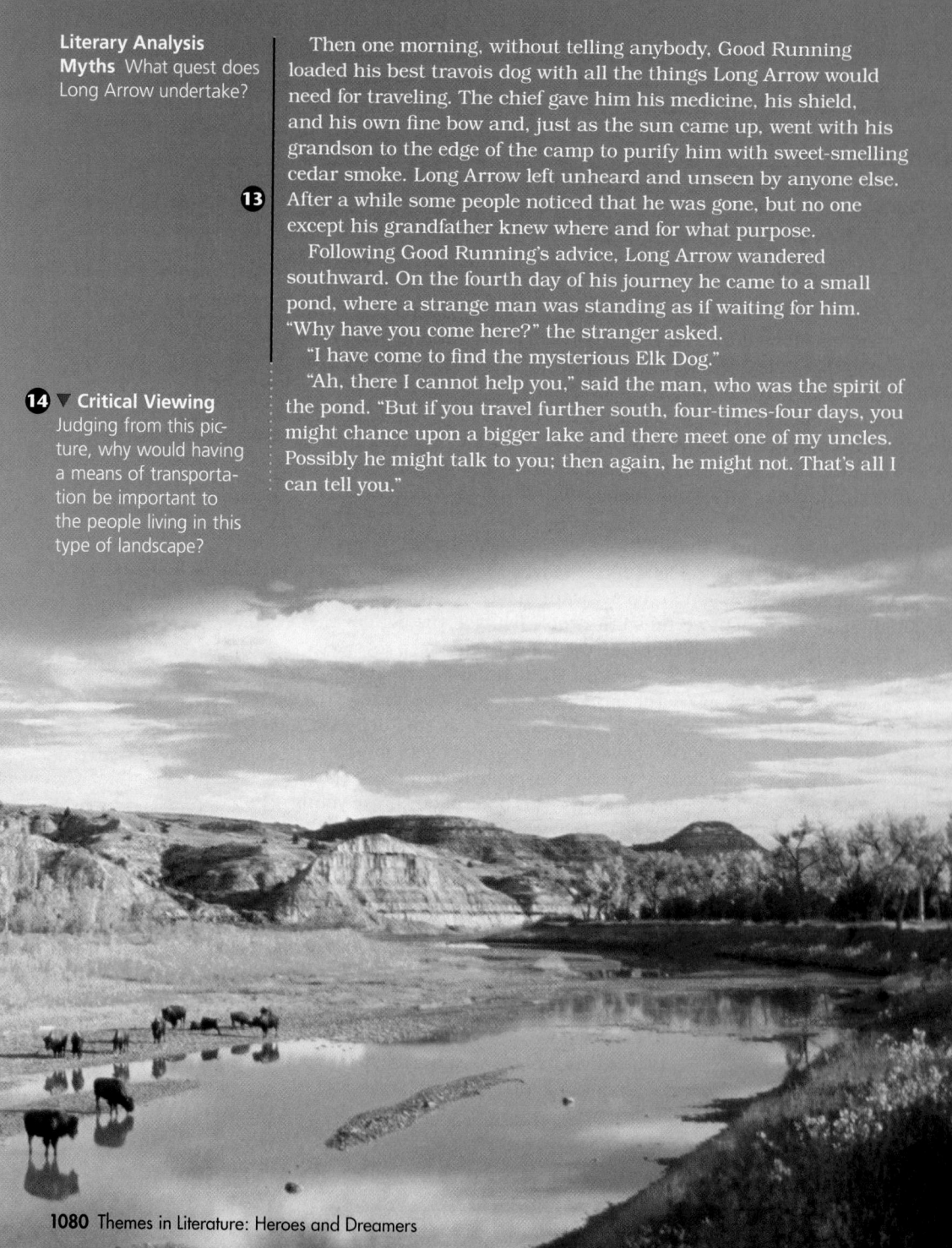

⓮ ▼ **Critical Viewing** Judging from this picture, why would having a means of transportation be important to the people living in this type of landscape?

Vocabulary Development

Selection Vocabulary Reinforcement

Students will benefit from additional examples and practice with the selection vocabulary words. Reinforce their comprehension with "show-you-know" sentences. The first part of the sentence uses the vocabulary word in an appropriate context. The second part of the sentence—the "show-you-know" part—clarifies the first. Model the strategy with this example for *humble:*

After landing a role on a popular sitcom, Anna was no longer *humble*; she bragged about her talents to anyone who would listen.

Then, give students these sentence prompts, and coach them in creating the clarification part:

1. Matthew ate his food with *relish*; ________.
   Sample answer: he licked his fingers and smacked his lips after every bite.
2. Christina did everything she could to *stifle* her laughter; ________.
   Sample answer: she covered her mouth with both hands and turned away from the comical sight.

Long Arrow thanked the man, who went down to the bottom of the pond, where he lived.

Long Arrow wandered on, walking for long hours and taking little time for rest. Through deep canyons and over high mountains he went, wearing out his moccasins and enduring cold and heat, hunger and thirst.

Finally Long Arrow approached a big lake surrounded by steep pine-covered hills. There he came face to face with a tall man, fierce and scowling and twice the height of most humans. This stranger carried a long lance with a heavy spearpoint made of shining flint. "Young one," he growled, "why did you come here?"

"I came to find the mysterious Elk Dog."

The stranger, who was the spirit of the lake, stuck his face right into Long Arrow's and shook his mighty lance. "Little one, aren't you afraid of me?" he snarled.

"No, I am not," answered Long Arrow, smiling.

The tall spirit man gave a hideous grin, which was his way of being friendly. "I like small humans who aren't afraid," he said, "but I can't help you. Perhaps our grandfather will take the trouble to listen to you. More likely he won't. Walk south for four-times-four days, and maybe you'll find him. But probably you won't." With that the tall spirit turned his back on Long Arrow and went to the bottom of the lake, where he lived.

Long Arrow walked on for another four-times-four days, sleeping and resting little. By now he staggered and stumbled in his weakness, and his dog was not much better off. At last he came to the biggest lake he had ever seen, surrounded by towering snow-capped peaks and waterfalls of ice. This time there was nobody to receive him. As a matter of fact, there seemed to be no living thing around. "This must be the Great Mystery Lake," thought Long Arrow. Exhausted, he fell down upon the shortgrass meadow by the lake, fell down among the wild flowers, and went to sleep with his tired dog curled up at his feet.

When Long Arrow awoke, the sun was already high. He opened his eyes and saw a beautiful child standing before him, a boy in a dazzling white buckskin robe decorated with porcupine quills of many colors. The boy said, "We have been expecting you for a long time. My grandfather invites you to his lodge. Follow me."

Telling his dog to wait, Long Arrow took his medicine shield and his grandfather's bow and went with the wonderful child.

15 LITERATURE IN CONTEXT

Culture Connection

Traditional Great Plains Culture

Before the westward push of white settlers ended their traditional way of life, the Blackfeet and other Native American tribes of the Great Plains shared a common culture.

- The lives of the Plains peoples revolved around the buffalo—they ate buffalo meat, slept in tipis made from buffalo hides, sewed with thread made from buffalo sinews, and carried water in buffalo stomachs.
- Plains tribes prized the virtues of a warrior—bravery, the ability to endure pain, skill with a bow, and masterful horsemanship.
- Young men sought spiritual assistance by fasting and going on vision quests.

Connect to the Literature

Which details in the story illustrate these elements of Plains culture?

16 Reading Check

Who has directed Long Arrow to the Great Mystery Lake?

15 Literature in Context

Culture Connection The Plains Indians included a number of tribes in addition to the Blackfeet, among them the Sioux, the Arapahoe, and the Cheyenne. One key religious ritual among many of the Plains Indians is the vision quest, which is a rite of passage undertaken by boys around ages ten or eleven. Mature men and some women might also renew themselves in a vision quest.

In the traditional vision quest, the seeker asks the holy men to set aside a particular day for his or her vision quest. The seeker enters a sweat lodge with the holy men to purify himself or herself. Then, the seeker goes to a chosen place to pray and meditate with a pipe; while praying, the seeker faces north, south, east, and west.

Connect to the Literature After discussing the cultures of the Great Plains, **ask** the Connect to the Literature question: Which details in the story illustrate these elements of Plains culture?

Answer: The Blackfeet live in tipis and follow the buffalo. Long Arrow carries a bow and is stoic and brave. He learns from holy men and goes on a vision quest.

16 Reading Check

Answer: The tall man with the hideous grin and long lance directs Long Arrow to the Great Mystery Lake.

Differentiated Instruction for Universal Access

Support for Less Proficient Readers
Have students read paragraphs 3–8 while you play the ***Hear It!* Audio CD.** Pause the recording after each paragraph to give students the chance to summarize each paragraph in their own words. Lead students in a discussion about the plot developments, using their summaries as discussion prompts.

Enrichment for Gifted/Talented Students
Suggest that students choose scenes from "The Orphan Boy and the Elk Dog" that lend themselves to illustration. Encourage students to choose different scenes and mediums for creating illustrations. Tell them to use visual media to express the heroic and mythic qualities in the narrative. Display students' artwork in the classroom in sequential order.

17 Reading Skill

Analyze Cultural Context

1. Have a student read aloud the bracketed passage.
2. **Ask** students to list the things that Long Arrow notices during the meal.
   Answer: Long Arrow notices the food they eat, the interior decorations of the tipi, the beautifully crafted possessions, and the wise power of the grandfather.
3. Then, **ask** students to respond to the Reading Skill question: What question about Blackfeet culture might be answered with the details in this paragraph?
   Answer: Questions this paragraph answers include *Which foods make up the Blackfeet diet? What kinds of artwork and decorations are enjoyed by the Blackfeet? Are elders respected in the Blackfeet culture?*

They came to the edge of the lake. The spirit boy pointed to the water and said, "My grandfather's lodge is down there. Come." The child turned himself into a kingfisher[4] and dove straight to the bottom.

Afraid, Long Arrow thought, "How can I follow him and not be drowned?" But then he said to himself, "I knew all the time that this would not be easy. In setting out to find the Elk Dog, I already threw my life away." And he boldly jumped into the water. To his surprise, he found it did not make him wet, that it parted before him, that he could breathe and see. He touched the lake's sandy bottom. It sloped down, down toward a center point.

Vocabulary
emanating (em′ ə nāt′ iŋ) *v.* coming forth, as from a source
relish (rel′ ish) *n.* enjoyment

Long Arrow descended this slope until he came to a small flat valley. In the middle of it stood a large tipi of tanned buffalo hide. The images of two strange animals were drawn on it in sacred vermilion[5] paint. A kingfisher perched high on the top of the tipi flew down and turned again into the beautiful boy, who said, "Welcome. Enter my grandfather's lodge."

Reading Skill
Analyze Cultural Context What question about Blackfeet culture might be answered with the details in this paragraph?

17 Long Arrow followed the spirit boy inside. In the back at the seat of honor sat a black-robed old man with flowing white hair and such power **emanating** from him that Long Arrow felt himself in the presence of a truly Great One. The holy man welcomed Long Arrow and offered him food. The man's wife came in bringing dishes of buffalo hump, liver, tongues, delicious chunks of deer meat, the roasted flesh of strange, tasty water birds, and meat pounded together with berries, chokecherries, and kidney fat. Famished after his long journey, Long Arrow ate with **relish**. Yet he still looked around to admire the furnishings of the tipi, the painted inner curtain, the many medicine shields, wonderfully wrought weapons, shirts and robes decorated with porcupine quills in rainbow colors, beautifully painted rawhide containers filled with wonderful things, and much else that dazzled him.

After Long Arrow had stilled his hunger, the old spirit chief filled the pipe and passed it to his guest. They smoked, praying silently. After a while the old man said, "Some came before you from time to time, but they were always afraid of the deep water, and so they went away with empty hands. But you, grandson, were brave enough to plunge in, and therefore you are chosen to receive a wonderful gift to carry back to your people. Now, go outside with my grandson."

18 The beautiful boy took Long Arrow to a meadow on which some strange animals, unlike any the young man had ever seen, were galloping and gamboling, neighing and nickering. They were truly

4. **kingfisher** *n.* type of water bird that dives for its food.
5. **vermilion** (vər mil′ yən) *n.* bright red.

Vocabulary Development

Expressive Vocabulary

To help students broaden their expressive vocabulary, encourage them to use the following words as they discuss the selection: *rely*, *transport*, *convenience*, and *powerful*. Have them complete these sentence starters:

1. In contrast to the people described in this myth, people in the modern world have come to *rely* on . . .
2. Without motor vehicles to *transport* us, we would have to . . .
3. Is the *convenience* of being able to travel quickly worth . . .
4. Our more *powerful* modes of transportation have . . .

18 wonderful to look at, with their glossy coats fine as a maiden's hair, their long manes and tails streaming in the wind. Now rearing, now nuzzling, they looked at Long Arrow with gentle eyes which belied their fiery appearance.

"At last," thought Long Arrow, "here they are before my own eyes, the Pono-Kamita, the Elk Dogs!"

"Watch me," said the mystery boy, "so that you learn to do what I am doing." Gracefully and without effort, the boy swung himself onto the back of a jet-black Elk Dog with a high, arched neck. Larger than any elk Long Arrow had ever come across, the animal carried the boy all over the meadow swiftly as the wind. Then the boy returned, jumped off his mount, and said, "Now you try it." A little timidly Long Arrow climbed up on the beautiful Elk Dog's back. Seemingly regarding him as feather-light, it took off like a flying arrow. The young man felt himself soaring through the air as a bird does, and experienced a happiness greater even than the joy he had felt when Good Running had adopted him as a grandson.

When they had finished riding the Elk Dogs, the spirit boy said to Long Arrow, "Young hunter from the land above the waters, I want you to have what you have come for. Listen to me. You may have noticed that my grandfather wears a black medicine robe as long as a woman's dress, and that he is always trying to hide his feet. Try to get a glimpse of them, for if you do, he can refuse you nothing. He will then tell you to ask him for a gift, and you must ask for these three things: his rainbow-colored quilled belt, his black medicine robe, and a herd of these animals which you seem to like."

"At last," thought Long Arrow, "here they are before my own eyes, the Pono-Kamita, the Elk Dogs!"

19 **Reading Check**

What creatures does Long Arrow find in the spirit chief's lake?

18 Critical Thinking

Speculate

1. Have students name synonyms for the adjectives Long Arrow uses to describe the Elk Dogs' actions, coats, and eyes.
   Possible responses: Students may list synonyms such as *odd, unique, amazing, shiny, delicate, kind,* and *feisty.*
2. **Ask** students to recall why the Blackfeet call horses "Elk Dogs."
   Answer: Horses remind the Blackfeet of elks because of their size and grace. The horses remind the people of dogs because of their strength and ability to haul things.
3. Point out to students that the statement "they looked at Long Arrow with gentle eyes" is personification. **Ask** students why the Blackfeet may describe horses with human qualities and sensibilities.
   Answer: The Blackfeet live close to the natural world; they respect their dogs. It seems natural that they would personify horses, which are responsive animals capable of not only being domesticated but also of communicating their likes and dislikes.

19 Reading Check

Answer: Long Arrow finds the strange and beautiful Elk Dogs—horses.

Differentiated Instruction for Universal Access

Culturally Responsive Instruction

Culture Connection Explain to students that in the past, the Blackfeet relied heavily on buffalo. From providing shelter to clothing to nourishment, buffalo were essential to ensuring the success and survival of the Blackfeet people.

Prompt students to reflect on what resources may have been essential to their ancestors when they first came to the United States. If students are recent immigrants, have them discuss the resources their families needed in their home countries and compare them to what they now need in the United States. Discuss the resources as a class, noting which resources are specific to a geographical area, like the buffalo were to the Plains Indians.

20 Critical Viewing

Answer: Someone might find their strength, beauty, grace, and size striking.

21 THE BIG ? Connecting to the Big Question

1. Explain that the way an individual deals with hardship reveals much about his or her character.
2. Have students read the bracketed passage. **Ask:** What role do Long Arrow's hardships play in his development as a hero?
   Possible response: Long Arrow is presented with many hardships, including being deaf and shunned by his people. Instead of remaining passive, however, he faces his hardships with patience, persistence, and courage. These hardships then allow him to develop heroic attributes, making him a stronger and wiser individual.
3. **Ask:** Do you think Long Arrow has possessed heroic attributes for his entire life? Explain.
   Possible response: Yes, Long Arrow just needed the confidence to demonstrate his heroic abilities.

20 ▲ **Critical Viewing** Based on this painting, what qualities of horses might impress someone who has never seen one before?

Vocabulary
stifle (stī´ fəl) *v.* smother; hold back

Long Arrow thanked him and vowed to follow his advice. For four days the young man stayed in the spirit chief's lodge, where he ate well and often went out riding on the Elk Dogs. But try as he would, he could never get a look at the old man's feet. The spirit chief always kept them carefully covered. Then on the morning of the fourth day, the old one was walking out of the tipi when his medicine robe caught in the entrance flap. As the robe opened, Long Arrow caught a glimpse of a leg and one foot. He was awed to see that it was not a human limb at all, but the glossy leg and firm hoof of an Elk Dog! 21 He could not **stifle** a cry of surprise, and the old man looked over his shoulder and saw that his leg and hoof were exposed. The chief seemed a little embarrassed, but shrugged and said, "I tried to hide this, but you must have been fated to see it. Look, both of my feet are those of an Elk Dog. You may as well ask me for a gift. Don't be timid; tell me what you want."

Long Arrow spoke boldly: "I want three things: your belt of rainbow colors, your black medicine robe, and your herd of Elk Dogs."

Vocabulary Development

Vocabulary Knowledge Rating

When students have completed reading and discussing "The Orphan Boy and the Elk Dog," have them take out their **Vocabulary Knowledge Rating Chart** for this selection. Read the words aloud once more and have students rate their knowledge of the words again in the After Reading column. Clarify any words that are still problematic. Have students write their own definition or example in the appropriate column. Then, have students complete the Vocabulary Practice at the end of the selection. Encourage students to use the words in further discussion and written work about this selection. Remind them that they will be accountable for these words on the **Selection Test**, ***Unit 6 Resources***, pp. 56–58 or 59–61.

22 "Well, so you're really not timid at all!" said the old man. "You ask for a lot, and I'll give it to you, except that you cannot have all my Elk Dogs; I'll give you half of them. Now I must tell you that my black medicine robe and my many-colored belt have Elk Dog magic in them. Always wear the robe when you try to catch Elk Dogs; then they can't get away from you. On quiet nights, if you listen closely to the belt, you will hear the Elk Dog dance song and Elk Dog prayers. You must learn them. And I will give you one more magic gift: this long rope woven from the hair of a white buffalo bull. With it you will never fail to catch whichever Elk Dog you want."

23 The spirit chief presented him with the gifts and said, "Now you must leave. At first the Elk Dogs will not follow you. Keep the medicine robe and the magic belt on at all times, and walk for four days toward the north. Never look back—always look to the north. On the fourth day the Elk Dogs will come up beside you on the left. Still don't look back. But after they have overtaken you, catch one with the rope of white buffalo hair and ride him home. Don't lose the black robe, or you will lose the Elk Dogs and never catch them again."

Long Arrow listened carefully so that he would remember. Then the old spirit chief had his wife make up a big pack of food, almost too heavy for Long Arrow to carry, and the young man took leave of his generous spirit host. The mysterious boy once again turned himself into a kingfisher and led Long Arrow to the surface of the lake, where his faithful dog greeted him joyfully. Long Arrow fed the dog, put his pack of food on the travois, and started walking north.

On the fourth day the Elk Dogs came up on his left side, as the spirit chief had foretold. Long Arrow snared the black one with the arched neck to ride, and he caught another to carry the pack of food. They galloped swiftly on, the dog barking at the big Elk Dogs' heels.

When Long Arrow arrived at last in his village, the people were afraid and hid. They did not recognize him astride his beautiful Elk Dog but took him for a monster, half man and half animal. Long Arrow kept calling, "Grandfather Good Running, it's your grandson. I've come back bringing Elk Dogs!"

Recognizing the voice, Good Running came out of hiding and wept for joy, because he had given Long Arrow up for lost. Then all the others emerged from their hiding places to admire the wonderful new animals.

Long Arrow said, "My grandfather and grandmother who adopted me, I can never repay you for your kindness. Accept these wonderful Elk Dogs as my gift. Now we no longer need to be **humble** footsloggers, because these animals will carry us swiftly everywhere we want to go. Now buffalo hunting will be easy. Now our tipis will be larger, our possessions will be greater, because

Reading Skill
Analyze Cultural Context Given the details in this paragraph, what questions might you ask about Blackfeet ceremonies and songs?

Vocabulary
humble (hum′ bəl) *adj.* showing an awareness of one's shortcomings; modest

24 **Reading Check**

What gifts does Long Arrow request from the chief?

22 Reading Skill
Analyze Cultural Context

1. Have a student read aloud the bracketed paragraph.
2. **Ask** students to respond to the Reading Skill question: Given the details in this paragraph, what questions might you ask about Blackfeet ceremonies and songs?
   Possible responses: Students may ask such questions as *Do Blackfeet ceremonies involve special dress or costume? Are Blackfeet ceremonies and songs always related to animals or other elements of nature? From whom do Blackfeet tribe members learn ceremonies and songs? Do the Blackfeet believe ceremonies function in the same way as prayers, meditation, or goal-setting?*

23 Literary Analysis
Myths

1. **Ask** students to recall and explain the definition of a quest myth.
   Answer: Quest myths feature a character who searches for knowledge or an important object; they also express the values of a culture.
2. Have a volunteer read aloud the bracketed passage.
3. **Ask** students to describe the chief in the spirit world and his treatment of Long Arrow.
   Answer: The chief is wise, generous, and compassionate. He gives Long Arrow gifts and advice to use in the future.
4. **Ask** students to identify the values expressed in Long Arrow's encounter with the chief.
   Possible responses: The chief reveals the Blackfeet's values of generosity, respect for tradition, and compassion.

24 Reading Check

Answer: Long Arrow requests the spirit chief's rainbow-colored belt, his black medicine robe, and his herd of Elk Dogs.

Concept Connector

Anticipation Guide
Have students return to their **Anticipation Guides** and respond to the statements again in the After Reading column. They may do this individually or in their original pairs or groups. Then, lead a class discussion probing for what students have learned that confirms or invalidates each statement. Encourage students to cite specific details, quotations, or other evidence from the text to support their responses to each statement.

Writing About the Big Question
Have students compare their responses to the sentence starter they completed before reading "The Orphan Boy and the Elk Dog" with their ideas afterward. Ask them to explain whether their thoughts have changed.

Reading Skill Graphic Organizer
Ask students to review the graphic organizers they completed to analyze cultural context while reading. Show them the partially completed **Reading Skill Graphic Organizer A** (*Graphic Organizer Transparencies*, p. 197) as an example. Then, have students share their graphic organizers.

25 Literary Analysis
Myths

Ask students to respond to the Literary Analysis question: What does this myth explain?

Answer: This myth explains how horses become part of the Blackfeet people's lives. Because the horse is understood to be a magical animal, the myth also shows the Blackfeet people's reverence for the utility, strength, and beauty of horses.

ASSESS

Answers

Critical Thinking

1. Some students may say yes; they see the journey as an exciting trek.
2. (a) The villagers shun Long Arrow because he cannot hear, so they think he is stupid. (b) The villagers are intolerant.
3. (a) He wants to make his grandfather proud of him and gain the respect of the villagers. (b) **Possible response:** Long Arrow loves and admires Good Running.
4. (a) Long Arrow faces a hard journey, frightening beings, and the ordeal of plunging into a lake. (b) In each case, courage and determination enable Long Arrow to persist and succeed.
5. (a) **Possible response:** The myth suggests that everyone—even people who are not well liked—deserve to be helped. (b) Students should expand their answers to reflect their partners' ideas.

Can anyone be a hero?

(a) Possible response: Long Arrow seems an unlikely hero at the beginning of the story because superficially he doesn't seem to reflect the values that are important to the Blackfeet people. Instead of being strong, able-bodied, and intelligent, the others see him as weak, skinny, and dumb. **(b)** Later in the story, Long Arrow displays bravery, inner strength, devotion, and persistence.

an Elk Dog travois can carry a load ten times bigger than that of a dog. Take them, my grandparents. I shall keep for myself only this black male and this black female, which will grow into a fine herd."

"You have indeed done something great, grandson," said Good Running, and he spoke true. The people became the bold riders of the Plains and soon could hardly imagine how they had existed without these wonderful animals.

After some time Good Running, rich and honored by all, said to Long Arrow, "Grandson, lead us to the Great Mystery Lake so we can camp by its shores. Let's visit the spirit chief and the wondrous boy; maybe they will give us more of their power and magic gifts." 25

Long Arrow led the people southward and again found the Great Mystery Lake. But the waters would no longer part for him, nor would any of the kingfishers they saw turn into a boy. Nor, gazing down into the crystal-clear water, could they discover people, Elk Dogs, or a tipi. There was nothing in the lake but a few fish.

Literary Analysis Myths What does this myth explain?

Critical Thinking

1. **Respond:** Would you like to travel with Long Arrow? Explain.
2. **(a)** Why do the villagers shun Long Arrow at the beginning of the story? **(b) Analyze:** What does this behavior suggest about the villagers?
3. **(a)** What reason does Long Arrow give for asking Good Running for a "great" thing to do? **(b) Infer:** What does his reason show about Long Arrow's feelings for Good Running?
4. **(a) Summarize:** List three obstacles Long Arrow faces on his journey. **(b) Analyze:** Explain how he overcomes each one.
5. **(a) Interpret:** What lesson does this myth teach about helping others? **(b) Discuss:** Share and discuss responses with a partner. Work together to formulate a response that presents both your opinions. Share your idea with the class.

Can anyone be a hero?
(a) Identify two reasons to explain why Long Arrow seems an unlikely hero at the beginning of the story. **(b)** What heroic traits does Long Arrow display later in the story?

Assessment Resources

Unit 6 Resources

L1 L2 EL **Selection Test A**, pp. 56–58. Administer Test A to less advanced readers and English learners.

L3 L4 **Selection Test B**, pp. 59–61. Administer Test B to on-level and more advanced students.

L3 L4 **Open-Book Test**, pp. 53–55. As an alternative, give the Open-Book Test.

All **Customizable Test Bank**

All **Self-tests**

Students may prepare for the **Selection Test** by taking the **Self-test** online.

PHLit Online! All assessment resources are available at **www.PHLitOnline.com.**

After You Read | The Orphan Boy and the Elk Dog

Literary Analysis: Myths

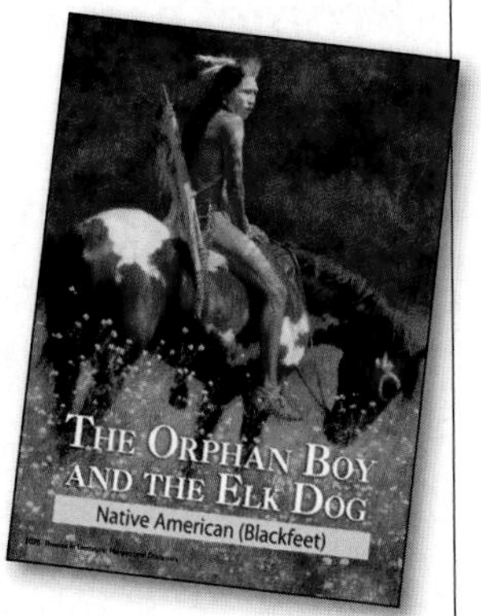

1. Using a chart like the one shown, identify which characteristics of **myths** are found in "The Orphan Boy and the Elk Dog." Support your choices by supplying examples from the text.

What the Story Explains	Exceptional or Fantastic Characters	Quest	Transgression

2. **(a)** What qualities help Long Arrow overcome the obstacles he faces on his quest? Support your answer with details from the text. **(b)** Working from your answer, draw a conclusion about the qualities the Blackfeet valued in a person.
3. **(a)** What advice does Good Running give Long Arrow before his journey? **(b)** Draw a conclusion about the customs and beliefs of the Blackfeet based on this advice.

Reading Skill: Analyze Cultural Context

4. **(a)** Give two examples of questions you might ask to **analyze the cultural context** of the myth. **(b)** Explain the answers that the myth suggests, and provide details from the text.

Vocabulary

Practice Copy each of the following word pairs. If the words have similar meanings, write *S* for **synonyms.** If the words have opposite meanings, write *A* for **antonyms.** Explain each of your choices.

1. surpassed, failed
2. emanating, absorbing
3. relish, pleasure
4. stifle, conceal
5. refuse, rubbish
6. humble, arrogant

Word Study Use the context of the sentences and what you know about the **Latin root *-fus-*** to explain your answer to each question.

1. Is *diffuse* flooding usually concentrated in one spot?
2. Would you feel appreciated if you received *effusive* praise?

Word Study

The **Latin root *-fus-*** means "to pour."

Challenge Explain how the root *-fus-* contributes to the meanings of these words. Consult a dictionary if necessary.

infusion
profuse
suffuse

Answers

Literary Analysis

1. The story explains how horses became part of the Blackfeet way of life. Exceptional characters include Long Arrow himself, the extremely tall man, and the Great One. The quest is a search for the Elk Dogs. In rejecting the orphan the people of the tribe commit a transgression.

   For other sample answers, see *Graphic Organizer Transparencies,* **Literary Analysis Graphic Organizer A**, p. 197, and the **Additional Answers** section.
2. (a) Long Arrow has courage, intelligence, and great physical endurance, for he walked days upon days to find the Great Mystery Lake. (b) **Possible response:** The Blackfeet seem to admire someone who has physical strength, mental agility, and courage.
3. (a) Long Arrow must learn to be a man, purify himself in a sweat bath, and use the pipe.
   (b) **Possible response:** These events suggest that the Blackfeet believe that success in life depends on respecting tribal traditions and purifying mind and body.

Reading Skill

4. (a) **Possible response:** Students may ask how Long Arrow's tribe acquires their food. Students may also ask about the role of women. (b) **Possible response:** A passage in the story states that when nearby game is "hunted out," the tribe moves. This suggests that Long Arrow's people depend largely on game for food. The way Good Running speaks to his wife reveals that women are not considered equal to men.

Vocabulary

Practice

Sample answers:

1. A; Surpassed means "to have exceeded expectations or capacity," the opposite of *failed.*
2. A; Emanating means "issuing forth from a source." *Absorbing* means "taking in."

Answers continued

3. S; *Relish* means "enjoyment in something." *Pleasure* means "enjoyment and satisfaction."
4. S; To *stifle* is "to smother someone or something." To *conceal* is "to hide or cover up something."
5. S; *Refuse* and *rubbish* both mean "trash or waste."
6. A; *Humble* means "modest" while *arrogant* means "conceited or egotistic."

Word Study

Sample answers:

1. No, the root *-fus-* means "to pour" and *diffuse* means "poured out or spread." If flooding is diffuse, it is spread all over.
2. Yes, the root *-fus-* means "to pour," and *effusive* means "pouring or overflowing." I would feel appreciated if praise poured into me.

Word Study: Challenge

Sample answers: An *infusion* is a product that is created by pouring together other ingredients. When something is *profuse,* it is plentiful or pours forth. To *suffuse* is to pour something into something else.

EXTEND/ASSESS

Answers

Grammar

Introduce and discuss the skill, using the instruction on the student page.

Teaching the Skill

1. Present these two examples for students to compare:

    Independent clause: Wild horses roam parts of the U.S.

    Dependent clause: where the land is untouched by humans

    Have students identify the subject and verb in each clause. Then, prompt students to explain why the sample dependent clause cannot stand alone.
2. Remind students that a compound sentence combines ideas that are independent but related in content.

WG **Writing and Grammar, Grade 10**

Students will find further instruction on and practice with simple and compound sentences in Chapter 20.

Practice A

1. subject: Epimetheus; verb: gave; simple
2. subjects: Prometheus, gods; verbs: stole, were not; compound
3. subject: Pandora; verb: was; simple
4. subjects: flood, people; verbs: covered, remained; compound

Challenge

Sample answers: Thus, the two at last were friends. (simple) Finally, Zeus determined to destroy the race of men altogether, and the other gods agreed. (compound)

Practice B

Sample answers:

1. simple
2. compound; Good Running was kind. He adopted Long Arrow.
3. simple
4. compound; Spirit people kept the Elk Dogs. The animals worked hard.

Challenge

Sample answer: The painting has vibrant colors. The painting has a simple composition. Compound: The painting has vibrant colors, and it has a simple composition.

Integrated Language Skills

Prometheus and the First People • The Orphan Boy and the Elk Dog

Grammar: Simple and Compound Sentences

A **clause** is a group of words with a subject and a verb. An **independent clause** is a clause that can stand on its own as a sentence. Clauses form different types of sentences.

- A **simple sentence** consists of a single independent clause.
- A **compound sentence** contains two or more independent clauses linked by a semicolon or coordinating conjunction, such as *and, but, or, for, nor, so* and *yet*.

In the following examples, subjects are underlined once and verbs are underlined twice.

Simple Sentence: The myth of Prometheus explains the early origins of fire.

Compound Sentence: Myths explain the world; legends record great deeds.

Compound Sentence: You can compare the Greek myths and the Native American myths, but they come from different cultures.

Practice A Underline the subjects and circle the verbs in each sentence. Then, tell whether the sentence is a simple or a compound sentence.

1. Epimetheus gave gifts to all the animals.
2. Prometheus stole fire from the gods; the gods were not happy.
3. Pandora was beautiful and curious.
4. A great flood covered the earth, but two people remained alive.

Challenge In "Prometheus and the First People," find an example of a simple sentence and an example of a compound sentence.

Practice B Identify each of the following sentences as *simple* or *compound*. Rewrite each compound sentence as two simple sentences.

1. People treated Long Arrow cruelly.
2. Good Running was kind, and he adopted Long Arrow.
3. Elk Dogs are swift, beautiful, and mysterious.
4. Spirit people kept the Elk Dogs; the animals worked hard.

Challenge Write two simple sentences about the painting on page 1076. Then, combine the two sentences into a compound sentence.

WG **Writing and Grammar Connection:** Chapter 3, Sections 1

Extend the Lesson

Sentence Modeling

Choose the sentence given from the selection students have read:

Wolves swam in the midst of flocks of sheep, but the sheep were not frightened by them, and the wolves never thought of their natural prey. ("Prometheus and the First People")

Then there was a snap in his right ear and a wormlike thing came out of it, and on his right side he could hear the rushing waters of a stream. ("The Orphan Boy and the Elk Dog")

Ask students what they notice about the sentence. Elicit from them that it is a compound sentence. Then, ask what else they notice. ("Prometheus": the compound sentence emphasizes the connection among the animals and events. "The Orphan Boy": the compound sentence stresses a fluid progression of actions.)

Have students imitate the sentence in a sentence on a topic of their own choosing, matching each grammatical and stylistic feature discussed. Collect and share the sentences.

Writing

In a small group, write a contemporary **myth**. You may write about the origin of some aspect of human life, such as how gossip or forgiveness entered the world *or* you may describe the origin of some feature of your everyday world, such as television, computers, or automobiles. Follow these steps:

- Agree on a topic that group members find interesting.
- Make a plan for writing that addresses your purpose, identifies a logical sequence, and sets a time frame for completion.
- Have one member write an opening sentence.
- With your planned sequence in mind, each group member should take a turn writing a paragraph that follows from the one before until the myth is complete.
- As a group, review the story as it progresses, and make any revisions agreed upon by the group members.

Present your myth to the class.

Writing Workshop: *Work in Progress*

Prewriting for a Technical Document For a Technical Document you may write, make a list of tasks that you do every day such as cooking a meal or playing a computer game. Select one of the tasks and list the basic steps that go into the task. Save your Task List in your writing portfolio.

Use this prewriting activity to prepare for the **Writing Workshop** on page 1146.

Listening and Speaking

Locate another Greek myth about the gods and humans *or* another Native American myth that explains the origin of an animal. Present your own **retelling** of the myth to your class. As you prepare your retelling, make sure you do the following:

- engage your audience with an exciting introduction to the story.
- **present the sequence of events** in a logical order and **explain the importance** of the narrative's action.
- accurately and vividly describe important scenes, action, and characters, using **sensory details** whenever possible.
- **pace** your narrative to **reflect the action and mood** of the story.
- include a **conclusion** that helps listeners understand the important lesson your myth illustrates.

Afterward, have classmates summarize the myth you have retold. Then, lead a discussion in which you compare and contrast the myth to either "Prometheus and the First People" or "The Orphan Boy and the Elk Dog."

PHLit Online!
www.PHLitOnline.com
- Interactive graphic organizers
- Grammar tutorial
- Interactive journals

EXTEND/ASSESS

Writing

1. Review the assignment, using the instruction on the student page.
2. To guide students in writing a myth, give them **Support for Writing**, p. 51 in ***Unit 6 Resources***.
3. To evaluate students' myths, use the Short Story rubric on pages 226–227 in ***Professional Development Guidebook.***

Six Traits Focus

✔	Ideas	✔	Word Choice
✔	Organization		Sentence Fluency
	Voice		Conventions

Writing and Grammar, Grade 10

Students will find guidance on writing a myth in Chapter 5.

Writing Workshop
Work in Progress

Have students save their completed Task List in their portfolios. They will use the Task List later as they continue this Work-in-Progress assignment (see p. 1118). These assignments prepare them to complete the Writing Workshop assignment (see pp. 1146–1151).

Listening and Speaking

1. Review the assignment, using the instruction on the student page.
2. Have students complete the **Support for Extend Your Learning** page (***Unit 6 Resources***, p. 52).

Teaching Resources

Unit 6 Resources
L3 L4 **Integrated Language Skills: Grammar,** p. 50
L3 L4 **Support for Writing,** p. 51
L3 L4 **Support for Extend Your Learning,** p. 52
L4 **Enrichment,** pp. 31, 49

Enriched Online Student Edition
Available under After You Read for this selection:
All **Interactive Grammar Tutorial**
L3 L4 **Internet Research Activity**

Professional Development Guidebook
Rubrics for Short Stories, pp. 226–227

PHLit Online! All print and digital resources are available online at **www.PHLitOnline.com.** Online resources accessible by students are noted on the student page.

TIME AND RESOURCE MANAGER

from Sundiata: An Epic of Old Mali • Rama's Initiation *from the* Ramayana

Lesson Pacing Guide

DAY 1 Preteach

- Administer the Reading and Vocabulary Warm-ups (*Unit 6 Resources*, pp. 62–65 or 80–83) as necessary.
- Introduce the Reading Skill: Analyze Cultural Context. FT
- Introduce the Literary Analysis concept: Epic and Epic Hero. FT
- Distribute copies of the appropriate graphic organizer for the Reading Skill (*Graphic Organizer Transparencies*, pp. 199–201). CRI
- Distribute copies of the appropriate graphic organizer for Literary Analysis (*Graphic Organizer Transparencies*, pp. 202–204). CRI
- Teach the selection vocabulary. FT CRI
- Introduce the Word Study skill.

DAYS 2–3 Preteach/Teach

- Build background with the Background feature. CRI
- Develop thematic vocabulary and thematic thinking with Writing About the Big Question.
- Prepare students to read with the Activating Prior Knowledge activities (TE). CRI
- Informally monitor comprehension while students read. FT
- Use the Reading Check questions to confirm comprehension.
- Develop students' ability to analyze cultural context using the Reading Skill questions. CRI
- Develop students' understanding of epic and epic hero using the Literary Analysis questions. CRI
- Reinforce vocabulary with the Vocabulary notes. CRI

DAY 4 Assess

- Assess students' comprehension and mastery of the skills by having them answer the Critical Thinking, Reading Skill, and Literary Analysis questions. FT
- Have students complete the Vocabulary Practice activities. FT
- Have students complete the Word Study activities.

DAY 5 Extend/Assess

- Have students complete the Grammar lesson. CRI
- Have students complete the Writing activity and write a newspaper report. (You may assign as homework.) FT
- Extend learning by having students complete the Listening and Speaking activity, an improvised dialogue. As an alternative, assign them "The Youngest Heroes" or "Equality on the Playing Field" in *Reality Central*. CRI
- Administer Selection Test A or B (*Unit 6 Resources*, pp. 74–79 or 95–100). FT

The excerpts from the epic *Sundiata: An Epic of Old Mali* are unedited. The excerpt "Rama's Initiation" from the epic *The Ramayana* is unedited.

Meeting Your Standards

Students will

1. analyze and respond to literary elements.
   - Literary Analysis: Epic and Epic Hero
2. read, comprehend, and analyze epics.
   - Reading Skill: Analyze Cultural Context
   - Reading Check questions
   - Apply the Skills questions
   - Assessment Practice
3. develop vocabulary.
   - Vocabulary
   - Word Study
4. apply grammar skills.
   - Complex and Compound-Complex Sentences
5. Develop writing proficiency.
   - Work in Progress: Technical Document
   - newspaper report
6. strengthen listening and speaking skills.
   - improvised dialogue

CRI For a full explanation of Culturally Responsive Instruction opportunities in this lesson, see p. T86–T87.

FT For an accelerated lesson, use the Fast Track strategies and activities.

Managing Differentiated Instruction

This leveled selection pairing groups a more accessible with a more challenging selection. Choose either one to teach the lesson skills. For classroom management suggestions for using the pairing in a mixed-ability class, see pp. T68–T69.

Daily Block Scheduling

Each day in this Lesson Pacing Guide represents a 40–50 minute period. Teachers using block scheduling may combine days to revise pacing. In addition, teachers may differentiate and support core instruction by integrating components for extended and intensive support as students require. See the Guide to Selected Leveled Resources (facing page).

Guide to Selected Leveled Resources

EL English Learners

			from Sundiata: An Epic of Old Mali	Rama's Initiation *from the* Ramayana
CORE COURSE	*Unit 6 Resources*	Selection Test A	pp. 74–76	pp. 95–97
	Graphic Organizer Transparencies	Reading Skill Graphic Organizer A	p. 199	p. 200
		Literary Analysis Graphic Organizer A	p. 202	p. 203
EXTENDED SUPPORT (Level 2)	*Unit 6 Resources*	Reading and Vocabulary Warm-ups A or B	pp. 62–65	pp. 80–83
	Reader's Notebook: English Learner's Version		adapted instruction and adapted selection	adapted instruction and summary
	Hear It! Audio CD		selection and summaries	selection and summaries
	Hear It! Audio CD (adapted text)		adapted selection and summaries	—
INTENSIVE SUPPORT (Level 1)	*Reality Central*		"The Youngest Heroes"	"Equality on the Playing Field"
	Real-World Writing Journal		Lesson 3, pp. 164–167	Lesson 4, pp. 168–171

L2 Below-Level Students

			from Sundiata: An Epic of Old Mali	Rama's Initiation *from the* Ramayana
CORE COURSE	*Unit 6 Resources*	Selection Test A	pp. 74–76	pp. 95–97
	Graphic Organizer Transparencies	Reading Skill Graphic Organizer A	p. 199	p. 200
		Literary Analysis Graphic Organizer A	p. 202	p. 203
EXTENDED SUPPORT (Level 2)	*Unit 6 Resources*	Reading and Vocabulary Warm-ups A or B	pp. 62–65	pp. 80–83
	Reader's Notebook		adapted instruction and full selection	adapted instruction and summary
	Hear It! Audio CD		selection and summaries	selection and summaries
INTENSIVE SUPPORT (Level 1)	*Reality Central*		"The Youngest Heroes"	"Equality on the Playing Field"
	Real-World Writing Journal		Lesson 3, pp. 164–167	Lesson 4, pp. 168–171
	Reading Kit		Reteaching worksheets	Reteaching worksheets

L1 Special Needs Students

			from Sundiata: An Epic of Old Mali	Rama's Initiation *from the* Ramayana
CORE COURSE	*Unit 6 Resources*	Selection Test A	pp. 74–76	pp. 95–97
	Graphic Organizer Transparencies	Reading Skill Graphic Organizer A	p. 199	p. 200
		Literary Analysis Graphic Organizer A	p. 202	p. 203
EXTENDED SUPPORT (Level 2)	*Unit 6 Resources*	Reading and Vocabulary Warm-ups A or B	pp. 62–65	pp. 80–83
	Reader's Notebook: Adapted Version		adapted instruction and adapted selection	adapted instruction and summary
	Hear It! Audio CD (adapted text)		adapted selection and summaries	—
INTENSIVE SUPPORT (Level 1)	*Reality Central*		"The Youngest Heroes"	"Equality on the Playing Field"
	Real-World Writing Journal		Lesson 3, pp. 164–167	Lesson 4, pp. 168–171
	Reading Kit		Reteaching worksheets	Reteaching worksheets

The program includes resources for these students: L3 On-Level L4 Advanced All All
For a complete guide to selection support, see pp. T106–T108.

NOTE: All print materials are also available online at *www.PHLitOnline.com.*

VISUAL GUIDE to Featured Selection Resources

• *from* Sundiata: An Epic of Old Mali
• Rama's Initiation *from the* Ramayana

RESOURCES FOR:

- EL English Learners
- L1 Special Needs Students
- L2 Below-Level Students
- L3 On-Level Students
- L4 Advanced Students
- All All Students

Vocabulary/Fluency/Prior Knowledge

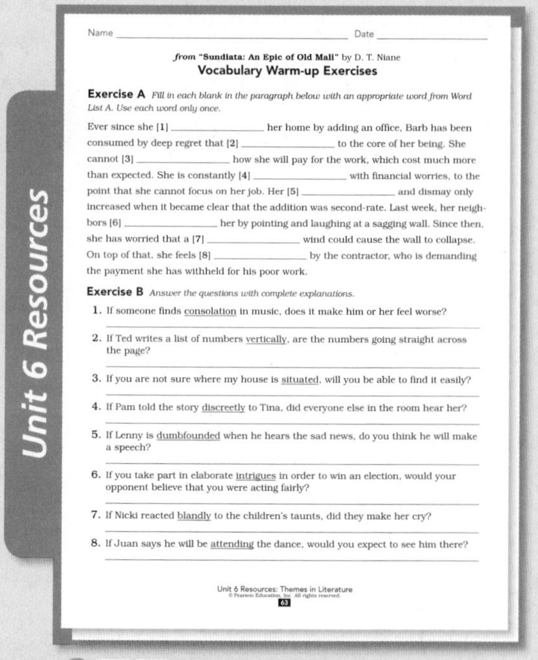
Unit 6 Resources

Name ______ Date ______

from **"Sundiata: An Epic of Old Mali"** by D. T. Niane
Vocabulary Warm-up Exercises

Exercise A *Fill in each blank in the paragraph below with an appropriate word from Word List A. Use each word only once.*

Ever since she [1] ______ her home by adding an office, Barb has been consumed by deep regret that [2] ______ to the core of her being. She cannot [3] ______ how she will pay for the work, which cost much more than expected. She is constantly [4] ______ with financial worries, to the point that she cannot focus on her job. Her [5] ______ and dismay only increased when it became clear that the addition was second-rate. Last week, her neighbors [6] ______ her by pointing and laughing at a sagging wall. Since then, she has worried that a [7] ______ wind could cause the wall to collapse. On top of that, she feels [8] ______ by the contractor, who is demanding the payment she has withheld for his poor work.

Exercise B *Answer the questions with complete explanations.*

1. If someone finds consolation in music, does it make him or her feel worse?
2. If Ted writes a list of numbers vertically, are the numbers going straight across the page?
3. If you are not sure where my house is situated, will you be able to find it easily?
4. If Pam told the story discreetly to Tina, did everyone else in the room hear her?
5. If Lenny is dumbfounded when he hears the sad news, do you think he will make a speech?
6. If you take part in elaborate intrigues in order to win an election, would your opponent believe that you were acting fairly?
7. If Nicki reacted blandly to the children's taunts, did they make her cry?
8. If Juan says he will be attending the dance, would you expect to see him there?

Unit 6 Resources: Themes in Literature
© Pearson Education, Inc. All rights reserved.
63

EL L1 L2 Vocabulary Warm-ups A and B, pp. 62–63, 80–81

Also available for these selections:

- **EL L1 L2 Reading Warm-ups A and B, pp. 64–65, 82–83**
- **All Writing About the Big Question, pp. 66, 84**
- **All Vocabulary Builder, pp. 69, 87**

Reader's Notebooks

Pre- and postreading pages for both selections, as well as from *Sundiata: An Epic of Old Mali,* appear in an interactive format in the *Reader's Notebooks*. Each *Notebook* is differentiated for a different group of learners.
The selections in the Adapted and English Learner's versions are abridged.

L2 L3 *Reader's Notebook*

L1 *Reader's Notebook: Adapted Version*

EL *Reader's Notebook: English Learner's Version*

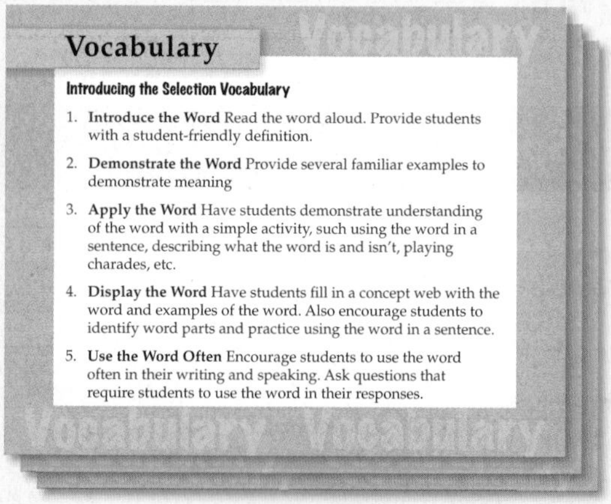
Vocabulary

Introducing the Selection Vocabulary

1. **Introduce the Word** Read the word aloud. Provide students with a student-friendly definition.
2. **Demonstrate the Word** Provide several familiar examples to demonstrate meaning
3. **Apply the Word** Have students demonstrate understanding of the word with a simple activity, such using the word in a sentence, describing what the word is and isn't, playing charades, etc.
4. **Display the Word** Have students fill in a concept web with the word and examples of the word. Also encourage students to identify word parts and practice using the word in a sentence.
5. **Use the Word Often** Encourage students to use the word often in their writing and speaking. Ask questions that require students to use the word in their responses.

Classroom Strategies and Teaching Routines

- core classroom routines outlined step-by-step
- convenient format for easy reference while teaching

Selection Support

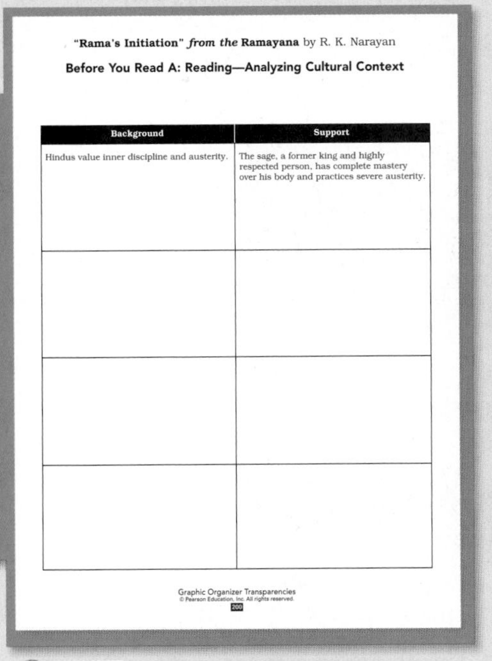
"Rama's Initiation" *from the* Ramayana by R. K. Narayan

Before You Read A: Reading—Analyzing Cultural Context

Background	Support
Hindus value inner discipline and austerity.	The sage, a former king and highly respected person, has complete mastery over his body and practices severe austerity.

Graphic Organizer Transparencies
© Pearson Education, Inc. All rights reserved.
200

EL L1 L2 **Reading: Graphic Organizer A, pp. 199, 200 (partially filled in)**

Also available for these selections:

EL L1 L2 Literary Analysis: Graphic Organizer A, pp. 202, 203 (partially filled in)

L3 Literary Analysis: Graphic Organizer B, p. 204

L3 Reading: Graphic Organizer B, p. 201

Skills Development/Extension

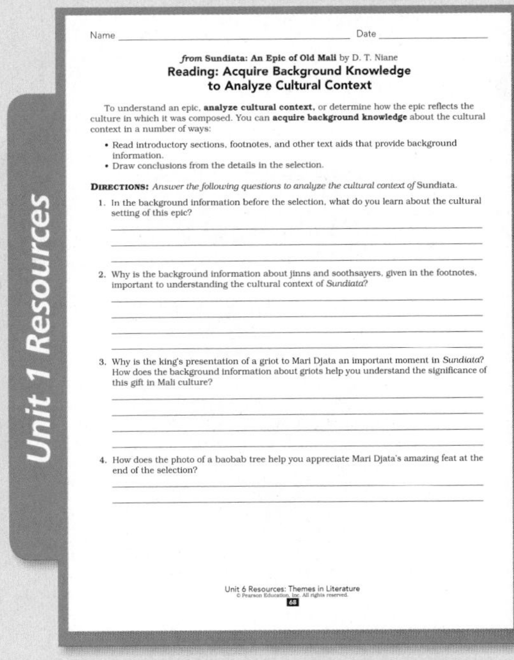
Name ________ Date ________

from Sundiata: An Epic of Old Mali by D. T. Niane

Reading: Acquire Background Knowledge to Analyze Cultural Context

To understand an epic, **analyze cultural context**, or determine how the epic reflects the culture in which it was composed. You can **acquire background knowledge** about the cultural context in a number of ways:

- Read introductory sections, footnotes, and other text aids that provide background information.
- Draw conclusions from the details in the selection.

Directions: *Answer the following questions to analyze the cultural context of* Sundiata.

1. In the background information before the selection, what do you learn about the cultural setting of this epic?
2. Why is the background information about jinns and soothsayers, given in the footnotes, important to understanding the cultural context of *Sundiata*?
3. Why is the king's presentation of a griot to Mari Djata an important moment in *Sundiata*? How does the background information about griots help you understand the significance of this gift in Mali culture?
4. How does the photo of a baobab tree help you appreciate Mari Djata's amazing feat at the end of the selection?

Unit 6 Resources: Themes in Literature
© Pearson Education, Inc. All rights reserved.
68

All **Reading: Analyze Cultural Context, pp. 68, 86**

Also available for these selections:

All Literary Analysis: Epic and Epic Heroes, pp. 67, 85

L4 Enrichment, pp. 70, 88

L3 L4 Grammar, p. 89

L3 L4 Support for Writing, p. 90

L3 L4 Support for Extend Your Learning, p. 91

Assessment

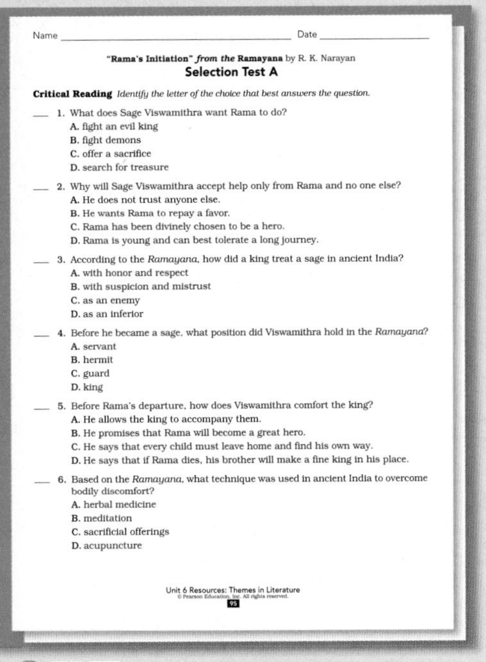
Name ________ Date ________

"Rama's Initiation" *from the* Ramayana by R. K. Narayan

Selection Test A

Critical Reading *Identify the letter of the choice that best answers the question.*

___ 1. What does Sage Viswamithra want Rama to do?
A. fight an evil king
B. fight demons
C. offer a sacrifice
D. search for treasure

___ 2. Why will Sage Viswamithra accept help only from Rama and no one else?
A. He does not trust anyone else.
B. He wants Rama to repay a favor.
C. Rama has been divinely chosen to be a hero.
D. Rama is young and can best tolerate a long journey.

___ 3. According to the *Ramayana*, how did a king treat a sage in ancient India?
A. with honor and respect
B. with suspicion and mistrust
C. as an enemy
D. as an inferior

___ 4. Before he became a sage, what position did Viswamithra hold in the *Ramayana*?
A. servant
B. hermit
C. guard
D. king

___ 5. Before Rama's departure, how does Viswamithra comfort the king?
A. He allows the king to accompany them.
B. He promises that Rama will become a great hero.
C. He says that every child must leave home and find his own way.
D. He says that if Rama dies, his brother will make a fine king in his place.

___ 6. Based on the *Ramayana*, what technique was used in ancient India to overcome bodily discomfort?
A. herbal medicine
B. meditation
C. sacrificial offerings
D. acupuncture

Unit 6 Resources: Themes in Literature
© Pearson Education, Inc. All rights reserved.
95

EL L1 L2 **Selection Test A, pp. 74–76, 95–97**

Also available for these selections:

L3 L4 Selection Test B, pp. 77–79, 98–100

L3 L4 Open-Book Test, pp. 71–73, 92–94

PHLit Online!
www.PHLitOnline.com

- complete narrated selection text
- a thematically related video with writing prompt
- an interactive graphic organizer
- highlighting feature
- access to all student print resources, adapted to individual student needs
- Spanish and English summaries

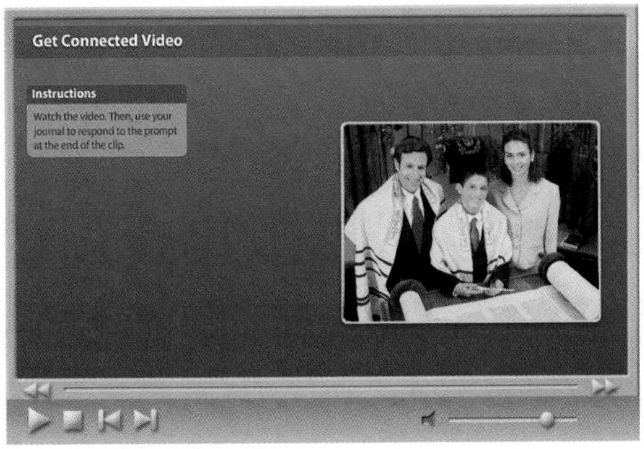

Get Connected! (thematic video with writing prompt)

Also available:

Background video

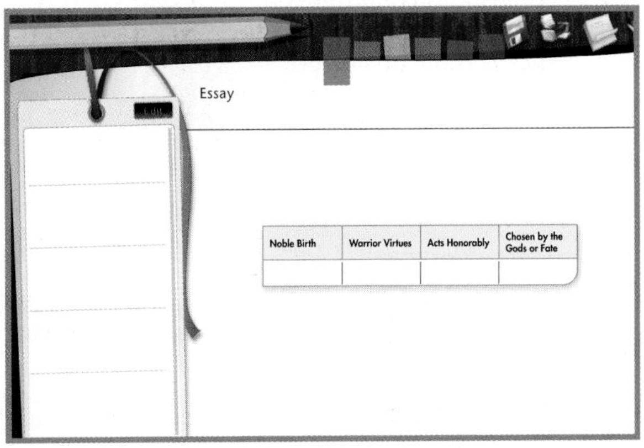

Writer's Journal (with graphics feature)

Also available:

Vocabulary Central (tools, activities, and songs for studying vocabulary)

DIFFERENTIATE/PRETEACH

❶ Selection Choices

You may use either the selection from *Sundiata: An Epic of Old Mali* or "Rama's Initiation" from *The Ramayana* to meet the lesson standards. Skills instruction for both selections appears on p. 1091. Choose one selection to teach (or choose to teach both). The Accessibility at a Glance chart at the bottom of this page will help you determine which of the two selections is more appropriate for your students.

❷ Selection Skills

1. With the class, preview the selection skills. (The lesson meets the lesson objectives given on p. 1090a.)
2. Explain that students will develop the skill of analyzing cultural context (introduced on p. 1063) as they read to better understand and enjoy the selection you choose. By examining epics and epic heroes as they read, they will gain deeper insight into themes in literature: heroes and dreamers.
3. To introduce the Writing and Listening and Speaking activities (p. 1119), tell students that when they have finished reading the selection, they will write a newspaper report and an outline related to the selection.
4. Tell students that they will also study a grammar concept: complex and compound-complex sentences. By mastering this concept, they will improve their reading fluency and the quality of their own writing.

Before You Read

from **Sundiata: An Epic of Old Mali • Rama's Initiation** *from the* **Ramayana**

❶ Selection Choices

▲ Read the excerpt from ***Sundiata: An Epic of Old Mali*** to find out how a boy who is the subject of ridicule defends his mother's honor.

▲ Read **"Rama's Initiation"** from the ***Ramayana*** to learn how a young man accepts his destiny by going on a perilous journey.

❷ Selection Skills Guide

Practice these skills with either the excerpt from ***Sundiata: An Epic of Old Mali*** (p. 1094) or **"Rama's Initiation"** (p. 1108).

- Understand epics and epic heroes
- Analyze cultural context
- Acquire background knowledge
- Identify complex and compound-complex sentences
- Write a newspaper report
- Present an improvised dialogue

Differentiated Instruction for Universal Access

Accessibility at a Glance: Selection Choices

	Sundiata		Ramayana	
Context	African epic		Indian epic	
Language/ Vocabulary	Difficult names		Difficult names	
Concept Level	Accessible (logical plot)		Challenging (background information regarding religion and culture essential to understanding)	
Literary Merit	Cross-cultural		Cross-cultural	
Lexile/Length	Lexile: 920L	Word Count: 2,791	Lexile: 880L	Word Count: 2,451
Overall Rating	**More accessible**		**More challenging**	

Because a number of factors determine the relative accessibility of paired selections, in some cases the Lexile rating of the more challenging selection will be lower than that of the more accessible selection.

❸ Literary Analysis: Epic and Epic Hero

An **epic** is an extended narrative poem about the deeds of heroes. The typical **epic hero** is a warrior, and his character may be based on a historic or a legendary figure. In a number of epics, the hero strives to win immortality or undying fame through great deeds, especially in combat. The typical hero has the following characteristics:

- He has a high position in society and the virtues of a warrior, such as strength, courage, and perseverance.
- He defends his family's honor, and he behaves ethically—fighting evil and striving for justice.
- He may be marked by the gods or by fate and so may benefit from special blessings or suffer from special burdens.

An epic often reflects the culture that created it, celebrating that culture's values and reinforcing its ideals.

PHLit Online!
www.PHLitOnline.com

Hear It!
- Selection summary audio
- Selection audio

See It!
- Get Connected video
- Background video
- More about the author
- Vocabulary flashcards

Do It!
- Interactive journals
- Interactive graphic organizers
- Self-test
- Internet activity
- Grammar tutorial
- Interactive vocabulary games

❹ Reading Skill: Analyze Cultural Context

To understand an epic, **analyze cultural context,** or determine ways in which the epic reflects the ideas and values of the historical period and the culture in which it was composed. You can **acquire background knowledge** about the culture in these ways:

- Read text features such as introductory sections, footnotes, and other text aids.
- Draw conclusions from the details in the selection.

❺ Using the Strategy: Cultural Context Chart

Take notes on a **cultural context chart** like the one shown.

Background	Support
At age twelve, boys in this culture are initiated as full members of the tribe.	Footnote 3
Men in this culture are free to express their emotions.	The two friends cry when they part.

Differentiated Instruction for Universal Access

Preparing Students for the More Challenging Selection

If you wish to prepare lower level readers to read "Rama's Initiation," the more challenging selection, follow these steps:

- Review the background information with students about Hinduism and Hindu culture on p. 1107. Clarify and discuss any difficult concepts. Encourage students to keep these ideas in mind as they read.
- Students might have difficulty with some of the terms and references in the selection related to Hinduism and Hindu culture (e.g. *yagna*, p. 1110). Remind students to use the footnotes at the bottom of the page as they read to determine the meaning of these unfamiliar words and references.
- Due to the challenging names of the characters in the selection, students might have difficulty keeping track of who is who. Encourage students to make a list of characters as they read, noting the character's name, role, and relationship to others in the story.

PRETEACH

❸ Literary Analysis

1. Introduce the skill, using the instruction on the student page.
2. Tell students that they will practice identifying epic heroes as they read.

Think Aloud: Model the Skill

Model the skill of identifying and understanding epics and epic heroes, using the following "think aloud." Say to students:

> Suppose I am reading a story about a warrior who is on a journey to slay a monster that is threatening his village. I know it is an *epic* because it tells the deeds of a hero. As I read, I learn that the warrior shows virtues such as courage and strength; he fights the evil monster for the greater good; and he is fated to defeat the monster. Thus, I conclude that he is an *epic hero*.

❹ Reading Skill

1. Introduce the skill, using the instruction on the student page.
2. Tell students that they will analyze cultural context as they read.

Think Aloud: Model the Skill

Model the skill of analyzing cultural context, using the following "think aloud." Say to students:

> To analyze the cultural context of an epic, I acquire background information from the introduction and footnotes. For example, suppose I am reading an ancient Jewish epic. I learn in the introduction that it was customary for Jewish people to wash their hands before entering a temple as part of ritual cleansing. Thus, when I read about a Jewish man who is scorned for not washing his hands upon entering a temple, I understand why.

❺ Using the Strategy

Give students a copy of either **Reading Skill Graphic Organizer A** or **B** (*Graphic Organizer Transparencies*, pp. 199–201) to record details of analyzing cultural context as they read. Use the examples in **Reading Skill Graphic Organizer A,** which is partially filled in, to model the process of completing the organizer.

❶ Writing About the Big Question

1. Review the assignment with the class.
2. Remind students that *adversity* means "a state of misfortune or distress." Then ask students to give an example of adversity they have seen, heard about, or experienced. What do they think is the key to overcoming adversity?
3. Have students complete the sentence starter. Review responses as a class. (**Possible response:** Showing determination and courage in the face of adversity is heroic because it shows strength of character.)
4. Remind students that their answers will help them think about the Big Question, "Can anyone be a hero?"

While You Read

Tell students that as they read, they should look for examples of behavior that made Mari Djata an unlikely hero.

❷ Vocabulary

1. Have students preview the selection vocabulary.
2. For each word, have students say the word aloud.
3. Then, use the word in a sentence that defines the word.
4. Finally, repeat your definitional sentence or a similar sentence with the word missing and have the class "fill in the blank" chorally. For example:

   To fathom is to understand completely. His friend's irrational behavior was so unusual and unbelievable that it was impossible for the boy to [students say "fathom"].

❸ Word Study

1. Introduce the skill, using the instruction in the box.
2. Ask students to think of three words ending in *-ive*. Have them define the words using their knowledge of the suffix *-ive*. (**Sample answer:** *active:* having the quality of action; *aggressive:* having the quality of aggression; *attractive:* having the quality of attraction)

Can anyone be a hero?

❶ Writing About the Big Question

In the excerpt from *Sundiata: An Epic of Old Mali,* a young man's determination allows him to overcome his infirmity and regain his family's honor. Use this sentence starter to develop your ideas about the Big Question.

Showing **determination** and **courage** in the face of adversity is heroic because _______________.

While You Read Look for examples of behavior that made Mari Djata an unlikely hero.

❷ Vocabulary

Read each word and its definition. Decide whether you know the word well, know it a little bit, or do not know it at all. After you read, see how your knowledge of each word has increased.

- **fathom** (fa*th*ˊ əm) *v.* understand thoroughly (p. 1095) ***I cannot fathom why he behaved so strangely.*** *fathomable adj.*
- **innuendo** (inˊ yo͞o enˊ dō) *n.* indirect insult or accusation; insinuation (p. 1096) ***She will not accuse him directly, but her innuendo let him know she suspects him.***
- **estranged** (e strānjdˊ) *adj.* kept apart; in the condition of having had affection turn into indifference or hostility (p. 1096) ***The two friends became estranged after an especially bitter quarrel.*** *estrange v. estrangement n.*
- **derisively** (di rīˊ siv lē) *adv.* in a mocking and ridiculing manner (p. 1100) ***He commented derisively on our poster which hurt our feelings.*** *derision n. derisive adj.*
- **affront** (ə fruntˊ) *n.* open insult (p. 1100) ***Their nasty laughter was an affront to her pride.*** *affront v.*
- **efface** (ə fāsˊ) *v.* rub or blot out (p. 1102) ***In order to efface the memory of that day, we never spoke of it again.*** *effaced v. effacement n.*

❸ Word Study

The **Latin suffix** ***-ive*** means "belonging to" or "quality of."

In this story, a character chuckles **derisively,** or in a manner filled with scorn and ridicule.

Vocabulary Development

Vocabulary Knowledge Rating

Create a **Vocabulary Knowledge Rating Chart** (***Professional Development Guidebook***, p. 33) for this selection. Include the selection vocabulary and the Big Question words that appear in the Writing About the Big Question sentence starter on this page. (The Big Question vocabulary is introduced on pp.1046–1047.)

Give students a copy of the chart. Read the words aloud, and have students mark their rating in the Before Reading column. Urge them to be alert to these words as they read and discuss the selection.

Tally how many students think they know a word to gauge how much instruction to provide. As students read and discuss the selection, point out the words and their context.

PHLit Online! **Vocabulary Central**, featuring tools, activities, and songs for studying vocabulary, is available at **www.PHLitOnline.com**.

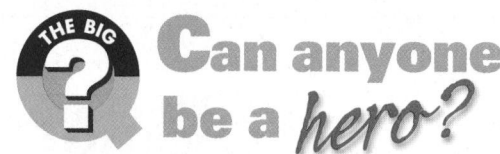

Meet D. T. Niane, (b. 1932) Mamadou Kouyaté, and the Malinke

Author of *Sundiata*: AN EPIC OF OLD MALI

Sundiata's people, the Malinke, are one of the Mande peoples of West Africa. Mande society is divided into different classes of people, from nobles to commoners. In his day, Sundiata's people traded in gold. After his victory over Sumanguru, Sundiata conquered neighboring lands and built an extensive kingdom known as the Mali empire.

The Griot Tradition Sundiata's achievements were celebrated over the centuries by West African oral historians known as griots (grē´ ōz). The twentieth-century griot Mamadou Kouyaté (mä´ mä do͞o ko͞o ya´ tā) continued this tradition. "I derive my knowledge from my father, Djeli Kedian, who also got it from his father," Kouyaté explained. "History holds no mystery for us." The scholar **D. T. Niane** (nī´ yan) wrote an account of Sundiata based on Kouyaté's retellings.

Did You Know!

Kouyaté belongs to the same clan as the kings of Old Mali.

❹ BACKGROUND FOR THE EPIC

A Great Leader

Sundiata tells the tale of Mari (or Sogolon) Djata, also known as Sundiata. Nearly 1,000 years ago, a warrior named Sumanguru took control of the area around Mali in West Africa and oppressed its Malinke people. A hero arose to unite the people, defeat Sumanguru, and usher in a period of peace. That hero was Sundiata.

Daily Bellringer

For each class during which you will teach this selection, have students complete one of the five Sentence Modeling activities for Week 32 in the *Daily Bellringer Activities* booklet.

❹ Background

The Mali Empire

The East African Mali Empire rose out of the decline of the Ghana Empire, which had flourished in earlier centuries. The area of western Africa where the story unfolds was a very unstable place at the time. Rival kings fought for power, land, and trade routes. Eventually, Sumanguru from Ghana gained control and oppressed the Mandinka people of Mali. Just when the land most needed a leader, the hero Dogolon-Djata (Sundiata) united his people, defeated the tyrant, and ushered in a period of prosperity. He also gained control of the trade routes through the Sahara and the gold mines of Bouré (in present-day Guinea). With riches from the gold trade, Sundiata and his successors built alliances, conquered more peoples, and expanded the empire.

Multidraft Reading

This icon ● marks natural pauses in the selection. To assist struggling readers and to deepen reading for all, assign the text in "chunks," following the icons, and apply multidraft reading protocols. For each reading, have students set the purpose indicated:

- **First reading**—literal comprehension: answering the Reading Check questions.
- **Second reading**—application of skills: answering the Epic and Epic Hero and Analyze Cultural Context prompts.
- **Third reading**—interpretation: answering the end-of-selection questions.

For more guidance, refer to the *Classroom Strategies and Teaching Routines* card on multidraft reading.

Differentiated Instruction — Additional Instruction

EL Extended Support—English Learners

Have students complete the **Reading and Vocabulary Warm-ups, *Unit 6 Resources,*** pp. 62–65 before they read. Assign the prereading pages and the adapted selection in the ***Reader's Notebook: English Learner's Version***. Then, have students listen to portions of the selection on the ***Hear It!* Audio CD.**

L1 L2 Extended Support—Struggling Readers

Have students complete the **Reading and Vocabulary Warm-ups, *Unit 6 Resources,*** pp. 62–65, before they read. Assign the pre-reading pages and the adapted selection in the ***Reader's Notebook: Adapted Version***. Then, have students listen to portions of the selection on the ***Hear It!* Audio CD** (adapted text).

L1 L2 Extended Support—Reluctant Readers

To build motivation and engagement before assigning the selection, have students read "The Youngest Heroes," a thematically related selection in ***Reality Central.*** Then, use the questions at the conclusion of the related selection to guide discussion.

PHLit Online!

For more about the author, practice with the selection vocabulary, and more background, go to **www.PHLitOnline.com.**

1 2

from Sundiata

AN EPIC OF OLD MALI

D. T. NIANE

3 ▲ **Critical Viewing**
Contrast this depiction of Mari (or Sogolon) Djata with the child described in the opening paragraphs. **[Contrast]**

1 Activating Prior Knowledge

Many political leaders use brain, not brawn, to settle problems. Action heroes, however, often use brawn over brain to fight evil. Ask students for examples of each—politicians who resolve problems intellectually and fictional superheroes who use extraordinary physical powers to influence the world. Then, let students know that the storytellers, or griots, of Mali told of political leaders who were like action heroes. The excerpt from *Sundiata* describes a person who is both a great leader and the possessor of superhuman powers.

Concept Connector ⟶

Students will return to these points of discussion after reading *Sundiata*.

Small-Group Activity

Have students work with partners to practice pronouncing characters' names and to draw family trees for Sundiata's family, using the Characters list on page 1095. Students can then quiz each other on characters' names and identities.

2 About the Selection

This excerpt from *Sundiata* begins the story of an unlikely hero: a taciturn boy with a huge head who cannot stand upright. How Mari Djata overcomes his infirmity and regains his honor is an exciting and instructive tale based on true events.

3 Critical Viewing

Answer: The art portrays Mari Djata as a powerful, admirable warrior on horseback who is in the act of throwing a spear. The artwork conveys physical strength, confidence, grace, and beauty. In contrast, the text describes a greedy, lazy boy with a disproportionate, malformed body.

Vocabulary Development

Thematic Vocabulary: The Big Question

As students are discussing the excerpt from *Sundiata*, encourage them to use the thematic vocabulary presented in Introducing the Big Question, pp. 1046–1047. You might encourage them with sentence starters like these:

1. At first, Mari Djata's *conduct* made him seem . . .
2. To avenge a blow to his mother's *honor*, Mari Djata decides to . . .
3. With enormous *determination*, Mari Djata grabs the iron bar and . . .
4. The soothsayers had predicted that Sogolon's son would be a *legendary* . . .

4 Reading Check

Answer: Mari Djata is partially crippled; he is unable or unwilling to walk upright. Others dislike him because he is strange and uncommunicative.

CHARACTERS IN SUNDIATA

Balla Fasséké (bä´ lä fä sā´ kä): Griot and counselor of Sundiata

Boukari (bo͞o kä´ rē): Son of the king and Namandjé, one of his wives; also called Manding (män´ diŋ) Boukari

Dankaran Touman (dän´ kä rän to͞o´ män): Son of the king and his first wife, Sassouma, who is also called Sassouma Bérété

Djamarou (jä mä´ ro͞o): Daughter of Sogolon and the king; sister of Sundiata and Kolonkan

Farakourou (fä rä ko͞o´ ro͞o): Master of the forges

Gnankouman Doua (nän ko͞o´ män do͞o´ ə): The king's griot; also called, simply, Doua

Kolonkan (kō lōn´ kən): Sundiata's eldest sister

Namandjé (nä män´ jē): One of the king's wives

Naré Maghan (nä´ rā mäg´ hän): Sundiata's father; the king of Mali before Sundiata

Nounfaïri (no͞on´ fä ē´ rē): Soothsayer and smith; father of Farakourou

Sassouma Bérété (sä so͞o´ mä be´ re te): The king's first wife

Sogolon (sô gô lōn´): Sundiata's mother; also called Sogolon Kedjou (kā´ jo͞o)

Sundiata (so͞on dyä´ tä): Legendary king of Mali; referred to as Djata (dyä´ tä) and Sogolon Djata ("son of Sogolon"), and Mari (mä´ rē) Djata.

CHILDHOOD

God has his mysteries which none can fathom. You, perhaps, will be a king. You can do nothing about it. You, on the other hand, will be unlucky, but you can do nothing about that either. Each man finds his way already marked out for him and he can change nothing of it.

Vocabulary
fathom (fath´ əm) *v.* understand thoroughly

Sogolon's son had a slow and difficult childhood. At the age of three he still crawled along on all-fours while children of the same age were already walking. He had nothing of the great beauty of his father Naré Maghan. He had a head so big that he seemed unable to support it; he also had large eyes which would open wide whenever anyone entered his mother's house. He was taciturn[1] and used to spend the whole day just sitting in the middle of the house. Whenever his mother went out he would crawl on all-fours to rummage about in
5 the calabashes[2] in search of food, for he was very greedy.

4 **Reading Check**
Why is Mari (or Sogolon) Djata's childhood difficult?

1. **taciturn** (tas´ ə turn´) *adj.* almost always silent; not liking to talk.

Differentiated Instruction for Universal Access

Strategy for Special Needs Students
Help students gain a solid understanding of Mari Djata's childhood. Have students read the first three paragraphs of the selection while you play the ***Hear It!* Audio CD**. Pause the recording after characters' names, new vocabulary, and the footnote. Help students pronounce names and clarify the vocabulary word definitions. Tell students to reread the paragraphs on their own after listening to the recording. Summarize the beginning of the story as a class.

Enrichment for Advanced Readers
The heroes in the selections in this unit are larger than life; they exist outside the realm of human limitation. Encourage students to define what heroism is in the "real world." Invite students to make lists of heroes and heroic actions in the modern world. Prompt students with questions such as these: What constitutes an authentic hero? What kinds of achievements are truly heroic? Do they think the term is used too freely? Have students explain their answers.

PHLit Online!
This selection is available in interactive format in the **Enriched Online Student Edition**, **www.PHLitOnline.com**, which includes a thematically related video and writing prompt and an interactive graphic organizer.

5 Reading Skill

Analyze Cultural Context

1. Have students read footnote 2, explaining to them any part of the footnote they do not understand.
2. **Ask** students the Reading Skill question: What detail does the background information in footnote 2 help you understand?
   Answer: The footnote makes it clear that calabashes are fruits with rinds suitable for use as containers. The boy pokes through the calabashes because his mother stores food in them.
3. **Ask** students how this detail characterizes the boy.
   Answer: It emphasizes Mari Djata's apparent lack of dignity and status.

6 Literary Analysis

Epic and Epic Hero

1. Have students read the bracketed passage.
2. **Ask** students the Literary Analysis question: In what two ways is Mari (or Sogolon) Djata set apart from other children?
   Answer: He neither walks nor talks. He also hits other children.
3. **Ask:** What quality of an epic hero is demonstrated in Mari Djata's condition as a child?
   Answer: He faces great physical, and perhaps mental, obstacles.

7 Critical Thinking

Analyze

1. **Ask:** Why might Sassouma be the "first to rejoice" at Mari Djata's infirmity?
   Answer: Sassouma is the king's first wife, and she has a son. She may be happy about Mari Djata's condition because it means her son's position as future king is secure.
2. **Ask:** Why is it important to note Sogolon's experiences?
   Answer: Mari Djata is the epic hero of the story; as Mari Djata's mother, Sogolon's honor and position in society are important because an epic hero defends the honor of his family.

Reading Skill 5
Analyze Cultural Context What detail does the background information in footnote 2 help you understand?

Malicious tongues began to blab. What three-year-old has not yet taken his first steps? What three-year-old is not the despair of his parents through his whims and shifts of mood? What three-year-old is not the joy of his circle through his backwardness in talking? Sogolon Djata (for it was thus that they called him, prefixing his mother's name to his), Sogolon Djata, then, was very different from others of his own age. He spoke little and his severe 6 face never relaxed into a smile. You would have thought that he was already thinking, and what amused children of his age bored him. Often Sogolon would make some of them come to him to keep him company. These children were already walking and she hoped that Djata, seeing his companions walking, would be tempted to do likewise. But nothing came of it. Besides, Sogolon Djata would brain the poor little things with his already strong arms and none of them would come near him any more.

Literary Analysis
Epic and Epic Hero In what two ways is Mari (or Sogolon) Djata set apart from other children?

The king's first wife was the first to rejoice at Sogolon Djata's infirmity. Her own son, Dankaran Touman, was already eleven. He was a fine and lively boy, who spent the day running about the village with those of his own age. He had even begun his initiation in the bush.[3] The king had had a bow made for him and he used to go behind the town to practice archery with his companions. Sassouma was quite happy and snapped her fingers at Sogolon, 7 whose child was still crawling on the ground. Whenever the latter happened to pass by her house, she would say, "Come, my son, walk, jump, leap about. The jinn didn't promise you anything out of the ordinary,[4] but I prefer a son who walks on his two legs to a lion that crawls on the ground." She spoke thus whenever Sogolon went by her door. The **innuendo** would go straight home and then she would burst into laughter, that diabolical laughter which a jealous woman knows how to use so well.

Vocabulary
innuendo (in′ yo͞o en′ dō) *n.* indirect insult or accusation; insinuation
estranged (e strānjd′) *adj.* kept apart; in the condition of having had affection turn into indifference or hostility

Her son's infirmity weighed heavily upon Sogolon Kedjou; she had resorted to all her talent as a sorceress to give strength to her son's legs, but the rarest herbs had been useless. The king himself lost hope.

How impatient man is! Naré Maghan became imperceptibly **estranged** but Gnankouman Doua never ceased reminding him of the hunter's words. Sogolon became pregnant again. The king hoped for a son, but it was a daughter called Kolonkan. She

2. **calabashes** (kal′ ə bash′ əz) *n.* dried, hollow shells of gourds (squashlike fruits), used as bowls, cups, and so on.
3. **initiation in the bush** education in tribal lore given to twelve-year-old West African boys so they can become full members of the tribe.
4. **The jinn . . . ordinary** Jinn are supernatural beings said to influence human affairs. They promised that the son of Sogolon would make Mali a great empire.

Vocabulary Development

Word Forms

Give students a blank **Word Form Chart** (***Professional Development Guidebook***, p. 42), with *fathom, estranged,* and *affront* in the correct columns. Work with the class, or have students work with a partner, to determine the related forms. The final chart should look like the one shown.

Noun	Verb	Adjective	Adverb
fathom	**fathom**	fathomable	
estrangement	estrange	**estranged**	
affront	affront	affronted	

resembled her mother and had nothing of her father's beauty. The disheartened king debarred Sogolon from his house and she lived in semi-disgrace for a while. Naré Maghan married the daughter of one of his allies, the king of the Kamaras. She was called Namandjé and her beauty was legendary. A year later she brought a boy into the world. When the king consulted soothsayers[5] on the destiny of this son he received the reply that Namandjé's child would be the right hand of some mighty king. The king gave the newly-born the name of Boukari. He was to be called Manding Boukari or Manding Bory later on.

What three-year-old has not yet taken his first steps!

Naré Maghan was very perplexed. Could it be that the stiff-jointed son of Sogolon was the one the hunter soothsayer had foretold?

"The Almighty has his mysteries," Gnankouman Doua would say and, taking up the hunter's words, added, "The silk-cotton tree emerges from a tiny seed."

One day Naré Maghan came along to the house of Nounfaïri, the blacksmith seer of Niani. He was an old, blind man. He received the king in the anteroom which served as his workshop. To the king's question he replied, "When the seed germinates growth is not always easy; great trees grow slowly but they plunge their roots deep into the ground."

8 "But has the seed really germinated?" said the king.

"Of course," replied the blind seer. "Only the growth is not as quick as you would like it; how impatient man is."

This interview and Doua's confidence gave the king some assurance. To the great displeasure of Sassouma Bérété the king restored Sogolon to favor and soon another daughter was born to her. She was given the name of Djamarou.

However, all Niani talked of nothing else but the stiff-legged son of Sogolon. He was now seven and he still crawled to get about. In spite of all the king's affection, Sogolon was in despair. Naré Maghan aged and he felt his time coming to an end. Dankaran Touman, the son of Sassouma Bérété, was now a fine youth.

One day Naré Maghan made Mari Djata come to him and he spoke to the child as one speaks to an adult. "Mari Djata, I am growing old and soon I shall be no more among you, but before death takes me off I am going to give you the present each king gives his successor. In Mali every prince has his own griot. Doua's father was my father's griot, Doua is mine and the son of Doua, Balla Fasséké here, will be your griot. Be inseparable friends from

Reading Skill
Analyze Cultural Context What does the background information on page 1093 suggest about how powerful Mari Djata will one day become?

9 **Reading Check**
What advice does the blind seer give to the king?

5. **soothsayers** (so͞oth′ sā′ ərz) *n.* people who profess to foretell the future.

8 Reading Skill

Analyze Cultural Context

1. Have students read the bracketed text.
2. **Ask** students the Reading Skill question: What does the background information on page 1093 suggest about how powerful Mari Djata will one day become?
   Answer: The information reveals that Mari Djata will eventually become a powerful king, but that his ascendancy will take more time than his father expects.
3. **Ask** what aspects of the Mali culture are suggested by the king's exchanges with Doua and Nounfaïri? Have students record their responses on **Reading Skill Graphic Organizer B** (*Graphic Organizer Transparencies*, p. 201.)
   Answer: The society's powerful people respect the words of griots, soothsayers, and seers as sacred predictions. The image of the seed germinating also suggests that the society is agricultural and familiar with different patterns of growth in nature.

9 Reading Check

Answer: The blind seer tells the king not to be impatient, because "great trees grow slowly."

Differentiated Instruction for Universal Access

Strategy for Less Proficient Readers
Students will benefit from writing a page-by-page summary of the narrative. Have students reread the previous pages and write two or three sentences summarizing what happens on each page of the narrative. Have them underline important plot developments in their summaries, such as Balla Fasséké becoming Mari Djata's griot. Then, have students repeat the process as they read the rest of the selection.

EL Strategy for English Learners
Students may not be familiar with the term *germinated*. Help them to define the word through context clues by pointing out that the griot says several times that the seed has germinated but that the plant's growth is not yet apparent. **Ask** students to apply this image to what is happening with Mari Djata. **Answer:** The griot is saying that something is going on inside the boy that is not yet visible to the outside world.

⑩ Humanities

Glass paintings such as this one are a very popular art form in Africa. The highly patterned artwork resembles tapestry but is actually created on glass. The painting, done on the inside face of the glass, is sometimes called "reverse-glass painting." Senegalese artists imported the art of painting on glass from North Africa in the late nineteenth century.

Use this question for discussion:

How does the painting of Mari Djata differ from the way he is described in the story?
Possible answer: The painting depicts a child standing on his own two legs; in the story, Mari Djata cannot yet stand or walk.

Vocabulary Development

Vocabulary Reinforcement

Reinforce students' comprehension with "show-you-know" sentences. The first part of the sentence uses the vocabulary word in an appropriate context. The second part of the sentence—the "show-you-know" part—clarifies the first.

It is difficult to *fathom* calculus; _______.
Sample answer: the advanced mathematical concepts are difficult to understand.

Then give students these sentence prompts, and coach them in creating the clarification part.

1. That woman made an *innuendo* about my dog; _______.
   Sample answer: she should keep her rude thoughts to herself.
2. Her friend's family was *estranged* for many years after an argument over money; _______.
   Sample answer: they finally reunited today.
3. My grandmother said my clothing was a personal *affront* to her; _______.
   Sample answer: I did not mean to insult her with my concert T-shirt, however.

this day forward. From his mouth you will hear the history of your ancestors, you will learn the art of governing Mali according to the principles which our ancestors have bequeathed to us. I have served my term and done my duty too. I have done everything which a king of Mali ought to do. I am handing an enlarged kingdom over to you and I leave you sure allies. May your destiny be accomplished, but never forget that Niani is your capital and Mali the cradle of your ancestors."

The child, as if he had understood the whole meaning of the king's words, beckoned Balla Fasséké to approach. He made room for him on the hide he was sitting on and then said, "Balla, you will be my griot."

"Yes, son of Sogolon, if it pleases God," replied Balla Fasséké.

The king and Doua exchanged glances that radiated confidence.

11 ◀ **Critical Viewing** What relationship in the epic might this picture illustrate? Explain. **[Connect]**

THE LION'S AWAKENING

A short while after this interview between Naré Maghan and his son the king died.

Sogolon's son was no more than seven years old. The council of elders met in the king's palace. It was no use Doua's defending the king's will which reserved the throne for Mari Djata, for the council took no account of Naré Maghan's wish. With the help of Sassouma Bérété's intrigues, Dankaran Touman was proclaimed king and a regency council[6] was formed in which the queen mother was all-powerful. A short time after, Doua died.

12 As men have short memories, Sogolon's son was spoken of with nothing but irony and scorn. People had seen one-eyed kings, one-armed kings, and lame kings, but a stiff-legged king had never been heard tell of. No matter how great the destiny promised for Mari Djata might be, the throne could not be given to someone who had no power in his legs; if the jinn loved him, let them begin by giving him the use of his legs. Such were the remarks that Sogolon heard every day. The queen mother, Sassouma Bérété, was the source of all this gossip.

Having become all-powerful, Sassouma Bérété persecuted Sogolon because the late Naré Maghan had preferred her. She banished Sogolon and her son to a back yard of the palace. Mari

Reading Skill
Analyze Cultural Context What do the details here indicate about the way in which West African society was ruled?

13 **Reading Check**

After the king's death, who takes power in the kingdom?

6. **regency** (rē´ jən sē) **council** group that rules instead of the king or queen when the king or queen is still a child or is otherwise incapable of ruling.

11 Critical Viewing

Answer: The picture might illustrate the relationship between Mari Djata and the king, his father. The man is speaking earnestly to the boy, the same way Mari Djata's father speaks to Mari Djata about receiving a griot.

12 Reading Skill

Analyze Cultural Context

1. Have students discuss whether the council of elders does the right thing on the occasion of Naré Maghan's death.
   Possible response: Students may say that the council should respect the king's wishes and appoint a temporary leader until Mari Djata comes of age; others may say that a country needs a leader, so the elders are right.
2. **Ask** students the Reading Skill question: What do the details here indicate about the way in which West African society was ruled?
   Answer: The passage reveals that although heredity was important in determining the line of succession, so was physical strength. A man with an infirmity like Mari Djata's was not acceptable as a king. This attitude suggests that the culture greatly valued physical strength.

▶ **Monitor Progress:** To assess students' ability to analyze cultural context, **ask:** Why might physical strength be so important in the Mali culture?
Possible response: Life is hard in this region; food, water, and protection from other tribes are necessary for survival. In such conditions, physical weakness is a danger.

▶ **Reteach:** If students have trouble assessing the importance of strength to Mali culture, have them first suggest ways in which life in Mali is different from life here. Have them use **Reading Skill Graphic Organizer B** (*Graphic Organizer Transparencies*, p. 201) to record their ideas.

13 Reading Check

Answer: After the king's death, the council of elders names Dankaran Touman as the next king and places his mother Sassouma in power until he is old enough to rule.

Differentiated Instruction for Universal Access

Enrichment for Gifted/Talented Students
Have students create outlines for epics about real or fictional American heroes. Have them pattern their epic after *Sundiata* by creating a central problem or conflict, serious obstacles that must be overcome, supporting characters, and, most importantly, heroes who overcome the obstacles and solve the problems. Then, divide students into small discussion groups, and tell them to analyze each other's epics. To start their discussions, give them such questions as *What values are revealed by this epic? What culture does this epic portray? In what ways are the heroes warriors? Which special burdens or blessings do the heroes have?* Treat students' myths as literature, and create a library shelf for them in the classroom. Encourage students to use each other's myths as examples in class discussions or writing assignments.

⓮ Literary Analysis
Epic and Epic Hero

1. Have students read the bracketed passage.
2. **Ask:** How does Sassouma treat Mari Djata's family when she becomes the queen mother?
   Answer: She treats them cruelly. She banishes Sogolon and Mari Djata's family to live in a hut. Then she allows people to view Mari Djata.
3. **Ask** students the Literary Analysis question: In what way is the honor of Mari Djata's family threatened?
   Answer: The family's honor is threatened because the queen mother allows Mari Djata to become a target of ridicule. The exposure also makes Sogolon, Mari Djata's mother, vulnerable to scorn and loss of status as the mother of a prince.

⓯ THE BIG ? Connecting to the Big Question

1. Point out that Mari Djata has few of the features we associate with heroes. He is slow, ugly, dull, and greedy.
2. Have students read the bracketed passage. **Ask** how Mari Djata responds to the insult to his mother.
   Answer: He declares that he will walk today.
3. **Ask** students to explain why this response might be heroic.
   Possible response: It seems very unlikely that he should suddenly be able to walk, but it is heroic of Mari Djata to try to counter the insult to Sogolon.
4. As they continue reading, have students look for ways Mari Djata changes from an unlikely hero to a hero indeed.

Djata's mother now occupied an old hut which had served as a lumber-room of Sassouma's.

Literary Analysis
Epic and Epic Hero In what way is the honor of Mari Djata's family threatened? ⓮

The wicked queen mother allowed free passage to all those inquisitive people who wanted to see the child that still crawled at the age of seven. Nearly all the inhabitants of Niani filed into the palace and the poor Sogolon wept to see herself thus given over to public ridicule. Mari Djata took on a ferocious look in front of the crowd of sightseers. Sogolon found a little consolation only in the love of her eldest daughter, Kolonkan. She was four and she could walk. She seemed to understand all her mother's miseries and already she helped her with the housework. Sometimes, when Sogolon was attending to the chores, it was she who stayed beside her sister Djamarou, quite small as yet.

Sogolon Kedjou and her children lived on the queen mother's leftovers, but she kept a little garden in the open ground behind the village. It was there that she passed her brightest moments looking after her onions and gnougous.[7] One day she happened to be short of condiments and went to the queen mother to beg a little baobab leaf.[8]

"Look you," said the malicious Sassouma, "I have a calabash full. Help yourself, you poor woman. As for me, my son knew how to walk at seven and it was he who went and picked these baobab leaves. Take them then, since your son is unequal to mine." Then she laughed **derisively** with that fierce laughter which cuts through your flesh and penetrates right to the bone.

Vocabulary
derisively (di rī′siv lē) *adv.* in a mocking and ridiculing manner
affront (ə frunt′) *n.* open insult

Sogolon Kedjou was dumbfounded. She had never imagined that hate could be so strong in a human being. With a lump in her throat she left Sassouma's. Outside her hut Mari Djata, sitting on his useless legs, was blandly eating out of a calabash. Unable to contain herself any longer, Sogolon burst into sobs and seizing a piece of wood, hit her son.

⓯ "Oh son of misfortune, will you never walk? Through your fault I have just suffered the greatest **affront** of my life! What have I done, God, for you to punish me in this way?"

Mari Djata seized the piece of wood and, looking at his mother, said, "Mother, what's the matter?"

"Shut up, nothing can ever wash me clean of this insult."

"But what then?"

"Sassouma has just humiliated me over a matter of a baobab leaf. At your age her own son could walk and used to bring his mother baobab leaves."

7. **gnougous** (nōō′ gōōz′) *n.* root vegetables.
8. **baobab** (bā′ ō bab′) **leaf** The baobab is a thick-trunked tree; its leaves are used to flavor foods.

Think Aloud

Vocabulary: Using Context
Help students use context clues to define unfamiliar words. Say to students:

> In the first full paragraph on this page, Sogolon "found a little consolation" in the love of her eldest daughter, Kolonkan. If I did not know the meaning of *consolation*, I could use the context in sentences before and after the word to figure it out. I know that Sogolon is upset, because the sentences before the word tell me that she "wept to see herself thus given over to public ridicule." I know from the sentences after the word that Kolonkan can walk, that she seems to understand all her mother's miseries, and that she already helped with the housework—all helpful, positive things. I can guess that Kolonkan's love helps Sogolon feel better or get over being upset. *Consolation* must mean "comfort."

15 "Cheer up, Mother, cheer up."

"No. It's too much. I can't."

"Very well then, I am going to walk today," said Mari Djata. "Go and tell my father's smiths to make me the heaviest possible iron rod. Mother, do you want just the leaves of the baobab or would you rather I brought you the whole tree?"

"Ah, my son, to wipe out this insult I want the tree and its roots at my feet outside my hut."

Balla Fasséké, who was present, ran to the master smith, Farakourou, to order an iron rod.

Sogolon had sat down in front of her hut. She was weeping softly and holding her head between her two hands. Mari Djata went calmly back to his calabash of rice and began eating again as if nothing had happened. From time to time he looked up discreetly at his mother who was murmuring in a low voice, "I want the whole tree, in front of my hut, the whole tree."

All of a sudden a voice burst into laughter behind the hut. It was the wicked Sassouma telling one of her serving women about the scene of humiliation and she was laughing loudly so that Sogolon could hear. Sogolon fled into the hut and hid her face under the blankets so as not to have before her eyes this heedless boy, who was more preoccupied with eating than with anything else. With her head buried in the bedclothes Sogolon wept and her body shook violently. Her daughter, Sogolon Djamarou, had come and sat down beside her and she said, "Mother, Mother, don't cry. Why are you crying?"

Mari Djata had finished eating and, dragging himself along on his legs, he came and sat under the wall of the hut for the sun was scorching. What was he thinking about? He alone knew.

18 The royal forges were situated outside the walls and over a hundred smiths worked there. The bows, spears, arrows and shields of Niani's warriors came from there. When Balla Fasséké came to order the iron rod, Farakourou said to him, "The great day has arrived then?"

"Yes. Today is a day like any other, but it will see what no other day has seen."

16 ▼ Critical Viewing
Why might Mari Djata have difficulty gathering leaves from a baobab tree like this one? **[Analyze]**

17 Reading Check
What incident provokes Mari Djata to order an iron bar?

16 Critical Viewing

Answer: The leaves are fairly high on the tree. Someone who does not stand upright and is not agile enough to climb well would not be able to reach them.

17 Reading Check

Answer: Mari Djata is provoked by his mother's rage over the insult she receives from Sassouma regarding Mari Djata's inability to pick baobab leaves.

Fluency

Have individual students take turns reading this page from "Sogolon had sat down" to "'Why are you crying?'" As they read, take notes on any hesitations and miscues.

- If students have difficulty with multisyllabic words (*humiliation, preoccupied, bedclothes*), encourage them to break the words into manageable or familiar chunks (*humiliate + -ion, pre- + occupied, bed + clothes*).
- If students stumble over compound-complex sentences, ask them to distinguish the separate parts of the troublesome sentence before rereading it aloud. For example, *It was the wicked Sassouma/telling one of her serving women about the scene of humiliation/and she was laughing loudly/so that Sogolon could hear.*

18 Reading Skill

Analyze Cultural Context

1. Have students read aloud the passage that describes the royal forges, beginning on p. 1101.
2. **Ask** students the Reading Skill question: What do these details suggest about the role of blacksmiths and warriors in West African culture?
   Answer: The details indicate that the principal weapons of Mali's warriors are made of iron by the blacksmiths. Therefore, the warriors and the blacksmiths must work together.
3. Point out that Nounfaïri and his son Farakourou are both soothsayers who work at the forges. Then **ask** how this further connects blacksmiths and warriors.
   Answer: Blacksmiths arm the Mali warriors. If they are soothsayers as well, with the power to foresee the future, it is possible that Mali warriors value the smiths not just for the weapons, but also for their instincts about how and when the weapons will be used.
4. **Ask** what the fact that there are more than a hundred smiths suggests about the fighting capabilities of Mali.
   Answer: It suggests that the Mali are extremely well-armed people.

19 Humanities

View of Kamalia from *Mungo Park: Travels in the Interior Districts of Africa*

Tell students that Mungo Park was a Scottish explorer who visited Africa in the early 1800s and became the first European to explore along the Niger River. He wrote a book about his journey that was widely read, and the book's illustrations allowed many Europeans their first glimpse into life in that neighboring continent.

Use this question for discussion:

What could a European reader learn about Kamalia from this illustration?
Possible response: People live in villages comprised of small, round huts with thatched roofs; based on the way people are dressed, it seems that the climate is hot; people grow crops and hunt with spears.

19

Reading Skill
Analyze Cultural Context 18 What do these details suggest about the role of blacksmiths and warriors in West African culture?

Vocabulary
efface (ə fās′) *v.* rub or blot out

The master of the forges, Farakourou, was the son of the old Nounfaïri, and he was a soothsayer like his father. In his workshops there was an enormous iron bar wrought by his father, Nounfaïri. Everybody wondered what this bar was destined to be used for. Farakourou called six of his apprentices and told them to carry the iron bar to Sogolon's house.

When the smiths put the gigantic iron bar down in front of the hut the noise was so frightening that Sogolon, who was lying down, jumped up with a start. Then Balla Fasséké, son of Gnankouman Doua, spoke.

"Here is the great day, Mari Djata. I am speaking to you, Maghan, son of Sogolon. The waters of the Niger can efface the stain from the body, but they cannot wipe out an insult. Arise, young lion, roar, and may the bush know that from henceforth it has a master."

20 The apprentice smiths were still there, Sogolon had come out and everyone was watching Mari Djata. He crept on all-fours and came to the iron bar. Supporting himself on his knees and one hand, with the other hand he picked up the iron bar without any effort and stood it up vertically. Now he was resting on nothing but his knees and held the bar with both his hands. A deathly silence had gripped all those present. Sogolon Djata closed his eyes, held tight, the muscles in his arms tensed. With a violent jerk he threw his weight on to it and his knees left the ground. Sogolon Kedjou was all eyes and watched her son's legs which were trembling as though

Vocabulary Development

Vocabulary Knowledge Rating

When students have completed reading and discussing *Sundiata*, have them take out their **Vocabulary Knowledge Rating Chart** for this selection. Read the words aloud once more, and have students rate their knowledge of the words again in the After Reading column. Clarify any words that are still problematic. Have students write their own definition and example or sentence in the appropriate column. Then have students complete the Vocabulary Practice activities at the end of the selection. Encourage students to use the words in further discussion and written work about this selection. Remind them that they will be accountable for these words on the **Selection Test**, ***Unit 6 Resources***, pp. 74–76 or 77–79.

from an electric shock. Djata was sweating and the sweat ran from his brow. In a great effort he straightened up and was on his feet at one go—but the great bar of iron was twisted and had taken the form of a bow!

Then Balla Fasséké sang out the "Hymn to the Bow," striking up with his powerful voice:

"Take your bow, Simbon,
Take your bow and let us go.
Take your bow, Sogolon Djata."

When Sogolon saw her son standing she stood dumb for a moment, then suddenly she sang these words of thanks to God, who had given her son the use of his legs:

"Oh day, what a beautiful day,
Oh day, day of joy;
Allah[9] Almighty, you never created a finer day.
So my son is going to walk!"

Literary Analysis
Epic and Epic Hero
What qualities of an epic hero does Mari Djata display here?

21 **Reading Check**
What causes both Mari Djata's mother and his griot to sing?

9. **Allah** (al´ ə) Muslim name for God.

22 **LITERATURE IN CONTEXT**

Culture Connection

Griot: The Mind of the People

In West Africa, the griot (pronounced "gree-oh") was the storyteller and historian of the village. The griot memorized the births, deaths, marriages, hunts, and wars of the people and its ancestors. Sometimes speaking or singing for days, the griot recited these events as stories, often to musical accompaniment. To the Mandinka, the griot was the "mind" of the people, an oral library of history and culture.

Many griots use talking drums, like this one, as they tell their stories.

Children gather closely around a griot to hear a story.

Connect to the Literature Given this information, explain why Naré Maghan's decision to appoint a griot for Mari Djata shows his confidence in his son.

20 Literary Analysis

Epic and Epic Hero

1. Have students read the bracketed passage.
2. **Ask** students the Literary Analysis question: What qualities of an epic hero does Mari Djata display here?
   Answer: The passage reveals that Mari Djata has the ability to concentrate and persevere; it also shows that Mari Djata has superhuman strength, since the iron bar is bent into a bow by the pressure he applies.
3. **Ask** students what other epic hero attributes can be inferred from this passage.
   Possible responses: The fact that Mari Djata has to exert such an effort suggests that he has to overcome a tremendous obstacle in standing. Also, he makes the effort to defend his honor and that of his family.

21 Reading Check

Answer: They are moved to sing because they are thankful for Mari Djata's amazing feat, which means that he will restore his family's honor and take his rightful place in the kingdom.

22 Literature in Context

Cultural Connection Although African history has been recorded for centuries in Arabic and in European languages since the 1800s, griots have served as the keepers of African history for a millennium. Griots, or griottes, as female storytellers are called, traditionally serve as historians, genealogists, advisors, entertainers, and praise singers. Through songs and the spoken word, griots carry vital cultural information from one generation to the next.

Connect to the Literature After students discuss the role of the griot, **ask** them to respond to the Connect to the Literature prompt: Given this information, explain why Naré Maghan's decision to appoint a griot for Mari Djata shows his confidence in his son.
Possible response: By appointing a griot while Mari Djata is still a disabled child, the king shows a serene confidence that the boy will become king.

Concept Connector

Activating Prior Knowledge

Have students return to the points they raised in their discussion about the relative values of physical and mental strength. After reading the excerpt from *Sundiata*, **ask** students to re-evaluate their perspectives. Encourage students to cite specific details, quotations, or other evidence from the text to support the way the epic maintains or changes their points of view about the value of each kind of strength.

Writing About the Big Question

Have students compare their responses to the sentence starter they completed before reading the excerpt with their ideas afterward. Ask them to explain whether their thoughts have changed.

Reading Skill Graphic Organizer

Ask students to review the graphic organizers they completed to use background knowledge to interpret cultural context. Show them **Reading Skill Graphic Organizer A** (*Graphic Organizer Transparencies*, p. 202). Then have students share their graphic organizers.

23 Reading Skill
Analyze Cultural Context

1. Have students read the griot's song.
2. **Ask** students the Reading Skill question: What do the images in the griot's song indicate about the region in which the Malinke live?
   Answer: Balla's song suggests that lions and antelopes live in the region.
3. **Ask** students how bringing Sogolon a baobab tree gives her power and honor in the Mali culture.
   Answer: Every part of the baobab tree is used by the Malinke. Now that Sogolon has one, she has the power to help others by giving them leaves or other parts of the tree.

ASSESS
Answers

Critical Thinking

1. Most students are likely to enjoy Mari Djata's triumph of the underdog.
2. (a) He cannot walk. (b) His mother loses favor with the king as a result of her son's infirmity.
3. (a) The king wishes that Mari Djata will one day succeed him as ruler. (b) The soothsayers predict that Namandje's son will aid another man who is king. This gives the king confidence in Mari Djata.
4. (a) She banishes the boy and his mother to a hut in the backyard of the palace. (b) She probably resents the fact that the king had actually favored Mari Djata and his mother.

Can anyone be a hero?
Possible responses:
(a) Sogolon's humiliation by Sassouma finally prompts Mari Djata to get over his lazy ways and stand up.
(b) His actions can be considered heroic because it costs him a great effort to stand, so great that he bends an iron bar into a bow.

Standing in the position of a soldier at ease, Sogolon Djata, supported by his enormous rod, was sweating great beads of sweat. Balla Fasséké's song had alerted the whole palace and people came running from all over to see what had happened, and each stood bewildered before Sogolon's son. The queen mother had rushed there and when she saw Mari Djata standing up she trembled from head to foot. After recovering his breath Sogolon's son dropped the bar and the crowd stood to one side. His first steps were those of a giant. Balla Fasséké fell into step and pointing his finger at Djata, he cried:

Reading Skill
Analyze Cultural Context 23 What do the images in the griot's song indicate about the region in which the Malinke live?

"Room, room, make room!
The lion has walked;
Hide antelopes,
Get out of his way."

Behind Niani there was a young baobab tree and it was there that the children of the town came to pick leaves for their mothers. With all his might the son of Sogolon tore up the tree and put it on his shoulders and went back to his mother. He threw the tree in front of the hut and said, "Mother, here are some baobab leaves for you. From henceforth it will be outside your hut that the women of Niani will come to stock up."

Critical Thinking

1. **Respond:** Did you enjoy Mari Djata's triumph? Explain.
2. **(a)** What is Mari Djata's main difficulty? **(b) Infer:** How does this problem affect the way people treat his mother?
3. **(a)** What does the king specify as his wish for Mari Djata? **(b) Analyze Cause and Effect:** How do the soothsayers' predictions help prompt the king's wishes?
4. **(a)** After the king's death, where does Sassouma Bérété force Sogolon and Mari Djata to live? **(b) Infer:** Why does Sassouma Bérété treat Mari Djata and Sogolon as she does?

THE BIG ? **Can anyone be a hero?**
(a) What event finally prompts Mari Djata to transcend his own problems for the sake of his mother? **(b)** Why would his actions be considered "heroic"?

Assessment Resources

Unit 6 Resources

L1 L2 EL **Selection Test A,** pp. 74–76. Administer Test A to less advanced readers and English learners.

L3 L4 **Selection Test B,** pp. 77–79. Administer Test B to on-level and more advanced students.

L3 L4 **Open-Book Test,** pp. 71–73. As an alternative, give the Open-Book Test.

All **Customizable Test Bank**

All **Self-tests**
Students may prepare for the **Selection Test** by taking the **Self-test** online.

PHLit Online! All assessment resources are available at **www.PHLitOnline.com.**

After You Read | *from* Sundiata: An Epic of Old Mali

Literary Analysis: Epic and Epic Hero

1. Some heroes battle dragons or warriors. Explain two ways in which the challenges Mari Djata faces differ from other **epic** struggles.
2. Using a chart like the one shown, give specific examples showing which qualities of an **epic hero** Mari Djata possesses.

Noble Birth	Warrior Virtues	Acts Honorably	Chosen by the Gods or Fate

3. What values or beliefs are conveyed through this tale? Support your response with details from the text.

Reading Skill: Analyze Cultural Context

4. **(a)** List three things that you learned about West African **cultural context** from the features that appear before the selection. **(b)** List two things you learned about West African culture from the selection or from the footnotes. **(c)** For each item of context you list, briefly explain how knowing that item helps you to understand *Sundiata*. Give specific examples.

Vocabulary

Practice Write a sentence about each situation described below, using a word from the vocabulary list for *Sundiata*, on page 1092.

1. ceasing to socialize with a group of friends
2. surprise and confusion about the purchase of a large python and a kitten to keep as pets
3. an exchange of snide remarks
4. an effort to harm someone's reputation
5. to laughingly make fun of someone
6. attempt to wipe away graffiti

Word Study Use the context of the sentences and what you know about the **Latin suffix *-ive*** to explain your answer to each question.

1. Is someone who is *combative* usually the peacemaker?
2. If a plant is *native* to North America, did it come from overseas?

Word Study

The **Latin suffix *-ive*** means "belonging to" or "quality of."

Challenge Explain how the suffix *-ive* contributes to the meanings of these words. Consult a dictionary if necessary.

elusive
persuasive
restorative

ASSESS/EXTEND

Answers

Literary Analysis

1. Mari Djata battles infirmity and scorn. These are actually "real-world" obstacles, unlike the monsters battled by other epic heroes.
2. Mari Djata comes from noble birth, since he is the son of a king. He shows a warrior's courage, strength, and determination when he avenges his mother. He is prompted to action by the need to defend his mother's honor. The songs and the words of the soothsayer and the griot suggest that Mari Djata has been chosen by higher powers.

   For other sample answers, see ***Graphic Organizer Transparencies,* Literary Analysis Graphic Organizer A**, p. 202, and the **Additional Answers** section.
3. **Possible response:** Physical strength is valued; Mari Djata becomes a hero when he overcomes a physical obstacle and tears the baobab tree out of the ground. The belief in fate is also reflected; the King consults a seer to find out which of his sons will become king.

Reading Skill

4. (a) The background about Mali's land and people and the fact that they were gold traders provides context for the story of Mari Djata's culture. The information about Sundiata's becoming a king and conqueror reveals what will happen beyond his inauspicious beginnings. The information about griot traditions explains why the king gives so much weight to what his griot says. The list of characters' names is a helpful reference and gives a sense of the social structure of the Malinke. (b) and (c) **Possible responses:** Students may note that the footnotes give information about calabashes, initiations, and the role of soothsayers.

Vocabulary

Practice

Sample answers:

1. After insulting them, John became estranged from his group of friends.
2. I cannot fathom why someone would purchase a python and a cat to keep as pets together.

Answers continued

3. Even though she did not insult me directly, her innuendo hurt my feelings.
4. The nasty rumors the girls were spreading were an affront to her character and a detriment to her reputation.
5. The teenagers made fun of their friend by commenting derisively on his new haircut.
6. Most attempts to efface graffiti are fruitless because the paint is permanent.

Word Study

Sample answers:

1. No. The suffix *-ive* means "belonging to" or "quality of" and *combative* means "having the quality of combat." Someone who is combative will fight often.
2. No. The suffix *-ive* means "belonging to" or "quality of" and *native* means "belonging to a place by birth." A plant native to North America originated in North America.

Word Study: Challenge

Sample answers: If something is *elusive*, it has the quality of eluding. Someone who is *persuasive* possesses the quality of persuading. To be *restorative* is to have the quality of restoration.

PRETEACH

Skills instruction for the ***Reading Skill*** *and* ***Literary Analysis*** *concept for this selection appears on p. 1091.*

1 Writing About the Big Question

1. Review the assignment with the class.
2. Ask students to think about and discuss the following question: Under what circumstances would they sacrifice something personal for the greater good?
3. Have students complete the sentence starters. Review responses as a class. (**Possible response:** Being able to sacrifice something important to you for the greater good can be considered heroic because it is an honorable action that helps others. Having courage and faith in oneself can help a person accomplish a difficult task such as overcoming a fear.)
4. Remind students that their answers will help them think about the Big Question, "Can anyone be a hero?"

While You Read

Tell students that as they read, they should note challenges Rama faces.

2 Vocabulary

1. Have students preview the selection vocabulary.
2. For each word, have students say the word aloud.
3. Then, use the word in a sentence that defines the word.
4. Finally, repeat your definitional sentence or a similar sentence with the word missing and have the class "fill in the blank" chorally. For example:

   To be secular is to not be religious. The music the high school choir sang was not religious but [students say "secular"].

3 Word Study

1. Introduce the skill, using the instruction in the box.
2. Ask students for a word ending in *-tude* that means "great size or extent" using their knowledge of the suffix. (**Answer:** *magnitude*)

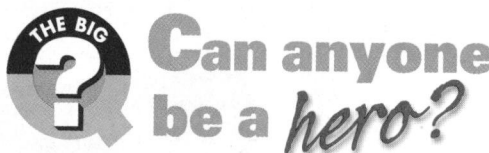

Making Connections

Rama's Initiation
from the **Ramayana**

Can anyone be a *hero?*

1 Writing About the Big Question

In "Rama's Initiation," a young boy discovers the importance of bravery and strength as he becomes a hero in a fight against evil. Use these sentence starters to develop your ideas about the Big Question.

Being able to **sacrifice** something important to you for the greater good can be considered heroic because ______________.
Having **courage** and faith in oneself can help a person accomplish a difficult task such as ______________.

While You Read Look for the challenges Rama faces on his journey and decide what role faith plays in his growth.

2 Vocabulary

Read each word and its definition. Decide whether you know the word well, know it a little bit, or do not know it at all. After you read, see how your knowledge of each word has increased.

- **renounced** (ri nounst´) *v.* to have given up formally (p. 1110) ***We renounced our claim to the prize because we did not follow the rules of the contest.*** *renouncement n.*
- **decrepitude** (dē krep´ ə to͞od´) *n.* feebleness; condition of being worn out by age or illness (p. 1110) ***His love for the ratty old chair blinded him to its extreme decrepitude.*** *decrepit adj.*
- **secular** (sek´ yə lər) *adj.* of wordly, as opposed to religious, matters (p. 1112) ***The singer sang both religious and secular songs.*** *secularism n.*
- **exuberance** (eg zo͞o´ bər əns) *n.* good health and high spirits (p. 1114) ***Her exuberance was apparent in the way she laughed and danced.*** *exuberant adj. exuberantly adv.*
- **adversaries** (ad´ vər ser´ ēz) *n.* opponents (p. 1116) ***Our adversaries attacked us.*** *adversarial adj. adversary n.*
- **esoteric** (es´ ə ter´ ik) *adj.* beyond the understanding or knowledge of most people (p. 1116) ***Since Quantum Mechanics is esoteric, the class sizes are often small.*** *esoterically adv.*

3 Word Study

The **Latin suffix *-tude*** means "condition of" or "quality of."

In this story, a character is not affected by **decrepitude,** or the condition of being worn out by age or illness.

Vocabulary Development

Vocabulary Knowledge Rating

Create a **Vocabulary Knowledge Rating Chart** (***Professional Development Guidebook***, p. 33) for this selection. Include the selection vocabulary and the Big Question words that appear in the Writing About the Big Question sentence starters. (The Big Question vocabulary is introduced on pp. 1046–1047.)

Give students a copy of the chart. Read the words aloud, and have students mark their rating in the Before Reading column. Urge them to be alert to these words as they read and discuss the selection.

Tally how many students think they know a word to gauge how much instruction to provide. As students read and discuss the selection, point out the words and their context.

PHLit Online! **Vocabulary Central**, featuring tools, activities, and songs for studying vocabulary, is available at **www.PHLitOnline.com.**

Meet R. K. Narayan (1906–2001)

Author of

Rama's Initiation *from the* Ramayana

The foundations of Hindu culture were laid around 1500 B.C., when a warrior people, the Aryans, invaded northern India. The Aryans enforced the caste system, in which society is rigidly divided into castes, or groups, each with its own occupation and duties. The caste system supports Hindu emphasis on righteous behavior and spiritual self-improvement.

From Poet-Sage to Modern Novelist The earliest surviving version of Rama's story, credited to the poet-sage Valmiki, dates to perhaps 300 B.C. Among the story's most recent retellers is Indian novelist **R. K. Narayan.** According to Narayan, "All imaginative writing in India has had its origin in . . . the 10,000-year-old epics of India."

Did You Know?

To this day, Hindus take Rama as their model for conduct.

❹ BACKGROUND FOR THE EPIC

Hinduism

The *Ramayana*, the great Hindu epic telling of Prince Rama, is one of the sacred books of Hinduism, the major religion of India. Hinduism involves a belief in many gods, each representing an aspect of life and nature. The most important gods are Brahma, the creator; Vishnu, the preserver; and Siva, the destroyer.

Daily Bellringer

For each class during which you will teach this selection, have students complete one of the five Sentence Modeling activities for Week 32 in the ***Daily Bellringer Activities*** booklet.

❹ Background

Hinduism

One of the oldest religions in the world, Hinduism, based on its many sacred scriptures, is the major religion of India. Two such scriptures are the Hindu epics the *Mahabharata* and the *Ramayana.* The *Ramayana* tells of Prince Rama, believed by many followers to be another incarnation of the Hindu god Vishnu.

Hindus believe that when the body dies, the soul is reborn, or reincarnated, in a continuous process. The soul of someone who leads a good life will be reborn into a person with higher status, while the soul of someone who leads a bad life will be reborn into a person or creature of a more lowly condition.

Multidraft Reading

This icon ● marks natural pauses in the selection. To assist struggling readers and to deepen reading for all, assign the text in "chunks," following the icons, and apply multidraft reading protocols. For each reading, have students set the purpose indicated:

- **First reading**—literal comprehension: answering the Reading Check questions.
- **Second reading**—application of skills: answering the Epic and Epic Hero and Analyze Cultural Context prompts.
- **Third reading**—interpretation: answering the end-of-selection questions.

For more guidance, refer to the ***Classroom Strategies and Teaching Routines*** card on multidraft reading.

Differentiated Instruction Additional Instruction

EL Extended Support—English Learners

Have students complete the **Reading and Vocabulary Warm-ups, *Unit 6 Resources,*** pp. 80–83, before they read. Assign the prereading pages for the selection in the ***Reader's Notebook: English Learner's Version***. Then, have students listen to portions of the selection on the ***Hear It!* Audio CD.**

L1 L2 Extended Support—Struggling Readers

Have students complete the **Reading and Vocabulary Warm-ups, *Unit 6 Resources,*** pp. 80–83, before they read. Assign the prereading pages for the selection in the ***Reader's Notebook: Adapted Version***. Then, have students listen to portions of the selection on the ***Hear It!* Audio CD** (adapted text).

L1 L2 Extended Support—Reluctant Readers

To build motivation and engagement before assigning the selection, have students read "Equality on the Playing Field," a thematically related selection in ***Reality Central.*** Then, use the questions at the conclusion of the related selection to guide discussion.

PHLit Online!

For more about the author, practice with the selection vocabulary, and more background, go to **www.PHLitOnline.com**.

TEACH

❶ Activating Prior Knowledge

Write the following statement on the board: "Superheroes from all times and cultures possess common traits." Then, have students generate a list of superheroes from ancient to present times, including figures in popular culture. Examples may include Hercules, King Arthur, Spiderman, and Wonder Woman. Discuss with students the characteristics that some of these heroes have in common, such as courage, loyalty, and integrity.

Concept Connector →

Students will return to these discussion points after completing the story.

Small-Group Activity

Tell students that an *initiation* is a rite of passage ceremony or ritual that marks acceptance into a group, into a new role, into a new life stage, or into a new spiritual phase. Have groups brainstorm for a list of initiations that they know of from their own culture or from their reading. Examples might include the Quinceañera initiation into womanhood, fraternity initiations, or the many fairy tales' use of the dragon-slaying quest as a prince's initiation into kingly duties.

❷ About the Selection

In "Rama's Initiation," the young prince Rama accepts his calling to defend a sage and perform a sacrifice in a faraway sacred place. He proves himself by defeating a demon, thus beginning his adventures as an epic hero. His adventures demonstrate the importance of bravery, strength, and respect for wisdom in Indian culture.

Rama's Initiation

from the Ramayana

R. K. Narayan

Rama and Sita, 1740. Victoria and Albert Museum, London.

❶ ❷

Vocabulary Development

Thematic Vocabulary: The Big Question

As students are discussing "Rama's Initiation" encourage them to use the thematic vocabulary presented in Introducing the Big Question, pp. 1046–1047. You might encourage them with sentence starters like these:

1. When Viswamithra came to speak to the King, he expressed a *resolute* desire to . . .
2. Thataka's sons' terrible *conduct* caused . . .
3. One example of Rama's heroic *attributes* is . . .
4. At the end of the story, Rama shows *courage* when he . . .

Steeped in the Hindu religion of India, the **Ramayana** *is the story of Prince Rama* (rä′ mə), *son of King Dasaratha* (dä sä rä′ tä). *With the guidance of several Hindu sages, or wise men, Rama confronts and overcomes many obstacles, including a test of strength to win his wife Sita. Just as he is about to inherit his throne, he is banished and spends fourteen years in exile before returning to his kingdom. Through the challenges he meets, he reaches a spiritual and moral state so perfect that many associate him with Krishna, the incarnation, or embodiment, of the Hindu god Vishnu* (vēsh′ no͞o).

This excerpt tells of adventures from Rama's childhood that occur before his fourteen-year banishment. Even as boys, he and his brother Lakshmana (läks mä′nä) *show extraordinary strength and skill.*

3 The new assembly hall, Dasaratha's latest pride, was crowded all day with visiting dignitaries, royal emissaries, and citizens coming in with representations or appeals for justice. The King was always accessible, and fulfilled his duties as the ruler of Kosala without grudging the hours spent in public service.

4 ◄ **Critical Viewing** What details in this painting indicate that Rama is an epic hero? **[Analyze]**

3 Humanities

The* Ramayana *of Valmiki (detail)

This illustration of an episode from Rama's later life, with his wife, Sita, is done in the Pahari style, a style of painting practiced in the hill communities of the Himalaya Mountains. The style became popular in the seventeenth century, highlighting human figures that were portrayed according to certain conventions: they had long, fish-shaped eyes, small foreheads, and long noses. Backgrounds were usually red, yellow, green, or brown. Vegetable colors were used to create the paintings, and the backgrounds did not include much detail, allowing the human figures to dominate. From the mid-eighteenth century, this style gave way to a more naturalistic look, with more landscape detail added. The women in Pahari paintings were noted for their beauty. In this painting, as is often the case, Rama is painted blue to indicate his divine origin.

Use this question for discussion:

What is the relationship between Rama and Sita in this painting?

Possible response: Rama is gently protecting Sita. There is also the suggestion of affection because he holds her hand and is smiling.

4 Critical Viewing

Possible response: Rama is shown as a hunter or warrior. His position is one of an active leader. His bearing and clothing are regal.

Differentiated Instruction for Universal Access

Culturally Responsive Instruction

Culture Connection Explain that the sages, or wise men, who guided Rama are Hindu *rishis* (as in the title *Maharishi*), who might be great poets, spiritual advisors, seers, or all three. They were traditionally sent to guide young princes along the path to greatness.

Sages appear in a variety of cultures. In the Bible, the three wise men are often called *Magi*, or sages from the Zoroastrian tradition of ancient Persia. In West African tales, sages are *griots*, the storytellers who pass along the history of their people. In medieval literature, the wise man is often a wizard. Judaism has the wise rabbis, and Taoism has the Seven Sages of the Bamboo Grove.

Have students name some *rishis* in their own lives, encouraging them to name wise women as well as wise men who have influenced their journeys through life.

PHLit Online!

This selection is available in interactive format in the **Enriched Online Student Edition**, **www.PHLitOnline.com**, which includes a thematically related video and writing prompt and an interactive graphic organizer.

❺ Reading Skill

Analyze Cultural Context

1. Have students read the bracketed passage.
2. **Ask** the Reading Skill question: What background information on page 1107 helps explain the king's treatment of the sage?
   Answer: The background information indicates that Hinduism has a strict code of righteous behavior, valuing a highly structured society. These doctrines explain why the king values the wise man.
3. **Ask** students what additional information from the story explains the king's attitude.
   Answer: The sage is, himself, a former king, so he is worthy of special respect.

❻ Literary Analysis

Epic and Epic Hero

1. Have students read the bracketed passage.
2. **Ask** students the Literary Analysis question: What typical epic conflict does the sage describe here?
   Answer: The sage presents a challenging battle against evil that will "please the gods above."
3. **Ask:** Which qualities will the epic hero need in order to triumph in this battle?
   Possible response: The epic hero will need courage, determination, a sense of duty and honor, and physical strength.

Reading Skill
Analyze Cultural Context What background information on page 1107 helps explain the king's treatment of the sage? ❺

Vocabulary
renounced (ri nounst′) *v.* to have given up formally
decrepitude (dē krep′ ə to͞od′) *n.* feebleness; condition of being worn out by age or illness

Literary Analysis
Epic and Epic Hero What typical epic conflict does the sage describe here? ❻

On a certain afternoon, messengers at the gate came running in to announce, "Sage Viswamithra" [vish wä′ mē trä]. When the message was relayed to the King, he got up and hurried forward to receive the visitor. Viswamithra, once a king, a conqueror, and a dreaded name until he **renounced** his kingly role and chose to become a sage (which he accomplished through severe austerities[1]), combined in himself the sage's eminence and the king's authority and was quick tempered and positive. Dasaratha led him to a proper seat and said, "This is a day of glory for us; your gracious presence is most welcome. You must have come from afar. Would you first rest?"

"No need," the sage replied simply. He had complete mastery over his bodily needs through inner discipline and austerities, and was above the effects of heat, cold, hunger, fatigue, and even **decrepitude**. The King later asked politely, "Is there anything I can do?" Viswamithra looked steadily at the King and answered, "Yes. I am here to ask of you a favor. I wish to perform, before the next full moon, a *yagna*[2] at Sidhasrama [sēd häs rä′ mä]. Doubtless you know where it is?"

"I have passed that sacred ground beyond the Ganges many times."

The sage interrupted. "But there are creatures hovering about waiting to disturb every holy undertaking there, who must be overcome in the same manner as one has to conquer the five-fold evils[3] within before one can realize holiness. Those evil creatures are endowed with immeasurable powers of destruction. But it is our duty to pursue our aims undeterred. The yagna I propose to perform will strengthen the beneficial forces of this world, and please the gods above."

"It is my duty to protect your sublime[4] effort. Tell me when, and I will be there."

The sage said, "No need to disturb your august self. Send your son Rama with me, and he will help me. He can."

"Rama!" cried the King, surprised, "When I am here to serve you."

Viswamithra's temper was already stirring. "I know your greatness," he said, cutting the King short. "But I want Rama to go with me. If you are not willing, you may say so."

The air became suddenly tense. The assembly, the ministers and officials, watched in solemn silence. The King looked miserable. "Rama is still a child, still learning the arts and practicing the use of arms." His sentences never seemed to conclude, but trailed away

1. **austerities** (ô ster′ ə tēz) *n.* acts or habits of self-denial.
2. **yagna** (yäg nä′) *n.* Sanskrit term for sacrifice.
3. **five-fold evils** In Hindu belief, the five evils are lust, anger, miserliness, egoism, and envy.
4. **sublime** (sə blīm′) *adj.* noble; grand.

Vocabulary Development

Word Forms

Give students a blank **Word Form Chart** (***Professional Development Guidebook***, p. 42), with *exuberance, esoteric,* and *secular* in the correct columns. Work with the class, or have students work with a partner, to determine the related forms. The final chart should look like the one shown.

Noun	Verb	Adjective	Adverb
exuberance		exuberant	exuberantly
		esoteric	esoterically
secularity		**secular**	secularly

as he tried to explain. "He is a boy, a child, he is too young and tender to contend with demons."

"But I know Rama," was all that Viswamithra said in reply.

"I can send you an army, or myself lead an army to guard your performance. What can a stripling[5] like Rama do against those terrible forces . . . ? I will help you just as I helped Indra[6] once when he was harassed and deprived of his kingdom."

8 Viswamithra ignored his speech and rose to leave. "If you cannot send Rama, I need none else." He started to move down the passage.

The King was too stricken to move. When Viswamithra had gone half way, he realized that the visitor was leaving unceremoniously and was not even shown the courtesy of being escorted to the door. Vasishtha [vä sē´ shtä], the King's priest and

5. **stripling** (strip´ liŋ) *n.* young boy passing into manhood.
6. **Indra** (in´ drə) Hindu god associated with rain and thunderbolts.

Literary Analysis
Epic and Epic Hero
In what way is Rama singled out as an epic hero?

9 **Reading Check**
What does Viswamithra ask of the king?

7 Humanities

The Marriage of Rama and His Brothers from the "Sangri Ramayana," c. 1760

This colorful painting from the Pahari school of miniature paintings is done in the style known as "Basohli." To distinguish this style from other Himalayan styles, viewers must look at the use of color and the forming of facial features. Many of the paintings have dark red borders and use primary colors with the addition of orange and green. As usual, Rama is shown with a blue face to indicate his connection to the gods.

Use this question for discussion:

How can you tell that a wedding is taking place?
Possible response: Couples are standing under a canopy with a crowd surrounding them; musicians are playing; everyone is dressed up.

8 Literary Analysis
Epic and Epic Hero

1. Have a student read aloud the bracketed passage.
2. **Ask** students the Literary Analysis question: In what way is Rama singled out as an epic hero?
Answer: The sage Viswamithra says that he wants Rama and only Rama for his mission.
3. **Ask:** Besides being singled out by the sage, what else in the narrative supports the idea that Rama will be an epic hero?
Answer: The sage describes a very dangerous but necessary mission that Rama alone can perform; Rama is considered by the sage to be more powerful than King Dasaratha and stronger than an army.

9 Reading Check

Answer: The sage asks the king to allow Rama to accompany the sage on a mission in which an extremely dangerous and evil enemy must be defeated.

Differentiated Instruction for Universal Access

Strategy for Special Needs Students
Use (and if necessary adapt and simplify) the phonetic spellings throughout the excerpt to help students pronounce the names of the main characters so that they will not spend too much time struggling on their own. Have students work in pairs to create a characters list, identifying the major characters and showing any relationships between them. Suggest that they also label characters with terms such as *king, hero, sage,* and *villain.* (For example: Rama—hero, son of King Dasaratha). Have them list these characters in alphabetical order.

Enrichment for Advanced Readers
After they have read the excerpt, invite students to write another episode focusing on Viswamithra, Rama, Lakshmana, and Rama's initiation. Ask students to focus the episode on portraying some other heroic quality Rama might develop, such as wisdom or resistance to temptation. Encourage them to share their writing with the class.

⑩ Reading Skill

Analyze Cultural Context

1. Read aloud the bracketed passage.
2. **Ask** students why the sage wants to be known as a Brahma Rishi.
   Answer: The status of a sage is higher than that of a king because the Brahma caste includes priests. Also, Viswamithra trained for years to become a Brahma Rishi and identifies himself as such rather than as a king.
3. Point out that Vasishtha, the King's own priest and guide, is worried about not granting the sage his wish. **Ask** students why this priest may be so concerned.
   Answer: The sage says the battle will please the gods. Perhaps the priest wants the King and the sage to come to an agreement because he wants the right decision, meaning the holiest decision, to be made.

⑪ Critical Thinking

Analyze

1. **Ask** students why Rama's father is reluctant to let Rama go on the mission.
   Answer: Rama's father is worried that his son is too young and unprepared to fight the dangerously evil creatures that the sage describes.
2. Have a student read aloud the sentence within the bracketed passage about the seed.
3. **Ask:** What does the sage tell the King through this image?
   Answer: The sage compares Rama to a young plant who must make his own way from underneath his father's shadow. If he is not allowed to grow, he will not reach his full potential.

guide, whispered to Dasaratha, "Follow him and call him back," and hurried forward even before the King could grasp what he was saying. He almost ran as Viswamithra had reached the end of the hall and, blocking his way, said, "The King is coming; please don't go. He did not mean . . ."

A wry smile played on Viswamithra's face as he said without any trace of bitterness, "Why are you or anyone agitated? I came here for a purpose; it has failed: no reason to prolong my stay."

Vocabulary
secular (sek´ yə lər) *adj.* of worldly, as opposed to religious, matters

"Oh, eminent one, you were yourself a king once."

"What has that to do with us now?" asked Viswamithra, rather irked, since he hated all reference to his **secular** past and wanted always to be known as a Brahma Rishi.[7] ⑩

Vasishtha answered mildly, "Only to remind you of an ordinary man's feelings, especially a man like Dasaratha who had been childless and had to pray hard for an issue . . ."

"Well, it may be so, great one; I still say that I came on a mission and wish to leave, since it has failed."

"It has not failed," said Vasishtha, and just then the King came up to join them in the passage; the assembly was on its feet.

Dasaratha made a deep obeisance and said, "Come back to your seat, Your Holiness."

"For what purpose, Your Majesty?" Viswamithra asked.

"Easier to talk seated . . ."

"I don't believe in any talk," said Viswamithra; but Vasishtha pleaded with him until he returned to his seat.

When they were all seated again, Vasishtha addressed the King: "There must be a divine purpose working through this seer, who may know but will not explain. It is a privilege that Rama's help should be sought. Do not bar his way. Let him go with the sage."

"When, oh when?" the King asked anxiously.

"Now," said Viswamithra. The King looked woebegone and desperate, and the sage relented enough to utter a word of comfort. "You cannot count on the physical proximity of someone you ⑪ love, all the time. A seed that sprouts at the foot of its parent tree remains stunted until it is transplanted. Rama will be in my care, and he will be quite well. But ultimately, he will leave me too. Every human being, when the time comes, has to depart and seek his fulfillment in his own way."

"Sidhasrama is far away . . .?" began the King.

"I'll ease his path for him, no need for a chariot to take us there," said Viswamithra, reading his mind.

---

7. **Brahma Rishi** (brä´ mä ri´ shē) enlightened wise person.

Think Aloud

Analyzing Cultural Context

Help students interpret the agricultural metaphor used by the sage to persuade the King. Say to students:

> The sage comforts the King by saying "A seed that sprouts at the foot of its parent tree remains stunted until it is transplanted." Because he expects the King to understand him, I can tell that the culture must be fairly rural and agricultural—so that even a King understands that small plants must be transplanted to thrive. The sage uses this agricultural metaphor to show the King that his sons must move out of his shadow to achieve their manhood.

(If you are using both selections, you might wish to compare the sage's words to those of the blind seer to the king in *Sundiata*: "When the seed germinates growth is not always easy; great trees grow slowly but they plunge their roots deep into the ground." Both the culture of old Mali and that of India at the time of the *Ramayana* were rural and agricultural.)

"Rama has never been separated from his brother Lakshmana. May he also go with him?" pleaded the King, and he looked relieved when he heard Viswamithra say, "Yes, I will look after both, though their mission will be to look after me. Let them get ready to follow me; let them select their favorite weapons and prepare to leave."

Dasaratha, with the look of one delivering hostages into the hand of an enemy, turned to his minister and said, "Fetch my sons."

12

13 Following the footsteps of their master like his shadows, Rama and Lakshmana went past the limits of the city and reached the Sarayu River, which bounded the capital on the north. When night fell, they rested at a wooded grove and at dawn crossed the river. When the sun came over the mountain peak, they reached a pleasant grove over which hung, like a canopy, fragrant smoke from numerous sacrificial fires. Viswamithra explained to Rama, "This is where God Shiva[8] meditated once upon a time and reduced to ashes the god of love when he attempted to spoil his meditation. From time immemorial saints praying to Shiva come here to perform their sacrifices, and the pall of smoke you notice is from their sacrificial fires."

A group of hermits emerged from their seclusion, received Viswamithra, and invited him and his two disciples to stay with them for the night. Viswamithra resumed his journey at dawn and reached a desert region at midday. The mere expression "desert" hardly conveys the absolute aridity of this land. Under a relentless sun, all vegetation had dried and turned to dust, stone and rock crumbled into powdery sand, which lay in vast dunes, stretching away to the horizon. Here every inch was scorched and dry and hot beyond imagination. The ground was cracked and split, exposing enormous fissures everywhere. The distinction between dawn, noon, and evening did not exist here, as the sun seemed to stay overhead and burn the earth without moving. Bleached bones

Reading Skill
Analyze Cultural Context What background information helps explain details in this paragraph?

14 **Reading Check**
Whom does the king send to accompany Rama and Viswamithra?

8. **Shiva** (shē′ və) Hindu god of destruction and reproduction; along with Vishnu and Brahma, one of the three most important gods in Hinduism.

12 Humanities

Lakshmana Consulting the Heads of the Monkey Armies from the *Ramayana*

Tell students that in one famous episode from the *Ramayana*, Rama and Lakshmana fight demons with the help of an army of monkeylike creatures called *Vaanaras*.

Use this question for discussion:

Based on this illustration, what "favorite weapons" did the brothers apparently select for their journey?
Answer: They chose bows and arrows.

13 Reading Skill

Analyze Cultural Context

1. Have students read the bracketed passage.
2. **Ask** students the Reading Skill question: What background information helps explain details in this paragraph? They may record their responses on **Reading Skill Graphic Organizer B** (***Graphic Organizer Transparencies***, p. 201).
   Answer: The background information on Hinduism explains that the god Shiva is one of the most important Hindu gods. The fact about Shiva meditating emphasizes the value Hindus place on the practice of meditation.
3. **Ask:** How might background information influence a reader's view of the importance of Viswamithra's quest?
   Answer: The background information helps the reader understand the sacredness of the site where the evil creatures are hovering. A reader may consider the quest worthy of a Hindu holy man and a young hero.

14 Reading Check

Answer: The King sends Rama's brother Lakshmana to accompany Rama and Viswamithra.

Differentiated Instruction for Universal Access

EL Strategy for English Learners
Students may have some difficulty understanding the metaphor of a tree and its seedlings that Viswamithra references in his discussion with Rama's father. Explain to students that a metaphor compares two things so that one takes on characteristics of the other. Then, tell students that in the metaphor, Rama is the seed, and his father is the parent tree. Ask them to explain the remaining part of the metaphor: "remains stunted until it is transplanted." Guide them to understand that Viswamithra thinks Rama needs to take new risks without his father.

Strategy for Less Proficient Readers
Students may have difficulty understanding the shift in the story that comes on the following page. Have students stop at the end of this page, and explain to them that "Thataka's Story," which they will encounter soon, is a "story within a story." Such a structure is a common narrative technique in epics. Explain that it is like a flashback in a movie, showing how something becomes a certain way. Make sure that students understand and can summarize the story up to the point of "Thataka's Story" before they continue with the selection.

15 Connecting to the Big Question

1. Remind students that heroism is often connected to the overcoming of obstacles, or challenges. Have them name some examples of this from literature they have read.
2. Have students read the bracketed passage. **Ask** what challenge Rama faces in this episode of the story.
   Answer: The landscape is terribly hot and dry.
3. **Ask** students to explain how the problem is solved.
   Answer: Viswamithra gives the young men two mantras to recite that make their passage through the harsh land bearable.
4. As they continue reading, have students note other challenges that Rama must overcome on his journey.

16 Humanities

Rama the 7th Avatar of Vishnu Slays Maricha Who Has Assumed the Form of a Deer by K. Venkatappa

K. Venkatappa was a painter, sculptor, and teacher of art who gained fame in the early part of the twentieth century. In this painting, he carries on the traditions that stem from the miniature painting of three centuries earlier. In this episode from the *Ramayana*, Rama fights the leader of the demons, who has assumed the form of a golden deer and attempted to abduct Rama's wife, Sita.

Use this question for discussion:

How does the artist indicate that the deer is not what it seems?
Answer: He uses shadows to suggest a demon form hidden behind the deer.

17 Critical Viewing

Answer: He is quick, athletic, and a good hunter.

16

17 ▲ **Critical Viewing** Based on this painting, what traits does Rama possess? **[Infer]**

lay where animals had perished, including those of monstrous serpents with jaws open in deadly thirst; into these enormous jaws had rushed (says the poet) elephants desperately seeking shade, all dead and fossilized, the serpent and the elephant alike. Heat haze rose and singed the very heavens. While traversing this ground, Viswamithra noticed the bewilderment and distress on the faces of the young men, and transmitted to them mentally 15
two mantras[9] (called "Bala" and "Adi-Bala"). When they meditated on and recited these incantations, the arid atmosphere was transformed for the rest of their passage and they felt as if they were wading through a cool stream with a southern summer breeze blowing in their faces. Rama, ever curious to know the country he was passing through, asked, "Why is this land so terrible? Why does it seem accursed?"

"You will learn the answer if you listen to this story—of a woman fierce, ruthless, eating and digesting all living creatures, possessing the strength of a thousand mad elephants."

Thataka's Story

Vocabulary
exuberance (eg zōō ´bər əns) *n.* good health and high spirits

The woman I speak of was the daughter of Suketha [sōō kä´ tä] a *yaksha*,[10] a demigod of great valor, might, and purity. She was beautiful and full of wild energy. When she grew up she was married to a chieftain named Sunda. Two sons were born to them—Mareecha [mä´ rē chä] and Subahu [sä bä´ hōō]—who were endowed with enormous supernatural powers in addition to physical strength; and in their conceit and exuberance they laid waste their surroundings. Their father, delighted at their pranks and infected by their mood, joined in their activities. He pulled out ancient trees by their roots and flung them about, and he slaughtered all

9. **mantras** (man´ trəz) *n.* sacred syllables or hymns chanted in prayer.
10. ***yaksha*** Sanskrit term for a good nature spirit.

Vocabulary Development

Vocabulary Knowledge Rating

When students have completed reading and discussing "Rama's Initiation," have them take out their **Vocabulary Knowledge Rating Chart** for this selection. Read the words aloud once more, and have students rate their knowledge of the words again in the After Reading column. Clarify any words that are still problematic. Have students write their own definition and example or sentence in the appropriate column. Then have students complete the Vocabulary Practice at the end of the selection. Encourage students to use the words in further discussion and written work about this selection. Remind them that they will be accountable for these words on the **Selection Test**, ***Unit 6 Resources***, pp. 95–97 or 98–100.

creatures that came his way. This depredation came to the notice of the great savant[11] Agasthya [ä gus tē yä́] (the diminutive[12] saint who once, when certain demoniac beings hid themselves at the bottom of the sea and Indra appealed for his help to track them, had sipped off the waters of the ocean). Agasthya had his hermitage in this forest, and when he noticed the destruction around, he cursed the perpetrator of this deed and Sunda fell dead. When his wife learned of his death, she and her sons stormed in, roaring revenge on the saint. He met their challenge by cursing them. "Since you are destroyers of life, may you become *asuras*[13] and dwell in the nether worlds." (Till now they had been demigods. Now they were degraded to demonhood.) The three at once underwent a transformation; their features and stature became forbidding, and their natures changed to match. The sons left to seek the company of superdemons. The mother was left alone and lives on here, breathing fire and wishing everything ill. Nothing flourishes here; only heat and sand remain. She is a scorcher. She carries a trident with spikes; a cobra entwined on her arm is her armlet. The name of this fearsome creature is Thataka [tä tä́ kä]. Just as the presence of a little *loba* (meanness) dries up and disfigures a whole human personality, so does the presence of this monster turn into desert a region which was once fertile. In her restlessness she constantly harasses the hermits at their prayers; she gobbles up anything that moves and sends it down her entrails.

18

Touching the bow slung on his shoulder, Rama asked, "Where is she to be found?"

Before Viswamithra could answer, she arrived, the ground rocking under her feet and a storm preceding her. She loomed over them with her eyes spitting fire, her fangs bared, her lips parted revealing a cavernous mouth; and her brows twitching in rage. She raised her trident and roared, "In this my kingdom, I have crushed out the minutest womb of life and you have been sent down so that I may not remain hungry."

19

Rama hesitated; for all her evil, she was still a woman. How could he kill her? Reading his thoughts, Viswamithra said, "You shall not consider her a woman at all. Such a monster must receive no consideration. Her strength, ruthlessness, appearance, rule her out of that category. Formerly God Vishnu himself killed Kyathi [kyä́ tē], the wife of Brigu [brḗ go͞o], who harbored the *asuras* fleeing his wrath, when she refused to yield them. Mandorai, [mänd rä́ ē] a woman bent upon destroying all the worlds, was vanquished by

Literary Analysis
Epic and Epic Hero Why is Thataka a suitable opponent for an epic hero?

Reading Skill
Analyze Cultural Context What do the details in this paragraph suggest about the place of women in Hindu culture?

20 **Reading Check**
Why does nothing grow in the land where Thataka lives?

11. **savant** (sə vänt́) *n.* learned person.
12. **diminutive** (də miń yo͞o tiv) *adj.* much smaller than ordinary or average.
13. ***asuras*** (ä so͞ó räz) in Hindu belief, group of demons at war with gods and human beings.

18 Literary Analysis

Epic and Epic Hero

1. **Ask** students to describe Thataka.
   Possible responses: In her youth, Thataka was beautiful, pure, energetic, and strong. Later, she loses her husband and watches her sons become demons, while becoming one herself; these experiences make her incredibly angry and volatile.
2. **Ask** students the Literary Analysis question: Why is Thataka a suitable opponent for an epic hero?
   Answer: She is a suitable opponent because she is powerful and evil.

19 Reading Skill

Analyze Cultural Context

1. Have students read the bracketed passage.
2. **Ask** students the Reading Skill question: What do the details in this paragraph suggest about the place of women in Hindu culture?
   Answer: Rama's hesitancy to kill Thataka suggests that women are viewed with respect and honor; however, it also suggests that women need to be protected because they are less capable than men. The idea that a woman could be a powerful warrior and an evil villain is alien to the culture.

Monitor Progress: To assess students' ability to analyze cultural context, have them suggest three things they learn about Indian values from Thataka's story.
Possible responses: Destructive behavior is bad. Meanness is a curse. Strength should be used wisely.

Reteach: If students cannot identify values in Thataka's story, have them find support in the story for each value listed above under "Possible responses."

20 Reading Check

Answer: Nothing grows because Suketha breathes fire on the land and wishes everything ill.

Concept Connector

Activating Prior Knowledge

Have students return to the discussion points raised before reading the story regarding the qualities of superheroes. How do students compare Rama to other superheroes? During this discussion, tell students to cite examples from the selection to support their ideas.

Writing About the Big Question

Have students compare their responses to the sentence starters they completed before reading the story with their ideas afterward. Ask them to explain whether their thoughts have changed.

Reading Skill Graphic Organizer

Ask students to review the graphic organizers they completed to use background knowledge to interpret cultural context. Show them **Reading Skill Graphic Organizer A** (*Graphic Organizer Transparencies*, p. 200) as an example. Then have students share their graphic organizers.

ASSESS

Answers

Critical Thinking

1. Many students will be relieved at the death of this monster.
2. (a) He asks the King to allow Rama to accompany Viswamithra and vanquish a powerful spirit. (b) The sage knows that Rama has the makings of a hero.
3. (a) The sun is hot and pitiless. The ground is split into many cracks. Bleached bones lie all around. (b) The land is no longer forbidding and arid but green and pleasant. (c) This episode suggests that the sage has enormous gifts of vision and power.
4. (a) Rama defeats the evil Thataka by shooting her in the throat with his arrow. (b) Rama is initiated into the life of a hero who will fight against horrifying evils.

Can anyone be a hero?

Possible response: (a) To become a hero, a person needs support from the people around him or her, which may come in the form of faith. (b) Vasistha has faith that the seer has a divine purpose, which convinces the King to allow Rama to go on the journey. Viswamithra has faith in the abilities of Rama to survive and succeed, which is what has sent him to the King in the first place.

Indra and he earned the gratitude of humanity. These are but two instances. A woman of demoniac tendencies loses all consideration to be treated as a woman. This Thataka is more dreadful than Yama, the god of death, who takes a life only when the time is ripe. But this monster, at the very scent of a living creature, craves to kill and eat. Do not picture her as a woman at all. You must rid this world of her. It is your duty."

Rama said, "I will carry out your wish."

Thataka threw her three-pronged spear at Rama. As it came flaming, Rama strung his bow and sent an arrow which broke it into fragments. Next she raised a hail of stones under which to crush her **adversaries**. Rama sent up his arrows, which shielded them from the attack. Finally Rama's arrow pierced her throat and ended her career; thereby also inaugurating Rama's life's mission of destroying evil and demonry in this world. The gods assembled in the sky and expressed their joy and relief and enjoined Viswamithra, "Oh, adept and master of weapons, impart without any reserve all your knowledge and powers to this lad. He is a savior." Viswamithra obeyed this injunction and taught Rama all the **esoteric** techniques in weaponry. Thereafter the presiding deities of various weapons, *asthras* [äs′ träz], appeared before Rama submissively and declared, "Now we are yours: command us night or day."

Vocabulary

adversaries (ad′vər ser′ ēz) *n.* opponents

esoteric (es′ ə ter′ ik) *adj.* beyond the understanding or knowledge of most people

Critical Thinking

1. **Respond:** What was your reaction to the killing of Thataka? Why?
2. **(a)** What favor does Viswamithra ask of King Dasaratha? **(b) Hypothesize:** Why does he want Rama, rather than the king, to perform the favor?
3. **(a)** List three details describing the region through which Rama, Lakshmana, and Viswamithra pass. **(b) Analyze:** How does the land seem different to Rama and Lakshmana when they use Viswamithra's mantras? **(c) Draw Conclusions:** What does this episode suggest about the sage's power?
4. **(a)** Summarize the outcome of Rama's first battle. **(b) Interpret:** This part of the epic is called "Rama's Initiation." Into what activity or way of life is he initiated?

Can anyone be a hero?
(a) What role does faith have in the creation of a hero?
(b) Identify two people in the story who had to have faith in order for Rama to succeed, and explain why that faith was important.

Assessment Resources

Unit 6 Resources

L1 L2 EL **Selection Test A,** pp. 95–97. Administer Test A to less advanced readers and English learners.

L3 L4 **Selection Test B,** pp. 98–100. Administer Test B to on-level and more advanced students.

L3 L4 **Open-Book Test,** pp. 92–94. As an alternative, give the Open-Book Test.

All **Customizable Test Bank**

All **Self-tests**

Students may prepare for the **Selection Test** by taking the **Self-test** online.

PHLit Online! All assessment resources are available at **www.PHLitOnline.com.**

After You Read

Rama's Initiation
from the **Ramayana**

Literary Analysis: Epic and Epic Hero

1. **(a)** What is the goal of the sage's **epic** journey? **(b)** What is Rama's goal in accompanying the sage? **(c)** Compare and contrast these goals with the goals of heroes who fight for honor or glory.
2. Using a chart like the one shown, give specific examples showing which qualities of an **epic hero** Rama possesses.

Noble Birth	Warrior Virtues	Acts Honorably	Chosen by the Gods or Fate

3. **(a)** Why does Rama hesitate before fighting Thataka? **(b)** Does his hesitation suit the character of an epic hero? Explain.

Reading Skill: Analyze Cultural Context

4. **(a)** List three things that you learned about Hindu **cultural context** from the features that appear before the selection. **(b)** List two things you learned about Hindu culture from the selection or from the footnotes. **(c)** For each item of context you list, briefly explain how knowing that item helps you to understand the *Ramayana*. Give specific examples.

Vocabulary

Practice Write a sentence about each of the following situations by using a word from the vocabulary list for the *Ramayana* on page 1106.

1. a building with peeling paint, a sagging door, and a broken fence
2. a successful lawyer who is also very spiritual
3. a scientist's most difficult theory
4. a girl who is excited about winning a soccer game
5. someone who is concerned about his opponents in an election
6. a leader who leaves her political party

Word Study Use the context of the sentences and what you know about the **Latin suffix *-tude*** to explain your answer to each question.

1. Is there a large crowd if a *multitude* of fans greet the author?
2. If you like *solitude*, would you like reading in a deserted library?

Word Study

The **Latin suffix *-tude*** means "condition of" or "quality of."

Challenge Explain how the suffix *-tude* contributes to the meanings of these words. Consult a dictionary if necessary.

aptitude
fortitude
latitude

ASSESS/EXTEND

Answers

Literary Analysis

1. (a) The goal of the sage's journey is to perform a *yagna*, or sacrifice to the gods. (b) Rama's goal is to look after Viswamithra and protect him from any demons. (c) Rama is not concerned with honor, glory, or personal achievement. Rather, he is selflessly concerned with protecting the life of another.
2. *Noble Birth*—Rama is the son of the King. *Warrior Virtues*—Rama is strong, skilled, and determined. *Acts Honorably*— He is selfless and protects the sage by destroying the demon. *Chosen by the Gods or Fate*—It is Rama's duty to destroy the demon. The sage only accepts Rama for the challenge.

   For other sample answers, see ***Graphic Organizer Transparencies*, Literary Analysis Graphic Organizer A**, p. 203, and the **Additional Answers** section.
3. (a) He hesitates because he does not want to harm a woman.
   (b) Yes, an epic hero will have honorable qualities, such as the desire to not harm others.

Reading Skill

4. (a) The Hindu culture was divided into a caste system. Hinduism involves a belief in multiple gods, the most important of which are Brahma, the creator; Vishnu, the preserver; and Siva, the destroyer. (b) There are five evils in the Hindu belief that one must conquer: lust, anger, miserliness, egoism, and envy. Hindus believe in *asuras*, a group of demons at war with humans. (c) **Possible response:** Understanding the caste system makes Rama's social position clear; he is part of a noble caste and is expected to achieve greatness. The belief in conquering the evil within helps explain the importance of Rama's selfless and moral actions.

Vocabulary

Practice

Sample answers:

1. Even though the newlyweds' house had a sagging door, a broken fence, and peeling paint, they loved it and did not mind its decrepitude.
2. Although the lawyer's job was secular, he felt a strong connection to the spiritual world.

Answers continued

3. Einstein's Theory of Relativity is esoteric and is difficult for most people to understand.
4. After her soccer team won the championship game, the girl's exuberance was obvious.
5. The politician was concerned about beating his adversaries in the upcoming debate.
6. Sandra renounced her position as leader of the political party because she no longer agreed with its beliefs.

Word Study

1. Yes. The suffix *-tude* means "condition of" or "quality of" and *multitude* means "condition of being many." If there is a multitude of people to greet an author, there is a large crowd.
2. Yes. The suffix *-tude* means "condition of" or "quality of" and *solitude* means "condition of being solitary or alone." If you like solitude, the library is an excellent place to read because you can be alone.

Word Study: Challenge

Sample answers:

Aptitude is the quality of being apt or able to learn. *Fortitude* is the quality of having strength. *Latitude* is the quality of being free of narrow restrictions.

EXTEND/ASSESS

Answers

Grammar

Introduce the skill, using the instruction on the student page.

Think Aloud: Model the Skill

Model the skill of identifying complex and compound-complex sentences. Say to students:

Since both complex and compound-complex sentences have a subordinate clause, I need to count the number of independent clauses to distinguish between the two types. The sentence, "Before I did my homework, I ate dinner," has one independent clause:" I ate dinner." Thus, it is a complex sentence. The sentence, "Before I did my homework, I ate dinner and I called my friend," has two independent clauses: "I ate dinner" and "I called my friend." Thus, it is compound-complex.

Practice A

1. Complex. Although he was born to a king; which made his mother sad—subordinate. Mari Djata had a difficult childhood—independent.
2. Compound-complex. When the king was about to die—subordinate. He called Mari Djata to him; he spoke as if the child were an adult—independent.
3. Compound-complex. When Mari Djata could not walk—subordinate. His mother was worried; her enemies were cruel—independent.

Challenge

Students' responses should include a complex sentence and a compound-complex sentence from the selection.

Practice B

Sample answers:

1. The boy was chosen for the journey, which was extremely dangerous.
2. Although the sage was usually even-tempered, he became angry with the king and he left quickly.
3. The king was protective of his two sons, though they were grown.
4. The young boy, who people thought was weak and foolish, trained very hard and he became a hero.

Challenge

Students' answers should include a complex sentence and a compound-complex sentence.

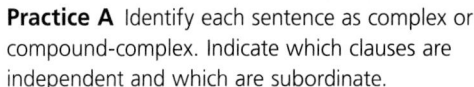

Integrated Language Skills

from Sundiata: An Epic of Old Mali • Rama's Initiation *from the* Ramayana

Grammar: Complex and Compound-Complex Sentences

- An **independent clause** contains a subject and verb and can stand alone as a complete sentence.
- A **subordinate clause** has a subject and verb but cannot stand alone as a complete sentence. It includes a subordinating conjunction such as *while, although, when, after* or *because.*

A **complex sentence** contains one independent clause and one or more subordinate clauses. **Compound-complex sentences** contain as least one subordinate clause and at least two independent clauses.

In these examples, the independent clauses are underlined once and the subordinate clauses are underlined twice.

Complex: After reading about knights, Don Quixote became a knight.

Complex: Sancho Panza, who accompanied Don Quixote, was a simple peasant, although Don Quixote called Panza his squire.

Compound-complex: When Cervantes wrote about Don Quixote, the age of knighthood was over, and Spain had become a power.

Practice A Identify each sentence as complex or compound-complex. Indicate which clauses are independent and which are subordinate.

1. Although he was born to a king, Mari Djata had a difficult childhood, which made his mother sad.
2. When the king was about to die, he called Mari Djata to him, and he spoke as if the child were an adult.
3. When Mari Djata could not walk, his mother was worried, and her enemies were cruel.

Challenge In the excerpt from *Sundiata: An Epic of Old Mali*, find an example of a complex and a compound-complex sentence.

Practice B Use each phrase below and create a either a complex or compound-complex sentence. You may add words to the phrase if necessary.

1. the boy was chosen for a journey (complex)
2. the sage became angry at the king (compound-complex)
3. the king was protective of his two sons(complex)
4. who went on to become a hero (compound-complex)

Challenge Write a simple sentence about the painting on page 1111. Add a subordinate clause to make it a complex sentence. Then, add another independent clause to make it a compound-complex sentence.

Writing and Grammar Connection: Chapter 28

Extend the Lesson

Sentence Modeling

Choose the sentence given from the selection students have read:

"The queen mother had rushed there and . . . trembled from head to foot." (from "*Sundiata: An Epic of Old Mali*")

"Agasthya had his hermitage in this forest, . . . Sunda fell dead." ("Rama's Initiation" from the *Ramayana*)

Ask students what they notice about the sentence. Elicit from them the type of sentence. Have students identify the clauses. Then, ask them what else they notice. (*Sundiata: An Epic of Old Mali:* Niane describes the most noteworthy events in the independent clauses. "Rama's Initiation" from the *Ramayana:* Narayan describes the dramatic and pivotal events in the independent clauses.)

Have students imitate the sentence in a sentence on a topic of their own choosing, matching each grammatical and stylistic feature discussed. Collect the sentences, and share them with the class.

Writing

The main characters in these two stories each perform heroic feats. Write a **newspaper report** of events at the end of the selection. First, take notes in which you identify main characters and outline story events. As you draft, include the following elements:

- a catchy headline
- information on *who, what, where, when, how,* and *why*
- believable quotations from participants and onlookers
- comments on the significance of the events

After finishing your draft, use a computer's publishing software or a graphic program to design your report. Choose readable headline and text fonts and set the news report in a double-column layout.

Writing Workshop: *Work in Progress*

Prewriting for a Technical Document Use the the Task List from your writing portfolio to create an outline. Fill in and briefly describe additional steps that are necessary to accomplish the task you have. Review your outline to make sure you have listed all the necessary steps. Save the Outline in your writing portfolio.

Use this prewriting activity to prepare for the **Writing Workshop** on page 1146.

Listening and Speaking

With two classmates, present an **improvised dialogue** about one of the following situations:

- A queen of Mali, her son, a rival queen, and a sage discuss an insult the rival queen delivered to the queen.
- An Indian king, his son, and a sage consult about venturing forth against the demons of the world.

Apply what you have learned about West African or Hindu culture, and be sure that characters speak in a manner suited to their position.

- As you prepare, take **concise notes,** concentrating on key words and ideas, so you can incorporate those important points into your dialogue.
- Take 10 minutes to prepare and no more than 10 minutes for the presentation.
- While you present your dialogue, use appropriate **eye contact** and **language choices** to keep your **audience engaged.**
- Stay true to the character you represent, speaking and responding in a way that reflects his or her attitudes and beliefs.

PHLit Online!
www.PHLitOnline.com
- Interactive graphic organizers
- Grammar tutorial
- Interactive journals

EXTEND/ASSESS

Writing

1. Review the assignment, using the instruction on the student page.
2. To guide students in writing a newspaper report, give them **Support for Writing**, p. 90 in ***Unit 6 Resources***.
3. To evaluate students' reports, use the Narrative rubrics on pp. 263–264 in ***Professional Development Guidebook***. In addition, evaluate how well students use strong verbs to portray actions.

Six Traits Focus

✔	Ideas	✔	Word Choice
✔	Organization	✔	Sentence Fluency
	Voice		Conventions

Writing and Grammar, Grade 10

Students will find guidance on narrative writing in Chapter 5.

Writing Workshop
Work in Progress

Have students save their completed outline in their portfolios. They will use the outline later as they complete the Writing Workshop assignment (see pp. 1146–1151).

Listening and Speaking

1. Review the assignment, using the instruction on the student page.
2. To support students' work on the assignment, have students complete the **Support for Extend Your Learning** page (***Unit 6 Resources***, p. 91).

Teaching Resources

All *Unit 6 Resources*
L3 L4 **Integrated Language Skills: Grammar,** p. 89
L3 L4 **Support for Writing,** p. 90
L3 L4 **Support for Extend Your Learning,** p. 91
L4 **Enrichment,** pp. 70, 88

All **Enriched Online Student Edition**
Available under After You Read for this selection:
All **Interactive Grammar Tutorial**
L3 L4 **Internet Research Activity**

Professional Development Guidebook
Rubrics for Technical Document, pp. 261–262

PHLit Online! All print and digital resources are available at **www.PHLitOnline.com.** Online resources accessible by students are noted on the student page.

MONITORING PROGRESS

Using the Test Practice

In this two-page Test Practice, students apply the reading skill for the first half of Unit 6 to a passage of fiction and a passage of nonfiction.

Review this skill, understanding cultural context, and then administer the test. For more guidance, consult the ***Classroom Strategies and Teaching Routines*** card on **Administering Timed Tests.**

ASSESS

Answers

Answers With Explanations

1. **B**—Sentence 4 names specific animals hunted. *Incorrect answers:* A—No details contain dates or places. C—Sentences 4 through 6 mention animal spirits, but not gods. D—Sentences 10 through 12 tell about cooperation, not competition.
2. **A**—Sentences 10 through 12 show that painting was considered crucial to hunting success. *Incorrect answers:* B—Details suggest a primitive culture that could not have developed historical perspective. C—Young people aren't mentioned. D—same explanation as for A.
3. **D**—Sentences 4 through 6 show belief in animal spirits. *Incorrect answers:* A—The passage describes painting, not habitation, in the caves. B—Sentences 10 through 12 show that the paintings were about survival, not enjoyment. C— The passage describes pictures of hunting, not actual hunting in the caves.
4. **A**—Sentences 10 through 12 show that they were early hunters. *Incorrect answers:* B—The story shows one artist, but sentences 10 through 12 show they were a hunting clan. C— The passage describes people who settled, rather than explored, in the cave area. D— Sentence 10 describes a cooperative people who worked together.

Test Practice: Reading

Analyze Cultural Context

Fiction Selection

Directions: *Read the selection. Then, answer the questions.*

Logane lifted the small torch. Darkness surrounded him ahead and behind the small circle of light as he crawled through the damp cave. At last he reached the open cavern. The dim lamplight revealed paintings on the walls—horses, bison, woolly mammoths: the spirits of animals hunted by Logane's people. The flickering flame made the animals seem to move. Logane paused, overwhelmed by the power of the spirits. At last, he removed the stone pots from his skin bag. Each pot contained a different color—black, red, yellow—mixed with animal fat. Logane touched the paint with his brushes, twigs whose ends had been pounded to fine threads. Hunters of Logane's clan were getting ready for the great hunt before the long winter. Logane had to renew the herds through his painting. Only that would ensure success in the hunt.

1. Which of the following questions is answered in this passage?

A. Where and when did Logane's people live?
B. What was an important source of food for Logane's community?
C. What gods did Logane's community worship?
D. How competitive were the members of Logane's community?

2. The details in this passage suggest that, in this culture, cave paintings are considered—

A. necessary for survival because they lead to a successful hunt.
B. a historical record of the accomplishments of the community.
C. valuable ways to teach young people myths and legends.
D. important for their beauty alone.

3. What does the passage show about cultural practices of Logane's people?

A. They lived deep inside caves.
B. They painted animals for enjoyment.
C. They hunted in caves.
D. They believed in animal spirits.

4. Which statement *best* portrays the life of Logane's people?

A. They were prehistoric hunters.
B. They were highly skilled artists.
C. They were brave explorers.
D. They were shy cave dwellers.

Writing for Assessment

Based on the details in this passage, make a list of three values you believe are important in this culture. Write a paragraph in which you explain how you reached your conclusions.

Writing for Assessment

Students should first list several details from the paragraph. Then they should ask themselves the following question about each detail: "Does this detail tell us anything about what these people believed to be important in their lives?" If the answer is "yes," they should use the detail and explain its importance.

Strategies for Test Taking

Suggest that students number each sentence in the passage. As they review each answer choice, they should look for support in the passage. If the choice is correct, they should be able to name one or more sentences that contain the details which support it.

Nonfiction Selection

Directions: *Read the selection. Then, answer the questions.*

The prehistoric people called "Cro-Magnon" were the first known people to practice art. Cro-Magnons were early modern humans who lived in caves and rock shelters throughout Spain and France from 35,000 years ago to about 10,000 years ago. Many of the rock shelters and caves show signs of habitation over long periods of time. Cro-Magnon people carved and sculpted figures of animals as well as humans. The Cro-Magnons also created beautiful cave paintings of animals, which probably related to their ritual beliefs and practices. Cro-Magnon art is highly sophisticated, showing that they were not amateurs but had long been experimenting with creating art in various mediums. They decorated their weapons and tools as well.

1. Which question about Cro-Magnon culture is *not* answered by this passage?

A. Who created art before the Cro-Magnons did?
B. Where did Cro-Magnons live?
C. Why did Cro-Magnons decorate their weapons and tools?
D. What types of art did Cro-Magnons create?

2. Based on this passage, what could you conclude about the lifestyle of Cro-Magnons?

A. They had enough surplus food and time to create art.
B. They were all highly skilled hunters.
C. They were primitive people who feared animals.
D. They appreciated music.

3. Cro-Magnons lived in Europe for about 25,000 years. Based on this and other details in the passage, what do you think this indicates about their culture?

A. Their culture was the only one in Europe at the time.
B. Cro-Magnon culture was constantly changing.
C. Cro-Magnon culture was relatively stable over a long period of time.
D. They were bloodthirsty, powerful, and able to drive out other culture groups.

4. Based on this passage, one can infer that the Cro-Magnon people—

A. believed animals were for food only.
B. placed a high value on animals.
C. worshiped animals as gods.
D. used animals for food and clothing.

Writing for Assessment

Connecting Across Texts
What details in the second passage might lead you to conclude that Logane is one of the Cro-Magnon people? Write a detailed paragraph in which you support your answer.

PHLit Online!
www.PHLitOnline.com
- Online practice
- Instant feedback

ASSESS

Answers

Answers With Explanations

1. C—The last sentence says they had weapons but does not tell why they decorated them. *Incorrect answers:* A—The first sentence answers the question: The Cro-Magnons were first. B—The second sentence answers the question: They lived in Spain and France. D— The last four sentences answer this question.
2. A—The fact that artists decorated the caves suggests surplus food and time. *Incorrect answers:* B—They were not all hunters; some were artists. C—The fact that they hunted animals suggests they did not fear them. D—No detail mentions music.
3. C—Sentence 2 names a long time span, and sentence 3 points to signs of long habitation. *Incorrect answers:* A—The passage doesn't say whether or not they were the only cultural group. B—Sentences 2 and 3 suggest stability rather than change. D—Other contemporary groups are not mentioned.
4. B— Sentences 4 and 5 suggest that animals were highly valued. *Incorrect answers:* A—Sentence 5 suggests animals figured in their religious rituals; they were not just food. C— Sentence 5 suggests animals figured in their religious rituals, not that they were worshipped. D— The passage doesn't suggest the uses of animals.

Writing for Assessment

Students should list the important details from the passage related to Cro-Magnon life. Then they should circle any details from the list which also appear in the story. They can use these as the basis for their writing.

PHLit Online!

Students may take the test in interactive format with instant feedback online at **www.PHLitOnline.com**.

Differentiated Instruction for Universal Access

Strategy for Less Proficient Readers
Most of the difficult vocabulary in the nonfiction selection relates to *Cro-Magnon art*. Create a word web with the words Cro-Magnon art in a middle circle. Invite students to find words and phrases from the passage related to their art (*carved figures, sculpted figures, animals, humans, cave paintings, rituals, sophisticated, various mediums, decorated weapons, tools*).

Strategy for Special Needs Students
Have students close their eyes as you read aloud the story of Logane on page 1120. Ask them to visualize each thing he saw or did. Then have small groups reread the passage and then create a graphic comic showing each thing he saw and did. Finally, have them answer the questions together.

PRETEACH

Meeting Your Standards

Students will

1. generate questions.
2. read and understand an interview and a public document.

*Log on at **www.PHLitOnline.com** for a detailed lesson plan for Informational Texts.*

Reading Skill

1. Introduce the skill, using the instruction on the student page.
2. Review the chart.
3. Tell students that they will generate questions as they read.

Think Aloud: Model the Skill

Model the skill of generating questions, using the following "think aloud." Say to students:

Let's say that I read an interview with the new Chief of Police. I preview the interview and see that the questions focus on the chief's years of service, policies, and plans for public safety. I will think of questions I have and look for answers to them as I read. As I find the answers, I will think of other questions that I can find the answers to on my own.

Can anyone be a hero?

Have students look for qualities that contribute to making someone a hero.

Multidraft Reading

Have students follow a multidraft reading protocol after they read.

- **First reading:** Have students read for general understanding.
- **Second reading:** Have students generate questions about the text.
- **Third reading:** Have students look for qualities that contribute to making someone a hero.

Informational Texts

Real-Life Reading

Interview
Careers in Science: Firefighter

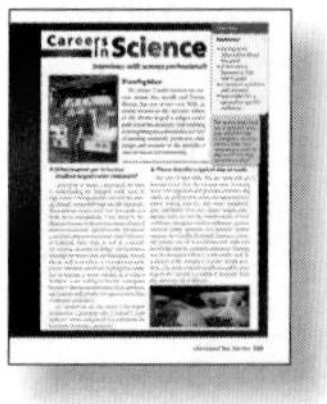

Public Document
Firefighters Physical Agility Test

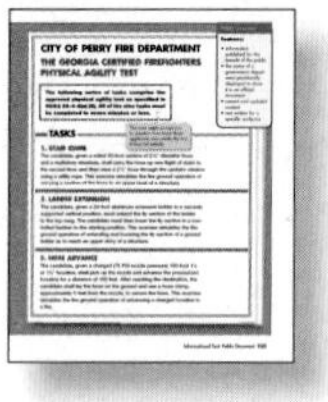

Reading Skill: Generate Questions

To better understand informational texts, read actively and engage the text by **generating questions.** First, preview the text and use your background knowledge to make predictions about its content, formulating questions that you expect to have answered. Then, as you read, look for answers to those questions, and generate additional relevant questions about the issues discussed in the text that you can research later. Use a chart like this one to help you generate questions.

What I Know	What I Learned	Relevant Questions
You need a high school diploma to become a firefighter.	A college degree is required for some firefighting positions.	What additional education and training is necessary to advance in a firefighting career?

THE BIG ?

Can anyone be a *hero?*

The interview and the public document suggest that firefighters must be dedicated, courageous, and strong. Consider what qualities might contribute to making someone a hero.

Differentiated Instruction for Universal Access

Reading Support
Give students reading support with the appropriate version of the ***Reader's Notebooks***:

- L2 L3 ***Reader's Notebook***
- L1 ***Reader's Notebook: Adapted Version***
- EL ***Reader's Notebook: English Learner's Version***

PHLit Online! All student resources, are available at **www.PHLitOnline.com.**

Careers in Science

Interviews with science professionals

Interview

Features:

- background information about the guest
- a discussion between a host and a guest
- a series of questions and answers
- text written for a general or specific audience

Firefighter

The Science Teacher focuses on success stories this month and Denise Dierich has one of her own. With an innate interest in the dynamic nature of life, Denise forged a unique career path. From biochemistry and teaching, to firefighting and paramedics, her love of learning constantly yields new challenges and rewards as she provides a vital service to her community.

This section might lead you to generate questions about the lives of firefighters working 24-hour shifts: *How many days a week do they work? Can they rest while on duty?*

1. What inspired you to become involved in your career endeavors?

Growing up in Alaska, I appreciated the value of understanding the biological world. Later, in high school, a biology teacher extended this interest through various field trips and lab demonstrations—science became more than just words in a book. As an undergraduate, I was drawn to biochemistry because it offered explanations of natural phenomena and how organisms work. (Denise has a bachelor's degree in biochemistry from University of California, Santa Cruz, as well as a secondary teaching credential in biology and chemistry.) Although the science itself was fascinating, I found the lab work to be tedious so I pursued a career in science education, which was anything but boring. Just as teaching is service-oriented, so is being a firefighter. I left teaching to become a firefighter because it also incorporates many of my ambitions and interests and provides the opportunity to help people and communities.

As I worked on aid calls (when a fire engine accompanies a paramedic unit), I realized I could apply my science background and enthusiasm for learning by becoming a paramedic.

2. Please describe a typical day at work.

We work 24-hour shifts. The day starts with an informal report from the previous crew involving issues with equipment and potential problems. Rig checks are performed to ensure the apparatus is in proper working order (i.e., fuel, fluids, equipment, gear, and lights). Next, our captain assigns training and duties for the day, which consist of hose evolutions, emergency medical technician practice scenarios, pump operation, and hydraulic system exercises, for example. Continual training is essential; because the job is so multifaceted, skills and knowledge must be constantly reinforced. Training may be interrupted if there is a call, which could be a medical or fire emergency, a motor vehicle accident, a fire alarm, a hazardous spill, or a public assist request. We respond to a variety of situations. Each day, and every call, is different.

TEACH

About Interviews

1. Direct students' attention to the Features box on Interviews. Explain that an interview includes the interviewer's questions and direct quotes from the interviewee.
2. Invite students to discuss interviews they have read.
   Possible response: Students may say that they have read interviews in their favorite magazines or newspapers about current actors, athletes, or politicians.
3. **Ask** students what expectations they have when they read an interview.
   Possible response: When I read an interview, I expect to learn more about the subject, or guest, than I knew before I read it.

Generate Questions

1. Remind students that it is important to consider what they know about a topic when they read an interview.
2. Invite students to preview the interview and use what they know to list questions they think will be answered in the text. Then, **ask** volunteers to share questions from their lists.
   Possible response: Students may say that they expect to learn about how Denise Dierich became a firefighter and how the experience and knowledge of being a science teacher helped her succeed.
3. Have students read the interview and the side notes. Remind them to look for answers to their questions as they read.
4. **Ask** students to discuss whether their questions about the text were answered.
   Possible response: Students may say that their questions were answered and that they have further questions that they want answered. Others may say that their questions were not answered and that they need to preview and read the interview again.

Differentiated Instruction for Universal Access

Support for Special Needs Students
Students who are struggling to generate relevant questions may benefit from working with the chart from p. 1122 in the student text. Display the **Three-column Chart**, ***Graphic Organizer Transparencies*** p. 237, and label it *What I Know*, *What I Learned*, and *Relevant Questions*. Ask students to offer information from the text for the first two columns. Then, work with students to help them generate questions based on the information listed.

Enrichment for Advanced Readers
Challenge students to research the history of firefighters. They might visit a local firehouse or set up an interview with a firefighter. Direct students to fill in a three-column chart similar to the one in the student text. When they have finished their research, have students present their findings to the class and discuss the methods they plan to use to answer their relevant questions.

Generate Questions

1. Remind students that they should think about ways to further their understanding of information they learn in a text.
2. **Ask** students to offer questions they still have after reading the interview.
   Possible response: How long does it take to become a firefighter? What is the most challenging aspect of being a firefighter?
3. Discuss with students how they would find answers to their questions.
   Possible response: Students may say that they will research firefighting at the local library or on the Internet.

ASSESS/EXTEND

Answers

Can anyone be a hero?

(a) Denise Dierich became a firefighter because it is a dynamic job that allows her to provide a service to the community.
(b) **Possible response:** Heroes are motivated to do what is right and put the interest of others ahead of their own.

3. *How do you use your science background in the fire service?*

The problem-solving skills developed through my science education have been very beneficial in my career as a firefighter. No fire or aid call is the same; we have to constantly evaluate situations and react appropriately. My background in biochemistry and study skills acquired through college science classes have been instrumental in preparing for the academic portion of the paramedic program—a commitment that involves several courses and certification tests.

When previewing, you might scan this boldface question and want to find out what kind of science background could be used in the fire service. When reading, you would discover the answer.

4. *What advice would you give to an interested high school student?*

The more education obtained, the better—it will only help a career in the fire service. The only specific requirement for eligibility is a high school diploma; however, a bachelor's degree shows self-discipline and the ability to complete tasks. Firefighting has become a very popular and competitive field—600 people tested for five openings in our last round. For some areas of advancement, a bachelor's degree is required (for example, a college degree is needed to become a battalion chief). Also, most firefighting tests include a fitness component, which can be quite demanding.

When reading, you might note that you'd like to research the fitness component of the firefighting test: *What is involved? Why is it considered demanding?*

Investigate the possibilities for a ride-along with local fire departments. Many firefighters and paramedics allow civilians to ride a medic unit or engine for part of a day. Consider joining a volunteer fire department; they will provide training and valuable experience. Some volunteer districts even provide housing at the station and help finance college tuitions.

5. *Is there anything else you would like to share?*

One of the things I like best about this job is that, like science, it is dynamic. There are always new things to learn. The best preparation is to enjoy learning. Firefighting is an honorable field that is respected by the community, and I enjoy the camaraderie and teamwork that are essential to the job.

Can anyone be a hero?

(a) According to the interview, what motivated Denise Dierich to become a firefighter? (b) How is this motivation similar to the qualities that motivate heroes?

CITY OF PERRY FIRE DEPARTMENT

THE GEORGIA CERTIFIED FIREFIGHTERS PHYSICAL AGILITY TEST

The following series of tasks comprise the approved physical agility test as specified in OCGA 25-4-8(a) (5). All of the nine tasks must be completed in seven minutes or less.

This note might prompt you to question how many times applicants may retake the test if they fail initially.

Public Document

Features:

- information published for the benefit of the public
- the name of a government department prominently displayed to show it is an official document
- current and updated content
- text written for a specific audience

TASKS

1. STAIR CLIMB

The candidate, given a rolled 50-foot section of 2½" diameter hose and a multistory structure, shall carry the hose up one flight of stairs to the second floor and then raise a 2½" hose through the upstairs window using a utility rope. This exercise simulates the fire ground operation of carrying a section of fire hose to an upper level of a structure.

2. LADDER EXTENSION

The candidate, given a 24-foot aluminum extension ladder in a securely supported vertical position, must extend the fly section of the ladder to the top rung. The candidate must then lower the fly section in a controlled fashion to the starting position. This exercise simulates the fire ground operation of extending and lowering the fly section of a ground ladder as to reach an upper story of a structure.

3. HOSE ADVANCE

The candidate, given a charged (75 PSI nozzle pressure) 150-foot 1½" or 1¾" hoseline, shall pick up the nozzle and advance the pressurized hoseline for a distance of 100 feet. After reaching the destination, the candidate shall lay the hose on the ground and use a hose clamp, approximately 5 feet from the nozzle, to secure the hose. This exercise simulates the fire ground operation of advancing a charged hoseline to a fire.

About Public Documents

1. Review the list of public document features on the student page with the class. Point out that public documents are official documents published for the general public, containing current informative material.
2. Invite students to list instances when they use public documents. Then, **ask** them to explain why public documents are helpful on these occasions.
   Possible response: Students may say that they use public documents when they are interested in services that are available to the public because all of the information they need is located in one place.

Generate Questions

1. Remind students that they should preview a text so they can set expectations for what they think will be covered.
2. Have students review the first three tasks on this page. Then, **ask** them to offer expectations they have about the document.
   Possible response: Students may say that they expect to learn details about the tasks in the physical agility tests, and the number of tasks a candidate must complete.
3. Reminds students that they may not find answers to all of their questions. **Ask** them to discuss methods they could use to find answers to any of their unanswered questions.
   Possible response: Students may say they could contact the governing body that issued the document and request any information that was not covered.
4. Point out any methods for obtaining answers to their questions or other questions students may have overlooked.

Differentiated Instruction for Universal Access

Enrichment for Gifted and Talented Students

Challenge students to work in pairs to prepare a dramatization of an oral interview between an interviewer and a person hoping to become a firefighter. Instruct each pair to begin by brainstorming for relevant questions they think would be asked during an interview. Have each pair decide which student will be the interviewer and the interviewee. Encourage them to create a draft of their interview and prepare a brief performance for the class. Allow time for the pairs to present their interviews to the class.

EL Strategy for English Learners

Students may benefit from reviewing the format of the public document before reading it. Walk them through the pages of the document, and point out the headings and subheads. You may also want to offer students examples of questions they might expect to have answered. Ask students to write those questions on a separate sheet of paper and place a check mark next to each when they find the answer in the text.

Generate Questions

1. Direct students to the second part of the physical agility test.
2. Have students preview the section and then read it.
3. **Ask** students to discuss relevant questions they generated as they read.
   Possible response: Students may say that they want to know how someone might prepare for this test and how many times a person can retake the test.

Reflecting on the Skill

After students have read both selections, **ask** them to consider what they found most interesting when applying the skill.
Possible response: Students may say that they found it interesting to see how many times a selection did or did not meet their expectations.

ASSESS/EXTEND

Answers

Can anyone be a hero?

Sample answer: A person needs to be honest, intelligent, possess a great deal of integrity, and be able to endure the physical demands required to be a firefighter.

4. BOX FAN CARRY

The candidate, given a gas generated box fan, shall use proper lifting techniques, and carry the box fan for a distance of 50 feet. After reaching the destination, the candidate shall set the box fan on the ground. This exercise simulates carrying bulky objects on the fire scene, to and from the structure.

5. UPPER SLED HIT

The candidate, given a 12-pound sledgehammer, shall hit an object placed on top of the sled for a distance of 2 feet. The candidate then shall go to the other side of the sled and hit the same object in the opposite direction 2 feet. This exercise simulates using tools on the fire ground in a standing position using upper torso strength.

Most items in the list include an explanation that answers questions about the purpose of each task.

6. CONE COURSE

The candidate shall walk through a cone course that is approximately 50 feet in length.

7. VENTILATION EXERCISE

Given a fire department axe and standing on level ground with a target (such as a wooden pallet) placed on the ground in front of them, the candidate must strike the target with the axe 20 times. The axe must be brought completely over the shoulder to simulate a chopping motion as if cutting a ventilation hole.

8. LADDER REMOVAL/REPLACEMENT

The candidate, given a 14-foot roof ladder placed in a horizontal position at a height of 5 feet and with the ladder rungs in a vertical position, shall lift the ladder from its support and place it on the ground then pick it up and return it to its original position. This exercise simulates the fire ground operation of removing from and replacing a ladder on its mounting bracket on the fire apparatus.

9. RESCUE DRAG

The candidate, given a 165-pound dummy on a level paved surface, shall drag the dummy a distance of 50 feet. This exercise simulates the fire ground operation of an emergency removal from a hazardous area of a team member or victim who may be rendered incapacitated.

Can anyone be a hero?
According to the document, what qualities does someone need to become a firefighter in Georgia?

Vocabulary Development

Vocabulary from Public Documents

Point out that public documents often use vocabulary that is specific to a particular subject, in this case firefighting. Guide students to understand the meaning of the following words that are used in the public document:

simulates: imitates
ventilation: the act of providing fresh air in place of air that has been used or contaminated
apparatus: a complex instrument or mechanism for a particular purpose
incapacitated: unable to act or respond

PHLit Online! **Vocabulary Development**, featuring tools, activities and songs for studying vocabulary, is available at **www.PHLitOnline.com.**

Test Practice: Informational Texts

Comparing Informational Texts

(a) Make a list of questions generated by scanning the headings and subheadings in the interview and public document. List at least three questions for each text. **(b)** Which text's headings and subheadings were more helpful in prompting you to **generate questions?** Explain.

Timed Writing

Write a Letter

Format and Audience
The prompt directs you to write a letter to a firefighter. Therefore, be sure you properly format your response and use formal language that is appropriate for your audience.

Write a letter to a firefighter in which you request additional information about firefighting as a career. In your letter, cite specific passages from the interview and public document, and ask questions based on those passages. (35 minutes)

Academic Vocabulary
When you *cite* a passage, you refer to it as an example.

5-Minute Planner

Complete these steps before you begin to write:

1. Read the prompt carefully and completely. Notice key words, like the ones highlighted, that give specific instructions about the assignment.
2. Review the interview and public document to identify aspects of firefighting that interest you. Note the passages in which those topics are covered, and generate questions that are not answered in either of the texts. **TIP** To help organize your notes, create a two-column chart. List your questions in the left column of the chart. In the right column, list the passages that deal with the topics of your questions.
3. Decide how you will structure your letter. For example, you might include a brief introductory paragraph in which you explain that you are researching firefighting as a career and would like to request information on the subject.
4. Prepare a quick outline, based on the structure you have chosen for your letter. Then, refer to your outline and your notes as you write.

Extend the Lesson

Connecting to the Students' World

To help students enhance their understanding of interviews and public documents and to help them apply the lesson to their own world, divide students into pairs. Have each pair choose a safety agency in their community. Have students research a profession in the agency by finding public documents. Then, have them conduct a mock interview with their partner, having one person pretend to be in that profession. Instruct them to generate relevant questions that a person interested in joining the agency might have.

Comparing Informational Texts

(a) Possible response: Interview: What are the age requirements for becoming a firefighter? What type of science background is useful for a firefighter? How much education does a person need to become a firefighter? **Public document:** How can someone prepare for the agility test? How many times can a person retake the test? Can a person who does not know how to swim become a firefighter?

(b) Possible response: Students may say that the headings and subheadings in the interview were more helpful because they allowed students to generate questions regarding Denise's decision to become a firefighter. Others may say that the headings and subheadings in the public document were more helpful because each focuses on a particular aspect of the agility test.

Timed Writing

1. Before students complete the activity, guide them in identifying and analyzing key words and phrases in the prompt, highlighted on the student page.
2. Work with students to draw up guidelines for their responses based on the key words in the prompt:
   - **Focus** The letter should request information about firefighting as a career.
   - **Organization** The letter should present a request and cite passages from the selections.
   - **Elaboration** The letter should provide supporting details and information from cited passages, as well as questions about the passages.
   - **Style** The audience is a firefighter, so a formal style is suitable.
3. Have students use the 5-Minute Planner to structure their time.
4. Allow students 35 minutes to complete the assignment. Evaluate their work using the guidelines they have developed.

PRETEACH

Meeting Your Standards

Students will

1. analyze and respond to archetypal narrative patterns.
2. compare the effects of archetypal narrative patterns in two works of fiction.
3. write a comparison of archetypal narrative patterns.

Log on at ***www.PHLitOnline.com*** *for a detailed lesson plan for Comparing Literary Works.*

1 Comparing Archetypal Narrative Patterns

1. Introduce the skill using the instruction on the student page.
2. Give students a copy of Comparing **Archetypal Narrative Patterns Graphic Organizer B,** ***Graphic Organizer Transparencies,*** p. 206. Tell them they will fill it in with details as they read.

Think Aloud: Model the Skill

Model a way to identify archetypal narrative patterns. Say to students:

I know that romance novels often follow a pattern: boy gets girl, boy loses girl, and boy does something to get girl again. This plot line appears in so many romance novels that they become archetypal patterns for this kind of story. Stories that began as oral literature have patterns, too. I identify those patterns by looking at their plots for similarities.

2 Vocabulary

1. Have students say each word aloud.
2. Then, use the word in a sentence that defines the word. Repeat the sentence, now with the word missing, and have the class "fill in the blank" chorally.

For more guidance, see the ***Classroom Strategies and Teaching Routines*** card, **Introducing Selection Vocabulary.**

Comparing Literary Works

Cupid and Psyche • Ashputtle

1 Comparing Archetypal Narrative Patterns

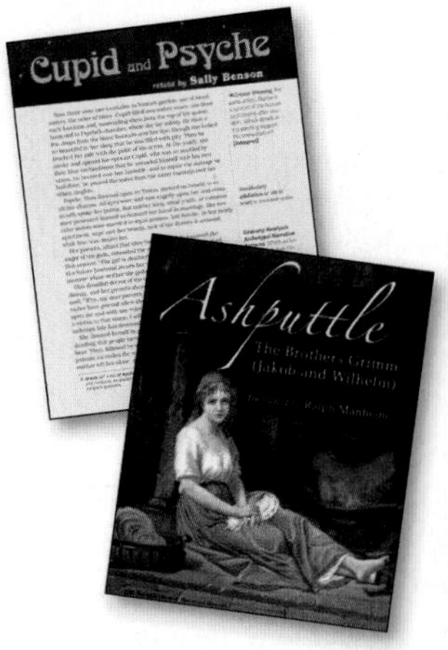

Archetypal narrative patterns are basic storytelling patterns found in the stories of cultures around the world. These patterns often appear in stories originally passed along orally, such as fairy tales and myths. Like familiar routines, patterns make the stories easier to remember and retell. Common archetypal narrative patterns include the following:

- a series of tests that a character must pass
- a quest or task a character must perform
- characters, events, or objects that come in threes
- a greedy, cruel, or jealous relative who behaves unfairly
- a hero who triumphs over stronger forces through cleverness or virtue
- a just end that rewards good or punishes evil

By analyzing and comparing patterns in stories, literary critics attempt to study literature in an objective way. Their results may also reveal something about the way human beings organize and understand information. As you read the selections, analyze the narrative patterns in each story using a chart like the one shown.

Story Detail	Archetypal Pattern
three sisters	characters that come in threes
help from the birds	

2 Vocabulary

- **adulation** (a´ jo͞o lā´ shən) *n.* excessive praise (p. 1131) *Rock stars may grow used to the adulation of fans.* adulate *v.*
- **allay** (a lā´) *v.* relieve; lessen; calm (p. 1134) *One look at the dog's sweet face will allay your fear of him.* allaying *v.* allayer *n.*
- **plague** (plāg) *v.* pester; harass; torment (p. 1139) *She is studying for a test, so do not plague her with questions.* plague *n.*
- **jeered** (jird) *v.* made fun of (p. 1139) *The fans jeered when the opposing outfielder dropped the ball.* jeer *v.* jeers *n.* jeering *adj.*

PHLit Online! www.PHLitOnline.com

- Vocabulary flashcards
- Interactive journals
- More about the authors
- Selection audio
- Interactive graphic organizers

Vocabulary Development

Vocabulary Knowledge Rating

Create a **Vocabulary Knowledge Rating Chart** (***Professional Development Guidebook***, p. 33) for this selection. Include the selection vocabulary and the Big Question word that appears in the Writing About the Big Question sentence starter. (The Big Question vocabulary is introduced on pp.1046–1047.)

Give students a copy of the chart. Read the words aloud, and have students mark their rating in the Before Reading column. Urge them to be alert to these words as they read and discuss the selection.

Tally how many students think they know a word to gauge how much instruction to provide. As students read and discuss the selection, point out the words and their context.

PHLit Online! **Vocabulary Central**, featuring tools, activities, and songs for studying vocabulary, is available online at **www.PHLitOnline.com.**

Can anyone be a *hero?*

3 Writing About the Big Question

In both "Cupid and Psyche" and "Ashputtle," the main characters face unusual obstacles. As you read the selections, you can decide if their actions in the face of these challenges are heroic. Use this sentence starter to develop your ideas about the Big Question.

In the face of an unusual obstacle, a true hero would show **attributes** such as _______________ and _______________.

Meet the Authors

Lucius Apuleius (ca. A.D. 124–170)
Sally Benson (1900–1972)

Authors of "Cupid and Psyche"

Although the tale of Cupid and Psyche goes back to Greek mythology, the best-known version is in the *Metamorphoses* by the ancient Roman writer Lucius Apuleius (lo͞o′ shəs ap′ yo͞o lē′ əs). This work is often considered the world's first novel.

A Modern Reteller Sally Benson won fame with her short stories. Her collection *Meet Me in St. Louis,* based on her own Missouri childhood, was adapted as a movie musical.

Jakob Grimm (1785–1863)
Wilhelm Grimm (1786–1859)

Authors of "Ashputtle"

Born in the German state of Hesse, Jakob and Wilhelm Grimm grew up in poverty after their father died. Although both studied law, they were most interested in language and literature. Eventually both brothers found work as librarians.

A National Literature The brothers began collecting tales that people told in Hesse and neighboring places. They also wrote books on literature, and Jakob made contributions to linguistics. Today, they are most remembered for the folktales they preserved, including "Rumpelstiltskin" and "Snow White."

Daily Bellringer

For each class during which you will teach this selection, have students complete one of the five Vocabulary activities for Week 33 in the ***Daily Bellringer Activities*** booklet.

3 Writing About the Big Question

1. Review the assignment with the class.
2. Explain that heroism does not necessarily involve actions that place a person in physical danger. Sometimes people show heroism by standing up for others or acting according to principle.
3. Have students complete the sentence starter. Review responses as a class.
(**Possible response:** In the face of an unusual obstacle, a true hero would show attributes such as perseverance and adherence to basic values.)
4. Remind students that their answers will help them think about the Big Question, "Can anyone be a hero?"
Tell students that as they read, they should look for ways the characters handle the obstacles they face.

Concept Connector

Tell students that they will return to their sentence starter after they have concluded reading.

Multidraft Reading

To assist struggling readers and to deepen reading for all, apply multidraft reading protocols. For each reading, have students set the purpose intended:

- **First reading**—literal comprehension: answering the Reading Check questions
- **Second reading**—application of skills: responding to the side-column notes
- **Third reading**—interpretation: answering the end-of-selection questions

For more guidance, refer to the ***Classroom Strategies and Teaching Routines*** card on multidraft reading.

Teaching Resources

The following resources can be used to enrich, extend, or differentiate the instruction.

All *Unit 6 Resources,* pp. 101–117
All *Professional Development Guidebook,* pp. 33, 44
All *Graphic Organizer Transparencies,* pp. 205–208
All Enriched Online Student Edition

PHLit Online! All resources, including print and audio, are available online at **www.PHLitOnline.com.**

PHLit Online!

For more about the authors, practice with the selection vocabulary, and more background, go online at **www.PHLitOnline.com.**

❶ Background

Roman mythology Ancient Roman mythology borrowed heavily from its Greek counterpart. Before the Romans came into contact with the Greeks and other cultures, they had a religious system in place, but the basis of the Roman myths can be traced to Greek mythology. Many of the gods and goddesses found in each tradition share the same characteristics but have different names; for example, the Greeks named their goddess of love Aphrodite, and the Romans called their goddess of love Venus. The Romans kept some Greek names, however; in fact, Psyche is a Greek name that means "soul."

❷ Activating Prior Knowledge

Before students read the myth, in which envy or jealousy motivates several characters, remind them that envy or jealousy is often referred to as "the green-eyed monster." Suggest that students draw their own interpretations of "the green-eyed monster," incorporating words into their drawings that suggest the people or items of which others sometimes feel envious or jealous. Tell students to include words that capture the consequences of envy or jealousy as well. Invite students to share their monsters with the class.

Concept Connector ⟶

Students will follow up on this activity after completing the selection.

❸ About the Selection

Psyche, a beautiful mortal woman, inadvertently draws attention and admiration away from Venus, the goddess of love. Venus sends her son, Cupid, the god of love, to exact her revenge. As the story unfolds, Psyche learns about the value of trust and the power of true love to persevere through difficult circumstances. This myth contains archetypal patterns that students may recognize. Some students may see similarities between this selection and the tale of "Beauty and the Beast."

Cupid

❶ ❷ ❸

There once lived a king and queen who had three daughters. The two elder daughters were beautiful, but the youngest daughter, Psyche,[1] was the loveliest maiden in the whole world. The fame of her beauty was so great that strangers from neighboring countries came in crowds to admire her, paying her the homage which is only due Venus[2] herself. In fact, Venus found her altars deserted, as men turned their devotion to the exquisite young girl. People sang her praises as she walked the streets, and strewed chaplets and flowers before her.

This **adulation** infuriated Venus. Shaking her silken locks in indignation, she exclaimed, "Am I then to be eclipsed by a mortal girl? In vain did that royal shepherd whose judgment was approved by Jupiter himself give me the palm of beauty over my illustrious rivals, Minerva and Juno.[3] I will give this Psyche cause to repent of so unlawful a beauty."

She complained to her son, Cupid, and led him to the land where Psyche lived, so that he could see for himself the insults the girl unconsciously heaped upon his mother. "My dear son," said Venus, "punish that beauty. Give thy mother a revenge as sweet as her injuries are great. Infuse into the bosom of that haughty girl a passion for some low, mean, unworthy being, so that she may reap a shame as great as her present joy and triumph."

1. **Psyche** (sī′ kē) a beautiful princess in Roman mythology.
2. **Venus** (vē′ nəs) the Roman goddess of love and beauty.
3. **royal shepherd. . . Minerva** (mi nur′ və) **and Juno** (jo͞o′ nō) In Greek and Roman mythology, Paris, a prince who lived as a shepherd, was called to judge who was most beautiful of three goddesses: Juno, queen of the gods; Minerva, goddess of wisdom; or Venus, goddess of love.

❹

Vocabulary Development

Word Forms

Give students a blank **Word Form Chart** (***Professional Development Guidebook,*** p. 42) with *adulation* and *allay* in the correct columns. Work with the class, or have students work with a partner, to determine the related forms. The final chart should look like the one shown.

Noun	Verb	Adjective	Adverb
adulation	adulate	adulatory	
allayment	**allay**		

and Psyche

retold by **Sally Benson**

Now, there were two fountains in Venus's garden, one of sweet waters, the other of bitter. Cupid filled two amber vases, one from each fountain and, suspending them from the top of his quiver, hastened to Psyche's chamber, where she lay asleep. He shed a few drops from the bitter fountain over her lips, though she looked so beautiful in her sleep that he was filled with pity. Then he touched her side with the point of his arrow. At the touch, she awoke and opened her eyes on Cupid, who was so startled by their blue enchantment that he wounded himself with his own arrow. He hovered over her, invisible, and to repair the damage he had done, he poured the water from the sweet fountain over her silken ringlets.

6 Psyche, thus frowned upon by Venus, derived no benefit from all her charms. All eyes were still cast eagerly upon her and every mouth spoke her praise, but neither king, royal youth, or common man presented himself to demand her hand in marriage. Her two elder sisters were married to royal princes, but Psyche, in her lonely apartment, wept over her beauty, sick of the flattery it aroused, while love was denied her.

Her parents, afraid that they had unwittingly incurred the anger of the gods, consulted the oracle of Apollo,[4] and received this answer: "The girl is destined for the bride of no mortal lover. Her future husband awaits her on the top of the mountain. He is a monster whom neither the gods nor men can resist."

This dreadful decree of the oracle filled all the people with dismay, and her parents abandoned themselves to grief. But Psyche said, "Why, my dear parents, do you now lament me? You should rather have grieved when the people showered undeserved honors upon me and with one voice called me 'Venus.' I now perceive I am a victim to that name. I submit. Lead me to that rock to which my unhappy fate has destined me."

She dressed herself in gorgeous robes, and her beauty was so dazzling that people turned away as it was more than they could bear. Then, followed by wailing and lamenting crowds, she and her parents ascended the mountain. On the summit, her father and mother left her alone, and returned home in tears.

4. oracle (ôr´ ə kəl) **of Apollo** (ə päl´ ō) Apollo was the Greek and Roman god of light, music, and medicine. An oracle was a person who revealed the will of the gods in answer to people's questions.

5 ◀ **Critical Viewing** For some artists, Psyche is a symbol of the human soul striving after wisdom. Which details in this painting support this interpretation? **[Interpret]**

Literary Analysis
Archetypal Narrative Patterns Which archetypal pattern does the fact that there are three sisters illustrate?

Vocabulary
adulation (a´ jo͞o lā´ shən) *n.* excessive praise

7 **Reading Check**
Why is Venus angry with Psyche?

4 Humanities

Psyche Gazes in Despair at Cupid Flying Away, by Sir Edward Burne-Jones

This painting, by Pre-Raphaelite painter Edward Burne-Jones, dramatically depicts Cupid's abandonment of Psyche. Its bright colors and simplicity are characteristic of the Pre-Raphaelite movement.

Ask students how this painting emphasizes the trauma of Cupid and Psyche's separation.
Possible response: Cupid and Psyche are depicted in two panels that illustrate their split. Also, the artist uses perspective to emphasize their separation: the larger Psyche appears very close, and the smaller Cupid appears farther away.

5 Critical Viewing

Possible response: Cupid symbolizes wisdom as he leaves Psyche behind in the dark. She is human and he is a god, so she cannot know what he knows. She seems to be striving after him, but since she cannot fly, she cannot catch him.

6 Literary Analysis

Archetypal Narrative Patterns

1. Remind students that they may recognize patterns in a selection because they have read or heard similar patterns in other stories.
2. **Ask** the Literary Analysis question. **Answer:** In the oral tradition, characters often come in threes.
3. **Ask** students to think of tales in which characters appear in threes. **Possible responses:** "The Three Little Pigs"; "Three Blind Mice"
4. Explain that the number three can symbolize birth, life, and death.

7 Reading Check

Answer: Venus is angry because the people who admire Psyche's beauty are deserting Venus' altars.

Differentiated Instruction for Universal Access

Accessibility at a Glance

Use this information to guide your teaching of "Cupid and Psyche."

Context	Mythological story of Cupid and his wife Psyche
Language/Vocabulary	• Mythological and ancient Roman vocabulary defined • Above-grade vocabulary
Concept Level	Accessible (love and envy)
Literary Merit	Classic mythology
Lexile/Length	Lexile: 1240L Word Count: 3,178

PHLit Online!

This selection is available in interactive format in the **Enriched Online Student Edition, www.PHLitOnline.com,** which includes an interactive graphic organizer.

❽ Humanities

Cupid and Psyche, by Sir Edward Burne-Jones

This painting is also by the Pre-Raphaelite painter Sir Edward Burne-Jones. Medieval and religious themes are the subjects of many Pre-Raphaelite paintings, and Burne-Jones found inspiration in the stories of medieval chivalry, the legends of King Arthur, and myths like that of Cupid and Psyche. *Cupid and Psyche*'s painstaking detail and vibrant colors are characteristic of the Pre-Raphaelite school.

Ask: How is the scene depicted here different from Cupid and Psyche's first encounter in the selection?
Answer: In the selection, Psyche is asleep in her room when Cupid arrives. In the painting, Cupid gazes on Psyche as she dozes outdoors in a garden.

❾ Critical Viewing

Answer: Cupid seems to gaze upon Psyche lovingly. Also, his arrows are not pointed at her.

❿ Literary Analysis

Archetypal Narrative Patterns

1. Read aloud the bracketed passage. Remind students that a common characteristic of archetypal narratives is a test that a character must pass.
2. **Ask** the Literary Analysis question: What test does Cupid set for Psyche?
   Answer: Cupid asks Psyche to make no attempt to see him.
3. **Ask** students why Cupid thinks this test is necessary.
   Possible response: Students may say that Cupid wants to test Psyche's ability to trust.

9 ▲ **Critical Viewing** Which details of this painting suggest Cupid's love for Psyche? **[Analyze]**

While Psyche stood on the ridge of the mountain, panting with fear and sobbing aloud, the gentle Zephyrus[5] raised her from the earth and bore her with an easy motion into a flowery dale. There she lay down on a grassy bank and fell asleep. She awoke refreshed, and saw near by a pleasant grove of tall and stately trees. She entered it, and discovered a fountain sending forth clear and crystal waters, and near it stood a magnificent palace that was too stupendous to have been the work of mortal hands. Drawn by admiration and wonder, she walked through the huge doors. Inside, golden pillars supported the vaulted roof, and the walls were hung with delightful paintings. She wandered through the empty rooms marveling at what she saw, when suddenly a voice addressed her. "Sovereign lady," it said, "all that you see is yours. We whose voices you hear are your servants and shall obey all your commands with the utmost care and diligence. Retire, therefore, to your chamber and repose on your bed of down, and when you see fit, repair to the bath. Supper awaits you in the adjoining alcove when it pleases you to take your seat there." ❽

Psyche listened with amazement, and, going to her room, she lay down and rested. Then, after a refreshing bath, she went to the alcove, where a table wheeled itself into the room without any visible aid. It was covered with the finest delicacies and the most wonderful wines. There even was music from invisible performers.

❿ She had not yet seen her destined husband. He came only in the hours of darkness and fled before dawn, but his accents were full of love and inspired a like passion in her. She often begged him to stay and let her behold him, but he would not consent. On the contrary, he charged her to make no attempt to see him, for it was his pleasure, for the best of reasons, to remain concealed. "Why should you wish to behold me?" he asked. "Have you any doubt of my love? If you saw me, perhaps you would fear me, perhaps adore me. But all I ask of you is to love me. I would rather have you love me as an equal than adore me as a god."

This reasoning satisfied Psyche for a time and she lived quite happily alone in the huge palace. But at length she thought of her

Literary Analysis Archetypal Narrative Patterns What test does Cupid set for Psyche?

5. **Zephyrus** (zef´ ə rəs) in Greek mythology, god of the west wind.

Think Aloud

Vocabulary: Using Context
Model the way to define unfamiliar words by using context with this "think aloud." Say to students:

> I'm going to show you how I use context to understand the meaning of the unfamiliar word *repose* in the first paragraph. In the text, the voice tells Psyche to retire to her chamber and "repose" and then, after bathing, she will be fed. In the next paragraph, the narrator explains that Psyche went to her room and rested. After resting, she took a bath and then went to the alcove to eat. I see that these actions follow the sequence of events the voice outlined. The only difference is that the voice told Psyche to "repose" and the narrator says she "rested." From these context clues, I can see that *repose* means "to rest."

parents who were in ignorance of her fate, and of her sisters with whom she wished to share the delights of her new home. These
10 thoughts preyed on her mind and made her think of her splendid mansion as a prison. When her husband came one night, she told him of her distress, and at last drew from him an unwilling consent that her sisters should be brought to see her.

So, calling Zephyrus, she told him of her husband's command, and he soon brought them across the mountain down to their sister's valley. They embraced her, and Psyche's eyes filled with tears of joy. "Come," she said, "enter my house and refresh yourselves." Taking them by their hands, she led them into her golden palace and committed them to the care of her numerous train[6] of attendant voices, to refresh themselves in her baths and at her table, and to show them all her treasures. The sight of all these splendid things filled her sisters with envy, and they resented the thought that she possessed such splendor which far exceeded anything they owned.

They asked her numberless questions, and begged her to tell them what sort of person her husband was. Psyche replied that he was a beautiful youth who generally spent the daytime in hunting upon the mountains. The sisters, not satisfied with this reply,
11 soon made her confess that she had never seen him. They then proceeded to fill her bosom with dire suspicions. "Call to mind," they said, "the Pythian oracle[7] that declared that you were destined to marry a direful and tremendous monster. The inhabitants of this valley say that your husband is a terrible and monstrous serpent, who nourishes you for a while with dainties that he may by and by devour you. Take our advice. Provide yourself with a lamp and a sharp knife. Put them in concealment so that your husband may not discover them, and when he is sound asleep, slip out of bed, bring forth your lamp and see for yourself whether what they say is true or not. If it is, hesitate not to cut off the monster's head, and thereby recover your liberty."

Psyche resisted these persuasions as well as she could, but they did not fail to have their effect on her mind, and when her sisters were gone, their words and her own curiosity were too strong for her to resist. She prepared her lamp and a sharp knife, and hid them out of sight of her husband. When he had fallen into his first sleep, she silently arose, and uncovering her lamp beheld him. He lay there, the most beautiful and charming of the gods, with his golden ringlets wandering over his snowy neck and crimson cheek. On his shoulders were two dewy wings, whiter than snow, with shining feathers.

12 **Reading Check**

What do Psyche's sisters persuade her to do?

---

6. **train** (trān) *n.* group of followers, such as servants.
7. **Pythian** (pith´ ē ən) **oracle** oracle of Apollo, called Pythian after Python, the monstrous snake that Apollo killed.

11 Connecting to the Big Question

1. Have students reread the bracketed passage. Then, **ask** them what they think of Psyche's behavior toward her sisters.
   Possible response: She is very generous to let them enjoy the wonderful life she has. She must love them because she invites them to share in her luxurious life.
2. **Ask** students to explain what motivates the sisters to respond as they do and whether Psyche is aware of their feelings.
   Answer: The end of the paragraph that begins "So, calling Zephyrus," explains that they envy Psyche. She seems to be unaware of these feelings, however, and trusts her sisters.
3. Finally, have students focus on how Psyche responds to her sisters. **Ask** how they would characterize this response and whether they think it is heroic.
   Possible response: She is persuaded by her sisters even though it means violating the direct instructions of her husband. It is not heroic, because a true hero would resist being pressured into doing something or violating a direction for no good reason.

   Tell students to look as they read for other examples of the way characters respond to obstacles and to think about which responses they consider heroic and why they think so.

12 Reading Check

Answer: Psyche's sisters persuade her to look at her husband while he is sleeping and, if he is indeed a monster, to cut off his head.

Differentiated Instruction for Universal Access

Strategy for Special Needs Students

Students may not understand the sibling rivalry described in the story. Draw students' attention to the word *envy*, and explain to them that this is a synonym for *jealousy*. Have students reread the paragraph that begins "So, calling Zephyrus," and write down the details of Psyche's house and what the sisters do while they are there. Then, have students write a sentence or two explaining why Psyche's sisters are envious.

Strategy for Less Proficient Readers

Students may not understand that Psyche's sisters want her to expose her husband not out of fear for her safety but because they are jealous. Have students reread the paragraph that begins "So, calling Zephyrus," and the one that follows, paying attention to how Psyche's sisters behave when they visit her. Ask students to write down details that describe the sisters' actions and attitudes. Then, have students write a sentence or two describing what they think the sisters might gain by having Psyche look at her husband's face.

13 Literary Analysis

Archetypal Narrative Patterns

1. Read aloud the bracketed passage. Point out that the magical palace has disappeared.
2. Then, **ask** the Literary Analysis question: In what other stories have you encountered a mysterious building like the palace?
   Possible response: Students may note that they have read about mysterious buildings in "Beauty and the Beast," "Hansel and Gretel," and "Jack and the Beanstalk."

14 Literary Analysis

Archetypal Narrative Patterns

1. Ask students to describe how the sisters treat Psyche in the story.
   Answer: The sisters, because of greed over Psyche's mysterious castle and wealth, convince Psyche to find out who her husband is. Once Cupid leaves Psyche, the sisters are happy because they think that they can convince him to choose one of them for his wife.
2. Explain that relatives who behave cruelly is another characteristic of archetypal narratives.
3. **Ask** students to identify how the sisters' fates express an archetypal narrative pattern.
   Answer: In archetypal narratives, evil or villainous behavior is usually punished. In this case, the cruel sisters die when their greed leads each to try to win Cupid for herself.

As she leaned over with the lamp to have a closer view of his face, a drop of burning oil fell on his shoulder, and made him wince with pain. He opened his eyes and fixed them full upon her. Then, without saying a word, he spread his white wings and flew out of the window. Psyche cried out and tried to follow him, falling from the window to the ground. Cupid, beholding her as she lay in the dust, stopped his flight for an instant and said, "O foolish Psyche! Is it thus you repay my love? After having disobeyed my mother's commands and made you my wife, will you think me a monster and cut off my head? But go. Return to your sisters whose advice you seem to think better than mine. I inflict no other punishment on you than to leave you forever. Love cannot dwell with suspicion."

He soared into the air, leaving poor Psyche prostrate on the ground.

Literary Analysis
Archetypal Narrative Patterns In what other stories have you encountered a mysterious building like the palace?

(13) When she recovered some degree of composure, she looked around her. The palace and gardens had vanished, and she found herself in an open field not far from the city where her sisters dwelt. She went to them and told them the whole story of her misfortune, at which, pretending to grieve, they inwardly rejoiced. "For now," they said, "he will perhaps choose one of us." With this idea, (14) without saying a word of her intentions, each of them rose early the next morning and ascended the mountain and, having reached the top, called upon Zephyrus to receive her and bear her to his lord. Then, leaping into space, and not being sustained by Zephyrus, they fell down the precipice and were dashed to pieces.

Psyche, meanwhile, wandered day and night, without food or rest, in search of her husband. One day, seeing a lofty mountain in the distance, she sighed and said to herself, "Perhaps my love, my lord, inhabits there."

On the mountain top was a temple and she no sooner entered it than she saw heaps of corn, some in loose ears and some in sheaves,[8] with mingled ears of barley. Scattered about lay sickles and rakes, and all the instruments of harvest, without order, as if thrown carelessly out of the weary reapers' hands in the sultry hours of the day.

Psyche put an end to this unseemly confusion by separating and sorting everything to its proper place and kind, believing that she ought to neglect none of the gods, but endeavor by her piety to engage them all in her behalf. The holy Ceres,[9] whose temple it was, finding her so religiously employed, spoke to her, "O Psyche, truly worthy of our pity, though I cannot shield you from the frowns of Venus, yet I can teach you how to best allay her displeasure. Go then, and voluntarily surrender yourself to her, and try by modesty and submission to win her forgiveness, and perhaps her favor will restore you to the husband you have lost."

Vocabulary
allay (a lā´) *v.* relieve; lessen; calm

8. **sheaves** (shēvz) *n.* bundles of stalks of grain.
9. **Ceres** (sir´ ēz´) Roman goddess of farming.

Think Aloud

Vocabulary: Using Context

Direct students' attention to the word *sultry* on this page. Model how to use context to infer the meaning of an unknown word with this "think aloud." Say to students:

> In this sentence, *sultry* is being used to describe a time of day when tired harvesters carelessly throw down their tools. I can guess that the harvesters would probably put their tools away carefully at the end of the day rather than carelessly, so I know that it is not quitting time. I also know that it is not the beginning of the day, because the harvesters are tired. I ask myself: for what other reason would harvesters want to stop working? Since I know that days get warmer as the hours pass, I can guess that they might take a break when it was too hot to work. I think that *sultry* means "hot."

Psyche obeyed the commands of Ceres and journeyed to the temple of Venus. Venus received her in a fury of anger. "Most undutiful and faithless of servants," she said, "do you at last remember that you really have a mistress? Or have you come to see your sick husband, yet laid up with the wound given him by his loving wife? You are so ill-favored and disagreeable that the only way you can merit your lover must be by dint of industry and diligence. I will make trial of your housewifery."

She ordered Psyche to be led to the storehouse of her temple, where a great quantity of wheat, barley, millet, beans and lentils, which was used as food for her pigeons, lay scattered about the floors. Then Venus said, "Take and separate all these grains into their proper parcels, and see that you get it done before evening."

15 Psyche, in consternation over the enormous task, sat stupid and silent. While she sat despairing, Cupid stirred up the little ant, a native of the fields, to take compassion on her. The leader of the ant-hill, followed by whole hosts of his six-legged subjects, went to work and sorted each grain to its parcel. And when all was done, the ants vanished out of sight.

At twilight, Venus returned from the banquet of the gods, crowned with roses. Seeing the task done, she exclaimed, "This is no work of yours, wicked one, but his, whom to your own and his misfortune you have enticed." So saying, she threw her a piece of black bread for her supper and went away.

Next morning Venus ordered Psyche to be called and said to her, "Behold yonder grove which stretches along the margin of the water. There you will find sheep feeding without a shepherd, with gold-shining fleeces on their backs. Go, fetch me a sample of that precious wool from every one of their fleeces."

Psyche obediently went to the river side, prepared to do her best to execute the command. But the river god inspired the reeds with harmonious murmurs, which seemed to say, "O maiden, severely tried, tempt not the dangerous flood, nor venture among formidable rams on the other side, for as long as they are under the influence of the rising sun they burn with a cruel rage to destroy mortals with their sharp horns or rude teeth. But when the noontide sun has driven the cattle to the shade, and the serene spirit of the flood has lulled them to rest, you may then cross in safety, and you will find the woolly gold sticking to the bushes and the trunks of the trees."

17 She followed the compassionate river god's instructions and soon returned to Venus with her arms full of the golden fleece. Venus, in a rage, cried, "I know very well it is by none of your own doings that you have succeeded in this task. And I am not satisfied yet that you have any capacity to make yourself useful. But I have another task for you. Here, take this box, and go your way to the infernal shade

16 **Reading Check**

What does Cupid do after Psyche exposes his identity?

15 Critical Thinking

Predict

1. Remind students that they can use prior knowledge of patterns to predict characters' actions.
2. Discuss the two tasks that Venus assigns Psyche. **Ask** students to predict, according to archetypal narrative patterns, what will happen next.
   Possible response: Because many narratives contain patterns of threes, students may predict that Psyche will complete the second task only to be given a third.

16 Reading Check

Answer: Cupid abandons Psyche and banishes her from his palace.

Differentiated Instruction for Universal Access

EL Strategy for English Language Learners

The descriptions of the tasks that Venus assigns Psyche involve vibrant images: The ants help Psyche sort the grain, and Psyche gathers the golden wool and goes on an errand to the Underworld. To help students decipher the language and appreciate the imagery, invite students to use the details to create a series of visuals illustrating events in the story. Post students' drawings or collages in the classroom.

Enrichment for Advanced Readers

Many students will show a keen interest in Roman mythology. Encourage them to develop that interest by researching other Roman gods and goddesses on the Internet, in encyclopedias, or by reading other translations of Roman myths. Have students make charts that describe the areas of domain, prominent symbols, characteristics, and representative stories about one of the major Roman gods and goddesses.

17 Literary Analysis

Archetypal Narrative Patterns

1. Read aloud the bracketed passage. Then, **ask** students to describe the tasks that Venus has given Psyche to perform.
   Answer: Psyche has been told to separate grain, collect fleece, and go to the Underworld.
2. **Ask** students to respond to the Literary Analysis prompt: Identify an archetypal pattern developed here.
   Answer: Psyche is being forced to perform a series of tasks, which is a common pattern in archetypal narratives. Also, there are three tasks, and the number three frequently appears in archetypal narratives. Finally, one of those tasks is a journey to the Underworld, which is another archetypal pattern.

18 Critical Thinking

Predict

1. **Ask** students: When characters are warned not to do something, how do they often react?
   Possible response: Students may say that characters often do exactly what they have been warned not to do.
2. Considering this pattern, **ask** students to predict what Psyche will do next.
   Possible response: Students may say that Psyche will open the box that she has been told not to open.
3. **Ask** students to name other stories that contain this same pattern.
   Possible response: Students may say that Pandora opens the box that she is also not supposed to, Snow White eats the poisoned apple, and Pinocchio joins the group of bad boys.

Literary Analysis Archetypal Narrative Patterns Identify an archetypal pattern developed here. 17

and give this box to Proserpina[10] and say, 'My mistress, Venus, desires you to send her a little of your beauty, for in tending her sick son, she has lost some of her own.' Be not too long on your errand, for I must paint myself with it to appear at the circle of gods and goddesses this evening."

Psyche was now sure that her destruction was at hand, being obliged to go with her own feet down to the deathly regions of Erebus.[11] So as not to delay, she went to the highest tower prepared to hurl herself headlong from it down to the shades below. But a voice from the tower said to her, "Why, poor unlucky girl, dost thou design to put an end to thy days in so dreadful a manner? And what cowardice makes thee sink under this last danger who hast been so miraculously supported in all thy former perils?"

Then the voice told her how she might reach the realms of Pluto[12] by way of a certain cave, and how to avoid the perils of the road, how to pass by Cerberus,[13] the three-headed dog, and prevail on Charon,[14] the ferryman, to take her across the black river and bring her back again. And the voice added, "When Proserpina has given you the box filled with her beauty, of all things this is chiefly to be observed by you, that you never once open or look into the box, nor allow your curiosity to pry into the treasure of the beauty of the goddesses." 18

Psyche, encouraged by this advice, obeyed in all things, and traveled to the kingdom of Pluto. She was admitted to the palace of Proserpina, and without accepting the delicate seat or delicious banquet that was offered her, but content with coarse bread for her food, she delivered her message from Venus. Presently the box was returned to her, shut, and filled with the precious commodity. She returned the way she came, happy to see the light of day once more.

Having got so far successfully through her dangerous task, a desire seized her to examine the contents of the box. "What," she said to herself, "shall I, the carrier of this divine beauty, not take the least bit to put on my cheeks to appear to more advantage in the eyes of my beloved husband!" She carefully opened the box, and found nothing there of any beauty at all, but an infernal and truly Stygian[15] sleep, which, being set free from its prison, took possession of her. She fell down in the road, unconscious, without sense or motion.

---

10. **infernal shade . . . Proserpina** (prō sur′ pi nə) In Greek and Roman mythology, the dead inhabit an "infernal shade," or dark region under the earth. Proserpina, daughter of Ceres, is the wife of Pluto, the god who rules this region.
11. **Erebus** (er′ ə bəs) in Greek mythology, the place under the earth through which the dead pass before entering the underworld.
12. **Pluto** (plo͞ot′ ō) Roman god of the underworld.
13. **Cerberus** (sur′ bər əs) in Greek and Roman mythology, the three-headed dog guarding the entrance to the underworld.
14. **Charon** (ker′ ən) in Greek mythology, the ferryman who carried the dead over the river Styx into the underworld.
15. **Stygian** (stij′ ē ən) *adj.* of the river Styx, a mythological river crossed by the dead on their way to the underworld.

Vocabulary Development

Thematic Vocabulary: The Big Question

As students are discussing "Cupid and Psyche," ask them to use the thematic vocabulary presented in Introducing the Big Question, pp. 1046–1047. You might encourage them with sentence starters such as these:

1. The *conduct* of Psyche's sisters toward her was . . .
2. An important part of Psyche's *character* is her . . .
3. Some readers might think that Psyche is not very *resolute* because . . .
4. Psyche shows little *courage* when faced with the task of . . .

Cupid had recovered from his wound and was no longer able to bear the absence of his beloved Psyche. He slipped through the smallest crack in the window of his chamber and flew to the spot where Psyche lay. He gathered up the sleep from her body and closed it again in the box. Then he waked Psyche with a light touch from one of his arrows.

"Again," he said, "hast thou almost perished by the same curiosity. But now perform exactly the task imposed on you by my mother, and I will take care of the rest."

Swift as lightning, he left the earth and penetrated the heights of heaven. Here he presented himself before Jupiter with his supplication. The god lent a favoring ear, and pleaded the cause of the lovers so earnestly with Venus that he won her consent. Then he sent Mercury to bring Psyche up to the heavenly assemblage, and when she arrived, he handed her a cup of ambrosia[16] and said, "Drink this, Psyche, and be immortal. Nor shall Cupid ever break away from the knot in which he is tied, but these nuptials[17] shall be perpetual."

Psyche became at last united to Cupid forever.

---

16. **ambrosia** (am brō´ zhə) *n.* food of the gods.
17. **nuptials** (nup´ shəlz) *n.* wedding.

Critical Thinking

1. **Respond:** Do you think Psyche was wrong to disobey Cupid by uncovering his identity? Explain.
2. **(a)** What reason does Venus give for sending Cupid to Psyche? **(b) Compare and Contrast:** Compare her plan with its actual outcome.
3. **(a) Summarize:** What tasks does Venus require Psyche to perform? **(b) Connect:** In the third task, in what way does Psyche repeat her earlier mistake with Cupid?
4. **(a) Interpret:** What does Cupid mean when he says, "Love cannot dwell with suspicion"? **(b) Draw Conclusions:** What lesson does the story suggest about love? Explain.

THE BIG ?

Can anyone be a hero?
Do you think that Psyche could be considered a hero? If your answer is *yes,* explain in what way you think she is heroic. If your answer is *no,* what do you think she could have done differently that would have made her a hero?

Concept Connector

Have students compare their Activating Prior Knowledge responses before reading the selection with their ideas afterwards.

ASSESS

Answers

Critical Thinking

1. **Possible responses:** Some students will say that Psyche should have been more trustful. Others will argue that curiosity is only human.
2. (a) Venus wants her son to force Psyche to fall in love with a lowly man because she is jealous of the attention that Psyche's beauty is attracting. (b) Instead of forcing her to fall in love with an undeserving mortal, Cupid takes Psyche as his wife.
3. (a) Psyche sorts grain, gathers wool, and goes on an errand to the Underworld on Venus's behalf. (b) Psyche disobeys instructions because of her curiosity and opens the box that she is told not to open.
4. (a) Cupid means that love requires trust. (b) **Possible response:** The story suggests that true love can overcome great obstacles. It also suggests that trust is an essential component of love.

THE BIG ?

Can anyone be a hero?
Possible responses: Psyche is not heroic because she shows weak character in not resisting her sisters' pressure and in twice letting her curiosity overcome her better judgment. Psyche is a hero because she is initially punished for something that is no fault of her own and because she completes several tests.

Differentiated Instruction for Universal Access

Culturally Responsive Instruction

Culture Focus The oral tradition is important in many cultures, as adults in the culture use stories to pass on their values, beliefs, and traditions to children. Invite students to recall a story from their ethnic heritage. If students cannot recall such a story, they could do research in a library or online to find one that is part of the oral tradition of any ethnic group.

After students have located a story, invite them to retell it to the rest of the class. Encourage them to use strong expression when telling the story to gain listeners' interest. Suggest that they practice telling their stories beforehand so they can tell them smoothly in class.

After all students have told their stories, discuss similarities. What kinds of archetypal narrative patterns do the stories exhibit?

Ashputtle

19 20 21 22

The Brothers Grimm (Jakob and Wilhelm)

translated by Ralph Manheim

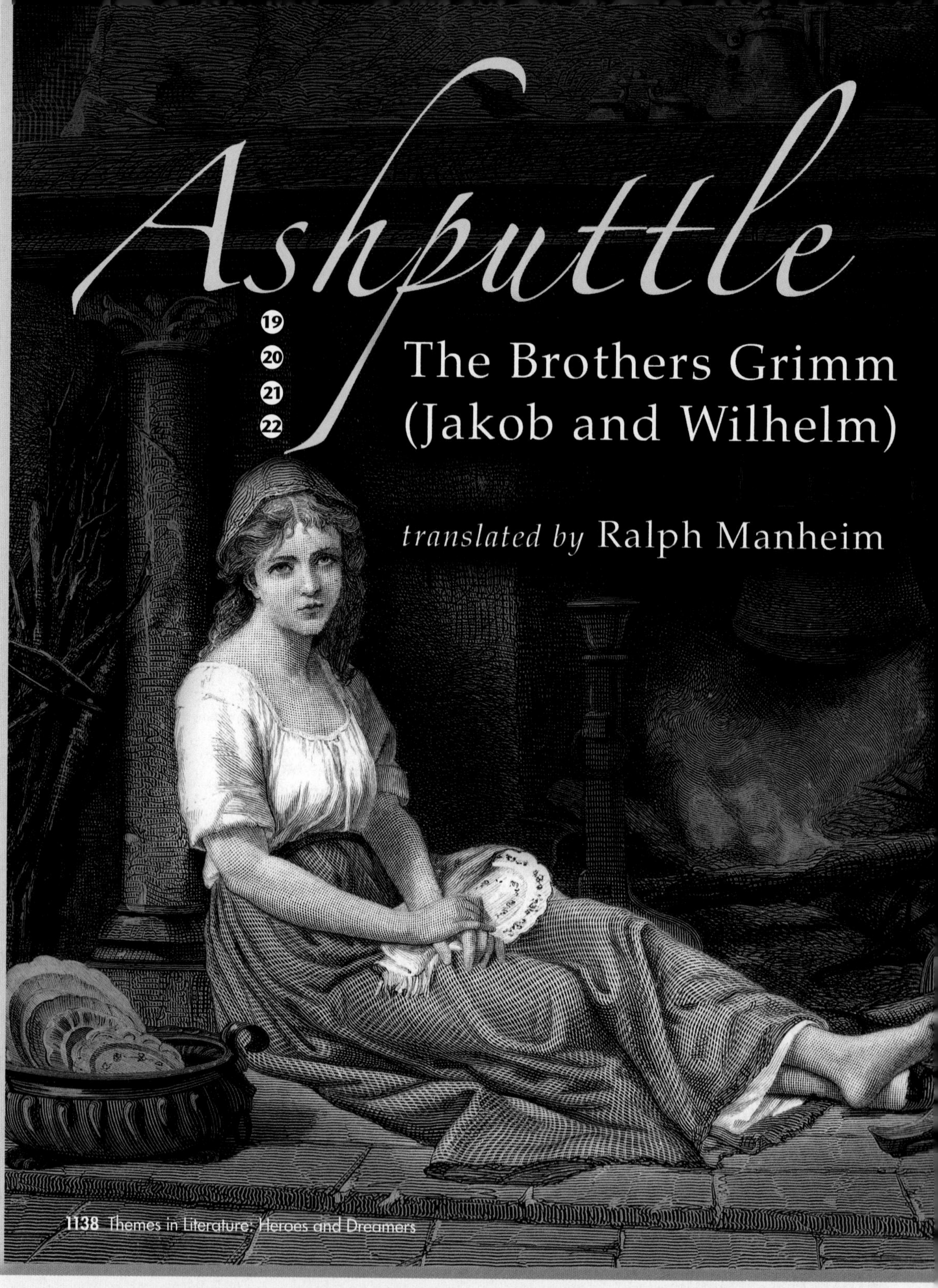

19 Background

Grimm's Fairy Tales Jakob and Wilhelm Grimm published their first collection of fairy tales, entitled *Children's and Household Tales* (trans.), in 1812. Over the next four decades, the collection was printed six more times and grew from 86 to 200 tales. While the Grimms gathered their stories from the German oral tradition and (in some cases) from printed sources, it is now believed that the brothers made changes to the tales, often to illustrate their personal opinions on religion and politics. These stories are still considered a cornerstone of children's literature, although modern editions often leave out the gruesome details found in the originals.

20 Activating Prior Knowledge

Lead students in a discussion about the purpose of fairy tales. Use these questions for discussion: Why might parents want their children to hear stories about characters such as Cinderella, Pinocchio, or Snow White? What messages do these stories have for young children? Are the messages useful? What do these stories teach children about gender roles?

Many students will recognize the similarities and differences between "Ashputtle" and "Cinderella." Provide students with copies of Venn diagrams, and have them complete the diagrams as they read the story.

Concept Connector →

Students will return to this activity after completing the selection.

21 About the Selection

Ashputtle, whose mother dies while she is still a young girl, ends up in an unhappy home where her stepmother and stepsisters treat her terribly. Not only is Ashputtle required to serve their every need, she is forced to do pointless yet grueling tasks. These tasks establish Ashputtle as the good-hearted heroine and the stepfamily as evil and cruel. In the end, Ashputtle's good heart is rewarded when she finds true love with the prince, and her relatives learn a valuable lesson about the consequences of dishonesty and cruelty.

Vocabulary Development

Selection Vocabulary Reinforcement

To reinforce and assess students' comprehension of selection vocabulary words, give them sentences using the words in which the word may or may not be used correctly. Students must tell whether the use is correct and explain their answer. Use these sentences:

1. The audience *jeered* the unpopular athlete.
   Answer: Yes, *jeered* is used correctly. People, unfortunately, might make fun of someone they do not like.
2. This illness has *plagued* me for the last five years.
   Answer: Yes, *plagued* is used correctly because it means "tormented."

A rich man's wife fell sick and, feeling that her end was near, she called her only daughter to her bedside and said: "Dear child, be good and say your prayers; God will help you, and I shall look down on you from heaven and always be with you." With that she closed her eyes and died. Every day the little girl went out to her mother's grave and wept, and she went on being good and saying her prayers. When winter came, the snow spread a white cloth over the grave, and when spring took it off, the man remarried.

24 His new wife brought two daughters into the house. Their faces were beautiful and lily-white, but their hearts were ugly and black. That was the beginning of a bad time for the poor stepchild. "Why should this silly goose sit in the parlor[1] with us?" they said. "People who want to eat bread must earn it. Get into the kitchen where you belong!" They took away her fine clothes and gave her an old gray dress and wooden shoes to wear. "Look at the haughty princess in her finery!" they cried and, laughing, led her to the kitchen. From then on she had to do all the work, getting up before daybreak, carrying water, lighting fires, cooking and washing. In addition the sisters did everything they could to plague her. They jeered at her and poured peas and lentils[2] into the ashes, so that she had to sit there picking them out. At night, when she was tired out with work, she had no bed to sleep in but had to lie in the ashes by the hearth. And they took to calling her Ashputtle because she always looked dusty and dirty.

One day when her father was going to the fair, he asked his two stepdaughters what he should bring them. "Beautiful dresses," said one. "Diamonds and pearls," said the other. "And you, Ashputtle. What would you like?" "Father," she said, "break off the first branch that brushes against your hat on your way home, and bring it to me." So he bought beautiful dresses, diamonds and pearls for his two stepdaughters, and on the way home, as he was riding through a copse,[3] a hazel branch brushed against him and knocked off his hat. So he broke off the branch and took it home with him. When he got home, he gave the stepdaughters what they had asked for, and gave Ashputtle the branch. After thanking him, she went to her mother's grave and planted the hazel sprig over it and cried so hard that her tears fell on the sprig and watered it. It grew and became a beautiful tree. Three times a day Ashputtle went and sat under it and wept and prayed. Each time a little white bird came and perched on the tree, and when Ashputtle made a wish the little bird threw down what she had wished for.

Now it so happened that the king arranged for a celebration. It was to go on for three days and all the beautiful girls in the

1. **parlor** (pär´ lər) *n.* room set aside for entertaining guests; living room.
2. **lentils** (lent´ 'lz) *n.* pea-like, edible seeds of the lentil, a plant in the pea family.
3. **copse** (käps) *n.* group of small trees growing thickly together.

23 ◀ **Critical Viewing**
Based on this illustration, predict what Ashputtle's personality will be like in the story. **[Predict]**

Vocabulary
plague (pläg) *v.* pester; harass; torment
jeered (jird) *v.* made fun of

Literary Analysis
Archetypal Narrative Patterns What other stories do you know that feature a heroine faced with cruel relatives?

25 **Reading Check**
Describe the way that Ashputtle's stepsisters treat her.

22 Humanities

Cinderella in the Corner

This illustration depicts Cinderella, Ashputtle's contemporary counterpart. She sits on the hearth among the ashes and has a faraway look on her face, as if she is imagining what life would be like away from her chores.

Ask students which details in the drawing reveal some of the difficulties in Ashputtle's life?
Answer: The figure is poorly clothed, which suggests that she is not treated well. Additionally,she looks to be tire from hard work.

23 Critical Viewing

Possible response: In the picture, the girl looks tired and lonely. Students may say that they expect Ashputtle to be the same.

24 Literary Analysis

Archetypal Narrative Patterns

1. After students read the bracketed passage, **ask** them to describe Ashputtle's stepsisters.
   Answer: The sisters, while beautiful, have "ugly and black" hearts and are cruel to Ashputtle.
2. Remind students that archetypal narratives often feature evil relatives as important characters.
3. **Ask** the Literary Analysis question: What other stories do you know that feature a heroine faced with cruel relatives?
   Possible response: Students may remember that Snow White and Cinderella had evil stepmothers.

25 Reading Check

Answer: Ashputtle's stepsisters treat her cruelly; they make her stay in the kitchen and do chores; they take away her nice clothes; and they make fun of her for being dirty.

Differentiated Instruction for Universal Access

Accessibility at a Glance
Use this information to guide your teaching of "Ashputtle."

Context	"Cinderella" tale about a girl who overcomes cruel relatives
Language/Vocabulary	• Accessible; some poetry/songs • Below-grade vocabulary
Concept Level	Accessible (familiar characters and plot)
Literary Merit	Classic fairy tale
Lexile/Length	Lexile: 900L Word Count: 2,537

PHLit Online!
This selection is available in interactive format in the **Enriched Online Student Edition, www.PHLitOnline.com,** which includes an interactive graphic organizer.

26 Literary Analysis

Archetypal Narrative Patterns

1. Remind students that archetypal narratives often feature tasks that a character must perform.
2. **Ask** the first Literary Analysis question: What task does Ashputtle's stepmother set for her?
   Answer: She says that Ashputtle must pick a bowlful of lentils from a pile of ashes within two hours.
3. Next, **ask** students wheter they think such a task is fair. Have them explain their answer.
   Possible response: It is not fair, because lentils are small and difficult to pick up. In addition, the stepmother put them there deliberately. There is no purpose served by doing this task except meeting her whims.
4. Finally, **ask** students to consider why characters are given such tasks in these types of narratives.
   Possible response: Students may say that characters are given such tasks in order to illustrate their perseverance and to show that they deserve the rewards they win in the end.

27 Literary Analysis

Archetypal Narrative Patterns

1. Remind students that archetypal narratives often feature characters that receive supernatural assistance.
2. **Ask** the second Literary Analysis question: What does the fact that the birds help her suggest about Ashputtle's character?
   Possible response: The birds' help suggests that Ashputtle respects nature. Also, white doves, one type of bird that comes to help, symbolize peace. Their assistance suggests that Ashputtle is virtuous and kind.

kingdom were invited, in order that his son might choose a bride. When the two stepsisters heard they had been asked, they were delighted. They called Ashputtle and said: "Comb our hair, brush our shoes, and fasten our buckles. We're going to the wedding at the king's palace." Ashputtle obeyed, but she wept, for she too would have liked to go dancing, and she begged her stepmother to let her go. "You little sloven!"[4] said the stepmother. "How can you go to a wedding when you're all dusty and dirty? How can you go dancing when you have neither dress nor shoes?" But when Ashputtle begged and begged, the stepmother finally said: "Here, I've dumped a bowlful of lentils in the ashes. If you can pick them out in two hours, you may go." The girl went out the back door to the garden and cried out: "O tame little doves, O turtledoves, and all the birds under heaven, come and help me put

Literary Analysis 26 Archetypal Narrative Patterns What task does Ashputtle's stepmother set for her?

the good ones in the pot,
the bad ones in your crop."[5]

Two little white doves came flying through the kitchen window, and then came the turtledoves, and finally all the birds under heaven came flapping and fluttering and settled down by the ashes. The doves nodded their little heads and started in, peck peck peck peck, and all the others started in, peck peck peck peck, and they sorted out all the good lentils and put them in the bowl. Hardly an hour had passed before they finished and flew away. Then the girl brought the bowl to her stepmother, and she was happy, for she thought she'd be allowed to go to the wedding. But the stepmother said: "No, Ashputtle. You have nothing to wear and you don't know how to dance; the people would only laugh at you." When Ashputtle began to cry, the stepmother said: "If you can pick two bowlfuls of lentils out of the ashes in an hour, you may come." And she thought: "She'll never be able to do it." When she had dumped the two bowlfuls of lentils in the ashes, Ashputtle went out the back door to the garden and cried out: "O tame little doves, O turtledoves, and all the birds under heaven, come and help me put

the good ones in the pot,
the bad ones in your crop."

Literary Analysis 27 Archetypal Narrative Patterns What does the fact that the birds help her suggest about Ashputtle's character?

Then two little white doves came flying through the kitchen window, and then came the turtledoves, and finally all the birds under heaven came flapping and fluttering and settled down by the ashes. The doves nodded their little heads and started in, peck peck peck peck, and all the others started in, peck peck peck peck, and they sorted out all the good lentils and put them in the bowls.

4. **sloven** (sluv´ ən) *n.* dirty or untidy person.
5. **crop** (kräp) *n.* part of a bird's throat in which it stores food.

Vocabulary Development

Word Forms

Give students a blank **Word Form Chart** (*Professional Development Guidebooks*, p. 44), with *plague* and *jeered* in the correct columns.

Work with the class, or have students work with a partner, to determine the related forms. The final chart should look like the one shown.

Noun	Verb	Adjective	Adverb
jeer	**jeered**		jeeringly
plague	**plague**	plaguey	plaguily

28

Before half an hour had passed, they had finished and they all flew away. Then the girl brought the bowls to her stepmother, and she was happy, for she thought she'd be allowed to go to the wedding. But her stepmother said: "It's no use. You can't come, because you have nothing to wear and you don't know how to dance. We'd only be ashamed of you." Then she turned her back and hurried away with her two proud daughters.

When they had all gone out, Ashputtle went to her mother's grave. She stood under the hazel tree and cried:

> *"Shake your branches, little tree,*
> *Throw gold and silver down on me."*

Whereupon the bird tossed down a gold and silver dress and slippers embroidered with silk and silver. Ashputtle slipped into the dress as fast as she could and went to the wedding. Her sisters and stepmother didn't recognize her. She was so beautiful in her golden dress that they thought she must be the daughter of some foreign king. They never dreamed it could be Ashputtle, for they thought she was sitting at home in her filthy rags, picking lentils out of the ashes. The king's son came up to her, took her by the hand and danced with her. He wouldn't dance with anyone else and he never let go her hand. When someone else asked for a dance, he said: "She is my partner."

She danced until evening, and then she wanted to go home. The king's son said: "I'll go with you, I'll see you home," for he wanted to find out whom the beautiful girl belonged to. But she got away from him and slipped into the dovecote.[6] The king's son waited until her father arrived, and told him the strange girl had slipped into the dovecote. The old man thought: "Could it be Ashputtle?" and he sent for an ax and a pick and broke into the dovecote, but there was no one inside. When they went indoors, Ashputtle was lying in the ashes in her filthy clothes and a dim oil lamp was burning on the chimney piece, for Ashputtle had slipped out the back end of the dovecote and run to the hazel tree. There she had taken off her fine clothes and put them on the grave, and the bird had taken them away. Then she had put her gray dress on again, crept into the kitchen and lain down in the ashes.

Next day when the festivities started in again and her parents and stepsisters had gone, Ashputtle went to the hazel tree and said:

29 ▲ **Critical Viewing**
Name another fairy tale that this picture might illustrate. Explain. **[Connect]**

30 **Reading Check**
How does it come about that Ashputtle is able to attend the wedding?

6. **dovecote** (duv′ kōt′) *n.* small house with compartments for nesting birds.

28 Humanities

Cinderella leaving the ball in a coach, illustration for *Cinderella* by Charles Perrault

Charles Perrault was a French writer who, like the Brothers Grimm, adapted traditional, oral folk tales for a more literary audience. "Cinderella," "Sleeping Beauty," and "Little Red Riding Hood" are some of his most famous works; they are considered the basis for modern versions of the tales. The original Ashputtle did not have a coach; it is a modern addition to the Cinderella story. Use the following questions for discussion:

1. **Ask:** Who is the woman in the window?
   Possible response: Students may say that the woman is Ashputtle's stepmother.
2. In what ways is she depicted as evil?
   Answer: The woman's side of the illustration is far darker in color, making her seem sinister. Also, she is with a black cat, a traditional symbol of evil, and the downspout above her head is in the shape of a dragon's head, another sinister symbol.

29 Critical Viewing

Possible response: Students may say that this picture could illustrate "Cinderella" because the version of the story that most students have heard describes Cinderella going to the ball in a coach.

30 Reading Check

Answer: Ashputtle is given a dress and shoes by the birds. She attends the wedding without telling her stepmother or stepsisters.

Differentiated Instruction for Universal Access

EL Strategy for English Learners

Many cultures have their own versions of the Cinderella story. Invite students to share versions of the Cinderella story from their own cultures. You may also ask a local or school librarian to help you locate different versions of the Cinderella story to share with students. Lead students in a discussion about the popularity of this story.

Strategy for Advanced Readers

Using various versions of the Cinderella story as a starting point, challenge students to plan a Cinderella storytelling event for younger students in your school or district. In addition to storytelling circles, students might act the story out or present it in a reader's theater version.

31 Critical Thinking

Predict

1. Have students summarize what has happened so far regarding the celebration. Then, **ask** how many tasks Venus set for Psyche.
   Answer: Venus set three tasks for Psyche.
2. **Ask** students how the results of the three tests varied.
   Answer: Psyche was able to pass the first two tests because she received help. She also had help on the last test, but her curiosity caused her to ruin the result. Still, she received additional help and was able to have her problem resolved to live happily thereafter.
3. **Ask** what has happened to Ashputtle after her first two trips to the festival.
   Answer: She had a wonderful time dancing with the prince but managed to escape after the festivities so that her identity would not be discovered.
4. Finally, **ask** them, based on the patterns they have seen, to predict what will happen to Ashputtle when she goes to the festival the third time.
   Possible response: Students will probably say that the third trip to the festival, like Psyche's third test, will have a different result from the first two and that this result will lead to her happiness.

"Shake your branches, little tree,
Throw gold and silver down on me."

Whereupon the bird threw down a dress that was even more dazzling than the first one. And when she appeared at the wedding, everyone marveled at her beauty. The king's son was waiting for her. He took her by the hand and danced with no one but her. When others came and asked her for a dance, he said: "She is my partner." When evening came, she said she was going home. The king's son followed her, wishing to see which house she went into, but she ran away and disappeared into the garden behind the house, where there was a big beautiful tree with the most wonderful pears growing on it. She climbed among the branches as nimbly as a squirrel and the king's son didn't know what had become of her. He waited until her father arrived and said to him: "The strange girl has got away from me and I think she has climbed up in the pear tree." Her father thought: "Could it be Ashputtle?" He sent for an ax and chopped the tree down, but there was no one in it. When they went into the kitchen, Ashputtle was lying there in the ashes as usual, for she had jumped down on the other side of the tree, brought her fine clothes back to the bird in the hazel tree, and put on her filthy gray dress.

He took her by the hand and danced with no one but her.

On the third day, after her parents and sisters had gone, Ashputtle went back to her mother's grave and said to the tree:

"Shake your branches, little tree,
Throw gold and silver down on me."

Whereupon the bird threw down a dress that was more radiant than either of the others, and the slippers were all gold. When she appeared at the wedding, the people were too amazed to speak. The king's son danced with no one but her, and when someone else asked her for a dance, he said: "She is my partner." 31

32 When evening came, Ashputtle wanted to go home, and the king's son said he'd go with her, but she slipped away so quickly that he couldn't follow. But he had thought up a trick. He had arranged to have the whole staircase brushed with pitch,[7] and as she was running down it the pitch pulled her left slipper off. The king's son picked it up, and it was tiny and delicate and all gold. Next morning he went to the father and said: "No girl shall be my wife but the one this golden shoe fits." The sisters were overjoyed,

7. **pitch** (pich) *n.* sticky substance used for waterproofing.

Vocabulary Development

Thematic Vocabulary: The Big Question

As students are discussing "Ashputtle," ask them to use the thematic vocabulary presented in Introducing the Big Question, pp. 1046–1047. You might encourage them with sentence starters such as these:

1. Ashputtle shows *selflessness* in enduring . . .
2. Ashputtle is *resolute* in her goal of . . .
3. Some readers might think that Ashputtle's father has a weak *character* because . . .
4. The prince shows *determination* in trying to find the identity of . . .
5. Some readers might be surprised that the stepsisters are willing to *sacrifice* . . .

32 for they had beautiful feet. The eldest took the shoe to her room to try it on and her mother went with her. But the shoe was too small and she couldn't get her big toe in. So her mother handed her a knife and said: "Cut your toe off. Once you're queen you won't have to walk any more." The girl cut her toe off, forced her foot into the shoe, gritted her teeth against the pain, and went out to the king's son. He accepted her as his bride-to-be, lifted her up on his horse,
33 and rode away with her. But they had to pass the grave. The two doves were sitting in the hazel tree and they cried out:

"Roocoo, roocoo,
There's blood in the shoe.
The foot's too long, the foot's too wide,
That's not the proper bride."

He looked down at her foot and saw the blood spurting. At that he turned his horse around and took the false bride home again. "No," he said, "this isn't the right girl; let her sister try the shoe on." The sister went to her room and managed to get her toes into the shoe, but her heel was too big. So her mother handed her a knife and said: "Cut off a chunk of your heel. Once you're queen you won't have to walk any more." The girl cut off a chunk of her heel, forced her foot into the shoe, gritted her teeth against the pain, and went out to the king's son. He accepted her as his bride-to-be, lifted her up on his horse, and rode away with her. As they passed the hazel tree, the two doves were sitting there, and they cried out:

"Roocoo, roocoo,
There's blood in the shoe.
The foot's too long, the foot's too wide,
That's not the proper bride."

He looked down at her foot and saw that blood was spurting from her shoe and staining her white stocking all red. He turned his horse around and took the false bride home again. "This isn't the right girl, either," he said. "Haven't you got another daughter?" "No," said the man, "there's only a puny little kitchen drudge[8] that my dead wife left me. She couldn't possibly be the bride." "Send her up," said the king's son, but the mother said: "Oh no, she's much too dirty to be seen." But he insisted and they had to call her. First she washed her face and hands, and when they were clean, she went upstairs and curtseyed to the king's son. He handed her the golden slipper and sat down on a footstool, took her foot out of her heavy wooden shoe, and put it into the slipper. It fitted perfectly.

8. **drudge** (druj) *n.* person whose job consists of hard, unpleasant work.

Literary Analysis
Archetypal Narrative Patterns How does the number of dances Ashputtle attends reflect an archetypal narrative element?

34 **Reading Check**
How does the prince propose to find the woman he wishes to marry?

Differentiated Instruction for Universal Access

Strategy for Special Needs Students
Explain that the birds' assistance is a pattern of supernatural intervention. Explain that *supernatural* means "something that is beyond normal or does not follow the rules of the universe." Have students reread the page, asking themselves if what the birds are doing is something that real birds can do. Then, have students write a short sentence or two describing how the birds' assistance counts as supernatural intervention.

Enrichment for Gifted/Talented Students
Throughout this tale, the doves play an important role, including here, where their short verse alerts the prince to the stepsisters' deception. Ask students to extend the birds' verse into a longer poem, or have them set the verse to music. Ask volunteers to share their finished work with the class.

32 Literary Analysis
Archetypal Narrative Patterns

1. Read aloud the bracketed passage. Emphasize that the story involves repetition—Ashputtle attends the festival several evenings in a row.
2. **Ask** the Literary Analysis question: How does the number of dances Ashputtle attends reflect an archetypal narrative element?
   Answer: Ashputtle attends three dances; events tend to come in threes in archetypal narratives.

33 Critical Thinking
Analyze

1. Have students reread the first page of Ashputtle. **Ask** them to describe Ashputtle's mother and what Ashputtle asks her father to bring her from the fair.
   Answer: Ashputtle's mother dies but says that she will always look down on her daughter from heaven. Ashputtle asks her father to bring her a branch. She takes the hazel branch and plants it on her mother's grave.
2. **Ask** students to describe how the hazel tree is important throughout the rest of the story.
   Answer: It is from the hazel tree that Ashputtle gets her dresses and where the birds that help her roost.
3. Finally, **ask** students to explain how the hazel tree functions symbolically in the story.
   Possible response: The tree, planted with love, becomes a link between Ashputtle and her dead mother. The animals in the tree help Ashputtle overcome obstacles; the tree grants her wishes; and the doves in the tree reveal the evil stepsisters to be false at the end of the story. Some students may say that the tree protects Ashputtle as a mother would.

34 Reading Check

Answer: The prince proposes to find the woman by using the golden shoe that she left behind.

35 Literary Analysis

Archetypal Narrative Patterns

1. Read aloud the bracketed passage. Remind students that archetypal narratives usually end with rewards for the hero and punishment for the villains.
2. **Ask** the Literary Analysis question: Which events show that evil is punished in the story?
   Answer: Ashputtle, the heroine, is rewarded with marriage to the prince. Her stepsisters, who are evil, are punished with blindness.

Concept Connector

Have students compare their responses to Writing About the Big Question and their Venn diagrams from before reading the selection with their ideas afterwards.

ASSESS

Answers

Critical Thinking

1. **Possible responses:** Some students may say that they sympathize with Ashputtle because she is in a hopeless situation; others may say that she does not stick up for herself enough.
2. (a) Ashputtle plants the gift, a hazel-tree branch, on her mother's grave. (b) Her actions suggest that she values nature, that she is not materialistic, and that she loves her mother. (c) Ashputtle is simple and kind, while her stepmother and stepsisters are materialistic and cruel.
3. (a) The birds help Ashputtle do the tasks she is given and give her dresses. (b) That Ashputtle receives this help suggests that the world favors good, kind people.
4. (a) The birds recognize the stepmother and stepsisters' deceit and eventually peck out the stepsisters' eyes. (b) These events suggest that bad things happen to evil people.

Can anyone be a hero?

Possible responses: Students might say that since Ashputtle puts up with hardship without complaint, she is a hero. Others might say that the outside help she receives makes her less heroic.

And when she stood up and the king's son looked into her face, he recognized the beautiful girl he had danced with and cried out: "This is my true bride!" The stepmother and the two sisters went pale with fear and rage. But he lifted Ashputtle up on his horse and rode away with her. As they passed the hazel tree, the two white doves called out:

"Roocoo, roocoo,
No blood in the shoe.
Her foot is neither long nor wide,
This one is the proper bride."

Then they flew down and alighted on Ashputtle's shoulders, one on the right and one on the left, and there they sat.

On the day of Ashputtle's wedding, the two stepsisters came and tried to ingratiate themselves and share in her happiness. On the way to church the elder was on the right side of the bridal couple and the younger on the left. The doves came along and pecked out one of the elder sister's eyes and one of the younger sister's eyes. Afterward, on the way out, the elder was on the left side and the younger on the right, and the doves pecked out both the remaining eyes. So both sisters were punished with blindness to the end of their days for being so wicked and false.

Literary Analysis Archetypal Narrative Patterns Which events show that evil is punished in the story? 35

Critical Thinking

1. **Respond:** Do you sympathize with Ashputtle, or do you think she should have stood up for herself more? Explain.
2. **(a)** What does Ashputtle do with her father's gift? **(b) Infer:** What do her actions suggest about her character? **(c) Contrast:** Contrast Ashputtle with her stepmother and stepsisters.
3. **(a)** What type of help does Ashputtle receive? **(b) Connect:** What lesson about life is suggested by the fact that a person like Ashputtle receives this help?
4. **(a) Support:** In what way do the schemes of the stepmother and stepsisters lead to their punishment? **(b) Connect:** In what way do these events support the lesson of "Ashputtle"?

Can anyone be a hero?
Do you think that Ashputtle is in some way a hero? If your answer is *yes,* explain in what way you think she is heroic. If your answer is *no,* what do you think she could have done differently that would have made her a hero?

Vocabulary Development

Vocabulary Knowledge Rating

When students have completed reading and discussing "Cupid and Psyche" and "Ashputtle," have them take out their **Vocabulary Knowledge Rating Chart.** Read the words aloud once more, and have students rate their knowledge of the words again in the After Reading column. Clarify any words that are still problematic. Have students write their own definition and example or sentence in the appropriate column. Then, have students complete the Vocabulary Practice activities. Encourage students to use the words in further discussion and written work about the selections. Remind them that they will be accountable for these words on the **Selection Test** (*Unit 6 Resources*, pp. 112–114 or 115–117).

After You Read

Cupid and Psyche • Ashputtle

Comparing Archetypal Narrative Patterns

1. Using a chart like this one, identify the **archetypal narrative patterns** in "Cupid and Psyche" and "Ashputtle."

Heroine	Powerful Older Woman	Ideal Lover	Rivals for Love	Supernatural Assistance

2. Compare the special tasks that Psyche must perform with the special tasks that Ashputtle must perform. Consider each of these structural elements: **(a)** the number of tasks; **(b)** who assigns the task and why; **(c)** the difficulty of the task; and **(d)** by what means the character completes the task.
3. Explain how your comparison of the tasks shows that the stories follow archetypal narrative patterns.

Writing to Compare Archetypal Narrative Patterns

Write an essay to compare archetypal narrative patterns in the two stories. Use these questions to get started:

- What was similar and what was different in the archetypal patterns in each story?
- What lesson does each story convey using archetypal patterns?
- What effect did the use of archetypal characters and narrative patterns have on your appreciation of each story?

Vocabulary

Practice Given the meaning of the italicized words, explain whether each of the following sentences is likely to be true.

1. His complete failure won him much *adulation*.
2. To *allay* his fear of snakes, I told him the story of how Aunt Mae was eaten by a python.
3. We *jeered* at the team to show our support.
4. You have already called him five times about the party; do not *plague* him.

ASSESS

Answers

Comparing Archetypal Narrative Patterns

1. *Heroine:* Psyche, Ashputtle; *Powerful Older Woman:* Venus, stepmother; *Ideal Lover:* Cupid, prince; *Rivals for Love:* sisters, stepsisters; *Supernatural Assistance:* voices and gods, birds

   Other sample answers appear in ***Graphic Organizer Transparencies*, Comparing Archetypal Narrative Patterns Graphic Organizer A (After You Read)**, p. 207, and in the **Additional Answers** section.
2. (a) Psyche and Ashputtle perform three tasks. (b) Venus assigns tasks to Psyche to prove her loyalty to Cupid. The stepmother and stepsisters assign tasks to Ashputtle out of cruelty. (c) Psyche's tasks seem impossible; Ashputtle's are tedious. (d) Psyche completes the tasks with supernatural aid, and Ashputtle is helped by birds.
3. Tasks are assigned by someone wanting to harm the heroine; the heroine gets supernatural assistance in completing the tasks; the tasks come in sets of three. The comparison shows that both stories follow extremely similar patterns, despite the fact that they originate from very different times, places, and cultures.

Writing to Compare Literary Works

1. Review the assignment criteria with students.
2. As they draft, have students refer to their completed **Comparing Archetypal Narrative Patterns Graphic Organizers** or to the chart in item 1, above.

Six Traits Focus

✔	Ideas		Word Choice
✔	Organization		Sentence Fluency
	Voice		Conventions

Vocabulary

1. Not likely; failure does not inspire praise.
2. Not likely; the story would probably heighten his fear.
3. Not likely; you would not jeer at a team to show support.
4. Likely; *plague* means "harass."

Assessment Resources

Unit 6 Resources

- L1 L2 EL **Selection Test A**, pp. 112–114
- L3 L4 **Selection Test B**, pp. 115–117
- L3 L4 **Open Book Test**, pp. 109–111

PHLit Online! All assessment resources are available at **www.PHLitOnline.com**.

PREARTEACH

Meeting Your Standards

Students will

1. write a technical document.
2. use writing strategies to generate ideas and to plan, organize, evaluate, and revise a technical document.
3. organize to explain the process.
4. apply grammar skills.

Introducing the Writing Assignment

Review the assignment and the criteria, using the instruction on the student page.

Connecting to Real-Life Writing

Point out that many careers involve writing technical documents. For examples, guidelines and procedures are developed and used in most offices.

Writing Workshop
Work in Progress

If students have done the Work-in-Progress assignments on pages 1089 and 1119, suggest that they examine their recorded ideas as they begin prewriting. They may wish to develop these ideas in a technical document.

TEACH

Prewriting Strategies

1. Introduce the prewriting strategy, using the instruction on the student page.
2. Have students apply the strategy to gather details for their technical documents.

Six Traits Focus

✔	Ideas		Word Choice
✔	Organization		Sentence Fluency
	Voice		Conventions

Writing Workshop

Technical Document

Defining the Form A **technical document** provides information and instruction on how to perform an action. You might use elements of the technical document in manuals for how to conduct a meeting, take minutes of a meeting, or how to assemble or operate an appliance.

Assignment Write a technical document that explains a process to readers. For example, you may explain: the procedures for conducting a meeting such as a student organization or a student club; the best way to practice a sports skill; or the process of setting up a fish tank. Include these elements:

- ✔ information and ideas that are conveyed *logically* and *correctly*
- ✔ detailed and accurate instructions
- ✔ *scenarios*, *definitions*, and *examples* to help understanding
- ✔ *discussion of possible problems, mistakes, and misunderstandings* readers may have
- ✔ accurate use of *technical terms*
- ✔ error-free grammar, especially focusing on *revising sentence fragments and run-on sentences*

To preview the criteria on which your technical document may be judged, see the rubric on page 1151.

Writing Workshop: *Work in Progress*

Review the work you did on pages 1089 and 1119.

Prewriting Strategy

Consider your audience. Think about your audience—the people who will be reading your technical document. Answer the following questions to help you determine what level of detail you need to include in your writing.

- **How much does my audience know about this topic?** Do they need a lot of background, or just a little? Will they need definitions of any special terms I use?
- **What is the age of my audience?** Do I need to use simple vocabulary and sentence structure for children, or can I use a style appropriate for people my age or older?
- **What skills might my audience have?** Do they have the basic skills needed to learn what I am teaching?

Teaching Resources

The following resources can be used to enrich or extend the instruction.

All *Unit 6 Resources*
Writing Workshop, pp. 118–119

All *Professional Development Guidebook*
Rubric for Self-Assessment: Technical Document, pp. 261–262

All *Graphic Organizer Transparencies*
Technical Document, p. 209

PHLit Online! All resources are available online at **www.PHLitOnline.com.**

Explaining the Process

Organization is the order in which you present your directions or process in your technical document. Technical writers should use a type of organization that clearly explains what to do and how to do it. Technical writing not only presents the "how-to" but the "how to prepare" and "what happens if." For example, a manual explaining how to assemble a bicycle includes the tools that will be needed, the step-by-step instructions, and the troubleshooting guide to use if something is not working properly.

Use a timeline to organize details. A logical organization for a technical document is chronological order. Because one step usually affects the following steps, explaining the steps in time order will help readers follow the logical sequence. Organize the steps you wish to explain by creating a timeline. Leave wide spaces between steps so you can add sub-steps as needed. Look at this example:

Timeline

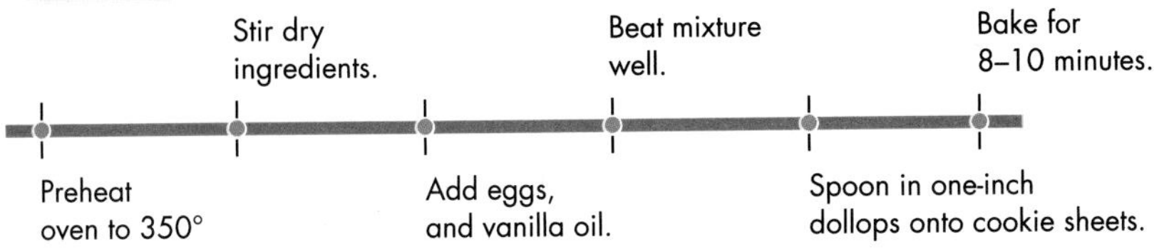
Preheat oven to 350°
Stir dry ingredients.
Add eggs, and vanilla oil.
Beat mixture well.
Spoon in one-inch dollops onto cookie sheets.
Bake for 8–10 minutes.

Add a glossary of technical terms. For users who may be inexperienced, you might want to include a glossary defining technical terms and phrases. For example, for a manual about conducting meetings you might define *adjournment, agenda, making a motion, tabling an issue, voice vote,* and so on. In most cases, glossaries appear at the end of a document.

Explaining the Process

1. Introduce the writing skills, using the instruction on the student page.
2. Discuss the examples, strategies, and timeline.

Teaching the Writing Skill

1. Ask students to brainstorm ideas for technical documents. Write their responses on the board.
2. Remind students to use language that is appropriate for their audience—the people who would need to refer to their documents. Have students assess their audience to determine if formal or informal language should be used. For example, a meeting of camp counselors is not likely to use expressions such as "making a motion."
3. Point out that a detailed timeline can make an excellent outline for a technical document. Encourage students to add illustrations to their timelines and suggest that they use the timelines as visuals to enrich their technical documents.
4. To help students develop the skill of writing concisely, you may wish to have students write drafts. Then, have them revise to make their writing as succinct as possible without deleting any essential information.
5. Assign small groups of students who are writing about similar subjects. Have them work together to brainstorm and define appropriate technical terms. Allow them to use the Internet to check their definitions or to find more appropriate technical terms.
6. Have group members work together to brainstorm for possible problems for each student to address in the troubleshooting section.

OES Online Essay Scorer

A writing prompt for this mode of writing can be found on the *PH Essay Scorer* at **www.PHLitOnline.com.**

Strategies for Using Technology in Writing

Encourage students to use word-processing software to format their technical documents in a clear and professional way. Remind them that people reading a technical document often need only part of the information presented, so a well-formatted technical document will make it easy for them to find the specific information for which they are looking. Encourage students to use bullets to clarify separate points, as in the Student Model, or to use numbering to clarify steps. An outline format can help the reader find pertinent information that may be in the middle of the document. Boldface or underlined heads quickly call the attention of the reader to important words or ideas.

Students can also use thesaurus software or an online thesaurus that will allow them to find and use the most specific and concise language possible.

TEACH

Drafting Strategies

1. Introduce the drafting strategies, using the instruction on the student page.
2. Have students apply the strategies as they draft.

Teaching the Strategies

Ask students to trade papers with partners. Have partners read each other's papers and mark places where definitions, scenarios, examples, and visuals would be helpful. Remind them that technical documents should be concise, so they should not add unnecessary text.

Six Traits Focus

✔	Ideas		Word Choice
✔	Organization		Sentence Fluency
	Voice		Conventions

Writing and Grammar, Grade 10

Students will find additional instruction on drafting technical documents in Chapter 15.

Revising Strategies

1. Introduce the revising strategies, using the instruction on the student page.
2. Have students apply the strategies as they revise.

Teaching the Strategies

1. Point out that when a writer is explaining a familiar process, it is easy to skip a step without realizing it. Have students trade papers with partners to check that there are no missing categories or steps and that everything is written in a logical order.
2. Remind students that their introductions should capture their readers' interest so that they will continue reading.

Six Traits Focus

✔	Ideas		Word Choice
✔	Organization		Sentence Fluency
	Voice		Conventions

Drafting Strategies

Provide elaboration. As your writing takes shape, you may find that parts of your explanation need more detail. Through elaboration—the adding of details—you can help your readers understand exactly what is required at each step. Look for places where adding details will help. Consider answering these kinds of questions:

- How much?
- Why?
- For how long?
- How?
- In what order?
- What will it look like?

Use definitions, scenarios, and examples. Use a variety of methods to help your readers understand your instructions.

- Define all technical terms, or refer readers to a glossary.
- Describe scenarios to aid understanding, especially when discussing troubleshooting.
- Use examples when appropriate, such as an example of an agenda.
- Include visuals, graphs or diagrams as needed, labeling key parts.

Revising Strategies

Revise for organization. Reread your draft. If you use a step-by-step organization, clearly explain each step in the order it is to be completed. Make sure the subjects you discuss are in a logical place. For example, instructions for preparing an agenda should go near the beginning of the document.

Revise for clarification. Review your document, underlining information that needs further explanation or words that need to be defined.

Write a strong introduction. Begin with an image or an idea that leads your reader into the document. Look through your prewriting notes to find details that remind you why you enjoy the activity, why it is important, or why you decided to write about it. The details that grabbed your interest may spark your audience's interest as well. Use one of these ideas to make your first sentence sell the process or product.

Understanding by Design

Clarifying Expected Outcomes: Using Rubrics

- Before students begin working on this assignment, have them preview the Rubric for Self-Assessment (p. 1151) to learn what qualities their technical documents must have. A copy of this rubric appears in ***Graphic Organizer Transparencies***, p. 209.
- Review the criteria in the rubric with the class. Before students use the rubric to assess their writing, work with them to rate the student model (p. 1150) using the rubric.
- If you wish to assess students' technical documents with either a 4-point or a 6-point scoring rubric, see ***Professional Development Guidebook***, pp. 261–262.

WRITER'S TOOLBOX

Sentence Fluency | Voice | Organization | Word Choice | Ideas | Conventions

Revising to Correct Fragments and Run-on Sentences

Fragments and run-on sentences can make your writing confusing and difficult for readers to understand.

Identifying and Correcting Fragments and Run-ons A complete sentence contains a subject and a verb and expresses a complete thought.

Fragment A fragment is a group of words that does not express a complete thought, but it is punctuated as if it were a sentence. To correct fragments, combine them with nearby sentences or add words to complete the sentence.

Fragments: She felt relieved. *After passing the test.*

Combined: *After passing the test,* she felt relieved.

Run-on A *run-on* is two or more complete sentences that are not properly joined or separated.

Fused: They hiked quickly they stopped to eat lunch.

Comma splice: They hiked quickly, they stopped to eat lunch.

Correcting a Run-on Sentence

Run-on: They wandered through the store they bought a novel.

Use a period to separate a run-on into two sentences. Begin each with a capital letter.	They wandered through the store. They bought a novel.
Use a comma and a coordinating conjunction, such as *and, but, or, for,* or *nor,* to combine two related independent clauses.	They wandered through the store, and they bought a novel.

Fixing Errors Use the following steps to correct fragments and run-ons.

1. **Decide if a problematic sentence is a fragment or a run-on.**
2. **If it is a fragment, add information to make a complete thought or combine the fragment with another sentence.**
3. **If it is a run-on, split it into two sentences. You might also add a comma or a conjunction to make it a correct single sentence.**

Grammar in Your Writing

Review the sentences in your draft to find fragments and run-ons. Neatly correct any errors using the strategies that have been presented.

WG Prentice Hall Writing and Grammar Connection: Chapter 21, Section 4

Revising to Correct Fragments and Run-on Sentences

1. Introduce the grammar skill, using the instruction on the student page.
2. Discuss the examples and the strategies for correcting fragments and run-on sentences.
3. Have students follow the instruction under Grammar in Your Writing to correct errors in their drafts.

Teaching the Grammar Skill

1. On the board, write the phrase *If he ate.* Guide students to find the subject, *he,* and the verb, *ate.* Explain that although the phrase contains a subject and a verb, it expresses only part of a thought, so it is a fragment.
2. Next, write on the board *After passing the test.* **Ask** students if this phrase is an example of a fragment or a sentence and explain why.
   Answer: It is a fragment, because it does not have a subject and it does not express a complete thought.
3. Have students work in small groups. Have each group write ten phrases, making some fragments and others sentences. Have groups trade papers and identify one another's fragments and sentences.
4. Explain that a *fused* sentence is a run-on that lacks punctuation. Another type of run-on is a *comma splice,* in which only a comma is used to combine two independent clauses.
5. Using the fused sentence example on the student page, model how to identify the independent clauses. On the board, model how to correct the run-on by dividing it into two sentences, inserting a comma and a conjunction, or inserting a semicolon.
6. Have each group write eight run-ons, some fused and some comma splices. Have groups exchange papers and correct the run-ons.

WG **Writing and Grammar, Grade 10**

Students will find additional instruction on revising fragments in Chapter 21, Section 4.

Strategies for Test Taking

Point out that students are especially likely to write fragments and run-ons when writing under pressure during in-class essay tests.

Before they submit their essays, suggest that students proofread for these errors. One quick method for checking if a sentence is a run-on is to turn it into a *yes* or *no* question.

Example: He ate fruit he drank water.

Did he eat fruit he drink water?

The single *yes* or *no* question makes no sense.

If the sentence is presented as two questions, however, the questions reveal that the sentence contains two complete thoughts.

Did he eat fruit? Did he drink water?

The sentence can be revised to read *He ate fruit, and he drank water.*

Student Model

Review the Student Model with the class, using the annotations to analyze the writer's use of the elements of a technical document.

Teaching From the Student Model

1. Explain that the Student Model is a sample and students' own technical documents may be longer or shorter.
2. Point out that the Student Model uses mostly imperative sentences. **Ask** students: Are imperative sentences appropriate for this kind of writing? Explain.
   Possible response: Yes, imperative sentences are appropriate because the purpose of a technical document is to tell the reader what to do in a specific situation.
3. **Ask:** In what other writing contexts are imperatives appropriate? When are they inappropriate?
   Possible response: Imperatives are appropriate when giving someone orders, instructions, or warnings. They are inappropriate when trying to persuade someone or summarize information.

Connecting to Real-Life Writing

Point out that technical documents are not just for the workplace. Provide these examples:

- When you write directions to get to your house, you are writing a technical document.
- You might write a packing list and instructions for a friend who has never gone camping.
- If you are involved in a volunteer organization or another group activity, you might write technical documents to help organize events.

Student Model: Amanda Scarcella, San Diego, CA

How to Run a Meeting

A successful meeting is important to groups and organizations because it helps people to set goals and stay on track. Meetings are the best way to formulate ideas and collaborate with others. To have a successful meeting there are general guidelines that should be followed.

> The first paragraph provides an introduction and overview of the steps that follow.

Basic Steps To A Successful Meeting:

Agenda:
- This document consists of the date and topics of the meeting being held.
- The topics being presented on the agenda should be numbered and titled.
- Each topic should be given a specific amount of time, to keep the meeting moving.
- A leader should make and share copies of agenda with every person attending the meeting.

> Here, Amanda provides concise information on how to prepare an agenda.

Leaders:
- Select a speaker to oversee and run the meeting in an orderly and timely way.
- Choose a person to take notes on discussions and decisions.

Guidelines:
- Establish guidelines about how the meeting will be run, and decide what will and will not happen during the meeting.
- Reinforce the practice of being respectful while others are talking.
- Encourage group members to be open to the voices and opinions of others.

Preparing:
- Everyone who attends a meeting should be prepared. It is important that group members and guests have a general idea of what decisions will be discussed.
- Provide materials such as paper and pens for the people attending the meeting.
- Group leaders should be organized and ready. For example, they might bring extra copies of the agenda and other important documents.

> Notice that Amanda has chosen to organize the technical document by subject—leaders; guidelines; and preparing, for example.

Trouble-shooting:
- To be sure that decisions and action steps are clear, the note-taker should distribute notes before the next meeting, and group members should read and correct them if necessary.
- While an agenda is useful, people should realize that a meeting may not follow it exactly if an urgent matter arises. In this case, the leader should keep the group informed about why the order of discussion may change.
- It is a good rule to end meetings on time even if agenda is not finished. This is respectful to the people who attended. Be polite and thank everyone for coming.

> Amanda provides a troubleshooting section to address possible misunderstandings.

Following these basic steps will result in a successful meeting—people will feel positive about their participation and the meeting will be efficient.

Strategies for Using Technology in Writing

If students are allowed to use computers for their tests, they may want to make use of styling features such as boldface to introduce subheads that emphasize the organizational plan of the essay. They can also highlight their thesis statements and topic sentences to ensure that they have supplied them and placed them effectively. If test constraints allow, they can use thesaurus, dictionary, and spell-checking functions to edit and revise their work. Students can also use the organizing tools and revision checkers available on the **Writing and Grammar Interactive Textbook Online.**

Editing and Proofreading

Check your draft for errors in grammar, spelling, and punctuation.

Focus on Spelling: Look for homophone errors, such as *who's* and *whose* or *their, there,* and *they're.* Review word formation rules, like those that cover adding prefixes and suffixes. Know the words that give you trouble, and check to be sure you have spelled them correctly.

Publishing and Presenting

Consider one of the following ways to share your writing:

Create a podcast. Podcasts are recordings that can be distributed through the Internet and downloaded as MP3 files. Find information on the Internet on how to create a podcast of your manual.

Present your manual to a school club or organization. Share your manual with a club or student organization to which you belong. Discuss the procedures in your manual with the club members, and request their feedback.

Reflecting on Your Writing

Writer's Journal Jot down your answers to this question:

How did writing about the task you choose help you understand it better?

Rubric for Self-Assessment

Find evidence in your writing to address each category. Then, use the rating scale to grade your work.

Criteria	Rating Scale (not very — very)				
Focus: How clear and accurate are your instructions?	1	2	3	4	5
Organization: How logically and correctly are your procedures conveyed?	1	2	3	4	5
Support/Elaboration: How clear are your scenarios and examples? How clearly do you explain possible problems and misunderstandings readers may have?	1	2	3	4	5
Style: How well do you avoid fragments and run-ons?	1	2	3	4	5
Conventions: How correct is your grammar and spelling?	1	2	3	4	5

Differentiated Instruction for Universal Access

Support for Special Needs Students

On the board, have students list groups that hold meetings and topics the groups might discuss. Then, assign groups. Each group should examine the lists and decide what kind of group they will be and what topic they will discuss. Next, have them stage meetings using the guidelines in the Student Model. Afterward, discuss how the guidelines worked. Ask them to think about what the student could have added, explained further, or deleted to make the guidelines more useful.

Editing and Proofreading

1. Introduce the editing and proofreading focus, using the instruction on the student page.
2. Have students edit and proofread their technical documents, correcting grammar, spelling, punctuation, and word choice. Make sure they check for errors of the type noted on the student page.

Teaching the Editing Focus

1. Have students brainstorm sets of homophones and list them on the board. Then, generate and write a brief definition beside each word.
2. Ask students to proofread their papers for correct homophone use.
3. Have partners trade papers and proofread each other's spelling. Then, ask students to make personal lists of frequently misspelled words. Encourage them to create mnemonic devices for their words and to continue studying their lists, adding words as needed.

Six Traits Focus

	Ideas	✔	Word Choice
	Organization		Sentence Fluency
	Voice	✔	Conventions

ASSESS

Publishing and Presenting

1. Ask a volunteer to briefly explain to the class what a podcast is, how it is made, and how it is distributed.
2. Point out that students can put their manuals to use by offering them to clubs or organizations. Advise students that they might have to modify their directions to fit a particular group's needs.

Reflecting on Your Writing

Once students have answered the question posed on the student page, ask them to consider whether the assignment was easier or more difficult than they expected. Discuss responses as a class.

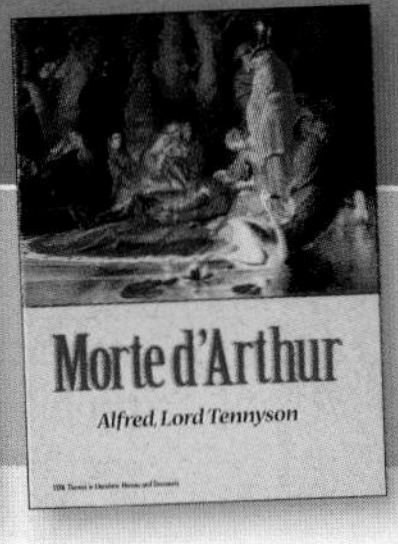

TIME AND RESOURCE MANAGER

Arthur Becomes King of Britain • Morte d'Arthur

Lesson Pacing Guide

DAY 1 Preteach

- Administer the Reading and Vocabulary Warm-ups (*Unit 6 Resources*, pp. 62–65 or 80–83) as necessary.
- Introduce the Reading Skill: Compare Worldviews FT
- Introduce the Literary Analysis concept: Legends and Legendary Heroes FT
- Distribute copies of the appropriate graphic organizer for the Reading Skill (*Graphic Organizer Transparencies*, pp. 210–212). CRI
- Distribute copies of the appropriate graphic organizer for Literary Analysis (*Graphic Organizer Transparencies*, pp. 213–215). CRI
- Teach the selection vocabulary. FT CRI
- Introduce the Word Study skill.

DAYS 2–3 Preteach/Teach

- Build background with the Background feature. CRI
- Develop thematic vocabulary and thematic thinking with Writing About the Big Question.
- Prepare students to read with the Activating Prior Knowledge activities (TE). CRI
- Informally monitor comprehension while students read. FT
- Use the Reading Check questions to confirm comprehension.
- Develop students' ability to compare worldviews using the Reading Skill questions. CRI
- Develop students' understanding of legends and legendary heroes using the Literary Analysis questions. CRI
- Reinforce vocabulary with the Vocabulary notes. CRI

DAY 4 Assess

- Assess students' comprehension and mastery of the skills by having them answer the Critical Thinking, Reading Skill, and Literary Analysis questions. FT
- Have students complete the Vocabulary Practice activities. FT
- Have students complete the Word Study activities.

DAY 5 Extend/Assess

- Have students complete the Grammar lesson. CRI
- Have students complete the Writing activity and write a script. (You may assign as homework.) FT
- Extend learning by having students complete the Research and Technology activity, a chart. (You may assign as homework.) As an alternative, assign them "Our Hero!" or "Peace Keepers" in *Reality Central*. CRI
- Administer Selection Test A or B (*Unit 6 Resources*, pp. 139–144 or 160–165). FT

"Arthur Becomes King of Britain" is an unedited excerpt from the novel *The Once and Future King*. "Morte d'Arthur" is a poem that appears unedited and in its entirety.

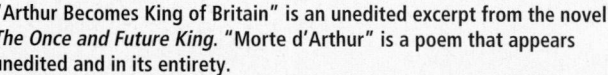

Meeting Your Standards

Students will

1. analyze and respond to literary elements.
   - Literary Analysis: Legends and Legendary Heroes
2. read, comprehend, and analyze legends.
   - Reading Skill: Compare Worldviews
   - Reading Check questions
   - Apply the Skills questions
   - Assessment Practice
3. develop vocabulary.
   - Vocabulary
   - Word Study
4. apply grammar skills.
   - Commas and Dashes
5. Develop writing proficiency.
   - Work in Progress: Comparison-and-Contrast Essay
   - script
6. strengthen research and technology skills.
   - "influences" chart

CRI For a full explanation of Culturally Responsive Instruction opportunities in this lesson, see p. T86–T87.

FT For an accelerated lesson, use the Fast Track strategies and activities.

Managing Differentiated Instruction
This leveled selection pairing groups a more accessible with a more challenging selection. Choose either one to teach the lesson skills. For classroom management suggestions for using the pairing in a mixed-ability class, see pp. T68–T69.

Daily Block Scheduling
Each day in this Lesson Pacing Guide represents a 40–50 minute period. Teachers using block scheduling may combine days to revise pacing. In addition, teachers may differentiate and support core instruction by integrating components for extended and intensive support as students require. See the Guide to Selected Leveled Resources (facing page).

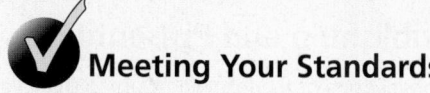

Guide to Selected Leveled Resources

EL English Learners

			Arthur Becomes King of Britain *from* the Once and Future King	Morte d'Arthur
CORE COURSE	*Unit 6 Resources*	Selection Test A	pp. 139–141	pp. 160–162
	Graphic Organizer Transparencies	Reading Skill Graphic Organizer A	p. 210	p. 211
		Literary Analysis Graphic Organizer A	p. 213	p. 214
EXTENDED SUPPORT (Level 2)	*Unit 6 Resources*	Reading and Vocabulary Warm-ups A or B	pp. 62–65	pp. 80–83
	Reader's Notebook: English Learner's Version		adapted instruction and adapted selection	adapted instruction and summary
	Hear It! Audio CD		selection and summaries	selection and summaries
	Hear It! Audio CD (adapted text)		adapted selection and summaries	—
INTENSIVE SUPPORT (Level 1)	*Reality Central*		"Our Hero!"	"Peace Keepers"
	Real-World Writing Journal		Lesson 5, pp. 172–175	Lesson 6, pp. 176–179

L2 Below-Level Students

			Arthur Becomes King of Britain *from* the Once and Future King	Morte d'Arthur
CORE COURSE	*Unit 6 Resources*	Selection Test A	pp. 139–141	pp. 160–162
	Graphic Organizer Transparencies	Reading Skill Graphic Organizer A	p. 210	p. 211
		Literary Analysis Graphic Organizer A	p. 213	p. 214
EXTENDED SUPPORT (Level 2)	*Unit 6 Resources*	Reading and Vocabulary Warm-ups A or B	pp. 62–65	pp. 80–83
	Reader's Notebook		adapted instruction and full selection	adapted instruction and summary
	Hear It! Audio CD		selection and summaries	selection and summaries
INTENSIVE SUPPORT (Level 1)	*Reality Central*		"Our Hero!"	"Peace Keepers"
	Real-World Writing Journal		Lesson 5, pp. 172–175	Lesson 6, pp. 176–179
	Reading Kit		Reteaching worksheets	Reteaching worksheets

L1 Special Needs Students

			Arthur Becomes King of Britain *from* the Once and Future King	Morte d'Arthur
CORE COURSE	*Unit 6 Resources*	Selection Test A	pp. 139–141	pp. 160–162
	Graphic Organizer Transparencies	Reading Skill Graphic Organizer A	p. 210	p. 211
		Literary Analysis Graphic Organizer A	p. 213	p. 214
EXTENDED SUPPORT (Level 2)	*Unit 6 Resources*	Reading and Vocabulary Warm-ups A or B	pp. 62–65	pp. 80–83
	Reader's Notebook: Adapted Version		adapted instruction and adapted selection	adapted instruction and summary
	Hear It! Audio CD (adapted text)		adapted selection and summaries	—
INTENSIVE SUPPORT (Level 1)	*Reality Central*		"Our Hero!"	"Peace Keepers"
	Real-World Writing Journal		Lesson 5, pp. 172–175	Lesson 6, pp. 176–179
	Reading Kit		Reteaching worksheets	Reteaching worksheets

The program includes resources for these students: L3 On-Level L4 Advanced All All
For a complete guide to selection support, see pp. T106–T108.

NOTE: All print materials are also available online at *www.PHLitOnline.com.*

VISUAL GUIDE to Featured Selection Resources

• Arthur Becomes King of Britain
• Morte d'Arthur

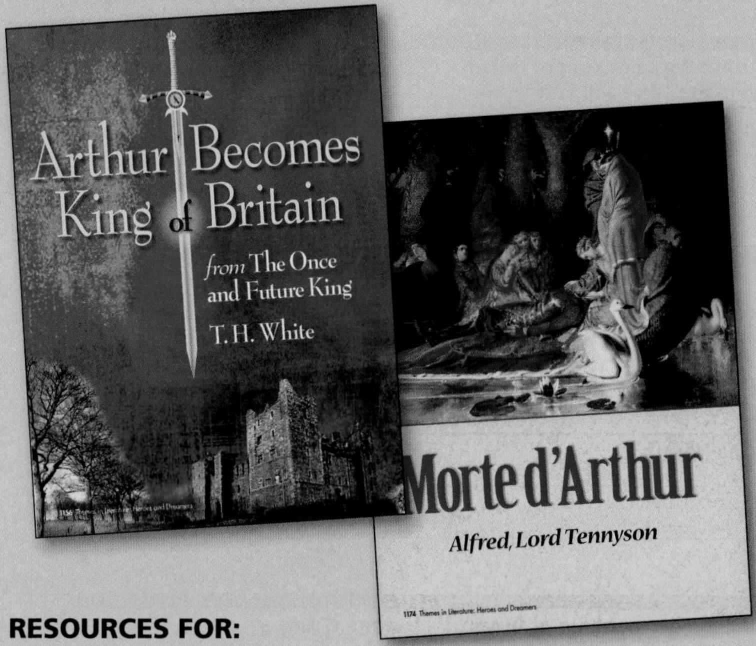

RESOURCES FOR:

- EL English Learners
- L1 Special Needs Students
- L2 Below-Level Students
- L3 On-Level Students
- L4 Advanced Students
- All All Students

Vocabulary/Fluency/Prior Knowledge

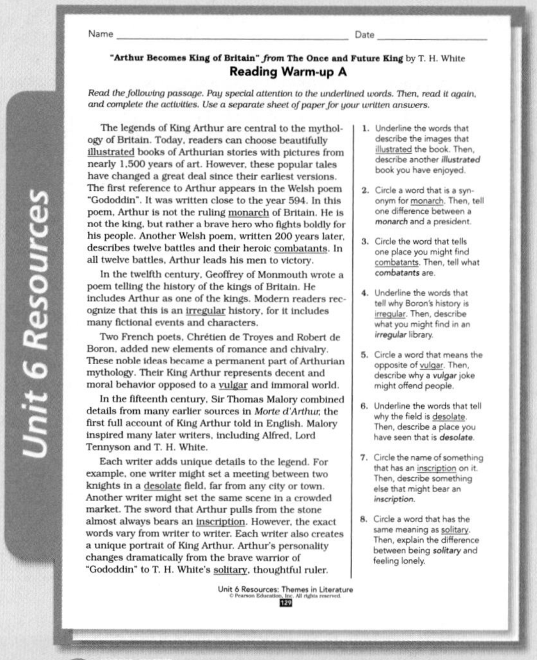

Unit 6 Resources

Name ______________________ Date ______________

"Arthur Becomes King of Britain" ***from*** **The Once and Future King** by T. H. White

Reading Warm-up A

Read the following passage. Pay special attention to the underlined words. Then, read it again, and complete the activities. Use a separate sheet of paper for your written answers.

The legends of King Arthur are central to the mythology of Britain. Today, readers can choose beautifully illustrated books of Arthurian stories with pictures from nearly 1,500 years of art. However, these popular tales have changed a great deal since their earliest versions. The first reference to Arthur appears in the Welsh poem "Gododdin". It was written close to the year 594. In this poem, Arthur is not the ruling monarch of Britain. He is not the king, but rather a brave hero who fights boldly for his people. Another Welsh poem, written 200 years later, describes twelve battles and their heroic combatants. In all twelve battles, Arthur leads his men to victory.

In the twelfth century, Geoffrey of Monmouth wrote a poem telling the history of the kings of Britain. He includes Arthur as one of the kings. Modern readers recognize that this is an irregular history, for it includes many fictional events and characters.

Two French poets, Chrétien de Troyes and Robert de Boron, added new elements of romance and chivalry. These noble ideas became a permanent part of Arthurian mythology. Their King Arthur represents decent and moral behavior opposed to a vulgar and immoral world.

In the fifteenth century, Sir Thomas Malory combined details from many earlier sources in *Morte d'Arthur*, the first full account of King Arthur told in English. Malory inspired many later writers, including Alfred, Lord Tennyson and T. H. White.

Each writer adds unique details to the legend. For example, one writer might set a meeting between two knights in a desolate field, far from any city or town. Another writer might set the same scene in a crowded market. The sword that Arthur pulls from the stone almost always bears an inscription. However, the exact words vary from writer to writer. Each writer also creates a unique portrait of King Arthur. Arthur's personality changes dramatically from the brave warrior of "Gododdin" to T. H. White's solitary, thoughtful ruler.

1. Underline the words that describe the images that illustrated the book. Then, describe another *illustrated* book you have enjoyed.
2. Circle a word that is a synonym for monarch. Then, tell one difference between a *monarch* and a president.
3. Circle the word that tells one place you might find combatants. Then, tell what *combatants* are.
4. Underline the words that tell why Boron's history is irregular. Then, describe what you might find in an *irregular* library.
5. Circle a word that means the opposite of vulgar. Then, describe why a *vulgar* joke might offend people.
6. Underline the words that tell why the field is desolate. Then, describe a place you have seen that is *desolate*.
7. Circle the name of something that has an inscription on it. Then, describe something else that might bear an *inscription*.
8. Circle a word that has the same meaning as solitary. Then, explain the difference between being *solitary* and feeling lonely.

Unit 6 Resources: Themes in Literature
© Pearson Education, Inc. All rights reserved.
129

EL L1 L2 **Reading Warm-ups A and B, pp. 129–130, 147–148**

Also available for these selections:

EL L1 L2 **Vocabulary Warm-ups A and B, pp. 127–128, 145–146**

All **Writing About the Big Question, pp. 131, 149**

All **Vocabulary Builder, pp. 134, 152**

L2 L3 ***Reader's Notebook***

L1 ***Reader's Notebook: Adapted Version***

EL ***Reader's Notebook: English Learner's Version***

Reader's Notebooks

Pre- and postreading pages for both selections, as well as "Arthur Becomes King of Britain," appear in an interactive format in the *Reader's Notebooks*. Each *Notebook* is differentiated for a different group of learners.
The selections in the Adapted and English Learner's versions are abridged.

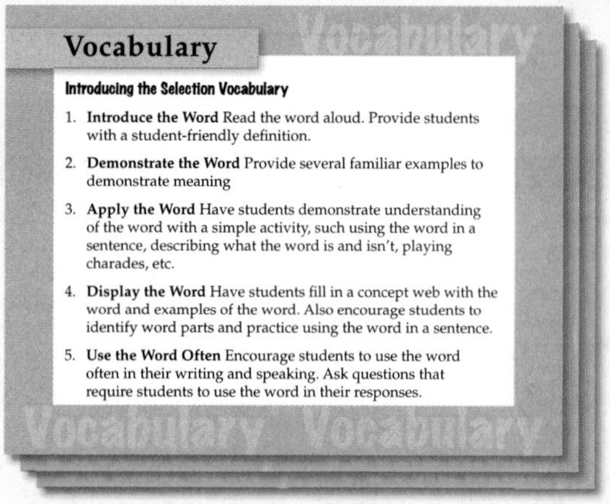

Vocabulary

Introducing the Selection Vocabulary

1. **Introduce the Word** Read the word aloud. Provide students with a student-friendly definition.
2. **Demonstrate the Word** Provide several familiar examples to demonstrate meaning
3. **Apply the Word** Have students demonstrate understanding of the word with a simple activity, such using the word in a sentence, describing what the word is and isn't, playing charades, etc.
4. **Display the Word** Have students fill in a concept web with the word and examples of the word. Also encourage students to identify word parts and practice using the word in a sentence.
5. **Use the Word Often** Encourage students to use the word often in their writing and speaking. Ask questions that require students to use the word in their responses.

Classroom Strategies and Teaching Routines

- core classroom routines outlined step-by-step
- convenient format for easy reference while teaching

Selection Support

Graphic Organizer Transparencies

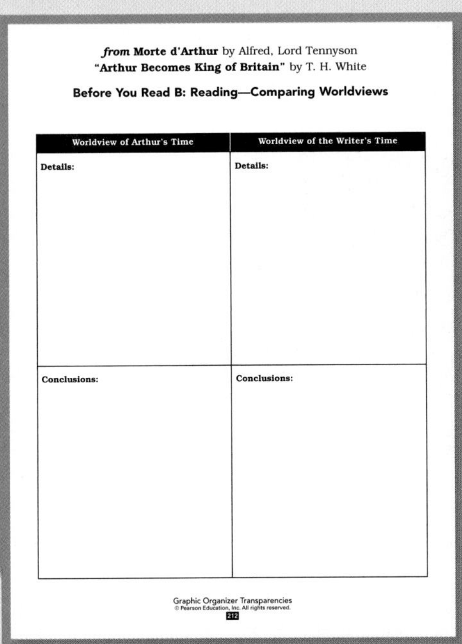

from **Morte d'Arthur** by Alfred, Lord Tennyson
"Arthur Becomes King of Britain" by T. H. White

Before You Read B: Reading—Comparing Worldviews

Worldview of Arthur's Time	Worldview of the Writer's Time
Details:	**Details:**
Conclusions:	**Conclusions:**

Graphic Organizer Transparencies
© Pearson Education, Inc. All rights reserved.
212

L3 Reading: Graphic Organizer B, p. 212

Also available for these selections:

- EL L1 L2 Literary Analysis: Graphic Organizer A, pp. 213, 214 (partially filled in)
- L3 Literary Analysis: Graphic Organizer B, p. 215
- EL L1 L2 Reading: Graphic Organizer A, pp. 210, 211 (partially filled in)

Skills Development/Extension

Unit 6 Resources

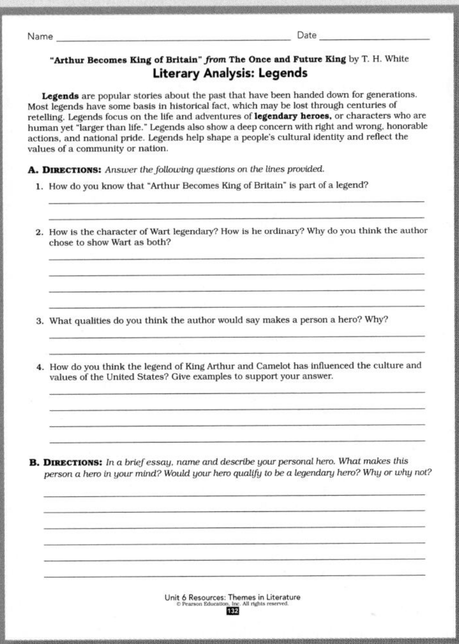

Name ______________________ Date ____________

"Arthur Becomes King of Britain" *from* **The Once and Future King** by T. H. White

Literary Analysis: Legends

Legends are popular stories about the past that have been handed down for generations. Most legends have some basis in historical fact, which may be lost through centuries of retelling. Legends focus on the life and adventures of **legendary heroes,** or characters who are human yet "larger than life." Legends also show a deep concern with right and wrong, honorable actions, and national pride. Legends help shape a people's cultural identity and reflect the values of a community or nation.

A. Directions: *Answer the following questions on the lines provided.*

1. How do you know that "Arthur Becomes King of Britain" is part of a legend?
2. How is the character of Wart legendary? How is he ordinary? Why do you think the author chose to show Wart as both?
3. What qualities do you think the author would say makes a person a hero? Why?
4. How do you think the legend of King Arthur and Camelot has influenced the culture and values of the United States? Give examples to support your answer.

B. Directions: *In a brief essay, name and describe your personal hero. What makes this person a hero in your mind? Would your hero qualify to be a legendary hero? Why or why not?*

Unit 6 Resources: Themes in Literature
© Pearson Education, Inc. All rights reserved.
132

All Literary Analysis: Legends and Legendary Heroes, pp. 132, 150

Also available for these selections:

- All Reading: Compare Worldviews, pp. 133, 151
- L4 Enrichment, pp. 135, 153
- L3 L4 Grammar, p. 154
- L3 L4 Support for Writing, p. 155
- L3 L4 Support for Extend Your Learning, p. 156

Assessment

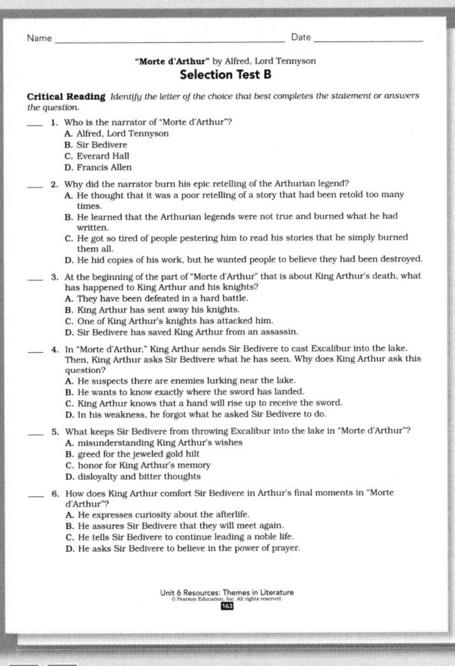

Name ______________________ Date ____________

"Morte d'Arthur" by Alfred, Lord Tennyson

Selection Test B

Critical Reading *Identify the letter of the choice that best completes the statement or answers the question.*

___ 1. Who is the narrator of "Morte d'Arthur"?
A. Alfred, Lord Tennyson
B. Sir Bedivere
C. Everard Hall
D. Francis Allen

___ 2. Why did the narrator burn his epic retelling of the Arthurian legend?
A. He thought that it was a poor retelling of a story that had been retold too many times.
B. He learned that the Arthurian legends were not true and burned what he had written.
C. He got so tired of people pestering him to read his stories that he simply burned them all.
D. He hid copies of his work, but he wanted people to believe they had been destroyed.

___ 3. At the beginning of the part of "Morte d'Arthur" that is about King Arthur's death, what has happened to King Arthur and his knights?
A. They have been defeated in a hard battle.
B. King Arthur has sent away his knights.
C. One of King Arthur's knights has attacked him.
D. Sir Bedivere has saved King Arthur from an assassin.

___ 4. In "Morte d'Arthur," King Arthur sends Sir Bedivere to cast Excalibur into the lake. Then, King Arthur asks Sir Bedivere what he has seen. Why does King Arthur ask this question?
A. He suspects there are enemies lurking near the lake.
B. He wants to know exactly where the sword has landed.
C. King Arthur knows that a hand will rise up to receive the sword.
D. In his weakness, he forgot what he asked Sir Bedivere to do.

___ 5. What keeps Sir Bedivere from throwing Excalibur into the lake in "Morte d'Arthur"?
A. misunderstanding King Arthur's wishes
B. greed for the jeweled gold hilt
C. honor for King Arthur's memory
D. disloyalty and bitter thoughts

___ 6. How does King Arthur comfort Sir Bedivere in Arthur's final moments in "Morte d'Arthur"?
A. He expresses curiosity about the afterlife.
B. He assures Sir Bedivere that they will meet again.
C. He tells Sir Bedivere to continue leading a noble life.
D. He asks Sir Bedivere to believe in the power of prayer.

Unit 6 Resources: Themes in Literature
© Pearson Education, Inc. All rights reserved.
163

L3 L4 Selection Test B, pp. 142–144, 163–165

Also available for these selections:

- EL L1 L2 Selection Test A, pp. 139–141, 160–162
- L3 L4 Open-Book Test, pp. 136–138, 157–159

PHLit Online!
www.PHLitOnline.com

- complete narrated selection text
- a thematically related video with writing prompt
- an interactive graphic organizer
- highlighting feature
- access to all student print resources, adapted to individual student needs
- Spanish and English summaries

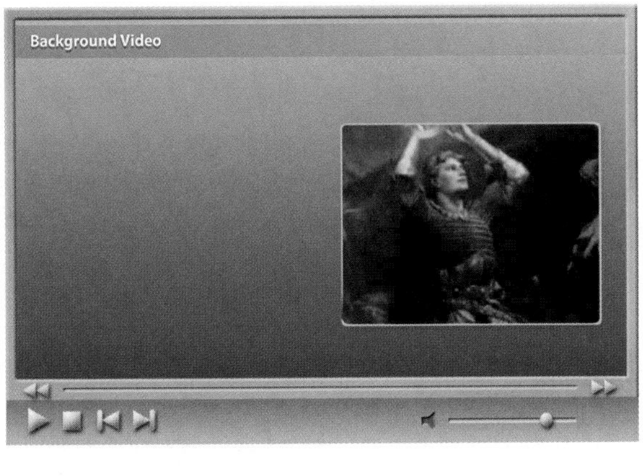
Background Video

Background video

Also available:
Get Connected! (thematic video with writing prompt)

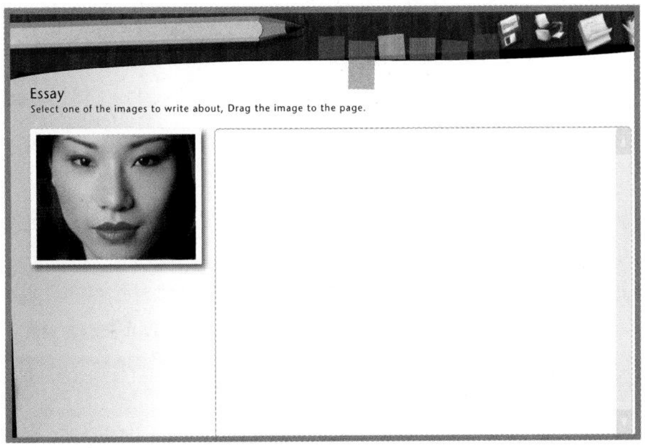
Essay
Select one of the images to write about. Drag the image to the page.

Writer's Journal (with graphics feature)

Also available:
Vocabulary Central (tools, activities, and songs for studying vocabulary)

DIFFERENTIATE/PRETEACH

❶ Selection Choices

You may use either the selection "Arthur Becomes King of Britain" or "Morte d'Arthur" to meet the lesson standards. Skills instruction for both selections appears on p. 1153. Choose one selection to teach (or choose to teach both). The Accessibility at a Glance chart at the bottom of this page will help you determine which of the two selections is more appropriate for your students.

❷ Selection Skills

1. With the class, preview the selection skills. (The lesson meets the lesson objectives given on p. 1152a.)
2. Explain that students will learn to use the skill of comparing worldviews as they read to better understand and enjoy the selection you choose. By examining legends and legendary heroes as they read, they will gain deeper insight into the genre: themes in literature.
3. To introduce the Writing and Research and Technology activities (p. 1187), tell students that when they have finished reading the selection, they will write a script for a television news report and an "influences" chart related to the selection.
4. Tell students that they will also study a grammar concept: commas and dashes. By mastering this concept, they will improve their reading fluency and the quality of their own writing.

Before You Read

Arthur Becomes King of Britain • Morte d'Arthur

❶ Selection Choices

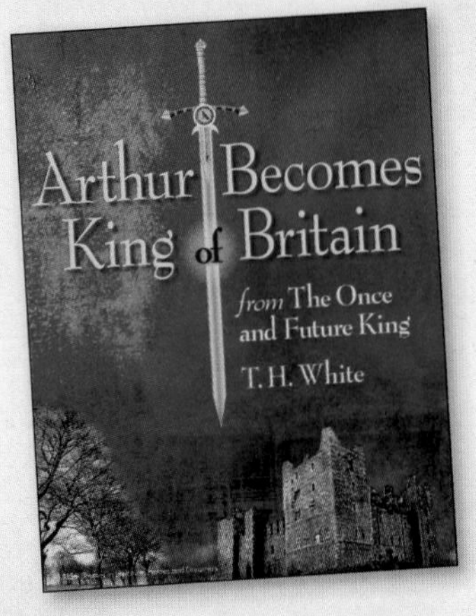

▲ Read **"Arthur Becomes King of Britain"** to find out how a legendary king of England is revealed.

▲ Read **"Morte d'Arthur"** to learn about the death and legacy of England's legendary King Arthur.

❷

Selection Skills Guide

Practice these skills with either **"Arthur Becomes King of Britain"** (p. 1156) or **"Morte d'Arthur"** (p. 1174).

- Understand legends and legendary heroes
- Compare and contrast worldviews
- Identify details
- Draw conclusions
- Use commas and dashes correctly
- Write a brief script
- Complete an "influences" chart

Differentiated Instruction for Universal Access

Accessibility at a Glance: Selection Choices

	from The Once and Future King: Arthur Becomes King of Britain	Morte d'Arthur
Context	Excerpt from novel that takes a humorous look at medieval life and the legend of Arthur	Poetic retelling of Arthur's death from a late-Victorian perspective
Language/ Vocabulary	• Mixture of medieval and contemporary language • Some subject-specific vocabulary	• Difficult • Archaic language defined • Above-level vocabulary
Concept Level	Accessible (Arthur as young boy)	Challenging (archaic language, complex structure)
Literary Merit	Humorous take on legend	Classic
Lexile/Length	Lexile: 790L Word Count: 4,723	Lexile: 1,180L Word Count: 2,853
Overall Rating	**More accessible**	**More challenging**

Because a number of factors determine the relative accessibility of paired selections, in some cases the Lexile rating of the more challenging selection will be lower than that of the more accessible selection.

❸ Literary Analysis: Legends and Legendary Heroes

Legends are popular stories about the past that have been handed down for generations. Most legends have some basis in historical fact. Legends share the following characteristics:

- A focus on the life and adventures of **legendary heroes,** or characters who are human yet "larger than life"
- A deep concern with right and wrong
- Support for feelings of national pride

Legends help shape a people's cultural identity and reflect the values of a community or nation.

❹ Reading Skill: Compare Worldviews

A **worldview** consists of values and beliefs held by a culture. When a writer retells a legend, the retelling may reflect two worldviews—that of the writer and that of the original tale. To understand a retelling, **compare and contrast** worldviews.

- **Identify details** that indicate characters' beliefs and their reasons for acting or feeling as they do. Then, identify details suggesting the writer's attitudes.
- Think about ways in which these worldviews are alike and different.
- **Draw a conclusion** about the values and basic beliefs of the different characters and of the writer. What **theme,** or insight about life, is revealed?

❺ Using the Strategy: Worldview Diagram

Record details on a **worldview diagram** to help draw conclusions.

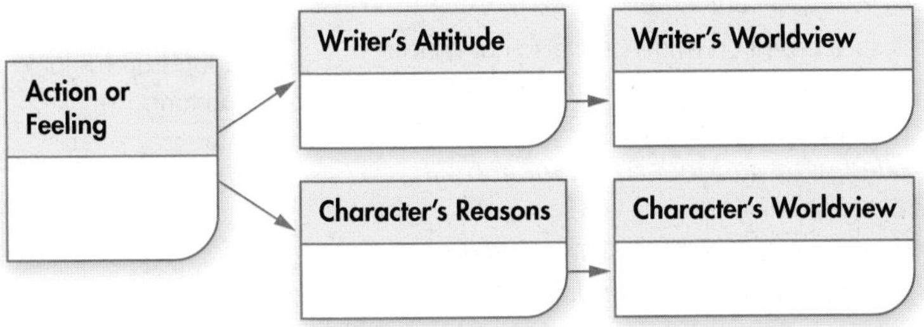

PHLit Online!
www.PHLitOnline.com

Hear It!
- Selection summary audio
- Selection audio

See It!
- Get Connected video
- Background video
- More about the author
- Vocabulary flashcards

Do It!
- Interactive journals
- Interactive graphic organizers
- Self-test
- Internet activity
- Grammar tutorial
- Interactive vocabulary games

PRETEACH

❸ Literary Analysis

1. Introduce the skill, using the instruction on the student page.
2. Tell students that they will practice identifying legendary heroes as they read.

Think Aloud: Model the Skill

Model the skill of identifying legends and legendary heroes, using the following "think aloud." Say to students:

> The Greek god Zeus, Hansel and Gretel, and Robin Hood are all heroes in stories passed down through the ages. From what I know about legends—the actual heroes existed long ago—I know only one character in this list is a legendary hero: Robin Hood. I know the story of Robin Hood is a legend because some form of the Robin Hood we know today existed hundreds of years ago in England.

❹ Reading Skill

1. Introduce the skill, using the instruction on the student page.
2. Tell students that they will compare worldviews as they read.

Think Aloud: Model the Skill

Model the skill of comparing worldviews, using the following "think aloud." Say to students:

> Suppose the story of *Cinderella* is retold so that the fairy tale takes place in the twenty-first century. Because the story will contain elements from the original story but also include details from contemporary times, there will be two worldviews—the values and beliefs of a culture—represented in that one story. For example, the movie *Miss Congeniality* presents an unlikely woman whose looks, like Cinderella's, are transformed in a culturally specific way.

❺ Using the Strategy

Give students a copy of either **Reading Skill Graphic Organizer A** or **B** (*Graphic Organizer Transparencies,* pp. 210–212) to compare worldviews as they read. Use the examples in **Reading Skill Graphic Organizer A,** which is partially filled in, to model the process of completing the organizer.

Differentiated Instruction for Universal Access

Preparing Students for the More Challenging Selection

If you wish to prepare lower-level readers to read "Morte d'Arthur," the more challenging selection, follow these steps:

- To help students better follow the events in the poem, review with them the legend of King Arthur. Discuss the mythical sword Excalibur, particularly its origins from the Lady of the Lake. For additional background, show clips from movies related to the legend, such as *King Arthur* (2005), *Excalibur* (1981), or *The Mists of Avalon* (2001).
- Many terms in this poem are archaic, and thus students may not be familiar with many of them. Present to students a list of these words, along with their definitions or translations into standard English. Include words such as *'twas, nay, nigh, spake, whereof, sware, morn, thou, thee, thy, art, seest, lightly, athwart, o'er, hast, beseemed, lief, wrought, woe, wouldst, lest, 'tis, whither,* and *changeth.* Display the list in the class for all students to see.

PRETEACH

❶ Writing About the Big Question

1. Review the assignment with the class.
2. Prompt students to list the values they think are prevalent in American culture. (**Possible responses:** freedom, independence, equality, democracy, capitalism, family, faith, wealth, diversity) Then, discuss with students the values which they find the most important to embody.
3. Have students complete the sentence starters. Review responses as a class. (**Possible response:** An example of how a person's character can reflect the values of his or her culture is *forming a diversity club at school that promotes equality for all people.*)
4. Remind students that their answers will help them think about the Big Question.

While You Read

Tell students that as they read, they should look for hints that reveal aspects of Wart's personality.

❷ Vocabulary

1. Have students preview the selection vocabulary.
2. For each word, have students say the word aloud.
3. Then, use the word in a sentence that defines the word.
4. Finally, repeat your definitional sentence or a similar sentence with the word missing and have the class "fill in the blank" chorally. Here is an example:

   Something sumptuous is costly or lavish. The expensive velvet curtains, imported textiles, and valuable artwork decorating the Banks' living room made it a [students say "sumptuous"] *sight.*

❸ Word Study

1. Introduce the skill, using the instruction in the box.
2. Ask students to think of three words ending in *-ate* and define these words using their knowledge of the suffix. (**Sample answer:** *Irate:* "showing anger"; *separate:* "characterized by being disconnected or detached"; *desperate:* "characterized by despair")

Can anyone be a *hero?*

❶ Writing About the Big Question

In "Arthur Becomes King of Britain," a nation must mourn a lost king and look toward its next leader. Use these sentence starters to develop your ideas about the Big Question.

An example of how a person's **character** can reflect the values of his or her culture is _______________.

An official leader such as a king or president should be heroic because _______________.

While You Read Notice the way people treat the character called "the Wart." Look for clues that reveal the facets of Wart's personality that might reveal his potential for leadership and heroism.

❷ Vocabulary

Read each word and its definition. Decide whether you know the word well, know it a little bit, or do not know it at all. After you read, see how your knowledge of each word has increased.

- **stickler** (stik´ lər) *n.* person who insists on strict obedience to rules or standards (p. 1158) *She is a stickler for perfect grammar.*
- **petulantly** (pech´ ə lənt lē) *adv.* in a manner that expresses impatience or irritation, especially over a minor matter (p. 1158) *The child petulantly refuses to let anyone tie her shoes.* petulance *n.* petulant *adj.*
- **skeptically** (skep´ ti kəl lē) *adv.* with doubt; questioningly (p. 1160) *She shook her head as she listened skeptically to his questionable explanation.* skeptic *n.* skeptical *adj.* skepticism *n.*
- **surmise** (sər mīz´) *n.* guess; idea based on evidence that is not conclusive (p. 1161) *His surmise about how I felt was wrong.* surmise *v.*
- **sumptuous** (sump´ cho͞o əs) *adj.* costly; lavish (p. 1162) *The dollhouse was sumptuous, filled with designer furniture and silk curtains.* sumptuously *adv.* sumptuousness *n.*
- **desolate** (des´ ə lit) *adj.* empty; solitary (p. 1163) *The desolate farmhouse was the only thing visible on the prairie.* desolated *v.* desolation *n.*

❸ Word Study

The **Latin suffix *-ate*** means "characterized by" or "showing."

In this story, the landscape is described as being **desolate,** characterized by barren land and a lack of inhabitants.

Vocabulary Development

Vocabulary Knowledge Rating

Create a Vocabulary Knowledge Rating Chart (***Professional Development Guidebook,*** p. 33) for this selection. Include the selection vocabulary and the Big Question words that appear in the Writing About the Big Question sentence starters on this page. (The Big Question vocabulary is introduced on pp. 1046–1047.)

Give students a copy of the chart. Read the words aloud and have students mark their rating in the Before Reading column. Urge them to be alert to these words as they read and discuss the selection.

Tally how many students think they know a word to gauge how much instruction to provide. As students read and discuss the selection, point out the words and their context.

PHLit Online! **Vocabulary Central,** featuring tools, activities, and songs for studying vocabulary, is available at **www.PHLitOnline.com.**

Meet T. H. White

(1906–1964)

Author of

Arthur Becomes King of Britain

Terence Hanbury White is widely known for his tales of Britain's national hero, King Arthur, but he was not born in England. He was born in India when it was still a British colony. White was educated at Cambridge University in England, where he received first-class honors in English.

Finding a Passion After school, White went to work as a teacher. When his autobiographical work *England Have My Bones* met with success, the thirty-year-old White became a full-time writer. The four-part novel *The Once and Future King,* a retelling of the King Arthur legends, is White's most famous work.

DID YOU KNOW?

White's version of the Arthur legends has inspired movies as well as the musical *Camelot* (1960)

❹ **BACKGROUND FOR THE LEGEND**

Legends of King Arthur

Tales of King Arthur, legendary ruler of Britain, and of the knights of his Round Table have been retold for centuries. Sir Thomas Malory wrote the first English prose version of the legends, *Le Morte d'Arthur,* in 1470. In "Arthur Becomes King of Britain," an excerpt from his series *The Once and Future King,* T. H. White modernizes Malory's version of the legends.

Daily Bellringer

For each class during which you will teach this selection, have students complete one of the five Revision activities for Week 34 in the ***Daily Bellringer Activities*** booklet.

❹ Background

Legends of King Arthur

The task of unearthing information about King Arthur has not been easy. There are a few references to a great leader called Arthur in a handful of texts from the sixth to eighth centuries. However, these references usually mention his name in passing. Arthur, it seems, is claimed as the king of nearly every Briton kingdom known. The sixth century saw many men named Arthur born into the Celtic royal families of Britain but, despite attempts to identify the great man himself amongst them, there can be little doubt that most of these people were only named in his honor.

Multidraft Reading

This icon ● marks natural pauses in the selection. To assist struggling readers and to deepen reading for all, assign the text in "chunks," following the icons, and apply multidraft reading protocols. For each reading, have students set the purpose indicated:

- **First reading**—literal comprehension: answering the Reading Check questions.
- **Second reading**—application of skills: answering the Legends and Legendary Heroes and Compare Worldviews prompts.
- **Third reading**—interpretation: answering the end-of-selection questions.

For more guidance, refer to the ***Classroom Strategies and Teaching Routines*** card on multidraft reading.

Differentiated Instruction — Additional Instruction

EL Extended Support—English Learners
Have students complete the **Reading and Vocabulary Warm-ups, *Unit 6 Resources,*** pp. 127–130, before they read. Assign the prereading pages and the adapted selection in the ***Reader's Notebook: English Learner's Version.*** Then, have students listen to portions of the selection on the ***Hear It!* Audio CD** (adapted text).

L1 L2 Extended Support—Struggling Readers
Have students complete the **Reading and Vocabulary Warm-ups, *Unit 6 Resources,*** pp. 127–130, before they read. Assign the prereading pages and the adapted selection in the ***Reader's Notebook: Adapted Version.*** Then, have students listen to portions of the selection on the ***Hear It!* Audio CD** (adapted text).

Extended Support—Reluctant Readers
To build motivation and engagement before assigning the selection, have students read "Our Hero!" a thematically related selection in ***Reality Central.*** Then, use the questions at the conclusion of the related selection to guide discussion.

PHLit Online!

For more about the author, practice with the selection vocabulary, and more background, go online at **www.PHLitOnline.com.**

TEACH

❶ Activating Prior Knowledge

1. Prepare an **Anticipation Guide** (see ***Professional Development Guidebook,*** pp. 36–38) with the following statements:
   - Legends are to be taken seriously.
   - Children should not strive to be better than their parents.
   - We all have destinies from which we cannot waver.
   - Modern people have little to learn from those who lived in the past.
2. Give students copies of the prepared **Anticipation Guide.** Have students mark their responses in the Me column. Then, have students discuss the statements in pairs or groups and mark the Guides again, this time in the Group column.
3. For further guidance, use the ***Classroom Strategies*** and ***Teaching Routines*** card for **Anticipation Guides.**

Concept Connector →

Students will return to the **Anticipation Guide** after completing the excerpt from *The Once and Future King.*

Whole-Class Activity

Many strong knights attempted to pull the sword from the anvil and stone. Ask students to explain or even demonstrate how they would use their strength to attempt to pull the sword from the stone. What posture would they assume? How would they use leverage to their advantage?

❷ About the Selection

While other versions of the Arthurian legend see Arthur as a heroic embodiment of ancient goodness and virtue, T. H. White views young Arthur in a more accessible way. The characters in White's version of the Arthurian story live, breathe, and blunder. In fact, this excerpt from *The Once and Future King* tells how Arthur became king because Sir Kay forgot his sword.

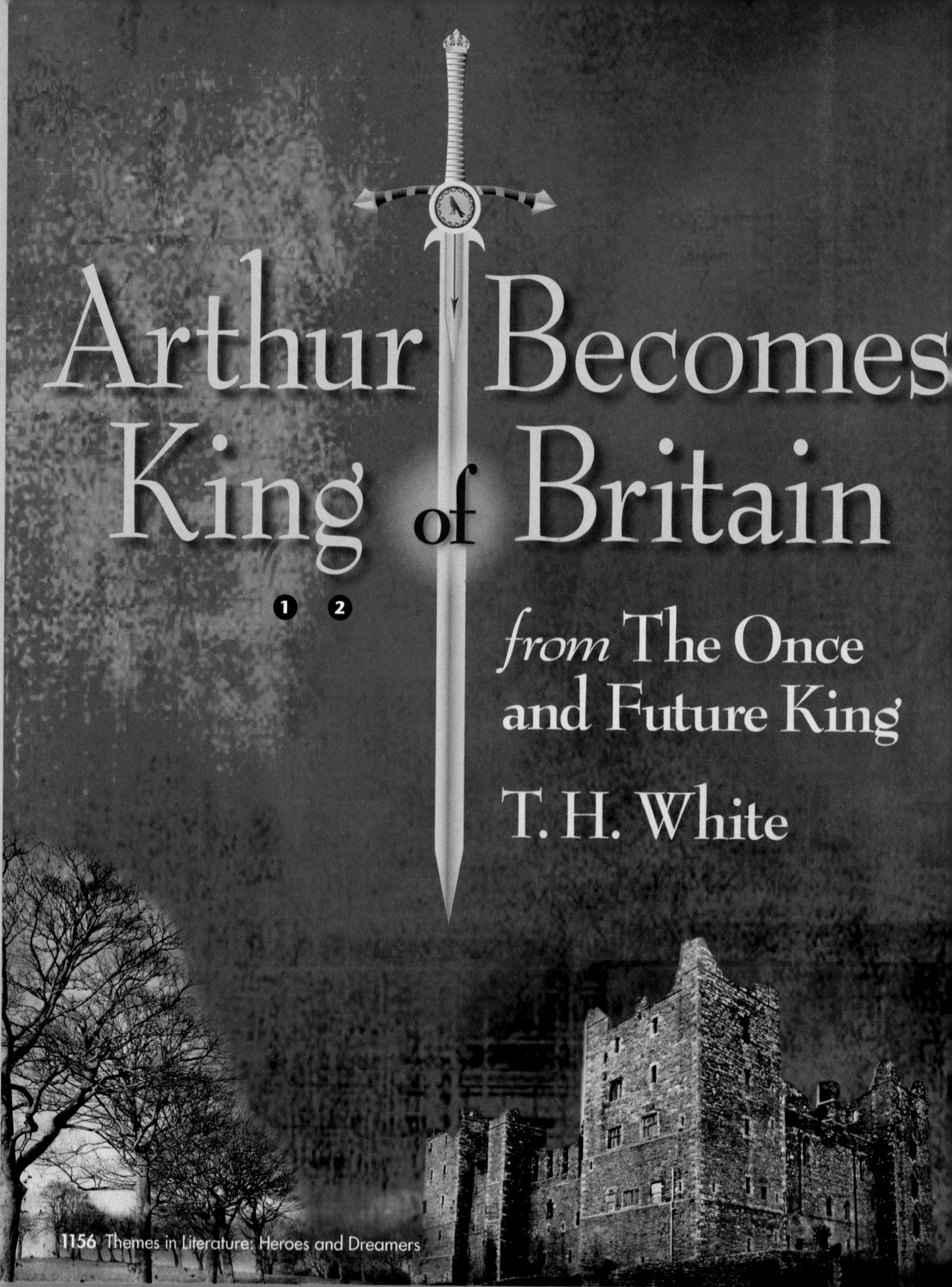

Arthur Becomes King of Britain

❶ ❷

from The Once and Future King

T. H. White

1156 Themes in Literature: Heroes and Dreamers

Vocabulary Development

Thematic Vocabulary: The Big Question
As students are discussing "Arthur Becomes King of Britain" from *The Once and Future King,* encourage them to use the thematic vocabulary presented in Introducing the Big Question, pp. 1046–1047. You might encourage them with sentence starters like these:

1. White takes the *legendary* story of King Arthur and transforms it into . . .
2. The nurse's reaction to the King's death is *humorous* because she . . .
3. Wart's *character* can be described as . . .
4. Wart's *determination* to pull the sword from the stone reveals that he . . .

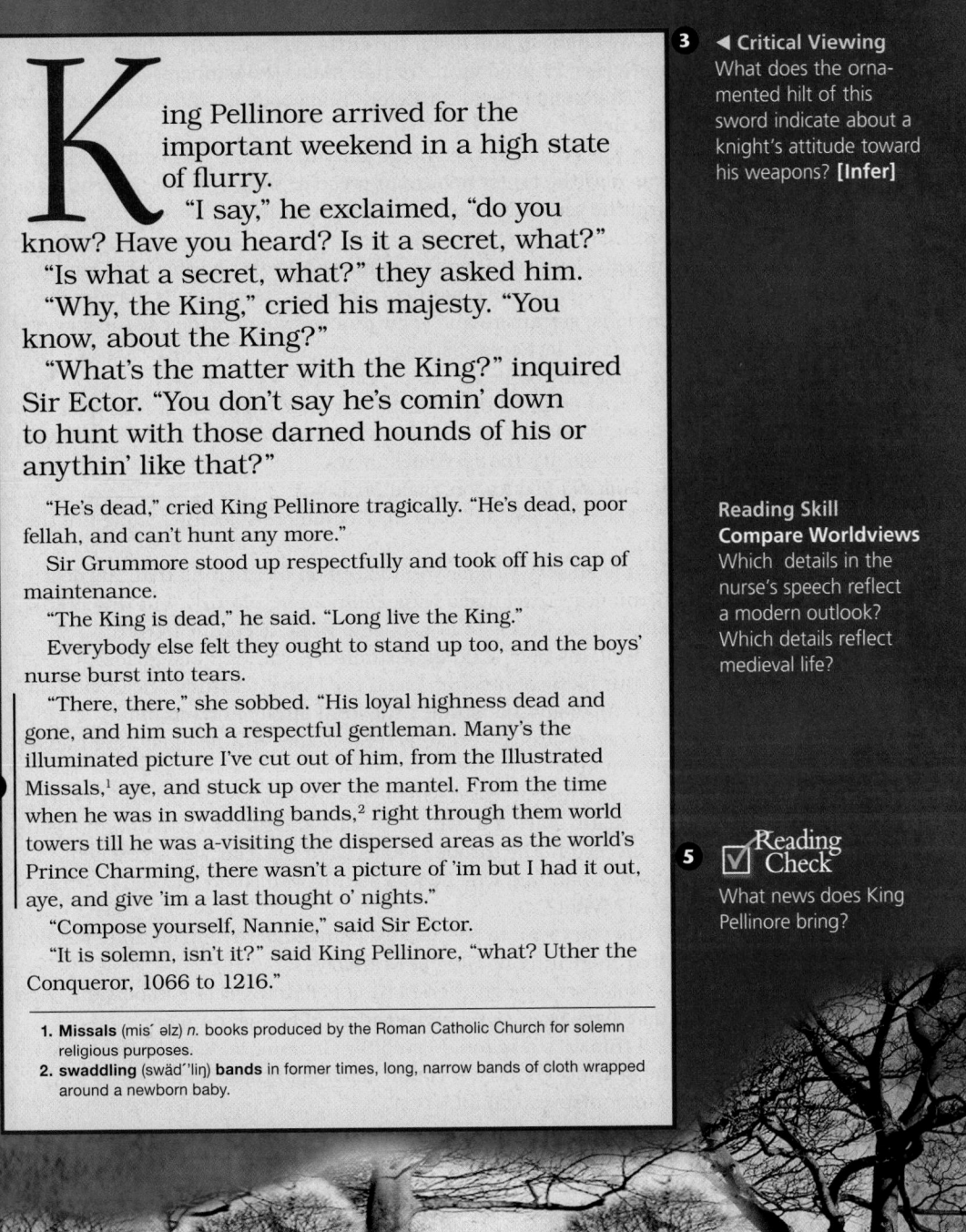

King Pellinore arrived for the important weekend in a high state of flurry.

"I say," he exclaimed, "do you know? Have you heard? Is it a secret, what?"

"Is what a secret, what?" they asked him.

"Why, the King," cried his majesty. "You know, about the King?"

"What's the matter with the King?" inquired Sir Ector. "You don't say he's comin' down to hunt with those darned hounds of his or anythin' like that?"

"He's dead," cried King Pellinore tragically. "He's dead, poor fellah, and can't hunt any more."

Sir Grummore stood up respectfully and took off his cap of maintenance.

"The King is dead," he said. "Long live the King."

Everybody else felt they ought to stand up too, and the boys' nurse burst into tears.

4 "There, there," she sobbed. "His loyal highness dead and gone, and him such a respectful gentleman. Many's the illuminated picture I've cut out of him, from the Illustrated Missals,[1] aye, and stuck up over the mantel. From the time when he was in swaddling bands,[2] right through them world towers till he was a-visiting the dispersed areas as the world's Prince Charming, there wasn't a picture of 'im but I had it out, aye, and give 'im a last thought o' nights."

"Compose yourself, Nannie," said Sir Ector.

"It is solemn, isn't it?" said King Pellinore, "what? Uther the Conqueror, 1066 to 1216."

1. **Missals** (mis´ əlz) *n.* books produced by the Roman Catholic Church for solemn religious purposes.
2. **swaddling** (swäd´'lin) **bands** in former times, long, narrow bands of cloth wrapped around a newborn baby.

3 **◄ Critical Viewing** What does the ornamented hilt of this sword indicate about a knight's attitude toward his weapons? **[Infer]**

Reading Skill
Compare Worldviews
Which details in the nurse's speech reflect a modern outlook? Which details reflect medieval life?

5 **Reading Check**
What news does King Pellinore bring?

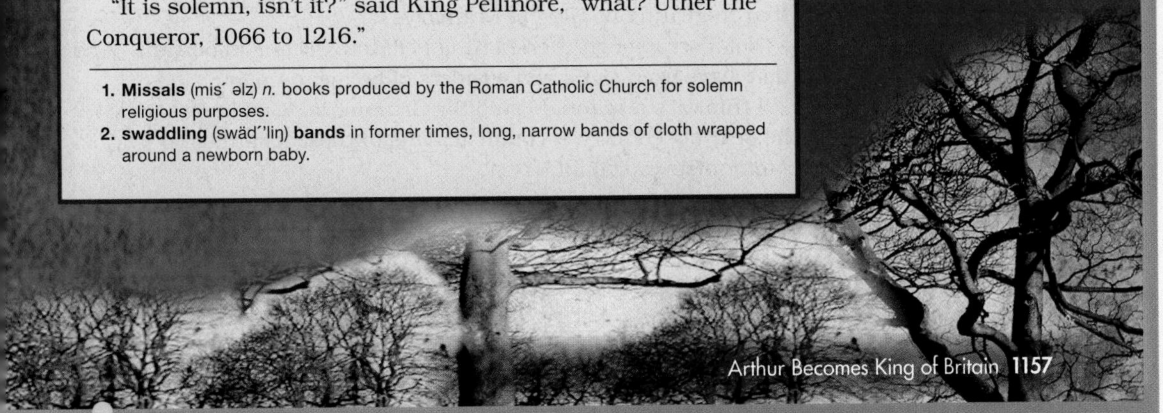

❸ Critical Viewing

Possible response: The richness of the carving and detail on the hilt shows that knights treasured their weapons.

❹ Reading Skill

Compare Worldviews

1. Read aloud the bracketed passage.
2. **Ask** students the Reading Skill question: Which details in the nurse's speech reflect a modern outlook? Which details reflect medieval life?
   Possible response: A medieval life is reflected in the references to an illuminated manuscript and swaddling bands, in the nurse's use of "loyal highness" (meaning "royal highness"), and in her reverence for the king who she thinks of every night before she goes to bed. The modern outlook is reflected in the humor of the paragraph, including the nurse misusing words and cutting out and pasting up pictures of a famous person.

❺ Reading Check

Possible response: King Pellinore brings the news of the death of the renowned King (Arthur's father and predecessor as King of England).

Differentiated Instruction for Universal Access

EL Pronunciation for English Learners

Some students may have difficulty pronouncing the final "m" sound, as in *him* and *them,* and instead might substitute the "n" sound. The following strategies can help students to pronounce the final "m" sound.

- Post these word pairs: *them, then* and *time, tine.* Pronounce each word in turn, stressing the final consonant, as students echo.
- Pair English learners with fluent speakers to practice discriminating the final "m" sound from the final "n" sound. If English learners err, fluent speakers should pronounce the word carefully, leading the way to the correct pronunciation.
- Pronounce the word *solemn.* Have students repeat and then write out the word. Discuss results with the class, examining what might have led to discrepancies between spellings.

PHLit Online!

This selection is available in interactive format in the **Enriched Online Student Edition** at **www.PHLitOnline.com,** which includes a thematically related video with writing prompt and an interactive graphic organizer.

6 Literary Analysis

Legends and Legendary Heroes

1. Read the bracketed passage aloud. Tell student to listen for examples of humor. **Ask** students to describe what they find humorous in the passage.
   Possible response: Pellinore's repetition of the Nurse's misuse of "hair" for "heir" and his changing Ector's "next-of-kin" to "next-of-skin."
2. **Ask** students the Literary Analysis question: Why is humor like this surprising in a retelling of a legend?
   Possible response: This humor not only shows a lighthearted look at Pellinore but also pokes fun at the most sacred aspect of royalty, the passing of the kingship through bloodlines. Legends usually assume a serious tone about such a historically serious subject.

Vocabulary

stickler (stik´ lər) *n.* person who insists on strict obedience to rules or standards

petulantly (pech´ ə lənt lē) *adv.* in a manner that expresses impatience or irritation, especially over a minor matter

"A solemn moment," said Sir Grummore. "The King is dead. Long live the King."

"We ought to pull down the curtains," said Kay, who was always a **stickler** for good form, "or half-mast[3] the banners."

"That's right," said Sir Ector. "Somebody go and tell the sergeant-at-arms."

It was obviously the Wart's[4] duty to execute this command, for he was now the junior nobleman present, so he ran out cheerfully to find the sergeant. Soon those who were left in the solar[5] could hear a voice crying out, "Nah then, one-two, special mourning fer 'is lite majesty, lower awai on the command Two!" and then the flapping of all the standards, banners, pennons, pennoncells, banderolls, guidons, streamers and cognizances[6] which made gay the snowy turrets of the Forest Sauvage.

"How did you hear?" asked Sir Ector.

"I was pricking through the purlieus[7] of the forest after that Beast, you know, when I met with a solemn friar of orders gray, and he told me. It's the very latest news."

"Poor old Pendragon," said Sir Ector.

"The King is dead," said Sir Grummore solemnly. "Long live the King."

"It is all very well for you to keep on mentioning that, my dear Grummore," exclaimed King Pellinore **petulantly**, "but who is this King, what, that is to live so long, what, accordin' to you?"

"Well, his heir," said Sir Grummore, rather taken aback.

"Our blessed monarch," said the Nurse tearfully, "never had no hair. Anybody that studied the loyal family knowed that."

"Good gracious!" exclaimed Sir Ector. "But he must have had a next-of-kin?"

Literary Analysis
Legends and Legendary Heroes 6
Why is humor like this surprising in a retelling of a legend?

"That's just it," cried King Pellinore in high excitement. "That's the excitin' part of it, what? No hair and no next of skin, and who's to succeed to the throne? That's what my friar was so excited about, what, and why he was asking who could succeed to what, what? What?"

"Do you mean to tell me," exclaimed Sir Grummore indignantly, "that there ain't no King of Gramarye?"

"Not a scrap of one," cried King Pellinore, feeling important. "And there have been signs and wonders of no mean might."

"I think it's a scandal," said Sir Grummore. "God knows what the dear old country is comin' to. Due to these lollards and communists, no doubt."

3. **half-mast** *v.* lower a flag halfway down a pole as a sign of mourning.
4. **the Wart** nickname for Arthur.
5. **solar** (sō´ lər) *n.* sun room.
6. **standards . . . cognizances** (käg´ nə zən´ səz) banners or flags.
7. **purlieus** (pʉrl´ yo͞oz´) *n.* outlying part of a forest, in which forest laws were not enforced.

Vocabulary Development

Relevant Topical Vocabulary

Direct students' attention to the words and phrases related to monarchy and the legend of Arthur on p. 1158, beginning with "The King is dead. . . ." Have students read the following five paragraphs and record the words on the board.

Possible response: Students will recognize "King . . . live so long" as a reference to "Long live the King," a phrase frequently used to honor a monarch at public occasions. The words, "heir," "next-of-kin," and "succeed to the throne" underscore the importance of the line of succession. "Monarch" refers to a king. "Loyal family" is the Nurse's malapropism for "Royal family." The reference to "signs and wonders" and the church underscore the divinity of kings, the belief that the king was chosen by God.

"What sort of signs and wonders?" asked Sir Ector.

"Well, there has appeared a sort of sword in a stone, what, in a sort of a church. Not in the church, if you see what I mean, and not in the stone, but that sort of thing, what, like you might say."

"I don't know what the Church is coming to," said Sir Grummore.

"It's in an anvil,"[8] explained the King.

"The Church?"

7 "No, the sword."

"But I thought you said the sword was in the stone?"

"No," said King Pellinore. "The stone is outside the church."

"Look here, Pellinore," said Sir Ector. "You have a bit of a rest, old boy, and start again. Here, drink up this horn of mead[9] and take it easy."

"The sword," said King Pellinore, "is stuck through an anvil which stands on a stone. It goes right through the anvil and into the stone. The anvil is stuck to the stone. The stone stands outside a church. Give me some more mead."

"I don't think that's much of a wonder," remarked Sir Grummore. "What I wonder at is that they should allow such things to happen. But you can't tell nowadays, what with all these Saxon agitators."[10]

"My dear fellah," cried Pellinore, getting excited again, "it's not where the stone is, what, that I'm trying to tell you, but what is written on it, what, where it is."

"What?"

"Why, on its pommel."[11]

"Come on, Pellinore," said Sir Ector. "You just sit quite still with your face to the wall for a minute, and then tell us what you are talkin' about. Take it easy, old boy. No need for hurryin'. You sit still and look at the wall, there's a good chap, and talk as slow as you can."

"There are words written on this sword in this stone outside this church," cried King Pellinore piteously, "and these words are as follows. Oh, do try to listen to me, you two, instead of interruptin' all the time about nothin', for it makes a man's head go ever so."

"What are these words?" asked Kay.

"These words say this," said King Pellinore, "so far as I can understand from that old friar of orders gray."

"Go on, do," said Kay, for the King had come to a halt.

8. **anvil** (an′ vəl) *n.* iron or steel block on which a blacksmith rests metal to hammer it into shape.

9. **mead** (mēd) *n.* drink made of fermented honey and water.

10. **Saxon** (sak′ sən) *agitators* (aj′ i tāt′ ərz) The Saxons were Germanic people who conquered parts of England in ancient times. Agitators are those who stir up people for a cause.

11. **pommel** (päm′ əl) *n.* knob at the end of the hilt of some swords.

8 **Reading Check**

Why is there no new king once the King is dead?

7 Reading Skill

Compare Worldviews

1. **Ask** students to describe some of the humor they have read so far in the selection.
   Possible response: Students may say that most of the humor they have encountered so far is silly language and people misunderstanding one another.
2. **Ask** students to describe what the humor they have read so far tells them about White's worldview.
   Possible response: The humor suggests that White does not take the Arthurian legends too seriously and that he finds a human connection in the story.

8 Reading Check

Answer: The sword is stuck in an anvil, which is stuck in a stone.

Differentiated Instruction for Universal Access

EL Strategy for English Learners

White uses humor to help establish his worldview and his characters speak everything from Cockney dialect ("Nah then, one-two, special mourning fer 'is lite majesty, lower awai on the command Two!" and then the flapping of all the standards. . . .") to upper-class chitchat. Help students translate the sergeant's dialect: "Nah" (Now), "fer" (for), "'is" (his), "lite" (late, or recently deceased), "awai" (away). Throughout the selection, have English learners work with students proficient in English to identify unfamiliar turns of phrase and speech patterns.

Enrichment for Gifted/Talented Students

These students may be the first to grasp the humor of the nurse's collection of pictures of the king she has cut out of hand-illustrated, or illuminated, manuscripts. These documents would have been valuable in medieval times; today they would be nearly priceless. Have students make a photocopy of a reproduction of a manuscript illumination and write a short text telling how it represents the medieval worldview.

❾ Literary Analysis

Legends and Legendary Heroes

1. **Ask** a volunteer to read aloud the bracketed passage, keeping in mind that it should be read in "capital letters," or as if it is very important.
2. Then, **ask** the Literary Analysis question: Why is the formal sound of the words on the stone suitable to a legend?
   Possible response: The formal language points out the ancient origin of the legend and creates an amusing contrast to the every-day, comic world that most of the characters inhabit.

❿ Reading Skill

Compare Worldviews

1. Remind students that according to the legend, the next king will be chosen when someone is able to pull the sword from the stone.
2. **Ask** students the Reading Skill question: How do these details about the choosing of the next king suggest a belief in mysterious powers guiding human affairs?
   Possible response: The gold-lettered wording on the sword announces that the king is the "Rightwise King Born," which suggests that the person who is able to pull the sword from the stone is born to be king. No one knows who the next king will be, but the people trust that the sword will tell them, suggesting a belief in supernatural powers.

⓫ Reading Skill

Compare Worldviews

1. Have students read the bracketed passage. Then, **ask** the Reading Skill question: What modern values are reflected in Kay's request?
   Possible response: Kay is less interested in being king than he is in the tournament and being in a big city filled with people. He wants adventure, excitement, and to be the center of attention.
2. **Ask** students to explain how White's description of Kay makes Kay a more accessible character.
   Possible response: Students may say that they can relate to Kay here because he sounds like a contemporary teenager who wants to be part of the action instead of a "larger than life" character.

Literary Analysis
Legends and Legendary Heroes ❾
Why is the formal sound of the words on the stone suitable to a legend?

Vocabulary
skeptically (skep′ ti kəl lē) *adv.* with doubt; questioningly

Reading Skill
Compare Worldviews
How do these details about the choosing of the next king suggest a belief in mysterious powers guiding human affairs? ❿

Reading Skill
Compare Worldviews
What modern values are reflected in Kay's request? ⓫

"Go on," said Sir Ector, "what do these words on this sword in this anvil in this stone outside this church, say?"

"Some red propaganda, no doubt," remarked Sir Grummore.

King Pellinore closed his eyes tight, extended his arms in both directions, and announced in capital letters, "Whoso Pulleth Out This Sword of this Stone and Anvil, is Rightwise King Born of All England."

"Who said that?" asked Sir Grummore.

"But the sword said it, like I tell you."

"Talkative weapon," remarked Sir Grummore **skeptically**.

"It was written on it," cried the King angrily. "Written on it in letters of gold."

"Why didn't you pull it out then?" asked Sir Grummore.

"But I tell you that I wasn't there. All this that I am telling you was told to me by that friar I was telling you of, like I tell you."

"Has this sword with this inscription been pulled out?" inquired Sir Ector.

"No," whispered King Pellinore dramatically. "That's where the whole excitement comes in. They can't pull this sword out at all, although they have all been tryin' like fun, and so they have had to proclaim a tournament all over England, for New Year's Day, so that the man who comes to the tournament and pulls out the sword can be King of all England forever, what, I say?"

"Oh, father," cried Kay. "The man who pulls the sword out of the stone will be the King of England. Can't we go to the tournament, father, and have a shot?"

"Couldn't think of it," said Sir Ector.

"Long way to London," said Sir Grummore, shaking his head.

"My father went there once," said King Pellinore.

Kay said, "Oh, surely we could go? When I am knighted I shall have to go to a tournament somewhere, and this one happens at just the right date. All the best people will be there, and we should see the famous knights and great kings. It does not matter about the sword, of course, but think of the tournament, probably the greatest there has ever been in Gramarye, and all the things we should see and do. Dear father, let me go to this tourney, if you love me, so that I may bear away the prize of all, in my maiden fight."

"But, Kay," said Sir Ector, "I have never been to London."

"All the more reason to go. I believe that anybody who does not go for a tournament like this will be proving that he has no noble blood in his veins. Think what people will say about us, if we do not go and have a shot at that sword. They will say that Sir Ector's family was too vulgar and knew it had no chance."

Vocabulary Development

Expressive Vocabulary
To help students broaden their expressive vocabulary, encourage them to use the following words as they discuss the selection: *respond, focus,* and *adapt*. Have them complete these sentence starters:

1. Kay is hoping his father will *respond* to his wishes by . . .
2. The man who will become king will have to *focus* when he . . .
3. On his first trip to London, King Pellinore will have to *adapt* to . . .

"We all know the family has no chance," said Sir Ector, "that is, for the sword." 12

"Lot of people in London," remarked Sir Grummore, with a wild **surmise**. "So they say."

He took a deep breath and goggled at his host with eyes like marbles.

"And shops," added King Pellinore suddenly, also beginning to breathe heavily.

"Dang it!" cried Sir Ector, bumping his horn mug on the table so that it spilled. "Let's all go to London, then, and see the new King!"

They rose up as one man.

"Why shouldn't I be as good a man as my father?" exclaimed King Pellinore.

"Dash it all," cried Sir Grummore. "After all, it is the capital!"

"Hurray!" shouted Kay.

"Lord have mercy," said the nurse.

13 At this moment the Wart came in with Merlyn, and everybody was too excited to notice that, if he had not been grown up now, he would have been on the verge of tears.

"Oh, Wart," cried Kay, forgetting for the moment that he was only addressing his squire, and slipping back into the familiarity of their boyhood. "What do you think? We are all going to London for a great tournament on New Year's Day!"

"Are we?"

"Yes, and you will carry my shield and spears for the jousts, and I shall win the palm[12] of everybody and be a great knight!"

"Well, I am glad we are going," said the Wart, "for Merlyn is leaving us too."

"Oh, we shan't need Merlyn."

"He is leaving us," repeated the Wart.

"Leavin' us?" asked Sir Ector. "I thought it was we that were leavin'?"

"He is going away from the Forest Sauvage."

Sir Ector said, "Come now, Merlyn, what's all this about? I don't understand all this a bit."

12. **win the palm** be the winner. A palm leaf is a symbol of victory.

14 ▲ **Critical Viewing**
Which details in this illustration suggest the importance of Arthur's sword as a symbol of England? **[Interpret]**

Vocabulary
surmise (sər mīz′) *n.* guess; idea based on evidence that is not conclusive

15 **Reading Check**
What is written on the sword?

12 Humanities

How Arthur Drew Forth the Sword
by Louis Rhead (1857–1926)

This illustration of Arthur pulling Excalibur from the stone was originally printed in 1923 in *King Arthur and his Knights* written for young readers by Sir James Knowles. Louis Rhead is known for his work in the American Art Nouveau movement, and his posters are still highly popular and frequently reprinted. Use this question for discussion:

How does this depiction of Arthur pulling the sword from the stone differ from the description of the scene in White's *Once and Future King?*
Possible response: Arthur looks older and more sure of himself than Wart does in the selection. He is surrounded by many people in a formal scene under an ornate canopy rather than scurrying around a churchyard by himself as in the story.

13 Literary Analysis

Legends and Legendary Heroes

1. Have students read the bracketed passage, then **ask** them what effect Wart's coming into the room on the verge of tears in the middle of a comic scene has on the development of the reader's sense of his character.
   Possible response: Wart's concern with losing his friend and mentor in the midst of everyone else's excitement indicates a serious, human side. For the first time in the story, the reader, like Kay, forgets that Wart is only a squire.
2. **Ask** students: What does this scene say about how White wants to portray Wart?
   Possible response: Students may say that White wants to show Arthur as a real person rather than as an unreachable legend.

14 Critical Viewing

Answer: The sword, which radiates light as though it has special, even divine, powers, is the focus of everyone's attention, illustrating its importance as a symbol of kingship.

15 Reading Check

Answer: "Whoso Pulleth Out This Sword of this Stone and Anvil, is Rightwise King Born of All England."

Differentiated Instruction for Universal Access

Culturally Responsive Instruction

Culture Connection Point out Sir Grummore's remark, "Some red propaganda, no doubt," at the top of p. 1160. Discuss the context of this remark, emphasizing Sir Grummore's suspicion of the sword's mysterious origins and its role in choosing a new king. Provide students with a cultural context for *red propaganda,* the deliberate spread of information by Communists. Explain to students that at the time *The Once and Future King* was published (1958), the United States was grappling with "The Red Scare," a period of high anti-communist sentiments lasting from the late 1940s to the late 1950s. During this period, government officials, as well as the public, feared infiltration of Communists in the United States government from countries such as the former Soviet Union, China, and Korea. Although T. H. White was British, the United States and Britain had been allies throughout the World Wars; Britain, then, also opposed communism and the proliferation of communist ideas. That White inserted this phrase in his book reveals how strongly cultural sentiments influenced his own telling of King Arthur.

16 Literature in Context

History Connection Tournaments were held in outlying areas of the kingdom, just as in London. In a poor and remote area such as King Pellinore's realm, however, there would not have been a permanent site for tournaments. An area would be cleared and the necessary facilities set up on a temporary basis.

Connect to the Literature After reviewing the information on tournaments, **ask** students the Connect to the Literature question: In light of these facts, should Kay be nervous about his first jousting tournament? Explain.

Possible response: Even if Kay is not likely to die in the jousting matches (if Pellinore's 1216 date of death for Pendragon is true, by then real battles had been replaced by mock jousts), he would be nervous about having knights and ladies watching him in his first tournament. He is as yet untried in combat, and if he were to be knocked from his horse, even the common people would see his shame.

17 Literary Analysis

Legends and Legendary Heroes

1. **Ask** students to compare Merlyn's words and attitude with those of Sir Ector.
   Possible response: Ector makes jokes about Merlyn leaving and brings readers back to the present when he tells Merlyn he cannot go, "not without a month's notice." Merlyn, however, does not joke. He shows wisdom; his words foretell the future, and he says he "must" go, as though a force beyond himself is commanding him.
2. **Ask** students: Which character is more closely connected with the traditions of a legend?
   Answer: Merlyn is clearly the more dramatic and legendary of the two characters.

16 **LITERATURE IN CONTEXT**

History Connection

Tournaments

The first tournaments were held in France in the 1100s. Groups of knights would split into two sides and fight each other. Death and injury often resulted. In the 1200s, the real battles were replaced with mock ones called *jousts.* In a joust, two horsemen would charge at each other with blunt weapons. Each would try to knock the other from his horse. Jousting tournaments were social gatherings attended by ladies and common people as well as by knights.

Connect to the Literature

In light of these facts, should Kay be nervous about his first jousting tournament? Explain.

"I have come to say Goodbye, Sir Ector," said the old magician. "Tomorrow my pupil Kay will be knighted, and the next week my other pupil will go away as his squire. I have outlived my usefulness here, and it is time to go."

"Now, now, don't say that," said Sir Ector. "I think you're a jolly useful chap whatever happens. You just stay and teach me, or be the librarian or something. Don't you leave an old man alone, after the children have flown." 17

"We shall all meet again," said Merlyn. "There is no cause to be sad."

"Don't go," said Kay.

"I must go," replied their tutor. "We have had a good time while we were young, but it is in the nature of Time to fly. There are many things in other parts of the kingdom which I ought to be attending to just now, and it is a specially busy time for me. Come, Archimedes,[13] say Goodbye to the company."

"Goodbye," said Archimedes tenderly to the Wart.

"Goodbye," said the Wart without looking up at all.

"But you can't go," cried Sir Ector, "not without a month's notice."

"Can't I?" replied Merlyn, taking up the position always used by philosophers who propose to dematerialize. He stood on his toes, while Archimedes held tight to his shoulder—began to spin on them slowly like a top—spun faster and faster till he was only a blur of grayish light—and in a few seconds there was no one there at all.

"Goodbye, Wart," cried two faint voices outside the solar window.

"Goodbye," said the Wart for the last time—and the poor fellow went quickly out of the room.

The knighting took place in a whirl of preparations. Kay's **sumptuous** bath had to be set up in the box room, between two towel-horses and an old box of selected games which contained a wornout straw dart-board—it was called fléchette in those days—because all the other rooms were full of packing. The nurse spent the whole time constructing new warm pants for everybody, on the principle that the climate of any place outside the Forest Sauvage must be treacherous to the extreme, and, as for the sergeant, he polished all the armor till it was quite brittle and sharpened the swords till they were almost worn away.

Vocabulary
sumptuous (sump´ cho͞o əs) *adj.* costly; lavish

13. **Archimedes** (är´ kə mē´ dēz´) Merlin's owl, who is able to talk.

At last it was time to set out.

8 Perhaps, if you happen not to have lived in the Old England of the twelfth century, or whenever it was, and in a remote castle on the borders of the Marches at that, you will find it difficult to imagine the wonders of their journey.

The road, or track, ran most of the time along the high ridges of the hills or downs, and they could look down on either side of them upon the **desolate** marshes where the snowy reeds sighed, and the ice crackled, and the duck in the red sunsets quacked loud on the winter air. The whole country was like that. Perhaps there would be a moory marsh on one side of the ridge, and a forest of a hundred thousand acres on the other, with all the great branches weighted in white. They could sometimes see a wisp of smoke among the trees, or a huddle of buildings far out among the impassable reeds, and twice they came to quite respectable towns which had several inns to boast of, but on the whole it was an England without civilization. The better roads were cleared of cover for a bow-shot on either side of them, lest the traveler should be slain by hidden thieves.

They slept where they could, sometimes in the hut of some cottager who was prepared to welcome them, sometimes in the castle of a brother knight who invited them to refresh themselves, sometimes in the firelight and fleas of a dirty little hovel with a bush tied to a pole outside it—this was the signboard used at that time by inns—and once or twice on the open ground, all huddled together for warmth between their grazing chargers. Wherever they went and wherever they slept, the east wind whistled in the reeds, and the geese went over high in the starlight, honking at the stars.

London was full to the brim. If Sir Ector had not been lucky enough to own a little land in Pie Street, on which there stood a respectable inn, they would have been hard put to it to find a lodging. But he did own it, and as a matter of fact drew most of his dividends from that source, so they were able to get three beds between the five of them. They thought themselves fortunate.

On the first day of the tournament, Sir Kay managed to get them on the way to the lists at least an hour before the jousts could possibly begin. He had lain awake all night, imagining how he was going to beat the best barons in England, and he had not been able to eat his breakfast. Now he rode at the front of the cavalcade, with pale cheeks, and Wart wished there was something he could do to calm him down. 19

Reading Skill
Compare Worldviews
How does this section connect past and present views of the world?

Vocabulary
desolate (des´ ə lit) *adj.* empty; solitary

19 **Reading Check**
Where are Sir Ector, Wart, and Kay traveling?

18 Reading Skill

Compare Worldviews

1. Encourage discussion of how the medieval worldview of the royalty of kings connects with the current worldview of leaders. **Ask** students whether any leaders of the last century have taken on the status of legends, and, if so, ask students to explain their answers.
Possible responses: Students may say that John F. Kennedy and Martin Luther King are legendary. Their deaths brought their lives to early ends, and both men are revered. John F. Kennedy's presidency is referred to as Camelot, and Martin Luther King had "a dream."
2. **Ask** students the Reading Skill question: How does this section connect past and present views of the world?
Possible response: White uses second person (you) to address the reader, suggesting that the reader does not happen "to have lived in the Old England of the twelfth century." By directly addressing the reader and suggesting that the reader would have to "imagine the wonders of their journey," White draws the imagination of the contemporary reader into the description of the past.

19 Reading Check

Possible response: Sir Ector, Wart, and Kay leave the Forest Sauvage and travel through the English countryside on their way to London.

Differentiated Instruction for Universal Access

Strategy for Less Proficient Readers

Students may have difficulty understanding Wart's actions concerning Merlyn's departure. Have students reread the page and then point out that Wart barely looks up to say goodbye to Merlyn. **Ask** students why Wart would not say goodbye to such a good friend.
Possible response: Students may say that Wart is too sad and does not want to accept that Merlyn is leaving him. To help students better understand Wart's response, encourage them to write a journal entry from Wart's point of view expressing how he feels at saying goodbye to his beloved tutor.

Enrichment for Advanced Readers

Have students pay attention to White's mixture of modern idioms with medieval scenes. Kay asks his father whether they can go to the tournament so that they can "have a shot" at it. When Sir Ector decides to go to the tournament, he says, "Dang it!" Have students analyze the effect that the mixture of modern idioms in medieval scenes has on the selection. As a writing prompt, ask students why White would do this. What effect does he wish it to have?

20 Humanities

Beaumains Overthrows Two Knights at the Stream by Louis Rhead

This illustration originally was printed in 1923 in *King Arthur and his Knights,* written for young readers by Sir James Knowles. Beaumains, dubbed "fair hands" by Sir Kay, who doubted his lineage, became known as the "kitchen knight." This illustration depicts him in a fight while on a quest to rid the damsel behind him of a treacherous knight in her own land. She later becomes Beaumains' wife. The illustration is an example of the "Golden Age of Illustration," the period between the late 1880s and the early 1920s when advances in printing and technology resulted in better art reproduction than ever before. Use these questions for discussion:

1. How would illustrations such as this one affect last century's young readers of the Arthurian legends?
   Possible response: Prior to television and film, these illustrations would provide the young readers with a sense of place and time and would provide details of costume and weapons that the words might not completely convey. The richness of the colors would allow the reader's imagination to fully enter the scene.
2. Does illustration of literary works play as important a role today as it did for readers of the past?
   Possible response: Most students will say that illustrations are still important. Some might bring up the example of this textbook, while others might mention comic book or graphic novel art. Others may say that an artist's depiction interferes with their own imagination in seeing a story.

20

Vocabulary Development

Selection Vocabulary Reinforcement

Students will benefit from additional examples and practice with the selection vocabulary words. Reinforce their comprehension with "show-you-know" sentences. The first part of the sentence uses the vocabulary word in an appropriate context. The second part of the sentence—the "show-you-know" part—clarifies the first. Model the strategy with this example for *surmise:*

I could only *surmise* whether the king had his subjects' best interests at heart; I had never seen evidence of how he felt about us.

Then, give students these sentence prompts and coach them in creating the clarification part:

1. A squire had to be a *stickler* for care of weapons and horses; ___________.
   Sample answer: his knight's life depended upon it.
2. Although squires were young, there was no room for them to act *petulantly;* ___________.
   Sample answer: they had to do as the knight commanded without question or back talk.

22 For country people, who only knew the dismantled tilting ground[14] of Sir Ector's castle, the scene which met their eyes was ravishing. It was a huge green pit in the earth, about as big as the arena at a football match. It lay ten feet lower than the surrounding country, with sloping banks, and the snow had been swept off it. It had been kept warm with straw, which had been cleared off that morning, and now the close-worn grass sparkled green in the white landscape. Round the arena there was a world of color so dazzling and moving and twinkling as to make one blink one's eyes. The wooden grandstands were painted in scarlet and white. The silk pavilions of famous people, pitched on every side, were azure and green and saffron and checkered. The pennons and pennoncells which floated everywhere in the sharp wind were flapping with every color of the rainbow, as they strained and slapped at their flagpoles, and the barrier down the middle of the arena itself was done in chessboard squares of black and white. Most of the combatants and their friends had not yet arrived, but one could see from those few who had come how the very people would turn the scene into a bank of flowers, and how the armor would flash, and the scalloped sleeves of the heralds jig in the wind, as they raised their brazen trumpets to their lips to shake the fleecy clouds of winter with joyances[15] and fanfares.

"Good heavens!" cried Sir Kay. "I have left my sword at home."

"Can't joust without a sword," said Sir Grummore. "Quite irregular."

"Better go and fetch it," said Sir Ector. "You have time."

"My squire will do," said Sir Kay. "What an awful mistake to make! Here, squire, ride hard back to the inn and fetch my sword. You shall have a shilling[16] if you fetch it in time."

The Wart went as pale as Sir Kay was, and looked as if he were going to strike him. Then he said, "It shall be done, master," and turned his ambling palfrey[17] against the stream of newcomers. He began to push his way toward their hostelry[18] as best he might.

23 "To offer me money!" cried the Wart to himself. "To look down at this beastly little donkey-affair off his great charger and to call me Squire! Oh, Merlyn, give me patience with the brute, and stop me from throwing his filthy shilling in his face."

When he got to the inn it was closed. Everybody had thronged to see the famous tournament, and the entire household had followed after the mob. Those were lawless days and it was not safe to leave your house—or even to go to sleep in it—unless you were certain

14. **tilting ground** ground on which a joust takes place.
15. **joyances** (joi´ əns iz) *n.* old word meaning "rejoicing."
16. **shilling** (shil´ iŋ) *n.* British silver coin.
17. **palfrey** (pôl´ frē) *n.* old term for a saddle horse, especially one for women.
18. **hostelry** (häs´ təl rē) *n.* inn.

21 ◀ Critical Viewing
Contrast the idea of knighthood conveyed by this illustration with the concerns of Pellinore and Kay. **[Contrast]**

Literary Analysis
Legends and Legendary Heroes
What does Wart's reaction have in common with the reaction a legendary hero would have in these circumstances?

24 Reading Check
How does Kay feel on the morning of his first tournament?

Differentiated Instruction for Universal Access

Strategy for Special Needs Students
Students may need assistance with understanding how Wart and the others feel on first seeing London and the jousting fields. Encourage students to empathize with Wart and the others in the group by comparing their own impressions on first seeing a very large city or a dazzling setting, such as a large amusement park, with those of the characters in the story. Have students write recollections of their impressions.

Enrichment for Gifted/Talented Students
Have students create a mixed-media mural showing what the tournament ground looked like. Encourage them to follow the description in the story while adding their own details. Encourage them to display their finished product in the classroom or a school display case.

21 Critical Viewing
Possible response: The knight on the white horse has unseated, and possibly killed, his opponent, and he is brandishing his sword to protect the lady following him from danger. For Kay and Pellinore, the tournament is only a festival, not a matter of life and death. The ladies are observers and are not in danger.

22 Literary Analysis
Legends and Legendary Heroes
1. Have the students read the bracketed passage. **Ask** students how the description of the jousting area sets the stage for a legendary scene.
   Possible response: The arena is a huge green pit, the flags are snapping in the wind, the grass sparkles, and everything is very colorful. White builds a glorious sense of sight and sound to set the stage for an important event.
2. Then **ask:** How does Sir Kay's exclamation "Good heavens! I have left my sword at home" contrast with the previous paragraphs and the idea of legend?
   Answer: By forgetting his sword, the newly dubbed Sir Kay does not behave like a knight. "At home" makes Kay sound as if he is a young boy who forgot his lunch rather than a legendary figure.

23 Literary Analysis
Legends and Legendary Heroes
1. Remind students that while legendary heroes are larger than life, they remain humans who are deeply concerned with right and wrong, or honorable and dishonorable, action.
2. **Ask** the Literary Analysis question: What does Wart's reaction have in common with the reaction a legendary hero would have in these circumstances?
   Possible response: Wart, though he is a squire, is offended by Sir Kay's offer of money and by his air of superiority. Wart is reacting as a common man who has been unjustly insulted by an unworthy authority figure.

24 Reading Check
Answer: Kay is very scared and miserable.

25 Reading Skill

Compare Wordviews

1. Discuss with students how the world is viewed through the values and beliefs that people hold in common. Guide students to recognize that not everyone thinks alike, but often in the past, generations have held common values.
2. **Ask** students to give examples of worldviews of decades of the recent past.
   Possible response: Students might cite the selfless service of the World War II generation and the rebellion and questioning of authority of the 1960s.
3. **Ask** the Reading Skill question: Which details here reflect modern attitudes and which reflect the world of legend?
   Possible response: Wart shows a legendary attitude when he determines to fulfill Kay's request by any means. Wart shows modern attitudes when he wonders whether he could steal a sword and then thinks of buying a sword.

26 Connecting to the Big Question

1. Remind students that legendary heroes, though they have performed some memorable and extraordinary deed, do not have to be one-dimensional characters. Heroes, as Wart is portrayed in this excerpt, come to life when they are given a range of human traits.
2. Have students read the bracketed text.
   Ask: How is Wart's attitude toward the sword different from what you might expect?
   Possible response: Wart treats the sword as if it were an ordinary object, taking it for a "war memorial."
3. **Ask:** How does Wart's naiveté contribute to your understanding of heroes?
   Possible response: Wart's innocence and ignorance of his own destiny present him not as an infallible hero but as a normal human boy, which makes him more emotionally accessible, realistic, and likable as a character. Because Wart experiences ordinary human emotion—specifically, naiveté, fear, and skepticism—he shows that heroes can be vulnerable, modest human beings.

Reading Skill
Compare Worldviews
Which details here reflect modern attitudes and which reflect the world of legend?

that it was impregnable.[19] The wooden shutters bolted over the downstairs windows were two inches thick, and the doors were double-barred.

"Now what do I do," asked the Wart, "to earn my shilling?"

He looked ruefully at the blind little inn, and began to laugh.

"Poor Kay," he said. "All that shilling stuff was only because he was scared and miserable, and now he has good cause to be. Well, he shall have a sword of some sort if I have to break into the Tower of London.

(25) "How does one get hold of a sword?" he continued. "Where can I steal one? Could I waylay some knight, even if I am mounted on an ambling pad, and take his weapons by force? There must be some swordsmith or armorer in a great town like this, whose shop would be still open."

He turned his mount and cantered off along the street. There was a quiet churchyard at the end of it, with a kind of square in front of the church door. In the middle of the square there was a heavy stone with an anvil on it, and a fine new sword was stuck through the anvil.

(26) "Well," said the Wart, "I suppose it is some sort of war memorial, but it will have to do. I am sure nobody would grudge Kay a war memorial, if they knew his desperate straits."

He tied his reins round a post of the lych gate,[20] strode up the gravel path, and took hold of the sword.

"Come, sword," he said. "I must cry your mercy and take you for a better cause.

"This is extraordinary," said the Wart. "I feel strange when I have hold of this sword, and I notice everything much more clearly. Look at the beautiful gargoyles[21] of the church, and of the monastery which it belongs to. See how splendidly all the famous banners in the aisle are waving. How nobly that yew[22] holds up the red flakes of its timbers to worship God. How clean the snow is. I can smell something like fetherfew and sweet briar—and is it music that I hear?"

It was music, whether of pan-pipes or of recorders, and the light in the churchyard was so clear, without being dazzling, that one could have picked a pin out twenty yards away.

"There is something in this place," said the Wart. "There are people. Oh, people, what do you want?"

Nobody answered him, but the music was loud and the light beautiful.

---

19. **impregnable** (im preg´ nə bəl) *adj.* not capable of being captured or entered by force.
20. **lych** (lich) **gate** roofed gate at the entrance to a churchyard.
21. **gargoyles** (gär´ goilz´) *n.* grotesque sculptures of animals or fantastic creatures decorating a building.
22. **yew** (yo͞o) *n.* type of evergreen tree with red cones.

Vocabulary Development

Word Forms

Give students a blank **Word Form Chart** (***Professional Development Guidebook***, p. 42), with *stickler, petulantly,* and *surmise* in the correct columns. Work with the class, or have students work with a partner, to determine the related forms. The final chart should look like the one shown below.

Hold students accountable for integrating the related forms of the words in their speaking and writing.

Noun	Verb	Adjective	Adverb
stickler	stickle		
petulance		petulant	**petulantly**
surmise	surmise		

27

"People," cried the Wart, "I must take this sword. It is not for me, but for Kay. I will bring it back."

There was still no answer, and Wart turned back to the anvil. He saw the golden letters, which he did not read, and the jewels on the pommel, flashing in the lovely light.

"Come, sword," said the Wart.

He took hold of the handles with both hands, and strained against the stone. There was a melodious consort[23] on the recorders, but nothing moved.

28 The Wart let go of the handles, when they were beginning to bite into the palms of his hands, and stepped back, seeing stars.

"It is well fixed," he said.

He took hold of it again and pulled with all his might. The music played more strongly, and the light all about the churchyard glowed like amethysts; but the sword still stuck.

"Oh, Merlyn," cried the Wart, "help me to get this weapon."

There was a kind of rushing noise, and a long chord played along with it. All round the churchyard there were hundreds of old friends. They rose over the church wall all together, like the Punch-and-Judy[24] ghosts of remembered days, and there were badgers and nightingales and vulgar crows and hares and wild geese and falcons and fishes and dogs and dainty unicorns and
30 solitary wasps and corkindrills and hedgehogs and griffins and the thousand other animals he had met. They loomed round the church wall, the lovers and helpers of the Wart, and they all spoke solemnly in turn. Some of them had come from the banners in the

23. **consort** (kän´ sôrt´) *n.* piece of music composed for a small group.

24. **Punch-and-Judy** puppets of the quarrelsome Punch and his wife, Judy, who fight constantly in a comical way.

Literary Analysis
Legends and Legendary Heroes
How does the mysterious music here add to the legendary quality of events?

29 **Reading Check**
What does Kay send Wart to do?

PROFESSIONAL DEVELOPMENT

Use Lit Logs to Honor Difficulty and Identify Passages for Re-reading: Have students write a lit log entry about any confusing language or events in "Arthur Becomes King of Britain." Then, have them read the logs aloud, or collect the logs and read them outside of class.

Through these logs, identify where students are having trouble understanding the selection. Then, choose a few troublesome spots and have students re-read these pages. Encourage students to answer as many questions as they can through re-reading. Clarify and discuss any remaining questions as a class. Finally, discuss the elements of the story that make it difficult.

For more of this author's strategies, see the Professional Development essay, pp. 1046c–1046d.

27 Humanities

Merlin the Magician by Howard Pyle (1853–1911)

Howard Pyle was a noted American author and illustrator who founded the American Brandywine School of Art. This drawing is part of the 1902 *King Arthur and His Knights,* which Pyle wrote and illustrated. Here Merlin (referred to as *Merlyn* in the selection) is reading a book, a description of the past; a crystal ball sits beside him to see the future. Merlin's power came in part from his living backward in time. He knows the future because he has been there; he does not know the past because that is his future. An accurate book would give him foresight into his own future. Use these questions for discussion:

1. Merlin lives backward in time. If he is reading a book, is he reading the past or the future?
   Possible response: He is reading his future as he reads of the past.
2. Ask students if knowing the future but being unable to change it would be an advantage for an advisor to a leader?
   Possible response: If he or she were believed, it could be an advantage.

28 Literary Analysis

Legends and Legendary Heroes

1. Remind students that legendary characters carry with them a sense of destiny that encompasses the history of the nation they represent.
2. After students read the bracketed passage, **ask** the Literary Analysis question: How does the mysterious music here add to the legendary quality of events?
   Possible response: The mystical music Wart hears suggests that an unearthly presence is witnessing the events. As the King is believed to be ordained by God, the implication is that this heavenly music recognizes the rightful heir to the throne.

29 Reading Check

Answer: Kay tells Wart to ride back to the inn and fetch his sword.

30 Reading Skill

Compare Worldviews

1. Have students review their earlier comments about the medieval worldview and the role of the King as the center of the culture.
2. **Ask** the Reading Skill question: Which details in this paragraph suggest the worldview of legendary times?
   Possible response: The rushing and chiming sounds and the real and imaginary animals speaking suggest a worldview in which the magical is considered "normal."

31 Literary Analysis

Legends and Legendary Heroes

- After students read the bracketed passage, **ask** the Literary Analysis question: How does this event mark Wart as a legendary hero?
  Possible response: Wart successfully removes the sword on his third try, thus becoming the rightful King of England, but he is unaware of the significance of his act.

Monitor Progress Ask students to explain how removing the sword makes Arthur legendary.
Answer: No one else can remove the sword, so when Wart removes it, he is shown to be "better than the average human" and a king.

Reteach Remind students that legendary heroes are human but are "larger than life." Have students create a two-column chart with one column labeled "human," and the other labeled "legendary." Direct students to list in one column the aspects of Arthur that suggest he is just like everybody else. Students should list in the other column the aspects of Arthur that are superhuman.

32 Literary Analysis

Legends and Legendary Heroes

1. Remind students that while legendary heroes are larger than life, they remain human.
2. **Ask** students to respond to the Literary Analysis item: Contrast Wart's everyday language with the significance of the event he describes.
   Possible response: Wart's everyday language paints him as a boy who does not realize what has just happened to him.

Reading Skill **30**
Compare Worldviews
Which details in this paragraph suggest the worldview of legendary times?

church, where they were painted in heraldry, some from the waters and the sky and the fields about—but all, down to the smallest shrew mouse, had come to help on account of love. Wart felt his power grow.

"Put your back into it," said a luce (or pike) off one of the heraldic banners, "as you once did when I was going to snap you up. Remember that power springs from the nape of the neck."

"What about those forearms," asked a badger gravely, "that are held together by a chest? Come along, my dear embryo,[25] and find your tool."

A merlin sitting at the top of the yew tree cried out, "Now then, Captain Wart, what is the first law of the foot? I thought I once heard something about never letting go."

"Don't work like a stalling woodpecker," urged a tawny owl affectionately. "Keep up a steady effort, my duck, and you will have it yet."

A white-front said. "Now, Wart, if you were once able to fly the great North Sea, surely you can coordinate a few little wing-muscles here and there? Fold your powers together, with the spirit of your mind, and it will come out like butter. Come along, Homo sapiens,[26] for all we humble friends of yours are waiting here to cheer."

Literary Analysis **31**
Legends and Legendary Heroes
How does this event mark Wart as a legendary hero?

The Wart walked up to the great sword for the third time. He put out his right hand softly and drew it out as gently as from a scabbard.

There was a lot of cheering, a noise like a hurdy-gurdy[27] which went on and on. In the middle of this noise, after a long time, he saw Kay and gave him the sword. The people at the tournament were making a frightful row.

"But this is not my sword," said Sir Kay.

"It was the only one I could get," said the Wart. "The inn was locked."

Literary Analysis **32**
Legends and Legendary Heroes
Contrast Wart's everyday language with the significance of the event he describes.

"It is a nice-looking sword. Where did you get it?"

"I found it stuck in a stone, outside a church."

Sir Kay had been watching the tilting nervously, waiting for his turn. He had not paid much attention to his squire.

"That is a funny place to find one," he said.

"Yes, it was stuck through an anvil."

"What?" cried Sir Kay, suddenly rounding upon him. "Did you just say this sword was stuck in a stone?"

---

25. **embryo** (em´ brē ō´) *n.* anything in an early stage of development.
26. **Homo sapiens** (hō´ mō sā´ pē enz´) scientific name for human beings.
27. **hurdy-gurdy** (hʉr´ dē gʉr´ dē) *n.* musical instrument played by turning a crank.

Vocabulary Development

Vocabulary Knowledge Rating

When students have completed reading and discussing "Arthur Becomes King of Britain," have them take out their **Vocabulary Knowledge Rating Chart** for this selection. Read the words aloud once more and have students rate their knowledge of the words again in the After Reading column. Clarify any words that are still problematic. Have students write their own definition and example or sentence in the appropriate column. Then, have students complete the Vocabulary Practice at the end of the selection. Encourage students to use the words in further discussion and written work about this selection. Remind them that they will be accountable for these words on the **Selection Test, *Unit 6 Resources,*** pp. 139–141 or 142–144.

"It was," said the Wart. "It was a sort of war memorial."

Sir Kay stared at him for several seconds in amazement, opened his mouth, shut it again, licked his lips, then turned his back and plunged through the crowd. He was looking for Sir Ector, and the Wart followed after him.

"Father," cried Sir Kay, "come here a moment."

"Yes, my boy," said Sir Ector. "Splendid falls these professional chaps do manage. Why, what's the matter, Kay? You look as white as a sheet."

"Do you remember that sword which the King of England would pull out?"

"Yes."

"Well, here it is. I have it. It is in my hand. I pulled it out."

Sir Ector did not say anything silly. He looked at Kay and he looked at the Wart. Then he stared at Kay again, long and lovingly, and said, "We will go back to the church."

33 "Now then, Kay," he said, when they were at the church door. He looked at his firstborn kindly, but straight between the eyes. "Here is the stone, and you have the sword. It will make you the King of England. You are my son that I am proud of, and always will be, whatever you do. Will you promise me that you took it out by your own might?"

Kay looked at his father. He also looked at the Wart and at the sword.

Then he handed the sword to the Wart quite quietly.

He said, "I am a liar. Wart pulled it out."

As far as the Wart was concerned, there was a time after this in which Sir Ector kept telling him to put the sword back into the stone—which he did—and in which Sir Ector and Kay then vainly tried to take it out. The Wart took it out for them, and stuck it back again once or twice. After this, there was another time which was more painful.

He saw that his dear guardian was looking quite old and powerless, and that he was kneeling down with difficulty on a gouty[28] knee.

"Sir," said Sir Ector, without looking up, although he was speaking to his own boy.

"Please do not do this, father," said the Wart, kneeling down also. "Let me help you up, Sir Ector, because you are making me unhappy."

35 "Nay, nay, my lord," said Sir Ector, with some very feeble old tears. "I was never your father nor of your blood, but I wote[29] well ye

Reading Skill
Compare Worldviews
What details of the conversation between Sir Ector and Kay reflect both modern and medieval values?

34 **Reading Check**
What does Sir Kay tell his father about the sword?

28. **gouty** (gout′ ē) *adj.* having gout, a disease causing swelling and severe pain in the joints.
29. **wote** (wōt) *v.* old world meaning "know."

33 Reading Skill

Compare Worldviews

- **Ask** students to discuss how they view archaic language.
  Possible response: Students may say that people in the past spoke formally and used correct grammar all of the time.
- **Ask** the Reading Skill question: What details of the conversation between Sir Ector and Kay reflect both modern and medieval values?
  Possible response: Kay's first inclination is to claim that he pulled the sword from the stone, a dreadful lie in the medieval worldview. Sir Ector refrains from saying anything *"silly,"* and *silly* is a word inappropriate to a legendary moment. The honor with which Sir Ector approaches the issue suits the high moral tone of the medieval setting, but students may be surprised at the loving, patient, and kindly manner in which he resolves the matter with his son because of its modernity.

34 Reading Check

Answer: First, Kay tells his father that he pulled the sword out himself. Then, he tells the truth—that Wart pulled it out.

Concept Connector

Anticipation Guide

Have students return to their **Anticipation Guides** and respond to the statements again, this time in the After Reading column. They may do this individually, or you may wish to have them work in their original pairs or groups. Then, lead a class discussion. Start by putting responses from the Me and Group columns on the board. Guide students to recognize how their responses have changed—or remained the same—after reading the excerpt from *The Once and Future King*. Encourage students to cite specific details or evidence from the text to support their new responses to the statements.

Writing About the Big Question

Have students compare their responses to the sentence starters they completed before reading the selection with their ideas afterward. Ask them to explain whether their thoughts have changed.

Reading Skill Graphic Organizer

Ask students to review the graphic organizers they completed to investigate worldview while reading. You may want to use the partially completed **Reading Skill Graphic Organizer A** (p. 211 in *Graphic Organizer Transparencies*) as an example. Then, have students share their graphic organizers.

35 Literary Analysis

Legends and Legendary Heroes

- **Ask** students the Literary Analysis question: How does the change in the kind of words Sir Ector uses emphasize the legendary importance of the event?
  Possible response: When Sir Ector reverts to the formal language of medieval England, White signals to the reader that he or she is leaving the contemporary world of humor and witnessing a legendary moment.

ASSESS

Answers

Critical Thinking

1. Students may choose Wart, as he is sensible and honorable.
2. (a) The new king will be the knight who pulls the sword from the stone. (b) **Possible response:** Men become kings because of special ability.
3. (a) Kay asks Wart to fetch his sword from the inn. (b) At first Wart is angry. He then becomes dedicated to bringing Kay a sword. (c) Kay abuses his friendship and shows off. Wart is hurt but keeps his anger to himself and demonstrates humility.
4. (a) A variety of animals offer advice to Wart, including a merlin and an owl. (b) **Possible response:** The presence of the animals may suggest that Wart is to be king not only of the realm but also of all creatures.

THE BIG ? Can anyone be a hero?

Possible responses: (a) Sir Ector treats Wart differently once he realizes that it was Wart, not his son, who extracted the sword from the stone. Now that Wart is to be king, Sir Ector treats him with respect and deference.
(b) The opinions and responses of others make it possible for a hero to be anyone; he or she does not necessarily have to come from royal blood.

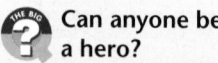

Literary Analysis
Legends and Legendary Heroes 35
How does the change in the kind of words Sir Ector uses emphasize the legendary importance of the event?

are of an higher blood than I wend[30] ye were."

"Plenty of people have told me you are not my father," said the Wart, "but it does not matter a bit."

"Sir," said Sir Ector humbly, "will ye be my good and gracious lord when ye are King?"

"Don't!" said the Wart.

"Sir," said Sir Ector, "I will ask no more of you but that you will make my son, your foster-brother, Sir Kay, seneschal[31] of all your lands?"

Kay was kneeling down too, and it was more than the Wart could bear.

"Oh, do stop," he cried. "Of course he can be seneschal, if I have got to be this King, and, oh, father, don't kneel down like that, because it breaks my heart. Please get up, Sir Ector, and don't make everything so horrible. Oh, dear, oh, dear, I wish I had never seen that filthy sword at all."

And the Wart also burst into tears.

30. **wend** (wend) *v.* thought (past tense of *ween,* an old word meaning "think").
31. **seneschal** (sen´ ə shəl) *n.* steward, or manager, in the house of a medieval noble.

Critical Thinking

1. **Respond:** Who is your favorite character in this retelling of the Arthur legend? Why?
2. **(a)** How is the new king of England to be chosen?
   (b) Draw Conclusions: What does this method suggest about the reason men become kings in the world of the story?
3. **(a)** What does Kay ask Wart to do when Kay discovers his sword is missing? **(b) Analyze:** Describe the reactions Wart has to Kay's request. **(c) Contrast:** Based on this incident, contrast the characters of Wart and Kay.
4. **(a)** Who or what offers advice to Wart as he attempts to pull the sword from the stone? **(b) Interpret:** How does this episode add to the sense of the importance of Wart's action?

THE BIG ? Can anyone be a hero?
(a) Which characters treat Wart differently at the end of the story? Why? **(b)** How do the responses of others help define the role of a hero?

Assessment Resources

Unit 6 Resources

L1 L2 EL **Selection Test A,** pp. 139–141. Administer Test A to less advanced readers and English Learners.

L3 L4 **Selection Test B,** pp. 142–144. Administer Test B to on-level and more advanced students.

L3 L4 **Open-Book Test,** pp. 136–148. As an alternative, give the Open-Book Test.

All **Customizable Test Bank**

All **Self-tests**
Students may prepare for the **Selection Test** by taking the **Self-test** online.

PHLit Online! All assessment resources are available at **www.PHLitOnline.com.**

After You Read | Arthur Becomes King of Britain

Literary Analysis: Legends and Legendary Heroes

1. Which features of **legends** are present in this excerpt? Use a chart like the one shown to gather examples from the text.

Life Story of Legendary Hero	Concern with Right and Wrong	Reflections of National Pride

2. What point about heroes might the author be making by mixing ordinary and legendary characteristics in Wart? Explain.

Reading Skill: Compare Worldviews

3. **(a)** Based on King Pellinore's tales of "'signs and wonders,'" draw a conclusion about his basic beliefs. **(b)** Describe Sir Grummore's reaction to the report. **(c) Compare and contrast** Pellinore's and Grummore's **worldviews.**
4. **(a)** Find three examples in which characters speak casually or in slang about legendary events. **(b)** What might these examples suggest about the difference between the author's worldview and the worldview of those who originally told the legend of Arthur?

Vocabulary

Practice Answer each of the following questions. Explain your response.

1. Will a *stickler* for cleanliness complain when you spill milk?
2. If you want to impress someone, should you behave *petulantly*?
3. Is it fair to jail a person based on a neighbor's *surmise*?
4. Will a trusting person respond *skeptically* to a friend's excuse?
5. Would a *sumptuous* house have silk pillows and velvet drapes?
6. Is a *desolate* road a convenient place to get a flat tire?

Word Study Use the context of the sentences and what you know about the **Latin suffix *-ate*** to explain your answer to each question.

1. Would a *moderate* climate generally have very high temperatures?
2. Is an *articulate* person likely to be troubled by speaking in public?

Word Study

The **Latin suffix *-ate*** means "characterized by" or "showing."

Challenge Explain how the suffix *-ate* contributes to the meanings of these words. Consult a dictionary if necessary.

collegiate
delicate
desperate

ASSESS/EXTEND

Answers

Literary Analysis

1. **Life Story:** Wart starts out as a squire, then becomes a king; **Right and Wrong:** Sir Kay abuses his power, Wart tries to find Kay a sword, Kay confesses his lie; **Pride:** everyone mourns for Pendragon, there is an England-wide tournament to find the rightful king, the animal kingdom recognizes Wart as king.

   For other sample answers, see ***Graphic Organizer Transparencies,* Literary Analysis Graphic Organizer A**, p. 214, and the **Additional Answers** section.
2. **Possible response:** By mixing characteristics, White might be showing that heroes are men who have greatness thrust upon them and who rise to the challenge.

Reading Skill

3. (a) Pellinore believes in the supernatural selection of a new king. (b) Sir Grummore is a skeptic who disparages the report about the sword in the stone. (c) Pellinore is a believer in spite of his silliness; his world is full of wonder and hope. Grummore, however, doubts the power of signs and wonders.
4. **Possible responses:** (a) King Pellinore speaks "of no hair and next of skin"; Grummore calls Excalibur a "talkative weapon"; and Wart refers to "some sort of war memorial." (b) White is having fun with the legend, creating silly characters who use contemporary slang to describe legendary events. In the end his characters—and his story—show honor and respect to Arthur.

Vocabulary

Practice
Sample answers:

1. Yes, because a stickler for cleanliness wants everything clean and orderly at all times.
2. No, because if you behave petulantly, people will find you annoying.
3. No, because a surmise is a guess, which could be wrong.

Answers continued

4. No, a trusting person will not respond skeptically to a friend's excuse, because that would suggest that he didn't believe the friend.
5. Yes, a sumptuous house would have silk pillows and velvet drapes, because they are luxurious.
6. No, because on a desolate road, you are not likely to find people or resources to help you.

Word Study
Sample answers:

1. No, the suffix *-ate* means "characterized by" or "showing," so a *moderate* climate is "characterized by" mild weather.
2. No, the suffix *-ate* means "characterized by" or "showing," so an *articulate* person is "characterized by" his ease with words.

Word Study: Challenge
Sample answers:

If someone is *collegiate,* she is showing membership to a college. Something *delicate* is characterized by the quality of tenderness. Someone who is *desperate* is characterized by despair.

PRETEACH

*Skills instruction for the **Reading Skill** and **Literary Analysis** concepts appears on p. 1153.*

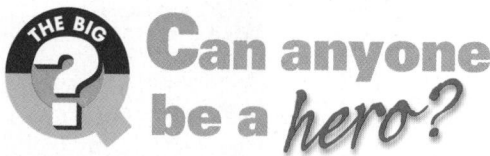

❶ Writing About the Big Question

1. Review the assignment with the class.
2. Prompt students to think about heroes they have seen depicted in movies, comic books, and video games. Discuss with students the traits, human or superhuman, these heroes possess that students find appealing.
3. Have students complete the sentence starter. Review responses as a class. (**Possible response:** A reader can more easily identify with a legendary hero who displays attributes such as fear, love, and vulnerability.)
4. Remind students that their answers will help them think about the Big Question, "Can anyone be a hero?"

While You Read

Tell students that as they read, they should look for examples of Arthur's and Sir Bedivere's behavior that show them not only as heroes but as flawed human beings.

❷ Vocabulary

1. Have students preview the selection vocabulary.
2. For each word, have students say the word aloud.
3. Then, use the word in a sentence that defines the word.
4. Finally, repeat your definitional sentence or a similar sentence with the word missing, and have the class "fill in the blank" chorally. Here is a an example:

   Something brandished is waved or shown as a threat. To prevent attack from the wasp, the tarantula [students say "brandished"] *its fangs.*

❸ Word Study

1. Introduce the skill, using the instruction in the box.
2. Ask students for a word ending in *-ment* that means "the act of praising or admiring" using their knowledge of the suffix. (**Answer:** *compliment*)

Making Connections | **Morte d'Arthur**

Can anyone be a *hero?*

❶ Writing About the Big Question

In "Morte d'Arthur," a poet shows the human, flawed side of a legendary hero who is facing death. Use this sentence starter to develop your ideas about the Big Question.

A reader can more easily identify with a **legendary** hero who displays **attributes** such as ______________ than one who demonstrates ______________.

While You Read Look for examples of Arthur's and Sir Bedivere's behavior that show them not just as heroes, but as humans with flaws.

❷ Vocabulary

Read each word and its definition. Decide whether you know the word well, know it a little bit, or do not know it at all. After you read, see how your knowledge of each word has increased.

- **disparagement** (di spar´ ij mənt) *n.* comments expressing a low opinion of or lack of respect for (p. 1176) *The critic's disparagement of her painting upset her.* disparage *v.* disparagingly *adv.*
- **bore** (bôr) *v.* carried (p. 1176) *We bore the injured player to the sidelines on a stretcher.* bear *v.*
- **reverence** (rev´ ə rəns) *n.* a feeling of deep respect, love, or awe (p. 1179) *The queen's subjects showed reverence toward her by bowing.* reverent *adj.* reverently *adv.* revere *v.*
- **brandished** (bran´ disht) *v.* showed, waved, or shook in a threatening or triumphant manner (p. 1180) *As he ran home, he brandished his excellent report card.*
- **wistfully** (wist´ fəl lē) *adv.* showing vague yearnings (p. 1181) *She looked wistfully at her old house, remembering the time she had lived there.* wistful *adj.* wistfulness *n.*
- **languid** (laŋ´ gwid) *adj.* without energy (p. 1181) *His languid arms dangled by his side.* languidly *adv.* languidness *n.* languish *v.*

❸ Word Study

The **Latin suffix *-ment*** means "act" or "state of." It often indicates a noun.

In this poem, the speaker shows his **disparagement,** or state of disappointment or disregard for the work he is about to read.

Vocabulary Development

Vocabulary Knowledge Rating

Create a **Vocabulary Knowledge Rating Chart** (*Professional Development Guidebook,* p. 33) for this selection. Include the selection vocabulary and the Big Question words that appear in the Writing About the Big Question sentence starter on this page. (The Big Question vocabulary is introduced on pp. 1046–1047.)

Give students a copy of the chart. Read the words aloud and have students mark their rating in the Before Reading column. Urge them to be alert to these words as they read and discuss the selection.

Tally how many students think they know a word to gauge how much instruction to provide. As students read and discuss the selection, point out the words and their context.

PHLit Online! **Vocabulary Central,** featuring tools, activities, and songs for studying vocabulary, is available online at **www.PHLitOnline.com.**

Meet

Alfred, Lord Tennyson

(1809–1892)

Author of

Morte d'Arthur

Alfred, Lord Tennyson was born in eastern Lincolnshire in England. His work was immensely popular during his lifetime and won him the friendship of Queen Victoria. In 1850, Tennyson was appointed poet laureate of England.

A Life's Work It took Tennyson more than forty years to complete *The Idylls of the King,* his epic retelling of the King Arthur legends. By conjuring up a golden Arthurian age—and the problems that doomed it—Tennyson expressed the questions people of his own time had about life.

DID YOU KNOW?

Tennyson was known as "the poet of the people."

❹ BACKGROUND FOR THE LEGEND

Legends of King Arthur

The figure of King Arthur, the legendary ruler of England, may be based on a historical Welsh ruler who resisted Germanic invaders of Britain in the 500s. The first English prose version of the legends, *Le Morte d'Arthur,* was written around 1470 by Sir Thomas Malory. In "Morte d'Arthur," Alfred, Lord Tennyson adapts the tale of Arthur's passing.

Daily Bellringer

For each class during which you will teach this selection, have students complete one of the five Revision activities for Week 34 in the *Daily Bellringer Activities* booklet.

❹ Background

Legends of King Arthur

The author frames the telling of "Morte d'Arthur" in his own era. The poem opens late on Christmas Eve after the festivities are done. A group of friends is sad that in modern times, the serious aspects of Christmas are neglected in favor of games and lighter interests. The friends include the narrator (Tennyson), Holmes (a parson), and Everard Hall (the poet who will read his tale of King Arthur).

Multidraft Reading

This icon ● marks natural pauses in the selection. To assist struggling readers and to deepen reading for all, assign the text in "chunks," following the icons, and apply multidraft reading protocols. For each reading, have students set the purpose indicated:

- **First reading**—literal comprehension: answering the Reading Check questions.
- **Second reading**—application of skills: answering the Legends and Legendary Heroes and Compare Worldviews prompts.
- **Third reading**—interpretation: answering the end-of-selection questions.

For more guidance, refer to the *Classroom Strategies and Teaching Routines* card on multidraft reading.

Differentiated Instruction — Additional Instruction

EL Extended Support—English Learners

Have students complete the **Reading and Vocabulary Warm-ups,** ***Unit 6 Resources,*** pp. 80–83, before they read. Assign the prereading pages for the selection in the ***Reader's Notebook: English Learner's Version.*** Then, have students listen to portions of the selection on the ***Hear It!*** **Audio CD.**

L1 L2 Extended Support—Struggling Readers

Have students complete the **Reading and Vocabulary Warm-ups,** ***Unit 6 Resources,*** pp. 80–83, before they read. Assign the prereading pages for the selection in the ***Reader's Notebook: Adapted Version.*** Then, have students listen to portions of the selection on the ***Hear It!*** **Audio CD** (adapted text).

Extended Support—Reluctant Readers

To build motivation and engagement before assigning the selection, have students read "Our Hero!" a thematically related selection in ***Reality Central.*** Then, use the questions at the conclusion of the related selection to guide discussion.

PHLit Online!

For more about the author, practice with the selection vocabulary, and more background, go online at **www.PHLitOnline.com.**

❶ Activating Prior Knowledge

1. Prepare an **Anticipation Guide** (see ***Professional Development Guidebook,*** pp. 36–38) with the following statements:
   - The values of the past are superior to those of the present.
   - One is bound to honor promises made to a dying friend.
   - Legends show only the virtues of a society.
2. Give students copies of the prepared **Anticipation Guide.** Have students mark their responses in the Me column. Then, have students discuss the statements in pairs or groups and mark the Guides again, this time in the Group column.
3. For further guidance, use the ***Classroom Strategies and Teaching Routines*** card for **Anticipation Guides.**

Concept Connector ⟶

Students will return to the **Anticipation Guide** after completing "Morte d'Arthur."

Small-Group Activity

To familiarize students with the tone and rhythm of the poem, have small groups read lines 1–51. Assign each student a character from the poem for which to read that character's dialogue. Make sure there are enough students in the group so that the lines of each speaker can be read. Have students read the lines aloud, taking their appropriate turns. Then, discuss students' reactions to the tone and rhythm.

❷ About the Selection

Several friends, while sitting around the fire on Christmas Eve, prevail upon the poet in the group to share his retelling of the Arthurian legend. The poet tells the story of Arthur's death and Sir Bedivere's obedience to the dying king's last request.

❸

❶ ❷

Morte d'Arthur

Alfred, Lord Tennyson

Vocabulary Development

Thematic Vocabulary: The Big Question

As students are discussing "Morte d'Arthur," encourage them to use the thematic vocabulary presented in Introducing the Big Question, pp. 1146–1147. You might encourage them with sentence starters like these:

1. The poem begins with the reflection that *honor* has become . . .
2. An epic poem highlights the *integrity* of heroes by . . .
3. By using dialogue to give voice to the dying Arthur, Tennyson shows that Arthur's *character* is . . .
4. The friends seem to long for the *courage* displayed long ago because . . .

The Epic

At Francis Allen's on the Christmas eve—
The game of forfeits[1] done—the girls all kissed
Beneath the sacred bush and passed away—
The parson Holmes, the poet Everard Hall,
The host, and I sat round the wassail bowl,[2]
Then halfway ebbed; and there we held a talk,
How all the old honor had from Christmas gone,
Or gone or dwindled down to some odd games
In some odd nooks like this; till I, tired out
With cutting eights[3] that day upon the pond,
Where, three times slipping from the outer edge,
I bumped the ice into three several stars,
Fell in a doze; and half-awake I heard
The parson taking wide and wider sweeps,
Now harping on the church commissioners,
Now hawking at geology and schism;[4]
5 Until I woke, and found him settled down
Upon the general decay of faith
Right through the world: "at home was little left,
And none abroad; there was no anchor, none,
To hold by." Francis, laughing, clapped his hand
On Everard's shoulder, with "I hold by him."
"And I," quoth Everard, "by the wassail-bowl."
"Why yes," I said, "we knew your gift that way
At college; but another which you had—
I mean of verse (for so we held it then)—
What came of that?" "You know," said Frank, "he burnt
His epic, his King Arthur, some twelve books"—
And then to me demanding why: "O, sir,
He thought that nothing new was said, or else
Something so said 'twas nothing—that a truth
Looks freshest in the fashion of the day;
God knows; he has a mint of reasons; ask.
It pleased *me* well enough." "Nay, nay," said Hall,

1. **forfeits** (fôr´ fits) *n.* game in which something is taken away as a penalty for making a mistake.
2. **wassail** (wäs´ əl) **bowl** *n.* punch bowl.
3. **cutting eights** ice-skating in such a way that the skates cut figure eights in the ice.
4. **schism** (siz´ əm) *n.* division within an organization, especially a church, because of a difference of opinion.

4 ◀ **Critical Viewing**
Based on the details in this painting, what do you predict will be the mood of the poem? **[Predict]**

Reading Skill
Compare Worldviews
What do lines 13–21 show about people's worldview in the poet's time?

6 **Reading Check**
What has Everard written?

3 Humanities

The Lamentation of King Arthur by William Bell Scott (1811–1890)

Scott was a British poet and painter. In his early twenties, he established himself as an artist and was appointed to an academic position as a teacher of design. In addition to his decorative work, he also focused on painting portraits and historical scenes.

4 Critical Viewing

Possible response: The mood of the poem will be serious and melancholy.

5 Reading Skill

Compare Worldviews

1. Remind students that they will explore two worldviews: that of Tennyson's time and that of Arthur's time.
2. **Ask** students the Reading Skill question: What do lines 13–21 show about people's worldview in the poet's time?
   Answer: The group of friends is sad that in their time the serious aspects of Christmas are neglected in favor of games and lighter interests. The parson, who believes that faith has decayed and that there are no values to cherish, is complaining about a "schism" or division in the church when it comes to matters of science.

6 Reading Check

Answer: Everard has written a twelve-volume epic of King Arthur in verse.

Differentiated Instruction for Universal Access

Strategy for Less Proficient Readers
Students may have difficulty following the story of Arthur because of the stylized language of the poem. Direct students to keep running summaries of the poem and lists of puzzling words and phrases as they read. They should also list the numbers of the lines where the words appear to review after they have finished the legend.

Enrichment for Advanced Readers
Students may enjoy imitating Tennyson's style to retell a different event. Have students follow Everard Hall's example and write a brief passage of unrhymed blank verse (iambic pentameter) describing some historical moment that other students will recognize. Challenge them to use *thou* and *thee* with the correct verb forms. Have them read their verses to the class.

PHLit Online!
This selection is available in interactive format in the **Enriched Online Student Edition** at **www.PHLitOnline.com,** which includes a thematically related video with writing prompt and an interactive graphic organizer.

❼ Literary Analysis
Legends and Legendary Heroes

1. Have a volunteer read aloud lines 57–63. Then, **ask** students to summarize the action in the passage.
   Answer: Sir Bedivere, King Arthur's last remaining knight, takes the wounded king into a ruined church.
2. Next, **ask** students to describe how the setting of the passage complements the final hours of a legend.
   Possible response: Students may say that taking Arthur into a ruined church creates the feeling that Arthur's defeat is also the defeat of goodness and virtue. Also, because Sir Bedivere is the last remaining knight, the solitude of the two men gives the scene a mysterious air, befitting of a legend.

"Why take the style of those heroic times?
For nature brings not back the mastodon,
Nor we those times; and why should any man
Remodel models? these twelve books of mine
Were faint Homeric echoes,[5] nothing-worth,
Mere chaff and draff, much better burnt." "But I,"
Said Francis, "picked the eleventh from this hearth,
And have it; keep a thing, its use will come.
I hoard it as a sugarplum for Holmes."
He laughed, and I, though sleepy, like a horse
That hears the corn-bin open, pricked my ears;
For I remembered Everard's college fame
When we were freshmen. Then at my request
He brought it; and the poet, little urged,
But with some prelude of disparagement,
Read, mouthing out his hollow o's and a's,
Deep-chested music, and to this result. •

Vocabulary
disparagement (di spar′ ij mənt) *n.* comments expressing a low opinion of or lack of respect for
bore (bôr) *v.* carried

Morte d'Arthur

So all day long the noise of battle rolled
Among the mountains by the winter sea,
Until King Arthur's table, man by man,
Had fallen in Lyonnesse[6] about their lord,
King Arthur; then, because his wound was deep,
The bold Sir Bedivere uplifted him,
Sir Bedivere, the last of all his knights,
❼ And bore him to a chapel nigh the field,
A broken chancel[7] with a broken cross,
That stood on a dark strait of barren land.
On one side lay the ocean, and on one
Lay a great water, and the moon was full.
Then spake King Arthur to Sir Bedivere:
"The sequel of today unsolders[8] all
The goodliest fellowship of famous knights
Whereof this world holds record. Such a sleep
They sleep—the men I loved. I think that we

5. **Homeric** (hō mer′ ik) **echoes** imitations of the Greek poet Homer (of the eighth century B.C.).
6. **Lyonnesse** (lī′ ə nes′) *n.* legendary country off the southwestern coast of England, supposed to have sunk beneath the sea.
7. **chancel** (chan′ səl) *n.* part of a church around the altar.
8. **unsolders** (un säd′ ərz) *v.* separates.

Vocabulary Development

Medieval Vocabulary

Many of these medieval words are derived from the Germanic language. *Brand* is an Old High German word for sword (and is also the source for the word *brandish*). Tennyson's use of words of medieval origin to name parts of a knight's armor and weapons makes the legend seem more authentic. Ask students to watch for these words as they read:

helm: helmet
brand: sword
haft: handle or hilt of a sword
casque: helmet
greaves: armor for the legs below the knee
cuisses: armor for the thigh

Shall never more, at any future time,
Delight our souls with talk of knightly deeds,
Walking about the gardens and the halls
Of Camelot, as in the days that were.
I perish by this people which I made—
Though Merlin[9] sware that I should come again
To rule once more—but let what will be be,
I am so deeply smitten through the helm
That without help I cannot last till morn.
Thou therefore take my brand Excalibur,
Which was my pride; for thou rememberest how
In those old days, one summer noon, an arm
Rose up from out the bosom of the lake,
Clothed in white samite,[10] mystic, wonderful,
Holding the sword—and how I rowed across
And took it, and have worn it, like a king;
And, wheresoever I am sung or told
In aftertime, this also shall be known.
But now delay not; take Excalibur,
And fling him far into the middle mere;[11]
Watch what thou seest, and lightly[12] bring me word."
To him replied the bold Sir Bedivere:
"It is not meet,[13] Sir King, to leave thee thus,
Aidless, alone, and smitten through the helm.
A little thing may harm a wounded man.
Yet I thy hest will all perform at full,[14]
Watch what I see, and lightly bring thee word."
So saying, from the ruined shrine he stepped
And in the moon athwart the place of tombs,
Where lay the mighty bones of ancient men,
Old knights, and over them the sea wind sang

How Sir Bedivere Cast the Sword Excalibur Into the Water, Aubrey Beardsley. Houghton Library, Harvard University.

Reading Skill
Compare Worldviews
What does Sir Bedivere's response show about the importance of obedience in Arthurian times?

Reading Check
What does Arthur ask Bedivere to do?

9. **Merlin** sorcerer who advised King Arthur.
10. **samite** (sam´ it) *n.* heavy silk fabric worn in the Middle Ages.
11. **mere** (mir) *n.* old or poetic word for "lake."
12. **lightly** *adv.* old or poetic word for "quickly."
13. **meet** *adj.* old or poetic word for "proper."
14. **I thy hest will all perform at full** I will carry out your order completely.

8 Humanities

How Sir Bedivere Cast the Sword Excalibur Into the Water by Aubrey Beardsley (1872–1898)

Aubrey Beardsley was a major figure in the 1890s Art Nouveau movement, which was marked by the use of an elegant style that featured flowing curves and elaborate decorative elements. This illustration is one of 500 drawings by Beardsley for an edition of Sir Thomas Malory's fifteenth-century book, *Le Morte d'Arthur,* the source used by Tennyson for *The Idylls of the King.* Use this question for discussion:

- How does the picture contrast with Tennyson's description of the event? **Possible response:** Students may say that Tennyson emphasizes action and movement, while the illustration presents a stylized, motionless scene. Also, Tennyson's setting seems wilder, colder, and more barren than Beardsley's barren lake.

9 Reading Skill
Compare Worldviews

1. Discuss with students the absolute power of a king in a culture where the phrase "your will is my command" was true. **Ask** students to share where they would draw the line if asked by a military or political leader to do something that went against their consciences.
   Possible responses: Students may say that they would hesitate to commit a crime, even if commanded to by a leader. Students may bring up examples of military crimes committed in modern wars.
2. Have students read the bracketed passage. **Ask** students the Reading Skill question: What does Sir Bedivere's response show about the importance of obedience in Arthurian time?
   Possible response: Bedivere's anxiety about leaving the dying Arthur's side in spite of his fears that further harm may come to Arthur shows the power of Arthur's authority.

10 Reading Check

Answer: Arthur asks Bedivere to take the sword Excalibur, fling it into the middle of the lake, watch what happens, and report what he sees.

Differentiated Instruction for Universal Access

EL Strategy for English Learners

Students may need discussion prompts to better understand Sir Bedivere's actions in the selection. Encourage students to discuss Sir Bedivere's dilemma and how they feel about it. What would they do if they were Sir Bedivere? Why would they follow that course of action? What do they think Sir Bedivere will eventually do? Will he hold out against his king or end up doing as Arthur wishes? Have students record their answers so that they may refer to them later in the selection.

Enrichment for Gifted/Talented Students

Encourage students who enjoy graphic arts to illustrate the scene of Sir Bedivere at the lakeside, torn by his dilemma of whether to throw the sword into the lake or disobey his king's command. Before they begin, encourage students to think about which aspect of the scene they wish to highlight—Sir Bedivere's indecision or the beauty of Excalibur.

11 Critical Viewing

Answer: The manuscript page is written in French, showing that the Arthurian legend spread throughout Europe.

12 Reading Skill

Compare Worldviews

1. Point out to students that a knight's duty to his king was absolute; they owed fealty (loyalty and allegiance) to their king.
2. Instruct students to read the bracketed passage. Have them summarize why Arthur is critical of Bedivere.
   Possible response: The knight disobeys Arthur and fails to execute his order to throw the sword into the lake.
3. **Ask** students the Reading Skill question: To what values does Arthur appeal in lines 124–126?
   Possible response: Arthur appeals to the values of honesty and obedience when he says that Bedivere betrays his nature and his name. Bedivere lies, an act that violates his vows of knighthood and brings shame on his manhood.

11 ▶ **Critical Viewing** Judging from the manuscript on page 1179, were the Arthur stories told only in England? Explain. **[Draw Conclusions]**

Shrill, chill, with flakes of foam. He, stepping down
By zigzag paths and juts of pointed rock,
Came on the shining levels of the lake.
There drew he forth the brand Excalibur,
And o'er him, drawing it, the winter moon,
Brightening the skirts of a long cloud, ran forth
And sparkled keen with frost against the hilt;
For all the haft twinkled with diamond sparks,
Myriads of topaz-lights, and jacinth-work[15]
Of subtlest jewelry. He gazed so long
That both his eyes were dazzled, as he stood,
This way and that dividing the swift mind,
In act to throw; but at the last it seemed
Better to leave Excalibur concealed
There in the many-knotted water flags,[16]
That whistled stiff and dry about the marge.[17]
So strode he back slow to the wounded king.
Then spake King Arthur to Sir Bedivere:
"Hast thou performed my mission which I gave?
What is it thou hast seen, or what hast heard?"
And answer made the bold Sir Bedivere:
"I heard the ripple washing in the reeds,
And the wild water lapping on the crag."
To whom replied King Arthur, faint and pale:
"Thou hast betrayed thy nature and thy name,
Not rendering[18] true answer, as beseemed
Thy fealty,[19] nor like a noble knight;
For surer sign had followed, either hand,
Or voice, or else a motion of the mere.
This is a shameful thing for men to lie.
Yet now, I charge thee, quickly go again
As thou art lief and dear, and do the thing
I bade thee, watch, and lightly bring me word."
Then went Sir Bedivere the second time
Across the ridge, and paced beside the mere,
Counting the dewy pebbles, fixed in thought;
But when he saw the wonder of the hilt,
How curiously and strangely chased,[20] he smote

Reading Skill 12
Compare Worldviews
To what values does Arthur appeal in lines 124–126?

15. **topaz-lights, and jacinth-work** yellow and reddish-orange jewels.
16. **water flags** marsh plants.
17. **marge** (märj) *n.* margin; edge.
18. **rendering** (ren´ dər iŋ) *v.* giving.
19. **beseemed** (bē sēm´ əd) / **Thy fealty** (fē´ əl tē) was suitable to the loyalty you owe your lord.
20. **chased** *adj.* decorated by engraving or embossing.

Vocabulary Development

Expressive Vocabulary

To help students broaden their expressive vocabulary, encourage them to use the following words as they discuss the selection: *appeals, differentiate,* and *diminish*. Have them complete these sentence starters:

1. Bedivere *appeals* to what he believes is his own better judgment when he . . .
2. Bedivere is struggling to *differentiate* between . . .
3. Bedivere is afraid that history will *diminish* Arthur's legacy without . . .

His palms together, and he cried aloud:
"And if indeed I cast the brand away;
Surely a precious thing, one worthy note,
Should thus be lost forever from the earth,
Which might have pleased the eyes of many men.
What good should follow this, if this were done?
What harm, undone? deep harm to disobey,
Seeing obedience is the bond of rule.
Were it well to obey then, if a king demand
An act unprofitable, against himself?
The king is sick, and knows not what he does.
What record, or what relic of my lord
Should be to aftertime, but empty breath
And rumors of a doubt? But were this kept,
Stored in some treasure-house of mighty kings,
Some one might show it at a joust of arms,
Saying, 'King Arthur's sword, Excalibur,
Wrought by the lonely maiden of the lake;
Nine years she wrought it, sitting in the deeps
Upon the hidden bases of the hills.'
So might some old man speak in the aftertime
To all the people, winning reverence;
But now much honor and much fame were lost."
So spake he, clouded with his own conceit,
And hid Excalibur the second time,
And so strode back slow to the wounded king.
Then spoke King Arthur, breathing heavily:
"What is it thou hast seen, or what hast heard?"
And answer made the bold Sir Bedivere:
"I heard the water lapping on the crag,
And the long ripple washing in the reeds."
To whom replied King Arthur, much in wrath:
"Ah, miserable and unkind, untrue,
Unknightly, traitor-hearted! Woe is me!
Authority forgets a dying king,
Laid widowed of the power in his eye
That bowed the will. I see thee what thou art,
For thou, the latest-left of all my knights,
In whom should meet the offices[21] of all,
Thou wouldst betray me for the precious hilt;
Either from lust of gold, or like a girl

Vocabulary
reverence (rev´ ə rəns) *n.* a feeling of deep respect, love, or awe

Reading Check
Why does Sir Bedivere disobey Arthur?

21. **offices** *n.* duties.

Differentiated Instruction for Universal Access

Strategy for Special Needs Students
Students may have difficulty following the dialogue between King Arthur and Sir Bedivere on these pages. To help students keep track of who is speaking, have them make a copy of the poem and then circle places where the poem describes who is talking. Then, have students underline King Arthur's dialogue with one line and Sir Bedivere's dialogue with two lines.

Enrichment for Advanced Readers
The rigors of knighthood were intense. Besides the skill required for sword fighting and jousting, the knights spent a great deal of time on horseback and carried the weight of their armor. Have students research the type and amount of physical training required for a knight in medieval times and present their findings to the class.

13 Humanities

Gifflet returns Excalibur to the lake at the dying Arthur's command, a hand rises from the water to receive the sword. France ca. 1316

This miniature is part of the lavishly illuminated manuscript *La Mort le Roi Artus,* the text of which was written by a single scribe in France in the fourteenth century. The manuscript includes 164 illustrations that capture scenes from Arthurian romances, and this particular miniature is distinguished by figures outlined in black against a burnished gold background with lush reds, blues, and greens. Use this question for discussion:

- Why is it ironic that Sir Bedivere in the poem *Morte d'Arthur* is worried that the sword will be a necessary physical symbol to keep Arthur's legend alive?
  Possible response: The Arthurian legend lives on in spite of the scant physical evidence that Arthur and his court existed. The many artistic renditions of the scene as well as the poem itself preserve the legend even without the sword.

14 Literary Analysis
Legends and Legendary Heroes

1. Encourage students to remember that though legends are often magical and mysterious stories, they also contain within them characters who encounter situations that question the values of the culture. Readers are meant to take with them the values that the legends illustrate.
2. **Ask:** How does Bedivere's debate with himself emphasize a concern with right and wrong?
   Possible response: Bedivere wants to do what is right, but he thinks that Arthur may be ill and not thinking clearly about the importance of this sword to his legacy. Bedivere is weighing the importance of obeying his king against the responsibility of history.

15 Reading Check

Answer: He does not want such a revered relic of King Arthur's glorious reign to be lost forever.

16 Connecting to the Big Question

1. Remind students that a common theme in legends is a deep concern with right and wrong. Often, it is the hero who upholds such values, but even the strongest and most determined heroes can fail, thus revealing their weaknesses.
2. Have a volunteer read the bracketed passage aloud. Then, **ask:** What emotions does Arthur reveal in this passage? Why?
   Possible response: Arthur is angry, disappointed, and despairing. Bedivere has disobeyed Arthur's dying wish again by failing to throw Excalibur into the lake.
3. **Ask:** Using Bedivere's second failure and Arthur's response in this passage, what human flaws do Arthur and Bedivere seem to possess?
   Possible response: Because Bedivere has deliberately disobeyed his dying king, he reveals that, in choosing wrong over right, he is selfish and greedy. As much as Arthur strives to uphold right over wrong, he has placed too much trust in his knight. His resulting anger—with himself for his poor judgment and with Bedivere for his betrayal—arouses him to a rage in which he threatens to kill Bedivere himself.
4. **Ask** students: Do Arthur's flaws make him any more or less a hero?
   Possible response: Arthur's flaws add a very human quality to his legendary heroism, which allows the reader to connect more deeply with a character with whom he or she can empathize.

17 Critical Viewing

Possible response: Arthur's warrior life would have been full of blood and death, but in the painting he is clean and surrounded by women. The painting, with the women playing instruments and the foreground full of flowers, captures a time of peace and beauty in contrast to the violence and brutality required to preserve the civilization depicted by the women.

17 ▶ Critical Viewing
Which details in the painting on page 1181 contrast Arthur's warrior life with the civilized life he fought to protect? **[Contrast]**

Vocabulary
brandished (bran´ disht) *v.* showed, waved, or shook in a threatening or triumphant manner

16
Valuing the giddy pleasure of the eyes.
Yet, for a man may fail in duty twice,
And the third time may prosper, get thee hence;
But, if thou spare to fling Excalibur,
I will arise and slay thee with my hands."
    Then quickly rose Sir Bedivere, and ran,
And, leaping down the ridges lightly, plunged
Among the bulrush beds,[22] and clutched the sword,
And strongly wheeled and threw it. The great brand
Made lightnings in the splendor of the moon,
And flashing round and round, and whirled in an arch,
Shot like a streamer of the northern morn,[23]
Seen where the moving isles of winter shock[24]
By night, with noises of the northern sea.
So flashed and fell the brand Excalibur;
But ere he dipped the surface, rose an arm
Clothed in white samite, mystic, wonderful,
And caught him by the hilt, and **brandished** him
Three times, and drew him under in the mere.
And lightly went the other to the king.
    Then spoke King Arthur, drawing thicker breath:
"Now see I by thine eyes that this is done.
Speak out; what is it thou hast heard, or seen?"
    And answer made the bold Sir Bedivere:
"Sir King, I closed mine eyelids, lest the gems
Should blind my purpose, for I never saw,
Nor shall see, here or elsewhere, till I die,
Not though I live three lives of mortal men,
So great a miracle as yonder hilt.
Then with both hands I flung him, wheeling him;
But when I looked again, behold an arm,
Clothed in white samite, mystic, wonderful,
That caught him by the hilt, and brandished him
Three times, and drew him under in the mere."
    And answer made King Arthur, breathing hard:
"My end draws nigh; 'tis time that I were gone.
Make broad thy shoulders to receive my weight,
And bear me to the margin; yet I fear
My wound hath taken cold, and I shall die."
    So saying, from the pavement he half rose,

22. **bulrush** (bool´ rush´) **beds** growth of marsh plants.
23. **a streamer of the northern morn** northern lights; the aurora borealis.
24. **the moving isles of winter shock** icebergs crash.

Think Aloud

Vocabulary: Using Context
Direct students' attention to the word *dint* in line 241 on p. 1181. Using the following "think aloud," model how to use context to infer the meaning of an unknown word. Say to students:

I'm going to think aloud to show you how I would figure out the meaning of *dint* from its context.

In this line, *dint* is used to tell what causes the sound of Bedivere's feet on the rocky landscape as he carries Arthur to his final resting place. When he steps onto the rock, his feet make a loud noise from the contact. Because Bedivere is a knight, I know he must be wearing armor on his entire body, even his feet. I know that knights wear armor to protect themselves from getting wounded in battle, but the way Bedivere's foot is described—"armèd heel"—suggests that Bedivere's armored foot is a weapon. So, the "armèd heel" is like a weapon used against the rock. When Bedivere's armored foot hits the rock, the rock rings sharply from the blow. From these clues, then, I can infer that *dint* is a hit or a strike with a weapon.

Slowly, with pain, reclining on his arm,
And looking **wistfully** with wide blue eyes
As in a picture. Him Sir Bedivere
Remorsefully regarded through his tears,
And would have spoken, but he found not words,
Then took with care, and kneeling on one knee,
O'er both his shoulders drew the **languid** hands,
And rising bore him through the place of tombs.
    But, as he walked, King Arthur panted hard,
Like one that feels a nightmare on his bed
When all the house is mute. So sighed the king,
Muttering and murmuring at his ear, "Quick, quick!
I fear it is too late, and I shall die."
But the other swiftly strode from ridge to ridge,
Clothed with his breath, and looking, as he walked,
Larger than human on the frozen hills.
He heard the deep behind him, and a cry
Before. His own thought drove him like a goad.[25]
Dry clashed his harness[26] in the icy caves
And barren chasms, and all to left and right
The bare black cliff clanged round him, as he based
His feet on juts of slippery crag that rang
Sharp-smitten with the dint of armèd heels—
And on a sudden, lo! the level lake,
And the long glories of the winter moon.
    Then saw they how there hove a dusky barge,
Dark as a funeral scarf from stem to stern,
Beneath them; and descending they were ware
19 That all the decks were dense with stately forms
Black-stoled, black-hooded, like a dream—by these
Three queens with crowns of gold—and from them rose
A cry that shivered to the tingling stars,
And, as it were one voice, an agony
21 Of lamentation, like a wind that shrills
All night in a waste land, where no one comes,
Or hath come, since the making of the world.
    Then murmured Arthur, "Place me in the barge,"
And to the barge they came. There those three queens
Put forth their hands, and took the king, and wept.

18

The Dream of Arthur in Avalon (detail), Sir Edward Burne-Jones. The Museo de Arte de Ponce. The Luis A. Ferré Foundation Inc. Ponce, Puerto Rico.

Vocabulary

wistfully (wist′ fəl lē) *adv.* showing vague yearnings

languid (laŋ′ gwid) *adj.* without energy

Literary Analysis
Legends and Legendary Heroes
Why is the arrival of the mysterious barge appropriate to the death of a legendary hero?

20 **Reading Check**
What does Sir Bedivere do on his third visit to the shore?

25. **goad** (gōd) *n.* sharp-pointed stick used to drive oxen.
26. **harness** (här′ nis) *n.* armor.

18 Humanities

The Dream of Arthur in Avalon
by Sir Edward Coley Burne-Jones (1833–1898)

It is not surprising that the British Pre-Raphaelite painter Sir Edward Burne-Jones chose this scene from Arthurian legend as a painting subject—he was known for his enthusiasm for the medieval. The subject of this painting is taken from Malory's *Morte d'Arthur.* Burne-Jones's dreamy, romantic "literary" style, executed in a flat technique, was effective not only in painting but in stained glass, tapestry, mosaic, and relief—all media that interested medieval artists as well. Use this question for discussion:

- What seems to be happening to King Arthur in this picture? How do you know?
  Answer: Arthur may be on his deathbed. The people around him seem to be mourning.

19 Literary Analysis

Legends and Legendary Heroes

1. After students read the bracketed passage, **ask** them to describe the mood and to identify details that contribute to the mood of the scene.
   Possible response: The black barge, hooded figures, and the three queens giving a shivering cry contribute to the somber, eerie, and mysterious mood.
2. **Ask** the Literary Analysis question: Why is the arrival of the mysterious barge appropriate to the death of a legendary hero?
   Possible response: The barge creates a sense of mystery and wonder, befitting the strange powers associated with Arthur.

20 Reading Check

Answer: Bedivere throws the sword into the water, where an arm in white silk catches it by the hilt, brandishes it three times and disappears into the lake with it.

㉑ Reading Skill
Compare Worldviews

1. **Ask** the Reading Skill question: How does the arrival of the three queens reflect a belief in supernatural forces or mystical events?
   Possible response: The three women on the barge must have some magical or divine power to know of Arthur's approaching death.
2. Explain to students that the use of the number three is an archetypal narrative pattern, or a pattern that is found throughout tales from many cultures and places. The use of three queens follows this pattern.

㉒ Literary Analysis
Legends and Legendary Heroes

1. **Ask** students to share examples of times when great leaders have challenged Americans to fulfill the ideals on which the country was founded.
   Possible response: Students may cite John F. Kennedy's "Ask not what your country can do for you; ask what you can do for your country" speech. Others may cite Martin Luther King's "I have a dream" speech.
2. **Ask** the Literary Analysis question: Which ideas in Bedivere's speech encourage English national pride?
   Possible response: Though Bedivere laments the passing of an age in which knights perform the good deeds, this passage encourages national pride, because England is the place where these brave men lived. The English may feel obligated to answer such a call when it comes again.

㉓ Reading Skill
Compare Worldviews

Ask the Reading Skill question: What is the main difference in Sir Bedivere's and Arthur's views of the world?
Possible response: Sir Bedivere believes the glory days of England have passed and that only dark days loom ahead. Arthur believes that the world is ever changing and encourages Bedivere to pray and to hope because the world is "Bound by gold chains about the feet of God."

Reading Skill
Compare Worldviews ㉑
How does the arrival of the three queens reflect a belief in supernatural forces or mystical events?

But she that rose the tallest of them all
And fairest laid his head upon her lap,
And loosed the shattered casque, and chafed his hands,
And called him by his name, complaining loud,
And dropping bitter tears against his brow
Striped with dark blood; for all his face was white
And colorless, and like the withered moon
Smote by the fresh beam of the springing east;
And all his greaves and cuisses dashed with drops
Of onset; and the light and lustrous curls—
That made his forehead like a rising sun
High from the dais-throne—were parched with dust;
Or, clotted into points and hanging loose,
Mixed with the knightly growth that fringed his lips.
So like a shattered column lay the king;
Not like that Arthur who, with lance in rest,
From spur to plume a star of tournament,
Shot through the lists at Camelot, and charged
Before the eyes of ladies and of kings.
    Then loudly cried the bold Sir Bedivere:
"Ah! my Lord Arthur, whither shall I go?
Where shall I hide my forehead and my eyes?
For now I see the true old times are dead,
When every morning brought a noble chance,
And every chance brought out a noble knight.
Such times have been not since the light that led
The holy Elders with the gift of myrrh.[27]
But now the whole ROUND TABLE is dissolved
Which was an image of the mighty world;
And I, the last, go forth companionless,
And the days darken round me, and the years,
Among new men, strange faces, other minds."
    And slowly answered Arthur from the barge:
"The old order changeth, yielding place to new,
And God fulfills himself in many ways,
Lest one good custom should corrupt the world.
Comfort thyself: what comfort is in me?
I have lived my life, and that which I have done
May He within himself make pure! but thou,
If thou shouldst never see my face again,

Literary Analysis
Legends and Legendary Heroes ㉒
Which ideas in Bedivere's speech encourage English national pride?

Reading Skill
Compare Worldviews ㉓
What is the main difference between Bedivere's and Arthur's view of the world?

27. **the light . . . of myrrh** (mur) star that guided the three kings ("the holy Elders") with their gifts of myrrh (a gum from plants, used to make incense and perfume), to Bethlehem at the birth of Jesus.

Vocabulary Development

Vocabulary Knowledge Rating

When students have completed reading and discussing "Morte d'Arthur," have them take out their **Vocabulary Knowledge Rating Chart** for this selection. Read the words aloud once more and have students rate their knowledge of the words again in the After Reading column. Clarify any words that are still problematic. Have students write their own definition and example or sentence in the appropriate column. Then, have students complete the Vocabulary Practice at the end of the selection. Encourage students to use the words in further discussion and written work about this selection. Remind them that they will be accountable for these words on the **Selection Test, *Unit 6 Resources*,** pp. 160–162 or 163–165.

Pray for my soul. More things are wrought by prayer
Than this world dreams of. Wherefore, let thy voice
Rise like a fountain for me night and day.
For what are men better than sheep or goats
That nourish a blind life within the brain,
23 If, knowing God, they lift not hands of prayer
Both for themselves and those who call them friend?
For so the whole round earth is every way
Bound by gold chains about the feet of God.
But now farewell. I am going a long way
With these thou seest—if indeed I go—
For all my mind is clouded with a doubt—
To the island-valley of Avilion;[28]
Where falls not hail, or rain, or any snow,
Nor ever wind blows loudly, but it lies
Deep-meadowed, happy, fair with orchard lawns
And bowery[29] hollows crowned with summer sea,
Where I will heal me of my grievous wound."
So said he, and the barge with oar and sail
Moved from the brink, like some full-breasted swan
that, fluting a wild carol ere her death,
Ruffles her pure cold plume, takes the flood
With swarthy webs. Long stood Sir Bedivere
Revolving many memories, till the hull
Looked one black dot against the verge of dawn,
And on the mere the wailing died away.

Here ended Hall, and our last light, that long
Had winked and threatened darkness, flared and fell;
At which the parson, sent to sleep with sound,
And waked with silence, grunted "Good!" but we
25 Sat rapt: it was the tone with which he read—
Perhaps some modern touches here and there
Redeemed it from the charge of nothingness—
Or else we loved the man, and prized his work;
I know not; but we sitting, as I said,
The cock crew loud, as at that time of year
The lusty bird takes every hour for dawn.
Then Francis, muttering, like a man ill-used,
"There now—that's nothing!" drew a little back,

24

26 ▲ **Critical Viewing**
What important qualities of a knight does this drawing depict? **[Interpret]**

27 **Reading Check**
Who comes to take Arthur away?

28. island-valley of Avilion According to ancient British myth, heroes were taken after death to the island paradise of Avalon, called "Avilion" here.
29. bowery (bou´ ər ē) *adj.* enclosed by overhanging boughs of trees or by vines.

24 Humanities

Young Knight

This pen and ink drawing of a young knight resides at the Victoria and Albert Museum in London.

25 Reading Skill

Compare Worldviews

1. Have students reread the bracketed passage, and then **ask** them to explain what the narrator is saying with the line "it was the tone with which he read—/Perhaps some modern touches here and there/Redeemed it from the charge of nothingness."
   Possible response: The narrator is saying that Everard's rendition of the legendary tale is better than he expected because of the modern touches.
2. Next, **ask** students how the description of most of the listeners sitting "rapt" through the night to hear the tale illustrates Tennyson's worldview concerning legends.
   Possible response: The listeners' attention to the tale shows that Tennyson considers legends important, even in modern times.

26 Critical Viewing

Possible response: It depicts the importance of nature to the knight, as he is surrounded by trees.

27 Reading Check

Answer: Three queens on a mystical barge come to take Arthur away.

Concept Connector

Anticipation Guide

Have students return to their **Anticipation Guides** and respond to the statements again, this time in the After Reading column. They may do this individually, or you may wish to have them work in their original pairs or groups. Then, lead a class discussion. Start by putting responses from the Me and Group columns on the board. Guide students to recognize how their responses have changed—or remained the same—after reading "Morte d'Arthur." Encourage students to cite specific details or evidence from the text to support their new responses to the statements.

Writing About the Big Question

Have students compare their responses to the sentence starter they completed before reading the selection with their ideas afterward. Ask them to explain whether their thoughts have changed.

Reading Skill Graphic Organizer

Ask students to review the graphic organizers they completed to investigate worldview while reading. You may want to use the partially completed **Reading Skill Graphic Organizer A** (p. 210 in *Graphic Organizer Transparencies*) as an example. Then, have students share their graphic organizers.

28 Literary Analysis

Legends and Legendary Heroes

Ask the Literary Analysis question: In what way do lines 344–351 suggest that faith and the opportunity for noble action might return in modern times, as strong as in the Arthur legend?

Possible response: The lines express the belief in England that Arthur will come again and usher in a time of peace and prosperity for England. This passage imagines the returning king as a modern gentleman; he is three times as fair as he was before. These lines foresee a time of Arthur's return and with it "all good things, and war shall be no more."

ASSESS

Answers

Critical Thinking

1. Students may have obeyed Arthur's request out of duty to a dying king.
2. (a) Friends are celebrating Christmas Eve. (b) **Possible response:** The parson complains about the decay of faith and values.
3. (a) The knights, except for Bedivere, have been killed; Arthur is dying. (b) **Possible response:** Bedivere fears that the old order of honor, bravery, and loyalty is vanishing.
4. (a) Arthur asks Bedivere to throw Excalibur in the lake, to watch what happens, and to return and report what he sees to Arthur. (b) **Possible response:** Bedivere is afraid that without concrete evidence of Arthur's reign, people will forget its lessons. (c) **Possible response:** Both men feel that the days of honor are over.

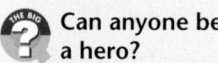

Can anyone be a hero?

Possible responses: (a) At the beginning of the poem, they seem to believe that heroism is impossible in the present age, devoted as it is to easy pleasures. (b) By the end of the poem, they seem to believe that heroism is possible. As the speaker says, "Arthur is come again: he cannot die."

And drove his heel into the smoldered log,
That sent a blast of sparkles up the flue.
And so to bed, where yet in sleep I seemed
To sail with Arthur under looming shores,
Point after point; till on to dawn, when dreams
Begin to feel the truth and stir of day,
To me, methought, who waited with the crowd,
There came a bark that, blowing forward, bore
King Arthur; like a modern gentleman
Of stateliest port;[30] and all the people cried,
"Arthur is come again: he cannot die."
Then those that stood upon the hills behind
Repeated—"Come again, and thrice as fair";
And, further inland, voices echoed—"Come
With all good things, and war shall be no more."
At this a hundred bells began to peal,
That with the sound I woke, and heard indeed
The clear church bells ring in the Christmas morn.

Literary Analysis
Legends and Legendary Heroes 28
In what way do lines 344–351 suggest that faith and the opportunity for noble action might return in modern times, as strong as in the Arthur legend?

30. **Of stateliest port** who carried himself in a most majestic or dignified manner.

Critical Thinking

1. **Respond:** If you had been in Sir Bedivere's position, would you have obeyed Arthur's request? Explain.
2. **(a)** What occasion is celebrated at the opening of the poem? **(b) Interpret:** What complaint does the parson make on this occasion?
3. **(a)** In Everard's poem, what has happened to Arthur and his knights? **(b) Interpret:** When Bedivere says that "'the true old times are dead,'" what does he imply will vanish from the world?
4. **(a)** What does Arthur specifically request of Bedivere? **(b) Interpret:** Why does Bedivere fear that if he obeys Arthur's request, "much honor and much fame were lost"? **(c) Connect:** What attitude toward the past do Bedivere and the parson share?

Can anyone be a hero?
(a) What attitude toward heroes and honor do the men at the beginning of the poem have? **(b)** Do their opinions change by the end of the poem? Explain.

Assessment Resources

Unit 6 Resources

L1 L2 EL **Selection Test A**, pp. 160–162. Administer Test A to less advanced readers and English learners.

L3 L4 **Selection Test B**, pp. 163–165. Administer Test B to on-level and more advanced students.

L3 L4 **Open-Book Test**, pp. 157–159. As an alternative, give the Open-Book Test.

All **Customizable Test Bank**

All **Self-tests**
Students may prepare for the **Selection Test** by taking the **Self-test** online.

PHLit Online! All assessment resources are available at **www.PHLitOnline.com.**

After You Read | Morte d'Arthur

Literary Analysis: Legends and Legendary Heroes

1. Which features of **legends** are present in this poem? Use a chart like the one shown to gather examples from the selection.

Life Story of Legendary Hero	Concern with Right and Wrong	Reflections of National Pride

2. In what way does the end of the poem suggest that King Arthur still unites the people of England, past and present?

Reading Skill: Compare Worldviews

3. Arthur says, "The old order changeth, yielding place to new." **(a)** Describe the "old order" of Arthur's reign, using details from the poem. **(b)** What do the parson's complaints show about the "new order" of modern times? **(c) Compare and contrast** the parson's **worldview** with the worldview of the old order.
4. In the narrator's dream, the people cry, "'Arthur is come again: he cannot die.'" Based on this dream, explain what basic values or beliefs Tennyson might hold.

Vocabulary

Practice Answer each of the following questions. Explain your response.

1. Are football players noted for their *languid* movements?
2. Should you make a *disparagement* about a friend's clothes?
3. Why scold a child who *brandished* a pair of scissors while running?
4. If you *bore* a heavy backpack up a mountain, did you push it?
5. Would dedicating a memorial to a soldier be a sign of *reverence*?
6. Why might you sigh *wistfully* while looking through old photos?

Word Study Use the context of the sentences and what you know about the **Latin suffix *-ment*** to explain your answer to each question.

1. If you were upset with your grades, would you feel *contentment*?
2. Does a receipt of purchase show your *entitlement* to that object?

Word Study

The **Latin suffix *-ment*** means "act" or "state of."

Challenge Explain how the suffix *-ment* contributes to the meanings of these words. Consult a dictionary if necessary.

atonement
embodiment
government

ASSESS/EXTEND

Answers

Literary Analysis

1. **Possible responses:** (a) **Life Story:** The poem is the story of King Arthur, the greatest legendary hero in English literature. (b) **Concern:** Bedivere wants to do the right thing for his king and for history; Arthur insists upon his knight doing what is right. (c) **Pride:** The British see Arthur as the emblem of what is best about England.

   For other sample answers, see *Graphic Organizer Transparencies,* **Literary Analysis Graphic Organizer A**, p. 213, and the **Additional Answers** section.
2. **Possible response:** The belief that King Arthur will return and with his return will come the good, noble, brave, and honorable to celebrate a time of peace, links the people of the present with the people of the past.

Reading Skill

3. **Possible responses:** (a) The dying Arthur laments the end of "the goodliest fellowship of famous knights." (b) The parson complains that there is nothing left of value. (c) Even at his death, Arthur remembers all that was good; the parson does not see possibility and spends his time complaining.
4. **Possible response:** The dream reflects Tennyson's patriotism and optimism for the future of England.

Vocabulary

Practice

Sample answers:

1. No, because languid movements are slow and lack energy. Football players are known for their speed and enthusiasm.
2. No, you should not make a disparagement about a friend's clothes because he or she might be insulted.
3. You should scold the child because scissors brandished while running might cause injury to the child or others.
4. No, if you bore a backpack, you carried it.

Answers continued

5. Yes, it would be a sign of reverence because the memorial would honor the soldier.
6. You might sigh wistfully because you are remembering happier times.

Word Study

Sample answers:

1. No. To feel contentment is to feel the "state of" happiness, which you wouldn't feel if you received poor marks.
2. Yes. *Entitlement* means the "act of possessing." If you paid for something, you would possess it.

Word Study: Challenge

Sample answers:

Atonement is the act of forgiving. The *embodiment* of something is the state of its core. *Government* is the act of governing.

Answers

Grammar

1. Introduce the skill, using the instruction on the student page.
2. Discuss the definitions, rules, and examples.

Think Aloud: Model the Skill

Model the skill of distinguishing commas from dashes. Say to students:

> I know that commas are used to separate three or more words and to set off nonessential or descriptive information, as in the sentence, "Hungry and impatient, Jean quickly made scrambled eggs." I would use a dash to give a summary statement or a sudden change in thought, as in the sentence, "The eggs—surprisingly good, actually—were organic."

WG Writing and Grammar, Grade 10

Students will find further instruction on and practice with commas and dashes in Chapter 28, Sections 2 and 5.

Practice A

1. Wart is thoughtful, kind, and diligent.
2. Merlyn, who has been Wart's tutor, disappears into thin air.
3. Sir Kay takes Wart to London—only to treat him meanly.
4. Wart returns to the inn, riding on his little donkey to fetch Kay's sword.

Challenge

Sample answers: *Comma:* "There was still no answer, and Wart turned back to the anvil."; compound sentence; *Dash:* "I can smell something like fetherfew and sweet briar—and is it music I hear?"; change of thought

Practice B

Sample answers:

1. Finally, Sir Bedivere throws the sword into the lake.
2. Arthur is wounded, and he prepares to die.
3. Correct
4. The narrator, who finally fell asleep, dreamed of a heroic future.

Challenge

Sample answer: People—all from different places—are circled around Arthur. One, a woman, admires his features. Another woman, perhaps thirty years old, tends to him.

Integrated Language Skills

Arthur Becomes King of Britain • Morte d'Arthur

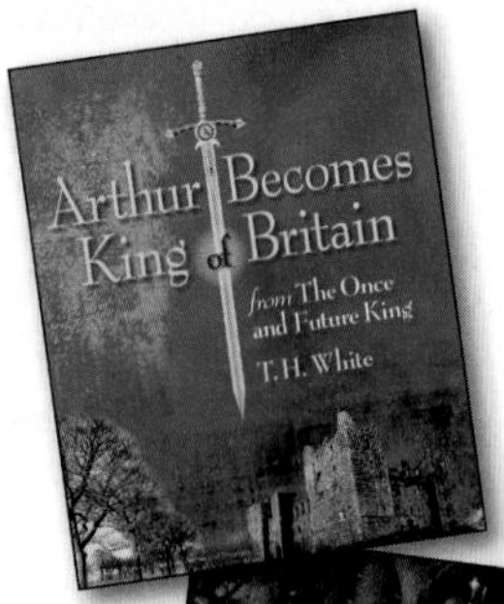

Grammar: Commas and Dashes

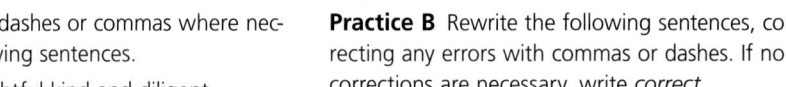

Commas are used to separate or join similar sentence elements and to show the relationship between ideas. **Dashes** are used to create longer, more emphatic pauses than commas.

- Use commas to separate three or more words or phrases in a series.
- Use a comma and a coordinating conjunction (*and, but, or, nor, for, so,* and *yet*) to link two independent clauses in a compound sentence.
- Use commas to set off introductory, parenthetical, and nonessential words, phrases, and clauses.
- Use dashes to indicate an abrupt change of thought, a dramatic interrupting idea, or a summary statement.

COMMAS: The king, **who ruled for a long time,** was very wise.

DASHES: The legend**—and there are some outlandish versions of the story—**has endured for many years.

Practice A Insert dashes or commas where necessary in the following sentences.

1. Wart is thoughtful kind and diligent.
2. Merlin who has been Wart's tutor disappears into thin air.
3. Sir Kay takes Wart to London only to treat him meanly.
4. Wart returns to the inn riding on his little donkey to fetch Kay's sword.

Challenge Find an example of commas and an example of dashes in "Arthur Becomes King of Britain." Explain why the punctuation marks were used in each case.

Practice B Rewrite the following sentences, correcting any errors with commas or dashes. If no corrections are necessary, write *correct.*

1. Finally—Sir Bedivere throws the sword into the lake.
2. Arthur is wounded and he prepares to die.
3. Three magnificent queens—weeping bitter tears—tended to the king.
4. The narrator who finally fell asleep, dreamed of a heroic future.

Challenge Write a brief paragraph about the painting on page 1181. Use commas and dashes to set off pieces of information where appropriate.

WG Writing and Grammar Connection: Chapter 28, Sections 2 & 5

Extend the Lesson

Sentence Modeling

Choose the sentence given from the selection students have read:

No hair and no next of skin, and who's to succeed to the throne? (from "Arthur Becomes King of Britain")

It is not meet, Sir King, to leave thee thus/Aidless, alone, and smitten through the helm. (from "Morte d'Arthur")

Ask students what they notice about the sentence. Elicit from them that it contains commas. Then, ask them what else they notice. ("Arthur Becomes King of Britain": White uses humor through a play on words with "no hair and next of skin," in place of "no heir and next of kin." "Morte d'Arthur": the serial adjectives serve to emphasize Arthur's vulnerability)

Have students imitate the sentence in a sentence on a topic of their own choosing, matching each grammatical and stylistic feature discussed. Collect the sentences and share them with the class.

Writing

In the fictional world where the Arthurian legend takes place, the discovery that Wart will be king of England and the death of King Arthur are two big news stories. Write a brief **script** for a television news report in which you present one of these stories to the nation. Follow these tips:

- First, take notes on *who* is involved, *what* happened, and *where, when, why,* and *how* it happened.
- Outline the various perspectives you will offer. For example, you might open with a news anchor, cut next to footage of Wart's sword or King Arthur's barge, and conclude with a discussion among commentators.
- As you draft, clearly identify each speaker and describe the visuals you would incorporate.
- Revise your draft, making sure the tone of your report fits your audience and purpose.

Writing Workshop: *Work in Progress*

Prewriting for a Comparison-and-Contrast Essay For a comparison-and-contrast essay you may write, choose two literary works. Freewrite about each piece separately for two to four minutes. Then, circle the ideas that are similar in your freewrites and underline the ideas that are different. Save these Freewrites in your writing portfolio.

Use this prewriting activity to prepare for the **Writing Workshop** on page 1242.

Research and Technology

The legend of King Arthur has inspired several film versions. Watch a movie based on the legends of King Arthur. As you watch, fill out a two-column **"influences" chart** that reflects the choices the director made in creating the film. Follow these steps to complete your chart:

- Discuss with classmates the **role of the director** in making a film. Identify choices the director might make, such as which characters to include, whether to make the story happy or sad, or whether to write an original story or to represent an existing tale.
- **Watch and listen** carefully to achieve your specific **purpose**—to find similarities and differences between the film and the text.
- In one column, note aspects of the film that the director probably took directly from the legends.
- In the other column, note aspects that probably represent modern influences.

Present your findings to the class.

PHLit Online!
www.PHLitOnline.com
- Interactive graphic organizers
- Grammar tutorial
- Interactive journals

EXTEND/ASSESS

Writing

1. Review the assignment, using the instruction on the student page.
2. To guide students in writing a script for a television news report, give them **Support for Writing,** p. 155 in ***Unit 6 Resources.***
3. To evaluate students' news scripts, use the Holistic rubrics, pp. 256–257 in ***Professional Development Guidebook.*** In addition, evaluate the news scripts on how effectively they use detail and vocabulary to convey the appropriate tone for the solemnity and importance of the event.

Six Traits Focus

✔	Ideas	✔	Word Choice
	Organization		Sentence Fluency
✔	Voice	✔	Conventions

Writing Workshop
Work in Progress

Have students save their completed Freewrites in their portfolios. They will use it as they continue this Work-in-Progress assignment (see p. 1219). These assignments prepare them to complete the Writing Workshop assignment (see pp. 1242–1249).

Research and Technology

1. Review the assignment, using the instruction on the student page.
2. Have students complete the **Support for Extend Your Learning** page (***Unit 6 Resources,*** p. 156).

Teaching Resources

Unit 6 Resources
- L3 L4 **Integrated Language Skills: Grammar,** p. 154
- L3 L4 **Support for Writing,** p. 155
- L3 L4 **Support for Extend Your Learning,** p. 156
- L4 **Enrichment,** pp. 135, 153

Enriched Online Student Edition
Available under After You Read for this selection:
- All **Interactive Grammar Tutorial**
- L3 L4 **Internet Research Activity**

Professional Development Guidebook
Rubics for News Script, pp. 256–257

PHLit Online! All print and digital resources are available at **www.PHLitOnline.com.** Online resources accessible by students are noted on the student page.

TIME AND RESOURCE MANAGER

from A Connecticut Yankee in King Arthur's Court • *from* Don Quixote

Lesson Pacing Guide

DAY 1 Preteach

- Administer the Reading and Vocabulary Warm-ups (*Unit 6 Resources*, pp. 166–169 or 184–187) as necessary.
- Introduce the Reading Skill: Compare Worldviews. FT
- Introduce the Literary Analysis concept: Parody. FT
- Distribute copies of the appropriate graphic organizer for the Reading Skill (*Graphic Organizer Transparencies*, pp. 216–218). CRI
- Distribute copies of the appropriate graphic organizer for Literary Analysis (*Graphic Organizer Transparencies*, pp. 219–222). CRI
- Teach the selection vocabulary. FT CRI
- Introduce the Word Study skill.

DAYS 2–3 Preteach/Teach

- Build background with the Background feature. CRI
- Develop thematic vocabulary and thematic thinking with Writing About the Big Question.
- Prepare students to read with the Activating Prior Knowledge activities (TE). CRI
- Informally monitor comprehension while students read. FT
- Use the Reading Check questions to confirm comprehension.
- Develop students' ability to compare worldviews using the Reading Skill questions. CRI
- Develop students' understanding of parody using the Literary Analysis questions. CRI
- Reinforce vocabulary with the Vocabulary notes. CRI

DAY 4 Assess

- Assess students' comprehension and mastery of the skills by having them answer the Critical Thinking, Reading Skill, and Literary Analysis questions. FT
- Have students complete the Vocabulary Practice activities. FT
- Have students complete the Word Study activities.

DAY 5 Extend/Assess

- Have students complete the Grammar lesson. CRI
- Have students complete the Writing activity and write a parody. (You may assign as homework.) FT
- Extend learning by having students complete the Research and Technology activity, a parody. As an alternative, assign them "Leaping into the Fire" or "The Sport Entertainment Hero" in *Reality Central*. CRI
- Administer Selection Test A or B (*Unit 6 Resources*, pp. 178–183 or 199–204). FT

The excerpt from the novel *A Connecticut Yankee in King Arthur's Court* has been edited for sensitivity issues. The excerpt from the novel *Don Quixote* is unedited.

Meeting Your Standards

Students will

1. analyze and respond to literary elements.
   - Literary Analysis: Parody
2. read, comprehend, and analyze parodies.
   - Reading Skill: Compare Worldviews
   - Reading Check questions
   - Apply the Skills questions
   - Assessment Practice
3. develop vocabulary.
   - Vocabulary
   - Word Study
4. apply grammar skills.
   - Semicolons, Colons, and Ellipsis Points
5. Develop writing proficiency.
   - Work in Progress: Comparison-and-Contrast Essay
   - parody
6. strengthen research and technology skills.
   - biographical brochure

CRI For a full explanation of Culturally Responsive Instruction opportunities in this lesson, see p. T86–T87.

FT For an accelerated lesson, use the Fast Track strategies and activities.

Managing Differentiated Instruction
This leveled selection pairing groups a more accessible with a more challenging selection. Choose either one to teach the lesson skills. For classroom management suggestions for using the pairing in a mixed-ability class, see pp. T68–T69.

Daily Block Scheduling
Each day in this Lesson Pacing Guide represents a 40–50 minute period. Teachers using block scheduling may combine days to revise pacing. In addition, teachers may differentiate and support core instruction by integrating components for extended and intensive support as students require. See the Guide to Selected Leveled Resources (facing page).

Guide to Selected Leveled Resources

EL English Learners

			from A Connecticut Yankee in King Arthur's Court	*from* Don Quixote
CORE COURSE	*Unit 6 Resources*	Selection Test A	pp. 178–180	pp. 199–201
	Graphic Organizer Transparencies	Reading Skill Graphic Organizer A	p. 216	p. 217
		Literary Analysis Graphic Organizer A	p. 219	p. 221
EXTENDED SUPPORT (Level 2)	*Unit 6 Resources*	Reading and Vocabulary Warm-ups A or B	pp. 166–169	pp. 184–187
	Reader's Notebook: English Learner's Version		adapted instruction and adapted selection	adapted instruction and summary
	Hear It! Audio CD		selection and summaries	selection and summaries
	Hear It! Audio CD (adapted text)		adapted selection and summaries	—
INTENSIVE SUPPORT (Level 1)	*Reality Central*		"Leaping into the Fire"	"The Sport Entertainment Hero"
	Real-World Writing Journal		Lesson 7, pp. 180–183	Lesson 8, pp. 184–187

L2 Below-Level Students

			from A Connecticut Yankee in King Arthur's Court	*from* Don Quixote
CORE COURSE	*Unit 6 Resources*	Selection Test A	pp. 178–180	pp. 199–201
	Graphic Organizer Transparencies	Reading Skill Graphic Organizer A	p. 216	p. 217
		Literary Analysis Graphic Organizer A	p. 219	p. 221
EXTENDED SUPPORT (Level 2)	*Unit 6 Resources*	Reading and Vocabulary Warm-ups A or B	pp. 166–169	pp. 184–187
	Reader's Notebook		adapted instruction and full selection	adapted instruction and summary
	Hear It! Audio CD		selection and summaries	selection and summaries
INTENSIVE SUPPORT (Level 1)	*Reality Central*		"Leaping into the Fire"	"The Sport Entertainment Hero"
	Real-World Writing Journal		Lesson 7, pp. 180–183	Lesson 8, pp. 184–187
	Reading Kit		Reteaching worksheets	Reteaching worksheets

L1 Special Needs Students

			from A Connecticut Yankee in King Arthur's Court	*from* Don Quixote
CORE COURSE	*Unit 6 Resources*	Selection Test A	pp. 178–180	pp. 199–201
	Graphic Organizer Transparencies	Reading Skill Graphic Organizer A	p. 216	p. 217
		Literary Analysis Graphic Organizer A	p. 219	p. 221
EXTENDED SUPPORT (Level 2)	*Unit 6 Resources*	Reading and Vocabulary Warm-ups A or B	pp. 166–169	pp. 184–187
	Reader's Notebook: Adapted Version		adapted instruction and adapted selection	adapted instruction and summary
	Hear It! Audio CD (adapted text)		adapted selection and summaries	—
INTENSIVE SUPPORT (Level 1)	*Reality Central*		"Leaping into the Fire"	"The Sport Entertainment Hero"
	Real-World Writing Journal		Lesson 7, pp. 180–183	Lesson 8, pp. 184–187
	Reading Kit		Reteaching worksheets	Reteaching worksheets

The program includes resources for these students: L3 On-Level L4 Advanced All All
For a complete guide to selection support, see pp. T106–T108.

NOTE: All print materials are also available online at *www.PHLitOnline.com.*

VISUAL GUIDE to Featured Selection Resources

• *from* A Connecticut Yankee in King Arthur's Court
• *from* Don Quixote

RESOURCES FOR:

- EL English Learners
- L1 Special Needs Students
- L2 Below-Level Students
- L3 On-Level Students
- L4 Advanced Students
- All All Students

Vocabulary/Fluency/Prior Knowledge

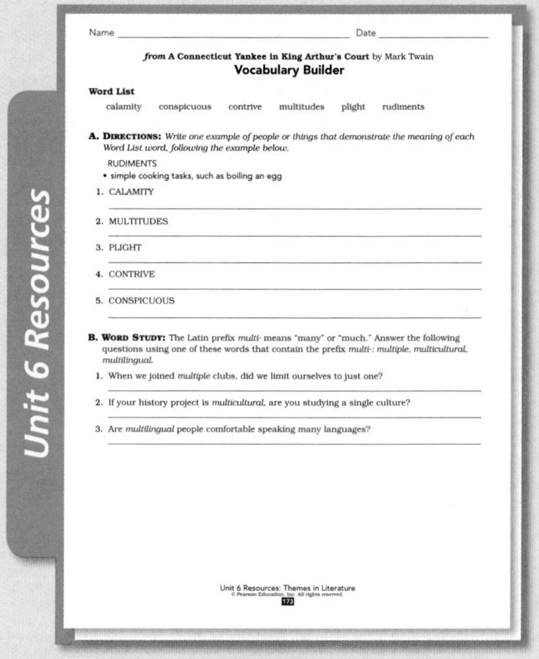

Name ______ Date ______

from **A Connecticut Yankee in King Arthur's Court** by Mark Twain
Vocabulary Builder

Word List

calamity conspicuous contrive multitudes plight rudiments

A. Directions: *Write one example of people or things that demonstrate the meaning of each Word List word, following the example below.*

RUDIMENTS
• simple cooking tasks, such as boiling an egg

1. CALAMITY
2. MULTITUDES
3. PLIGHT
4. CONTRIVE
5. CONSPICUOUS

B. Word Study: The Latin prefix *multi-* means "many" or "much." Answer the following questions using one of these words that contain the prefix *multi-*: *multiple, multicultural, multilingual.*

1. When we joined *multiple* clubs, did we limit ourselves to just one?
2. If your history project is *multicultural*, are you studying a single culture?
3. Are *multilingual* people comfortable speaking many languages?

Unit 6 Resources: Themes in Literature
© Pearson Education, Inc. All rights reserved.
173

All **Vocabulary Builder, pp. 173, 191**

Also available for these selections:

EL L1 L2 Vocabulary Warm-ups A and B, pp. 166–167, 184–185

EL L1 L2 Reading Warm-ups A and B, pp. 168–169, 186–187

All Writing About the Big Question, pp. 170, 188

Reader's Notebooks

Pre- and postreading pages for both selections, as well as the selection from *A Connecticut Yankee in King Arthur's Court*, appear in an interactive format in the *Reader's Notebooks*. Each *Notebook* is differentiated for a different group of learners.

The selections in the Adapted and English Learner's versions are abridged.

L2 L3 ***Reader's Notebook***

L1 ***Reader's Notebook: Adapted Version***

EL ***Reader's Notebook: English Learner's Version***

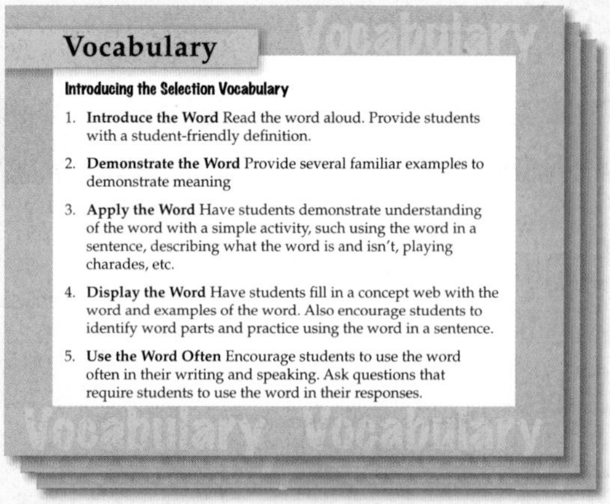

Vocabulary

Introducing the Selection Vocabulary

1. **Introduce the Word** Read the word aloud. Provide students with a student-friendly definition.
2. **Demonstrate the Word** Provide several familiar examples to demonstrate meaning
3. **Apply the Word** Have students demonstrate understanding of the word with a simple activity, such using the word in a sentence, describing what the word is and isn't, playing charades, etc.
4. **Display the Word** Have students fill in a concept web with the word and examples of the word. Also encourage students to identify word parts and practice using the word in a sentence.
5. **Use the Word Often** Encourage students to use the word often in their writing and speaking. Ask questions that require students to use the word in their responses.

Classroom Strategies and Teaching Routines

- core classroom routines outlined step-by-step
- convenient format for easy reference while teaching

Selection Support

Graphic Organizer Transparencies

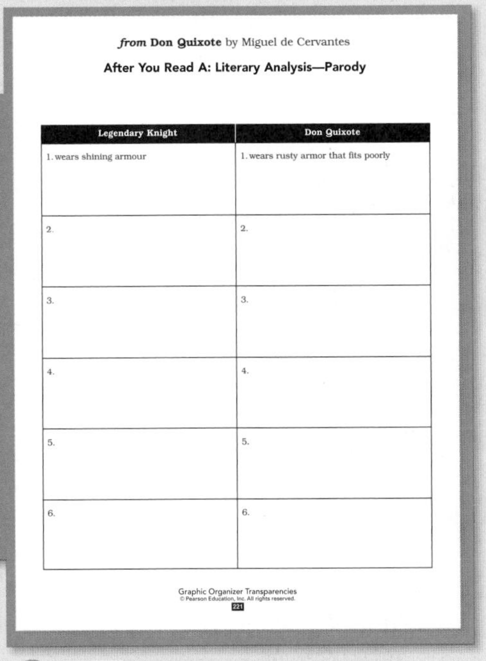
from **Don Quixote** by Miguel de Cervantes

After You Read A: Literary Analysis—Parody

Legendary Knight	Don Quixote
1. wears shining armour	1. wears rusty armor that fits poorly
2.	2.
3.	3.
4.	4.
5.	5.
6.	6.

Graphic Organizer Transparencies
© Pearson Education, Inc. All rights reserved.
221

EL L1 L2 **Literary Analysis: Graphic Organizer A,** pp. 219, 221 (partially filled in)

Also available for these selections:

- L3 Literary Analysis: Graphic Organizer B, pp. 220, 222
- EL L1 L2 Reading: Graphic Organizer A, pp. 216, 217 (partially filled in)
- L3 Reading: Graphic Organizer B, p. 218

Skills Development/Extension

Unit 6 Resources

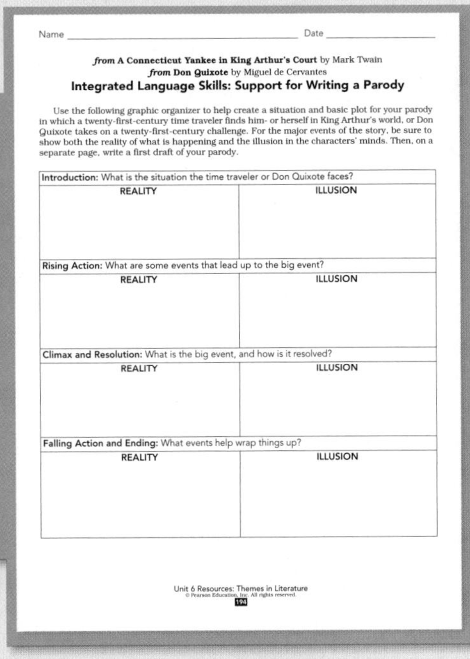
Name ______ Date ______

from **A Connecticut Yankee in King Arthur's Court** by Mark Twain
from **Don Quixote** by Miguel de Cervantes

Integrated Language Skills: Support for Writing a Parody

Use the following graphic organizer to help create a situation and basic plot for your parody in which a twenty-first-century time traveler finds him- or herself in King Arthur's world, or Don Quixote takes on a twenty-first-century challenge. For the major events of the story, be sure to show both the reality of what is happening and the illusion in the characters' minds. Then, on a separate page, write a first draft of your parody.

Introduction: What is the situation the time traveler or Don Quixote faces?
REALITY | ILLUSION

Rising Action: What are some events that lead up to the big event?
REALITY | ILLUSION

Climax and Resolution: What is the big event, and how is it resolved?
REALITY | ILLUSION

Falling Action and Ending: What events help wrap things up?
REALITY | ILLUSION

Unit 6 Resources: Themes in Literature
© Pearson Education, Inc. All rights reserved.
194

L3 L4 **Support for Writing,** p. 194

Also available for these selections:

- All Reading: Compare Worldviews, pp. 172, 190
- All Literary Analysis: Parody, pp. 171, 189
- L4 Enrichment, pp. 174, 192
- L3 L4 Grammar, p. 193
- L3 L4 Support for Extend Your Learning, p. 195

Assessment

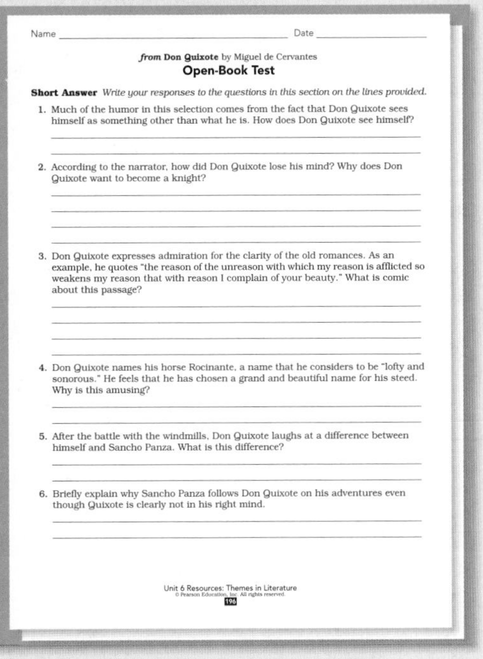
Name ______ Date ______

from **Don Quixote** by Miguel de Cervantes

Open-Book Test

Short Answer *Write your responses to the questions in this section on the lines provided.*

1. Much of the humor in this selection comes from the fact that Don Quixote sees himself as something other than what he is. How does Don Quixote see himself?
2. According to the narrator, how did Don Quixote lose his mind? Why does Don Quixote want to become a knight?
3. Don Quixote expresses admiration for the clarity of the old romances. As an example, he quotes "the reason of the unreason with which my reason is afflicted so weakens my reason that with reason I complain of your beauty." What is comic about this passage?
4. Don Quixote names his horse Rocinante, a name that he considers to be "lofty and sonorous." He feels that he has chosen a grand and beautiful name for his steed. Why is this amusing?
5. After the battle with the windmills, Don Quixote laughs at a difference between himself and Sancho Panza. What is this difference?
6. Briefly explain why Sancho Panza follows Don Quixote on his adventures even though Quixote is clearly not in his right mind.

Unit 6 Resources: Themes in Literature
© Pearson Education, Inc. All rights reserved.
196

L3 L4 **Open-Book Test,** pp. 175–177, 196–198

Also available for these selections:

- EL L1 L2 Selection Test A, pp. 178–180, 199–201
- L3 L4 Selection Test B, pp. 181–183, 202–-204

PHLit Online!
www.PHLitOnline.com

- complete narrated selection text
- a thematically related video with writing prompt
- an interactive graphic organizer
- highlighting feature
- access to all student print resources, adapted to individual student needs
- Spanish and English summaries

Get Connected Video
Instructions
Watch the video. Then, use your journal to respond to the prompt at the end of the clip.

Get Connected! (thematic video with writing prompt)

Also available:

Background video

Vocabulary Central

Vocabulary Central (tools, activities, and songs for studying vocabulary)

Also available:

Writer's Journal (with graphics feature)

DIFFERENTIATE/PRETEACH

❶ Selection Choices

You may use either the selection from *A Connecticut Yankee in King Arthur's Court* or *Don Quixote* to meet the lesson standards. Skills instruction for both selections appears on p. 1189. Choose one selection to teach (or choose to teach both). The Accessibility at a Glance chart at the bottom of this page will help you determine which of the two selections is more appropriate for your students.

❷ Selection Skills

1. With the class, preview the selection skills. (The lesson meets the lesson objectives given on p. 1188a.)
2. Explain that students will develop the skill of comparing worldviews (introduced on p. 1153) as they read to better understand and enjoy the selection you choose. By examining parody as they read, they will gain deeper insight into the genre: themes in literature.
3. To introduce the Writing and Research and Technology activities (p. 1219), tell students that when they have finished reading the selection, they will write a parody and a biographical brochure related to the selection.
4. Tell students that they will also study a grammar concept: semicolons, colons, and ellipsis points. By mastering this concept, they will improve their reading fluency and the quality of their own writing.

Before You Read

from A Connecticut Yankee in King Arthur's Court • *from* Don Quixote

❶ Selection Choices

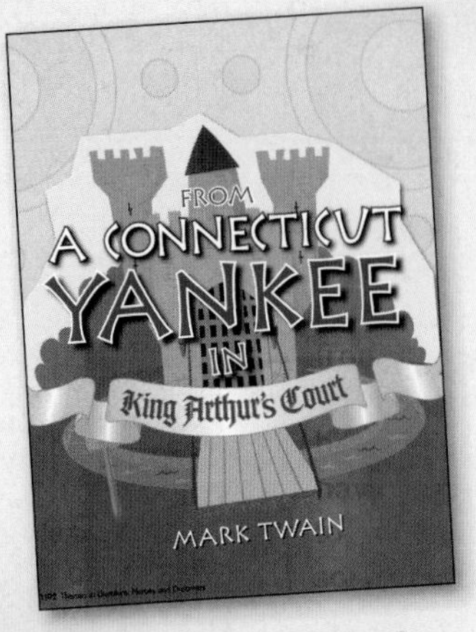

▲ Read the excerpt from ***A Connecticut Yankee in King Arthur's Court*** to find out how a reluctant time traveler gets in and out of trouble.

▲ Read the excerpt from ***Don Quixote*** to find out what happens when a well-meaning gentleman decides to become a legendary hero.

❷ Selection Skills Guide

Practice these skills with either the excerpt from ***A Connecticut Yankee in King Arthur's Court*** (p. 1192) or the excerpt from ***Don Quixote*** (p. 1208)

- Understand parody
- Compare and contrast worldviews
- Understand colons, semicolons, and ellipsis points
- Write a parody
- Create a biographical brochure

Differentiated Instruction for Universal Access

Accessibility at a Glance: Selection Choices

	from A Connecticut Yankee in King Arthur's Court	*from* Don Quixote	
Context	Nineteenth-century man time travels to King Arthur's England	Man lives the illusion that he is a great knight	Because a number of factors determine the relative accessibility of paired selections, in some cases the Lexile rating of the more challenging selection will be lower than that of the more accessible selection.
Language/ Vocabulary	• Dialogue • Parody of archaic language • Grade-level vocabulary	• Some complex sentences • Parody of archaic language • Above-level vocabulary	
Concept Level	Challenging (man disregarding the past, making fun of ignorance of others)	Accessible (man living in his imagination)	
Literary Merit	Well-known author	Classic	
Lexile/Length	Lexile: 1030L Word Count: 4,281	Lexile: 1350L Word Count: 3,070	
Overall Rating	**More challenging**	**More accessible**	

❸ Literary Analysis: Parody

A **parody** is a humorous work in which the author's purpose is to imitate the style or ideas of other works in an exaggerated or a ridiculous way. For example, the following passage parodies the style, conflict, and characters typically found in sports stories:

> John was tense as he flipped the final peanut into the air. Then, he exploded into action. In one flawless move, he snapped his head back, and the peanut dropped neatly into his mouth.

Although parodies are humorous, they often have a deeper purpose: to convey the writer's perspective on a subject. Through the use of exaggeration, parodies point out the faulty attitudes, ideals, and values of past and current society. When you read a parody, think about the **theme** or insight about life that it conveys.

PHLit Online!
www.PHLitOnline.com

Hear It!
- Selection summary audio
- Selection audio

See It!
- Get Connected video
- Background video
- More about the author
- Vocabulary flashcards

Do It!
- Interactive journals
- Interactive graphic organizers
- Self-test
- Internet activity
- Grammar tutorial
- Interactive vocabulary games

❹ Reading Skill: Compare Worldviews

A serious work of literature reflects the writer's **worldview,** or basic beliefs and values. Very often, those beliefs and values stem directly from the time period and culture of the work's author. In a parody, another writer may portray the original author's worldview as an illusion and therefore open to ridicule.

As you read, **compare and contrast** illusion and reality in the narrative as shown in the different characters' beliefs and actions.

❺ Using the Strategy: Worldview Diagram

Record details from the selections on a **worldview diagram** like this one.

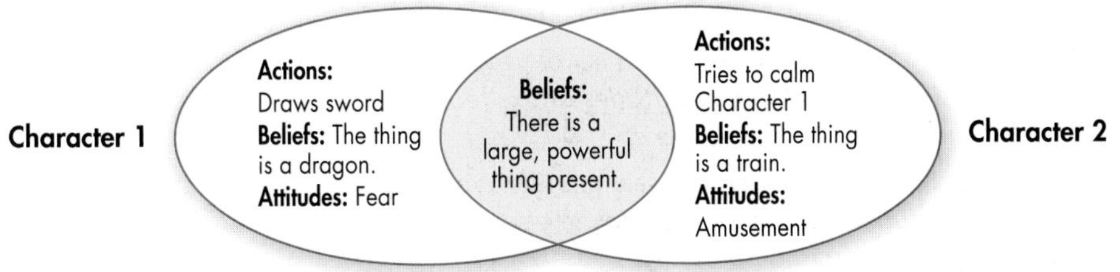

Differentiated Instruction for Universal Access

Preparing Students for the More Challenging Selection

If you wish to prepare lower-level readers to read the selection from *A Connecticut Yankee in King Arthur's Court,* the more challenging selection, follow these steps:

- Students might have difficulty with the main concept of the story: disregarding the past. Discuss why someone would disregard or ignore the past. What might the consequences of this action be?
- Explain to students that as part of the parody, the author uses archaic language. Point out examples (e.g. "Prithee, what dream?" p. 1193). Encourage students to use the footnotes provided while reading to determine the meaning of unfamiliar archaic words.
- Students might have difficulty with the heavy dialogue in the story. Encourage students to pause after reading long sections of dialogue. Have them consider what has been said and what it implies about the speakers.

❸ Literary Analysis

1. Introduce the skill, using the instruction on the student page.
2. Tell students that they will examine parody as they read.

Think Aloud: Model the Skill

Model the skill of identifying parody. Say to students:

> To identify a parody and to appreciate its humor, I need to be familiar with the original work of which it parodies. I can watch a movie such as *Spaceballs, Austin Powers,* or *Scary Movie* and find it funny. If I recognize, however, that its characters, plot, and notable quotes make fun of those in movies in its own genre—science fiction, spy, or horror—then I will appreciate the humor more.

❹ Reading Skill

1. Introduce the skill, using the instruction on the student page.
2. Tell students that they will compare and contrast worldviews as they read.

Think Aloud: Model the Skill

Model the skill of comparing and contrasting worldviews. Say to students:

> I know that a parody is based on a particular worldview, and in order to be funny, the parody must present this worldview as ridiculous. Suppose I am watching a comedy about an upcoming dog show. Different dog owners are asked serious questions about their dog's breed and training, all questions that represent the worldview that dog shows are prestigious, serious events. However, it is the least likely dog owners—clumsy and unrefined—as well as their scruffy terrier, who win the show, which suggests a different worldview about dog shows.

❺ Using the Strategy

Give students a copy of either **Reading Skill Graphic Organizer A** or **B** (*Graphic Organizer Transparencies,* pp. 216–218) to compare worldviews as they read. Use the examples in **Reading Skill Graphic Organizer A,** which is partially filled in, to model the process of completing the organizer.

PRETEACH

❶ Writing About the Big Question

1. Review the assignment with the class.
2. Ask students to think of the personality trait that is the most important when overcoming difficult obstacles. Have students discuss their answers.
3. Have students complete the sentence starter. Review responses as a class. (**Possible response:** When faced with seemingly insurmountable obstacles, a person with <u>determination</u> can <u>persevere</u> because despite any difficulties, he or she will continue until the goal is accomplished.)
4. Remind students that their answers will help them think about the Big Question, "Can anyone be a hero?"

While You Read

Tell students that as they read, they should look for the pros and cons in Hank's plan for escape.

❷ Vocabulary

1. Have students preview the selection vocabulary.
2. For each word, have students say the word aloud.
3. Then, use the word in a sentence that defines the word.
4. Finally, repeat your definitional sentence or a similar sentence with the word missing and have the class "fill in the blank" chorally. Here are some examples:

   A <u>calamity</u> is a terrible disaster. The powerful tornado that destroyed hundreds of homes and injured many people was considered a [students say "calamity"].

   Something <u>conspicuous</u> is easy to see. Amid the crowd of people wearing black and gray, the man in the bright green jumpsuit was very [students say " conspicuous"].

❸ Word Study

1. Introduce the skill, using the instruction in the box.
2. Ask students to think of a word with the prefix *multi-* that means "a person with many millions of dollars." (**Answer:** multimillionaire)

Making Connections

from A Connecticut Yankee in King Arthur's Court

Can anyone be a *hero?*

❶ Writing About the Big Question

In the excerpt from *A Connecticut Yankee in King Arthur's Court,* a man's resourcefulness and ingenuity help him out in a "unique" circumstance. Use this sentence starter to develop your ideas about the Big Question.

When faced with seemingly insurmountable obstacles, a person with **determination** can **persevere** because _______________.

While You Read Look for positive and negative points in the man's plan for escape. Decide if any of his actions are heroic.

❷ Vocabulary

Read each word and its definition. Decide whether you know the word well, know it a little bit, or do not know it at all. After you read, see how your knowledge of each word has increased.

- **plight** (plīt) *n.* a distressing situation (p. 1193) ***The <u>plight</u> of the cat was eased when we rescued her from the tree.***
- **contrive** (kən trīv′) *v.* bring about; manage (p. 1195) ***We must <u>contrive</u> a plan to get everyone home in time for the surprise party.*** *contrivance n. contriver n.*
- **rudiments** (ro͞o′ də mənts) *n.* basics; slight beginning (p. 1195) ***First graders learn only the <u>rudiments</u> of arithmetic.*** *rudimental adj. rudimentary adj.*
- **calamity** (kə lam′ ə tē) *n.* terrible misfortune; disaster (p. 1196) ***The powerful hurricane was a great <u>calamity</u>.*** *calamitous adj.*
- **multitudes** (mul′ tə to͞odz) *n.* crowds; large number of people or things (p. 1199) ***Outside the stadium, <u>multitudes</u> of excited fans swarmed.*** *multitudinous adj.*
- **conspicuous** (kən spik′ yo͞o əs) *adj.* easy to see (p. 1199) ***We were <u>conspicuous</u> in our bright clothes when everyone else wore black.*** *conspicuously adv. conspicuousness n.*

❸ Word Study

The Latin **prefix *multi-*** means "many" or "much."

In this story, **multitudes**, or a crowd of many people, fill the court of the castle.

Vocabulary Development

Vocabulary Knowledge Rating

Create a **Vocabulary Knowledge Rating Chart** (***Professional Development Guidebook,*** p. 33) for this selection. Include the selection vocabulary and the Big Question words that appear in the Writing About the Big Question sentence starter on this page. (The Big Question vocabulary is introduced on pp. 1046–1047.)

Give students a copy of the chart. Read the words aloud and have students mark their rating in the Before Reading column. Urge them to be alert to these words as they read and discuss the selection.

Tally how many students think they know a word to gauge how much instruction to provide. As students read and discuss the selection, point out the words and their context.

PHLit Online! **Vocabulary Central,** featuring tools, activities, and songs for studying vocabulary, is available at **www.PHLitOnline.com.**

Meet
Mark Twain
(1835–1910)

Author of
A CONNECTICUT YANKEE IN KING ARTHUR'S COURT

Samuel Clemens, who later won fame as Mark Twain, grew up in the small Mississippi River port of Hannibal, Missouri. He left school early to learn the printing trade and later found work as a steamboat pilot. After the Civil War, he headed west, hunting for silver in Nevada and gold in California while writing accounts of his travels.

A Connecticut Writer In 1870, Twain married Olivia Langdon and began to raise a family. Settling in Hartford, Connecticut, he penned his popular boyhood tale *The Adventures of Tom Sawyer* and a string of other bestsellers.

DID YOU KNOW?

Twain took his pen name from a riverboat cry, "Mark twain!," meaning the water was deep enough for safe passage.

4

BACKGROUND FOR THE PARODY

Yankees and Knights

The days of King Arthur are typically depicted as a time of great deeds and noble characters. Twain paints a different picture of this time. Hank Morgan, the hero of Twain's *A Connecticut Yankee in King Arthur's Court,* is a nineteenth-century "Yankee," or New Englander. Hank has all the shrewdness often associated with New Englanders. His ingenuity is tested, though, in King Arthur's court.

Daily Bellringer

For each class during which you will teach this selection, have students complete one of the five Research activities for Week 35 in the *Daily Bellringer Activities* booklet.

4 Background
Yankees and Knights

What we call *technology* Mark Twain's Yankee would call *machinery* or *inventions.* In Twain's time, steam engines, electricity, and even early automobiles were redefining the world. Twain's decision to invest in a typesetting machine led to financial disaster for him, but he remained fascinated by the promise of America's industrial future. Hank Morgan's first official act as King Arthur's minister is to start a patent office. He then lays telephone and telegraph wires across Arthur's England and brings electric lights and printing presses to a reluctant medieval England.

Multidraft Reading

This icon ● marks natural pauses in the selection. To assist struggling readers and to deepen reading for all, assign the text in "chunks," following the icons, and apply multidraft reading protocols. For each reading, have students set the purpose indicated:

- **First reading**—literal comprehension: answering the Reading Check questions.
- **Second reading**—application of skills: answering the Parody and Compare Worldviews prompts.
- **Third reading**—interpretation: answering the end-of-selection questions.

For more guidance, refer to the ***Classroom Strategies and Teaching Routines*** card on multidraft reading.

Differentiated Instruction   Additional Instruction

EL Extended Support—English Learners
Have students complete the **Reading and Vocabulary Warm-ups, *Unit 6 Resources,*** pp. 166–169, before they read. Assign the prereading pages and the adapted selection in the ***Reader's Notebook: English Learner's Version.*** Then, have students listen to portions of the selection on the ***Hear It!* Audio CD.**

L1 L2 Extended Support—Struggling Readers
Have students complete the **Reading and Vocabulary Warm-ups, *Unit 6 Resources,*** pp. 166–169, before they read. Assign the prereading pages and the adapted selection in the ***Reader's Notebook: Adapted Version.*** Then, have students listen to portions of the selection on the ***Hear It!* Audio CD** (adapted text).

Extended Support—Reluctant Readers
To build motivation and engagement before assigning the selection, have students read "Leaping Into the Fire," a thematically related selection in ***Reality Central.*** Then, use the questions at the conclusion of the related selection to guide discussion.

PHLit Online!
For more about the author, practice with the selection vocabulary, and more background, go online at **www.PHLitOnline.com.**

❶ Activating Prior Knowledge

Ask students to imagine that time travel is a reality. Have students brainstorm for ideas of where they would like to visit, as well as during which time periods. Once students have completed the list, ask the following questions: What dangers might you encounter during your visit and how would you avoid them? What knowledge do you have that would help you in the past? How would you handle culture shock? How would you communicate with the people of the time? Is it a good idea to use your knowledge of the past and present to try to change people or events?

Concept Connector ⟶

Students will reconsider their ideas after reading the excerpt from *A Connecticut Yankee in King Arthur's Court.*

Small-Group Activity

Hank Morgan is able to determine what day England witnessed a total eclipse hundreds of years in the past. Have small groups research the pattern of total eclipses and determine how accurately the appearance of an eclipse could be plotted in the past or into the future. Have groups present their findings to the class.

❷ About the Selection

A Connecticut Yankee in King Arthur's Court satirizes the utopian days of King Arthur. The story of Hank Morgan, a nineteenth-century American who time-travels to sixth-century England, is a powerful analysis of such issues as monarchy versus democracy, but the novel is also fresh and funny. Hank, a resourceful mechanic with a can-do Yankee spirit, is concerned with the inequities he sees between the aristocracy and commoners of medieval England. Using democratic values and technology, he attempts to transform the country in spite of Merlin's jealousy, animosity from the Knights of the Round Table, and the ignorance and superstition of the people. Because of a spell Merlin casts, Hank sleeps for thirteen hundred years before he reawakens in nineteenth-century Connecticut.

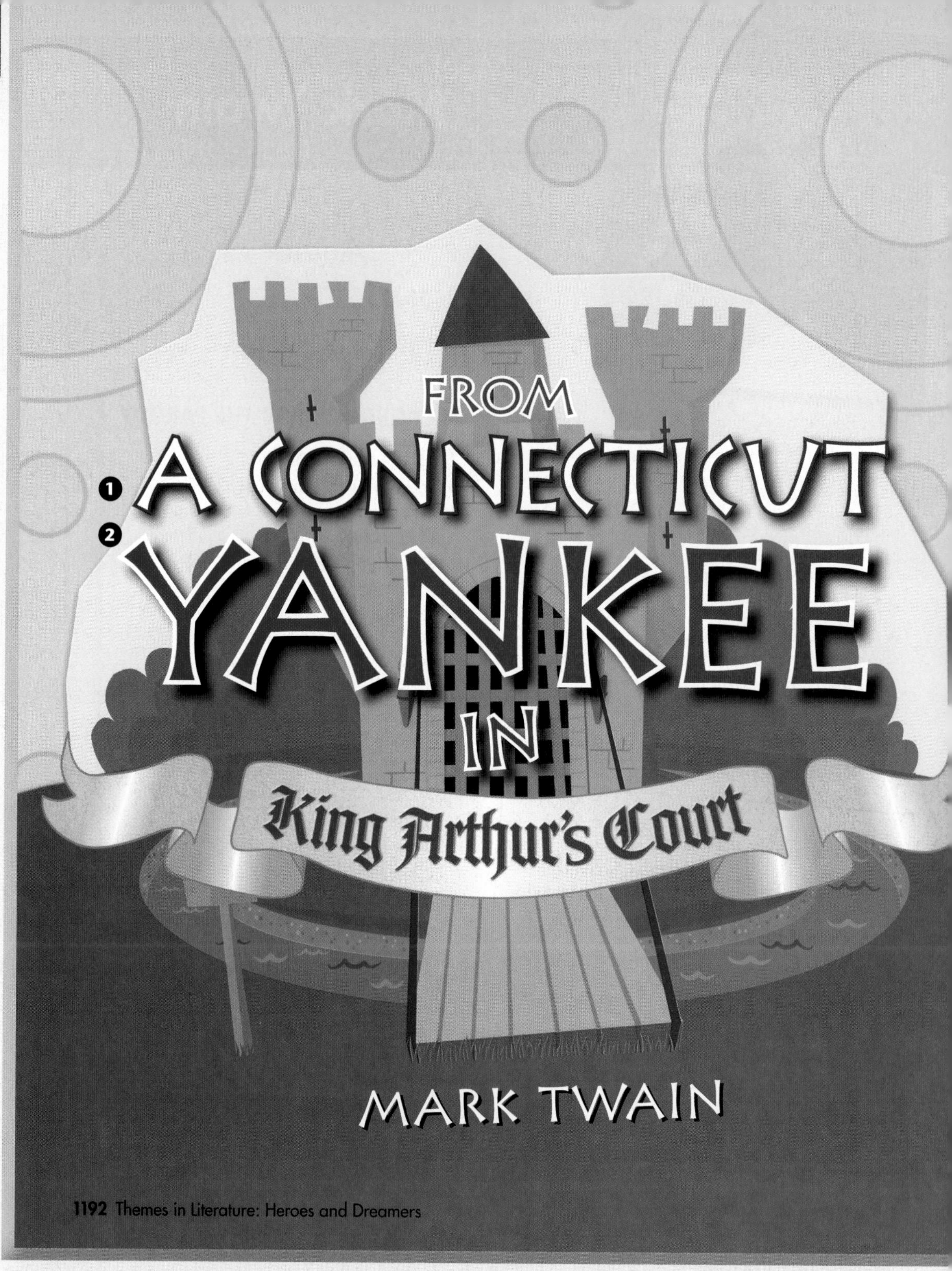

FROM
❶ A CONNECTICUT
❷ YANKEE
IN
King Arthur's Court
MARK TWAIN
1192 Themes in Literature: Heroes and Dreamers

Vocabulary Development

Thematic Vocabulary: The Big Question

As students are discussing the excerpt from *A Connecticut Yankee in King Arthur's Court,* encourage them to use the thematic vocabulary presented in Introducing the Big Question, pp. 1046–1047. You might encourage them with sentence starters like these:

1. Hank does not have an *inherent* belief in magic because . . .
2. Clarence displays *honorable* attributes such as . . .
3. Unwilling to *sacrifice* his life, Hank uses his knowledge of the solar eclipse to . . .
4. The solar eclipse will be remembered by the people of King Arthur's Court as a *legendary* event because . . .

The practical Hank Morgan is manager of an arms factory in Connecticut in 1879. One day, in a fight with an employee named Hercules, he is knocked unconscious. Awakening in a strange place, he finds himself the prisoner of a knight in armor, Sir Kay. On their way to King Arthur's court, Hank meets Clarence, a friendly young page. Hank is unsure of where he is, and he is astonished when Clarence tells him that it is June 19 in the year 528. Hank knows that a solar eclipse occurred at noon on June 21 in the year 528 but that no eclipse is predicted for his own year. If an eclipse occurs, he reasons, it will confirm that he has traveled in time. In the meantime, he is taken to a dungeon to await execution.

CHAPTER V—AN INSPIRATION

I was so tired that even my fears were not able to keep me awake long.

When I next came to myself, I seemed to have been asleep a very long time. My first thought was, "Well, what an astonishing dream I've had! I reckon I've waked only just in time to keep from being hanged or drowned or burned or something. . . . I'll nap again till the whistle blows, and then I'll go down to the arms factory and have it out with Hercules."

But just then I heard the harsh music of rusty chains and bolts, a light flashed in my eyes, and that butterfly,[1] Clarence, stood before me! I gasped with surprise; my breath almost got away from me.

"What!" I said, "you here yet? Go along with the rest of the dream! scatter!"

But he only laughed, in his light-hearted way, and fell to making fun of my sorry **plight**.

"All right," I said resignedly, "let the dream go on; I'm in no hurry."

"Prithee[2] what dream?"

3 "What dream? Why, the dream that I am in Arthur's court—a person who never existed; and that I am talking to you, who are nothing but a work of the imagination."

"Oh, la, indeed! and is it a dream that you're to be burned to-morrow? Ho-Ho—answer me that!"

The shock that went through me was distressing. I now began to reason that my situation was in the last degree serious, dream or

1. **butterfly** *n.* sociable, lighthearted person.
2. **Prithee** (prith´ ē) *interjection* old term for "please."

4 ◄ **Critical Viewing** Based on this illustration, predict whether this selection will be serious or humorous. Explain your reasoning. **[Predict]**

Vocabulary
plight (plīt) *n.* a distressing situation

Reading Skill
Compare Worldviews
What illusion does Hank think he has? What illusion does Clarence think Hank has?

5 **Reading Check**
What danger is Hank facing?

3 Reading Skill

Compare Worldviews

1. **Ask** students whether dreams are given credibility today. Are they part of a contemporary worldview?
   Possible response: Students may say that some people still understand dreams as a means of foretelling the future. However, most people now understand dreams as a reflection of a person's psyche.
2. **Ask** students the Reading Skill question: What illusion does Hank think he has? What illusion does Clarence think Hank has?
   Possible response: Hank thinks he is having a dream about being in King Arthur's court and that Clarence is a figment of his imagination. Clarence laughs and thinks that Hank is imagining dreaming because he does not want to face being burned at the stake.

4 Critical Viewing

Possible response: The selection will be humorous because the illustration is cartoon-like and the background and the lettering suggest playfulness.

5 Reading Check

Answer: Hank is to be burned at the stake the next day.

Differentiated Instruction for Universal Access

Strategy for Special Needs Students
Students may have difficulty understanding the prior knowledge necessary for this parody to work. To help them recognize the parallels of the original and this parody, have students familiarize themselves with the King Arthur story, either by reading "Morte d'Arthur" in this edition or another short example if they have not yet done so.

PHLit Online!
This selection is available in interactive format in the **Enriched Online Student Edition** at **www.PHLitOnline.com**, which includes a thematically related video and writing prompt and an interactive graphic organizer.

❻ Reading Skill

Compare Worldviews

1. **Ask** students to read the bracketed passage and to describe what Hank and Clarence are discussing.
   Answer: Hank wants Clarence to help him escape. Clarence is explaining that an escape is impossible given the number of men guarding the prison.
2. **Ask** students how the attitudes of the two men reflect the worldviews of their cultures.
   Answer: Hank knows that there is a solution to every impossible problem and that he will find a way out. Clarence lives under the authority of the knights and, based on his subservient position, cannot imagine outwitting the system.

❼ Literary Analysis

Parody

1. Explain that language plays an important role in most parodies. Authors ridicule the language of an original work by using its vocabulary and phrasing in a heightened, burlesque way.
2. **Ask** students the Literary Analysis question: Which phrases in Clarence's speech imitate the style of tales of knights?
   Possible response: The pronouns *thee* and *thou* would be the most obvious words in the parody. The words and phrases *bides not, to essay to cross, god pity me,* and *an thou* are also examples. The entire speech includes language that is too formal for a page to use.

no dream; for I knew by past experience of the lifelike intensity of dreams, that to be burned to death, even in a dream, would be very far from being a jest, and was a thing to be avoided, by any means, fair or foul, that I could contrive. So I said beseechingly:

"Ah, Clarence, good boy, only friend I've got—for you *are* my friend, aren't you?—don't fail me; help me to devise some way of escaping from this place!"

"Now do but hear thyself! Escape? Why, man, the corridors are in guard and keep of men-at-arms."

"No doubt, no doubt. But how many, Clarence? Not many, I hope?"

❻ "Full a score.[3] One may not hope to escape." After a pause—hesitatingly: "and there be other reasons—and weightier."

"Other ones? What are they?"

"Well, they say—oh, but I daren't, indeed and indeed, I daren't!"

"Why, poor lad, what is the matter? Why do you blench? Why do you tremble so?"

"Oh, in sooth, there is need! I do want to tell you, but—"

"Come, come, be brave, be a man—speak out, there's a good lad!"

He hesitated, pulled one way by desire, the other way by fear; then he stole to the door and peeped out, listening; and finally crept close to me and put his mouth to my ear and told me his fearful news in a whisper, and with all the cowering apprehension of one who was venturing upon awful ground and speaking of things whose very mention might be freighted with death.

Literary Analysis
Parody Which phrases in Clarence's speech imitate the style of tales of knights? ❼

"Merlin, in his malice, has woven a spell about this dungeon, and there bides not the man in these kingdoms that would be desperate enough to essay to cross its lines with you! Now God pity me, I have told it! Ah, be kind to me, be merciful to a poor boy who means thee well; for an thou betray me I am lost!"

I laughed the only really refreshing laugh I had had for some time; and shouted:

"Merlin has wrought a spell! *Merlin*, forsooth! That cheap old humbug,[4] that maundering old ass? Bosh, pure bosh, the silliest bosh in the world! Why, it does seem to me that of all the childish, idiotic, chuckleheaded, chicken-livered superstitions that ev—oh, [curse] Merlin!"

❽ But Clarence had slumped to his knees before I had half finished, and he was like to go out of his mind with fright.

"Oh, beware! These are awful words! Any moment these walls may crumble upon us if you say such things. Oh, call them back before it is too late!"

---

3. **a score** twenty.
4. **humbug** *n.* con artist; impostor; one who misrepresents himself or herself in order to take advantage of others.

Think Aloud

Vocabulary: Using Context

Direct students' attention to Hank's description of Clarence's *apprehension* on this page. Using a think-aloud process, model how to use context to infer the meaning of an unknown word. Say to students:

> Hank describes Clarence whispering in his ear with *cowering apprehension. Cowering* means "crouching down in fear." I know that one meaning of *apprehend* is "capture," as in apprehending a criminal. In spite of the prison setting, I do not think that this definition fits Clarence's situation. Clarence tells Hank "fearful news in a whisper." Clarence is fearful of his own knowledge, as if uttering them will bring about his death. Clarence is afraid of giving the information to Hank for fear of the consequences of doing so. *Apprehension*, then, means "fear that something bad will happen."

8 Now this strange exhibition gave me a good idea and set me to thinking. If everybody about here was so honestly and sincerely afraid of Merlin's pretended magic as Clarence was, certainly a superior man like me ought to be shrewd enough to **contrive** some way to take advantage of such a state of things. I went on thinking, and worked out a plan. Then I said:

"Get up. Pull yourself together; look me in the eye. Do you know why I laughed?"

"No—but for our blessed Lady's sake, do it no more."

"Well, I'll tell you why I laughed. Because I'm a magician myself."

"Thou!" The boy recoiled a step, and caught his breath, for the thing hit him rather sudden; but the aspect which he took on was very, very respectful. I took quick note of that; it indicated that a humbug didn't need to have a reputation in this asylum; people stood ready to take him at his word, without that. I resumed.

"I've known Merlin seven hundred years, and he—"

"Seven hun—"

10 "Don't interrupt me. He has died and come alive again thirteen times, and traveled under a new name every time: Smith, Jones, Robinson, Jackson, Peters, Haskins, Merlin—a new alias every time he turns up. I knew him in Egypt three hundred years ago; I knew him in India five hundred years ago—he is always blethering around in my way, everywhere I go; he makes me tired. He don't amount to shucks, as a magician; knows some of the old common tricks, but has never got beyond the **rudiments**, and never will. He is well enough for the provinces[5]—one-night stands and that sort of thing, you know—but dear me, *he* oughtn't to set up for an expert—anyway not where there's a real artist. Now look here, Clarence, I am going to stand your friend, right along, and in return you must be mine. I want

5. **for the provinces** (präv´ ins iz) for unsophisticated audiences in places far from a big city.

Vocabulary
contrive (kən trīv´) *v.* bring about; manage

Vocabulary
rudiments (ro͞o´ də mənts) *n.* basics; slight beginning

9 **Reading Check**
What does Hank claim to be?

8 Reading Skill
Compare Worldviews

1. **Ask** students to read the bracketed passage and to describe Clarence's reaction to Hank's cursing Merlin.
Answer: Clarence slumps to his knees and quivers in fear, warning Hank to take it all back.
2. **Ask** what this action shows about Clarence's worldview.
Answer: Clarence believes in Merlin's power to cast spells.
3. **Ask** students: What does Hank reveal about his values here?
Possible response: Hank shows that he believes himself to be superior to Clarence. Hank will take advantage of Clarence's ignorance.

9 Reading Check
Answer: Hank claims to be a magician.

Differentiated Instruction for Universal Access

Strategy for Less Proficient Readers
Students may have trouble understanding Clarence's dialogue. Tell students that Twain is intentionally making Clarence's dialogue difficult because he is making fun of the elaborate language used in Arthurian legends. Have students work in pairs to break the sentences into smaller sections and to look up any unknown words. Then, have them reread the dialogue, watching for examples of Twain's use of exaggerated language for humor.

EL Strategy for English Learners
Students may find the elaborate English used by Clarence especially difficult. Explain to students that these exclamations are used for humor and that no one uses these phrases any more except jokingly. Have students list exclamatory words they have never heard before, such as *forsooth! beware! wrought a spell!* and *Thou!* Give students time to find the meaning of each word before asking them to explain how these exclamations might be used for humor.

⑩ Literary Analysis

Parody

1. Remind students that when they analyze a parody, they should draw on their prior knowledge of the Arthurian legend.
2. Have students pause after finishing the bracketed passage. **Ask** the Literary Analysis question: Which phrases in Hank's speech are humorously out of step with traditional ideas of a mighty sorcerer?
   Possible responses: Students might include "Supreme Grand High-yu-Muckamuck," which is a slang expression that someone might use to make fun of a person in authority. Another example, "Will you get that to the king for me?" sounds like office jargon. In each case, Hank sounds nothing like a wise wizard.

⑪ Reading Skill

Compare Worldviews

1. Have students read the bracketed passage. **Ask** students whether they believe that the harshness of Hank's assessment of the medieval people is related to Hank's worry over having made a mistake.
   Possible response: Students may say that it does seem as if Hank is being harsh because he feels foolish for making a mistake.
2. **Ask** students the Reading Skill question: What do Hank's thoughts reveal about his worldview? What do they suggest about the worldview of Clarence and others of his time?
   Possible responses: Students may say that Hank sees the medieval people as being unable to think and reason, showing that he sees his modern world as far superior to the medieval one.

Literary Analysis
Parody Which phrases in Hank's speech are humorously out of step with traditional ideas of a mighty sorcerer? ⑩

Vocabulary
calamity (kə lam′ ə tē) *n.* terrible misfortune; disaster

Reading Skill ⑪
Compare Worldviews What do Hank's thoughts reveal about his worldview? What do they suggest about the worldview of Clarence and others of his time?

you to do me a favor. I want you to get word to the king that I am a magician myself—and the Supreme Grand High-yu-Muckamuck and head of the tribe, at that; and I want him to be made to understand that I am just quietly arranging a little **calamity** here that will make the fur fly in these realms if Sir Kay's project is carried out and any harm comes to me. Will you get that to the king for me?"

The poor boy was in such a state that he could hardly answer me. It was pitiful to see a creature so terrified, so unnerved, so demoralized. But he promised everything; and on my side he made me promise over and over again that I would remain his friend, and never turn against him or cast any enchantments upon him. Then he worked his way out, staying himself with his hand along the wall, like a sick person.

Presently this thought occurred to me: how heedless I have been! When the boy gets calm, he will wonder why a great magician like me should have begged a boy like him to help me get out of this place; he will put this and that together, and will see that I am a humbug.

I worried over that heedless blunder for an hour, and called myself a great many hard names, meantime. But finally it occurred to me all of a sudden that these animals didn't reason; that *they* never put this and that together; that all their talk showed that they didn't know a discrepancy when they saw it. I was at rest, then.

But as soon as one is at rest, in this world, off he goes on something else to worry about. It occured to me that I had made another blunder: I had sent the boy off to alarm his betters with a threat—I intending to invent a calamity at my leisure; now the people who are the readiest and eagerest and willingest to swallow miracles are the very ones who are hungriest to see you perform them; suppose I should be called on for a sample? Suppose I should be asked to name my calamity? Yes, I had made a blunder; I ought to have invented my calamity first. "What shall I do? what can I say, to gain a little time?" I was in trouble again; in the deepest kind of trouble: . . . "There's a footstep!—they're coming. If I had only just a moment to think. . . . Good, I've got it. I'm all right."

You see, it was the eclipse. It came into my mind, in the nick of time, how Columbus, or Cortez, or one of those people, played an eclipse as a saving trump once, on some savages, and I saw my chance. I could play it myself, now; and it wouldn't be any plagiarism, either, because I should get it in nearly a thousand years ahead of those parties.

Vocabulary Development

Expressive Vocabulary

To help students broaden their expressive vocabulary, encourage them to use the following words as they discuss the selection: *accommodate, withdraw, violate, react,* and *perceive.* Have them complete these sentence starters:

1. Hank seems unwilling to *accommodate* Clarence's . . .
2. Hank might make peace with Merlin if he would only *withdraw* his . . .
3. Perhaps because he feels superior, Hank tends to *violate* . . .
4. The reader is anticipating how the medieval people will *react* to . . .
5. Because he himself is in danger, Hank seems unable to *perceive* that . . .

Clarence came in, subdued, distressed, and said:

"I hasted the message to our liege the king, and straightway he had me to his presence. He was frighted even to the marrow, and was minded to give order for your instant enlargement,[6] and that you be clothed in fine raiment and lodged as befitted one so great; but then came Merlin and spoiled all; for he persuaded the king that you are mad, and know not whereof you speak; and said your threat is but foolishness and idle vaporing. They disputed long, but in the end, Merlin, scoffing, said, 'Wherefore hath he not *named* his brave calamity? Verily it is because he cannot.' This thrust did in a most sudden sort close the king's mouth, and he could offer naught to turn the argument; and so, reluctant, and full loth to do you the discourtesy, he yet prayeth you to consider his perplexed case, as noting how the matter stands, and name the calamity—if so be you have determined the nature of it and the time of its coming. Oh, prithee delay not; to delay at such a time were to double and treble the perils that already compass thee about. Oh, be thou wise—name the calamity!"

I allowed silence to accumulate while I got my impressiveness together, and then said:

"How long have I been shut up in this hole?"

"Ye were shut up when yesterday was well spent. It is nine of the morning now."

"No! Then I have slept well, sure enough. Nine in the morning now! And yet it is the very complexion of midnight, to a shade. This is the 20th, then?"

"The 20th—yes."

"And I am to be burned alive to-morrow." The boy shuddered.

"At what hour?"

"At high noon."

"Now then, I will tell you what to say." I paused, and stood over that cowering lad a whole minute in awful silence; then, in a voice deep, measured, charged with doom, I began, and rose by dramatically graded stages to my colossal climax, which I delivered in as sublime and noble a way as ever I did such a thing in my life: "Go back and tell the king that at that hour I will smother the whole world in the dead blackness of midnight; I will blot out the sun, and he shall never shine again; the fruits of the earth shall rot for lack of light and warmth, and the peoples of the earth shall famish and die, to the last man!" 13

I had to carry the boy out myself, he sunk into such a collapse. I handed him over to the soldiers, and went back.

6. **enlargement** *n.* old term for "release."

Literary Analysis
Parody Given the nature of the argument Clarence describes, why does the formality of his language seem exaggerated?

Reading Check
How do the king and Merlin respond to Hank's threat of a "calamity"?

Differentiated Instruction for Universal Access

Enrichment for Advanced Readers
Students can manipulate language and context to explore how both elements lend themselves to parody. To model how to use language as humor, have students work in groups to rewrite the lyrics to a song or the words to a rap (appropriate to a school setting) by using elaborate language, or language more formal than the songwriter or rap artist used. For example, "Mary had a little lamb" could be rewritten as "Mary was in possession of a diminutive infant sheep."

12 Literary Analysis

Parody

1. Instruct students to pause before they begin reading the bracketed passage. **Ask** students to explain how the language Clarence uses becomes a central part of the success of Twain's parody.
Possible response: Clarence is an uneducated page who believes in the supernatural, yet he speaks in the most elaborate language of his day.
2. Then, **ask** the Literary Analysis question: Given the nature of the argument Clarence describes, why does the formality of his language seem exaggerated?
Possible response: The king's fear and Merlin's disdain would produce a pointed argument, and yet Clarence's telling of it lessens the directness through his use of elaborate language, which makes the exchange more comic than real. Clarence is in a panic, so it seems funny that he would take the time to use such formal language to say that Hank is in danger.

Monitor Progress Lead students in a discussion regarding how Twain's use of language creates the parody of the Arthurian legends. Have students complete Venn diagrams that compare a specific passage from "Morte d'Arthur," such as a line of dialogue in which Bedivere talks to Arthur, to a specific passage in *Connecticut Yankee,* such as when Hank talks to Arthur.

Reteach Remind students that language is an important part of literary parodies. Explain to students that the humor lies in the differences; in "Morte d'Arthur," Bedivere is speaking in all seriousness, while in *Connecticut Yankee,* Hank is making fun of and exaggerating the language.

13 Reading Check

Answer: The king panics and wants to accommodate Hank by releasing him from prison and treating him as a great magician. Merlin says that Hank is mad and is faking his abilities.

14 Reading Skill

Compare Worldviews

1. **Ask** students to read the bracketed passage, watching for references to light, color, and temperature that would compare Hank's shifting mood to an eclipse.
   Answer: In the "darkness," realization hits Hank that he is in "deadly danger." This realization "crept inch by inch" and turns him "cold." Once the cold drops to a certain point, he rallies. Hope and cheerfulness come "with a bound." He knows the eclipse will save him, and he is happy and impatient for the next day.
2. **Ask** the Reading Skill question: What does Hank indicate about his values in the last sentence of this paragraph?
   Possible responses: The Yankee can-do spirit kicks in, and the capitalism that defines Hank's world reasserts its importance.

15 Reading Skill

Compare Worldviews

1. Before students read the bracketed passage, **ask** them whether it is fair to use superstitions against superstitious people.
   Possible response: Students may say that it is not fair to play on the ignorance of others.
2. **Ask** students the Reading Skill question: What reasoning does Hank follow to determine that he will not succeed in creating his illusion?
   Possible response: Hank uses inductive reasoning to determine that he will not succeed. He lists specific details: the stake, the piled wood, a monk, a crowd, the king and queen on their thrones. This leads to his conclusion that he will die at the stake.

CHAPTER VI—THE ECLIPSE

In the stillness and the darkness, realization soon began to supplement knowledge. The mere knowledge of a fact is pale; but when you come to *realize* your fact, it takes on color. It is all the difference between hearing of a man being stabbed to the heart, and seeing it done. In the stillness and the darkness, the knowledge that I was in deadly danger took to itself deeper and deeper meaning all the time; a something which was realization crept inch by inch through my veins and turned me cold.

But it is a blessed provision of nature that at times like these, as soon as a man's mercury[7] has got down to a certain point there comes a revulsion, and he rallies. Hope springs up, and cheerfulness along with it, and then he is in good shape to do something for himself, if anything can be done. When my rally came, it came with a bound. I said to myself that my eclipse would be sure to save me, and make me the greatest man in the kingdom besides; and straightway my mercury went up to the top of the tube, and my solicitudes all vanished. I was as happy a man as there was in the world. I was even impatient for tomorrow to come, I so wanted to gather in that great triumph and be the center of all of the nation's wonder and reverence. Besides, in a business way it would be the making of me; I knew that.

Reading Skill
Compare Worldviews
What does Hank indicate about his values in the last sentence of this paragraph?

Meantime there was one thing which had got pushed into the background of my mind. That was the half-conviction that when the nature of my proposed calamity should be reported to those superstitious people, it would have such an effect that they would want to compromise. So, by and by when I heard footsteps coming, that thought was recalled to me, and I said to myself, "As sure as anything, it's the compromise. Well, if it is good, all right, I will accept; but if it isn't, I mean to stand my ground and play my hand for all it is worth."

The door opened, and some men-at-arms appeared. The leader said:

"The stake is ready. Come!"

The stake! The strength went out of me, and I almost fell down. It is hard to get one's breath at such a time, such lumps come into one's throat, and such gaspings; but as soon as I could speak, I said:

"But this is a mistake—the execution is tomorrow."

"Order changed; been set forward a day. Haste thee!"

I was lost. There was no help for me. I was dazed, stupefied; I had

Reading Skill
Compare Worldviews
What reasoning does Hank follow to determine that he will not succeed in creating his illusion?

7. **mercury** referring to the liquid metal used in a thermometer; the mercury rises and falls in the thermometer with the temperature.

Vocabulary Development

Word Forms

Give students a blank **Word Form Chart** (***Professional Development Guidebook***, pp. 41–42) with *multitudes, rudiments,* and *calamity* listed in the correct column. Work with the class, or have students work in pairs, to determine the related forms.

Hold students accountable for integrating the related forms of the words into their speaking and writing.

Noun	Verb	Adjective	Adverb
multitude		multitudinous	multitudinously
rudiments		rudimentary	rudimentarily
calamity		calamitous	calamitously

16 **LITERATURE IN CONTEXT**

Science Connection

Eclipses

An eclipse occurs when one heavenly body blocks our view of another. In a lunar eclipse, the earth comes between the sun and the moon, casting its shadow on the moon. In a solar eclipse, the moon comes between the Earth and the sun, blocking our view of the sun. In a famous incident to which Twain refers, Christopher Columbus, who knew that a lunar eclipse was to occur on February 29, 1504, won the cooperation of natives on Jamaica by predicting that the moon would change color and lose its light.

In a solar eclipse, the moon's shadow falls on Earth, turning day into night.

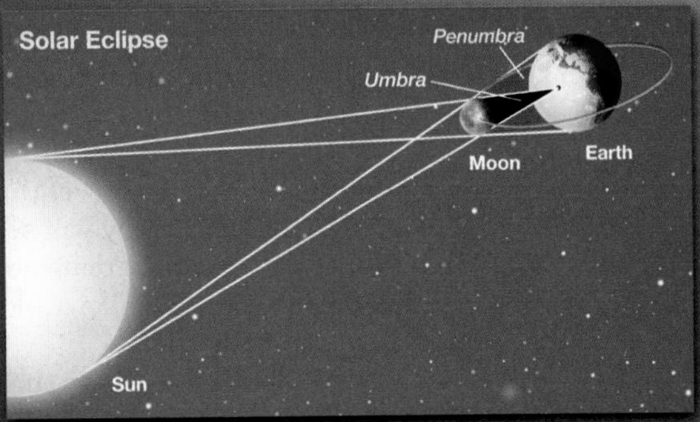

Connect to the Literature How might a solar eclipse affect people, like those in this story, who lack a scientific understanding of the solar system?

15 no command over myself; I only wandered purposelessly about, like one out of his mind; so the soldiers took hold of me, and pulled me along with them, out of the cell and along the maze of underground corridors, and finally into the fierce glare of daylight and the upper world. As we stepped into the vast inclosed court of the castle I got a shock; for the first thing I saw was the stake, standing in the center, and near it the piled fagots[8] and a monk. On all four sides of the court the seated **multitudes** rose rank above rank, forming sloping terraces that were rich with color. The king and the queen sat in their thrones, the most **conspicuous** figures there, of course.

To note all this, occupied but a second. The next second Clarence had slipped from some place of concealment and was pouring news into my ear, his eyes beaming with triumph and gladness. He said:

18 19 "'Tis through *me* the change was wrought! And main hard have I worked to do it, too. But when I revealed to them the calamity in store, and saw how mighty was the terror it did engender, then saw I also that this was the time to strike! Wherefore I diligently

Vocabulary

multitudes (mul′ tə to͞odz′) *n.* crowds; large number of people or things

conspicuous (kən spik′ yo͞o əs) *adj.* easy to see

17 **Reading Check**

What new problem upsets Hank's plans?

8. **fagots** (fag′ əts) *n.* bundles of sticks used as fuel.

16 Literature in Context

Science Connection In *A Connecticut Yankee in King Arthur's Court*, Hank travels back in time from 1879 to 528. Hank knows that a solar eclipse is supposed to take place on June 21 of that year. According to NASA scientists, 251 solar eclipses occurred in the sixth century, 65 of them total eclipses.

Connect to the Literature After reviewing the information on eclipses, **ask** students the Connect to Literature question: How might a solar eclipse affect people, like those in this story, who lack a scientific understanding of the solar system?

Possible response: Such people are likely to be terrified, believing that their gods are angry or that the world is ending.

17 Reading Check

Possible response: Hank's execution has been moved up one day, a change that he believes will be fatal.

Fluency

Students might have difficulty with reading due to a high frequency of challenging vocabulary and complex sentence structure. Have students read aloud the text beginning with "But it is a blessed provision . . ." (p. 1198) and ending with ". . . time to strike!" (p. 1199). Look for these problem spots:

- If students have difficulty with the word *solicitudes* (p. 1198), remind them to use context clues. Point out that reading the rest of the sentence containing the word, as well as the sentence immediately after, will help them to understand the word.
- If students have difficulty with complex sentences such as the one that begins "I was dazed…" (p. 1198), point out that they can break the complex sentence down into smaller ones. Suggest logical breakdowns that maintain the intended meaning. Help students realize that the semicolons can serve as logical breaking points since they separate complete ideas.

18 Literary Analysis

Parody

1. Remind students that Hank believes that Clarence and the others in the kingdom are without the ability to reason. **Ask** students how he has been proven wrong.
   Answer: Clarence has reasoned in much the same way as Hank.
2. **Ask** students the Literary Analysis question: In what way is Clarence's scheming a parody of Hank's?
   Possible responses: Clarence is playing on the superstition of his people much as Hank does. He has unwittingly outwitted Hank by scaring the king into moving up Hank's execution.

19 THE BIG ? Connecting to the Big Question

1. Remind students that the combination of an unlikely hero in a sticky situation helps to make a story humorous and suspenseful.
2. Have students read the bracketed text. **Ask** students: How does Clarence's speech reveal a negative point in Hank's plan?
   Possible response: Though Hank's plan made sense as a way to save his life, Hank underestimated Clarence's ability to reason and the gravity of his worldview—that magical forces govern the natural world. Clarence is so terrified of Hank's calamity that he proposes to the king to execute Hank a day earlier than planned, which would give Hank the opportunity to perform his calamity, albeit a much weakened version, and would thus save the kingdom from apocalyptic ruin. Hank's miscalculated judgment about Clarence and his worldview, then, has brought Hank closer to his death.
3. **Ask** students: How does Hank's mistake make his situation more comical? Explain.
   Possible response: It is Clarence's worldview—the strict belief in superstition that Hank mocks and disregards—that brings Hank's death prematurely closer.

Literary Analysis
Parody In what way is Clarence's scheming a parody of Hank's?

pretended, unto this and that and the other one, that your power against the sun could not reach its full until the morrow; and so if any would save the sun and the world, you must be slain today, while your enchantments are but in the weaving and lack potency. 18 Odsbodikins, it was but a dull lie, a most indifferent invention, but you should have seen them seize it and swallow it, in the frenzy 19 of their fright, as it were salvation sent from heaven; and all the while was I laughing in my sleeve the one moment, to see them so cheaply deceived, and glorifying God the next, that He was content to let the meanest[9] of His creatures be His instrument to the saving of thy life. Ah, how happy has the matter sped! You will not need to do the sun a *real* hurt—ah, forget not that, on your soul forget it not! Only make a little darkness—only the littlest little darkness, mind, and cease with that. It will be sufficient. They will see that I spoke falsely—being ignorant, as they will fancy—and with the falling of the first shadow of that darkness you shall see them go mad with fear; and they will set you free and make you great! Go to thy triumph, now! But remember—ah, good friend, I implore thee remember my supplication, and do the blessed sun no hurt. For *my* sake, thy true friend."

I choked out some words through my grief and misery; as much as to say I would spare the sun; for which the lad's eyes paid me back with such deep and loving gratitude that I had not the heart to tell him his good-hearted foolishness had ruined me and sent me to my death.

As the soldiers assisted me across the court the stillness was so profound that if I had been blindfold I should have supposed I was in a solitude instead of walled in by four thousand people. There was not a movement perceptible in those masses of humanity; they were as rigid as stone images, and as pale; and dread sat upon every countenance. This hush continued while I was being chained to the stake; it still continued while the fagots were carefully and tediously piled about my ankles, my knees, my thighs, my body. Then there was a pause, and a deeper hush, if possible, and a man knelt down at my feet with a blazing torch; the multitude strained forward, gazing, and parting slightly from their seats without knowing it; the monk raised his hands above my head, and his eyes toward the blue sky, and began some words in Latin; in this attitude he droned on and on, a little while, and then stopped. I waited two or three moments; then looked up; he was standing there petrified. With a common impulse the multitude rose slowly up and stared into the sky. I followed their eyes; as sure as guns,

9. **meanest** *adj.* lowest; least significant.

Vocabulary Development

Selection Vocabulary Reinforcement

Reinforce students' comprehension with "show-you-know" sentences. The first part of the sentence uses the vocabulary word in an appropriate context. The second part of the sentence—the "show-you-know" part—clarifies the first. Model the strategy with this example:

Small school children learn only the *rudiments* of reading and math in kindergarten: ______________.
Sample answer: they are too young to understand much more than the basics.

1. Even a light rain can be the source of a great *calamity:* ______________.
   Sample answer: the slick roads can lead to car accidents.
2. We can expect a *multitude* of mosquitoes this summer: ________.
   Sample answer: we had a mild winter and a wet, rainy spring.

there was my eclipse beginning! The life went boiling through my veins; I was a new man! The rim of black spread slowly into the sun's disk, my heart beat higher and higher, and still the assemblage and the priest stared into the sky, motionless. I knew that this gaze would be turned upon me, next. When it was, I was ready. I was in one of the most grand attitudes I ever struck, with my arm stretched up pointing to the sun. It was a noble effect. You could see the shudder sweep the mass like a wave. Two shouts rang out, one close upon the heels of the other:

"Apply the torch!"

"I forbid it!"

The one was from Merlin, the other from the king. Merlin started from his place—to apply the torch himself, I judged. I said:

"Stay where you are. If any man moves—even the king—before I give him leave, I will blast him with thunder, I will consume him with lightnings!"

The multitude sank meekly into their seats, and I was just expecting they would. Merlin hesitated a moment or two, and I was on pins and needles that

21

20 ◀ **Critical Viewing**
How do the emotions expressed in this illustration compare to those expressed by the king in the story? **[Compare and Contrast]**

22 **Reading Check**
What surprising event occurs just before Hank is about to be executed?

20 Critical Viewing

Possible response: The illustration compares to the king's expressions because it shows fear, desperation, helplessness, and shock.

21 Humanities

Drawing of King Arthur and his Court Viewing an Eclipse

This drawing, or cartoon, depicts the moment when King Arthur and his court see the sun begin to disappear during an eclipse. The word *cartoon* can be used to describe animated movies, comic books, and even single-cell political satire drawings found in newspapers. Use this question for discussion:

How can this cartoon be described as a parody of a moment when medieval people see an eclipse?
Possible response: Students may say that the exaggerated facial expressions of the people, and the fact that they all seem to be tripping over one another to run away from the sun, makes this a parody.

22 Reading Check

Answer: Just before Hank is to be executed, a total eclipse begins.

PROFESSIONAL DEVELOPMENT | **Mark Twain**

APPLY THE STRATEGY

Use Lit Logs to Reveal a Range of Responses and the Difference Between Fact and Interpretation: Ask students to write lit log entries about the problematic or unconventional "hero" in the selection from *A Connecticut Yankee in King Arthur's Court*. Afterwards, have them share their entries with the class.

Then, encourage students to discuss the similarities and differences in their responses. Distinguish between the facts of the story and how readers can respond to or interpret those facts. Point out that though students' responses reveal differences in interpretation, they still agree on the story's basic facts and the hero's actions.

For more of this author's strategies, see the Professional Development essay, pp. 1046c–1046d.

㉓ Reading Skill
Compare Worldviews

1. **Ask** students what doubts are raised for Hank about the date, the year, the century, and whether he is dreaming.
Answer: He is to be killed on June 21. If that date is off even by one day, he is not in the sixth century and is dreaming.
2. **Ask:** How does Hank resolve the question of whether he is suffering from an illusion of his own?
Possible responses: Hank asks the monk, the person in the crowd most likely to keep track of dates, what day it is. When the monk tells him it is June 21, Hank uses this fact to determine that he is not dreaming.

little while. Then he sat down, and I took a good breath; for I knew I was master of the situation now. The king said:

"Be merciful, fair sir, and essay no further in this perilous matter, lest disaster follow. It was reported to us that your powers could not attain unto their full strength until the morrow; but—"

"Your Majesty thinks the report may have been a lie? It *was* a lie."

That made an immense effect; up went appealing hands everywhere, and the king was assailed with a storm of supplications that I might be bought off at any price, and the calamity stayed.

The king was eager to comply. He said:

"Name any terms, reverend sir, even to the halving of my kingdom; but banish this calamity, spare the sun!"

My fortune was made, I would have taken him up in a minute, but I couldn't stop an eclipse; the thing was out of the question. So I asked time to consider. The king said:

"How long—ah, how long, good sir? Be merciful; look, it groweth darker, moment by moment. Prithee how long?"

"Not long. Half an hour—maybe an hour."

There were a thousand pathetic protests, but I couldn't shorten
㉓ up any, for I couldn't remember how long a total eclipse lasts. I was in a puzzled condition, anyway, and wanted to think. Something was wrong about that eclipse, and the fact was very unsettling. If this wasn't the one I was after, how was I to tell whether this was the sixth century, or nothing but a dream? Dear me, if I could only prove it was the latter! Here was a glad new hope. If the boy
㉔ was right about the date, and this was surely the 20th, it *wasn't* the sixth century. I reached for the monk's sleeve, in considerable

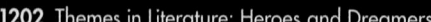

"HOW LONG—AH, HOW LONG, GOOD SIR? BE MERCIFUL; LOOK, IT GROWETH DARKER, MOMENT BY MOMENT. PRITHEE HOW LONG?"

Vocabulary Development

Vocabulary Knowledge Rating

When students have completed reading and discussing the excerpt from *A Connecticut Yankee in King Arthur's Court,* have them take out their **Vocabulary Knowledge Rating Chart** for this selection. Read the words aloud once more and have students rate their knowledge of the words again in the After Reading column. Clarify any words that are still problematic. Have students write their own definition and example or sentence in the appropriate column. Then, have students complete the Vocabulary Practice at the end of the selection. Encourage students to use the words in further discussion and written work about this selection. Remind them that they will be accountable for these words on the **Selection Test, *Unit 6 Resources,*** pp. 178–180 or 181–183.

excitement, and asked him what day of the month it was.

Hang him, he said it was the *twenty-first*! It made me turn cold to hear him. I begged him not to make any mistake about it; but he was sure; he knew it was the 21st. So, that feather-headed boy had botched things again! The time of the day was right for the eclipse; I had seen that for myself, in the beginning, by the dial[10] that was near by. Yes, I *was* in King Arthur's court, and I might as well make the most of it I could.

24 The darkness was steadily growing, the people becoming more and more distressed. I now said:

25 "I have reflected, Sir King. For a lesson, I will let this darkness proceed, and spread night in the world; but whether I blot out the sun for good, or restore it shall rest with you. These are the terms, to wit: You shall remain king over all your dominions, and receive all the glories and honors that belong to the kingship; but you shall appoint me your perpetual minister and executive, and give me for my services one per cent. of such actual increase of revenue[11] over and above its present amount as I may succeed in creating for the state. If I can't live on that, I sha'n't ask anybody to give me a lift. Is it satisfactory?"

There was a prodigious roar of applause, and out of the midst of it the king's voice rose, saying:

26 "Away with his bonds, and set him free! and do him homage, high and low, rich and poor, for he is become the king's right hand, is clothed with power and authority, and his seat is upon the highest step of the throne! Now sweep away this creeping night, and bring the light and cheer again, that all the world may bless thee."

But I said:

"That a common man should be shamed before the world, is nothing; but it were dishonor to the *king* if any that saw his minister naked should not also see him delivered from his shame. If I might ask that my clothes be brought again—"

"They are not meet," the king broke in. "Fetch raiment of another sort; clothe him like a prince!"

My idea worked. I wanted to keep things as they were till the eclipse was total, otherwise they would be trying again to get me to dismiss the darkness, and of course I couldn't do it. Sending for the clothes gained some delay, but not enough. So I had to make another excuse. I said it would be but natural if the king should change his mind and repent to some extent of what he had done under excitement; therefore I would let the darkness grow awhile,

10. **dial** *n.* sundial, or device used to measure time by the position of the sun in the sky.
11. **revenue** (rev′ ə no͞o′) *n.* money taken in by a government in the form of taxes, fees, and penalties.

Reading Skill
Compare Worldviews What are the differing ways in which Hank and the crowd interpret the eclipse?

Literary Analysis
Parody What two types of language does Hank mix together in this speech? Explain.

Literary Analysis
Parody Which elements of the situation make the king's solemn words into a parody?

27 **Reading Check**
What does Hank ask for in return for bringing back the sun?

24 Reading Skill
Compare Worldviews

1. **Ask** students how the people's interpretation of the eclipse is consistent with the Dark Ages, the era in which King Arthur was alleged to have lived.
Answer: The Dark Ages were a time of ignorance, superstition, and dread. That people would have believed a man could make the sky turn dark is consistent with the beliefs of that era.
2. **Ask** the Reading Skill question: What are the differing ways in which Hank and the crowd interpret the eclipse?
Answer: While Hank seems to derive power from the eclipse, the people are scared and stare motionless at the sky, not knowing what to do.

25 Literary Analysis
Parody

Ask the Literary Analysis question: What two types of language does Hank mix together in this speech? Explain.
Possible responses: Hank mixes the exaggerated court language of medieval England, such as "Sir King" and "to wit" with the language of the business world from which he comes, such as "one percent or such actual increase of revenue."

26 Literary Analysis
Parody

Ask the Literary Analysis question: Which elements of the situation make the king's solemn words into a parody?
Possible response: The king uses such flowery language that he sounds as if he is being magnanimous when, in fact, he has no power over the eclipse and is afraid of Hank's "power." By using such language, the king hopes that the people will again be respectful of his power.

27 Reading Check

Answer: Hank asks to be appointed the king's perpetual minister and executive with payment of one percent of the revenue.

Concept Connector

Activating Prior Knowledge
Have students return to the Activating Prior Knowledge questions. Ask students if they have changed their minds about how they would act if they found themselves in another time. Encourage students to cite specific details or evidence from the text to support their new responses to the questions.

Writing About the Big Question
Have students compare their response to the sentence starter they completed before reading the excerpt with their ideas afterward. Ask them to explain whether their thoughts have changed.

Reading Skill Graphic Organizer
Ask students to review the graphic organizers they completed to follow worldview while reading. You may want to use the partially completed **Reading Skill Graphic Organizer A** (*Graphic Organizer Transparencies,* p. 219) as an example. Then, have students share their graphic organizers.

ASSESS

Answers

Critical Thinking

1. Students may sympathize with Clarence because he is trying to help Hank.
2. (a) Hank is to be burned at the stake. (b) He has experienced "the lifelike intensity of dreams" before.
3. (a) Merlin has woven a spell around the dungeon. (b) Hank tells Clarence that he is a magician himself.
4. (a) Hank shows that he is an enterprising businessman. (b) **Possible response:** No, because tricking people who do not know any better is cruel.

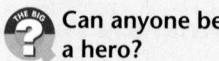

Can anyone be a hero?

Possible responses: (a) Hank could use his advanced understanding of science to perform further "heroic" acts. His knowledge of history—the future where he is now—could help him continue to fool the members of King Arthur's court. (b) Hank possesses no true magic in a world in which magic is highly valued and respected. Merlin could continue to be a threat to Hank, possibly revealing Hank's secret. Maintaining his heroic status may be difficult, since Hank is only a hero due to good luck and the unique knowledge he possesses.

and if at the end of a reasonable time the king had kept his mind the same, the darkness should be dismissed. Neither the king nor anybody else was satisfied with that arrangement, but I had to stick to my point.

It grew darker and darker and blacker and blacker, while I struggled with those awkward sixth-century clothes. It got to be pitch-dark, at last, and the multitude groaned with horror to feel the cold uncanny night breezes fan through the place and see the stars come out and twinkle in the sky. At last the eclipse was total, and I was very glad of it, but everybody else was in misery; which was quite natural. I said:

"The king, by his silence, still stands to the terms." Then I lifted up my hand—stood just so a moment—then I said, with the most awful solemnity: "Let the enchantment dissolve and pass harmless away!"

There was no response, for a moment, in that deep darkness and that graveyard hush. But when the silver rim of the sun pushed itself out, a moment or two later, the assemblage broke loose with a vast shout and came pouring down like a deluge to smother me with blessings and gratitude.

And Clarence was not the last of the wash, to be sure.

Critical Thinking

1. **Respond:** Do you sympathize with Clarence? Why or why not?
2. **(a)** What threat does Hank face? **(b) Infer:** Why does he think he may be dreaming?
3. **(a)** What does Clarence say Merlin has woven? **(b) Analyze:** What story about himself does this information prompt Hank to tell?
4. **(a) Interpret:** What does the deal Hank strikes with King Arthur show about his character? **(b) Make a Judgment:** Is Hank's manipulation of Clarence and the king justified? Why or why not?

Can anyone be a hero?
(a) List two reasons why Hank could continue to be successful as a "hero" in King Arthur's court. **(b)** List two reasons why Hank might not be successful.

Assessment Resources

Unit 6 Resources

L1 L2 EL **Selection Test A,** pp. 178–180. Administer Test A to less advanced readers and English learners.

L3 L4 **Selection Test B,** pp. 181–183. Administer Test B to on-level and more advanced students.

L3 L4 **Open-Book Test,** pp. 175–177. As an alternative, give the Open-Book Test.

All **Customizable Test Bank**

All **Self-tests**
Students may prepare for the **Selection Test** by taking the **Self-test** online.

PHLit Online! All assessment resources are available at **www.PHLitOnline.com.**

After You Read | *from* A Connecticut Yankee in King Arthur's Court

Literary Analysis: Parody

1. (a) Identify the main personality traits of Clarence, Merlin, and King Arthur. **(b)** Of these traits, which would the characters in the original King Arthur legends probably not display? Explain.

2. Using a chart like the one shown, give examples that show specific ways in which Hank is a **parody** of a heroic figure.

Arthurian Hero	Hank Morgan
1. wins with great strength or supernatural power	1.
2. desires glory	2.
3. serves his king out of loyalty	3.
4. other ____________	4.

3. What attitudes, values, or beliefs of Twain's are suggested in this parody?

Reading Skill: Compare Worldviews

4. (a) Compare and contrast two of Hank's and Clarence's reactions to danger. **(b)** What does the contrast suggest about common illusions in Arthur's day?

Vocabulary

Practice Replace the italicized word in each sentence with its **antonym,** or word of opposite meaning, from the vocabulary list on page 1190. Then, explain which version of the sentence works better.

1. To master the *subtleties* of the saxophone, take advanced lessons.
2. The entire nation mourned his *success*.
3. The band was successful, so *handfuls* of people came to the show.
4. She is concerned about the *benefits* of stray dogs and cats.
5. She needed to *destroy* a way to win the election.
6. The bland color of his outfit makes him *unnoticeable*.

Word Study Use the context of the sentences and what you know about the **Latin prefix *multi-*** to explain your answer to each question.

1. Is a *multilingual* teacher limited to speaking only in English?
2. If a person is good at *multitasking*, can he or she do several things at once?

Word Study

The **Latin prefix *multi-*** means "many" or "much."

Challenge Explain how the prefix *multi-* contributes to the meanings of these words. Consult a dictionary if necessary.

multicultural
multipurpose
multisyllabic

Answers

Literary Analysis

1. (a) Clarence is good-natured and simple. Merlin is malicious and resentful of Hank. Arthur is indecisive and easily duped. (b) The characters in the original stories would not be fearful, particularly Arthur, who is courageous.
2. **Hank Morgan:** 1. wins through trickery; 2. desires his freedom, wealth, and to be feared; 3. serves his king by having "power" over him.
   For other sample answers, see ***Graphic Organizer Transparencies,* Literary Analysis Graphic Organizer A,** p. 219, and the **Additional Answers** section.
3. **Possible response:** This parody suggests that Twain values freedom of speech, which, as it is presented in the worldview of medieval times, is nonexistent. Twain also reveals that technology—and a willingness to be open-minded—is advantageous to those who embrace it.

Reading Skill

(a) **Possible response:** Hank is shocked by the fact that he is to be burned to death, while Clarence regards that as routine. Hank laughs at the news that Merlin has cast a spell on the jail, while Clarence is horrified. (b) The people of Arthur's day believed that nobles deserved obedience and homage. They also believe in the illusions that are promised by magic.

Vocabulary

Practice

Sample answers:

1. rudiments; it makes more sense to master subtleties in advanced lessons, not in basic lessons.
2. calamity; it makes more sense to mourn a calamity, not a success.
3. multitudes; *multitudes* makes more sense, because a successful band would attract many people.
4. plight; it makes more sense to be concerned about animals' plight, not their benefits.
5. contrive; *contrive* makes more sense because she would want to bring about a plan, not destroy one.

Answers continued

6. conspicuous; *unnoticeable* makes more sense because bland colors are not conspicuous.

Word Study

Sample answers:

1. No, the prefix *multi-* means "many" or "much," so *multilingual* means "able to speak many languages." A multilingual teacher can speak many languages so is not limited to speaking English.
2. Yes, the prefix *multi-* means "many" or "much," so *multitasking* means "doing many tasks at the same time." A person who can multitask can do several things at once.

Word Study: Challenge

Sample answers:

Something *multicultural* pertains to many different cultures. Something *multipurpose* has many different purposes. A word that is *multisyllabic* has many syllables.

PRETEACH

*Skills instruction for the **Reading Skill** and **Literary Analysis** concepts for this selection appears on p. 1189.*

❶ Writing About the Big Question

1. Review the assignment with the class.
2. Ask students to describe a hero from a story. Then, ask them describe a real-life hero they have heard of. Discuss the similarities and differences between fictional heroes and real-life heroes.
3. Have students complete the sentence starters. Review responses as a class. (**Possible responses:** Someone dreaming about being a legendary hero might imagine that it is important to be daring. However, the most useful attributes for a hero in real life are intelligence and determination.)
4. Remind students that their answers will help them think about the Big Question.

While You Read

Tell students that as they read, they should identify Don Quixote's actions that reveal his idea of a hero.

❷ Vocabulary

1. Have students preview the selection vocabulary.
2. For each word, have students say the word aloud.
3. Then, use the word in a sentence that defines the word.
4. Finally, repeat your definitional sentence or a similar sentence with the word missing and have the class "fill in the blank" chorally. For example:

   Ingenuity is cleverness or resourcefulness. That the woman was able to fix the actor's costume using only a hairpin and an elastic band showed her [students say "ingenuity"].

❸ Word Study

1. Introduce the skill, using the instruction in the box.
2. Have students think of an *ex-* word that means to drive out. (**Sample answer:** *expel.*)

Making Connections | *from* Don Quixote

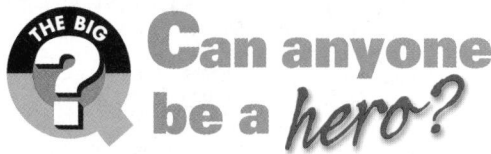

THE BIG ? Can anyone be a *hero?*

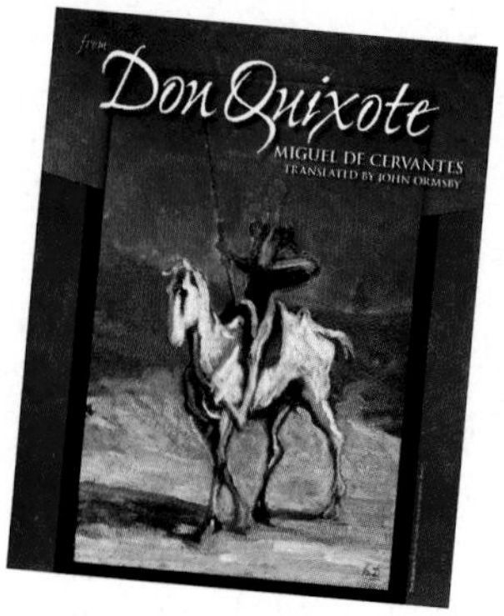

❶ Writing About the Big Question

In the excerpt from *Don Quixote,* a gentleman sets out to become a hero. Use these sentence starters to develop your ideas about the Big Question.

Someone dreaming about being a **legendary** hero might imagine that it is important to ______________. However, the most useful **attributes** for a hero in real life are ______________.

While You Read Examine Don Quixote's actions and ideas to discover what he thinks a hero should do.

❷ Vocabulary

Read each word and its definition. Decide whether you know the word well, know it a little bit, or do not know it at all. After you read, see how your knowledge of each word has increased.

- **lucidity** (lo͞o sid′ ə tē) *n.* clarity; quality of being readily understood (p. 1209) ***We built the model well because of the lucidity of the instructions in the manual.*** *lucid adj. lucidly adv.*
- **affable** (af′ ə bəl) *adj.* pleasant; friendly (p. 1210) ***Because she was so affable, she had many friends.*** *affability n. affably adv.*
- **ingenuity** (in′jə no͞o′ ə tē) *n.* cleverness (p. 1211) ***His ingenuity was apparent when he mended the chair with only tape and string.*** *genius n. ingenious adj.*
- **sonorous** (sə nôr′ əs) *adj.* having a rich or impressive sound (p. 1212) ***His sonorous voice echoed across the room.*** *sonority n. sonorously adv.*
- **veracious** (və rā′ shəs) *adj.* truthful; honest (p. 1212) ***Her veracious account of the accident left no doubt as to who was at fault.*** *verify v. veracity n.*
- **extolled** (ek stōld′) *adj.* praised (p. 1213) ***The joys of country living are often extolled.*** *extol v. extoller n.*

❸ Word Study

The **Latin prefix *ex-*** means "up" or "out."

In this story, a character thinks his accomplishments have not been adequately **extolled,** or praised highly enough.

Vocabulary Development

Vocabulary Knowledge Rating

Create a **Vocabulary Knowledge Rating Chart** (***Professional Development Guidebook,*** p. 33) for this selection. Include the selection vocabulary and the Big Question words that appear in the Writing About the Big Question sentence starters on this page. (The Big Question vocabulary is introduced on pp. 1046–1047.)

Give students a copy of the chart. Read the words aloud and have students mark their rating in the Before Reading column. Urge them to be alert to these words as they read and discuss the selection.

Tally how many students think they know a word to gauge how much instruction to provide. As students read and discuss the selection, point out the words and their context.

PHLit Online! **Vocabulary Central,** featuring tools, activities, and songs for studying vocabulary, is available at **www.PHLitOnline.com.**

Meet

Miguel de Cervantes

(1547–1616)

Author of

Don Quixote

Born near Madrid, Spain, Miguel de Cervantes (mē gel′ də sər vän′ tēz) joined the army as a young man. Returning to Spain from a war, he was captured by pirates, who enslaved him for five years. Even after returning home, Cervantes's troubles were not over: Financial problems eventually led to fines and imprisonment.

A Change of Fortune Cervantes's luck changed when he published his novel *Don Quixote* (dän′ kē hōt′ ē). Although the book did not make him rich, it did ease his debts and win him fame. Cervantes is widely regarded as Spain's greatest writer.

DID YOU KNOW?

Tradition has it that Cervantes wrote at least part of *Don Quixote* while he was in prison.

4 BACKGROUND FOR THE PARODY

The Age of Chivalry

The days of knights were long gone when Miguel de Cervantes wrote *Don Quixote,* his parody of medieval romance—tales of knightly adventure. In these stories, knights live by the code of chivalry, rules for conduct that stress courage and courtesy.

Daily Bellringer

For each class during which you will teach this selection, have students complete one of the five Research activities for Week 35 in the ***Daily Bellringer Activities*** booklet.

4 Background

The Age of Chivalry

Cervantes understood Don Quixote's passionate desire to be something that he could not be. All through his life, Cervantes wanted to be a great poet. He wrote twenty to thirty plays in verse in the years immediately following 1585, but he was not pleased with any of them. By the time he wrote *Don Quixote,* he believed that he lacked poetic gifts. The absurdity and appeal of this great character at the center of a masterpiece derives not only from Cervantes's graceful style but also from his identification with his hero.

Multidraft Reading

This icon ● marks natural pauses in the selection. To assist struggling readers and to deepen reading for all, assign the text in "chunks," following the icons, and apply multidraft reading protocols. For each reading, have students set the purpose indicated:

- **First reading**—literal comprehension: answering the Reading Check questions.
- **Second reading**—application of skills: answering the Parody and Compare Worldviews prompts.
- **Third reading**—interpretation: answering the end-of-selection questions.

For more guidance, refer to the ***Classroom Strategies*** and ***Teaching Routines*** card on multidraft reading.

Differentiated Instruction — Additional Instruction

EL Extended Support—English Learners
Have students complete the **Reading and Vocabulary Warm-ups, *Unit 6 Resources,*** pp. 184–187, before they read. Assign the prereading pages for the selection in the ***Reader's Notebook: English Learner's Version.*** Then, have students listen to portions of the selection on the ***Hear It!* Audio CD.**

L1 L2 Extended Support—Struggling Readers
Have students complete the **Reading and Vocabulary Warm-ups, *Unit 6 Resources,*** pp. 184–187, before they read. Assign the prereading pages for the selection in the ***Reader's Notebook: Adapted Version.*** Then, have students listen to portions of the selection on the ***Hear It!* Audio CD** (adapted text).

Extended Support—Reluctant Readers
To build motivation and engagement before assigning the selection, have students read "The Sport Entertainment Hero," a thematically related selection in ***Reality Central.*** Then, use the questions at the conclusion of the related selection to guide discussion.

PHLit Online!
For more about the author, practice with the selection vocabulary, and more background, go online at **www.PHLitOnline.com.**

TEACH

❶ Activating Prior Knowledge

Ask students to describe some of the superheroes they have seen in films. Then, invite them to brainstorm for episodes in a film of their own invention that makes fun of superheroes. Encourage them to use exaggeration and distortion to heighten the humor of their scenes. Finally, point out that they are using techniques similar to those that Cervantes used in his parody.

Concept Connector →

Students will reconsider their ideas after reading the excerpt from *Don Quixote.*

Whole-Class Activity

Tell students to imagine that reports have reached the town council of a goofy old man pretending to be a knight who is attacking buses with a broken lance, because he thinks that they are monsters who go about the city kidnapping people. With the class, convene a meeting of the town council to discuss the situation. Is the man dangerous? Why or why not? What action should be taken?

❷ About the Selection

Cervantes's main character is Don Quixote, an old gentleman who has gone crazy reading books of chivalry and now tries to emulate the knights of former times. Through Quixote, Cervantes humorously and touchingly contrasts romantic ideals with life's realities.

❸ Humanities

Don Quixote and Sancho Panza by Honoré Daumier (1808–1879)

Honoré Daumier was a renowned lithographer who portrayed scenes and events of everyday life, revealing his reverence for humanity and his masterful skills as a satirist. After years of working as the most feared and esteemed political cartoonist in France, Daumier experimented with different styles of art including watercolors, sculptures, and oils, the latter of which resulted in many works on the theme of Don Quixote.

from Don Quixote

❶ ❷ ❸ MIGUEL DE CERVANTES

TRANSLATED BY JOHN ORMSBY

Don Quixote, Honoré Daumier. Neue Pinakothek, Munich.

Vocabulary Development

Thematic Vocabulary: The Big Question

As students are discussing the excerpt from *Don Quixote,* encourage them to use the thematic vocabulary presented in Introducing the Big Question, pp. 1046–1047. You might encourage them with sentence starters like these:

1. Don Quixote believes that to be like the *legendary* storybook heroes, he must . . .
2. Don Quixote's actions in the first chapter show he is *resolute* about . . .
3. In contrast to Don Quixote, Sancho displays the *attributes* of . . .
4. Although Don Quixote thinks his *conduct* at the end of the story is heroic, in reality, it is . . .

CHAPTER I

Which Treats of the Character and Pursuits of the Famous Gentleman Don Quixote[1] of La Mancha[2]

In a village of La Mancha, which I prefer to leave unnamed, there lived not long ago one of those gentlemen that keep a lance in the lance-rack, an old shield, a lean hack, and a greyhound for hunting. A stew of rather more beef than mutton, hash on most nights, bacon and eggs on Saturdays, lentils on Fridays, and a pigeon or so extra on Sundays consumed three quarters of his income. The rest went for a coat of fine cloth and velvet breeches and shoes to match for holidays, while on weekdays he cut a fine figure in his best homespun. He had in his house a housekeeper past forty, a niece under twenty, and a lad for the field and marketplace, who saddled the hack as well as handled the pruning knife. The age of this gentleman of ours was bordering on fifty. He was of a hardy constitution, spare, gaunt-featured, a very early riser, and fond of hunting. Some say that his surname was Quixada or Quesada (for there is no unanimity among those who write on the subject), although reasonable conjectures tend to show that he was called Quexana. But this scarcely affects our story; it will be enough not to stray a hair's breadth from the truth in telling it.

You must know that the above-named gentleman devoted his leisure (which was mostly all the year round) to reading books of chivalry—and with such ardor and avidity that he almost entirely abandoned the chase and even the management of his property. To such a pitch did his eagerness and infatuation go that he sold many an acre of tillage land to buy books of chivalry to read, bringing home all he could find.

But there were none he liked so well as those written by the famous Feliciano de Silva, for their lucidity of style and complicated conceits[3] were as pearls in his sight, particularly when in his reading he came upon outpourings of adulation[4] and courtly challenges. There he often found passages like "*the reason of the unreason with which my reason is afflicted so weakens my reason that with reason I complain of your beauty*"; or again, "*the high heavens, that of your divinity divinely fortify you with the stars, render you deserving of the desert your greatness deserves.*"

Over this sort of folderol[5] the poor gentleman lost his wits, and he used to lie awake striving to understand it and worm

1. **Don Quixote** (dän´ kē hōt´ ē).
2. **La Mancha** province (region) in south-central Spain.
3. **conceits** (kən sēts´) *n.* elaborate comparisons or metaphors.
4. **adulation** (a´ jo͞o lā´ shən) *n.* intense or excessive praise or admiration.
5. **folderol** (fäl´ də räl´) *n.* mere nonsense.

Literary Analysis
Parody Which details in this paragraph make the formal-sounding chapter title seem ridiculous?

Vocabulary
lucidity (lo͞o sid´ ə tē) *n.* clarity; quality of being readily understood

Literary Analysis
Parody What qualities of the language of heroic tales are mocked in the quotations in this paragraph?

6 **Reading Check**
To what activity does Quixada devote most of his time?

4 Literary Analysis
Parody

1. Remind students that one of the characteristics of parody is that it mocks the language of its subject.
2. **Ask** students the first Literary Analysis question: Which details in this paragraph make the formal-sounding chapter title seem ridiculous?
Answer: The famous gentleman's name is probably wrong; he is not famous, and he is not a gentleman. Instead, he is not wealthy, has modest weapons, eats simple foods, has a poor horse, has only one fine suit, is bordering on age fifty, and is not well-attended.

5 Literary Analysis
Parody

1. Have students read the bracketed passage. Instruct them to pay close attention to the language the author uses to imitate the style of books about chivalry.
2. **Ask** students the second Literary Analysis question: What qualities of the language of heroic tales are mocked in the quotations in this paragraph?
Possible responses: Cervantes is using exaggeration to ridicule the artificiality and convoluted language of the typical heroic novel.

6 Reading Check
Answer: Quixada devotes most of his time to reading books about chivalry.

Differentiated Instruction for Universal Access

Strategy for Special Needs Students
Because of Cervantes's florid and elaborate style, students may have trouble understanding the excerpts and appreciating their humor. Summarize passages for them and play the ***Hear It!* Audio CD** while they follow along in the textbook.

Enrichment for Advanced Readers
Ask students whether they know anyone who uses lofty language to achieve a comic effect. Have them discuss the humor of using such language to describe ordinary events. Then, encourage students to describe a common, everyday event, such as going to school, in uncommon language. Ask for volunteers to share their examples with the class.

PHLit Online!
This selection is available in interactive format in the **Enriched Online Student Edition** at **www.PHLitOnline.com,** which includes a thematically related video and writing prompt and an interactive graphic organizer.

7 Critical Viewing

Possible response: Don Quixote would associate this armor with the famous knights about whom he reads.

8 Reading Skill

Compare Worldviews

1. Explain to students that sometimes an author will use a parody to ridicule a trivial subject by ludicrously overstating it. The characteristics of the original classic form are used to contrast the ideal with the real.
2. **Ask** students to identify characteristics of a classic tale about knights that an author could use to ridicule a lesser subject.
   Possible responses: Students may say that an author can use the daring deeds of a hero, references to his elaborate weapons and armor, and the hero's noble steed, among other examples.
3. Have students read the bracketed passage. Then, **ask** students the Reading Skill question: Why might Don Quixote's illusion be so appealing to him?
   Possible response: Don Quixote has become absorbed in his books because his own life does not compare to the life of imaginary worlds and legends.

7 ▲ **Critical Viewing** What feelings or ideas might Don Quixote associate with this image? Explain. **[Connect]**

out its meaning; though Aristotle[6] himself could have made out or extracted nothing, had he come back to life for that special purpose. He was rather uneasy about the wounds which Don Belianís gave and received, because it seemed to him that, however skilled the surgeons who had cured him, he must have had his face and body covered all over with seams and scars. He commended, however, the author's way of ending his book, with a promise to go on with that interminable adventure, and many a time he felt the urge to take up his pen and finish it just as its author had promised. He would no doubt have done so, and succeeded with it too, had he not been occupied with greater and more absorbing thoughts.

Many an argument did he have with the priest of his village (a learned man, and a graduate of Sigüenza[7]) as to which had been the better knight, Palmerín of England or Amadís of Gaul. Master Nicolás, the village barber, however, used to say that neither of them came up to the Knight of Phœbus, and that if there was any that could compare with *him* it was Don Galaor, the brother of Amadís of Gaul, because he had a spirit equal to every occasion, and was no wishy-washy knight or a crybaby like his brother, while in valor he was not a whit behind him.

In short, he became so absorbed in his books that he spent his nights from sunset to sunrise, and his days from dawn to dark, poring over them; and what with little sleep and much reading his brain shriveled up and he lost his wits. His imagination was stuffed with all he read in his books about enchantments, quarrels, battles, challenges, wounds, wooings, loves, agonies, and all sorts of impossible nonsense. It became so firmly planted in his mind that the whole fabric of invention and fancy he read about was true, that to him no history in the world was better substantiated. He used to say the Cid Ruy Díaz[8] was a very good knight but that he was not to be compared with the Knight of the Burning Sword who with one backstroke cut in half two fierce and monstrous giants. He thought more of Bernardo del Carpio because at Roncesvalles he slew Roland in spite of enchantments, availing himself of Hercules' trick when he strangled Antæus the son of Terra in his arms. He approved highly of the giant Morgante, because, although of the giant breed which is always arrogant and ill-mannered, he alone was affable and well-bred. But above all he admired Reinaldos of

Reading Skill
Compare Worldviews
Why might Don Quixote's illusion be so appealing to him? 8

Vocabulary
affable (af′ ə bəl) *adj.* pleasant; friendly

6. **Aristotle** (ar′ is tät′'l) ancient Greek thinker and scientist.
7. **Siguenza** (sē gwän′ sä) one of a group of "minor universities" granting degrees that were often laughed at by Spanish humorists.
8. **Cid Ruy Díaz** (sēd ro͞o′ ē dē′ äs) famous Spanish soldier Ruy Díaz de Vivar; called "the Cid," a derivation of the Arabic word for "lord."

Vocabulary Development

Mock Heroic Terminology

Cervantes describes the household and life of Don Quixote using references that his contemporaries would understand as being more characteristic of commoners than of a knight.

mutton: flesh of a grown sheep, having a stronger taste than lamb
homespun: coarse, loosely woven plain cloth made of yarn spun at home
hack: an old, worn-out horse
lentils: seeds of an Old World legume

Have students note any other words that may be used to create a more thorough description of Don Quixote as a commoner and not a gentleman.

Montalbán, especially when he saw him sallying forth from his castle and robbing everyone he met, and when beyond the seas he stole that image of Mohammed which, as his history says, was entirely of gold. To have a bout of kicking at that traitor of a Ganelon he would have given his housekeeper, and his niece into the bargain.

In a word, his wits being quite gone, he hit upon the strangest notion that every madman in this world hit upon. He fancied it was right and requisite, no less for his own greater renown than in the service of his country, that he should make a knight-errant of himself, roaming the world over in full armor and on horseback in quest of adventures. He would put into practice all that he had read of as being the usual practices of knights-errant: righting every kind of wrong, and exposing himself to peril and danger from which he would emerge to reap eternal fame and glory. Already the poor man saw himself crowned by the might of his arm Emperor of Trebizond[9] at least. And so, carried away by the intense enjoyment he found in these pleasant fancies, he began at once to put his scheme into execution.

The first thing he did was to clean up some armor that had belonged to his ancestors and had for ages been lying forgotten in a corner, covered with rust and mildew. He scoured and polished it as best he could, but the one great defect he saw in it was that it had no closed helmet, nothing but a simple morion.[10] This deficiency, however, his ingenuity made good, for he contrived a kind of half-helmet of

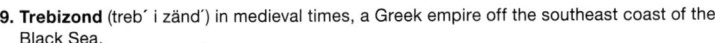

9. **Trebizond** (treb´ i zänd´) in medieval times, a Greek empire off the southeast coast of the Black Sea.

10. **morion** (mōr´ ē än´) *n.* old-fashioned soldier's helmet with a brim, covering the top part of the head.

9 ▲ Critical Viewing
In this illustration, what elements convey Don Quixote's condition? **[Analyze]**

Vocabulary
ingenuity (in´ jə no͞o´ ə tē) *n.* cleverness

11 Reading Check
What effect does Don Quixote's reading have on his mind?

9 Critical Viewing

Possible responses: As he reads, Don Quixote is absorbed in the world of his imagination. Evil and danger are all around him, and he must defend himself and innocent others from the imaginary dangers with his real sword.

10 Reading Skill

Compare Worldviews

1. **Ask** students what notion Don Quixote decides he must follow.
   Answer: He determines that he must become a knight-errant and roam the world looking for adventures.
2. Instruct students to read the bracketed passage. Have them summarize the information about Don Quixote's cleaning of the armor.
   Answer: He begins to clean the armor of his ancestors that is covered with rust and mildew. He tries to fix the defect in his helmet.
3. **Ask** what the cleaning of the armor shows about his awareness of his current state.
   Answer: He knows the world of his ancestor's past is part of his imaginary world and that the defects are a part of his real world.

11 Reading Check

Answer: Don Quixote has gone mad from reading all of the stories.

Differentiated Instruction for Universal Access

Enrichment for Advanced Readers
Don Quixote's name has entered the language as an adjective, *quixotic,* which describes behavior like his: excessively idealistic or impractical. Have students use a dictionary to search for other adjectives based on proper names and no longer capitalized, such as *oedipal, platonic, gargantuan,* and *mercurial.* Encourage them to share their findings with the class.

⓬ Reading Skill
Compare Worldviews

1. **Ask** students to return to the illustration of the helmet and to describe its qualities.
   Answer: The helmet in the illustration is elaborate with feathers and ironwork. The helmet is complete, in good working order, and would protect a knight's face and head.
2. **Ask** the Reading Skill question: How does the narrator's view of the helmet differ from Don Quixote's?
   Possible response: The author knows that the helmet is old-fashioned and broken, while Don Quixote decides to consider the helmet perfect.

⓭ Literary Analysis
Parody

1. Remind students that playing with language is a tool most authors use in creating a parody.
2. **Ask** the Literary Analysis question: How does the contrast between the "lofty, sonorous name" and the horse's actual qualities add to the parody?
   Possible response: Rocinante is skin and bones, has cracked hoofs, and is blemished. The name recalls what a knight's horse might have been, but the actual horse does not support the image.

▶**Monitor Progress** Have students make two-column parody charts. On the left, have them write details from the imaginary world of knights-errant. On the right, have them write the details of Don Quixote's real life. Students should explain the connections between the legend and reality.

▶**Reteach** If students are having difficulty understanding the parallels between the legendary world and the real world, present sample details: Don Quixote's armor, in the real world, is very old, rusty, and mildewed; the helmet is an open helmet. In his imaginary life, though, he wears fine armor, and his helmet is a fancy closed helmet like the one pictured on page 1210.

Reading Skill
Compare Worldviews How does the narrator's view of the helmet differ from Don Quixote's?

pasteboard which, fitted on to the morion, looked like a whole one. It is true that, in order to see if it was strong and fit to withstand a cut, he drew his sword and gave it a couple of slashes, the first of which undid in an instant what had taken him a week to do. The ease with which he had knocked it to pieces disconcerted him somewhat, and to guard against the danger he set to work again, fixing bars of iron on the inside until he was satisfied with its strength. Then, not caring to try any more experiments with it, he accepted and commissioned it as a helmet of the most perfect construction. ⓬

He next proceeded to inspect his nag, which, with its cracked hoofs and more blemishes than the steed of Gonela, that "*tantum pellis et ossa fuit*,"[11] surpassed in his eyes the Bucephalus of Alexanderia or the Babieca of the Cid.[12] Four days were spent in thinking what name to give him, because (as he said to himself) it was not right that a horse belonging to a knight so famous, and one with such merits of its own, should be without some distinctive name. He strove to find something that would indicate what it had been before belonging to a knight-errant, and what it had now become. It was only reasonable that it should be given a new name to match the new career adopted by its master, and that the name should be a distinguished and full-sounding one, befitting the new order and calling it was about to follow. And so, after having composed, struck out, rejected, added to, unmade, and remade a multitude of names out of his memory and fancy, he decided upon calling it Rocinante. To his thinking this was a lofty, **sonorous** name that nevertheless indicated what the hack's[13] status had been before it became what now it was, the first and foremost of all the hacks in the world. ⓭

Literary Analysis
Parody How does the contrast between the "lofty, sonorous name" and the horse's actual qualities add to the parody?

Vocabulary
sonorous (sə nôr´ əs) *adj.* having a rich or impressive sound
veracious (və rā´ shəs) *adj.* truthful; honest

Having got a name for his horse so much to his taste, he was anxious to get one for himself, and he spent eight days more pondering over this point. At last he made up his mind to call himself Don Quixote—which, as stated above, led the authors of this **veracious** history to infer that his name quite assuredly must have been Quixada, and not Quesada as others would have it. It occurred to him, however, that the valiant Amadís was not content to call himself Amadís and nothing more but added the name of his kingdom and country to make it famous and called himself Amadís of Gaul. So he, like a good knight, resolved to add on the name of his own region and style himself Don Quixote of La Mancha. He believed that this accurately described his origin and country, and

11. **"*tantum pellis et ossa fuit*"** (tän´ tum pel´ is et äs´ ə fo͞o´ it) "creature made of skin and bones" (Latin).
12. **Bucephalus** (byo͞o sef´ ə ləs) **of Alexander or the Babieca** (bäb ē ā´ kä) **of the Cid** Bucephalus was Alexander the Great's war horse; Babieca was the Cid's war horse.
13. **hack's** An old, worn-out horse.

Vocabulary Development

Expressive Vocabulary

To help students broaden their expressive vocabulary, encourage them to use the following words as they discuss the selection: *achieve, enhance, dedicate,* and *appreciate*. Have them complete these sentence starters:

1. Don Quixote believes he can *achieve* the look of a knight by . . .
2. To *enhance* the strength of the helmet, Don Quixote . . .
3. In his madness, Don Quixote has determined that he will *dedicate* his life to . . .
4. His extensive reading of the tales of knighthood has led Don Quixote to *appreciate* . . .

that he did it honor by taking its name for his own.

So then, his armor being furbished, his morion turned into a helmet, his hack christened, and he himself confirmed, he came **14** to the conclusion that nothing more was needed now but to look for a lady to be in love with, for a knight-errant without love was like a tree without leaves or fruit, or a body without a soul.

"If, for my sins, or by my good fortune," he said to himself, "I come across some giant hereabouts, a common occurrence with knights-errant, and knock him to the ground in one onslaught, or cleave him asunder at the waist, or, in short, vanquish and subdue him, will it not be well to have someone I may send him to as a present, that he may come in and fall on his knees before my sweet lady, and in a humble, submissive voice say, 'I am the giant Caraculiambro, lord of the island of Malindrania, vanquished in single combat by the never sufficiently **extolled** knight Don Quixote of La Mancha, who has commanded me to present myself before your grace, that your highness may dispose of me at your pleasure'?"

Oh, how our good gentleman enjoyed the delivery of this speech, especially when he had thought of someone to call his lady! There was, so the story goes, in a village near his own a very good-looking farm-girl with whom he had been at one time in love, though, so far as is known, she never knew it nor gave a thought to the matter. Her name was Aldonza Lorenzo, and upon her he thought fit to confer the title of Lady of his Thoughts. Searching for a name not too remote from her own, yet which would aim at and bring to mind that of a princess and great lady, he decided upon calling her Dulcinea del Toboso, since she was a native of El Toboso. To his way of thinking, the name was musical, uncommon, and significant, like all those he had bestowed upon himself and his belongings. ●

Don Quixote, **Pablo Picasso**. Bridgeman Art Library, London/New York. © 2004 Estate of Pablo Picasso/Artists Rights Society, (ARS), New York.

15 ▲ Critical Viewing
In this painting, how does the physical contrast between Sancho Panza and Don Quixote reflect different views of the world? **[Connect]**

Vocabulary
extolled (ek stōld′) *adj.* praised

16 Reading Check
What three steps has Don Quixote taken to transform himself into a knight?

14 Humanities

Don Quixote by Pablo Picasso (1881–1973)

Pablo Picasso created this drawing on August 10, 1955 for the cover of a French journal in celebration of the 350th anniversary of the publication of *Don Quixote*. The black-on-white sketch was completed quickly, as so many of Picasso's sketches were. The icon of the lanky knight and his round companion under the heat of the Spanish sun brings together two of Spain's finest artists, Cervantes and Picasso. Use this question for discussion:

This print has sold throughout the world and remains one of Picasso's most frequently reproduced works. What qualities of the sketch might explain its popularity?
Possible response: The elegant simplicity of the work and the black upon white rendering make it accessible. The almost childlike quality is universal, yet the complexity of the rendition of the skin-and-bones horse is masterful. The sympathy the artist shows for his subjects elicits sympathy from the viewer.

15 Critical Viewing

Possible response: Don Quixote understands the world to be an adventure, a beautiful and challenging setting for great deeds and valiant heroes to play out their grand destinies. Sancho Panza understands the smallness of life, its mundane and predictable events, and its visible truths.

16 Reading Check

Answer: Don Quixote cleans some old armor, renames his horse Rocinante, and renames himself Don Quixote de la Mancha.

Differentiated Instruction for Universal Access

EL Pronunciation for English Learners

Some students might have difficulty pronouncing words with the initial "th" sound, as in *then, this,* and *there,* replacing it with the "d" or "z" sounds. The following strategies can help students to pronounce the "th" sound:

- Write these word pairs on the board: *then, den; though, dough;* and *there, dare.* Pronounce each word in the pair, emphasizing the difference in the "d" and "th" sounds. Then, have students repeat after you.
- Pronounce *then, this, though,* and *there* with students. Then, call out a word and have students write the word. Have students compare and discuss results, noting what might have led to any discrepancies in their spellings.

17 Critical Thinking
Predict

1. Have students read the chapter title for Chapter VIII. Remind students that when making predictions, they should rely on prior knowledge.
2. Based upon what the students know from the previous chapter title and what happens in the chapter, **ask** them to anticipate what will and will not happen in the upcoming chapter.
   Possible response: "Good Fortune" will translate in Don Quixote's world to bad luck. Rather than being "valiant," he will be foolish. The "Terrible and Undreamed of Adventure of the Windmills" will not be terrible in the sense of fearful. The "Adventure" will not be an adventure a knight might undertake. "Worthy" would suggest silly, and "fitly recorded" would be not for posterity, but for humor.

18 Connecting to the Big Question

1. Elicit from students qualities they think a hero should possess.
2. Have students read the bracketed text. **Ask** students: How do Don Quixote's words and actions express what he thinks a hero should do?
   Possible response: Because fortune has conveniently arrayed the conflict before him, Quixote cannot refuse to take part in "righteous warfare," as a knight would have felt compelled to do. Just as knights would have done for their kings, Quixote believes that, as a servant of God, he must vanquish the "evil" that lurks on the landscape.
3. **Ask:** Do Don Quixote's words and actions make him an actual hero?
   Possible response: Though there are no real dangers threatening Quixote, his words and actions reveal that he adheres to what he believes in—even if what he believes in is false or absurd. Quixote is not heroic, because he does not do anything extraordinary; he does, however, deserve credit for his "honorable intentions."

CHAPTER VIII

17 Of the Good Fortune Which the Valiant Don Quixote Had in the Terrible and Undreamed-of Adventure of the Windmills, With Other Occurrences Worthy to Be Fitly Recorded

At this point they came in sight of thirty or forty windmills that are on that plain.

"Fortune," said Don Quixote to his squire, as soon as he had seen them, "is arranging matters for us better than we could have hoped. Look there, friend Sancho Panza,[14] where thirty or more monstrous giants rise up, all of whom I mean to engage in battle and slay, and with whose spoils we shall begin to make our fortunes. For this is righteous warfare, and it is God's good service to sweep so evil a breed from off the face of the earth."

"What giants?" said Sancho Panza.

"Those you see there," answered his master, "with the long arms, and some have them nearly two leagues[15] long."

Reading Skill 18
Compare Worldviews
What different ideas about the windmills do Sancho Panza and Don Quixote have?

"Look, your worship," said Sancho. "What we see there are not giants but windmills, and what seem to be their arms are the vanes that turned by the wind make the millstone go."

"It is easy to see," replied Don Quixote, "that you are not used to this business of adventures. Those are giants, and if you are afraid, away with you out of here and betake yourself to prayer, while I engage them in fierce and unequal combat."

So saying, he gave the spur to his steed Rocinante, heedless of the cries his squire Sancho sent after him, warning him that most certainly they were windmills and not giants he was going to attack. He, however, was so positive they were giants that he neither heard the cries of Sancho, nor perceived, near as he was, what they were.

"Fly not, cowards and vile beings," he shouted, "for a single knight attacks you."

A slight breeze at this moment sprang up, and the great vanes began to move.

"Though ye flourish more arms than the giant Briareus, ye have to reckon with me!" exclaimed Don Quixote, when he saw this.

So saying, he commended himself with all his heart to his lady Dulcinea, imploring her to support him in such a peril. With lance braced and covered by his shield, he charged at Rocinante's fullest gallop and attacked the first mill that stood in front of him. But as he drove his lance-point into the sail, the wind whirled it around with

---

14. **Sancho Panza** a simple countryman whom Don Quixote takes as his squire. In contrast to Don Quixote, Panza is practical and has common sense.
15. **leagues** (lēgz) *n.* A league is a distance of about three miles in English-speaking countries.

Vocabulary Development

Vocabulary Knowledge Rating

When students have completed reading and discussing the excerpt from *Don Quixote,* have them take out their **Vocabulary Knowledge Rating Chart** for this selection. Read the words aloud once more and have students rate their knowledge of the words again in the After Reading column. Clarify any words that are still problematic. Have students write their own definition and example or sentence in the appropriate column. Then, have students complete the Vocabulary Practice at the end of the selection. Encourage students to use the words in further discussion and written work about this selection. Remind them that they will be accountable for these words on the **Selection Test,** ***Unit 6 Resources,*** pp. 199–201 or 202–204.

such force that it shivered the lance to pieces. It swept away with it horse and rider, and they were sent rolling over the plain, in sad condition indeed. (19)

Sancho hastened to his assistance as fast as the animal could go. When he came up he found Don Quixote unable to move, with such an impact had Rocinante fallen with him.

"God bless me!" said Sancho. "Did I not tell your worship to watch what you were doing, because they were only windmills? No one could have made any mistake about it unless he had something of the same kind in his head."

"Silence, friend Sancho," replied Don Quixote. "The fortunes of war more than any other are liable to frequent fluctuations. Moreover I think, and it is the truth, that that same sage Frestón who carried off my study and books, has turned these giants into mills in order to rob me of the glory of vanquishing them, such is the enmity he bears me. But in the end his wicked arts will avail but little against my good sword."

"God's will be done," said Sancho Panza, and helping him to rise got him up again on Rocinante, whose shoulder was half dislocated. Then, discussing the adventure, they followed the road to Puerto Lápice, for there, said Don Quixote, they could not fail to find adventures in abundance and variety, as it was a well-traveled thoroughfare. For all that, he was much grieved at the loss of his lance, and said so to his squire.

"I remember having read," he added, "how a Spanish knight, Diego Pérez de Vargas by name, having broken his sword in battle, tore from an oak a ponderous bough or branch. With it he did such things that day, and pounded so many Moors, that he got the surname of Machuca, and he and his descendants from that day forth were called Vargas y Machuca. I mention this because from the first oak I see I mean to tear such a branch, large and stout. I am determined and resolved to do such deeds with it that you may deem yourself very fortunate in being found worthy to see them and be an eyewitness of things that will scarcely be believed."

"Be that as God wills," said Sancho, "I believe it all as your worship says it. But straighten yourself a little, for you seem to be leaning to one side, maybe from the shaking you got when you fell."

(20) ▲ **Critical Viewing**
Which details in this painting capture the humor of Don Quixote's "battle" with the windmills? **[Analyze]**

Literary Analysis
Parody How does the contrast between Don Quixote's ridiculous defeat and these brave words contribute to the humor in this parody?

(22) **Reading Check**
Which "enemy" does Don Quixote decide to battle?

(19) Humanities

Don Quixote and the Windmill
by Francisco J. Torrome

This artwork captures the comedy of the decisive moment in the "Terrible and Undreamed-of Adventure of the Windmills." Don Quixote loses his battle with the windmill and is dashed to the ground while a dismayed Sancho Panza clutches his head in the distance. Use this question for discussion:

How does this illustration contrast Don Quixote and Sancho Panza?
Answer: Don Quixote sees the windmills as monsters, while Sancho sees them for what they are. Quixote pays for his folly, while Sancho is dismayed but unharmed.

(20) Critical Viewing

Possible response: Don Quixote, an old man in bad armor, is caught mid-fall, highlighting the slapstick quality of the moment when he falls from his horse.

(21) Literary Analysis
Parody

1. **Ask** a volunteer to read the bracketed passage. Ask students to give examples of knightly language Don Quixote uses to boast about his next adventure.
   Possible response: Don Quixote is "determined and resolved" to do deeds of such great note that Panza will "deem" himself "fortunate in being found worthy to see them."
2. **Ask** the Literary Analysis question: How does the contrast between Don Quixote's ridiculous defeat and these brave words contribute to the humor in this parody?
   Possible response: Don Quixote has been defeated by a windmill and now says that Sancho Panza will be "an eyewitness of things that will scarcely be believed." This statement is already true because Panza has witnessed a man fighting a windmill.

(22) Reading Check

Answer: Don Quixote fights his most famous battle against a windmill.

Concept Connector

Activating Prior Knowledge
Have students return to the Activating Prior Knowledge activity. Ask students if they have come up with some new scenes for a parody film about superheroes. Encourage students to cite specific details or evidence from the text to support their new ideas.

Writing About the Big Question
Have students compare their responses to the sentence starters they completed before reading the excerpt with their ideas afterward. Ask them to explain whether their thoughts have changed.

Reading Skill Graphic Organizer
Ask students to review the graphic organizers they completed to follow worldview while reading. You may want to use the partially completed **Reading Skill Graphic Organizer A** (p. 221 in ***Graphic Organizer Transparencies***) as an example. Then, have students share the graphic organizers they did and the examples of worldview they found in the selection.

23 Reading Skill
Compare Worldviews

Ask the Reading Skill question: What contrasting views of bodily comfort do Don Quixote and Sancho Panza have?

Answer: Sancho Panza is of this world. He eats when he is hungry, drinks when he is thirsty, and complains when he is in pain. Don Quixote is of the imaginary world of ideals where pain is not permitted, but he allows his squire to complain because he knows of no stories in which a squire is held to the standards of a knight.

ASSESS
Answers

Critical Thinking

1. Students may choose Don Quixote's attack on the windmills, because it is absurd and pointless.
2. (a) Don Quixote reads his life away. (b) His own life is empty, yet he reads of adventures and conquests. In his delusion, he believes that he, too, can make a difference.
3. (a) Don Quixote believes the windmills to be giants. (b) He explains that a spell was put on the giants. (c) **Possible response:** Admitting the truth would destroy the illusion Don Quixote has built for himself.
4. **Possible response:** Sancho Panza probably goes adventuring to take care of a demented old man he is fond of.

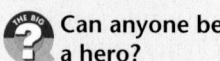

THE BIG ? Can anyone be a hero?

Possible response: (a) Yes, I think Don Quixote displays heroic qualities, such as fearlessness, because he charges the windmill—though it is only an imaginary threat. (b) Don Quixote upholds an illusion in which he believes the world contains evil that only he can vanquish through his knightly virtues. This illusion blurs his judgment and exposes him to real dangers, such as fighting the "giants," or windmills. Additionally, this illusion sets him apart from others, which has the potential to physically and emotionally isolate him.

"That is the truth," said Don Quixote, "and if I make no complaint of the pain it is because knights-errant are not permitted to complain of any wound, even though their bowels be coming out through it."

"If so," said Sancho, "I have nothing to say. But God knows I would rather your worship complained when anything ailed you. For my part, I confess I must complain however small the ache may be, unless this rule about not complaining applies to the squires of knights-errant also."

23 Don Quixote could not help laughing at his squire's simplicity, and assured him he might complain whenever and however he chose, just as he liked. So far he had never read of anything to the contrary in the order of knighthood.

Sancho reminded him it was dinner time, to which his master answered that he wanted nothing himself just then, but that Sancho might eat when he had a mind. With this permission Sancho settled himself as comfortably as he could on his beast, and taking out of the saddlebags what he had stowed away in them, he jogged along behind his master munching slowly. From time to time he took a pull at the wineskin with all the enjoyment that the thirstiest tavernkeeper in Málaga might have envied. And while he went on in this way, between gulps, he never gave a thought to any of the promises his master had made him, nor did he rate it as hardship but rather as recreation going in quest of adventures, however dangerous they might be.

Reading Skill
Compare Worldviews
What contrasting views of bodily comfort do Don Quixote and Sancho Panza have?

Critical Thinking

1. **Respond:** Which of Don Quixote's ideas or actions did you find most amusing? Why?
2. **(a)** What does Don Quixote spend most of his time doing before he decides to become a knight? **(b) Analyze Cause and Effect:** In what way does this activity bring about his decision?
3. **(a)** Why does Don Quixote attack the windmills? **(b) Connect:** How does he explain his failure to conquer them? **(c) Hypothesize:** What would happen to his dreams of knightly adventure if he admitted the truth about the windmills?
4. **Speculate:** Why do you think Sancho agrees to go adventuring with Don Quixote?

THE BIG ? Can anyone be a hero?
(a) Do you think Don Quixote displays heroic qualities? Explain. **(b)** What are the advantages and dangers of Don Quixote's illusion of being a legendary hero?

Assessment Resources

Unit 6 Resources

L1 L2 EL **Selection Test A,** pp. 199–201. Administer Test A to less advanced readers and English learners.

L3 L4 **Selection Test B,** pp. 202–204. Administer Test B to on-level and more advanced students.

L3 L4 **Open-Book Test,** pp. 196–198. As an alternative, give the Open-Book Test.

All **Customizable Test Bank**

All **Self-tests**
Students may prepare for the **Selection Test** by taking the **Self-test** online.

PHLit Online! All assessment resources are available at **www.PHLitOnline.com.**

After You Read *from* Don Quixote

Literary Analysis: Parody

1. In what way is Don Quixote's adventure with the windmills a **parody** of an episode in a romance or legend?
2. Using a chart like the one shown, give examples showing specific ways in which Don Quixote is a parody of a heroic knight.

Legendary Knight	Don Quixote
1. wears shining armour	1.
2. rides a great steed	2.
3. pledges love to a lady	3.
4. conquers giants	4.
5. other ______	5.

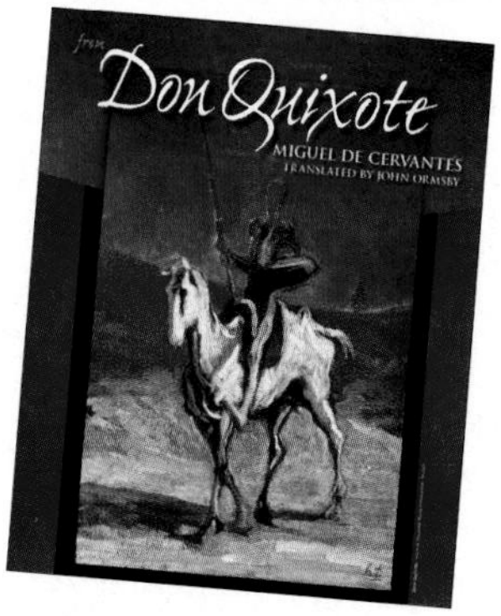

3. What attitudes, values, or beliefs of Cervantes' are suggested in this parody?

Reading Skill: Compare Worldviews

4. **(a) Compare and contrast** Don Quixote's responses with Sancho Panza's in two situations. **(b)** In what way do these contrasts emphasize the fact that Don Quixote's beliefs are illusions?

Vocabulary

Practice Replace the italicized word in each sentence with its **antonym,** or word of opposite meaning, from the vocabulary list on page 1206. Then, explain which version of the sentence works better.

1. The *vagueness* of his idea convinced other scientists to accept it.
2. The speaker's *squeaky* voice soothed his listeners.
3. I knew we had similar tastes when she *criticized* my favorite poet.
4. Everyone liked her because of her *unpleasant* personality.
5. Her clear and original science project showcased her *inability.*
6. She was *dishonest* to a fault and always said what she meant.

Word Study Use the context of the sentences and what you know about the **Latin prefix *ex-*** to explain your answer to each question.

1. If you *excavate* a hole, are you filling it in?
2. If a store charges *exorbitant* prices, are its prices normal?

Word Study

The **Latin prefix *ex-*** means "up" or "out."

Challenge Explain how the prefix *ex-* contributes to the meanings of these words. Consult a dictionary if necessary.

excel
exalt
expansion

ASSESS/EXTEND

Answers

Literary Analysis

1. Don Quixote's absurd charge on the windmills is a comic inversion of the brave deeds of knights.
2. **Don Quixote:** polishes rusty armor; rides a gaunt hack with split hoofs; pledges love to a bewildered farm girl; fails to conquer a windmill.

   For other sample answers, see ***Graphic Organizer Transparencies,* Reading Skill Graphic Organizer A**, p. 221, and the **Additional Answers** section.
3. Possible response: Cervantes suggests that romanticizing chivalry, a long-dead worldview, is absurd.

Reading Skill

4. (a) Don Quixote believes windmills are giants; Sancho Panza sees them as windmills. Don Quixote believes it is wrong to complain about pain; Sancho Panza revels in complaint. (b) In a realist's world the windmills are as real as pain. In an idealist's world, windmills can be transfigured and pain can be ignored.

Vocabulary

Practice

Sample answers:

1. lucidity; *lucidity* makes more sense because scientists would not accept an idea that was vague.
2. sonorous; a sonorous voice would be more likely to soothe visitors.
3. extolled; *extolled* makes more sense because someone with similar tastes would not criticize another.
4. affable; people are more likely to like someone who is affable and friendly, not unpleasant.
5. ingenuity; *ingenuity* makes more sense because if something is original and clear, it would not lack skill.
6. veracious; *veracious* makes more sense because someone who says what she means is honest, not dishonest.

Answers continued

Word Study

Sample answers:

1. No. If the prefix *ex-* means "up" or "upward," then *excavate* means "to make hollow or dig up," not "fill in."
2. No. The prefix *ex-* means "up" or "upward" and *exorbitant* means "excessive or high up," so exorbitant prices are higher than normal.

Word Study: Challenge

Sample answers:

To *excel* is to do extremely well or perform upwards of others. To *exalt* is to raise or move up in rank or power. An *expansion* is something that has increased or moved up in size.

Answers

Grammar

1. Introduce the skill, using the instruction on the student page.
2. Discuss the definitions and examples.

Think Aloud: Model the Skill

Model the skill of using semicolons, colons, and ellipsis points. Say:

> I use semicolons, colons, and ellipses to create pauses in my sentences. I determine what to use based on the sentence. To join two independent clauses, I use a semicolon, as in the sentence, "The man had a menacing laugh; he was terrifying." To introduce a list or example, I use a colon: "I need three things: a pencil, an eraser, and a piece of paper." I use ellipses to represent a gap in a sentence.

WG Writing and Grammar, Grade 10

Students will find further instruction on and practice with semicolons, colons, and ellipsis points in Chapter 28, Section 3.

Practice A

1. Hank was a manager in a factory; he did not believe in time travel.
2. Clarence had many good qualities: loyalty, honesty, and courage.
3. Hank was sure all was well . . . until he saw the stake and wood for the fire.

Challenge

Sample answer:

Colon: "So I said beseechingly: 'Ah, Clarence, good boy, only friend I've got . . .' "

Practice B

Sample answers:

1. Don Quixote collected the necessary items: armor, a helmet, his sword, and his horse.
2. They decided to fight a great foe: windmills.
3. Don Quixote conquers the windmills . . . although Sancho does not help him.

Challenge

Sample answer: Don Quixote is reading his book; he is not paying attention to the world around him.

Integrated Language Skills

from A Connecticut Yankee in King Arthur's Court • *from* Don Quixote

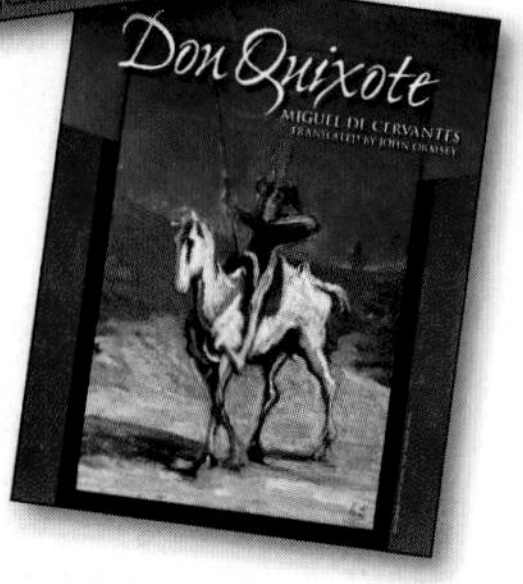

Grammar: Semicolons, Colons, and Ellipsis Points

Semicolons, colons, and **ellipsis points** are three forms of punctuation that suggest pauses in a sentence.

Use a **semicolon** to join independent clauses not already joined by a coordinating conjunction (*and, but, or, nor, for, so,* and *yet*). Use semicolons to separate items in a series when one or more of the items includes a comma or the word "and."

- **Example:** Ivan devised a plan; he was confident of success.
- A **colon** directs the reader's attention to the text that follows it. Use a colon to introduce a list, a quotation, or an example.
- **Example:** The list only contained a few items: milk, soap, and eggs.

The three spaced periods that form **ellipsis points** represent a gap or a pause in a sentence. Ellipsis points may also show that something has been omitted.

- **Example:** As I read about Don Quixote, I counted the imaginary giants, "One, two, three . . . "

Practice A Copy each of the following sentences, adding semicolons, colons, or ellipsis points where necessary.

1. Hank was a manager in a factory he did not believe in time travel.
2. Clarence had many good qualities loyalty, honesty, and courage.
3. Hank was sure all was well until he saw the stake and wood for the fire.

Challenge Find an example of a semicolon, a colon, and ellipsis points in *A Connecticut Yankee in King Arthur's Court.*

Practice B Rewrite the following sentences, correcting any errors by inserting or deleting semicolons, colons, or ellipsis points. If no corrections are necessary, write "correct."

1. Don Quixote collected the necessary items; armor, a helmet, his sword, and a horse.
2. They decided to: fight a great foe . . . windmills.
3. Don Quixote conquers the windmills; although Sancho does not help him.

Challenge Write three sentences about the painting on page 1211. Use a semicolon, a colon, or ellipsis points in each sentence.

WG Writing and Grammar Connection: Chapter 28, Section 3

Extend the Lesson

Sentence Modeling

Choose the sentence given from the selection students have read:

> If I had only a just a moment to think. . . . Good, I've got it. (from *A Connecticut Yankee in King Arthur's Court*)

> But this scarcely affects our story; it will be enough not to stray a hair's breadth from the truth in telling it. (from *Don Quixote*)

Elicit from students that the sentence contains ellipsis points or a semicolon. Then, ask what else they notice. (From *A Connecticut Yankee in King Arthur's Court:* the sentence reveals Hank's halting thinking process. From *Don Quixote:* the semicolon balances and makes more formal the two similar clauses.)

Have students imitate the sentence in a sentence on a topic of their own choosing, matching each grammatical and stylistic feature discussed. Collect and share with the class.

Writing

Write a **parody** in which a twenty-first-century time traveler lands in King Arthur's world *or* a parody in which Don Quixote takes on a twenty-first-century challenge. Follow these tips:

- Choose a situation that causes problems for your time traveler or that Don Quixote might misunderstand.
- Outline the events of your story.
- Decide on your story's narrator and his or her attitudes about the story's characters and events.
- As you draft, clearly depict both the reality of what is happening and the illusions in the characters' minds.
- To help the reader better understand the characters, write interior monologues expressing the characters' feelings and opinions.
- Use exaggeration to convey the humor of the plot events and characters reactions.

Writing Workshop: *Work in Progress*

Prewriting for a Comparison-and-Contrast Essay Use the Freewrites from your writing portfolio to develop a **Venn diagram** of similarities and differences. List the similarities you circled in the left-hand oval and differences you underlined in the right-hand oval. Write any points that apply to both literary works in the overlapping part of the diagram. Save the Venn Diagram in your writing portfolio.

Use this prewriting activity to prepare for the **Writing Workshop** on page 1242.

Research and Technology

Working with a group, create a **biographical brochure** on Mark Twain or Miguel de Cervantes. Brainstorm several research questions to guide your work. Then, use biographical dictionaries, the Internet, the library, and other reliable sources to find answers to your research questions.

- Include the key details of the author's life that would be important for your reader to learn.
- Consider creating a timeline of the author's life and works.
- Use publishing software to **design and publish** your document in an attractive format.
- Include **principles of design** such as accurate margins, tabs, spacing, and columns. Select a readable font and limit the number of words on each page for ease of use.
- Incorporate drawings and graphics into your finished work.

PHLit Online!
www.PHLitOnline.com
- Interactive graphic organizers
- Grammar tutorial
- Interactive journals

EXTEND/ASSESS

Writing

1. Review the assignment, using the instruction on the student page.
2. To guide students in writing a parody, give them **Support for Writing**, p. 194 in ***Unit 6 Resources.***
3. To evaluate students' parodies, use the Short Story rubrics, pp. 226–227.

Six Traits Focus

✔	Ideas		Word Choice
✔	Organization		Sentence Fluency
✔	Voice		Conventions

Writing Workshop
Work in Progress

Have students save their completed Venn diagram in their portfolios. They will use the diagram later as they complete the Writing Workshop assignment (see pp. 1242–1249).

Research and Technology

1. Review the assignment, using the instruction on the student page.
2. Have students complete the **Support for Extend Your Learning** page (***Unit 6 Resources,*** p. 195).

Teaching Resources

Unit 6 Resources
- L3 L4 **Integrated Language Skills: Grammar,** p. 193
- L3 L4 **Support for Writing,** p. 194
- L3 L4 **Support for Extend Your Learning,** p. 195
- L4 **Enrichment,** pp. 174, 192

Enriched Online Student Edition
Available under After You read for this selection:
- All **Interactive Grammar Tutorial**
- L3 L4 **Internet Research Activity**

Professional Development Guidebook
Rubrics for Narration: Short Stories, pp. 226–227

PHLit Online! All print and digital resources are available at **www.PHLitOnline.com.** Online resources accessible by students are noted on the student page.

MONITORING PROGRESS

Using the Test Practice

In this two-page Test Practice, students apply the reading skill for the second half of Unit 6 to a passage of fiction and a passage of nonfiction.

Review this skill, comparing worldviews, and then administer the test. For more guidance, consult the *Classroom Strategies and Teaching Routines* card, **Administering Timed Tests.**

ASSESS

Answers

Answers With Explanations

1. C—Alex could "feel the fear crawling up his back." *Incorrect answers:* A— Randy thinks it's cool, but Alex is fearful. B— Alex feels fear (sentence 7), not boredom. D— Alex says that they "must have gone back in time," not that they had gotten lost.
2. A—Alex jumps to the irrational conclusion that they've gone back in time; but Randy reminds him rationally that they are in a museum. *Incorrect answers:* B—The story only shows the boys' reactions in one situation; not enough to determine "always" or "never". C—same explanation as for B. D—The story does not suggest that Randy believes dinosaurs are imaginary; only that he did not believe they were hearing real dinosaurs.
3. C—Alex says they "must have gone back in time." (paragraph 4) *Incorrect answers:* A—Alex thinks they have gone back in time, not forward. B— Alex tells Randy it isn't funny, because Randy isn't taking his fear seriously. D— Alex thinks they have gone back in time, not to a new exhibit.
4. D—Randy knew they hadn't gone back in time, because he had read the brochure. *Incorrect answers:* A—Alex would have made the same mistake at any time, because he didn't read the brochure and then jumped to conclusions. B—He wasn't playing a trick on Randy. C— The problem wasn't his knowledge of dinosaurs, but the fact that he did not read the brochure and then jumped to conclusions.

Test Practice: Reading

Compare Worldviews

Fiction Selection

Directions: ***Read the selection. Then, answer the questions.***

Alex and Randy stepped through the broad wooden doors into a thick forest. Alex gasped. A moment ago they had been in a museum. Alex turned around, but the doors had disappeared. "Cool," said Randy casually. Alex had promised Randy he would see the dinosaur exhibit, but this must be real. Alex could feel the fear crawling up his back. Just then, a deep roar shook the ground. "Very cool," said Randy with a big grin.

"Randy, this isn't funny! Where are we?"

"We're in a museum! Think rationally! This is an exhibit." said Randy.

"No. We must have gone back in time or something. The doors have disappeared! I can hear a dinosaur! We've got to get out of here!" cried Alex.

Randy laughed. "You always jump to conclusions!" He pushed a button set into a nearby tree trunk. The screen of trees slid back, revealing the doors. "See?" Randy said. "*I* read the brochure. It's just an illusion!"

1. Which of the following *best* describes Randy's reaction to the exhibit?

A. He jokes that it is cool.
B. He believes it is boring.
C. He thinks it is scary.
D. He wonders if he is lost.

2. What *best* describes the difference between Alex's and Randy's worldview?

A. Alex jumps to unrealistic conclusions; Randy believes in thinking rationally.
B. Alex is always fearful and afraid; Randy reads instructions carefully.
C. Alex believes in having fun; Randy believes in being cautious.
D. Alex believes in dinosaurs; Randy believes dinosaurs are imaginary creatures.

3. At the exhibit Alex is under the impression that he has—

A. traveled to the future.
B. frightened Randy with a trick.
C. entered the ancient world of dinosaurs.
D. discovered a new exhibit at the museum.

4. Alex could have avoided this misconception by—

A. entering the exhibit later.
B. playing a different trick on Randy.
C. learning more about dinosaurs.
D. reading the museum's brochure.

Writing for Assessment

In a brief paragraph, describe how Randy and Alex's different worldviews influenced their reactions after they entered the exhibit Support your response with details.

Writing for Assessment

Students should first write a statement about each character's worldview. Then they should summarize how each reacted to the exhibit. Finally, they should connect the two. Their responses should include at least two details for each character

Strategies for Test Taking

Students should read each question carefully, so that they do not mix up characters, who in this story, are Alex and Randy. Only item 2 refers to both characters. The other items all ask about Alex's reactions and impressions.

Nonfiction Selection

Directions: *Read the selection. Then, answer the questions.*

Long before scientists knew about the existence of dinosaurs, ancient people knew about dinosaur bones. Many legends surrounded the fossils of dinosaurs and other prehistoric beasts. The ancient Chinese believed that these fossils were "dragon bones" and "dragon teeth" and ground them up for use as medicines. Dinosaur fossils may have been the basis for ancient Greek myths about the griffin, a mythic creature that looked like a lion but had wings and a beak. Greek historian Herodotus wrote about griffins from Central Asia, where the skeleton of a dinosaur the size of a lion with a beak and frilled neck fringe was found.

Even as recently as the 17th century, dinosaur bones were misunderstood. Robert Plot, a chemist, discovered a huge dinosaur fossil in England in 1676. He identified it as the leg bone of a giant human and published a drawing of it in his book on natural history. Though views of dinosaur bones have changed over the years, people have always found them fascinating.

1. According to this passage, the ancient Chinese believed that—

A. dragons had ruled the earth.
B. fossils they found had medicinal powers.
C. giant humans lived in ancient Greece.
D. ancient bones came from the gods.

2. According to both the ancient Chinese and the ancient Greek worldviews,—

A. dangerous, gigantic flying monsters had once lived on Earth.
B. griffins originated in Asia.
C. ancient bones had medicinal properties.
D. dinosaur bones were proof that strange creatures had existed.

3. What did Robert Plot's view of fossils have in common with the view of scientists today?

A. a belief that fossils should be studied
B. a desire to display fossils in museums
C. a concern about preserving fossils
D. a fear that fossils belong to giant humans

4. People from all times in history have found dinosaur bones to be—

A. signs that dragons exist.
B. useful as medicine.
C. very interesting.
D. worthless.

Writing for Assessment

Connecting Across Texts
Imagine a conversation in which Alex and Randy describe their view of dinosaur bones to a person from ancient China. Write a ten-line script in which you reveal each person's worldview. Use details from both selections.

PHLit Online!
www.PHLitOnline.com
- Online practice
- Instant feedback

Differentiated Instruction for Universal Access

Strategy for Special Needs Students
Students might create a quick chart comparing the two characters in the fiction selection. Their charts should include Alex's and Randy's reactions at the exhibit, as well as their ideas about what was going on. Then they should use these charts to help them with answering the questions and with the Writing for Assessment item.

Strategy for Less Proficient Readers
Remind students that many test questions are in the form of incomplete sentences or ideas and require them to find the answer choice that best completes the sentence. Suggest that students read the question stem first and think about what would make the most sense as a conclusion to the sentence before looking at the choices. Students should then identify the answer choice that most closely matches their idea.

ASSESS

Answers

Answers With Explanations

1. i—Sentence 3 indicates that they used dinosaur fossils as medicine. *Incorrect answers:* A—Sentence 3 indicates their belief in dragons, but not in dragons' past supremacy. C—Sentence 3 indicates their belief in dragons, not in giant humans. D—Sentence 3 states they believed the bones came from dragons, not gods.
2. D—The Chinese saw the bones as evidence of dragons; the Greeks believed they were bones of mythic griffins. *Incorrect answers:* A—They both saw them as evidence of strange creatures, not huge flying monsters. B—Only the Greeks wrote about griffins from Asia. C—Only the Chinese believed in the bones' medicinal powers.
3. A—Plot's inclusion of a fossil in his natural history book shows this belief. *Incorrect answers:* B—The passage says Plot included the bone in a book, not a museum. C—The passage says Plot included the bone in a book, not that he preserved it. D—The passage says that was Plot's belief, not his fear.
4. C—The examples from the passage show that an interest in dinosaurs goes back to ancient times. *Incorrect answers:* A—The Chinese believed the bones had belonged to dragons. B—Only the Chinese believed the bones had medicinal powers. D—The examples show the opposite: a belief in the value of those bones.

Writing for Assessment

Suggest that students put themselves into each character's shoes. They might brainstorm a two-to-three-sentence monologue for each individual character, beginning with the words, "I believe". Then students could put these mini-scripts together into an extended dialogue among the three characters that is supported with details from each selection.

PHLit Online!
Students may take the test in interactive format with instant feedback online at **www.PHLitOnline.com**.

PRETEACH

Meeting Your Standards

Students will

1. critique generalizations and evidence.
2. read and critique a book review and a movie review.

Log on at ***www.PHLitOnline.com*** *for a detailed lesson plan.*

Reading Skill

1. Introduce the skill, review the chart.
2. Tell students that they will critique generalizations and evidence in reviews as they read.

Think Aloud: Model the Skill

Model the skill of critiquing generalizations and evidence in a review, using the following "think aloud." Say to students:

> I read a negative review about a band's new album. The reviewer writes that the music sounds identical to that of another band. If specific songs are cited as examples, I will probably trust the review.

Can anyone be a hero?

Have students look for heroic characters. Remind them that heroic deeds do not necessarily involve risking one's wellbeing.

Multidraft Reading

Have students follow a multidraft reading protocol after they preview.

- **First reading**—Have students read for general understanding.
- **Second reading**—Have students critique generalizations and evaluate evidence for credibility.
- **Third reading**—Have students look for descriptions of heroic characters.

Informational Texts

Real-Life Reading

Book Review
Mothers and Daughters

Movie Review
The Joy Luck Club

Reading Skill: Critique Generalizations and Evidence

When reading a review, **evaluate the credibility of the author's argument** or opinion by **critiquing,** or judging, **generalizations.** Generalizations are broad statements or inferences. Consider whether the author presents sufficient **evidence** to support his or her generalizations. If there is little evidence, or if the evidence is weak, consider what impact this has on the credibility of the text. Poorly-supported arguments may lead you to draw the conclusion that the author's argument is not valid or reliable. Use a chart like this one to keep track of your evaluations.

What does the author say?	How does the author support this claim?	Are the author's generalizations credible?

THE BIG ? Can anyone be a *hero?*

Both reviews discuss the characters in *The Joy Luck Club* and the way they handle the tragedies and difficulties in their lives. Consider whether being a hero might sometimes mean dealing with the ups and downs of normal, everyday life.

Differentiated Instruction for Universal Access

Reading Support
Give students reading support with the appropriate version of the ***Reader's Notebooks***:

L2 L3 ***Reader's Notebook***

L1 ***Reader's Notebook: Adapted Version***

EL ***Reader's Notebook: English Learner's Version***

PHLit Online! All student resources, are available at **www.PHLitOnline.com.**

Mothers and Daughters

A dazzling first novel illuminates two generations of Chinese-American life.

Reviewed by MICHAEL DORRIS, An author whose new book, The Broken Cord, *will be published this summer.*
Copyright Chicago Tribune Co.
Mar 12, 1989
The Joy Luck Club By Amy Tan Putnam, 277 pages, $18.95

Book Review

Features:

- a summary of the work
- background information about the writer
- quotations or excerpts from the book
- the reviewer's analysis and evaluation of the work
- text written for a general audience

The review begins by stating the reviewer's opinion. In a credible review, the following paragraphs will offer sufficient evidence to support this opinion.

The Joy Luck Club is that rare, mesmerizing novel one always seeks but seldom finds. Tracing the poignant destinies of two generations of tough, intelligent women, each gorgeously written page welcomes the reader and leads to an enlightenment that, like all true wisdom, sometimes brings pleasure and sometimes sadness.

The book's four aging mothers, born in a pre-World War II China just embarked on a major cultural transition, are migrants who interpret life through the vivid eyes of their youth, through the experience and example of their own mothers. Their four daughters, first-generation Californians, stand at the midpoint of a seesaw. If they inch in one direction, they are traditional Chinese; if they inch in the other, they are Americans. Theirs is an ongoing quest for balance between the past and the future.

The reviewer offers details as evidence that his opinion is valid.

To tell this complex story, Amy Tan, a writer of dazzling talent, has created an intricate tapestry of a book—one tale woven into the other, a panorama of distinctive voices that call out to each other over time.

Tan's characters, regardless of their cultural orientation or age, speak with authority and authenticity. The details of their lives, unfamiliar to most American readers, are rendered with such conviction that almost immediately their rules seem to become the adages and admonitions with which we ourselves grew up. From the mainland China of the '30s and '40s to the San Francisco Bay area of today, the settings are so beautifully visualized that when we finish *The Joy Luck Club* we know the right bakeries in which to shop for dim sum and the best park in which to watch the old men play chess, and we have glimpsed the hidden meaning of carved jade.

The book opens and closes with the voice of Jing-mei "June" Woo, whose mother, Suyuan, had decades before, in a war-torn refugee center in interior China, initiated the Joy Luck Club.

"My idea," Suyuan confides, "was to have a gathering of four women, one for each corner of my mah jong table." She invited An-mei Hsu, Lindo Jong, and Ying-Ying, who was later to marry an American named St. Clair, to join her. They were a disparate group, uprooted from different regions and economic strata, but had in common their youth and their "wishful faces," their anxiety and their loneliness. Each week one of the women hosted a party, served special though simple delicacies and defied the depression their precarious circumstances might dictate.

"What was worse, we asked among ourselves," Suyuan says. "To sit and wait for our own deaths with proper somber faces? Or to choose our own happiness?

"So we decided to hold parties and pretend each week had become the new year. . . . We feasted, we laughed, we played games, lost and won, we told the best stories. And each week, we could hope to be lucky. That was our only joy. And that's how we came to call our little parties Joy Luck."

About Book Reviews

1. Review the Features listed in the Book Review box with students. Make sure they understand that a book review gives the reviewer's opinion of a published book.
2. Invite students to discuss their experiences with book reviews. **Possible response:** Students may say that they read book reviews to help them decide whether they should read a newly published book.
3. Speak with students about how they approach a book review. Students may say that if they are reading a book review, they will pay attention to how well the reviewer provides evidence that supports his or her position.

Critique Generalizations and Evidence

1. Point out that reliable reviews begin with the reviewer's opinion and then proceed to offer evidence supporting the opinion.
2. Invite a volunteer to read aloud the opening paragraph of the review. **Ask** students to restate the reviewer's opinion in their own words.
   Possible response: *The Joy Luck Club* is a beautifully written novel that comes around once in a great while, offering brilliant insight by examining the lives of the characters.
3. Have students finish reading "Mothers and Daughters." Invite them to think about the evidence the reviewer presents to support his opinion. Then, **ask** them to discuss how well the quotations on this page support the reviewer's opinion.
   Possible response: The quotations support the reviewer's opinion. They serve as both an indication of Tan's writing ability as well as a glimpse into the enlightenment that the reviewer mentions in the opening paragraph.

Differentiated Instruction for Universal Access

Strategy for Less Proficient Readers

As students read the selection, have them identify sections of the text that they find difficult to comprehend. Encourage them to use a separate sheet of paper to note challenging parts in the text, jotting down a question, concern, or thought for explanation. This technique will help students organize their questions and thoughts for class discussion and clarification. After students have finished reading the selection, discuss the trouble spots they noted while reading.

EL Background for English Learners

Before students read the selection, they may benefit from a written summary of the key ideas of the review. As students read, encourage them to place a check next to each key idea. Students may also record any ideas they have that are not listed in the written summary. After students have finished reading the selection, ensure that all students have placed checks next to the ideas on the written summary. If any student fails to check each idea, point out the idea in the selection. Discuss any ideas students noted that are not present on the written summary.

Critique Generalizations and Evidence

1. Remind students that reviewer's might make generalizations, or judgments, without providing adequate evidence to support them.
2. Read aloud the last paragraph of the review and the corresponding side note.
3. Have students think about the reviewer's generalization about literature. Then, **ask** students to consider whether the lack of evidence weakens the credibility of the reviewer's argument.
   Possible response: Some students may say that they agree with the statement because the reviewer confirms his opinion that *The Joy Luck Club* leaves the reader with new knowledge. Others may say that they do not agree with this generalization, citing their own experiences with literature.
4. **Ask** students to draw a conclusion about the overall credibility of the reviewer's opinion of *The Joy Luck Club*.
   Possible response: The reviewer presents a well-supported examination of *The Joy Luck Club*. He provides several excerpts from the text to support his positive opinion of the novel.

ASSESS/EXTEND

Answers

Can anyone be a hero?

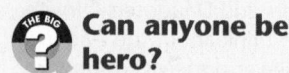

Possible responses: (a) June agrees to meet her sisters and tell them about their mother. In the process, she honors her mother's memory, proves something to the aunties, and learns about herself. **(b)** No, June believes that she is doing what has to be done.

The Club, and the friendships it reflects, endured. It expanded to include the women's spouses; it became the clearing house for news about their children. Eventually all money won or lost was shared in common, an emergency bank on which any member could draw. Joy Luck remains their stable center despite the turbulence of immigration and social change; and when Suyuan dies, June is invited to take her mother's place ("on the East, where things begin") at the mah jong table.

It seems at first an uncomfortable and artificial wedding of generations grown apart, until, at the conclusion of the first evening's session, the existence of June's two half-sisters—lost as infants and believed dead—is revealed. June is instructed to go to Shanghai, meet her siblings and answer their inevitable questions.

"'See my sisters and tell them about my mother?' June says, nodding. 'What will I say? What can I tell them about my mother? I don't know anything. She was my mother.'

> The reviewer provides quotations, excerpts, and details from the book as evidence for his opinion.

'Not know your mother?' cries Auntie An-mei with disbelief. 'How can you say? Your mother is in your bones!'

'Tell them stories of your family here. How she became success,' offers Auntie Lin.

'Tell them stories she told you, lessons she taught, what you know about her mind that has become your mind,' says Auntie Ying. 'Your mother very smart lady.'"

There follows a litany of specific suggestions of what to convey: Suyuan's kindness, her intelligence, her hopes, the good food she knew how to cook. Finally June understands.

"They are frightened. In me, they see their own daughters, just as ignorant, just as unmindful of all the truths and hopes they have brought to America. They see daughters who grow impatient when their mothers talk in Chinese, who think they are stupid when they explain things in fractured English. They see that joy and luck do not mean the same to their daughters, that to these closed American-born minds "joy luck" is not a word, it does not exist. They see daughters who will bear grandchildren grown without any connecting hope passed from generation to generation."

"I will tell them everything," June says simply, and the aunties look at her with "doubtful faces."

They need not have worried. Not only does June fulfill her promise, but also, before she deplanes at the Shanghai airport, eight lives have been meticulously revealed. In exquisite passages, each of the senior women reflects on the formative events in her past; then, in counterpoint, each of their daughters—June, Rose, Waverly and Lena—examines her own path to maturity.

It is a large cast for a first novelist to direct, and *The Joy Luck Club* is an ambitious book. But Tan performs the miracle of making every character, even the minor and disagreeable ones, ultimately sympathetic. We understand their obsessions, the sources of their weaknesses and strengths, the quiet love or desperate fear that underpins their sacrifices. Elements of Chinese-American culture that often have often been distorted or ignorantly stereotyped are here illuminated, burnished, made fresh.

Literature is writing that makes a difference, that alters the way we understand the world and ourselves.By that standard, *The Joy Luck Club* is the real thing. Without a hint of polemic, the book leaves the reader changed, more cognizant of subtleties, anxious to explore the confusions of any parent's motivation, any child's rebellion. Tan succeeds not only in her careful language, not only in the vista she opens before us, but also in the heart with which she invests this generous book. *The Joy Luck Club* is well-named; it is a pure joy to read.

> Here, the reviewer makes a generalization about literature and offers no evidence to support it.

Can anyone be a hero?
(a) How does the character June act heroically? (b) Do you think she considers her actions to be heroic? Explain.

Vocabulary Development

Vocabulary from Book Reviews

Point out that book reviews often use vocabulary that is specific to literary analysis. Guide students to understand the meaning of the following words that are used in the selection:

poignant: deeply moving
disparate: dissimilar
precarious: uncertain
formative: pertaining to development
burnished: made smooth
polemic: a controversial argument

PHLit Online! **Vocabulary Central**, featuring tools, activities, and songs for studying vocabulary, is available at **www.PHLitOnline.com.**

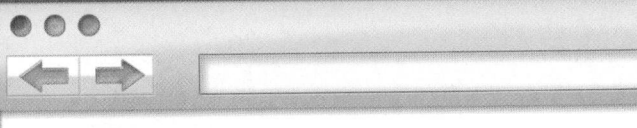

THE JOY LUCK CLUB

Movie Review

Features:

- information about the film, including release date, running time, and cast
- a summary of the plot
- evaluations of the actors' performances
- text written for a general audience

A Film Review by JAMES BERARDINELLI

- Rating: 3 stars (out of 4 stars)
- United States, 1993
- U.S. Release Date: 9/24/93 (limited); 10/1/93 (general)
- Running Length: 2:19
- MPAA Classification: R
- Theatrical Aspect Ratio: 1.85:1

CAST: Ming-Na Wen, Tamlyn Tomita, Lauren Tom, Rosalind Chao, Kieu Chinh, Tsai Chin, France Nuyen, Lisa Lu

DIRECTOR: Wayne Wang

PRODUCERS: Wayne Wang, Amy Tan, Ronald Bass, and Patrick Markey

SCREENPLAY: Amy Tan and Ronald Bass based on the novel by Amy Tan

CINEMATOGRAPHY: Amir M. Mokri

MUSIC: Rachel Portman

U.S. DISTRIBUTOR: Hollywood Pictures

In English and Chinese with English subtitles

The review begins with a summary of the plot and a description of the characters in the movie. This information will help the reader understand how the reviewer arrived at his opinion.

THE JOY LUCK CLUB, as stated in the movie's opening narrative, is a collection of four aging Chinese women bound together more by hope than joy or luck. The four women—Suyuan (Kieu Chinh), Lindo (Tsai Chin), Ying Ying (France Nuyen), and An Mei (Lisa Lu)—came to America many years ago to escape China's feudal society for the promise of the United States' democracy. Now, however, Suyuan has died and the three surviving members of the club invite her daughter June (Ming-Na Wen) to take her place. June belongs to the "new" generation, those of Chinese heritage who grew up speaking English and learning American customs. Also of roughly the same age are Waverly (Tamlyn Tomita), Lindo's daughter; Lena (Lauren Tom), Ying Ying's daughter; and Rose (Rosalind Chao), An Mei's daughter. *The Joy Luck Club* tells of the varied difficulties and tragedies involved in these mother/daughter relationships.

About Movie Reviews

1. Direct students' attention to the Features on the Movie Review box. Explain that a movie review includes information about the film, a synopsis of the plot, and critiques of actors' performances.
2. **Ask** students to think about occasions when they have read a movie review. Then, **ask** students to explain whether the movie review was helpful.
   Possible response: Students may say that they read a movie review when they were trying to decide whether they should see a new film and, based on the review, they decided to see the film.

Critique Generalizations and Evidence

1. Have students read the review of the movie *The Joy Luck Club*.
2. Explain that a movie review, unlike a book review, focuses on a variety of aspects: not just the execution of the filmmaker. The reviewer presents information about the film in the beginning of the review and goes on to share his or her opinion about the film.
3. Invite students to reread the first paragraph of the review. Then, **ask** them to discuss what the reviewer will base his critique on.
   Possible response: The reviewer's critique of the film will be based on the actors' performances and how well the film depicts the relationships between the mothers and daughters.

Differentiated Instruction for Universal Access

Strategy for Less Special Needs Students

On the board, draw the graphic organizer for tracking evaluations on page 1222. As a group, use the graphic organizer to evaluate the book review. Help students identify some of the author's generalizations, evidence used to support those generalizations, and whether the author's generalizations are credible.

Enrichment for Advanced Readers

Challenge students to find other movie reviews of *The Joy Luck Club*. Encourage them to use the graphic organizer on page 1222 to aid them in evaluating the credibility of each source. Then, have each student write a brief essay in which they compare and contrast the opinions of each reviewer. Provide time in class for each student to read his or her essay.

Critique Generalizations and Evidence

1. Explain to students that movie reviews sometimes include quotations from individuals involved with the production of the film.
2. Read the quotation from the first paragraph aloud. Have students think about the validity of the quotation. Then, **ask** them to discuss whether this quotation supports the reviewer's opinion. **Possible response:** The quotation shows that the filmmakers, like the reviewer, believe that the relationships between the mothers and daughters should be an essential theme of the film.

ASSESS/EXTEND

Answers

Can anyone be a hero?

Possible response: Yes, the mothers make a conscious decision to leave China and establish a better life in America.

Reflecting on the Skill

After students have read both selections, **ask** them to consider what they found most challenging when applying the skill.
Possible response: Students may say that they found it difficult to determine whether a review provided sufficient evidence to support a particular generalization.

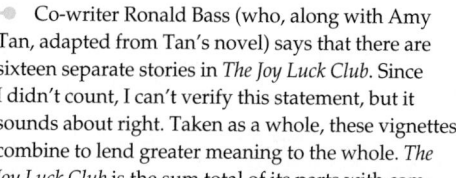

The reviewer quotes one of the film's writers about the structure of the movie. This evidence helps support the reviewer's opinion.

Co-writer Ronald Bass (who, along with Amy Tan, adapted from Tan's novel) says that there are sixteen separate stories in *The Joy Luck Club*. Since I didn't count, I can't verify this statement, but it sounds about right. Taken as a whole, these vignettes combine to lend greater meaning to the whole. *The Joy Luck Club* is the sum total of its parts with common themes giving solid grounding and greater resonance to the overall film. As Bass comments, "I saw all the mothers' and daughters' stories as facets of the same experience. Put together, they formed a mosaic. That's the genius of the book, and if we cut it down to just a couple of stories it would be like any other movie."

The stories are not related in such a manner as to seem pared down or truncated, nor is their presentation confusing, thanks to a cleverly-orchestrated framing scene with the principal characters gathered together. However, it is apparent that a lot more could have been told, and we're left wondering about all that we didn't get to see. The characters are mostly well-developed, but it's tantalizing to consider how much fuller some of them could have been with a different plot structure.

Here the reviewer makes generalizations about the dialogue and story and does not offer any specific evidence as support.

The Joy Luck Club is clearly — perhaps too clearly — an adaptation of a book. The dialogue is often too poetic to be real, and the story too clearly plotted to be acceptable as anything more than an imperfect reflection of the world we live in. The line between drama and melodrama is a fine one, and, while *The Joy Luck Club* most often successfully navigates the tightrope, there are times when it slips and comes across as heavy-handed. This film is no stranger to moments of manipulation.

The characters are *The Joy Luck Club's* real strength. Many are played by more than one actor (as children then adults, for example), but all transitions are smooth and seamless. It's as easy to accept both a little girl and the beautiful, sophisticated-looking Tamlyn Tomita as Waverly, and that's because the characters transcend the performers portraying them.

It's fascinating and satisfying the way the diverse threads are knitted together into a single tapestry. *The Joy Luck Club's* message is one of hope—that catharsis and emotional fulfillment often come through tragedy. Sure, a lot of bad things happen during the course of this film, but at the end, the tears are of happiness and new beginnings, not loss.

Can anyone be a hero?
Based on this review, do you think the four mothers in the book and film could be considered heroes? Explain.

Test Practice: Informational Texts

Comparing Informational Texts

(a) In what ways is the **evidence** that supports the **generalizations** of the book review similar to the evidence that supports the generalizations of the movie review? **(b)** In what ways is the evidence different?

Timed Writing

Write an Essay

Format
The prompt directs you to write an essay. Therefore, be sure your response includes an introduction, several supporting paragraphs, and a conclusion.

Write an essay in which you evaluate the credibility of each reviewer's arguments and opinions. Critique the evidence in each review, and decide whether it is sufficient to support the writer's generalizations. Then, decide which review you judge to be more credible, and explain your choice. Use details from the text to support your ideas. (40 minutes)

Academic Vocabulary
When you *critique* something, you make judgments about its strengths and weaknesses.

5-Minute Planner

Complete these steps before you begin to write:

1. Read the prompt carefully and completely. Pay special attention to key words and phrases that are highlighted in color. **TIP** Note that the prompt directs you to **evaluate the credibility** of arguments, **critique** evidence, and decide which review is more credible. Be sure you understand and address all parts of the prompt in your response.
2. Skim the reviews to find generalizations and the evidence used to support them. Make notes about your observations.
3. Review your notes and consider whether the evidence sufficiently supports the generalizations. Also note whether you think the generalizations and evidence are strong enough to support the author's opinions.
4. Decide which review you find to be more credible.
5. Use your notes to create a rough outline for your essay. Then, refer to your notes and outline as you write.

ASSESS/EXTEND

Answers

Comparing Informational Texts

(a) Both reviews provide evidence that address the reviewer's position. Both reviews offer subjective generalizations that are presented without any supporting evidence.

(b) Possible response: The book review includes specific evidence from the book, such as quotations, excerpts, and details, which support the author's generalizations. The movie review does not include specific evidence from the movie; it includes a general quote from one of the film's writers.

Timed Writing

1. Before students complete the activity, guide them in identifying and analyzing key words and phrases in the prompt, highlighted on the student page.
2. Work with students to draw up guidelines for their essays based on the key words in the prompt:
   - **Focus** The essay should clearly evaluate how well the evidence supports the reviewer's opinion.
   - **Organization** The essay should evaluate the evidence and then draw a conclusion about the validity of the text.
   - **Elaboration** The essay should use details from the reviews to support its critique.
   - **Style** The audience is not specified, so a formal style is suitable.
3. Have students use the 5-Minute Planner to structure their time.
4. Allow students 40 minutes to complete the assignment. Evaluate their work using the guidelines they have developed.

Extend the Lesson

Connecting to the Students' World

To help students enhance their understanding of book reviews and movie reviews and to help them apply the lesson to their own world, divide students into pairs. Have each pair choose a book they have recently read or a film they have recently seen. Instruct them to list three opinions they have about it. Remind them to offer opinions that can be easily supported by evidence. Have each pair present their reviews to the class. When all pairs have finished presenting, have students draw conclusions about the validity or reliability of each argument.

PRETEACH

Meeting Your Standards

Students will

1. analyze and respond to theme and worldview in fiction.
2. compare the effects of theme and worldview in two works of fiction.
3. write a comparison of a themes and worldviews.

Log on at ***www.PHLitOnline.com*** *for a detailed lesson plan for Comparing Literary Works.*

❶ Comparing Style

1. Introduce the skill using the instruction on the student page.
2. Give students a copy of **Comparing Themes and Worldviews Graphic Organizer B,** ***Graphic Organizer Transparencies,*** p. 224. Tell them they will fill it in with details as they read.

Think Aloud: Model the Skill

Model a way to identify theme and worldview. Say to students:

> Let's say I read a story about a girl that succeeds in gaining the acceptance of her classmates. I know the theme is that people want acceptance from others. I can determine that the author believes people can bridge their differences and accept others. I know that the way authors see the world affects the story they tell.

❷ Vocabulary

1. Have students say each word aloud.
2. Then, use the word in a sentence that defines the word. Repeat the sentence, now with the word missing, and have the class "fill in the blank" chorally.

   For more guidance, see the ***Classroom Strategies and Teaching Routines*** card, **Introducing Selection Vocabulary.**

Comparing Literary Works

Damon and Pythias • Two Friends

❶ Comparing Themes and Worldviews

The **theme** of a literary work is the idea about life that it conveys. Many themes are universal, or found in the literature of different times and places. The struggle between good and evil, for example, is a universal theme. A particular writer's expression of a theme will reflect a specific worldview—basic beliefs that shape the writer's outlook.

In past times, many writers portrayed a well-ordered world in which every event happens for a reason, a world defended by true heroes. Such writers might show good people being rewarded while bad people are punished. In modern times, many writers depict a chaotic or an indifferent world filled with ordinary, limited people. Writers may show good people triumphing over terrible odds, or they may show bad people succeeding.

Both "Damon and Pythias," an ancient legend, and "Two Friends," a more modern short story, center on the theme of friendship. Yet, in each work, the theme is filtered through a different worldview. As you read, identify the central message in each story. Then, use a chart like the one shown to compare the different worldviews revealed in each.

Theme:			
	expressed through...		
Type of Characters	**Language They Speak**	**Challenge They Face**	**Ending**
❑ "larger-than-life" ❑ ordinary	❑ eloquent; formal ❑ everyday	❑ "larger-than-life" ❑ ordinary	❑ Justice is done. ❑ Justice is not done.

❷ Vocabulary

- **dire** (dīr) *adj.* calling for quick action (p. 1230) ***The dire problem must be solved at once.*** *direness n. direly adv. direst adj.*
- **serenity** (sə ren′ ə tē) *n.* state of calm or peace (p. 1231) ***The stream created a mood of serenity.*** *serene adj. serenely adv.*
- **ardent** (är′ dənt) *adj.* intensely enthusiastic (p. 1234) ***She is an ardent soccer fan and goes to every game.*** *ardently adv.*
- **relent** (ri lent′) *v.* to become less strong or intense (p. 1239) ***I hope the downpour will relent soon.*** *relentless adj. unrelenting adj.*

PHLit Online! www.PHLitOnline.com

- Vocabulary flashcards
- Interactive journals
- More about the authors
- Selection audio
- Interactive graphic organizers

Vocabulary Development

Vocabulary Knowledge Rating

Create a **Vocabulary Knowledge Rating Chart** (***Professional Development Guidebook,*** p. 33) for this selection. Include the selection vocabulary and the Big Question word that appears in the Writing About the Big Question sentence starter on the next page. (The Big Question vocabulary is introduced on pp. 1046–1047.)

Give students a copy of the chart. Read the words aloud and have students mark their rating in the Before Reading column. Urge them to be alert to these words as they read and discuss the selection.

Tally how many students think they know a word to gauge how much instruction to provide. As students read and discuss the selection, point out the words and their context.

PHLit Online! **Vocabulary Central,** featuring tools, activities, and songs for studying vocabulary, is available online at **www.PHLitOnline.com.**

Can anyone be a *hero?*

❸ Writing About the Big Question

In both "Damon and Pythias" and "Two Friends," the loyalty between two men is put to an extreme test. Such a test might bring out the hero in a person, but it also raises more questions. Can anyone who faces life's tests with strength and courage be a hero? Use this sentence starter to develop your ideas.

The best way to discover a person's true **character** is ________.

Meet the Authors

Ancient Greek Legends and Their Retellers

Like other legends, "Damon and Pythias" exaggerates the characteristics of people to provide examples of the best—and the worst—conduct. In this way, a legend serves as a cultural how-to manual, showing people which virtues they should honor and cultivate.

Retelling the Tales Over the centuries, the legend of Damon and Pythias has been retold and adapted in many forms, including plays. William F. Russell, a recent reteller of this and many other myths and legends, is also the author of a widely read newspaper column on education.

Guy de Maupassant (1850–1893)

Author of "Two Friends"

In his short stories, Guy de Maupassant often focuses on the environment in which his characters live. The outcome of events in his work is determined by forces beyond a character's control, such as family history, social circumstances, and the character's basic disposition. His stories provide a fascinating record of nineteenth-century life.

A Productive Life Maupassant seemed destined for success. A gifted writer born into an aristocratic family, he won the attention of famous authors while he was still a young man. He soon became famous in his own right. Unfortunately, his career was cut short by illness. Maupassant died while still in his early forties. Yet, he left a fortune to every future reader: 300 short stories.

Teaching Resources

The following resources can be used to enrich, extend, or differentiate the instruction.

- All *Unit 6 Resources*, pp. 202–221
- All *Professional Development Guidebook*, pp. 33, 36–38, 42
- All *Graphic Organizer Transparencies*, pp. 224, 226, 240
- All Enriched Online Student Edition

PHLit Online! All resources, including print and audio, are available at **www.PHLitOnline.com.**

Daily Bellringer

For each class during which you will teach this selection, have students complete one of the five Sentence Combining activities for Week 36 in the *Daily Bellringer Activities* booklet.

❸ Writing About the Big Question

1. Review the assignment with the class.
2. Remind students that heroism does not necessarily involve visible actions. People can act heroically even when nobody knows what they are facing.
3. Have students complete the sentence starter. Review responses as a class. (**Possible response:** The best way to discover a person's true character is to see how that person acts under pressure.)
4. Remind students that their answers will help them think about the Big Question."

   Tell students that as they read, they should look for how the individuals reveal their character.

Concept Connector →

Tell students that they will return to their sentence starters after they have concluded reading.

Multidraft Reading

To assist struggling readers and to deepen reading for all, apply multidraft reading protocols. For each reading, have students set the purpose intended:

- **First reading**—literal comprehension: answering the Reading Check questions
- **Second reading**—application of skills: responding to the side-column notes
- **Third reading**—interpretation: answering the end-of-selection questions

For more guidance, refer to the *Classroom Strategies and Teaching Routines* card on multidraft reading.

PHLit Online!

For more about the authors, practice with the selection vocabulary, and more background, go online at **www.PHLitOnline.com.**

❶ Background

Dionysius the Elder An important character in "Damon and Pythias" is Dionysius, the tyrant of Syracuse. The real Dionysius, known as Dionysius the Elder, began his rule of Syracuse in 406 B.C.E. He was an active expansionist and a militaristic leader. A playwright and a patron, Dionysius had a taste for tragedies.

❷ Activating Prior Knowledge

1. Prepare an **Anticipation Guide** (see ***Professional Development Guidebook,*** pp. 36–39) with the following statements:
    - Friends should always support one another, no matter the situation.
    - Doing good deeds always has a positive impact on people.
    - People should accept punishment without a fight.
    - Risking one's life for a friend is selfless.
2. Give students a copy of the prepared **Anticipation Guide** and have students mark their responses in the Me column. Have students discuss the statements in pairs or groups and mark the Guides again in the Group column.

Concept Connector ➞

Students will return to the **Anticipation Guide** after completing the story.

❸ About the Selection

When the cruel tyrant Dionysius demands that Pythias be executed, Damon agrees to risk his own life while his friend settles his affairs. When the tyrant finally realizes how nobly the two friends behave, he spares them.

❹ Literary Analysis
Theme and Worldview

1. Read aloud the bracketed text. Emphasize to students that authors imbed references to their theme throughout a literary work.
2. **Ask** the Literary Analysis question.
Answer: The subject is friendship, and its value is indicated by the admiration of the city's people for Damon and Pythias.

DAMON AND PYTHIAS

retold by **William F. Russell, Ed.D.**

❶ ❷ ❸

Literary Analysis
Theme and Worldview What subject or theme is suggested in the first paragraph of the story?

❹

Damon [dā′ mən] and Pythias [pith′ ē əs] were two noble young men who lived on the island of Sicily in a city called Syracuse. They were such close companions and were so devoted to each other that all the people of the city admired them as the highest examples of true friendship. Each trusted the other so completely that nobody could ever have persuaded one that the other had been unfaithful or dishonest, even if that had been the case.

Now it happened that Syracuse was, at that time, ruled by a famous tyrant named Dionysius [dī ə nis′ ē əs],[1] who had gained the throne for himself through treachery, and who from then on flaunted his power by behaving cruelly to his own subjects and to all strangers and enemies who were so unfortunate as to fall into his clutches. This tyrant, Dionysius, was so unjustly cruel that once, when he awoke from a restless sleep during which he dreamt that a certain man in the town had attempted to kill him, he immediately had that man put to death.

It happened that Pythias had, quite unjustly, been accused by Dionysius of trying to overthrow him, and for this supposed crime of treason Pythias was sentenced by the king to die. Try as he might, Pythias could not prove his innocence to the king's satisfaction, and so, all hope now lost, the noble youth asked only for a few days' freedom so that he could settle his business affairs and see to it that his relatives would be cared for after he was executed. Dionysius, the hardhearted tyrant, however, would not believe Pythias' promise to return and would not allow him to leave unless he left behind him a hostage, someone who would be put to death in his place if he should fail to return within the stated time.

Vocabulary
dire (dīr) *adj.* calling for quick action

Pythias immediately thought of his friend Damon, and he unhesitatingly sent for him in this hour of **dire** necessity, never thinking for a moment that his trusty companion would refuse his request. Nor did he, for Damon hastened straightaway to the palace—much to the amazement of King Dionysius—and gladly

1. **Dionysius** Dionysius the Elder (ca. 430 B.C.–367 B.C.), ruler of ancient Syracuse.

Vocabulary Development

Selection Vocabulary Reinforcement

To reinforce and assess students' comprehension of selection vocabulary words, give them sentences in which the word may or may not be used correctly. Students must tell whether the use is correct and explain their answer. Use these sentences:

1. The poverty-stricken family was in *dire* need of assistance.
Answer: Yes, *dire* is used correctly. A poverty-stricken family would urgently require assistance.
2. Everything was perfect because there were many *impediments* to my enjoyment of the meal.
Answer: No, *impediments* is not used correctly. They would prevent enjoyment, not cause it.
3. For some people, meditation is a way to achieve *serenity*.
Answer: Yes, *serenity* is used correctly. It means "state of calm."

offered to be held hostage for his friend, in spite of the dangerous condition that had been attached to this favor. Therefore, Pythias was permitted to settle his earthly affairs before departing to the Land of the Shades,[2] while Damon remained behind in the dungeon, the captive of the tyrant Dionysius.

After Pythias had been released, Dionysius asked Damon if he did not feel afraid, for Pythias might very well take advantage of the opportunity he had been given and simply not return at all, and then he, Damon, would be executed in his place. But Damon replied at once with a willing smile: "There is no need for me to feel afraid, O King, since I have perfect faith in the word of my true friend, and I know that he will certainly return before the appointed time—unless, of course, he dies or is held captive by some evil force. Even so, even should the noble Pythias be captured and held against his will, it would be an honor for me to die in his place."

6 Such devotion and perfect faith as this was unheard of to the friendless tyrant; still, though he could not help admiring the true nobility of his captive, he nevertheless determined that Damon should certainly be put to death should Pythias not return by the appointed time.

And, as the Fates would have it, by a strange turn of events, Pythias *was* detained far longer in his task than he had imagined. Though he never for a single minute intended to evade the sentence of death to which he had been so unjustly committed, Pythias met with several accidents and unavoidable delays. Now his time was running out and he had yet to overcome the many impediments that had been placed in his path. At last he succeeded in clearing away all the hindrances, and he sped back the many miles to the palace of the king, his heart almost bursting with grief and fear that he might arrive too late.

Meanwhile, when the last day of the allotted time arrived, Dionysius commanded that the place of execution should be readied at once, since he was still ruthlessly determined that if one of his victims escaped him, the other should not. And so, entering the chamber in which Damon was confined, he began to utter words of sarcastic pity for the "foolish faith," as he termed it, that the young man of Syracuse had in his friend.

In reply, however, Damon merely smiled, since, in spite of the fact that the eleventh hour had already arrived, he still believed that his lifelong companion would not fail him. Even when, a short time later, he was actually led out to the site of his execution, his serenity remained the same.

2. **Land of the Shades** in Greek mythology, place where people go when they die.

5 ▲ **Critical Viewing** As he appears on this coin, does Dionysius seem to have the characteristics of the man in the legend? Explain. **[Interpret]**

Vocabulary
serenity (sə ren´ ə tē) *n.* state of calm or peace

7 **Reading Check**
What does Damon agree to do for his friend Pythias?

5 Critical Viewing

Possible response: Students may say that the severity of the man's expression suggests a harsh personality similar to the man in the myth.

6 Critical Thinking
Predict

1. Invite volunteers to summarize what has happened so far in the story. **Ask** them what clues the storyteller gives about the character of Dionysius.
   Possible response: He is a cruel tyrant who gained the throne by trickery. He seems unable to understand the deep friendship that Damon and Pythias have for each other, though he does seem intrigued by it since he questions Damon about how he feels facing death.
2. Then, **ask** them, based on what they know about Dionysius, how they think the story will end.
   Possible responses: Some students may say that the cruelty of Dionysius will lead him to kill one of the two friends. Others may infer that Dionysius will relent since the story reflects the values of an age that treasured heroes.

7 Reading Check

Answer: Damon agrees to be held as a hostage while Pythias settles his business affairs.

Differentiated Instruction for Universal Access

Accessibility at a Glance
Use this information to guide your teaching of "Damon and Pythias."

Context	Mythological story of friendship
Language/Vocabulary	• Some names difficult to pronounce • Above-grade vocabulary
Concept Level	Accessible (friendship and trust)
Literary Merit	Classic; mythological tale
Lexile/Length	Lexile: 1550L — Word Count: 1,094

PHLit Online!
This selection is available in interactive format in the **Enriched Online Student Edition**, online at **www.PHLitOnline.com**, which includes an interactive graphic organizer.

8 Literary Analysis
Theme and Worldview

1. **Ask** the Literary Analysis question. **Answer:** Because Dionysius spares Pythias' life, goodness is clearly rewarded.
2. **Ask** students to summarize what the story's conclusion conveys about the theme and worldview. **Answer:** The conclusion suggests that friendship is important and that the world recognizes and responds to goodness in people.

Concept Connector

Have students return to their **Anticipation Guides** and respond to the statements again in the After Reading column. Then, lead a class discussion on the statements.

ASSESS

Answers

Critical Thinking

1. **Possible response:** Students may say that they are most anxious just before Pythias returns.
2. (a) Damon risks his life for Pythias. (b) Damon's decision demonstrates his trust in and devotion to his friend.
3. (a) Damon is not fearful because he believes that Pythias will honor his promise to return. (b) **Possible responses:** Students may say that the friendship is idealistic and therefore does not exist. Others may argue that such a friendship may exist in any time period.
4. (a) He is impressed by Damon's willingness to sacrifice himself and by Pythias' determination to save his friend. (b) **Possible response:** The ending suggests that the Greeks valued honor and believed that heroic action can convince cruel people to do good.

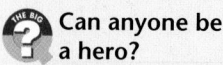

Can anyone be a hero?

(a) **Possible response:** Damon was more heroic because he put his life at risk when he did not have to. (b) **Possible response:** Dionysius is not a hero because it was his cruelty that caused the problem in the first place.

Great excitement stirred the crowd that had gathered to witness the execution, for all the people had heard of the bargain that had been struck between the two friends. There was much sobbing and cries of sympathy were heard all around as the captive was brought out, though he himself somehow retained complete composure even at this moment of darkest danger.

Presently the excitement grew more intense still as a swift runner could be seen approaching the palace courtyard at an astonishing speed, and wild shrieks of relief and joy went up as Pythias, breathless and exhausted, rushed headlong through the crowd and flung himself into the arms of his beloved friend, sobbing with relief that he had, by the grace of the gods, arrived in time to save Damon's life.

Literary Analysis
Theme and Worldview What details here show the belief that good people are rewarded? 8

This final exhibition of devoted love and faithfulness was more than even the stony heart of Dionysius, the tyrant, could resist. As the throng of spectators melted into tears at the companions' embrace, the king approached the pair and declared that Pythias was hereby pardoned and his death sentence canceled. In addition, he begged the pair to allow him to become their friend, to try to be as much a friend to them both as they had shown each other to be.

Thus did the two friends of Syracuse, by the faithful love they bore to each other, conquer the hard heart of a tyrant king, and in the annals of true friendship there are no more honored names than those of Damon and Pythias—for no person can do more than be willing to lay down his life for the sake of his friend.

Critical Thinking

1. **Respond:** When were you most anxious about the legend's outcome? Explain.
2. **(a)** What does Damon risk for Pythias? **(b) Interpret:** What does his decision show you about their friendship?
3. **(a) Infer:** Why is Damon patient and not fearful as he waits for Pythias? **(b) Take a Position:** Could a friendship like the one between Damon and Pythias exist today? Why or why not?
4. **(a)** What changes Dionysius' mind about executing one of the young men? **(b) Infer:** What does this ending suggest about the world view of the ancient Greeks? Explain.

Can anyone be a hero?
(a) Who do you think was more of a hero—Damon or Pythias? Explain. **(b)** Does Dionysius' decision to spare both men make him a hero? Why or why not?

Vocabulary Development

Thematic Vocabulary: The Big Question

As students are discussing "Damon and Pythias," ask them to use the thematic vocabulary presented in Introducing the Big Question, pp. 1046–1047. You might encourage them with sentence starters such as these:

1. Damon shows great *selflessness* when he . . .
2. The *determination* of Pythias to save Damon is shown when he . . .
3. The change in Dionysius shows that a person's *character* can be . . .
4. It is not surprising that the Greeks would *honor* the two friends because . . .

Two Friends

9 10 11

Guy de Maupassant

translated by Gordon R. Silber

The following story is set during the Franco-Prussian War, a conflict between France and Germany that began on July 19, 1870. The Germans won a series of victories, one of which ended in the capture of the French leader, Napoleon III. On September 19, 1870, the German army established a blockade around Paris. Movement in and out of the city was severely restricted. Led by a provisional government and plagued by famine and hopelessness, Paris managed to hold out until January 28, 1871, when the city surrendered. As Maupassant's story begins, the city is on the verge of surrender.

12 ▲ **Critical Viewing**
What insight into friendship does this painting convey? **[Interpret]**

Differentiated Instruction for Universal Access

Accessibility at a Glance
Use this information to guide your teaching of "Two Friends."

Context	Friends take a risk to enjoy a day of fishing
Language/Vocabulary	• Some complex sentences; dialogue • Grade-appropriate vocabulary
Concept Level	Challenging (power does not defeat friendship)
Literary Merit	Classic; noted author
Lexile/Length	Lexile: 1060L Word Count: 2,153

9 Background

Guy de Maupassant Guy de Maupassant experienced the devastation of the Franco-Prussian War firsthand when his family's wealth was obliterated and he was forced to become an office clerk. Later in life, he became a writer and follower of the naturalist movement, which strived to show human behavior in a true light. Maupassant quickly developed a reputation as a master of the short story form. His pessimistic worldview permeated his work. Maupassant attempted suicide toward the end of his life and spent the rest of his days in a sanitarium.

10 Activating Prior Knowledge

1. Prepare an **Anticipation Guide** (see ***Professional Development Guidebook***, pp. 36–39) with the following statements:
   - Good people are always rewarded in the end.
   - War justifies behavior that is not acceptable during times of peace.
   - Keeping quiet in the face of harm is heroic.
2. Give students a copy of the prepared **Anticipation Guide** and have them mark their responses in the Me column. Have students discuss the statements in pairs or groups and mark the Guides again in the Group column.

Concept Connector →

Students will follow return to the **Anticipation Guide** after completing the story.

11 About the Selection

Two friends attempt to recapture the happiness they felt before the start of the Franco-Prussian War. Avid fishermen, the pair decides that a blissful afternoon of angling is worth risking a trip into enemy territory. The events that follow paint a bleak picture of the prospects for peace and happiness in a world moved only by violence.

12 Critical Viewing

Answer: The painting suggests that friends can enjoy time together without talking or otherwise interacting.

⓭ Critical Thinking
Compare

1. Have students read the bracketed text. Then, **ask** them to describe the setting of the story.
   Answer: The story is set in Paris during the war; conditions are harsh, and people are desperate for food.
2. Then, **ask** them how that setting contrasts to the description of past times, when the two friends used to meet.
   Possible response: Maupassant creates a strong contrast between the idyllic days of fishing and the strife-filled days of war.

⓮ Literary Analysis
Theme and Worldview

1. Read aloud the bracketed text. Then, **ask** the Literary Analysis question: What idea of friendship does this paragraph suggest?
   Answer: The paragraph suggests that good friends can sit in comfortable silence if they understand each other.
2. Remind students that while two authors can address the same theme, they may have different worldviews which affect the way their stories develop.
3. Then, **ask** them what tone Maupassant sets in the beginning of this story and how that tone contrasts with the tone in the prior selection.
   Answer: The tone of "Two Friends" is dark: it is wartime, and people are suffering. The tone of "Damon and Pythias" was much more elevated, with the characters viewed in terms of their nobility.
4. Finally, **ask** them what this difference in tone suggests about the worldview of this story compared to that of the first selection.
   Possible response: Students may say that the dark tone suggests that Maupassant has a much more negative worldview.

Paris was blockaded, starved, in its death agony. Sparrows were becoming scarcer and scarcer on the rooftops and the sewers were being depopulated. One ate whatever one could get.

⓭ As he was strolling sadly along the outer boulevard one bright January morning, his hands in his trousers pockets and his stomach empty, M.[1] Morissot [mô rē sō´], watchmaker by trade but local militiaman for the time being, stopped short before a fellow militiaman whom he recognized as a friend. It was M. Sauvage [sō väzh´], a riverside acquaintance.

Every Sunday, before the war, Morissot left at dawn, a bamboo pole in his hand, a tin box on his back. He would take the Argenteuil [är zhän tē´y'] railroad, get off at Colombes, and walk to Marante Island. As soon as he arrived at this ideal spot he would start to fish; he fished until nightfall.

Vocabulary
ardent (är´ dənt) *adj.* intensely enthusiastic or devoted

Every Sunday he would meet a stout, jovial little man, M. Sauvage, a haberdasher[2] in Rue Notre-Dame-de-Lorette, another **ardent** fisherman. Often they spent half a day side by side, line in hand and feet dangling above the current. Inevitably they had struck up a friendship.

Literary Analysis
Theme and Worldview
What idea about friendship does this paragraph suggest?

Some days they did not speak. Sometimes they did; but they understood one another admirably without saying anything because they had similar tastes and responded to their surroundings in exactly the same way.

⓮ On a spring morning, toward ten o'clock, when the young sun was drawing up from the tranquil stream wisps of haze which floated off in the direction of the current and was pouring down its vernal warmth on the backs of the two fanatical anglers,[3] Morissot would sometimes say to his neighbor, "Nice, isn't it?" and M. Sauvage would answer, "There's nothing like it." And that was enough for them to understand and appreciate each other.

On an autumn afternoon, when the sky, reddened by the setting sun, cast reflections of its scarlet clouds on the water, made the whole river crimson, lighted up the horizon, made the two friends look as ruddy as fire, and gilded the trees which were already brown and beginning to tremble with a wintery shiver, M. Sauvage would look at Morissot with a smile and say, "Fine sight!" And Morissot, awed, would answer, "It's better than the city, isn't it?" without taking his eyes from his float.

As soon as they recognized one another they shook hands energetically, touched at meeting under such changed circumstances. M. Sauvage, with a sigh, grumbled, "What goings-on!"

1. **M.** abbreviation for Monsieur (mə syʉr´), "Mister" or "Sir" in French.
2. **haberdasher** (hab´ ər dash´ ər) *n.* person in the business of selling men's clothing.
3. **anglers** (aŋ´ glərz) *n.* people who fish with hook and line.

Vocabulary Development

Selection Vocabulary Reinforcement

Reinforce students' comprehension of the selection vocabulary with "show-you-know" sentences. The first part of the sentence uses the vocabulary word in an appropriate context. The second part of the sentence—the "show-you-know" part—clarifies the first. Model the strategy with this example for *ardent:*

The *ardent* fans screamed wildly; they were clearly excited to see the star.

Then, give students these sentence prompts, and coach them in creating the clarification part:

1. His *jauntiness* may seem exaggerated to those who do not know him; ________.
   Possible response: his friends know that he is simply a carefree person.
2. As the questioning continued, the lawyer would not *relent;* ________.
   Possible response: her refusal to back down paid off when the witness broke down.

15

Morissot groaned dismally, "And what weather! This is the first fine day of the year."

The sky was, in fact, blue and brilliant.

They started to walk side by side, absent-minded and sad. Morissot went on, "And fishing! Ah! Nothing but a pleasant memory."

"When'll we get back to it?" asked M. Sauvage.

They went into a little café and had an absinthe,[4] then resumed their stroll along the sidewalks.

Morissot stopped suddenly, "How about another, eh?" M. Sauvage agreed, "If you want." And they entered another wine shop.

On leaving they felt giddy, muddled, as one does after drinking on an empty stomach. It was mild. A caressing breeze touched their faces.

The warm air completed what the absinthe had begun. M. Sauvage stopped. "Suppose we went?"

"Went where?"

"Fishing, of course."

"But where?"

"Why, on our island. The French outposts are near Colombes. I know Colonel Dumoulin; they'll let us pass without any trouble."

16 ▲ **Critical Viewing**
What does this painting suggest about the pace of life in the French countryside? Explain.
[Interpret]

17 **Reading Check**
What pleasure do M. Morissot and M. Sauvage share?

---

4. absinthe (ab´ sinth´) *n.* type of liqueur.

15 Humanities

Les Maisons Cabassud a la Ville D'Avray (the Cabassud Houses in the Town of Avray) by Camille Corot

Camille Corot (1796–1875), a native of Paris, painted French landscapes almost exclusively. Classically trained, he traveled throughout Europe, painting pastures, villages, and mountainsides. One reason that his work is so celebrated is that he avoided the romantic tendency of landscape painters to idealize country life. **Ask** students to compare and contrast this landscape with the one described in the story.

Answer: It is January in the story, but many of the trees in the painting have leaves and the grass is green. The painting is a country scene, and the men are in Paris, a city; however, the flashbacks so far describe the men fishing in spring and autumn in the country.

16 Critical Viewing

Possible response: The absence of vehicles and bustling activity suggests that life in the French countryside follows a slow, relaxed pace.

17 Reading Check

Answer: Morissot and Sauvage share a love of fishing.

Differentiated Instruction for Universal Access

Strategy for Special Needs Students

Students may have trouble differentiating between the prewar setting and the postwar setting. To help students with shifts in time, give them a blank Two-column Chart (***Graphic Organizer Transparencies,*** p. 240), and have them create charts with one column labeled *before* and the other labeled *after*. Ask students to identify setting details that describe each time period, recording each in the proper column. When they are finished, have them write sentences that contrast the two settings.

EL Vocabulary for English Learners

As students read, they will encounter words that relate to the Franco-Prussian War. Help students make a list of these words, such as *blockaded, militiamen, outpost, Republic, password,* and *spies.* Define each one, and have students enter the words and definitions in their notebooks. Tell students to use each word in a sentence.

PHLit Online!

This selection is available in interactive format in the **Enriched Online Student Edition,** online at **www.PHLitOnline.com,** which includes an interactive graphic organizer.

18 Literary Analysis
Theme and Worldview

1. Remind students that the two friends in "Damon and Pythias" are depicted as heroes.
2. Read aloud the bracketed text. Then, **ask** the Literary Analysis question: Which details here show that the men are not exceptional heroes?
   Answer: The men are afraid of the Prussians, as shown by their uneasiness, their fear at the silence, and the way they try to avoid being seen when moving to the river.
3. Point out that while both stories place a high value on friendship, only one story characterizes the friends as conventional heroes.

19 Critical Thinking
Predict

1. Have students consider the friends' attitude toward the Prussians, the risk the men are taking to fish, and Maupassant's worldview as they understand it so far.
2. Then, **ask** students what they predict will happen next in the story.
   Possible responses: Students may say that, in all likelihood, the men will come face-to-face with the Prussians. Some may suggest that Maupassant's dark worldview means that the meeting will have bad consequences for the friends.

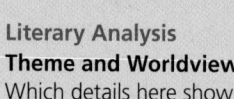

Morissot trembled with eagerness: "Done! I'm with you." And they went off to get their tackle.

An hour later they were walking side by side on the highway. They reached the villa which the Colonel occupied. He smiled at their request and gave his consent to their whim. They started off again, armed with a pass.

Soon they passed the outposts, went through the abandoned village of Colombes, and reached the edge of the little vineyards which slope toward the Seine. It was about eleven.

Opposite, the village of Argenteuil seemed dead. The heights of Orgemont and Sannois dominated the whole countryside. The broad plain which stretches as far as Nanterre was empty, absolutely empty, with its bare cherry trees and its colorless fields.

18 Pointing up to the heights, M. Sauvage murmured, "The Prussians are up there!" And a feeling of uneasiness paralyzed the two friends as they faced this deserted region.

"The Prussians!" They had never seen any, but for months they had felt their presence—around Paris, ruining France, pillaging, massacring, starving the country, invisible and all-powerful. And a kind of superstitious terror was superimposed on the hatred which they felt for this unknown and victorious people.

19 Morissot stammered, "Say, suppose we met some of them?"

His Parisian jauntiness coming to the surface in spite of everything, M. Sauvage answered, "We'll offer them some fish."

But they hesitated to venture into the country, frightened by the silence all about them.

Literary Analysis
Theme and Worldview Which details here show that the men are not exceptional heroes?

Finally M. Sauvage pulled himself together: "Come on! On our way! But let's go carefully." And they climbed over into a vineyard, bent double, crawling, taking advantage of the vines to conceal themselves, watching, listening.

A stretch of bare ground had to be crossed to reach the edge of the river. They began to run, and when they reached the bank they plunged down among the dry reeds.

Morissot glued his ear to the ground and listened for sounds of anyone walking in the vicinity. He heard nothing. They were indeed alone, all alone.

Reassured, they started to fish.

Opposite them Marante Island, deserted, hid them from the other bank. The little building which had housed a restaurant was shut up and looked as if it had been abandoned for years.

M. Sauvage caught the first gudgeon.[5] Morissot got the second, and from then on they pulled in their lines every minute or two with a silvery little fish squirming on the end, a truly miraculous draught.

5. **gudgeon** (guj´ ən) *n.* small European freshwater fish.

Vocabulary Development

Word Forms

The vocabulary words for "Two Friends" have related forms. Give students a blank **Word Forms Chart** (***Professional Development Guiebook***, p. 42) with *ardent, jauntiness,* and *relent* in the correct columns. Work with the class, or have students work with a partner, to determine the related forms. The final chart should look like the one shown. Hold students accountable for integrating the related forms of the words into their speaking and writing.

Noun	Verb	Adjective	Adverb
ardency		**ardent**	ardently
jauntiness	jaunt	jaunty	jauntily
relentlessness	**relen**t	relentless	relentlessly

Skillfully they slipped the fish into a sack made of fine net which they had hung in the water at their feet. And happiness pervaded their whole being, the happiness which seizes upon you when you regain a cherished
20 pleasure of which you have long been deprived.

The good sun was pouring down its warmth on their backs. They heard nothing more; they no longer thought about anything at all; they forgot about the rest of the world—they were fishing!

But suddenly a dull sound which seemed to come from underground made the earth tremble. The cannon were beginning.

Morissot turned and saw, over the bank to the left, the great silhouette of Mount Valérien wearing a white plume on its brow, powdersmoke which it had just spit out.

And almost at once a second puff of smoke rolled from the summit, and a few seconds after the roar still another explosion was heard.

Then more followed, and time after time the mountain belched forth death-dealing breath, breathed out milky-white vapor which rose slowly in the calm sky and formed a cloud above the summit.

M. Sauvage shrugged his shoulders. "There they go again," he said.

As he sat anxiously watching his float bob up and down, Morissot was suddenly seized by the wrath which a peace-loving man will feel toward madmen who fight, and grumbled, "Folks sure are stupid to kill one another like that."

M. Sauvage answered, "They're worse than animals."

And Morissot, who had just pulled in a bleak,[6] went on, "And to think that it will always be like this as long as there are governments."

M. Sauvage stopped him: "The Republic[7] wouldn't have declared war—"

Morissot interrupted: "Under kings you have war abroad; under the Republic you have war at home."

And they started a leisurely discussion, unraveling great political problems with the sane reasonableness of easygoing, limited individuals, and found themselves in agreement on the point that men would never be free. And Mount Valérien thundered

They heard nothing more; they no longer thought about anything at all; they forgot about the rest of the world—they were fishing!

Literary Analysis
Theme and Worldview What goals or ideals do the men seem to have?

22 **Reading Check** What risk do the men decide to take?

6. **bleak** *n.* small European freshwater fish with silvery scales.
7. **The Republic** the temporary republican government that assumed control of France when Napoleon III was captured by the Prussians.

Differentiated Instruction for Universal Access

Strategy for Less Proficient Readers
Maupassant's description of Morissot and Sauvage going fishing is full of sensory images, or images that refer to one of the five senses. Have students identify the details that help them imagine this scene. They can create a chart with columns for *see, hear, smell, touch,* and *taste* to help them keep track of the details. Then, encourage them to describe the two friends' outing in their own words.

Enrichment for Advanced Readers
Point out that Morissot and Sauvage have a heated political discussion, found at the bottom of this page, in which they conclude that war is futile and destructive. Have students write a few paragraphs arguing for or against this position. Call on volunteers to share their short essays with the class.

20 Literary Analysis
Theme and Worldview

1. Before reading aloud the bracketed text, remind students that an author's worldview is revealed through details in a story.
2. **Ask** the Literary Analysis question: What goals or ideals do the men seem to have?
   Answer: The men seem to care only for fishing. They want to live simply and enjoy life.
3. Emphasize the contrast between the men's ideals and the cannon in the last sentence. **Ask** students to explain what the sound of the cannon represents.
   Possible response: Students may say that the cannon's boom represents the conflict between the men's ideals and the reality of the outside world.

21 Connecting to the Big Question

1. Remind students that the two friends are in the midst of a difficult war in which their home, Paris, is surrounded by a powerful army, and people have little or no food. **Ask** them what kinds of actions they would expect in wartime from someone they would consider a hero.
   Possible responses: Students might say that heroes in wartime risk death while taking actions that help the side for which they are fighting or that save their fellow soldiers.
2. Read the bracketed text aloud. Then, **ask** students what the two friends do when confronted by reminders of the war.
   Answer: They feel reawakened fear but continue fishing while complaining about governments, which they think cause war.
3. Finally, **ask** students if they think the two friends are heroic.
   Possible responses: Students are likely to say that their actions and attitudes are hardly heroic. Some might credit them with courage for not running away when the cannons opened fire.

   Tell students to think about whether the characters' subsequent actions in the story are heroic.

22 Reading Check

Answer: The men risk going into enemy territory to fish.

㉓ Humanities

Infantry Officer, Full Dress by Frederic Remington (1861–1909)

American painter Frederic Remington was best known for his paintings of the American West. He was also a correspondent for the Spanish-American War, an experience that probably influenced this painting.

Ask these questions to prompt discussion:

1. What does the officer in the painting have in common with the Prussian officer in the story?
   Answer: Both men are smoking a pipe.
2. In what way is the officer in the story different from the one in the painting?
   Answer: While the officer in the painting shows military bearing, the officer in the story is introduced as being hairy and sitting "astride" a chair, not a very officer-like image.

㉔ Critical Viewing

Answer: The officer's stiff posture indicates that he is severe and formal.

㉕ Literary Analysis
Theme and Worldview

1. Read aloud the bracketed text. Point out that the officer interprets the friends' efforts to live happily as a crime: spying.
2. **Ask** students whether his assessment is reasonable.
   Possible responses: Some students may say that the assessment is unreasonable because the men are doing nothing wrong. Others may say that the assessment is reasonable because the men were found near enemy lines, and the officer knows nothing about their history or views.
3. **Ask** students what this situation says about Maupassant's worldview.
   Possible response: Students may say that the officer reinforces the worldview that men cannot live happily because of war.

㉓ ㉔ ▼ **Critical Viewing** What does this officer's posture suggest about his attitude and training? Explain. **[Interpret]**

unceasingly, demolishing French homes with its cannon, crushing out lives, putting an end to the dreams which many had dreamt, the joys which many had been waiting for, the happiness which many had hoped for, planting in wives' hearts, in maidens' hearts, in mothers' hearts, over there, in other lands, sufferings which would never end.

"That's life for you," opined M. Sauvage.

"You'd better say 'That's death for you,'" laughed Morissot.

But they shuddered in terror when they realized that someone had just come up behind them, and looking around they saw four men standing almost at their elbows, four tall men, armed and bearded, dressed like liveried[8] servants, with flat caps on their heads, pointing rifles at them.

The two fish lines dropped from their hands and floated off down stream.

In a few seconds they were seized, trussed up,[9] carried off, thrown into a rowboat and taken over to the island.

And behind the building which they had thought deserted they saw a score of German soldiers.

A kind of hairy giant who was seated astride a chair smoking a porcelain pipe asked them in excellent French: "Well, gentlemen, have you had good fishing?"

Then a soldier put down at the officer's feet the sack full of fish which he had carefully brought along. The Prussian smiled: "Aha! I see that it didn't go badly. But we have to talk about another little matter. Listen to me and don't get excited.

"As far as I am concerned, you are two spies sent to keep an eye on me. I catch you and I shoot you. You were pretending to fish in order to conceal your business. You have fallen into my hands, so much the worse for you. War is like that. ㉕

8. **liveried** (liv′ ər ēd) *adj.* uniformed
9. **trussed up** tied up.

Think Aloud

Vocabulary: Using Context

Model the way to determine the meaning of unfamiliar words by using context with this "think aloud." Say to students:

> I'm going to show you how I can find the meaning of the word *pardon* by using context. In the last paragraph on p. 1238, the officer tells the two friends that he will shoot them as spies. Then, in the first paragraph on p. 1239, he offers a deal. If they tell him the password, he will do something they want for them in return. Since they are threatened with being shot, I figure that what they want most is to be released. Based on these context clues, I infer that *pardon* means something like "forgiving a crime." Two paragraphs later, the officer says that if they tell him the password, they will be allowed to "go back." That statement confirms my definition of *pardon:* the officer is offering to forgive them and set them free.

26 "But—since you came out past the outposts you have, of course, the password to return. Tell me that password and I will pardon you."

The two friends, side by side, pale, kept silent. A slight nervous trembling shook their hands.

The officer went on: "No one will ever know. You will go back placidly. The secret will disappear with you. If you refuse, it is immediate death. Choose."

They stood motionless, mouths shut.

The Prussian quietly went on, stretching out his hand toward the stream: "Remember that within five minutes you will be at the bottom of that river. Within five minutes! You have relatives, of course?"

Mount Valérien kept thundering.

The two fishermen stood silent. The German gave orders in his own language. Then he moved his chair so as not to be near the prisoners and twelve men took their places, twenty paces distant, rifles grounded.

The officer went on: "I give you one minute, not two seconds more."

Then he rose suddenly, approached the two Frenchmen, took Morissot by the arm, dragged him aside, whispered to him, "Quick, the password? Your friend won't know. I'll pretend to **relent**."

Morissot answered not a word.

The Prussian drew M. Sauvage aside and put the same question.

M. Sauvage did not answer.

They stood side by side again.

And the officer began to give commands. The soldiers raised their

27 rifles.

Then Morissot's glance happened to fall on the sack full of gudgeons which was lying on the grass a few steps away.

A ray of sunshine made the little heap of still squirming fish gleam. And he almost weakened. In spite of his efforts his eyes filled with tears.

He stammered, "Farewell, Monsieur Sauvage."

M. Sauvage answered, "Farewell, Monsieur Morissot."

They shook hands, trembling from head to foot with a shudder which they could not control.

The officer shouted, "Fire!"

The twelve shots rang out together.

M. Sauvage fell straight forward, like a log. Morissot, who was taller, tottered, half turned, and fell crosswise on top of his comrade, face up, as the blood spurted from his torn shirt.

The German gave more orders.

Vocabulary
relent (ri lent′) *v.* to become less strong or intense

Literary Analysis
Theme and Worldview Which actions show the heroism of M. Morissot and M. Sauvage?

28 **Reading Check**
What does the German officer order the men to do?

26 Critical Thinking
Analyze

1. Have students reread the second paragraph on page 1236. **Ask** students: How are the men able to go fishing?
   Answer: A colonel who Sauvage knows gives them a pass.
2. Point out to students that nowhere before the German officer asks for a password is one mentioned. Then, **ask** students whether it is likely that the men have a password. If not, why don't the friends deny knowledge of a password?
   Possible response: Whether the friends have a password or not becomes inconsequential in a futile situation. They are going to die regardless of their response.
3. What does this detail say about the friends, the future, and Maupassant's worldview?
   Possible response: Death and tragedy are inevitable.

27 Literary Analysis
Theme and Worldview

1. Read aloud the bracketed text. Point out that while the two friends are not conventionally fearless heroes, they bravely face death.
2. **Ask** the Literary Analysis question: Which actions show the heroism of M. Morissot and M. Sauvage?
   Answer: The men bid one another farewell in a relatively normal manner. While they are clearly frightened, they do not openly weep or cower but face their fate with honor.

28 Reading Check

Answer: The German officer orders the men to reveal the password to the French outpost.

Differentiated Instruction for Universal Access

EL Pronunciation for English Learners
Some students might have difficulty with the /th/ digraph that appears in the words *the, that,* and *Then.* To help them, write several other /th/ words on the board, such as *this, though, through,* and *thus.* Then, pronounce each word in turn, calling on the students to repeat each pronunciation. Next, call out the words at random. Have student volunteers circle the word on the board. Discuss the results with the class. Were there any incorrect choices? If so, what led to those errors?

29 Literary Analysis
Theme and Worldview

Ask the Literary Analysis question: What details of this ending emphasize the injustice of the heroes' fate?
Answer: It is ironic that the bodies of the men are thrown in the river that brought them such pleasure in life. Also, it is ironic that the soldiers will enjoy the fish that the men are killed for catching.

Concept Connector

Have students compare their Writing About the Big Question and **Anticipation Guide** responses before reading the story with their ideas afterward.

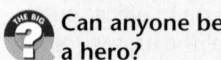

ASSESS
Answers

Critical Thinking

1. **Possible response:** Some students may be shocked because the men were innocent. Others may not be surprised because of the story's dark worldview.
2. (a) They fished. (b) Paris is under siege, and movement is restricted.
3. (a) Drink and nice weather encourage the men to take the risk. (b) The men enjoy the sun on their backs and the way that fishing clears their minds.
(c) Fishing represents the happiness and pleasure of life.
4. (a) The men are similar in character and enjoy the same activities.
(b) Each knows the other will not betray the password; they are ready to die together.

Can anyone be a hero?

(a) **Possible response:** Students are likely to say that they are not stereotypical heroes because they are simple men who only want to enjoy life. (b) **Possible responses:** Students may say that difficult situations can cause ordinary people to act in heroic ways. Some may say that some rare individuals set out on paths that require them to act heroically.

His men scattered, then returned with rope and stones which they tied to the dead men's feet. They carried them to the bank.

Mount Valérien continued to roar, its summit hidden now in a mountainous cloud of smoke.

Two soldiers took Morissot by the head and the feet, two others seized M. Sauvage. They swung the bodies for a moment then let go. They described an arc and plunged into the river feet first, for the weights made them seem to be standing upright. 29

There was a splash, the water trembled, then grew calm, while tiny wavelets spread to both shores.

A little blood remained on the surface.

The officer, still calm, said in a low voice: "Now the fish will have their turn."

And he went back to the house.

And all at once he caught sight of the sack of gudgeons in the grass. He picked it up, looked at it, smiled, shouted, "Wilhelm!"

A soldier in a white apron ran out. And the Prussian threw him the catch of the two and said: "Fry these little animals right away while they are still alive. They will be delicious."

Then he lighted his pipe again.

Literary Analysis
Theme and Worldview What details of this ending emphasize the injustice of the heroes' fate?

Critical Thinking

1. **Respond:** Were you shocked by the ending of the story? Explain.
2. **(a)** Before the siege, what did Morissot and Sauvage do together on Sundays? **(b) Analyze Cause and Effect:** Why does the situation in Paris force them to change their habits?
3. **(a) Analyze Cause and Effect:** What circumstances lead the two friends to risk going outside town? **(b) Support:** Identify two details that show the pleasure the two experience when fishing.
(c) Interpret: What aspects of life does fishing represent for them?
4. **(a) Analyze:** Use details from the story to describe the friendship of the two men. **(b) Draw Conclusions:** What role does friendship play in the decision each man makes in the ending?

Can anyone be a hero?
(a) Do M. Morissot and M. Sauvage fit your image of stereotypical heroes? Why or why not? **(b)** Do you believe that situations make heroes, or do you think some people are naturally heroic? Explain your answer.

Vocabulary Development

Vocabulary Knowledge Rating

When students have completed reading and discussing "Damon and Pythias" and "Two Friends," have them take out their **Vocabulary Knowledge Rating Chart.** Read the words aloud once more and have students rate their knowledge of the words again in the After Reading column. Clarify any words that are still problematic. Have students write their own definition and example or sentence in the appropriate column. Then, have students complete the Vocabulary Practice activities on the next page. Encourage students to use the words in further discussion and written work about the selections. Remind them that they will be accountable for these words on the **Selection Test** (*Unit 6 Resources,* pp. 216–218 or 219–221).

After You Read

Damon and Pythias • Two Friends

Comparing Theme and Worldview

1. **(a)** For each story, complete a chart like the one shown.

Friends	Powerful Person	Test of Loyalty	Result of Test?

   (b) Use your chart to draw a conclusion about the theme of each story. **(c)** Explain what the themes of these stories have in common.
2. What is the relationship between loyalty and power in the worldview of each story?
3. **(a)** Describe the way in which Damon and Pythias each face probable death. **(b)** Compare the way in which they face death with Morrisot and Sauvage's final goodbye.
4. **(a)** What is the difference between heroism in Maupassant's worldview and heroism in the worldview of the legend? **(b)** Which view makes heroism seem most "heroic"? Explain.

Writing to Compare Theme and Worldview

Write an essay and a brief letter to a friend evaluating the themes and worldviews reflected in "Damon and Pythias" and "Two Friends." First, write an essay stating which writer's views most strongly resemble your own. Then, state your own views about friendship in a letter to one of your friends. Use these questions to get started:

- In which story is friendship presented more realistically?
- Which story does a better job of teaching a clear lesson?
- Which story shows the forces opposing friendship?
- Which worldview is closer to your own perspective? Why?
- What is your view of friendship?

Vocabulary

Practice Give an example of the items described. Explain your answers.

1. a *dire* emergency
2. music that inspires *serenity*
3. the actions of an *ardent* fan
4. signs that a storm will *relent*

Assessment Resources

The following resources can be used to assess students' knowledge and skills.

Unit 6 Resources

L1 L2 EL **Selection Test A,** pp. 216–218

L3 L4 **Selection Test B,** pp. 219–221

L3 L4 **Open-Book Test,** pp. 213–215

PHLit Online! All assessment resources are available at **www.PHLitOnline.com**

Vocabulary continued

3. An intensely enthusiastic fan might yell loudly during a game.
4. Clearing skies might signal that a storm is weakening.

ASSESS

Answers

Comparing Theme and Worldview

1. (a) *Friends:* Damon, Pythias; Morissot, Sauvage. *Powerful Person:* Dionysius; German officer. *Test:* Damon must trust Pythias to return; Morissot and Sauvage must trust each other to keep the password. *Result:* Dionysius changes; Morissot and Sauvage are killed.

   Other sample answers appear in ***Graphic Organizer Transparencies,* Comparing Theme and Worldview Graphic Organizer A,** p. 225, and in the **Additional Answers** section.

   (b) In "Damon and Pythias," friendship is a virtue that can change the world. In "Two Friends," friendship is helpless.
   (c) Both stories place a high value on friendship.
2. Dionysius changes his ways in the face of the friends' loyalty, but the officer is unmoved.
3. (a) Damon and Pythias face death bravely. (b) Morrisot and Sauvage are frightened, but stay true.
4. (a) In Maupassant's worldview, heroism is powerless. The legend is more positive, suggesting that heroism can affect the world.
   (b) **Possible response:** The unsung, pointless bravery of "Two Friends" seems more heroic.

Writing to Compare

1. Review the assignment criteria with students.
2. As they draft, have students refer to their completed **Comparing Theme and Worldview Graphic Organizers** or to the chart in item 1, above.

Six Traits Focus

✓	Ideas		Word Choice
✓	Organization		Sentence Fluency
	Voice		Conventions

Vocabulary

1. A car accident would be an urgent emergency.
2. Instrumental music is calming to many people.

PRETEACH

Meeting Your Standards

Students will

1. write a comparison-and-contrast essay.
2. use writing strategies to generate ideas and to plan, organize, evaluate, and revise the essay.
3. apply grammar skills.

Introducing the Writing Assignment

Review the assignment and the criteria, using the instruction on the student page.

Connecting to Real-Life Writing

Explain to students that elements of a comparison-and-contrast essay are often incorporated into other types of writing. Point out these examples:

- Standardized test essays and scholarship applications may require student to compare and contrast experiences.
- The comparison-and-contrast technique can be used in persuasive writing as well as research writing.

John Phillip Santos on Comparison and Contrast

Show students Segment 3 on John Phillip Santos on ***See It!*** **DVD** or from this page in the **Enriched Online Student Edition**, at **www.PHLitOnline.com**.

Writing Workshop *Work in Progress*

If students have done the Work-in-Progress assignments on pp. 1187 and 1219, suggest that they examine their recorded ideas as they begin prewriting. They may wish to develop these ideas in a comparison-and-contrast essay.

OES Online Essay Scorer

A writing prompt for this mode of writing can be found on the *PH Essay Scorer* at **www.PHLitOnline.com**.

Writing Workshop

Comparison-and-Contrast Essay

Defining the Form A **comparison-and-contrast** essay explores the similarities and differences between or among two or more topics, thus bringing both into clearer focus. You might use elements of the comparison-and-contrast essay in profiles of historical figures, reviews of literature or performances, or descriptive essays.

Assignment Write a comparison-and-contrast essay about two literary characters, two concepts, or two events. Include these elements:

✔ a clear *thesis statement* that reveals your purpose for writing

✔ *supporting evidence*, including facts and examples that show similarities and differences between two or more subjects

✔ a clear and logical *organizational pattern*

✔ *transitions* that show clear relationships between ideas

✔ error-free grammar, including *varied sentence structure and length*

To preview the criteria on which your comparison-and-contrast essay may be judged, see the rubric on page 1249.

Writing Workshop: *Work in Progress*

If you have completed the Work-in Progress assignments on pages 1187 and 1219, you already have many ideas to use in your comparison-and-contrast essay. Work with these ideas, or explore a new idea as you complete the Writing Workshop.

Teaching Resources

The following resources can be used to enrich or extend the instruction.

All *Unit 6 Resources*
Writing Workshop, pp. 222–223

All *Professional Development Guidebook*
Rubric for Self-Assessment: Comparison-and-Contrast Essay, pp. 234–235

All *Graphic Organizer Transparencies*
Rubric for Self-Assessment: Comparison-and-Contrast Essay, p. 227

All *See It!* **DVD**
John Phillip Santos, Segments 3 and 4

PHLit Online! All resources, including print and video, are available at **www.PHLitOnline.com**.

Prewriting Strategies

Your comparison-and-contrast essay should explore subjects that share traits but are significantly different. Use these strategies to find a topic:

List related topics. Think of a broad subject area, such as music, sports, or fictional characters. Then, list specific items. For example, you might list favorite athletes or unusual places. Look for similarities—and differences—between two or more items on your list. Choose one set as your subject.

Fill in a sentence frame. Find at least three ways to complete a sentence frame. Then, choose your best idea to explore in your essay.

Sample Sentence Frame

I often confuse _______ and _______ because they are both _______. However, they are also different because of _______ and _______.

Consider your purpose. The comparisons and contrasts you explore should fulfill a larger purpose or idea, such as one of the following:

- **To persuade**—You believe one of your subjects is better than the other and you want to convince your readers to share your opinion.
- **To reflect**—Both subjects are meaningful to you, but in different ways, and you want to explore why this is the case.
- **To describe**—The similarities and differences in your subjects are very striking and you want to portray them.

Evaluate your topic. Be sure your topics offer enough interesting similarities and differences. To evaluate your topic choices, use a Venn diagram like the one shown.

Apply It!

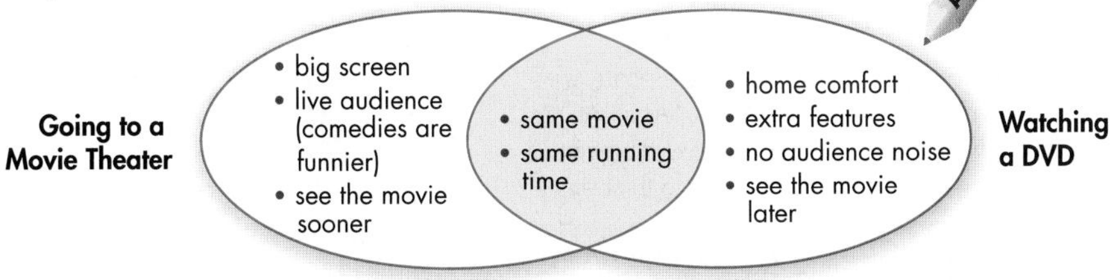

Conduct research. Consider conducting research to further explore your analysis. For example, after creating a Venn diagram, a writer might read movie industry journals to find the average time between a movie's release into theaters and its release onto DVD.

Formulate a thesis statement. Write a *thesis statement* that incorporates a sense of your larger purpose. You will include this thesis statement in your introduction

PHLit Online!
www.PHLitOnline.com
- Author video: Writing Process
- Author video: Rewards of Writing

Understanding by Design

Clarifying Expected Outcomes: Using Rubrics

- Before students begin working on this assignment, have them preview the Rubric for Self-Assessment (p. 1249) to learn what qualities their comparison-and-contrast essays must have. A copy of this rubric appears in ***Graphic Organizer Transparencies***, p. 227.
- Review the criteria in the rubric with the class. Before students use the rubric to assess their writing, work with them to rate the Student Model (p. 1248) using the rubric.
- If you wish to assess students' comparison-and-contrast essays with either a 4-point or a 6-point scoring rubric, see ***Professional Development Guidebook***, pp. 234–235.

TEACH

Prewriting Strategies

1. Introduce the Prewriting Strategies, using the instruction on the student page.
2. Have students apply the strategies to choose a topic.

Teaching the Strategies

1. Complete the sentence frame, using *bees* and *wasps*. Both are yellow and black insects. Bees are plump, mild, and eat nectar, while wasps are thin, aggressive, and eat other insects.
2. Provide these sample thesis statements to show purposes:

   Persuade: Huckleberry Finn is more clever than Tom Sawyer.

   Reflect: Summer camp friendships differ from school friendships.

   Describe: Proms in 1950 were different from those today.

Think Aloud: Choosing a Purpose

Model how to choose a purpose, using this "think aloud":

I want to compare and contrast playing guitar and playing piano. I could *persuade* my reader that piano is more fun to play; I could *reflect* on my varying experiences with both instruments; or I could *describe* the surprising similarities and vast differences between them.

Six Traits Focus

✔	Ideas	Word Choice
	Organization	Sentence Fluency
	Voice	Conventions

Writing and Grammar, Grade 10

Students will find additional instruction on prewriting for a comparison-and-contrast essay in Chapter 9, Section 2.

Writing and Grammar Interactive Textbook Online

Students can use the following tools at **www.pearsonsuccessnet.com** as they complete their comparison-and-contrast essays:

- Topic Bin
- Sentence Length Revising Tool

Drafting Strategies

1. Introduce the Drafting Strategies, using the instruction on the student page.
2. Have students apply the strategies as they draft.

Teaching the Strategies

1. Explain that a point-by-point organization is best when an essay is technical or very detailed. This structure will help the reader remember and keep track of complicated details. A subject-by-subject organization is better when the two subjects can be easily remembered and understood as the reader moves from paragraph to paragraph.
2. Ask the class to suggest different points for a comparison-and-contrast essay on the similarities and differences between two musical groups. Brainstorm for subjects such as popularity, backup singers, themes of the lyrics, and so on. Then have them decide which of the two organizational plans fits the essay best.

Think Aloud: Model Choosing an Organization

Model how to choose an organization, using the following "think aloud":

Suppose I want to write an essay in which I compare and contrast the efficiency of a gasoline engine with a hydrogen fuel cell engine. To determine the most effective way of presenting my information, I need to consider my purpose first. If my purpose is to persuade the reader that one engine is better, I need to emphasize how well each engine processes its fuel. To present these details in a way that the reader will understand, I can use point-by-point organization. For example, my first body paragraph might compare the costs of both fuels; the second might compare the waste products of the engines; and the third might compare the costs to make each engine.

Six Traits Focus

✔	Ideas	✔	Word Choice
✔	Organization		Sentence Fluency
✔	Voice		Conventions

WG Writing and Grammar, Grade 10

Students will find additional instruction on drafting a comparison-and-contrast essay in Chapter 9, Section 3.

Drafting Strategies

Choose an organization. Most comparison-and-contrast essays are organized in one of two ways. In **subject-by-subject organization,** you analyze all of the features of one subject and then all the features of the second subject. In **point-by-point organization,** you discuss one point about both subjects and then move on to a second point. Select an organizational structure that best suits your subjects.

Types of Organization

Subject-by-Subject	Point-by-Point
Subject A • Point 1 • Point 2 Subject B • Point 1 • Point 2	Point A • Subject 1 • Subject 2 Point B • Subject 1 • Subject 2

Use your thesis statement and purpose. Include your thesis in your introduction. Check that the ideas you include in each body paragraph connect directly to your thesis statement and purpose. Restate or reevaluate your thesis statement in your conclusion.

Support opinions. Using a wide variety of evidence can make your ideas more convincing and add interest to your essay.

- **Examples:** Illustrations help clarify similarities and differences.
- **Facts:** Hard evidence helps readers understand each subject.
- **Quotations:** The exact words of experts add authority.

Use transitions. Help readers follow the logic of your comparisons and contrasts by using effective transitions to show the relationships between ideas. These transitional words and phrases are especially useful:

similarly	*on the other hand*	*conversely*	*however*
although	*nevertheless*	*in contrast*	*whereas*

Model: Using Transitions to Clarify Connections

If you have to choose one sport in which to participate, the three most popular are basketball, soccer, and volleyball. All are fast-moving sports that require being in good physical condition, a commitment of time and energy, and an ability to think and react quickly.

Despite the similarities in the physical demands they make, each sport has its own special requirements.

The writer uses a transitional phrase to signal a shift from comparison to contrast.

Strategies for Test Taking

When taking a test that includes a comparison-and-contrast writing prompt, students should be aware that the implied audience is well-educated adults, unless otherwise specified. Students should choose points of comparison and supporting details that are appropriate for this audience. They should also use a formal tone and formal language, unless the test gives different instructions.

John Phillip Santos

On Making Comparisons

In the following passage from my book, I wanted to find a way to illuminate the history of Mexican Americans by comparing and contrasting my family's name—Santos—with its literal meaning in Spanish and earlier versions of the name that had been used in the past.

"You're part of a long tradition of writers."
—John Philip Santos

Professional Model:

from *"Places Left Unfinished at the Time of Creation"*

It is ~~It's~~ a common name my family carries, ~~through a skyful of generations~~ out of our Mexican past. It is a name that invokes the saints and embroiders daily prayers of Latinos in North and South America. The old ones in the family say the name was once *de Los Santos*. "From the saints." But no one remembers when or why it was shortened. There were Santos in San Antonio two hundred years ago. In the records for the year 1793 at the Mission San Antonio de Valero, which later became the Alamo, you find the names of Manuel and Jorge de Los Santos, referred to as "Indios," but it's not clear whether they are our ancestors.

It sometimes seems as if Mexicans are to forgetting what the Jews are to remembering. We have made selective forgetting a sacramental obligation. Leave it all in the past, all that you were, and all that you could not be. There is pain enough in the present to go around. Some memories cannot not be abandoned. Let the past reclaim all the rest forever, and let stories come to their fitting end.

In this early section of the book, by asking readers to move between English and Spanish, I am slowly preparing them for the mix of the two languages that I use in telling the story to come.

By adding this passage, I was able to establish the broader historical background of our Mexican families from San Antonio. This allowed me to compare our experience to the storied legacy of Jewish people.

After comparing traditions of remembering and forgetting to a sacramental obligation, I wanted the rest of the paragraph to have a chant-like quality. The final sentences are short, written with short words, making the passage seem solemn and ceremonial.

John Phillip Santos on Making Comparisons

Review the passage on the student page with the class, using John Phillip Santos's comments to deepen students' understanding of the process of writing a comparison-and-contrast essay.

Teaching From the Professional Model

1. Show students Segment 4 on John Phillip Santos on the ***See It!* DVD** or from this page in the **Enriched Online Student Edition** at **www.PHLitOnline.com.**
2. Point out that most last names—called *surnames*—are passed from generation to generation, connecting us to our ancestors. For many Americans, these names often help to remind us of our families' countries of origin.
3. **Ask** students: What evidence does Santos use to support the idea that Mexicans prefer forgetting?
   Possible response: His Mexican family remembers that their name was shortened but forgets when and why. They've also forgotten who their ancestors are. Additionally, he describes their philosophy of forgetting: There is pain enough in the present, so forget the pain of the past.
4. Discuss with students how Santos compares and contrasts Mexicans with Jews.
   Possible response: Both see their relationship to memory as a sacred obligation. The contrast is that Jews try to remember and Mexicans try to forget.
5. Point out that it is important to avoid stereotypes when discussing cultures or ethnicities, as they can be offensive. Even positive-sounding stereotypes can be offensive. In this case, Santos compares his own experience as a Mexican with important values in the Jewish tradition, so he is not stereotyping.

Differentiated Instruction for Universal Access

Strategy for Less Proficient Readers
Ask students to underline Santos's edits in the passage. Discuss with students why Santos might have made these changes.

Point out the unusual construction of the sentence: *Mexicans are to forgetting what Jews are to remembering.* Explain that the format is from mathematics and means that the relationship between Mexicans and forgetting is the same as the relationship between Jews and remembering.

Strategy for Advanced Students
Ask students to interview family members to research their ancestors, their surnames, and their families' ideas about remembering and forgetting. Have students write journal entries to compare and contrast their family's ideas with Santos's. Have them reflect on their findings.

PHLit Online!
Enriched Online Student Edition
Show or assign the video online at **www.PHLitOnline.com.**

Revising Strategies

1. Introduce the revising strategies, using the instruction on the student page.
2. Have students apply the strategies as they revise.

Teaching the Strategies

1. Tell students that in addition to evaluating the amount of support they have provided for each topic, they should check the types of support they used. For example, if they used only anecdotes, they should consider adding statistics or quotations from experts.
2. Ask students to make sure every detail in each paragraph supports the paragraph's main idea.
3. On the board, write *people*, *a lot*, *things*, and *everything*. Ask students for other examples of vague language, and add them to the list. Have students find such words in their essays and consider replacing them with more specific words.
4. Invite students to use thesauruses to find vivid words. Caution them to check exact definitions in dictionaries to make sure they are choosing words with the desired connotations.

Think Aloud: Model Adding Description

Model how specific descriptions can strengthen a comparison-and-contrast essay, using the following "think aloud":

Though I'm not writing fiction, I can still make my essay creative and engaging by using vivid descriptions to enhance similarities and differences. Say I have the sentence "Bees eat nectar, but wasps eat other insects." It's informative but dull. I can change it to "Bees land on fragrant flowers to sip sweet nectar, while wasps dart among the leaves, searching for hidden caterpillars to attack and devour." My description not only adds interest, but also highlights the different behaviors of bees and wasps.

Six Traits Focus

✔	Ideas	✔	Word Choice
✔	Organization		Sentence Fluency
	Voice		Conventions

WG Writing and Grammar, Grade 10

Students will find additional instruction on revising a comparison-and-contrast essay in Chapter 9, Section 4.

Revising Strategies

Revise to balance your organization. An effective comparison-and-contrast essay provides a thorough analysis of each subject being compared. Follow these steps to check the balance of your coverage:

- First, use one color to highlight places where you discuss one subject. Use another color to highlight places where you discuss a different subject. Use other colors for any additional subjects.
- Next, review your highlighted draft to determine whether you have addressed each subject equally. Add details to support underdeveloped subjects.

Revise for precision. When you compare and contrast, you discuss subjects that share many traits. To clearly distinguish one from the other, use words that are specific and precise.

Vague: The effects used in the first *Star Wars* movies were *good*, but today's computerized images *are also good.*

Specific: The effects used in the first *Star Wars* movies were *convincing*, but today's computerized images *are truly lifelike.*

Peer Review

Ask a partner to read your essay and evaluate how well you have presented details about your subjects of comparison. Discuss whether or not you need to provide additional support for either subject. Consider developing an idea further or adding details to provide more thorough comparisons and contrasts.

Model: Revising to Create Balance

Basketball requires the ability to turn, pivot, start, and stop suddenly. It also requires the ability to instantaneously read and react to the opponents' moves. Soccer requires the ability to predict the ball's movement, be aware of the location of team members, and to quickly intervene in plays. Volleyball also requires quick reflexes. ^ Players must be prepared to make snap judgments about whether a ball is going out of bounds or requires a return.

The writer adds information about her third topic to create a better balance.

Strategies for Using Technology in Writing

If students are using word-processing software to draft and revise their comparison-and-contrast essays, suggest that they use the Find feature of the software to locate conjunctions such as *and, but,* and *yet*. When they find a conjunction, have them examine the sentence to determine whether it is a compound sentence. If it is, have students make sure that it has a comma before the conjunction.

Students can also use features of the **Writing and Grammar Interactive Textbook Online** to draft or revise their essays.

SIX TRAITS WRITER'S TOOLBOX SIX TRAITS

Sentence Fluency | Voice | Organization | Word Choice | Ideas | Conventions

Revising to Vary Sentence Structure and Length

A sequence of too many sentences of the same length and structure can be monotonous. Vary sentence lengths, sentence beginnings, and subject-verb order to create an engaging flow in your writing.

Vary sentence length. The constant use of short sentences can make your writing seem undeveloped and choppy. Work to identify whether you have too many short sentences in sequence and combine some to create a better flow. Reserve a short, punchy sentence for an idea you want to emphasize.

Choppy: I like lakes more than the ocean. It is easier to swim. You can fish. You can water ski. Lakes are nice at all times of day. They are pretty in all weather. I feel at home on a lake.

Flowing: I like lakes more than the ocean because it is easier to swim, fish, and water ski. Lakes are beautiful at all times of day and in all weather. I feel at home on a lake.

Vary sentence beginnings. Avoid using the same parts of speech to start a series of sentences. Vary your sentence beginnings by using different parts of speech, phrases, and clauses.

Adjective: *Blue* skies always remind her of home.
Prepositional phrase: *Until then,* she was not sure she would make friends at her new school.
Adverb clause: *Wherever she went,* she still thought about the people she had left.
Gerund phrase: *Spending lunchtime alone* was most distressing to her.

You can also vary subject-verb order to add interest. Create variety in your sentences by reversing the usual subject-verb order.

Original: The statue stood outside the theater.

Inverted: Outside the theater stood the statue.

Grammar in Your Writing

Review three body paragraphs of your draft, highlighting sequences of sentences that have similar length and structure. Add variety to your sentences by changing sentence lengths, altering sentence beginnings, or inverting subject-verb order.

WG

Prentice Hall Writing and Grammar Connection: Chapter 21, Section 3

Differentiated Instruction for Universal Access

EL Strategy for English Learners

English learners may have difficulty varying sentence beginnings. Review the examples on the student page, defining each part of speech with which the sentences begin. Have each student write three original sentences beginning with an adjective, three beginning with a prepositional phrase, and so on. Sentences should be related to students' essay topics and may be incorporated into their essays.

Strategy for Less Proficient Readers

Have students count the words in each sentence of the Professional Model. Point out how Santos uses short sentences at the end to create a particular effect. Use this as an example of how short sentences can add emphasis if they are used carefully. Ask each student to write a brief paragraph that ends with a short, powerful sentence.

Revising to Vary Sentence Structure and Length

1. Introduce the writing skill, using the instruction on the student page.
2. Discuss the examples and the strategies for varying sentence length and structure.
3. Have students follow the instruction under Grammar in Your Writing to correct errors in their drafts.

Teaching the Writing Skill

1. Explain that using short sentences is an effective way to emphasize an idea. If a short sentence lies among long sentences, it interrupts the rhythm of the text, forcing the reader to stop and consider this important idea.
2. Have students skim their papers, noting the general sentence length and structure. **Ask:** Why shouldn't there be equal numbers of long and short sentences?
   Answer: If short sentences are not reserved for important points, they will not create as much emphasis. Too many long sentences will sound boring and long-winded.
3. Ask students to revise the following choppy paragraph.
   Original: The Westminster Kennel Club holds the most prestigious dog show in the country. One category is Working Dogs. They also show Toy Dogs. Hounds are another category. Dogs in the Terrier category have won Best of Show most often.
   Possible Revision: The prestigious Westminster Kennel Club Dog Show features dogs that fall into the categories of Working Dogs, Toy Dogs, Hounds, and Terriers. Terriers have won Best of Show most often.

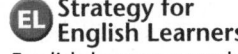

WG Writing and Grammar, Grade 10

Students will find additional instruction on revising to vary sentence structure and length in Chapter 21, Section 3.

Student Model

Review the Student Model with the class, using the annotations to analyze the writer's use of the elements of a comparison-and-contrast essay.

Teaching from the Student Model

1. Explain that the Student Model is a sample, and students' own comparison-and-contrast essays may be longer.
2. **Ask** students to name the topic, the thesis statement, and the organization.
   Answer: The topic is a comparison of letters, telephone calls, and e-mails. The thesis statement is "While the three modes of communication have a lot in common, there are differences that let each stand out on its own." The organization is point by point, or similarity then difference.
3. Point out that the writer uses the transitional word *Despite* at the beginning of her third paragraph to move the essay from similarities to differences.
4. Have students notice the way that the writer organizes her essay. The entire essay supports her original thesis statement. Within the essay, she begins each paragraph with a topic sentence, which she then supports with examples. Finally, her last paragraph, the conclusion, explains why the topic is important.

Connecting to Real-Life Writing

Explain to students that the ability to write effective comparison-and-contrast material is important in a variety of occupations. For example, archaeologists, doctors, and civic engineers might need to answer questions such as the following:

- How is the newly discovered dinosaur like or unlike those already unearthed?
- How is this new medical treatment different, or better, than previous treatments?
- What are the similarities and differences between two recycling programs?

Student Model: Amanda Goodman, Glen Rock, NJ

You've Got Mail

Personal communications have gone through a major evolution in modern times. The letter gave way to the telephone call, and now they have both been overwhelmed in popularity by e-mail. While the three modes of communication have a lot in common, there are differences that let each stand out on its own.

> In her introduction, Amanda identifies the subjects she will compare.

Letters, phone calls, and e-mail are similar because they all involve personal communication. They allow people to share ideas and feelings with other people. Communicators do not have to be face to face; they can be across the world and get the same points across. Letter writers, phone callers, and e-mailers are generally not limited by time either. They can create and share their communications round the clock.

> In this paragraph, Amanda discusses the similarities that the three formats share.

Despite their similarities, letters, phone calls, and e-mail communicate differently. Letters convey a personal touch and make recipients especially happy when received. They can be saved, to be reread (often over and over) at a later time. Unlike a letter, e-mail is usually more spontaneous and less likely to be reread. Phone call messages quickly fade. Of all three modes, letters take the longest time between the sender and the receiver. If time is important, letters are probably the worst format to use.

E-mail is seldom personal. It is more convenient than "snail mail," though. You never have to move away from your computer. Plus, you can edit without cross-outs. Once you send an e-mail, it is delivered instantly. This speed has its disadvantages. Because people create e-mails with such haste, they often do not stop to think carefully about what they want to say—or correct grammar or spelling mistakes—before they click an e-mail on its way.

> In the third, fourth, and fifth paragraphs, Amanda addresses the unique qualities of each form.

A phone call is extremely personal, and it shows that you have set aside time for the other person. You are able to hear the tone of voice and expression of the other person. Phone calls may be expensive, temporary, and time-sensitive—unlike a letter or an e-mail, which a recipient can read when he or she has the time. Another problem with the phone is that once you say something, you cannot take it back, in contrast to the way you can edit writing.

> Transitions help clarify the contrasts between subjects.

There is a time and a place for all three types of communication. People are often so busy that they have time only for e-mail, but maybe people should set aside some time to write a letter or call a friend.

Strategies for Test Taking

Point out that comparison-and-contrast questions are common in essay tests. When writing under pressure, many students forget to use transitions to organize their thoughts clearly. Have students circle all of the comparison-and-contrast transitions in the Student Model. Then, read the essay aloud without these transitions and discuss the difference.

Editing and Proofreading

Review your draft to correct errors in grammar, spelling, and punctuation.

Focus on Transitional Words: Double-check the meanings of the transitional words you have used, and make sure they are punctuated correctly. If you start a sentence with a coordinating conjunction, such as *however* or *nevertheless*, follow it with a comma.

Publishing and Presenting

Consider one of the following ways to share your writing:

Present a shared reading. With a partner, deliver an oral presentation of your essay. First, present to a small group. Read the paragraphs that discuss one subject, while your partner reads the paragraphs that discuss the other subject. Ask for listeners' comments to improve your presentation before sharing it with another group.

Create a class book. Compile a collection of comparison-and-contrast essays. Devise a title that reflects the content of the collection and place the finished book in your classroom or school library.

Reflecting on Your Writing

Writer's Journal Jot down your answers to this question:

How did comparing and contrasting your subjects about the work help you understand them?

WG *Prentice Hall Writing and Grammar Connection: Chapter 9*

Rubric for Self-Assessment

Find evidence in your writing to address each category. Then, use the rating scale to grade your work.

Criteria	Rating Scale (not very – very)
Focus: How clear is your purpose and thesis?	1 2 3 4 5
Organization: How effectively does your organization show comparisons and contrasts?	1 2 3 4 5
Support/Elaboration: How varied and convincing is your evidence?	1 2 3 4 5
Style: How well do you use transitions to connect ideas?	1 2 3 4 5
Conventions: How correct is your grammar? How consistently and well do you vary sentence lengths and structures?	1 2 3 4 5

Differentiated Instruction for Universal Access

EL Strategy for English Learners

English learners may not be familiar with some transition words. On the board, write these words: *similarly, but, however, likewise, although, still, as, also, even though, otherwise, like,* and *yet*. Have students make two-column charts, labeling them *Compare* and *Contrast*. Point to the words on the board, using each in a sentence. Then, have students identify whether you are using the word to compare or contrast ideas. Have students add each transition word to the correct column of their charts. Help them to write new sentences containing each word. Encourage students to keep their charts for later use, continuing to add words as they work.

Editing and Proofreading

1. Introduce the editing and proofreading focus, using the instruction on the student page.
2. Have students edit and proofread their comparison-and-contrast essays, correcting grammar, spelling, punctuation, and word choice. Make sure they check for errors of the type noted on the student page.

Teaching the Editing Focus

Have students proofread one another's essays, focusing on transition words and punctuation.

Six Traits Focus

	Ideas	✔	Word Choice
	Organization		Sentence Fluency
	Voice	✔	Conventions

ASSESS

Publishing and Presenting

1. For shared readings, have students practice in pairs, alternating the reading of paragraphs or sentences that describe the two topics. Highlighting their parts will help students script the reading.
2. If students will be collaborating on a class book, suggest they choose topics that address particular themes or topics of interest to the entire class.

Reflecting on Your Writing

After answering the question in the student text, have students write about the ways their opinions of their subjects have changed or have been reinforced as a result of writing this essay.

WG **Writing and Grammar, Grade 10**

Students will find additional guidance on editing and proofreading, publishing and presenting, and reflecting on comparison-and-contrast essays in Chapter 9, Sections 5 and 6.

MONITORING PROGRESS

Think About It

1. Remind students that the unit Big Question is "Can anyone be a hero?"
2. Point out that students have read selections in this unit about different kinds of heroes. Guide students to consider how these heroic characters are similar to heroes they know about in real life.
3. Point out that it is important to look at different factors that affect heroism. Review the Example from Literature shown in the chart. Point out that despite Long Arrow's handicap, his heroic characteristics led to heroic accomplishments.
4. Explain that the Big Question is relevant not only in literature, but in other areas as well. For example, students might remember that Rosa Parks was an ordinary person who decided one day that she didn't want to give up her seat on a segregated bus. Parks found herself in the midst of the Civil Rights Movement and became one of its champions.
5. Review the headings on the chart. Remind students that not every hero starts out as a hero. Encourage students to consider the ways in which circumstances create heroes.
6. Have students copy and complete the chart shown on the student page. If they have difficulty finding examples from real life, suggest these starting points:
   - Which career fields have more than their share of heroes? (For example: firefighters)
   - What human interest stories in the news reveal the courage of average citizens?

   Have volunteers read aloud their completed charts. Invite the class to discuss their examples.

Applying the Big Question

THE BIG Q

Can anyone be a *hero?*

Think About It

Think about what you have read in this unit and what you know about heroes from your other classes and from your own experiences. Copy and complete the chart below to apply what you have learned about the different ways different people can be heroes. One row has been completed for you.

Example	Person	Does he or she start out as a hero?	Heroic characteristics	Heroic accomplishments or actions	What I learned
From Literature	Long Arrow from "The Orphan Boy and the Elk Dog"	No, Long Arrow is a poor orphan who cannot hear.	perseverance, bravery, and loyalty	He discovers and introduces horses to his tribe.	Even someone who was looked down upon by society can go on to do great things.
From Literature					
From Science					
From Social Studies					
From Real Life					

Teaching Resources

Unit 6 Resources

All **Applying the Big Question,** p. 5

PHLit Online!

All print resources are also available online at **www.PHLitOnline.com.**

Talk About It

Working with a partner, write and conduct a mock **interview** with one of the people listed in the second column of your heroes chart. On note cards, write questions you would like to ask the person about the challenges and rewards of being a hero. On another set of note cards, write answers to the questions. Make sure your questions and answers convey maturity and respect. Decide who will be the hero and who will be the interviewer. Practice asking and answering the questions. Then, present your interview to the class. Discuss any questions when you have finished and evaluate the effectiveness of the interview.

Write About It

At the beginning of Unit 6, you wrote a response to the Big Question. Now that you have completed the unit, see how your understanding of the question has deepened. Write a new response in which you discuss whether your initial ideas have changed or been validated.

- ❑ Anyone can be a hero.
- ❑ Not everyone can be a hero.
- ❑ My own response: __________.

Support your response with at least one example from literature and one example from an additional subject area or your own life. You can draw on your chart for examples or complete these sentences to help you organize your response.

- In this unit, a story character overcame obstacles in order to become a hero by __________.
- One example of a hero in the field of Science is __________ because __________.
- A historical figure who some people consider to be a hero, but who others do not is __________.
- I felt like a hero when __________. I felt that I was not heroic when __________.
- Sometimes it is hard to be a hero because __________.
- An example of a hero in the world today is __________ because __________.

Challenge What issues does this question still raise for you? How could you continue your exploration?

☆ shows an **Academic Vocabulary** word.

Big Question Vocabulary

attributes
☆ character
☆ conduct
courage
determination
honor
☆ inherent
☆ integrity
legendary
persevere
☆ principles
☆ resolute
☆ responsibility
sacrifice
selflessness

Strategies for Listening and Speaking

Review with students how to conduct themselves during oral presentations.

For listeners:

- Remind students to be quiet and attentive during classmates' presentations. Encourage students to take notes.

For speakers:

- Guide interviewers to refer to notecards as they speak, but not to read directly from them.
- Encourage "heroes" to behave as they imagine the character would behave. Students being interviewed might hold a prop or wear an article of clothing that helps to identify them.
- Both speakers should be prepared to defend their questions and answers.

MONITORING PROGRESS

Talk About It

1. Have students complete the assignment, following the instruction on the student page.
2. Encourage students to answer questions "in character." For contemporary heroes, students might access national publications on the Internet that have published features about the person.

Write About It

1. Introduce the assignment, using the instruction on the student page.
2. Review the thematic vocabulary with the class (see pp. 1046–1047).

Teaching Prewriting

1. Suggest that students may have read a selection that changed their opinions of the Big Question.
2. Have students respond to the Big Question, completing the sentences on the student page. Then, refer students to their responses in Introducing the Big Question, pp. 1046–1047, to see how their thinking may have changed.

Teaching Drafting

1. Have students use their charts or completed sentences for ideas.
2. Remind students to include topic sentences. Their completed sentences can serve as opening topic sentences, or they can serve as supporting details.
3. Encourage students to organize their paragraphs so that they are clear and to the point.

Teaching Revising/Editing

1. Remind students to remove information that is not relevant and to add additional details to support their main ideas.
2. After students have revised their drafts, have them reread their edited versions.

Guiding Student Publishing

Students might compile their responses in a class notebook entitled "Exploring Heroism."

Answers

Meeting Your Standards

Students will

1. understand idioms, technical terms, and jargon.
2. understand where and when to use idioms, technical terms, and jargon.
3. identify and use the literal and figurative meanings of words.

Idioms, Jargon, and Technical Terms

1. Introduce the skill, using the instruction on the student page.
2. Review the examples in chart.

Teaching the Skill

1. On the board, draw a similar chart to the one shown on p. 1252. Elicit from students idioms with which they might be familiar. Write the idioms and their meanings in the chart for students' reference.
2. Emphasize that students might already know jargon, particularly computer and Internet jargon. Discuss terms such as *download, hyperlink, log on, log in, search engine, spam, surfing,* and *upload.*
3. **Ask:** How might these terms help us to communicate?
   Answer: These terms allow us to communicate more quickly and conveniently.
4. Then, **ask** students: How might terms such as these make communication more difficult?
   Possible response: If a person familiar with these terms uses them in a conversation with a person who does not know them, the terms might confuse him or her.

Practice A

Sample answers:

1. Jargon: "Bringing up that topic," "will have a negative impact." Rewrite: Discussing that topic will be bad for our relationship.
2. Jargon: "friendly fire," "rendered nonviable"; Rewrite: Civilians were accidentally shot and killed by soldiers on their own side.
3. Jargon: "it was necessary to downsize"; Rewrite: The business owner said she needed to fire many employees.

Vocabulary Workshop

Idioms, Jargon, and Technical Terms

Words have *literal meanings,* which are the denotative or actual meanings of the words. Many words and phrases in English also have a figurative meaning. *Figurative language* is language that is not meant to be understood literally. **Idioms** are expressions that are characteristic of a language, region, community or class of people. They cannot be understood literally. Many dictionaries list idioms with the entry for the main word in the phrase. Look at these examples of idioms:

Idiom	Meaning
It *beats me.*	I don't know.
Let's *call it a day.*	Let's stop working for today.
Amy should *brush up on* her Spanish.	Amy should refresh her knowledge Spanish.
The thief tried to *cover her tracks.*	The thief tried to hide what she had done.

Technical terms are the words used by people in specific fields to describe their activities. The words themselves may be familiar, but they have specialized meanings in a particular profession. Examples from the field of theater include *stage left, curtain time, fly space,* and *apron.* Technical terms help those with knowledge of the field communicate effectively.

Jargon, like technical terminology, is the specialized language used in a specific field. However, when jargon is used with people outside the field, it results in confusion. Try to figure out what this means: *When you get the proof, stet the correx.* It means that the corrections should not be made on a page print-out. In most writing jargon should generally be avoided.

Practice A Identify the jargon in each sentence. Then, rewrite the sentence using more understandable language. Use a dictionary if necessary.

1. Bringing up that topic will have a negative impact on our relationship.
2. Civilians were caught in friendly fire and rendered non-viable.
3. The business owner said it was necessary to downsize.

1252

Teaching Resources

Unit 6 Resources

Idioms, Jargon, and Technical Terms, pp. 224–225

PHLit Online! **Vocabulary Central,** featuring definitions, audio pronunciations, Word Families, and activities, is available online at **www.PHLitOnline.com.**

4. Occasioned by an increase in the number of the involuntarily undomiciled, the city council opened new shelter units.

5. We will hold the decision in abeyance until we have heard from all members of the council.

PHLit Online!
www.PHLitOnline.com
- Illustrated vocabulary words
- Interactive vocabulary games
- Vocabulary flashcards

Practice B Identify the idiom in each sentence and write a definition for each. If you are unsure of the meaning of the word or phrase, check your definition in a dictionary.

1. Let's fan out and try to find Sarah's lost earring.
2. I think you had better be quiet, if you catch my drift.
3. The sound of nails on a chalkboard drove her up the wall.
4. I'll go on record in support of the new proposal.
5. George left no stone unturned as he searched for his car keys.
6. Jordan's little sister is a pain in the neck.
7. They were taken to the principal's office and given the third degree.
8. Your mother started tearing her hair out when you didn't answer your cell phone.
9. Three hundred people in the box factory got the axe.
10. The district will break ground on the new high school tomorrow.

Challenge
Working with one or two classmates, research a profession and the jargon typically used in that field. For example, you might interview a sports coach to learn jargon associated with gymnastics or swimming. Compile a glossary and share with classmates.

Activity Prepare five note cards like this one. Write each of the following words and its definition on a card. Look the word up in a dictionary and find a technical meaning for the word. Write the field it comes from and the technical meaning on the card.

case strike term pitch pin

Word:

Definition:

Field:

Technical Definition:

Differentiated Instruction for Universal Access

Strategy for Less Proficient Readers
Give each student a list of the following idioms:

He's a loose cannon.
Rise and shine.
Read the writing on the wall.
She pulled the wool over his eyes.
It's no skin off my back.

Guide students through a literal translation of each idiom and discuss why it doesn't make sense. Then, discuss what the figurative translation of each sentence might be. Finally, write the correct figurative translations on the board.

Enrichment for Gifted and Talented Students
Have students work with partners. Each pair should write a paragraph containing idioms and jargon. Then, have pairs trade paragraphs and use dictionaries and prior knowledge to translate each other's paragraphs into plain English.

ASSESS/EXTEND

Answers

Practice A
Sample answers (continued):

4. Jargon: "occasioned by an increase," "involuntarily undomiciled," "shelter units"; Rewrite: Because the number of homeless people is growing, the city council opened new shelters.
5. Jargon: "hold the decision in abeyance"; Rewrite: We won't decide until we've heard from everyone in the council.

Practice B
Sample answers:

1. *Fan out* means "spread out."
2. *If you catch my drift* means "if you understand me."
3. *Drove her up the wall* means "greatly annoyed" her.
4. *Go on record in support* means "let it be known that I support."
5. *Left no stone unturned* means "searched in every single place."
6. *Pain in the neck* means "annoying."
7. *Given the third degree* means "questioned as though they were suspected of wrongdoing."
8. *Tearing her hair out* means "getting worried."
9. *Got the axe* means "were fired from their jobs."
10. *Break ground* means "begin construction."

Activity
Provide each student with five notecards and a dictionary.
Sample answer:
Word: *case*; Definition: an instance of something; Field: law; Technical Definition: a set of facts supporting a legal claim

Challenge
Allow students to choose partners who share common interests. For each word, glossaries should include the field definition and an example sentence. Urge students to illustrate where appropriate. Have students share their favorite glossary entries with the class.

Meeting Your Standards

Students will

1. compare media coverage of the same event in two reports.
2. compare the emphasis and techniques of the two reports.
3. evaluate the reports for factual and objective reporting.

Introducing Comparing Media Coverage

Introduce the assignment and the strategies, using the instruction on the student page.

Evaluate Coverage

1. Tell students that determining the purpose of each report is the first step in comparing the coverage.
2. Tell students that they can use the Internet to check the background of a reporting agency to determine reliability.
3. Emphasize that facts can be proven beyond doubt. While opinions may be supported by facts, they are subject to interpretation. Suggest that students underline facts and circle opinions in written reports.

Compare Coverage

1. Suggest that students record questions regarding missing facts in the margin of each report.
2. Have students write a statement about the tone of each report.
3. In their statements, tell students to cite examples from each report to support their claims.

Assess the Activity

To evaluate students' delivery, use the **Listening: Evaluating a Media Presentation** rubric, p. 267 in the *Professional Development Guidebook.*

Communications Workshop

Comparing Media Coverage

The same event can be described in varying ways. The rising number of media sources presents a challenge: People must analyze coverage to fully understand issues and events. The following techniques will help you assess different media presentations and compare the delivery of information.

Evaluate Coverage

Choose two different reports of the same event. Consider print, television and web sources. Evaluate each report separately to start the comparison.

Purpose Is the report attempting to persuade or entertain? The techniques used in the report should be appropiate to the purpose.

Background Does the reporter have an agenda—a particular viewpoint or opinion to support? Knowing the background of the person or group structuring the information allows you to actively listen for *propaganda* and potential *bias,* a tendency to favor unfairly one side of an issue.

Facts and Opinions Are the items presented as facts verifiable? Are facts accompanied by music or images that add an emotional dimension? Does the reporter add comments that are not facts of the story?

Actively Listen and Watch Is the language factual and objective, or emotional and subjective? Is the pacing of speech designed to elicit an emotional response from the audience?

Compare Coverage

After you evaluate the reports separately, compare them.

Focus on Emphasis Note the facts that each report highlights. Which points are omitted from one, but not the other? Which report contains more opinions? Compare the items that each reporter chose to emphasize.

Analyze Techniques Compare the techniques each presentation uses to convey information. Note the use of music, pictures, and colors that might evoke emotional responses from the audience. Compare how each report uses language and pacing to convey a specific tone or attitude.

Evaluate Results After you have compared the two reports, write a statement explaining which one is more factual and objective.

Activity: Compare Media Coverage

Evaluate a story as presented by two different media sources. Use the checklist to analyze the basic elements of the two presentations.

Comparing Media Coverage

For each report, note the following:

Purpose ____________

Background ____________

The majority of information is factual

____

The majority of information is opinion

____

There is a balance of fact and opinion

____

___ Visuals are neutral
___ Visuals are dramatic
___ Language is factual
___ Language is emotional

Differentiated Instruction for Universal Access

EL Strategy for English Learners

Before students begin their projects, review with them the differences between fact and opinion. Point out that facts are verifiable or will be the same in any report. Opinions are an individual's beliefs or conclusions that cannot be proved. Point out to students that there are clue words that may signal an opinion such as *think, believe, suppose, ought, may, possibly,* and *sometimes.*

Strategy for Less Proficient Learners

Review the Comparison Media Coverage form with students before they begin the Activity. Clarify each of the items on the form, and have students reword any of the items which are unclear. Particularly focus on the difference between *neutral* and *dramatic, factual* and *emotional,* and *fact* and *opinion.* Provide students with copies of the form for note taking.

Independent Reading

Can anyone be a *hero?*

The Once and Future King
T. H. White
Ace, 1987

Escape into the legendary world of Camelot, where chivalry defines the age. This novel describes in vivid detail the rise of King Arthur, his idealistic kingdom, and its eventual collapse. These stories of allegiance, betrayal, love, and adventure have lived for centuries, as has the image of Arthur as the ultimate king and hero.

A Connecticut Yankee in King Arthur's Court
Mark Twain
Signet, 1963

After being knocked out by a blow to the head, nineteenth-century Connecticut resident Hank Morgan wakes up in King Arthur's England. In styles ranging from light humor to searing satire, Twain's classic novel describes what happens when an American man comes face to face with the dark underside of seemingly perfect Camelot.

Places Left Unfinished at the Time of Creation
John Phillip Santos
Penguin, 2000

John Phillip Santos traces his Mexican American family's history in this epic tale. From Madrina, a girl gifted with prophecy when she saw a soul leave its body, to Teofilo, who was kidnapped and raised by the Kikapu Indians, you will meet compelling characters whose adventures span generations.

Early Irish Myths and Sagas
Translated by Jeffrey Gantz
Penguin, 1981

These ancient stories were first written down around the eighth century, but, for centuries, they were passed orally from generation to generation. Capturing a mystical world of battle and beauty, these stories provide a glimpse into the mind and soul of the Celtic world.

Beowulf
Globe Fearon, 2000

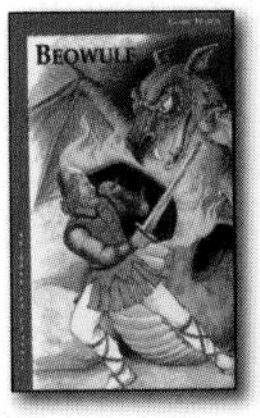

Deep under a bloody lake, a ferocious monster lies in wait. Beowulf, a heroic prince with incredible strength and skill, is the only one who can defeat this monster and overcome other terrifying threats. In the story of *Beowulf* you will meet this legendary hero and accompany him on his courageous quests.

Consult your teacher before choosing one of these titles.

Planning Students' Further Reading

Have students choose a book for independent reading from those listed on the student page. Before recommending a work to students, preview it, taking into account the values of your community as well as the maturity of your students. The following notes offer some guidance for the titles on the student page.

Because a variety of factors play a role in determining the accessibility of a work, a book with a higher readability rating may be deemed more accessible than a book with a lower rating.

L1 ***The Once and Future King*** This book contains jousts between knights that result in deaths and injuries. There is also some cruelty to animals. There are no explicit sexual scenes; however, some readers may be offended by implications of sexual relations among unmarried people. Morgause bears Arthur's son Mordred, and Lancelot has an illicit affair with Guinevere, Arthur's wife. **Lexile: 1080L**

L3 ***A Connecticut Yankee in King Arthur's Court*** The novel contains violence and incidents of prejudice. **Lexile: 1080L**

L4 ***Places Left Unfinished at the Creation of Time*** Some students may be sensitive to the central idea of the memoir, which is the apparent suicide of the author's grandfather, an act kept secret by the family. Some may find the graphic description of killing a deer to be upsetting. **Level suitable for high school students.**

L3 ***Early Irish Myths and Sagas*** These myths and sagas include graphic descriptions of violence. They also include references to sexual relations, intimate body parts, pregnancy, incest, drunkenness, as well as to the magic of druids. To prepare students to read these tales, discuss the contrasts characteristic of the world of Irish myth: on the one hand, an unashamed acquaintance with life at its most brutal; on the other, lyrical descriptions and a deep idealization of love.

L2 ***Beowulf*** The work contains violence, descriptions of ancient rituals and religions and drinking. Grendel and the dragon may be considered supernatural creatures by some. **Level suitable for high school students**

Connecting to the Big Question

Have students form literature circles in which to discuss the books they read independently. See Professional Development Guidebook, pp. 47–49, for guidance in running literature circles.

Suggest that students discuss these questions:

- Are the characters "typical" heroes? Are the main characters heroes at all?
- Does a hero have to do something for society or just for one person?

Challenge

The following titles for advanced readers are available in the Penguin Literature Library.

***Cyrano de Bergerac* by Edmond Rostand** No sensitive issues.

***In the Time of the Butterflies* by Julia Alvarez** The novel contains violence.

MONITORING PROGRESS

Using the Unit Review

In this Test Practice workshop (pp. 1256–1261), students apply the skills in Unit 6. The practice is divided into four sections.

1. Before assigning each section, review the relevant Unit skills with students.
2. Set a time limit for the multiple choice items in each section, allowing a little over one minute per question. Allow ten to fifteen minutes for any Writing for Assessment questions.
3. Administer each section. Have students write the starting time at the top of their papers. When half the time for the multiple choice items has run out, ask students to write the time next to an answer on which they are working. Have them do the same when time is three quarters through and again when time is up. Have them note the start and end times for any Writing for Assessment questions as well.
4. Review with students the pacing reflected in their notes.

Reteaching Skills

1. For each practice, use the Reteach chart on the same page as the answers to determine which skills require reteaching, based on which items students answered incorrectly.
2. Reteach these skills prior to assigning the **Benchmark Test** for the second half of Unit 6 (***Unit 6 Resources***, pp. 226–232).

Test Practice: Unit 6 Review

I. Literary Skills

Directions: *Read the passage. Then, answer each question that follows.*

Jane Babbitt and the Cordless Phone

Everyone from Pennsbury, Pennsylvania, has heard stories of Jane Babbitt. Some say that Jane saved the school music program by making instruments for all the students. Others say that mighty Jane single-handedly defeated the Brookline High School basketball team by playing all positions when the rest of the team was ill. I do not know about those stories, but I do know that Jane invented the cordless phone.

Jane's best friend, Molly Kubrick, had fifty brothers and sisters. Imagine trying to have a private conversation with one hundred prying sibling ears around you! Molly grew more frustrated every day. When Jane saw how annoyed her best friend was, she knew she had to help.

One day after school, Jane went over to Molly's house to have a look at her phone. "Listen, phone," she said to the black phone connected to the wall, "Molly's got to be able to have private conversations. Your cord will just have to stretch." Apparently, even Molly's phone had heard about Jane. The phone resolved to let its cord stretch as far as possible.

Molly took the phone off the receiver and left the house. "Hi Molly!" her sister Veronica yelled from the yard. "Who are you calling?" Molly kept walking down the street. She got the to end of the block.

"Hi Molly!" shouted her brothers Rich and Eddie. "Are you calling your boyfriend?" She rolled her eyes and kept going. The cord stretched and stretched. Molly had to walk all the way to the other side of town before she was finally free of the eyes of her many brothers and sisters.

She looked down at the phone. The cord had snapped along the way. Molly's eyes filled with tears. Suddenly, she heard Jane come up behind her. "Did you make your call?" Jane said affably, with a smile.

"I can't. The phone is broken," Molly said sadly.

"No way. This phone will still work. Right, phone?" said Jane to the phone. Suddenly, Molly heard the dial tone. She started to dial and made her first private call.

I lived across the street at the time, and saw Molly make her call. That's how I know we all have Jane to thank for the cordless phone.

Strategies for Test Taking

Remind students that, when faced with options such as "All of the above" or "None of the above," they need to be sure that each of the other three options fits the question criterion. If not, the "All" or "None" answer option cannot be correct. Direct their attention to question 9 on p. 1257 and to answer option D. Point out that if one of the other options is *not* correct, then D cannot be correct.

1. This selection shares all of the following characteristics with **myths** except—
   A. it includes a character with exceptional skills.
   B. it explains how something originated.
   C. it has a protagonist.
   D. it explains the actions of the gods.

2. Which statement characterizes Molly's **worldview?**
   A. Share everything with your family.
   B. Forgive and forget.
   C. Do not trust your friends too much.
   D. Everyone deserves to have some privacy.

3. What does the first paragraph tell you about the **cultural context** of this selection?
   A. The selection is set in modern times.
   B. The selection is set in the Midwest.
   C. The telephone has just been invented.
   D. It is unusual for females to attend school.

4. In what way is Jane similar to an **epic hero?**
   A. Her story has been passed down for hundreds of years.
   B. She goes on a long journey to foreign lands.
   C. She struggles against the gods.
   D. Her amazing skills make her larger-than-life.

5. Which of these **narrative patterns** does this selection follow?
   A. Someone has a need, and a hero helps that person.
   B. A hero desires power and uses others to get it.
   C. A protagonist struggles with an antagonist, and the antagonist triumphs.
   D. Someone challenges a hero to a duel, and the hero accepts.

6. **Vocabulary in Context** What is the *best* definition for the underlined word *affably?*
   A. angrily
   B. cheerfully
   C. wisely
   D. sadly

7. Why does the author include the detail that Molly has fifty siblings?
   A. to convince the reader that gigantic families are beneficial for everyone
   B. to confuse the reader with extra information
   C. to prove that Molly complains too much
   D. to emphasize Molly's difficulties in finding privacy in a humorous way

8. What does the author say to suggest that Jane is a **legendary hero** in her community?
   A. The author saw Molly make her phone call.
   B. The author claims that Jane defeated a basketball team without anyone else's help.
   C. The author states that everyone in the community knows about Jane's adventures.
   D. The author went to high school with Jane.

9. This story fits the characteristics of a **folk tale** because—
   A. it describes human deeds.
   B. no gods appear in the story.
   C. it expresses values.
   D. All of the above.

Writing for Assessment

10. **Identify** one **universal theme** in this selection. In a paragraph, **explain** how this theme is developed. **Support** your answer with details from the selection.

GO ON

Answers continued

9. D—All three characteristics are common to folk tales. *Incorrect answers:* A—see explanation for D. B—see explanation for D. C—see explanation for D.

Writing for Assessment

10. Students' paragraphs should identify and analyze the use of animals in myths and support their opinion with details from the story.

Reteach

Question	Instructional Pages to Reteach
1	1063
2	1153
3	1063
4	1091
5	1128
7	1189
8	1153
9	1051
10	1228

Answers

Answers With Explanations

1. D—The story includes no gods. *Incorrect answers:* A—Jane has exceptional skills. B—The story explains the origins of cordless phones. C—Jane is the protagonist.
2. D—Molly wants privacy, which is difficult to find in her home. *Incorrect answers:* A—Molly wishes to have the chance not to share. B—This issue does not enter into the story. C—same explanation as for B.
3. A—Details about high school, basketball, and telephones set the story in modern times. *Incorrect answers:* B—Pennsylvania, the setting, is not in the Midwest. C—The telephone might have been around for a long time; only cordless phones are new. D—Nothing in the story suggests this conclusion.
4. D—Jane's amazing skills are similar to the abilities of epic heroes. *Incorrect answers:* A—Since the story is set in modern times, that cannot be the case. B—Jane does not leave her community in any of the stories about her. C—The gods do not appear.
5. A—Jane helps Molly gain the privacy she wants. *Incorrect answers:* B—Jane does not seek or obtain power in this story. C—The story includes no antagonist. D—Jane does not duel anyone.
6. B—Jane's cheerfulness is shown by her smile. *Incorrect answers:* A—If Jane felt this way, she would not be smiling. C—Jane is simply curious if Molly made the call. D—same explanation as for A.
7. D—The exaggeration is a mark of humor. *Incorrect answers:* A—The author does not advocate large families. B—The information explains why Molly cannot have privacy, and later figures in the issue of how far she walks. C—Given the number of siblings she has, Molly seems justified in feeling it is hard to gain privacy.
8. C—That Jane's adventures are so well known suggests that she is legendary. *Incorrect answers:* A—This does not establish the legendary nature of Jane's character. B—This is only one example of the stories about Jane. D—same explanation as for A.

Answers With Explanations

1. **D**—Researching this issue would not provide more information on the life of *Homo erectus. Incorrect answers:* A—This topic would identify possible sources of food and competing hunters. B—This topic is directly about *Homo erectus.* C—This topic clearly addresses lifestyle.
2. **B**—The logical inference that nomads had to be able to produce fire since they moved about supports this claim. *Incorrect answers:* A—No details in the passage support this conclusion. C—The text states that when humans adopted fire is unknown. D—The text states that they must have had fire in order to survive.
3. **C**—Nomads move from place to place in search of food. *Incorrect answers:* A—Nomads still exist today. B—Nomads also gather foods; they do not only hunt. D—Human groups can lie nomadically.
4. **B**—The scientists found that the bones were burned at higher temperatures than would occur in natural fires. *Incorrect answers:* A—In some parts of prehistory, people did not use fire. C—This is the technique used to establish the fact, but not the fact. D—Scientists do not know if this is true.
5. **D**—Knowing this would help fix the use of fire in time. *Incorrect answers:* A—The kinds of animals hunted is not germane to the issue of use of fire. B—This might be helpful to know once the period of the Ice Age was known. C—If they knew how to use fire, the location of campsites is not relevant.
6. **B**—These statements support the idea that Ice Age humans needed fire and must have known how to create it. *Incorrect answers:* A—Without knowing that these animals were cooked by fire, this statement provides no support. C—This does not support the idea that Ice Age humans could create fire. D—same explanation as for C.

II. Informational Reading Skills

Directions: *Read the passage. Then, answer each question that follows.*

The Fire Makers

The use and production of fire is one of humanity's most distinctive traits. As long as 1.5 million years ago, one of our earliest ancestors—*Homo erectus*—may have been using fire. U.S. and South African researchers have found evidence of burnt bones in South Africa. Using a method called "electron spin resonance," the scientists have determined that the bones had been heated to high temperatures, leading them to believe that the bones were burnt in a hearth fire. According to Dr. Anne Skinner, "These bones could have been burnt in a forest fire or brush fire, but that's generally a low temperature flame. These had been heated to a very high temperature."

There is little evidence that to tell us exactly when humans learned this skill. Scientists have determined that prehistoric people commonly used caves as shelters and have found the remains of communal campfires. These sites include bones of extinct animals such as cave bears and saber-toothed tigers, indicating these sites are very old. *Using* fire, however, is not *making* fire, and whether the fires were created or were "stolen" from natural brush fires remains uncertain. Because carrying fire can be hazardous and fires can easily go out, though, it seems likely that nomadic hunter-gatherers must have learned to make fires themselves, as they did not remain in one place. Additionally, being without fire in Ice Age Europe would almost certainly have meant death; people would have had to know how to create their own fires to survive.

1. If you wanted to learn more about how *Homo erectus* lived, which of the following questions would *not* help to guide your research?

A. What other creatures existed 1.5 million years ago?
B. What did *Homo erectus* look like?
C. What foods did *Homo erectus* eat?
D. How does electron spin resonance work?

2. Which claim about fire is most strongly supported in this passage?

A. Fire originated in South Africa.
B. Ancient hunter-gatherers could create fire.
C. *Homo erectus* used fire.
D. European Ice Age hunters did not use fire.

3. Vocabulary in Context What is the *best* definition of the underlined word *nomadic*?

A. ancient
B. related to hunting
C. wandering
D. pre-human

4. Which detail provides support for the writer's claim that ancient people in South Africa used fire?

A. Prehistoric people commonly used fire.
B. Scientists determined that the bones had been burnt in hearth fires.
C. Scientists used "electron spin resonance."
D. Nomadic people worried about fire.

Reteach

Question	Instructional Pages to Reteach
1	1122
2	1222
4	1222
5	1222
6	1222

5. Which of the following questions would be helpful in locating more information on when early modern humans started to use fire?

A. What animals did modern prehistoric humans hunt?
B. Is there any evidence that humans 30,000 years ago created fire?
C. Where are most of the campsites for early humans located?
D. When did the Ice Age in which humans lived begin?

6. Which statement *best* supports the generalization that people in the Ice Age created fire?

A. Bones from extinct animals have been discovered at campsites.
B. Fire can easily be lost, and it was essential for survival in the Ice Age.
C. Earlier people had already developed the means to use fire.
D. Scientists discovered evidence that fire was used in South African caves.

III. Vocabulary

Directions: *Read each sentence. Choose the synonym for the italicized word.*

1. Juan's *conduct* toward his teacher is respectful.

A. resolution
B. principle
C. behavior
D. character

2. The judge's *integrity* was never called into question.

A. honesty
B. selflessness
C. courage
D. responsibility

3. Jared was *resolute* in his refusal to surrender.

A. courageous
B. unusual
C. determined
D. principled

4. Humor is Janet's most attractive *attribute*.

A. responsibility
B. legend
C. principle
D. characteristic

5. Paula's stubbornness seems to be an *inherent* characteristic.

A. conduct
B. resolute
C. inborn
D. attribute

6. The volunteer's *selfless* acts inspired others.

A. unselfish
B. responsible
C. individual
D. courageous

7. *Perseverance* is important for achieving goals.

A. luck
B. sacrifice
C. persistence
D. honesty

8. King Arthur's *courage* in battle is legendary.

A. sacrifice
B. principle
C. valor
D. fear

GO ON

Answers With Explanations

1. C—The sentence describes how Juan acts. *Incorrect answers:* A—A resolution is a commitment to do something, not behavior. B—A principle is a value on which behavior might be based, but not the behavior. D—Character refers to the traits one possesses, not the actions one performs.
2. A—Someone with integrity is honest. *Incorrect answers:* B—*Selflessness* means "putting others first," not "honesty." C—Courage refers to bravery. D—Responsibility measures acting according to duty.
3. C—Resolution shows determination. *Incorrect answers:* A—While a refusal to surrender might be courageous, Jared's resolution shows his strength of will. B—Jared might be rare in this quality, but that is not what *resolution* means. D—Jared might be standing on principle, but his determination is what matters.
4. D—An attribute is a facet of someone's character. *Incorrect answers:* A—Responsibilities are duties, not character traits. B—A legend is a story about someone, not a character trait. C—A principle is a value, not a character trait.
5. C—Something inherent is central to a person's character. *Incorrect answers:* A—*Conduct* means "behavior," not "inborn." B—*Resolute* means "determined," not "inborn." D—*Attribute* means the same as *characteristic* and cannot modify it.
6. A—A selfless act involves sacrificing oneself for others. *Incorrect answers:* B—Acting responsibly generally does not offer the inspiration that selflessness does. C—*Individual* means "alone," not "unselfish." D—*Courageous* means "brave," not "unselfish."
7. C—Someone who perseveres persists despite obstacles. *Incorrect answers:* A—Perseverance is a character trait; luck is external. B—*Sacrifice* means "giving something up," not "determination." D—Some people achieve goals dishonestly.

Answers continued

8. C—Valor is another word for *bravery*. *Incorrect answers:* A—*Sacrifice* means "giving something up," not "bravery." B—A principle is a value, of which valor might be one. D—Some people show fear in battle, but usually not legendary heroes.

Reteach

Question	Instructional Pages to Reteach
1	1046–1047
2	1046–1047
3	1046–1047
4	1046–1047
5	1046–1047
7	1046–1047
8	1046–1047

ASSESS

Answers

Answers With Explanations

1. **A**—You must check for tags first, and then compare the tags to the list. *Incorrect answers:* B—Sentence 1 is important. C—Sentence 1 should come first as it describes a condition that must be met before any actions are taken. D—Sentence 3 is an important step.
2. **D**—The informality of this sentence violates the professional tone. *Incorrect answers:* A—The sentence is consistent with a professional tone. B—same explanation as for A. C—same explanation as for A.
3. **A**—The addition will give the statement the needed subject and verb. *Incorrect answers:* B—The statement would still lack a subject and verb. C—The statement would remain a fragment. D—The two sentences address different steps and should remain separate.
4. **B**—The list that follows details the activities. *Incorrect answers:* A—This placement would separate subject from verb. C—This placement would incorrectly break up the list. D—Some punctuation is needed after "activities."
5. **B**—The change would unite the two actions to perform at the end of the event. *Incorrect answers:* A—Checking name tags does not logically flow from helping children reboard the bus. C—A comma after the introductory phrase is correct. D—The original is choppy.
6. **A**—This version shows the proper sequence of events. *Incorrect answers:* B—This version is a compound, not a complex, sentence C—This version is also a compound sentence, and it puts the actions out of sequence. D—This version is also a compound sentence as well a having a brusque tone.

Reteach

Question	Instructional Pages to Reteach
1	1148
2	1186
3	1149
4	1218
5	1149
6	1088

IV. Writing and Language Conventions

Technical Document

Directions: *Read the passage. Then, answer each question that follows.*

Guidelines for Volunteer Counselors

(1) All children will be pre-registered. (2) When they arrive at the facility, escort them directly to Room 12B. (3) Check tags against the master list. (4) First, make sure each child has a name tag. (5) Once you organize the children, bring them to the buses. (6) List of activities to conduct while on the bus. (7) When you arrive at the site park rangers will have lighted the campfire. (8) Adult counselors will be present to conduct activities singing songs, learning rhymes, and playing games. (9) Your job is to see that no child wanders away from the site or gets too near the fire. (10) At end of event, help children reboard the bus; check name tags against the list. (11) Arrive at the facility. (12) Make sure each parent signs his or her child out of camp. (13) You'll have a total blast!

1. Which revision should be made to this passage to improve its **organization**?

A. Switch sentences 3 and 4.
B. Delete sentence 1.
C. Switch sentences 1 and 2.
D. Delete sentence 3.

2. Which sentence should be deleted to maintain a consistent professional **tone?**

A. sentence 1
B. sentence 3
C. sentence 9
D. sentence 13

3. What is the *best* way to correct the **fragment** in sentence 6?

A. Add "You will have a" to the beginning.
B. Change "to conduct" to "conducting."
C. Delete "on the."
D. Combine sentences 6 and 7.

4. Where should a **colon** be added in sentence 8?

A. after "counselors"
B. after "activities"
C. after "rhymes"
D. Leave as is.

5. In what way should sentence 10 be revised?

A. Replace the semicolon with the word "so."
B. Replace the semicolon with the word "and."
C. Add another semicolon after "event."
D. Leave as is.

6. What is the *best* way to combine sentences 11 and 12 into a single **complex sentence?**

A. After you arrive at the facility, make sure each parent signs his or her child out of camp.
B. Arrive back at the facility and make sure each parent signs his or her child out of camp.
C. Make sure that each parent signs his or her child out of camp, but you can only do that after you arrive back.
D. Arrive back, find parent, and sign child out.

Differentiated Instruction for Universal Access

Strategy for Special Needs Students

Review skills and warm up for the test by walking students through item 6. Ask a volunteer to read item 6 aloud. Call on students to define a complex sentence. (A sentence with at least one dependent and independent clause.) Next, guide students in eliminating incorrect choices.

- **A**—"After you arrive at the facility" is a dependent clause; the remainder of the sentence is an independent clause.
- **B**—The sentence has two independent clauses. (Eliminate.)
- **C**—The sentence has two independent clauses and puts the actions in reverse order. (Eliminate.)
- **D**—The sentence has three independent clauses and an unfriendly tone as well. (Eliminate.)

Guide students in seeing that **A** is the best choice. Have them complete the remaining items, encouraging them to apply a similar strategy to each. First, define key terms in the prompt and then eliminate incorrect choices.

Exposition: Comparison-and-Contrast Essay

Directions: *Read the passage. Then, answer each question that follows.*

(1) Both theater and the movies have advantages. (2) In the theater, the experience is immediate. (3) In the theater, living human beings speak in real time. (4) A flat screen and speakers cannot compete with the electricity of live actors. (5) Most theaters do not permit eating during the performance. (6) No rustling bags and crunching popcorn can distract the audience.

(7) Movies offer a wider range of setting, action, and special effects. (8) The movie screen is so big that the annoyance of audience members coming and going is minor. (9) As you can see live theater or movies is a matter of personal taste. (10) Crunching popcorn can be a distraction, but many people enjoy the extra pleasure of popcorn and soft drinks.

1. Which title would you add to this essay to best convey its **purpose?**
   - **A.** Real Life, Real Actors, Real Experience
   - **B.** Choosing Activities You Enjoy
   - **C.** Live Theater or the Movies?
   - **D.** Why I Love Movies

2. Which sentences should be combined to prevent choppiness?
   - **A.** sentences 1 and 2
   - **B.** sentences 2 and 3
   - **C.** sentences 3 and 4
   - **D.** sentences 4 and 5

3. Which sentences should be reversed so the passage is **organized** more clearly?
   - **A.** sentences 6 and 7
   - **B.** sentences 7 and 8
   - **C.** sentences 8 and 9
   - **D.** sentences 9 and 10

4. Where should a **comma** be added in sentence 9?
   - **A.** After "you."
   - **B.** After "see."
   - **C.** After "movies."
   - **D.** Leave as is.

5. Which **transitional word** should be used to combine sentences 5 and 6?
   - **A.** nevertheless
   - **B.** therefore
   - **C.** however
   - **D.** similarly

Writing for Assessment

6. Write an essay in which you **compare** two activities you enjoyed when you were young. Explain why you would choose one over the other. **Support** your claims using **details.**

STOP

Reteach

Question	Instructional Pages to Reteach
1	1249
2	1247
3	1244
4	1186
5	1244
6	1242–1244, 1246

Benchmark

Reteach skills as indicated by students' performance, following the Reteach charts on pp. 1257–1261 to administer the end-of-unit **Benchmark Test** (*Unit 6 Resources*, pp. 226–232). Follow the **Interpretation Guide** for the test (*Unit 6 Resources*, pp. 233–238) to assign reteaching pages as necessary in the *Reading Kit.* Use **Success Tracker** online to automatically assign these pages.

Answers With Explanations

1. C—Since the author asserts the superiority of neither art form, this title is appropriate. *Incorrect answers:* A—This title only refers to one art form, making it undesirable. B—This title is so general as to be unsuitable. D—same explanation as for A.
2. D—Since Sentence 4 seems to be a non sequitur, combining these sentences would be useful. *Incorrect answers:* A—Sentence 1, which sets up the essay, needs to remain separate. B—While these sentences could be combined, joining 4 and 5 is preferable. C—The two sentences address different topics.
3. D—Sentence 9 should conclude the essay. *Incorrect answers:* A—Sentence 6 belongs in the first paragraph, and Sentence 7 belongs in the second. B—Sentence 7, which introduces movies, belongs first. C—Sentence 9 belongs at the end, not near the beginning of the paragraph.
4. B—This placement would correctly punctuate the introductory phrase. *Incorrect answers:* A—This placement would incorrectly interrupt subject and verb in a clause. C—same explanation as for A. D—The comma is needed.
5. B—The effect in Sentence 6 is a logical result of the cause in Sentence 5. *Incorrect answers:* A—The lack of noise is because of the absence of food, not in spite of it. C—same explanation as for A. D—The lack of noise is a result, not a comparable phenomenon.

Writing for Assessment

6. Students' essays should use a correct comparison-and-contrast organization and have supporting details. Students may create a comparison-and-contrast chart to organize their ideas before writing.

PHLit Online!

The **Benchmark Tests** and **Success Tracker** are available online at **www.PHLitOnline.com.**

Resources

Glossary

GLOSSARY

Big Question vocabulary appears in **blue type**. High-utility Academic Vocabulary is **underlined.**

A

abruptly (uh BRUHPT lee) *adv.* happening suddenly; unexpectedly

abysmal (uh BIHZ muhl) *adj.* immeasurably bad or extreme; terrible

accomplices (uh KOM plihs uhz) *n.* people who help another person commit a crime

adamant (AD uh mant) *adj.* not giving in; unyielding; firm

adapt (uh DAPT) *v.* change or adjust

adept (uh DEHPT) *adj.* expert; highly skilled

adulation (aj uh LAY shuhn) *n.* high or excessive praise; intense admiration

adversaries (AD vuhr sehr eez) *n.* opponents

adversity (ad VUR suh tee) *n.* state of difficulty or misfortune

affable (AF uh buhl) *adj.* pleasant; friendly

affront (uh FRUHNT) *n.* open insult

aggregate (AG ruh giht) *n.* a group of distinct things gathered into a whole; a sum

aggrieved (uh GREEVD) *adj.* wronged; suffering grief or injury

allay (uh LAY) *v.* relieve; lessen; calm

alleviate (uh LEE vee ayt) *v.* to lighten; relieve

amenable (uh MEE nuh buhl) *adj.* responsive; open

amiably (AY mee uh blee) *adv.* in a cheerful, friendly way

anguish (ANG gwihsh) *n.* extreme suffering, as from grief or pain

anticipate (an TIHS uh payt) *v.* look forward to

apathy (AP uh thee) *n.* lack of interest or emotion

apprehension (ap rih HEHN shuhn) *n.* anxious feeling; fear

arable (AR uh buhl) *adj.* suitable for growing crops

ardent (AHR duhnt) *adj.* intensely enthusiastic; devoted

aspirations (as puh RAY shuhnz) *n.* strong ambitions

assuage (uh SWAYJ) *v.* lessen (pain or distress); satisfy (thirst or hunger)

attributes (AT rihb yoots) *n.* characteristics of a person or thing

audaciously (aw DAY shuhs lee) *adv.* in a bold manner

augmented (awg MEHNT ihd) *adj.* made greater; enhanced

august (aw GUHST) *adj.* impressive; majestic

awareness (uh WAIR nuhs) *n.* having knowledge

B

background (BAK grownd) *n.* conditions that surround or come before something

bias (BY uhs) *n.* point of view one has before the facts are known

blemished (BLEHM ihsht) *adj.* damaged; spoiled

bore (bohr) *v.* carried

brandished (BRAN dihsht) *v.* showed, waved, or shook in a threatening or triumphant manner

brazen (BRAY zuhn) *adj.* shameless; bold

buffer (BUHF uhr) *v.* lessen a shock; cushion

C

cajoling (kuh JOHL ihng) *n.* coaxing with flattery

calamity (kuh LAM uh tee) *n.* terrible misfortune; disaster

candid (KAN dihd) *adj.* honest; direct

canopied (KAN uh peed) *adj.* covered by a cloth suspended from poles or a framework

catalyst (KAT uh lihst) *n.* person or thing that triggers an event or action

cessation (seh SAY shuhn) *n.* halt; stopping

change (chaynj) *v.* become different; transform

character (KAR ihk tuhr) *n.* moral strength; self-discipline

chastisement (chas TYZ muhnt) *n.* severe criticism; punishment

choleric (KOL uhr ihk) *adj.* quick tempered; inclined to anger

circuit (SUR kiht) *n.* act of going around something; route

clenching (KLEHNCH ihng) *v.* closing; holding tightly

clustering (KLUHS tuhr ihng) *adj.* gathering; forming in a group

commemorates (kuh MEHM uh rayts) *v.* honors a memory

commences (kuh MEHNS ez) *v.* begins

commiserate (kuh MIHZ uh rayt) *v.* sympathize with; show sorrow for

comprehend (kom prih HEHND) *v.* grasp mentally; understand

compromise (KOM pruh myz) *n.* agreement where both sides give something up

compulsory (kuhm PUHL suhr ee) *adj.* required; mandatory

comrade (KOM rad) *n.* close companion; friend

concession (kuhn SEHSH uhn) *n.* act of granting or giving; allowance

concrete (KON kreet) *adj.* something specific or tangible

condemn (kuhn DEHM) *v.* disapprove of; pass unfavorable judgment on

condemned (kuhn DEHMD) *v.* declared to be guilty of wrongdoings; convicted

conduct (KON duhkt) *n.* the way a person acts; behavior

configuration (kuhn FIHG yuh RAY shuhn) *n.* arrangement of parts; pattern

confirm (kuhn FURM) *v.* establish the truth or correctness of something

confounded (kon FOWND ihd) *adj.* made to feel confused

confrontation (kon fruhn TAY shuhn) *n.* clashing of forces or ideas

confusion (kuhn FYOO zhuhn) *n.* state of disorder or distraction

conjured (KON juhrd) *v.* summoned as if by magic

connection (kuh NEHK shuhn) *n.* relationship between things

consigned (kuhn SYND) *v.* handed over; gave up or delivered

conspicuous (kuhn SPIHK yu uhs) *adj.* easy to see

constricting (kuhn STRIHKT ihng) *adj.* preventing freedom of movement; limiting

contempt (kuhn TEHMPT) *n.* scorn; the attitude of someone who looks down on something or someone else

contested (KON tehst uhd) *v.* tried to disprove or invalidate something; disputed

context (KON tehkst) *n.* environment or situation in which something is found

context (KON tehkst) *n.* circumstances that form the setting of an event

contrive (kuhn TRYV) *v.* to bring about; manage

convalesce (kon vuh LEHS) *v.* to regain strength and health

converge (kuhn VURJ) *v.* to come together

convey (kuhn VAY) *v.* communicate or make known

convoluted (kon vuh LOOT uhd) *adj.* twisted in a complicated way

counsel (KOWN suhl) *n.* advice; discussion

countenance (KOWN tuh nuhns) *n.* face; the look of a face, showing a person's nature

courage (KUR ihj) *n.* willingness to deal with something dangerous

credulity (kruh DOO luh tee) *n.* tendency to believe too readily

customarily (kuhs tuh MEHR ih lee) *adv.* usually; by habit or tradition

D

debate (dih BAYT) *v.* argue or discuss

debut (day BYOO) *n.* first public appearance

decorum (dih KAWR uhm) *n.* behavior that is polite and is correct for an occasion

decrepitude (dih KREHP uh tood) *n.* feebleness; condition of being worn out by age or illness

deference (DEHF uhr uhns) *n.* a yielding to the ideas, wishes, and so on of another

deficiency (dih FIHSH uhn see) *n.* lack of something essential

deflects (dih FLEHKTS) *v.* wards off; turns aside

deftness (dehft nehs) *n.* skillfulness

defunct (dih FUHNGKT) *adj.* no longer in use or existence; dead

dejectedly (dih JEHK tihd lee) *adv.* in a depressed way

delusion (dih LOO zhuhn) *n.* an erroneous belief that is held despite evidence to the contrary

demeanor (dih MEE nuhr) *n.* way of conducting oneself; behavior

derisively (dih RY sihv lee) *adv.* in a mocking and ridiculing manner

derived (dih RYVD) *v.* reached by reasoning

desolate (DEHS uh liht) *adj.* empty; solitary

destitute (DEHS tuh toot) *adj.* lacking the basic necessities of life; poverty-stricken

determination (dih TUR muh NAY shuhn) *n.* firmness of purpose

detestable (dee TEHS tuh buhl) *adj.* deserving hate or scorn; offensive

dexterous (DEHKS tuhr uhs) *adj.* having or showing mental or physical skill; deft

differentiate (dihf uh REHN shee ayt) *v.* distinguish between

dignity (DIHG nuh tee) *n.* quality of deserving respect and honor; self-respect

dilapidated (duh LAP uh dayt ihd) *adj.* shabby; broken down

diligence (DIHL uh juhns) *n.* constant, careful effort

dimpled (DIHM puhld) *adj.* marked with small hollows or indentations

dingy (DIHN jee) *adj.* dirty-looking; shabby

dire (dyr) *adj.* urgent; terrible; calling for quick action

discern (duh ZURN) *v.* tell the difference between two or more things; perceive

disconsolate (dihs KON suh liht) *adj.* so unhappy that nothing brings comfort; miserable

discord (DIHS kawrd) *n.* conflict; disagreement

discourse (DIHS kawrs) *v.* speak (on a topic) formally and at length

discourse (DIHS kawrs) *n.* ongoing communication of ideas and information

disdain (dihs DAYN) *n.* disgust for something or someone; scorn

disembarked (DIHS ehm BAHRKT) *v.* left a ship to go ashore

disparagement (dihs PAR ihj muhnt) *n.* comments expressing a low opinion of or lack of respect for

disreputable (dihs REHP yuh tuh buhl) *adj.* not respectable; having or deserving a bad reputation

dissent (dih SEHNT) *n.* refusal to accept a common belief or opinion; disagreement

distinct (dihs TIHNGKT) *adj.* clearly different; separate

distortion (dihs TAWR shuhn) *n.* anything that shows something in an untrue way

dogged (DAWG ihd) *adj.* stubborn

E

earnest (UR nihst) *adj.* serious and intense; not joking

eased (eezd) *v.* freed from pain or trouble; lessened

ebony (EHB uh nee) *adj.* black

edict (EE dihkt) *n.* public order; decree

edifying (EHD uh fy ihng) *adj.* instructive in such a way as to improve morally or intellectually

efface (uh FAYS) *v.* rub or blot out

elude (ih LOOD) *v.* avoid; escape by quickness or cleverness

elusive (ih LOO sihv) *adj.* hard to grasp mentally

emanating (EHM uh nayt ihng) *v.* coming forth, as from a source

embodied (ehm BOD eed) *v.* gave form to; made concrete

emigrants (EHM uh gruhnts) *n.* people who leave their country or region to settle elsewhere

emotion (ih MOH shuhn) *n.* strong feeling, such as love

empathy (EHM puh thee) *n.* sharing in another person's feelings

encroaching (ehn KROHCH ihng) *adj.* intruding on, especially in a gradual way

endeavored (ehn DEHV uhrd) *v.* tried to achieve a set goal

endure (ehn DUR) *v.* hold up under pain or hardship

engaging (ehn GAYJ ihng) *adj.* attractive; pleasant

enlighten (ehn LY tuhn) *v.* make clear through knowledge

enthralls (ehn THRAWLZ) *v.* captivates; fascinates

entreated (ehn TREET uhd) *v.* begged; pleaded with

ephemeral (ih FEHM uhr uhl) *adj.* short-lived

equilibrium (ee kwuh LIHB ree uhm) *n.* a state of balance

esoteric (ehs uh TEHR ihk) *adj.* beyond the understanding or knowledge of most people

estranged (ehs TRAYNJD) *adj.* kept apart; in the condition of having had affection turn into indifference or hostility

eternal (ih TUR nuhl) *adj.* without beginning or end; everlasting

evaluate (ih VAL yoo ayt) *v.* determine the worth of something

evidence (EHV uh duhns) *n.* information that indicates whether something is true or valid

evoking (ih VOHK ihng) *v.* to draw forth emotions or responses

evolve (ih VOLV) *v.* develop through gradual changes

exorbitant (ehg ZAWR buh tuhnt) *adj.* going beyond what is reasonable; excessive

expectations (ehks pehk TAY shuhnz) *n.* something looked forward to

explanation (ehks pluh NAY shuhn) *n.* clarifying statement

expound (ehk SPOWND) *v.* explain in detail

extolled (ehk STOHLD) *adj.* praised

extricating (EHKS truh kayt ihng) *n.* setting free; removing from a difficult situation

exuberance (ehg ZOO buhr uhns) *n.* good health; high spirits

F

falteringly (FAWL tuhr ihng lee) *adv.* spoken hesitatingly or with a wavering voice

fate (fayt) *n.* destiny; what happens to a person or thing; final outcome

fathom (FATH uhm) *v.* understand thoroughly

fawned (fawnd) *v.* flattered; act with excessive concern for the wishes and moods of another, as a servant might

flourishes (FLUR ihsh uhz) *v.* grows vigorously; thrives

fluttered (FLUHT uhrd) *v.* flapped or vibrated rapidly

foe (foh) *n.* enemy

forbore (fawr BAWR) *v.* prevented oneself from doing something; refrained from

foreboding (fawr BOHD ihng) *n.* a feeling that something bad will happen; premonition

formidable (FAWR muh duh buhl) *adj.* causing fear or dread

fraud (frawd) *n.* deceit; trickery

furtively (FUR tihv lee) *adj.* secretively; sneakily; stealthily

futile (FYOO tuhl) *adj.* not successful; useless

G

gauge (gayj) *v.* measure the size, amount, extent, or capacity of

grave (grayv) *adj.* very serious and worrying

grimacing (GRIHM ihs ihng) *v.* making a twisted face showing disgust or pain

growth (grohth) *n.* the process of developing

H

haphazardly (hap HAZ uhrd lee) *adv.* in an unplanned or a disorganized way

haste (hayst) *n.* quickness of motion; rapidity

heedless (HEED lihs) *adj.* careless; thoughtless

history (HIHS tuhr ee) *n.* account of what has happened

honor (ON uhr) *n.* strong sense of right and wrong

humble (HUHM buhl) *adj.* showing an awareness of one's shortcomings; modest

hypocrisy (hih POK ruh see) *n.* a pretending to be what one is not, or to feel what one does not feel

I

idealistic (y dee uh LIHS tihk) *adj.* representing things as they should be rather than how they are

identity (y DEHN tuh tee) *n.* qualities of a person that make up who they are

idle (Y duhl) *adj.* useless; not busy

ignorance (IHG nuhr uhns) *n.* lack of knowledge or education

immaterial (ihm uh TIHR ee uhl) *adj.* not consisting of matter

imminent (IHM uh nuhnt) *adj.* about to happen

impeded (ihm PEED uhd) *v.* blocked; obstructed

impediments (ihm PEHD uh muhnts) *n.* things that slow something or someone down or that get in the way; barriers

impending (ihm PEHN dihng) *adj.* about to happen

imperceptibly (ihm puhr SEHP tuh blee) *adv.* so slowly or slightly as to be barely noticeable

imperiously (ihm PIHR ee uhs lee) *adv.* arrogantly

impervious (ihm PUR vee uhs) *adj.* not affected by (used with to)

impetuosity (ihm pehch oo OS uh tee) *n.* quality of acting suddenly, with great force and little thought; rashness

impression (ihm PREHSH uhn) *n.* an effect produced on the mind

improbable (ihm PROB uh buhl) *adj.* not likely to happen or be true

inaudibly (ihn AW duh blee) *adv.* in a way that cannot be heard

incessant (ihn SEHS uhnt) *adj.* not stopping; constant

incredulity (ihn kruh DOO luh tee) *n.* unwillingness to believe

indigence (IHN duh juhns) *n.* poverty

indignant (ihn DIHG nuhnt) *adj.* feeling anger, especially at injustice

indignation (IHN dihg NAY shuhn) *n.* anger that is a reaction to injustice or meanness

individual (ihn duh VIHJ oo uhl) *adj.* relating to a single person or thing

indulgence (ihn DUHL juhns) *n.* leniency; readiness to tolerate or forgive bad behavior

inexorably (ihn EHK suhr uh blee) *adv.* without the possibility of being delayed or stopped; unalterable

infinite (IHN fuh niht) *adj.* beyond measure or comprehension; endless

infirm (ihn FURM) *adj.* weak; feeble

infirmity (ihn FUR muh tee) *n.* weakness; physical defect

influence (IHN floo uhns) *n.* the power of people to change others

ingenuity (ihn juh NOO uh tee) *n.* cleverness

ingratiating (ihn GRAY shee ayt ihng) *adj.* acting in a way intended to win someone's favor

inhabit (ihn HAB iht) *v.* live in

inherent (ihn HIHR uhnt) *adj.* existing naturally in something

inheritance (ihn HEHR uh tuhns) *n.* gift handed down to a later generation in a family

innuendo (ihn yoo EHN doh) *n.* indirect insult or accusation; insinuation

insight (ihn syt) *n.* clear idea of the nature of things

instinct (IHN stihngkt) *n.* an inborn pattern of behavior, as opposed to a learned skill

insurrection (ihn suh REHK shuhn) *n.* rebellion

integrity (ihn TEHG ruh tee) *n.* willingness to stand by moral principles

interact (ihn tuhr AKT) *v.* relate to one another; affect another

interminable (ihn TUR muh nuh buhl) *adj.* seemingly endless

interpretation (ihn tur pruh TAY shuhn) *n.* explanation of the meaning of something

interred (ihn TURD) *v.* buried (said of a dead body)

intertidal (ihn tuhr TY duhl) *adj.* pertaining to a shore zone bounded by the levels of low and high tide

intervened (ihn tuhr VEEND) *v.* came between

intrigues (ihn TREEGZ) *n.* plots; schemes

irascible (ih RAS uh buhl) *adj.* irritable

irreproachable (ihr ih PROH chuh buhl) *adj.* above criticism

irretrievable (IHR ih TREE vuh buhl) *adj.* impossible to regain or recover

isolation (y suh LAY shuhn) *n.* being alone or set apart

itinerary (y TIHN uh rehr ee) *n.* route; travel plan

J

jauntiness (JAWN tee nuhs) *n.* carefree, easy attitude

jeered (jihrd) *v.* made fun of; mocked; taunted

jurisdiction (jur ihs DIHK shuhn) *n.* sphere of authority or power

K

keenest (KEEN uhst) *adj.* sharpest; most cutting

knowledge (NOL ihj) *n.* awareness and understanding of information

L

lacquered (LAK uhrd) *adj.* covered in tough, sticky varnish

lamentation (lam uhn TAY shuhn) *n.* act of crying out in grief; wailing; weeping

language (LANG gwihj) *n.* system used for expressing or communicating; word choice

languid (LANG gwihd) *adj.* without energy

lavished (LAV ihsht) *v.* gave with extreme generosity

lease (lees) *n.* contract by which something is rented for a specified period of time; rental

legacies (LEHG uh seez) *n.* money, property, or position left in a will to someone

legendary (LEHJ uhn DEHR ee) *adj.* extraordinary; memorable

livid (LIHV ihd) *adj.* discolored, as by a bruise; red with anger

lofty (LAWF tee) *adj.* elevated in rank or character; noble

looming (LOOM ihng) *adj.* appearing unclearly but in a threatening form; threatening to occur

lowly (LOH lee) *adj.* humble; of low rank

lucidity (loo SIHD uh tee) *n.* quality of being readily understood

lucrative (LOO kruh tihv) *adj.* producing wealth; profitable

lunar (LOO nuhr) *adj.* of the moon

M

maligned (muh LYND) *adj.* spoken ill of

manifestations (man uh fehs TAY shuhnz) *n.* appearances; forms

manipulate (muh NIHP yuh layt) *v.* control by use of influence, often in an unfair way

manipulated (muh NIHP yuh layt uhd) *v.* managed or controlled through clever moves

marginal (MAHR juh nuhl) *adj.* at, on, or near the edge

meager (MEE guhr) *adj.* of poor quality or small amount

meaning (MEE nihng) *n.* significance of something

meditates (MEHD uh tayts) *v.* thinks deeply

melancholy (MEHL uhn kol ee) *adj.* sad and depressed

millennial (muh LEHN ee uhl) *adj.* of 1,000 years

mirth (murth) *n.* joyfulness; merriment

misconstrued (mihs kuhn STROOD) *v.* misinterpreted

misinterpret (mihs ihn TUR priht) *v.* not understand correctly

modified (MOD uh fyd) *v.* changed; altered slightly

monotonously (muh NOT uh nuhs lee) *adv.* in a dull, unvarying way

motive (MOH tihv) *n.* something that causes a person to act in a certain way

multitudes (MUHL tuh toodz) *n.* large number of people or things

mutable (MYOO tuh buhl) *adj.* changeable

N

negotiate (nih GOH shee ayt) *v.* bargain with the hope of reaching an agreement

nevertheless (nehv uhr thuh LEHS) *adv.* in spite of that; however

nimbly (NIHM buh lee) *adv.* in a quick, easy, light way; with agility

nomadic (noh MAD ihk) *adj.* moving from place to place; without a permanent home

nonchalantly (NON shuh luhnt lee) *adv.* casually; indifferently

O

objective (uhb JEHK tihv) *adj.* not dependent on another's point of view

oblivious (uh BLIHV ee uhs) *adj.* unaware

obscured (uhb SKYURD) *v.* made dark; blocked from view; hid

oppose (uh POHZ) *v.* to set against; disagree with

oppressive (uh PREHS ihv) *adj.* causing great discomfort; distressing

oratory (AWR uh tawr ee) *n.* act of public speaking; strategies used in such speaking

overcome (oh vuhr KUHM) *v.* to master or prevail over

P

pallor (PAL uhr) *n.* lack of color; unnatural paleness

paradox (PAR uh doks) *n.* a statement or situation that seems contradictory

paranoia (par uh NOY uh) *n.* mental disorder characterized by delusions

perception (puhr SEHP shuhn) *n.* the way one understands the world through the senses

perpetually (puhr PEHCH oo uhl ee) *adv.* continuing forever; constantly

persevere (PUR suh VIHR) *v.* continue despite opposition; persist

perspective (puhr SPEHK tihv) *n.* the way one sees things; viewpoint

petulantly (PEHCH uh luhnt lee) *adv.* in a manner that expresses impatience or irritation

piety (PY uh tee) *n.* loyalty and devotion to family, the divine, or some other object of respect

piqued (peekt) *adj.* annoyed or upset

plague (playg) *v.* pester; harass; torment

plausibility (PLAW zuh BIHL uh tee) *n.* believability; seeming truth

plight (plyt) *n.* distressing situation

poignant (POY nuhnt) *adj.* emotionally moving; piercing

portentous (pawr TEHN tuhs) *adj.* ominous; giving signs of evil to come

presume (prih ZOOM) *v.* rely too much on; take advantage of

presumptuous (prih ZUHMP choo uhs) *adj.* overstepping appropriate bounds; too bold

pretense (prih TEHNS) *n.* a pretending; a false show of something

principles (PRIHN suh puhlz) *n.* rules for right conduct; basics

prodigious (pruh DIHJ uhs) *adj.* of great size or power

profuse (pruh FYOOS) *adj.* giving or pouring forth freely, often to excess; plentiful

progress (PROG rehs) *n.* development; improvement

prostrate (PROS trayt) *adj.* lying flat

prudent (PROO duhnt) *adj.* exercising sound judgment; cautious

purified (PYUR uh fyd) *v.* rid of impurities or pollution; made pure

Q

quench (kwehnch) *v.* satisfy; to fulfill the needs or desires of something

question (KWEHS chuhn) *v.* express uncertainty about; ask

R

radical (RAD uh kuhl) *adj.* extreme change

rash (rash) *adj.* too hasty in speech or action; reckless

rave (rayv) *v.* to talk incoherently or wildly

reality (ree AL uh tee) *n.* quality of being true to life

reapers (REE puhrz) *n.* people who gather or harvest grain

reciprocity (rehs uh PROS uh tee) *n.* relations of exchange; interdependence

reconciliation (rehk uhn sihl ee AY shuhn) *n.* restoring friendship and harmony

reflect (rih FLEHKT) *v.* think seriously about something

refuse (REHF yoos) *n.* waste; trash

rejoiced (rih JOYST) *v.* showed happiness

rejuvenation (rih joo vuh NAY shuhn) *n.* making new, youthful, or energetic again; revitalization

relent (rih LEHNT) *v.* become less strong, severe, or intense; ease up

relish (REHL ihsh) *n.* enjoyment

renounced (rih NOWNST) *v.* gave up formally

repertoire (REHP uhr twahr) *n.* stock of works, such as songs, that a performer is prepared to present

replenished (rih PLEHN ihsht) *v.* made complete or full again

replication (rehp luh KAY shuhn) *n.* duplicate; reproduction

resolute (REHZ uh loot) *adj.* showing a fixed purpose

resolution (rehz uh LOO shuhn) *n.* strong determination; a plan or decision

resolve (rih ZOLV) *v.* reach a conclusion or decision

respond (rih SPOND) *v.* answer

responsibility (rih spon suh BIHL uh tee) *n.* having to answer to someone or something else; being accountable for success or failure

reveling (REHV uhl ihng) *v.* taking great pleasure; celebrating

reverence (REHV uhr uhns) *n.* a feeling of deep respect, love, or awe

revise (rih VYZ) *v.* reconsider; modify

rudiments (ROO duh muhnts) *n.* basics; slight beginnings

S

sacrifice (SAK ruh fys) *v.* give up

sated (SAYT uhd) *adj.* satisfied; provided with more than enough

scrutinized (SKROO tuh nyzd) *v.* examined carefully

secular (SEHK yuh luhr) *adj.* of worldly, as opposed to religious, matters

self-expression (sehlf ehk SPREHSH uhn) *n.* sharing one's personality or emotions

selflessness (SEHLF lihs nuhs) *n.* being devoted to others' interests rather than one's own

self-sufficiency (sehlf suh FIHSH uhn see) *n.* independence

sententiously (sehn TEHN shuhs lee) *adv.* in a way that shows excessive fondness for wise sayings; in lecturing tones

serenity (suh REHN uh tee) *n.* state of calm or peace

servile (SUR vuhl) *adj.* slavelike; humbly submissive to authority

silhouette (sihl oo EHT) *n.* outline drawing filled in with a solid color

simulating (SIHM yuh layt ihng) *v.* giving the appearance of

skeptically (SKEHP tuh kuhl ee) *adv.* with doubt; questioningly

slumbering (SLUHM buhr ihng) *adj.* sleeping

sonorous (suh NAWR uhs) *adj.* having a rich or impressive sound

spare (spair) *adj.* lean; thin

spectacle (SPEHK tuh kuhl) *n.* strange or remarkable sight

squalid (SKWOL ihd) *adj.* foul; unclean

staidness (STAYD nuhs) *n.* state of being settled; calm

stance (stans) *n.* the way one stands, especially the placement of the feet

stark (stahrk) *adj.* bare; harsh

staunch (stawnch) *adj.* steadfast; loyal

steady (STEHD ee) *adj.* firm; sure in movement

stereotype (STEHR ee uh typ) *n.* overly broad and often incorrect notion of a group

stickler (STIHK luhr) *n.* person who insists on strict obedience to rules or standards

stifle (STY fuhl) *v.* smother; hold back

stipulates (STIHP yuh layts) *v.* includes specifically as part of an agreement

strife (stryf) *n.* struggle; conflict

struggle (STRUHG uhl) *v.* face difficulty

subdued (suhb DOOD) *adj.* quiet; lacking energy

subjective (suhb JEHK tihv) *adj.* based on or influenced by a person's feelings or point of view

subordinate (suh BAWR duh niht) *adj.* below another in importance or rank

subtle (SUH tuhl) *adj.* fine; delicate

subversion (suhb VUR zhuhn) *n.* activity meant to overthrow something established; rebellion

successive (suhk SEHS ihv) *adj.* following one after another in sequence

succinct (suhk SIHNGKT) *adj.* clearly and briefly stated

sullen (SUHL uhn) *adj.* gloomy and showing resentment

sumptuous (SUHMP choo uhs) *adj.* costly; lavish

supercilious (soo puhr SIHL ee uhs) *adj.* expressing an attitude of superiority; contemptuous

surmise (suhr MYZ) *n.* guess; idea based on evidence that is not conclusive

surpassed (suhr PAST) *v.* went beyond; excelled

T

tactile (TAK tuhl) *adj.* related to the sense of touch

tangible (TAN juh buhl) *adj.* able to be touched; actual

temperate (TEHM puhr iht) *adj.* mild; kept within limits

tempering (TEHM puhr ihng) *n.* changing to make more suitable, usually by mixing with something

tentative (TEHN tuh tihv) *adj.* hesitant; not confident

tenuous (TEHN yoo uhs) *adj.* not strong

threshold (THREHSH ohld) *n.* the bottom of a doorway; entrance or a point of beginning

titanic (ty TAN ihk) *adj.* powerful; of great size

toil (toyl) *n.* hard, tiring work

trace (trays) *n.* tiny amount; hint

transcends (tran SEHNDZ) *v.* goes beyond the limits of; exceeds

tremulous (TREHM yuh luhs) *adj.* trembling; quivering

tumult (TOO muhlt) *n.* noisy commotion

twinges (TWIHNJ uhz) *n.* sharp, sudden pains, either physical or mental

U

ulterior (uhl TIHR ee uhr) *adj.* further; beyond what is openly stated or implied

uncertainty (uhn SUR tuhn tee) *n.* inability to be sure

understanding (uhn duhr STAN dihng) *n.* power to comprehend and discern

unify (YOO nuh fy) *v.* combine into one

universal (yoo nuh VUR suhl) *adj.* existing in all things

unorthodox (uhn AWR thuh doks) *adj.* not typical; breaking with tradition

unwieldy (uhn WEEL dee) *adj.* hard to manage because of shape or weight; awkward

V

vagaries (vuh GAIR eez) *n.* erratic or unpredictable actions; whims

venerable (VEHN uhr uh buhl) *adj.* worthy of respect because of age or character

venturing (VEHN chuhr ihng) *v.* taking the risk of

veracious (vuh RAY shuhs) *adj.* truthful; honest

verbal (VUR buhl) *adj.* relating to words

verified (VEHR uh fyd) *v.* proved to be true

verify (VEHR uh fy) *v.* prove that something is true

vile (vyl) *adj.* evil; low; extremely disgusting

W

waver (WAY vuhr) *v.* show indecision; fluctuate

wistfully (WIHST fuhl ee) *adv.* showing vague yearnings

wither (WIHTH uhr) *v.* dry up; shrivel from loss of moisture

wrathfully (RATH fuhl ee) *adv.* with intense anger

Spanish Glossary

El vocabulario de Gran Pregunta aparece en **azul**. El Vocabulario Academico de alta utilidad esta **subraydo**.

A

abruptly / abruptamente *adv.* que sucede de repente; inesperadamente

abysmal / abismal *adj.* inmensamente malo o extremo; terrible

accomplices / cómplices *s.* personas que ayudan a otros a cometer un crimen

adamant / obstinado *adj.* que no cede; inflexible; firme

adapt / adaptar *v.* cambiar o ajustar

adept / adepto *adj.* experto; altamente calificado

adulation / adulación *s.* grandes o excesivos elogios; intensa admiración

adversaries / adversarios *s.* opositores

adversity / adversidad *s.* estado de dificultad o infortunio

affable / afable *adj.* agradable; amistoso

affront / afrenta *s.* insulto abierto

aggregate / agregado *s.* grupo de cosas concretas que unidas forman un todo; una suma

aggrieved / agraviado *adj.* que sufre perjuicio; afligido o herido

allay / aliviar *v.* mitigar; reducir; calmar

alleviate / mitigar *v.* alivianar; aliviar

amenable / receptivo *adj.* sensible; abierto

amiably / amigablemente *adv.* de manera jovial y amistosa

anguish / angustia *s.* sufrimiento extremo, como de pena o dolor

anticipate / anticipar *v.* aguardar con interés

apathy / apatía *s.* falta de interés o sentimiento

apprehension / aprensión *s.* sentimiento ansioso; temor

arable / arable *adj.* apto para cultivar cosechas

ardent / ferviente *adj.* intensamente entusiasta; devoto

aspirations / aspiraciones *s.* ambiciones fuertes

assuage / aplacar *v.* aminorar (dolor o aflicción); satisfacer (sed o hambre)

attributes / atributos *s.* características de una persona o cosa

audaciously / audazmente *adv.* de manera intrépida

augmented / aumentado *adj.* hecho más grande; realzado

august / augusto *adj.* impresionante; majestuoso

awareness / conciencia *s.* tener conocimiento

B

background / antecedentes *s.* condiciones que rodean o preceden a algo

bias / prejuicio *s.* el punto de vista que uno tiene antes de conocer los hechos

blemished / manchado *adj.* dañado; estropeado

bore / portó *v.* cargó

brandished / blandió *v.* mostró, esgrimió o batió de manera amenazante o triunfante

brazen / descarado *adj.* sin vergüenza; audaz

buffer / amortiguar *v.* aminorar un golpe; suavizar

C

cajoling / lisonjeo *s.* persuasión de alguien con lisonjas

calamity / calamidad *s.* desgracia terrible; desastre

candid / candoroso *adj.* franco; directo

canopied / entoldado *adj.* cubierto por una tela suspendida de postes o una estructura

catalyst / catalizador *s.* persona o cosa que desata un evento o acción

cessation / cesación *s.* detención; alto

change / cambiar *v.* convertirse en algo distinto; transformar

character / temperamento *s.* fortaleza moral; autodisciplina

chastisement / castigo *s.* crítica severa; corrección

choleric / colérico *adj.* malgeniado; irascible

circuit / circuito *s.* acción de girar alrededor de algo; ruta

clenching / apretar *v.* cerrar; agarrar firmemente

clustering / amontonado *adj.* reunido; formado en un grupo

commemorates / conmemora *v.* honra la memoria de

commences / comienza *v.* inicia

commiserate / compadecer *v.* apiadarse de; tener lástima por

comprehend / comprender *v.* captar mentalmente; entender

compromise / acuerdo *s.* convenio donde ambas partes ceden algo

compulsory / obligatorio *adj.* requerido; exigido

comrade / camarada *s.* compañero cercano; amigo

concession / concesión *s.* acción de otorgar o dar; indulgencia

concrete / concreto *adj.* algo específico o tangible

condemn / condenar *v.* desaprobar de; emitir un juicio desfavorable sobre

condemned / condenado *v.* que ha sido declarado culpable de fechorías; sentenciado por un juez

conduct / conducta *s.* la forma de actuar de una persona; comportamiento

configuration / configuración *s.* disposición de partes; patrón

confirm / confirmar *v.* establecer la verdad o precisión de algo

confounded / aturdido *adj.* sentirse confundido

confrontation / confrontación *s.* choque de fuerzas o ideas

confusion / confusión *s.* estado de desorden o distracción

conjured / invocado *v.* llamado como por acto de magia

connection / conexión *s.* relación entre cosas

consigned / consignado *v.* entregado; cedido o entregado

conspicuous / conspicuo *adj.* fácil de ver

constricting / restrictivo *adj.* que evita la libertad de movimiento; limitante

contempt / desprecio *s.* desdén; la actitud de alguien que tiene a menos a algo o a alguien

contested / disputó *v.* que intentó refutar o invalidar algo; impugnó

context / contexto *s.* circunstancias que crean el entorno de un evento

context / contexto *s.* entorno o situación en la que algo se encuentra

contrive / ingeniar *v.* procurar hacer; lograr

convalesce / convalecer *v.* recuperar fuerza y salud

converge / converger *v.* unirse

convey / transmitir *v.* comunicar o dar a conocer

convoluted / intrincado *adj.* retorcido de manera complicada

counsel / consejo *s.* orientación; discusión

countenance / semblante *s.* rostro; la expresión de una cara que muestra la naturaleza de una persona

courage / valor *s.* la voluntad de lidiar con algo peligroso

credulity / credulidad *s.* tendencia a creer con demasiada facilidad

customarily / habitualmente *adv.* comúnmente; por hábito o tradición

D

debate / debatir *v.* argumentar o discutir

debut / debut *s.* primera aparición pública

decorum / decoro *s.* comportamiento cortés y apropiado para cierta ocasión

decrepitude / decrepitud *s.* debilidad; condición de estar desgastado por edad o enfermedad

deference / deferencia *s.* el ceder a las ideas, deseos, etc. de otra persona

deficiency / deficiencia *s.* falta de algo esencial

deflects / desvía *v.* que detiene algo; que rechaza algo

deftness / habilidad *s.* destreza

defunct / difunto *adj.* que ya no está en uso o existencia; muerto

dejectedly / abatidamente *adv.* estar desalentado; de forma deprimida

delusion / ilusión *s.* una creencia errónea que se mantiene a pesar de haber evidencia en contra

demeanor / comportamiento *s.* manera de comportarse; conducta

derisively / burlonamente *adv.* de manera irónica y ridiculizante

derived / derivado *v.* que se obtuvo mediante razonamiento

desolate / desolado *adj.* vacío; solitario

destitute / indigente *adj.* carente de las necesidades básicas de la vida; de gran pobreza

determination / determinación *s.* firmeza de propósito

dexterous / diestro *adj.* tener o mostrar destreza mental o física; experto

differentiate / diferenciar *v.* distinguir entre

dignity / dignidad *s.* cualidad de merecer respeto y honor; respeto de sí mismo

dilapidated / dilapidado *adj.* estado ruinoso; raído

diligence / diligencia *s.* esfuerzo constante y esmerado

dimpled / con hoyuelos *adj.* marcado con pequeños hoyos o hendiduras

dingy / manchado *adj.* de aspecto sucio; deslustrado

dire / abrumador *adj.* urgente; terrible; que exige una acción rápida

discern / discernir *v.* distinguir la diferencia entre dos o más cosas; percibir

disconsolate / desconsolado *adj.* tan infeliz que nada le reconforta; miserable

discord / discordia *s.* conflicto; desacuerdo

discourse / discurso *s.* comunicación continua de ideas e información

discourse / disertar *v.* hablar (sobre un tema) formal y detalladamente

disdain / desdeño *s.* disgusto por alguien o algo; desprecio

disembarked / desembarcó *v.* abandonó un buque para ir a tierra

disparagement / menosprecio *s.* comentarios que expresan una mala opinión o falta de respeto por alguien

disreputable / desacreditado *adj.* no respetable; que tiene o merece mala reputación

dissent / desacuerdo *s.* renuencia a aceptar una creencia u opinión común; desavenencia

distinct / distinto *adj.* claramente diferente; separado

distortion / distorsión *s.* cualquier cosa que muestra algo de manera engañosa

dogged / obstinado *adj.* terco

SPANISH GLOSSARY

E

earnest / formal *adj.* serio e intenso; sin bromear

eased / alivió *v.* liberó de dolor o dificultad; alivianó

ebony / ébano *adj.* de color negro

edict / edicto *s.* mandato público; decreto

edifying / edificante *adj.* algo educativo que permite que la persona mejore moral o intelectualmente

efface / tachar *v.* borrar o suprimir

elude / eludir *v.* evitar; escapar con celeridad o astucia

elusive / elusivo *adj.* difícil de comprender

emanating / emanar *v.* brotar hacia afuera, como de una fuente

embodied / materializó *v.* dio forma a; concretó

emigrants / emigrantes *s.* personas que abandonan su país o región para establecerse en otro lugar

emotion / emoción *s.* sentimiento fuerte, como el amor

empathy / empatía *s.* compartir los sentimientos de otra persona

encroaching / invadir *adj.* cometer una intrusión, especialmente de manera gradual

endeavored / se esforzó por *v.* trató de alcanzar una meta fijada

endure / soportar *v.* aguantar con dolor o penuria

engaging / cautivador *adj.* atractivo; agradable

enlighten / ilustrar *v.* aclarar algo mediante el conocimiento

enthralls / encantar *v.* que cautiva; fascina

entreated / suplicó *v.* imploró; rogó

ephemeral / efímero *adj.* pasajero

equilibrium / equilibrio *s.* estado de balance

esoteric / esotérico *adj.* más allá de la comprensión o conocimiento de la mayoría de las personas

estranged / apartado *adj.* que se mantiene separado; condición en la que el afecto se torna en indiferencia u hostilidad

eternal / eterno *adj.* sin principio ni fin; sempiterno

evaluate / evaluar *v.* determinar el valor de algo

evidence / evidencia *s.* información que indica si algo es veraz o válido

evoking / evocar *v.* hacer salir las emociones o reacciones

evolve / evolucionar *v.* desarrollarse a través de cambios graduales

exorbitant / exorbitante *adj.* más allá de lo razonable; excesivo

expectations / expectativas *s.* algo que se aguarda con interés

explanation / explicación *s.* declaración aclaratoria

expound / enunciar *v.* explicar en detalle

extolled / elogiado *adj.* alabado

extricating / liberar *v.* dejar libre; sacar de una situación difícil

exuberance / exuberancia *s.* buena salud; vivacidad

F

falteringly / titubeante *adv.* dicho con titubeo o con voz trémula

fate / sino *s.* destino; lo que le sucede a una persona o cosa; resultado final

fathom / desentrañar *v.* comprender a fondo

fawned / aduló *v.* lisonjeó; actuó con preocupación excesiva por los deseos y antojos de otro, como lo haría un sirviente

flourishes / florece *v.* que crece vigorosamente; que prospera

fluttered / revoloteó *v.* agitó o vibró rápidamente

foe / adversario *s.* enemigo

forbore / abstuvo *v.* que desistió de realizar algo; que renunció a algo

foreboding / presentimiento *s.* una sensación de que algo malo ocurrirá; premonición

formidable / temible *adj.* que causa temor o pánico

fraud / fraude *s.* engaño; embuste

futile / fútil *adj.* ineficaz; inútil

G

gauge / aforar *v.* medir el tamaño, cantidad, alcance o capacidad de algo

grave / grave *adj.* que requiere de consideración seria; importante e inquietante

grimacing / haciendo muecas *v.* haciendo un gesto que muestre disgusto o dolor

growth / crecimiento *s.* el proceso del desarrollo

H

haphazardly / al azar *adv.* de manera no planeada o desorganizada

haste / apuro *s.* con rapidez de movimiento; prisa

heedless / desatento *adj.* descuidado; imprudente

history / historia *s.* relato de lo que ha pasado

honor / honor *s.* fuerte sentido del bien y del mal

humble / humilde *adj.* que muestra estar consciente de sus propios defectos; modesto

hypocrisy / hipocresía *s.* fingir ser o sentir lo que uno no es o siente

I

idealistic / idealista *adj.* que representa las cosas como deberían ser en lugar de como son en realidad

identity / identidad *s.* cualidades de una persona que representan lo que es

idle / ocioso *adj.* inútil; desocupado

ignorance / ignorancia *s.* falta de conocimiento o educación

immaterial / inmaterial *adj.* que no consiste de materia

imminent / inminente *adj.* a punto de suceder

impeded / impidió *v.* bloqueó; obstruyó

impediments / impedimentos *s.* cosas que retrasan a alguien o a algo, o que obstaculizan; barreras

impending / inminente *adj.* a punto de suceder

imperceptibly / imperceptiblemente *adv.* tan lento o leve que casi no se nota

imperiously / imperiosamente *adv.* arrogantemente

impervious / impenetrable *adj.* que no lo afecta algo

impetuosity / impetuosidad *s.* calidad de actuar repentinamente, con gran fuerza y poca consideración; temeridad

impression / impresión *s.* efecto que se produce sobre la mente

improbable / improbable *adj.* que no es factible que suceda o sea verdad

inaudibly / inaudiblemente *adv.* de forma que no se pueda oír

incessant / incesante *adj.* que no se detiene; constante

incredulity / incredulidad *s.* renuencia a creer

indigence / indigencia *s.* pobreza

indignant / indignado *adj.* que siente ira, especialmente por una injusticia

indignation / indignación *s.* ira en reacción a la injusticia o mezquindad

individual / individual *adj.* relativo a una sola persona o cosa

indulgence / indulgencia *s.* lenidad; estar dispuesto a tolerar o perdonar la mala conducta

inexorably / inexorablemente *adv.* sin la posibilidad de que lo atrasen o detengan; inalterable

infinite / infinito *adj.* más allá de medida o comprensión; interminable

infirm / enfermo *adj.* débil; endeble

infirmity / enfermedad *s.* debilidad; defecto físico

influence / influencia *s.* el poder de las personas para cambiar a otras

ingenuity / ingenio *s.* inventiva

ingratiating / congraciado *adj.* que actúa de cierta manera para ganarse el favor de alguien

inhabit / habitar *v.* residir en

inherent / inherente *adj.* que existe naturalmente en algo

inheritance / herencia *s.* dote que es pasada a la siguiente generación de una familia

innuendo / alusión *s.* insulto o acusación indirecta; insinuación

insight / discernimiento *s.* idea clara de la naturaleza de las cosas

instinct / instinto *s.* un patrón innato de comportamiento, en contraposición a una destreza aprendida

insurrection / insurrección *s.* rebelión

integrity / integridad *s.* voluntad para cumplir con los principios morales

interact / interactuar *v.* relacionarse entre sí, afectar a otro

interminable / interminable *adj.* que parece no tener fin

interpretation / interpretación *s.* explicación del significado de algo

interred / sepultó *v.* enterró (dícese de un cuerpo)

intertidal / entre marea alta y baja *adj.* característico de una zona litoral sujeta a los niveles de mareas alta y baja

intervened / intervino *v.* se interpuso entre

intrigues / intrigas *s.* tramas; maquinaciones

irascible / irascible *adj.* irritable

irreproachable / irreprochable *adj.* por encima de la crítica

irretrievable / irrecuperable *adj.* imposible de alcanzar de nuevo o recobrar

isolation / aislamiento *s.* estar solo o aislado

itinerary / itinerario *s.* ruta; plan de viaje

J

jauntiness / garbo *s.* actitud libre y desenvuelta

jeered / burló *v.* escarneció; mofó; ridiculizó

jurisdiction / jurisdicción *s.* esfera de autoridad o poder

K

keenest / más agudo *adj.* el más penetrante; cortante

knowledge / conocimiento *s.* conciencia y comprensión de información

L

lacquered / laqueado *adj.* cubierto con un barniz resistente y pegajoso

lamentation / lamento *s.* acto de vociferar con aflicción; gemido; llanto

language / lenguaje *s.* sistema usado para expresarse o comunicar; escogencia de palabras

languid / lánguido *adj.* falto de energía

lavished / derrochó *v.* dio con extrema generosidad

lease / arrendamiento *s.* contrato mediante el cual algo es alquilado por un plazo determinado de tiempo; alquiler

legacies / legados *s.* dinero, propiedades o posición que se deja a alguien en un testamento

legendary / legendario *adj.* extraordinario; memorable

livid / lívido *adj.* pálido, como por haber sufrido una herida; enrojecido por la ira

lofty / eminente *adj.* elevado en rango o temperamento; noble

looming / que aparece *adj.* que se asoma en forma vaga, indistinta, pero amenazante; que amenaza con ocurrir

lowly / inferior *adj.* humilde; de baja posición

lucidity / lucidez *s.* cualidad de ser fácilmente entendido

SPANISH GLOSSARY

lucrative / lucrativo *adj.* que produce riqueza; rentable

lunar / lunar *adj.* de la luna

M

maligned / difamado *adj.* que se habló mal de

manifestations / manifestaciones *s.* apariciones; formas

manipulate / manipular *v.* controlar mediante el uso de influencia, a menudo de forma injusta

manipulated / manipuló *v.* que manejó o controló mediante jugadas astutas

marginal / marginal *adj.* en o cerca del borde

meager / escaso *adj.* de mala calidad o poca cantidad

meaning / significado *s.* el sentido de algo

meditates / medita *v.* que piensa profundamente

melancholy / melancólico *adj.* triste y deprimido

millennial / milenario *adj.* de 1.000 años

mirth / regocijo *s.* alegría; júbilo

misconstrued / malinterpretó *v.* entendió mal

misinterpret / malinterpretar *v.* no entender correctamente

modified / modificó *v.* cambió; alteró ligeramente

monotonously / monótonamente *adv.* de forma aburrida e invariable

motive / motivo *s.* lo que causa que una persona actúe de cierta manera

multitudes / multitudes *s.* gran cantidad de personas o cosas

mutable / mutable *adj.* cambiable

N

negotiate / negociar *v.* pactar con la esperanza de llegar a un acuerdo

nevertheless / sin embargo *adv.* a pesar de eso; no obstante

nimbly / ágilmente *adv.* de forma rápida, fácil y liviana; con agilidad

nomadic / nómada *adj.* que se traslada de un lugar a otro; sin hogar permanente

nonchalantly / indiferentemente *adv.* casualmente; imperturbablemente

O

objective / objetivo *adj.* que no está sujeto al punto de vista de otro

oblivious / olvidadizo *adj.* absorto

obscured / oscureció *v.* hizo oscuro; obstruyó la vista; escondió

oppose / oponer *v.* ponerse en contra; estar en desacuerdo con

oppressive / opresivo *adj.* que causa gran incomodidad; angustiante

oratory / oratoria *s.* acto de hablar en público; estrategias usadas en disertaciones

overcome / vencer *v.* conquistar o prevalecer sobre

P

pallor / palor *s.* carencia de color; palidez poco natural

paradox / paradoja *s.* declaración o situación que parece contradictoria

paranoia / paranoia *s.* trastorno mental que se caracteriza por delirios

perception / percepción *s.* la forma en que uno entiende el mundo a través de los sentidos

perpetually / perpetuamente *adv.* que continua para siempre; constantemente

persevere / perseverar *v.* continuar a pesar de la oposición; persistir

perspective / perspectiva *s.* la forma en que uno ve las cosas; punto de vista

petulantly / petulantemente *adv.* de forma que expresa impaciencia o irritación

piety / piedad *s.* lealtad y devoción hacia la familia, lo divino o algún otro objeto de respeto

piqued / molesto *adj.* enojado o irritado

plague / importunar *v.* molestar; fastidiar; atormentar

plausibility / admisibilidad *s.* credibilidad; verdad aparente

plight / aprieto *s.* situación difícil

poignant / conmovedor *adj.* que afecta emocionalmente; desgarrador

portentous / portentoso *adj.* ominoso; que da señales de cosas nefastas por venir

presume / presumir *v.* depender demasiado de; abusar de

presumptuous / descarado *adj.* que traspasa los límites de lo correcto; demasiado imprudente

pretense / pretensión *s.* jactancia; simulación fingida de algo

principles / principios *s.* reglas para una conducta correcta; normas

prodigious / prodigioso *adj.* de gran tamaño o poder

profuse / profuso *adj.* dar o vaciar libremente, a menudo en exceso; abundante

progress / progreso *s.* desarrollo; mejoras

prostrate / postrado *adj.* yacer tendido

prudent / prudente *adj.* practicar un razonamiento acertado; cauteloso

purified / purificó *v.* libró de impurezas o contaminación; hizo puro

Q

quench / aplacar *v.* satisfacer; llenar las necesidades o deseos de algo

question / preguntar *v.* expresar incertidumbre sobre algo; formular una pregunta

R

radical / radical *adj.* cambio extremo

rash / imprudente *adj.* demasiado apresurado en el dicho o en el hecho; precipitado

rave / desvariar *v.* hablar incoherentemente o decir disparates

reality / realidad *s.* calidad de ser conforme a la verdad

reapers / segadores *s.* personas que recogen o cosechan los granos

reciprocity / reciprocidad *s.* relaciones de intercambio; interdependencia

reconciliation / reconciliación *s.* reestablecer la amistad y la armonía

reflect / reflexionar *v.* pensar seriamente sobre algo

refuse / desechos *s.* desperdicios; basura

rejoiced / regocijó *v.* mostró alegría

rejuvenation / rejuvenecimiento *s.* hacer nuevo, más joven o energético una vez más; revitalización

relent / ceder *v.* volverse menos fuerte, severo o intenso; ablandarse

relish / deleite *s.* goce

renounced / renunció *v.* se rindió formalmente

repertoire / repertorio *s.* lista de obras, por ejemplo, canciones que un artista está preparado para presentar

replenished / reabasteció *v.* completó o llenó de nuevo

replication / réplica *s.* duplicado; reproducción

resolute / resuelto *adj.* que muestra un propósito fijo

resolution / resolución *s.* fuerte determinación; plan o decisión firme

resolve / resolver *v.* llegar a una conclusión o decisión

respond / responder *v.* contestar

responsibility / responsabilidad *s.* tener que responder ante alguien o algo; rendir cuentas por el éxito o el fracaso

reveling / deleitarse *v.* disfrutar; celebrar

reverence / reverencia *s.* un sentimiento de profundo respeto, amor o admiración

revise / revisar *v.* reconsiderar; modificar

rudiments / rudimentos *s.* fundamentos; inicios modestos

S

sacrifice / sacrificar *v.* ceder

sated / saciado *adj.* satisfecho; provisto con más que suficiente

scrutinized / escudriñó *v.* examinó detenidamente

secular / seglar *adj.* relativo a asuntos mundanos, en comparación con religiosos

self-expression / expresión del carácter propio *s.* compartir con otros la personalidad o las emociones

selflessness / desprendimiento *s.* tener devoción por los intereses de los demás por encima de los propios

self-sufficiency / autosuficiencia *s.* independencia

sententiously / sentenciosamente *adv.* que muestra un gusto excesivo por los proverbios; en tono de disertación

serenity / serenidad *s.* estado de calma o paz

servile / servil *adj.* semejante a un esclavo; humildemente sumiso a la autoridad

silhouette / silueta *s.* dibujo de un perfil relleno con un color sólido

simulating / simular *v.* dar la apariencia de

skeptically / escépticamente *adv.* con duda; interrogativamente

slumbering / soñoliento *adj.* adormecido

sonorous / sonoro *adj.* tener un sonido rico o impresionante

spare / frugal *adj.* enjuto; descarnado

spectacle / espectáculo *s.* presenciar algo extraño o extraordinario

squalid / escuálido *adj.* impuro; sucio

staidness / sobriedad *s.* estado de estar tranquilo; sosegado

stance / postura *s.* la forma en que uno se para, especialmente en cuanto a la colocación de los pies

stark / desolado *adj.* desierto; severo

staunch / firme *adj.* constante; leal

steady / estable *adj.* firme; de movimiento seguro

stereotype / estereotipo *s.* noción de un grupo que es demasiado amplia y a menudo incorrecta

stickler / rigorista *s.* persona que insiste en la obediencia estricta a las reglas o normas

stifle / sofocar *v.* asfixiar; reprimir

stipulates / estipula *v.* que incluye específicamente como parte de un acuerdo

strife / refriega *s.* lucha; conflicto

struggle / luchar *v.* enfrentar dificultades

subdued / alicaído *adj.* quieto; que le falta energía

subjective / subjetivo *adj.* basado en o influenciado por los sentimientos o punto de vista de una persona

subordinate / subordinado *adj.* inferior a otro en importancia o rango

subtile / sutil *adj.* fino; delicado

subversion / subversión *s.* actividad con intención de derrocar algo establecido; rebelión

successive / sucesivo *adj.* que uno le sigue al otro en secuencia

succinct / sucinto *adj.* expresado clara y brevemente

sullen / taciturno *adj.* adusto y que muestra resentimiento

sumptuous / suntuoso *adj.* costoso; espléndido

supercilious / altanero *adj.* que muestra una actitud de superioridad; desdeñoso

surmise / suposición *s.* conjetura; idea basada en evidencia que no es concluyente

surpassed / sobrepasó *v.* que fue más allá; superó

T

tactile / táctil *adj.* relativo al sentido del tacto

tangible / tangible *adj.* capaz de ser tocado; real

temperate / temperado *adj.* moderado; que se mantiene dentro de los límites

tempering / temperar s. cambiar para hacer más apto, generalmente al mezclarlo con otra cosa

tentative / tentativo *adj.* vacilante; incierto

tenuous / tenue *adj.* sin fuerza

threshold / umbral *s.* la parte inferior de un portal; entrada o punto de inicio

titanic / titánico *adj.* poderoso; de gran tamaño

toil / labor *s.* trabajo arduo y cansado

trace / trazo *s.* pequeña cantidad; pizca

transcends / trasciende *v.* que va más allá de los límites de; excede

tremulous / trémulo *adj.* tembloroso; que se estremece

tumult / tumulto *s.* conmoción ruidosa

twinges / punzadas *s.* dolores agudos y repentinos, ya sea físicos o mentales

U

ulterior / ulterior *adj.* subsecuente; más allá de lo que está abiertamente expresado o implícito

uncertainty / incertidumbre *s.* incapacidad de estar seguro

understanding / entendimiento *s.* poder de comprender y discernir

unify / unificar *v.* combinar en uno solo

universal / universal *adj.* que existe en todas las cosas

unorthodox / no ortodoxo *adj.* atípico; que rompe con la tradición

unwieldy / abultado *adj.* difícil de manejar debido a su forma o peso; incómodo

V

vagaries / caprichos *s.* acciones erráticas o impredecibles; antojos

venerable / venerable *adj.* digno de respeto debido a edad o posición

venturing / atreverse *v.* tomar el riesgo de

veracious / veraz *adj.* verdadero; honesto

verbal / verbal *adj.* relativo a las palabras

verified / verificó *v.* demostró que es cierto

verify / verificar *v.* probar que algo es cierto

vile / vil *adj.* malo; bajo; extremadamente detestable

W

waver / vacilar *v.* mostrar indecisión; titubear

wistfully / anhelantemente *adv.* mostrando vagos deseos

wither / marchitar *v.* secar; que se encoge por falta de humedad

wrathfully / coléricamente *adv.* con intenso enojo

Literary Terms

ACT See ***Drama.***

ALLEGORY An ***allegory*** is a story or tale with two or more levels of meaning—a literal level and one or more symbolic levels. The events, setting, and characters in an allegory are symbols for ideas and qualities.

ALLITERATION ***Alliteration*** is the repetition of initial consonant sounds. Writers use alliteration to give emphasis to words, to imitate sounds, and to create musical effects. In the following line from Theodore Roethke's "The Waking" (p. 685), there is alliteration of the *f* sound:

> I *f*eel my *f*ate in what I cannot *f*ear.

ALLUSION An ***allusion*** is a reference to a well-known person, place, event, literary work, or work of art. The title of the story "By the Waters of Babylon" (p. 314) is an allusion to the Bible's Psalm 137, in which the Hebrew people lament their exile in Babylon. It begins, "By the rivers of Babylon, there we sat down, yea, we wept. . . ."

ANALOGY An ***analogy*** makes a comparison between two or more things that are similar in some ways but otherwise unalike.

ANECDOTE An anecdote is a brief story about an interesting, amusing, or strange event told to entertain or to make a point. In the excerpt from "The Way to Rainy Mountain" (p. 595), N. Scott Momaday tells anecdotes about his grandmother to reveal her character and provide a glimpse into a vanishing way of life.

See also ***Narrative.***

ANTAGONIST An ***antagonist*** is a character or force in conflict with a main character, or protagonist.

ANTICLIMAX Some stories end in an ***anticlimax.*** Like a climax, an *anticlimax* is the turning point in a story. However, an anticlimax is always a letdown. It is the point at which you learn that the story will not turn out in a way that truly resolves the problem or satisfies the reader.

ARCHETYPE An ***archetype*** is a type of character, detail, image, or situation that appears in literature from around the world and throughout history. Some critics believe that archetypes reveal deep truths about human experience.

ASIDE An ***aside*** is a short speech delivered by a character in a play in order to express his or her thoughts and feelings. Traditionally, the aside is directed to the audience and is presumed not to be heard by the other characters.

ASSONANCE ***Assonance*** is the repetition of vowel sounds followed by different consonants in two or more stressed syllables. Assonance is found in this phrase from Elizabeth Bishop's "The Fish" (p. 650): "frayed and wavering."

ATMOSPHERE See ***Mood.***

AUTOBIOGRAPHICAL ESSAY See ***Essay.***

AUTOBIOGRAPHY An ***autobiography*** is a form of nonfiction in which a writer tells his or her own life story. An autobiography may tell about the person's whole life or only a part of it. An example of an autobiography is Erik Weihenmayer's *Touch the Top of the World* (p. 449).

See also ***Biography*** and ***Nonfiction.***

BALLAD A ***ballad*** is a songlike poem that tells a story, often one dealing with adventure and romance. Most ballads are written in four- to six-line stanzas and have regular rhythms and rhyme schemes. A ballad often features a *refrain*—a regularly repeated line or group of lines.

See also ***Oral Tradition.***

BIOGRAPHY A ***biography*** is a form of nonfiction in which a writer tells the life story of another person. Biographies have been written about many famous people, historical and contemporary, but they can also be written about "ordinary" people.

See also ***Autobiography*** and ***Nonfiction.***

BLANK VERSE ***Blank verse*** is poetry written in unrhymed iambic pentameter lines. This verse form was widely used by William Shakespeare.

CHARACTER A ***character*** is a person or an animal who takes part in the action of a literary work. The main character, or protagonist, is the most important character in a story. In Chinua Achebe's story "Civil Peace" (p. 358), Jonathan Iwegbu is the protagonist. This character often changes in some important way as a result of the story's events.

Characters are sometimes classified as round or flat, dynamic or static. A ***round character*** shows many different traits—faults as well as virtues. A *flat character* shows only one trait. A *dynamic character* develops and grows

during the course of the story; a ***static character*** does not change.

See also ***Characterization*** and ***Motivation.***

CHARACTERIZATION ***Characterization*** is the act of creating and developing a character. In direct characterization, the author directly states a character's traits. For example, in "The Masque of the Red Death" (p. 372), Poe directly characterizes Prince Prospero: "But the Prince Prospero was happy and dauntless and sagacious."

In indirect characterization, an author gives clues about a character by describing what a character looks like, does, and says, as well as how other characters react to him or her. It is up to the reader to draw conclusions about the character based on this indirect information.

The most effective indirect characterizations usually result from showing characters acting or speaking.

See also ***Character.***

CLIMAX The ***climax*** of a story, novel, or play is the high point of interest or suspense. The events that make up the rising action lead up to the climax. The events that make up the falling action follow the climax.

See also ***Conflict; Plot;*** and ***Anticlimax.***

COMEDY A ***comedy*** is a literary work, especially a play, that has a happy ending. Comedies often show ordinary characters in conflict with society. These conflicts are introduced through misunderstandings, deceptions, and concealed identities. When the conflict is resolved, the result is the correction of moral faults or social wrongs. Types of comedy include *romantic comedy,* which involves problems among lovers, and the *comedy of manners,* which satirically challenges the social customs of a sophisticated society. Comedy is often contrasted with tragedy, in which the protagonist meets an unfortunate end.

COMIC RELIEF ***Comic relief*** is a technique that is used to interrupt a serious part of a literary work by introducing a humorous character or situation.

CONFLICT A ***conflict*** is a struggle between opposing forces. Characters in conflict form the basis of stories, novels, and plays.

There are two kinds of conflict: external and internal. In an *external conflict,* the main character struggles against an outside force. This force may be another character, as in "Civil Peace" (p. 358), in which Jonathan Iwegbu struggles with the leader of the thieves. The outside force could also be the standards or expectations of a group, such as the oppression and censorship that Juan struggles against in "The Censors" (p. 410). The outside force may be nature itself, as when Erik Weihenmayer struggles to climb Mt. Everest in *Touch the Top of the World* (p. 449).

An *internal conflict* involves a character in conflict with himself or herself. In *Julius Caesar* (p. 892), Brutus experiences an internal conflict when trying to decide whether to assassinate Caesar.

See also ***Plot.***

CONNOTATION The ***connotation*** of a word is the set of ideas associated with it in addition to its explicit meaning.

See also ***Denotation.***

CONSONANCE ***Consonance*** is the repetition of final consonant sounds in stressed syllables with different vowel sounds, as in *hat* and *sit.*

CONTEMPORARY INTERPRETATION A ***contemporary interpretation*** is a literary work of today that responds to and sheds new light on a well-known, earlier work of literature. Such an interpretation may refer to any aspect of the older work, including plot, characters, settings, imagery, language, and theme. T. H. White's *The Once and Future King* (p. 1156) provides a modern version of the legend of King Arthur.

COUPLET A ***couplet*** is a pair of rhyming lines, usually of the same length and meter. In the following couplet from Sonnet 29 by William Shakespeare, the speaker comforts himself with the thought of his love:

> For thy sweet love remember'd such wealth brings
> That then I scorn to change my state with kings.

See also ***Stanza.***

DENOTATION The ***denotation*** of a word is its dictionary meaning, independent of other associations that the word may have. The denotation of the word *lake,* for example, is "an inland body of water." "Vacation spot" and "place where the fishing is good" are connotations of the word *lake.*

See also ***Connotation.***

DESCRIPTION A ***description*** is a portrait in words of a person, place, or object. Descriptive writing uses sensory details, those that appeal to the senses: sight, hearing, taste, smell, and touch. Description can be found in all types of writing. Anita Desai's "Games at Twilight" (p. 138) has vivid descriptive passages.

DESCRIPTIVE ESSAY See ***Essay.***

DIALECT ***Dialect*** is a special form of a language, spoken by people in a particular region or group. It may involve changes to the pronunciation, vocabulary, and sentence structure of the standard form of the language. Rudyard Kipling's "Danny Deever" (p. 652) is a poem written in the Cockney dialect of English, used by working-class Londoners.

DIALOGUE A ***dialogue*** is a conversation between characters that may reveal their traits and advance the action of a narrative. In fiction or nonfiction, quotation marks indicate a speaker's exact words, and a new paragraph usually indicates a change of speaker. Following is an exchange between two characters in "The Monkey's Paw" (p. 32):

> "*What's that?*" cried the old woman, starting up.
> "A rat," said the old man in shaking tones—"a rat. It passed me on the stairs."

Quotation marks are not used in *script*, the printed copy of a play. Instead, the dialogue follows the name of the speaker, as in this example from *Julius Caesar* (p. 892):

> **PORTIA.** Is Caesar yet gone to the Capitol?

DICTION ***Diction*** refers to an author's choice of words, especially with regard to range of vocabulary, use of slang and colloquial language, and level of formality. This sentence from "The Masque of the Red Death" (p. 372) is an example of formal diction containing many words derived from Latin: "This was an extensive and magnificent structure, the creation of the prince's own eccentric yet august taste."

See also ***Connotation*** and ***Denotation.***

DIRECT CHARACTERIZATION
See ***Characterization.***

DRAMA A ***drama*** is a story written to be performed by actors. The script of a drama is made up of ***dialogue***—the words the actors say—and ***stage directions,*** which are descriptions of how and where action happens.

The drama's ***setting*** is the time and place in which the action occurs. It is indicated by one or more sets, including furniture and backdrops, that suggest interior or exterior scenes. *Props* are objects, such as a sword or a cup of tea, that are used onstage.

At the beginning of most plays, a brief *exposition* gives the audience some background information about the characters and the situation. Just as in a story or novel, the plot of a drama is built around characters in conflict.

Dramas are divided into large units called acts, which are divided into smaller units called *scenes.* A long play may include many sets that change with the scenes, or it may indicate a change of scene with lighting. *Julius Caesar* (p. 892) is a play in five acts.

See also ***Dialogue; Genre; Stage Directions;*** and ***Tragedy.***

DRAMATIC IRONY See ***Irony.***

DRAMATIC MONOLOGUE A ***dramatic monologue*** is a poem in which a character reveals himself or herself by speaking to a silent listener or thinking aloud.

DRAMATIC POETRY ***Dramatic poetry*** is poetry that utilizes the techniques of drama. The dialogue between the bride and the bridegroom at the end of "The Bridegroom" (p. 642) is an example.

END RHYME See ***Rhyme.***

EPIC An ***epic*** is a long narrative poem about the deeds of gods or heroes. *Sundiata: An Epic of Old Mali* (p. 1094) and the *Ramayana* (p. 1108) are examples of the genre.

An epic is elevated in style and usually follows certain patterns. In Greek epics and in the epics modeled after them, the poet begins by announcing the subject and asking a Muse—one of the nine goddesses of the arts, literature, and sciences—to help.

An *epic hero* is the larger-than-life central character in an epic. Through behavior and deeds, the epic hero displays qualities that are valued by the society in which the epic originated.

See also ***Epic Simile*** and ***Narrative Poem.***

EPIC SIMILE An ***epic simile,*** also called ***Homeric simile,*** is an elaborate comparison of unlike subjects. In this example from the *Odyssey*, Homer compares the bodies of men killed by Odysseus to a fisherman's catch heaped up on the shore:

> Think of a catch that fishermen haul in to a
>   half-moon bay
> in a fine-meshed net from the whitecaps of the sea:
> how all are poured out on the sand, in throes
>   for the salt sea,
> twitching their cold lives away in Helios' fiery air:
> so lay the suitors heaped on one another.

See also ***Figurative Language*** and ***Simile.***

EPIPHANY An ***epiphany*** is a character's sudden flash of insight into a conflict or situation. At the end of the poem "The Fish" (p. 6650), the speaker has an epiphany that causes her to release the fish.

LITERARY HANDBOOK

ESSAY An ***essay*** is a short nonfiction work about a particular subject. While classification is difficult, five types of essays are sometimes identified.

A *descriptive essay* seeks to convey an impression about a person, place, or object. (In "Flood" (p. 396), Annie Dillard describes scenes from a flood.)

An *expository essay* gives information, discusses ideas, or explains a process. In "The Spider and the Wasp"(p. 464), Alexander Petrunkevitch compares and contrasts the two creatures mentioned in the title.

A *narrative essay* tells a true story. In "The Dog That Bit People" (p. 525), James Thurber tells the story of a troublesome pet. An autobiographical essay is a narrative essay in which the writer tells a story from his or her own life.

A *persuasive essay* tries to convince readers to do something or to accept the writer's point of view. In "Keep Memory Alive" (p. 548), Elie Wiesel argues the importance of speaking out against evil.

See also ***Description; Exposition; Genre; Narration; Nonfiction;*** and ***Persuasion.***

EXPOSITION ***Exposition*** is writing or speech that explains a process or presents information. In the plot of a story or drama, the exposition is the part of the work that introduces the characters, the setting, and the basic situation.

See also ***Plot.***

EXPOSITORY ESSAY See ***Essay.***

EXTENDED METAPHOR In an ***extended metaphor,*** as in regular metaphor, a writer speaks or writes of a subject as though it were something else. An extended metaphor sustains the comparison for several lines or for an entire poem. In *Julius Caesar* (p. 892), Brutus uses an extended metaphor in Act II, Scene i, lines 21–27, when he speaks of "ambition's ladder."

See also ***Figurative Language*** and ***Metaphor.***

FALLING ACTION See ***Plot.***

FANTASY A ***fantasy*** is a work of highly imaginative writing that contains elements not found in real life. Examples of fantasy include stories that involve supernatural elements, such as fairy tales, and stories that deal with imaginary places and creatures.

See also ***Science Fiction.***

FICTION ***Fiction*** is prose writing that tells about imaginary characters and events. The term is usually used for novels and short stories, but it also applies to dramas and narrative poetry. Some writers rely on their imaginations alone to create their works of fiction. Others base their fiction on actual events and people, to which they add invented characters, dialogue, and plot situations.

See also ***Genre; Narrative;*** and ***Nonfiction.***

FIGURATIVE LANGUAGE ***Figurative language*** is writing or speech not meant to be interpreted literally. It is often used to create vivid impressions by setting up comparisons between dissimilar things.

Some frequently used figures of speech are *metaphors, similes*, and *personifications*.

See also ***Literal Language.***

FLASHBACK A ***flashback*** is a means by which authors present material that occurred earlier than the present time of the narrative. Authors may include this material in the form of a characters' memories, dreams, or accounts of past events, or they may simply shift their narrative back to the earlier time.

FOIL A ***foil*** is a character who provides a contrast to another character. In *Julius Caesar* (p. 892), the impetuous and resentful Cassius is a foil for the cooler and more rational Brutus.

FOOT See ***Meter.***

FORESHADOWING ***Foreshadowing*** is the use in a literary work of clues that suggest events that have yet to occur. This technique helps to create suspense, keeping readers wondering about what will happen next.

FREE VERSE ***Free verse*** is poetry not written in a regular pattern of meter or rhyme. Cornelius Eady's "The Poetic Interpretation of the Twist" (p. 633) is an example.

GENRE A ***genre*** is a category or form of literature. Literature is commonly divided into three major types of writing: poetry, prose, and drama. For each type, there are several distinct genres, as follows:

1. Poetry: Lyric Poetry, Concrete Poetry, Dramatic Poetry, Narrative Poetry, and Epic Poetry
2. Prose: Fiction (Novels and Short Stories) and Nonfiction (Biography, Autobiography, Letters, Essays, and Reports)
3. Drama: Serious Drama and Tragedy, Comic Drama, Melodrama, and Farce

See also ***Drama, Poetry,*** and ***Prose.***

R18

HAIKU The ***haiku*** is a three-line verse form. The first and third lines of a haiku each have five syllables. The second line has seven syllables. A haiku seeks to convey a single vivid emotion by means of images from nature.

HOMERIC SIMILE See ***Epic Simile.***

HYPERBOLE A ***hyperbole*** is a deliberate exaggeration or overstatement. In Mark Twain's "The Notorious Jumping Frog of Calaveras County," the claim that Jim Smiley would follow a bug as far as Mexico to win a bet is a hyperbole. As this example shows, hyperboles are often used for comic effect.

IAMB See ***Meter.***

IDIOM An ***idiom*** or ***idiomatic expression*** is an expression that is characteristic of a language, region, community or class of people. Idiomatic expressions mean something more than or different from the meaning of the words making them up. Following is an example of an idiom from T. H. White's *The Once and Future King* (p. 1156): "Think what people will say about us, if we do not go and *have a shot* at that sword."

See also ***Dialect.***

IMAGE An ***image*** is a word or phrase that appeals to one or more of the five senses—sight, hearing, touch, taste, or smell. Writers use images to re-create sensory experiences in words.

See also ***Description.***

IMAGERY ***Imagery*** is the descriptive or figurative language used in literature to create word pictures for the reader. These pictures, or images, are created by details of sight, sound, taste, touch, smell, or movement.

INDIRECT CHARACTERIZATION
See ***Characterization.***

INTERNAL RHYME See ***Rhyme.***

IRONY ***Irony*** is the general term for literary techniques that portray differences between appearance and reality, or expectation and result. In ***verbal irony,*** words are used to suggest the opposite of what is meant. In ***dramatic irony,*** there is a contradiction between what a character thinks and what the reader or audience knows to be true. In *irony of situation*, an event occurs that directly contradicts the expectations of the characters, the reader, or the audience.

LITERAL LANGUAGE ***Literal language*** uses words in their ordinary senses. It is the opposite of ***figurative language.*** If you tell someone standing on a diving board to jump in, you speak literally. If you tell someone on the street to "go jump in a lake," you are speaking figuratively.

See also ***Figurative Language.***

LYRIC POEM A ***lyric poem*** is a poem written in highly musical language that expresses the thoughts, observations, and feelings of a single speaker.

MAIN CHARACTER See ***Character.***

METAPHOR A ***metaphor*** is a figure of speech in which one thing is spoken of as though it were something else. Unlike a simile, which compares two things using *like* or *as*, a metaphor implies a comparison between them. In "A Tree Telling of Orpheus" (p. 659), the speaker is a tree and describes music as if it were water: "my roots felt music moisten them."

See also ***Extended Metaphor*** and ***Figurative Language.***

METER The ***meter*** of a poem is its rhythmical pattern. This pattern is determined by the number and arrangements of stressed syllables, or beats, in each line. To describe the meter of a poem, you must scan its lines. Scanning involves marking the stressed and unstressed syllables, as shown with the following two lines from *Julius Caesar* (p. 824):

> Wĕ bóth hăve féd ăs wéll, ănd wé căn bóth
>
> Ĕndúre thĕ wíntĕr's cóld ăs wéll ăs hé . . .

As you can see, each stressed syllable is marked with a slanted line (´) and each unstressed syllable with a horseshoe symbol (˘). The stressed and unstressed syllables are then divided by vertical lines (|) into groups called *feet*. The following types of feet are common in English poetry:

1. *Iamb:* a foot with one unstressed syllable followed by a stressed syllable, as in the word "again"
2. *Trochee:* a foot with one stressed syllable followed by an unstressed syllable, as in the word "wonder"
3. *Anapest:* a foot with two unstressed syllables followed by one strong stress, as in the phrase "on the beach"
4. *Dactyl:* a foot with one strong stress followed by two unstressed syllables, as in the word "wonderful"
5. *Spondee:* a foot with two strong stresses, as in the word "spacewalk"

Depending on the type of foot that is most common in them, lines of poetry are described as *iambic, trochaic, anapestic,* and so forth.

Lines are also described in terms of the number of feet that occur in them, as follows:

1. *Monometer:* verse written in one-foot lines
   All things
   Must pass
   Away.
2. *Dimeter:* verse written in two-foot lines
   Thomas | Jefferson
   What do | you say
   Under the | gravestone
   Hidden | away?

   —Rosemary and Stephen Vincent Benét,
   "Thomas Jefferson, 1743–1826"
3. *Trimeter:* verse written in three-foot lines
   I know | not whom | I meet
   I know | not where | I go.
4. *Tetrameter:* verse written in four-foot lines
5. *Pentameter:* verse written in five-foot lines
6. *Hexameter:* verse written in six-foot lines
7. *Heptameter:* verse written in seven-foot lines

Blank verse, used by Shakespeare in *Julius Caesar* (p. 892), is poetry written in unrhymed iambic pentameter.

Free verse, used by Cornelius Eady in "The Poetic Interpretation of the Twist" (p. 633), is poetry that does not follow a regular pattern of meter and rhyme.

MONOLOGUE A ***monologue*** in a play is a long speech by one character that, unlike a *soliloquy,* is addressed to another character or characters. An example from Shakespeare's *Julius Caesar* (p. 892) is the famous speech by Antony to the Roman people in Act III, Scene ii. It begins, "Friends, Romans, countrymen, lend me your ears. . . ." (line 74).

See also ***Soliloquy.***

MOOD ***Mood,*** or ***atmosphere,*** is the feeling created in the reader by a literary work or passage. The mood is often suggested by descriptive details. Often the mood can be described in a single word, such as lighthearted, frightening, or despairing. Notice how this passage from Edgar Allan Poe's "The Masque of the Red Death" (p. 372) contributes to an eerie, fearful mood:

> And now was acknowledged the presence of the Red Death. He had come like a thief in the night. And one by one dropped the revelers in the blood-bedewed halls of their revel, and died each in the despairing posture of his fall.

See also ***Tone.***

MORAL A ***moral*** is a lesson taught by a literary work, especially a fable—many fables, for example, have a stated moral at the end. It is customary, however, to discuss contemporary works in terms of the themes they explore, rather than a moral that they teach.

MOTIVATION ***Motivation*** is a reason that explains or partially explains why a character thinks, feels, acts, or behaves in a certain way. Motivation results from a combination of the character's personality and the situation he or she must deal with. In *Antigone* (p. 814), the protagonist is motivated by loyalty to her dead brother and reverence for the laws of the gods.

See also ***Character*** and ***Characterization.***

MYTH A ***myth*** is a *fictional* tale that describes the actions of gods and heroes or explains the causes of natural phenomena. Unlike legends, myths emphasize supernatural rather than historical elements. Many cultures have collections of myths, and the most familiar in the Western world are those of the ancient Greeks and Romans. "Prometheus and the First People"(p. 1066) is a retelling of a famous ancient Greek myth.

See also ***Oral Tradition.***

NARRATION ***Narration*** is writing that tells a story. The act of telling a story in speech is also called narration. Novels and short stories are fictional narratives. Nonfiction works—such as news stories, biographies, and autobiographies—are also narratives. A narrative poem tells a story in verse.

See also ***Anecdote, Essay, Narrative Poem, Nonfiction, Novel,*** and ***Short Story.***

NARRATIVE A ***narrative*** is a story told in fiction, nonfiction, poetry, or drama.

See also ***Narration.***

NARRATIVE ESSAY See ***Essay.***

NARRATIVE POEM A ***narrative poem*** is one that tells a story. Alexander Pushkin's "The Bridegroom" (p. 642)

is a narrative poem that tells how Natasha, a merchant's daughter, outwits a thief and murderer.

See also ***Dramatic Poetry; Epic;*** and ***Narration.***

NARRATOR A ***narrator*** is a speaker or character who tells a story. The writer's choice of narrator determines the story's *point of view*, or the perspective from which the story is told. By using a consistent point of view, a writer controls the amount and type of information revealed to the reader.

When a character in the story tells the story, that character is a *first-person narrator.* This narrator may be a major character, a minor character, or just a witness. Readers see only what this character sees, hear only what he or she hears, and so on. Stephen Vincent Benét's "By the Waters of Babylon" (p. 314) is told by a first-person narrator. Viewing unfolding events from this character's perspective, the reader shares in his discoveries and feels more suspense than another point of view would provide.

When a voice outside the story narrates, the story has a *third-person narrator.* An *omniscient*, or all-knowing, third-person narrator can tell readers what any character thinks and feels. For example, in "The Monkey's Paw" (p. 32), we know the thoughts of the father, the wife, and the son. A *limited third-person narrator* sees the world through one character's eyes and reveals only that character's thoughts. In Jack Finney's "Contents of the Dead Man's Pocket" (p. 118), the narrator reveals only Tom's thoughts and feelings.

See also ***Speaker.***

NONFICTION ***Nonfiction*** is prose writing that presents and explains ideas or that tells about real people, places, ideas, or events. To be classified as nonfiction, a work must be true. Dorothy West's "The Sun Parlor" (p. 490) is a true account of events related to a particular room in a house.

See also ***Autobiography; Biography;*** and ***Essay.***

NOVEL A ***novel*** is a long work of fiction. It has a plot that explores characters in conflict. A novel may also have one or more subplots, or minor stories, and several themes.

OCTAVE See ***Stanza.***

ONOMATOPOEIA ***Onomatopoeia*** is the use of words that imitate sounds. *Whirr, thud, sizzle,* and *hiss* are typical examples. Writers can deliberately choose words that contribute to a desired sound effect.

ORAL TRADITION The ***oral tradition*** is the retelling of songs, stories, and poems passed orally, or by spoken word, from generation to generation. Many folk songs, ballads, fairy tales, legends, and myths originated in the oral tradition.

See also ***Myth.***

OXYMORON An ***oxymoron*** is a combination of words that contradict each other. Examples are "deafening silence," "honest thief," "wise fool," and "bittersweet." This device is effective when the apparent contradiction reveals a deeper truth.

PARADOX A ***paradox*** is a statement that seems contradictory but that actually may express a deeper truth. Because a paradox is surprising, it catches the reader's attention.

PARALLELISM See ***Rhetorical Devices.***

PERSONIFICATION ***Personification*** is a type of figurative language in which a nonhuman subject is given human characteristics. Denise Levertov personifies a tree in her poem "A Tree Telling of Orpheus" (p. 659). In fact, the tree is the speaker in this poem: "I listened, and language came into my roots . . ."

See also ***Figurative Language.***

PERSUASION ***Persuasion*** is writing or speech that attempts to convince the reader to adopt a particular opinion or course of action.

PERSUASIVE ESSAY See ***Essay.***

PLOT ***Plot*** is the sequence of events in a literary work. In most novels, dramas, short stories, and narrative poems, the plot involves both characters and a central conflict. The plot usually begins with an *exposition* that introduces the setting, the characters, and the basic situation. This is followed by the *inciting incident*, which introduces the central conflict. The conflict then increases during the *development* until it reaches a high point of interest or suspense, the *climax*. All the events leading up to the climax make up the *rising action*. The climax is followed by the *falling action*, which leads to the *denouement*, or *resolution*, in which the conflict is resolved and in which a general insight may be conveyed.

POETRY ***Poetry*** is one of the three major types of literature, the others being prose and drama. Most poems make use of highly concise, musical, and emotionally charged

R21

language. Many also make use of imagery, figurative language, and special devices of sound such as rhyme. Poems are often divided into lines and stanzas and often employ regular rhythmical patterns, or meters. Poetry that does not follow a regular metrical pattern is called *free verse.*

See also ***Genre.***

POINT OF VIEW See ***Narrator.***

PROSE ***Prose*** is the ordinary form of written language. Most writing that is not poetry, drama, or song is considered prose. Prose is one of the major categories of literature and occurs in two forms: fiction and nonfiction.

See also ***Fiction; Genre;*** and ***Nonfiction.***

PROTAGONIST The ***protagonist*** is the main character in a literary work.

See also ***Antagonist*** and ***Character.***

PUN A ***pun*** is a play on words involving a word with two or more different meanings or two words that sound alike but have different meanings. In *Julius Caesar* (p. 892), there is a pun on the phrase *mend you* (Act I, Scene i, lines 17-18): "yet if you be out [angry], sir, I can mend you." The speaker is a cobbler and by *mend you* he means both "mend your shoes" and "improve your disposition."

QUATRAIN A ***quatrain*** is a stanza, or section, of a poem made up of four lines, usually with a definite rhythm and rhyme scheme.

REPETITION ***Repetition*** is the use of any element of language—a sound, a word, a phrase, a clause, or a sentence—more than once.

Poets use many kinds of repetition. *Alliteration, assonance, consonance, rhyme,* and *rhythm* are repetitions of certain sounds and sound patterns. A *refrain* is a repeated line or group of lines. In both prose and poetry, repetition is used for musical effects and for emphasis.

See also ***Alliteration; Assonance; Consonance; Rhyme;*** and ***Rhythm.***

RESOLUTION See ***Plot.***

RHETORICAL DEVICES ***Rhetorical devices*** are special patterns of words and ideas that create emphasis and stir emotion, especially in speeches or other oral presentations. *Parallelism,* for example, is the repetition of a grammatical structure in order to create a rhythm and make words more memorable. In "Keep Memory Alive" (p. 548), Elie Wiesel uses parallelism: "Neutrality helps the oppressor, never the victim. Silence encourages the tormentor, never the tormented."

Other common rhetorical devices include *restatement,* expressing the same idea in different words, and *rhetorical questions,* questions with obvious answers.

RHYME ***Rhyme*** is the repetition of sounds at the ends of words. *End rhyme* occurs when the rhyming words come at the ends of lines, as in "The Desired Swan Song" by Samuel Taylor Coleridge:

> Swans sing before they die—'twere no bad thing
> Should certain persons die before they sing.

Internal rhyme occurs when one of the rhyming words appears within a line, as in these lines from "The Waking" (p. 685):

> God bless the Ground! I shall walk softly *there,*
> And learn by going *where* I have to go.

Exact rhyme involves the repetition of the same final vowel and consonant sounds in words like *ball* and *hall. Slant rhyme* involves the repetition of words that sound alike but do not rhyme exactly, like *grove* and *love.*

See also ***Repetition*** and ***Rhyme Scheme.***

RHYME SCHEME A ***rhyme scheme*** is a regular pattern of rhyming words in a poem. The rhyme scheme of a poem is indicated by using different letters of the alphabet for each new rhyme. In an aabb stanza, for example, line 1 rhymes with line 2 and line 3 rhymes with line 4. "Meeting at Night" (p. 744) uses an abccba rhyme scheme in each of its two stanzas:

> The gray sea and the long black land; a
> And the yellow half-moon large and low; b
> And the startled little waves that leap c
> In fiery ringlets from their sleep, c
> As I gain the cove with pushing prow, b
> And quench its speed i' the slushy sand. a

Many poems use the same pattern of rhymes, though not the same rhymes, in each stanza.

See also ***Rhyme.***

RHYTHM ***Rhythm*** is the pattern of *beats,* or *stresses,* in spoken or written language. Some poems follow a very specific pattern, or meter, whereas prose and free verse may use the natural rhythms of everyday speech.

See also ***Meter.***

RISING ACTION See ***Plot.***

ROUND CHARACTER See ***Character.***

SATIRE A ***satire*** is a literary work that ridicules the foolishness and faults of individuals, an institution, society, or even humanity in general.

SCENE See ***Drama.***

SCIENCE FICTION ***Science fiction*** is writing that tells about imaginary events involving science or technology. Many science-fiction stories are set in the future. C. J. Cherryh's science-fiction story "The Threads of Time" (p. 229) plays with the dimension of time.

See also ***Fantasy.***

SENSORY LANGUAGE ***Sensory language*** is writing or speech that appeals to one or more of the senses.

See also ***Image.***

SESTET See ***Stanza.***

SET See ***Drama.***

SETTING The ***setting*** of a literary work is the time and place of the action. Time can include not only the historical period—past, present, or future—but also a specific year, season, or time of day. Place may involve not only the geographical place—a region, country, state, or town—but also the social, economic, or cultural environment.

In some stories, setting serves merely as a backdrop for action, a context in which the characters move and speak. In others, however, setting is a crucial element.

See also ***Mood.***

SHORT STORY A ***short story*** is a brief work of fiction. In most short stories, one main character faces a conflict that is resolved in the plot of the story. Great craftsmanship must go into the writing of a good story, for it has to accomplish its purpose in relatively few words.

See also ***Fiction*** and ***Genre.***

SIMILE A ***simile*** is a figure of speech in which the words like or as are used to compare two apparently dissimilar items. The comparison, however, surprises the reader into a fresh perception by finding an unexpected likeness. In "The Guitar" (p. 648), for example, García Lorca says that the guitar "weeps monotonously / As weeps the water, / As weeps the wind / Over snow."

SOLILOQUY A ***soliloquy*** is a long speech expressing the thoughts of a character alone on stage. In William Shakespeare's *Julius Caesar* (p. 892), Brutus delivers a soliloquy in which he confirms and justifies his participation in the plot to assassinate Caesar (Act II, Scene i, lines 10–34): "It must be by his death . . ."

See also ***Monologue.***

SONNET A ***sonnet*** is a fourteen-line lyric poem, usually written in rhymed iambic pentameter. The *English*, or *Shakespearean*, sonnet consists of three quatrains (four-line stanzas) and a couplet (two lines), usually rhyming *abab cdcd efef gg.* The couplet usually comments on the ideas contained in the preceding twelve lines. The sonnet is usually not printed with the stanzas divided, but a reader can see distinct ideas in each. (See the Sonnet 18 by William Shakespeare on page 686.)

The *Italian*, or *Petrarchan*, sonnet consists of an octave (eight-line stanza) and a sestet (six-line stanza). Often, the octave rhymes *abbaabba* and the sestet rhymes *cdecde.* The octave states a theme or asks a question. The sestet comments on the theme or answers the question.

See also ***Lyric Poem; Meter;*** and ***Stanza.***

SPEAKER The ***speaker*** is the imaginary voice assumed by the writer of a poem. In many poems, the speaker is not identified by name. When reading a poem, remember that the speaker within the poem may be a person, an animal, a thing, or an abstraction. The speaker in the following stanza by Emily Dickinson is a person who has died:

> Because I could not stop for Death—
> He kindly stopped for me—
> The Carriage held but just Ourselves—
> And Immortality.

STAGE DIRECTIONS *Stage directions* are notes included in a drama to describe how the work is to be performed or staged. These instructions are printed in italics and are not spoken aloud. They are used to describe sets, lighting, sound effects, and the appearance, personalities, and movements of characters.

See also ***Drama.***

STANZA A ***stanza*** is a repeated grouping of two or more lines in a poem that often share a pattern of rhythm and rhyme. Stanzas are sometimes named according to the number of lines they have—for example, a *couplet,* two lines; a *quatrain,* four lines; a *sestet,* six lines; and an *octave,* eight lines.

See also Sonnet.

STATIC CHARACTER See ***Character.***

STYLE ***Style*** refers to an author's unique way of writing. Elements determining style include diction; tone; characteristic use of figurative language, dialect, or rhythmic devices; and typical grammatical structures and patterns.

See also ***Diction*** and ***Tone.***

SURPRISE ENDING A ***surprise ending*** is a conclusion that violates the expectations of the reader but in a way that is both logical and believable.

O. Henry's "One Thousand Dollars" (p. 308) and Saki's "The Open Window" (p. 195) have surprise endings. Both authors were masters of this form.

SYMBOL A ***symbol*** is a character, place, thing or event that stands for something else, often an abstract idea. For example, a flag is a piece of cloth, but it also represents the idea of a country. Writers sometimes use conventional symbols like flags. Frequently, however, they create symbols of their own through emphasis or repetition. In "The Garden of Stubborn Cats" (p. 384), for example, the cats come to symbolize nature's stubborn resistance to human development.

THEME A ***theme*** is a central message or insight into life revealed through a literary work.

The theme of a literary work may be stated directly or implied. When the theme of a work is implied, readers think about what the work suggests about people or life.

Archetypal themes are those that occur in folklore and literature across the world and throughout history. The hero who makes civilization possible, the theme of "Prometheus and the First People" (p. 1066), is an example of an archetypal theme.

TONE The ***tone*** of a literary work is the writer's attitude toward his or her audience and subject. The tone can often be described by a single adjective, such as *formal* or *informal, serious* or *playful, bitter* or *ironic*. When Valenzuela discusses the fate of Juan in "The Censors" (p. 410), she uses an ironic tone: ". . . another victim of his devotion to his work."

See also ***Mood.***

TRAGEDY A ***tragedy*** is a work of literature, especially a play, that tells of a catastrophe, a disaster or great misfortune, for the main character. In ancient Greek drama, the main character was always a significant person—a king or a hero—and the cause of the tragedy was often a tragic flaw, or weakness, in his or her character. In modern drama, the main character can be an ordinary person, and the cause of the tragedy can be some evil in society itself. Tragedy not only arouses fear and pity in the audience, but also, in some cases, conveys a sense of the grandeur and nobility of the human spirit.

Shakespeare's *Julius Caesar* (p. 892) is a tragedy. Brutus suffers from the tragic flaw of blindness to reality and people's motives. His noble-mindedness is almost a form of arrogance. This flaw ultimately leads to his death.

See also ***Drama.***

UNDERSTATEMENT An ***understatement*** is a figure of speech in which the stated meaning is purposely less than (or "under") what is really meant. It is the opposite of ***hyperbole,*** which is a deliberate exaggeration.

UNIVERSAL THEME A ***universal theme*** is a message about life that can be understood by most cultures. Many folk tales and examples of classic literature address universal themes such as the importance of courage, the effects of honesty, or the danger of greed.

VERBAL IRONY See ***Irony.***

VILLANELLE A ***villanelle*** is a nineteen-line lyric poem written in five three-line stanzas and ending in a four-line stanza. It uses two rhymes and repeats two refrain lines that appear initially in the first and third lines of the first stanza. These lines then appear alternately as the third line of subsequent three-line stanzas and, finally, as the last two lines of the poem. Theodore Roethke's "The Waking" (p. 684) is a villanelle.

VOICE ***Voice*** is a writer's distinctive "sound" or way of "speaking" on the page. It is related to such elements as word choice, sentence structure, and tone. It is similar to an individual's speech style and can be described in the same way—fast, slow, blunt, meandering, breathless, and so on.

Voice resembles ***style,*** an author's typical way of writing, but style usually refers to a quality that can be found throughout an author's body of work, while an author's voice may sometimes vary from work to work.

See also ***Style.***

Tips for Discussing Literature

As you read and study literature, discussion with other readers can help you understand, enjoy, and develop interpretations of what you read. Use the following tips to practice good speaking and listening skills while participating in group discussions of literature.

- ## Understand the purpose of your discussion

  When you discuss literature, your purpose is to broaden your understanding and appreciation of a work by testing your own ideas and hearing the ideas of others. Stay focused on the literature you are discussing and keep your comments relevant to that literature. Starting with one focus question will help to keep your discussion on track.

- ## Communicate effectively

  Effective communication requires thinking before speaking. Plan the points that you want to make and decide how you will express them. Organize these points in logical order and cite details from the work to support your ideas. Jot down informal notes to help keep your ideas focused.

  Remember to speak clearly, pronouncing words slowly and carefully so that others can understand your points. Also, keep in mind that some literature touches readers deeply—be aware of the possibility of counterproductive emotional responses and work to control them. Negative emotional responses can also be conveyed through body language, so work to demonstrate respect in your demeanor as well as in your words.

- ## Encourage everyone to participate

  While some people are comfortable participating in discussions, others are less eager to speak up in groups. However, everyone should work to contribute thoughts and ideas. To encourage the entire group's participation, try the following strategies:

  - If you enjoy speaking, avoid monopolizing the conversation. After sharing your ideas, encourage others to share theirs.
  - Try different roles. For example, have everyone take turns being the facilitator or host of the discussion.
  - Use a prop, such as a book or gavel. Pass the prop around the group, allowing whomever is holding the prop to have the floor.

- ## Make relevant contributions

  Especially when responding to a short story, a poem, or a novel, avoid simply summarizing the plot. Instead, consider *what* you think might happen next, *why* events take place as they do, or *how* a writer provokes a response in you. Let your ideas inspire deeper thought or discussion about the literature.

- ## Consider other ideas and interpretations

  A work of literature can generate a wide variety of responses in different readers—and that can make your discussions exciting. Be open to the idea that many interpretations can be valid. To support your own ideas, point to the events, descriptions,

characters, or other literary elements in the work that produced your interpretation. To consider someone else's ideas, decide whether details in the work support the interpretation he or she presents. Be sure to convey your criticism of the ideas of others in a respectful and supportive manner.

- **Ask questions and extend the contributions of others**

  Get in the habit of asking questions to help you clarify your understanding of another reader's ideas. You can also use questions to call attention to possible areas of confusion, to points that are open to debate, or to errors.

  In addition, offer elaboration of the points that others make by providing examples and illustrations. To move a discussion forward, pause occasionally to summarize and evaluate tentative conclusions reached by the group members. Then, continue the discussion with a fresh understanding of the material and ideas you have already covered.

- **Manage differing opinions and views**

  Each participant brings his or her own personality, experiences, ideas, cultural background, likes and dislikes to the experience of reading, making disagreement almost inevitable. As differences arise, be sensitive to each individual's point of view. Do not personalize disagreements, but keep them focused on the literature or ideas under discussion.

  When you meet with a group to discuss literature, use a chart like the one shown to analyze the discussion.

Work Being Discussed:	
Focus Question:	
Your Response:	Another Student's Response:
Supporting Evidence:	Supporting Evidence:

Literary Criticism

Criticism is writing that explores the meaning and techniques of literary works, usually in order to evaluate them. Writing criticism can help you think through your experience of a work of literature and can also help others deepen their own understanding. All literary criticism shares similar goals:

- ***Making Connections*** within or between works, or between a work of literature and its context
- ***Making Distinctions*** or showing differences between elements of a single work or aspects of two or more works
- ***Achieving Insights*** that were not apparent from a superficial reading
- ***Making a Judgment*** about the quality or value of a literary work

Critics use various ***theories of literary criticism*** to understand, appreciate, and evaluate literature. Some theories focus on the context of the work while others focus on the work itself. Sometimes critics combine one or more theories. These charts show a few examples of the many theories of criticism:

Focus on Contexts	
Human Experience	**Mythic Criticism** Explores universal situations, characters, and symbols called archetypes as they appear in a literary work.
Culture and History	**Historic Criticism** Analyzes how circumstances or ideas of an era influence a work
Author's Life	**Biographical Criticism** Explains how the author's life sheds light on the work

Focus on the Work Itself
Formal Criticism Shows how the work reflects characteristics of the genre, or literary type, to which it belongs

Examples of Literary Theories in Action

- ***Mythic Criticism:*** discussing how the Greek myth "Prometheus and the First People," p. 1066, reveals Prometheus as an archetypal character
- ***Historical Criticism:*** showing how William Shakespeare was influenced by Elizabethan concepts of nature and politics in *Julius Caesar*, p. 892
- ***Biographical Criticism:*** showing James Thurber's family relationships influenced the theme of "The Dog That Bit People," p. 525
- ***Formal Criticism:*** analyzing how "Contents of the Dead Man's Pocket," p. 118, combines short-story elements like plot, suspense, setting, character, and theme

Literary Movements

Our literary heritage has been shaped by a number of ***literary movements,*** directions in literature characterized by shared assumptions, beliefs, and practices. This chart shows, in chronological order, some important literary movements. While these movements developed at particular historical moments, all of them may still influence individual writers working today.

Movement	Beliefs and Practices	Examples
Classicism Europe during the Renaissance (c. 1300–1650)	• Looks to classical literature of ancient Greece and Rome as models • Values logic, clarity, balance, and restraint • Prefers "ordered" nature of parks and gardens	the clarity and restraint of Robert Frost's verse ("The Road Not Taken," p.659)
Romanticism Europe during the late 1700s and the early 1800s	• Rebels against Classicism • Values imagination and emotion • Focuses on Everyday life	the celebration of the natural world in Rachel carson's writings ("Silent Spring," p. 153)
Realism Europe and America from the mid–1800s to the 1890s	• Rebels against Romanticism's search for the ideal • Focuses on everyday life	the faithful rendering of Pueblo life in Leslie Mamon Silko's fiction ("The Man to Send Rain Clouds," p. 268)
Naturalism Europe and America during the late 1800s and early 1900s	• Assumes people cannot choose their fate but are shaped by psychological and social forces • Views society as a competitive jungle	the portrayal of characters as victims of social pressures and psychology in Guy de Maupassant's fiction ("The Necklace," p. 294)
Modernism World-wide between 1890 and 1945	• In response to WWI, questions human reason • Focuses on studies of the unconscious and the art of primitive peoples • Experiments with language and form	the experiments with language in E. E. Cummings's poetry ("maggie and mily and molly and may," p. 668)
Post-Modernism World-wide after 1945; still prevalent today	• Believes works of art comment on themselves • Finds inspiration in information technology	the self-commentary in Scott McLoud's work ("Understanding Comics," p. 172)

Tips for Improving Reading Fluency

When you were younger, you learned to read. Then, you read to expand your experiences or for pure enjoyment. Now, you are expected to read to learn. As you progress in school, you are given more and more material to read. The tips on these pages will help you improve your reading fluency, or your ability to read easily, smoothly, and expressively.

Keeping Your Concentration

One common problem that readers face is the loss of concentration. When you are reading an assignment, you might find yourself rereading the same sentence several times without really understanding it. The first step in changing this behavior is to notice that you do it. Becoming an active, aware reader will help you get the most from your assignments. Practice using these strategies:

- Cover what you have already read with a note card as you go along. Then, you will not be able to reread without noticing that you are doing it.
- Set a purpose for reading beyond just completing the assignment. Then, read actively by pausing to ask yourself questions about the material as you read.
- Use the Reading Strategy instruction and notes that appear with each selection in this textbook.
- Stop reading after a specified period of time (for example, 5 minutes) and summarize what you have read. To help you with this strategy, use the Reading Check questions that appear with each selection in this textbook. Reread to find any answers you do not know.

Reading Phrases

Fluent readers read phrases rather than individual words. Reading this way will speed up your reading and improve your comprehension. Here are some useful ideas:

- Experts recommend rereading as a strategy to increase fluency. Choose a passage of text that is neither too hard nor too easy. Read the same passage aloud several times until you can read it smoothly. When you can read the passage fluently, pick another passage and keep practicing.
- Read aloud into a tape recorder. Then, listen to the recording, noting your accuracy, pacing, and expression. You can also read aloud and share feedback with a partner.
- Use the *Prentice Hall Listening to Literature* audiotapes or CDs to hear the selections read aloud. Read along silently in your textbook, noticing how the reader uses his or her voice and emphasizes certain words and phrases.

Understanding Key Vocabulary

If you do not understand some of the words in an assignment, you may miss out on important concepts. Therefore, it is helpful to keep a dictionary nearby when you are reading. Follow these steps:

- Before you begin reading, scan the text for unfamiliar words or terms. Find out what those words mean before you begin reading.
- Use context—the surrounding words, phrases, and sentences—to help you determine the meanings of unfamiliar words.
- If you are unable to understand the meaning through context, refer to the dictionary.

Paying Attention to Punctuation

When you read, pay attention to punctuation. Commas, periods, exclamation points, semicolons, and colons tell you when to pause or stop. They also indicate relationships between groups of words. When you recognize these relationships, you will read with greater understanding and expression. Look at the chart below.

Punctuation Mark	Meaning
comma	brief pause
period	pause at the end of a thought
exclamation point	pause that indicates emphasis
semicolon	pause between related but distinct thoughts
colon	pause before giving explanation or examples

Using te Reading Fluency Checklist

Use the checklist below each time you read a selection in this textbook. In your Language Arts journal or notebook, note which skills you need to work on and chart your progress each week.

Reading Fluency Checklist
❑ Preview the text to check for difficult or unfamiliar words.
❑ Practice reading aloud.
❑ Read according to punctuation.
❑ Break down long sentences into the subject and its meaning.
❑ Read groups of words for meaning rather than reading single words.
❑ Read with expression (change your tone of voice to add meaning to the word).

Reading is a skill that can be improved with practice. The key to improving your fluency is to read. The more you read, the better your reading will become.

Types of Writing

Writing is a process that begins with the exploration of ideas and ends with the presentation of a final draft. Often, the types of writing are grouped into modes according to form and purpose.

Narration

Whenever writers tell any type of story, they are using **narration.** Most narratives share certain elements, such as characters, a setting, a sequence of events, and, often, a theme. Following are some types of narration:

Autobiographical Writing Autobiographical writing tells a true story about an important period, experience, or relationship in the writer's life. Effective autobiographical writing includes

- A series of events that involve the writer as the main character
- Details, thoughts, feelings, and insights from the writer's perspective
- A conflict or an event that affects the writer
- A logical organization that tells the story clearly
- Insights that the writer gained from the experience

Types of autobiographical writing include personal narratives, autobiographical sketches, reflective essays, eyewitness accounts, and memoirs.

Short Story A short story is a brief, creative narrative. Most short stories include

- Details that establish the setting in time and place
- A main character who undergoes a change or learns something during the course of the story
- A conflict or a problem to be introduced, developed, and resolved
- A plot, the series of events that make up the action of the story
- A theme or message about life

Types of short stories include realistic stories, fantasies, historical narratives, mysteries, thrillers, science-fiction stories, and adventure stories.

Description

Descriptive writing is writing that creates a vivid picture of a person, place, thing, or event. Most descriptive writing includes

- Sensory details—sights, sounds, smells, tastes, and physical sensations
- Vivid, precise language
- Figurative language or comparisons
- Adjectives and adverbs that paint a word picture
- An organization suited to the subject

Types of descriptive writing include description of ideas, observations, travel brochures, physical descriptions, functional descriptions, remembrances, and character sketches.

Persuasion

Persuasion is writing or speaking that attempts to convince people to accept a position or take a desired action. Following are some types of persuasion:

Persuasive Essay A persuasive essay presents a position on an issue, urges readers to accept that position, and may encourage a specific action. An effective persuasive essay

- Explores an issue of importance to the writer
- Addresses an issue that is arguable
- Uses facts, examples, statistics, or personal experiences to support a position
- Tries to influence the audience through appeals to the readers' knowledge, experiences, or emotions
- Uses clear organization to present a logical argument

Forms of persuasion include editorials, position papers, persuasive speeches, grant proposals, advertisements, and debates.

Advertisements An advertisement is a planned communication meant to be seen, heard, or read. It attempts to persuade an audience to buy a product or service, accept an idea, or support a cause. Advertisements may appear in printed or broadcast form. An effective advertisement includes

- A memorable slogan to grab the audience's attention
- A call to action
- Persuasive and/or informative text
- Striking visual or aural images
- Information about price, location, date, and time

Several common types of advertisements are public-service announcements, billboards, merchandise ads, service ads, and political campaign literature.

Expostion

Exposition is writing that relies on facts to inform or explain. Effective expository writing reflects a well-thought-out organization—one that includes a clear introduction, body, and conclusion. Here are some types of exposition:

Comparison-and-Contrast Essay A comparison-and-contrast essay analyzes the similarities and differences between or among two or more things. An effective comparison-and-contrast essay

- Identifies a purpose for comparison and contrast
- Identifies similarities and differences between or among two or more things, people, places, or ideas
- Gives factual details about the subjects
- Uses an organizational plan suited to the topic and purpose

Cause-and-Effect Essay A cause-and-effect essay examines the relationship between events, explaining how one event or situation causes another. A successful cause-and-effect essay includes

- A discussion of a cause, event, or condition that produces a specific result
- An explanation of an effect, outcome, or result
- Evidence and examples to support the explanation
- A logical organization that makes the explanation clear

Problem-and-Solution Essay A problem-and-solution essay describes a problem and offers one or more solutions to it. It describes a clear set of steps to achieve a result. An effective problem-and-solution essay includes

- A clear statement of the problem, with its causes and effects summarized for the reader
- The most important aspects of the problem
- A proposal of at least one realistic solution
- Facts, statistics, data, or expert testimony to support the solution
- A clear organization that makes the relationship between problem and solution obvious

Research Research Writing

Research writing is based on information gathered from outside sources. A research paper—a focused study of a topic—helps writers explore and connect ideas, make discoveries, and share their findings with an audience. An effective research paper

- Focuses on a specific, narrow topic, which is usually summarized in a thesis statement
- Presents relevant information from a wide variety of sources
- Uses a clear organization that includes an introduction, body, and conclusion
- Includes a bibliography or works-cited list that identifies the sources from which the information was drawn

Other types of writing that depend on accurate and insightful research include multimedia presentations, statistical reports, annotated bibliographies, and experiment journals.

Response to Literature

When you write a **response-to-literature essay,** you give yourself the opportunity to discover *what, how,* and *why* a piece of writing affected you. An effective response

- Contains a reaction to a poem, story, essay, or other work of literature
- Analyzes the content of a literary work, its related ideas, or the work's effect on the reader
- Presents a thesis statement to identify the nature of the response
- Focuses on a single aspect of the work or gives a general overview
- Supports opinion with evidence from the work addressed

The following are just a few of the ways you might respond in writing to a literary work: reader's response journals, literary letters, and literary analyses.

Workplace Writing

Workplace writing is the format you will use most after you finish school. In general, workplace writing is fact-based and meant to communicate specific information in a structured format. Effective workplace writing

- Communicates information concisely
- Includes details that provide necessary information and anticipate potential questions
- Is error-free and neatly presented

Common types of workplace writing include business letters, memorandums, résumés, forms, and applications.

Writing Friendly Letters

Writing Friendly Letters

A friendly letter is an informal letter to a friend, a family member, or anyone with whom the writer wants to communicate in a personal way. Most friendly letters are made up of five parts:

- ✔ the heading
- ✔ the salutation, or greeting
- ✔ the body
- ✔ the closing
- ✔ the signature

The purpose of a friendly letter is often one of the following:

- ✔ to share personal news and feelings
- ✔ to send or to answer an invitation
- ✔ to express thanks

Model Friendly Letter

In this friendly letter, Betsy thanks her grandparents for a birthday present and gives them some news about her life.

11 Old Farm Road
Topsham, Maine 04011

April 14, 20—

The **heading** includes the writer's address and the date on which he or she wrote the letter.

Dear Grandma and Grandpa,

Thank you for the sweater you sent me for my birthday. It fits perfectly, and I love the color. I wore my new sweater to the carnival at school last weekend and got lots of compliments.

The weather here has been cool but sunny. Mom thinks that "real" spring will never come. I can't wait until it's warm enough to go swimming.

School is going fairly well. I really like my Social Studies class. We are learning about the U.S. Constitution, and I think it's very interesting. Maybe I will be a lawyer when I grow up.

When are you coming out to visit us? We haven't seen you since Thanksgiving. You can stay in my room when you come. I'll be happy to sleep on the couch. (The TV is in that room!!)

Well, thanks again and hope all is well with you.

The **body** is the main part of the letter and contains the basic message.

Love,

Betsy

Some common **closings** for personal letters include "Best Wishes", "Love "Sincerely", and "Yours Truly".

Writing Business Letters

Formatting Business Letters

Business letters follow one of several acceptable formats. In **block format,** each part of the letter begins at the left margin. A double space is used between paragraphs. In **modified block format,** some parts of the letter are indented to the center of the page. No matter which format is used, all letters in business format have a heading, an inside address, a salutation, or greeting, a body, a closing, and a signature. These parts are shown and annotated on the model business letter below, formatted in modified block style.

Model Business Letter

In this letter, Yolanda Dodson uses modified block format to request information.

Students for a Cleaner Planet
c/o Memorial High School
333 Veteran's Drive
Denver, CO 80211

January 25, 20—

Steven Wilson, Director
Resource Recovery Really Works
300 Oak Street
Denver, CO 80216

Dear Mr. Wilson:

Memorial High School would like to start a branch of your successful recycling program. We share your commitment to reclaiming as much reusable material as we can. Because your program has been successful in other neighborhoods, we're sure that it can work in our community. Our school includes grades 9–12 and has about 800 students.

Would you send us some information about your community recycling program? For example, we need to know what materials can be recycled and how we can implement the program.

At least fifty students have already expressed an interest in getting involved, so I know we'll have the people power to make the program work. Please help us get started.

Thank you in advance for your time and consideration.

Sincerely,

Yolanda Dodson

Yolanda Dodson

The **inside address** indicates where the letter will be sent.

A **salutation** is punctuated by a colon. When the specific addressee is not known, use a general greeting such as "To whom it may concern:"

The **body** of the letter states the writer's purpose. In this case, the writer requests information.

The **closing** "Sincerely" is common, but "Yours truly" or "Respectfully yours" are also acceptable. To end the letter, the writer types her name and provides a signature.

Writing a Résumé

Writing a Résumé

A résumé summarizes your educational background, work experiences, relevant skills, and other employment qualifications. It also tells potential employers how to contact you. An effective résumé presents the applicant's name, address, and phone number. It follows an accepted résumé organization, using labels and headings to guide readers.

A résumé should outline the applicant's educational background, life experiences, and related qualifications using precise and active language.

Model Résumé

With this résumé, James, a college student, hopes to find a full-time job.

James H. McSweeney
1234 Greene Street, Apt. #3
Charlotte, NC 28223
jamesmcswe@email.com

> Put contact information such as name, address, telephone number, and e-mail address at the top of the résumé.

EDUCATION

University of North Carolina; Charlotte, NC
Bachelor of Science in Administrative Information Management
Expected; June 20, _ _

WORK EXPERIENCE

> James uses heads with capital letters to identify each section of his résumé.

P.E.S. Engineering; Charlotte, NC
Summer 2005
Intern
Designed a customized record management system for the engineers; trained in the data entry department.

Gen X Wireless Services; Paramus, NJ
2003–2005 (summers and breaks)
Receivables Management Representative
Handled incoming accounts-receivable call for cellular phone accounts in the New York, New Jersey, and Connecticut markets; trained other representatives.

Computer Services Department; University of North Carolina, Charlotte, NC
Fall 2004
Computer Lab Technician
Assisted students in the use of software and hardware; responded to user questions and problems.

> Entries on résumé should be short and to the point.

COMPUTER SKILLS
HTML, XML, Excel, Microsoft Access, and Microsoft Office.

REFERENCES
Furnished on request.

Citing Sources and Preparing Manuscript

In research writing, cite your sources. In the body of your paper, provide a footnote, an endnote, or a parenthetical citation, identifying the sources of facts, opinions, or quotations. At the end of your paper, provide a bibliography or a works-cited list, a list of all the sources you cite. Follow an established format, such as Modern Language Association (MLA) Style.

Works-Cited List (MLA Style)

A works-cited list must contain accurate information sufficient to enable a reader to locate each source you cite. The basic components of an entry are as follows:

- Name of the author, editor, translator, or group responsible for the work
- Title of the work
- Place and date of publication
- Publisher

For print materials, the information required for a citation generally appears on the copyright and title pages of a work. For the format of works-cited list entries, consult the examples at right and in the chart on page R34.

Parenthetical Citations (MLA Style)

A parenthetical citation briefly identifies the source from which you have taken a specific quotation, factual claim, or opinion. It refers the reader to one of the entries on your works-cited list. A parenthetical citation has the following features:

- It appears in parentheses.
- It identifies the source by the last name of the author, editor, or translator.
- It gives a page reference, identifying the page of the source on which the information cited can be found.

Punctuation A parenthetical citation generally falls outside a closing quotation mark but within the final punctuation of a clause or sentence. For a long quotation set off from the rest of your text, place the citation at the end of the excerpt without any punctuation following.

Special Cases

- If the author is an organization, use the organization's name, in a shortened version if necessary.
- If you cite more than one work by the same author, add the title or a shortened version of the title.

Sample Works Cited Lists

Carwardine, Mark, Erich Hoyt, R. Ewan Fordyce, and Peter Gill. *The Nature Company Guides: Whales, Dolphins, and Porpoises.* New York: Time-Life Books, 1998.

Whales in Danger. "Discovering Whales." 18 Oct 1999. <http://whales.magna.com.au/DISCOVER>

Neruda, Pablo. *"Ode to Spring." Odes to Opposites.* Trans Ken Krabbenhoft. Ed. and illus. Ferris Cook. Boston: Little, Brown and Company, 1995.

The Saga of the Volsungs. Trans. Jesse L. Byock. London: Penguin Books, 1990.

List an anonymous work by title.

List both the title of the work and the collection in which it is found.

Sample Parenthetical Citations

It makes sense that baleen whales such as the blue whale, the bowhead whale, the humpback whale, and the sei whale (to name just a few) grow to immense sizes (Carwardine, Hoyt, and Fordyce 19–21). The blue whale has grooves running from under its chin to partway along the length of its underbelly. As in some other whales, these grooves expand and allow even more food and water to be taken in (Ellis 18–21).

Author's last name

Page numbers where information can be found

LA Style for Listing Sources

Book with one author	Pyles, Thomas. *The Origins and Development of the English Language.* 2nd ed. New York: Harcourt Brace Jovanovich, Inc., 1971.
Book with two or three authors	McCrum, Robert, William Cran, and Robert MacNeil. *The Story of English.* New York: Penguin Books, 1987.
Book with an editor	Truth, Sojourner. *Narrative of Sojourner Truth.* Ed. Margaret Washington. New York: Vintage Books, 1993.
Book with more than three authors or editors	Donald, Robert B., et al. *Writing Clear Essays.* Upper Saddle River, NJ: Prentice Hall, Inc., 1996.
Single work from an anthology	Hawthorne, Nathaniel. "Young Goodman Brown." *Literature: An Introduction to Reading and Writing.* Ed, Edgar V. Roberts and Henry E. Jacobs. Upper Saddle River, NJ: Prentice Hall, Inc., 1998. 376–385. [Indicate pages for the entire selection.]
Introduction in a published edition	Washington, Margaret. Introduction. *Narrative of Sojourner, Truth.* By Sojourner Truth. Ed. Margaret Washington. New York: Vintage Books, 1993, pp. v–xi.
Signed article in a weekly magazine	Wallace, C. (2000, February 14). A Vodacious Deal. *Time,* 155, 63.
Signed article in a monthly magazine	Gustaitis, Joseph. "The Sticky History of Chewing Gum." *American History* Oct. 1998: 30–38.
Unsigned editorial or story	"Selective Silence." Editorial. *Wall Street Journal* 11 Feb. 2000: A14. [If the editorial or story is signed, begin with the author's name.]
Signed pamphlet or brochure	[Treat the pamphlet as though it were a book.]
Pamphlet with no author, publisher, or date	*Are You at Risk of Heart Attack?* n.p. n.d. [n.p. n.d. indicates that there is no known publisher or date.]
Filmstrips, slide programs, videocassettes, DVDs, and other audiovisual media	*The Diary of Anne Frank.* Dir. George Stevens. Perf. Millie Perkins, Shelly Winters, Joseph Schildkraut, Lou Jacobi, and Richard Beymer. Twentieth Century Fox, 1959.
Radio or television program transcript	*"The First Immortal Generation." Ockam's Razor.* Host Robyn Williams. Guest Damien Broderick. National Public Radio. 23 May 1999. Transcript.
Internet	"Fun Facts About Gum." NACGM site. National Association of Chewing Gum Manufacturers. 19 Dec. 1999 <http://www.nacgm.org/consumer/funfacts.html> [Indicate the date you accessed the information. Content and addresses at Web sites change frequently.]
Newspaper	Thurow, Roger. "South Africans Who Fought for Sanctions Now Scrap for Investors." *Wall Street Journal* 11 Feb. 2000: A1+ [For a multipage article, write only the first page number on which it appears, followed by a plus sign.]
Personal interview	Smith, Jane. Personal interview. 10 Feb. 2000.
CD (with multiple publishers)	Simms, James, ed. *Romeo and Juliet.* By William Shakespeare. CD-ROM. Oxford: Attica Cybernetics Ltd.; London: BBC Education; London: HarperCollins Publishers, 1995.
Signed article from an encyclopedia	Askeland, Donald R. (1991). "Welding." *World Book Encyclopedia.* 1991 ed.

Guide to Rubrics

What is a rubric?

A rubric is a tool, often in the form of a chart or a grid, that helps you assess your work. Rubrics are particularly helpful for writing and speaking assignments.

To help you or others assess, or evaluate, your work, a rubric offers several specific criteria to be applied to your work. Then, the rubric helps you or an evaluator indicate your range of success or failure according to those specific criteria. Rubrics are often used to evaluate writing for standardized tests.

Using a rubric will save you time, focus your learning, and improve the work you do. When you know what the rubric will be before you begin writing a persuasive essay, for example, you will be aware as you write of specific criteria that are important in that kind of an essay. As you evaluate the essay before giving it to your teacher, you will focus on the specific areas that your teacher wants you to master—or on areas that you know present challenges for you. Instead of searching through your work randomly for any way to improve it or correct its errors, you will have a clear and helpful focus on specific criteria.

How are rubrics constructed?

Rubrics can be constructed in several different ways.

- Your teacher may assign a rubric for a specific assignment.
- Your teacher may direct you to a rubric in your textbook.
- Your teacher and your class may construct a rubric for a particular assignment together.
- You and your classmates may construct a rubric together.
- You may create your own rubric with criteria you want to evaluate in your work.

How will a rubric help me?

A rubric will help you assess your work on a scale. Scales vary from rubric to rubric but usually range from 6 to 1, 5 to 1, or 4 to 1, with 6, 5, or 4 being the highest score and 1 being the lowest. If someone else is using the rubric to assess your work, the rubric will give your evaluator a clear range within which to place your work. If you are using the rubric yourself, it will help you make improvements to your work.

What are the types of rubrics?

- A holistic rubric has general criteria that can apply to a variety of assignments. See p. R-40 for an example of a holistic rubric.
- An analytic rubric is specific to a particular assignment. The criteria for evaluation address the specific issues important in that assignment. See p. R-39 for examples of analytic rubrics.

Sample Analytic Rubrics

Rubric With a 4-point Scale

The following analytic rubric is an example of a rubric to assess a persuasive essay. It will help you evaluate focus, organization, support/elaboration, and style/convention.

	Focus	Organization	Support/Elaboration	Style/Convention
4	Demonstrates highly effective word choice; clearly focused on task.	Uses clear, consistent organizational strategy.	Provides convincing, well-elaborated reasons to support the position.	Incorporates transitions; includes very few mechanical errors.
3	Demonstrates good word choice; stays focused on persuasive task.	Uses clear organizational strategy with occasional inconsistencies.	Provides two or more moderately elaborated reasons to support the position.	Incorporates some transitions; includes few mechanical errors.
2	Shows some good word choices; minimally stays focused on persuasive task.	Uses inconsistent organizational strategy; presentation is not logical.	Provides several reasons, but few are elaborated; only one elaborated reason.	Incorporates few transitions; includes many mechanical errors.
1	Shows lack of attention to persuasive task.	Demonstrates lack of organizational strategy.	Provides no specific reasons or does not elaborate.	Does not connect ideas; includes many mechanical errors.

Rubric With a 6-point Scale

The following analytic rubric is an example of a rubric to assess a persuasive essay. It will help you evaluate presentation, position, evidence, and arguments.

	Presentation	Position	Evidence	Arguments
6	Essay clearly and effectively addresses an issue with more than one side.	Essay clearly states a supportable position on the issue.	All evidence is logically organized, well presented, and supports the position.	All reader concerns and counterarguments are effectively addressed.
5	Most of essay addresses an issue that has more than one side.	Essay clearly states a position on the issue.	Most evidence is logically organized, well presented, and supports the position.	Most reader concerns and counterarguments are effectively addressed.
4	Essay adequately addresses issue that has more than one side.	Essay adequately states a position on the issue.	Many parts of evidence support the position; some evidence is out of order.	Many reader concerns and counterarguments are adequately addressed.
3	Essay addresses issue with two sides but does not present second side clearly.	Essay states a position on the issue, but the position is difficult to support.	Some evidence supports the position, but some evidence is out of order.	Some reader concerns and counterarguments are addressed.
2	Essay addresses issue with two sides but does not present second side.	Essay states a position on the issue, but the position is not supportable.	Not much evidence supports the position, and what is included is out of order.	A few reader concerns and counterarguments are addressed.
1	Essay does not address issue with more than one side.	Essay does not state a position on the issue.	No evidence supports the position.	No reader concerns or counterarguments are addressed.

Sample Holistic Rubric

Holistic rubrics such as this one are sometimes used to assess writing assignments on standardized tests. Notice that the criteria for evaluation are focus, organization, support, and use of conventions.

Points	Criteria
6 Points	• The writing is strongly focused and shows fresh insight into the writing task. • The writing is marked by a sense of completeness and coherence and is organized with a logical progression of ideas. • A main idea is fully developed, and support is specific and substantial. • A mature command of the language is evident, and the writing may employ characteristic creative writing strategies. • Sentence structure is varied, and writing is free of all but purposefully used fragments. • Virtually no errors in writing conventions appear.
5 Points	• The writing is clearly focused on the task. • The writing is well organized and has a logical progression of ideas, though there may be occasional lapses. • A main idea is well developed and supported with relevant detail. • Sentence structure is varied, and the writing is free of fragments, except when used purposefully. • Writing conventions are followed correctly.
4 Points	• The writing is clearly focused on the task, but extraneous material may intrude at times. • Clear organizational pattern is present, though lapses may occur. • A main idea is adequately supported, but development may be uneven. • Sentence structure is generally fragment free but shows little variation. • Writing conventions are generally followed correctly.
3 Points	• Writing is generally focused on the task, but extraneous material may intrude at times. • An organizational pattern is evident, but writing may lack a logical progression of ideas. • Support for the main idea is generally present but is sometimes illogical. • Sentence structure is generally free of fragments, but there is almost no variation. • The work generally demonstrates a knowledge of writing conventions, with occasional misspellings.
2 Points	• The writing is related to the task but generally lacks focus. • There is little evidence of organizational pattern, and there is little sense of cohesion. • Support for the main idea is generally inadequate, illogical, or absent. • Sentence structure is unvaried, and serious errors may occur. • Errors in writing conventions and spellings are frequent.
1 Point	• The writing may have little connection to the task and is generally unfocused. • There has been little attempt at organization or development. • The paper seems fragmented, with no clear main idea. • Sentence structure is unvaried, and serious errors appear. • Poor word choice and poor command of the language obscure meaning. • Errors in writing conventions and spelling are frequent.
Unscorable	The paper is considered unscorable if: • The response is unrelated to the task or is simply a rewording of the prompt. • The response has been copied from a published work. • The student did not write a response. • The response is illegible. • The words in the response are arranged with no meaning. • There is an insufficient amount of writing to score.

Student Model

Persuasive Writing

This persuasive letter, which would receive a top score according to a persuasive rubric, is a response to the following writing prompt, or assignment:

With the increased use of technology in the workplace, the skills that high-school graduates must possess have changed. Write a letter to your principal advocating new technology courses that could give high-school graduates a competitive edge.

Dear Principal:

I am writing to alert you to an urgent need in our school's curriculum. We need computer graphics courses!

> The letter begins with an engaging introduction that clearly states the persuasive focus.

Although you would have to find funds to buy the equipment, I've concluded that setting up this course would well be worth it. By adding this course, you would be adding many high paying career options for students. Computer graphics is a type of art, and businesses all around us involve art in some form. You see computer graphics in commercials, movies, news broadcasts, weather broadcasts, architectural design, and business presentations. Workers with computer graphics skills are well paid because they are in such high demand.

You may argue that the school already has computer science classes. Good point! I'm in a computer science class and it is mainly programming. Once we did have an assignment to design a graphic of a pumpkin. You wouldn't believe how much coding it takes to get a simple, animated drawing. In order to get a really creative image with definite lines, shading, lifelike colors, and texture, you need to use computer graphics software designed especially for that purpose. With software, you can make images that move and talk smoothly and environments with realistic colors and lighting. This is the same graphics software that businesses use for commercials, movies, and brochures. Students should be learning how to use this software.

> The author effectively counters an opposing argument to increase the persuasive power of her own argument.

Most importantly, computer graphics is a subject area that allows students to express their creativity. Adding a computer graphics course would have a positive effect on students. Course participates would enjoy doing their assignments, so they would earn good grades and turn in creative work. The energy and enthusiasm they would bring to their projects would catch the attention of the community at large. As a result, they would make the school and the principal look good.

> A positive argument that is well supported enhances the letter's persuasive appeal.

As you can see, adding a computer graphics course could be a very profitable idea for you, the students, and the community. You would be ensuring the success of the students who desire an art or computer career. You would be opening hundreds of different career pathways. Wouldn't it be great to know you were the reason for these students' success? Thanks for your time and consideration.

Sincerely,
Dawn Witherspoon

21st Century Skills

New technology has created many new ways to communicate. Today, it is easy to contribute information to the Internet and send a variety of messages to friends far and near. You can also share your ideas through photos, illustrations, video, and sound recordings. *21st Century Skills* gives you an overview of some ways you can use today's technology to create, share, and find information. Here are the topics you will find in this section.

- ✔ Blogs
- ✔ Social Networking
- ✔ Widgets & Feeds
- ✔ Multimedia Elements
- ✔ Podcasts
- ✔ Wikis

BLOGS

A **blog** is a common form of online writing. The word *blog* is a contraction of *Web log.* Most blogs include a series of entries known as *posts.* The posts appear in a single column and are displayed in reverse chronological order. That means that the most recent post is at the top of the page. As you scroll down, you will find earlier posts.

Blogs have become increasingly popular. Researchers estimate that 75,000 new blogs are launched every day. Blog authors are often called *bloggers.* They can use their personal sites to share ideas, songs, videos, photos, and other media. People who read blogs can often post their responses with a comments feature found in each new post.

Because blogs are designed so that they are easy to update, bloggers can post new messages as often as they like, often daily. For some people blogs become a public journal or diary, in which they share their thought about daily events.

Types of Blogs

Not all blogs are the same. Many blogs have a single author, but others are group projects. These are some common types of blog:

- ✔ Personal blogs often have a general focus. Bloggers post their thoughts on any topic they find interesting in their daily lives.
- ✔ Topical blogs focus on a specific theme, such as movie reviews, political news, class assignments, or health care opportunities.

Web Safety

Always be aware that information you post on the Internet can be read by everyone with access to that page. Once you post a picture or text, it can be saved on someone else's computer, even if you later remove it.

Using the Internet safely means keeping personal information personal. Never include your address (e-mail or real), last name, or telephone numbers. Avoid mentioning places you can be frequently found. Never give out passwords you use to access other web sites and do not respond to e-mails from people you do not know.

Anatomy of a Blog

Here are some of the features you can include in a blog.

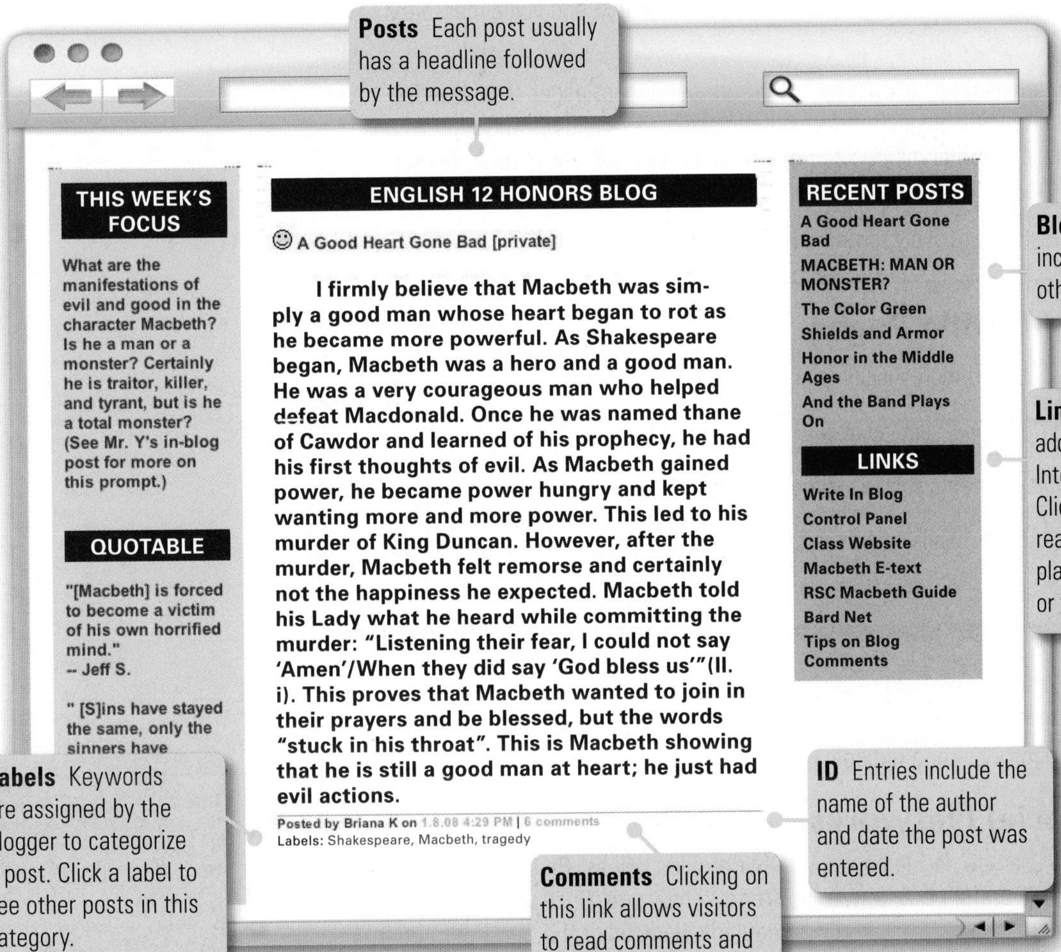
THIS WEEK'S FOCUS
What are the manifestations of evil and good in the character Macbeth? Is he a man or a monster? Certainly he is traitor, killer, and tyrant, but is he a total monster? (See Mr. Y's in-blog post for more on this prompt.)
QUOTABLE
"[Macbeth] is forced to become a victim of his own horrified mind."
-- Jeff S.
" [S]ins have stayed the same, only the sinners have
ENGLISH 12 HONORS BLOG
A Good Heart Gone Bad [private]
I firmly believe that Macbeth was simply a good man whose heart began to rot as he became more powerful. As Shakespeare began, Macbeth was a hero and a good man. He was a very courageous man who helped defeat Macdonald. Once he was named thane of Cawdor and learned of his prophecy, he had his first thoughts of evil. As Macbeth gained power, he became power hungry and kept wanting more and more power. This led to his murder of King Duncan. However, after the murder, Macbeth felt remorse and certainly not the happiness he expected. Macbeth told his Lady what he heard while committing the murder: "Listening their fear, I could not say 'Amen'/When they did say 'God bless us'"(II. i). This proves that Macbeth wanted to join in their prayers and be blessed, but the words "stuck in his throat". This is Macbeth showing that he is still a good man at heart; he just had evil actions.
Posted by Briana K on 1.8.08 4:29 PM | 6 comments
Labels: Shakespeare, Macbeth, tragedy
RECENT POSTS
A Good Heart Gone Bad
MACBETH: MAN OR MONSTER?
The Color Green
Shields and Armor
Honor in the Middle Ages
And the Band Plays On
LINKS
Write In Blog
Control Panel
Class Website
Macbeth E-text
RSC Macbeth Guide
Bard Net
Tips on Blog Comments

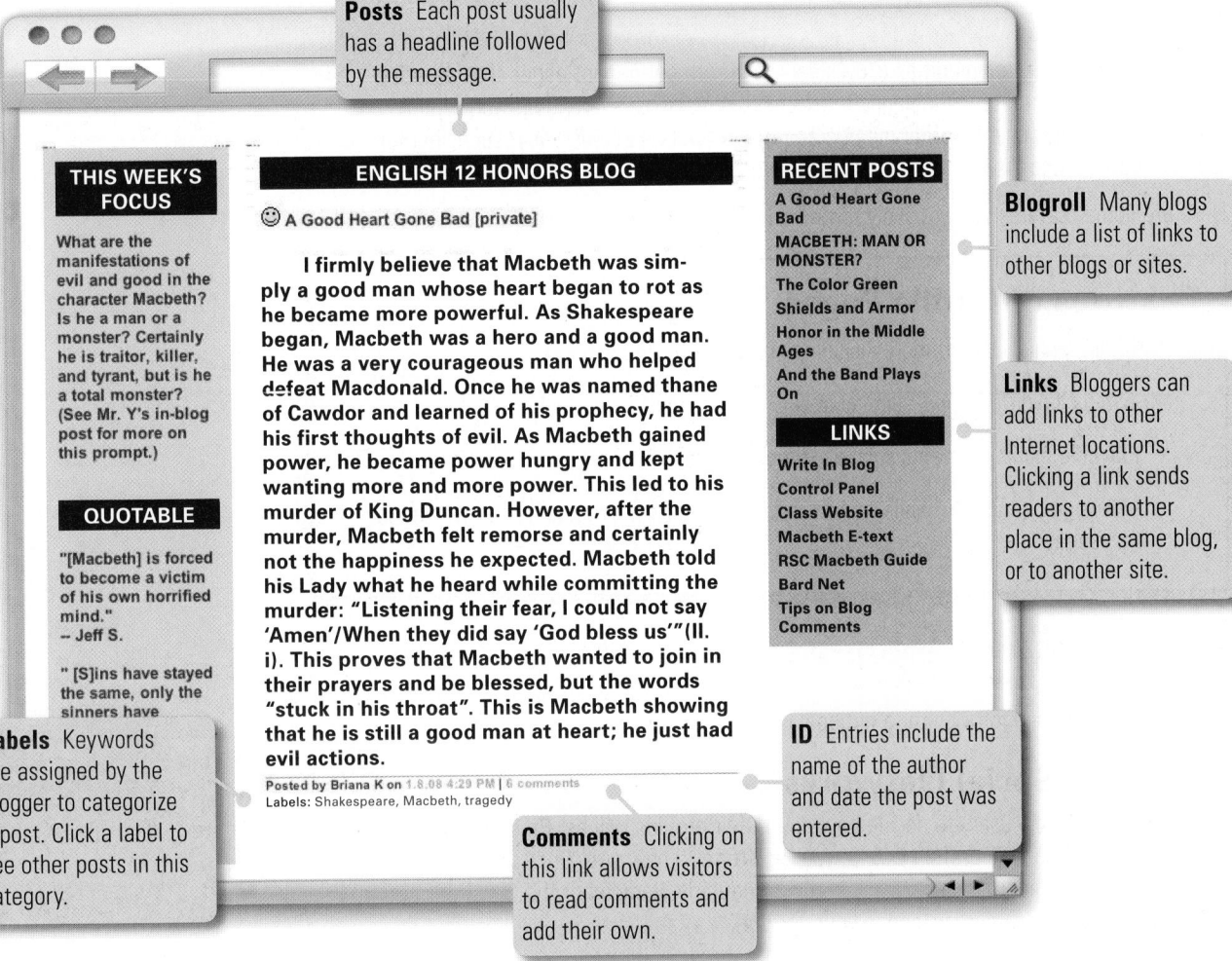

Posts Each post usually has a headline followed by the message.

Blogroll Many blogs include a list of links to other blogs or sites.

Links Bloggers can add links to other Internet locations. Clicking a link sends readers to another place in the same blog, or to another site.

Labels Keywords are assigned by the blogger to categorize a post. Click a label to see other posts in this category.

ID Entries include the name of the author and date the post was entered.

Comments Clicking on this link allows visitors to read comments and add their own.

Creating a Blog

Keep these hints and strategies in mind to help you create an interesting and fair blog:

- ✔ Focus each blog entry on a single topic.
- ✔ Vary the length of your posts. Sometimes, all you need is a line or two to share a quick thought. Other posts will be much longer.
- ✔ Choose font colors and styles that can be read easily.
- ✔ Many people scan blogs rather than read them closely. You can make your main ideas pop out by using clear or clever headlines and boldfacing key terms.
- ✔ Give credit to other people's work and ideas. State the names of people whose ideas you are quoting or add a link to take readers to that person's blog or site.
- ✔ If you post comments, try to make them brief and polite.

SOCIAL NETWORKING

Social networking means any interaction between members of an online community. People can exchange many different kinds of information, from text and voice messages to video images.

Many social network communities allow users to create permanent pages that describe themselves. Users create home pages to express themselves, share ideas about their lives, and post messages to other members in the network. Each user is responsible for adding and updating the content on his or her profile page.

Here are some features you are likely to find on a social network profile:

Features of Profile Pages

- A biographical description, including photographs and artwork.
- Lists of favorite things, such as books, movies, music, and fashions.
- Playable media elements such as videos and sound recordings.
- Message boards, or "walls" in which members of the community can exchange messages.

You can create a social network page for an individual or a group, such as a school or special interest club. Many hosting sites do not charge to register, so you can also have fun by creating a page for a pet or a fictional character.

Privacy in Social Networks

Social networks allow users to decide how open their profiles will be. Be sure to read introductory information carefully before you register at a new site. Once you have a personal profile page, monitor your privacy settings regularly. Remember that any information you post will be available to anyone in your network.

Users often post messages anonymously or using false names, or *pseudonyms*. People can also post using someone else's name. Judge all information on the net critically. Do not assume that you know who posted some information simply because you recognize the name of the post author. The rapid speed of communication on the Internet can make it easy to jump to conclusions—be careful to avoid this trap.

Tips for Sending Effective Messages

Technology makes it easy to share ideas quickly, but writing for the Internet poses some special challenges, as well. The writing style for blogs and social networks is often very conversational. In blog posts and comments, instant messages, and e-mails, writers often express themselves very quickly, using relaxed language, short sentences, and abbreviations. However, in a conversation, we get a lot of information from a speaker's tone of voice and body language. On the Internet, those clues are missing. As a result, Internet writers often use italics or bracketed labels to indicate emotions. Another alternative is using emoticons—strings of characters that give visual clues to indicate emotion:

:-) smile (happy)	**:-(** frown (unhappy)	**;-)** wink (light sarcasm)

Use these strategies to communicate effectively when using technology:

- ✔ Reread your messages. Before you click *Send,* read your message through and make sure that your tone will be clear to the reader.
- ✔ Do not jump to conclusions—ask for clarification first. Make sure you really understand what someone is saying before you respond.
- ✔ Use abbreviations your reader will understand.

WIDGETS & FEEDS

A **widget** is a small application performs a specific task. You might find widgets that give weather predictions, offer dictionary definitions or translations, provide entertainment such as games, or present a daily word, photograph, or quotation.

A **feed** is a special kind of widget. It displays headlines taken from the latest content on a specific media source. Clicking on the headline will take you to the full article.

Many social network communities and other web sites allow you to personalize your home page by adding widgets and feeds.

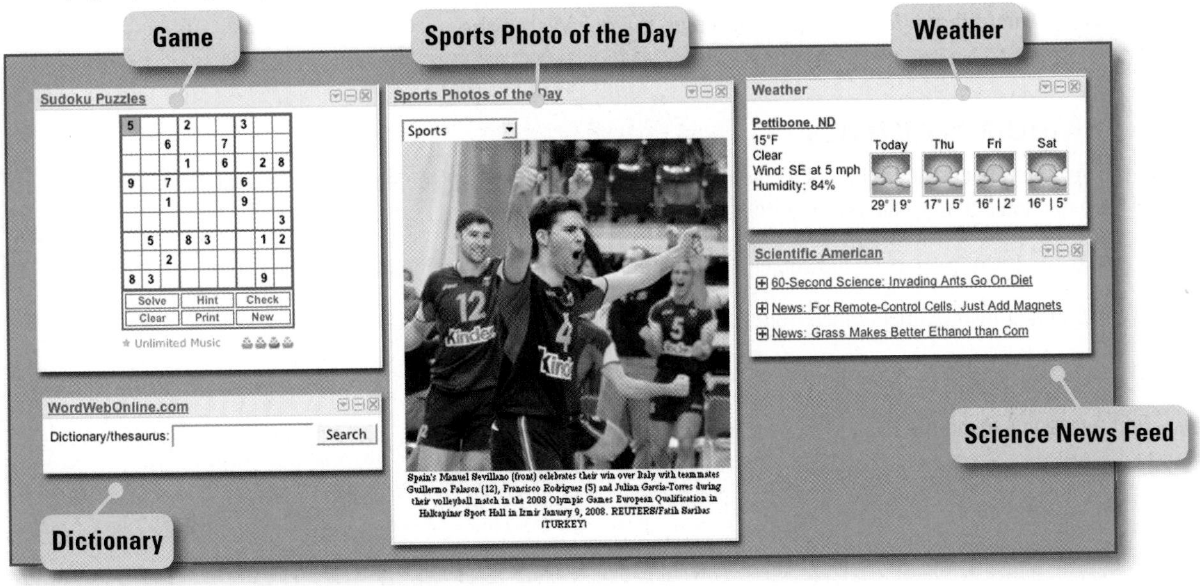

MULTIMEDIA ELEMENTS

One of the great advantages of communicating on the Internet is that you are not limited to using text only. When you create a web profile or blog, you can share your ideas using a wide variety of media. In addition to widgets and feeds (see page R31), these media elements can make your Internet communication more entertaining and useful.

Graphics	
Photographs	You can post photos taken by digital cameras.
Illustrations	Artwork can be created using computer software. You can also use a scanner to post a digital image of a drawing or sketch.
Charts, Graphs, and Maps	Charts and graphs can make statistical information clear. Use spreadsheet software to create these elements. Use Internet sites to find maps of specific places.

Video	
Live Action	Digital video can be recorded by a camera or recorded from another media source.
Animation	Animated videos can also be created using software.

Sound	
Music	Many social network communities make it easy to share your favorite music with people who visit your page.
Voice	Use a microphone to add your own voice to your Web page.

Editing Media Elements

You can use software to customize media elements. Open source software is free and available to anyone on the Internet. Here are some things you can do with software:

- ✔ Crop a photograph to focus on the subject or brighten an image that is too dark.
- ✔ Transform a drawing's appearance from flat to three-dimensional.
- ✔ Insert a "You Are Here" arrow on a map.
- ✔ Edit a video or sound file to shorten its running time.
- ✔ Add background music or sound effects to a video.

PODCASTS

A **podcast** is a digital audio or video recording of a program that is made available on the Internet. Users can replay the podcast on a computer, or download it and replay it on a personal audio player. You might think of podcasts as radio or television programs that you create yourself. They can be embedded on a website or fed to a webpage through a podcast widget.

Creating an Effective Podcast

To make a podcast, you will need a recording device, such as a microphone or digital video camera, as well as editing software. Open source editing software is widely available and free of charge. Most audio podcasts are converted into the MP3 format. Here are some tips for creating a podcast that is clear and entertaining:

- ✔ Listen to several podcasts by different authors to get a feeling for the medium. Make a list of features and styles you like and also those you want to avoid.
- ✔ Test your microphone to find the best recording distance. Stand close enough to the microphone so that your voice sounds full, but not so close that you create an echo.
- ✔ Create an outline that shows your estimated timing for each element.
- ✔ Be prepared before you record. Rehearse, but do not create a script. Podcasts are best when they have a natural, easy flow.
- ✔ Talk directly to your listeners. Slow down enough so they can understand you.
- ✔ Use software to edit your podcast before publishing it. You can edit out mistakes or add additional elements.

WIKIS

A **wiki** is collaborative website that lets visitors create, add, remove, and edit content. The term comes from the Hawaiian phrase *wiki wiki,* which means "quick." Web users at a wiki are both the readers and the writers of the site. Some wikis are open to contributions from anyone. Others require visitors to register before they can edit the content.

All of the text in these collaborative websites was written by people who use the site. Articles are constantly changing, as visitors find and correct errors and improve texts.

Wikis have both advantages and disadvantages as sources of information. They are valuable open forums for the exchange of ideas. The unique collaborative writing process allows entries to change over time. However, entries can also be modified incorrectly. Careless or malicious users can delete good content and add inappropriate or inaccurate information.

You can change the information on a wiki, but be sure your information is correct and clear before you add it. Wikis keep track of all changes, so your work will be recorded and can be evaluated by other users.

Rules of Debate

A **debate** is a structured contest based on a formal discussion of opinion. In essence, it is a battle of intellect and verbal skill. The goal is mastering the art of persuasion. Who can best express, argue, and support opinions on a given topic? Who can best refute an argument, showing that the opponent's points are invalid? Which team, in the end, can convince the judges that their argument is the most sound?

Teams

A **formal debate** is conducted with two teams—an Affirmation team and a Negative team. As the names suggest, the Affirmation team is responsible for presenting the "pro" side of an issue, while the Negative team presents the "con" side of the issue. Each team has a main purpose and will offer both constructive and rebuttal speeches, practicing the art of persuasion and debate.

Affirmation team The Affirmation team as a whole carries the burden of proof for the debate. They must prove there is a problem. To do so, they need to cite credible sources, include relevant details, and present and support valid points. Each team member has a specific job. The first speaker has the most responsibility. He or she must

- define the issue or problem
- introduce the team line—a one line summary of the team's position on the issue
- identify the point of the argument each speaker will discuss

The remaining team members have the job of presenting and supporting the main points of the argument.

Negative team Though the Negative team does not carry the burden of proof, the team must show that there is no problem or that the Affirmation team's solutions are invalid. Though their purpose is to rebut an argument, the rebuttal technique calls for a formation of their own argument. They must argue against the Affirmation team. To construct their argument, they must use—like the Affirmation team—credible sources, relevant details, and valid points. They should incorporate any available statistics, pertinent facts, or applicable testimonies to bolster their argument. Even though the first speaker of the Affirmation team lays out each point of the argument, the Negative team speakers cannot address points that have not been thoroughly discussed by an Affirmation team member.

Structure

Just like most other contests, debates have a set structure. Debates are divided into halves. The first half begins with the the constructive speeches from both team, which last ten minutes each.

After the first half, there is a short intermission. Then, the second half begins with the Negative team. This half is reserved for the rebuttal speeches, which last five minutes each and include rebuttals and refutations. This is each team's chance to rebuild their arguments that the other team broke down (rebuttal), and put forth evidence to show the other team is wrong (refutation). Although the Negative team begins the argument in the second half, every debate begins and ends with the Affirmation team.

Structure of Debate

1st Half: Constructive Speeches (10 minutes each)	1st Half: Rebuttal Speeches (5 minutes each)
1st Affirmative Team Speaker	1st Negative Team Speaker
1st Negative Team Speaker	1st Affirmative Team Speaker
2nd Affirmative Team Speaker	2nd Negative Team Speaker
2nd Negative Team Speaker	2nd Affirmative Team Speaker
3rd Affirmative Team Speaker	3rd Negative Team Speaker
3rd Negative Team Speaker	3rd Affirmative Team Speaker

Speeches—Content, Organization, and Delivery

Debate speeches are the result of practicing the art of persuasion. To be effective, speakers must include pertinent content, use clear and logical organization, and have a powerful delivery. These combined elements make a strong speech.

Content Debates often focus on concrete issues that can be proved or disproved. The basis for a debate speech is its content. The Affirmation team should first determine their position. They should be sure to include any facts and/or statistics that concretely support the argument. Speech writers should cite specific instances and occurrences that solidify their position. Writers might also include testimonies or ideas from professionals. Finally, the Affirmation team needs to propose possible solutions to the problem or issue and examine the costs and effects of those solutions.

Though the Negative team does not have to state a position—their position is automatically the opposing position—they still need to include facts, statistics, testimony, and descriptions of specific instances or occurrences to make their counterpoints. They need to analyze the Affirmation team's proposed solutions and explain why they will not work. In essence, the Negative team must construct an argument around the Affirmation team's argument.

Organization Debate speeches are organized like other speeches and essays. They should have an introduction, transitions, body, and conclusion. The speeches should have clear main points and supporting details for those points. Because a debate is a structured discussion, there will be a specific order of points and the speakers who present them must be identified. Speakers can use note cards to help them stick to the planned organization, but they should only use brief notes, never reading directly from the cards.

Delivery The manner in which a speech is delivered can make or break the argument. The impression the speaker makes on the audience, including the judges, is key. To make a good impression, the speaker must present the material with confidence. He or she can portray confidence by forming a connection with the audience through eye contact, glancing away only briefly to consult notes. A speaker should focus on his or her voice, varying the tone, volume, and pace appropriately. Body movements should not include fidgeting or nervous movement. They should only be used if they are deliberate and help express or underscore a point. Finally, speakers should be concise, focusing on vivid and clear word choice and using words that emphasize the point.

Scoring

Debates are scored much like other contests. Each side is judged on the content and delivery of their speeches. Judges contemplate different elements of content and delivery in order to determine the number of points to give each team. They might ask themselves these questions in order to determine score:

Finally, judges look at the observation of debate etiquette. Speakers are expected to be mature and respectful of their opponents. Speakers should never attack an opponent, but instead should attack the argument. Judges will deduct points for personal attacks.

Scoring Criteria

Content	Delivery
Were arguments convincing?	Were speakers able to speak extemporaneously?
Were arguments supported with credible, valid and relevant reasons?	Were body movements deliberate and effective?
Were refutations and rebuttals effective?	Did speakers make a connection with the audience?
Were speakers confident and knowledgeable?	Did speakers stay within their time limits?

Parts of Speech

Nouns A **noun** is the name of a person, place, or thing. A **common noun** names any one of a class of people, places, or things. A **proper noun** names a specific person, place, or thing.

Common Nouns	***Proper Nouns***
city	Washington, D.C.

Pronouns A **pronoun** is a word that stands for a noun or for a word that takes the place of a noun.

A **personal pronoun** refers to (1) the person speaking, (2) the person spoken to, or (3) the person, place, or thing spoken about.

	Singular	***Plural***
First Person	I, me, my, mine	we, us, our, ours
Second Person	you, your, yours	you, your, yours
Third Person	he, him, his, she, her, hers, it, its	they, them, their, theirs

Antecedents are nouns (or words that take the place of nouns) for which pronouns stand. In the following sentence, the pronoun *it* stands for the noun *Florida*.

Florida is popular because it has a warm climate.

A **reflexive pronoun** ends in *-self* or *-selves* and adds information to a sentence by pointing back to a noun or a pronoun earlier in the sentence.

"If you were honest folk *yourselves* you wouldn't let a thief go free."

— Leo Tolstoy, p. 308

An **intensive pronoun** ends in *-self* or *-selves* and simply adds emphasis to a noun or a pronoun in the same sentence.

After a time, I *myself* was allowed to go into the dead houses and search for metal.

— Stephen Vincent Benét, p. 282

A **demonstrative pronoun** directs attention to a specific person, place, or thing.

this these that those

These are the juiciest pears I have ever tasted.

A **relative pronoun** begins a subordinate clause and connects it to another idea in the sentence.

The poet *who* wrote "Fear" is Gabriela Mistral.

An **interrogative pronoun** is used to begin a question. The five interrogative pronouns are *what, which, who, whom,* and *whose.*

An **indefinite pronoun** refers to a person, place, or thing, often without specifying which one.

all anyone each everyone few one someone

And then, for a moment, *all* is still, . . .

— Edgar Allan Poe, p. 340

Verbs A **verb** is a word that expresses time while showing an action, a condition, or the fact that something exists.

An **action verb** indicates the action of someone or something.

An action verb is **transitive** if it directs action toward someone or something named in the same sentence.

He *dusted* his hands, muttering.

— Jack Finney, p. 110

An action verb is **intransitive** if it does not direct action toward something or someone named in the same sentence.

I *smiled* and looked up at the crew . . .

— Lynne Cox, p. 58

A **linking verb** is a verb that connects the subject of a sentence with a noun or a pronoun that renames or describes the subject. The noun, pronoun, or phrase acting as a noun that renames the subject is called a **predicate nominative.**

Romance at short notice was her specialty.

— Saki, p. 1160

A **helping verb** is a verb that can be added to another verb to make a verb phrase.

Nor *did* I suspect that these experiences could be part of a novel's meaning.

Adjectives An **adjective** describes a noun or a pronoun or gives a noun or a pronoun a more specific meaning. Adjectives answer these questions:

What kind?	*blue* lamp, *large* tree
Which one?	*this* table, *those* books
How many?	*five* stars, *several* buses
How much?	*less* money, *enough* votes

The articles *the, a,* and *an* are adjectives. *An* is used before a word beginning with a vowel sound.

A noun may sometimes be used as an adjective.

diamond necklace *summer* vacation

Adverbs An **adverb** modifies a verb, an adjective, or another adverb. Adverbs answer the questions *where, when, in what way,* or *to what extent.*

He could stand *there.* (modifies verb *stand*)

He was *blissfully* happy. (modifies adjective *happy*)

It ended *too* soon. (modifies adverb *soon*)

Prepositions A **preposition** relates a noun or a pronoun that appears with it to another word in the sentence.

before the end *near* me *inside* our fence

Conjunctions A **conjunction** connects words or groups of words.

A **coordinating conjunction** connects similar kinds or groups of words.

mother *and* father   simple *yet* stylish

Correlative conjunctions are used in pairs to connect similar words or groups of words.

both Sue *and* Meg   *neither* he *nor* I

A **subordinating conjunction** connects two complete ideas by placing one idea below the other in rank or importance.

You would know him *if* you saw him.

Sentences, Phrases, and Clauses

Sentences A **sentence** is a group of words with a subject and a predicate. Together, these parts express a complete thought.

A **fragment** is a group of words that does not express a complete thought.

The Four Structures of Sentences There are two kinds of clauses: independent and subordinate. An independent clause can stand by itself as a sentence; a subordinate clause cannot. These can be used to form four basic sentence structures: *simple, compound, complex*, and *compound-complex*.

A **simple sentence** consists of a single independent clause.

A **compound sentence** consists of two or more independent clauses.

The clauses in a compound sentence can be joined by a comma and a coordinating conjunction *(and, but, for, nor, or, so, yet)* or by a semicolon (;).

A **complex sentence** consists of one independent clause and one or more subordinate clauses.

The independent clause in a complex sentence is often called the *main clause* to distinguish it from the subordinate clause or clauses.

A **compound-complex sentence** consists of two or more independent clauses and one or more subordinate clauses.

Phrases A **phrase** is a group of words, without a subject and a verb, that functions in a sentence as one part of speech.

A **prepositional phrase** is a group of words that includes a preposition and a noun or a pronoun that is the object of the preposition.

outside my window   below the counter

An **adjective phrase** is a prepositional phrase that modifies a noun or a pronoun by telling *what kind* or *which one*.

The wooden gates *of that lane* stood open.

An **adverb phrase** is a prepositional phrase that modifies a verb, an adjective, or an adverb by pointing out *where, when, in what way*, or *to what extent*.

On a sudden impulse, he got to his feet. . . .
— Jack Finney, p. 110

An **appositive phrase** is a noun or a pronoun with modifiers, placed next to a noun or a pronoun to identify it or add information and details.

M. Morissot, watchmaker by trade but local militiaman for the time being, stopped short. . . .
— Guy de Maupassant, p. 1137

A **participial phrase** is a participle with its modifiers or complements. The entire phrase acts as an adjective.

Choosing such a tide, I hoped for a glimpse of the pool.
— Rachel Carson, p. 155

A **gerund** is a form of a verb that is used as a noun. It ends in *-ing*. A **gerund phrase** is a gerund with modifiers or a complement, all acting together as a noun.

. . . *moving along the ledge* was quite as easy as he had thought it would be.
— Jack Finney, p. 110

An **infinitive** is the form of a verb using to. It acts as a noun, adjective, or adverb. An **infinitive phrase** is an infinitive with modifiers, complements, or a subject, all acting together as a single part of speech.

To be dead, and never again behold my city!
—Dreams, p. 630

Clauses A **clause** is a group of words with a subject and a verb.

An **independent clause** has a subject and a verb and can stand by itself as a complete sentence.

A **subordinate clause** has a subject and a verb but cannot stand by itself as a complete sentence; it can only be part of a sentence.

An **adjective clause** is a subordinate clause that modifies a noun or a pronoun by telling *what kind* or *which one*.

The people *who read the book* loved it.

An **adverb clause** modifies a verb, an adjective, an adverb, or a verbal by telling *where, when, in what way, to what extent, under what condition*, or *why*.

They read it as soon *as it was published*.

A **noun clause** is a subordinate clause that acts as a noun.

Whoever reads it is overcome with joy.

Parallelism **Parallelism** is the placement of equal ideas in words, phrases, or clauses of similar type.

Parallel Words: The camp has excellent facilities for *riding, hiking,* and *swimming.*

Parallel Phrases: Jennings had gone to the country *to rest, to think,* and *to catch a few fish.*

Parallel Clauses: A news story should tell *what happened, when it happened,* and *who was involved.*

Verb Usage

The Four Principal Parts of Verbs A verb has four **principal parts:** the *present*, the *present participle*, the *past*, and the *past participle.*

Regular verbs form the past and past participle by adding *-ed* to the present form.

Present: walk
Present Participle: (am) walking
Past: walked
Past Participle: (have) walked

The past and past participle of an **irregular verb** are not formed by adding *-ed* or *-d* to the present form. Irregular verbs form the past and past participle by changing form. Whenever you are in doubt about the principal parts of an irregular verb, use a dictionary to check them.

Present: go
Present Participle: (am) going
Past: went
Past Participle: (have) gone

Pronoun Usage

Pronoun Case The **case** of a pronoun is the form it takes to show its use in a sentence. There are three pronoun cases: *nominative, objective,* and *possessive.*

The **nominative case** is used to rename the subject of the sentence. The nominative case pronouns are *I, you, he, she, it, we, you, they.*

As the subject: *She* is brave
Renaming the subject: The leader is *she.*

The **objective case** is used as the direct object, indirect object, or object of the preposition. The objective case pronouns are *me, you, him, her, it, us, you, them.*

As a direct object: Tom called me.
As an indirect object: My friend gave *me* advice.
As an object of preposition: The coach gave pointers to *me.*

The **possessive case** is used to show ownership. The possessive pronouns are *my, your, his, her, its, our, their, mine, yours, his, hers, its, ours, theirs.*

Agreement

Subject and Verb Agreement To make a subject and verb agree, make sure that both are singular or both are plural.

Many *storms are* the cause of beach erosion.

In the case of a plural and a singular subject joined by *or* or *nor*, choose the form of the verb that agrees with the closer of the two.

Either the *cats* or the *dog is* hungry.
Neither *Angie* nor *her sisters were* present.

Pronoun-Antecedent Agreement Pronouns must agree with their antecedents in number and gender. Use singular pronouns with singular antecedents and plural pronouns with plural antecedents. Many errors in pronoun-antecedent agreement occur when a plural pronoun is used to refer to a singular antecedent for which the gender is not specified.

Incorrect: Everyone did their best.
Correct: Everyone did his or her best.

The following indefinite pronouns are singular: *anybody, anyone, each, either, everybody, everyone, neither, nobody, no one, one, somebody, someone.*

The following indefinite pronouns are plural: *both, few, many, several.*

The following indefinite pronouns may be either singular or plural: *all, any, most, none, some.* Treat these pronouns as singular when the antecedent is singular.

All of the gold is gone, and we do not know who took *it.*

Treat these pronouns as plural when the antecedent is plural.

Most of my friends are going, and *they* will have a good time.

Using Modifiers

Degrees of Comparison Most adjectives and adverbs have three different forms to show degrees of comparison—the *positive*, the *comparative*, the *superlative.*

Use *-er* or *more* to form the comparative degree and *-est* or *most* to form the superlative degree of most one- and two-syllable modifiers.

Use *more* and *most* to form the comparative and superlative degrees of all modifiers with three or more syllables.

The irregular comparative and superlative forms of certain adjectives and adverbs must be memorized.

The form of some irregular modifiers differs only in the positive degree. The modifiers *bad, badly,* and *ill*, for example, all have the same basic form in the comparative and superlative degrees (*worse, worst*).

Capitalization and Punctuation

Capitalization Capitalize the first word of a sentence and also the first word in a quotation if the quotation is a complete sentence.

"No matter," he concluded, "I'll go toward the rising sun." — Leo Tolstoy, p. 308

Capitalize all proper nouns and adjectives.

W. W. Jacobs Flanders Fields African writers

Capitalize a person's title when it is followed by the person's name or when it is used in direct address.

Reverend Tallboys Mrs. Prothero "Hello, Major."

Capitalize titles showing family relationships when they refer to a specific person and are used with a name or as a name.

Aunt Mae Let's ask Grandmother. *but* his father

Capitalize the first word and all other key words in the titles of books, periodicals, poems, stories, plays, paintings, and other works of art.

Lord of the Flies "Spring and All"

End Marks Use a **period** to end a declarative sentence, an imperative sentence, an indirect question, and most abbreviations.

The class will meet at noon.

Use a **question mark** to end a direct question, an incomplete question, or a statement that is intended as a question.

Did you prepare your assignment?

Use an **exclamation mark** after a statement showing strong emotion, an urgent imperative sentence, or an interjection expressing strong emotion.

Wait until you hear the news!

Commas Use a **comma** before the coordinating conjunction to separate two independent clauses in a compound sentence.

His arms had begun to tremble from the steady strain of clinging to this narrow perch, and he did not know what to do now. . . . — Jack Finney, p. 110

Use commas to separate three or more words, phrases, or clauses in a series.

. . . he produced about fifteen hundred *drawings, prints, pastels,* and *oil paintings* with ballet themes.
— Richard Mühlberger, p. 520

Use commas to separate adjectives of equal rank. Do not use commas to separate adjectives that must stay in a specific order.

With *pink, dimpled* knees, Henri, not yet a year old, sprawls on the lap of his nurse. . . .
[In Degas's painting], the *creamy white* tones of the passengers stand out.
— Richard Mühlberger, p. 520

Use a comma after an introductory word, phrase, or clause.

When Marian Anderson again returned to America, she was a seasoned artist.
— Langston Hughes, p. 88

Use commas to set off parenthetical and nonessential expressions.

Now, *yes, now,* it was about to set!
— Leo Tolstoy, p. 308

Use commas with places, dates, and titles.

Poe was raised in Richmond, Virginia.
August 4, 2026
Alfred, Lord Tennyson

Use a comma to indicate the words left out of an elliptical sentence, to set off a direct quotation, and to prevent a sentence from being misunderstood.

Vincent Canby writes for *The New York Times*; Roger Ebert, for the *Chicago Sun Times*.

Semicolons Use a **semicolon** to join independent clauses that are not already joined by a conjunction.

They could find no buffalo; they had to hang an old hide from the sacred tree.
— N. Scott Momaday, p. 545

Use a semicolon to join independent clauses separated by either a conjunctive adverb or a transitional expression.

James Thurber wrote many books; moreover, he was a cartoonist and a journalist.

Use semicolons to avoid confusion when independent clauses or items in a series already contain commas.

Thurber is remembered for his character Walter Mitty; for his cartoons, many of which illustrated his books; and for his terrifically funny essays.

Colons Use a **colon** in order to introduce a list of items following an independent clause.

The authors we are reading include a number of poets: Robert Frost, Octavio Paz, and Emily Dickinson.

Use a colon to introduce a formal quotation.

The next day Howard Taubman wrote enthusiastically in The New York Times: "Marian Anderson has returned to her native land one of the great singers of our time. . . ."
— Langston Hughes, p. 88

Quotation Marks A **direct quotation** represents a person's exact speech or thoughts and is enclosed in quotation marks.

"Clara, my mind is made up."

An **indirect quotation** is a restatement or paraphrase of what a person said or thought and does not require quotation marks.

The cops suggested that it might be a good idea to tie the dog up, but mother said that it mortified him to be tied up. . . . — James Thurber, p. 481

Always place a comma or a period inside the final quotation mark.

"Eh, you're a stranger," she said. "I thought so."
— Josephina Niggli, p. 246

Place a question mark or an exclamation mark inside the final quotation mark if the end mark is part of the quotation; if it is not part of the quotation, place it outside the final quotation mark.

He asked, "Which poetry do you like best?"

Have you ever read the poem "Africa"?

Use single quotation marks for a quotation within a quotation.

Use quotation marks around the titles of short written works, episodes in a series, songs, and titles of works mentioned as parts of a collection.

"Making a Fist" "These Are Days"

Underline or italicize titles of longer works, such as plays, movies, or novels.

Dashes Use **dashes** to indicate an abrupt change of thought, a dramatic interrupting idea, or a summary statement.

It made her so mad to see Muggs lying there, oblivious of the mice—they came running up to her—that she slapped him and he slashed at her, but didn't make it. — James Thurber, p. 481

Parentheses Use **parentheses** to set off asides and explanations only when the material is not essential or when it consists of one or more sentences.

When I finished (What a lot of facts I found out!), I turned in my report.

Hyphens Use a **hyphen** with certain numbers, after certain prefixes, with two or more words used as one word, and with a compound modifier coming before a noun.

fifty-two greenish-blue water

Apostrophes Add an **apostrophe** and s to show the possessive case of most singular nouns.

Prospero's castle the playwright's craft

Add an apostrophe to show the possessive case of plural nouns ending in *-s* and *-es.*

the sailors' ships the babies' mothers

Add an apostrophe and *-s* to show the possessive case of plural nouns that do not end in *-s* or *-es.*

the children's games the people's friend

Use an apostrophe in a contraction to indicate the position of the missing letter or letters.

I *didn't* love any one of you more than any other.
— William Melvin Kelley, p. 220

Glossary of Common Usage

among, between: *Among* is usually used with three or more items. *Between* is generally used with only two items.

Among the poems we read this year, Eve Merriam's "Metaphor" was my favorite.

"Like the Sun" tells of the conflict *between* telling the truth and telling white lies.

around: In formal writing, *around* should not be used to mean *approximately* or *about.* These usages are allowable, however, in informal writing or in colloquial dialogue.

Romeo and Juliet had its first performance in *approximately* 1595.

Shakespeare was *about* thirty when he wrote it.

as, because, like, as to: The word *as* has several meanings and can function as several parts of speech. To avoid confusion, use *because* rather than *as* when you want to indicate cause and effect.

Because Cyril was interested in African American poetry, he wrote his report on Langston Hughes.

Do not use the preposition *like* to introduce a clause that requires the conjunction *as.*

James Thurber conversed as he wrote—wittily.

The use of *as to* for *about* is awkward and should be avoided.

Rosa has a theory *about* Edgar Allan Poe's style.

beside, besides: *Beside* is a preposition meaning "at the side of" or "close to." Do not confuse *beside* with *besides,* which means "in addition to." *Besides* can be a preposition or an adverb.

As the men cross the lawn and approach the open window, a brown spaniel trots *beside* them.

There are many other Indian oral epics *besides* the *Ramayana.*

can, may: The verb *can* generally refers to the ability to do something. The verb *may* generally refers to permission to do something.

Dylan Thomas describes his childhood Christmases so vividly that most readers can visualize the scenes.

Creon's edict states that no one may bury Polyneices.

different from, different than: The preferred usage is *different from.*

The structure and rhyme scheme of a Shakespearean sonnet are *different from* the organization of a Petrarchan sonnet.

farther, further: Use *farther* when you refer to distance. Use *further* when you mean "to a greater degree" or "additional."

The *farther* the ants travel, the more ominous and destructive they seem.

The storm in Act I of *The Tragedy of Julius Caesar* *further* hints at the ominous deeds to come.

fewer, less: Use *fewer* for things that can be counted. Use *less* for amounts or quantities that cannot be counted.

Poetry often uses *fewer* words than prose to convey ideas and images.

It takes *less* time to perform a Greek tragedy than to perform a Shakespearean play.

good, well: Use the adjective *good* after linking verbs such as *feel, look, smell, taste,* and *seem.* Use *well* whenever you need an adverb or as an adjective describing health.

Caesar remarks that Cassius does not look *good*; on the contrary, his appearance is "lean."

Twain wrote especially *well* when he described eccentric characters.

hopefully: Do not attach this adverb to a sentence loosely, as in "*Hopefully*, the rain will stop by noon." Rewrite the sentence so that *hopefully* modifies a specific verb. Other possible ways of revising such sentences include using the adjective *hopeful* or a phrase such as *everyone hopes that.*

Dr. Martin Luther King, Jr., wrote and spoke *hopefully* about his dream of racial harmony.

Mr. White was *hopeful* that the monkey's paw would bring him good fortune.

Everyone hopes that the class production of *Antigone* will be a big success.

its, it's: Do not confuse the possessive pronoun its with the contraction *it's*, used in place of "it is" or "it has."

In *its* very first lines, "The Stolen Child" establishes an eerie mood.

In "The Street of the Cañon," Pepe Gonzalez knows that *it's* dangerous to attend the party.

just, only: When you use *just* as an adverb meaning "no more than," be sure you place it directly before the word it logically modifies. Likewise, be sure you place *only* before the word it logically modifies.

Just one wish changed the Whites' lives forever.

A short story can usually develop *only* a few characters, whereas a novel can include many.

kind of, sort of: In formal writing, you should not use these colloquial expressions. Instead, use a word such as *rather* or *somewhat.*

Poe portrays Prince Prospero as *rather* arrogant.

The tone of the biography is *somewhat* harsh.

lay, lie: Do not confuse these verbs. *Lay* is a transitive verb meaning "to set or put something down." Its principal parts are *lay, laying, laid, laid. Lie* is an intransitive verb meaning "to recline." Its principal parts are *lie, lying, lay, lain.*

They laid the monkey's paw on the table for a while before anyone dared to pick it up.

La Belle Dame sans Merci enchants the knight as he *lies* in her "elfin grot."

leave, let: Be careful not to confuse these verbs. *Leave* means "to go away" or "to allow to remain." *Let* means "to permit."

Threatening Antigone not to disobey his orders, Creon angrily *leaves* the stage.

Creon did not want to *let* Antigone bury her brother.

raise, rise: *Raise* is a transitive verb that usually takes a direct object. *Rise* is an intransitive verb and never takes a direct object.

In his speech, Antony unexpectedly *raises* the subject of Caesar's will.

When the Cabuliwallah comes to call, Mini *rises* from her chair and runs to greet him.

set, sit: Do not confuse these verbs. *Set* is a transitive verb meaning "to put (something) in a certain place." Its principal parts are *set, setting, set, set. Sit* is an intransitive verb meaning "to be seated." Its principal parts are *sit, sitting, sat, sat.*

Antigone's conduct *sets* a high standard for us.

Jerry's mother *sits* in her beach chair while Jerry swims in the ocean.

so, so that: Be careful not to use the coordinating conjunction *so* when your context requires *so that. So* means "accordingly" or "with the result that" and expresses a cause-and-effect relationship. *So that* expresses purpose—what someone intends to achieve.

He wanted to do well on the test, *so* he read *The Tragedy of Julius Caesar* again.

Antony uses eloquent rhetoric to stir up the people *so that* they will rebel.

than, then: The conjunction *than* is used to connect the two parts of a comparison. Do not confuse *than* with the adverb *then,* which usually refers to time.

I enjoyed "The Marginal World" more *than* "Flood."

Marian Anderson gave a triumphant singing recital in New York that evening, and she *then* embarked on a coast-to-coast American tour.

that, which, who: Use the relative pronoun *that* to refer to things. Use *which* only for things and *who* only for people.

The poem *that* Cheryl liked the most was "The street."

Haiku, *which* consists of only seventeen syllables, is often built around one or two vivid images.

The assassin *who* strikes Caesar first is Casca.

unique: Because *unique* means "one of a kind," you should not use it carelessly to mean "interesting" or "unusual." Avoid such illogical expressions as "most unique," "very unique," and "extremely unique."

Emily Dickinson's bold experiments with form make her *unique* in the history of nineteenth-century American poetry.

when, where: Do not directly follow a linking verb with *when* or *where*. Be careful not to use *where* when your context requires *that*.

Faulty: The exposition is *when* an author provides the reader with important background information.

Revised: In the exposition, an author provides the reader with important background information.

Faulty: Madras, India, is *where* R. K. Narayan was born.

Revised: R. K. Narayan was born in Madras, India.

Faulty: We read *where* the prizes were worth hundreds of dollars.

Revised: We read *that* the prizes were worth hundreds of dollars.

R56

Index of Skills

Boldface numbers indicate pages where terms are defined.

Literary Analysis

Reading

Reading Informational Texts

Reading Skills

Vocabulary

Grammar, Usage, and Mechanics

Practice

Word Origins/Meanings

Writing

Writing Applications

Writing Strategies

Prewriting:

More Skills

Critical Thinking

Critical Viewing

R67

Listening and Speaking

Activities:

Steps/Tips:

Research and Technology

Activities:

Steps/Tips:

FCAT Practice

Informational Texts:

Reading:

Tips:

INDEX OF SKILLS

Index of Features

Boldface numbers indicate pages where terms are defined.

Communications Workshop

Comparing Literary Works

FCAT Practice

Informational Texts:

Reading:

Tips:

Independent Reading

Informational Texts

Literature in Context

Architecture Connection

Culture Connection

Geography Connection

History Connection

Humanities Connection

Language Connection

Literature Connection

Mythology Connection

Science Connection

World Events Connection:

Unit Introduction

Vocabulary Workshop

Writing Workshop: Work in Progress

Index of Authors and Titles

Notes: Page numbers in *italics* refer to biographical information; Nonfiction and informational text appears in red; Featured authors appear in **boldface** text. For a complete listing of the informational texts in this program, please see page xxxii.

M

N

O

P

R

S

T

U

V

W

Acknowledgements

Grateful acknowledgment is made to the following for copyrighted material:

Atlanta-Fulton Public Library System "Atlanta-Fulton Public Library System: Library Cards / AFPLS Logo" from Atlanta-Fulton Public Library System One Margaret Mitchell Square Atlanta GA 30303. Copyright © 2006 Atlanta-Fulton Public Library System. All Rights Reserved. Used by permission.

The Bancroft Library, Admin Offices From "Desert Exile: The Uprooting of a Japanese-American Family" pp. 69-78 by Yoshiko Uchida. Copyright © 1982 by University of Washington Press: Seattle. Courtesy of the Bancroft Library, University of California, Berkeley. Used by permission.

James Berardinelli "The Joy Luck Club: A Film Review" by James Berardinelli from *www.reelviews.net*. Copyright © 1993 by James Berardinelli.

Susan Bergholz Literary Services From "In Commemoration: One Million Volumes" by Rudolfo A. Anaya from *A Million Stars*. Copyright © 1995 by Rudolfo Anaya. First published as "In Commemoration: One Million Volumes" in A Mill Stars; Millionth Acquisition for U. of NM General Library, U. of NM Press, 1982. "Tepeyac" by Sandra Cisneros from *Woman Hollering Creek*. Copyright © 1991 by Sandra Cisneros. Published by Vintage Books, a division of Random House, Inc., New York and originally in hardcover by Random House, Inc. Used by permission of Susan Bergholz Literary Services, New York, NY and Lamy, NM. All rights reserved.

Brandt & Hochman Literary Agents, Inc. "By the Waters of Babylon" by Stephen Vincent Benét from *The Selected Works of Stephen Vincent Benet*. Copyright © 1937 by Stephen Vincent Benet Copyright renewed © 1965 by Thomas C. Benet, Stephanic Mahin and Rachel B. Lewis. Used by permission of Brandt & Hochman Literary Agents, Inc.

Brooks Permissions "The Bean Eaters" by Gwendolyn Brooks from *Blacks*. Copyright © 1991 by Gwendolyn Brooks, published by Third World Press, Chicago. Used by Consent of Brooks Permissions.

Curtis Brown Ltd. "The Leader in the Mirror" by Pat Mora from *Teaching Tolerance*. Copyright © 1994 by Pat Mora. First published in *Teaching Tolerance*, published by Southern Poverty Law Center. Used by permission of Curtis Brown, Ltd.

California State University, Fullerton "California State University, Fullerton Catalog: Music" from *http://www.fullerton.edu/catalog*

Charlotte County Board of County Commissioners "Charlotte-Glades Library System: About the Library / CGLS Logo" from *http://www.charlottecountyfl.com/Library*.

Chicago Tribune "Mothers and daughters: A dazzling first novel illuminations two generations of Chinese-American life" by Michael Dorris from *Chicago Tribune, March 12 1989*.

City of Berkeley Fire Department "Berkeley Fire Department Recruitment Information / City of Berkeley Logo" from *http://www.ci.berkeley.ca.us/fire*

City of Boca Raton "The City of Boca Raton Volunteer Application & Volunteer Service Agreement" from *http://www.ci.boca-raton.fl.us*.

City of Fort Lauderdale "City of Fort Lauderdale Paramedic/Firefighter Examination Process" from *http://ci.ftlaud.fl.us/*

City of Perry Fire Department "City of Perry Firefighter Application/Perry, GA Fire Dept. Seal" from *www.perry-ga.gov*. Used by permission.

Frances Collin, Literary Agent "The Marginal World' from *The Edge of the Sea* by Rachel Carson. Copyright © 1955 by Rachel L. Carson. Used by permission of Frances Collin, Trustee. Any electronic copying or distribution of this text is expressly forbidden.

Don Congdon Associates, Inc. "Contents of the Dead Man's Pockets" by Jack Finney from Collier's, 1950. Copyright © 1956 by Crowell Publishing, renewed 1984 by Jack Finney. Used by permission.

Dial Books for Young Readers, a division of Penguin Young Readers Group "Cupid and Psyche" by Sally Benson from *Stories of the Gods and Heroes*. Copyright © 1940 by Sally Benson. Copyright © renewed 1968 by Sally Benson. All rights reserved.

Doubleday, a division of Random House, Inc. "The Sun Parlor" by Dorothy West from *The Richer, The Poorer*. Copyright © 1995 by Dorothy West. "The Waking" by Theodore Roethke from *The Collected Poems of Theodore Roethke*. Copyright © 1953 by Theodore Roethke. Used by permission of Doubleday, a division of Random House, Inc.

Cornelius Eady "The Empty Dance Shoes" by Cornelius Eady from *Victims of the Latest Dance Craze: Poems by Cornelius Eady*. Copyright © 1985 by Cornelius Eady. "The Poetic Interpretation of the Twist" by Cornelius Eady from *Victims of the Latest Dance Craze: Poems by Cornelius Eady*. Copyright © 1985 by Cornelius Eady. All rights reserved.

Eastman & Eastman o/b/o Billy Joel "Hold Fast Your Dreams–and Trust Your Mistakes" by Billy Joel from *Hold Fast Your Dreams: Twenty Commencement Speeches*. Copyright © 1996 by Carrie Boyko and Kimberly Colen. All rights reserved.

Farrar, Straus & Giroux, LLC "The Fish" by Elizabeth Bishop from *The Complete Poems 1927-1979*. Copyright © 1979, 1983 by Alice Helen Methfessel. From "Nobel Lecture" by Alexander Solzhenitsyn translated by F.D. Reeve. Translation copyright © 1972 by Farrar, Straus & Giroux, LLC. Copyright © 1972 by the Nobel Foundation. Used by permission of Farrar, Straus and Giroux, LLC.

Estate of Robert Fitzgerald "The Antigone of Sophocles" an English version by Dudley Fitts and Robert Fitzgerald. Used by the permission of the Estate of Robert Fitzgerald, Penelope Laurans Fitzgerald, Executor.

Dr. Renee Friedman "Archaeology's Interactive Dig - Narmer's Temple: Week 1" by Renee Friedman from *http://www.archaeology.org* Copyright © 2003 Archaeological Institute of America.

Garmin International, Inc. "GPS Quick Start Guide" from *www.garmin.com*. Copyright © 2004 Garmin Ltd. or its subsidiaries. Used by permission.

Joi Gresham From "A Raisin in the Sun, Act I, Scene ii" by Lorraine Hansberry from *A Raisin in the Sun.* Copyright © 1984 by Robert Nemiroff, as an unpublished work. Copyright © 1959, 1966, 1984 by Robert Nemiroff. All rights reserved.

Sanford J. Greenburger Associates "The Threads of Time" by C.J. Cherryh from *The Collected Short Fiction of C.J. Cherryh*. First Printing, February 2004. All rights reserved. Used by permission.

Grove/Atlantic, Inc. "Tanka: The Clustering Clouds" from *Anthology of Japanese Literature* by Minamoto no Toshiyori, translated by Donald Keene. Copyright © 1965 by Grove Atlantic, Inc. Used by permission.

Harcourt, Inc. "How to React to Familiar Faces" from *How to Travel with a Salmon & Other Essays* by Umberto Eco, copyright © Gruppo Editoriale Fabbri, Bompiani, Sonzogno, Etas S.p.A., English translation by William Weaver copyright © 1994 by Harcourt, Inc. "Jazz Fantasia" by Carl Sandburg from *Smoke and Steel*. Copyright © 1920 by Harcourt, Inc. and renewed 1948 by Carl Sandburg. Used by permission of Harcourt, Inc. This material may not be reproduced in any form or by any means without the prior written permission of the publisher.

Harper's Magazine "The Leap" by Louise Erdrich from *Harper's Magazine*. Copyright © 1990 by Harper's Magazine Foundation. Used from the March issue by special permission.

Harvard University Press "Tell all the Truth but tell it slant (#1129)", "The Wind-tapped like a tired man (#436)" by Emily Dickinson from *The Poems of Emily Dickinson*, Thomas H. Johnson, ed., Cambridge, Mass.: The Belknap Press of Harvard University Press, Copyright © 1951, 1955, 1979, 1983 by the President and Fellows of Harvard College. Used by permission of the publishers and the Trustees of Amherst College. Copyright © 1951, 1955, byt the President and Fellows of Harvard College. © Copyright 1914, 1914, 1918, 1919, 1924, 1929, 1930, 1932, 1935, 1937, 1942 by Martha Dickinson Bianchi.

Healdsburg Jazz Festival "Healdsburg Jazz Festival Winter 2007 Newsletter" from *www.healdsburgjazzfestival.org*. Used by permission.

Thomas A. Hill "The History of the Guitar" by Thomas A. Hill from *The Guitar: An Introduction of the Instrument*. Copyright © 1973 by Thomas A. Hill. All rights reserved. Used with permission of Thomas A. Hill.

Hispanic Society of America "The Guitar" by Federico García Lorca from *Translations From Hispanic Poets*. Copyright 1938 by The Hispanic Society of America. Used with permission of the Hispanic Society of America.

The Barbara Hogenson Agency, Inc. "The Dog That Bit People" by James Thurber from *My Life and Hard Times*. Copyright © 1933, 1961 by James Thurber. Used by arrangement with Rosemary Thurber and The Barbara Hogenson Agency. All rights reserved.

Houghton Mifflin Company, Inc. "Prometheus and the First People" (originally titled "The Creation of Man" and "The Coming of Evil") from *Greek Myths* by Olivia E. Coolidge. Copyright 1949 by Olivia E. Coolidge; copyright renewed (c) 1977 by Olivia E. Coolidge. Adapted by permission of Houghton Mifflin Company. Text © 1949 by Olivia E. Coolidge. Used by permission of Houghton Mifflin Co. All rights reserved.

David Henry Hwang From "Tibet Through the Red Box" from Act II" by David Henry Hwang. Used by permission.

The Jazz Society of Pensacola "The Jazz Society of Pensacola, March 2007 Newsletter" by Andrew R. Metzger from *http://www.jazzpensacola.com*. Copyright © 2001 Jazz Society of Pensacola. Used by permission.

Johnson & Alcock Ltd., London "The Bridegroom" by Alexander Pushkin translated by D.M. Thomas from *The Bronze Horseman and Other Poems*, London: Secker & Warburg UK 1982. Used by permission of Johnson and Alcock Ltd., London.

Johnson Outdoors Inc. "Compass Directions and Warranty" by Staff from *www.silvacompass.com* Copyright 2002 Johnson Outdoors Inc. All rights reserved. Used by permission.

Martha Kaplan Agency From "Swimming to Antarctica: Tales of a Long-Distance Swimmer" by Lynne Cox. Copyright © 2004 by Lynne Cox. Used by permission.

Liveright Publishing Corporation "Reapers" by Jean Toomer from *Cane*. Copyright 1923 by Boni & Liveright, renewed 1951 by Jean Toomer. Used by permission of Liveright Publishing Corporation.

Los Angeles Public Library "Los Angeles Public Library: Borrower Services" from *http://www.lapl.org*

The Jennifer Lyons Literary Agency, LLC "Fear" by Gabriela Mistral from *Selected Poems of Gabriela Mistral*, translated by Doris Dana. Copyright 1961, 1964, 1970, 1971 by Doris Dana. Used by permission.

Metropolitan Museum of Modern Art From *What Makes a Degas a Degas* by Richard Muhlberger. Copyright © Metropolitan Museum of Modern Art

Marco Mielcarek "Voices from the Wall: Ich bin ein Berliner" by Marco Mielcarek. Used by permission.

Edna St. Vincent Millay Society "Conscientious Objector" by Edna St. Vincent Millay from *Collected Poems*. Copyright © 1934, 1962 by Edna St. Vincent Millay and Norma Millay Ellis. All rights reserved. Copyright © 1917, 1921, 1923, 1928, 1931, 1933, 1934, 1936, 1937, 1938, 1939, 1940, 1941, 1950 by Edna St. Vincent Millay. Copyright © 1945, 1946, 1947, 1951, 1952, 1953, 1954, 1956 by Norma Millay Ellis. Used by permission of Elizabeth Barnett, literary executor.

Navarre Scott Momaday From "The Way to Rainy Mountain" by N. Scott Momaday. Copyright © 1969 by The University of New Mexico Press. Used by permission.

William Morris Agency "A Visit to Grandmother" by William Melvin Kelley from *Dances on the Shore*. Copyright © 1964, 1992 by William Melvin Kelley. Used by permission of William Morris Agency, LLC on behalf of the author.

National Aeronautics and Space Administration "Black Water Turns the Tide on Florida Coral" from *http://www.nasa.gov*

National Science Teachers Assocation Publications "An Interview with Firefighter Denise Dierich" by Megan Sullivan from *http://newsite.nsta.org* Copyright © 2003 NSTA.

New American Library, a division of Penguin From "An Enemy of the People" by Henrik Ibsen translated by Rolf Fjelde from *Henrik*

Ibsen: The Complete Major Prose Plays. Copyright © 1965, 1970, 1978 by Rolf Fjelde. All rights reserved. Used by permission.

New Directions Publishing Corporation "Spring and All" by William Carlos Williams from *Collected Poems, 1909-1939, Volume I*. Copyright © 1938 by New Directions Publishing Corp. "A Tree Telling of Orpheus" by Denise Levertov from *Poems, 1968-1972*. Copyright © 1965, 1966, 1967,1968, 1969, 1970, 1971 by Denise Levertov Goodman. Copyright © 1970, 1971, 1972, 1987 by Denise Levertov. Used by permission of New Directions Publishing Corp.

The New York Times "Mr. Gorbachev's Role" by Staff from *The New York Times (Late Edition)* November 10, 1999. Copyright © 1999 by The New York Times Inc. All rights reserved. Used by permission and protected by the Copyright Laws of The United States. The printing, copying, redistribution, or retransmission of the Material without express written permission is prohibited.

The New York Times Agency "Feel the City's Pulse? It's Be-bop, Man!" by Ann Douglas from *The New York Times August 28, 1998*. Copyright © 1998 by the New York Times. All rights reserved. Used by permission and protected by the Copyright Laws of The United States. The printing, copying, redistribution, or retransmission of the Material without express written permission is prohibited.

North Point Press, div of Farrar, Straus & Giroux "All" by Bei Dao translated by Donald Finkel and Xueliang Chen from *A Splintered Mirror: Chinese Poetry From the Democracy Movement*. Translation copyright © 1991 by Donald Finkel. Used by permission of North Point Press, a division of Farrar, Straus and Giroux, LLC. "Also All" by Shu Ting, translated by Donald Finkel and Jinsheng Yi from *A Splintered Mirror: Chinese Poetry From the Democracy Movement*. Translation copyright © 1991 by Donald Finkel.

Norwegian Nobel Institute Keep Memory Alive" by Elie Wiesel from *Elie Wiesel's Nobel Prize Acceptance Speech*. Used with permission from the Norwegian Nobel Institute. Copyright © 1986 by the Nobel Foundation.

Naomi Shihab Nye "Making a Fist" by Naomi Shihab Nye from *Hugging the Jukebox*. Copyright © 1982 by Dutton: New York. Used by permission of the author, Naomi Shihab Nye.

Harold Ober Associates, Inc. From *Marian Anderson: Famous Concert Singer* by Langston Hughes. Copyright © 1954 by Langston Hughes. Renewed 1982 by George Houston Bass. "Do Not Go Gentle Into That Good Night" by Dylan Thomas, from *The Poems of Dylan Thomas*. Copyright © 1952 by Dylan Thomas. "The Weary Blues" by Langston Hughes. From *The Collected Poems of Langston Hughes* by Langston Hughes, copyright © 1994 by The Estate of Langston Hughes. Used by permission of Harold Ober Associates Incorporated.

Oxford University Press, UK "How Much Land Does a Man Need?" by Leo Tolstoy translated by Louise and Aylmer Maude from *The Raid and Other Stories*. Edited by Maude, Louise & Aylmer. Copyright © 1935 Oxford University Press. Used with permission of Oxford University Press.

Pantheon Books, a div of Random House Inc. "The Orphan Boy and the Elk Dog" by Blackfoot from *American Indian Myths and Legends* by Richard Erdoes and Alfonso Ortiz. Copyright © 1984 by Richard Erdoes and Alfonso Ortiz.

Pearson Education "Tides" by Staff from *Prentice Hall Science Explorer: Earth Science*. Copyright © 2001 by Pearson Education, Inc., publishing as Pearson Prentice Hall. All rights reserved. Used by permission.

Pearson Education Ltd. From "Sundiata: An Epic of Old Mali: Childhood, The Lion's Awakening" by D.T. Niane translated by G.D. Pickett from *Sundiata: An Epic of Old Mali*. Copyright © Longman Group Limited 1965, used by permission of Pearson Education Limited. Copyright © Presence Africaine 1960 (original French version: Soundjata, ou L'Epopee Mandingue) © Longman Group Ltd. (English Version) 1965.

Penguin Group (USA) Inc. "Everest" from *Touch the Top of the World: A Blind Man's Journey to Climb Farther than the Eye Can See* by Erik Weihenmayer. Copyright © 2002 by Erik Weihenmayer. All rights reserved.

Penguin Putnam, Inc From "Places Left Unfinished at the Time of Creation" by John Phillip Santos. Copyright © 1999 by John Philip Santos. All rights reserved.

G.P. Putnam's Sons, a division of Penguin "Arthur Becomes King" Part I, Chapter XXII from *The Once and Future King* by T.H. White. Copyright © 1938, 1939, 1940, © 1958 by T. H. White, renewed.

Random House, Inc. "Occupation: Conductorette from *I Know Why the Caged Bird Sings* by Maya Angelou. Copyright © 1969 by Maya Angelou. All rights reserved. Used by permission.

Random House Children's Books "Ashputtle" by Jakob and Wilhelm Grimm translated by Ralph Manheim from *Grimm's Tales for Young and Old: The Complete Stories*, copyright © 1977 by Ralph Manheim. Translation copyright © 1977 by Ralph Manheim. All rights reserved. Used by permission of Random House Children's Books, a division of Random House, Inc.

Marian Reiner, Literary Agent "Metaphor" by Eve Merriam from *It Doesn't Always Have to Rhyme*. Copyright © 1964, 1970, 1973, 1986 by Eve Merriam. Copyright renewed 1964 by Eve Merriam. Used by permission of Marian Reiner.

Rogers, Coleridge and White, Ltd. "Games at Twilight" by Anita Desai from *Games at Twilight and Other Stories*. Copyright © 1978 by Anita Desai. Used by permission of the author c/o Rogers, Coleridge & White Ltd., 20 Powis Mews, London W11 1JN.

Heyden White Rostow "The American Idea" by Theodore H. White from *The New York Times Magazine, July 6, 1986*. Copyright © 1986 by Theodore H. White. Copyright © 1986 by The New York Times Company. All rights reserved. Used by permission.

William F. Russell, Ed.D "Damon and Pythias" from *Classic Myths to Read Aloud* by William F. Russell, Copyright © 1988 by William F. Russell.

Scientific American "The Spider and the Wasp" by Alexander Petrunkevitch from *Scientific American, August, 1952*. Copyright © 1952 by Scientific American, Inc.

The Sheep Meadow Press "Pride" by Dahlia Ravikovitch translated by Chana Bloch and Ariel Bloch from *The Window*. Copyright © 1987 by Chana Bloch. All rights reserved. Used by permission.

Elyse Sommer "A Curtain Up Review: Antigone As Acted and Played by the Three Fates on the Way to Becoming the Three Graces". Review by Elyse Sommer in www.curtainup.com, the online theater magazine. Copyright 2004, Elyse Sommer. Used by permission.

Sonoma County "The County of Sonoma Volunteer Application" from *http://www.sonoma-county.org*

Emma Sweeney Agency, LLC "Civil Peace" by Chinua Achebe from *Girls at War and Other Stories*. Copyright © 1972, 1973 by Chinua Achebe. Used by permission of Doubleday, a division of Random House, Inc.

Talkin' Broadway "Antigone (Theatre Review)" by Matthew Murray from www.talkinbroadway.com. Used by permission.

Jeremy P. Tarcher/Putnam "Making History with Vitamin C (originally titled: Ascorbic Acid)" by Penny Le Couteur and Jay Burreson from *Napoleon's Buttons: How 17 Molecules Changed History*. Copyright © 2003 by Micron Geological Ltd. and Jay Burreson. All rights reserved.

Anthony Thwaite "Tanka: "Was it that I went to sleep"" by Ono no Komachi translated and co-edited by Geoffrey Bownas and Anthony Thwaite from *The Penguin Book of Japanese Verse*. "When I went to visit" by Ki no Tsurayuki translated by Bownas & Thwaite from *The Penguin Book of Japanese Verse*. "One cannot ask loneliness" by Priest Jakuren translated by Bownas & Thwaite from *The Penguin Book of Japanese Verse*. Penguin Books copyright © 1964, revised edition 1998. Translation copyright © Geoffrey Bownas and Anthony Thwaite, 1964, 1998. Used by permission.

University of North Carolina Press The Street of the Canon" by Josefina Niggli from *Mexican Village*. Copyright © 1945 by the University of North Carolina Press, renewed 1972 by Josefina Niggli. Used by permission of the publisher.

U.S. News & World Report Will All the Blue Men End Up in Timbuktu?" by Stefan Lovgren from *US News and World Report, December 7, 1998*. Copyright © 1998 U.S. News & World Report, L.P. All rights reserved. Used by permission.

UCLA Office of Media Relations "Strong Earth Tides Can Trigger Earthquakes" from *http://www.newsroom.ucla.edu/*. Courtesy of UCLA. Used by permission.

David Unger "The Censors" by Luisa Valenzuela translated by Hortense Carpentier from *Open Door: Stories*. Copyright © translation by David Unger. Used by permission.

University of North Carolina Press "The Street of the Canon" by Josefina Niggli from *Mexican Village*. Copyright © 1945 by the University of North Carolina Press, renewed 1972 by Josefina Niggli. Used by permission of the publisher.

Viking Penguin, Inc. "Like the Sun" by R.K. Narayan, from *Under the Banyan Tree*. Copyright © 1985 by R. K. Narayan. Copyright © 1985 by R.K. Narayan. "My City" by James Weldon Johnson from *Saint Peter Relates an Incident*. Copyright © 1935 by James Weldon John, © renewed 1963 by Grace Nail Johnson. All rights reserved.

Susan Vreeland "Artful Research" by Susan Vreeland from *The Writer, January 2002*. Copyright © 2001. "Magdalena Looking" by Susan Vreeland from *Girl in Hacinth Blue*. Copyright © 1999 by Susan Vreeland. Available in hardback: MacAdam-Cage; paperback: Penguin. Used with permission.

W. W. Norton & Company, Inc. "Don Quixote", excerpt from *Don Quixote: A Norton Critical Edition: The Ormbsby Translation, Revised*, by Miguel de Cervantes, edited by Joseph Jones and Kenneth Douglas. Copyright © 1981 by W.W. Norton & Company, Inc. Used by permission of W.W. Norton & Company, Inc.

Walker Publishing Company "Imaginary Lines" by Dava Sobel from *Longitude: The True Story of a Lone Genius Who Solved the Greatest Scientific Problem of His Time*. Copyright © Dava Sobel, 1995. All rights reserved. Used by permission.

Wallace Literary Agency, Inc. "Rama's Initiation" from *The Ramayana* by R.K. Narayan. Published by Penguin Books. Copyright © 1972 by R.K. Narayanan. Used by permission of the Wallace Literary Agency, Inc.

Wesleyan University Press "Glory" by Yusef Komunyakaa from *Magic City* (Wesleyan University Press, 1992) Copyright © 1992 by Yusef Komunyakaa and used by permission of Wesleyan University Press.

The Wylie Agency, Inc. "The Garden of Stubborn Cats" by Italo Calvino from *Marcovaldo or the Seasons in the City*. Copyright © 1963 by Guilio Einaudi editore s.p.a., used with the permission of the Wylie Agency Inc. English translation copyright © 1983 by Harcourt Brace Jovanovich, Inc. and Martin Secker & Warburg Limited.

Note: Every effort has been made to locate the copyright owner of material reproduced on this component. Omissions brought to our attention will be corrected in subsequent editions.

Credits

AP/Wide World Photos; **357:** b. Campbell William/CORBIS **358:** t. Betty Press/Woodfin Camp & Associates; **360:** t. ©The Stock Market/John Curtis **361:** b. Campbell William/CORBIS **363:** r. Corel Professional Photos CD-ROM **371:** t. Bettmann/CORBIS **372:** © Stefan Grambart **375:** t. © Stefan Grambart **376:** © Stefan Grambart **379:** b. © Stefan Grambart **380:** t. © Stefan Grambart **383:** t. ©Ulf Andersen/Getty Images **384:** Frank Siteman/Stock, Boston; **386:** b. Jane Burton (c) Dorling Kindersley **387:** *M.C. Escher's Relativity.* Copyright ©2004 The M.C. Escher Company - Baarn - Holland. All rights reserved. **389:** r. ©Russell Illig/PhotoDisc/ Getty Images **392:** t. istockphoto.com **395:** t. Ingram Publishing/ SuperStock **396:** t. istockphoto.com **403:** b. David Turnley/CORBIS **404:** t. Alexandra Avakian/Getty Images **404:** t. ©Diane Cook and Len Jenshel/ TIB/Getty Images **405:** b. © AP Photos **405-405:** Bkgrnd istockphoto.com **406:** t. © Bernard Bisson & Thierry Orban/Sygma/CORBIS **409:** t. Diaz-Piferrer **409:** b. Cheron Bayna **410:** t. © Smithsonian American Art Museum, Washington, DC / Art Resource **411:** t. *Man Writing*, 2004 (oil on canvas) by Ruth Addinall (Contemporary Artist)Private Collection/ The Bridgeman Art Library **412:** © Patti Mollica/SuperStock **414:** r. istock-photo.com **414:** m. istockphoto.com **414:** tr. istockphoto.com **414:** tl. istockphoto.com **414:** Bkgrnd istockphoto.com **414:** Bkgrnd istockphoto. com **416:** m. ©Bob Daemmrich **416-417:** b. ©Felicia Martinez/PhotoEdit Inc. **420:** b. Will Hart/PhotoEdit Inc. **428:** t. © Stefano Bianchetti/CORBIS **430:** b. © Mike Booth/Alamy **gr10 U3** **442:** t. © Ian Shaw/Alamy; **443:** b. © JAUBERT BERNARD/Alamy **445:** t. ©Images.com/CORBIS **446:** m. PEANUTS reprinted by permission of United Feature Syndicate, Inc. **447:** b. ©Michael Newman/PhotoEdit Inc. **449:** t. Getty Images **450-451:** b. Courtesy of Didrik Johnck **453:** t. Courtesy of Didrik Johnck **454:** Courtesy of Didrik Johnck **456:** b. Courtesy of Didrik Johnck **463:** Time Life Pictures/Getty Images **464:** l. Brian P. Kenney/Animals Animals **465:** t. ©Minden Pictures, Inc. **467:** t. ©Dorling Kindersley **468:** Getty Images **469:** t. ©OSF/M. Fogden/Animals Animals **470:** ©Geoff Dann/ Dorling Kindersley **473:** t. AP/Wide World Photos **474-475:** © Mike Agliolo/ CORBIS **475:** t. istockphoto.com **476:** b. Les Stone/CORBIS **479:** t. *'As for Resolution'* (oil on canvas), Brooks, Robin (Contemporary Artist) / Private Collection, / The Bridgeman Art Library International **480:** b. *Portrait of George III* (1738-1820) *in his Coronation Robes*, c.1760 (oil on canvas), Ramsay, Allan (1713-84) / Private Collection, / The Bridgeman Art Library International **481:** tl. The Bridgeman Art Library, London/ New York **481:** tr. The Bridgeman Art Library, London/New York **489:** t. AP/Wide World Photos **490:** t. ©Connie Hayes/Images.com **493:** t. © Colin Bootman/Bridgeman Art Library/Getty Images **495:** ©Connie Hayes/Images.com **499:** t. Courtesy of the author **500:** t. © Alberto Ruggieri/Illustration Works/CORBIS **503:** Rt. Michael Newman/PhotoEdit Inc. **503:** t. Vic Bider/PhotoEdit Inc. **504:** t. © Paul Vismara/Images.com **519:** m. Courtesy of the Library of Congress **519:** b. Bettmann/CORBIS **520:** t. istockphoto.com **521:** tl. istockphoto.com **521:** tm. istockphoto. com **521:** tr. istockphoto.com **522:** t. istockphoto.com **525:** t. *My Life and Hard Times* Copyright ©1933 by James Thurber. Copyright © renewed 1961 by James Thurber. Reprinted by arrangement with Rosemary A. Thurber and The Barbara Hogenson Agency.; **528:** t. *My Life and Hard Times* Copyright ©1933 by James Thurber. Copyright © renewed 1961 by James Thurber. Reprinted by arrangement with Rosemary A. Thurber and The Barbara Hogenson Agency.; **541:** t. Bettmann/CORBIS **542:** b. © Bettmann/ CORBIS **543:** t. © CORBIS **544:** t. © Alain Nogues/ CORBIS SYGMA **547:** t. ©Lesegretain/CORBIS SYGMA **548:** t. Jacques Langevin/CORBIS SYGMA **548:** ml. Penguin Signet Classics **548:** mr. © Bettmann/CORBIS **550:** m. Private Collection/The Bridgeman Art Library, London/New York **550:** tr. Dean Conger/CORBIS **551:** b. Hulton Archive/Getty Images Inc. **559:** tl. Carl Mydans/Time Life Pictures/Getty Images **560:** istockphoto.com **561:** b. istockphoto.com **562:** b. © SuperStock, Inc./SuperStock **563:** tr. *John Adams* (oil on canvas), Otis, Bass (1784-1861) (attr.to)/ © Collection of the New-York Historical Society, USA,/The Bridgeman Art Library International **563:** tl. *Thomas Jefferson* (1743-1826) (colour litho), Peale, Rembrandt (1778-1860) / Private Collection, Peter Newark American Pictures/The Bridgeman Art Library International **568:** t. Image copyright ©The Metropolitan Museum of Art/Art Resource, NY **570-571:** Photograph © 2008 Museum of Fine Arts, Boston. All Rights Reserved. **572:** t. *Self Portrait* (oil on canvas), Degas, Edgar (1834-1917)/Private Collection,/The Bridgeman Art Library International **585:** t. NO CREDIT NECESSARY **585:** b. Thomas Victor **586:** t. Bettmann/CORBIS **586-587:** border istockphoto.com **588-589:** Bkgrnd istockphoto.com **589:** b. © CORBIS **590-591:** border istockphoto. com **591:** r. © Zen Shui / SuperStock **592:** b. © Seattle Post-Intelligencer Collection; Museum of History and Industry / CORBIS **592-593:** border istockphoto.com **593:** r. © Bettmann/ CORBIS **594:** border istockphoto. com **595:** rt. © Stapleton Collection/CORBIS **596:** t. ©CORBIS **599:** t. © Joseph Sohm; Visions of America/CORBIS **600:** b. © Lindsay Hebberd/ CORBIS **604:** b. Jose Luis Palaez, Inc./CORBIS **607:** t. Prentice Hall **612:** t. © Ian Shaw / Alamy **614:** ©Myrleen Ferguson Cate/PhotoEdit Inc. **Gr10 U4** **626:** t. ©Spencer Grant/PhotoEdit Inc. **627:** b. © wsr /Alamy **629:** b. Prentice Hall **630:** m. CALVIN AND HOBBES © 1999 Watterson. Reprinted with permission of UNIVERSAL PRESS SYNDICATE. All rights reserved. **631:** b. ©David Young-Wolff / PhotoEdit Inc. **633:** © Hulton-Deutsch Collection/CORBIS **633:** © Hulton-Deutsch Collection/ CORBIS **634:** Bettmann/CORBIS **635:** t. **641:** t. The Granger Collection, New York **641:** ml. Art Resource, NY **641:** ml. AP/Wide World Photos **641:** b. Courtesy of the Library of Congress **642:** *The Lights of Marriage*, (detail) Marc Chagall, Kunsthaus, Zurich, ©1998 Artists Rights Society (ARS), New York/ADAGP, Paris; **645:** r. Giraudon / Art Resource, NY **646:** l. Smithsonian Banque d'Images, ADAGP/Art Resource, NY **648:** *The Old Guitarist*, 1903, Pablo Picasso, Spanish, 1881-1973, oil on panel 122.9 x 82.6 cm, Helen Birch Bartlett Memorial Collection, 1926.253. Reproduction, The Art Institute of Chicago, ©2004 Estate of Pablo Picasso/Artists Rights Society (ARS), New York; **649:** Bkgrnd © John Woodcock **650:** *The Black Carp* (woodblock print), Harunobu, Gakutei (fl.1818-30)/ Private Collection, Photo © Held Collection/The Bridgeman Art Library International **650-651:** Bkgrnd © Micha Pawlitzki/zefa/CORBIS **652:** © Bettmann/CORBIS **654:** m. *The Royal Fusiliers*, 1876 (w/c on paper), Simkin, Richard (1840-1926) / Private Collection, © Malcolm Innes Gallery, London, UK/The Bridgeman Art Library International **657:** ml. AP/Wide World Photos **657:** b. William Carlos Williams (detail), The National Portrait Gallery, Smithsonian Institution, Washington, D.C./Art Resource, NY; **657:** t. Time Life Pictures/Getty Images **657:** ml. photo by James Evans **658:** t. *Haymaking*, 1898, Alfred Glendenning, Tate Gallery, London/Art Resource, NY **659:** *The Oak of Flagey*, called Vercingetorix, Courbet, Gustave (1819-77)/ Pennsylvania Academy of the Fine Arts, Philadelphia, USA,/The Bridgeman Art Library International **660:** l. *Attic red-figure hydria*, decorated with a scene of the Thracian bard Thamyris being deprived of sight and voice, from the Group of Polygnotus, from Greece, c.440-420 Bc (ceramic),/© Ashmolean Museum, University of Oxford, UK, /The Bridgeman Art Library International **661:** *Reconstruction of the Queen's Lyre*, from Ur, c.2600-2400 BC, Mesopotamian/British Museum, London, UK,/The Bridgeman Art Library International **662:** © Stefan Klein/istockphoto.com **663:** b. Corel Professional Photos CD-ROM; **664:** Kamil Vojnar **665:** © Catherine Hazard/SuperStock **675:** t. The Granger Collection, New York **675:** ml. *Dylan Thomas* (1914-53), c.1937-38 (oil on canvas), John, Augustus Edwin (1878-1961)/© National Museum and Gallery of Wales, Cardiff/ www.bridgeman.co.uk **676:** © Patti Mollica/SuperStock **678:** *Old Man in Sorrow (On the Threshold of Eternity)* 1890 (oil on canvas), Gogh, Vincent van (1853-90)/Rijksmuseum Kroller-Muller, Otterlo, Netherlands, /The Bridgeman Art Library International **683:** t. Bentley Historical Library **683:** ml. SuperStock **684:** *Cumberland Hills*, 1948 (oil on board), Nicholson, Winifred (1893-1981) /Arts Council Collection, Hayward Gallery, London, UK,/The Bridgeman Art Library International **686:** Frances Howard, Isaac Oliver, Victoria and Albert Museum/Art Resource, NY; **686:** border Lisa Thornberg /istockphoto.com **687:** Bkgrnd istockphoto.com **688:** t. *View of the Summer Palace*, Peking (colour on silk), Chinese School/ Bibliotheque Nationale, Paris, France/The Bridgeman Art Library International **701:** t. Bettmann/CORBIS **701:** m.

Bettmann/CORBIS **702:** © Christie's Images/SuperStock **703:** t. Scala/Art Resource, NY **717:** m. Time Life Pictures/Getty Images Inc. **717:** b. Photo by Bachrach. Used by permission of Marian Reiner **718:** b. /istockphoto.com **719:** © Howard J. Winter/zefa/CORBIS **720:** m. © Lew Robertson/Corbis **720:** © Michael A. Keller/CORBIS **721:** © Robert Michael/CORBIS **722:** ©Russell Tate/istockphoto.com **725:** b. Amherst College Archives and Special Collections, by permission of the Trustees of Amherst College **725:** t. National Portrait Gallery, Smithsonian Institution/Art Resource, NY **725:** m. Dina Gona **725:** b. Amherst College Archives and Special Collections, by permission of the Trustees of Amherst College **726:** © Regien Paassen **727:** b. *The Cliffs of Moher*, 2003 (oil on board), Warmoth, Pip Todd (b.1962) /Private Collection, Kings Road Galleries/ The Bridgeman Art Library International **728:** t. © Joel Barr/SuperStock 1658-117-A-P7B **735:** t. Photograph © The Estate of Carl Van Vechten Gravure and Compilation © Eakins Press Foundation **735:** m. The Granger Collection, New York; **735:** b. The Granger Collection, New York **736:** *Autumn Lamp* (Guitar Player, 1983), Romare Bearden, From the Mecklenburg Autumn Series, oil with collage, 40" x 31", Private collection, ©1997 Romare Bearden Foundation/Licensed by VAGA, New York, New York **738:** t. © Oksana Struk/ istockphoto.com **739:** t. ©istockphoto.com **739:** tr. © Aliaksandr Stsiazhyn/istockphoto.com **739:** tl. © Aliaksandr Stsiazhyn/istockphoto.com **739:** mr. © Aliaksandr Stsiazhyn/istockphoto.com **739:** m. © Aliaksandr Stsiazhyn/istockphoto.com **743:** m. Michael Nicholson/CORBIS **743:** m. Bettmann/CORBIS **743:** b. The Granger Collection, New York **744:** t. Smithsonian American Art Museum, Washington, DC/Art Resource, NY **745:** *Terror from the Deep* (gouache on paper), Frey, Oliver (b.1948)/ Private Collection, © Look and Learn/The Bridgeman Art Library International **746:** t. © SuperStock, Inc./SuperStock 900-117358-I-P22B **759:** m. Dorothy Alexander **759:** b. Dorothy Alexander **759:** t. ©Kuntz Doug/CORBIS SYGMA **760:** Getty Images **761:** tr. ©Retna, LTD **761:** tl. Courtesy of Columbia Records **764:** t. AP/Wide World Photos **765:** m. AP/Wide World Photos **765:** t. One of a series of paintings of birds and fruit, late 19th century (w/c on paper), Wang Guochen (19th century)/School of Oriental & African Studies Library, Uni. of London,/The Bridgeman Art Library International **766:** t. One of a series of paintings of birds and fruit, late 19th century (w/c on paper), Wang Guochen (19th century)/ School of Oriental & African Studies Library, Uni. of London,/The Bridgeman Art Library International **776:** t. ©Spencer Grant/PhotoEdit Inc. **778:** b. © Bettmann/ CORBIS **Gr10 U5** **792:** b. Time Life Pictures/Getty Images Inc. **797:** m. ©Chris Bennion/Seattle Children's Theater **797:** Bkgrnd istockphoto.com **800:** r. ©Chris Bennion/Seattle Children's Theater **803:** b. © Peter Turnley/CORBIS **804-805:** ©Chris Bennion/Seattle Children's Theater **813:** b. Images Courtesy of Old Dominion University Theatre Program. *ANTIGONE*, 2000. Directed by Dr. Erlene Hendrix. Designed & Photographed by Konrad Winters. **813:** Vatican Museum/ Scala/Art Resource, NY; **814:** Images Courtesy of Old Dominion University Theatre Program. *ANTIGONE*, 2000. Directed by Dr. Erlene Hendrix. Designed & Photographed by Konrad Winters. **817:** t. Images Courtesy of Old Dominion University Theatre Program. *ANTIGONE*, 2000. Directed by Dr. Erlene Hendrix. Designed & Photographed by Konrad Winters. **819:** Images Courtesy of Old Dominion University Theatre Program. *ANTIGONE*, 2000. Directed by Dr. Erlene Hendrix. Designed & Photographed by Konrad Winters. **821:** Images Courtesy of Old Dominion University Theatre Program. *ANTIGONE*, 2000. Directed by Dr. Erlene Hendrix. Designed & Photographed by Konrad Winters. **823:** Liz McAulay/© Dorling Kindersley **824:** b. Images Courtesy of Old Dominion University Theatre Program. *ANTIGONE*, 2000. Directed by Dr. Erlene Hendrix. Designed & Photographed by Konrad Winters. **828:** Images Courtesy of Old Dominion University Theatre Program. *ANTIGONE*, 2000. Directed by Dr. Erlene Hendrix. Designed & Photographed by Konrad Winters. **830:** Bildarchiv Preussischer Kulturbesitz/Art Resource, NY **839:** b. Images Courtesy of Old Dominion University Theatre Program. *ANTIGONE*, 2000. Directed by Dr. Erlene Hendrix. Designed & Photographed by Konrad Winters. **842:** Images Courtesy of Old Dominion University Theatre Program. *ANTIGONE*, 2000. Directed by Dr. Erlene Hendrix. Designed & Photographed by Konrad Winters. **846:** Images Courtesy of Old Dominion University Theatre Program. *ANTIGONE*, 2000. Directed by Dr. Erlene Hendrix. Designed & Photographed by Konrad Winters. **849:** Images Courtesy of Old Dominion University Theatre Program. *ANTIGONE*, 2000. Directed by Dr. Erlene Hendrix. Designed & Photographed by Konrad Winters. **854:** Images Courtesy of Old Dominion University Theatre Program. *ANTIGONE*, 2000. Directed by Dr. Erlene Hendrix. Designed & Photographed by Konrad Winters. **857:** Images Courtesy of Old Dominion University Theatre Program. *ANTIGONE*, 2000. Directed by Dr. Erlene Hendrix. Designed & Photographed by Konrad Winters. **869:** b. Bettmann/CORBIS **870:** AP/Wide World Photos **874:** Robbie Jack/ CORBIS **886:** Illustration by Hugh Dixon from "Shakespeare in Performance" courtesy of Salamander Books, London; **887:** b. Adam Woolfitt/CORBIS **892:** tl. SuperStock **894:** istockphoto.com **894:** l. © Bettmann/CORBIS **894:** Bkgrnd Roman **895:** istockphoto.com **897:** *Painting from the Villa Boscoreale* (fresco), Roman, (1st century BC)/ Museo Archeologico Nazionale, Naples, Italy, Giraudon/www.bridgeman.co.uk **898:** Picture Post/Hulton Archive/Getty Images **901:** Sunset Boulevard/CORBIS SYGMA **902:** Scala / Art Resource, NY **905:** The Art Archive/Jan Vinchon Numismatist Paris/Dagli Orti **908:** Scala/ Art Resource **910:** The Art Archive/Provinciaal Museum G M Kam Nijmegen Netherlands/Dagli Orti **913:** Nimatallah/Art Resource, NY **916:** Reunion des Musees Nationaux/Art Resource **917:** istockphoto.com **918:** b. **922:** Culver Pictures, Inc. **926:** Hulton Archive/Getty Images **930:** Prisma/Ancient Art and Architecture Coll, Ltd I19HB5-PR **931:** t. The Art Archive/Museo Nazionale Terme Rome/Dagli Orti **933:** Reunion de Musees Nationaux/Art Resource, NY **934:** Doug Pearson/Corbis **940:** *Death of Julius Caesar* (100-44 BC) (oil on canvas) by Vincenzo Camuccini (1773-1844). Museo e Gallerie Nazionali di Capodimonte, Naples, Italy/The Bridgeman Art Library **941:** istockphoto.com **943:** Timothy McCarthy/Art Resource, NY **944:** MGM / THE KOBAL COLLECTION **951:** John Springer Collection/CORBIS **958:** MGM/ Photofest **961:** *Extispicium relief* (inspection of entrails) from the Forum of Trajan, Rome. Early Hadrianic. Louvre, Paris, France, Alinari/Art Resource, NY; **966:** Bettmann/CORBIS **967:** istockphoto.com **969:** Hulton Archive/Getty Images Inc. **973:** The Art Archive/ Rheinischeslandesmuseum Bonn/Dagli Orti **974:** Hulton Archive/Getty Images Inc. **976:** Erich Lessing/Art Resource, NY **982:** The Art Archive/ Jan Vinchon Numismatist Paris/Dagli Orti **986:** *Bust of Brutus* (85-42 BC) c.1540 (marble) (see also 244606) by MIchelangelo Buonarroti (1475-1564). Museo Nzaionale del Bargello, Florence,Italy/Alinari/The Bridgeman Art Library. **987:** istockphoto.com **991:** t. *A Roman Triumph*, 1838 (oil on canvas) by Frank Topham (1838-1924). New Walk Museum, Leicester City Museum Service. UK/The Bridgeman Art Library **993:** Hulton Archive/Getty Images Inc. **999:** Hulton Archive/Getty Images Inc. © Bob Daemmrich /PhotoEdit Inc. **1015:** CORBIS **1016:** t. Joan Marcus Photography **1016:** b. **1020:** Bluestone Productions/SuperStock **1024:** t. Time Life Pictures/Getty Images Inc. **Gr10 U6** **1049:** Prentice Hall **1050:** *NON SEQUITUR* © 1999 Wiley Miller. Dist. By UNIVERSAL PRESS SYNDICATE. Reprinted with permission. All rights reserved. **1051:** © Bob Daemmrich / PhotoEdit Inc. **1053:** border **1054:** tl. Library of Congress **1054:** bl. Photodisc/Getty Images **1054:** br. **1054:** ml. The Institute of Texan Cultures, San Antonio, Texas **1055:** t. Courtesy of John Philip Santos **1057:** m. New Mexico Department of Tourism **1057:** b. **1058:** t. Schalkwijk / Art Resource, NY **1060:** b. **1065:** Mimmo Jodice/CORBIS **1066:** *Prometheus Carrying Fire*, Jan Cossiers, Art Resource, NY **1068:** Wolfgang Kaehler/ CORBIS **1069:** Private Collection/The Bridgeman Art Library **1070:** tefano Bianchetti/CORBIS **1075:** t. Courtesy of the Library of Congress **1075:** b. Jeff Vanuga/CORBIS **1076:** *The Color of Sun*, Howard Terpning, oil, 26 x 26, © 2002 Howard Terpning, licensed by The Greenwich Workshop, Inc. **1078:** Bildarchiv Preussischer Kulturbesitz / Art Resource, NY **1080:** Jason Lindsey / Alamy **1081:** b. Steve Kaufman/CORBIS **1083:** Jeff Vanuga/CORBIS **1084:** Private Collection/The Bridgeman Art Library

1086: Mark J. Barrett / Alamy **1093:** t. Werner Forman/Art Resource, NY **1093:** b. Cover from *SUNDIATA*. Copyright ©1992 by David Wisniewski. Reprinted by permission of Clarion Books/Houghton Mifflin Co. All rights reserved. **1094:** Cover from *SUNDIATA*. Copyright ©1992 by David Wisniewski. Reprinted by permission of Clarion Books/Houghton Mifflin Co. All rights reserved. **1098:** Leather painting of *"An Elder Wearing Otuogwu Cloth Talking to a Teen Boy"*, John Mainga, LAMU, The Gallery of Contemporary African Art, photo by John Lei/Omni-Photo Communications, Inc. **1101:** Dea/Dani-Jeski/Getty Images, Inc. **1102:** The Granger Collection, New York **1103:** M. & E. Bernheim/Woodfin Camp & Associates **1107:** Victoria & Albert Museum, London/Art Resource, NY **1107:** b. AP/Wide World Photos **1108:** Victoria & Albert Museum, London/Art Resource, NY **1111:** Angelo Hornak/CORBIS **1113:** Private Collection, Archives Charmet/The Bridgeman Art Library **1114:** Mary Evans Picture Library/Alamy **1129:** t. Courtesy of Barbara Benson Golseth **1129:** b. The Granger Collection, New York **1130:** *Psyche Gazes in Despair at Cupid Flying Away*, Sir Edward Burne-Jones/The Bridgeman Art Library, London/New York **1132:** t. *Cupid and Psyche*, Sir Edward Burne-Jones/The Bridgeman Art Library, London/New York **1138:** Bettmann/CORBIS **1141:** t. Carl Offterdinger/The Bridgeman Art Library, London/New York **1155:** Getty Images Inc. **1156:** Inset Ivan Gusev/istockphoto.com **1156-1157:** b. Duncan Walker/istockphoto.com **1156-1157:** Bkgrnd **1159:** b. istockphoto.com **1161:** The Granger Collection, New York **1162:** Pete Dancs/Getty Images Inc. **1164:** The Granger Collection, New York **1173:** Bettmann/CORBIS **1174:** t. *The Lamentation of King Arthur* by William Bell Scott (1811-90) ©Private Collection/ © Whitford & Hughes, London, UK/ The Bridgeman Art Library **1175-1184:** border Shutterstock, Inc. **1176-1184:** border Shutterstock, Inc. **1177:** The Granger Collection, New York **1179:** Courtesy of the Trustees of British Library **1181:** *The Dream of Arthur in Avalon*, detail, Sir Edward Burne-Jones, The Museo de Arte de Ponce, The Luis A. FerrÈ Foundation, Inc. Ponce, Puerto Rico; **1183:** Victoria & Albert Museum, London/Art Resource **1191:** t. Courtesy of the Library of Congress **1192:** istockphoto.com **1195:** b. istockphoto.com **1199:** David Nunuk/Photo Researchers, Inc. **1201:** b. *The Eclipse of the Sun Predicted* by Hank Morgan, illustration for *'A Connecticut Yankee in King Arthur's Court'*, by Mark Twain (1835-1910), published 1988 (engraving) (see 193780), Belomlinsky, Mikhail (Contemporary Artist)/Private Collection/www.bridgeman.co.uk **1202:** b. istockphoto.com **1207:** t. The Granger Collection, New York; **1208:** Giraudon/Art Resource, NY **1210:** t. location of photographs, eg name of museum, collection, or copyright holder/Bridgeman Art Library, London/New York **1211:** t. Leonard e Selva/CORBIS **1213:** *Don Quixote*, Pablo Picasso, Bridgeman Art Library, London/New York, ©2004 Estate of Pablo Picasso/Artists Rights Society (ARS), New York; **1215:** *Don Quixote and the Windmill*, Francisco J. Torrome (fl. 1890-1908), Bonhams, London/Bridgeman Art Library, London/New York; **1229:** b. Getty Images **1230:** t. Culver Pictures, Inc. **1231:** Bildarchiv Preussischer Kulturbesitz/Art Resource, NY **1233:** *The Anglers, Study for "La Grand-Jatte"*, 1883, Georges Seurat, Oil on panel, 16 x 25cm. Musee Nat. d'Art Moderne, Troyes, France, Giraudon/Art Resource, NY; **1235:** t. Les Maisons Cabassud la Ville d'Avray, Jean Baptiste Camille Corot, The Louvre, Paris, Scala, Art Resource, New York; **1238:** *Infantry Officer*, Full Dress, oil on canvas, Frederic Remington/Christie's Images **1245:** t. Prentice Hall